ENCYCLOPEDIA OF AMERICAN CARS

BY THE AUTO EDITORS OF CONSUMER GUIDE®

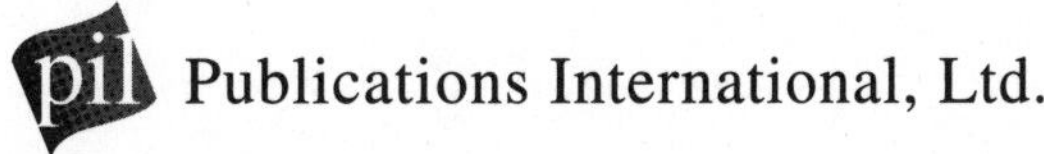
Publications International, Ltd.

Louis Weber, CEO
Publications International, Ltd.
7373 North Cicero Avenue
Lincolnwood, Illinois 60712

ISBN-13: 978-1-4127-1354-2
ISBN-10: 1-4127-1354-4

Manufactured in China.

8 7 6 5 4 3 2 1

Library of Congress Control Number: 2006902818

Photo Credits

Owners:
Special thanks to the owners of the cars featured in this book for their enthusiastic cooperation. They are listed below along with the page number(s) on which their cars appear:

William E. Harrah Foundation, National Automobile Museum – 13, 145; **Bob and Phyllis Leach** – 14, 145; **Dave Holls** – 38; **Bill and Daubney** – 41; **Avanti Motor Corporation** – 41; **Eugene Fattore, Jr.** – 103, 154; **Bill Woodman** – 103; **Herb Kromback** – 140; **Jeff Tranberg** – 146; **James and Robert Lojewski** – 146; **Brad and Barb Hillick** – 147; **Jerry Richman** – 147; **R.C. "Buzz" Pitzen** – 148; **Ray Somers** – 149; **Robert Zaitlin** – 149; **Ted Onufryk** – 150; **Kit Lee** – 150; **Les Raye** – 151; **Howard Engerman** – 151; **Richard Stanley** – 152; **Thomas Hollfelder** – 152; **Harry Nicks** – 153; **Gene and Magdalena Asbury** – 153; **Steven D. Wilson** – 155; **Carmine A. Palazzo** – 156; **Chuck Misetich** – 156; **Steve Bergin** – 157; **Bill and Rita Malik** – 157; **Mike Kuhn** – 158; **Jeff Rupert** – 159; **Barry Waddell** – 159; **Jim and Chris Ross** – 160; **Dennis Helferich** – 179; **Chevrolet Motor Division** – 230; **Jeanne C. Finister** – 289; **Edward Zukiel** – 289; **Bill and Pat Locke** – 290; **Corvette Connections/Mike Scott and Jack Gersh** – 290; **Ray Sherr** – 291; **Lloyd and Martha Mayes** – 292; **James McLeod** – 292; **James Harland** – 293; **Stephan M. Thomas** – 294; **Esther Day Candies Corporation** – 294; **Walter G. Serviss** – 295; **Bob Johnson** – 295; **Michael A. Porto** – 296, 583, 590; **Alex and Beverly Dow** – 296; **S. Ray Miller, Jr.** – 297, 300, 730; **Art Astor** – 297; **Larry Martin** – 298; **Thomas J. Sory** – 298; **Scott Swaydrak** – 299; **Mike Riefer** – 299; **Alfred Ferrara** – 301; **The Nethercutt Collection/Skip Marketti** – 301, 370; **Cliff Felpel** – 302; **Jim Perrault** – 302; **George Carretto** – 303; **John Webber** – 304; **Dick Colarossi** – 304; **Tom Eganhouse, MD** – 305; **Joseph B. Folladori** – 368; **Excalibur** – 380; **Charles Hibert** – 392; **Sherm Smith** – 433; **Sandra Simpkin** – 433; **Robert M. Forker** – 434; **Anthony A. Lucarz** – 434; **Allan St. Jacques** – 435; **Luis A. Chanes** – 436; **Sigfried Grunze** – 436; **Judy Bruggenthies** – 437; **Neil Swartz** – 438; **Rob and Dottie Sharkey** – 438; **Bill Hubert** – 440, 446; **Neil Greener** – 440, 492; **James P. Manak** – 441; **Steve Carey** – 442; **Eldon and Esta Hostetler** – 442; **Steve Blake** – 443; **Bill Hill – 443; Billy F. Wilson – 444;** **Michael W. Riebe** – 444; **Henry Hopkins** – 445; **Allan S. Murray** – 445; **Rosemary and Duane Sell** – 446; **Jim Mueller** – 447; **Ed Johnson** – 447; **Larry Klein** – 448; **Nicola Bulgari** – 448, 531, 817; **Alexander Marshall** – 488; **Arthur Sabin** – 491; **Hudson J. Firestone** – 498; **Jerry Johnson** – 498; **Frederick J. Roth** – 506; **James Godo** – 513; **Glenn and Sylvia Coffey** – 513; **Tom Hincz** – 514; **Ray Menefee** – 530; **Warren and Sylvia Lauridsen** – 530; **Ed and Judy Schoenthaler** – 562, 668; **Lee Gurvey** – 577; **Thomas F. Lerch** – 577; **Len Berman** – 578; **Richard Krist** – 579; **Nick Alexander** – 580; **Thomas Amendola, Sr.** – 580; **Linda Wade** – 581; **Judge Lewis Weinstein** – 581; **Melvin R. Hull** – 582, 615; **Bob Clarke** – 583, 617; **Clarence Becker** – 584; **Glen Patch** – 584; **Bud Dutton** – 585; **Glenn Eisenhamer** – 585; **Ed Musial** – 586; **Peter's Motorcars** – 586; **Mike and Charlene Izzo** – 587; **Kenneth C. Wessel** – 588; **Neil Torrence** – 588, 589; **Mark and Jan Hilbert** – 589; **Thomas Derro** – 590; **Harris Laskey** – 591; **John Thomas** – 591; **Carroll and Dawn Bramble** – 592; **Ralph Neubauer** – 592; **Richard Zeider, MD** – 669; **Craig Karr** – 683; **The Blackhawk Collection** – 683; **P. Alvin Zamba** – 684; **Richard and Linda Kughn** – 684; **David Guthery** – 684; **Carl Sable** – 721; **Donald Phillips** – 721; **Phil Newcomb** – 722; **Plymouth Motor Corporation** – 722; **Jim McGrew** – 723; **Kyle J. Wood** – 723; **Gary J. Kistinger** – 724; **Robert J. and Charlene Matteoli** – 724; **Greg Minor** – 725; **Don and Linda Davis** – 725; **Cliff Mathos** – 726; **Anthony Fusco** – 726; **Ted Hinkle** – 727; **Frank McLiesh** – 728; **Joe Hayes** – 729; **Wilbert Endres** – 731; **Burt Van Flue** – 731; **Mr. and Mrs. Ken Mooney** – 732; **Robert Thornton** – 732; **Ronald Benach** – 733; **Bruce McBroom** – 734; **Dick Mahn** – 734; **Dave Cammack** – 735; **Jim Flicek** – 735; **David M. Kronk** – 736; **Roy Umberger** – 736; **James Bronson** – 794; **Darryl Schleger, MD** – 810; **Ed Barwick** – 818; **George W. Mills** – 818; **William L. Plunkett** – 819; **Terry D. Sanders** – 840; **David Hans** – 840; **Thomas R. Coady, Jr.** – 845; **Petersen Automotive Museum** – 845; **Ed Henning** – 846; **Jeff Cromeens** – 847, 849; **David Lawrence** – 847; **David Hill** – 854; **Brooks Stevens Automobile Collection, Inc.** – 857; **Dave Diedrics** – 864; **Zimmer Motors/Wendy Fiske** – 864; **James Kozbelt** – 908.

Photography:
The editors gratefully acknowledge the cooperation of the following people who supplied photography to help make this book possible:

Nicky Wright – 13, 145, 297, 300, 445, 498, 584, 732, 846; **Joe Wherry** – 14, 145; **Gary Smith** – 38, 513; **Dan Lyons** – 41, 302, 442, 724, 731; **Doug Mitchel** – 41, 151, 157, 175, 230, 290, 293, 299, 434, 437, 439, 441, 447, 514, 530, 562, 577, 581, 585, 586, 592, 668, 721, 729, 730, 733, 736, 845; **Sam Griffith** – 103, 146, 154, 230, 294, 491, 498; **Mark Sincavage** – 140; **Thomas Glatch** – 146, 380, 727, 840, 857; **Mark Garcia** – 147; **Don Heiny** – 147, 444, 580, 581, 590, 726; **Avanti Motor Corporation** – 148; **Vince Manocchi** – 148, 149, 150, 152, 156, 157, 160, 289, 290, 291, 292, 295, 296, 297, 301, 304, 370, 392, 433, 438, 506, 579, 580, 583, 585, 587, 588, 589, 590, 668, 669, 722, 725, 847, 864; **Phil Toy** – 150, 445, 683, 840; **Milton Gene Kieft** – 151, 179, 294, 301, 368, 444, 446, 488, 577, 578, 584, 586, 588, 684, 736; **Joe Joliet** – 155; **W.C. Waymack** – 158, 298, 433, 434, 440, 442, 443, 446, 591, 592, 726, 730; **Mike Mueller** – 159, 289; **Nina Padgett-Russin** – 292, 732; **Jay Peck** – 295; **Darrel Arment** – 299; **Jeff Rose** – 302, 864; **Robert Nicholson** – 303; **David Newhardt** – 435, 436; **Rick Lenz** – 440, 492; **Paul Hostetler** – 441; **Bud Juneau** – 443, 448, 530, 583, 591, 617, 724, 725, 728, 734, 818; **Gary Greene** – 447; **John Heilig** – 448, 531, 817; **Ford Photographic Services** – 483, 485, 439, 643, 646; **Chan Bush** – 506, 819; **Neil Nissing** – 578, 845; **GM Photographic** – 651, 806, 808, 809; **Randy Lorentzen** – 684; **David Temple** – 721, 723; **Jim Frenak** – 722; **Jay Peck** – 723; **David Gooley** – 733, 822; **Jim Thompson** – 735; **Willoughby Photo** – 735; **Guy Bernhardt** – 794; **Richard Spiegelman** – 818, 854; **Jerry Heasley** – 847, 849; **Don Stokum** – 908.

Very special thanks to the following: American Automobile Manufacturers Association; Jon Bill, Auburn–Cord–Duesenberg Museum; Buick Public Relations; Cadillac Public Relations; Chevrolet Public Relations; Pamela Clark, Oldsmobile History Center; Randy Ema; Kelley Enright, DaimlerChrysler Public Relations; Ford Division Public Affairs; Ford Photographic Services; GM Design Staff; John A. Leverett, Panoz Auto Development Co.; Dean E. McKaig, General Motors; Pontiac Public Relations; Dan Schwartz, Avanti Motor Corporation; Wieck Media Services.

Table of
Contents

Introduction

In the dawn of its age, the automobile took many forms. Internal combustion engines vied with steam and electricity as a source of motive power, while chassis designs varied greatly as to engine placement, steering mechanisms, and the number of wheels.

By some counts, there were more than 2500 "manufacturers" in the early part of the twentieth century, but a great many were backyard tinkerers who bought a proprietary engine and placed it in a chassis bearing their own name. Many went under when the first mass-produced car, the Ford Model T, was introduced at a starting price of $825—far less than it took for most people to build one themselves.

While the Model T wasn't the first horseless carriage manufactured by the Ford Motor Company, it certainly had the most impact. During its 19-year production run, it not only put America on wheels by selling more than 15 million copies, it also established the four-wheeled, gasoline-powered, front engine/rear-drive, left-hand steering layout that is still the national standard on most American cars more than 80 years later.

Ironically, once this standard was accepted, cars began to look markedly alike. In the 1920s, even the most car-crazed youngster must have had difficulty distinguishing one make from another. Body designs seemed to follow the same pattern, exceptions existing mainly in high-priced cars like Cadillac and Lincoln—though that was due more to their sheer size and adornment than to any distinction of line. It wasn't until the early 1930s that styling became distinguishable between the popularly priced makes, a trend started largely by General Motors with its Art and Colour Section headed by Harley Earl. By 1933, even the "low-priced three"—Chevy, Ford, and Plymouth—sported distinct faces.

In looking back over the development of the automobile, one can't help noting how world events have had a hand in shaping its history. World War I prompted our engineers to accelerate mechanical technology, advancements that soon found their way into production cars. The Depression forced many companies out of business, narrowing our choices and muting the flamboyant attitude of the Roaring '20s. World War II virtually halted development for half a decade—longer, really, since few cars changed much in the first four years after production resumed.

A nationwide recession in 1958 not only helped kill off venerable Packard and newcomer Edsel, it also prompted a resurgence of economical compacts, which had been tried before and were abandoned due to lack of buyer interest. Their popularity this time around started the turn to "niche" vehicles, from which came muscle cars, ponycars, and personal coupes, along with the first automobiles to find commercial success despite (or perhaps because of) the fact that they deviated from the basic design principles set down by the Model T more than 50 years before. The result was an automotive free-for-all in Detroit, a period in which the horsepower race that had begun in the '50s ramped-up with reckless abandon with seemingly no end in sight.

But the line was soon to be drawn. By the late 1960s, government safety and emission regulations were playing a growing part in automotive design, and together with the insurance lobby, conspired to dump a heavy rain on Detroit's parade. A final blow was dealt by the Arab oil embargo in fall 1973, when OPEC became a four-letter word. What had been a rosy picture just five years earlier had now turned decidedly gray.

It is said, however, that necessity is the mother of invention, and the 1970s proved to be a decade of transformation, if not excitement. Some of the greatest changes in the history of the automobile took place during this period, as manufacturers learned to cope with a much more restrictive environment. While few automotive aficionados look back on the '70s with a great sense of longing, it did bring about some interesting experimentation with technologies that would be refined as time went on: turbocharging, alternate materials, electronics, and the science of aerodynamics. All these came at a price, however, and the decade would also bring extraordinary increases in the cost of buying, owning, and manufacturing cars.

If the 1970s go down in history as a decade of discouragement, then the '80s and '90s must be considered nothing less than the renaissance of the automobile. As auto manufacturers learned to cope with emissions rules through fuel injection and electronic engine controls, power once again began to creep upward. Impact-absorbing bumpers became more subtle and integrated, styling dispatched with the gaudy tape stripes and opera windows, and silhouettes bore the smooth mark of aerodynamics. By century's end, it looked as though the American auto industry was once again producing the kind of cars that one day would be coveted classics.

The 75-plus years covered in this encyclopedia represent what many consider to be the golden age of the automobile. Almost all of the people collecting and restoring old cars today are concerned with the post-1930 period, as the pre-1930 antiques that once dominated the hobby have, to a large extent, long since been relegated to museums. Meanwhile, collector focus has moved forward with time and the addition of younger enthusiasts. People generally tend to be interested in the cars they remember from their youth, which explains the current high popularity of late-'60s muscle cars.

In the first edition of this book we suggested that the "age of collectible cars" might actually end with 1970, but we have since come to think otherwise. Collectors have expressed much interest in the cars of the '70s. The latest domestic models, many the product and expression of fascinating new technology, are arguably the best cars ever built in this country. Undoubtedly they will one day be collectible as well.

America has produced some of the most unique and coveted automobiles manufactured anywhere in the world. All of these classics—and classics yet to be—are celebrated within the pages of this book. We hope you enjoy it.

Genesis of an Era: The 1930s

Ironically, the automotive styling and engineering developments of 1940-75 were almost wholly the result of lessons learned during the greatest economic disaster in modern history. The Depression may have meant the end for many automobile producers, but it forced the survivors to think, plan, and invent. In so doing, they altered the shape of the American automobile almost completely.

During the 1930s, the industry parted company with unsynchronized manual transmissions, wood-framed bodies, mechanical brakes, and solid front axles. In their place came synchromesh gears, semiautomatic and fully automatic transmissions, all-steel bodies composed of fewer and larger panels welded together, hydraulic brakes, and independent front suspension. As roads improved, buyers demanded more speed, so higher-revving engines were needed. This led to new foundry and engine-building techniques that guaranteed high-rpm reliability. Cars could then be geared higher to travel faster. The advent of automatic shiftless transmissions made it less important to gear and "cam" a car so the lazy driver could pull away from a crawl without changing out of "High." As we learned how independent front suspensions and rubber engine mounts could help absorb road shocks, we were able to design stiffer chassis, which made overall construction tighter and more solid. Compared to its 1930 forebear—an upright box on artillery wheels wheezing along on four or six small cylinders—the automobile of 1940 was a sleek torpedo on slotted steel wheels, with more room inside, a longer wheelbase, and a vibration-free, rubber-mounted engine—and it was a good 20 mph faster.

In the process of thinning out industry ranks, the Depression years largely determined the nature of the major producers as we know them today—and selected those independents strong enough to survive. Ever since its founding by W.C. Durant in 1908, General Motors had been striving for managerial and creative decentralization through its division structure. While Henry Ford ruled his strongly centralized company almost single-handedly, the division concept put GM ahead in production during the early 1920s. Only after Henry Ford II took over his grandfather's troubled firm in 1945 did Ford begin to decentralize—and rebuild.

Walter P. Chrysler was an old GM man, and saw the light very early on. Although Chrysler Corporation was founded in the '20s, it came of age during the '30s. Following a division structure not unlike GM's, Chrysler built the second-largest car company in the nation during the decade, and it remained so until the early 1950s.

By 1940, only a few independent manufacturers were left. After the war, only four major independents remained, all with high hopes: Hudson, Nash, Packard, and Studebaker. Together with newcomer Kaiser-Frazer and later joined by Crosley and Willys, the independents enjoyed as much as a 15-percent market share in the late '40s and early '50s. But it didn't last. Nash's president George Mason was the only high-ranking executive among the independents who could envision the benefits of a merger. He had managed to add Hudson to his empire in '54, thus forming American Motors, but died before he could meld in Packard and Studebaker. One by one, the other independents vanished, though Studebaker-Packard lasted longer than most. Only AMC hung on longer, though even it faded away when the struggling company was purchased by Chrysler Corporation in 1987.

The 1940s

Although classic four-square styling was largely abandoned after World War II, some of its finest expressions appeared in 1940-42: the senior Packards, the Hupp Skylark and Graham Hollywood, and the last production LaSalle. Other cars, like the sleek Fords and Mercurys of 1940, offered near perfection in line and form. Chrysler's 1949 products, boxy and upright, symbolized that corporation's concern for ample interior space within compact exterior dimensions.

The modern V-8 engine was perhaps the most significant engineering development of the decade. Of course, V-8s had been around for years—at Cadillac since 1915, and at Ford since 1932. But these were relatively heavy, long-stroke, low-compression engines, known for smoothness rather than performance. In 1949, Cadillac and Oldsmobile pioneered a new generation of V-8s, the forerunners of the powerplants found in most large U.S. cars today. America's light, efficient, and powerful V-8 soon became famous worldwide for its performance and reliability. The '40s also offered traditionally designed engines for those who preferred them. Packard's magnificent 356-cubic-inch straight eight and Cadillac's 346-cid V-8 were L-head units known for quietness and smooth operation. Both are highly prized by collectors.

Most engines of the '40s, however, were workaday inline sixes and eights that may not have been revolutionary, but were dependable and economical. The 230- and 170-cid sixes sold by Plymouth and Studebaker, respectively, served their makers well right on through the '50s, and were well-known for thriftiness. Studebaker's powerplant was a traditional winner in the Mobilgas Economy Run.

Racing was not emphasized by the industry as a whole during the '40s, but many individuals recorded performances that indicated the competition potential of certain production models. The supercharged Graham of 1940-41 was among the fastest cars powered by a conventional sidevalve six. The Hudson Super Six, the Graham's postwar counterpart, could reach speeds that far exceeded what was normally expected from six cylinders. Oldsmobile and Cadillac achieved early competition success with their overhead-valve V-8s. Cadillac scored unbelievable 10th- and 11th-place finishes at the grueling 1950 24 Hours of Le Mans. Oldsmobile's fast, lightweight 88 dominated stock car racing from 1949 through 1951.

Another extremely important engineering highlight of the '40s was the increasing use of the modern automatic transmission. Before, there had been only semiautomatics. Oldsmobile offered one for 1938, then dropped it the next year for Hydra-Matic—the most successful completely shift-free transmission of all time. Chrysler enthusiastically marketed its Fluid Drive (which eliminated most shift motions) well into the 1950s. Ford was conservative, and stayed with the manual gearshift (both with and without overdrive) for all 1940-49 Fords and Mercurys. Ford offered the GM-built Hydra-Matic for the 1949 Lincoln, but did not manufacture an automatic of its own until 1951. Nash and Kaiser-Frazer stayed with stickshifts until 1950, then gave in and also purchased the Hydra-Matic.

Two independents that did strike out with automatics of their own were Packard and Studebaker. Packard's Ultramatic was the only such unit developed entirely by an independent without any help from a transmission firm. It was a smooth-shifting gearbox, but not amenable to the extra power delivered by later Packard engines. Studebaker teamed up with Detroit Gear to create a fine three-speed automatic, but it didn't arrive until 1950.

GM really had the automatic market to itself in the 1940s. Cadillac began offering Hydra-Matic in 1948; Buick debuted its Dynaflow Drive the same year. Though smooth in operation, Dynaflow was not in the same performance league as Hydra-Matic.

The '40s were years of attrition and false starts for the smaller automakers. American Bantam, Hupmobile, and Graham all ceased production well before World War II—and did not return afterward. Willys-Overland, which offered conventional passenger cars through the 1942 model year, came back after the war with an interesting line of Jeep-like vehicles. These included the unique Jeepster that appeared for 1948—the last true touring car in the American industry. The decade's best-known failure was the Tucker—a brilliant concept that nevertheless saw no more than 50 copies. For years, the assumption was that the Tucker had been killed—prematurely—by General Motors and its cohorts. Yet even though its admirable design caused the big manufacturers a bit of concern, it was not actually a serious threat to them. Whether the car could have been realistically produced at the price Preston Tucker claimed will probably never be known.

The 1950s

A lot of people think the cars of the '50s are responsible for the sorry state of the automotive scene today. Critics tell us they were heavy, ungainly, dumb-looking beasts with no—or at best few—redeeming virtues. Yet, they were nowhere near as uniformly bad as skeptics like to insist. In fact, several important advances were made between 1950 and 1960.

Consider, for example, short-stroke V-8s, efficient automatic transmissions, and unit-body construction—which we tried and liked—and air suspension, tailfins, and push-button transmissions—which we tried, disliked, and discarded. Notwithstanding the emphasis on chrome-laden gimmickry, the 1950s also brought some innovative new body styles such as the two- and four-door pillarless hardtop, and the all-steel station wagon that became (for the first time in its history) more like a car than a truck.

If these years are remembered for some of the industry's worst styling excesses, they were also marked by some of the finest automotive designs of all time: the Studebaker "Loewy coupes," the Continental Mark II, the Darrin-styled Kaisers, and the two-seat Thunderbirds.

There's something else about these automobiles that even their admirers often fail to mention, perhaps because it's so obvious. These cars have an intrinsic character—a special appeal—which the industry somehow lost in the late '60s. They were different—vastly different—from the cars of today. This was probably the last decade when a manufacturer dared sell something clearly unique, like the "Step-down" Hudson, the tiny Nash Metropolitan, or the fiberglass Woodill Wildfire. Cars of the '50s were also built differently: Interiors were trimmed in comfortable mohair or genuine leather; bodies were made of heavy-gauge steel. Their makers shunned things like plastic, cardboard, and decals. While the average family car of 1950-59 probably handled as sloppily as everyone said it did, it was also built with more pure integrity than its more nimble successors. Every piece of trim met every other piece precisely where intended. Each door, trunklid, and hood closed with a resounding clunk, swinging shut on vaultlike hinges. Collectors still discover rust-free examples with six-figure mileage, and interiors, paint, and mechanical components in roughly the same shape as when the car left the factory. And this, despite the industry's reputation for haphazard assembly quality.

The 1960s

This turbulent era in American history produced memorable automobiles. It's not at all difficult to remember the cars: the 18-foot-long luxury hardtops, the bucket-seat sporty compacts, the personal cars, the ponycars, and the muscle cars. An incredibly diverse assortment of automobiles streamed out of the factory gates in those years, a car for every taste and budget; anything from the $1700 Metropolitan to the $18,500 Crown Imperial limousine.

Government demands that the industry clean up exhaust emissions and make cars safer were good ideas, even if the legislation that followed was often controversial. But the mandates that took effect in the late '60s also guaranteed an end to the uninhibited experimentation that characterized the early years of the decade.

In a way, the public had as much to do with the decline of innovation as the government. What incentive was there for automakers to develop something really new or different when buyers seemed interested mainly in performance, styling, and pizzazz? Consider the record. After generating high initial interest, the sophisticated Corvair was soon forgotten—long before Ralph Nader came along. Buyers yawned at the first Pontiac Tempest, not sure what to make of its all-independent suspension and rear-mounted trans-axle. The Tempest sold well, but it might have done even better with a more ordinary drivetrain. In 1966, Oldsmobile introduced its radical, superbly engineered front-wheel-drive Toronado, which was consistently outsold by the conventionally designed Buick Riviera. Pontiac's overhead-cam six of 1966, an engine that offered as good a balance between economy and performance as any on the market, was almost completely ignored as most customers insisted on V-8s. Sales records aside, there is something significant about the technological *tours de force* of the '60s: Nearly all of them came from General Motors. There are many reasons for this. The decline of the independents after World War II (the mergers and demise of Hudson and Nash, Packard and Studebaker, plus the disappearance of Kaiser and Willys) radically altered the nature of the industry. Soon, the high-volume manufacturers discovered there were not just one or two kinds of buyers, but many. The result was a raft of new sizes and concepts designed for distinct segments of the market—and new categories like compact, sporty compact, intermediate, standard, luxury, and personal specialty. Yet ironically, all this variety gradually blurred the distinction in price or status between makes. What had happened was that the market began subdividing after about 1955, but it wasn't really expanding. This can be seen in the production figures. Chevrolet, for example, wasn't actually turning out any more cars in 1970 than it did in 1960, but it was building a far greater variety of models.

General Motors was best able to adapt to this new atmosphere. Although Ford had its successes—the Mustang and Continental Mark III for instance—they were triumphs of packaging or marketing, not technology. But GM had grown so large by the mid '60s that it could just as easily produce either unusual, technically interesting designs like the Corvair or Toronado or boringly ordinary cars like the Chevy II or Impala.

Despite the domination of the market by GM and Ford, a few specialty manufacturers operated profitably during the '60s by appealing to small but significant groups of buyers overlooked by the industry giants. The Avanti II continued to occupy its own market niche for years after its parent company fell apart. The original Shelby GT 350 was little more than a reengineered Mustang designed by a former racer who believed there was a tiny—but vocal—market for all-out performance. Checker still sold cars to practical folk looking for taxicab toughness and simplicity. Brooks Stevens found that others shared his dream of driving a "modern classic," and therefore they would buy an Excalibur.

Buyers did not always react enthusiastically to important engineering advances in the 1960s, but they did become more discriminating in their judgments of gimmicky or useless features. As the decade began, the public started rejecting such things as tailfins, pushbutton transmissions, and chrome-encrusted super-cruisers. Rapidly, new models appeared from the likes of Chevrolet, Dodge, Lincoln, and Pontiac—cars that illustrated that good design meant more than a five-pound hood ornament. The early compacts proved that the industry could still build practical cars—and that they could be designed to sell—after a generation of offering impractical ones. The sporty compacts brought home a point the Europeans had long accepted: The best car is not necessarily the biggest. Heading into the 1970s, it was clear that America's automotive values were slowly beginning to change. As events were to prove, the changes could not have been more timely.

The 1970s

In the early 1970s. the industry was beset by a lengthening list of government regulations, complicated by a new set of equally stark realities resulting from the Arab oil embargo. With the sudden recognition of how interdependent the world had become, Detroit executives made key decisions that would change the nature of the American car more dramatically and more swiftly than ever before. General Motors would lead the way—and where GM went, the rest would follow. Reacting quickly to the change in consumer needs, GM embarked on a daring long-term program to downsize its entire fleet. The first results appeared on the 1977 B- and C-body full-sized models. It represented a huge gamble even for the number one producer, for "standards" were still crucially important to profits. But it worked: The new cars were as large or larger than their predecessors on the inside yet astonishingly smaller on the outside—and up to 800 pounds lighter. More importantly, they sold quite well. GM went on to apply the same formula to its intermediates, specialty cars, and compacts in rapid succession, while other makers rushed to follow. Meanwhile, there were advances in allied areas. Ford designer Bill Boyer told us that 96 inches is about as short as a wheelbase should be. "When you can't downsize any more," he declares, "you improve efficiency by more complicated means: aerodynamics, front-drive/transverse engines." And you can provide performance through turbocharging a smaller engine rather than relying on a big V-8 with a surfeit of power.

The 1980s

It is often said that every cloud has a silver lining, and however black the cloud of government regulations appeared in the 1970s, the technology that it spawned in the '80s made the interim suffering seem ultimately worthwhile. One result of the drain on horsepower that accompanied tightening EPA and CAFE requirements was that the focus of performance switched from straightline acceleration to more-adroit handling and braking. The resulting automobiles became more capable all-around performers.

Yet around 1982, horsepower began making a comeback. One of the first signs that the slump was over appeared in that year's Mustang GT, which was fitted with a 157-bhp version of the venerable 302-cid small-block V-8—up from a 120-bhp 255 which was the '81 ponycar's most potent V-8. This engine got stronger each year, and was joined by increasingly sophisticated turbocharged fours. GM's offerings likewise began building muscle: The Z28 Camaro's top engine went from 165 bhp in 1982 to 215 by '85. And these weren't exceptions to the rule.

Another indication that the sober '70s were at an end also occurred in 1982 with the rebirth of the ragtop. Convertibles had been discontinued by '76 due to waning popularity and anticipation of government rollover standards that never materialized. Chrysler Corporation usually takes the kudos for reviving "wind-in-your-hair" motoring, though Buick introduced a ragtop Riviera the same year. Other manufacturers followed suit, and by decade's end there were nine American droptops from which to choose, with more on the way.

The 1990s

The trials experienced by the American auto industry in the previous two decades proved to be character builders. During the '90s, Detroit saw something of a renaissance. Staid General Motors—of all companies—shook up the way the industry did business with the 1991 introduction of the Saturn. Prior to its 1996 redesign, the Ford Taurus returned a domestic nameplate to the top of the U.S. sales rankings. Chrysler, meanwhile, came out with a slew of cutting-edge models built around "cab-forward" design and walked on the wild side with cars like the ferocious Dodge Viper and playful Plymouth Prowler. In 1998, Chrysler surprised everyone by merging with Daimler-Benz. Ford and GM acquired or formed alliances with foreign automakers. Foreign design and engineering would prove to have more influence on domestic products during this decade.

The 2000s

The new century got off to a rocky start with a recession. Ford was hit hard by a scandal involving Firestone tire blow-outs on its best-selling Explorer line. The Daimler/Chrysler merger created losses instead of the "synergy" promised at its announcement, though new cars such as the Chrysler 300 and Dodge Charger helped turn things around. General Motors continued to lose market share. However, it was hoped that Bob Lutz, in charge of new-product development, would do for GM what he had done for Chrysler in the '90s. William Ford had taken control of the family firm and promised to bring stability as well as get Ford back on track. For all their efforts, the domestic carmakers continued to lose market share to foreign manufacturers—most of whom had opened American factories. Mid-decade gas crises revealed the folly of depending on gas-guzzling SUVs for profits while neglecting cars. The American auto industry has survived and learned lessons from wars and recessions. Undoubtedly, this new challenge will result in innovation and more exciting cars.

Qualifications and Exceptions

Even the best system of terminology and classification has its exceptions. For the Major Makes section, the intent was to include every volume manufacturer that did business in America between 1930 and 2006. Thus, makes like Essex, Franklin, and Marmon are listed even though all were active only briefly in the early '30s. Similarly, there is a listing for AMC, which was activated as a separate nameplate in 1966.

Several makes usually considered "minor" by the industry are the first exceptions. Avanti II, Checker, Duesenberg, Excalibur, Panoz, and Shelby are treated as majors even though their production was a mere fraction of total industry volume. The reasoning is subjective; though their volume was never substantial, we felt these cars warranted more than a mere notation among the "minors." Shelby as a marque saw only sporadic production since its formation in 1965, but in some years its volume was quite considerable for a tiny company—not to mention its impact. The last is reason enough to include Duesenberg.

Canadian-market models are not officially covered here, but again there is an exception; namely, the 1965-66 Studebaker, which was nominally a Canadian product in those years. This decision was made on the grounds that Studebaker had been too much a part of the American scene in previous years to leave out its final offerings. Also, many American-market cars are made in Canada and Mexico. The problem is that if these cars are listed, then Canadian-market Plymouths, for example, should be included, too. An argument can be made for including American cars built in Canada and Mexico, but lumping in Canadian-market Plymouths would have exceeded the scope of the book.

A different problem arose in deciding how to treat major models of certain makes, cars substantially different in technology or character from the marque's usual products. For improved clarity and coverage, the rear-engine Corvair and the singular Corvette have their own chapters apart from the main Chevrolet entry. Likewise, Mustang and Thunderbird are treated separately from Ford. But this led to more exceptions. The Kaiser-Darrin is not listed separately from Kaiser, for example. Another reason for treating the aforementioned models individually is that the main Chevrolet and Ford entries were already enormous. The Nash Metropolitan involved two more exceptions. Because of its individual character, it is considered distinct from other Nash models by many authorities. Yet it was labeled a Nash until 1958, when that nameplate disappeared and Metropolitan became a make in its own right. To avoid confusing the issue any further, we have included it in the Nash chapter—appropriate, we feel, considering its origins. We have treated similar cases in the same manner. Clipper was a Packard model before it became a distinct marque for 1956, but since it was little different than the Packard product and only lasted one year on its own, we included it with its parent company. Likewise the Valiant, officially a separate make upon its introduction in 1960, but a Plymouth model thereafter.

In other cases, we follow industry practice. For example, Continental was a distinct Ford Motor Company make in 1956-1958, and there was no problem separating the appropriate models from Lincoln in the period covered. The same principle applies to AMC (the make, not the corporation). The company used the Rambler nameplate exclusively from 1957 through 1965, and the '65 Ambassador and Marlin both bore the appropriate script and emblems. For 1966-67, however, these models had new "AMC" identification, and the AMX and Javelin appeared for 1968 as AMC products, not Ramblers. For 1970, the Rambler name disappeared entirely in favor of AMC. Thus, the reader will find the 1965 Marlin, for example, discussed under "Rambler," and the 1966-67 models under "AMC."

Willys posed some of the most serious problems encountered. Officially, the Willys passenger car ended after 1955 with the expiration of the domestic Aero-based models. But a steel-bodied station wagon continued to be offered through 1961—variously called a Willys, a Kaiser-Jeep, and a Jeep. From 1963 on, Jeep Corporation marketed the four-wheel-drive Wagoneer much like a passenger model and, in 1967, Kaiser-Jeep Corporation released the Jeepster 2, designed in the image of the 1948 original. Most industry sources and the collector hobby consider the 1948-51 Jeepster a passenger car, but none list the Jeep wagons, Wagoneer, or Jeepster 2, which are all defined as "trucks." Including the original Jeepster might seem to imply including these other products as well. The problem was that by leaving in those models, the book would be opened up to similar contemporary competitors like the Ford Bronco or International Scout, which were definitely beyond our scope. Ultimately, it was decided to make two more exceptions: The original Jeepster and Aero passenger cars are the only postwar Willys models discussed.

Finally, during the 1990s, trucks and SUVs became an increasingly important part of the American market. Though this is an encyclopedia of American cars, we mention trucks, SUVs, and minivans in the text because they are important parts of the industry's story. We include a few minivan and SUV pictures, but cover only cars in the tables.

Chapter Texts

The general text of each entry presents a detailed account of the make's history. There is, we think, sound reason for this even in a reference work. Too often, "encyclopedias" simply report statistics. But to understand what was done, it is essential to know how and why it was done and what the results were. Therefore, we have included information on the designers, engineers, and executives who shaped these cars; the reasons they did what they did; the alternative plans they rejected; and the successes or failures that followed. Each chapter is intended to offer a concise, yet complete, description of each major manufacturer—a basic outline for the casual user, a quick education for the uninitiated, and a solid review for the expert. In the process of writing these entries, we have attempted to puncture many hoary automotive legends—that the Corvair was torpedoed by Ralph Nader, for example, or that Studebaker was a victim of a plot at Ford. You'll find the real stories no less interesting.

Photographs

Selecting photographs for a work like this can be more difficult than editing the text. Limited space and the great variety of cars offered by the larger companies dictate that it is not always possible to provide a truly representative sample for each model year over such a broad time span. While this book cannot contain the detailed photographic references of a single-make history, the most important and influential models are shown.

Unlike some other automotive encyclopedias, this one includes pictures of selected prototypes, experimentals, and show cars, as well as production models—all clearly labeled as such. The reasons are the inordinate interest in such nonproduction designs among today's enthusiasts, and the importance of these proposals as benchmarks. While there are hundreds, even thousands, of styling studies for each model, there are interesting or key design ideas that either evolved into production or were abruptly dismissed. The prototypes selected represent the industry at its best and worst in line with the major goal of this book: to present a broad, clear, and factual account of the American automobile industry.

Tables

At the end of each chapter is a series of tables listing every model and body style offered by that make in the 1930-2006 period. Again, however, there are exceptions. The Duesenberg and Tucker entries have no accompanying charts because the former built chassis that were then fitted with custom bodywork, and the latter produced only prototypes that are adequately described in the text.

Of all the elements in a book like this, charts are the most time-consuming and pose the greatest problems of style and accuracy. Space naturally played a part in the choice of material shown. The object was to provide, at a glance, the data most readers would be likely to require in a hurry: models, wheelbases, body styles, weights, prices, model-year production, and engine availability. In using the tables, the reader should keep the following in mind:

Series or Model Entries

Each group of body styles is listed under a series or model heading. This indicates the factory model or series code number (where applicable), name, and wheelbase (in inches). Code numbers posed many problems. On several occasions, it was unclear whether a code applied to the series or model line as a whole, to specific body styles, or both. In instances where they were misleading or irrelevant, the code numbers were omitted. Where a code applies to both the model/series and to the body style, the first part is shown with the model/series and the second with the body style. An example is found in the 1959 Dodge chart. Officially, that year's Coronet six-cylinder club sedan was designated by the factory as MD1-L21, but "MD1-L" applied to all Coronet sixes, and "21" only to the club sedan. The number is therefore divided accordingly.

In the '60s, some code systems became more complex, so numbers are listed as the situation required. In 1961, for example, codes for the Dodge Lancer followed '59 practice. But the 1961 Dart Six series consisted of Seneca, Pioneer, and Phoenix subseries. In this case, only the series number "RD3" is shown in the heading, the rest of the designation appearing alongside the corresponding body styles. In reality, a 1961 Dart Six Phoenix hardtop sedan went by the code RD3-H434; here, however, it is shown as model RD3, body style H434.

Abbreviations

For best readability, it was important to limit each entry to one line. To do this, the following standard abbreviations were adopted for the body-style listings:

abbreviation	meaning
A/S	auxiliary seats
A/W	all-weather
brghm/b'ham	brougham (sedan, convertible, etc.)
bus	business, as in coupe
cab	cabriolet
comm/comcl	commercial
conv cpe	two-door convertible
conv sdn	four-door convertible
cpe	coupe
CQ	closed rear roof quarters
div	division window (limousine)
fstbk	fastback ("torpedo")
form	formal, as in sedan
FQ	formal rear roof quarters
htchbk	hatchback
htp cpe	two-door pillarless hardtop
htp sdn	four-door pillarless hardtop
htp wgn	pillarless station wagon
J/B	"jetback" (fastback)
lndu	landau
limo	limousine
phtn	phaeton
proto	prototype
rdstr	two-passenger roadster
R/S	rumble seat, as in roadster
sdn	sedan
SQ	solid rear roof quarters
spdstr	speedster
spt	sport, as in coupe
T/B	"trunkback"
tng	touring
util	utility, usually a two-door sedan
wgn	station wagon

Generally, all body styles except sports cars and very small models like American Bantam have five- or six-passenger capacity; exceptions are specified. There are also cases where it is necessary to differentiate between otherwise similar types. These abbreviations are:

P (7P, 8P, etc.)	passenger capacity
S (2S, 3S)	number of seats (wagons)
W (4W, 6W)	number of side windows
FW	fixed window

Engine abbreviations also follow a consistent pattern: block configuration is followed by the number of cylinders and, where needed, a suffix letter. The letters are as follows:

I (I-6, I-8, etc.)	inline or straight
V (V-6, V-8, etc.)	V-block
S	supercharged
T	turbocharged
D	diesel

Manufacturers differ widely in how they treat engine options. Some group both standard and extra-cost engines under the same model code; others distinguish between them and even give them separate model numbers. The charts follow the practice each manufacturer used for a given model year. The Pontiac Six and Eight, for example, were distinct models and are shown as such. Plymouth engines were usually listed as options for a given model and are combined. This difference is emphasized by spelling out and capitalizing the words "Six" and "Eight" in cases like Pontiac and by using the abbreviations "I-6" and "V-8" in cases like Plymouth.

Where options are combined, prices shown are for base-engine models. Production figures shown are for the total number of that model built, regardless of engine.

Weight

The column marked "wght" provides the initial advertised curb weight (not adjusted for passengers, fuel, or cargo) for each body style as listed in industry sources, usually National Automobile Dealers Association (NADA) guides. The reader may expect these to differ slightly from other published figures, because weights varied depending on equipment fitted or even the scales used.

It is important to note, however, that before 1990 when more than one engine was standard for a given model, curb weights shown are averages, deemed necessary for maximum readability. For example, the 1955 Chevrolet Bel Air convertible weighed 3315 pounds with the six and 3285 pounds with the V-8. Our listed weight is the average: 3300 pounds. Previously, many manufacturers only quoted weight for cars with the standard engine and today that is the normal practice. Usually, the choice of engine did not change curb weight by more than 100-150 pounds.

Prices

Figures shown in the "Price" column are based on initial advertised prices (as delivered) according to NADA and similar sources, and represent contemporary dollars ("as-new" price). Oftentimes, prices varied during the model year. When more than one standard engine was available, however, we have not averaged prices; the figure for the least expensive power unit is shown instead.

Model-Year Production

The question most often asked about older cars—and one of the most important in a reference work about them—is "How many did they make?" The answer is not always clear-cut, and in some cases production has been a subject of research—and dispute—among automotive historians for decades. However, the figures listed are the most recent and accurate available and have been thoroughly researched and cross-checked. Note that mainly model-year, not calendar-year, figures are used in both the tables and the text. The reason for this is that calendar-year totals always include some portion of two model years, which creates confusion when comparing one make with another. Model-year figures normally represent production of cars marketed as the 1939, 1949, 1959, 1969, etc. models. For makes and/or years where precise model-year totals were not available, registrations or calendar-year figures are given and are always identified as such. These exceptions apply mainly to the early years of the '30s, before the model-year concept had been universally adopted by the industry, and to low-volume independents like Duesenberg, where the idea had relatively little meaning in the context of company operations. Starting in the '90s, manufacturers were more likely to publish calendar-year totals and model-year figures were sometimes not available.

Production received long and painstaking analysis in preparing this book. Too often, published totals have been based on company handouts that are often misleading and sometimes inaccurate. The 1953 Buick Skylark, for example, is listed by the division (and at least one other source) as the "Roadmaster Anniversary Convertible." The contradictions and false trails of factory lists were fully explored and compared to other lists from a dozen different sources. Sometimes, it was discovered that there were cars built that weren't "officially" listed; in other cases, models were listed but not actually produced.

There were a few cases where it was possible to go beyond known information by estimating, such as when a company provided only a combined total for two or three model years. In those cases where we felt confident to do so, production was proportioned over individual model years. The usual standard for these breakdowns was calendar-year output in cases where it very nearly coincided with model-year output (usually when a model year began in January rather than September or October).

In some instances, available factory figures included nonproduction models, usually styles intended for production but not produced in volume. These are retained in the charts and are clearly labeled as nonproduction. While not all records documented nonproduction models, the ones available are shown for completeness.

There were a few cases where even estimating proved impossible, or where a large group of models or body styles were lumped together. Through research, we were able to add a number of previously missing figures to this latest edition; it is hoped that we will be able to add even more to the next edition.

Engine

Under each model year roster is a list of standard (S) and optional (O) engines and their model or series availability. Other basic information provided includes block configuration, number of cylinders, displacement (to the nearest 0.1 cubic inch), bore and stroke (to the nearest .01 inch), and SAE gross horsepower (SAE net starting in 1972). In cases where there was more than one standard engine, all are shown as "S."

Additions and Corrections

Much care has been taken in compiling this book to ensure a high degree of accuracy. Nevertheless, additional research may yield data or conclusions other than those presented here. The publishers welcome additions and suggestions. They may be addressed to *Encyclopedia of American Cars*, c/o Consumer Guide® Publications, 7373 North Cicero Avenue, Lincolnwood, Illinois, 60712, or send an e-mail to: jstewart@pubint.com.

—The Auto Editors of Consumer Guide®

Allstate

Imagine Chrysler selling shirts, Ford merchandising mattresses, or GM pushing power tools. Sound strange? No more so than retailing giant Sears, Roebuck getting into the car business, which it did for a brief time in the '50s.

The story begins in the late '40s with Theodore V. Houser, then vice president of merchandising for Sears, but also on the board of Kaiser-Frazer, the upstart postwar automaker. In 1949, Houser broached the idea of marketing a K-F product under Sears' familiar Allstate name—a complete car to be sold along with parts and accessories for it at the new auto shops Sears was then opening up next to its retail stores. A hookup with K-F was a natural. At the time, Houser was buying Homart enamelware from Kaiser Metals Company in which Sears held a 45-percent interest.

The first thought was simply to put Allstate logos on Kaiser-Frazer's large 1949 models, but Sears was dubious. Then the compact Henry J came along for 1951 (*see entry*), exactly the car Houser had been looking for: simple, inexpensive, and easy to service.

Somehow, K-F president Edgar F. Kaiser managed to convince his dealers to accept a chain department store as a competitor, and the Allstate was announced that November. It was the only new American make for 1952, and the first car Sears had offered since its high-wheeler of 40 years earlier. In an apparent attempt to feel out the market, Sears initially concentrated promotion in the Southeast, though the Allstate was ostensibly available nationwide through the Sears catalog.

Though obviously a Henry J, the Allstate sported a distinctive front end designed by Alex Tremulis (lately involved with the Tucker fiasco), plus a major interior upgrade in line with Sears' policy of improving on proprietary products. K-F interior specialist Carleton Spencer used quilted saran plastic combined with a coated-paper fiber encapsulated in vinyl, a material he'd discovered in use on the transatlantic telegraph cable. Seemingly impervious to normal wear, it was superior to the upholstery of most Henry Js.

Not surprisingly, Sears specified its own Allstate batteries, spark plugs, and tube tires, each with the appropriate guarantee. The entire vehicle was covered for 90 days or 4000 miles, K-F's standard warranty. Allstate's Deluxe models had trunklids and dashboard gloveboxes, items found less often on Henry Js,

1952 fastback two-door sedan

though basic and standard Allstates lacked the opening trunk. The costlier Deluxe Six also had armrests and a horn ring that weren't available on lesser versions even at extra cost.

Otherwise, everything else was the same. That meant K-F's pudgy-looking little two-door fastback sedan with a choice of two L-head Willys engines: a four and a six. Sears' marketing was more aggressive, though, with five Allstate models to four Henry Js. The cheapest '52 Allstate, the basic Four, was priced just below the standard Henry J.

There was little change for '53. A full-width rubber-covered pad was added to the dash, taillights were relocated to the rear fenders, and models reduced to two Fours and the Six.

But by then, it was clear the Allstate had failed. Whether it was because people didn't take to buying cars in department stores or because of the narrow marketing approach is difficult to determine. Both factors probably contributed. Only 1566 Allstates were built for 1952. The count was 797 when Sears canceled the project in early '53, leaving plans for future models stillborn. Among these was a pair of proposals for a two-door station wagon, one by industrial designer Brooks Stevens, the other by Gordon Tercey of K-F Styling.

Allstates are extremely rare today, and thus more desired by collectors than comparable Henry Js. In 1971, Allstate Insurance purchased an Allstate car for historical purposes. In the '60s it would have been hard to convince the folks at Sears' parts counters that the car had ever existed.

Specifications

1952 - 1,566 built				
A2304 Four (wb 100.0)		**Wght**	**Price**	**Prod**
110	basic sdn 2d	2,300	1,395	200
111	std sdn 2d	2,300	1,486	500
113	Deluxe sdn 2d	2,300	1,539	200
A2404 Six (wb 100.0)				
—	basic sdn 2d	2,325	1,594	200
115	Deluxe sdn 2d	2,325	1,693	466
1952 Engines	**bore×stroke**	**bhp**	**availability**	
I-4, 134.2	3.11×4.38	68	S-Allstate Four	
I-6, 161.0	3.13×3.50	80	S-Allstate Six	

1953 - 797 built				
A3304 Four (wb 100.0)		**Wght**	**Price**	**Prod**
210	std sdn 2d	2,405	1,528	200
213	Deluxe sdn 2d	2,405	1,589	225
A3404 Six (wb 100.0)				
215	Deluxe sdn 2d	2,455	1,785	372
1953 Engines	**bore×stroke**	**bhp**	**availability**	
I-4, 134.2	3.11×4.38	68	S-Allstate Four	
I-6, 161.0	3.13×3.50	80	S-Allstate Six	

Note: Model-by-model production totals are estimated.

1952 fastback two-door sedan

American Austin

1930 Model A 2-passenger coupe

1930 Model A roadster

When Sir Herbert Austin came to America in 1929, the well-known English manufacturer had many people excited over his plan to build cars in the USA. After a tour of the country, he announced that the American Austin would be built in Butler, Pennsylvania. Detroit shook its collective head, but Butler wasn't such a strange choice. It had access to industrial services and an eager work force, and it was close enough to East Coast ports to make importing components from England quite feasible. The basic concept of the car itself seemed promising, too, and as production started in May 1930, the company claimed it had close to 200,000 orders for its new ultralight, ultra-economical car.

The American Austin was built through 1934, and the same engine was used throughout the production run. It was an L-head four that displaced 46 cubic inches, had only two main bearings, and developed 13-14 brake horsepower at 3200 rpm. A roadster and coupe were initially offered. In 1931, a business coupe, Deluxe coupe, and 2/4 passenger cabriolet were added. Once production fired up, some of the original prices were cut, and the figures were reduced again in 1933 in an effort to boost sales.

For a while, prospects for the American Austin looked good—but only for a while. The 1930 output of 8558 units would never be exceeded. Two factors were largely responsible for the lackluster reception. One was the general business decline brought on by the Depression. The other was the fact that, even in bad times, Americans didn't take to midget cars. To be sure, the American Austin was a midget. Its 75-inch wheelbase was fully 16 inches less than that of the future VW Beetle. Also, the Austin weighed only 1100-1200 pounds, and Americans were notoriously leery about light cars in those years, as many still are. It was an attractive little car, designed in part by Alexis de Sakhnoffsky, but that didn't seem to matter, and production ground to a halt in 1935.

Austins provided a welcome touch of amusement in a drab period for America. And, for a few people, they became a sort of reverse status symbol, much like the Beetle would be in the 1950s. Al Jolson, who loved cars and usually drove Packards or Lincolns, bought the first Austin coupe delivered to a private buyer. He was followed by numerous other Hollywood stars: Buster Keaton, Slim Summerville, and the "Our Gang" kiddies. Austins even starred in a movie. They were used as "steeds" for a knightly battle in Will Rogers' *A Connecticut Yankee in King Arthur's Court.* It made for a great movie scene, but it didn't help to sell Austins.

Specifications

1930 - 8,558 built*

Model A (wb 75.0)	Wght	Price	Prod
rdstr	1,100	445	—
cpe 2P	1,130	465	—

1930 Engine	bore×stroke	bhp	availability
I-4, 46.0	2.20×3.00	14	S-all

*Calendar year

1931 - 1,279 built*

Model A (wb 75.0)	Wght	Price	Prod
rdstr	1,040	395	—
bus cpe	1,130	330	—
cpe 2P	1,130	395	—
DeLuxe cpe 2P	1,130	525	—
cabriolet 2-4P	1,175	550	—

1931 Engine	bore×stroke	bhp	availability
I-4, 46.0	2.20×3.00	14	S-all

*Calendar year

1932 - 3,846 built*

Model A (wb 75.0)	Wght	Price	Prod
rdstr	1,040	395	—
bus cpe	1,130	330	—
cpe 2P	1,130	395	—

1932 Engine	bore×stroke	bhp	availability
I-4, 46.0	2.20×3.00	14	S-all

*Calendar year

1933 - 4,726 built*

Model 2-75 (wb 75.0)	Wght	Price	Prod
rdstr	1,020	315	—
bus cpe	1,100	275	—
Special bus cpe	1,100	295	—
cpe 2P	1,130	315	—
Model 3-75 (wb 75.0)			
rdstr	1,929	365	—
bus cpe	1,100	295	—
cpe 2P	1,130	345	—
DeLuxe cpe	1,130	365	—

1933 Engine	bore×stroke	bhp	availability
I-4, 46.0	2.20×3.00	13	S-all

*Calendar year

1934 - 1,300 built (est.)*

Model 375 (wb 75.0)	Wght	Price	Prod
rdstr	1,020	365	—
bus cpe	1,130	295	—
cpe 2P	1,130	345	—
DeLuxe cpe 2P	1,130	365	—

1934 Engine	bore×stroke	bhp	availability
I-4, 46.0	2.20×3.00	13	S-all

*Calendar year

1935-36

Models listed in industry records, but no production.

American Bantam

Small cars never made it big in prewar America, but that didn't stop people from pushing them. Among the more energetic proponents was Roy S. Evans, who took over the moribund American Austin Car Company in 1935 with hopes of succeeding where Sir Herbert Austin had failed.

Evans' hopes were tempered by the Depression, which still seemed endless, and Austin's formidable debts: $75,000 in back taxes and interest, plus a $150,000 property mortgage to the Pullman Standard Company. But the federal court overseeing American Austin's bankruptcy felt Evans might salvage things, and gave him the place for only $5000 cash—a mere 1/2000th of its appraised value. Evans secured a $250,000 loan from the Reconstruction Finance Corporation, then hired the necessary talent to help him create a new car called American Bantam.

Like American Austin, the Bantam was styled by the artistic Alexis de Sakhnoffsky, who conjured a new front with a smooth hood and rounded grille, plus reworked fenders and rear deck. His bill was only $300, and Evans was able to retool the entire line for a mere $7000. Indy race-car builder Harry Miller was hired to improve mechanicals, but lack of funds confined him to a redesigned manifold. Butler's own engineers replaced the Austin's expensive roller bearings with cheap babbitt bearings, and added full-pressure lubrication, a new three-speed transmission, Hotchkiss final drive, and Ross cam-and-lever steering. They also devised a heavier frame. Engine size was unchanged, but three main bearings were used instead of two after 1939. Wheel diameter shrank from 18 to 16 inches for 1937 and to 15 inches for 1938.

The debut 1936 Bantam line comprised a roadster and five coupes in the $295-$385 range. Two roadsters and three coupes were listed for '37 at somewhat higher prices ($385-$492). Several new models arrived for 1938, including a Speedster with pretty "Duesenberg sweep" side panels, and the novel Boulevard Delivery with a rear half-roof. For 1939 came a smart Riviera convertible, designed by the young Alex Tremulis, who later recalled that it could cruise at 75-80 mph and average 42.5 mpg—a rather questionable claim.

Bantam production continued into 1941, but not even the dynamic Evans could convince Americans of the value in his tiny package. Output was about 2000 units in 1938, just 1229 the following year, under 1000 in 1940-41, then none. The firm found temporary salvation by winning a contract to design what became the World War II Army Jeep. Bantam built the first prototype, but the army was concerned about its ability to produce Jeeps in the quantities needed. Ford and Willys were supplied with Bantam's blueprints and asked to submit their own versions. Bantam received contracts for only 2,643 units, while Ford and Willys built more than 600,000 during the war. Bantam did get a contract to build two-wheel Jeeptrailers. The company produced utility trailers until 1956.

1938 Model 60 Speedster 4 passenger

1939 Model 62 coupe

Specifications

1936

Model 575 (wb 75.0)	Wght	Price	Prod*
rdstr 2P	1,040	385	—
bus cpe 1P	1,130	295	—
bus cpe 2P	1,130	307	—
Standard cpe	1,130	355	—
DeLuxe cpe	1,130	385	—

1936 Engine	bore×stroke	bhp	availability
I-4, 46.0	2.20×3.00	13	all

*Under 500, all models

1937 - 3,500 built (est.)

Model 575 (wb 75.0)	Wght	Price	Prod
rdstr	1,100	431	—
Custom rdstr	1,100	492	—
bus cpe	1,100	385	—
cpe 2P	1,100	411	—
DeLuxe cpe 2P	1,100	431	—

1937 Engine	bore×stroke	bhp	availability
I-4, 46.0	2.20×3.00	20	S-all

1938 - 2,000 built (est.)

Model 60 (wb 75.0)	Wght	Price	Prod
Special rdstr	1,130	449	—
rdstr	1,140	479	—
DeLuxe rdstr	1,160	525	—
bus cpe	1,230	399	—
cpe 2P	1,230	399	—
Master cpe 2P	1,250	439	—
DeLuxe cpe 2P	1,250	465	—
Foursome spdstr 4P	1,265	497	—
wgn 2d	1,434	565	—

1938 Engine	bore×stroke	bhp	availability
I-4, 46.0	2.20×3.00	20	S-all

1939 - 1,229 built*

Model 62 (wb 75.0)	Wght	Price	Prod
rdstr	1,130	449	—
Special rdstr	1,140	479	—
DeLuxe rdstr	1,160	525	—
cpe 2P	1,230	399	—
Special cpe 2P	1,240	439	—
DeLuxe cpe 2P	1,250	469	—
Sunair cpe 2P	1,250	479	—
Foursome spdstr 4P	1,265	497	—
DeLuxe Foursome spdstr 4P	1,280	549	—
wgn 2d	1,434	565	—

1939 Engine	bore×stroke	bhp	availability
I-4, 46.0	2.20×3.00	20	S-all

1940 - 800 built

Series 65 (wb 75.0)		Wght	Price	Prod
65	cpe	1,261	399	—
65	Master cpe	1,275	449	—
65	conv cpe	1,340	525	—
65	Master rdstr	1,211	449	—
65	conv sdn	1,296	549	—
65	wgn 2d	1,400	565	—

1940 Engine	bore×stroke	bhp	availability
I-4, 50.1	2.26×3.13	22	S-all

1941 - 138 built*

Series 65 (wb 75.0)		Wght	Price	Prod
65	cpe	1,261	399	—
65	Master cpe	1,275	449	—
65	conv cpe	1,340	525	—
65	Master rdstr	1,211	449	—
65	conv sdn	1,296	549	—
65	wgn 2d	1,400	565	—

1941 Engine	bore×stroke	bhp	availability
I-4, 50.1	2.26×3.13	22	S-all

*Calendar-year figures.

AMC

AMC became a distinct make for 1966, as American Motors substituted this badge for Rambler nameplates on the full-size Ambassador and midsize fastback Marlin. The intermediate Rambler Rebel followed suit for '68, when the Javelin ponycar and two-seat AMX arrived as new AMC models. Rambler disappeared after the final, 1969 edition of the 1964-vintage American compact, which was replaced for 1970 by the AMC Hornet and Gremlin.

The 1966 Ambassador was a face-lifted version of the redesigned '65 Rambler model, one of the better efforts from the studios of AMC design vice president Richard A. Teague. Squarish but clean, it spanned a 116-inch wheelbase, four inches longer than the '64 Ambassador's. A new special edition for '66 was the DPL hardtop coupe, elegantly appointed with reclining bucket seats, fold-down center armrests, pile carpeting, and many other standards.

Ranked below were Ambassador sedans, wagons, and hardtops in 880 and 990 trim, plus a 990 convertible. All offered the long-running 232-cubic-inch Typhoon six or optional 287- and 327-cid V-8s. Only the 270-horsepower 327 required premium fuel. Most Ambassadors were ordered with automatic, but a few carried a three-speed manual transmission or AMC's "Twin-Stick" overdrive. A four-speed manual was also listed for 990s and the DPL.

1966 Ambassador DPL hardtop coupe

1966 Ambassador DPL hardtop coupe

1966 Rambler Classic Rebel hardtop coupe

1967 Ambassador DPL hardtop coupe

1966 Ambassador 660 station wagon

1966 Ambassador 880 two-door sedan

1967 Ambassador 990 four-door sedan

1967 Ambassador DPL convertible coupe

1967 Rambler Rebel SST hardtop coupe

1967 Rambler Rebel 770 Cross Country station wagon

The big Ambassador evolved nicely through the late '60s. Wheelbase was stretched two inches for '67, when semifastback styling with more-rounded contours was adopted. The '68s were little changed save a slightly altered hood and a revised model sequence: standard, DPL, and SST. New frontal styling with a more-sculpted hood, plastic grille, and horizontal quad headlights marked the '69s, riding a new 122-inch wheelbase and sporting standard air conditioning. A minor restyle for 1970 brought new rear fenders and taillamps to sedans and hardtops, and new roof panels and taillamps to wagons.

AMC made an unsuccessful first stab at the booming personal-car market with the radically styled 1965 Rambler Marlin, renamed AMC Marlin for 1966-67. This was a big fastback hardtop coupe, initially based on the midsize 1965-66 Rambler Classic, with the same 112-inch wheelbase and similar front sheetmetal. Teague penned sweeping, elliptical rear side windows so the C-pillars wouldn't look heavy, but the overall styling was somewhat clumsy nonetheless. The '66 changed only in detail: revised grille, standard front antiroll bar on six-cylinder models, and newly optional vinyl roof treatment.

The '67 Marlin was switched to that year's new Ambassador platform and ended up much better proportioned on its longer wheelbase. Teague helped with handsome lower-body lines of the same hippy sort applied to that year's Ambassador and Rebel. Measuring 6.5-inches longer than previous Marlins, the '67 was perhaps the best of this school, but it arrived too late to save the day. Sales had been low from the start, and 1965-66 sales were less than 5000 and 3000, respectively. Marlin offered some sports-car features (optional four-speed gearbox, tachometer, bucket seats, and V-8s with up to 280 bhp) but lacked a sports car's taut, precise handling and manageable size.

Replacing Marlin for 1968 was the smaller and far more popular Javelin, a "ponycar" in the image of Ford's wildly successful Mustang. Beautifully shaped and exciting, the Javelin sold like

1967 Rambler Rebel SST convertible coupe

1967 Marlin fastback hardtop coupe

1967 Marlin fastback hardtop coupe

1968 Ambassador SST hardtop coupe

1968 Ambassador SST four-door sedan

1968 Rebel 770 four-door sedan

1968 Rebel SST convertible coupe

1968 Javelin SST fastback hardtop coupe

1968 Javelin SST fastback hardtop coupe

1968 AMX 2-passenger coupe

hotcakes. Over 56,000 of the '68s were built, helping AMC out of a four-year sales slump. With standard 232 six, a Javelin cruised at 80 mph; the optional 290 V-8 boosted top speed to 100 mph. An optional "Go Package" offered a 343 V-8 with four-barrel carburetor and dual exhausts, plus power front-disc brakes, heavy-duty suspension, and wide tires—good for eight seconds in the 0-60-mph dash and a top speed approaching 120 mph. On its 109-inch wheelbase, Javelin was a bit roomier, larger, and longer than the rival Mustang, Chevy Camaro, and Plymouth Barracuda. Its styling was arguably the cleanest of the lot.

Javelin was face-lifted for 1969, mainly via an altered grille. A "twin-venturi" nose, revised wheel covers, and a new hood with simulated air scoops arrived for 1970. But sales failed to match

1968 Javelin SST hardtop coupe

1968 Javelin fastback hardtop coupe

1968 AMX 2-passenger coupe

1968 AMX 2-passenger coupe

the first-year total because of additional ponycar competition—notably a sleek new Camaro.

An exciting mid 1968 newcomer was the AMX, a two-seat coupe created by sectioning the Javelin bodyshell to a trim 97-inch wheelbase. This car introduced a new 390-cid V-8 with forged-steel crankshaft and connecting rods. Output was a healthy 315 bhp and 425 pound-feet of torque. AMX's standard engine was a 290-cid V-8; a 343 was optional. Tight suspension, bucket seats, and extra-cost four-speed gearbox made for a capable semisports car; the AMC also did well in competition. As with the Marlin, the most handsome AMX was the last, the 1970 edition looking more-integrated and "serious" than the others. But again, demand was always much lower than company management hoped, with production for all three model years combined failing to top 20,000 units.

As mentioned, Rebel switched to an AMC nameplate for 1968, though the basic car had appeared the previous year as a Rambler, taking over from the old Classic. It remained AMC's midsize, however, riding a 114-inch wheelbase and offering a variety of sixes and V-8s. Prices were competitive, starting at around $2500. Sedans, hardtop coupes, and wagons were available in three series—550, 770, and SST. Rebel also offered AMC's sole 1968 convertibles, but few were built: just 377 in the 550 series and another 823 SSTs. They would be AMC's last factory droptops (not counting the later Renault-based Alliance models). The '69 Rebel line was trimmed to just basic and SST series. A wider track and a new grille, plus a restyled rear deck and taillights, were the only changes of note.

For 1970, Rebel sedans and hardtops were lengthened two inches to accommodate redesigned roof panels and rear fenders, and new taillights appeared. Series stayed the same, but AMC again went after the performance crowd with "The Machine." A Rebel with a cause, this hardtop coupe packed the company's most-potent V-8, plus four-speed manual gearbox with Hurst linkage and a 3.54:1 rear axle. Providing easy exterior identification were a bold, functional hood air scoop, special red-white-and-blue paint, and 15-inch mag wheels with raised-white-letter tires. An 8000-rpm tachometer, dual exhausts with low-restriction mufflers, and a definite front-end rake completed this expensive package ($3475). The Machine certainly looked like a hot performer, but Javelin won the competition laurels. Mark Donohue, piloting a Javelin, came within one point of winning the Sports Car Club of America's 1970 Trans-Am road series. The 1970 racing chassis was fitted with Javelin's new 1971 sheet metal and won Trans-Am in '71 and '72.

AMC spent $40 million, a million man-hours and three years on its new 1970 Hornet compact, which revived a time-honored name not seen since the last Hudsons of 1957. It bowed as two- and four-door notchback sedans on a 108-inch wheelbase (two inches up on the predecessor American) with a choice of two sixes and base or SST trim. First-year sales were 92,458, a strong showing that helped AMC's sagging finances. Still, Kenosha lost money that year—$58.2 million on sales of over $1 billion.

April 1970 brought the clever Gremlin, America's first subcompact. With AMC's thriftiest six and base prices below $2000,

1969 Ambassador SST four-door sedan

1969 Rebel SST station wagon

1969 Rebel hardtop coupe

1969 Javelin SST fastback hardtop coupe

1969 Javelin SST fastback hardtop coupe

1969 AMX 2-passenger coupe

1970 AMX 2-passenger coupe

1970 Ambassador SST hardtop coupe

1970 Rebel SST hardtop coupe

1970 Rebel hardtop coupe

1970 Rebel SST hardtop coupe

1970 Rebel "The Machine" hardtop coupe

1970 Hornet SST two-door sedan

1970 Hornet two-door sedan

1970 Javelin SST fastback hardtop coupe

1970 Javelin SST hardtop coupe

1970 Javelin SST Mark Donohue Edition

1970 Gremlin hatchback coupe

1970 Gremlin hatchback coupe

1971 Matador station wagon

1971 Hornet SC/360 two-door sedan

1971 Javelin SST fastback hardtop coupe

1971 Hornet SC/360 two-door sedan

1971 Javelin AMX fastback hardtop coupe

this import-fighter initially sold well: over 26,000 for its abbreviated first model year. Gremlin related to Hornet as AMX did to Javelin. Sheetmetal was similar ahead of the B-posts, but Gremlin wheelbase was trimmed to 96 inches to match a severely truncated rear body with lift-up wagon-style rear window. Though this styling proved controversial, designer Teague insisted it was the only way to go. "Nobody would have paid it any attention if it had looked like one of the Big Three," he said.

With Hornet and Gremlin, AMC gave up trying to be a "full-line" automaker slugging toe-to-toe with the Big Three, returning to its original role as a "niche" marketer specializing in small cars. But the transition took a long time, and it wasn't until model-year '79 that AMC fully returned to the formula it had found so profitable in the late '50s and early '60s. In a way, it was strange that this tiny outfit would have ever tried to match the giants model-for-model, but president Roy Abernethy and even market-wise chairman Roy D. Chapin, Jr., were somehow persuaded to abandon the course pursued long before by George Romney.

An important development toward more specialized products was the February 1970 acquisition of Toledo-based Kaiser-Jeep Corporation, which instantly made AMC the nation's leading builder of four-wheel-drive vehicles. Though uncharted territory for AMC, Jeep's long experience in the field would prove

1971 Javelin AMX fastback hardtop coupe

1972 Ambassador Brougham station wagon

1972 Hornet SST two-door sedan

1971 Gremlin hatchback coupe

1972 Matador hardtop coupe

valuable, eventually finding its way into the passenger-car line.

Though it took nearly a decade to complete, AMC's market reorientation was evident as early as 1971. The jazzy Rebel Machine and slow-selling AMX were dropped, though the latter's name was applied to a new top-line Javelin. The ponycar was given heavy—and not altogether successful—sheetmetal surgery on an inch-longer wheelbase, with crisper lines highlighted by pronounced bulges over the front wheel openings in the manner of the contemporary Chevrolet Corvette. Inside was a reworked dash curved inward at the center, as in Pontiac's then-current Grand Prix, so as to bring minor controls closer to the driver.

Javelin stumbled along in this form through 1974, a vestige of the past. Annual production never broke 30,000 in this period, reflecting the general fast decline in ponycar demand after 1970. AMC decided against a direct replacement—reasonable, considering the only such cars still selling in decent numbers by then were the Chevrolet Camaro/Pontiac Firebird. Still, Javelin remained faithful to the cause. For example, the big 401-cid V-8 introduced for '71 was optionally available through

1972 Hornet Sportabout Gucci Edition sedan/wagon

1972 Javelin SST fastback hardtop coupe

the end, though with diminished power both on paper (with the 1971 industry switch to more realistic SAE net power ratings) and in fact (due to detuning for lower exhaust emissions).

Another AMC nameplate, Ambassador, disappeared after 1974. Continued with only minor trim and equipment changes in its final years, the firm's full-size was ultimately done in by lack of interest. Sales had never been great, and though its aging 1967 design was more sensible in some ways than that of concurrent Big Three rivals, the lack of change increasingly weighed against it. The crowning blow was probably the Middle East oil embargo of 1973-74, which triggered America's first energy crisis and temporarily crippled sales of most all full-size cars.

Another holdover fared only slightly better. This was the midsize Matador, a renamed, restyled Rebel appearing for 1971 as a continuation of that basic 1967 design. Offered in the same three body styles through 1973, it was pretty ordinary stuff and failed to generate much showroom traffic. In later years, AMC tacitly acknowledged the line's near on-road invisibility with a series of humorous television commercials that asked "What's a Matador?" Few buyers apparently cared.

An attempt to perk up Matador's staid image arrived for 1974, when the notchback hardtop coupe gave way to a completely different pillared fastback that AMC boldly announced would race in NASCAR. Designer Teague gave it smooth, curvaceous contours and an unusual front with the hood shaped to form the upper portions of huge headlamp nacelles. Despite special "designer" interiors (then a favored AMC marketing ploy) and sporty options like the X package, the fastback provided only temporary relief and Matador sales remained underwhelming. Like Ambassador, the midsize suffered in the aftermath of the first energy crisis. By 1978 it was quite passé, even the coupes, which had been progressively hoked up in the interim. After that, it was *adios*, Matador.

Gremlin was one "sow's ear" that Teague made into the proverbial silk purse. In fact, it was generally AMC's number-two seller in the '70s, after Hornet. Special trim options appeared almost yearly to help keep interest alive. Among the most popular was the X package, which typically delivered tape stripes, black grille, slotted wheels, wider tires, custom bucket-

1972 Javelin SST Pierre Cardin Edition

1972 Gremlin X hatchback coupe

1972 Gremlin X hatchback coupe

1973 Matador station wagon

1973 Matador four-door sedan

1973 Hornet Sportabout D/L sedan/wagon

1973 Ambassador Brougham station wagon

1973 Hornet hatchback coupe

1973 Gremlin X "Levi's" hatchback coupe

1974 Matador four-door sedan

1974 Hornet Sportabout D/L sedan/wagon

1973 Ambassador Brougham hardtop coupe

1973 Javelin SST fastback hardtop coupe

1974 Ambassador Brougham station wagon

1974 Matador X fastback coupe

1974 Hornet two-door sedan

seat interior, sports steering wheel, and similar dress-up items. Prices were reasonable, about $300 at first. The "LEVI's®" edition, new for '73, sported seats and door panels done up in blue spun nylon with copper rivets to look just like the cotton denim of Levi Strauss & Company, which happily collaborated on the package, even allowing use of its distinctive red jeans label. This was probably the most winsome Gremlin, and it may well be the most collectible.

Gremlin vanished after 1978 but lived on in Spirit—the same thing with smoother, more-conventional styling. Joining the familiar chopped-tail two-door was a slick new hatchback coupe with a particularly graceful superstructure for such a short car. Both body styles offered three trim levels, and the AMX tag was revived for a special "paint-on performance" coupe in 1980. Spirits moved via a standard 2.5-liter (151-cid) four purchased from Pontiac or, at extra cost, the long-lived AMC six. A heavy emphasis on quality made Spirits generally better-built than Gremlins, if not Big Three rivals. But there was no escaping the aged '60s-style design, and while the four was fairly thrifty, it had very little power; the six was quicker but thirstier.

In a similar transformation, the compact Hornet became the Concord for 1978. Reflecting AMC's limited new-model development funds, it wasn't all that different structurally or mechanically, but it looked more "important" and, like its linemates, benefited from an urgent stress on workmanship prompted by the growing success of Japanese imports. Concord was AMC's volume seller from the time it appeared. By 1980 it boasted a thriftier standard engine, cleaner looks, more comfort and convenience extras, and a broader antirust warranty.

Not to be overlooked are three early-'70s Hornet developments. One was the SC/360, a performance-oriented two-door offered only for 1971. As the name suggested, it packed AMC's 360-cid small-block V-8, rated at 245 bhp with standard two-barrel carb or 285 bhp with extra-cost four-pot induction. Acceleration was quite vivid, and a large functional hood

1974 Javelin fastback hardtop coupe

1974 Javelin AMX fastback hardtop coupe

1974 Javelin fastback hardtop coupe

1974 Gremlin X "Levi's" hatchback coupe

1975 Matador fastback coupe

1975 Hornet D/L four-door sedan

1975 Hornet hatchback coupe

1975 Hornet Sportabout sedan/wagon

scoop, heavy-duty suspension, styled wheels, fat tires, tape stripes, and Hurst four-speed were either standard or available. But as had so often been the case, AMC was a day late and a dollar short: only 784 were built, making the SC/360 one of the '70s rarest production Detroiters and thus something of a collector's item.

A more sensible and successful innovation was the Hornet Sportabout, a graceful four-door wagon with a one-piece tailgate. Another '71 newcomer, it would prove uncommonly long-lived. Even lovelier was the new-for-'73 Hornet hatchback coupe. Offering vast load space, it could be quite sporty with an optional X package. Needless styling gimmicks made some versions quite tacky by the time the Concord came in, and the hatchback was discontinued after '79. There was also a special AMX model with this bodyshell, a limited 1977-78 offering.

Concord spawned a novel offshoot for 1980, the four-wheel-drive Eagle, reviving a name that AMC owned via the Jeep takeover and, with it, the dregs of Willys-Overland. A natural for a firm with AMC's particular, but limited, resources, Eagle was essentially the Concord platform equipped with a new full-time 4WD system called Quadra-Trac, whose transfer case apportioned driving torque between front and rear wheels via a

1975 Pacer D/L hatchback coupe

1975 Gremlin hatchback coupe

1976 Matador Brougham fastback coupe

1976 Matador Brougham fastback coupe

1976 Hornet Sportabout sedan/wagon

1976 Hornet D/L four-door sedan

1976 Gremlin hatchback coupe

1976 Gremlin X hatchback coupe

1977 Matador four-door sedan

1977 Matador fastback coupe

1977 Hornet hatchback coupe

1977 Hornet D/L two-door sedan

1977 Hornet D/L four-door sedan

1977 Hornet AMX hatchback coupe

center differential with clutches running in a slip-limiting silicone compound.

Eagle arrived with Concord's three body styles and a nominal 1.3-inch-longer wheelbase. Its ride height was greater too, thanks to larger tires and the required extra ground clearance for the differentials. The drivetrain comprised the firm's well-known 258-cid six (a stroked 232, first offered for 1971) mated to three-speed Torque Command automatic transmission (actually Chrysler TorqueFlite). Power steering and brakes and all-season radial tires were standard. Eagles flew with prominent (and necessary) wheel-arch flares made of color-keyed Krayton plastic, and a Sport-package option offered black extensions and other trim, plus Goodyear Tiempo tires.

Predictably, the Eagle drove and felt much like any Concord. AMC didn't intend it for off-road use, stressing the safety advantages of 4WD traction for everyday driving, particularly in the snowbelt. A full range of luxury and convenience features was offered, but there was no V-8 option for the sake of fuel economy—and the government's corporate average fuel-economy (CAFE) mandates. The Spirit/Concord Pontiac-built four became available for '81.

AMC's biggest '70s disappointment was the Pacer, announced for 1975 as "the first wide small car." It was planned for a lightweight Wankel rotary engine that GM was developing in the early '70s but quickly shelved. Designer Teague penned distinctive lines with acres of glass, a short nose, and a hatchback body that looked nearly as wide as it was long.

Unhappily, cancellation of the GM Wankel forced AMC into patchwork engineering alterations that seriously compromised the original concept. While the rotary would have provided decent performance and fuel economy, AMC had to use its relatively big and weighty six, to the detriment of both as well as handling. With that and all its heavy glass, Pacer ended up quite portly for a subcompact, and its styling seemed frankly odd to

1977 Pacer D/L two-door station wagon

1977 Pacer X hatchback coupe

1977 Pacer D/L two-door station wagon

1977 Gremlin X hatchback coupe

1978 Matador station wagon

1978 Matador Barcelona four-door sedan

1978 Matador Barcelona fastback coupe

1978 Concord D/L two-door sedan

1978 AMX fastback coupe

1978 Concord D/L sedan/wagon

1978 Concord D/L sedan/wagon

1978 Concord D/L two-door sedan

1978 Pacer D/L wagon

1978 Pacer D/L hatchback coupe

1978 Gremlin hatchback coupe

1978 Gremlin hatchback coupe

many eyes (though doors wrapped into the roof were predictive of '80s design). By 1979, annual sales were down to only 10,000 or so despite the interim addition of wagons and an optional V-8, and Pacer was unceremoniously dumped after 1980.

An aging product line that didn't generate sufficient sales for funding more-modern replacements proved an increasingly vicious cycle for AMC as the '70s wore on. Eagle, for instance, owed much to Concord, which dated from the then decade-old Hornet. At decade's end, mounting losses were aggravated by a deep national recession that cut sales further, and AMC soon found itself the object of a takeover bid by Renault of France, which acquired a controlling interest by 1982.

Thus was born what some were quick to call "Franco-American Motors." Renault executives came in to run things alongside AMC officials, and the old Nash factory in Kenosha was retooled at great expense to produce an Americanized version of the European Renault 9 subcompact, which was aptly renamed Alliance.

Trouble was, acquiring AMC made Renault no wiser about the American market, and it had little more impact as a back-door "domestic" than it had as an independent import. Odd Renault products like the tinny-tiny Le Car and lumpy Fuego coupe

1978 Gremlin GT hatchback coupe

1979 Concord DL hatchback coupe

1979 Pacer DL two-door station wagon

1979 Spirit Liftback coupe

1979 Concord Limited two-door sedan

1979 Pacer DL two-door station wagon

1979 Spirit Limited hatchback coupe

1979 AMX hatchback coupe

didn't help AMC dealers very much. The Alliance did, but not for long. As a car, it was no more than adequate, and not really up to the huge task of improving Renault's second-rate image among U.S. buyers.

Still, Alliance seemed just what the doctor ordered: modern two- and four-door front-drive sedans with a 97.8-inch wheelbase and a thrifty, transverse 85-cid four-cylinder engine. And for a time it sold well: over 142,000 of the debut 1983 models. Bolstered by two- and four-door hatchback derivatives called Encore, sales zoomed to over 208,000 the following year.

But mechanical problems and indifferent workmanship were as evident here as on French-built Renaults. Once word got around,

1980 Concord DL two-door sedan

1980 Concord DL four-door sedan

1980 Concord Limited sedan/wagon

1980 AMX hatchback coupe

1980 Pacer DL two-door station wagon

1980 Pacer DL hatchback coupe

1981 Eagle Limited two-door sedan

1981 Eagle sedan/wagon

1981 Eagle SX/4 Sport hatchback coupe

1982 Spirit GT Liftback coupe

1985 Renault Encore GS hatchback coupe

1985 Renault Alliance DL two-door sedan

1986 Renault Alliance DL convertible coupe

1986 Renault Alliance DL four-door sedan

1986 Renault Encore S hatchback sedan

1986 Renault Encore Electronic hatchback coupe

sales tumbled: to 150,000 for '85, then to 65,000 and finally to only some 35,000. AMC tried to stop the slide for '85 with an optional 105-cid/78-bhp engine and a brace of new Alliance convertibles—Kenosha's first droptops since '68—but to no avail.

By 1987, with AMC's continued losses and several years of withering home-market sales, Renault was in financial trouble and ready to pull out. Fortunately, Lee Iacocca, the miracle worker who'd lately turned Chrysler Corporation from penniless to prosperous, was willing to take over, mainly to get his hands on AMC's lucrative Jeep business. Thus did America's last sizable independent automaker pass into history, transformed almost overnight into a new Chrysler division called Jeep-Eagle.

AMC's own products departed much earlier, dropped after 1983 in the rush to Renaults. The sole exceptions were the Eagle wagon and four-door sedan, which hung on until the Chrysler takeover, then disappeared with Alliance.

Before the end, AMC slipped the Eagle's full-time 4WD under the Spirit coupe and ex-Gremlin two-door bodies to create a pair of "Eaglets." The most interesting of these was the SX/4 Sport, Teague's pretty little fastback bedecked with foglights, distinctive striping, rear spoiler, and plush bucket-seat interior. Though pleasant and distinctive, it was no sprinter, and buyers continued to prefer "real" 4WDs—like Jeep CJs and Wagoneers—to these passenger-car pretenders.

Still, low production, a drivetrain unique among American cars, and status as AMC's last attempt at something different makes the short-lived junior Eagles a minor collector's item. Only about 37,500 Eagles of all kinds were sold for 1981 and less than half that number for '82 and '83; exact breakdowns aren't available, but the smaller ones probably accounted for no more than a third of each year's total. After 1983, the big Eagles carried on alone, virtually unchanged and garnering some 6000-7000 annual sales—too paltry for industry statisticians to even bother with.

For 1988, Chrysler began to re-establish Eagle as an "upscale" brand aimed at would-be import buyers—but with only inherited front-drive Renault's: the competent but dull midsize Premier (built in Canada) and the compact Medallion (imported from France). The latter didn't last past 1989, but the former carried on with minor success through 1991 (and as the 1990-91 Dodge Monaco). Medallion gave way to rebadged designs by Mitsubishi of Japan, but Premier's successor would be an all-American Eagle, the exciting 1993 Vision, one of Chrysler's breakthrough "LH" sedans with "cab-forward" styling (see *Eagle*).

Chrysler's Eagle was no more successful as a niche make than AMC was in its later years and was dropped after 1998—proof that in the auto business at least, history can and often *does* repeat itself.

Specifications

(also see Rambler) **Note:** Some prod. figures approx.

1966

Marlin (wb 112.0)	Wght	Price	Prod
6659-7 fstbk cpe	3,050	2,601	4,547
Ambassador 880 (wb 116.0)			
6685-2 sdn 4d	3,006	2,455	13,974
6686-2 sdn 2d	2,970	2,404	1,493
6688-2 wgn 4d	3,160	2,759	4,791
Ambassador 990 (wb 116.0)			
6685-5 sdn 4d	3,034	2,574	25,986
6687-5 conv cpe	3,462	2,968	1,814
6688-5 wgn 4d	3,180	2,880	8,852
6689-5 htp cpe	3,056	2,600	4,324
Ambassador DPL (wb 116.0)			
6689-7 htp cpe	3,090	2,756	10,458

1966 Engines	bore × stroke	bhp	availability
I-6, 232	3.75 × 3.50	145	S-Marlin
I-6, 232	2.75 × 3.50	155	S-Ambassador
V-8, 287	3.75 × 3.25	198	O-all
V-8, 327	4.00 × 3.25	250/270	O-all

1967

Marlin (wb 118.0)	Wght	Price	Prod
6759-7 fstbk cpe	3,342	2,963	2,545
Ambassador 880 (wb 118.0)			
6785-2 sdn 4d	3,279	2,657	9,772
6786-2 cpe	3,310	2,519	3,623
6788-2 wgn 4d	3,486	2,962	3,540
Ambassador 990 (wb 118.0)			
6785-5 sdn 4d	3,324	2,776	18,033
6788-5 wgn 4d	3,545	3,083	7,919
6789-5 htp cpe	3,376	2,803	6,140
Ambassador DPL (wb 118.0)			
6787-7 conv cpe	3,434	3,143	1,260
6789-7 htp cpe	3,394	2,958	12,552

1967 Engines	bore × stroke	bhp	availability
I-6, 232	3.75 × 3.50	145	S-Marlin
I-6, 232	3.75 × 3.50	155	S-Amb; O-Marl
V-8, 290	3.75 × 3.28	200	S-Amb conv; O-others
V-8, 343	4.08 × 3.28	235	O-all
V-8, 343	4.08 × 3.28	280	O-all

1968

Rebel 550 (wb 114.0)	Wght	Price	Prod
6815 sdn 4d	3,062	2,443	11,329
6817 conv 2d	3,195	2,736	377
6818 wgn 4d	3,301	2,729	7,228
6819 htp cpe	3,117	2,454	7,385
Rebel 770 (wb 114.0)			
6815-5 sdn 4d	3,074	2,542	19,640
6818-5 wgn 4d	3,306	2,854	11,169
6819-5 htp cpe	3,116	2,556	4,428
Rebel SST (wb 114.0)			
6817-7 conv cpe	3,427	2,999	823
6819-7 htp cpe	3,348	2,775	11,516
AMX (wb 97.0)			
6839-7 fstbk cpe 2S	3,097	3,245	6,725
Javelin (wb 109.0) - 56, 462 built			
6879-5 fstbk cpe	2,826	2,482	29,097
6879-7 SST fstbk cpe	2,836	2,587	27,347
Ambassador (wb 118.0)			
6885-2 sdn 4d	3,193	2,820	6,272
6889-2 htp cpe	3,258	2,892	3,360
Ambassador DPL (wb 118.0)			
6885-5 sdn 4d	3,265	2,920	9,362
6888-5 wgn 4d	3,475	3,207	10,698
6889-5 htp cpe	3,321	2,947	3,696
Ambassador SST (wb 118.0)			
6885-7 sdn 4d	3,496	3,151	13,387
6889-7 htp cpe	3,530	3,172	7,876

1968 Engines	bore × stroke	bhp	availability
I-6, 232	3.75 × 3.50	145	S-Jav, Reb exc SST
I-6, 232	3.75 × 3.50	155	S-Amb exc SST
V-8, 290	3.75 × 3.28	200	S-Rebel SST, Amb SST; O-all
V-8, 290	3.75 × 3.28	225	S-AMX; O-Jav
V-8, 343	4.08 × 3.28	235	O-Rebel, Amb
V-8, 343	4.08 × 3.28	280	O-AMX Jav, Reb, Amb
V-8, 390	4.17 × 3.57	315	O-All

1969

Rebel (wb 114.0)	Wght	Price	Prod
6915 sdn 4d	3,062	2,484	10,885
6918 wgn 4d	3,301	2,817	8,569
6919 htp cpe	3,117	2,496	5,396
Rebel SST (wb 114.0)			
6915-7 sdn 4d	3,074	2,584	20,595
6918-7 wgn 4d	3,306	2,947	9,256
6919-7 htp cpe	3,140	2,598	5,405
AMX (wb 97.0)			
6939-7 fstbk cpe 2S	3,097	3,297	8,293
Javelin (wb 109.0)			
6979-5 fstbk cpe	2,826	2,512	17,389
6979-7 SST fstbk cpe	2,836	2,633	23,286
Ambassador (wb 122.0)			
6985-2 sdn 4d	3,276	2,914	14,617
Ambassador DPL (WB 122.0)			
6985-5 sdn 4d	3,358	3,165	12,665
6988-5 wgn 4d	3,561	3,504	8,866
6989-5 htp cpe	3,403	3,182	4,504
Ambassador SST (wb 122.0)			
6985-7 sdn 4d	3,508	3,605	18,719
6988-7 wgn 4d	3,732	3,998	7,825
6989-7 htp cpe	3,566	3,622	8,998

1969 Engines	bore × stroke	bhp	availability
I-6, 232	3.75 × 3.50	145	S-Jav, Rebel
I-6, 232	3.75 × 3.50	155	S-Amb, Amb DPL; O-Rebel
V-8, 290	3.75 × 3.28	200	S-Amb SST; O-Ambassador, Rebel, Javelin
V-8, 290	3.75 × 3.28	225	S-AMX; O-Jav
V-8, 343	4.08 × 3.28	235	O-Rebel, Amb
V-8, 343	4.08 × 3.28	280	O-AMX, Javelin, Rebel, Ambassador
V-8, 390	4.17 × 3.57	315	O-AMX, Javelin SST, Amb SST

1970*

Hornet (wb 108.0)	Wght	Price	Prod
7005-0 sdn 4d	2,748	2,072	—
7006-0 sdn 2d	2,677	1,994	—
Hornet SST (wb 108.0)			
7005-7 sdn 4d	2,765	2,221	—
7006-7 sdn 2d	2,705	2,144	—
Rebel (wb 114.0)			
7015-0 sdn 4d	3,129	2,636	—
7018-0 wgn 4d	3,356	2,766	—
7019-0 htp cpe	3,148	2,660	—
Rebel SST (wb 114.0)			
7015-7 sdn 4d	3,155	2,684	—
7018-0 wgn 4d	3,375	3,072	—
7019-7 htp cpe	3,206	2,718	—
Rebel Machine (wb 114.0)			
7019-0 htp cpe	3,650	3,475	2,326
AMX (wb 97.0) - 4,116 built			
7039-7 fstbk cpe 2S	3,126	3,395	—

Gremlin (wb 96.0)	Wght	Price	Prod
7046-0 sdn 2d	2,497	1,879	—
7046-5 sdn 2d	2,557	1,959	—
Javelin (wb 109.0) - 28,210 built			
7079-5 fstbk cpe	2,845	2,720	—
7079-7 SST fstbk cpe	2,863	2,848	—
7079-7 SST/Trans-Am fstbk cpe	3,340	3,995	—
Ambassador (wb 122.0)			
7085-2 sdn 4d	3,328	3,020	—
Ambassador DPL (wb 122.0)			
7085-5 sdn 4d	3,523	3,588	—
7088-5 wgn 4d	3,817	3,946	—
7089-5 htp cpe	3,555	3,605	—
Ambassador SST (wb 122.0)			
7085-7 sdn 4d	3,557	3,722	—
7088-5 wgn 4d	3,852	4,122	—
7089-5 htp cpe	3,606	3,739	—

* Total 1970 calendar year: 276,110

1970 Engines	bore × stroke	bhp	availability
I-6, 199	3.75 × 3.00	128	S-Hornet, Grem
I-6, 232	3.75 × 3.50	145	S-Hornet SST, Rebel, Jav; O-Horn,Grem
I-6, 232	3.75 × 3.50	155	S-Amb; O-Horn,Reb
V-8, 304	3.75 × 3.44	210	S-DPL, SST; O-all exc AMX
V-8, 360	4.08 × 3.44	245	O-Reb, Amb, Jav
V-8, 360	4.08 × 3.44	290	S-AMX;O-Reb;Amb
V-8, 390	4.17 × 3.57	325	O-AMX, Jav, Reb SST, Amb SST
V-8, 390	4.17 × 3.57	340	S-Reb Machine; O-all

1971

Gremlin (wb 96.0)	Wght	Price	Prod*
7146-0 sdn 2d 2P	2,503	1,899	53,480
7146-5 sdn 2d 4P	2,552	1,999	
Hornet (wb 108.0)			
7105-0 sdn 4d I-6	2,731	2,234	23,500**
7106-0 sdn 2d V-8	2,654	2,174	
7105-7 SST sdn 4d I-6	2,732	2,334	
7106-7 SST sdn 2d V-8	2,691	2,274	49,500***
7108-7 Sportabout wgn 4d	2,827	2,594	
7106-1 SC/360 sdn 2d	3,057	2,663	784
Javelin (wb 110.0)			
7179-5 htp cpe I-6	2,887	2,879	3,500
7179-7 SST htp cpe I-6	2,890	2,999	1,000
7179-5 htp cpe V-8	3,144	2,980	4,000
7179-7 SST htp cpe V-8	3,147	3,100	17,000
7979-8 AMX htp cpe V-8	3,244	3,432	2,054
Matador (wb 118.0) - 45,789 built (approx. 30,000 I-6)			
7155-7 sdn 4d I-6	3,165	2,770	—
7119-7 htp cpe I-6	3,201	2,799	—
7118-7 wgn 4d I-6	3,437	3,163	6,800
7115-7 sdn 4d V-8	3,324	3,100	—
7119-7 htp cpe V-8	3,360	3,129	—
7118-7 wgn 4d V-8	3,596	3,493	4,200
Ambassador (wb 122.0)			
7185-2 DPL sdn 4d I-6	3,315	3,616	650
7185-2 DPL sdn 4d V-8	3,488	3,717	6,000
7185-5 SST sdn 4d V-8	3,520	3,852	7,500
7189-5 SST htp cpe V-8	3,561	3,870	
7188-5 SST wgn 4d V-8	3,815	4,253	8,000
7185-7 Brghm sdn 4d V-8	3,541	3,983	10,000
7189-7 Brghm htp cpe V-8	3,580	3,999	
7188-7 Brghm wgn 4d V-8	3,862	4,430	10,000

*Estimates **Includes 500 V-8s ***Includes 9,500 V-8s

1971 Engines	bore × stroke	bhp	availability
I-6, 232.0	3.75 × 3.50	135	S-Grem, Hrnt, Jav, Mat
I-6, 258.0	3.75 × 3.90	150	S-Amb; O-Grem, Hrnt, Jav, Mat
V-8, 304.0	3.75 × 3.44	210	S-Jav, Mat, Amb; O-Hrnt
V-8, 360.0	4.08 × 3.44	245	S-Hrnt SC; O-Jav, Mat, Amb
V-8, 360.0	4.08 × 3.44	285	O-Hrnt SC, Jav, Mat, Amb
V-8, 401.0	4.17 × 3.68	330	O-Amb

1972

Gremlin (wb 96.0) - 61,717 blt		Wght	Price	Prod*
46-5	sdn 2d I-6	2,494	1,999	53,000
46-5	sdn 2d V-8	2,746	2,153	8,500
Hornet SST (wb 108.0) - 71,056 blt				
05-7	sdn 4d I-6	2,691	2,265	35,000
06-7	sdn 2d I-6	2,627	2,199	
08-7	Sprtabt wgn 4d I-6	2,769	2,587	30,000
05-7	sdn 4d V-8	2,925	2,403	2,000
06-7	sdn 2d V-8	2,861	2,337	
08-7	Sprtabt wgn 4d V-8	2,998	2,725	5,000
Javelin (wb 110.0)				
79-7	SST htp cpe I-6	2,876	2,807	23,455
79-7	SST htp cpe V-8	3,118	2,901	
79-8	AMX htp cpe V-8	3,149	3,109	2,729
Matador (wb 118.0) - 54,813 built				
15-7	sdn 4d I-6	3,171	2,784	11,000
19-7	htp cpe I-6	3,210	2,818	
18-7	wgn 4d I-6	3,480	3,140	3,000
15-7	sdn 4d V-8	3,355	2,883	34,000
19-7	htp cpe V-8	3,394	2,917	
18-7	wgn 4d V-8	3,653	3,239	7,500
Ambassador (wb 122.0) - 44,364 built				
85-5	SST sdn 4d	3,537	3,885	18,000
89-5	SST htp cpe	3,579	3,902	
88-5	SST wgn 4d	3,833	4,270	5,500
85-7	Brougham sdn 4d	3,551	4,002	15,000
89-5	Brougham htp cpe	3,581	4,018	
88-5	Brougham wgn 4d	3,857	4,437	5,500

*Estimates

1972 Engines	bore × stroke	bhp	availability
I-6, 232.0	3.75 × 3.50	100	S-Grem, Hrnt, Jav, Mat exc wgn
I-6, 258.0	3.75 × 3.90	110	S-Mat wgn, Grem, Hrnt; O-Jav, Mat
V-8, 304.0	3.75 × 3.44	150	S-all base V-8s
V-8, 360.0	4.08 × 3.44	175	O-all exc Grem
V-8, 360.0	4.08 × 3.44	195	O-Jav, Mat, Amb
V-8, 401.0	4.17 × 3.68	255	O-Jav, Mat, Amb

1973

Gremlin (wb 96.0)		Wght	Price	Prod
46-5	sdn 2d I-6	2,642	2,098	—
46-5	sdn 2d V-8	2,867	2,252	—
Hornet (wb 108.0)				
05-7	sdn 4d I-6	2,854	2,343	—
06-7	sdn 2d I-6	2,777	2,298	—
03-7	htchbk cpe I-6	2,818	2,449	—
08-7	Sprtabt wgn 4d I-6	2,921	2,675	—
05-7	sdn 4d V-8	3,067	2,481	—
06-7	sdn 2d V-8	2,990	2,436	—
03-7	htchbk cpe V-8	3,031	2,587	—
08-7	Sprtabt wgn 4d V-8	3,134	2,813	—
Javelin (wb 110.0)				
79-7	htp cpe I-6	2,868	2,889	22,556
79-7	htp cpe V-8	3,104	2,983	
79-8	AMX htp cpe V-8	3,170	3,191	4,980
Matador (wb 118.0)				
15-7	sdn 4d I-6	3,289	2,853	—
19-7	htp cpe I-6	3,314	2,887	—
18-7	wgn 4d I-6	3,627	3,179	—
15-7	sdn 4d V-8	3,502	2,952	—
19-7	htp cpe V-8	3,527	2,986	—
18-7	wgn 4d V-8	3,815	3,278	—
Ambassador Brougham (wb 122.0)				
85-7	sdn 4d	3,763	4,461	—
89-7	htp cpe	3,774	4,477	—
88-7	wgn 4d	4,054	4,861	—

1973 Engines	bore × stroke	bhp	availability
I-6, 232.0	3.75 × 3.50	100	S-Grem, Hrnt, Jav, Mat exc wgn
I-6, 258.0	3.75 × 3.90	110	S-Mat wgn; O-Grem, Hrnt, Jav, Mat
V-8, 304.0	3.75 × 3.44	150	S-all base V-8s
V-8, 360.0	4.08 × 3.44	175	O-all exc Grem
V-8, 360.0	4.08 × 3.44	195	O-Jav, Mat, Amb
V-8, 360.0	4.08 × 3.44	220	O-Jav, Mat, Amb
V-8, 401.0	4.17 × 3.68	255	O-Jav, Mat, Amb

1974

Gremlin (wb 96.0)		Wght	Price	Prod
46-5	sdn 2d I-6	2,649	2,481	119,642
46-5	sdn 2d V-8	2,888	2,635	12,263
Hornet (wb 108.0)				
05-7	sdn 4d I-6	2,833	2,824	
06-7	sdn 2d I-6	2,767	2,774	70,052
03-7	htchbk cpe I-6	2,791	2,849	
08-7	Sprtabt wgn 4d I-6	2,900	3,049	57,414
05-7	sdn 4d V-8	3,077	2,962	
06-7	sdn 2d V-8	3,011	2,912	7,697
03-7	htchbk cpe V-8	3,035	2,987	
08-7	Sprtabt wgn 4d V-8	3,144	3,187	10,295
Javelin (wb 110.0)				
79-7	htp cpe I-6	2,869	2,999	5,036
79-7	htp cpe V-8	3,116	3,093	19,520
79-8	AMX htp cpe V-8	3,184	3,299	4,980
Matador (wb 118.0; cpe 114.0) - 99,922 built				
15-7	sdn 4d I-6	3,425	3,052	25,826
16-7	cpe I-6	3,437	3,096	
18-7	wgn 4d I-6	3,739	3,378	2,975
15-7	sdn 4d V-8	3,632	3,151	35,000
16-7	cpe V-8	3,634	3,195	
18-7	wgn 4d V-8	3,925	3,477	6,734
16-9	Brougham cpe I-6	3,456	3,249	28,000
16-9	Brougham cpe V-8	3,663	3,348	
16-8	X htp cpe V-8	3,672	3,699	1,500
Ambassador Brougham (wb 122.0)				
85-7	sdn 4d	3,851	4,559	17,901
88-7	wgn 4d	4,125	4,960	7,070

1974 Engines	bore × stroke	bhp	availability
I-6, 232.0	3.75 × 3.50	100	S-Grem, Hrnt, Jav, Mat wgn
I-6, 258.0	3.75 × 3.90	110	S-Mat wgn; O-Grem, Hrnt, Javelin, Matador
V-8, 304.0	3.75 × 3.44	150	S-all base V-8s
V-8, 360.0	4.08 × 3.44	175	O-all exc Grem
V-8, 360.0	4.08 × 3.44	195	O-Jav, Mat, Amb
V-8, 401.0	4.17 × 3.68	235	O-Jav, Mat, Amb

1975

Gremlin (wb 96.0)		Wght	Price	Prod
46-5	sdn 2d I-6	2,694	2,798	42,630
46-5	sdn 2d V-8	2,952	2,952	3,218
Hornet (wb 108.0)				
05-7	sdn 4d I-6	2,881	3,124	
06-7	sdn 2d I-6	2,815	3,074	36,305
03-7	htchbk cpe I-6	2,839	3,174	
08-7	Sprtabt wgn 4d I-6	2,948	3,374	3,016
05-7	sdn 4d V-8	3,127	3,262	
06-7	sdn 2d V-8	3,061	3,212	20,369
03-7	htchbk cpe V-8	3,085	3,312	
08-7	Sprtabt wgn 4d V-8	3,194	3,512	4,223
Pacer (wb 100.0)				
66-7	htchbk sdn 2d	2,995	3,299	72,158
Matador (wb 118.0; cpe 114.0)				
85-7	sdn 4d I-6	3,586	3,452	9,390
16-7	cpe I-6	3,562	3,446	
88-7	wgn 4d I-6	3,878	3,844	1,575
85-7	sdn 4d V-8	3,746	3,551	40,500
16-7	cpe V-8	3,734	3,545	
88-7	wgn 4d V-8	4,038	3,943	8,117

1975 Engines	bore × stroke	bhp	availability
I-6, 232.0	3.75 × 3.50	100	S-Grem, Hrnt, Pcr
I-6, 258.0	3.75 × 3.90	110	S-Mat; O-Grem, Hornet, Pacer
V-8, 304.0	3.75 × 3.44	150	S-Grem, Hrnt, Matador
V-8, 360.0	4.08 × 3.44	175	O-Matador

1976

Gremlin (wb 96.0)		Wght	Price	Prod
46-3	sdn 2d I-6	2,771	2,889	52,115
46-5	Cus sdn 2d I-6	2,774	2,998	
46-3	sdn 2d V-8	3,020	3,051	826
46-5	Cus sdn 2d V-8	3,023	3,160	
Pacer (wb 100.0)				
66-7	htchbk sdn 2d	3,114	3,499	117,244

Hornet (wb 108.0)		Wght	Price	Prod
05-7	sdn 4d I-6	2,971	3,199	
06-7	sdn 2d I-6	2,909	3,199	41,025
03-7	htchbk cpe I-6	2,920	3,199	
08-7	Sprtabt wgn 4d I-6	3,040	3,549	26,787
05-7	sdn 4d V-8	3,220	3,344	
06-7	sdn 2d V-8	3,158	3,344	789
03-7	htchbk cpe V-8	3,169	3,344	
08-7	Sprtabt wgn 4d V-8	3,289	3,694	2,976

Matador (wb 118.0; cpe 114.0)		Wght	Price	Prod
85-7	sdn 4d I-6	3,589	3,627	4,993
16-7	cpe I-6	3,562	3,621	
85-7	sdn 4d V-8	3,838	3,731	25,471
16-7	cpe V-8	3,811	3,725	
88-7	wgn 4d V-8	4,015	4,373	11,049

1976 Engines	bore × stroke	bhp	availability
I-6, 232.0	3.75 × 3.50	90	S-all exc Mat
I-6, 258.0	3.75 × 3.90	95	S-Matador; O-others
I-6, 258.0	3.75 × 3.90	120	O-Pacer
V-8, 304.0	3.75 × 3.44	120	S-all exc Pacer
V-8, 360.0	4.08 × 3.44	140/180	O-Matador sedan/wagon

1977

Gremlin (wb 96.0)		Wght	Price	Prod
46-4	sdn 2d I-4	2,654	3,248	7,558
46-5	sdn 2d I-6	2,811	2,995	8,613
36-7	Custom sdn 2d I-6	2,824	3,248	

Pacer (wb 100.0)		Wght	Price	Prod
66-7	htchbk sdn 2d	3,156	3,649	20,265
68-7	wgn 2d	3,202	3,799	37,999

Hornet (wb 108.0)		Wght	Price	Prod
05-7	sdn 4d I-6	3,035	2,449	
06-7	sdn 2d I-6	2,971	3,399	73,752
03-7	htchbk cpe I-6	3,012	3,419	
08-7	wgn 4d I-6	3,100	3,699	
05-7	sdn 4d V-8	3,268	3,613	
06-7	sdn 2d V-8	3,204	3,563	4,091
03-7	htchbk cpe V-8	3,245	3,662	
08-7	wgn 4d V-8	3,333	3,863	

Matador (wb. 118.0; cpe 114.0)		Wght	Price	Prod
85-7	sdn 4d I-6	3,713	4,549	2,447
16-7	cpe I-6	3,704	4,499	
85-7	sdn 4d V-8	3,876	4,669	17,322
16-7	cpe V-8	3,872	4,619	
88-7	wgn 4d V-8	4,104	4,899	11,078

1977 Engines	bore × stroke	bhp	availability
I-4, 121.0	3.41 × 3.32	80	S-Gremlin
I-6, 232.0	3.75 × 3.50	88	S-all exc Mat
I-6, 258.0	3.75 × 3.90	98	S-Matador
I-6, 258.0	3.75 × 3.90	114	O-all exc Mat
V-8, 304.0	3.75 × 3.44	121	S-Hornet
V-8, 304.0	3.75 × 3.44	126	S-Matador
V-8, 360.0	4.08 × 3.44	129	O-Matador

1978

Gremlin (wb 96.0)		Wght	Price	Prod
46-4	sdn 2d I-4	2,656	3,789	6,349
46-5	sdn 2d I-6	2,834	3,539	15,755
46-7	Custom sdn 2d I-6	2,822	3,789	

Concord (wb 108.0)		Wght	Price	Prod
05-7	sdn 4d I-6	3,099	3,849	
06-7	sdn 2d I-6	3,029	3,749	110,972
03-7	htchbk cpe I-6	3,051	3,849	
08-7	wgn 4d I-6	3,133	4,049	
05-7	sdn 4d V-8	3,332	4,099	
06-7	sdn 2d V-8	3,262	3,999	6,541
03-7	htchbk cpe V-8	3,284	4,099	
08-7	wgn 4d V-8	3,366	4,299	

Note: A total of 3,780 4-cyl Concords were produced.

Pacer (wb 100.0)		Wght	Price	Prod
66-7	htchbk sdn 2d I-6	3,197	4,048	18,717
68-7	wgn 2d I-6	3,245	4,193	
66-7	htchbk sdn 2d V-8	3,430	4,298	2,514
68-7	wgn 2d V-8	3,478	4,443	

AMX (wb 108.0)		Wght	Price	Prod
03-9	htchbk cpe I-6	3,159	4,649	2,540
03-9	htchbk cpe V-8	3,381	4,899	

Matador (wb 118.0; cpe 114.0)		Wght	Price	Prod
85-7	sdn 4d I-6	3,718	4,849	23
16-7	cpe I-6	3,709	4,799	
85-7	sdn 4d V-8	3,921	5,039	6,807
16-7	cpe V-8	3,916	4,989	
88-7	wgn 4d V-8	4,146	5,299	3,746

1978 Engines	bore × stroke	bhp	availability
I-4, 121.0	3.41 × 3.32	80	S-Grem, Con
I-6, 232.0	3.75 × 3.50	90	S-all exc Mat, AMX
I-6, 258.0	3.75 × 3.90	120	S-Mat, AMX; O-others
V-8, 304.0	3.75 × 3.44	130	S-Con, Pcr, AMX
V-8, 360.0	4.08 × 3.44	140	S-Mat wgn; O-Mat

1979

Spirit (wb 96.0)		Wght	Price	Prod
43-7	htchbk cpe I-4	2,545	3,953	
46-7	sdn 2d I-4	2,489	3,853	
43-7	DL htchbk cpe I-4	2,635	4,190	16,237
46-7	DL sdn 2d I-4	2,579	4,090	
43-7	Lmtd htchbk cpe I-4	2,732	5,190	
46-7	Limited sdn 2d I-4	2,676	5,090	
43-7	htchbk cpe I-6	2,762	4,133	
46-7	sdn 2d I-6	2,706	4,033	
43-7	DL htchbk cpe I-6	2,852	4,370	36,241
46-7	DL sdn 2d I-6	2,798	4,270	
43-7	Lmtd htchbk cpe I-6	2,949	5,370	
46-7	Limited sdn 2d I-6	2,893	5,270	

Concord (wb 108.0)		Wght	Price	Prod
05-7	sdn 4d I-6	2,939	4,489	
06-7	sdn 2d I-6	2,873	4,389	
03-7	htchbk cpe I-6	2,888	4,324	
08-7	wgn 4d I-6	2,977	4,689	
05-7	DL sdn 4d I-6	3,040	4,788	
06-7	DL sdn 2d I-6	2,982	4,688	91,842
03-7	DL htchbk cpe I-6	3,003	4,623	
08-7	DL wgn 4d I-6	3,072	4,988	
05-7	Limited sdn 4d I-6	3,146	5,788	
06-7	Limited sdn 2d I-6	3,090	5,688	
08-7	Limited wgn 4d I-6	3,177	5,988	
05-7	sdn 4d V-8	3,146	4,889	
06-7	sdn 2d V-8	3,080	4,789	
03-7	htchbk cpe V-8	3,095	4,724	
08-7	wgn 4d V-8	3,184	5,089	
05-7	DL sdn 4d V-8	3,247	5,188	
06-7	DL sdn 2d V-8	3,189	5,088	4,656
03-7	DL htchbk cpe V-8	3,210	5,023	
08-7	DL wgn 4d V-8	3,279	5,388	
05-7	Limited sdn 4d V-8	3,353	6,188	
06-7	Limited sdn 2d V-8	3,297	6,088	
08-7	Limited wgn 4d V-8	3,384	6,888	

Note: 6,355 4-cyl Concords were produced.

Pacer (wb 100.0)		Wght	Price	Prod
66-7	DL htchbk sdn 2d I-6	3,133	5,039	
68-7	DL wgn 2d I-6	3,170	5,189	9,201
66-7	Lmtd htchbk sdn 2d I-6	3,218	6,039	
68-7	Limited wgn 2d I-6	3,255	6,189	
66-7	DL htchbk sdn 2d V-8	3,360	5,439	
68-7	DL wgn 2d V-8	3,397	5,589	1,014
66-7	Lmtd htckbk sdn 2d V-8	3,445	6,439	
68-7	Limited wgn 2d V-8	3,482	6,589	

AMX (wb 96.0)		Wght	Price	Prod
43-9	htchbk cpe I-6	2,899	6,090	3,657*
43-9	htchbk cpe V-8	3,092	6,465	

* Included in Spirit total.

1979 Engines	bore × stroke	bhp	availability
I-4, 121.0	3.41 × 3.32	80	S-Sprt; O-Con exc wgn
I-6, 232.0	3.75 × 3.50	90	S-Con; O-Spirit
I-6, 258.0	3.75 × 3.90	100	S-Pacer
I-6, 258.0	3.75 × 3.90	110	S-Sprt, AMX; O-Con
V-8, 304.0	3.75 × 3.44	125	S-all V-8s

1980

Spirit (wb 96.0)		Wght	Price	Prod
43-0	htchbk cpe I-4	2,556	4,605	
46-0	sdn 2d I-4	2,512	4,505	
43-5	DL htchbk cpe I-4	2,656	5,004	37,799
46-5	DL sdn 2d I-4	2,611	4,904	
43-7	Lmtd htckbk cpe I-4	2,675	5,451	
46-7	Limited sdn 2d I-4	2,630	5,351	

Spirit (wb 96.0)		Wght	Price	Prod
43-0	htchbk cpe I-6	2,758	4,734	
46-0	sdn 2d I-6	2,714	4,634	
43-5	DL htchbk cpe I-6	2,858	5,133	33,233
46-5	DL sdn 2d I-6	2,813	5,033	
43-7	Lmtd htckbk cpe I-6	2,877	5,580	
46-7	Limited sdn 2d I-6	2,832	5,480	

Concord (wb 108.0)		Wght	Price	Prod
05-0	sdn 4d I-4	2,712	5,219	
06-0	sdn 2d I-4	2,646	5,094	
08-0	wgn 4d I-4	2,741	5,419	
05-5	DL sdn 4d I-4	2,834	5,618	
06-5	DL sdn 2d I-4	2,764	5,493	9,949
08-5	DL wgn 4d I-4	2,855	5,818	
05-7	Limited sdn 4d I-4	2,859	6,065	
06-7	Limited sdn 2d I-4	2,789	5,940	
08-7	Limited wgn 4d I-4	2,886	6,265	
05-0	sdn 4d I-6	2,910	5,348	
06-0	sdn 2d I-6	2,844	5,223	
08-0	wgn 4d I-6	2,939	5,548	
05-5	DL sdn 4d I-6	3,032	5,747	
06-5	DL sdn 2d I-6	2,962	5,622	70,507
08-5	DL wgn 4d I-6	3,053	5,947	
05-7	Limited sdn 4d I-6	3,057	6,194	
06-7	Limited sdn 2d I-6	2,987	6,069	
08-7	Limited wgn 4d I-6	3,084	6,394	

Pacer (wb 100.0)		Wght	Price	Prod
66-5	DL htckbk 2d I-6	3,147	5,407	405
68-5	DL wgn 2d I-6	3,195	5,558	1,341
66-7	Limited htchbk 2d I-6	3,172	6,031	—
68-7	Limited wgn 2d I-6	3,220	6,182	—

AMX (wb 96.0)		Wght	Price	Prod
43-9	htchbk cpe I-4	2,901	5,653	—

Eagle (wb 109.3)		Wght	Price	Prod
35-5	sdn 4d I-6	3,450	7,418	9,956
36-5	sdn 2d I-6	3,382	7,168	10,616
38-5	wgn 4d I-6	3,470	7,718	25,807
35-7	Limited sdn 4d I-6	3,465	7,815	—
36-7	Limited sdn 2d I-6	3,397	7,565	—
38-7	Limited wgn 4d I-6	3,491	8,115	—

1980 Engines	bore × stroke	bhp	availability
I-4, 151.0	4.00 × 3.00	90	S-all 4-cylinder models
I-6, 258.0	3.75 × 3.90	110	S-all 6-cylinder models

1981

Spirit (wb 96.0)		Wght	Price	Prod
43-0	htckbk cpe I-4	2,587	5,190	
43-0	htchbk cpe I-6	2,716	5,326	42,252
43-5	DL htckbk cpe I-4	2,673	5,589	
43-5	DL htchbk cpe I-6	2,802	5,725	
46-0	sdn 2d I-4	2,543	5,090	
46-0	sdn 2d I-6	2,671	5,226	2,367
46-5	DL sdn 2d I-4	2,627	5,489	
46-5	DL sdn 2d I-6	2,756	5,625	

Concord (wb 108.0)		Wght	Price	Prod
05-0	sdn 4d I-4	2,738	5,944	
05-0	sdn 4d I-6	2,864	6,080	
05-5	DL sdn 4d I-4	2,837	6,343	24,403
05-5	DL sdn 4d I-6	2,963	6,479	
05-7	Limited sdn 4d I-4	2,859	6,790	
05-7	Limited sdn 4d I-6	2,985	6,926	
06-0	sdn 2d I-4	2,672	5,819	
06-0	sdn 2d I-6	2,798	5,955	
06-5	DL sdn 2d I-4	2,767	6,218	15,496
06-5	DL sdn 2d I-6	2,893	6,354	
06-7	Limited sdn 2d I-4	2,789	6,665	
06-7	Limited sdn 2d I-6	2,915	6,801	
08-0	wgn 4d I-4	2,768	6,144	
08-0	wgn 4d I-6	2,894	6,280	
08-5	DL wgn 4d I-4	2,852	6,543	15,198
08-5	DL wgn 4d I-6	2,978	6,679	
08-7	Limited wgn 4d I-4	2,880	6,990	
08-7	Limited wgn 4d I-6	3,006	7,126	

Eagle 50 (wb 97.2)		Wght	Price	Prod
53-0	SX/4 liftbk cpe 2d I-4	2,967	6,717	
53-0	SX/4 liftbk cpe 2d I-6	3,123	6,853	17,340
53-5	DL SX/4 liftbk cpe 2d I-4	3,040	7,119	
53-5	DL SX/4 liftbk cpe 2d I-6	3,196	7,255	

Eagle 50 (wb 97.2)		Wght	Price	Prod
56-0	Kambk sdn 2d I-4	2,919	5,995	
56-0	Kambk sdn 2d I-6	3,015	6,131	
56-5	DL Kambk sdn 2d I-4	2,990	6,515	5,603
56-5	DL Kambk sdn 2d I-6	3,146	6,651	

Eagle 30 (wb 109.3)		Wght	Price	Prod
35-5	sdn 4d I-4	3,172	8,097	
35-5	sdn 4d I-6	3,328	8,233	
35-7	Limited sdn 4d I-4	3,180	8,494	1,737
35-7	Limited sdn 4d I-6	3,336	8,630	
36-5	sdn 2d I-4	3,104	7,847	
36-5	sdn 2d I-6	3,260	7,983	
36-7	Limited sdn 2d I-4	3,114	8,244	2,378
36-7	Limited sdn 2d I-6	3,270	8,380	
38-5	wgn 4d I-4	3,184	8,397	
38-5	wgn 4d I-6	3,340	8,533	
38-7	Limited wgn 4d I-4	3,198	8,794	10,371
38-7	Limited wgn 4d I-6	3,354	8,930	

1981 Engines	bore × stroke	bhp	availability
I-4, 151.0	4.00 × 3.00	82	S-all 4-cylinder models
I-6, 258.0	3.75 × 3.90	110	S-all 6-cylinder models

1982

Spirit (wb. 96.0)		Wght	Price	Prod
43-0	htchbk cpe I-4	2,588	5,576	
43-0	htchbk cpe I-6	2,687	5,726	
43-5	DL htchbk cpe I-4	2,666	5,959	20,063
43-5	DL htchbk cpe I-6	2,765	6,109	
46-0	sdn 2d I-4	2,538	5,476	
46-0	sdn 2d I-6	2,637	5,626	
46-5	DL sdn 2d I-4	2,614	5,859	119
46-5	DL sdn 2d I-6	2,713	6,009	

Concord (wb 108.0)		Wght	Price	Prod
05-0	sdn 4d I-4	2,752	6,254	
05-0	sdn 4d I-6	2,842	6,404	
05-5	DL sdn 4d I-4	2,841	6,761	
05-5	DL sdn 4d I-6	2,931	6,911	25,572
05-7	Limited sdn 4d I-4	2,862	7,258	
05-7	Limited sdn 4d I-6	2,952	7,408	
06-0	sdn 2d I-4	2,683	5,954	
06-0	sdn 2d I-6	2,773	6,104	
06-5	DL sdn 2d I-4	2,768	6,716	
06-5	DL sdn 2d I-6	2,858	6,866	6,132
06-7	Limited sdn 2d I-4	2,790	7,213	
06-7	Limited sdn 2d I-6	2,880	7,363	
08-0	wgn 4d I-4	2,786	7,013	
08-0	wgn 4d I-6	2,876	7,163	
08-5	DL wgn 4d I-4	2,940	7,462	12,106
08-5	DL wgn 4d I-6	3,030	7,612	
08-7	Limited wgn 4d I-4	2,892	7,959	
08-7	Limited wgn 4d I-6	2,982	8,109	

Eagle 50 (wb 97.2)		Wght	Price	Prod
53-0	SX/4 liftbk cpe 2d I-4	2,972	7,451	
53-0	SX/4 liftbk cpe 2d I-6	3,100	7,601	
53-5	DL SX/4 liftbk cpe 2d I-4	3,041	7,903	10,445
53-5	DL SX/4 liftbk cpe 2d I-6	3,169	8,053	
56-0	Kambk sdn 2d I-4	2,933	6,799	
56-0	Kambk sdn 2d I-6	3,061	6,949	
56-5	DL Kambk sdn 2d I-4	3,000	7,369	520
56-5	DL Kambk sdn 2d I-6	3,128	7,519	

Eagle 30 (wb 109.3 in.)		Wght	Price	Prod
35-5	sdn 4d I-4	3,172	8,869	
35-5	sdn 4D I-6	3,310	9,019	
35-7	Limited sdn 4d I-4	3,180	9,316	4,091
35-7	Limited sdn 4d I-6	3,308	9,466	
36-5	sdn 2d I-4	3,107	8,719	
36-5	sdn 2d I-6	3,235	8,869	
36-7	Limited sdn 2d I-4	3,115	9,166	1,968
36-7	Limited sdn 2d I-6	3,243	9,316	
38-5	wgn 4d I-4	3,299	9,566	
38-5	wgn 4d I-6	3,327	9,716	20,899
38-7	Limited wgn 4d I-4	3,213	10,013	
38-7	Limited wgn 4d I-6	3,341	10,163	

1982 Engines	bore × stroke	bhp	availability
I-4, 151.0	4.00 × 3.00	82	S-all 4-cylinder models
I-6, 258.0	3.75 × 3.90	110	S-all 6-cylinder models

1983

Alliance (wb 97.8)		Wght	Price	Prod
96-0	sdn 2d	1,945	5,595	
96-3	L sdn 2d	1,945	6,020	
96-6	DL sdn 2d	1,945	6,655	55,556
96-6	MT sdn 2d	—	7,450	
95-3	L sdn 4d	1,980	6,270	
95-6	DL sdn 4d	1,980	6,905	86,649
95-8	Limited sdn 4d	1,980	7,470	
95-6	MT sdn 4d	—	7,700	

Spirit (wb 96.0)		Wght	Price	Prod
43-5	DL htchbk cpe I-6	2,810	5,995	
43-9	GT htchbk cpe I-6	2,817	6,495	3,491

Concord (wb 108.0)		Wght	Price	Prod
05-0	sdn 4d I-6	2,904	6,724	
05-5	DL sdn 4d I-6	2,999	6,995	4,433
08-0	wgn 4d I-6	2,948	7,449	
08-5	DL wgn 4d I-6	3,037	7,730	867
08-7	Limited wgn 4d I-6	3,061	8,117	

Eagle 50 (wb 97.2)		Wght	Price	Prod
53-0	SX/4 liftbk cpe 2d I-4	3,034	7,697	
53-0	SX/4 liftbk cpe 2d I-6	3,165	7,852	
53-5	DL SX/4 liftbk cpe 2d I-4	3,094	8,164	2,259
53-5	DL SX/4 liftbk cpe 2d I-6	3,225	8,319	

Eagle 30 (wb 109.3)		Wght	Price	Prod
35-5	sdn 4d I-4	3,265	9,162	
35-5	sdn 4d I-6	3,396	9,317	3,093
38-5	wgn 4d I-4	3,285	9,882	
38-5	wgn 4d I-6	3,416	10,037	
38-7	Limited wgn 4d I-4	3,301	10,343	12,378
38-7	Limited wgn 4d I-6	3,432	10,498	

1983 Engines	bore × stroke	bhp	availability
I-4, 85.2	2.99 × 3.03	56	S-Alliance
I-4, 151.0	4.00 × 3.00	84	S-early Eagle
I-4, 150.0	3.88 × 3.19	—	S-late Eagle
I-6, 258.0	3.75 × 3.90	110	S-Sprt, Conc; O-Egl

1984

Encore (wb 97.8)		Wght	Price	Prod
93-0	htchbk sdn 2d	2,010	5,755	
93-3	S htchbk sdn 2d	2,021	6,365	
93-6	LS htchbk sdn 2d	2,069	6,995	55,343
93-9	GS htchbk sdn 2d	2,079	7,547	
93-6	Dimnd Ed htchbk sdn 2d	—	7,570	
99-3	S htchbk sdn 4d	2,044	6,615	
99-6	LS htchbk sdn 4d	2,095	7,195	32,266
99-6	Dimnd Ed htchbk sdn 4d	—	7,770	

Alliance (wb 97.8)		Wght	Price	Prod
96-0	sdn 2d	1,970	5,959	
96-3	L sdn 2d	1,972	6,465	
96-6	DL sdn 2d	2,011	7,065	50,978
96-6	Diamond Ed sdn 2d	—	7,715	
95-3	L sdn 4d	2,000	6,715	
95-6	DL sdn 4d	2,038	7,365	70,037
95-6	Diamond Ed sdn 4d	—	8,015	
95-8	Limited sdn 4d	2,055	8,027	

Eagle 30 (wb 109.3 in.)		Wght	Price	Prod
35-5	sdn 4d I-4	3,273	9,495	
35-5	sdn 4d I-6	3,391	9,666	4,241
38-5	wgn 4d I-4	3,304	10,225	
38-5	wgn 4d I-6	3,422	10,396	
38-7	Limited wgn 4d I-4	3,320	10,695	21,294
38-7	Limited wgn 4d I-6	3,438	10,866	

1984 Engines	bore × stroke	bhp	availability
I-4, 85.2	2.99 × 3.03	56	S-Allnce, Encore
I-4, 150.0	3.88 × 3.19	NA	S-Eagle
I-6, 258.0	3.75 × 3.90	110	O-Eagle

1985

Encore (wb 97.8)		Wght	Price	Prod
93-0	htchbk sdn 2d	1,982	5,895	
93-3	S htchbk sdn 2d	2,021	6,360	
93-6	LS htchbk sdn 2d	2,069	7,060	38,623
93-9	GS htchbk sdn 2d	2,079	7,560	
99-3	S htchbk sdn 4d	2,044	6,610	
99-6	LS htchbk sdn 4d	2,095	7,310	19,902

Alliance (wb 97.8)		Wght	Price	Prod
96-0	sdn 2d	1,958	5,995	
96-3	L sdn 2d	1,965	6,400	33,617
96-6	DL sdn 2d	1,998	7,000	
95-3	L sdn 4d	2,000	6,650	
95-6	DL sdn 4d	2,037	7,250	50,906
95-8	Limited sdn 4d	2,087	7,750	
97-3	L conv cpe	2,189	10,295	
97-6	DL conv cpe	2,226	11,295	7,141

Eagle 30 (wb 109.3)		Wght	Price	Prod
35-5	sdn 4d I-6	3,390	10,457	2,655
38-5	wgn 4d I-6	3,421	11,217	
38-7	Limited wgn 4d I-6	3,452	11,893	13,535

1985 Engines	bore × stroke	bhp	availability
I-4, 85.2	2.99 × 3.03	56	S-Alliance, Encore
I-4, 105.0	3.19 × 3.29	77	S-Alliance conv, Encore GS; O-Alliance, Encore
I-6, 258.0	3.75 × 3.90	110	S-Eagle

1986

Encore (wb 97.8)		Wght	Price	Prod
93-3	S htchbk sdn 2d	2,006	6,710	
93-6	LS htchbk sdn 2d	2,010	7,310	
93-9	GS htchbk sdn 2d	2,013	7,968	12,239
93-4	Elect htchbk sdn 2d	2,051	7,498	
99-3	S htchbk sdn 4d	2,039	6,960	
99-6	LS htchbk sdn 4d	2,043	7,560	6,870

Alliance (wb 97.8)		Wght	Price	Prod
96-0	sdn 2d	1,959	5,999	
96-3	L sdn 2d	1,964	6,510	23,204
96-6	DL sdn 2d	1,971	7,110	
95-0	sdn 4d	1,993	6,199	
95-3	L sdn 4d	1,998	6,760	41,891
95-6	DL sdn 4d	2,005	7,360	
97-3	L conv cpe	2,222	10,557	
97-6	DL conv cpe	2,228	11,557	2,015

Eagle 30 (wb 109.3)		Wght	Price	Prod
35-5	sdn 4d I-6	3,391	10,719	1,274
38-5	wgn 4d I-6	3,425	11,489	
38-7	Limited wgn 4d I-6	3,456	12,719	6,943

1986 Engines	bore × stroke	bhp	availability
I-4, 85.2	2.99 × 3.03	56	S-Allnce, Encore
I-4, 105.0	3.19 × 3.29	77	S-Alliance conv, Encr Elect/GS; O-Alliance, Encore
I-6, 258.0	3.75 × 3.90	110	S-Eagle

1987

Alliance (wb 97.8)		Wght	Price	Prod
96-0	sdn 2d	1,959	6,399	
96-3	L sdn 2d	1,965	6,925	13,132
96-6	DL sdn 2d	2,000	7,625	
96-7	GTA sdn 2d	2,104	8,999	
95-0	sdn 4d	1,997	6,599	
95-3	L sdn 4d	2,003	7,200	16,214
95-8	DL sdn 4d	2,038	7,900	
97-3	L conv cpe	2,206	11,099	
97-6	DL conv cpe	2,239	12,099	1,991
97-7	GTA conv cpe	2,298	12,899	
93-0	htchbk sdn 2d	1,985	6,599	
93-3	L htchbk sdn 2d	1,991	6,975	
93-6	DL htchbk sdn 2d	2,028	7,675	2,857
93-9	GS htckbk sdn 2d	2,057	8,499	
99-3	L htchbk sdn 4d	2,039	7,250	
99-6	DL htchbk sdn 4d	2,081	7,950	2,142

Eagle (wb 109.3)		Wght	Price	Prod
35-5	sdn 4d I-6	3,383	11,150	751
38-5	wgn 4d I-6	3,417	11,943	
38-7	Limited wgn 4d I-6	3,431	12,653	4,452

1987 Engines	bore × stroke	bhp	availability
I-4, 85.2	2.99 × 3.03	56	S-Alliance
I-4, 105.0	3.19 × 3.29	77	S-Alliance conv; O-Alliance
I-4, 120.0	3.23 × 3.66	95	S-Alliance GTA
I-6, 258.0	3.75 × 3.90	112	S-Eagle

Note: Production totals that were unavailable from AMC have been compiled from industry sources.

Auburn

Though the Auburns best remembered today were built in the '30s and late '20s, the marque was established way back in 1903. That's when brothers Frank and Morris Eckhart, buggy-builders in the northeast Indiana town of Auburn, began selling an $800 chain-drive runabout with a single-cylinder engine. Two-, four-, and six-cylinder models followed quickly in the years through 1912. Like other small, marginally capitalized automakers of the time, Auburn offered "assembled cars" built from a variety of proven, but brought-in, components.

As a result, Auburn was nearly stagnant by 1919, when the Eckharts sold out to a Chicago group headed by chewing-gum king William K. Wrigley, Jr. New capital and more-aggressive marketing were put behind a new model, the "Beauty Six," with streamlined body, disc wheels, step plates instead of running boards, and windshield vent wings—all very advanced for the day. But a deep post-World War I recession cut greatly into car sales. With annual output below 4000 units, Auburn was on the ropes again by 1924.

Then came a second savior, Errett Lobban Cord, a brash young entrepreneur described as both "boy wonder" and "profane, bespectacled capitalist." Salesmanship was his claim to fame. Responsible for the selling and distribution of the majority of Moon Motor Car Company's production in the Chicago market alone, Cord attracted the attention of Auburn's Chicago owners. Wanting to try the production end of the car business, Cord accepted the position of Auburn general manager. After promptly disposing of some 700 leftover 1924s, which netted enough cash to pay off Auburn's debts, he was made vice president. By 1926, he was both the firm's president and its chief stockholder.

Auburn prospered under Cord, gaining a modest competition image, greatly increasing exports, expanding its dealer body, and adding eight-cylinder models in 1925. With fast, handsome, and reliable cars priced incredibly low, Auburn passed the 20,000 mark in annual production by 1929. Though Eights naturally offered more vivid performance than Sixes, all Auburns were appreciated for their good looks and high value.

Deciding to concentrate on Eights and, ultimately, a Twelve, Cord dropped the Auburn Six after 1930. That year's final 6-85 series offered just a cabriolet, sedan, and sport sedan. Power was supplied by Lycoming, a Pennsylvania company Cord had purchased in 1929. The sturdy 185-cubic-inch engine produced 70 horsepower at 3400 rpm. Despite modest $1000-$1100 pricing, the 6-85 was by no means dull: smooth and clean on a 120-inch wheelbase. Even so, Auburn sales dropped almost 50 percent for calendar 1930, and model-year volume declined to 14,360. With the Depression hitting hard, management concluded that the Six was just not profitable enough to retain, though it would return.

There were two Auburn Eights for 1930. The lower-priced 125-inch-wheelbase 8-95 was an unquestioned bargain, offering four models (the six-cylinder trio plus a five-seat phaeton) in the $1200-$1400 range. Its 247-cid inline engine was basically the 6-85 unit with two more cylinders and 100 bhp. For $1500-$1700 you could have the same foursome as Custom Eight 125s, with that many horses from 298.6 cid. Mounting a 130-inch chassis, they weighed some 3900 pounds but could do almost 90 mph—astonishing for the day. In 1929, this engine had powered a 3000-pound speedster to 100 mph—a first for Auburn.

Auburn was one of the few automakers to see higher sales *after* the 1929 Wall Street Crash. Calendar-year 1931 production zoomed to a record of over 32,000 on the strength of more dealers and a line of fleet, luxurious, bargain-priced Eights. Reflecting Cord's cagey sales strategy, the bigger eight was dropped along with the six, the smaller eight bored to 268.6 cid and 98 bhp. Larger, more-rakish bodies were placed on longer 127-inch wheelbases for identical Eight and Custom Eight series. The latter featured standard freewheeling, but both lines offered speedster, coupe, cabriolet, brougham, phaeton-sedan, and closed-sedan bodies, plus seven-seat sedans on a special 136-inch chassis. All this moved *Business Week* to hail Auburn as "more car for the money than the public had ever seen."

1930 Custom Eight Cabriolet 2/4 passenger

1932 Custom Eight Cabriolet 2/4 passenger

1932 12-160 Speedster

1932 Custom Eight four-door sedan

1934 Eight Cabriolet 2/4 passenger

If the 1931 Eight was a remarkable buy, the 1932 Twelve was even more so: the least-costly V-12 on the market at prices ranging from $975 for the Standard coupe to $1275 for the top-line Custom Speedster. The engine, a 391-cid Lycoming designed by Auburn chief engineer George Kublin, packed a healthy 160 bhp at 3500 rpm. It was mounted in an X-braced frame spanning a kingly 133-inch wheelbase. Custom Twelves featured the well-known Columbia dual-ratio rear axle with 4.55 and 3.04:1 gear sets that could be selected below 40 mph, which effectively provided six forward speeds. Eights continued as before, as did the usual body types, including eight-cylinder long sedans. The beautiful V-12 boattail speedsters, so rare today, were the best expressions of that year's Auburn styling.

Yet despite these peerless cars, sales plunged in 1932 to a calendar-year output of just over 11,000. Red ink continued gushing in 1933, as volume fell to under 5000. While all this mystified E.L. Cord, hindsight reveals that a V-12 at any price just couldn't interest many buyers in the depths of the Depression. Unsold '33 V-12s were retitled and sold as '34s. Auburn's Eight, which had exhausted what demand it had enjoyed in 1931, was little changed for '32 and '33.

Worse, Cord was now spread very thin building his far-flung business empire. He'd bought Duesenberg in 1926, launched the front-drive Cord L-29 three years later, then acquired Lycoming, the Ansted engine company, several midwestern corporations, and even Checker Cab—plus shipbuilding and aviation interests. Perhaps to avoid a brewing scandal over his management of these enterprises, Cord fled to England in 1934 and promptly dropped from sight. Eventually, his conglomerate's fortunes were handed over to Duesenberg president Harold T. Ames.

The 1934 line featured all-steel bodies with more-streamlined, but less-distinctive styling by Alan Leamy of L-29 renown. The Six was revived with a 210-cid Lycoming engine making 85 bhp at 3500 rpm. Eights used a revised, 280-inch version of the previous straight eight developing 100 bhp with a cast-iron head or 115 bhp with a high-compression aluminum head. Standard and Custom models on a 119-inch (Six) or 126-inch Eight chassis were offered for as little as $695 (Standard Six) in an effort to win Depression-depleted dollars. But these cars didn't sell. Poorly received styling (especially the "shovel front") often get the blame, but 1934 wasn't a good sales year for any make.

The '35 Auburns benefited from the talents of two automotive legends—designer Gordon Buehrig and engineer August Duesenberg. Buehrig was given a modest $50,000 and told to do what he could to improve Auburn styling. Adding a bold grille and massive hood to the existing body did the trick. Augie, meantime, was asked to adapt a Schwitzer-Cummins supercharger to the eight. Horsepower jumped to a hefty 150 horsepower. Supercharged cars were identified by external exhausts. The six and 115-bhp eight were carried over. The result was a line of very pretty cars that would include Auburn's final glory—the superb 851/852 speedster.

Buehrig didn't have enough money for a complete redesign so he worked with the midsection of leftover '33 Speedsters, giving the old bodies the new front-end treatment, beautifully curved pontoon fenders, and a new boattail. All Speedsters were supercharged and could hit 100 mph right out of the showroom, yet they sold for as little as $2245. Once again Auburn was offering truly unbelievable value.

But 1935 proved a confused and ultimately disappointing year, so the 1936 Auburns were predictably almost unchanged. The six-cylinder 653 became Series 654, still offered in standard form as well as Custom and Salon "Dual Ratio" models. The same arrangement, plus supercharged models, applied to the 1936 Series 852. Yet despite this still-brilliant fleet of cabriolets, broughams, phaetons, sedans, and the 852 Supercharged Speedster, sales refused to improve. Speedster production, for instance, came to less than 500 for both years.

Like a prodigal son, E. L. Cord returned from England in 1936 to salvage his crumbling empire, only to find the IRS and

1935 851 Speedster

1936 Supercharged Eight Dual Ratio four-door sedan

the Securities and Exchange Commission ready to launch major investigations of his doings. One result was the cancellation of planned 1937 Auburns. The make was dead.

Cord would manage to keep most of his fortune, and in later years got involved in western land speculation. Though he is not remembered fondly by Auburn fans, it's doubtful the make would have risen so high without him. It's a shame that its life at the pinnacle was so short.

Specifications

1930

6-85 Six (wb 120.0)		Wght	Price	Prod*
685A	sdn 4d	3,300	1,095	—
685B	spt sdn 2W	3,300	995	—
685F	cab, 204P	3,125	1,095	—
8-95 Eight (wb 125.0)				
895A	sdn 4d	3,590	1,295	—
895B	spt sdn 2W	3,590	1,195	—
895F	cab 2-4P	3,410	1,295	—
895H	phtn sdn 5P	3,600	1,395	—
125 Custom Eight (wb 130.0)				
125A	sdn 4d	3,995	1,595	—
125B	spt sdn 2W	3,995	1,495	—
125F	cab 2-4P	3,800	1,595	—
125H	phtn sdn 5P	3,990	1,695	—

1930 Engines	bore×stroke	bhp	availability
I-6, 185.0	2.88×4.75	70	6-85
I-8, 247.0	2.88×4.75	100	8-95
I-8, 298.6	3.25×4.50	125	125

* Calendar-year production: 11,357

1931

8-98 Eight (wb 127.0; 7P-136.0)	Wght	Price	Prod*
b'ham 2d 5P	3,580	945	—
spdstr 2P	3,320	945	—
sdn 4d	3,700	995	—
cpe 2P	3,460	995	—
cab 2-4P	3,540	1,045	—
phtn sdn 5P	3,650	1,145	—
sdn 7P	3,990	1,195	—
8-98A Custom Eight (wb 127.0; 7P-136.0)			
b'ham 2d 5P	3,630	1,145	—
sdn 4d	3,750	1,195	—
cpe 2P	3,510	1,195	—
cab 204P	3,490	1,245	—
phtn sdn 5P	3,700	1,345	—
spdstr 2P	3,370	1,395	—
sdn 7P	4,040	1,395	—

1931 Engine	bore×stroke	bhp	availability
I-8, 268.6	3.00×4.75	98	8-98, 8-98A

*Calendar-year production: 32,301

1932

8-100 Eight (wb 127.0; 7P-136.0)	Wght	Price	Prod*
cpe 2P	3,485	675	—
b'ham 2d 5P	3,605	725	—
sdn 4d	3,725	775	—
cab 2-4P	3,495	795	—
phtn sdn 5P	3,675	845	—
spdstr 2P	3,345	845	—
sdn 7P	4,015	875	—
8-100A Custom Eight Dual Ratio (wb 127.0; 7P-136.0)			
cpe 2P	3,575	805	—
b'ham 2d 5P	3,695	855	—
sdn 4d	3,815	905	—
cab 2-4P	3,585	925	—
phtn sdn 5P	3,765	975	—
spdstr 2P	3,435	975	—
sdn 7P	4,105	1,005	—
12-160 Twelve (wb 133.0)			
cpe 2P	4,275	975	—
b'ham 2d 5P	4,395	1,025	—
sdn 4d	4,515	1,075	—
cab 2-4P	4,285	1,095	—
phtn sdn 5P	4,465	1,145	—
spdstr 2P	4,135	1,145	—
12-160A Custom Twelve Dual Ratio (wb 133.0)			
cpe 2P	4,375	1,105	—
b'ham 2d 5P	4,495	1,155	—
sdn 4d	4,615	1,205	—
cab 2-4P	4,385	1,225	—
phtn sdn 5P	4,565	1,275	—
spdstr 2P	4,235	1,275	—

1932 Engines	bore×stroke	bhp	availability
I-8, 268.6	3.00×4.75	100	all Eights
V-12, 391.6	3.13×4.25	160	all Twelves

* Total 1932 registrations: 11,345

1933

8-101 Eight (wb 1276.0; 7P-136.0)	Wght	Price	Prod*
cpe 2P	3,485	745	—
b'ham 2d 5P	3,605	795	—
sdn 4d	3,725	845	—
cab 2-4P	3,495	895	—
phtn sdn 5P	3,675	945	—
spdstr 2P	3,345	945	—
sdn 7P	4,015	945	—
8-101A Custom Eight			
cpe 2P	3,575	895	—
b'ham 2d 5P	3,695	945	—
sdn 4d	3,815	995	—
cab 2-4P	3,585	1,045	—
phtn sdn 5P	3,765	1,095	—
spdstr 2P	3,435	1,095	—
sdn 7P	4,105	1,095	—
8-105 Salon Eight Dual Ratio (wb 127.0)			
b'ham 2d 5P	3,800	1,045	—
sdn 4d	3,920	1,095	—
cab 2-4P	3,640	1,145	—
phtn sdn 5P	3,835	1,195	—
spdstr 2P	3,510	1,195	—
12-161 Twelve (wb 133.0)			
cpe 2P	4,275	1,145	—
b'ham 2d 5P	4,395	1,195	—
sdn 4d	4,515	1,245	—
cab 2-4P	4,285	1,295	—
phtn sdn 5P	4,465	1,345	—
spdstr 2P	4,135	1,345	—
12-161A Custom Twelve Dual Ratio (wb 133.0)			
cpe 2P	4,355	1,295	—
b'ham 2d 5P	4,495	1,345	—
sdn 4d	4,615	1,395	—
cab 2-4P	4,385	1,445	—
phtn sdn 5P	4,565	1,495	—
spdstr 2P	4,235	1,495	—
12-165 Salon Twelve Dual Ratio (wb 133.0)			
b'ham 2d 5P	4,715	1,595	—
sdn 4d	4,870	1,645	—
cab 2-4P	4,570	1,695	—
phtn sdn 5P	4,710	1,745	—
spdstr 2P	4,440	1,745	—

1933 Engines	bore×stroke	bhp	availability
I-8, 268.6	3.00×4.75	100	all Eights
V-12, 391.6	3.13×4.25	160	all Twelves

* Calendar-year production: 4,813

1934

652X Six (wb 119.0)	Wght	Price	Prod*
b'ham 2d 5P	3,215	695	—
sdn 4d	3,263	745	—
cab 2-4P	3,105	795	—
652Y Custom Six Dual Ratio (wb 119.0)			
b'ham 2d 5P	3,305	795	—
sdn 4d	3,353	845	—
cab 2-4P	3,195	895	
phtn sdn 5P	3,375	945	—
850X Eight (wb 126.0)			
b'ham 2d 5P	3,628	945	—
sdn 4d	3,668	995	—
cab 2-4P	3,603	1,045	—
850Y Custom Eight Dual Ratio (wb 126.0)			
b'ham 2d 5P	3,688	1,075	—
sdn 4d	3,755	1,125	—
cab 2-4P	3,653	1,175	—
phtn sdn 5P	3,773	1,225	—
1250 Salon Twelve Dual Ratio (wb 133.0)			
b'ham 2d 5P	4,715	1,395	—
sdn 4d	4,870	1,445	—
cab 2-4P	4,570	1,495	—
phtn sdn 5P	4,710	1,545	—

1934 Engines	bore×stroke	bhp	availability
I-6, 210.0	3.06×4.75	85	all Sixes
I-8, 280.0	3.06×4.75	100	850X
I-8, 280.0	3.06×4.75	115	850Y
V-12, 391.6	3.13×4.25	160	1250

*Calendar-year production: 7,770

1935 and 1936

653/654 Six (wb 120.0)	Wght	Price	Prod*
b'ham 2d 5P	3,214	745	—
sdn 4d	3,279	795	—
cpe 2P	3,105	835	—
cab 2-4P	3,182	945	—
phtn sdn 5P	3,248	995	—
653 Custom Six Dual Ratio (from February 1935)(wb 120.0)			
b'ham 2d 4P	3,321	852	—
cpe 2P	3,201	942	—
sdn 4d	3,388	952	—
cab 2-4P	3,282	1,052	—
phtn sdn 5P	3,248	1,102	—
653 Salon Six Dual Ratio (wb 120.0)			
b'ham 2d 4P	3,471	932	—
sdn 4d	3,533	982	—
cpe 2P	3,371	990	—
cab 2-4P	3,432	1,100	—
phtn sdn 5P	3,498	1,182	—
851/852 Eight (wb 127.0)			
b'ham 2d 5P	3,475	995	—
cpe 2P	3,395	1,085	—
sdn 4d	3,580	1,095	—
cab 2-4P	3,415	1,225	—
phtn sdn 5P	3,565	1,275	—
sdn 7P	3,870	1,195	—
851/852 Custom Eight Dual Ratio (wb 127.0)			
b'ham 2d 5P	3,574	1,088	—
cpe 2P	3,493	1,173	—
sdn 4d	3,679	1,188	—
cab 2-4P	3,511	1,313	—
phtn sdn 5P	3,664	1,368	—
sdn 7P	3,969	1,288	—
851/852 Salon Eight Dual Ratio (wb 127.0)			
b'ham 2d 5P	3,724	1,168	—
cpe 2P	3,643	1,221	—
sdn 4d	3,835	1,268	—
cab 2-4P	3,641	1,361	—
phtn sdn 5P	3,814	1,448	—
sdn 7P	4,125	1,368	—
851/852 Supercharged Eight Dual Ratio (wb 127.0)			
b'ham 2d 5P	3,655	1,445	—
sdn 4d	3,729	1,545	—
cpe 2P	3,565	1,545	—
cab 2-4P	3,633	1,675	—
phtn sdn 5P	3,714	1,725	—
spdstr 2P	3,706	2,245	—

1935/36 Eng.	bore×stroke	bhp	availability
I-6, 210.0	3.06×4.75	85	all Sixes
I-8, 280.0	3.06×4.75	115	Eights exc Suprchd
I-8S, 280.0	3.06×4.75	150	Supercharged

* 1935 cal-year prod: 6,316; '36 cal-year prod: 1,263

Avanti /Avanti II

Studebaker fled to Canada in late 1963 and left the auto business three years later. By that time, Leo Newman and Nathan Altman had resurrected the Avanti, Studebaker's most interesting car of the '60s.

Designed by a team under Raymond Loewy, the Avanti had failed Studebaker in the marketplace but succeeded greatly with enthusiasts—the only Studebaker in two generations to inspire such interest. Before its phaseout upon Studebaker's departure from South Bend, the Avanti had broken virtually every major U.S. Auto Club speed record (*see* Studebaker).

Newman and Altman were partners in a South Bend Studebaker dealership, one of the oldest. Knowing the Avanti was too good to lose, they bought the name, production rights, tooling, and a portion of the century-old South Bend plant where the Avanti had been built. In 1965, they began turning out a revised version called Avanti II. They hoped to make 300 a year, which they'd never manage, but output was adequate and consistent.

Unlike the original, Avanti II was a commercial success. Its fiberglass body meant no expensive sheetmetal dies to maintain. And because Newman and Altman had conceived their Avanti as more exclusive than Studebaker's, they could build it carefully and largely by hand on a small assembly line. That meant they could tailor each car to the customer's wishes.

Well-heeled buyers could push the $6550 base price beyond $10,000. Options included Hurst four-speed manual transmission, power steering, air conditioning, electric window lifts, tinted glass, AM/FM radio, Eppe fog or driving lights, limited-slip differential, Magnum 500 chrome wheels, and Firestone bias-ply or Michelin radial tires. Early Avanti IIs had vinyl interiors, but textured "Raphael vinyl" could be ordered for $200. Genuine leather seat and door trim added $300, full leather $500. Paint colors were anything a buyer wanted, as were interior trims in later years. Though this led to some bizarre cars, it was part of the "custom-built" aura and it helped sales.

Early IIs retained the original Avanti's modified Lark convertible frame, but Studebaker V-8s were gone by the time Newman and Altman started, so they followed Studebaker's own lead by adopting the same 327-cubic-inch Chevrolet small-block in 300-horsepower Corvette tune. Chevy then introduced a 350-cid enlargement, and Avantis got it in 1969, though rated power was unchanged. Transmissions were either a fully synchronized Borg-Warner four-speed manual or a "Power-Shift" automatic that permitted manual hold of first and second gears.

These new mechanicals resided in a body almost identical to the original Avanti's. The main visual differences were a more level stance (Altman's customers disliked the Studebaker's marked front-end rake), Avanti logos with suffix Roman-numeral IIs, and reduced-radius wheel openings.

Corvette power made for fine performance in the sleek four-place Avanti. The typical automatic car could run 0-60 mph in under nine seconds and hit 125 mph with a 3.54:1 rear axle. Better still, the Chevy engines were lighter than the old Studebaker V-8, so front/rear weight balance improved from 59/41 percent to 57/43. Power front-disc/rear-drum brakes resisted fade admirably, while providing quick deceleration of nearly 1g in 80-mph panic stops. Obviously, Newman and Altman cared about safety as much as straight-line performance.

Being custom-built, the Avanti II necessarily cost more than Studebaker's version, competing in Cadillac Eldorado territory instead of Chrysler country like the $4,445 original. Realizing this meant a change in market orientation, Newman and Altman pitched the II more on "personal-luxury" than performance.

And indeed, the car was in its element on the open road. Magazine testers gave it points for safety, quietness, structural rigidity, and a firm but comfortable ride. "In this day of great concern over automotive safety," wrote John R. Bond in 1966, "the Avanti II should make new friends, for obviously there was more thought given to safety in its conception than in most American cars... It's a better car than it was three years ago."

Avanti II saw few changes in the 1970s save those needed to meet federal safety and emissions rules. Among the more obvious—and depressing—was the ugly, rubber-tipped "cow catcher" grafted on to meet 1973's new five-mph bumper standard, although Avanti Motor Corporation was small enough to win exemption from the required 2½-mph side-impact door beams. Also for '73, the engine was changed to Chevrolet's new detoxed 400 V-8. With net horsepower ratings in force for '74, the 400 came in at an anemic 180-bhp SAE net (245 gross). The 350 returned for '77 and would remain standard into the early '80s.

With Nate Altman's untimely death in 1976, Avanti seemed to lose direction, at times appearing half-hearted about its product and its future. Workmanship declined even as prices, spurred by inflation, galloped upward (breaking $12,000 in '76 and pushing $23,000 in '82). Federal dictates prompted detail interior changes (mainly to switchgear) wrought with an afterthought carelessness suggesting less-than-professional engineering and design work. On the plus side, the firm reduced its plethora of paint and trim choices in the interest of higher build quality and lower inventory costs. But little money and effort were going into updating the concept, as Altman had done. Both car and company were surviving, but hardly thriving.

That was about to change. After rebuffing several buyout offers over the years, the Altman family and other Avanti board members gave audience to Stephen Blake, a young Washington, D.C., construction tycoon. Alas, Altman's death came only days after the parties agreed to serious negotiations, and another seven years would pass before Blake became owner, president, and CEO of Avanti Motor Corporation in October 1982.

Blake blew into South Bend like a tornado, rearranging work flow in the crumbling remains of the old Studebaker plant for improved efficiency and quality. He also resisted the UAW and dismissed many dealers, inking more businesslike contracts with established Cadillac stores in major markets. Recruiting needed engineering talent soon resulted in several improvements: a switch to premium DuPont Imron paint (as on Indy race cars), greater use of GM components, optional body-color bumpers and black trim, square headlights, revamped interior, minor chassis tweaks, and an optional 190-bhp 305-cid V-8 (versus 155 bhp standard) from the Chevy Camaro Z28. The name lost it's Roman numeral "II" and returned to plain "Avanti." Most of these changes came together in a special 20th Anniversary 1983 coupe offered in solid black, white, red, or silver.

Bolder still were Blake's plans for the first Avanti convertible (unveiled as a prototype in late '83) and a new drop-floor chassis with independent rear suspension designed by Herb Adams. Blake even made a stab at racing, entering an Avanti "GT" in the 1983 Pepsi Challenge 24-hour enduro at Daytona. Though it finished only 27th out of 30 survivors from a starting field of 79, its merely showing up suggested Avanti was moving forward again.

Sadly, Blake tried to do too much too fast, and unexpected peeling problems with the new race-car paint cost a bundle to fix. By early 1985, Blake had spent himself into a credit crunch

1970s Avanti II sport coupe

1981 Avanti II coupe

1981 Avanti II coupe

1984 Avanti coupe

with his prime lender, a South Bend bank, and was forced to sell.

Avanti might have died right there had it not been for Michael Kelly, a 36-year-old Texas ethanol baron who acquired Blake's interests for just $725,000 in April 1985. Operating as New Avanti Motor Corporation, Kelly's regime began building Blake's convertible alongside the familiar coupe in 1987. Both models received new seats, a "cockpit" dash, altered bumpers, and improved cooling and climate systems. The coupe still listed for about $30,000; the convertible was some $10,000 more. With this changing of the guard, no 1986 Avantis were built.

Even more ambitious than Blake, Kelly moved production to a new plant in Youngstown, Ohio. This occurred in August 1987, thus closing the old Studebaker factory at last. Avantis would still be mostly hand-built, but the modern facilities promised great strides in quality—and volume, which Kelly predicted would eventually reach an unprecedented 1000 cars a year.

To achieve that, Kelly literally stretched the Avanti line by adding three new models: a 117-inch-wheelbase Luxury Sport Coupe, an even longer four-door Luxury Touring Sedan on a 123-inch chassis, and a jumbo limousine on a huge 174-inch span. Purists moaned, though designer Loewy (who died in late 1987) had mocked up a pair of "Avanti-styled" sedans as '65-66 Studebakers. At least the LSC looked as good as the standard coupe, a tribute to the "rightness" of the original design.

Besides 40 LSCs, Kelly's company managed 50 Silver Anniversary coupes in 1988 to honor Avanti's 25th birthday. These carried Chevy 305 V-8s that were muscled up to 250 bhp (from 170 standard) via Paxton superchargers supplied by the Granatelli brothers, just as in Studebaker days. Appropriately, the anniversary models were painted pearl silver. Interiors featured black or red leather, an "entertainment center" with TV, power moonroof, compact-disc player, and cellular telephone. There was also a fortified suspension with fat tires on handsome alloy wheels, and bodies gained a front spoiler with fog lamps, rocker-panel skirts, and reshaped bumpers.

Exceeding projected first-year production by 50 percent, New Avanti built 300 cars in 1987, the level Blake had hoped to attain but didn't. But Kelly, too, soon overreached himself, and this (plus legal hassles from one-time backers) forced him to sell in August 1988. The buyer turned out to be his principal partner, shopping-mall developer J. J. Cafaro, who changed the company name once again, this time to Avanti Automotive Corporation.

Both LSC and the planned limo were forgotten, but Cafaro did introduce a four-door Touring Sedan for 1990, though on a trimmer 116-inch wheelbase. Improbably, he claimed its body was molded directly from one of the old Loewy sedan mockups that had sat for years in the South Bend attic gathering dust and pigeon droppings. Though distinctive, the four-door wasn't as handsome as the classic coupe, but was definitely built better. High-tech composites replaced steel for its roof and (belatedly adopted) door beams, and Kevlar was substituted for fiberglass in the floorpan, bumpers, and seatbelt and body mounts.

Cafaro's operation managed 150 Avantis in 1988 and some 350 in '89. Most were the standard coupe. The 1990 target was 500 cars, but actual output was much lower. There were heady plans for '91, including a switch to the 245-bhp Corvette L98 engine, plus a new chassis (engineered by Callaway Technologies) with all-independent suspension and the four-wheel disc brakes from Ford's Thunderbird Super Coupe. But these plans were derailed by a sharp recession that hurt sales industrywide. Instead of building its planned 1000 cars in '91, Avanti Automotive Corporation filed for bankruptcy. The firm produced only 15 cars that year, mostly convertibles with a few cosmetic changes and body-material substitutions like those on the sedan.

A postscript to the Cafaro bankruptcy concerns one Robert Lucarell, who stayed as caretaker for the Youngstown plant.

Lucarell sold handfuls of assorted leftover parts to die-hard owners, all the while insisting that the car and the company he loved would rise yet again. "Avanti is still a going business," he told *Automotive News* in May 1994. "I am here selling parts and helping people fix their cars over the telephone every day."

Among those customers was Jim Bunting, a retired advertising executive in Lancaster, Pennsylvania, who'd bought his first Avanti in the mid '80s and became a fan. Bunting was intrigued by a two-seat Avanti drawn by the late Bob Andrews, a member of the Loewy team, and decided to build a real one. But no crude hatchet job would do, so he contacted Tom Kellogg, the team member who had done considerable detail work and most of the renderings for the Avanti project. Kellogg obliged with drawings of how the two-seater should look, but sent along a sketch with a playful note reading, "Let's do this one next." It showed a modernized Avanti of the sort Kellogg had been doodling for years, with the basic look evolved just as Studebaker might have done had it not folded.

Bunting loved Kellogg's "Avanti for the '90s," and decided to make it real. To keep costs reasonable, he started with a '94 Pontiac Firebird—a good choice, as its outer body panels were easily swapped for a new Avanti-look fiberglass skin custom-tailored by Kellogg. The transformation took place at the Harrisburg, Pennsylvania, shop of hot-rod builder Bill Lang and was finished in January 1996. By that point, other people had seen the car and wanted one, too. Bunting then showed it—still in primer and a bit rough—at a major swap meet, where more favorable inquiries convinced him to offer copies. After further tweaks by Kellogg, the finished car was unveiled in June 1997 at the combined meet of the Studebaker and Avanti clubs. Because rights to the Avanti name were in limbo, the car was christened AVX—"AVanti eXperimental."

Incorporating AVX Cars in Lancaster, Bunting contracted with Lang's Custom Auto to convert post-'92 Firebirds at the rate of two a month. The initial price was $33,900, plus the donor coupe or convertible. Echoing Newman & Altman, AVX owners could have their car most anyway they liked. "Nothing is too outrageous," Bunting told *Collectible Automobile®* magazine. Several ready-made packages were contemplated: two for brakes, three for suspension, and four engine upgrades, including a Paxton-supercharged Corvette LS1 V-8 with 455 bhp up to an incredible 650.

While the AVX was well-timed for the late-1990s luxury-car sales boom, Bunting quickly found that running a car company, even a tiny one, was more than he bargained for. Thus, after overseeing the build of three prototypes (a coupe, a T-top coupe, and a convertible), he sold AVX Cars to investor John Seaton. Surprisingly, Seaton soon teamed up with none other than Michael Kelly, who had never lost his enthusiasm for things Avanti. In August 1999, they formed a new Avanti Motor Corporation in Villa Rica, Georgia, just west of Atlanta, with Kelly as chairman and Seaton as CEO. To the undoubted delight of Avanti enthusiasts, the new concern managed to acquire the assets of all the preceding Avanti companies and even artifacts from the Studebaker days. It also held title to the Avanti name and logo, which would soon grace converted Firebirds based on the AVX design.

After setting up in a 74,000-square-foot former hosiery mill, the Kelly/Seaton enterprise turned out its first cars as 2001 models, selling 52 convertibles and T-top coupes for that calendar year. All used a 305-bhp GM 350-cid V-8 allied to a four-speed automatic or a five-speed manual transmission. Antilock brakes were included along with other stock Firebird features. Base prices were $79,000 for the coupe, $83,000 for the convertible. A supercharger option, pegged at a heroic $10,000, was added for 2002, swelling horsepower to 470. Though GM canceled the Firebird after model-year '02, Avanti stockpiled enough rolling chassis to continue production for several more years with no major change. This it did in true "custom car" fashion worthy of the Newman/Altman days—and with sales to match: 77 in '02, another 88 in '03, and 102 in 2004. Predictably, perhaps, most were convertibles.

1989 Avanti sport convertible coupe

1989 Avanti sport coupe

1989 Avanti four-door sedan

For 2005, the Avanti was reengineered around the new S197 Ford Mustang platform. Michael Kelly himself headed the effort, which involved most of the company's small workforce (just 36 employees)—everyone from accountants to craftspersons. And so much the better. As sales manager Dan Schwartz later said, "We're all cross-trained." The result was almost indistinguishable from the Firebird-based Avanti, a tribute to the team's skill and passion. So, too, was a new and unique Avanti instrument panel with airbags, one of many changes necessitated by the government's latest safety and emissions rules. By this time, Seaton had left (in late 2001) and

1998 AVX coupe

1998 AVX coupe

2005 Avanti convertible coupe

2006 Lister

Leonard Kelly, Michael's father, had been installed as president.

Only a convertible was offered for 2005, equipped with a 300-bhp Mustang 4.6-liter V-8, manual or automatic transmission, plus all-wheel antilock disc brakes, traction control, Ford Traction-Lok limited-slip rear differential, 17-inch polished

2006 Avanti Studebaker XUV prototype

wheels, leather interior, and full power accessories. Though the base price was slashed to $63,000, just 46 cars were sold that calendar year. Then again, Avanti sales were still mainly a word-of-mouth customer-to-factory proposition, and many would-be buyers likely didn't know the car was still around.

To reach a broader audience, a V-8 coupe was added for 2006, plus a lower-priced coupe and convertible using the base Mustang's 210-hp 4.0-liter V-6. Prices were adjusted, ranging from around $65,000 to near $76,000. At this writing, Avanti hoped to sell 75 to 100 units total, including a special GT model, possibly supercharged to around 390 bhp, slated for introduction in July 2006.

Meantime, Michael Kelly, doubtless with an eye to history, realized that his new Avanti concern wouldn't likely survive, let alone thrive, with just one basic product. Accordingly, he formed a division called SVO to create a pair of "component cars," sports-racers very closely modeled on the late '50s Lister-Jaguar and early '60s Porsche 904. Engineered by Chuck Beck, famed for his authentic, high-quality Porsche Spyder and Speedster replicas, both employ Avanti-fabricated frames, with Corvette C4 suspension and GM small-block V-8s. As "owner-assembled" cars, they're exempt from certain costly federal regulations, a major plus for tiny Avanti, and they help the bottom line, even though each is planned to see only about 25 copies a year. Though intended largely for vintage racing and other off-road use, both the Lister and 904 are easily licensed and usable on the street.

The replicas are beyond the scope of this book, as is the latest twist in the Avanti story: a big new sport-utility wagon reviving the historic Studebaker name. Planned to start sale in mid 2006, this Avanti Studebaker is based on Ford's Super Duty truck chassis and is thus about the same size as the GM-marketed Hummer H2. It also looks much like the military-influenced Hummer—boxy and purposeful—a resemblance that caused no small legal hassle when Avanti showed a concept model in 2004. But the wrangling has been settled, leaving the SUV to go forward with a choice of a gasoline V-10 or turbodiesel V-8, both Ford sourced. Ironically, the newest Studebaker is pitched at the very top of its market, tentatively tagged at $75,000-$80,000. But that's only to be expected from a company that aims to produce "unique, handcrafted automobiles of the finest quality, for the most discerning clients, providing them the utmost expression of their individuality."

With all this, Avanti survives into the twenty-first century with a brighter future than at any time since Leo Newman and Nate Altman picked up where Studebaker left off. Considering all that's happened since then, that's a most remarkable achievement.

Specifications

1965

(wb 109.0)	Wght	Price	Prod
spt cpe	3,217	6,550	21

1965 Engine	bore×stroke	bhp	availability
V-8, 327.0	4.00×3.25	300	S-all

1966

(wb 109.0)	Wght	Price	Prod
spt cpe	3,181	7,200	98

1966 Engine	bore×stroke	bhp	availability
V-8, 327.0	4.00×3.25	300	S-all

1967

(wb 109.0)	Wght	Price	Prod
spt cpe	3,217	7,200	60

1967 Engine	bore×stroke	bhp	availability
V-8, 327.0	4.00×3.25	300	S-all

1968

(wb 109.0)	Wght	Price	Prod
spt cpe	3,217	6,645	89

1968 Engine	bore×stroke	bhp	availability
V-8, 327.0	4.00×3.25	300	S-all

1969

(wb 109.0)	Wght	Price	Prod
spt cpe	3,217	7,145	103

1969 Engines	bore×stroke	bhp	availability
V-8, 327.0	4.00×3.25	300	S-all
V-8, 350.0	4.00×3.48	300	O-all

1970

(wb 109.0)	Wght	Price	Prod
spt cpe	3,342	7,500	111

1970 Engine	bore×stroke	bhp	availability
V-8, 350.0	4.00×3.48	300	S-all

1971

(wb 109.0)	Wght	Price	Prod
spt cpe	3,217	7,645	107

1971 Engine	bore×stroke	bhp	availability
V-8, 350.0	4.00×3.48	270	S-all

1972

(wb 109.0)	Wght	Price	Prod
spt cpe	3,217	8,145	127

1972 Engine	bore×stroke	bhp	availability
V-8, 400.0	4.13×3.75	270	S-all

1973

(wb 109.0)	Wght	Price	Prod
spt cpe	3,250	8,145	106

1973 Engine	bore×stroke	bhp	availability
V-8, 400.0	4.13×3.75	—	S-all

1974

(wb 109.0)	Wght	Price	Prod
spt cpe	3,250	8,645	123

1974 Engine	bore×stroke	bhp	availability
V-8, 400.0	4.13×3.75	180	S-all

1975

(wb 109.0)	Wght	Price	Prod
spt cpe	3,250	9,945	125

1975 Engine	bore×stroke	bhp	availability
V-8, 400.0	4.13×3.75	175	S-all

1976

(wb 109.0)	Wght	Price	Prod
spt cpe	3,500	12,195	175

1976 Engine	bore×stroke	bhp	availability
V-8, 400.0	4.13×3.75	175	S-all

1977

(wb 109.0)	Wght	Price	Prod
spt cpe	3,500	13,195	180

1977 Engine	bore×stroke	bhp	availability
V-8, 350.0	4.00×3.48	180	S-all

1978

(wb 109.0)	Wght	Price	Prod
spt cpe	3,500	15,980	190

1978 Engine	bore×stroke	bhp	availability
V-8, 350.0	4.00×3.48	180	S-all

1979

(wb 109.0)	Wght	Price	Prod
spt cpe	3,570	17,670	195

1979 Engine	bore×stroke	bhp	availability
V-8, 350.0	4.00×3.48	185	S-all

1980

(wb 109.0)	Wght	Price	Prod
spt cpe	3,570	18,995	190

1980 Engine	bore×stroke	bhp	availability
V-8, 350.0	4.00×3.48	190	S-all

1981

(wb 109.0)	Wght	Price	Prod
spt cpe	3,570	20,495	200*

1981 Engine	bore×stroke	bhp	availability
V-8, 305.0	3.74×3.48	155	S-all

1982

(wb 109.0)	Wght	Price	Prod
spt cpe	3,570	22,995	200*

1982 Engine	bore×stroke	bhp	availability
V-8, 305.0	3.74×3.48	155	S-all

1983

(wb 109.0)	Wght	Price	Prod
spt cpe	3,690	24,995	—

1983 Engine	bore×stroke	bhp	availability
V-8, 305.0	3.74×3.48	155	S-all

1984

(wb 109.0)	Wght	Price	Prod
spt cpe	3,680	31,860	287

1984 Engines	bore×stroke	bhp	availability
V-8, 305.0	3.74×3.48	155	S-all
V-8, 305.0	3.74×3.48	190	O-all

1985

(wb 109.0)	Wght	Price	Prod
spt cpe	3,680	37,995	—
GT cpe	3,210	37,995	—

1985 Engines	bore×stroke	bhp	availability
V-8, 305.0	3.74×3.48	190	S-cpe
V-8, 305.0	3.74×3.48	205	S-GT

1987

(wb 109.0; luxury spt cpe 117.0)	Wght	Price	Prod
spt cpe	—	29,995	300*
conv cpe	—	39,995	
luxury spt cpe	—	55,900	

1987 Engine	bore×stroke	bhp	availability
V-8, 305.0	3.74×3.48	155	S-all

1988

(wb 109.0; luxury spt cpe 117.0)	Wght	Price	Prod
spt cpe	3,750	35,000	150*
conv cpe	—	45,000	
luxury cpe	—	53,000	

1988 Engines	bore×stroke	bhp	availability
V-8, 305.0	3.74×3.48	170	S-all
V-8S, 305.0	3.74×3.48	250	S-Silver Anniv, suprchrgd

1989

(wb 109.0; luxury cpe 117.0)	Wght	Price	Prod
spt cpe	—	—	350*
conv cpe	—	—	
luxury cpe	—	—	

1989 Engine	bore×stroke	bhp	availability
V-8, 305.0	3.74×3.48	—	S-all

1990

(wb 109.0; sdn 116.0)	Wght	Price	Prod
spt cpe	—	—	—
conv cpe	—	—	—
sdn 4d	—	—	—

1990 Engine	bore×stroke	bhp	availability
V-8, 305.0	3.74×3.48	—	S-all

1991

(wb 109.0)	Wght	Price	Prod
spt cpe	—	—	15
conv cpe	—	—	

1991 Engine	bore×stroke	bhp	availability
V-8, 305.0	3.74×3.48	—	S-all

1998-99 AVX

(wb 101.1)	Wght	Price	Prod
T-top cpe	—	33,900**	—
conv cpe	—	33,900**	—

1998-99 Eng.	bore×stroke	bhp	availability
V-8, 350.0	4.00×3.48	—	S-all

2001

(wb 101.1)	Wght	Price	Prod
T-top cpe	—	69,000	52
conv cpe	—	83,000	

2001 Engines	bore×stroke	bhp	availability
V-8, 350.0	4.00×3.48	305	S-all
V-8S, 350.0	4.00×3.48	470	O-all

2002

(wb 101.1)	Wght	Price	Prod
T-top cpe	3,640	79,000	77
conv cpe	—	83,000	

2002 Engines	bore×stroke	bhp	availability
V-8, 350.0	4.00×3.48	305	S-all
V-8S, 350.0	4.00×3.48	470	O-all

2003

(wb 101.0)	Wght	Price	Prod
T-top cpe	—	79,000	88
conv cpe	—	83,000	

2003 Engines	bore×stroke	bhp	availability
V-8, 350.0	4.00×3.48	305	S-all
V-8, 350.0	4.00×3.48	470	O-all

2004

(wb 101.0)	Wght	Price	Prod
T-top cpe	—	79,000	102
conv cpe	—	83,000	

2004 Engines	bore×stroke	bhp	availability
V-8, 350.0	4.00×3.48	305	S-all
V-8, 350.0	4.00×3.48	470	O-all

2005

(wb 101.3)	Wght	Price	Prod
conv cpe	—	63,000	46

2005 Engines	bore×stroke	bhp	availability
V-8, 281.0	3.55×3.54	300	S-all

2006

(wb 101.3)	Wght	Price	Prod
V-6 cpe	—	64,950	—
V-6 conv cpe	—	69,950	—
V-8 cpe	—	70,950	—
V-8 conv cpe	—	75,950	—

2006 Engines	bore×stroke	bhp	availability
V-6, 245.0	3.95×3.32	210	S-V-6
V-8, 281.0	3.55×3.54	300	S-V-8

2006 Prod. figures not available at time of publication.

* Estimated production

** Donor Pontiac Firebird required

Buick

David Dunbar Buick was a canny Scottish industrialist but an unlikely auto builder. After making his mark with a process for annealing porcelain to steel for bathtubs, he turned to the profit opportunities of the horseless-carriage phenomenon. His first car, appearing in 1903, was a simple little chain-drive runabout with flat-twin power. One engine feature, overhead valves, was a rarity then, but has been a hallmark of almost all Buicks since.

In 1904, Buick moved from Detroit to Flint, Michigan, where it soon came under the control of William C. Durant. Buick prospered, and in 1908 Durant formed General Motors with Buick as its foundation and chief source of revenue. Six-cylinder engines arrived in 1914, and were the only type Buick offered from 1925 to '30. By that point, Buick buyers were mostly upper middle-class professional types who'd moved up from a Chevrolet, Oakland, or Oldsmobile—hence the "doctor's car" sobriquet of the make's early years. The Depression considerably reduced the size of this clientele—and Buick sales—but the division would bounce back strongly, reaching fourth in industry production for model-year 1938 (from a decade-low seventh in 1934-36).

The decision to offer costlier eight-cylinder cars came before the Wall Street crash, so Buick's sales problems in the early '30s, stemmed mainly from bad timing. At least the 1930 line corrected the bulged "pregnant" beltline styling that had been decidedly unpopular in 1929. Buicks were conventional cars, arrayed in three series: the low-priced "40" on a 118-inch wheelbase, the midrange "50" on a 124-inch span, and the deluxe "60" on a 132-inch chassis. All carried "valve-in-head" sixes, the last six-cylinder engines at Buick until the 1960s. The 40 used a 257.5-cubic-incher with 81 horsepower, the 50 and 60 a 331.3-cid engine with 99 bhp. The 50 offered just four-door sedan and four-place sport coupe; 40 and 60 listed a full range of models, some quite scarce (only 836 seven-seat Series 60 limousines, for instance). Despite the deepening Depression, Buick finished third in industry production for the model year, mainly because competitors fared far worse.

For 1931 came an expanded lineup powered by the first Buick eights, among the most-advanced engines of their day: smooth and reliable five-main-bearing units designed by division chief engineer F.A. Bower. They included a 77-bhp 220.7 for the 50, now the least-costly Buick; a 272.6 with 90 bhp for the 60, the new midranger; and a 104-bhp 344.8-cid engine for new top-echelon Series 80 and 90. The lengthened model roster again included sedans, coupes, phaetons, convertibles, and roadsters, plus Series 90 seven-seat sedan and limousine. The 50, which included a "second-series" group announced in early '31, rode the 114-inch wheelbase applied to the 1930 Marquette, Buick's short-lived junior make; 60, 80, and 90 spanned 118, 124, and 132 inches, respectively.

Straight eights would be Buick's mainstay for the next 22 years. The new 1931 engine proved its mettle at that year's Indianapolis 500 by powering a racer that Phil Shafer qualified at 105.1 mph; for the race he averaged 86.4 mph. Any '31 Buick was quick in showroom tune; 10-60 mph took about 25 seconds, quite speedy for the day, and 90 mph was possible.

The big news for 1932 was "Silent Second SynchroMesh" transmission, plus more horsepower for all engines. Power and most wheelbases went up again for 1933, but sales did not. As a partial consequence, Harlow H. Curtice was appointed Buick president in October that year.

Curtice believed in "more speed for less money," and backed it up with an all-new 117-inch-wheelbase Series 40 for 1934. The result was a sales upturn aided by more modern, streamlined styling that broke sharply with "Roaring '20s" squarishness. Also featured linewide in '34 was GM's new "Knee-Action" (Dubonnet-type) independent front suspension, then a great step forward. Though the 40 omitted flashy soft tops to empha-

1930 Series 60 7-passenger sedan

1932 Series 90 sport phaeton

1931 Series 50 business coupe

1932 Series 90 convertible phaeton

1932 Series 60 business coupe

1933 Series 60 Victoria coupe

size far more popular coupes and sedans, its masterful blend of an inexpensive, Chevrolet-size platform and "important" Buick styling helped boost the division's 1934 output from some 47,000 to over 71,000. Buick then jumped way over 100,000 for model-year '36, and would reach even greater heights a few years hence.

Also in 1934, Curtice launched a $64 million factory modernization program that wasn't completed until 1940. However, plowing receipts back into facilities left little money for product improvements, so the 1935 Buicks weren't changed much. Offerings again comprised 40, 50, 60, and 90 with straight eights of 233, 235, 278, and 344 cid, respectively. There was one belated addition, though: a Series 40 convertible coupe.

More extensive changes occurred for 1936, as Buick adopted GM's all-steel "Turret Top" construction that eliminated the traditional fabric roof insert, gaining sleek all-new styling with it. The division also boasted more-potent engines with aluminum pistons. Series numbers began giving way to names that would last all the way through 1958—from the bottom, Special (40), Century (60), Roadmaster (80), and Limited (90). Respective wheelbases were 118, 122, 131, and 138 inches.

Styling was a big factor in Buick's 1936 resurgence. It was, of course, the work of Harley J. Earl, founder and head of GM's Art & Colour Section, the first formal styling department at a major automaker. Earl liked streamlining, and Buick had it for '36. Lines were rounder than ever, set off by more swept-back windshields, fully integrated trunks (instead of separate, detachable fixtures), and massive vertical-bar grilles. The public responded to this package by buying over 168,000 Buicks for the model year. Calendar-1936 production reached near 180,000 as division volume returned to its pre-Depression level.

Engines choices were reduced for '36 from four to just two. Special retained its 93-bhp 233-cid eight. Other '36s carried a new 320-cid unit with 120 bhp. The latter would be a Buick mainstay through the '50s. Putting it in the lighter Special body made the new '36 Century a fast car, with genuine 100-mph top speed and 10-60 acceleration of 18-19 seconds. Besides good performance and sleek good looks, Century was attractively priced: as little as $1035 for the sport coupe and $1135 for the rakish convertible. It quickly became known as a "factory hot rod" (arguably Detroit's first)—about the fastest thing you could buy for $1000 or so.

Such triumphs didn't imply much change for 1937. But Harley Earl wasn't satisfied, so Flint's Turret-Tops gained longer fenders with blunt trailing edges, plus horizontal grille bars and complementing side hood vents. Buick was perhaps GM's best-looking '37 car, and still an industry style-setter.

Mechanically, the bigger eight returned unchanged, but a

1934 Series 60 convertible coupe

1937 Series 60 Century two-door sedan

1936 Series 60 Roadmaster four-door sedan

1938 Series 90 Limited 8-passenger sedan

1939 Series 40 Special convertible coupe

1940 Series 40 Special convertible coupe

1940 Series 60 Century sport coupe

1941 Series 40A Special sport coupe

1941 Series 90 Limited limousine

1941 Series 60 Century business coupe

longer stroke boosted Special's engine to 248 cid, horsepower to an even 100. Factory figures suggested a '37 Special could scale 10-60 mph in 19.2 seconds—fine performance for the class and only a second behind the hot Century. New for all '37s were hypoid rear axle, improved generator, standard windshield defroster, front/rear antiroll bars, and a *claimed* industry first: a steering-wheel horn ring (Cord introduced it in '36).

The top-line Limited became almost Cadillac-exclusive in 1936-37, so it's puzzling they'd be long overlooked as collector's items. All late-'30s Limiteds were of "trunkback" configuration and carried dual spare tires in long "pontoon" front fenders. The elegant formal sedan of 1936-37 came with a glass division between front and rear compartments, plus the expected *grand luxe* trim. Through 1939, the series included six- and eight-passenger sedans and a limousine. Limited chassis were supplied in fair numbers to custom coachbuilders such as Eureka, Miller, Sayers & Scoville, and Flexible for hearse, ambulance, and flower-car applications.

A new grille with fewer but thicker horizontal bars was the chief styling cue for 1938, but more mechanical changes made a good car even better. All-coil suspension—another Buick first—delivered a much-improved ride, aided by shock absorbers four times the typical size. Domed, high-compression pistons boosted horsepower on both engines, now dubbed "Dynaflash." A new item for Special was a four-speed semi-automatic transmission, though it proved troublesome and was dropped after one year. Flint wouldn't attempt another clutchless drive until fully automatic Dynaflow about a decade later.

Buick by now had expanded to encompass a broad market. Prices ranged from $945 for the 1938 Special business coupe to near $2500 for the opulent eight-passenger Limited limo. For big spenders, Brunn still offered custom-bodied Limiteds, though far fewer than in the halcyon pre-Depression days.

Flint closed out the decade with lower-looking 1939 models mildly face-lifted with "waterfall" grilles, "streamboards" (optional concealed running boards), and a sunroof option on some models. Sidemount spare tires were still available, but not as frequently ordered. Special's 122-inch wheelbase (from 1937-38) shrank two inches. Other spans were unchanged from '38: 126-inch Century, 133-inch Roadmaster, 140-inch Limited. Body choices were as plentiful as ever, prices as moderate. The natty Century convertible sport phaeton sold for just $1713, the sport coupe for $1175. Buick abandoned the increasingly unpopular rumble-seat ragtop for '39, but scored a safety innovation with flashing turn signals, installed at the rear as part of the trunk emblem. Also new were column-mounted gearshift and refillable shock absorbers.

Buick's buyers were quite loyal, and in the '40s the division would be GM's number-two seller, after Chevrolet. Throughout the decade, Buick usually ran fourth behind the "Low-Price Three" (Chevy, Ford, Plymouth), building upwards of 300,000 cars a year. GM endured an extended strike after World War II and Flint took awhile to regain momentum, but was back to over 324,000 cars for 1949. Buicks of the '40s reflected the division's period slogan "Valve in Head—Ahead in Value": big but reasonably priced cars that were a bit ostentatious. For those who felt status was everything, there was always Cadillac.

The early-'40s lineup was one of the widest in Buick history and wouldn't be matched until the mid '50s. Model groups expanded from four to six for 1940 with the addition of the Series 50 Super (another enduring name). It bowed with fewer models than the Special priced just below it, but included a handsome wood-bodied Estate wagon. Super and Special both rode a 121-inch wheelbase and carried the respected 248-cid straight eight, still with 107 bhp (as since 1938). Priced above

1942 Series 40B Special four-door sedan

1946 Roadmaster four-door sedan

1942 Series 40A Special convertible coupe

1947 Special Sedanet fastback

1942 Series 40 Special station wagon

1947 Roadmaster convertible coupe

1946 Series 40 Special sedanet

1948 Super station wagon

them—and still with the brawny 320.2-cid eight—were Century (60) and Roadmaster (now Series 70) on 126-inch chassis, plus two Limited lines: 133-inch-wheelbase Series 80 and 140-inch Series 90 (the latter confined to long sedans and limousines).

Buick again cataloged several interesting wares for 1940, but some were in their last season. Low sales had been thinning the ranks of convertible sedans. This year saw the final Century model; Super and Roadmaster versions would run one year more. "Streamlined Sedans" with fastback styling reminiscent of the Lincoln-Zephyr saw just 14 copies in the Series 80. More popular was the $1952 Series 80 convertible sedan (phaeton) with conventional lines, though only 250 were called for. Custom styles were still around, but not as "factory" models. One rakish town car by Brewster on the Series 90 chassis would be the first Buick named a "Classic" by the Classic Car Club of America. Buffalo's Brunn was also still doing customs in 1940, including one fairly conventional town car on the Roadmaster platform.

Flint had a banner 1941, with model-year production soaring to 374,000. Leading that year's line were beautiful and opulent Brunn customs on the Limited chassis: phaeton, town car, landau brougham, and full landau. Most flamboyant was the convertible coupe, offered to dealers for $3500. At that price, only the prototype sold, but it was significant for a "sweep-spear" side motif that prefigured a postwar Buick hallmark.

Among production '41s, the two Limited lines were combined into a single Series 90 on a 139-inch wheelbase. Century was shorn of its convertible, convertible sedan, and club coupe. The Estate wagon shifted from Super to Special but cost some $200 more than in 1940. Reflecting its strong sales, Special split into two subseries: 121-inch-wheelbase 40 and 118-inch 40A. Styling was evolutionary, with a bolder, heavier grille and

1949 Roadmaster convertible coupe

1949 Super Sedanet fastback

1949 Roadmaster Riviera hardtop coupe

1949 Roadmaster four-door sedan

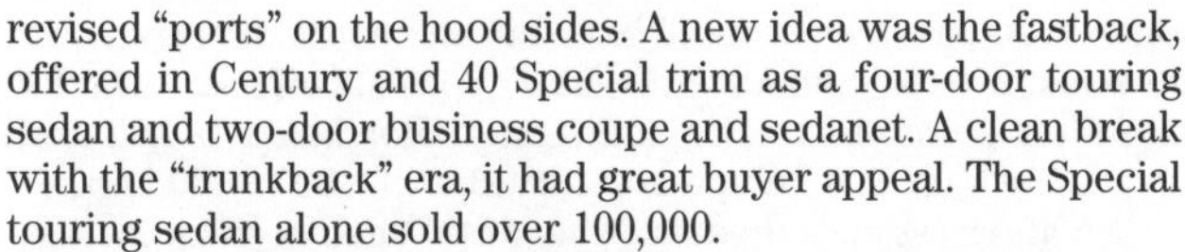

revised "ports" on the hood sides. A new idea was the fastback, offered in Century and 40 Special trim as a four-door touring sedan and two-door business coupe and sedanet. A clean break with the "trunkback" era, it had great buyer appeal. The Special touring sedan alone sold over 100,000.

The 1941 Special/Super engine gained new-design high-compression pistons for more-efficient combustion that lifted horsepower to 115. Available for the 40 touring sedan and sedanet was "Compound Carburetion"—two carburetors with a progressive linkage that added 10 bhp. This was standard on other '41s, resulting in 165 bhp for the 320 engine. Chassis were carryovers for all but Limited, which used a new X-member design.

World War II came at precisely the wrong time for Buick, which completely restyled for 1942 *a la* Harley Earl's 1939 "Y-Job" show car. The result was Flint's sleekest cars ever, with a wide, low, vertical-bar grille theme that would continue postwar. Fastback "torpedo" styling was more popular than ever. Century, which would go into postwar limbo until 1954, was down to only two models, both fastbacks. Their Special counterparts continued to dominate sales of that two-series line (realigned into 40A and 40B on 118- and 121-inch wheelbases, respectively). Two-door sedanets were new for Super and Roadmaster. Most '42 Buicks wore Earl's new "Airfoil" front fenders swept back through almost the entire length of the car to meet the rear-fender leading edges. Limiteds and Specials lacked this, but had front fenders extended well into the doors.

As elsewhere in Detroit, Buicks built after January 1, 1942, used painted metal instead of chromed parts per government order. For the same reason, Specials and Supers exchanged aluminum pistons for cast-iron slugs. This, plus lowered compression, dropped horsepower to 110 (118 with Compound Carburetion). Production ground to a halt in early February after some 92,000 units, and wouldn't begin again until October 1945.

But thanks to its '42 redesign, Buick resumed civilian production in fine fettle. While nearly all makes were forced to issue warmed-over prewar models, Flint's styling was technically but a year old in 1945, and thus still fairly fresh. Packard, by contrast, returned with the two-year-old styling of its very handsome 1941-42 Clipper, then felt obliged to undertake a severe facelift for 1948. Buick stretched its '42 tooling through the 1949 Special, then came back with a brand-new Special for 1950. (One year can make a big difference in the car business.) Exotic customs did not return; they simply weren't needed. A mere 2482 Buicks were built in the closing months of 1945, but output surged to more than 153,000 for model-year '46.

While the first postwar Buicks were basically '42s, there were fewer of them: Special, Super, and Roadmaster sedans and sedanets; Super and Roadmaster convertibles; Super Estate wagon; no Centurys or Limiteds; only one Special series. Styling was cleaned up via single instead of double side moldings, simpler grille, and the first of Buick's distinctive "gunsight" hood ornaments. Wheelbases were 121 inches for Special (as for 1942's Series 40B), 124 for Super, 129 for Roadmaster. Compound Carburetion didn't return either, so Special/Super remained at 110 bhp. This array of models, wheelbases, and engines would endure through 1948 with only minor changes.

Appearance alterations were also minor through '48, as GM was planning its first all-postwar models for 1949. The '47s gained a "wing-top" grille conferring a lower look; a new, more-elaborate crest appeared above it. The only changes for '48 were full-length belt moldings on Specials and chrome fender nameplates on Super/Roadmaster.

But Flint made big news for '48 with Dynaflow, its excellent new fully automatic transmission, arriving as a $244 option for Roadmaster only. Demand for this torque-converter unit proved so strong that Buick had to double planned installations. By 1951, Dynaflow was ordered by 85 percent of Buick buyers.

The all-new '49 models swelled Buick volume to 324,276 units—again right behind Chevy-Ford-Plymouth. These were sleek and graceful cars next to the 1946-48s, and reviewers agreed they were worth the great attention they got. Harley Earl's team successfully translated aircraft themes to an automobile, and only a hint of the old separate rear fenders remained on Super and Roadmaster. Also new was the first of Buick's trademark "portholes" or "VentiPorts," an idea from designer Ned Nickles.

Buick's most eye-catching '49 was the Roadmaster Riviera, introduced at midyear along with Cadillac's Coupe de Ville and

1950 Roadmaster Riviera four-door sedan

1950 Special Jetback fastback sedan

1950 Super Riviera hardtop coupe

1951 Super four-door sedan

Oldsmobile's Holiday. As Detroit's first modern mass-produced "hardtop convertibles," they began a trend that would eventually render real convertibles obsolete. The '49 Riviera was a handsome, luxurious brute with a beautiful pillarless roofline. It was sold with either conventional straight side moldings or "sweep-spear" trim, soon to join VentiPorts as a make trademark.

With the main emphasis on styling, the '49 Buicks changed little mechanically, though Dynaflow-equipped Supers got higher, 6.9:1 compression that improved horsepower to 120. Roadmaster had been similarly raised to 150 in 1948, and continued that way with Dynaflow standard. Body styles stayed the same, save the new hardtop. The woody wagon was reworked to fit '49 styling, but sales remained modest. Roadmaster was put on a 126-inch wheelbase and Super reassigned to the 121-inch Special chassis.

Buick would maintain this basic lineup through 1953. All 1950 models, Special now included, wore a new look dominated by big, "toothy" vertical-bar grilles and fuller body contours. This, too, would persist through '53. Specials also received a half-inch longer wheelbase. Though still attractively priced, the 1950s were a bit utilitarian. Offerings comprised standard and DeLuxe fastback and "Touring" notchback four-doors, fastback sedanet coupe, and a revived business coupe. With fastbacks quickly falling from buyer favor, the Special sedanet was Buick's only "jetback" for '51, when the Special received a Riviera hardtop, as had the Super for 1950.

The Riviera name also graced well-proportioned 1950-51 Super and Roadmaster four-door sedans with special long wheelbases (125.5 and 130.3 inches, respectively). Both lines also included woody Estate wagons through '53, with structural body parts of mahogany and white ash. These were big and expensive. The '53 Roadmaster Estate cost a hefty $4031 and weighed 4315 pounds.

Super was Buick's volume seller in the early '50s, offering standard and Riviera sedans, a convertible, Riviera hardtop and the Estate, plus a 1950 sedanet and a handful of notchback '52 two-door sedans. Roadmaster styles essentially duplicated these.

All 1950-52 Buicks and the '53 Special continued to rely on aging but proven valve-in-head straight eights. Displacement, compression, and power varied with model and year. The 1950 Special engine delivered 115 bhp (120 bhp with Dynaflow) from its usual 248 cid. Supers and 1951-53 Specials offered up to 130 bhp from a bored-out 263.3-cid version. Roadmasters still used the 320, which was bumped up for '52 from 152 to 170 bhp.

Dynaflow (some called it "Dyna-slush") had been an increasingly popular Super/Special option since 1950 (it remained standard on Roadmaster). It multiplied torque via a drive turbine induced to rotate through an oil bath by a facing crankshaft-driven turbine. Dynaflow was smooth, but gave poor performance. The successor Twin-Turbine Dynaflow of 1953 was more positive and gave better oomph. By decade's end an even better Triple-Turbine transmission was offered across the

1951 Roadmaster Riviera four-door sedan

1951 Roadmaster station wagon

board at $296 extra. But no Dynaflow could deliver acceleration like the Cadillac/Oldsmobile Hydra-Matic, and was thus handicapped in the burgeoning '50s "horsepower race."

Golden Anniversary 1953 brought first-time availability of power steering and a 12-volt electrical system, but the highlight was a fine new overhead-valve V-8 for Super and Roadmaster. An oversquare design of 322 cid, this "Fireball" engine packed up to 188 bhp on industry-topping 8.5:1 compression. Roadmasters were demoted to a 121.5-inch wheelbase save the Riviera sedan, which shared the Super's 125.5-inch span.

Also highlighting Buick's 50th year was a flashy new limited-edition Roadmaster convertible. Called Skylark, it was perfect for Hollywood types and Texas oil barons. Only 1690 were sold that year, largely because of the extraordinary $5000 price.

Skylark was another of those long-famous Harley Earl styling projects, but was planned for the broadest possible appeal. Instead of being a two-seat sports car—which accounted for only 0.27 percent of the '53 market—it was a luxurious and sporty "personal" four-seater similar to Ford's post-1957 Thunderbirds. Like 1953's corresponding Olds Fiesta and Cadillac Eldorado, Skylark was basically a customized standard convertible, with four-inch lower windshield and top, plus fully radiused rear wheel cutouts. Though bereft of the trademark portholes, it sported Kelsey-Hayes chrome wire wheels, then becoming fashionable throughout Detroit.

Along with Olds and Cadillac, Buick switched to longer, more-massively square bodies for 1954, but also revived its prewar "hot rod" with a new Century line offering the bigger Buick engine in the smaller Buick body. All models wore inverted-U grilles with fine vertical bars set under oval nacelles cradling headlamps and parking lamps. Windshields were newly wrapped as on recent GM showmobiles, and rear fenders kicked up to carry vertical pairs of bullet taillamps high in the trailing edges. Offerings regrouped to include convertibles, hardtops, and sedans in each series. Century and Special also offered new all-steel four-door Estate wagons (remarkably with no *ersatz* wood). A two-door sedan was exclusive to Special, and was the price-leader at $2207.

Special belatedly received its own Fireball V-8 for '54, a 264-cid unit with 143/150 bhp. Other models carried the 322 with power ratings of 177 (manual-shift Super) to 200 (Roadmaster and Skylark). Wheelbases were realigned once more: 122 inches for Special/Century, 127 for Super/Roadmaster.

Skylark also returned for '54, but was much less "custom" than the '53, though that enabled Buick to trim price down to $4483. Now more Century than Roadmaster, the '54 stood apart with tacked-on tailfins and huge chrome-plated diecast taillight housings, plus the circular rear wheel openings. Overall, it somewhat resembled Buick's '54 Wildcat II show car, but was evidently less-impressive than the '53 Skylark, for only 836 were sold before the model was dropped.

Much of Buick's 1954 styling was previewed by the XP-300 and 1951 LeSabre show cars, rolling testbeds for numerous postwar GM ideas. Both used an experimental 215-cid aluminum V-8, a very special job unrelated to Buick's same-size early-'60s engine. With exactly square dimensions (3.25-inch bore and stroke), 10:1 compression, and a Roots-type supercharger, it produced over 300 bhp—phenomenal for the day. However, it ran on a methanol/gasoline blend, not exactly common at local filling stations. Both showpieces were futuristic. The 116-inch-wheelbase LeSabre sported a wrapped windshield and "Dagmar" bumpers. The XP-300, on an inch-shorter wheelbase, prefigured production '54 Buicks in its frontal treatment.

Speaking of production, Buick had been pushing relentlessly toward number-three, breaking its all-time record in calendar 1950 with more than 550,000 cars. The 1954 tally of 531,000 left Buick trailing only Chevrolet and Ford, a position it hadn't held since the '40s. The division's 1955 volume was another record: 781,000, nearly 50 percent higher than the previous best.

1951 Super Jetback fastback coupe

1952 Special sport coupe

1952 Roadmaster convertible coupe

1953 Roadmaster station wagon

This success was owed largely to the Special, which had become one of America's most popular cars. Over 380,000 were built for 1955, Detroit's banner year of the decade, including 155,000 Riviera two-door hardtops, that season's single best-selling Buick. A deft '55 restyle kept sales booming, aided by even-more-potent V-8s delivering 188 bhp on Specials, 236 bhp elsewhere. For mid-'55 came four-door Riviera hardtop sedans in the Special and Century series; Super and Roadmaster versions followed for '56. These (along with the Oldsmobile Holiday) were the first four-door hardtops, GM once again forcing the rest of the industry to play catch-up.

The '56 Buicks didn't sell as well as the '55s—but then, '56

1954 Wildcat II show car

1953 Roadmaster Riviera hardtop coupe

1954 Roadmaster Riviera four-door sedan

1954 Century four-door sedan

1955 Century Riviera hardtop sedan

1956 Roadmaster Riviera hardtop sedan

1956 Roadmaster four-door sedan

1956 Special Riviera hardtop sedan

was a "breather" for most everyone. Another facelift introduced model-year designation to exterior nameplates, which Buick would abandon after 1957 amid customer complaints that it made the cars obsolete that much sooner. The "horsepower race" was at full gallop, and the '56s were the most-powerful Buicks yet. The Special now offered 220 bhp, other models 255. A Century could leap from 0-60 mph in 10.5 seconds and top 110 mph, and every '56 Buick could do at least 100 mph.

Longer and lower new bodies arrived for '57 wearing slightly exaggerated '56 styling. Though division general manager Ed Ragsdale never said how much this makeover cost, it must have run several hundred million. Yet despite the most-sweeping alterations since '49, Buick's '57s didn't sell that well, mainly because rivals were pressing hard for industry design leadership. Chrysler, in fact, took over with its new fleet of longer, lower, glassier, and tailfinned cars created under Virgil Exner.

Still, Flint's '57s were dashing and fairly clean for the age. And horsepower was higher still: 250 for Special, an even 300 elsewhere, thanks to a bore/stroke job taking V-8 displacement to 364 cubes. Model changes were few but interesting: pillarless four-door wagons for Century and Special, plus a Series 75 Roadmaster Riviera hardtop coupe and sedan. The latter, just upmarket versions of the regular Series 70 models, had every possible standard luxury save air conditioning: Dynaflow, power steering and brakes, dual exhausts, automatic windshield washers, backup lights, clock, special interior with deep-pile carpeting, and more. But though 1957 was a decent year for Buick, it was even better for Plymouth, which pushed Flint

1957 Super Riviera hardtop sedan

1957 Century Caballero hardtop station wagon

1957 Century Riviera hardtop coupe

1957 Roadmaster convertible coupe

1958 Century convertible coupe

from third to fourth in sales for the first time in three years.

Sales were far worse for 1958, notable for the gaudiest Buicks ever. From contrived chrome-draped fins to a monster grille holding 160 shiny little squares, Flint's "B-58" models looked overtly ornate—especially the heroically over-decorated Limited, newly revived: The '58s were also the fattest Buicks since the war—some 400 pounds heavier than the 1950s and three to four inches longer than the '57s—so performance suffered with unchanged horsepower.

No '58 Buick sold well, though the year's flash recession was as much to blame as the garish styling. Model-year production stopped at some 240,000, and Flint dropped behind Olds to fifth in sales. Air suspension was offered, but seldom ordered. In all, '58 was a very bad year for Buick.

So was 1959. But where the '58s were ostentatious, the '59s were tasteful. Though again dominated by omnipresent tailfins—bigger than ever now, and newly canted—the '59s were smooth, clean, and fairly dignified, with huge windshields, fewer chrome grille squares—and no sweep-spears. Buick now shared corporate A- and B-bodies with sister GM makes, but it wasn't obvious. Nor was the fact that '59 styling was a hasty reply to Chrysler's successful '57s. But thank goodness for it. Original '59 plans called for face-lifted '58s, which were gruesome.

For the first time in two decades, Buick retitled its series for '59. Special became LeSabre, Invicta replaced Century, and Super and Roadmaster were now Electra and Electra 225. The last two rode a 126.3-inch wheelbase, trimmed 1.2 inches from 1957-58. LeSabre/Invicta shared a 123-inch chassis and Special/Century body styles save hardtop wagons, which were dropped due to low sales. Electras were priced quite a bit lower than counterpart '58s, spanning a $3800-$4300 range. Buick was called 1959's most-changed car, and the changes were for the better.

On the mechanical side, 1959 brought a new 401-cid V-8 with 325 bhp for the upper three series; LeSabre stayed with the last Special's 364. Power brakes and steering were standard on Electras, a $150 option elsewhere. Air conditioning was $430 across the board. Air suspension (for the rear only) was still nominally available—and still almost never ordered due to unresolved reliability problems.

Significantly, Buick dealers sold more Opels than ever in '59. The "captive import" from GM's German subsidiary had been assigned to Buick in '58, and soon nabbed a fair number of customers weary of oversized, overweight cars. But Buick was already planning its own compact, and its star would rise again.

Indeed, Buick volume soared from about 250,000 cars and ninth place in 1960 to more than 665,000 and a tight hold on fifth by '69. This success was due partly to the advent of compacts and partly to increased demand for traditional Buicks. Electra sales, for instance, were only some 56,000 in 1960 but nearly 159,000 by '69. Corresponding LeSabre figures were about 152,000 and nearly 198,000. Wildcat, which replaced Invicta for '63, began at about 35,000 but was almost double that by decade's end.

The aforementioned compact appeared for 1961 as the smallest Buick in 50 years. Reviving the Special name, it was one of three "second-wave" GM compacts—the Buick-Olds-Pontiac models that followed Chevy's Corvair (and borrowed some of its body engineering). Riding a 112-inch wheelbase, Special offered base and DeLuxe coupe, sedan, and four-door wagon in the $2300-$2700 range. All carried a new 215-cid aluminum-block V-8 with 155 bhp—light, smooth, and efficient. (Amazingly, production lasted into the 21st century. GM sold manufacturing rights to Rover, which used it in Rover cars and Land Rover utility vehicles beginning in the late '60s.)

Responding quickly to the sporty-car craze begun by the 1960 Corvair Monza, Buick fielded a more special Special DeLuxe

1958 Century Caballero hardtop station wagon

1960 Electra 225 hardtop sedan

1960 Electra 225 Riviera hardtop sedan

1960 Invicta hardtop coupe

coupe for mid '61. This one resurrected another familiar name: Skylark. No-cost bucket seats, optional vinyl roof, and a 185-bhp V-8 helped sell more than 12,000 in that short debut season. For 1962 came Skylark and Special DeLuxe convertibles, an optional Borg-Warner four-speed gearbox—and more than 42,000 Buick compact sales.

The big Buicks changed dramatically after the 1960 models, which were basically toned-down '59s. The '61s rode unchanged wheelbases but weighed 100-200 pounds less, looked much cleaner, and boasted fewer gimmicks. For 1962, Buick unleashed the Wildcat as a specialty Invicta: a two-ton, 123-inch-wheelbase luxury hardtop priced around $4000 and sporting bucket seats, vinyl roof, and unique exterior badging. First-year sales were so good that Wildcat replaced Invicta on all midrange senior Buicks for '63 save a single wagon (fewer than 3500 sold), after which the Invicta name disappeared.

1961 Electra 225 convertible coupe

1961 Invicta hardtop coupe

As noted, the premium Electras attracted increased sales right away. Two series continued for 1960-61: standard Electra and the posher Electra 225, named for its overall length in inches and soon popularly known as the "Deuce-and-a-Quarter." This setup didn't last, however, as all Electras became 225s for '62. Buick then concentrated on fewer offerings. Electra's standard engine through 1966 was a 325-bhp 401 V-8. A bored-out 425 with 340/360 bhp became optionally available by 1964. Both then gave way to a standard 430 with 360 horses.

Buick styling wasn't exceptional in this decade, with one singular exception: the new-for-'63 Riviera (recycling yet another well-known Flint moniker). This svelte personal-luxury hardtop coupe changed Buicks' stodgy image almost overnight. Many people felt that GM styling chief William L. Mitchell (who'd succeeded Harley Earl on his retirement back in '58) had fathered one of the best automotive shapes of all time.

This new Riviera was first conceived as a LaSalle, reviving Cadillac's lower-priced nameplate of 1927-40. (It wasn't the first attempt. Buick head designer Ned Nickles had penned an experimental "LaSalle II" roadster and hardtop sedan for the 1955 Motorama, both with trademark vertical-themed grille.) The impetus was Ford's highly successful four-seat Thunderbird that bowed for 1958. At one time, a convertible, four-door hardtop, and even a convertible sedan were considered. Ultimately, the hardtop-coupe clay model approved in early 1961 was assigned to Buick to give it a shot in the sales arm. Not that there was much choice. Cadillac didn't have facilities to build the car (and didn't need it), Chevrolet was enjoying record sales, and Oldsmobile and Pontiac had other fish to fry.

Mitchell freely admitted to borrowing some of the '63 Riviera's design elements. Its razor-edge roof styling, for instance, was inspired by certain 1950s English custom bodywork. But the finished product was handsome and individual.

1961 Special DeLuxe four-door sedan

1962 Invicta Wildcat hardtop sport coupe

1962 Invicta Estate wagon

1963 Electra 225 hardtop sedan

1962 Special Skylark hardtop coupe

1963 Wildcat hardtop sedan

1962 Electra 225 hardtop coupe

1963 Riviera hardtop coupe

As scheduled, model-year production was exactly 40,000.

Riding a 117-inch wheelbase, Riviera was about 14 inches shorter and 200-300 pounds lighter than other big '63 Buicks. At first, Electra's 325-bhp 401 V-8 was standard and the new 340-bhp 425 optional, but the latter became base power for '64, when optional horses increased to 360. Standard two-speed Turbine Drive was used for '63, three-speed Hydra-Matic thereafter. Handling was up to performance, which was strong. The typical 325-bhp Riv ran the quarter-mile in 16 seconds at 85 mph; a 360-bhp car managed 15.5 seconds and 90-plus mph.

For 1964, Buick joined Olds and Pontiac in offering larger, restyled compacts with GM's new midsize A-body platform, also used by Chevy's new Chevelle. Wheelbase stretched to 115 inches for all body styles except the new Skylark Sport Wagon, which had a 120-inch wheelbase. The Sport Wagon (and Olds Vista Cruisers) featured a raised rear roof section with glass insets on three sides. There were new engines, too: a 225-cid V-6 (a novelty for Detroit) with 155 bhp, and a cast-iron 300-cid V-8 with 210/250 bhp. With that, the plush Skylark rapidly became the most-popular smaller Buick. Skylark/Special production was about 9-to-10 for '64, but Skylark had reached a near 5-to-1 ratio by 1969.

Flint's 1964 standards were longer overall but unchanged in wheelbase. The compacts' new 300 V-8 became base LeSabre power. Like the Century of yore, Wildcat was the division's hot rod, carrying the Electra 401 in the lighter, shorter LeSabre chassis. Reflecting its popularity, a four-door sedan joined the convertible and two hardtops that year. All '64 seniors retained their '63 look, but with corners and edges rounded off. Riviera was little changed, but production dropped by about 2500 units.

The division's 1965 production was 50 percent above its 1960 total, putting Buick fifth in the annual industry race. An expanded lineup in general and the unique Riviera in particular were responsible, but so was a very strong overall market that bought Detroit cars in record numbers: over 9.3 million for the calendar year, the best since '55.

1963 LeSabre convertible coupe

1964 Special Skylark convertible coupe

1964 Wildcat hardtop sport coupe

1965 Wildcat hardtop sport coupe

1964 LeSabre hardtop sedan

1965 LeSabre four-door sedan

1964 Riviera hardtop coupe

1965 Electra 225 hardtop sport coupe

Like everyone else in 1965, Buick proliferated trim and model variations so buyers could virtually custom-build their cars. That year's junior line comprised V-6 and V-8 Skylarks and standard and DeLuxe Specials priced from about $2350 to $3000, plus V-8 Special "Sportwagons" in the $3000-$3200 range. Wildcat returned with three body types in standard, DeLuxe, and Custom trim, plus DeLuxe and Custom convertibles. LeSabre and Electra 225 offered the same in standard and Custom versions. At $4440 base, the Electra 225 Custom convertible was the priciest '65 Buick, with the elegant Riviera close behind at $4408. Engine assignments stood pat. Riviera gained added distinction via hidden headlights, the four beams moving from the main grille to stack vertically behind front-fender subgrilles reworked into "clamshells." Taillights moved down into the rear bumper.

A memorable new option arrived for '65: the Gran Sport package for Riviera and Skylark. It delivered some $250 worth of performance goodies, including oversize tires, Super-Turbine 300 automatic, and Wildcat 401 V-8. The Skylark Gran Sport was every inch a grand tourer, though it was really Buick's "muscle car" reply to Pontiac's hot-selling year-old GTO. The Riviera GS was even grander in its way, capable of 125 mph flat out. *Motor Trend* magazine said it "goes and handles better than before, and that's quite an improvement."

The big attraction for 1966 was a second-generation Riviera, a cousin to that year's new E-body front-drive Olds Toronado. The Riv retained rear drive and looked much more massive than the crisp 1963-65, yet wheelbase was only two inches longer. More-curvaceous contours, wide hidden-headlamp grille, and a sleek semifastback roof with vestiges of the previous razor edges made it impressive to the eye. Yet it sold for only about $4400, which today seems unbelievably low. Other '66 Buicks were mainly carryovers, but a stroked 340 version of the 300 V-8 was made standard for LeSabres and Skylark Sportwagons.

Modestly redone grilles, side trim, and taillights were again the principal alterations for '67 juniors, but that year's seniors

1965 Electra 225 convertible coupe

1966 LeSabre four-door sedan

1966 Riviera hardtop coupe

1967 Skylark GS 400 hardtop sport coupe

1967 Electra 225 hardtop coupe

got new GM B- and C-bodies with flowing semifastback profiles on hardtop coupes and more voluptuous lines everywhere else. Identifying the '67 Riviera was a horizontal-crossbar grille and revamped parking lights.

Specials and Skylarks continued with the 225 V-6 and 300/340 V-8s for '67, but a new 430 V-8—Buick's biggest engine—was now standard for Wildcat, Electra, and Riviera. Though no more potent than the 425, it was smoother and quieter. A new Special/Skylark option was a cast-iron 400, a bored-and-stroked 340. This formed the heart of a new Skylark subseries called GS 400 offering convertible, two-door hardtop, and pillared coupe with handling suspension, bucket seats, and other sporty touches. A similar hardtop with the 340 engine bowed as the GS 340. Model-year sales were excellent, exceeding 560,000.

Skylark sold in record numbers for 1968, partly because Specials were trimmed to just three DeLuxe models. Like other '68 GM intermediates, junior Buicks adopted a new "split-wheelbase" A-body making for 112-inch Special/Skylark two-doors, 116-inch Special four-doors and DeLuxe wagons, and 121-inch Sportwagons (versus 120 inches in 1964-67). The hot GS 400 returned minus coupe, while GS 340 gave way to a GS 350 with a bored 350-cid V-8 packing 280 bhp. A 230-bhp version was a new Special/Skylark option and standard for Sportwagon, Skylark Custom, and LeSabres; all these offered the tuned unit at extra cost. The 225 V-6 gave way to a Chevy-built 250 inline six with lower compression, reflecting 1968's new federal emissions rules.

Like the '67s, the big '68 Buicks had side sculpturing (traced with moldings on some models) recalling the '50s "sweepspear," plus divided grilles, big bumpers, and, new that season, hidden wipers. The rebodied midsizers wore similar downsloped side "character" lines, plus new grilles, the hide-away wipers, pointy rear fenders, and taillamps in big back bumpers. Riviera got a heavy-handed divided grille that made it look more contrived than in 1966-67. Many Buicks returned to tradition with stylized front-fender "ventiports." Exceptions were Wildcats, GS 400s, and Skylark Customs, where rectangular trim was used to suggest air vents of various types.

No engine changes occurred for record-breaking 1969, when Buick built more than 665,000 cars, its decade high, though it still ran fifth in the industry. Seniors again received new bodies, this time with ventless side glass and a squarer, more-formal look. The year-old junior line displayed the expected minor trim shuffles; Gran Sports and Sportwagons remained separate series, as in '68. LeSabre still rode a 123-inch wheelbase, but so did Wildcat for the first time in four years.

This hot-selling line continued into 1970, but without Specials—the smaller workaday models were now Skylarks—and with Estate wagons in a separate series. The latter remained big upper-class two- and three-seat haulers battling the likes of Chrysler's Town & Country. All full-sizers acquired new grilles, bumpers, and taillights; intermediates received longer hoods, bulkier lower-body contours, and different grilles for each series. Riviera also gained a longer hood, reverted to exposed headlamps astride a thin-line vertical-bar grille, sported a wider rear window and altered bumpers, and offered rear fender skirts as a first-time option. The result was more dignified, if a tad stuffy.

Buick's main mechanical development was an enormous 455 V-8. An outgrowth of the 430 it supplanted, this monster gulped premium gas at the rate of 12 mpg on compression ratios of at least 10:1. The last mammoth V-8 Buick would build, the 455 bowed in '70 with 350, 360, or 370 bhp, and was standard for the GS and LeSabre 455s, Riviera, Electra 225, Wildcat, and Estates.

Flint would remain staunchly committed to big cars throughout the '70s, but energy economics and government mandates inevitably prompted smaller models as time passed. Nevertheless, full-size cars remained Buick's bread-and-butter through 1975, accounting for over 40 percent of total division sales.

GM completely redesigned its full-size models for 1971, and that year's big Buicks were the largest and heaviest yet—as big as American cars would ever get. Styling was more rounded, with smoothly curved "fuselage" bodysides, massive hoods, and broader expanses of glass. Wildcat was retitled Centurion (recalling a mid-'50s Buick show car), and shared its B-body platform with the popular LeSabre. The upmarket Electra remained a C-body cousin to Olds Ninety-Eight and Cadillac de Ville. Estate wagons moved up to its 127-inch wheelbase.

Big Buicks continued in this form through 1976, becoming busier and somewhat bulkier each year, but not significantly changed except where needed to satisfy blossoming safety and emissions rules. All were thirsty. The last 455-cid Electra, for example, was good for only 8.7 mpg in the Environmental Protection Agency's city-fuel-economy ratings.

Riviera also bulked up for '71, gaining three inches between wheel centers (to 122). It also gained about 120 needless pounds, though it looked like more. Dominating swoopy new Bill Mitchell styling was a dramatic "boattail" deck that proved controversial and was thus short-lived—gone after '73. The GS option, a last vestige of sport, vanished after 1975, but Buick tried to keep enthusiasts interested with a "Rallye" package offering reinforced front antiroll bar, a new rear bar, and heavy-duty springs and shocks. This was claimed to provide even better ride and handling than the GS, and probably should have been standard to handle the size and weight of these beasts. Oddball styling and outsize heft must have contributed to Riviera's sagging fortunes in this period; by 1975, sales were less than half of what they'd been five years before.

The last of the 1968-vintage Skylarks appeared for 1971-72. They remained solid, good-looking middleweights, though their engines were being emasculated by power-sapping emission-control devices, which meant Gran Sports weren't so hot anymore. Signaling the imminent demise of midsize Buick convertibles (ragtop sales were down to a trickle industrywide), Skylark hardtop coupes offered a fold-back cloth sunroof as a new '72 option. Trim packages created a bevy of models: base,

1968 GS 400 hardtop sport coupe

1968 Electra 225 hardtop coupe

1968 Sportwagon

1968 Electra 225 Custom hardtop sedan

1968 Wildcat Custom convertible coupe

1969 Wildcat Custom hardtop sport coupe

1969 Skylark Custom convertible coupe

1969 Special DeLuxe coupe

1969 Riviera hardtop coupe

1970 Wildcat Custom hardtop sport coupe

1970 Riviera hardtop coupe

1970 GSX hardtop sport coupe

1971 GS 455 hardtop sport coupe

1971 Riviera GS hardtop sport coupe

350 and Custom Skylarks, plus Sportwagons and Gran Sports.

Buick's last true muscle cars were also 1970-72 models. They've since become coveted collectibles for their performance and miniscule production. A prime example is the 1970 GSX, a bespoilered GS 455 hardtop with new "Stage I" engine tuning; it saw only 678 copies; the GS 455 convertible was little higher at 1416. Both were back for '71 (GSX as an option package) with bold black body stripes and hood paint, special grille, chrome wheels, and fat tires. Figures aren't available for the '71 GSX, but only 902 GS ragtops were built and just 8268 hardtops, reflecting the big drop in performance-car demand after 1969.

For 1973, the respected Century name returned once more, this time on redesigned intermediate Buicks with unchanged wheelbases. All employed a new-generation A-body with so-called "Colonnade" styling that did away with pillarless coupes and sedans. Convertibles were no more, GM reacting to a proposed federal rule on rollover protection that would have outlawed ragtops but which ironically never materialized. Bolstered by spiffy Luxus and Regal submodels (the latter made a separate series after '74), the midsize Centurys sold well through 1977, providing an important "safety net" at times when inflation and rising fuel prices sent would-be big-car buyers scurrying for thriftier alternatives.

A compact also returned to Buick, its first in 10 years. Arriving for mid '73 as the Apollo, it was just a rebadged clone of the 111-inch-wheelbase X-body Chevrolet Nova from 1968, with the same three body styles (two- and four-door sedans and a hatchback two-door) plus, initially, the same 250-cid Chevy straight six as standard power. It was a definite asset during the big-car sales slump touched off by the Middle East oil embargo late that year, but intermediates would remain more important to Buick's overall health.

Confusing buyers for 1975 was the return of the Skylark name at the top of the compact line, where it would eventually supplant Apollo. In common with all X-body variants that year, Buick's version gained heavily revised outer panels that gave it something like European "sports sedan" flair.

A genuine surprise was the new-for-'75 Skyhawk, the smallest Buick in living memory. A near twin to the Vega-based Chevrolet Monza, this 97-inch-wheelbase subcompact "hatchcoupe" took a bit more than eight percent of total division sales in its first six months. Though not light for its size, Skyhawk offered a decent performance/economy blend thanks to a new 90-degree 231-cid V-6 engine, the only one available. Rated at 110 bhp, and also standard power for the '75 Skylark, Century, and Regal, this would be a significant engine in years to come.

Model-year 1977 brought the first of GM's downsized cars. Sometime before the first energy crisis, management had decided to move to smaller, lighter, more-economical designs in every size and price category. Its largest cars were the logical starting point, and they were rendered even more timely by the government corporate average fuel economy standards (CAFE) that took effect for '78.

The first fruits of this program were dramatically evident at Buick, where LeSabre and Electra shrank to almost Century size. Wheelbases contracted to 116 and 119 inches, respectively (Estate wagons rode the shorter one); curb weights dropped several hundred pounds. This made smaller engines feasible, yet interiors were within inches of the old behemoths' size. Riviera wasn't left out, becoming a high-spec version of the new B-body LeSabre (though it would soon return to the corporate E-body).

1971 Centurion hardtop coupe

1974 LeSabre Luxus coupe

1972 Riviera hardtop coupe

1974 Riviera GS coupe

1973 Apollo hatchback coupe

1974 Electra 225 Limited hardtop sedan

Electras through 1979 relied on a standard Chevy-built 350 V-8; a new 403 with 185 bhp was optional, courtesy of Olds. Convertibles were no more (killed after '75), but two- and four-door sedans were offered in LeSabre, LeSabre Custom, Electra 225, and 225 Limited series. The following year brought even fancier Electra Park Avenue models. An interesting 1978 addition was the LeSabre sport coupe, powered by that year's new 165-bhp turbocharged version of the Buick V-6.

Big Buicks entered the '80s with subtly restyled sheetmetal said to reduce wind resistance as an aid to fuel economy. Toward the same end, more extensive use of lighter materials also netted an average 150-pound weight savings, about half that achieved with the '77s. It's odd how perspective changes. GM's first downsized big cars seemed quite small next to Big Three rivals of the day. Now they look just as large as their outsized predecessors.

Intermediates were next on the corporate slenderizing schedule, so a smaller Century bowed for 1978 along with a separate Regal series of personal-luxury coupes, all built on a new 108.1-inch-wheelbase A-body. Regal sold well from the start, but Century didn't. Sloped-roof "aeroback" styling on the two- and four-door sedans was out of phase with buyer tastes, though there was nothing wrong with the handsome wagon. Buick corrected this mistake for 1980 with a more-formal-looking notchback four-door bearing a faint resemblance to the first-generation Cadillac Seville, and sales took off. Buick had turbocharged its V-6 with the new midsize line in mind, offering it in sporty Century and Regal sport coupe models. But the sales pattern was the same, and the blown Century vanished with aerobacks.

Riviera was downsized a second time for '79. Styling was crisper and tighter, and front-wheel drive finally put the model in line with its Toronado and Cadillac Eldorado cousins. A turbo V-6 was available here, too. Though most buyers opted for standard powerplants, the blown Riv was a fine performer—able to leap from 0-60 mph in under 12 seconds while averaging close to 20 mpg in more-restrained driving, this despite a still-bulky 3800-pound curb weight. The 1980 Riviera was basically a reprise but introduced a long-time Cadillac feature: "Twilight Sentinel," the automatic on/off headlamp control with delay timer (for keeping the lights on for up to three minutes after switching off the ignition to illuminate your path).

Though it promised much, the little Skyhawk hatch-coupe was never a big seller and disappeared after 1980. One interesting 1979-80 variation was the Road Hawk, a package aimed at younger buyers more interested in sports-car looks than genuine ability. Fore and aft spoilers, special paint and tape stripes, identifying decals, mag-style wheels, and larger tires were included, but there was little action to back up the brag.

An important new Buick arrived in the spring of '79 as an

1974 Century Luxus Colonnade coupe

1975 Riviera coupe

1975 Electra 225 Limited hardtop sedan

1976 Skylark S/R Landau coupe

1976 Riviera S/R coupe

early-1980 entry. This was a front-drive replacement for the long-running rear-drive Skylark, sharing GM's technically advanced new 104.9-inch-wheelbase X-body platform with siblings Chevrolet Citation, Pontiac Phoenix, and Oldsmobile Omega. Buick had learned its styling lesson, so this new, smaller compact was offered only in traditional notchback form. Design highlights included rack-and-pinion steering, all-coil suspension, and transversely mounted engines—either 2.5-liter Pontiac-built inline-four or an optional 2.8-liter 60-degree V-6 from Chevrolet. Skylark performed well with the latter, and tastefully done sport coupe and sport sedan models offered firmer suspension and sportier appointments for more-serious drivers. Likely on the strength of the Buick name, Skylark became the second-best-selling X-car after the higher-volume, lower-priced Citation. Unfortunately, execution left much to be desired on all X-cars, which soon supplanted the Dodge Aspen/Plymouth Volare as the most-recalled cars from Detroit.

Yet despite the occasional flawed product and market miscalculation, Buick had moved with changing buyer demands in the '70s, reaping the benefit of good sales while some other makes faltered. Per tradition, Buick anticipated most market trends and responded with cars that, if not on the leading edge of design, were at least in tune with the times. Strong sales year after year were proof that Buick not only knew its market but how to satisfy it.

Flint continued doing that into the '80s. But though Buick suffered from rising sales of Japanese cars as much as any Detroit make, it could not escape the cumulative effects of misguided corporate policies that severely eroded GM's market share by 1990.

Buick began the '80s by again reaching out to the younger, more-affluent types who'd bought Gran Sports in the "flower power" era. This reflected the product policies of Lloyd Reuss, a former division chief engineer who became Buick general manager in 1980. A genuine "car guy," Reuss wanted some Buicks to be American-style BMWs, and he got his way. By 1983, there were sporty T type editions of every Buick save for the LeSabre and plush Electra, featuring black exterior trim, firmer chassis, more-potent engines, and "driver-oriented" interiors. Buick also mounted an Indy-car racing program for its V-6 and offered over-the-counter hop-up parts to cement its hoped-for image as a more youthful, performance-oriented outfit.

This strategy worked well for a time, but ultimately backfired. Buick jumped to third in industry production for 1982-83 and ran fourth in model years '81 and 1984-86. Even so, '86 volume was well down on '85's, and the slide continued into 1987, when Buick fell to fifth, behind Oldsmobile. A significant factor was strong new competition from Pontiac, which offered many of the same basic cars but had recently returned to its '60s-style performance theme and returned to third for the first time since 1970. Trying to be all things to all people, Reuss later conceded, only confused Buick's image—and its customers.

In the end, it didn't matter. Chairman Roger Smith's wholesale corporate reorganization, ordained in 1984 to reverse GM's withering market share and in evidence by '87, called for returning each GM make to its distinct rung on the price-and-prestige ladder fashioned back in the '30s by legendary president Alfred P. Sloan. At Flint, this meant a hasty retreat from T types and turbo V-6s, and by decade's end the division had mostly returned to its traditional brand of upper-middle-class luxury—a "doctor's car" once more.

Buick's generally strong sales in the '80s reflected a consistent model lineup, which evolved in step with those of other GM divisions but was, perhaps, more clear-cut to buyers from year to year. Some individual models certainly seemed ageless. The big 1977-vintage Electra and LeSabre, for example, hardly

1976 Regal Landau Colonnade coupe

1978 Century fastback sport coupe

1977 Riviera coupe

1978 Riviera coupe

1977 Regal Landau coupe

1979 Riviera S Type Turbo coupe

1977 Electra four-door sedan

1979 LeSabre sport coupe

1977 Estate wagon Limited

1980 Skyhawk Road Hawk fastback coupe

changed at all after their 1980 update, receiving only minor styling and equipment shuffles through mid-decade while accounting for about a quarter of division output each year.

The full-size Estate wagons continued in this vein through 1990, garnering fewer sales as time passed, but coupe and sedan models gave way to more-efficient and popular front-drive successors, beginning with 1985's new C-body Electra. A similar H-body LeSabre arrived the following year.

Announcing a second wave of GM downsizing, these smaller big Buicks shared a 110.8-inch wheelbase and measured some two feet shorter and 400 pounds lighter than the 1977-84 models. Yet they hardly sacrificed any passenger room and were vastly more pleasurable to drive, thriftier with fuel, and adequately quick. Transverse-mounted V-6s mated to four-speed over-drive automatic transaxles across the board. Initially, 3.0-liter gasoline and 4.3-liter diesel engines were offered, but soon vanished in favor of the old reliable 3.8-liter gas unit, though updated with sequential multiport electronic fuel injection and, from '86, roller valve lifters. A modified "3800" engine with 165 bhp (versus 150) arrived on certain '88s. Electra coupes disap-

1980 Skylark sport coupe

1980 Riviera S Type turbo coupe

1980 Century fastback sport coupe

1980 Regal sport coupe

1981 Century Limited four-door sedan

1981 Regal sport coupe

1981 Electra Estate wagon (diesel)

1981 Riviera coupe

peared after 1987, when the top-line Park Avenue became a separate model and a laudable new antilock brake system (announced for '86) became more widely available for both series. Electra offered a subtly sporty T Type sedan, LeSabre a T Type coupe. But, as always, the traditional Custom and Limited lines sold better by far. And those sales were good: around 100,000-150,000 a year.

The same could not be said for the sixth-generation Riviera. New for '86, the third downsized personal-luxury Buick in 10 years laid a gigantic egg. Sales plunged to an 11-year Riviera low, the '86 tally off a whopping 70 percent from model-year '85. The 1987-88 results were even poorer.

In a way, this was curious. On a tighter 108-inch wheelbase, this new Riviera was far more nimble than the old, and its quiet, well-mannered drivetrain was basically the same as found in Electra/LeSabre. But it was evidently a bit *too* small for Riviera customers. An unfortunate styling resemblance to Buick's N-body Somerset/Skylark didn't help, and hardly anyone liked the gimmicky Graphic Control Center, a touch-sensitive TV-type screen that needlessly complicated even simple tasks like changing radio stations.

Hoping to turn things around, Buick made the '89 Riviera look more "important," adding 11 inches to overall length, ladling on chrome, and restyling the tail to resemble that of the 1979-85 models. Did it work? Yes and no. Production leaped from about 8600 for '88 to over 21,000 for '89, but the latter wasn't even half the total of a decade before. The 1990s sold only about 1300 units better. A more-conventional dash was a welcome change that season.

All this must have greatly disappointed Flint executives, who'd seen the 1981-84 Riviera average 50,000 model-year sales and the '85 over 65,000 (the increase no doubt due to buyers learning of the shrunken '86). Like the last rear-drive Buicks, these cars changed little after 1980. There was a mild facelift for '84, and an optional Olds-built 350 V-8 was offered through '82, but turbo and nonturbo V-6s were available all along (the latter a new 4.1-liter from '81), as was a 350 Olds diesel V-8 (a troublesome beast, and thus rarely ordered), and choice of standard and T Type coupes.

Riviera's most interesting '80s development was the advent

1981 Regal sport coupe

1982 Skylark Limited four-door sedan

1982 Century Custom coupe

1982 LeSabre F/E (Formal Edition) coupe

1982 Skylark sport coupe

1982 Riviera convertible coupe

1982 Regal Grand National coupe

1983 Skylark T Type coupe

of its first convertible, bowing at mid 1982. A coupe conversion performed by an outside contractor, it was a handsome rig, fairly solid for a droptop and as luxurious as any Riv. But it was heavier and slower with its standard 4.1 V-6 (fitted to most examples, though the turbo 3.8 was ostensibly available) and found few takers at $25,000-plus. Production was predictably limited—just 1248, 1750, 500, and 400, respectively, for 1982-85—scarcity that guarantees this as a minor future collectible at least. Of course, the ragtop Riv died with the '86 E-body, which was deemed too small to be a practical four-seater in convertible form (though Buick later showed a prototype of just such a car).

Two more collectible '80s Buicks are found among the rear-drive Regal coupes, which were reskinned for '81 with crisper, more-aerodynamic lines that persisted through the end of series production in December 1987. These are the hot turbo-powered T Type and Grand National.

The new-for-'82 Regal T Type replaced the previous sport coupe as Flint's "factory hot rod," offering fat tires, beefier chassis, attention-getting exterior, and plush interior. Horsepower was rated at 175-180 bhp at first, then boosted to 200 bhp for 1984 via sequential-port fuel injection. The GN bowed at mid '82 as a low-volume commemorative car (named for the Chevy-powered Regals then starting to clean up on the NASCAR circuit), but in reality, it was just a fancy T Type.

After a one-year hiatus, though, Grand National returned with a mean all-black exterior and more unique touches. For 1986 came a turbo intercooler that swelled horses by 35 for both T Type and GN. Recalibrated engine electronics gave the '87s 10 bhp more—and truly phenomenal acceleration. In fact, these Buicks bid fair as the fastest cars in the land, able to bound from 0 to 60 in about six seconds.

Quicker still was the 1987 GNX, a $30,000 end-of-the-line limited edition (547 built, by contractor ASC) with higher turbo boost, "smarter" electronics, cleaner porting, bigger tires, meaner looks, a claimed 300 bhp (276 actual) and a mighty 355-420 pound-feet of torque. Magazine testers clocked 0-60 in the mid-fives and the quarter-mile in about 14.5 seconds at 95 mph.

1983 Riviera convertible coupe

1983 Riviera T Type coupe

1983 Regal T Type turbo coupe

1983 Century Limited four-door sedan

1983 Skyhawk Limited station wagon

For all this grandstanding, the Regal T Type was always a peripheral seller and the GN almost invisible (only 215 of the '82s, about 2000 for '84, even fewer for 1985-87). Still, they were great fun, even if Buick wasn't the place one expected to find a modern muscle car.

Smaller cars, particularly intermediates, were far more important to Buick's fortunes in the '80s. For 1981 these comprised the workaday Regal coupes and a mostly carryover group of Century sedans and wagons. All continued the 1978 A-body design that was renamed G-body for '82, when the Centurys became Regals and Buick's 4.1-liter V-6 replaced a 4.3 V-8 option. Model-year volume was some 384,500 for 1981 and over 328,000 for '82, not bad for two very difficult industry years. Production eased to some 226,000 for 1983-84, by which time four-speed automatic transmissions had been adopted as a much better bet for improved mileage.

Meantime, Buick had introduced the first front-drive Century, a notchback coupe and sedan built on the new 1982 A-body used by sister Chevy, Olds, and Pontiac models. Like them, this Century was just a "deluxe" X-car with more expansive sheet-metal and plusher interiors on the same 104.9-inch wheelbase. Initial engine choices were a 2.5-liter Pontiac four; a new 3.0-liter Buick V-6 (destroked from 3.8); and a 4.3-liter Olds diesel V-6. Euro-style T Types were added for '83. The following year brought a 3.8-liter option (standard for T Types) and new five-door Custom and Limited Estate wagons (replacing the old Regal models).

Though little changed for '85, Century displaced Regal (now down to coupes only) as Buick's best-seller, with annual production through 1987 of over a quarter-million units. The '86s were modestly restyled via a curiously unaerodynamic undercut nose. The T Type coupe vanished, Chevy's familiar 2.8 V-6 ousted Buick's 3.0 as the step-up engine, and the 3.8 gained 25 horses (for 150 total) via low-friction roller valve lifters, sequential-port injection, and distributorless triple-coil ignition. For 1987, the T Type became a package option, and both the four and 2.8 V-6 received "Generation II" improvements conferring slightly more power. More standard equipment eased the sticker shock of 1988 prices that were up to the $12,000-$15,000 range (versus $10,000-$12,000 five years before). The 1989s received a minor facelift and a new 160-bhp 3.3-liter V-6 derived from the veteran 3.8 (to replace the 2.8). Nevertheless, volume withered to some 150,000 for '88, then dropped below 90,000 for '89, thanks to a worsening national economy and other factors. Still, this was highly important business for Flint—and highly creditable for such an elderly basic design.

A notch below the front-drive Century was the compact Skylark, which was an X-body for 1981-85, an N-body thereafter. For all the recalls and attendant bad publicity that plagued GM's X-cars in these years, the Skylark continued to sell well. Buick built over a quarter-million of the '81s and more than 100,000 a year for 1982-84. The '85s ended the line at around 93,000. Changes in styling, engineering, and models were strictly evolutionary. There were always 2.5 four and 2.8 V-6 coupes and sedans (except '85, sedans only) in base/Custom and Limited trim. Sport versions through '82 and the two-door 1983-85 T Type could be had with a high-output V-6 (port-injected for '85) and came with distinctive exteriors and Buick's firmer "Gran Touring" suspension package. In all, this Skylark served Buick well.

Buick still peddled a subcompact Skyhawk in the '80s, though quite different from the same-named late-'70s hatch coupe. Bowing for '82, this was one of GM's five front-drive J-body models, riding a 101.2-inch-wheelbase chassis with all-coil suspension via front MacPherson struts and a rear beam axle on trailing arms. Buick wouldn't get a convertible version like Chevy and Pontiac, but did offer their two- and four-door notchback styles plus 5-door wagons from '83 and a "fasthatch" coupe from '86. Engines were the same four-cylinder fare used by sister Js: Chevy-built overhead-valve 2.0-liter (abandoned after '87) and a Brazilian-built overhead-cam unit. The latter, initially a 1.8, was also offered as a more-potent turbocharged version from 1984; both grew to 2.0 liters for '87, after which the blown engine was cancelled. Custom and plusher Limited trim was cataloged all along. The inevitable T Types arrived for '83—notchback two-doors first, then fasthatch coupes too. Styling changed little through the final '89 models save an optional hidden-headlamp nose from 1986. Coupes, turbos, and T Types were all dropped after '87 due to dwindling sales and the division's return to its more-traditional "Premium American Motorcars" thrust.

In sales, Skyhawk typically ran in the middle of the J-car pack—behind Chevy Cavalier and Pontiac's 2000/Sunbird but ahead of Olds Firenza and Cadillac Cimarron. While none of these cars matched certain Japanese rivals for refinement, workmanship, and economy, they were at least competent and sometimes pleasant. Skyhawk probably benefited as much from the Buick corporate badge as any design feature, but would surely have sold better without so much intramural competition. As it was, production peaked with the '84 models—

1983 Skyhawk T Type coupe

1984 Skylark T Type coupe

1983 Regal four-door sedan

1984 LeSabre Custom four-door sedan

1983 LeSabre Estate wagon (diesel)

1984 Regal Grand National coupe

1984 Century Estate wagon

1984 Regal T Type turbo coupe

over 145,000 built. After dropping for '85, volume recovered to some 91,500 for industry banner-year '86. But that spurt was a fluke. By '89, Skyhawk sales were down below 30,000.

Much of the J-car's basic engineering appeared in the 1985 Somerset Regal, a notchback two-door heralding the arrival of GM's new N-body. Buick wasn't able to trade on the popular Regal name the way Olds did with Cutlass, so this car soon became just Somerset. Companion N-body four-doors arrived for '86 under the Skylark, finishing off the last X-body models; Somersets became Skylarks two years later.

Through 1987, Somerset/Skylark engines comprised the familiar 2.5 four (updated to "Generation II" specs that season) and extra-cost Buick 3.0 V-6. An added option for '88 was Oldsmobile's new "Quad 4," a dual-overhead-cam 2.3-liter four with four valves per cylinder, an aluminum head, and a cast-iron block. With a healthy 150 bhp even in mild initial tune, the Quad-4 promised much. But it wasn't in the same league with similar Japanese engines for smoothness, quietness, and lugging power. Buick was thus wise to retain the V-6 (unlike Pontiac, which dropped it for the '88 Grand Am).

The N-body Buick got off to a good start. Some 86,000 were built for the abbreviated debut model year, followed by nearly 138,000 of the '86s. Like Skyhawk, this was not a state-of-the-art competitor, but it kept getting better. Among the more-notable

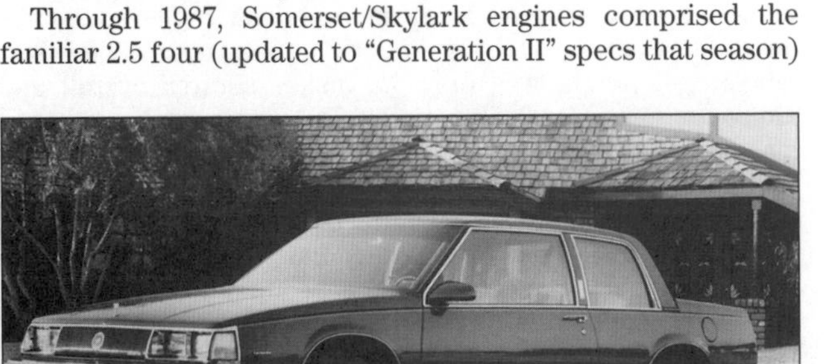

1985 Electra Park Avenue coupe

1985 Riviera coupe

1985 LeSabre Limited four-door sedan

1985 Regal Grand National coupe

1985 Skyhawk T Type coupe

1985 Somerset Regal coupe

1986 LeSabre Limited coupe

1986 Skylark Limited four-door sedan

improvements was the 1989 exchange of 3.0 V-6 for the torquier 160-bhp "3300" unit. The following year brought more logical ergonomics to all Skylarks, plus a new Luxury Edition four-door and a Gran Sport coupe.

Having learned with the J-cars that too many corporate clones spoil the sales broth, GM returned to more individual styling for a trio of 1988 midsize coupes. At Buick, this new front-drive GM10 or W-body design replaced the rear-drive Regal, but retained make appearance "cues" to stand apart more clearly from the related Pontiac Grand Prix and Olds Cutlass Supreme. Significantly, wheelbase was cut just 0.6-inch from the previous Regal's, to the benefit of passenger space; base curb weight slimmed some 250 pounds and overall length by 8.4 inches, to the benefit of economy and handling. The usual Custom and Limited versions were on hand, and a Gran Sport appearance/handling package offered front "bib" spoiler, rocker-panel skirts, black grille, aluminum road wheels, and other "Euro" touches.

All models initially carried a transverse, port-injected 2.8 Chevy V-6 of 125 bhp and four-speed overdrive automatic trans-axle, plus all-disc brakes—uncommon in mass-market Detroiters. Equally laudable was the all-independent suspension with the expected front struts and coil springs, plus rear struts on single trailing links and dual lateral links connected by a single transverse plastic leaf spring, as on the big C/H-bodies.

Despite such technical finesse, Regal finished well-down on the midsize sales chart for 1988. The reason, said many pundits, was GM's delay in introducing planned four-door models, a style far preferred in this class. GM remedied its mistake for 1991, and Buick added Regal sedans with the same trim levels and wheelbase as its W-body coupes. By that point, the 2.8 V-6 had been enlarged to a 3.1 with 10 more bhp, and a praiseworthy antilock braking system (ABS) was offered optionally on Limited and GS models. Despite all this, Regal sales continued to disappoint.

Another '88 newcomer was a more telling sign of Buick's late-decade fortunes. It was Flint's first production two-seater, named Reatta (derived from an American Indian word for lariat). Though basically a Riviera cut down to a 98.5-inch wheelbase, Reatta was only 4.5 inches shorter overall and almost as heavy (at 3350 pounds). Powertrain and dashboard also came from the Riv, but styling was Reatta's own: smooth, rounded, "friendly."

Buick took pains to note that Reatta was not a sports car but a "mature" two-seater emphasizing luxury, comfort, even practicality. Extensive standard equipment limited options to just an electric sliding sunroof and a driver's seat with no fewer than 16 power adjustments. You had to contend with the dubious Graphic Control Center in 1988-89 models, but the roomy two-place cabin and a largish trunk with drop-down pass-through panel invited long-distance touring. Even better, Reatta was shrewdly priced: around $25,000 initially, about half as much as Cadillac's slow-selling Italian-bodied Allanté convertible. An open-air Reatta bowed for 1990 as Buick's first "in-

1986 Riviera T Type coupe

1987 LeSabre T Type coupe

1987 Skylark Custom four-door sedan

1987 Riviera T Type coupe

1987 Regal Grand National coupe

1988 Regal Custom coupe

1988 Riviera coupe

1988 Reatta 2-passenger coupe

1988 LeSabre Limited coupe

1988 Electra T Type four-door sedan

1989 Skyhawk SE coupe

house" ragtop in 15 years. (It would have appeared in early '89 but for last-minute production troubles.) Both 1990 Reattas gained a standard driver-side airbag and conventional audio and climate controls. The '91s boasted a further-improved 3800 V-6, new electronic shift control for the four-speed automatic transmission, standard touring tires, and a shorter final drive for sprightlier pickup.

Yet for all its appealing qualities, the Reatta was a fish out of water: conceived in the heady days of Buick sportiness but born to a division fast returning to "The Great American Road." It did have the handcrafted aura of a genuine limited edition, built at a special new "Reatta Craft Centre" (though that was situated at Olds in Lansing, not at Flint). Yet Riviera offered the same basic car for less money—plus the bonus of a back seat. Worse, Reatta workmanship was erratic, especially on the convertible, which not only made do with a manual top but was downright pricey at an initial $34,995—$6700 above the coupe. With all this, Reatta failed to meet even its minimum yearly sales goal of 10,000 units and was thus dropped after 1991. Total production was precisely 21,850, including a mere 2437 ragtops (only 305 of which were built to '91 specs).

Reatta was a sad loss for those who appreciate interesting cars, but it died in a good cause. The aging of America's vast "baby-boom" generation implied growing demand for the sort of "modern conservatism" traditional from Flint.

Indeed, the division enjoyed something close to prosperity in the early '90s, running third in calendar-year sales among domestic makes before yielding to a resurgent Pontiac in 1993. Still, this success was only relative, as Buick volume was down to barely half its mid '80s level—about half-a-million cars per year. Worse, GM as a whole was losing money by the ton: $2 billion in 1990 alone, a massive $4.5 billion in '91.

Analysts found no mystery in that. Quite simply, they said, GM still had too many factories with too much capacity to build too many vehicles for too few customers. By contrast, Ford and Chrysler had become leaner and more efficient in the '80s. GM merely redrew its organizational chart to enter the '90s with the highest overhead and lowest per-unit profit of the Big Three (not to mention the Japanese "transplant" operations that now loomed large in the total U.S. picture). By 1993, GM's net losses over four years had reached a towering $18 billion.

By that point, GM had endured another painful reorganization and numerous plant closings, plus an unprecedented 1992 "palace coup" that summarily ousted chairman Robert Stempel and president Lloyd Reuss after just two years in office. GM was making money again just two years later, thanks to the efforts of new president John F. "Jack" Smith, who'd recently turned things around for GM Europe, and John Smale, the former CEO of Proctor & Gamble.

In a sense, Buick had long been showing the way to GM's future. As the purveyor of "Premium American Motorcars," it entered the '90s with one of Detroit's stronger "brand images," thanks to a well-established lineup of cars that made no apologies for being smooth, lush, and Detroit-traditional. Buick worked hard to strengthen its position even further in the '90s. Dropping Reatta had been but a first step.

A second one was the '91 debut of the first Roadmaster in 35 years. It was only that year's restyled Chevy Caprice in Buick dress, built on the same rear-drive B-body chassis from '77. But this new "Roadie" was big, spacious, and well-equipped in the best tradition of full-size Detroiters. In other words, it was a lot of car for the money, considering it was cheaper than the smaller, more efficient front-drive Park Avenue. An Estate wagon bowed first with fake-wood siding, eight-passenger seating, handy two-way tailgate with separate lift-up window, and a $21,500 price tag. Six-passenger standard and Limited sedans followed for '92 in the $22,000-$24,000 range. That same year, the base 170-hp 5.0-liter V-8 was bolstered by a much torquier 5.7-liter option. The '94s could run close to $27,000, but they also ran with a standard 350 LT1 V-8 from Chevy's latest Corvette sports car, though in low-stress, 260-bhp tune. *Car and Driver* clocked one at 7.8 seconds 0-60, but pulling power, not sheer acceleration, was the name of this game—as in towing trailers and boats.

The reborn Roadmaster pulled a fair number of customers, all things considered: a best of 85,500 for '92, 30,000 to 40,000 for 1993-95. Though that wasn't much compared to the levels of 10 and 20 years before, each sale was almost pure gravy, as the elderly platform and other major components had been paid for long ago. But the Roadmaster would die after '96 to make room for more-profitable sport-utility vehicle production at the Arlington, Texas, factory that also built the Caprice. Like Reatta, the '90s Roadmaster served a purpose, but it was clearly a car of Buick's past, not its future.

How, then, to explain the aging front-drive Century as one of Flint's most profitable assets in this period? Again, there was no mystery. Buick increased quality and added features that customers wanted while keeping the lid on price. While holding on to an old design might seem questionable, Buick couldn't afford to let this one die, because the Century had come to have great appeal for rental-car companies and other fleet buyers; in fact, they now accounted for the majority of sales. The improved workmanship was just a timely bonus, the result of a gradual but wholesale reengineering effort for both Century and Oldsmobile's related Cutlass Ciera. And it paid off. In 1993, the influential J. D. Power organization ranked this elderly duo near the top of the industry for initial vehicle quality.

Sales, of course, were the most important payoff, and Century model-year production remained well above 100,000 for 1990-95. This was achieved with remarkably few changes: a more-orthodox face for '91, new downpriced Special models for '92 (recycling yet another familiar Buick name), a new 2.2-liter base four for '93 (ousting the old Iron Duke at last). A standard driver-side airbag and ABS arrived for '94, when offerings thinned to Custom and Special sedans and a Special wagon. By that point, Buick was into "value pricing" (like other GM divisions), which meant selling well-equipped cars for several hundred dollars less than if they were "optioned up" the usual way. Yet Century's price spread hadn't changed that much, with stickers still in the affordable $16,000-$18,000 range. Even more than Roadmaster, Buick's "old dog" A-body had learned some profitable new tricks—enough to earn a complete redesign for '97.

Century's one-time successor, the front-drive Regal, could be as quick and pleasant as any rival—and more so than some. Even so, production tumbled 27 percent from model-year '92 to just over 83,000 for '93, then to 78,600 before recovering to the

1989 Century Custom four-door sedan

1990 Reatta 2-passenger convertible coupe

1989 Regal Gran Sport coupe

1992 Skylark coupe

1990 Skylark Luxury Edition four-door sedan

1993 Riviera coupe with Gran Touring Package

1993 Roadmaster Estate station wagon

1994 Park Avenue Ultra four-door sedan

1996 Century Custom four-door sedan

1996 Roadmaster Limited four-door sedan

100,000 level for '95. Likely factors in this see-saw performance were styling that didn't age gracefully, a complete lack of airbags until '94 (the '95s got standard dual restraints), and the fact that the $15,000 Regals of 1990 cost well over $20,000 by '95. Happily, ABS was standard by then, even on base-trim Customs, and the natty Gran Sport had been promoted from 1990-91 option package to separate coupe and sedan models.

Continuing as Buick's top-seller by far, the full-size H-body LeSabre drew well over 150,000 orders each model year in 1992-94. Its stellar second-place finish in J.D. Power's 1989 quality survey prompted Buick to bill itself as "the new symbol for quality in America." LeSabre also earned "best family car" honors from *Family Circle* magazine and a string of yearly Best Buy endorsements from Consumer Guide®. Helping the cause was a thorough 1992 redesign featuring a more rounded and contemporary look, a smoother 3800 V-6, standard driver-side airbag, and useful no-cost extras like power windows and GM's "PASS-Key" antitheft ignition. Coupes disappeared, but Custom and Limited sedans kept moving out the door on the strength of appealing high-teens starting prices and considered yearly feature upgrades like standard power door locks ('93), passenger airbag and heat-reflecting "solar control" glass ('94) and high-value "Select Series" models ('95). Though LeSabre had no more allure for enthusiasts than a Century or Regal, it offered solid family transport with a modicum of luxury at a fair price, a combination many folks found hard to resist.

Buick's flagship C-body line received a similar makeover for 1991, gaining more-fulsome lines inspired by the '89 Essence show car, plus plastic front fenders and eight inches in overall length (wheelbase was unchanged). Models thinned to a $24,385 Park Avenue sedan and a posh new $27,420 Park Avenue Ultra. Both carried 3800 V-6s with tuned-port injection and 170 bhp, plus four-speed automatic transaxles with electronic shift control newly integrated with the engine computer. Also on hand: standard driver-side airbag, ABS, solar-control windshield glass, and full power assists.

Befitting its name, the Ultra came with a leather-trimmed interior and a few unique styling touches. Come 1992, it added a supercharged V-6, the only such engine in U.S. production other than Ford's Thunderbird SC unit. Unlike Buick turbos of the '70s and '80s, Ultra's supercharged engine was tuned for low-speed torque, not high-end power. Still, its 205 bhp wasn't exactly puny, so neither was performance. Where the regular Park Avenue took 9.2 seconds 0-60, the Ultra needed about eight. Also new for '92 was optional traction control for both models (later extended to LeSabre as well). This praiseworthy feature was appreciated even more when the Ultra went to 225 bhp for 1994—good for seven seconds flat in the benchmark sprint to 60. The 1995 base model got a reengineered "Series II" 3800 with vibration-quelling "balance shafts." The blown V-6 followed suit for '96 and muscled up to 240 bhp—not bad for a lowly pushrod engine then over 20 years old.

Like their linemates, Park Avenue/Ultra added a few standard features each year. While that necessarily pushed up prices, customers seemed willing to go along. That was especially true for '91, when the series doubled its model-year production to over 100,000. Annual volume then settled to between 55,000 and 68,000 through mid-decade.

The compact N-body Skylark was much less important to Buick in the early '90s than it was in the '80s. Indeed, sales declined most every model year even as Pontiac's similar Grand Am steadily drew up to four times as many buyers. Skylark's 1992 redesign didn't help, with a flashy, sharp-lined exterior and an oddly drawn dash worthy of Salvador Dali.

Skylark offered coupes and sedans in base and Gran Sport trim for '92, then in Custom, Limited, and GS guise, through '95. GS models always had a standard V-6: a Buick 3.3 through '93, then a Chevy-built 3.1. Either was preferable to the otherwise-standard Quad-4, which remained a rough-and-rowdy runner despite GM's best efforts to civilize it (including the belated addition of twin balance shafts for '95, when it was prosaically retitled Twin Cam). A three-speed automatic was still the lone transmission and thus quite passé even for a compact. An optional four-speed unit arrived for '94, when all Skylarks gained a driver-side airbag as well as standard air conditioning, cruise control, tilt steering wheel, power windows, and automatic power door locks. By that point, Skylark had added special "value-priced" models in the hotly contested $14,000-$18,000 bracket. Yet despite such tactics and worthy interim changes, this was still one of those cars that seemed to aim more at Hertz and Avis than Joe and Jane America.

Buick tried bolstering Skylark's showroom appeal with a 1996 facelift featuring a toned-down exterior and a more orthodox dashboard with standard passenger's airbag. At the same time, the base four was enlarged to 2.4 liters, mostly for better low-speed torque (horsepower was unchanged), and was teamed with the four-speed automatic like the V-6. And all models boasted standard traction control. But none of this helped sales, which actually declined to the 50,000-unit level. With that and a new cost-cutting push by GM managers, Buick exited the compact field after 1997.

A changing market and GM's steadily declining share of it—down to less than 30 percent by the mid '90s—would eventually claim another Buick, the once-proud Riviera. Its future certainly looked bleak as the decade opened, as the restyled '89 was left to soldier on for four model years without significant change. Though there were laudable technical advances like electronic transmission control and standard ABS, they only kept the car current without making it more compelling. Worse, the luxury-coupe market started to nosedive in an early-decade recession. As a result, Riv sales were flat for 1991-92 at some 12,000-13,000 per year, then plunged to a paltry 4555 for '93. And there were no '94s at all.

But that's only because Buick had prepared an all-new Riviera for a spring '94 debut. Artfully detailed and refreshingly different, the 1995 model marked a renaissance for the personal-luxury Buick—arguably the most-exciting Riviera in a quarter-century. Styling was a major attraction. Developed under studio chief Bill Porter, it had begun as a variation on the curvy Lucerne showmobile, but ended up like no Buick before. Some saw a hint of trendy "cab forward" proportioning, others a touch of Jaguar and even Ferrari Dino in the smoothly carved nose, tail, and profile. Even if you didn't like the new look—and not everyone did—you had to admire its audacity. *Car and Driver*, for one, praised "the boldness and coherence of the Riviera's design, [though] the shape somehow doesn't make our hearts flutter instantly. But neither did we tire of it quickly, for there's a wealth of visual detail that was gradually revealed to us as we spent time with the car."

The reborn Riviera was definitely larger and more "substantial" than the 1989-93 generation, growing nine inches longer, 1.9 inches wider, and 238 pounds heavier. The weight gain partly reflected the use of a new "G-car" platform, claimed to be the stiffest in GM history. It was the same structure used for Oldsmobile's new '95 Aurora sedan, but aside from sharing a few underskin components and a 113.8-inch wheelbase, the

1996 Regal Limited four-door sedan

1996 Skylark Gran Sport coupe

1997 Century Custom four-door sedan

1997 LeSabre Limited four-door sedan

1998 Park Avenue Ultra four-door sedan

1998 Regal GS four-door sedan

two cars were nothing alike.

The move from E-body to G-car gave Riviera a modern independent rear suspension with semitrailing arms, toe-control links, coil springs and antiroll bar. Together with a strut-type front end and Buick chassis tuning, the Riv handled with confidence, if not Euro firmness, and delivered a great American-style ride. The interior enhanced comfort by offering space enough for six—five with available front buckets—plus the expected upscale decor and a handsome reverse-slant instrument panel that prompted faint memories of 1963.

Early '95 Rivieras carried the 225-bhp supercharged V-6 from that season's Park Avenue Ultra. Despite fair heft (nearly 3800 pounds) and mandatory four-speed autobox, the blown Riv clocked a brisk 7.9 seconds in 0-60 runs by *Consumer Guide®*. A less-expensive, standard model soon followed with the unblown 205-bhp Series II engine. Both versions packed standard four-wheel ABS, full power, dual-zone climate control, a remote-keyless-entry system and many other amenities now expected in the class. Even so, the base Riv stickered at just over $28,000, thousands less than pricey foreign luxury coupes, not to mention domestic rivals. The supercharged model was only some $1100 upstream, and even a full option load wouldn't push it much beyond $32 grand.

Enthusiasts must have been happy to see Riviera not only alive and well but more elegant and desirable than it had been in a long, long time. Buick was happy to see sales go through the roof, relatively speaking, turning out 41,442 for the extended 1995 run. But that would be the peak. With buyers fast deserting big coupes for upscale sport-utility vehicles (SUVs) and luxury import-brand sedans, Riviera sales dropped to just over 18,000 for '96, inched up to almost 19,000 for '97, then plunged to 10,953 for '98. There were few changes along the way though, the supercharged engine was boosted to 240 bhp for '96 and was the only engine available for '98, when bucket seats were standardized too. But the market had spoken, and Riviera was consigned to history after a token 2000-unit run for 1999. Of those, about 200 were specially trimmed Silver Arrow models, a nostalgic nod to the Bill Mitchell show car previewing the classic '63 Riviera. Though the valedictory edition may emerge one day as a minor collector's item, it was a sad finale for what had been one of the most glamorous of all Buicks.

Losing Riviera and Skylark did not seriously affect Buick business in the late '90s, which stayed fairly steady with some 400,000 or more sales each calendar year through 2000. Timely redesigns were a big help, with 1997 a pivotal model year. Century and Regal were recast on a new corporate W-body platform shared with Pontiac Grand Prix and Oldsmobile's new midsize '98 Intrigue. Coupes were forgotten, but sedans got smooth, handsome lines on longer wheelbases that made for roomier interiors. Century targeted the family market with six-passenger Custom and Limited models using a 3.1-liter V-6. Regal catered to luxury seekers with LS and bucket-seat GS sedans using 3.8-liter V-6s—a 195-bhp version for LS, a hot 240-bhp supercharged version for GS, which also boasted leather upholstery, sporty styling accents, and handling-oriented Gran Touring suspension. Centurys base-priced some $2000-$3000 less than Regals and, perhaps as a result, were far more popular, drawing well over 100,000 calendar-year sales in 1998-2000 versus 65,000-75,000 for Regal. To its credit, Buick generally held the price line while adding features most every season. The '99 Centurys, for example, got standard traction control and a useful tire-pressure monitor, while GM's new OnStar communications system moved from optional to standard for 2001 GS Regals and Limited Centurys. Century and Regal were good values for traditional sedan buyers. Despite few changes to an aging design, sales remained strong for the first few years

1998 Skylark four-door sedan

1999 Riviera coupe

2000 Century four-door sedan

2001 Park Avenue Ultra four-door sedan

2001 Regal Olympic Edition four-door sedan

2002 Century Limited four-door sedan

2002 LeSabre Custom four-door sedan

2002 Rendezvous four-door wagon

of the twenty-first century. However, volume fell rapidly preceding their demise during the 2004 season.

The admirable G-platform was the basis for redesigned big Buicks, starting with 1997's Park Avenue and Park Avenue Ultra. Here, too, styling was more curvaceous, though still Buick-conservative, and interiors became more spacious thanks to a longer wheelbase (by three inches), though overall length was little changed. Predictably, Flint's flagships offered a pile of new features, including front shoulder belts conveniently integrated with the seat, an aircraft-style head-up display projecting speed and other data onto the windshield at driver eye level, and "rain-sensing" wipers that varied intermittent sweeps according to moisture detected on the windshield. Arriving a bit later was Cadillac's praiseworthy "StabiliTrak" electronic antiskid system, which throttled back power and/or applied brakes to individual wheels to keep you on course. With all this, plus reasonable prices of $30,000-$35,000, Park Avenue calendar-year sales improved a healthy 44 percent in '97 and held in the 58,000-62,000 range for '98 and '99. Buick revived a tradition with the addition of portholes to the front fenders of the 2003 Park Avenue Ultra. Last seen on '83 Electras, the portholes returned as part of Buick's 100th anniversary celebration. For its last year in 2005, all Park Avenues (not just Ultras) proudly displayed portholes. Model-year sales dwindled to just 9,363 for that final year.

LeSabre got a mild cosmetic freshening for 1997 before it, too, became a G-car. The introduction of the new LeSabre transferred production to Detroit and marked the end of Buick

2003 LeSabre Celebrity Edition four-door sedan

2003 Park Avenue Ultra four-door sedan

2004 Park Avenue Ultra four-door sedan

2004 Century four-door sedan

2004 Regal Abboud GS four-door sedan

2005 Century four-door sedan

2005 LaCrosse four-door sedan

2005 LaCrosse four-door sedan

2005 LeSabre four-door sedan

2005 Park Avenue Ultra four-door sedan

production in Flint, where most Buicks had been built since 1904. Buick moved its headquarters from Flint to Detroit's Renaissance Center the previous year. Thus ended nearly a century of association between Buick and Flint. Appropriately, the redesigned 2000 models bowed in early 1999, the 40th anniversary of the LeSabre nameplate—on production Buicks, that is. Interior room improved via a longer wheelbase, plus a little extra width and even height, yet overall length and weight were again little changed. Styling was more closely aligned with Park Avenue's, and many of the flagship's features were on hand. Even the sophisticated StabiliTrak system was available in a new "Driver Confidence" package that also included the head-up display and self-sealing tires, though it required the Gran Touring suspension option. Yet for all the changes—including more nimble handling, a benefit of the stout G-car structure—LeSabre remained a resolutely conservative, upper-middle-class Buick with a family-friendly character and value pricing in low-$20,000 territory. Trouble was, many families had long since preferred minivans and SUVs over full-size sedans, which partly explains why LeSabre calendar-year sales remained essentially flat at just under 150,000 per year through 2000. To mark Buick's 100th year in 2003, LeSabre added a Celebration Edition which featured StabilTrak antiskid control, head-up instrument display, and unique trim. The G-car LeSabre went out of production after the 2005 season.

For 2005, both Century and Regal were replaced by a single nameplate: LaCrosse. CX and CXL versions, aimed at the traditional Buick buyer, had a soft ride and were powered by GM's venerable 3.8-liter V-6 with 200 horsepower. CXS was aimed at import buyers with firmer suspension and a 240-bhp 3.6-liter twincam V-6 that had been introduced in the 2004 Cadillac CTS and SRX. The new engine was not only quicker than the 3.8-liter, but was also smoother. Styling was cleaner and showed the new direction of Buick design. The interior design also moved forward with better materials and assembly. The LaCrosse was a significant improvement over the models it replaced. All versions were comfortable and the CXS offered good handling as well. However, LaCrosse failed to match the combined sales of its two predecessors.

Just as LaCrosse replaced two familiar nameplates, so did Lucerne in 2006. Taking over for both LaSabre (a Buick staple since 1959) and Park Avenue, the Lucerne shared a platform with the Cadillac DTS. Occupying a middle ground between the aggressive Chrysler 300 and the conservative Toyota Avalon, Lucerne redefined traditional Buick values for the twenty-first century. Ride was soft in the Buick tradition, but some complained that the boulevard ride was gained at the price of boat-like handling. Silence was also a Buick tradition and Buick put a renewed effort into the quietness of its new models. The 3.8-liter V-6 with 197 bhp from the previous cars was joined by Cadillac's Northstar V-8 engine with 275 horsepower—Buick's first passenger-car V-8 in more than a decade. Interiors were more luxurious with fit and materials to match any car in its class.

Light-truck demand grew at a phenomenal pace throughout the 1990s, one of the most important market trends of the decade. Another was GM's steady loss of market share, which withered to only some 25 percent by the start of the new millennium. Attempting to turn things around, GM embraced "brand management," a philosophy that said good products were less important to sales than a good name with a good image. It was a new twist on the old "sell the sizzle, not the steak" idea, and it didn't work in the much more competitive late-'90s market. Worse for Buick, brand management was a distraction that left the division on the sidelines of the profitable light-truck action.

GM finally corrected the oversight with the 2002 Rendezvous, Buick's first truck in 70 years. Actually, this was one of a new

2005 Park Avenue four-door sedan

2005 Rendezvous CX four-door wagon

2006 LaCrosse CXS four-door sedan

2006 Lucerne four-door sedan

2006 Lucerne four-door sedan

breed of "crossover" vehicles that were raking in big money by combining truck-type styling and utility with carlike refinement and driving ease. Rendezvous was related to Pontiac's similarly conceived Aztek, which bowed about a year before it, but was far more attractive, as most critics said. Both amounted to clever reskins of GM's basic 1997 front-drive minivan design, with different outer sheetmetal giving a quasi-SUV appearance, plus four conventional side doors. As a Buick, Rendezvous one-upped Aztek with better standard trim and equipment, not to mention a four-inch longer wheelbase that made room for available three-row seating for up to seven, a must feature for this new kind of vehicle. Each offered models with front-wheel drive or GM's new "VersaTrak" all-wheel drive, but the only engine was the corporation's hoary 3.4-liter pushrod V-6, which sent 185 bhp through a four-speed automatic transmission.

A much needed boost in power came in 2004 with the availability of a 245-bhp twincam 3.6-liter V-6. For 2006 a new base engine added ten horsepower. Despite the pedestrian underpinnings, Rendezvous emerged as a pleasant, well-equipped package that expanded Buick's market reach.

That reach was expanded further with a truck-based SUV in 2004 and a minivan in '05. The Rainier was Buick's version of GM's much-cloned midsize sport ute. Other variations were the Chevrolet TrailBlazer, GMC Envoy, Oldsmobile Bravada, Isuzu Ascender, and Saab 9-7X. The Buick's standard engine was a 275-bhp inline six; a 290-bhp V-8 was optional. Rainier included luxuries expected of a Buick—leather upholstery, power front seats, and automatic climate control. Buick also added extra insulation and laminated glass for a quieter ride.

Terraza was a General Motors minivan with an SUV-style nose added to create what GM called a "crossover sport van." The Chevrolet Uplander, Pontiac Montana SV6, and Saturn Relay shared the same design. Terraza was the most expensive and luxurious of the group.

Buick entered its second century with declining sales and market share. However, a renewed focus on comfort and silence was evident in the Lucerne. The crossover Enclave concept is expected as a 2007 production model and promises to be a stronger SUV entry than Rendezvous or Rainier. After a rocky start to a new century, Buick seems to be finding direction and building better vehicles.

2006 Terraza minivan

2007 Enclave four-door wagon prototype

Specifications

1930

Series 40 (wb 118.0)		Wght	Price	Prod
30-40	sdn 2d	3,600	1,270	6,144
30-44	spt rdstr 2P	3,420	1,310	3,639
30-45	phtn 4P	3,410	1,310	1,100
30-46	bus cpe	3,540	1,260	5,716
30-46S	special cpe 4P	3,600	1,300	10,748
30-47	sdn 4d	3,700	1,330	47,496
—	chassis	—	—	3,288

Series 50 (wb 124.0)		Wght	Price	Prod
30-57	sdn 4d	4,235	1,540	23,139
30-58	cpe 4P	4,120	1,510	5,275

Series 60 (wb 132.0)		Wght	Price	Prod
30-60	sdn 7P	4,415	1,910	6,650
30-60L	limo 7P	4,475	2,070	836
30-61	special sdn 4d	4,330	1,760	12,557
30-64	rdstr 2P	4,015	1,585	2,009
30-64C	special cpe 4P	4,225	1,695	5,381
30-68	cpe 5P	4,220	1,740	10,216
30-69	phtn 7P	4,110	1,595	1,618
—	chassis	—	—	924

1930 Engines	bore×stroke	bhp	availability
I-6, 257.5	3.44×4.63	81	S-40
I-6, 331.3	3.75×5.00	99	S-50, 60

1931

Series 50 (wb 114.0)		Wght	Price	Prod
8-50	sdn 2d	3,065	1,035	combined
8-54	spt rdstr 2-4P	2,840	1,055	below
8-55	phtn 5p	2,840	1,055	
8-56	bus cpe	2,980	1,025	
8-56S	spt cpe 2-4P	3,060	1,055	
8-57	sdn 4d	3,170	1,095	

Series 50 (wb 114.0; intro. 1/31)		Wght	Price	Prod
8-50	sdn 2d	3,145	1,035	3,677
8-54	spt rdstr 2-4P	2,935	1,055	977
8-55	phtn 5P	2,970	1,055	388
8-56	bus cpe	3,055	1,025	2,782
8-56C	conv cpe 4P	3,095	1,095	1,540
8-56S	spt cpe 2-4P	3,135	1,055	5,757
8-57	sdn 4d	3,265	1,095	33,358
—	chassis	—	—	2,008

Series 60 (wb 118.0)		Wght	Price	Prod
8-64	spt rdstr 2-4P	3,465	1,335	1,078
8-65	phtn 5P	3,525	1,335	495
8-66	bus cpe	3,615	1,285	2,732
8-66S	spt cpe 2-4P	3,695	1,325	30,775
8-67	sdn 4d	3,795	1,355	30,775
—	chassis	—	—	1,692

Series 80 (wb 124.0)		Wght	Price	Prod
8-86	cpe 4P	4,120	1,535	3,579
8-87	sdn 4d	4,255	1,565	14,769

Series 90 (wb 132.0)		Wght	Price	Prod
8-90	sdn 7P	4,435	1,935	4,202
8-90L	limo 7P	4,505	2,035	620
8-91	brgm 4d 5P	4,340	1,785	7,858
8-94	spt rdstr 4P	4,010	1,610	843
8-95	phtn 7P	4,125	1,620	450
8-96	cpe 5P	4,260	1,765	7,715
8-96C	conv cpe	4,195	1,785	1,070
8-96S	spt cpe 2-4P	4,250	1,720	2,993
—	chassis	—	—	290

1931 Engines	bore×stroke	bhp	availability
I-8, 220.7	2.88×4.25	77	S-50
I-8, 272.6	3.06×4.63	90	S-60
I-8, 344.8	3.13×5.00	104	S-80, 90

1932

Series 50 (wb 114.0)		Wght	Price	Prod
32-55	spt phtn 5P	3,270	1,155	116
32-56	bus cpe	3,275	935	1,726
32-56C	conv cpe-rdstr 4P	3,335	1,080	643
32-56S	special cpe 4P	3,395	1,040	1,914
32-57	sdn 4d	3,450	995	10,803
32-57S	special sdn 4d	3,510	1,080	9,941
32-58	victoria cpe 5P	3,420	1,060	2,196

Series 50 (wb 114.0)		Wght	Price	Prod
32-58C	conv phtn 5P	3,425	1,080	400
—	chassis	—	—	664

Series 60 (wb 118.0)		Wght	Price	Prod
32-65	spt phtn 5P	3,795	1,390	103
32-66	bus cpe	3,795	1,250	636
32-66C	cpe-rdstr 4P	3,795	1,310	452
32-66S	special cpe 4P	3,860	1,270	1,684
32-67	sdn 4d	3,980	1,310	9,060
32-68	victoria cpe 5P	3,875	1,290	1,514
32-68C	conv phtn 5P	3,880	1,310	384
—	chassis	—	—	408

Series 80 (wb 126.0)		Wght	Price	Prod
32-86	victoria cpe 5P	4,335	1,540	1,800
32-87	sdn 4d	4,450	1,570	4,092

Series 90 (wb 134.0)		Wght	Price	Prod
32-90	sdn 7P	4,657	1,955	1,387
32-90L	limo 7P	4,740	2,055	190
32-91	club sdn 5P	4,620	1,820	2,238
32-95	spt phtn 7P	4,400	1,675	146
32-96	victoria cpe 5P	4,460	1,785	1,460
32-96C	cpe rdstr 4P	4,390	1,805	289
32-96S	Country Club cpe 4P	4,470	1,740	586
32-97	sdn 4d	4,565	1,805	1,485
32-98	conv phtn 5P	4,480	1,830	269
—	chassis	—	—	216

1932 Engines	bore×stroke	bhp	availability
I-8, 230.4	2.94×4.25	82	S-50
I-8, 272.6	3.06×4.63	95	S-60
I-8, 344.8	3.13×5.00	113	S-80, 90

1933

Series 50 (wb 119.0)		Wght	Price	Prod
33-56	bus cpe	3,520	995	1,321
33-56C	conv cpe 4P	3,525	1,115	350
33-56S	spt cpe 2-4P	3,585	1,030	1,653
33-57	sdn 4d	3,705	1,045	19,259
33-58	victoria cpe 5P	3,605	1,065	4,123
—	chassis	—	—	870

Series 60 (wb 127.0)		Wght	Price	Prod
33-66C	conv cpe 2-4P	3,940	1,365	152
33-66S	spt cpe 2-4P	3,975	1,270	1,000
33-67	sdn 4d	4,115	1,310	7,450
33-68	victoria cpe 5P	4,005	1,310	2,887
33-68C	conv phtn 5P	4,110	1,585	183
—	chassis	—	—	399

Series 80 (wb 130.0)		Wght	Price	Prod
33-86	victoria cpe 5P	4,420	1,540	758
33-86C	conv cpe 2-4P	4,325	1,575	90
33-86S	spt cpe 2-4P	4,355	1,495	401
33-87	sdn 4d	4,505	1,570	1,545
33-88C	conv phtn 5P	4,525	1,845	124
—	chassis	—	—	90

Series 90 (wb 138.0)		Wght	Price	Prod
33-90	sdn 7P	4,705	1,955	902
33-90L	limo 7P	4,780	2,055	338
33-91	club sdn 5P	4,595	1,820	1,639
33-96	victoria cpe 5P	4,520	1,785	557
33-97	sdn 4d	4,595	1,805	641
—	chassis	—	—	192

1933 Engines	bore×stroke	bhp	availability
I-8, 230.4	2.94×4.25	86	S-50
I-8, 272.6	3.06×4.63	97	S-60
I-8, 344.8	3.13×5.00	113	S-80, 90

1934

Series 40 (wb 117.0)		Wght	Price	Prod
34-41	club sdn T/B 5P	3,175	925	11,495
34-46	cpe 5P	2,995	795	1,808
34-46S	spt cpe 2-4P	3,085	855	1,279
34-47	sdn 4d	3,155	895	7,805
34-48	tng sdn 2d T/B	3,120	865	4,779
—	chassis	—	—	1,727

Series 50 (wb 119.0)		Wght	Price	Prod
34-56	bus cpe 2P	3,682	1,110	1,082
34-56C	conv cpe 2-4P	3,692	1,230	589
34-56S	spt cpe 2-4P	3,712	1,145	1,192
34-57	sdn 4d	3,852	1,190	12,805

Series 50 (wb 119.0)		Wght	Price	Prod
34-58	victoria cpe 5P	3,767	1,160	4,405
—	chassis	—	—	1,777

Series 60 (wb 128.0)		Wght	Price	Prod
34-61	club sdn 5P	4,318	1,465	5,629
34-66C	conv cpe 2-4P	4,133	1,495	263
34-66S	spt cpe 2-4P	4,193	1,375	825
34-67	sdn 4d	4,303	1,425	5,365
34-68	victoria T/B cpe 5P	4,213	1,395	1,966
34-68C	conv phtn 5P	4,353	1,675	587
—	chassis	—	—	717

Series 90 (wb 136.0)		Wght	Price	Prod
34-90	sdn 7P	4,806	2,055	1,234
34-90L	limo 7P	4,876	2,175	428
34-91	club sdn 5P	4,696	1,965	1,507
34-96C	conv cpe 4P	4,511	1,945	83
34-96S	spt cpe 2-4P	4,546	1,875	137
34-97	sdn 4d	4,691	1,945	654
34-98	victoria cpe 5P	4,571	1,895	348
34-98C	conv phtn 5P	4,691	2,145	138
—	chassis	—	—	405

1934 Engines	bore×stroke	bhp	availability
I-8, 233.0	3.09×3.88	93	S-40
I-8, 235.3	2.97×4.25	88	S-50
I-8, 278.1	3.09×4.63	100	S-60
I-8, 344.8	3.13×5.00	116	S-90

1935

Series 40 (wb 117.0)		Wght	Price	Prod
35-41	sdn T/B 4d	3,210	925	19,173
35-46	bus cpe	3,020	795	2,858
35-46C	conv cpe 2-4P	3,140	925	1,000
35-46S	spt cpe 2-4P	3,090	855	1,200
35-47	sdn 4d	3,180	895	6,641
35-48	sdn 2d T/B	3,160	865	5,027
—	chassis	—	—	2,621

Series 50 (wb 119.0)		Wght	Price	Prod
35-56	bus cpe	3,652	1,110	257
35-56C	conv cpe 2-4P	3,662	1,230	187
35-56S	spt cpe 2-4P	3,682	1,145	279
35-57	sdn 4d	3,822	1,190	3,998
35-58	victoria cpe 5P	3,737	1,160	1,618
—	chassis	—	—	197

Series 60 (wb 128.0)		Wght	Price	Prod
35-61	club sdn 5P	4,288	1,465	2,854
35-66C	conv cpe 2-4P	4,103	1,495	111
35-66S	spt cpe 2-4P	4,163	1,375	261
35-67	sdn 4d	4,273	1,425	1,792
35-68	victoria cpe 5P	4,183	1,395	603
35-68C	conv phtn 6W 5P	4,323	1,675	308
—	chassis	—	—	309

Series 90 (wb 136.0)		Wght	Price	Prod
35-90	sdn 7P	4,776	2,055	651
35-90L	limo 7P	4,846	2,175	296
35-91	club sdn 5P	4,666	1,965	580
35-96C	conv cpe 2-4P	4,481	1,945	11
35-96S	spt cpe 2-4P	4,516	1,875	42
35-97	sdn 4d	4,661	1,945	119
35-98	victoria cpe 5P	4,541	1,895	32
35-98C	conv phtn 6W 5P	4,661	2,145	43
—	chassis	—	—	181

1935 Engines	bore×stroke	bhp	availability
I-8, 233.0	3.09×3.88	93	S-40
I-8, 235.3	2.97×4.25	88	S-50
I-8, 278.1	3.09×4.63	100	S-60
I-8, 334.8	3.13×5.00	116	S-90

1936

Series 40 Special (wb 118.0)		Wght	Price	Prod
36-41	sdn 4d T/B	3,660	885	78,803
36-46	bus cpe	3,150	765	10,928
36-46C	conv cpe 2-4P	3,590	905	1,650
36-46S	spt cpe 3P	3,180	820	1,103
36-46S	spt cpe 2-4P R/S	3,180	820	1,494
36-48	victoria cpe T/B 5P	3,305	835	22,323
—	chassis	—	—	5,413

Series 60 Century (wb 122.0)		Wght	Price	Prod
36-61	sdn 4d T/B	3,780	1,090	18,203
36-66C	conv cpe 2-4P	3,595	1,135	766

Series 60 Century (wb 122.0)		Wght	Price	Prod
36-66S	spt cpe 3P T/B	3,195	1,035	1,079
36-66S	spt cpe 2-4P R/S	3,195	1,035	1,018
36-68	victoria cpe T/B 5P	3,730	1,055	3,799
—	chassis	—	—	1,115

Series 80 Roadmaster (wb 131.0)				
36-80C	conv phtn T/B 6P	4,100	1,565	1,230
36-81	sdn 4d T/B 6P	4,100	1,255	15,328
—	chassis	—	—	534

Series 90 Limited (wb 138.0)				
36-90	sdn T/B 8P	—	1,845	1,709
36-90L	limo T/B 8P	—	1,945	947
36-91	sdn T/B 6P	—	1,695	1,726
36-91F	form sdn T/B 4d	1,635	1,895	75
—	chassis	—	—	352

1936 Engines	bore×stroke	bhp	availability
I-8, 233.0	3.09×3.88	93	S-40
I-8, 320.2	3.44×4.31	120	S-60, 80, 90

1937

40 Special (wb 122.0)		Wght	Price	Prod
37-40C	conv phtn 5P	3,630	1,302	1,945
37-41	sdn 4d T/B	3,490	1,021	85,195
37-44	sdn 2d	3,490	959	9,342
37-46	bus cpe	3,380	913	13,773
37-46C	conv cpe 4P	3,480	1,056	2,399
37-46S	spt cpe 4P	3,445	975	5,284
37-47	sdn 4d	3,510	995	22,517
37-48	tng sdn T/B 2d	3,480	985	16,034
—	chassis	—	—	6,860

60 Century (wb 126.0)				
37-60C	conv phtn 5P	3,840	1,524	425
37-61	tng sdn T/B 4d	3,720	1,233	21,140
37-64	sdn 2d	3,720	1,172	1,118
37-66C	conv cpe 4P	3,715	1,269	843
37-66S	spt cpe 4P	3,660	1,187	2,873
37-67	sdn 4d	3,750	1,297	4,771
37-68	tng sdn T/B 2d	3,750	1,197	2,897
—	chassis	—	—	1,026

80 Roadmaster (wb 131.0)				
37-80C	conv phtn T/B 6P	4,214	1,856	1,155
37-81	sdn T/B 4d	4,159	1,518	14,981
37-81F	formal sdn 6P	4,229	1,641	489
—	chassis	—	—	606

90 Limited (wb 138.0)				
37-90	sdn T/B 8P	4,549	2,240	1,710
37-90L	limo T/B 8P	4,599	2,342	965
37-91	sdn T/B 4d	4,469	2,066	1,242
37-91F	form sdn T/B 4d	4,409	2,240	158
—	chassis	—	—	598

1937 Engines	bore×stroke	bhp	availability
I-8, 248.0	3.09×4.13	100	S-40
I-8, 320.2	3.44×4.31	130	S-60, 80, 90

1938

40 Special (wb 122.0)		Wght	Price	Prod
38-40C	conv phtn 5P	3,705	1,406	946
38-41	tng sdn 4d T/B	3,560	1,047	82,191
38-44	spt sdn 2d 5P	3,515	981	5,951
38-46	bus cpe	3,385	945	11,368
38-46C	conv cpe 4P	3,575	1,103	2,625
38-46S	spt cpe T/B 4P	3,425	1,001	5,574
38-47	spt sdn 4d	3,535	1,022	11,341
38-48	tng sdn T/B 2d	3,520	1,006	14,213
—	chassis	—	—	7,092

Series 60 Century (wb 126.0)				
38-60C	conv phtn 5P	3,950	1,713	219
38-61	tng sdn T/B 4d	3,780	1,297	12,673
38-66C	conv cpe 4P	3,815	1,359	694
38-66S	spt cpe T/B 4P	3,690	1,226	2,030
38-67	spt sdn 4d	3,785	1,272	1,516
38-68	tng sdn T/B 2d	3,760	1,256	1,393
—	chassis	—	—	762

Series 80 Roadmaster (wb 133.0)				
37-80C	conv phtn 6P	4,235	1,983	411
37-81	tng sdn T/B 4d	4,245	1,645	4,704
37-81F	form sdn 6P	4,305	1,758	296

Series 80 Rdmstr (wb 133.0)		Wght	Price	Prod
37-87	spt sdn 6P	4,245	1,645	466
—	chassis	—	—	223

Series 90 Limited (wb 140.0)				
37-90	tng sdn T/B 8P	4,585	2,350	706
37-90L	limo T/B 8P	4,665	2,453	577
37-91	tng sdn T/B 4d	4,580	2,176	441
—	chassis	—	—	277

1938 Engines	bore×stroke	bhp	availability
I-8, 248.0	3.09×4.13	107	S-40
I-8, 320.2	3.44×4.31	141	S-60, 80, 90

1939

Series 40 Special (wb 120.0)		Wght	Price	Prod
41	tng sdn T/B 4d	3,482	966	111,473
41C	spt phtn T/B 5P	3,642	1,406	830
46	bus cpe	3,322	894	14,609
46C	conv cpe T/B 4P	3,452	1,077	4,809
46S	spt cpe T/B 4P	3,372	950	10,276
48	tng sdn T/B 2d	3,417	955	27,290
—	chassis	—	—	6,281

Series 60 Century (wb 126.0)				
61	tng sdn T/B 4d	3,782	1,246	18,783
61C	spt phtn T/B 5P	3,917	1,713	269
66C	conv cpe T/B 4P	3,712	1,343	850
66S	spt cpe T/B 4P	3,637	1,175	3,470
—	chassis	—	—	518

Series 80 Roadmaster (wb 133.0)				
80C	spt phtn 4d 6P	4,237	1,983	3
81	tng sdn T/B 4d	4,247	1,543	5,619
81C	spt phtn T/B 4d	4,392	1,983	364
81F	form sdn T/B 6P	4,312	1,758	340
87	spt sdn 6P	4,262	1,543	20
—	chassis	—	—	143

Series 90 Limited (wb 140.0)				
90	tng sdn T/B 8P	4,608	2,350	686
90L	limo T/B 8P	4,653	2,453	543
91	tng sdn T/B 4d	4,568	2,074	382
—	chassis	—	—	176

1939 Engines	bore×stroke	bhp	availability
I-8, 248.0	3.09×4.13	107	S-40
I-8, 320.2	3.44×4.31	141	S-60, 80, 90

1940

Series 40 Special (wb 121.0)		Wght	Price	Prod
41	sdn 4d	3,660	996	68,816
41C	spt phtn	3,755	1,355	597
41T	taxi	3,700	1,000	48
46	bus cpe	3,505	895	12,382
46C	conv cpe	3,665	1,077	3,763
46S	spt cpe	3,540	950	8,401

Series 50 Super (wb 121.0)				
48	sdn 2d	3,605	955	20,768
51	sdn 4d	3,790	1,109	97,226
51C	spt phtn	3,895	1,549	534
56C	conv cpe	3,785	1,211	4,804
56S	spt cpe	3,735	1,058	26,462
59	wgn 4d	3,870	1,242	501

Series 60 Century (wb 126.0)				
61	sdn 4d	3,935	1,210	8,708
61C	spt phtn	4,050	1,620	203
66	bus cpe	3,800	1,128	44
66C	conv cpe	3,915	1,343	550
66S	spt cpe	3,765	1,175	96

Series 70 Roadmaster (wb 126.0)				
71	sdn 4d	4,045	1,359	13,733
71C	spt phtn	4,195	1,768	238
76C	conv cpe	4,055	1,431	612
76S	spt cpe	3,990	1,277	3,972

Series 80 Limited (wb 133.0)				
80C	Streamlined spt phtn	4,540	1,952	7
81	sdn 4d	4,440	1,553	3,898
81C	T/B spt phtn	4,540	1,952	250
81F	T/B form sdn	4,455	1,727	270
87	Strmlined spt sdn 4d	4,380	1,553	14
87F	Streamlined form sdn	4,455	1,727	7

Series 90 Limited (wb 140.0)		Wght	Price	Prod
90	sdn 4d, 8P, A/S	4,645	2,096	828
90L	limo 8P, A/S	4,705	2,199	634
91	sdn 4d	4,590	1,942	418

1940 Engines	bore×stroke	bhp	availability
I-8, 248.0	3.09×4.13	107	S-40, 50
I-8, 320.2	3.44×4.31	141	S-60, 70, 80, 90

1941

Series 40 Special (wb 121.0)		Wght	Price	Prod
41	sdn 4d	3,730	1,052	92,528
41SE	sdn 4d	3,790	1,134	13,402
46	bus cpe	3,630	935	9,201
46S	sedanet	3,700	1,006	88,148
46SSE	sedanet	3,690	1,063	9,614
49	wgn 4d	3,980	1,463	850

Series 40A Special (wb 118.0)				
44	bus cpe	3,530	915	3,261
44C	conv cpe	3,780	1,138	4,309
44S	spt cpe	3,590	980	5,290
47	sdn 4d	3,670	1,021	14,139

Series 50 Super (wb 121.0)				
51	sdn 4d	3,770	1,185	58,638
51C	conv phtn	4,014	1,555	508
56	bus cpe	3,620	1,031	2,452
56C	conv cpe	3,810	1,267	12,391
56S	spt cpe	3,670	1,113	19,876

Series 60 Century (wb 126.0)				
61	sdn 4d	4,025	1,288	15,136
66	bus cpe	3,870	1,195	222
66S	sedanet	3,920	1,241	5,547

Series 70 Roadmaster (wb 126.0)				
71	sdn 4d	4,010	1,364	10,553
71C	conv phtn	4,469	1,775	326
76C	conv cpe	4,045	1,457	1,869
76S	spt cpe	3,920	1,282	2,834

Series 90 Limited (wb 139.0)				
90	sdn 4d, 8P, A/S	4,680	2,360	906
90L	limo 8P, A/S	4,760	2,465	669
91	sdn 4d	4,575	2,155	1,231
91F	form sdn, A/S	4,665	2,310	296

1941 Engines	bore×stroke	bhp	availability
I-8, 248.0	3.09×4.13	115	S-40A, 40 exc SE
I-8, 248.0	3.09×4.13	125	S-50, 41SE, 46SSE
I-8, 320.2	3.44×4.31	165	S-60, 70, 90

1942

Series 40A Special (wb 118.)		Wght	Price	Prod
44	util cpe	3,510	990	461
44C	conv cpe	3,790	1,260	1,788
47	sdn 4d	3,650	1,080	1,652
48	bus sedanet	3,555	1,010	559
48S	fam sedanet	3,610	1,045	5,990

Series 40B Special (wb 121.0)				
41	sdn 4d	3,760	1,120	17,397
41SE	sdn 4d	3,785	1,200	2,288
46	bus sedanet	3,650	1,020	1,408
46S	fam sedanet	3,705	1,075	11,856
46SSE	fam sedanet	3,725	1,130	1,809
49	wgn 4d	3,925	1,450	327

Series 50 Super (wb 124.0)				
51	sdn 4d	3,890	1,280	16,265
56C	conv cpe	4,025	1,450	2,489
56S	sedanet	3,800	1,230	14,629

Series 60 Century (wb 126.0)				
61	sdn 4d	4,065	1,350	3,319
66S	sedanet	3,985	1,300	1,232

Series 70 Roadmaster (wb 129.0)				
71	sdn 4d	4,150	1,465	5,418
76C	conv cpe	4,300	1,675	511
76S	sedanet	4,075	1,395	2,475

Series 90 Limited (wb 139.0)				
90	sdn 4d, 8P, A/S	4,710	2,445	150
90L	limo 8P, A/S	4,765	2,545	250
91	sdn 4d	4,665	2,245	215
91F	form sdn	4,695	2,395	85

1942 Engines	bore×stroke	bhp	availability
I-8,248.0	3.09×4.13	110	S-40A, 40B exc SE
I-8,248.0	3.09×4.13	118	S-50, 46SSE, 41SE
I-8,320.2	3.44×4.31	165	S-60, 70, 90

1946

Series 40 Special (wb 121.0)		Wght	Price	Prod
41	sdn 4d	3,720	1,580	1,650
46S	sedanet	3,670	1,522	1,350
Series 50 Super (wb 124.0)				
51	sdn 4d	3,935	1,822	77,724
56C	conv cpe	4,050	2,046	5,987
56S	sedanet	3,795	1,741	34,425
59	wgn 4d	4,170	2,594	748
Series 70 Roadmaster (wb 129.0)				
71	sdn 4d	4,165	2,110	20,864
76C	conv cpe	4,345	2,347	2,587
76S	sedanet	4,095	2,014	8,292

1946 Engines	bore×stroke	bhp	availability
I-8,248.0	3.09×4.13	110	S-40, 50
I-8,320.2	3.44×4.31	144	S-70

1947

Series 40 Special (wb 121.0)		Wght	Price	Prod
41	sdn 4d	3,720	1,623	18,431
46S	sedanet	3,760	1,611	14,603
Series 50 Super (wb 124.0)				
51	sdn 4d	3,910	1,929	83,576
56C	conv cpe	4,050	2,333	28,297
56S	sedanet	3,795	1,843	46,917
59	wgn 4d	4,170	2,940	2,036
Series 70 Roadmaster (wb 129.0)				
71	sdn 4d	4,190	2,232	47,152
76C	conv cpe	4,345	2,651	12,074
76S	sedanet	4,095	2,131	19,212
79	wgn 4d	4,445	3,249	300

1947 Engines	bore×stroke	bhp	availability
I-8,248.0	3.09×4.13	110	S-40, 50
I-8,320.2	3.44×4.31	144	S-70

1948

Series 40 Special (wb 121.0)		Wght	Price	Prod
41	sdn 4d	3,705	1,809	14,051
46S	sedanet	3,635	1,735	11,176
Series 50 Super (wb 124.0)				
51	sdn 4d	3,855	2,087	53,447
56C	conv cpe	4,020	2,518	19,017
56S	sedanet	3,770	1,987	33,819
59	wgn 4d	4,170	3,127	2,018
Series 70 Roadmaster (wb 129.0)				
71	sedan 4d	4,160	2,418	47,569
76C	conv cpe	4,315	2,837	11,503
76S	sedanet	4,065	2,297	20,649
79	wgn 4d	4,460	3,433	350

1948 Engines	bore×stroke	bhp	availability
I-8, 248.0	3.09×4.13	110	S-40
I-8, 248.0	3.09×4.13	115	S-50
I-8, 320.2	3.44×4.31	144/150	S-70

1949

Series 40 Special (wb 121.0)		Wght	Price	Prod
41	sdn 4d	3,695	1,861	5,940
46S	sedanet	3,625	1,787	4,687
Series 50 Super (wb 121.0)				
51	sedan 4d	3,835	2,157	136,423
56C	conv cpe	3,985	2,583	22,110
56S	sedanet	3,735	2,059	66,250
59	wgn 4d	4,100	3,178	1,847
Series 70 Roadmaster (wb 126.0)				
71	sdn 4d	4,205	2,735	55,242
76C	conv cpe	4,370	3,150	8,244
76R	Riviera htp cpe	4,420	3,203	4,343
76S	sedanet	4,115	2,618	18,537
79	wgn 4d	4,490	3,734	653

1949 Engines	bore×stroke	bhp	availability
I-8, 248.0	3.09×4.13	110	S-40
I-8, 248.0	3.09×4.13	115/120	S-50
I-8, 320.2	3.44×4.31	150	S-70

1950

Series 40 Special (wb 121.5)		Wght	Price	Prod
41	sdn 4d	3,710	1,941	1,141
41D	DeLuxe sdn	3,735	1,983	141,396
43	J/B sdn 4d	3,715	1,809	58,700
43D	DeLuxe J/B sdn, 4d	3,720	1,952	14,335
46	J/B cpe	3,615	1,803	2,500
46D	DeLuxe J/B cpe	3,665	1,899	76,902
46S	J/B sedanet	3,655	1,856	42,935
Series 50 Super (wb 121.5)				
51	sdn 4d	3,745	2,139	55,672
56C	conv cpe	3,965	2,476	12,259
56R	Riviera htp cpe	3,790	2,139	56,030
56S	J/B sedanet	3,645	2,041	10,697
59	wgn 4d	4,115	2,844	2,480
Series 50 Super (wb 125.5)				
52	sdn 4d	3,870	2,212	114,745
Series 70 Roadmaster (wb 125.3; 72-130.3)				
71	sdn 4d	4,135	2,633	6,738
72	Riviera sdn 4d	4,220	2,738	54,212
75R	Riviera htp cpe	4,135	2,633	2,300
76R	Riv DeLuxe htp cpe	4,245	2,854	8,432
76C	conv cpe	4,345	2,981	2,964
76S	J/B sedanet	4,025	2,528	2,968
79	wgn 4d	4,470	3,407	420

1950 Engines	bore×stroke	bhp	availability
I-8, 248.0	3.09×4.13	115/120	S-40
I-8, 263.3	3.19×4.13	124/128	S-50
I-8, 320.2	3.44×4.31	152	S-70

1951

Series 40 Special (wb 121.5)		Wght	Price	Prod
41	sdn 4d	3,605	2,139	999
41D	DeLuxe sdn 4d	3,680	2,185	87,848
45R	Riviera sdn 2d	3,645	2,225	16,491
46C	conv cpe	3,830	2,561	2,099
46S	spt cpe	3,600	2,046	2,700
48D	DeLuxe sdn 2d	3,615	2,127	54,311
Series 50 Super (wb 121.5; 52-125.5)				
51	sdn 4d	3,755	2,356	10,000
52	Riviera sdn 4d	3,845	2,437	92,886
56C	conv cpe	3,965	2,728	8,116
56R	Riviera sdn 2d	3,765	2,356	54,512
56S	DeLuxe sdn 2d	3,685	2,248	1,500
59	wgn 4d	4,100	3,133	2,212
Series 70 Roadmaster (wb 126.3; 72R-130.3)				
72R	Riviera sdn 4d	4,240	3,044	48,758
76C	conv cpe	4,355	3,283	2,911
76MR	Riviera htp cpe	4,185	3,051	809
76R	Riv htp cpe, hydrlic cntrls	4,235	3,143	12,901
79R	wgn 4d	4,470	3,780	679

1951 Engines	bore×stroke	bhp	availability
I-8, 263.3	3.19×4.13	120/128	S-40
I-8, 263.3	3.19×4.13	124/128	S-50
I-8, 320.2	3.44×4.31	152	S-70

1952

Series 40 Special (wb 121.5)		Wght	Price	Prod
41	sdn 4d	3,650	2,209	137
41D	DeLuxe sdn 4d	3,665	2,255	63,346
45R	Riviera htp cpe	3,665	2,295	21,180
46C	conv cpe	3,850	2,634	600
46S	spt cpe	3,605	2,115	2,206
48D	sdn 2d	3,620	2,197	32,684
Series 50 Super (wb 121.5; 52-125.5)				
52	sdn 4d	3,825	2,563	71,387
56C	conv cpe	3,970	2,869	6,904
56R	Riviera htp cpe	3,775	2,478	55,400
59	wgn 4d	4,105	3,296	1,641
Series 70 Roadmaster (wb 126.3; 72R-130.3)				
72R	sdn 4d	4,285	3,200	32,069
76C	conv cpe	4,395	3,453	2,402
76R	Riviera htp cpe	4,235	3,306	11,387
79R	wgn 4d	4,505	3,977	359

1952 Engines	bore×stroke	bhp	availability
I-8, 263.3	3.19×4.13	120/128	S-40
I-8, 263.3	3.19×4.13	124/128	S-50
I-8, 320.2	3.44×4.31	170	S-70

1953

Series 40 Special (wb 121.5)		Wght	Price	Prod
41D	DeLuxe sdn 4d	3,710	2,255	100,312
45R	Riviera htp cpe	3,705	2,295	58,780
46C	conv cpe	3,815	2,553	4,282
48D	DeLuxe sdn 2d	3,675	2,197	53,796
Series 50 Super (wb 121.5; 52-125.5)				
52	Riviera sdn 4d	3,905	2,696	90,685
56C	conv cpe	4,035	3,002	6,701
56R	Riviera htp cpe	3,845	2,611	91,298
59	wgn 4d	4,150	3,430	1,830
Series 70 Roadmaster (wb 121.5; 72R-125.5)				
72R	Riviera sdn 4d	4,100	3,254	50,523
76C	conv cpe	4,250	3,506	3,318
76R	Riviera htp cpe	4,125	3,358	22,927
76X	Skylark conv cpe	4,315	5,000	1,690
79R	wgn 4d	4,315	4,031	670

1953 Engines	bore×stroke	bhp	availability
I-8, 263.3	3.19×4.13	125/130	S-40
V-8, 322.0	4.00×3.20	164/170	S-50
V-8, 322.0	4.00×3.20	188	S-70

1954

Series 40 Special (wb 122.0)		Wght	Price	Prod
41D	DeLuxe sdn 4d	3,735	2,265	70,356
46C	conv cpe	3,810	2,563	6,135
46R	Riviera htp cpe	3,740	2,305	71,186
48D	DeLuxe sdn 2d	3,690	2,207	41,557
49	DeLuxe wgn 4d	3,905	3,163	1,650
Series 50 Super (wb 127.0)				
52	Riviera sdn 4d	4,105	2,711	41,756
56C	conv cpe	4,145	2,964	3,343
56R	Riviera htp cpe	4,035	2,626	73,531
Series 60 Century (wb 122.0)				
61	sdn 4d	3,805	2,520	31,919
66C	conv cpe	3,950	2,963	2,790
66R	Riviera htp cpe	3,795	2,534	45,710
69	wgn 4d	3,975	3,470	1,563
Series 70 Roadmaster (wb 127.0)				
72R	Riviera sdn 4d	4,250	3,269	26,862
76C	conv cpe	4,355	3,521	20,404
76R	Riviera htp cpe	4,215	3,373	3,305
Series 100 Skylark (wb 122.0)				
100M	conv cpe	4,260	4,483	836

1954 Engines	bore×stroke	bhp	availability
V-8, 264.0	3.63×3.20	143/150	S-40
V-8, 322.0	4.00×3.20	177/182	S-50
V-8, 322.0	4.00×3.20	195/200	S-60
V-8, 322.0	4.00×3.20	200	S-70, 100

1955

Series 40 Special (wb 122.0)		Wght	Price	Prod
41	sdn 4d	3,745	2,291	84,182
43	Riviera htp sdn	3,820	2,409	66,409
46C	conv cpe	3,825	2,590	10,009
46R	Riviera htp cpe	3,720	2,332	155,818
48	sdn 2d	3,715	2,233	61,879
49	wgn 4d	3,940	2,974	2,952
Series 50 Super (wb 127.0)				
52	sdn 4d	4,140	2,876	43,280
56C	conv cpe	4,280	3,225	3,527
56R	Riviera htp cpe	4,075	2,831	85,656
Series 60 Century (wb 122.0)				
61	sdn 4d	3,825	2,548	13,269
63	Riviera htp sdn	3,900	2,733	55,088
66C	conv cpe	3,950	2,991	5,588
66R	Riviera htp cpe	3,805	2,601	80,338
68	sdn 2d	3,795	2,490	270
69	wgn 4d	3,995	3,175	4,243
Series 70 Roadmaster (wb 127.0)				
72	sdn 4d	4,300	3,349	31,717
76C	conv cpe	4,415	3,552	4,739
76R	Riviera htp cpe	4,270	3,453	28,071

1955 Engines	bore×stroke	bhp	availability
V-8, 264.0	3.63×3.20	188	S-40
V-8, 322.0	4.00×3.20	236	S-50, 60, 70

1956

Series 40 Special (wb 122.0)		Wght	Price	Prod
41	sdn 4d	3,790	2,416	66,977
43	Riviera htp sdn	3,860	2,528	91,025
46C	Special conv cpe	3,880	2,740	9,712
46R	Riviera htp cpe	3,775	2,457	113,861
48	sdn 2d	3,750	2,357	38,672
49	wgn 4d	3,945	2,775	13,770
Series 50 Super (wb 127.0)				
52	sdn 4d	4,200	3,250	14,940
53	Riviera htp sdn	4,265	3,340	34,029
56C	conv cpe	4,340	3,544	2,889
56R	Riviera htp cpe	4,140	3,204	29,540
Series 60 Century (wb 122.0)				
61	sdn 4d	3,930	export	1
63	Riviera htp sdn	4,000	3,025	20,891
63D	Riviera DeLx htp sdn	4,000	3,041	35,082
66C	conv cpe	4,045	3,306	4,721
66R	Riviera htp cpe	3,890	2,963	33,334
69	wgn 4d	4,080	3,256	8,160
Series 70 Roadmaster (wb 127.0)				
72	sdn 4d	4,280	3,503	11,804
73	Riviera htp sdn	4,355	3,692	24,779
76C	conv cpe	4,395	3,704	4,354
76R	Riviera htp cpe	4,235	3,591	12,490

1956 Engines	bore×stroke	bhp	availability
V-8, 322.0	4.00×3.20	220	S-40
V-8, 322.0	4.00×3.20	255	S-50, 60, 70

1957

Series 40 Special (wb 122.0)		Wght	Price	Prod
41	sdn 4d	4,012	2,660	59,739
43	Riviera htp sdn	4,041	2,780	50,563
46C	conv cpe	4,082	2,987	8,505
46R	Riviera hpt cpe	3,956	2,704	64,425
48	sdn 2d	3,955	2,596	23,180
49	wgn 4d	4,292	3,047	7,013
49D	Riviera Est wgn 4d	4,309	3,167	6,817
Series 50 Super (wb 127.5)		**Wght**	**Price**	**Prod**
53	Riviera htp sdn	4,356	3,681	41,665
56C	conv cpe	4,414	3,981	2,056
56R	Riviera htp cpe	4,271	3,536	26,529
Series 60 Century (wb 122.0)				
61	sdn 4d	4,137	3,234	8,075
63	Riviera htp sdn	4,163	3,354	26,589
66C	conv cpe	4,234	3,598	4,085
66R	Riviera htp cpe	4,081	3,270	17,029
68	sdn 2d	4,080	export	2
69	Caballero wgn 4d	4,423	3,706	10,186
Series 70 Roadmaster (wb 127.5)				
73	Riviera htp sdn	4,469	4,053	11,401
73A	Riviera htp sdn, 1-pc bcklt	4,455	4,053	10,526
76C	conv cpe	4,500	4,066	4,363
76R	Riviera htp cpe	4,374	3,944	3,826
76A	Riviera htp cpe, 1-pc bcklt	4,370	3,944	2,812
Series 75 Roadmaster (wb 127.5)				
75	Riviera htp sdn	4,539	4,483	12,250
75R	Riviera htp cpe	4,427	4,373	2,404

1957 Engines	bore×stroke	bhp	availability
V-8, 364.0	4.13×3.40	250	S-40
V-8, 364.0	4.13×3.40	300	S-50, 60, 70, 75

1958

Series 40 Special (wb 122.0)		Wght	Price	Prod
41	sdn 4d	4,115	2,700	48,238
43	Riviera htp sdn	4,180	2,820	31,921
46C	conv cpe	4,165	3,041	5,502
46R	Riviera htp cpe	4,058	2,744	34,903
48	sdn 2d	4,063	2,636	11,566
49	wgn 4d	4,396	3,154	3,663
49D	Riviera Est htp wgn 4d	4,408	3,261	3,420
Series 50 Super (wb 127.5)				
53	Riviera htp sdn	4,500	3,789	28,460
56R	Riviera htp cpe	4,392	3,644	13,928
Series 60 Century (wb 122.0)				
61	sdn 4d	4,241	3,316	7,241
63	Riviera htp sdn	4,267	3,436	15,171

Series 60 Cntry (wb 122.0)		Wght	Price	Prod
66C	conv cpe	4,302	3,680	2,588
66R	Riviera htp cpe	4,182	3,368	8,110
68	sdn 2d	4,189	export	2
69	Caballero htp wgn 4d	4,498	3,831	4,456
Series 75 Roadmaster (wb 127.5)				
75	Riviera htp sdn	4,668	4,667	10,505
75C	conv cpe	4,676	4,680	1,181
75R	Riviera htp cpe	4,568	4,557	2,368
Series 700 Limited (wb 127.5)				
750	Riviera htp sdn	4,710	5,112	5,571
755	Riviera htp cpe	4,691	5,002	1,026
756	conv cpe	4,603	5,125	839

1958 Engines	bore×stroke	bhp	availability
V-8, 364.0	4.13×3.40	250	S-40
V-8, 364.0	4.13×3.40	300	S-50, 60, 75, 700

1959

4400 LeSabre (wb 123.0)		Wght	Price	Prod
4411	sdn 2d	4,159	2,740	13,492
4419	sdn 4d	4,229	2,804	51,379
4435	wgn 4d	4,565	3,320	8,286
4437	htp cpe	4,188	2,849	35,189
4439	htp sdn	4,266	2,925	46,069
4467	conv cpe	4,216	3,129	10,489
4600 Invicta (wb 123.0)				
4619	sdn 4d	4,331	3,357	10,566
4635	wgn 4d	4,660	3,841	5,231
4637	htp cpe	4,274	3,447	11,451
4639	htp sdn	4,373	3,515	20,156
4667	conv cpe	4,317	3,620	5,447
4700 Electra (wb 126.3)				
4719	sdn 4d	4,557	3,856	12,357
4737	htp cpe	4,465	3,818	11,216
4739	htp sdn	4,573	3,963	20,612
4800 Electra 225 (wb 126.3)				
4829	Riviera htp sdn	4,632	4,300	6,324
4839	htp sdn	4,641	4,300	10,491
4867	conv cpe	4,562	4,192	5,493

1959 Engines	bore×stroke	bhp	availability
V-8, 364.0	4.13×3.40	250	S-LeSabre
V-8, 401.0	4.19×3.64	325	S-others

1960

4400 LeSabre (wb 123.0)		Wght	Price	Prod
4411	sdn 2d	4,139	2,756	14,388
4419	sdn 4d	4,219	2,870	54,033
4435	wgn 4d, 2S	4,568	3,386	5,331
4437	htp cpe	4,163	2,915	26,521
4439	htp sdn	4,269	2,991	35,999
4445	wgn 4d, 3S	4,574	3,493	2,222
4467	conv cpe	4,233	3,145	13,588
4600 Invicta (wb 123.0)				
4619	sdn 4d	4,324	3,357	10,839
4635	wgn 4d, 2S	4,644	3,841	3,471
4637	htp cpe	4,255	3,447	8,960
4639	htp sdn	4,365	3,515	15,300
4645	wgn 4d, 3S	4,679	3,948	1,605
4667	conv cpe	4,347	3,620	5,236
4700 Electra (wb 126.3)				
4719	sdn 4d	4,544	3,856	13,794
4737	htp cpe	4,453	3,818	7,416
4739	htp sdn	4,554	3,963	14,488
4800 Electra 225 (wb 126.3)				
4829	Riviera htp sdn	4,653	4,300	8,029
4839	htp sdn	4,650	4,300	5,841
4867	conv cpe	4,571	4,192	6,746

1960 Engines	bore×stroke	bhp	availability
V-8, 364.0	4.13×3.40	235/250	S-LeSabre
V-8, 364.0	4.13×3.40	300	O-LeSabre
V-8, 401.0	4.19×3.40	325	S-others

1961

4000 Special (wb 112.0)		Wght	Price	Prod
4019	sdn 4d	2,610	2,384	18,339
4027	spt cpe	2,579	2,330	4,232
4035	wgn 4d	2,775	2,681	6,101
4045	wgn 4d, 3S	2,844	2,762	798
4119	DeLuxe sdn 4d	2,632	2,519	32,986
4135	DeLuxe wgn 4d	2,794	2,816	11,729
4317	Skylark spt cpe	2,687	2,621	12,683
4400 LeSabre (wb 123.0)				
4411	sdn 2d	4,033	2,993	5,959
4435	wgn 4d	4,450	3,623	5,628
4437	htp cpe	4,054	3,152	14,474
4439	htp sdn	4,129	3,228	37,790
4445	wgn 4d, 3S	4,483	3,730	2,423
4467	conv cpe	4,186	3,382	11,951
4469	sdn 4d	4,102	3,107	35,005
4600 Invicta (wb 123.0)				
4637	htp cpe	4,090	3,447	6,382
4639	htp sdn	4,179	3,515	18,398
4667	conv cpe	4,206	3,620	3,953
4700 Electra (wb 126.0)				
4719	sdn 4d	4,298	3,825	13,818
4737	htp cpe	4,260	3,818	4,250
4739	htp sdn	4,333	3,932	8,978
4800 Electra 225 (wb 126.0)				
4829	Riviera htp sdn	4,417	4,350	13,719
4867	conv cpe	4,441	4,192	7,158

1961 Engines	bore×stroke	bhp	availability
V-8, 215.0	3.50×2.80	155	S-Special (Skylark 185 bhp)
V-8, 364.0	4.13×3.40	235/250	S-LeSabre
V-8, 401.0	4.19×3.64	325	S-others

1962

Special (wb 112.1)		Wght	Price	Prod
4019	sdn 4d	2,666	2,358	23,249
4027	cpe	2,638	2,304	19,135
4035	wgn 4d	2,876	2,655	7,382
4045	wgn 4d, 3S	2,896	2,736	2,814
4067	conv cpe	2,858	2,587	7,918
4119	Del sdn 4d	2,648	2,593	31,660
4135	Del wgn 4d	2,845	2,890	10,380
4167	Del conv cpe	2,820	2,879	8,332
4347	Skylark htp cpe	2,707	2,787	34,060
4367	Skylark conv cpe	2,871	3,012	8,913
LeSabre (wb 123.0)				
4411	sdn 2d	4,041	3,091	7,418
4439	spt sdn	4,156	3,369	37,518
4447	htp cpe	4,054	3,293	25,479
4469	sdn 4d	4,104	3,227	56,783
Invicta (wb 123.0)				
4435	wgn 4d	4,471	3,836	9,131
4639	htp sdn	4,159	3,667	16,443
4645	wgn 4d, 3S	4,505	3,917	4,617
4647	Wildcat spt cpe	4,150	3,927	2,000*
4647	spt cpe	4,077	3,733	10,355
4667	conv cpe	4,217	3,617	13,471
*Estimated				
Electra 225 (wb 126.0)				
4819	sdn 4d	4,304	4,051	13,523
4829	Riviera htp sdn 6W	4,390	4,448	15,395
4839	htp sdn	4,309	4,186	16,734
4847	htp cpe	4,235	4,062	8,922
4867	conv cpe	4,396	4,366	7,894

1962 Engines	bore×stroke	bhp	availability
V-6, 198.0	3.63×3.20	135	S-Special
V-8, 215.0	3.50×2.80	155	S-Special DeLx
V-8, 215.0	3.50×2.80	190	S-Skyl; O-Spec
V-8, 401.0	4.19×3.64	265/280	S-LeSabre
V-8, 401.0	4.19×3.64	325	S-Invicta, Electra

1963

Special (wb 112.1)		Wght	Price	Prod
4019	sdn 4d	2,696	2,363	21,733
4027	cpe	2,661	2,309	21,886
4035	wgn 4d	2,866	2,659	5,867
4045	wgn 4d, 3S	2,903	2,740	2,415
4067	conv cpe	2,768	2,591	8,082
4119	Del sdn 4d	2,720	2,521	37,695
4135	Del wgn 4d	2,854	2,818	8,771
4347	Skylark spt cpe	2,757	2,857	32,109

Special (wb 112.1)		Wght	Price	Prod
4367	Skylark conv cpe	2,810	3,011	10,212
LeSabre (wb 123.0)				
4411	sdn 2d	3,905	2,869	8,328
4435	wgn 4d	4,320	3,526	5,566
4439	htp sdn	4,007	3,146	50,420
4445	wgn 4d, 3S	4,340	3,606	3,922
4447	htp cpe	3,924	3,070	27,977
4467	conv cpe	4,052	3,339	9,975
4469	sdn 4d	3,970	3,004	64,995
Wildcat (wb 123.0)				
4639	htp sdn	4,222	3,871	17,519
4647	htp cpe	4,123	3,849	12,185
4667	conv cpe	4,228	3,961	6,021
Invicta (wb 123.0)				
4635	wgn 4d	4,397	3,969	3,495
Electra 225 (wb 126.0)				
4819	sdn 4d	4,241	4,051	14,268
4829	pillarless sdn	4,284	4,254	11,468
4839	htp sdn	4,272	4,186	19,714
4847	htp cpe	4,153	4,062	6,848
4867	conv cpe	4,297	4,365	6,367
Riviera (wb 117.0)				
4747	htp cpe	3,988	4,333	40,000

1963 Engines	bore×stroke	bhp	availability
V-6, 198.0	3.63×3.20	135	S-Spec, Spec DeL
V-8, 215.0	3.50×2.80	155	O-Spec, Spec DeL, Skylark
V-8, 215.0	3.50×2.80	200	S-Skylark; O-all Specials
V-8, 401.0	4.19×3.64	265/280	S-LeSabre
V-8, 401.0	4.19×3.64	325	S-Invicta, Wildcat, Electra, Riviera
V-8, 425.0	4.31×3.64	340	O-Riviera

1964

Special (wb 115.0; Sptwgns-120.0)		Wght	Price	Prod
4027	cpe	2,991	2,343	15,030
4035	wgn	3,266	2,689	6,270
4067	conv cpe	3,108	2,605	6,308
4069	sdn 4d	3,008	2,397	17,983
4127	Del cpe	3,006	2,457	11,962
4135	Del wgn 4d	3,285	2,787	9,467
4169	Del sdn 4d	3,026	2,490	31,742
4337	Skylark spt cpe	3,057	2,680	42,356
4367	Skylark conv cpe	3,175	2,834	10,225
4369	Skylark sdn 4d	3,070	2,669	19,635
4255	Skylark Spt Wgn	3,557	2,989	2,709
4355	Skylark Cstm Spt Wgn	3,595	3,161	3,913
4265	Skylark Spt Wgn 4d 3S	3,689	3,124	2,586
4365	Skyl Cstm Spt Wgn 3S	3,727	3,286	4,446
LeSabre (wb 123.0)				
4439	htp sdn	3,730	3,122	37,052
4447	htp cpe	3,629	3,061	24,177
4467	conv cpe	3,787	3,314	6,685
4469	sdn 4d	3,693	2,980	56,729
4635	wgn 4d	4,352	3,554	6,517
4645	wgn 4d, 3S	4,362	3,635	4,003
Wildcat (wb 123.0)				
4639	htp sdn	4,058	3,327	33,358
4647	htp cpe	4,003	3,267	22,893
4667	conv cpe	4,076	3,455	7,850
4669	sdn	4,021	3,164	20,144
Electra 225 (wb 126.0)				
4819	sdn 4d	4,212	4,059	15,968
4829	pillarless sdn	4,238	4,261	11,663
4839	htp sdn	4,229	4,194	24,935
4847	htp cpe	4,149	4,070	9,045
4867	conv cpe	4,280	4,374	7,181
Riviera (wb 117.0)				
4747	htp cpe	3,951	4,385	37,658

1964 Engines	bore×stroke	bhp	availability
V-6, 225.0	3.75×3.40	155	S-Special
V-8, 300.0	3.75×3.40	210/250	S-LeSabre 4400; O-Spec
V-8, 401.0	4.19×3.64	325	S-LeS 4600, Wildcat, Elec
V-8, 425.0	4.31×3.64	340/360	S-Riv; O-LeS 4600, Wldct, Elec

1965

Special (wb 115.0)		Wght	Price	Prod
43327	cpe	2,977	2,343	12,945
43335	wgn 4d	3,258	2,688	2,868
43367	conv cpe	3,087	2,605	3,357
43369	sdn 4d	3,010	2,397	13,828
43427	cpe V-8	3,080	2,414	5,309
43435	wgn 4d V-8	3,365	2,759	3,676
43467	conv cpe V-8	3,197	2,676	3,365
43469	sdn 4d V-8	3,117	2,468	8,121
43535	Del wgn 4d	3,242	2,787	1,677
43569	Del sdn 4d	3,016	2,669	11,033
43635	Del wgn 4d	3,369	2,858	9,123
43669	Del sdn 4d	3,143	2,561	26,299
Skylark (wb 115.0; wgns-120.0)				
44255	Sptwgn 4d	3,642	2,989	4,226
44265	Sptwgn 4d, 3S	3,750	3,123	4,664
44327	cpe	3,035	2,537	4,195
44337	htp cpe	3,057	2,680	4,549
44367	conv cpe	3,149	2,834	1,181
44369	sdn 4d	3,086	2,669	3,385
44427	GS cpe	3,146	2,608	11,877
44437	GS htp cpe	3,198	2,751	47,034
44455	Cus Sptwgn 4d	3,690	3,160	8,300
44465	Cus Sptwgn 3S	3,802	3,285	11,166
44467	GS conv cpe	3,294	2,905	10,456
44469	sdn 4d	3,194	2,740	22,335
LeSabre (wb 123.0)				
45237	htp cpe	3,753	3,030	15,786
45239	htp sdn	3,809	3,090	18,384
45269	sdn 4d	3,788	2,948	37,788
45437	Cus htp cpe	3,724	3,100	21,049
45439	Cus htp sdn	3,811	3,166	23,394
45467	Cus conv cpe	3,812	3,325	6,543
45469	Cus sdn 4d	3,777	3,024	22,052
Wildcat (wb 126.0)				
46237	htp cpe	3,988	3,286	6,031
46239	htp sdn	4,089	3,346	7,499
46269	sdn 4d	4,058	3,182	10,184
46437	Del htp cpe	4,014	3,340	11,617
46439	Del htp sdn	4,075	3,407	13,903
46467	Del conv cpe	4,069	3,502	4,616
46469	Del sdn 4d	4,046	3,285	9,765
46637	Cus htp cpe	4,047	3,566	15,896
46639	Cus htp sdn	4,160	3,626	14,878
46667	Cus conv cpe	4,087	3,727	4,398
Electra 225 (wb 126.0)				
48237	htp cpe	4,208	4,082	6,302
48239	htp sdn	4,284	4,206	12,842
48269	sdn 4d	4,261	4,071	12,459
48437	Cus htp cpe	4,228	4,265	9,570
48439	Cus htp sdn	4,344	4,389	29,932
48467	Cus conv cpe	4,325	4,440	8,505
48469	Cus sdn 4d	4,272	4,254	7,197
Riviera (wb 117.0)				
49447	htp cpe	4,036	4,408	34,586

1965 Engines	bore×stroke	bhp	availability
V-6, 225.0	3.75×3.40	155	S-Spec, Skyl
V-8, 300.0	3.75×3.40	210/250	S-LeSabre; O-Spec, Skyl
V-8, 401.0	4.19×3.64	325	S-Wildcat, Electra, Riv; O-LeSabre
V-8, 425.0	4.31×3.64	340/360	O-Wildcat, Electra, Riv

1966

Special (wb 115.0)		Wght	Price	Prod
43307	cpe	3,009	2,348	9,322
43335	wgn 4d	3,296	2,695	1,451
43367	conv cpe	3,092	2,604	1,357
43369	sdn 4d	3,046	2,401	8,797
43407	cpe V-8	3,091	2,418	5,719
43435	wgn 4d V-8	3,399	2,764	3,038
43467	conv cpe V-8	3,223	2,671	2,036
43469	sdn 4d V-8	3,148	2,471	9,355
43507	Del cpe	3,009	2,432	2,359
43517	Del htp cpe	3,038	2,504	2,507
43535	Del wgn 4d	3,290	2,783	824
43569	Del sdn 4d	3,045	2,485	5,573
43607	Del cpe V-8	3,112	2,502	4,908
43617	Del htp cpe V-8	3,130	2,574	10,350
43635	Del wgn 4d V-8	3,427	2,853	7,592
43669	Del sdn 4d V-8	3,156	2,555	27,909
Skylark (wb 115.0; wgns-120.0)				
44255	Sptwgn 4d	3,713	3,025	2,469
44265	Sptwgn 4d, 3S	3,811	3,173	2,667
44307	cpe V-6	3,034	2,624	1,454
44317	htp cpe	3,069	2,687	2,552
44339	htp sdn	3,172	2,846	1,422
44367	conv cpe	3,158	2,837	608
44407	cpe V-8	3,145	2,694	6,427
44417	htp cpe V-8	3,152	2,757	33,326
44439	htp sdn V-8	3,285	2,916	18,873
44455	Cus Sptwgn 4d	3,720	3,155	6,964
44465	Cus Sptwgn 4d, 3S	3,844	3,293	9,510
44467	conv cpe V-8	3,259	2,904	6,129
44607	GS cpe	3,479	2,956	1,835
44617	GS htp cpe	3,428	3,019	9,934
44667	GS conv cpe	3,532	3,167	2,047
LeSabre (wb 123.0)				
45237	htp cpe	3,751	3,022	13,843
45239	htp sdn	3,828	3,081	17,740
45269	sdn 4d	3,796	2,942	39,146
45437	Cus htp cpe	3,746	3,109	18,830
45439	Cus htp sdn	3,824	3,174	21,914
45467	Cus conv cpe	3,833	3,326	4,994
45469	Cus sdn 4d	3,788	3,035	25,932
Wildcat (wb 126.0)				
46437	htp cpe	4,003	3,326	9,774
46439	htp sdn	4,108	3,391	15,081
46467	conv cpe	4,065	3,480	2,690
46469	sdn 4d	4,070	3,233	14,389
46637	Cus htp cpe	4,018	3,547	10,800
46639	Cus htp sdn	4,176	3,606	13,060
46667	Cus conv cpe	4,079	3,701	2,790
Electra 225 (wb 126.0)				
48237	htp cpe	4,176	4,032	4,882
48239	htp sdn	4,271	4,153	10,792
48269	sdn 4d	4,255	4,022	11,740
48437	Cus htp cpe	4,230	4,211	10,119
48439	Cus htp sdn	4,323	4,332	34,149
48467	Cus conv cpe	4,298	4,378	7,175
48469	Cus sdn 4d	4,292	4,201	9,368
Riviera (wb 119.0)				
49487	htp cpe	4,180	4,424	45,348

1966 Engines	bore×stroke	bhp	availability
V-6, 225.0	3.75×3.40	160	S-Special, Skyl
V-8, 300.0	3.75×3.40	210	O-Special, Skyl
V-8, 340.0	3.75×3.85	220	S-4440 wgn, LeS
V-8, 401.0	4.19×3.64	325	S-Skylark GS, Wildcat, Electra
V-8, 425.0	4.31×3.64	340	S-Riv; O-Wldct, Elect

1967

Special (wb 115.0; wgns-120.0)		Wght	Price	Prod
43307	cpe	3,071	2,411	6,989
43335	wgn 4d	3,343	2,742	908
43369	sdn 4d	3,077	2,462	4,711
43407	cpe	3,173	2,481	8,937
43435	wgn 4d	3,425	2,812	1,688
43469	sdn 4d	3,196	2,532	5,793
43517	Del htp cpe	3,127	2,566	2,357
43569	Del sdn 4d	3,142	2,545	3,650
43617	Del htp cpe	3,202	2,636	14,408
43635	Del wgn 4d	3,317	2,901	6,851
43669	Del sdn 4d	3,205	2,615	26,057
Skylark (wb 115.0; wgns-120.0)				
34017	GS 340 htp cpe	3,283	2,845	3,692
44307	cpe V-6	3,137	2,665	894
44407	cpe V-8	3,229	2,735	3,165
44417	htp cpe	3,199	2,798	41,084

Skylark (wb 115.0; wgns-120.0)		Wght	Price	Prod
44439	htp sdn	3,373	2,950	13,721
44455	Sptwgn 4d	3,713	3,025	5,440
44465	Sptwgn 4d, 3S	3,811	3,173	5,970
44455	Cust Sptwgn 4d	3,772	3,202	3,114
44465	Cust Sptwgn 4d, 3S	3,876	3,340	4,559
44467	conv cpe	3,335	2,945	6,319
44469	sdn 4d	3,324	2,767	9,213
44607	GS 400 cpe	3,439	2,956	1,014
44617	GS 400 htp cpe	3,500	3,019	10,659
44667	GS 400 conv cpe	3,505	3,167	2,140
LeSabre (wb 123.0)				
45239	htp sdn	3,878	3,142	17,464
45269	sdn 4d	3,847	3,002	36,220
45287	htp cpe	3,819	3,084	13,760
45439	Cus htp sdn	3,873	3,236	32,526
45467	Cus conv cpe	3,890	3,388	4,624
45469	Cus sdn 4d	3,855	3,096	27,930
45487	Cus htp cpe	3,853	3,172	22,666
Wildcat (wb 126.0)				
46439	htp sdn	4,069	3,437	15,110
46467	conv cpe	4,064	3,536	2,276
46469	sdn 4d	4,008	3,277	14,579
46487	htp cpe	4,021	3,382	10,585
46639	Cus htp sdn	4,119	3,652	13,547
46667	Cus conv cpe	4,046	3,757	2,913
46687	Cus htp cpe	4,055	3,603	11,871
Electra 225 (wb 126.0)				
48239	htp sdn	4,293	4,184	12,491
48257	htp cpe	4,197	4,075	6,845
48269	sdn 4d	4,246	4,054	10,787
48439	Cus htp sdn	4,336	4,363	40,978
48457	Cus htp cpe	4,242	4,254	12,156
48467	Cus conv cpe	4,304	4,421	6,941
48469	Cus sdn 4d	4,312	4,270	10,106
Riviera (wb 119.0)				
49487	htp cpe	4,189	4,469	42,799

1967 Engines	bore×stroke	bhp	availability
V-6, 225.0	3.75×3.40	160	S-Spec, Skyl
V-8, 300.0	3.75×3.40	210	O-Spec, Skyl
V-8, 340.0	3.75×3.85	220/260	S-4400 wgn, LeS; O-Skyl
V-8, 400.0	4.04×3.90	340	S-GS 400
V-8, 430.0	4.19×3.90	360	S-Wildcat, Electra, Riv

1968

Special DeLuxe (wb 116; 2d-112)		Wght	Price	Prod
43327	cpe	3,185	2,513	21,988
43369	sdn 4d	3,277	2,564	16,571
43435	wgn 4d	3,670	3,001	10,916
Skylark (wb 116.0; 2d-112.0)				
43537	htp cpe	3,240	2,688	32,795
43569	sdn 4d	3,278	2,666	27,387
44437	Cus htp cpe	3,344	2,956	44,143
44439	Cus htp sdn	3,481	3,108	12,984
44467	Cus conv cpe	3,394	3,098	8,188
44469	Cus sdn 4d	3,377	2,924	8,066
Sportwagon (wb 121.0)				
44455	Cust Sptwgn 4d	3,975	3,341	10,530
44465	Cust Sptwgn 4d, 3S	4,118	3,499	12,358

Note: Sportwagon production includes 4,614 2-seat and 3,869 3-seat series 48000 woodgrain models.

Gran Sport (wb 112.0)		Wght	Price	Prod
43437	GS 350 htp cpe	3,375	2,926	8,317
44637	GS 400 htp cpe	3,514	3,127	10,743
44667	GS 400 conv cpe	3,547	3,271	2,454
LeSabre (wb 123.0)				
45239	htp sdn	3,980	3,281	18,058
45269	sdn 4d	3,946	3,141	37,433
45287	htp cpe	3,923	3,223	14,992
45439	Cus htp sdn	4,007	3,375	40,370
45467	Cus conv cpe	3,966	3,504	5,257
45469	Cus sdn 4d	3,950	3,235	34,112
45487	Cus htp cpe	3,932	3,311	29,596
Wildcat (wb 126.0)				
46439	htp sdn	4,133	3,576	15,153
46469	sdn 4d	4,076	3,416	15,201
46487	htp cpe	4,065	3,521	10,708
46639	Cus htp sdn	4,162	3,791	14,059
46667	Cus conv cpe	4,118	3,873	3,572
46687	Cus htp cpe	4,082	3,742	11,276
Electra 225 (wb 126.0)				
48239	htp sdn	4,270	4,330	15,376
48257	htp cpe	4,180	4,221	10,705
48269	sdn 4d	4,253	4,200	12,723
48439	Cus htp sdn	4,314	4,509	50,846
48457	Cus htp cpe	4,223	4,400	16,826
48467	Cus conv cpe	4,285	4,541	7,976
48469	Cus sdn 4d	4,304	4,415	10,910
Riviera (wb 119.0)				
49487	htp cpe	4,222	4,615	49,284

1968 Engines	bore×stroke	bhp	availability
I-6, 250.0	3.88×3.53	155	S-Special Del, Skylark
V-8, 350.0	3.80×3.85	230	S-Swgn, Sky Cus, LeS; O-Spec, Sky
V-8, 350.0	3.80×3.85	280	S-GS 350; O-Sp Del, Sky, LeS,Swgn
V-8, 400.0	4.04×3.90	340	S-GS 400; Sprtwagn 400
V-8, 430.0	4.19×3.90	360	S-Wldct, Elect, Riv

1969

Special DeLuxe (wb 116; 2d-112)		Wght	Price	Prod
43327	cpe	3,216	2,562	15,268
43369	sdn 4d	3,182	2,613	11,113
43435	wgn 4d	3,736	3,092	2,590
43436	luxury wgn 4d	3,783	3,124	6,677
Skylark (wb 116.0; 2d-112.0)				
43537	htp cpe	3,240	2,736	38,658
43569	sdn 4d	3,270	2,715	22,349
44437	Cus htp cpe	3,341	3,009	35,639
44439	Cus htp sdn	3,477	3,151	9,609
44467	Cus conv cpe	3,398	3,152	6,552
44469	Cus sdn 4d	3,397	2,978	6,423
Sportwagon (wb 121.0)				
44456	Cust Sptwgn 4d	4,106	3,465	9,157
44466	Cust Sptwgn 4d,3S	4,321	3,621	11,513
Gran Sport (wb 112.0)				
43437	GS 350 htp cpe	3,406	2,980	4,933
44637	GS 400 htp cpe	3,549	3,181	6,356
44667	GS 400 conv cpe	3,594	3,325	1,776
LeSabre (wb 123.2)				
45237	htp cpe	3,936	3,298	16,201
45239	htp sdn	3,983	3,356	17,235
45269	sdn 4d	3,966	3,216	36,664
45437	Cus htp cpe	4,018	3,386	38,887
45439	Cus htp sdn	4,073	3,450	48,123
45467	Cus conv cpe	3,958	3,579	3,620
45469	Cus sdn 4d	3,941	3,310	37,136
Wildcat (wb 123.2)				
46437	htp cpe	3,926	3,596	12,416
46439	htp sdn	4,304	3,651	13,805
46469	sdn 4d	4,102	3,491	13,126
46637	Cus htp cpe	4,134	3,817	12,136
46639	Cus htp sdn	4,220	3,866	13,596
46667	Cus conv cpe	4,152	3,948	2,374
Electra 225 (wb 126.2)				
48239	htp sdn	4,294	4,432	15,983
48257	htp cpe	4,203	4,323	13,128
48269	sdn 4d	4,238	4,302	14,521
48439	Cus htp sdn	4,328	4,611	65,240
48457	Cus htp cpe	4,222	4,502	27,018
48467	Cus conv cpe	4,309	4,643	8,294
48469	Cus sdn 4d	4,281	4,517	14,434
Riviera (wb 119.0)				
49487	htp cpe	4,199	4,701	52,872

1969 Engines	bore×stroke	bhp	availability
I-6, 250.0	3.88×3.53	155	S-SD cpe/sdn, Sky
V-8, 350.0	3.80×3.85	230	S-SD wgn, Sky Cus, Swgn, LeS
V-8, 350.0	3.80×3.85	280	S-GS 350; O-LeS, SW, SD, Skyl
V-8, 400.0	4.04×3.90	340	S-GS 400; O-LeS, Sprtwgn
V-8, 430.0	4.19×3.90	360	S-Riv, Elct, Wldct

1970

Skylark (wb 116.0; 2d-112.0)		Wght	Price	Prod
43327	cpe	3,250	2,685	18,620
43369	sdn 4d	3,311	2,736	13,420
43537	350 htp cpe	3,277	2,859	70,918
43569	350 sdn 4d	3,320	2,838	30,281
44437	Cus htp cpe	3,435	3,132	36,367
44439	Cus htp sdn	3,565	3,220	12,411
44467	Cus conv cpe	3,499	3,275	4,954
44469	Cus sdn 4d	3,499	3,101	7,113
Sportwagon (wb 116.0)				
43435	wgn 4d	3,775	3,210	2,239
43436	luxury wgn 4d	3,898	3,242	10,002
Gran Sport (wb 112.0)				
43437	htp cpe	3,434	3,098	9,948
44637	455 htp cpe	3,562	3,283	8,732
44667	455 conv cpe	3,619	3,469	1,416
LeSabre (wb 124.0)				
45237	htp cpe	3,866	3,419	14,163
45239	htp sdn	4,018	3,477	14,817
45269	sdn 4d	3,970	3,337	35,404
45437	Cus htp cpe	3,921	3,507	35,641
45439	Cus htp sdn	3,988	3,571	43,863
45467	Cus conv cpe	3,947	3,700	2,487
45469	Cus sdn 4d	3,950	3,431	36,682
46437	Cus 455 htp cpe	4,066	3,675	5,469
46439	Cus 455 htp sdn	4,143	3,739	6,541
46469	Cus 455 sdn 4d	4,107	3,599	5,555
Estate wagon (wb 124.0)				
46036	wgn 4d	4,691	3,923	11,427
46046	wgn 4d, 3S	4,779	4,068	16,879
Wildcat Custom (wb 124.0)				
46637	htp cpe	4,099	3,949	9,447
46639	htp sdn	4,187	3,997	12,924
46667	conv cpe	4,214	4,079	1,244
Electra 225 (wb 127.0)				
48239	htp sdn	4,296	4,592	14,338
48257	htp cpe	4,214	4,482	12,013
48269	sdn 4d	4,274	4,461	12,580
48439	Cus htp sdn	4,385	4,771	65,114
48457	Cus stp cpe	4,297	4,661	26,002
48467	Cus conv cpe	4,341	4,802	6,045
48469	Cus sdn 4d	4,283	4,677	14,109
Riviera (wb 119.0)				
49487	htp cpe	4,216	4,854	37,336

1970 Engines	bore×stroke	bhp	availability
I-6, 250.0	3.88×3.53	155	S-Sky, Sky 350
V-8, 350.0	3.80×3.85	260	S-LeS, Sky Cus, SW; O-Skylark
V-8, 350.0	3.80×3.85	285	O-LeS, Skyl, Sportwagon
V-8, 350.0	3.80×3.85	315	S-GS; O-LeS, Sky, Sprtwgn
V-8, 455.0	4.31×3.90	350/360	S-GS 455
V-8, 455.0	4.31×3.90	370	S-Wldct, Est Wgn, LeS 455, Elec, Riv

1971

Skylark (wb 116.0; 2d 112.0)		Wght	Price	Prod
43327	cpe	3,254	2,847	14,500
43337	htp cpe	3,272	2,918	61,201
43369	sdn 4d	3,326	2,897	34,037
44437	Custom htp cpe	3,391	2,317	29,536
44439	Custom htp sdn	3,547	3,397	10,814
44467	Custom conv cpe	3,431	3,462	3,993
44469	Custom sdn 4d	3,455	3,288	8,299
Sportwagon (wb 116.0)				
43436	wgn 4d	3,928	3,515	12,525
Gran Sport (wb 112.0)				
43437	htp cpe	3,461	3,285	8,268

Gran Sport (wb 112.0)		Wght	Price	Prod
43467	conv cpe	3,497	3,476	902
LeSabre (wb 124.0)				
45239	htp sdn 4d	4,109	4,119	14,234
45257	htp cpe	4,049	4,061	13,385
46269	sdn 4d	4,078	3,992	26,348
45439	Custom htp sdn	4,147	4,213	41,098
45457	Custom htp cpe	4,095	4,149	29,944
45467	Custom conv cpe	4,086	4,342	1,856
45469	Custom sdn 4d	4,107	4,085	26,970
Estate wagon (wb 127.0)				
46035	wgn 4d 2S	4,906	4,640	8,699
46045	wgn 4d 3S	4,965	4,786	15,335
Centurion (wb 124.0)				
46639	htp sdn	4,307	4,564	15,345
46647	htp cpe	4,195	4,678	11,892
46667	conv cpe	4,227	4,678	2,161
Electra 225 (wb 127.0)				
48237	htp cpe	4,345	4,801	8,662
48239	htp sdn	4,381	4,915	17,589
48437	Custom htp cpe	4,359	4,980	26,831
48439	Custom htp sdn	4,421	5,093	72,954
Riviera (wb 122.0)				
49487	htp cpe	4,325	5,253	33,810

1971 Engines	bore×stroke	bhp	availability
I-6, 250.0	3.88×3.53	145	S-Skylark
V-8, 350.0	3.80×3.85	230	S-SW, LeS, O-Sky
V-8, 350.0	3.80×3.85	260	S-Sky GS; O-Sky, LeS
V-8, 455.0	4.31×3.90	315	S-Cent, Elec, Est Wgn; Riv, O-Sky, LeS, GS
V-8, 455.0	4.31×3.90	330	O-Cent, Riv
V-8, 455.0	4.31×3.90	345	O-Sky, LeS, GS

1972

Skylark (wb 116.0; 2d 112.0)		Wght	Price	Prod
4D69	sed 4d	3,475	2,973	42,206
4D69	350 sdn 4d	3,600	3,104	
4D27	cpe	3,420	2,925	14,552
4D37	htp cpe	3,426	2,993	84,868
4D37	350 htp cpe	3,600	3,124	
4G37	GS htp cpe	3,471	3,225	7,723
4G67	GS conv cpe	3,525	3,406	852
4H69	Custom sdn 4d	3,516	3,228	9,924
4H39	Custom htp sdn	3,609	3,331	12,925
4H37	Custom htp cpe	3,477	3,255	34,271
4H67	Custom conv cpe	3,534	3,393	3,608
4F36	Sportwagon 4d 2S	3,987	3,444	14,417
LeSabre (wb 124.0)				
4L69	sdn 4d	4,201	3,958	29,505
4L39	htp sdn	4,211	4,079	15,160
4L57	htp cpe	4,166	4,024	14,011
4N69	Custom sdn 4d	4,221	4,047	35,295
4N39	Custom htp sdn	4,226	4,168	50,804
4N57	Custom htp cpe	4,181	4,107	36,510
4N67	Custom conv cpe	4,235	4,291	2,037
Estate wagon (wb 127.0)				
4R45	wgn 4d 3S	5,060	4,728	18,793
4R35	wgn 4d 2S	4,975	4,589	10,175
Centurion (wb 124.0)				
4P39	htp sdn	4,406	4,508	19,852
4P47	htp cpe	4,336	4,579	14,187
4P67	conv cpe	4,396	4,616	2,396
Electra 225 (wb 127.0)				
4U39	htp sdn	4,515	4,890	19,433
4U37	htp cpe	4,445	4,782	9,961
4V39	Custom sdn 4d	4,530	5,060	104,754
4V37	Custom htp cpe	4,455	4,952	37,974
Riviera (wb 122.0)				
4Y87	htp cpe	4,343	5,149	33,728

1972 Engines	bore×stroke	bhp	availability
V-8, 350.0	3.80×3.85	150	S-Skyl, LeS
V-8, 350.0	3.80×3.85	190	S-GS, O-Skyl, LeS
V-8, 455.0	4.31×3.90	225	S-Cent, Elec, EWgn; O-Sky GS, LeSabre
V-8, 455.0	4.31×3.90	250	S-Riviera; O-Cent, LeS
V-8, 455.0	4.31×3.90	270	O-GS

1973

Apollo (wb 111.0)		Wght	Price	Prod
B69	sdn 4d	3,239	2,628	8,450
B27	sdn 2d	3,195	2,605	14,475
B17	htchbk sdn 2d	3,297	2,754	9,868
Century (wb 116.0; 2d 112.0)				
D29	Colonnade sdn 4d	3,780	3,057	38,202
D37	Colonnade cpe	3,713	3,057	56,154
F35/45	wgn 4d 2S/3S	4,156*	3,486*	7,760*
H29	Luxus Clnnde sdn 4d	3,797	3,326	22,438
H57	Luxus Colonnade cpe	3,718	3,331	71,712
K35/45	Luxus wgn 4d 2S/3S	4,190*	3,652*	10,645*
J57	Regal Colonnade cpe	3,743	3,470	91,557
LeSabre (wb 124.0)				
L69	sdn 4d	4,234	3,998	29,649
L39	htp sdn	4,259	4,125	13,413
L57	htp cpe	4,210	4,067	14,061
N69	Custom sdn 4d	4,264	4,091	42,854
N39	Custom htp sdn	4,284	4,217	55,879
N57	Custom htp cpe	4,225	4,154	41,425
Centurion (wb 124.0)				
P39	htp sdn	4,329	4,390	22,354
P57	htp cpe	4,260	3,336	16,883
P67	conv cpe	4,316	4,534	5,739
Estate wagon (wb 127.0)				
R35	wgn 4d 2S	4,952	4,645	12,282
R45	wgn 4d 3S	5,021	4,790	23,513
Electra 225 (wb 127.0)				
T39	htp sdn	4,581	4,928	17,189
T37	htp cpe	4,488	4,815	9,224
V39	Custom htp sdn	4,603	5,105	107,031
V37	Custom htp cpe	4,505	4,993	44,328
Riviera (wb 122.0)				
Y87	htp cpe	4,486	5,221	34,080

1973 Engines	bore×stroke	bhp	availability
I-6, 250.0	3.87×3.50	100	S-Apollo
V-8, 350.0	3.80×3.85	150	S-Apllo, Cnty, LeS
V-8, 350.0	3.80×3.85	175	S-Cnty; O-Ap, LeS
V-8, 455.0	4.31×3.90	225	S-Ewgn, Elec; O-Cnty, LeS
V-8, 455.0	4.31×3.90	250	S-Riv; O-LeS; Ewgn, Elec
V-8, 455.0	4.31×3.90	260/270	O-Riviera

*Figures for 2S (2-seat) wgns shown; for 3S wgns add approx. 40 lbs and $125. Production combined.

1974

Apollo (wb 111.0)		Wght	Price	Prod
B69	sdn 4d	3,362	3,060	16,779
B27	sdn 2d	3,322	3,037	28,286
B17	htchbk sdn 2d	3,428	3,160	11,644
Century (wb 116.0; 2d 112.0)				
D29	350 Clnnde sdn 4d	3,890	3,836	22,856
D37	350 Colonnade cpe	3,845	3,790	33,166
D37	Grnd Sprt Clnnde cpe	3,937	3,904	
F35/45	wgn 4d 2S/3S	4,272*	4,205*	4,860*
H29	Luxus Clnnde sdn 4d	3,910	4,109	11,159
H57	Luxus Colonnade cpe	3,835	4,089	44,930
K35/45	Luxus wgn 4d 2S/3S	4,312*	4,371*	6,791*
J29	Regal Clnnde htp sdn	3,930	4,221	9,333
J57	Regal Clnnde htp cpe	3,900	4,201	57,512
LeSabre (wb 124.0)				
N69	sdn 4d	4,337	4,355	18,572
N39	htp sdn	4,387	4,482	11,879
N57	htp cpe	4,297	4,424	12,522
P69	Luxus sdn 4d	4,352	4,466	16,039
P39	Luxus htp sdn	4,397	4,629	23,910
P57	Luxus htp cpe	4,307	4,575	27,243
P67	Luxus conv cpe	4,372	4,696	3,627
Estate wagon (wb 127.0)		**Wght**	**Price**	**Prod**
R35	wgn 4d 2S	5,082	5,019	4,581
R45	wgn 4d 3S	5,182	5,163	9,831
Electra 225 (wb 127.0)		**Wght**	**Price**	**Prod**
T39	htp sdn	4,682	5,373	5,750
T37	htp cpe	4,607	5,260	3,339
V39	Custom htp sdn	4,702	5,550	29,089
V37	Custom htp cpe	4,627	5,438	15,099
X39	Limited htp sdn	4,732	5,921	30,051
X37	Limited htp cpe	4,682	5,886	16,086
Riviera (wb 122.0)				
Y87	htp cpe	4,572	5,678	20,129

1974 Engines	bore×stroke	bhp	availability
I-6, 250.0	3.87×3.50	100	S-Apollo
V-8, 350.0	3.80×3.85	150	S-Apllo, Cnty, LeS
V-8, 350.0	3.80×3.85	175	O-Cnty; O-Ap, LeS
V-8, 455.0	4.31×3.90	175	O-Cnty, EWgn
V-8, 455.0	4.31×3.90	210	S-EWgn, Elec, Riviera; O-Cnty
V-8, 455.0	4.31×3.90	245	O-EWgn, Electra, Riviera, Cnty

*Figures for 2S wgns shown; for 3S wgs add approx. 30 lbs and $125. Production combined.

1975

Skyhawk (wb 97.0)		Wght	Price	Prod
S07	htchbk cpe 2d	2,891	4,173	29,448
T07	S htchbk cpe 2d	2,851	3,860	
Apollo/Skylark (wb 111.0)*				
B69	Apollo sdn 4d I-6	3,438	3,436	21,138
W27	Skylark "S" cpe V-6	3,405	3,234	27,689
B27	Skylark cpe V-6	3,438	3,463	
B17	Skyl htckbk sdn 2d V-6	3,512	3,586	6,814
C69	Apollo S/R sdn 4d I-6	3,478	4,092	2,241
C27	Skylark S/R cpe V-6	3,404	4,136	3,746
C17	Skyl S/R htckbk V-6	3,514	4,253	1,505
Century (wb 116.0; 2d 112.0)*				
D37	Colonnade cpe	3,762	3,894	39,556
E37	Spec Clnnde cpe V-6	3,613	3,815	
D29	Colonnade sdn 4d	3,818	3,944	22,075
F35	wgn 4d 2S V-8	4,320	4,636	4,416
F45	wgn 4d 3S V-8	4,370	4,751	
H29	Cust Clnnde sdn 4d	3,851	4,211	9,995
H57	Cust Clnnde cpe	3,759	4,154	32,966
K35	Custom wgn 4d 2S	4,350	4,802	7,078
K45	Custom wgn 4d 3S	4,400	4,917	
Regal (wb 116.0; 2d 112.0)*				
J29	Clnnde sdn 4d V-6	3,888	4,311	10,726
J57	Colonnade cpe V-6	3,821	4,257	56,646
LeSabre (wb 123.5)				
N69	sdn 4d	4,355	4,771	14,088
N39	htp sdn	4,411	4,898	9,119
N57	htp cpe	4,294	4,840	8,647
P69	Custom sdn 4d	4,388	4,934	17,026
P39	Custom htp sdn	4,439	5,061	30,005
P57	Custom htp cpe	4,316	5,007	25,016
P67	Custom conv cpe	4,392	5,133	5,300
Estate wagon (wb 127.0)				
R35	wgn 4d 2S	5,055	5,447	4,128
R45	wgn 4d 3S	5,135	5,591	9,612
Electra 225 (wb 127.0)				
V39	Custom htp sdn	4,706	6,201	27,357
V37	Custom htp cpe	4,582	6,041	16,145
X39	Limited htp sdn	4,762	6,516	33,778
X37	Limited htp cpe	4,633	6,352	17,750
Riviera (wb 122.0)				
Z87	htp cpe	4,539	6,420	17,306

1975 Engines	bore×stroke	bhp	availability
V-6, 231.0	3.80×3.40	110	S-Skh, Skylark, Century, Regal
I-6, 250.0	3.87×3.50	105	S-Apollo
V-8, 260.0	3.50×3.39	110	S-Apollo, Skyl,
V-8, 350.0	3.80×3.85	145	S-Cnty exc wgns
V-8, 350.0	3.80×3.85	165	S-Cnty wgns, LeS; O-Cnty, Rgl
V-8, 400.0	4.12×3.75	185	S-LeSabre (CA)
V-8, 455.0	4.31×3.90	205	S-EWgn, Elec, Riviera; O-LeS

*Six & V-8 weights averaged. Prices for sixes shown; for V-8s add approx. $80 to I-6 or $20-30 to V-6 models.

1976

Skyhawk (wb 97.0)		Wght	Price	Prod
S07	htchbk cpe 2d	2,889	4,216	15,768
T07	S htchbk cpe 2d	2,857	3,903	
Skylark (wb. 111.0)				
W27	S cpe	3,416	3,435	51,260
B27	cpe	3,426	3,549	
B69	sdn 4d	3,384	3,609	48,157
B17	htchbk cpe 2d	3,494	3,687	6,703
C69	S/R sdn 4d	3,406	4,324	3,243
C27	S/R cpe	3,410	4,281	3,880
C17	S/R htchbk cpe 2d	3,430	4,398	1,248
Century (wb 116.0; 2d 112.0)				
D37	Colonnade cpe	3,748	4,070	59,448
E37	Spec Clnnde cpe V-6	3,508	3,935	
D29	Colonnade sdn 4d	3,567	4,105	33,632
H29	Cust Clnnde sdn 4d	3,817	4,424	19,728
H57	Cust Clnnde cpe	3,705	4,346	34,036
K35	Custom wgn, 2S V-8	4,363	4,987	16,625
K45	Cust wgn, 4d 3S V-8	4,413	5,099	
Regal (wb 116.0; 2d 112.0)				
J29	Clnnde sdn 4d V-8	4,104	4,825	17,118
J57	Clnnde cpe V-6	3,866	4,465	124,498
LeSabre (wb 124.0)				
N69	sdn 4d V-6	4,170	4,747	4,315
N39	htp sdn V-6	4,059	4,871	2,312
N57	htp cpe V-6	4,129	4,815	3,861
P69	Custom sdn 4d V-8	4,328	5,046	34,841
P39	Custom htp sdn V-8	4,386	5,166	46,109
P57	Custom htp cpe V-8	4,275	5,144	45,669
Estate wagon (wb 127.0)				
R35	wgn 4d 2S	5,013	5,591	5,990
R45	wgn 4d 3S	5,139	5,731	14,384
Electra 225 (wb 127.0)				
V39	htp sdn	4,641	6,527	26,655
V37	htp cpe	4,502	6,367	18,442
X39	Limited htp sdn	4,709	6,852	51,067
X37	Limited htp cpe	4,521	6,689	28,395
Riviera (wb 122.0)				
Z87	htp cpe	4,531	6,798	20,082

1976 Engines	bore×stroke	bhp	availability
V-6, 231.0	3.80×3.40	110	S-Skh, Skylark, Cnty, Rgl, LeS
V-8, 260.0	3.50×3.39	110	S-Skylark
V-8, 350.0	3.80×3.85	145	S-Rgl, Cnty exc wgn; O-Skl
V-8, 350.0	3.80×3.85	165	S-Cnty wgn, LeS Cus; O-Skl, Cnty, Rgl
V-8, 455.0	4.31×3.90	205	S-EWgn, Elec, Riv; O-LeS Cus

1977

Skyhawk (wb 97.0)		Wght	Price	Prod
S07	htchbk cpe 2d	2,817	4,294	12,345
T07	S htchbk cpe 2d	2,805	3,981	
Skylark (wb 111.0)*				
W27	S cpe	3,286	3,642	49,858
B27	cpe	3,286	3,765	
B69	sdn 4d	3,324	3,825	48,121
B17	htchbk cpe 2d	3,408	3,942	5,316
C69	S/R sdn 4d	3,324	4,587	4,000
C27	S/R cpe	3,330	4,527	5,023
C17	S/R htchbk cpe	3,358	4,695	1,154
Century (wb 116.0; 2d 112.0)*				
D37	cpe	3,582	4,304	52,864
E37	Special cpe	3,590	4,170	
D29	sdn 4d	3,754	4,364	29,065
H29	Custom sdn 4d	3,750	4,688	13,645
H57	Custom htp cpe	3,610	4,628	20,834
K35	Cust wgn 4d 2S V-8	4,260	5,219	19,282
K45	Cust wgn 4d 3S V-8	4,310	5,271	
Regal (wb 116.0; 2d 112.0)*				
J29	sdn 4d V-8	3,928	5,244	17,946
J57	cpe V-6	3,612	4,713	174,560
LeSabre (wb 115.9)*				
N69	sdn 4d	3,560	5,093	19,827
N37	cpe	3,522	5,033	8,455
P69	Custom sdn 4d	3,572	5,382	103,855
P37	Custom cpe	3,530	5,322	58,589
F37	Custom cpe V-8	3,634	5,819	
Estate wagon (115.9)				
R35	wgn 4d 2S	4,015	5,903	25,075
R45	wgn 4d 3S	4,141	6,078	
Electra 225 (wb 119.0)				
V-69	sdn	3,814	6,866	25,633
V37	cpe	3,761	6,673	15,762
X69	Limited sdn	3,839	7,226	82,361
X37	Limited cpe	3,785	7,033	37,871
Riviera (wb 116.0)				
Z37	htp cpe	3,784	7,385	26,138

1977 Engines	bore×stroke	bhp	availability
V-6, 231.0	3.80×3.40	105	S-Skh, Skl, Century, Regal, LeSabre
V-8, 301.0	4.00×3.00	135	S-Skl, LeS
V-8, 305.0	3.74×3.48	145	O-Skl, Cnty wgn
V-8, 350.0	3.80×3.85	140	S-Cnty exc wgn, Rgl; O-Skl
V-8, 350.0	3.80×3.85	155	S-Cnty wgn, Elec, Riv; O-Skylark, Century, Regal
V-8, 350.0	4.06×3.39	170	S-EWgn; O-LeS, Elec, Riv
V-8, 403.0	4.35×3.38	185	O-Cnty, LeS, Elec, Riv

*Six & V-8 weights averaged. Prices for sixes shown; for V-8s add $150

1978

Skyhawk (wb 97.0)		Wght	Price	Prod
S07	htchbk cpe 2d	2,707	4,414	24,589
T07	S htchbk cpe 2d	2,678	4,146	
Skylark (wb 111.0)*				
W27	S cpe	3,285	3,911	42,087
B27	cpe	3,287	4,035	
B69	sdn 4d	3,318	4,120	40,951
B17	htchbk cpe 2d	3,397	4,217	2,642
C69	Custom sdn 4d	3,303	4,367	14,523
C27	Custom cpe	3,270	4,282	12,740
C17	Cust htchbk cpe 2d	3,369	4,464	1,277
Century (wb 108.1)*				
E09	Special sdn 4d	3,087	4,520	12,533
E87	Special sdn 2d	3,096	4,413	10,818
E37	Special wgn 4d 2S	3,231	5,021	9,586
H09	Custom sdn 4d	3,111	4,768	18,361
H87	Custom sdn 2d	3,084	4,658	12,434
H35	Custom wgn 4d 2S	3,265	5,233	24,014
G87	sport coupe sdn 2d	3,124	5,051	—
L09	Limited sdn 4d	3,148	5,127	—
L87	Limited sdn 2d	3,171	4,017	—
Regal (wb 108.1)*				
J47	cpe	3,065	4,885	236,652
M47	Limited cpe	3,114	5,268	—
K47	sport coupe turbo V-6	3,153	5,958	—
LeSabre (wb 115.9)*				
N69	sdn 4d	3,522	5,536	23,354
N37	cpe	3,531	5,451	8,265
P69	Custom sdn 4d	3,534	6,045	86,638
P37	Custom cpe	3,496	5,727	53,675
F37	sport cpe turbo V-6	3,559	6,346	—
Estate wagon (wb 115.9)				
R35	wgn 4d 2S V-8	4,063	6,394	25,964
Electra 225 (wb 119.0)				
V-69	sdn 4d	3,730	7,431	14,590
V37	cpe	3,682	7,252	8,259
X69	Limited sdn 4d	3,757	7,817	65,335
X37	Limited cpe	3,710	7,638	33,365
U69	Park Avenue sdn 4d	3,777	8,208	—
U37	Park Avenue cpe	3,730	7,952	—
Riviera (wb 116.0)				
Z37	cpe	3,701	9,224	20,535

1978 Engines	bore×stroke	bhp	availability
V-6, 196.0	3.50×3.40	90	S-Century exc wgn, Rgl exc S/C
V-6, 231.0	3.80×3.40	105	S-Skh, Skylark, Cnty wgn, LeS; O-Rgl exc S/C, Century
V-6T, 231.0	3.80×3.40	150	S-Rgl & LeS S/Cs; O-Rgl
V-6T, 231.0	3.80×3.40	165	O-Rgl & LeS S/Cs
V-8, 301.0	4.00×3.00	140	S-LeS exc wgn
V-8, 305.0	3.74×3.48	145	S-Skl, Cnty wgn, Rgl exc S/C; O-Cnty
V-8, 305.0	3.74×3.48	160	O-Century, Regal exc S/C
V-8, 350.0	3.80×3.85	155	S-EWgn, Elec, Riv; O-LeS
V-8, 350.0	4.00×3.48	170	O-Skl, Cnty
V-8, 403.0	4.35×3.38	185	O-LeS, Elec, Riv

*Six & V-8 weights averaged. Prices for sixes shown; for V-8s add $175.

1979

Skyhawk (wb 97.0)		Wght	Price	Prod
S07	htchbk cpe 2d	2,740	4,778	23,139
T07	S htchbk cpe 2d	2,724	4,560	
Skylark (wb 111.0)				
W27	S cpe	3,164	4,082	10,201
B27	cpe	3,174	4,208	
B69	sdn 4d	3,218	4,308	10,849
B17	htchbk cpe 2d	3,254	4,357	608
C69	Custom sdn 4d	3,226	4,562	3,822
C27	Custom cpe	3,182	4,462	3,546
Century (wb 108.1)				
E09	Special sdn 4d	3,105	5,021	7,363
E87	Special sdn 2d	3,090	4,921	4,805
E35	Special wgn 4d 2S	3,222	5,492	10,413
H09	Custom sdn 4d	3,123	5,290	9,681
H87	Custom sdn 2d	3,103	5,165	2,474
H37	Custom wgn 4d 2S	3,258	5,806	21,100
G87	sport coupe sdn 2d	3,099	5,473	1,653
L09	Limited sdn 4d	3,156	5,658	2,694
Regal (wb 108.1)				
J47	cpe	3,081	5,407	157,228
M47	Limited cpe	3,123	5,814	94,748
K47	sport cpe turbo V-6	3,190	6,497	21,389
LeSabre (wb 115.9)				
N69	sdn 4d	3,523	6,110	25,431
N37	cpe	3,492	6,010	7,542
P69	Limited sdn 4d	3,567	6,620	75,939
P37	Limited cpe	3,518	6,495	38,290
F37	sport cpe turbo V-6	3,545	6,953	3,582
Estate wagon (wb 115.9)				
R35	wgn 4d 2S V-8	4,021	7,169	21,312
Electra 225 (wb 119.0)				
V-69	sdn 4d	3,831	8,878	11,055
V37	cpe	3,767	8,703	5,358
X69	Limited sdn 4d	3,853	9,278	76,340
X37	Limited cpe	3,789	9,103	28,878
U69	Park Avenue sdn 4d	3,860	9,959	—
U37	Park Avenue cpe	3,794	9,784	—
Riviera (wb 114.0)				
Z57	cpe V-8	3,759	10,684	52,181
Y57	S-Type cpe	3,774	10,960	

1979 Engines	bore×stroke	bhp	availability
V-6, 196.0	3.50×3.40	105	S-Cnty exc wgn, Rgl exc S/C
V-6, 231.0	3.80×3.40	115	S-Skh, Skl, Cnty wgn, LeS; O-Cnty, Rgl
V-6T, 231.0	3.80×3.40	170-185	S-Riviera S; O-Cnty/Rgl/LeS Spt
V-8, 301.0	4.00×3.00	140	S-Cnty, Rgl, LeS
V-8, 301.0	4.00×3.00	150	O-Cnty, Rgl
V-8, 305.0	3.74×3.48	130	S-Skylark

1979 Engines	bore×stroke	bhp	availability
V-8, 305.0	3.74×3.48	155	O-Cnty, Rgl
V-8, 350.0	3.80×3.85	155	S-EWgn, Elec; O-LeS
V-8, 350.0	4.00×3.48	165	O-Sky, Cent wgn
V-8, 350.0	4.06×3.39	170	S-Riv; O-Riv S
V-8, 403.0	4.35×3.38	185	O-EWgn, Elec

1980

Skyhawk (wb 97.0)		Wght	Price	Prod
S07	htchbk cpe 2d	2,754	5,211	8,322
T07	S htchbk cpe 2d	2,754	4,993	

Skylark (wb 104.9)		Wght	Price	Prod
B69	sdn 4d	2,458	5,488	80,940
B37	sdn 2d	2,430	5,342	55,114
C69	Limited sdn 4d	2,498	5,912	86,948
C37	Limited sdn 2d	2,458	5,765	42,652
D69	Sport Sedan 4d	2,490	6,102	—
D37	sport cpe 2d I-4/V-6	2,450	5,955	—

Century (wb 108.1)**		Wght	Price	Prod
H69	sdn 4d	3,158	5,858	129,740
L69	Limited sdn 4d	3,202	6,344	—
H87	sdn 2d	3,138	5,758	1,074
G87	sport coupe sdn 2d	3,202	6,275	—
H35	Estate wgn 4d 2S	3,311	6,432	11,122
E35	wgn 4d 2S	3,300	6,134	6,493

Regal (wb 108.1)**		Wght	Price	Prod
J47	cpe 2d	3,179	6,506	214,735
M47	Limited cpe 2d	3,282	6,925	
K47	sprt cpe turbo V-6 2d	3,194	7,203	

LeSabre (wb 115.9)**		Wght	Price	Prod
N69	sdn 4d	3,433	6,940	23,873
N37	cpe 2d	3,380	6,845	8,342
P69	Limited sdn 4d	3,439	7,242	37,676
P37	Limited cpe 2d	3,391	7,100	20,561
F37	sport cpe turbo V-6	3,430	8,003	—
R35	wgn 4d 2S V-8	3,898	7,844	9,318
R35	wgn 4d 3S V-8	3,982	8,037	

Electra 225 (wb 119.0; wgns 115.9)**		Wght	Price	Prod
X69	Limited sdn 4d	3,670	9,580	54,422
W69	Park Ave sdn 4d	3,670	10,676	—
X37	Limited cpe 2d	3,664	9,425	14,058
W37	Park Ave cpe 2d	3,692	10,537	—
V35	Est wgn 4d 2S V-8	4,105	10,806	—
V35	Est wgn 4d 3S V-8	4,135	10,999	—

Riviera (wb 114.0)		Wght	Price	Prod
Z57	cpe V-8	3,633	11,640	48,621
Y57	S-Type cpe	3,734	12,151	

1980 Engines	bore×stroke	bhp	availability
I-4, 151.0	4.00×3.00	90	S-Skylark
V-6, 173.0	3.50×3.00	115	O-Skylark
V-6, 231.0	3.80×3.40	110	S-Skyh, Cnty, Rgl, LeS
V-6T, 231.0	3.80×3.40	170	S-Rgl S/C, LeS S/C; O-Cnty
V-6T, 231.0	3.80×3.40	175	S-Cnty S/C
V-6T, 231.0	3.80×3.40	185	S-Riv "S"; O-Riv
V-6, 252.0	3.97×3.40	125	S-Elec; O-LeS
V-8, 265.0	3.75×3.00	120	S-Cnty, Rgl
V-8, 301.0	4.00×3.00	140	S-LeS, Elec, EWgn, O-Cnty, Rgl
V-8, 305.0	3.74×3.48	155	O-Cnty, Rgl
V-8, 350.0	3.80×3.85	155	O-LeS, Elec, EWgn
V-8, 350.0	4.06×3.39	160	S-Elec, Riv; O-LeS, Riv S, EWgn
V-8D, 350.0	3.88×3.53	105	O-EWgn, Elec

* I-4, V-6 wghts avrgd. Prices for L4s; V-6s add $225 ** V-6 & V-8 wghts avrgd. Prices for V-6s; V-8s add $105

1981

Skylark (wb 104.9)		Wght	Price	Prod
B69	sdn 4d	2,479	6,551	104,091
B37	sdn 2d	2,453	6,405	46,515
C69	Limited sdn 4d	2,513	7,007	81,642
C37	Limited sdn 2d	2,482	6,860	30,080
D69	Sport Sedan 4d	2,512	7,186	—
D37	sport coupe 2d	2,486	7,040	—

Century (wb 108.1)		Wght	Price	Prod
H69	sdn 4d	3,224	7,094	127,119
L69	Limited sdn 4d	3,249	7,999	
H35	Estate wgn 4d 2S	3,368	7,735	11,659
E35	wgn 4d 2S	3,321	7,391	5,489

Regal (wb 108.1)		Wght	Price	Prod
J47	cpe 2d	3,245	7,555	123,848
K47	sprt cpe turbo V-6 2d	3,261	8,528	
M47	Limited cpe 2d	3,382	8,024	116,352

LeSabre (wb 115.9)		Wght	Price	Prod
N69	sdn 4d	3,573	7,805	19,166
N37	cpe 2d	3,544	7,715	4,909
P69	Limited sdn 4d	3,595	8,101	39,006
P37	Limited cpe 2d	3,562	7,966	14,862
R35	Est wgn 4d 2S V-8	4,118	8,722	4,934

Electra (wb 118.9; wgn 115.9)		Wght	Price	Prod
X69	Limited sdn 4d	3,802	10,368	58,832
W69	Park Avenue sdn 4d	3,818	11,396	
X37	Limited cpe 2d	3,686	10,237	10,151
W37	Park Avenue cpe 2d	3,808	11,267	
V35	Est wgn 4d 2S V-8	4,290	11,291	6,334

Riviera (wb 114.0)		Wght	Price	Prod
Z57	cpe 2d	3,643	12,147	52,007
Y57	T Type cpe turbo V-6	3,651	13,091	

1981 Engines	bore×stroke	bhp	availability
I-4, 151.0	4.00×3.00	90	S-Skylark
V-6, 173.0	3.50×3.00	115	O-Skylark
V-6, 231.0	3.80×3.40	110	S-Cnty, Rgl, LeS
V-6T, 231.0	3.80×3.40	170	S-Rgl S/C
V-6T, 231.0	3.80×3.40	180	S-Riviera T; O-Riviera
V-6, 252.0	3.97×3.40	125	S-Elec, Riv; O-LeS, Riv T
V-8, 265.0	3.75×3.00	119	O-Cnty, Rgl
V-8, 307.0	3.80×3.39	140	S-EWgn; O-LeSabre, Electra, Riviera
V-8D, 350.0	4.06×3.39	105	O-LeS, Elec, EWgn, Riv

1982

Skyhawk (wb 101.2)		Wght	Price	Prod
S69	Custom sdn 4d	2,385	7,489	22,540
T69	Limited sdn 4d	2,411	7,931	
S27	Custom cpe 2d	2,327	7,297	25,378
T27	Limited cpe 2d	2,349	7,739	

Skylark (wb 104.9)		Wght	Price	Prod
B69	sdn 4d	2,521	7,647	65,541
B37	cpe 2d	2,490	7,477	21,017
C69	Limited sdn 4d	2,547	8,079	44,290
C37	Limited cpe 2d	2,517	7,917	13,712
D69	Sport Sedan 4d	2,552	8,219	1,295*
D37	sport coupe 2d	2,522	8,048	

Century (wb 104.9)		Wght	Price	Prod
H19	Custom sdn 4d	2,671	9,141	83,250
L19	Limited sdn 4d	2,683	9,581	
H27	Custom cpe 2d	2,643	8,980	19,715
L27	Limited cpe 2d	2,654	9,417	

Regal (wb 108.1)		Wght	Price	Prod
J47	cpe 2d	3,152	8,712	134,237
M47	Limited cpe 2d	3,192	9,266	
K47	sprt cpe turbo V-6 2d	3,265	9,738	2,022
J69	sdn 4d	3,167	8,862	74,428
M69	Limited sdn 4d	3,205	9,364	
J35	wgn 4d	3,410	9,058	14,732

LeSabre (wb 115.9)		Wght	Price	Prod
N69	Custom sdn 4d	3,594	8,876	23,220
N37	Custom cpe 2d	3,565	8,774	5,165
P69	Limited sdn 4d	3,666	9,331	47,224
P37	Limited cpe 2d	3,583	9,177	16,062
R35	Est wgn 4d 2s V-8	4,228	10,668	7,149

Electra (wb 118.9; wgn 115.9)		Wght	Price	Prod
X69	Limited sdn 4d	3,807	11,884	59,601
W69	Park Avenue sdn 4d	3,888	13,559	
X37	Limited cpe 2d	3,747	11,713	8,449
W37	Park Avenue cpe 2d	3,824	13,408	
V35	Est wgn 4d 2s V-8	4,229	12,911	8,182

Riviera (wb 114.0)		Wght	Price	Prod
Z57	cpe 2d	3,680	14,272	42,823
Y57	T Type cpe turbo V-6	—	14,940	
Z67	conv cpe	—	23,994	1,248

1982 Engines	bore×stroke	bhp	availability
I-4, 112.0	3.50×2.91	88	S-Skyhawk
I-4, 112.0	3.33×3.12	80	O-Skyhawk
I-4, 121.0	3.50×3.15	90	O-Skyhawk
I-4, 151.0	4.00×3.00	90	O-Skyl, Century
V-6, 173.0	3.50×3.00	112	O-Skylark
V-6, 173.0	3.50×3.00	135	O-Skylark
V-6, 181.0	3.80×2.66	110	O-Century
V-6, 231.0	3.80×3.40	110	S-Rgl, LeS
V-6T, 231.0	3.80×3.40	175/180	S-Rgl S/C, Riv T
V-6, 252.0	3.96×3.40	125	S-Elec, Riv; O-Rgl, LeS
V-6D, 262.5	4.06×3.39	85	O-Cnty, Rgl
V-8, 307.0	3.80×3.38	140	S-EWgn; O-LeS, Elec, Riv
V-8D, 350.0	4.06×3.39	105	O-Rgl, LeS, Elec, EWgn, Riv

* Sport model prod. included in basic Skylark totals.

1983

Skyhawk (wb 101.2)		Wght	Price	Prod
S69	Custom sdn 4d	2,369	7,166	19,847
T69	Limited sdn 4d	2,411	7,649	
S27	Custom cpe 2d	2,316	6,958	27,557
T27	Limited cpe 2d	2,333	7,457	
S35	Custom wgn 4d	2,439	7,492	10,653
T35	Limited wgn 4d	2,462	7,934	
E27	T Type cpe 2d	2,336	7,961	5,095

Skylark (wb 104.9)		Wght	Price	Prod
B69	Custom sdn 4d	2,521	7,718	51,950
B37	Custom cpe 2d	2,492	7,548	11,671
C69	Limited sdn 4d	2,549	8,150	30,674
C37	Limited cpe 2d	2,519	7,988	7,863
D37	T Type cpe 2d V-6	2,608	9,337	2,489

Century (wb 104.9)		Wght	Price	Prod
H19	Custom sdn 4d	2,692	9,002	50,296
H27	Custom cpe 2d	2,644	8,841	
L19	Limited sdn 4d	2,705	9,425	73,030
L27	Limited cpe 2d	2,662	9,261	
G27	T Type cpe 2d V-6	2,749	10,017	4,600*
G19	T Type sdn 4d V-6	2,801	10,178	

Regal (wb 108.1)		Wght	Price	Prod
J47	cpe 2d	3,123	9,100	147,935
M47	Limited cpe 2d	3,164	9,722	
K47	T Typ trb V-6 cpe 2d	3,194	10,366	3,732
J69	sdn 4d	3,139	9,279	61,285
M69	Limited sdn 4d	3,177	9,856	
J35	wgn 4d	3,289	9,550	15,287

LeSabre (wb 115.9)		Wght	Price	Prod
N69	Custom sdn 4d	3,574	9,394	31,196
N37	Custom cpe 2d	3,545	9,292	6,974
P69	Limited sdn 4d	3,613	9,990	66,547
P37	Limited cpe 2d	3,579	9,836	22,029
R35	Est wgn 4d 2S V-8	4,105	11,187	9,306

Electra (wb 118.9; wgn 115.9)		Wght	Price	Prod
X69	Limited sdn 4d	3,794	12,586	79,700
W69	Park Avenue sdn 4d	3,871	14,245	
X37	Limited cpe 2d	3,734	12,415	8,885
W37	Park Avenue cpe 2d	3,806	14,094	
V35	Est wgn 4d 2S V-8	4,175	13,638	9,581

Riviera (wb 114.0)		Wght	Price	Prod
Z57	cpe 2d	3,689	15,238	47,153
Y57	T Type cpe turbo V-6	3,593	15,906	1,331
Z67	conv cpe	3,875	24,960	1,750

1983 Engines	bore×stroke	bhp	availability
I-4, 112.0	3.34×3.13	84	O-Skyhawk
I-4, 121.0	3.50×3.15	86	S-Skyhawk
I-4, 151.0	4.00×3.00	90	S-Skylark, Century
V-6, 173.0	3.50×2.99	112	O-Skylark
V-6, 173.0	3.50×2.99	135	S-Skylark T; O-Skylark
V-6, 181.0	3.80×2.66	110	O-Century
V-6, 231.0	3.80×3.40	110	S-Rgl, LeS

1983 Engines	bore×stroke	bhp	availability
V-6T, 231.0	3.80×3.40	180	S-Regal T, Riviera T
V-6, 252.0	3.97×3.40	125	S-Elec, Riv; O-Rgl, LeS
V-6D, 262.5	4.06×3.39	85	O-Cnty, Rgl
V-8, 307.0	3.80×3.39	140	S-EWgn; O-LeS, Elec, Riv
V-8D, 350.0	4.06×3.39	105	O-Rgl, LeS, Electra, EWgn, Riviera

* T Type production included in basic totals.

1984

Skyhawk (wb 101.2)		Wght	Price	Prod
S69	Custom sdn 4d	2,436	7,345	45,648
T69	Limited sdn 4d	2,471	7,837	
S27	Custom cpe 2d	2,383	7,133	74,760
T27	Limited cpe 2d	2,424	7,641	
S35	Custom wgn 4d	2,507	7,677	13,668
T35	Limited wgn 4d	2,536	8,127	
E27	T Type cpe 2d	2,399	8,152	11,317
Skylark (wb 104.9)				
B69	Custom sdn 4d	2,593	7,707	56,495
B37	Custom cpe 2d	2,561	7,545	12,377
C69	Limited sdn 4d	2,618	8,283	33,795
C37	Limited cpe 2d	2,587	8,119	7,621
D37	T Type cpe 2d V-6	2,676	9,557	923
Century (wb 104.9)				
H19	Custom sdn 4d	2,790	9,274	178,454
L19	Limited sdn 4d	2,811	9,729	
H27	Custom cpe 2d	2,742	9,110	15,429
L27	Limited cpe 2d	2,763	9,562	
H35	Custom wgn 4d	2,958	9,660	25,975
L35	Limited wgn 4d	2,976	10,087	
G27	T Type cpe 2d V-6	2,855	10,510	3,477*
G19	T Type sdn 4d V-6	2,903	10,674	
Regal (wb 108.1)				
J47	cpe 2d	3,172	9,487	160,638
M47	Limited cpe 2d	3,210	10,125	
K47	T Typ trb V-6 cpe 2d	3,254	12,118	5,401
J69	sdn 4d	3,219	9,671	58,715
M69	Limited sdn 4d	3,254	10,263	
LeSabre (wb 115.9)				
N69	Custom sdn 4d	3,717	10,129	36,072
N37	Custom cpe 2d	3,684	9,984	3,890
P69	Limited sdn 4d	3,763	10,940	86,418
P37	Limited cpe 2d	3,730	10,780	28,332
Electra (wb 118.9; wgn 115.9)				
R69	Limited sdn 4d	3,944	13,332	52,551
U69	Park Avenue sdn 4d	3,994	15,044	
R37	Limited cpe 2d	3,884	13,155	4,075
U37	Park Avenue cpe 2d	3,928	14,888	
V35	Estate wgn 4d 2s V-8	4,295	14,483	17,563
Riviera (wb 114.0)				
Z57	cpe 2d	3,766	15,967	56,210
Y57	T Type cpe turbo V-6	3,666	17,050	1,153
Z67	conv cpe	3,873	25,832	500

1984 Engines	bore×stroke	bhp	availability
I-4, 112.0	3.34×3.13	84	O-Skyhawk
I-4T, 112.0	3.34×3.13	150	S-Skyhawk T; O-Skyhawk
I-4, 121.0	3.50×3.15	86	S-Skyhawk
I-4, 151.0	4.00×3.00	92	S-Skyl, Century
V-6, 173.0	3.50×2.99	112	O-Skylark
V-6, 173.0	3.50×2.99	135	S-Skyl T; O-Skyl
V-6, 181.0	3.80×2.66	110	O-Century
V-6, 231.0	3.80×3.40	110	S-Rgl, LeS
V-6, 231.0	3.80×3.40	125	S-Cent T; O-Cent
V-6T, 231.0	3.80×3.40	200	S-Rgl T
V-6T, 231.0	3.80×3.40	190	S-Riv T
V-6, 252.0	3.97×3.40	125	S-Elec, Riv; O-Rgl, LeS
V-6D, 262.5	4.06×3.39	85	O-Cnty, Rgl
V-8, 307.0	3.80×3.39	140	S-EWgn; O-LeS, Elec, Riv
V-8D, 350.0	4.06×3.39	105	O-LeS, EWgn, Riv

* T Type production included in basic totals.

1985

Skyhawk (wb 101.2)		Wght	Price	Prod
S69	Custom sdn 4d	2,392	7,581	27,906
T69	Limited sdn 4d	2,424	8,083	
S27	Custom cpe 2d	2,347	7,365	44,804
T27	Limited cpe 2d	2,380	7,883	
S35	Custom wgn 4d	2,469	7,919	5,285
T35	Limited wgn 4d	2,496	8,379	
E27	T Type cpe 2d	2,362	8,437	4,521
Skylark (wb 104.9)				
B69	Custom sdn 4d	2,618	7,707	65,667
C69	Limited sdn 4d	2,655	8,283	27,490
Somerset Regal (wb 103.4)				
J27	Custom cpe 2d	2,567	8,857	48,470
M27	Limited cpe 2d	2,571	9,466	37,601
Century (wb 104.9)				
H19	Custom sdn 4d	2,790	9,545	215,928
L19	Limited sdn 4d	2,812	10,012	
H27	Custom cpe 2d	2,742	9,377	13,043
L27	Limited cpe 2d	2,764	9,841	
H35	Custom wgn 4d	2,958	9,941	28,221
L35	Limited wgn 4d	2,975	10,379	
G27	T Type cpe 2d V-6	2,881	11,249	4,043*
G19	T Type sdn 4d V-6	2,930	11,418	
Regal (wb 108.1)				
J47	cpe 2d	3,172	9,928	60,597
M47	Limited cpe 2d	3,199	10,585	59,780
K47	T Typ trb V-6 cpe 2d	3,349	12,640	2,067
K47	Grnd Nat V-6 cpe 2d	—	13,315	2,102
LeSabre (wb 115.9)				
N69	Custom sdn 4d	3,683	10,603	32,091
N37	Custom cpe 2d	3,672	10,455	5,156
P69	Limited sdn 4d	3,729	11,916	84,432
P37	Limited cpe 2d	3,696	11,751	22,211
R35	Estate wgn 4d	4,153	12,704	5,597
Electra (wb 110.8; wgn 115.9)				
X69	sdn 4d	3,250	14,331	131,011
W69	Park Avenue sdn 4d	3,269	16,240	
X11	cpe 2d	3,205	14,149	5,852
W11	Park Avenue cpe 2d	3,223	16,080	
F69	T Type sdn 4d V-6	3,261	15,568	4,644*
F11	T Type cpe 2d V-6	3,216	15,386	
V35	Est wgn 4d 2s V-8	4,231	15,323	7,769
Riviera (wb 114.0)				
Z57	cpe 2d	3,857	16,710	63,836
Y57	T Type cpe turbo V-6	3,668	17,654	1,069
Z67	conv cpe	3,977	26,797	400

1985 Engines	bore×stroke	bhp	availability
I-4, 112.0	3.43×3.13	84	S-Skyh T; O-Skyh
I-4T, 112.0	3.34×3.13	150	O-Skyhawk T
I-4, 121.0	3.50×3.15	86	S-Skyhawk
I-4, 151.0	4.00×3.00	92	S-Skylark, Cnty, Somerset
V-6, 173.0	3.50×2.99	112	O-Skyl, Century
V-6, 173.0	3.50×2.99	125	O-Skylark
V-6, 181.0	3.80×2.66	110	S-Elect; O-Cnty
V-6, 181.0	3.80×2.66	125	O-Somerset
V-6, 231.0	3.80×3.40	110	S-Rgl, LeS
V-6, 231.0	3.80×3.40	125	S-Cnty T, Electra T/Park; O-Cnty, Electra
V-6T, 231.0	3.80×3.40	200	S-Rgl T
V-6T, 231.0	3.80×3.40	190	S-Riv T
V-6D, 262.5	4.06×3.39	85	O-Century, Regal, Electra
V-8, 307.0	3.80×3.39	140	S-EWgn, Riv; O-LeSabre
V-8D, 350.0	4.06×3.39	105	O-LeS, EWgn, Riv

*T Type production included in basic totals.

1986

Skyhawk (wb 101.2)		Wght	Price	Prod
S69	Custom sdn 4d	2,392	8,073	29,959
T69	Limited sdn 4d	2,425	8,598	
S27	Custom cpe 2d	2,343	7,844	45,884
T27	Limited cpe 2d	2,381	8,388	
S35	Custom wgn 4d	2,469	8,426	6,079
T35	Limited wgn 4d	2,498	8,910	
E27	T Type cpe 2d	2,440	8,971	6,071
E77	T Type htchbk 2d	2,526	9,414	
S77	Sport htchbk 2d	2,433	8,184	—
Skylark (wb 103.4)				
J69	Custom sdn	2,601	9,620	62,235
M69	Limited sdn 4d	2,608	10,290	
Somerset (wb 103.4)				
J27	Custom cpe 2d	2,557	9,425	72,062
M27	Limited cpe 2d	2,577	10,095	
K27	T Type cpe 2d	2,562	11,390	3,558
Century (wb 104.9)				
H19	Custom sdn 4d	2,773	10,228	229,066
L19	Limited sdn 4d	2,795	10,729	
H27	Custom cpe 2d	2,726	10,052	13,752
L27	Limited cpe 2d	2,748	10,544	
—	Gran Sport cpe 2d	—	—	1,029
H35	Custom wgn 4d	2,938	10,648	25,374
L35	Limited wgn 4d	2,955	11,109	
G19	T Type sdn 4d V-6	2,941	12,223	5,286
Regal (wb 108.1)				
J47	cpe 2d	3,289	10,654	39,734
M47	Limited cpe 2d	3,315	11,347	43,599
K47	T Typ trb V-6 cpe 2d	3,380	13,714	7,896
K47	Grnd Nat V-6 cpe 2d	—	14,349	5,512*
LeSabre (wb 110.8; wgn 115.9)				
P69	Custom sdn 4d	3,150	12,511	30,235
P37	Custom cpe 2d	3,108	12,511	7,191
R69	Limited sdn 4d	3,161	13,633	43,215
R37	Limited cpe 2d	3,119	13,633	14,331
R35	Estate wgn 4d	4,206	13,597	7,755
Electra (wb 110.8; wgn 115.9)				
X69	sdn 4d	3,256	15,588	109,042
W69	Park Avenue sdn 4d	3,305	17,338	
X11	cpe 2d	3,205	15,396	4,996
W11	Park Avenue cpe 2d	3,250	17,158	
F69	T Type sdn 4d V-6	3,278	16,826	5,816
V35	Est wgn 4d 2s V-8	4,242	16,402	10,371
Riviera (wb 108.0)				
Z57	cpe 2d	3,298	19,831	20,096
Y57	T Type cpe	3,329	21,577	2,042

1986 Engines	bore×stroke	bhp	availability
I-4, 112.0	3.34×3.13	88	S-Skyhawk T; O-Skyhawk
I-4T, 112.0	3.34×3.13	150	O-Skyhawk T
I-4, 121.0	3.50×3.15	88	S-Skyhawk
I-4, 151.0	4.00×3.00	92	S-Skylark, Cnty, Somerset
V-6, 173.0	3.50×2.99	112	O-Century
V-6, 181.0	3.80×2.66	125	S-Smrst T, LeS; O-Smrset, Sky
V-6, 231.0	3.80×3.40	110	S-Regal
V-6, 231.0	3.80×3.40	140	S-Elec, Riv
V-6, 231.0	3.80×3.40	150	S-Century T; O-Century, LeS
V-6T 231.0	3.80×3.40	235	S-Regal T
V-8, 307.0	3.80×3.39	140	S-EWgn; O-Regal

*Production included in basic Regal total.

1987

Skyhawk (wb 101.2)		Wght	Price	Prod
S69	Custom sdn 4d	2,385	8,559	15,778
T69	Limited sdn 4d	2,423	9,503	2,200
S27	Custom cpe 2d	2,336	8,522	19,814
T27	Limited cpe 2d	2,345	9,445	1,556
S35	Custom wgn 4d	2,463	9,249	3,061
T35	Limited wgn 4d	2,498	9,841	498
S77	Sport htchbk 2d	2,396	8,965	3,757
Skylark (wb 103.4)				
J69	Custom sdn 4d	2,535	9,915	26,173
M69	Limited sdn 4d	2,609	11,003	7,532
Somerset (wb 103.4)				
J27	Custom cpe 2d	2,489	9,957	34,916
M27	Limited cpe 2d	2,574	11,003	11,585
Century (wb 104.9)				
H19	Custom sdn 4d	2,783	10,989	88,445

Century (wb 104.9)		Wght	Price	Prod
L19	Limited sdn 4d	2,811	11,593	71,340
H27	Custom cpe 2d	2,736	10,844	2,878
L27	Limited cpe 2d	2,765	11,397	4,384
H35	Custom wgn 4d	2,866	11,478	10,141
L35	Limited Est wgn 4d	2,866	11,998	6,990
Regal (wb 108.1)				
J47	cpe 2d	3,286	11,562	44,844
M47	Limited cpe 2d	3,315	12,303	20,441
J47/Y56	T Type V-6 cpe 2d	—	14,857	8,541*
J47/WE2	Grnd Nat V-6 cpe 2d	—	15,136	20,193*
J47/T26	GNX cpe	—	—	547*
LeSabre (wb 110.8)				
H69	sdn 4d	3,141	13,438	6,243
P69	Custom sdn 4d	3,140	13,616	60,392
R69	Limited sdn 4d	3,171	14,918	70,797
P37	Custom cpe 2d	3,104	13,616	5,035
R37	Limited cpe 2d	3,137	14,918	7,741
L37	T Type cpe 2d	—	15,521	4,123
Electra (wb 110.8)				
X69	sdn 4d	3,269	16,902	7,787
W69	Park Avenue sdn 4d	3,338	18,769	75,600
W11	Park Avenue cpe 2d	3,236	18,577	4,084
F69	T Type sdn 4d	3,278	18,224	2,570
Estate wagons (wb 115.9)				
R35	LeSabre wgn 4d	4,160	14,724	5,251
V35	Electra wgn 4d	4,239	17,697	7,508
Riviera (wb 108.0)				
Z57	cpe 2d	3,320	20,337	12,636
Z57/Y50	T Type cpe	3,360	22,181	2,587

1987 Engines	bore×stroke	bhp	availability
I-4, 121.0	3.50×3.15	90	S-Skyhawk
I-4, 121.0	3.39×3.39	96	O-Skyhawk
I-4T, 121.0	3.39×3.39	165	O-Skyhawk
I-4, 151.0	4.00×3.00	98	S-Skylark, Cnty, Somerset
V-6, 173.0	3.50×2.99	125	O-Century
V-6, 181.0	3.80×2.66	125	O-Somerset, Skylark
V-6, 231.0	3.80×3.40	110	S-Regal
V-6, 231.0	3.80×3.40	150	S-LeS, Elec, Riv; O-Cnty
V-6T, 231.0	3.80×3.40	245	S-Rgl Grnd Nat; O-Regal
V-6T, 231.0	3.80×3.40	276	S-GNX
V-8, 307.0	3.80×3.39	140	S-EWgn; O-Rgl

*Production included in basic Regal total.

1988

Skyhawk (wb 101.2)		Wght	Price	Prod
S69	sdn 4d	2,396	8,884	14,271
S27	cpe 2d	2,336	8,884	9,857
S35	wgn 4d	2,474	9,797	1,707
S27/WN2	S/E cpe 2d	—	9,979	3,299
Skylark (wb 103.4)				
C69	Custom sdn 4d	2,601	10,399	24,940
D69	Limited sdn 4d	2,622	11,721	5,316
J27	Custom cpe 2d	2,555	10,684	19,590
M27	Limited cpe 2d	2,576	11,791	4,946
Century (wb 104.9)				
H19	Custom sdn 4d	2,796	11,793	62,214
L19	Limited sdn 4d	2,803	12,613	39,137
H27	Custom cpe 2d	2,725	11,643	1,322
L27	Limited cpe 2d	2,732	12,410	1,127
H35	Custom wgn 4d	2,945	12,345	5,312
L35	Limited Est wgn 4d	2,949	13,077	4,146
Reatta (wb 98.5)				
C97	cpe 2d	3,350	25,000	4,708
Regal (wb 107.5)				
B57	Custom cpe 2d	2,953	12,449	64,773
D57	Limited cpe 2d	2,972	12,782	65,224
LeSabre (wb 110.8)				
P37	cpe 2d	3,192	14,560	2,403
P69	Custom sdn 4d	3,239	14,405	67,213
R69	Limited sdn 4d	3,291	15,745	57,524
R37	Limited cpe 2d	3,242	16,350	2,474
P37/WE2	T Type cpe 2d	—	16,518	6,426
Electra (wb 110.8)				
X69	Limited sdn 4d	3,288	17,479	5,791
W69	Park Avenue sdn 4d	3,326	19,464	84,853
F69	T Type sdn 4d	3,333	20,229	1,869
Estate wagons (wb 115.9)				
R35	LeSabre wgn 3S 4d	4,156	16,040	3,723
V35	Electra wgn 3S 4d	4,217	18,954	5,901
Riviera (wb 108.0)				
Z57	cpe 2d	3,364	21,615	6,560
Z57/Y50	T Type cpe	—	23,380	2,065

1988 Engines	bore×stroke	bhp	availability
I-4, 121.0	3.39×3.39	96	S-Skyhawk
I-4, 138.0	3.62×3.35	150	O-Skylark (dohc)
I-4, 151.0	4.00×3.00	98	S-Skyl, Century
V-6, 173.0	3.50×2.99	125	O-Cnty, Regal
V-6, 181.0	3.80×2.66	125	O-Skylark
V-6, 231.0	3.80×3.40	150	S-LeS; O-Cnty
V-6, 231.0	3.80×3.40	165	S-LeS T, Elec, Riviera; O-LeS
V-6T, 231.0	3.80×3.40	245	S-Rgl Grnd Nat
V-8, 307.0	3.80×3.39	140	S-Estate Wgn

1989

Skyhawk (wb 101.2)		Wght	Price	Prod
S69	sdn 4d	2,469	9,285	13,841
S27	cpe 2d	2,420	9,285	7,837
S35	wgn 4d	2,551	10,230	1,688
Skylark (wb 103.4)				
C69	Custom sdn 4d	2,640	11,115	42,636
D69	Limited sdn 4d	—	12,345	4,774
J27	Custom cpe 2d	2,583	11,115	12,714
M27	Limited cpe 2d	—	12,345	1,416
Century (wb 104.9)				
H69	Custom sdn 4d	2,769	12,429	89,281
L69	Limited sdn 4d	—	13,356	49,839
H37	Custom cpe 2d	2,725	12,199	6,953
H35	Custom wgn 4d	2,905	13,156	5,479
L35	Limited Est wgn 4d	—	13,956	3,980
Reatta (wb 98.5)				
C97	cpe 2d	3,394	26,700	7,009
Regal (wb 107.5)				
B57	Custom cpe 2d	3,144	14,214	56,057
D57	Limited cpe 2d	—	14,739	32,700
LeSabre (wb 110.8)				
P37	cpe 2d	3,227	15,425	7,219
P69	Custom sdn 4d	3,267	15,330	78,738
R69	Limited sdn 4d	—	16,730	61,328
R37	Limited cpe 2d	—	16,630	2,287
Electra (wb 110.8)				
X69	Limited sdn 4d	3,289	18,525	5,814
W69	Park Avenue sdn 4d	—	20,460	71,786
U69	Pk Ave Ultra sdn 4d	—	—	4,815
F69	T Type sdn 4d	—	21,325	1,151
Estate wagons (wb 115.9)				
R35	LeSabre wgn 3S 4d	4,209	16,770	2,971
V35	Electra wgn 3S 4d	4,273	19,860	4,560
Riviera (wb 108.0)				
Z57	cpe 2d	3,436	22,540	21,189

1989 Engines	bore×stroke	bhp	availability
I-4, 121.0	3.50×3.15	90	S-Skyhawk
I-4, 138.0	3.62×3.35	150	O-Skylark (dohc)
I-4, 151.0	4.00×3.00	98	S-Century
I-4, 151.0	4.00×3.00	110	S-Skylark
V-6, 173.0	3.50×2.99	130	S-Regal
V-6, 191.0	3.50×3.31	140	S-late Regal
V-6, 204.0	3.70×3.16	160	O-Skyl, Century
V-6, 231.0	3.80×3.40	165	S-LeSabre, Elect, Reat, Riv
V-8, 307.0	3.80×3.39	140	S-Estate Wgn

1990

Skylark (wb 103.4)		Wght	Price	Prod
V-69	sdn 4d	2,636	10,465	46,705
C69	Custom sdn 4d	—	11,460	24,469
D69	Lxry Edition sdn 4d	—	13,145	3,019
V27	cpe 2d	2,636	10,565	4,248
J27	Custom cpe 2d	2,583	11,115	5,490
M27	Gran Sport cpe 2d	—	12,935	1,637
Century (wb 104.9)				
H69	Custom sdn 4d	2,776	13,150	88,309
L69	Limited sdn 4d	—	14,075	35,248
H37	Custom cpe 2d	2,754	13,250	1,944
H35	Custom wgn 4d	2,924	14,570	4,383
L35	Limited Est wgn 4d	—	15,455	2,837
Reatta (wb 98.5)				
C97	cpe 2d	3,379	28,335	6,383
C67	conv cpe 2d	3,562	34,995	2,132
Regal (wb 107.5)				
B57	Custom cpe 2d	3,108	15,200	39,036
D57	Limited cpe 2d	—	15,860	15,787
LeSabre (wb 110.8)				
P37	cpe 2d	3,242	16,145	2,406
P69	Custom sdn 4d	3,269	16,050	96,616
R69	Limited sdn 4d	—	17,400	62,504
R37	Limited cpe 2d	—	16,300	1,855
Electra (wb 110.8)				
X69	Limited sdn 4d	3,288	20,225	2,621
W69	Park Avenue sdn 4d	—	21,750	44,072
U69	Pk Ave Ultra sdn 4d	—	27,825	1,967
F69	T Type sdn 4d	—	23,025	478
Estate wagon (wb 115.9)				
R35	wgn 3S 4d	4,281	17,940	7,838
Riviera (wb 108.0)				
Z57	cpe 2d	3,464	23,040	22,526

1990 Engines	bore×stroke	bhp	availability
I-4, 138.0	3.62×3.35	160	O-Skylark (dohc)
I-4, 151.0	4.00×3.00	110	S-Century, Skylark
V-6, 191.0	3.50×3.31	135	S-Regal
V-6, 204.0	3.70×3.16	160	O-Skyl, Cnty
V-6, 231.0	3.80×3.40	165	S-LeS, Elec, Reatta, Riviera
V-6, 231.0	3.80×3.40	170	O-Regal
V-8, 307.0	3.80×3.39	140	S-Estate Wgn

1991

Skylark (wb 103.3)		Wght	Price	Prod
V-69	sdn 4d	2,654	10,725	57,323
C69	Custom sdn 4d	2,692	12,020	11,582
D69	Luxury Ed sdn 4d	2,716	13,865	928
V27	cpe 2d	2,593	10,825	5,108
J27	Custom cpe 2d	2,628	12,020	1,706
M27	Gran Sport cpe 2d	2,659	13,665	693
Century (wb 104.9)				
G69	Special sdn 4d	2,869	13,240	13,045
H69	Custom sdn 4d	2,869	13,685	81,424
L69	Limited sdn 4d	2,870	14,795	15,273
H37	Custom cpe 2d	2,832	13,785	1,951
H35	Custom wgn 4d	3,071	15,310	3,102
L35	Limited wgn 4d	3,072	16,230	1,729
Reatta (wb 98.5)				
C97	cpe 2d	3,392	29,300	1,214
C67	conv cpe 2d	3,593	35,965	305
Regal (wb 107.5)				
B19	Custom sdn 4d	3,321	15,910	56,315*
D19	Limited sdn 4d	3,324	16,735	48,081
B57	Custom cpe 2d	3,247	15,960	16,333*
D57	Limited cpe 2d	3,251	16,455	5,903

* Includes Gran Sport.

LeSabre (wb 110.8)		Wght	Price	Prod
P69	Custom sdn 4d	3,269	17,080	56,231
R69	Limited sdn 4d	3,301	18,430	33,344
P37	cpe 2d	3,231	17,180	695
R37	Limited cpe 2d	3,264	18,330	486
Park Avenue (wb 110.8)				
W69	sdn 4d	3,580	24,385	87,461
U69	Ultra sdn 4d	3,662	27,420	22,030
Roadmaster (wb 115.9)				
R35	Estate wgn 4d	4,415	21,445	7,291
Riviera (wb 108.0)				
Z57	cpe 2d	3,496	24,560	13,166

1991 Engines	bore×stroke	bhp	availability
I-4, 138.0	3.62×3.92	160	O-Skylark (dohc)
I-4, 151.0	4.10×3.10	110	S-Skylark, Century
V-6, 191.0	4.00×3.00	140	S-Regal
V-6, 204.0	3.70×3.16	160	O-Skylark, Century
V-6, 231.0	3.80×3.40	165	S-LeSabre
V-6, 231.0	3.80×3.40	170	S-Riv, Reatta, Park Ave, O-Regal
V-8, 305.0	3.74×3.48	170	S-Roadmaster

1992

Skylark (wb 103.4)		Wght	Price	Prod
J69	sdn 4d	2,846	13,560	43,630
M69	Gran Sport sdn 4d	2,965	15,555	4,480
J37	cpe 2d	2,782	13,560	7,788
M37	Gran Sport cpe 2d	2,901	15,555	4,748
Century (wb 104.9)				
G69	Special sdn 4d	2,914	13,795	68,361
H69	Custom sdn 4d	2,914	14,755	42,745
L69	Limited sdn 4d	2,930	15,695	8,829
H37	Custom cpe 2d	2,862	14,550	627
H35	Custom wgn 4d	3,054	15,660	5,029
L35	Limited wgn 4d	3,080	16,395	1,784
Regal (wb 107.5)				
B19	Custom sdn 4d	3,320	16,865	60,921
D19	Limited sdn 4d	3,320	18,110	20,220
F19	Gran Sport sdn 4d	3,380	19,300	10,754
B57	Custom cpe 2d	3,236	16,610	12,152
D57	Limited cpe 2d	3,236	17,790	4,921
F57	Gran Sport cpe 2d	3,236	18,600	5,925
LeSabre (wb 110.8)				
H69	Custom sdn 4d	3,417	18,695	101,139
R69	Limited sdn 4d	3,457	20,775	70,412
Park Avenue (wb 110.7)				
W69	sdn 4d	3,536	25,285	57,443
U69	Ultra sdn 4d	3,640	28,780	11,499
Roadmaster (wb 115.9)				
N69	sdn 4d	4,073	21,865	30,415
T69	Limited sdn 4d	—	24,195	43,402
R35	Estate wgn 4d	4,468	23,040	11,491
Riviera (wb 108.0)				
Z57	cpe 2d	3,497	24,415	12,585

1992 Engines	bore×stroke	bhp	availability
I-4, 138.0	3.62×3.35	120	S-Skylark (ohc)
I-4, 151.0	4.10×3.10	110	S-Century
V-6, 191.0	3.51×3.31	140	S-Regal
V-6, 204.0	3.70×3.16	160	O-Skyl, Century
V-6, 231.0	3.80×3.40	170	S-LeS, Riviera, Pk Ave, O-Regal,
V-6S, 231.0	3.80×3.40	205	S-Pk Ave Ultra
V-8, 350.0	4.00×3.48	180	S-Roadmaster

1993

Skylark (wb 103.4)		Wght	Price	Prod
V-69	Custom sdn 4d	2,846	12,995	41,625
J69	Limited sdn 4d	2,965	13,875	6,903
M69	Gran Sport sdn 4d	2,965	15,760	1,627
V37	Custom cpe 2d	2,782	12,995	5,691
J37	Limited cpe 2d	2,965	13,875	894
M37	Gran Sport cpe 2d	2,901	15,760	1,442
Century (wb 104.9)				
G69	Special sdn 4d	2,949	14,205	100,012
H69	Custom sdn 4d	2,948	15,905	14,673
L69	Limited sdn 4d	2,948	16,865	4,846
H37	Custom cpe 2d	2,903	15,620	566
G35	Special wgn 4d	3,103	14,960	7,216
H35	Custom wgn 4d	3,102	16,865	2,751
Regal (wb 107.5)				
B19	Custom sdn 4d	3,340	16,865	54,113
D19	Limited sdn 4d	3,362	18,460	7,494
F19	Gran Sport sdn 4d	3,472	19,310	7,625
B57	Custom cpe 2d	3,250	16,610	7,443
D57	Limited cpe 2d	3,258	18,260	2,523
F57	Gran Sport cpe 2d	3,388	19,095	4,109
LeSabre (wb 110.8)				
P69	Custom sdn 4d	3,433	19,935	99,518
R69	Limited sdn 4d	3,454	21,735	51,416
Park Avenue (wb 110.8)				
W69	sdn 4d	3,536	26,040	40,468
U69	Ultra sdn 4d	3,639	29,395	14,738
Roadmaster (wb 115.9)				
N69	sdn 4d	3,973	22,555	13,233
T69	Limited sdn 4d	3,988	24,920	17,725
R35	Estate wgn 4d	4,508	23,850	9,541
Riviera (wb 108.0)				
Z57	cpe 2d	3,504	26,320	4,555

1993 Engines	bore×stroke	bhp	availability
I-4, 133.0	3.50×3.46	110	S-Century
I-4, 138.0	3.62×3.92	115	S-Skylark (ohc)
V-6, 191.0	3.51×3.31	140	S-Regal
V-6, 204.0	3.70×3.16	160	O-Skyl, Century
V-6, 231.0	3.80×3.40	170	S-LeS, Riviera, Pk Ave, O-Regal
V-6S, 231.0	3.80×3.40	205	S-Pk Ave Ultra
V-8, 350.0	4.00×3.48	180	S-Roadmaster

1994

Skylark (wb 103.4)		Wght	Price	Prod
V-69	Custom sdn 4d	2,855	13,599	46,548
J69	Limited sdn 4d	2,939	16,199	2,010
M69	Gran Sport sdn 4d	3,038	18,299	857
V37	Custom cpe 2d	2,791	13,599	9,024
M37	Gran Sport cpe 2d	2,985	18,299	626
Century (wb 104.9)				
G69	Special sdn 4d	2,974	15,495	122,916
H69	Custom sdn 4d	2,976	16,695	5,853
G35	Special wgn 4d	3,134	16,345	9,100
Regal (wb 107.5)				
B19	Custom sdn 4d	3,338	18,299	47,293
D19	Limited sdn 4d	3,362	19,799	4,672
F19	Gran Sport sdn 4d	3,429	20,299	8,528
B57	Custom cpe 2d	3,240	17,999	10,828
F57	Gran Sport cpe 2d	3,335	19,999	7,236
LeSabre (wb 110.8)				
P69	Custom sdn 4d	3,449	20,860	113,834
R69	Limited sdn 4d	3,449	24,420	45,416
Park Avenue (wb 110.8)				
W69	sdn 4d	3,533	26,999	52,034
U69	Ultra sdn 4d	3,637	31,699	12,630
Roadmaster (wb 115.9)				
N69	sdn 4d	4,191	23,999	15,311
T69	Limited sdn 4d	4,279	26,399	14,831
R35	Estate wgn 4d	4,572	25,599	8,767

1994 Engines	bore×stroke	bhp	availability
I-4, 133.0	3.50×3.46	120	S-Century
I-4, 138.0	3.62×3.35	115	S-Skylark
V-6, 191.0	3.51×3.31	155	O-Skylark
V-6, 191.0	3.51×3.31	160	S-Regal, O-Cnty
V-6, 231.0	3.80×3.40	170	S-LeS, Pk Ave; O-Rgl
V-6S, 231.0	3.80×3.40	225	S-Pk Ave Ultra
V-8, 350.0	4.00×3.48	260	S-Roadmaster

1995

Skylark (wb 103.4)		Wght	Price	Prod
V-69	Custom sdn 4d	2,941	14,320	53,860
V-69SK	Limited sdn 4d	2,941	15,195	
V-69SL	Gran Sport sdn 4d	3,058	16,895	
V37	Custom cpe 2d	2,888	14,320	
V37SK	Limited cpe 2d	2,888	15,195	
V37SL	Gran Sport cpe 2d	3,005	16,895	
Century (wb 104.9)				
G69	Special sdn 4d	2,968	16,360	113,699
G69SL	Limited sdn 4d	2,968	17,995	
H69	Custom sdn 4d	2,993	17,965	
G35	Special wgn 4d	3,130	17,080	
Regal (wb 107.5)				
B19	Custom sdn 4d	3,335	19,920	100,169
D19	Limited sdn 4d	3,463	21,235	
F19	Gran Sport sdn 4d	3,406	21,870	
B57	Custom cpe 2d	3,261	19,603	
B57SE	Gran Sport cpe 2d	3,328	19,995	
LeSabre (wb 110.8)				
P69	Custom sdn 4d	3,442	21,735	171,783
R69	Limited sdn 4d	3,442	25,465	
Park Avenue (wb 110.8)				
W69	sdn 4d	3,532	28,244	62,994
U69	Ultra sdn 4d	3,642	33,084	
Roadmaster (wb 115.9)				
N69	sdn 4d	4,211	25,265	30,508
R69	Limited sdn 4d	4,244	27,555	
R35	Estate wgn 4d	4,563	27,070	
Riviera (wb 113.8)				
D07	cpe 2d	3,748	27,632	41,442

1995 Engines	bore×stroke	bhp	availability
I-4, 133.0	3.50×3.46	120	S-Century
I-4, 138.0	3.62×3.35	150	S-Skylark (dohc)
V-6, 191.0	3.51×3.31	155	O-Skylark
V-6, 191.0	3.51×3.31	160	S-Rgl, O-Cnty
V-6, 231.0	3.80×3.40	170	S-LeS, O-Regal
V-6, 231.0	3.80×3.40	205	S-Pk Ave, Riv
V-6S, 231.0	3.80×3.40	225	S-Pk Ave Ult, O-Riviera
V-8, 350.0	4.00×3.48	260	S-Roadmaster

1996

Skylark (wb 103.4)		Wght	Price	Prod
J69	Custom sdn 4d	2,948	15,495	36,360
J69	Limited sdn 4d	2,948	16,518	
J69	Gran Sport sdn 4d	—	17,701	
J37	Custom cpe 2d	2,917	15,495	6,782
J37	Limited cpe 2d	2,917	16,518	
J37	Gran Sport cpe 2d	—	17,701	
Century (wb 104.9)				
G69	Special sdn 4d	2,950	16,720	86,758
G69	Custom sdn 4d	—	18,383	
G69	Limited sdn 4d	—	19,406	
G35	Special wgn 4d	3,118	18,135	7,663
Regal (wb 107.5)				
B19	Custom sdn 4d	3,331	19,740	107,056
B19SE	Limited sdn 4d	—	21,195	
F19SE	Gran Sport sdn 4d	—	21,800	
B57	Custom cpe 2d	3,232	19,445	5,991
B57	Gran Sport cpe 2d	—	21,340	
LeSabre (wb 110.8)				
P69	Custom sdn 4d	3,430	21,380	40,220
R69	Limited sdn 4d	—	25,385	13,963
Park Avenue (wb 110.8)				
W69	sdn 4d	3,536	28,205	41,016
U69	Ultra sdn 4d	3,629	32,820	7,757
Roadmaster (wb 115.9)				
N69	sdn 4d	4,211	25,560	6,411
T69	Limited sdn 4d	4,244	27,490	7,493
R35	Estate wgn 4d	4,563	27,575	9,085
Z27	Limited Est wgn 4d	—	29,445	
Riviera (wb 113.8)				
D07	cpe 2d	3,690	29,475	18,036

1996 Engines	bore×stroke	bhp	availability
I-4, 134.0	3.50×3.46	120	S-Century
I-4, 146.0	3.54×3.70	150	S-Skylark (dohc)
V-6, 191.0	3.51×3.31	155	O-Skylark
V-6, 191.0	3.51×3.31	160	S-Rgl, O-Cnty
V-6, 231.0	3.80×3.40	205	S-LeS, Prk Ave, Rivi; O-Regal
V-6S, 231.0	3.80×3.40	240	S-Park Avenue Ultra, O-Riviera
V-8, 350.0	4.00×3.48	260	S-Roadmaster

1997

Skylark (wb 103.4)		Wght	Price	Prod
J69	Custom sdn 4d	2,985	15,970	53,863
J37	Custom cpe 2d	2,945	15,970	4,041
Century (wb 109.0) - 58,728 built				
G69	Custom sdn 4d	3,348	17,845	—
G69	Limited sdn 4d	3,359	19,220	—
Regal (wb 107.5) - 24,257 built				
B19	LS sdn 4d	3,331	20,545	—
F19	GS sdn 4d	—	22,945	—

LeSabre (wb 110.8) - 223,398 blt		Wght	Price	Prod
P69	Custom sdn 4d	3,441	22,015	—
R69	Limited sdn 4d	3,462	25,565	—
Park Avenue (wb 113.8) - 62,591 built				
W69	sdn 4d	3,788	29,995	—
U69	Ultra sdn 4d	3,879	34,995	—
Riviera (wb 113.8)				
D07	cpe 2d	3,720	30,110	18,827

1997 Engines	bore×stroke	bhp	availability
I-4, 146.0	3.54×3.70	150	S-Skylark (dohc)
V-6, 191.0	3.51×3.31	155	O-Skylark
V-6, 191.0	3.51×3.31	160	S-Century
V-6, 231.0	3.80×3.40	195	S-Regal
V-6, 231.0	3.80×3.40	205	S-LeS, Pk Av, Riv
V-6S, 231.0	3.80×3.40	240	S-Pk Av Ult, O-Rgl, Riviera

1998

Century (wb 109.0) - 138,220 blt		Wght	Price	Prod
G69	Custom sdn 4d	3,335	18,215	—
G69	Limited sdn 4d	3,354	19,575	—
Regal (wb 109.0) - 76,174 built				
B19	LS sdn 4d	3,447	20,945	—
F19	GS sdn 4d	3,562	23,690	—
LeSabre (wb 110.8) - 149,418 built				
P69	Custom sdn 4d	3,443	22,465	—
R69	Limited sdn 4d	3,465	25,790	—
Park Avenue (wb 113.8) - 63,811 built				
W69	sdn 4d	3,740	30,675	—
U69	Ultra sdn 4d	3,837	35,550	—
Riviera (wb 113.8)				
D07	cpe 2d	3,699	32,500	10,953

1998 Engines	bore×stroke	bhp	availability
V-6, 191.0	3.51×3.31	160	S-Century
V-6, 231.0	3.80×3.40	195	S-Regal
V-6, 231.0	3.80×3.40	205	S-LeS, Pk Ave
V-6S, 231.0	3.80×3.40	240	S-Park Avenue Ultr, Riv, O-Rgl

1999

Century (wb 109.0) - 160,028		Wght	Price	Prod
G69	Custom sdn 4d	3,365	18,775	—
G69	Limited sdn 4d	3,375	20,145	—
Regal (wb 109.0) - 77,848				
B19	LS sdn 4d	3,450	21,695	—
F19	GS sdn 4d	3,545	24,395	—
LeSabre (wb 110.8) - 105,523				
P69	Custom sdn 4d	3,430	22,725	—
R69	Limited sdn 4d	—	25,990	—
Park Avenue (wb 113.8) - 61,416				
W69	sdn 4d	3,790	31,130	—
U69	Ultra sdn 4d	3,880	36,025	—
Riviera (wb 113.8)				
D07	cpe 2d	3,720	33,820	2,154

1999 Engines	bore×stroke	bhp	availability
V-6, 191.0	3.51×3.31	160	S-Century
V-6, 231.0	3.80×3.40	200	S-Regal
V-6, 231.0	3.80×3.40	205	S-LeS, Prk Ave
V-6S, 231.0	3.80×3.40	240	S-Prk Ave Ultra, Riviera, O-Regal

2000

Century (wb 109.0) - 155,748		Wght	Price	Prod
G69	Custom sdn 4d	3,368	19,602	—
G69	Limited sdn 4d	3,371	21,737	—
Regal (wb 109.0) - 67,219				
B19	LS sdn 4d	3,439	22,220	—
F19	GS sdn 4d	3,543	25,065	—
LeSabre (wb 112.2)				
P69	Custom sdn 4d	3,567	23,235	134,492
R69	Limited sdn 4d	3,591	27,340	66,291
Park Avenue (wb 113.8)				
W69	sdn 4d	3,778	31,725	42,725
U69	Ultra sdn 4d	3,884	36,800	9,545

2000 Engines	bore×stroke	bhp	availability
V-6, 191.0	3.51×3.31	175	S-Century
V-6, 231.0	3.80×3.40	200	S-Regal
V-6, 231.0	3.80×3.40	205	S-LeSabre, Park Avenue
V-6S, 231.0	3.80×3.40	240	S-Pk Ave Ultra, O-Regal

2001

Century (wb 109.0) - 138,150 blt		Wght	Price	Prod
G69	Custom sdn 4d	3,368	19,840	—
G69	Limited sdn 4d	3,371	22,871	—
Regal (wb 109.0) - 57,133 built				
B19	LS sdn 4d	3,438	22,845	—
F19	GS sdn 4d	3,543	26,095	—
LeSabre (wb 112.2)				
P69	Custom sdn 4d	3,567	24,107	107,331
R69	Limited sdn 4d	3,591	28,796	37,737
Park Avenue (wb 113.8)				
W69	sdn 4d	3,778	32,980	30,939
U69	Ultra sdn 4d	3,884	37,490	6,091

2001 Engines	bore×stroke	bhp	availability
V-6, 191.0	3.51×3.31	175	S-Century
V-6, 231.0	3.80×3.40	200	S-Regal
V-6, 231.0	3.80×3.40	205	S-LeSabre, Park Avenue
V-6S, 231.0	3.80×3.40	240	S-Pk Ave Ultr, O-Regal

2002

Century (wb 109.0) - 157,897 blt		Wght	Price	Prod
G69	Custom sdn 4d	3,353	20,285	—
G69	Limited sdn 4d	3,391	23,285	—
Regal (wb 109.0) - 43,939 built				
B19	LS sdn 4d	3,461	23,230	—
F19	GS sdn 4d	3,536	27,285	—
LeSabre (wb 112.2)				
P69	Custom sdn 4d	3,567	24,290	104,365
R69	Limited sdn 4d	3,591	29,990	38,285
Park Avenue (wb 113.8)				
W69	sdn 4d	3,778	33,420	28,261
U69	Ultra sdn 4d	3,884	37,930	4,033

2002 Engines	bore×stroke	bhp	availability
V-6, 191.0	3.51×3.31	175	S-Century
V-6, 231.0	3.80×3.40	200	S-Regal
V-6, 231.0	3.80×3.40	205	S-LeSabre, Park Avenue
V-6S, 231.0	3.80×3.40	240	S-Park Avenue Ultra, O-Regal

2003

Century (wb 109.0)		Wght	Price	Prod
S69	sdn 4d	3,353	20,720	160,504
Regal (wb 109.0) - 39,042 built				
B69	LS sdn 4d	3,461	23,740	—
F69	GS sdn 4d	3,543	27,685	—
LeSabre (wb 112.2) - 128,228 built				
P69	Custom sdn 4d	3,567	25,135	—
R69	Limited sdn 4d	3,591	30,835	—
Park Ave (wb 113.8) - 29,209 built				
W69	sdn 4d	3,778	34,075	—
U69	Ultra sdn 4d	3,884	39,145	—

2003 Engines	bore×stroke	bhp	availability
V-6, 191.0	3.51×3.31	175	S-Century
V-6, 231.0	3.80×3.40	200	S-Regal
V-6, 231.0	3.80×3.40	205	S-LeSabre, Park Ave
V-6S, 231.0	3.80 x 3.40	240	S-Pk Ave Ultra, O-Regal

2004

Century (wb 109.0)		Wght	Price	Prod
S69	sdn 4d	3,342	21,645	61,558
Regal (wb 109.0) - 29,594 built				
B69	LS sdn 4d	3,461	24,235	—
F69	GS sdn 4d	3,524	28,685	—
LeSabre (wb 112.2) - 122,667 built				
P69	Custom sdn 4d	3,567	25,745	—
R69	Limited sdn 4d	3,591	31715	—
Park Ave (wb 113.8) - 17,159 blt				
W69	sdn 4d	3,778	34,975	—
U69	Ultra sdn 4d	3,884	40,150	—

2004 Engines	bore×stroke	bhp	availability
V-6, 191.0	3.51×3.31	175	S-Century
V-6, 231.0	3.80×3.40	200	S-Regal
V-6, 231.0	3.80×3.40	205	S-LeSabre, Park Avenue
V-6S, 231.0	3.80 x 3.40	225	O-Regal
V-6S, 231.0	3.80 x 3.40	230	S-Park Avenue Ultra

2005

LaCrosse (wb 110.5) - 81,931 blt		Wght	Price	Prod
C19	CX sdn 4d	3,495	22,835	—
D19	CXL sdn 4d	3,502	25,335	—
E19	CXS sdn 4d	3,568	28,335	—
LeSabre (wb 112.2) - 107,960 built				
P69	Custom sdn 4d	3,567	26,545	—
R69	Limited sdn 4d	3,591	32205	—
Park Avenue (wb 113.8) - 9,363 built				
W69	sdn 4d	3,778	35,555	—
U69	Ultra sdn 4d	3,884	40,730	—

2005 Engines	bore×stroke	bhp	availability
V-6, 217.0	3.70×3.37	240	O-LaCrosse (dohc)
V-6, 231.0	3.80×3.40	200	S-LaCrosse
V-6, 231.0	3.80×3.40	205	S-LeSabre, Park Avenue
V-6S, 231.0	3.80 x 3.40	240	S-Pk Ave Ultra

2006

LaCrosse (wb 110.5)		Wght	Price	Prod*
C19	CX sdn 4d	3,495	22,835	—
D19	CXL sdn 4d	3,502	25,335	—
E19	CXS sdn 4d	3,568	28,335	—
Lucerne (wb 115.6)				
P69	CX sdn 4d	3,764	26,265	—
D69	CXL sdn 4d	3,969	28,265	—
E69	CXS sdn 4d	4,013	35265	—

2006 Engines	bore×stroke	bhp	availability
V-6, 217.0	3.70×3.37	240	O-LaCrosse (dohc)
V-6, 231.0	3.80×3.40	200	S-LaCrosse
V-6, 231.0	3.80×3.40	197	S-Lucerne
V-8, 279.0	3.66×3.31	275	O-Lucerne

*Production figures not available at time of publication.

Cadillac

Cadillac was founded in late 1902 by Henry Martyn Leland, a brilliant engineer who'd worked at Ford and Oldsmobile. His first cars were simple "one-lung" runabouts, but he soon developed a more civilized four-cylinder model, the successful Cadillac "30" of 1909-15. Leland's passion for precision craftsmanship and standardized parts, born of his experience as a gunmaker, was evident early on. In England in 1908, three Cadillacs were disassembled, their components mixed up, then reassembled into three cars that ran perfectly. This feat won Cadillac its first Dewar Trophy and inspired the make's now long-familiar slogan, "Standard of the World."

The following year, Cadillac became part of fledgling General Motors. As an upper-middle-priced car in those days, it didn't compete directly with Packard or Pierce-Arrow, but was always a high-quality item. Cadillac's pioneering 1915 V-8 set new standards for smoothness, power, and reliability, and sales increased steadily from the late Teens through the end of the '20s, when the make turned to luxury cars exclusively.

Had it not been part of GM, Cadillac might have perished in the Depression, a time when few could afford—or wanted to be seen in—big, expensive automobiles no matter how superb. Unlike independent Packard, which was forced to survive with medium-priced products, Cadillac was protected by GM's vast size and enormous financial strength. Then, too, the division already had a medium-priced car, the LaSalle, introduced in 1927 (*see entry*). All this helped Cadillac endure "hard times" without squandering its blue-chip image even as it built ultra-luxury cars selling only in small numbers.

Foremost among them was that magnificent 1930 surprise, the Sixteen, carrying an overhead-valve, 452-cubic-inch engine producing 165 horsepower and 320 pound-feet of torque. Horsepower was increased to 185 in '34. An undoubted great in an era of greats, the Sixteen was ostensibly available in 33 different models, submodels or trim variations ranging from a $5350 two-passenger roadster to a $9700 town brougham. The typical example could return about eight miles to a 15-cent gallon of gas and 150 miles to a quart of oil, plus cruise at 70 and top 90 mph. But brute performance wasn't its forte. Rather, the Sixteen was intended to elevate Cadillac into the rarefied realm of Packard, Peerless, and Pierce-Arrow. That it did, offering superb luxury and smooth, effortless power with minimal shifting. Cadillac advertised its performance as "a continuous flow... constantly at full-volume efficiency... flexible... instantly responsive."

The Sixteen was only nine months old when Cadillac introduced another multicylinder engine, a 368-cid V-12. Essentially a V-16 with four fewer cylinders, it delivered 135 horsepower and 285 pound-feet of torque. The cars it powered also weren't quite as large the Sixteens, riding the Cadillac Eight's 140-inch wheelbase instead of an enormous 148-inch span. Predictably, the Twelve also wasn't as fast, but its free-revving engine was renowned for smooth, even power. And that power was quite ample. A roadster could do about 85 mph with standard rear-axle ratio, and most Twelves could cruise all day at 70. Of course, the Twelve was cheaper than the Sixteen—by far—offered with 11 body choices in the $3795-$4985 range.

But despite their refined performance and majestic proportions, the multicylinder Cadillacs were anachronisms in the devastated Depression market, and none sold in significant numbers. The peak was 1930-31 with exactly 3250 Sixteens and 5725 Twelves. Production was only fair for '32, then declined to about 700 and 400 units per year, respectively. Both models were dropped after 1937, but Cadillac made one more try starting the following year with an L-head V-16. At 431 cid and 185 bhp, this engine was smaller and lighter yet more potent than the earlier ohv design, but only 508 cars were so equipped through 1940, its final year.

There were two reasons why these grand Cadillacs fared so poorly. As noted, staggeringly expensive cars with more than eight cylinders seemed socially inappropriate to many people in the early '30s. After their initial sales spurt, these models were shunned by most customers for the cheaper, less-showy, but by no means inferior Cadillac Eights. Later, the big engines were simply outmoded by advancing technology. The introduction of precision-insert connecting-rod bearings helped eliminate knock and high-speed wear in engines with fewer than 12 cylinders, so there was little reason for Cadillac buyers to choose a Twelve or Sixteen over an Eight.

Fortunately for Cadillac, its V-8 line sold consistently and fairly well through the '30s. Model-year production hung around 10,000 units for 1930-31, plunged to 2000-3000 for 1932-33, then recovered rapidly. With the introduction of the low-priced Series 60 for 1936, V-8 volume passed 10,000, then reached over 13,000 by 1939. This highly creditable performance was owed to a reliable cast-iron L-head engine, competitive prices, and a wide range of body styles.

Cadillac's early-'30s V-8 was based on a 341-cid unit introduced in 1928. Sized at 353 cid for 1930-35, it delivered 95-130 bhp. A completely redesigned 346 with 135 bhp replaced it for 1936. That year's new Series 60 used a 322-cid version, then adopted the 346. This respected powerplant would remain in

1930 Sixteen touring

1930 Series 353 Eight town sedan

1931 Series 355 Eight 2-passenger coupe

1932 Series 355-B Eight 5-passenger coupe

1932 Series 355-B Eight four-door sedan

1933 Twelve Imperial 7-passenger four-door sedan

production until Cadillac launched its new short-stroke ohv V-8 for 1949. Though the L-head had limits, it delivered excellent performance and reasonable economy. The lighter 1938-39 models could do nearly 100 mph and run 0-60 in 15-16 seconds—no mean feat for 4500-pound luxury liners before World War II.

Unlike luxury rivals, Cadillac designed and built most of its bodies in-house via Fisher and Fleetwood, two respected coach-makers that GM had acquired. (Cadillac also supplied chassis in fair numbers to independent body builders. This arrangement enabled designer Harley Earl to maintain a consistent look throughout the car instead of in just the radiator and hood. "Classic" Cadillac styling was undoubtedly epitomized by the 1930-31 models with their opulent, thick-collar vertical radiators; beautifully rounded hoods; and clean, flowing lines. Body styles were bewildering. The 1930 Fisher line spanned seven types in the $3300-$4000 range. Fleetwood Custom models numbered no fewer than 14, priced from $3450 to $5145. Most elegant of all were the several "Madame X"—after a stage play of the era—styles with their slender chrome door and windshield moldings.

Square-rigged styling began to dissolve with the more-rounded 1932 Cadillacs, but true streamlining wasn't evident until the 1933 models. While these retained the basic '32 bodies, Earl modernized appearance with items like skirted fenders, Vee'd radiators, and more-swept-back windshields. A notable innovation was front-door ventwing windows, called "No-Draft Ventilation," a feature shared with sister GM divisions that year. All early-'30s Cadillacs have long been prized by enthusiasts as some of the best designs of the late Classic era.

Styling for 1934 was fully revised along the lines of the exotic, experimental "Aerodynamic" fastback coupe presented at the 1933 Chicago World's Fair. Earl now moved away completely from upright forms into the realm of pontoon fenders, sloped radiators, "bullet" headlights, and rakish rear decks. He also conjured novel two-piece front and rear bumpers likely inspired by the biplane configuration, but they proved fragile and unpopular, and were thus abandoned after one season. The 1935-36 models were relatively dumpy by comparison, with roundness prevailing over squareness throughout.

Everything changed again for 1938, when young William L. Mitchell, an Earl protégé, drew up the Sixty Special sedan as an addition to the 124-inch-wheelbase Series 60. Square yet crisply elegant and quite compact for a Cadillac, Mitchell's creation stood apart with chrome-edged side windows, square-back fenders, concealed running boards and a low profile on a wheelbase three inches longer than on other 60s—a coupe, a

1934 Eight Fleetwood Aero-Dynamic 5-passenger coupe

1934 Series 355-D Eight convertible sedan

1934 Series 355-D Eight 2-passenger convertible coupe

1935 Series 355-D Eight 5-passenger four-door sedan

1936 Series Sixty 2/4-passenger convertible coupe

1936 Series Seventy-Five Fleetwood convertible sedan

1936 Eight Series Sixty 2-passenger coupe

1937 Series Sixty convertible sedan

1937 Series Seventy Fleetwood touring sedan

sedan, and two convertibles. It's long been judged one of the all-time design greats.

Cadillac's produced 10,000 units more for 1939 than for '38 (which had suffered in a national recession). Only mild facelifts occurred and engines were unchanged, but the division now blanketed the luxury field. A new 126-inch-wheelbase Series 61 offered four models priced from $1610 to $2170, while the Sixty Special returned as a series of its own priced from $2090 to $2315. The Series 75 listed the usual plethora of Fleetwood bodies on a 141-inch span, Cadillac's longest V-8 wheelbase yet.

The 1930s saw vast technical progress at Cadillac. Having introduced clashless "Syncro-Mesh" transmission in 1929, the division followed up for '32 with "Triple-Silent" Syncro-Mesh (helical-cut gears for all three forward speeds). "No-Draft" and vacuum-assisted brakes appeared for 1933, independent front suspension for '34. For 1935 came GM's all-steel "Turret Top" construction that eliminated fabric roof inserts. Hydraulic brakes arrived on all but Sixteens for 1936. Column-mounted gearshift arrived in '38 and optional turn signals one year later.

As mentioned, a "second-series" Sixteen arrived for 1938, and again led the Cadillac fleet for 1939-40. Its new short-stroke engine was smaller than the earlier V-16, but made the same 185 bhp. Like Cadillac's V-8, it featured rugged cast-iron construction and side valves, as well as nine main bearings and separate manifolds, carburetor, water pump, and distributor for each cylinder bank. Chassis was shared with the 75, as were body styles: two coupes, a convertible, touring sedans with and without division window, a "trunkback" convertible sedan, formal sedans seating five or seven, and several seven-passenger sedans. The big difference was price. The basic five-passenger sedan of 1940 sold for $1745 with V-8 but $5140 with V-16—a premium no longer really justified, as Cadillac's V-8 was one of

1937 Series Seventy Fleetwood convertible coupe

1938 Series Sixty-Five touring sedan

1937 Series Seventy-Five Fleetwood convertible sedan

1938 Sixty Special touring sedan

1938 Series Seventy-Five Fleetwood town sedan

1938 Series Seventy-Five Fleetwood convertible coupe

1938 Series Seventy-Five Fleetwood convertible sedan

1939 Sixty Special touring sedan

the smoothest engines anywhere. With sales no better than in 1930-37, the opulent Sixteen was dropped for good after 1940—a relic of a grand age we would not see again.

Some of Cadillac's most important engineering developments—and some of its most beautiful cars—appeared in the '40s. Like Buick, the division face-lifted for 1940-41, then issued completely new styling for '42 that left it in a good market position when civilian car production resumed after World War II.

Most 1940 Cadillacs were relatively plain—in front, almost Chevrolet-like with their simple bar grilles. The exception was the splendid Sixteen, which wore the eggcrate radiator theme first seen for 1937, soon to be a Cadillac fixture. All models wore sealed-beam headlamps, as did most cars from Detroit that year.

Ranked below the 90 and 75 for 1940 was a new Series 72 with a 138-inch wheelbase and slightly fewer models, but also lower prices ($2670-$3695). Though impressive and well designed, it would be a one-year-only line, with sales limited by competition from the more luxurious 75. Yet, even counting 75s and Sixteens, Cadillac built only a little over 2500 long-wheelbase 1940 cars.

The crisp Sixty Special returned with minor styling tweaks in the same four models offered for '39. A predictive, if rarely ordered, new option (Cadillac sold only 1500 between 1938 and '41) was a sliding metal sunroof (called "Sunshine Turret Top Roof"). It was available on both the standard Sixty Special "town sedan" and division-window Imperial. There was also a "town car" offered with painted-metal or leather-covered roof. Just 15 were built; most 1940 Sixty Specials were the standard sedan (4472 units).

1940 Sixty Special Fleetwood touring sedan

1940 Series Seventy-Five Fleetwood coupe

1941 Series Sixty-Two convertible coupe

1941 Series Sixty-Two touring sedan

1942 Series Sixty-Three four-door sedan

Displacing the 61 as 1940's most-affordable Cadillac was the Series 62, another future Cadillac fixture. Initial offerings comprised coupe, touring sedan, convertible coupe, and convertible sedan on a 129-inch wheelbase. Prices ranged from $1685 to $2195. As in later years, the 62 garnered the most sales by far of any 1940 Cadillac line.

The division's 1940 V-8 retained its familiar monoblock construction (unitized block and crankcase), three main bearings with counterweights, and two-barrel downdraft carb. Though heavy, it was reliable and exceptionally smooth. As in '39, it was tuned for 135 horsepower in the 62 and Sixty Special, 140 for the 72 and 75.

A significant and attractive design change occurred for 1941, when Cadillac revived the Series 61 to replace its junior LaSalle line. This was a marketing decision based on the success of Lincoln-Zephyr and Packard's One Ten/One Twenty, and it worked. While Packard continued to rely on medium-priced cars long after World War II, Cadillac (and Lincoln) returned to the luxury field exclusively, thus bolstering its "fine car" reputation—and sales—at Packard's expense.

The '41 Cadillacs wore a fresh face: a complex eggcrate grille with central bulge (carried down from the hood). Taillights were also more prominent, and one even concealed the gas filler, yet another feature destined for a long life. Departure of both the Sixteen and 72 reduced wheelbases to three: 136 inches for the 75, 139 on four new Series 67 sedans, and 126 for others.

Cadillac's big mechanical news for 1941 was a first in the luxury class: fully shiftless Hydra-Matic Drive. Developed by Oldsmobile, which had introduced it a year earlier, this excellent automatic transmission would remain an option for all models through 1949. Also, higher compression lifted the V-8 to 150 bhp. This combined with revised axle ratios to permit most '41 Caddys to reach a genuine 100 mph and scale 0-60 in about 14 seconds—impressive for the day.

Improved performance, the new Hydra-Matic, and a still-broad price span ($1345-$4045) pushed Cadillac production to a new high for the '41 model year: 66,130. That was only some 6700 short of Packard, which was selling a much higher proportion of less-costly cars. Most of the gain was owed to the revived 61, which was every inch a Cadillac despite its lower price. But the 62 was up dramatically, the Sixty Special scored a healthy 4100 sales, and a new Series 63 four-door attracted some 5000 customers all by itself.

The 1942 lineup was mostly the same but had a new look, dominated by big bullet-shape fenders front and rear, plus fastback rooflines (debuted on the '41 Series 61) for a Series 62 coupe named "sedanet." Unfortunately, this year's Sixty Special was more like other Cadillacs—far less "special." Cadillac built a total 16,511 of its '42s before war halted production in February 1942. The division then turned out tanks, aircraft engines, and munitions until V-J Day.

Resuming civilian operations took several months, so Cadillac managed only 1142 Series 62 sedans before the end of 1945 and 29,194 cars total for model-year '46. These were only slightly changed from '42, but the 63, 67, and division-window 60 Special were all dropped. What remained were fastback 61s, fastback and notchback 62s, a lone Sixty Special, and five 75s.

The '47s were little changed: round instead of rectangular parking lights (when large optional fog lamps weren't designated), script instead of block-letter fender nameplates, a five-bar grille theme in place of the six bars used the previous year, and the famed "sombrero" wheelcovers were first offered. Postwar inflation swelled prices by $150-$200, but production now regained its prewar stride, nearing 62,000 for the model year. As before, the 62 accounted for most of it with just under 40,000 units.

1946 Series Sixty-One four-door sedan

1946 Sixty Special four-door sedan

1947 Series Sixty-Two sedanet (club coupe)

1947 Series Sixty-Two convertible coupe

1948 Series Sixty-One sedanet (club coupe)

1948 Series Sixty-Two four-door sedan

1948 Series Sixty-One four-door sedan

1949 Series Sixty-Two Coupe de Ville hardtop

Then came 1948, "The Year of the Tailfin." Before the war, designers Earl, Mitchell, Franklin Q. Hershey, and Art Ross had been shown the then-secret Lockheed P-38 "Lightning" pursuit fighter. During the war, a skeleton crew played with ideas for postwar styling inspired by some of the plane's design elements: pontoon front fenders, pointy front, cockpitlike curved windshields—and tailfins. This influence would be seen at other GM divisions. Olds, for example, adopted the P-38's engine air-scoop motif for the headlamp bezels on its 1949 "Futuramic" models. But the fin had the most lasting impact. As Mitchell later said: "From a design standpoint, the fins gave definition to the rear of the car for the first time. They made the back end as interesting as the front, and established a long-standing Cadillac-styling hallmark."

Tailfins were the crowning touch for Cadillac's masterful '48 design, which was executed by a small team working under Hershey at his farm in suburban Detroit. The make's traditional grille became more aggressive via larger eggcrates, complemented by a more-shapely hood. Roof and fenderlines were curvaceously beautiful from every angle. Inside was a new dashboard dominated by a huge "drum" housing gauges and controls. This lasted only a year, however, as it was complex and costly to produce. The '49s used a simpler instrument board that echoed the grille shape, a theme that would persist for the next eight years.

Models, body styles, and wheelbases stood pat for '48, but Series 75s wouldn't get the new look until 1950 (low production precluded early amortization of their prewar dies). The '49 line was a rerun too—except for two stunning developments. One was the Coupe de Ville, a $3497 entry in the Series 62 that

1949 Series Sixty-Two convertible coupe

1950 Sixty Special four-door sedan

1950 Series Sixty-One four-door sedan

1951 Series Sixty-Two Coupe de Ville hardtop

1951 Series Sixty-Two convertible coupe

shares honors with that year's new Oldsmobile 98 Holiday and Buick Roadmaster Riviera as Detroit's first volume hardtop. Cadillac sold 2150 of the '49s, a higher percentage of its total production than either Buick or Olds. Of course, the idea behind all three was convertible airiness combined with closed-car comfort and solidness, and it proved enormously popular, starting a trend that would dominate Detroit by the mid-'50s. (Cadillac also built one 1949 Coupe de Ville on the 133-inch Sixty Special chassis, strictly an experiment.)

Equally revolutionary was Cadillac's exciting new 1949 overhead-valve V-8, the second blow of a potent one-two punch delivered directly to Packard, Lincoln, and Chrysler's Imperial. The product of 10 years' research and development, this engine was designed by Ed Cole, Jack Gordon, and Harry Barr, who aimed for less weight and higher compression (to take advantage of the higher-octane fuels promised after the war). This dictated valve rearrangement, a stroke shorter than bore, wedge-shape combustion chambers, and "slipper" pistons. The last, devised by Byron Ellis, traveled low between the crankshaft counterweights to allow for short connecting rods and, thus, low reciprocating mass.

Sized at 331 cid, the new V-8 arrived with 160 horsepower, 10 bhp more than the old 346 L-head despite less displacement, testifying to its efficiency. The ohv had other advantages. Though a cast-iron job like the L-head, it weighed nearly 200 pounds less. Compression was just 7.5:1, yet could be pushed up to 12:1; the L-head couldn't. The ohv also delivered more torque and 14-percent better mileage. It was no less durable nor reliable. And it had room enough to be greatly enlarged—as indeed it was. In a relatively light 1949-50 Series 62, it could produce 0-60 mph in around 13 seconds and an easy 100 mph.

Further proof of this V-8's prowess was provided by sportsman Briggs Cunningham, who entered a near-stock 1950 Cadillac in that year's Le Mans 24-Hour race in France. Driven by Sam and Miles Collier, it finished 10th overall, an achievement unmatched by any other luxury car. It tore down the Mulsanne Straight at around 120 mph and averaged 81.5 mph for the race. Cunningham himself drove a streamlined Cadillac-powered special that the French called *Le Monstre*. He went even faster than the Colliers, but lost top gear and finished right behind them.

This brilliant V-8 combined with best-in-class styling to put Cadillac firmly atop the luxury heap by 1950. Though the 331 would continue through '55, it would gain over 100 bhp in the interim.

Though Cadillac styling would deteriorate to chrome-laden glitter in the late '50s, its basic '48 design was good enough to remain popular—and thus largely intact—through 1953. As Mitchell once noted: "A traditional look is always preserved. If a grille is changed, the tail end is left alone; if a fin is changed, the grille is not monkeyed with."

And so it was: a new one-piece windshield and revamped grille for 1950, small auxiliary grilles under the headlamps for '51, a winged badge in that spot for '52, one-piece rear windows and suggestive "Dagmar" front bumper guards for '53. However, Cadillac gave up on fastbacks much earlier than sister GM makes, switching all of its 1950 coupes to notchback profiles with hardtop rooflines *a la* Coupe de Ville.

Models also didn't change much through '53. Still accounting for most sales, the 62 offered four-door sedan, hardtop coupe, Coupe de Ville, and convertible, all on the usual 126-inch wheelbase. Sixty Special remained a solitary super-luxury four-door on its own wheelbase, which was now 130 inches versus the 133 of 1942-48. The Series 75 again offered its customary array of limousines and long-wheelbase sedans on a 146.8-inch chassis. Cadillac also continued supplying chassis for various coach-

1952 Sixty Special four-door sedan

1953 Series Seventy-Five Fleetwood 8-passenger sedan

1953 Sixty Special four-door sedan

1953 Series Sixty-Two Coupe de Ville hardtop

1953 Series Sixty-Two convertible coupe

1954 Sixty Special Fleetwood four-door sedan

1954 Series Sixty-Two hardtop coupe

1954 Series Sixty-Two convertible coupe

1954 Series Seventy-Five Fleetwood 8-passenger sedan

1956 Series Sixty-Two Coupe de Ville hardtop

1957 Series Sixty-Two hardtop coupe

1957 Eldorado Brougham hardtop sedan

1957 Eldorado Seville hardtop coupe

1957 Eldorado Biarritz convertible coupe

builders, averaging about 2000 a year through 1959.

The "entry-level" Series 61 was still around in 1950, but its sedan and De Ville-inspired coupe were demoted to a 122-inch wheelbase (from 126 in the '40s). Manual shift was still standard here (and on 75s), but other Caddys now came with Hydra-Matic at no extra cost. The 61s still lacked chrome rocker moldings and had plainer interiors, but also lower prices (by about $575). But with record 1950 sales of 100,000-plus, Cadillac no longer needed a "price leader," so the 61 was cancelled after 1951, this time for good.

After observing its golden anniversary in 1952, Cadillac issued a flashy limited-edition convertible, the 1953 Series 62 Eldorado. Like that year's new Buick Skylark and Olds 98 Fiesta, it boasted features previewed on recent GM Motorama show cars: custom interior, special cut-down "Panoramic" wraparound windshield, a sporty "notched" beltline, and a metal lid instead of a canvas boot to cover the lowered top. A striking piece, the Eldorado was a preview of Cadillacs to come, but only 532 of the '53s were built, largely because price was a towering $7750.

Model-year '54 ushered in longer, lower, and wider Caddys with more power and an all-new GM C-body bearing the trendy wrapped windshield. Wheelbase lengthened to 129 inches on Series 62s and to 149.8 on 75s. The V-8 was boosted to 230 bhp, and power steering and windshield washers became standard linewide. Four-way power seat was a new option. Eldorado returned with standard gold-color trim and genuine wire wheels, but was much more like the standard 62 ragtop and thus far cheaper than the '53: $4738. Predictably, sales rose to 2150 for the model year. That improved to 3950 for '55, then rose 65 percent for '56, when Eldorados doubled to include a Seville hardtop coupe with the same $6556 base price as the ragtop, which was retitled Biarritz.

Eldorado became more-distinctive again after 1954, sprouting pointy "shark" fins above round taillights. Other models retained the small taillight-and-fin motif from prior years. Cadillac's basic '54 styling persisted through effective, if evolutionary, face-lifts for 1955 and '56. The latter year brought the division's first four-door hardtop, the Sedan de Ville, which immediately scored almost as many sales as the Coupe de Ville and standard 62 hardtop combined.

Division sales continued upward, reaching 140,777 for banner '55. But even that was a temporary plateau. Despite challenges from an all-new '56 Lincoln and revitalized '57 Imperial, Cadillac remained America's luxury sales leader by far. Combined Lincoln/Imperial volume never exceeded 40,000 cars a year in this era; at Cadillac, that was good quarterly output.

Horsepower seemed to climb right along with sales. For 1955 it reached 250 standard via higher compression and improved manifolding; Eldorado now boasted 270 bhp courtesy of dual four-barrel carburetors, optional for other models. For 1956, the milestone V-8 received the first of several enlargements, being bored to 365 cid. It now produced 285 bhp in standard models, 305 for Eldorado.

The ratings were 300/325 for 1957, when compression reached 10:1 and the line was again rebodied, emerging with blockier but still evolutionary styling inspired by the Orleans, Eldorado Brougham, and Park Avenue show cars of 1954-55. Reaching into the luxury stratosphere was a production Eldorado Brougham priced at a princely $13,074. One of the most-interesting '50s Cadillacs, this low-slung pillarless sedan on a "compact" 126-inch wheelbase featured center-opening doors and a brushed stainless-steel roof, the latter one of Harley Earl's favorite touches. Standard quad headlights were an industry first shared with that year's Nash.

The Brougham's most-intriguing mechanical feature was air suspension, the work of engineers Lester Milliken and Fred Cowin. Based on systems used for commercial vehicles since 1952, this employed an air "spring" at each wheel comprising a domed air chamber, rubber diaphragm, and pistons. Fed by a central air compressor, the domes continually adjusted for load and road conditions (via valves and solenoids) for a smooth, level ride. Cadillac's system differed from "air ride" options at other GM divisions in being "open" (taking in air from outside) rather than "closed." Unhappily, cost and complexity were high relative to benefits. The air domes leaked, and replacements were frequent, leading many owners to junk the system in favor of conventional coil springs. Following 1960, Cadillac and GM abandoned air suspension altogether.

After two years and 704 units, the Brougham was fully restyled, and assembly was farmed out to Pininfarina in Italy. Only 99 were built for '59, another 101 of the near-identical '60s. Though appearance was clean (and a preview of Cadillac's 1961 styling), these were larger (130-inch wheelbase) and heavier cars that weren't put together very well (bodies contained lots of lead filler). They're collector's items now, but restoring one is a chore.

Back to the volume Cadillacs, which were heavily face-lifted for 1958 in a manner typical of GM that year. The most-garish Caddys yet, they dripped with chrome and were far-less stylish than previous postwar models. Sales were poor, though a nationwide recession was probably more to blame than the styling, which was, after all, in vogue. At 121,778 units, model-year production was the lowest since 1954. Horsepower ratings, however, continued upward. The 365 V-8 was coaxed to 310 bhp on all but the Eldorado, where it was 335.

Forecasting the future, De Ville became a 62 subseries for '58, and pillared sedans were eliminated. The 62 line also gained a hardtop sedan with extended rear deck. All models were available with cruise control, high-pressure cooling system, two-speaker signal-seeking radio, and automatic parking brake release. A special show Eldorado introduced a "thinking" convertible top that raised itself and the side windows when a sensor detected raindrops; this gimmick allegedly saw limited production, though probably less than air suspension.

Another new GM C-body arrived for 1959, bringing more curvaceous Cadillac styling devised as a hurried reply to Chrysler's resurgent '57 Imperial. Hallmarks included huge windshields,

1957 Fleetwood Sixty Special hardtop sedan

1957 Series Seventy-Five limousine

1958 Series Sixty-Two Coupe de Ville hardtop

thin-section rooflines, slim pillars—and soaring fins of ridiculous proportions, ending in bullet taillamps. Offsetting these excesses were some worthy suspension changes, improved power steering, and a V-8 stroked to 390 cid. Predictably, horsepower rose again, to 345 on Eldorados; other models were up to 325.

De Ville now became a distinct series, offering hardtop sedans with flat-top four-window styling and a curvier six-window roofline, plus a hardtop coupe. The Series 62 duplicated these, and added a convertible. Also still pillarless (as it had been since '57) was the lush Sixty Special, now on a 130-inch wheelbase shared with other standard models including the line-topping Eldorado Seville, Biarritz, and Brougham.

Prices were generally higher for '59, with 62s at around $5000 and Eldos going for $7400 and up. Still, Cadillac built over 142,000 cars, a fair gain on 1958. Though not appreciated then, these Caddys are sought-after today as the epitome of '50s styling with their massive size, sparkling trim, and especially those overblown fins.

Cadillac displayed several two-seat idea cars in the '50s. First came the 1953 Le Mans, which looked much like the '54 Eldorado but on a trim 115-inch wheelbase. That same dimension was used on the following year's El Camino coupe and La Espada convertible, which previewed '55 styling. A restyled Le Mans was also shown at the '55 Motorama. Wildest of all was the 1959 Cyclone, a rocketlike machine with 104-inch wheelbase,

1959 Coupe de Ville hardtop

1959 Cyclone show car

all-independent suspension, unit construction, and a clear-plastic "bubble" top. The canopy was coated inside with vaporized silver to resist the sun's rays, and slid away as the door was opened. And those doors were sliding types, as on the late Kaiser-Darrin, though they worked electrically. Cyclone was a parting gift from GM design chief Harley Earl, who retired in 1958. His successor was longtime understudy Bill Mitchell, who would return Cadillac to more-dignified styling in the '60s.

Indeed, Cadillac immediately backed away from wretched excess with a more-restrained 1960 line bearing cleaner grilles and lowered fins. Offerings stayed the same, as did prices, ranging from $4892 for the Series 62 hardtop coupe to $9748 for the big Series 75 limousine. Mechanical specifications also stood pat. Cadillac had run ninth in model-year production for 1956-57, then dropped to 10th, where it would remain through 1964. Still, that was impressive going for a luxury make.

Carrying another new GM C-body, the '61s were the cleanest Cadillacs in years. This reflected the influence of Bill Mitchell, who favored a more-chiseled look and less chrome than Harley Earl. The grille was reduced to a modest grid, and wrapped windshields were abandoned (except on 75s), though Mitchell contrived to improve visibility. The Eldorado Seville and Brougham disappeared, while the Biarritz convertible was

1961 Coupe de Ville hardtop

1960 Fleetwood Sixty Special hardtop sedan

downgraded to the 325-bhp engine.

GM settled into a styling groove under Mitchell, so Cadillac's '62s were basically toned-down '61s. Highlights included still-lower fins, front-fender cornering lights as a new option, and backup/turn/stop lights combined behind a single white lens. Four-window sedans received more-orthodox rooflines but still included a pair of short-deck variants, now called Series 62 town sedan and De Ville Park Avenue. A new braking system with dual master cylinder and separate front and rear hydraulic lines appeared. Model-year output rose to nearly 161,000, up some 23,000 over '61.

The long-running Cadillac V-8 got its first major revision in 14 years for 1963. Cylinder size was unchanged, as were valves, rocker arms, heads, compression (still 10.5:1), and connecting rods. But everything else was different: lighter, stronger crankshaft; a stiffer block weighing 50 pounds less; accessories relocated to improve service access. While all this did little for performance, the revised 390 was smoother and quieter by far. And performance was already good. The typical '63 Cadillac could reach 115-120 mph, do 0-60 mph in 10 seconds, return about 14 miles per gallon, and was near-silent at high speed. In fact, for refinement, many testers held Cadillac superior to Rolls-Royce. Styling departed from recent practice. Fins were lower than ever, the grille bulkier, new outer body panels and side moldings created a more slab-sided effect, and a more-massive rear end carried long vertical tail/backup lights.

Prices rose only slightly for '63, so Cadillac remained an excellent value for the money. No-cost features expanded to include self-adjusting power brakes and remote-control door mirror. A six-way power seat became standard on Eldorado, and power windows were standard for all except Series 62 sedans and coupes. Even power vent windows were offered. So were vinyl roof coverings, a new option. Remarkably, a 62 still cost as little as $5026; the Eldorado Biarritz was only $6608. With all this, Cadillac set another model-year production record, topping 163,000.

Revisions were minor for 1964. Even lower tailfins created

1962 Series Sixty-Two convertible coupe

1963 Sedan de Ville four-window hardtop

1962 Sedan de Ville six-window hardtop

1963 Coupe de Ville hardtop

an unbroken beltline, accentuating length; grilles got a body-color horizontal divider bar; and taillamp housings were reshaped. A newly optional automatic heating/air-conditioning system maintained a set temperature regardless of outside conditions. It's been a Cadillac staple ever since. Perhaps more significantly, the 390 was enlarged to 429 cid, good for 340 bhp. Unit volume improved once more, this time to near 166,000.

Cadillac had a resounding 1965, producing close to 200,000 cars. But it was a great year in general for Detroit, so that volume was only good for 11th place. The mainstay Series 62 was renamed Calais, while Eldorado and Sixty Special officially became Fleetwoods, like the Series 75, bearing the requisite nameplates, wreath-and-crest medallions, broad rocker panel and rear-quarter brightwork, and rectangular-pattern rear appliques. A new Fleetwood Brougham sedan (actually a Sixty Special trim option) offered a vinyl roof with "Brougham" script on the rear pillars.

Another body change gave '65 Caddys a longer, lower silhouette, with fins planed absolutely flat, though a hint of them remained in a recontoured rear deck. Also new were a straight back bumper and vertical lamp clusters. Up front, headlight pairs switched from horizontal to vertical, making for an even wider grille. Curved side windows appeared, six-window hardtop sedans disappeared, and pillared sedans returned in Calais, De Ville and Sixty Special guise. The Special also reverted to its exclusive 133-inch wheelbase (last used from 1954 to 1958).

Despite an unchanged V-8, the slightly lighter '65 Caddys boasted the luxury field's best power-to-weight ratio. "Dual driving range" Turbo Hydra-Matic and full-perimeter frames (replacing the X-type used since '57) arrived except on 75s, and all models came with a new "sonically balanced" exhaust system. Amazingly, prices weren't too far above what they'd been in 1961.

Cadillac enjoyed its first 200,000-car year for calendar '66, breaking the barrier by exactly 5001 units. A mild facelift brought a new front bumper and grille, plus more smoothly integrated taillights. Perimeter frames now supported Series 75s, which were also fully rebodied for the first time since 1959. Variable-ratio power steering, which "speeded up" the more the wheel was turned from straight-ahead, was a new option along with carbon-cloth seat heating pads. The Fleetwood Brougham became a separate model, more luxuriously trimmed than the plain-roof Sixty Special and priced about $320 higher.

Arriving for 1967 was the most-significant Cadillac of the decade: an all-new Eldorado with front-wheel drive. Based on Oldsmobile's new 1966 Toronado, it was a daring concept for the luxury field, though with six years of careful planning and research behind it. Front drive gave it outstanding roadability; Bill Mitchell gave it magnificent styling.

It had originated in 1959 with the XP-727 program, which underwent several rethinks through early 1962. Management then settled on front-wheel drive, and further prototypes

1964 Series Seventy-Five Fleetwood limousine

1964 Series Sixty-Two hardtop coupe

1964 Sedan de Ville four-window hardtop

1965 Coupe de Ville hardtop

1965 Sixty-Special Fleetwood Brougham four-door sedan

1965 Calais hardtop coupe

1965 Series Seventy-Five Fleetwood Landau limousine

1965 Calais four-door sedan

1965 Fleetwood Eldorado convertible coupe

1966 Sixty Special Fleetwood Brougham four-door sedan

evolved with that in mind. For awhile, Cadillac considered calling it LaSalle, but ultimately chose Eldorado as a name with higher recognition. A clay model called XP-825, with razor-edge lines and formal roof treatment, was essentially the final production design.

Unlike Toronado, the '67 Eldorado was a very low-key announcement. This was typical of Cadillac, which used the one-year delay to improve on Oldsmobile's package. The Eldo thus rode better, yet handled at least as well despite the same basic suspension (torsion bars, A-arms, and telescopic shocks up front; a beam axle on semi-elliptic leaf springs and four shock absorbers—two horizontal, two vertical—in back). Two unique additions were self-leveling control and optional radially vented caliper front-disc brakes.

On its own relatively compact 120-inch wheelbase, the '67 Eldorado was announced at $6277 and targeted for 10 percent of Cadillac's total 1967 model-year production—about 20,000 units. The final figure was 17,930. For 1968-70, sales ran 23,000-28,000. A technological tour de force, it quickly established itself as the ultimate Cadillac. And unlike the old Brougham, it made money from day one.

Cadillac didn't forget its bread-and-butter "standards" for 1967, applying an extensive restyle marked by a front-end ensemble thrust forward at the top. New linewide features included printed mylar instrument-panel circuits, automatic level control (standard on all Fleetwoods), cruise control, and tilt steering wheel. Bolstered by the new Eldorado, also part of the Fleetwood series, Cadillac built precisely 200,000 cars for the model year.

The 1968 spotlight was on motive power: an all-new 472-cid V-8 with 375 bhp. Designed to meet the new government emissions standards that took effect that year, it was extensively tested in the laboratory, running the equivalent of 500,000 miles. Though not as fuel-efficient as the 429, the 472 could launch a Coupe de Ville from 0 to 100 mph in under 30 seconds.

Designwise, the '68 Eldorado gained side-marker lights (also newly required) plus larger taillights, combined turn signal/parking lamps in the front-fender caps, and a hood extended at the rear to conceal the windshield wipers. Standards also got the hidden wipers and side markers, plus a revised grille and a

1966 Series Seventy-Five Fleetwood limousine

1966 Coupe de Ville hardtop

1967 Series Seventy-Five Fleetwood 9-passenger sedan

1967 Coupe de Ville hardtop

1967 Sixty Special Fleetwood Brougham four-door sedan

1967 Fleetwood Eldorado hardtop coupe

1968 Sixty Special Fleetwood Brougham four-door sedan

1968 Fleetwood Eldorado hardtop coupe

trunklid reshaped for increased cargo space. Calais lost its pillared four-door sedan.

Cadillac built a record 266,798 cars for calendar '69, breezing past Chrysler and American Motors to grab ninth in the industry rankings. For the model year, though, it remained 11th at a little over 223,000, down almost 7000 units from '68.

The Eldorado was again little changed for 1969, save for exposed headlights. Standards, however, were fully restyled via squarer new bodyshells. Headlamps reverted to horizontal, while parking lights wrapped around to flank a higher grille, still prominently Vee'd. A somewhat dubious change was the elimination of front vent windows. Per Washington edict, no-cost equipment again expanded to include front-seat headrests, energy-absorbing steering column, ignition-key warning buzzer, and antitheft steering-column/transmission lock. Prices ran from just above $5400 for a Calais to well over $10,000 for the 75 limousine.

Eldorado got a new engine for 1970, and a badge reading "8.2 litres" to prove it. At 500 cubic inches, this was the world's largest production-car engine, developing 400 bhp and a monumental 550 pound-feet of torque. Other models retained the 375 horsepower 472. All 1970 Cadillacs boasted new integral steering knuckles, fiberglass-belted tires, and a radio antenna imbedded in the windshield.

Senior styling was touched up for 1970: a new grille with bright vertical accents over a cross-hatch background, horizontal bright trim on parking lights, winged crests instead of V's on De Ville and Calais hoods, and new taillamps. Eldorado sported a narrowed grille separate from the headlamps, plus slimmer taillamps. Production results were mixed. Though model-year volume rose to near 239,000 units, Cadillac again finished 10th, but calendar output dropped by over 100,000 cars for 1970, and the division fell back to 11th behind Chrysler and AMC. Still, in a generally quiet year for the industry, Cadillac out-produced Lincoln 3-1 and Imperial by no less than 15-1. "The Standard of the World" still reigned supreme as America's luxury favorite.

Cadillac stayed with its successful late-'60s lineup through 1976, though styling didn't change much after '71 and Calais sales were 6000-8000 annually. Forecasting the '80s was the

1968 Sedan de Ville hardtop

1969 Sixty Special Fleetwood Brougham four-door sedan

1968 De Ville convertible coupe

1969 Fleetwood Eldorado hardtop coupe

1968 Fleetwood Eldorado hardtop coupe

1970 Sedan de Ville hardtop

1969 Sedan de Ville hardtop

1970 Coupe de Ville hardtop

1969 Coupe de Ville hardtop

1970 De Ville convertible coupe

new compact Seville of 1975, the smallest Cadillac in 50 years, followed by a decisively downsized big-car range for 1977.

Along with its E-body Buick Riviera and Oldsmobile Toronado stablemates, the Eldorado became bulkier for 1971, though not drastically heavier. It would continue through 1978 with few changes apart from government-mandated safety and emissions equipment that, along with inflation, escalated prices each year. Though they accounted for upwards of 40,000 annual sales, these outsized cruisers were not svelte, good-handling cars like the 1967-70 models.

Arriving with the '71 redesign was the first front-drive Eldorado convertible, a body style not offered by its corporate cousins and the first open-air Eldo since 1966. By 1976, eroding ragtop sales and high attrition throughout Detroit rendered it the only factory-built convertible on the market. This prompted a special run of 2000 all-white "last convertibles" and a promise to build no more. Rabid opportunists bid prices to the skies in the hope of making a killing on the collector market with what looked like a gilt-edged investment. The division kept its word, but only for a while. As time would prove, the droptop's demise was only temporary, and the '76 Eldos were not Detroit's "last" convertibles—nor, by the mid-'80s, particularly worth keeping.

In what was a busy Cadillac year, 1971 also brought a smoother but larger new C-body for the standard line, with "fuselage" flanks and softer, more-massive contours. Calais remained the latter-day equivalent of the old Series 61, though it wasn't that much cheaper than the better-equipped De Ville. Perhaps because of this, sales declined to below 10,000 units by 1974, prompting Calais' cancellation for 1977. Only two- and four-door hardtops were listed in these years, with the two-door becoming a fixed-pillar style after '73.

The money-spinning De Ville was reduced to that same twosome after 1970. Its convertible was judged superfluous with the revived Eldorado ragtop; the pillared four-door was merely put on hold until 1977. Considering the history of the name, a pillared Coupe de Ville was a contradiction in terms and, possibly for that reason, proved less popular than the pillarless Sedan de Ville after 1973.

Though still low-volume specialty items, the premium Fleetwoods got a new GM D-body for '71, and thus fresh styling for the first time since 1966. The Sixty Special remained a four-door sedan on a unique 133-inch wheelbase, but there was only one version now. Called Fleetwood Sixty Special Brougham, it shared the Series 75's new roof styling with more distinctly separate side windows. It, too, would see little appearance change through 1976.

The main reason Cadillac styling evolved so slowly in this period is that engineering and design talent was engaged with the more-pressing concerns of the day: fuel economy, emissions, and occupant crash protection. As it was very difficult to reconcile those last two with the first, Cadillac's engineering emphasis fell on the emissions side with both of its V-8s. For example, exhaust-gas recirculation was added for 1973 to reduce oxides of nitrogen (NOx) emissions, while the air-injection pump and engine pulleys were altered to lessen noise.

Big-car sales slipped badly with the 1973-74 oil embargo. Cadillac was no exception, but it recovered smartly by 1975, when the Eldo's huge 500 V-8—by then down to a measly 190 bhp in SAE net measure—became standard for other Cadillacs save one.

And that one marked a big departure from tradition: a brand-new four-door sedan that was not only much smaller than anything else in the line, but also more expensive—outpriced only by the 75. It arrived in the spring of 1975 as the Seville, from Eldorado lineage. Cadillac had considered "Leland," to honor its founder, but decided most buyers were too young to make that connection. LaSalle (again!) was also in the running, but was ultimately rejected for the same reason—and because Cadillac's '30s companion make was still felt to have a "loser" image. But this Seville was no loser, being carefully planned for the one area of the luxury market that Cadillac had yet to exploit: the quality intermediate typified by Mercedes-Benz.

The Seville bowed to mixed reviews. Clean and trim on its 114.3-inch wheelbase, it compared favorably with German rivals for interior space. But styling struck some as unimaginative, and it was an open secret that this "baby Cadillac" was actually a heavily reengineered version of GM's workaday X-body compact, a serious deficit in the prestige class.

But the driving left little to criticize. Power came from a 350-cid V-8 built by Olds to Cadillac specifications, which included a new Bendix electronic-fuel-injection system exclusive to this

1970 Fleetwood Eldorado hardtop coupe

1971 Fleetwood Sixty Special Brougham four-door sedan

1971 Fleetwood Eldorado convertible coupe

1971 Fleetwood Eldorado coupe

1972 Fleetwood Eldorado convertible coupe

1973 Fleetwood Eldorado coupe

1973 Fleetwood Eldorado convertible coupe

1973 Coupe de Ville hardtop

1974 Fleetwood Sixty Special Brougham four-door sedan

1974 Fleetwood Eldorado convertible coupe

1975 Coupe de Ville

1976 Seville four-door sedan

1976 Fleetwood Sixty Special Brougham four-door sedan

1977 Sedan de Ville

1977 Coupe de Ville

1977 Fleetwood Eldorado coupe

1977 Seville four-door sedan

1978 Coupe de Ville d'Elegance

1978 Seville Elegante four-door sedan

model. The result was brisk, turbinelike performance, with typical 0-60 acceleration of 10-11 seconds and a top speed of over 110 mph. Seville weighed 1000 pounds less and was 27 inches shorter than a '75 De Ville, yet its ride was as cloudlike as buyers expected. And it was the best-handling Cadillac since the '67 Eldorado—much closer to M-B and BMW than those makers might have admitted. To be sure, it wouldn't glide over washboard surfaces with the disdain of a big Mercedes, but it didn't cost nearly so much either. Buyers responded with enthusiasm. Seville sales totalled 43,000 in its first full model year, 1976, a healthy 15 percent of division output.

Other Cadillacs were mostly unchanged for '76, but improving energy supplies and a reviving economy spurred sales across the board, and the division broke 300,000 units for the first time since '73. Things were even better for 1977-78 despite cancellation of Calais and the Eldo convertible: about 350,000 per year. A second energy crisis depressed 1979-80 calendar-year volume, but Cadillac kept its usual two-three percent of the total industry, the share it had claimed for many years.

Perhaps only Cadillac could so drastically change its cars while setting new sales records. Its 1977 standards were fresh from the ground up—8½ inches shorter and nearly 1000 pounds lighter on average than the '76s. Wheelbases were now 121.5 inches for De Ville/Fleetwood Brougham, 144.5 for the Fleetwood limo. They also had a cleaner, more-efficient new engine: a fuel-injected 425 V-8 with 180 bhp; a 195-bhp version was optional except for limos. Upmarket "D'Elegance" trim options continued for De Villes, along with new pseudo-convertible "Cabriolet" roof coverings.

The story was much the same for 1979, when Eldorado was downsized to lose 1100 pounds, 20 inches in length, and 12.3 inches in wheelbase (to 114). An unusual touch for an upmarket domestic was independent rear suspension, more compact than the previous beam axle, which made it possible to reduce wheelbase with little loss of passenger room. Options for all '79 Cadillacs included dual electric remote-control door mirrors, integrated 40-channel CB radio, and "Tripmaster" on-board travel computer. First offered on the '78 De Ville, Tripmaster provided digital readouts for average mpg and speed, miles to destination and estimated arrival time, plus engine rpm, coolant temperature, and electrical system voltage.

Attention for 1980 focused on a completely overhauled second-generation Seville. Its most controversial aspect was a sloped "trunkback" rear, executed by designer Wayne Cady but also a parting shot for GM styling chief Bill Mitchell. Reminiscent of certain 1950s Rolls-Royce bodies, it made for the most-distinctive Cadillac since the tailfinned '48s, though not everyone liked it. For cost reasons, Seville now shared the latest Eldorado chassis, thus shifting from rear to front drive and gaining the same all-independent suspension with automatic self-leveling. As had been true since 1978, a spiffy Elegante version, usually two-toned, was a higher-cost alternative to the standard article.

A telling feature of the '80 Seville was its standard engine: a "dieselized" version of the existing Oldsmobile 350 gasoline V-8, built in Lansing for use by other GM divisions. Cadillac had first offered this as a 1978 option for the Seville; it was optional across-the-board for '79. Smooth and quiet for a diesel, it gave Cadillac a direct reply to compression-ignition Mercedes models. More importantly, it helped the division contribute to GM's compliance with the corporate average fuel economy (CAFE) mandates that took effect with model-year 1978.

As time went on, however, it became clear that most people bought diesel Mercedes not for their economy or longevity but the snob appeal of their three-pointed star. And unhappily for Cadillac's image, the Olds engine suffered early and persistent reliability problems that GM never could seem to fix. By the mid-'80s, a glut of cheap gasoline would wash away memories of the second "energy crisis" that played havoc with the market in 1979-82. Once buyers began rushing back to big cars and big engines, Cadillac had no trouble abandoning diesels. Neither did most anyone else who'd been peddling them in the U.S.

Before this came a further blow to Cadillac's reputation for quality: the problematic "V-8-6-4" variable-displacement gasoline engine, a costly stopgap also prompted by CAFE. Displacing 6.0 liters (368 cid) and tuned for a modest 140 bhp, it arrived as a 1981 option for Seville and was made standard elsewhere.

At its heart was an electromechanical system, developed by the Eaton Corporation, that opened and closed the valves on two or four cylinders (hence the name) when signaled by an electronic module controlling the engine's digital fuel injection. The aim, of course, was improved economy, the cylinders shutting down under part-throttle, low-load conditions when you didn't need all eight, such as in medium-speed highway cruising. It was a good idea, but too complex to be reliable, and Cadillac paid a big price in both image and dollars once angry consumers began suing for redress. Few mourned when the V-8-6-4 was terminated after just one year (though it persisted in limos through '82).

A better bet was Buick's 125-bhp 4.1-liter V-6, newly optional across the '81 board (except limousines) and the first six in

1978 Eldorado Custom Biarritz Classic coupe

1979 Seville Elegante four-door sedan

1979 Eldorado coupe

1979 Eldorado coupe

1980 Seville Elegante four-door sedan

1981 Fleetwood Brougham coupe

1980 Eldorado Biarritz coupe

1981 Coupe de Ville

Cadillac history. Another new extra was an electronic "memory" power seat that assumed one of two preset positions at the touch of a button—shades of Mercury's mid-'50s "Seat-O-Matic."

There were a couple more surprises for '82. The biggest one was a Cadillac even smaller than the '75 Seville. Called Cimarron, it was just a high-zoot version of GM's new 101.2-inch wheelbase J-body subcompact, loaded to the gills but otherwise much like sister four-doors at every other GM division—except for price: initially $12,000. That looked very steep when a similar Chevy Cavalier or Pontiac J2000 could be had for half as much with comparable equipment. Cimarron did have a few J-car exclusives like leather upholstery and optional sliding-glass "Astroroof," but its humble origins were so obvious that nobody took it for a real Cadillac.

Cimarron was a frank embarrassment to Cadillac, caught in a flagrant act of "badge-engineering." Still, it was a logical development: needed to boost the division's fleet-average economy until its larger cars could be downsized again, and also to help stem a rising tide of upscale imports (typified by the BMW 3-Series) beginning to erode Cadillac sales. But the decision to field this gilded J came at the 11th hour, and it showed. The resulting criticism stung.

As a result, Cadillac immediately began distancing Cimarron from lesser Js, adding more standard features, ringing in a mild facelift and a lush "D'Oro" submodel for '83, making Chevy's 2.8 V-6 an option from mid-'85 and standard for '87 (replacing the

1981 Seville four-door sedan (diesel)

1981 Eldorado Biarritz coupe

1981 Eldorado coupe

1982 Cimarron four-door sedan

1982 Fleetwood Brougham Coupe d'Elegance

1982 Eldorado Touring Coupe

1982 Coupe de Ville

1982 Seville Elegante four-door sedan

1983 Eldorado Biarritz coupe

1983 Fleetwood Brougham coupe

1983 Seville Elegante four-door sedan

1984 Coupe de Ville

1984 Fleetwood Brougham Sedan d'Elegance

original weak and noisy 2.0-liter four), tinkering with suspension to impart a more "European" feel. But buyers always stayed away in droves, and Cadillac struggled to move an average 20,000 Cimarrons per year through 1986. Demand then slid to less than 15,000, and the model was belatedly killed after the 1988 model year.

Not that Cadillac cried much on its way to the bank, because total output rose steadily from 1982 through '85—from about 235,500 to nearly 335,000. Though Cimarron and troublesome engines may have blotted its enviable engineering record, Cadillac still dominated the luxury market.

Which brings us back to 1982's other surprise, yet another new engine. This was a small 4.1-liter (249-cid) V-8 with a cast-iron head atop a lightweight aluminum block, plus digital fuel injection. Dubbed "HT4100," it was standard for all '82s (save Cimarron and limos). Initial rated output was 125 bhp, same as for the Buick 4.1 V-6, which remained as an option for that year, then disappeared entirely. However, the V-8 actually produced a bit less torque than the V-6. It was certainly far less torquey than the old 425 or even the V-8-6-4, so the big Cadillacs were far less rapid.

Happier '82 news involved a Touring Coupe package for Eldorado with blackout moldings, fatter tires on aluminum wheels, and standard buckets-and-console interior with unique trim. Traditionalists still had their usual choices of two- and four-door De Villes and Fleetwoods in plain and D'Elegance trim, plus standard and Biarritz Eldorados and base and Elegante Sevilles—all available with fake wire wheels and convertible-look tops.

The big Caddys changed little over the next two years. HT4100 horsepower and torque rose by 10 each for '83, when Eldo and Seville offered a new acoustically tailored sound system developed by GM's Delco Electronics Division in concert with the Bose speaker people.

All was again mostly quiet for '84 except for the return of an open-air Eldorado (though all the "last convertible" nonsense had already been silenced). Actually, Buick had issued a ragtop Riviera back in '82, which made Cadillac seem rather slow to follow suit with its related Eldo. The likely reason was not the no-more-convertibles promise but the Riviera's slow sales, which must have made Cadillac managers hesitate.

But they finally did it, and they did it big. Offered only in uplevel Biarritz trim (a staple option for coupes since the late '70s), the reborn ragtop Eldo base-priced at $31,286—in raw dollars the costliest U.S. production convertible ever offered. But like the open Riviera, it would die after 1985. Price didn't kill it as much as the advent of a smaller new E-body and the luxury market's continuing desertion to imports.

Model-year '85 was pivotal for Cadillac, as its best-selling De Ville was downsized again and given front-wheel drive for the first time. Its new GM C-body was shared with that year's similarly revised Buick Electra and Olds Ninety-Eight. So was the 110.8-inch-wheelbase chassis with all-independent coil-spring/strut suspension and power rack-and-pinion steering. Dimensionally, this trimmest De Ville ever was two feet shorter and some 600 pounds lighter than its rear-drive predecessor. There was also a new Seventy-Five limousine on a 134.4-inch platform. The 4.1 V-8 was turned sideways to provide comparable cabin space within the smaller new package, but necessary manifolding changes brought horsepower back to 125 and torque to 190 pound-feet. Still, Cadillac could claim the world's only transverse V-8.

Even better, the new Coupe and Sedan de Ville and their lush Fleetwood counterparts quickly outsold the popular rear-drive series. Cadillac built over 197,000 for the first full model year, versus an annual 137,000-175,000 of the 1981-84 C-bodies.

1984 Seville four-door sedan (cabriolet roof)

1984 Seville four-door sedan

1984 Eldorado Biarritz convertible coupe

1985 Seville Elegante four-door sedan

1984 Eldorado Biarritz coupe

1985 Fleetwood Brougham four-door sedan

1984 Eldorado Touring Coupe

1985 Cimarron four-door sedan

But before buyers had given this approval, Cadillac had decided to retain some rear-drive models as a hedge. This proved a shrewd move once the market began its strong recovery from the doldrums of '82. Badged Fleetwood Brougham through 1986, then just plain Brougham, these cars continued with few changes through the end of the decade, garnering about 50,000 orders a year, each one pure gravy. We should note the passing of the big Brougham coupe and the diesel V-8 option after 1985. The latter wouldn't be missed. Nor was it really needed for CAFE, since the government had relaxed those requirements somewhat. Indeed, Cadillac saw fit to switch these cars to a 5.0-liter (307-cid) Olds V-8 with 140 bhp for the 1986 model year.

As planned, the Cadillac line's second wholesale downsizing since '77 was completed when a new-generation Eldorado and Seville appeared for 1986. Remaining twins under the skin, they shared the new 108-inch-wheelbase E-body platform (technically, Seville was still GM's K-body) of that year's Riviera and Olds Toronado. The Cadillacs, of course, had a 4.1 V-8 (again situated transversely rather than longitudinally) instead of the others' Buick V-6. Designers again managed similar interior space within smaller envelopes, here trimmed 16 inches in length and 350-plus pounds in curb weight, and Seville shed its controversial "bustle" for a conventional notchback profile.

1985 Sedan de Ville

1985 Fleetwood four-door sedan

1985 Coupe de Ville

1985 Fleetwood Seventy-Five limousine

1985 Eldorado coupe (diesel)

1986 Eldorado Biarritz coupe

1986 Sedan de Ville

Both had a raft of interesting new features: floor-mounted shifters (for the mandatory four-speed overdrive automatic transaxle), flush-mount "composite" headlamps, and more electronic gadgets than ever.

Sadly, these cars proved even bigger sales disasters than ill-conceived Cimarron. Seville volume, a strong 40,000 a year for 1984-85, dropped by half; Eldorado, which garnered an annual 76,000-plus orders in the same period, plunged by more than two-thirds.

The reasons were obvious enough: bland styling that was too close to that of GM's much cheaper N-body compacts (which began arriving the previous year) and dimensions that just weren't impressive enough for the cars' regular clientele. A 1987 *Newsweek* article on GM's declining fortunes graphically highlighted the design problem by picturing a Seville tail-to-tail with an N-body Olds Calais; it was tough to tell them apart. Worse, workmanship slipped badly due to equipment problems at the highly automated new Detroit-Hamtramck plant dedicated solely to E/K production. Typical of the woes: robots painting each other instead of cars.

There was nothing to do but soldier on, so the '87s received only minor suspension tweaks. For 1988, Cadillac tried to rectify its styling mistake via time-honored methods. Seville thus gained a "power dome" hood and a more "important" grille. Eldorado was similarly treated but also received new squared-up lower-body sheetmetal that stretched overall length by three inches at the rear—shades of the '50s.

Happier developments included first-time availability of an antilock brake system (ABS) and a more-potent engine. The former was the same laudable option announced for the 1986 De Ville/Fleetwood—though not readily available until '87. The 4.1 V-8 was enlarged to 4.5 liters (273 cid), and this plus a new two-stage intake manifold, larger throttle bores, and other changes lifted horsepower by 25 (to 155 total) and torque by 40 pound-feet (to 240). The '88 Eldorado and Seville were thus usefully quicker off the line than the 1986-87s—quite punchy, in fact—and ABS made panic stops shorter and more controlled. A "touring" suspension package was still available for those seeking crisper handling with little sacrifice in ride comfort.

The bread-winning De Ville and Fleetwood were improving, too. Besides a slight power increase, the '86 line offered new Touring Coupe and Sedan de Villes with firm suspension, husky blackwall tires on aluminum wheels, a front airdam with built-in foglights, plus less chrome outside and special trim inside. The '87s were lengthened 1.5 inches via extended rear fender caps and got a new grille, while the Sixty Special designation returned on a stretched, 115.8-inch-wheelbase Fleetwood four-door—a nod to the "executive car" market. The front-drive Seventy-Five was in its last year. As Chrysler had lately realized, factory-built limousines were unprofitable and thus better left to aftermarket converters, of which there were plenty. The main changes for '88 involved the more-potent 4.5 V-8 and standardization of several former options including the timed

Twilight Sentinel headlamp system, tilt/telescope steering wheel, illuminated entry system, and cruise control.

The De Ville and Fleetwood then finished out the '80s with a major revamping that produced a major sales gain. Again looking to the "longer-is-better" ploy, Cadillac stretched sedan models 8.8 inches in overall length, and increased wheelbase by three inches to 113.8. Coupes were 5.9 inches longer overall on an unchanged wheelbase. Styling on both body types was modified to suit the new dimensions, trunk space improved by some two cubic feet, and front fenders were rendered in a rust-free "nylon composite alloy" to save a little weight. Offerings also expanded with the return of a two-door Fleetwood after a two-year hiatus. Also returning (and again recalling the '50s) were rear fender skirts on the Fleetwoods, which again included a Sixty Special that actually lost two inches of wheelbase.

Several new linewide options also appeared for '89, including a supplemental air bag housed in the steering-wheel hub, "ElectriClear" heated windshield (to match the now-standard rear-window defroster), and GM's clever new "PASS-Key" theft-deterrent system. The powertrain was unchanged, but so was performance, as weight increases averaged only 100 pounds despite the added inches.

Those inches translated directly into higher sales, and total De Ville/Fleetwood production jumped by nearly 26,000 units—over 17 percent—to nearly 179,000 for the model year. The 1990s weren't greatly changed, but performance benefited by a switch from single-point to multipoint fuel injection that lifted the 4.5 V-8 from 155 to 180 bhp and improved torque by five pound-feet to 245 total. Safety-conscious customers applauded a newly standard driver-side air bag on all models, plus no-cost ABS on Fleetwoods. Series sales continued strong despite the start of a deep new recession, falling by only some 2300 units.

The 1990 Seville and Eldorado also carried the more-potent V-8, which was welcome, because both were becoming decidedly sporty. Still seeking to beat back imported sports sedans, Cadillac offered a limited-edition Seville Touring Sedan package in late '88, then made it a full-fledged option for 1989. Its chief attractions were a quieter monochrome exterior, beefy tires on handsome alloy rims, Touring Suspension, and a shorter final-drive for quicker acceleration.

The STS proved popular enough to rate separate-model status for 1990, when both Seville and Eldorado received a minor

1986 De Ville Touring Sedan

1986 De Ville Touring Coupe

1986 Eldorado coupe

1986 Seville Elegante four-door sedan

1987 Cimarron four-door sedan

1987 Presidential Limousine

1987 Allanté two-passenger convertible coupe

1987 Seville four-door sedan

1987 Eldorado coupe

facelift, standard driver-side air bag and some miscellaneous no-cost extras. The STS also came with ABS now. Sales were better than they'd been a few years earlier, but still not what Cadillac wanted. Eldorado volume dropped from near 31,000 for '89 to about 22,000 for 1990. Seville, however, more than made up for this loss, soaring better than 40 percent from 23,000 to 33,000.

Cadillac's most ambitious car of the '80s—certainly its most publicized—was the Allanté, a sharp two-seat convertible aimed squarely at the big-bucks Mercedes 560SL. The first two-seat Caddy since 1941, it bowed with great fanfare for 1987 on a front-drive Eldorado chassis shortened to a 99.4-inch wheelbase. Power initially came from a tuned 4.1 V-8 with multi-point (instead of single- or dual-point) injection, roller valve lifters, high-flow cylinder heads, and tuned intake manifold, good for 170 bhp. Italy's renowned Pininfarina was contracted for the styling and to build the bodywork—more snob appeal that way. Modified Eldo understructures were flown in special 747 jets to a new PF plant set up in Turin especially for Allanté production; fully trimmed shells (galvanized unit hulls with aluminum hood and trunklid) were then air-shipped back to Detroit-Hamtramck for drivetrain installation and final assembly. Standard equipment included a lift-off hardtop to supplement the manual soft top. A cellular telephone was the lone option.

Though a pleasant, capable tourer and an entirely new breed of Cadillac, the Allanté failed to make the hoped-for impression. Cadillac predicted calendar-'87 sales of 4000 units, but moved only 1651 (of 3363 built); deliveries for the first full production year totaled just 3065 versus a planned 7000. Model-year production was just 2569. The results: an embarrassing pile-up of unsold cars, hefty rebates to clear it—and a further blow to Cadillac prestige. In fact, trade weekly *Automotive News* named Allanté its 1987 "Flop of the Year." Division chief John O. Grettenberger dismissed that dubious honor—and wide coverage of the car's slow start—as "just the latest round of GM bashing."

Still, for what it was, Allanté was judged too expensive: $54,000 at announcement, $56,500 for the little-changed '88. And it depreciated by a third the minute it left a showroom, whereas a Mercedes SL actually went up in value. An assortment of niggling troubles—wind and water leaks, squeaks and rattles, horns that didn't work, and heaters that worked too well—hardly helped matters.

Cadillac scrambled, installing its bigger 4.5 V-8 for 1989, then tuning for a smashing 200 bhp and 270 pound-feet. Alas, that and a shorter final drive sufficiently lowered EPA mileage to incur a $650 Gas Guzzler penalty, which upped actual delivered price to $57,183. But 0-60 acceleration dropped from 10 seconds to 8.5 or less, and Cadillac kept things safe at every speed with new speed-sensitive power steering, bigger wheels and tires, and three-mode "speed-dependent damping" (auto-adjusting shock absorbers). Other improvements included comfier seats, a revised top mechanism (always manual), and PASS-Key anti-theft protection. Model-year production rose from 2569 to 3298, which was encouraging. But Allanté sales were now being propped up by a "guaranteed resale" scheme pegged to the SL's higher residual values; Cadillac promised to pay the difference if an Allanté owner traded for another new Cadillac.

Having fumbled its original mission as division flagship, Allanté got a new role for 1990: technology showcase. High-tech it had. The big news was a standard traction-control system—a first for a front-drive car—plus a revised "Speed Sensitive Suspension" (SSS) that stayed in "soft" mode up to 40 mph (instead of 25) for a smoother low-speed ride; as before, it then selected "normal," going into "firm" only above 60 mph. "Firm" also kicked in during hard acceleration, braking, or cornering.

1988 Cimarron four-door sedan

1988 Fleetwood d'Elegance four-door sedan

1988 Allanté two-passenger convertible coupe

1988 Fleetwood Sixty Special four-door sedan

1988 Fleetwood Brougham four-door sedan

1989 Coupe de Ville

1988 Seville Touring Sedan (STS)

1989 Fleetwood four-door sedan

1989 Allanté two-passenger convertible coupe

1989 Seville Touring Sedan (STS)

1990 Eldorado Touring Coupe (ETC)

1989 Eldorado coupe

1990 Coupe de Ville

A no-cost driver-side airbag served safety, and a compact disc player lengthened the standard-equipment list.

Straining to keep the price attractive, Cadillac offered a 1990 Allanté *sans* hardtop for $51,500, $6313 below the "full" version, which was hiked to $57,813. Yet despite the arrival of new-design Mercedes SLs starting in the mid-$70,000s, Allanté sales only got worse, model-year output easing to 3101.

Allanté held on for three more seasons. Like some other GM cars that had been put to death too soon, the last one was the best. For one thing, the '93 packed Cadillac's new all-aluminum, dual-overhead-cam "Northstar" V-8 with 4.6 liters and a resounding 295 bhp. Also on hand were more-sophisticated traction control and a faster-acting "Road Sensing Suspension" (RSS). But by this point, a brilliant new Seville and Eldorado had done much to polish Cadillac's image, and Allanté was no longer needed to prove that "Standard of the World" still meant something. For the benefit of collectors—and make no mistake: Allantés *will* be collected—model-year volumes were 2500 for '91, just 1931 for '92, and 4670 for swan-song '93.

Meantime, other Cadillacs were doing quite nicely, both technically and commercially. Though the division lost about 45,000 calendar-year sales between 1990 and '91, demand then stabilized at around 214,000 through mid-decade (save for 1993's modest 10,000-unit dip). That was an admirable showing given GM's numerous troubles of the day, not to mention continued aggressive competition from Lincoln. On that score, Cadillac remained comfortably ahead of its perennial rival, though Lincoln narrowed Cadillac's lead down to 30,500 units in 1993 despite offering fewer models.

But Cadillac had more to worry about than just Lincoln. European luxury cars had not only multiplied, but were selling better than ever to the younger, affluent "baby boom" generation that still mostly ignored Cadillac. Then, too, the Japanese had lately weighed in with upscale coupes and sedans under the Acura, Infiniti, and Lexus banners. All these competitors were technically sophisticated, and most were outstanding to drive. To protect its position as the luxury leader, Cadillac had to respond—and fast.

Cadillac did, starting with an upsized iron-head V-8 for 1991. Now at 4.9 liters (300 cid), this engine was newly standard for all models except Allanté and the big old Brougham. Horsepower stood at 200, and newly integrated electronic transmission controls insured smooth, efficient delivery. That same year, ABS went from optional to standard status for De Ville, Eldorado, and the base Seville. The De Ville/Fleetwood line was also lightly face-lifted, mainly by a new grille and more-prominent hood bulge.

With one eye on the imports, Cadillac revived the De Ville Touring Sedan for 1991 after a three-year absence. Priced at around $35,200, it stood apart from sister De Villes with a subdued "monochromatic" exterior, stout 16-inch alloy wheels shod with blackwall performance tires, shorter final gearing for better pickup, thicker stabilizer bars for tighter handling, and posh wood-and-leather interior.

Taking even closer aim at the imports were the all-new 1992 Eldorado and Seville. Both were smooth and curvy, clean and elegant, a refreshing break with their recent boxy past. Styling, however, was no longer so similar between the two, and there were greater differences elsewhere as well. For example, Seville now strode its own 111-inch wheelbase, while the Eldo stuck to a 108-inch span. Both models grew some 12 inches longer and 2.5 inches wider, but the new Seville was taut, purposeful, even bold for a Cadillac—enough to make the Eldo seem cautious to some eyes.

Prices opened some eyes. The Eldo now started at $32,000, while the Seville was up in $35,000-$38,000 territory. Then again, inflation had taken a toll, and both new models were really fine values against comparable imports. As before, the more-enthusiastic buyer opted for the Seville Touring Sedan or an Eldorado with extra-cost Touring Coupe package—which made an "ETC." Either choice meant firm suspension, wider tires on 16-inch wheels, less exterior chrome, and a more driver-oriented cabin with console, front buckets, and analog instead of electronic digi-graphic instruments.

The STS and ETC became more exciting for '93, as the pushrod 4.9 V-8 gave way to the sterling all-aluminum Northstar. As in the final Allantés, this 32-valver packed a 295-bhp punch that knocked 0-60 times down to 7.5 seconds or so in *Consumer Guide*® tests—more than a second quicker than before. Both models also gained speed-sensitive power steering and optional Road Sensing Suspension. Arriving for the base Eldo was a $3000 Sport Coupe package with a special 270-bhp Northstar tuned for 10 extra pound-feet (300 versus 290) at lower rpm—all the better for low-speed lugging power. An alternative new Sport Appearance option offered ETC-style looks and interior for just $875. All '93 Eldos and Sevilles benefited from standard passenger airbags, minor rear-suspension tweaks, and improved traction control that could throttle back on engine power as well as apply the brakes to keep you on the straight and narrow.

Eldorado's Sport Coupe package was dropped for '94, but the Touring Coupe became a separate model, the base Seville got the high-torque Northstar to become the SLS ("Seville Luxury Sedan"), and RSS was made standard for ETC and STS. For '95, both versions of the Northstar gained five horsepower, and there were subtle styling changes for all Eldos and Sevilles, including a body-color grille for ETC (thus matching the four-door STS). Typical of Cadillac was a new standard feature: headlamps that switched on automatically with the wipers.

In all, the new "personal" Cadillacs were everything expected of the marque—and more. Fittingly, they sold well. In fact, both almost doubled their model-year production from '91 to '92, the Eldorado exceeding 31,000, the Seville reaching almost 44,000. The '93s skidded to about 21,500 and 37,240, respectively, doubtless due to higher sticker prices reflecting the costlier Northstar engines. But 1994 brought a modest recovery, Seville climbing back to nearly 47,000 and Eldo to nearly 25,000. Though such numbers weren't great compared to early-'80s

1991 Brougham four-door sedan

1991 Fleetwood Sixty Special four-door sedan

1991 Allanté two-passenger convertible coupe

1991 Seville Touring Sedan (STS)

1991 Eldorado coupe

1992 Eldorado Touring Coupe (ETC)

1992 Sedan de Ville

1992 Fleetwood coupe

1992 Brougham four-door sedan

1993 Sedan de Ville

sales, they were a darn sight better than late-'80s volume. Just as important, these cars proved that at least some Cadillacs could set an American standard for an automotive world now vastly and forever changed.

The big rear-drive Brougham sedan hardly changed at all through 1992. As a late-'70s holdover it was now quite an anachronism, heroically overdecorated and obviously underdamped. But Cadillac was loath to let it go because some buyers wouldn't have a front-drive car—and because the Brougham made more money per sale than other Cadillacs. Besides, it was the longest car in American production, as the division was proud to advertise.

An old design long since paid for allowed Cadillac to keep updating the Brougham without eating into profits. Accordingly, the 1990 model gained standard antilock brakes while answering requests for more power with a newly optional 5.7-liter V-8, the biggest engine for this car in years. It came from Chevy and required an extra-cost trailering package, but its healthy 175 bhp was welcomed by "stretch limo" converters. Base powerplants switched for '91, going from a 140-bhp Olds 307 (last descendant of the fabled '49 "Rocket") to Chevy's evergreen 305, now up to 170 horsepower. At the same time, the 5.7 was pushed to 185 bhp and made a freestanding option. No other major changes occurred—except for a worrisome 60-percent sales plunge from nearly 34,000 for 1990 to just under 14,000 for '92.

But Cadillac was still devoted to "traditional" cars, and proved it by launching a big new Fleetwood for '93. This was basically a rebodied Brougham *a la* the '91 Chevy Caprice and Buick's reborn Roadmaster, though the Brougham name lived on for a spiffy interior-trim option. Styling remained "formal" but curvier and more contemporary, with plenty of applied trim and the usual expansive eggcrate face. Overall length stretched 4.1 inches to 225, but wheelbase was unchanged. Curb weight rose only 90 pounds despite the extra sheetmetal and added standards like the "Airbank"—dual airbags wide enough to protect all three occupants of the still-standard front bench seat. A plastic fuel tank helped minimize weight gain, while newly standard traction control helped drivers stay safely on course in foul weather.

The 5.7 was also standard for the '93 Fleetwood, but '94 brought even better performance with adoption of the new 260-bhp version of Chevrolet's LT1 5.7, with sequential multipoint fuel injection (instead of single-point). Electronic transmission control was also added. Only detail changes occurred for '95.

For so much opulence, the new-wave Fleetwood was reasonably priced in the mid-$30,000 area, and thus quite a bargain against comparably sized luxury imports. Buyers responded, and 1993 model-year production almost doubled to nearly 32,000 units. The '94s found fewer takers (just over 27,000), and calendar-year output was back to Brougham levels by 1995 at around 13,400 (off 7000 from calendar '94). But the sales issue was soon rendered moot, as GM dropped all of its rear-drive cars after 1996 so its Texas factory could build more SUVs. That prompts one to wonder whether the final Fleetwoods will be scooped up by collectors someday as the last big Cadillacs of the grand old school. Stranger things have happened.

There was nothing strange about the mainstay front-drive Cadillacs of this period, which evolved through two distinct phases. The first ended the familiar square-rigged series after 1993 with no further changes of consequence. Among lesser but laudable improvements were standard traction control for '92 Fleetwoods and the De Ville Touring Sedan, followed by speed-sensitive steering and suspension for all '93s. When the Fleetwood name moved to the big rear-drive car, the front-drive Fleetwood coupe was dropped, leaving the Sixty Special sedan

1993 Allanté two-passenger convertible coupe

1993 Fleetwood four-door sedan

1993 Eldorado Touring Coupe (ETC)

1994 Seville Touring Sedan (STS)

1994 De Ville Concours four-door sedan

1994 Eldorado Touring Coupe (ETC)

1994 Fleetwood four-door sedan

1995 Sedan de Ville

1995 Eldorado coupe

1995 Seville Touring Sedan (STS)

as the lone uplevel '93.

The Special disappeared the next year, as did the Coupe de Ville, thus ending those once-proud model names. But the Sedan de Ville returned with a thorough redesign, and there was a new Concours (borrowing an old Chevy name) to replace the De Ville Touring Sedan. Motive power was the main difference. Sedan de Ville used the 200-bhp pushrod 4.9 V-8, Concours the 270-bhp twincam Northstar. Both looked like slightly smaller versions of the '93 Fleetwood, so few would have guessed they were built on a new K-Special version of the Seville platform. Wheelbase grew 2.8 inches to 113.8 (to match the previous De Ville sedan stretch) and overall length extended 3.4 inches to 209.7, thus increasing passenger and parcel space. Styling had bit more "crease in the pants" than Fleetwood, but was conservatively handsome except for rather chubby rear flanks (slim vertical taillamps didn't help).

Predictably, the new De Ville/Concours were even more impressive than their predecessors: smooth, quiet performers with noticeably less engine and road noise. There was also new reassurance in a standard "Airbank" system, plus the usual arm-long list of comfort and convenience goodies. The Concours proved a virtual hot rod, *Consumer Guide*® clocking 0-60 at a very swift 6.8 seconds, and its standard traction control and Road Sensing Suspension struck a happy balance between Euro-style handling and American-style ride. As ever, Sedan de Ville aimed at older, less-energetic drivers, but was hardly the barge the Fleetwood was. Either model used fair amounts of premium gas, but that still didn't concern most Cadillac buyers. Amazingly, De Ville's base price remained unchanged for '94 at $32,990; the Concours started little higher, a reasonable $36,950.

With all this, many felt Cadillac had worked minor miracles with the De Ville/Concours, so the division was doubtless dismayed to see sales go down instead of up. The '94 loss wasn't huge—about 10,000 units for the model year to just over 120,000—but calendar-year output dropped 20,000 units between '94 and '95 to around 111,000.

And to GM's undoubted frustration, the downward trend continued into the new millennium, with sales and production declining most every year through 2001. In a way, this was curious. The '92 Seville and Eldorado and '94 De Ville represented solid technical and design progress, and Cadillac was planning bold new initiatives intended to further defend against unprecedented competition, chiefly from foreign makes but also a suddenly and surprisingly resurgent Lincoln. Yet somehow, Cadillac couldn't put together a winning formula.

There were several problems, starting with a stale image. Journalists by now liked to quip that Cadillac buyers were typically "somewhere between 60 and death," meaning the make wasn't appealing to the younger upscale trendsetters who pre-

1995 Fleetwood four-door sedan

1996 Seville Luxury Sedan (SLS)

1996 Eldorado coupe

1996 De Ville four-door sedan

1996 Seville Touring Sedan (STS)

1996 Fleetwood four-door sedan

1997 Eldorado Touring Coupe (ETC)

1997 Seville Touring Sedan (STS)

1997 De Ville four-door sedan

1998 Seville Touring Sedan (STS)

1999 Catera four-door sedan

ferred BMWs, Mercedes, and Toyota's upstart Lexuses for their superior workmanship, cachet, and performance. And once customers are lost, they're awfully hard to win back. GM compounded this problem with "brand management," attempting to win sales more by clever marketing than imaginative design or superior quality. Though Cadillac did pioneer several praiseworthy innovations in the late '90s and began exploring new markets, the efforts were often too little, too late. As a result, the division's calendar-year sales plunged nearly 23 percent between 1995 and '99, and were down to around 130,500 by 2001. After decades as America's luxury leader, Cadillac was a mere also-ran.

A perfect symbol of Cadillac's plight was Eldorado, which languished with no further change of consequence before being summarily dropped after the 2002 model run. To be sure, demand for big luxury coupes had been withering since the early '90s—enough to claim Lincoln's Mark VIII after 1998—yet the Eldorado returned each year as one of the old-fogey cars that Cadillac said it wanted to get away from. What Cadillac really wanted was to attract younger buyers without turning off its older customers, but the company ended up satisfying neither group entirely.

Still, Eldorado was hardly ignored in its later years. Model-year '96, for example, introduced optional "Rainsense" wipers that automatically activated when sensors detected moisture on the windshield (recalling a certain 1958 Eldo show car). For '97, the sporty ETC added a new Continuously Variable Road Sensing Suspension (CVRSS), which largely involved shock absorbers that automatically adjusted firmness according to input from sensors on road speed, wheel movement, steering angle and so forth. The '98 ETC introduced "Stabilitrak," Cadillac's new antiskid system. Also standard for that year's Seville STS and later standard or optional for other front-drive Cadillacs, Stabilitrak took the CVRSS idea a step further, using sensor input to brake either or both front wheels to keep the car on its intended path—a great boon for "dynamic" safety. Curiously, though, Eldorado would never get the "passive" safety benefit of front side airbags like other Caddys. However, the '99s did share an exclusive with Seville in optional "active" power front seats. These provided a gentle message via small powered rollers in the cushion and backrest, plus a series of air bladders that periodically inflated and deflated. The idea was to relieve pressure points that could induce body aches on long trips, and it worked tolerably well.

But creature comforts and moderate year-to-year price changes couldn't halt Eldorado's steady slide toward oblivion. By 2002, volume was only about a third of what it was a decade before—under 10,500 units. Approximately 1600 were Eldorado Collector Series (ECS) cars, which had the usual "Collector Edition" badges and extra trim, plus an exhaust system tuned to mimic the original 1953 Eldorado. With Eldorado's passing went a hallowed Cadillac name that's not likely to be revived, the division having decided that future models will have "letter" names like ETC or, as on post-1999 base Eldorados, ESC (Eldorado Sport Coupe).

Seville, the "international" Cadillac, retained its new-for-'92 design only through 1997, when the Continuously Variable Road Sensing Suspension became standard for the base SLS as well as the sporty STS. The latter was further upgraded for '97 with standard Stabilitrak, and both Sevilles offered GM's new OnStar communications system as a dealer-installed option. Using a cellular phone link to a satellite-based navigation system and a 24-hour staffed operations center, OnStar could provide "live" route and location assistance, track a stolen car, even remotely open the doors should you lock yourself out. The system would also automatically summon emergency help if the airbags deployed in an accident. Most people found OnStar much easier to use than the video-type in-car navigation systems then coming into vogue, and its emergency services were unique. OnStar eventually became a semi-independent company whose basic hardware and services, both steadily improved, would spread to other GM divisions and even a few other automakers. But Cadillac offered it first on '97 Sevilles, De Villes, and Eldorados.

Seville base prices were trimmed $2500-$3000 for '97 in an effort to spark sales, but model-year production disappointed at just over 45,000. Even more disappointing, output fell nearly 11,000 units for '98 despite a full redesign. It should have gone up. Notwithstanding cautiously evolutionary styling and carryover powertrains, the '98 was the best Seville yet. Built on a new G-car platform, the stiffest in GM history, it gained 1.2 inches in wheelbase, yet stood 3.1 inches shorter overall. The result was a roomier yet tighter-handling Seville that ceded little, if anything, to comparable import rivals in performance, dynamic ability, ride, comfort, and luxury.

Audaciously, Cadillac earmarked 20 percent of Seville production for a special model to be sold in Europe, a bid to establish itself as a true "world-class" competitor; there was even a right-hand-drive STS for Britain. Yet despite being the most un-American Cadillac ever, the Seville bombed in Europe, judged unacceptably big and thirsty for local conditions and lacking the build quality of BMW and Mercedes. Said Britain's *CAR* magazine in November 2001: "The STS is massive, brash and worringly vague to drive. [Its] V-8 engine is nice, but the rest of the experience feels like a bad copy of a Lexus LS... Owning this car is a sign of terminally bad taste."

Back home, Seville volume recovered to near 42,500 for 1999, but shrank by nearly 8000 units in 2000 before thudding to just over 28,000 for '01. And more's the pity. Judged on its own merits, this Seville was a darn good car. It just wasn't quite as good as Cadillac needed it to be.

And so it would remain through end-of-the-line 2004, despite modest yearly sticker price hikes (all but irrelevant in a market long addicted to rebates) and the addition of a few new features. Notable among the latter was the '03 debut of GM's Magnetic Ride Control shock absorbers for the STS model's Road-Sensing Suspension. An innovation shared with that year's 50th Anniversary Chevrolet Corvette, these dampers were filled with a special "magnetorheological" fluid that could almost instantly change viscosity—and thus firmness—when acted on by an electrical current. MRC was highly effective, but did nothing to change the less-than-electric image of the STS, let alone the unsporting SLS model. Thus, to Cadillac's undoubted dismay, Seville sales continued to wither each year, with model-year production finally reduced to just 6514 units.

Another *fin de siecle* disappointment was the Catera. It, too, aimed at giving Cadillac international credibility, only in the even more-competitive "near luxury" class. The approach was the opposite of the G-based Seville's, Catera being basically a upscale "Cadillac-ized" version of the 1995-vintage Opel Omega from GM's German subsidiary. It was even built in Germany, allowing Cadillac to claim genuine European breeding. And indeed, Catera seemed to have the right stuff for a modern sports sedan: trim size, a smooth 3.0-liter twincam V-6, all-independent suspension, tasteful design, and full-house equipment. It even dared depart from other contemporary Caddys in being rear-wheel drive. Trouble was, Catera was rather heavier than rivals BMW 3-Series and Mercedes C-Class, while being relatively short on power. To make matters worse, it didn't offer a manual transmission as a "proper" Eurosedan should. Initial advertising strained at youth appeal, using a cartoon duck and the tag line "Catera is the Cadillac that zigs," but critics were

1999 Eldorado Touring Coupe (ETC)

1999 Seville Touring Sedan (STS)

2000 DeVille DHS four-door sedan

2000 DeVille DHS four-door sedan

2000 Catera Sport four-door sedan

2001 DeVille DTS four-door sedan

2002 Escalade four-door wagon

2002 Seville STS four-door sedan

quick to dismiss the campaign as ineffective and, given Cadillac's aims, rather juvenile. Later ads downplayed the duck, and a year-2000 update ushered in a more-serious Catera Sport model with larger wheels and tires, rear spoiler, firmer suspension and, belatedly, standard front side airbags. But despite this, plus a couple of interim price cuts and attractive lease deals, Catera never really caught on. Sales peaked in '98 at over 30,000, dropped below 15,000 the following model year, then limped along in the 12,000-16,000 area through 2001. Catera then vanished in favor of a new home-grown entry-level Cadillac that we'll discuss shortly.

The full-size DeVille was Cadillac's one real success in the late '90s, scoring over 100,000 sales for most every model year through 1999. Thoughtful yearly improvements played a part. Optional OnStar arrived for '97, when a discreet facelift omitted rear fender skirts, allowing a wider rear track for more-stable handling. Also new that season was a luxury D'Elegance version priced between the base sedan and the sporty Concours. For '98, the Concours' standard Stabilitrak was made optional for other DeVilles. A standard tip computer and optional massaging front seats were added for '99.

DeVille was then redesigned for 2000 on the Seville's capable G-car platform, yet sales dropped below 100,000 in another reversal that was hard to understand. For one thing, the new DeVille not only looked trimmer, it was, giving up two inches in width and length but adding 1.5 inches in wheelbase, again for more interior space. Then too, prices were surprisingly little-changed for the three models. D'Elegance was retitled DHS (for "DeVille High-luxury Sedan"), while Concours became the DTS ("DeVille Touring Sedan"). All boasted standard OnStar, front side airbags, newly available rear torso side airbags, plus ever-pleasing Northstar power. Also on hand were LED taillamps that lit up faster than traditional incandescent bulbs—a change Cadillac said might preclude a rear-end crunch. The DHS was a near limousine. Rear passengers were coddled with heated seats, power lumbar adjustment, rear and side sunshades, and illuminated vanity mirrors. High-tech options abounded for DHS and DTS, including a touch-screen navigation system, an ultrasonic warning system to signal the presence of obstacles when backing up, and an industry first called Night Vision. The last, employing infrared technology proven in the Persian Gulf War, used a grille-mounted camera to detect the heat signatures of objects beyond headlight range, which were projected as "virtual" images onto the windshield near driver eye level. No other car offered anything like it, and though not popular at a hefty $2000, Night Vision was the type of technical innovation that had served Cadillac so well in the '50s and '60s.

Yet all this gizmology tended to obscure the virtues of a mighty impressive big luxury sedan. Even the base DeVille offered adroitly balanced ride and handling, and *Motor Trend* praised the DTS as "a technological *tour de force*, an efficient, elegant, and uniquely American approach to fine motoring and a true Cadillac."

But the public either didn't get that message or didn't care, because DeVille lost favor as time passed just like Seville. A dearth of change didn't help. The line—though not the basic design—bowed out after '05 and ending model-year production of 59,750, a huge letdown from late-'90s volume.

By this point, though, Cadillac had charted a new course, yet another effort to regain its former greatness. The master plan was slow to gel, but it eventually came to include a new design signature called "Art & Science" for its hard, angular, somewhat disjointed lines that were meant to look as if they'd come from a computer, not a stylist's hand.

Meantime, Cadillac's image got an unexpected boost from, of all things, a truck, the nameplate's first. This was the 1999 Escalade, an upscale clone of the already posh Yukon Denali sport-utility wagon at sister-division GMC. Cadillac execs were publicly baffled but privately delighted as big-name sports heroes, bad-boy recording artists and even some movie stars fast made the "'Slade" their ride of choice, often customized with gold trim and outsized wheels (typically 20-inchers at first, soon dubbed "dubs" in urban street lingo). Despite such debatable alterations—or maybe because of them—the Escalade made it cool again to be seen in a Caddy, and a planned 2001 Art & Science facelift only stoked sales. Responding for '02, Cadillac issued a similarly styled Escalade EXT, a full-bling take on Chevrolet's new multipurpose Avalanche four-door SUV/pickup. Following for '03 was a companion ESV wagon derived from the Chevy Suburban/GMC Yukon XL. This trio not only upped Cadillac "buzz" but brought in vital "plus" business. Indeed, the Escalade line accounted for nearly 40 percent of division sales by 2004.

But cars, not trucks, were Cadillac's heart and soul, and GM managers wholeheartedly backed the development of a new-generation fleet intended partly to herald a renaissance for all of GM. A recent string of boldly styled concepts had suggested Cadillac would again reach for luxury-class leadership, but in new ways so as to stand apart from the European and Japanese brands that had lately stolen so much of its thunder. The result was a quick succession of new cars that, like the Escalade, made people take a fresh look at Cadillac.

First up was the 2003 CTS, a U.S.-built replacement for the Catera, but far more ambitious. Significantly, it introduced the premium rear-drive Sigma platform that was also designed to accept all-wheel-drive powertrains and would underpin other vital new near-term models. The only engine at first was a more-powerful 3.2-liter version of Catera's V-6, but an even stronger 3.6 came online for 2004. The 3.2 was dropped the next year, when a lower-priced, lower-power 2.8-liter derivative of the 3.6 V-6 was added as a new model.

Staking its claim as a true sports sedan, the CTS was the first Cadillac in over 50 years to offer a manual transmission as well as an automatic. And both were five-speed units, Cadillac's first. To the same end, engineers spent much time tuning the chassis on Germany's demanding Nürburgring race circuit. As a result, most reviews found little lacking in the handling department, especially with the optional firm damping and 17-inch wheel/tire package. Actually, even the base CTS suspension might have been a bit too Teutonic for some buyers, as the 2004 setup was softened a bit to enhance ride comfort. The sharp-edged styling was unlike anything from anyone else, but took a while to catch on with the public (and, earlier, some GM bigwigs). Some evident interior cost cutting also drew criticism. Yet overall, the first of Cadillac's new guard was a fine effort right out of the box. *Consumer Guide®* initially judged the CTS "an upper-echelon driving machine... a solid and sporty sedan [that] delivers good near-luxury value, listing for around $36,000 popularly equipped. ... There's more here than meets the eye."

A good many buyers evidently agreed, as CTS sales got off to a strong start, helped by attractive base prices in the $30,000 range. Cadillac built nearly 75,700 for the extra-long debut model year. The tally dipped below 60,000 for '04, but recovered slightly the next model year. This was good going in light of the brash styling and an increasingly difficult market. At last, Cadillac seemed to be on the right track.

New dreams of the *racetrack*, following a short-lived late-'90s assault on LeMans, prompted Cadillac to work up a hot CTS-V as both road-burner and hoped-for competition star. An early 2004 arrival, it was the first in a planned series of high-performance models that would be to GM's finest what the M Division was to BMW and AMG to Mercedes. Cadillacs had usually offered good speed, but mostly in a straight line. Not this time. To the already capable CTS chassis, engineers at GM's then-new Performance Division added heavier-gauge steel suspension cradles, thicker front and rear stabilizer bars, high-rate shocks, and a crossbrace atop the front-suspension towers to bolster rigidity. Some steel suspension pieces were swapped for lighter aluminum components, but the basic geometry was unchanged. Other upgrades included a massive four-piston Brembo-brand disc brake at each corner and meaty 245/45ZR18 Goodyear run-flat tires on special seven-spoke alloy wheels spreading 8.5 inches wide.

But the most exciting upgrade was underhood, where Cadillac found room for the 5.7-liter LS6 V-8 from the contemporary C5-generation Corvette Z06. The transplant cost a little power, but not much, with rated outputs of 400 bhp at a zingy 6000 rpm and 395 beefy pound-feet of torque peaking at 4800. The result was the most potent production Cadillac ever, proof that the division was dead serious about cracking the enthusiast market. So, too, the mandatory six-speed manual transmission, the same Tremec T56 unit used in the 'Vette, but moved from the rear to just behind the engine. Cadillac hardly missed a trick, specifying a heavier-than-stock driveshaft, a limited-slip rear differential with strong but light cast-aluminum housing, and fairly tight gearing (3.73:1).

For a factory hot rod, the CTS-V was quite restrained outside, limited to more-aggressive lower fascias front and rear, a distinctive wire-mesh grille insert, subtle "aero" rocker panel skirts, and telltale dual exhausts. Interior exclusives involved satin-chrome-finish trim instead of the usual wood, plus bright-ringed gauges and, for exuberant cornering, grippy suede seat inserts. Even the central armrest was lowered some four inches to ease shifting.

2003 CTS four-door sedan

2003 CTS four-door sedan

2003 Seville STS four-door sedan

2004 CTS-V four-door sedan

Here it seemed was a Cadillac that begged comparison with Europe's best sports sedans, and "car buff" magazines wasted little time doing just that. *Car and Driver* first pitted the CTS-V against a BMW M3 coupe and new M5 sedan, judging the Cadillac equal or better in most respects, especially

2004 SRX four-door wagon

2004 XLR hardtop convertible

for value. The CTS-V wasn't cheap at an initial $49,300 base, but the M5 cost $23,000 more. Later, *Car and Driver* judged the CTS-V a close second to the Audi S4 quattro and ahead of Mercedes' C55 AMG in a three-way comparo. "[W]e emerged with a unanimous sense of the CTS-V as the road-course champ," said the editors. Yet they found straightline go no less impressive, clocking just 4.8 seconds 0-60 mph and a standing quarter-mile of 13.2 seconds at 109 mph.

Such dragworthy stats suggested the V-Series CTS was ready to race, and Cadillac backed a two-car team for the 2004 season of the Sports Car Club of America's Speed World Challenge series for production-based cars. Against the formidable likes of modified Corvettes, Dodge Vipers, and Porsche 911s, the Cadillac tallied four pole starts and three wins—not bad for a beginner.

Cadillac built 2401 CTS-Vs for 2004 and another 4194 for '05, when the only changes were monetary: a $190 bump in starting price (there were still no options) and a tacked-on $1300 Gas-Guzzler Tax. The '06 models nominally broke the $50,000 barrier, but some of the increase reflected an engine swap, as the 6.0-liter LS2 V-8 from the year-old C6-generation Corvette was installed. Interestingly, no more power or torque were claimed for the bigger engine. Boy, Cadillac really had changed.

But the CTS was just a warm-up. For 2004, Cadillac unwrapped a new two-seat convertible, a car that made everyone forget the hapless Allanté ever existed. Called XLR, in line with the brand's adopted three-letter naming scheme, it was basically a C6 Corvette engineered to Cadillac standards of quality and refinement. Actually, the XLR was created by Team Corvette before it began working in earnest on the C6, and the lessons learned benefited the Corvette.

Though the XLR was easy to dismiss as just a Caddy in Corvette clothing, there were many key differences. For starters, the XLR design was new school Cadillac if a bit old news, having been previewed with the 1999 Evoq concept. Also, the XLR came only as a hardtop convertible, with a power-retractable solid roof that pirouetted into the trunk like that of main rivals Mercedes SL and Lexus SC 430 (and it left as little luggage space). Other distinctions included specific suspension tuning, slightly slower steering (again by GM's Magnasteer system), and slimmer 18-inch tires. The XLR also differed dimensionally, being a bit longer, taller, slightly narrower, and some 450 pounds heavier than a ragtop C6.

And then there was the all-Cadillac powertrain. What else for the division's latest image-leader? A heavily revised "Gen II" version of Cadillac's respected 4.6 Northstar V-8 boasted new cylinder heads with freer-flow ports and higher compression (10.5:1), plus a stiffer block and crank, redesigned manifolds, and "by-wire" electronic throttle control. The result was 320 bhp at 6400 rpm and 310 pound-feet of torque maxing at 4400. The only transmission was a five-speed automatic with a separate manual shift gate vs. the C6's initial four-speed automatic or available six-speed manual.

Naturally, the XLR inherited the Corvette's much-lauded "uniframe" structure, with composite body panels draped around an inner skeleton featuring a stiff central "backbone," hydroformed side rails, aluminum windshield frame, a cross-cowl magnesium reinforcing bar, and aluminum "sandwich" floors with light balsa-wood cores. Even so, the XLR was clearly a luxury tourer, not a 'Vette-style sports car. And there was nothing wrong with that—not with 0-60 mph available in less than 6.0 seconds and sticky 0.88g skidpad acceleration. The price was right, too. Though the debut $76,000 tab was almost twice that of a base Corvette coupe, the XLR came with most every known amenity in the automotive world: power everything, heated/cooled seats, OnStar, a navigation system, "smart" cruise control that automatically maintained a safe following distance, and Cadillac's new Keyless Access system with engine-start button and no external keylocks. The only option was satellite radio, and that became standard for 2006, along with steering-linked xenon headlamps.

In all, the XLR was arguably the most exciting new Cadillac since the 1967 Eldorado. *Car and Driver* greeted it as "a strong entry in the prestigious roadster class," while *Road & Track* deemed it a sign that "Cadillac is heading in the right direction." And while the XLR wasn't intended to be an everyday sight, initial demand must have gratified division planners, with 4387 built for '04 and 4190 for '05.

A V-Series XLR was a foregone conclusion, and it arrived for 2006 hewing to the CTS-V formula: understated exterior, "tech-look" interior, big power, even more-dynamic handling. This time, though, Cadillac looked to its own engine laurels with a new supercharged 4.4-liter Northstar that exceeded pundits' expectations by spinning out 443 bhp (at 6400 rpm) and 414 pound-feet of torque, some 90 percent of which was on call from 2200 to 6000 rpm. Again, engineers pulled out many stops, conjuring a new intake system, a unique and stronger block casting, oil-cooled pistons, even a redesigned accessory drive. The only transmission was a new six-speed automatic, also with manual shift gate. Chassis tweaks involved wider 19-inch run-flat tires, a solid front stabilizer bar, the addition of a rear bar, revised tuning for the MRC shocks, and larger brakes borrowed from the Corvette Z51.

Car and Driver timed an XLR-V at a mere 4.7 seconds 0-60 mph and a standing-quarter of 13 seconds at 110 mph—a noticeable improvement on the base model. Skidpad performance was curiously little-changed at 0.87g, but handling, steering, and braking all drew praise from *Car and Driver*'s testers. Still, the V-Series treatment didn't change the XLR's comfortable touring-car persona; it only made for a faster, more agile tour. "As high-performance roadsters go," *C/D* summed up, "the XLR-V is quite well-suited to the quotidian requirements of your less-extreme motorist... [It] has all the creature comforts technology can provide, and its unique mesh grille, supercharged badge and four shiny tailpipes tell everyone this Cadillac is a cut above. For those who think 100 grand is a reasonable amount of money to spend on a car, this Cadillac is certainly worth a look."

A Seville replacement was next on the to-do list, and it emerged for 2005 as the STS. As expected, it was basically a stretched CTS, though with slightly softer body lines. Against its predecessor, the STS measured 4.7 inches shorter overall but an inch taller on a 4.2-inch-longer wheelbase, to the benefit of interior room. Engine choices comprised a base 255-bhp 3.6-liter V-6 or the new "Gen II" Northstar tuned for 320 bhp, both teamed with a five-speed automatic. But in a rather large surprise, all-wheel drive was a $1900 option for the V-8 model, then for the V-6 as well. Respective base prices were $40,300 and $46,800, but that only bought a fairly traditional Cadillac drive. Sportier types had to shell out a whopping $11,000-$13,000 for a Preferred Equipment Group with Z-rated performance tires on 18-inch wheels (17s were stock), plus Magnetic Ride Control and uprated brakes and steering. Even with that, the STS lacked the agility of most import-brand rivals, coming seventh in an eight-way *Car and Driver* comparison test. "The STS is agonizingly close to meeting the challenge of the best [midsize sport sedans]," said the editors, "but we think the sensibilities of its makers could use a little fine-tuning." *Consumer Guide*®, by contrast, liked the dynamics, but chided "subpar rear-seat space and cargo room. Interior materials and assembly are not up to the best-in-class standard, either. We're [also] disappointed that $62,500 is the price of admission for all-wheel drive... "

The expected STS-V muscled in for 2006 at a stiff $74,270, but it came fully loaded (no options)—and loaded for bear. The treatment was comprehensive, much like that of the V-Series XLR, but here the supercharged Northstar made a thumping 469 bhp and 439 pound-feet of torque, delivered to the rear wheels only via a six-speed automatic. A three-way *Car and Driver* matchup ranked the raciest STS between the BMW M5 and Mercedes' CLS 55 AMG, mainly because of relatively "softer" dynamics and a plusher, less driver-oriented character. But as the editors observed: "... the STS-V's price nets you a no-apologies supersedan with big money left over—almost 16 large versus the CLS 55. That's a huge advantage—especially since the STS-V has this group's most comprehensive allocation of features and amenities... "

As if to hedge its bets with the new STS, Cadillac freshened the stalwart front-drive DeVille for 2006 and changed the name to DTS. Optional Night Vision was canned, but the Gen II Northstar was specified, the G-body structure strengthened, and the chassis tweaked for improved handling and refinement. Appearance was modernized too, with an edgy Art & Science-style lower-body reskin and improved dashboard ergonomics. Like other GM divisions, Cadillac stressed value, offering Luxury I, Luxury II, and Luxury III versions with 275 bhp in the $42,000-$48,000 range, plus a sportier $47,000 Performance model with 291 horses and many DeVille DTS features. *Consumer Guide*® put the new line in perspective by noting that "Cadillac leaves any sporting pretensions to its [STS models. DTS] aims for the traditional American luxury-car buyer and scores. It's powerful, roomy, and refined, and matches most rivals for standard safety features."

Cadillac was a bit slow to answer the fast-growing clamor for carlike "crossover" SUVs, but its first effort was one of the best. Arriving for 2004, the SRX was a clever variation on

2005 STS four-door sedan

2005 STS four-door sedan

2006 STS-V four-door sedan

2006 DTS four-door sedan

2006 DTS four-door sedan

the Sigma car platform, offering the same V-6 and V-8 rear-drive and all-wheel-drive powertrains as the STS that followed it. The edgy "Art & Science" look was well-suited to this wagon, which hewed to Cadillac tradition with a healthy helping of standard luxuries, including a posh leather-lined interior and power everything, plus a power-operated liftgate for '06. V-8s added real-wood accents, heated seats, and power-adjustable pedals, all available for V-6 models. A high level of safety was standard, too, encompassing antilock brakes, traction control, front torso side airbags, and curtain side airbags. Buyers had a choice of five-passenger seating with a fore/aft sliding back bench or an available seven-passenger package with the convenience of a power-folding third-row seat. Other options included Magnetic Ride Control suspension, navigation system, rear-seat DVD entertainment, and a novel "UltraView" sunroof with multiple glass panels that slid back at the touch of a button to let in 5.6 square feet of the great outdoors. Keenly priced in the $40,000-$47,000, the SRX impressed road-testers with its sprightly performance, adroit handling, and refinement. *Consumer Guide*® bestowed a Recommended ribbon in the first year and Best Buy medals for 2005-06. "Against similarly priced premium midsize SUVs, SRX is among the best in performance, features, and accommodations, if not always in the quality of cabin appointments. Unless you off-road or tow heavy loads, the SRX's road manners and efficient packaging make it preferable to most truck-type rivals. Add AWD security and it's a thoughtful alternative to a traditional luxury sedan." That's just what Cadillac was aiming for, and sales in the first two calendar years were pretty much on target at just over 53,000—all welcome "plus" business.

That's the Cadillac story so far, and it seems far from over despite much dire news in 2005 about GM and Detroit in general. Indeed, there's the strong near-term prospect of a grand, new V-12 Cadillac as America's representative in the surprisingly robust $100,000 ultraluxury market. Meantime, Cadillac can take pride in its dramatic early century comeback, confounding critics who had written its obituary so many times in the 1980s and '90s. Rising calendar-year sales confirm the turnaround, improving from 199,800 (including trucks) in 2002 to over 235,000 in '05.

But today's brutally competitive global auto market allows no manufacturer to be self-satisfied, and Cadillac knows this better than most. Though it may never be the luxury power it was in GM's glory days, Cadillac seems likely to keep moving forward with confidence and courage.

2006 XLR-V hardtop convertible

Specifications

1930

353 Eight (wb 140.0) - 11,005 blt	Wght	Price	Prod
Fisher:			
cpe 2P	4,940	3,295	—
conv cpe 2P	4,845	3,595	—
cpe 5P	4,930	3,595	—
town sdn 5P	5,025	3,495	—
sdn 5P	5,055	3,695	—
sdn 7P	5,155	3,795	—
Imperial sdn 7P	5,195	3,995	—
Fleetwood:			
rdstr 2P	4,610	3,450	—
sdn 5P	5,135	4,195	—
sdn cab 5P	5,185	4,245	—
Imperial sdn 5P	5,205	4,395	—
Imperial cab 5P	5,225	4,445	—
sdn 7P	5,265	4,295	—
Imperial sdn 7P	5,305	4,595	—
sdnt 5P	5,055	4,500	—
sdnt 4P	5,055	4,595	—
phtn A/W 4P	4,975	4,700	—
town cab	5,215	4,995	—
town cab "Fleetmont"	5,135	5,145	—
town cab "Fleetcrest"	5,135	5,145	—
Limo b'ham	5,305	5,145	—

370 Twelve (wb 140.0; 7P-143.0) - 5,725 blt (1930-31)	Wght	Price	Prod
Fisher:			
rdstr 2P	4,910	3,945	—
phtn 5P	4,950	4,055	—
A/W phtn 5P	5,290	4,895	—
cpe 2P	5,035	3,795	—
conv cpe 2P	5,005	4,045	—
cpe 5P	5,055	3,895	—
sdn 5P	5,215	3,895	—
town sdn 5P	5,230	3,945	—
sdn 7P	5,345	4,195	—
Imperial sdn 7P	5,420	4,345	—
touring 7P	5,005	4,295	—

370 Twelve	Wght	Price	Prod
Fleetwood:			
sdn 5P	5,350	4,995	—
Imperial sdn 5P	5,420	5,200	—
sdn cab 5P	5,400	5,095	—
Imperial cab 5P	5,440	5,300	—
sdn 7P	5,480	5,075	—
Imperial sdn 7P	5,520	5,275	—
town cab 5P	5,430	5,750	—
town cab 5P CQ	5,350	5,800	—
limo b'ham 7P	5,520	5,800	—

Sixteen (wb 148.0) - 3,250 built (1930-31)		Wght	Price	Prod
4100	*Madam X:*			
4108C	Imp landau cab 5P	5,925	—	4
4130	Imperial sdn 5P	5,905	7,300	17
4130S	sdn 5P	5,835	6,950	49
4155	Imperial cab 5P	5,925	7,350	10
4155S	sdn cabriolet 5P	5,885	7,125	7
4155C	Imp landau cab 5P	5,925	—	5
4155SC	landau sdn cab 5P	5,885	—	2
4161	Imperial club sdn 5P	5,725	—	1
4161S	club sdn 5P	5,655	6,950	43
4175	Imperial sdn 7P	6,005	7,525	110
4175S	sdn 7P	5,965	7,225	47
4200 series:				
4200	statnry sdn cab 7P	—	—	1
4206	statnry cpe cab 2P	—	—	1
4207	statnry cpe cab 2P	—	—	3
4208	Imperial cab 5P	5,885	—	7
4212	trnsfrm twn cab 5P	6,005	8,750	6
4212C	trnsfrm town cab CQ 5P	6,005	—	1
4220	4121C leather roof	6,006	8,750	9
4220B	4212C painted roof	6,005	—	1
4225	4212C SQ	6,005	8,750	6
4225C	4212C CQ	6,005	—	1
4235	conv cpe 2P	5,655	6,900	94
4257A	touring 5P	—	—	1
4257H	touring 7P	—	—	1
4260	phtn 5P	—	6,500	85
4260A	phtn 5p	—	—	1

Sixteen		Wght	Price	Prod
4262	Imperial cab 7P	—	—	1
4264	trnsfrm town b'ham 5P	6,005	9,200	4
4264B	trnsfrm town b'ham 5P	6,005	9,700	6
4275	Imperial sdn 7P	6,005	6,525	1
4275C	Imperial Lnd sdn 7P	6,005	7,525	2
4276	cpe 2P	5,750	6,850	70
4280	A/W phtn 4P	5,675	7,350	8
4285	A/W spt cab 5P	—	—	2
4291	trnsfrm limo b'ham 7P	6,005	8,750	14
4300 series:				
4302	rdstr 2P	5,310	5,350	105
4312	trnsfrm town cab 5P	—	6,525	24
4320	trnsfrm twn cab 7P Q/W	—	7,150	25
4325	trnsfrm twn cab 7P SQ	—	7,150	35
4325C	transformable CQ	—	—	3
4330	Imperial sdn 5P	5,905	6,300	50
4330S	sdn 5P	5,835	5,950	394
4335	conv cpe 2P	5,655	5,900	100
4355	Imperial cab 5P	5,925	6,350	52
4355S	sdn cab 5P	5,885	6,125	81
4355C	Imp landau cab 5P	—	—	1
4361	Imp club sdn 5P	—	—	2
4361S	club sdn 5P	5,725	5,950	258
4375	Imperial sdn 7P	6,005	6,525	438
4375S	sdn 7P	5,965	6,225	501
4375C	Imp landau sdn 7P	—	—	2
4376	cpe 2P	5,750	5,800	98
4380	A/W phtn 4P	—	6,650	250
4381	cpe 5P	5,740	5,950	98
4391	trnsfrm limo b'ham 7P	6,005	7,150	30
Misc. Fisher:				
30-152	town sdn 5P	—	—	3
30-158	cpe 2P	—	—	3
30-158	sdn 5P	—	—	5
30-168	conv cpe 2p	—	—	17
30-172	cpe 5P	—	—	2
2901LX	sdn 7P	—	—	1
2951LX	sdn 7P	—	—	1

Sixteen	Wght	Price	Prod
30-X sdn test car 7P	—	—	1
LX 2905 town sdn 5P	—	—	1
LX 2913 cpe 5P	—	—	1
Misc. Fleetwood:			
3289B trnsfrm town cab 7P	—	—	1
3981 sdnt cab 4P	—	6,450	1
3991 trnsfrm limo b'ham	—	—	1
4412 trnsfrm town cab 5P	—	—	1
4476 cpe 2P	5,750	5,800	11
2950X special sdn 7P	—	—	1
Misc. chassis and unknown	—	—	37

1930 Engines	bore×stroke	bhp	availability
V-8, 353.0	3.63×4.94	95	S-Eight
V-12, 368.0	3.13×4.00	135	S-Twelve
V-16, 452.6	3.00×4.00	165	S-Sixteen

Editor's note: Cadillac Sixteens appeared in a broad number of body styles. This analysis, the clearest ever published, appears in *Sixteen Cylinder Motorcars* by Roy S. Schneider, Heritage House, 430 W. Longden Avenue, Arcadia, California 91006, with production figures researched from company records by Carl L. Steig.

1931

355 Eight (wb 134.0) - 10,709 blt	Wght	Price	Prod
rdstr 2P	4,355	2,845	—
phtn 5P	4,395	2,945	—
cpe 2P	4,480	2,695	—
conv cpe 2P	4,450	2,945	—
cpe 5P	4,500	2,795	—
sdn 4d 5P	4,660	2,795	—
town sdn 5P	4,675	2,845	—
A/W phtn 5P	4,685	3,795	—
sdn 4d 7P	4,760	2,945	—
Imperial sdn 7P	4,835	3,095	—
touring 7P	4,450	3,195	—

370A Twelve (wb 140.0; 7P-143.0) (see 1930)

Sixteen (wb 148.0) (see 1930)

1931 Engines	bore×stroke	bhp	availability
V-8, 353.0	3.63×4.94	95	S-Eight
V-12, 368.0	3.13×4.00	135	S-Twelve
V-16, 452.6	3.00×4.00	165	S-Sixteen

1932

355B Eight (wb 134.0) - 2,693 blt*	Wght	Price	Prod
rdstr 2P	4,635	2,895	—
cpe 2P	4,705	2,795	—
conv cpe 2P	4,675	2,945	—
sdn 5P	4,885	2,895	—
355B Eight (wb 140.0)			
Fisher:			
phtn 5P	4,700	2,995	—
Special phtn 5P	4,750	3,095	—
spt phtn 5P	4,800	3,245	—
A/W phtn 5P	5,070	3,495	—
cpe 5P	4,715	2,995	—
special sdn 5P	4,965	3,045	—
town sdn 5P	4,980	3,095	—
sdn 7P	5,110	3,145	—
Imperial sdn 7P	5,150	3,295	—
Fleetwood:			
sdn 5P	4,965	3,395	—
town cpe 5P	4,915	3,395	—
sdn 7P	5,110	3,545	—
limo 7P	5,150	3,745	—
town cab 5P	4,990	4,095	—
town cab 7P	5,100	4,245	—
limo b'ham 7P	5,100	4,245	—
370B Twelve (wb 134.0) - 1,709 built*			
rdstr 2P	4,870	3,595	—
cpe 2P	5,085	3,495	—
conv cpe 2P	5,060	3,645	—
sdn 5P	5,175	3,595	—
370B Twelve (wb 140.0)			
Fisher:			
phtn 5P	5,240	3,695	—
Special phtn 5P	5,290	3,795	—
spt phtn 5P	5,340	3,945	—
A/W phtn 5P	5,385	4,195	—

370B Twelve	Wght	Price	Prod
cpe 5P	5,220	3,695	—
Special sdn 5P	5,345	3,745	—
town sdn 5P	5,370	3,795	—
sdn 7P	5,460	3,845	—
Imperial sdn 7P	5,500	3,995	—
Fleetwood:			
town cpe 5P	5,225	4,095	—
sdn 5P	5,345	4,095	—
sdn 7P	5,460	4,245	—
limo 7P	5,500	4,445	—
town cab 5P	5,380	4,795	—
town cab 7P	5,580	4,945	—
limo b'ham 7P	5,580	4,945	—
452B Sixteen (wb 143.0) - 296 built**			
rdstr 2P	5,065	4,595	3
cpe 2P	5,530	4,495	—
conv cpe 2P	5,505	4,645	—
sdn 5P	5,625	4,595	—
452B Sixteen (wb 149.0)			
Fisher:			
phtn 5P	5,400	4,695	1
Special phtn 5P	5,450	4,795	3
spt phtn 5P	5,500	4,945	2
A/W phtn 5P	5,525	5,195	13
Fleetwood:			
town cpe 5P	5,605	5,095	24
sdn 5P	5,735	5,095	—
conv cpe 5p	5,505	4,645	1
sdn 7P	5,865	5,245	47
limo 7P	5,935	5,445	—
Imp cabriolet sedan	—	—	4
Imp landaulette	—	—	1
town cab 5P	5,775	5,795	4
town cab 7P	5,935	5,945	2
limo b'ham 7P	5,935	5,945	7

* Includes 140.0-in wb; ** Includes 149.0-in wb.

1932 Engines	bore×stroke	bhp	availability
V-8, 353.0	3.63×4.94	115	S-Eights
V-12, 368.0	3.13×4.00	135	S-Twelves
V-16, 452.6	3.00×4.00	165	S-Sixteens

Note: weights listed for five wire wheels, all models.

1933

355C Eight (wb 134.0) - 2,906 blt*	Wght	Price	Prod
rdstr 2P	4,695	2,795	—
cpe 2P	4,855	2,695	—
conv cpe 2P	4,825	2,845	—
355 C Eight (wb 140.0)			
Fisher:			
phtn 5P	4,865	2,895	—
A/W phtn 5P	5,110	3,395	—
cpe 5P	4,850	2,895	—
sdn 5P	5,000	2,895	—
town sdn 5P	5,060	2,995	—
sdn 7P	5,105	3,045	—
Imperial sdn 7P	5,140	3,195	—
Fleetwood:			
sdn 5P	5,000	3,295	—
sdn 7P	5,105	3,445	—
limo 7P	5,140	3,645	—
town cab 5P	5,010	3,395	—
town cab 7P	5,200	4,145	—
limo b'ham 7P	5,225	4,145	—
370C Twelve (wb 134.0) - 952 built*			
rdstr 2P	5,030	3,495	—
cpe 2P	5,165	3,395	—
conv cpe 2P	5,125	3,545	—
370C Twelve (wb 140.0)			
Fisher:			
phtn 5P	5,200	3,595	—
A/W phtn 5P	5,405	4,095	—
cpe 5P	5,200	3,595	—
sdn 5P	5,335	3,595	—
town sdn 5P	5,385	3,695	—
sdn 7P	5,440	3,745	—
Imperial sdn 7P	5,500	3,895	—

370C Twelve	Wght	Price	Prod
Fleetwood:			
sdn 5P	5,335	3,995	—
sdn 7P	5,440	4,145	—
limo 7P	5,500	4,345	—
town cab 5P	5,375	4,695	—
town cab 7P	5,575	4,845	—
limo b'ham 7P	5,575	4,845	—
452C Sixteen (wb 149.0) - 125 built			
Fleetwood:			
A/W phtn 5P	6,110	8,000	—
conv cpe 5P	5,910	7,500	2
town cpe 5P	6,000	6,250	4
Imperial cab 5P	6,100	5,540	1
sdn 5P	6,070	6,250	—
sdn 7P	6,200	6,400	—
limo 7P	6,270	6,600	—
town cab 5P	6,110	6,850	—
town cab 7P	6,270	6,850	—
limo b'ham 7P	6,300	6,850	—
Sport phaeton	—	—	1
Imperial town sdn	—	—	1

* Includes 140-in. wb.

1933 Engines	bore×stroke	bhp	availability
V-8, 353.0	3.38×4.94	115	S-Eights
V-12, 368.0	3.13×4.00	135	S-Twelves
V-16, 452.0	3.00×4.00	165	S-Sixteens

1934

355D Eight Series 10 (wb 128.0) - 2,015 built	Wght	Price	Prod
702 town sdn 5P	4,735	2,695	—
709 sdn 5P	4,715	2,645	—
718 conv cpe 2P	4,515	2,645	—
721 conv sdn 5P	4,750	2,845	—
722 town cpe 5P	4,630	2,695	—
728 cpe 2P	4,550	2,545	—
355D Eight Series 20 (wb 136.0) - 2,729 built			
652 town sdn 5P	4,815	2,895	—
659 sdn 5P	4,825	2,845	—
662 sdn 7P	4,945	2,995	—
663 Imperial sdn 7P	4,970	3,145	—
668 conv cpe 2P	4,625	2,845	—
671 conv sdn 5P	4,860	3,045	—
678 cpe 2P	4,660	2,745	—
355D Eight Series 30 (wb 146.0) - 336 built			
Fleetwood (straight windshield):			
6030FL Imperial cab 5P	5,500	3,895	—
6030S sdn 5P	5,465	3,495	—
6033S town sdn 5P	5,415	3,545	—
6075 limo 7P	5,580	3,845	—
6075FL Imperial cab 7P	5,580	4,045	—
6075S sdn 7P	5,545	3,645	—
Fleetwood (mod. V windshield):			
5612 town cab 5P	5,540	5,695	—
5630FL Special Imp cab 5P	5,500	4,345	—
5630S Special sdn 5P	5,465	3,945	—
5625 town cab 7P	5,650	5,795	—
5633S Special town sdn 5P	5,415	3,995	—
5635 conv cpe 4P	5,115	4,245	—
5675 Special limo 7P	5,580	4,295	—
5675FL Imperial cab 7P	5,580	4,495	—
5675S Special sdn 7P	5,545	4,095	—
5676 cpe 4P	5,150	4,095	—
5680 Imperial conv sdn 5P	5,465	4,495	—
5691 limo b'ham 7P	5,580	5,695	—
370D Twelve Series 40 (wb 146.0) - 683 built			
Fleetwood (straight windshield):			
6130FL Imperial cab 5P	5,765	4,595	—
6130S sdn 5P	5,735	4,195	—
6133S town sdn 5P	5,700	4,245	—
6175 limo 7P	5,790	4,545	—
6175FL Imperial cab 7P	5,790	4,745	—
6175S sdn 7P	5,760	4,345	—
Fleetwood (V windshield):			
5712 town cab 5P	5,990	6,395	—
5725 town cab 7P	6,040	6,495	—
5730FL Special Imp cab 5P	5,765	5,045	—
5730S Special sdn 5P	5,735	4,645	—
5733S Special town sdn 5P	5,700	4,695	—

370D Twelve		Wght	Price	Prod
5735	conv cpe 4P	5,485	4,945	—
5775	Special limo 7P	5,790	4,995	—
5775FL	Special Imp cab 7P	5,790	5,195	—
5775S	Special sdn 7P	5,760	4,795	—
5776	cpe 4P	5,520	4,795	—
5780	Imperial conv sdn 5P	5,800	5,195	—
5791	limo b'ham 7P	6,030	6,395	—
452D Sixteen Series 60 (wb 154.0) - 56 built				
Fleetwood (straight windshield):				
6275	limo 7P	6,210	7,300	10
6275S	sdn 7P	6,190	7,100	5
Fleetwood (V windshield):				
5825	town cab 7P	6,390	9,250	4
5830	Imperial sdn 5P	—	—	1
5833	Imperial town sdn 5P	—	—	1
5833S	town sdn 5P	6,085	7,350	2
5835	conv cpe 2P	5,900	7,900	2
5875	limo 7P	6,210	7,950	9
5875S	Special sdn 7P	6,190	7,750	5
5875FL	Special Imp sdn 7P	—	8,150	1
5876	stationary cpe 2P	5,840	7,750	5
5880	Imperial conv sdn 5P	6,100	8,150	5
5880S	conv sdn 5P	—	7,950	1
5885	conv cpe 5P	—	8,150	1
5899	Aero cpe 5P	—	8,150	3
—	Chassis	—	—	1

1934 Engines	bore×stroke	bhp	availability
V-8, 353.0	3.38×4.94	130	S-Eights
V-12, 368.0	3.13×4.00	150	S-Twelves
V-16, 452.0	3.00×4.00	185	S-Sixteens

1935

355D Eight Series 10 (wb 128.0) - 1,130 built		Wght	Price	Prod
702	town sdn 5P	4,735	2,495	—
709	sdn 5P	4,715	2,445	—
718	conv cpe 2/4P	4,515	2,445	—
721	conv sdn 5P	4,750	2,755	—
722	town cpe 5P	4,630	2,495	—
728	cpe 2/4P	4,550	2,345	—
355D Eight Series 20 (wb 136.0) - 1,859 built				
652	town sdn 5P	4,815	2,695	—
659	sdn 5P	4,825	2,645	—
662	sdn 7P	4,945	2,995	—
663	Imperial sdn 7P	4,970	2,945	—
668	conv cpe 2/4P	3,625	2,645	—
671	conv sdn 5P	4,860	2,955	—
678	cpe 2/4P	4,660	2,545	—
355D Eight Series 30 (wb 146.0) - 220 built				
Fleetwood (straight windshield):				
6030FL	Imperial cab	5,500	3,695	—
6030S	sdn 5P	5,465	2,295	—
6033S	town sdn 5P	5,415	3,345	—
6075	limo 7P	5,580	3,645	—
6075 FL	Imperial cab 7P	5,580	3,845	—
6075S	sdn 7P	5,545	3,445	—
Fleetwood (V windshield):				
5612	town cab 5P	5,540	5,495	—
5625	town cab 7P	5,650	5,595	—
5630FL	Special Imp cab 5P	5,500	4,145	—
5630S	Special sdn 5P	5,465	3,745	—
5633S	Special cab sdn 5P	5,415	3,795	—
5635	conv cpe 4P	5,115	4,045	—
5675FL	Special Imp cab 7P	5,580	4,295	—
5675S	Special sdn 7P	5,545	3,895	—
5675	Special limo 7P	5,580	4,095	—
5676	cpe 4P	5,150	3,895	—
5680	Imperial conv sdn 5P	5,465	4,295	—
5691	limo b'ham 7P	5,580	5,495	—
370D Twelve Series 40 (wb 146.0) - 377 built				
Fleetwood (straight windshield):				
6130FL	Imperial cab 5P	5,765	4,395	—
6130S	sdn 5P	5,735	3,995	—
6133S	town sdn 5P	5,700	4,045	—
6175	limo 7P	5,790	4,345	—
6175FL	Imperial cab 7P	5,790	4,545	—
6175S	sdn 7P	5,760	4,145	—
Fleetwood (V windshield):				
5712	town cab 5P	5,990	6,195	—

370D Twelve		Wght	Price	Prod
5725	town cab 7P	6,040	6,295	—
5730FL	Special Imp cab 5P	5,765	4,845	—
5730S	Special sdn 5P	5,735	4,445	—
5733S	Special town sdn 5P	5,700	4,495	—
5735	conv cpe 4P	5,485	4,745	—
5775	Special limo 7P	5,790	4,795	—
5775FL	Special Imp cab 7P	5,790	4,995	—
5775S	Special sdn 7P	5,760	4,595	—
5776	cpe 4P	5,520	4,595	—
5780	Imperial conv sdn 5P	5,800	4,995	—
5791	limo b'ham 7P	6,030	6,195	—
452D Sixteen Series 60 (wb 154.0) - 50 built				
Fleetwood (straight windshield):				
6233S	town sdn 5P	6,085	6,800	2
6275	limo 7P	6,210	7,100	6
6275S	sdn 7P	6,190	6,900	3
6275B	Imperial sdn 7P	—	—	2
6275H3	limo (extra hdrm) 7P	—	—	1
Fleetwood (V windshield):				
5825	town cab 7P	6,390	9,050	2
5830S	Special sdn 5P	6,240	7,400	1
5833	Imperial town sdn 5P	—	8,000	2
5833S	town sdn 5P	6,085	7,450	4
5875	limo 7P	6,210	7,750	15
—	cpe 2p	5,840	7,550	2
5875S	sdn 7P	6,190	7,550	2
5875FL	Imperial cab 7P	6,100	7,950	4
5876	stationary cpe 2P	5,840	7,550	2
5880	conv sdn 5P	6,100	7,950	4
5885	conv cpe 5P	—	8,150	2
5891B	limo b'ham 7P	—	8,950	1
Chassis		—	—	1

1935 Engines	bore×stroke	bhp	availability
V-8, 353.0	3.38×4.94	130	S-Eights
V-12, 368.0	3.13×4.00	150	S-Twelves
V-16, 452.0	3.00×4.00	185	S-Sixteens

1936

Series 60 (wb 121.0)-6,700 blt		Wght	Price	Prod
6019	touring sdn 5P	4,010	1,695	—
6067	conv cpe 2/4P	3,985	1,725	—
6077	cpe 2P	3,830	1,645	—
Series 70 (wb 131.0) - 2,000 built				
7019	touring sdn 5P	4,670	2,445	—
7029	conv sdn 5P	4,710	2,745	—
7057	cpe 2P	4,620	2,595	—
7067	conv cpe 2/4P	4,690	2,695	—
Series 75 Fleetwood (wb 138.0) - 3,227 built				
7503	sdn 7P	4,885	2,795	—
7509	sdn 5P	4,805	2,645	—
7513	Imperial sdn 7P	5,045	2,995	—
7519	touring sdn 5P	4,805	2,645	—
7523	touring sdn 7P	4,885	2,795	—
7529	conv sdn 5P	5,040	3,395	—
7519F	formal sdn 5P	4,805	3,395	—
7533	Imp touring sdn 5P	5,045	2,995	—
7539	town sdn 5P	4,840	3,145	—
7543	town car 7P	5,115	4,445	—
Series 80 Fleetwood (wb 131.0) - 250 built				
8019	touring sdn 5P	4,945	3,145	—
8029	conv sdn 5P	4,990	3,445	—
8057	cpe 2P	4,690	3,295	—
8067	conv cpe 2/4P	4,800	3,395	—
Series 85 Fleetwood (wb 138.0) - 651 built				
8503	sdn 7P	5,195	3,495	—
8509	sdn 5P	5,115	3,345	—
8513	Imperial sdn 7P	5,230	3,695	—
8519	touring sdn 5P	5,115	3,345	—
8519F	formal sdn 5P	5,115	4,095	—
8523	touring sdn 7P	5,195	3,495	—
8529	conv sdn 5P	5,230	4,095	—
8533	Imp touring sdn 7P	5,230	3,695	—
8539	town sdn 5P	5,065	3,845	—
8543	town car 7P	5,300	5,145	—
Series 90 Fleetwood (wb 154.0) - 52 built				
5825	town cab	6,390	8,850	1
5825C	town cab 7P CQ	6,450	—	1
5830S	Special sdn 5P	—	7,600	1

Series 90 Fltwd		Wght	Price	Prod
5830FL	Special Imperial cab	—	8,000	3
5833S	town sdn 5P	6,085	7,250	3
5835	conv cpe 2P	—	7,900	2
5875	limo 7P	6,190	7,750	24
5875S	sdn 7P	6,190	7,550	2
5875FL	Imperial cab 7P	6,210	7,850	1
5876	stationary cpe 2P	—	7,750	1
5880	conv sdn 5P	6,100	7,850	6
5899	Aero cpe 5P	—	8,150	4
—	Chassis	—	6,250	3

1936 Engines	bore×stroke	bhp	availability
V-8, 322.0	3.38×4.50	125	S-60
V-8, 346.0	3.50×4.50	135	S-70, 75
V-12, 368.0	3.13×2.00	150	S-80, 85
V-16, 452.0	3.00×4.00	185	S-90

1937

Series 60 (wb 124.0)-7,000 blt*		Wght	Price	Prod
—	club cpe 2P	—	1,710	
6019	touring sdn 5P	3,845	1,760	
6027	cpe 2P	3,710	1,655	
6049	conv sdn 5P	3,885	2,120	
6067	conv cpe 2P	3,745	1,790	
Series 65 (wb 131.0)				
6519	touring sdn 5P	4,385	2,190	2,401
Series 70 Fleetwood (wb 131.0) - 1,001 built				
7019	touring sdn 5P	4,420	2,695	—
7029	conv sdn 5P	4,460	3,060	—
7057	spt cpe 2P	4,285	2,905	—
7067	conv cpe 2P	4,325	3,005	—
Series 75 Fleetwood (wb 138.0) - 3,227 built**				
7509F	formal sdn 5P	4,745	3,785	
7519	touring sdn 5P	4,745	2,915	
7523	touring sdn 7P	4,825	3,070	
7523S	touring spt sdn 7P	4,825	2,710	
7523SL	touring bus sdn 8P	4,825	2,845	
7529	conv sdn 5P	4,980	3,730	
7533	Imp touring sdn 7P	4,985	3,270	
7533S	tour Spl Imp sdn 7P	4,985	2,910	
7533SL	Imp tour bus sdn 8P	4,985	3,050	
7539	town sdn 5P	4,780	3,425	
7543	town car 7P	5,055	4,855	
Series 85 Fleetwood (wb 138.0) - 474 built				
8509F	formal sdn 5P	5,050	4,500	—
8519	touring sdn 5P	5,050	3,635	—
8523	touring sdn 7P	5,130	3,790	—
8529	conv sdn 5P	5,165	4,450	—
8533	Imp touring sdn 7P	5,165	3,990	—
8539	town sdn 5P	5,000	4,145	—
8543	town car 7P	5,230	5,575	—
Series 90 (wb 154.0) - 49 built				
5825	town cab	6,390	9,230	2
5833S	town sdn 5P	6,085	7,595	2
5875	limo 7P	6,190	7,900	24
5875S	sdn 7P	6,190	7,645	2
5875SF	sdn 7P SQ	6,200	—	1
5875FL	Imperial cab 7P	6,210	8,155	3
5876	stationary cpe 2P	5,840	7,745	4
5880	conv sdn 5P	6,100	8,205	5
5885	conv cpe 5P	—	8,150	2
5891	limo b'ham	—	9,150	1
5899	Aero cpe 5P	—	8,150	1
—	Chassis	—	—	2

*Includes commercials on 160-in. wheelbase

**Includes commercials on 155-in. wheelbase

1937 Engines	bore×stroke	bhp	availability
V-8, 346.0	3.50×4.50	135	S-60, 65, 70, 75
V-12, 368.0	3.13×4.00	150	S-85
V-16, 452.0	3.00×4.00	185	S-90

1938

Series 60 (wb 124.0)		Wght	Price	Prod
6119	sdn 4d	3,940	1,730	1,295
6119	sdn 4d CKD	—	—	12
6127	cpe 2P	3,855	1,695	438
6149	conv sdn 5P	3,980	2,215	60
6167	conv cpe 2P	3,845	1,815	145
—	comm chas (wb 159.0)	—	—	101
Series Sixty Spcl (wb 127.0)		**Wght**	**Price**	**Prod**
6019S	sdn 4d	4,170	2,090	3,587

Series Sixty Spcl (wb 127.0)		Wght	Price	Prod
6019S	sdn 4d CKD	—	—	108
—	chassis	—	—	8
Series 65 (wb 132.0)				
6519	sdn 4d	4,540	2,290	1,178
6519F	Imperial div sdn 5P	4,580	2,360	110
6549	conv sdn 5P	4,5801	2,605	110
—	chassis	—	—	3
Series 75 (wb 141.3)				
7519	sdn 5P	4,865	3,080	475
7519F	Imperial div sdn 5P	4,925	3,155	34
7523	sdn 7P	4,945	3,210	380
7523L	bus sdn 7P	4,945	3,105	25
7529	conv sdn 5P	—	—	58
7533	Imperial sdn 7P	5,105	3,360	479
7533	Imperial sdn 7P CKD	—	—	84
7533F	formal sdn 7P	5,105	3,995	40
7533L	Imperial bus sdn 7P	5,105	3,260	25
7539	town sdn 5P	4,900	3,635	56
7553	town car 7P	5,175	5,115	17
7557	cpe 2P	4,675	3,280	52
7557B	cpe 5P	4,775	3,380	42
7559	formal sdn 5P	5,105	3,995	63
7567	conv cpe	4,665	3,380	44
—	chassis (inc. 8 CKD)	—	—	24
—	comm chas (wb 161.0)	—	—	11
Series 90 (wb 141.3)				
9019	sdn 5P	5,105	5,140	43
9019F	Imperial sdn 5P	5,165	5,215	5
9023	sdn 7P	5,185	5,270	65
9029	conv sdn 5P	5,350	6,000	13
9033	Imperial sdn 7P	5,345	5,420	95
9033F	formal sdn 7P	5,345	6,055	17
9039	town sdn 5P	5,140	5,695	20
9053	town car 7P	5,415	7,175	11
9057	cpe 2P	4,915	5,340	11
9057B	cpe 5P	5,015	5,440	8
9059	formal sdn 5P	5,105	6,055	8
9067	conv cpe 2P	4,905	5,440	10
9006	Pres limo (wb 161.0)	—	—	2
—	chassis	—	—	3

1938 Engines	bore×stroke	bhp	availability
V-8, 346.0	3.50×4.50	135	S-60, 65, 70
V-8, 346.0	3.50×4.50	140	S-75
V-16, 431.0	3.25×3.25	185	S-90

1939

Series 61 (wb 126.0)		Wght	Price	Prod
6119	sdn 4d	3,770	1,680	3,955
6119	sdn 4d CKD	—	—	196
6119A	sunroof sdn 4d	—	—	43
6119F	Imperial sdn 5P	—	—	30
6127	cpe 2/4P	3,685	1,610	1,023
6129	conv sdn 5P	3,810	2,170	140
6167	conv cpe 2/4P	3,765	1,770	350
—	comm chas (wb 156.0)	—	—	237
Series Sixty Special (wb 127.0)				
6019S	sdn 4	4,110	2,090	5,135
6019S	sdn 4d CKD	—	—	84
6019SA	sunroof sdn 4d	—	—	225
6019SAF	Imp sunroof sdn 4d	—	—	55
—	chassis	—	—	7
Series 75 (wb 141.3)				
7519	sdn 5P	4,785	2,995	543
7519F	Imperial div sdn 5P	4,845	3,155	53
7523	sdn 7P	4,865	3,210	412
7523L	bus sdn 7P	4,865	3,105	33
7529	conv sdn 5P	5,030	3,945	36
7533	Imperial sdn 7P	5,025	3,360	638
7533	Imp sdn 7P CKD	—	—	60
7533F	formal sdn 7P	5,025	3,995	44
7533L	Imperial bus sdn 7P	5,025	3,260	2
7539	town sdn 5P	4,820	3,635	51
7553	town car 7P	5,095	5,115	13
7557	cpe 2P	4,595	3,280	36
7557B	cpe 5P	4,695	3,380	23
7559	formal sdn 5P	4,785	3,995	53
7567	conv cpe 2P	4,675	3,380	27
—	chassis	—	—	13
—	comm chas (wb 161.0)	—	—	28
Series 90 (wb 141.3)				
9019	sdn 5P	5,190	5,140	13
9019F	Imperial sdn 5P	5,265	5,215	2
9023	sdn 7P	5,215	5,270	18
9029	conv sdn 5P	5,220	6,000	4
9033	Imperial sdn 7P	5,260	5,420	60
9033F	formal sdn 7P	5,260	6,055	8
9039	town sdn 5P	5,230	5,695	2
9053	town car 7P	5,330	7,175	5
9057	cpe 2P	4,830	5,340	6
9057B	cpe 5P	4,930	5,440	5
9059	formal sdn 5P	5,190	6,055	4
9067	conv cpe 2P	4,970	5,440	7
—	chassis	—	—	2

1939 Engines	bore×stroke	bhp	availability
V-8, 346.0	3.50×4.50	135	S-60, 61
V-8, 346.0	3.50×4.50	140	S-75
V-16, 431.0	3.25×3.25	185	S-90

1940

Series 62 (wb 129.0)		Wght	Price	Prod
6219	sdn 4d	4,065	1,745	4,302
6227	cpe 2/4P	3,975	1,685	1,322
6229	conv sdn	4,265	2,195	75
6267	conv cpe	4,080	1,795	200
62	chassis	—	—	1
Series Sixty Special (wb 127.0)				
6019F	division sdn	4,110	2,230	110
6019S	sdn 4d	4,070	2,090	4,472
6053LB	twn car-leather bck	4,365	3,820	6
6053MB	twn car-metal bck	4,365	3,465	9
Series 72 (wb 138.0)				
7219	sdn 4d	4,670	2,670	455
7219F	division sdn	4,710	2,740	100
7223	sdn 4d, 7P	4,700	2,785	305
7223L	livery sdn 7P	4,700	2,690	25
7233	Imperial sdn 7P	4,740	2,915	292
7233F	formal sdn 7P	4,780	3,695	20
7233L	livery imp sdn 7P	4,740	2,825	36
7259	formal sdn	4,670	3,695	18
72	comm chas (wb 165.0)	—	—	275
Series 75 (wb 141.3)				
7519	sdn 4d	4,900	2,995	155
7419F	division sdn	4,940	3,155	25
7523	sdn 4d, 7P	4,930	3,210	166
7529	conv sdn 7P,T/B	5,110	3,945	45
7533	Imperial sdn 7P	4,970	3,360	338
7533F	formal sdn 7P	4,970	3,995	42
7539	town sdn	4,935	3,635	14
7553	town car 7P	5,195	5,115	14
7557	cpe 2/4P	4,785	3,280	15
7557B	cpe	4,810	3,380	12
7559	formal sdn, T/B	4,900	3,995	48
7567	conv cpe	4,915	3,380	30
75	chassis	—	—	3
75	comm chas (wb 161.0)	—	—	52
Series 90 Sixteen (wb 141.3)				
9019	sdn 4d	5,190	5,140	4
9023	sdn 4d, 7P	5,215	5,270	4
9029	conv sdn, T/B	5,265	5,795	2
9033	Imperial sdn 7P	5,260	5,225	20
9033F	formal sdn 7P, T/B	5,260	5,845	20
9039	town sdn, T/B	5,220	5,495	1
9053	town car 7P, T/B	5,330	6,945	2
9057	cpe 2/4P	4,830	5,145	2
9057B	cpe	4,930	5,245	1
9059	formal sdn, T/B	5,190	5,845	2
9067	conv cpe 2/4P	4,970	5,245	2
90	chassis	—	3,700	1

1940 Engines	bore×stroke	bhp	availability
V-8, 346.0	3.50×4.50	135	S-62, 60S
V-8, 346.0	3.50×4.50	140	S-72, 75
V-16, 431.0	3.25×3.25	185	S-Sixteen

1941

Series 61 (wb 126.0)		Wght	Price	Prod
6109	sdn 4d	4,065	1,445	10,925
6109D	del sdn 4d	4,085	1,535	3,495
6127	cpe	3,985	1,345	11,812
6127D	del cpe	4,005	1,435	3,015
61	chassis	—	—	3
Series 62 (wb 126.0)				
6219	sdn 4d	4,030	1,495	8,012
6219D	del sdn 4d	4,050	1,585	7,850
6227	cpe 2/4P	3,950	1,420	1,985
6227D	del cpe 2/4P	3,970	1,510	1,900
6229D	conv sdn	4,230	1,965	400
6267D	conv cpe	4,055	1,645	3,100
62	chassis	—	—	4
62	comm chas (wb 163.0)	—	—	1,475
Series 63 (wb 126.0)				
6319	sdn 4d	4,140	1,695	5,050
Series Sixty Special (wb 126.0)				
6019	sdn 4d	4,230	2,195	3,878
6019F	division sdn	4,290	2,345	220
6053LB	town car	4,485	—	1
60	chassis	—	—	1
Series 67 (wb 139.0)				
6719	sdn 4d	4,555	2,595	315
6719F	division sdn	4,615	2,745	95
6723	sdn 4d, 7P	4,630	2,735	280
6733	Imperial sdn 7P	4,705	2,890	210
Series 75 (wb 136.0)				
7519	sdn 4d	4,750	2,995	422
7519F	division sdn	4,810	3,150	132
7523	sdn 4d, 7P	4,800	3,140	405
7523L	business sdn 9P	4,750	2,895	54
7533	Imperial sdn 7P	4,860	3,295	757
7533F	formal sdn 7P	4,915	4,045	98
7533L	business imp sdn 7P	4,810	3,050	6
7559	formal sdn	4,900	3,920	75
75	chassis	—	—	5
75	comm chas (wb 163.0)	—	—	150

1941 Engine	bore×stroke	bhp	availability
V-8, 346.0	3.50×4.50	150	S-all

1942

Series 61 (wb 126.0)		Wght	Price	Prod
6107	club cpe	4,035	1,450	2,482
6109	sdn 4d	4,115	1,530	3,218
Series 62 (wb 129.0)				
6207	club cpe	4,105	1,545	515
6207D	club cpe	4,125	1,630	530
6267D	conv cpe	4,365	1,880	308
6269	sdn 4d	4,185	1,630	1,780
6269D	sdn 4d	4,205	1,705	1,827
Series 63 (wb 126.0)				
6319	sdn 4d	4,115	1,745	1,750
Series Sixty Special (wb 133.0)				
6069	sdn 4d	4,310	2,265	1,684
6069F	division sdn	4,365	2,415	190
60	chassis	—	—	1
Series 67 (wb 138.0)				
6719	sdn 4d	4,605	2,700	200
6719F	division sdn	4,665	2,845	50
6723	sdn 7P	4,680	2,845	260
6733	Imperial sdn 7P	4,755	2,995	190
Series 75 (wb 136.0)				
7519	sdn 4d	4,750	3,080	205
7519F	division sdn	4,810	3,230	65
7523	sdn 4d, 7P	4,800	3,230	225
7523L	business sdn 9P	4,750	2,935	29
7533	Imperial sdn 7P	4,860	3,375	430
7533F	formal sdn 7P	4,915	4,215	80
7533L	business imp sdn 9P	4,860	3,080	6
7559	formal sdn	4,900	4,060	60
75	chassis	—	—	1
75	comm chas (wb 163.0)	—	—	425

1942 Engine	bore×stroke	bhp	availability
V-8, 346.0	3.50×4.50	150	S-all

1946

Series 61 (wb 126.0)		Wght	Price	Prod
6107	club cpe	4,145	2,052	800
6109	sdn 4d	4,225	2,176	2,200

Series 61 (wb 126.0)		Wght	Price	Prod
61	chassis	—	—	1

Series 62 (wb 129.0)				
6207	club cpe	4,215	2,284	2,323
6267D	conv cpe	4,475	2,556	1,342
6269	sdn 4d	4,295	2,359	14,900
62	chassis	—	—	1

Series Sixty Special (wb 133.0)				
6069	sdn 4d	4,420	3,095	5,700

Series 75 (wb 136.0)				
7519	sdn 4d	4,860	4,298	150
7523	sdn 4d, 7P	4,905	4,475	225
7523L	business sdn 9P	4,920	4,153	22
7533	Imperial sdn 7P	4,925	4,669	221
7533L	business imp sdn 9P	4,925	4,346	17
75	comm chas (wb 163.0)	—	—	1,292

1946 Engine	bore×stroke	bhp	availability
V-8, 346.0	3.50×4.50	150	S-all

1947

Series 61 (wb 126.0)		Wght	Price	Prod
6107	club cpe	4,080	2,200	3,395
6109	sdn 4d	4,165	2,324	5,160

Series 62 (wb 129.0)				
6207	club cpe	4,145	2,446	7,245
6267	conv cpe	4,455	2,902	6,755
6269	sdn 4d	4,235	2,523	25,834
62	chassis	—	—	1

Series Sixty Special (wb 133.0)				
6069	sdn 4d	4,370	3,195	8,500

Series 75 (wb 136.0)				
7519	sdn 4d	4,875	4,471	300
7523	sdn 4d, 7P	4,895	4,686	890
7523L	business sdn 9P	4,790	4,368	135
7533	Imperial sdn 7P	4,930	4,887	1,005
7533L	business imp sdn 9P	4,800	4,560	80
75	chassis	—	—	3
75	comm & bus chas (wb 163.0)	—	—	2,623

1947 Engine	bore×stroke	bhp	availability
V-8, 346.0	3.50×4.50	150	S-all

1948

Series 61 (wb 126.0)		Wght	Price	Prod
6107	club cpe	4,068	2,728	3,521
6169	sdn 4d	4,150	2,833	5,081
61	chassis	—	—	1

Series 62 (wb 126.0)				
6207	club cpe	4,125	2,912	4,764
6267	conv cpe	4,449	3,442	5,450
6259	sdn 4d	4,179	2,996	23,997
62	chassis	—	—	2

Series Sixty Special (wb 133.0)				
6069	sdn 4d	4,356	3,820	6,561

Series 75 (wb 136.0)				
7519	sdn 4d	4,875	4,779	225
7523	sdn 4d, 7P	4,878	4,999	499
7523L	business sdn 9P	4,780	4,679	90
7533	Imperial sdn 7P	4,959	5,199	382
7533L	bus imperial sdn 9P	—	—	64
75	chassis	—	—	2
75	comm chas (wb 163.0)	—	—	2,067

1948 Engine	bore×stroke	bhp	availability
V-8, 346.0	3.50×4.50	150	S-all

1949

Series 61 (wb 126.0)		Wght	Price	Prod
6107	club cpe	3,838	2,788	6,409
6169	sdn 4d	3,915	2,893	15,738
61	chassis	—	—	1

Series 62 (wb 126.0)				
6207	club cpe	3,862	2,966	7,515
6237	Cpe de Ville htp cpe	4,033	3,497	2,150
6267	conv cpe	4,218	3,523	8,000
6269	sdn 4d	3,956	3,050	37,977
62	chassis	—	—	1

Series Sixty Spec (wb 133.0)		Wght	Price	Prod
6037	Cpe de Ville htp cpe	4,200	—	1
6069	sdn 4d	4,129	3,828	11,399

Series 75 (wb 136.0)				
7519	sdn 4d	4,579	4,750	220
7523	sdn 4d, 7P	4,626	4,970	595
7523L	business sdn 9P	4,522	4,650	35
7533	Imperial sdn 7P	4,648	5,170	626
7533L	business imp sdn 9P	4,573	4,839	25
75	chassis	—	—	1
86	comm chas (wb 163.0)	—	—	1,861

1949 Engine	bore×stroke	bhp	availability
V-8, 331.0	3.81×3.63	160	S-all

1950

Series 61 (wb 122.0)		Wght	Price	Prod
6137	htp cpe	3,829	2,761	11,839
6169	sdn 4d	3,822	2,866	14,931
61	chassis	—	—	2

Series 62 (wb 126.0)				
6219	sdn 4d	4,012	3,234	41,890
6237	htp cpe	3,933	3,150	6,434
6237D	Cpe de Ville htp cpe	4,074	3,523	4,507
6267	conv cpe	4,316	3,654	6,986
62	chassis	—	—	1

Series Sixty Special (wb 130.0)				
6019	sdn 4d	4,136	3,797	13,755

Series 75 (wb 146.8)				
7523	sdn 4d, 7P	4,555	4,770	716
7523L	business sdn 9P	4,235	export	1
7533	Imperial sdn 7P	4,586	4,959	743
86	comm chas (wb 157.0)	—	—	2,052

1950 Engine	bore×stroke	bhp	availability
V-8, 331.0	3.81×3.63	160	S-all

1951

Series 61 (wb 122.0)		Wght	Price	Prod
6137	htp cpe	3,829	2810	2,400
6189	sdn 4d	3,827	2,917	2,300

Series 62 (wb 126.0)				
6219	sdn 4d	4,062	3,528	55,352
6237	htp cpe	4,081	3,436	10,132
6237D	Cpe de Ville htp cpe	4,156	3,843	10,241
6267	conv cpe	4,377	3,987	6,117
62-126	chassis	—	—	2

Series Sixty Special (wb 130.0)				
6019	sdn 4d	4,234	4,142	18,631

Series 75 (wb 146.8)				
7523	sdn 4d, 8P	4,621	5,200	1,090
7523L	business sdn 9P	4,300	—	30
7533	Imperial sdn 8P	4,652	5,405	1,085
86	comm chas (wb 157.0)	—	—	2,960

1951 Engine	bore×stroke	bhp	availability
V-8, 331.0	3.81×3.63	160	S-all

1952

Series 62 (wb 126.0)		Wght	Price	Prod
6219	sdn 4d	4,140	3,684	42,625
6237	htp cpe	4,173	3,587	10,065
6237D	Cpe de Ville htp cpe	4,203	4,013	11,165
6267	conv cpe	4,416	4,163	6,400

Series Sixty Special (wb 130.0)				
6019	sdn 4d	4,255	4,323	16,110

Series 75 (wb 146.8)				
7523	sdn 4d, 8P	4,698	5,428	1,400
7533	Imperial sdn 8P	4,733	5,643	800
8680S	comm chas (wb 157.0)	—	—	1,694

1952 Engine	bore×stroke	bhp	availability
V-8, 331.0	3.81×3.63	190	S-all

1953

Series 62 (wb 126.0)		Wght	Price	Prod
6219	sdn 4d	4,225	3,666	47,640
6237	htp cpe	4,230	3,571	14,353
6237D	Cpe de Ville htp cpe	4,340	3,995	14,550
6267	conv cpe	4,500	4,144	8,367
6267S	Eldorado conv cpe	4,800	7,750	532
62	chassis	—	—	4

Series Sixty Spec (wb 130.0)		Wght	Price	Prod
6019	sdn 4d	4,415	4,305	20,000

Series 75 (wb 146.8)				
7523	sdn 4d, 8P	4,830	5,408	1,435
7533	Imperial sdn 8P	4,850	5,621	765
8680S	comm chas (wb 157.0)	—	—	2,005

1953 Engine	bore×stroke	bhp	availability
V-8, 331.0	3.81×3.63	210	S-all

1954

Series 62 (wb 129.0)		Wght	Price	Prod
6219	sdn 4d	4,370	3,933	34,252
6219S	De Ville htp sdn	—	proto	1
6237	htp cpe	4,365	3,838	17,460
6237D	Cpe de Ville htp cpe	4,405	4,261	17,170
6267	conv cpe	4,610	4,404	6,310
6267S	Eldorado conv cpe	4,815	5,738	2,150
62	chassis	—	—	1

Series Sixty Special (wb 133.0)				
6019	sdn 4d	4,500	4,863	16,200

Series 75 (wb 149.8)				
7523	sdn 4d, 8P	5,055	5,875	889
7533	Imperial sdn 8P	5,105	6,090	611
8680S	comm chas (wb 158.0)	—	—	1,635

1954 Engine	bore×stroke	bhp	availability
V-8, 331.0	3.81×3.63	230	S-all

1955

Series 62 (wb 129.0)		Wght	Price	Prod
6219	sdn 4d	4,370	3,977	45,300
6237	htp cpe	4,358	3,882	27,879
6237D	Cpe de Ville htp cpe	4,424	4,305	33,300
6267	conv cpe	4,627	4,448	8,150
6267S	Eldorado conv cpe	4,809	6,286	3,950
62	chassis	—	—	7

Series Sixty Special (wb 133.0)				
6019	sdn 4d	4,540	4,728	18,300

Series 75 (wb 149.8)				
7523	sdn 4d, 8P	5,020	6,187	1,075
7533	limo 8P	5,113	6,402	841
8680S	comm chas (wb 158.0)	—	—	1,975

1955 Engines	bore×stroke	bhp	availability
V-8, 331.0	3.81×3.63	250	S-62, 60S, 75
V-8, 331.0	3.81×3.63	270	S-Eldorado

1956

Series 62 (wb 129.0)		Wght	Price	Prod
6219	sdn 4d	4,430	4,296	26,666
6237	htp cpe	4,420	4,201	26,649
6237D	Cpe de Ville htp cpe	4,445	4,624	24,086
6237S	EldoSeville htp cpe	4,665	6,556	3,900
6239D	Sdn de Ville htp sdn	4,550	4,753	41,732
6267	conv cpe	4,645	4,766	8,300
6267S	Eldo Biarritz conv cpe	4,880	6,556	2,150
62	chassis	—	—	19

Series Sixty Special (wb 133.0)				
6019	sdn 4d	4,610	5,047	17,000

Series 75 (wb 149.8)				
7523	sdn 4d, 8P	5,050	6,613	1,095
7533	limo 8P	5,130	6,828	955
8680S	comm chas (wb 158.0)	—	—	2,025

1956 Engines	bore×stroke	bhp	availability
V-8, 365.0	4.00×3.63	285	S-62, 60S, 75
V-8, 365.0	4.00×3.63	305	S-Eldorado

1957

Series 62 (wb 129.5)		Wght	Price	Prod
6237	htp cpe	4,565	4,677	25,120
6237D	Cpe de Ville htp cpe	4,620	5,116	23,813
6237S	Eldo Seville htp cpe	4,810	7,286	2,100
6239	htp sdn	4,595	4,781	32,342
6239D	Sdn de Ville htp sdn	4,655	5,256	23,808
6239S	Eldo Seville htp sdn	4,810	7,286	4
6267	conv cpe	4,730	5,293	9,000
6267S	Eldo Biarritz conv cpe	4,930	7,286	1,800
62	chassis & export sdn	—	—	385

Series Sixty Special (wb 133.0)				
6039	htp sdn	4,735	5,614	24,000

Series 70 Eldo Brghm (wb 126.0)		Wght	Price	Prod
7059	htp sdn	5,315	13,074	400

Series 75 (wb 149.8)		Wght	Price	Prod
7523	sdn 4d, 8P	5,340	7,440	1,010
7533	limo 8P	5,390	7,678	890
8680S	comm chas (wb 156.0)	—	—	2,169

1957 Engines	bore×stroke	bhp	availability
V-8, 365.0	4.00×3.63	300	S-62, 60S
V-8, 365.0	4.00×3.63	325	S-70, O-62, Eldo

1958

Series 62 (wb 129.5)		Wght	Price	Prod
6237	htp cpe	4,630	4,784	18,736
6237D	Cpe de Ville htp cpe	4,705	5,251	18,414
6237S	Eldo Seville htp cpe	4,910	7,500	855
6239	htp sdn	4,675	4,891	13,335
6239E	htp sdn (ext. deck)	4,770	5,079	20,952
6239	Sdn de Ville htp sdn	4,855	5,497	23,989
6267	conv cpe	4,856	5,454	7,825
6267S	Eldo Biarritz conv cpe	5,070	7,500	815
62	chassis & exp sdn	—	—	206

Series Sixty Special (wb 133.0)		Wght	Price	Prod
6039	htp sdn	4,930	6,232	12,900

Series 70 Eldorado Brougham (wb 126.0)		Wght	Price	Prod
7059	htp sdn	5,315	13,074	304

Series 75 (wb 149.8)		Wght	Price	Prod
7523	sdn 4d, 9P	5,360	8,460	802
7533	limo 9P	5,425	8,675	730
8680S	comm chas (wb 156.0)	—	—	1,915

1958 Engines	bore×stroke	bhp	availability
V-8, 365.0	4.00×3.63	310	S-all exc Eldo
V-8, 365.0	4.00×3.63	335	S-Eldo; O-all

1959

Series 62 (wb 130.0)		Wght	Price	Prod
6229	htp sdn 6W	4,835	5,080	23,461
6237	htp cpe	4,690	4,892	21,947
6239	htp sdn 4W	4,770	5,080	14,138
6267	conv cpe	4,855	5,455	11,130
62	export htp sdn 6W	4,835	5,080	60

De Ville (wb 130.0)		Wght	Price	Prod
6329	htp sdn 6W	4,850	5,498	19,158
6337	htp cpe	4,720	5,252	21,924
6339	htp sdn 4W	4,825	5,498	12,308

Eldorado (wb 130.0)		Wght	Price	Prod
6437	Seville htp cpe	—	7,401	975
6467	Biarritz conv cpe	—	7,401	1,320
6929	Brougham htp sdn	—	13,075	99

Series Sixty Special (wb 130.0)		Wght	Price	Prod
6039	htp sdn	4,890	6,233	12,250

Series 75 (wb 149.8)		Wght	Price	Prod
6723	sdn 4d, 9P	5,490	9,533	710
6733	limo 9P	5,570	9,748	690
6890	comm chas (wb 156.0)	—	—	2,102

1959 Engines	bore×stroke	bhp	availability
V-8, 390.0	4.00×3.88	325	S-62, De Ville, 60S, 75
V-8, 390.0	4.00×3.88	345	S-Eldorado

1960

Series 62 (wb 130.0)		Wght	Price	Prod
6229	htp sdn 6W	4,805	5,080	26,824
6237	htp cpe	4,670	4,892	19,978
6239	htp sdn 4W	4,775	5,080	9,984
6267	conv cpe	4,850	5,455	14,000
62	chassis & export sdn	—	—	38

De Ville (wb 130.0)		Wght	Price	Prod
6329	htp sdn 6W	4,835	5,498	22,579
6337	htp cpe	4,705	5,252	21,585
6339	htp sdn 4W	4,815	5,498	9,225

Eldorado (wb 130.0)		Wght	Price	Prod
6437	Seville htp cpe	—	7,401	1,075
6467	Biarritz conv cpe	—	7,401	1,285
6929	Brougham htp sdn	—	13,075	101

Series Sixty Special (wb 130.0)		Wght	Price	Prod
6039	htp sdn	4,880	6,233	11,800

Series 75 (wb 149.8)		Wght	Price	Prod
6723	sdn 4d, 9P	5,475	9,533	718
6733	limo 9P	5,560	9,748	832
6890	comm chas (wb 156.0)	—	—	2,160

1960 Engines	bore×stroke	bhp	availability
V-8, 390.0	4.00×3.88	325	S-62, De Ville, 60S, 75
V-8, 390.0	4.00×3.88	345	S-Eldorado

1961

Series 62 (wb 129.5)		Wght	Price	Prod
6229	htp sdn 6W	4,680	5,080	26,216
6237	htp cpe	4,560	4,892	16,005
6239	htp sdn 4W	4,660	5,080	4,700
6267	conv	4,720	5,455	15,500
62	chassis	—	—	5
6399	town sedan hpt 6W	—	—	3,756

De Ville (wb 129.5)		Wght	Price	Prod
6329	hpt sdn 6W	4,710	5,498	26,415
6337	hpt cpe	4,595	5,252	20,156
6339	hpt sdn 4W	4,715	5,498	4,847

Eldorado (wb 129.5)		Wght	Price	Prod
6367	Biarritz conv cpe	—	6,477	1,450

Series Sixty Special (wb 129.5)		Wght	Price	Prod
6039	htp sdn	4,770	6,233	15,500

Series 75 (wb 149.8)		Wght	Price	Prod
6723	sdn 4d, 9P	5,390	9,533	699
6733	limo 9P	5,420	9,748	926
6890	comm chas (wb 156.0)	—	—	2,204

1961 Engine	bore×stroke	bhp	availability
V-8, 390.0	4.00×3.88	325	S-all

1962

Series 62 (wb 129.5)		Wght	Price	Prod
6229	htp sdn 6W	4,640	5,213	16,730
6239	htp sdn 4W	4,645	5,213	17,314
6247	htp cpe	4,530	5,025	16,833
6267	conv cpe	4,630	5,588	16,800
6289	town sedan htp sdn	4,590	5,213	2,600

De Ville (wb 129.5)		Wght	Price	Prod
6329	htp sdn 6W	4,660	5,631	16,230
6339	htp sdn 4W	4,675	5,631	27,378
6347	htp cpe	4,595	5,385	25,675
6389	Park Avenue htp sdn	4,655	5,631	2,600

Eldorado (wb 129.5)		Wght	Price	Prod
6367	Biarritz conv cpe	4,620	6,610	1,450

Series Sixty Special (wb 129.5)		Wght	Price	Prod
6039	htp sdn 6W	4,710	6,366	13,350

Series 75 (wb 149.8)		Wght	Price	Prod
6723	sdn 4d, 9P	5,325	9,722	696
6733	limo 9P	5,390	9,937	904
6890	comm chas (wb 156.0)	—	—	2,280

1962 Engine	bore×stroke	bhp	availability
V-8, 390.0	4.00×3.88	325	S-all

1963

Series 62 (wb 129.5)		Wght	Price	Prod
6229	htp sdn 6W	4,610	5,214	12,929
6239	htp sdn 4W	4,595	5,214	16,980
6257	htp cpe	4,505	5,026	17,786
6267	conv cpe	4,545	5,590	17,600
62	chassis	—	—	3

De Ville (wb 129.5)		Wght	Price	Prod
6329	htp sdn 6W	4,650	5,633	15,146
6339	htp sdn 4W	4,605	5,633	30,579
6357	htp cpe	4,520	5,386	31,749
6389	Park Avenue htp sdn	4,590	5,633	1,575

Eldorado (wb 129.5)		Wght	Price	Prod
6367	Biarritz conv cpe	4,640	6,608	1,825

Series Sixty Special (wb 129.5)		Wght	Price	Prod
6039	htp sdn	4,690	6,366	14,000

Series 75 (wb 149.8)		Wght	Price	Prod
6723	sdn 4d, 9P	5,240	9,724	680
6733	limo 9P	5,300	9,939	795
6890	comm chas (wb 156.0)	—	—	2,527

1963 Engine	bore×stroke	bhp	availability
V-8, 390.0	4.00×3.88	325	S-all

1964

Series 62 (wb 129.5)		Wght	Price	Prod
6229	htp sdn 6W	4,575	5,236	9,243
6239	htp sdn 4W	4,550	5,236	13,670
6257	htp cpe	4,475	5,048	12,166
6267	conv cpe	4,545	5,612	17,900

De Ville (wb 129.5)		Wght	Price	Prod
6329	htp sdn 6W	4,600	5,655	14,627
6339	htp cpe 4W	4,575	5,655	39,674
6357	htp cpe	4,495	5,408	38,195

Eldorado (wb 129.5)		Wght	Price	Prod
6367	Biarritz conv cpe	4,605	6,630	1,870

Series Sixty Special (wb 129.5)		Wght	Price	Prod
6039	htp sdn	4,680	6,388	14,550

Series 75 (wb 149.8)		Wght	Price	Prod
6723	sdn 4d, 9P	5,215	9,746	617
6733	limo 9P	5,300	9,960	808
6890	comm chas (wb 156.0)	—	—	2,639

1964 Engine	bore×stroke	bhp	availability
V-8, 429.0	4.13×4.00	340	S-all

1965

Calais (wb 129.5)		Wght	Price	Prod
68239	htp sdn	4,500	5,247	13,975
68257	htp cpe	4,435	5,059	12,515
68269	sdn 4d	4,490	5,247	7,721

De Ville (wb 129.5)		Wght	Price	Prod
68339	htp sdn	4,560	5,666	45,535
68357	htp cpe	4,480	5,419	43,345
68367	conv cpe	4,690	5,639	19,200
68369	sdn 4d	4,555	5,666	15,000

Eldorado (wb 129.5)		Wght	Price	Prod
68467	conv cpe	4,660	6,738	2,125

Sixty Special (wb 133.0)		Wght	Price	Prod
68069	sdn 4d	4,670	6,479	18,100

Seventy-Five (wb 149.8)		Wght	Price	Prod
69723	sdn 4d, 9P	5,190	9,746	455
69733	limo 9P	5,260	9,960	795
69890	comm chas (wb 156.0)	—	—	2,669

1965 Engine	bore×stroke	bhp	availability
V-8, 429.0	4.13×4.00	340	S-all

1966

Calais (wb 129.5)		Wght	Price	Prod
68239	htp sdn	4,465	5,171	13,025
68257	htp cpe	4,390	4,986	11,080
68269	sdn 4d	4,460	5,171	4,575

De Ville (wb 129.5)		Wght	Price	Prod
68339	htp sdn	4,515	5,581	60,550
68357	htp cpe	4,460	5,339	50,580
68367	conv cpe	4,445	5,555	19,200
68369	sdn 4d	4,535	5,581	11,860

Eldorado (wb 129.5)		Wght	Price	Prod
68467	conv cpe	4,500	6,631	2,250

Sixty Special (wb 133.0)		Wght	Price	Prod
68069	sdn 4d	4,615	6,378	5,455
68169	Fltwd Brghm sdn 4d	4,665	6,695	13,630

Seventy-Five (wb 149.8)		Wght	Price	Prod
69723	sdn 4d, 9P	5,320	10,312	980
69733	limo 9P	5,435	10,521	1,037
69890	comm chas (wb 156.0)	—	—	2,463

1966 Engine	bore×stroke	bhp	availability
V-8, 429.0	4.13×4.00	340	S-all

1967

Calais (wb 129.5)		Wght	Price	Prod
68247	htp cpe	4,447	5,040	9,085
68249	htp sdn	4,495	5,215	9,880
68269	sdn 4d	4,499	5,215	2,865

De Ville (wb 129.5)		Wght	Price	Prod
68347	htp cpe	4,486	5,392	52,905
68349	htp sdn	4,532	5,625	59,902
68367	conv cpe	4,479	5,608	18,200

De Ville (wb 129.5)	Wght	Price	Prod
68369 sdn 4d	4,534	5,625	8,800
Eldorado (wb 120.0)			
69347 htp cpe	4,500	6,277	17,930
Sixty Special (wb 133.0)			
68069 sdn 4d	4,678	6,423	3,550
68169 Fltwd Brghm sdn 4d	4,715	6,739	12,750
Seventy-Five (wb 149.8)			
69723 sdn 4d, 9P	5,344	10,360	835
69733 limo 9P	5,436	10,571	965
68490 comm chas (wb 156.0)	—	—	2,333

1967 Engine	bore×stroke	bhp	availability
V-8, 429.0	4.13×4.00	340	S-all

1968

Calais (wb 129.5)	Wght	Price	Prod
68247 htp cpe	4,570	5,315	8,165
68249 htp sdn	4,640	5,491	10,025
De Ville (wb 129.5)			
68347 htp cpe	4,595	5,552	63,935
68349 htp sdn	4,675	5,785	72,662
68367 conv cpe	4,600	5,736	18,025
68369 sdn 4d	4,680	5,785	9,850
Eldorado (wb 120.0)			
69347 htp cpe	4,580	6,605	24,528
Sixty Special (wb 133.0)			
68069 sdn 4d	4,795	6,583	3,300
68169 Fltwd Brghm sdn 4d	4,805	6,899	15,300
Seventy-Five (wb 149.8)			
69723 sdn 4d, 9P	5,300	10,629	805
69733 limo 9P	5,385	10,768	995
69890 comm chas (wb 156.0)	—	—	2,413

1968 Engine	bore×stroke	bhp	availability
V-8, 472.0	4.30×4.06	375	S-all

1969

Calais (wb 129.5)	Wght	Price	Prod
68247 htp cpe	4,555	5,484	5,600
68349 htp sdn	4,630	5,660	6,825
De Ville (wb 129.5)			
68347 htp cpe	4,595	5,721	65,755
68349 htp sdn	4,660	5,954	72,958
68367 conv cpe	4,590	5,905	16,445
68369 sdn 4d	4,640	5,954	7,890
Eldorado (wb 120.0)			
69347 htp cpe	4,550	6,711	23,333
Sixty Special (wb 133.0)			
68069 sdn 4d	4,765	6,779	2,545
68169 Fltwd Brghm sdn 4d	4,770	7,110	17,300
Seventy-Five (wb 149.8)			
69723 sdn 4d, 9P	5,430	10,841	880
69733 limo 9P	5,555	10,979	1,156
69890 comm chas (wb 156.0)	—	—	2,550

1969 Engine	bore×stroke	bhp	availability
V-8, 472.0	4.30×4.06	375	S-all

1970

Calais (wb 129.5)	Wght	Price	Prod
68247 htp cpe	4,620	5,637	4,724
68249 htp sdn	4,680	5,813	5,187
De Ville (wb 129.5)			
68347 htp cpe	4,650	5,884	76,043
68349 htp sdn	4,725	6,118	83,274
68367 conv cpe	4,660	6,068	15,172
68369 sdn 4d	4,690	6,118	7,230
Eldorado (wb 120.0)			
69347 htp cpe	4,630	6,903	23,842
Sixty Special (wb 133.0)			
68089 sdn 4d	4,830	6,953	1,738
68189 Fltwd Brghm sdn 4d	4,835	7,284	16,913
Seventy-Five (wb 149.8)			
69723 sdn 4d, 9P	5,530	11,039	876
69733 limo 9P	5,630	11,178	1,240
69890 comm chas (wb 156.0)	—	—	2,506

1970 Engines	bore×stroke	bhp	availability
V-8, 472.0	4.30×4.06	375	S-all exc Eldo
V-8, 500.0	4.30×4.30	400	S-Eldorado

1971

Calais (wb 129.5)	Wght	Price	Prod
68247 htp cpe	4,635	5,899	3,360
68249 htp sdn	4,710	6,075	3,569
De Ville (wb 130.0)			
68347 htp cpe	4,685	6,264	66,081
68349 htp sdn	4,730	6,498	69,345
Eldorado (wb 120.0)			
69346 htp cpe	4,675	7,383	20,568
69367 conv	4,730	7,751	6,800
Sixty Special Brougham (wb 133.0)			
68169 Fleetwood sdn 4d	4,815	7,763	15,200
Seventy-Five (wb 151.5)			
69723 sdn 4d	5,510	11,869	752
69733 limo 9P	5,570	12,008	848
69890 comm chas (wb 157.5)	—	—	2,014

1971 Engines	bore×stroke	bhp	availability
V-8, 472.0	4.30×4.06	345	S-all exc Eldo
V-8, 500.0	4.30×4.30	365	S-Eldorado

1972

Calais (wb 130.0)	Wght	Price	Prod
68247 htp cpe	4,642	5,771	3,900
68249 htp sdn	4,698	5,938	3,875
De Ville (wb 130.0)			
68347 htp cpe	4,682	6,168	95,280
Calais (wb 130.0)			
68349 htp sdn	4,762	6,390	99,531
Eldorado (wb 126.3)			
69347 htp cpe	4,682	7,230	32,099
69367 conv	4,772	7,546	7,975
Sixty Special Brougham (wb 133.0)			
68169 Fltwd sdn 4d	4,858	7,637	20,750
Seventy-Five (wb 151.5)			
69723 sdn 4d	5,515	11,748	955
69733 limo 9P	5,637	11,880	960
69890 comm chas (wb 157.5)	—	—	2,462

1972 Engines	bore×stroke	bhp	availability
V-8, 472.0	4.30×4.06	220	S-all exc Eldo
V-8, 500.0	4.30×4.30	235	S-Eldorado

1973

Calais (wb 130.0)	Wght	Price	Prod
68247 htp cpe	4,900	5,866	4,275
68249 htp sdn	4,953	6,038	3,798
De Ville (wb 130.0)			
68347 htp cpe	4,925	6,268	112,849
68349 htp sdn	4,985	6,500	103,394
Eldorado (wb 126.3)			
69347 hpt cpe	4,880	7,360	42,136
69367 conv	4,966	7,681	9,315
Sixty Special Brougham (wb 133.0)			
68169 Fleetwood sdn 4d	5,102	7,765	24,800
Seventy-Five (wb 151.5)			
69723 sdn 4d	5,620	11,948	1,043
69733 limo 9P	5,742	12,080	1,017
69890 comm chas (wb 157.5)	—	—	2,212

1973 Engines	bore×stroke	bhp	availability
V-8, 472.0	4.30×4.06	220	S-all exc Eldo
V-8, 500.0	4.30×4.30	235	S-Eldorado

1974

Calais (wb 130.0)	Wght	Price	Prod
68247 cpe	4,900	7,371	4,559
68249 htp sdn 4d	4,979	7,545	2,324
De Ville (wb 130.0)			
68347 cpe	4,924	7,867	112,201
68349 htp sdn 4d	5,032	8,100	60,419
Eldorado (wb 126.3)			
69347 htp cpe	4,960	9,110	32,812
69367 conv	5,019	9,437	7,600
Sixty Spec Brghm (wb 133.0)			
68169 Fleetwood sdn 4d	5,143	9,537	18,250
Seventy-Five (wb 151.5)			
69723 sdn 4d	5,719	13,120	895
69733 limo 9P	5,883	13,254	1,005
69890 comm chas (wb 157.5)	—	—	2,265

1974 Engines	bore×stroke	bhp	availability
V-8, 472.0	4.30×4.06	205	S-all exc Eldo
V-8, 500.0	4.30×4.30	210	S-Eldorado

1975

Seville (wb 114.3)	Wght	Price	Prod
S69 sdn 4d	4,232	12,479	16,355
Calais (wb 130.0)			
68247 cpe	5,003	8,184	5,800
68249 htp sdn 4d	5,087	8,377	2,500
De Ville (wb 130.0)			
68347 cpe	5,049	8,600	110,218
68349 htp sdn 4d	5,146	8,801	63,352
Eldorado (wb 126.3)			
69347 cpe	5,108	9,935	35,802
69367 conv	5,167	10,354	8,950
Fleetwood Brougham (wb 133.0)			
68169 sdn 4d	5,242	10,414	18,755
Seventy-Five (wb 151.5)			
69723 sdn 4d	5,720	14,218	876
69733 limo 9P	5,862	14,557	795
69890 comm chas (wb 157.5)	—	—	1,329

1975 Engines	bore×stroke	bhp	availability
V-8, 350.0	4.06×3.39	180	S-Seville
V-8, 500.0	4.30×4.30	190	S-all exc Seville

1976

Seville (wb 114.3)	Wght	Price	Prod
S69 sdn 4d	4,232	12,479	43,772
Calais (wb 130.0)			
68247 cpe	4,989	8,629	4,500
68249 htp sdn 4d	5,083	8,825	1,700
De Ville (wb 130.0)			
68347 cpe	5,025	9,067	114,482
68349 htp sdn 4d	5,127	9,265	67,677
Eldorado (wb 126.3)			
69347 cpe	5,085	10,586	35,184
69367 conv	5,153	11,049	14,000
Fleetwood Brougham (wb 133.0)			
68169 sdn 4d	5,213	10,935	24,500
Seventy-Five (wb 151.5)			
69723 sdn 4d	5,746	14,889	981
69733 limo 9P	5,889	15,239	834
69890 comm chas (wb 157.5)	—	—	1,509

1976 Engines	bore×stroke	bhp	availability
V-8, 350.0	4.06×3.39	180	S-Seville
V-8, 500.0	4.30×4.30	190	S-all exc Seville
V-8, 500.0	4.30×4.30	215	O-all exc Seville

1977

Seville (wb 114.3)	Wght	Price	Prod
S69 sdn 4d	4,192	13,359	45,060
De Ville (wb 121.5)			
68347 cpe	4,186	9,810	138,750
68349 sdn 4d	4,222	10,020	95,421
Eldorado (wb 126.3)			
69347 cpe	4,955	11,187	47,344
Fleetwood Brougham (wb 121.5)			
68169 sdn 4d	4,340	11,546	28,000
Fleetwood limousine (wb 144.5)			
69723 sdn 4d	4,738	18,349	1,582
69773 formal sdn 4d	4,806	19,014	1,032
69890 comm chas (wb 157.5)	—	—	1,299

1977 Engines	bore×stroke	bhp	availability
V-8, 350.0	4.06×3.39	180	S-Seville
V-8, 425.0	4.08×4.06	180	S-all exc Seville
V-8, 425.0	4.08×4.06	195	O-Brgm, DeVil, Eldorado

1978

Seville (wb 114.3)		Wght	Price	Prod
S69	sdn 4d	4,179	14,161	56,985
De Ville (wb 121.5)				
68347	cpe	4,163	10,584	117,750
68349	sdn 4d	4,236	10,924	88,951
Eldorado (wb 126.3)				
69347	cpe	4,906	12,401	46,816
Fleetwood Brougham (wb 121.5)				
68169	sdn 4d	4,314	12,842	36,800
Fleetwood limousine (wb 144.5)				
69723	sdn 4d	4,772	20,007	848
69773	formal sdn 4d	4,858	10,742	682
69890	comm chas (wb 157.5)	—	—	852

1978 Engines	bore×stroke	bhp	availability
V-8, 350.0	4.06×3.39	170	S-Seville
V-8D, 350.0	4.06×3.39	120	O-Seville
V-8, 425.0	4.08×4.06	180	S-all exc Seville
V-8, 425.0	4.08×4.06	195	S-Brgm, DeVil, Eldorado

1979

Seville (wb 114.3)		Wght	Price	Prod
S69	sdn 4d	4,179	16,224	53,487
Eldorado (wb 114.0)				
L57	cpe	3,792	14,668	67,436
De Ville (wb 121.5)				
D47	cpe	4,143	11,728	121,890
D69	sdn 4d	4,212	12,093	93,211
Fleetwood Brougham (wb 121.5)				
B69	sdn 4d	4,240	14,102	42,200
Fleetwood limo (wb 144.5)				
F23	sdn 4d	4,782	21,869	2,025
F33	formal sdn 4d	4,866	22,640	2,025
—	comm chas (wb 157.5)	—	—	864

1979 Engines	bore×stroke	bhp	availability
V-8, 350.0	4.06×3.39	170	S-Seville, Eldo
V-8D, 350.0	4.06×3.39	125	O-all, exc limo
V-8, 425.0	4.08×4.06	180	S-all exc Seville
V-8, 425.0	4.08×4.06	195	O-Brgm, DeVil

1980

Eldorado (wb 114.0)		Wght	Price	Prod
L57	cpe	3,806	16,141	52,685
De Ville (wb 121.5)				
D47	cpe	4,048	12,899	55,490
D69	sdn 4d	4,084	13,282	49,188
Fleetwood Brougham (wb 121.5)				
B47	cpe	4,025	15,307	2,300
B69	sdn 4d	4,092	15,564	29,659
Fleetwood limousine (wb 144.5)				
F23	sdn 4d	4,629	23,509	1,612
F33	formal sdn 4d	4,718	24,343	—
—	comm chas (wb 157.5)	—	—	750
Seville (wb 114.3)				
S69	sdn 4d	3,911	20,477	39,344

1980 Engines	bore×stroke	bhp	availability
V-8D, 350.0	4.06×3.39	105	S-Sevil; O-Fleet Brgm, Eldo
V-8, 350.0	4.06×3.39	160	O-Seville, Eldo
V-8, 368.0	3.80×4.06	150	S-DeV, Fltwd
V-8, 368.0	3.80×4.06	145	S-Eldo; O-Sevil

1981

Seville (wb 114.0)		Wght	Price	Prod
S69	sdn 4d	4,167	21,088	28,631
Eldorado (wb 114.0)				
L57	cpe	3,930	16,492	60,643
De Ville (wb 121.4)				
D47	cpe	4,151	13,450	54,145
D69	sdn 4d	4,202	13,847	55,100
Fleetwood Brougham (wb 121.4)				
B47	cpe	4,204	15,942	8,300
B69	sdn 4d	4,250	16,365	31,500
Fleetwood limo (wb 144.5)				
F23	sdn 4d	4,629	24,464	610
F33	formal sdn 4d	4,717	25,323	590
	commercial chassis	—	—	670

1981 Engines	bore×stroke	bhp	availability
V-6, 252.0	3.97×3.40	125	O-all exc limos
V-8D, 350.0	4.06×3.39	105	S-Seville; O-DeVil, Brgm, Eldorado
V-8-6-4, 368.0	3.80×4.06	140	S-DeV, Brgm, Eldo; O-Seville
V-8, 368.0	3.80×4.06	150	S-comm chas

1982

Cimarron (wb 101.2)		Wght	Price	Prod
G69	sdn 4d	2,594	12,131	25,968
Seville (wb 114.0)				
S69	sdn 4d	4,167	23,433	19,998
Eldorado (wb 114.0)				
L57	cpe	3,930	18,716	52,018
De Ville (wb 121.4)				
D47	cpe	3,923	15,249	44,950
D69	sdn 4d	3,979	15,699	53,870
Fleetwood Brougham (wb 121.4)				
B47	cpe	3,965	18,096	5,180
B69	sdn 4d	4,006	18,567	32,150
Fleetwood limousine (wb 144.5)				
F23	sdn 4d	4,628	27,961	514
F33	formal sdn 4d	4,718	28,941	486
	commercial chassis	—	—	450

1982 Engines	bore×stroke	bhp	availability
I-4, 112.0	3.50×2.90	88	S-Cimarron
V-8, 249.0	3.46×3.31	125	S-Sev, Eldo, De Ville, Fltwd
V-6, 252.0	3.97×3.40	125	O-Sev, Eldo, De Ville, Fltwd
V-8D, 350.0	4.06×3.39	105	O-Seville, Eldo, De Ville, Fltwd
V-8-6-4, 368.0	3.80×4.06	140	S-limousines
V-8, 368.0	3.80×4.06	150	S-comm chas

1983

Cimarron (wb 101.2)		Wght	Price	Prod
G69	sdn 4d	2,639	12,215	19,294
Seville (wb 114.0)				
S69	sdn 4d	3,844	21,440	30,430
Eldorado (wb 114.0)				
L57	cpe	3,748	19,334	67,416
De Ville (wb 121.5)				
D47	cpe	3,935	15,970	60,300
D69	sdn 4d	3,993	16,441	70,423
Fleetwood Brougham (wb 121.5)				
B47	cpe	3,986	18,688	5,200
B69	sdn 4d	4,029	19,182	38,300
Fleetwood limousine (wb 144.5)				
F23	sdn 4d	4,765	29,323	492
F33	formal sdn 4d	4,852	30,349	508
	commercial chassis	—	—	451

1983 Engines	bore×stroke	bhp	availability
I-4, 121.0	3.50×3.15	88	S-Cimarron
V-8, 249.0	3.46×3.30	135	S-Sev, Eldo, DeVil, Fltwd
V-8D, 350.0	4.06×3.39	105	O-Seville, Eldo, DeVil, Fltwd
V-8-6-4, 368.0	3.80×4.06	140	S-limousines
V-8, 368.0	3.80×4.06	150	S-comm chas

1984

Cimarron (wb 101.2)		Wght	Price	Prod
G69	sdn 4d	2,583	12,614	21,898
Seville (wb 114.0)				
S69	sdn 4d	3,804	22,468	39,997
Eldorado (wb 114.0)				
L57	cpe	3,734	20,342	74,506
L67	Biarritz conv cpe	3,926	31,286	3,300
De Ville (wb 121.5)				
M47	cpe	3,940	17,140	46,340
M69	sdn 4d	3,981	17,625	68,270
Fleetwood Brougham (wb 121.5)				
W47	cpe	3,990	19,942	4,500
W69	sdn 4d	4,034	20,451	39,650
Fleetwood limousine (wb 144.5)				
F23	sdn 4d	4,765	30,454	462
F33	formal sdn 4d	4,855	31,512	631
	commercial chassis	—	—	746

1984 Engines	bore×stroke	bhp	availability
I-4, 121.0	3.50×3.15	88	S-Cimarron
V-8, 249.0	3.46×3.30	135	S-Sev, Eldo, DeVil, Fltwd
V-8D, 350.0	4.06×3.39	105	O-Seville, Eldo, DeVil, Fltwd
V-8-6-4, 368.0	3.80×4.06	140	S-limousines

1985

Cimarron (wb 101.2)		Wght	Price	Prod
G69	sdn 4d	2,583	12,962	19,890
Seville (wb 114.0)				
S69	sdn 4d	3,803	23,259	39,755
Eldorado (wb 114.0)				
L57	cpe	3,724	20,931	74,101
L67	conv cpe	3,915	22,105	2,300

Note: Production total includes 2,463 Commemorative Edition models.

De Ville (wb 110.8)		Wght	Price	Prod
D47	cpe	3,324	17,990	39,500*
D69	sdn 4d	3,396	18,571	101,366*
Fleetwood (wb 110.8)				
B47	cpe	3,346	21,069	*
B69	sdn 4d	3,422	21,040	*

* Fleetwood prod. included in De Ville cpe and sdn totals.

Fleetwood Brougham RWD (wb 121.5)		Wght	Price	Prod
W47	cpe	3,977	20,798	3,000
W69	sdn 4d	4,020	21,402	52,450
Fleetwood limousine (wb 134.4)				
H23	sdn 4d	3,583	32,640	405
H33	formal sdn 4d	3,642	—	—

1985 Engines	bore×stroke	bhp	availability
I-4, 121.0	3.50×3.15	88	S-Cimarron
V-6, 173.0	3.50×2.99	125	O-Cimarron
V-8, 249.0	3.46×3.30	125	S-DeV, Fltwd, limo
V-8, 249.0	3.46×3.30	135	S-Sev, Eldo, Brgm
V-6D, 262.0	4.06×3.39	85	O-DeV, Fltwd
V-8D, 350.0	4.06×3.39	105	O-Sev, Eldo, Brgm

1986

Cimarron (wb 101.2)		Wght	Price	Prod
G69	sdn 4d	2,583	13,128	24,534
Seville (wb 108.0)				
S69	sdn 4d	3,428	26,756	19,098
Eldorado (wb 108.0)				
L57	cpe	3,365	24,251	21,342
	American II cpe	—	—	1,500
De Ville (wb 110.8)				
D47	cpe	3,319	19,669	36,350*
D69	sdn 4d	3,378	19,990	129,857*
Fleetwood (wb 110.8)				
	cpe	—	23,443	*
	sdn 4d	—	23,764	*

* Fleetwood (option package) production included in De Ville coupe and sedan totals.

Fleetwood Brougham RWD (wb 121.5)		Wght	Price	Prod
W69	sdn 4d	4,020	21,265	49,137
Fleetwood Seventy-Five limousine (wb 134.4)				
H23	sdn 4d	3,637	33,895	650
H33	formal sdn 4d	3,736	35,895	350
	commercial chassis	—	—	365

1986 Engines	bore×stroke	bhp	availability
L4, 121.0	3.50×3.15	85	S-Cimarron
V-6, 173.0	3.50×2.99	120	O-Cimarron

1986 Engines	bore×stroke	bhp	availability
V-8, 249.0	3.46×3.30	130/135	S-Sev, Eldo, DeVil, Fltwd
V-8, 249.0	3.46×3.30	135	S-limo
V-8, 307.0	3.80×3.39	140	S-Brgm

1987

Cimarron (wb 101.2)		Wght	Price	Prod
G69	sdn 4d	2,659	15,032	14,561
Allanté (wb 99.4)				
R67	cpe	3,494	54,700	3,363
Seville (wb 108.0)				
S69	sdn 4d	3,420	26,326	18,578
Eldorado (wb 108.0)				
L57	cpe	3,360	23,740	17,775
De Ville (wb 110.8)				
D47	cpe	3,312	21,316	32,700
D69	sdn 4d	3,370	21,659	129,521
Fleetwood d'Elegance (wb 110.8)				
B69	sdn 4d	3,421	26,104	—
Fleetwood Sixty Special (wb 115.8)				
S19	sdn 4d	3,408	34,850	—
Fleetwood Brougham RWD (wb 121.5)				
W69	sdn 4d	4,046	22,637	65,504
Fleetwood Seventy-Five limousine (wb 134.4)				
H23	sdn 4d	3,678	36,510	302
H33	formal sdn 4d	3,798	38,580	
	commercial chassis	—	—	577

1987 Engines	bore×stroke	bhp	availability
V-6, 173.0	3.50×2.99	125	S-Cimarron
V-8, 249.0	3.46×3.30	130	S-Sev, Eldo, DeVil, Fltwd, limo
V-8, 249.0	3.46×3.30	170	S-Allanté
V-8, 307.0	3.80×3.39	140	S-Brgm

1988

Cimarron (wb 101.2)		Wght	Price	Prod
G69	sdn 4d	2,756	16,071	6,454
Allanté (wb 99.4)				
R67	cpe	3,489	56,533	2,569
Seville (wb 108.0)				
S69	sdn 4d	3,449	27,627	22,968
Eldorado (wb 108.0)				
L57	cpe	3,399	24,891	33,210
De Ville (wb 110.8)				
D47	cpe	3,397	23,049	152,513*
D69	sdn 4d	3,437	23,404	
Fleetwood d'Elegance (wb 110.8)				
B69	sdn 4d	3,463	28,024	*
Fleetwood Sixty Special (wb 115.8)				
S19	sdn 4d	3,547	34,750	*

* Fleetwood production included with De Ville.

Fleetwood Brougham RWD (wb 121.5)		Wght	Price	Prod
W69	sdn 4d	4,156	23,846	53,130

1988 Engines	bore×stroke	bhp	availability
V-6, 173.0	3.50×2.99	125	S-Cimarron
V-8, 249.0	3.46×3.30	170	S-Allanté
V-8, 273.0	3.62×3.31	155	S-Sev, Eldo, DeVil, Fltwd
V-8, 307.0	3.80×3.39	140	S-Brgm

1989

Allanté (wb 99.4)		Wght	Price	Prod
R67	conv cpe	3,492	57,183	3,296
Seville (wb 108.0)				
S69	sdn 4d	3,422	29,750	22,909
Eldorado (wb 108.0)				
L57	cpe	3,422	26,738	30,925
De Ville (wb 110.8; sdn 113.8)				
D47	cpe	3,397	24,960	23,294
D69	sdn 4d	3,470	25,435	122,693
Fleetwood (wb 110.8; sdn 113.8)				
847	cpe	3,459	29,825	4,108
869	sdn 4d	3,545	30,300	26,641*
Fleetwood Sixty Special (wb 113.8)				
S69	sdn 4d	3,598	34,230	*
Fleetwood Brougham RWD (wb 121.5)				
W69	sdn 4d	4,190	25,699	40,264

1989 Engines	bore×stroke	bhp	availability
V-8, 273.0	3.62×3.31	155	S-Sev, Eldo, DeVil, Fltwd
V-8, 273.0	3.62×3.31	200	S-Allanté
V-8, 307.0	3.80×3.39	140	S-Brgm

* Sixty Special production included with Fleetwood sdn.

1990

Allanté (wb 99.4)		Wght	Price	Prod
R67	conv cpe	3,466	51,500	3,101
Seville (wb 108.0)				
S69	sdn 4d	3,480	31,830	33,128
Eldorado (wb 108.0)				
L57	cpe	3,426	28,885	22,291
De Ville (wb 110.8; sdn 113.8)				
D47	cpe	3,466	26,960	17,569
D69	sdn 4d	3,546	27,540	131,717
Fleetwood (wb 110.8; sdn 113.8)				
847	cpe	—	32,400	2,438
869	sdn 4d	—	32,980	22,889*
Fleetwood Sixty Special (wb 113.8)				
S69	sdn 4d	—	36,980	*
Brougham RWD (wb 121.5)				
W69	sdn 4d	4,283	27,400	33,741

1990 Engines	bore×stroke	bhp	availability
V-8, 273.0	3.62×3.31	180	S-Sev, Eldo, DeVil, Fltwd
V-8, 273.0	3.62×3.31	200	S-Allanté
V-8, 307.0	3.80×3.39	140	S-Brgm
V-8, 350.0	4.00×3.48	175	O-Brgm

* Sixty Special production included with Fleetwood sdn.

1991

Allanté (wb 99.4)		Wght	Price	Prod
S67	conv cpe	3,479	57,260	2,500
R67	conv/htp cpe	3,536	62,810	
Seville (wb 108.0)				
S69	sdn 4d	3,512	34,195	26,431
Y69	STS sdn 4d	3,564	37,395	
Eldorado (wb 108.0)				
L57	cpe 2d	3,469	31,495	16,212
De Ville (wb 110.8; sdn 113.8)				
D69	sdn 4d	3,622	30,455	
D69TS	Touring Sedan 4d	—	33,455	147,998
D47	sdn 2d	3,545	30,455	
Fleetwood (wb 110.8; sdn 113.8)				
B69	sdn 4d	3,675	35,195	*
B47	cpe 2d	3,593	35,195	*
Fleetwood Sixty Special (wb 113.8)				
G69	sdn 4d	3,706	38,695	*
Brougham (wb 121.5)				
W69	sdn 4d	4,281	30,455	27,231

1991 Engines	bore×stroke	bhp	availability
V-8, 273.0	3.62×3.31	200	S-Allanté
V-8, 300.0	3.62×3.62	200	S-DeVil, Fltwd, Sixty Spc, Eldo, Sev
V-8, 305.0	3.74×3.48	170	S-Brougham
V-8, 350.0	4.00×3.48	185	O-Brougham

*Fleetwood production included with De Ville.

1992

Allanté (wb 99.4)		Wght	Price	Prod
S67	conv cpe	3,402	58,470	1,931
R67	conv/htp cpe	3,462	64,090	
Seville (wb 111.0)				
S69	sdn 4d	3,648	34,975	43,954
Y69	STS sdn 4d	3,721	37,975	
Eldorado (wb 108.0)				
L57	cpe 2d	3,604	32,470	31,151
De Ville (wb 110.8; sdn 113.8)				
D69	sdn 4d	3,591	31,740	
T69	Touring Sedan 4d	3,627	35,190	142,328
D47	sdn 2d	3,519	31,740	
Fleetwood (wb 110.8; sdn 113.8)				
B69	sdn 4d	3,642	36,360	*
B47	cpe 2d	3,566	36,360	*
Fleetwood Sixty Special (wb 113.8)				
G69	sdn 4d	3,653	39,860	*
Brougham (wb 121.5)				
W69	sdn 4d	4,277	31,740	13,761

1992 Engines	bore×stroke	bhp	availability
V-8, 273.0	3.62×3.31	200	S-Allanté
V-8, 300.0	3.62×3.62	200	S-De Ville, Fltwd, Sixty Spc, Eldo, Seville
V-8, 305.0	3.74×3.48	170	S-Brougham
V-8, 350.0	4.00×3.48	185	O-Brougham

*Fleetwood production included with De Ville.

1993

Allanté (wb 99.4)		Wght	Price	Prod
S67	conv cpe	3,776	61,675	4,670
Seville (wb 111.0)				
S69	sdn 4d	3,648	36,990	37,239
Y69	STS sdn 4d	3,721	41,990	
Eldorado (wb 108.0)				
L57	cpe 2d	3,640	33,990	21,473
De Ville (wb 110.8; sdn 113.7)				
D69	sdn 4d	3,605	32,990	
T69	Touring Sedan 4d	3,651	36,310	130,714
D47	sdn 2d	3,519	33,915	
Sixty Special (wb 113.8)				
G69	sdn 4d	3,649	37,230	*

*Sixty Special production included with De Ville.

Fleetwood (wb 121.5)		Wght	Price	Prod
W69	sdn 4d	4,367	33,990	31,773

1993 Engines	bore×stroke	bhp	availability
V-8, 279.0	3.66×3.31	295	S-Allanté
V-8, 279.0	3.66×3.31	270	O-Eldorado
V-8, 279.0	3.66×3.31	295	O-Eldo, Seville
V-8, 299.0	3.62×3.62	200	S-De Ville, Sixty Spc, Eldo, Sev
V-8, 350.0	4.00×3.48	185	O-Fleetwood

1994

Seville (wb 111.0)		Wght	Price	Prod
S69	sdn 4d	3,830	40,990	46,714
Y69	STS sdn 4d	3,892	44,890	
Eldorado (wb 108.0)				
L57	cpe 2d	3,773	37,290	24,970
T57	TC cpe 2d	3,818	40,590	
De Ville (sdn 113.7)				
D69	sdn 4d	3,757	32,990	120,352
F69	Concours sdn 4d	3,984	36,950	
Fleetwood (wb 121.5)				
W69	sdn 4d	4,478	33,990	27,473

1994 Engines	bore×stroke	bhp	availability
V-8, 279.0	3.66×3.31	270	S-Eldo, Seville, Concours
V-8, 279.0	3.66×3.31	295	O-Eldo, Seville
V-8, 300.0	3.62×3.62	200	S-De Ville
V-8, 350.0	4.00×3.48	260	O-Fleetwood

1995

Seville (wb 111.0)		Wght	Price	Prod
S69	sdn 4d	3,832	41,935	38,931
Y69	STS sdn 4d	3,869	45,935	
Eldorado (wb 108.0)				
L57	cpe 2d	3,765	38,220	25,230
T57	TC cpe 2d	3,801	41,535	

De Ville (wb 113.7)		Wght	Price	Prod
D69	sdn 4d	3,761	34,900	91,501
F69	Concours sdn 4d	3,988	37,570	

Fleetwood (wb 121.5)		Wght	Price	Prod
W69	sdn 4d	4,351	35,595	16,180

1995 Engines	bore×stroke	bhp	availability
V-8, 279.0	3.66×3.31	275	S-Eldo, Sev, Con
V-8, 279.0	3.66×3.31	300	O-Eldo, Seville
V-8, 299.0	3.62×3.62	200	S-De Ville
V-8, 350.0	4.00×3.48	260	O-Fleetwood

1996

Seville (wb 111.0)		Wght	Price	Prod
S69	sdn 4d	3,832	42,995	38,241
Y69	STS sdn 4d	3,869	47,495	
Eldorado (wb 108.0)				
L57	cpe 2d	3,765	39,595	20,816
T57	TC cpe 2d	3,801	42,995	
De Ville (wb 113.7)				
D69	sdn 4d	3,981	35,995	111,279
F69	Concours sdn 4d	3,959	40,495	
Fleetwood (wb 121.5)				
W69	sdn 4d	4,461	36,995	15,109

1996 Engines	bore×stroke	bhp	availability
V-8, 279.0	3.66×3.31	275	S-Eldo, Sev, DeVil
V-8, 279.0	3.66×3.31	300	O-Eldo, Sev, Con
V-8, 350.0	4.00×3.48	260	S-Fleetwood

1997

Catera (wb 107.4)		Wght	Price	Prod
M69	sdn 4d	3,770	29,995	28,704
Seville (wb 111.0)				
S69	SLS sdn 4d	3,900	39,995	23,127
Y69	STS sdn 4d	3,900	44,995	22,156
Eldorado (wb 108.0)				
L57	cpe 2d	3,821	37,995	11,521
T57	TC cpe 2d	3,863	41,395	8,626
De Ville (wb 113.8)				
D69	sdn 4d	4,009	36,995	77,603
E69	d'Elegance sdn 4d	4,009	39,995	14,095
F69	Concours sdn 4d	4,052	41,995	9,665

1997 Engines	bore×stroke	bhp	availability
V-6, 181.0	3.40×3.40	200	S-Catera
V-8, 279.0	3.66×3.31	275	S-Eldo, Sev, DeVil
V-8, 279.0	3.66×3.31	300	O-Eldo, Sev, Con

1998

Catera (wb 107.4)		Wght	Price	Prod
M69	sdn 4d	3,770	29,995	20,512
R69	leather int. sdn 4d	—	33,610	9,635
Seville (wb 112.2)				
S69	SLS sdn 4d	3,972	42,495	16,460
Y69	STS sdn 4d	—	46,995	18,061
Eldorado (wb 108.0)				
L57	cpe 2d	3,843	38,495	11,666
T57	TC cpe 2d	3,876	42,695	6,749
DeVille (wb 113.8)				
D69	sdn 4d	4,012	37,695	83,798
E69	d'Elegance sdn 4d	4,052	41,295	16,417
F69	Concours sdn 4d	4,063	42,995	10,052

1998 Engines	bore×stroke	bhp	availability
V-6, 181.0	3.40×3.40	200	S-Catera
V-8, 279.0	3.66×3.31	275	S-Eldo, Seville, DeVille
V-8, 279.0	3.66×3.31	300	O-Eldo, Sev, Con

1999

Catera (wb 107.4)		Wght	Price	Prod
R69	sdn 4d	3,770	34,180	14,495
Seville (wb 112.2)				
S69	SLS sdn 4d	3,970	43,355	20,891
Y69	STS sdn 4d	4,001	47,850	21,561
Eldorado (wb 108.0)				
L57	cpe 2d	3,843	39,235	9,637
T57	TC cpe 2d	3,876	43,495	6,535
DeVille (wb 113.8)				
D69	sdn 4d	4,012	38,630	85,561
E69	d'Elegance sdn 4d	4,052	42,730	17,335
F69	Concours sdn 4d	4,063	43,230	9,357

1999 Engines	bore×stroke	bhp	availability
V-6, 181.0	3.40×3.40	200	S-Catera
V-8, 279.0	3.66×3.31	275	S-Eldo, Seville, DeVille
V-8, 279.0	3.66×3.31	300	O-Eldo, Seville, Concours

2000

Catera (wb 107.4)		Wght	Price	Prod
R69	sdn 4d	3,770	31,010	16,072
Seville (wb 112.2)				
S69	SLS sdn 4d	3,970	43,880	16,904
Y69	STS sdn 4d	4,001	48,480	17,688
Eldorado (wb 108.0)				
L57	ESC cpe 2d	3,843	39,120	8,396
T57	ETC cpe 2d	3,876	42,695	5,597
DeVille (wb 115.3)				
D69	sdn 4d	3,978	39,500	69,085
E69	DHS sdn 4d	—	44,700	12,365
F69	DTS sdn 4d	—	44,700	17,006

2000 Engines	bore×stroke	bhp	availability
V-6, 181.0	3.40×3.40	200	S-Catera
V-8, 279.0	3.66×3.31	275	S-Eldo, Seville, DeVille
V-8, 279.0	3.66×3.31	300	O-Eldo, Sev, DTS

2001

Catera (wb 107.5)		Wght	Price	Prod
R69	sdn 4d	3,770	31,305	12,097
Seville (wb 112.2)				
S69	SLS sdn 4d	3,986	41,935	14,626
Y69	STS sdn 4d	4,027	48,245	13,430
Eldorado (wb 108.0)				
L57	ESC cpe 2d	3,814	40,346	5,745
T57	ETC cpe 2d	3,865	44,011	4,652
DeVille (wb 115.3)				
D69	sdn 4d	3,978	38,630	63,778
E69	DHS sdn 4d	4,049	42,730	13,550
F69	DTS sdn 4d	4,047	43,230	14,516

2001 Engines	bore×stroke	bhp	availability
V-6, 181.0	3.40×3.40	200	S-Catera
V-8, 279.0	3.66×3.31	275	S-Eldo, Sev, DeVil
V-8, 279.0	3.66×3.31	300	O-Eldo, Sev, DTS

2002

Seville (wb 112.2)-26,577 blt		Wght	Price	Prod
S69	SLS sdn 4d	3,992	43,524	—
Y69	STS sdn 4d	4,027	49,080	—
Eldorado (wb 108.0) - 7105 built				
L57	ESC cpe 2d	3,814	41,865	—
T57	ETC cpe 2d	3,865	45,000	—
C5T	ECS cpe 2d	3,865	47,660	—
DeVille (wb 115.3) - 95,877 built				
D69	sdn 4d	3,984	42,325	—
E69	DHS sdn 4d	4,048	47,255	—
F69	DTS sdn 4d	4,044	47,255	—

2002 Engines	bore×stroke	bhp	availability
V-8, 279.0	3.66×3.31	275	S-Eldo, Sev, DeVil
V-8, 279.0	3.66×3.31	300	O-Eldo, Sev, DTS

2003

CTS (wb 113.4) - 75,687 blt		Wght	Price	Prod
M69	sdn 4d	3,509	29,350	—
Seville (wb 112.2) - 19,836 built				
S69	Luxury sdn 4d	3,989	45,535	—
Y69	Touring sdn 4d	4,050	51,650	—
DeVille (wb 115.3) - 82,085 built				
D69	sdn 4d	3,978	44,400	—
E69	DHS sdn 4d	4,049	49,150	—
F69	DTS sdn 4d	4,047	49,150	—

2003 Engines	bore×stroke	bhp	availability
V-6, 194.0	3.44×3.46	220	S-CTS
V-8, 279.0	3.66×3.31	275	S-DeV, Seville
V-8, 279.0	3.66×3.31	300	O-DeV, Seville

2004

CTS (wb 113.4) - 59,587 built		Wght	Price	Prod
M69	sdn 4d	3,568	30,140	—
N69	CTS-V sdn 4d	3,850	49,300	—
Seville (wb 112.2) - 6514 built				
S69	SLS sdn 4d	3,969	45,825	—
DeVille (wb 115.3) - 77,205 built				
D69	sdn 4d	3,978	44,650	—
E69	DHS sdn 4d	4,049	49,800	—
F69	DTS sdn 4d	4,047	49,800	—
XLR (wb 105.7) - 4,387 built				
V67	conv	3,647	75,385	—

2004 Engines	bore×stroke	bhp	availability
V-6, 194.0	3.44×3.46	220	S-CTS
V-6, 217.0	3.70×3.37	255	O-CTS
V-8, 279.0	3.66×3.31	275	S-DeV, Seville
V-8, 279.0	3.66×3.31	300	O-DeVille
V-8, 279.0	3.66×3.31	320	S-XLR
V-8, 346.0	3.90×3.62	400	S-CTS-V

2005

CTS (wb 113.4) - 69,444 blt		Wght	Price	Prod
M69	2.8 sdn 4d	3,509	30,190	—
P69	3.6 sdn 4d	3,509	31,850	—
N69	CTS-V sdn 4d	3,850	49,300	—
STS (wb 116.4) - 39,806 built				
W29	V-6 sdn 4d	3,960	40,300	—
C29	V-8 sdn 4d	4,026	46,800	—
DeVille (wb 115.3) - 59,750 built				
D69	sdn 4d	3,978	45,695	—
E69	DHS sdn 4d	4,049	51,250	—
F69	DTS sdn 4d	4,047	51,200	—
XLR (wb 105.7) - 4,190 built				
V67	conv	3,647	75,385	—

2005 Engines	bore×stroke	bhp	availability
V-6, 170.0	3.50×2.94	210	S-CTS
V-6, 217.0	3.70×3.37	255	S-STS, O-CTS
V-8, 279.0	3.66×3.31	275	S-DeVille
V-8, 279.0	3.66×3.31	290	O-DeVille
V-8, 279.0	3.66×3.31	320	S-XLR, O-STS
V-8, 346.0	3.90×3.62	400	S-CTS-V

2006

CTS (wb 113.4)		Wght	Price	Prod*
M69	2.8 sdn 4d	3,509	30,515	—
P69	3.6 sdn 4d	3,509	33,160	—
N69	CTS-V sdn 4d	3,850	50,675	—
STS (wb 116.4)				
W29	V-6 sdn 4d	3,960	41,020	—
C29	V-8 sdn 4d	4,026	47,250	—
X29	STS-V sdn 4d	4,295	74,270	—
DTS (wb 115.6)				
D69	sdn 4d	4,009	41,195	—
XLR (wb 105.7)				
V67	conv	3,647	76,480	—
X67	conv	3,810	—	—

2006 Engines	bore×stroke	bhp	availability
V-6, 170.0	3.50×2.94	210	S-CTS
V-6, 217.0	3.70×3.37	255	S-STS, O-CTS
V-8S, 267.0	3.58×3.31	469	S-STS-V, XLR-V
V-8, 279.0	3.66×3.31	275	S-DTS
V-8, 279.0	3.66×3.31	291	O-DTS
V-8, 279.0	3.66×3.31	320	S-XLR, O-STS
V-8, 364.0	4.00×3.62	400	S-CTS-V

*Prod numbers not available at time of publication.

Checker

Founded in 1922, Checker was long-famous for specially designed taxicabs and airport limousines when it began selling "civilian" models in 1959. Some sources say Checker offered "pleasure cars" as early as 1948, but the Kalamazoo factory always said 1959 was the first year for private sales.

Assuming one could find a Checker dealer (they were never very numerous), civilians bought what was initially called Superba, a four-door sedan or wagon in standard or Special trim. Specials were more deluxe inside, but not much. All were the same tanklike affairs familiar to anyone who ever hailed a cab from the mid-'50s to the mid-'80s. The A8 hit the streets in 1956 with a wheelbase of 120 inches—fairly compact for the time. Average curb weights were 3400 pounds for the sedans, and nearly 3800 for the boxy wagons.

Morris Markin, Checker's founder and president, was steadfast: There'd be no change to this dumpy but practical design so long as there were buyers for reliable, durable, "taxi-tough" cars. Not that there'd been many changes before. Aside from noncommercial paint jobs and leaving off the "hire light," the Superba differed from the A8 only in a front-end facelift with trendy quad headlamps.

Superba power came from Continental Motor Company, basically the same 226-cubic-inch L-head six once used by Kaiser (*see entry*). Here, though, it was available in side-valve and overhead-valve versions at no difference in price. The former had 7.3:1 compression and produced a mere 80 horsepower, so it must have been meant for areas where gas was of very poor quality. The ohv unit had a more-modern 8:1 squeeze and a more-respectable 122 bhp. Transmissions were the expected three-speed column-shift manual and Borg-Warner automatic.

True to its taxi traditions, the Superba sedan could be equipped with a pair of rear jump seats for carrying up to eight. The wagon, which came with a roll-down tailgate window, had the same roomy back seat, which folded down to make a truly voluminous cargo deck. Unusually, though, the seat-folding was accomplished by an electric servo. This gimmick and the different bodywork made the wagon some $350 more expensive than the sedan.

At a time when mainstream American cars rolled on 14-inch wheels, Checker stuck with 15s, which made for smoother taxi rides over the increasingly cratered streets of urban America. Also reflecting its taxi origins, the Superba boasted tall doors and ruler-flat floors for easy entry/exit and plenty of foot space. It did not, however, boast much in the way of luxury: rubber mats where carpeting might have been, pedestrian hardboard headliner, and a conspicuous absence of late-'50s safety features like padded dash and sun visors, dished steering wheel, and seatbelts. Plain round gauges nestled within a flat-faced dashboard that looked like something from a '51 Plymouth, a design that would be absolutely unchanged through the very last cars Checker built.

Seeking higher nonfleet sales, Checker applied the Marathon name to the Superba Special for 1961, substituted 14-inch wheels on both Superba and Marathon sedans, and standardized the ohv engine for wagons. Prices stood pat: $2542 for the base Superba sedan to $3004 for the Marathon wagon. Air conditioning cost $411 extra, power steering $64. The model quartet returned for 1962, the only change being a return to 15-inch wheels for sedans. But Checker now further plied the consumer market with a special new Town Custom limousine on a 129-inch wheelbase. Optimistically priced at $7500, it came with vinyl roof and a division window between front and rear compartments; there was also a full range of power options. But production was limited by low demand—understandable, as even the most-expensive nonlimousine Cadillac cost less. The only change for '63 was boosting the ohv engine to 141 bhp for all models.

In 1964, prices rose about $100 and Superba was dropped from the Checker line. The following year, Checker switched to more-modern Chevrolet engines: standard 140-bhp, 230-cid six and optional 283 and 327 V-8s with 195 and 250 bhp, respectively. The Town Custom limo was still around, but only by special order. The 283 cost $110 extra, automatic transmission $248, overdrive $108.

For 1966, Checker added a Marathon Deluxe sedan and a lower-priced limousine ($4541), thus re-establishing a four-model line. Both were dropped the following year, but the Deluxe sedan returned for '68, the limousine for 1969.

The Chevy V-8s naturally made post-1964 Checkers much faster than the earlier six-cylinder cars. And there was more power to come. The 283 was dropped for '67, and a 307-cid replacement with 200 bhp was available for 1968 only. For 1969, the 327 was joined by a new 350 Chevy small-block with 300 bhp. Emissions tuning cut horses to 250 for 1970. Prices for the optional engines were usually low: in 1968, $108 for the 307 and $195 for the 327.

Checker sales were always moderate in the '60s, though adequate to sustain the firm's desired annual volume of 6000-7000 units. Checker's best year of the decade was 1962, when it built 8173 cars, though most were taxis.

Markin never wavered from his mission of building taxi-tough cars. It isn't widely known, but Nathan Altman once approached Checker about building his Avanti II (*see entry*). Markin replied that the Avanti was too ugly to bother with.

David Markin took over the helm in Kalamazoo on his father's death in 1970, but he didn't much change the company or its products until the mid-'70s. That's when Edward N. Cole, having retired as GM president in 1974, joined Checker to launch a new-model development program. Sadly, Cole was killed in a plane crash before his efforts reached fruition.

1961 Superba four-door sedan

1963 Marathon station wagon

1964 Marathon four-door sedan

1965 Marathon four-door sedan

1965-67 Marathon DeLuxe Limousine

1980 Marathon four-door sedan

Checker began a long, steady decline in 1970. The main problem was increased competition for fleet sales from the major Detroit makers who needed this important outlet when passenger-car sales slowed in the mid-'70s (during the OPEC oil embargo) and again at decade's end. With its low fixed volume and relatively high overhead, tiny Checker just couldn't compete with the Big Three on price. As a result, its passenger-car volume was dramatically lower after 1969: fewer than 400 for 1970, a more encouraging 600-1000 units a year through 1974, less than 500 thereafter.

Relentless inflation-fueled price escalation didn't help. The standard sedan was up to almost $4000 by '73, to near $5400 by '75, over $6000 in '77, and close to $8000 by 1980. That was Chrysler or Buick money, and a lot to ask for such a dull car that wasn't put together all that well.

These difficulties were reflected in Checker's dwindling number of models and sales as the '70s wore on. The decade began with the usual Marathon sedan and wagon and long-wheelbase Deluxe sedan and limo. The latter proved unprofitable and was dropped after '71.

The wagon disappeared after 1974, but the sedan and long-wheelbase Deluxe sedan carried on to the end. The standard six after 1970 was the stroked 250 version of the Chevy 230, rated at 145 horsepower through '71, 100-115 thereafter. The 350 V-8 remained optional, down-rated to 145-170 bhp SAE net for 1972-79. A 145-bhp, 305-cid small-block became an additional option after 1976 and a 105 horsepower, 350-cid diesel was offered in 1980-82.

Through all of this, Checker clung to its extremely dated basic design, resisting all suggestions that it needed to be replaced. The addition of federal "crash" bumpers for 1974—big girderlike lumps of steel—rendered quite ugly a car that had once simply looked old. The famed Ghia coachworks in Italy devised a prototype for a handsome new-generation Checker in 1970, but it was refused. The same fate awaited "Galva II," a 1975 proposal by Autodynamics of Madison Heights, Michigan. This had extremely simple, rectilinear styling to keep tooling costs to an absolute minimum. It likely failed for lack of money, though managerial stubbornness was still a factor.

But that began to change once the dynamic Ed Cole started planning yet another new Checker soon after his arrival. Targeted for production sometime during 1983, this was a boxy, square-lined, four-door hatchback sedan with front-drive mechanicals borrowed from the GM X-car compacts, which Cole knew were in the works when he joined Checker. A sturdy new box-section chassis of undisclosed design was planned for three models: a 109-inch-wheelbase six-passenger version, a 122-inch eight-seater, and a 128-inch nine-seater. A variety of low-cost, easily replaced plastic body panels was contemplated, as was an interesting rear suspension with solid rubber springs. Design work progressed as far as a single full-scale mockup.

But it made no difference in the end. The project lost momentum with Cole's untimely death, and by that time even Checker's taxi business had become marginal. With that, Kalamazoo ceased all production in mid-1982.

Intriguingly, Checkers show signs of becoming minor collector's items, especially the low-volume Town Limousines and the huge multidoor "Aerobus" wagons built for airport shuttle service. Checkers, collectible? Morris Markin would be amazed.

Specifications

1960 - 6,980 built, including taxis

Superba (wb 120.0)	Wght	Price	Prod
sdn 4d	3,410	2,542	—
Special sdn 4d	3,410	2,650	—
wgn 4d	3,780	2,896	—
Special wgn 4d	3,780	3,004	—

1960 Engines	bore×stroke	bhp	availability
I-6, 226.0	3.31×4.38	80	S-all
I-6, 226.0	3.31×4.38	122	O-all

1961 - 5,683 built, including taxis

Superba (wb 120.0)	Wght	Price	Prod
sdn 4d	3,320	2,542	—
wgn 4d	3,570	2,896	—
Marathon (wb 120.0)			
sdn 4d	3,345	2,650	—
wgn 4d	3,615	3,004	—

1961 Engines	bore×stroke	bhp	availability
I-6, 226.0	3.31×4.38	80	S-all
I-6, 226.0	3.31×4.38	122	S-wgn; O-sdn

1962 - 8,173 built, including taxis

Superba (wb 120.0)	Wght	Price	Prod
sdn 4d	3,320	2,642	—
wgn 4d	3,570	2,991	—
Marathon (wb 120.0)			
sdn 4d	3,345	2,793	—

Marathon (wb 120.0)				
	wgn 4d	3,615	3,140	—
Town Custom (wb 129.0)				
	limo 8P	5,000	7,500	—

1962 Engines	bore×stroke	bhp	availability
I-6, 226.0	3.31×4.38	80	S-all
I-6, 226.0	3.31×4.38	122	O-all

1963 - 7,050 built, including taxis

Superba (wb 120.0)		Wght	Price	Prod
	sdn 4d	3,485	2,642	—
	wgn 4d	3,625	2,991	—
Marathon (wb 120.0)				
	sdn 4d	3,485	2,773	—
	wgn 4d	3,625	3,140	—
Town Custom (wb 129.0)				
	limo 8P	5,000	7,500	—

1963 Engines	bore×stroke	bhp	availability
I-6, 226.0	3.31×4.38	80	S-all
I-6, 226.0	3.31×4.38	141	O-all

1964 - 6,310 built, including taxis

Marathon (wb 120.0)		Wght	Price	Prod
	sdn 4d	3,625	2,814	—
	wgn 4d	3,720	3,160	—
Town Custom (wb 129.0)				
	limo 8P	5,000	8,000	—

1964 Engines	bore×stroke	bhp	availability
I-6, 226.0	3.3×4.38	80	S-all
I-6, 226.0	3.31×4.38	141	O-all

1965 - 6,136 built, including taxis

Marathon (wb 120.0)		Wght	Price	Prod
A12	sdn 4d	3,360	2,793	—
A12W	wgn 4d	3,450	3,140	—
Town Custom (wb 129.0)				
A12E	limo 8P	4,800	8,000	—

1965 Engines	bore×stroke	bhp	availability
I-6, 230.0	3.88×3.20	140	S-all
V-8, 283.0	3.88×3.00	195	O-all
V-8, 327.0	4.00×3.25	250	O-all

1966 - 1,056 built; 5,761 including taxis

Marathon (wb 120.0)		Wght	Price	Prod
A12	sdn 4d	3,400	2,874	—
A12E	Deluxe sdn 4d	3,800	3,567	—
A12E	limo 8P	3,800	4,541	—
A12W	wgn 4d	3,500	3,500	—

1966 Engines	bore×stroke	bhp	availability
I-6, 230.0	3.88×3.25	140	S-all
V-8, 283.0	3.88×3.00	195	O-all
V-8, 327.0	4.00×3.25	250	O-all

1967 - 935 built; 5,822 including taxis

Marathon (wb 120.0)		Wght	Price	Prod
A12	sdn 4d	3,400	2,874	—
A12W	wgn 4d	3,500	3,075	—

1967 Engines	bore×stroke	bhp	availability
I-6, 230.0	3.88×3.25	140	S-all
V-8, 327.0	4.00×3.25	250	O-all

1968 - 992 built; 5,477 including taxis

Marathon (wb 120.0)		Wght	Price	Prod
A12	sdn 4d	3,390	3,221	—
A12E	Deluxe sdn 4d	3,590	3,913	—
A12W	wgn 4d	3,480	3,491	—

1968 Engines	bore×stroke	bhp	availability
I-6, 230.0	3.88×3.25	140	S-all
V-8, 307.0	3.88×3.25	200	O-all
V-8, 327.0	4.00×3.25	275	O-all

1969 - 760 built; 5,417 including taxis

Marathon (wb 120.0)		Wght	Price	Prod
A12	sdn 4d	3,390	3,290	—
A12W	wgn 4d	3,480	3,560	—
Deluxe (wb 129.0)				
A12E	sdn 4d	3,590	3,984	—
A12E	limo 8P	3,802	4,969	—

1969 Engines		bore×stroke	bhp	availability
I-6,	230.0	3.88×3.25	155	S-all
V-8,	327.0	4.00×3.25	235	O-all
V-8,	350.0	4.00×3.48	300	O-all

1970 - 397 built

Marathon (wb 120.0)		Wght	Price	Prod
A12	sdn 4d	3,268	3,671	—
A12W	wgn 4d	3,470	3,941	—
Marathon Deluxe (wb 129.0)				
A12E	sdn 4d	3,378	4,364	—
A12E	limo 8P	3,578	5,338	—

1970 Engines		bore×stroke	bhp	availability
I-6,	230.0	3.88×3.25	155	S-all
V-8,	350.0	4.00×3.48	250	O-all

1971

Marathon (wb 120.0)		Wght*	Price*	Prod*
A12	sdn 4d	3,400	3,843	500
A12W	wgn 4d	3,600	4,113	
Marathon Deluxe (wb 129.0)				
A12E	sdn 4d	3,700	4,536	100
A12E	limo 8P	3,975	5,510	

1971 Engines		bore×stroke	bhp	availability
I-6,	250.0	3.88×3.53	145	S-all
V-8,	350.0	4.00×3.48	245	O-all

* I-6 weight/price given; V-8 adds 100 lbs & $110. Production estimated.

1972

Marathon (wb 120.0)		Wght*	Price*	Prod*
A12	sdn 4d	3,400	3,654	750
A12W	wgn 4d	3,600	3,910	
Marathon Deluxe (wb 129.0)				
A12E	sdn 4d	3,700	4,312	100

1972 Engines		bore×stroke	bhp	availability
I-6,	250.0	3.88×3.53	110	S-all
V-8,	350.0	4.00×3.48	165	O-all

*I-6 weight/price given; V-8 adds 100 lbs & $250. Production estimated.

1973

Marathon (wb 120.0)		Wght*	Price*	Prod*
A12	sdn 4d	3,622	3,955	800
A12W	wgn 4d	3,825	4,211	
Marathon Deluxe (wb 129.0)				
A12E	sdn 4d 8P I-6	3,822	4,612	100
A12E	sdn 4d 8P V-8	3,923	4,727	

1973 Engines		bore×stroke	bhp	availability
I-6,	250.0	3.88×3.53	100	S-all
V-8,	350.0	4.00×3.48	145	O-Marathon

*I-6 weight/price given; V-8 adds 100 lbs & $115. Production estimated.

1974

Marathon (wb 120.0)		Wght*	Price*	Prod*
A12	sdn 4d	3,720	4,453	900
A12W	wgn 4d	3,925	4,710	
Marathon Deluxe (wb 129.0)				
A12E	sdn 4d 8P	3,920	5,394	50

1974 Engines		bore×stroke	bhp	availability
I-6,	250.0	3.88×3.53	100	S-all
V-8,	350.0	4.00×3.48	145	O-all

*I-6 weight/price given; V-8 adds 100 lbs & $150. Production estimated.

1975

Marathon (wb 120.0; DeL 129.0)		Wght	Price	Prod*
A12	sdn 4d I-6	3,774	5,394	450
A12	sdn 4d V-8	3,839	5,539	
A12E	Deluxe sdn 4d V-8	4,137	6,216	

1975 Engines		bore×stroke	bhp	availability
I-6,	250.0	3.88×3.53	105	S-sixes
V-8,	350.0	4.00×3.48	145	S-V-8s

*Production estimated.

1976

Marathon (wb 120.0)		Wght	Price	Prod*
A12	sdn 4d I-6	3,774	5,749	400
A12	sdn 4d V-8	3,839	5,894	
Marathon Delux (wb 129.0)				
A12E	sdn 4d V-8	4,137	6,736	—

1976 Engines		bore×stroke	bhp	availability
I-6,	250.0	3.88×3.53	105	S-sixes
V-8,	350.0	4.00×3.48	165	S-V-8s

* Production estimated.

1977

Marathon (wb 120.0)		Wght	Price	Prod*
A12	sdn 4d I-6	3,765	6,156	300
A12	sdn 4d V-8	3,830	6,301	
Marathon Deluxe (wb 129.0)				
A12E	sdn 4d V-8	4,137	—	—

1977 Engines		bore×stroke	bhp	availability
I-6,	250.0	3.88×3.53	110	S-sixes
V-8,	305.0	3.74×3.48	145	S-V-8s
V-8,	350.0	4.00×3.48	170	O-V-8s

* Production estimated.

1978

Marathon (wb 120.0)		Wght	Price	Prod*
A12	sdn 4d I-6	3,765	6,814	300
A12	sdn 4d V-8	3,830	6,959	
Marathon Deluxe (wb 129.0)				
A12E	sdn 4d V-8	4,062	7,867	—

1978 Engines		bore×stroke	bhp	availability
I-6,	250.0	3.88×3.53	110	S-sixes
V-8,	305.0	3.74×3.53	145	S-V-8s
V-8,	350.0	4.00×3.48	170	O-V-8s

* Production estimated.

1979

Marathon (wb 120.0)		Wght	Price	Prod*
A12	sdn 4d I-6	3,765	7,314	200
A12	sdn 4d V-8	3,830	7,515	
Marathon Deluxe (wb 129.0)				
A12E	sdn 4d V-8	3,999	8,389	—

1979 Engines		bore×stroke	bhp	availability
I-6,	250.0	3.88×3.53	115	S-Sixes
V-8,	305.0	3.74×3.48	130	S-V-8s
V-8,	350.0	4.00×3.48	170	O-V-8s

* Production estimated.

1980

Marathon (wb 120.0)		Wght	Price	Prod*
A12	sdn 4d I-6	3,765	7,800	250
A12	sdn 4d V-8	3,830	8,000	
Marathon Deluxe (wb 129.0)				
A12E	sdn 4d V-8	3,999	9,192	—

1980 Engines		bore×stroke	bhp	availability
V6,	229.0	3.74×3.48	115	S-sixes
V-8,	267.0	3.50×3.48	120	S-Del; O-all
V-8,	305.0	3.74×3.48	155	O-V-8s
V-8D,	350.0	4.06×3.39	105	O-V-8s

* Production estimated.

1981 - 2,950 built, including taxis

Marathon (wb 120.0)		Wght	Price	Prod
A12	sdn 4d V6	3,680	9,632	—
A12	sdn 4d V-8	—	9,869	—
Marathon Deluxe (wb 129.0)				
A12E	sdn 4d V-8	3,999	10,706	—

1981 Engines		bore×stroke	bhp	availability
V6,	229.0	3.73×3.48	110	S-sixes
V-8,	267.0	3.50×3.48	115	S-V-8s
V-8,	305.0	3.74×3.48	150	O-V-8s
V-8D,	350.0	4.06×3.39	105	O-V-8s

1982 - 2,000 built, including taxis

Marathon (wb 120.0)		Wght	Price	Prod
A12	sdn 4d V6	3,680	10,950	—
A12	sdn 4d V-8	—	11,187	—
Marathon Deluxe (wb 129.0)				
A12E	sdn 4d V-8	3,839	12,025	—

1982 Engines		bore X stroke	bhp	availability
V6,	229.0	3.73×3.48	110	S-sixes
V-8,	267.0	3.50×3.48	115	S-V-8s
V-8D,	350.0	4.06×3.39	105	O-V-8s

Chevrolet

William C. Durant founded General Motors in 1908 but was ousted two years later, so he formed Chevrolet in 1911, intending to make it a powerful lever for regaining control. He did. By 1915, Chevrolet was a force to be reckoned with; by 1918 it was part of General Motors; by the mid-'20s, it was GM's largest volume division—and has been ever since.

Early Chevys were largish, medium-price cars with six-cylinder and even V-8 power. The make's historic turn to the low-price field came with the four-cylinder "490" of 1915, named for its advertised list price. It was a big success, outflanking Ford's Model T with more attractive styling and more features. Its closely related successors were Chevy's mainstay products into the late '20s.

However, Chevy didn't pass Ford in production until 1927, the year Dearborn stopped building the aged T to retool for the Model A. Then, in 1929, Chevrolet introduced its new "Stovebolt Six," also known as the "Cast-Iron Wonder." The nicknames stemmed from the engine's cast-iron pistons and numerous ¼-inch slotted bolts—hardly esoteric, but wonderfully effective and reliable as Old Faithful.

1930 AD Universal phaeton

1932 BA Confederate 2/4-passenger sport roadster

1933 CA Eagle 2/4-passenger sport coupe

The Stovebolt was engineered by Ormond E. Hunt from an earlier design by Henry M. Crane that had evolved into the 1926 Pontiac engine. By 1930, it produced an even 50 brake horsepower from 194 cubic inches. With various improvements, this solid, overhead-valve engine would remain Chevrolet's only powerplant for nearly three decades. For 1934, new combustion chambers prompted the name "Blue Flame," and two versions would be offered through 1935: 60-bhp, 181 cid and 80-bhp, 206.8 cid. The six was then redesigned for 1937 to be shorter and lighter. It also gained nearly "square" cylinder dimensions as well as four (versus three) main bearings. The result was 85 bhp from 216.5 cid. It was with this engine in 1940 that a young Juan Manuel Fangio won the car-breaking 5900-mile round-trip road race between Buenos Aires, Argentina, and Lima, Peru, at an average speed of 53.6 mph. Fangio continued to race Chevrolets after World War II, but eventually switched to Grand Prix cars and became a legend as the first five-time world champion driver.

Throughout most of its history, Chevrolet has made the right moves at the right time. To follow the Stovebolt, division general manager William "Big Bill" Knudsen and GM design director Harley Earl cooked up an elegant line of Cadillac-style cars for 1929-32. The 1930-31 line comprised a single series offering roadsters for two or four passengers, a phaeton, three coupes, and two sedans. Prices were attractively low: $495-$685.

The 1930-33 Chevys carried a different series name each year: in order, Universal, Independence, Confederate, then Eagle (deluxe) and Mercury (standard). This practice was ended for 1934, when models were grouped into Master and Standard lines. Master tacked on the "DeLuxe" handle for '35, and Standards became Masters for 1937-39.

Chevy styling in these years evolved along the lines of costlier GM cars. The '33s, with their skirted fenders and graceful lines, were perhaps the most-attractive Chevrolets of the decade. Body styles proliferated, and by 1932 included such exotics as a $625 landau phaeton. The 1933 Eagles offered many features designed to win buyers from Ford: a Fisher body with "No-Draft Ventilation" front-door ventwing windows, airplane-type instruments, Cadillac-style hood doors, a cowl vent, synchromesh transmission, selective free-wheeling, safety plate glass, adjustable driver's seat, even an octane selector. Many of these also appeared on the standard Mercury models. Wheelbases gradually lengthened, going from 1930's 107 inches to 109 for 1931-32, then to 107/110 for the '33 Mercury/Eagle; the '34 Master/Standard split 112/107.

Chevy fared well in this period despite the prevailing Depression. Production outpaced Ford's each year in 1931-33, bottoming to 313,000 units for '32, but recovering to 486,000 for '33. Volume then soared to nearly a million by 1936, though Ford was nearer.

Along with more-streamlined styling, 1934 brought new "Knee-Action" independent front suspension (IFS) to Master models, Bill Knudsen's last major decision before leaving Chevy in October 1933. According to writer Karl Ludvigsen, engineer Maurice Olley tried to discourage Knudsen from using it, saying there weren't enough centerless grinding machines in America to produce all the coil springs. Knudsen replied this was just what the machine-tool industry needed to get back on its feet. Still, he limited the new suspension to the one line.

1934 Master Six town sedan

1934 Master Six coach two-door

1935 Master DeLuxe coach two-door

1936 Master DeLuxe 2/4-passenger sport coupe

1937 Master DeLuxe sport sedan

1938 Master DeLuxe four-door sedan

1939 Master DeLuxe 4-passenger sport coupe

Knee-Action wasn't universally liked, so Standard/Master retained solid front axles through 1940, after which all Chevys had IFS.

The 1935s were the last Chevys with any styling kinship to the "classic" era. Master DeLuxe added an inch of wheelbase to suit sleeker new bodies with Vee'd windshield, streamlined fenders, and a raked-back radiator with cap concealed beneath the hood, then an innovation. Also new was the corporate all-steel "Turret Top" construction without the traditional fabric roof insert.

Modernization continued for 1936 as Chevrolet adopted still-rounder styling of the streamlined school, highlighted by die-cast "waterfall" grilles, steel-spoke wheels (wires remained optional), and sleeker fenders. As ever, Chevy relied on extra features to win sales from Ford. A big plus for '36 was hydraulic brakes, which Ford wouldn't offer until 1939 (thanks mainly to old Henry's stubbornness). Chevy was also quicker than Ford to drop body styles without roll-up windows, abandoning both roadsters and phaetons for 1936. The two series became more alike, as both used the 80-bhp 206.8-cid Stovebolt.

The redesigned 85-bhp engine of 1937 made Chevrolet particularly well equipped for the sales battle. However, styling became rather dull, as it did for other GM cars, with skinny, uninteresting grilles and high, bulky bodies that looked clumsy next to the increasingly streamlined Fords. Despite that, Chevy regained production supremacy for model-year '38, and until the '90s, at least, rarely surrendered it to Dearborn.

Renewed competitiveness was evident in an expanded 1940 line with what Chevy called "Royal Clipper" styling. Though not a drastic change from 1939, this facelift was sufficiently thorough to make the cars look much newer. Wheelbase was 113 inches, up from 1937-39's 112.3. Master 85 returned from '39 as the cheaper Chevy, with Master DeLuxe above it. Each offered business coupe, two-door town sedan, and four-door sport sedan; the 85 also listed a woody wagon, the DeLuxe line a sport coupe. A new top-line Special DeLuxe series had all these

1940 Special DeLuxe two-door town sedan

1940 Special DeLuxe station wagon

1941 Special DeLuxe Fleetline four-door sedan

1941 Special DeLuxe cabriolet coupe

1942 Fleetline Aerosedan fastback coupe

1942 Special DeLuxe four-door sport sedan

1946 Fleetline Aerosedan fastback coupe

1946 Fleetmaster cabriolet coupe

1947 Fleetline Sportmaster four-door sedan

1948 Fleetline Sportmaster four-door sedan

plus Chevy's first true convertible coupe, which was quite successful (nearly 12,000 model-year sales). Specials and Master DeLuxes came with Knee-Action; Master 85s carried Chevy's last solid front axles. Model-year production soared from some 577,000 to nearly 765,000 as Chevrolet bested Ford by over 220,000 cars.

The gap widened to more than 300,000 for 1941 as Chevrolet scored its first million-car model year. Though no one knew it then, this year's substantial redesign would carry the make through 1948: 116-inch wheelbase, Knee-Action linewide, attractive new styling by Harley Earl's Art & Colour Section, and five extra horsepower achieved with higher compression (6.5:1); new pistons; and revised combustion chambers, valves, rocker arms, and water pump. Master 85s were dropped, but Special DeLuxe added a sleek Fleetline four-door sedan at midyear. Distinguished by a more-formal roofline with closed-in rear quarters *a la* the Cadillac Sixty Special, the newcomer managed a creditable 34,000 sales for its shortened debut model year.

Styling refinements marked the war-shortened '42s. Fenders were extended back into the front doors, as on costlier GM makes, and a smart, clean grille replaced the somewhat busy '41 face. Models stayed the same except for five-passenger coupes replacing business coupes, and series names continued as Master DeLuxe and Special DeLuxe. The latter now contained a Fleetline subseries with a new "torpedo-style" two-door Aerosedan that proved an instant hit and a conventional Sportmaster four-door, both bearing triple chrome bands on front and rear fenders.

By the time the government halted civilian car production in February 1942, Chevy's model-year total was over a quarter-million units, of which less than 50,000 were built in calendar '42. Convertibles and wagons numbered only about 1000 each. Like all 1942 Detroit cars, rarity has since rendered these Chevys coveted collector's items.

Strikes and material shortages hampered GM's postwar production startup, allowing Ford to outpace Chevy for '46. But Chevy was again "USA-1" for 1947-48 even though it followed most other makes (Ford included) by offering slightly modified '42s. The few differences involved grille treatments, medallions and other exterior trim. Models and specifications stood pat, but now Stylemaster and Fleetmaster names came in.

Meanwhile, Chevy contemplated a smaller companion model evolved under a program called "Cadet." Though different configurations were considered, the final prototype was an orthodox four-door sedan with smooth "bathtub" styling, 108-inch wheelbase, and a scaled-down Stovebolt Six. But after spending a few million dollars, management decided there was no need for a compact in the booming postwar seller's market, especially as the Cadet would have cost as much to build as a standard Chevy. Ford reached the same conclusions at about the same time. Still, the Cadet is significant as the first application of engineer Earle S. MacPherson's simple, effective strut-type front suspension, today almost universal among small cars. Ford would be the first to use it in production, however, as MacPherson went to Dearborn soon after the Cadet project was cancelled.

If production Chevys didn't change much in this period, management did, and new models were floated for the future: sports cars, hardtop-convertibles, all-steel station wagons. These and other ideas gained impetus with the June 1946 arrival of Cadillac chief Nicholas Dreystadt to replace M.E. Coyle as Chevrolet general manager. Dreystadt also encouraged a forceful engineering program that would ultimately breathe new life into a make that had acquired a respectable but stodgy image. Unfortunately, he died after just two years in office, and his successor, W.E. Armstrong, resigned early because of illness. Then came Thomas H. Keating, who continued Dreystadt's policies. Soon after he took charge, Edward N. Cole came over from Cadillac to be Chevy chief engineer.

1949 Styleline DeLuxe four-door sport sedan

1949 Styleline DeLuxe station wagon

Their first order of business was to make Chevys look more "with it." In a happy bit of timing, GM had scheduled most of its all-new postwar models for 1949, and Chevy's were among the best. Though wheelbase was actually cut an inch, to 115, the cleanly styled '49s contrived to look much longer than the 1946-48 models. They were definitely lower, accented by a newly curved two-piece windshield trimmed two inches in height, fenders swept back smoothly through the cowl and doors, and rear fenders rolled gracefully forward. Suspension revisions and a lower center of gravity made for the best-handling Chevys yet—and probably better than that year's Plymouth and Ford. The '49s were also beautifully put together, testifying that engineers and production people had taken great care to make them "right."

Matching all this newness was an equally new four-series model line. It began with an "entry-level" Special series of two- and four-door Fleetline fastback sedans and notchback Styleline town and sport sedans, sport coupe, and business coupe. All but the last were offered with more-luxurious DeLuxe trim, as was a Styleline convertible and eight-passenger station wagon. There were actually two wagons: an "early" '49 with vestigial wood in its body construction, and a midyear all-steel replacement. Fleetlines initially sold well, but the fastback fad soon faded, so offerings dwindled. The last was a lone 1952 DeLuxe two-door.

Having regained its production stride in 1947-48, Chevy rolled out a record 1,010,000 cars for 1949. Ford, however, managed about 108,000 more, thanks to a popular all-new design and an early introduction (in June '48).

No make better reflected the exuberant '50s than Chevrolet, which evolved from family freighter to hot hauler in just a few short years. Again, in this decade the division mostly made the right moves at the right times. By 1960, Chevrolet was no longer just one of the "low-priced three" but an alternative to Dodge, Mercury, and Pontiac.

1950 Styleline DeLuxe four-door sport sedan

1951 Special Styleline two-door sedan

1952 Styleline DeLuxe four-door sedan

1952 Styleline DeLuxe convertible coupe

1953 Two-Ten DeLuxe four-door sedan

1953 Bel Air convertible coupe

1954 Two-Ten DeLuxe two-door sedan

1955 Bel Air hardtop sport coupe

The 1950-52 models were the last of the traditional low-cost, low-suds Chevys, though DeLuxes accounted for 80-85 percent of production. The hoary old 216.5 Stovebolt was coaxed up to 92 bhp for 1950, when a new 105-bhp 235.5-cid version arrived for cars equipped with optional two-speed Powerglide. The last was Chevy's new fully automatic transmission, thus beating Ford, whose Ford-O-Matic was still a year off, and Plymouth, which wouldn't have a true self-shifter until '55. A torque-converter automatic similar to Buick's Dynaflow, Powerglide was a big reason why Chevy beat Ford in model-year car production by no less than 290,000, with a total of near 1.5 million.

Another factor was the new 1950 Bel Air, America's first low-priced hardtop coupe. Buyers couldn't get enough of it. Like the pioneering 1949 Buick, Cadillac, and Olds hardtops, this junior edition sported lush trim that included simulated convertible-top bows on the headliner. It debuted as a top-shelf Styleline DeLuxe priced at $1741, about $100 below the ragtop, but it outpaced the convertible by better than 2-to-1 with over 76,000 first-year sales.

Chevy took a breather the next two years, with no mechanical developments and only bulkier sheetmetal for '51, followed by detail trim revisions for '52. Yet Chevy remained "USA-1" for both years. The '51 total was 1.23 million to Ford's 1.01 million. Korean War restrictions forced industrywide cutbacks for '52,

▲ 1952 Allstate two-door sedan

▼ 1938 American Bantam panel delivery

▲ 1966 AMC Ambassador 990 convertible coupe

▼ 1968 AMC AMX hardtop coupe

▲ 1970 AMC Javelin Trans Am hardtop coupe

▼ 1931 Auburn boattail speedster

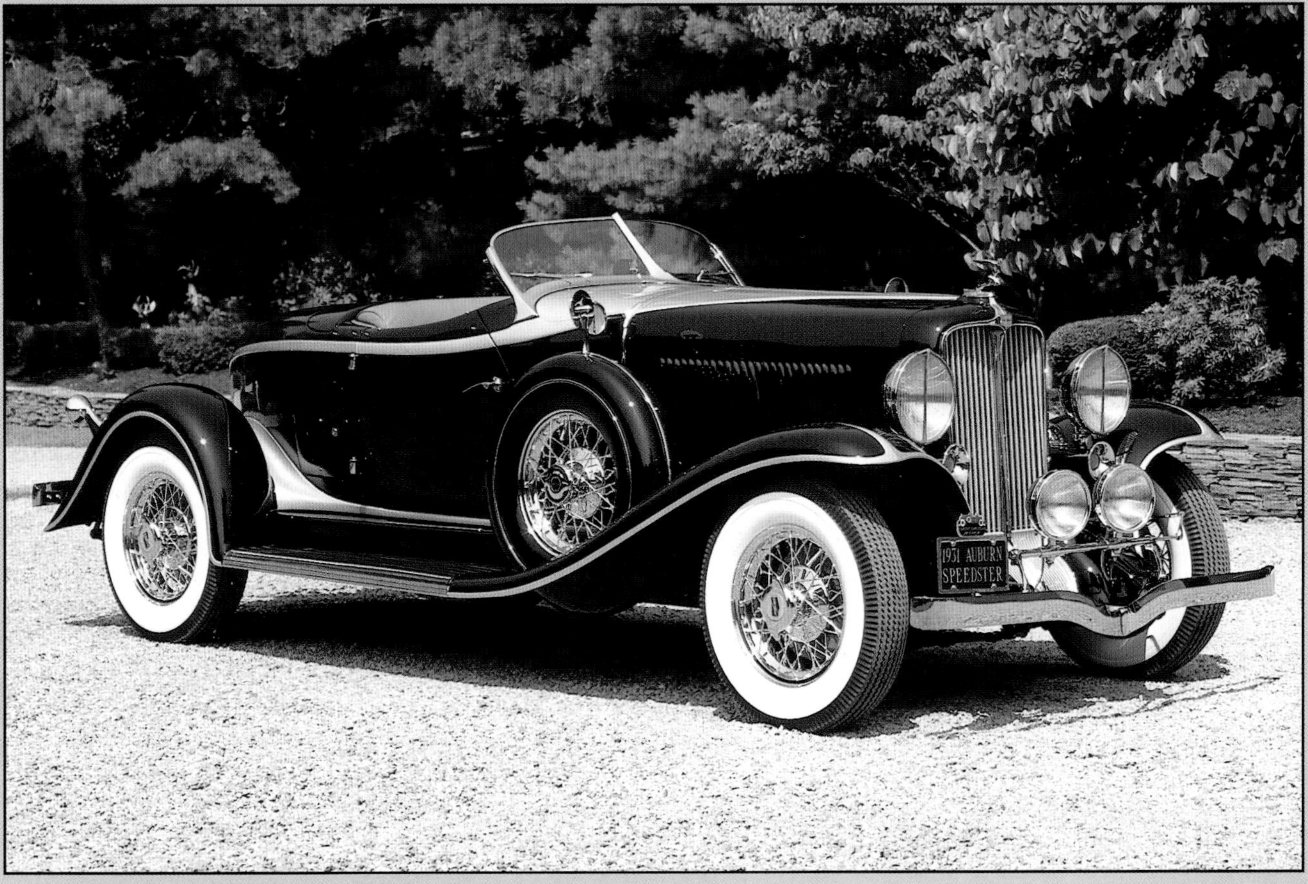

▲ 1989 Avanti convertible coupe and coupe

▼ 1931 Buick 95 phaeton

▲ 1935 Buick Series 60 convertible sedan

▼ 1953 Buick Skylark convertible coupe

▲ 1956 Buick Special convertible coupe

▼ 1961 Buick LeSabre convertible coupe

▲ 1963 Buick Riviera hardtop coupe

▼ 1966 Buick Rivera GS hardtop coupe

▲ 1932 Cadillac Twelve all-weather phaeton

▼ 1938 Cadillac Sixty Special four-door sedan

▲ 1947 Cadillac Series Sixty-Two convertible coupe

▼ 1959 Cadillac Series Sixty-Two hardtop coupe

▲ 1967 Cadillac Eldorado hardtop coupe

▼ 1972 Cadillac Fleetwood Brougham four-door sedan

▲ 2004 Cadillac CTS-V four-door sedan

▼ 1972 Checker station wagon

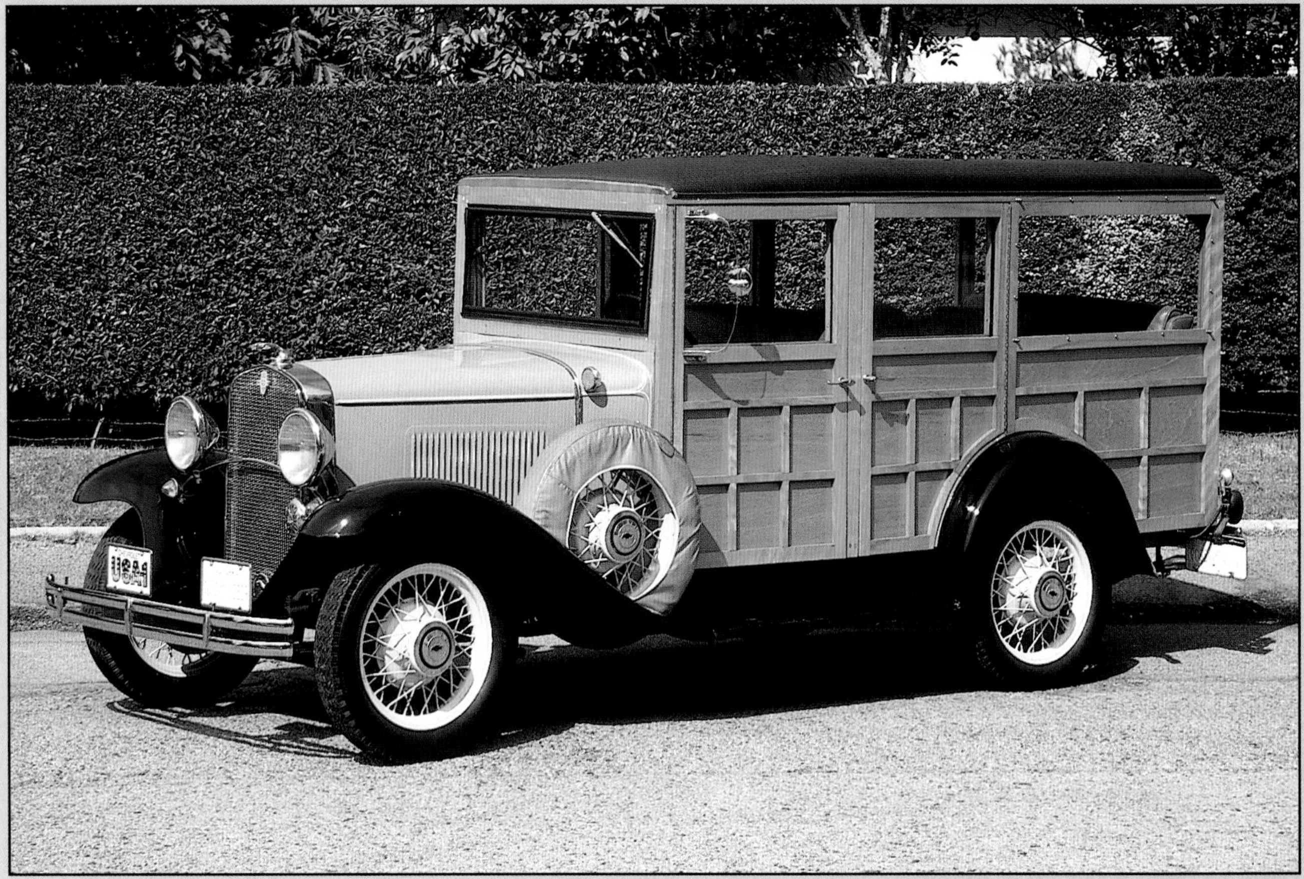

▲ 1931 Chevrolet station wagon

▼ 1947 Chevrolet Fleetline two-door Aerosedan

▲ 1951 Chevrolet Fleetline Deluxe four-door sedan

▼ 1957 Chevrolet Bel Air convertible coupe

▲ **1965 Chevrolet Chevelle Super Sport hardtop coupe**

▼ **1967 Chevrolet Impala hardtop coupe**

▲ 1970 Chevrolet Camaro Z28 coupe

▼ 1970 Chevrolet Chevelle Super Sport LS-6 hardtop coupe

▲ 1970 Chevrolet Monte Carlo SS 454 hardtop coupe

▼ 2006 Chevrolet Impala SS four-door sedan

1955 Bel Air Beauville station wagon

1955 Two-Ten hardtop sport coupe

1956 Bel Air hardtop sport sedan

1956 Bel Air hardtop sport coupe

1956 Bel Air Nomad two-door station wagon

1956 Two-Ten hardtop sport coupe

1957 Bel Air Nomad two-door station wagon

1957 Bel Air hardtop sport coupe

but Chevy's 800,000-plus still beat Ford's 671,000.

Though the Corvette sports car was Chevy's big news for '53 (*see entry*), passenger models got a major facelift. The bottom-end Special series was retitled One-Fifty, DeLuxe became Two-Ten, and Bel Air was applied to a full range of models as the new top of the line. Higher compression brought the Blue Flame Six to 108 bhp with manual transmission or 115 bhp with Powerglide. The figures were 115/125 for 1954, when styling became a bit flashier. Chevy continued to set the production pace. With war restrictions over, volume soared to over 1.3 million units for '53 and to near 1.17 million for '54. But though sound and reliable, Chevys still weren't very exciting. All-new styling and a landmark V-8 would take care of that.

Without question, the new 265 V-8 of 1955 was one of Detroit's milestone engines. Though designed for efficiency and low unit cost, it was really one of those "blue sky" projects that comes along only once or twice in an engineer's career. As principal designer Ed Cole later recalled: "I had worked on V-8 engines all my professional life. I had lived and breathed engines. [Engineer Harry F.] Barr and I were always saying how we would do it if we could ever design a new engine. You just know you want five main bearings—there's no decision to make. We knew that a certain bore/stroke relationship was the most compact. We knew we'd like a displacement of 265 cubic inches . . . And we never changed any of this. We released our engine for tooling direct from the drawing boards. That's how wild and crazy we were."

They had reason to be enthusiastic. The 265 boasted low reciprocating mass allowing high rpm; die-cast heads with integral, interchangeable valve guides; aluminum "slipper" pistons;

a crankshaft of forged pressed-steel instead of alloy iron—and much more. Best of all, it weighed less than the old six yet was far more potent, initially pumping out 162/170 bhp (manual/Powerglide) in standard tune or 180 bhp with optional Power-Pak (four-barrel carburetor and dual exhausts).

Of course, it could give a lot more—and did for '57 when bored to 283 cid and offered with optional fuel injection. Chevrolet developed a new 348-cid "big-block" for 1958 and beyond. It was a good one, but the small-block remains one of the best-known, best-loved engines of all time, earning Chevy a performance reputation the way sixes never could.

At just under $200, Powerglide became an increasingly popular option in the '50s—a smooth operator well-suited to all but high-power models. Standard three-speed manual and extra-cost stick-overdrive were offered throughout the decade, and an all-synchromesh four-speed manual came on board in 1959. Late '57 brought a second automatic option, three-speed Turboglide, but this was complex, costly, and short-lived. Powerglide would be *the* Chevy automatic until the mid-'60s.

The 1955-57 Chevys are coveted collectibles now, and styling has as much to do with this as engineering. Design principals Clare MacKichan (then Chevy studio chief), Carl Renner, Chuck Stebbins, Bob Veryzer, and others worked under Harley Earl's dictum of "Go all the way, then back off." Though the '55 didn't reach showrooms looking like their fanciful renderings, it wasn't far off, wearing Earl's hallmark beltline "dip," wrapped windshield, and a simple eggcrate grille inspired by Ferrari. The last became broader, brighter, and more conventional for '56 in line with buyer tastes.

Other elements in Chevy's winning '55 package included a more-capable suspension, bigger brakes, better steering, more interior and trunk room, better visibility—the list was almost endless. Even the old six was improved: boosted to 123/136 bhp (manual/Powerglide). With all this, plus attractive prices that weren't changed much from '54 (mostly in the $1600-$2260 range), Chevy led the industry in a record Detroit year with over 1.7 million cars, a new make high and a quarter-million better than Ford.

An interesting '55 newcomer was the Bel Air Nomad, America's first "hardtop wagon." A Carl Renner idea adapted from his 1954 Motorama show Corvette, the Nomad didn't sell that well, mainly because two-door wagons were less popular than four-doors, though water leaks were also a problem. Then, too, it was relatively expensive ($2600-$2700). Had anybody else built it, the Nomad probably would have seen minuscule production, but a respectable 8386 were built for 1955, 7886 for '56, and 6103 for 1957.

Chevy called its '55 "The Hot One." Ads said the '56 was even

1957 Two-Ten Delray club coupe

1958 Impala hardtop sport coupe

1957 Bel Air convertible coupe

1958 Biscayne two-door sedan

1958 Bel Air Impala convertible coupe

1958 Bel Air hardtop sport coupe

hotter. It was. The old Stovebolt, now offered with manual shift only, was up to 140 bhp, while the V-8 delivered up to 225 bhp with Power-Pak. A $40-million restyle made all models look more like Cadillacs, and four-door hardtop sport sedans joined the Two-Ten and Bel Air lines. Despite a broad industry retreat, Chevy managed record market penetration of close to 28 percent on just 88 percent of its '55 volume—about 1.5 million units. Ford repeated at around 1.4 million.

Ford (and Plymouth) counterpunched with all-new styling for '57. Chevy had to make do with another substantial facelift, but it was deftly done and quite popular. In fact, this Chevy is still regarded by many as the definitive '50s car. There were now eight engine choices, up three from '56, including no fewer than six 283 V-8s with 185 up to 283 bhp. The last was courtesy of "Ramjet" fuel injection, a new option that found few takers at $500, but enabled the division to claim "1 hp per cu. in." (though Chrysler had achieved that magic figure with its '56 300B). Yet even without the "fuelie," a '57 Chevy could be quite fast. For example, a Bel Air sport sedan with the four-barrel 270-bhp engine could do 0-60 mph in 9.9 seconds, the quarter-mile in 17.5, and over 110 mph flat out.

Properly equipped, the 1955-57 Chevy was a formidable track competitor. Before the Automobile Manufacturers Association voted to withdraw from organized racing in June 1957, Chevy did very well in NASCAR and other stock-car events. At that year's Daytona Speed Weeks, Chevy took the first three places in the two-way flying-mile for Class 4 (213-259 cid); in Class 5 (259-305 cid) it took 33 out of 37 places, the fastest car averaging 131.076 mph. Chevy also won the 1957 Pure Oil Manufacturers Trophy with 574 points against 309 for runner-up Ford.

While the AMA racing "ban" didn't deter Chevy and others from providing under-the-table racing support, it seemed to be reflected in the softer, more-luxurious Chevys of 1958. Riding a new 117.5-inch-wheelbase X-member chassis, they were longer, lower, wider, and heavier, but not really slower than the lighter '57s. Bodies were naturally all-new, too—and shinier, looking more "important" and Cadillac-like than ever. As it turned out, they'd be one-year-only jobs. Not so the new 348 big-block V-8, a modified truck engine (which Chevy was understandably loath to mention) offering 250 to 315 bhp. That year's base V-8 was a 185-bhp 283.

Underscoring all this change was the new line-leading 1958 Impala (a name dreamed up by designer Robert Cadaret), a lush Bel Air subseries offering convertible and hardtop sport coupe with six or V-8 in the $2600-$2800 range. Below was a rearranged model group. One-Fifty was renamed Delray (borrowed from a spiffy 1954-57 Two-Ten two-door sedan), Biscayne replaced Two-Ten, and "Station Wagon" was a separate line with no fewer than five models: two-door Yeoman and four-door Yeoman, Brookwood (in six- and nine-seat form), and Nomad. Unlike the 1955-57 Nomad, the '58 was conventionally styled.

Chevy was now clearly reaching for buyers it had never sought before: solid, substantial Pontiac types who cared more about size and comfort than performance or handling. The division's grasp did not exceed that reach. In a rough year for the economy in general and Detroit in particular, Chevy managed over 1.1 million cars. Impala was a big success, accounting for fully 15 percent of the total.

If Chevrolet showed restraint in bucking tailfins for '58, it more than made up for that the following year with another all-new body bearing huge "cat's-eye" taillamps and a "batwing" rear deck that tester Tom McCahill said was "big enough to land a Piper Cub." It could have been worse. Several 1959 proposals envisioned ugly, Edsel-like vertical grilles. Ford had shaded Chevy in model-year '57 production and came within 12,000

1959 Impala convertible coupe

1959 Bel Air two-door sedan

1959 Impala hardtop sport coupe

1960 Impala convertible coupe

1960 Nomad station wagon

1960 Impala hardtop coupe

1961 Impala convertible coupe

1961 Bel Air four-door sedan

1961 Bel Air hardtop sport coupe

1962 Chevy II Nova 400 convertible coupe

1962 Impala hardtop sport coupe

1962 Bel Air hardtop sport coupe

1963 Impala SS convertible coupe

1963 Impala SS hardtop sport coupe

1963 Chevy II Nova 400 SS hardtop sport coupe

1964 Chevelle Malibu SS convertible coupe

1964 Impala convertible coupe

1964 Chevelle Malibu SS hardtop sport coupe

units of doing it again for '59. Dearborn's more-conservative styling no doubt played a part. But future Chevys would be far more-tasteful under William L. Mitchell, who replaced Harley Earl as GM design chief on the latter's retirement in 1958.

Delray disappeared from the '59 line and a new full-range Impala series displaced Bel Air at the top, pushing other non-wagon series down a notch. All models rode a new 119-inch wheelbase, Chevy's longest yet. The growth between 1957 and 1959 was amazing: length up by nearly 11 inches, width by seven inches, weight by 300 pounds. The '59s were the first of the overstuffed "standard" Chevys that would endure for the next 15 years, though they made sense at the time. Buyers demanded ever-bigger cars in the '50s, so even the low-priced three grew to about the size of late-'40s Cadillacs and Lincolns.

Though Chevrolet would mostly follow Ford's marketing initiatives in the '60s, it continued to lead in production, winning every model year except 1961 and 1966. Like its arch rival, Chevy expanded into compacts (Corvair and Chevy II), intermediates (Chevelle), "muscle cars" (Impala SS, Malibu SS) and "ponycars" (Camaro). Each was carefully conceived to fill a specific need, and all succeeded save the singular rear-engine Corvair, which is different enough to merit a separate entry.

Such increasing specialization might imply increasing production, but though Chevy did set some records, its 1969 volume was "only" some 500,000 cars ahead of 1960's despite the introduction of four new model lines. This proliferation reflected a market that had subdivided, generating more "niche" competition than in the '50s. As a result, Chevy often competed less against rivals than against itself or other GM makes.

Its lineup certainly became quite broad by 1969, when it spanned no fewer than five wheelbases: 98 inches for Corvette, 108 for Corvair/Camaro, 111 for Chevy II/Nova, 116 for Chevelle, and 119 inches for full-size Chevrolets. An exception was the post-'67 Chevelle which, like other GM intermediates, went to a 112-inch wheelbase for two-door models and 116 for four-doors, an arrangement that would persist through 1977.

With no change in wheelbase, what became known as the "standard" (full-size) Chevrolet moved from overstyled outrageousness to clean, crisp elegance. The pattern was set immediately, the 1960 edition being a more-subdued version of the wild '59. A taut new package bereft of fins and wrapped windshields bowed for '61, reflecting the first direct influence of Bill Mitchell. For '63 came a more-sculptured look. Another complete redesign brought more-flowing lines for '65, followed by even curvier '67s with semifastback hardtop coupes and more-pronounced "Coke bottle" fenders. The '69s had a fuller, squarer look, emphasized by bodyside bulges and elliptical wheel openings. The decade's prettiest big Chevy might well be the '62, with its straight, "correct" lines and, for Impala hardtop coupes, a rear roof sculptured to resemble a raised convertible top.

Nineteen sixty-two also saw Chevy enlarge the 283 small-block V-8 to 327 cid for an initial 250 or 300 bhp in full-size models. But 283s would continue to power a variety of Chevys through 1967, when a stroked 350 more amenable to emission controls began to be phased in.

Biscayne remained Chevy's full-size price leader in the '60s, but buyer interest quickly tapered off. The midpriced Bel Air also waned, but the top-line Impala rapidly became Detroit's single-most-popular model line. Its best sales year in this decade was 1964, when some 889,600 were built.

By far the most-collectible Impala is the performance-bred Super Sport, an option package for mid-1961 and 1968-69, an Impala subseries in other years. Body styles were always limited to convertible and hardtop coupe. The concept was simple: the smooth big Chevy with sporty styling touches and available performance and handling options. Sixes were available but

1965 Chevelle Malibu SS convertible coupe

1965 Chevy II Nova SS hardtop sport coupe

1965 Impala Super Sport convertible coupe

1965 Impala hardtop sport coupe

1965 Impala hardtop sport sedan

1966 Impala Super Sport convertible coupe

not often ordered (only 3600 of the '65s, for instance). Typical features ran to special SS emblems, vinyl bucket seats, central shift console, and optional tachometer. A variety of V-8s was offered, including big-blocks, beginning with the famous 409 of 1961, an enlarged 348 delivering 360 horsepower initially and up to 425 bhp by '63.

With options like stiffer springs and shocks, sintered metallic brake linings, four-speed manual gearbox, and ultra-quick power steering, the SS Impalas were the best-performing big Chevys in history. But they couldn't last forever. Government regulations and the advent of midsize muscle cars combined to do in sporty big cars of all kinds. Yet Impala SS remained exciting right to the end. Even the final 1967-69 models could be ordered with "Mark IV" 427 big-blocks packing 385-425 bhp.

A far-more-lucrative full-size Chevy was the Caprice, an Impala dolled up with the best grades of upholstery and trim. A mid-1965 reply to Ford's quiet-as-a Rolls LTD, Caprice garnered a healthy 181,000 sales for model-year '66, when it became a separate line and the initial hardtop sedan was joined by wagons and a hardtop coupe. Production through the rest of the decade ranged from 115,500 to nearly 167,000. Obviously, Cadillac luxury at a Chevy kind of price still appealed as much in the '60s as it had in the days of the first Impala.

One rung below the full-size Chevy was the intermediate Chevelle, introduced for 1964 in answer to Ford's popular Fairlane. Though conventional in design, Chevelle offered almost as much interior room as Impala within more-sensible exterior dimensions—effectively a return to the ideally proportioned 1955-57 "classic" Chevy. Sales went nowhere but up—from 328,400 in the first year to nearly 440,000 by 1969. Helping

1966 Caprice Custom hardtop coupe

1966 Chevelle Super Sport 396 hardtop sport coupe

1966 Chevy II Nova Super Sport hardtop coupe

1967 Impala SS convertible coupe

1967 Impala hardtop sport coupe

1967 Chevelle SS 396 hardtop sport coupe

1967 Chevy II Nova Super Sport hardtop coupe

1967 Camaro SS 350 hardtop coupe (with RS package)

things along were numerous performance options and bucket-seat Malibu SS convertible and hardtop models.

Third down the size scale was the Chevy II, an orthodox compact rushed out for 1962 to answer Ford's Falcon, which had been handily trimming the radical Corvair. Initial engine choices were a 90-bhp, 153-cid four and a 120-bhp, 194-cid six. (Falcon had only sixes through mid-1963, then added a V-8 option.) It was a good move, but through 1966, Chevy IIs outnumbered Falcons only once: model-year '63. Sales dropped nearly 50 percent for '64, due partly to intramural competition from Chevelle. A spate of Super Sport models didn't help. Nor did a heavy facelift for '66.

What did help was a 1968 Chevy II pumped up to near intermediate size via an all-new 111-inch-wheelbase GM X-body platform. Convertibles, wagons, and hardtop coupes were deleted, leaving four-door sedans and two-door pillared coupes. The latter were available with an SS package option. Backed by a strong ad campaign and competitive prices, Chevy's compact posted soaring sales of 201,000 for '68 and over a quarter-million for 1970, when the name was changed to Nova (originally, the premium Chevy II series).

Adding new spice to Chevy's '67 line was Camaro, which would eventually succeed the ailing Corvair as the division's sporty compact. Despite the beautiful styling and impressive performance of the all-new '65 Corvair, the rear-engine Chevy was no threat to Ford's incredibly successful Mustang in the burgeoning ponycar market. Worse, it was costly to build—entirely different in concept and technology from other Chevys. Six months after the '65s debuted, division managers decided Corvair would be allowed to fade away in favor of the conven-

1967 Chevelle Malibu hardtop sedan

1968 Caprice hardtop coupe

1968 Chevelle SS 396 hardtop sport coupe

1968 Chevy II Nova coupe (sans side-marker lights)

1968 Camaro Z-28 Rally Sport prototype

1969 Camaro Z-28 hardtop sport coupe

1969 Camaro Rally Sport convertible coupe

1969 Chevelle SS 396 hardtop sport coupe

1969 Impala Custom hardtop coupe

1969 Kingswood Estate station wagon

1970 Nova coupe

1970 Caprice hardtop coupe

1970 Chevelle SS 396 hardtop sport coupe

1970 Monte Carlo hardtop sport coupe

tional Camaro, which was deliberately designed as a direct Mustang-fighter.

Created under the omnipresent eye of GM design chief Bill Mitchell, Camaro styling was exactly right: long-hood/short-deck proportions; low, chiseled profile; flowing, slightly "hippy" lines. Like Mustang, Camaro aimed at those who wanted a sporty four-seater that could be equipped as an economy run-about, vivid straight-line performer, or something in-between, so it offered a Mustang-style plethora of options: some 81 factory items and 41 dealer-installed accessories.

Camaro's 1967 prices started at $2466 for the basic hardtop coupe and $2704 for the convertible with standard 140-bhp, 230-cid six. A 155-bhp, 250-cid six cost $26 extra; a 210-bhp 327 V-8 was $106. Next on the list was a 350 V-8 with 295 bhp, exclusive to Camaro in '67 but more-widely available beginning in '68. To get it you had to order a $211 Super Sports package comprising stiffer springs and shocks, D70-14 Firestone Wide-Oval tires, performance hood with extra sound insulation, SS emblems, and "bumblebee" nose stripes. A 396 big-block V-8 became available during the year at nearly $400.

Also tempting '67 Camaro customers were custom carpeting; bucket seats; fold-down rear seat; luxury interior; full instrumentation; and console shifters for the optional Turbo Hydra-Matic, heavy-duty three-speed manual, and four-speed manual. For $105, a Rally Sport package added a hidden-headlight grille, "RS" badges, and other touches. Additional extras ran to tinted glass, radio, air conditioning, clock, cruise control, and a vinyl roof covering for hardtops. Mechanical options included sintered metallic brake linings, ventilated front disc brakes, vacuum brake booster, power steering, fast-ratio manual steering, stiff suspension, Positraction limited-slip differential, and a dozen different axle ratios. With all this, a Camaro could easily be optioned to $5000.

Though two years behind Mustang, Camaro was a big hit. Production topped 220,000 the first year, 235,000 for '68, and 240,000 for '69. There were no major changes through mid-1970. The '68s carried a horizontal grille treatment, ventless side glass, Chevy's new "Astro Ventilation" system, and restyled taillights; the '69s were more-thoroughly face-lifted via a recontoured lower body with front and rear creaselines atop the wheel openings, plus a Vee'd grille and new rear styling.

Available for the street but aimed squarely at the track was Camaro RPO (Regular Production Option) Z-28, a tailor-made competition package for hardtops announced during 1967. With it, Camaro won 18 of 25 events in the Sports Car Club of America's new Trans-American road-racing series for production "sedans." Camaro then claimed the class championship in 1968 and '69.

Veteran Chevy engineer Vincent W. Piggins had designed the Z-28 expressly for the Trans-Am—then convinced management to sell it to the public. To meet the prevailing displacement limit, he combined the 327 block with the 283 crankshaft to produce a high-winding 302.4-cid small-block with a nominal 290 bhp—it was more like 350—and 290 pound-feet of torque. Completing the Z-28 package were heavy-duty suspension, 11-inch-diameter clutch, quick steering, hood air ducts feeding big carburetors, close-ratio four-speed gearbox, front disc brakes, metallic rear-brake linings, a "ducktail" rear spoiler, broad dorsal racing stripes, and Rally wheels with wide-tread tires. All this listed for about $400, but actual price was more like $800 because the four-speed, power front discs, special headers, and metallic rear-drum linings were all "mandatory" extras.

Nevertheless, the Z-28 was a whale of high-performance buy. It wasn't for everyone, of course, but production climbed quickly, going from 602 for '67 to 7199 for '68 and then to 20,302 for '69. All are now coveted collectibles, not only as the first of a great

1970 Nova coupe

1970 Camaro SS 350 hardtop coupe (early series)

1970 Camaro Rally Sport coupe (late series)

1970 Camaro Rally Sport coupe (late series)

1971 Chevelle SS 454 hardtop sport coupe

1971 Camaro SS coupe

1971 Kingswood Estate station wagon

1971 Monte Carlo SS 454 hardtop sport coupe

breed, but because, unfortunately, the Z would become less-special in future years.

Chevrolet fielded an all-new Camaro for 1970 and entered the personal-luxury market with the Monte Carlo. A 65-day strike kept the division from outproducing Ford, but its 12-month total of nearly 1.5 million cars was hardly bad. For the model year, Chevy built 1.46 million cars to its arch rival's two million-plus.

A kissin' cousin of Pontiac's all-new '69 Grand Prix, the cleanly styled Monte Carlo rode the Chevelle's 116-inch four-door chassis but came only as a hardtop coupe with the longest hood in Chevy history. A 250-bhp 350 V-8 teamed with Turbo-Hydra-Matic as standard, and all sorts of luxury options were offered. Alternative engines ran to a 300-bhp 350 and a new 400 V-8 with 330 bhp. Base-priced just below $3000, the Monte Carlo sold well: over 145,000 for 1970 (against only 50,000 for Ford's considerably costlier Thunderbird). Among them were a mere 3823 equipped with the optional SS 454 package—an iron fist in a velvet glove if ever there was one.

Listed as RPO Z20, the Monte SS package delivered the division's huge new 454 big-block engine, a stroked 427 tuned for 360 bhp in this application, plus square-tip dual exhausts and a chassis fortified with auto-leveling rear shocks, stiffer front shocks, and power front disc brakes. Discreet badges and black rocker-panel trim were the only clues as to what lay beneath that long hood. Acceleration was vivid: just 7.5 seconds for 0-60 mph. But luxury was this car's forte—after 1919 more in '71, the Monte Carlo wouldn't take another run at performance until years later.

Corvair's demise after 1969 left Nova as Chevy's only compact. The 1970 edition was mildly face-lifted, but saw no substantive change. That year's Chevelle, still on the split-wheelbase 1968 A-body platform, was restyled to look more like full-size Chevys, gaining a divided grille, bulges around each wheel opening, and a more-rounded, massive look. Super Sport packages were again offered for both Nova and Chevelle, the former built around a 350 V-8, the latter around the big-block 454 and 396 (which was actually a 402 now). None saw very high sales, what with rising fuel prices and insurance rates putting a big damper on muscle-car demand throughout Detroit. The big-car sales emphasis was still on the luxurious Impala and Caprice; Biscayne and Bel Air were now reduced to just one four-door

1971 Chevelle with Heavy Chevy option

1971 Vega 2300 hatchback coupe

1971 Vega 2300 Kammback two-door station wagon

1971 Nova SS coupe

1972 Kingswood Estate station wagon

1972 Chevelle Malibu hardtop sport sedan

1972 Impala Custom coupe

1973 Chevelle Laguna coupe

1973 Chevelle Malibu coupe

1973 Monte Carlo coupe

sedan each.

Arriving in the spring of 1970 was a brilliant new second-generation Camaro ('69s were sold as '70s through the previous December). With dramatic, European-inspired GT styling, it sold nearly 125,000 copies despite the abbreviated 1970 run. The ragtop was no more, another victim of fading demand, but a smooth new coupe offered the usual arm-long list of extras, including two SS packages, like Chevelle's, plus a separate Rally Sport trim group and the still-potent Z28 option. Wheelbase was unchanged, but most everything else was. If the result was heavier and less-efficient, it was also a smoother-riding and better-handling Chevy ponycar.

Chevrolet would remain "USA-1" throughout the '70s despite a few product blunders and the vexing problems that plagued all Detroit in that turbulent decade. In model-year production, it ran second to Ford only in 1970 and '71. After that, Chevy was the consistent industry leader with at least 2 million cars a year except for troubled '75, when depressed big-car demand after the 1973-74 energy crisis dropped the tally to about 1.75 million.

Such strength enabled Chevrolet to endure mistakes that would have crippled most any other brand save Ford. Even the subcompact Vega, long viewed as the division's biggest folly of the period, hung on for seven model years and sold respectably in every one.

Vega certainly seemed a good idea when it bowed for 1971. Riding a 97-inch wheelbase, the shortest in Chevy history, it carried an all-new, 140-cid four with 90 or 110 bhp. Pert styling marked by a Camaro-like front was offered in three practical body styles: two-door notchback sedan, hatchback coupe, and a nifty little two-door "Kammback" wagon.

Chevrolet spent vast sums designing, launching, and promoting this latest attempt at beating back small imports—not to mention Ford's new Pinto—and on a special factory to build it. But like the Corvair, Vega missed its intended target: bought not as basic transport but as a small sporty car, abetted by a GT coupe and wagon. Worse, it quickly became notorious for early, severe body rust, and its alloy-block engine (which made do without cylinder liners) suffered persistent oil leaks and head warping. By 1976, when the even smaller Chevette was ready, Vega was being trounced by a number of domestic and foreign rivals. Though the name was dropped after '77, the basic car—minus the problematic engine—continued through 1979 in the Monza line.

An intriguing Vega offshoot was the Cosworth-Vega of 1975-76, quite "foreign" for a U.S. car and thus something of a collector's item now. Its main attraction was a destroked, 122-cid Vega engine wearing a special 16-valve twincam aluminum cylinder head designed by England's Cosworth Engineering. Fuel was fed by Bendix electronic injection actuated by a glovebox-mounted computer.

Available only as a hatchback coupe, the "CosVeg" initially came only in black with special gold striping and cast-aluminum wheels. Completing the package were wide radial tires, full instrumentation in an engine-turned panel, front/rear anti-roll bars, four-speed gearbox, quick steering, and discreet badges. Unfortunately, the engine yielded only 111 bhp, so this wasn't the BMW-beater Chevy had planned. The '76 version offered any Vega body color and an optional five-speed gearbox, but many were unsold at year's end. Respective production was just 2061 and 1447.

Monza proved a far-more-successful Vega variant. New for '75, it rode the same chassis, but carried a handsome 2+2 coupe body with lift-up rear hatch and a fastback roofline reminiscent of certain Ferraris. A notchback "Towne Coupe" was added during the year. The Vega four was base power, but a new 262-cid small-block V-8 was optional, mildly tuned for 110 bhp.

1974 Caprice convertible coupe

1974 Monte Carlo coupe

1974 Vega Estate Wagon two-door

1974 Nova Custom four-door sedan

1974 Camaro Type LT sport coupe

Enthusiasts could opt for several interesting RPOs such as a Z01 performance and handling package and, for 2+2s, a "Spyder" appearance group.

After 1977, the Vega wagon became a Monza, and all three models got a new standard engine: the 151-cid Pontiac "Iron Duke" four (so named to reassure buyers stung by the Vega unit). That same year, the blunt-front Towne Coupe was optionally available with the 2+2's "droop snoot." Monza then saw only minor changes through early 1981, when it departed to make way for an even better small Chevy.

After a mostly stand-pat 1970, the full-size Chevys ballooned to as big as they'd ever get, thanks to 1971's new "fuselage-style" GM B-body and a longer 121.5-inch wheelbase. As ever, promotion focused on Impala and Caprice. The Biscayne and Bel Air sedans were now relegated to the fleet market, and would be discontinued after 1972 and '75, respectively. Mid-price Impala Customs, new for '68, continued finding favor among those who liked, but couldn't quite afford, a Caprice. The Caprice itself was similarly upgraded as more Classic models were added year by year.

Big-Chevy engine choices through 1976 revolved around 350, 400, and 454 V-8s, though a 145-bhp 305 was rushed out as standard for '76 (except on wagons), a post-oil-embargo economy move. Emissions tuning rendered all decreasingly potent, as did the added weight of "crash" bumpers after 1972, plus other federally required measures. Styling became progressively more ornate and "formal," and threatened rollover standards prompted hardtop coupes to be replaced by "pillared" 1974 models with huge rear side windows. For the same reason, the Caprice convertible (an Impala through '72) disappeared after 1975. Despite their limitations, these big Chevys always sold in large numbers—as ever, the epitome of middle-class American motoring.

Then, a revolution: the first wave of GM's corporatewide downsizing program, which saw the 1977 Caprice/Impala trimmed by 5½ inches in wheelbase and 600-800 pounds in gas-wasting bulk. It seemed like a huge gamble then, and Ford tried to take advantage by extolling the "road-hugging weight" of its still-enormous full-sizers. But Chevrolet, as usual, knew exactly what it was doing, and Caprice/Impala sales actually improved (despite the departure of hardtop sedans). And why not? The new models were not only lighter but more-agile, easier on gas and, to some, better-looking.

In the intermediate ranks, Chevelle and Monte Carlo were switched to GM's new "Colonnade" A-body for 1973, which meant fresh styling and no more convertibles or closed pillarless models. The Monte divided into S and plusher Landau offerings, both with rather baroque, "French curve" styling. The blockier Chevelles included base, Malibu and ritzy Malibu Classic coupes and sedans, plus a plethora of wagons in base, Classic, and Classic Estate trim. An interesting 1974-76 concoction was the Laguna S-3 coupe. A cross between a luxury tourer and the now-departed Malibu SS, it sported body-color grille surround and bumpers, plus a posh vinyl interior available for

1975 Chevelle Malibu Classic coupe

1975 Vega LX two-door sedan

1975 Nova LN four-door sedan

1976 Caprice Classic hardtop sport sedan

1975 Monte Carlo coupe

1976 Monte Carlo Landau coupe

a time with optional swiveling front seats—a revival of a '50s Chrysler idea.

When the big Chevys shrank to intermediate stature, it was obvious that the midsizers would get smaller, too. They did, for 1978. Chevelles became Malibus, and shared a new 108.1-inch-wheelbase platform with Monte Carlo. The latter retained generally florid looks, but the Malibus were crisp and clean. Again, sales didn't suffer—to Chevy's undoubted relief.

A consistently high seller since its '68 overhaul, the compact Nova saw little change through 1973, when a minor facelift occurred and hatchback two-door sedans arrived in the usual base and Custom trim. An extensive 1975 reskin ushered in new rooflines and more glass, fancy LN ("Luxury Nova") models (renamed Concours for '76), and steering and front suspension borrowed from Camaro. Nova captured 15 percent of Chevy's total 1975 sales to become the year's most-popular American compact. Engine offerings simplified for '76. The "performance" option was now a 305 V-8, a debored 350 replacing both that engine and the little 262. Standard power through 1979 remained the workhorse 250-cid inline six, after which both engine and car were scrubbed in favor of fours and V-6s in a new compact called Citation, "the first Chevy of the '80s."

Unveiled in April 1979, Citation was a runaway success its first year, helped by another fuel crisis. Body styles comprised two- and four-door hatchback sedans and a pillared "slantback" two-door unique among the four versions of this corporate design. On a 104.9-inch wheelbase, Citation's new X-body platform afforded excellent space at moderate weight, which averaged around 2500 pounds. Pontiac's well-proven "Iron Duke" four was standard; the only power option was a new Chevy-built 60-degree V-6 displacing 2.8 liters (173 cid). Both engines were mounted transversely to take advantage of the space-saving front-drive mechanicals. A four-speed manual transaxle was standard, three-speed automatic optional. For a sporty Citation, you ordered a two-door with an X-11 package comprising uprated suspension and other chassis modifications, plus brash exterior graphics. The lightweight X-11 was a capable performer with the V-6.

Like most new designs, however, Citation had a hefty helping of engineering and quality-control problems, and would be recalled many times. But overall balance and livability made it a hot number for awhile, and Chevrolet was hard pressed to meet demand.

Camaro almost expired after 1974 as sales sagged in the wake of the first energy crisis. But a determined effort by enthusiastic GMers saved the striking second generation from a premature end.

The 1971-72 Camaros were much like the inaugural "1970½" models save minor changes dictated by federal regulations. For '73, the macho SS was replaced by a less-pretentious LT (Luxury Touring) model with standard 145-bhp V-8, variable-ratio power steering, and appearance touches like hidden wipers, black rockers, Rally wheels, and woodgrain dash trim.

Prices started to gallop with the '74s, which were face-lifted at each end to accommodate required five-mph impact bumpers. A wraparound rear window marked the '75s, which began Camaro's sales revival after a four-year dry spell. Capitalizing on renewed interest in ponycars, Chevy reinstated the Rally Sport package as a midseason option. This included matte-black hood and front fender tops, special paint, and the further option of color-matched Z28 wheels. The '74 facelift kept going for 1976-77 as Camaro reached, then exceeded, its '60s sales record.

The big Camaro event in 1977 was a revived Z28, only with the emphasis now on refined road manners rather than raw power. Chassis engineer Jack Turner took a straightforward

1976 Cosworth Vega hatchback coupe

1976 Nova coupe

1977 Monza Spyder hatchback coupe

1977 Caprice Classic four-door sedan

1977 Impala coupe

1977 Vega GT hatchback coupe

1978 Monte Carlo coupe

1978 Nova Custom four-door sedan

1978 Monza two-door station wagon

1978 Camaro Z28 sport coupe

1978 Monza coupe

1979 Monte Carlo sport coupe

1979 Malibu Classic two-door sedan

1979 Chevette hatchback sedan

approach: tighter springs, thicker front antiroll bar, a more-flexible rear bar, larger wheels and tires. New exterior graphics and colors were well suited to the smooth lines. A midyear introduction limited '77 sales, but the reborn Z then zoomed in popularity.

Picking up where Vega left off was Chevette, the smallest Chevrolet ever, announced for bicentennial 1976. Derived from the 1974 German Opel Kadett, the first of GM's "world car" T-body models, it rode a modest 94.3-inch wheelbase, measured 17 inches shorter than Vega, and weighed in at just under a ton. Its mission, of course, was economy, which it delivered: 35 mpg or so on the highway. Engines were small: initially a 1.4-liter/85-cid overhead-cam four with 52 bhp and a 60-bhp 1.6-liter/98-cid version. The former was gone by '78, when the 1.6 was tuned to deliver a slightly more-respectable 63-68 bhp.

Chevette bowed as a single two-door hatchback sedan, but a four-door on a three-inch-longer wheelbase was added for '78. Options were numerous, as the car had been built "down" to a low price. Yet, like so many Chevys before it, Chevette was exactly right for its time, and quite competitive in the increasingly hard-fought subcompact market.

The entire market would be hard-fought in the 1980s. Detroit found itself battling not only a deep national recession early in the decade, but also a horde of Japanese competitors, which had already captured lots of U.S. sales territory with low prices, top-notch workmanship, and superior reliability. Though the economy began recovering after 1982, import penetration reached record levels by mid-decade—some 35-40 percent of the total U.S. car market—despite price increases prompted by a weakening dollar. Much of the Japanese gains came at the expense of AMC, Chrysler, and Ford, but GM had problems of its own and suffered lower volume, too. Chevrolet's withered to

1980 Citation X-11 notchback

1980 Citation hatchback sedan

1980 Camaro Z28 coupe

1980 Impala four-door sedan

1980 Monte Carlo Sport Turbo coupe

1980 Citation notchback coupe

1980 Malibu Classic Estate wagon

1981 Caprice sport coupe

about 1.6 million units for 1981, when the market was still relatively good, then to a bit under 1.4 million for 1985-87.

Meantime, the division had decided to switch rather than fight, and began selling a pair of small Japanese models with bowtie badges. But in domestic production, Chevrolet maintained its traditional number-one rank only through 1987. It was then overhauled by an increasingly aggressive Ford Division. Dearborn as a whole out-earned the General for the first time in 40 years—and on only half the volume.

Chevy's mixed fortunes in the '80s certainly weren't for lack of product or canny marketing. GM's long-term downsizing program ushered in a spate of smaller, more-efficient new Chevys, yet old standbys were allowed to carry on so long as sales were decent. Continuing modernization saw fuel injection (both single- and multi-point) replace carburetors on many engines, which increasingly became V-6s and inline-fours. Yet V-8s were still part of the picture, as were performance cars—once demand for them returned around 1984.

Reflecting these trends were those three division staples of the '80s, the Monte Carlo, Chevette, and Caprice/Impala. The last saw little change following a mild 1980 "aero" reskin that freshened the basic '77 styling even if it did little for mileage as claimed. Hoods were lower, rear decks higher, and coupes exchanged their sharply creased wraparound backlights for flat panes. Sedans used V-6s, either 229-cid Chevy or 231-cid Buick, as base power though 1984, then a 4.3-liter (262-cid) Chevy V-6. There was also a diesel V-8 option, the trouble-prone 350 Olds engine, canceled after '85 as Americans bathed again in a sea of cheap gasoline. Most of these big Chevys carried the reliable 305 small-block V8 (usually standard on wagons). Coupes were dropped for '83, revived for '84, then dropped again four years later. The venerable Impala name was gone by '86, as Caprices

1981 Chevette hatchback sedan (diesel)

1981 Citation hatchback sedan

1982 Monte Carlo sport coupe

1982 Camaro Z28 sport coupe

1982 Cavalier hatchback coupe

had proliferated into base, Classic, Classic Brougham, and Classic LS Brougham models.

Chevy was wise to retain big rear-drive cars once Buick, Olds, and for a time, Pontiac dropped them, for they were strong sellers even in the worst of times. And when times got better, so did Caprice/Impala sales, rising from a decade low of about 185,000 units for 1982 to nearly a quarter-million a year for 1983-87. Production then dropped below 200,000, though that was still far from shabby.

The humble Chevette was similarly little changed through the '80s, an increasing sales handicap in the fast-moving small-car sector. Model-year '81 was the production peak—nearly 434,000 units—after which assemblies tapered off steadily each year. Yet even the swan-song '86s managed over 100,000 sales, and the lack of change enabled Chevy to keep the lid on prices. Appearance updates were confined to a full-width grille and square headlamps for '79, bigger taillights for '80. Major mechanical changes were limited to a five-speed manual option from 1983 and an extra-cost four-cylinder diesel (from Isuzu) that was rarely ordered, probably because it made a slow car even slower. Though few mourned its passing, the Chevette had done an able job. It was simply time for better things.

The same could be said of the 1978-vintage Monte Carlo, which departed during 1988. Here, though, there was reason to mourn. A handsome '81 facelift, similar to the big Chevys', was followed at mid-1983 by a revived SS bearing a smoothly raked new nose and a 305 V-8 tuned for 175 bhp (later upped to 180). You also got a beefy suspension with fat raised-white-letter tires, plus bold exterior graphics and trunklid spoiler. Things were pretty plain inside, but luxury options weren't long in coming.

If far removed from late-'60s muscle, this new SS was hardly your typical mid-'80s Monte. In fact, it was the starting point for Chevy's latest racing stockers, which began cleaning up in NASCAR and elsewhere. To help its teams do even better, Chevy released an SS "Aerocoupe" at mid-1986 bearing a huge, compound-curve backlight that allegedly added a few more mph on the long supertracks. It only lasted through 1987, and only some 6200 were built—which only makes this a gilt-edged future collectible.

As ever, the most-popular Montes were the luxury sort; they were even called Luxury Sport from 1986. All sold well: more than 187,000 for '81, over 90,000 for 1982 and '83, an average 120,000 a year thereafter. Chevy might well have kept the decade-old coupe going a little longer but, again, it was time to move on.

"Moving on" at the bottom of the line meant moving to smaller, more-efficient front-drive models. The compact Citation had been the first. Cavalier and Celebrity would follow for the sub-compact and midsize segments, respectively.

Celebrity was one of four GM A-body lines announced for '83 in early 1982. All were essentially X-cars in tailored suits. Inner structure, chassis, even drivetrains were all the same, but squarer, more-formal notchback styling contrived to make Celebrity look more expensive than the slopeback Citation—which it was, by some \$1500-\$2000. Two- and four-door sedans were the only body styles at first, but an attractive wagon arrived for '84. All could be dressed up with trim packages variously called Custom, CL, and Classic. Also new for '84 was a Eurosport option group, available for any model. A gesture to enthusiasts, this delivered Chevy's firmer F41 handling suspension, plus special emblems, less exterior chrome, and sporty accents inside. It gilded a very middle-class lily, but the result was good enough to beg comparison with much costlier European sports sedans.

Planned to replace Malibu, Celebrity ran alongside the old

1982 Celebrity two-door sedan

1984 Monte Carlo SS sport coupe

1983 Camaro Z28 sport coupe

1984 Citation II hatchback sedan

1983 Celebrity four-door sedan

1983 Cavalier Type 10 hatchback coupe

1983 Cavalier Cadet four-door sedan

1984 Cavalier Type 10 convertible coupe

rear-drive line through 1983, then soldiered on alone. Not that Chevy needed to worry, for the Celebrity handily surpassed Malibu's peak sales in this decade (278,000 for '80) by averaging 350,000 a year for 1984-87 peaking at nearly 405,000 for '86. Sales dwindled thereafter as the two-door was killed after '88 and the mainstay four-door departed after '89. But this was only because a replacement was at hand. Overall, Celebrity was a winner.

The same could not be said for the Citation that spawned it. Buyers spurned the first front-drive Chevy in rapidly growing numbers amidst a welter of safety recalls, drivability problems, and damaging publicity about weak brakes that locked up too early in panic stops. The division tried to stem the tide for '84 with detail changes and "Citation II" badges, but fooled no one. A high-output, 135-bhp V-6 arrived for the 1982 X-11 package, then became optional for any model, but that didn't help either. In unit volume, debut 1980 would be Citation's best year: over 811,000. The tally plunged nearly 50 percent for '81, dropped under 166,000 for '82, then fell well below 100,000 through the last-of-the-line '85s. It only seemed to prove what some critics had been saying—that GM left final "shakedown" testing to its unwitting customers.

Far fewer complaints attended the front-drive Cavalier subcompact. Replacing Monza for '82, it rode the new 101.2-inch-wheelbase J-body platform, the first ever offered by all five GM divisions. Cavalier was basically "right" from the start. Nobody much liked the original engine—a new Chevy-built 2.0-liter four with old-fashioned overhead-valve head (some called it the "junkyard engine")—and the four-speed manual transaxle wasn't the slickest around, but that was about it. And there were some tangible strengths: decent room for four, neat styling, initial choice of four body styles—two- and four-door sedans, four-door wagon, and two-door "fasthatch" coupe—and competitive prices, initially less than $6000 base.

Customers responded strongly to Cavalier, snapping up better than 195,000 for the extra-long '82 model year, over 462,000 of the '84s and some 432,000 of the '86s. Steady improvement helped: a five-speed manual option, throttle-body fuel injection, more power, a neat convertible for '83, new frontal styling for '84, "mini-muscle" V-6 Z24 coupes for '85, a major facelift and a Z24 convertible for '88, and detail changes most every year.

Sales continued strong through 1994, last year for the original J-body. Demand throttled back some in the face of fresh competition, yet Cavalier did no worse than 225,000 for 1992. Even the '94s managed almost 274,000, not bad for a basic design in its 13th season. Evolutionary changes helped. Budget-priced VL ("Value Leader") models bowed for 1988. A larger 3.1-liter V-6 making 135 bhp was added in '90. For '91, the pushrod four grew to 2.2 liters and 95 bhp; by '94 it was up to 120 bhp thanks to multipoint fuel injection and other improvements. The '91 Cavs also sported a minor facelift, a more-ergonomic dash, and better-equipped base models tagged RS. Later years brought more cosmetic touchups and extra standard features like larger wheels and tires for some models, plus cupholders, extra instruments, automatic door locks, and GM's ABS VI antilock brake system. Still, starting prices remained comfortably below $10,000, though the natty Z24 convertible was pushing $20,000 by mid-decade.

Succeeding Citation as Chevy's compact were the Corsica sedan and Beretta coupe, introduced in March '87 as early '88 models. Both used a new 103.4-inch-wheelbase L-body platform exclusive to Chevrolet, though with engineering that owed much to the J-car and the front-drive N-body models at Buick, Olds and Pontiac. Among other things, that meant coil-spring suspension with front struts and a twist beam rear axle on trailing arms, rack-and-pinion steering, and front-disc/rear-drum brakes. Standard power at first was the latest Cavalier four, with the division's 130-bhp 2.8 V-6 optional. Styling was also unique to Chevy—and a welcome change from GM's earlier "cloning:" smooth, rounded, aerodynamically efficient. Best of all, these cars reflected Chevy's strongest efforts yet to ensure tight, thorough fit and finish. Corsica/Beretta got off to a strong sales start, with 225,000 built in calendar '87 alone. The "true" '88s saw only running changes. So would most later models.

A Euro-style Corsica called LTZ arrived for 1989, along with a four-door hatchback that was hard to tell from the normal notchback. That same year, Beretta's sporty GT option became a separate model and gained many appearance features of the racy GTU package from mid-'88. The GTU (named for the under-2.0-liter Grand Touring class in the International Motor Sports Association) was distinguished by 16-inch aluminum wheels, "ground effects" lower-body skirting, a five-speed manual gear-box designed by Getrag in Germany, and a tinted upper-wind-shield band with "Beretta" in big, bold letters.

1984 Celebrity Eurosport four-door sedan

1985 Monte Carlo SS sport coupe

1985 Citation II X-11 hatchback coupe

1986 Monte Carlo SS "Aerocoupe"

1985 Camaro IROC-Z sport coupe

1986 Celebrity Classic four-door sedan

Beretta GT, GTU, and the Corsica LTZ all came with a V-6. A firm Z51 handling option made Berettas corner as slick as they looked. A similar Z52 setup did the same for '91 Corsicas, though it killed the LTZ.

The GTU bids fair as a minor collector's item, being a low-volume short-timer with only 3814 built for '88 and 9813 for '89. Its 1990 replacement was the Beretta GTZ, identified by a neat grilleless face instead of a broad eggcrate. Under the hood sat the High-Output version of Oldsmobile's vaunted new 2.3-liter "Quad-4," a genuine Euro-style twincam engine with four valves per cylinder and an excellent 180 bhp. But though faster than a GTU, the GTZ was far noisier and stiffer-riding. As if to acknowledge its shortcomings, Chevy offered a credit-option V-6 for '91 GTZs, a 140-bhp 3.1-liter unit.

Chevy made an odd bit history by announcing a 1990 Beretta convertible that never made it to showrooms. A handful were built for Indy 500 pace-car duty, but all were prototypes. Like Oldsmobile's new 1990 Cutlass Supreme ragtop, which did see series production, the open Beretta was basically a roofless coupe with a structural metal "hoop" bridging the B-posts. The hoop helped restore some lost torsional rigidity and preserved the coupe's pillar-mounted outside door handles. Chevy dropped Cavalier convertibles to make way for the soft-top Beretta, only to revive them when quality-control problems proved insurmountable on the Beretta. It was a minor but embarrassing episode symbolic of larger troubles.

Spring 1989 ushered in the belated 1990 replacement for Celebrity. Named Lumina, it rode the front-drive GM10 platform first used for 1988 coupes at Buick, Olds, and Pontiac. This time, though, there was no delaying the planned sedan. Base Luminas carried a humble 2.5-liter four—the old "Iron Duke" still hanging on—and offered the 3.1 V-6 at extra cost. The latter was standard for a sporty Euro coupe and sedan with black exterior trim, sport suspension, and wider 16-inch wheels and tires (versus 14s or 15s). All Luminas naturally boasted the GM10's laudable all-independent suspension and four-wheel disc brakes. But the Euro, as *Car and Driver* observed, was really quite "Amero" in ride, handling, performance, and interior treatment.

That wasn't necessarily bad, of course, but Ford's Taurus remained a much more-popular midsize. Even into the '90s, Lumina was handily outsold by Taurus and Japanese rivals Honda Accord and Toyota Camry. Styling was a likely factor. Even Charles M. Jordan, then GM design chief, admitted that Lumina sales suffered because the design sat on a shelf for some seven years before the public saw it, by which time it was no longer "clear" or "up to date."

There were no such problems with Camaro. Effectively facelifted for 1978, the durable second generation ran three final years in four models: base, Rally Sport, Z28 and new-for-'79

1986 Cavalier RS convertible coupe

1986 Camaro Z28 sport coupe

1987 Cavalier Z24 club coupe

1987 IROC-Z convertible coupe

1987 Caprice Classic four-door sedan

1988 Beretta GTU coupe

luxury Berlinetta (replacing LT). V-6s ousted straight sixes as standard power for 1980, when an interim 267-cid V-8 option joined the 305 and 350 engines. Sales held up well, all things considered: 152,000 for 1980, a bit more than 126,000 for '81.

A smaller Camaro was a foregone conclusion by then, and it duly arrived for 1982 on a trim 101-inch wheelbase. Though retaining the traditional format, the third generation was nearly 10 inches shorter, three inches narrower, and almost 300 pounds lighter, yet looked terrific. Chevy design chief Jerry Palmer precisely tailored styling to the smaller package: chiseled yet obviously aerodynamic. A new liftup rear hatch provided luggage access, and its compound-curve backlight was said to be the largest, most-complex piece of car glasswork ever. Beneath the swoopy new body was a more-modern all-coil suspension with front struts, and rear disc brakes were optionally available to complement the standard front discs.

The Rally Sport temporarily departed as the base '82 sport coupe became the first Camaro with a standard four, the aged 90-bhp "Iron Duke." A 2.8 V-6 was standard for Berlinetta. As ever, the hunky Z28 got the most attention. It packed only 305 V-8s: a four-barrel 150-bhp unit or a 165-bhp version with "Cross Fire" twin-throttle-body electronic fuel injection, as on that year's Corvette. Four-speed manual gearbox was standard except on the 165-bhp 228, where it was three-speed automatic only (optional elsewhere). The base Camaro could be ordered with V-6, Berlinetta with the carbureted 305.

Once again, Chevy scored big with a smaller car, the new Camaro garnering 50,000 more model-year sales than its '81 predecessor. By 1984, it was up past a quarter-million. But 1985-86 production plunged to some 185,000, the '87 tally was 50,000 units below that, and 1988 volume was under 100,000. New competition from all quarters contributed to the decline, but so did indifferent assembly and persistent mechanical troubles.

Nonetheless, the third-generation Camaro—Z28 especially—was very much in the ponycar spirit of the '60s. Changes through 1992 were evolutionary but well timed. For example, a

1988 Beretta GT coupe

1988 Cavalier Z24 coupe

1988 Cavalier Z24 convertible coupe

1988 Nova sedan

1988 Corsica four-door sedan

1988 Camaro IROC-Z sport coupe

1989 Camaro RS sport coupe

1989 Corsica hatchback sedan

T-bar roof option appeared for '83, when the Z28 switched to a fuel-saving four-speed automatic and other engines became available with a five-speed manual option. The Cross-Fire V-8 disappointed, so a high-output 190-bhp carbureted engine replaced it for '84. That year's Berlinetta acquired a gimmicky dash with hard-to-read electronic digital/graphic instruments and spacey minor controls; thankfully, these didn't last long.

Providing genuine excitement for 1985 was a hot new IROC-Z performance package for Z28, honoring the Camaros used in the revived International Race of Champions "top gun" driver's contests. The H.O. V-8 was exclusive to the IROC and available with a five-speed manual transmission, now standard for all Camaros. More-efficient "Tuned Port Injection" (TPI) yielded a new 215-bhp option for Z28s. IROC hunkered down on 16 × 8 five-spoke aluminum wheels wearing meaty Goodyear Eagle performance tires, came with its own handling suspension and high-effort power steering, and looked ready to race with its full-perimeter lower-body "skirts."

1989 Camaro IROC-Z sport coupe

1990 Lumina Euro four-door sedan

1990 Camaro IROC-Z sport coupe

1990 Lumina coupe

Chevy again turned up the wick for '87. The IROC got the TPI V-8 and could be ordered with the 350 Corvette engine packing 225 bhp (delayed from a promised mid-'86 debut). Z28 returned with standard four-barrel 305. The underpowered four was gone and Berlinetta reverted to being an LT. But the real treat was the first Camaro convertible in 18 years. A mid-'87 arrival, it was quite a head-turner in IROC trim, but could be had in other lines, too. They were crafted "out of house" to Chevy specs, making these "semi-factory" models, but hardly anyone cared when blasting top-down on a winding two-lane.

Then suddenly, the Z28 vanished—a big surprise—though the 1988 sport coupe was much the same thing save a standard V-6. The LT disappeared too. Minor tweaking added five horses to all three V-8s, though you lost 25 on the injected 305 when teamed with automatic. Base prices had risen some $2000-$3000 in five years, a rather modest increase, really. The ragtop IROC was the costliest '88 Camaro with a starting tariff around 18-grand.

The hallowed RS designation returned for 1989 on a V-6 coupe marketed the previous season only in California. It looked a lot like the IROC, but had its own suspension tuning and equipment mix. The RS also came as a convertible with a standard V-8. The IROC itself could now be had with 16-inch wheels and new Z-rated tires certified safe for sustained speeds above 149 mph. Production hit nearly 111,000 for the model year in a modest sales recovery, though there was no particular reason for it.

The 1990 Camaros comprised RS and IROC coupes and convertibles with some extra standard features. Among the goodies: 16-inch wheel/tire package for IROCs, a torquier 3.1-liter V-6 with 140 bhp for RS, and a tilt steering wheel, driver-side airbag and GM "PASS-Key" antitheft ignition for all models. A deliberately shortened model year held production to just under 35,000.

Camaro's 1991 began in the spring of 1990. Z28s took over for IROCs. The reason? Dodge now sponsored the IROC series and owned rights to that name. At least Z coupes could be quicker now with a new 245-bhp 350 option, the extra power reflecting a switch to more-sophisticated sequential multipoint injection. The 305 also got that and rose to 230 bhp. Reworked front and back ends freshened all models, and Z28s wore a higher-flying rear spoiler that looked faintly ludicrous. For all the recent additions to standard equipment, Camaro was still a bargain performance buy, ranging from $12,000 for the RS V-6 coupe to just under $21,000 for ragtop Z28. To Chevrolet's delight, sales more than tripled, '91 production soaring beyond 100,000.

Volume then faded to 70,000, likely because a new Camaro was known to be coming for 1993. The third generation thus closed out after '92 with only one further change: a $175 "Heritage Appearance" package to mark Camaro's 25th birthday. Available in white, red, or black, it involved only badges and some hood and decklid stripes. It was a feeble gesture, but at least Chevy didn't forget its ponycar's anniversary.

Any chance to celebrate was doubtless welcome by now, for the '80s had not been kind to Chevrolet. True, the division had more models than ever, but it wasn't selling that many more cars. Worse, Ford was entrenched as number one, and seemed destined to remain so.

Nevertheless, Chevrolet was a strong "USA-2" through the mid-'90s, with yearly domestic car sales of around one million units. As with the '80s Nova, the California-built Geo Prizm was counted in those results, but not other Geo cars, which were classed as imports on the basis of "domestic content" even though some came from Canada instead of Japan.

Chevy had launched the Geo nameplate for 1989 as a marketing umbrella for Japanese-designed models like Prizm. The

1991 Caprice Classic four-door sedan

1991 Corsica LT four-door sedan

1991 Lumina Z34 coupe

1991 Beretta GT coupe

idea was to distinguish these products from "real" Chevrolets in the minds of those most likely to buy them—what marketing types called "import intenders." But the ploy worked only in the beginning, and Geo sales dropped steadily. A big blow was losing the popular Isuzu-built Storm sporty coupe after model-year '93. By '98 the remaining Geos were badged Chevrolets. The Toyota Corolla-based Prizm was redesigned that year and continued through 2002.

Though Chevy had been "The Heartbeat of America" since 1987 (an ad slogan adopted for the make's 75th anniversary), its mainstream cars of the early '90s offered little to raise anyone's pulse. Indeed, motor-noters began chiding GM for building mostly "rental cars": dependable but dull underachievers compared to class rivals. Nevertheless, the Chevys most-popular with buyers were the least interesting to enthusiasts: Cavalier, Lumina, and Beretta/Corsica, usually in that order. Each was typically good for more than 200,000 model-year sales, sometimes a bit more.

Yet there were flashes of interest in this mundane group. The Beretta GTZ was one, as was its 1994 successor, called Z26. Also replacing the Beretta GT, the Z26 was usefully more-refined, thanks to an updated Quad-4 with 170 bhp. In the Lumina line, 1991 introduced a sporty Z34 coupe, named for its new 3.4-liter "Twin Dual Cam" V-6. This engine, the latest version of Chevy's venerable 60-degree pushrod design, delivered a punchy 210 bhp with five-speed manual or 200 with optional four-speed automatic. Also included were firm suspension, fat tires on alloy wheels, a louvered hood, "ground effects" body add-ons and a more-driver-oriented interior. The result was a lively package many enthusiasts could warm to. Lumina sedans from 1992 were similarly entertaining when ordered with the "Euro 3.4" option, though it was limited to automatic.

Otherwise, both these model lines evolved pretty much like Cavalier. Corsica lost its sporty LTZ after 1990 and its four-door hatchback body after '91, but both Corsica and Beretta gained progressively stronger 2.2-liter base engines, a more-coherent dash (from '91), larger front brakes with standard antilock control (1992), and more-aggressive "value" pricing. Luminas also benefited from better base engines, as well as ABS, automatic power door locks, and other improvements.

A very different Lumina was the APV ("All Purpose Vehicle"), premiering for 1990 as Chevrolet's first front-drive minivan and one of three "G200" models (the others were Pontiac Trans Sport and Olds Silhouette). Unlike Chevy's rear-drive Astro, APV was a direct reply to the hot-selling Chrysler minivans that owned at least 50 percent of the market, thanks to their carlike convenience and road manners. Accordingly, APV was sized roughly between the standard and extended Chrysler models, riding a 109.8-inch wheelbase and boasting the comfort advantage of all-independent suspension. Body construction was novel, with outer panels of plasticlike composites attached to a steel inner "skeleton," as on Pontiac's late two-seat Fiero. Equally novel was optional "modular" seating for seven, with lightweight individual buckets that could be easily moved or removed to create a variety of useful configurations.

Only Chevy offered a blank-side cargo model, but all GM200s arrived with a 120-bhp 3.1 V-6 and three-speed automatic. That made for weak performance, especially with a full passenger or cargo load, so an optional 3.8-liter Buick V-6 was added for '92, bringing 165 bhp and a more-responsive four-speed automatic. Befitting a Chevy, APV prices were the lowest of the three corporate cousins, initially in a narrow $14,000-$16,000 range.

Unfortunately, APV's pointy-nose styling was too radical for most buyers. Critics typically likened it to an "anteater" or "Dustbuster." Worse, the design dictated a massive dashtop and huge windshield that made for lots of unwanted reflections; a wide extra set of front roof pillars only hampered vision further. The APV also suffered a relatively low-roof interior that compromised both load volume and rear-cabin access.

Hoping to improve sales with an improved product, Chevy bobbed the nose of the '94 APV and offered a new option: a unique power right sliding door (operated by remote control). Chevy also changed the name to Lumina Minivan and capped base prices at $16,800-$17,500. But nothing seemed to help, and the APV/Minivan was no more a threat to Chrysler's minivan dominance than the Astro. Sales languished mostly in the 50,000-60,000 area, about a tenth of Chrysler's volume. There seemed nothing to do but try again, and Chevy did for '97 with the conventionally styled all-steel Venture. Though a competent competitor, it was never a threat to the top-selling Chrysler and Dodge models—or some import-brand rivals.

Minivans had all but eliminated demand for traditional full-size station wagons, so it was rather surprising to see one among the redesigned Caprices of 1991. Even more surprising was the big rear-drive Chevy's new shape. Clean but blimpy, it reminded some of a Step-Down Hudson—and that wasn't meant as a compliment.

There was no denying the new Caprices looked heavier. And they were, the sedan by 200 pounds, the wagon by about 150. Extra sheetmetal was partly to blame, as overall width bulged two inches and overall length added two-three inches. An unchanged wheelbase implied the vintage-'77 B-car chassis was still underneath. It was, but modernized a bit with revised suspension geometry and standard antilock control for the usual front-disc/rear-drum brakes. Returning unchanged was a single powerteam comprising four-speed automatic transmission and a 170-bhp 305 V-8 with throttle-body injection. Inside was a new, if rather uninspired dash with standard driver's airbag, plus a bit more room for heads, legs, and elbows.

The '91 Caprice was an early starter, reaching showrooms in the spring of 1990. Sedans initially offered base and ritzier Classic trim, both six-seaters with a bench front and rear. The wagon was a plain Caprice, but included a roof rack, rear wiper, and a nifty two-way tailgate (swing-out or drop-down) with separate liftup window. An optional foldaway third seat gave eight-passenger capacity. In all, these new Caprices were just old wine in more-contemporary bottles, but they offered a lot of metal for the money at $16,500-$18,000. Perhaps even to Chevy's surprise, model-year sales almost doubled to a over 200,000, though it obviously helped that the '91 run was much longer than usual.

Included in that tally were a relative handful of Classics with a sporty option package, another LTZ. A late addition to the roster at $825, it delivered wider wheels and tires, a firmer suspension than the famous F41 setup (still available), heavy-duty brakes and cooling system, and additional gauges including a digital speedometer to replace the normal strip-type analog device. Most of these items were borrowed from the Caprice police package (law enforcement having become a major sales venue for these cars), but the result wasn't pleasing. Handling was little better than stock, yet ride was stiff to the point of irritation. And there was no more power to pull the near two-ton curb weight, so 0-60 proved a leisurely 10.1-second affair in Consumer Guide® tests. Nevertheless, the Caprice LTZ was *Motor Trend's* 1991 "Car of the Year."

Caprice carried into '92 with minor changes: transmission safety interlock (you had to press the brake pedal to get out of Park, as on a growing number of cars), standard tilt steering wheel, and no-cost power rear vent windows for the wagon. Also new for the wagon was an optional 350 V-8; it made only 10 more horses than the 305 but packed an extremely useful 45 extra pound-feet of torque—300 in all. The 350 became an LTZ

1991 Cavalier RS four-door sedan

1991 Camaro Z28 convertible

1991 Lumina APV minivan

1992 Caprice station wagon

1992 Lumina Euro four-door sedan

1992 Corsica LT four-door sedan

1992 Cavalier RS convertible coupe

1993 Camaro Z28 coupe

1992 Camaro RS coupe

1994 Caprice Classic four-door sedan

1993 Lumina Euro four-door sedan

1994 Lumina Euro four-door sedan

1993 Corsica four-door sedan

1994 Corsica four-door sedan

1993 Cavalier VL coupe

1994 Beretta coupe

standard for '93, when base models were retitled Classic and the Classic was tagged LS. At the same time, Chevy answered styling critics by giving sedans a lighter look, achieved with fully radiused wheel openings, broader taillamps and a 1.6-inch wider rear track. Sales eased to just under 100,000.

Just for fun, Chevy displayed a special Caprice sedan at early '93 auto shows. A mean, solid-black thing, it crouched two inches lower on five-spoke 17-inch alloy wheels with fat Goodyear Eagle GS-C tires. Most chrome was erased, a new honeycomb grille installed, and a deft C-pillar insert imparted a jaunty kickup to the rearmost side glass. Inside were leather-trimmed front bucket seats and center console. Under the hood: the same new 300-bhp LT1 V-8 that powered the latest Corvette. Chevy called it Impala SS, and showgoers went wild. "Build it," they pleaded. Replied Chevy general manager Jim Perkins, "You got it."

The first of the reborn big muscle Chevys rolled off the line in February 1994, thus putting the LTZ to rest. Tires were now Goodrich Comp T/As, ride height was lifted to within an inch of stock Caprice spec, and the LT1 was tuned for 260 bhp but no less torque. Otherwise, the new Impala SS was just like the show car. That included a heavy-duty police chassis with quick-ratio steering, rear disc brakes (with massive 12-inch rotors), rear antiroll bar, uprated body mounts and premium de Carbon gas-pressure shocks. Full power and luxury trim completed another amazing Chevy value in modern performance: $21,290 base, just $327 more than an ordinary Caprice Classic LS at the time of the SS's introduction.

Encouraged by rave "buff book" reviews, demand for the new Super Sport was super-strong. Chevy had planned 4000 of the '94s but ending up selling more than 6000—the most the plant could build. Production was upped to over 20,000 for '95, when dark cherry and green-gray metallic were added to the paint chart. The '96s carried on with a new standard analog tach and console shift (instead of column lever) for the mandatory four-speed automatic. Impala outsold Caprice that year with sales of almost 42,000.

Meantime, Caprices picked up a new dual-airbag dash for '94 (as did the SS). They also got a new 200-bhp base V-8, a 350 cut down to original 1955 size (4.3 liters/265 cid). The '95s were unchanged except that sedans acquired the Impala's kicked-up rear side-window styling—and looked miles better for it.

But by that point, both Caprice and the brawny Impala were doomed. Having decided there was more money to be made with big sport-utility trucks, GM sacrificed the full-size Chevys after 1996 to free up space at their Texas plant for truck production (a move that also claimed the related Buick Roadmaster and Cadillac Fleetwood). Few mourned the Caprice, but it was sad losing the Impala so soon. Though an anachronism in the '90s, it was the kind of car a whole generation understood—a happy throwback to the glory days of Chevy performance.

A ground-up fresh Camaro promised some new glory days. Arriving for '93 in base and Z28 coupe models, it was about the same size as its well-liked predecessor (wheelbase was unchanged) but more-sculptured and futuristically swoopy, patterned on the recent "California Camaro" show car—and not that much more-subdued. Yet the new fourth-generation design was unmistakably Camaro, carefully preserving hallowed appearance "cues" like tunneled headlamps, broad taillights, a low Vee'd nose, even optional T-tops for the coupe.

1994 Cavalier Z24 coupe

1995 Cavalier four-door sedan

1994 Camaro Z28 convertible coupe

1995 Monte Carlo LS coupe

1995 Monte Carlo LS coupe

1996 Caprice Classic station wagon

Despite added standard features, the '93 was only some 150 pounds heavier than previous Camaros. One reason was a lighter, yet stronger, unit body/chassis with steel-reinforced composite panels over a steel framework as on GM200 minivans and the small Saturn. The nominal weight gain bode well for performance, especially on the Z28, which now packed a 350 LT1 V-8 with 275 bhp, 30 more than before. The base Camaro also muscled up via a new overhead-valve 3.4-liter V-6 with a creditable 160 horses. Transmission choices comprised standard five-speed manual for the base model, a new six-speed for Z28 (again borrowed from Corvette), and optional four-speed automatic for both. Front suspension reverted to Detroit-traditional twin A-arms, though with unique geometry and premium gas-pressure, coil-over de Carbon shocks. The latter were also featured in back, where the live axle was now located by a torque rod and trailing arms. Each end had a hefty stabilizer bar. Antilock brakes were standard, with rear discs on Z28. A tantalizing new option was RPO 1LE, an ultrastiff performance suspension package for Z28. It was "not recommended for street use" but worked wonders on the track.

With 70 more horses than a Mustang GT and a starting price on the right side of $17-grand, the '93 Z28 was immediately hailed as the new best buy in Detroit performance. That came from "buff books," who typically reported 0-60 at just over five seconds with manual. For buyers of all stripes, Camaro appealed with standards like dual airbags, full instrumentation, and a good sound system (with even better ones available). Options were still fairly numerous but easier to comprehend, being grouped into sensible packages.

A deliberately slow "ramp-up" limited '93 Camaros to just 40,224, all coupes, but they were the tightest, most solid-feeling Camaros in history. Production then hit full stride to pass 125,000 for '94, when promised base and Z28 convertibles went on sale with standard power top; glass backlight; and a low, tidy "top stack." Six-speed Z28s became a bit quicker that year thanks to shorter final gearing (3.42:1 vs. 2.73/3.23). Unhappily, their shifter acquired CAGS, the Computer Aided Gear Selection feature first used on Corvettes. Electronic watchdogs "forced" a short-shift from 1st to 4th at certain speeds and throttle openings, a bit of nonsense prompted by government fuel-economy standards. But enthusiasts found that CAGS could be defeated by pulling a little wire, and many did pull it.

As ever, the torquey Z28 was a prodigious tire-smoker off-the-line, and a standard limited-slip differential was no substitute for modern traction control. Chevy finally obliged for '95 by offering the Corvette's ASR (Acceleration Slip Reduction) as a Z28 option. ASR would restore lost grip by braking a spinning wheel and/or throttling back on engine power as needed—a boon for wet-road control. And when the road was dry, you could switch it off if you wanted. Street racers loved that.

Though a new Mustang had galloped away with the ponycar market, Camaro mostly held its own for 1995, slipping to 110,595. Arriving late that year was a stronger "3800" V-6 option for base models sold in California. This became standard for all '96s, bringing a useful 40 extra horsepower and 25 more pound-feet of torque over the displaced 3.4. With that, a base Camaro could at least keep up with a Z28 on winding roads, though not on a dragstrip, of course.

Working hard to reclaim "USA-1," Chevy redesigned two of its biggest sellers for 1995. The Lumina sedan got more of a reskin than a total revamping, and a rather conservative one at that, but the similarly restyled coupe resurrected the Monte Carlo name in an effort to stand more clearly apart. Each offered plain and fancy models: base and LS for Lumina, LS and Z34 for Monte. The usual 3.1 V-6 was standard for all but Z34, whose 210-bhp 3.4-liter twincam engine was optional for

1996 Impala SS four-door sedan

1996 Lumina LS four-door sedan

1996 Monte Carlo Z34 coupe

1996 Corsica four-door sedan

1996 Beretta Z26 coupe

Lumina LS. Recalling the "baby Cadillac" Chevys of 1955-57, Monte Carlo looked faintly like Cadillac's latest Eldorado, but even the sporty Z34 wasn't exactly "eye candy." Nor was it that thrilling to drive despite the usual firm chassis and "enthusiast" appointments. At least these Chevys finally had dual airbags (which the market much preferred over motorized "mouse-belts" to meet the government's 1994 mandate for front passive restraints). They were also aggressively priced: as little as $15,500 for a Lumina, about $16,800 for a Monte. Critics initially felt Chevy had done too little with its midsize cars—until the new '96 Ford Taurus came along with controversial looks and much higher prices.

Cavalier was not only way overdue for an overhaul, it needed a very good one to stay competitive in the bruising small-car sales battle. Chevy came through with fresh, clean styling that looked good despite being a tad taller and two inches shorter than previous models. Wheelbase grew by 2.8 inches to help open up extra room inside. Wagons vanished, leaving base coupe and sedan, LS sedan and convertible, and Z24 coupe (the last two bowing in spring '95). V-6 power was also gone, as Z24 switched to the latest 150-bhp "balance shaft" version of the twincam Quad-4. LS models could be had with this engine. Base Cavs stuck with the familiar pushrod 2.2. Transmissions comprised a five-speed manual and an optional three-speed automatic (still). For '96, Quad-4 Cavaliers gained a little displacement and 10 pound-feet of torque (to 2.4 liters and 150), and were available in LS trim. Apart from that, newly standard PASSLock ignition, daytime running lights, and optional low-speed traction control (included with a newly available four-speed automatic), Cavalier was unchanged for '96. Though production snags hampered early sales, output remained quite substantial at well over 229,000 units for calendar '95.

As with archrival Ford, trucks loomed ever larger in Chevrolet's total business picture during the 1990s and into the twenty-first century. Indeed, car sales at both makes were eclipsed by demand for light-duty pickups, sport-utility vehicles (SUVs), and minivans as early as 1990. This reflected a change in buyer preferences that would see light trucks surpass cars in total U.S. sales for calendar 2001.

Chevrolet fought the truck wars well. All-new full-size pickups arrived for 1999 under the Silverado banner, followed by a separate new line of more competitive heavy-duty pickups, tagged Silverado HD, and redesigned Tahoe and Suburban SUVs. For 2002 came a larger new midsize SUV, the TrailBlazer, though some of the older Blazer models hung on as price-leaders for that segment. Also new for '02 was the Avalanche, basically a Suburban with an open cargo box instead of a closed cargo bay, plus "tough guy" styling touches. The box was a short 5.3 feet long, but a "midgate" could be folded down with the rear seats to extend load length to 8.1 feet. Avalanche answered a question no one was really asking, but proved fairly popular. Not so for Chevy's 1984-vintage Astro minivan, which steadily waned in popularity until its 2005 exit. The newer front-drive Venture minivan languished, too. On the other hand, the compact Tracker SUV, sourced from GM affiliate Suzuki of Japan, did good business, especially once redesigned for 1999.

Trouble was, the market clamor for trucks led Chevy (Ford as well) to put less apparent effort into cars—understandable, what with the car/truck sales gap widening each year. As a result, Chevy's replacement car models in this period were usually judged underwhelming against class rivals. And though they generally sold well, they sold more to rental and corporate fleets than retail buyers, to the detriment of both image and trade-in value. Either way, discounts were deep in a market long accustomed to "deal of the week" incentives.

But a sale is a sale no matter who the customer is, and Chevy was happy to keep building around a quarter-million Cavaliers each model year through 2004. Highlights in the Cav's later years included the 1998 return of a Z24 convertible, replacing the LS version, and a mild 2000-model revamp featuring added standard equipment. The ragtop body style was dropped altogether for 2001, reflecting continued lack of buyer interest. Collectors may one day note the low yearly production for all Cavalier convertibles, which never exceeded 10,000 and was often less than half that (just 4108 of the 1985 Type 10s, 5011 of the '98 Z24s, to cite but two examples).

The Z24 coupe was canned for 2002, but lived on in a similar LS Sport model with GM's new 2.2-liter "Ecotec" twincam four-cylinder, good for 140 bhp and shared with a new LS Sport sedan. Other models adopted this engine for 2003, shedding the old overhead-valve unit, and all got modest styling revisions. Tellingly, though, the recently standardized antilock brakes moved to the options list (joining newly available front side airbags protecting both head and torso, plus GM Onstar assistance and satellite radio). Chevy was trying to maintain price parity with small cars from import brands that could set prices more aggressively because they had far less overhead to cover than did GM. This largely explains why Chevy returned to sell-

1996 Camaro convertible coupe

ing rebadged imports for 2004, adding the little Aveo four-door sedan and hatchback as new bottom-rung offerings pitched below Cavalier. Sourced from low-wage South Korea and a GM subsidiary recently formed from the remains of bankrupt Daewoo Motors, Aveo was a fair sales success. Meanwhile, "buy domestic" diehards could opt for a $10,135 Cavalier coupe with no frills and no options.

Chevy shored up its position among midsize sedans with two models, each reviving a great name from Chevrolet's past. Replacing Corsica for '97 was a very different new Malibu, offering front-wheel drive in a sedate-looking package sized closer to Lumina than Cavalier. In fact, while Malibu stood 10.5 inches shorter than Lumina, it was only a half-inch trimmer in wheelbase, resulting in a spacious interior. Both the base and LS models came with a good load of expected standard features, plus an optional 155-bhp, 3.1-liter V-6 with the size and power that most competitors either didn't match or offered at a hefty surcharge. A 150-bhp 2.4-liter Twin Cam four was standard, but vanished for 2000 in the face of strong buyer preference for the V-6, which added 15 horses that season. Like Cavalier, this Malibu offered no thrills, just honest value, with base prices in the $16,000-$20,000 range. Buyers responded to the tune of around 200,000 in most model years after the shortened inaugural season. The name changed to Malibu Classic for 2004, when the advent of a redesigned Malibu relegated the older car mainly to fleet sales.

Though the 1997-2004 Malibu was arguably a better buy than Lumina, Chevy's older midsize car showed surprising sales strength before its departure, drawing more than 200,000 annual orders through 1999. An interesting new addition for '97 was a sporty LTZ version with front bucket seats, rear disc brakes, and an optional 215-bhp 3.4-liter twincam V-6. Chevy upped its appeal for '98 by substituting GM's veteran "3800" pushrod V-6, which made only 200 bhp but had more usable low-end torque. That same year, Lumina joined Monte Carlo in offering GM's then-new OnStar communications system as an $895 option. Basically, OnStar tied the car by cell phone and a satellite link to a 24-hour staffed operations center that could provide route guidance and other assistance, including summoning emergency help. OnStar was a boon to owner peace-of-mind, with particularly high appeal among women. It soon spread throughout the Chevrolet lineup, cars and trucks alike, as either standard or optional equipment. The LTZ lost its rear disc brakes for '99, but added the 3.8-liter V-6 as standard. Total Lumina sales plunged 33 percent that model year, but that was partly in anticipation of a bigger, better successor. Lumina thus made a final stand for model-year 2000 with a lone model aimed at the fleet market.

Its replacement was another Impala, a very different sedan from the rear-drive biggies of a few years before. For starters, it shared a much revised GM W-body platform with the latest Buick Century/Regal and Oldsmobile Intrigue, which made it the first Impala with front-wheel drive. That also meant a more rational size, with overall length of 200 inches (about the same, incidentally, as GM's rear-drive 1980s intermediates) and a rangy 110.5-inch wheelbase providing ample rear-seat room and a capacious trunk. Powertrains were familiar fare, with a four-speed automatic the only transmission. The base Impala used a pushrod 3.4-liter V-6 with 180 bhp; the uplevel LS carried the 200-bhp "3800." Both came well-equipped with four-wheel disc brakes, 16-inch wheels, air conditioning, and power windows and locks. The LS added antilock brakes, traction control, a firm-ride suspension for tighter handling, and a side airbag for the driver, all of which were available for the base model when optioned with the 3.8 V-6. The LS also sported front bucket seats in lieu of a three-person bench. A rear spoiler

1997 Malibu four-door sedan

1997 Lumina LTZ four-door sedan

1997 Camaro coupe

1997 Camaro 35th Anniversary Edition convertible coupe

1997 Venture minivan

1998 Cavalier Z24 convertible coupe

1998 Camaro coupe

1998 Metro LSi coupe

1998 Prizm four-door sedan

1999 Lumina LS four-door sedan

and other trim options gave it a passing resemblance to the 1994-96 Impala SS.

But that's where the similarities ended. Though much easier to thread along tight, twisty two-lanes, even 3.8-liter Impalas had nowhere near the sizzle of their V-8 predecessors. They were quick enough, thanks to a favorable power-to-weight ratio. In fact, Chevy claimed real-world performance suitable for police duty, and even developed a police package for the new Impala. John Law wasn't much interested. though. He still preferred the extra perceived ruggedness of the old rear-drive Caprice—enough that one Southern California entrepreneur profited hugely by restoring used squad cars for law-enforcement agencies as a money-saving alternative to a new Ford Crown Victoria. The front-drive Impala also took heat for styling, especially the use of two taillamps instead of the traditional three. At least they were round again, not oblong.

Despite such debates, the front-drive Impala was a solid success, topping 200,000 model-year sales each season through 2003 and an impressive 300,000 for '04. Like Malibu, it offered no-nonsense family transportation at attractive prices in the Chevrolet tradition. But Chevy couldn't resist spicing things up a bit, hence a new Impala SS for 2004, this time with a supercharged 3.8 V-6 cranking out 240 horses. Though not a sports sedan of the European stripe, this SS was a fast and capable tourer, helped by a firmed-up suspension and grippier tires on standard 17-inch alloy wheels. All that, plus special trim, black-only paint, and other exclusive touches, made the $27,355 asking price seem like a darned good deal

Arriving slightly ahead of the front-drive Impala was a redesigned 2000 Monte Carlo with the same platform, powertrains, general size, and features. The base model was again tagged LS, but the sporty Z34 was retitled SS and given a standard 200-bhp 3800 V-6. Further emphasizing high value, Chevy gave both models standard four-wheel antilock disc brakes, air conditioning, and a tire-pressure monitor. The SS added firmer suspension, performance tires, and larger alloy wheels. Styling was more elaborate, with curved upper-body character lines intended to evoke 1973-77 Montes, though it's doubtful many younger folks made the connection. Enthusiasts still didn't much connect with the performance or handling, though both were more than acceptable. Indeed, *Consumer Guide*® said the "SS shines on twisty roads" and found its ride "compliant enough on bumpy city streets." Summing up, the editors felt the latest Monte Carlo "trounces [compact coupes] in size, comfort, and performance, and beats [rival Honda and Toyota] coupes on a features-per-dollar basis. It isn't as polished as those... rivals and won't hold its value as well, but this new Chevy does have its own brand of American-car character."

Alas, it proved no more popular than the previous Monte. In fact, model-year 2000 production fell more than 5000 units from the '99 tally. Volume then rallied to some 71,000—and stayed there until 2005, when it dipped below 65,000. A near-zero market for midsize coupes didn't help. Neither did a lack of year-to-year change.

But there were two interesting Montes in this period that merit mention. One was the 2002 Dale Earnhardt Signature Edition SS, of which just 3333 were built between October 2001 and March 2002. This model was created to honor legendary NASCAR driver Dale Earnhardt, who was tragically killed just short of the finish line in the 2001 Daytona 500. Like the "Intimidator's" own racing Montes, the Earnhardt Signature Edition was finished in black. It also sported silver metallic "ground effects" lower-body skirting, "diamond-cut" alloy wheels, and graphics of Dale's signature, his famous No. 3 ID, and the logo of team owner Richard Childress Racing. The graphics were repeated inside on a commemorative plaque and

1999 Astro minivan

2000 Cavalier coupe

elsewhere on the dashboard. The interior also featured ebony bucket seats with pewter leather inserts and embroidered bow tie emblems on the headrests. Several regular SS options were part of the package, including power moonroof, heated six-way power bucket seats, and a free year of OnStar service. If any turn-of-millennium Monte stands to be a future collector car, this may be it.

Unless it's the Supercharged SS of 2004-05. Predictably, this was much like the "blown" Impala, with the same forced-induction V-6 and chassis upgrades including standard ABS with traction control. Like its sedan sister, this Monte was a good performance deal at just over $28,000 base, but even Chevy's NASCAR fans weren't that impressed.

Enthusiasts had always been fond of the Camaro, so many were surprised and shocked when Chevy announced that 2002 would be the end of the line for its storied ponycar. But industry analysts had expected the move. After all, Ford's Mustang regularly outsold Camaro in the 1990s, and the gap grew each year even though most critics judged the Chevy superior for go-power, handling, and, arguably, appearance. Of course, people don't always buy based on what critics say, and some sales were likely lost to pickups and SUVs. In any event, Camaro model-year production fell steadily, dropping some two-thirds between 1996 and 2001. By that point, GM was struggling to cut costs and regain market share (then under 30 percent, a historic low that would go even lower). The ailing Camaro was an obvious target for the budgetary axe. (Ditto sibling Pontiac Firebird with its even lower volume.)

Accordingly, Camaro was not fundamentally altered after 1993, though there were developments with definite collector interest. For example, Z28s added 10 horsepower for '96, and you could up that to 305 via a new SS package available late in the model year. Created and supplied by outside contractor SLP Engineering, the option also included a functional hood scoop (which contributed to the power boost), uprated suspension with bigger wheels and performance tires, a racy rear-deck spoiler, broad dorsal striping and other special trim, all for

2000 Impala four-door sedan

2000 Monte Carlo LS coupe

2000 Malibu four-door sedan

2001 Impala LS four-door sedan

2002 Camaro Z28 SS 35th Anniversary Edition convertible coupe

2002 Monte Carlo Dale Earnhardt Edition coupe

2002 Cavalier coupe

2003 Cavalier coupe

2003 SSR pickup truck

a reasonable $3000. That year's base models offered a new RS package with spoiler and "aero" lower-body skirts, as well as a performance group comprising the Z28's limited-slip differential, four-wheel disc brakes, quicker steering, and dual-outlet exhaust, provided you ordered optional 16-inch wheels. The RS made a one-year stand as separate coupe and convertible models for '97, when the SS option went to $4000. Priced at just $575 that year was a special 30th Anniversary Package for Z28s, including SS-equipped models. Recalling 1969, this delivered white paint, orange striping, and white alloy wheels, plus white upholstery with the requisite houndstooth-check cloth inserts.

A reshaped nose updated styling for '98, when V-8 Camaros got a power boost by exchanging their iron-block LT1 engine for the all-aluminum LS1 unit from that year's new "C5" Corvette. Displacement was still 350 cid, 5.7 liters, but Z28s muscled up to 305 bhp, the SS option to 320. Base models became a bit safer for '99 by offering optional traction control previously restricted to V-8s. For 2000, all three engines were retuned to cleaner LEV (Low Emissions Vehicle) standards, a laudable achievement that Chevy topped for '01 by extracting five more horses from each V-8. Swan song 2002 brought another Camaro milestone, observed with a 35th Anniversary Package for Z28s. Included were the 325-bhp SS engine, Rally Red paint, checkered-flag hood/decklid stripes, anodized brake calipers, unique alloy wheels, and an ebony/pewter leather interior with strategically placed birthday logos. Chevy even threw in an "owner's portfolio" chronicling Camaro history.

That chronicle may soon need updating. In January 2006, at the North American International Auto Show in Detroit, Chevy wowed the crowds with a concept Camaro that looked all but ready for the showroom. It was like 1967 all over again. Ford's new Mustang had been a sales smash since its 2005-model debut, and GM wasn't about to let Dearborn have the field to itself. What's more, Dodge was showing a concept for a revival of its Challenger ponycar—and all but promising production within three years.

Will Camaro be reborn too? The odds at this writing look very good. It's known to be on the wish list of key GM executives, and sales numbers for the newest Mustang help them make a business case with the bean counters.

But much depends on how quickly and well the company tackles a number of serious problems that came to a head in 2005, when GM bled $8.6 billion in red ink, its worst loss since crisis 1992. Even before that, some financial gurus had said

2004 Monte Carlo Supercharged SS coupe

2004 Aveo four-door sedan

2004 Impala SS four-door sedan

2004 Malibu four-door sedan

2004 Monte Carlo Supercharged SS coupe

GM's situation was so bad that declaring bankruptcy might be the only way out. While this isn't the place for a Harvard Business School-type analysis, GM had basically lost its competitiveness. Though still the world's largest vehicle maker, it was also a bloated company building too many vehicles for too few buyers—and buyers had been deserting for years. In addition, huge "legacy" costs—pensions and health-care obligations per UAW contracts—left GM with a significant price disadvantage of $1500 per vehicle versus comparable Toyotas and other import-brand models. One wag remarked that GM had evolved into a health-care provider that made vehicles as a sideline. Workers, for their part, were understandably reluctant to make concessions. After all, they'd made plenty since the early 1980s as GM closed plants, laid off workers, and reorganized itself time and again.

A final conundrum involved the high-cost incentives (rebates, low-interest loans, cut-rate lease deals) that buyers expected because the Big Three kept offering them. In the brutally competitive market of the early 2000s, Detroit found it tough to move the metal without "cash on the hood," and the economics were such that keeping factories running, even at a fraction of their capacity, was cheaper than closing them down for any amount of time.

With all this and more, GM faced a crisis recalling the desperate Depression era, a once-unthinkable fight for survival.

2005 Cobalt SS Supercharged coupe

2004 Venture minivan

2005 Equinox four-door wagon

We hope a future edition of this book will record that the company succeeded in turning itself around.

Assuming that happens, a new Camaro should too. And it's likely to be a "gotta-have" not very different from the '06 concept. That design, penned by Tom Peters of Cadillac XLR and C6 Corvette fame, reinterpreted '69 Camaro styling to achieve a thoroughly modern look, with angular lines and a muscular stance accented by 20-inch wheels in front, 21s at the rear. The interior was also retro-modern, but the powertrain was state of the art. A 6.0-liter, 400-bhp Corvette LS2 V-8 resided under the hood. The show car featured all-independent suspension; massive 15-inch four-wheel disc brakes; and a modified, 110.5-inch-wheelbase version of the Pontiac GTO's Zeta platform. Should GM decide to build the Camaro, it looks like it will be well worth the wait, with a 2008 or 2009 debut most strongly rumored as we write.

Meanwhile, the bow tie brand moved to be a stronger player in the mainstream car market with four fresh entries starting with the 2004 model year. First up was a redesigned Malibu sharing a new Epsilon front-drive platform with near-luxury 9-3 models at GM-owned Saab. Somewhat daringly, bread-and-butter sedans were joined by extended-body Maxx hatchbacks riding a six-inch-longer wheelbase. The Chevy Malibu Maxx was actually hatched in Europe, which knew it as the Opel/Vauxhall Signum—and didn't like it much. At least Chevy was trying to woo more-active buyers over here, equipping the Maxx with a fore/aft sliding back seat for apportioning cargo space and rear leg room as needed. Reclining rear seatbacks were also standard, as was a fixed "skylight" above. Another exclusive was optional DVD entertainment for keeping the kids happy "back there."

Both new 2004 Malibu body styles listed LS and nicer LT versions with a 200-hp 3.5-liter V-6 and four-speed automatic transmission. A price-leader sedan used the 145-bhp 2.2-liter Ecotec four-cylinder, but that was mainly for advertising. Laudably, Chevy standardized ABS, traction control, and curtain side airbags for all but the base sedan, and rear disc brakes for Maxxes. Options were fairly upscale for a family midsize, with power-adjustable pedals, a remote control engine-starting system, and satellite radio among the choices. Front torso side airbags were added for '05 as standard on LTs, optional otherwise. Styling, arguably a bit disjointed, became more coherent for '06, when leather-trimmed LTZ and sporty SS versions were added. The SS pair was notable for a new 240-bhp 3.9-liter pushrod V-6, plus a manual shiftgate for the automatic transmission, uprated suspension with 18-inch alloy wheels, a rear-spoiler, and a spiffed-up interior with leather/cloth upholstery.

A deliberately modest production ramp-up limited model-year '04 Malibu sales to 150,640, but '05 volume was back to

2006 Impala LTZ four-door sedan

2005 Cobalt four-door sedan

2005 Uplander minivan

previous levels at nearly 242,000. There was no mystery in that. The new-generation Malibu was keenly priced in the $18,000-$25,000 range, and it was a noticeably better car than its predecessor: stronger, tighter, more refined, and more pleasant to drive.

The same can be said for the Cavalier-replacing Cobalt. With a 2005 debut, it was two years behind the Saturn Ion despite sharing GM's front-drive Delta small-car platform. Chevy used the extra time to pen more orthodox styling and improve refinement. Helping the latter was the use of sound-deadening "Quiet Steel" for some body panels—no Saturn plastic skin here—and some evident attention to engine mounts and similar details. Of course, the engines themselves were also shared: workhorse 2.2-liter Ecotec for base and LS sedans and coupes, and a 171-hp 2.4 for sporty SS models added as early '06s.

A genuine eye-opener was Cobalt's SS Supercharged coupe, Chevy's lob at the fast-growing "sport compact" youth market. This delivered a class-competitive 205 bhp from a blown 2.0-liter Ecotec, plus mandatory five-speed manual gearbox, standard 18-inch wheels (vs. 16s or 17s), appropriate chassis upgrades including rear disc brakes (shared with regular SSs), plus a high-flying rear spoiler and other racy exterior add-ons. SS Supercharged buyers were well-advised to order the $1500 Performance Package for its limited-slip differential, a near necessity maintaining control of the front wheels under power. Its genuine Recaro seats and trendy A-pillar-mounted instruments (including a boost gauge) were just a bonus.

All Cobalts offered the safety of optional curtain and front side airbags, plus OnStar assistance and satellite radio. A luxury-oriented LTZ sedan with standard automatic transmission, heated leather seats, and premium audio highlighted an otherwise stand-pat 2006 season.

All this marked a change in Chevy's small-car strategy. With the imported Aveo catering to price-conscious shoppers, Cobalt was pitched one rung higher as a "premium" subcompact with world-class fit-and-finish, performance, and features—or so Chevy said. Refreshingly, the cars lived up to that claim on the road. From the sedate LS sedan to the eager Supercharged SS, Chevy had finally produced worthy alternatives to the likes of Toyota Corollas and Honda Civics. *Consumer Guide®* bestowed its Recommended ribbon on Cobalt as a "pleasant, solid, well-equipped compact with many appealing features...If you can live with subpar rear-seat room and comfort, Cobalt merits a look." A good many buyers also liked it: nearly 161,000 for model-year '05—encouraging in that *annus horribilus* for old GM.

The jury is still out on three new 2006 models, but all suggest that Chevy is once again dead-serious about building truly desirable cars. Perhaps the shakiest of the three in terms of longevity is also, unsurprisingly, the trendiest: the Cobalt-based HHR wagon. The initials stand for "Heritage High Roof," a veiled reference to styling allegedly in the mold of Chevy's circa-1950 Suburban wagon. The resemblance may be strained, but there is no mistaking Chevy's intent: a youth-oriented "lifestyle accessory" in the mold of Chrysler's retro-look PT Cruiser, which still sold respectably in its sixth season. Celebrated GM product czar Robert Lutz bridled at that comparison, but some journalists couldn't help but see the HHR as a "Me-Too Cruiser."

Still, imitation is flattery, sincerely meant or not, and the HHR, as *Consumer Guide*® observed, was no less "a practical blend of look-at-me style and utility in a not-too-large package." Handling wasn't the best, and neither was performance with the Cobalt's mainstream 2.2- and 2.4-liter fours, even with a standard five-speed manual transmission. But the HHR was well-equipped for its midteens base price, and all the right safety, convenience, and appearance options were available, yet wouldn't much damage your pocketbook. Not one of Chevy's best efforts, perhaps, but a welcome sign of life on the car side of the business.

So, too, the extensive 2006 makeover for Impala and Monte Carlo. The update was particularly crucial for the top-selling Impala. GM literally couldn't afford to get it wrong. And at first glance, it didn't. Though the old W-body persisted, Chevy gave the sedans and coupes clean new styling, modernized interiors, and a much revised suspension that aimed to up

2006 HHR four-door wagon

2006 Monte Carlo SS coupe

2006 Malibu Maxx SS four-door sedan

2006 Monte Carlo SS coupe

2006 Camaro coupe concept

driving fun without compromising comfort. Parallel lineups listed base LS and LS 3.5 models with a 211-bhp 3.5 V-6, plus LT 3.9 and luxury LTZ versions with a 242-bhp 3.9-liter V-6.

But the real news was the return of V-8 power for the SS Impala and Monte Carlo. This was the 5.3-liter overhead-valve unit already familiar in midsize Chevy trucks, enhanced by GM's new Active Fuel Management system, once known as Displacement on Demand. Recalling Cadillac's "V-8-6-4" engine of 25 years before, AFM was designed to save fuel under light throttle loads by automatically shutting down cylinders—four in this case. But unlike the hapless Caddy engine, the AFM 5.3 was glitch-free and virtually seamless in operation, reflecting huge advances in electronic engine controls since the early 1980s. Though AFM couldn't make the V-8 yield minicar fuel thrift—an Impala SS tested by *Consumer Guide*® logged 20.3 mpg in mostly highway driving versus the EPA estimated 18/28 city/highway—it was a selling point at a time when record gas prices had people looking for the best mileage they could get.

Just as timely, GM tuned the 3.5-liter V-6 to run on E85, a mix of 15 percent gasoline and 85 percent ethanol. E85 not only tended to be cheaper than regular gas, it also burned cleaner, a fact that appealed to the environmentally conscious. And because ethanol is made from corn and other renewable sources, it promised to reduce the country's dependence on foreign oil, another selling point in an age of increasingly tight oil supplies.

E85 aside, however, there was frankly little to get excited about in the latest Impala and Monte Carlo. *Consumer Guide*® judged Impala "affordable, relatively roomy, and has competent road manners. Powertrains are improved for 2006, and curtain side airbags are available for the first time. But this sedan still feels dated compared to midsize-car-class pacesetters, the Honda Accord and Toyota Camry. In the same vein, Monte Carlo is a throwback to the era of the midsize domestic coupe." Harsh words, but perhaps mitigated by the likelihood of clean-sheet replacements with rear-wheel drive by 2010, perhaps sooner.

Critics can argue that Chevrolet and the GM still have much catching up to do, and the sooner, the better for GM workers, stakeholders, and customers. But Rome wasn't rebuilt in a day, and GM is making progress. At Chevrolet it takes the form of needed new full-size SUVs and pickups for 2007, refinements to popular newer fare like the Equinox "crossover" SUV, and weeding out peripheral products, however attention-getting, like SSR (born 2003, terminated after 2006). We should also note that Chevrolet was again "USA-1" in 2005, besting a faltering Ford in total calendar-year car and truck sales for the first time in two decades. That's got to count for something.

Specifications

1930

AD Universal (wb 107.0)	Wght	Price	Prod
rdstr 2P	2,195	495	5,684
spt rdstr 2-4P	2,250	515	27,651
phtn 5P	2,265	495	1,713
cpe 2P	2,415	565	100,373
spt cpe 2-4P	2,525	615	45,311
coach 5P	2,515	565	255,027
club sdn 5P	2,575	625	24,888
sdn 5P	2,615	675	135,193
Special sdn 5P	2,625	685	35,929
cpe 2P R/S	2,540	—	9,211

1930 Engine	bore×stroke	bhp	availability
I-6, 194.0	3.13×3.75	50	S-all

1931

AE Independence (wb 109.0)	Wght	Price	Prod
rdstr 2P	2,275	475	2,939
spt rdstr 2P	2,330	495	24,050
DeLuxe phtn 5P	2,370	510	852
cpe 2P 3W	2,490	535	57,741
spt cpe 2-4P	2,565	575	66,029
cpe 2P 5W	2,490	545	28,379
coach 5P	2,585	545	228,316
sdn 5P	2,685	635	52,465
Special sdn 5P	2,725	650	109,775
cpe 5P	2,610	595	20,297
cab 2-4P	2,520	615	23,077
conv sdn 5P	2,610	650	5,634

1931 Engine	bore×stroke	bhp	availability
I-6, 194.0	3.13×3.75	50	S-all

1932

BA Confederate (wb 109.0)	Wght	Price	Prod
rdstr 2P	2,410	445	1,118
cpe 2P 3W	2,580	490	8,874
coach 5P	2,665	495	132,109
sdn 5P	2,750	590	27,718
spt cpe 2-4P	2,645	535	26,623 (combined)
DeLuxe spt cpe 2-4P	2,695	550	
cpe 2P 5W	2,580	490	34,796 (combined)
DeLuxe cpe 2P 5W	2,630	505	
cpe 5P	2,700	575	7,566 (combined)
DeLuxe cpe 5P	2,700	590	
landau phtn 5P	2,700	625	1,602 (combined)
DeLx landau phtn 5P	2,750	640	
DeLuxe phtn 5P	2,520	495	419
DeLx spt rdstr 2-4P	2,530	500	8,552
DeLuxe cpe 2P	2,630	510	2,226
DeLuxe coach 5P	2,715	515	9,346
DeLx Special sdn 5P	2,850	630	52,446

1932 Engine	bore×stroke	bhp	availability
I-6, 194.0	3.13×3.75	60	S-all

1933

CA Eagle (wb 110.0)	Wght	Price*	Prod
spt rdstr 2P	2,675	485	2,876
phtn 5P	2,715	515	543
cpe 2P	2,715	495	60,402
spt cpe 2-4P	2,780	535	26,691
coach 5P	2,820	515	162,629
Town sdn 2d 5P	—	545	30,657
sdn 5P	2,880	565	162,361
cab 2-4P	2,715	565	4,276

* All models $15 extra with 6-wire wheel equipment.

CC Mercury (wb 107.0)	Wght	Price	Prod
cpe 2p	2,335	445	8,909
cpe 2-4P	2,395	475	1,903
coach 5P	2,425	455	25,033

1933 Engines	bore×stroke	bhp	availability
I-6, 181.0	3.31×3.50	60	S-Merc series
I-6, 206.8	3.31×4.00	65	S-Eagle series

1934

DA Master (wb 112.0)	Wght	Price*	Prod
spt rdstr 2-4P	2,815	540	1,974
cpe 2P	2,935	560	53,018
spt cpe 2-4P	2,995	600	18,365
cab 2-4P	2,990	665	3,276
coach 5P	2,995	580	163,948
sdn 5P	3,080	640	124,754
Town sdn 2d 5P	3,020	615	49,431
spt sdn 4d 5P	3,155	675	37,646

DC Standard (wb 107.0)	Wght	Price	Prod
spt rdstr 2-4P	2,380	465	1,038
phtn 5P	2,400	495	234
cpe 2P	2,470	485	16,765
sdn 2d	2,580	495	69,082
sdn 4d	2,655	540	11,840

* All DA/DC models exc DC sdn 4d $30 extra with 6-wire wheel equipment.

1934 Engines	bore×stroke	bhp	availability
I-6, 181.0	3.31×3.50	60	S-Standard
I-6, 206.8	3.31×4.00	80	S-Master

1935

EC Standard (wb 107.0)	Wght	Price	Prod
spt rdstr 2-4P	2,430	465	1,176
phtn 5P	2,495	485	217
cpe 2P	2,540	475	32,193
coach 5P	2,645	485	126,138
sdn 5P	2,700	550	42,049

ED/EA Master DeLuxe (wb 113.0)*	Wght	Price	Prod
cpe 2P 5W	2,910	560	40,201
spt cpe 2-4P 3W	2,940	600	11,904
coach 5P	3,010	580	102,996
sdn 5P	3,055	640	57,771
Town sdn 2d 5P	3,055	615	66,231
spt sdn 4d 5P	3,130	675	67,339

* ED no Knee-Action. EA Knee-Action, add 60 lbs & $20.

1935 Engines	bore×stroke	bhp	availability
I-6, 181.0	3.31×3.50	74	S-Standard
I-6, 206.8	3.31×4.00	80	S-Master DeLx

1936

FC Standard (wb 109.0)	Wght	Price	Prod
cpe 2P	2,645	495	59,356
cab 2-4P	2,745	595	3,629
coach 5P	2,750	510	76,646
sdn 5P	2,775	575	11,142
Town sdn 2d 5P	2,775	535	220,884
spt sdn 4d 5P	2,805	600	46,760

FD/FA Master DeLuxe (wb 113.0)*	Wght	Price	Prod
cpe 2P 5W	2,895	560	49,319
spt cpe 2-4P	2,940	590	10,985
coach 5P	2,985	580	40,814
sdn 5P	3,060	640	14,536
Town sdn 2d 5P	3,030	605	244,134
spt sdn 4d 5P	3,080	665	140,073

* FD no Knee-Action. FA Knee-Action, add 50 lbs & $20.

1936 Engine	bore×stroke	bhp	availability
I-6, 206.8	3.31×4.00	79	S-all

1937

GB Master (wb 112.3)	Wght	Price	Prod
bus cpe 2P	2,770	619	54,683
cab 2-4P	2,790	725	1,724
coach 5P	2,800	637	15,349

GB Master	Wght	Price	Prod
Town sdn 2d 5P T/B	2,830	655	178,645
sdn 4d 5P	2,845	698	2,755
spt sdn 4d 5P T/B	2,885	716	43,240

GA Master DeLuxe (wb 112.3)	Wght	Price	Prod
cpe 2P	2,840	685	56,166
spt cpe 2-4P	2,870	724	8,935
coach 5P	2,910	703	7,260
Town sdn 2d 5P T/B	2,935	721	300,332
sdn 4d 5P	2,935	770	2,221
spt sdn 4d 5P T/B	2,960	788	144,110

1937 Engine	bore×stroke	bhp	availability
I-6, 216.5	3.50×3.75	85	S-all

1938

HB Master (wb 112.3)	Wght	Price	Prod
cpe 2P	2,770	648	39,793
cab 2-4P	2,790	755	2,787
coach 5P	2,795	668	3,326
Town sdn 2d T/B	2,825	689	95,050
sdn 4d	2,840	730	522
spt sdn 4d T/B	2,845	750	20,952

HA Master DeLuxe (wb 112.3)	Wght	Price	Prod
cpe 2P	2,840	714	36,106
spt cpe 4P	2,855	750	2,790
coach 5P	2,900	730	1,038
Town sdn 2d T/B	2,915	750	186,233
sdn 4d	2,915	796	236
spt sdn 4d T/B	2,940	817	76,323

1938 Engine	bore×stroke	bhp	availability
I-6, 216.5	3.50×3.75	85	S-all

1939

JB Master 85 (wb 112.3)	Wght	Price	Prod
cpe 2P	2,780	628	41,770
coach 5P	2,795	648	1,404
Town sdn 2d T/B	2,820	669	124,059
sdn 4d	2,805	689	336
spt sdn 4d T/B	2,845	710	22,623
wgn 4d	3,010	848	430*

* 229 with folding end gates, 201 with rear door

JA Master DeLuxe (wb 112.3)	Wght	Price	Prod
bus cpe 2P	2,845	684	33,809
spt cpe 4P	2,845	715	20,908
coach 5P	2,865	699	180
Town sdn 2d T/B	2,875	720	220,181
sdn 4d	2,875	745	68
spt sdn 4d T/B	2,910	766	110,521
wgn 4d	3,060	883	989

1939 Engine	bore×stroke	bhp	availability
I-6, 216.5	3.50×3.75	85	S-all

1940

KB Master 85 (wb 113.0)	Wght	Price	Prod
bus cpe	2,865	659	25,734
town sedan 2d, T/B	2,915	699	66,431
sport sedan 4d, T/B	2,930	740	11,468
wgn 4d, 8P	3,106	903	411

KH Master DeLuxe (wb 113.0)	Wght	Price	Prod
bus cpe	2,920	684	28,090
sport coupe	2,925	715	17,234
town sedan 2d, T/B	2,965	725	143,125
sport sedan 4d, T/B	2,990	766	40,924

KA Special DeLuxe (wb 113.0)	Wght	Price	Prod
bus cpe	2,930	720	25,537
sport coupe	2,945	750	46,628
conv cpe	3,160	898	11,820
town sedan 2d, T/B	2,980	761	205,910
sport sedan 4d, T/B	3,010	802	138,811
wgn 4d, 8P	3,158	934	2,493*

*367 with double rear doors

1940 Engine	bore×stroke	bhp	availability
I-6, 216.5	3.50×3.75	85	S-all

1941

AG Master DeLx (wb 116.0)	Wght	Price	Prod
bus cpe	3,020	712	48,763
cpe	3,025	743	79,124
town sedan 2d	3,050	754	219,438
sport sedan 4d	3,090	795	59,538

AH Special DeLx (wb 116.0)	Wght	Price	Prod
bus cpe	3,040	769	17,602
cpe	3,050	800	155,889
conv cpe	3,285	949	15,296
town sedan 2d	3,095	810	228,458
sport sedan 4d	3,127	851	148,661
wgn 4d, 8P	3,410	995	2,045
Fleetline sdn 4d	3,130	877	34,162

1941 Engine	bore×stroke	bhp	availability
I-6, 216.5	3.50×3.75	90	S-all

1942

BG Master DeLx (wb 116.0)	Wght	Price	Prod
cpe 2P	3,055	760	8,089
cpe 5P	3,060	790	17,442
town sedan 2d	3,090	800	41,872
sport sedan 4d	3,110	840	14,093

BH Special DeLuxe (wb 116.0)	Wght	Price	Prod
cpe 2P	3,070	815	1,716
cpe 5P	3,085	845	22,187
conv cpe	3,385	1,080	1,182
town sedan 2d	3,120	855	39,421
sport sedan 4d	3,145	895	31,441
wgn 4d, 8P	3,425	1,095	1,057

BH Fleetline (wb 116.0)	Wght	Price	Prod
Aerosedan 2d	3,105	880	61,855
Sportmaster sdn 4d	3,165	920	14,530

1942 Engine	bore×stroke	bhp	availability
I-6, 216.5	3.50×3.75	90	S-all

1946

DJ Stylemaster (wb 116.0)	Wght	Price	Prod
sport sedan 4d	3,175	1,205	75,349
town sedan 2d	3,170	1,152	61,104
spt cpe	3,130	1,137	19,243
bus cpe	3,105	1,098	14,267

DK Fleetmaster (wb 116.0)	Wght	Price	Prod
sport sedan 4d	3,225	1,280	73,746
town sedan 2d	3,190	1,225	56,538
spt cpe	3,145	1,212	27,036
conv cpe	3,445	1,476	4,508
wgn 4d, 8P	3,465	1,712	804

DK Fleetline (wb 116.0)	Wght	Price	Prod
Sportmaster sdn 4d	3,240	1,309	7,501
Aerosedan 2d	3,165	1,249	57,932

1946 Engine	bore×stroke	bhp	availability
I-6, 216.5	3.50×3.75	90	S-all

1947

EJ Stylemaster (wb 116.0)		Wght	Price	Prod
1503	sport sedan 4d	3,130	1,276	42,571
1502	town sedan 2d	3,075	1,219	88,534
1524	spt cpe	3,060	1,202	34,513
1504	bus cpe	3,050	1,160	27,403

EK Fleetmaster (wb 116.0)		Wght	Price	Prod
2103	sport sedan 4d	3,185	1,345	91,440
2102	town sedan 2d	3,125	1,286	80,128
2124	spt cpe	3,090	1,281	59,661
2134	conv cpe	3,390	1,628	28,443
2109	wgn 4d, 8P	3,465	1,893	4,912

EK Fleetline (wb 116.0)		Wght	Price	Prod
2113	Sportmaster sdn 4d	3,150	1,371	54,531
2144	Aerosedan 2d	3,125	1,313	159,407

1947 Engine	bore×stroke	bhp	availability
I-6, 216.5	3.50×3.75	90	S-all

1948

FJ Stylemaster (wb 116.0)		Wght	Price	Prod
1502	town sedan 2d	3,095	1,313	70,228
1503	sport sedan 4d	3,115	1,371	48,456
1504	bus cpe	3,045	1,244	18,396
1524	spt cpe	3,020	1,323	34,513

FK Fleetmaster (wb 116.0)		Wght	Price	Prod
2102	town sedan 2d	3,110	1,381	66,208
2103	sport sedan 4d	3,150	1,439	93,142
2109	wgn 4d, 8P	3,430	2,013	10,171
2124	spt cpe	3,050	1,402	58,786
2134	conv cpe	3,340	1,750	20,471

FK Fleetline (wb 116.0)		Wght	Price	Prod
2113	Sportmaster sdn 4d	3,150	1,492	64,217
2144	Aerosedan 2d	3,100	1,434	211,861

1948 Engine	bore×stroke	bhp	availability
I-6, 216.5	3.50×3.75	90	S-all

1949

GJ Styleline Specl (wb 115.0)		Wght	Price	Prod
1502	town sedan 2d	3,070	1,413	69,398
1503	sport sedan 4d	3,090	1,460	46,334
1504	bus cpe	3,015	1,339	20,337
1524	spt cpe	3,030	1,418	27,497

GJ Fleetline Special (wb 115.0)		Wght	Price	Prod
1552	sdn 2d	3,060	1,413	58,514
1553	sdn 4d	3,095	1,460	36,317

GK Styleline DeLuxe (wb 115.0)		Wght	Price	Prod
2102	town sedan 2d	3,100	1,492	147,347
2103	sport sedan 4d	3,125	1,539	191,357
2109	wgn 4d, wood body	3,485	2,267	3,342
2119	wgn 4d, steel body	3,465	2,267	2,664
2124	spt cpe	3,065	1,508	78,785
2134	conv cpe	3,375	1,857	32,392

GK Fleetline DeLuxe (wb 115.0)		Wght	Price	Prod
2152	sdn 2d	3,100	1,492	180,251
2153	sdn 4d	3,135	1,539	130,323

1949 Engine	bore×stroke	bhp	availability
I-6, 216.5	3.50×3.75	90	S-all

1950

HJ Styleline Specl (wb 115.0)		Wght	Price	Prod
1502	town sedan 2d	3,085	1,403	89,897
1503	sport sedan 4d	3,120	1,450	55,644
1504	bus cpe	3,025	1,329	20,984
1524	spt cpe	3,050	1,408	28,328

HJ Fleetline Special (wb 115.0)		Wght	Price	Prod
1552	sdn 2d	3,080	1,403	43,682
1553	sdn 4d	3,115	1,450	23,277

HJ Styleline DeLuxe (wb 115.0)		Wght	Price	Prod
2102	town sedan 2d	3,100	1,482	248,567
2103	sport sedan 4d	3,150	1,529	316,412
2119	wgn 4d, steel body	3,460	1,994	166,995
2124	spt cpe	3,090	1,498	81,536
2134	conv cpe	3,380	1,847	32,810
2154	Bel Air htp cpe	3,225	1,741	76,662

HK DeLuxe Fleetline (wb 115.0)		Wght	Price	Prod
2152	sdn 2d	3,115	1,482	189,509
2153	sdn 4d	3,145	1,529	124,287

1950 Engines	bore×stroke	bhp	availability
I-6, 216.5	3.50×3.75	92	S-all
I-6, 235.5	3.56×3.94	105	S-Powerglide

1951

JJ Styleline Specl (wb 115.0)		Wght	Price	Prod
1502	sdn 2d	3,095	1,540	75,566
1503	sdn 4d	3,130	1,595	63,718
1504	bus cpe	3,040	1,460	17,020
1524	spt cpe	3,060	1,545	18,981

JJ Fleetline Special (wb 115.0)		Wght	Price	Prod
1552	sdn 2d	3,090	1,540	6,441
1553	sdn 4d	3,130	1,594	3,364

JK Styleline DeLuxe (wb 115.0)		Wght	Price	Prod
2102	sdn 2d	3,110	1,629	262,933
2103	sdn 4d	3,140	1,680	380,270
2119	wgn 4d	3,470	2,191	23,586
2124	spt cpe	3,115	1,647	64,976
2134	conv cpe	3,380	2,030	20,172
2154	Bel Air htp cpe	3,225	1,914	103,356

JK Fleetline DeLuxe (wb 115.0)		Wght	Price	Prod
2152	sdn 2d	3,125	1,629	131,910
2153	sdn 4d	3,155	1,680	57,693

1951 Engines	bore×stroke	bhp	availability
I-6, 216.5	3.50×3.75	92	S-all
I-6, 235.5	3.56×3.94	105	S-Powerglide

1952

KJ Styleline Specl (wb 115.0)		Wght	Price	Prod
1502	sdn 2d	3,085	1,614	54,781
1503	sdn 4d	3,115	1,670	35,460
1504	bus cpe	3,045	1,530	10,359
1524	spt cpe	3,050	1,620	8,906

KK Styleline DeLuxe (wb 115.0)		Wght	Price	Prod
2102	sdn 2d	3,110	1,707	215,417
2103	sdn 4d	3,145	1,761	319,736

KK Styleline DeLuxe		Wght	Price	Prod
2119	wgn 4d	3,475	2,297	12,756
2124	spt cpe	3,100	1,726	36,954
2134	conv cpe	3,380	2,128	11,975
2154	Bel Air htp cpe	3,215	2,006	74,634
KK Fleetline DeLuxe (wb 115.0)				
2152	sdn 2d	3,110	1,707	37,164

1952 Engines	bore×stroke	bhp	availability
I-6, 216.5	3.50×3.75	92	S-manual shift
I-6, 235.5	3.56×3.94	105	S-Powerglide

1953

150 Special (wb 115.0)		Wght	Price	Prod
1502	sdn 2d	3,180	1,613	79,416
1503	sdn 4d	3,215	1,670	54,207
1504	bus cpe	3,140	1,524	13,555
1509	Handyman wgn 4d	3,420	2,010	22,408
1524	club cpe	3,140	1,620	6,993
210 DeLuxe (wb 115.0)				
2102	sdn 2d	3,215	1,707	247,455
2103	sdn 4d	3,250	1,761	332,497
2109	Handyman wgn 4d	3,450	2,123	18,258
2119	Townsmn wgn 4d, 8P	3,495	2,273	7,988
2124	club cpe	3,190	1,726	23,961
2134	conv cpe	3,435	2,093	5,617
2154	htp cpe	3,295	1,967	14,045
240 Bel Air (wb 115.0)				
2402	sdn 2d	3,230	1,820	144,401
2403	sdn 4d	3,275	1,874	247,284
2434	conv cpe	3,470	2,175	24,047
2454	htp cpe	3,310	2,051	99,028

1953 Engines	bore×stroke	bhp	availability
I-6, 235.5	3.56×3.94	108	S-manual shift
I-6, 235.5	3.56×3.94	115	S-Powerglide

1954

150 Special (wb 115.0)		Wght	Price	Prod
1502	sdn 2d	3,165	1,680	64,855
1503	sdn 4d	3,210	1,623	32,430
1509	Handyman wgn 4d	3,455	2,020	21,404
1512	Utility sdn 2d, 3P	3,145	1,539	10,770
210 DeLuxe (wb 115.0)				
2102	sdn 2d	3,185	1,717	195,498
2103	sdn 4d	3,230	1,771	235,146
2109	Handyman wgn 4d	3,470	2,133	27,175
2124	Delray cpe	3,185	1,782	66,403
240 Bel Air (wb 115.0)				
2402	sdn 2d	3,220	1,830	143,573
2403	sdn 4d	3,255	1,884	248,750
2419	Townsmn wgn 4d, 8P	3,540	2,283	8,156
2434	conv cpe	3,445	2,185	19,383
2454	sport coupe htp cpe	3,300	2,061	66,378

1954 Engines	bore×stroke	bhp	availability
I-6, 235.5	3.56×3.94	115	S-manual
I-6, 235.5	3.56×3.94	125	S-Powerglide

1955

150 (wb 115.0)		Wght	Price	Prod
1502	sdn 2d	3,145	1,685	66,416
1503	sdn 4d	3,150	1,728	29,898
1512	Util sdn	3,070	1,593	11,196
1529	Handyman wgn 4d	3,275	2,030	17,936
210 (wb 115.0)				
2102	sdn 2d	3,130	1,775	249,105
2103	sdn 4d	3,165	1,819	317,724
2109	Townsman wgn 4d	3,355	2,127	82,303
2124	Delray cpe	3,130	1,835	115,584
2129	Handyman wgn 2d	3,315	2,079	28,918
2154	htp cpe	3,158	1,959	11,675
Bel Air (wb 115.0)				
2402	sdn 2d	3,140	1,888	168,313
2403	sdn 4d	3,185	1,932	345,372
2409	Beauville wgn 4d	3,370	2,262	24,313
2429	Nomad wgn 2d	3,285	2,472	8,386
2434	conv cpe	3,300	2,206	41,292
2454	sport coupe htp cpe	3,180	2,067	185,562

1955 Engines	bore×stroke	bhp	availability
I-6, 235.5	3.56×3.94	123/136	S-manual/ Powerglide
V-8, 265.0	3.75×3.00	162	O-manual
V-8, 265.0	3.75×3.00	180	O-all

1956

150 (wb 115.0)		Wght	Price	Prod
1502	sdn 2d	3,154	1,826	82,384
1503	sdn 4d	3,196	1,869	51,544
1512	Util sdn	3,117	1,734	9,879
1529	Handyman wgn 2d	3,299	2,171	13,487
210 (wb 115.0)				
2102	sdn 2d	3,167	1,912	205,545
2103	sdn 4d	3,202	1,955	283,125
2109	Townsman wgn 4d	3,371	2,263	113,656
2113	Sport htp sdn	3,252	2,117	20,021
2119	Beauville wgn 4d, 9P	3,490	2,348	17,988
2124	Delray cpe	3,172	1,971	56,382
2129	Handyman wgn 2d	3,334	2,215	22,038
2154	Sport htp cpe	3,194	2,063	18,616
Bel Air (wb 115.0)				
2402	sdn 2d	3,187	2,025	104,849
2403	sdn 4d	3,221	2,068	269,798
2413	Sport htp sdn	3,270	2,230	103,602
2419	Beauville wgn 4d, 9P	3,506	2,482	13,279
2429	Nomad wgn 2d	3,352	2,608	7,886
2434	conv cpe	3,330	2,344	41,268
2454	Sport htp cpe	3,222	2,176	128,382

1956 Engines	bore×stroke	bhp	availability
I-6, 235.5	3.56×3.94	140	S-all
V-8, 265.0	3.75×3.00	162/170	S-manual/ Powerglide
V-8, 265.0	3.75×3.00	205	O-all
V-8, 265.0	3.75×3.00	225	O-all

1957

150 (wb 115.0)		Wght	Price	Prod
1502	sdn 2d	3,211	1,996	70,774
1503	sdn 4d	3,236	2,048	52,266
1512	Util sdn 2d	3,163	1,885	8,300
1529	Handyman wgn 2d	3,406	2,307	14,740
210 (wb 115.0)				
2102	sdn 2d	3,225	2,122	160,090
2103	sdn 4d	3,270	2,174	260,401
2109	Townsman wgn 4d	3,461	2,456	127,803
2113	Sport htp sdn	3,320	2,270	16,178
2119	Beauville wgn 4d	3,561	2,563	21,083
2124	Delray cpe	3,220	2,162	25,644
2129	Handyman wgn 2d	3,406	2,402	17,528
2154	Sport htp cpe	3,260	2,204	22,631
Bel Air (wb 115.0)				
2402	sdn 2d	3,232	2,238	62,751
2403	sdn 4d	3,276	2,290	254,331
2409	Townsman wgn 4d	3,460	2,580	27,375
2413	Sport htp sdn	3,340	2,364	137,672
2429	Nomad wgn 2d	3,465	2,757	6,103
2434	conv cpe	3,409	2,511	47,562
2454	Sport htp cpe	3,278	2,299	166,426

1957 Engines	bore×stroke	bhp	availability
I-6, 235.5	3.56×3.94	140	S-all
V-8, 265.0	3.75×3.00	162	O-all manual
V-8, 283.0	3.88×3.00	185	S-all automatic
V-8, 283.0	3.88×3.00	220	O-all
V-8, 283.0	3.88×3.00	245/250	O-all
V-8, 283.0	3.88×3.00	270/283	O-manual shift

1958

Delray (wb 117.5) - 178,000* blt		Wght	Price	Prod
1121	Util sdn 2d, I-6	3,351	2,013	—
1141	sdn 2d, I-6	3,396	2,101	—
1149	sdn 4d, I-6	3,439	2,155	—
1221	Util sdn 2d, V-8	3,356	2,120	—
1241	sdn 2d, V-8	3,399	2,208	—
1249	sdn 4d, V-8	3,442	2,262	—
Biscayne (wb 117.5) - 100,000* built exc 1541				
1541	sdn 2d, I-6	3,404	2,236	76,229
1549	sdn 4d, I-6	3,447	2,290	—
1641	sdn 2d, V-8	3,407	2,343	—
1649	sdn 4d, V-8	3,450	2,397	—
Bel Air (wb 117.5) - 592,000* built				
1731	Sport htp cpe, I-6	3,455	2,447	—
1739	Sport htp sdn, I-6	3,511	2,511	—

Bel Air		Wght	Price	Prod
1741	sdn 2d, I-6	3,424	2,386	—
1747	Impala htp cpe, I-6	3,458	2,586	—
1749	sdn 4d, I-6	3,467	2,440	—
1767	Impala conv cpe, I-6	3,522	2,734	—
1831	Sport htp cpe, V-8	3,458	2,554	—
1839	Sport htp sdn, V-8	3,514	2,618	—
1841	sdn 2d, V-8	3,427	2,493	—
1847	Impala htp cpe, V-8	3,459	2,693	—
1849	sdn 4d, V-8	3,470	2,547	—
1867	Impala conv cpe, V-8	3,523	2,841	—
Station Wagon (wb 117.5) - 187,063 built				
1191	Yeoman 2d, I-6	3,693	2,413	—
1193	Yeoman 4d, I-6	3,740	2,467	—
1291	Yeoman 2d, V-8	3,696	2,520	—
1293	Yeoman 4d, V-8	3,743	2,574	—
1593	Brookwd 4d, 6P, I-6	3,748	2,571	—
1594	Brookwd 4d, 9P, I-6	3,837	2,678	—
1693	Brookwd 4d, 6P, V-8	3,751	2,678	—
1694	Brookwd 4d, 9P, V-8	3,839	2,785	—
1793	Nomad 4d, I-6	3,768	2,728	—
1893	Nomad 4d, V-8	3,771	2,835	—

* To nearest 100. Impalas approximately 60,000.

1958 Engines	bore×stroke	bhp	availability
I-6, 235.5	3.56 ×3.94	145	S-six
V-8, 283.0	3.88×3.00	185	S-V-8
V-8, 283.0	3.88×3.00	230/250	O-all
V-8, 283.0	3.88×3.00	290	O-all manual
V-8, 348.0	4.13×3.25	250	O-all
V-8, 348.0	4.13×3.25	280/315	O-all

1959

Biscayne (wb 119.0) - 311,800* blt		Wght	Price	Prod
1111	sdn 2d, I-6	3,535	2,247	—
1119	sdn 4d, I-6	3,605	2,301	—
1121	Util sdn 2d, I-6	3,480	2,160	—
1211	sdn 2d, V-8	3,530	2,365	—
1219	sdn 4d, V-8	3,600	2,419	—
1221	Util sdn 2d, V-8	3,490	2,278	—
Bel Air (wb 119.0) - 447,100* built				
1511	sdn 2d, I-6	3,515	2,386	—
1519	sdn 4d, I-6	3,600	2,440	—
1539	Sport htp sdn, I-6	3,660	2,556	—
1611	sdn 2d, V-8	3,510	2,504	—
1619	sdn 4d, V-8	3,615	2,558	—
1639	Sport htp sdn, V-8	3,630	2,674	—
Impala (wb 119.0) - 407,200 built exc 1867				
1719	sdn 4d, I-6	3,625	2,592	—
1737	Sport htp cpe, I-6	3,570	2,599	—
1739	Sport htp sdn, I-6	3,665	2,664	—
1767	conv cpe, I-6	3,660	2,849	—
1819	sdn 4d, V-8	3,620	2,710	—
1837	Sport htp cpe, V-8	3,580	2,717	—
1839	Sport htp sdn, V-8	3,670	2,782	—
1867	conv cpe, V-8	3,650	2,967	65,800
Station Wagon (wb 119.0) - 195,583 blt* exc 1215				
1115	Brookwood 2d, I-6	3,870	2,571	—
1135	Brookwood 4d, I-6	3,955	2,638	—
1215	Brookwood, 2d, V-8	3,860	2,689	18,800
1235	Brookwood, 4d, V-8	3,955	2,756	—
1535	Parkwood 4d, I-6	3,965	2,749	—
1545	Kingswd, 4d, 9P, I-6	4,020	2,852	—
1635	Parkwood 4d, V-8	3,970	2,867	—
1645	Kingswd 4d, 9P, V-8	4,015	2,970	—
1735	Nomad 4d, I-6	3,980	2,891	—
1835	Nomad 4d, V-8	3,975	3,009	—

* To nearest 100.

1959 Engines	bore×stroke	bhp	availability
I-6, 235.5	3.56×3.94	135	S-six
V-8, 283.0	3.88×3.00	185	S-V-8
V-8, 283.0	3.88×3.00	230-290	O-all
V-8, 348.0	4.13×3.25	250-315	O-all

1960

Biscayne (wb119.0) - 287,700* blt		Wght	Price	Prod
1111	sdn 2d, I-6	3,485	2,262	—
1119	sdn 4d, I-6	3,555	2,316	—
1121	Util sdn 2d, I-6	3,455	2,175	—
1211	sdn 2d, V-8	3,500	2,369	—
1219	sdn 4d, V-8	3,570	2,423	—
1221	Util sdn 2d, V-8	3,470	2,282	—

Biscayne Fltmstr (wb 119.0) - prod incl with Biscayne				
1311	sdn 2d, I-6	3,480	2,230	—
1319	sdn 4d, I-6	3,545	2,284	—
1411	sdn 2d, V-8	3,495	2,337	—
1419	sdn 4d, V-8	3,560	2,391	—
Bel Air (wb 119.0) - 381,500* built				
1511	sdn 2d, I-6	3,490	2,384	—
1519	sdn 4d, I-6	3,565	2,438	—
1537	Sport htp cpe, I-6	3,515	2,489	—
1539	Sport htp sdn, I-6	3,605	2,554	—
1611	sdn 2d, V-8	3,505	2,491	—
1619	sdn 4d, V-8	3,500	2,545	—
1637	Sport htp cpe, I-6	3,530	2,596	—
1639	Sport htp sdn, V-8	3,620	2,661	—
Impala (wb 119.0) - 411,000* built exc 1867				
1719	sdn 4d, I-6	3,575	2,590	—
1737	Sport htp cpe, I-6	3,530	2,597	—
1739	Sport htp sdn, I-6	3,625	2,662	—
1767	conv cpe, I-6	3,625	2,847	—
1819	sdn 4d, V-8	3,580	2,697	—
1837	Sport htp cpe, V-8	3,540	2,704	—
1839	Sport htp sdn, V-8	3,625	2,769	—
1867	conv cpe, V-8	3,635	2,954	79,903
Station Wagon (wb 119.0) - 212,700* built				
1115	Brookwood 2d, I-6	3,845	2,586	—
1135	Brookwood 4d, I-6	3,935	2,653	—
1215	Brookwood 2d, V-8	3,855	2,693	—
1235	Brookwood 4d, V-8	3,935	2,760	—
1535	Parkwood 4d, I-6	3,945	2,747	—
1545	Kingswd, 4d, 9P, I-6	3,990	2,850	—
1635	Parkwood 4d, V-8	3,950	2,854	—
1645	Kingswd 4d, 9P, V-8	4,000	2,957	—
1735	Nomad 4d, I-6	3,955	2,889	—
1835	Nomad 4d, V-8	3,960	2,996	—

* To nearest 100.

1960 Engines	bore×stroke	bhp	availability
I-6, 235.5	3.56×3.94	135	S-six
V-8, 283.0	3.88×3.00	170	S-V-8
V-8, 283.0	3.88×3.00	230	O-all
V-8, 348.0	4.13×3.25	250-335	O-all

1961

Biscayne (wb 119.0) - 201,000* blt		Wght	Price	Prod
1111	sdn 2d, I-6	3,415	2,262	—
1121	Util sdn 2d, I-6	3,390	2,175	—
1169	sdn 4d, I-6	3,500	2,316	—
1211	sdn 2d, V-8	3,425	2,369	—
1221	Util sdn 2d, V-8	3,395	2,282	—
1269	sdn 4d, V-8	3,505	2,423	—
Biscayne Fleetmaster (wb 119.0) - 3,000* built				
1311	sdn 2d, I-6	3,410	2,230	—
1369	sdn 4d, I-6	3,495	2,284	—
1411	sdn 2d, V-8	3,415	2,337	—
1469	sdn 4d, V-8	3,500	2,391	—
Bel Air (wb 119.0) - 330,000* built				
1511	sdn 2d, I-6	3,430	2,384	—
1537	Sport htp cpe, I-6	3,475	2,489	—
1539	Sport htp sdn, I-6	3,550	2,554	—
1569	sdn 4d, I-6	3,515	2,438	—
1611	sdn 2d, V-8	3,435	2,491	—
1637	Sport htp cpe, V-8	3,480	2,596	—
1639	Sport htp sdn, V-8	3,555	2,661	—
1669	sdn 4d, V-8	3,520	2,545	—
Impala (wb 119.0) - 426,400* built exc 1867				
1711	sdn 2d, I-6	3,445	2,536	—
1737	Sport htp cpe, I-6	3,485	2,597	—
1739	Sport htp sdn, I-6	3,575	2,662	—
1767	conv cpe, I-6	3,605	2,847	—
1769	sdn 4d, I-6	3,530	2,590	—
1811	sdn 2d, V-8	3,440	2,643	—
1837	Sport htp cpe, V-8	3,480	2,704	—
1839	Sport htp sdn, V-8	3,570	2,769	—
1867	conv cpe, V-8	3,600	2,954	64,600
1869	sdn 4d, V-8	3,525	2,697	—
Station Wagon (wb 119.0) - 168,900 built**				
1135	Brookwood 4d, I-6	3,850	2,653	—
1145	Brookwd 4d, 9P, I-6	3,900	2,756	—
1235	Brookwood 4d, V-8	3,845	2,760	—
1245	Brookwd 4d, 9P, V-8	3,895	2,864	—
1535	Parkwood 4d, I-6	3,865	2,747	—

Station Wagon		Wght	Price	Prod
1545	Parkwood 4d, 9P, I-6	3,910	2,850	—
1635	Parkwood 4d, V-8	3,860	2,854	—
1645	Parkwood 4d, 9P, V-8	3,905	2,957	—
1735	Nomad 4d, I-6	3,885	2,889	—
1745	Nomad 4d, 9P, I-6	3,935	2,992	—
1835	Nomad 4d, V-8	3,880	2,996	—
1845	Nomad 4d, 9P, V-8	3,930	3,099	—

* To nearest 100.

** Included with models above.

1961 Engines	bore×stroke	bhp	availability
I-6, 235.5	3.56×3.94	135	S-six
V-8, 283.0	3.88×3.00	170	S-V-8
V-8, 283.0	3.88×3.00	230	O-all
V-8, 348.0	4.13×3.25	250-350	O-all
V-8, 409.0	4.31×3.50	360	O-Impala SS

1962

Chevy II 100 (wb 110.0)		Wght	Price	Prod
0111	sdn 2d, I-4	2,410	2,003	
0135	wgn 4d, I-4	2,665	2,399	11,500*
0169	sdn 4d, I-4	2,445	2,041	
0211	sdn 2d, I-6	2,500	2,063	
0235	wgn 4d, I-6	2,755	2,399	35,500*
0269	sdn 4d, I-6	2,535	2,101	
Chevy II 300 (wb 110.0)				
0311	sdn 2d, I-4	2,425	2,084	—
0345	wgn 4d, 9P, I-4	2,765	2,517	—
0369	sdn 4d, I-4	2,460	2,122	—
0411	sdn 2d, I-6	2,515	2,144	
0445	wgn 4d, 9P, I-6	2,855	2,577	92,800*
0469	sdn 4d, I-6	2,550	2,182	
Chevy II Nova 400, I-6 (wb 110.0)				
0435	wgn 4d	2,775	2,497	—
0437	Sport htp cpe	2,550	2,254	59,586
0441	sdn 2d	2,540	2,198	44,390
0449	sdn 4d	2,575	2,336	139,004
0467	conv cpe	2,745	2,475	23,741
Biscayne (wb 119.0) - 160,000 built**				
1111	sdn 2d, I-6	3,405	2,324	—
1135	wgn 4d, I-6	3,845	2,725	—
1169	sdn 4d, I-6	3,480	2,378	—
1211	sdn 2d, V-8	3,400	2,431	—
1235	wgn 4d, V-8	3,840	2,832	—
1269	sdn 4d, V-8	3,475	2,485	—
Bel Air (wb 119.0) - 365,000 built**				
1511	sdn 2d, I-6	3,410	2,456	—
1535	wgn 4d, I-6	3,845	2,819	—
1537	Sport htp cpe, I-6	3,445	2,561	—
1545	wgn 4d, 9P, I-6	3,895	2,922	—
1569	sdn 4d, I-6	3,480	2,510	—
1611	sdn 2d, V-8	3,405	2,563	—
1635	wgn 4d, V-8	3,840	2,926	—
1637	Sport htp cpe, V-8	3,440	2,668	—
1645	wgn 4d, 9P, V-8	3,890	3,029	—
1669	sdn 4d, V-8	3,475	2,617	—
Impala (wb119.0) - 704,900 blt**		**Wght**	**Price**	**Prod**
1735	wgn 4d, I-6	3,870	2,961	—
1739	Sport htp sdn, I-6	3,540	2,734	—
1745	wgn 4d, 9P, I-6	3,925	3,064	—
1747	Sport htp cpe, I-6	3,455	2,669	—
1767	conv cpe, I-6	3,565	2,919	—
1769	sdn 4d, I-6	3,510	2,662	—
1835	wgn 4d, V-8	3,865	3,068	—
1839	Sport htp sdn, V-8	3,535	2,841	—
1845	wgn 4d, 9P, V-8	3,920	3,171	—
1847	Sport htp cpe, V-8	3,450	2,776	—
1867	conv cpe, V-8	3,560	3,026	—
1869	sdn 4d, V-8	3,505	2,769	—

* To nearest 100.

** Not incl wagons (187,600 built), includes SS models.

1962 Engines	bore×stroke	bhp	availability
I-4, 153.0	3.88×3.25	90	S-Chevy II 100, 300
I-6, 194.0	3.56×3.25	120	S-Chevy II all
I-6, 235.5	3.56×3.94	135	S-Chev I-6
V-8, 283.0	3.88×3.00	170	S-Chev V-8
V-8, 327.0	4.00×3.25	250/300	O-V-8 all Chev
V-8, 409.0	4.31×3.50	380/409	O-V-8 all Chev

1963

Chevy II 100 (wb110) - 50,400* blt		Wght	Price	Prod
0111	sdn 2d, I-4	2,430	2,003	—
0135	wgn 4d, I-4	2,725	2,338	—
0169	sdn 4d, I-4	2,455	2,040	—
0211	sdn 2d, I-6	2,520	2,062	—
0235	wgn 4d, I-6	2,810	2,397	—
0269	sdn 4d, I-6	2,545	2,099	—
Chevy II 300 (wb 110.0) - 78,800* built				
0311	sdn 2d, I-4	2,440	2,084	—
0345	wgn 4d, 9P, I-4	2,810	2,516	—
0369	sdn 4d, I-4	2,470	2,121	—
0411	sdn 2d, I-6	2,530	2,143	—
0445	wgn 4d, 9P, I-6	2,900	2,575	—
0469	sdn 4d, I-6	2,560	2,180	—
Chevy II Nova 400, I-6 (wb 110.0)				
0435	wgn 4d	2,835	2,494	—
0437	Sport htp cpe	2,590	2,267	87,415
0449	sdn 4d	2,590	2,235	58,862
0467	conv cpe	2,760	2,472	24,823
Biscayne (wb 119.0) - 186,500* built				
1111	sdn 2d, I-6	3,205	2,322	—
1135	wgn 4d, I-6	3,685	2,723	—
1169	sdn 4d, I-6	3,280	2,376	—
1211	sdn 2d, V-8	3,340	2,429	—
1235	wgn 4d, V-8	3,810	2,830	—
1269	sdn 4d, V-8	3,415	2,483	—
Bel Air (wb 119.0) - 354,100* built				
1511	sdn 2d, I-6	3,215	2,454	—
1535	wgn 4d, I-6	3,685	2,818	—
1545	wgn 4d, 9P, I-6	3,720	2,921	—
1569	sdn 4d, I-6	3,280	2,508	—
1611	sdn 2d, V-8	3,345	2,561	—
1635	wgn 4d, V-8	3,810	2,925	—
1645	wgn 4d, 9P, V-8	3,850	3,028	—
1669	sdn 4d, V-8	3,415	2,615	—
Impala (wb 119) - 832,600* blt (incl 153,271 SS models)				
1735	wgn 4d, I-6	3,705	2,960	—
1739	Sport htp sdn, I-6	3,350	2,732	—
1745	wgn 4d, 9P, I-6	3,745	3,063	—
1747	Sport htp cpe, I-6	3,265	2,667	—
1767	conv cpe, I-6	3,400	2,917	—
1769	sdn 4d, I-6	3,310	2,661	—
1835	wgn 4d, V-8	3,835	3,067	—
1839	Sport htp sdn, V-8	3,475	2,839	—
1845	wgn 4d, 9P, V-8	3,870	3,170	—
1847	Sport htp cpe, V-8	3,390	2,774	—
1867	conv cpe, V-8	3,525	3,024	—
1869	sdn 4d, V-8	3,435	2,768	—

* To nearest 100; does not include wagons.
Total wagons 198,542; Chevy II wagons 75,274.

1963 Engines	bore×stroke	bhp	availability
I-4, 153.0	3.88×3.25	90	S-Chevy II
I-6, 194.0	3.56×3.25	120	S-Chevy II
I-6, 230.0	3.87×3.25	140	S-Chevrolet
V-8, 283.0	3.88×3.00	195	S-Chevrolet
V-8, 327.0	4.00×3.15	250-340	O-Chevrolet
V-8, 409.0	4.31×3.50	340-425	O-Chevrolet

1964

Chevy II 100 (wb110) - 53,100 blt*		Wght	Price	Prod
0111	sdn 2d, I-4	2,455	2,011	—
0169	sdn, I-4	2,495	2,048	—
0211	sdn 2d, I-6	2,540	2,070	—
0235	wgn 4d, I-6	2,840	2,406	—
0269	sdn 4d, I-6	2,580	2,108	—
Chevy II Nova 400, I-6 (wb 110.0) - 102,900* blt (incl SS)				
0411	sdn 2d	2,560	2,206	—
0435	wgn 4d	2,860	2,503	—
0437	Sport htp cpe	2,660	2,271	—
0469	sdn 4d	2,595	2,243	—
Chevy II Nova SS, I-6 (wb 110.0)				
0447	Sport htp cpe	2,675	2,433	10,576
Chevelle 300 (wb 115.0) - 68,300* built				
5311	sdn 2d, I-6	2,825	2,231	—
5315	wgn 2d, I-6	3,050	2,528	—
5335	wgn 4d, I-6	3,130	2,566	—
5369	sdn 4d, I-6	2,850	2,268	—
5411	sdn 2d, V-8	2,995	2,339	—

Chevelle 300		Wght	Price	Prod
5415	wgn 2d, V-8	3,170	2,636	—
5435	wgn 4d, V-8	2,250	2,674	—
5469	sdn 4d, V-8	2,980	2,376	—
Chevelle Malibu (wb 115.0) - 149,000* built				
5535	wgn 4d, I-6	3,140	2,647	—
5537	Sport htp cpe, I-6	2,850	2,376	—
5545	wgn 4d, 9P, I-6	3,240	2,744	—
5567	conv cpe, I-6	2,995	2,587	—
5569	sdn 4d, I-6	2,870	2,349	—
5635	wgn 4d, V-8	3,265	2,755	—
5637	Sport htp cpe, V-8	2,975	2,484	—
5645	wgn 4d, 9P, V-8	3,365	2,852	—
5667	conv cpe, V-8	3,120	2,695	—
5669	sdn 4d, V-8	2,996	2,457	—
Chevelle Malibu SS (wb 115.0) - 76,860 built				
5737	Sport htp cpe, I-6	2,875	2,538	—
5767	conv cpe, I-6	3,020	2,749	—
5837	Sport htp cpe, V-8	3,000	2,646	—
5867	conv cpe, V-8	3,145	2,857	—
Biscayne (wb 119.0) - 173,900* built				
1111	sdn 2d, I-6	3,230	2,363	—
1135	wgn 4d, I-6	3,700	2,763	—
1169	sdn 4d, I-6	3,300	2,417	—
1211	sdn 2d, V-8	3,365	2,471	—
1235	wgn 4d, V-8	3,820	2,871	—
1269	sdn 4d, V-8	3,430	2,524	—
Bel Air (wb 119.0) - 318,100* built				
1511	sdn 2d, I-6	3,235	2,465	—
1535	wgn 4d, I-6	3,745	2,828	—
1545	wgn 4d, 9P, I-6	3,705	2,931	—
1569	sdn 4d, I-6	3,305	2,519	—
1611	sdn 2d, V-8	3,370	2,573	—
1635	wgn 4d, V-8	3,825	2,935	—
1645	wgn 4d, 9P, V-8	3,865	3,039	—
1669	sdn 4d, V-8	3,440	2,626	—
Impala (wb 119.0) - 889,600* built				
1735	wgn 4d, I-6	3,725	2,970	—
1739	Sport htp sdn, I-6	3,370	2,742	—
1745	wgn 4d, 9P, I-6	3,770	3,073	—
—	Sport htp cpe, I-6	3,265	2,667	—
1767	conv cpe, I-6	3,400	2,927	—
1769	sdn 4d, I-6	3,340	2,671	—
1835	wgn 4d, V-8	3,850	3,077	—
1839	Sport htp sdn, V-8	3,490	2,850	—
1845	wgn 4d, 9P, V-8	3,895	3,181	—
1847	Sport htp cpe, V-8	3,415	2,786	—
1867	conv cpe, V-8	3,525	3,025	—
1869	sdn 4d, V-8	3,460	2,779	—
Impala SS (wb 119.0)				
1347	htp cpe, I-6	3,325	2,839	1,998
1367	conv cpe, I-6	3,435	3,088	316
1447	Sport htp cpe, V-8	3,450	2,947	97,753
1467	conv cpe, V-8	3,555	3,196	19,099

* Nearest 100; does not include wagons. Wagon prod: Chevy II 35,700; Chevelle 44,000; others 192,800.

1964 Engines	bore×stroke	bhp	availability
I-4, 153.0	3.88×3.25	90	S-Chevy II 100
I-6, 194.0	3.56×3.25	120	S-Chevy II 100/400, Chvlle
I-6, 230.0	3.87×3.25	140	S-Chev;O-others
I-6, 230.0	3.87×3.25	155	O-all
V-8, 283.0	3.88×3.00	195	S-V-8 Chvlle, Chev; O-Chev II
V-8, 283.0	3.88×3.00	220	O-Chevelle
V-8, 327.0	4.00×3.25	250/300	O-Chev, Chvlle
V-8, 409.0	4.31×3.50	340-425	O-Chevrolet

1965

Chevy II 100 (wb 110.0)		Wght	Price	Prod
11111	sdn 2d, I-4	2,505	2,011	1,300*
11169	sdn 4d, I-4	2,520	2,048	
11311	sdn 2d, I-6	2,605	2,077	
11335	wgn 4d, I-6	2,875	2,413	39,200*
11369	sdn 4d, I-6	2,620	2,115	
Chevy II Nova 400, I-6 (wb 110.0) - 51,700* built				
11535	wgn 4d	2,880	2,510	—
11537	htp cpe	2,645	2,270	—
11569	sdn 4d	2,645	2,243	—

Chevy II Nova SS, I-6 (wb 110.0)		Wght	Price	Prod
11737	htp cpe	2,690	2,433	9,100
Chevelle 300 (wb 115.0)-31,600* blt (plus 41,600* DeLx)				
13111	sdn 2d, I-6	2,870	2,156	—
13115	wgn 2d, I-6	3,140	2,453	—
13169	sdn 4d, I-6	2,900	2,193	—
13211	sdn 2d, V-8	3,010	2,262	—
13215	wgn 2d, V-8	3,275	2,561	—
13269	sdn 4d, V-8	3,035	2,301	—
13311	Del sdn 2d, I-6	2,870	2,231	—
13335	Del wgn 4d, I-6	3,185	2,567	—
13369	Del sdn 4d, I-6	2,910	2,269	—
13411	Del sdn 2d, V-8	3,010	2,339	—
13435	Del wgn 4d, V-8	3,320	2,674	—
13469	Del sdn 4d, V-8	3,050	2,377	—
Chevelle Malibu (wb 115.0) - 152,200* built				
13535	wgn 4d, I-6	3,225	2,647	—
13537	htp cpe, I-6	2,930	2,377	—
13567	conv cpe, I-6	3,025	2,588	—
13569	sdn 4d, I-6	2,945	2,250	—
13635	wgn 4d, V-8	3,355	2,755	—
13637	htp cpe, V-8	3,065	2,485	—
13667	conv cpe, V-8	3,160	2,696	—
13669	sdn 4d, V-8	3,080	2,458	—
Chevelle Malibu SS (wb 115.0)-101,577 blt (201 SS 396)				
13737	htp cpe, I-6	2,980	2,539	—
13767	conv cpe, I-6	3,075	2,750	—
13837	htp cpe, V-8	3,115	2,647	—
13867	conv cpe, V-8	3,210	2,858	—
Biscayne (wb 119.0)				
15311	sdn 2d, I-6	3,305	2,363	
15335	wgn 4d, I-6	3,765	2,764	107,700*
15369	sdn 4d, I-6	3,365	2,417	
15411	sdn 2d, V-8	3,455	2,470	
15435	wgn 4d, V-8	3,900	2,871	37,600*
15469	sdn 4d, V-8	3,515	2,524	
Bel Air (wb 119.0)				
15511	sdn 2d, I-6	3,310	2,465	
15535	wgn 4d, I-6	3,765	2,828	107,800*
15545	wgn 4d, 9P, I-6	3,810	2,931	
15569	sdn 4d, I-6	3,380	2,519	
15611	sdn 2d, V-8	3,460	2,573	
15635	wgn 4d, V-8	3,905	2,936	163,600*
15645	wgn 4d, 9P, V-8	3,950	3,039	
15669	sdn 4d, V-8	3,530	2,626	
Impala (wb 119.0) - 803,400* built (incl Caprice pkg)				
16335	wgn 4d, I-6	3,825	2,970	
16337	htp cpe, I-6	3,385	2,678	
16339	htp sdn, I-6	3,490	2,742	56,600*
16345	wgn 4d, 9P, I-6	3,865	3,073	
16367	conv cpe, I-6	3,470	2,943	
16369	sdn 4d, I-6	3,460	2,672	
16435	wgn 4d, V-8	3,960	3,078	
16437	htp cpe, V-8	3,525	2,785	
16439	htp sdn, V-8	3,630	2,850	746,800*
16445	wgn 4d, 9P, V-8	4,005	3,181	
16467	conv cpe, V-8	3,605	3,051	
16469	sdn 4d, V-8	3,595	2,779	
Impala SS (wb 119.0) - 243,114 built				
16537	htp cpe, I-6	3,435	2,839	—
16567	conv cpe, I-6	3,505	3,104	—
16637	htp cpe, V-8	3,570	2,947	—
16667	conv cpe, V-8	3,655	3,212	—

* Nearest 100; does not include wagons. Wagon prod: Chevy II, 21,500; Chevelle, 37,600; others, 184,400. Convertible prod: Malibu 19,765; Impala SS, 27,842.

1965 Engines	bore×stroke	bhp	availability
I-4, 153.0	3.88×3.25	90	S-Chevy II 100
I-6, 194.0	3.56×3.25	120	S-Chevy II, Chevelle
I-6, 230.0	3.87×3.25	140	S-Chev; O-others
I-6, 250.0	3.87×3.53	150	O-Chevrolet
V-8, 283.0	3.88×3.00	195	S-Chev, Chvlle; O-Chevy II
V-8, 283.0	3.88×3.00	220	O-all
V-8, 327.0	4.00×3.25	250/300	O-all
V-8, 327.0	4.00×3.25	350	O-Chevelle
V-8, 396.0	4.09×3.75	325-425	O-Chev, Chvlle
V-8, 409.0	4.31×3.50	340/400	O-Chevrolet

1966

Chevy II 100 (wb 110.0)		Wght	Price	Prod
11111	sdn 2d, I-4	2,520	2,028	
11169	sdn 4d, I-4	2,535	2,065	
11311	sdn 2d, I-6	2,620	2,090	44,500*
11335	wgn 4d, I-6	2,855	2,430	
11369	sdn 4d, I-6	2,635	2,127	
11411	sdn 2d, V-8	2,775	2,197	
11435	wgn 4d, V-8	2,990	2,536	2,500*
11469	sdn 4d, V-8	2,790	2,234	
Chevy II Nova (wb 110.0)				
11535	wgn 4d, I-6	2,885	2,518	
11537	htp cpe, I-6	2,675	2,271	54,300*
11569	sdn 4d, I-6	2,640	2,245	
11635	wgn 4d, V-8	3,010	2,623	
11637	htp cpe, V-8	2,830	2,377	19,600*
11669	sdn 4d, V-8	2,800	2,351	
Chevy II Nova SS (wb 110.0)				
11737	htp cpe, I-6	2,740	2,430	6,700*
11837	htp cpe, V-8	2,870	2,535	16,300*
Chevelle 300 (wb 115.0)				
13111	sdn 2d, I-6	2,895	2,156	23,300*
13169	sdn 4d, I-6	2,935	2,202	
13211	sdn 2d, V-8	3,040	2,271	5,300*
13269	sdn 4d, V-8	3,080	2,308	
13311	Del sdn 2d, I-6	2,910	2,239	
13335	Del wgn 4d, I-6	3,210	2,575	
13369	Del sdn 4d, I-6	2,945	2,276	
13411	Del sdn 2d, V-8	3,060	2,345	37,600*
13435	Del wgn 4d, V-8	3,350	2,681	
13469	Del sdn 4d, V-8	3,095	2,382	
Chevelle Malibu (wb 115.0) - 241,600* built				
13517	htp cpe, I-6	2,935	2,378	—
13535	wgn 4d, I-6	3,235	2,651	—
13539	htp sdn, I-6	3,035	2,458	—
13567	conv cpe, I-6	3,030	2,588	—
13569	sdn 4d, I-6	2,960	2,352	—
13617	htp cpe, V-8	3,075	2,484	—
13635	wgn 4d, V-8	3,375	2,766	—
13639	htp sdn, V-8	3,180	2,564	—
13667	conv cpe, V-8	3,175	2,693	—
13669	sdn 4d, V-8	3,110	2,456	—
Chevelle Malibu SS, V-8 (wb 115.0) - 72,300* built				
13817	htp cpe	3,375	2,776	—
13867	conv cpe, V-8	3,470	2,984	—
Biscayne (wb 119.0)				
15311	sdn 2d, I-6	3,310	2,379	
15335	wgn 4d, I-6	3,770	2,772	83,200*
15369	sdn 4d, I-6	3,375	2,431	
15411	sdn 2d, V-8	3,445	2,484	
15435	wgn 4d, V-8	3,895	2,877	39,200*
15469	sdn 4d, V-8	3,519	2,537	
Bel Air (wb 119.0)				
15511	sdn 2d, I-6	3,315	2,479	
15535	wgn 4d, 2S, I-6	3,770	2,835	
15545	wgn 4d, 3S, I-6	3,815	2,948	72,100*
15569	sdn 4d, I-6	3,390	2,531	
15611	sdn 2d, V-8	3,445	2,584	
15635	wgn 4d, 2S, V-8	3,895	2,940	164,500*
15645	wgn 4d, 9P, V-8	3,940	3,053	
15669	sdn 4d, V-8	3,525	2,636	
Impala (wb 119.0)				
16335	wgn 4d, 2S, I-6	3,805	2,971	
16337	htp cpe, I-6	3,430	2,684	
16339	htp sdn, I-6	3,525	2,747	33,100*
16345	wgn 4d, 3S, I-6	3,860	3,083	
16367	conv cpe, I-6	3,484	2,935	
16369	sdn 4d, I-6	3,435	2,678	
16435	wgn 4d, 2S, V-8	3,990	3,076	
16437	htp cpe, V-8	3,555	2,789	
16439	htp sdn, V-8	3,650	2,852	621,800*
16445	wgn 4d, 3S, V-8	4,005	3,189	
16467	conv cpe, V-8	3,610	3,041	
16469	sdn 4d, V-8	3,565	2,783	
Impala SS (wb 119.0) - 119,314 built				
16737	htp cpe, I-6	3,460	2,842	—
16767	conv cpe, I-6	3,505	3,093	—
16837	htp cpe, V-8	3,585	2,947	—
16867	conv cpe, V-8	3,630	3,199	—

Caprice, V-8 (wb 119.0)-181,000* blt		Wght	Price	Prod
16635	wgn 4d, 2S	3,970	3,234	—
16639	htp sdn	3,675	3,063	—
16645	wgn 4d, 3S	4,020	3,347	—
16647	htp cpe	3,600	3,000	—

* Nearest 100; does not include wagons. Wagon prod: Chevy II, 21,400; Chevelle 31,900; others, 185,500. Impala SS convertible coupe, 15,872.

1966 Engines	bore×stroke	bhp	availability
I-4, 153.0	3.88×3.25	90	S-Chevy II 100
I-6, 194.0	3.56×3.25	120	S-Chevy II, Chevelle
I-6, 230.0	3.87×3.25	140	O-Chev II, Chvlle
I-6, 250.0	3.87×3.53	155	S-Chevrolet; O-Chevy II
V-8, 283.0	3.88×3.00	195	S-Chevelle, Chevrolet
V-8, 283.0	3.88×3.00	220	O-Chevrolet
V-8, 327.0	4.00×3.25	275/300	O-all
V-8, 327.0	4.00×3.25	350	O-Chev II, Chvlle
V-8, 396.0	4.09×3.76	325	S-Chvlle 396; O-Chev, Chvlle
V-8, 396.0	4.09 × 3.76	360/375	O-Chevelle
V-8, 427.0	4.25 × 3.76	390/425	O-Chevrolet

1967

Chevy II 100 (wb 110.0)		Wght	Price	Prod
11111	sdn 2d, I-4	2,555	2,090	
11169	sdn 4d, I-4	2,560	2,120	
11311	sdn 2d, I-6	2,640	2,152	34,200*
11335	wgn 4d, I-6	2,865	2,478	
11369	sdn 4d, I-6	2,650	2,182	
11411	sdn 2d, V-8	2,770	2,258	
11435	wgn 4d, V-8	2,985	2,583	1,700*
11469	sdn 4d, V-8	2,780	2,287	
Chevy II Nova (wb 110.0)				
11535	wgn 4d, I-6	2,890	2,566	
11537	htp cpe, I-6	2,660	2,330	34,400*
11569	sdn 4d I-6	2,660	2,298	
11635	wgn 4d, V-8	3,015	2,671	
11637	htp cpe, V-8	2,790	2,435	13,200*
11669	sdn 4d, V-8	2,790	2,403	
Chevy II Nova SS (wb 110.0)				
11737	htp cpe, I-6	2,690	2,487	1,900*
11837	htp cpe, V-8	2,820	2,590	8,200*
Camaro (wb 108.1) (includes 602 Z28s)				
12337	htp cpe, I-6	2,770	2,466	58,808
12367	conv cpe, I-6	3,025	2,704	
12437	htp cpe, V-8	2,920	2,572	162,109
12467	conv cpe, V-8	3,180	2,809	
Chevelle 300 (wb 115.0)				
13111	sdn 2d, I-6	2,935	2,221	19,900*
13169	sdn 4d, I-6	2,955	2,250	
13211	sdn 2d, V-8	3,070	2,326	4,800*
13269	sdn 4d, V-8	3,090	2,356	
13311	Del sdn 2d, I-6	2,955	2,295	
13335	Del wgn 4d, I-6	3,230	2,619	19,300*
13369	Del sdn 4d, I-6	2,980	2,324	
13411	Del sdn 2d, V-8	3,090	2,400	
13435	Del wgn 4d, V-8	3,360	2,725	7,000*
13469	Del sdn 4d, V-8	3,110	2,430	
Chevelle Malibu (wb 115.0)				
13517	htp cpe, I-6	2,980	2,434	
13535	wgn 4d, I-6	3,260	2,695	
13539	htp sdn, I-6	3,065	2,506	40,600*
13567	conv cpe, I-6	3,050	2,637	
13569	sdn 4d, I-6	3,000	2,400	
13617	htp cpe, V-8	3,115	2,540	
13635	wgn 4d, V-8	3,390	2,801	
13639	htp sdn, V-8	3,200	2,611	187,200*
13667	conv cpe, V-8	3,185	2,743	
13669	sdn 4d, V-8	3,130	2,506	
Chevelle Concours (wb 115.0)				
13735	wgn 4d, I-6	3,270	2,827	5,900
13835	wgn 4d, V-8	3,405	2,933	21,400
Chevelle Super Sports (wb 115.0) - 63,000* built				
13817	htp cpe	3,415	2,825	—
13867	conv cpe, V-8	3,485	3,033	—

Biscayne (wb 119.0)		Wght	Price	Prod
15311	sdn 2d, I-6	3,335	2,442	
15335	wgn 4d, I-6	3,765	2,817	54,200*
15369	sdn 4d, I-6	3,395	2,484	
15411	sdn 2d, V-8	3,465	2,547	
15435	wgn 4d, V-8	3,885	2,923	38,600*
15469	sdn 4d, V-8	3,525	2,589	
Bel Air (wb 119.0)				
15511	sdn 2d, I-6	3,340	2,542	
15535	wgn 4d, 2S, I-6	3,770	2,881	41,500*
15545	wgn 4d, 3S, I-6	3,825	2,993	
15569	sdn 4d, I-6	3,410	2,584	
15611	sdn 2d, V-8	3,470	2,647	
15635	wgn 4d, 2S, V-8	3,890	2,986	138,200*
15645	wgn 4d, 9P, V-8	3,940	3,098	
15669	sdn 4d, V-8	3,535	2,689	
Impala (wb 119.0)				
16335	wgn 4d, 2S, I-6	3,805	3,016	
16339	htp sdn, I-6	3,540	2,793	
16345	wgn 4d, 3S, I-6	3,868	3,129	
16367	conv cpe, I-6	3,515	2,991	18,800*
16369	sdn 4d, I-6	3,455	2,723	
16387	htp cpe, I-6	3,475	2,740	
16435	wgn 4d, 2S, V-8	3,920	3,122	
16439	htp sdn, V-8	3,660	2,899	
16445	wgn 4d, 3S, V-8	3,990	3,234	556,800*
16467	conv cpe, V-8	3,625	3,097	
16469	sdn 4d, V-8	3,575	2,828	
16487	htp cpe, V-8	3,590	2,845	
Impala SS (wb 119.0) - 76,055 blt (incl 2,124 SS427)				
16767	conv cpe, I-6	3,535	3,149	400*
16787	htp cpe, I-6	3,500	2,898	
16867	conv cpe, V-8	3,650	3,254	73,600*
16887	htp cpe, V-8	3,615	3,003	
Caprice, V-8 (wb 119.0) - 124,500* built				
16635	wgn 4d, 2S	3,935	3,301	—
16639	htp sdn	3,710	3,130	—
16645	wgn 4d, 3S	3,990	3,413	—
16647	htp cpe	3,605	3,078	—

* Nearest 100; does not incl wagons. Wagon prod: Chevy II 12,900; Chevelle 27,300; others 155,100. Convertible prod: Camaro 25,141; Impala SS 9,545.

1967 Engines	bore×stroke	bhp	availability
I-4, 153.0	3.88×3.25	90	S-Chev II 100 sdn
I-6, 194.0	3.56×3.25	120	S-Chevy II, Chevelle
I-6, 230.0	3.88×3.25	140	S-Camaro
I-6, 250.0	3.88×3.53	155	S-Chev exc Capr; O-others
V-8, 283.0	3.88×3.00	195	S-all exc Cam
V-8, 302.0	4.00×3.00	290	O-Cam (Z28)
V-8, 327.0	4.00×3.25	210	O-Camaro
V-8, 327.0	4.00×3.25	275	O-all
V-8, 327.0	4.00×3.25	325	O-Chevelle
V-8, 350.0	4.00×3.48	295	O-Camaro
V-8, 396.0	4.09×3.76	325	S-Chvlle 396; O-Cam, Chev
V-8, 396.0	4.09×3.76	350	O-Chvlle 396
V-8, 427.0	4.25×3.76	385	O-Chevrolet

1968

Chevy II Nova (wb 111) - 201,000* blt (incl 6,571 SS cps)		Wght	Price	Prod
11127	cpe I-4	2,760	2,222	—
11169	sdn 4d, I-4	2,790	2,252	—
11327	cpe I-6	2,860	2,284	—
11369	sdn 4d, I-6	2,890	2,314	—
11427	cpe, V-8	2,995	2,390	—
11469	sdn 4d, V-8	3,025	2,419	—
Camaro (wb 108.1) (includes 7,199 Z28s)				
12337	htp cpe, I-6	2,810	2,588	50,937
12367	conv cpe, I-6	3,110	2,802	
12437	htp cpe, V-8	2,955	2,694	184,178
12467	conv cpe, V-8	3,245	2,908	
Chevelle 300 (wb 112.0; 4d-116.0) (incl 62,785 SS)				
13127	cpe, I-6	3,020	2,341	2,900*
13135	Nomad wgn 4d, I-6	3,370	2,625	
13227	cpe, V-8	3,155	2,447	9,700*
13235	Nomad wgn 4d, V-8	3,500	2,731	

Chevelle 300		Wght	Price	Prod
13327	Del cpe, I-6	3,035	2,415	
13335	Cus Nmd wgn 4d, I-6	3,415	2,736	25,500*
13337	Del htp cpe, I-6	3,050	2,479	
13369	Del sdn 4d, I-6	3,105	2,445	
13427	Del cpe, V-8	3,170	2,521	
13435	Cus Nmd wgn 4d, V-8	3,545	2,841	17,700*
13437	Del htp cpe, V-8	3,185	2,584	
13469	Del sdn 4d, V-8	3,240	2,550	
Chevelle Malibu (wb 112.0; 4d-116.0)				
13535	wgn 4d, I-6	3,440	2,846	
13537	htp cpe, I-6	3,070	2,558	
13539	htp sdn, I-6	3,185	2,629	33,100*
13567	conv cpe, I-6	3,135	2,757	
13569	sdn 4d, I-6	3,125	2,524	
13635	wgn 4d, V-8	3,575	2,951	
13637	htp cpe, V-8	3,204	2,663	
13639	htp sdn, V-8	3,315	2,735	233,200*
13667	conv cpe, V-8	3,260	2,863	
13669	sdn 4d, V-8	3,255	2,629	
Chevelle Concours (wb 116.0)				
13735	wgn 4d, I-6	3,450	2,978	—
13835	wgn 4d, V-8	3,580	3,083	—
Chevelle SS 396 (wb 112.0)				
13837	htp cpe	3,550	2,899	60,499
13867	conv cpe	3,570	3,102	2,286
Biscayne (wb 119.0)				
15311	sdn 2d, I-6	3,400	2,581	
15335	wgn 4d, I-6	3,790	2,957	44,500*
15369	sdn 4d, I-6	3,465	2,623	
15411	sdn 2d, V-8	3,520	2,686	
15435	wgn 4d, V-8	3,900	3,062	37,600*
15469	sdn 4d, V-8	3,585	2,728	
Bel Air (wb 119.0)				
15511	sdn 2d, I-6	3,405	2,681	
15535	wgn 4d, 2S, I-6	3,800	3,020	28,800*
15545	wgn 4d, 3S, I-6	3,845	3,133	
15569	sdn 4d, I-6	3,470	2,723	
15611	sdn 2d, V-8	3,525	2,786	
15635	wgn 4d, 2S, V-8	3,910	3,125	123,400*
15645	wgn 4d, 3S, V-8	3,955	3,238	
15669	sdn 4d, V-8	3,590	2,828	
Impala (wb 119.0) - 38,210 SS blt (incl 1,778 SS427)				
16339	htp sdn, I-6	3,605	2,917	
16369	sdn 4d, I-6	3,520	2,846	11,400*
16387	htp cpe, I-6	3,250	2,863	
16435	wgn 4d, 2S, V-8	3,850	3,245	—
16439	htp sdn, V-8	3,715	3,022	—
16445	wgn 4d, 3S, V-8	3,905	3,358	—
16447	Cus htp cpe, V-8	3,645	3,021	
16467	conv cpe, V-8	3,680	3,197	699,500*
16469	sdn 4d, V-8	3,630	2,951	
16487	htp cpe, V-8	3,630	2,968	
Caprice (wb 119.0) - 115,500* built				
16635	wgn 4d, 2S	3,950	3,458	—
16639	htp sdn	3,755	3,271	—
16645	wgn 4d, 3S	4,005	3,570	—
16647	htp cpe	3,660	3,219	—

* Nearest 100; does not incl wagons. Wagon prod: Chvlle 45,500; others 175,600. Cam conv cpe 20,440.

1968 Engines	bore×stroke	bhp	availability
I-4, 153.0	3.88×3.25	90	S-Chevy II
I-6, 230.0	3.88×3.25	140	S-Chevy II, Cam, Chvlle
I-6, 250.0	3.88×3.53	155	S-Chevrolet; O-Cam, Chvlle
V-8, 302.0	4.00×3.00	290	O-Cam (Z28)
V-8, 307.0	3.88×3.25	200	S-Chevy II, Chvlle, Chev
V-8, 327.0	4.00×3.25	210	S-Camaro
V-8, 327.0	4.00×3.25	250	O-Chevelle, Chevrolet
V-8, 327.0	4.00×3.25	275	O-all
V-8, 327.0	4.00×3.25	325	O-Chevelle
V-8, 350.0	4.00×3.48	295	O-Chev II, Cam
V-8, 396.0	4.09×3.76	325	S-Chvlle 396; O-Cam, Chev
V-8, 396.0	4.00×3.00	350/375	O-Cam, Chvlle
V-8, 427.0	4.25×3.76	385/425	O-Chevrolet

1969

Chevy II Nova (wb 111.0)		Wght	Price	Prod
17,564 SS coupes built				
11127	cpe, I-4	2,785	2,237	6,100*
11169	sdn 4d, I-4	2,810	2,267	
11327	cpe I-6	2,895	2,315	10,200*
11369	sdn 4d, I-6	2,920	2,345	
11427	cpe, V-8	3,035	2,405	89,900*
11469	sdn 4d, V-8	3,065	2,434	

Camaro (wb 108.1) (includes 20,302 Z28s)				
12337	htp cpe, I-6	3,040	2,638	65,008**
12367	conv cpe, I-6	3,160	2,852	
12437	htp cpe, V-8	3,050	2,726	178,087**
12467	conv cpe, V-8	3,295	2,940	

Note: Wagon desig. "CT" refers to convent. tailgate, open from top. Most wagons had dual-action tailgates, opening from top or from side, from 1969 onward.

Chevelle Nomad (wb 116.0)				
13135	wgn 4d, CT, I-6	3,390	2,668	—
13136	wgn 4d, I-6	3,475	2,710	—
13235	wgn 4d, CT, V-8	3,515	2,758	—
13236	wgn 4d, V-8	3,600	2,800	—

Chevelle 300 Del (wb 112.0;4d-116.0)				
13327	cpe, I-6	3,035	2,458	
13337	htp cpe, I-6	3,075	2,521	11,000*
13369	sdn 4d, I-6	3,100	2,488	
13427	cpe, V-8	3,165	2,548	
13437	htp cpe, V-8	3,205	2,611	31,000*
13469	sdn 4d, V-8	3,230	2,577	

Chevelle Grnbrier (wb 116.0)				
13335	wgn 4d, CT, I-6	3,445	2,779	7,400*
13336	wgn 4d, I-6	3,530	2,821	
13435	wgn 4d, CT, V-8	3,585	2,869	
13436	wgn 4d, 2S, V-8	3,665	2,911	38,500*
13446	wgn 4d, 3S, V-8	3,740	3,020	

Chevelle Malibu (wb 112.0; 4d-116.0) (incl 86,307 SS)				
13537	htp cpe, I-6	3,095	2,601	
13539	htp sdn, I-6	3,205	2,672	23,500*
13567	conv cpe, I-6	3,175	2,800	
13569	sdn 4d, I-6	3,130	2,567	
13637	htp cpe, V-8	3,230	2,690	
13639	htp sdn, V-8	3,340	2,762	343,600*
13667	conv cpe, V-8	3,300	2,889	
13669	sdn 4d, V-8	3,265	2,657	

Chevelle Concours (wb 116.0)				
13536	wgn 4d, I-6	3,545	2,931	—
13636	wgn 4d, 2S, V-8	3,685	3,021	—
13646	wgn 4d, 3S, V-8	3,755	3,141	—
13836	del wgn 4d, 2S, V-8	3,680	3,153	—
13846	del wgn 4d, 3S, V-8	3,730	3,266	—

Biscayne (wb 119.0)				
15311	sdn 2d, I-6	3,530	2,645	
15336	Brookwd wgn 4d, I-6	4,045	3,064	27,400*
15369	sdn 4d, I-6	3,590	2,687	
15411	sdn 2d, V-8	3,670	2,751	
15436	Brookwd wgn 4d, V-8	4,170	3,169	41,300*
15469	sdn 4d, V-8	3,725	2,793	

Bel Air (wb 119.0)				
15511	sdn 2d, I-6	3,540	2,745	16,000*
15569	sdn 4d, I-6	3,590	2,787	
15611	sdn 2d, V-8	3,675	2,851	
15636	Twnsmn wgn 4d, 2S, V-8	4,175	3,232	139,700*
15646	Twnsmn wgn 4d, 3S, V-8	4,230	3,345	
15669	sdn 4d, V-8	3,725	2,893	

Impala (wb 119.0) - 2,455 SS427 built				
16337	htp cpe, I-6	3,650	2,927	
16339	htp sdn, I-6	3,735	2,981	8,700*
16369	sdn 4d, I-6	3,640	2,911	
16436	Kngswd wgn 4d, 2S, V-8	4,225	3,352	
16437	htp cpe, V-8	3,775	3,033	
16439	htp sdn, V-8	3,855	3,056	
16446	Kngswd wgn 4d, 3S, V-8	4,285	3,465	768,300*
16447	Cus htp cpe, V-8	3,800	3,085	
16467	conv cpe, V-8	3,835	3,261	
16469	sdn 4d, V-8	3,760	3,016	

Caprice, V-8 (wb 119.0) - 166,900* built				
16636	Kngswd Est wgn 4d, 2S	4,245	3,565	—
16639	htp sdn	3,895	3,346	—
16646	Kngswd Est wgn 4d, 3S	4,300	3,678	—

Caprice, V-8		Wght	Price	Prod
16647	htp cpe	3,815	3,294	—

* Nearest 100. ** Includes 1970 ext. of 1969 model. Wagon production: Chevelle 45,900; others 59,300. Camaro convertible coupe, 17,573.

1969 Engines	bore×stroke	bhp	availability
I-4, 153.0	3.88×3.25	90	S-Chevy II
I-6, 230.0	3.88×3.25	140	S-Chvlle, Chev II, Cam
I-6, 250.0	3.88×3.53	155	S-Chv; O-Chvl, Chev II, Cam
V-8, 302.0	4.00×3.00	350	O-Cam (Z28)
V-8, 307.0	3.88×3.25	200	S-Chev II, Chvlle
V-8, 327.0	4.00×3.25	210	S-Camaro
V-8, 327.0	4.00×3.25	235	S-Chevrolet
V-8, 350.0	4.00×3.48	255	O-all
V-8, 350.0	4.00×3.48	300	O-Chev, Chvlle, Nov SS, Cam SS
V-8, 396.0	4.09×3.76	265	S-Chvlle 396; O-Chevrolet
V-8, 396.0	4.09×3.76	325	O-Chvlle 396, Camaro SS
V-8, 396.0	4.09×3.76	350/375	O-Chvlle/ Nov/ Cam SS
V-8, 427.0	4.25×3.76	335-425	O-Chevrolet

Note: Station wagon engines—for wb 116 read Chevelle; for wb 119 read Chevrolet.

1970

Nova (wb 111.0) - 254,242 blt (incl 19,558 SS models)		Wght	Price	Prod
11127	htp cpe, I-4	2,820	2,335	—
11169	sdn 4d, I-4	2,843	2,365	—
11327	cpe, I-6	2,919	2,414	—
11369	sdn 4d, I-6	2,942	2,443	—
11427	cpe, V-8	3,048	2,503	—
11469	sdn 4d, V-8	3,071	2,533	—

Camaro (wb 108.1) (includes 8,733 Z28s)				
12387	spt cpe, I-6	3,076	2,749	12,566
12487	spt cpe, V-8	3,190	2,839	112,323

Chevelle (wb 112.0; 4d-116.0) - 354,855 blt (incl Malibu)				
13337	htp cpe, I-6	3,142	2,620	—
13369	sdn 4d, I-6	3,196	2,585	—
13437	htp cpe, V-8	3,260	2,710	—
13469	sdn 4d, V-8	3,312	2,679	—

Chev Malibu (wb 112.0; 4d 116.0) (53,599 SS; 3,733 w/454 V-8)				
13537	htp cpe, I-6	3,197	2,719	—
13539	htp sdn, I-6	3,302	2,790	—
13567	conv cpe, I-6	3,243	2,919	—
13569	sdn 4d, I-6	3,221	2,685	—
13637	htp cpe, V-8	3,307	2,809	—
13639	htp sdn, V-8	3,409	2,881	—
13667	conv cpe, V-8	3,352	3,009	—
13669	sdn 4d, V-8	3,330	2,775	—

Station Wagon (wb 116.0)				
13136	Nomad 4d, 2S, I-6	3,615	2,835	—
13236	Nomad 4d, 2S, V-8	3,718	2,925	—
13336	Greenbrier 4d, 2S, I-6	3,644	2,946	—
13436	Greenbrier 4d, 2S, V-8	3,748	3,100	—
13446	Greenbrier 4d, 3S, V-8	3,794	3,213	—
13536	Concours 4d, 2S, I-6	3,687	3,056	—
13636	Concours 4d, 2S, V-8	3,794	3,210	—
13646	Concours 4d, 3S, V-8	3,836	3,323	—
13836	Cncurs del wgn 4d, 2S, V-8	3,821	3,342	—
13846	Cncurs del wgn 4d, 3S, V-8	3,880	3,455	—

Biscayne (wb 119.0)				
15369	sdn 4d, I-6	3,600	2,787	12,300*
15469	sdn 4d, V-8	3,759	2,898	23,100*

Bel Air (wb 119.0)				
15569	sdn 4d, I-6	3,604	2,887	9,000*
15669	sdn 4d, V-8	3,763	2,998	66,800*

Impala (wb 119.0) - 495,909 built exc 16467				
16337	htp cpe, I-6	3,641	3,038	—
16369	sdn 4d, I-6	3,655	3,021	—
16437	htp cpe, V-8	3,788	3,149	—
16439	htp sdn, V-8	3,871	3,203	—
16447	Cus htp cpe, V-8	3,801	3,266	—
16467	conv cpe, V-8	3,843	3,377	9,562
16469	sdn 4d, V-8	3,802	3,132	—

Caprice (wb 119.0) - 92,000* built				
16639	htp sdn	3,905	3,527	—
16647	htp cpe	3,821	3,474	—

Monte Carlo (wb 116.0) (incl 3,823 w/SS454 pkg.)				
13857	htp cpe	3,460	3,123	145,976

Station Wagon (wb 119.0)				
15436	Brookwood 4d, 2S	4,204	3,294	—
15636	Townsman 4d, 2S	4,208	3,357	—
15646	Townsman 4d, 3S	4,263	3,469	—
16436	Kingswood 4d, 2S	4,269	3,477	—
16446	Kingswood 4d, 3S	4,329	3,589	—
16636	Kingswd del 4d, 2S	4,295	3,753	—
16646	Kingswd del 4d, 3S	4,361	3,886	—

* Nearest 100; does not include wagons.

1970 Engines	bore×stroke	bhp	availability
I-4, 153.0	3.88×3.25	90	S-Nova
I-6, 230.0	3.88×3.25	140	S-Cam; O-Nov
I-6, 250.0	3.88×3.53	155	S-Chev exc Caprice & Imp cpe, Chevelle; O-Nova, Cam
V-8, 307.0	3.88×3.25	200	S-Nova, Cam; O-Chevelle
V-8, 350.0	4.00×3.48	250	S-Chev, MC; O-others
V-8, 350.0	4.00×3.48	300	O-Chev, MC; Chvlle, Cam, Nova SS
V-8, 350.0	4.00×3.48	360	O-Cam (Z28)
V-8, 402.0*	4.13×3.76	375	O-Cam, Chvlle
V-8, 402.0*	4.13×3.76	350	O-Cam, Chvlle
V-8, 400.0	4.12×3.75	265	O-Chev, MC
V-8, 400.0	4.12×3.75	330	O-MC, Chvlle
V-8, 454.0	4.25×4.00	345	O-Chevrolet
V-8, 454.0	4.25×4.00	360	O-Monte Carlo
V-8, 454.0	4.25×4.00	390	O-Chevrolet

Note: Station Wagon engines—for wb 116 read Chevelle; for wb 119 read Chevrolet.

* Commonly known as "396," actual displacement 402 cid.

1971

Vega (wb 97.0)		Wght	Price	Prod
14111	sdn 2d	2,146	2,090	58,804
14177	htchbk cpe 2d	2,190	2,196	168,308
14115	Kammback wgn 2d	2,230	2,328	42,793

Nova (wb 111.0)				
11327	cpe I-6	2,952	2,376	65,891
11369	sdn 4d I-6	2,976	2,405	29,037
11427	cpe V-8	3,084	2,471	77,344
11469	sdn 4d V-8	3,108	2,501	22,606

Camaro (wb 108.1; incl. 4,862 Z28s)				
12387	spt cpe I-6	3,094	2,921	11,178
12487	spt cpe V-8	3,218	3,016	103,452

Chevelle (wb 112.0; 4d-116.0) (incl 19,293 SS454s)				
11337	htp cpe I-6	3,166	2,712	6,660
11369	sdn 4d I-6	3,210	2,677	6,621
13437	htp cpe V-8	3,296	2,807	17,117
13469	sdn 4d V-8	3,338	2,773	9,042
13537	Malibu htp cpe I-6	3,212	2,885	6,220
13569	Malibu sdn 4d I-6	3,250	2,851	4,241
13637	Malibu htp cpe V-8	3,342	2,980	180,117
13639	Malibu htp sdn V-8	3,450	3,052	20,775
13667	Malibu conv V-8	3,390	3,260	5,089
13669	Malibu sdn 4d V-8	3,380	2,947	37,385

Chevelle Wagon (wb 116.0)				
13136	Nomad 4d 2S I-6	3,632	2,997	2,801
13236	Nomad 4d 2S V-8	3,746	3,097	6,528
13436	Greenbrier 4d 2S V-8	3,820	3,228	6,128
13446	Greenbrier 4d 3S V-8	3,882	3,340	2,129
13636	Concours 4d 2S V-8	3,864	3,337	12,716
13646	Concours 4d 3S V-8	3,908	3,450	4,276
13836	Cncrs Est 4d 2S V-8	3,892	3,514	4,502
13846	Cncrs Est 4d 3S V-8	3,944	3,626	3,219

Biscayne (wb 121.5)				
15369	sdn 4d I-6	3,732	3,096	5,846
15469	sdn 4d V-8	3,888	3,448	16,463

Bel Air (wb 121.5)				
15569	sdn 4d I-6	3,732	3,233	3,452
15669	sdn 4d V-8	3,888	3,585	38,534

Impala (wb 121.5)		Wght	Price	Prod
16357	htp cpe I-6	3,742	3,408	939
16369	sdn 4d I-6	3,760	3,391	1,606
16439	htp sdn V-8	3,978	3,813	140,300
16447	Custom htp cpe V-8	3,912	3,826	139,437
16457	htp cpe V-8	3,896	3,759	52,952
16467	conv V-8	3,960	4,021	4,576
16469	sdn 4d V-8	3,914	3,742	135,334
Caprice (wb 121.5)				
16639	htp sdn 4d	4,040	4,134	64,093
16647	htp cpe	3,964	4,081	46,404
Monte Carlo (wb 116.0) (incl 1,919 w/SS454 pkg.)				
13857	htp cpe	3,488	3,416	128,600
Chevrolet Wagon (wb 125.0)				
15435	Brookwood 4d 2S	4,542	3,929	5,314
15635	Townsman 4d 2S	4,544	4,020	12,951
15645	Townsman 4d 3S	4,598	4,135	6,870
16435	Kingswood 4d 2S	4,588	4,112	26,638
16445	Kingswood 4d 3S	4,648	4,227	32,311
16635	Kingswood Est 4d 2S	4,678	4,384	11,913
16645	Kingswood Est 4d 3S	4,738	4,498	19,010

1971 Engines	bore×stroke	bhp	availability
I-4, 140.0	3.50×3.63	90	S-Vega
I-4, 140.0	3.50×3.63	110	O-Vega
I-6, 250.0	3.88×3.53	145	S-Nova, Chevl, Cam, Chev
V-8, 307.0	3.88×3.25	200	S-Nova, Chvlle, Cam
V-8, 350.0	4.00×3.48	245	S-MC, Chev exc K/Est & Cap; O-Nov, Chvlle, Camaro
V-8, 350.0	4.00×3.48	270	O-Chevelle, Cam, MC, Chev
V-8, 350.0	4.00×3.48	330	O-Cam (Z28)
V-8, 400.0	4.12×3.75	255	S-Chev K/Est & Cap; O-Chev
V-8, 402.0*	4.13×3.76	300	O-Chevelle, Cam, MC, Chev
V-8, 454.0	4.25×4.00	365	O-Chvlle, MC, Chevrolet
V-8, 454.0	4.25×4.00	425	O-Chvlle, MC

Note: "Chev" for 1971-80 means full-size Chevrolets, incl Biscayne, Bel Air, Impala, Caprice, and full-size (125-in. wb) wagons.

* Commonly known as "396," actual displacement 402 cid.

1972

Vega (wb 97.0)		Wght	Price	Prod
1V11	sdn 2d	2,158	2,060	55,839
1V15	wgn 2d	2,333	2,285	71,957
1V77	htchbk cpe 2d	2,294	2,160	262,682
Nova (wb 111.0)				
1X27	cpe I-6	2,949	2,351	96,740
1X27	cpe V-8	3,083	2,441	163,475
1X69	sdn 4d I-6	2,982	2,379	43,029
1X69	sdn 4d V-8	3,116	2,469	46,489
Camaro (wb 108.1; includes 2,575 Z28s)				
1Q87	spt cpe I-6	3,121	2,730	4,824
1Q87	spt cpe V-8	3,248	2,820	63,832
Chevelle (wb 112.0;4d-116.0)				
1C37	htp cpe I-6	3,172	2,669	6,993
1C37	htp cpe V-8	3,300	2,759	22,714
1C69	sdn 4d I-6	3,204	2,636	6,764
1C69	sdn 4d V-8	3,332	2,726	12,881
1D37	Malibu htp cpe I-6	3,194	2,833	4,790
1D37	Malibu htp cpe V-8	3,327	2,923	207,598
1D39	Malibu htp sdn V-8	3,438	2,991	24,192
1D67	Malibu conv V-8	3,379	3,187	4,853
1D69	Malibu sdn 4d I-6	3,240	2,801	3,562
1D69	Malibu sdn 4d V-8	3,371	2,891	45,013
Chevelle Wagon (wb 116.0)				
1B36	Nomad 4d 2S I-6	3,605	2,926	2,956
1B36	Nomad 4d 2S V-8	3,732	3,016	7,768
1C36	Greenbrier 4d 2S V-8	3,814	3,140	6,975
1C46	Greenbrier 4d 3S V-8	3,870	3,247	2,370
1D36	Concours 4d 2S V-8	3,857	3,244	17,968
1D46	Concours 4d 3S V-8	3,909	3,351	6,560
1H36	Cncrs Est 4d 2S V-8	3,887	3,431	5,331
1H46	Cncrs Est 4d 3S V-8	3,943	3,538	4,407

Chevrolet (wb 122.0)		Wght	Price	Prod
1K69	Biscayne sdn 4d I-6	3,857	3,074	1,504
1K59	Biscayne sdn 4d V-8	4,045	3,408	19,034
1L69	Bel Air sdn 4d I-6	3,854	3,204	868
1L69	Bel Air sdn 4d V-8	4,042	3,538	41,020
1M39	Impala htp sdn V-8	4,150	3,771	170,304
1M47	Imp Cus htp cpe V-8	4,053	3,787	183,493
1M57	Impala htp cpe I-6	3,864	3,385	289
1M57	Impala htp cpe V-8	4,049	3,720	52,403
1M67	Impala conv V-8	4,125	3,979	6,456
1M69	Impala sdn 4d I-6	3,928	3,369	1,235
1M69	Impala sdn 4d V-8	4,113	3,708	183,361
1N39	Caprice htp sdn V-8	4,203	4,076	78,768
1N47	Caprice htp cpe V-8	4,102	4,026	65,513
1N69	Caprice sdn 4d	4,166	4,009	34,174
Chevrolet Station Wagon (wb 125.0)				
1K35	Brookwood 4d 2S	4,686	3,882	8,150
1L35	Townsman 4d 2S	4,687	3,969	16,482
1L45	Townsman 4d 3S	4,769	4,078	8,667
1M35	Kingswood 4d 2S	4,734	4,056	43,152
1M45	Kingswood 4d 3S	4,817	4,165	40,248
1N35	Kingswood Est 4d 2S	4,798	4,314	20,281
1N45	Kingswood Est 4d 3S	4,883	4,423	34,723
Monte Carlo (wb 116.0)				
1H57	htp cpe V-8	3,506	3,362	180,819

1972 Engines	bore×stroke	bhp	availability
I-4, 140.0	3.50×3.63	80	S-Vega
I-4, 140.0	3.50×3.63	90	O-Vega
I-6, 250.0	3.88×3.53	110	S-Nov, Chvlle, Cam, Chev exc Cap & K/Est
V-8, 307.0	3.88×3.25	130	S-Nova, Chvlle & Cam exc Cal
V-8, 350.0	4.00×3.48	165	S-Chvlle & Cam in Calif. O-Nov, Chvlle, Chevrolet
V-8, 350.0	4.00×3.48	175	O-Chvlle, MC
V-8, 350.0	4.00×3.48	200	O-Cam, Chev
V-8, 350.0	4.00×3.48	255	O-Cam (Z28)
V-8, 400.0	4.12×3.75	170	S-Chev Cap & K/Est; O-Chev
V-8, 402.0	4.13×3.76	210	O-Chevrolet
V-8, 402.0	4.13×3.76	240	O-Chvlle, Cam, MC
V-8, 454.0	4.25×4.00	270	O-Chvlle, MC, Chevrolet

1973

Vega (wb 97.0)		Wght	Price	Prod
V11	sdn 2d	2,219	2,087	58,425
V15	wgn 2d	2,317	2,323	102,751
V77	htchbk cpe 2d	2,313	2,192	266,124
Nova (wb 111.0)				
X17	htchbk cpe 2d I-6	3,145	2,528	11,005
X17	htchbk cpe 2d V-8	3,274	2,618	33,949
X27	cpe I-6	3,033	2,377	54,140
X27	cpe V-8	3,162	2,467	81,679
X69	sdn 4d I-6	3,065	2,407	27,440
X69	sdn 4d V-8	3,194	2,497	32,843
Y17	Cus htchbk cpe 2d I-6	3,152	2,701	3,172
Y17	Cus htchbk cpe 2d V-8	3,281	2,792	42,886
Y27	Custom cpe I-6	3,073	2,551	6,336
Y27	Custom cpe V-8	3,202	2,741	52,042
Y69	Custom sdn 4d I-6	3,105	2,580	4,344
Y69	Custom sdn 4d V-8	3,234	2,671	19,673
Camaro (wb 108.1; incl. 11,574 Z28s)				
Q87	spt cpe I-6	3,119	2,781	3,614
Q87	spt cpe V-8	3,238	2,872	60,810
S87	Type LT spt cpe V-8	3,349	3,268	32,327
Chevelle (wb 112.0; 4d-116.0)				
C29	DeLx Clnde sdn 4d I-6	3,435	2,719	5,253
C29	DeLx Clnde sdn 4d V-8	3,585	2,835	15,502
C37	DeLx Colnde cpe I-6	3,423	2,743	6,332
C37	DeLx Colnde cpe V-8	3,580	2,860	15,045
D29	Malib Clnde sdn 4d I-6	3,477	2,871	2,536
D29	Malib Clnde sdn 4d V-8	3,627	2,987	58,143
D37	Malib Colnde cpe I-6	3,430	2,894	3,157
D37	Malib Colnde cpe V-8	3,580	3,010	165,627
E29	Lgna Clnde sdn 4d V-8	3,627	3,179	13,095
E37	Lgna Clnde cpe V-8	3,678	3,203	42,941

Chevelle Wagon (wb 116.0)		Wght	Price	Prod
C35	DeLuxe 4d 2S I-6	3,849	3,106	1,870
C35	DeLuxe 4d 3S V-8	4,054	3,331	1,316
C37	DeLuxe 4d 2S V-8	4,006	3,198	7,754
D37	Malibu 4d 3S V-8	4,075	3,423	5,961
D35	Malibu 4d 2S V-8	4,027	3,290	18,592
G35	Malibu Est 4d 3S V-8	4,080	3,608	4,099
G35	Malibu Est 4d 2S V-8	4,032	3,475	5,527
E35	Laguna 4d 3S V-8	4,158	3,616	2,200
E35	Laguna 4d 2S V-8	4,110	3,483	4,419
H35	Laguna Est 4d 3S V-8	4,189	3,795	3,709
H35	Laguna Est 4d 2S V-8	4,141	3,662	3,661
Chevrolet (wb 121.5)				
K69	Bel Air sdn 4d I-6	3,895	3,247	1,394
K69	Bel Air sdn 4d V-8	4,087	3,595	40,438
L39	Impala htp sdn V-8	4,162	3,822	139,143
L47	Impala Cus cpe V-8	4,110	3,836	176,824
L57	Impala cpe V-8	4,096	3,769	42,979
L69	Impala sdn 4d	4,138	3,752	190,536
N39	Cap Clsic htp sdn V-8	4,208	4,134	70,155
N47	Cap Clsic htp cpe V-8	4,103	4,082	77,134
N67	Cap Clsic conv cpe V-8	4,191	4,345	7,339
N69	Cap Clsic sdn 4d V-8	4,176	4,064	58,126
Chevrolet Station Wagon (wb 125.0)				
K47	Bel Air 4d 3S	4,770	4,136	6,321
K35	Bel Air 4d 2S	4,717	4,022	14,549
L35	Impala 4d 2S	4,742	4,119	46,940
L45	Impala 4d 3S	4,807	4,233	43,664
N35	Caprice Estate 4d 2S	4,779	4,382	22,969
N45	Caprice Estate 4d 3S	4,858	4,496	39,535
Monte Carlo (wb 116.0)				
H57	spt cpe	3,713	3,415	4,960
H57	S spt cpe	3,720	3,562	177,963
H57	Landau spt cpe	3,722	3,806	107,770

1973 Engines	bore×stroke	bhp	availability
I-4, 140.0	3.50×3.63	72	S-Vega
I-4, 140.0	3.50×3.63	85	O-Vega
I-6, 250.0	3.88×3.53	100	S-Nov, Chvlle, Cam exc LT, Chevrolet
V-8, 307.0	3.88×3.25	115	S-Nova, Chvlle exc Lag, Cam exc LT
V-8, 350.0	4.00×3.48	145	S-Lag, CamLT, MC, Chev exc Caprice; O-Nova, Chvlle exc Lag, Cam exc LT, Chev exc Caprice
V-8, 350.0	4.00×3.48	175	O-Nov, Chvlle, Camaro, MC
V-8, 350.0	4.00×3.48	245	O-Cam (Z28)
V-8, 400.0	4.12×3.75	150	O-Chevrolet
V-8, 454.0	4.25×4.00	215	O-Caprice
V-8, 454.0	4.25×4.00	245	O-Chvlle, MC, Caprice

1974

Vega (wb 97.0)		Wght	Price	Prod
V11	sdn 2d	2,369	2,505	58,724
V11	LX sdn 2d	—	2,833	5,996
V15	wgn 2d 2S	2,514	2,748	88,248
V15	Estate wgn 2d 2S	—	2,976	27,089
V77	hatchback cpe	—	—	276,028
Nova (wb 111.0)				
X17	htchbk cpe I-6	3,260	2,935	13,722
X17	htckbk cpe V-8	3,398	3,034	20,627
X27	cpe I-6	3,150	2,811	87,399
X27	cpe V-8	3,288	2,919	72,558
X69	sdn 4d I-6	3,192	2,841	42,105
X69	sdn 4d V-8	3,330	2,949	32,017
Y17	Cus htchbk cpe I-6	3,299	3,108	9,631
Y17	Cus htchbk cpe V-8	3,437	3,217	36,653
Y27	Custom cpe I-6	3,206	2,985	11,115
Y27	Custom cpe V-8	3,344	3,093	39,912
Y69	Custom sdn 4d I-6	3,233	3,014	7,458
Y69	Custom sdn 4d V-8	3,371	3,123	17,340
Camaro (wb 108.1; incl 13,802 Z28s)				
Q87	spt cpe I-6	3,309	3,162	22,210

Camaro		Wght	Price	Prod
Q87	spt cpe V-8	3,450	3,366	79,835
S87	Type LT spt cpe V-8	3,566	3,713	48,963
Chevelle (wb 112.0; 4d-116.0)				
C29	Malib sdn Clnde 4d I-6	3,638	3,049	11,399
C29	Malib sdn Clnde 4d V-8	3,788	3,340	26,841
C37	Malib Clnde cpe I-6	3,573	3,054	15,790
C37	Malib Clnde cpe V-8	3,723	3,345	37,583
D29	Malib Classic Col I-6	3,695	3,304	4,457
D29	Malib Classic Col V-8	3,845	3,595	51,468
D37	Malib Classic Col I-6	3,609	3,307	4,132
D37	Malib Classic Col V-8	3,759	3,598	116,962
D37	Malib Clsic lan cpe I-6	—	3,518	351
D37	Malib Clsic lan cpe V-8	3,911	3,800	27,490
E37	Lag S3 Clnde cpe V-8	3,951	3,723	21,902
Chevelle Wagon (wb 116.0) (all V-8)				
C35	Malibu 4d 3S	4,223	3,834	2,583
C37	Malibu 4d 2S	4,191	3,701	12,408
D35	Malibu Classic 4d 3S	4,315	4,251	4,909
D35	Malibu Classic 4d 2S	4,283	4,118	13,986
G35	Malib Clsic Est 4d 3S	4,338	4,424	4,742
G35	Malib Clsic Est 4d 2S	4,306	4,291	5,480
Chevrolet (wb 121.5)				
K69	Bel Air sdn 4d	4,148	3,960	24,778
L39	Impala spt sdn 4d	4,256	4,215	76,492
L47	Impala Custom cpe	4,169	4,229	98,062
L57	Impala spt cpe	4,167	4,162	50,036
L69	Impala sdn 4d	4,205	4,135	133,164
N39	Cap Clsic spt sdn 4d	4,344	4,534	48,387
N47	Cap Classic Cus cpe	4,245	4,483	59,484
N67	Cap Classic conv cpe	4,308	4,745	4,670
N69	Cap Classic sdn 4d	4,294	4,465	43,367
Chevrolet Wagon (wb 125.0)				
K35	Bel Air 4d 2S	4,829	4,464	6,437
K45	Bel Air 4d 3S	4,884	4,578	2,913
L35	Impala 4d 2S	4,891	4,561	23,455
L45	Impala 4d 3S	4,936	4,675	23,259
N35	Caprice Estate 4d 2S	4,960	4,800	12,280
N45	Caprice Estate 4d 3S	5,004	4,914	23,063
Monte Carlo (wb 116.0)				
H57	S spt cpe	3,926	3,885	184,873
H57	Landau spt cpe	3,928	4,129	127,344

1974 Engines	bore×stroke	bhp	availability
I-4, 140.0	3.50×3.63	75	S-Vega
I-4, 140.0	3.50×3.63	85	O-Vega
I-6, 250.0	3.88×3.53	100	S-Nov, Chvlle, Camaro
V-8, 350.0	4.00×3.48	145	S-Nov, Chvlle, Camaro, MC, Chev exc Cap
V-8, 350.0	4.00×3.48	160	O-as above
V-8, 350.0	4.00×3.48	185	O-Nova, Cam
V-8, 350.0	4.00×3.48	245	O-Cam (Z28)
V-8, 400.0	4.12×3.75	150	S-Cap exc wgns
V-8, 400.0	4.12×3.75	180	S-wagons; O-Chvlle, MC
V-8, 454.0	4.25×4.00	235	O-Chevelle, MC, Caprice

1975

Vega (wb 97.0)		Wght	Price	Prod
V11	sdn 2d	2,415	2,786	33,878
V11	LX sdn 2d	—	3,119	1,255
V15	wgn 2d 2S	2,531	3,016	47,474
V15	Estate wgn 2d 2S	2,541	3,244	8,659
V77	htchbk cpe	2,478	2,899	112,912
V77	Cosworth htchbk cpe	2,173	5,916	2,061
Monza (wb 97.0)				
M27	Towne cpe	2,675	3,570	69,238
R07	S htchbk cpe	—	3,648	9,795
R07	2+2 htchbk cpe	2,753	3,953	57,170
Nova (wb 111.0)				
X17	htchbk cpe I-6	3,391	3,347	7,952
X17	htchbk cpe V-8	3,493	3,422	8,421
X27	cpe I-6	3,276	3,205	48,103
X27	S cpe I-6	—	3,099	16,655
X27	cpe V-8	3,378	3,280	33,921
X27	S cpe V-8	—	3,174	5,070
X69	sdn 4d I-6	3,306	3,209	43,760
X69	sdn 4d V-8	3,408	3,284	22,587

Nova		Wght	Price	Prod
Y17	Cus htckbk cpe I-6	3,421	3,541	3,812
Y17	Cus htchbk cpe V-8	3,523	3,616	11,438
Y27	Custom cpe I-6	3,335	3,402	7,214
Y27	LN Cpe I-6	—	3,782	1,138
Y27	Custom cpe V-8	3,437	3,477	19,074
Y27	LN cpe V-8	—	3,857	11,395
Y69	Custom sdn 4d I-6	3,367	3,415	8,959
Y69	LN sdn 4d I-6	—	3,795	1,286
Y69	Custom sdn 4d V-8	3,469	3,490	13,221
Y69	LN sdn 4d V-8	—	3,870	8,976
Camaro (wb 108.1)				
Q87	spt cpe I-6	3,421	3,540	29,749
Q87	spt cpe V-8	3,532	3,685	76,178
S87	Type LT spt cpe V-8	3,616	4,057	39,843
Chevelle (wb 112.0; 4d-116.0)				
C29	Malibu sdn 4d I-6	3,713	3,402	12,873
C29	Malibu sdn 4d V-8	3,833	3,652	24,989
C37	Malibu cpe I-6	3,642	3,407	13,292
C37	Malibu cpe V-8	3,762	3,657	23,708
D29	Malib Clsic sdn 4d I-6	3,778	3,695	1
D29	Malib Clsic sdn 4d V-8	3,898	3,945	51,070
D37	Malib Classic cpe I-6	3,681	3,698	4,330
D37	Malib Classic cpe V-8	3,801	3,948	76,607
D37	Malib Clsic Lan cpe I-6	—	3,930	378
D37	Malib Clsic Lan cpe V-8	3,903	4,180	22,691
E37	Laguna S3 cpe V-8	3,908	4,113	7,788
Chevelle Malibu Wagon (wb 116.0)				
C35	4d 3S	4,237	4,463	2,377
C35	4d 2S	4,207	4,318	11,600
D36	Classic 4d 3S	4,305	4,701	6,394
D36	Classic 4d 2S	4,275	4,556	15,974
G35	Classic Estate 4d 3S	4,331	4,893	4,600
G35	Classic Estate 4d 2S	4,301	4,748	4,637
Chevrolet (wb 121.5)				
K69	Bel Air sdn 4d	4,179	4,345	15,871
L39	Impala spt sdn 4d	4,265	4,631	47,125
L47	Impala Custom cpe	4,190	4,626	49,455
L47	Impala Landau cpe	—	4,901	2,465
L57	Impala spt cpe	4,207	4,575	21,333
L69	Impala sdn 4d	4,218	4,548	91,330
N39	Cap Clsic spt sdn 4d	4,360	4,891	40,482
N47	Cap Clsic cpe	4,275	4,837	36,041
N47	Cap Clsic Lan cpe	—	5,075	3,752
N67	Cap Clsic conv cpe	4,343	5,113	8,349
N69	Cap Clsic sdn 4d	4,311	4,819	33,715
Chevrolet Wagon (wb 125.0)				
K35	Bel Air 4d 2S	4,856	4,878	4,032
K45	Bel Air 4d 3S	4,913	4,998	2,386
L35	Impala 4d 2S	4,910	5,001	17,998
L45	Impala 4d 3S	4,959	5,121	19,445
N35	Caprice Estate 4d 2S	4,978	5,231	9,047
N45	Caprice Estate 4d 3S	5,036	5,351	18,858
Monte Carlo (wb 116.0)				
H57	S spt cpe	3,927	4,249	148,529
H57	Landau spt cpe	3,930	4,519	110,380

1975 Engines	bore×stroke	bhp	availability
I-4, 122.0	3.50×3.16	111	S-Cos Vega
I-4, 140.0	3.50×3.63	78	S-Vega, Monza exc 2+2
I-4, 140.0	3.50×3.63	87	S-Monza 2+2; O-Vega
I-6, 250.0	3.88×3.53	105	S-Nov, Chvlle, Camaro
V-8, 262.0	3.67×3.10	110	O-Nov, Monza
V-8, 350.0	4.00×3.48	125	O-Monza
V-8, 350.0	4.00×3.48	145	S-Nov, Chvlle, Camaro, Monte Carlo, Chev exc wgns
V-8, 350.0	4.00×3.48	155	O-Nov, Chvlle, Camaro, MC, Chevrolet
V-8, 400.0	4.12×3.75	175	S-Chevrolet wagons; O-Chvlle, MC, Chevrolet
V-8, 454.0	4.25×4.00	235	O-Chevlle, Monte Carlo, Chevrolet

1976

Chevette (wb 94.3)		Wght	Price	Prod
B08	htchbk sdn 2d	1,927	3,098	178,007
J08	Scooter htchbk sdn 2d	1,870	2,899	9,810
Vega (wb 97.0)				
V11	sdn 2d	2,443	2,984	27,619
V15	wgn 2d 2S	2,578	3,227	46,114
V15	Estate wgn 2d 2S	—	3,450	7,935
V77	htchbk cpe	2,534	3,099	77,409
V77	Cos htchbk cpe 2d	—	6,066	1,447
Monza (wb 97.0)				
M27	Towne cpe	2,625	3,359	46,735
R07	2+2 htchbk cpe	2,668	3,727	34,170
Nova (wb 111.0)				
X17	htchbk cpe I-6	3,391	3,417	10,853
X17	htchbk cpe V-8	3,475	3,579	7,866
X27	cpe I-6	3,188	3,248	87,438
X27	cpe V-8	3,272	3,413	44,421
X69	sdn 4d I-6	3,221	3,283	86,600
X69	sdn 4d V-8	3,305	3,448	37,167
Y17	Cncrs htchbk cpe I-6	3,401	3,972	2,088
Y17	Cncrs htchbk cpe V-8	3,485	4,134	5,486
Y27	Concours cpe I-6	3,324	3,795	6,568
Y27	Concours cpe V-8	3,408	3,960	15,730
Y69	Concours sdn 4d I-6	3,367	3,830	10,151
Y69	Concours sdn 4d V-8	3,451	3,995	20,360
Camaro (wb 108.1)				
Q87	spt cpe I-6	3,421	3,762	38,047
Q87	spt cpe V-8	3,511	3,927	92,491
S87	Type LT spt cpe V-8	3,576	4,320	52,421
Chevelle (wb 112.0; 4d-116.0)				
C29	Malibu sdn 4d I-6	3,729	3,671	13,116
C29	Malibu sdn 4d V-8	3,834	4,201	25,353
C37	Malibu cpe I-6	3,650	3,636	12,616
C37	Malibu cpe V-8	3,755	4,166	17,976
D29	Malib Clsic sdn 4d I-6	3,827	4,196	4,253
D29	Malib Clsic sdn 4d V-8	3,932	4,490	73,307
D37	Malib Clsic cpe I-6	3,688	3,926	5,791
D37	Malib Clsic cpe V-8	3,793	4,455	76,843
D37	Malib Clsic Lan cpe I-6	—	4,124	672
D37	Malib Clsic Lan cpe V-8	—	4,640	29,495
E37	Laguna S3 cpe V-8	3,978	4,621	9,100
Chevelle Malibu Wagon (wb 116.0)				
C35	4d 3S	4,268	4,686	2,984
C35	4d 2S	4,238	4,543	13,581
D35	Classic 4d 3S	4,330	4,919	11,617
D35	Classic 4d 2S	4,300	4,776	24,635
G35	Malib Clsic Est 4d 3S	4,356	5,114	6,386
G35	Malib Clsic Est 4d 2S	4,326	4,971	5,518
Chevrolet (wb 121.5)				
L39	Impala spt sdn 4d	4,245	4,798	39,849
L47	Impala Custom cpe	4,175	4,763	43,219
L47	Impala Landau cpe	—	5,058	10,841
L69	Impala S spt sdn 4d	—	4,507	18,265
L69	Impala sdn 4d	4,222	4,706	86,057
N39	Cap Clsic spt sdn 4d	4,314	5,078	55,308
N47	Caprice Classic cpe	4,244	5,043	28,161
N47	Cap Clsic Lan cpe	—	5,284	21,926
N69	Cap Clsic sdn 4d	4,285	5,013	47,411
Chevrolet Wagon (wb 125.0)				
L35	Impala 4d 2S	4,912	5,166	19,657
L45	Impala 4d 3S	4,972	5,283	21,329
N35	Caprice Estate 4d 2S	4,948	5,429	10,029
N45	Caprice Estate 4d 3S	5,007	5,546	21,804
Monte Carlo (wb 116.0)				
H57	S spt cpe	3,907	4,673	191,370
H57	Landau spt cpe	—	4,966	161,902

1976 Engines	bore×stroke	bhp	availability
I-4, 85.0	3.23×2.61	52	S-Chevette
I-4, 97.6	3.23×2.98	60	O-Chevette
I-4, 122.0	3.50×3.15	111	S-Cos Vega
I-4, 140.0	3.50×3.63	70	S-Vega, Monza
I-4, 140.0	3.50×3.63	84	O-Vega, Monza
I-6, 250.0	3.88×3.53	105	S-Nov, Chvlle, Camaro
V-8, 262.0	3.67×3.10	110	O-Monza
V-8, 305.0	3.74×3.48	140	S-Nov, Chvlle, Camaro, MC; O-Monza

1976 Engines	bore×stroke	bhp	availability
V-8, 305.0	3.74×3.48	145	S-Chvlle wgn, Chev; O-MC
V-8, 350.0	4.00×3.48	165	O-Nov, Chvlle, Camaro, MC, Chevrolet
V-8, 400.0	4.12×3.75	175	S-Chev wgn; O-Chvlle, MC, Chevrolet
V-8, 454.0	4.25×4.00	225	O-Chevrolet

1977

Chevette (wb 94.3)		Wght	Price	Prod
B08	htchbk sdn 2d	1,958	3,225	120,278
J08	Scooter htchbk sdn 2d	1,898	2,999	13,191

Vega (wb 97.0)				
V11	sdn 2d	2,459	3,249	12,365
V15	wgn 2d 2S	2,571	3,522	25,181
V15	Estate wgn 2d 2S	—	3,745	3,461
V77	htchbk cpe	2,522	3,359	37,395

Monza (wb 97.0)				
M27	Town cpe	2,580	3,560	34,133
R07	2+2 htchbk cpe	2,671	3,840	39,215

Nova (wb 111.0)				
X17	htchbk cpe I-6	3,217	3,646	18,048
X17	htchbk cpe V-8	3,335	3,766	
X27	cpe I-6	3,139	3,482	132,833
X27	cpe V-8	3,257	3,602	
X69	sdn 4d I-6	3,174	3,532	141,028
X69	sdn 4d V-8	3,292	3,652	
Y17	Cncrs htchbk cpe I-6	3,378	4,154	5,481
Y17	Cncrs htchbk cpe V-8	3,486	4,274	
Y27	Concours cpe I-6	3,283	3,991	28,602
Y27	Concours cpe V-8	3,391	4,111	
Y69	Concours sdn 4d I-6	3,329	4,066	39,272
Y69	Concours sdn 4d V-8	3,437	4,186	

Camaro (wb 108.1)				
Q87	spt cpe	3,369	4,113	131,717
S87	Type LT spt cpe	3,422	4,478	72,787
Q87	Z28 spt cpe V-8	—	5,170	14,349

Chevelle Malibu (wb 112.0; 4d-116.0)				
C29	sdn 4d I-6	3,628	3,935	39,064
C29	sdn 4d V-8	3,737	4,055	
C37	cpe I-6	3,551	3,885	28,793
C37	cpe V-8	3,650	4,005	
D29	Classic sdn 4d I-6	3,725	4,475	76,776
D29	Classic sdn 4d V-8	3,824	4,595	
D37	Classic cpe I-6	3,599	4,125	73,739
D37	Classic cpe V-8	3,698	4,245	
D37	Classic Lan cpe I-6	—	4,353	37,215
D37	Classic Lan cpe V-8	—	4,473	

Chevelle Malibu Wagon (wb 116.0)				
C35	4d 3S	4,169	4,877	4,014
C35	4d 2S	4,139	4,734	18,023
D35	Classic 4d 3S	4,263	5,208	19,053
D35	Classic 4d 2S	4,233	5,065	31,539

Chevrolet (wb 116.0)				
L35	Imp wgn 4d 3S V-8	4,072	5,406	28,255
L35	Imp wgn 4d 2S V-8	4,042	5,289	37,108
L47	Imp Custom cpe I-6	3,533	4,876	55,347
L47	Imp Custom cpe V-8	3,628	4,996	
L47	Impala Landau cpe	—	—	2,745
L69	Impala sdn 4d I-6	3,564	4,901	196,824
L69	Impala sdn 4d V-8	3,659	5,021	
N35	Cap Cl wgn 4d 3S V-8	4,118	5,734	33,639
N35	Cap Cl wgn 4d 2S V-8	4,088	5,617	22,930
N47	Cap Clsic cpe I-6	3,571	5,187	62,366
N47	Cap Clsic cpe V-8	3,666	5,307	
N69	Cap Clsic sdn 4d I-6	3,606	5,237	212,840
N69	Cap Clsic sdn 4d V-8	3,701	5,357	
N69	Cap Landau cpe	—	—	9,607

Monte Carlo (wb 116.0)				
H57	S spt cpe	3,852	4,968	224,327
H57	Landau spt cpe	—	5,298	186,711

1977 Engines	bore×stroke	bhp	availability
I-4, 85.0	3.23×2.61	57	S-Chevette
I-4, 97.6	3.23×2.98	63	O-Chevette
I-4, 140.0	3.50×3.15	84	S-Vega, Monza
I-6, 250.0	3.88×3.53	110	S-Nov, Chvlle, Camaro, Chev
V-8, 305.0	3.74×3.48	145	S-Nov, Chvlle exc Clsic wgn, Camaro, MC, Chev; O-Monza
V-8, 350.0	4.00×3.48	170	S-Chvlle Clsic wgn; O-Nov, Chvlle, Cam, MC, Chevrolet

1978

Chevette (wb 94.3; 4d-97.3)		Wght	Price	Prod
B08	htchbk sdn 2d	1,965	3,644	118,375
B68	htchbk sdn 4d	2,035	3,764	167,769
J08	Scooter htchbk sdn 2d	1,932	3,149	12,829

Monza (wb 97.0)				
M07	2+2 htchbk cpe	2,732	3,779	36,227
M15	wgn 2d	2,723	3,868	24,255
M15	Estate wgn 2d	—	4,102	2,478
M27	cpe	2,688	3,622	37,878
M77	S htchbk cpe	2,643	3,697	2,326
R07	2+2 htchbk cpe	2,777	4,247	28,845
R27	spt cpe	2,730	4,100	6,823

Nova (wb 111.0)				
X17	htchbk cpe I-6	3,258	3,866	12,665
X17	htchbk cpe V-8	3,403	4,051	
X27	cpe I-6	3,132	3,702	101,858
X27	cpe V-8	3,277	3,887	
X69	sdn 4d I-6	3,173	3,777	123,158
X69	sdn 4d V-8	3,318	3,962	
Y27	Custom cpe I-6	3,261	3,960	23,953
Y27	Custom cpe V-8	3,396	4,145	
Y69	Custom sdn 4d I-6	3,298	4,035	26,475
Y69	Custom sdn 4d V-8	3,443	4,220	

Camaro (wb 108.1)				
Q87	spt cpe	3,300	4,414	134,491
Q87	Rally sport cpe	—	4,784	11,902
S87	Type LT spt cpe	3,352	4,814	65,635
S87	Type LT Rally sprt cpe	—	5,065	5,696
Q87	Z28 spt cpe V-8	—	5,604	54,907

Malibu (wb 108.1)				
T19	sdn 4d V-6	3,006	4,276	44,426
T19	sdn 4d V-8	3,143	4,469	
T27	cpe V-6	3,001	4,204	27,089
T27	cpe V-8	3,138	4,394	
T35	wgn 4d 2S V-6	3,169	4,516	30,850
T35	wgn 4d 2S V-8	3,550	4,706	
W19	Classic sdn 4d V-6	3,039	4,561	102,967
W19	Classic sdn 4d V-8	3,175	4,751	
W27	Classic spt cpe V-6	3,031	4,461	60,992
W27	Classic spt cpe V-8	3,167	4,651	
W27	Classic Lan cpe V-6	—	4,684	29,160
W27	Classic Land cpe V-8	—	4,874	
W35	Clsic wgn 4d 2S V-6	3,196	4,714	63,152
W35	Clsic wgn 4d 2S V-8	3,377	4,904	

Chevrolet (wb 116.0)				
L35	Imp wgn 4d 3S V-8	4,071	5,904	28,518
L35	Imp wgn 4d 2S V-8	4,037	5,777	40,423
L47	Impala cpe I-6	3,511	5,208	33,990
L47	Impala cpe V-8	3,619	5,393	
L47	Imp Landau cpe I-6	—	5,598	4,652
L47	Imp Landau cpe V-8	—	5,783	
L69	Impala sdn 4d I-6	3,530	5,283	183,161
L69	Impala sdn 4d V-8	3,638	5,468	
N35	Cap Clsic wgn 4d 3S V-8	4,109	6,151	32,952
N35	Cap Clsic wgn 4d 2S V-8	4,079	6,012	24,792
N47	Cap Clsic cpe I-6	3,548	5,526	37,301
N47	Cap Clsic cpe V-8	3,656	5,711	
N47	Cap Landau cpe I-6	—	5,830	22,771
N47	Cap Landau cpe V-8	—	6,015	
N69	Cap Clsic sdn 4d I-6	3,578	5,628	203,837
N69	Cap Clsic sdn 4d V-8	3,686	5,811	

Monte Carlo (wb 108.1)				
Z37	spt cpe V-6	3,040	4,785	216,730
Z37	spt cpe V-8	3,175	4,935	
Z37	Landau spt cpe V-6	—	5,678	141,461
Z37	Landau spt cpe V-8	—	5,828	

1978 Engines	bore×stroke	bhp	availability
I-4, 97.6	3.23×2.98	63	S-Chevette
I-4, 97.6	3.23×2.98	68	O-Chevette
I-4, 151.0	4.00×3.00	85	S-Monza
V-6, 196.0	3.50×3.40	90	O-Monza
V-6, 200.0	3.50×3.48	95	S-Malibu
V-6, 231.0	3.80×3.40	105	S-MC; O-Mal, Mon
I-6, 250.0	3.88×3.53	110	S-Nova, Cam exc Z28, Chev
V-8, 305.0	3.74×3.48	145	S-Nov, Malibu, Cam exc Z28, MC, Chev; O-Monza
V-8, 350.0	4.00×3.48	170	O-Nov, Mali wgns, Cam, Chev
V-8, 350.0	4.00×3.48	185	S-Camaro Z28

1979

Chevette (wb 94.3;4d-97.3)		Wght	Price	Prod
B08	htchbk sdn 2d	1,978	3,948	136,145
B68	htchbk sdn 4d	2,057	4,072	208,865
J08	Scooter htchbk sdn 2d	1,929	3,437	24,099

Monza (wb 97.0)				
M07	2+2 htchbk cpe	2,630	4,161	56,871
M15	wgn 2d	2,631	4,167	15,190
M27	cpe	2,577	3,850	61,110
R07	2+2 htchbk cpe	2,676	4,624	30,662

Nova (wb 111.0)				
X17	htchbk cpe I-6	3,264	4,118	4,819
X17	htchbk cpe V-8	3,394	4,353	
X27	cpe I-6	3,135	3,955	36,800
X27	cpe V-8	3,265	4,190	
X69	sdn 4d I-6	3,179	4,055	40,883
X69	sdn 4d V-8	3,309	4,290	
Y27	Custom cpe I-6	3,194	4,164	7,529
Y27	Custom cpe V-8	3,324	4,399	
Y69	Custom sdn 4d I-6	3,228	4,264	7,690
Y69	Custom sdn 4d V-8	3,358	4,499	

Camaro (wb 108.0)				
Q87	spt cpe	3,305	5,163	111,357
Q87	Rally sport cpe	—	5,572	19,101
S87	Berlinetta cpe	3,358	5,906	67,236
Q87	Z28 spt cpe V-8	—	6,748	84,877

Malibu (wb 108.1)				
T19	sdn 4d V-6	2,988	4,915	59,674
T19	sdn 4d V-8	3,116	5,180	
T27	cpe V-6	2,983	4,812	41,848
T27	cpe V-8	3,111	5,077	
T35	wgn 2d 2S V-6	3,155	5,078	50,344
T35	wgn 2d 2S V-8	3,297	5,343	
W19	Classic sdn 4d V-6	3,024	5,215	104,222
W19	Classic sdn 4d V-8	3,152	5,480	
W27	Classic cpe V-6	3,017	5,087	60,751
W27	Classic cpe V-8	3,145	5,352	
W27	Classic Lan cpe V-6	—	5,335	25,213
W27	Classic Lan cpe V-8	—	5,600	
W35	Classic wgn 4d V-6	3,183	5,300	70,095
W35	Classic wgn 4d V-8	3,325	5,565	

Chevrolet (wb 116.0)				
L35	Imp wgn 4d 3S V-8	4,045	6,636	28,710
L35	Imp wgn 4d 2S V-8	4,013	6,497	39,644
L47	Impala cpe V-6	3,495	5,828	26,589
L47	Impala cpe V-8	3,606	6,138	
L47	Impala Lan cpe I-6	—	6,314	3,247
L47	Impala Lan cpe V-8	—	6,624	
L69	Impala sdn 4d I-6	3,513	5,928	172,717
L69	Impala sdn 4d V-8	3,624	6,238	
N35	Cap Clsic wgn 4d 3S V-8	4,088	6,960	32,693
N35	Cap Clsic wgn 4d 2S V-8	4,056	6,800	23,568
N37	Cap Classic cpe I-6	3,538	6,198	36,629
N37	Cap Classic cpe V-8	3,649	6,508	
N47	Cap Clsic Lan cpe I-6	—	6,617	21,824
N47	Cap Clsic Lan cpe V-8	—	6,927	
N69	Cap Clsic sdn 4d I-6	3,564	6,323	203,017
N69	Cap Clsic sdn 4d V-8	3,675	6,633	

Monte Carlo (wb 108.1)				
Z37	spt cpe V-6	3,039	5,333	225,073
Z37	spt cpe V-8	3,169	5,598	
Z37	Landau spt cpe V-6	—	6,183	91,850
Z37	Landau spt cpe V-8	—	6,448	

1979 Engines	bore×stroke	bhp	availability
I-4, 97.6	3.23×2.98	70	S-Chevette

1979 Engines	bore×stroke	bhp	availability
I-4, 97.6	3.23×2.98	74	O-Chevette
I-4, 151.0	4.00×3.00	90	S-Monza I-4
V-6, 196.0	3.50×3.40	105	S-Monza V-6
V-6, 200.0	3.50×3.48	94	S-Malibu, MC
V-6, 231.0	3.80×3.40	115	O-Mal, Mnz, MC
I-6, 250.0	3.88×3.53	115	S-Nova, Cam exc Z28, Chev exc wgns
V-8, 267.0	3.50×3.48	125	S-Malibu, MC
V-8, 305.0	3.74×3.48	130	S-Nova, Cam exc Z28, Chev; O-Monza
V-8, 305.0	3.74×3.48	160	O-Monte Carlo, Malibu
V-8, 350.0	4.00×3.48	170	O-Nov, Mal, Chev
V-8, 350.0	4.00×3.48	175	S-Cam Z28; O-Camaro

1980

Chevette (wb 94.3;4d-97.3)		Wght	Price	Prod
B08	htchbk sdn 2d	1,989	4,601	148,686
B68	htchbk sdn 4d	2,048	4,736	261,477
J08	Scooter htchbk	1,935	4,057	40,998
Monza (wb 97.0)				
M07	2+2 htchbk cpe	2,672	4,746	53,415
M27	cpe	2,617	4,433	95,469
R07	Sport 2+2 htchbk cpe	2,729	5,186	20,534
Citation (wb 104.9)				
H11	cpe I-4	2,391	4,800	42,909
H11	cpe V-6	2,428	4,925	
X08	htchbk sdn 2d I-4	2,417	5,422	210,258
X08	htchbk sdn 2d V-6	2,454	5,547	
X11	club cpe I-4	2,397	5,214	100,340
X11	club cpe V-6	2,434	5,339	
X68	htchbk sdn 4d I-4	2,437	5,552	458,033
X68	htchbk 4d V-6	2,474	5,677	
Camaro (wb 108.1)				
P87	spt cpe	3,218	5,843	68,174
P87/Z85	RS cpe	—	6,086	12,015
S87	Berlinetta cpe	3,253	6,606	26,679
P87	Z28 spt cpe V-8	—	7,363	45,137
Malibu (wb 108.1)				
T19	sdn 4d V-6	3,001	5,617	67,696
T19	sdn 4d V-8	3,122	5,697	
T27	spt cpe V-6	2,996	5,502	28,425
T27	spt cpe V-8	3,117	5,582	
T35	wgn 4d 2S V-6	3,141	5,778	30,794
T35	wgn 4d 2S V-8	3,261	5,858	
W19	Classic sdn 4d V-6	3,031	5,951	77,938
W19	Classic sdn 4d V-8	3,152	6,031	
W27	Classic spt cpe V-6	3,027	5,816	28,425
W27	Classic spt cpe V-8	3,148	5,896	
W27/Z03	Classic Lan cpe V-6	—	6,009	9,342
W27/Z03	Classic Lan cpe V-8	—	6,149	
W35	Clsic wgn 4d 2S V-6	3,167	6,035	35,730
W35	Clsic wgn 4d 2S V-8	3,307	6,115	
Full-size Chevrolet (wb 116.0)				
L35	Imp wgn 4d 3S V-8	3,924	7,186	6,767
L35	Imp wgn 4d 2S V-8	3,892	7,041	11,203
L47	Impala spt cpe V-6	3,344	6,535	10,756
L47	Impala spt cpe V-8	3,452	6,615	
L69	Impala sdn 4d V-6	3,360	6,650	70,801
L69	Impala sdn 4d V-8	3,468	6,730	
N35	Cap Clsic wgn 4d 3S V-8	3,962	7,536	13,431
N35	Cap Clsic wgn 4d 2S V-8	3,930	7,369	9,873
N47	Caprice Clsic cpe V-6	3,376	6,946	13,919
N47	Caprice Clsic cpe V-8	3,484	7,026	
N47/Z03	Cap Clsic Lan cpe V-6	—	7,400	8,857
N47/Z03	Cap Clsic Lan cpe V-8	—	7,480	
N69	Cap Clsic sdn 4d V-6/V-8	—	—	91,208
Monte Carlo (wb 108.1)				
Z37	spt cpe V-6	3,104	6,524	116,580
Z37	spt cpe V-8	3,219	6,604	
Z37/Z03	Landau cpe V-6	—	6,772	32,262
Z37/Z03	Landau cpe V-8	—	6,852	

1980 Engines	bore×stroke	bhp	availability
I-4, 97.6	3.23×2.98	70	S-Chevette
I-4, 97.6	3.23×2.98	74	O-Chevette
I-4, 151.0	4.00×3.00	86	S-Monza
I-4, 151.0	4.00×3.00	90	S-Citation
V-6, 173.0	3.50×3.00	115	O-Citation
V-6, 229.0	3.74×3.48	115	S-Mali, Cam, MC, Chev exc wgn
V-6, 231.0	3.80×3.40	110	O-Cam, Monz, MC, Chev exc wgn
V-6T, 231.0	3.80×3.40	170	O-MC
V-8, 267.0	3.50×3.48	120	S-Mal, Cam, MC, Chevrolet
V-8, 305.0	3.74×3.48	155	O-Mal, Cam, MC, Chev
V-8, 350.0	4.00×3.48	190	S-Cam Z28; O-other Cam
V-8D, 350.0	4.06×3.39	105	O-Chev wgn

1981

Chevette (wb 94.3; 4d-97.3)		Wght	Price	Prod
B08	htchbk sdn 2d	2,000	5,255	114,621
B68	htchbk sdn 4d	2,063	5,394	250,616
J08	Scooter htchbk 2d	1,945	4,695	55,211
B08	Diesel htchbk sdn 2d	—	—	4,252
B68	Diesel htchbk sdn 4d	—	—	8,900
Citation (wb 104.9)				
X08	htchbk sdn 2d I-4	2,404	6,270	113,983
X08	htchbk sdn 2d V-6	2,459	6,395	
X68	htchbk sdn 4d I-4	2,432	6,404	299,396
X68	htchbk sdn 4d V-6	2,487	6,529	
Camaro (wb 108.0)				
P87	spt cpe V-6	3,222	6,780	62,614
P87	spt cpe V-8	3,392	6,830	
S87	Berlinetta cpe V-6	3,275	7,576	20,253
S87	Berlinetta cpe V-8	3,445	7,626	
P87	Z28 spt cpe V-8	—	8,263	43,272
Malibu (wb 108.1)				
T69	sdn 4d V-6	3,028	6,614	60,643
T69	sdn 4d V-8	3,194	6,664	
T27	spt cpe V-6	3,037	6,498	15,834
T27	spt cpe V-8	3,199	6,548	
T35	wgn 4d 2S V-6	3,201	6,792	29,387
T35	wgn 4d 2S V-8	3,369	6,842	
W69	Classic sdn 4d V-6	3,059	6,961	80,908
W69	Classic sdn 4d V-8	3,225	7,011	
W27	Classic spt cpe V-6	3,065	6,828	14,255
W27	Classic spt cpe V-8	3,227	6,878	
W27/Z03	Classic Lan cpe V-6	—	7,092	4,622
W27/Z03	Classic Lan cpe V-8	—	7,142	
W35	Classic wgn 4d 2S V-6	3,222	7,069	36,798
W35	Classic wgn 4d 2S V-8	3,390	7,119	
Full-size Chevrolet (wb 116.0)				
L35/AQ4	Imp wgn 4d 3S V-8	—	7,765	8,462
L35	Imp wgn 4d 2S V-8	3,897	7,624	11,345
L47	Impala spt cpe V-6	3,326	7,129	6,067
L47	Impala spt cpe V-8	3,458	7,179	
L69	Impala sdn 4d V-6	3,354	7,241	60,090
L69	Impala sdn 4d V-8	3,486	7,291	
N35/AQ4	Cap Clsic wgn 4d 3S V-8	—	8,112	16,348
N35	Cap Clsic wgn 4d 2S V-8	3,940	7,948	11,184
N47	Cap Clsic cpe V-6	3,363	7,534	9,741
N47	Cap Clsic cpe V-8	3,495	7,584	
N47/Z03	Cap Clsic Lan cpe V-6	—	7,990	6,615
N47/Z03	Cap Clsic Lan cpe V-8	—	8,040	
N69	Cap Clsic sdn 4d V-6	3,400	7,667	89,573
N69	Cap Clsic sdn 4d V-8	3,532	7,717	
Monte Carlo (wb 108.1)				
Z37	spt cpe V-6	3,102	7,299	149,659
Z37	spt cpe V-8	3,228	7,349	
Z37/Z03	Landau cpe V-6	—	8,006	38,191
Z37/Z03	Landau cpe V-8	—	8,056	

1981 Engines	bore×stroke	bhp	availability
I-4, 97.6	3.23×2.98	70	S-Chevette
I-4D, 111.0	3.31×3.23	51	O-late Chvtte
I-4, 151.0	4.00×3.00	84	S-Citation
V-6, 173.0	3.50×2.99	110	O-Citation
V-6, 173.0	3.50×2.99	135	O-Citation
V-6, 229.0	3.74×3.48	110	S-Cam, Mal, MC, Chev cpe/sdn
V-6, 231.0	3.80×3.40	110	S-CA, Cam, Mal, MC, Chev cpe/sdn
V-6T, 231.0	3.80×3.40	170	O-Monte Carlo
V-8, 267.0	3.50×3.48	115	O-Cam, Mal, MC, Chev
V-8, 305.0	3.74×3.48	150	S-Chev wgn; O-Cam, Mal, MC, Chev
V-8, 305.0	3.74×3.48	165	S-Camaro Z28
V-8, 350.0	4.00×3.48	175	O-Camaro Z28
V-8D, 350.0	4.06×3.39	105	O-Chevrolet

1982

Chevette (wb 94.3; 4d-97.3)		Wght	Price	Prod
B08	htchbk sdn 2d	2,004	5,513	51,431
B68	htchbk sdn 4d	2,064	5,660	111,661
J08	Scooter htchbk 2d	1,959	4,997	31,281
J68	Scooter htchbk 4d	2,006	5,238	21,742
B08/Z90	Diesel htchbk sdn 2d	—	6,579	4,874
B68/Z90	Diesel htchbk sdn 4d	—	6,727	11,819
Cavalier (wb 101.2)				
D27	cpe	2,318	6,966	30,245
E77	htchbk cpe	2,389	7,199	22,114
D69	sdn 4d	2,372	7,137	52,941
D35	wgn 4d	2,432	7,354	30,853
D27/Z11	Cadet cpe	—	6,278	2,281
D69/Z11	Cadet sdn 4d	—	6,433	9,511
D35/Z11	Cadet wgn 4d	—	6,704	4,754
D27/Z12	CL cpe	2,315	7,944	6,063
E77/Z12	CL htchbk cpe	2,381	8,281	12,792
D69/Z12	CL sdn 4d	2,362	8,137	15,916
D35/Z12	CL wgn 4d	2,422	8,452	7,587
Citation (wb 104.9)				
H11	cpe I-4	—	6,297	9,102
H11	cpe V-6	—	6,515	
X08	htchbk sdn 2d I-4	2,442	6,754	29,613
X08	htchbk sdn 2d V-6	—	6,972	
X68	htchbk sdn 4d I-4	2,409	6,899	126,932
X68	htchbk sdn 4d V-6	—	7,024	
Camaro (wb 101.0)				
P87	spt cpe I-4	—	7,631	
P87	spt cpe V-6	—	7,755	78,761
P87	spt cpe V-8	—	7,925	
S87	Berlinetta cpe V-6	2,940	9,266	39,744
S87	Berlinetta cpe V-8	—	9,436	
P87	Z28 spt cpe V-8	2,870	9,700	63,563
Celebrity (wb 104.9)				
W27	cpe I-4	2,691	8,313	19,629
W27	cpe V-6	2,751	8,438	
W19	sdn 4d I-4	2,734	8,463	72,701
W19	sdn 4d V-6	2,794	8,588	
Malibu (wb 108.1)				
W69	Classic sdn 4d V-6	3,091	8,137	70,793
W69	Classic sdn 4d V-8	—	8,207	
W35	Clsic wgn 4d 2S V-6	3,240	8,265	45,332
W35	Clsic wgn 4d 2S V-8	—	8,335	
Full-size Chevrolet (wb 116.0)				
L35/AQ4	Imp wgn 4d 3S V-8	4,050	8,670	6,245
L35	Imp wgn 4d 2S V-8	3,930	8,516	10,654
L69	Impala sdn 4d V-6	3,361	7,918	47,780
L69	Impala sdn 4d V-8	—	7,988	
N35/AQ4	Cap Clsic wgn 4d 3S V-8	4,010	9,051	25,385
N47	Cap Clsic spt cpe V-6	3,373	8,221	11,999
N47	Cap Clsic spt cpe V-8	—	8,291	
N69	Cap Clsic sdn 4d V-6	3,410	8,367	86,126
N69	Cap Clsic sdn 4d V-8	—	8,437	
Monte Carlo (wb 108.1)				
Z37	spt cpe V-6	3,190	8,177	92,392
Z37	spt cpe V-8	—	8,247	

1982 Engines	bore×stroke	bhp	availability
I-4, 97.6	3.23×2.98	65	S-Chevette
I-4D, 111.0	3.36×3.28	51	O-Chevette
I-4, 112.0	3.50×2.91	88	S-Cavalier
I-4, 151.0	4.00×3.00	90	S-Citation, Cam, Celebrity
I-4, 122.0	3.50×2.15	90	O-Cavalier
V-6, 173.0	3.50×2.99	112	O-Cit, Celeb
V-6, 173.0	3.50×2.99	135	O-Citation
V-6, 229.0	3.74×3.48	110	S-Malibu, MC, Chev cpe/sdn
V-6, 231.0	3.80×3.40	110	S-Calif, Chev
V-6D, 262.0	4.06×3.39	85	O-Malibu, MC
V-8, 267.0	3.50×3.48	115	S-Chevr wag; O-Mal, MC, Chev

1982 Engines	bore×stroke	bhp	availability
V-8, 305.0	3.74×3.48	150	S-Cam Z28; O-Cam, Mal, MC, Chevrolet
V-8, 305.0	3.74×3.48	165	O-Camaro Z28
V-8D, 350.0	4.06×3.39	105	O-Chev, Mal, MC

1983

Chevette (wb 94.3; 4d-97.3)		Wght	Price	Prod
B08	htchbk sdn 2d	2,088	5,469	37,537
B68	htchbk sdn 4d	2,148	5,616	81,297
J08	Scooter htchbk 2d	2,029	4,997	33,488
J68	Scooter htchbk 4d	2,098	5,333	15,303
B08/Z90	Diesel htchbk sdn 2d	—	6,535	439
B68/Z90	Diesel htchbk sdn 4d	—	6,683	1,501

Cavalier (wb 101.2)		Wght	Price	Prod
C27	cpe	2,384	5,888	23,028
C69	sdn 4d	2,403	5,999	33,333
C35	wgn 4d	2,464	6,141	27,922
D27	CS cpe	2,374	6,363	22,172
E77	Type 10 htckbk cpe	2,440	6,549	25,869
D69	CS sdn 4d	2,425	6,484	52,802
D35	CS wgn 4d	2,486	6,633	32,834
D27/Z08	CS conv cpe	—	10,990	627

Citation (wb 104.9)		Wght	Price	Prod
H11	cpe I-4	2,471	6,333	6,456
H11	cpe V-6	2,526	6,483	
X08	htchbk sdn 2d I-4	2,463	6,788	14,323
X08	htchbk sdn 2d V-6	2,518	6,938	
X68	htchbk sdn 4d I-4	2,511	6,934	71,405
X68	htchbk sdn 4d V-6	2,566	7,084	

Camaro (wb 101.0)		Wght	Price	Prod
P87	spt cpe I-4	—	8,036	
P87	spt cpe V-6	2,959	8,186	63,806
P87	spt cpe V-8	3,116	8,386	
S87	Berlinetta cpe V-6	2,944	9,881	27,925
S87	Berlinetta cpe V-8	3,136	10,106	
P87	Z28 spt cpe V-8	3,061	10,336	62,100

Celebrity (wb 104.9)		Wght	Price	Prod
W27	cpe I-4	2,710	8,059	19,221
W27	cpe V-6	2,770	8,209	
W19	sdn 4d I-4	2,730	8,209	120,608
W19	sdn 4d V-6	2,790	8,359	

Malibu (wb 108.1)		Wght	Price	Prod
W69	Classic sdn 4d V-6	3,199	8,084	61,534
W69	Classic sdn 4d V-8	3,307	8,309	
W35	Clsic wgn 4d 2S V-6	3,343	8,217	55,892
W35	Clsic wgn 4d 2S V-8	3,470	8,442	

Full-size Chevrolet (wb 116.0)		Wght	Price	Prod
L69	Impala sdn 4d V-6	3,490	8,331	45,154
L69	Impala sdn 4d V-8	3,594	8,556	
N35	Cap Clsic wgn 4d 3S V-8	4,092	9,518	53,028
N69	Cap Clsic sdn 4d V-6	3,537	8,802	122,613
N69	Cap Clsic sdn 4d V-8	3,641	9,027	

Monte Carlo (wb 108.1)		Wght	Price	Prod
Z37	spt cpe V-6	3,220	8,552	91,605
Z37	spt cpe V-8	3,328	8,777	
Z37/Z65	SS spt cpe V-8	—	10,474	4,714

1983 Engines	bore×stroke	bhp	availability
I-4, 97.6	3.23×2.98	65	S-Chevette
I-4D, 111.0	3.31×3.23	51	O-Chevette
I-4, 121.0	3.50×3.15	88	S-Cavalier
I-4, 151.0	4.00×3.00	92	S-Cit, Cam, Celeb
V-6, 173.0	3.50×2.99	112	S-Cam Berl; O-Cam, Cit, Celeb
V-6, 173.0	3.50×2.99	135	O-Citation
V-6, 229.0	3.74×3.48	110	S-Mal, MC, Chev cpe/sdn
V-6, 231.0	3.80×3.40	110	S-CA. Chev
V-6D, 262.0	4.06×3.39	85	O-Mal, MC, Celeb
V-8, 305.0	3.74×3.48	150	S-Cam Z28, Chev wgn; O-Cam, Malibu, MC, Chev
V-8, 305.0	3.74×3.48	175	S-MC SS; O-Cam
V-8D, 350.0	4.06×3.39	105	O-Chev, Mal, MC

1984

Chevette (wb 94.3; 4d-97.3)		Wght	Price	Prod
J08	htchbk sdn 2d	1,999	4,997	66,446
J68	htchbk sdn 4d	2,051	5,333	28,466
B08	CS htchbk 2d	2,038	5,489	47,032
B68	CS htchbk 4d	2,102	5,636	94,897
J08/Z90	Dsel htchbk sdn 2d	—	5,500	1,495
J68/Z90	Dsel htchbk sdn 4d	—	5,851	1,180
B08/Z90	CS dsel htchbk sdn 2d	2,261	5,999	1,000
B68/Z90	CS dsel htchbk sdn 4d	2,320	6,161	3,384

Cavalier (wb 101.2)		Wght	Price	Prod
C69	sdn 4d	2,386	6,222	90,023
C35	wgn 4d	2,455	6,375	50,718
D69	CS sdn 4d	2,398	6,666	110,295
D35	CS wgn 4d	2,468	6,821	58,739
E27	Type 10 cpe	2,367	6,477	103,204
E77	Type 10 htchbk cpe	2,418	6,654	44,146
E27/Z08	Type 10 conv cpe	2,583	11,299	5,486

Citation II (wb 104.9)		Wght	Price	Prod
H11	cpe I-4	2,454	6,445	4,936
H11	cpe V-6	2,529	6,695	
X08	htchbk sdn 2d I-4	2,494	6,900	8,783
X08	htchbk sdn 2d V-6	2,569	7,150	
X68	htchbk sdn 4d I-4	2,506	7,046	83,486
X68	htchbk sdn 4d V-6	2,581	7,296	

Camaro (wb 101.0)		Wght	Price	Prod
P87	spt cpe I-4	2,899	7,995	127,292
P87	spt cpe V-6	2,932	8,245	
P87	spt cpe V-8	3,112	8,545	
S87	Berlinetta cpe V-6	2,944	10,895	33,400
S87	Berlinetta cpe V-8	3,126	11,270	
P87	Z28 spt cpe V-8	3,135	10,620	100,416

Celebrity (wb 104.9)		Wght	Price	Prod
W27	cpe I-4	2,663	7,711	29,191
W27	cpe V-6	2,781	7,961	
W19	sdn 4d I-4	2,703	7,890	200,259
W19	sdn 4d V-6	2,816	8,140	
W35	wgn 4d 2S I-4	2,857	8,214	48,295
W35	wgn 4d 2S V-6	2,964	8,464	
W35/AQ4	wgn 4d 3S I-4	—	8,429	31,543
W35/AQ4	wgn 4d 3S V-6	—	8,679	

Full-size Chevrolet (wb 116.0)		Wght	Price	Prod
L69	Impala sdn 4d V-6	3,489	8,895	55,296
L69	Impala sdn 4d V-8	3,628	9,270	
N35	Cap Clsic wgn 4d 3S V-8	4,053	10,210	65,688
N47	Cap Clsic spt cpe V-6	3,633	9,253	19,541
N47	Cap Clsic spt cpe V-8	3,834	9,628	
N69	Cap Classic sdn 4d V-6	3,532	9,400	135,970
N69	Cap Clsic sdn 4d V-8	3,662	9,775	

Monte Carlo (wb 108.1)		Wght	Price	Prod
Z37	spt cpe V-6	3,176	8,936	112,730
Z37	spt cpe V-8	3,292	9,311	
Z37/Z65	SS spt cpe V-8	3,434	10,700	24,050

1984 Engines	bore×stroke	bhp	availability
I-4, 97.6	3.23×2.98	65	S-Chevette
I-4D, 111.0	3.31×3.23	51	O-Chevette
I-4, 121.0	3.50×3.15	86	S-Cavalier
I-4, 151.0	4.00×3.00	92	S-Cit, Cam, Celeb
V-6, 173.0	3.50×2.99	107	S-Cam, Berl; O-Cam
V-6, 173.0	3.50×2.99	112	O-Cit, Celeb
V-6, 173.0	3.50×2.99	130/135	O-Cit, Celeb
V-6, 229.0	3.74×3.48	110	S-MC, Chev cpe/sdn
V-6, 231.0	3.80×3.40	110	S-CA. Chev
V-6D, 262.0	4.06×3.39	85	O-Celebrity
V-8, 305.0	3.74×3.48	150	S-Cam Z28, Chev wagon; O-Cam, MC, Chev
V-8, 305.0	3.74×3.48	180	S-MC SS
V-8, 305.0	3.74×3.48	190	O-Cam Z28
V-8D, 350.0	4.06×3.39	105	O-Chev, MC

1985

Chevette (wb 94.3; 4d-97.3)		Wght	Price	Prod
B08	CS htchbk 2d	2,085	5,340	57,706
B68	CS htchbk 4d	2,145	5,690	65,128
B08/Z90	CS dsel htchbk sdn 2d	2,261	5,850	203
B68/Z90	CS dsel htchbk sdn 4d	2,320	6,215	462

Cavalier (wb 101.2)		Wght	Price	Prod
C69	sdn 4d	2,339	6,477	86,597
C35	wgn 4d	2,409	6,633	34,581
D69	CS sdn 4d	2,352	6,900	93,386
D35	CS wgn 4d	2,420	7,066	33,551
E27	Type 10 cpe	2,320	6,737	106,021
E77	Type 10 htchbk cpe	2,382	6,919	25,508
E27/Z08	Type 10 conv cpe	2,458	11,693	4,108

Citation II (wb 104.9)		Wght	Price	Prod
X08	htchbk sdn 2d I-4	2,499	6,940	7,443
X08	htchbk sdn 2d V-6	2,568	7,200	
X68	htchbk sdn 4d I-4	2,535	7,090	55,279
X68	htchbk sdn 4d V-6	2,603	7,350	

Camaro (wb 101.0)		Wght	Price	Prod
P87	spt cpe I-4	2,881	8,363	
P87	spt cpe V-6	2,977	8,698	97,966
P87	spt cpe V-8	3,177	8,998	
S87	Berlinetta cpe V-6	3,056	11,060	13,649
S87	Berlinetta cpe V-8	3,221	11,360	
P87/Z28	Z28 spt cpe V-8	3,251	11,060	47,022
P87/B4Z	IROC-Z spt cpe V-8	3,319	11,739	21,177

Celebrity (wb 104.9)		Wght	Price	Prod
W27	cpe I-4	2,689	8,102	29,010
W27	cpe V-6	2,790	8,362	
W19	sdn 4d I-4	2,722	8,288	239,763
W19	sdn 4d V-6	2,827	8,548	
W35	wgn 4d 2S I-4	2,857	8,479	45,602
W35	wgn 4d 2S V-6	2,953	8,739	
W35/AQ4	wgn 4d 3S I-4	—	8,699	40,547
W35/AQ4	wgn 4d 3S V-6	—	8,959	

Full-size Chev (wb 116.0)		Wght	Price	Prod
L69	Impala sdn 4d V-6	3,508	9,519	53,438
L69	Impala sdn 4d V-8	3,634	9,759	
N35	Cap Clsic wgn 4d 3S V-8	4,083	10,714	55,886
N47	Caprice Clsic cpe V-6	3,525	9,888	16,229
N47	Cap Classic cpe V-8	3,651	10,128	
N69	Cap Clsic sdn 4d V-6	3,549	10,038	139,240
N69	Cap Clsic sdn 4d V-8	3,674	10,278	

Monte Carlo (wb 108.0)		Wght	Price	Prod
Z37	spt cpe V-6	3,139	9,540	83,573
Z37	spt cpe V-8	3,245	9,780	
Z37/Z65	SS spt cpe V-8	3,385	11,380	35,484

1985 Engines	bore×stroke	bhp	availability
I-4, 97.6	3.23×2.98	65	S-Chevette
I-4D, 111.0	3.31×3.23	51	O-Chevette
I-4, 121.0	3.50×3.15	85	S-Cavalier
I-4, 151.0	4.00×3.00	88/92	S-Cit, Cam, Celeb
V-6, 173.0	3.50×2.99	112	O-Cit, Celeb
V-6, 173.0	3.50×2.99	125/135	S-Cam Berl; O-late Cav, Cit, Cam, Celeb
V-6, 262.0	4.00×3.48	130	S-MC, Chev
V-6D, 262.0	4.06×3.39	85	O-Celeb
V-8, 305.0	3.74×3.48	150/165	S-Cam Z28, Caprice wgn; O-Cam, MC, Chev
V-8, 305.0	3.74×3.48	180	S-MC SS
V-8, 305.0	3.74×3.48	190	O-Cam IROC-Z
V-8, 305.0	3.74×3.48	215	O-Cam Z28 /IROC-Z
V-8D, 350.0	4.06×3.39	105	O-Chevrolet

1986

Chevette (wb 94.3; 4d-97.3)		Wght	Price	Prod
B08	CS htchbk 2d	2,080	5,645	48,756
B68	CS htchbk 4d	2,140	5,959	54,164
B08/Z90	CS diesel sdn 2d	2,261	6,152	124
B68/Z90	CS diesel sdn 4d	2,320	6,487	200

Nova (wb 95.7)		Wght	Price	Prod
K19	sdn 4d	2,163	7,435	124,961*
K68	htchbk sdn 4d	2,205	7,669	42,788*

*27,945 additional Novas built late in 1985 model year.

Cavalier (wb 101.2)		Wght	Price	Prod
C27	cpe I-4	2,299	6,706	57,370
C27	cpe V-6	—	7,316	
C69	sdn 4d I-4	2,342	6,888	86,492
C69	sdn 4d V-6	—	7,498	
C35	wgn 4d I-4	2,412	7,047	30,490
C35	wgn 4d V-6	—	7,657	
D77	CS htchbk cpe I-4	2,375	7,373	8,046
D77	CS htchbk cpe V-6	—	7,983	
D69	CS sdn 4d I-4	2,355	7,350	89,168
D69	CS sdn 4d V-6	—	7,960	

Cavalier		Wght	Price	Prod
D35	CS wgn 4d I-4	2,423	7,525	23,101
D35	CS wgn 4d V-6	—	8,135	
E27	RS cpe I-4	2,325	7,640	53,941
E27	RS cpe V-6	—	8,250	
E77	RS htckbk cpe I-4	2,387	7,830	7,504
E77	RS htckbk cpe V-6	—	8,440	
E69	RS sdn 4d I-4	2,367	7,811	17,361
E69	RS sdn 4d V-6	—	8,451	
E35	RS wgn 4d I-4	2,440	7,979	6,252
E35	RS wgn 4d V-6	—	8,589	
E67	RS conv cpe I-4	2,444	12,530	5,785
E67	RS conv cpe V-6	2,642	13,140	
F27	Z24 spt cpe V-6	2,519	8,878	36,365
F77	Z24 htchbk cpe V-6	2,581	9,068	10,226
Camaro (wb 101.0)				
P87	spt cpe I-4	2,900	8,935	99,517
P87	spt cpe V-6	2,994	9,285	
P87	spt cpe V-8	3,116	9,685	
S87	Berlinetta cpe V-6	3,063	11,902	4,479
S87	Berlinetta cpe V-8	3,116	12,302	
P87/Z28	Z28 spt cpe V-8	3,201	11,902	38,547
P87/B4Z	IROC-Z spt cpe V-8	3,278	12,561	49,585
Celebrity (wb 104.9)				
W27	cpe I-4	2,689	8,735	29,223
W27	cpe V-6	2,794	9,170	
W19	sdn 4d I-4	2,719	8,931	291,760
W19	sdn 4d V-6	2,824	9,366	
W35	wgn 4d 2S I-4	2,847	9,081	36,655
W35	wgn 4d 2S V-6	2,912	9,516	
W35/AQ4	wgn 4d 3S I-4	2,850	9,313	47,245
W35/AQ4	wgn 4d 3S V-6	—	9,748	
Caprice (wb 116.0)				
L69	sdn 4d V-6	3,535	10,243	50,751
L69	sdn 4d V-8	3,628	10,633	
N35	Clsic wgn 4d 3S V-8	4,095	11,511	45,183
N47	Classic spt cpe V-6	3,546	10,635	9,869
N47	Classic spt cpe V-8	3,638	11,025	
N69	Classic sdn 4d V-6	3,564	10,795	67,772
N69	Classic sdn 4d V-8	3,656	11,185	
N69/B45	Clsic Brgm sdn 4d V-6	3,574	11,429	69,320
N69/B45	Clsic Brgm sdn 4d V-8	3,667	11,819	
N69/B45	Clsic LS Brgm sdn 4d V-6	—	—	2,117
N69/B45	Clsic LS Brgm sdn 4d V-8	—	—	
Monte Carlo (wb 108.0)				
Z37	spt cpe V-6	3,138	10,241	50,418
Z37	spt cpe V-8	3,244	10,631	
Z37/Z09	LS cpe V-6	3,138	10,421	27,428
Z76/Z09	LS cpe V-8	—	10,841	
Z37/Z65	SS spt cpe V-8	3,387	12,466	41,164
Z37/Z65	SS Aerocoupe V-8	3,440	14,191	200

1986 Engines	bore×stroke	bhp	availability
I-4, 97.0	3.19×3.03	74	S-Nova
I-4, 97.6	3.23×2.98	65	S-Chevette
I-4D, 111.0	3.31×3.23	51	O-Chevette
I-4, 121.0	3.50×3.15	85	S-Cavalier
I-4, 151.0	4.00×3.00	88/92	S-Cam, Cele
V-6, 173.0	3.50×2.99	112	O-Celebrity
V-6, 173.0	3.50×2.99	120/135	S-Cam Berl, Cav Z24; O-Cav, Cam, Celeb
V-6, 262.0	4.00×3.48	140	S-MC, Caprice
V-8, 305.0	3.74×3.48	150/155/165	S-Cam Z28, Caprice wgn; O-Cam, MC, Cap
V-8, 305.0	3.74×3.48	180	S-MC SS
V-8, 305.0	3.74×3.48	190	O-Cam IROC-Z
V-8, 305.0	3.74×3.48	215	O-Camaro Z28/IROC-Z

1987

Chevette (wb 94.3; 4d-97.3)		Wght	Price	Prod
B08	CS htchbk 2d	2,078	4,995	26,135
B68	CS htchbk 4d	2,137	5,495	20,073
Nova (wb 95.7)				
K19	sdn 4d	2,206	8,258	123,782
K68	htchbk sdn 4d	2,253	8,510	26,224
Cavalier (wb 101.2)				
C27	cpe I-4	2,300	7,255	53,678
C27	cpe V-6	—	7,915	

Cavalier		Wght	Price	Prod
E27	RS cpe I-4	2,360	8,318	36,353
E27	RS cpe V-6	—	8,978	
F27	Z24 spt cpe V-6	2,511	9,913	42,890
D77	CS htchbk cpe I-4	2,359	7,978	3,480
D77	CS htchbk cpe V-6	—	8,638	
E77	RS htchbk cpe I-4	2,408	8,520	2,818
E77	RS htchbk cpe V-6	—	9,180	
F77	Z24 htchbk cpe V-6	2,560	10,115	4,517
C69	sdn 4d I-4	2,345	7,449	84,445
C69	sdn 4d V-6	—	8,109	
D69	CS sdn 4d I-4	2,355	7,953	50,625
D69	CS sdn 4d V-6	—	8,613	
E69	RS sdn 4d I-4	2,397	8,499	15,482
E69	RS sdn 4d V-6	—	9,159	
C35	wgn 4d I-4	2,401	7,615	25,542
C35	wgn 4d V-6	—	8,275	
D35	CS wgn 4d I-4	2,411	8,140	15,023
D35	CS wgn 4d V-6	—	8,800	
E35	RS wgn 4d I-4	2,460	8,677	5,575
E35	RS wgn 4d V-6	—	9,337	
E67	RS conv cpe I-4	2,519	13,446	5,826
E67	RS conv cpe V-6	—	14,106	
Camaro (wb 101.0)				
P87	spt cpe V-6	3,062	9,995	83,890
P87	spt cpe V-8	3,181	10,395	
P87	LT cpe V-6	—	11,517	—
P87	LT cpe V-8	—	11,917	—
P87/Z28	Z28 spt cpe V-8	3,228	12,819	52,863
P87/Z28	IROC-Z spt cpe V-8	—	13,488	
P67	conv cpe V-8	—	14,794	263
P67/Z28	Z28 conv cpe V-8	—	17,218	744
P67/Z28	IROC-Z conv cpe V-8	—	17,917	
Corsica (wb 103.4)* - 8,973 built				
T69	sdn 4d I-4	2,491	8,995	—
T69	sdn 4d V-6	2,609	9,655	—
Beretta (wb 103.4)* - 8,072 built				
V37	cpe I-4	2,550	9,555	—
V37	cpe V-6	2,648	10,215	—
Celebrity (wb 104.9)				
W27	cpe I-4	2,685	9,995	18,198
W27	cpe V-6	2,769	10,605	
W19	sdn 4d I-4	2,715	10,265	273,864
W19	sdn 4d V-6	2,799	10,875	
W35	wgn 4d 2S I-4	2,847	10,425	33,894
W35	wgn 4d 2S V-6	2,931	11,035	
W35/AQ4	wgn 4d 3S I-4	—	10,672	36,568
W35/AQ4	wgn 4d 3S V-6	—	11,382	
Caprice (wb 116.0)				
L35	wgn 4d 3S V-8	4,114	11,995	11,953
N35	Clsic wgn 4d 3S V-8	4,125	12,586	28,387
N47	Classic cpe V-6	3,512	11,392	3,110
N47	Classic cpe V-8	3,605	11,802	
L69	sdn 4d V-6	3,510	10,995	56,266
L69	sdn 4d V-8	3,603	11,435	
N69	Classic sdn 4d V-6	3,527	11,560	53,802
N69	Classic sdn 4d V-8	3,620	12,000	
U69	Clsic Brgm sdn 4d V-6	3,576	12,549	51,341
U69	Clsic Brgm sdn 4d V-8	3,669	12,989	
U69/B6N	Clsic LS Brgm sdn 4d V-6	—	13,805	23,641
U69/B6N	Clsic LS Brgm sdn 4d V-8	—	14,245	
Monte Carlo (wb 108.0)				
Z37	LS cpe V-6	3,283	11,306	39,794
Z37	LS cpe V-8	3,389	11,746	
Z37/Z65	SS spt cpe V-8	3,473	13,463	33,199
Z37/Z16	SS Aerocoupe V-8	3,526	14,838	6,052

1987 Engines	bore×stroke	bhp	availability
I-4, 97.0	3.19×3.03	74	S-Nova
I-4, 97.6	3.23×2.98	65	S-Chevette
I-4, 121.0	3.50×3.15	90	S-Cav, Cors, Ber
I-4, 151.0	4.00×3.00	98	S-Celeb
V-6, 173.0	3.50×2.99	125/130	S-Cam, Cav Z24; O-Cav, Celeb, Cors, Ber
V-6, 262.0	4.00×3.48	140/145	S-MC, Cap cpe/sdn
V-8, 305.0	3.74×3.48	150/170	S-Cam Z28; O-Cam, MC, Cap
V-8, 305.0	3.74×3.48	180	S-MC SS
V-8, 305.0	3.74×3.48	215	O-Cam Z28 /IROC-Z
V-8, 307.0	3.80 × 3.38	140	S-Capr wgn
V-8, 350.0	4.00 × 3.48	225	O-Cam IROC-Z

* Corsica and Beretta were actually early 1988 models, introduced during the 1987 model year.

1988

Nova (wb 95.7)		Wght	Price	Prod
K19	sdn 4d	2,211	8,795	87,263
K68	htchbk sdn 4d	2,257	9,050	18,570
L19	twin-cam sdn 4d	—	11,395	3,300
Cavalier (wb 101.2)				
C37	cpe I-4	2,359	8,120	34,470
C69	sdn 4d I-4	2,363	8,195	107,438
C35	wgn 4d I-4	2,413	8,490	29,806
C35	wgn 4d V-6	—	9,150	
C37/WV9	VL cpe	—	6,995	43,611
E37	RS cpe I-4	2,371	9,175	24,359
E69	RS sdn 4d I-4	2,414	9,385	18,852
F37	Z24 cpe V-6	2,558	10,725	55,658
F67	Z24 conv cpe V-6	2,665	15,990	8,745
Camaro (wb 101.0)				
P87	spt cpe V-6	3,054	10,995	66,605
P87	spt cpe V-8	3,228	11,395	
P87/Z28	IROC-Z spt cpe V-8	3,229	13,490	24,050
P87/Z08	conv cpe V-8	3,350	16,255	1,859
P87/Z08	IROC-Z conv cpe V-8	3,352	18,015	3,761
Corsica (wb 103.4) - 291,163 built				
T69	sdn 4d I-4	2,589	9,555	—
T69	sdn 4d V-6	2,688	10,215	—
Beretta (wb 103.4) (incl 3,814 GTUs)		**Wght**	**Price**	**Prod**
V37	cpe I-4	2,608	10,135	275,098
V37	cpe V-6	2,707	10,795	
Celebrity (wb 104.9)				
W27	cpe I-4	2,727	10,585	11,909
W27	cpe V-6	2,793	11,195	
W19	sdn 4d I-4	2,765	11,025	195,205
W19	sdn 4d V-6	2,833	11,025	
W35/B5E	wgn 4d 2S I-4	2,903	11,350	23,759
W35/B5E	wgn 4d 2S V-6	2,970	11,960	
W35/AQ4	wgn 4d 3S I-4	—	11,590	27,583
W35/AQ4	wgn 4d 3S V-6	—	12,200	
Caprice (wb 116.0)				
L69	sdn 4d V-6	3,540	12,030	60,900
L69	sdn 4d V-8	3,633	12,470	
N69	Classic sdn 4d V-6	3,556	12,575	42,292
N69	Classic sdn 4d V-8	3,649	13,015	
U69	Clsic Brgm sdn 4d V-6	3,607	13,645	33,685
U69	Clsic Brgm sdn 4d V-8	3,700	14,085	
U69/B6N	Clsic LS Brgm sdn 4d V-6	—	14,820	21,586
U69/B6N	Clsic LS Brgm sdn 4d V-8	—	15,260	
N35	Clsic wgn 4d 3S V-8	4,158	14,340	30,645
Monte Carlo (wb 108.0)				
Z37	LS cpe V-6	3,212	12,330	13,970
Z37	LS cpe V-8	3,267	12,770	
Z37/Z65	SS cpe V-8	3,239	14,320	16,204

1988 Engines	bore×stroke	bhp	availability
I-4, 97.0	3.19×3.03	74	S-Nova
I-4, 97.0	3.19×3.03	110	O-Nov twin-cam
I-4, 121.0	3.50×3.15	90	S-Cav, Cors, Beretta
I-4, 151.0	4.00×3.00	98	S-Celebrity
V-6, 173.0	3.50×2.99	120/135	S-Cam, Cav Z24; O-Cav wgn, Celeb, Cors, Beretta
V-6, 262.0	4.00×3.48	140/145	S-MC, Cap cpe/sdn
V-8, 305.0	3.74×3.48	150/170	S-Cam IROC-Z; O-Cam, MC, Caprice
V-8, 305.0	3.74×3.48	180	S-MC SS
V-8, 305.0	3.74×3.48	220	O-Cam IROC-Z
V-8, 307.0	3.80×3.38	140	S-Caprice wgn
V-8, 350.0	4.00×3.48	230	O-Cam IROC-Z

1989

Cavalier (wb 101.2)		Wght	Price	Prod
C37	cpe I-4	2,418	8,395	65,971
C69	sdn 4d I-4	2,423	8,595	107,569

Cavalier	Wght	Price	Prod
C35 wgn 4d I-4	2,478	8,975	28,549
C35 wgn 4d V-6	2,566	9,635	
C37/WV9 VL cpe I-4	—	7,375	91,931
F37 Z24 cpe V-6	—	11,325	69,531
F67 Z24 conv cpe V-6	2,729	16,615	13,075

Camaro (wb 101.0)			
P87 RS htchbk cpe V-6	3,082	11,495	83,487
P87 RS htchbk cpe V-8	3,285	11,895	
P87/Z28 IROC-Z cpe V-8	3,264	14,145	20,067
P67 RS conv cpe V-8	3,116	16,995	3,245
P67/Z28 IROC-Z conv cpe V-8	—	18,945	3,940

Corsica (wb 103.4)			
T69 sdn 4d I-4	2,595	9,985	190,236
T69 sdn 4d V-6	2,690	10,645	
T68 htchbk sdn 4d I-4	2,648	10,375	26,578
T68 htchbk sdn 4d V-6	—	11,035	
Z69 LTZ sdn 4d V-6	—	12,825	14,353

Beretta (wb 103.4)			
V37 cpe I-4	2,631	10,575	91,197
V37 cpe V-6	2,727	11,235	
W37 GT cpe V-6	—	12,685	89,045
W37 GTU cpe V-6	—	—	9,813

Celebrity (wb 104.9)			
W19 sdn 4d I-4	2,751	11,495	162,482
W19 sdn 4d V-6	2,819	12,280	
W35/B5E wgn 4d 2S I-4	2,888	11,925	17,940
W35/B5E wgn 4d 2S V-6	2,928	12,710	
W35/AQ4 wgn 4d 3S I-4	—	12,175	21,239
W35/AQ4 wgn 4d 3S V-6	—	12,960	

Caprice (wb 116.0)			
L69 sdn 4d V-8	3,693	13,865	69,908
N69 Classic sdn 4d V-8	—	14,445	42,971
U69 Clsic Brgm sdn 4d V-8	—	15,615	32,343
U69/B6N Clsic LS Brgm sdn 4d V-8	—	16,835	28,033
N35 Clsic wgn 4d 3S V-8	4,192	15,025	23,789

1989 Engines	bore×stroke	bhp	availability
I-4, 121.0	3.50×3.15	90	S-Cav, Cors, Beretta
I-4, 151.0	4.00×3.00	98	S-Celebrity
V-6, 173.0	3.50×2.99	125/135	S-Cam RS, Cav Z24; Ber GT/GTU, O-Cav wgn, Celeb, Cors, Ber
V-8, 305.0	3.74×3.48	170	S-Cam RS conv, IROC-Z, Cap; O-Camaro RS
V-8, 305.0	3.74×3.48	220/230	O-Cam IROC-Z
V-8, 307.0	3.80×3.38	140	S-Caprice wgn
V-8, 350.0	4.00×3.48	230/240	O-Cam IROC-Z

1990

Cavalier (wb 101.2)	Wght	Price	Prod
C37 cpe I-4	2,436	8,620	35,121
C69 sdn 4d I-4	2,444	8,820	64,405
C35 wgn 4d I-4	—	9,195	13,812
C35 wgn 4d V-6	—	9,880	
C37/WV9 VL cpe I-4	—	7,577	111,476
C69/WV9 VL sdn I-4	—	7,777	39,429
C35/WV9 VL wgn I-4	—	8,165	8,234
F37 Z24 cpe V-6	—	11,505	38,474

Camaro (wb 101.0)			
P87 RS htchbk cpe V-6	3,077	10,995	28,750
P87 RS htchbk cpe V-8	—	11,345	
P87/Z28 IROC-Z cpe V-8	—	14,555	4,213
P67 RS conv cpe V-8	3,263	16,880	729
P67/Z28 IROC-Z conv cpe V-8	—	20,195	1,294

Corsica (wb 103.4)			
T69 sdn 4d I-4	2,491	9,495	170,545
T69 sdn 4d V-6	—	10,180	
T68 htchbk sdn 4d I-4	2,609	9,895	13,001
T68 htchbk sdn 4d V-6	—	10,580	
Z69 LTZ sdn 4d V-6	—	12,795	10,975

Beretta (wb 103.4)			
V37 cpe I-4	3,000	10,320	46,082
V37 cpe V-6	3,126	11,005	
W37 GT cpe V-6	—	12,500	35,785
W37 Indy GT cpe V-6	—	—	4,615
Z37 GTZ cpe I-4	—	13,750	13,239

Celebrity (wb 104.9)	Wght	Price	Prod
W35/B5E wgn 4d 2S I-4	2,888	12,395	11,324
W35/B5E wgn 4d 2S V-6	—	13,655	
W35/AQ4 wgn 4d 3S I-4	—	12,645	17,881
W35/AQ4 wgn 4d 3S V-6	—	13,305	

Lumina (wb 107.5)			
L27 cpe I-4	3,042	12,140	10,209
L27 cpe V-6	—	12,800	
N27 Euro cpe V-6	—	14,040	33,703
L69 sdn 4d I-4	3,122	12,340	164,171
L69 sdn 4d V-6	—	13,000	
N69 Euro sdn 4d V-6	—	14,240	86,924

Caprice (wb 116.0)			
L69 sdn 4d V-8	3,693	14,525	53,276
N69 Clsic sdn 4d V-8	—	15,125	15,679
U69 Clsic Brgm sdn 4d V-8	—	16,325	16,291
U69/B6N Clsic LS Brgm sdn 4d V-8	—	17,525	11,977
N35 Clsic wgn 4d 3S V-8	4,192	15,725	12,305

1990 Engines	bore×stroke	bhp	availability
I-4, 133.0	3.50×3.46	95	S-Cav, Cors, Ber
I-4, 138.0	3.62×3.35	180	S-Beretta GTZ
I-4, 151.0	4.00×3.00	110	S-Celeb, O-Lum
V-6, 191.0	3.51×3.31	135/140	S-Cam RS, Cav Z24; O-Cav wgn, Celeb, Cors, Ber, Lum
V-8, 305.0	3.74×3.48	170	S-Cam RS conv, IROC-Z, Cap; O-Camaro RS
V-8, 305.0	3.74×3.48	220	O-Cam IROC-Z
V-8, 307.0	3.80×3.38	140	S-Caprice wgn
V-8, 350.0	4.00×3.48	230	O-Cam IROC-Z

1991

Cavalier (wb 101.3)	Wght	Price	Prod
C37/WV9 VL cpe	2,480	7,995	171,759
C37 RS cpe	2,465	9,065	
F37 Z24 cpe	2,688	12,050	
C67 RS conv cpe	2,753	15,214	5,882
C69/WV9 VL sdn 4d	2,491	8,270	70,786
C69 RS sdn 4d	2,444	9,265	
C35/WV9 VL wgn 4d	2,587	9,225	19,685
C35 RS wgn 4d	2,587	10,270	

Camaro (wb 101.0)			
P87 RS cpe	3,103	12,180	92,306
P87/Z28 Z28 cpe	3,319	15,445	
P67 RS conv cpe	3,203	17,960	8,532
P67/Z28 Z28 conv cpe	3,400	20,815	

Corsica (wb 103.4)			
T69 LT sdn 4d	2,638	10,070	187,981
T68 LT htchbk sdn 4d	2,742	10,745	2,525

Beretta (wb 103.4) - 69,868 built			
V37 cpe	2,649	10,365	—
W37 GT cpe	2,797	13,150	—
Z37 GTZ cpe	2,795	14,550	—

Lumina (wb 107.5)			
L69 sdn 4d	3,192	12,870	159,482
N69 Euro sdn 4d	3,321	14,995	
L27 cpe	3,111	12,670	36,345
N27 Euro cpe	3,239	14,795	
P27 Z34 cpe	3,374	17,275	

Caprice (wb 115.9)			
L19 sdn 4d	3,907	16,515	201,880
N19 Classic sdn 4d	3,945	18,470	
L35 wgn 4d	4,354	17,875	15,582

1991 Engines	bore×stroke	bhp	availability
I-4, 133.0	3.50×3.46	95	S-Cav, Cors, Ber
I-4, 138.0	3.63×3.35	180	O-Ber (dohc)
I-4, 151.0	4.00×3.00	110	S-Lumina
V-6, 191.0	3.51×3.31	140	S-Cam, O-Cav, Cors, Ber, Lum
V-6, 207.0	3.62×3.31	210	O-Lum (dohc)
V-8, 305.0	3.74×3.48	170	S-Cap, O-Cam
V-8, 305.0	3.74×3.48	230	O-Camaro
V-8, 350.0	4.00×3.48	245	O-Camaro

1992

Cavalier (wb 101.3)	Wght	Price	Prod
C37/WV9 VL cpe	2,465	8,899	126,117
C37 RS cpe	2,436	9,999	
F37 Z24 cpe	2,689	12,995	

Cavalier	Wght	Price	Prod
C69/WV9 VL sdn 4d	2,471	8,999	70,786
C69 RS sdn 4d	2,444	10,199	
C35/WV9 VL wgn 4d	2,617	10,099	19,685
C35 RS wgn 4d	2,617	11,199	
C67 RS conv cpe	2,672	15,395	9,045
F67 Z24 conv cpe	2,826	18,305	

Camaro (wb 101.0)			
P87 RS cpe	3,103	12,075	66,191
P87/Z28 Z28 cpe	3,319	16,055	
P67 RS conv cpe	3,203	18,055	3,816
P67/Z28 Z28 conv cpe	3,400	21,500	

Corsica (wb 103.4)			
T69 LT sdn 4d	2,638	10,999	144,833

Beretta (wb 103.4) - 52,451 built			
V37 cpe	2,649	10,999	—
W37 GT cpe	2,749	12,575	—
Z37 GTZ cpe	2,795	15,590	—

Lumina (wb 107.5)			
L27 cpe	3,115	13,200	38,037
N27 Euro cpe	3,224	15,600	
P27 Z34 cpe	3,402	18,400	
L69 sdn 4d	3,220	13,400	198,269
W69/BYP Euro sdn 4d	3,328	15,800	

Caprice (wb 115.9)			
L19 sdn 4d	3,907	17,300	103,381
N19 Classic sdn 4d	3,951	19,300	
N19/B4U Classic LTZ sdn 4d	4,080	20,125	
L35 wgn 4d	4,354	18,700	13,400

1992 Engines	bore×stroke	bhp	availability
I-4, 133.0	3.50×3.46	110	S-Cav, Cors, Ber
I-4, 138.0	3.63×3.35	180	O-Ber (dohc)
I-4, 151.0	4.00×3.00	105	S-Lumina
V-6, 191.0	3.51×3.31	140	S-Cam, O-Cav, Cors, Ber, Lum
V-6, 207.0	3.62×3.31	210	O-Lum (dohc)
V-8, 305.0	3.74×3.48	170	S-Cap, O-Cam
V-8, 305.0	3.74×3.48	230	O-Camaro
V-8, 350.0	4.00×3.48	180	O-Caprice
V-8, 350.0	4.00×3.48	245	O-Camaro

1993

Cavalier (wb 101.3)	Wght	Price	Prod
C37/WV9 VL cpe	2,509	8,520	127,229
C37 RS cpe	2,526	9,520	
F37 Z24 cpe	2,695	12,500	
C67 RS conv cpe	2,678	15,395	8,609
F67 Z24 conv cpe	2,678	18,305	
C69/WV9 VL sdn 4d	2,520	8,620	96,545
C69 RS sdn 4d	2,515	9,620	
C35/WV9 VL wgn 4d	2,623	9,735	19,207
C35 RS wgn 4d	2,698	10,785	

Camaro (wb 101.1) - 39,103 built			
P87 RS cpe	3,241	13,399	—
P87/Z28 Z28 cpe	3,373	16,779	—

Corsica (wb 103.4)			
T69 LT sdn 4d	2,665	11,395	148,232

Beretta (wb 103.4) - 42,263 built			
V37 cpe	2,649	11,395	—
W37 GT cpe	2,749	12,995	—
Z37 GTZ cpe	2,795	15,995	—

Lumina (wb 107.5)			
L27 cpe	3,169	14,690	30,166
N27 Euro cpe	3,193	15,600	
P27 Z34 cpe	3,374	18,400	
L69 sdn 4d	3,288	14,010	191,189
W69 Euro sdn 4d	3,312	15,800	

Caprice (wb 115.9)			
L19 sdn 4d	3,995	17,995	90,041
N19 Classic sdn 4d	3,988	19,995	
L35 wgn 4d	4,471	19,575	10,607

1993 Engines	bore×stroke	bhp	availability
I-4, 133.0	3.50×3.46	110	S-Cav, Corsica, Beretta, Lumina
I-4, 138.0	3.63×3.35	175	O-Ber (dohc)
V-6, 191.0	3.51×3.31	140	O-Cav, Corsica, Beretta, Lumina
V-6, 207.0	3.62×3.31	160	S-Camaro
V-6, 207.0	3.62×3.31	210	O-Lum (dohc)

1993 Engines	bore×stroke	bhp	availability
V-8, 305.0	3.74×3.48	170	S-Caprice
V-8, 350.0	4.00×3.48	180	O-Caprice
V-8, 350.0	4.00×3.48	275	O-Camaro

1994

Cavalier (wb 101.3)	Wght	Price	Prod
C37/WV9 VL cpe	2,509	8,845	
C37 RS cpe	2,526	10,715	147,528
F37 Z24 cpe	2,695	13,995	
C67 RS conv cpe	2,678	16,995	7,932
F67 Z24 conv cpe	2,753	19,995	
C69/WV9 VL sdn 4d	2,520	8,995	
C69 RS sdn 4d	2,515	11,315	98,966
C35 wgn 4d	2,623	11,465	18,149

Camaro (wb 101.1)	Wght	Price	Prod
P87 cpe	3,247	13,399	112,529
P87/Z28 Z28 cpe	3,436	16,779	
P67 conv cpe	3,342	18,745	7,260
P67/Z28 Z28 conv cpe	3,524	22,075	

Corsica (wb 103.4)	Wght	Price	Prod
D69 LT sdn 4d	2,665	13,145	143,296

Beretta (wb 103.4) - 64,277 built	Wght	Price	Prod
V37 cpe	2,649	12,415	—
W37 Z26 cpe	2,795	15,310	—

Lumina (wb 107.5)	Wght	Price	Prod
N27 Euro cpe	3,269	16,875	3,860
P27 Z34 cpe	3,440	19,310	
L69 sdn 4d	3,333	15,305	82,766
W69 Euro sdn 4d	3,369	16,515	

Caprice (wb 115.9)	Wght	Price	Prod
L19 Classic sdn 4d	4,036	18,995	90,026
N19 LS sdn 4d	4,045	21,435	
L35 wgn 4d	4,541	20,855	7,719
L19/W×3 Impala SS sdn 4d	4,036	21,920	6,303

1994 Engines	bore×stroke	bhp	availability
I-4, 133.0	3.50×3.46	120	S-Cav, Cors, Ber
I-4, 138.0	3.63×3.35	170	O-Ber (dohc)
V-6, 191.0	3.51×3.31	140	S-Lum, O-Cav
V-6, 191.0	3.51×3.31	160	O-Cors, Beretta
V-6, 207.0	3.62×3.31	160	S-Camaro
V-6, 207.0	3.62×3.31	200	O-Lum (dohc)
V-8, 265.0	3.74×3.00	200	S-Caprice
V-8, 350.0	4.00×3.48	260	S-Imp SS, O-Cap
V-8, 350.0	4.00×3.48	275	O-Camaro

1995

Cavalier (wb 104.1)	Wght	Price	Prod
C37 cpe	2,617	10,060	88,909
F37 Z24 cpe	2,788	13,810	
F67 LS conv cpe	2,838	17,210	6,060
C69 sdn 4d	2,676	10,265	56,700
F69 LS sdn 4d	2,736	12,465	

Camaro (wb 101.1)	Wght	Price	Prod
P87 cpe	3,251	14,250	115,365
P87/Z28 Z28 cpe	3,390	17,915	
P67 conv cpe	3,342	19,495	7,360
P67/Z28 Z28 conv cpe	3,480	23,095	

Corsica (wb 103.4)	Wght	Price	Prod
D69 LT sdn 4d	2,745	13,890	142,073

Beretta (wb 103.4) - 71,762 built	Wght	Price	Prod
V37 cpe	2,756	12,995	—
W37 Z26 cpe	2,990	16,295	—

Lumina (wb 107.5) - 242,112 built	Wght	Price	Prod
L69 sdn 4d	3,330	15,460	—
N69 LS sdn 4d	3,372	16,960	—

Monte Carlo (wb 107.5) - 93,150 built	Wght	Price	Prod
W27 LS cpe	3,306	16,760	—
X27 Z34 cpe	3,436	18,960	—

Caprice (wb 115.9)	Wght	Price	Prod
L19 Classic sdn 4d	4,061	20,310	54,273
L19/WX3 Impala SS sdn 4d	4,036	22,910	21,434
L35 wgn 4d	4,473	22,840	5,030

1995 Engines	bore×stroke	bhp	availability
I-4, 133.0	3.50×3.46	120	S-Cav, Cors, Ber
I-4, 138.0	3.63×3.35	150	O-Cav (dohc)
V-6, 191.0	3.51×3.31	155	O-Corsica
V-6, 191.0	3.51×3.31	160	S-Lumina, MC, O-Beretta
V-6, 207.0	3.62×3.31	160	S-Camaro
V-6, 207.0	3.62×3.31	210	O-Lum, MC dohc
V-8, 265.0	3.74×3.00	200	S-Caprice
V-8, 350.0	4.00×3.48	260	S-Imp SS, O-Cap
V-8, 350.0	4.00×3.48	275	O-Camaro

1996

Cavalier (wb 104.1)	Wght	Price	Prod
C37 cpe	2,617	10,500	145,229
F37 Z24 cpe	2,788	14,200	
F67 LS conv cpe	2,838	17,500	7,073*
C69 sdn 4d	2,676	10,700	116,447
F69 LS sdn 4d	2,736	12,900	

Camaro (wb 101.1)	Wght	Price	Prod
P87 cpe	3,306	14,990	
P87/R7R RS cpe	—	17,490	54,525
P87/Z28 Z28 cpe	3,466	19,390	
P67 conv cpe	3,440	21,270	
P67/R7R RS conv cpe	—	22,720	6,837
P67/Z28 Z28 conv cpe	3,593	24,490	

Corsica (wb 103.4)	Wght	Price	Prod
D69 LT sdn 4d	2,745	14,385	148,652

Beretta (wb 103.4) - 42,476 built	Wght	Price	Prod
V37 cpe	2,756	13,490	—
W37 Z26 cpe	2,990	16,690	—

Lumina (wb 107.5) - 224,573 built	Wght	Price	Prod
L69 sdn 4d	3,330	16,355	—
N69 LS sdn 4d	3,372	18,055	—

Monte Carlo (wb 107.5) - 80,717 built	Wght	Price	Prod
W27 LS cpe	3,306	17,255	—
X27 Z34 cpe	3,436	19,455	—

Caprice (wb 115.9)	Wght	Price	Prod
L19 Classic sdn 4d	4,061	19,905	27,155
L19/WX3 Impala SS sdn 4d	4,036	24,405	41,941
L35 wgn 4d	4,473	22,405	485

1996 Engines	bore×stroke	bhp	availability
I-4, 133.0	3.50×3.46	120	S-Cav, Cors, Ber
I-4, 146.0	3.54×3.70	150	O-Cav (dohc)
V-6, 191.0	3.51×3.31	155	O-Cors, Beretta
V-6, 191.0	3.51×3.31	160	S-Lum, MC
V-6, 207.0	3.62×3.31	215	O-Lum, Monte Carlo (dohc)
V-6, 231.0	3.80×3.40	200	S-Camaro
V-8, 265.0	3.74×3.00	200	S-Caprice
V-8, 350.0	4.00×3.48	260	S-Imp SS; O-Cap
V-8, 350.0	4.00×3.48	285**	O-Camaro

* Cav conv sales fig. ** 305 bhp with SS package.

1997

Cavalier (wb 104.1)	Wght	Price	Prod
C37 cpe	2,584	10,980	
C37/WP2 RS cpe	2,617	12,225	171,225
F37 Z24 cpe	2,788	14,465	
F67 LS conv cpe	2,899	17,765	1,108
C69 sdn 4d	2,630	11,180	142,803
F69 LS sdn 4d	2,729	13,380	

Camaro (wb 101.1)	Wght	Price	Prod
P87 cpe	3,294	16,215	
P87/R7R RS cpe	3,307	17,970	48,292
P87/Z28 Z28 cpe	3,433	20,115	
P67 conv cpe	3,446	21,770	
P67/R7R RS conv cpe	3,455	23,170	6,680
P67/Z28 Z28 conv cpe	3,589	25,520	

Malibu (wb 107.0) - 100,266 built	Wght	Price	Prod
D69 sdn 4d	3,051	15,470	—
E69 LS sdn 4d	3,077	18,190	—

Lumina (wb 107.5) - 234,626 built	Wght	Price	Prod
L69 sdn 4d	3,360	16,945	—
N69 LS sdn 4d	3,388	19,145	—
— LTZ sdn 4d	—	19,455	—

Monte Carlo (wb 107.5) - 72,555 built	Wght	Price	Prod
W27 LS cpe	3,320	17,445	—
X27 Z34 cpe	3,455	19,945	—

1997 Engines	bore×stroke	bhp	availability
I-4, 133.0	3.50×3.46	120	S-Cavalier
I-4, 146.0	3.54×3.70	150	S-Malibu, O-Cav (dohc)
V-6, 191.0	3.51×3.31	160	S-Lum, MC
V-6, 207.0	3.62×3.31	215	O-Lum, MC (dohc)
V-6, 231.0	3.80×3.40	200	S-Camaro
V-8, 350.0	4.00×3.48	285*	O-Camaro

* 305 horsepower with SS package.

1998

Prizm (wb 97.0) - 45,000 blt	Wght	Price	Prod
K19 sdn 4d	2,359	12,045	—
K19/WP2 LSi 4d	—	14,615	—

Cavalier (wb 104.1)	Wght	Price	Prod
C37 cpe	2,584	11,610	126,599
C37/WP2 RS cpe	2,584	12,870	
F37 Z24 cpe	2,749	15,710	25,879
F67 Z24 conv cpe	2,899	19,410	5,011
C69 sdn 4d	2,630	11,810	117,224
F69 LS sdn 4d	2,630	14,250	55,838

Camaro (wb 101.1)	Wght	Price	Prod
P87 cpe	3,331	16,625	49,515
P87/Z28 Z28 cpe	3,349	20,470	
P67 conv cpe	3,468	22,125	4,505
P67/Z28 Z28 conv cpe	3,574	27,450	

Malibu (wb 107.0)	Wght	Price	Prod
D69 sdn 4d	3,100	15,670	167,951
E69 LS sdn 4d	—	18,470	100,537

Lumina (wb 107.5)	Wght	Price	Prod
L69 sdn 4d	3,330	17,245	172,884
N69 LS sdn 4d	3,372	19,245	35,743
— LTZ sdn 4d	3,420	19,745	

Monte Carlo (wb 107.5)	Wght	Price	Prod
W27 LS cpe	3,239	17,795	54,395
X27 Z34 cpe	3,452	20,295	14,995

1998 Engines	bore×stroke	bhp	availability
I-4, 109.5	3.11×3.60	120	S-Prizm
I-4, 133.0	3.50×3.46	115	S-Cavalier
I-4, 146.0	3.54×3.70	150	S-Mal, O-Cav (dohc)
V-6, 191.0	3.51×3.31	150	O-Malibu
V-6, 191.0	3.51×3.31	160	S-Lumina, MC
V-6, 231.0	3.80×3.40	200	S-Cam, O-Lum, MC
V-8, 350.0	4.00×3.48	305	O-Camaro
V-8, 350.0	4.00×3.48	320	O-Camaro

1999

Prizm (wb 97.0) - 50,000 blt	Wght	Price	Prod
K19 sdn 4d	2,403	12,268	—
K19/WP2 LSi 4d	—	14,839	—

Cavalier (wb 104.1)	Wght	Price	Prod
C37 cpe	2,617	11,871	116,893
C37/WP2 RS cpe	—	13,131	
F37 Z24 cpe	—	15,791	17,432
F67 Z24 conv cpe	2,838	19,751	8,755
C69 sdn 4d	2,676	11,971	101,863
F69 LS sdn 4d	—	14,411	33,105

Camaro (wb 101.1)	Wght	Price	Prod
P87 cpe	3,306	16,625	37,514
P87/Z28 Z28 cpe	3,349	20,870	
P67 conv cpe	3,500	22,125	4,584
P67/Z28 Z28 conv cpe	3,574	27,850	

Malibu (wb 107.0)	Wght	Price	Prod
D69 sdn 4d	3,051	15,950	148,691
E69 LS sdn 4d	3,077	18,910	97,924

Lumina (wb 107.5)	Wght	Price	Prod
L69 sdn 4d	3,330	18,190	127,600
N69 LS sdn 4d	—	19,920	11,498
— LTZ sdn 4d	3,372	20,360	

Monte Carlo (wb 107.5)	Wght	Price	Prod
W27 LS cpe	3,306	18,510	49,354
X27 Z34 cpe	3,436	20,535	20,245

1999 Engines	bore×stroke	bhp	availability
I-4, 109.5	3.11×3.60	120	S-Prizm
I-4, 133.0	3.50×3.46	115	S-Cavalier
I-4, 146.0	3.54×3.70	150	S-Malibu, O-Cav (dohc)
V-6, 191.0	3.51×3.31	150	O-Malibu
V-6, 191.0	3.51×3.31	160	S-Lumina, MC
V-6, 231.0	3.80×3.40	200	S-Camaro, O-Lumina, MC
V-8, 346.0	3.90×3.62	305	O-Camaro
V-8, 346.0	3.90×3.62	320	O-Camaro

2000

Prizm (wb 97.0) - 38,921 blt		Wght	Price	Prod
K19	sdn 4d	2,403	13,960	—
K19/WP2	LSi 4d	2,431	16,010	—
Cavalier (wb 104.1)				
C37	cpe	2,584	13,160	115,751
F37	Z24 cpe	2,749	16,365	26,104
F67	Z24 conv cpe	2,899	19,830	5,293
C69	sdn 4d	2,630	13,260	126,491
F69	LS sdn 4d	2,729	14,805	39,624
Camaro (wb 101.1)				
P87	cpe	3,317	17,040	39,527
P87/Z28	Z28 cpe	3,424	21,615	
P67	conv cpe	3,454	24,340	5,934
P67/Z28	Z28 conv cpe	3,561	28,715	
Malibu (wb 107.0)				
D69	sdn 4d	3,051	16,535	146,780
E69	LS sdn 4d	3,077	19,215	105,739
Lumina (wb 107.5)				
L69	sdn 4d	3,327	18,890	37,493
Impala (wb 110.5)				
F19	sdn 4d	3,389	18,890	141,223
H19	LS sdn 4d	3,466	22,790	79,950
Monte Carlo (wb 110.5)				
W27	LS cpe	3,306	19,390	31,210
X27	SS cpe	3,436	21,935	33,137

2000 Engines	bore×stroke	bhp	availability
I-4, 109.5	3.11×3.60	125	S-Prizm
I-4, 133.0	3.50×3.46	115	S-Cavalier
I-4, 146.0	3.54×3.70	150	O-Cav (dohc)
V-6, 191.0	3.51×3.31	170	S-Malibu
V-6, 191.0	3.51×3.31	175	S-Lumina
V-6, 205.0	3.62×3.31	180	S-Impala, MC
V-6, 231.0	3.80×3.40	200	S-Cam, O-Imp, MC
V-8, 346.0	3.90×3.62	305	O-Camaro
V-8, 346.0	3.90×3.62	320	O-Camaro

2001

Prizm (wb 97.0) - 50,141 blt		Wght	Price	Prod
K19	sdn 4d	2,403	14,155	—
K19/WP2	LSi 4d sdn	2,431	16,220	—
Cavalier (wb 104.1)				
C37	cpe	2,617	13,260	92,232
F37	Z24 cpe	2,676	16,465	18,260
C69	sdn 4d	2,676	13,360	125,476
F69	LS sdn 4d	2,729	14,955	34,597
Camaro (wb 101.1)				
P87	cpe	3,306	17,305	23,691
P87/Z28	Z28 cpe	3,439	21,875	
P67	conv cpe	3,500	24,600	5,318
P67/Z28	Z28 conv cpe	3,574	28,980	
Malibu (wb 107.0)				
D69	sdn 4d	3,051	17,150	141,819
E69	LS sdn 4d	3,077	19,410	71,189
Impala (wb 110.5)				
F19	sdn 4d	3,466	19,269	137,143
H19	LS sdn 4d	3,466	23,345	69,845
Monte Carlo (wb 110.5)				
W27	LS cpe	3,340	19,690	31,988
X27	SS cpe	3,391	22,520	39,280

2001 Engines	bore×stroke	bhp	availability
I-4, 109.5	3.11×3.60	125	S-Prizm
I-4, 133.0	3.50×3.46	115	S-Cavalier
I-4, 146.0	3.54×3.70	150	O-Cav (dohc)
V-6, 191.0	3.51×3.31	170	S-Malibu
V-6, 205.0	3.62×3.31	180	S-Impala, MC
V-6, 231.0	3.80×3.40	200	S-Cam, O-Imp, MC
V-8, 346.0	3.90×3.62	310	O-Camaro
V-8, 346.0	3.90×3.62	325	O-Camaro

2002

Prizm (wb 97.0) - 28,198 built		Wght	Price	Prod
K19	sdn 4d	2,403	14,330	—
K19/WP2	LSi 4d	2,431	16,395	—
Cavalier (wb 104.1) - 327,495 built				
C37	cpe	2,617	13,860	—
S37	LS cpe	2,617	14,910	—
F37	Z24 cpe	2,749	16,480*	—
H37	LS Sport cpe	2,676	16,280**	—
C69	sdn 4d	2,676	13,960	—
F69	LS sdn 4d	2,729	15,010	—
H69	Z24 sdn 4d	2,676	16,580*	—
H69	LS Sport sdn 4d	—	16,380**	—
Camaro (wb 101.1) - 41,776 built				
P87	cpe	3,323	18,080	—
P87/Z28	Z28 cpe	3,524	22,495	—
P67	conv cpe	3,524	26,075	—
P67/Z28	Z28 conv cpe	3,577	29,590	—
Malibu (wb 107.0) - 170,101 built				
D69	sdn 4d	3,053	17,535	—
E69	LS sdn 4d	3,077	19,740	—
Impala (wb 110.5) - 221,219 built				
F19	sdn 4d	3,389	19,960	—
H19	LS sdn 4d	3,389	23,660	—
Monte Carlo (wb 110.5) - 70,781 built				
W27	LS cpe	3,340	20,060	—
X27	SS cpe	3,395	22,860	—

2002 Engines	bore×stroke	bhp	availability
I-4, 109.5	3.11×3.60	125	S-Prizm
I-4, 133.0	3.50×3.46	115	S-Cavalier
I-4, 134.0	3.39×3.72	140	O-Cav LS Sport (dohc)
I-4, 146.0	3.54×3.70	150	O-Cav Z24 (dohc)
V-6, 191.0	3.51×3.31	170	S-Malibu
V-6, 205.0	3.62×3.31	180	S-Impala, Monte Carlo
V-6, 231.0	3.80×3.40	200	S-Camaro, O-Impala, MC
V-8, 346.0	3.90×3.62	310	O-Camaro
V-8, 346.0	3.90×3.62	325	O-Camaro

* Z24 discontinued early in model year.
** LS Sport replaced Z24.

2003

Cavalier - 299,581 built		Wght	Price	Prod
C37	cpe	2,617	14,030	—
F37	LS cpe	2,617	15,480	—
H37	LS Sport cpe	2,676	16,680	—
C69	sdn 4d	2,676	14,180	—
F69	LS sdn 4d	2,749	15,630	—
H69	LS Sport sdn 4d	—	16,830	—
Malibu (wb 107.0) - 202,588 built				
D69	sdn 4d	3,106	17,785	—
E69	LS sdn 4d	3,101	20,085	—
Impala (wb 110.5) - 284,118 built				
F19	sdn 4d	3,389	20,655	—
H19	LS sdn 4d	3,389	23,825	—
Monte Carlo (wb 110.5) - 71,129 built				
W27	LS cpe	3,340	20,655	—
X27	SS cpe	3,395	23,095	—

2003 Engines	bore×stroke	bhp	availability
I-4, 134.0	3.39×3.72	140	S-Cavalier
V-6, 191.0	3.51×3.31	170	S-Malibu
V-6, 205.0	3.62×3.31	180	S-Imp, MC
V-6, 231.0	3.80×3.40	200	O-Imp, MC

2004

Cavalier - 242,418 built		Wght	Price	Prod
C37	cpe	2,617	10,135	—
F37	LS cpe	2,617	15,820	—
H37	LS Sport cpe	2,749	17,325	—
C69	sdn 4d	2,676	14,245	—
F69	LS sdn 4d	2,676	16,020	—
H69	LS Sport sdn 4d	2,808	17,525	—
Malibu (wb 106.3; htchbk-112.3) - 150,640 built				
S69	sdn 4d	3,174	18,370	—
T69	LS sdn 4d	3,297	20,370	—
U69	LT sdn 4d	3,315	22,870	—
T68	LS htchbk sdn 4d	3,458	21600	—
U68	LT htchbk sdn 4d	3,476	24,100	—
Impala (wb 110.5) - 302,569 built				
F19	sdn 4d	3,465	21,400	—
H19	LS sdn 4d	3,476	24,505	—
P19	SS sdn 4d	3,606	27335	—
Monte Carlo (wb 110.5) - 64,771 built				
W27	LS cpe	3,340	21,335	—
X27	SS cpe	3,434	23,730	—
Z27	SS Sprchgd cpe	3,522	27,135	—

2004 Engines	bore×stroke	bhp	availability
I-4, 134.0	3.39×3.72	140	S-Cavalier
I-4, 134.0	3.39×3.72	145	S-Malibu
V-6, 205.0	3.62×3.31	180	S-Imp, MC
V-6, 213.0	3.70×3.31	200	O-Malibu
V-6, 231.0	3.80×3.40	200	O-Imp, MC
V-6S, 231.0	3.80×3.40	240	O-Imp, MC

2005

Cavalier (wb 104.1)-111,748 blt		Wght	Price	Prod
C37	cpe	2,617	10,325	—
F37	LS cpe	2,617	16,090	—
H37	LS Sport cpe	2,749	17,510	—
C69	sdn 4d	2,676	14,610	—
F69	LS sdn 4d	2,676	16,290	—
H69	LS Sport sdn 4d	2,808	17,710	—
Cobalt (wb 103.3) - 160,862 built				
K37	cpe	2,808	13,625	—
L37	LS cpe	2,824	15,290	—
P37	SS Sprchgd cpe	2,806	21,430	—
K69	sdn 4d	2,868	13,625	—
L69	LS sdn 4d	2,895	15,290	—
Z69	LT sdn 4d	2,989	18,195	—
Malibu (wb 106.3; htchbk-112.3) - 241,965 built				
S69	sdn 4d	3,174	19,085	—
T69	LS sdn 4d	3,297	21,150	—
U69	LT sdn 4d	3,315	23,945	—
T68	LS htchbk sdn 4d	3,458	21,350	—
U68	LT htchbk sdn 4d	3,476	24,495	—
Impala (wb 110.5) - 259,014 built				
F19	sdn 4d	3,389	22,220	—
H19	LS sdn 4d	3,466	25,330	—
P19	SS sdn 4d	3,606	28,425	—
Monte Carlo (wb 110.5) - 37,143 built				
W27	LS cpe	3,340	22,150	—
X27	LT cpe	3,434	24,560	—
Z27	SS Sprchgd cpe	3,522	28,225	—

2005 Engines	bore×stroke	bhp	availability
I-4S, 122.0	3.39×3.39	205	O-Cobalt
I-4, 134.0	3.39×3.72	140	S-Cav, Cobalt
I-4, 134.0	3.39×3.72	145	S-Malibu
V-6, 205.0	3.62×3.31	180	S-Imp, MC
V-6, 213.0	3.70×3.31	200	O-Malibu
V-6, 231.0	3.80×3.40	200	O-Imp, MC
V-6S, 231.0	3.80 x 3.40	240	O-Imp, MC

2006

Cobalt (wb 103.3)		Wght	Price	Prod*
K37	LS cpe	2,730	13,900	—
L37	LT cpe	2,742	16,200	—
M37	SS cpe	2,815	18,200	—
P37	SS Sprchgd cpe	2,925	21,400	—
K69	LS sdn 4d	2,780	13,900	—
L69	LT sdn 4d	2,793	16,200	—
Z69	LTZ sdn 4d	2,905	18,400	—
M69	SS sdn 4d	2,871	18,200	—
Malibu (wb 106.3; htchbk-112.3)				
S69	LS sdn 4d	3,174	17,365	—
T69	LT sdn 4d	3,297	19,365	—
U69	LTZ sdn 4d	3,315	24,205	—
W69	SS sdn 4d	3,415	23,865	—
T68	LT htchbk sdn 4d	3,476	21,025	—
U68	LTZ htchbk sdn 4d	3,476	24,755	—
W68	SS htchbk sdn 4d	3,620	24,065	—
Impala (wb 110.5)				
B19	LS sdn 4d	3,553	21,330	—
T19	LT sdn 4d	3,637	24,760	—
U19	LTS sdn 4d	—	26,870	—
D19	SS sdn 4d	3,712	27,130	—
Monte Carlo (wb 110.5)				
J27	LS cpe	3,354	21,330	—
M27	LT cpe	3,396	21,860	—
N27	LTZ cpe	—	25,975	—
L27	SS cpe	3,490	27,130	—

2006 Engines	bore×stroke	bhp	availability
I-4S, 122.0	3.39×3.39	205	O-Cobalt
I-4, 134.0	3.39×3.72	145	S-Cobalt, Malibu
I-4, 145.0	3.46×3.85	171	O-Cobalt
V-6, 213.0	3.70×3.31	201	O-Malibu
V-6, 213.0	3.90×2.99	211	S-Imp, MC
V-6, 237.0	3.90×3.31	242	O-Mali, Imp, MC
V-8, 325.0	3.78×3.62	303	O-Imp, MC

*Figures not available at time of publication.

Chevrolet Corvair

Corvair was the most-controversial Chevrolet since the abortive "Copper-Cooled" model of 1923. Of course, neither was *supposed* to stir up trouble. Each was merely a response to a particular market situation in its day.

The problem with Corvair was a radical design that made it too costly for its original economy-car mission and too "foreign" for its target audience. Had it not opened up an entirely new market—and almost by accident at that—Corvair wouldn't have lasted even half of the ten years it did hang on. And there's the irony, for it was Corvair's success as a *sporty* compact that spawned the car that ultimately helped do it in: the Ford Mustang. A young lawyer-on-the-make named Ralph Nader did the rest.

Chevrolet's interest in a smaller companion car was evident as early as the late '40s, when it contemplated the Cadet, a prototype 2200-pound four-door sedan of conventional design begun right after World War II. Powered by a short-stroke 133-cid version of the division's famous "Stovebolt Six," this 108-inch-wheelbase compact was intended to sell at rock-bottom prices in anticipation of a postwar recession. Instead, the market boomed, rendering the Cadet unnecessary. What's more, it would have cost as much to build as a regular Chevy, and so was deemed unprofitable at the targeted $1000 retail price. The project was thus canceled in mid-1947.

Things were far different by the late '50s. Led by Volkswagen and Renault, sales of economy imports were becoming too large to ignore, particularly once a national recession hit in mid-1957. American Motors responded with its compact 1958 American, a warmed-over '55 Nash Rambler. Studebaker chimed in with the '59 Lark, a full-size car cut down to compact size. So successful was the Lark that it temporarily halted Studebaker's ultimate slide to oblivion. Both these independent efforts would soon have Big Three rivals. Ford was readying its Falcon and Chrysler its Valiant for model-year 1960. General Motors had peddled its so-called "captive imports," British Vauxhalls and German Opels, in 1958-59. For 1960, GM would rely on Corvair.

Initiated in 1956, the Corvair was largely the brainchild of Chevy chief engineer (and future GM president) Edward N. Cole, who became division general manager in July of that year. It was predictably a technician's car, by far the most-radical of the new Big Three compacts. Perhaps inspired by Cole's interest in airplanes—but more likely by the popular VW Beetle—it was planned around a 140-cid air-cooled flat six developing 80 or 95 horsepower in initial form and—just as uncommon—mounted at the rear ("where an engine belongs," as Corvair ads would claim). It was a relatively complicated engine, with six separate cylinder barrels and a divided crankcase. Yet despite a lightweight aluminum block, it ended up at 366 pounds, some 78 pounds above the target weight, a miscalculation that would have negative consequences for handling.

All-independent suspension and unit construction were equally unusual for a U.S. car. Corvair's trim 108-inch-wheelbase Y-body platform was all new, but its all-coil suspension was perhaps too basic: conventional wishbones in front, VW Beetle-style semitrailing swing axles in back. Antiroll bars were omitted to keep retail price as low as possible, but this saved only $4 a car, and GM was well aware they were needed to achieve acceptable handling with rear swing axles and the tail-heavy weight distribution. This decision, as well as management's desire to standardize assembly, precluded more-sophisticated suspension geometry until 1962, when a Regular Production Option including stiffer springs, shorter rear-axle limit straps, and a front sway bar became available. A major suspension improvement occurred for 1964: a transverse rear camber-compensating spring.

Nevertheless, the initial Corvair suspension of 1960-63 did not create a "dangerous, ill-handling car" as later lawsuits claimed. It did oversteer to be sure, but the tail-wag tendency wasn't severe—*provided* that recommended tire pressures were observed (15 psi front, 26 rear). The problem was that most owners didn't pay attention to that, and some got into trouble. When Ralph Nader found out and wrote *Unsafe at Any Speed*, Corvair handling became a *cause celebre* that wasn't put to rest until a 1972 congressional investigation cleared the 1960-63 models. Of course, this came far too late. Corvair was already three years gone.

Corvair's decade-long model run divides into two design generations: 1960-64 and 1965-69. Initial offerings comprised quite spartan four-door sedans in "500" and more-deluxe "700" trim selling at $2000-$2100. Three-speed floorshift manual transaxle was standard; Chevy's two-speed Powerglide was optional. Two-door 500 and 700 coupes arrived at midseason, but the real attention-getter was the new "900" Monza coupe, which boasted an even spiffier interior with bucket seats.

Bolstered by a newly optional four-speed gearbox for 1961, the Monza caught fire, uncovering a huge latent demand for sporty, fun-to-drive compacts. This was fortunate, because Ford's much simpler and cheaper Falcon was handily outselling other Corvairs in the economy market. From here on, the rear-engine Chevy would aim increasingly at enthusiast drivers.

But it was too late to change some plans, so a brace of Corvair Lakewood station wagons arrived for '61 as scheduled, as did a Monza sedan. The Lakewood offered a surprising amount of cargo space—58 cubic feet behind the front seat, 10 more under the front "hood"—more than other compact wagons and even some larger models. It didn't sell well, though, with first-year production barely topping 25,000. Chevy also issued the interesting Corvair-based Greenbrier window van, Corvan panel, and Rampside pickup, all "forward control" models inspired by VW's Type 2 Microbus and forerunners of today's popular minivans. Finally, the flat six was bored out to 145 cid. Standard power remained at 80, but a $27 "Turbo Air" option lifted that to 98.

For 1962, the 500 series was trimmed to a lone coupe, and the Monza line expanded to include a wagon (no longer called Lakewood) and a new convertible. The Monza wagon was plush, but only about 6000 were built before the body style was dropped entirely to make assembly-line room for the Chevy II, the resolutely orthodox Falcon-style compact rushed out to do what Corvair had failed to in the economy market.

Mid-1962 brought what has become the most highly prized first-generation Corvair: the turbocharged Monza Spyder. Initially, this was a $317 option package for Monza two-doors comprising a 150-bhp engine with lots of chrome dressup, a shorter final drive for sprightlier acceleration, heavy-duty suspension, and a multigauge instrument panel with tachometer and brushed-metal trim. The four-speed and sintered-metallic brake linings were "mandatory" options. The Spyder wasn't cheap—a minimum price of $2600—but it was the next best thing to a Porsche. Total production ran about 40,000 units through 1964.

First-generation Corvair styling saw only minor year-to-year changes, mostly at the front. The original winged Chevy bowtie gave way to a smaller emblem on a slim full-width chrome bar for '61. The '62s substituted dummy air slots. A wide single chevron replaced those for '63. Then came a double-bar version of the '61 treatment. Aside from the aforementioned rear camber compensator, the big news for '64 was a stroked 164-cid engine with 95 or 110 bhp in normally aspirated form. Spyder power was unchanged.

With 1965 came a design revolution. The sleek, second-generation Corvair looked good even from normally unflattering angles, a tribute to the work of GM Design under chief William L. Mitchell. It was something an Italian coachbuilder might do—as Pininfarina did with a specially bodied '64 Corvair of generally similar lines. Not only was the 1965 Corvair nicely shaped, it had just the right amount of chrome trim. Closed models were now pillarless hardtops, and a four-door returned to the 500 series.

The '65s were equally new under their handsome bodies. The turbo six was up to 180 bhp, but the best all-around engine was the new 140-bhp nonturbo version that was standard for the top-line Corsa coupe and convertible, replacing Monza Spyder. Its extra power came from new cylinder heads, redesigned manifolds, and four progressively linked carburetors. The "140" was an option for lesser Corvairs, which continued with 95 standard and 110 optional bhp.

The 1960 Corvair had been the first mass-produced American car with swing-axle rear suspension. The '65 was the first with fully independent suspension, not counting the '63 Corvette. The sole difference was that where Corvette linked rear wheels with a single transverse leaf spring, Corvair used individual coils. Both systems employed upper and lower control arms at each rear wheel. The uppers were actually the axle halfshafts; the lowers were unequal-length nonparallel trailing arms (two per side). Together, these controlled all wheel motion. Small rubber-mounted rods extended from each lower arm to the main rear crossmember to absorb longitudinal movement at the pivot points.

No question now about tricky behavior "at the limit": Corvair handling was near-neutral with mild initial understeer. With rear wheels nearly vertical at all times, the car could be pushed around corners with fine stability. Attention was also paid to the front suspension, which was tuned to complement the new rear end and provide additional roll stiffness.

Like the Monza Spyder before it, the 1965-66 Corsa was the most-desirable second-generation Corvair—as it still is among collectors. Base-priced at $2519 for the coupe and $2665 as a convertible, it came with full instrumentation, special exterior accents (including a bright rear-panel appliqué for instant recog-

1960 700 four-door sedan

1961 700 Lakewood station wagon

1961 Greenbrier Sports Wagon passenger van

1962 900 Monza club coupe

1965 Corsa convertible coupe

1969 Monza hardtop sport coupe

nition), deluxe all-vinyl bucket-seat interior, and the 140-bhp engine. With the $158 turbo-six option, Corsa was squarely in the performance league: less than 11 seconds 0-60 mph, 18 seconds at 80 mph for the standing quarter-mile. Given enough room, a blown Corsa could hit 115 mph.

Unfortunately, Corsa didn't sell well against Ford's instant smash-hit Mustang, which had bowed about six months before and could also better the Chevy's on-road performance. More critical was the decline in Monza sales then setting in. Though the most-popular Corvair rallied slightly for '65, production plunged by some two-thirds the following year. Sales were definitely being affected by Nader's book—and GM's embarrassing admission that it had put Nader under surveillance. But damning charges and damaging publicity were beside the point. GM had already sealed Corvair's fate in April 1965 with an internal memo that said, in effect, "No more development work. Do only enough to meet federal requirements."

When Chevy's true Mustang-fighter, the Camaro, arrived for 1967, Corvair was trimmed to just 500 sedan and coupe and Monza sedan, coupe, and convertible. The turbo engine was also dropped, and hardtop sedans were in their final year.

The 1968-69 models were the rarest Corvairs. Comprising just 500 and Monza hardtops and Monza convertibles, they're readily spotted by federally mandated front side-marker lights—clear on the '68s, amber for '69. Monza convertibles were scarcest of all: respectively, just 1386 and 521 built.

With so little change in light of fast-falling sales, Corvair was looking terminal by 1968, so many were surprised that Chevy even bothered with the '69 models. Some dealers wouldn't sell them and others refused to service them, so the division offered what few buyers remained a $150 credit on the purchase of another Chevy through 1974. With that, the Corvair was dead.

In retrospect, Corvair was a victim of its own success. Had it not been for the Monza, we might not have had the Mustang—and ultimately, the Camaro. Left stillborn by the no-more-development edict was a project dubbed XP-849, which went at least as far as a pair of clay mockups: one apparently a rear-engine design, the other with *front-wheel* drive. Intriguingly, both were badged "Corvair 2." A possible prelude to Chevy's unfortunate 1971 Vega, though likely for overseas consumption, XP-849 would never materialize. But it showed that at least some GMers still remembered the adventuresome spirit of the original Corvair despite years of corporate miscues and public controversy.

Specifications

1960

500 (wb 108.0)		Wght	Price	Prod
0527	cpe	2,270	1,984	14,628
0569	sdn 4d	2,305	2,038	47,683
700 (wb 108.0)				
0727	cpe	2,290	2,049	36,562
0769	sdn 4d	2,315	2,103	139,208
900 Monza (wb 108.0)				
0927	cpe	2,280	2,238	11,926

1960 Engines	bore×stroke	bhp	availability
flat 6, 140.0	3.38 × 2.60	80	S-all
flat 6, 140.0	3.38 × 2.60	95	O-all

1961

500 (wb 108.0)		Wght	Price	Prod
0527	cpe	2,320	1,920	16,857
0535	Lakewood wgn 4d	2,530	2,266	5,591
0569	sdn 4d	2,355	1,974	18,752
700 (wb 108.0)				
0727	cpe	2,350	1,985	24,786
0735	Lakewood wgn 4d	2,555	2,331	20,451
0769	sdn 4d	2,380	2,039	51,948
900 Monza (wb 108.0)				
0927	cpe	2,395	2,201	109,945
0969	sdn 4d	2,420	2,201	33,745

1961 Engines	bore × stroke	bhp	availability
flat 6, 145.0	3.44 × 2.60	80	S-all
flat 6, 145.0	3.44 × 2.60	98	O-all

1962

500 (wb 108.0)		Wght	Price	Prod
0527	cpe	2,350	1,992	16,245
700 (wb 108.0)				
0727	cpe	2,390	2,057	18,474
0735	wgn 4d	2,590	2,407	3,716
0769	sdn 4d	2,410	2,111	35,368
900 Monza (wb 108.0)				
0927	cpe	2,440	2,273	144,844
0927	Spyder cpe	2,465	2,636	6,894
0935	wgn 4d	2,590	2,569	2,362
0967	conv cpe	2,625	2,483	13,995
0967	Spyder conv cpe	2,650	2,846	2,574
0969	sdn 4d	2,455	2,273	48,059

1962 Engines	bore×stroke	bhp	availability
flat 6, 145.0	3.44 × 2.60	80	S-all exc Spyd
flat 6, 145.0	3.44 × 2.60	102	O-all exc Spyd
flat 6T, 145.0	3.44 × 2.60	150	S-Monza Spyd

1963

500 (wb 108.0)		Wght	Price	Prod
0527	cpe	2,330	1,992	16,680
700 (wb 108.0)				
0727	cpe	2,355	2,056	12,378
0769	sdn 4d	2,385	2,110	20,684
900 Monza (wb 108.0)				
0927	cpe	2,415	2,272	117,917
0927	Spyder cpe	2,440	2,589	11,627
0967	conv cpe	2,525	2,481	36,693
0967	Spyder conv cpe	2,550	2,798	7,472
0969	sdn 4d	2,450	2,326	31,120

1963 Engines	bore×stroke	bhp	availability
flat 6, 145.0	3.44 × 2.60	80	S-all exc Spyd
flat 6, 145.0	3.44 × 2.60	102	O-all exc Spyd
flat 6T, 145.0	3.44 × 2.60	150	S-Monza Spyd

1964

500 (wb 108.0)		Wght	Price	Prod
0527	cpe	2,365	2,000	22,968
600 Monza Spyder (wb 108.0)				
0627	cpe	2,470	2,599	6,480
0667	conv cpe	2,580	2,811	4,761
700 (wb 108.0)				
0769	sdn 4d	2,415	2,119	16,295
900 Monza (wb 108.0)				
0927	cpe	2,445	2,281	88,440
0967	conv cpe	2,555	2,492	31,045
0969	sdn 4d	2,470	2,335	21,926

1964 Engines	bore×stroke	bhp	availability
flat 6, 164.0	3.44 × 2.94	95	S-all exc 600
flat 6, 164.0	3.44 × 2.94	110	O-all exc 600
flat 6T, 164.0	3.44 × 2.94	150	S-600

1965

500 (wb 108.0)		Wght	Price	Prod
10137	htp cpe	2,385	2,066	36,747
10139	htp sdn	2,405	2,142	17,560
Monza (wb 108.0)				
10537	htp cpe	2,440	2,347	88,954
10539	htp sdn	2,465	2,422	37,157
10567	conv cpe	2,675	2,493	26,466
Corsa (wb 108.0)				
10737	htp cpe	2,475	2,519	20,291
10767	conv cpe	2,710	2,665	8,353

1965 Engines	bore×stroke	bhp	availability
flat 6, 164.0	3.44 × 2.94	95	S-all exc Corsa
flat 6, 164.0	3.44 × 2.94	110	O-all exc Corsa
flat 6, 164.0	3.44 × 2.94	140	S-Crs; O-others
flat 6T, 164.0	3.44 × 2.94	180	O-Corsa

1966

500 (wb 108.0)		Wght	Price	Prod
10137	htp cpe	2,400	2,083	24,045
10139	htp sdn	2,445	2,157	8,779
Monza (wb 108.0)				
10537	htp cpe	2,445	2,350	37,605
10539	htp sdn	2,495	2,424	12,497
10567	conv cpe	2,675	2,493	10,345
Corsa (wb 108.0)				
10737	htp cpe	2,485	2,519	7,330
10767	conv cpe	2,720	2,662	3,142

1966 Engines	bore×stroke	bhp	availability
flat 6, 164.0	3.44 × 2.94	95	S-all except Corsa
flat 6, 164.0	3.44 × 2.94	110	O-all except Corsa
flat 6, 164.0	3.44 × 2.94	140	S-Crs; O-others
flat 6T, 164.0	3.44 × 2.94	180	O-Corsa

1967

500 (wb 108.0)		Wght	Price	Prod
10137	htp cpe	2,435	2,128	9,257
10139	htp sdn	2,470	2,194	2,959
Monza (wb 108.0)				
10537	htp cpe	2,465	2,398	9,771
10539	htp sdn	2,515	2,464	3,157
10567	conv cpe	2,695	2,540	2,109

1967 Engines	bore×stroke	bhp	availability
flat 6, 164.0	3.44 × 2.94	95	S-all
flat 6, 164.0	3.44 × 2.94	110/140	O-all

1968

500 (wb 108.0)		Wght	Price	Prod
10137	htp cpe	2,470	2,243	7,206
Monza (wb 108.0)				
10537	htp cpe	2,500	2,507	6,807
10567	conv cpe	2,725	2,626	1,386

1968 Engines	bore × stroke	bhp	availability
flat 6, 164.0	3.44 × 2.94	95	S-all
flat 6, 164.0	3.44 × 2.94	110/140	O-all

1969

500 (wb 108.0)		Wght	Price	Prod
10137	htp cpe	2,515	2,528	2,762
Monza (wb 108.0)				
10537	htp cpe	2,545	2,522	2,717
10567	conv cpe	2,770	2,641	521

1969 Engines	bore × stroke	bhp	availability
flat 6, 164.0	3.44 × 2.94	95	S-all
flat 6, 164.0	3.44 × 2.94	110/140	O-all

Chevrolet Corvette

America's most-enduring sports car debuted in January 1953 as a production-ready Motorama showmobile, the culmination of a 30-month development effort between Harley Earl's Art & Colour Studio and the Chevrolet Division Engineering Staff. Enthusiastic public response prompted management to okay production of the two-seat convertible—a brave decision as sales of import sports cars then amounted to less than one percent of the market. Production commenced June 30 on a small line at Chevy's Flint, Michigan, plant.

All Corvettes through 1962 rode a 102-inch wheelbase, identical with that of the Jaguar XK-120, one of Earl's favorite sports cars. The chassis was initially a cut-down and modified Chevrolet passenger-car frame. Body construction was unique: the first use of fiberglass in a series-production car by a major automaker. Styling was vintage Harley Earl show car: rounded and rather bulbous, with extended pod-type taillights, a toothy grille, and trendy wraparound windshield—hardly timeless, though it looked great at the time.

Ironically, in view of what lay ahead, Corvette almost expired after 1955 due to very low sales. Just 315 were built for '53 (most reserved for promotion and favored VIPs), followed by 3640 for '54—when production was shifted to St. Louis—and a mere 700 of the '55s. Some blamed this disappointing performance on the car's rather odd mix of features. Boulevardier types disliked the plastic side curtains, clumsy cloth top, and the lack of both back seat and exterior door handles. Enthusiasts chided the gimmicky styling and plodding drive-train—two-speed Powerglide automatic and Chevy's 235.5-cubic-inch "Stovebolt Six"—though triple carbs, high-lift cam, higher compression, and other changes brought the aged engine to a commendable 150 horsepower.

Thanks to pleas from Earl and Chevy chief engineer Ed Cole, GM decided in late 1954 to give Corvette a second chance. And Cole had what would prove to be its salvation: the brilliant 265-cid overhead-valve V-8 he'd designed with Harry Barr, John Gordon, and others for Chevy's all-new 1955 passenger cars. Arriving with 195 horsepower, it vastly improved Corvette performance, and all but seven of the '55 examples were so equipped. A newly optional three-speed floorshift manual gearbox further shifted the car's image from "plastic bathtub" to serious sporting machine. However, Chevrolet had 1100 unsold '54s at the start of '55 production, which hampered sales in spite of a much improved car.

The restyled '56 was even sportier, and Chevy rightly billed it as "America's only true sports car." A rounded rump and beautifully sculptured bodysides with curving, concave "coves" just aft of the front-wheel openings marked a stunning improvement over the stubby, slab-sided original. Proper roll-up windows and an optional lift-off hardtop (both previewed on a 1954 Motorama Corvette) made motoring more civilized, as did pushbutton door handles outside. Dropping the six and tuning the V-8 for 210 or 225 horsepower (the latter via a high-lift camshaft, twin four-barrel carburetors, and dual exhausts) made for thrilling performance; adept chassis changes by newly hired engineer Zora Arkus-Duntov made handling more than capable. The close-ratio three-speed manual replaced standard Powerglide, which shifted to the options sheet. The most-potent '56 could nail 60 mph from rest in just 7.5 seconds and top 120 mph.

There was no need to change the handsome styling for '57, but Chevy upped performance by boring the V-8 to 283 cid. This came in five versions offering 220 horsepower up to an amazing 283 horsepower, the latter courtesy of new "Ramjet" fuel injection. A four-speed manual transmission arrived in April at $188 extra, and combined with axle ratios as low as 4.56:1 to make "fuelie" '57s thunderingly fast. Published road tests showed 0-60 in 5.7 seconds, 0-100 mph in 16.8 seconds, the standing quarter-mile in 14.3 seconds at 96 mph, and a maximum speed of 132-plus mph. Unfortunately, mechanical bugs and a steep $500 price limited Ramjet installations to only 1040 units that year. Chevy also offered a $725 "heavy-duty racing suspension" with high-rate springs and shocks, front antiroll bar, quick steering, and metallic brake linings with finned drums. With this and one of the high-power engines, a '57 'Vette was virtually ready to race off the showroom floor.

And indeed, Corvette now began making its mark in international competition. Dr. Richard Thompson won the national Sports Car Club of America (SCCA) C-Production championship in 1956, then took the '57 crown in B-Production, where the 'Vette qualified by dint of its larger engine. John Fitch's '56 was the fastest modified car at that year's Daytona Speed Week, a Corvette finished 9th in the grueling 12 Hours of Sebring in '56, and another came home 2nd at Pebble Beach. Chevy's 1957 Sebring assault saw production Corvettes finish 1-2 in the GT class and 12th and 15th overall.

This success was all symbolic of a dramatic metamorphosis. Said one European writer: "Before Sebring... the Corvette was regarded as a plastic toy. After Sebring, even the most biased were forced to admit that [it was] one of the world's finest sports cars..." That included buyers, who happily took 3467 of the '56s and 6339 of the '57s. Corvette's future was assured.

Nineteen fifty-eight brought a busier, shinier Corvette measuring 10 inches longer, more than two inches wider, and a few pounds heavier. The basic shape was broadly the same as 1956-

1954 Corvette convertible roadster

1955 Corvette Six convertible roadster

1955 Corvette V-8 convertible roadster

1956 Corvette convertible coupe

1957 Corvette convertible coupe

1958 Corvette convertible coupe with optional hardtop

57 except for quad headlamps (all the rage that year), a dummy air scoop ahead of each bodyside "cove," simulated hood louvers, and equally silly longitudinal chrome strips on the trunklid. Yet there were genuine improvements, including sturdier bumpers and a redesigned cockpit with passenger grab bar, locking glovebox, and all of the instruments directly ahead of the driver (instead of spread all the way across the dash panel, as before).

Despite the added heft, performance remained vivid because '58 engines were little changed. In fact, the top fuel-injected 283 gained seven horsepower to reach 290, thus exceeding the hallowed "1 hp per cu. in." benchmark reached the previous year. Inflation plagued the national economy in '58, yet base price remained reasonable at $3631, up just $118 from their debut in '53. Critics generally liked the '58. So did buyers. Model-year production gained 2829 units over the '57 tally as Corvette turned a profit for the first time.

Volume rose by another 500 units for '59, when Chevy smoothed out the hood, deleted the chrome trunk trim, and added trailing radius rods (the year's only noteworthy mechanical change) to counteract rear-axle windup in hard acceleration. This basic package carried into 1960 as Corvette production broke the magic 10,000-unit barrier for the first time.

That year brought a larger 24-gallon fuel tank as a new extra, and the optional heavy-duty suspension was replaced by a larger front antiroll bar and a new standard rear bar. An extra inch of wheel travel in rebound further contributed to a smoother ride and more-neutral handling. Aluminum radiators were newly offered, but announced cast-aluminum cylinder heads didn't make it.

Though Corvette was fast moving from *pur sang* sports car to plush GT, it was no less a competitor on the track. Highlights include a GT-class win and 12th overall at Sebring '58, national SCCA B-Production championships in 1958-59, fastest sports car at the 1958 Pike's Peak Hill Climb, and a slew of victories by privateers. Thanks to the Automobile Manufacturers Association mid-1957 edict, Chevy was officially "out of racing" now, though not above lending under-the-table support to those campaigning its cars. Among them was sportsman Briggs Cunningham, who gave Corvette one of its finest racing hours when one of his three team cars (driven by John Fitch and Bob Grossman) finished 8th in the 1960 running of the fabled 24 Hours of Le Mans.

The 1960 Corvette might have been very different. Beginning in 1957, Chevy contemplated a smaller, lighter car based on the prototype "Q-model," with rear transaxle, independent rear suspension, and inboard disc brakes. A full-size mockup soon took shape bearing a remarkable resemblance to the production Sting Ray then six years distant, but the project was abandoned because of the '58 recession and the time and money

1958 Corvette convertible coupe

1959 Corvette convertible coupe

1960 Corvette convertible coupe

1961 Corvette convertible coupe

1962 Corvette convertible coupe

1963 Sting Ray "split window" sport coupe

1963 Sting Ray convertible coupe with optional hardtop

being expended to bring out Chevy's rear-engine Corvair compact for 1960.

There was nothing to do but soldier on with the existing Corvette while designers and engineers set about creating a less radical replacement. Meantime, GM styling chief Harley Earl had retired in 1958, and his successor, William L. Mitchell, had an idea for breathing new life into the old Corvette.

It took the form of a 1961 model restyled behind the doors along the lines of Mitchell's 1959 Stingray racer (built on the "mule" chassis salvaged from 1957's unsuccessful Corvette SS prototype effort at Sebring). A new flowing "ducktail" not only increased luggage space some 20 percent but mated handsomely with the 1958-60 front, which Mitchell simplified by substituting mesh for the familiar chrome grille "teeth."

Horsepower for the top fuel-injected engine jumped to 315 for '61. Chevy continued to come up with refinements: standard sunvisors, higher-capacity aluminum-core radiator, side-mount expansion tanks, a wider choice of axle ratios. Base price was up to $3934, but that dough got you a lot of go. Even the mildest 283 with Powerglide was good for 7.7 seconds 0-60 mph and nearly 110 mph flat out; figures for the optional 315-bhp "fuelie" V-8 and four-speed manual were 5.5 seconds and 130-plus mph. In case anyone still doubted Corvette's track prowess, a near-stock model finished 11th at Sebring '61 against much-costlier and more-exotic racing machinery.

Refinement was again the keynote for '62, but Chevy gave a hint of things to come by offering the next Corvette's engines in the last "traditional" models. There were four in all—one fuelie and three with carburetors—all 283s bored and stroked to 327 cid, good for 250 up to a thumping 360 horsepower. The fuel-injection system was modified, a new 3.08:1 final-drive ratio gave quieter cruising with the two lowest-power engines, and the heavy-duty suspension option returned from '59. Styling was cleaner than ever. Mitchell eliminated the chrome outline around the "coves" and their optional two-toning, blacked-in the grille, and added ribbed aluminum appliques to rocker panels and the dummy reverse front-fender scoops.

Corvette continued its winning ways on the track and in the showroom for '62. Dick Thompson, the "flying dentist," won that year's national A-Production crown in SCCA, Don Yenko the B-P title. More important to GM managers, production was still climbing, from 1961's record 10,000-plus to over 14,500. No question now: The 'Vette was here to stay.

And how. Nineteen sixty-three brought the all-new Sting Ray, the first complete revision of Chevrolet's sports car in 10 years—a revolution and a revelation. Apart from four wheels and two seats, the only things the new 'Vette shared with the '62 were steering, front suspension, the four 327 V-8s, and fiberglass bodywork. Most everything else was changed—definitely for the better.

Dimensional changes involved slightly shorter overall length, a two-inch narrower rear track, and a wheelbase pared four inches (to 98). Curb weight was also reduced, thanks to a new ladder-type frame (replacing the heavy old X-member affair) and despite a new steel-reinforced "cage" that made for a stronger, safer cockpit. In fact, the Sting Ray had almost twice as much steel support in its main body structure as previous Corvettes, and less fiberglass in its body. Brakes remained drums but were now self-adjusting, and the fronts were wider.

The big mechanical news for '63 was independent rear suspension, a first for a modern U.S. production car. Duntov's clever thinking produced a frame-mounted differential with U-jointed halfshafts acting on a single transverse leaf spring; differential-mounted control arms ran laterally and slightly forward to the hub carriers to limit fore/aft movement, and a pair of trailing radius rods was fitted behind. This arrangement was elegantly simple, relatively cheap, and highly effective. Front/rear weight distribution was now 48/52 percent versus the former 53/47. New recirculating-ball steering combined with a dual-arm, three-link ball-joint front suspension for quicker steering. With all this, Corvette ride and handling were better than ever.

Engines were unchanged from '62, but the '63 versions carried alternators instead of generators, positive crankcase ventilation, and smaller flywheels. Competition options included stiff suspension, metallic brake linings, and a 36.5-gallon long-distance fuel tank. Handsome cast-alumium wheels with genuine knock-off hubs were listed as an option, but were withdrawn because they tended to leak air with tubeless tires. It is doubtful if any were put on a production car at the factory, but they were available over the counter at Chevy dealers.

Sting Ray styling was equally new and quite dramatic, evolved from the experimental XP-720 coupe of late 1959. The customary convertible gained a sleek fastback coupe companion—a first for Corvette—with rear window split by a vertical divider. Duntov lobbied against the last, saying it hampered outward vision. Mitchell huffed in reply that "if you take that off, you might as well forget the whole thing." Duntov ultimately won, and a one-piece backlight was substituted after '63, leaving the split-window coupe a one-year model—and today all the more highly prized because of it.

Both '63 Sting Rays carried hidden headlights (in rotating pods that fit flush with the pointy nose when the lamps were off), an attractive beltline dip at the doors' trailing edges, humped front and rear fenders, slim L-shape half-bumpers at each end, a slightly different "ducktail," and a sharp full-perimeter "character line" at midbody height. Inside was a new "dual cockpit" dashboard with complete set of big gauges and Corvette's first proper glovebox. Coupe interior access was facilitated by doors cut into the roof. An optional lift-off hardtop was still available for the convertible.

Because of work on the stillborn Q-model, the Sting Ray coupe was developed first, then the convertible. A 2+2 coupe was considered, progressing as far as a full-size mockup, but was rejected as being out of character for Corvette. Prototypes received intensive wind-tunnel testing that resulted in frontal area being trimmed by a square foot. Despite the shorter wheelbase, interior space was at least as good as it had been in previous Corvettes.

The Sting Ray quickly proved the fastest and most-roadable

1963 Sting Ray convertible coupe

1964 Sting Ray sport coupe

1964 Sting Ray convertible coupe

1965 Sting Ray sport coupe

'Vette, yet. It was also the most popular: 1963 sales were nearly twice the record '62 total, about 10,000 for each body style. Performance had less to do with this than the wider market appeal of new extra-cost creature comforts: leather upholstery, power steering, power brakes (at last), AM/FM radio, air conditioning, and more.

Over the next four years, the Sting Ray was progressively cleaned up. Chevrolet removed what little nonsense there was or made it functional, as with the fake hood louvers (erased) and coupe rear quarter vents (opened up) for '64. The following year, the sculptured hood was smoothed out and the dummy front-fender slots were made into working vents. The design

1965 Sting Ray convertible coupe

1966 Sting Ray sport coupe

1967 Sting Ray sport coupe

was virtually perfected by 1967, when the only changes were a single oblong backup light above the license plate, bolt-on instead of knock-off aluminum wheels, revised front-fender louvers, and an optional vinyl covering for the convertible's accessory hardtop.

Naturally, there were important mechanical improvements in the Sting Ray years. The fuelie 327 was boosted to as high as 375 horsepower for 1964. The following year brought standard four-wheel disc brakes for stopping power to match the steadily escalating performance. Also new for '65 was Corvette's first big-block V-8, the 425-bhp "Mark IV." This was initially sized at 396 cid, then enlarged to 427 for '66. To handle its brute force, Chevy specified stiffer suspension, extra-heavy-duty clutch, and larger radiator and fan. With the 4.11:1 rear axle, a '66 Mark IV could do 0-60 in less than five seconds and more than 140 mph flat out—not bad for a civilized, fully equipped machine selling for around $4500. Fuel injection was dropped after 1965, mainly due to high production costs and low sales.

But Corvette sales as a whole set new records in all but one of the Sting Ray years, peaking at nearly 28,000 for '66. Horsepower seemed to set yearly records, too. That peak was reached with the stupendous L88 option of 1967: an aluminum-head 427 with 12.5:1 compression, wild cam, and big four-barrel carb, putting out no less than 560 horsepower, but conservatively rated at 430. Only 20 cars were so equipped, but they symbolized how far the 'Vette had come.

Of course, many of the high-power Sting Rays went racing, though they often bowed to Carroll Shelby's stark, super-quick Cobras. Still, there were bright spots. Don Yenko was SCCA national B-Production champ in 1963, a Roger Penske car won its class at Nassau '65, and 1966 saw Sting Rays place 12th overall in the Daytona Continental and 9th at Sebring.

The Sting Ray was a tough act to follow, and not everyone liked its 1968 replacement. Arriving for the first year of federal safety and emissions standards, it combined a new seven-inch-longer body (most of the increase in front overhang) with essentially carryover engines and chassis. Styling, previewed by the 1965 Mako Shark II show car, was all humpy and muscular, with fulsome front and rear fenders housing seven-inch-wide wheels for better roadholding. Flip-up headlamps and modest "lip" spoilers at each end were also featured but, like the Sting Rays, there was still no opening trunklid. And the name wasn't Sting Ray anymore, just Corvette. Coupe and convertible returned, the former a new notchback style with an innovative "T-top" design: twin panels could be removed to create a semiconvertible. Mechanical upgrades were limited to substituting General Motors' fine three-speed Turbo Hydra-Matic transmission for the archaic Powerglide and moving the battery from under the hood to behind the seats for better weight distribution.

This third-generation Corvette would have bowed for 1967 had Zora Arkus-Duntov not delayed it to work out some kinks. Still, the '68s had plenty of problems. The most glaring was poor workmanship that led one motor-noter to label his press car "unfit to road test." Other writers judged the new design needlessly gimmicky, with a dashboard awash in winking lights and a trouble-prone pop-up cowl panel hiding the wipers. A narrower cockpit, a penalty of the wasp-waisted styling, and less luggage space didn't win any friends. Neither did inadequate cooling on big-block cars, nor did an average 150 pounds of extra weight. Yet, in spite of all that, the '68 set another Corvette sales record at more than 28,500 units.

The tally was nearly 38,800 for '69, when the Stingray name reappeared—this time as one word on front fenders. Duntov did his best to correct inherent flaws in the year-old design, finding a little more cockpit space (smaller steering wheel, slimmer door panels), adding an override so the wiper panel could be left up in freezing weather, and reworking other assorted bits. Detail styling changes comprised neater outside door handles, black instead of chrome grille bars, and backup lights integrated within the inner taillights. Handling improved via wider wheels, and the frame was stiffened. Emissions considerations prompted lower compression ratios and a small-block V-8 stroked to 350 cid, while a fourth 427 option appeared with a nominal 430 horsepower and available axle ratios from 4.56:1 to 2.75:1. Even wilder was the all-aluminum ZL-1 big-block, a virtual Can-Am racing engine priced at a formidable $4718. Production? Just two. But Corvette celebrated a production benchmark that year as number 250,000 came off the St. Louis line.

Volume promptly plunged some 50 percent for 1970, thanks to a two-month auto-workers strike. The main news that season was a big-block punched out to 454 cid, again to meet emissions standards that were increasingly sapping power from all Detroit engines. Even so, lower compression left the big-block LS-5 at 390 horsepower. A more-powerful LS-7 version rated at 460 horsepower was advertised and prototype Corvettes so equipped were produced, but the engine was never actually offered for public sale because it couldn't be made "clean" enough. The rest of the car was again little changed—a fine-check grille and front-fender vents provided visual ID—but Chevrolet cleaned up more details and offered a 370-bhp solid-lifter LT-1 small-block V-8.

Corvette was little-changed for 1971. The big-block LS-7 attempted for 1970, but not produced, returned as an emissions-friendly LS-6 putting out 425 bhp.

Inflation, rising gas prices, and soaring insurance rates were putting a big crimp in performance-car sales. Corvette was no exception, its 1972 volume not even equaling '69's. That year's switch to more-realistic SAE net power ratings made engines seem punier—which they were—and the LS-6 was canceled along with the fiber-optic exterior light monitors available since '68. However, the once-optional antitheft alarm system was now standard, a belated nod to the 'Vette's high "thievability."

The '73s gained a body-color nose of pliable plastic in line with the government's new five-mph impact-protection rule, plus more insulation and new chassis mounts for quietness. The coupe's removable rear window, a feature since '68, went away. So did all engines save a pair of 350s and one 454. Rear-impact standards dictated a matching body-color tail for the '74s, which arrived with the Middle East oil embargo, still higher gas prices, and long lines at the pumps. Yet, while other cars suffered sales drops, Corvette kept climbing.

But it kept slipping, too. Both the LT-1 and the last big-block options were banished after '74, as was the traditional convertible after '75, a victim of steadily falling demand. Changes were few through 1977 (when Stingray badges came off again), yet sales remained strong. The '76 tally broke the 1969 record with over 46,550. The '77s sold an improbable 49,000-plus.

Clearly, Chevy had made a silk purse of the sow's-ear '68 and reaped the rewards. Government's heavy hand made a change in the car's character inevitable, but that was hardly bad. By 1975, the Corvette had become more balanced, less outlandish, and arguably more pleasant. A juvenile straightline screamer had matured into a suave, high-speed gran turismo.

Still, enthusiasts had been long clamoring for an all-new Vette. A pair of 1972 Wankel-engine show cars strongly hinted it could be a midengine design. Perhaps in time for Corvette's silver anniversary in 1978? No, but it came close for 1980. Its basis would have been the Aerovette, the renamed V-8-powered iteration of the four-rotor 1972 experiment. Bill Mitchell lobbied hard for a production version, and GM president Tom Murphy actually approved one very similar to the show-car design. By late '77, Aerovette-style clay models were complete and tooling was ready to be ordered. But the plan foundered when Mitchell retired that year. Zora Duntov, another booster, had retired at the end of '74, and his successor as Corvette chief engineer, David R. McLellan, wanted to keep the "front mid-engine" format for reasons of packaging, manufacturing, performance, and cost.

Indeed, cost finally killed the production Aerovette—never mind that midengine designs had not proven the wave of the sports-car future as some predicted back in the '60s. Chevy duly regrouped. By mid-1978, McLellan and company were working on a more-conventional new Corvette.

Meantime, the third generation would have to hold on awhile—no big problem, what with sales still strong. Nevertheless, GM decided to splurge on rejuvenating the old warrior

1968 Corvette convertible coupe

1968 Corvette sport coupe

1969 Stingray coupe

1970 Stingray coupe

for Corvette's 25th birthday year.

The '78 thus received one big change—a new fastback roofline with a huge compound-curve rear window *a la* Sting Ray—and a host of minor ones (mostly to the cockpit). Corvette was named pace car for that year's Indy 500, and Chevrolet issued 6502 replicas with special paint, leather interior, and owner-applied pace-car decals. To the division's chagrin, quick-buck artists were quick to convert standard 'Vettes into bogus replicas, creating no little confusion. There was also a Silver Anniversary model, actually a trim package and not all that different from stock. Engine choices were down to two 350s: standard 185-bhp L48 and extra-cost 220-bhp L82.

Corvette mostly marked time for '79. It was now quite plush for a sports car. Power windows, air, tilt steering wheel, power door locks, and AM/FM/cassette were available. Despite high cost and poor mileage, sales leaped to over 50,000.

Chevy finally put its sports car on a diet for 1980, removing some 150 pounds via wider use of plastics and by substituting aluminum for steel in the differential housing and front frame crossmember. Aerodynamics improved via a new sloped nose with integral spoiler, plus a faired-in rear spoiler.

More weight-saving occurred for '81, mostly from a fiberglass rear leaf spring and thinner glass for door windows and the optional see-through T-tops. There was now just one 350, a new L81 version with magnesium rocker covers, stainless-steel exhaust manifold, and GM's Computer Command Control engine-management system. Horsepower was 190. Government fuel-economy mandates dictated a lockup torque converter for the optional automatic transmission. Inflation pushed base price past $15,000, but that included Cadillac-style front cornering lights. This year saw the historic transfer of production from St. Louis to a new high-tech plant in Bowling Green, Kentucky, built exclusively for Corvette. With it came promises of improved workmanship.

The move to Kentucky also suggested that an all-new Corvette was imminent at last. It was—and sorely needed. Volume had withered since the all-time high of 1979, dropping to the 40,000 level for 1980 and '81. The following year, when the old "shark" design made its 15th and final appearance, production crumbled to a 10-year low of 25,407. A second energy crisis and a deep new national recession hardly helped.

That final "shark" previewed the next-generation drivetrain in a revised L83 engine with fuel injection—the first "fuelie" Corvette since 1965. And for the first time since 1955, there was no manual gearbox, just a new four-speed automatic with torque-converter lockup on all forward gears save first. But the real kicker was another limited-production job tellingly named Collector Edition, with lift-up rear window (belatedly) and unique trim. It was the costliest 'Vette yet at a towering $22,537, a far cry from the $4663 it took to buy a '68. This time, Chevy avoided forgeries by building as many Collectors as customers demanded, which ended up at 6759.

Historians huffed when the much-anticipated fourth generation bowed in early '83 as a 1984 model (a decision made mainly

1972 Stingray coupe

1974 Stingray coupe

1975 Stingray coupe

to ease emissions certification)—thus skipping Corvette's 30th model year. Some observers (including former design chief Bill Mitchell) criticized appearance as bland, but most people liked it. Created under the direction of Jerry Palmer, it was clean, contemporary, recognizably Corvette, and 23.7 percent more aerodynamic—in all, quite a feat. A lift-up hatch window returned from the Collector Edition, but the T-top gave way to a one-piece roof panel, and a new front-hinged "clamshell" hood/fender assembly offered superb engine access.

That engine was a 205-bhp L83 with "Cross-Fire" dual-throttle-body injection, initially mated to four-speed converter-lock-up Turbo Hydra-Matic. But the autobox soon became an optional alternative to a new "4+3 Overdrive" manual. The work of 'Vette specialist Doug Nash, this was basically the normal four-speed with a second planetary gearset actuated by engine electronics to provide gas-saving overdrive ratios in all gears but first.

The rest of the '84 was equally new, starting with its "uni-frame" construction: a Lotus-like backbone chassis welded to an upper "birdcage." Front suspension was modified with a single transverse plastic leaf spring replacing individual coils. At the rear was new five-link geometry comprising upper and lower longitudinal links, twin lateral strut rods from differential to hub carriers, and the usual tie rods, halfshafts, and transverse plastic leaf spring. Steering switched to rack-and-pinion, and there were new-design disc brakes. Tires were Goodyear's new ultrasticky Eagle VR50s with unidirectional "gatorback" tread, worn on wide cast-alloy wheels.

Weight-saving was again a priority, so the '84 had more lightweight materials than any previous Corvette (including beautiful aluminum forgings for suspension components). Though 150 pounds lighter than the '82, the '84 ended up some 300 pounds heavier than expected despite reductions of two inches in wheelbase (to 96.2) and 8.8 inches in overall length.

Still, the '84 offered more passenger and cargo space, better outward vision, and all the comfort and luxury expected in a thoroughbred GT. Unfortunately, it introduced a dazzling digital/graphic electronic gauge cluster that was hard to read, especially on sunny days. A harsh ride—even harsher with the Z51 handling option—emphasized the new structure's surprising flex. A record base price—$23,360—also drew barbs. But that was about all anyone could fault. Few sports cars could rival the Corvette's performance. Buyers evidently thought it as a good value, for model-year production roared back to near the '79 level, ending at over 51,500.

Chevy tended to details for 1985, gaining 25 horsepower by switching from "Cross-Fire" to "Tuned Port" injection, softening both the standard and optional suspensions, and adding an oil cooler and gas-pressurized shock absorbers. The '86s were even better. The brakes received standard Bosch antilock control for stopping power to match the now-stupendous corner-

1976 Stingray coupe

1977 Corvette coupe

1978 Corvette Silver Anniversary coupe

1979 Corvette coupe

1980 Corvette coupe

1981 Corvette coupe

1982 Corvette coupe

1984 Corvette coupe

1984 Corvette coupe

1985 Corvette coupe

1986 Corvette Indianapolis 500 Pace Car convertible coupe

ing grip. Though horsepower posted only a modest gain to 235, the small-block 350 (now designated L98) V-8 received aluminum cylinder heads, higher compression (9.5:1 versus 9.0), and dual exhaust. However, the new heads weren't available until midyear and most '86s had iron heads with 230 bhp.

But the big event of 1986 was the midseason return of the Corvette convertible after a 10-year absence. To no one's great surprise, it arrived just in time to be selected Indianapolis 500 pace car—which meant another batch of replicas, all yellow ragtops. Because the fourth generation had been designed to be topless, structural stiffening was straightforward: an X-member below the floorpan and reinforcements around the cockpit.

The main change for '87 was roller valve lifters that added another 5 horses for a total of 240. Chevrolet also announced an optional in-cockpit tire-pressure monitoring system, similar to that of the otherworldly Porsche 959, but development problems would delay this until 1989. Seeking still more cornering power, Chevy offered the '88s with optional 17-inch wheels wearing fat P275/40ZR Goodyear Eagle tires. Both these and the standard 16-inch rims were newly styled. The suspension was modified to better resist rear-end squat in hard acceleration and nosedive in panic braking, which was now handled by larger, thicker, all-disc brakes with dual-piston front calipers. Freer-breathing heads and a reprofiled camshaft boosted horsepower to 245.

Another milestone Corvette birthday rolled around in '88—the 35th—and Chevy celebrated with specially trimmed anniversary coupes (actually an optional appearance package, RPO Z01). This was done mostly in white—including interior and even nameplates—accented by black roof pillars and blue-tint glass roof panel. Automatic climate system, all-leather cockpit trim, power driver's seat, heated rear window and door mirrors, and a Sport Handling Package were included, too. Though just 2050 were built, it was a nice way for America's sports car to enter middle age with a 35-year production total approaching 900,000.

But it was only a warm up to 1990's amazing new "King of the Hill" Corvette, a constant subject of "buff book" spy reports since late '87. Though delayed from a planned '89 launch, the ZR-1 was well worth waiting for—another Chevy option code destined to make history. Available only in coupe form, it boasted an all-new, all-aluminum V-8 designated LT5. It was still a 350 but with a smaller bore and longer stroke than the existing L98—plus dual overhead camshafts actuating four valves per cylinder.

LT5 specs read like a competition textbook: forged-steel crank and conrods, diecast pistons, stellite-faced valves, sequential-port fuel injection, "Direct Fire" all-coil ignition, high 11.25:1 compression, and more. The result was 375 horsepower—astounding for a modern emissions-controlled street engine claimed to deliver up to 22.5 mpg. A unique feature was three-stage throttle control providing "stepped" power delivery via the engine's electronic control module. To keep lesser-skilled—or unauthorized—drivers from getting into trouble, the system included a "power mode" that precluded full power at full throttle without a special key. The LT5 was carefully engineered so the engine bay wouldn't need alteration, but the ZR-1 was easily spotted from behind by its square taillights and subtly bulged bodywork draped over super-wide tires.

Two ZR-1 innovations premiered on '89 Corvettes. One was a six-speed manual gearbox designed by Chevy and Germany's ZF. It had vastly better shift action than the never-liked "4+3" it replaced, but also a rather odd thing called computer-aided gear selection (CAGS) that "forced" a 1-4 shift at light throttle between 12 and 19 mph. Here was another subtle extreme dictated by EPA fuel-economy test procedures and Chevy's desire

1986 Corvette convertible coupe

1987 Corvette coupe

1987 Corvette convertible coupe

that Corvette avoid the government's dreaded new gas-guzzler tax. But though CAGS seemed to spoil the fun, it scarcely ever activated in the kind of driving done by most 'Vette owners.

Corvette's other '89 innovation was Selective Ride Control (RPO FX3), restricted to cars with the new six-speed and the Z51 handling package. Like some Japanese setups, this electro-mechanical system provided three selectable damping levels—Touring, Sport, and Competition—via electric motors that varied the size of the proportioning-valve orifice in each shock absorber. Each level also had six progressively firmer settings that automatically cut in with increasing speed, and a high-speed override automatically switched settings for optimum handling. Developed by Bilstein and GM's Delco Division, SRC claimed to improve both ride and cornering, which it did, though not dramatically.

Other '89 developments began with making the 17-inch wheel/tire option and a modified Z52 handling package newly standard for all models. The latter included strengthened front chassis (introduced with the '86 convertible), faster-ratio steering, Delco/Bilstein gas-filled shocks and, for six-speed cars, engine-oil cooler, heavy-duty radiator, and auxiliary cooling fan. Finally, rearranged top latches made the convertible more-convenient, and Chevy returned to tradition by offering a detachable hardtop for it (priced at $2000).

ZR-1 aside, the main 1990 Corvette news involved two laud-

1988 Corvette coupe

1988 Corvette 35th Anniversary Edition coupe

1989 Corvette convertible coupe with optional hardtop

able standard safety features: a driver-side air bag (hidden in the steering-wheel hub) and Bosch "ABS II" antilock braking system. The latter was especially worthwhile on the ZR-1, which could do a blistering 4.5 seconds 0-60 and top 175 mph. Not laudable at all was the new "aircraft-inspired" instrument panel given all 1990 Vettes, a planned change that was largely responsible for delaying the ZR-1. It was definitely not for the better: a plasticky mish-mash of shapes and colors more outrageous than ergonomic.

On balance, though, the fourth-series Corvette evolved nicely through 1990. The same could not be said for sales after 1984. Model-year production dropped below 40,000 for '85, then sank to less than 31,000 in '87 before bottoming out at fewer than 23,000 for 1988. There was a modest recovery for '89, but the tally was down again for 1990 to some 23,646. The onset of yet another sharp recession played a part, but so did escalating prices. By 1990, the base coupe was $32,000; the convertible over $37,000. Then there was the ZR-1, the costliest GM car ever with a delivered retail price of just under $59,000. Rabid speculators and fools with money gladly bid that up to over $100-grand—but not for long. Within 18 months the ZR-1 was selling for well under retail amid reports of surplus LT5s and rumors that Chevy would soon kill the "King of the Hill."

In a way, Chevy did precisely that with a 1991 "taillift" for regular 'Vettes. To the outrage of those who'd rushed to buy ZR-1s, the standard article now wore a similar convex back panel and square taillights. Though Chevy never explained this move, the likely reason was to boost overall Corvette sales with ZR-1 style. If so, the plan backfired, as model-year volume slipped to a little over 20,600. Of these, a mere 2044 were ZR-1s, a drop from 3049 the previous season. By the way, the King was now technically a package option, not a separate model, adding $31,683 to the normal coupe's $32,455 base sticker.

Nineteen ninety-one also brought the fourth-generation's first facelift, as all models, ZR-1 included, wore a smoother, slimmer nose with wrapped turn-signal/fog-lamp assemblies. In addition, the twin front-fender "gills" gave way to four horizontal "strakes." Mechanical changes were of the detail sort: a standard power-steering cooler, a new Z07 package combining the FX3 and Z51 options, first-time FX3 availability for the convertible, and a new "retained power" feature that allowed operating accessories for a few minutes after shutting off.

Dave Hill took over as Corvette chief engineer in September 1992. He was a good choice, having played the same role for Cadillac's short-lived Allanté. Hill was no less committed than Dave McClelland to traditional 'Vette values, including rear drive and a unique platform. But with two-seater sales increasingly tough—and with GM facing a huge cash crisis—he also knew that Corvette would have to "pull its own weight" as never before. That meant not only improving sales but making each one more profitable by taking cost out of the car—without spoiling it, of course. GM was known to be thinking about spinning future 'Vettes from a higher-volume platform, but Hill wouldn't have that. As he told the press in 1993: "I can assure you, the last thing on our minds is a hot version of the Camaro replacing the Corvette."

As if to signal renewed faith in its sports car, Chevy again reworked the hallowed small-block V-8 for 1992 to give base Corvettes an extra 55 horsepower. The rejuvenated engine, titled LT1, was also quicker to wind and had a higher rev limit, though it wasn't as torquey as the L98, with 330 pound-feet peaking at 4000 rpm (versus 340 at 3200). Nevertheless, the LT1 was cheered by the press and enthusiasts alike, many of whom felt that it rendered the ZR-1 almost superfluous. And in fact, with its 5.4-second 0-60 capability, the LT1 wasn't that much slower than the King, especially given the price difference.

The ZR-1 itself added front-fender nameplates for '92, but all Corvettes now boasted Acceleration Slip Regulation, a new Bosch-designed traction-control system. Like similar setups at Porsche, BMW, and Mercedes, this one used the ABS sensors to detect wheelspin, in which event it would either brake the offending wheels and/or throttle back power to keep you from slip-sliding away. To back it up, all '92s wore grippier tires, Goodyear's new asymmetric-tread Eagle GS-C.

Those tires grew wider on standard '93s, and wider aft than fore. In fact, they were now close to King size: at the back, 285/40ZR17s on 9.5-inch-wide rims; in front, 255/45ZR17s on 8.5s. Also for '93, the LT1 was retuned for 10 extra pound-feet of torque, but the LT5 was attended to as well, internal changes boosting horsepower to 405 at 5800 rpm (up 30 bhp) and torque to 385 pound-feet at 5200 (up 15). With that, the ZR-1 was again the power king of American production cars after bowing to Dodge's spartan new Viper RT/10 in 1991-92.

Unfortunately, the extra muscle didn't do much for the King's 0-60 kick—about 0.2-second at most, according to *Car and Driver*. Top speed, however, was up six mph to a shattering 179, and the new tires improved skidpad cornering from 0.88g to a race-carlike 0.92. Yet all this was quite academic, for ZR-1 sales were just a trickle now: a mere 448 for '93, down from 502 the previous model year. On the other hand, overall Corvette sales went up for the first time in four years. Though an improvement of only a little over 1000 units, the '93 upsurge to 21,590 was heartening in Corvette's 40th year.

Yes, it was birthday time again, and as everyone knew it would, Chevrolet issued another anniversary special. A $1455 package option available for any '93, it comprised Ruby Red paint and wheel centers, a color-matched leather-trimmed interior, embroidered "40th" logos on headrests, and corresponding bright insignia on nose, deck, and front fenders. Available separately was a new gadget, the Passive Keyless Entry system. This used a pair of small transmitters to generate a low-power electromagnetic field within a few feet of the car's perimeter; walking up to or away from the car interrupted the field to lock or unlock the doors and hatch. It was a gimmick worthy of Cadillac, Mercedes, or Lexus, but only Corvette had it. Of course, the 'Vette had been picking up such do-dads for years, yet even the posh '93 was still no less the red-blooded all-American sports car loved by millions all over the world.

A good many of those folks got together in September 1994 for a genuine lovefest: the opening of the National Corvette Museum. Located in Bowling Green, not far from the factory, this shrine to America's sports car was built with private funds—and no blessing from Chevy at first. But the division soon recognized it as—ahem—a concrete expression of Corvette fandom and thus a potential gold mine of corporate goodwill. Accordingly, Chevy raided its attic for exhibits, making "permanent loans" of various historic Corvettes, engines and other memorabilia, including the '59 Mitchell Sting Ray and the Mako II show car. Zora Duntov was persuaded to attend the museum's opening ceremonies, as was Dave McClelland. Both were doubtless moved by the sight of some 2000 vintage Corvettes driven in from around the U.S. (and a few foreign countries) by loyal owners who just had to be present for a signal moment in automotive history.

1989 Corvette coupe

1989 Corvette ZR-1 prototype

1990 Corvette convertible coupe with optional hardtop

Chevy, meantime, cheered a second consecutive gain in Corvette volume, the '94s attracting 23,330 sales despite being little changed. Still, what few changes they had were welcome: a modified dash with knee bolsters and passenger airbag; electronic controls and safety-shift interlock for automatic models; standard heated glass backlight for ragtops; new-design five-spoke wheels for ZR-1; softer damping for the FX3 option; a new steering wheel, seats, and door panels. The ZR-1 package was downpriced a bit to $31,258, but managed only 448 orders.

The King was belatedly buried after 1995 and a final 448 examples. It would have died sooner, but Chevy was obliged to buy so many LT5 engines from contract builder Mercury Marine, and the condition was only met that year. Happily, other '95 Corvettes got the ZR-1's heavy-duty brakes as standard, plus revised fender "gills" and, on automatic models, a transmission-fluid temperature gauge. Base prices were the highest ever, though not exorbitant for the day at $36,785 for the coupe and $43,665 for the ragtop.

A near-stock LT1 convertible paced the 1995 Indy 500, the third such honor for Corvette and the 10th for a Chevrolet. Predictably, Chevy ran off a few replicas: this time, exactly 527. All were painted Dark Purple Metallic over Arctic White and came with "79th Indianapolis 500" decals for owner application, plus complimentary embroidered logos on the seats.

Magazine testers had been noticing steady improvements in Corvette workmanship and ride comfort, and the '95s were the best yet. Though Chevy couldn't seem to exorcise certain squeaks and rattles, the fourth generation was by now acceptably tight and solid on rough roads, which no longer chattered your teeth so much except with the hard-riding Z51 suspension.

Meantime, the division confirmed what spies were reporting: a brand-new 1997 Corvette that promised to be simpler, lighter, stronger, and more affordable. With that, the fourth series made a final stand for 1996. Signaling the end of this line was another Collector Edition, a $1250 package that dressed a coupe or convertible with pearlescent Sebring Silver paint, bright five-spoke alloys, and special emblems and trim.

More intriguing was a new limited-edition Grand Sport package (RPO Z16), a successor of sorts to the ZR-1. Priced at $3250 for coupes and $2880 for convertibles, it delivered the King's wheels and tires, showy black brake calipers, and a pair of red "hashmarks" on the left fender. Coupes also came with tacked-on rear fender flares. A specific color scheme combined Admiral Blue paint with a broad, white dorsal stripe, recalling the trio of original GS Sting Rays raced by John Mecom at Nassau in '63.

But the Grand Sport's big attraction was its new LT4 engine. Optional for other '96s at $1450, it was essentially a higher-output LT1 with wider ports, bigger valves with hollow stems and stronger springs, reshaped pistons giving 10.8:1 compression (versus 10.4), wilder cam, high-flow fuel injectors, and a sturdier crank. The result was 330 horsepower peaking at a higher 5800 rpm, plus five extra pound-feet of torque.

Rounding out GS features were six-way power sport seats with embroidered "Grand Sport" legends and a leather-lined interior in all-black or black and blinding red. Future trivia hounds should note that the coupe's lift-off roof-panel option was *verboten* with the GS group, and that white was the only top color for GS convertibles. Available for all '96s was new "Selective Real-Time Damping," essentially a faster-acting FX3 setup priced at $1695.

GS production was quite low, comprising 810 coupes and just 190 convertibles. That rarity, plus a unique blend of features, implies one of the more collectible 'Vettes of this generation—second only, perhaps, to the mythic ZR-1.

Though not widely appreciated, the 'Vette again came close to extinction in the early '90s. The reason was General Motors' huge $4.5 million loss of 1991, which led to a management shakeup that ousted Robert Stempel as company chairman and prompted a temporary freeze on new-model programs through 1996—including a new-generation Corvette. Within days, however, GM's new leaders saw proposals for Chevy's next sports car and gave it the green light, though there was no way it would debut as planned for 1993 in time for Corvette's 40th anniversary.

1990 Corvette ZR-1 coupe

1991 Corvette coupe

1991 Corvette convertible coupe

1992 Corvette coupe

1992 Corvette convertible coupe

1993 Corvette 40th Anniversary Edition convertible coupe

1994 Corvette convertible coupe

1993 Corvette ZR-1 coupe

1994 Corvette coupe

The new 'Vette was called "C5" (rather inaccurately, we think) for Corvette fifth generation. This went against the tradition chronology that would have named the new series "C7." But though some four years late, it was well worth waiting for—whatever you called it. For starters, it was the first all-new design in Corvette history, with virtually no borrowed or carryover components. New it had to be, because Chevy wanted to dramatically expand Corvette's market reach while reducing production costs. Team Corvette succeeded admirably on both counts under Dave Hill. The result was the most technically advanced 'Vette yet—and by most all accounts the best Corvette ever.

Desired gains in passenger space, luggage room, and structural rigidity dictated a clean-sheet design and altered dimensions. Against its predecessor, the C5 was a sizable 8.3 inches longer in wheelbase (a Corvette record at 104.5 inches), nearly three inches wider, and 1.4 inches taller; yet stretched only 1.2 inches longer overall and actually weighed some 80 pounds less in initial hatch coupe form. Beneath the slinky new fiberglass body, which boasted a lower, 0.29 drag factor, was an entirely new structural skeleton built around a much-stiffer frame with a central "backbone" measuring 12 inches high, nine inches wide and four feet long. Immensely rigid, this chassis featured full-length "hydroformed" side rails diecast by a high-pressure water process into stout 4×6-inch members. Providing further reinforcement were a windshield/cowl structure of welded aluminum castings and extrusions, attached to a pair of sturdy rectangular steel members rising from the front frame rails. A cast-magnesium steering column/pedal box added more strength without excess weight. A new steel superstructure provided better support for the coupe's liftup rear window and takeoff roof panel, the latter newly framed in magnesium and attached by convenient latches instead of bolts and a wrench.

Despite the sturdy side rails, sill height was dropped four inches, making for much easier entry/exit than in a C4. Footwells were usefully wider, helped by Corvette's first rear-mounted transmission, which was either four-speed automatic or optional six-speed manual. This wasn't a true rear transaxle, as the differential remained separate, but it didn't impinge on luggage space, which more than doubled in the hatch coupe to 25 cubic feet. More importantly, the tail-mounted transmission helped improve fore/aft weight distribution to 51.5/48.5 percent, all the better for handling.

So, too, the suspension, which applied to new geometry to basic C4 elements. For example, unequal-length A-arms returned up front and an antiroll bar and plastic transverse leaf spring reprised at each end, but all suspension pieces now mounted to noise-isolating cast-aluminum subframes. In addition, rear A-arms with toe-control links relieved the halfshafts of suspension duty, bushings were changed all-round, and shocks were repositioned and revalved for tighter wheel control. Steering changed to GM's new computer-managed "Magnasteer II" system that varied effort according to road speed via electromagnets instead of hydraulics. All-disc antilock brakes returned, slightly smaller in diameter but thicker. In another departure, tires were slightly narrower but larger aft than fore—respectively, P275/40ZR18 and P245/45ZR17. And they were unique to Corvette, being specially developed Goodyear Eagle F1 GS EMTs designed to run safely without air pressure for up to 200 miles, thus eliminating the need for a space-robbing spare tire and jack.

As if all this weren't enough, the C5 got a new engine, too. Dubbed LS1, it looked superficially like an update of the LT1/LT4, with two overhead valves per cylinder and nominal 5.7-liter displacement. In fact, though, only bore spacing was shared. Besides a deeper-skirted new block made of aluminum instead of cast iron, the LS1 boasted new cylinder heads, freer-flow intake and exhaust systems, and Corvette's first "drive-by-wire" throttle. The last replaced the normal mechanical linkage with an electric motor that worked the throttle by computer control according to input from an accelerator position sensor. The throttle was tied through the engine computer to standard cruise and traction control functions for precise power delivery under all conditions, plus fewer parts and easier installation.

At 346 cid, the LS1 has fewer cubes than its iron-block forebears, but was also lighter, physically smaller, and more-potent, turning out 345 horsepower and 350 pound-feet of torque. Even better, it rated slightly higher EPA mileage of 18 mpg city, 28 highway with manual shift. Who said you can't have it all?

Interestingly, the C5 claimed 34 percent fewer parts than a corresponding C4. Team Corvette had overlooked nothing to make their new baby not only more efficient and practical but also easier to build to a high quality standard. But no one's perfect. The first 1400 C5s had to be recalled for rear suspension fixes, and early road tests complained of windows that pushed out from their seals at high speed—and more of those pesky,

1995 Corvette Indianapolis 500 Pace Car convertible coupe

1996 Corvette convertible coupe

1997 Corvette convertible coupe

1996 Corvette Grand Sport convertible coupe

1997 Corvette convertible coupe

unwanted squeaks and rattles.

But the rough edges were mostly smoothed out within six months, and they did nothing to dampen the C5's enthusiastic reception. Some thought the styling a bit tame, but there was no doubting this new Corvette's ability. Most magazines timed 0-60 mph at a swift five seconds with the manual transmission, while praising the near-flat, grippy cornering (0.85g in *Car and Driver's* test); effortless, stable, high-speed cruising; the comfortable new cabin and its refreshingly no-nonsense gauges and controls; greater on-road solidity; and, yes, better workmanship throughout. Best of all, the '97 coupe started at $37,945, just $770 above its '96 counterpart. *Automobile* magazine's David E. Davis, Jr., aptly summed up the C5 as "a home run in every way, and it could not have come at a more opportune time for Chevrolet and General Motors."

A deliberately slow production build-up held 1997-model output to just 9752 units, but the C5 hit stride the following year with 31,084, the 'Vette's best one-year total since 1986. The C5 was designed as a convertible first, and sun-lovers cheered its return for '98. Thanks to the super-stiff structure, virtually no shoring-up was required, though the convertible was necessarily a tad more willowy than the coupe. Some groused that only a manual top was available, but it was easy to operate and visibly better made. Trunk space was only about half that of the hatch coupe's but double that of the droptop C4. And wonder of wonders, it was accessible from outside via the first proper trunklid on a 'Vette since 1962.

Car and Driver proclaimed the latest convertible "the most desirable 'Vette since 1967." Chevrolet got one placed as pace car for the 1998 Indy 500, and again rolled out the expected replicas for retail sale, 1158 in all. *Motor Trend* had passed over the 'Vette for 1997 Car of the Year honors, choosing Chevy's new family Malibu sedan instead, but made up for it by giving the '98 trophy to the entire Corvette "line."

Two new options arrived: magnesium wheels (soon withdrawn due to supplier problems) and, at midseason, an "Active Handling" antiskid system. The latter supplemented the traction control with additional sensor input allowing more-precise selective braking of individual wheels to keep the car on course. Like the C5 coupe, the convertible offered three suspension choices: base, firm-ride Z51($350), and an evolved F45 "Selective Real-Time Damping" option (a pricey $1695), basically computer-controlled auto-adjusting shock absorbers with driver-selectable Tour, Sport, and Performance modes. Opinions divided on the effectiveness of these setups, but most critics, including ourselves, thought the F45 too harsh on most roads. We preferred the base calibrations, though *Car and Driver* felt the Z51 delivered better handling with only a slight loss in ride comfort, being "nowhere near as punishing as the C4 Z51 was."

That's just as well, because the Z51 was mandatory for 1999's new fixed-roof "hardtop" version of the convertible. This third model was not unexpected, having been rumored in the press and even pictured in Chevrolet publicity for the preceding two years. Originally, the hardtop was supposed to double yearly Corvette sales by offering just the basics (manual cloth seats, smaller footwear, no chip-controlled suspension tricks) at a much lower price, once whispered at around $25,000. But the idea bombed in customer "focus groups," and there was no need for a "stripper" anyway, as Chevy was selling every C5 it could build. Accordingly, the hardtop was recast as a more performance-oriented machine, sold only with manual transmission, the Z51 chassis, and few options. Chevy did restore traction control, 18-inch rolling stock, and leather upholstery; but extras were limited to the antiskid system, power driver's seat, and Bose audio.

The hardtop itself was made of fiberglass and bonded to the convertible bodyshell. With that and fewer frills, the new model aimed to be a lighter, stiffer Corvette with consequently better acceleration and handling. Stiffer it was, but it only weighed some 90 pounds less, so it was barely faster than a well-driven manual coupe or convertible. *Car and Driver* reported 0-60 mph at 4.8 seconds, while *Road & Track* scored a rather more believable 5.3. The "buff" magazines loved it. "We had great fun in the hardtop," *Car and Driver* enthused, "[and] we applaud Chevy's tactic of making the quickest Corvette the cheapest." Still, a base price of $38,197 was hardly in budget-car land, and the better-equipped hatchback cost only $400 more.

But the hardtop was a heartening sign that Chevy was again really serious about the Corvette. Another clue was the $3.5 million spent to develop the C5-R, an all-out racing version with a 6.0-liter V-8 making some 600 horsepower for an assault on the fabled 24 Hours of Le Mans. For 2000, however, the only Corvettes at the French enduro were a pair of stock-based pace cars, though the C5-R did get a shakedown in several long-distance U.S. races. But Corvette made history in 2001 as a pair of C5-Rs ran 10th and 11th overall in France (first and second in the GTS Class), the first Le Mans finish for factory supported 'Vettes in 40 years.

Meantime back in 1999, Chevy introduced more options for the coupe and convertible: a power telescopic steering column and an aircraft-style head-up display (HUD). The latter projected speed and other data onto the windshield at driver eye level. It could be distracting, but it could also be turned off. Buyers were still turned on by the C5, as model-year production rose seven percent to near 33,270.

The 2000 total was only 89 units higher, but prices weren't much higher either. The hardtop could now be optioned like other models with the HUD, dual-zone climate control, and

1998 Corvette coupe

1998 Corvette Indianapolis 500 Pace Car convertible coupe

1999 Corvette hardtop coupe

1999 Corvette hardtop coupe

1999 Corvette convertible coupe

1999 Corvette coupe

2000 Corvette convertible coupe

2000 Corvette coupe

2001 Corvette coupe

2001 Corvette Z06 hardtop coupe

2001 Corvette convertible coupe

fog lamps, but buyers were unmoved, as the model's sales dropped almost 50 percent.

In response, Chevy muscled up the hardtop for 2001, and now it really was the fastest, best-handling Corvette of all. Tagged Z06, recalling the option code of a rare 1963 racing package, it boasted a heavily reworked V-8 reviving another legendary Corvette option number, LS6. Higher compression (10.5:1 vs. 10.1); a hotter cam; new heads; and smoother, higher-capacity intake and exhaust systems helped extract 385 horsepower and 385 pound-feet, up 40 horses and 35 pound-feet from the previous LS1, which got some of the same refinements this year to add five horsepower and 25 pound-feet. To match Z06 power, Chevy engineers specified a stronger six-speed gearbox, a firmer FE4 suspension with thicker antiroll bars, and one-inch-wider wheels wearing 265/40ZR17 tires in front and 295/35ZR18s in back. The beefy tires were purpose-designed Goodyear F1 SCs, but they weren't run-flats, so a small inflator was provided for emergencies. The new wheels and tires shaved some 23 pounds off curb weight. Thinner windshield and rear-window glass erased six pounds more, and mufflers went from aluminum to titanium for a final 18-pound saving. Net curb weight was 3116 pounds, which *Car and Driver* noted was over 50 pounds lighter than the old hardtop and only 77 more than a BMW M3 coupe. Z06 cosmetic alterations were subtle but effective: mesh grille inserts, red-painted brake calipers, a functional brake-cooling duct ahead of each rear wheel, and an arresting black-and-red interior with more heavily bolstered seats.

In most every way, the Z06 was a world-beating performer. Despite a "green" engine, *Car and Driver's* example dispatched 0-60 in just 4.3 seconds, and its 0.98g skidpad tour bested those of a street Viper GTS and Ferrari's 360 Modena. *AutoWeek* reported near-identical acceleration and the shortest stops it had ever recorded. After a few laps on the racetrack, *Car and Driver's* Csaba Csere reported that "the Z06 feels very much like the Corvette showroom-stock endurance cars that several of us raced in the mid-'80s. A smooth touch on the controls was rewarded with beautiful balance and great stability." Yet this was no high-strung terror on the street. It wasn't exactly quiet, especially at full throttle, but the noise was music to enthusiast ears, the ride firm but not punishing, the engine ever unfussed and supremely tractable. All this for $43,855, just $500 more than a 'Vette ragtop. "When we recall that the old ZR-1 cost about twice as much as a garden-variety Corvette," said Csere, "[the Z06 is] a bargain—and the perfect model to take the Corvette into the 21st century."

Total 'Vette production improved to 35,622 for model-year '01, but the 5768 souls who bought Z06s were doubtless peeved by the even hotter 2002 edition. Further engine refining added 20 horsepower and 15 pound-feet of torque to reach ZR-1 power levels, and suspension was again retuned for even more predictable handling and a less-agitated rough-road ride. Chevy said some of these improvements weren't ready in time for '01, so those who waited were amply rewarded. Volume improved once again for '02 but not by much, reaching 37,230.

A slight production retreat, to 35,469 units, was a small downer for Corvette's 50th birthday year, but 2003 did bring developments worth celebrating. Besides commemorative insignia for all models, the convertible and hatchback offered an optional 50th Anniversary Package announced by special red paint, champagne-colored wheels, and unique trim. It looked expensive at $5000, but also included a new suspension trick called Magnetic Selective Ride Control. An innova-

2002 Corvette coupe

2002 Corvette Z06 hardtop coupe

2003 Corvette Indianapolis 500 Pace Car coupe

tion shared with Cadillac, MSRC used special shock absorbers filled with a fluid containing tiny metal particles. When acted on by an electric current, this "magnetorheological" fluid could change viscosity—and thus damping firmness—in the wink of an eye. A suspension computer determined the exact damping rate based on sensor data that measured suspension movement, steering angle, and other factors. Drivers could select "Tour" or firmer "Sport" modes to suit road conditions. Judged highly effective in most magazine tests, MSRC was available as a freestanding option for base models at a reasonable $1695. Finally, the coupe and convertible made several options standard for '03, including fog lamps, sport seats, and dual-zone climate control. The Z06 was largely a carryover. Base prices, still creeping up, went to $43,255 for the coupe, $49,700 for the ragtop, $50,485 for the Z06.

The C5 did well to hold its existing sales level, as 2003 ushered in a raft of strong rivals bracketing Corvette's price range. Dodge offered a redesigned V-10 Viper, and a reborn Nissan Z-car, the 350Z, made headlines with its slick looks, 'Vette-like handling, and $26,269 starting price. Mazda chimed in for 2004 with the RX-8, a new-generation rotary-engine sports car pitched in the high-$20,000 area. And Porsche's midengine Boxster, though just as old a design as the C5, remained a formidable foe at prices that almost exactly duplicated the 'Vette's.

By now, though, the rumor mill had long been abuzz about the successor C6, and Chevy suggested an imminent changing of the Corvette guard with tellingly named Commemorative Edition packages as the main news for 2004. The title referred not to the C5's imminent departure but a sterling 2003 racing season for the factory-supported C-5Rs, which notched a third straight manufacturer's title in the American LeMans Series after just missing a "three-peat" at the LeMans 24 Hours. The Commemorative Packages must have been good-luck charms, because Corvette C5-Rs won every race they entered in 2004, nabbing a fourth ALMS crown and an unprecedented third double victory in France (first in class and first overall).

There were actually two Commemorative packages for 2004: a $3700 ensemble for the coupe and convertible, and a more elaborate $4335 kit for the Z06. Both delivered vivid LeMans Blue paint contrasted by wide, red-edged silver stripes on the hood, roof, and rear deck. Special "LeMans 24 Hours" cross-flag emblems appeared on the nose and tail, and as embroidered logos on the headrests within a specific shale-colored cockpit. Polished alloy wheels completed this 1SC option, which also included all features of the regular 1SB Preferred Equipment Group.

To this, the Z06 package (also called 1SB) added a unique carbon-fiber hood taking a useful 10.6 pounds off the nose, plus special clearcoat-finish wheels with hubs reading "Commemorative 24:00 Heures du Mans." Moreover, testing on Germany's fabled Nürburgring circuit prompted revised damping for the Sachs gas-pressure shock absorbers, stiffer bushings for the front upper-control arms, and softer bushings for the rear antiroll bar. Together, these tweaks aimed to "settle" the car more quickly in fast transitions—which they did. *Car and Driver* praised the Commemorative Z06 for "steering response [now] so much quicker it's hard to believe the ratio is the same [as other Corvettes']. Its weight is with-

2003 Corvette 50th Anniversary Edition coupe

2003 Corvette 50th Anniversary Edition convertible coupe

2004 Corvette Commemorative Edition coupe

in 141 pounds [of theirs], yet it feels like hundreds less. Its structure also feels twice as rigid." Recording a leechlike skidpad grip of 0.98 g, *Car and Driver* found the chassis "exceptionally well tuned to the active handling system's competitive driving mode…" For straightline competition, the Commemorative Z06 proved the fastest stock Corvette ever tested by *Motor Trend*, clocking just 4.2 seconds 0-60 mph and a standing quarter-mile of 12.4 seconds at 117 mph. And all with GM's usual three-year/36,000-mile bumper-to-bumper warranty.

Unfortunately for collectors, Chevy followed tradition by deliberately holding back on Commemorative model production: about 2000 Z06s, around twice that many coupes and convertibles. But whatever one may think of "factory collector cars," these '04s were a fine send-off for a Corvette generation that earned such accolades as: 1998 North American Car of the Year, *Car and Driver*'s "10 Best" list in 1999 and 2002-04, and perennial *Consumer Guide*® Best Buy in the sports class. The C5 would be a tough act to follow. Yet some people evidently waited to see how good the next Corvette would be, as '04 production dipped to 34,064.

The wait was worthwhile, because the 2005 C6 was a better Corvette in most every way. Significantly, it was the first developed in concert with another GM car, the 2004 Cadillac XLR. It wasn't a clean-sheet job like C5, but only because Team Corvette decided it didn't need to be. Much was changed, nevertheless, the C6 ending up 85 percent new by weight, according to Dave Hill, chief engineer for GM's performance car group. "We had really stretched to upgrade the C5 each year," he told us. "Now we wanted to stretch again and annihilate the compromises we had been living with." The team identified 100 "dissatisfiers," as Hill called them—things to be changed and/or improved based on feedback from C5 owners and the team's own standards. Toward that end, lessons learned in making the XLR a world-class luxury tourer were applied to improving fit and finish, powertrain and road-noise isolation, and interior design, materials, and assembly. Yet the C6 was also developed with an eye to the racing C6-R version, and ideas flowed freely between the Corvette competition group and the production-car team.

With Tad Jeuchter as assistant chief engineer and Tom Peters as head designer, the C6 emerged five inches shorter and an inch narrower than the C5, but with a wheelbase stretched 1.2 inches to 106. The last was dictated by XLR packaging requirements, but enhanced a purposeful new "wheels at the corners" stance. The wheels themselves were larger, now 18 inches up front and 19 at the rear as standard for the hatchback and convertible.

Exposed headlamps—the first on a 'Vette since 1962—saved weight and made aerodynamics fractionally slicker. Peters also restored a "port" grille, a slim air intake at the base of the nose; increased the "double bubble" contour of the coupe's liftoff roof panel; and gave both body styles a "boattail" decklid character line, recalling the '63 Sting Ray split-window coupe. None of the composite body panels was left untouched, and an adept blending of curves and creases made for a look more chiseled and muscular.

The cockpit also got a thorough going-over, gaining a simplified dashboard with more convenient minor controls, aluminum and metal-look accents, new seats with longer cushions and larger side bolsters, even small door map pockets and proper cupholders. A $1400 navigation system arrived as

2005 Corvette Indianapolis 500 Pace Car convertible coupe

a first-time Corvette option, and new touch-activated electric door latches (with mechanical inside releases) were part of a standard keyless entry system with pocket transmitter and dashboard engine-start switch, a "gift" from the XLR.

That switch fired up a Chevy small-block V-8 so thoroughly modified as to warrant the new tag LS2. Besides a bore stretch upping displacement to 6.0 liters—364 cubes—the new engine sported higher compression (10.9:1 vs. 10.1:1), redesigned high-flow intake and exhaust systems, and various internal changes that reduced pumping losses. Icing the cake, the LS2 was 15 pounds lighter than the LS1, helped by a smaller water pump and a new aluminum oil pan providing superior lubrication despite one-quarter less capacity. With all this, the LS2 was mighty impressive, making 400 bhp at 6000 rpm and 400 pound-feet peak torque at 4400. That put it just five horses shy of the previous Z06's LS6 engine, and it made equal torque at slightly lower rpm.

As before, transmissions comprised six-speed Tremec T56 manual and four-speed GM automatic, both still mounted at the rear. A revised shift linkage gave the manual more positive action, while the automatic got Cadillac-style shift programming. A six-speed automatic replaced it for 2006.

The C5's "Uniframe" structure was already quite light and plenty stiff, but the C6 benefited from welded extruded-aluminum members that were bolted and bonded to strengthen the door-hinge pillars. An underdash brace made of hydroformed steel, like the chassis siderails, tied those pillars more solidly to the central chassis tunnel. Ragtops gained extra rigidity from a fiberglass tub that not only served as the trunk but provided a rear cockpit wall lacking on the C5. Also new was an optional $1995 power top with hardware that weighed just 15 pounds and took up no more trunk space than the manual roof. The top itself—in your choice of black, gray, or beige—was reshaped to reduce wind noise and fully lined. As on some German convertibles, the C6's side windows automatically dropped a bit when opening a door, then snugged up against the top for a tight seal.

Chassis changes were extensive. Though unchanged in concept, the all-independent suspension was treated to all-new components, highlighted by longer-stroke shock absorbers for increased wheel travel, plus stiffer sway bar mounts, revised bushings, and recalibrated springs. The base FE1 suspension adopted Goodyear's new-generation Eagle F1 GS run-flat tires. So did the Magnetic Ride Control option, repriced to $1695. The handling-focused Z51 Performance Package, now at $1495, substituted asymmetric-tread Eagle F1 Supercar shoes in the same EEE sizes: P245/40ZR18 front, P285/35ZR19 rear. All C6s sported larger brakes than C5s, but retained standard Active Handling traction/antiskid control.

Options were more extensive than ever: torso side airbags for the coupe (newly standard for the ragtop), the aforementioned navigation system, OnStar assistance ($695), satellite radio ($325), and various packages with such niceties as perforated leather upholstery, heated power seats and power telescopic steering column adjustment. Yet for all their many improvements, C6s cost little more than the final C5s, the convertible going up less than $1000 and the coupe not at all.

Unsurprisingly, the C6 got rave reviews. *Car and Driver* named it one of 2005's "10 Best" automobiles and gave it a slim one-point victory over a newly updated Porsche 911. *Road & Track* put the C6 first in a nine-way sports car showdown for having "no real weaknesses and many strengths. It possesses world-class performance, a high level of comfort and dashing good looks. And it's available for nearly half the price of a Porsche Carrera S...America's sports car is now back in its rightful place atop the sports car mountain."

Though journalists chose Chrysler's reborn 300 sedan as 2005 North American Car of the Year, it certainly wasn't for lack of Corvette performance. Depending on body style, options, and gearing, a C6 could run 0-60 mph in as little as

2005 Corvette coupe

2006 Corvette Z06 coupe

2006 Corvette Z06 coupe

4.1 seconds (Chevy claimed 4.2) and standing quarter-miles as low as 12.6 seconds at 114 mph. Skidpad pull was in race car territory at 0.98g with the Z51 package, yet real-world fuel economy was in the family sedan league at 18-20 mpg. No wonder *Consumer Guide*® said the newest Corvette "delivers thrilling acceleration, handling, and braking [yet] costs tens of thousands less than rivals with similar performance. If you like your sports cars bold and brawny, there's no better high-performance value and no stronger Best Buy in this class."

A new Z06 promised even higher performance, and it didn't disappoint. Blasting onto the scene in spring 2005 as an early '06 model, it was more or less a street-legal racing 'Vette incorporating many lessons from the C-5R program. For starters, it was based on the sloped-roof coupe, which had better high-speed aerodynamics than the old Z06 notchback. A fixed roof panel was specified for racing-level rigidity. More significantly, the C6 Uniframe was reengineered in aluminum as another Z06 exclusive, more than offsetting the fastback body's greater weight. "It's like a whole different car," proclaimed Dave Hill. "It was an extremely large stretch to take 136 pounds out of something that only weighed about 350 to begin with... a revolutionary improvement." Also saving weight were a magnesium engine cradle (replacing an aluminum piece) and the use of carbon fiber for the floorboard skins and noticeably bulged fenders.

But what really set tongues flapping was the new Z06's mighty LS7 V-8 and its rated 505 bhp. Though sized like the fabled big-blocks of yore—7.0 liters, 428 cid—this pushrod engine used the same "Gen IV" small-block architecture as the LS2. Yet the LS7 differed in most every respect beyond extra cubes. Primo engineering features abounded: forged-steel crank, flat-top forged pistons giving 11.0:1 compression, sodium-filled exhaust valves, high-lift cam, racing-style dry-sump lubrication, specific low-restriction intake and exhaust systems. Even so, *Car and Driver* noted that save "titanium connecting rods and intake valves, there's nothing in this engine's parts list to suggest it's a monster motor. The genius here is in the details, with careful attention paid to maximum airflow and valvetrain [lightness] and stiffness. The result is a big engine that revs like a small one to 7000 rpm with a 6300-rpm horsepower peak. The torque curve is wide and flat with more than 400 pound-feet available between 2400 and 6400 rpm." Max twist was a burly 470 pound-feet at 4800.

Like its predecessor, the C6 Z06 came only with a six-speed manual gearbox, plus power-handling upgrades to the clutch, U-joints, rear halfshafts, and limited-slip differential. Brakes were also beefed up, with huge cross-drilled rotors of 14 inches fore and 13 aft clamped by six-piston front calipers and four-pot rears, all painted bright Corvette Red. Wheel diameters were C6 stock, but rim widths were increased to accommodate ultrafat 275/35 front and 325/30 rear run-flat tires. Other distinctive Z06-only visuals included a working cold-air scoop in the nose, radiused rear wheel openings, a wider grille, an air "splitter" below it, a small brake-cooling duct ahead of each rear wheel, and deeper aero-enhancing perimeter body skirts. Interior changes were confined to a two-tone color scheme, a slightly smaller steering wheel, and different seats with larger, nonadjustable bolsters.

Bowing at five bucks shy of $70,000 to start, the 2006 Z06 was an incredible buy in ultrahigh performance. Though *Car and Driver* thought at-limit handling a tad nervous on the racetrack, it judged the car "very well balanced" overall. "It won't do anything that will surprise the driver." Except, perhaps, when putting the pedal to the metal. *Car and Driver*'s tester "ripped to 60 mph in only 3.6 seconds, hit 100 in 7.9 and 150 in 17.5. That's on par with or better than the performance of the $153,345 Ford GT (and good luck getting that price) and $180,785 Ferrari F430... Spending double the Z06's price does not guarantee you'll have a car that can beat it... When you experience this thrilling car... it seems reasonable to say that we're in the golden age of Corvette."

We couldn't agree more, especially given the C6 generation's first-year run of 37,372 units, one of the higher totals in recent Corvette history. But can that golden age continue given the many crushing problems General Motors faces at this writing? (See Chevrolet for details.) We earnestly hope so. After all, Corvette is an American icon, and the automotive world would be a much poorer place without it.

Specifications

1953

290 (wb 102.0)		Wght	Price	Prod
2934	conv rdstr	2,705	3,513	300

1953 Engine	bore×stroke	bhp	availability
I-6, 235.5	3.56 × 3.94	150	S-all

1954

290 (wb 102.0)		Wght	Price	Prod
2934	conv rdstr	2,705	3,523	3,640

1954 Engine	bore×stroke	bhp	availability
I-6, 235.5	3.56 × 3.94	150/155	S-all

1955

290 (wb 102.0)		Wght	Price	Prod
2934	conv rdstr	2,650	2,934	700

1955 Engines	bore×stroke	bhp	availability
I-6, 235.5	3.56 × 3.94	155	S-all
V-8, 265.0	3.75 × 3.00	195	O-all

1956

290 (wb 102.0)		Wght	Price	Prod
2934	conv rdstr	2,764	3,149	3,467

1956 Engine	bore×stroke	bhp	availability
V-8, 265.0	3.75 × 3.00	210/225	S-all

1957

290 (wb 102.0)		Wght	Price	Prod
2934	conv rdstr	2,730	3,465	6,339

1957 Engines	bore×stroke	bhp	availability
V-8, 283.0	3.88 × 3.00	220	S-all
V-8, 283.0	3.88 × 3.00	245/270	O-all
V-8, 283.0	3.88 × 3.00	250/283	O-all (FI)

1958

290 (wb 102.0)		Wght	Price	Prod
867	conv rdstr	2,793	3,631	9,168

1958 Engines	bore×stroke	bhp	availability
V-8, 283.0	3.88 × 3.00	230	S-all
V-8, 283.0	3.88 × 3.00	245/270	O-all
V-8, 283.0	3.88 × 3.00	250/290	O-all (FI)

1959

290 (wb 102.0)		Wght	Price	Prod
867	conv rdstr	2,840	3,875	9,670

1959 Engines	bore×stroke	bhp	availability
V-8, 283.0	3.88 × 3.00	230	S-all
V-8, 283.0	3.88 × 3.00	245/270	O-all
V-8, 283.0	3.88 × 3.00	250/290	O-all (FI)

1960

290 (wb 102.0)		Wght	Price	Prod
0867	conv rdstr	2,840	3,872	10,261

1960 Engines	bore×stroke	bhp	availability
V-8, 283.0	3.88 × 3.00	230	S-all
V-8, 283.0	3.88 × 3.00	245/270	O-all
V-8, 283.0	3.88 × 3.00	250/290	O-all (FI)

1961

290 (wb 102.0)		Wght	Price	Prod
0867	conv rdstr	2,905	3,934	10,939

1961 Engines	bore×stroke	bhp	availability
V-8, 283.0	3.88 × 3.00	230	S-all
V-8, 283.0	3.88 × 3.00	245/270	O-all
V-8, 283.0	3.88 × 3.00	275/315	O-all (FI)

1962

290 (wb 102.0)		Wght	Price	Prod
0867	conv rdstr	2,925	4,038	14,531

1962 Engines	bore×stroke	bhp	availability
V-8, 327.0	4.00 × 3.25	250	S-all
V-8, 327.0	4.00 × 3.25	300/340	O-all
V-8, 327.0	4.00 × 3.25	360	O-all (FI)

1963

Sting Ray (wb 98.0)		Wght	Price	Prod
0837	cpe	2,859	4,252	10,594
0867	conv rdstr	2,881	4,037	10,919

1963 Engines	bore×stroke	bhp	availability
V-8, 327.0	4.00 × 3.25	250	S-all
V-8, 327.0	4.00 × 3.25	300/340	O-all
V-8, 327.0	4.00 × 3.25	360	O-all (FI)

1964

Sting Ray (wb 98.0)		Wght	Price	Prod
0837	cpe	2,960	4,252	8,304
0867	conv rdstr	2,945	4,037	13,925

1964 Engines	bore×stroke	bhp	availability
V-8, 327.0	4.00 × 3.25	250	S-all
V-8, 327.0	4.00 × 3.25	300-365	O-all
V-8, 327.0	4.00 × 3.25	375	O-all (FI)

1965

Sting Ray (wb 98.0)		Wght	Price	Prod
19437	cpe	2,975	4,321	8,186
19467	conv rdstr	2,985	4,106	15,376

1965 Engines	bore×stroke	bhp	availability
V-8, 327.0	4.00 × 3.25	250	S-all
V-8, 327.0	4.00 × 3.25	300-365	O-all
V-8, 327.0	4.00 × 3.25	375	O-all (FI)
V-8, 396.0	4.09 × 3.75	425	O-all

1966

Sting Ray (wb 98.0)		Wght	Price	Prod
19437	cpe	2,985	4,295	9,958
19467	conv rdstr	3,005	4,084	17,762

1966 Engines	bore×stroke	bhp	availability
V-8, 327.0	4.00 × 3.25	300	S-all
V-8, 327.0	4.00 × 3.25	350	O-all
V-8, 427.0	4.25 × 3.76	390/425	O-all

1967

Sting Ray (wb 98.0)		Wght	Price	Prod
19437	cpe	3,000	4,353	8,504
19467	conv rdstr	3,020	4,141	14,436

1967 Engines	bore×stroke	bhp	availability
V-8, 327.0	4.00 × 3.25	300	S-all
V-8, 327.0	4.00 × 3.25	350	O-all
V-8, 427.0	4.25 × 3.76	390-435	O-all

1968

Sting Ray (wb 98.0)		Wght	Price	Prod
19437	cpe	3,055	4,663	9,936
19467	conv rdstr	3,065	4,320	18,630

1968 Engines	bore×stroke	bhp	availability
V-8, 327.0	4.00 × 3.25	300	S-all
V-8, 327.0	4.00 × 3.25	350	O-all
V-8, 427.0	4.25 × 3.76	390-435	O-all

1969

Sting Ray (wb 98.0)		Wght	Price	Prod
19437	cpe	3,140	4,781	22,129
19467	conv rdstr	3,145	4,438	16,633

1969 Engines	bore×stroke	bhp	availability
V-8, 350.0	4.00 × 3.48	300	S-all
V-8, 350.0	4.00 × 3.48	350	O-all
V-8, 427.0	4.25 × 3.76	390-435	O-all

1970

Sting Ray (wb 98.0)		Wght	Price	Prod
19437	cpe	3,184	5,192	10,668
19467	conv rdstr	3,196	4,849	6,648

1970 Engines	bore×stroke	bhp	availability
V-8, 350.0	4.00 × 3.48	300	S-all
V-8, 350.0	4.00 × 3.48	350/370	O-all
V-8, 454.0	4.25 × 4.00	390/460*	O-all

Note: 1967-70 racing engines not listed. * Never sold.

1971

Sting Ray (wb 98.0)		Wght	Price	Prod
19437	cpe	3,202	5,533	14,680
19467	conv rdstr	3,216	5,296	7,121

1971 Engines	bore×stroke	bhp	availability
V-8, 350.0	4.00 × 3.48	270	S-all
V-8, 350.0	4.00 × 3.48	330	O-all
V-8, 454.0	4.25 × 4.00	365/425	O-all

1972

Sting Ray (wb 98.0)		Wght	Price	Prod
1Z37	cpe	3,215	5,472	20,496
1Z67	conv rdstr	3,216	5,246	6,508

1972 Engines	bore×stroke	bhp	availability
V-8, 350.0	4.00 × 3.48	200	S-all
V-8, 350.0	4.00 × 3.48	255	O-all
V-8, 454.0	4.25 × 4.00	270	O-all

1973

Sting Ray (wb 98.0)		Wght	Price	Prod
Z37	cpe	3,326	5,635	25,521
Z67	conv rdstr	3,333	5,399	4,943

1973 Engines	bore×stroke	bhp	availability
V-8, 350.0	4.00 × 3.48	190	S-all
V-8, 350.0	4.00 × 3.48	250	O-all
V-8, 454.0	4.2534.001	275	O-all

1974

Sting Ray (wb 98.0)		Wght	Price	Prod
Z37	cpe	3,309	6,082	32,028
Z67	conv rdstr	3,315	5,846	5,474

1974 Engines	bore×stroke	bhp	availability
V-8, 350.0	4.00 × 3.48	195	S-all
V-8, 350.0	4.00 × 3.48	250	O-all
V-8, 454.0	4.25 × 4.00	270	O-all

1975

Sting Ray (wb 98.0)	Wght	Price	Prod
Z37 cpe	3,433	6,797	33,836
Z67 conv rdstr	3,446	6,537	4,629

1975 Engines	bore×stroke	bhp	availability
V-8, 350.0	4.00 × 3.48	165	S-all
V-8, 350.0	4.00 × 3.48	205	O-all

1976

Sting Ray (wb 98.0)	Wght	Price	Prod
Z37 cpe	3,445	7,605	46,558

1976 Engines	bore×stroke	bhp	availability
V-8, 350.0	4.00 × 3.48	180	S-all
V-8, 350.0	4.00 × 3.48	210	O-all

1977

(wb 98.0)	Wght	Price	Prod
Z37 cpe	3,448	8,648	49,213

1977 Engines	bore×stroke	bhp	availability
V-8, 350.0	4.00 × 3.48	180	S-all
V-8, 350.0	4.00 × 3.48	210	O-all

1978

(wb 98.0)	Wght	Price	Prod
Z87 cpe	3,401	9,645	41,274*
Z87/Z78 Pace Car Repl cpe	3,450	13,653	6,502

* Includes 2,500 Silver Anniversary editions.

1978 Engines	bore×stroke	bhp	availability
V-8, 350.0	4.00 × 3.48	185	S-all
V-8, 350.0	4.00 × 3.48	220	O-all

1979

(wb 98.0)	Wght	Price	Prod
Z87 cpe	3,372	12,313	53,807

1979 Engines	bore×stroke	bhp	availability
V-8, 350.0	4.00 × 3.48	195	S-all
V-8, 350.0	4.00 × 3.48	225	O-all

1980

(wb 98.0)	Wght	Price	Prod
Z87 cpe	3,206	13,965	40,614

1980 Engines	bore×stroke	bhp	availability
V-8, 350.0	4.00 × 3.48	190	S-all
V-8, 350.0	4.00 × 3.48	230	O-all
V-8, 305.0	3.74 × 3.48	180	O-all

1981

(wb 98.0)	Wght	Price	Prod
Y87 cpe	3,179	15,248	40,606

1981 Engine	bore×stroke	bhp	availability
V-8, 350.0	4.00 × 3.48	190	S-all

1982

(wb 98.0)	Wght	Price	Prod
Y87 cpe	3,232	18,290	18,648
Y07 Collect Ed htchbk cpe	3,233	22,537	6,759

1982 Engine	bore×stroke	bhp	availability
V-8, 350.0	4.00 × 3.48	200	S-all

1983

No Corvette model was produced.

1984

(wb 96.2)	Wght	Price	Prod
Y07 cpe	3,087	23,360	51,547

1984 Engine	bore×stroke	bhp	availability
V-8, 350.0	4.00 × 3.48	205	S-all

1985

(wb 96.2)	Wght	Price	Prod
Y07 htchbk cpe	3,191	24,873	39,729

1985 Engine	bore×stroke	bhp	availability
V-8, 350.0	4.00 × 3.48	230/235	S-all

1986

(wb 96.2)	Wght	Price	Prod
Y07 htchbk cpe	3,239	27,027	27,794
Y67 conv cpe	—	32,032	7,315

1986 Engine	bore×stroke	bhp	availability
V-8, 350.0	4.00 × 3.48	230	S-all

1987

(wb 96.2)	Wght	Price	Prod
Y07 htchbk cpe	3,216	27,999	20,007
Y67 conv cpe	3,279	33,172	10,625

1987 Engine	bore×stroke	bhp	availability
V-8, 350.0	4.00 × 3.48	240	S-all

1988

(wb 96.2)	Wght	Price	Prod
Y07 htchbk cpe	3,229	29,480	15,382
Y67 conv cpe	3,299	34,820	7,407

1988 Engine	bore×stroke	bhp	availability
V-8, 350.0	4.00 × 3.48	245	S-all

1989

(wb 96.2)	Wght	Price	Prod
Y07 htchbk cpe	3,229	31,545	16,663
Y67 conv cpe	3,269	36,785	9,749

1989 Engine	bore×stroke	bhp	availability
V-8, 350.0	4.00 × 33.48	240/245	S-base models

1990

(wb 96.2)	Wght	Price	Prod
Y67 conv cpe	3,263	37,264	7,630
Y07 htchbk cpe	3,223	31,979	12,967
Z07 ZR-1 htchbk cpe	3,465	58,995	3,049

1990 Engines	bore×stroke	bhp	availability
V-8, 350.0	4.00 × 3.48	245	S-base models
V-8, 350.0	3.90 × 3.66	375	S-ZR-1 (dohc)

1991

Corvette (wb 96.2)	Wght	Price	Prod
Y07 htchbk cpe	3,223	32,455	12,923
Y67 conv cpe	3,263	38,770	5,672
Z07* ZR-1 htchbk cpe	3,503	64,138	2,044

1991 Engines	bore×stroke	bhp	availability
V-8, 350.0	4.00 × 3.48	245	S-base
V-8, 350.0	3.90 × 3.66	375	O-ZR-1 (dohc)

*Though listed as a separate model, the ZR-1 was technically an option package beginning in 1991.

1992

Corvette (wb 96.2)	Wght	Price	Prod
Y07 htchbk cpe	3,223	33,635	14,102
Y67 conv cpe	3,269	40,145	5,875
Z07 ZR-1 htchbk cpe	3,503	65,318	502

1992 Engines	bore×stroke	bhp	availability
V-8, 350.0	4.00 × 3.48	300	S-base
V-8, 350.0	3.90 × 3.66	375	O-ZR-1 (dohc)

1993

Corvette (wb 96.2)	Wght	Price	Prod
Y07 htchbk cpe	3,333	34,595	15,450
Y67 conv cpe	3,383	41,195	5,692
Z07 ZR-1 htchbk cpe	3,503	66,278	448

1993 Engines	bore×stroke	bhp	availability
V-8, 350.0	4.00 × 3.48	300	S-base
V-8, 350.0	3.90 × 3.66	405	O-ZR-1 (dohc)

1994

Corvette (wb 96.2)	Wght	Price	Prod
Y07 htchbk cpe	3,309	36,185	17,536
Y67 conv cpe	3,361	42,960	5,346
Z07 ZR-1 htchbk cpe	3,512	67,443	448

1994 Engines	bore×stroke	bhp	availability
V-8, 350.0	4.00 × 3.48	300	S-base
V-8, 350.0	3.90 × 3.66	385	O-ZR-1 (dohc)

1995

Corvette (wb 96.2)	Wght	Price	Prod
Y07 htchbk cpe	3,203	36,785	15,323
Y67 conv cpe	3,360	43,665	4,971
Z07 ZR-1 htchbk cpe	3,512	68,043	448

1995 Engines	bore×stroke	bhp	availability
V-8, 350.0	4.00 × 3.48	300	S-base
V-8, 350.0	3.90 × 3.66	405	O-ZR-1 (dohc)

1996

Corvette (wb 96.2)	Wght	Price	Prod
Y07 htchbk cpe	3,298	37,225	16,357
Y07 GS htchbk cpe	3,298	40,475	810
Y67 conv cpe	3,360	45,060	4,179
Y67 GS conv cpe	3,360	47,940	190

1996 Engines	bore×stroke	bhp	availability
V-8, 350.0	4.00 × 3.48	300	S-all
V-8, 350.0	4.00 × 3.48	330	O-all

1997

Corvette (wb 104.5)	Wght	Price	Prod
Y07 htchbk cpe	3,229	37,945	9,752

1997 Engine	bore×stroke	bhp	availability
V-8, 346.0	3.90 × 3.62	340	S-all

1998

Corvette (wb 104.5)	Wght	Price	Prod
Y07 htchbk cpe	3,245	37,995	19,235
Y67 conv cpe	3,246	44,425	11,849

1998 Engine	bore×stroke	bhp	availability
V-8, 346.0	3.90 × 3.62	345	S-all

1999

Corvette (wb 104.5)	Wght	Price	Prod
Y37 hrdtp cpe	3,153	38,197	4,031
Y07 htchbk cpe	3,245	38,591	18,078
Y67 conv cpe	3,246	44,999	11,161

1999 Engine	bore×stroke	bhp	availability
V-8, 346.0	3.90 × 3.62	345	S-all

2000

Corvette (wb 104.5)	Wght	Price	Prod
Y37 hrdtp cpe	3,173	38,705	2,090
Y07 htchbk cpe	3,245	39,280	18,113
Y67 conv cpe	3,246	45,705	13,479

2000 Engine	bore×stroke	bhp	availability
V-8, 346.0	3.90 × 3.62	345	S-all

2001

Corvette (wb 104.5)	Wght	Price	Prod
Y07 htchbk cpe	3,214	39,830	15,681
Y37 Z06 hrdtp cpe	3,116	46,855	5,768
Y67 conv cpe	3,210	46,355	14,173

2001 Engines	bore×stroke	bhp	availability
V-8, 346.0	3.90 × 3.62	350	S-all
V-8, 346.0	3.90 × 3.62	385	S-Z06

2002

Corvette (wb 104.5)	Wght	Price	Prod
Y07 htchbk cpe	3,214	41,005	14,760
Y37 Z06 hrdtp cpe	3,116	49,705	8,297
Y67 conv cpe	3,210	47,530	12,710

2002 Engines	bore×stroke	bhp	availability
V-8, 346.0	3.90 × 3.62	350	S-all
V-8, 346.0	3.90 × 3.62	405	S-Z06

2003

Corvette (wb 104.5)	Wght	Price	Prod
Y07 htchbk cpe	3,214	43,895	12,812
Y37 Z06 hrdtp cpe	3,116	51,155	8,635
Y67 conv cpe	3,210	50,370	14,022

2003 Engines	bore×stroke	bhp	availability
V-8, 346.0	3.90×3.62	350	S-All
V-8, 346.0	3.90×3.62	405	S-Z06

2004

Corvette (wb 104.5)	Wght	Price	Prod
Y07 htchbk cpe	3,214	44,535	16,165
Y37 Z06 hrdtp cpe	3,116	52,385	5,683
Y67 conv cpe	3,210	51,535	12,216

2004 Engines	bore×stroke	bhp	availability
V-8, 346.0	3.90×3.62	350	S-All
V-8, 346.0	3.90×3.62	405	S-Z06

2005

Corvette (wb 105.7)	Wght	Price	Prod
Y07 htchbk cpe	3,179	44,245	26,728
Y67 conv cpe	3,199	52,245	10,644

2005 Engines	bore×stroke	bhp	availability
V-8, 364.0	4.00×3.62	400	S-All

2006

Corvette (wb 105.7)	Wght	Price	Prod*
Y07 htchbk cpe	3,179	43,800	—
Y87 Z06 hrdtp cpe	3,130	65,000	—
Y67 conv cpe	3,199	51,535	—

2006 Engines	bore×stroke	bhp	availability
V-8, 364.0	4.00×3.62	400	S-All
V-8, 427.0	4.13×4.00	505	S-Z06

*Production figures not available at time of publication.

Chrysler

Walter Percy Chrysler honed his native mechanical skills on the great Midwestern railroads, then learned about cars by tinkering with a $5000 Locomobile he bought in 1908. Within a few years he became plant manager at Buick under Charles W. Nash, then took over for him as Buick president. But Chrysler didn't get along with GM's Billy Durant, so he left to run his own car company (as did Nash). After being hired to straighten out faltering Maxwell/Chalmers, Chrysler acquired control of the company by 1924, the year he introduced a new car under his own name. Thus was born the last of America's "Big Three" automakers (though it wasn't formally incorporated until 1925).

That first Chrysler was the foundation of the company's early success. It was designed with instrumental assistance from three superb engineers: Fred Zeder, Carl Breer, and Owen Skelton, the "Three Musketeers" who would dominate the design of Chrysler Corporation products throughout the '30s. Power came from a high-compression 202-cubic-inch L-head six with seven main bearings and 68 brake horsepower—0.3 bhp per cubic inch, outstanding for the day. Also featured were four-wheel hydraulic brakes (well ahead of most rivals), full-pressure lubrication, attractive styling, and competitive prices around $1500. It couldn't miss, and it didn't. By 1927, production was up from 32,000 to some 182,000.

Sixes remained Chrysler's mainstay through 1930, when the make offered four different engines ranging from 195.6 to 309.3 cid. The smallest was the four-main-bearing job in the cheap CJ-Series; the others were derived from the original 1924 design. That year's lineup comprised no fewer than 38 models priced from $795 for the least-costly CJ to $3000-plus for the imposing Imperial.

The Chrysler line then moved rapidly upmarket in price, prestige, and power. The reason was the company's 1928 expansion via the acquisition of Dodge and introduction of DeSoto and Plymouth. Given his GM experience, it's no surprise that Walter Chrysler wanted a similar make "ladder" running from low-priced Plymouths to premium Chryslers to keep customers in his corporate camp. At first, DeSoto, not Dodge, was the step up from Plymouth; their price positions wouldn't be reversed until the mid-'30s.

Imperial had arrived in 1926 to answer Cadillac, though this would always be more of a prestige leader than high money-earner. Also unlike GM's luxury make, Imperials built through 1954 weren't the products of a separate division, just the finest Chryslers, though they usually rivaled Cadillac in most every way. A notable exception is that Imperial didn't try to match Cadillac's costly V-12 and V-16 engines of the '30s—wise, considering how poorly those sold in the devastated Depression market.

Imperial reached a pinnacle in 1931, when Chrysler introduced its first eights. The largest was naturally reserved for Imperial: a smooth, low-revving 385-cid L-head with nine main bearings and 125 bhp. Despite weighing nearly 5000 pounds, these majestic cars could reach 96 mph and do 0-60 mph in 20 seconds. Styling (heavily influenced by the Cord L-29), was distinctive: long and low, with gracefully curved fenders and a rakish grille. Hard times made sales scarce, but these Imperials provided glorious motoring at relatively modest prices. They remain among the most beautiful Chryslers ever built—particularly the custom-bodied examples from the likes of Locke, Derham, Murphy, Waterhouse, and especially LeBaron. Though most coachbuilders perished in the Depression, Chrysler hired Ray Dietrich, one of the partners in LeBaron, to head its styling department (such as it was) in the late '30s.

Chrysler also offered an eight-cylinder 1931 CD-Series priced about half as much as Imperials, with engines of 240.3 cid and 82 bhp or 260.8 cid and 90 bhp. There was also a DeLuxe Eight with 95 bhp from 282.1 cid. But sixes still anchored the line, as they would through 1954. In the '30s these became progressively larger and more potent, reaching 241.5 cid and 93 bhp by 1934.

Meantime, Chrysler cemented its reputation for advanced engineering with the 1931 debut of "Floating Power" rubber engine mounts. They were standard on all models, as were automatic spark control, free-wheeling, and rustproofed bodies. Welded steel bodies were an innovation from the previous year. To prove their strength, Chrysler persuaded a five-ton elephant to climb atop a sedan at Coney Island in one of the firm's many famous period publicity stunts. Fortunately, the body held.

1930 77 Royal four-door sedan

1931 custom-bodied close-coupled two-door

1931 Series CG Imperial roadster

1932 Series CH Imperial town car by LeBaron

1932 Series C16 Six 2/4-passenger roadster

1933 Series CL Imperial convertible sedan

1934 Series CA Six Brougham two-door

1934 Series CX Airflow Imperial Eight four-door sedan

Chrysler also offered an optional four-speed manual transmission, basically a three-speed unit with an extra-low first gear. But hardly anyone used "emergency low," so this was dropped after 1933. Interiors were lavish during these years, especially on Imperials and Chrysler Eights, which came with full instrumentation in a polished walnut panel.

After making few changes through 1933, Chrysler made a major one, summoning the future with the most-radical production car yet attempted by a U.S. maker. Widely recognized as the first truly modern automobile, the 1934 Airflow was an "engineer's" car, which was hardly surprising. What *was* curious is that normally canny Walter Chrysler approved its daring concept without much regard for whether the public would like it.

As the story goes, Carl Breer spotted a squadron of Army Air Corps planes flying overhead in 1927, which inspired him to push with Zeder and Skelton for a streamlined automobile employing aircraft-type design principles. Wind-tunnel tests suggested a modified teardrop shape (and ultimately the Airflow name). Placing the eight-cylinder engines over the front axles made for considerable passenger space. Seats were an industry-leading 50 inches across, and there was more than enough interior room for even the burly Walter P. Chrysler. What's more, the forward drivetrain positioning enabled all passengers to sit within the wheelbase, thus improving ride comfort for those in back. A beam-and-truss body engineered along aircraft principles provided great strength with less weight. Oliver Clark followed all these dictates with exterior styling that seemed downright strange. The Custom Imperial looked best, its long wheelbase allowing the rounded lines to be stretched out more—and they needed every inch of stretch they could get.

But there was no denying Airflow performance. At the Bonneville Salt Flats a '34 Imperial coupe ran the flying-mile at 95.7 mph, clocked 90 mph for 500 miles, and set 72 new national speed records. Airflows were strong, too. In Pennsylvania, one was hurled off a 110-foot cliff (another publicity stunt); it landed wheels down and was driven away.

Unfortunately, the massive cost and effort of retooling delayed Airflow sales until January 1934 (June for Custom Imperials). Then, jealous competitors—mainly GM—began running "smear" advertising that claimed the cars were unsafe. All this blunted public interest that was initially quite favorable despite the newfangled styling, and prompted rumors that the Airflow was flawed. Save for a group of traditional Series CA and CB Sixes, the 1934 Chrysler line was all Airflow, and sales were underwhelming. While most makes boosted volume by up to 60 percent from rock-bottom '33, Chrysler rose only 10 percent. It could have been worse—and was for DeSoto, which banked entirely on Airflows that year (all sixes).

Yet the Airflow wasn't nearly the disaster it's long been portrayed to be. Though Chrysler dropped from eighth to tenth in model-year output for 1932, it went no lower through '37, the Airflow's final year, when it rose to ninth. And though the cars did lose money, the losses were far from crippling. The Airflow's most-lasting impact was to discourage Chrysler from fielding anything so adventurous for a very long time. Not until 1955 would the firm again reach for industry design leadership.

There were also two immediate results of the 1934 sales experience. First, planned Airflow-style Plymouths and Dodges were abruptly canceled. Second, Chrysler Division regrouped around more-orthodox "Airstream" Sixes and Eights for 1935 and '36. Though not pure Airflow, this design's "pontoon" fenders, raked-backed radiators, and teardrop-

1936 Series C9 Airflow Eight four-door sedan

1938 Series C19 Imperial four-door sedan

1936 Series C7 Airstream Six business coupe

1938 Series C19 New York Special four-door sedan

1937 Series C16 Royal Six rumble-seat coupe

1939 Chrysler Custom Imperial parade phaeton

1937 Series C17 Airflow Eight four-door sedan

1939 Series C24 Custom Imperial 7-passenger sedan

shape headlamp pods provided a strong family resemblance, yet wasn't so wild that it discouraged customers. Airstreams literally carried Chrysler in those years.

Most 1937 Chryslers and all '38s had transitional styling of the period "potato school," carrying barrel grilles, rounded fenders, and pod-type headlamps. Ornate dashboards grouped gauges in front of the driver on '37s, in a central panel for '38. Offered in both years were revamped non-Airflow models comprising six-cylinder Royals and eight-cylinder standard and Custom Imperials. An interesting 1938 hybrid was the New York Special combining the year's new 119-inch-wheelbase Royal chassis with Imperial's 298.7-cid eight. Distinguished by a color-keyed interior, it came only as a four-door sedan (a business coupe was planned, but it's doubtful any were produced). All eights were now five-main-bearing side-valve engines (the nine-main unit was dropped after '34). Volume recovered from the 1934 low of some 36,000 to over 106,000 by 1937, only to drop by half for recession '38; still Chrysler remained ninth.

The division fell back to 11th place for 1939 despite improved volume of near 72,500—and handsome new Ray Dietrich styling. Headlamps moved stylishly into the fenders above a lower grille composed of vertical bars, and all fenders were lengthened. Adding to the list of Chrysler engineering firsts was "Superfinish," a new process of mirror-finishing engine and chassis components to minimize friction.

Several familiar model names bowed for 1939: Windsor (as a Royal subseries), New Yorker, and Saratoga. The C-22 Royal/Royal Windsor line carried the 241.5-cid six from 1938 and rode an unchanged wheelbase,though a long sedan and limousine were added on a 136-inch platform. The 125-inch C-23 Imperial included New Yorker coupes and sedans and a brace of Saratogas. Topping the line was the C-24 Custom Imperial: two long sedans and one limo on a 144-inch-wheelbase. All eight-cylinder offerings used the same 323.5-cid powerplant, with 130-138 bhp depending on the model. Dating from 1934, it would remain in production until the breakthrough hemispherical-head V-8 of 1951.

1940 Series C25 Royal coupe

1941 Thunderbolt show car

1941 Series C33 Crown Imperial 8-passenger sedan

Walter Chrysler died in August 1940 after turning over the presidency to his chosen successor, K. T. Keller, in 1935. But engineers continued running Chrysler with Keller's whole-hearted support. Styling remained conservative, construction sound, value good. Chrysler Division fared well in the immediate prewar years, rising to 10th place on over 92,000 units for 1940, then to 8th for '41 with nearly 162,000. Much of this was owed to a now very broad range of models and prices. The 1940 line, for instance, ranged from an $895 Royal Six coupe to a $2445 eight-passenger Crown Imperial limo.

Longer wheelbases accompanied new 1940 Chrysler bodies with notchback profiles, separate fenders, and smooth lines. The result, as one wag said, "wouldn't knock your eyes out, but wouldn't knock your hat off either." Models again grouped into six- and eight-cylinder ranks. Royal and Windsor Sixes rode a 122.5-inch chassis (139.5 for eight-seat sedans and limos). Eights began with the new Traveler, New Yorker, and Saratoga on a 128.5-inch span (the last two also offered formal sedans). A 145.5-inch chassis carried Crown Imperial sedans and limousine. The eight now delivered 135-143 bhp, the six produced 108 or 112 bhp.

Two striking show cars from LeBaron (by then owned by Briggs Manufacturing, Chrysler's longtime body supplier) appeared during 1940; six of each were built. The Newport, designed by Ralph Roberts, was an Imperial-based dual-cowl phaeton with "melted-butter" streamlining. It paced the 1941 Indianapolis 500. The Thunderbolt, penned by Briggs' Alex Tremulis and built on the New Yorker chassis, had even sleeker flush-fender styling, plus a three-person bench seat and a novel, fully retracting hard top. Both cars hid their headlamps behind metal doors, a preview of 1942 DeSotos.

The most-interesting 1941 Chrysler was Dave Wallace's unique Town & Country, the make's first station wagon. Unlike other period "woodies," this one was fairly graceful—and functional, with "clamshell" center-opening rear doors. Riding the Royal chassis, the T&C offered six- or nine-passenger seating for a remarkably low $1412/$1492. Still, only 997 were built for the model year, mostly the nine-seat type. A new variation on the familiar four-door was the attractive 1941 Town Sedan. Available in each series, it bore rear-roof quarters *sans* side windows, plus front- instead of rear-hinged back doors.

Wheelbases were trimmed an inch for all '41 Chryslers save Crown Imperials. Grilles became simpler, taillamps more ornate. The Traveler departed, but Saratogas expanded to include club and business coupes, two- and four-door sedans, and Town Sedan. Several interesting new upholstery choices arrived: Highlander, a striking combination of Scots plaid and leatherette; Saran, a woven plastic and leatherette created for certain open models; and Navajo, a pattern resembling the blankets of those Southwest Indians. The year's main new technical gimmick was optional "Vacamatic" transmission, a semiautomatic with two Low and two High gears; you shifted only to go between the ranges. Vacamatic was combined with Fluid Drive (introduced in '39), which allowed the driver to start and stop without using the clutch.

A major facelift achieved a smoother look for '42 by wrapping the horizontal grille bars right around to the front fenders. A sleeker hood opened from the front instead of the sides, and running boards were newly hidden beneath flared door bottoms. Highlander Plaid returned along with a new upholstery option called Thunderbird, also inspired by Indian motifs. Town & Country was upgraded to the Windsor chassis. Increased bore brought the six to 250.6 cid and 120 bhp; the eight cylinder was offered only in a 140-bhp version.

Like other Detroit cars, Chryslers built after January 1, 1942 used painted metal instead of chrome trim per government order. For the same reason, Chrysler ended civilian production in early February 1942 for the duration of World War II. The division built only 5292 cars that calendar year and close to 36,000 for the model year. It then turned out anti-aircraft guns, Wright Cyclone aero engines, land-mine detectors, radar units, marine engines, and "Sea Mule" harbor tugs; tanks were its most famous wartime product.

When they could during the war, small teams of designers and engineers would work on ideas for postwar Chryslers—largely smoother versions of the 1940-42 models with fully wrapped bumpers and grilles, thinner A- and B-pillars, and skirted rear fenders. But like most every other Detroit producer, Chrysler needed only warmed-over '42s to satisfy the huge seller's market that developed postwar, and that's what it offered through early 1949.

These cars wore less fender brightwork but a new eggcrate grille—one of Detroit's shiniest faces. All prewar offerings returned save Crown Imperial sedans, and engines were slightly detuned. A more significant change involved the Town & Country, which was no longer a wagon but a separate series of six- and eight-cylinder sedans and convertibles. Chrysler had promised a full line of nonwagon T&Cs, including a two-door brougham sedan and even a true roadster and a hardtop coupe. But only a handful of each were built, all basically prototypes. Hardtops, numbering just seven, were created by grafting an elongated coupe roof onto the T&C convertible. All were built in 1946, a good three years before General Motors began making sales hay with "hardtop convertibles." The eight-cylinder T&C sedan was dropped after '46 and just 100 copies.

Postwar inflation pushed prices up dramatically. For example, a Royal business coupe that had cost a little more than $1000 in 1942 was over $1400 in '46. Prices would continue rising through decade's end, when a Crown Imperial went for nearly double its 1940 figure. Even so, Chrysler ranked among the top-10 in industry production for 1947-48.

Only detail alterations occurred for 1947: fender trim, wheels/hubcaps, colors, carburetion, instruments, plus low-pressure Goodyear "Super Cushion" tires. The Traveler name returned for a luxurious Windsor utility sedan with special paint and interior and an attractive wood luggage rack. Unlike DeSoto's similar Suburban, it had a separate trunk instead of fold-down triple seats and wood rear floorboards. Also making a belated comeback was the eight-passenger Crown Imperial sedan.

The '48 Chryslers were just carryover '47s, though the six-cylinder T&C sedan was dropped at midyear, leaving the straight-eight convertible to carry on alone. The latter would prove the most numerous early T&C, with total 1946-48 production of 8380 units. Like all T&Cs through 1950, they've long been bona fide collectibles.

1942 New Yorker convertible coupe

1942 Series C36N New Yorker with "blackout" trim

1946-48 New Yorker "Zippo"

1946-48 Saratoga four-door sedan

1946-48 Town & Country convertible coupe

Chrysler planned a redesigned Silver Anniversary line for late '48, but ran into delays. Thus, existing models—save the ragtop T&C—were sold through March 1949 at unchanged prices, though none of these "first-series" '49s were built in that calendar year. Though streamlined styling with integral, skirted fenders had been considered for the all-postwar "second-series" '49s, Keller insisted on bolt-upright bodies with vast interior space. He got them, but with some loss in sales appeal. Output fell to some 124,200 for model-year '49, and Chrysler slipped back to 12th in the industry race.

Overall, the '49 Chryslers were ornate, with massive chrome-laden grilles, prominent brightwork elsewhere, and curious vertical taillights except on Crown Imperials (which were spared the gaudy devices). Gimmicky names were used for certain desirable features: "Safety-Level Ride," "Hydra-Lizer" shock absorbers, "Safety-Rim" wheels, "Full-Flow" oil filter, "Cycle-Bonded" brake linings. Wheelbases were generally longer. Royals and Windsors now spanned 125.5 inches, though a 139.5-inch chassis continued for long models. Saratogas, New Yorkers, convertible T&C, and an Imperial sedan got a 131.5-inch chassis; Crowns remained at 145.5. Engines were largely unchanged.

Chrysler-based customs were still around in the late '40s, many built by Derham of Rosemont, Pennsylvania. In 1946-48 Derham offered a Crown Imperial town limousine, as well as numerous one-offs such as a dual-cowl Imperial phaeton and a New Yorker coupe that resembled a Lincoln Continental with a Chrysler front end. Derham also tried the padded-top treatment on a handful of '49 New Yorker sedans. Chrysler itself built custom formal sedans, and A. J. Miller of Ohio did a long-wheelbase limousine/hearse. Wildest of all was a promotional 1946-48 New Yorker parade car done up as a giant Zippo lighter.

Chrysler entered the '50s as a lower-medium-price make with seven series and 24 models. By 1959 it was an upper-medium line with 15 models spanning four series. Styling and engineering improved rapidly, and the dowdy L-head cars of 1950 gave way to exciting high-performance machines by mid-decade. Chrysler also had some of the best-looking tailfins of the age.

Those fins, which premiered as tack-ons for '55, were the work of Virgil M. Exner, who came from Studebaker to head corporate styling in 1949. Exner favored "classic" design elements: upright grilles, circular wheel openings, rakish silhouettes. But the practical, boring boxes of K.T. Keller (then preparing for retirement) weren't selling, and before Exner could get out anything completely new, Chrysler Division's yearly volume had dropped from 180,000 to barely 100,000.

Predictably, the 1950 Chryslers were repeats of the all-new postwar '49 models save the usual trim shuffles and a broader chrome eggcrate smile. A Deluxe Imperial sedan with custom interior was added, but the big news was Chrysler's first volume hardtop coupe. Called Newport, it was offered as a Windsor, New Yorker, and wood-trimmed Town & Country (the last replacing the convertible).

Six-cylinder Royals were in their last year for 1950, selling for $2100-$3100. The T&C was no longer needed to glamorize an unglamorous group of cars as it had done in the early postwar period. After '50, T&C would apply only to station wagons. Before leaving, the Town & Country hardtop would pioneer a form of four-wheel disc brakes. Unlike later systems, this one employed two discs expanding inside a drum.

1949 New Yorker four-door sedan

1950 New Yorker Newport hardtop coupe

1951 New Yorker Newport hardtop coupe

1951 New Yorker Official Pace Car convertible coupe

1951 New Yorker four-door sedan

1952 Saratoga four-door sedan

Saratoga, another peripheral seller, would depart after 1952 (though it would be back). So would a revived 1950-51 Traveler, a Deluxe-trim Windsor utility sedan (something of a contradiction). Standard and Deluxe Windsors and New Yorkers then carried on until 1955's "Hundred Million Dollar Look," when only Deluxes were offered *sans* remaining long sedans and Imperials; the latter were newly marketed as a separate make (*see Imperial*).

With one singular exception, Chryslers didn't change much from 1951 through '54. Wheelbases stayed the same throughout, as did basic styling, though a more conservative grille marked the '51s. The '52s were all but identical; the firm didn't even keep separate production figures. Taillights are the only way to tell them apart: the '52s had built-in backup lamps. The '53s gained slightly bulkier lower-body sheetmetal, more chrome, and one-piece windshields. The '54s were a little "brighter" still. Body and series assignments also stood pat, though 1953-54 brought a revived Custom Imperial line with sedan and limousine on a 133.5-inch wheelbase, plus a standard-length Newport.

The above-mentioned exception was 1951's new hemispherical-head V-8, Chrysler's greatest achievement of the decade. Highland Park's early-'50s styling may have been bland, but its engineering was still anything but. The brilliant "Hemi" was simply the latest example. Still, the Chrysler six had long dominated division sales, so its complete disappearance after 1954 surprised some. But it was part of a plan instigated by Keller's successor, Lester Lum "Tex" Colbert. Then, too, the Hemi left fewer buyers for the six: well over 100,000 in 1950, but only some 45,000 by '54.

Colbert took over as company president in 1950 with several goals. The main ones were decentralized division management, a total redesign for all makes as soon as possible, and an ambitious program of plant expansion and financing. Giving the divisions freer reign meant that people close to retail sales would have more say in mapping policy.

The Hemi polished Chrysler's image in a big way, and quickly spread to other company nameplates. First offered on the '51 Saratoga, New Yorker, and Imperial, it wasn't really a new idea, but it did have exceptional volumetric efficiency and delivered truly thrilling performance. Despite lower compression that allowed using lower-octane fuel than most other postwar overhead-valve V-8s, the Hemi produced far more power for a given displacement.

And it had plenty of power even in initial 331-cid form. An early prototype recorded 352 bhp on the dynamometer after minor modifications to camshaft, carburetors, and exhaust. Drag racers would later extract up to 1000 bhp. But the Hemi was complex and costly to build, requiring twice as many rocker shafts, pushrods, and rockers; heads were heavy, too. All versions were thus phased out by 1959 in favor of more-conventional "wedge-head" V-8s. But the Hemi was too good to lose, and it would return in Highland Park's great midsize muscle cars of the '60s.

Of course, the Hemi made for some very hot Chryslers in the '50s. By dint of its lighter Windsor chassis, the Hemi Saratoga was the fastest in the line up to 1955, able to scale 0-60 mph in as little as 10 seconds and reach nearly 110 mph flat-out—straight from the showroom. Bill Sterling's Saratoga won the Stock Class and finished third overall—behind a Ferrari—in the 1951 Mexican Road Race. Chryslers also did well as NASCAR stockers, but were eclipsed by Hudson's "fabulous" Hornets in 1952-54. However, millionaire Briggs Cunningham began building rakish Hemi-powered sports cars for European road races, and his C-5R ran third overall at Le Mans '53 at an average of 104.14 mph (against 105.85

1953 New Yorker DeLuxe Newport hardtop coupe

1953 Custom Imperial Newport hardtop coupe

1954 New Yorker DeLuxe convertible coupe

1954 New Yorker DeLuxe four-door sedan

1955 New Yorker DeLuxe convertible coupe

1955 C300 hardtop coupe

1956 New Yorker convertible coupe

1955 New Yorker DeLuxe four-door sedan

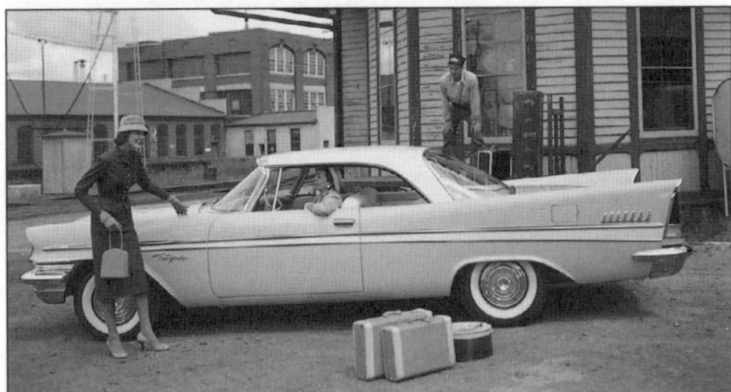

1957 New Yorker hardtop coupe

1955 Windsor DeLuxe four-door sedan

1957 New Yorker four-door sedan

mph for the winning Jaguar C-Type). Then came Chrysler's own mighty 1955 C-300 packing a stock Hemi tuned for 300 bhp—the most ever offered in a regular-production U.S. car. The 300 dominated NASCAR in 1955-56, and might have continued to do so had the Automobile Manufacturers Association not agreed to de-emphasize racing after 1957.

The 300 was part of the all-new Exner-styled '55 line that cost $100 million to develop, hence the "Hundred Million Dollar Look" advertising hype. But it was worth the expense, boosting model-year volume to over 150,000 units and bringing appearance up to par with performance at last. Evolved from an early-'50s series of Exner-designed, Ghia-built Chrysler "idea cars," the '55s were clean and aggressive-looking on a slightly longer 126-inch wheelbase. Windsor DeLuxe was treated to a new 301-cid Hemi with 188 bhp. New Yorker retained a 331 rated at 250 bhp.

The '56s looked even better—rare for a period facelift—and offered even more power. Windsors moved up to the 331 with 225 bhp standard and 250 optional. New Yorker offered 280 bhp via a bored-out 354 Hemi. That year's 300B used the same engine tweaked to 340 bhp; with a hot multicarb option it delivered 355 bhp—making this the first Detroit V-8 to break the magic "1 hp per cu. in." barrier. Chevy would manage the trick for '57, but only with fuel injection.

Exner's work was never better than on the '57 Chryslers: longer, much lower, wider, and sleeker, with modest grilles and graceful fins. They still look good today. That year's 300C was breathtaking: big and powerful yet safe and controllable—and offered as a convertible for the first time. A unique trapezoidal grille set it apart from other models.

Supplementing Newport hardtops for 1955-56 were the Windsor Nassau and New Yorker St. Regis, conservatively two-toned and boasting slightly ritzier interiors than standard Newports. Neither returned for '57, but the previous year's Newport hardtop sedans, a hasty answer to GM, would carry on well into the '70s. The '57 Town & Country wagons, Windsor and New Yorker, seated six, but could hold nine from 1958 on via a novel, optional rear-facing third seat.

Saratoga returned as Chrysler's midrange '57 series and promptly sold more than 37,000 copies. It again offered a performance premium in its 295-bhp, 354-cid Hemi. Windsors boasted 285 horses. New Yorkers moved up to an enlarged 392 with 325 bhp; in the 300C this engine delivered an incredible 375 or 390 bhp. Nobody ran the period "horsepower race" better than Chrysler.

The division had merely caught up in the "transmission race" with fully automatic two-speed PowerFlite, which bowed in late 1953 to replace semiautomatic "Fluid Drive." But Chrysler pulled ahead in mid-'56 by adding three-speed TorqueFlite, one of the finest automatics ever built. Also that year, both transmissions switched to the now-famous—or infamous—pushbutton controls, mounted in a handy pod to

1958 300D hardtop coupe

1958 New Yorker hardtop sedan

1958 Windsor "Dartline" hardtop sedan (spring model)

1959 Windsor hardtop coupe

1959 New Yorker Town & Country station wagon

1959 Chrysler 300E hardtop coupe

the left of the steering wheel. PowerFlite-equipped '55s used a slender wand to the right of the helm. Though this looked stiletto-lethal, it crumpled harmlessly on impact.

Chrysler's '57 styling was superb, but offering a second all-new design in three years led to hasty, sub-standard workmanship and a tendency to early body rust—one reason relatively few of these cars survive today. A series of plant strikes didn't help. Even so, Chrysler moved close to 125,000 cars for the model year, down from the 128,000 of '56 but still good for 10th in industry production.

No discussion of Chrysler in the '50s is complete without mentioning "Torsion-Aire Ride," a corporate staple from 1957 until the early '80s. Packard had its excellent four-wheel "Torsion Level" system for 1955-56, so the idea wasn't really new. But Torsion-Aire was in far more driveways, and proved once and for all that American cars could be made to handle. Instead of sending road shock into the chassis or body like coil or leaf springs, torsion bars absorbed most of it by twisting against their mounts. Chrysler used them only at the front, likely more for engine-compartment space than improved geometry, but it complemented them with a conventional rear end specially calibrated to maximize the bars' effectiveness.

A deep national recession and continuing subpar quality made 1958 a terrible year for Chrysler Division. Volume plunged to less than 64,000, and the make dropped to 11th, still trailing Cadillac (as it had since '56). A mild facelift was generally not for the better except on the 300D, which was all but identical to the '57 C-model. Windsor gained a convertible, but was demoted to the 122-inch Dodge/DeSoto platform. Horsepower kept climbing. Windsors were up to 290 and Saratogas to 310, courtesy of 354-cid Hemis; New Yorkers packed 345 bhp and the 300D a rousing 380/390, all from 392s.

A more substantial restyle marked the "lion-hearted" '59s. Though arguably less graceful in appearance, they scored close to 70,000 sales in a mild Detroit recovery. The switch to wedge-head V-8s introduced a 383 with 305 bhp for Windsor and 325 for Saratoga; a bigger-bore 413 gave 350 in New Yorker and 380 bhp in the 300E. Though not as efficient as the Hemi, the wedge was much simpler and cheaper to build.

The 300E has been long chided as a weakling next to its Hemi-powered predecessors, but road tests said it was just as quick as a 300D. With 10.1:1 compression, TorqueFlite, and 3.31:1 axle, the E could run 0-60 mph in under 8.5 seconds and reach 90 mph in 17.5. Even so, production was just 550 hardtops and a mere 140 convertibles, a record low that would stand until '63.

After flirting with a GM-style five-division structure in the '50s, Highland Park was back to just Dodge and Chrysler-Plymouth by 1960. The firm introduced its first compact that year, the Valiant, but it wasn't badged a Chrysler. Indeed, C-P repeatedly declared throughout the '60s that there would

1960 300F hardtop coupe

1960 New Yorker hardtop sedan

1961 300G hardtop coupe

1961 New Yorker hardtop sedan

1961 Newport convertible coupe

never be a small Chrysler. Let Buick, Olds, and Pontiac rush to compacts. Dodge and Plymouth would field—and sometimes suffer with—smaller cars; Chryslers would remain big, brawny, and luxurious. And so they would, all the way into the mid-'70s.

The 1960-61 models were the last of the outlandishly finned Exner-styled Chryslers and the first to employ full unit construction instead of traditional body-on-frame (even the old Airflow had body panels welded to a separate cage frame). Since "unibodies" were held together more by welds than nuts and bolts, they didn't suffer so much from looseness or rattles. But they were definitely more prone to rust—as many a sad owner found out.

Stylewise, the 1960 models were highly sculptured but as clean as the deft '57s. Chrome was tastefully handled, superstructures were glassy (especially windshields), and inverted trapezoid grilles conferred an aggressive 300-like appearance. Returning from '59 were optional swiveling front seats that pivoted outward through an automatic latch release when a door was opened.

Wheelbases and engines stood pat for 1960. The Saratoga was in its last year. Windsor would also depart for good, after '61. Top-liners were confined to six varieties of luxury New Yorker and the 300F. By decade's end, New Yorker regularly scored over 30,000 annual sales. Prices were just below Imperial's but about equal to those of the larger Buicks.

By far the most-exciting 1960 Chrysler was the sixth-edition "letter-series" 300 with a racy yet simple new "cross-hair" grille, four-place bucket-seat interior, road-hugging suspension, and newly optional French-made Pont-a-Mousson four-speed gear-box. The F rode hard, but cornered better than any other car of its size. And it was a flyer. New "ram-induction" manifolding lifted its 413 V-8 to 375 or 400 bhp, good for standing quarter-miles of 16 seconds at 85 mph. A half-dozen different axle ratios were available for even greater speed. With the 3.03 cog plus a tuned engine and some body streamlining, Andy Granatelli came close to 190 mph in one flying-mile run. The 300F wasn't cheap at $5411 for the hardtop and $5841 for the convertible, but it had a lot of style and sizzle.

The '61 line was mostly a repeat of 1960 save somewhat more contrived styling. Windsor moved up to replace Saratoga; taking its place was a downpriced base series called Newport. The latter fast became the make's bread-and-butter, thanks to very competitive pricing of just under $3000 through 1964, a point repeatedly emphasized in Chrysler ads. By 1965, Newport's annual sales were exceeding 125,000. The '61 carried a 265-bhp 361 V-8; Windsor and New Yorker retained their previous engines. That year's 300G didn't offer the four-speed option, but returned to 15-inch wheels (versus 14s) for the first time since 1956.

Though Highland Park's fortunes were shaky in these years, Chrysler Division actually improved its volume and industry rank. After sinking to 12th with over 77,000 cars for 1960, it finished 11th on better than 96,000 units for '61.

Nevertheless, the company's general sales difficulties hastened a management shakeup that had an immediate effect on products. At the end of July 1961, a beleaguered "Tex" Colbert retired as president, a role he had resumed in 1960 when William Newberg quit the post after two months amid allegations of having financial interests in several Chrysler suppliers. This ushered in former administrative vice-president Lynn A. Townsend, who then became chairman in January 1967, with Virgil Boyd as president through early 1970. These changes also prompted Exner, who was often blamed for the sales woes, to leave in late 1961 after shaping the '63 corporate line. His replacement was Elwood Engel, recruited from Ford and part of the design team on the elegant '61 Lincoln Continental.

Thus began a new direction for Chrysler styling. For 1962, the division fielded what Exner called the "plucked chickens": basically '61s shorn of fins. The 1963-64s had "the crisp, clean custom look"—chiseled but chunky. For 1965 came Engel's smooth, squarish bodies with fenders edged in bright metal, one of his signatures.

Among the finless '62s was a new four-model group of "non-letter" 300s: convertible, hardtop coupe, and four-doors with and without B-pillars. All carried the same engine as the now-departed Windsor and could be optioned with sporty features like center console and front bucket seats. Save the pillared sedan (only 1801 built, all for export), these 300s were quite popular at prices in the $3300-$3800 range. But they hurt that year's 300H, which cost $1600-$1800 more yet looked almost the same. As a result, letter-series volume dropped from about 1600 for '61 to just 558.

New Yorker was downgraded to the junior 122-inch wheelbase for 1963-64, becoming the same general size as the less-costly Chryslers, yet sales were strong in both years. Arriving as 1963 "spring specials" were a 300 Pace Setter hardtop and convertible and the New Yorker Salon hardtop sedan. The former, commemorating Chrysler's selection as pace car for that year's Indianapolis 500, was identified by crossed checkered-flag emblems and special trim. The Salon came with such standard luxuries as air conditioning; AM/FM radio; "Auto Pilot" speed control; power brakes, steering, seats, and windows; TorqueFlite (what else?); and color-keyed wheel covers and vinyl roof. Minus the Pace Setters, this lineup repeated for '64 with largely untouched engines and styling.

The 1963-64 300J/300K (the letter "I" was skipped to avoid confusion with the number "1") were big, solid performance cars in the letter-series tradition. The J came only as a hardtop; the convertible was reinstated with the K. Just 400 Js were built in all, a record low for Chrysler's limited edition, but the K saw a healthy 3600-plus. All ran 413s with 360/390 bhp, down slightly from 300H ratings. The last of the true letter-series cars was the 300L of 1965. It saw 2845 copies, including a mere 440 convertibles. None of these were quite the stormers that previous 300s were, but they remained the most roadable Chryslers and among the best handling of all big Detroiters. Sales lost to the non-letter 300s is what killed them, of course.

Chrysler did very well for 1965, selling over 125,000 Newports, nearly 30,000 non-letter 300s and almost 50,000 New Yorkers. Things were even better for '66: the 300 nearly doubled and Newport climbed by 42,000 units.

The post-1964 Engel Chryslers were shorter than their Exner forebears but just as spacious inside. Wheelbase was 124 inches for all models except wagons (121 through '66, then 122 inches). Expanding the '67 line were the Newport

1962 New Yorker hardtop sedan

1963 New Yorker Salon hardtop sedan

1962 300H convertible coupe

1965 New Yorker hardtop coupe

1963 300 hardtop coupe

1965 300L hardtop coupe

1966 New Yorker hardtop sedan

1967 New Yorker hardtop sedan

1967 Newport Custom hardtop coupe

1968 300 hardtop coupe

1969 Newport Custom hardtop sedan

Custom two- and four-door hardtops and four-door sedan. Tagged some $200 above comparable standard Newports, Customs were trumpeted as "a giant step in luxury, a tiny step in price." Deluxe interiors were the big attraction: jacquard cloth and textured vinyl, plus pull-down center armrests. Like other '67 Chryslers, the Custom dash sprouted no fewer than eight toggle switches, three thumbwheels, 16 pushbuttons, three sliding levers, and 12 other assorted controls. Vinyl-covered lift handles appeared on Custom trunklids, and there were "over 1000 chrome accents along the sides, plus 15 gold crown medallions."

Meanwhile, the luxurious New Yorker Town & Country wagon disappeared after 1965 (sales had been slow for years), but six- and nine-passenger Newport wagons continued through '68, after which T&C became a separate wagon series. All typically came with vinyl upholstery instead of the cloth-and-vinyl of Newport sedans.

Spring 1968 brought the interesting $126 "Sportsgrain" option: wagon-type simulated-wood side paneling for the Newport convertible and hardtop coupe. It didn't catch on and thus was dropped after '69. Sportsgrain convertibles must be rare indeed, as Chrysler built only 2847 total ragtop Newports for '68. More popular that year were the added Newport Special two- and four-door hardtops with a turquoise color scheme, later extended to 300s.

Engine choices for '65 involved 270- and 315-bhp 383s for Newport and 300, a 413 with 340 or 360 bhp for New Yorker and 300L. The more-potent 383 gained 10 horses for '66, when a huge 440 big-block arrived as standard New Yorker fare, rated at 350 bhp. The 300s adopted it for 1967, when a 375-hp version was added. The 440s stood pat for 1968-69, but the 383s were retuned to 290 and 330 bhp, this despite the advent of federal emissions standards.

These moves and the conservative Engel styling paid off in vastly higher volume: 206,000-plus for '65, nearly 265,000 the following year. Though sales dipped to some 219,000 for '67, Chrysler ran 10th in industry output in each of these years, then claimed ninth with 1968 production that just topped the '66 record.

The all-new "fuselage-styled" '69s did almost as well. If not the most beautiful Chryslers of the decade, they were at least handsome with their great looping bumper/grille combinations, fulsome bodysides, and low rooflines. Despite remaining on the 124-inch wheelbase, all models were bigger than ever: almost 225 inches long and nearly 80 inches wide—about as big as American cars would ever get.

Predictably, the 1970s changed only in detail, but midyear introduced the first Cordobas: a Newport hardtop coupe and sedan with paint, vinyl roof, bodyside moldings, wheels, and grille all colored gold, plus unique "Aztec Eagle" upholstery. A well-equipped Newport 440 hardtop also arrived with TorqueFlite, vinyl roof, and other extras as standard.

A reminder, but not a revival, of the great letter-series in 1970 was the 300-H. The "H" stood for Hurst, maker of the floor-mounted shifter used for the TorqueFlite automatic. Performance goodies abounded—special road wheels, white-letter tires, a tuned 440 V-8, heavy-duty suspension—set off by a gold-and-white paint job, custom hood, trunklid spoiler, special grille, pinstriping, and unique interior. Only 501 were built. Also appearing for 1970 were Chrysler's last big convertibles, a Newport and 300 that saw respective production of just 1124 and 1077 units. They've since become minor collector's items.

Vast changes in corporate administration were evident by 1969-70. Quality control had become an end in itself as engineers struggled to correct Chrysler Corporation's poor reputation in that area. On the administrative side, Townsend had consolidated Colbert's old decentralized structure and moved to strengthen divisional identities between Dodge and Chrysler-Plymouth. Still, the firm would travel a very rocky road in the '70s.

The Chrysler brand stayed with its basic 1969-70 formula through 1973. Style variations through '72 came via easy-change items that became a bit tackier with time. The '73s gained blockier lower-body sheetmetal and a more-conventional front, with bigger bumpers per federal requirement.

New for '71 was a low-priced Newport Royal subseries with standard 255-bhp 360 V-8, an enlarged version of the corporate small-block engine introduced in the mid-'60s. A stroked 400-cid version of the 383, more adaptable to emissions tuning, replaced it for '72, then disappeared with the 360 and all Royal models. Other Chryslers relied on the 440 with added emission controls that sapped power, which was down to 215 bhp by '73—though that was in more-realistic SAE net measure, not the old gross rating. A popular new addition for '72 was the New Yorker Brougham: two hardtops and a sedan with lusher interiors and a $300-$400 price premium over the standard issue.

Overall, Chrysler did fairly well in this period. Sales fell to around 177,000 for 1970-71, but recovered to nearly 205,000 for '72, then to 234,000-plus. Nevertheless, Chrysler still couldn't seem to beat Cadillac, trailing GM's flagship every year in 11th place.

Sales sank mightily in the wake of the first energy crisis despite a completely redesigned crop of 1974 models, still on a 124-inch wheelbase but about five inches shorter than the "fuselage" generation. Styling was crisper but more slab-sided, announced by pseudo-classic square grilles, a period fad that Chrysler had studiously avoided before. Engine options and horsepower were down: 185/205-bhp 400 V-8s for Newport and Newport Custom, 230/275-bhp 440s for T&C wagons, New Yorker, and New Yorker Brougham. The last was now quite like the Imperial, which was again being marketed as a Chrysler but was still registered as a separate make (and is so treated here). After '75, Imperial actually became a Brougham via the badge-engineering so long practiced by Chrysler—to the confusion of customers up and down the corporate line.

Few in Highland Park had foreseen the energy crisis, which only accelerated the buyer resistance to big cars that had been building as a result of galloping sticker prices. Sales of the record-priced 1974s dropped to 1970 levels, and a two-month backlog quickly piled up, yet chairman Townsend refused to slash prices. Instead, he slashed production. By early November 1974, corporate sales were down 34 percent—not as bad as GM's 43 percent loss, but more serious, as Chrysler's fixed costs were spread over much smaller volume. The results were employee layoffs and an unsold inventory of 300,000 units by early 1975.

Finally, Chrysler offered something no one in Detroit ever had: cash rebates—essentially paying people to buy. Other automakers had little choice but to follow. It amounted to throwing money away in an attempt to lose less on the balance sheets, but it was a necessary, if drastic, step. That big backlog cost Chrysler $300,000 a week.

These sharp reversals prompted a complete rethink that must have seemed quite alien for a make that had solemnly promised never to build a smaller car. But a new philosophy was emerging that echoed some 1958 remarks of then-outgoing president K.T. Keller, who suggested Chrysler should "get back to design for function, with more stress on utility."

The most visible evidence of the new order was the 1975

1970 New Yorker hardtop sedan

1970 Chrysler 300 convertible coupe

1970 Newport hardtop coupe

1972 Town & Country station wagon

1973 New Yorker four-door sedan

Cordoba. Though this personal-luxury coupe broke new ground for the marque, it wasn't at all daring: largely a twin to that year's revamped Dodge Charger, with styling that looked like a cross between the sleek Jaguar XJ6 and semi-baroque Chevrolet Monte Carlo. On a 115-inch wheelbase, this new Cordoba was the shortest Chrysler since the war—and only 2.5 inches longer than the very first 1924 Six.

Cordoba was billed as "the new small Chrysler," which it was, and something of a road car, which it wasn't despite standard antiroll bars and steel-belted radial tires. Reflecting its true character were interiors upholstered in crushed velour or vinyl with brocade cloth. "Fine Corinthian leather," extolled on TV by actor Ricardo Montalban, cost extra.

Save higher prices, the rest of the line was little changed for 1975-76. The accent was now strictly on luxury with a modicum of "efficiency" thrown in. The opulent New Yorker Brougham boasted standard leather, velour, or brocade upholstery, plus shag carpeting, "test-tube" walnut appliques, and filigree moldings. Economy, such as it was, got a little help from numerically lower axle ratios and a new "Fuel Pacer" option—an intake manifold-pressure sensor hooked to a warning light that glowed during heavy-footed moments.

Chrysler fielded something even smaller for 1977: the mid-size, 3500-pound, M-body LeBaron. Cleanly styled in the boxy Mercedes idiom on a 112.7-inch wheelbase, it came in standard and upmarket Medallion trim as either a coupe or four-door sedan. Despite its origins in the workaday A-body Dodge Aspen/Plymouth Volare compacts, it sold quite well, providing timely sales assistance in a market again clamoring for smaller cars. The full-size line was mildly facelifted, and Newport Custom departed. Cordoba soldiered on in two little-changed models.

LeBaron got greater emphasis for 1978 with the addition of downpriced S versions and a brace of Town & Countrys, the latter replacing full-size Chrysler wagons. All offered 90- and 110-bhp versions of the hoary 225-cid "Slant Six" as alternatives to optional 140- and 155-bhp 318-cid V-8s. The slow-selling full-sizers were further reduced by dropping pillared four-doors. The 440 V-8 was still available for them, but most were ordered with the standard 400. LeBaron had bowed with square headlamps newly approved by Washington. Cordoba now got them, too.

For 1979, Chrysler issued downsized big sedans on a 118.5-inch wheelbase: six and V-8 Newport and V-8-only New Yorker and New Yorker Fifth Avenue. Built on the firm's 1971-vintage intermediate platform, these ostensibly "new" R-body models were considerably smaller and lighter than the old mastodons, but still looked big and heavy—which they were. Sales were underwhelming: about 133,000 in a record Detroit year. The LeBaron line now listed base, Medallion, and new midrange Salon models plus woody-look T&C wagons, none substantially altered. Reviving the spirit of the great letter-series 300 was a midyear option group for Cordoba comprising unique trim, bucket seats, cross-hair grille, and a 195-bhp 360-cid V-8.

By this point, a gathering financial crisis was threatening Chrysler Corporation's very existence. But help was already onboard in the person of newly named chairman Lee A. Iacocca, the recently ousted president of Ford who'd arrived in late 1978. He arrived none too soon. Not only was Chrysler near bankruptcy, it was in "a state of anarchy," as Iacocca wrote later in his best-selling autobiography. "There was no real committee setup, no cement in the organizational chart, no system of meetings to get people talking to each other... I took one look at the system and almost threw up. That's when I knew I was in really deep trouble."

"Chrysler had no overall system of financial controls," he said. "Nobody in the whole place seemed to fully understand what was going on when it came to financial planning and projecting. I couldn't find out anything. I already knew about the lousy cars, the bad morale, and the deteriorating factories. But I simply had no idea that I wouldn't even be able to get hold of the right numbers so that we could begin to attack some basic problems."

New products to answer some of those problems were nearing completion when Iacocca came in; others were further away. None would have appeared without the federal loan guarantees Iacocca managed to coax from a reluctant

1975 New Yorker Brougham hardtop sedan

1975 Cordoba coupe

1976 New Yorker Brougham hardtop sedan

1977 Cordoba coupe with Crown roof

United States Congress in mid-1980.

For the Chrysler line, this situation dictated a holding action for 1980-81, though with a few game attempts at something different. Prime among the latter was a second-generation Cordoba, a crisply reskinned LeBaron coupe on the same 112.7-inch wheelbase. It was a fair success its first year at some 54,000 units, but annual volume then fell to less than half of that through '83, after which Cordoba said *adios*. A 185-bhp 360 V-8 was optional for 1980; choices then thinned to a standard 85-bhp, 225-cid Slant-Six or a 130-bhp 318 V-8. A less-expensive LS edition for 1981-83 again tried to evoke letter-series memories, but few were sold.

The big R-body Newport/New Yorker provided little sales help in this period, and was dropped after much-reduced 1981 volume of fewer than 11,000 (including a high proportion of taxi and police sales). A much happier fate awaited the M-body LeBaron, which also looked terminal but would run a good deal longer. It was facelifted for 1980 with bolder grilles, more-sharply creased fenders and, save wagons, blockier rooflines. Making room for the downsized Cordoba, LeBaron coupes moved to the 108.7-inch Aspen/Volare wheelbase and gained a more close-coupled look.

What ultimately prolonged this design appeared as a mid-1980 special called LeBaron Fifth Avenue Edition, a loaded four-door with throwback styling in the image of the like-named R-body New Yorker. When the latter was canceled and a new front-drive LeBaron instituted for '82, this one model, kept on as a "downsized" New Yorker, showed increasing sales strength as the market recovered from its early-decade doldrums. By 1984, it was simply Fifth Avenue and up to over 79,000 produced—a figure that neared 110,000 the next year. Remarkably, the Fifth Avenue was still bringing in over 70,000

1977 New Yorker Brougham hardtop sedan

1977 Cordoba coupe with Crown roof

1977 LeBaron Medallion coupe

1978 LeBaron Town & Country station wagon

1978 Newport hardtop coupe

1978 Cordoba coupe with Crown roof

1979 New Yorker Fifth Avenue four-door sedan

1979 Cordoba coupe

1980 Cordoba Crown coupe

1981 LeBaron Medallion four-door sedan

1981 New Yorker Fifth Avenue four-door sedan

1982 Cordoba LS coupe with Carriage roof

1982 Cordoba coupe with Landau roof

1982 LeBaron four-door sedan

1982 New Yorker four-door sedan

1982 LeBaron Mark Cross convertible coupe

1983 LeBaron Mark Cross Town & Country convertible coupe

1983 New Yorker Fifth Avenue four-door sedan

1983 Cordoba coupe

1983 E-Class four-door sedan

1984 LeBaron Town & Country station wagon

1984 Laser Turbo coupe

1984 LeBaron convertible coupe

orders per year as late as 1987.

There was no mystery in this. A lot of folks still craved traditional rear-drive American luxury. This one offered plenty of standard amenities at attractive prices that began around $13,000 and finished the decade only some $5000 higher. Yes, the Fifth Avenue was terribly outmoded by 1989, but as tooling costs had long been amortized, Chrysler could keep prices reasonable (despite pressures to the contrary), which hardly dampened demand. In all, this car was a pleasant surprise success for Chrysler.

Meanwhile, Iacocca presided over a remarkable resurgence that put Chrysler Corporation solidly back in the black by 1983. The company even paid all its creditors ahead of time, without ever resorting to federal backup. The return to prosperity came almost entirely on clever—and seemingly endless—permutations of the front-wheel-drive K-car compact, introduced for 1981 as the Dodge Aries/Plymouth Reliant. Chrysler versions followed for '82; by decade's end they'd constitute virtually the entire line.

First up were smaller LeBarons: base and Medallion coupes and sedans on the 99.9-inch K-car wheelbase. Power came from Chrysler's own newly designed 2.2-liter (135-cid) single-overhead-cam four or an optional 2.6-liter "balancer" four supplied by longtime Japanese partner Mitsubishi. A turbocharged 2.2 spinning out 142-146 bhp arrived for '84 and was relatively popular. Replacing the old M-body LeBarons, these "CV" models were joined at mid-1982 by a woody-look Town & Country wagon and America's first factory convertibles since the mid-'70s. The latter can be fairly credited to Iacocca and were a brilliant stroke, offered in plain and nostalgic T&C trim.

Iacocca also issued CV-based long models recalling the 1940s and '50s. These comprised a five-passenger Executive Sedan on a 124-inch wheelbase and a seven-seat limousine on a 131-inch chassis—the first "carriage trade" Chryslers since the last Stageway Imperial limousines of 1970. They sold in modest numbers through 1986, mainly to fancy hotels and airport limo services. Chrysler then gave up on them as just so much bother.

The CV LeBarons continued through 1986 with only minor styling and mechanical changes. A stroked 2.5-liter (153-cid) engine with 100 bhp became available that season, a year after TorqueFlite automatic was made standard and the five-speed manual transmission was dropped. The line quickly established itself as Chrysler's top period seller, garnering around 100,000 orders annually. The notchback four-door and T&C wagon lasted through 1988.

Next in the line of K-based Chryslers was a stretched four-door, originally named "Gran LeBaron" but announced for 1983 under the prosaic title of E-Class, a reference to its E-body platform. Though riding a three-inch longer wheelbase, the E-Class was much like the CV LeBaron save revised rear-quarter styling, a roomier back seat, and slightly higher prices. But it failed to catch on—at least as a Chrysler product. After 1984 and some 80,000 examples, it was badge-engineered into Plymouth and Dodge models that sold somewhat better as "new-age" family cars.

A more-successful spinoff was the first front-drive New Yorker. Bowing at mid-1983, this was an E-Class with more class—or what passed for it at the time. Taking a cue from Fifth Avenue sales, stylists gave the E-body a blind-quarter padded vinyl roof, a more-upright vertical-bar grille, extra chrome accents, even "opera lamps" (a '70s throwback). There was also a more-uptown interior with Mark Cross leather upholstery (introduced with the LeBaron convertible) and high-tech tricks like an irritating Electronic Voice Alert, a

1985 New Yorker Turbo four-door sedan

1985 Executive Limousine

1985 LeBaron GTS Turbo hatchback sedan

1985 Fifth Avenue four-door sedan

1986 LeBaron coupe

1986 New Yorker Turbo four-door sedan

1986 LeBaron Town & Country convertible coupe

1986 Laser coupe

1987 LeBaron Town & Country station wagon

1987 LeBaron Turbo convertible coupe

"back-seat driver" with a synthesized voice that nagged you from within the instrument panel when your "key is in the ignition" or "a door is ajar." New Yorker wasn't the only Chrysler afflicted by this ill-conceived device, which was soon dropped anyway. The car itself lasted longer, generating some 60,000 sales through 1987, after which it departed for a more-impressive New Yorker.

The two most interesting Chryslers of the 1980s were the Laser coupe and LeBaron GTS sedan. The former, new for '84, was a sleek "fasthatch" design on an abbreviated 97.0-inch-wheelbase K-car platform (internally dubbed "G24"). A near-identical twin to the reborn Dodge Daytona introduced alongside it, the Laser was a sporty, if somewhat crude performer in turbo form and practical in any guise. But it may have been a little much for most Chrysler types, because the Daytona always outsold it. As Dodge was reasserting its claim as the corporation's "performance" division, Chrysler-Plymouth dealers lost the Laser after 1986, though they got something more salable to replace it.

GTS, a 1985 addition, was a very different LeBaron: a smooth hatchback four-door aimed at America's increasingly affluent baby-boomers and their growing preference for premium European sedans. As usual, there was a duplicate Dodge, the Lancer. Both shared the same new H-body and the usual K-car underpinnings on a 103.1-inch wheelbase. Available engines were the now-familiar assortment of Chrysler-built four-cylinder units teamed with five-speed overdrive manual and TorqueFlite automatic transaxles.

Though no threat to the likes of BMW and Mercedes, the LeBaron GTS was a competent all-around tourer, surprisingly roomy and quite versatile (like Laser, its back seat folded down for extra cargo space). Over 135,000 found buyers in the first two years at base prices running $9000-$11,000. Unfortunately, volume dropped by almost 50 percent for '87, reflecting tough competition from the popular new Ford Taurus/Mercury Sable. For 1989, GTS referred only to a top-spec 2.2 turbo model, the base and midrange offerings becoming just plain LeBarons.

As if buyers weren't already bewildered by so many LeBarons, Chrysler introduced two more for 1987: a new J-body coupe and convertible to replace the previous CV styles. Chrysler's design staff, under new chief Tom Gale, gave them rounded, GTS-type contours, a clean yet dignified hidden-headlamp nose, and a shapely tail with full-width light panel. From the rear, the coupe was nicely reminiscent of Studebaker's Avanti. The convertible looked great from any angle, especially with the top down.

Though the CV wheelbase was retained, the J-model's inner structure related more to Daytona than K-car. By now, corporate planners were seeking to reestablish Chrysler as their premium make, so there were no divisional doubles of these LeBarons. Instead, Chrysler gave up the Laser, and the Daytona continued as a Dodge exclusive. This strategy helped the Daytona less than the LeBaron Js, which got off to a strong sales start at nearly 83,500 units.

New Yorker figured in another name game for 1988: fully revised on the new 104.3-inch-wheelbase C-body platform shared with Dodge's Dynasty. There were no major chassis innovations at first, but there was a new engine: a smooth 136-bhp 3.0-liter (181-cid) Mitsubishi V-6 with electronic-port fuel injection (by now almost universal at Highland Park). Styling was clean but archly conservative—really a cautious update of the Fifth Avenue and, again, reportedly dictated by chairman Iacocca himself. Base and better-equipped Landau sedans (the latter with vinyl rear quarter-roof) were listed from around $17,500. A first for Chrysler was availability of

1987 LeBaron coupe

1988 New Yorker Landau four-door sedan

1988 New Yorker four-door sedan

1988 Chrysler's TC by Maserati convertible coupe

1988 Fifth Avenue four-door sedan

1989 Chrysler's TC by Maserati with removable hardtop

1989 LeBaron GTS Turbo hatchback sedan

1989 LeBaron GTC Turbo coupe

1989 LeBaron GTC Turbo convertible coupe

1989 Fifth Avenue four-door sedan

1990 New Yorker Fifth Avenue four-door sedan

1990 New Yorker Landau four-door sedan

1990 Town & Country minivan

1990 LeBaron GTC Turbo convertible coupe

1990 LeBaron four-door sedan

antilock brakes, a $1000 option but worth every penny in peace of mind. Handling and performance were nothing special, but these were merely traditional luxury cars of a trimmer, more-efficient sort—really, no bad thing to be.

And Chrysler made them better for 1989 with standard all-disc brakes and a new four-speed automatic transaxle that gave Highland Park another industry first with its fully adaptive electronic shift control. Other new features for the New Yorker nameplate's 50th year included options such as antitheft alarm system, power front seatback recliners, and two-position "memory" power driver's seat, plus a revised electronic instrument cluster.

Plymouth's new 1989 Acclaim compact implied an upscale Chrysler version. Sure enough, it arrived in January 1990 to take over for the departed LeBaron hatchback. A blocky "trunked" four-door with smoothed-off edges, it was essentially a gussied-up Acclaim that could pass as a pint-size New Yorker with optional bright trim, vinyl-roof toppings, and a standard 141-bhp V-6. The K-car's 2.2-liter four had grown to 2.5 liters and 100 bhp, and it was now standard for all '89 two-door LeBarons. The only option was a 150-bhp turbo version for LeBaron coupes and convertibles. Those J-body cars received a modernized dash for 1990. Designed by Trevor Creed, lately of Citroën, it was flashy, but less than ideal for ergonomics. Also new for the Js was a 2.2-liter "Turbo IV" option with Chrysler's new Variable Nozzle Technology. Power was unchanged from the previous "Turbo II" (174 bhp), but VNT reduced throttle lag by optimizing exhaust-gas flow to the turbocharger with a set of radial vanes that could be angled by computer control according to throttle position and engine speed.

Symbolic of Chrysler's 1980s fortunes was its first-ever production two-seater. Awkwardly named Chrysler's TC by Maserati, it was first shown in mid-1986 (as the "Q-coupe") but was delayed by numerous problems to a late-1988 debut as an '89 model. Maserati, of course, is the well-known Italian sports-car maker in which Chrysler had lately acquired a minority interest, but its main role in this joint venture was simply to build Chrysler's design.

Almost too predictably, the TC was yet another K-clone: a shortened 93.3-inch-wheelbase version of that ubiquitous platform topped by a wedgy convertible body looking much like the open LeBaron J (though the TC was actually created first). Powerteams involved a special 200-bhp turbocharged 2.2 with intercooler, port injection, and a new Maserati-design 16-valve twincam cylinder head, available only with five-speed manual; and a single-cam 160-bhp "Turbo II" engine for buyers preferring three-speed automatic. The customer's only other choice was paint color, since the TC was conceived as a fully equipped "one-price" model. Included were the expected leather upholstery and full power assists, but also all-disc antilock brakes, manual soft top with heated-glass rear window, and a removable hardtop (made of sheet-molding compound). The last had a nostalgic styling touch: rear-quarter portholes, recalling the '56 Thunderbird and the earliest days of Iacocca's career at Ford.

Despite all this, the TC bombed. Its similarity to the much cheaper LeBaron convertible was too obvious; and handling, refinement, and performance were undistinguished for a car of its price. Adding injury to insult, the announced $30,000 base sticker was hiked $3000 within three months. Thus did trade weekly *Automotive News* name the TC its 1988 "Flop of the Year," the same "honor" it accorded Cadillac's Allanté the previous year. The 1990 edition was unchanged except for adding a wood-rimmed steering wheel with airbag and a 3.0-liter Mitsubishi V-6 to replace the Turbo II engine with auto-

1991 New Yorker Salon four-door sedan

1991 Town & Country minivan

1991 Chrysler's TC by Maserati convertible coupe

1991 Imperial four-door sedan

1992 New Yorker Fifth Avenue four-door sedan

1992 LeBaron convertible coupe

1992 Town & Country minivan

1993 New Yorker Fifth Avenue four-door sedan

1993 Concorde four-door sedan

matic. Production soon ended at some 7300 total units. A few 1990s were retailed into '91, again at fire-sale prices.

Meanwhile, the old rear-drive M-body Fifth Avenue was finally retired for a new Y-body 1990 model, essentially the latest front-drive New Yorker stretched to a 109.3-inch wheelbase. Styling displayed the usual "formal" cues, though hidden headlamps were a nice change and there were gadgets galore. Under the hood sat a new Chrysler V-6: a 3.3-liter overhead-valve design with port injection and 147 bhp. But the real surprise was yet another reborn Imperial, this one a more-deluxe Fifth Avenue measuring four inches longer (203 overall). An upright grille announced it, and the familiar Imperial eagle badges appeared on the tail and roof. But prices were stiff for what amounted to luxury K-cars: $21,395 for Fifth Avenue, $25-grand for Imperial. Worse, both were narrower and less roomy than Cadillac's recently enlarged DeVille. And Chrysler charged extra for antilock brakes that Lincoln included on its Continental sedan. With all this, the Y-body twins were not huge sellers. The Fifth Avenue claimed a respectable 44,400 model-year sales, but Imperial managed fewer than 15,000.

There was a new Town & Country for 1990, the first in two years. To no one's surprise, it was a minivan. Chrysler had pioneered this concept with its '84 Dodge Caravan/Plymouth Voyager, and had kept sales roaring with useful yearly updates, especially the '87 introduction of extended "Grand" models on a spacious 119.1-inch wheelbase. With every minivan an easy sale—and often loaded with profitable extras—a luxury version was a logical addition to the Chrysler lineup.

The minivan T&C bowed as a single long-chassis model with numerous comfort and convenience features including leather interior. Base price was a bit startling at $25,000, but the only extras were whitewall tires and a front license-plate bracket. A vertical-bar grille and pseudo-wood bodysides distinguished T&C from less-costly Dodge/Plymouth minivans. The sole powertrain was a 150-bhp 3.3 pushrod V-6 and four-speed automatic, the latter a new option for Caravan/Voyager. Though model-year sales were modest at under 3500 units, Chrysler hoped for better T&C results in the future.

Assuming there was a future, which many were doubting in 1990. Incredibly, Chrysler was again flirting with disaster in a market turned sour once more, but this time there was no question of a government rescue. Chrysler's latest woes were clearly of its own doing.

They stemmed from a mid-'80s spending spree amid windfall earnings, mainly from minivans. Optimistically, Iacocca decided that if GM could acquire Hughes Electronics, Chrysler should buy its own aerospace company—say, Gulfstream Aviation. Trouble was, Chrysler's purchase cost far more than GM's in relation to total assets, and Gulfstream ultimately proved of little direct benefit. Chrysler spent billions more to acquire American Motors in 1987, landing the lucrative Jeep franchise, but assuming a mountain of debt it could ill-afford. Worse, these and other overreaching moves diverted funds that might have been better used to improve Chrysler's own products and plants. As a result, the company was woefully unprepared when a sharp recession hit in 1990, and sales, earnings, and cash reserves all dropped alarmingly.

As part of its 1980s "diversification," Chrysler split off its vehicle business as a separate Chrysler Motors unit in 1985. But this was an organizational indulgence, and it lasted only five years. In the meantime, the firm began losing the key executives who'd helped engineer its early-'80s comeback, the former Iacocca colleagues from Ford who'd been serving as presidents and chairmen of Chrysler Motors. First to go was minivan "father" Harold Sperlich in 1988; financial whiz Gerald Greenwald and Bennett Bidwell resigned two years later. These departures ushered in Robert Lutz as president of Chrysler Motors in 1988. Three years later, he became overall president of a reunified Chrysler Corporation.

Lutz arrived in the nick of time. A knowledgeable "car guy" with top-level executive experience at Opel, BMW, and Ford Europe, he knew even better than Iacocca that consumer tastes had changed greatly and that Chrysler had to change with them—fast. That not only meant more-contemporary, "international" vehicles but a whole new way of designing, building, and selling them. With Iacocca's endorsement, Chrysler began shedding noncore businesses like Gulfstream while forming "cross-functional platform teams" charged with creating superior cars and trucks—and getting them to market in three years or less instead of the usual four or five.

Under the "team concept," designers, engineers, production experts, and marketing talent would work together from day one to ensure their products were on target with buyers for features, cost, and quality. The idea was to minimize the delays, mistakes, confusion, and "turf battles" that often arise when people work on separate pieces of the same project. The decision to produce the hot Dodge Viper sports car provided a timely opportunity to test the new approach on a manageably small scale. It worked beautifully, and the team concept was quickly adopted for all future-product programs. Chrysler also began forging closer alliances with its many suppliers by including them as members of the various teams.

With these and other departures from Detroit tradition, the company liked to say it was "reinventing" itself, hoping to become a "New New Chrysler Corporation" able to make timely, right moves to survive and even thrive in a now vastly changed automotive world. Toward that end, chairman Iacocca was finally persuaded to step down, something he'd resisted for years. Though Lutz was the obvious heir apparent, Iacocca got in one last surprise by handing the job to Robert Eaton in early 1993. Eaton was a shrewd choice. He came directly from GM Europe, which had recently come back strong under his command, and his low-key manner made a nice contrast with the often outspoken Lutz. To his credit, Lutz agreed to stay on and give his all for the new chairman. They made a formidable team.

Of course, massive change doesn't happen overnight, so the early '90s were transition years for the Chrysler line. Existing models were kept on only until replacements were ready, which would be remarkably soon.

Some of the old stuff was treated with "benign neglect." The Y-body, for example, vanished after 1993 and only two interim changes of note: a 3.8-liter V-6 for '91 (standard for Imperial, optional on Fifth Avenue) and a mild Fifth Avenue facelift for '92. Sales faded in both cases. Imperial dropped under 12,000 for '91, then to 7600 and a final 7000 or so. Fifth Avenue held up better, scoring no worse than just under 30,000 in its last model year. Still, against Cadillac and Lincoln, these cars were only a token luxury presence for the Chrysler brand, and in looks and driving feel they were about as modern as a leisure suit.

The same could be said for the C-body New Yorker, which lost its spiffy Landau version for 1991, then got a nearly imperceptible facelift before closing out as a single '93 model all but identical with the Dodge Dynasty. Despite base prices that never exceeded $20,000, this New Yorker couldn't match the sales of the costlier Fifth Avenue, managing just 20,000-23,000 a year after 1990.

LeBarons were fiddled with during this period, but not drastically changed. The J-body line was rearranged for '91, then added optional antilock brakes for '92, when the A-body sedan expanded to base, LX, and Landau models. Two-doors got a nice facelift for '93, showing new grilles and exposed headlamps. Turbo engines were dropped, but the Mitsubishi V-6 was now standard for midline LX and sporty GTC coupes and convertibles. At the same time, the LX sedan departed and the base model was renamed LE. Coupes and four-cylinder power disappeared for '94, leaving the two sedans and one GTC convertible with standard V-6. Only the ragtop returned for '95, after which the LeBaron name was finally put to rest (at least so far). Though sales declined with all models, the J-body two-doors fared a little better.

Heralding Chrysler's next generation was the front-drive Concorde sedan, the 1993 replacement for the C-body New Yorker. Though billed as an intermediate car, it was really a full-size, standing nearly 17 feet long on a rangy 113-inch wheelbase. All-independent suspension and no-cost antilock brakes recalled Chrysler's glory days. So did appearance. With its new "LH" platform (still a "unibody," of course), Concorde introduced "cab forward" styling that made for vast interior space and a sleek, even daring, new look—a refreshing break from boxiness. For the first time in nearly 40 years, Chrysler could claim industry design leadership. Though Concorde's form was shared by divisional sisters Dodge Intrepid and Eagle Vision, Chrysler wisely made sure there

1994 New Yorker four-door sedan

1995 Cirrus LXi four-door sedan

1994 LeBaron GTC convertible coupe

1995 Sebring coupe

1996 Town & Country LXi minivan

1996 Sebring LX coupe

1996 LHS four-door sedan

1996 Concorde LXi four-door sedan

were enough differences among the three to avoid the possibility of buyer confusion.

Essentially, cab-forward lengthened the greenhouse and pushed the wheels out closer to the car's corners, resulting in a stubby deck, foreshortened nose, and purposeful wide-track stance (though a longitudinal engine dictated lengthy front overhang). General design thinking had been moving in this direction, so cab-forward was not entirely new or unique to Chrysler. But nobody would it use more. In fact, cab-forward was the company's new design signature.

Concorde bowed in a single, well-equipped model base-priced at $18,341. Included were front bucket seats, shift console, tachometer, dual airbags, full power assists, and other amenities. Power came from one of two V-6s. The pushrod 3.3 was standard, tuned for 153 bhp. Optional was a new 3.5-liter unit with dual-overhead camshafts, four valves per cylinder and 214 bhp. Both were mated with four-speed automatic transaxle. Key options included electronic traction control, a firmer "touring" suspension with performance tires, leather interior, and an innovative built-in child safety seat that flipped out from the rear backrest.

Though advertised as "the renaissance of the American car," Concorde was assembled in Canada, as Chrysler was obliged to note in fine print. It was just another sign that the auto world had become a small one after all.

The LH cars had been branded by some as the "Last Hope" for Chrysler's survival. Fortunately, they were the solid success the company needed. Concorde alone scored debut model-year production of 56,218, and its 1994 volume was nearly 86,000. The sophomore edition creeped up to $19,500, but gained the touring suspension as standard, revised transmission controls, eight more horses for the 3.3 engine, power steering that increased effort with road speed, and a power moonroof option. No big changes occurred for '95, though trim levels expanded to LX and posher LXi.

Next on the new-model menu were an LH-based New Yorker and a premium companion called LHS, arriving in spring '93 as the 1994 successors to the starchy Y-body Imperial/Fifth Avenue. Both rode the Concorde wheelbase but stretched nearly five inches longer overall, hence their internal designation "207." Styling was naturally in the wedgy cab-forward mold, but a more-orthodox face and upright rear roofline imparted formality without stuffiness. Graceful reverse-curve C-posts, allegedly inspired by late-'30s Bugattis, combined with a setback rear seat for near-limousine legroom. LHS was the sporty version, aiming at affluent "boomers" with front buckets, shift console, leather interior, firmer touring suspension and less exterior flash. New Yorker was for more-conservative folks, delivering a front bench seat, column shift, cloth trim, relatively soft damping, and a little more outside chrome. Both models carried the twincam 3.5-liter V-6.

At just over $30-grand, the LHS was some $5000 above the new New Yorker, yet outsold it from day one. Combined volume was excellent at nearly 83,000 for debut '94, far above anything the Y-body had managed. Ads playfully admitted that some past Chryslers had been "barges"—but not these two. Like Concorde, the LHS/New Yorker was taut and responsive on twisty roads, peppy enough, smooth and refined (save rather excessive tire noise) and, of course, eminently spacious. Not since the '50s had Chryslers changed so much in just one year—or so much for the better.

The 207s carried into 1995 essentially unchanged. LHS added an optional power moonroof during the '94 run. New Yorker got a standard premium audio system and touring suspension for '95. But with sales still greatly favoring LHS, Chrysler decided to drop the New Yorker after a short 1996-model run, thus ending a veteran American nameplate after 57 eventful years.

A new link with Chrysler's past appeared on 1995 models, as the corporate pentastar gave way to the make's original "rose" emblems, revived after a 41-year absence. It was a pleasant surprise, but no less so than that year's new Cirrus, the cab-forward replacement for the A-body LeBaron sedan. Once again, Chrysler played fast and loose with semantics, labeling Cirrus a compact even though dimensions were close to intermediate and even full-size. A 108-inch wheelbase, for example, put Cirrus just 2.8 inches shy of a Buick Park Avenue or Oldsmobile Ninety-Eight. Its overall length of

1997 LHS four-door sedan

1997 Concorde LXi four-door sedan

1997 Sebring convertible coupe

1997 Cirrus LXi four-door sedan

186 inches wasn't that "compact," either.

All this made Cirrus relatively vast inside, and it looked even bolder than bigger cab-forwards, though not everyone liked the low, jutting, vertical-bar grille. What people did approve was the taut, assured handling of its new wide-stance "JA" platform, again with all-independent suspension, standard antilock brakes and speed-variable power steering. The powerteam sat transversely here, and four-speed automatic was again mandatory. The only engine for '95 was a Mitsubishi-based 2.5-liter (152-cid) V-6, another twincam multivalve unit, good for 164 bhp. This continued on the posh LXi but was optional for the '96 LX, which switched to a standard twincam four, a new Chrysler-designed 2.4-liter with 150 bhp. Both Cirruses were fully equipped with standard air conditioning, tilt steering wheel, good-quality sound system and power windows/mirrors/door locks. The LXi added power driver's seat in a leather-trimmed interior, remote keyless entry, and antitheft alarm, plus touring suspension with performance tires on alloy wheels. In all, Cirrus was another impressive new Chrysler—and appealing value with base prices in the mid-to-high teens.

A rather different '95 newcomer was the Sebring coupe, a luxury edition of the year-old Dodge Avenger. Replacing the J-body LeBaron coupe, it wasn't technically an American car, as its foundation was the Japanese-designed 1994-98 Mitsubishi Galant sedan platform with 103.7-inch wheelbase. But the snazzy two-door body was styled with Chrysler input, and the base LX model came with a Chrysler's own 2.0-liter four as used in the small 1994-95 Dodge/Plymouth Neon. (Mitsubishi's 2.5-liter V-6 featured in the uplevel LXi.) The Sebring coupe was also American-made, built exclusively for the U.S. market at the Illinois factory that Chrysler set up with Mitsubishi in 1989 as Diamond-Star Motors. But sales were never impressive, even though Sebring coupes offered a good many standard features at affordable mid-teens to low-$20,000s prices. A shrinking coupe market didn't help, but neither did the few changes that occurred over five model years, the most visible being a modest 1997 facelift. As a result, calendar-year sales ran 25,000-35,000 through 1999, then plunged below 13,000.

More successful was the Sebring convertible that bowed in early 1996 to replace the drop-top LeBaron. Unlike the coupe, this Sebring was pure Chrysler, sharing powertrains and a basic platform with the Cirrus sedan. Here, too, cab-forward styling contributed to uncommon interior space, with genuinely comfortable rear seating for two adults, the best of most any affordable ragtop around. Though no sports car, the Sebring convertible was a pleasant driver on highway and byway alike. There was curiously little difference in power between the two models: 150 bhp from a 2.4-liter four in the base JX, 163 from a 2.5 V-6 in the uplevel JXi. Performance was sedate either way, thanks in part to mandatory automatic transmission, but Chrysler upped the fun quotient a bit for '97 by adding a new "AutoStick" feature to its V-6 models. A separate slot on the selector quadrant allowed the driver to move the gears up and down manually.

Though changed little more year-to-year than Sebring coupes, the convertibles sold better and more consistently, pulling in around 50,000 orders each calendar year through 2000. Like its LeBaron predecessor, a good many went to rental companies in sunbelt areas like Florida, Southern California, and Arizona, so Chrysler retained title to America's most-popular "rent-a-vertible." Among the few noteworthy changes in this period were the addition of a posh LXi Limited version for 1998 with leather-and-wood interior, chrome wheels, V-6, and AutoStick, and Sebring's first traction-control system.

Cirrus, too, seemed stuck in a time warp, its six-year run marked by annual equipment shuffles—including a here today, gone tomorrow four-cylinder engine. An exception was the '99 edition, which sported a larger grille adorned with a broad winged badge in bright chrome, a new Chrysler-brand signature being phased-in throughout the line. Calendar-year sales see-sawed from the low to high 30,000s, a fairly lackluster showing for a mainstream sedan. The related Dodge Stratus did much better business, helped by lower prices and more-aggressive marketing.

We shouldn't forget Town & Country, if only because Chrysler Corporation had become the "minivan company" in more ways than one. Like sister Dodge/Plymouth models, the T&C got a smoother exterior and redesigned dash for '91, plus a standard driver's airbag and exclusive digi-graphic instrumentation (dubious at best). Optional all-wheel drive arrived for 1992, a boon for "snowbelt" mobility that attracted few orders. Only new-design wheels marked the '93s. For '94, the optional 3.8 V-6 became standard and the dash was again modified to accommodate a no-cost passenger airbag. Chrysler also installed door guard beams per new federal rules for side-impact protection, and offered the industry's first integrated child safety seat at extra cost. T&C then carried into '95 with few other changes pending release of redesigned 1996 models. Though base price was then nearing $30,000, T&C sales had also climbed steadily: from just 6400 of the '91s to over 40,000 by middecade, more than respectable for a gilded people-mover.

Adding safety features, especially airbags, were a big sales help to all Chrysler minivans in these years. The government may have mandated front "passive restraints," but there were several ways to meet the requirement, and the public showed a marked preference for airbags over motorized front shoulder belts or "passive" three-point harnesses. Chrysler recognized this sooner than Ford or GM, and was quicker to offer airbags throughout its corporate fleet without waiting until model replacement time. It was a particularly shrewd thing to do for minivans, many of which were purchased by parents who naturally wanted the safest possible vehicle for their children. Other makers had no choice but to follow Chrysler's lead, something that hadn't occurred in decades.

Chrysler kept up its product offensive in the late '90s, starting with fully redesigned 1996 T&Cs, Dodge Caravans, and Plymouth Voyagers. Though not a breakthrough like the 1984 originals, the new "NS" models preserved all their winning attributes and added some of their own, including sleeker styling, more available power, and thoughtful family-oriented features like "Easy-Out" second- and third-row seats with built-in rollers and the industry's first driver's-side sliding rear door. The latter proved so popular that the company eventually built all its minivans that way. T&C sales remained steady and fairly strong, running 70,000-76,000 each calendar year through 2000. As ever, minivans remained vital to the health of the Chrysler marque, amounting to 22-40 percent of the brand's total car sales in this period.

Demand for nonminivan Chryslers jumped 25 percent in calendar 1998, and a dramatically redesigned Concorde was one reason. Wheelbase was not changed, but most everything else was. A wide, Ferrari-like eggcrate grille announced handsome new cab-forward styling that added 7.5 inches to overall length, making a roomy trunk even more so. Yet despite that and a much stiffer structure, the new Concorde weighed about the same as the old, thanks to the use of aluminum for the hood, some rear suspension components, and two new Chrysler-bred V-6s. The base LX model used a 2.7-liter with dual overhead camshafts and 200 bhp, the uplevel LXi a related single-cam 3.2 with 225. Engineers worked hard to reduce the noise, vibration, and harshness criticized in previous LH models, but didn't entirely succeed. And workmanship, though visibly improved, still wasn't up to snuff. Prices held steady, but only with skimping on the quality of some materials, especially inside. Overall, though, the '98 Concorde was an impressive effort—enough that *Consumer Guide*® named it a Best Buy each year through 2003. But though sales jumped more than 67 percent for calendar '98 to nearly 65,000, buyers seemed to lose interest after that, and volume steadily declined, skidding to under 26,000 by calendar 2003. An increasingly rough market was partly to blame, but so were some new public-relations gaffes described further on.

A new Concorde implied a redesigned LHS, and it arrived as an early-1999 entry. But the big surprise was a sportier sister audaciously reviving the famed letter-series 300 line after nearly 35 years. Called 300M, it wore specific front and rear styling that made it 10 inches shorter overall than the LHS. And instead of being a luxury cruiser, the M presented itself a serious "driver's car" of the European sports sedan school. It was even designed for sale in Europe, where regulations dic-

1998 Concorde LXi four-door sedan

1998 Cirrus LXi four-door sedan

1998 Sebring JXi convertible coupe

1999 300M four-door sedan

tated the trimmer size. Both models came with front bucket seats and an automatic transmission married to a new single-cam 3.5-liter V-6 with 253 bhp (basically a big-bore version of the Concorde's 3.2), but the 300M added the AutoStick manual-shift feature and was even more athletic than the LHS off the straight and narrow. An optional $255 Performance and Handling Package made it even more so, providing higher-effort power steering, firmer damping, uprated all-disc antilock brakes, and stiffer 16-inch tires vs. comfort-oriented 17s (also standard for LHS).

Despite all this, the 300M was nothing like the "beautiful brutes" of old. Not only was it slower—a so-so 7.7 seconds 0-60 mph in *Road & Track*'s test—it was a sedan, not a glamour-puss convertible or pillarless coupe. But the M could "out-stop" any of its forebears and leave them gasping on a twisty road. It was also built miles better, if nowhere near as well as the Eurosedans it sought to challenge. Then again, it didn't cost like they did, delivering for a reasonable $30,000 or so, about the same as a like-equipped LHS.

The 300M immediately outsold the LHS, by more than 2-to-1 in calendar '99 and 2000 with some 107,000 units combined. Heeding the market, Chrysler dropped the LHS after 2001, though it gave '02 Concordes a similar nose treatment, plus a top-line Limited model offering most LHS features at a lower price. The 300M maintained its sales pace into calendar 2000, then fell nearly 28 percent in '01. That suggested buyers might like something even sportier, so 2002 ushered in a 300M Special with slightly more power, a few extra frills, the Performance/Handling option as standard, and high-speed tires on chunky 18-inch wheels. But that was no help, and calendar-year sales showed double-digit losses through 2004. The cab-forward Ms then stepped aside for very different 300s that we'll come to in due course.

The '98 Concorde and '99 LHS/300M rolled out amidst the understandable ballyhoo surrounding Chrysler Corporation's historic marriage to Germany's Daimler-Benz, announced in November 1998 and finalized during '99. Consolidation was sweeping the industry. Ford had purchased Britain's Jaguar and lately Volvo of Sweden. General Motors controlled several Japanese makers and the automotive operations of Sweden's Saab. With the big fish getting bigger, Chrysler chairman Bob Eaton began seeking a strategic partner to insure his company's survival. The deal was all but sealed when he chanced to mention the idea to D-B's hard-driving chairman, Jurgen Schrempp.

On paper, the Chrysler/Daimler union seemed a heavenly match. Chrysler was the industry's most-cost-efficient producer, a recognized leader in design and innovation, loaded with talent, and had a strong asset in Jeep. Daimler boasted a formidable image, worldwide resources, and the engineering prowess of Mercedes-Benz. Both companies were profitable, and getting together promised numerous cost-saving "synergies" as well as lots of nifty new cars and trucks.

But what the parties proclaimed as a "merger of equals" was really a Trojan-horse takeover. Though Eaton and Schrempp were nominal co-chairs of the new DaimlerChrysler, the merger terms clearly favored Daimler. This contributed to a culture clash that delayed combining operations beyond obvious functions like purchasing. Within a year, some Chrysler hands said the American company was being "Germanized" into a mere division, something Schrempp later conceded was part of his original plan—which only aggravated ill feelings in Michigan. Meantime, a number of Chrysler's best executives, designers, and engineers jumped ship, including manufacturing wizard Dennis Pauley, president Tom Stallkamp, design chief Tom Gale and, tellingly, former president Bob

1999 LHS four-door sedan

2000 Sebring convertible coupe

2000 Concorde LXi four-door sedan

2000 LHS four-door sedan

2000 Town & Country minivan

2001 Sebring LX four-door sedan

2001 LHS four-door sedan

2001 PT Cruiser four-door wagon

2002 300M Special four-door sedan

2002 Sebring LX convertible

Lutz, who had largely masterminded Chrysler's early-'90s turnaround and opposed the merger. Eaton, for his part, said he always believed the merger *was* of equals, yet he, too, left, stepping down some 18 months before his term expired.

That left Schrempp to tackle a growing pile of vexing problems. First, sales of the cash-cow Jeep Grand Cherokee sport-utility began slipping. Then minivans started lagging, forcing Chrysler to offer more rebates and other costly consumer incentives to clear 2000-model inventories. But that only stole sales that might have gone to the company's redesigned 2001 minivans, which offered more features but cost more to build and thus carried higher prices. That was not what buyers wanted, especially since the new models didn't look very different from the old ones. Chrysler dangled more lures to spark sales, but competition was stronger than ever, so the new minivans were a fairly tough sell. With all this and more, DC stock tumbled, losing half its value by the end of 2000 versus its merger-time price, and some members of the DC board began demanding that Schrempp be fired.

Schrempp temporarily dodged that bullet and soon dispatched a trusted deputy, Dieter Zetsche, to turn things around as the new CEO of what was now called Chrysler Group. Joining him as COO was another Mercedes veteran, Wolfgang Bernhard. They moved decisively, shedding more plants and workers while haggling for every last penny with parts suppliers. But they also made friends throughout the Chrysler camp—Zetsche in particular. Most of all, they put the rush on a stream of new cars and trucks, plus show-stopping concepts that kept Chrysler in the news year after year.

The result was another dramatic Chrysler comeback that culminated in 2005 with a solid $1.7 billion group operating profit, this in a year when General Motors lost more than twice that sum. Trouble was, the Mercedes-Benz division, once a perpetual profit machine, was now losing money too. A weak dollar was partly to blame, but so was a series of image-tarnishing reliability and workmanship troubles that hampered M-B sales in the vital U.S. market. Adding to the red ink was a costly expansion of the Mercedes model line into mass-market price territory, especially the money-losing European minicar misadventure ironically called Smart. With all this, Schrempp lost critical support on DC's Supervisory Board, and Zetsche was summoned back to Stuttgart in late 2005 to take over as CEO *and* to head the Mercedes car unit. Bernhard had been in line for the latter post, but was passed over at the last minute and ended up at Volkswagen in Wolfsburg. Replacing Zetsche at DC's Michigan complex was a canny Chrysler hand, Tom LaSorda.

Plymouth had been one of the first victims of the Chrysler-Daimler union, consigned to history after the 2001 model run as a money-saving measure. But the make lived on in spirit for a time, as its Voyager minivans and Prowler neo hot rod were promptly rebadged as Chryslers. Of course, they were still sold by the same dealers, who were fast changing their signs to read Chrysler-Jeep.

Collectors may wish to note that the last Prowler was built on February 15, 2002, bringing total production to 11,676. The following May, that very car was auctioned off for charity at an eye-popping $175,000. *Car and Driver* reported that was $129,378 over sticker, but did include a small, matching Mopar-cataloged luggage trailer. As one might expect, the buyer was a true Prowler fanatic, already possessing no fewer than 14 other examples—"one in every color," he said.

A far more affordable and practical retro-style Chrysler was the new-for-2001 PT Cruiser. Beginning sale in mid-2000 after a cagey 18-month publicity buildup, it was, to quote *Road & Track*, "part street rod, part minivan, totally unlike anything else." Chrysler called it a "category buster," and the PT ("Personal Transportation") was indeed hard to pigeonhole. Older folks tended to see a useful compact wagon that looked faintly like a late-'30s Ford. The younger crowd simply saw a way-cool ride. The EPA saw it two ways, classifying the Cruiser as a truck for corporate fuel-economy purposes, a car for safety and emissions standards.

But that was the beauty of it. The PT Cruiser could be most anything to most anyone. Not surprisingly, it sold faster than any Chrysler in history, racking up more than 273,000 orders through the end of 2001, never mind DaimlerChrysler's mounting, well-publicized troubles at the time. Budget-friendly prices helped: about $16,000 to start, $18,000 "nicely equipped." Still, a good many early Cruisers sold well above sticker, as rabid demand bid up delivered prices by thousands. Chrysler strained to keep up, expanding capacity at the PT plant in Mexico only a few months after sales began.

The PT Cruiser would have been a dandy way to revitalize Plymouth. In fact, its basic concept originated with 1997's Plymouth Pronto show car. A 1998 follow-up, the two-door Pronto Cruzer, previewed the eventual production design, attributed to a young whiz named Brian Nesbitt working with Bill Dayton and John Bucci. Overseeing the project (begun long before the merger) were Tom Gale, then Chrysler's vice president for product development; John Herlitz, then design director; and design execs Trevor Creed (who later replaced Gale) and Neil Walling. Interior design was supervised by veteran designer and respected auto historian Jeff Godshall. But Nesbitt tended to get all the glory, and the PT's instant sales success largely explains why he was soon recruited by General Motors to work similar magic there.

The PT Cruiser wasn't big on mechanical magic, just sound, modern engineering. For example, the sole powerplant at first was Chrysler's now-familiar 150-bhp 2.4-liter 16-valve twincam four, mated to an optional four-speed automatic transmission or a standard five-speed with the tightest, most-precise linkage yet on a front-drive Mopar. Parts of the floorpan and some chassis components originated with the subcompact Dodge/Plymouth Neon, but the PT ended up sharing very little with other Chrysler Group vehicles.

Offered in base, Touring, and leather-trimmed Limited versions, the Cruiser scored for its high versatility, funky looks, and obvious potential for personalization. Compact sport-utility size afforded fine room for four adults and all manner of stuff. Chrysler claimed 26 possible configurations for the seats and multiposition rear cargo shelf; the latter could even double as a picnic table. Acceleration was nothing special—initially around nine seconds 0-60 mph with manual—but the PT was pleasantly nimble and easy on the bumps. It also belied the notion that Chrysler couldn't deliver quality. Even early examples were solid and well-finished inside and out. Not all people liked the styling, but most did, including a few professional designers. A more-contemporary look was considered, but likely wouldn't have had as much impact. "Some of what we did was very conscious," Gale told *Collectible Automobile* magazine, but "we were not consciously trying to be retro... [T]he space and mechanical packages somehow naturally led to the form."

The PT almost begged for hop-up parts and '50s-style customizing, and aftermarket companies obliged with a slew of bolt-on performance and dress-up components. Chrysler joined in for '02, offering a "flame" decal package, a "Woodie" version with simulated timber on the bodysides and liftgate, and a limited-production "Dream Cruiser" with Inca Gold paint, chrome wheels, and a numbered dashboard plaque.

2002 Prowler convertible coupe

2002 Concorde LX four-door sedan

2002 Sebring LXi coupe

2002 PT Cruiser four-door wagon with "Woodie package"

2002 Voyager minivan

2003 Crossfire coupe

2003 Crossfire coupe

For 2003, Chrysler answered leadfoot pleas with a turbocharged GT Cruiser—a.k.a. PT Turbo—packing 215 bhp (later listed at 220) and a mandatory AutoStick transmission. Also on hand were a firmed-up suspension with 17-inch wheels (versus other models' 15s or 16s), four-wheel disc brakes with antilock control (optional for Touring and Limited), street-savvy monochrome exterior, sport front seats, and specific interior trim. Though the price wasn't unreasonable at a bit over $22,000, the GT was apparently too rich for some buyers. Chrysler responded for '04 with a 180-bhp turbo engine as a $1280 option for Touring and Limited PTs. The quick one-two power play helped liven sales, which went from a low-100,000 plateau to nearly 116,000 for calendar '04.

Included in that total were the first PT Cruiser convertibles, introduced as early '05 models after a concept preview back in 2001. Offered in the same trim levels as wagons, the droptop two-doors boasted a power-folding top with heated glass window, split folding rear seat—and far less luggage space. A integrated structural hoop soared overhead behind the front seats; it looked ungainly, but helped make up for slicing off the roof. Rigidity, in fact, was quite good for a modern convertible. Just as nice, this was one of the few ragtops that could seat four without breaking the buyer's bank account, base prices ranging from around $19,500 to $27,600.

PT volume improved again for calendar 2005, reaching nearly 134,000. Full-year convertible sales helped, but a bigger boost likely came from price cuts on the mainstay wagons—a sizable $2555-$4190, depending on model—achieved by moving some standard features to the options column. For 2006, the Cruiser got its first facelift, a subtle redo involving the headlights, front fascia, and dashboard. Prices remained stable, running $14,000-$29,000 or so, reflecting intense market competition and relentless cost cutting.

Overshadowed by "PT Mania" in 2001 were redesigned midsize Chryslers that now encompassed the sedans previously known as Cirrus. *Car and Driver* likened the new four-door Sebring to a scaled-down 300M, but sportiness wasn't its mission. Instead, refinement was the watchword, with a beefier, quieter structure; a more-supple ride; and the safety of available curtain side airbags, which dropped from just above the windows to protect occupants' heads in a side impact. Though styling became a bit less cab forward, interior space remained exceptional for the class. A massaged 2.4-liter four provided the base power, but the optional V-6 was now Chrysler's own 200-bhp twincam 2.7, and the mandatory automatic could be had with optional AutoStick for the first time. Helped by an extra-long debut season, Sebring sedan sales almost doubled those of the final Cirrus at more than 67,000 through the end of calendar 2001.

Sebring convertibles were less visibly changed for '01 despite mostly new outer sheetmetal, but they got the same engines as sedans and, more important, a thorough structural shoring-up. The result was good enough to finish third in a five-way *Car and Driver* convertible test, ahead of a Ford Mustang GT and Toyota Solara. At under $30,000 for their test Limited, "the Sebring emerged as our value champ," said the editors, "and also won as best to behold." About the only thing lacking was enough horsepower to make performance vivid instead of merely brisk. Calendar-year sales slipped to a little over 45,000 units, but that wasn't bad for what proved to be a turbulent year for Chrysler Group and the nation.

Though also redesigned for 2001, Sebring coupes remained more Mitsubishi than Chrysler, sharing the 1999-2000 platform of the Japanese company's latest Galant sedans and sporty Eclipse models. That also meant the V-6 option was a 3.0-liter Mitsubishi engine. Dodge still offered its own versions, but now called them Stratus, not Avenger. As with the Sebring line, the aim was to simplify marketing—and maybe reduce buyer confusion at last. For all the changes, however, Sebring coupe sales remained modest at some 16,600 for calendar '01, though that was actually a bit above the '00 tally.

Chrysler then seemed to forget the Sebrings through 2006, bothering only to shuffle features, names, and occasionally styling elements while the Toyota Camry and Honda Accord nabbed the lion's share of midsize-car sales year after year. The only signs of "progress" were a moderate facelift and optional front side airbags for 2003 coupes and a bold new "big-mouth" face for 2004 sedans and ragtops. The coupes, always very slow sellers, were discarded after '05, while other Sebrings carried into '06 with hardly any change from 2004. Was Chrysler ceding the midsize war to its American-made Japanese-brand rivals? It sure seemed so. But perhaps the company was only biding its time until a more competitive replacement could be readied for around 2007.

A far more interesting Chrysler arrived in 2003: a slick two-seat semisports car marking the first tangible result of the Daimler-Benz takeover. Like the PT Cruiser and Dodge Viper, the 2004-model Crossfire hewed closely to a well-received concept (the '01 Crossfire). But its sharp Chrysler styling was just a new wrapper for an older Mercedes, the 1998-vintage SLK, which was about to be replaced by a clean-sheet design. Critics chided both Daimler and Chrysler for this evident hand me down, but the Crossfire had much to recommend it. One big plus was price: initially $33,600 to start, some $6000 less than a base SLK. Of course, it helped that the Crossfire had a fixed fastback roof instead of an expensive retractable hardtop, though Chrysler quickly catered to fresh-air fiends by issuing a power-soft-top model in calendar '04.

It also helped that Mercedes had mostly amortized the costs of powertrain and chassis components. And if those were no longer new, they were still pretty impressive. As in the SLK, a 215-bhp 3.2-liter V-6 drove the rear wheels through

2003 PT Cruiser GT four-door wagon

2003 Sebring Xi coupe

2004 PT Cruiser convertible

2004 PT Cruiser convertible

2004 Sebring convertible coupe

a six-speed manual gearbox or an optional five-speed, manually shiftable automatic. (The latter was preferred for drivability reasons, and most U.S. buyers ordered it anyway.) Chrysler claimed it had made numerous technical tweaks for the Crossfire, but the all-independent suspension, all-disc antilock brakes, recirculating-ball power steering, and standard torso side airbags were all essentially the same as those of the SLK. One notable upgrade concerned wheel diameters: 18 inches front and 19 rear versus 16s or 17s for SLKs. There was no room for a spare, though, so a plug-in air compressor and a can of sealant were provided. Another Crossfire distinction was the rear spoiler that popped up automatically—and rather noisily—above 40 mph to aid high-speed stability; below 50 mph, it snugged itself back into the deck.

Because Mercedes had lately added a supercharged SLK, the Crossfire was expected to follow. Sure enough, model-year 2005 introduced "blown" SRT-6 versions with the same 330 bhp. The initials stood for Street and Racing Technology, the recently formed in-house team charged with developing higher-performance versions of chosen Chrysler Group products, not unlike Mercedes' AMG. To handle their greater speed, SRT-6s were treated to an ultrafirm suspension and "summer" tires (versus all-season) on specific multispoke wheels. Completing the package were a cockpit trimmed in leather and suedelike Alcantara, plus a fixed rear spoiler of tastefully modest size.

By this point, nonsupercharged Crossfires offered a choice of base and Limited trim. The latter, costing $4000-$4700 more, delivered full-leather upholstery, heated power seats, tire-pressure monitor, premium audio system, and other goodies. The SRT-6s had these too, but started $11,000 higher, listing at $45,000-$49,000.

Chrysler hoped for 20,000 Crossfire sales each calendar year in America (plus a few more in Europe), but ended up with rather less: a mere 4000 in the abbreviated 2003 season, around 14,700 in '04 and again in '05. Though the "used Mercedes" hardware might have turned off more-knowledgeable buyers, sales were probably hobbled more by pricing that looked out of whack for a Chrysler, with all the bad vibes many people still attached to that name. Lukewarm press reviews hurt, too. Though Chrysler resisted incentives on its new "halo" car, a nine-month backlog by early 2005 forced deep discounts, which only further tarnished the car's image. With all this, Crossfire will likely be allowed to fade away, though it continued with little change into 2006.

As with most every Detroit brand, trucks had assumed critical sales importance for Chrysler by the early 2000s, though this brand always sold more cars than trucks, at least through 2005. Still, Town & Country minivans remained big money-spinners for Chrysler dealers, and they became even more sellable for 2005 by exchanging their "Easy Out" rear seats—which weren't really so easy to move—for "Stow 'n Go" seats that folded neatly into floorwells with no wrenches and no sweat. The feature was costly to engineer, requiring a completely new undercarriage and leaving no room for optional all-wheel drive, but this Chrysler Group exclusive was understandably popular, a timely innovation in the face of freshly hatched import-brand competition.

Meantime, Chrysler joined the fast-growing market for so-called "crossover" wagons with Pacifica, arriving in 2003 as an early '04 entry. Like others in this new category, it blended attributes of cars and sport-utility vehicles, but emphasized comfort, convenience, and luxury more than most. Essentially, Pacifica was a reconfigured Chrysler minivan (and thus generally classified as a truck) with a high-profile wagon-style four-door body offering three-row seating for six in a

2-2-2 format. Stow 'n Go was absent here, but the seats did fold easily to form a long, flat cargo deck. Unfortunately, Pacifica ended up too heavy for its 250-bhp 3.5-liter V-6 and four-speed AutoStick transmission, especially with the all-wheel drive available in lieu of front drive. Price was another issue, as most early units were loaded with options such as leather upholstery, heated first- and second-row seats, power liftgate (a recent minivan addition), navigation system, satellite radio, and rear DVD entertainment. Initial sales were thus as tepid as performance. Chrysler had simply misread the market, perhaps blinded by its stated ambition to become a more-upscale "premium" brand. But sales turned around once production was adjusted to include more front-drive models with fewer extras. Chrysler then broadened offerings for 2005, adding a base-trim model and a top-line Limited to bracket the original version, which was renamed Touring. The base Pacifica was a five-passenger price-leader with a second-row bench seat, a 215-bhp 3.8-liter V-6, and front-drive only, but its $29,000 sticker looked a lot less scary than the mid-$30,000 tags of some other models.

The initial marketing miscues tended to obscure a pleasant, practical, family friendly vehicle. And to Chrysler's credit, every Pacifica came with antilock brakes and load-leveling rear suspension. AWDs added standard curtain side airbags, power-adjustable pedals, and tire-pressure monitor, all of which were also available for front-drivers. Still, looking at sales through calendar '05, it's unclear whether this "sports tourer" can earn a permanent place in the lineup. Perhaps it will, once people understand exactly what it is.

There was no misunderstanding the new 300 sedans that barged in as early 2005 entries. Big, bold, and brawny, they were cars any die-hard Detroit fan devotee could endorse—"a complete about-face from the LH cars they replace," as *Road & Track* observed. Rear-wheel drive was back. So was a Hemi V-8, though its only links to the past were half-spherical combustion chambers and two pushrod-operated valves per cylinder. Styling, directed by young hotshot Ralph Gillies, was in your face and proud of it: blocky, slab sided, and not a little menacing, with a low "chopped-top" roof and a big, square eggcrate grille intended to evoke memories of 1950s letter-series 300s. It was a sweeping departure from cab forward design, and the public loved it. Virtually overnight, the new 300 became one of Detroit's hottest sellers, flying out the door at a rate matched only by Ford's redesigned '05 Mustang—more than 147,000 in the first 13 months of production. It became so popular that fully one fifth of Chrysler Group's solid $1.7 billion 2005 operating profit came from this one line, according to *Business Week*. It was a key reason why Dieter Zetsche was promoted from Chrysler Group CEO at year's end to head all of DaimlerChrysler.

Tearing up your own rulebook can be fraught with hazards, but Zetsche and company knew what they were doing. Confirming the benefits of the much-derided merger was a clean-sheet LX platform shared with Dodge's equally arresting 2005 Magnum wagons and '06 Dodge Charger sedans. It was an open secret that much LX engineering came from the respected Mercedes E-Class, but Chrysler took pains to point out that all of its components were unique and would not bolt into an E-Class. Not that it mattered, because the 300 chassis had all the "right stuff." The front suspension, for example, comprised upper and lower control arms, coil-over shocks, and an antiroll bar. Out back was a five-link setup with separate shocks and coil springs. Steering was controlled via a power rack-and-pinion unit. All-disc antilock brakes and a Mercedes-style Electronic Stability Program (antiskid/traction-control system) were standard for all but the base model,

2004 Sebring four-door sedan

2005 300C four-door sedan

2005 300 Touring four-door sedan

2005 300C SRT8 four-door sedan

2005 Town & Country minivan with Stow 'n Go

2005 Crossfire convertible coupe

2005 Crossfire SRT6 convertible coupe

2005 Crossfire SRT6 coupe

where they were optional. A final bonus from the German connection was the all-wheel-drive setup that was offered on two of the six models.

Actually, the only major carryover components were two V-6 engines and an associated four-speed automatic transmission, and even those were modified to suit their surroundings. The base rear-drive 300 used a 190-bhp, 2.7-liter V-6. An equally familiar 250-bhp 3.5-liter V-6 moved the midlevel Tourings, rear drive and AWD, the latter priced some $2300 higher. But what everyone wanted—and mostly bought—was the Hemi. Designated 300C (another '50s echo), the Hemi models boasted a five-speed automatic with rear or AWD, the latter carrying a $1325 surcharge, and the big attraction, a thumping 340 bhp and a muscular 390 pound-feet of torque.

Sized at 5.7 liters, equal to 345 cid, this new Hemi was a modern marvel: smooth, efficient, strong at most any speed, and a treat for enthusiast ears. Most road tests easily beat Chrysler's 6.3-second 0-60-mph claim with rear drive. *Road & Track* clocked just 5.6 seconds, impressive for a 4150-pound sedan. So, too, the magazine's observed fuel economy of 18.3 mpg, despite much hard driving. Assisting with that was a new "Multi Displacement System" exclusive to the 5.7 Hemi among Chrysler Group engines. Like GM's similar Active Fuel Management, MDS would automatically deactivate four cylinders under light throttle loads to reduce fuel consumption (wear and tear, too). It wasn't a huge fuel-saver, but it did work and was almost undetectable in operation.

V-6s were naturally tame by comparison. *Car and Driver*'s rear-drive Touring clocked 7.3 seconds 0-60 mph, while a base 300 needed a lengthy 11 seconds, according to Chrysler. Yet there wasn't much payback in actual fuel economy, suggesting the V-6s were overmatched by the two-ton weight.

But whether Hemi hot or V-6 sedate, every 300 offered quiet, comfortable cruising allied to confident road manners, and big interior space (helped by a rangy 120-inch wheelbase). Craftsmanship marked a new high for Chrysler and equaled most anything in the near-luxury class, foreign or domestic—let alone the large-sedan competition. All this for $23,000-$34,000. No wonder *Consumer Guide®* named the new 300 a Best Buy, thanks to a "combination of performance, roominess, and value. It's a worthy rival for a variety of family cars and sporty sedans."

Even more spectacular was the 300C SRT-8, arriving in early 2005 as the newest factory hot rod from Chrysler's Street and Racing Technology shop. Hunkering a half-inch lower on 20-inch wheels (versus 18s), the SRT-8 packed a much-modified, higher-compression Hemi grown to 6.1 liters (370 cid), 425 horses and 420 pound-feet of twist. SRT wasn't given to halfway measures, so most all the hardware was beefed-up or redesigned: engine block, engine internals, intake and exhaust systems, transmission, rear-axle gearing (no AWD here), brakes, steering, and suspension. Even the antiskid control was reprogrammed to be less controlling at the driver's discretion—and the traction control could now be fully switched off, again to up the fun factor. Completing the package were deeper front and rear fascias and added amenities such as xenon headlamps, rear spoiler, rear obstacle detection, leather/suede upholstery, and power-adjustable pedals. Options were few, with curtain side airbags, navigation system, sunroof, and satellite radio the major items.

Starting at just below $40,000, the 300C SRT-8 was an unbeatable high-performance deal, and testers loudly sang its praises. *Road & Track* clocked a blazing 4.9 seconds 0-60 mph, pipping Chrysler's claim, and a dragstrip-worthy quarter-mile of 13.3 seconds at 108.2 mph. The car could stop just as well, and though handling was even tauter and more assured, ride comfort was scarcely affected. There were only two drawbacks, mainly for those prone to guilty consciences: no Multi Displacement System and a $1300 Gas-Guzzler Tax. For everyone else, the SRT-8 was, as *R&T* concluded, "a car blessed with an American Hemi heart and a European feel and sophistication to its driving dynamics. Think of [it] as an American [Mercedes] E55, for a savings of about $30-grand."

Chrysler further expanded the 300 line for 2007, adding two limousinelike Long Wheelbase models. The 300 Touring Long Wheelbase featured the 3.5-liter V-6, while the 300C Long Wheelbase came with the ubiquitous Hemi V-8. Both models were stretched six inches behind the front doors, creating extensive rear legroom. Modified by Accubuilt, an Ohio-based specialty vehicle manufacturer, the cars could be ordered with personalized features such as rear footrests, lighted rear writing tables, 12-volt power ports for computers or cell phones, and reading lights for rear passengers.

Though our story must end here, the reborn 300s are the kind of Chryslers old Walter P. would endorse: stylish, innovative, solid, and affordable. They suggest a bright future for the marque. Of course, nothing is certain in this world, and complacency is an enemy of success, but we hope the 300s are just the first in a long line of great new Chryslers.

2006 300C AWD four-door sedan

2006 PT Cruiser convertible

2005 Pacifica four-door wagon

2007 300 Touring Long Wheelbase four-door sedan

Specifications

1930

Model CJ6 (wb 109.0)	Wght	Price	Prod*
rdstr 2-4P	2,390	805	1,616
touring 5P	2,455	835	279
bus cpe 2P	2,560	795	2,267
Royal cpe 2-4P	2,590	835	3,593
Royal sdn 4d 5P	2,695	845	20,748
conv cpe	—	—	705
chassis	—	—	31
Model 66 (wb 112.8)			
rdstr 2-4P	2,625	1,025	1,213
phtn 5P	2,695	1,025	26
bus cpe 2P	2,750	995	2,014
Royal cpe 2-4P	2,850	1,075	3,257
brougham 5P	2,850	995	2,343
Royal sdn 5P	2,930	1,095	3,753
Model 70 (wb 116.5)			
rdstr 2-4P	3,205	1,345	1,431
phtn 5P	3,235	1,295	279
bus cpe 2P	3,410	1,345	766
Royal cpe 2-4P	3,490	1,395	3,135
brougham 5P	3,490	1,345	1,204
Royal sdn 5P	3,590	1,445	11,213
conv cpe 2-4P	3,450	1,545	705
Model 77 (wb 124.0)			
rdstr 2-4P	3,370	1,665	1,729
phtn 5P	3,495	1,795	173
bus cpe 2P	3,560	1,395	230
Royal cpe 2-4P	3,615	1,495	2,954
Crown cpe 4P	3,580	1,575	883
conv cpe 2-4P	3,580	1,825	418
Royal sdn 5P	3,750	1,495	7,211
Town sdn 5P	3,720	1,445	436
Crown sdn 5P	3,760	1,595	2,654

Imperial (wb 136.0)			
rdstr 2-4P	3,955	2,995	—
spt phtn 4P	4,225	3,955	—
phtn 7P	3,925	3,195	15**
cpe 2P	4,025	3,095	—
conv cpe 2-4P	4,120	3,095	50**
sdn 5P	4,335	3,075	300**
Town sdn 5P	4,310	3,075	100**
sdn 7P	4,460	3,195	150**
sdn limo 7P	4,510	3,575	—

* Some figures include later years; see 1931, 1932.
** Est based on one-third of 1929-30 model year prod .

1930 Engines	bore×stroke	bhp	availability
I-6, 195.6	3.13×4.25	62	S-CJ6
I-6, 195.6	3.13×4.25	65	S-66s blt 1929
I-6, 218.6	3.13×4.75	75	S-70s blt 1929
I-6, 218.6	3.13×4.75	68	S-66s blt 1930
I-6, 268.4	3.38×5.00	93	S-70s blt '30, 77
I-6, 309.3	3.63×5.00	100	S-Imperial

1931

Model CJ6 (wb 109.0)

Production was carried over from 1930, with 1931 model output commencing July 1, 1930. Production figures combined with 1930 CJ6 models. Body styles and weights identical; prices $20-$50 below 1930 prices.

Model 66 (wb 112.8)

Production was carried over from 1930 commencing July 1, 1930. Production figures combined with 1930 Model 66. Body styles and weights identical; prices $5 above 1930 prices.

Model 70 (wb 116.5)

Production was carried over from 1930 commencing July 1, 1930. Production figures combined with 1930 Model 70. Body styles and weights identical. Open-car prices unchanged; closed-car prices lowered $100 except for Royal sedan, which was lowered $150.

CM6 New Six (wb 116.0)	Wght	Price	Prod
rdstr 2-4P	2,565	885	2,281
cpe 2-4P	2,700	885	5,327
sdn 4d	2,815	895	28,620
phtn 5P	2,740	915	196
bus cpe 2P	2,730	865	802
conv cpe 2-4P	2,750	935	1,492
chassis	—	—	99
CD8 New Eight (wb 124.0)*			
rdstr 2-4P	3,100	1,495	1,462
spt rdstr 2-4P	3,225	1,595	
Royal Standard cpe	3,235	1,495	3,000
Royal Sport cpe	3,235	1,535	
conv cpe 2-4P	3,195	1,665	700
Royal Standard sdn	3,365	1,525	9,000
Royal Special sdn	3,365	1,565	
phtn 5P	3,490	1,970	85
chassis	—	—	108

* First series commenced July 1930. Second series commenced January 1931; discontinued April 1931, replaced by Deluxe Eight.

DeLuxe Eight (wb 124.0)			
rdstr 2-4P	3,330	1,545	511
phtn 5P	3,545	1,970	113
cpe 2-4P	3,525	1,525	1,506
conv cpe 2-4P	3,445	1,585	501
cpe 5P	3,575	1,565	500
sdn 5P	3,640	1,565	5,843
chassis	—	—	126
CG Imperial (wb 145.0)			
Custom rdstr 2-4P	4,530	3,220	100
Custom spt phtn 5P	4,645	3,575	85
Custom cpe 2-4P	4,605	3,150	135
Custom conv cpe	4,570	3,320	10
sdn 5P	4,705	2,745	909

CG Imperial (wb 145.0)	Wght	Price	Prod
close-coupled sdn 5P	4,685	2,845	1,195
sdn 7P	4,825	2,945	403
sdn limo 8P	4,915	3,145	271
conv sdn	4,825	3,995	25
chassis	—	—	95

1931 Engines	bore×stroke	bhp	availability
I-6, 195.6	3.13×4.25	62	S-CJ6
I-6, 217.8	3.25×4.38	78	S-CM6
I-6, 218.6	3.13×4.75	68	S-66
I-6, 268.4	3.38×5.00	93	S-70
I-8, 240.3	3.00×4.25	82	S-CD8s blt '30
I-8, 260.8	3.13×4.25	90	S-CD8s blt '31
I-8, 282.1	3.25×4.25	95	S-DeLx Eight
I-8, 384.8	3.50×5.00	125	S-CG

1932

Model 70 (wb 116.5) Wght Price Prod

Listed by Chrysler for 1932, although production ceased in May 1931. Engine numbers from V-29414. Production combined with 1930 and 1931 (see entries).

Model CM6 (wb 116.0)

Production continued from 1931, commencing July 1, ending in December. Engine numbers from CM-30829. Production combined with 1931 (see entry).

Model CD DeLuxe Eight (wb 124.0)

Production continued from 1931, commencing July 1, ending in November. Engine numbers from CD-21141. Production combined with 1931 (see entry).

CG Imperial (wb 145.0)

Production continued from 1931, commencing July 1, ending in December. Engine numbers from CG-3752.

CI6 "Second Series" Six (wb 116.0)			
rdstr 2-4P	2,830	885	474
phtn 5P	2,905	915	59
bus cpe 2P	2,915	865	354
cpe 2-4P	3,040	885	2,913
conv cpe 2-4P	2,970	935	1,000
sdn 5P	3,135	895	13,772
conv sdn 5P	3,160	1,125	322
chassis	—	—	70
CP8 Eight (wb 125.0)			
cpe 2-4P	3,735	1,435	718
conv cpe 2-4P	3,705	1,495	396
cpe 5P	3,810	1,475	502
sdn 5P	3,885	1,475	3,198
conv sdn 5P	4,090	1,695	251
chassis	—	—	48
CH Imperial (wb 135.0)			
cpe 2-4P	4,480	1,925	239
sdn 5P	4,645	1,945	1,002
conv sdn 5P	4,890	2,195	152
chassis	—	—	9
CL Imperial (wb 146.0)			
conv cpe	4,930	3,295	28
phtn 5P	5,065	3,395	14
close-coupled sdn 5P	5,150	2,895	57
conv sdn 5P	5,125	3,595	49
sdn 8P	5,295	2,995	35
sdn limo 7P	5,330	3,295	32
chassis	—	—	5

1932 Engines	bore×stroke	bhp	availability
I-6, 217.8	3.25×4.38	78	S-CM6
I-6, 224.0	3.25×4.50	82	S-CI6
I-6, 268.4	3.38×5.00	93	S-70
I-8, 282.1	3.25×4.25	95	S-CD
I-8, 298.6	3.25×4.50	100	S-CP8
I-8, 384.8	3.50×5.00	125	S-CG, CH, CL

1933

CO Six (wb 117.0)	Wght	Price	Prod
bus cpe 2P	2,968	745	587
cpe 2-4P	3,018	775	1,454
conv cpe 2-4P	3,013	795	677
brougham 5P	3,078	745	1,207
sdn 5P	3,143	785	13,264
sdn 7P (spcl interior)	3,200	845	51
conv sdn 5P	3,212	945	205
sdn 7P	—	—	151
chassis	—	—	267
CT Royal Eight (wb 120.0)	**Wght**	**Price**	**Prod**
bus cpe 2P	3,303	895	226
cpe 2-4P	3,343	915	1,033
conv cpe 2-4P	3,363	945	539
sdn 5P	3,483	925	7,993
conv sdn 5P	3,617	1,085	257
sdn 7P	3,658	1,125	246
chassis	—	—	95
CQ Imperial Eight (wb 126.0)			
cpe 2-4P	3,734	1,275	364
conv cpe 2-4P	3,754	1,325	243
cpe 5P	3,754	1,295	267
sdn 5P	3,864	1,295	2,584
conv sdn 5P	4,144	1,495	364
chassis	—	—	16
CL Imperial Custom (wb 146.0)			
rdstr 2-4P	4,910	3,295	9
phtn 5P	4,890	3,395	36
close-coupled sdn 5P	5,045	2,895	43
sdn 7P	5,240	2,995	21
limo sdn 7P	5,245	3,295	22
conv sdn	5,135	3,395	11
stationary cpe	—	—	3
chassis	—	—	6

1933 Engines	bore×stroke	bhp	availability
I-6, 224.0	3.25×4.50	83/89	S-CO
I-8, 273.8	3.25×4.13	90/98	S-CT
I-8, 298.7	3.25×4.50	108/100	S-CQ
I-8, 384.8	3.50×5.00	135/125	S-CL

1934

CA Six (wb 118.0)	Wght	Price	Prod
bus cpe 2P	2,868	740	1,650
cpe 2-4P	2,903	815	1,875
conv cpe 2-4P	—	850	700
brougham 5P	3,019	760	1,575
sdn 5P	3,123	820	17,617
chassis	—	—	385
CB Custom Six (wb 121.0)			
close-coupled sdn 5P	—	900	980
conv sdn 5P	—	970	450
chassis	—	—	20
CU Airflow Eight (wb 123.0)			
cpe 5P	—	1,345	732
brougham 5P	3,741	1,345	306
sdn 6P	3,760	1,345	7,226
Town sdn 6P	—	1,345	125
CV Airflow Imperial Eight (wb 128.0)			
cpe 5P	3,929	1,625	212
sdn 6P	3,974	1,625	1,997
Town sdn 6P	3,969	1,625	67
chassis	—	—	1
CX Airflow Imperial Eight (wb 137.5)			
sdn 5P	4,154	2,245	25
Town sdn 5P	4,160	2,245	1
sdn limo 8P	4,299	2,345	78
Town sdn limo	4,304	2,345	2
CW Airflow Imperial Custom Eight (wb 146.0)			
sdn 8P	5,780	5,000	17
Town sdn 8P	5,815	5,000	28
limo sdn 8P	5,900	5,145	20
Town limo sdn 8P	5,935	5,145	2

1934 Engines	bore×stroke	bhp	availability
I-6, 241.5	3.38×4.50	93	S-CA, CB
I-6, 241.5	3.38×4.50	100	O-CA, CB
I-8, 298.7	3.25×4.50	122	S-CU
I-8, 323.5	3.25×4.98	130	S-CV, CX
I-8, 384.8	3.50×5.00	150	S-CW

1935

C6 Airstream Six (wb 118.0)	Wght	Price	Prod
bus cpe 2P	2,863	745	1,975
cpe 2-4P	2,953	810	861
touring brougham 5P	2,988	820	1,901
fstbk sdn 4d 5P	3,013	830	6,055
touring sdn 5P	3,048	860	12,790
fstbk sdn 2d 5P	2,990	820	400
chassis	—	—	476
CZ Airstream Eight (wb 121.0; lwb-133.0)	**Wght**	**Price**	**Prod**
bus cpe 2P	3,103	910	100
Deluxe bus cpe 2P	3,138	930	
cpe 2-4P	3,138	935	550
Deluxe cpe 2-4P	3,233	955	
touring brougham 2d	3,203	960	500
Delux tour brghm 2d	3,293	980	
sdn 4d	3,213	975	2,958
Deluxe sdn 4d	3,333	985	
touring sdn 4d	3,263	995	4,394
Deluxe tour sdn 4d	3,338	1,015	
Delux conv cpe 2-4P	3,298	1,015	101
Delux Travler sdn 5P	3,513	1,235	245
Deluxe lwb sdn 7P	3,538	1,235	212
chassis	—	—	237
C1 Airflow 8 (wb 123.0)			
bus cpe 2P	3,823	1,245	72
cpe 6P	3,883	1,245	307
sdn 6P	3,828	1,245	4,617
C2 Imperial Airflow 8 (wb 128.0)			
cpe 6P	4,003	1,475	200
sdn 4d 6P	3,998	1,475	2,398
C3 Custom Imperial Airflow 8 (wb 137.5)			
sdn 4d 6P	4,208	2,245	69
Town sdn 4d 6P	4,308	2,245	1
sdn limo 8P	4,378	2,345	53
Town sdn limo 8P	4,478	2,345	2
CW Custom Imperial Airflow 8 (wb 146.5)			
sdn 8P	4,785	5,000	15
sdn limo 8P	5,990	5,145	15
Town sdn limo 8P	5,090	5,145	2

1935 Engines	bore×stroke	bhp	availability
I-6, 241.5	3.38×4.50	93	S-C6
I-6, 241.5	3.38×4.50	100	O-C6
I-8, 273.8	3.25×4.13	105	S-CZ
I-8, 273.8	3.25×4.13	110	O-CZ
I-8, 323.5	3.25×4.88	115	S-C1
I-8, 323.5	3.25×4.88	120	O-C1
I-8, 323.5	3.25×4.88	130	S-C2, C3
I-8, 323.5	3.25×4.88	138	O-C2, C3
I-8, 384.8	3.50×5.00	150	S-CW

1936

C7 Airstream (wb 118.0)	Wght	Price	Prod
bus cpe 2P	2,963	760	3,703
cpe 2-4P	3,037	825	759
conv cpe 2-4P	3,053	925	650
touring brougham 5P	3,082	825	3,177
conv sdn 5P	3,282	1,125	497
touring sdn 4d	3,137	875	34,099
chassis	—	—	586
C8 Airstream Deluxe (wb 121.0; lwb-133.0)			
bus cpe 2P	3,155	925	520
cpe 2-4P	3,220	995	325
conv cpe 2-4P	3,350	1,075	240
touring brougham 5P	3,330	995	268
conv sdn 5P	3,495	1,265	362
touring sdn 4d	3,345	1,045	6,547
Traveler sdn 5P	3,500	1,255	350
lwb sdn 7P	3,550	1,245	619
lwb sdn limo 7P	3,595	1,865	67
lwb Town sdn 7P	3,550	4,995	8
chassis	—	—	196
C9 Airflow Eight (wb 123.0)			
cpe 6P	3,997	1,395	110
sdn 4d 6P	4,102	1,345	1,590
C10 Airflow Imperial (wb 128.0)			
cpe 6P	4,105	1,475	240
sdn 4d 6P	4,175	1,475	4,259
chassis	—	—	1
C11 Airflow Custom Imperial (wb 137.0; lwb-146.5)			
sdn 4d 5P	5,900	2,475	38
sdn limo 7P	6,000	2,575	37
lwb sdn 4d 8P	6,200*	5,000*	10
lwb limo 8P	6,250*	5,000*	

*Estimated

1936 Engines	bore×stroke	bhp	availability
I-6, 241.5	3.38×4.50	93	S-C7

1936 Engines	bore×stroke	bhp	availability
I-6, 241.5	3.38×4.50	100	O-C7
I-8, 273.8	3.25×4.13	105	S-C8
I-8, 273.8	3.25×4.13	110	O-C8
I-8, 323.5	3.25×4.88	115	S-C9
I-8, 323.5	3.25×4.88	130	S-C10, C11

1937

C16 Royal (wb 116.0; lwb-133.0)	Wght	Price	Prod
bus cpe 2P	3,049	810	9,830
cpe 2-4P	3,099	860	1,050
conv cpe 2-4P	3,274	1,020	767
brougham 5P F/B	3,114	870	750
touring brougham 5P	3,094	880	7,835
fstbk sdn 4d 5P	3,124	910	1,200
touring sdn 4d 5P	3,134	920	62,408
conv sdn 5P	3,484	1,355	642
lwb sdn 7P	3,544	1,145	856
lwb sdn limo 7P	3,550	1,245	138
chassis	—	—	524
C14 Imperial (wb 121.0)			
bus cpe 2P	3,374	1,030	1,075
cpe 2-4P	3,449	1,070	225
conv cpe 2-4P	3,609	1,170	351
touring brougham 5P	3,544	1,070	430
touring sdn 5P	3,564	1,100	11,796
conv sdn 5P	3,824	1,500	325
chassis	—	—	118
C17 Airflow (wb 128.0)			
cpe 6P	4,225	1,610	230
sdn 4d 6P	4,300	1,610	4,370
C15 Custom Imperial (wb 140.0)			
sdn 4d	4,500	2,060	187
sdn 7P	4,522	2,060	721
sdn limo 7P	4,644	2,160	276
chassis	—	—	16

1937 Engines	bore×stroke	bhp	availability
I-6, 228.0	3.38×4.25	93	S-C16
I-6, 228.0	3.38×4.25	100	O-C16
I-8, 273.8	3.25×4.13	110	S-C14
I-8, 273.8	3.25×4.13	115	O-C14
I-8, 323.5	3.25×4.88	130	S-C17, C15
I-8, 323.5	3.25×4.88	138	O-C17, C15

1938

C18 Royal (wb 119.0; lwb-136.0)	Wght	Price	Prod
bus cpe 2P	3,090	918	4,840
cpe 2-4P	3,135	963	363
conv cpe 2-4P	3,250	1,085	480
fstbk brougham 5P	3,160	963	88
touring brougham 5P	3,165	975	3,802
fstbk sdn 5P	3,170	998	112
touring sdn 5P	3,180	1,010	31,991
conv sdn 5P	3,450	1,425	177
chassis	—	—	564
lwb sdn T/B 7P	3,450	1,235	722
limo T/B 7P (lwb)	3,545	1,325	161
C19 Imperial (wb 125.0; NY Spl-119.0)			
bus cpe 2P	3,450	1,123	766
NY Spl bus cpe 2P	3,475	1,255	
touring sdn 5P	3,565	1,198	8,554
NY Spl trng sdn 5P	3,600	1,378	
cpe 2-4P	3,515	1,160	80
conv cpe 2-4P	3,630	1,275	189
touring brougham 5P	3,560	1,165	245
conv sdn 5P	3,950	1,595	113
chassis	—	—	55
C20 Custom Imperial (wb 144.0)			
sdn 5P	4,495	2,295	252
sdn 7P	4,510	2,295	122
sdn limo 7P	4,635	2,395	145
chassis	—	—	11

1938 Engines	bore×stroke	bhp	availability
I-6, 241.5	3.38×4.50	95	S-C18
I-6, 241.5	3.38×4.50	102	O-C18
I-8, 298.7	3.25×4.50	110	S-C19
I-8, 298.7	3.25×4.50	122	O-C19
I-8, 323.5	3.25×4.88	130	S-C20
I-8, 323.5	3.25×4.88	138	O-C20

1939

C22 Royal (wb 119.0; lwb-136.0)	Wght	Price	Prod
cpe 2P	3,120	918	4,780
Windsor cpe 2P	3,130	983	
Victoria cpe 4P	3,160	970	239
Wndsr Vict cpe 4P	3,165	1,065	
brougham 5P	3,200	975	4,838
sdn 4d	3,265	1,010	45,955
Windsor sdn 4d	3,275	1,075	
Windsor club cpe 5P	3,245	1,185	2,983
lwb sdn 7P	3,520	1,235	621
lwb sdn limo 7P	3,625	1,325	191
chassis	—	—	394
C23 Imperial/New Yorker/Saratoga (wb 125.0)			
Imperial bus cpe 2P	3,520	1,123	492
Imp Victoria cpe 4P	3,555	1,160	35
Imp brougham 5P	3,610	1,165	185
Imperial sdn 4d	3,640	1,198	10,536
New Yorker sdn 4d	3,695	1,298	
Saratoga sdn 4d	3,720	1,443	
NY Victoria cpe 4P	3,665	1,395	99
NY bus cpe 2P	3,540	1,223	606
NY club cpe 5P	3,550	1,260	
Saratoga club cpe 5P	3,665	1,495	134
chassis	—	—	48
C24 Custom Imperial (wb 144.0)			
sdn 5P	4,590	2,595	88
sdn 7P	4,620	2,595	95
sdn limo 7P	4,665	2,695	117
chassis	—	—	7

1939 Engines	bore×stroke	bhp	availability
I-6, 241.5	3.38×4.50	100	S-C22
I-6, 241.5	3.38×4.50	107	O-C22
I-8, 323.5	3.25×4.88	130	S-C23
I-8, 323.5	3.25×4.88	132	S-C24
I-8, 323.5	3.25×4.88	138	O-C24

1940

C25 (wb 122.5; 8P-139.5)	Wght	Price	Prod
Royal sdn 4d	3,175	995	23,274
Windsor sdn 4d	3,210	1,025	28,477
Royal sdn 2d	3,150	960	9,851
Windsor sdn 2d	3,175	995	
Royal bus cpe	3,075	895	5,117
Windsor bus cpe	3,095	935	
Royal cpe	3,110	960	4,315
Windsor cpe	3,135	995	
Wndsr Highl cpe	3,135	1,020	2,275
Windsor conv cpe	3,360	1,160	
Wndsr Highl conv cpe	3,360	1,185	
Royal sdn 4d, 8P	3,550	1,235	439
Windsor sdn 4d, 8P	3,575	1,275	
Royal limo	3,640	1,310	98
Windsor limo	3,660	1,350	
chassis	—	—	152
C26 (wb 128.5)			
Traveler sdn 4d	3,590	1,180	14,603
New Yorker sdn 4d	3,635	1,260	
Saratoga sdn 4d	3,790	1,375	
Traveler cpe	3,525	1,150	1,117
New Yorker cpe	3,570	1,230	
NY Highlander cpe	3,570	1,255	
Traveler bus cpe	3,475	1,095	731
New Yorker bus cpe	3,490	1,175	
Traveler sdn 2d	3,555	1,150	275
New Yorker sdn 2d	3,610	1,230	
New Yorker conv cpe	3,775	1,375	845
NY Hlndr conv cpe	3,775	1,400	
C27 Crown Imperial (wb 145.5)			
sdn 4d	4,340	2,245	355
sdn 4d, 8P	4,330	2,345	284
limo, 8P	4,365	2,445	210
chassis	—	—	1

1940 Engines	bore×stroke	bhp	availability
I-6, 241.5	3.38×4.50	108	S-Royal, Wind
I-6, 241.5	3.38×4.50	112	O-Royal, Wind
I-8, 323.5	3.25×4.88	135	S-Trav, NY, Sartga
I-8, 323.5	3.25×4.88	143	O-Trav, NY, Sartga
I-8, 323.5	3.25×4.88	132	S-Crown Imp
I-8, 323.5	3.25×4.88	143	O-Crown Imp

1941

C-28S Royal (wb 121.5; 8P-139.5)	Wght	Price	Prod
sdn 4d	3,300	1,091	51,378
club cpe	3,260	1,085	10,830
luxury brougham 2d	3,270	1,066	8,006
bus cpe	3,170	995	6,846
town sdn 4d	3,320	1,136	1,277
sdn 4d, 8P	3,650	1,345	297
limo 8P	3,695	1,415	31
chassis	—	—	3
T & C wgn 4d, 6P	3,540	1,412	200
T & C wgn 4d, 9P	3,595	1,492	797
C-28W Windsor (wb 121.5; 8P-139.5)			
sdn 4d	3,300	1,165	36,396
club cpe	3,260	1,142	8,513
conv cpe	3,470	1,315	4,432
luxury brougham 2d	3,270	1,128	2,898
town sdn 4d	3,315	1,198	2,704
bus cpe	3,170	1,045	1,921
sdn 4d, 8P	3,575	1,410	116
limo, 8P	3,660	1,487	54
C-30K/30N (wb 127.5)			
Saratoga sdn 4d	3,755	1,320	15,868
New Yorker sdn 4d	3,775	1,389	
Saratoga club cpe	3,685	1,299	2,845
New Yorker club cpe	3,690	1,369	
Saratoga town sdn 4d	3,750	1,350	2,326
NY town sdn 4d	3,785	1,399	
Saratoga bus cpe	3,600	1,245	771
New Yorker bus cpe	3,635	1,325	
Srtoga lxry brghm 2d	3,715	1,293	293
NY luxury broug 2d	3,745	1,369	
NY conv cpe	3,945	1,548	1,295
T & wgn 4d	—	proto	1
chassis	—	—	9
C-33 Crown Imperial (wb 145.5)			
sdn 4d	4,435	2,595	179
sdn 4d, 8P	4,495	2,696	205
limo 8P	4,560	2,795	316
special town sdn 4d*	3,900	1,760	894
chassis	—	—	1

* C-30 body and chassis, C-33 engine and nameplates.

1941 Engines	bore×stroke	bhp	availability
I-6, 241.5	3.38×4.50	108/112	S-Royal, Wind
I-6, 241.5	3.38×4.50	115	O-Royal, Wind
I-8, 323.5	3.25×4.88	137	S-Srtoga, NY
I-8, 323.5	3.25×4.88	140	O-Srtoga, NY
I-8, 323.5	3.25×4.88	143	S-Crown Imp

1942

C-34S Royal (wb 121.5; 8P-139.5)	Wght	Price	Prod
bus cpe	3,331	1,075	479
club cpe	3,406	1,168	779
brougham 2d	3,431	1,154	709
sdn 4d	3,476	1,177	7,424
town sdn 4d	3,481	1,222	73
sdn 4d, 8P	3,854	1,535	79
limo 8P	3,895	1,605	21
C-34W Windsor (wb 121.5; 8P-139.5)			
bus cpe	3,351	1,140	250
club cpe	3,426	1,228	1,713
conv cpe	3,661	1,420	574
brougham 2d	3,441	1,220	317
sdn 4d	3,496	1,255	10,054
town sdn, 4d	3,506	1,295	479
T & C wgn 4d, 6P	3,614	1,595	150
T & C wgn 4d, 9P	3,699	1,685	849
sdn 4d, 8P	3,879	1,605	29
limo 8P	3,900	1,685	12
C-36K Saratoga (wb 127.5)			
bus cpe	3,703	1,325	80
club cpe	3,788	1,380	193
brougham 2d	3,798	1,365	36
sdn 4d	3,833	1,405	1,239
town sdn 4d	3,843	1,450	46
chassis	—	—	2
C-36N New Yorker (wb 127.5)			
bus cpe	3,728	1,385	158
club cpe	3,783	1,450	1,234
conv cpe	4,033	1,640	401

C-36N New Yorker	Wght	Price	Prod
brougham 2d	3,798	1,440	62
T & C wgn 4d, 9P	—	proto	1
sdn 4d	3,873	1,475	7,045
town sdn 4d	3,893	1,520	1,648

C-33 Crown Imperial (wb 145.5)			
sdn 4d	4,565	2,815	81
sdn 4d, 8P	4,620	2,915	152
limo 8P	4,685	3,065	215
chassis	—	—	2

1942 Engines	bore×stroke	bhp	availability
I-6, 250.6	3.44×4.50	120	S-Royal, Wind
I-8, 323.5	3.25×4.88	140	S-others

1946

C-38S Royal (wb 121.5; 8P-139.5)*	Wght	Price	Prod
sdn 4d	3,523	1,561	—
sdn 2d	3,458	1,526	—
club cpe	3,443	1,551	—
bus cpe	3,373	1,431	—
sdn 4d, 8P	3,997	1,943	—
limo 8P	4,022	2,063	—
chassis	—	—	—

C-38W Windsor (wb 121.5; 8P-139.5)*			
sdn 4d	3,528	1,611	—
sdn 2d	3,468	1,591	—
club cpe	3,448	1,601	—
bus cpe	3,383	1,481	—
conv cpe	3,693	1,861	—
sdn 4d, 8P	3,977	1,993	—
limo 8P	4,052	2,113	—
Traveler sdn 4d	3,610	1,746	—

C-39K Saratoga (wb 127.5)*			
sdn 4d	3,972	1,863	—
sdn 2d	3,932	1,838	—
club cpe	3,892	1,848	—
bus cpe	3,817	1,753	—

C-39N New Yorker (wb 127.5)*			
sdn 4d	3,973	1,963	—
sdn 2d	3,932	1,938	—
club cpe	3,897	1,948	—
bus cpe	3,837	1,853	—
conv cpe	4,132	2,193	—
chassis	—	—	—

C-38/39 Town & Country (wb 121.5; I-8-127.5)*			
sdn 4d, I-6	3,917	2,366	124
brougham 2d, I-6	—	proto	1
conv cpe, I-6	—	proto	1
sdn 4d, I-8	4,300	2,718	100
conv cpe, I-8	4,332	2,743	1,935
htp cpe, I-8	—	proto	7

C-40 Crown Imperial (wb 145.5)*			
limo 8P	4,814	3,875	—

1946 Engines	bore×stroke	bhp	availability
I-6, 250.6	3.44×4.50	114	S-Royal, Wind, T&C six
I-8, 323.5	3.25×4.88	135	S-others

*Factory combined production figures for 1946 through First Series 1949.

1947

C-38S Royal (wb 121.5; 8P-139.5)*	Wght	Price	Prod
sdn 4d	3,523	1,661	—
sdn 2d	3,458	1,626	—
club cpe	3,443	1,651	—
bus cpe	3,373	1,561	—
sdn 4d, 8P	3,997	2,043	—
limo 8P	4,022	2,163	—

C-38W Windsor (wb 121.5; 8P-139.5)*			
sdn 4d	3,528	1,711	—
Traveler sdn 4d	3,610	1,846	—
sdn 2d	3,468	1,691	—
club cpe	3,448	1,701	—
bus cpe	3,383	1,611	—
conv cpe	3,693	2,075	—
sdn 4d, 8P	3,977	2,093	—
limo 8P	4,052	2,213	—

C-39K Saratoga (wb 127.5)*	Wght	Price	Prod
sdn 4d	3,972	1,973	—
sdn 2d	3,900	1,948	—
club cpe	3,930	1,958	—
bus cpe	3,817	1,873	—

C-39N New Yorker (wb 127.5)*			
sdn 4d	3,987	2,073	—
sdn 2d	3,932	2,048	—
club cpe	3,940	2,058	—
bus cpe	3,837	1,973	—
conv cpe	4,132	2,447	—

C-38/39 Town & Country (wb 121.5; I-8-127.5)			
sdn 4d, I-6	3,955	2,713	2,651
conv cpe, I-8	4,332	2,998	3,136

C-40 Crown Imperial (wb 145.5)*			
sdn 4d, 8P	4,865	4,205	—
limo 8P	4,875	4,305	—

1947 Engines	bore×stroke	bhp	availability
I-6, 250.6	3.44×4.50	114	S-Royal, Wind, T&C six
I-8, 323.5	3.25×4.88	135	S-others

* Factory combined production figures for 1946 through First Series 1949.

1948 - First Series 1949

C-38S Royal (wb 121.5; 8P-139.5)*	Wght	Price	Prod
sdn 4d	3,523	1,955	—
sdn 2d	3,485	1,908	—
club cpe	3,475	1,934	—
bus cpe	3,395	1,819	—
sdn 4d, 8P	3,925	2,380	—
limo 8P	4,022	2,506	—

C-38W Windsor (wb 121.5; 8P-139.5)*			
sdn 4d	3,528	2,021	—
Traveler sdn 4d	3,610	2,163	—
sdn 2d	3,510	1,989	—
club cpe	3,475	2,000	—
bus cpe	3,395	1,884	—
conv cpe	3,693	2,414	—
sdn 4d, 8P	3,935	2,434	—
limo 8P	4,035	2,561	—

C-39K Saratoga (wb 127.5)*			
sdn 4d	3,972	2,291	—
sdn 2d	3,900	2,254	—
club cpe	3,930	2,265	—
bus cpe	3,817	2,165	—

C-39N New Yorker (wb 127.5)*			
sdn 4d	3,987	2,411	—
sdn 2d	3,932	2,374	—
club cpe	3,940	2,385	—
bus cpe	3,837	2,285	—
conv cpe	4,132	2,815	—

C-38/39 Town & Country (wb 121.5; I-8-127.5)			
sdn 4d, I-6	3,955	2,860	1,175
conv cpe, I-8	4,332	3,420	3,309

C-40 Crown Imperial (wb 145.5)*			
sdn 4d, 8P	4,865	4,662	—
limo 8P	4,875	4,767	—

1948 Engines	bore×stroke	bhp	availability
I-6, 250.6	3.44×4.50	114	S-Royal, Wind, T&C six
I-8, 323.5	3.25×4.88	135	S-others

Note: First Series 1949 models sold December 1948 through March 1949; identical in weight/price to 1948 models and comprised about 15 percent of total prod.

* Factory combined production figures for 1946 through First Series 1949; breakdowns are not available from Chrysler archives. However, since the Town & Country figures have been obtained (by historian Donald Narus), it is very likely that breakdowns exist for other models.

Combined 1946-1949 First Series Production

C-38S Royal (wb 121.5; 8P-139.5)*	Prod
sdn 4d	24,279
sdn 2d	1,117
club cpe	4,318
bus cpe	1,221
sdn 4d, 8P	626
limo 8P	169
chassis	1

C-38W Windsor (wb 121.5; 8P-139.5)	Prod
sdn 4d	161,139
Traveler sdn 4d	4,182
sdn 2d	4,034
club cpe	26,482
bus cpe	1,980
conv cpe	11,200
sdn 4d, 8P	4,390
limo 8P	1,496

C-39K Saratoga (wb 127.5)	
sdn 4d	4,611
sdn 2d	155
club cpe	765
bus cpe	74

C-39N New Yorker (wb 127.5)	
sdn 4d	52,036
sdn 2d	545
club cpe	10,735
bus cpe	701
conv cpe	3,000
chassis	2

C-38/39 Town & Country (wb 121.5; I-8-127.5)	
sdn 4d, I-6	4,049
brougham 2d, I-6 (proto)	1
conv cpe, I-6 (proto)	1
sdn 4d, I-8	100
conv cpe, I-8	8,368
htp cpe, I-8 (proto)	7

C-40 Crown Imperial (wb 145.5)	
sdn 4d, 8P	650
limo 8P	750

1949 Second Series

C-45-1 Royal (wb 125.5; 8P-139.5)			Prod
sdn 4d	3,550	2,134	13,192
club cpe	3,495	2,114	4,849
wgn 4d, 9P	4,060	3,121	850
sdn 4d, 8P	4,200	2,823	185

C-45-2 Windsor (wb 125.5; 8P-139.5)			
sdn 4d	3,681	2,329	55,879
club cpe	3,631	2,308	17,732
conv cpe	3,845	2,741	3,234
sdn 4d, 8P	4,290	3,017	373
limo 8P	4,430	3,144	73

C-46-1 Saratoga (wb 131.5)			
sdn 4d	4,103	2,610	1,810
club cpe	4,037	2,585	465

C-46-2 New Yorker (wb 131.5)			
sdn 4d	4,113	2,726	18,779
club cpe	4,048	2,700	4,524
conv cpe	4,277	3,206	1,137
chassis	—	—	1

C-46-2 Town & Country (wb 131.5)			
conv cpe	4,630	3,970	1,000

C-46-2 Imperial (wb 131.5)			
sdn 4d	4,300	4,665	50

C-47 Crown Imperial (wb 145.5)			
sdn 4d, 8P	5,250	5,229	40
limo 8P	5,295	5,334	45

1949 Engines	bore×stroke	bhp	availability
I-6, 250.6	3.44×4.50	116	S-Royal, Wind
I-8, 323.5	3.25×4.88	135	S-others

1950

C-48-1 Royal (wb 125.5; 8P-139.5)	Wght	Price	Prod
sdn 4d	3,610	2,134	17,713
club cpe	3,540	2,114	5,900
T&C wgn 4d, wood	4,055	3,163	599
T&C wgn 4d, steel	3,964	2,735	100
sdn 4d, 8P	4,190	2,855	375

C-48-2 Windsor (wb 125.5; 8P-139.5)			
sdn 4d	3,765	2,329	78,199
Traveler sdn 4d	3,830	2,560	900
club cpe	3,670	2,308	20,050
Newport htp cpe	3,875	2,637	9,925
conv cpe	3,905	2,741	2,201
sdn 4d, 8P	4,295	3,050	763
limo 8P	4,400	3,176	174
chassis	—	—	1

C-49-1 Saratoga (wb 131.5)	Wght	Price	Prod
sdn 4d	4,170	2,642	1,000
club cpe	4,110	2,616	300
C-49-2 New Yorker (wb 131.5)			
sdn 4d	4,190	2,758	22,633
club cpe	4,110	2,732	3,000
Newport htp cpe	4,370	3,133	2,800
conv cpe	4,360	3,232	899
wgn 4d, wood	—	proto	1
chassis	—	—	2
C-49-2 Town & Country (wb 131.5)			
Newport htp cpe	4,670	4,003	700
C-49-2 Imperial (wb 131.5)			
sdn 4d	4,245	3,055	9,500
Deluxe sdn 4d	4,250	3,176	1,150
C-50 Crown Imperial (wb 145.5)			
sdn 4d, 8P	5,235	5,229	209
limo 8P	5,305	5,334	205
chassis	—	—	1

1950 Engines	bore×stroke	bhp	availability
I-6, 250.6	3.44×4.50	116	S-Royal, Wind
I-8, 323.5	3.25×4.88	135	S-others

1951

C-51W Windsor (wb125.5; 8P-139.5)	Wght	Price	Prod
sdn 4d	3,527	2,390	10,151*
club cpe	3,570	2,368	4,243*
T & C wgn 4d	3,965	3,063	1,239*
sdn 4d, 8P	4,145	3,197	399*
ambulance (spl order)	—	—	153
Deluxe sdn 4d	3,775	2,608	47,573*
Delux Travlr sdn 4d	3,890	2,867	850
Deluxe club cpe	3,700	2,585	8,365
Delux Nwprt htp cpe	3,855	2,953	6,426*
Deluxe conv cpe	3,945	3,071	2,646*
Deluxe sdn 4d, 8P	4,295	3,416	720
Deluxe limo 8P	4,415	3,557	152
C-55 Saratoga (wb 125.5; 8P-139.5)			
sdn 4d	4,018	3,016	22,375*
club cpe	3,948	2,989	5,355*
Newport htp cpe	—	proto	1
T C wgn 4d	4,310	3,681	818*
sdn 4d, 8P	4,465	3,912	115*
ambulance (spl order)	—	—	1
C-52 New Yorker (wb 131.5)			
sdn 4d	4,260	3,378	25,461*
club cpe	4,145	3,348	3,533
Newport htp cpe	4,330	3,798	3,654*
conv cpe	4,460	3,916	1,386*
T&C wgn 4d (4 C51s)	4,455	4,026	251
chassis	—	—	1
C-54 Imperial (wb 131.5)			
sdn 4d	4,350	3,674	13,678*
club cpe	4,230	3,661	749*
Newport htp cpe	4,380	4,042	2,174*
conv cpe	4,570	4,402	650
C-53 Crown Imperial (wb 145.5)			
sdn 4d, 8P	5,360	6,573	227*
limo 8P	5,450	6,690	213*
chassis	—	—	2

1951 Engines	bore×stroke	bhp	availability
I-6, 250.6	3.44×4.50	116	S-Windsor
V-8, 331.1	3.81×3.63	180	S-others

1952

C-51W Windsor (wb125.5; 8P-139.5)	Wght	Price	Prod
sdn 4d	3,640	2,498	5,961*
club cpe	3,550	2,475	2,492*
T & C wgn 4d	4,015	3,200	728*
sdn 4d, 8P	4,145	3,342	234*
Deluxe sdn 4d	3,775	2,727	27,940*
Delux Nwprt htp cpe	3,855	3,087	3,774*
Deluxe conv cpe	3,990	3,210	1,554*
C-55 Saratoga (wb 125.5; 8P-139.5)			
sdn 4d	4,010	3,215	13,141*
club cpe	3,935	3,187	3,145*
T & C wgn 4d, 8P	4,345	3,925	481*
sdn 4d, 8P	4,510	4,172	68*
C-52 New Yorker (wb 131.5)			
sdn 4d	4,205	3,530	14,954*
Newport htp cpe	4,325	3,969	2,146*
conv cpe	4,450	4,093	814*
C-54 Imperial (wb 131.5)			
sdn 4d	4,315	3,839	8,033*
club cpe	4,220	3,826	440*
Newport htp cpe	4,365	4,224	1,276*
C-53 Crown Imperial (wb 145.5)			
sdn rd, 4P	5,395	6,872	133*
limo 8P	5,430	6,994	125*

1952 Engines	bore×stroke	bhp	availability
I-6, 264.5	3.44×4.75	119	S-Windsor
V-8, 331.1	3.81×3.63	180	S-others

* As with other corporate makes, Chrysler combined model-year prod. for 1951-52. However, prod. figures are known for several 1951-only body styles, making prod. estimates of remaining body styles (spanning both years) more accurate. In the above cases (*), estimates are based on the known percentages of the two-year run: 63 percent for 1951 and 37 percent for 1952.

1953

C-60-1 Windsor (wb125.5; 8P-139.5)	Wght	Price	Prod
sdn 4d	3,660	2,462	18,879
club cpe	3,600	2,442	11,646
T & C wgn 4d	3,960	3,259	1,242
sdn 4d, 8P	4,170	3,403	425
C-60-2 Windsor Deluxe (wb 125.5)			
sdn 4d	3,775	2,691	45,385
Newport htp cpe	3,775	2,995	5,642
conv cpe	4,005	3,217	1,250
C-56-1 New Yorker (wb 125.5; 8P-139.5)			
sdn 4d	4,005	3,150	37,540
club cpe	3,925	3,121	7,749
Newport htp cpe	4,020	3,487	2,525
T & C wgn 4d	4,265	3,898	1,399
sdn 4d, 8P	4,510	4,334	100
C-56-2 New Yorker Deluxe (wb 125.5)			
sdn 4d	4,025	3,293	20,585
club cpe	3,925	3,264	1,934
Newport htp cpe	4,025	3,653	3,715
conv cpe	4,295	3,945	950
chassis	—	—	21
C-58 Custom Imperial (wb 133.5; htp cpe-131.5)			
sdn 4d	4,305	4,225	7,793
town limo 6P	4,525	4,762	243
Newport htp cpe	4,290	4,525	823
C-59 Crown Imperial (wb 145.5)			
sdn 4d, 8P	5,235	6,872	48
limo 8P	5,275	6,994	111
chassis	—	—	1

1953 Engines	bore×stroke	bhp	availability
I-6, 264.5	3.44×4.75	119	S-Windsor
V-8, 331.1	3.81×3.63	180	S-others

1954

C-62 Wndsr Dlx (wb125.5; 8P-139.5)	Wght	Price	Prod
sdn 4d	3,655	2,562	33,563
club cpe	3,565	2,541	5,659
Newport htp cpe	3,685	2,831	3,655
conv cpe	3,915	3,046	500
T & C wgn 4d	3,955	3,321	650
sdn 4d, 8P	4,185	3,492	500
C-63-1 New Yorker (wb 125.5; 8P-139.5)			
sdn 4d	3,970	3,229	15,788
club cpe	3,910	3,202	2,079
Newport htp cpe	4,005	3,503	1,312
T & C wgn 4d	4,245	4,024	1,100
sdn 4d, 8P	4,450	4,368	140
C-63-2 New Yorker Deluxe (wb 125.5)			
sdn 4d	4,065	3,433	26,907
club cpe	4,005	3,406	1,861
Newport htp cpe	4,095	3,707	4,814
conv cpe	4,265	3,938	724
chassis	—	—	17
C-64 Custom Imperial (wb 133.5)			
sdn 4d	4,355	4,260	4,324
town limo 6P	4,465	4,797	83
special town limo 6P	4,475	—	2

C-64 Custom Imperial	Wght	Price	Prod
Newport htp cpe	4,345	4,560	1,249
conv cpe	—	proto	1
chassis	—	—	2
C-66 Crown Imperial (wb 145.5)			
sdn 4d, 8P	5,220	6,922	23
limo 8P	5,295	7,044	77

1954 Engines	bore×stroke	bhp	availability
I-6, 264.5	3.44×4.75	119	S-Wind Deluxe
V-8, 331.1	3.81×3.63	195	S-NY
V-8, 331.1	3.81×3.63	235	S-others

1955

C-67 Windsor Dlx (wb 126.0)	Wght	Price	Prod
sdn 4d	3,925	2,660	63,896
Nassau htp cpe	3,930	2,703	18,474
Newport htp cpe	3,925	2,818	13,126
conv cpe	4,075	3,090	1,395
T & C wgn 4d	4,295	3,332	1,983
C-68 New Yorker Deluxe (wb 126.0)			
sdn 4d	4,160	3,494	33,342
Newport htp cpe	4,140	3,652	5,777
St. Regis htp cpe	4,125	3,690	11,076
conv cpe	4,285	3,924	946
T & C wgn 4d	4,430	4,209	1,036
chassis	—	—	1
C-68 300 (wb 126.0)			
htp cpe	4,005	4,110	1,725

1955 Engines	bore×stroke	bhp	availability
V-8, 301.0	3.63×3.63	188	S-Wind Deluxe
V-8, 331.1	3.81×3.63	250	S-NY Deluxe
V-8, 331.1	3.81×3.63	300	S-300

1956

C-71 Windsor (wb 126.0)	Wght	Price	Prod
sdn 4d	3,900	2,870	53,119
Newport htp sdn	3,990	3,128	7,050
Nassau htp cpe	3,910	2,905	11,400
Newport htp cpe	3,920	3,041	10,800
conv cpe	4,100	3,336	1,011
T & C wgn 4d	4,290	3,598	2,700
C-72 New Yorker (wb 126.0)			
sdn 4d	4,110	3,779	24,749
Newport htp sdn	4,220	4,102	3,599
Newport htp cpe	4,175	3,951	4,115
St. Regis htp cpe	4,175	3,995	6,686
conv cpe	4,360	4,243	921
T & C wgn 4d	4,460	4,523	1,070
C-72 300B (wb 126.0)			
htp cpe	4,145	4,419	1,102

1956 Engines	bore×stroke	bhp	availability
V-8, 331.1	3.81×3.63	225	S-Windsor
V-8, 331.1	3.81×3.63	250	O-Windsor
V-8, 354.0	3.94×3.63	280	S-NY
V-8, 354.0	3.94×3.63	340	S-300B
V-8, 354.0	3.94×3.63	355	O-300B

1957

C-75-1 Windsor (wb 126.0)	Wght	Price	Prod
sdn 4d	3,995	3,088	17,639
htp sdn	4,030	3,217	14,354
htp cpe	3,925	3,153	14,027
T & C wgn 4d	4,210	3,575	2,035
C-75-2 Saratoga (wb 126.0)			
sdn 4d	4,165	3,718	14,977
htp sdn	4,195	3,832	11,586
htp cpe	4,075	3,754	10,633
C-76 New Yorker (wb 126.0)			
sdn 4d	4,315	4,173	12,369
htp sdn	4,330	4,259	10,948
htp cpe	4,220	4,202	8,863
conv cpe	4,365	4,638	1,049
T & C wgn 4d	4,490	4,746	1,391
C-76 300C (wb 126.0)			
htp cpe	4,235	4,929	1,767
conv cpe	4,390	5,359	484

1957 Engines	bore×stroke	bhp	availability
V-8, 354.0	3.94×3.63	285	S-Windsor
V-8, 354.0	3.94×3.63	295	S-Saratoga
V-8, 392.0	4.00×3.90	325	S-NY

1957 Engines	bore×stroke	bhp	availability
V-8, 392.0	4.00×3.90	375	S-300C
V-8, 392.0	4.00×3.90	390	O-300C

1958

LC-1-L Windsor (wb 122.0)		Wght	Price	Prod
	sdn 4d	3,895	3,129	12,861
	htp sdn	3,915	3,279	6,254
	htp cpe	3,860	3,214	6,205
	T & C wgn 4d, 9P	4,245	3,803	862
	T & C wgn 4d, 6P	4,155	3,616	791
	conv cpe	—	—	2
LC-2-M Saratoga (wb 126.0)				
	sdn 4d	4,120	3,818	8,698
	htp sdn	4,145	3,955	5,322
	htp cpe	4,045	3,878	4,466
LC-3-H New Yorker (wb 126.0)				
	sdn 4d	4,195	4,295	7,110
	htp sdn	4,240	4,404	5,227
	htp cpe	4,205	4,347	3,205
	conv cpe	4,350	4,761	666
	T & C wgn 4d, 9P	4,445	5,083	775
	T & C wgn 4d, 6P	4,435	4,868	428
LC-3-S 300D (wb 126.0)				
	htp cpe	4,305	5,173	618
	conv cpe	4,475	5,603	191

1958 Engines	bore×stroke	bhp	availability
V-8, 354.0	3.94×3.63	290	S-Windsor
V-8, 354.0	3.94×3.63	310	S-Saratoga
V-8, 392.0	4.00×3.90	345	S-NY
V-8, 392.0	4.00×3.90	380	S-300D
V-8, 392.0	4.00×3.90	390	O-300D

1959

MC-1-L Windsor (wb 122.0)		Wght	Price	Prod
512	htp cpe	3,830	3,289	6,775
513	sdn 4d	3,800	3,204	19,910
514	htp sdn	3,735	3,353	6,084
515	conv cpe	3,950	3,620	961
576	T & C wgn 4d, 6P	4,045	3,691	751
577	T & C wgn 4d, 9P	4,070	3,878	992
MC-2-M Saratoga (wb 126.0)				
532	htp cpe	3,970	4,026	3,753
533	sdn 4d	4,010	3,966	8,783
534	htp sdn	4,035	4,104	4,934
MC-3-H New Yorker (wb 126.0)				
552	htp cpe	4,080	4,476	2,435
553	sdn 4d	4,120	4,424	7,792
554	htp sdn	4,165	4,533	4,805
555	conv cpe	4,270	4,890	286
578	T & C wgn 6P	4,295	4,997	444
579	T & C wgn 9P	4,360	5,212	564
—	chassis	—	—	3
MC-C-H 300E (wb 126.0)				
592	htp cpe	4,290	5,319	550
595	conv cpe	4,350	5,749	140

1959 Engines	bore×stroke	bhp	availability
V-8, 383.0	4.03×3.75	305	S-Windsor
V-8, 383.0	4.03×3.75	325	S-Saratoga
V-8, 413.0	4.18×3.75	350	S-NY
V-8, 413.0	4.18×3.75	380	S-300E

1960

PC-1-L Windsor (wb 122.0)		Wght	Price	Prod
23	htp cpe	3,855	3,279	6,496
27	conv cpe	3,855	3,623	1,467
41	sdn 4d	3,815	3,194	25,152
43	htp sdn	3,850	3,343	5,897
46	T & C wgn 4d, 6P	4,235	3,733	1,120
46	T & C wgn 4d, 9P	4,390	3,814	1,026
PC-2-M Saratoga (wb 126.0)				
23	htp cpe	4,030	3,989	2,963
41	sdn 4d	4,010	3,939	8,463
43	htp sdn	4,035	4,067	4,099
PC-3-H New Yorker (wb 126.0)				
23	htp cpe	4,175	4,461	2,835
27	conv cpe	4,185	4,875	556
41	sdn 4d	4,145	4,409	9,079
43	htp sdn	4,175	4,518	5,625
46	T & C wgn, 6P	4,515	5,022	624
46	T & C wgn, 9P	4,535	5,131	671
PC-3-H 300F (wb 126.0)				
23	htp cpe	4,270	5,411	964
27	conv cpe	4,310	5,841	248

1960 Engines	bore×stroke	bhp	availability
V-8, 383.0	4.03×3.75	305	S-Windsor
V-8, 383.0	4.03×3.75	325	S-Saratoga
V-8, 413.0	4.18×3.75	350	S-NY
V-8, 413.0	4.18×3.75	375	S-300F
V-8, 413.0	4.18×3.75	400	O-300F

1961

RC-1-L Newport (wb 122.0)		Wght	Price	Prod
812	htp cpe	3,690	3,025	9,405
813	sdn 4d	3,710	2,964	34,370
814	htp sdn	3,730	3,104	7,789
815	conv cpe	3,760	3,442	2,135
858	T & C wgn 4d, 6P	4,070	3,541	1,832
859	T & C wgn 4d, 9P	4,155	3,622	1,571
RC-2-M Windsor (wb 122.0)				
822	htp cpe	3,710	3,303	2,941
823	sdn 4d	3,730	3,218	10,239
824	htp sdn	3,765	3,367	4,156
RC-3-H New Yorker (wb 126.0)				
832	htp cpe	4,065	4,175	2,541
833	sdn 4d	4,055	4,123	9,984
834	htp sdn	4,100	4,261	5,862
835	conv cpe	4,070	4,592	576
878	T & C wgn 4d, 6P	4,425	4,764	676
879	T & C wgn 4d, 9P	4,455	4,871	760
RC-4-P 300G (wb 126.0)				
842	htp cpe	4,260	5,411	1,280
845	conv cpe	4,315	5,841	337

1961 Engines	bore×stroke	bhp	availability
V-8, 361.0	4.12×3.38	265	S-Newport
V-8, 383.0	4.25×3.38	305	S-Windsor
V-8, 413.0	4.18×3.75	350	S-NY
V-8, 413.0	4.18×3.75	375	S-300G
V-8, 413.0	4.18×3.75	400	O-300G

1962

SC1-L-Newport (wb 122.0)		Wght	Price	Prod
812	htp cpe	3,650	3,027	11,910
813	sdn 4d	3,690	2,964	54,813
814	htp sdn	3,715	3,106	8,712
815	conv cpe	3,740	3,399	2,051
858	T & C wgn 4d, 6P	4,060	3,478	3,271
859	T & C wgn 4d, 9P	4,090	3,586	2,363
SC2-M 300 (wb 122.0)				
822	htp cpe	3,750	3,323	11,341
823	sdn 4d	—	3,258	1,801
824	htp sdn	3,760	3,400	10,030
825	conv cpe	3,815	3,883	1,848
SC3-H New Yorker (wb 126.0)				
833	sdn 4d	3,925	4,125	12,056
834	htp sdn	4,005	4,263	6,646
878	T & C 4d, 6P	4,225	4,766	728
879	T & C 4d, 9P	4,455	4,873	793
SC2-M 300H (wb 122.0)				
842	htp cpe	4,010	5,090	435
845	conv cpe	4,080	5,461	123

1962 Engines	bore×stroke	bhp	availability
V-8, 361.0	4.12×3.38	265	S-Newport
V-8, 383.0	4.25×3.38	305	S-300
V-8, 413.0	4.18×3.75	340	S-NY
V-8, 413.0	4.18×3.75	380	S-300H
V-8, 413.0	4.18×3.75	405	O-300H

1963

TC1-L Newport (wb 122.0)		Wght	Price	Prod
812	htp cpe	3,760	3,027	9,809
813	sdn 4d	3,770	2,964	49,067
814	htp sdn	3,800	3,106	8,437
815	conv cpe	3,825	3,399	2,093
858	T & C wgn 4d, 6P	4,200	3,478	3,618
859	T & C wgn 4d, 9P	4,215	3,586	2,948
TC2-M 300 (wb 122.0)				
802	Pace Setter htp cpe	3,790	3,769	306
822	htp cpe	3,790	3,430	9,423
805	Pace Setter conv cpe	3,840	4,129	1,861
825	conv cpe	3,845	3,790	1,535
TC2-M 300				
823	sdn 4d	3,790	—	1,625
824	htp sdn	3,815	3,400	9,915
TC3-H New Yorker (wb 122.0)				
833	sdn 4d	3,910	4,981	14,884
834	htp sdn	3,950	4,118	10,289
884	Salon htp sdn	4,290	5,860	593
878	T & C wgn 4d, 6P	4,350	4,708	950
879	T & C wgn 4d, 9P	4,370	4,815	1,244
TC2-M 300J (wb 122.0)				
842	htp cpe	4,000	5,184	400

1963 Engines	bore×stroke	bhp	availability
V-8, 361.0	4.12×3.38	265	S-Newport
V-8, 383.0	4.25×3.38	305	S-300
V-8, 413.0	4.19×3.75	340	S-NY
V-8, 413.0	4.19×3.75	360	O-300
V-8, 413.0	4.19×3.75	390	S-300J

1964

VC1-L Newport (wb 122.0)		Wght	Price	Prod
812	htp cpe	3,760	2,962	10,579
813	sdn 4d	3,805	2,901	55,957
814	htp sdn	3,795	3,042	9,710
815	conv cpe	3,810	3,334	2,176
858	T & C wgn 4d, 6P	4,175	3,414	3,720
859	T & C wgn 4d, 9P	4,200	3,521	3,041
VC2-M 300 (wb 122.0)*				
822	htp cpe	3,850	3,443	18,379
824	htp sdn	3,865	3,521	11,460
823	sdn 4d	—	—	2,078
825	conv cpe	4,120	3,803	1,401
VC3-H New Yorker (wb 122.0)				
832	htp cpe	—	—	300
833	sdn 4d	4,015	3,994	15,443
834	htp sdn	4,035	4,131	10,887
878	T & C wgn 4d, 6P	4,385	4,721	1,190
879	T & C wgn 4d, 9P	4,395	4,828	1,603
884	Salon htp sdn	4,280	5,860	1,621
VC2-M 300K (wb 122.0)*				
842	htp cpe	3,965	4,056	3,022
845	conv cpe	3,995	4,522	625

*Silver 300 models: 300–2,152; 300K–255.

1964 Engines	bore×stroke	bhp	availability
V-8, 361.0	4.12×3.38	265	S-Newport
V-8, 383.0	4.25×3.38	305	S-300
V-8, 413.0	4.19×3.75	340	S-NY; O-300
V-8, 413.0	4.19×3.75	360	S-300K; O-300
V-8, 413.0	4.19×3.75	390	O-300K

1965

AC1-L Newport (wb 124; wgns-121)		Wght	Price	Prod
C12	htp cpe	4,035	3,070	23,655
C13	sdn 4d, 4W	4,045	3,009	61,054
C14	htp sdn	4,050	3,149	17,062
C15	conv cpe	4,025	3,442	3,192
C18	sdn 4d, 6W	4,000	3,146	12,411
C56	T & C wgn 4d, 6P	4,360	3,521	4,683
C57	T & C wgn 4d, 9P	4,455	3,629	3,738
AC2-M 300 (wb 124.0)				
C22	htp cpe	4,085	3,551	11,621
C24	htp sdn	4,150	3,628	12,452
C25	conv cpe	4,140	3,911	1,418
C28	sdn 4d, 6W	—	—	2,187
AC3-H New Yorker (wb 124.0; wgns-121.0)				
C32	htp cpe	4,270	4,161	9,357
C34	htp sdn	4,295	4,238	21,110
C38	sdn 4d, 6W	4,265	4,104	16,339
C76	T & C wgn 4d, 6P	4,650	4,827	1,368
C77	T & C wgn 4d, 9P	4,745	4,935	1,697
AC2-P 300L (wb 124.0)				
C42	htp cpe	4,245	4,153	2,405
C45	conv cpe	4,170	4,618	440

1965 Engines	bore×stroke	bhp	availability
V-8, 383.0	4.25×3.38	270	S-Nwprt; O-300
V-8, 383.0	4.25×3.38	315	S-300; O-Nwprt
V-8, 413.0	4.19×3.75	340	S-NY
V-8, 413.0	4.19×3.75	360	S-300L; O-300, NY

1966

BC1-L Newport (wb124; wgns-121)		Wght	Price	Prod
23	htp cpe	3,920	3,112	37,622
27	conv cpe	4,020	3,476	3,085
41	sdn 4d, 4W	3,875	3,052	74,964
42	sdn 4d, 6W	3,910	3,183	9,432
43	htp sdn	4,010	3,190	24,966
45	wgn 4d, 6P	4,370	4,086	9,035
46	wgn 4d, 9P	4,550	4,192	8,567
BC2-M 300 (wb 124.0)				
23	htp cpe	3,940	3,583	24,103
27	conv cpe	4,015	3,936	2,500
41	sdn 4d	3,895	3,523	2,353
43	htp sdn	4,000	3,659	20,642
BC3-H New Yorker (wb 124.0)				
23	htp cpe	4,095	4,157	7,955
42	sdn 4d	4,100	4,101	13,025
43	htp sdn	4,140	4,233	26,599

1966 Engines	bore×stroke	bhp	availability
V-8, 383.0	4.25×3.38	270	S-Newport
V-8, 383.0	4.25×3.38	325	S-300; O-Nwprt
V-8, 440.0	4.32×3.75	350	S-NY

1967

CC1-E Newport (wb124; wgns-122)		Wght	Price	Prod
23	htp cpe	3,920	3,219	26,583
27	conv cpe	3,970	3,583	2,891
41	sdn 4d	3,955	3,159	48,945
43	htp sdn	3,980	3,296	14,247
45	wgn 4d, 6P	4,495	4,264	7,183
46	wgn 4d, 9P	4,550	4,369	7,520
CC1-L Newport Custom (wb 124.0)				
23	htp cpe	3,935	3,407	14,193
41	sdn 4d	3,975	3,347	23,101
43	htp sdn	3,995	3,485	12,728
CC2-M 300 (wb 124.0)				
23	htp cpe	4,070	3,936	11,556
27	conv cpe	4,105	4,289	1,594
43	htp sdn	4,135	4,012	8,744
CC3-H New Yorker (wb 124.0)				
23	htp cpe	4,170	4,264	6,885
41	sdn 4d	4,185	4,208	10,907
43	htp sdn	4,240	4,339	21,665

1967 Engines	bore×stroke	bhp	availability
V-8, 383.0	4.25×3.38	270	S-Newport
V-8, 383.0	4.25×3.38	325	O-Newport
V-8, 440.0	4.32×3.75	350	S-300, NY; O-wgns
V-8, 440.0	4.32×3.75	375	O-all exc wgns

1968

DC1-E Newport (wb124; wgns-122)		Wght	Price	Prod
CE23	htp cpe*	3,840	3,366	36,768
CE27	conv cpe*	3,910	3,704	2,847
CE41	sdn 4d	3,850	3,306	61,436
CE43	htp sdn	3,865	3,444	20,191
CE45	T & C wgn 4d, 6P	4,340	4,418	9,908
CE46	T & C wgn 4d, 9P	4,410	4,523	12,233
DC1-L Newport Custom (wb 124.0)				
CL23	htp cpe	3,890	3,552	10,341
CL41	sdn 4d	3,855	3,493	16,915
CL43	htp sdn	3,860	3,631	11,460
DC2-M 300 (wb 124.0)				
CM23	htp cpe	3,985	4,010	16,953
CM27	conv cpe	4,050	4,337	2,161
CM43	htp sdn	4,015	4,086	15,507
DC3-H New Yorker (wb 124.0)				
CH23	htp cpe	4,060	4,424	8,060
CH41	sdn 4d	4,055	4,367	13,092
CH43	htp sdn	4,090	4,500	26,991

*Sportsgrain models: htp cpe 965; conv cpe 175.

1968 Engines	bore×stroke	bhp	availability
V-8, 383.0	4.25×3.38	290	S-Nwprt, T&C
V-8, 383.0	4.25×3.38	330	O-Nwprt, T&C
V-8, 440.0	4.32×3.75	350	S-300,NY;O-T&C
V-8, 440.0	4.32×3.75	375	O-all exc T&C

1969

EC-E Newport (wb 124.0)*		Wght	Price	Prod
CE23	htp cpe	3,891	3,485	33,639
CE27	conv cpe	4,026	3,823	2,169
CE41	sdn 4d	3,941	3,414	55,083
CE43	htp sdn	4,156	3,549	20,608
EC-L Newport Custom (wb 124.0)				
CL23	htp cpe	3,891	3,652	10,955
CL41	sdn 4d	3,951	3,580	18,401
CL43	htp sdn	3,971	3,730	15,981
EC-P Town & Country (wb 122.0)				
CP45	wgn 4d, 6P	4,435	4,583	10,108
CP46	wgn 4d, 9P	4,485	4,669	14,408
EC-M 300 (wb 124.0)				
CM23	htp cpe	3,965	4,104	16,075
CM27	conv cpe	4,095	4,450	1,933
CM43	htp sdn	4,045	4,183	14,464
EC-H New Yorker (wb 124.0)				
CH23	htp cpe	4,070	4,539	7,537
CH41	sdn 4d	4,135	4,487	12,253
CH43	htp sdn	4,165	4,615	27,157

*Sportsgrain models:195.

1969 Engines	bore×stroke	bhp	availability
V-8, 383.0	4.24×3.38	290	S-Nwprt, T&C
V-8, 383.0	4.25×3.38	330	O-Nwprt, T&C
V-8, 440.0	4.32×3.75	350	S-300,NY;O-T&C
V-8, 440.0	4.32×3.75	375	O-all exc T&C

1970

FC-E Newport (wb 124.0)		Wght	Price	Prod
CE23	htp cpe*	4,030	3,589	21,664
CE27	conv cpe	4,085	3,925	1,124
CE41	sdn 4d	4,080	3,514	39,285
CE43	htp sdn*	4,110	3,652	16,940
FC-L Newport Custom (wb 124.0)				
CL23	htp cpe	4,035	3,781	6,639
CL41	sdn 4d	4,091	3,710	13,767
CL43	htp sdn	4,125	3,861	10,873
FC-P Town & Country (wb 122.0)				
CP45	wgn 4d, 6P	4,490	4,738	5,686
CP46	wgn 4d, 9P	4,555	4,824	9,583
FC-M 300 (wb 124.0)				
CM23	htp cpe*	4,135	4,234	10,084
CM27	conv cpe	4,175	4,580	1,077
CM43	htp sdn	4,220	4,313	9,846
FC-H New Yorker (wb 124.0)				
CH23	htp cpe	4,235	4,681	4,917
CH41	sdn 4d	4,310	4,630	9,389
CH43	htp sdn	4,335	4,761	19,903

*CE23 includes 1,868 Cordoba htp cpes; CE43 includes 1,873 Cordoba htp sdns; CM23 includes 501 300-H "Hurst" htp cpes.

1970 Engines	bore×stroke	bhp	availability
V-8, 383.0	4.25×3.38	290	S-Nwprt, T&C
V-8, 383.0	4.25×3.38	330	O-Nwprt, T&C
V-8, 440.0	4.32×3.75	350	S-NY, 300; O-T&C
V-8, 440.0	4.32×3.75	375	O-all exc T&C

1971

CE Newport (wb 124.0)		Wght	Price	Prod
23	Royal htp cpe	4,121	4,153	8,500
23	htp cpe	4,121	4,265	13,549
41	Royal sdn 4d	4,171	4,078	19,662
41	sdn 4d	4,171	4,190	24,834
43	Royal htp sdn	4,191	4,216	5,188
43	htp sdn	4,191	4,265	10,800
CP Town & Country (wb 122.0)				
45	wgn 4d 2S	4,525	4,951	5,697
46	wgn 4d 3S	4,580	5,037	10,993
CL Newport Custom (wb 124.0)				
23	htp cpe	4,126	4,391	5,527
41	sdn 4d	4,181	4,319	11,254
43	htp sdn	4,211	4,471	10,207
CS 300 (wb 124.0)				
23	htp cpe	4,246	4,608	7,256
43	htp sdn	4,321	4,687	6,683
CH New Yorker (wb 124.0)				
23	htp cpe	4,250	4,961	4,485
41	sdn 4d	4,335	4,910	9,850
43	htp sdn	4,355	5,041	20,633

1971 Engines	bore×stroke	bhp	availability
V-8, 360.0	4.00×3.58	255	S-CE
V-8, 383.0	4.25×3.38	275	S-CL, CP; O-CE Royal
V-8, 383.0	4.25×3.38	300	O-CL, CP, CE Royal
V-8, 440.0	4.32×3.75	335	S-CS, CH; O-all others
V-8, 440.0	4.32×3.75	370	O-all

1972

CL Newport Royal (wb 124.0)		Wght	Price	Prod
23	htp cpe	4,035	4,124	22,622
41	sdn 4d	4,095	4,051	47,437
43	htp sdn	4,100	4,186	15,185
CM Newport Custom (wb 124.0)				
23	htp cpe	4,130	4,357	10,326
41	sdn 4d	4,185	4,435	19,278
43	htp sdn	4,195	4,435	15,457
CP Town & Country (wb 122.0)				
45	wgn 4d 2S	4,610	5,055	6,473
46	wgn 4d 3S	4,665	5,139	14,116
CH New Yorker (wb 124.0)				
23	htp cpe	4,270	4,915	5,567
41	sdn 4d	4,335	4,865	7,296
43	htp sdn	4,365	4,993	10,013
CS New Yorker Brougham (wb 124.0)				
23	htp cpe	4,270	5,271	4,635
41	sdn 4d	4,335	5,222	5,971
43	htp sdn	4,365	5,350	20,328

1972 Engines	bore×stroke	bhp	availability
V-8, 360.0	4.00×3.58	175	S-CL
V-8, 400.0	4.34×3.38	190	S-CM, CP; O-CL
V-8, 440.0	4.32×3.75	225	S-CH, CS; O-all

1973

CL Newport (wb 124.0)		Wght	Price	Prod
23	htp cpe	4,160	4,254	27,456
41	sdn 4d	4,200	4,181	54,147
43	htp sdn	4,210	4,316	20,175
CM Newport Custom (wb 124.0)				
23	htp cpe	4,145	4,484	12,293
41	sdn 4d	4,200	4,419	20,092
43	htp sdn	4,225	4,567	20,050
CP Town & Country (wb 122.0)				
45	wgn 4d 2S	4,670	5,241	5,353
46	wgn 4d 3S	4,725	5,266	14,687
CH New Yorker (wb 124.0)				
41	sdn 4d	4,355	4,997	7,991
43	htp sdn	4,375	5,125	7,619
CS New Yorker Brougham (wb 124.0)				
23	htp cpe	4,335	5,413	9,190
41	sdn 4d	4,425	5,364	8,541
43	htp sdn	4,440	5,492	26,635

1973 Engines	bore×stroke	bhp	availability
V-8, 400.0	4.34×3.38	185	S-CL, CM
V-8, 440.0	4.32×3.75	215	S-CP, CH, CS; O-CL, CM

1974

CL Newport (wb 124.0)		Wght	Price	Prod
23	htp cpe	4,380	4,752	13,784
41	sdn 4d	4,430	4,677	26,944
43	htp sdn	4,440	4,816	8,968
CM Newport Custom (wb 124.0)				
23	htp cpe	4,430	5,105	7,206
41	sdn 4d	4,480	5,038	10,569
43	htp sdn	4,500	5,190	9,892
CP Town & Country (wb 124.0)				
45	wgn 4d 2S	4,915	5,767	2,236
46	wgn 4d 3S	4,970	5,896	5,958
CH New Yorker (wb 124.0)				
41	sdn 4d	4,560	5,554	3,072
43	htp sdn	4,595	5,686	3,066
CS New Yorker Brougham (wb 124.0)				
23	htp cpe	4,540	5,982	7,980
41	sdn 4d	4,640	5,931	4,533
43	htp sdn	4,655	6,063	13,165

1974 Engines	bore×stroke	bhp	availability
V-8, 400.0	4.34×3.38	185	S-CL, CM
V-8, 400.0	4.34×3.38	205	O-CL, CM
V-8, 440.0	4.32×3.75	230	S-CP, CH, CS; O-CL, CM
V-8, 440.0	4.32×3.75	275	O-CH, CS

1975

SS Cordoba (wb 115.0)		Wght	Price	Prod
22	cpe	3,975	5,072	150,105

CL Newport (wb 124.0)		Wght	Price	Prod
23	htp cpe	4,395	4,937	10,485
41	sdn 4d	4,440	4,854	24,339
43	htp sdn	4,475	5,008	6,846

CM Newport Custom (wb 124.0)		Wght	Price	Prod
23	htp cpe	4,450	5,329	5,831
41	sdn 4d	4,500	5,254	9,623
43	htp sdn	4,520	5,423	11,626

CP Town & Country (wb 124.0)		Wght	Price	Prod
45	wgn 4d 2S	5,015	6,099	1,891
46	wgn 4d 3S	5,050	6,244	4,764

CS New Yorker Brougham (wb 124.0)		Wght	Price	Prod
23	htp cpe	4,650	6,334	7,567
41	sdn 4d	4,630	6,277	5,698
43	htp sdn	4,690	6,424	12,774

1975 Engines	bore×stroke	bhp	availability
V-8, 318.0	3.91×3.31	150	O-SS
V-8, 360.0	4.00×3.58	180	S-SS; O-CL, CM
V-8, 360.0	4.00×3.58	190	O-CL, CM
V-8, 400.0	4.34×3.38	165	O-SS
V-8, 400.0	4.34×3.38	175	S-CL, CM, CS
V-8, 400.0	4.34×3.38	190	O-SS
V-8, 400.0	4.34×3.38	195	O-CL, CM, CS
V-8, 400.0	4.34×3.38	235	O-SS
V-8, 440.0	4.32×3.75	215	S-CP, CS; O-others
V-8, 440.0	4.32×3.75	260	O-CP

1976

SS Cordoba (wb 115.0)		Wght	Price	Prod
22	cpe	4,130	5,392	120,462

CL Newport (wb 124.0)		Wght	Price	Prod
23	htp cpe	4,455	5,076	6,109
41	sdn 4d	4,490	4,993	16,370
43	htp sdn	4,525	5,147	5,908

CM Newport Custom (wb 124.0)		Wght	Price	Prod
23	htp cpe	4,530	5,479	6,448
41	sdn 4d	4,565	5,407	11,587
43	htp sdn	4,585	5,576	9,893

CP Town & Country (wb 124.0)		Wght	Price	Prod
45	wgn 5d 2S	5,045	6,084	1,770
46	wgn 5d 3S	5,075	6,244	3,769

CS New Yorker Brougham (wb 124.0)		Wght	Price	Prod
23	htp cpe	4,865	6,641	11,510
43	htp sdn	4,950	6,737	28,327

1976 Engines	bore×stroke	bhp	availability
V-8, 318.0	3.91×3.31	150	O-SS
V-8, 360.0	4.00×3.58	170/175	O-SS, CL, CM
V-8, 400.0	4.34×3.38	175	S-SS, CL, CM; O-CS
V-8, 400.0	4.34×3.38	210	O-all
V-8, 400.0	4.34×3.38	240	O-SS
V-8, 440.0	4.32×3.75	205	S-CP, CS; O-CL, CM

1977

FH LeBaron (wb 112.7) - 54,851 blt		Wght	Price	Prod
22	cpe	3,510	5,066	—
41	sdn 4d	3,560	5,224	—

FP LeBaron Medallion (wb 112.7) Prod incl above.				
22	cpe	3,615	5,436	—
41	sdn 4d	3,675	5,594	—

SS Cordoba (wb 115.0) - 183,146 built				
SP22	cpe	—	5,368	—
SS22	cpe	4,045	5,418	—

CL Newport (wb 124.0)		Wght	Price	Prod
23	htp cpe	4,400	5,374	16,227
41	sdn 4d	4,455	5,280	39,424
43	htp sdn	4,485	5,433	20,738

CP Town & Country (wb 124.0)		Wght	Price	Prod
45	wgn 5d 2S	5,025	6,461	2,488
46	wgn 5d 3S	5,060	6,647	6,081

CS New Yorker Brougham (wb 124.0)		Wght	Price	Prod
23	htp cpe	4,685	7,090	19,732
43	htp sdn	4,770	7,215	56,610

1977 Engines	bore×stroke	bhp	availability
V-8, 318.0	3.91×3.31	135	O-Cordoba
V-8, 318.0	3.91×3.31	145	S-LeB; O-Cordoba
V-8, 360.0	4.00×3.58	155	O-Crdba, Nwpt
V-8, 360.0	4.00×3.58	170	O-Crdba
V-8, 400.0	4.34×3.38	190	S-Crdba, Nwpt; O-T&C, NY
V-8, 440.0	4.32×3.75	195	S-T&C, NY; O-Newport

1978

LeBaron (wb 112.7)		Wght	Price	Prod
FM22	"S" cpe I-6	3,335	4,894	—
FM22	"S" cpe V-8	3,415	5,080	—
FM41	"S" sdn 4d I-6	3,400	5,060	—
FM41	"S" sdn 4d V-8	3,485	5,246	—
FH22	cpe I-6	3,420	5,144	16,273
FH22	cpe V-8	3,505	5,330	
FH41	sdn 4d I-6	3,465	5,310	22,732
FH41	sdn 4d V-8	3,550	5,496	
FP22	Medallion cpe I-6	3,495	5,526	37,138
FP22	Medallion cpe V-8	3,580	5,712	
FP41	Medallion sdn 4d I-6	3,550	5,692	44,291
FP41	Medallion sdn 4d V-8	3,635	5,878	
FH45	T&C wgn 5d 2S I-6	3,600	5,724	22,256
FH45	T&C wgn 5d 2S V-8	3,685	5,910	

Cordoba (wb 114.9)		Wght	Price	Prod
SS22	cpe	4,020	5,811	124,825
SS22	S cpe	—	5,611	

Newport (wb 123.9)		Wght	Price	Prod
CL23	htp cpe	4,395	5,804	8,877
CL43	htp sdn	4,460	5,888	30,078

New Yorker Brougham (wb 123.9)		Wght	Price	Prod
CS23	htp cpe	4,620	7,702	11,469
CS43	htp sdn	4,670	7,831	33,090

1978 Engines	bore×stroke	bhp	availability
I-6, 225.0	3.40×4.12	90	O-LeBaron
I-6, 225.0	3.40×4.12	110	S-LeBaron
V-8, 318.0	3.91×3.31	140	S-LeBaron; O-Cordoba
V-8, 318.0	3.91×3.31	155	O-LeB, Crdba
V-8, 360.0	4.00×3.58	155	S-Crdba S; O-others
V-8, 360.0	4.00×3.58	170	O-all
V-8, 400.0	4.34×3.38	190	S-Cordoba, Newport, NY; O-Cordoba S
V-8, 440.0	4.32×3.75	185/195	O-Nwpt, NY

1979

LeBaron (wb 112.7)		Wght	Price	Prod
FM22	cpe I-6	3,270	5,381	10,987
FM22	cpe V-8	3,365	5,692	
FM41	sdn 4d I-6	3,330	5,479	14,297
FM41	sdn 4d V-8	3,425	5,790	
FH22	Salon cpe I-6	3,285	5,623	17,637
FH22	Salon cpe V-8	3,385	5,934	
FH41	Salon sdn 4d I-6	3,350	5,851	18,843
FH41	Salon sdn 4d V-8	3,450	6,162	
FP22	Medallion cpe I-6	3,345	6,017	21,762
FP22	Medallion cpe V-8	3,440	6,328	
FP41	Medallion sdn 4d I-6	3,425	6,425	25,041
FP41	Medallion sdn 4d V-8	3,520	6,556	
FH45	T&C wgn 4d 2S I-6	3,585	6,331	19,932
FH45	T&C wgn 4d 2S V-8	3,675	6,642	

Cordoba (wb 114.9)		Wght	Price	Prod
SS22	cpe	3,680	6,337	88,015
SP22	"300" cpe	3,880	8,034	

Newport (wb 118.5)		Wght	Price	Prod
TH42	sdn 4d I-6	3,530	6,405	78,296
TH42	sdn 4d V-8	3,605	6,720	

New Yorker (wb 118.5)		Wght	Price	Prod
TP42	sdn 4d	3,800	10,026	54,640

1979 Engines	bore×stroke	bhp	availability
I-6, 225.0	3.40×4.12	100	S-LeBaron
I-6, 225.0	3.40×4.12	110	S-Nwpt; O-LeB
V-8, 318.0	3.91×3.31	135	S-LeB, Cordoba, Newport; O-New Yorker
V-8, 360.0	4.00×3.58	150	S-NY; O-others
V-8, 360.0	4.00×3.58	195	S-"300"; O-others

1980

LeBaron (wb 112.7; cpe 108.7)		Wght	Price	Prod
FL41	Special sdn 4d I-6	3,260	5,995	—
FM22	cpe I-6	3,220	6,362	8,181
FM22	cpe V-8	3,300	6,457	
FM41	sdn 4d I-6	3,300	6,518	8,470
FM41	sdn 4d V-8	3,385	6,613	
FM45	wgn 4d 2S I-6	3,455	6,723	1,887
FM45	wgn 4d 2S V-8	3,535	6,818	
FH22	Salon cpe I-6	3,230	6,643	18,538
FH22	Salon cpe V-8	3,310	6,738	
FH41	Salon sdn 4d I-6	3,325	6,764	10,762
FH41	Salon sdn 4d V-8	3,405	6,859	
FP22	Medallion cpe I-6	3,285	7,185	10,448
FP22	Medallion cpe V-8	3,360	7,280	
FP41	Medallion sdn 4d I-6	3,400	7,329	13,079
FP41	Medallion sdn 4d V-8	3,485	7,424	
FH45	T&C wgn 5d 2S I-6	3,525	7,324	11,100
FH45	T&C wgn 5d 2S V-8	3,610	7,419	

Cordoba (wb 112.7)		Wght	Price	Prod
SH22	cpe I-6	3,270	6,978	31,238
SH22	cpe V-8	3,355	7,073	
SP22	Crown cpe I-6	3,320	7,428	22,233
SP22	Crown cpe V-8	3,400	7,523	
SS22	LS cpe I-6	3,270	6,745	
SS22	LS cpe V-8	3,365	6,840	
SP22	"300" cpe V-8	—	—	

Newport (wb 118.5)		Wght	Price	Prod
TH42	sdn 4d I-6	3,545	7,247	15,061
TH42	sdn 4d V-8	3,630	7,343	

New Yorker (wb 118.5)		Wght	Price	Prod
TP42	sdn 4d	3,810	10,872	13,513

1980 Engines	bore×stroke	bhp	availability
I-6, 225.0	3.40×4.12	90	S-all sixes
V-8, 318.0	3.91×3.31	120	S-all V-8s exc "300"
V-8, 360.0	4.00×3.58	130	O-Nwpt, NY
V-8, 360.0	4.00×3.58	185	S-Crdba "300"

Note: Chrysler production through 1980 includes export models, which makes figures in this book somewhat higher than those quoted elsewhere.

1981

LeBaron (wb 112.7; cpe-108.7)		Wght	Price	Prod
FL45	Special cpe I-6	—	6,672	11,890
FL45	Special cpe V-8	—	6,734	
FL41	Special sdn 4d I-6	3,275	6,495	
FL41	Special sdn 4d V-8	—	6,557	
FM45	sdn 4d I-6	3,470	7,346	2,136
FH22	Salon cpe I-6	3,200	7,263	17,485
FH22	Salon cpe V-8	3,325	7,325	
FH41	Salon sdn 4d I-6	3,305	7,413	
FH41	Salon sdn 4d V-8	3,430	7,475	
FP22	Medallion cpe I-6	3,255	7,768	7,635
FP22	Medallion cpe V-8	3,380	7,830	
FP41	Medallion sdn I-6	3,365	7,917	
FP41	Medallion sdn V-8	3,490	7,979	
FH45	T&C wgn 5d 2S I-6	3,545	8,008	3,987
FH45	T&C wgn 5d 2S V-8	3,665	8,070	

Cordoba (wb 112.7)		Wght	Price	Prod
SP22	cpe I-6	3,355	7,969	12,978
SP22	cpe V-8	3,495	8,033	
SS22	LS cpe I-6	3,300	7,199	7,315
SS22	LS cpe V-8	3,420	7,263	

Newport (wb 118.5)		Wght	Price	Prod
TH42	sdn 4d I-6	3,515	7,805	3,622
TH42	sdn 4d V-8	3,635	7,869	

New Yorker (wb 118.5)		Wght	Price	Prod
TP42	sdn 4d V-8	3,805	10,463	6,548

1981 Engines	bore×stroke	bhp	availability
I-6, 225.0	3.40×4.12	85	S-all sixes
V-8, 318.0	3.91×3.31	130	S-all V-8s
V-8, 318.0	3.91×3.31	165	O-Nwpt, NY

1982

LeBaron (wb 100.3)	Wght	Price	Prod
CH22 cpe	2,470	8,143	14,295
CH41 sdn 4d	2,455	8,237	19,619
CH27 conv cpe	2,485	11,698	3,045
CP22 Medallion cpe	2,475	8,408	12,856
CP41 Medallion sdn	2,465	8,502	22,915
CP27 Medallion conv cpe	2,660	13,998	9,780
CP45 T & C wgn 5d 2S	2,660	9,425	7,809
Cordoba (wb 112.7)			
SP22 cpe I-6	3,370	9,197	11,762
SP22 cpe V-8	3,520	9,267	
SS22 LS cpe I-6	3,315	8,258	3,136
SS22 LS cpe V-8	3,465	8,328	
New Yorker (wb 112.7)			
FS41 sdn 4d I-6	3,510	10,781	50,509
FS41 sdn 4d V-8	3,655	10,851	

1982 Engines	bore×stroke	bhp	availability
I-4, 135.0	3.44×3.62	84	S-LBrn, exc T&C
I-4, 156.0	3.59×3.86	92	S-LeB T&C; O-LeBaron
I-6, 225.0	3.40×4.12	90	S-Cordoba, NY sixes
V-8, 318.0	3.91×3.31	130	S-Cordoba, NY V-8s
V-8, 318.0	3.91×3.31	165	S-CA. Cordoba, NY V-8

1983

LeBaron (wb 100.3)	Wght	Price	Prod
CP22 cpe	2,464	8,514	18,331
CP41 sdn 4d	2,531	8,790	30,869
CP27 conv cpe	2,532	12,800	9,891
CP27 MC conv cpe	—	14,595	
CP27 MC T&C conv cpe	—	15,595	
CP45 T & C wgn 5d 2S	2,656	9,731	10,994
E Class (wb 103.3)			
TH41 sdn 4d	2,583	9,341	39,258
New Yorker (wb 103.3)			
TP41 sdn 4d	2,580	10,950	33,832
Cordoba (wb 112.7)			
SP22 cpe I-6	3,467	9,580	13,471
SP22 cpe V-8	3,605	9,805	
New Yorker Fifth Avenue (wb 112.7)			
FS41 sdn 4d I-6	3,631	12,487	83,501
FS41 sdn 4d V-8	3,781	12,712	
Executive (wb 124.0; limo 131.0)			
CP48 sdn 4d	—	18,900	—
CP49 limo 4d	—	21,900	—

1983 Engines	bore×stroke	bhp	availability
I-4, 135.0	3.44×3.62	94	S-LeB, E Cl, NY
I-4, 156.0	3.59×3.86	93	O-LeB, E Cl, NY
I-6, 225.0	3.40×4.12	90	S-Cordoba, Fifth Ave six
V-8, 318.0	3.91×3.31	130	S-Cordoba, Fifth Ave V-8

1984

Laser (wb 97.0)	Wght	Price	Prod
GCH24 htchbk cpe 3d	2,525	8,648	33,976
GCP24 XE htchbk cpe 3d	2,545	10,546	25,882
LeBaron (wb 100.3)			
KCP22 cpe	2,445	8,783	24,963
KCP41 sdn 4d	2,495	9,067	47,664
KCP27 conv cpe	2,530	11,595	6,828
KCP27 MC conv cpe	—	15,495	8,275
KCP27 MC T&C conv cpe	—	16,495	1,105
KCP45 T & C wgn 5d 2S	2,665	9,856	11,578
E Class (wb 103.3)			
ETH41 sdn 4d	2,530	9,565	32,237
New Yorker (wb 103.3)			
ETP41 sdn 4d	2,675	12,179	60,501
Fifth Avenue (wb 112.7)			
MFS41 sdn 4d	3,660	13,990	79,441
Executive (wb 124.0; limo 131.0)			
KCP48 sdn 4d	2,945	18,975	196
KCP49 limo 4d	—	21,975	594

1984 Engines	bore×stroke	bhp	availability
I-4, 135.0	3.44×3.62	99	S-Laser, LeB, E Class, NY
I-4T, 135.0	3.44×3.62	142	O-Laser, LeB, E Class, NY
I-4, 156.0	3.59×3.86	101	S-Exec; O-LeB, E Class, NY
V-8, 318.0	3.91×3.31	130	S-Fifth Ave

1985

Laser (wb 97.0)	Wght	Price	Prod
GCH24 htchbk cpe 3d	2,613	8,854	32,673
GCP24 XE htchbk cpe 3d	2,665	10,776	18,193
LeBaron (wb 100.3)			
KCP22 cpe	2,533	9,460	24,970
KCP41 sdn 4d	2,559	9,309	43,659
KCP27 conv cpe	2,616	11,889	9,196
KCP27 MC conv cpe	—	15,994	6,684
KCP27 MC T&C conv cpe	—	16,994	595
KCP45 T & C wgn 5d 2S	2,721	10,363	7,711
LeBaron GTS (wb 103.1)			
HCH44 spt sdn 5d	2,660	9,024	33,176
HCP44 LS spt sdn 5d	2,706	9,970	27,607
New Yorker (wb 103.3)			
ETP41 sdn 4d	2,583	12,865	60,700
Fifth Avenue (wb 112.7)			
MFS41 sdn 4d	3,741	13,978	109,971
Limousine (wb 131.3)			
KCP49 limo 4d	3,206	26,318	759

1985 Engines	bore×stroke	bhp	availability
I-4, 135.0	3.44×3.62	99	S-Lsr, LeB, GTS
I-4T, 135.0	3.44×3.62	146	O-Lsr, LeB, GTS, NY
I-4, 156.0	3.59×3.86	101	S-NY, Limo; O-LeB
V-8, 318.0	3.91×3.31	140	S-Fifth Ave

1986

Laser (wb 97.0)	Wght	Price	Prod
GCH24 htchbk cpe 3d	2,547	9,364	21,123
GCP24 XE htchbk cpe 3d	2,599	11,501	8,560
GCP24/AGB XT htchbk cpe 3d	2,695	11,854	6,989
LeBaron (wb 100.3)			
KCP22 cpe	2,525	9,977	24,761
KCP41 sdn 4d	2,559	10,127	40,116
KCP27 conv cpe	2,625	12,695	12,578
KCP27 Mark Cross conv cpe	2,751	16,595	6,905
KCP27 MC T&C conv cpe	2,774	17,595	501
KCP45 T & C wgn 5d 2S	2,702	11,370	6,493
LeBaron GTS (wb 103.1)			
HCH44 spt sdn 5d	2,601	9,754	42,841
HCP44 Premium spt sdn 5d	2,647	11,437	30,716
New Yorker (wb 103.3)			
ETP41 sdn 4d	2,655	13,409	51,099
Fifth Avenue (wb 112.7)			
MFS41 sdn 4d	3,740	14,910	104,744
Limousine (wb 131.3)			
KCP49 limo 4d	3,206	27,495	138

1986 Engines	bore×stroke	bhp	availability
I-4, 135.0	3.44×3.62	97	S-Lsr, LeB,GTS
I-4T, 135.0	3.44×3.62	146	S-Limo; O-Lsr, LeB, GTS, NY
I-4, 153.0	3.44×4.09	100	S-Lsr XE, LeB T&C wgn, NY; O-Lsr, LeB,GTS
V-8, 318.0	3.91×3.31	140	S-Fifth Ave

1987

LeBaron (wb 100.3)	Wght	Price	Prod
JCH21 cpe	2,690	11,295	44,124
JCP21 Premium cpe	2,731	12,288	31,291
JCP27 conv cpe	2,786	13,974	8,025
KCP41 sdn 4d	2,582	10,707	54,678
KCP45 T & C wgn 5d 2S	2,759	12,019	5,880
LeBaron GTS (wb 103.1)			
HCH44 spt sdn 5d	2,641	9,774	23,772
HCP44 Premium spt sdn 5d	2,709	11,389	15,278
New Yorker (wb 103.3)			
ETP41 sdn 4d	2,757	14,193	68,279
Fifth Avenue (wb 112.7)			
MFS41 sdn 4d	3,741	15,422	70,579

1987 Engines	bore×stroke	bhp	availability
I-4, 135.0	3.44×3.62	97	S-LeB sdn, GTS
I-4T, 135.0	3.44×3.62	146	S-limo; O-LeB, GTS, NY
I-4, 153.0	3.44×4.09	100	S-LeB exc sdn, NY; O-GTS
V-8, 318.0	3.91×3.31	140	S-Fifth Ave

1988

LeBaron (wb 100.3)	Wght	Price	Prod
JCH21 cpe	2,769	11,473	38,733
JCP21 Premium cpe	2,875	13,830	9,938
JCH27 conv cpe	2,860	13,959	23,150
JCP27 Premium conv cpe	2,964	18,079	15,037
KCP41 sdn 4d	2,559	11,286	24,452
KCP45 T & C wgn 5d 2S	2,702	12,889	2,136
LeBaron GTS (wb 103.1)			
HCH44 spt sdn 5d	2,641	10,798	9,607
HCP44 Premium spt sdn 5d	2,709	12,971	4,604
New Yorker Turbo (103.3)			
ETP41 sdn 4d	2,826	17,373	8,805
New Yorker (wb 104.3)			
CCH41 sdn 4d	3,214	17,416	23,568
CCS41 Landau sdn 4d	3,276	19,509	47,400
Fifth Avenue (wb 112.7)			
MFS41 sdn 4d	3,759	17,243	43,486

1988 Engines	bore×stroke	bhp	availability
I-4, 135.0	3.44×3.62	97	S-LeB sdn, GTS
I-4T, 135.0	3.44×3.62	146	S-NY Turbo; O-LeB,GTS
I-4, 153.0	3.44×4.09	100	S-LeB exc sdn
I-4, 153.0	3.44×4.09	96	S-GTS Prem; O-GTS
V-6, 181.4	3.59×2.99	136	S-NY
V-8, 318.0	3.91×3.31	140	S-Fifth Ave

1989

LeBaron (wb 100.3) - 99,633 blt	Wght	Price	Prod
JCH21 Highline cpe	2,810	11,495	—
JCP21 Premium cpe	2,945	14,695	—
JCH27 conv cpe	2,929	13,995	—
JCP27 Premium conv cpe	3,038	18,195	—
JCH21 GT cpe	—	14,795	—
JCH27 GT conv cpe	—	17,195	—
JCH21 GTC turbo cpe	—	17,435	—
JCH27 GTC turbo conv cpe	—	19,666	—
LeBaron Sedan (wb 103.1) - 6,549 built			
HCH44 htchbk spt sdn 5d	2,714	11,495	—
HCP44 Prem htchbk spt sdn 5d	2,827	13,495	—
HCX44 GTS trbo htchbk spt sdn 5d	2,926	17,095	—
New Yorker (wb 104.3)			
CCH41 sdn 4d	3,214	17,416	100,461
CCS41 Landau sdn 4d	3,276	19,509	
Fifth Avenue (wb 112.7)			
MFS41 sdn 4d	3,741	18,345	17,454

1989 Engines	bore×stroke	bhp	availability
I-4, 135.0	3.44×3.62	93	S-LeBaron sdn
I-4T 135.0	3.44×3.62	174	S-LeBaron GTC, GTS
I-4, 153.0	3.44×4.09	100	S-LeB cpe/conv, prem sdn; O-LeBaron Sdn
I-4T, 153.0	3.44×4.09	150	O-LeBaron GTC/GTS
V-6, 181.4	3.59×2.99	140	S-NY
V-8, 318.0	3.91×3.31	140	S-Fifth Ave

1990

LeBaron (wb 100.3) - 65,220 blt	Wght	Price	Prod
JCH21 Highline cpe	2,810	12,495	—
JCP21 Premium cpe	2,945	16,415	—
JCH27 conv cpe	2,929	14,995	—
JCP27 Premium conv cpe	3,038	19,595	—
JCH21 GT cpe	—	15,725	—
JCH27 GT conv cpe	—	17,799	—

LeBaron (wb 100.3)	Wght	Price	Prod
JCH21 GTC cpe	—	18,238	—
JCH27 GTC conv cpe	—	20,406	—
LeBaron Sedan (wb 103.3)			
sdn 4d	2,854	15,995	8,074
New Yorker (wb 104.3)			
CCH41 Salon sdn 4d	3,066	16,395	41,581
CCS41 Landau sdn 4d	3,276	18,795	
New Yorker Fifth Avenue (wb 109.3)			
sdn 4d	3,452	21,395	44,423
Imperial (wb 109.3)			
sdn 4d	3,570	24,995	14,968

1990 Engines	bore×stroke	bhp	availability
I-4T 135.0	3.44×3.62	174	S-LeBaron GTC
I-4, 153.0	3.44×4.09	100	S-LeB cpe/conv
I-4T, 153.0	3.44×4.09	150	O-LeB cpe/conv
V-6, 181.4	3.59×2.99	141	S-LeBaron Sdn, LeB Prem/GT cpe/conv
V-6, 201.5	3.66×3.19	147	S-Imp, NY, NY 5th Ave

1991

LeBaron (wb 100.3)		Wght	Price	Prod
JCH21	cpe 2d	2,853	12,995	
JCP21	LX cpe 2d	—	15,520	7,770
JCH21/GTC	GTC cpe 2d	—	15,595	
JCH27	conv cpe 2d	2,991	15,976	
JCP27	LX conv cpe 2d	—	19,226	31,979
JCH27/GTC	GTC conv cpe 2d	—	18,151	
LeBaron Sedan (wb 103.3)				
	sdn 4d	3,040	16,501	17,741
New Yorker Salon (wb 104.5)				
	sdn 4d	3,348	17,971	14,337
New Yorker Fifth Avenue (wb 109.3)				
	sdn 4d	3,452	20,875	40,892
Imperial (wb 109.3)				
	sdn 4d	3,570	26,978	10,146

1991 Engines	bore×stroke	bhp	availability
I-4, 153.0	3.44×4.09	100	S-LeB cpe/conv
I-4T, 153.0	3.44×4.09	152	O-LeB cpe/conv
V-6, 181.4	3.59×2.99	141	S-LeB Sedan; O-LeB cpe/conv
V-6, 201.5	3.66×3.19	147	S-NY Salon /Fifth Avenue
V-6, 230.5	3.78×3.42	150	S-Imp; O-NY /Fifth Avenue

1992

LeBaron (wb 100.5)		Wght	Price	Prod
JCH21	cpe 2d	2,863	13,488	
JCP21	LX cpe 2d	—	16,094	5,595
JCH21/GTP	GTC cpe 2d	—	16,164	
JCH27	conv cpe 2d	3,010	16,734	
JCP27	LX conv cpe 2d	—	20,130	40,239
JCH27/GTC	GTC conv cpe 2d	—	18,985	
LeBaron Sedan (wb 103.5) - 33,854 blt				
	sdn 4d	2,972	13,998	—
	LX sdn 4d	—	15,287	—
	Landau sdn 4d	—	15,710	—
New Yorker Salon (wb 104.5)				
	sdn 4d	3,346	18,849	17,231
New Yorker Fifth Avenue (wb 109.5)				
	sdn 4d	3,425	21,874	34,349
Imperial (wb 109.5)				
	sdn 4d	3,534	28,453	7,069

1992 Engines	bore×stroke	bhp	availability
I-4, 153.0	3.44×4.09	100	S-all LeBaron
I-4T, 153.0	3.44×4.09	152	O-LeB cpe/conv
V-6, 181.4	3.59×2.99	141	O-all LeBaron
V-6, 201.5	3.66×3.19	147	S-NY Salon /Fifth Avenue
V-6, 230.5	3.78×3.42	150	S-Imp; O-5th Ave

1993

LeBaron (wb 100.5 cpe, 100.6 conv)		Wght	Price	Prod
JCH21	cpe 2d	2,863	13,999	
JCP21	LX cpe 2d	—	16,676	6,460
JCH21/GTP	GTC cpe 2d	—	16,840	
JCH27	conv cpe 2d	3,010	17,399	
JCP27	LX conv cpe 2d	—	21,165	28,800
JCH27/GTP	GTC conv cpe 2d	—	19,815	
LeBaron Sedan (wb 103.5) - 29,454 built				
	LE sdn 4d	2,880	14,497	—
	Landau sdn 4d	2,906	17,119	—
New Yorker Salon (wb 104.5)				
	sdn 4d	3,273	18,705	22,323
New Yorker Fifth Avenue (wb 109.6)				
	sdn 4d	3,365	21,948	29,805
Imperial (wb 109.6)				
	sdn 4d	3,519	29,381	7,064
Concorde (wb 113.0)				
HLP41	sdn 4d	3,327	18,341	56,218

1993 Engines	bore×stroke	bhp	availability
I-4, 153.0	3.44×4.09	100	S-all LeBaron
V-6, 181.4	3.59×2.99	141	O-all LeBaron
V-6, 201.4	3.66×3.19	147	S-NY Saln/Fifth Ave
V-6, 201.5	3.66×3.19	153	S-Concorde
V-6, 214.7	3.78×3.19	214	O-Cncrde (ohc)
V-6, 230.5	3.78×3.42	150	S-Imp; O-NY Fifth Avenue

1994

LeBaron (wb 100.6)	Wght	Price	Prod
JCH27 GTC conv cpe 2d	3,122	16,999	37,844
LeBaron Sedan (wb 103.5) - 28,678 built			
LE sdn 4d	2,971	16,551	—
Landau sdn 4d	—	17,993	—
Concorde (wb 113.0)			
HLP41 sdn 4d	3,379	19,457	85,636
New Yorker/LHS (wb 113.0)			
HCH41 New Yorker sdn 4d	3,457	25,386	34,283
HCP41 LHS sdn 4d	3,483	30,283	49,335

1994 Engines	bore×stroke	bhp	availability
V-6, 181.4	3.59×2.99	141	S-LeBaron conv
V-6, 181.4	3.59×2.99	142	S-LeB Sedan
V-6, 201.5	3.66×3.19	161	S-Concorde
V-6, 214.7	3.78×3.19	214	S-NY, LHS; O-Cncrde (ohc)

1995

LeBaron (100.6 conv)	Wght	Price	Prod
JCH27 GTC conv cpe 2d	3,122	17,469	36,227
Sebring (wb 103.7) - 20,611 built			
JCS22 LX cpe 2d	2,816	15,434	—
JCP22 LXi cpe 2d	2,980	19,029	—
Cirrus (wb 108.0) - 79,275 built			
ACP41 LX sdn 4d	3,145	17,435	—
ACP41/K LXi sdn 4d	—	19,365	—
Concorde (wb 113.0)			
HLP41 sdn 4d	3,376	20,550	60,613
New Yorker/LHS (wb 113.0)			
HCH41 New Yorker sdn 4d	3,592	25,596	23,624
HCP41 LHS sdn 4d	3,628	29,595	32,002

1995 Engines	bore×stroke	bhp	availability
I-4, 121.8	3.44×3.27	140	S-Sebr (dohc)
V-6, 152.3	3.29×2.99	155	O-Sebring (ohc)
V-6, 152.3	3.29×2.99	164	S-Cirrus (ohc)
V-6, 181.4	3.59×2.99	141	S-LeBaron
V-6, 201.5	3.66×3.19	161	S-Concorde
V-6, 214.7	3.78×3.19	214	S-NY, LHS; O-Cncrde (ohc)

1996

Sebring (wb cpe 103.7, conv 106)	Wght	Price	Prod
JCS22 LX cpe 2d	2,908	16,441	32,527
JCP22 LXi cpe 2d	3,157	20,150	
XCH27 JX conv cpe 2d	3,340	19,490	47,809
XCP27 JXi conv cpe 2d	3,432	24,675	
Cirrus (wb 108.0)			
ACP41 LX sdn 4d	3,148	17,560	43,367
ACP41/K LXi sdn 4d	3,153	20,430	
Concorde (wb 113.0)			
HLP41 LX sdn 4d	3,492	19,445	49,994
HLP41 LXi sdn 4d	—	24,100	
New Yorker (wb 113.0)			
HCH41 sdn 4d	3,587	27,300	3,295
LHS (wb 113.0)			
HCP41 sdn 4d	3,596	30,255	34,900

1996 Engines	bore×stroke	bhp	availability
I-4, 121.8	3.44×3.27	140	S-Sebring cpe
I-4, 148.2	3.44×3.98	150	S-Cirs, Seb conv
V-6, 152.3	3.29×2.99	163	O-Sebring cpe
V-6, 152.3	3.29×2.99	168	O-Cirs, Seb conv
V-6, 201.5	3.66×3.19	161	S-Concorde
V-6, 214.7	3.78×3.19	214	S-NY, LHS; O-Concorde

1997

Sebring (wb cpe 103.7, conv 106)	Wght	Price	Prod
JCS22 LX cpe 2d	2,888	16,540	33,140
JCP22 LXi cpe 2d	3,197	21,020	
XCH27 JX conv cpe 2d	3,350	20,150	55,887
XCP27 JXi conv cpe 2d	3,365	24,660	
Cirrus (wb 108.0)			
ACP41 LX sdn 4d	3,099	18,030	27,913
ACP41/K LXi sdn 4d	—	20,365	
Concorde (wb 113.0)			
HLP41 LX sdn 4d	3,468	20,435	50,913
HLP41 LXi sdn 4d	—	24,665	
LHS (wb 113.0)			
HCP41 sdn 4d	3,625	30,255	36,525

1997 Engines	bore×stroke	bhp	availability
I-4, 121.8	3.44×3.27	140	S-Sebring cpe
I-4, 148.2	3.44×3.98	150	S-Cirrus, Sebring conv
V-6, 152.3	3.29×2.99	163	O-Sebring cpe
V-6, 152.3	3.29×2.99	168	O-Cirs, Seb conv
V-6, 214.7	3.78×3.19	214	S-LHS, Conc

1998

Sebring (wb cpe 103.7, conv 106)	Wght	Price	Prod
JCS22 LX cpe 2d	2,888	16,840	35,010
JCP22 LXi cpe 2d	3,197	20,775	
XCH27 JX conv cpe 2d	3,344	20,575	50,814
XCP27 JXi conv cpe 2d	3,406	25,840	
Cirrus (wb 108.0)			
ACP41 LXi sdn 4d	3,181	19,460	37,290
Concorde (wb 113.0)			
HLP41 LX sdn 4d	3,451	21,305	46,535
HLP41 LXi sdn 4d	3,531	24,220	

1998 Engines	bore×stroke	bhp	availability
I-4, 121.8	3.44×3.27	140	S-Sebring cpe
I-4, 148.2	3.44×3.98	150	S-Sebring conv
V-6, 152.3	3.29×2.99	163	O-Sebring cpe
V-6, 152.3	3.29×2.99	168	S-Cirrus; O-Seb conv
V-6, 167.0	3.38×3.09	200	S-Concorde
V-6, 197.0	3.62×3.19	225	O-Concorde

1999

Sebring (wb cpe 103.7, conv 106)	Wght	Price	Prod*
JCS22 LX cpe 2d	2,967	17,225	24,859
JCP22 LXi cpe 2d	3,203	21,325	
XCH27 JX conv cpe 2d	3,331	23,970	55,206
XCP27 JXi conv cpe 2d	3,382	26,285	
Cirrus (wb 108.0)			
ACP41 LXi sdn 4d	3,146	19,460	49,526
Concorde (wb 113.0) - 61,403 built			
HLP41 LX sdn 4d	3,446	21,510	—
HLP41 LXi sdn 4d	3,556	25,235	—
300M (wb 113.0)			
HYS41 sdn 4d	3,567	28,700	75,191
LHS (wb 113.0)			
HCP41 sdn 4d	3,689	28,700	27,720

* Calendar-year production

1999 Engines	bore×stroke	bhp	availability
I-4, 121.8	3.44×3.27	140	S-Sebring cpe
V-6, 152.3	3.29×2.99	163	O-Sebring cpe
V-6, 152.3	3.29×2.99	168	S-Cir, Seb conv
V-6, 167.0	3.38×3.09	200	S-Concorde
V-6, 197.0	3.62×3.19	225	O-Concorde
V-6, 215.0	3.78×3.19	253	S-300M, LHS

2000

Sebring (wb cpe 103.7, conv 106)		Wght	Price	Prod*
JCS22	LX cpe 2d	3,155	19,765	33,778
JCP22	LXi cpe 2d	3,203	22,100	
XCH27	JX conv cpe 2d	3,440	24,245	38,361
XCP27	JXi conv cpe 2d	3,444	26,560	
Cirrus (wb 108.0)				
ACH41	LX sdn 4d	2,911	16,230	40,241
ACP41	LXi sdn 4d	3,168	20,085	
Concorde (wb 113.0)				
HLP41	LX sdn 4d	3,452	22,145	72,352**
HLP41	LXi sdn 4d	3,532	26,385	
300M (wb 113.0)				
HYS41	sdn 4d	3,567	29,085	57,933
LHS (wb 113.0)				
HCP41	sdn 4d	3,564	28,240	—

2000 Engines	bore×stroke	bhp	availability
I-4, 121.8	3.44×3.27	140	S-Cirrus
V-6, 152.3	3.29×2.99	163	S-Sebring cpe
V-6, 152.3	3.29×2.99	168	S-Sebring conv; O-Cirrus
V-6, 167.0	3.38×3.09	200	S-Concorde
V-6, 197.0	3.62×3.19	225	O-Concorde
V-6, 215.0	3.78×3.19	253	S-300M, LHS

*Calendar-year production **Includes LHS

2001

Sebring (wb cpe 103.7, conv 106.0, sdn 108.0)		Wght	Price	Prod*
TCS22	LX cpe 2d	3,155	19,910	82,108
TCP22	LXi cpe 2d	3,204	21,475	
RCH41	LX sdn 4d	3,250	17,945	
RCP41	LXi sdn 4d	—	20,830	
RCH27	JX conv cpe 2d	3,489	24,370	50,587
RCP27	JXi conv cpe 2d	—	26,830	
RCS27	Limited conv cpe 2d	—	28,915	
Concorde (wb 113.0)				
HCH41	LX sdn 4d	3,449	22,510	72,352**
HCM41	LXi sdn 4d	3,548	26,755	
300M (wb 113.0)				
HYS41	sdn 4d	3,574	29,640	37,098
LHS (wb 113.0)				
HCP41	sdn 4d	3,557	28,680	—

2001 Engines	bore×stroke	bhp	availability
I-4, 143.4	3.41×3.94	142	S-Sebring cpe
I-4, 148.2	3.44×3.98	150	S-Sebring conv, Sebring sdn
V-6, 167.0	3.38×3.09	200	S-Concorde; O-Sebring sdn, Sebring conv
V-6, 181.4	3.59×2.99	200	O-Sebring cpe
V-6, 197.0	3.62×3.19	222	O-Concorde
V-6, 215.0	3.78×3.19	253	S-300M, LHS

*Calendar-year production **Includes LHS

2002

Sebring (wb cpe 103.7, conv 106.0, sdn 108.0)		Wght	Price	Prod*
TCS22	LX cpe 2d	3,099	20,020	10,284
TCP22	LXi cpe 2d	3,183	21,710	
RCH27	LX conv cpe 2d	3,394	23,075	50,020
RCP27	LXi conv cpe 2d	3,474	26,160	
RCX27	GTC conv cpe 2d	3,452	25,115	
RCS27	Limited conv cpe 2d	3,491	28,795	
RCH41	LX sdn 4d	3,201	17,705	84,803
RCP41	LXi sdn 4d	3,273	20,280	
Concorde (wb 113.0) - 40,522 built				
HCH41	LX sdn 4d	3,479	22,370	—
HCM41	LXi sdn 4d	3,548	24,975	—
HCP41	Limited sdn 4d	3,567	27,870	—
300M (wb 113.0) - 36,118 built				
HYS41	sdn 4d	3,581	28,340	—
HYX41	Special sdn 4d	3,650	31,940	—
Prowler (wb 113.3) - 329 built				
RCS27	conv cpe 2d	2,864	44,625	—

2002 Engines	bore×stroke	bhp	availability
I-4, 143.4	3.41×3.94	142	S-Sebring cpe
I-4, 148.2	3.44×3.98	150	S-Sebring conv, Sebring sdn
V-6, 167.0	3.38×3.09	200	S-Cncrd; O-Seb sdn, Seb conv
V-6, 181.4	3.59×2.99	200	O-Sebring cpe
V-6, 215.0	3.78×3.19	234	O-Concorde
V-6, 215.0	3.78×3.19	250	O-Concorde
V-6, 215.0	3.78×3.19	253	S-300M, Prwler

* Calendar-year production

2003

Sebring (wb cpe 103.7, conv 106.0, sdn 108.0)		Wght	Price	Prod*
STCS22	LX cpe 2d	2,973	22,460	9,332
STCP22	LXi cpe 2d	3,115	22,460	
JRCH27	LX conv 2d	3,303	23,775	46,158
JRCX27	GTC conv 2d	3,325	25,610	
JRCP27	LXi conv 2d	3,362	26,860	
JRCS27	Lmtd conv 2d	3,380	29,495	
JRCH41	LX sdn 4d	3,106	18,170	64,308
JRCP41	LXi sdn 4d	3,167	20,745	
Concorde (wb 113.0) - 29,303 built				
LHCH41	LX sdn 4d	3,365	22,940	—
LHCM41	LXi sdn 4d	3,392	25,670	—
LHCP41	Limited sdn 4d	3,459	28565	—
300M (wb 113.0) - 27,130 built				
LHYS41	sdn 4d	3,461	28,645	—
LHYX41	Spec sdn 4d	3,545	32,215	—

2003 Engines	bore×stroke	bhp	availability
I-4, 143.4	3.41×3.94	147	S-Sebring cpe
I-4, 148.2	3.44×3.98	150	S-Sebring conv, Sebring sdn
V-6, 167.0	3.38×3.09	200	S-Conc; O-Sebr sdn, Sebr conv
V-6, 181.4	3.59×2.99	200	O-Sebring cpe
V-6, 215.0	3.78×3.19	234	O-Concorde
V-6, 215.0	3.78×3.19	250	S-300M; O-Conc
V-6, 215.0	3.78×3.19	255	O-300M

* Calendar-year production

2004

Sebring (wb cpe 103.7, conv 106.0, sdn 108.0)		Wght	Price	Prod*
STCS22	LX cpe 2d	3,064	21,145	12,103
STCP22	Limited cpe 2d	3,206	23,420	
JRCH27	LX conv 2d	3,357	24,590	39,388
JRCX27	GTC conv 2d	3,391	26,190	
JRCP27	LXi conv 2d	3,419	27,515	
JRCS27	Lmtd conv 2d	3,448	30,325	
JRCH41	LX sdn 4d	3,181	18,640	77,269
JRCP41	LXi sdn 4d	3,273	21,215	
Concorde (wb 113.0)**				
LHCH41	LX sdn 4d	3,495	23,480	—
LHCM41	LXi sdn 4d	3,566	26,210	—
LHCP41	Limited sdn 4d	3,574	29,105	—
300M (wb 113.0)**				
LHYS41	sdn 4d	3,591	29,185	—
LHYX41	Spec sdn 4d	3,650	32,615	—
Crossfire (wb 94.5)				
ZHCS29	htchbk cpe	3,061	33620	—

2004 Engines	bore×stroke	bhp	availability
I-4, 143.4	3.41×3.94	147	S-Sebring cpe
I-4, 148.2	3.44×3.98	150	S-Seb cnv, Seb sdn
V-6, 167.0	3.38×3.09	200	S-Conc; O-Sebr sdn, Sebr conv
V-6, 181.4	3.59×2.99	200	O-Sebring cpe
V-6, 195.2	3.54×3.31	215	S-Crossfire
V-6, 215.0	3.78×3.19	234	O-Concorde
V-6, 215.0	3.78×3.19	250	S-300M; O-Conc
V-6, 215.0	3.78×3.19	255	O-300M

* Calendar-year production ** Produced during 2003

2005

Sebring (wb cpe 103.7, conv 106.0, sdn 108.0)		Wght	Price	Prod*
STCS22	cpe 2d	3,064	22,145	345
STCP22	Lmtd cpe 2d	3,264	24,520	
JRCH27	conv 2d	3,276	25,410	34,439
JRCX27	GTC conv 2d	3,327	26,885	
JRCP27	Tour conv 2d	3,340	28,210	
JRCS27	Lmtd conv 2d	3,365	31,020	
JRCH41	sdn 4d	3,094	19,350	62,255
JRCP41	Touring sdn 4d	3,128	20,070	
JRCS41	Limited sdn 4d	3,164	22,360	
JRCM41	TSi sdn 4d	3,273	23,780	
300 (wb 120.0) - 142,504 blt		**Wght**	**Price**	**Prod**
LXCH48	sdn 4d	3,623	23,295	—
LXCP48	Tour sdn 4d	3,651	27,095	—
LXFP48	Tr AWD sdn 4d	3,934	29,370	—
LXCS48	300C sdn 4d	3,980	32,870	—
LXFS48	300C AWD sdn 4d	4,166	34,195	—
LXCX48	SRT-8 sdn 4d	4,043	39,370	—
Crossfire (wb 94.5) - 14,665 sold**				
ZHCP29	htchbk cpe	3,006	29,045	—
ZHCP27	conv 2d	3,040	34,085	—
ZHCS29	Lmtd htchbk cpe	3,006	33,745	—
ZHCS27	Lmtd conv 2d	3,095	38,045	—
ZHCX29	SRT-6 htchbk cpe	3,161	44,820	—
ZHCX27	SRT-6 conv 2d	3,250	49,120	—

2005 Engines	bore×stroke	bhp	availability
I-4, 143.4	3.41×3.94	142	S-Sebring cpe
I-4, 148.2	3.44×3.98	150	S-Sebr conv, Sebr sdn
V-6, 167.0	3.38×3.09	190	S-300
V-6, 167.0	3.38×3.09	200	O-Sebr sdn, Sebr conv
V-6, 181.4	3.59×2.99	198	O-Sebring cpe
V-6, 195.2	3.54×3.31	215	S-Crossfire
V-6S, 195.2	3.54×3.31	330	S-Cross SRT-6
V-6, 215.0	3.78×3.19	250	S-300 Touring
V-8, 345.0	3.92×3.58	340	S-300C
V-8, 370.0	4.06×3.58	425	S-300 SRT-8

* Calendar-year production ** Calendar-year sales

2006

Sebring (wb conv 106.0, sdn 108.0)		Wght	Price	Prod*
JRCH27	conv 2d	3,394	25,765	—
JRCX27	GTC conv 2d	3,452	27,240	—
JRCP27	Tour conv 2d	3,474	28,565	—
JRCS27	Lmtd conv 2d	3,491	31,375	—
JRCH41	sdn 4d	3,273	19,705	—
JRCP41	Tour sdn 4d	3,273	20,425	—
JRCS41	Lmtd sdn 4d	3,173	22,715	—
JRCM41	TSi sdn 4d	3,273	23,990	—
300 (wb 120.0)				
LXCH48	sdn 4d	3,712	23,525	—
LXCP48	Tour sdn 4d	3,758	27,525	—
LXFP48	Tr AWD sdn 4d	4,041	29,525	—
LXCS48	300C sdn 4d	4,046	33,425	—
LXFS48	300C AWD sdn 4d	4,251	34,750	—
LXCX48	SRT8 sdn 4d	4,046	39,920	—
Crossfire (wb 94.5)				
ZHCP29	htchbk cpe	3,061	—	—
ZHCP27	conv 2d	3,040	—	—
ZHCS29	Lmtd htchbk cpe	3,061	—	—
ZHCS27	Lmtd conv 2d	3,040	—	—
ZHCX29	SRT6 htchbk cpe	3,240	—	—
ZHCX27	SRT6 conv 2d	3,328	—	—

2006 Engines	bore×stroke	bhp	availability
I-4, 148.2	3.44×3.98	150	S-Sebr conv, Sebr sdn
V-6, 167.0	3.38×3.09	190	S-300
V-6, 167.0	3.38×3.09	200	O-Sebr sdn, Sebr conv
V-6, 181.4	3.59×2.99	198	O-Sebring cpe
V-6, 195.2	3.54×3.31	215	S-Crossfire
V-6S, 195.2	3.54×3.31	330	S-Cross SRT-6
V-6, 215.0	3.78×3.19	250	S-300 Touring
V-8, 345.0	3.92×3.58	340	S-300C
V-8, 370.0	4.06×3.58	425	S-300 SRT-8

* Production figures not available at time of publication

Continental

Officially, the Continental "Marks" of 1956-58 were not Lincolns but the products of a separate division created to establish Ford Motor Company at the very top of the market—even above Cadillac. Only one model was offered for 1956-57: the flawlessly styled, beautifully crafted Mark II, worth every penny of its stratospheric $10,000 price. Yet Ford lost about $1000 on every one, because this was primarily an "image" car—more ego trip than calculated profit-maker. Dearborn then attempted to put Continental in the black with a lower-priced 1958-60 line based on the giant "unibody" Lincoln of those years, but it never sold particularly well.

Dealers and customers had pleaded with Ford to revive the Lincoln Continental since the last of the original line in 1948. But there was no money until 1953, when profits were looking up and Dearborn managers, determined to outflank arch-rival General Motors in every market sector, approved a development program to create a new Continental in the contemporary idiom.

This came under the auspices of a new Special Products Division headed by William Clay Ford, the younger brother of company president Henry Ford II. After calling in five outside consultants, management reviewed 13 different proposals and unanimously selected the one submitted by Special Products.

It was, nevertheless, an excellent choice. Harley F. Copp, Special Products' chief engineer, gave it a unique "cowbelly" chassis dipped low between the front and rear axles to permit high seating without a high roofline. The roomy cabin was starkly simple, but richly appointed in a choice of three cloths (including fine broadcloth) or Scottish "Bridge of Weir" leather. The dash echoed locomotive and aircraft motifs with full, brushed-finished instrumentation and large toggle-type switches.

Chosen power was the 368-cubic-inch V-8 destined for the all-new '56 Lincolns, with the same 285 horsepower. However, Mark II units were specially selected and individually adjusted before installation. The same applied to the transmission, Lincoln's three-speed Turbo-Drive automatic, also new for '56, and the 3.07:1 rear axle.

Actually, great pains were taken throughout the assembly process, as Mark IIs were built in a special "go-slow" plant. Bodies, for instance, were first trial-fitted to chassis, then painted, sanded, and polished by hand. Chrome plating exceeded industry standards. Nuts and bolts were torqued by people, not machines. Finally, each car was given a 12-mile preshipment road test, followed by a detailed inspection and correction of any defects.

Appearing on a 126-inch wheelbase, the sleek and timeless Mark II measured 218.5 inches overall and weighed over 4800 pounds. It came only as a hardtop coupe, though the original plan was for a retractable hardtop-convertible (an idea quickly evolved by Ford Division into the 1957-59 Skyliner). The price may have been breathtaking, but it reflected the unusual amount of hand labor and high luxury content. Indeed, air conditioning was the sole option ($740).

The Mark II bowed to thunderous applause from both sides of the Atlantic, and was immediately hailed as a design landmark. But the euphoria didn't last. The Mark II made little impression on the ultra-luxury market. Production came to approximately 2500 of the '56s and a mere 444 of the near-identical '57s. With that, Ford canceled not only the Mark II, but also

1956 Mark II hardtop coupe

1958 Mark III convertible coupe

a beautiful four-door sedan and a convertible that were planned as 1958 "line extensions" (though not before a couple of prototype convertibles were built in 1957).

Years later, one Ford executive declared the Mark II was, on balance, a big mistake. "What we had going for us . . . was literally a revival of the Duesenberg concept. What we ended up with was something much less—and even that didn't last long. It was a project that for a time broke Bill Ford's heart, and I guess you could say that in many ways it broke ours, too."

In line with an upper-management decision, price was cut drastically for 1958's "new" Continental, the Mark III. The result of recommendations from a Mercury cost analyst, this square-rigged Lincoln-based leviathan had a 131-inch wheelbase, elongated fenders, large chrome appliques, canted quad headlamps, a reverse-slant roofline, and a huge new 430-cid V-8 with 375 horsepower. Convertible, four-door sedan, hardtop coupe, and Landau hardtop sedan were offered in the $5800-$6200 range. Closed models sported a rear window that dropped down electrically for flow-through interior ventilation. Standard luxuries abounded once more, but not hand craftsmanship. The Mark III was "built to a price," and those reduced prices increased sales to 12,550 cars—respectable for that difficult, recessionary model year.

But the luxury market had shriveled badly, so Ford canceled Continental as a separate marque after 1958, though a little-changed Mark III returned in the Lincoln line as the 1959 Mark IV. Continental Division was folded into Lincoln-Mercury, which also absorbed the fast-faltering Edsel Division, thus ending Ford's dream of a GM-like five-division hierarchy.

A decade later came a new Mark III, so numbered to signal its "official" status as the Mark II's lineal successor. This was never anything but a Lincoln, however. Also unlike its forebear, it was an immediate sales success. (*See* Lincoln for the Continental story before and after 1956-58.)

1958 Mark III Landau hardtop sedan

Specifications

1956				
Mark II (wb 126.0)		**Wght**	**Price**	**Prod**
60A	htp cpe	4,825	9,695	2,556
1956 Engine	**bore×stroke**	**bhp**	**availability**	
V-8, 368.0	4.00×3.66	285	S-all	
1957				
Mark II (wb 126.0)		**Wght**	**Price**	**Prod**
60A	htp cpe	4,800	9,966	444
1957 Engine	**bore×stroke**	**bhp**	**availability**	
V-8, 368.0	4.00×3.66	300	S-all	
1958				
Mark III (wb 131.0)		**Wght**	**Price**	**Prod**
54A	sdn 4d	4,800	6,072	1,283
65A	htp cpe	4,865	5,825	2,328
68A	conv cpe	5,040	6,283	3,048
75A	Landau htp sdn	4,965	6,072	5,891
1958 Engine	**bore×stroke**	**bhp**	**availability**	
V-8, 430.0	4.30×3.70	375	S-all	

Cord

It's been said that one can avoid criticism only by saying nothing, doing nothing, and being nothing. Errett Lobban Cord avoided those pitfalls and was criticized a lot. He jumped from car salesman in 1924, to president and chief stockholder of Auburn in 1926. At age 31, he was the youngest president of an American automaker. By the early '30s he'd also acquired Duesenberg and many other enterprises. His method was only too clear: dump large amounts of common stock until its value was so low that he could buy controlling shares for a song. Cord's empire included aviation, shipping, taxicabs, among other interests. While distracted by these other ventures, Cord's auto companies suffered. Heavy losses forced Cord to sell his holdings in 1937. Auto production was the first to be shut down by the new owners. Some enthusiasts have never really forgiven him for that.

During 10 years of wheeler-dealer success, E.L. Cord was behind some of the most-magnificent cars ever built. In 1928, he ushered in the beautiful Auburn Speedster. The following year introduced the mighty Duesenberg Model J and the Cord L-29. The last proved less than hoped for, but it led to the 1936-37 Cord 810/812, one of the most-memorable and influential cars of all time.

The unbridled optimism of the late '20s prompted many new models and a few new makes to fill specific market niches. E.L. Cord decided to fill the price gap between his eight-cylinder Auburns and exotic Duesenbergs with a rakish new car bearing his own name and the then-novel feature of front-wheel drive.

The resulting L-29 was chiefly engineered by race-car builder Harry Miller and one Cornelius Van Ranst, both avid proponents of "horse-pulls-cart." Its powerplant began as the 298.6-cubic-inch Auburn straight eight, but ended up quite different. For the Cord's front drive it had to be mounted backward so that clutch and transmission could face forward. The cylinder head was altered to put the water outlet up front, and the crankcase was modified for a rear engine mount. According to one Cord authority, the L-29 engine had over 70 unique parts. Advertised at 125 horsepower, its actual output was 115 until 1932 when a larger bore increased horsepower to a truthful 125.

Sending its power to the front wheels was a three-speed sliding-pinion gearbox mounted behind the differential as on a Miller-designed 1927 Indianapolis racer. Front brakes were mounted inboard, against the differential instead of on the wheels. This reduced unsprung weight for improved ride and handling. Quarter-elliptic leaf springs appeared fore, semielliptics aft, Houdaille-Hershey shock absorbers all around. Driveshafts employed premium Cardan constant-velocity universal joints.

This layout was not without problems. The main one was excessive drivetrain length that dictated a tremendous 137.5-inch wheelbase, yet put more than half of the car's weight over the rear wheels—where it did nothing for traction on hills, icy roads, or gravel surfaces. Worse, the U-joints couldn't stand braking, plus the pounding of wheels that drove as well as steered, and they wore out with merciless frequency. Though these problems could have been licked with time, Cord was adamant that the car debut before 1930 (which it did, though only by six months).

But, oh, what that layout did for looks. The super-long front allowed Auburn chief designer Al Leamy (with help from body engineer John Oswald) to craft a flowing hood/fenders ensemble that only accented that impressive length and the lowness conferred by front-wheel drive. Capping the front end was a sheetmetal grille completely enclosing the radiator—an industry first. In all, the L-29 looked sensational in its four "factory" body types: sedan, brougham, phaeton, and cabriolet, all supplied by subsidiary Cord companies. Numerous celebrities bought L-29s, and coachbuilders at home and abroad created stunning custom bodies. Standard models were fairly priced in the $3100-$3300 range, so the L-29 should have been a success.

It wasn't. Even without the poor traction and U-joint woes, front drive was an unproven commodity and thus a tough sell in the conservative $3000 market. And late 1929 was hardly the best time to launch any car, what with Wall Street types launching themselves out of windows. Furthermore, compared to contemporary Packards, Lincolns, and Cadillacs, the L-29 was a slug. Its 0-60 time was around 25 seconds, top speed barely 75 mph. One writer euphemistically termed this "pleasant tepidity," and it was almost excusable given the brilliant styling.

But there was no way the L-29 could make money. It thus limped along through 1932 with virtually no changes. Total production came to 5010. By 1935, one used-car guide listed the cash value of the L-29 convertible at just $145. Although a failure in its time, the L-29 has since been widely appreciated—including certification as a Classic by the Classic Car Club of America.

After three years in limbo, the Cord name returned in 1936 on

1930 L-29 convertible sedan

1930 L-29 Cabriolet 2/4 passenger

1936 810 Cabriolet

a dashing and predictive new car, the 810. This model retained front-wheel drive, but with a big difference. Where the L-29 had a long straight eight behind the transmission and mounted both far behind the front axle, the 810 used a V-8 that was half as long and could thus sit just aft of the axle; its differential/clutch assembly extended forward to the transmission, which was located slightly ahead of the axle. The results were much better weight distribution and traction than in the L-29, abetted by a trimmer 125-inch wheelbase.

Advanced features abounded in the 810. Front suspension, for instance, comprised independent trailing arms joined by a single transverse leaf spring. The transmission had four forward ratios instead of the usual three, plus Bendix "Electric Hand" preselector. With this, you first chose the desired gear via a switchlike lever on an extension of the steering column, then shifted by stabbing the clutch.

The 810 V-8 was a 288.6-cid unit made by Lycoming, another of Cord's companies. This packed 125 horsepower, which was good, but an available Schwitzer-Cummins centrifugal supercharger (similar to late Auburns) swelled that to an eye-opening 170. The total was soon 190 via a higher-boost blower. Standard 810s would reach 90 mph and run 0-60 in 20 seconds. The supercharged version would do 110 mph and hit 60 in 11-13 seconds—one of the fastest production cars in prewar America.

But performance seems almost secondary next to 810 styling, the work of Gordon Buehrig, assisted by Dale Cosper, Dick Robertson, and Paul Laurenzen. Initially conceived for a stillborn "baby Duesenberg," it was unforgettable: smoothly formed "coffin-nose" hood, striking wraparound horizontal louvers instead of a radiator, minimal trim, pontoon fenders, and, on blown models, racy exposed exhaust pipes. Concealed headlamps flipped up when needed (via manual cranks)—another industry first. Equally futuristic for the time were a unit-body construction, front-opening hood, separate license-plate light, full wheel covers, and concealed gas cap. Inside were a turned-metal dash awash in needle gauges and a ceiling-mounted radio speaker (sedans). Amazingly, Buehrig cobbled up many appearance items from proprietary bits and pieces, including some Auburn leftovers.

Like the L-29, the 810 bowed with four models: Westchester and Beverly sedans (upholstery patterns were the main difference) and two-seat Cabriolet and four-passenger Phaeton convertibles. Prices, however, were much lower: as little as $2000. Prices were hiked some $500 for 1937's little-changed 812 line, which added two long sedans on a 132-inch wheelbase, the Custom Beverly and Custom Berline, priced at $2,960-$3,575.

Sadly, the 810/812 had even more problems than the L-29. This reflected the fast-fading fortunes of the Cord Corporation that dictated a shoestring budget, cost-cutting engineering in places, and too much hand labor for consistent or even good build quality. Not that any of this mattered in the end. E. L. Cord's empire collapsed in 1937, and the Cord automobile followed Auburn and Duesenberg down the road to oblivion.

Though the L-29 was long ignored by collectors, the 810/812 began appreciating in value almost immediately after production ended (at 1629/1278 units). As with Duesenberg Js and Auburn Speedsters, peerless styling would be a motivation for several postwar revival attempts and shoddy replicas, but none would have even the original's modest success.

1937 812 Supercharged Westchester four-door sedan

1937 812 Phaeton convertible

Specifications

1930 - 1,700 registered

L29 (wb 137.5)	Wght	Price	Prod
cabriolet 2-4P	4,300	3,295	—
sdn 4d 5P	4,530	3,095	—
phaeton sdn 5P	4,500	3,295	—
brougham 5P	4,500	3,095	—

1930 Engine	bore×stroke	bhp	availability
I-8, 298.6	3.25×4.50	125	S-all

1931 - 1,433 built

L29 (wb 137.5)	Wght	Price	Prod
cabriolet 2-4P	4,300	2,495	—
sdn 4d 5P	4,530	2,395	—
phaeton sdn 5P	4,500	2,595	—
brougham 5P	4,500	2,395	—

1931 Engine	bore×stroke	bhp	availability
I-8, 298.6	3.25×4.50	125	all

1932 - 335 registered*

L29 (wb 137.5)	Wght	Price	Prod
cabriolet 2-4P	4,300	2,495	—
sdn 4d 5P	4,560	2,395	—
phaeton sdn 5P	4,500	2,595	—
brougham 5P	4,560	2,395	—

1932 Engine	bore×stroke	bhp	availability
I-8, 322.0	3.38×4.50	125	all

*Total L29 production 5,010; began in 1929.

1936 - 1,629 built*

810 (wb 125.0)	Wght	Price	Prod
Westchester sdn 4d	3,715	1,995	—
Beverly sdn 4d	3,740	2,095	—
cabriolet	3,815	2,145	—
phaeton	3,864	2,195	—

1936 Engine	bore×stroke	bhp	availability
V-8, 288.6	3.50×3.75	125	S-all

1937

812 (wb 125.0; Custom-132.0)	Wght	Price	Prod
Westchester sdn 4d	3,715	2,445	590**
Beverly sdn 4d	3,800	2,545	
cabriolet	3,815	2,595	
phaeton	3,864	2,645	
Cstm Beverly sdn 4d	3,900	2,960	
Custom Berline	4,120	3,060	

*Estimated

812 Supercharged (wb 125.0; Custom-132.0)	Wght	Price	Prod
Westchester sdn 4d	3,765	2,860	688**
Beverly sdn 4d	3,850	2,960	
cabriolet	3,865	3,010	
phaeton	3,914	3,060	
Cstm Beverly sdn 4d	3,950	3,375	
Custom Berline	4,170	3,575	

1937 Engines	bore×stroke	bhp	availability
V-8, 288.6	3.50×3.75	125	S-812
V-8S, 288.6	3.50×3.75	170/190	S-Schgd 812

** Estimated

Crosley

Powel Crosley, Jr., built one crude small car while a teenager at the turn of the century, then became a radio and refrigerator magnate in the '20s and '30s. But cars remained his first love, and in 1939 he entered the auto business in a big way with a very small product. Dreaming of an American "volkswagen," he offered a tiny 80-inch-wheelbase two-cylinder job at the lowest price in the land: $325-$350. Measuring just 10 feet long and weighing less than half a ton, it garnered a modest 2017 sales for '39. To buy one, you visited a local hardware store or appliance shop—a novel but shortsighted marketing scheme. Crosley Motors built about 5000 cars by 1942, when the government halted civilian production for the duration of World War II.

There were just two Crosley models for 1939: a two-passenger convertible coupe and a four-passenger convertible sedan. Prices dropped as low as $299 for 1940, when offerings expanded to include standard and DeLuxe convertible sedans, a convertible coupe, a wood-body station wagon, a "covered wagon" with full canvas top, and several commercial types. Styling was little changed and very basic, dominated by low, freestanding fenders and a prominent hood bulged out ahead of small horizontal grilles in the front apron. Headlamps attached to the sides of the hood. Interiors were barren—just a central speedometer flanked by fuel and water gauges.

Crosley power through 1942 came from an air-cooled, two-main-bearing Waukesha twin producing 13½ horsepower from 38.9 cubic inches. Performance wasn't quite as bad as those figures imply, since gearing was ultralow. Top speed was about 50 miles an hour, though the factory recommended cruising at no more than 40. Crosley claimed up to 60 miles per gallon, though few owners likely exceeded 50 mpg.

Completing this bare-bones package were unsynchronized three-speed gearbox, cable-operated mechanical brakes, six-gallon fuel tank, sliding (instead of roll-down) door windows, a single hand-operated windshield wiper, and petite 4.25×12-inch tires on simple disc wheels. The customary universal joints were eliminated as a further cost-cutting measure, flexible rubber engine mounts supposedly making them unnecessary. But they were necessary, as owners found out. They also discovered that Crosley dealers were far better equipped to fix refrigerators than cars. With this, 1940 volume fell by more than three-fourths despite the expanded lineup.

To fix things up for '41, Crosley called in engineer Paul Klotsch, late of the Briggs Manufacturing Company. Klotsch redesigned the motor mounts, added U-joints to the driveshaft, revised the lubrication system, shortened the stroke, and increased main-bearing surface area—the last two to improve engine durability. The revised engine ended up at 35.3 cid and 12 horsepower, but it powered a greatly improved Crosley and sales went up—to 2289—despite higher prices ($339-$496). The cars were now sold through separate automobile dealers in addition to Crosley's appliance outlets. There were no technical changes for '42, but prices rose again (to $468-$582) and the "covered wagon" was dropped. Crosley built 1029 cars that war-shortened model year.

For a wartime U.S. Navy project, Crosley developed an overhead-cam four-cylinder engine with a block made of brazed copper and sheet steel. Called "CoBra," it was selected to power the first postwar Crosleys. This five-main-bearing unit had been fairly successful in a variety of wartime machinery from truck refrigerators to Mooney Mite airplanes, but was less than happy in a car. The copper-steel block was subject to electrolysis that developed holes in the cylinder bores, thus necessitating early rebuilds. Crosley soon rectified the fault by offering a cast-iron version—called CIBA, for Cast-Iron Block Assembly—of the same 44-cid size and 26.5 horsepower output. Significantly, used-car price guides of the day gave a higher trade-in value for cars with the cast-iron engine, including retrofitted 1946-48 models.

Production of the '46 Crosleys began in June of that year: initially a four-seat closed sedan, then a convertible, too. A wagon returned for '47, a delivery sedan for '48. All were two-door styles. Commercial bodies were also offered. Wheelbase was unchanged, but new styling literally made the cars more "grown up": 28 inches longer than prewar Crosleys. Prices were more than double what they'd been in '39, but the Crosley was

1939 convertible coupe

1939 convertible coupe

1946 Four two-door sedan

1947 convertible sedan

1947 pickup truck

still quite inexpensive. A '47 was yours for as little as $888.

For a time, things went well. Production totaled almost 5000 for '46, more than 19,000 for '47, and close to 29,000 for '48. Powel Crosley grandly predicted 80,000 a year in the near future, but his firm would never do so well again. New postwar designs from other independents and the Big Three, plus a nagging reputation for engine problems, caused '49 volume to tumble below 7500.

This was ironic, because the '49 was a much better Crosley. New styling made it look something like a scaled-down '49 Ford, with a smooth hood and integral front fenders bearing sealed-beam headlights. Sedans and convertibles also received remote-control door handles and turn indicators—positively

1948 Four two-door station wagon

1949 Series CD Four Hotshot roadster

civilized features for a Crosley. In addition, the firm fielded a surprising newcomer: a smart little "bugeye" roadster called Hotshot on an 85-inch wheelbase, priced at just $849.

Seeking to turn things around for 1950, Crosley offered wagon, convertible, and sedan in standard and Super trim, plus the doorless Hotshot and a slightly better-trimmed version called Super Sports, which had conventional doors. Crosley was still in a class by itself on price—$872-$984 that year—and for engineering. Disc brakes, for example, had arrived for 1949-50, a first for series production shared with Chrysler's 1950 Town & Country Newport. Unfortunately, hasty development caused the Crosley brakes to deteriorate quickly after exposure to road salt and grime, causing tremendous service headaches. Since the firm was still smarting from the woes of its unlamented sheetmetal engine, this new problem was the last thing dealers—or customers—needed. Conventional drum brakes were reinstituted for 1951.

Though the little roadsters failed to sell, they were tremendous class competitors in racing. Both could do up to 90 mph, and handling was excellent thanks to a crude but effective semielliptic- and coil-spring front suspension and quarter-elliptic-spring rear suspension. The Hotshot's greatest accomplishment was winning the Index of Performance at Sebring in 1951.

At the other extreme was Crosley's 1950 "FarmORoad," a bare-bones, Jeep-like utility vehicle on a minuscule 63-inch wheelbase. Base price was just $795, and available accessories let it do everything from towing a hay wagon to digging ditches.

But by now, buyers were unmoved by anything Crosley did, so the firm was forced to abandon vehicles in July 1952. It was ultimately acquired by General Tire and Rubber, which disposed of automotive operations after Powel Crosley spent some $3 million trying to save them.

▲ 1966 Chevrolet Corvair Monza convertible coupe

▼ 1956 Chevrolet Corvette convertible coupe

▲ 1967 Chevrolet Corvette Sting Ray coupe

▼ 1969 Chevrolet Corvette Stingray coupe

▲ 2006 Chevrolet Corvette Z06 coupe

▼ 1932 Chrysler Imperial CL convertible coupe

▲ 1947 Chrysler Town and Country four-door sedan

▼ 1956 Chrysler New Yorker St. Regis hardtop coupe

▲ 1971 Chrysler 300 hardtop sedan

▼ 2005 Chrysler 300C SRT8 four-door sedan

▲ 1956 Continental Mark II hardtop coupe

▼ 1931 Cord L-29 convertible sedan

▲ 1937 Cord 812 Supercharged Phaeton convertible coupe

▼ 1950 Crosley Hotshot roadster

▲ 1932 DeSoto SC Custom convertible coupe

▼ 1956 DeSoto Fireflite hardtop sedan

▲ 1934 Dodge convertible coupe

▼ 1948 Dodge Custom convertible coupe

▲ 1957 Dodge Custom Royal Lancer hardtop sedan

▼ 1968 Dodge Charger hardtop coupe

▲ 1970 Dodge Challenger R/T convertible coupe

▼ 1971 Dodge Charger R/T hardtop coupe

▲ 2003 Dodge Viper RT/10 convertible coupe

▼ 1930 Duesenberg J convertible coupe

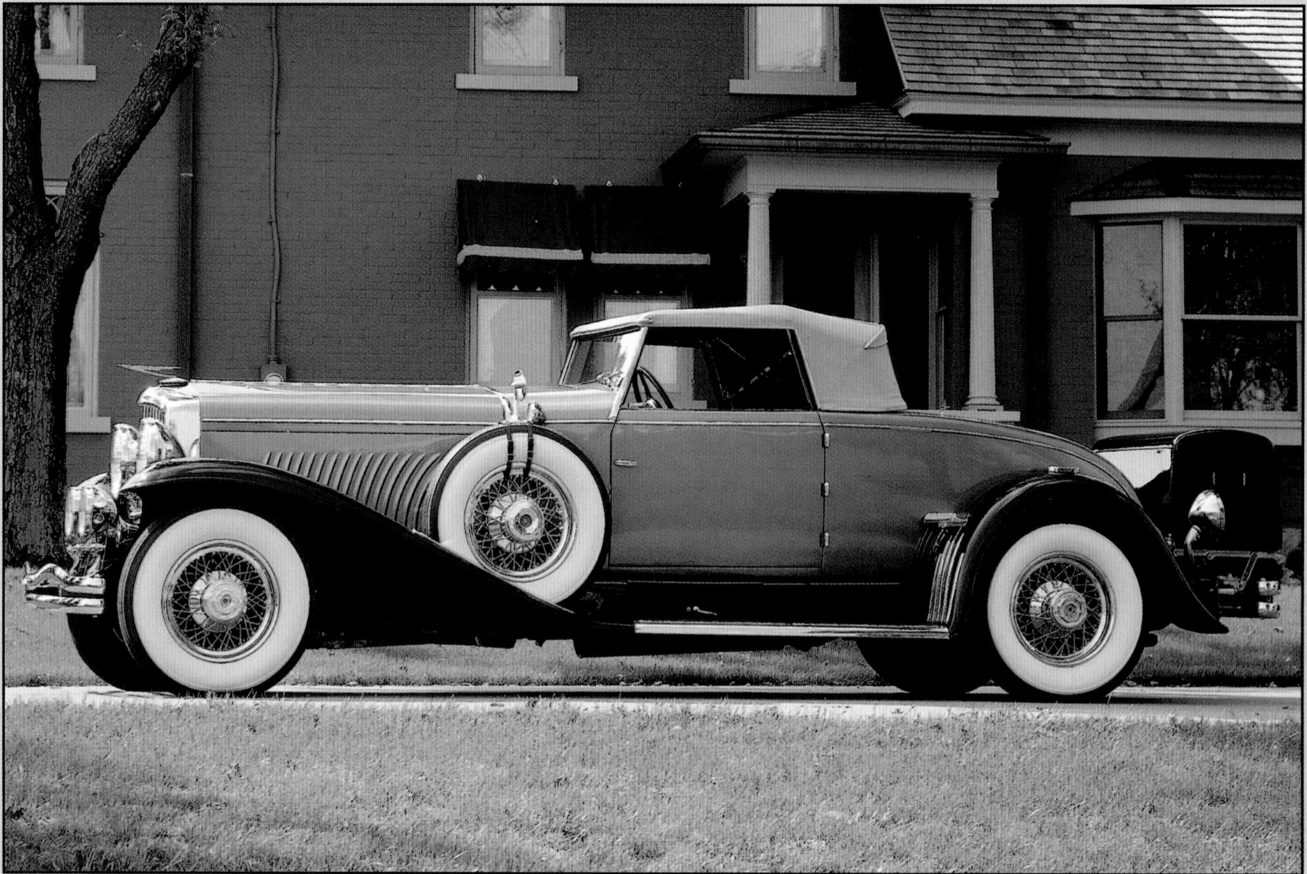

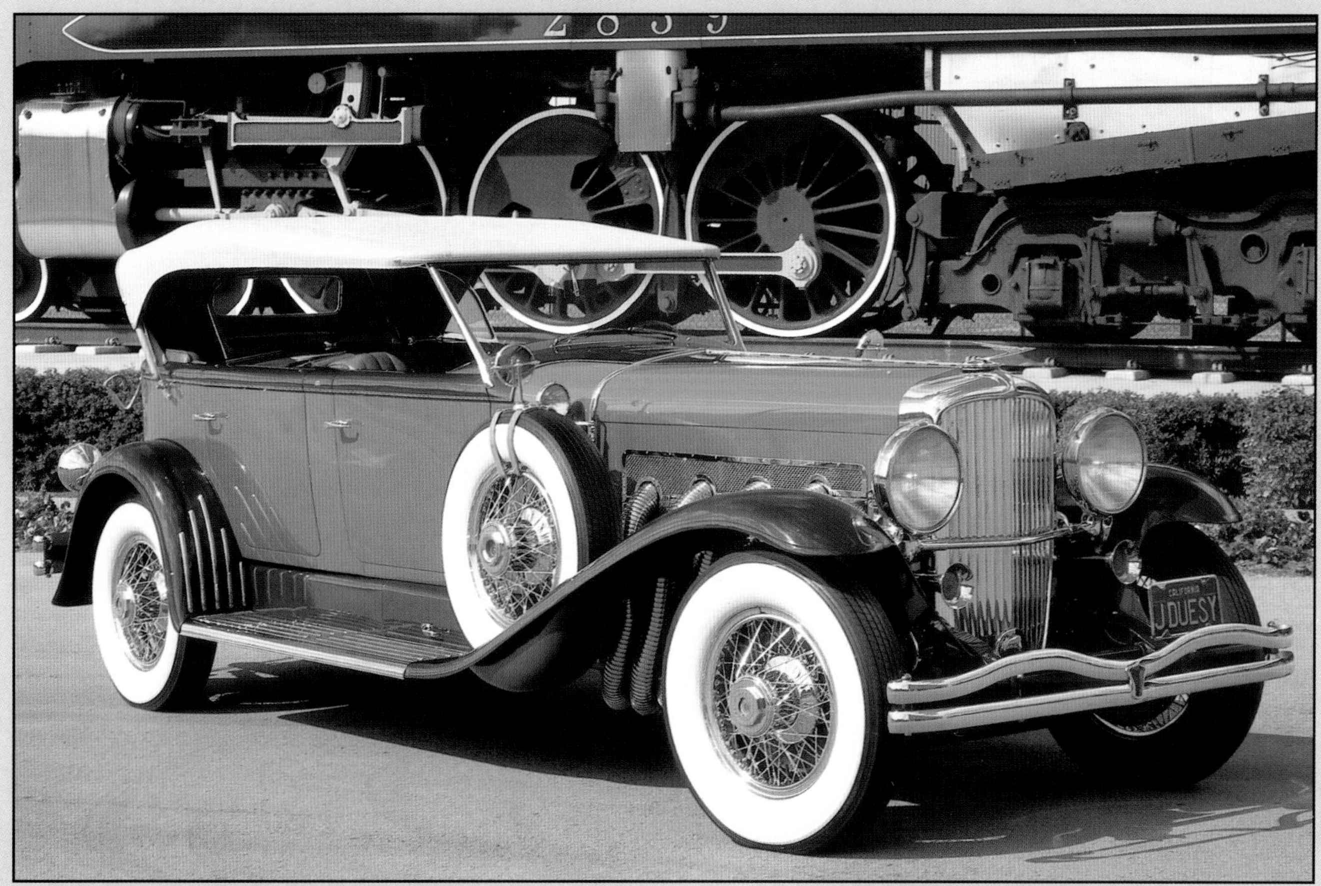

▲ 1934 Duesenberg J dual-cowl phaeton

▼ 1935 Duesenberg SJ short-wheelbase roadster

▲ 1959 Edsel Corsair convertible coupe

▼ 1960 Edsel Villager station wagon

▲ 1985 Excalibur Series IV phaeton

▼ 1931 Ford Victoria coupe

▲ 1932 Ford Deluxe roadster

▼ 1940 Ford Deluxe convertible coupe

1949-50 Series CD Four two-door sedan

1950 FarmORoad

1950 Series CD Four Super Sports roadster

1950 Series CD Four Hotshot with doors

Specifications

1939

Series 1A (wb 80.0) - 2,017 blt	Wght	Price	Prod
conv cpe, 2P	925	325	—
conv sdn, 4P	925	350	—

1939 Engine	bore×stroke	bhp	availability
I-2, 38.9	3.00×2.75	13.5	S-all

1940

Series 2A (wb 80.0) - 422 blt	Wght	Price	Prod
sdn 2d	975	349	—
Deluxe sdn 2d	975	359	—
conv cpe	950	299	—
covered wgn 2d	1,125	399	—
wgn 2d	1,160	450	—

1940 Engine	bore×stroke	bhp	availability
I-2, 38.9	3.00×2.75	13.5	S-all

1941

Series CB41 (wb 80.0) - 2,289 blt	Wght	Price	Prod
sdn 2d	975	390	—
Deluxe sdn 2d	975	400	—
conv cpe	950	339	—
covered wgn 2d	1,125	441	—
wgn 2d	1,160	496	—

1941 Engine	bore×stroke	bhp	availability
I-2, 38.9	3.00×2.75	13.5	S-all

1942

Series CB42 (wb 80.0) - 1,029 blt	Wght	Price	Prod
sdn 2d	975	468	—
Deluxe sdn 2d	1,050	516	—
conv cpe	975	413	—
wgn 2d	1,105	582	—

1942 Engine	bore×stroke	bhp	availability
I-2, 38.9	3.00×2.75	13.5	S-all

1946

CC Four (wb 80.0)	Wght	Price	Prod
sdn 2d	1,145	905	4,987
conv cpe	1,150	proto	12

1946 Engine	bore×stroke	bhp	availability
I-4, 44.0	2.50×2.25	26.5	S-all; O-cast-iron block

1947

CC Four (wb 80.0)	Wght	Price	Prod
sdn 2d	1,555	888	14,090
conv cpe	1,150	949	4,005
wgn 2d	1,305	929	1,249

1947 Engine	bore×stroke	bhp	availability
I-4, 44.0	2.50×2.25	26.5	S-all; O-cast-iron block

1948

CC Four (wb 80.0)	Wght	Price	Prod
sdn 2d	1,280	869	2,760
Sport Utility sdn 2d	1,160	799	
conv cpe	1,210	899	2,485
wgn 2d	1,305	929	23,489

1948 Engine	bore×stroke	bhp	availability
I-4, 44.0	2.50×2.25	26.5	S-all; O-cast-iron block

1949

CD Four (wb 80.0; rdstr-85.0)	Wght	Price	Prod
DeLuxe sdn 2d	1,363	866	2,231
conv cpe	1,320	866	645
wgn 4d	1,403	894	3,803
Hotshot rdstr	1,175	849	752

1949 Engine	bore×stroke	bhp	availability
I-4, 44.0	2.50×2.25	26.5	S-all; O-cast-iron block

1950

CD Four (wb 80.0; rdstr-85.0)	Wght	Price	Prod
sdn 2d	1,363	882	1,367
Super sdn 2d	1,363	951	
conv cpe	1,320	882	478
Super conv cpe	1,320	954	
wgn 2d	1,403	916	4,204
Super wgn 2d	1,403	984	
Hotshot rdstr	1,175	872	742
Super Sports rdstr	1,175	925	

1950 Engine	bore×stroke	bhp	availability
I-4, 44.0	2.50×2.25	26.5	S-all

1951

CD Four (wb 80.0; rdstr-85.0)	Wght	Price	Prod
bus cpe	1,355	943	1,077
Super sdn 2d	1,370	1,033	
wgn 2d	1,420	1,002	4,500
Super wgn 2d	1,450	1,077	
Super conv cpe	1,310	1,035	391
Hotshot rdstr	1,180	952	646
Super Sports rdstr	1,180	1,029	

1951 Engine	bore×stroke	bhp	availability
I-4, 44.0	2.50×2.25	26.5	S-all

1952

CD Four (wb 80.0; rdstr-85.0)	Wght	Price	Prod
Standard bus cpe	1,355	943	216
Super sdn 2d	1,400	1,033	
Standard wgn 2d	1,430	1,002	1,355
Super wgn 2d	1,480	1,077	
Super conv cpe	1,400	1,035	146
Hotshot rdstr	1,240	952	358
Super Sports rdstr	1,240	1,029	

1952 Engine	bore×stroke	bhp	availability
I-4, 44.0	2.50×2.25	25.5	S-all

DeSoto

Prosperity seemed endless in 1928 when the fast-rising new Chrysler Corporation purchased Dodge and issued its first DeSoto and Plymouth. Though good times soon turned to "hard times," DeSoto would be one of the few pre-Depression "expansion" makes to survive them. DeSoto went on to build its most-exciting cars in the '50s, only to die in late 1960 after a flash recession and sibling rivalry obliterated its narrow, well-defined price niche. In between, DeSoto did good and sometimes great business as the medium-price "bridge" between Dodge and Chrysler, with design and engineering that usually owed more to the latter than the former.

Early DeSotos, though, were pitched just above Plymouth in size, power, and price. The make didn't settle into its long-familiar "middle-middle" role until the late '30s. Even so, DeSoto history generally parallels Chrysler's with one key exception: While Chrysler offered a group of conventionally styled Sixes for 1934, DeSoto relied exclusively on that year's radical new Airflow. The result was a sales disaster that briefly threatened DeSoto's existence.

The 1930-33 DeSotos reflected general Chrysler Corporation trends. Styling was bolt-upright formal through '31, then smoothed a bit with barrel-like grilles. Sixes and eights were available through 1931. All were orthodox side-valve designs with cast-iron construction. The five-main-bearing eight was smoother and quieter than the four-main six, but neither was a powerhouse. Eights cost around $1000, early-'30s Sixes around $800-$850. But Eights appealed to only about one in three buyers, so DeSoto offered nothing but sixes from 1932 until its hemi-head "FireDome" V-8 of 1952. Actually, the six was but a single engine that was periodically enlarged—essentially a smaller version of Chrysler's six.

DeSoto started the '30s in the middle of the industry production pack, but moved upward through 1933 despite building fewer cars each year. Model-year volume totaled some 32,000 for 1930-31, then fell below 25,000 for '32. The tally dropped under 23,000 for 1933, by which time DeSoto had climbed from 15th in a field of 31 makes to 10th out of 26.

Reflecting this sales decline, DeSoto cut prices for 1933: as low as $665 for a standard sedan or coupe and $875 for the top-line Custom convertible sedan. All models carried an 82-horsepower 217.8-cubic-inch six. This became a 100-horsepower, 241.5-cid for 1934-36, after which a destroked 228.1 with 93 or 100 horsepower took over. Though never exciting, DeSoto's six was sturdy and reliable, happily running for long spells with little maintenance other than an occasional quart of oil. It was also fairly thrifty, returning up to 22 mpg with gentle use. These traits made later six-cylinder DeSotos quite popular as taxicabs.

DeSoto first observed a model year with the January 1932 introduction of its SC-Series "All New Six." This wore chunky but attractive styling as a standard sedan, seven-passenger sedan, and Custom sedan, convertible, and phaeton. Additional coupes and a new brougham two-door sedan arrived for '33.

All the pros and cons of the 1934 Chrysler Airflow naturally held for the DeSoto versions, only they came in a single four-model series versus a multiplicity of Chryslers. Output now bottomed out to a prewar low of just under 14,000.

Following Chrysler in a hasty retreat from Airflows, DeSoto introduced more-conventional—and salable—"Airstream" styling for 1935. It appeared on seven companion models bearing a Plymouth-like raked grille, slab sides, and rounded deck. Sedans were sold with either outside spare tire or "trunkback" styling that enclosed the spare in an integral luggage compartment. There was also a $35 two-tone paint option. Thanks to the Airstreams, production rebounded to 26,800, yet DeSoto dropped to 13th in the wake of Packard's highly successful new medium-priced One Twenty.

DeSoto Division rode out the last half of the '30s with increasingly larger and duller cars. Airflows disappeared after 1936, a year ahead of Chrysler's, but long sedans and limousines arrived that year on a 130-inch wheelbase; this grew to 136 inches for 1938. The great Ray Dietrich of coachbuilding fame was hired to direct Chrysler's corporate design in this period, so DeSoto looked as conservative as its sister makes, though in tune with contemporary tastes. A national recession limited 1938 output to just under 39,000, but DeSoto still finished 12th. The industry recovered in 1939, but fared much better than DeSoto, which again ran 13th despite higher volume of over 54,000.

The DeSoto lineup assumed a consistent pattern by 1938:

1930 Series CF Eight convertible coupe

1931 Series SA Six 2/4-passenger roadster

1932 Series SC New Six Custom 2/4-passenger roadster

DeLuxe and Custom models selling at around $900 and $1000, respectively. Both rode the same orthodox chassis with standard 119-inch wheelbase. Open styles were conspicuously absent for 1939, though a sliding sunroof was offered on selected closed models. Styling still left something to be desired. A '39 DeSoto looked like a Plymouth with goiter. Dumpy appearance would remain one of the make's sales handicaps until well after World War II.

For 1940 came more-attractive Dietrich styling abetted by longer wheelbases of 122.5 inches standard, 139.5 extended. Chrysler's Fluid Drive, which allowed the driver to start and stop without using the clutch, became available on DeSotos. The Custom convertible coupe was reinstated, but not the convertible sedan. Though model-year output rose some 11,000 units, DeSoto again placed 13th. Like other Chrysler makes, it might have done better had the firm not suffered a crippling strike at the start of 1940 production.

Volume soared for '41, jumping from 65,500 to over 97,000 and moving DeSoto up to tenth—its best placing ever. Much of this success was owed to a heavy facelift that made for good-looking cars with lower hoods and bolder fronts. Grilles smiled with the prominent vertical "teeth" that would remain a DeSoto hallmark through 1955. Standard-chassis models lost an inch in wheelbase but measured 5.5 inches longer overall than the '40s; they were lower and wider, too. There was a new model: the Custom Town Sedan, a formal but pretty adaptation of the standard issue with closed or "blind" rear-roof quarters, priced about $50 higher. DeSoto wooed buyers with numerous extras including underseat heater, pushbutton radio, and streamlined fender skirts.

1933 Series SD 7-passenger sedan

1934 Series SE Airflow 5-passenger coupe

1936 Custom Airstream convertible coupe

A more-extensive restyle for 1942 introduced "Airfoil" hidden headlamps that were "out of sight, except at night." Though not an industry first (the 1936-37 Cord 810/812 had something similar), they were Detroit's only hidden lamps that year, and imparted a cleaner look. Emphasizing them was a grille placed entirely on the lower half of the car's "face." A sculpted lady was introduced as a hood mascot.

Model choices held firm for '42, but there was a "squarer" six, bored out to 236.6 cid. Somewhat detuned and rated at 115 horsepower, it would continue through the rest of the decade. There wasn't much time for specials in that war-shortened model year, but DeSoto managed a plush Custom Town Sedan called "Fifth Avenue" (a name much later resurrected at Chrysler). Identified outside only by small nameplates and inside by luxurious leather and Bedford cloth trim, it sold for about $75 more than the regular Town Sedan. Production was low everywhere in Detroit for '42, and DeSoto was no exception at less than 25,000—fewer than 1000 of some individual models.

DeSoto returned to civilian sales with an abbreviated 1946 line, though drivetrain and chassis combinations were the same as '42. Cancelation of the long-wheelbase DeLuxe sedan left only three extended-chassis models, all Customs: limousine, seven-seat sedan, and an intriguing newcomer called Suburban. The last was designed for the ultimate in stylish hauling for hotels, airports, and well-heeled individuals. A fold-down rear seat sans trunk partition made for a huge cargo hold. Completing the package was a metal-and-wood roof rack. Not surprisingly, the Suburban was the costliest '46 DeSoto at $2093, a healthy $200 above the seven-seat sedan.

As with all Chrysler makes, the 1947-48 DeSotos were largely the same as the '46s; serial numbers are the only guide to model years. All wore a mild facelift of prewar styling with headlamps reexposed, fenders extended back into the front doors, a wider and heavier-looking grille, and reshuffled medallions and parking lights. Rated horsepower was 109, down six from '42, though this reflected a new rating method, not mechanical changes. Besides "civilian" cars, DeSoto built 11,600 taxicabs in these years—its fifth best-selling model. Suburban production was also quite satisfactory: 7500 for the period.

DeSoto was fully redesigned for '49, as were other Chrysler makes that year. Standard wheelbase was four inches longer at 125.5, but boxy, upright styling hid the fact. This was typical of Chrysler's new postwar look, which was very dull compared to Ford's and GM's. A vertical-bar grille was retained, similar to the 1942-48 design, but the lady mascot was replaced by a bust of Hernando DeSoto. Like any "proper" hood ornament of the time, it glowed when the parking lamps or headlights were on. Horsepower rose by three, to 112. Fluid Drive with "Tip-Toe" semiautomatic shift became standard on Customs and a $121 option for DeLuxes.

The '49 DeSotos arrived in March of that year after a brief run of old-style cars to fill the gap. Among them were some interesting new utility models. Besides a $2959 woody wagon, the DeLuxe line included the all-steel Carry-All, similar to the Custom Suburban but on the standard wheelbase. It was also quite a bit cheaper at $2191. The Suburban itself returned at $3179, up over $500 from '48 (postwar inflation was affecting car prices all over). As before, the Suburban shared the long chassis with an eight-passenger Custom sedan (but not the limo, which was dropped), and offered vast cargo space, rooftop luggage rack, plus rear jump seats giving true nine-passenger capacity. The Carry-All handily sold 2690 copies for the model year, but the wagon did only 850, the Suburban a mere 129. The woody lasted only through 1950, the Suburban and Carry-All through '52.

Overall, 1949 was a less-than-spectacular DeSoto year. Volume remained at the '48 level—about 92,500—and the make again finished 12th. However, Customs outsold DeLuxes by 3-to-1, a sign of growing buyer preference for greater luxury.

The 1950 line arrived with somewhat sleeker rear ends and two new models. DeSoto bowed its first hardtop coupe, the Custom Sportsman, at $2489, and moved the DeLuxe woody wagon up to Custom trim before replacing it with a slightly cheaper all-steel model at midyear. Despite the relative lack of change, model-year production leaped to nearly 134,000 for 1950, a gain of almost 45 percent.

Styling was touched up again for '51, when the venerable L-head six was stroked to 250.6 cid, though that yielded only four extra horses. Chrome was very evident, perhaps more than on any other Chrysler line, especially in those toothy fronts. Production eased to 106,000, dropping DeSoto from 12th to 15th, as Kaiser sailed past with its beautiful new '51 design and Hudson did the same with its powerful new six-cylinder Hornets. Government-ordered production cutbacks for the Korean War also played a part.

DeSoto's big event for 1952 was its first-ever V-8. Called "FireDome," it was an overhead-valve hemi-head design—a smaller, 276.1-cid version of the brilliant Chrysler 331 introduced the previous year. Packing 160 horsepower, it put DeSoto firmly in Detroit's escalating "horsepower race."

The FireDome powered a new like-named top-of-the-line 1952 series that duplicated Custom offerings save the Suburban. Though it immediately garnered nearly 50,000 sales, DeSoto as a whole could do no better than 88,000 for the model year. However, it rose a bit in the production ranks, finishing 13th.

For 1953, remaining Custom/DeLuxe models were combined into a new Powermaster Six series that still lagged behind FireDome in sales, this time by a margin of 2-1. Both lines

1936 Series S2 Airflow III 5-passenger coupe

1936 Series S1 Custom Airstream touring sedan

1937 Series S3 Six 3/5-passenger convertible coupe

1938 Series S5 Six touring sedan

1939 Series S6 Custom coupe with optional sunroof

1939 Series S6 Custom touring sedan

1939 Series S6 Custom club coupe

1940 Series S-7 DeLuxe 3-passenger coupe

1942 Series S-10C Custom four-door sedan

1941 Series S-8C Custom four-door sedan

1942 Series S-10C Custom club coupe

included Sportsman hardtops. The growing influence of newly recruited styling chief Virgil Exner was evident in an update of DeSoto's more-massive '52 look, with new one-piece windshields and more-liberal chrome accents. Model-year volume jumped back to 130,000 and DeSoto moved up to 11th, its best finish since banner '41.

Adding much-needed pizzazz to DeSoto's dour image in 1954 was the interesting Adventurer I, one in the series of Exner-styled show cars begun with the Plymouth XX-500 of 1950. Most were built by Ghia in Italy. Riding a shortened 111-inch wheelbase, Adventurer I was an off-white, close-coupled coupe sporting outside exhausts, wire wheels, and full instrumentation. It came close to production—closer than any other Exner special. "Had it been mass-produced," the designer later said, "it would have been the first four-passenger sports car made in this country. It was better than a 2+2—and, of course, it had the DeSoto Hemi. It was my favorite car." Adventurer II followed in '55, a standard-chassis four-seat fastback shaped more by Ghia than Exner. Painted deep red and lacking bumpers, it was very sleek but not quite as integrated as Adventurer I, and wasn't seriously considered for production.

Meanwhile, the first of Exner's new "Forward Look" production models was due for 1955, so DeSoto's old '49 bodyshell was modestly reworked one last time for '54. The V-8 was tweaked to 170 horsepower, but the big news was the midyear debut of two-speed PowerFlite, Chrysler's first fully automatic transmission. This would be standard on many DeSotos through 1960. Fluid Drive ($130 extra) was on the way out, as was overdrive ($96), long sedans, and the Powermaster Six. Reflecting Chrysler Corporation's 1954 sales nightmare, DeSoto's model-year output dropped below 77,000 and the make fell back to 12th place in the industry.

Much bolder, fully up-to-date new Exner styling and more-powerful engines stood to turn things around for 1955. Firedome (the "d" no longer capitalized) now played "second banana" to a new uplevel Fireflite line. Both shared a 126-inch wheelbase with that year's Chryslers, and carried a Hemi bored out to 291 cid. Rated horsepower was 185 for Firedomes, 200 for Fireflites. No '55 Chrysler product was sedate, but DeSoto looked possibly busiest of all—though still attractive, with a much lower silhouette; wrapped windshield; the last of the toothy grilles; "gullwing" dash; and broad, optional two-toning. This package appealed greatly, boosting division output to nearly 115,000. Still, even that was good for only 13th in a year when most every Detroit car sold very well.

Firedome offered DeSoto's only '55 wagon, along with a detrimmed Special hardtop priced some $110 below its Sportsman counterpart. The plush Coronado sedan, a mid-1954 addition to the Firedome line, returned as a 1955 "spring special" Fireflite at $100 above the $2800 regular sedan. It's now a minor collector's item, mainly for having one of the industry's first three-tone paint jobs (turquoise, black, and white). Convertibles were available in both '55 DeSoto series but saw minuscule sales: just 625 Firedomes and 775 Fireflites.

For 1956, a longer stroke took DeSoto's Hemi to 330.4 cid, lifting Firedome to 230 horsepower and Fireflite to 255. Wire mesh replaced the trademark grille teeth, and unreadable gold-on-white instruments appeared. But as on other Chrysler lines, the big change was tailfins, though they were pretty modest for '56. DeSoto's carried distinctive "tri-tower" taillamps—stacked pairs of round red lenses separated by a matching backup lamp—which would persist through 1959.

Following GM's lead in '55, DeSoto introduced three four-door hardtops for '56: a Sportsman in each series and a low-priced Firedome Seville. A Seville hardtop coupe replaced the previous Firedome Special. (Cadillac's new-for-'56 Eldorado two-door hardtop was also called Seville, but no legal battles ensued.) A midseason highlight was the limited-edition Adventurer hardtop coupe, a supercar awash in gold-anodized aluminum trim. Carrying a new 341-cid, 320-horsepower Hemi, it was part of that year's expanded Highland Park performance squadron along with the Chrysler 300B, Plymouth Fury, and Dodge D-500. DeSoto was selected as the 1956 Indy 500 pace car, and the division celebrated by reeling off about 400

1946 Custom Suburban 8-passenger sedan

1946 Deluxe sedan

1947 Custom club coupe

1949 Custom convertible coupe

1950 Custom Sportsman hardtop coupe

1951 Custom four-door sedan

1953 Firedome Sportsman hardtop coupe

1953 Firedome convertible coupe

1954 Firedome four-door sedan

"Pacesetter" replicas, all Fireflite convertibles with Adventurer-style trim, priced at $3615 apiece.

DeSoto shared in the industry's general 1956 retreat, building about 4300 fewer cars. However, it returned to 11th place due to fast-fading sales at Nash and Hudson, Studebaker and Packard. The division finished in that spot again for '57 even though volume jumped to about 110,500—as near as DeSoto ever came to passing Chrysler (ending about 7200 units behind).

No wonder. The '57s were not only all-new for the second time in three years, but superbly engineered and strikingly styled. A low-cost Firesweep series based on the 122-inch Dodge platform joined the line in an effort to extend DeSoto's market territory. It helped. The Firesweep sedan sold for only $2777, where the cheapest Firedome was $2958. Firesweeps also included two-and four-door hardtops and six-seat Shopper and nine-passenger Explorer four-door wagons. Fireflite offered all these plus a convertible; Firedome was the same but had no wagons.

All were big, heavy, powerful cars. The two upper series used the 341 V-8 from the '56 Adventurer with 270 and 295 horsepower, respectively. Firesweeps had the previous year's 330 debored to 325 cid and tuned for 245 horsepower standard, 260 horsepower optional. Last but not least, a soft-top Adventurer joined the hardtop coupe in a separate series above Fireflite. They packed 345 bhp from a modestly bored 345 Hemi.

Virgil Exner's dramatic new styling made finned fantasies of all '57 Chrysler products. DeSoto's version of this second-generation Forward Look was quite handsome: dartlike profile, tri-tower taillamps attractively integrated into the soaring rear fenders, simple but pleasant side moldings, prominent bumper/grille, and acres more glass. DeSoto also benefited from Chrysler's corporatewide switch to torsion-bar front suspension, which made these heavyweights uncannily good handlers. Aiding performance was the arrival of quick, responsive three-speed TorqueFlite automatic as an optional alternative to PowerFlite. Also controlled by Highland Park's pushbuttons, it was a great transmission that would way outlive DeSoto.

Indeed, for all this excitement, DeSoto was now threatened again, only this time by an upwardly mobile Dodge and a downward expansion of the Chrysler line. As if on cue, production plunged to 50,000 units the following year—the make's lowest total since 1938. A sharp national recession, poor workmanship after '56, and several marketing mistakes all contributed to a downward spiral from which DeSoto would never recover.

Predictably, the '58 DeSotos were much like the '57s save busier grilles and trim, and standard quad headlights. (Some states hadn't approved "quadrilights" for '57, so DeSoto front fenders were designed to accept one or two lamps each, the latter where law permitted. By '58, four-lamp systems were legal nationwide.) The '58 lineup returned along with a new Firesweep convertible. At $4369, the '58 Adventurer ragtop was the most-expensive DeSoto ever, though Chrysler's convertible 300D cost nearly $1300 more.

Engines and power ratings swelled, but the complex Hemi was ever costly to build, so Chrysler began switching to cheaper wedgehead V-8s for '58. Among them were two new "Turboflash" DeSoto engines. Firesweeps had a 350-inch mill with 280 horsepower standard or 295 with optional four-barrel carb. Other models carried a big-bore 361 with 295 bhp in standard Firedome tune, 305 with twin four-barrels in Fireflites (optional on Firedomes), 345 in high-compression Adventurer guise, and a smashing 355 for Adventurers with optional Bendix fuel injection. Injection cost a hefty $637.20 and few were ordered. Fraught with problems, all were probably replaced with carburetors. With all this, the '58 DeSotos were quite quick even without the Hemi, helped by fast-shifting TorqueFlite, now standard on Fireflites and Adventurers. (Firesweeps again came with three-speed manual and offered Firedome's standard PowerFlite at extra cost.) A 305-horsepower Firedome could scale 0-60 in 7.7 seconds, 0-80 mph in 13.5 seconds, and reach 115 mph.

DeSoto claimed its towering tailfins of this era "added stability at speed," but that was pure propaganda. The fins did little from an aerodynamic standpoint under 80 mph. Their main purpose was to make Chrysler products stand out from the crowd—which they most definitely did.

Despite the return of the same broad lineup, 1959 marked the beginning of DeSoto's end. Firesweeps were upgraded to the 361 wedge in just one 295-horsepower version. Other models

1955 Fireflite Sportsman hardtop coupe

1956 Firedome Seville hardtop coupe

1955 Fireflite Coronado four-door sedan

1957 Fireflite four-door sedan

1955 Fireflite convertible coupe

1957 Fireflite Shopper station wagon

1956 Fireflite convertible coupe

1957 Firedome convertible coupe

got an even bigger-bore new 383 with 305 horsepower for Firedome, 325 for Fireflite, and 350 for Adventurer. The last saw slightly improved sales, but total model-year production of just over 46,000 was hardly the sort that had sustained DeSoto earlier in the decade.

Rumors of DeSoto's imminent demise began cropping up in '59, and naturally affected sales. Though calendar-year output was up slightly from '58, volume for both years was less than half that of 1957's near 120,000 units. Plainly, the recession had put DeSoto in the same kind of trouble as Oldsmobile, Buick, and Mercury, but those makes started at higher levels and thus had further to fall. Moreover, all were planning smaller models for 1960-61. Although DeSoto's 1962 plans included "downsized" standard cars, there was no program for a compact.

The real problem, though, was a change in corporate marketing strategy. Previously, company franchises split into Chrysler-Plymouth, DeSoto-Plymouth, and Dodge-Plymouth dealers. The advent of Imperial as a separate make for 1955 prompted Chrysler Division to expand in the lower end of its price territory, while Dodge moved upward with larger, more-luxurious cars. DeSoto had nowhere to go—except the grave.

At first, Chrysler strongly denied that DeSoto would be terminated, and even staged a 1959 celebration marking production of the two-millionth DeSoto. Press releases noted that almost a million DeSotos were still registered and that $25 million had been earmarked for future models—$7 million for 1960 alone. Officials also said commitments had been made for '61, and that work was underway toward 1962-63. They also pointed out that Chrysler had regularly made a profit on DeSoto.

But then Chrysler combined DeSoto and Plymouth Divisions in 1960, with the new compact Valiant an ostensibly separate make. Valiant sold very well and Plymouth did fairly well, but DeSoto fared badly. Sales in the first two months of 1960 were just 4746—a mere 0.51 percent of the industry—down substantially from the 1959 period (6134 units and 0.72 percent).

DeSoto's 1960 line reflected these developments: cut to just a sedan, hardtop sedan, and hardtop coupe in two series. The upper was called Adventurer, but sold for a few hundred dollars below '59 Fireflites and was much-less-special than previous Adventurers. Fireflite was now in the $3000 area formerly occupied by Firesweep. The year's most-popular DeSoto was the Fireflite sedan, but even it failed to exceed 10,000 units.

All 1960 DeSotos shared a 122-inch wheelbase with that year's Chrysler Windsor and Dodge Matador/Polara. They also adopted the new "unibody" construction that arrived corporate-wide (except on Imperial). Adventurers carried the 305-horsepower 383 from the now-departed Firedome; Fireflites had the 295-horsepower 361 from the '59 Firesweep. Styling was all but identical with the 1960 Chrysler's, announced by a blunt, trapezoidal grille composed of small horizontal bars atop a huge vee'd bumper with rubber-capped guards. Fins flew as high as ever, but performance was down. A 1960 Adventure could stay with a Windsor away from a stoplight, but would lose to a Chrysler Saratoga or the lighter 383 Dodge Dart Phoenix.

DeSoto's appearance for 1961 was brief—token really. Production was understandably low: a mere 3034. There was but one nameless series (the cars were simply "DeSotos"), and four-door pillared sedans were eliminated. Minimal advertising focused on the individual styling. "Odd" was a more-apt adjective—especially in front, where diagonally stacked quad headlights flanked a curious "double" grille with a latticelike lower

1957 Fireflite Sportsman hardtop coupe

1958 Adventurer hardtop coupe

1959 Fireflite Sportsman hardtop coupe

1960 Adventurer hardtop coupe

1960 Adventurer four-door sedan

1961 hardtop coupe

1961 hardtop coupe

section; above was a large oval holding the DeSoto name in unreadable stylized letters against a fine mesh. The rest of the effort was equally uninspired.

But DeSoto's fate had long been sealed, so Chrysler wound down production by Christmas 1960, filling what few orders remained with mostly '61 Windsors. Some DeSoto-Plymouth dealers then became Chrysler-Plymouth stores—to the chagrin of existing C-P dealers nearby. Left stillborn were the smaller '62 DeSotos based on the planned new corporate "S-series" platform—though that was no great loss considering their dumpy looks.

It was a sad finale for a marque that had generated much business for Chrysler over more than three decades. And ironically, it was premature. Less than a year later, DeSoto was effectively resurrected at Dodge to bolster sales of its unpopular 1962 standard line, which had been shrunk to near-compact size. Called Custom 880, this reborn full-size Dodge was much like the '61 DeSoto, and even cost about the same, but sold much better with its smoother styling and more model choices. One suspects, then, that DeSoto's rapid decline, like Edsel's, stemmed from a "loser" image as much as from a changed market.

Specifications

1930

Model K Six (wb 109.0) - 29,860 built**	Wght	Price	Prod
rdstr 2-4P	2,350	845	—
touring (phaeton) 5P	2,445	845	—
bus cpe 2P	2,465	845	—
DeLuxe cpe 2-4P	2,525	885	—
sdn 2d 5P	2,580	845	—
sdn 4d 5P	2,645	885	—
DeLuxe sdn 4d 5P	2,655	955	—
Model CF Eight (wb 114.0) - 19,525 built (est.)**			
rdstr 2-4P	2,720	985	1,457*
phaeton 5P	2,800	1,035	179*
bus cpe 2P	2,835	965	1,015*
DeLuxe cpe 2-4P	2,875	1,025	2,735*
conv cpe 2-4P	2,845	1,075	524*
sdn 4d 5P	2,965	995	9,653*
DeLuxe sdn 4d 5P	2,975	1,065	4,139*
chassis	—	—	373*
Model CK Finer Six (wb 109.0) - 7,443 built (est.)**			
rdstr 2-4P	2,385	810	1,086*
DeLuxe rdstr 2-4P	2,520	835	
touring (phaeton) 5P	2,475	830	209*
bus cpe 2P	2,515	830	858*
DeLuxe cpe 2-4P	2,585	860	1,521*
conv cpe 2-4P	2,540	945	184*
sdn 4d	2,705	875	8,248*
chassis	—	—	94*

* Combined 1930-31 individual model exact production
** Available Model K figures include 1929 production. 1930-model production began August 15. Engine number span for 1930: K83241 to K11310. If no engine numbers were skipped, total 1930 Model K production was 29,860. Available Model CF and CK figures include 1931 production. 1930 Model CF production began January 1, 1930. Model CK production began April 29. Sources of serial number spans suggest that of 20,075 Model CFs built, approximately 19,575 were 1930s and 550 1931s. Same sources indicate 7,443 CKs were 1930s and 4,757 1931s.

1930 Engines	bore×stroke	bhp	availability
I-6, 174.9	3.00×4.13	57	S-K
I-8, 207.7	2.88×4.00	70	S-CF
I-6, 189.8	3.13×4.13	60	S-CK

1931

Model CF Eight (wb 114.0) - 550 built (est.)

Production was carried over from 1930, with 1931-model output commencing July 1. Production figures combined with 1930 CF Eight. Body styles, weights, and prices identical.

Model CK Finer Six (wb 109.0) - 4,757 built (est.)

Production was carried over from 1930, with 1931-model output commencing July 1. Production figures combined with 1930 CK Finer Six. Body styles, weights, and prices identical.

Model SA Six (wb 109.0)	Wght	Price	Prod*
rdstr 2-4P	2,465	795	1,949
touring (phaeton) 5P	2,580	795	100
bus cpe 2P	2,585	740	1,309
cpe 2-4P	2,635	775	2,663
conv cpe 2-4P	2,630	825	638
sdn 2d 5P	2,680	695	2,349
sdn 4d 5P	2,695	775	17,866
DeLuxe sdn 4d 5P	2,834	825	1,450
chassis	—	—	32

Model CF Eight Second Series (wb 114.0)	Wght	Price	Prod
rdstr 2-4P	2,785	995	73
touring (phaeton) 5P	2,800	1,035	22
bus cpe 2P	2,915	965	102
DeLuxe cpe 2-4P	2,970	995	486
conv cpe 2-4P	2,970	1,110	48
sdn 4d 5P	3,025	995	3,490
DeLuxe sdn 4d 5P	3,115	1,065	
chassis	—	—	3

* Model SA and CF Second Series production continued into 1932; production figures are for 1931-32 combined. Approximately one-third of total SA models were 1931s, the rest 1932s. Second Series Model CF production began January 1,1931.

1931 Engines	bore×stroke	bhp	availability
I-8, 207.7	2.88×4.00	70	S-CF
I-6, 189.8	3.13×4.13	60	S-CF
I-6, 205.3	3.25×4.13	67	S-SK
I-8, 220.7	2.88×4.25	77	S-CF 2nd Series

1932

Model SA Six (wb 109.0)

Production was carried over from 1931, with 1932-model output commencing July 23. Production figures combined with 1931 SA Six. Body styles, weights, and prices identical.

Model SC New Six (wb 112.4)	Wght	Price	Prod
Standard rdstr 2P	2,725	675	894
Custom rdstr 2-4P	2,748	775	
phaeton 5P	—	775	30
Standard cpe 2P	2,778	695	1,691
Standard cpe 2-4P	2,848	735	2,897
Custom cpe 2-4P	2,908	790	
sdn 2d (brougham)	2,883	695	3,730
Cstm conv cpe 2-4P	2,848	845	960
Standard sdn 4d	2,978	775	8,924
Custom sdn 4d	3,018	835	4,791
Custom conv sdn 5P	3,175	975	275
sdn 7P	3,175	925	221
chassis	—	—	83

Model CF Eight Second Series (wb 114.0)

Production carried over from 1931, with 1932-model output commencing July 23. Production figures combined with 1931 CF Second Series. Body styles, weights, and prices identical.

1932 Engines	bore×stroke	bhp	availability
I-6, 205.3	3.25×4.13	67	S-SA
I-8, 220.7	2.88×4.25	77	S-CF 2nd Series
I-6, 211.5	3.25×4.25	75	S-SC

1933

Model SD (wb 114.4)	Wght	Price	Prod
bus cpe 2P	2,930	665	800
Standard cpe 2-4P	2,940	705	2,705
Custom cpe 2-4P	2,995	750	
Standard sdn 2d	2,995	665	2,436
Special sdn 2d	3,000	725	
Cstm conv cpe 2-4P	2,990	775	412
Standard sdn 4d	3,060	735	7,890
Custom sdn 4d	3,150	795	8,133
Custom conv sdn 5P	—	875	132
sdn 7P(export only)	—	—	104
chassis	—	—	124

1933 Engine	bore×stroke	bhp	availability
I-6, 217.8	3.25×4.38	82	S-all

1934

Model SE Airflow (wb 115.5)	Wght	Price	Prod
cpe 5P	3,323	995	1,584
brougham 6P	3,323	995	522
sdn 4d	3,378	995	11,713
Town sdn 6P	3,343	995	119
chassis	—	—	2

1934 Engine	bore×stroke	bhp	availability
I-6, 241.5	3.38×4.50	100	S-all

1935

Model SF Airstream Six (wb 116.0)	Wght	Price	Prod
bus cpe 2P	2,840	695	1,760
cpe 2-4P	2,925	760	900
conv cpe 2-4P	3,035	835	226
sdn 2d	2,915	745	1,350
touring sdn 2d	2,960	775	2,035
sdn 4d	2,990	795	5,714
touring sdn 4d	3,035	825	8,018
Model SG Airflow Six (wb 115.5)			
bus cpe 3P	3,390	1,015	70
cpe 5P	3,390	1,015	418
sdn 4d	3,390	1,015	6,269
Town sdn 6P	3,400	1,015	40

1935 Engine	bore×stroke	bhp	availability
I-6, 241.5	3.38×4.50	100	S-all

1936

S1 Airstream DeLx (wb 118.0)	Wght	Price	Prod
bus cpe 2P	2,941	695	2,592
touring brougham 5P	3,051	770	2,207
touring sdn 5P	3,111	810	13,093
chassis	—	—	99
S1 Airstream Custom (wb 118; lwb-130.0)			
bus cpe 2P	—	745	940
cpe 2-4P	—	795	641
conv cpe 2-4P	3,031	895	350
touring brougham 5P	3,031	825	1,120
touring sdn 4d	3,126	865	13,801
conv sdn 5P	—	1,095	215
Traveler sdn 4d*	—	1,075	23
lwb sdn 7P	—	1,075	208
limo 7P (lwb)	—	—	10
S2 Airflow II (wb 115.5)			
cpe 5P	—	1,095	250
sdn 4d	—	1,095	4,750

1936 Engine	bore×stroke	bhp	availability
I-6, 241.5	3.38×4.50	100	S-all

1937

S3 Six (wb 116.0; lwb-133.0)	Wght	Price	Prod
bus cpe 3P	3,038	770	11,050
cpe 3-5P	3,088	820	1,030
conv cpe 3-5P	3,225	975	992
brghm F/B 6P	3,123	830	1,200
touring 6P	3,148	840	11,660
sdn F/B 4d	3,123	870	2,265
touring sdn 4d	3,148	880	51,889
conv sdn 5P	3,441	1,300	426
lwb sdn 7P	3,451	1,120	695
limo sdn 7P (lwb)	3,475	1,220	71
chassis	—	—	497

1937 Engine	bore×stroke	bhp	availability
I-6, 228.1	3.38×4.25	93	S-all

1938

S5 Six (wb 119.0; lwb-136.0)	Wght	Price	Prod
bus cpe 3P	3,039	870	5,160
conv cpe 3-5P	3,229	1,045	431
touring brougham 6P	3,119	930	5,367
sdn F/B 4d 6P	3,134	958	498
touring sdn 4d 6P	3,139	970	23,681
conv sdn 5P	3,394	1,375	88
lwb sdn 7P	3,439	1,195	513
sdn limo 7P (lwb)	3,524	1,285	81
Cstm Trvlr sdn 4d (lwb)	—	—	2,550
cpe 2-4P	—	—	38
fstbk brougham	—	—	11
chassis	—	—	413

1938 Engines	bore×stroke	bhp	availability
I-6, 228.1	3.38×4.25	93	S-all
I-6, 228.1	3.38×4.25	100	O-all

1939

S6 DeLx (wb 119.0; lwb-136.0)	Wght	Price	Prod
bus cpe 2P	3,064	870	5,176
cpe A/S 2-4P	3,089	925	2,124
touring sdn 2d 5P	3,129	930	7,472
touring sdn 4d 5P	3,174	970	31,513
lwb touring sdn 7P	3,454	1,195	425
sdn limo 7P	3,549	1,285	84
chassis	—	—	154
S6 Custom (wb 119.0; lwb-136.0)			
cpe 2P	3,069	923	498
cpe A/S 2-4P	3,094	978	287
club cpe 4P	3,164	1,145	264
touring sdn 2d 5P	3,134	983	424
touring sdn 4d 5P	3,179	1,023	5,993
lwb touring sdn 7P	3,459	1,248	30
sdn limo 7P	3,554	1,338	5

1939 Engines	bore×stroke	bhp	availability
I-6, 228.1	3.38×4.25	93	S-all
I-6, 228.1	3.38×4.25	100	O-all

1940

S-7S DeLx (wb 122.5; 7P-139.5)	Wght	Price	Prod
bus cpe	3,001	845	3,650
cpe, A/S	3,026	905	2,098
sdn 2d	3,066	905	7,072
sdn 4d	3,086	945	18,666
sdn 4d, 7P	3,490	1,175	142
S-7C Custom (wb 122.5; 7P-139.5)			
bus cpe	3,024	885	1,898
pe, A/S	3,044	945	2,234
conv cpe	3,329	1,095	1,085
sdn 2d	3,084	945	3,109
sdn 4d	3,104	985	25,221
sdn 4d, 7P	3,490	1,215	206
limo 7P	3,550	1,290	34
chassis	—	—	52

1940 Engines	bore×stroke	bhp	availability
I-6, 228.1	3.38×4.25	100	S-all
I-6, 228.1	3.38×4.25	105	O-all

1941

S-8S DeLx (wb 121.5; 7P-139.5)	Wght	Price	Prod
bus cpe	3,134	945	4,449
club cpe	3,219	1,025	5,603
sdn 2d	3,224	1,008	9,228
sdn 4d	3,254	1,035	26,417
sdn 4d, 7P	3,629	1,270	101
S-8C Custom (wb 121.5; 7P-139.5)			
bus cpe	3,144	982	2,033
club cpe	3,239	1,080	6,726
conv cpe	3,494	1,240	2,937
brougham 2d	3,264	1,060	4,609
sdn 4d	3,269	1,085	30,876
town sdn	3,329	1,133	4,362
sdn 4d, 7P	3,649	1,310	120
limo 7P	3,700	1,390	35
chassis	—	—	1

1941 Engine	bore×stroke	bhp	availability
I-6, 228.1	3.38×4.25	105	S-all

1942

S-10S DeLx (wb121.5;7P-139.5)	Wght	Price	Prod
bus cpe	3,190	1,010	469
club cpe	3,270	1,092	1,968
conv cpe	3,500	1,250	79
sdn 2d	3,270	1,075	1,781
sdn 4d	3,315	1,103	6,463
town sdn	3,335	1,147	291
sdn 4d, 7P	3,705	1,455	49
S-10C Custom (wb 121.5; 7P-139.5)			
bus cpe	3,205	1,046	120
club cpe	3,270	1,142	2,236
conv cpe	3,510	1,317	489
sdn 2d	3,305	1,142	913
sdn 4d	3,330	1,152	7,974
town sdn	3,365	1,196	1,084
sdn 4d, 7P	3,725	1,504	79
limo 7P	3,820	1,580	20

1942 Engine	bore×stroke	bhp	availability
I-6, 236.6	3.44×4.25	115	S-all

1946

S-11S DeLuxe (wb 121.5)	Wght	Price	Prod*
bus cpe	3,302	1,331	—
club cpe	3,392	1,451	—
sdn 2d	3,397	1,426	—
sdn 4d	3,427	1,461	—
S-11C Custom (wb 121.5; 7-8P-139.5)			
club cpe	3,378	1,501	—
conv cpe	3,618	1,761	—
sdn 2d	3,423	1,491	—
sdn 4d	3,433	1,511	—
sdn 4d, 7P	3,837	1,893	—
limo 8P	3,937	2,013	—
Suburban sdn 4d, 8P	4,012	2,093	—

1946 Engine	bore×stroke	bhp	availability
I-6, 236.6	3.44×4.25	109	S-all

* Factory comb. prod.figures for '46 through '49 First Series.

1947

S-11S DeLuxe (wb 121.5)	Wght	Price	Prod*
bus cpe	3,323	1,451	—
club cpe	3,413	1,541	—
sdn 2d	3,418	1,516	—
sdn 4d	3,448	1,551	—
S-11C Custom (wb 121.5; 7-8P-139.5)			
club cpe	3,398	1,591	—
conv cpe	3,618	1,965	—
sdn 2d	3,443	1,581	—
sdn 4d	3,453	1,601	—
sdn 4d, 7P	3,837	1,983	—
limo 7P	3,995	2,013	—
Suburban sdn 4d, 8P	4,012	2,283	—

1947 Engine	bore×stroke	bhp	availability
I-6, 236.6	3.44×4.25	109	S-all

* Factory comb. prod.figures for '46 through '49 First Series.

1948

S-11S DeLuxe (wb 121.5)	Wght	Price	Prod*
bus cpe	3,285	1,699	—
club cpe	3,385	1,815	—
sdn 2d	3,375	1,788	—
sdn 4d	3,435	1,825	—
S-11C Custom (wb 121.5; 7-9P-139.5)			
club cpe	3,389	1,874	—
conv cpe	3,599	2,296	—
sdn 2d	3,399	1,860	—
sdn 4d	3,439	1,892	—
sdn 4d, 7P	3,819	2,315	—
limo 7P	3,995	2,442	—
Suburban sdn 4d, 9P	3,974	2,631	—

1948 Engine	bore×stroke	bhp	availability
I-6, 236.6	3.44×4.25	109	S-all

* Factory comb. prod.figures for '46 through '49 First Series.

1949 First Series

S-11S DeLuxe (wb 121.5)	Wght	Price	Prod*
bus cpe	3,285	1,699	—
club cpe	3,385	1,815	—
sdn 2d	3,375	1,788	—
sdn 4d	3,435	1,825	—
S-11C Cstm (wb 121.5;7-9P-139.5)			
club cpe	3,389	1,874	—
conv cpe	3,599	2,296	—
sdn 2d	3,399	1,860	—
sdn 4d	3,439	1,892	—
sdn 4d, 7P	3,819	2,315	—
limo 7P	3,995	2,442	—
Suburban 4d, 9P	3,974	2,631	—

1949(1) Eng.	bore×stroke	bhp	availability
I-6, 236.6	3.44×4.25	109	S-all

* Factory combined prod figs for '46 through '49 First Series.

Combined 1946-1949 First Series Production:

S-11S DeLuxe (wb 121.5)	Prod
bus cpe	1,950
club cpe	8,580
sdn 2d	12,751
sdn 4d	32,213
S-11C Custom (wb121.5;7-9P-139.5)	
club cpe	38,720
conv cpe	8,100
sdn 2d	1,600
sdn 4d	126,226
sdn 4d, 7P	3,530
limo 7P	120
Suburban 4d, 8-9P	7,500
chassis	105

1949 Second Series

S-13-1 DeLuxe (wb 125.5)	Wght	Price	Prod
club cpe	3,455	1,976	6,807
sdn 4d	3,520	1,986	13,148
Carry-All sdn 4d, 6P	3,565	2,191	2,690
wgn 4d, 9P	3,915	2,959	850
S-13-2 Custom (wb 125.5; 8-9P-139.5)			
club cpe	3,585	2,156	18,431
conv cpe	3,785	2,578	3,385
sdn 4d	3,645	2,174	48,589
sdn 4d, 8P	4,200	2,863	342
Suburban 4d, 9P	4,410	3,179	129

1949(2) Eng.	bore×stroke	bhp	availability
I-6, 236.6	3.44×4.25	112	S-all

1950

S-14-1 DeLx (wb125.5;8P-139.5)	Wght	Price	Prod
club cpe	3,450	1,976	10,704
sdn 4d	3,525	1,986	18,489
Carry-All sdn 4d, 5P	3,600	2,191	3,900
sdn 4d, 8P	3,995	2,676	235
chassis	—	—	1
S-14-2 Custom (wb 125.5; 8-9P-139.5)			
club cpe	3,575	2,156	18,302
Sportsman htp cpe	3,735	2,489	4,600
conv cpe	3,815	2,578	2,900
sdn 4d	3,640	2,174	72,664
wgn 4d (wood)	4,035	3,093	600
wgn 4d (steel)	3,900	2,717	100
sdn 4d, 8P	4,115	2,863	734
Suburban 4d, 9P	4,400	3,179	623
chassis	—	—	2

1950 Engine	bore×stroke	bhp	availability
I-6, 236.6	3.44×4.25	112	S-all

1951

S-15-1 DeLx (wb 125.5; 8P-139.5)	Wght	Price	Prod*
club cpe	3,475	2,215	—
sdn 4d	3,570	2,227	—
Carry-All sdn 4d	3,685	2,457	—
sdn 4d, 8P	4,045	3,001	—
S-15-2 Custom (wb 125.5;8-9P-139.5)			
club cpe	3,585	2,418	—
Sportsman htp cpe	3,760	2,761	—
conv cpe	2,862	2,840	—
sdn 4d	3,685	2,438	—
wgn 4d	3,960	3,047	—
sdn 4d, 8P	4,122	3,211	—
Suburban 4d, 9P	4,395	3,566	—

1951 Engine	bore×stroke	bhp	availability
I-6, 250.6	3.44×4.50	116	S-all

* Factory comb. '51-'52 Deluxe and Custom prod. figs.

1952

S-15-1 DeLx (wb 125.5; 8P-139.5)	Wght	Price	Prod*
club cpe	3,435	2,319	—
sdn 4d	3,540	2,333	—
Carry-All sdn 4d	3,650	2,572	—
sdn 4d, 8P	4,035	3,142	—
S-15-2 Custom (wb 125.5; 8-9P-139.5)			
club cpe	3,565	2,531	—
Sportsman htp cpe	3,720	2,890	—
conv cpe	3,865	2,996	—
sdn 4d	3,660	2,552	—
wgn 4d	4,020	3,189	—
sdn 4d, 8P	4,155	3,362	—
Suburban 4d, 9P	4,370	3,734	—
S-17 Firedome (wb 125.5; 8P-139.5)			
club cpe	3,675	2,718	5,699
Sportsman htp cpe	3,850	3,078	3,000
conv cpe	3,950	3,183	850
sdn 4d	3,760	2,740	35,651
wgn 4d	4,080	3,377	550
sdn 4d, 8P	4,325	3,547	50

1952 Engines	bore×stroke	bhp	availability
I-6, 250.6	3.44×4.50	116	S-Deluxe, Custom
V-8, 276.1	3.63×3.34	160	S-Firedome

* Factory comb. '51-'52 Deluxe and Custom prod. figs.

1951-1952 Deluxe and Custom Production:

S-15-1 DeLx (wb 125.5; 8P-139.5)	Prod
club cpe	6,100
sdn 4d	13,506
Carry-All sdn 4d	1,700
sdn 4d, 8P	343
S-15-2 Custom (wb 125.5; 8-9P-139.5)	
club cpe	19,000
Sportsman htp cpe	8,750
conv cpe	3,950
sdn 4d	88,491
wgn 4d	1,440
sdn 4d, 8P	769
Suburban 4d, 9P	600

1953

S-18 Pwrmstr (wb 125.5; 8P-139.5)	Wght	Price	Prod
club cpe	3,480	2,334	8,063
Sportsman htp cpe	3,585	2,604	1,470
sdn 4d	3,535	2,356	33,644
wgn 4d	3,845	3,078	500
sdn 4d, 8P	4,080	3,251	225
S-16 Firedome (wb 125.5; 8P-139.5)			
club cpe	3,655	2,622	14,591
Sportsman htp cpe	3,740	2,893	4,700
conv cpe	3,990	3,114	1,700
sdn 4d	3,720	2,643	64,211
wgn 4d	3,995	3,351	1,100
sdn 4d, 8P	4,270	3,529	200

1953 Engines	bore×stroke	bhp	availability
I-6, 250.6	3.44×4.50	116	S-Powermaster
V-8, 276.1	3.63×3.34	160	S-Firedome

1954

S-20 Pwrmstr (wb 125.5; 8P-139.5)	Wght	Price	Prod
club cpe	3,505	2,364	3,499
Sportsman htp cpe	3,590	2,635	250
sdn 4d	3,570	2,386	14,967
wgn 4d	3,855	3,108	225
sdn 4d, 8P	4,100	3,281	263
S-19 Firedome (wb 125.5; 8P-139.5)			
club cpe	3,735	2,652	5,762
Sportsman htp cpe	3,815	2,923	4,382
conv cpe	4,015	3,144	1,025
sdn 4d	3,790	2,673	45,095
wgn 4d	4,045	3,381	946
sdn 4d, 8P	4,305	3,559	165
chassis	—	—	1

1954 Engines	bore×stroke	bhp	availability
I-6, 250.6	3.44×4.50	116	S-Power-master
V-8, 276.1	3.63×3.34	170	S-Firedome

1955

S-22 Firedome (wb 126.0)	Wght	Price	Prod
Special htp cpe	3,801	2,541	28,944
Sportsman htp cpe	3,805	2,654	
conv cpe	4,010	2,824	625
sdn 4d	3,870	2,498	46,388
wgn 4d	4,185	3,170	1,803
S-21 Fireflite (wb 126.0)			
Sportsman htp cpe	3,890	2,939	10,313
conv cpe	4,115	3,151	775
sdn 4d (inc. Crnado)	3,940	2,727	26,637

1955 Engines	bore×stroke	bhp	availability
V-8, 291.0	3.72×3.34	185	S-Firedome
V-8, 291.0	3.72×3.34	200	S-Fireflite

1956

S-23 Firedome (wb 126.0)	Wght	Price	Prod
Seville htp cpe	3,800	2,684	19,136
Seville htp sdn	3,920	2,833	4,030
Sportsman htp cpe	3,835	2,854	4,589
Sportsman htp sdn	3,945	2,953	1,645
conv cpe	4,080	3,081	646
sdn 4d	3,780	2,678	44,909
wgn 4d	4,095	3,371	2,950
S-24 Fireflite (wb 126.0)			
Sportsman htp cpe	3,905	3,346	7,479
Sportsman htp sdn	3,970	3,431	3,350
conv cpe	4,075	3,544	1,085*
Pacesetter conv cpe	4,070	3,615	400*
sdn 4d	3,860	3,119	18,207
Adventurer htp cpe	3,870	3,728	996

* Estimated; total convertible coupes: 1,485.

1956 Engines	bore×stroke	bhp	availability
V-8, 330.4	3.72×3.80	230	S-Firedome
V-8, 330.4	3.72×3.80	255	S-Fireflite exc Adventurer
V-8, 341.4	3.78×3.80	320	S-Adventurer

1957

S-27 Firesweep (wb 122.0)	Wght	Price	Prod
Sportsman htp cpe	3,645	2,836	13,333
Sportsman htp sdn	3,720	2,912	7,168
sdn 4d	3,675	2,777	17,300
Shopper wgn 4d, 6P	3,965	3,169	2,270
Explorer wgn 4d, 9P	3,970	3,310	1,198
S-25 Firedome (wb 126.0)			
Sportsman htp cpe	3,910	3,085	12,179
Sportsman htp sdn	3,960	3,142	9,050
conv cpe	4,065	3,361	1,297
sdn 4d	3,955	2,958	23,339
S-26 Fireflite (wb 126.0)			
Sportsman htp cpe	4,000	3,614	7,217
Sportsman htp sdn	4,125	3,671	6,726
conv cpe	4,085	3,890	1,151
sdn 4d	4,025	3,487	11,565
Shopper wgn 4d, 6P	4,290	3,982	837
Explorer wgn 4d, 9P	4,250	4,124	934
S-26A Adventurer (wb 126.0)			
htp cpe	4,040	3,997	1,650
conv cpe	4,235	4,272	300

1957 Engines	bore×stroke	bhp	availability
V-8, 325.0	3.69×3.80	245	S-Firesweep
V-8, 325.0	3.69×3.80	260	O-Firesweep
V-8, 341.0	3.78×3.80	270	S-Firedome
V-8, 341.0	3.78×3.80	290	S-Fireflite
V-8, 345.0	3.80×3.80	345	S-Adventurer

1958

LS1-L Firesweep (wb 122.0)		Wght	Price	Prod
23	Sportsman htp cpe	3,660	2,890	5,635
27	conv cpe	3,850	3,219	700
41	sdn 4d	3,660	2,819	7,646
43	Sportsman htp sdn	3,720	2,953	3,003
45A	Shopper wgn 4d, 6P	3,955	3,266	1,305
45B	Explorer wgn 4d, 9P	3,980	3,408	1,125
LS2-M Firedome (wb 126.0)				
23	Sportsman htp cpe	3,825	3,178	4,325
27	conv cpe	4,065	3,489	519
41	sdn 4d	3,855	3,085	9,505
43	Sportsman htp sdn	3,920	3,235	3,130
LS3-H Fireflite (wb 126.0)				
23	Sportsman htp cpe	3,920	3,675	3,284
27	conv cpe	4,105	3,972	474
41	sdn 4d	3,990	3,583	4,192
43	Sportsman htp sdn	3,980	3,731	3,243
45A	Shopper wgn 4d, 6P	4,225	4,030	318
45B	Explorer wgn 4d, 9P	4,295	4,172	609
LS3-S Adventurer (wb 126.0)				
23	htp cpe	4,000	4,071	350
27	conv cpe	4,180	4,369	82

1958 Engines	bore×stroke	bhp	availability
V-8, 350.0	4.06×3.38	280	S-Firesweep
V-8, 350.0	4.06×3.38	295	O-Firesweep
V-8, 361.0	4.13×3.38	295	S-Firedome
V-8, 361.0	4.13×3.38	305	S-Fireflite; O-Firedome
V-8, 361.0	4.13×3.38	345	S-Adventurer
V-8, 361.0	4.13×3.38	355	O-Adventurer

1959

MS1-L Firesweep (wb 122.0)		Wght	Price	Prod
23	Sportsman htp cpe	3,625	2,967	5,481
27	conv cpe	3,840	3,315	596
41	sdn 4d	3,670	2,904	9,649
43	Sportsman htp sdn	3,700	3,038	2,875
45A	Shopper wgn 4d, 6P	3,950	3,366	1,064
45B	Explorer wgn, 4d, 9P	3,980	3,508	1,179
MS2-M Firedome (wb 126.0)				
23	Sportsman htp cpe	3,795	3,341	2,862
27	conv cpe	4,015	3,653	299*
41	sdn 4d	3,840	3,234	9,171*
43	Sportsman htp sdn	3,895	3,398	2,744
MS3-H Fireflite (wb 126.0)				
23	Sportsman htp cpe	3,910	3,831	1,983
27	conv cpe	4,105	4,152	283
41	sdn 4d	3,920	3,763	4,480
43	Sportsman htp sdn	3,950	3,888	2,364
45A	Shopper wgn 4d, 6P	4,170	4,216	271
45B	Explorer wgn 4d, 9P	4,205	4,358	433
MS3-S Adventurer (wb 126.0)				
23	htp cpe	3,980	4,427	602
27	conv cpe	4,120	4,749	97

* Includes Seville htp cpe, conv cpe, sdn 4d, and htp sdn, trim variation introduced in Spring 1959 to mark DeSoto's 30th anniversary.

1959 Engines	bore×stroke	bhp	availability
V-8, 361.0	4.13×3.38	295	S-Firesweep
V-8, 383.0	4.25×3.38	305	S-Firedome
V-8, 383.0	4.25×3.38	325	S-Fireflite
V-8, 383.0	4.25×3.38	350	S-Adventurer; O-others

1960

PS1-L Fireflite (wb 122.0)		Wght	Price	Prod
23	htp cpe	3,885	3,102	3,494
41	sdn 4d	3,865	3,017	9,032
43	htp sdn	3,865	3,167	1,958
PS3-M Adventurer (wb 122.0)				
23	htp cpe	3,945	3,663	3,092
41	sdn 4d	3,895	3,579	5,746
43	htp sdn	3,940	3,727	2,759

1960 Engines	bore×stroke	bhp	availability
V-8, 361.0	4.13×3.38	295	S-Fireflite
V-8, 383.0	4.25×3.38	305	S-Adventurer
V-8, 383.0	4.25×3.38	325	O-all
V-8, 383.0	4.25×3.38	330	O-Adventurer

1961

RS1-L (wb 122.0)		Wght	Price	Prod
612	htp cpe	3,760	3,102	911
614	htp sdn	3,820	3,167	2,123

1961 Engine	bore×stroke	bhp	availability
V-8, 361.0	4.13×3.38	265	S-all

Dodge

The Dodge Brothers Company was 14 years old when it was bought by Walter Chrysler in 1928. As a new division of his corporation, Dodge built 125,000 cars in 1929. Then the Depression turned the nation's economy from sunny to gloomy. Though most makes bottomed out in 1933-34, Dodge averaged a healthy 100,000 cars a year, good for fourth behind Chevrolet, Ford, and sister-make Plymouth.

Brothers John and Horace Dodge were traditionalists who believed in practicality and honest dollar value, so their cars never made any gesture toward sport. This continued under Chrysler, with nothing to suggest the high-performance Dodges to come. Through 1954, Dodges were just solid, reliable, low-to-middle-priced cars. Famed World War I U.S. Army General John J. Pershing did as much as anyone to make "Dodge" synonymous with "dependable" by commanding a fleet of 250 Dodge touring cars during his Mexican border campaign against Pancho Villa in 1916.

Dodge changed rungs on the Chrysler price ladder in the early 1930s, sometimes standing above DeSoto, sometimes below. By 1933 it was decided that Dodge should occupy the attractive spot just above Plymouth and below DeSoto. Though the Great Depression delayed Chrysler's efforts to rebuild Dodge by several years, the division surged in 1935, reaching 159,000 cars for the model year. Dodge then soared to near 264,000 for '36 and reached its prewar peak with over 295,000 for 1937. A deep recession the next year temporarily halted the climb, and Dodge slipped out of the top five, but by 1941 it was back up to 237,000.

The Dodge Brothers (who both died in 1920) and their successors sold only four-cylinder cars through 1928, then announced their first six: 241.5-cubic inch L-head unit making 58-68 horsepower. Chrysler presided over the first Dodge Eight in 1930, which would continue through three different displacements for the next three years. Dodge then offered nothing but inline-sixes through 1952. That engine, a flathead cast-iron design introduced in 1933, ultimately evolved through displacements of 201-230 cid and rated horsepower of 75-138. And it wasn't finished even in 1952; it continued for seven years more.

Dodge styling in the 1930s was the most conservative of any Chrysler make, and the division was lucky to escape being saddled with an Airflow, as was planned for 1935. Dodge's long-famous ram hood mascot, a manifestation of the Chrysler

1930 Series DD New Six four-door sedan

1932 Series DK Eight 2/4-passenger coupe

1931 Series DH Six station wagon

1933 Series DO Eight four-door sedan

1932 Series DK Eight four-door sedan

1933 Series DP Six Salon Brougham sedan

takeover, arrived in '32. Lines were four-square through 1934 save a slight concession to the "streamlining" craze in a rakish 1933-34 grille. Then came a waterfall grille, skirted fenders, and much-more-rounded lines as part of the companywide "Airstream" look adopted for 1935-36. By 1939, Dodges had acquired extended "pontoon" fenders, elongated rear decks, and a sharp "prow-front" under the direction of company design chief Ray Dietrich, thus falling nicely in line with DeSoto and Chrysler.

Like most makes, and the Depression notwithstanding, Dodge cataloged numerous body types throughout the '30s, including all the popular open styles. Among the latter was a convertible sedan, which was absent for 1935 and then vanished after '38 due to diminishing sales. A long 128-inch-wheelbase chassis appeared for 1936 under seven-passenger sedans and limousines; by 1939 this was up to 134 inches. Dodge also made a strong effort to win custom-body business by selling chassis to hearse, ambulance, and station wagon builders.

Speaking of wheelbases, Dodge did much shuffling there, too. The short-lived Eights started at 114 inches, stretched to 118.5 for '31, then to 122. Sixes ranged from 109 to 120 inches through 1939, but were mostly 114-117 inches. Series names and positions also changed a lot, as did each year's advertising theme. Chrysler would name cars most anything if it helped sales, and it hyped the Dodge line under such prosaic banners as "New Standard" (1934), "New Value" ('35), "Beauty Winner" (1936), and "Luxury Liner" (1939). That last one is still part of auto "journalese," if not popular parlance.

Nineteen thirty-seven brought some of the more innovative period Dodges. Though not vastly altered from the "Air Styled" '36s, they boasted nonsnag door handles, recessed dash knobs, lower driveshaft tunnels, one-piece steel-roof construction (ending fabric inserts at last), and built-in windshield defroster vents. Dodge also claimed an industry first with fully insulated rubber body mounts.

Like other Chrysler products, the '39 Dodges were totally redesigned—fitting for the make's Silver Anniversary year. Also in evident celebration, the division returned to a two-series lineup for the first time since 1934: Special and DeLuxe, differing mainly in interior trim. DeLuxe also offered more models. Long sedans took a year off, but not the sturdy Dodge six: still pumping out 87 horsepower, as it had since '34. A "birthday present" of sorts was a limited-edition five-passenger DeLuxe Town Coupe with Hayes bodywork on the standard 117-inch wheelbase. Hayes built 1000 of these pretty, thin-pillared bodies for use among Dodge, DeSoto, and Chrysler. The Dodge version saw 363 copies of the one-year-only model, and led the "Luxury Liners" in glamour as well as price ($1055).

Continuity was Dodge's hallmark in the '40s, the division retaining its essential 1939 bodyshells all the way through "first-series" 1949 models, though exterior sheetmetal and some internal structure would change along the way. Standard wheel-

1933 Series DO Eight station wagon

1934 Series DS DeLuxe Six Special convertible sedan

1937 Series D5 convertible sedan

1936 Series D2 Beauty Winner Six two-door trunkback sedan

1936 Series D2 convertible coupe

1937 Series D5 four-door trunkback sedan

1938 Series D8 four-door trunkback sedan

1937 Series D5 two-door sedan

1938 Series D8 convertible coupe

1939 Series D11 Luxury Liner DeLuxe four-door sedan

base throughout was 119.5 inches. A long sedan and limousine returned for 1940 on a 139.5-inch chassis, which then shrunk a bit to 137.5. Styling was typical of Highland Park in this era: prominent fenders, increasingly gaudy grilles, and low rooflines with limited glass areas.

The 1940 line repeated '39 offerings: low-priced Special coupe and two- and four-door sedans; the same as DeLuxes plus convertible, five-seater coupe, and the aforementioned seven-place sedan and limousine (the last cost $1170). The upper series accounted for some 120,000 units, about 60 percent of the model-year total—though only 1000 were long models. Running boards were on the way out, now a $10 linewide option. A new 1940 extra was two-tone paint, though with fenders, hood, and deck in the contrasting color, this conferred a taxicab air and was not popular.

A clean facelift livened up looks for '41, announced by parking lights combined with the headlamps in a more horizontal heart-shaped grille. Chrysler's Fluid Drive clutch became optional, and higher compression booted the old-soldier six to 91 bhp. Two-door sedans were now Broughams, DeLuxe designated the inexpensive three-model line, and the upper series was renamed Custom. Expanding the last was a handsome four-door Town Sedan with blank rear-roof quarters. It was a modest success, garnering 16,074 orders. Long models continued selling in small numbers (just 654 this year). Total production divided between 106,000 DeLuxes and 131,000 Customs. Though Dodge had moved from ninth to sixth in the industry for 1940, it fell back a spot for '41. The following year, though, it reclaimed sixth from Oldsmobile.

With Pearl Harbor and America's entry into World War II, the government halted civilian production in February 1942. Dodges weren't as scarce as some other Detroit cars that year, though they're hard enough to come by now. Model-year production was about 68,500. Among standard-chassis models, the Custom convertible was rarest: just 1185 built.

A heavy facelift made the '42 Dodges look good, if not quite as radical as that year's hidden-headlamp DeSotos. Front fenders were broadened to accommodate a more-horizontal grille with a distinct eggcrate texture and bulged center. Optional fender skirts returned from '41 with bright moldings to match rear-fender trim, and five-passenger coupes gained more rakishly angled B-posts. The only mechanical change involved stroking the old six to 230.2 cid and substituting a Carter carb for the previous Stromberg. Horsepower stood at 105.

Sporadic wartime design work in Highland Park produced several interesting prototypes for postwar Dodges. These involved the basic 1940-42 body updated with smoother grilles, wraparound bumpers, thinner door pillars, and fully integrated fenders. But all were rendered stillborn because '42 tooling was far from amortized. Dodge thus resumed civilian production with warmed-over prewar cars for 1946-48, as did most other American makes.

The division was especially slow to do so, building only 420 cars by the end of 1945. But output zoomed in calendar '46, and Dodge finished the model year in fourth (behind the low-priced three) with nearly 164,000. The tally was over 243,000 for '47, but Dodge fell to fifth behind an equally resurgent Buick. The make regained fourth the next year, again on slightly more than 243,000 cars.

The facelift for the 1946-48 Dodges—all but identical save serial numbers, like divisional siblings—was created by A.B. "Buzz" Grisinger, John Chika, and Herb Weissinger, a trio soon to win fame at Kaiser-Frazer. Allowed bolt-on alterations only, they opted for a new grille with thick horizontal bars overlaid by thinner vertical ones. Square parking lights sat outboard of the bottom grille corners, and a prominent nameplate graced the hood. Technical improvements included dash-mounted pushbutton starter (replacing a foot pedal), front brakes with double wheel cylinders, revised transmission, inline fuel filter, and "Full-Flo" oil filter.

Like its corporate sisters, Dodge wasn't ready with its first all-new postwar cars in time for a 1949 announcement, so 1948s were sold through April as "first-series" '49s. The "second series" '49s were all-new save a rerated 103-horsepower six, and sold in record numbers: nearly 257,000 for the model year, though that was good for only eighth in industry volume.

Model offerings were considerably revised within two series. The inexpensive group was the 115-inch-wheelbase Wayfarer,

1940 Series D-14 DeLuxe Luxury Liner four-door sedan

1941 Series D-19 Custom Luxury Liner four-door sedan

1942 Series D-22 DeLuxe business coupe

1946 Series D-24C Custom convertible coupe

comprising a notchback business coupe, a fastback two-door sedan, and a novel three-passenger roadster with side curtains. Prices spanned $1611 to $1738. The "volume" models were a new Meadowbrook sedan and top-line Coronet sedan, coupe, convertible, and—new for Dodge—a four-door structural-wood wagon. All rode a 123.5-inch wheelbase and sported better trim and equipment than the spartan Wayfarers. Exclusive to the four-door Coronet was an $85 "Town Sedan" option with luxurious Bedford cord upholstery. The $1848 Meadowbrook sold for about $75 less than the standard Coronet sedan.

As with other Chrysler divisions, Dodge's new '49 styling was very square and slab-sided. A shiny latticework grille bore some resemblance to the 1946-48 affair, but looked more-massive. Bolt-on rear fenders were capped by three-sided taillights, but front fenders were fully flush for the first time. Collectors judge the Wayfarer roadster the most desirable '49 Dodge, and many of the original 5420 have been restored. The Coronet wagon was far less successful: only 800 were produced. After 600 more were built for early 1950, it departed for an all-steel Sierra wagon.

Gyro-Matic semiautomatic transmission became optional. This was an important sales point at a time when people were tiring of manual shifting. Fluid Drive with Gyro-Matic was a complex solution to a simple problem, combining a conventional clutch with a fluid coupling that multiplied torque like a torque converter; electrical shift circuits added to what one writer called a "full range of potential transmission trouble." The coupling performed the usual flywheel functions of storing energy, smoothing power impulses, and meshing the ring gear with the starter pinion. Lacking a clutch-plate contact, a clutch was mounted in tandem. The fluid coupling was a drum filled with low-viscosity mineral oil. Running the engine rotated a set of vanes attached to the inner face that threw oil outward onto a facing runner with another set of vanes. The oil turned the runner to provide a smooth flow of power while avoiding any metal-to-metal contact.

Fluid Drive had two gear positions: Low, governing first and second gears, High for third and fourth. Low was mainly for fast starts or towing. In most other driving you simply shifted into High and pressed the accelerator, then let up at 14 mph, when a "thump" announced the shift from third to fourth. Stops and starts required no clutching or shifting, hence Chrysler's claim that Fluid Drive Gyro-Matic eliminated 95 percent of all shift motions. The clutch was there, but was used only to change between Low and High or to back up.

Unusually for an all-new Detroiter, the 1949 Dodge got a heavy facelift for its second season. Coronet now featured Dodge's first hardtop coupe, dubbed Diplomat, and the Wayfarer roadster gained roll-down door glass to become the Sportabout convertible (still with a single bench seat for three). Other offerings returned from '49, including a seven-passenger sedan on a 137.5-inch wheelbase in the Coronet line. This would continue in very small numbers through 1952, mainly for taxi and limousine use.

Dodge fared well in the early 1950s despite ho-hum cars and government-ordered caps on civilian production due to the Korean War. Division car output was just over 343,000 for 1950 and 290,000 for '51, good for seventh in the industry. The division maintained that rank with only 206,000 cars for '52 and a more-satisfying 320,000 for '53, then dropped to eighth on 1954 volume of only 154,000.

Styling became a tad sleeker for 1951-52. Wheelbases were unchanged, but a lower grille opening, clean flanks, and faired-in taillights improved appearance. The most-visible '52 alteration was paint applied to the grille bar just above the bumper.

A revised 1953 lineup put a lone Meadowbrook Suburban wagon and other two-door models on the 114-inch Plymouth wheelbase—thus reviving a stubby look; a 119-inch chassis supported six-cylinder Meadowbrook, Meadowbrook Special, and Coronet sedans and club coupes. But windshields were now one-piece, rooflines restyled, and trim moved around, all of which helped improve what were still slab-sided boxes. As with all '53 Chrysler Corporation cars, this facelift marked the first direct influence of new styling chief Virgil Exner, who'd come to Highland Park from Studebaker a few years before.

But the big news for '53 was the Coronet Eight, a new top-line group that consisted of long-chassis club coupe and sedan and "shorty" convertible, Diplomat hardtop, and two-door

Sierra, all powered by Dodge's first-ever performance engine: the brilliant Red Ram V-8. Arriving at 241.3 cid, it delivered 140 horsepower but was capable of much more. In essence, it was a scaled-down version of 1951's new 331-cid Chrysler Hemi. The company had long experimented with hemispherical combustion chambers and was now cashing in on what it had learned. Against other V-8s, the Hemi offered the inherent advantages of smoother porting and manifold passages, larger valves set farther apart, better thermal efficiency, ample water jacketing, a nearly central spark-plug location, and low heat rejection into coolant. Its main drawback was cost: far more expensive to build than, say, the 1955 Chevrolet 265.

Even so, the Red Ram combined with surprisingly low weight to make the '53 Dodges terrific stormers and fine handlers. They were even frugal with fuel: A Red Ram scored 23.4 miles per gallon in the '53 Mobilgas Economy Run. Other V-8 Dodges broke 196 AAA stock-car records at Bonneville in '53, and Danny Eames drove one to a record 102.62 mph on California's El Mirage dry lake.

Several interesting show cars also contributed to Dodge's now increasingly youthful image. Like others at Chrysler in this period, these were Exner designs built by Ghia in Italy. The first was Firearrow, a nonrunning '53 roadster with a unique frameless windshield; a road-ready version appeared the following year. In late 1954 came the evolutionary Firearrow convertible and sport coupe whose lines inspired the limited-production Dual-Ghia of 1956-58. The coupe proved quite stable aerodynamically, achieving 143.44 mph on the banked oval at the Chrysler Proving Grounds in rural Chelsea, Michigan.

Only detail appearance changes occurred on Dodge's '54 production models, but the Red Ram became available across the board, and a luxurious new top-line Royal V-8 series offered club coupe, sedan, convertible, and Sport hardtop coupe. Meadowbrook now listed six and V-8 sedans and coupes on the 119-inch chassis; Coronet added long-chassis four-door Sierra wagons and short two-door Suburbans, plus convertible and Sport hardtop as before.

Dodge paced the 1954 Indianapolis 500, and trumpeted its selection with 701 replica pace-car convertibles called Royal 500. Priced at $2632 apiece, they sported Kelsey-Hayes chrome wire wheels, "continental" outside spare tire, special ornamentation, and a tuned 150-bhp Red Ram. A dealer-installed four-barrel Offenhauser manifold was also available, which must have made this a screamer, though Chrysler never quoted actual horsepower.

The Royal 500 symbolized Dodge's rapid emergence as Chrysler's "performance" outfit. And indeed, the division was rolling up more competition successes. Lincoln is famous for its dominance in the Mexican Road Race of these years. Less widely known is the fact that Dodge overwhelmed the event's Medium Stock class in 1954, finishing 1-2-3-4-6-9.

After suffering poor '54 sales along with sister divisions, Dodge came back with a vengeance. Bearing Exner's first-generation "Forward Look," the all-new '55s were flashy but not overdone, the work of Exner lieutenant Murray Baldwin. They were bigger as well as brighter, with all models on a 120-inch wheelbase. Series comprised six and V-8 Coronets and V-8 Royals and Custom Royals. The last, the new line-topper, offered four-door sedan and three Lancer submodels: sedan (a midyear arrival), convertible, and hardtop coupe. The old six, which had been coaxed to 110 horsepower for '54, now packed 123 bhp. The Red Ram was bored to 270.1 cid, good for 175/183 bhp; an optional "Power Package" with four-barrel carb delivered 193. Dodge prospered with greatly increased '55 volume of nearly 277,000 cars, but rivals also did well in that record industry year and Dodge couldn't budge from eighth place.

1948 Series D-24C Custom convertible coupe

1949 Coronet four-door sedan

1949 Wayfarer roadster

1950 Coronet four-door sedan

1951 Coronet Diplomat hardtop coupe

1952 Coronet four-door sedan

1952 Wayfarer two-door sedan

1953 Coronet Eight four-door sedan

1954 Royal four-door sedan

1954 Royal hardtop sport coupe

1954 Royal 500 convertible coupe

1954 Royal club coupe

1955 Royal Sierra station wagon

1955 Coronet Six two-door sedan

1955 Coronet V-8 four-door sedan

1955 Custom Royal Lancer hardtop coupe

1955 Custom Royal four-door sedan

1956 Custom Royal Lancer hardtop sedan

1956 Coronet V-8 two-door sedan

1956 Royal Sierra station wagon

1956 Royal Suburban two-door station wagon

1956 Coronet "Texan" Lancer hardtop coupe

1956 Custom Royal La Femme hardtop coupe

1956 Custom Royal four-door sedan

1957 Suburban two-door station wagon

An interesting '55 footnote was "La Femme," a Custom Royal Lancer hardtop coupe painted pink and white. As the name implied, it featured custom accoutrements for m'lady, including a folding umbrella and a fitted handbag in the backs of the front seats. La Femme returned for '56, but response was minimal and few of these cars were produced.

Most '55 Dodge Lancers wore tiny chrome rear-fender trim suggesting fins. For '56 Highland Park offered sharply uplifted fenders, and Dodge wore them as well as any. Two-speed PowerFlite, the firm's first fully automatic transmission, had arrived with lever control in '54. Now it had pushbuttons in a handy pod to the left of the wheel.

Besides revised frontal styling and new interiors, Dodge '56 also advertised a stroked "Super Red Ram" V-8 with 315 cid and 218 horsepower, versus 189 for the returning 270. The evergreen six now offered 131 horses. Available across the board was the first of the now-famous "D-500" options. For '56 this was just a four-barrel carb that provided 230 horsepower. However, a Chrysler historical publication also lists a four-barrel 315 with higher compression (9.25:1 vs. 8.0 elsewhere), good for 260 horsepower. Other '56 developments involved a new Lancer four-door hardtop sedan in each series, and a "spring special" Golden Lancer, a D-500 Custom Royal hardtop coupe with Sapphire White/Gallant Gold exterior and harmonizing white/black/gray interior.

Nineteen fifty-six was a down year for all Detroit, and Dodge built 240,000 cars to again run eighth. But helped by torsion-bar suspension, all-new styling, and more power for '57, Dodge would climb to seventh on volume of nearly 288,000.

Carrying Exner's "second-generation" Forward Look, the '57 Dodges were longer, lower, wider, and more aggressive-looking, with a massive bumper/grille, lots of glass, and high-flying fins (ads called all of this "Swept-Wing" styling). Wheelbase stretched to 122 inches, where it would remain through 1961. The Hemi was again enlarged: bored this time to 325 cid. The result, depending on compression and carbs, was 245-310 bhp. The '57 D-500 option was a 354 from junior Chryslers, tuned for 340 bhp. The old six got another seven horses for its ultimate total of 138.

The D-500 package was Dodge's answer to the limited-edition supercars at sister divisions—available for any model right down to the plain-Jane Coronet two-door. Shocks, springs, and the new-for-'57 front torsion bars were all suitably firmed up for what *Motor Trend* magazine called a "close liaison with the road"—handling that put D-500s at the head of their class. V-8s delivered brisk-to-blistering go. Even the relatively mild 245-bhp mill could scale 0-60 in about 9.5 seconds. For '58 the D-500 package replaced its complex Hemi with a less costly 361-cid wedgehead V-8. The wedgehead delivered 305 or 320 horsepower. Optional Bendix electronic fuel injection boosted power to 333, but it was unreliable and the few that were sold were probably replaced by carburetors.

A mild facelift with four headlamps and revised trim marked the '58 Dodges. The line was a rerun until February, when a spiffy Regal Lancer hardtop coupe was announced as one of the "spring specials" so long favored by Chrysler marketers. Some of its trim items were also available on lesser Dodges, including lancer-head grille medallion, blackout headlamp trim, and rather contrived bodyside/fin moldings. Sensibly left alone were 1957's new Torsion-Aire Ride and optional three-speed TorqueFlite automatic transmission that had earned near-universal praise—and buyer approval. Both would persist at Dodge and throughout the corporate camp for many years.

Now in its final season, Dodge's 325 Hemi packed 252/265 bhp for '58. A 350 wedgehead offered 295 standard horsepower in Custom Royals and V-8 wagons. Although 1958 was disas-

1957 Custom Royal Lancer convertible coupe

1957 Custom Royal Lancer hardtop coupe

1957 Custom Royal Lancer hardtop sedan

1957 Custom Sierra station wagon

1957 Custom Royal four-door sedan

1958 Custom Royal Lancer hardtop coupe

1958 Custom Royal Lancer hardtop sedan

1959 Custom Royal Lancer hardtop coupe

1959 Custom Royal four-door sedan

1960 Polara four-door sedan

trous for every Detroit make, Dodge fared worse than most. Model-year production plunged to 138,000 as the division barely finished ahead of Cadillac.

But Dodge shared in Detroit's modest 1959 recovery, building about 156,000 cars and rebounding from ninth to eighth in the volume stakes. Sales might have been better had it not been for a rather heavy-handed facelift marked by droopy hooded headlamps and misshapen fins above suggestive thrusting taillamps. Revised interiors could be newly furnished with swivel front seats, semibuckets that pivoted outward upon opening a door. The venerable flathead six was in its final year. V-8s, now wedgeheads only, comprised a new 326 with 255 bhp for Coronets; a 305-bhp 361 for other models; and a big new 383 with 320/345 bhp. The last-named was that year's D-500—and not cheap. Both were thirsty, but it was the age of 30-cent-a-gallon gas and the market still craved performance (if not quite as much as before the '58 recession).

The '60s would see Dodge strengthen its position in the high-performance field, push upward into price territory left vacant by DeSoto's cancelation after '61, and diversify with compacts and intermediates. Volume rose rapidly after 1964 to an annual average of more than half a million units, and the division set a new record with 633,000 cars built for '66. But competitors were up too, so Dodge's standing in the industry production stakes varied between fifth or sixth in its best years and seventh to ninth in the troubled years 1961-63.

Taking note of the growing buyer interest in smaller cars prompted by the '58 recession, Dodge entered the '60s with a much broader lineup divided into "junior" and "senior" groups. The former was the new Dart: sixes and V-8s on a 118-inch wheelbase save wagons, which rode a 122. Series were tagged Seneca, Pioneer, and Phoenix in ascending order of price and plush. Phoenix offered a convertible, hardtop coupe and sedan, and pillared four-door; lesser lines were limited to wagons, two- and four-door sedans, and a Pioneer two-door hardtop. The senior line comprised V-8 Matadors and Polaras on the 122-inch wheelbase. All 1960 Dodges employed unit body/chassis construction, new at Chrysler Corporation that year, and wore more-sculptured lines announced by bright, blunt, and busy front ends. Fins were still in evidence, ending well ahead of podlike taillights on Matador/Polara, near the rear of more-conventional fenders on Darts.

Despite appearances, most 1960 Dodges were relatively light and thus offered good performance with reasonable economy. That was even true of base-engine models, which carried the larger, 225-cid version of Chrysler Corporation's new "Slant Six." Initially rated at 145 bhp, this durable workhorse would carry on into the early '80s. Dart's V-8 was the solid, reliable 318

1960 Dart Phoenix convertible coupe

1960 Polara hardtop coupe

1961 Dart Phoenix hardtop coupe

1961 Dart Pioneer station wagon

1961 Polara hardtop sedan

1961 Dart Phoenix hardtop coupe

with 230/255 horsepower. Matadors used a 295-bhp Chrysler 361, optional on Dart Pioneer and Phoenix. Polaras had a standard 383 (available for Phoenix and Matador) with 325/330 horsepower. Helped greatly by the Dart, attractively priced in the $2300-$3000 range, Dodge scored impressively higher sales: up over 200,000 for the model year to nearly 368,000, good for sixth on the industry roster.

Per well-established Chrysler practice, the '61 line included a Dodge version of a Plymouth product: the 106.5-inch-wheelbase Valiant compact, new for 1960. Called Lancer, it shared the Valiant's "unibody" structure and basic styling but stood apart with a horizontal-bar grille and slightly better trim. Also like Valiant, there were two Lancer series, 170 and 770, each with two-door sedan, four-door sedan, and four-door wagon body styles. The 770 added a hardtop coupe that was also new to Valiant for '61, as was the pillared two-door. Power came from the smaller, 170-cid Slant Six with 101 bhp. The 225 Dart engine was optional.

The Dart itself was substantially facelifted for '61, gaining a deeply concave full-width grille cradling quad headlamps, plus curious reverse-slant tailfins. The senior Matador was dropped and remaining Polaras were restyled to be virtual Dart dead ringers. Engines mostly reprised the 1960 choices. Among these was Dodge's customary D-500 option, now a 383 with twin four-barrel carburetors and ram-induction manifolding (new for '60), good for an outstanding 330 horsepower. In a Dart, that translated to about 10 pounds for each horsepower, a super power-to-weight ratio that meant 120-mph flat out and acceleration to match. Torsion bar suspension and oversized Chrysler brakes made it as roadable as it was quick. It was even quicker when equipped with the Chrysler 413, a ram-induction wedge delivering 350 or 375 bhp as a new Dart option, though price was high and availability quite limited.

However, Dodge sales dropped by over 25 percent for '61, reflecting increased competition and an overall industry downtrend. Lancer didn't sell well, but it was a stopgap anyway. A successor was in the works, so the only notable changes for '62 were a busier grille and a smart bucket-seat GT hardtop (replacing the 770 model).

Meantime, a brand-new 116-inch-wheelbase Dart in base, 330, and 440 series arrived, measuring six inches shorter and 400 pounds lighter than corresponding '61s. Topping the line was a sporty bucket-seat Polara 500 group, offering hardtops with two and four doors, plus convertible. Chrysler design chief Virgil Exner thought that if Americans liked compacts, they'd go for downsized "standard" cars, too. But he was about 15 years ahead of his time, and these cars sold as poorly as the Lancer—aggravated by frankly odd Lancer-like looks.

But performance fans roundly applauded the smaller, lighter Darts, mainly because the big-block 413 returned with more

1961 Lancer 770 hardtop coupe

1962 Dart 440 hardtop sedan

1962 Polara 500 convertible coupe

1962 Polara 500 hardtop sedan

1962 Lancer GT hardtop coupe

muscle: 365, 380, 410, and a rollicking 420-bhp. Shoehorned into the lightest base-trim two-doors, these cars began terrorizing the nation's dragstrips, thus renewing Dodge's "hot car" reputation and setting the stage for even wilder doings. In fact, big-inch Dodge intermediates won the National Hot Rod Association Championship in 1962 and would reign supreme for the next few years on literally every quarter-mile. They were also strong contenders at Daytona.

But performance alone doesn't necessarily sell cars, and Dodge's total volume for '62 was down to about 240,500, off some 30,000 in a year when most rivals scored higher sales. Things would have been worse had it not been for the true full-size cars that were reinstated at midyear as the Custom 880. Effectively taking over for the now-departed DeSoto, they looked like the finless '61 Polaras they were, with '62 Chrysler-style "plucked chicken" tails and standard 265-bhp 361 V-8.

While Plymouth struggled on with its related downsized "standards," Dodge increased wheelbase to 119 inches for 1963—and pushed performance. What had been called Dart was now just "Dodge," comprising 330, 440, and Polara series. As before, the last included a swanky bucket-seat 500 convertible and hardtop coupe. Styling was cleaner and more conventional, though the "face" was still pretty odd. Engines remained broadly the same, but a bore job took the 413 wedge to 426 cubes and 370/375 horsepower. But the big news was the "Ramcharger," a super-performance 426 with aluminum pistons and high-lift cam punching out 415/425 horsepower.

Dodge did field a Dart for '63, but it was a very different car: a mostly new compact to replace Lancer. (The name change was a last-minute decision.) It was basically that year's redesigned Valiant with more crisply styled exterior and five extra inches in wheelbase (111 except wagons, still at 106). Sedans and wagons made up the 170 and 270 series, with convertibles offered in 270 and bucket-seat GT guise; there was also a GT hardtop coupe. At the other end of the scale, Custom 880s returned with new lower-priced 880 companions, all bearing grilles with fine vertical bars. With so much new, Dodge surged past Rambler to grab seventh in the industry on record volume of over 446,000 units.

The '64 lineup was much like '63's, with facelifts that continued Dodge's move back to more-orthodox looks. Darts became livelier, as Valiant's new 273-cid small-block V-8 was added to the options list, bringing 180 horsepower. That year's Ramcharger was Chrysler's fabled hemi-head V-8, returning to the performance wars in a new 426 version with 425 horsepower—but only for racing. The top showroom power options remained wedgehead 426s, now with 365 standard horsepower or 415 with high-compression heads. But Hemi-powered Dodge/Plymouth intermediates provided plenty of entertainment anyway, dominating the NASCAR season beginning with a 1-2-3 sweep at the Daytona 500. In the production race, Dodge swept back into sixth for the first time since 1960.

For 1965, the Coronet name returned on a revamped midsize line with more square-cut styling and a 117-inch wheelbase for all models but wagons (116 inches). These were essentially the 1962-64 "standards" logically repositioned to battle popular intermediates like Ford Fairlane and Chevy Chevelle. But there was also a much-altered 115-inch-wheelbase Coronet Hemi-Charger two-door sedan weighing just 3165 pounds. Intended strictly for drag racing and base-priced at $3165, it came with the reborn 426 Hemi, of course, plus heavy-duty springs and shocks, antiroll bar, four-on-the-floor manual transmission, and strong police brakes. Performance was more than ample: 0-60 mph in seven seconds or less. Buyers in less of a hurry flocked to a civilized new buckets-and-console Coronet 500 hardtop and convertible available with wedgehead V-8s up to 426 cubes

1962 Custom 880 hardtop sedan

1963 Custom 880 hardtop sedan

1964 Polara 500 convertible coupe

1964 Polara hardtop coupe

1964 Custom 880 hardtop coupe

and 365 horsepower.

Capping the '65 line was a completely redesigned group of 121-inch wheelbase Polaras and Custom 880s, plus a companion sports/luxury hardtop, the $3355 Monaco. All shared chassis and body structure with that year's Chryslers and full-size Plymouth Furys. Their conservatively square basic shape was dictated by design chief Elwood Engel, who'd been recruited from Ford to replace Virgil Exner in 1962. The Dodges were distinguished by a "dumbbell" grille and delta taillamps.

After a modest '65 restyle, Darts squared up for '66, via new front sheetmetal. Coronets returned in standard, Deluxe, 440, and 500 guise, also with blockier fronts as well as curvier rear fenders and wedgy taillights. Custom 880 was renamed Monaco, and the big bucket-seat hardtop became Monaco 500. Monacos and Polaras got wider taillights and crisper lower-body contours, plus Chrysler's new big-block 440 wedgehead with 350 horsepower as the top power option.

A midyear salvo in the division's 1966 "Dodge Rebellion" was Charger, essentially a fastback Coronet hardtop coupe with hidden-headlamp grille, full-width taillights, and a sporty four-seat interior with full-length center console and individual fold-down rear buckets. A mild 318 V-8 was standard, but you could order a mighty 425-bhp "Street Hemi," a new regular production option for all '66 Chrysler intermediates. Also on the Charger option sheet: manual transmission, "Rallye" suspension, and numerous luxury items.

In all, 1966 was a great year for Dodge. After easing to 489,000 units for '65, volume shot up to its aforementioned decade high, good for fifth in the industry. Dodge wouldn't rank as high again until '88.

For 1967, the Dart got an all-new unit structure on the existing wheelbase and lost its wagons. Styling was a bit curvier and more "important," though still pretty, if rather mainstream. Polara/Monaco also got a new structure: a full-size body/frame platform shared with that year's Chryslers and Plymouth Furys. Styling here was somewhat more contrived: lower and sleeker but with rear decks longer than hoods, plus a complex grille comprising a square vertical-bar section between openings split by horizontal bars. A belated facelift made Coronets look more like the Charger, which continued its '66 appearance but added two 383 V-8 options with 270 and 325 horsepower.

Continuing its performance push, Dodge issued a sportier Coronet for '67. Called R/T, for "Road/Track", it came as a convertible and hardtop coupe with a tuned 375-bhp 440 "Magnum" V-8, heavy-duty suspension, wide tires, and oversize brakes—Dodge's entry in the burgeoning "muscle-car" market uncov-

1964 Polara hardtop sedan

1964 Dart GT hardtop coupe

1964 Custom 880 convertible coupe

1965 Dart GT convertible coupe

1965 Monaco hardtop coupe

1965 Coronet 500 hardtop coupe

1966 Polara hardtop sedan

ered by the Pontiac GTO. A similar package was devised the following year for a new Charger R/T. The 426 Hemi remained optional for intermediates, still on a limited basis. Despite its appealing '67 line, Dodge fell back to seventh place on model-year volume of nearly 466,000 units.

Dart and full-size Dodges were facelifted for '68, as it was time for Coronet and Charger to be fully revised. The result was the best-looking midsize Dodges yet: long and low, with rounded "fuselage" lines and pleasingly simple grilles. Charger again featured hidden headlamps, but was now a notchback hardtop with a semifastback "flying buttress" roofline.

Sporty models continued multiplying. Dart added a plush GTS hardtop and convertible with standard 340-cid V-8, an enlarged 273 with 275 horsepower. A big 300-bhp 383 was optional—and bordered on overkill in a compact. Coronet offered the new budget-priced Super Bee, a no-frills two-door muscle coupe with special 335-bhp "Magnum" 383. These and the Coronet and Charger R/Ts made up what Dodge called the "Scat Pack." All wore "bumble-bee" tape stripes on their tails, and ranked among 1968's quickest and most-roadable performance machines.

Along with Chrysler and Plymouth Fury, the 1969 Polara/Monaco got "fuselage" styling of their own, but remained on a 122-inch wheelbase. Dart, Coronet, and Charger wore minor

1966 Coronet 500 hardtop coupe

1967 Coronet 500 Hemi hardtop coupe

1967 Monaco hardtop sedan

1967 Coronet R/T hardtop coupe

1967 Charger fastback hardtop coupe

1967 Polara 500 hardtop coupe

1967 Dart GT hardtop coupe

facelifts. Dart GTS was joined by a Swinger, a two-door hardtop with special trim, bright grille, and choice of 318 or 340 V-8s.

But the pride of Dodge's '69 fleet was unquestionably the Charger Daytona. Conceived for long-distance NASCAR races like the Daytona 500, it was an exercise in aerodynamics, marked by a unique bullet nose with hidden headlights and "bib" spoiler, plus a flush-window fastback roof and a huge trunklid wing on towering twin stabilizers. All this made the Daytona about 20-percent more "slippery" than previous racing Chargers, which gave it an advantage of 500 yards per lap. Dodge built only 505—just enough to qualify as "production" under NASCAR rules. A Daytona won the Talladega 500 in September 1969, though that was partly because the Ford contingent didn't show. In 1970, the Daytona's and Plymouth's similar Superbirds won 38 of 48 major NASCAR races. For shorter races, Dodge also had a wingless, blunt-nose Charger 500.

Appearing with Plymouth's third-generation Barracuda for 1970 was a Dodge relative, the division's belated reply to the Ford Mustang, Chevy Camaro, and other ponycars. Fittingly named Challenger, it was offered with a Slant-Six as standard power, plus V-8 options of 318, 383, 440, and even the Hemi. Models comprised hardtop coupe and convertible in plain and

1968 Coronet R/T hardtop coupe

1969 Coronet 500 hardtop coupe

1968 Charger hardtop coupe

1969 Charger Hemi hardtop coupe

1969 Polara 500 hardtop coupe

1968 Dart GTS hardtop coupe

1969 Charger Daytona hardtop coupe

1968 Monaco 500 hardtop coupe

1969 Dart GT hardtop coupe

sporty R/T trim. The hardtop could also be ordered as a Special Edition with padded vinyl roof and a smaller "formal" rear window. Priced attractively in the $3000-$3500 range and cataloging a broad list of options, Challenger sold very well its first year, but then tailed off rapidly. In 1970 sales, sixes outpaced V-8s, while hardtops outsold convertibles. Only about 10,000 SE coupes were built.

Specifications and dimensions for other 1970 Dodges were largely as for '69, but Coronets, Chargers, and Polara/Monaco received large "loop" bumper/grilles; Coronet's divided affair looked a bit swollen. More-massive rear bumpers also adorned the big cars, as well as Darts. Charger offered a six for the first time, while the exotic Daytona, having proven its point, was dropped (leaving Plymouth to carry the colors with its similar Superbird). Ignition/steering-column locks, fiberglass-belted tires, dual-action wagon tailgates, and a long list of federally mandated safety equipment completed the 1970 story. As in 1969, Dodge remained seventh in industry output, though volume fell from 611,000 to 543,000 for the model year.

Dodge's path through the '70s was strewn with the same obstacles that made life difficult for all U.S. automakers in those years: a growing number of ever-stricter government regulations and a dramatically altered business climate stemming from the OPEC oil embargo of 1973-74. The division was ill-prepared for both, its early-decade lines heavy with cars motivated by thirsty V-8s and wallowing on too-soft suspensions. Worse, Chrysler's steadily declining fortunes allowed most of these dinosaurs to hang on too long. Indifferent workmanship only further dampened sales, which culminated in the corporation's near-demise during 1980. But by that point, Dodge was through its trial by fire and building nothing remotely like its early-'70s dinosaurs, save the 118.5-inch-wheelbase St. Regis sedan and the Mirada personal-luxury coupe.

It didn't take much corporate contemplation to dispose of the poor Challenger: clumsy, poorly built, and never a serious sales threat to Camaro/Firebird or even Mustang II (if you call that one a ponycar). The overweight latecomer was put out to pasture after 1974, when only about 16,000 were sold. Collectors noted the rarity and desirability of convertibles, R/Ts, and big-inch engines after '71, and have been bidding up prices at auctions.

With the dawn of the first energy crisis, the brontosauruslike Polara/Monaco also seemed headed for the automotive tar pits, but Dodge tried hard to save them via discounts and cash rebates beginning in 1974, Polara vanished after '73. A blocky new Monaco arrived for '74, similar to that year's redesigned Chrysler but still on a 122-inch wheelbase. In 1977, it became the Royal Monaco—selling in decent numbers only by dint of police and taxi orders—while the Monaco name replaced Coronet on midsize cars.

Given such disappointments, it's no surprise that Dodge increasingly depended on Dart sales through mid-decade. Giving the compact line new appeal for '71 was the fastback Demon, a double to Plymouth's new-for-'70 Valiant Duster with the same 108-inch wheelbase and choice of Slant Six, 318 V-8, and optional 340 V-8. The last was reserved for a sporty Demon 340 decked out with bodyside tape stripes, matte-black hood with dual dummy scoops, and wide tires on special wheels as part of a specially beefed-up chassis.

With its trim size and 275 horsepower, the Demon 340 was nimble yet spirited—really the Dart GTS idea remade for changing times. But the name bothered some people, so Demon was prosaically retitled Dart Sport for '73, when all Darts gained a latticework grille and modest center hood bulge. The Sport 340 became a 360 for 1974-75, Dodge enlarging its small-block V-8 in deference to easier emissions tuning. A memorable

1970 Polara hardtop coupe

1970 Coronet 500 hardtop coupe

1970 Challenger hardtop coupe

1970 Dart Swinger 340 hardtop coupe

1970 Charger R/T hardtop coupe

1971 Charger 500 hardtop coupe

1971 Polara Brougham hardtop sedan

1971 Challenger R/T hardtop coupe

1971 Dart Demon "Sizzler" fastback coupe

1971 Monaco hardtop coupe

Sport option was the "Convertriple," which actually meant two separate extras: fold-down rear seat and sliding-steel sunroof. Ordered together, they made for something vaguely like a "three-way" car. Also making Dart more than just basic transportation were the plush Special Edition sedans and coupes of 1974-76. These offered vinyl tops, special emblems, velour interiors, and other extras for about $3800.

The ultra-reliable Dart remained a sales winner right to the end (mostly on the strength of workaday sedans), but its 1976 replacement was a letdown. This was the Aspen, in essence a slightly larger, roomier, and heavier Dart offering a wider range of luxury options—much like the Granada was to Maverick at Ford. Unfortunately, Aspen soon earned the dubious distinction of being the most-recalled car in history (along with its Volare twin at Plymouth), due to poor workmanship in general and early body rust in particular. (GM's X-cars soon wrested that sorry title.) But performance was good with the extra-cost 360-cid V-8 listed through '79, and furnishings were nicer than on most Darts. Aspen also revived a compact Dodge wagon, something Dart had lacked since its '67 redesign. There were pseudo-muscle R/T coupes and even a "finish it yourself" 1979 kit-car racer.

Despite its problems, Aspen was important for Dodge sales in the late '70s. It also exemplified one of the few things Detroit began doing well: putting big-car comfort in smaller packages (here, 108.7-inch-wheelbase coupes, 112.7-inch sedans and wagons). Aspen was advertised as the "family car of the future," which was hyperbole worthy of P.T. Barnum, but it would lead to the genuine article.

An unusual Aspen (and Volare) feature was its front suspension, which had torsion bars per Chrysler tradition, but situated crosswise instead of lengthwise. Some critics sneered that this was contrived merely so Chrysler could still advertise front torsion bars—and that it had no real advantage for ride or quietness; a few even claimed it actually hampered handling. Regardless, the transverse bars did allow for better suspension isolation, which made for smoother going than in the Dart. Aspen's mainstay engines, 225 Slant Six and 318 V-8, were by now hoary affairs, but proven. And the thrifty six (which could yield up to 25 mpg on the highway with manual shift) was about as bulletproof as Detroit engines ever got.

If Aspen didn't realize its sales potential, the larger Dodges fared even worse. The midsize Coronet/Monaco became more like the equivalent Plymouth Satellite/Fury with each passing year (all were built nose-to-tail at Chrysler's Lynch Road plant in Detroit) and was hardly a bargain at prices averaging $100 higher. It was also thirsty, and styling was forgettable. The Charger was simply watered down amidst name shuffles. For 1975 it became a twin to Chrysler's posh Cordoba, a car even the *Dukes of Hazzard* wouldn't have recognized.

This midsize generation began with fuselage-style '71 Charger coupes on a 115-inch wheelbase and 117-inch Coronet sedans and wagons. By 1978, they'd been heavily facelifted once—for '75—and trimmed to Charger SE and Magnum XE coupes, plus assorted Monacos and Monaco Broughams.

The reason for thinning those ranks was Diplomat. Launched for 1977, it was much like Chrysler's new LeBaron: a reskinned Aspen/Volare platform with coupes, sedans, and wagons on a 112.7-inch wheelbase. Diplomat sold well from the start, and its more-sensible design made the old-style intermediates unnecessary. The Coronet-turned-Monaco was thus transformed after 1978 into the St. Regis, all but identical with Chrysler's "downsized" R-body Newport/New Yorker sedan. The Cordoba-like Charger vanished at the same time; the related Magnum hung on through '79.

Then the smooth Mirada took over as the personal-luxury

Dodge. Mounting the Diplomat platform, it was a close cousin of 1980's new second-generation Chrysler Cordoba. One of the few true hardtop coupes left by that time, it bore a striking front end recalling the "coffin nose" of the late-'30s Cord 810/812—and the previous Magnum. Good looks won Mirada a lot of good copy in "buff" magazines. And considering how things had changed since the muscle-car days, it was decently quick—if you ordered the optional 185-bhp 360-cid V-8, Dodge's hairiest engine that year. Unhappily, this was another one that was just a shade too late to be of any real value, and Mirada's annual production averaged less than 7500 units through swan-song 1983.

Capping Dodge's enforced product renewal in the '70s was the L-body Omni, a sensible, front-drive subcompact announced for 1978. It was cut from the trend-setting pattern of the Volkswagen Rabbit, and was even powered at first by a slightly larger version of VW's single-overhead-cam four (also mounted transversely). Omni wasn't quite as much fun to drive, but had the same boxy, four-door hatchback styling and high practicality. Along with Plymouth's near-identical Horizon, Omni was one of the few bright spots in Chrysler's very gloomy sales picture at the time.

For 1979, Omni gained a slick companion coupe on a slightly shorter chassis (96.7-inch wheelbase versus 99.2). Called 024, it

1972 Dart Demon fastback coupe

1972 Charger hardtop coupe

1973 Monaco hardtop coupe

1973 Polara hardtop sedan

1974 Charger hardtop coupe

1974 Dart S.E. four-door sedan

1974 Monaco Brougham hardtop sedan

1975 Royal Monaco Brougham hardtop coupe

1975 Coronet Brougham hardtop coupe

1975 Charger SE (Special Edition) coupe

1976 Royal Monaco Brougham coupe

1976 Coronet Custom four-door sedan

1976 Charger Daytona coupe

1977 Charger Daytona coupe

1977 Monaco Brougham coupe

1977 Monaco Brougham four-door sedan

1977 Diplomat four-door sedan

1977 Aspen R/T coupe

won an immediate following, even managing a few conquest sales among import buyers seeking a sporty and nimble 2+2 that was easy on the pocketbook.

After a quiet 1980, Dodge followed Chrysler-Plymouth's lead by beginning another divisional overhaul, replacing old rear-drive models with smaller, more-efficient front-drive designs, most every one derived from the versatile 100.1-inch wheelbase K-car compact of 1981. Aided by a steadily expanding lineup marketed with a renewed emphasis on sporty performance, Dodge reaped the rewards with higher sales. Division volume rose from 309,000 for 1980 to nearly 341,000 for '81. By 1985, Dodge had achieved its goal of a half-million annual sales.

One model that wouldn't disappear was Diplomat, which got a crisp restyling for 1980, then took over for St. Regis as the traditional full-size Dodge through 1989. Though reduced after 1981 to just a single four-door sedan in two trim levels, Diplomat enjoyed steady, if modest, sales (again mainly to police and taxi fleets). Its standard Slant Six was discontinued after '83, leaving only the veteran 318 V-8.

Aries-K was the literal foundation of Dodge's 1980 line. Replacing Aspen, it was a well-engineered new-wave compact, though no more original than Omni. Design hallmarks included the choice of two transverse-mounted single-overhead-cam fours—Chrysler 2.2 liter (135 cid) or optional Mitsubishi 2.6 (156 cid)—plus rack-and-pinion steering, front-disc/rear-drum brakes, and all-coil suspension with front MacPherson struts and a twist-type rear beam axle doubling as an antiroll bar.

Most Aries were sold with optional TorqueFlite. The standard transaxle was a four-speed floorshift manual; a five-speed option arrived for 1982, then replaced the four-speed for '86, when a 2.5-liter version of the Chrysler "Trans-4" was added. Coupe, sedan, and a neat little five-door wagon were variously available in base, Custom, SE, and LE trim at competitive prices identical with those of Plymouth's twin Reliant. A smooth 1985 facelift made all Ks look more grown-up, and coupes could be ordered with sporty options like 14-inch cast-aluminum wheels, front bucket seats, and a center console.

Though Aries consistently lagged behind Reliant in sales, it sold consistently well: nearly 181,000 for debut '81, between 125,000 and 150,000 a year thereafter. Progressively improved workmanship, longer warranties (up to 7 years/70,000 miles on drivetrain components by 1987), and sensible product upgrades helped keep it competitive through 1989, when the line was trimmed to make room for the new A-body Spirit. By that time, critics had long chided Chrysler for not building anything truly new since 1981, but many buyers didn't seem to care much. The K sparked Chrysler's renaissance and no little innovation. Few cars can claim as much, let alone one so humble.

Dodge's first K-car derivatives appeared the year after Aries' launch. These were a personal-luxury twosome dubbed 400, a coupe and sedan with a front end like that of the Mirada. A 400 convertible arrived at mid-1982, the first open Dodge since the 1971 Challenger and a deft marketing move by Chrysler chairman Lee Iacocca. Like the LeBaron convertible, the 400 was built at first by an outside contractor, but proved so popular that Chrysler took over production itself. Mechanicals and dimensions for all 400s were nearly identical with Aries'.

Arriving for 1983 was a stretched 400 sedan called 600, using the new K-based 103.1-inch-wheelbase corporate E-body. A 400-like front differentiated it from Chrysler's E-Class and New Yorker. A sporty ES version bid for the burgeoning "Eurosedan" market with black exterior trim, handling package, and five-speed. It didn't win many buyers from Saab, BMW, or Mercedes, but was surprisingly capable, all things considered.

Shifting gears for 1984, Dodge dropped the 400 sedan and put 600 badges on the coupe and convertible. The latter was

1977 Diplomat coupe

1978 Monaco Brougham four-door sedan

1979 Magnum XE coupe

1979 St. Regis four-door sedan

1979 Diplomat station wagon

1979 Omni hatchback sedan

1979 Omni 024 hatchback coupe

1980 Diplomat Medallion four-door sedan

1981 Aries two-door sedan

1982 Charger 2.2 hatchback coupe

also newly available in ES trim, tied to the turbo 2.2. It was the raciest Dodge in years, but few were ordered. Still, the new approach helped series sales, which rose from 1983's combined 59,500 to over 72,000 for '84. The following year brought a more prosaic E-body SE sedan, and its strong initial sales pointed the way. After an Aries-like 1986 facelift, the 600 coupe and convertible were canceled, leaving the SE and a detrimmed base four-door to sell just as well all by themselves through 1988.

Dodge dealers bemoaned losing the 600 convertible, but at least their Daytona sports coupe had no more in-house competition from Chrysler's Laser after 1986. Both models had arrived for '84 on a much-modified 97-inch K-car chassis topped by slick, "fasthatch" styling. Corporate finances at the time dictated they be virtually identical, but the Daytona outsold Laser from the start, probably because it was geared more to Dodge's typical clientele. Daytona also had an edge with three models to Laser's two: initially base, Turbo, and the racy Turbo Z, the last distinguished by ground-hugging lower-body extensions, discreet hatchlid spoiler, and big wheels and tires.

With the sort of evolutionary improvements found in all Chrysler products in this decade, the Daytona rocked along at around 50,000 units a year through 1986. By that point it was available with a stroked and fuel-injected 2.5-liter four as base power, plus a T-top option (shared with Laser) and a "C/S" handling package named for Carroll Shelby, the old friend Iacocca had persuaded to "heat up" certain Dodges, as Shelby had done with Mustangs when both worked at Ford back in the '60s.

To compensate for the lost convertible, Dodge dealers got a restyled '87 Daytona. It boasted a smooth, hidden-headlamp "droop-snoot," and was offered in base, luxury Pacifica, and hot-rod Shelby Z models. Pacifica carried the familiar 146-bhp turbo 2.2, the Z a hot 174-bhp "Turbo II" engine; even the base model could be ordered with the 146-bhp unit as part of a C/S performance package. For 1989, Pacifica was replaced by ES and ES Turbo, the latter powered by a new 150-bhp turbocharged 2.5, and the Z was retitled Daytona Shelby. There were several styling and equipment adjustments, including standard four-wheel disc brakes across the board. Of interest to weekend racers was the C/S Competition Package for the base Daytona—basically the Shelby model with special exterior, 2.2-liter "Turbo II" power, and "maximum performance suspension" but few creature comforts so as to realize a 200-pound weight savings. All Daytonas sported a more-ergonomic dashboard and standard driver-side air bag for 1990, when the blown 2.2 received a new Variable Nozzle Technology (VNT) turbocharger that provided no more horsepower but did make driving much smoother. That year's base and ES models also offered Daytona's first V-6: the 3.0-liter (181-cid) 141-bhp Mitsubishi unit fast-spreading throughout the corporate camp.

Though Daytona generated only about a third as many sales as Mustang or Camaro, it symbolized Dodge's return to performance better than anything else in the line. And its sportiest models gave away little in acceleration or handling to those heavier, more-powerful rear-drive ponycars—proof that Chrysler engineering was still to be reckoned with.

Bowing alongside Daytona was a very different '84 Dodge: America's first "garageable" van. Aptly named Caravan, it was essentially a tall K-wagon on a special 112-inch wheelbase. Caravan had a very roomy interior that offered seating options for up to eight. Quick-release anchors made for easy removal of the second and third bench seats for cargo carrying. Front drive and astute packaging conferred a lower ride height than any rear-drive van, which eased entry/exit and contributed to a car-like driving position. In fact, aside from sitting a little higher and farther forward, driving a Caravan was much like driving

1982 400 coupe

1982 Diplomat four-door sedan

1983 400 coupe

1984 Caravan LE minivan

1984 600 ES four-door sedan

1984 Daytona Turbo Z hatchback coupe

an Aries wagon.

This as much as attractive pricing made the Caravan (and Plymouth's twin Voyager) an instant hit, generating upward of 200,000 annual sales. A fair number were windowless Ram Van commercials, but most were passenger models—initially base, SE, and woody-look LE.

Extending Caravan's appeal—literally—was the 1988 addition of 14-inch-longer "Grand" models on a 119.1-inch wheelbase. At the same time, the 3.0 Mitsubishi V-6 joined the options list, bringing 144 horsepower and a welcome gain in towing capacity over the four-cylinders. The main 1989 developments were optional availability of Chrysler's new 150-bhp turbocharged 2.5 four on standard-length SE and LE Caravans—somewhat surprising for this sort of rig—and "Ultradrive," a new electronically controlled four-speed automatic option for V-6 LEs and all Grand Caravans.

But Ultradrive had a shaky start, garnering some bad press that it was flawed. Chrysler stonewalled publicly while working quickly and quietly to amend the problems. The next year, Caravans offered a new 3.3-liter overhead-valve V-6 option: the first all-Chrysler engine since the 2.2-liter K-car four and the first in a family of corporate powerplants for the '90s.

Unquestionably, Caravan (and Voyager) was Chrysler's biggest coup of the '80s. For once, Detroit's perennial number-three outfit had delivered the right product at the right time.

Though Dodge canceled the 600 ES sport sedan after 1984, it didn't abandon the idea; it just substituted something better: the H-body Lancer (reviving the early-'60s compact name). This was another new Dodge similar to a new Chrysler, in this case the LeBaron GTS, but Lancer stood apart with the cross-bar grille then being adopted throughout the division (which must have confused Chrysler 300 enthusiasts) and by being offered in a more-overtly sporting ES rendition.

All that may be said of the GTS applies equally to Lancer—except sales, which ran about a third less. One suspects the Chrysler name and its luxury aura did more for GTS than the Dodge name did for Lancer despite similar pricing. Perhaps recognizing this, the division issued a bespoilered Lancer Shelby for 1988 with the 174-bhp "Turbo II" 2.2 and racy body addenda similar to those of the earlier Pacifica and Shelby Lancer limited editions. The '89 ES was sportier, too, gaining the new 150-bhp turbo 2.5 as standard equipment. But the H-body would prove something of a short-timer and would not return for 1990.

More successful was the P-body Shadow, intended to replace the aging Omni but introduced for 1987 as an additional, more-ambitious small sedan. Dodge wanted you to think of it as a junior BMW, but it was really more junior Lancer, with the same rounded "aerosedan" styling in three- and five-door notchback body styles on the Daytona wheelbase.

1984 600 ES Turbo convertible coupe

1985 Daytona Turbo hatchback coupe

1985 Caravan SE minivan

1985 Diplomat SE four-door sedan

1985 Omni GLH hatchback sedan

1986 Charger 2.2 hatchback coupe

K-car heritage was again evident in the Shadow chassis and drivetrains. The latter initially comprised the usual turbo and "atmospheric" 2.2-liter fours teamed with manual five-speed and automatic TorqueFlite transaxles. Unlike Plymouth with its similar Sundance, Dodge fielded enthusiast-oriented ES models with uprated suspension and a few "Euro" touches. For 1989, the corporate 2.5-liter "balancer-shaft" four was a new option for base models, and the 150-bhp turbo version was standard for ES (replacing the blown 2.2). The latter was also included in a new Daytona-style competition package for three-doors, along with handling suspension, bigger wheels and tires, "aero" body skirting, rear spoiler, and bucket seats. A minor facelift and reworked dashboards arrived for all 1990 Shadows; ES was treated to standard all-disc brakes, and its now-optional Turbo II engine was updated with a VNT blower.

Yet for all the emphasis on sport, it was the workaday Shadows that carried the sales load. And that load was considerable: over 76,000 for the first model year. Plymouth moved a like number of its Sundances.

The reason Omni didn't fade into the Shadow is that it was too good to lose. Despite relatively few changes after 1981, it averaged a remarkable 100,000 sales each year through 1983 and 58,500 or more thereafter.

The turning point was 1981, when the K-car's 2.2-liter "Trans-4" became optional for both Omni and the 024 coupe, improving acceleration and quietness with little or no loss in mileage. A smaller Peugeot-built 1.6-liter (replacing the VW 1.7 for '83) was technically standard through 1986, but almost nobody bought it. Likewise the stripped 1981 "Miser" models, which disappeared after the following year.

Sustaining the L-body line through its 1990 swan-song were an increasingly better-equipped Omni and ever-sportier coupes. The coupes began at mid-1982 with an overdecorated 2.2-liter model reviving the famous Charger name, signaling Dodge's return to interesting cars. The base 024 became a Charger for '83, and the 2.2 was joined at midyear by a dashing Shelby Charger with tuned 107-bhp engine, very stiff suspension, racy body add-ons, silver paint, and big blue stripes evocative of Carroll Shelby's late-'60s Mustang GTs. A wider choice of colors was offered for '84, and other Chargers acquired a nose job and the Shelby's cleaner rear-roof styling. The next year, the Shelby took on the blown, 146-bhp 2.2 to become the Turbo Charger.

But by 1987, a profusion of sporty Daytonas and Shadows were crowding all Chargers out of the market, so production ceased that March. The Shelby Chargers were fairly rare: about 30,000 for the five model years.

Omni, meantime, kept getting better, picking up a more-modern dashboard for '84 and additional standard features most every year. Workmanship improved too. The aging 1978 design should have been an increasing liability in the marketplace, but Chrysler took advantage of tooling costs long since amortized to keep prices down and sales up.

The company went even further for 1987 by replacing all Omnis with just one fully equipped "America" model, appealingly priced at $5799. Options were limited to reduce overhead and insure higher, more-consistent assembly quality—another cue taken from Europe and Japan. Value-minded shoppers rushed to buy, taking more than 152,000—more sales than the entire Omni/Charger line had ever generated in a single year. Chrysler paid heed and put Aries/Reliant on the "America plan" before closing out the original K-cars after 1989. With that, Omni sales fast declined after '87, but the L-body hung on into model-year 1990, when the America badge was dropped and a driver-side air bag added.

A short-lived exception to such crushing sensibility was the GLH, basically the wolfish Shelby Charger in sheepish Omni dress. The initials, attributed to Ol' Shel, meant "Goes Like Hell." It did. The debut '85 was sprightly enough with its 110-bhp engine, but the turbocharged 146-bhp GLH-S of 1986 was a genuine terror, though it suffered terrible torque-steer; one tester observed the accelerator functioned like a "lane-change switch." Still, like the Shelby Chargers, this Omni was great fun—crude but invigorating in the best muscle-car tradition. And as only a few thousand were built for 1984-86, the GLH/GLH-S bid fair as future collectibles.

Arriving for 1988 was Dynasty, a sort of latter-day Diplomat on the front-drive C-body platform of that year's new Chrysler New Yorker. The only body style was a square-lined unibody four-door on a 104.3-inch wheelbase, available in standard and uplevel LE trim levels. Unlike the Chrysler, though, Dynasty's standard engine was the corporate 2.5-liter four with 96 horsepower, a bit weak for the 3000-pound curb weight. Fortunately, the Daytona's 3.0-liter Mitsubishi V-6 was optional. Changes for '89 were confined to a slightly more-powerful, 150-bhp V-6 option teaming with Chrysler's new Ultradrive automatic, plus optional security system, two-position driver-seat "memory" feature, and all-disc antilock brakes (the last phased in during '88). The 150-bhp Japanese option was ousted by Chrysler's own 3.3 V-6 for 1990, when all Dynastys gained standard driver-side airbags.

Billed as a "contemporary family sedan," Dynasty made no gesture toward sport, but it didn't have to. With base prices of $11,500-$12,500, it offered fine value in a roomy, traditional-style car of the sort that still appealed mightily to many people. And numerous they were. Despite its unpretentious nature, Dynasty became Chrysler Corporation's most-popular car line. Model-year '89 production, for example, was close to 138,000—many for rent-a-car companies but a fine showing all the same.

Though Aries was down to two- and four-door Americas for 1989, their heir apparent bowed as the family Dodge for the early '90s. Called Spirit, this notchback sedan was built on the same 103.3-inch-wheelbase A-body platform as Plymouth's new Acclaim, and thus spelled the end for the like-length four-door 600. The now-expected trio of base, luxury LE, and sporty ES models was offered, the last with a standard 2.5-liter turbo four, the others with the nonturbo version of that engine. Dynasty's 3.0-liter V-6 was optional only for ES, again teamed with Ultradrive. Spirit styling echoed Aries', but was smoother and more "grown-up." ES was identified by body-color front- and rear-end caps and rocker extensions, plus integral fog lamps. Spirit returned for 1990 with standard driver-side air bag (Chrysler was now pushing hard with this laudable safety feature), no-cost all-disc brakes for ES, and numerous detail improvements.

Considering where it began, Dodge fared remarkably well in the '80s, resuming its traditional performance role within

1986 Omni GLH Turbo hatchback sedan

1986 600 ES Turbo convertible coupe

1986 Daytona Turbo Z hatchback coupe

1986 Lancer Pacifica hatchback sedan

1987 Caravan LE minivan (extended wheelbase)

1987 Daytona Shelby Z hatchback coupe

1988 Lancer ES Turbo hatchback sedan

1987 Aries LE two-door sedan

1988 Dynasty LE four-door sedan

1987 Diplomat SE four-door sedan

1988 Shadow ES hatchback sedan

Chrysler Corporation while remaining the firm's only "full-line" nameplate and thus its best-selling one. In another return to tradition, Dodge finished the decade a solid sixth in the industry, compared to a lackluster eighth in 1982.

Dodge then retreated to seventh in volume through 1994, passed by Mercury amid new woes for Chrysler Corporation and a timely shift to more salable new products (see Chrysler for more details on early-'90s corporate happenings). Still, sales declined only as far as some 260,000 in 1992 and were back above 342,000 two years later. By 1996, Dodge had replaced every car in its lineup—and many of its trucks, too.

Signaling the start of this product revolution was that stunning 1989 showmobile, the two-seat Viper RT/10 roadster. A stark but potent creature, it was freely created in the image of Carroll Shelby's legendary Cobra. But the real movers behind it were Chrysler president Bob Lutz and chief engineer Francois Castaing, who wanted to show their company was capable of far more than K-cars and minivans.

To no one's surprise, showgoers pleaded for a Viper they could buy. In May 1990, Chrysler said it would oblige them. But more than just an exciting image-booster for Dodge, this low-volume sports car would be the first test for the streamlined "team approach" to vehicle development that Lutz and Castaing wanted to implement companywide. Though the concept car had to be entirely reengineered for production on just $50 million, the showroom Viper was on time and on budget. Sales began in May 1992, just 36 months after project approval, a new record development time for a production MoPar.

If not exactly cheap at $50,000, the Viper cost far less than other contemporary "exotics"—or a genuine Cobra. Raw power and colossal acceleration were its reasons for being. Though based on a forthcoming truck engine, Viper's unusual new all-aluminum V-10 (hence RT/10) was engineered with assistance from Italy's Lamborghini (then owned by Chrysler). It wasn't a sophisticated mill, what with pushrods working two valves per cylinder, but it was huge: no less than 8.0 liters, a massive 488 cid. The result was a mighty 400 horsepower and 450 pound-feet of torque. With mandatory six-speed manual transmission and standard limited-slip differential, the Viper could rocket from 0 to 60 mph in about 4.5 seconds and rip through the standing quarter-mile in 13.1 seconds at 108 mph.

Unlike other recent Dodges, Viper had conventional rear-wheel drive and classic all-independent double-wishbone suspension. This was, after all, a "pure sport car," as Shelby called such machines, which also meant few concessions to civility. For example, brakes and steering were powered, but nothing else. There were no exterior door handles—and no windows, either; just clip-in side-curtains. The top was a rudimentary canvas toupee that didn't ward off rain too well. It did, however, trap much of the V-10's prodigious heat, which was noticed

1989 Spirit ES four-door sedan

1989 Lancer Shelby hatchback sedan

1990 Daytona ES hatchback coupe

1990 Omni hatchback sedan

1990 Shadow ES hatchback coupe

1990 Caravan ES minivan

even at speed with the top off and the takeout rear window removed. Trunk space? Barely enough for a gym bag. Yet despite its stark furnishings and lightweight body panels made of plasticlike materials, the Viper ended up a bit heavier than planned at around 3400 pounds, though that partly reflected a very stiff, separate tubular-steel chassis.

But why sweat the details? The Viper was all about fast fun on sunny days—not to mention looking great, as the voluptuous show-car styling survived completely intact. That included a nonstructural "sport bar" behind the cockpit and exposed, functional side exhaust pipes that were wonderfully "retro" but could fry errant legs and sounded quite odd. Huge disc brakes provided terrific stopping power within handsome tri-spoke 17-inch aluminum wheels. Ultra-wide Z-rated tires helped provide super-sticky cornering, though power-sliding oversteer was ever available with a well-timed slam on the hammer. Yet unlike the scary Cobra, the Viper was easy to drive fast and well.

A lot more people wanted Vipers than Dodge could build—which was exactly how Chrysler wanted it. The exoticar market was notoriously fickle, so why build too many Vipers too soon and risk depressing resale values? Production was slow to start anyway. Seeking top-notch quality for the costliest Dodge ever, Chrysler retooled its Detroit New Mack Avenue plant for turning out Vipers only as needed, which meant mostly by hand. Still, initial quality was somewhat less than world-class, and only 162 Vipers were built as '92 models, all painted bright red. But teething troubles couldn't dim the Viper's luster or the public's lust for Viper.

Viper roared into 1993 with only two changes: black as a second color choice and available dealer-installed air conditioning. Though some 3000 cars were planned that model year, unexpected molding troubles with the big one-piece front end held actual volume to about 1000. But the problems were soon fixed, and '94 production nearly tripled to 2892. Full factory air became optional that year, the transmission got an electric reverse-gear lockout, and color choices expanded to yellow and Emerald Green. The '95 was unchanged except for price, which Chrysler reluctantly raised by a relatively modest $1500.

A Viper paced the 1991 Indy 500, with Carroll Shelby himself driving the prerace parade lap. Though sales were still a year off, Dodge's new hot rod hardly needed this publicity, as "buff" magazines were breathlessly reporting every facet of its show car-to-showroom progress. And in fact, Viper wasn't the first choice. Dodge had bought pace-car privileges to promote its new '91 Stealth, an upscale V-6 sports coupe available with all-wheel drive and up to 300 turbocharged horses. But aside from styling, the Stealth was a Mitsubishi design built in Japan, and a Japanese pace car just wasn't "politically correct" for the premier American race. Dodge relented, prepared a Viper prototype to fill in, and relegated Stealths to the background.

Among other new '91 Dodges was an unexpected high-power edition of the workaday Spirit. Also branded R/T, it was strictly a showroom lure, as only some 1400 were built through 1992. Base price was $17,871, a weighty $4000 above the costliest standard Spirit. Under the hood sat a maxed-out 2.2-liter "Trans-4" with a new twincam cylinder head and other modifications that yielded an amazing (and very peaky) 224 horsepower. Manual five-speed was the only transmission, and Dodge threw in necessary chassis upgrades, including the rear disc brakes newly optional for lesser '91 Spirits. You also got a dechromed exterior in red, white, or black, adorned with a subtle decklid spoiler. Though it looked another torque-steer terror, the Spirit R/T handled with fair finesse, if no less noise than an Omni GLH. And it was undeniably quick, with 0-60 times of well under seven seconds.

There was nothing odd about the new '91 Shadow convertible, which carried on from the ragtop 600. This time, though, Dodge left construction chores to American Sunroof Corporation. Cost concerns dictated a manual top, and the conversion slimmed back-seat space, but the regular "Highline" model started at $12,995, and a sporty ES edition sold for very little more. At the other end of the line, Dodge revived the "America" ploy for three- and five-door Shadows priced from just $7699. Power steering was one of their few standard "luxuries," and the only engine offered was the lowly 93-bhp version of the tried and true 2.2.

Like Chrysler's other '91 minivans, Caravan got a timely and very adept update marked by smoother sheetmetal, a new dash (complete with glovebox), and optional all-wheel-drive for 3.3-liter V-6 models. Even more laudable was first-time availability of antilock brakes, initially limited to the upper SE and LE trim levels. Also bolstering Caravan's appeal were a standard driver-side airbag as a '91 running change, followed by America's first integrated child safety seat as a 1992 option. A passenger airbag and side-guard door beams arrived for '94, when LE and ES Grand models could be ordered with a torquier 3.8 V-6 making 162 horsepower. All this did nothing but help sales, which improved from about a quarter-million for 1991 to over 300,000 by '94—and that was just Caravan. Even after 10 years, America still preferred Highland Park's minivans above all others.

There was little left to do for the Daytona, short of a total redesign. With its humble K-car origins and disco-era looks, it was just too old by the early '90s to stand comparison with a host of newer-design rivals for refinement or quality. Still, Dodge tried to inject some of the Viper's venom, starting with a "High-Torque Turbo I" engine for 1991. Standard for the Shelby and optional in lesser Daytonas, it made only two more horses but a useful 30 extra pound-feet of torque over the previous 2.5 turbo. The raucous VNT 2.2 vanished, but wasn't greatly missed.

A slightly smoother look with exposed headlamps arrived for 1992 Daytonas, as did optional rear disc brakes. Dodge now sponsored the International Race of Champions, so the world's best drivers vied for "top gun" honors in Daytonas instead of Chevy Camaros. A new top-line IROC model was thus no surprise, though its mild 3.0-liter Mitsubishi V-6 arguably was. More interesting was the IROC R/T, a midyear '92 replacement for the Daytona Shelby packing the 224-bhp "Turbo III" engine from the Spirit R/T. Aside from that and deliberately limited production—only some 800 or so—this R/T was much like the regular IROC. But none of this racy stuff could stop Daytona sales from freefalling, and the model was belatedly retired after measly '93 model-year volume of 9677 units.

By this point, Dodge was ready to join C-P Division in introducing a succession of new models to rejuvenate its lineup for the late '90s and beyond. The changeover would be orderly but quite rapid, reflecting the efficient work of the "cross-functional platform teams" recently established in the image of Team Viper. As a result, Spirit, Shadow, and Dynasty were left to fade away with no further changes of note after 1992. All these cars had served Dodge well, but the new stuff was far better. First up was Intrepid, one of the much-discussed 1993 "LH" sedans. Though ostensibly a midsize, it was close to full-size, offering bountiful interior space thanks to a lengthy 113-inch wheelbase and radical "cab forward" styling. The related Chrysler Concorde and Eagle Vision had this too, but they targeted different buyers with their own visual cues and model/equipment mixes.

Intrepid was the most affordable of the LH trio, but also the most-aggressively styled, with a Viper-inspired face, sharper

1991 Spirit ES four-door sedan

1991 Dynasty LE four-door sedan

1991 Shadow ES convertible coupe

1992 Viper RT/10 roadster

1992 Spirit R/T four-door sedan

1993 Intrepid ES four-door sedan

1992 Grand Caravan ES minivan

1993 Daytona IROC R/T hatchback coupe

roofline, and a bolder rear end with "Intrepid" writ large on a wide central backup lamp. The base model used the corporate pushrod 3.3 V-6, tuned for 153 horsepower. The sportier ES substituted a new overhead-cam 3.5-liter unit with 24 valves and 214 horses. All Intrepids came with four-speed automatic transmission, dual airbags, a wide-track chassis with all-independent suspension, a fair helping of standard amenities, and worthy options like antilock brakes. ES achieved flatter, more-responsive handling with a firm "touring" suspension and wider tires on 16-inch alloys (versus 15-inch steel rims). It was also sportier inside, with shift console and higher-grade trim. Best of all, Intrepid cost about the same as the dull old Dynasty it replaced, the base model arriving at just under $16,000.

With all this, the standard-bearer for the "New Dodge" got off to a strong start, attracting over 81,000 sales for model-year '93. Intrepid jumped above 155,000 for '94 on the strength of standard air conditioning, a newly optional power moonroof, eight more horses for the 3.3 engine, and the advent of speed-variable power steering.

The spotlight then turned to Neon, which bowed in early 1994 to signal the end of Shadow for '95. Plymouth naturally sold it too, as in Omni/Horizon days, only Chrysler didn't bother with separate names, which saved some tooling and marketing money. In fact, Dodge's Neons differed from Plymouth's only in the color of their badges: divisional red instead of blue.

Such clever thinking was a hallmark of Neon's new "PL" platform, and was passed on to consumers as attractively low list prices: as early ads said, "about 95-hundred to start, 12-five nicely loaded." That was for the debut four-door sedan in barebones form. The nicer Highline and Sport versions cost a bit more; similarly priced Highline and Sport coupes arrived in the fall. Unfortunately, Chrysler's cost-consciousness also produced rather bargain-basement trim even for an economy car, though it also allowed room in the budget for standard dual airbags and niceties like cupholders and floor console.

Neon continued Chrysler's move to cab-forward styling (as suggested a few years earlier by a Neon concept car). Proportions were scaled down to a 104-inch wheelbase, which was still quite long for a subcompact and thus made for another relatively cavernous interior. Yet there was a winning cuteness to Neon not found in the bigger LH cars, particularly the friendly "face" with oval headlamps and a simple horizontal grille that almost seemed ready to grin. Announcement ads played up this charm with a fetching one-word headline: "Hi!"

Dodge built some 179,000 Neons as '95 models, but close to 131,000 for calendar '94. The latter is perhaps a more-accurate gauge of the car's popularity given its early introduction. The only engine at first was a new 132-bhp 2.0-liter overhead-cam four designed and built by Chrysler. A 16-valve twincam version with 150 horsepower was gradually phased in for Sport models. Transmissions comprised the usual manual five-speed or optional three-speed automatic. Though far from quiet, Neon was great fun to drive, thrifty, pretty reliable, and even speedy: a brisk 8.9 seconds for Consumer Guide®'s base-engine five-speed sedan. In all, Neon was a huge step forward from the old "Omnirizon," proof that Chrysler could still build an appealing small car on its own.

Next on the menu was a Spirit successor called Stratus, which went on sale in early 1995 as a lower-priced version of the new "JA" Chrysler Cirrus sedan introduced some six months before. Hewing to the new corporate formula, Stratus delivered wide-track cab-forward sleekness on a 108-inch wheelbase, plus standard antilock brakes, dual airbags, even air conditioning. Like Intrepid, there were base and sportier ES models. Engine options began with another new all-Chrysler engine, a twincam multivalve 2.4-liter four with 140 horsepower. ES sported a Mitsubishi-based 2.5-liter V-6 with 164 horsepower. Both these engines mated solely with four-speed automatic. The 132-bhp Neon engine with five-speed manual, a combo that proved livelier on the road than it looked on paper, was standard for all Stratus models. Prices were appealingly competitive at just under $14,000 for the standard Stratus and some $17-grand for the better-equipped ES. Roomy, responsive, and rock-solid, Stratus met a very favorable reception, and Dodge happily built over 58,000 for model-year '95.

Though Chrysler was now starting to sever ties with Mitsubishi, its longtime Japanese partner loomed large in the 1995 Avenger. A spiritual successor to Daytona, this was little more than a sporty coupe based on Mitsubishi's midrange Galant family sedan, with rather sedate styling on the same

103.7-inch wheelbase. Most American-market Galants were now built in Illinois, so Avengers were too, even though Chrysler had sold its interest in the plant to Mitsubishi. Chrysler did contribute to Avenger's styling, but though designers tried hard for a cab-forward look, it was less evident here than on the company's all-American products. At least the front maintained a Dodge identity by wearing the make's trademark crossed-bars grille motif. Once again, there were base and ES models. Respective power was the single-cam Neon 2.0-liter and the Mitsubishi V-6 (engines shared with the Stratus ES). The V-6 was limited to four-speed automatic.

At $17,191, the ES cost some $4000 more than the standard Avenger, but the extra money was well spent, bringing antilock brakes (optional for base), fatter tires on 16-inch alloy wheels, fog lamps, rear spoiler and other goodies. Yet even this Avenger was no excitement machine—just another pleasant, competent, Japanese-style car that bordered on anonymity. Most critics judged Avenger a big step forward from the weary Daytona, but that was surely damning with faint praise.

Dodge finished up its linewide makeover with a brilliant new second-generation Caravan for 1996. Viper had been around only five model years by then, yet was now the oldest car in the fleet. Dodge had indeed remade itself with unusual speed.

Not that Viper was neglected. By 1995, in fact, team leader Roy Sjoberg could claim over 1100 changes to the snaky sports car since the first '92 roadster. New ones joined them for '96, starting with 15 more horsepower (to 415 total) and an extra 23 pound-feet of torque (to 488). Higher compression and a hotter cam were responsible, as was eliminating the distinctive "shin burner" side exhausts for a less-restrictive setup routed beneath the car to a pair of center rear outlets. In addition, curb weight lightened some 60 pounds by changing suspension components from steel to aluminum, a newly optional lightweight hard top afforded much-better weather protection than the skimpy fabric "bikini," and there were new color schemes featuring broad nose and deck stripes hinting at a racing program. Equally significant, production shifted to a new plant on Detroit's Conner Avenue, which promised improved workmanship. Partly because of the move, model-year production was deliberately held to just 500 units.

Another reason was the spring 1996 debut of a fixed-roof Viper fastback as an early '97 entry. Though it looked much like the roadster, the GTS coupe was claimed to be 90 percent new. Standard were power windows, adjustable pedals, air conditioning (at last!), and a redesigned dash incorporating dual airbags, features that also showed up on '97 RT/10s. And there was yet more muscle, as Viper's V-10 was both lightened and fully reengineered to produce 450 horsepower (at 5200 rpm) and 500 pound-feet of torque (peaking at just 3600 revs).

The racy-looking GTS had obvious competition potential, and Dodge realized it with a squadron of GTS-Rs designed for Le Mans and other long-distance events. With factory backing and hard work by several outside teams, these Vipers proved almost unstoppable. In a trio of "three-peats" they claimed the FIA GT2 and GT World Championships in 1997-1999 and class victories at Le Mans in 1998-2000. At home, GTS-Rs won the 1999 American Le Mans Series (ALMS), scoring a class win in each race they entered, followed in 2000 by overall victory at the 24 Hours of Daytona. Dodge then left international sports-car racing to focus anew on NASCAR.

Meantime, roadgoing Vipers kept evolving nicely. The '99s, for example, exchanged 17-inch wheels for 18s, added power mirrors and aluminum-finish cockpit trim, and offered genuine British Connolly leather upholstery as a new option. Also new that year was an American Club Racing (ACR) package for the GTS with five-point competition seatbelts, special suspension, unique one-piece wheels, and a low-restriction air cleaner that helped liberate an extra 10 horsepower. The option wasn't cheap at $10,000, but weekend warriors loved it on their local racetracks, though they did without air conditioning, audio, and even fog lights Monday through Friday. The package was improved for 2000 with adjustable monotube shock absorbers and a "performance" oil pan providing better lubrication of the mighty engine's innards. For 2001, both roadster and coupe got standard antilock brakes, a great advance for "active" safety, though another step back from Viper's original uncompromising nature. Colors came and went each season through 2002 and the finale of the basic 1992 design. By that point, Viper

1993 Spirit four-door sedan

1994 Shadow ES hatchback coupe

1995 Neon Sport coupe

1995 Stratus four-door sedan

1995 Neon four-door sedan

1995 Avenger ES coupe

1996 Neon sport coupe

1996 Intrepid four-door sedan

1997 Stratus four-door sedan

owners numbered over 14,000, each a happy soul no doubt.

Yet with fewer than 1500 sales per year, Viper was a bit player in the Dodge drama of the 1990s, when minivans, light pickups and sport-utility vehicles (SUVs) increasingly upstaged cars in consumer affections. Indeed, Dodge was then selling way more cars than trucks each year—a record million-plus in 1998-2000, about three times its nontruck volume. The same was true to a lesser degree for Chevrolet and Ford, but Dodge had fewer car models, so its total business depended relatively more on trucks.

Though Dodge remained far behind its rivals in truck sales, a series of successful products helped close the gap some. First up was 1994's all-new full-size Ram pickup, whose broad-shouldered styling and available V-10 power (related to Viper's) helped pull in almost three times as many orders as previous models. A further sales boost came in 1998 with the "Quad Cab," an industry first adding two rear-hinged back doors to Ram's extended Club Cab for easier entry/exit. The idea proved so popular that rivals rushed to copy it. Dodge's midsize Dakota pickups also enjoyed much stronger sales after getting a Ram-inspired redesign (for '97) and their own Quad Cabs (for 2000) with four front-hinged doors. And after sitting on the sidelines for five years, Dodge launched the Dakota-based Durango for 1998 as a much more-competitive SUV than the ancient '70s-vintage Ramcharger.

As ever, though, Dodge's biggest strength was owning America's favorite minivan, its Caravans drawing at least a quarter-million sales each calendar year through 2000. Much of that success stemmed from the full redesign for 1996 marked by sleeker looks; roomier, quieter and stronger bodies; larger available engines with more power; and thoughtful new features like "Easy Out" back seats with built-in rollers and sliding rear doors for both sides, not just the right. While the related Plymouth Voyager and Chrysler Town & Country offered all this too, only Dodge tried for a measure of sportiness, fielding ES and Sport models with firmer suspension, youthful styling touches, even a manually shiftable automatic transmission.

Alas, heavy reliance on one product also remained Dodge's biggest weakness, aggravated by a growing public perception of minivans as uncool "soccer mom" transport. But though minivan demand did soften somewhat, Caravan sales weren't seriously affected. What did start to hurt was stronger competition, especially from Honda and Toyota, whose U.S.-bred minivans were stealing Caravan sales with superior workmanship and mechanical finesse. Dodge responded with mostly new 2001 Caravans, but they didn't look that new and were more expensive, in part because Chrysler's controls on production costs, once the envy of Detroit, had become rather lax. With all this, Caravan sales dropped to some 242,000 for calendar '01, still tops in class by far, but the lowest for Dodge in a decade. Then again, 2001 was a tough year for most businesses as the nation's decade-long boom economy ended and a frightening war on terrorism began.

Despite the market's growing preference for trucks, Dodge car sales were consistent and fairly strong in the late 1990s, totaling at least 360,000 each calendar year from '96 through 2000, after which the tally dipped to about 329,000. Leading the pack—though not as much as you might think—was the subcompact Neon, drawing 110,000-112,000 yearly orders through 2000 as a Dodge. Sales of Plymouth-badged Neons ran 25-30 percent lower, largely because of the Plymouth badge, said some analysts.

However, Dodge also did more than Plymouth to woo the younger buyers most attracted to small, low-priced cars. For example, coupes appeared in both lineups for '96, as did an available 150-bhp twincam version of Neon's 2.0-liter four, but only Dodge catered to weekend racers with a Competition

Package featuring uprated suspension and tires, all-disc brakes, heavy-duty five-speed gearbox, tachometer, and other go-faster stuff. What's more, it was optional for the workaday sedan (at $1575) as well as the sportier-looking coupe ($1745, including the twincam mill). Dodge followed up for '98 with an R/T package, also available for both body styles. This paired the twincam engine and the Competition group's basic chassis bits with more heavily bolstered front bucket seats, a rear spoiler, fog lights, broad dorsal racing stripes, and large "R/T" decals. It didn't make a fire-breather like the big-block R/Ts of old, but it did make a fun ride even more so—and quite popular among said weekend racers. But those were the highlights in the otherwise uneventful career of the first-generation Neon, which remained rather rough and rowdy next to newer rivals, especially those from Japan.

A full redesign for 2000 (arriving in early 1999) strove to enhance Neon's market appeal, yet failed to address basic shortcomings. The optional automatic, for example, was still an outmoded three-speed unit, and workmanship, though better, remained below par. Coupes were canned—their sales had always disappointed—but so was the twincam engine. Sedans were restyled around little-changed dimensions but lost their playful look, and the single-cam engine was scarcely quieter. Buyers must have noticed all this, for Dodge Neon sales fell to just over 107,000 for calendar '01. Pushing on for 2002, Dodge reinstated an R/T package and added an ACR option, both packing a tuned single-cam 2.0-liter with—you guessed it—150 horsepower. Leather upholstery and front side airbags were newly available, too. So was a four-speed automatic transmission, ousting the three-speeder at last.

Neon saw little change after this, falling ever-further behind the best small cars through swan song 2006. In fact, with one exception (detailed below), the only news of note in this period was dropping the ACR option and tagging the midline ES as SXT for '03, then discarding the R/T after '04. Despite so much sameness, sales held up surprisingly well, but only because fleet orders made up a high percentage. In the retail market, Neon appealed mainly as one of the cheapest cars in the class (around $13,000-$17,000), and it could be had even cheaper with the rebates and other incentives buyers expected.

Other Dodge cars also received only sporadic attention in the first years of the new century. With trucks so dominating division sales, it made sense to keep the product focus on high-margin minivans, pickups, and SUVs. One suspects, however, that Dodge and others only hurt their own car cause with this tactic, even if import brands seemed unstoppable in grabbing ever-larger slices of the nontruck pie.

These trends were evident by the late 1990s, when the first-generation Intrepid closed out with little further change: just more power for the '96 ES and the introduction of Chrysler's AutoStick manually shiftable automatic transmission.

The redesigned '98 Intrepids were something else, however: still "cab forward" outside and roomy inside, yet sleeker—real "dream car styling" come true. Length and width increased a bit, but wheelbase was unchanged. And unlike before, Intrepid shared no exterior body panels with Chrysler's related Concorde. Engines were new, too. The base Intrepid got a 2.7-liter V-6 with dual overhead camshafts and more ponies than the pushrod 3.3 it replaced. The sporty ES exchanged a single-cam 3.5 for a similar but more efficient 3.2, also with more power. Both models came with front buckets and console, but even the ES, which added standard antilock brakes, wasn't the speedy backroads runner its looks implied.

Dodge addressed that in early 2000 by adding an Intrepid R/T with wider tires on 17-inch wheels (versus 16s), an uprated suspension with thicker antiroll bars at each end, and a reinstated

1997 Avenger coupe

1998 Avenger ES coupe

1998 Neon R/T coupe

1998 Dodge Intrepid ES four-door sedan

1999 Avenger coupe

1999 Intrepid ES four-door sedan

2000 Stratus ES four-door sedan

2000 Neon four-door sedan

2001 Neon R/T four-door sedan

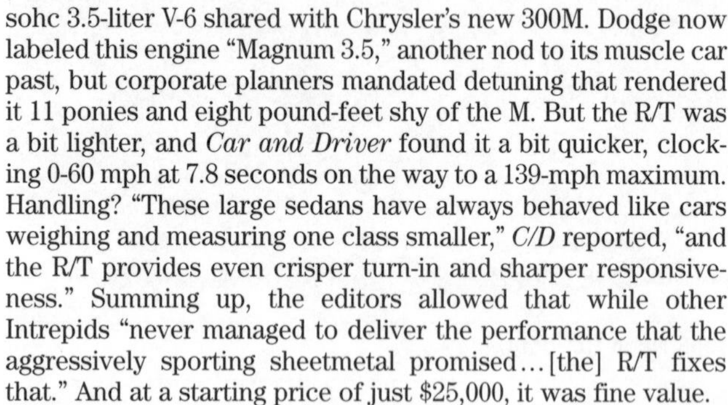

sohc 3.5-liter V-6 shared with Chrysler's new 300M. Dodge now labeled this engine "Magnum 3.5," another nod to its muscle car past, but corporate planners mandated detuning that rendered it 11 ponies and eight pound-feet shy of the M. But the R/T was a bit lighter, and *Car and Driver* found it a bit quicker, clocking 0-60 mph at 7.8 seconds on the way to a 139-mph maximum. Handling? "These large sedans have always behaved like cars weighing and measuring one class smaller," *C/D* reported, "and the R/T provides even crisper turn-in and sharper responsiveness." Summing up, the editors allowed that while other Intrepids "never managed to deliver the performance that the aggressively sporting sheetmetal promised...[the] R/T fixes that." And at a starting price of just $25,000, it was fine value.

But then, as with Neon, Dodge let Intrepid carry on with scarcely anything new to keep buyers interested. And some of the changes that did occur seemed retrograde; like replacing the R/T after just one year with a mundane SXT that had the same engine—and with six more horses—but offered neither AutoStick nor a handling-focused suspension. It seemed a curious move for a "performance" brand, but the R/T had never been a big draw. Besides, the Intrepid still sold mainly as the large, comfortable family four-door it was; sportiness just wasn't much of a factor. With all this, sales were OK through 2002, but then slid steadily through end-of-the-line 2004.

Dodge had less success in the midsize field as the century turned, again due to a relative lack of change, plus increasingly stiff class competition. On a calendar-year basis, Avenger coupe sales languished in the low 30,000s through 1999, then plummeted to a mere 5500 units with the year-2000 changeover to redesigned '01 models. The Stratus sedan ran in the mid to high 90,000s except for 1998, when it topped 106,000. But here, too, a good chunk of each year's production went to corporate and rental fleets to the detriment of Stratus' image and resale values on the retail market. Like Neon, these were competent, high-value cars, and Dodge struggled to keep them appealing with yearly touch-ups. But it wasn't enough, and finicky consumers found more to like at other dealerships.

The redesigned 2001 models aimed to lure them back with fresh styling, new features, and a more solid, refined driving experience within little-changed dimensions. Avenger was renamed Stratus coupe, but was still built in Illinois on a Mitsubishi platform, this one borrowed from the Japanese company's 1999-2000 Galant sedan and sporty Eclipse models. Sedans remained purely Chrysler creations, evident in their cab-forward proportions, but production now centered solely in Michigan (some prior models had been sourced from Mexico). Among the few shared features, other than the Stratus name, were a base 2.4-liter four-cylinder engine and a smooth, rounded nose with Dodge's trademark "crosshair" grille motif. Models comprised price-leader SE coupes and sedans, a new two-door R/T with Mitsubishi's latest 3.0-liter V-6 (replacing Avenger ES), and a four-door ES packing Chrysler's 2.7-liter V-6. Interestingly, both V-6s were rated at 200 bhp, perhaps to keep peace in the transpacific family. Automatic transmission was mandatory for sedans and optional for coupes in lieu of a five-speed manual. Enthusiasts were quick to note the V-6/manual combo, a first for Dodge's midsize coupe and not matched by sibling Chrysler Sebrings. Also available for the R/T was Chrysler's AutoStick feature, previously limited to ES sedans.

For all the changes, though, the new Stratuses were just more of the same: noticeably improved in many areas, yet still not quite good enough to threaten the competition's best. Sedans had standard all-disc brakes and offered curtain side airbags as a first-time option, but torso side airbags weren't available anywhere, and antilock brakes cost extra. And though the manual R/T coupe promised the most rewarding drive, *Road & Track* damned it with faint initial praise, judging it merely "well equipped to take on the Toyota Solaras and Honda Accord coupes of the world." *Car and Driver* was more upbeat, finding the R/T "nearly as delightful to flog as its Mitsubishi [Eclipse] cousin."

In any case, the Stratus would be another Dodge allowed to coast along with minimal change until its time was up. The 2002 line acquired a value-priced SE Plus sedan, and a sporty R/T sedan bowed at midseason to add some image spice, offering a five-speed manual or AutoStick self-shifter in a tempting

2001 Stratus four-door sedan

2002 Stratus R/T coupe

2001 Intrepid R/T four-door sedan

2002 Dodge Viper GTS coupe

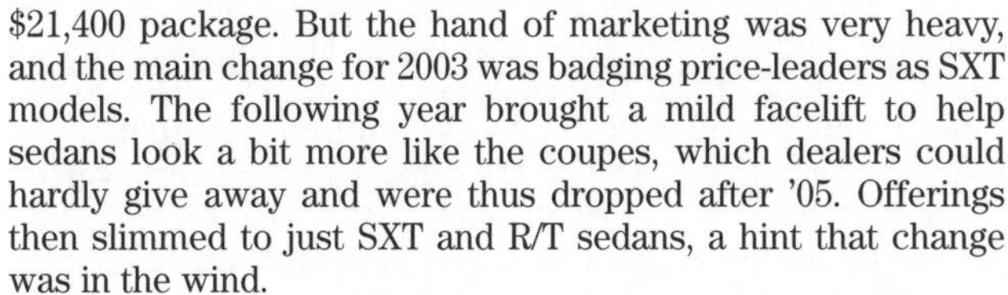

$21,400 package. But the hand of marketing was very heavy, and the main change for 2003 was badging price-leaders as SXT models. The following year brought a mild facelift to help sedans look a bit more like the coupes, which dealers could hardly give away and were thus dropped after '05. Offerings then slimmed to just SXT and R/T sedans, a hint that change was in the wind.

After an 11-year run, the iconic Viper finally changed for 2003, fully redesigned with a more mature demeanor but an even hairier chest. Initially offered as a newly named SRT-10 roadster, it spanned a 2.6-inch-longer wheelbase (98.8) and spread no less than nine inches wider, but was slightly shorter overall, thanks to trimmer front and rear overhangs. Styling, credited to former Toyota designer Osamu Shikado, was recognizably Viper but crisper, more squarish in proportions and, from some angles, more aggressive. Enhancing the appearance was a full manual-folding soft top that dispensed with the fixed rear "sport bar" while improving convenience and weather protection versus the old afterthought "bikini" top. One simple latch released it for stowing in a well behind the cockpit, one reason for the longer wheelbase. Side exhaust pipes returned, but were now inside the rocker panels, shielded to meet noise regulations—though that didn't prevent accidental fried legs. The cockpit itself was vastly upgraded, gaining better-quality plastics, some needed seating space, and a more orderly dashboard with a speedometer calibrated to 220 mph (which Dodge said was deliberate). The pedals now adjusted electrically, and lined up in axis with the steering wheel, thus eliminating the old model's irksome pedal offset. Despite these advances, most testers thought cockpit fit-and-finish weren't worthy of the price—initially $80,795, plus a $3000 Gas-Guzzler Tax.

Construction again involved a steel chassis and a body made of composite-plastic and aluminum. This time, though the windshield frame, door-pillar hinges, and front-fender supports were rendered in carbon fiber to hold the line on weight, which ended up at around 3400 pounds curbside. The four-wheel double-wishbone suspension stayed roughly the same, but wheel diameter swelled from 18 to 19 inches, allowing larger four-wheel antilock disc brakes. Traction and/or stability control were still nowhere in sight. Dodge wasn't about to change the Viper's "purity" as a driver's car. The rear tires did change, becoming broader at the rear, with 345/30s over 13 inches wide replacing 335/30s.

Viper's trademark pushrod aluminum V-10 continued, but displacement went to 8.3 liters and 505 cid. Power and torque were initially mooted at 500 each, but pound-feet ultimately settled at 525, and fiddling took bhp to 510 for 2006. A mandatory Tremec T56 six-speed manual gearbox returned with its previous gearing. The rear-axle ratio was also unchanged (3.07:1).

Despite adding a measure of civility, the '03 Viper was even more of a rip-snorting muscle machine than its previous incarnation. *Car and Driver* reported 0-60 mph at just 3.9 seconds and a dragsterlike quarter-mile of 12.9 seconds at 121 mph. Handling remained trackworthy as well, *C/D* measuring a full 1.00g on the skidpad. Sure, the ride remained buckboard hard, the cockpit would still heat up like a sauna, and control efforts would again challenge Mr. Universe, but Viper fans wouldn't have it any other way.

In fact, Viper owners liked the new one so much, they snapped up the entire 2003 model run, some 1500 units, in just two weeks. No one else had a chance. That's because Dodge mailed out presale certificates giving existing owners first dibs. Dealers, obliged to honor these guarantees, wailed loudly when certificate holders came in demanding to buy at just a few dollars over invoice, thus depriving dealers—and Chrysler Group—of thousands in potential profit. Would-be first-time Viper buyers were doubtless plenty sore at having to wait a year. Oh well, it must have seemed a good idea at the time.

A new Viper would have been a sellout anyway, and demand remained strong, with 1782 sales in calendar 2004 and 1652 in '05. Few changes occurred until 2006, when the Viper coupe returned by popular request. Dodge had developed a 2003 Competition Coupe as a turnkey proposition for weekend warriors, but the production coupe—also badged SRT-10, not GTS—was rather different. In fact, Dodge made some changes to a prototype design after getting feedback at a national Viper

2003 Viper SRT-10 convertible coupe

2003 Viper SRT-10 convertible coupe

2003 SRT-4 four-door sedan

2005 Magnum R/T AWD wagon

club convention. Viper fans are nothing if not passionate.

The result appeared for 2005 with unique rear-quarter panels, windshield frame, door glass, rear fascia, and taillamps, plus a "double bubble" fixed roof and specific trunklid. The coupe, though, could carry six cubic feet of stuff, four more than the roadster. Everything else was the same, including curb weight, so performance was virtually identical. Even so, *Car and Driver* found the coupe less prone to throttle-on tail sliding than the roadster. The editors also found it to be a more comfortable and thus more practical roadgoing Viper, even on day-long drives. Perhaps Dodge should have called it GTS after all.

The SRT in the new Viper's surname stood for Street and Racing Technology, a small in-house team recently formed to develop high-performance models for all Chrysler Group brands. SRT was a small but high-profile result of the controversial 1998 merger between Chrysler Corporation and Germany's Daimler-Benz (see *Chrysler* for more details), being comparable to parent Mercedes' AMG division.

SRT's second effort for Dodge was announced several months after the new Viper in response to the fast growing "sport compact" craze. Young, mostly urban enthusiasts had lately taken to transforming used Honda Civics, Acura Integras, and similar cars into striking custom street racers known as "tuner cars" or "sport compacts," implying a huge new market for performance parts and styling accessories. Automakers began conjuring sporty versions of their workaday small fries

2005 Magnum R/T wagon

to get in on this lucrative action—and hopefully hook some new buyers for life. The little Neon was already known as a demon handler, having racked up a number of autocross and road-racing championships, and it made a fine starting point for Dodge's sport compact contender, the SRT-4.

The biggest deal for the pumped-up Neon was swapping in a turbocharged version of the corporate 2.4-liter twincam four to net a startling, and as we'd soon find out underrated, 205 bhp. Allied to mandatory heavy-duty five-speed manual gearbox and a sub-3000-pound curb weight, the intercooled engine could deliver 0-60 mph in a claimed 5.9 seconds, making this the second-fastest car in the Dodge lineup after the mighty Viper. Starting price was no less eye-opening at just under $20,000. This was in line with SRT's aim of delivering maximum bang for the buck in a car ready for owner personalization. Even so, the SRT-4 was well-equipped, particularly for "stylin'" on the street. A large "basket handle" spoiler was a must, but there were also fat 17-inch tires, chrome-tipped exhaust, discreet lower-body cladding, a bolder nose with working hood scoop, a deeper bumper, and a gaping Dodge crosshair grille. The suspension was lowered and stiffened, and big disc brakes with ABS went behind standard alloy wheels. The cabin kept the street-racer theme with bolstered bucket seats, turbo-boost/vacuum gauge, 160-mph speedometer, metal-look accents, a unique three-spoke steering wheel, and a whimsical "cue ball" shift knob.

The SRT-4 was a wild and woolly beast: loud, hard-riding, and tough to drive well because of turbo throttle lag and so much power going through the front wheels. It was more at home on a smooth racetrack than on rough city pavement. The kids loved it, but they were about the only ones. Over-30 magazine testers found the SRT-4 unacceptably rude and crude, though great fun for about the first five minutes. SRT added standard limited-slip differential for '04, as well as 15 bhp. The power boost wasn't very noticeable, probably because it had been underrated at 205 bhp in the first place. The farewell '05 edition offered an $1195 ACR package comprising an even firmer suspension—"yeah, that's what it needs," moaned *Car and Driver*—plus wider tires on 16-inch alloy wheels.

The ACR version took on four rival sport compacts in a *C/D* comparison test. It finished midpack despite having the best weight-to-power ratio, the most go (5.6 seconds 0-60, 14.3 seconds at 99 mph in the quarter-mile, 150 mph all-out), the best braking, and the quickest autocross time. "This feisty little brute might have placed higher... were it not such a one-trick pony," *C/D* concluded. But winning isn't everything, and the SRT-4 did make an impression on Generation X-Box, even if the youngsters didn't buy many of them. Then, too, many single-purpose cars have become coveted collector's items, and that could well happen to the hyper-Neon some day.

Making an even bigger impression, at least on the public consciousness, were the replacements for the full-size Intrepid, the 2005 Magnum and '06 Charger. Reviving two such hallowed names gave some people pause, because the new Magnum was a station wagon, of all things, while the latest Charger was a sedan, not a slinky coupe like the one jumping around on TV's still-popular "Dukes of Hazzard." But Dodge correctly pointed out that wagons were starting to make a comeback of sorts and that coupe sales were generally "nowhere" in early twenty-first-century America.

There was no debating the new cars' worthiness, however, as both shared Chrysler Group's impressive new LX platform with the instant-hit '05 Chrysler 300 sedans. That meant a sophisticated chassis with rear-wheel drive—the first "traditional" mainstream Dodge cars in 16 years—plus all-independent suspension greatly influenced by new partner Mercedes' popular E-class. Equally laudable were four-wheel disc brakes and, save

2006 Charger R/T four-door sedan

2006 Charger R/T four-door sedan

2006 Charger SRT8 four-door sedan

2006 Charger Daytona R/T four-door sedan

2006 Magnum SRT8 wagon

2006 Viper SRT10 coupe

2006 Viper SRT10 coupe

2007 Dodge Caliber four-door hatchback

2007 Dodge Caliber SRT4 four-door hatchback

the base Magnum SE, standard antilock brake control and ESP antiskid/traction control. Still another surprise was the Magnum SXT with *all*-wheel drive, something no Detroit make had ever offered in the big-car class.

Big these new Dodges definitely were, both physically and visually. Wheelbase was a generous 120 inches, overall length around 200, width a brawny 74 or so. Styling emphasized this mass with low rooflines, high slab sides, and aggressive faces that could have fit a big Ram pickup. The designs polarized opinions, but Dodge had learned that trying to please the many usually ended up pleasing only the few. Moreover, the Charger/Magnum looked like no other cars around (300s excepted, of course). They were as bold a break with convention as cab forward was over a decade before.

Like sibling Chryslers, mainstream Chargers and Magnums relied on the corporate single-cam 250-bhp 3.5-liter V-6 allied to four-speed automatic transmission, with a 190-bhp 2.7 engine reserved for the base Magnum. But the real excitement was a brand-new Hemi V-8, a 5.7-liter/345-cid powerhouse making 340 horses and a burly 390 pound-feet of torque. Standard for both Charger and Magnum R/T, and linked to a five-speed automatic with sporty manual-shift gate, the Hemi gestured to fuel efficiency with its Multi Displacement System. Like GM's similar Active Fuel Management, MDS was designed to shut down four cylinders under light throttle loads to save a little gas. It didn't save much, especially since the Hemi encouraged a lot of foot-to-the-floor action, but it was better than nothing and was hard to detect doing its thing. As it turned out, the Hemi's EPA economy ratings were good enough to avoid triggering the Gas-Guzzler Tax, a potential liability for popularly priced vehicles.

Speaking of price, both lines showed up with base stickers in the $22,000-$31,000 range. Options were predictably ample. The Charger R/T pushed performance more than other models with two desired packages. A $1695 Road/Track Performance Group added 10 horses, uprated suspension with rear load leveling, firm-feel steering, and unique alloy wheels in stock 18-inch size, plus leather/suede upholstery and heated front seats. To this, the $2675 Daytona R/T package added a rear spoiler, 235/55 tires (replacing 225/60s), and broad swathes of matte-black finish on the hood and rear fenders, complete with reversed-out "Hemi" and "Charger" lettering, respectively. Daytona's colors also echoed the "Scat Pack" days, with the first 4000 finished in "Go ManGo," a coppery orange. The next 4000 were in "Top Banana" yellow. More colors were slated later, including the possible return of "Sub Lime" and "Plum Crazy."

Charger/Magnum ads naturally played up the V-8 models, depicting humorous encounters with unwary folks who were smoked by the Dodge, then asked, "That thing got a Hemi in it?" The phrase was soon on people's lips from coast to coast.

Meantime, the small dedicated band of gearheads at Street and Racing Technology couldn't resist taking the R/T models to a higher level. The result was SRT8 versions for both the Magnum and Charger, each with a 6.1-liter (370-cid) Hemi pumping out 425 bhp—the highest specific output in Chrysler V-8 history, said SRT—and walloping torque of 420 pound-feet. More than just a bore job, the 6.1 bristled with premium engineering, including its own block casting, flat-top pistons, higher compression (10.3:1 versus 9.6), larger ports, wider intake valves, sodium-filled exhaust valves, higher-lift cam, headers, and freer-flow intake and exhaust piping. SRT also lowered the suspension by half an inch from R/T spec, substituted harder suspension bushings, reprogrammed the ESP and transmission shift points, and bolted on 20-inch wheels. The SRT8 Charger was treated to a new rear spoiler and a hood scoop to help keep the engine bay cool. Last but not least were specially appointed interiors, plus deeper front and rear fascias that made both SRT8s look even hairier than "ordinary" R/Ts. The price for all this wasn't exactly cheap, yet the SRT8s, wagon and sedan, were undeniable high-performance bargains, starting at just under $40,000.

Despite their size and two-ton heft, the new Hemi Chargers and Magnums were very fast on the straights, but also Eurosedan-agile through the curves. R/Ts could run 0-60 mph in the mid-five-second bracket and standing quarter-miles in the low 14s at just over 100. Who said the muscle car era was gone forever? SRT8s were more thrilling yet, doing 0-60 lunges in five seconds or less, sub-14-second quarter-mile blasts, and 0-100 mph *and back to 0* in no more than 17 seconds. V-6s seemed

2006 Dodge Challenger coupe concept

like sluggards by comparison, posting 0-60s in the low nines, but they looked just as quick—and mean—as the Hemis.

Dodge must have been encouraged by the initial response. Magnum alone tallied nearly 92,000 sales from its mid-'04 launch through the end of '05, fewer than the Chrysler 300 but surprisingly good for a supposedly passé station wagon. The Charger seemed poised to do at least equally well.

Still, there's no denying that Dodge (Chrysler, too) seemed out of step flaunting such big, heavy, and thirsty cars in 2005. After all, that was the year many Americans first paid more than $3 a gallon for gas amid new concerns over world oil supplies, soaring demand for fuel-stingy gasoline/electric hybrid vehicles, and more strident calls by environmentalists for tougher fuel-economy standards to slow the pace of global warming. Though it's unclear how those factors will play out, you can bet they won't be going away anytime soon.

But Dodge has hardly lost a sense of social responsibility. In early 2006 Caliber arrived as an early '07 model. A compact wagon to replace the Neon sedan, it was built on a new platform developed with Mitsubishi. Caliber marked another brave step for Dodge, blending macho Magnum style with four-cylinder efficiency in a trio of American-made "world" engines, all with twin overhead camshafts and *de rigueur* variable valve timing. The base SE and SXT offered a 148-bhp 1.8-liter with manual transmission or a high-tech continuously variable automatic (CVT). Both also had an optional 158-bhp 2.0-liter, while the sporty R/T mated a 172-bhp 2.4 with CVT and standard AWD; a front-drive version with five-speed manual was scheduled to come later.

Caliber's tall-body styling over a 103.7-inch wheelbase provided good room for up to five adults, plus anywhere from 18.5 to 48 cubic feet of cargo space. With small-car buyers increasingly demanding upscale features, Caliber came sensibly calibrated with standards like curtain side airbags and options such as antilock brakes (included on CVT) models and ESP traction/stability control, plus the usual fancy trim, audio upgrades, and such. Yet prices started just south of $14,000, very competitive with class rivals. For all this practicality, Dodge didn't forget leadfoots, planning the inevitable SRT4

2006 Dodge Challenger coupe concept

version for a fall 2006 release. With a 2.4-liter turbocharged to no less than 300 bhp, the Caliber SRT4 upped the last Neon SRT-4 by 70 ponies. Due to extra girth, though, Dodge's claimed 0-60-mph time remained unchanged at 5.9 seconds. Reflecting SRT's usual throroughness, the hottest Caliber was set to boast a standard six-speed manual gearbox, a working hood scoop, big all-disc Charger/Magnum brakes, and a lowered suspension crouching over standard 19-inch wheels. Yet for all the go-fast goodies, the new SRT4 was rated at an estimated 28 mpg on the highway. The best of all worlds? Could be.

Also due from Dodge for 2007 is the much needed successor to the aging Stratus, plus attractive new truck models like the Jeep-based Nitro, Dodge's first compact SUV. There's also the prospect of a smaller-than-Caliber car for the European market, where Chrysler Group wants Dodge to be a major player.

Last but not least is the 2006 concept predicting a reborn Challenger ponycar on a modified LX platform. The concept was first shown at the early 2006 car shows, and it made quite a stir. Said to be offered sometime around '08, it promises to be a strong, er, challenger to Ford's highly popular Mustang.

All in all, things look pretty good for Dodge at this point in the story. Though its truck sales softened a bit in 2005—mainly due to some buyers having second thoughts about thirsty SUVs—car sales seemed healthy again, exceeding 300,000 calendar-year units in 2001, '02, and '05. While today is never a sure forecast of tomorrow, Dodge seems poised for further prosperity in the near future, especially with cars. After all, as the old adage says, nothing succeeds like success.

Specifications

1930

DA Six (wb 112.0) - 15,000 blt (est.)*	Wght	Price	Prod
rdstr 2-4P	2,687	995	—
phtn 5P	2,730	1,025	—
bus cpe 2P	2,750	945	—
DeLuxe cpe 2-4P	2,812	1,025	—
victoria 4P	2,846	1,025	—
brougham 5P	2,834	995	—
sdn 2d 5P	2,876	925	—
sdn 4d 5P	2,894	995	—
DeLuxe sdn 4d 5P	2,898	1,065	—

DB Six Senior (wb 120.0) - 7,000 built (est.)*	Wght	Price	Prod
rdstr 2-4P	3,303	1,615	—
cpe 2-4P	3,426	1,595	—
brougham 5P	3,419	1,545	—
sdn 4d	3,513	1,595	—
landau sdn 4d	3,525	1,645	—

DC Eight (wb 114.0) - 19,993 built**	Wght	Price	Prod
rdstr 2P	2,802	1,095	598
phtn 5P	2,690	1,225	234
cpe 2-4P	2,981	1,125	2,999
conv cpe 2-4P	2,938	1,195	728
sdn 4d	3,043	1,145	20,315
bus cpe	—	—	123
chassis	—	—	253

DD New Six (wb 109.0) - 29,651 built***	Wght	Price	Prod
rdstr 2-4P	2,462	855	772
phtn 5P	2,521	875	542
bus cpe 2P	2,534	835	3,877
cpe 2-4P	2,603	855	3,363
conv cpe 2-4P	2,605	935	620
sdn 4d	2,668	865	33,432
chassis	—	—	899

* Available 1930 figures combined with 1929 production.

** Total based on serial number spans. Individual model totals for 1930-32 combined. Approximately 80 percent of the individual model totals were 1930 models.

*** Total based on serial number spans. Individual model totals for 1930-32 combined. Approximately 70 percent of the individual model totals were 1930 models.

1930 Engines	bore×stroke	bhp	availability
I-6, 208.0	3.38×3.88	63	S-DA
I-6, 241.5	3.38×4.50	78	S-DB
I-6, 189.8	3.13×4.13	61	S-DD
I-8, 220.7	2.88×4.25	75	S-DC

1931

DC Eight (wb 114.0) - 4,268 built

Production was carried over from 1930, with 1931-model output commencing July 15. Prod figs combined with 1930 DC; total 1931 prod based on serial number spans. Body styles and weights identical. Prices $100 less except phaeton, which was $145 less than 1930.

DD New Six (wb 109.0) - 12,854 built

Production was carried over from 1930, with 1931-model output commencing July 15. Prod figs combined with 1930 DD; total 1931 prod based on serial number spans. Body styles and weights identical. Prices $100 less than 1930.

DG Eight (wb 118.5) - 9,520 blt*	Wght	Price	Prod
rdstr 2-4P	2,936	1,095	64
cpe 2-4P	3,094	1,095	2,181
conv cpe	3,240	1,170	500
sdn 4d	3,175	1,135	8,937
chassis	—	—	20

DH Six (wb 114.0) - 20,558 built**	Wght	Price	Prod
rdstr 2-4P	2,638	825	160
bus cpe 2P	2,661	815	3,178
cpe 2-4P	2,745	835	4,187
sdn 4d	2,820	845	33,090
chassis	—	—	47

* Total based on serial number spans. Individual model totals for 1931-32 combined (see also additional models under 1932). Approximately 80 percent of the individual model totals were 1932 models.

** Total based on serial number spans. Individual model totals for 1931-32 combined (see also additional models under 1932). Approximately 50 percent of the individual model totals were 1931 models.

1931 Engines	bore×stroke	bhp	availability
I-8, 220.7	2.88×4.25	75	S-DC
I-6, 189.8	3.13×4.13	61	S-DD
I-8, 240.3	3.00×4.25	84	S-DG
I-6, 211.5	3.25×4.25	68	S-DH

1932

DG Eight (wb118.5) - 2,344 blt*	Wght	Price	Prod
rdstr 2-4P	2,976	1,095	**
phtn 5P	—	1,155	43**
bus cpe 2P	3,003	1,095	119**
cpe 2-4P	3,094	1,095	**
conv cpe 5P	3,240	1,145	**
sdn 4d	3,175	1,135	**
chassis	—	—	**

* Total prod based on serial number spans for 1932.

** Prod combined with 1931 except for phaeton (43) and business coupe (119), which were new models for 1932.

DH Six (wb 114.0) - 20,268 built**	Wght	Price	Prod
rdstr 2-4P	2,638	850	**
phtn 5P	2,655	865	164
bus cpe 2P	2,661	815	**
cpe 2-4P	2,745	835	**
sdn 4d	2,820	845	**
chassis	—	—	**

* Total prod based on serial number spans for 1932.

** Production combined with 1931 except for phaeton (164), which was a new model for 1932.

DC Eight (wb 114.0) - 631 built

Leftover 1930-31 models sold as 1932s commencing July 1, 1931. Total volume based on serial number spans. Body styles, weights and prices as for 1931.

DD New Six (wb 109.0) - 1,000 built (est.)

Leftover 1930-31 models sold as 1932s commencing July 1, 1931. Total volume estimated. Body styles, weights and prices as for 1931.

DL Six (wb 114.3) - 21,042 built	Wght	Price	Prod
bus cpe 2P	2,928	795	1,963
cpe 2-4P	2,995	835	1,815
conv cpe 2-4P	2,988	895	224
sdn 4d	3,094	945	16,901
conv sdn	—	—	12
cpe 5P	—	—	1
chassis	—	—	126

DK Eight (wb 122.0) - 6,187 built	Wght	Price	Prod
cpe 2-4P	3,417	1,115	821
cpe 5P	3,504	1,145	651
conv cpe 2-4P	3,438	1,220	126
sdn 4d	3,527	1,145	4,422
conv sdn 5P	3,706	1,395	88
bus cpe 2P	—	—	57
chassis	—	—	22

1932 Engines	bore×stroke	bhp	availability
I-8, 220.7	2.88×4.25	75	S-DC
I-6, 189.8	3.13×4.13	61	S-DD
I-8, 240.3	3.00×4.25	84	S-DG
I-6, 211.5	3.25×4.25	74	S-DH
I-6, 217.8	3.25×4.38	79	S-DL
I-8, 282.1	3.25×4.25	90	S-DK

1933

DP Six (wb 111.3; lwb-115.0)	Wght	Price	Prod
bus cpe 2P	2,452	595	11,236
lwb bus cpe 2P	2,501	595	
cpe 2-4P	2,506	640	8,875
lwb cpe 2-4P	2,551	640	
conv cpe 2-4P	2,511	695	1,563
conv cpe 2-4P	2,556	695	
sdn 2d	2,591	630	8,523
lwb sdn 2d	2,636	630	
sdn 4d	2,632	670	69,074
lwb sdn 4d	2,661	675	
salon brougham 5P	2,651	660	4,200
lwb salon brghm 5P	2,678	660	
chassis	—	—	980

DO Eight (wb 122.0)	Wght	Price	Prod
cpe 2-4P	3,451	1,115	212
cpe 5P	3,540	1,145	159
conv cpe 2-4P	3,465	1,185	56
sdn 4d	3,580	1,145	1,173
conv sdn 5P	3,961	1,395	39
chassis	—	—	13

1933 Engines	bore×stroke	bhp	availability
I-6, 201.3	3.13×4.38	75	S-DP
I-8, 282.1	3.25×4.25	92	S-DO

1934

DR DeLuxe Six (wb 117.0)	Wght	Price	Prod
bus cpe 2P	2,695	665	8,723
cpe 2-4P	2,745	715	5,323
conv cpe 2-4P	2,845	765	1,239
sdn 2d	2,855	715	7,308
sdn 4d	2,940	765	53,479
sdns 4d 7P	—	—	710
chassis	—	—	1,475

DS DeLuxe Six (wb 121.0)	Wght	Price	Prod
Special brghm 4d 5P	2,905	845	1,397
Special conv sdn 5P	2,915	875	350
chassis	—	—	3

DRXX New Standard Six (wb 117.0)	Wght	Price	Prod
bus cpe 2P	2,695	645	2,284
cpe 2-4P	2,745	690	105
sdn 2d	2,855	695	3,133
sdn 4d	2,940	745	9,481
chassis	—	—	1

1934 Engine	bore×stroke	bhp	availability
I-6, 217.8	3.25×4.38	87	S-all

1935

DU New Value Six (wb 116.0; lwb-128.0)	Wght	Price	Prod
cpe 2P	2,731	645	17,800
cpe 2-4P	2,801	710	4,499
conv cpe 2-4P	2,883	770	950
fstbk sdn 2d	2,821	690	7,891
sdn T/B 2d	2,868	715	18,069
fstbk sdn 4d	2,861	735	33,118
sdn T/B 4d	2,868	760	74,203
Caravn sdn 4d 5P (lwb)	3,221	995	193
lwb sdn 4d 7P	3,118	995	1,018
chassis	—	—	1,258

1935 Engine	bore×stroke	bhp	availability
I-6, 217.8	3.25×4.38	87	S-all

1936

D2 Beauty Winner Six (wb 116.0; lwb-128.0)	Wght	Price	Prod
cpe 2P	2,773	640	32,952
cpe 2-4P	2,823	695	4,317
conv cpe 2-4P	2,887	795	1,525
fstbk sdn 2d	2,903	695	2,453
sdn T/B 2d	2,893	720	37,468
fstbk sdn 4d	2,923	735	5,996
sdn T/B 4d	2,958	760	174,334
conv sdn 5P	3,018	995	750
lwb sdn 4d 7P	3,238	975	1,942
chassis	—	—	1,910

1936 Engine	bore×stroke	bhp	availability
I-6, 217.8	3.25×4.38	87	S-all

1937

D5 (wb 115.0; lwb-132.0)	Wght	Price	Prod
bus cpe 2P	2,902	715	41,702
cpe 2-4P	2,967	770	3,500
conv cpe 2-4P	3,057	910	1,345
fstbk sdn 2d	2,992	780	5,302
sdn T/B 2d	2,997	790	44,750
fstbk sdn 4d	2,982	820	7,555
sdn T/B 4d	2,997	830	185,483
conv sdn 5P	3,262	1,230	473
lwb sdn 7P	3,367	1,075	2,207
limo 7P (lwb)	—	1,175	216
chassis	—	—	2,514

1937 Engine	bore×stroke	bhp	availability
I-6, 217.8	3.25×4.38	87	S-all

1938

D8 (wb 115.0; lwb-132.0)	Wght	Price	Prod
bus cpe 2P	2,877	808	15,552
cpe 2-4P	2,952	858	950

D8 (wb 115.0; lwb-132.0)	Wght	Price	Prod
conv cpe 2-4P	3,122	960	701
fstbk sdn 2d	2,977	858	999
sdn T/B 2d	2,957	870	17,282
fstbk sdn 4d	2,977	898	714
sdn T/B 4d	2,967	910	73,417
conv sdn T/B 5P	3,308	1,275	132
lwb sdn 7P	3,332	1,095	1,953
limo 7P (lwb)	—	1,185	153
wgn 4d	—	—	375
chassis	—	—	2,301

1938 Engine	bore×stroke	bhp	availability
I-6, 217.8	3.25×4.38	87	S-all

1939

D11 Luxury Liner Special (wb 117.0)	Wght	Price	Prod
bus cpe 2P	2,905	756	12,300
sdn 2d	2,955	815	26,700
sdn 4d	2,955	855	32,000
D11 Luxury Liner DeLuxe (wb 117.0)			
bus cpe 2P	2,940	803	12,800
Town cpe 5P	3,075	1,055	363
sdn 2d	3,010	865	17,608
sdn 4d	3,045	905	80,169
chassis	—	—	875

1939 Engine	bore×stroke	bhp	availability
I-6, 217.8	3.25×4.38	87	S-all

Note: Many sources also list a 2-4 passenger rumble-seat coupe (2,985 lbs/$860), and a 134-inch wheelbase 7-passenger sedan (3,440 lbs/$1,095) and limousine (3,545 lbs/$1,185). However, Dodge gives no prod figs for these models, and their prod in 1939 is in doubt.

1940

D-17 Special (wb 119.5)	Wght	Price	Prod
bus cpe	2,867	755	12,001
sdn 2d	2,942	815	27,700
sdn 4d	2,997	855	26,803
D-14 DeLuxe (wb 119.5; 7P-139.5)			
bus cpe	2,905	803	12,750
cpe, A/S	2,973	855	8,028
conv cpe	3,190	1,030	2,100
sdn 2d	2,990	860	19,838
sdn 4d	3,028	905	84,976
sdn 4d, 7P	3,460	1,095	932
limo 7P	3,500	1,170	79
chassis	—	—	298

1940 Engine	bore×stroke	bhp	availability
I-6, 217.8	3.25×4.38	87	S-all

1941

D-19 DeLuxe (wb 119.5)	Wght	Price	Prod
bus cpe	3,034	862	22,318
sdn 2d	3,109	915	34,566
sdn 4d	3,149	954	49,579
D-19 Custom (wb 119.5; 7P-137.5)			
club cpe	3,154	995	18,024
conv cpe	3,384	1,162	3,554
brougham 2d	3,169	962	20,146
sdn 4d	3,194	999	72,067
town sdn	3,234	1,062	16,074
sdn 4d, 7P	3,579	1,195	604
limo 7P	3,669	1,262	50
chassis	—	—	20

1941 Engine	bore×stroke	bhp	availability
I-6, 217.8	3.25×4.38	91	S-all

1942

D-22 DeLuxe (wb 119.5)	Wght	Price	Prod
bus cpe	3,056	895	5,257
club cpe	3,131	995	3,314
sdn 2d	3,131	958	9,767
sdn 4d	3,171	998	13,343
D-22 Custom (wb 119.5; 7P-137.5)			
club cpe	3,171	1,045	4,659
conv cpe	3,476	1,245	1,185
brougham 2d	3,171	1,008	4,685
sdn 4d	3,206	1,048	22,055
town sdn	3,256	1,105	4,047
sdn 4d, 7P	3,693	1,395	201
limo 7P	3,768	1,475	9

1942 Engine	bore×stroke	bhp	availability
I-6, 230.2	3.25×4.63	105	S-all

1946

D-24S DeLuxe (wb 119.5)	Wght	Price	Prod*
bus cpe	3,146	1,229	—
sdn 2d	3,236	1,299	—
sdn 4d	3,256	1,339	—
D-24C Custom (wb 119.5; 7P-137.5)			
club cpe	3,241	1,384	—
conv cpe	3,461	1,649	—
sdn 4d	3,281	1,389	—
town sdn	3,331	1,444	—
sdn 4d, 7P	3,757	1,743	—

1946 Engine	bore×stroke	bhp	availability
I-6, 230.2	3.25×4.63	102	S-all

* Factory combined production figures for 1946 through First Series 1949.

1947

D-24S DeLuxe (wb 119.5)	Wght	Price	Prod*
bus cpe	3,146	1,347	—
sdn 2d	3,236	1,417	—
sdn 4d	3,256	1,457	—
D-24C Custom (wb 119.5; 7P-137.5)			
club cpe	3,241	1,502	—
conv cpe	3,461	1,871	—
sdn 4d	3,281	1,507	—
town sdn	3,331	1,577	—
sdn 4d, 7P	3,757	1,861	—

1947 Engine	bore×stroke	bhp	availability
I-6, 230.2	3.25×4.63	102	S-all

* Factory combined production figures for 1946 through First Series 1949.

1948

D-24S DeLuxe (wb 119.5)	Wght	Price	Prod*
bus cpe	3,146	1,587	—
sdn 2d	3,236	1,676	—
sdn 4d	3,256	1,718	—
D-24C Custom (wb 119.5; 7P-137.5)			
club cpe	3,241	1,774	—
conv cpe	3,461	2,189	—
sdn 4d	3,281	1,788	—
town sdn	3,331	1,872	—
sdn 4d, 7P	3,757	2,179	—

1948 Engine	bore×stroke	bhp	availability
I-6, 230.2	3.25×4.63	102	S-all

* Factory combined production figures for 1946 through First Series 1949.

1949 First Series

D-24S DeLuxe (wb 119.5)	Wght	Price	Prod*
bus cpe	3,146	1,587	—
sdn 2d	3,236	1,676	—
sdn 4d	3,256	1,718	—
D-24C Custom (wb 119.5; 7P-137.5)			
club cpe	3,241	1,774	—
conv cpe	3,461	2,189	—
sdn 4d	3,281	1,788	—
town sdn	3,331	1,872	—
sdn 4d, 7P	3,757	2,179	—

1949(1) Eng.	bore×stroke	bhp	availability
I-6, 230.2	3.25×4.63	102	S-all

* Factory combined production figures for 1946 through First Series 1949.

1946-1949 Combined First Series Production:

D-24S DeLuxe (wb 119.5)	Prod
bus cpe	27,600
sdn 2d	81,399
sdn 4d	61,987
D-24C Custom (wb 119.5; 7P-137.5)	
club cpe	103,800
conv cpe	9,500
sdn 4d	333,911
town sdn	27,800
sdn 4d, 7P	3,698
limo 7P (proto)	2
chassis	302

1949 Second Series

D-29 Wayfarer (wb 115.0)	Wght	Price	Prod
cpe	3,065	1,611	9,342
sdn 2d	3,180	1,738	49,054
rdstr	3,145	1,727	5,420
D-30 (wb 123.5; 8P-137.5)			
Meadowbrook sdn 4d	3,355	1,848	144,390 (combined with Coronet sdn 4d)
Coronet sdn 4d	3,380	1,927	
Coronet club cpe	3,325	1,914	45,435
Coronet conv cpe	3,570	2,329	2,411
Coronet sdn 4d, 8P	4,070	2,635	—
Coronet wgn 4d, 9P	3,830	2,865	800
chassis	—	—	1

1949(2) Engine	bore×stroke	bhp	availability
I-6, 230.2	3.25×4.63	103	S-all

1950

D-33 Wayfarer (wb 115.0)	Wght	Price	Prod
bus cpe	3,095	1,611	7,500
sdn 2d	3,200	1,738	65,000
Sportabout rdstr	3,155	1,727	2,903
D-34 (wb 123.5; 8P-137.5)			
Meadowbrook sdn 4d	3,395	1,848	221,791 (combined with Coronet sdn 4d)
Coronet sdn 4d	3,405	1,927	
Coronet sdn 4d, 8P	4,070	2,635	1,300
Coronet club cpe	3,340	1,914	38,502
Coronet conv cpe	3,590	2,329	1,800
Crnt Diplomat htp cpe	3,515	2,223	3,600
Crnt wgn 4d-wood	3,850	2,865	600
Crnt Sirra wgn 4d-steel	3,726	2,485	100
chassis	—	—	1

1950 Engine	bore×stroke	bhp	availability
I-6, 230.2	3.25×4.63	103	S-all

1951

D-41 Wayfarer (wb 115.0)	Wght	Price	Prod*
bus cpe	3,125	1,795	—
sdn 2d	3,210	1,936	—
Sportabout rdstr	3,175	1,924	1,002
D-42 (wb 123.5; 8P-137.5)			
Meadowbrook sdn 4d	3,415	2,059	—
Coronet sdn 4d	3,415	2,148	—
Coronet club cpe	3,320	2,132	—
Crnt Diplomat htp cpe	3,515	2,478	—
Coronet conv cpe	3,575	2,568	—
Crnt Sierra wgn 4d	3,750	2,768	—
Coronet sdn 4d, 8P	3,935	2,916	—

1951 Engine	bore×stroke	bhp	availability
I-6, 230.2	3.25×4.63	103	S-all

* Factory combined 1951-1952 production.

1952

D-41 Wayfarer (wb 115.0)	Wght	Price	Prod*
bus cpe	3,053	1,886	—
sdn 2d	3,140	2,034	—
D-42 (wb 123.5; 8P-137.5)			
Meadowbrook sdn 4d	3,355	2,164	—
Coronet sdn 4d	3,385	2,256	—
Coronet club cpe	3,290	2,240	—
Coronet conv cpe	3,520	2,698	—
Crnt Diplomat htp cpe	3,475	2,602	—
Crnt Sierra wgn 4d	3,735	2,908	—
Coronet sdn 4d, 8P	3,935	3,064	—

1952 Engine	bore×stroke	bhp	availability
I-6, 230.2	3.25×4.63	103	S-all

* Factory combined 1951-1952 production.

Combined 1951-1952 production:

D-41 Wayfarer (wb 115.0)	Prod
bus cpe	6,702
sdn 2d	70,700
Sportabout rdstr (1951 only)	1,002
D-42 (wb 123.5; 8P-137.5)	
Meadowbrook/Coronet sdn 4d	329,202
Coronet club cpe	56,103
Coronet conv cpe	5,550
Coronet Diplomat htp cpe	21,600
Coronet Sierra wgn 4d	4,000
Coronet sdn 4d, 8P	1,150

1953

D-46 (wb 119.0)	Wght	Price	Prod
Meadwbrk Spec cpe	3,100	1,958	
Meadowbrook cpe	3,085	1,958	36,766
Coronet cpe	3,155	2,084	
Meadwbrk Spec sdn 4d	3,195	2,000	
Meadowbrook sdn 4d	3,175	2,000	84,158
Coronet sdn 4d	3,220	2,111	
D-47 Meadowbrook Suburban (wb 114.0)			
wgn 2d	3,190	2,176	15,751
D-44 Coronet Eight (wb 119.0)			
club cpe	3,325	2,198	32,439
sdn 4d	3,385	2,220	124,059
D-48 Coronet Eight (wb 114.0)			
conv cpe	3,438	2,494	4,100
Diplomat htp cpe	3,310	2,361	17,334
Sierra wgn 2d	3,425	2,503	5,400
chassis	—	—	1

1953 Engines	bore×stroke	bhp	availability
I-6, 230.2	3.25×4.63	103	S-D-46, D-47
V-8, 241.3	3.44×3.25	140	S-D-44, D-48

1954

D51-1 Meadwbrk I-6 (wb 119.0)	Wght	Price	Prod
club cpe	3,120	1,983	3,501
sdn 4d	3,195	2,025	7,894
D50-1 Meadowbrook V-8 (wb 119.0)			
club cpe	3,335	2,154	750
sdn 4d	3,390	2,176	3,299
D51-2 Coronet I-6 (wb 119.0)			
club cpe	3,165	2,109	4,501
sdn 4d	3,235	2,136	14,900
D52 Coronet I-6 (wb 119.0; 2d-114.0)			
Suburban wgn 2d	3,185	2,229	6,389
Sierra wgn 4d, 6P	3,430	2,719	312
Sierra wgn 4d, 8P	3,435	2,790	
D50-2 Coronet V-8 (wb 119.0)			
club cpe	3,345	2,223	7,998
sdn 4d	3,405	2,245	36,063
D53-2 Coronet V-8 (wb 114.0; 4d-119.0)			
Sport htp cpe	3,310	2,380	100
conv cpe	3,505	2,514	50
Suburban wgn 2d	3,400	2,517	3,100
Sierra wgn 4d, 6P	3,605	2,960	988
Sierra wgn 4d, 8P	3,660	3,031	
D50-3 Royal V-8 (wb 119.0)			
club cpe	3,365	2,349	8,900
sdn 4d	3,425	2,373	50,050
D53-3 Royal V-8 (wb 114.0)			
Sport htp cpe	3,355	2,503	3,852
conv cpe (incl. 701 500s)	3,575	2,632	2,000
chassis	—	—	1

1954 Engines	bore×stroke	bhp	availability
I-6, 230.2	3.25×4.63	110	S-Coronet 6s
V-8, 241.3	3.44×3.25	140	S-Mdwbrk V-8
V-8, 241.3	3.44×3.25	150	S-others (Offenhauser manifold available)

1955

D56-1 Coronet I-6 (wb 120.0)	Wght	Price	Prod
sdn 2d	3,235	2,013	13,277
sdn 4d	3,295	2,093	15,976
Suburban wgn 2d	3,410	2,349	3,248
Suburban wgn 4d, 6P	3,480	2,463	1,311
Suburban wgn 4d, 8P	3,595	2,565	
D55-1 Coronet V-8 (wb 120.0)			
sdn 2d	3,360	2,116	10,827
club sdn 2d	3,235	2,124	
sdn 4d	3,395	2,196	30,098
Lancer htp cpe	3,375	2,281	26,727
Suburban wgn 2d	3,550	2,452	4,867
Suburban wgn 4d, 6P	3,590	2,566	4,641
Suburban wgn 4d, 8P	3,695	2,668	
D55-2 Royal V-8 (wb 120.0)			
sdn 4d	3,425	2,310	45,323
Lancer htp cpe	3,425	2,395	25,831
Sierra wgn 4d, 6P	3,655	2,659	5,506
Sierra wgn 4d, 8P	3,730	2,761	
D55-3 Cstm Royal V-8 (wb 120.0)			
sdn 4d	3,485	2,473	55,503
Lancer sdn 4d	3,505	2,516	
Lancer htp cpe	3,480	2,543	30,499
Lancer conv cpe	3,610	2,748	3,302

1955 Engines	bore×stroke	bhp	availability
I-6, 230.2	3.25×4.63	123	S-Coronet 6s
V-8, 270.1	3.63×3.25	175	S-Crnt V-8, Ryl
V-8, 270.1	3.63×3.25	183	S-Cstm Royal
V-8, 270.1	3.63×3.25	193	O-Cstm Royal

1956

D62 Coronet I-6 (wb 120.0)	Wght	Price	Prod*
sdn 2d	3,250	2,194	10,509
sdn 4d	3,295	2,267	14,277
Suburban wgn 2d	3,455	2,491	2,025
D63-1 Coronet V-8 (wb 120.0)			
club sdn 2d	3,380	2,302	24,390
sdn 4d	3,435	2,375	50,106
Lancer htp sdn	3,560	2,552	3,502
Lancer htp cpe	3,430	2,438	21,105
conv cpe	3,600	2,678	1,913
Sierra wgn 4d, 6P	3,600	2,716	10,241
Sierra wgn 4d, 8P	3,715	2,822	
Suburban wgn 2d	3,605	2,599	3,476
D63-2 Royal V-8 (wb 120.0)			
sdn 4d	3,475	2,513	26,616
Lancer htp sdn	3,625	2,697	3,795
Lancer htp cpe	3,505	2,583	11,787
Sierra wgn 4d, 6P	3,710	2,869	4,473
Sierra wgn 4d, 8P	3,800	2,974	
Suburban wgn 2d	3,620	2,729	1,875
D63-3 Custom Royal V-8 (wb 120.0)			
sdn 4d	3,520	2,623	27,829
Lancer htp sdn	3,675	2,807	4,226
Lancer htp cpe	3,505	2,693	14,417
conv cpe	3,630	2,913	1,378

1956 Engines	bore×stroke	bhp	availability
I-6, 230.2	3.25×4.63	131	S-Coronet 6s
V-8, 270.1	3.63×3.25	189	S-Coronet V-8
V-8, 315.0	3.63×3.80	218	S-Ryl, Cstm Ryl
V-8, 315.0	3.63×3.80	230/260	O-all

*Includes Canadian exports.

1957

D72 Coronet I-6 (wb 122.0)	Wght	Price	Prod
club sdn 2d	3,400	2,370	7,175
sdn 4d	3,470	2,451	10,483
D66 Coronet V-8 (wb 122.0)			
club sdn 2d	3,530	2,478	21,132
sdn 4d	3,620	2,559	60,810
Lancer htp sdn	3,665	2,665	13,619
Lancer htp cpe	3,570	2,580	44,397
conv cpe	3,815	2,842	3,363
D501 Coronet D-500 V-8 (122.0)			
club sdn 2d	3,885	3,314	101
conv cpe	3,975	3,670	
D67-1 Royal V-8 (wb 122.0)			
sdn 4d	3,620	2,712	19,923
Lancer htp sdn	3,690	2,818	8,824
Lancer htp cpe	3,585	2,769	12,252
D67-2 Custom Royal V-8 (wb 122.0)			
sdn 4d	3,690	2,881	22,548
Lancer htp sdn	3,750	2,991	12,068
Lancer htp cpe	3,670	2,920	17,629
conv cpe	3,810	3,146	2,456
D70 Station Wagon V-8 (wb 122.0)			
Sierra wgn 4d, 6P	3,930	2,946	17,352
Sierra wgn 4d, 9P	4,015	3,073	
Suburban wgn 2d	3,830	2,861	7,163
D71 Custom Station Wgn V-8 (wb 122.0)			
Sierra wgn 4d, 6P	3,960	3,087	7,216
Sierra wgn 4d, 9P	4,030	3,215	

1957 Engines	bore×stroke	bhp	availability
I-6, 230.2	3.25×4.63	138	S-D72
V-8, 325.0	3.69×3.80	245	S-all exc D72, D67, D501
V-8, 325.0	3.69×3.80	260	S-D67-2
V-8, 325.0	3.69×3.80	285/310	O-all (D-500)
V-8, 354.0	3.94×3.63	340	O-all (D-500)

1958

LD-1 Coronet I-6 (wb 122.0)	Wght	Price	Prod
club sdn 2d	3,360	2,449	2,922
sdn 4d	3,410	2,530	4,592
Lancer htp cpe	3,400	2,572	715
LD-2 Coronet V-8 (wb 122.0)			
club sdn 2d	3,505	2,556	7,576
sdn 4d	3,555	2,637	31,707
Lancer htp sdn	3,605	2,764	7,117
Lancer htp cpe	3,540	2,679	21,032
Lancer conv cpe	3,725	2,942	1,718
LD-2-M Royal V-8 (wb 122.0)			
sdn 4d	3,570	2,797	7,515
Lancer htp sdn 4d	3,640	2,915	3,332
Lancer htp cpe	3,565	2,854	4,318
LD-3-H Custom Royal V-8 (wb 122.0)			
sdn 4d	3,640	3,030	9,981
Lancer htp sdn	3,670	3,142	5,747
Lancer htp cpe	3,610	3,071	7,172
conv cpe	3,785	3,298	1,139
Regal Lancer htp cpe	3,650	3,245	1,163
LD-3 Station Wagon V-8 (wb 122.0)			
Sierra wgn 4d, 6P	3,930	3,035	13,113
Sierra wgn 4d, 9P	3,990	3,176	
Suburban wgn 2d	3,875	2,970	1,300
Cstm Sierra wgn 4d, 6P	3,955	3,212	5,783
Cstm Sierra wgn 4d, 9P	4,035	3,354	

1958 Engines	bore×stroke	bhp	availability
I-6, 230.2	3.25×4.63	138	S-Coronet 6
V-8, 325.0	3.69×3.80	252	S-Coronet V-8
V-8, 325.0	3.69×3.80	265	S-Royal
V-8, 350.0	4.06×3.38	295	S-Cus Ryl, wgns
V-8, 361.0	4.12×3.38	305-333	O-all (D-500)

1959

	MD1-L Coronet I-6 (wb 122.0)	Wght	Price	Prod
21	club sdn 2d	3,375	2,516	5,432
23	Lancer htp cpe	3,395	2,644	2,151
41	sdn 4d	3,425	2,587	8,103
	MD2-L Coronet V-8 (wb 122.0)			
21	club sdn 2d	3,565	2,636	8,002
23	Lancer htp cpe	3,590	2,764	19,283
27	conv cpe	3,775	3,089	1,840
41	sdn 4d	3,615	2,707	43,025
43	Lancer htp sdn	3,620	2,842	8,946
	MD3-M Royal V-8 (wb 122.0)			
23	Lancer htp cpe	3,625	2,990	3,483
41	sdn 4d	3,640	2,934	8,389
43	Lancer htp sdn	3,690	3,069	2,935
	MD3-H Custom Royal V-8 (wb 122.0)			
23	Lancer htp cpe	3,675	3,201	6,278
27	conv cpe	3,820	3,422	984
41	sdn 4d	3,660	3,145	8,925
43	Lancer htp sdn	3,745	3,270	5,019
	MD3-L Sierra V-8 (wb 122.0)			
45A	wgn 4d, 6P	3,940	3,103	17,719
45B	Sierra wgn 4d, 9P	4,015	3,224	
	MD3-H Custom V-8 (wb 122.0)			
45A	wgn 4d, 6P	3,980	3,318	5,871
45B	wgn 4d, 9P	4,020	3,439	

1959 Engines	bore×stroke	bhp	availability
I-6, 230.2	3.25×4.63	138	S-Coronet 6
V-8, 326.0	3.95×3.31	255	S-Coronet V-8
V-8, 361.0	4.12×3.38	295/305	S-all exc Cmt
V-8, 383.0	4.25×3.38	320/345	O-all (D-500, Super D-500)

1960

	PD3 Dart I-6 (wb 118.0; wgns-122.0)	Wght	Price	Prod
L21	Seneca sdn 2d	3,385	2,278	
L41	Seneca sdn 4d	3,420	2,330	93,167
L45	Seneca wgn 4d	3,805	2,695	
M21	Pioneer sdn 2d	3,375	2,410	
M23	Pioneer htp cpe	3,410	2,488	
M41	Pioneer sdn 4d	3,430	2,459	36,434
M45A	Pioneer wgn 4d, 6P	3,820	2,787	
M45B	Pioneer wgn 4d, 9P	3,875	2,892	

PD3 Dart I-6		Wght	Price	Prod
H23	Phoenix htp cpe	3,410	2,618	
H27	Phoenix conv cpe	3,460	2,868	6,567
H41	Phoenix sdn 4d	3,420	2,595	
H43	Phoenix htp sdn	3,460	2,677	
PD4 Dart V-8 (wb 118.0; wgns-122.0)				
L21	Seneca sdn 2d	3,530	2,397	
L41	Seneca sdn 4d	3,600	2,449	45,737
L45	Seneca wgn 4d	3,975	2,815	
M21	Pioneer sdn 2d	3,540	2,530	
M23	Pioneer htp cpe	3,610	2,607	
M41	Pioneer sdn 4d	3,610	2,578	74,655
M45A	Pioneer wgn 4d, 6P	4,000	2,906	
M45B	Pioneer wgn 4d, 9P	4,065	3,011	
H23	Phoenix hpt cpe	3,605	2,737	
H27	Phoenix conv cpe	3,690	2,988	66,608
H41	Phoenix sdn 4d	3,610	2,715	
H43	Phoenix htp sdn	3,655	2,796	
PD1-L Matador (wb 122.0) - 27,908 built				
23	htp cpe	3,705	2,996	—
41	sdn 4d	3,725	2,930	—
43	htp sdn	3,820	3,075	—
45A	wgn 4d, 6P	4,045	3,239	—
44B	wgn 4d, 9P	4,120	3,354	—
PD2-H Polara (wb 122.0) - 16,728 built				
23	htp cpe	3,740	3,196	—
27	conv cpe	3,765	3,416	—
41	sdn 4d	3,735	3,141	—
43	htp sdn	3,815	3,275	—
45A	wgn 4d, 6P	4,085	3,506	—
45B	wgn 4d, 9P	4,220	3,621	—

1960 Engines	bore×stroke	bhp	availability
I-6, 225.0	3.40×4.13	145	S-Dart 6
V-8, 318.0	3.91×3.31	230	S-Seneca, Pioneer V-8
V-8, 318.0	3.91×3.31	255	S-Phoenix V-8
V-8, 361.0	4.12×3.38	295	S-Matador; O-Pionr, Phnix
V-8, 383.0	4.25×3.38	325	S-Polara; O-Mtdor, Phnix
V-8, 383.0	4.25×3.38	330	O-Polara, Matador, Phnix

1961

RW1-Lancer 170 (wb106.5)-25,508 blt		Wght	Price	Prod
711	sdn 2d	2,585	1,979	—
713	sdn 4d	2,595	2,041	—
756	wgn 4d	2,760	2,354	—
RW1-H Lancer 770 (wb 106.5) - 49,268 built				
723	htp cpe	2,595	2,164	—
731	spt cpe	2,643	2,075	—
733	sdn 4d	2,605	2,137	—
776	wgn 4d	2,775	2,449	—
RD3 Dart I-6 (118.0; wgns-122.0)*				
L411	Seneca sdn 2d	3,290	2,278	
L413	Seneca sdn 4d	3,335	2,330	60,527
L456	Seneca wgn 4d	3,740	2,695	
M421	Pioneer sdn 2d	3,290	2,410	
M422	Pioneer htp cpe	3,335	2,488	
M423	Pioneer sdn 4d	3,335	2,459	18,214
M466	Pioneer wgn 4d, 6P	3,740	2,787	
M467	Pioneer wgn 4d, 9P	3,825	2,892	
H432	Phoenix htp cpe	3,325	2,618	
H433	Phoenix sdn 4d	3,350	2,595	4,273
H434	Phoenix htp sdn	3,385	2,677	
RD4 Dart V-8 (wb 118.0; wgns-122.0)				
L511	Seneca sdn 2d	3,470	2,397	
L513	Seneca sdn 4d	3,515	2,449	27,174
L556	Seneca wgn 4d	3,920	2,815	
M521	Pioneer sdn 2d	3,460	2,530	
M522	Pioneer htp cpe	3,500	2,607	
M523	Pioneer sdn 4d	3,510	2,578	39,054
M566	Pioneer wgn 4d, 6P	3,940	2,906	
M567	Pioneer wgn 4d, 9P	4,005	3,011	
H532	Phoenix htp cpe	3,520	2,737	
H533	Phoenix sdn 4d	3,535	2,715	34,319
H534	Phoenix htp sdn	3,555	2,796	
H535	Phoenix conv cpe	3,580	2,988	
RD1-L Polara (wb 122.0) - 14,032 built				
542	htp cpe	3,690	3,032	—

RD1-L Polara		Wght	Price	Prod
543	sdn 4d	3,700	2,966	—
544	htp sdn	3,740	3,110	—
545	conv cpe	3,765	3,252	—
578	wgn 4d, 6P	4,115	3,294	—
579	wgn 4d, 9P	4,125	3,409	—

1961 Engines	bore×stroke	bhp	availability
I-6, 170.0	3.40×3.13	101	S-Lancer
I-6, 225.0	3.40×4.13	145	S-Dart 6; O-Lancer
V-8, 318.0	3.91×3.31	230	S-Dart V-8
V-8, 318.0	3.91×3.31	260	O-Dart V-8
V-8, 361.0	4.12×3.38	265	S-Polara
V-8, 361.0	4.12×3.38	305	O-Dart V-8 (D-500)
V-8, 383.0	4.25×3.38	325	O-Polara (D-500), Dart V-8
V-8, 383.0	4.25×3.38	330	O-Polara, Dart V-8 (ram ind)
V-8, 413.0	4.19×3.75	350/375	O-Dart

1962*

SL1-L Lancer 170 (wb 106.5) - 19,780 built		Wght	Price	Prod
711	sdn 2d	2,495	1,951	—
713	sdn 4d	2,525	2,011	—
756	wgn 4d	2,685	2,306	—
SL1-H Lancer 770 (wb 106.5) - 30,888 built				
731	sdn 2d	2,520	2,052	—
733	sdn 4d	2,540	2,114	—
776	wgn 4d	2,705	2,408	—
SL1-P Lancer GT (wb 106.5)				
742	htp cpe	2,560	2,257	13,683
SD1 Dart I-6 (wb 116.0)				
L401	Fleet Special sdn 2d	2,965	2,158	9,506
L411	sdn 2d	2,970	2,241	
L403	Fleet Special sdn 4d	2,995	2,214	26,470
L413	sdn 4d	3,000	2,297	
L456	wgn 4d	3,270	2,644	4,303
M421	330 sdn 2d	2,965	2,375	843
M422	330 htp cpe	2,985	2,463	1,592
M423	330 sdn 4d	3,000	2,432	6,299
M466	330 wgn 4d	3,275	2,739	860
H432	440 htp cpe	3,025	2,606	801
H433	440 sdn 4d	3,045	2,584	2,338
SD2 Dart V-8 (wb 116.0)				
L501	Fleet Special sdn 2d	3,130	2,316	2,184
L511	sdn 2d	3,135	2,348	
L503	Fleet Special sdn 4d	3,165	2,372	10,521
L513	sdn 4d	3,170	2,404	
L556	wgn 4d	3,435	2,571	4,085
M521	330 sdn 2d	3,135	2,482	899
M522	330 htp cpe	3,155	2,570	3,016
M523	330 sdn 4d	3,170	2,540	13,407
M566	330 wgn 4d, 6P	3,435	2,848	4,592
M567	330 wgn 4d, 9P	3,500	2,949	2,896
H532	440 htp cpe	3,185	2,713	7,119
H533	440 sdn 4d	3,205	2,691	16,065
H534	440 htp sdn	3,260	2,763	7,716
H535	440 conv cpe	3,285	2,945	3,166
H576	440 wgn 4d, 6P	3,460	2,989	3,606
H577	440 wgn 4d, 9P	3,530	3,092	3,708
SD2-P Polara 500 (wb 116.0)				
542	htp cpe	3,315	3,019	6,834
544	htp sdn	3,360	2,960	3,345
545	conv cpe	3,430	3,268	2,089
SD3-L Custom 880 (wb 122.0) - 17,505 built				
612	htp cpe	3,615	3,030	—
613	sdn 4d	3,655	2,964	—
614	htp sdn	3,680	3,109	—
615	conv cpe	3,705	3,251	—
658	wgn 4d, 6P	4,025	3,292	—
659	wgn 4d, 9P	4,055	3,407	—

1962 Engines	bore×stroke	bhp	availability
I-6, 170.0	3.40×3.13	101	S-Lancer
I-6, 225.0	3.40×4.13	145	S-Dart 6; O-Lancer
V-8, 318.0	3.91×3.31	230	S-Dart V-8
V-8, 318.0	3.91×3.31	260	O-Dart V-8
V-8, 361.0	4.12×3.38	265	S-Custom 880
V-8, 361.0	4.12×3.38	305	S-Polara 500; O-Dart V-8
V-8, 361.0	4.12×3.38	310	O-Dart V-8, Polara 500
V-8, 383.0	4.25×3.38	330/335	O-Dart V-8, Polara 500
V-8, 413.0	4.19×3.75	365/420	O-Dart V-8, Polara 500

* Dart does not include production for Canada/export.

1963*

TL1-L Dart 170 (wb 111.0; wgns-106.0) - 58,536 built		Wght	Price	Prod
711	sdn 2d	2,605	1,983	—
713	sdn 4d	2,625	2,041	—
756	wgn 4d	2,710	2,309	—
TL1-H Dart 270 (wb 110.0; wgns-106.0) - 61,159 built				
731	sdn 2d	2,610	2,079	—
733	sdn 4d	2,635	2,135	—
735	conv cpe	2,740	2,385	—
776	wgn 4d	2,735	2,433	—
TL1-P Dart GT (wb 111.0) - 34,227 built				
742	htp cpe	2,690	2,289	—
745	conv cpe	2,765	2,512	—
TD1-L 330 I-6 (wb 119.0; wgns-116.0) - 51,761 built				
401	Fleet Special sdn 2d	3,040	2,205	10,365
411	sdn 2d	3,050	2,245	
403	Fleet Special sdn 4d	3,065	2,261	29,746
413	sdn 4d	3,070	2,301	
456	wgn 4d, 2S	3,320	2,648	4,554
457	wgn 4d, 3S	3,380	2,749	942
TD1-M 440 I-6 (wb 119.0; wgns-116.0)				
421	sdn 2d	3,050	2,381	1,183
422	htp cpe	3,050	2,470	1,246
423	sdn 4d	3,075	2,438	7,434
TD1-H Polara I-6 (wb 119.0) - 68,262 built				
432	htp cpe	3,105	2,624	623
433	sdn 4d	3,105	2,602	1,698
TD2-L 330 V-8 (wb 119.0; wgns-116.0)				
601	Fleet Special sdn 2d	3,310	2,313	4,654
611	sdn 2d	3,220	2,352	
603	Fleet Special sdn 4d	3,335	2,369	19,330
613	sdn 4d	3,245	2,408	
656	wgn 4d, 2S	3,490	2,756	5,679
657	wgn 4d, 3S	3,550	2,857	2,332
TD2-M 440 V-8 (wb 119.0; wgns-116.0)				
621	sdn 2d	3,215	2,489	1,934
622	htp cpe	3,245	2,577	5,947
623	sdn 4d	3,250	2,546	26,247
666	wgn 4d, 2S	3,495	2,854	7,216
667	wgn 4d, 3S	3,555	2,956	5,501
TD2-H Polara V-8 (wb 119.0)				
632	htp cpe	3,255	2,732	8,234
633	sdn 4d	3,275	2,709	17,189
634	htp sdn	3,330	2,781	9,312
635	conv cpe	3,340	2,963	2,962
TD2-P Polara 500 V-8 (wb 119.0)				
642	htp cpe	3,375	2,965	5,676
645	conv cpe	3,455	3,196	1,580
TA3 880 V-8 (wb 122.0)				
E503	sdn 4d	3,800	2,815	
E556	wgn 4d, 6P	4,145	3,142	9,831
E557	wgn 4d, 9P	4,175	3,257	
L512	Custom htp cpe	3,825	3,030	
L513	Custom sdn 4d	3,815	2,964	
L514	Custom htp sdn	3,840	3,109	
L515	Custom conv cpe	3,845	3,251	18,435
L558	Cstm htp wgn 4d, 2S	4,160	3,292	
L559	Cstm htp wgn 4d, 3S	4,186	3,407	

1963 Engines	bore×stroke	bhp	availability
I-6, 170.0	3.40×3.13	101	S-Dart
I-6, 225.0	3.40×4.13	145	S-330/440/ Polara 6; O-Dart
V-8, 318.0	3.91×3.31	230	S-330, 440, Polara V-8s

1963 Engines	bore×stroke	bhp	availability
V-8, 361.0	4.13×3.38	265	S-880, Cstm 880
V-8, 383.0	4.25×3.38	305	S-Polara 500; O-others exc Dart
V-8, 383.0	4.25×3.38	330	O-all exc Dart
V-8, 413.0	4.19×3.75	360	O-880, Cstm 880
V-8, 426.0	4.25×3.75	370/425	O-330, 440, Polara (ram ind)

* Dart 330/440 and all Polaras do not include production for Canada/export.

1964

VL1-L Dart 170 (wb 111.0; wgns 106.0)		Wght	Price	Prod*
711	sdn 2d	2,615	1,988	
713	sdn 4d	2,640	2,053	77,134[1]
756	wgn 4d, 2S	2,740	2,315	
VL1-H Dart 270 (wb 111.0; wgns-106.0)				
731	sdn 2d	2,625	2,094	
733	sdn 4d	2,645	2,160	66,069[2]
735	conv cpe	2,735	2,389	
776	wgn 4d, 2S	2,745	2,414	
VL1-P Dart GT (wb 111.0)				
742	htp cpe	2,670	2,318	49,830[3]
745	conv cpe	2,770	2,536	
VD1-L 330 I-6 (wb 119.0; wgns-116.0)				
411	sdn 2d	3,115	2,264	9,514
413	sdn 4d	3,145	2,317	34,467
456	wgn 4d, 2S	3,400	2,654	4,111
457	wgn 4d, 3S	3,475	2,755	1,426
VD1-M 440 I-6 (wb 119.0)				
421	sdn 2d	3,110	2,401	886
422	htp cpe	3,120	2,483	2,163
423	sdn 4d	3,145	2,454	6,987
VD1-H Polara I-6 (wb 119.0)				
432	htp cpe	3,135	2,637	783
433	sdn 4d	3,170	2,615	1,611
VD2-L 330 V-8 (wb 119.0; wgns-116.0)				
—	sdn 2d	—	—	5,195
613	sdn 4d	3,325	2,424	28,891
656	wgn 4d, 2S	3,570	2,762	6,961
657	wgn 4d, 3S	3,620	2,863	2,899
VD2-M 440 V-8 (wb 119.0; wgns-116.0)				
621	sdn 2d	3,280	2,508	2,064
622	htp cpe	3,295	2,590	14,537
623	sdn 4d	3,330	2,562	32,143
666	wgn 4d, 2S	3,585	2,861	8,101
667	wgn 4d, 3S	3,640	2,962	6,673
667	wgn 4d, 3S	3,640	2,962	—
VD2-H Polara V-8 (wb 119.0)				
632	htp cpe	3,320	2,745	19,689
633	sdn 4d	3,365	2,722	25,054
634	htp sdn	3,395	2,794	13,229
645	conv cpe	3,435	2,994	3,478
VD2-P Polara 500 V-8 (wb 119.0) - 17,787 built				
642	htp cpe	3,340	2,978	15,163
645	conv cpe	3,550	3,227	2,624
VA3 880 V-8 (wb 122.0)				
E513	sdn 4d	3,795	2,826	
E556	wgn 4d, 6P	4,165	3,155	10,562
E557	wgn 4d, 9P	4,185	3,270	
L522	Custom htp cpe	3,765	3,043	
L523	Custom sdn 4d	3,825	2,977	
L524	Custom htp sdn	3,860	3,122	21,234
L525	Custom conv cpe	3,850	3,264	
L568	Cstm htp wgn 4d, 2S	4,155	3,305	
L569	Cstm htp wgn 4d, 3S	4,185	3,420	

1964 Engines	bore×stroke	bhp	availability
I-6, 170.0	3.40×3.13	101	S-Dart
I-6, 225.0	3.40×4.13	145	S-330/440/ Polara 6; O-Dart
V-8, 273.5	3.63×3.31	180	O-Dart
V-8, 318.0	3.91×3.31	230	S-330, 440, Polara V-8
V-8, 361.0	4.13×3.38	265	S-880, Cstm 880
V-8, 383.0	4.25×3.38	305/330	O-all exc Dart
V-8, 426.0	4.25×3.75	365	O-330, 440, Polara
V-8, 426.0	4.25×3.75	415/425	O-330, 440, Polara (ram ind)

* Dart 330/440 and all Polaras do not include production for Canada/export.

[1]VL1-L Dart 170 includes 74,625 I-6; 2,509 V-8. [2]VL1-H Dart 270 includes 58,972 I-6; 7,097 V-8. [3]VL1-P Dart GT includes 37,660 I-6; 12,170 V-8.

1965

AL1-L Dart 170 (wb 111.0; wgns-106.0) - 86,013 built		Wght	Price	Prod
L11	sdn 2d	2,645	2,074	—
L13	sdn 4d	2,660	2,139	—
L56	wgn 4d	2,770	2,407	—
AL1-H Dart 270 (wb 111.0; wgns 106.0) - 78,245 built				
L31	sdn 2d	2,650	2,180	—
L32	htp cpe	2,675	2,274	—
L33	sdn 4d	2,670	2,247	—
L35	conv cpe	2,765	2,481	—
L76	wgn 4d	2,770	2,506	—
AL1-P Dart GT (wb 111.0) - 45,118 built				
L42	htp cpe	2,715	2,404	—
L45	conv cpe	2,795	2,628	—
AW1-L Coronet I-6 (wb 117.0; wgns-116.0)*				
W11	Deluxe sdn 2d	3,090	2,257	—
W13	Deluxe sdn 4d	3,140	2,296	—
W21	sdn 2d	3,070	2,217	—
W23	sdn 4d	3,095	2,256	—
W56	Deluxe wgn 4d	3,390	2,592	—
AW1-H Coronet 440 I-6 (wb 117.0; wgns-116.0)*				
W32	htp cpe	3,100	2,403	—
W33	sdn 4d	3,125	2,377	—
W35	conv cpe	3,230	2,622	—
W76	wgn 4d	3,395	2,674	—
AW2-L Coronet V-8 (wb 117.0; wgns-116.0; H-C 115.0)*				
W01	Hemi-Charger sdn 2d	3,165	—	—
W11	Deluxe sdn 2d	3,160	2,353	—
W13	Deluxe sdn 4d	3,210	2,392	—
W21	sdn 2d	3,145	2,313	—
W23	sdn 4d	3,195	2,352	—
W56	Deluxe wgn 4d	3,470	2,688	—
AW2-H Coronet 440 V-8 (wb 117.0; wgns-116.0)*				
W32	htp cpe	3,180	2,499	—
W33	sdn 4d	3,230	2,473	—
W35	conv cpe	3,295	2,718	—
W76	wgn 4d, 6P	3,490	2,770	—
W77	wgn 4d, 9P	3,560	2,868	—
AW2-P Coronet 500 V-8 (wb 117.0) - 32,745 built				
W42	htp cpe	3,255	2,674	—
W45	conv cpe	3,340	2,894	—
AD2-L Polara V-8 (wb 121.0) - 12,705 built				
D12	htp cpe	3,850	2,837	—
D13	sdn 4d	3,905	2,806	—
D14	htp sdn	3,965	2,913	—
D15	conv cpe	3,940	3,131	—
D23	sdn 4d (318)	3,847	2,730	—
D56	wgn 4d, 6P	4,220	3,153	—
D57	wgn 4d, 9P	4,255	3,259	—
AD2-H Custom 880 V-8 (wb 121.0) - 44,496 built				
D32	htp cpe	3,945	3,085	—
D34	htp sdn	4,155	3,150	—
D35	conv cpe	3,965	3,335	—
D38	sdn 4d	3,915	3,010	—
D76	wgn 4d, 6P	4,270	3,422	—
D77	wgn 4d, 9P	4,355	3,527	—
AD2-P Monaco V-8 (wb 121.0)				
D42	htp cpe	4,000	3,355	13,096

* Combined I-6 and V-8 production: Coronet 71,880; Coronet 440 104,767.

1965 Engines	bore×stroke	bhp	availability
I-6, 170.0	3.40×3.13	101	S-Dart
I-6, 225.0	3.40×4.13	145	S-Coronet/440 6s; O-Dart
V-8, 273.5	3.63×3.31	180	S-Corn/440/500 V-8s; O-Dart
V-8, 273.5	3.63×3.31	235	O-Corn/440/500 V-8s, Dart
V-8, 318.0	3.91×3.31	230	S-Pol 318 sdn; O-Coronet/ 440/ 500/V-8s
V-8, 361.0	4.12×3.38	265	O-Coronet/ 440/500 V-8s
V-8, 383.0	4.25×3.38	315	S-Monaco; O-Coronets
V-8, 383.0	4.25×3.38	270	S-Polara, Custom 880
V-8, 383.0	4.25×3.38	330	O-Coronet/ 440/500 V-8s
V-8, 413.0	4.19×3.75	340	O-Polara, Cstm 880, Mnco
V-8, 426.0	4.25×3.75	365	O-all exc Dart
V-8, 426.0	4.25×3.75	425	S-Hem-Chrgr 425

1966

BLL Dart (wb 111.0; wgns-106.0) - 75,990 built		Wght	Price	Prod
1-21	sdn 2d, I-6	2,670	2,094	—
2-21	sdn 2d, V-8	2,860	2,222	—
1-41	sdn 4d, I-6	2,695	2,158	—
2-41	sdn 4d, V-8	2,895	2,286	—
1-45	wgn 4d, I-6	2,780	2,436	—
2-45	wgn 4d, V-8	2,990	2,564	—
BLH Dart 270 (wb 111.0; wgns 106.0) - 69,996 built				
1-23	htp cpe, I-6	2,720	2,307	—
2-23	htp cpe, V-8	2,890	2,435	—
1-27	conv cpe, I-6	2,805	2,570	—
2-27	conv cpe, V-8	2,995	2,698	—
1-21	sdn 2d, I-6	2,665	2,214	—
2-21	sdn 2d, V-8	2,860	2,342	—
1-41	sdn 4d, I-6	2,680	2,280	—
2-41	sdn 4d, V-8	2,895	2,408	—
1-45	wgn 4d, I-6	2,795	2,533	—
2-45	wgn 4d, V-8	3,020	2,661	—
BLP Dart GT (wb 111.0) - 30,041 built				
1-23	htp cpe, I-6	2,735	2,417	—
2-23	htp cpe, V-8	2,915	2,545	—
1-27	conv cpe, I-6	2,830	2,700	—
2-27	conv cpe, V-8	2,995	2,828	—
BWL Coronet (wb 117.0) - 66,161 built				
1-21	sdn 2d, I-6	3,055	2,264	—
2-21	sdn 2d, V-8	3,215	2,358	—
1-41	sdn 4d, I-6	3,077	2,306	—
2-41	sdn 4d, V-8	3,245	2,396	—
1-21	Deluxe sdn 2d, I-6	3,050	2,303	—
2-21	Deluxe sdn 2d, V-8	3,215	2,391	—
1-41	Deluxe sdn 4d, I-6	3,075	2,341	—
2-41	Deluxe sdn 4d, V-8	3,240	2,435	—
1-45	Deluxe wgn 2d, I-6	3,480	2,631	—
2-45	Deluxe wgn 2d, V-8	3,595	2,725	—
BWH Coronet 440 (wb 117.0) - 128,998 built				
1-23	htp cpe, I-6	3,075	2,457	—
1-23	htp cpe, V-8	3,235	2,551	—
1-27	conv cpe, I-6	3,185	2,672	—
2-27	conv cpe, V-8	3,310	2,766	—
1-41	sdn 4d, I-6	3,095	2,432	—
2-41	sdn 4d, V-8	3,220	2,526	—
1-45	wgn 4d, I-6	3,515	2,722	—
2-45	wgn 4d, 2S, V-8	3,585	2,816	—
2-46	wgn 4d, 3S, V-8	3,680	2,926	—
BWP Coronet 500 (wb 117.0) - 55,683 built				
1-23	htp cpe, I-6	3,115	2,611	—
2-23	htp cpe, V-8	3,275	2,705	—
1-27	conv cpe, I-6	3,180	2,827	—
2-27	conv cpe, V-8	3,345	2,921	—
1-41	sdn 4d, I-6	3,120	2,586	—
2-41	sdn 4d, V-8	3,280	2,680	—
BX2-P Charger (wb 117.0)				
29	fstbk htp cpe 4P	3,499	3,122	37,344
BD2-L Polara (wb 121.0) - 107,832 built				
23	htp cpe	3,820	2,874	—
27	conv cpe	3,885	3,161	—
41	sdn 4d	3,860	2,838	—
41	sdn 4d (318)	3,765	2,763	—
43	htp sdn	3,880	2,948	—
45	wgn 4d, 2S	4,265	3,183	—
46	wgn 4d, 3S	4,295	3,286	—

BD2-H Monaco (wb 121.0)		Wght	Price	Prod
23	htp cpe	3,855	3,107	
41	sdn 4d	3,890	3,033	
43	htp sdn	4,835	3,170	49,773
45	wgn 4d, 2S	4,270	3,436	
46	wgn 4d, 3S	4,315	3,539	

BD2-P Monaco 500 (wb 121.0)				
23	htp cpe	3,895	3,604	10,840

1966 Engines	bore×stroke	bhp	availability
I-6, 170.0	3.40×3.13	101	S-Dart 6s
I-6, 225.0	3.40×4.13	145	S-Coronet 6; O-Dart 6
V-8, 273.5	3.63×3.31	180	S-Coronet V-8, Dart V-8
V-8, 273.5	3.63×3.31	235	O-Dart V-8
V-8, 318.0	3.91×3.31	230	S-Charger, Pol 318 sdn; O-Cor V-8
V-8, 361.0	4.13×3.38	265	O-Charger, Coronet V-8
V-8, 383.0	4.25×3.38	270	S-Pol, Mon; O-Monaco 500
V-8, 383.0	4.25×3.38	325	S-Monaco 500; O-all exc Dart
V-8, 426.0	4.25×3.75	425	O-Chrgr (max perf cam avail)
V-8, 440.0	4.32×3.75	350	O-Pol, Mon, Monaco 500

1967

CLL Dart (wb111.0)-53,043 blt		Wght	Price	Prod
1-21	sdn 2d, I-6	2,710	2,187	—
2-21	sdn 2d, V-8	2,895	2,315	—
1-41	sdn 4d, I-6	2,725	2,224	—
2-41	sdn 4d, V-8	2,910	2,352	—

CLH Dart 270 (wb 111.0) - 63,227 built				
1-23	htp cpe, I-6	2,725	2,388	—
2-23	htp cpe, V-8	2,910	2,516	—
1-41	sdn 4d, I-6	2,735	2,362	—
2-41	sdn 4d, V-8	2,915	2,490	—

CLP Dart GT (wb 111.0)—38,225 built				
1-23	htp cpe, I-6	2,750	2,499	—
2-23	htp cpe, V-8	2,930	2,627	—
1-27	conv cpe, I-6	2,850	2,732	—
2-27	conv cpe, V-8	3,030	2,860	—

CWE Coronet (wb 117.0) - 4,933 built				
1-45	wgn 4d, I-6	3,485	2,622	—
2-45	wgn 4d, V-8	3,650	2,716	—

CWL Coronet Deluxe (wb 117.0) - 29,022 built				
1-21	sdn 2d, I-6	3,045	2,359	—
2-21	sdn 2d, V-8	3,210	2,453	—
1-41	sdn 4d, I-6	3,070	2,397	—
2-41	sdn 4d, V-8	3,235	2,491	—
1-45	wgn 2d, I-6	3,495	2,693	—
2-45	wgn 2d, V-8	3,625	2,787	—

CWH Coronet 440 (wb 117.0) - 106,368 built				
1-23	htp cpe, I-6	3,065	2,500	—
2-23	htp cpe, V-8	3,235	2,594	—
1-27	conv cpe, I-6	3,140	2,740	—
2-27	conv cpe, V-8	3,305	2,834	—
1-41	sdn 4d, I-6	3,060	2,475	—
2-41	sdn 4d, V-8	3,225	2,569	—
1-45	wgn 4d, I-6	3,495	2,771	—
2-45	wgn 4d, 2S, V-8	3,605	2,865	—
2-46	wgn 4d, 3S, V-8	3,705	2,975	—

CWP Coronet 500 (wb 117.0) - 39,260 built (incl. R/T)				
1-23	htp cpe, I-6	3,115	2,679	—
2-23	htp cpe, V-8	3,280	2,773	—
1-27	conv cpe, I-6	3,190	2,919	—
2-27	conv cpe, V-8	3,355	3,013	—
1-41	sdn 4d, I-6	3,075	2,654	—
2-41	sdn 4d, V-8	3,235	2,748	—

CW2-P Coronet R/T (wb 117.0)				
23	htp cpe, V-8	3,565	3,199	—
27	conv cpe, V-8	3,640	3,438	—

CW2-P Charger (wb 117.0)				
29	fstbk htp cpe 4P, V-8	3,480	3,128	15,788

CD2-L Polara (wb 122.0) - 69,798 built				
23	htp cpe	3,870	2,953	—

CD2-L Polara		Wght	Price	Prod
27	conv cpe	3,930	3,241	—
41	sdn 4d	3,885	2,915	—
41	sdn 4d (318)	3,765	2,843	—
43	htp sdn	3,920	3,028	—
45	wgn 4d, 2S	4,440	3,265	—
46	wgn 4d, 3S	4,450	3,368	—

CD2-M Polara 500 (wb 122.0) - 5,606 built				
23	htp cpe	3,880	3,155	—
27	conv cpe	3,940	3,443	—

CD2-H Monaco (wb 122.0) - 35,225 built				
23	htp cpe	3,885	3,213	—
41	sdn 4d	3,895	3,138	—
43	htp sdn	3,945	3,275	—
45	wgn 4d, 2S	4,425	3,543	—
46	wgn 4d, 3S	4,475	3,646	—

CD2-P Monaco 500 (wb 122.0)				
23	htp cpe	3,970	3,712	5,237

1967 Engines	bore×stroke	bph	availability
I-6, 170.0	3.40×3.13	115	S-Dart 6
I-6, 225.0	3.40×4.13	145	S-Coronet 6; O-Dart 6
V-8, 273.5	3.63×3.31	180	S-Dart V-8, Coronet V-8
V-8, 273.5	3.63×3.31	235	O-Dart V-8
V-8, 318.0	3.91×3.31	230	S-Charger, Polara 318; O-Cor V-8
V-8, 383.0	4.25×3.38	270	S-Pol, Mon; O-Cor, Mon 500
V-8, 383.0	4.25×3.38	325	S-Monaco 500; O-Cor, Chgr, Polara, Monaco
V-8, 426.0	4.25×3.75	425	O-Coronet R/T, Charger
V-8, 440.0	4.32×3.75	350	O-Polara, Mon
V-8, 440.0	4.32×3.75	375	S-Coronet R/T; O-Chrgr, Pol, Monaco

1968

DLL Dart (wb 111.0) - 60,250 built		Wght	Price	Prod
1-21	sdn 2d, I-6	2,705	2,323	—
2-21	sdn 2d, V-8	2,875	2,451	—
1-41	sdn 4d, I-6	2,725	2,360	—
2-41	sdn 4d, V-8	2,900	2,488	—

DLH Dart 270 (wb 111.0) - 76,497 built				
1-23	htp cpe, I-6	2,725	2,525	—
2-23	htp cpe, V-8	2,885	2,653	—
1-41	sdn 4d, I-6	2,710	2,499	—
2-41	sdn 4d, V-8	2,900	2,627	—

DLP Dart GT (wb 111.0) - 26,280 built				
1-23	htp cpe, I-6	2,715	2,637	—
2-23	htp cpe, V-8	2,895	2,675	—
1-27	conv cpe, I-6	2,790	2,831	—
2-27	conv cpe, V-8	2,970	2,959	—

DL2-S Dart GTS (wb 111.0) - 8,745 built				
23	htp cpe, V-8	3,065	3,189	—
27	conv cpe, V-8	3,150	3,383	—

DWL Coronet Deluxe (wb 117.0) - 46,299 built				
1-21	cpe, I-6	3,015	2,487	—
2-21	cpe, V-8	3,200	2,581	—
1-41	sdn 4d, I-6	3,035	2,525	—
2-41	sdn 4d, V-8	3,220	2,619	—
1-45	wgn 4d, I-6	3,455	2,816	—
2-45	wgn 4d, V-8	3,590	2,910	—

DWH Coronet 440 (wb117.0)-116,348 blt (incl. Super Bee)				
1-21	cpe, I-6	3,015	2,565	—
2-21	cpe, V-8	3,200	2,671	—
1-23	htp cpe, I-6	3,040	2,627	—
2-23	htp cpe, V-8	3,225	2,733	—
1-41	sdn 4d, I-6	3,035	2,603	—
2-41	sdn 4d, V-8	3,320	2,709	—
1-45	wgn 4d, I-6	3,450	2,924	—
2-45	wgn 4d, 2S, V-8	3,585	3,030	—
2-46	wgn 4d, 3S, V-8	3,680	3,140	—

DWH Coronet Super Bee (wb 117.0)				
M-21	cpe, V-8	3,395	3,027	—

DW2-P Coronet 500 (wb 117.0)		Wght	Price	Prod
23	htp cpe, V-8	3,260	2,879	
27	conv cpe, V-8	3,360	3,036	
41	sdn 4d, V-8	3,240	2,912	40,139
45	wgn 4d, 2S, V-8	3,610	3,212	
46	wgn 4d, 3S, V-8	3,700	3,322	

DW2-S Coronet R/T (wb 117.0) - 10,849 built				
23	htp cpe, V-8	3,530	3,379	—
27	conv cpe, V-8	3,630	3,613	—

DX1-S Charger (wb 117.0) - 96,108 built				
1P-29	htp cpe 4P, I-6	3,100	2,934	—
2P-29	htp cpe 4P, V-8	3,305	3,040	—
2X-29	R/T htp cpe, 4P, V-8	3,575	3,506	—

DD2-L Polara (wb 122.0) - 99,055 built				
23	htp cpe	3,700	3,027	—
27	conv cpe	3,755	3,288	—
41	sdn 4d	3,735	3,005	—
43	htp sdn	3,755	3,100	—
45	wgn 4d, 2S	4,155	3,388	—
46	wgn 4d, 3S	4,210	3,454	—

DD2-M Polara 500 (wb 122.0) - 4,983 built				
23	htp cpe	3,740	3,226	—
27	conv cpe	3,780	3,487	—

DD2-H Monaco (wb 122.0) - 37,412 built				
23	htp cpe	3,845	3,369	—
41	sdn 4d	3,885	3,294	—
43	htp sdn	3,910	3,432	—
45	wgn 4d, 2S	4,295	3,702	—
46	wgn 4d, 3S	4,360	3,835	—

DD2-P Monaco 500 (wb 122.0)				
23	htp cpe	3,885	3,869	4,568

1968 Engines	bore×stroke	bhp	availability
I-6, 170.0	3.40×3.13	115	S-Dart 6
I-6, 225.0	3.40×4.13	145	S-Coronet 6; O-Dart 6
V-8, 273.5	3.63×3.31	190	S-Dart V-8, Coronet V-8
V-8, 318.0	3.91×3.31	230	S-Chrgr, Pol; O-Dart V-8, Coronet V-8
V-8, 340.0	4.04×3.31	275	S-Dart GTS
V-8, 383.0	4.25×3.38	300	O-Dart GTS
V-8, 383.0	4.25×3.38	290	S-Monaco; O-Coronet V-8, Charger, Polara
V-8, 383.0	4.25×3.38	330	O-Coronet V-8, Chrgr, Pol, Mon
V-8, 383.0	4.25×3.38	335	S-Coronet Super Bee
V-8, 426.0	4.25×3.75	425	O-Coronet R/T, Charger R/T
V-8, 440.0	4.32×3.75	350	O-Polara & Monaco wgns
V-8, 440.0	4.32×3.75	375	S-Coronet R/T, Charger R/T; O-Pol, Mon

1969

LL Dart (wb 111.0)-106,329 blt (incl. Swinger 340)		Wght	Price	Prod
23	Swinger htp cpe	2,795	2,400	—
41	sdn 4d	2,810	2,413	—

LM Dart Swinger 340 (wb 111.0)				
23	htp cpe	3,097	2,836	—

LH Dart Custom (wb 111.0) - 63,740 built				
23	htp cpe	2,795	2,577	—
41	sdn 4d	2,810	2,550	—

LP Dart GT (wb 111.0) - 20,914 built				
23	htp cpe	2,800	2,672	—
27	conv cpe	2,905	2,865	—

LS Dart GTS V-8 (wb 111.0) - 6,702 built				
23	htp cpe	3,105	3,226	—
27	conv cpe	3,210	3,419	—

WL Coronet Deluxe (wb 117.0) - 23,988 built				
21	cpe	3,067	2,554	—
41	sdn 4d	3,097	2,589	—
45	wgn 4d	3,552	2,922	—

WH Coronet 440 (wb 117.0)		Wght	Price	Prod
21	cpe	3,067	2,630	
23	htp cpe	3,097	2,692	
41	sdn 4d	3,102	2,670	105,882
45	wgn 4d, 2S	3,557	3,033	
46	wgn 4d, 3S, V-8 only	3,676	3,246	
WM Coronet Super Bee V-8 (wb 117.0) - 27,846 built				
21	cpe	3,440	3,076	—
23	htp cpe	3,470	3,138	—
WP Coronet 500 V-8 (wb 117.0) - 32,050 built				
23	htp cpe	3,171	2,929	—
27	conv cpe	3,306	3,069	—
41	sdn 4d	3,206	2,963	—
45	wgn 4d, 2S	3,611	3,280	—
46	wgn 4d, 3S	3,676	3,392	—
WS Coronet R/T (wb 117.0) - 7,238 built				
23	htp cpe	3,601	3,442	—
27	conv cpe	3,721	3,660	—
XP/XS Charger (wb 117.0)				
XP29	htp cpe, I-6	3,103	3,020	69,142
XP29	htp cpe, V-8	3,256	3,126	
XS29	R/T htp cpe, V-8	3,646	3,592	20,057
—	Daytona htp cpe, V-8	—	4,000	505
XX Charger 500 V-8 (wb 117.0)				
XX29	htp cpe	3,671	3,860	*
DL Polara (wb 122.0) - 83,122 built				
23	htp cpe	3,646	3,117	—
27	conv cpe	3,791	3,377	—
41	sdn 4d	3,701	3,095	—
43	htp sdn	3,731	3,188	—
45	wgn 4d, 2S	4,161	3,522	—
46	wgn 4d, 3S	4,211	3,629	—
DM Polara 500 (wb 122.0) - 5,564 built				
23	htp cpe	3,681	3,314	—
27	conv cpe	3,801	3,576	—
DH Monaco (wb 122.0) - 38,566 built				
23	htp cpe	3,811	3,528	—
41	sdn 4d	3,846	3,452	—
43	htp sdn	3,891	3,591	—
45	wgn 4d, 2S	4,306	3,917	—
46	wgn 4d, 3S	4,361	4,046	—

* Production included with XP 29 models

1969 Engines	bore×stroke	bhp	availability
I-6, 170.0	3.40×3.13	115	S-Dart
I-6, 225.0	3.40×4.13	145	S-Coronet Del/440; O-Drt
V-8, 273.5	3.63×3.31	190	S-Dart V-8 exc. GTS, Swngr 340
V-8, 318.0	3.91×3.31	230	S-Coronet Del/440/500, Chgr, Pol; O-Dart
V-8, 340.0	4.04×3.31	275	S-GTS, Swinger 340
V-8, 383.0	4.25×3.38	290	S-Mon; O- Pol, Chgr, Coronet
V-8, 383.0	4.25×3.38	330	O-GTS, Cor V-8, Mon, Pol, Charger
V-8, 383.0	4.25×3.38	335	S-Coronet Super Bee
V-8, 426.0	4.25×3.75	425	O-Coronet R/T, Charger R/T& Daytona
V-8, 440.0	4.32×3.75	350	O-Monaco & Polara wgns
V-8, 440.0	4.32×3.75	375	S-Cor R/T, Chgr R/T& Day; O-Pol, Mon exc wagons
V-8, 440.0	4.32×3.75	390	O-Corn S B

1970

LL Dart (wb 111.0)		Wght	Price	Prod
23	Swinger htp cpe	2,903	2,261	119,883
41	sdn 4d	2,900	2,308	35,499
LH Dart Custom (wb 111.0)				
23	htp cpe	2,898	2,463	17,208
41	sdn 4d	2,905	2,467	23,779
LM Dart Swinger 340 (wb 111.0)		**Wght**	**Price**	**Prod**
23	htp cpe	3,130	2,631	13,785
JH Challenger (wb 110.0)				
23	htp cpe	3,028	2,851	53,337
27	conv cpe	3,103	3,120	3,173
29	S.E. htp cpe	3,053	3,083	6,584
JS Challenger R/T (wb 110.0)				
23	htp cpe (incl. T/A)	3,405	3,226	14,889
27	conv cpe	3,470	3,535	1,070
29	S.E. htp cpe	3,440	3,498	3,979
WL Coronet Deluxe (wb 117.0)				
21	cpe	3,150	2,669	2,978
41	sdn 4d	3,188	2,704	7,894
45	wgn 4d	3,675	3,048	3,694
WH Coronet 440 (wb 117.0)				
21	cpe	3,170	2,743	1,236
23	htp cpe	3,185	2,805	24,341
41	sdn 4d	3,190	2,783	33,258
45	wgn 4d	3,673	3,156	3,964
46	wgn 4d	3,775	3,368	3,772
WM Coronet Super Bee (wb 117.0)				
21	cpe	3,500	3,012	3,966
23	htp cpe	3,535	3,074	11,540
WP Coronet 500 (wb 117.0)				
23	htp cpe	3,235	3,048	8,247
27	conv cpe	3,345	3,188	924
41	sdn 4d	3,255	3,082	2,890
45	wgn 4d, 2S	3,715	3,404	1,657
46	wgn 4d, 3S	3,785	3,514	1,779
WS Coronet R/T (wb 117.0)				
23	htp cpe	3,545	3,569	2,319
27	conv cpe	3,610	3,785	296
XH/XP Charger (wb 117.0)				
XH29	htp cpe	3,293	3,001	39,431
XP29	500 htp cpe	3,293	3,139	
XS/XX Charger R/T (wb 117.0)				
XS29	htp cpe	3,610	3,711	10,337
XX29	Daytona htp cpe	3,710	3,993	
DE Polara (wb 122.0)*				
41	sdn 4d, I-6	3,775	2,960	—
45	wgn 4d, 2S, V-8	4,180	3,513	—
46	wgn 4d, 3S, V-8	4,235	3,621	—
DL Polara "Deluxe" V-8 (wb 122.0)*				
23	htp cpe	3,770	3,224	—
27	conv cpe	3,830	3,527	842
41	sdn 4d	3,805	3,222	—
43	htp sdn	3,850	3,316	—
45	wgn 4d, 2S	4,180	3,670	—
46	wgn 4d, 3S	4,235	3,778	—
DM Polara Custom V-8 (wb 122.0)*				
23	htp cpe	4,005	3,458	—
41	sdn 4d	3,975	3,426	—
43	htp sdn	3,925	3,528	—
DH Monaco (wb 122.0)				
23	htp cpe	3,950	3,679	3,522
41	sdn 4d	4,010	3,604	4,721
43	htp sdn	4,045	3,743	10,974
45	wgn 4d, 2S	4,420	4,110	2,211
46	wgn 4d, 3S	4,475	4,242	3,264

* Dodge combined production figures for most Polara models. Available figures are:

23	htp cpe (DL, DM)	15,243
27	conv cpe (DL)	842
41	sdn 4d (DE, DL, DM)	18,740
43	htp sdn (DL, DM)	19,223
45	wgn 4d, 2S (DE, DL)	3,074
46	wgn 4d, 3S (DE, DL)	3,546

1970 Engines	bore×stroke	bhp	availability
I-6, 198.0	3.40×3.64	125	S-Dart
I-6, 225.0	3.40×4.13	145	S-Chal/Cor/ Chrgr/Pol 6s; O-Dart
V-8, 318.0	3.91×3.31	230	S-Dart exc Swinger 340, Chal, Corn, Chrgr, Pol
V-8, 340.0	4.04×3.31	275	S-Swngr 340; O-Challenger
V-8, 383.0	4.25×3.38	290	S-Mon, Pol Cus; O-Chal/Cor/ Chrgr/ Pol V-8
V-8, 383.0	4.25×3.38	330	O-Chal, Cor, Pol, Pol Cstm, Monaco
V-8, 383.0	4.25×3.38	335	S-Super Bee, Challenger R/T; O-Challenger, Charger R/T
V-8, 426.0	4.25×3.75	425	O-Chal, Spr B, Cor/Chrgr R/Ts
V-8, 440.0	4.32×3.75	350	O-Mon, Polara, Polara Custom
V-8, 440.0	4.32×3.75	375	S-Charger/ Corn/Chal R/Ts
V-8, 440.0	4.32×3.75	390	O-Charger/ Corn/Chal R/Ts, Super Bee

1971

Dart (wb 111.0; fstbk cpes-108.0)		Wght	Price	Prod
LL29	Demon fstbk cpe	2,845	2,343	69,861
LL23	Swinger Spec htp cpe	2,900	2,402	13,485
LL41	sdn 4d	2,900	2,450	32,711
LH23	Swinger htp cpe	2,900	2,561	102,480
LH41	Custom sdn 4d	2,900	2,609	21,785
LM29	Dmn fstbk 340 cpe V-8	3,165	2,721	10,098
Challenger (wb 110.0)				
JL23	cpe	3,050	2,727	23,088
JH23	htp cpe	3,092	2,848	
JH27	conv cpe	3,180	3,105	2,165
JS23	R/T htp cpe V-8	3,495	3,273	4,630
Coronet (wb 118.0)				
WL41	sdn 4d	3,302	2,777	11,794
WL45	wgn 4d 2S	3,778	3,101	5,470
WH41	Custom sdn 4d	3,308	2,951	37,817
WH45	Custom wgn 4d 2S	3,812	3,196	5,365
WH46	Cstm wgn 4d 3S V-8	3,890	3,454	5,717
WP41	Brghm sdn 4d V-8	3,475	3,232	4,700
WP45	Crstwd wgn 4d 2S V-8	3,845	3,601	2,884
WP46	Crstwd wgn 4d 3S V-8	3,900	3,682	3,981
Charger (wb 115.0)				
WL21	cpe	3,270	2,707	46,183
WH23	htp cpe	3,138	2,975	
WP23	500 htp cpe V-8	3,350	3,223	11,948
WM23	Spr Bee htp cpe V-8	3,640	3,271	5,054
WP29	SE htp cpe V-8	3,375	3,422	15,811
WS23	R/T htp cpe V-8	3,685	3,777	3,118
Polara (wb 122.0)				
DE41	sdn 4d	3,788	3,298	16,444
DE23	htp cpe	3,755	3,319	11,500
DE43	htp sdn V-8	3,875	3,497	2,487
DL41	Custom sdn 4d V-8	3,835	3,593	13,850
DL43	Custom htp sdn V-8	3,875	3,681	17,458
DL23	Custom htp cpe V-8	3,805	3,614	9,682
DL45	Cstm wgn 4d 2S V-8	4,280	3,992	9,682
DL46	Cstm wgn 4d 3S V-8	4,335	4,098	
DM43	Brghm htp sdn V-8	4,035	3,884	2,570
DM23	Brghm htp cpe V-8	3,965	3,818	2,024
Monaco (wb 122.0)				
DH41	sdn 4d	4,050	4,223	16,900
DH43	htp sdn	4,080	4,362	
DH23	htp cpe	4,000	4,298	3,195
DH45	wgn 4d 2S	4,525	4,689	5,449
DH46	wgn 4d 3S	4,585	4,821	

1971 Engines	bore×stroke	bhp	availability
I-6, 198.0	3.40×3.64	125	S-Drt, Chal JL
I-6, 225.0	3.40×4.13	145	S-Chal JH, Cor, Chrgr, Pol; O-Dart, Chal JL
V-8, 318.0	3.91×3.31	230	S-Chal, Cor, Chrgr, Pol; O-Dart
V-8, 340.0	4.04×3.31	275	S-Demon 340; O-Chal
V-8, 360.0	4.00×3.58	275	O-Polara

1971 Engines	bore×stroke	bhp	availability
V-8, 383.0	4.25×3.38	275	S-Chal R/T, Chrgr S B, Pol B'ham, Mon; O-Chal, Cor, Chrgr, Pol
V-8, 383.0	4.25×3.38	300	O-Chal, Cor, Chrgr, Pol, Mon
V-8, 426.0	4.25×3.75	335	O-Pol, Monaco
V-8, 426.0	4.25×3.75	425	O-Chrgr, Chal
V-8, 440.0	4.32×3.75	335	O-Pol, Monaco
V-8, 440.0	4.32×3.75	370	S-Charger R/T; O-Charger
V-8, 440.0	4.32×3.75	385	O-Chal, Chrgr

1972

Dart (wb 111.0; fstbk cpes 108.0)		Wght	Price	Prod
LL29	Demon fstbk cpe	2,800	2,316	39,880
LL23	Swinger Spec htp cpe	2,845	2,373	19,210
LL41	sdn 4d	2,855	2,420	26,019
LH23	Swinger htp cpe	2,835	2,528	119,618
LH41	Custom sdn 4d	2,855	2,574	49,941
LM29	Dmn 340 fstbk cpe V-8	3,125	2,759	8,750
Challenger (wb 110.0)				
JH23	cpe	3,098	2,790	18,535
JS23	Rallye htp cpe V-8	3,225	3,082	8,123
Coronet (wb 118.0)				
WL41	sdn 4d	3,362	2,721	11,293
WL45	wgn 4d 2S V-8	3,795	3,209	
WH45	Cstm wgn 4d 2S V-8	3,800	3,382	5,452
WH46	Cstm wgn 4d 3S V-8	3,840	3,460	
WH41	Custom sdn 4d	3,370	2,998	43,132
WP45	Crstwd wgn 4d 2S V-8	3,810	3,604	6,471
WP46	Crstwd wgn 4d 3S V-8	3,850	3,683	
Charger (wb 115.0)				
WL21	cpe	3,278	2,652	7,803
WH23	htp cpe	3,292	2,913	45,361
WP29	SE htp cpe V-8	3,390	3,249	22,430
Polara (wb 122.0)				
DL41	sdn 4d	3,835	3,618	25,187
DL43	htp sdn	3,875	3,709	8,212
DL23	htp cpe	3,800	3,641	7,000
DM41	Custom sdn 4d	3,845	3,808	19,739
DM43	Custom htp sdn	3,890	3,898	22,505
DM23	Custom htp cpe	3,815	3,830	15,039
DM45	Custom wgn 4d 2S	4,320	4,262	3,497
DM46	Custom wgn 4d 3S	4,370	4,371	7,660
Monaco (wb 122.0)				
DP41	sdn 4d	3,980	4,095	6,474
DP43	htp sdn	4,030	4,216	15,039
DP23	htp cpe	3,960	4,153	7,786
DP45	wgn 4d 2S	4,445	4,627	2,569
DP46	wgn 4d 3S	4,490	4,756	5,145

1972 Engines	bore×stroke	bhp	availability
I-6, 198.0	3.40×3.64	100	S-Dart
I-6, 225.0	3.40×4.13	100	O-Dart
I-6, 225.0	3.40×4.13	110	S-Chal, Cor, Chrgr; O-Dart
V-8, 318.0	3.91×3.31	150	S-Chal, Cor, Chrgr, Pol; O-Drt
V-8, 340.0	4.04×3.31	240	S-Demon 340, O-Dart, Chal, Charger
V-8, 360.0	4.00×3.58	175	S-Mon; O-Pol
V-8, 400.0	4.34×3.38	190	O-Chrgr, Pol, Monaco
V-8, 400.0	4.34×3.38	250	O-Pol, Mon
V-8, 400.0	4.34×3.38	255	O-Charger
V-8, 440.0	4.32×3.75	230	O-Monaco
V-8, 440.0	4.32×3.75	235	O-Polara
V-8, 440.0	4.32×3.75	280	O-Monaco
V-8, 440.0	4.32×3.75	285	O-Pol, Mon
V-8, 440.0	4.32×3.75	330	O-Cor, Chrgr

1973

Dart (wb 111.0; fstbk cpes-108.0)		Wght	Price	Prod
LL29	Sport fstbk cpe	2,850	2,424	68,113
LL23	Swinger Spec htp cpe	2,895	2,462	17,480
LL41	sdn 4d	2,910	2,504	21,539
LH23	Swinger htp cpe	2,890	2,617	107,619
LH41	Custom sdn 4d	2,910	2,658	62,626
LM29	Sprt 340 fstbk cpe V-8	3,205	2,853	11,315
Challenger (wb 110.0)				
JH23	htp cpe V-8	3,155	3,011	32,596
Coronet (wb 118.0)				
WL41	sdn 4d	3,472	2,867	14,395
WL45	wgn 4d 2S V-8	3,955	3,314	4,874
WH41	Custom sdn 4d	3,962	3,017	46,491
WH45	Cstm wgn 4d 2S V-8	3,955	3,442	13,018
WH46	Cstm wgn 4d 3S V-8	4,000	3,560	
WP45	Crstwd wgn 4d 2S V-8	3,970	3,671	8,755
WP46	Crstwd wgn 4d 3S V-8	4,005	3,791	
Charger (wb 115.0)				
WL21	cpe	3,428	2,810	11,995
WH23	htp cpe	3,465	3,060	45,415
WP29	SE htp cpe V-8	3,540	3,375	61,908
Polara (wb 122.0)				
DL41	sdn 4d	3,865	3,729	15,015
DL23	htp cpe	3,835	3,752	6,432
DL45	wgn 4d 2S	4,420	4,186	3,327
DM41	Custom sdn 4d	3,870	3,911	23,939
DM43	Custom htp sdn	3,905	4,001	29,341
DM23	Custom htp cpe	3,835	3,928	17,406
DM45	Custom wgn 4d 2S	4,440	4,370	3,702
DM46	Custom wgn 4d 3S	4,485	4,494	8,839
Monaco (wb 122.0)				
DP41	sdn 4d	4,020	4,218	6,316
DP43	htp sdn	4,060	4,339	9,031
DP23	htp cpe	3,985	4,276	6,133
DP45	wgn 4d 2S	4,470	4,730	2,337
DP46	wgn 4d 3S	4,515	4,859	5,579

1973 Engines	bore×stroke	bhp	availability
I-6, 198.0	3.40×3.64	95	S-Dart
I-6, 225.0	3.40×4.13	105	S-Cor, Chrgr; O-Dart
V-8, 318.0	3.91×3.31	150	S-Chal, Cor, Charger, Pol exc wgns; O-Dart
V-8, 340.0	4.04×3.31	240	S-Drt Sprt 340; O-Chal, Cor, Charger
V-8, 360.0	4.00×3.58	170	S-Pol wgns, Mon; O-Pol
V-8, 400.0	4.34×3.38	175	O-Coronet, Charger
V-8, 400.0	4.34×3.38	185	S-Mon wgns; O-Pol, Mon
V-8, 400.0	4.34×3.38	220	O-Pol, Mon
V-8, 400.0	4.34×3.38	260	O-Corn, Chrgr
V-8, 440.0	4.32×3.75	220	O-Pol, Monaco
V-8, 440.0	4.32×3.75	280	O-Corn, Chrgr

1974

Dart (wb 111.0; fstbk cpes-108.0)		Wght	Price	Prod
LL29	Sport fstbk cpe	2,990	2,878	59,567
LL23	Swinger Spec htp cpe	3,035	2,918	16,155
LH23	Swinger htp cpe	3,030	3,077	89,242
LL41	sdn 4d	3,055	2,961	78,216
LH41	Custom sdn 4d	3,055	3,119	
LM29	Sprt 360 fstbk cpe V-8	3,330	3,320	3,951
LP41	Spec Edition sdn 4d	3,641	3,837	12,385
LP23	Spec Edition htp cpe	3,599	3,794	
Challenger (wb 110.0)				
JH23	htp cpe V-8	3,225	3,143	16,437
Coronet (wb 118.0)				
WL41	sdn 4d	3,548	3,271	8,752
WL45	wgn 4d 2S V-8	4,085	3,699	2,968
WH41	Custom sdn 4d	3,538	3,374	36,021
WH45	Cstm wgn 4d 2S V-8	4,090	3,882	2,975
WH46	Cstm wgn 4d 3S V-8	4,130	4,196	4,950
WP45	Crstwd wgn 4d 2S V-8	4,100	4,117	1,916
WP46	Crstwd wgn 4d 3S V-8	4,135	4,433	3,146
Charger (wb 115.0)				
WL21	cpe	3,510	3,212	8,876
WH23	htp cpe	3,528	3,412	29,101
WP29	SE htp cpe V-8	3,625	3,742	36,399
Monaco (wb 122.0; wgns-124.0)				
DM41	sdn 4d	4,170	4,259	9,101
DM23	htp cpe	4,150	4,283	3,347
DM45	wgn 4d 2S	4,760	4,706	1,583
DH41	Custom sdn 4d	4,175	4,446	12,655
DH43	.Custom htp sdn	4,205	4,539	10,585
DH23	Custom htp cpe	4,155	4,464	6,649
DH45	Custom wgn 4d 2S	4,770	4,839	1,253
DH46	Custom wgn 4d 3S	4,815	4,956	3,272
DP41	Brougham sdn 4d	4,410	4,891	3,954
DP43	Brougham htp sdn	4,445	4,999	5,649
DP23	Brougham htp cpe	4,370	4,951	4,863
DP45	Brougham wgn 4d 2S	4,860	5,360	1,042
DP46	Brougham wgn 4d 3S	4,905	5,477	2,718

1974 Engines	bore×stroke	bhp	availability
I-6, 198.0	3.40×3.64	95	S-Dart exc SE
I-6, 225.0	3.40×4.13	105	S-Dart SE, Cor; O-Dart
V-8, 318.0	3.91×3.31	150	S-Chal, Cor, Chrgr; O-Dart
V-8, 360.0	4.00×3.58	180	S-Mon exc Brham & wgns; O-Chrgr
V-8, 360.0	4.00×3.58	200	O-Cor, Chrgr, Mon exc Brham & wgns
V-8, 360.0	4.00×3.58	245	S-Dart 360; O-Chal, Chrgr
V-8, 400.0	4.34×3.38	185	S-Mon Brham, wgns; O-Cor, Charger
V-8, 400.0	4.34×3.38	205	O-Corn, Chrgr
V-8, 400.0	4.34×3.38	240	O-Monaco exc wagons
V-8, 400.0	4.34×3.38	250	O-Corn, Chrgr
V-8, 440.0	4.32×3.75	230	O-Mon exc wgns
V-8, 440.0	4.32×3.75	250	O-Mon wagons
V-8, 440.0	4.32×3.75	275	O-Corn, Chrgr

1975

Dart (wb 111.0; fstbk cpes-108.0)		Wght	Price	Prod
LL29	Sport fstbk cpe	2,980	3,297	50,312
LM29	Sprt 360 fstbk cpe V-8	3,335	4,014	1,043
LL23	Swinger Spec htp cpe	3,045	3,341	9,304
LL41	sdn 4d	3,060	3,269	24,193
LH23	Swinger htp cpe	3,035	3,518	45,495
LH41	Custom sdn 4d	3,060	3,444	60,818
LP23	Spec Edition htp cpe	3,260	4,232	5,680
LP41	Spec Edition sdn 4d	3,280	4,159	13,194
Coronet (wb 117.5; htps-115.0)				
WL41	sdn 4d	3,652	3,641	8,138
WL21	htp cpe	3,620	3,591	6,058
WL45	wgn 4d 2S V-8	4,185	4,358	2,852
WH41	Custom sdn 4d	3,692	3,754	26,219
WH23	Custom htp cpe	3,702	3,777	18,513
WH45	Cstm wgn 4d 2S V-8	4,240	4,560	2,623
WH46	Cstm wgn 4d 3S V-8	4,290	4,674	5,052
WP23	Brghm htp cpe V-8	3,800	4,154	10,292
WP45	Crstwd wgn 4d 2S V-8	4,230	4,826	1,784
WP46	Crstwd wgn 4d 3S V-8	4,290	4,918	2,967
Charger (wb 115.0)				
XS22	SE htp cpe	3,950	4,903	30,812
Monaco (wb 121.5; wgns-124.0)				
DM41	sdn 4d	4,280	4,605	7,097
DM23	htp cpe	4,225	4,631	2,116
DH41	Royal sdn 4d	4,285	4,848	10,126
DH43	Royal htp sdn	4,310	4,951	8,117
DH23	Royal htp cpe	4,240	4,868	4,001
DP41	Royal Brghm sdn 4d	4,455	5,262	5,126
DP43	Royal Brghm htp sdn	4,485	5,382	5,964
DP29	Royal Brghm htp cpe	4,370	5,460	
DM45	wgn 4d 2S	4,885	5,109	1,547
DH45	Royal wgn 4d 2S	4,905	5,292	1,279
DH46	Royal wgn 4d 3S	4,945	5,415	2,666
DP45	Ryl Brghm wgn 4d 2S	4,980	5,779	1,165
DP46	Ryl Brghm wgn 4d 3S	5,025	5,905	2,909

1975 Engines	bore×stroke	bhp	availability
I-6, 225.0	3.40×4.13	95	S-Dart, Corn
V-8, 318.0	3.91×3.31	135	O-Charger
V-8, 318.0	3.91×3.31	145	O-Dart
V-8, 318.0	3.91×3.31	150	S-Coronet; O-Chrgr, Mon

1975 Engines	bore×stroke	bhp	availability
V-8, 360.0	4.00×3.58	180	S-Chrgr, Mon exc Brham wgns; O-Corn, Royal Monaco Brougham
V-8, 360.0	4.00×3.58	190	O-Chrgr, Ryl Monaco Brham
V-8, 360.0	4.00×3.58	230	S-Dart 360
V-8, 400.0	4.34×3.38	165/ 190/235	O-Corn, Chrgr
V-8, 400.0	4.34×3.38	175	S-Royal Mon Brham; O-Mon
V-8, 400.0	4.34×3.38	185	O-Charger
V-8, 400.0	4.34×3.38	195	O-Monaco
V-8, 440.0	4.32×3.75	195	O-Monaco exc Royal Brham
V-8, 440.0	4.32×3.75	215	O-all Monaco

1976

Dart (wb 111.0; fstbk cpes-108.0)		Wght	Price	Prod
LL29	Sport fstbk cpe	2,990	3,258	18,873
LL23	Swinger Spec htp cpe	3,050	3,337	3,916
LL41	sdn 4d	3,070	3,295	34,864
LH23	Swinger htp cpe	3,035	3,510	10,885
Aspen (wb 112.7; cpes-108.7)				
NL41	sdn 4d	3,252	3,371	17,573
NL29	cpe	3,222	3,336	27,730
NL45	wgn 5d 2S	3,605	3,658	37,642
NH41	Custom sdn 4d	3,240	3,553	32,163
NH29	Custom cpe	3,232	3,518	23,782
NP41	SE sdn 4d	3,470	4,440	24,378
NP29	SE cpe	3,432	4,413	21,564
NH45	SE wgn 5d 2S	3,630	3,988	34,617
Coronet (wb 117.5)				
WL41	sdn 4d	3,742	3,770	15,658
WL45	wgn 4d 2S V-8	4,285	4,634	2,632
WL46	wgn 4d 3S V-8	4,350	4,776	3,336
WH41	Brougham sdn 4d	3,760	4,059	15,215
WH45	Crstwd wgn 4d 2S V-8	4,285	5,023	1,725
WH46	Crstwd wgn 4d 3S V-8	4,360	5,165	2,597
Charger (wb 115.0)				
WL23	htp cpe	3,712	3,736	9,906
WH23	cpe	3,718	4,025	13,826
XS22	SE htp cpe V-8	3,945	4,763	42,168
Monaco (wb 121.5; wgns-124.0)				
DM41	sdn 4d	4,160	4,388	6,221
DM45	wgn 4d 2S	4,910	4,948	1,116
DH41	Royal sdn 4d	4,325	4,763	11,320
DH23	Royal htp cpe	4,280	4,778	2,915
DH45	Royal wgn 4d 2S	4,915	5,241	923
DH46	Royal wgn 4d 3S	4,950	5,364	1,429
DP41	Ryl Brghm sdn 4d	4,520	5,211	5,111
DP29	Ryl Brghm htp cpe	4,430	5,382	4,076
DP46	Ryl Brghm wgn 4d 3S	4,995	5,869	2,480

1976 Engines	bore×stroke	bhp	availability
I-6, 225.0	3.40×4.13	100	S-all sixes
V-8, 318.0	3.91×3.31	150	S-Cor exc wgns, Chrgr, Mon exc wgns & Royal; O-Dart; Aspen
V-8, 360.0	4.00×3.58	170	S-Corn wgns, Royal Mon; O-Asp, Corn, Charger, Ryl Monaco Brham
V-8, 360.0	4.00×3.58	175	O-Corn, Chrgr
V-8, 360.0	4.00×3.58	220	O-Dart, Corn
V-8, 400.0	4.34×3.38	175	S-Mon wgns/ Ryl Brhams; O-Cor, Chrgr, Mon
V-8, 400.0	4.34×3.38	185/240	O-Corn, Chrgr
V-8, 400.0	4.34×3.38	210	O-Monaco
V-8, 400.0	4.34×3.38	255	O-Coronet
V-8, 440.0	4.32×3.75	205	O-Monaco

1977

Aspen (wb 112.7; cpes-108.7)		Wght	Price	Prod
NL41	sdn 4d	3,290	3,631	32,662
NL29	cpe	3,235	3,582	33,102
NL45	wgn 5d 2S	3,492	3,953	67,294
NH41	Custom sdn 4d	3,295	3,813	45,697
NH29	Custom cpe	3,240	3,764	29,946
NP41	SE sdn 4d	3,492	4,366	25,949
NP29	SE cpe	3,428	4,317	19,985
NH45	SE wgn 5d 2S	3,518	4,283	58,011
Charger (wb 115.0)				
XS22	SE htp cpe V-8	3,895	5,098	42,542
Monaco (wb 117.4; htps-115.0)				
WL41	sdn 4d	3,772	3,988	20,633
WL23	htp cpe	3,630	3,911	14,054
WS23	Special htp cpe	—	3,995	—
WL45	wgn 4d 2S V-8	4,335	4,724	3,896
WL46	wgn 4d 3S V-8	4,395	4,867	4,594
WH41	Brougham sdn 4d	3,782	4,217	17,224
WH23	Brougham htp cpe	3,752	4,146	14,430
WH45	Crstwd wgn 4d 2S V-8	4,330	5,224	1,948
WH46	Crstwd wgn 4d 3S V-8	4,405	5,367	3,301
Diplomat (wb 112.7)				
GH41	sdn 4d	3,560	5,101	9,647
GH22	cpe	3,510	4,943	14,023
GP41	Medallion sdn 4d	3,675	5,471	4,667
GP22	Medallion cpe	3,615	5,313	9,215
Royal Monaco (wb 121.5; wgns-124.0)				
DM41	sdn 4d	4,125	4,716	12,646
DM23	htp cpe	4,050	4,731	3,360
DM45	wgn 4d 2S	4,905	5,353	2,010
DH41	Brougham sdn 4d	4,270	4,996	21,440
DH23	Brougham htp cpe	4,205	5,011	8,309
DH45	Brougham wgn 4d 2S	4,900	5,607	1,418
DH46	Brougham wgn 4d 3S	4,935	5,730	4,251

1977 Engines	bore×stroke	bhp	availability
I-6, 225.0	3.40×4.13	100	S-Asp exc wgns
I-6, 225.0	3.40×4.13	110	S-Asp wgns, Mon; O-Aspen
V-8, 318.0	3.91×3.31	145	S-Dip, Mon exc wgns, Charger, Ryl Mon; O-Asp
V-8, 318.0	3.91×3.31	135	O-Mon, Chrgr
V-8, 360.0	4.00×3.58	155	S-Mon wgns, Ryl Mon Brham; O-Aspen, Mon, Chrgr, Ryl Mon
V-8, 360.0	4.00×3.58	170	O-Mon, Chrgr
V-8, 360.0	4.00×3.58	175	O-Aspen
V-8, 400.0	4.34×3.38	190	S-Ryl Mon wgns; O-Mon, Chrgr, Royal Mon
V-8, 440.0	4.32×3.75	195	O-Ryl Mon

1978

Omni (wb 99.2)		Wght	Price	Prod
ZL44	htchbk sdn 5d	2,145	3,976	81,611
Aspen (wb 112.7; cpe-108.7)				
NL41	sdn 4d	3,235	3,911	60,191
NL29	cpe	3,195	3,783	75,599
NL45	wgn 5d 2S	3,448	4,253	61,917
Charger/Magnum (wb 114.9)				
XP22	Chrgr SE htp cpe V-8	3,895	5,368	2,800
XS22	Mgnm XE htp cpe V-8	3,895	5,509	55,431
Monaco (wb 117.4; cpes-114.9)				
WL41	sdn 4d	3,760	4,344	20,292
SL23	htp cpe	3,738	4,254	10,291
WL45	wgn 4d 2S V-8	4,310	5,103	2,376
WL46	wgn 4d 3S V-8	4,375	5,246	2,944
WH41	Brougham sdn 4d	3,775	4,568	8,665
WH23	Brougham htp cpe	3,742	4,507	6,842
WH45	Crstwd wgn 4d 2S V-8	4,305	5,549	1,329
WH46	Crstwd wgn 4d 3S V-8	4,380	5,692	2,112
Diplomat (wb 112.7)				
GM41	S sdn 4d	3,438	4,937	1,667
GM22	S cpe	3,358	4,771	1,655
GH41	sdn 4d	3,508	5,187	21,094
GH22	cpe	3,462	5,021	19,000
GH45	wgn 5d 2S	3,598	5,538	11,226
GP41	Medallion sdn 4d	3,592	5,569	11,628
GP22	Medallion cpe	3,538	5,403	12,372

1978 Engines	bore×stroke	bhp	availability
I-4, 104.7	3.13×3.40	70/75	S-Omni
I-6, 225.0	3.40×4.13	90	O-Asp exc wgns, Dip
I-6, 225.0	3.40×4.13	100	S-Asp exc wgns
I-6, 225.0	3.40×4.13	110	S-Aspen wgns, Diplomat; O-Aspen, Mon
V-8, 318.0	3.91×3.31	140	S-Asp, Dip, Mag, Mon exc wgns; O-Aspen, Dip
V-8, 318.0	3.91×3.31	150	S-Charger
V-8, 318.0	3.91×3.31	155	O-Aspen, Dip, Mag, Monaco
V-8, 360.0	4.00×3.58	155	S-Mon wgns; O- Aspen, Dip, Mag, Monaco
V-8, 360.0	4.00×3.58	165	O-Aspen
V-8, 360.0	4.00×3.58	170	O-Dip, Mag, Mon, Chrgr
V-8, 360.0	4.00×3.58	175	O-Aspen, Chrgr
V-8, 400.0	4.34×3.38	190	O-Mag, Mon
V-8, 400.0	4.34×3.38	175/ 185/240	O-Charger
V-8, 440.0	4.32×3.75	195	O-Monaco

1979

Omni (wb 99.2; 024-96.7)		Wght	Price	Prod
ZL44	htchbk sdn 5d	2,135	4,469	84,093
ZL24	024 htchbk cpe 3d	2,195	4,864	57,384
Aspen (wb 112.7; cpe-108.7)				
NL41	sdn 4d	3,175	4,516	62,568
NL29	cpe	3,110	4,399	42,833
NL45	wgn 5d 2S	3,380	4,838	38,183
Magnum (wb 114.9)				
XS22	XE htp cpe V-8	3,675	6,039	30,354
Diplomat (wb 112.7)				
GM41	sdn 4d	3,378	5,336	10,675
GM22	cpe	3,318	5,234	8,733
GH41	Salon sdn 4d	3,400	5,714	5,479
GH22	Salon cpe	3,335	5,482	6,849
GH45	Salon wgn 5d 2S	3,588	6,127	9,511
GP41	Medallion sdn 4d	3,472	6,198	5,995
GP22	Medallion cpe	3,392	5,966	6,637
St. Regis (wb 118.5)				
EH42	sdn 4d	3,602	6,532	34,972

1979 Engines	bore×stroke	bhp	availability
I-4, 104.7	3.13×3.40	70	S-Omni
I-6, 225.0	3.40×4.13	100	S-Asp, Dip
I-6, 225.0	3.40×4.13	110	S-St. Regis; O-Asp, Dip
V-8, 318.0	3.91×3.31	135	S; O-Asp, Dip, St.Regis, Mag
V-8, 360.0	4.00×3.58	150	O-Dip, St. Reg, Magnum
V-8, 360.0	4.00×3.58	195	O-Asp, Dip, St.Reg, Mag

1980

Omni (wb 99.2; 024-96.7)		Wght	Price	Prod
ZL44	htchbk sdn 5d	2,095	5,681	76,505
ZL24	024 htchbk cpe 3d	2,135	5,526	61,650
Aspen (wb 112.7; cpes-108.7)				
NE41	Special sdn 4d I-6	3,210	5,151	19,225
NE29	Special cpe I-6	3,155	5,151	13,166
NL41	sdn 4d I-6/V-8	3,242	5,162	26,239
NL29	cpe I-6/V-8	3,185	5,045	11,895
NL45	wgn 5d 2S I-6/V-8	3,410	5,434	14,944
Diplomat (wb 112.7; cpes-108.7)				
GL22	Special spt cpe I-6	3,130	5,995	—
GM41	sdn 4d	3,342	6,202	7,941
GM22	spt cpe	3,260	6,048	5,884
GM45	wgn 4d 2S	3,495	6,346	2,093
GH41	Salon sdn 4d	3,205	6,501	5,479
GH22	Salon cpe	3,270	6,372	6,849
GH45	Salon wgn 5d 2S	3,525	7,041	2,664
GP41	Medallion sdn 4d	3,442	7,078	2,159
GP22	Medallion cpe	3,322	6,931	2,131
Mirada (wb 112.7)				
XS22	S htp cpe	3,328	6,645	32,746
XH22	htp cpe	3,230	6,850	

St. Regis (wb 118.5)	Wght	Price	Prod
EH42 sdn 4d	3,608	7,129	17,068

1980 Engines	bore×stroke	bhp	availability
I-4, 104.7	3.13×3.40	65	S-Omni
I-6, 225.0	3.40×4.13	90	S-Asp, Dip, St.Reg, Mirada
V-8, 318.0	3.91×3.31	120/155	O-Aspen exc Spcls, Dip, St.Reg, Mirada
V-8, 360.0	4.00×3.58	130/185	O-St. Reg, Mir

Note: Dodge production through 1980 includes export models, which makes figures in this book somewhat higher than those reported elsewhere.

1981

Omni (wb 99.1; 024-96.6)	Wght	Price	Prod
ZL44 htchbk sdn 5d	2,130	5,690	41,056
ZE44 Miser htchbk sdn 5d	2,060	5,299	
ZL24 024 htchbk cpe 3d	2,205	6,149	35,983
ZE24 Miser 024 htchbk cpe 3d	2,137	5,299	

Aries (wb 99.6)	Wght	Price	Prod
DL41 sdn 4d	2,300	5,980	47,679
DL21 sdn 2d	2,305	5,880	
DH41 Custom sdn 4d	2,310	6,448	46,792
DH21 Custom sdn 2d	2,315	6,315	
DH45 Custom wgn 5d	2,375	6,721	31,380
DP41 SE sdn 4d	2,340	6,933	20,160
DP21 SE sdn 2d	2,340	6,789	
DP45 SE wgn 5d	2,390	7,254	9,770

Diplomat (wb 112.7; cpes-108.7)	Wght	Price	Prod
GL41 sdn 4d	3,337	6,672	4,608
GL22 spt cpe	3,272	6,495	
GM45 wgn 5d 2S	3,530	7,089	1,806
GH41 Salon sdn 4d	3,367	7,268	15,023
GH22 Salon cpe	3,262	7,134	
GH45 Salon wgn 5d 2S	3,565	7,670	1,206
GP41 Medallion sdn 4d	3,427	7,777	1,527
GP22 Medallion cpe	3,317	7,645	

Mirada (wb 112.7)	Wght	Price	Prod
XS22 htp cpe	3,350	7,700	11,899

St. Regis (wb 118.5)	Wght	Price	Prod
EH42 sdn 4d	3,587	7,674	5,388

1981 Engines	bore×stroke	bhp	availability
I-4, 104.7	3.13×3.40	63	S-Omni
I-4, 135.0	3.44×3.62	84	S-Aries; O-Omni
I-4, 156.0	3.59×3.86	92	O-Aries
I-6, 225.0	3.40×4.12	85	S-Dip, Mirada, St. Regis
V-8, 318.0	3.91×3.31	130/165	O-Dip, Mir, St. Reg

1982

Omni (wb 99.1; 024-96.6)	Wght	Price	Prod
ZH44 Cstm htchbk sdn 5d	2,175	5,927	14,466
ZE44 Miser htchbk sdn 5d	2,110	5,499	16,105
ZP44 E-type 5d	2,180	6,636	639
ZH24 024 htchbk cpe 3d	2,205	6,421	11,287
ZE24 Miser 024 htchbk cpe 3d	2,180	5,799	14,947
ZP24 Chrgr 2.2 htchbk cpe 3d	2,315	7,115	14,420

Aries (wb 99.9)	Wght	Price	Prod
DL41 sdn 4d	2,310	6,131	28,561
DL21 sdn 2d	2,315	5,990	10,286
DH41 Custom sdn 4d	2,320	7,053	19,438
DH21 Custom sdn 2d	2,320	6,898	8,127
DH45 Custom wgn 5d	2,395	7,334	26,233
DP41 SE sdn 4d	2,385	7,736	4,269
DP21 SE sdn 2d	2,365	7,575	1,374
DP45 SE wgn 5d	2,470	8,101	6,375

400 (wb 99.9)	Wght	Price	Prod
VH41 sdn 4d	2,423	8,137	3,595
VH22 cpe 2d	2,470	8,043	12,716
VH27 conv cpe	2,485	12,300	5,541
VP41 LS sdn 4d	2,438	8,402	2,870
VP22 LS cpe 2d	2,475	8,308	6,727

Diplomat (wb 112.7)	Wght	Price	Prod
GL41 Salon sdn 4d	3,345	7,750	19,773
GH41 Medallion sdn 4d	3,375	8,799	3,373

Mirada (wb 112.7)	Wght	Price	Prod
XS22 htp cpe	3,380	8,619	6,818

1982 Engines	bore×stroke	bhp	availability
I-4, 104.7	3.13×3.40	63	S-Omni
I-4, 135.0	3.44×3.62	84	S-Aries, 400; O-Omni
I-4, 156.0	3.59×3.86	92	O-Aries, 400
I-6, 225.0	3.40×4.12	90	S-Dip, Mir
V-8, 318.0	3.91×3.31	130/165	O-Dip, Mir

1983

Omni (wb 99.1)	Wght	Price	Prod
ZE44 htchbk sdn 5d	2,093	5,841	33,264
ZH44 Cstm htchbk sdn 5d	2,124	6,071	9,290

Charger (wb 96.6)	Wght	Price	Prod
ZH24 htchbk cpe 3d	2,137	6,379	22,535
ZP24 2.2 htchbk cpe 3d	2,194	7,303	10,448
ZS24 Shelby htchbk cpe 3d	2,330	8,290	8,251

Aries (wb 100.1)	Wght	Price	Prod
DL41 sdn 4d	2,263	6,718	51,783
DL21 sdn 2d	2,257	6,577	14,218
DH45 Custom wgn 5d	2,372	7,636	29,228
DH41 SE sdn 4d	2,300	7,417	8,962
DH21 SE sdn 2d	2,273	7,260	4,325
DP45 SE wgn 5d	2,424	8,186	4,023

400 (wb 100.3)	Wght	Price	Prod
VP41 sdn 4d	2,482	8,490	9,560
VP22 cpe 2d	2,404	8,014	11,504
VP27 conv cpe	2,473	12,500	4,888

600 (wb 103.1)	Wght	Price	Prod
EH41 sdn 4d	2,524	8,841	21,065
ES41 ES sdn 4d	2,504	9,372	12,423

Diplomat (wb 112.7)	Wght	Price	Prod
GL41 Salon sdn 4d	3,387	8,248	21,368
GH41 Medallion sdn 4d	3,458	9,369	3,076

Mirada (wb 112.7)	Wght	Price	Prod
XS22 htp cpe	3,378	9,011	5,597

1983 Engines	bore×stroke	bhp	availability
I-4, 104.7	3.13×3.40	63	S-Omni, Chrgr
I-4, 97.3	3.17×3.07	62	S-late Omni, Charger
I-4, 135.0	3.44×3.62	94	S-Chgr 2.2, Aries, 400, 600; O-Omni, Chrgr
I-4, 135.0	3.44×3.62	107	S-Shlby Chrgr
I-4, 156.0	3.59×3.86	93	O-Aries, 400, 600
I-6, 225.0	3.40×4.12	90	S-Dip, Mirada
V-8, 318.0	3.91×3.31	130	O-Dip, Mirada

1984

Omni (wb 99.1)	Wght	Price	Prod
ZE44 htchbk sdn 5d	2,181	5,830	54,584
ZH44 Cstm htchbk sdn 5d	2,249	6,148	13,486
ZE44/AGBGLH sdn 5d	—	7,350	—

Charger (wb 96.6)	Wght	Price	Prod
ZH24 htchbk cpe 3d	2,222	6,494	34,763
ZP24 2.2 htchbk cpe 3d	2,360	7,288	11,949
ZS24 Shelby htchbk cpe 3d	2,388	8,541	7,552

Daytona (wb 97.0)	Wght	Price	Prod
VH24 htchbk cpe 3d	2,528	8,308	21,916
VS24 Turbo htchbk cpe 3d	2,596	10,227	27,431
VS24/AGSTrb Z htchbk cpe 3d	2,646	11,494	—

Aries (wb 100.3)	Wght	Price	Prod
DL41 sdn 4d	2,323	6,949	55,331
DL21 sdn 2d	2,317	6,837	11,921
DH45 Custom wgn 5d	2,432	7,736	31,421
DH41 SE sdn 4d	2,360	7,589	12,314
DH21 SE sdn 2d	2,333	7,463	4,231
DP45 SE wgn 5d	2,484	8,195	4,814

600 (wb 100.3)	Wght	Price	Prod
VP22 cpe 2d	2,465	8,376	13,296
VP27 conv cpe	2,533	10,595	10,960
VP27/AGTTurbo conv cpe	—	12,895	—

600 sedan (wb 103.3)	Wght	Price	Prod
EH41 sdn 4d	2,564	8,903	28,646
ES41 ES sdn 4d	2,564	9,525	8,735

Diplomat (wb 112.7)	Wght	Price	Prod
Gl-41 Salon sdn 4d	3,454	9,180	16,261
GP41 SE sdn 4d	3,584	9,828	5,902

1984 Engines	bore×stroke	bhp	availability
I-4, 97.3	3.17×3.07	64	S-Omni, Chrgr
I-4, 135.0	3.44×3.62	96	S-Chgr 2.2, Aries, 600 exc sdn; O-Om, Chrgr
I-4, 135.0	3.44×3.62	99	S-Day, 600 sdn
I-4, 135.0	3.44×3.62	110	S-Shl; O-Omni, Charger
I-4T, 135.0	3.44×3.62	142	S-Day turbo; O-Day, all 600
I-4, 156.0	3.59×3.86	101	O-Aries, all 600
V-8, 318.0	3.91×3.31	130	S-Diplomat

1985

Omni (wb 99.1)	Wght	Price	Prod
LZE44 htchbk sdn 5d	2,174	5,977	54,229
LZH44 SE htchbk sdn 5d	2,154	6,298	13,385
LZE44/AGBGLH htchbk sdn 5d	2,222	7,620	6,513

Charger (wb 96.5)	Wght	Price	Prod
LZH24 htchbk cpe 3d	2,215	6,584	38,203
LZP24 2.2 htchbk cpe 3d	2,366	7,515	10,645
LZS24 Shelby htchbk cpe 3d	2,457	9,553	7,709

Daytona (wb 97.0)	Wght	Price	Prod
GVH24 htchbk cpe 3d	2,611	8,505	29,987
GVS24 Turbo htchbk cpe 3d	2,688	10,286	9,509
GVS24/AGSTrb Z htchbk cpe 3d	2,744	11,620	8,023

Aries (wb 100.3)	Wght	Price	Prod
KDL41 sdn 4d	2,393	7,039	39,580
KDL21 sdn 2d	2,375	6,924	9,428
KDM41 SE sdn 4d	2,424	7,439	23,920
KDM21 SE sdn 2d	2,390	7,321	7,937
KDM45 SE wgn 5d	2,514	7,909	22,953
KDH41 LE sdn 4d	2,446	7,792	5,932
KDH21 LE sdn 2d	2,414	7,659	3,706
KDP45 LE wgn 5d	2,546	8,348	4,519

Lancer (wb 103.1)	Wght	Price	Prod
HDH44 spt sdn 5d	2,659	8,713	30,567
HDS44 ES sdn 5d	2,726	9,690	15,286

600 (wb 100.3; sdn-103.3)	Wght	Price	Prod
KVP22 cpe 2d	2,539	9,060	12,670
KVP27 conv cpe	2,601	10,889	8,188
KVP27/AGTES Trb conv cpe	—	13,995	5,621
EEH41 SE sdn 4d	2,591	8,953	32,368

Diplomat (wb 112.7)	Wght	Price	Prod
MGL41 Salon sdn 4d	3,558	9,399	25,398
MGP41 SE sdn 4d	3,628	10,418	13,767

1985 Engines	bore×stroke	bhp	availability
I-4, 97.3	3.17×3.07	64	S-Omni, Chrgr
I-4, 135.0	3.44×3.62	96	S-Aries; O-Om, Charger
I-4, 135.0	3.44×3.62	99	S-Day, Lancer, 600; O-Aries
I-4, 135.0	3.44×3.62	110	S-Omni GLH, Chgr 2.2; O-Om, Chrgr
I-4T, 135.0	3.44×3.62	146	S-Shel Chrgr, Day Turbos, 600ES; O-Om GLH, Daytona, Lancer, 600
I-4, 156.0	3.59×3.86	101	O-Aries, 600
V-8, 318.0	3.91×3.31	140	S-Diplomat

1986

Omni (wb 99.1)	Wght	Price	Prod
LZE44 htchbk sdn 5d	2,154	6,209	61,812
LZH44 SE htchbk sdn 5d	2,174	6,558	8,139
LZE44/AGBGLH htchbk sdn 5d	2,341	7,918	3,629

Charger (wb 96.5)	Wght	Price	Prod
LZH24 htchbk cpe 3d	2,215	6,787	38,172
LZP24 2.2 htchbk cpe 3d	2,366	7,732	4,814
LZS24 Shelby htchbk cpe 3d	2,382	9,361	7,669

Daytona (wb 97.0)	Wght	Price	Prod
GVH24 htchbk cpe 3d	2,546	9,013	26,771
GVS24 Trb Z htchbk cpe 3d	—	11,301	17,595

Aries (wb 100.3)	Wght	Price	Prod
KDL41 sdn 4d	2,402	7,301	14,445
KDL21 sdn 2d	2,395	7,184	2,437
KDM41 SE sdn 4d	2,429	7,759	40,254
KDM21 SE sdn 2d	2,412	7,639	9,084
KDM45 SE wgn 5d	2,513	8,186	17,757

Dodge

Aries	Wght	Price	Prod
KDH41 LE sdn 4d	2,444	8,207	5,638
KDH21 LE sdn 2d	2,427	8,087	2,475
KDH45 LE wgn 5d	2,549	8,936	5,278
Lancer (wb 103.1)			
HDH44 htchbk spt sdn 5d	2,650	9,426	34,009
HDS44 htchbk ES sdn 5d	2,702	10,332	17,888
600 (wb 100.3; sdn-103.3)			
KVP22 cpe 2d	2,523	9,577	11,714
KVP27 conv cpe	2,594	11,695	11,678
KVP27/AGTES Trb conv cpe	2,648	14,856	4,759
EEM41 sdn 4d	2,593	9,370	16,253
EEH41 SE sdn 4d	2,593	10,028	15,291
Diplomat (wb 112.7)			
MGL41 Salon sdn 4d	3,555	10,086	15,469
MGP41 SE sdn 4d	3,624	11,166	11,484

1986 Engines	bore×stroke	bhp	availability
I-4, 97.3	3.17×3.07	64	S-Om, Charger
I-4, 135.0	3.44×3.62	96	O-Om, Chrgr
I-4, 135.0	3.44×3.62	97	S-Aries, Day, Lancr, 600
I-4, 135.0	3.44×3.62	110	S-Omni GLH, Chgr 2.2; O-Om, Charger
I-4T, 135.0	3.44×3.62	146	S-Shelby, Day Turbos 600ES; O-Omni GLH, Day, Lncr, 600
I-4, 153.0	3.44×4.09	100	O-Ars, Day, Lncr, 600
V-8, 318.0	3.91×3.31	140	S-Diplomat

1987

Omni (wb 99.1)	Wght	Price	Prod
LZE44 Amer htchbk sdn 5d	2,237	5,499	66,907
Charger (wb 96.5)			
LZH24 htchbk cpe 3d	2,290	6,999	24,275
LZS24 Shelby htchbk cpe 3d	2,483	9,840	2,011
Daytona (wb 97.0)			
GVH24 htchbk cpe 3d	2,676	9,799	18,485
GVP24 Pcfca htchbk cpe 3d	2,862	13,912	7,467
GVS24 Shel Z htchbk cpe 3d	2,812	12,749	7,152
Shadow (wb 97.0)			
PDH44 htchbk sdn 5d	2,494	7,699	37,559
PDH24 htchbk sdn 3d	2,459	7,499	38,497
Aries (wb 100.3)			
KDL41 sdn 4d	2,415	7,655	4,710
KDM41 SE sdn 4d	2,484	8,134	66,506
KDL21 sdn 2d	2,409	7,655	204
KDM21 SE sdn 2d	2,468	8,134	7,517
KDM45 SE wgn 5d	2,588	8,579	20,362
Lancer (wb 103.1)			
HDH44 sdn 5d	2,645	9,474	17,040
HDS44 ES htchbk sdn 5d	2,692	10,428	9,579
600 (wb 103.3)			
EEM41 sdn 4d	2,594	9,891	20,074
EEH41 SE sdn 4d	2,601	10,553	20,317
Diplomat (wb 112.7)			
MGL41 Salon sdn 4d	3,566	10,598	11,256
MGP41 SE sdn 4d	3,627	11,678	9,371

1987 Engines	bore×stroke	bhp	availability
I-4, 135.0	3.44×3.62	96	S-Omni, Chrgr
I-4, 135.0	3.44×3.62	97	S-Aries, Shdw, Lancer, 600
I-4T, 135.0	3.44×3.62	146	S-(auto. trans.), Day Pacifica; O-Day, Shdw, Lancer, 600
I-4T, 135.0	3.44×3.62	174	S Shelby Z (man. trans.)
I-4, 153.0	3.44×4.09	100	S-Day; O-Aries, Lancer, 600
V-8, 318.0	3.91×3.31	140	S-Diplomat

1988

Omni (wb 99.1)	Wght	Price	Prod
LZE44 Amer htchbk sdn 5d	2,225	5,999	59,867
Daytona (wb 97.0)			
GVH24 htchbk cpe 3d	2,676	10,025	54,075
GVP24 Pacifica htchbk cpe 3d	2,862	14,513	4,752
GVS24 Shel Z htchbk cpe 3d	2,812	13,394	7,580
Shadow (wb 97.0)			
PDH44 htchbk sdn 5d	2,544	8,075	55,857
PDH24 htchbk sdn 3d	2,513	7,875	36,452
Aries America (wb 100.3)			
KDH41 sdn 4d	2,485	6,995	85,613
KDH21 sdn 2d	2,459	6,995	6,578
KDH45 wgn 5d	2,537	7,695	19,172
Lancer (wb 103.1)			
HDH44 htchbk sdn 5d	2,646	10,482	6,580
HDS44 ES htchbk sdn 5d	2,702	12,715	2,484
DS44/AFPShel htchbk sdn 5d	—	—	279
600 (wb 103.3)			
EEM41 sdn 4d	2,595	10,659	10,305
EEH41 SE sdn 4d	2,633	11,628	6,785
Dynasty (wb 104.3)			
CDH41 sdn 4d	2,956	11,666	26,653
CDP41 LE sdn 4d	2,966	12,226	28,897
Diplomat (wb 112.7)			
MGE41 sdn 4d	3,584	12,127	444
MGL41 Salon sdn 4d	3,567	11,407	12,992
MGP41 SE sdn 4d	3,634	14,221	5,737

1988 Engines	bore×stroke	bhp	availability
I-4, 135.0	3.44×3.62	93	S-Omni, Aries, Shdw, Lncr, 600
I-4T, 135.0	3.44×3.62	146	S-Day Pacif; O-Day, Shdw, Lancer, 600
I-4T, 135.0	3.44×3.62	174	S-Day Shel Z, Lancer Shelby
I-4, 153,0	3.44×4.09	96	S-Day, Dyn, Lancer ES; O-Aries, Shdw, Lancer, 600
V-6, 181.4	3.59×2.99	136	O-Dynasty
V-8, 318.0	3.91×3.31	140	S-Diplomat

1989

Omni (wb 99.1)	Wght	Price	Prod
LZE44 Amer htchbk sdn 5d	2,237	6,595	46,239
Daytona (wb 97.0) - 80,878 built			
GVL24 htchbk cpe 3d	2,751	9,295	—
GVH24 ES htchbk cpe 3d	2,822	10,395	—
GVS24 ES turbo cpe 3d	2,936	11,995	—
GVX24 Shelby htchbk cpe 3d	2,951	13,295	—
Shadow (wb 97.0) - 99,743 built			
PDH44 htchbk sdn 5d	2,558	8,595	—
PDH24 htchbk cpe 3d	2,520	8,395	—
Aries America (wb 100.3) - 36,932 built			
KDH41 sdn 4d	2,323	7,595	—
KDH21 sdn 2d	2,317	7,595	—
Lancer (wb 103.1) - 5,019 built			
HDH44 spt sdn 5d	2,646	11,195	—
HDS44 ES sdn 5d	2,702	13,695	—
HDX44 Shelby sdn 5d	2,838	17,395	—
Spirit (wb 103.3) - 68,181 built			
ADH41 sdn 4d	2,765	10,485	—
ADP41 ES sdn 4d	2,842	13,145	—
ADX41 LE sdn 4d	2,901	11,845	—
Dynasty (wb 104.3) - 137,718 built			
CDH41 sdn 4d	2,992	12,295	—
CDP41 LE sdn 4d	3,066	13,595	—
Diplomat (wb 112.7) - 6,429 built			
MGL41 Salon sdn 4d	3,582	11,995	—
MGP41 SE sdn 4d	3,732	14,795	—

1989 Engines	bore×stroke	bhp	availability
I-4, 135.0	3.44×3.62	93	S-Omni, Aries,
I-4, 135.0	3.44×3.62	93	S-Shdw, Lncr
I-4T, 135.0	3.44×3.62	174	S-Day/Lncr, Shel
I-4, 153.0	3.44×4.09	100	S-Day, Dyn, Spirit; O-Aries, Shdw, Lancer
I-4T, 153.0	3.44×4.09	150	S-Spirit ES, Lancer ES; O-Day, Lancer, Shdw ES, Sprt
V-6, 181.4	3.59×2.99	141	S-Dyn LE; O-Dyn, Spirit ES
V-8, 318.0	3.91×3.31	140	S-Diplomat

1990

Omni (wb 99.1)	Wght	Price	Prod
LZE44 htchbk sdn 5d	2,296	6,995	16,733
Daytona (wb 97.0) - 43,785 built			
GVL24 htchbk cpe 3d	2,751	9,795	—
GVH24 ES htchbk cpe 3d	2,822	10,995	—
GVS24 ES turbo cpe 3d	2,936	12,895	—
GVX24 Shelby htchbk cpe 3d	2,951	14,295	—
Shadow (wb 97.0) - 93,660 built			
PDH44 htchbk sdn 5d	2,642	8,935	—
PDH24 htchbk cpe 3d	2,606	8,735	—
Spirit (wb 103.3) - 99,319 built			
ADH41 sdn 4d	2,854	10,485	—
ADP41 ES sdn 4d	—	13,145	—
ADX41 LE sdn 4d	—	11,845	—
Dynasty (wb 104.3) - 112,833 built			
CDH41 sdn 4d	2,992	12,295	—
CDP41 LE sdn 4d	3,066	14,395	—

1990 Engines	bore×stroke	bhp	availability
I-4, 135.0	3.44×3.62	93	S-Shadow
I-4T, 135.0	3.44×3.62	174	S-Day Shel; O-Shadow
I-4, 153.0	3.44×4.09	100	S-Day, Dyn, Spirit; O-Shdw
I-4T, 153.0	3.44×4.09	150	S-Spirit ES; O-Spirit, Shdw, Daytona
V-6, 181.4	3.59×2.99	141	S-Dynasty LE; O-Dyn, Spirit, Daytona
V-6, 201.5	3.66×3.19	147	O-Dynasty

1991

Daytona (wb 97.0)-17,286 blt	Wght	Price	Prod
htchbk cpe 3d	2,777	10,500	—
ES htchbk cpe 3d	—	11,745	—
IROC htchbk cpe 3d	—	12,940	—
Shadow (wb 97.0)			
Amer htchbk sdn 3d	2,615	7,699	
Hghln htchbk sdn 3d	—	8,948	28,344
ES htchbk sdn 3d	—	10,424	
Amer htchbk sdn 5d	2,652	7,999	
Hghln htchbk sdn 5d	—	9,248	33,339
ES htchbk sdn 5d	—	10,724	
Highline conv cpe 2d	2,910	12,995	19,528
ES conv cpe 2d	—	14,068	
Spirit (wb 103.3) - 94,895 built			
sdn 4d	2,801	10,976	—
LE sdn 4d	—	12,976	—
ES sdn 4d	—	13,760	—
R/T sdn 4d	3,060	17,871	—
Dynasty (wb 104.3) - 11,320 built			
CDH41 sdn 4d	2,996	13,697	—
CDP41 LS sdn 4d	—	15,137	—

1991 Engines	bore×stroke	bhp	availability
I-4, 135.0	3.44×3.62	93	S-Shdw (ohc)
I-4T, 135.0	3.44×3.62	224	S-Spir R/T (dohc)
I-4, 153.0	3.44×4.09	100	S-Day, Spir, Dynasty; O-Shdw (ohc)
I-4T, 153.0	3.44×4.09	152	O-Day, Shdw, Spirit
V-6, 181.4	3.59×2.99	141	O-Day, Spirit, Dynasty (ohc)
V-6, 201.5	3.66×3.19	147	O-Dyn (ohv)

1992

Daytona (wb 97.2)-13,478 blt	Wght	Price	Prod
htchbk cpe 3d	2,779	10,469	—
ES htchbk cpe 3d	—	11,510	—
IROC htchbk cpe 3d	—	12,805	—
IROC R/T htchbk cpe 3d	—	19,185	—
Shadow (wb 97.0)			
Amer htchbk sdn 3d	2,615	7,869	
Hghln htchbk sdn 3d	—	9,246	45,786
ES htchbk sdn 3d	—	10,912	
Amer htchbk sdn 5d	2,652	8,269	
Hghln htchbk sdn 5d	—	9,646	44,201
ES htchbk sdn 5d	—	11,234	

Shadow	Wght	Price	Prod
Highline conv cpe 2d	2,910	13,457	3,152
ES conv cpe 2d	—	14,685	

Spirit (wb 103.5) - 89,697 built			
sdn 4d	2,788	11,470	—
LE sdn 4d	—	13,530	—
ES sdn 4d	—	14,441	—
R/T sdn 4d	3,089	18,674	—

Dynasty (wb 104.5) - 96,403 built			
CDH41 sdn 4d	3,026	14,277	—
CHP41 LS sdn 4d	—	15,767	—

Viper (96.2)			
RT/10 conv rdstr 2d	3476	50,000	162

1992 Engines	bore×stroke	bhp	availability
I-4, 135.0	3.44×3.62	93	S-Shdw (ohc)
I-4T, 135.0	3.44×3.62	224	S-Spirit R/T, Daytona IROC R/T (dohc)
I-4, 153.0	3.44×4.09	100	S-Day, Spir, Dyn; O-Shdw
I-4T, 153.0	3.44×4.09	152	O-Day, Shdw, Spirit
V-6, 181.4	3.59×2.99	141	O-Day, Shdw, Spir, Dyn (ohc)
V-6, 201.0	3.66×3.19	147	O-Dyn (ohv)
V-10, 488.0	4.00×3.88	400	S-Viper

1993

Daytona (wb 97.2) - 9,677 blt	Wght	Price	Prod
htchbk cpe 3d	2,779	10,874	—
ES htchbk cpe 3d	2,864	12,018	—
IROC htchbk cpe 3d	2,942	13,309	—
IROC R/T htchbk cpe 3d	2,942	19,185	—

Shadow (wb 97.0)			
htchbk sdn 3d	2,613	8,397	57,039
ES htchbk sdn 3d	—	9,804	
htchbk sdn 5d	2,884	8,797	52,498
ES htchbk sdn 5d	—	10,204	
Highline conv cpe 2d	2,910	14,028	6,307
ES conv cpe 2d	—	14,167	

Spirit (wb 103.5) - 90,607 built			
Highline sdn 4d	2,788	11,941	—
ES sdn 4d	—	14,715	—

Dynasty (wb 104.5) - 65,805 built			
CDH41 sdn 4d	2,971	14,736	—
CDP41 LS sdn 4d	—	16,267	—

Intrepid (wb 113.0) - 81,236 built			
HDH41 sdn 4d	3,217	15,930	—
HDP41 ES sdn 4d	3,315	17,189	—

Viper (96.2)			
RDS27 RT/10 conv rdstr 2d	3,476	50,000	1,043

1993 Engines	bore×stroke	bhp	availability
I-4, 135.0	3.44×3.62	93	S-Shdw (ohc)
I-4T, 135.0	3.44×3.62	224	S-Day IROC R/T (dohc)
I-4, 153.0	3.44×4.09	100	S-Day, Spir, Dyn O-Shdw
V-6, 181.4	3.59×2.99	141	O-Day, Shdw, Spirit, Dyn
V-6, 201.0	3.66×3.19	147	O-Dynasty
V-6, 201.4	3.66×3.19	153	S-Intrep (ohv)
V-6, 214.7	3.78×3.19	214	O-Intrep (ohc)
V-10, 488.0	4.00×3.88	400	S-Viper

1994

Shadow (wb 97.0)	Wght	Price	Prod
htchbk sdn 3d	2,608	8,806	50,910
ES htchbk sdn 3d	—	10,252	
htchbk sdn 5d	2,643	9,206	46,953
ES htchbk sdn 5d	—	10,652	

Spirit (wb 103.5)			
ADH41 sdn 4d	2,824	12,470	82,613

Intrepid (wb 113.0) - 155,170 built			
HDH41 sdn 4d	3,271	17,251	—
HDP41 ES sdn 4d	3,370	19,191	—

Viper (96.2)			
RDS27 RT/10 conv rdstr 2d	3,476	54,500	2,892

1994 Engines	bore×stroke	bhp	availability
I-4, 135.0	3.44×3.62	93	S-Shadow
I-4, 153.0	3.44×4.09	100	O-Shadow
I-4, 153.0	3.44×4.09	106	S-Spirit
V-6, 181.4	3.59×2.99	142	O-Shdw, Spir (ohc)
V-6, 201.4	3.66×3.19	161	S-Intrep (ohv)
V-6, 214.7	3.78×3.19	214	O-Intrep (ohc)
V-10, 488.0	4.00×3.88	400	S-Viper

1995

Neon (wb 104.0)	Wght	Price	Prod
LDL42 sdn 4d	2,338	9,500	145,095
LDH42 Highline sdn 4d	2,405	11,240	
LDS42 Sport sdn 4d	2,448	13,267	
LDH22 Highline cpe 2d	—	11,240	33,808
LDS22 Sport cpe 2d	—	13,567	

Avenger (wb 103.7)			
JDH22 cpe 2d	2,822	13,341	32,966
JDS22 ES cpe 2d	3,084	17,191	

Spirit (wb 103.5)			
ADH41 sdn 4d	2,863	14,323	28,412

Stratus (wb 108.0)			
ADH41 sdn 4d	2,937	13,965	58,550
ADP41 ES sdn 4d	3,153	17,430	

Intrepid (wb 113.0)			
HDH41 sdn 4d	3,310	17,974	178,679
HDP41 ES sdn 4d	3,372	20,884	

Viper (96.2)			
RDS27 RT/10 conv rdstr 2d	3,476	56,000	1,577

1995 Engines	bore×stroke	bhp	availability
I-4, 121.8	3.44×3.27	132	S-Neon, Stratus (ohc)
I-4, 121.8	3.44×3.27	140	S-Avngr (dohc)
I-4, 121.8	3.44×3.27	150	O-Neon (dohc)
I-4, 148.2	3.44×3.98	150	O-Strat (dohc)
V-6, 152.3	3.29×2.99	155	O-Avngr (ohc)
V-6, 152.3	3.29×2.99	164	O-Strat (ohc)
I-4, 153.0	3.44×4.09	100	S-Spirit (ohc)
V-6, 181.4	3.59×2.99	142	O-Spirit (ohc)
V-6, 201.4	3.66×3.19	161	S-Intrep (ohv)
V-6, 214.7	3.78×3.19	214	O-Intrep (ohc)
V-10, 488.0	4.00×3.88	400	S-Viper

1996

Neon (wb 104.0)	Wght	Price	Prod
LDL22 cpe 2d	2,384	9,495	34,641
LDH22 Highline cpe 2d	2,385	11,300	96,702
LDS22 Sport cpe 2d	2,469	12,500	
LDL42 sdn 4d	2,343	9,995	
LDH42 Highline sdn 4d	2,416	11,500	
LDS42 Sport sdn 4d	2,456	12,700	

Avenger (wb 103.7)			
JDH22 cpe 2d	2,879	14,040	38,828
JDS22 ES cpe 2d	3,124	16,829	

Stratus (wb 108.0)			
ADH41 sdn 4d	2,899	14,460	98,929
ADP41 ES sdn 4d	3,117	16,110	

Intrepid (wb 113.0)			
HDH41 sdn 4d	3,318	18,445	145,167
HDP41 ES sdn 4d	3,415	22,260	

Viper (wb 96.2)			
RDS27 R/T10 conv rdster 2d	3,445	58,600	1,234
RDS29 GTS cpe 2d	3,383	66,000	—

1996 Engines	bore×stroke	bhp	availability
I-4, 121.8	3.44×3.27	132	S-Neon, Strat
I-4, 121.8	3.44×3.27	140	S-Avngr (dohc)
I-4, 121.8	3.44×3.27	150	O-Neon (dohc)
I-4, 148.2	3.44×3.98	150	O-Stratus
V-6, 152.3	3.29×2.99	163	O-Avenger
V-6, 152.3	3.29×2.99	168	O-Stratus
V-6, 201.5	3.66×3.19	161	S-Intrepid
V-6, 214.7	3.78×3.19	214	O-Intrepid
V-10, 488.0	4.00×3.88	415	S-Viper

1997

Neon (wb 104.0)	Wght	Price	Prod
LDL22 cpe 2d	2,389	10,395	29,551
LDH22 Highline cpe 2d	2,416	12,470	
LDL42 sdn 4d	2,399	10,595	85,559
LDH42 Highline sdn 4d	2,459	12,670	

Avenger (wb 103.7)	Wght	Price	Prod
JDH22 cpe 2d	2,822	14,620	32,638
JDS22 ES cpe 2d	3,084	17,490	

Stratus (wb 108.0)			
ADH41 sdn 4d	2,911	14,960	96,757
ADP41 ES sdn 4d	2,968	16,665	

Intrepid (wb 113.0)			
HDH41 sdn 4d	3,349	19,405	151,404
HDP41 ES sdn 4d	3,440	22,910	

Viper (wb 96.2)			
RDS27 R/T10 conv rdster 2d	3,319	58,600	—
RDS29 GTS cpe 2d	3,383	66,000	954

1997 Engines	bore×stroke	bhp	availability
I-4, 121.8	3.44×3.27	132	S-Neon, Strat
I-4, 121.8	3.44×3.27	140	S-Avngr (dohc)
I-4, 121.8	3.44×3.27	150	O-Neon (dohc)
I-4, 148.2	3.44×3.98	150	O-Stratus
V-6, 152.3	3.29×2.99	163	O-Avenger
V-6, 152.3	3.29×2.99	168	O-Stratus
V-6, 201.5	3.66×3.19	161	S-Intrepid
V-6, 214.7	3.78×3.19	214	O-Intrepid
V-10, 488.0	4.00×3.88	415	S-Viper

1998

Neon (wb 104.0)	Wght	Price	Prod
LDH22 cpe 2d	2,470	11,155	29,886
LDL22 Sport cpe 2d	—	12,980	99,989
22 R/T cpe 2d	—	13,895	
LDH42 sdn 4d	2,507	11,355	
LDL42 Sport sdn 4d	—	13,160	
42 R/T sdn 4d	—	14,095	

Avenger (wb 103.7)			
JDH22 cpe 2d	2,888	14,930	29,603
JDS22 ES cpe 2d	2,989	17,310	

Stratus (wb 108.0)			
ADH41 sdn 4d	2,919	14,840	107,136
ADP41 ES sdn 4d	2,958	17,665	

Intrepid (wb 113.0)			
HDH41 sdn 4d	3,422	19,685	70,266
HDP41 ES sdn 4d	3,517	22,465	

Viper (wb 96.2)			
RDS27 R/T10 conv rdster 2d	3,319	64,000	74
RDS29 GTS cpe 2d	3,383	66,500	848

1998 Engines	bore×stroke	bhp	availability
I-4, 121.8	3.44×3.27	132	S-Neon, Strat
I-4, 121.8	3.44×3.27	140	S-Avngr (dohc)
I-4, 121.8	3.44×3.27	150	O-Neon (dohc)
I-4, 148.2	3.44×3.98	150	O-Stratus
V-6, 152.3	3.29×2.99	163	O-Avenger
V-6, 152.3	3.29×2.99	168	O-Stratus
V-6, 167.0	3.38×3.09	200	S-Intrepid
V-6, 197.0	3.62×3.19	225	O-Intrepid
V-10, 488.0	4.00×3.88	450	S-Viper

1999

Neon (wb 104.0) 165,229 - blt	Wght	Price	Prod*
LDH22 cpe 2d	2,470	10,550	—
LDL22 Sport cpe 2d	—	11,225	—
22 R/T cpe 2d	—	13,365	—
LDH42 sdn 4d	2,507	10,750	—
LDL42 Sport sdn 4d	—	11,425	—
42 R/T sdn 4d	—	13,565	—

Avenger (wb 103.7) - 15,801 built			
JDH22 cpe 2d	2,897	15,370	—
JDS22 ES cpe 2d	2,996	17,465	—

Stratus (wb 108.0) - 100,196 built			
ADH41 sdn 4d	3,007	15,140	—
ADP41 ES sdn 4d	3,169	18,960	—

Intrepid (wb 113.0) - 174,607 built			
HDH41 sdn 4d	3,423	19,890	—
HDP41 ES sdn 4d	3,518	22,640	—

Viper (wb 96.2) - 1,600 built			
RDS27 R/T10 conv rdster 2d	3,319	65,725	—
RDS29 GTS cpe 2d	3,383	68,225	—

1999 Engines	bore×stroke	bhp	availability
I-4, 121.8	3.44×3.27	132	S-Neon, Strat
I-4, 121.8	3.44×3.27	140	S-Avngr (dohc)
I-4, 121.8	3.44×3.27	150	S-Neon (dohc)
I-4, 148.2	3.44×3.98	150	O-Stratus

1999 Engines	bore×stroke	bhp	availability
V-6, 152.3	3.29×2.99	163	O-Avenger
V-6, 152.3	3.29×2.99	168	O-Stratus
V-6, 167.0	3.38×3.09	200	S-Intrepid
V-6, 197.0	3.62×3.19	225	O-Intrepid
V-10, 488.0	4.00×3.88	450	S-Viper

*Calendar-year production

2000

Neon (wb 105.0)		Wght	Price	Prod*
LDH41	sdn 4d	2,559	12,460	179,084
Avenger (wb 103.7)				
JDH22	cpe 2d	3,137	18,970	—
JDS22	ES cpe 2d	3,172	21,215	—
Stratus (wb 108.0)				
ADH41	SE sdn 4d	2,940	15,930	117,178
ADP41	ES sdn 4d	3,058	19,830	
Intrepid (wb 113.0)				
HDH41	sdn 4d	3,471	20,545	
HDP41	ES sdn 4d	3,489	22,235	161,599
HDX41	R/T sdn 4d	3,511	24,435	
Viper (wb 96.2)				
RDS27	R/T10 conv rdster 2d	3,440	67,225	1,726
RDS29	GTS cpe 2d	3,460	69,725	

2000 Engines	bore×stroke	bhp	availability
I-4, 121.8	3.44×3.27	132	S-Neon, Strat
I-4, 148.2	3.44×3.98	150	O-Stratus
V-6, 152.3	3.29×2.99	163	S-Avenger
V-6, 152.3	3.29×2.99	168	O-Stratus
V-6, 167.0	3.38×3.09	200	S-Intrepid
V-6, 197.0	3.62×3.19	225	O-Intrepid
V-6, 215.0	3.78×3.19	242	O-Intrepid
V-10, 488.0	4.00×3.88	450	S-Viper

*Calendar-year production

2001

Neon (wb 105.0)		Wght	Price	Prod*
LDH41	sdn 4d	2,585	12,715	145,718
Stratus (wb cpe 103.7, sdn 108.0)				
TDH22	SE cpe 2d	3,012	17,810	
TDS22	R/T cpe 2d	3,188	20,705	118,871
RDH41	SE sdn 4d	3,226	17,800	
RDP41	ES sdn 4d	3,297	20,435	
Intrepid (wb 113.0)				
HDH41	sdn 4d	3,471	20,910	
HDP41	ES sdn 4d	3,493	22,605	120,786
HDX41	R/T sdn 4d	3,563	24,975	
Viper (wb 96.2)				
RDS27	R/T10 conv 2d	—	69,225	1,887
RDS29	GTS cpe 2d	3,460	72,225	

2001 Engines	bore×stroke	bhp	availability
I-4, 121.8	3.44×3.27	132	S-Neon
I-4, 121.8	3.44×3.27	150	O-Neon
I-4, 143.4	3.41×3.94	147	S-Stratus cpe
I-4, 148.2	3.44×3.98	150	S-Stratus sdn
V-6, 167.0	3.38×3.09	200	S-Intrep, O-Strat
V-6, 181.4	3.59×2.99	200	O-Stratus cpe
V-6, 197.0	3.62×3.19	225	O-Intrepid
V-6, 215.0	3.78×3.19	242	O-Intrepid
V-10, 488.0	4.00×3.88	450	S-Viper

*Calendar-year production

2002

Neon (wb 105.0)-156,988 blt		Wght	Price	Prod*
LDL41	sdn 4d	2,604	12,240	—
LDS41	ACR sdn 4d	2,566	14,305	—
LDH41	SE sdn 4d	2,645	14,015	—
LDP41	ES sdn 4d	2,662	14,545	—
LDX41	R/T sdn 4d	2,643	16,190	—
Stratus (wb cpe 103.7, sdn 108.0)				
TDH22	SE cpe 2d	2,949	17,920	17,632
TDS22	R/T cpe 2d	3,100	20,940	
RDH41	SE sdn 4d	3,114	17,400	
RDH41	SE Plus sdn 4d	3,136	18,845	114,849
RDP41	ES sdn 4d	3,189	20,660	
RDX41	R/T sdn 4d	3,201	21,400	
Intrepid (wb 113.0) - 125,083 built				
HDH41	sdn 4d	3,373	20,370	—
HDP41	ES sdn 4d	3,418	22,530	—
HDX41	R/T sdn 4d	3,471	26,615	—
Viper (wb 96.2) - 1,478 built				
RDS27	R/T10 conv rdster 2d	3,340	71,725	—
RDS29	GTS cpe 2d	3,381	72,225	—

2002 Engines	bore×stroke	bhp	availability
I-4, 121.8	3.44×3.27	132	S-Neon
I-4, 121.8	3.44×3.27	150	O-Neon
I-4, 143.4	3.41×3.94	147	S-Stratus cpe
I-4, 148.2	3.44×3.98	150	S-Stratus sdn
V-6, 167.0	3.38×3.09	200	S-Intrep, O-Strat
V-6, 181.4	3.59×2.99	200	O-Stratus cpe
V-6, 197.0	3.62×3.19	234	O-Intrepid
V-6, 215.0	3.78×3.19	244	O-Intrepid
V-10, 488.0	4.00×3.88	450	S-Viper

* Calendar-year production

2003

Neon (wb 105.0)-150,957 blt		Wght	Price	Prod*
PLDL41	SE sdn 4d	2,587	12,665	—
PLDP41	SXT sdn 4d	2,639	14,975	—
PLDX41	R/T sdn 4d	2,651	16,815	—
PLDS41	SRT-4 sdn 4d	2,970	19,995	—
Stratus (wb cpe 103.7, sdn 108.0)				
STDH22	SXT cpe 2d	3,064	18,955	18,056
STDS22	R/T cpe 2d	3,206	21,800	
JRDM41	SE sdn 4d	3,207	17,920	
JRDH41	SXT sdn 4d	3,207	18,985	97,261
JRDP41	ES sdn 4d	3,245	21,430	
JRDX41	R/T sdn 4d	3,269	21,790	
Intrepid (wb 113.0) - 89,916 built				
LHDH41	SE sdn 4d	3,469	20,915	—
LHDP41	ES sdn 4d	3,487	24,235	—
LHDP41	SXT sdn 4d	3,548	24,235	—
Viper (wb 98.8) - 2,484 built				
ZBDS27	SRT-10 conv 2d	3,357	79,995	—

2003 Engines	bore×stroke	bhp	availability
I-4, 121.8	3.44×3.27	132	S-Neon
I-4, 121.8	3.44×3.27	150	O-Neon
I-4, 143.4	3.41×3.94	147	S-Stratus cpe
I-4, 148.2	3.44×3.98	150	S-Stratus sdn
I-4T, 148.2	3.44×3.98	215	O-Neon
V-6, 167.0	3.38×3.09	192	S-Intr; O-Strts sdn
V-6, 181.4	3.59×2.99	205	O-Stratus cpe
V-6, 215.0	3.78×3.19	234	O-Intrepid
V-6, 215.0	3.78×3.19	250	O-Intrepid
V-10, 505.0	4.03×3.96	500	S-Viper

* Calendar-year production

2004

Neon (wb 105.0)-139,004 blt		Wght	Price	Prod*
PLDL41	SE sdn 4d	2,584	13,200	—
PLDP41	SXT sdn 4d	2,634	15,510	—
PLDX41	R/T sdn 4d	2,647	17,350	—
PLDS41	SRT-4 sdn 4d	2,869	20,450	—
Stratus (wb cpe 103.7, sdn 108.0)				
STDH22	SXT cpe 2d	3,014	19,560	23,035
STDS22	R/T cpe 2d	3,104	22,405	
JRDM41	SE sdn 4d	3,088	18,420	
JRDH41	SXT sdn 4d	3,095	19,530	139,004
JRDP41	ES sdn 4d	3,148	21,975	
JRDX41	R/T sdn 4d	3,178	22,510	
Intrepid (wb 113.0)**				
LHDH41	SE sdn 4d	3,469	21,385	—
LHDP41	ES sdn 4d	3,487	24,705	—
LHDP41	SXT sdn 4d	3,548	24,705	—
Viper (wb 98.8) - 2,469 built				
ZBDS27	SRT-10 conv 2d	3,309	81,090	—

2004 Engines	bore×stroke	bhp	availability
I-4, 121.8	3.44×3.27	132	S-Neon
I-4, 121.8	3.44×3.27	150	O-Neon
I-4, 143.4	3.41×3.94	147	S-Stratus cpe
I-4, 148.2	3.44×3.98	150	S-Stratus sdn
I-4T, 148.2	3.44×3.98	230	O-Neon
V-6, 167.0	3.38×3.09	200	S-Intr; O-Strts sdn
V-6, 181.4	3.59×2.99	205	O-Stratus cpe
V-6, 215.0	3.78×3.19	234	O-Intrepid
V-6, 215.0	3.78×3.19	250	O-Intrepid
V-10, 505.0	4.03×3.96	500	S-Viper

* Calendar-year production

** 2004 Intrepid produced in calendar-year 2003.

2005

Neon (wb 105.0)-125,791 blt		Wght	Price	Prod*
PLDL41	SE sdn 4d	2,581	13,615	—
PLDP41	SXT sdn 4d	2,626	15,925	—
PLDS41	SRT-4 sdn 4d	2,900	20,650	—
Stratus (wb cpe 103.7, sdn 108.0)				
STDH22	SXT cpe 2d	3,051	20,025	1,427
STDS22	R/T cpe 2d	3,206	22,870	
JRDH41	SXT sdn 4d	3,182	20,145	100,517
JRDX41	R/T sdn 4d	3,230	21,625	
Magnum (wb 120.0) - 50,642 built				
LXDH49	SE wgn 4d	3,847	21,870	—
LXEH49	SXT AWD wgn 4d	4,159	27,900	—
LXDP49	RT wgn 4d	4,179	29,370	—
LXEP49	RT AWD wgn 4d	4,393	31,370	—
Viper (wb 98.8) - 2,025 built				
ZBDS27	SRT-10 conv 2d	3,310	81,495	—

2005 Engines	bore×stroke	bhp	availability
I-4, 121.8	3.44×3.27	132	S-Neon
I-4, 143.4	3.41×3.94	147	S-Stratus cpe
I-4, 148.2	3.44×3.98	150	S-Stratus sdn
I-4T, 148.2	3.44×3.98	230	O-Neon
V-6, 167.0	3.38×3.09	190	S-Magnum SE
V-6, 167.0	3.38×3.09	200	O-Stratus sdn
V-6, 181.4	3.59×2.99	205	O-Stratus cpe
V-6, 215.0	3.78×3.19	250	S-Mag SXT
V-8, 345.0	3.92×3.58	340	S-Magnum RT
V-10, 505.0	4.03×3.96	500	S-Viper

* Calendar-year production

2006

Stratus (wb 108.0)		Wght	Price	Prod*
JRDH41	SXT sdn 4d	3,182	20,465	—
JRDS41	R/T sdn 4d	3,230	23,445	—
Charger (wb 120.0)				
LXDH48	SE sdn 4d	3,685	22,320	—
LXDP48	R/T sdn 4d	3,995	29,320	—
LXDX48	SRT8 sdn 4d	4,088	35,320	—
Magnum (wb 120.0)				
LXDH49	SE wgn 4d	3,751	22,320	—
LXEH49	SXT AWD wgn 4d	4,055	28,790	—
LXDP49	R/T wgn 4d	4,083	30,235	—
LXEP49	R/T AWD wgn 4d	4,249	32,235	—
LXDX49	SRT8 wgn 4d	4,253	37,320	—
Viper (wb 98.8)				
ZBDS27	SRT10 conv 2d	3,336	81,895	—
ZBDS29	SRT10 cpe 2d	3,356	83,145	—

2006 Engines	bore×stroke	bhp	availability
I-4, 148.2	3.44×3.98	150	S-Stratus
V-6, 167.0	3.38×3.09	190	S-Magnum SE
V-6, 167.0	3.38×3.09	200	O-Stratus
V-6, 215.0	3.78×3.19	250	S-Charger SE, Magnum SXT
V-8, 345.0	3.92×3.58	340	S-Charger R/T, Magnum R/T
V-8, 370.0	4.06×3.58	425	S-Chrgr SRT8, Mag SRT8
V-10, 505.0	4.03×3.96	510	S-Viper

* Production figures not available at time of publication.

Note: Mitsubishi-built captive imports such as the Dodge Colt, Dodge Challenger, and Dodge Stealth, as well as the AMC/Renault-based Dodge Monoco are not included in the above tables.

Duesenberg

Fred and August Duesenberg built what many still consider the finest American automobiles of all time. Their great skills were evident early on. After the Duesenberg family emigrated from Germany to Iowa in the late 1800s, a twenty-something Fred built racing bicycles renowned for precision craftsmanship. The brothers then moved on to Des Moines and automobiles, where they designed the 1904 Mason, named for their backer. By 1912, they were putting together impressive engines for Mason's competition cars. The following year, they formed Duesenberg Motor Company to build both marine engines and racing cars bearing their name.

In 1917, the brothers set up in a larger plant at Elizabeth, New Jersey, to turn out aircraft and tractor engines as well. But this business was soon overshadowed by new triumphs in automobile racing. In 1919, a special 16-cylinder Duesenberg engine pushed a Land Speed Record car to 158 mph on the sands at Daytona Beach, Florida—astounding for the day. The following year, the brothers built a Bugatti-inspired 180-cubic-inch straight-eight with single overhead camshaft and three valves per cylinder. In 1921, this engine powered the only American car ever to win the French Grand Prix. Duesenberg-powered racers soon came to rival the great racing Millers at Indianapolis, winning the annual 500-miler no less than three times before 1930.

With their vast experience and growing reputation in racing, the Duesenbergs decided to move to Indianapolis and build a road car. Designated Model A, it appeared in late 1921 at the princely price of $6500. A genuine result of lessons learned on the track, it carried a potent 259.6-cid overhead-valve straight-eight that could deliver up to 85 mph. It also boasted a first among American cars: four-wheel hydraulic brakes, a system Fred had devised for racing as early as 1914.

Though brilliantly engineered and fastidiously crafted, the Model A was no style-setter. Nor were the brothers very good businessmen. Thus, after selling fewer than 500 cars through 1926, they sold Duesenberg Motors to the brash Errett Lobban Cord, who also gained control of Auburn that year. Fred and Augie stayed on, however, and in 1927 they built a dozen or so Model A derivatives called Model X. But this was only a stop-gap. E.L. Cord wanted something far more exotic.

He got it in the Duesenberg Model J, introduced to universal applause in December 1928. With characteristic immodesty, Cord proclaimed it "the world's finest motor car." And by most any measurement it was, the product of Cord's money and Fred's genius.

Any discussion of Duesenbergs invariably leads to engines and horsepower. The Model J arrived with a 420-cid straight-eight built by Lycoming to Fred's design. Horsepower was advertised as 265, mind-boggling for the time—easily over twice the power of the industry's previous best, Chrysler. Doubters have since argued that the actual figure was closer to 200, but there's evidence the factory didn't exaggerate. Though the stock engine had only 5.2:1 compression, a modified unit with 8:1 ratio allegedly showed 390 horsepower. There was also a fabled Lycoming chart listing a reject Model J engine with 208 horsepower at 3500 rpm, and the late John R. Bond, founder of *Road & Track*, projected 245-250 at the maximum 4250 rpm. So the odds are that production Model Js had at least 250, if not more.

But forget horsepower and consider some of the other specifications. In a day when side valves were usual and overhead valves "modern," the J had overhead camshafts—and not one but two. What's more, they were driven by hefty chains to operate not two but four valves per cylinder—32 in all. The engine itself was enameled in bright green, and fittings were finished in nickel, chrome, or stainless steel. Standard wheelbase was no less than 142.5 inches. Frame rails were a massive 8.5 inches deep and a quarter-inch thick. Brakes were oversized and hydraulic (vacuum-assisted after 1930). Use of aluminum alloy was extensive: in engine, dash, steering column, differential and flywheel housings, crankcase, timing-chain cover, water pump, intake manifold, brake shoes, even the gas tank. So despite their massive size, Model Js didn't weigh much over 5200 pounds. They could thus do a staggering 89 mph in second gear and 112-116 in High.

Interiors were opulent but functional. Instruments were the most numerous yet seen in an automobile: the usual speedometer (calibrated to 150 mph), ammeter, and water-temp and oil-pressure gauges, plus tachometer, brake-pressure gauge, split-second stopwatch, and altimeter/barometer. Warning lights reminded you to add chassis oil (the chassis lubricated itself every 75 miles), change engine oil, or replenish battery water. But all this was only typical of Fred Duesenberg's dedication to excellence—a passion that his cars be superior in every way.

1930 Model J Berline Sport by Murphy

Model J Victoria convertible (Greta Garbo's car)

1930 Model J roadster

Model J prices have long generated much confusion. Of course, you bought not a finished car but a bare chassis, which listed for a stupendous $8500 in 1929-30, $9500 thereafter. E. L. Cord was aiming only at those wealthy enough to afford such prices—and the lofty extra expense of bodywork custom-designed to presumably discriminating individual tastes. Though standard "factory" styles were announced as low as $2500, total cost with the least costly convertible coupe body, by Murphy of Pasadena, seems to have run at least $13,000. Most Model Js originally sold for under $17,000 complete. A few cost up to $20,000, a handful as much as $25,000. In 1929, that was equal to 50 Ford Model As.

Bodies were as regal as the Model J's drivetrain. These were, after all, grand luxe carriages, so only the finest woods, fabrics, and leathers were used. Vanity cases, radios, bars, and rear instrument panels were common owner-specified features. Less common was the town car upholstered in silk and given ebony, silver, and ivory fittings. Another car reportedly got solid-gold hardware and mosaic-wood inlays for the rear compartment. So despite its astonishing performance, the Model J was primarily a super-luxury conveyance able to run in eerie silence, as customers demanded.

And who were those demanding customers? Well, only 470 chassis and 480 engines were built between 1929 and 1936, so the clientele was, at least, exclusive. Some ads emphasized the fact. These contained not a word of hype, nor specifications—not even a picture of the car. Instead, there might be a yachtsman at the helm battling what looked like a 40-knot gale, or a well-dressed tycoon relaxing in a library worthy of a university. Regardless, there was but one line of type: "He Drives a Duesenberg." Not that the ads were chauvinistic. One showed an elegantly attired woman talking to her hat-in-hand gardener in front of an estate that would shame Versailles. Naturally, the headline declared, "She Drives a Duesenberg."

If the J was imposing, the supercharged SJ was awesome. Approximately 36 were built, with chassis priced at a prodi-

1930 Model J convertible sedan

1931 Model J Clear Vision sedan by Murphy

gious $11,750. Because the centrifugal blower delivered a six-psi boost at 4000 rpm, conrods were switched from aluminum alloy to sturdier tube-steel types. SJs developed no less than 320 horsepower, but Augie Duesenberg wanted more, so he half-heartedly tried a set of "ram's horn" manifolds with dual carburetors and was amazed to see 400 horsepower on the dynamometer. Only three cars were fitted with the 400-horsepower engine.

SJ performance is well-documented. A stock example could reach 104 mph in second and top 125. In 1935, the famed Ab Jenkins drove a aerodynamic speedster (later know as the Mormon Meteor) on the Bonneville Salt Flats in Utah for 24 hours at an average speed of 135 mph. Jenkins also ran 152 mph for one full hour and clocked one lap at 160! Naturally, the Mormon Meteor had the "ram's horn" engine. In spite of its speed, the car was still usable on the street. To put it mildly, the SJ was simply incredible.

Yet besides power and luxury, these Duesenbergs had surprising dynamic balance, without the heaviness of so many high-priced contemporaries. Model Js weren't "trucky," did not steer like tanks, and didn't demand huge leg muscles to operate their clutches or brakes. They did understeer, but this was easily checked by exquisitely accurate steering. A wide-open SJ with exhaust cut-out throbbed more than extroverts could endure, but with a closed exhaust cut-out it was little louder than a healthy Cadillac Sixteen.

Only two Model Js came close to being "sports cars," a pair of specials unofficially referred to as SSJ. Both were built by the Cord-owned Central Manufacturing Company, using the La Grande name, on "short" 125-inch wheelbases. Both were first driven by movie stars. The first was owned by Gary Cooper. The second was loaned to Clark Gable as a demonstrator, but was not purchased by Gable. Both cars survive today, though as museum pieces, and there's still no definitive information on their performance. But they must have been shattering, what with relatively lean bodies, 400-horse "ram's horn" engines, and

1932 Model SJ Torpedo Phaeton by Brunn

1934 Model J dual-cowl phaeton

1935 Model SJ speedster by J. Gurney Nutting

1935 SJ short-wheelbase roadster

1936 Model SJN convertible coupe

chassis 17 inches shorter than standard.

Another Model J offshoot was the JN—introduced in 1935. An attempt to give a more-modern look to an aging design, the JN was equipped with smaller 17-inch-diameter wheels (versus 19 inches), skirted fenders, bullet-shaped taillights, and bodies set on the frame rails for a lower look. Supercharged JNs gained the logical SJN designation. But again, confusion reigns. Blowers were later removed from some SJs, while others were added to originally unblown models. At least 45 cars had a supercharger at one time during their lives. Then there's the longtime misconception that any car with pipes snaking out from under its hood has to be supercharged. Duesenberg built cars with beautiful plumbing outside, but it wasn't always connected to a supercharger inside.

Under E.L. Cord, the company wasn't necessarily supposed to make a profit—just magnificent, cost-no-object cars as the flagships of Cord's industrial empire. The plan was for Duesenberg to sell a lot of 500 cars and come out with a new design. The Depression stretched out the time to sell that 500 cars. Cord's empire collapsed in 1937 before a new design was needed.

Sadly, Fred Duesenberg didn't live that long; he had been killed five years earlier in an auto accident—ironically, behind the wheel of an SJ. Brother August continued working, but failed with his plan to revive the marque in 1947. Several subsequent revival attempts proved equally fruitless. Among the more notable was a "modern" Duesenberg sedan floated by Fred's son "Fritz" in 1966 and an abortive 1980 Cadillac-based sedan cooked up by two of the brothers' nephews. There have also been numerous postwar replicas of original models ranging from splendid to schlocky.

But none of these efforts had the heart and soul of Fred himself. As the late Ken Purdy, pioneer automotive journalist, once wrote: "[Fred Duesenberg] died content... [He] had done what is given few men to do... chosen a good course and held unswervingly to it... With his mind and his two good hands he created something new and good and, in its way, immortal. And the creator is, when all is said and done, the most fortunate of men."

Eagle

Symbolizing power and nobility since Roman times, the name of America's national bird has been used over the years on products ranging from pencils to potato chips—and cars, of course. In fact, no fewer than six different automakers operated under the Eagle flag before World War I, four in the U.S. alone. Durant Motors produced its own Eagle in 1923-24, and Chevrolet used the name for its deluxe models of 1933. In the late '60s, Eagle was a natural choice for the competition cars built by the All-American Racers firm of driving legend Dan Gurney.

As a make, however, the only Eagle pertinent to this book is the one established by Chrysler Corporation from the remains of American Motors Corporation. Chrysler bought AMC from Renault of France in 1987, mainly to gain the lucrative Jeep franchise. But it also inherited the rights to use the Eagle name on cars, which had descended to AMC through a series of mergers and takeovers. This line of succession began with Jeep-builder Willys and its Aero-Eagle passenger cars of 1952-54. Willys (and Jeep) were then bought by Kaiser (*see entry*), which evolved into the Kaiser-Jeep Corporation acquired by AMC in 1970. Later, AMC briefly sold a Jeep Eagle, a fancy CJ-7, then put the Eagle name on its new 1980 line of four-wheel-drive passenger cars (*see* AMC).

Besides this name, Chrysler also inherited AMC's dealer body—which posed a problem. Those dealers were used to selling cars as well as Jeeps, and most still needed cars to sustain their business despite rising Jeep sales. Accordingly, most AMC operations—dealers included—were rolled into a new third Chrysler division called Jeep-Eagle, with Eagle now a full-fledged car make. To avoid "cannibalizing" sales from Dodge and Chrysler-Plymouth, Eagle was to be an upscale brand aimed at the fast-growing import market, where it would presumably win customers from the likes of Toyota, Honda, and Nissan.

Amid grand predictions for early success, Jeep-Eagle opened its doors for model-year '88. There was no question of continuing the outmoded AMC Eagles (which died early in the model year), nor the small, problematic Renault Alliance and Encore that AMC had built in Kenosha since 1983. That left just two remnants of the former Renault regime: the midsize V-6 Premier and the compact four-cylinder Medallion. Both were front-drive Renault designs like Alliance/Encore, but had been rushed to the U.S. just before the Chrysler buyout in a last-ditch effort to reverse sagging AMC sales. Medallion was a French import, basically a "federalized" Renault 21. Premier was a Canadian-built notchback based on the European Renault 30, complete with surprisingly dull styling by Giugiaro of Italy.

Both these cars became 1988 Eagles by the mere substitution of a new (and rather handsome) badge, but they sold no better as such, being conventional for Renaults but still too quirky for most Americans. Workmanship was also wanting, especially on the Medallion, which made a fast exit after 1989. Premier lasted through 1992, but only because Renault insisted that Chrysler keep building the car after taking over AMC. Chrysler tried hard to satisfy this condition, but it was a tough job, and Premier production peaked in calendar '88 at some 59,000 units. Sales then went fast downhill despite the 1990 addition of a Dodge duplicate reviving the Monaco name.

1988 Eagle Premier four-door sedan

1989 Eagle Medallion station wagon

1989 Eagle Summit LX four-door sedan

Drawing a tighter bead on "import intenders," Chrysler shifted Eagle to contemporary designs from Japanese partner Mitsubishi. All were "badge-engineered" front-drivers, and all but one were built in Japan—namely the subcompact Summit sedans sold from 1989 (cloned from the Mitsubishi Mirage) and the short-lived early-'90s "mini-minivan" Summit wagon (based on Mitsu's Expo LRV). The one "domestic" in this flock was the sharp Talon sports coupe, which bowed in early 1989 as a spin-off of the new 1990 Mitsubishi Eclipse and Plymouth Laser. All three versions were built in Illinois at the new Diamond-Star Motors plant that Chrysler and Mitsubishi had just set up as a 50/50 joint venture. But though Talon was an enthusiast's delight in top-line all-wheel-drive turbocharged form, it was really a Japanese car and thus another Eagle beyond our scope.

1992 Premier LX four-door sedan

1995 Vision TSi four-door sedan

1996 Talon ESi coupe

1996 Talon TSi coupe

1996 Vision four-door sedan

1997 Talon TSi coupe

1997 Talon ESi coupe

1997 Vision TSi four-door sedan

1998 Talon TSi coupe

A true American Eagle finally appeared in the new-for-'93 Vision. Though this, too, was built in Canada, it was designed in Detroit as one of the "cab-forward" LH sedans setting a bold new direction for Chrysler styling. Befitting Eagle's mission, Vision was conceived as more "European" than the Chrysler Concorde and Dodge Intrepid, but in the way of corporate cousins it achieved this largely through appropriate styling details and features. Like Intrepid, Vision bowed in regular and premium models, respectively labeled ESi (3.3-liter pushrod V-6) and TSi (twincam 3.5 V-6).

Far more than most home-grown four-doors, Vision was a credible Euro-style sports sedan, though it was no BMW. At best, performance was brisk rather than thrilling, but handling was crisp and responsive thanks to the wide-stance LH chassis with all-independent suspension. The TSi even boasted standard all-disc antilock brakes and, from 1994, speed-variable power steering. Vision also had the appealingly swoopy cab-forward shape that combined with a long 113-inch wheelbase to provide unusually spacious seating for five. Road noise was annoyingly high and some interior trim looked none too classy. Overall though, Vision was an impressive package, earning *Consumer Guide*® "Best Buy" honors (along with its Chrysler LH stablemates).

Unfortunately for product planners, Vision sales were disappointingly modest, running a poor third to Concorde on only 30-40 percent of Intrepid's volume. Production was around 30,000 for model-year '93 and stubbornly stuck to that level through '95. Price was a likely factor in this lackluster performance. Though Vision was carefully pitched between its LH sisters, Eagle dealers complained it was tough to sell because customers thought it overpriced. Chrysler countered that Visions came with more standard equipment than comparable Intrepids and Concordes, and urged dealers to make sure customers understood that. If buyers did understand, they didn't show it, for production of the 1996-97 models sagged to about 15,500 combined. It also didn't help that the car itself was little changed, though the '96 ESi received two worthy upgrades in standard 16-inch wheels (replacing 15s) and Chrysler's new AutoStick feature that allowed the automatic transmission to be shifted somewhat like a manual. But the '97 Visions were virtual reruns, and Talon sales were languishing, too.

With all this, no one was surprised when Chrysler dropped Vision after '97 and Talon after model year '98, thus ending a nameplate that had seemed a good idea 10 years before, but just didn't pan out. A prime motivation was Chrysler's desire to cut overhead by trimming its dealer body, which it did over the next few years by combining Jeep-Eagle stores with Chrysler-Plymouth outlets wherever practical. It proved a timely move. Sport-utility vehicles were Jeep's stock-in-trade, SUV sales were booming, and Jeep's image was forever golden. As a result, the new Chrysler-Plymouth-Jeep dealers were generally more-profitable than they'd been as either C-P or Jeep-Eagle stores. Company accountants cheered.

In the end, Eagle failed because neither Chrysler nor the public knew quite what to make of it. A hodge-podge lineup and spotty promotion implied Chrysler wasn't fully committed to the nameplate and also left consumers confused about what an Eagle was—if they knew the name at all. The cars were far from losers, yet no model achieved the desirability or clear image of import competitors and even some domestic rivals. Eagle was no Edsel, but Chrysler should have remembered a lesson from that unhappy Ford experience: Respect for any car is always earned, never bestowed.

Specifications

1988

Eagle (wb 109.3)	Wght	Price	Prod
wag 4d	3,502	12,995	2,305

1988 Engine	bore×stroke	bhp	availability
I-6, 258.0	3.75×3.90	110	S-all

1990

Talon (wb 97.2) - 32,708 built	Wght	Price	Prod
htchbk cpe	2,711	12,995	—
TSi htchbk cpe	2,777	14,753	—
TSi AWD htchbk cpe	3,101	16,437	—

1990 Engines	bore×stroke	bhp	availability
I-4, 121.9	3.35×3.46	135	S-Talon exc TSi
I-4T, 121.9	3.35×3.46	190/195	S-Talon TSi

1991

Talon (wb 97.2)	Wght	Price	Prod
htchbk cpe	2,711	12,990	20,080
TSi htchbk cpe	2,777	14,609	
TSi AWD htchbk cpe	3,101	16,513	12,016

1991 Engines	bore×stroke	bhp	availability
I-4, 121.9	3.35×3.46	135	S-Talon exc TSi
I-4T, 121.9	3.35×3.46	190/195	S-Talon TSi

1992

Talon (wb 97.2)	Wght	Price	Prod
htchbk cpe	2,712	13,631	21,551
TSi htchbk cpe	2,791	14,963	
TSi AWD htchbk cpe	3,108	16,905	8,106

1992 Engines	bore×stroke	bhp	availability
I-4, 121.9	3.35×3.46	135	S-Talon exc TSi
I-4T, 121.9	3.35×3.46	180/195	S-Talon TSi

1993

Talon (wb 97.2)	Wght	Price	Prod
DL htchbk cpe	2,550	11,752	
ES htchbk cpe	2,712	14,197	23,291
TSi htchbk cpe	2,791	15,703	
TSi AWD htchbk cpe	3,108	17,772	2,814

Vision (wb 113.0) - 30,676 blt	Wght	Price	Prod
HXP41 ESi sdn 4d	3,290	17,387	—
HXS41 TSi sdn 4d	3,422	21,104	—

1993 Engines	bore×stroke	bhp	availability
I-4, 107.1	3.17×3.39	92	S-Talon DL (ohc)
I-4, 121.9	3.35×3.46	135	S-Talon ES (dohc)
I-4T, 121.9	3.35×3.46	180/195	S-Talon TSi (dohc)
V-6, 201.4	3.66×3.19	153	S-Vis ESi (ohv)
V-6, 214.7	3.78×3.19	214	S-Vis TSi (ohc)

1994

Talon (wb 97.2)	Wght	Price	Prod
DL htchbk cpe	2,549	11,892	
ES htchbk cpe	2,712	14,362	20,545
TSi htchbk cpe	2,789	15,885	
TSi AWD htchbk cpe	3,109	17,978	635

Vision (wb 113.0) - 31,271 built	Wght	Price	Prod
HXP41 ESi sdn 4d	3,344	19,308	—
HXS41 TSi sdn 4d	3,486	22,773	—

1994 Engines	bore×stroke	bhp	availability
I-4, 107.1	3.17×3.39	92	S-Talon DL (ohc)
I-4, 121.9	3.35×3.46	135	S-Talon ES (dohc)
I-4T, 121.9	3.35×3.46	180/195	S-Talon TSi (dohc)
V-6, 201.4	3.66×3.19	161	S-Vis ESi (ohv)
V-6, 214.7	3.78×3.19	214	S-Vis TSi (ohc)

1995

Talon (wb 98.8)	Wght	Price	Prod
JXH24 ESi htchbk cpe	2,756	14,362	17,750
JXP24 TSi htchbk cpe	2,866	17,226	
JFS24 TSi AWD htchbk cpe	3,119	19,448	450

Vision (wb 113.0) - 29,821 built	Wght	Price	Prod
HXP41 ESi sdn 4d	3,408	19,697	—
HXS41 TSi sdn 4d	3,507	22,871	—

1995 Engines	bore×stroke	bhp	availability
I-4, 121.8	3.44×3.27	140	S-Talon ESi (dohc)
I-4T, 121.9	3.35×3.46	205/210	S-Talon TSi (dohc)
V-6, 201.4	3.66×3.19	161	S-Vis ESi (ohv)
V-6, 214.7	3.78×3.19	214	S-Vis TSi (ohc)

1996

Talon (wb 98.8) - 15,100 built	Wght	Price	Prod
JXL24 htchbk cpe	2,789	14,059	—
JXH24 ESi htchbk cpe	2,789	14,830	—
JXP24 TSi htchbk cpe	2,866	18,015	—
JFS24 TSi AWD htchbk cpe	3,120	20,271	—

Vision (wb 113.0) - 12,806 built	Wght	Price	Prod
HXP41 ESi sdn 4d	3,371	19,245	—
HSX41 TSi sdn 4d	3,494	23,835	—

1996 Engines	bore × stroke	bhp	availability
I-4, 121.8	3.44 × 3.27	140	S-Taln base, ESi
I-4T, 121.9	3.35 × 3.46	205/210	Talon TSi
V-6, 201.4	3.66 × 3.19	161	S-Vis ESi (ohv)
V-6, 214.7	3.78 × 3.19	214	S-Vis TSi (ohc)

1997

Talon (wb 98.8) - 9,788 built	Wght	Price	Prod
JXL24 htchbk cpe	2,729	14,594	—
JXH24 ESi htchbk cpe	2,745	15,365	—
JXP24 TSi htchbk cpe	2,899	18,550	—
JFS24 TSi AWD htchbk cpe	3,142	20,806	—

Vision (wb 113.0) - 5,874 built	Wght	Price	Prod
HXP41 ESi sdn 4d	3,439	20,305	—
HSX41 TSi sdn 4d	3,535	24,485	—

1997 Engines	bore × stroke	bhp	availability
I-4, 121.8	3.44 × 3.27	140	S-Taln base, ESi
I-4T, 121.9	3.35 × 3.46	210	S-Talon TSi
V-6, 201.4	3.66 × 3.19	161	S-Vis ESi (ohv)
V-6, 214.7	3.78 × 3.19	214	S-Vis TSi (ohc)

1998

Talon (wb 98.8) - 4,308 built	Wght	Price	Prod
JXL24 htchbk cpe	2,729	14,505	—
JXH24 ESi htchbk cpe	2,745	15,275	—
JXP24 TSi htchbk cpe	2,899	18,460	—
JFS24 TSi AWD htchbk cpe	3,142	20,715	—

1998 Engines	bore × stroke	bhp	availability
I-4, 121.8	3.44 × 3.27	140	S-Taln base, ESi
I-4T, 121.9	3.35 × 3.46	210	S-Talon TSi

Edsel

A comedy of errors or a good idea at the wrong time? The Edsel was both—proof that what seems sound today may not be so tomorrow. As one historian later wrote: "Its aim was right, but the target moved."

That target was sighted in the heady days of 1954, when Ford Motor Company was strongly recovering from its near-collapse in the late '40s. Led by board chairman Ernest R. Breech, optimistic Dearborn managers, determined to match General Motors model for model, laid expansionist plans for a GM-like five-make hierarchy involving a separate new Continental Division (*see entry*) and a second medium-price make to bolster Mercury. The latter made appealing sense at a time when the medium-price market was booming. In record-setting 1955, Pontiac, Buick, and Dodge built nearly two million cars combined.

But with the industry's usual three-year lead times, Edsel didn't arrive until late 1957, by which time the entire market was depressed and the medium-price segment had shriveled from 25 to 18 percent. Hoping to sell 100,000 of its debut '58 models, Edsel Division built only a little over 63,000, though that was fair going for an all-new line in a recession year. But from there it was all downhill. After fewer than 45,000 for '59 and a mere 3000 of the token 1960 models, the make was canceled at the end of November '59.

The name, of course, honored the only son of company founder Henry Ford and the father of then-president Henry Ford II. Not that it was supposed to be the choice. Ford solicited monikers from all over—including free/thinker poet Marianne Moore, who came up with stunners like "Mongoose Civique," "Turcotinga," and "Utopian Turtletop." Ranger, Pacer, Corsair, and Citation were the top finishers among 6000 names considered by the ad agency, and were ultimately adopted as series designations. But Breech didn't like these or any of the other suggestions. "Edsel" had popped up as an early prospect, probably because the project was widely known as the "E-car." But the Ford family was against it, and even publicly denied that Edsel would ever be used. But when a decision lagged, Breech stepped in. "I'll take care of Henry," he declared. He did, and Edsel it was.

Though originally conceived as a more-expensive and powerful "super Mercury," Edsel was positioned between Ford and Mercury. It was also far from the radical all-new design rumored for some two years before introduction, which might also have affected first-year sales.

The '58 line comprised entry-level Ranger and step-up Pacer series on the 118-inch wheelbase (116 for wagons) of the 1957-58 Ford; further up were Corsair and Citation on the 124-inch Mercury chassis. Bodyshells were similarly shared. Ranger offered two- and four-door sedans and hardtops, two-door Roundup wagon, and four-door Villager wagons with seating for six or nine. Pacer deleted the two-door wagon and sedan but added a convertible; its two wagons were tagged Bermuda. Corsair was confined to two- and four-door hardtops; Citation offered those plus a soft-top model. Prices ranged from $2500 to $3800.

Styling was the '58 Edsel's most unique aspect—and the most controversial, especially the "horse-collar" vertical grille and slim horizontal taillights (which one cynic termed "ingrown toenails"). But fins were mercifully absent, and the package was tastefully restrained next to the glittery '58 Buick and Olds. Typical of the day, gadgets abounded: optional "Teletouch Drive" automatic transmission controlled by pushbuttons in the steering-wheel hub, "cyclops eye" rotating-drum speedometer, and power assists for most everything but the rearview mirror.

1958 Pacer convertible coupe

1958 Pacer four-door sedan

1958 Citation hardtop coupe

1959 Corsair four-door hardtop

Power comprised two V-8s from Dearborn's new 1958 "FE-Series" big-block family. The two lower series carried a 361-cubic-incher with 303 horsepower; Corsair/Citation used a massive 410 with 345 horsepower. With that, Edsels were quite rapid, but roadability, braking, and workmanship left much to be desired—also typical of the times.

Disappointing first-year sales dictated a reduced platoon of '59 Edsels on a single 120-inch wheelbase—all basically reskinned Fords. Offerings comprised six- and nine-seater Villager wagons; Corsair convertible; Ranger two-door sedan; and Corsair/Ranger four-door sedans, hardtop coupes, and hardtop sedans. Engines proliferated. Ranger/Villager came with a 200-bhp 292 Ford V-8, but a 145-bhp 223 inline six, also borrowed from Ford, was a new no-charge option, a nod to the market's sudden concern for fuel economy with the '58 recession. Corsairs had a standard 225-bhp 332 V-8, again from Ford Division. The 361 returned unchanged as a $58 linewide option, but in the lighter '59s it delivered 0-60 mph in 10 seconds or less. Styling was toned-down from '58, with grille-mounted headlights, taller windshields, and more-conventional taillights moved into the back panel. Prices were trimmed along with models and weight. The costliest '59, the ragtop Corsair, started at about $3100.

Dearborn halted Edsel production in November 1959 after a halfhearted run of downpriced, "decontented" 1960 models that were even more Ford-like than the '59s. Corsairs and the 361 V-8 disappeared, leaving two Villagers, five Rangers, a 292 V-8 detuned to 185 horsepower, and a new 352 V-8 option with 300 bhp. Working with that year's all-new Ford design, stylists abandoned the vertical-grille motif for a split-horizontal affair looking suspiciously like that of the '59 Pontiac, though this was pure coincidence. A quartet of vertical ovals housed tail and backup lamps, and slim chrome moldings graced the upper bodysides. Two- and three-speed automatic transmissions, power steering, and air conditioning were all still available. The Ranger convertible listed at $3000, but could be optioned up to $3800. The inexpensive Ranger two-door started at $2643.

But everyone knew Edsel was finished, so it's a wonder that any of the '60s got built. Some almost didn't. The ragtop Ranger saw but 76 copies, the nine-passenger Villager a mere 59. Thus ended Detroit's biggest and most public flop since the Tucker.

"Edsel" now shows up in dictionaries as a synonym for "loser"—unfortunate considering the great legacy of Edsel Ford. But though Dearborn reportedly spent $250 million on the project, it wasn't a total loss. Expanding plants for Edsel production left Ford with surplus capacity that came in mighty handy when its new 1960 Falcon immediately ran away with the compact market.

Had it been a truly different car introduced three to five years either side of 1958, the Edsel might be with us yet. Instead, it's become a monument to the cynicism of an age when Detroit thought buyers didn't know—or care—about the difference between style and substance.

1959 Corsair convertible coupe

1960 Villager 6-passenger station wagon

Specifications

1958

Ranger (wb 118.0; wgns-116.0)		Wght	Price	Prod
21	sdn 2d	3,729	2,519	4,615
22	sdn 4d	3,805	2,592	6,576
23	htp cpe	3,724	2,593	5,546
24	htp sdn	3,796	2,678	3,077
26	Roundup wgn 2d	3,761	2,876	963
27	Villager wgn 4d, 6p	3,827	2,933	2,294
28	Villager wgn 4d, 9p	3,900	2,990	978
Pacer (wb 118.0; wgns-116.0)				
42	sdn 4d	3,826	2,375	6,083
43	htp cpe	3,773	2,805	6,139
44	htp sdn	3,857	2,863	4,959
45	conv cpe	3,909	3,028	1,876
47	Bermuda wgn 4d, 6p	3,853	3,190	1,456
48	Bermuda wgn 4d, 9p	3,919	3,247	779
Corsair (wb 124.0)				
63	htp cpe	4,134	3,346	3,312
64	htp sdn	4,235	3,425	5,880
Citation (wb 124.0)		**Wght**	**Price**	**Prod**
83	htp cpe	4,136	3,535	2,535
84	htp sdn	4,230	3,615	5,112
85	conv cpe	4,311	3,801	930

1958 Engines	bore×stroke	bhp	availability
V-8, 361.0	4.05×3.50	303	S-Rangr, Pacer
V-8, 410.0	4.20×3.70	345	S-Corsair, Citation

1959

Ranger (wb 120.0)		Wght	Price	Prod
57F	htp sdn	3,682	2,756	2,352
58D	sdn 4d	3,774	2,684	12,814
63F	htp cpe	3,591	2,691	5,474
64C	sdn 2d	3,547	2,629	7,778
Corsair (wb 120.0)				
57B	htp sdn	3,709	2,885	1,694
58B	sdn 4d	3,696	2,812	3,301
63B	htp cpe	3,778	2,819	2,315
76E	conv cpe	3,790	3,072	1,343
Station Wagon (wb 120.0)				
71E	Villager wgn 4d, 9P	3,930	3,055	2,133
Station Wagon		**Wght**	**Price**	**Prod**
71F	Villager wgn 4d, 6P	3,842	2,971	5,687

1959 Engines	bore×stroke	bhp	availability
I-6, 223.0	3.62×3.60	145	O-Rangr, Wag
V-8, 292.0	3.75×3.30	200	S-Rangr, Wag
V-8, 332.0	4.00×3.30	225	S-Cors; O-others
V-8, 361.0	4.05×3.50	303	O-all

1960

Ranger (wb 120.0)		Wght	Price	Prod
57A	htp sdn	3,718	2,770	135
58A	sdn 4d	3,700	2,697	1,288
63A	htp cpe	3,641	2,705	295
64A	sdn 2d	3,601	2,643	777
76B	conv cpe	3,836	3,000	76
Station Wagon (wb 120.0)				
71E	Villager wgn 4d, 9P	4,046	3,072	59
71F	Villager wgn 4d, 6P	4,029	2,989	216

1960 Engines	bore×stroke	bhp	availability
I-6, 223.0	3.62×3.50	145	O-all
V-8, 292.0	3.75×3.30	185	S-all
V-8, 352.0	4.00×3.50	300	O-all

Essex

Introduced in 1919, the Hudson-built Essex was a sales winner in its first two years, offering a lively four-cylinder engine and the first closed body types among popular-price mass-production cars. But when Essex adopted a less-reliable six in 1924, its image and popularity suffered accordingly. Though this engine was enlarged and improved in 1930-31, Essex failed to win back its early reputation for ruggedness and durability. Hudson Motor Company might have failed with it except for a happy accident that saved the day.

Roy D. Chapin, one of Hudson's founders, was still active in the company during 1930-32, even though he was working for the Hoover Administration. When Hoover was voted out of office, Chapin immediately returned to Hudson and prepared to make some long-needed changes in the price-leading Essex line. For 1932, he ordered the six enlarged from 160 to 193 cubic inches, which lifted horsepower from 58 to 70. This improved engine initially powered Pacemaker and Challenger models on a 113-inch wheelbase (unchanged since 1930). But at midyear, Chapin dumped it into a new 106-inch-wheelbase series dubbed Terraplane. Said one memorable ad: "In the air, it's aeroplaning; on the water, it's hydroplaning; on the ground, hot diggety dog, that's Terraplaning!"

The Essex Terraplane turned Hudson around in 1932-33. It was fast (up to 80 mph), economical (up to 25 mpg), and cheap (as little as $425). Adding to its appeal was the 1933 option of a 94-bhp 243.9-cid straight eight.

Essex Terraplanes set numerous speed marks, including over 100 stock-car records. The public responded with enthusiasm—so much so that Hudson dropped the Essex name after 1933 to make Terraplane a marque in its own right (*see entry*).

1930 Challenger Six Sun sedan two-door

1931 Challenger Six 2-passenger coupe

Specifications

1930 - 68,593 built

Challenger Six (wb 113.0)	Wght	Price	Prod
rdstr 2-4P	2,550	695	—
phtn 5P	2,620	695	—
cpe 2P	2,660	650	—
cpe 2-4P	2,700	685	—
coach 5P	2,730	650	—
Standard sdn 4d	2,805	715	—
Touring sdn 4d	2,850	775	—
brougham 4d	2,850	795	—
Sun sdn 4d	2,760	695	—

1930 Engine	bore×stroke	bhp	availability
I-6, 160.0	2.75×4.50	58	S-all

1931 - 47,418 built

Challenger Six (wb 113.0; 7P-119.0)	Wght	Price	Prod
rdstr 2-4P	2,400	725	—
cpe 2P	2,595	595	—
cpe 2-4P	2,645	645	—
Special cpe 2-4P	2,800	725	—
coach 5P	2,690	595	—
Standard sdn 4d	2,750	695	—
Touring sdn 4d	2,815	775	—
Town sdn 4d	2,815	735	—
Special sdn 4d	2,950	855	—
sdn 7P	2,945	895	—

1931 Engine	bore×stroke	bhp	availability
I-6, 160.0	2.75×4.50	58	S-all

1932 - 18,700 built

Pacemaker (wb 113.0)	Wght	Price	Prod
phtn 5P	—	765	—
bus cpe 2P	2,775	695	—
cpe 2-4P	2,840	745	—
Special cpe 2-4P	2,895	795	—
conv cpe 2-4P	2,760	845	—
coach 5P	2,860	705	—
Standard sdn 4d	2,980	775	—
Town sdn 4d	2,950	745	—
Special sdn 4d	3,010	845	—
Standard (wb 113.0)			
bus cpe	—	660	—
cpe 4P	2,750	710	—
coach 5P	2,785	665	—
Standard sdn 4d	2,870	735	—
Terraplane (wb 106.0) - 14,125 built			
rdstr 2P	2,010	425	—
phtn 5P	2,170	495	—
bus cpe 2P	2,135	470	—
cpe 2-4P	2,190	510	—
coach 5P	2,205	475	—
Standard sdn 4d	2,250	550	—
Sport rdstr 2-4P	2,110	525	—
Special bus cpe 2P	2,135	510	—
Special cpe 2-4P	2,190	550	—
Spec conv cpe 2-4P	2,145	610	—
Special coach 5P	2,205	515	—
Special sdn 4d	2,250	590	—

1932 Engine	bore×stroke	bhp	availability
I-6, 193.0	2.94×4.75	70	S-all

1933

Terraplane Six (wb 106.0)	Wght	Price	Prod*
rdstr 2P	2,135	425	—
phtn 5P	2,260	515	—
cpe 2P	2,220	485	—
cpe 2-4P	2,260	535	—
coach 5P	2,275	505	—
sdn 4d	2,345	555	—
Special rdstr 2-4P	2,220	505	—
Special cpe 2-4P	2,310	555	—
Spec conv cpe 2-4P	2,275	575	—
Special coach 5P	2,335	525	—
Special sdn 5P	2,415	575	—
Terraplane Special Six (wb 113.0)			
Spt rdstr 2-4P	2,290	505	—
phtn 5P	—	535	—
bus cpe 2P	2,320	505	—
cpe 2-4P	2,330	555	—
conv cpe 2-4P	—	575	—
coach 5P	2,270	525	—
sdn 4d	2,420	575	—
Terraplane DeLuxe Six (wb 113.0)			
cpe 2P	2,395	585	—
cpe 2-4P	2,405	635	—
conv cpe 2-4P	2,395	655	—
coach 5P	2,450	605	—
sdn 4d	2,500	655	—
Terraplane Eight (wb 113.0)			
rdstr 2P	2,410	565	—
rdstr 2-4P	2,455	625	—
cpe 2P	2,485	615	—
cpe 2-4P	2,545	655	—
conv cpe 2-4P	2,495	695	—
coach 5P	2,565	615	—
sdn 4d	2,640	675	—
Terraplane DeLuxe Eight (wb 113.0)			
cpe 2P	2,540	685	—
cpe 2-4P	2,600	725	—
conv cpe 2-4P	2,550	765	—
coach 5P	2,625	685	—
sdn 4d	2,700	745	—

* Production not available.

1933 Engines	bore×stroke	bhp	availability
I-6, 193.0	2.94×4.75	70	S-all Sixes
I-8, 243.9	2.94×4.50	94	S-all Eights

Note: Essex production figures shown above are based on serial number spans listed in industry sources and may be presumed reliable, though it is always possible that some numbers were skipped. For comparison, Essex calendar year production, as reported by Don Butler in *The History of Hudson*, was as follows:

1930	76,158	**1932**	34,007
1931	40,338	**1933**	38,150

See "Terraplane" for 1934-37 models and "Hudson" for 1938-39 Terraplane models.

Excalibur

Noted industrial designer Brooks Stevens has given us a number of interesting cars, none more exciting than his own Excalibur. The first was actually a series of light race-and-ride roadsters built in 1951 with "vintage-modern" bodywork on a 100-inch-wheelbase Henry J chassis. Though strictly a private effort, these "Excalibur Js" did well enough in competition for Stevens to hope that Kaiser-Frazer might build his design for sale to the public. But K-F had just failed with its fiberglass-bodied Darrin two-seater and would flee the U.S. market after 1955, leaving unfilled Stevens' dream of a new car with classic '30s styling.

The dream got a another chance in 1963 at Studebaker, where Stevens had been a design consultant for four years. Having completed clever, low-cost facelifts on the compact Lark and sporty Hawk coupe, he was asked by company president Sherwood Egbert to devise some 1964 show cars that would bolster Studebaker's public image in the face of steadily declining sales. The firm had just closed its century-old South Bend, Indiana, plant, canceled both the Hawk and Egbert's radical Avanti, and retreated with a reduced Lark line to Hamilton, Ontario, Canada. With things looking so terminal, Egbert hoped Stevens' specials would convince people that Studebaker still had a future.

Stevens did his best, but time permitted only a trio of dolled-up Larks that didn't make much of an impression at Chicago in February 1964. But for the next major event, the annual New York Auto Show in April, Stevens was determined to have something that would "get people to come to that damn booth." Though Egbert had departed (stricken by cancer), his successor, Byers Burlingame, agreed to cooperate.

The idea was a "contemporary classic," a new car that looked like the Mercedes SSK that Stevens once owned. "I wanted this to be a replica [for those] who could not play in the collector's market even then [and for those who wanted] a "two-way classic,' something that you can be sure will get you back home..." Stevens duly rendered a dashing neoclassic roadster body, and a Lark Daytona convertible chassis was delivered to his Milwaukee studios with power front-disc brakes and supercharged, 290-horsepower Studebaker 289 V-8. The result, labeled "Studebaker SS," was completed in just six weeks by Stevens and his sons, David and William.

No sooner did it reach New York than Studebaker backed out. A "contemporary classic," said company officials, conflicted with their newly embraced image of the "common-sense car." Undeterred, Stevens arranged to exhibit the SS in a separate space. Luckily, he wound up across from a hot-dog stand, but the cycle-fendered two-seater would have drawn crowds anyway. It was, in fact, a sensation, and dozens of inquiries from would-be owners prompted the Stevens sons to form SS Automobiles in August. By 1966, they had built 56 copies of a mildly modified version bearing the Stevens-registered name Excalibur and also called SS.

Studebaker, meanwhile, had ceased building cars at last, thus ending the availability of its 289 V-8, but General Motors friends Ed Cole and "Bunkie" Knudsen agreed to provide the Stevens family with Chevrolet 327s in 300-bhp Corvette tune. This change made the lithe 2100-pound Excalibur a blistering performer. Even with standard 3.31:1 rear axle, 0-60 mph took less than five seconds, a big improvement over the Studey-powered car's seven seconds. And projected top speed was 160 mph!

Though undeniably old, the 109-inch-wheelbase Studebaker chassis had several advantages for a "contemporary classic." Unlike newer torque-box designs, it was quite narrow and thus a perfect fit for the slim, '30s-style Excalibur body; and as a convertible platform, it was firmly X-braced. Still, it required considerable reworking to ensure safe handling with such a high power-to-weight ratio.

That task, and many others, fell to David Stevens. The vin-

1964 Studebaker SS roadster (Excalibur prototype)

1965-69 Series I SSK roadster

1966-69 Series I SS phaeton

1970-74 Series II SS phaeton

1975-79 Series III SS roadster

1975-79 Series III phaeton

1980-84 Series IV phaeton

tage-style cowl, for example, forced a lower steering column and pedals. He also had to decrease spring rates and alter caster and camber, but the result was a car as fast on curves as it was on straights. This modified chassis continued under all "Series I" Excaliburs built through 1969.

Brooks Stevens, of course, was responsible for the styling, which was deliberately planned as an evocative but not line-for-line rendition of the 1928 Mercedes SSK. Interestingly, though, initial sales literature was done in prewar Mercedes style.

Quality was uncompromising from the start, and would continue to distinguish Excalibur from the motley group of "replicars" it inspired. As just one example, Brooks Stevens turned to Mercedes-Benz's original German supplier for the simulated outside exhaust pipes and used French-built freestanding headlamps closely resembling original SSK equipment.

The earliest Excaliburs were bodied in hand-hammered aluminum, but fiberglass was soon substituted. Also for reasons of cost and practicality, the prototype's sheet-brass radiator was exchanged for a cast-aluminum affair. Atop it was Brooks' "sword-in-circle" mascot that simulated, but didn't infringe upon, M-B's jealously guarded three-pointed star. Dominating the cockpit was a full set of white-on-black Stewart-Warner gauges in a vintage-style dash with engine-turned metal appliqué. Seats were modified Studebaker buckets covered in vinyl. With all this, the Excalibur's announced price looked unbelievably low: $7250 for a hand-built car with one of the most-competent chassis in the business.

Encouraged by intense initial interest in the SS—and ready buyers—the Stevens family added two companion models in 1966: a more-elaborate roadster with full fenders and running boards, and, late in the year, a four-place "phaeton" convertible. The latter was surprisingly roomy. David Stevens proudly pointed to top-up headroom within an inch of a Cadillac Eldorado's and legroom that was actually greater. Also in '66, the firm changed its name to Excalibur Automobile Corporation.

Prices inevitably escalated, reaching a $10,000 minimum by '69, but Excaliburs remained a remarkable value. Not until 1976 would they become $20,000 automobiles, and then only because of inflation and the cost of federally mandated safety and emissions equipment. At least the hikes were made less painful by progressively upgraded materials and features. By 1969, no-cost features had expanded to include air conditioning, heater/defroster, variable-ratio power steering with tilt wheel, power front-disc brakes, steel-belted radial tires on chrome-plated wire wheels, the same as twin sidemount spares, luggage rack, AM/FM stereo, leather seats, air horns, driving lights, rear air shocks, "Positraction" limited-slip differential, and self-shift Turbo Hydra-Matic transmission (the last two from GM, of course).

Excalibur production would never be high, but was never intended to be. This was, after all, a labor of love, a gift from the Stevens family to enthusiasts of traditional motoring in the grand Classic manner. After the 56 SS roadsters of 1965 came 90 Series I models in 1966, but production never topped 100 per year through 1972.

Announced in 1970 were Series II Excaliburs with new 111-inch wheelbase and the Corvette's latest 350 V-8. The original roadster was dropped, but the other two models returned at higher $12,000 starting prices. A notable advance was a modern new box-section chassis purpose-designed by David Stevens around Corvette suspension components, thus ousting the old Lark frame (Excalibur's inventory had run out anyway). Turbo Hydra-Matic moved to the options list in favor of a GM "Muncie" four-speed manual gearbox. Independent rear suspension and standard all-disc power brakes combined with Goodyear Polyglas tires on specially designed wire wheels to provide a fine blend of ride comfort and adroit handling. Acceleration was a bit slower despite unchanged horsepower—but not much: A Series II could scale 0-60 in six seconds and reach a genuine 150 mph.

Prices and production began taking off with the Series III, which arrived in 1975 (Excalibur has never adhered to strict model years). This was basically the Series II design modified for tightening safety/emissions rules, but not so much as to compromise styling or roadability that were, by now, Excalibur hallmarks. Besides "shock mounted solid aluminum alloy [bumpers that] meet government standards for absorbing impact," Series IIIs boasted fuller clamshell-type fenders and standard high-back bucket seats covered in leather and made—like most of the car—by Excalibur itself. The main mechanical alteration was switching to Chevy's big-block 454 V-8, which could be emissions-tuned with less loss of power and torque than the small-block 350. Both roadster and phaeton carried identical 1975 starting prices of $18,900, more than double the original figure of a decade before. And prices would go much higher, reaching $28,600 by the end of this series in 1979.

By any standard, Excalibur was still a tiny automaker, but the Stevens brothers would not be rushed. Nor did they want to dilute their market with too much of a good thing. As it had since 1969, the more-practical four-place phaeton continued outselling the two-seat roadster, but total volume remained minuscule even for a specialty maker. The Series III saw but 1141 over five years, versus 342 for the Series II and 359 for the original Series I.

Excalibur had traveled far since David and William C. "Steve" Stevens built their first cars (the latter even worked on the assembly line until 1968). Striking evidence of their progress arrived in 1980 with an elegant new Series IV. More luxury tourer than lightweight sports machine, it was the most radically changed Excalibur in history. Wheelbase was stretched to a limousinelike 125 inches, and there were more standard accoutrements than any previous Excalibur. Styling, now by David Stevens, remained firmly "Classic," but was smoother and sleeker in the way that the late-'30s Mercedes 500/540K was evolved from the SS/SSK. The phaeton acquired a lift-off hardtop plus fully powered soft top; the roadster gained a rakish rumble seat.

Most engineering changes came per federal edicts. The most notable was a vastly smaller Chevy V-8, the well-known 5.0-liter/305-cid unit, linked to four-speed overdrive automatic as the sole transmission choice. Excalibur feared a larger engine would have lowered fuel mileage to the point of having to pay fines under Corporate Average Fuel Economy rules, something the tiny firm just couldn't afford. As a result, customers were saddled with a much bigger and heavier Excalibur that was far from exciting on either straights or curves.

With that plus the start of a severe recession and lofty new inflation-fueled prices—initially near $40,000—Excalibur sales nosedived. It couldn't have happened at a worse time for the Stevens family, who faced burdensome new overhead costs from a heavy revamping of their suburban Milwaukee plant (to improve quality). The result was a steadily worsening situation that forced the brothers to file for Chapter 11 bankruptcy in mid-1986. Ironically, this came just after Excalibur marked its 20th anniversary with its first commemoratives: 50 roadsters and 50 phaetons bearing two-tone exteriors with chrome sweepspears and pewter plaques, plus interiors trimmed in walnut and Connolly leather.

But then came help in the form of Henry Warner, president of Acquisition Company of Wisconsin, who bought the Stevens family's interests and reorganized the firm as Excalibur Marketing Corporation. By early 1987, Series IV roadsters and phaetons were again trickling out of Milwaukee as Series V models. Their main difference was a more-potent 350 Chevy V-8 option that partly redressed the weak performance of the standard 305. At midyear, EMC revealed a whopping four-door Touring Sedan on a 144-inch-wheelbase chassis (essentially a 20-inch stretch of the phaeton's square-tube ladder frame). Measuring 224 inches long and weighing 4400 pounds, the Touring Sedan was optimistically priced at the same $65,650 figure applied to both open Series Vs, with which it shared frontal styling. Interiors were opulent. A front bench replaced the phaeton's buckets, and the long wheelbase made for a rear compartment worthy of a '30s Cadillac Sixteen. Also announced was an even-more-extravagant 204-inch-wheelbase "grand limousine." David Stevens had earlier conceived both these closed models as sales-building "line extensions."

But none of this served to boost sales and thus attract needed capital to offset mounting debts in an economy again gone slack. Nor did a three-year, $9-million lease deal with a Chicago concern involving some 150 cars. As a result, Excalibur went bankrupt again, production ceasing in June 1990.

1980-84 Series IV phaeton

1981-86 Series IV roadster

1985 20th Anniversary Signature Series phaeton

But Excalibur wasn't quite dead. In November 1991, German Michael Timmer bought the firm for $1.33 million amid charges that the Warner regime engaged in odometer fraud, installed some used parts, failed to meet federal passive-restraint rules, and generally did its best to "kill" the company. Timmer seemed bent on saving it, putting $1 million toward plant improvements with an eye to resuming production by April 1992. There would be four models: Series V roadster, phaeton and sedan, plus, surprisingly, a revived Series III roadster. Prices were targeted for the $50,000-$75,000 range.

Unfortunately, Timmer ran out of money before he could build any cars, so Excalibur was again bankrupt by early '92. But it was still alive, thanks to a new rescue by the German father-and-son team of Udo and Jens Geitlinger, who'd made a fortune in real estate. With help from production boss Scott Dennison and some 33 other employees still hanging on from prior regimes, Jens picked up where Timmer left off, issuing an updated Series III roadster called the "Limited Edition 100."

Besides design changes for all the latest safety and emissions standards, including a driver-side air bag, the Geitlinger Series III carried the new 300-bhp Corvette LT1 V-8 teamed with four-speed automatic or optional six-speed ZF manual. Price was set at $89,842. At the same time, the big limo was to get a new dash and GM suspension to sell for a staggering $124,774. The other Series V cars weren't forgotten, being muscled up to L98 Corvette power and starting prices of $74,986 for the roadster and $77,691 for the phaeton. The Geitlingers eyed total first-year production of 60-80 units, and Dennison predicted 120 Excaliburs per year starting in 1993, with some two-thirds earmarked for export.

But the world market had also changed dramatically, and Excalibur could no longer do business as usual. Accordingly, the firm diversified in 1993, first by adding a replica Shelby-Cobra with some interesting deviations from the original, then by becoming a contract supplier of various "accessories" like luggage racks and "aero" cab extensions for trucks. Car production ended in 1997, but accessory production continued.

But the world market had also changed dramatically, and Excalibur could no longer do business as usual. Accordingly, the firm diversified in 1993, first by adding a replica Shelby-Cobra with some interesting deviations from the original, then by becoming a contract supplier of various "accessories" like luggage racks and "aero" cab extensions for trucks. Motorcycle trailers were also built. Car production ended in 1997, but accessory production continued until the early 2000s when Excalibur once again went into receivership.

In 2003, Alice Preston, who had worked with Brooks Stevens since 1963, purchased the assets of Excalibur Automobile Corp. The company continues selling parts and performing restorations on the 3200 Excaliburs produced. Excalibur hopes to someday resume auto production using its former body styles.

1985 20th Anniversary Signature Series Roadster

1993 Limited Edition roadster

1993 Series V phaeton

1994 Cobra roadster replica

1995 Excalibur Limousine

Specifications

1965

Series I (wb 109.0)*	Wght	Price	Prod
SSK rdstr	2,100	7,250	56

1965 Engine	bore×stroke	bhp	availability
V-8, 289.0	3.56×3.62	290	S-all

1966

Series I (wb 109.0)*	Wght	Price	Prod
SSK rdstr	2,100	7,250	87
rdstr	2,500	8,000	
phtn	2,500	7,950	3

1966 Engine	bore×stroke	bhp	availability
V-8, 327.0	4.00×3.25	300	S-all

1967

Series I (wb 109.0)*	Wght	Price	Prod
SSK rdstr	2,100	8,000	38
rdstr	2,500	8,500	
phtn	2,600	8,250	33

1967 Engines	bore×stroke	bhp	availability
V-8, 327.0	4.00×3.25	300	S-all
V-8, 327.0	4.00×3.25	300+	O-all

1968

Series I (wb 109.0)*	Wght	Price	Prod
SSK rdstr	2,300	8,650	37
rdstr	2,500	8,650	
phtn	2,600	9,850	20

1968 Engines	bore×stroke	bhp	availability
V-8, 327.0	4.00×3.25	300	S-all
V-8, 327.0	4.00×3.25	300+	O-all

1969

Series I (wb 109.0)*	Wght	Price	Prod
SSK rdstr	2,400	9,000	47
rdstr	2,550	9,000	
phtn	2,650	10,000	44

1969 Engines	bore×stroke	bhp	availability
V-8, 327.0	4.00×3.25	300	S-all
V-8, 327.0	4.00×3.25	300+	O-all

* Production 1965-69; SSK 168; rdstr 59; phtn 89.

1970

Series II (wb 111.0)	Wght	Price	Prod
SSK rdstr	2,750	12,000	11
SS rdstr	2,900	12,500	
SS phtn	3,000	12,900	26

1970 Engine	bore×stroke	bhp	availability
V-8, 350.0	4.00×3.48	300	S-all

1971

Excalibur records show no 1971 model production.

1972

Series II (wb 111.0)	Wght	Price	Prod
SS rdstr	2,900	12,500	13
SS phtn	3,000	13,500	52

1972 Engine	bore×stroke	bhp	availability
V-8, 454.0	4.25×4.00	—	S-all

1973

Series II (wb 111.0)	Wght	Price	Prod
SS rdstr	2,900	13,500	22
SS phtn	3,000	16,000	100

1973 Engine	bore×stroke	bhp	availability
V-8, 454.0	4.25×4.00	270	S-all

1974

Series II (wb 111.0)	Wght	Price	Prod
SS rdstr	2,900	17,000	26
SS phtn	3,000	17,000	92

1974 Engine	bore×stroke	bhp	availability
V-8, 454.0	4.25×4.00	275	S-all

1975

Series III (wb 112.0)	Wght	Price	Prod
SS rdstr	4,350	18,900	8
SS phtn	4,350	18,900	82

1975 Engine	bore×stroke	bhp	availability
V-8, 454.0	4.25×4.00	215	S-all

1976

Series III (wb 112.0)	Wght	Price	Prod
SS rdstr	4,350	21,500	11
SS phtn	4,350	21,500	173

1976 Engine	bore×stroke	bhp	availability
V-8, 454.0	4.25×4.00	215	S-all

1977

Series III (wb 112.0)	Wght	Price	Prod
SS rdstr	4,350	23,600	15
SS phtn	4,350	23,600	222

1977 Engine	bore×stroke	bhp	availability
V-8, 454.0	4.25×4.00	215	S-all

1978

Series III (wb 112.0)	Wght	Price	Prod
SS rdstr	4,350	25,600	15
SS phtn	4,350	25,600	248

1978 Engine	bore×stroke	bhp	availability
V-8, 454.0	4.25×4.00	215	S-all

1979

Series III (wb 112.0)	Wght	Price	Prod
SS rdstr	4,350	28,600	27
SS phtn	4,350	28,600	340

1979 Engine	bore×stroke	bhp	availability
V-8, 350.0	4.00×3.48	180	S-all

1980

Series IV (wb 125.0)	Wght	Price	Prod
SS rdstr	4,300	—	0
SS phtn	4,300	37,700	93

1980 Engine	bore×stroke	bhp	availability
V-8, 305.0	3.74×3.48	155	S-all

1981

Series IV (wb 125.0)	Wght	Price	Prod
rdstr	4,400	50,000	36
phtn	4,400	46,500	199

1981 Engine	bore×stroke	bhp	availability
V-8, 305.0	3.74×3.48	155	S-all

1982

Series IV (wb 125.0)	Wght	Price	Prod
rdstr	4,400	57,500	60
phtn	4,400	52,000	152

1982 Engine	bore×stroke	bhp	availability
V-8, 305.0	3.74×3.48	155	S-all

1983

Series IV (wb 125.0)	Wght	Price	Prod
rdstr	4,400	59,500	—
phtn	4,400	55,500	—

1983 Engines	bore×stroke	bhp	availability
V-8, 305.0	3.74×3.48	155	S-all

1984

Series IV (wb 125.0)	Wght	Price	Prod
rdstr	4,400	59,500	—
phtn	4,400	57,000	—

1984 Engine	bore×stroke	bhp	availability
V-8, 305.0	3.74×3.48	155	S-all

1985

Signature Series (wb 125.0)	Wght	Price	Prod
rdstr	4,400	62,000	—
phtn	4,400	59,500	—

1985 Engine	bore×stroke	bhp	availability
V-8, 305.0	3.74×3.48	155	S-all

1986

Series IV (wb 125.0)	Wght	Price	Prod
rdstr	—	65,000	*
phtn	—	65,000	*

1986 Engine	bore×stroke	bhp	availability
V-8, 305.0	3.74×3.48	155	S-all

* Specifications and prices were announced for 1986, but the Excalibur Company went into bankruptcy. Production resumed in December 1986 with the 1987 models.

1987

(wb 124.0)	Wght	Price	Prod
rdstr	4,400	—	—
phtn	4,400	—	—

1987 Engine	bore×stroke	bhp	availability
V-8, 305.0	3.74×3.48	170	S-all

1988

(wb 124.0; Touring Sdn 144.0)	Wght	Price	Prod
rdstr 2d	4,400	65,650	—
phtn 2d	4,400	65,650	—
touring sdn 4d	4,400	65,650	—

1988 Engines	bore×stroke	bhp	availability
V-8, 305.0	3.74×3.48	170	S-all
V-8, 350.0	4.00×3.48	—	O-all

1989

(wb 124.0; Touring Sdn 144.0)	Wght	Price	Prod
rdstr 2d	4,400	71,865	—
phtn 2d	4,400	71,865	—
touring sdn 4d	4,400	72,325	—

1989 Engines	bore×stroke	bhp	availability
V-8, 305.0	3.74×3.48	170	S-all
V-8, 350.0	4.00×3.48	—	O-all

1990

(wb 124.0; Touring Sdn 144.0)	Wght	Price	Prod
rdstr 2d	4,400	—	—
phtn 2d	4,400	—	—
touring sdn 4d	4,400	—	—

1990 Engines	bore×stroke	bhp	availability
V-8, 305.0	3.74×3.48	170	S-all
V-8, 350.0	4.00×3.48	—	O-all

1993

	Wght	Price	Prod
Cobra (wb 94.5)	2,500	—	21
Limited Edition (wb 112.0)	3,171	89,842	6
Phaeton (wb 125.1)	4,389	77,691	3
Roadster (wb 124.0)	4,356	74,986	1

1993 Engines	bore×stroke	bhp	availability
V-8, 302.0	4.00×3.00	215	S-Cobra
V-8, 350.0	4.00×3.48	245	S-Phtn, Rdstr
V-8, 350.0	4.00×3.48	300	S-Limited Ed.

1994

	Wght	Price	Prod
Cobra (wb 94.5)	2,500	—	35
Limited Edition (wb 112.0)	3,171	—	14
Roadster (wb 124.0)	4,356	—	2

1994 Engines	bore×stroke	bhp	availability
V-8, 302.0	4.00×3.00	215	S-Cobra
V-8, 350.0	4.00×3.48	245	S-Roadster
V-8, 350.0	4.00×3.48	300	S-Limited Ed.

1995

	Wght	Price	Prod
Cobra (wb 94.5)	2,500	—	46
Limited Edition (wb 112.0)	3,171	—	7
Phaeton (wb 125.1)	4,389	—	2
Roadster (wb 124.0)	4,356	—	1
Limousine (wb 172.0)	5,200	124,774	1

1995 Engines	bore×stroke	bhp	availability
V-8, 302.0	4.00×3.00	215	S-Cobra
V-8, 350.0	4.00×3.48	245	S-Phton, Rdstr, Limousine
V-8, 350.0	4.00×3.48	300	S-Limited Ed.

1996

	Wght	Price	Prod
Cobra (wb 94.5)	2,500	51,807	—
Limited Edition (wb 112.0)	3,171	74,897	—
Phaeton (wb 125.1)	4,389	98,897	—
Roadster (wb 124.0)	4,356	104,595	—
Limousine (wb 172.0)	5,200	159,000	—

1996 Engines	bore×stroke	bhp	availability
V-8, 302.0	4.00×3.00	215	S-Cobra
V-8S, 302.0	4.00×3.00	325	O-Cobra
V-8, 350.0	4.00×3.48	245	S-Phton, Rdstr, Limousine
V-8, 350.0	4.00×3.48	300	S-Limited Ed.

Ford

Founded in 1903, Ford Motor Company skyrocketed from obscurity to dominate the American auto industry in less than 12 years. The foundation of this unparalleled success was the world's first mass-produced car: the cheap, simple Model T, whose lovable quirkiness was matched only by that of its creator, company founder Henry Ford. Henry's decision to abandon his treasured "Tin Lizzie" after 19 years and a staggering 15-million cars—the last not very different from the first—came almost too late, and his company lost a lot in money and goodwill during the long changeover to the belated new Model A.

Yet despite keen competition from an aggressive Chevrolet and newcomer Plymouth, the Model A was a success, almost perfectly timed for the Great Depression that began soon after its 1928 debut. Ford built more than 1.1 million cars for 1930—almost twice as many as Chevrolet and more than 14 times as many as Plymouth.

The 1930 Ford Model A received a number of changes that seem minor now but were major at the time. All models retained the "little Lincoln" styling crafted by Henry's artistic son Edsel (who was named Ford Motor Company president in 1919), but the fenders were lower and wider, the hoodline was higher, and stainless steel replaced nickel plate on the radiator and headlight shells. Enhancing the lower look was a switch to balloon tires on smaller 19-inch wheels (replacing 21-inchers). Running changes made during the model year included a numerically higher steering ratio for less effort at the wheel, and standardization of vacuum-operated windshield wipers that had previously been an extra-cost accessory.

As before, the Model A spanned a wide range of body types: coupes, sport coupes, roadsters, and cabriolets with or without rumble seat; "Tudor" and "Fordor" sedans; a surprisingly dignified Town Sedan; and a wood-body station wagon. Most could be had with Standard or DeLuxe trim, the latter typically featuring brighter colors and spiffier interiors. Prices ranged from just $435 for the basic two-seat roadster to $660 for the Town Sedan. There was also a very deluxe Town Car with canvas-covered formal roof. Not many sold at $1200—a mere 96 for the model year. Arriving in June was a $625 DeLuxe two-door phaeton, a jaunty five-seater with standard left-sidemount spare, chrome trunk rack, leather upholstery, and lower steering wheel and windshield. Another new style, bowing in the autumn of 1930, was the Victoria coupe sporting a slanted windshield, soon to be commonplace throughout Detroit.

Little visible change occurred for 1931 save a painted section atop the front of the radiator shell, which made identification easy. Chevrolet was still pushing hard, and Ford yielded the top spot in 1931 model-year volume, though only by some 4100 cars. Ford wouldn't top Chevy again until 1934 despite scoring a coup with America's first low-priced V-8.

Henry Ford had once contemplated a radical X-8 engine for the long-overdue Model T replacement, but ultimately settled for a more-conventional V-8 on which Ford engineers discreetly began work in 1930. But it was delayed by the peculiar conditions Henry imposed on his engineers, so the Model A appeared

1930 Model A DeLuxe 2-passenger coupe

1931 Model A Victoria 5-passenger coupe

1931 Model A DeLuxe roadster

1931 Model A convertible sedan

1932 Model 18 V-8 DeLuxe Fordor sedan

1932 Model 18 V-8 2/4-passenger sport coupe

with only four-cylinder power as an interim measure. Model A production ended in autumn 1931, though sales continued through April 1932. Then came a revised four-cylinder car, the Model B. Both this and the new 1932 V-8 Model 18 shared evolutionary styling, a 106.5-inch wheelbase (up three inches from the A's), and the same broad body-style array. The big difference, of course, was under the hood. The V-8 was a tremendous bargain: Standard roadster, coupe, and phaeton all listed below $500. Still, many buyers were wary, so Ford kept four-cylinder cars through 1934.

Ford's first V-8 was that now-famous cast-iron flathead that initially delivered 65 horsepower from 221 cubic inches. That compared with 40/50 horsepower from the 200.5-cid Model A/B four. With a relatively sensational top speed of 78 mph, the peppy V-8 Ford caused a storm of public interest, garnering over 50,000 advance orders. Millions flocked to see it on its March 1932 unveiling.

The old man kept a close watch over the V-8's development, badgering his engineers and telling them what to do. His perceived need for getting the engine to market as soon as possible left insufficient time for durability testing, so troubles surfaced early. Cylinder-head cracks and excessive oil burning were the most common, but some engine mounts worked loose and ignition problems cropped up. Though Ford replaced pistons by the thousands to ease owner worries, the engine difficulties hurt sales. But they'd be cleared up soon enough, and the V-8 became known as a reliable powerplant that could stand considerable "heating up." Hot rodders loved it.

Fords looked more flowing for 1933, reflecting Detroit's swing to streamlining. Edsel Ford had been an important force in

1933 Model 40 V-8 DeLuxe Tudor sedan

1935 Model 48 V-8 DeLuxe 2-passenger coupe

1934 Model 40A V-8 convertible coupe

1935 Official Pace Car convertible sedan

Dearborn design for some time, and his tasteful new '33 Ford was universally applauded. The hood now extended back to the windshield, fenders were "skirted" and dipped low in front, sharp corners were rounded off, and rear-hinged doors appeared on closed models. Helping all this was a wheelbase lengthened to 112 inches (where it would remain through 1940) and a wheel diameter shrunk to 17. V-8 durability kept improving, and the frame was completely redesigned. With V-8 production at full strength, Ford's model-year volume rose by 100,000 cars—impressive for difficult 1933, but not enough to beat Chevrolet. Still, the speedy Ford V-8 was attracting a legion of fans. Among them was no less than John Dillinger, who wrote Henry to praise the product—an unsolicited testimonial from Public Enemy Number One.

Appearance became smoother still on 1934's 40A line. The V-8 itself got a new carburetor and manifold that increased advertised horsepower to 85—some claim actual power was 90. By now, most of its early problems were just bad memories. The four-cylinder engine was breathing its last. The Standard two-passenger coupe still sold for little more than $500, while the DeLuxe Fordor cost only $615. Safety glass was newly featured on closed models.

The Ford station wagon, introduced as a 1929 Model A, had a body constructed of birch or maple supplied by the Mingel Company of Kentucky; assembly was by Murray and Briggs in Detroit. Starting in 1935, Ford built these bodies itself in a plant at Iron Mountain on Michigan's Upper Peninsula, an ideal location because of nearby hardwood forests that minimized transportation costs.

A fuller look marked the 1935 Model 48 Fords, with smaller windows and a more prominently Vee'd grille than 1933-34. Also new was an integral trunk for sedans. It added a bulky "bustle," but erased the increasingly old-fashioned external trunk rack and spare tire. A new camshaft and better crankcase ventilation further enhanced the lively V-8, and the frame and rear axle were beefed up. Retained from Model T times was an exceedingly simple suspension: just a solid axle on a transverse leaf spring front and rear, an archaic setup that wouldn't be abandoned for another 13 years. This and the use of mechanical brakes through 1939 left Ford distinctly behind the times, but old Henry believed simpler was better, and he was nothing if not stubborn. Still, he did give in to steel wheels, which replaced traditional wires after 1935.

Ford made only minor styling changes for 1936, but they were good ones. The most obvious were a longer, more-pointed hood and a more sharply Vee'd grille to match. Industry design trends dictated hiding some previously exposed components, so horns now hooted from behind little covered holes astride the grille. Model choices were still numerous, but Standard and DeLuxe were now distinct series, with the latter listing twice as many body styles (seven to 14).

Offerings expanded for '37 with the addition of a small-bore 136-cid V-8, originally devised for the European market to take advantage of tax laws based on displacement. In America it came to be called the "V-8/60," as it produced that much horsepower. But though it made for cheaper new Model 74 Fords in a year of generally higher car prices, it didn't sell nearly as well as expected. Buyers evidently preferred higher performance over lower retail cost. Economy was supposed to be a strong point, but really wasn't. With this development, the familiar 221 flathead became known as the "V-8/85." For 1937 it benefited from improved cooling via relocated water pumps, plus larger insert bearings, and new cast-alloy pistons. It again powered Standards and DeLuxes now designated Model 78. V-8/60s were Standard-trim only.

Responding to GM's 1936 "Turret-Top" bodies, Ford adopted

1936 Model 68 V-8 DeLuxe 2/4-passenger roadster

1936 Model 68 V-8 DeLuxe Tudor sedan

1937 Model 78 V-8 DeLuxe Tudor sedan

all-steel construction for 1937 closed models, belatedly discarding the fabric roof inserts of old. But this was easily overshadowed by crisp new bodies with headlamps nestled firmly in the fenders and a prow-type grille composed of fine horizontal bars (stretched rearward at the top). This and a lighter overall look made the '37 Ford one of the prettiest cars of the decade. President Franklin D. Roosevelt liked it enough to buy a convertible sedan for use at his Warm Springs, Georgia, retreat. In a year of questionable styling throughout the industry, Ford was a standout—proof that streamlining didn't necessarily mean an end to distinctive, eye-pleasing automobiles.

The 1938 line ushered in "two-tier styling" for 60-bhp 82A and 85-bhp 81A series. Where Standards used slightly modified 1937 bodies, DeLuxes sported a different new look. The romantic roadster was history, and the equally old-fashioned phaeton (a throwback to touring-car days) was in its final season. Both

1938 Model 82A Standard 2-passenger coupe

1939 Model 91A DeLuxe 2-passenger coupe

1938 Model 81A DeLuxe Fordor sedan

1940 DeLuxe Fordor sedan

1939 Model 91A DeLuxe Fordor sedan

1941 Super DeLuxe Fordor sedan

body styles had long since lost whatever favor they once had, but Ford was far behind its rivals in realizing this fact (Plymouth's last roadster and phaeton appeared in 1932, Chevrolet's in '35). Closed rumble-seat types were also in their last year. With sales still slow, the V-8/60 line was reduced to just a coupe, Fordor, and Tudor. Styling for all models was a variation on 1937 themes, announced by more-bulbous faces.

DeLuxes were again fully restyled for 1939, bearing a lower Vee'd vertical-bar grille and clean front fenders with integral headlamps. As in recent years, this styling was created by E.T. "Bob" Gregorie under Edsel Ford's guidance. By contrast, that year's Ford Standards looked like warmed-over '38 DeLuxes. The convertible sedan made a final bow, again in the DeLuxe line. Prices rose slightly, now covering a $599-$921 spread. Mechanical changes included internal engine enhancements inspired by the new Mercury and hydraulic instead of mechanical brakes. Old Henry had finally given in on the latter point—three years after Chevrolet and 11 years behind Plymouth. But Ford still couldn't match their independent front suspension, and wouldn't until 1949.

Gregorie made Fords even prettier for 1940—so much so that the DeLuxes in particular have long been coveted collectibles. Sealed-beam headlamps arrived, as elsewhere in Detroit, neatly housed in more-upright fender nacelles. The fenders themselves were beautifully curved to complement body contours; rear fender skirts, long a popular accessory, imparted an even sleeker look. Standards carried a '39 DeLuxe-style vertical-bar grille. DeLuxes bore a chromed horizontal-bar center section flanked by painted subgrilles in the "catwalk" areas between nose and fenders.

Nineteen-forty was the last year for the little-loved V-8/60 and the first for a Standard-trim wood-body Ford wagon. Yet despite a broad model slate, pretty styling, and prices in the $620-$950 range, Ford trailed Chevy in model-year output by a substantial 222,720 cars. Ford had been "USA-1" for 1934-37, then bowed to Chevy by about 55,000 for recession-year '38 (410,200 to 465,000-plus).

Some dealers had been disappointed in Edsel Ford's new Mercury, feeling a six-cylinder Ford would have been a better idea (which was, in fact, the original concept). Edsel promised a six, then had to reckon with his father. But Henry approved it in one of those strange turnabouts for which he was infamous. Edsel went to work, and the new L-head six bowed for 1941. With 226 cid and 90 horsepower, it had five more cubic inches than the V-8 and a like number of extra horsepower—a bit embarrassing.

The '41s were the biggest, flashiest, and heaviest Fords yet. Wheelbase stretched two inches to 114, bodysides ballooned outward, and a stouter frame contributed to an average 100 pounds of added curb weight. Styling was evolutionary, with wider, more-integrated front fenders; a busy vertical-bar grille with tall center section flanked by low subgrilles; larger rear

1942 Super DeLuxe coupe

1942 Super DeLuxe station wagon

1946 Super DeLuxe Sportsman convertible coupe

1946 Super DeLuxe Fordor sedan

fenders; and more-rakish coupe rooflines. The lineup expanded, too: low-priced Special, midrange DeLuxe, and new Super DeLuxe, all offered with either six or V-8. Prices ranged from $684 for the six-cylinder Special coupe to $1013 for the V-8 DeLuxe woody wagon—the first factory-built Ford to break the $1000 barrier.

But none of this did much for sales. While Ford's total volume improved to near 691,500, it remained about two-thirds of Chevy's, which went up even more, to slightly over a million.

The 1942 Fords gained a lower, wider, vertical-bar grille surmounted by rectangular parking lamps in the vestigial catwalks. The V-8 was pushed up to the same 90 horsepower as the six—likely by the stroke of a engineer's pen. If the V-8 had to cost more, Ford reasoned, it should have at least as much power, even if only on paper. Specials were now sixes only, but the lineup was otherwise unchanged. Prices were hiked about $100 throughout. Ford built just 43,000 cars from January 1 through February 2, when the government ended civilian production for the duration of World War II. At that point, Ford's 1942 model-year total was just shy of 160,500 cars, versus Chevy's quarter-million-plus.

A renowned pacifist during World War I, Henry Ford was in his late 70s when the Japanese attacked Pearl Harbor on December 7, 1941. But he realized that the Second World War was a very different situation, and had already geared his firm to war production. Ford Motor Company duly turned out a variety of military vehicles including Jeeps (with American Bantam and Willys-Overland), and its new mile-long plant in Willow Run, Michigan, near Detroit, produced a variety of bombers through 1945.

Henry finally surrendered control of his company—but not to Edsel, who died a broken man in 1943 at age 49. Despite the end of the war, the doddering mogul stubbornly continued to manage an increasingly troubled Ford Motor Company until his family insisted he step down. That came in 1945, when he handed the reins to grandson Henry Ford II, who would hold them for the next 33 years, most of them successful. The great old man himself passed on in 1947.

Unlike his grandfather, "HFII" consistently sought and encouraged talented managers. However, he just as consistently encouraged their retirement—or fired them—when they reached a certain level of power. Though the Ford family no longer owns a majority of common stock, Ford is still very much a family operation.

Young Henry quickly returned Ford Motor Company to civilian production after V-J day. Ford Division was again the industry's volume leader for model-year 1946, but Chevrolet would be back to full speed the following year and would remain "USA-1" through 1948.

Like most other makes, Ford returned to peacetime with restyled '42 cars, though it bored its V-8 out to 239.4 cid for an extra 10 horsepower. Also, the low-priced Special Sixes were eliminated, leaving six- and eight-cylinder DeLuxe and Super DeLuxe. And there was now a second V-8 convertible, a novel variation on the standard item called Sportsman.

Developed from Bob Gregorie's wartime sketches, the Sportsman featured white ash and mahogany trim over its doors, rear body panels, and deck, as on the Chrysler Town & Country. This was an easy way to give an old design new appeal, and it boosted floor traffic at Ford dealers. But a $500 price premium over the all-steel convertible limited sales to just 1209 for '46, 2250 for '47, and just 28 for '48 (the last actually reserialed '47s).

Appearance alterations for 1947 involved shuffled nameplates and lower-mounted round parking lights. No changes at all occurred for '48, but the six was rerated to 95 horsepower, up five. Postwar inflation had pushed up prices, the increases averaging about $100 for 1947.

But nothing really new was needed in the car-starved early-postwar market, and Ford output exceeded 429,000 units for 1947. The total was only 248,000 the following year, but that only reflected an early end to 1948 production. The reason was the first all-new postwar Fords that went on sale with great anticipation in June 1948.

Styling for these 1949 models was a competitive process, as Ford solicited ideas from freelancers as well as in-house designers. One outside team was headed by George Walker, who hired onetime GM and Raymond Loewy employee Richard

1947½ Super DeLuxe Fordor sedan

1948 Super DeLuxe station wagon

1948 Super DeLuxe convertible coupe

1949 Custom convertible coupe

Caleal to join designers Joe Oros and Elwood Engel. When Caleal became disenchanted with the direction taken by the other members of the Walker team, he was given permission to pursue his own ideas at his home in Indiana. Working in his kitchen with clay modelers Joe Thompson and John Lutz, Caleal shaped his design.

Later, Henry Ford II and other Ford execs gathered at Walker's studio to view design proposals by Caleal, Ford styling head E.T. "Bob" Gregorie, and Oros and Engel. The executives selected Caleal's design, which went into production basically unchanged, except that his vertical taillights were made horizontal and bled into the rear quarter.

Though the 1949 Ford was nowhere near as radical as the 1950-51 Studebaker, it sold in numbers Ford hadn't seen since 1930: over 1.1 million for the extra-long model year. Reflecting this and later achievements, Walker was named design chief for all of Ford Motor Company in 1955.

The 1949 Ford was crucial to Dearborn's survival. Young Henry II was still scrambling to bring order to the organizational and fiscal chaos he inherited from his grandfather even as the company continued losing money by the bucketful. But the '49 was the most-changed Ford since the Model A, and was as much a hit.

Though wheelbase and engines were unchanged from the 1946-48 models, the '49 was three inches lower, fractionally shorter, and usefully lighter. Even better, it had a modern ladder-type frame with Dearborn's first fully independent front suspension (via coil springs and upper and lower A-arms), plus a modern rear end with open Hotchkiss drive (replacing torque-tube) and parallel longitudinal leaf springs supporting the live axle. It all added up to a sprightly performer that could run circles around rivals from Chevrolet and Plymouth. A '49 Ford couldn't quite reach 100 mph, but hopping up the flathead V-8 was still simple, cheap, and easy. Multiple carburetors, headers, dual exhausts, and other "speed parts" were as close as local auto stores.

Though Ford briefly considered retaining it, the low-selling Sportsman was dropped for '49 and other offerings regrouped into Standard and Custom series. The former offered six and V-8 Tudor and Fordor, along with business and club coupes. The better-trimmed V-8-only Custom deleted the business coupe but added a convertible and a new two-door structural-wood wagon (replacing the previous four-door style).

Prices rose again for 1949, the range now $1333-$2119. Overdrive was optional across the board at $97. Ford wouldn't have its own automatic transmission until 1951, though it tried to get one earlier. Studebaker had developed an excellent automatic

1949 Custom two-door station wagon

for 1950 in association with Warner Gear. Ford wanted to buy it for its cars, but Studebaker refused—much to its later regret.

The '49 Fords suffered handling and noise problems stemming from the rushed design program. Workmanship also suffered for the same reason, and a 24-day auto workers' strike in May 1948 didn't help either. Even so, these were very worthy automobiles—the first tangible evidence that Henry II was firmly in charge. Ably assisting him was the youthful "Whiz Kids" team of executives and engineers he'd recruited, including one Robert S. McNamara.

The stage was set for a smart comeback in the '50s. And indeed, by 1952, Ford Motor Company had passed a faltering Chrysler Corporation to regain the number-two spot in manufacturer volume. The reason? Interesting cars that sold well.

Efforts for 1950 aimed at quashing the bugs from '49. "50 Ways New, 50 Ways Better," blared the ads. And the 1950s were better: tighter and quieter in corners and rough-road driving alike. A new confection was the V-8 Crestliner, a special-edition Custom Tudor priced $100-$200 above the standard article. It was snazzy, with a padded canvas-covered top and sweeping contrast-color panel on the bodysides, but sales were only fair at 17,601 for 1950 and another 8703 for '51. Crestliner's real purpose was to counter Chevy's true "hardtop-convertible," the 1950 Bel Air.

Otherwise, the 1950 Fords were predictably much like the '49s, though a crest instead of Ford lettering above the "bullet" grille provided instant I.D. Prices held steady, running from $1333 for the DeLuxe business coupe to $2028 for the Squire. Though still without a hardtop and a fully automatic transmission like Chevrolet, Ford bested 1930's imposing model-year output, making more than 1.2 million cars. But Chevrolet managed nearly 1.5-million, and would remain "USA-1" through 1953.

Seeking greater competitiveness, Ford slightly downpriced its '51 models and applied an attractive facelift featuring a new grille with small twin bullets on a thick horizontal bar. The Custom wagon now bore Country Squire script, but would be the last true Ford woody. Ford finally offered a self-shift transmission in Ford-O-Matic Drive—a three-speed automatic to outdo Chevy's two-speed Powerglide. However, only second and third gears worked automatically; a shift to low had to be made manually. A redesigned dash gave the interior a more upscale look. Also new for '51 was Ford's first hardtop coupe, the Custom V-8 Victoria. Though it, too, was a bit late, the Vicky proved no less popular than Chevy's Bel Air, selling some 110,000 that debut season. Ford's model-year volume declined by about 200,000 cars, but Chevy's fell a similar amount, reflecting new government-ordered restrictions on civilian production prompted by the Korean War.

Model-year '52 introduced a clean, new, square-rigged Ford with a one-piece windshield, simple grille, small round tail-

1950 Custom Crestliner two-door sedan

1950 DeLuxe Six Fordor sedan

1951 Custom Fordor sedan

1951 Custom Victoria hardtop coupe

1951 Custom Country Squire two-door station wagon

1952 Crestline Victoria hardtop coupe

lamps, and an "air scoop" motif on the lower rear flanks. Only detail changes would occur to this basic design through 1954. Wheelbase crept up to 115 inches for a revised model slate that started with a cheap Mainline Tudor/Fordor, business coupe, and two-door Ranch Wagon, followed by Customline sedans, club coupe, and four-door Country Sedan wagon. Topping the range was the V-8 Crestline group of Victoria hardtop, newly named Sunliner convertible, and posh Country Squire four-door wagon. These wagons, by the way, were Ford's first all-steel models (the Squire switching from real wood to wood-look decals). Assisting in their design was Gordon Buehrig, the famed designer of Classic-era Auburns, Cords, and Duesenbergs who'd also had a hand in the '51 Victoria. Doing more with less, Ford introduced a new 215.3-cid overhead-valve six with 101 horsepower as standard for Mainline/Customline. The flathead V-8 was tweaked to 110 horsepower.

Dearborn observed its Golden Anniversary in 1953, proclaimed on Fords by special steering-wheel-hub medallions. But aside from that and a few other cosmetic details, the '53s were basically '52s with higher prices, now ranging from $1400-$2203. With the Korean conflict ended, Ford Division built 1.2 million cars to edge Chevrolet for the model year (Chevy consoled itself with calendar-year supremacy), but only by dumping cars on dealers in a production "blitz" so they could sell for "less than cost." Ironically, Chevrolet wasn't much affected by this onslaught, but Studebaker, American Motors, and Kaiser-Willys were, because they couldn't afford to discount as much. The Ford blitz is generally considered one of the key factors in the independents' mid-'50s decline.

The venerable flathead V-8 was honorably retired for 1954 in favor of a new overhead-valve "Y-block" V-8 (so-called because of its frontal appearance in cross-section). With 130 horsepower, this was easily the year's hottest engine in the low-price field. Together with ball-joint front suspension, also new, the Y-block greatly narrowed the engineering gap between expensive and inexpensive cars. Its initial 239 cid was the same as flathead displacement, but the ohv had different "oversquare" cylinder dimensions. Compression was 7.2:1 in base trim, but could be taken as high as 12:1 if required (which it wasn't).

The rest of the '54 story was basically 1953 save a larger, 223-cid overhead-valve six with 115 bhp. There was also a novel new hardtop called Skyliner, a Crestline Victoria with a transparent, green-tint Plexiglas roof insert over the front seat. This concept, suggested by Buehrig and realized by interior styling director L. David Ash, is a forerunner of today's moonroof. But it cast a strange light on the interior, and heat buildup was a major problem. That and a price identical with the Sunliner convertible's—$2164—held '54 Skyliner sales to 13,344. Only the Country Squire and Mainline business coupe fared worse.

Retaining the 1952-54 shell, the 1955 Ford was completely

1952 Crestline Sunliner convertible coupe

1953 Crestline Country Squire Station Wagon

1953 Crestline Sunliner Official Pace Car

1954 Mainline Tudor sedan

1953 Crestline Victoria hardtop coupe

1954 Crestline Skyliner (glasstop) hardtop coupe

1955 Fairlane town sedan four-door

1955 Fairlane Crown Victoria hardtop coupe

1955 Fairlane Crown Victoria hardtop coupe

1956 Customline Fordor sedan

1956 Fairlane Sunliner convertible (prototype)

1956 Fairlane Sunliner convertible coupe

1956 Fairlane Town Victoria hardtop sedan

1957 Custom 300 Tudor sedan

reskinned, emerging colorful if chromey, with a rakish look of motion and a modestly wrapped windshield. Styling was handled by Franklin Q. Hershey, who also gets credit for that year's new two-seat Thunderbird (*see separate entry*). Club coupes were abandoned, wagons grouped in a separate series, and Crestline was renamed Fairlane (after the Ford family estate in Dearborn). With the "horsepower race" at full gallop, the 239-cid V-8 was ousted for a 272 enlargement, packing 162/182 horsepower as an option for all models. The standard six gained five bhp to deliver 120 total.

Skyliner was also ousted for '55, but Ford had another idea. This was the Fairlane Crown Victoria, a hardtop-style two-door sedan with a bright metal roof band wrapped up and over from steeply angled B-posts. The "tiara" looked like a roll bar, but added no structural strength; a Plexiglas insert rode ahead of it, as on Skyliner. A full steel-roof model was also offered for $70 less than the "bubble-topper"; predictably, it sold much better: 33,000-plus to just 1999. The totals were 9209 and just 603 for '56, after which the Crown Vic was dumped.

But Ford as a whole did splendidly in banner 1955, shattering its postwar record of 1953 by building nearly 1.5 million cars. Still, the division was done in by an all-new Chevy, which tallied better than 1.7 million. Volume for both makes declined in the industry's overall retreat for '56, but Ford dropped by fewer

1957 Country Squire station wagon

1957 Fairlane 500 Skyliner retractable hardtop coupe

1957 Fairlane Victoria hardtop coupe

1957 Fairlane 500 Sunliner convertible coupe

than 50,000 versus Chevy's loss of nearly 200,000.

Ford's '56 line featured the expected mild facelift, plus more-potent engines and two new models: a Customline Victoria and the division's first four-door hardtop, the Fairlane Town Victoria. Ford also began selling "Lifeguard Design" safety features, equipping all models with dished steering wheel, breakaway rearview mirror, and crashproof door locks; padded dash and sunvisors cost $16 extra, factory-installed seatbelts $9. Buyers responded early in the model year, but the rush to seatbelts overtaxed Ford's supplier, so only 20 percent of the '56s got them. Ford continued to stress safety for a few more years, but put more emphasis on performance. Speaking of which, the 272 V-8 delivered 173 horsepower as a '56 Mainline/Customline option. A new 312-cid "Thunderbird" unit with 215/225 horsepower was optional across the board, and a midrange 292-cid V-8 offered 200 horsepower.

The 1957 Fords were all-new, offering a vast array of V-8s from a 190-bhp 272 up to a 245-bhp 312. The 223-cid six was standard for all but one model. There were now two wheelbases and no fewer than five series: 116 inches for Station Wagon and Custom/Custom 300 sedans (replacing Mainline/Customline), 118 inches for Fairlane and the new line-topping Fairlane 500. All were available with six or V-8 power. Both Fairlane series listed two- and four-door Victorias, plus thin-pillar equivalents that looked like hardtops with windows up. The glamorous droptop Sunliner was now a Fairlane 500 and came with the base V-8. Haulers comprised plain and fancier Del Rio two-door Ranch Wagons, a pair of four-door Country Sedans, and the wood-look four-door Squire—Ford's priciest '57 wagon at $2684.

Ford's '57 styling was particularly simple for the period: a blunt face with clean, full-width rectangular grille; tasteful side moldings; and tiny tailfins. More importantly, it was new against Chevy's second facelift in two years. Unfortunately, the Fords had some structural weaknesses (principally roof panels) and were prone to rust, one reason you don't see that many today. But though Plymouth arguably won the styling stakes with its finned "Forward Look," 1957 was a great Ford year. In fact, the division scored a substantial win in model-year output with close to 1.7 million cars to Chevy's 1.5 million. Some statisticians also had Ford ahead in calendar-year volume for the first time since 1935, though the final score showed Chevy ahead by a mere 130 cars.

The Skyliner name returned in mid-1957, but on a very different Ford: the world's first mass-produced retractable hardtop. An addition to the Fairlane 500 series, it stemmed from engineering work done a few years before at Continental Division, which had considered, but didn't produce, the 1956 Mark II as a "retrac." Ford sold 20,766 Skyliners for '57, but demand fast tapered to 14,713 for '58, then to 12,915. The model was duly axed after 1959, a victim of new division chief Bob McNamara's no-nonsense approach to products and profits. Skyliner "retracs" became prime collectibles, and the retractable-hardtop concept made a comeback in the new millennium.

For 1958, Ford countered all-new passenger Chevys and modestly restyled Plymouths with a glittery facelift featuring quad headlamps and taillamps, a massive bumper/grille a la '58 Thunderbird, and more anodized aluminum trim. V-8 choices expanded via two new "FE-series" big-blocks: a 332 offering 240/265 horsepower, and a 300-bhp 352. A deep national recession cut Ford volume to just under 988,000 cars. Chevrolet sold over 1.1 million, but spent much more money to do so.

Chevy then unveiled an all-new line of radical "bat-fin" cars for 1959. Ford replied with more-conservative styling that helped it close the model-year gap to less than 12,000 units. A major reskin of the basic 1957-58 bodyshells brought square lines; simple side moldings; a heavily sculptured "flying-V" back panel; and a low, rectangular grille filled with floating starlike ornaments. All previous models continued, though now on the 118-inch wheelbase. Come midseason, a new Galaxie series of two- and four-door pillared and pillarless sedans generated high buyer interest and strong sales with their square but stylish Thunderbird-inspired wide-quarter rooflines. At the same time, the Sunliner convertible and Skyliner retractable gained Galaxie rear-fender script (but retained Fairlane 500 ID at the rear). V-8s were down to a 200-bhp 292, 225-bhp 332, and 300-bhp 352. Also carried over from '58 was Cruise-O-Matic, Ford's smooth new three-speed automatic transmission that proved a sales plus against Chevrolet's Powerglide, if not Plymouth's

1958 Custom 300 Tudor sedan

1959 Country Squire 9-passenger station wagon

1958 Fairlane 500 Skyliner retractable hardtop

1959 Fairlane 500 Fordor sedan

1958 Fairlane 500 Victoria hardtop coupe

1959 Fairlane 500 Skyliner retractable hardtop

responsive three-speed TorqueFlite.

For Ford Motor Company as a whole, 1959 seemed to justify the strenuous efforts of Henry Ford II and board chairman Ernest R. Breech. Assuming control of a third-rate company in 1945, they'd turned it into something approaching General Motors in less than 15 years.

Ford's path through the 1960s closely parallels that of rival Chevrolet. At decade's end, it was also selling only about 400,000 more cars per year than in 1960—despite expansion into important new markets: economy compacts, intermediates, and sportier standard-size models. Also like Chevy, Ford built these diverse types on relatively few wheelbases. (See separate entries for the stories on the personal-luxury T-Bird and the new-for '65 Mustang "ponycar," the two most-specialized Fords of this period.)

Key management changes occurred early on. Lee A. Iacocca took charge as Ford Division general manager in 1960. George Walker left the following year and Eugene Bordinat became Dearborn's design chief. Iacocca soon put an end to the mundane people-movers favored by Bob McNamara, and by 1970 Ford was offering some exciting cars.

Ford also moved from "Chevy-follower" to "Chevy-leader" in the 1960s. Its compact Falcon far outsold the rival Corvair, its 1962 midsize Fairlane was two years ahead of Chevelle, and its phenomenally successful Mustang sent Chevrolet racing to the drawing board to come up with the Camaro.

The best way to summarize Fords of the '60s is by size. The smallest was Falcon, which bowed for 1960 as one of the new Big Three compacts (along with Corvair and Chrysler's Valiant). Wheelbase was a trim 109.5 inches through 1965, then 110.9 (113 for wagons). Two- and four-door sedans and four-door wagons were always offered, convertibles and hardtop coupes for 1963-65. All had unit construction.

To some, the pre-'66 Falcons were the ultimate "throwaway" cars: designed to sell at a low price—initially just under $2000—and to be discarded within five years (some said one year). To others, though, Falcon was the Model A reborn: cheap but cheerful, simple but not unacceptably spartan. A conventional suspension and cast-iron six—mostly a 170-cid unit of 101 horsepower—certainly looked dull next to Corvair engineering, but made for friendly, roomy little cars that rode well and delivered 20-25 mpg. Falcons were also easily serviced by "shadetree mechanics" who wouldn't go near the complicated Chevy compact. Though sales gradually declined due to competition from both inside and outside the division, Falcon was always profitable.

Falcon replied to the hot-selling Corvair Monza in the spring of 1961 with the bucket-seat Futura two-door. All Falcons were reskinned for 1964-65 with pointy front fenders and generally square, less-distinctive lines. The prime collector Falcon is the

1960 Galaxie Starliner hardtop coupe

1960 Galaxie Town Victoria hardtop sedan

1960 Falcon two-door sedan (DeLuxe trim)

1961 Galaxie club sedan four-door

1961 Galaxie Starliner hardtop coupe

1961 Falcon four-door sedan (DeLuxe trim)

Futura Sprint, a pretty convertible and hardtop coupe offered from mid-1963 through 1965. These were available with the lively "Challenger" small-block V-8 from the midsize Fairlane—initially a 260 with 164 horsepower, then a 289 with about 200 horsepower for '65. It was a fine engine, which helps explain why its 302 evolution continued all the way into the 1990s. It completely transformed Falcon performance without greatly affecting mileage. Sprints offered special exterior I.D., vinyl bucket seats, console, and 6000-rpm tachometer. When equipped with optional four-speed manual transmission, they were great fun to drive.

The 1966 Falcons were basically shorter versions of that year's rebodied Fairlanes, with the same sort of curvy GM-like contours and long-hood/short-deck proportions of Mustang. Falcon continued in this form through early 1970. In 1967, its last year before emissions controls, the 289 packed 225 horsepower in "Stage 2" tune with four-barrel carburetor, and made for some very fast Falcons, the sportiest of which was the pillared Futura Sport Coupe. The 289 was detuned to 195 horsepower for '68, when the aforementioned 302 arrived as a new option. This ran on regular gas with a two-barrel carb and delivered 210 bhp; with a four-barrel it made 230 horsepower on premium fuel, though emissions considerations soon put an end to that version.

Mid-1970 brought the final Falcons: a stark wagon and two sedans derived from the intermediate Torino (which had evolved from the Fairlane). These could be powered by everything from a 155-bhp 250-cid six to a big-block 429-cid V-8 with 360-370 horsepower. But the name had outlived its usefulness, and Ford had a new compact, the Maverick, so Falcon was consigned to history.

Back to 1962, Ford broke new ground with the midsize Fairlane, which was basically a bigger Falcon on a 115.5-inch wheelbase. In concept it was much like Virgil Exner's downsized '62 Plymouths and Dodges. But unlike Chrysler, Ford retained full-size Customs and Galaxies—a wise move even though Fairlane sold more than 297,000 units its first year and over 300,000 for '63. Helping the cause were attractive prices in the $2100-$2800 range.

The Fairlane was significant for introducing Ford's brilliant small-block V-8, the basis for some of its hottest '60s cars. Bored out to 289 cid as a '63 option, it packed up to 271 horsepower—almost one horsepower per cubic inch. Powerful and smooth yet surprisingly economical, it was the definitive small V-8. Tuned versions in sports-racers like the Ford GT40 and Shelby Cobra disproved the old adage about there being "no substitute for cubic inches." In fact, the GT40 nearly took the world GT Manufacturers Championship away from Ferrari in 1964, its first full season. Still, it was the big-block Ford GTs that won the LeMans 24-Hours, the world's most-prestigious

1962½ Falcon DeLuxe Futura sports coupe

1962 Falcon DeLuxe Futura sports coupe

1962 Galaxie 500/XL Sunliner convertible coupe

1962 Fairlane 500 four-door sedan

1962 Galaxie 500 Sunliner with Starlite top

1963½ Falcon Futura Sprint hardtop sports coupe

1963 300 four-door sedan

1963 Galaxie 500/XL "Scatback" hardtop coupe

1964 Fairlane 500 hardtop sports coupe

1964 Falcon Futura Sprint hardtop sports coupe

sports car endurance race, two years in a row, 1966-67.

Initially, Fairlane offered two- and four-door sedans in base and sportier 500 trim, plus a bucket-seat 500 Sport Coupe. Four-door Ranch and Squire wagons and a brace of two-door hardtops were added for '63. Beginning with the '64s, Ford offered a growing assortment of handling and performance options, including stiff suspensions and four-speed gearboxes.

Fairlane was completely rebodied for '66 on a 116-inch wheelbase (113 for wagons) gaining a sleek, tailored look via curved side glass and flanks, stacked quad headlamps, and tidy vertical taillights. Heading the line were the bucket-seat 500XL hardtop coupe and convertible in base and GT trim. Standard XLs came with a 120-bhp 200-cid six, but most were ordered with optional 289 V-8s. GTs carried a big-block 390 making a potent 335 horsepower. That engine could be ordered on any Fairlane, and racers were quick to put it in stripped two-door sedans, which earned respect for their competitive prowess.

With no change in wheelbases, Fairlane got another body and styling change for 1968. Joining the base and 500 lines was a new Torino series, Ford's lushest intermediates yet. A 115-bhp 200-cid six was standard for all but the Torino GT convertible, hardtop coupe, and new fastback hardtop (all duplicated in the 500 line), which came with the 210-bhp 302-cid V-8 as well as buckets-and-console interior, pinstriping, and more performance options than a salesman could memorize.

Ford's '69 midsizers were '68 repeats save for new fastback and notchback Torino hardtops called Cobra (after Carroll Shelby's muscular Ford-powered sports cars). These came with the 335-bhp 428 V-8 that had first appeared in the "1968½" Mercury Cyclone as the "Cobra Jet." A $133 option was "Ram-Air," a fiberglass hood scoop connecting to a special air-cleaner assembly with a valve that ducted incoming air directly into the carb. Four-speed manual gearbox, stiff suspension and racing-style hood locks were all standard. One magazine was actually disappointed when its Cobra ran 0-60 mph in 7.2 seconds and the quarter-mile in 15 seconds at 98.3 miles per hour! But most everyone admitted that of all the '69 "supercars"—Plymouth GTX, Dodge Charger R/T, Pontiac GTO, Chevelle 396, and Buick GS 400—the Torino Cobra was the tightest, best-built, and quietest.

Torino Cobras could be potent racing machines. Ford discovered that the styling of the counterpart Cyclone was slightly more aerodynamic, and thus usually ran the Mercurys in stock-car contests over 250 miles long. Nevertheless, a race-prepped Torino could achieve about 190 mph, and Lee Roy Yarborough drove one to win the '69 Daytona 500.

Ford's biggest cars of the 1960s were variously offered as Custom/Custom 500, Fairlane/Fairlane 500 (pre-'62), Galaxie/Galaxie 500, and station wagon. Their "standard" wheelbase swelled to 119 inches for 1960, then became 121 after 1968. These were heavy cars (3000-4000 pounds), and most weren't rewarding to drive except on an Interstate, but certain variations were surprisingly capable on winding roads.

What we now call the full-size Fords began the decade with all-new bodyshells that would persist through 1964. The '60s were much longer, lower, wider, and sleeker than the boxy '59s, and even mimicked Chevy's batfins a little, but they looked good with their chrome-edged beltlines and bigger glass areas. The Skyliner was gone, but there was a new fixed-roof Starliner hardtop coupe with sleek semifastback profile. Though less popular than square-roof Galaxies, the Starliner was just the thing for NASCAR racing by dint of its slipperier shape.

Starliner bowed out after 1961, when standards were facelifted via a full-width concave grille (with '59-style insert) and a return to round taillights capped by discreet blades. That year's top engine option was the new 390-cid version of the FE-series

1964 Galaxie 500/XL Sunliner convertible coupe

1965 Falcon Futura hardtop coupe

1965 Galaxie 500/XL hardtop coupe

1965 Ford Galaxie 500/XL convertible coupe

big-block. This packed 300 standard horsepower, but was available, though on a very limited basis, as a high-compression "Interceptor" with 375 and 401 horsepower.

Chunkier, more-"important" styling marked the '62 standards, which regrouped into Galaxie/Galaxie 500/Station Wagon lines spanning roughly the same models. Reflecting the buckets-and-console craze then sweeping Detroit were the midseason 500 XL Victoria hardtop coupe and Sunliner convertible. The "500" stood for the 500-mile NASCAR races the division was winning (Ford won every 500 in '63). "XL" purportedly stood for "Xtra Lively," though the standard powertrain was "just" a 170-bhp 292 V-8 and Cruise-O-Matic. But options could turn this sporty hunk into a real fire-breather. Besides Borg-Warner four-speed manual gearbox and 300-, 340-, 375-, and 401-bhp 390s, there was a larger-bore 406 big-block providing 385/405 horsepower. An even bigger bore for '63 produced a 427-cid powerhouse with 410/425 horsepower. High prices—around $400—made these engines relatively uncommon.

New lower-body sheetmetal gave the 1963 "Super-Torque" Galaxies a cleaner, leaner look, announced by a simple concave grille. A pair of cheap "300" sedans was added (renamed Custom/Custom 500 for '64), and there was more midyear excitement in a set of 500 and 500XL sports hardtops with thin-pillar "slantback" rooflines, a bit starchier than the old Starliner but again aimed right at the stock-car ovals.

The last, but most-substantial, restyle on the big 1960 body occurred for '64, bringing heavily sculptured lower-body sheetmetal, a complex grille, and slantback rooflines for all closed models. The entire Ford line won *Motor Trend* magazine's "Car of the Year" award, partly because of the division's ever-widening "Total Performance" campaign. Performance was just what the big Fords had, with available small-block and big-block V-8s offering from 195 up to a rousing 425 horsepower. Even a relatively mild 390 XL could scale 0-60 mph in 9.3 seconds; a 427 reduced that to just over 7 seconds. The one major complaint was a marked tendency to nosedive in "panic" stops, aggravated by overboosted power brakes.

Ford had its best NASCAR year ever in 1965, winning 48 of 55 events, including 32 straight at one point. Luxury, however, got most of the showroom emphasis. All-new except for engines, the '65s were distinguished by simpler, more-linear styling announced by stacked quad headlamps. Underneath was a stronger chassis with a completely new front suspension evolved from NASCAR experience. But arriving at midyear were the poshest big Fords ever, the $3300 Galaxie 500 LTD hardtop coupe and sedan, claimed to be "quiet as a Rolls-Royce." The times were indeed a-changin'. With intermediates taking over in competition, the big Fords no longer needed any sort of "performance" image to support sales.

The 1965 platform got a minor touch up for '66, and LTDs

1965 Fairlane 500 hardtop sports coupe

1966 Galaxy 500 LTD limousine (limited production)

1966 Ford Galaxie 500 convertible coupe

1966 Falcon Futura sports coupe

1966 Fairlane 500/XL hardtop coupe

1967 Galaxie 500/XL convertible coupe

gained "7-Litre" companions powered by the Thunderbird's big 345-bhp 428 engine. The following year brought new outer sheetmetal with more flowing lines and "faster" rooflines on hardtop coupes. LTD became a separate three-model series, adding four-door sedan but losing the slow-selling 7-Litre models. Hidden-headlamp grilles marked the '68 LTDs and Galaxie XLs as part of a lower-body restyle for all models.

A new bodyshell arrived for '69 with a two-inch longer wheelbase, a "tunneled backlight" for newly named "SportsRoof" fastbacks, and ventless door glass on hardtops and convertibles. LTD sales continued rising. Ford had built nearly 139,000 of the '68s; it built more than twice that number for '69.

Ford kept pace with Chevrolet in the '60s production race, and actually beat it for model years 1961 and '66. Ford would be number one again for 1970 and '71 at slightly over two-million cars to Chevy's 1.5/1.8 million. Ford enjoyed its first two-million-car year in 1965, though that was a great year for all domestic automakers.

Ford wouldn't lead Chevy again until the late '80s, but it generally fared well in the '70s. Still, Dearborn was the last of the Big Three to abandon traditional full-size cars—and the first to suffer for it. In the wake of the OPEC oil embargo and the first energy crisis, Chrysler pushed compacts while GM went forward with plans to downsize its entire fleet. Ford stubbornly resisted the winds of change, promoting its aging big cars on the basis of greater passenger space and the presumed safety of their "road-hugging weight." But the public didn't buy this cynical line—or as many of the cars.

In large measure, this denial reflected the personal view of chairman Henry Ford II, who decreed there would be no wholesale rush to smaller cars, no vast capital investment in new technology. As a result, Ford greeted 1980 a critical two to three years behind GM in the fuel efficiency and "space" races—and at a critical sales disadvantage next to its domestic foes and a horde of fast-rising Japanese makes. The firm would recover, but not before making drastic product changes.

Leading the 1970 line were modestly facelifted full-size Fords with "poke-through" center grille sections on LTDs and XLs, plus revamped rear ends on all models. Four series were offered: Custom, Galaxie 500, XL, and LTD. The sporty XLs were in their final year. Luxury was further emphasized with a new LTD Brougham hardtop coupe, hardtop sedan, and four-door sedan.

Broughams also featured in the 1970 Torino line, which shared new exterior panels "shaped by the wind" with a three-model Fairlane 500 series. Wheelbase grew an inch; profiles were lower and five inches longer. The Torino Cobra returned as Ford's "budget muscle car" with standard 360/375-bhp 429 V-8. It was a blistering performer and its new hardtop body with concave backlight was distinctive, but hot-car demand

1967 Fairlane 500/XL GTA convertible coupe

1968 Torino GT fastback hardtop coupe

1968 Torino GT 428 Cobra Jet Official Pace Car

1968 LTD hardtop sedan

1969 Galaxie 500 fastback hardtop coupe

1969 LTD hardtop sedan

1969 Fairlane Cobra 428 CJ SportsRoof hardtop coupe

1969 Torino GT convertible coupe

1970 Torino GT SportsRoof hardtop coupe

1970½ Falcon two-door sedan

1970 LTD Brougham hardtop sedan

was fast-waning everywhere, and only 7675 were built for the model year.

Ford scored much higher 1970 sales with its new compact Maverick, a semifastback two-door on a 103-inch wheelbase. Introduced in early '69, Maverick was much like the original Falcon in size, price, performance, and simplicity; even its basic chassis and powertrain were the same. Arriving just below $2000 and backed by an aggressive but light-hearted ad campaign, this import-fighter scored an impressive 579,000 model-year sales, contributing greatly to Ford's production victory over Chevy.

Bolstering Maverick's appeal for '71 was a notchback four-door on a 109.9-inch wheelbase (almost the same as the original Falcon's), a sportier two-door called Grabber, and a newly optional 302 V-8 as an alternative to the 100-bhp 170 six. With minor changes, Maverick would carry the division's compact sales effort through 1977, which it did tolerably well, though its old-fashioned engineering looked increasingly so with time and the arrival of more-capable domestic and foreign competitors.

Of course, there was little here to interest enthusiasts. The Grabber looked snazzy but was pretty tame even with V-8. And certain requisites like decent instruments and front-disc brakes were either late in coming (the latter didn't arrive until '76) or not available. Maverick's last gesture to the youth market was the Stallion, a 1976 trim package similar to those offered on the Pinto and Mustang II. The Maverick kit, which was strictly for two-doors, included black paint accents, twin door mirrors, styled steel wheels, raised-white-letter tires, and special badging. More popular was the Luxury Decor Option (LDO), a 1973 package available for either body style through the end of the line. It comprised upgraded interior appointments color-keyed to a special paint scheme crowned by a matching vinyl top.

Ford's major 1971 announcement was the four-cylinder Pinto, a 2000-pound, 94.2-inch-wheelbase subcompact with fastback styling in two-door and Runabout three-door hatchback models. A direct reply to Chevrolet's Vega, also new that year, it was smaller, less technically daring, less accommodating, and its performance and fuel economy were nothing special compared to that of many imports. Yet Pinto usually outsold the trouble-prone Vega as well as many overseas contenders. Offered with 98- and 122-cid engines through 1973, then 122- and 140-cid fours, it was progressively dressed-up and civilized with nicer trim and more convenience options. Three-door wagons arrived for 1972, including a woody-look Squire (some called it "Country Squirt"). By 1976, there was also a youthful "Cruising Wagon" with blanked-off side windows and cute little rear portholes. Still, Pinto remained primarily basic transportation throughout its long 10-year life.

Though Pinto served Ford well in a difficult period, it will forever be remembered as what one wag called "the barbecue that seats four." That refers to the dangerously vulnerable fuel tank and filler-neck design of 1971-76 sedan models implicated in a rash of highly publicized (and fatal) fires following rear-end collisions. Sadly, Ford stonewalled in a number of lawsuits all the way to federal court, which severely tarnished its public image, even if Pinto sales didn't seem to suffer much. What really put Pinto out to pasture after 1980 was not bad publicity but relative lack of change—and the advent of a much better small Ford.

The midsize Torino proved exceptionally popular in the early '70s, then fell from favor once fuel economy became a pressing consumer concern. The 14-model 1971 lineup was basically a carryover of the previous year's. The Cobra fastback coupe remained the most-exciting of this bunch, though its standard engine was downgraded to a 285-bhp version of the ubiquitous 351 small-block first seen for 1969. High-power and big-inch

1970 Maverick fastback coupe

1971 Torino Cobra SportsRoof coupe

1971 LTD Brougham hardtop coupe

1971 Pinto fastback coupe

1971 Torino Brougham "formal" hardtop coupe

1972 Gran Torino Brougham sedan

1972 Torino Sport fastback hardtop coupe

1972 Galaxie 500 hardtop sedan

engines began disappearing at Ford and throughout Detroit in 1972. By 1980, only a mildly tuned 351 remained as an option for full-size Fords.

Except for engines, the 1972 Torino was all-new—and a big disappointment. Like GM's post-1967 intermediates, models divided along two wheelbases: 114-inch two-door hardtops and fastbacks (including semisporty GT variants) and 118-inch sedans and wagons. Body-on-frame construction appeared for the first time, and dimensions ballooned close to those of late-'60s Galaxies and LTDs. Symbolic of most everything wrong with Detroit at the time, these Torinos were needlessly outsized, overweight, and thirsty, with limited interior room and soggy chassis. Ford tried to make them passably economical, then gave up and simply fitted a larger fuel tank. After getting just 13.5 mpg with a '76, the auto editors of *Consumer Guide*® decided that "the more buyers learn about the Torino, the more reasons they will find to opt for a Granada."

Equally dismal was the tarted-up Torino bowing at mid-1974 to answer Chevy's popular Monte Carlo. Sharing a coupe bodyshell and running gear with that year's new fat-cat Mercury Cougar, this Grand Torino Elite leaned heavily on "Thunderbird tradition" with most every personal-luxury cliche of the period: overstuffed velour interior, a square "formal" grille, stand-up hood ornament, and a vinyl-covered rear half-roof with dual "opera" windows. Initially priced at $4437, the Elite didn't sell as well as the Monte, though over 366,000 were built through 1976. After that point, a downsized, downpriced T-bird rendered it redundant.

Granada was a far more rational proposition and one of Ford's best-timed ideas of this decade. Introduced during 1975, it was conceived as just a slightly larger Maverick using the same chassis and drivetrains. But when the fuel crunch boosted small-car sales, Ford decided to retain Maverick and launch its erstwhile successor as a more-luxurious compact half a step up in price. This explains why the Granada appeared on the four-door Maverick's 109.9-inch wheelbase.

Adroitly keyed to the changing market, Granada blended American-style luxury with the mock-Mercedes look then in vogue. Buyers wholeheartedly approved, and Granada zoomed from nowhere to become Ford Division's top-seller, outdistancing the full-sizers and swollen Torinos by wide margins. It was soon a familiar sight on American roads. Not that it performed that well on those roads with its untidy cornering response and a roly-poly ride on rough sections. Nevertheless, Granada bridged a big market gap at a crucial time, appealing to both compact buyers with upscale aspirations and big-car owners now energy-conscious for the first time. Offerings through 1980 comprised six and V-8 four-door sedan and opera-window coupe in base and plusher Ghia trim (the last referring to the famed Italian coachbuilder bought by Ford in 1970). There was also a gesture toward sport in the 1978-80 ESS—for "European Sports Sedan"—but it was only a gesture.

Maverick's true successor bowed for 1978 with a name borrowed from Ford's Australian subsidiary: Fairmont. It was undoubtedly Dearborn's single-most-significant new product of the decade, although few knew that outside the company. Why? Because Fairmont's basic engineering would be the foundation for most Ford Motor Company cars introduced through the mid-'80s, including a new-generation Mustang and T-Bird.

Billed as the first FoMoCo car designed with the aid of computer analysis, the Fairmont (and its Zephyr twin at Mercury) was a common-sense car and pretty conventional. Though conceived around a traditional front-engine/rear-drive format, it was a big improvement over Maverick: clean-lined; sensibly boxy for good interior space on a shorter 105.5-inch wheelbase; lighter and thus thriftier than many expected. Engines were familiar—initially the 140-cid Pinto four, 200-cid six, and 302-cid V-8—but there was a new all-coil suspension with modified MacPherson-strut front end geometry, which mounted the coil springs on lower A-arms. Aside from better handling, this arrangement opened up more underhood space for easier servicing. A front stabilizer bar was standard, as was rack-and-pinion steering, offered at extra cost with variable-ratio power assist, a new item shared with several other Fords that year.

1973 Pinto Squire two-door station wagon

1974 Gran Torino Brougham hardtop coupe

1973 LTD Brougham hardtop sedan

1975 Granada coupe

1974 LTD Brougham sedan

1975 Maverick fastback coupe

The "Fox" program that produced Fairmont was one of Ford's first projects initiated after the 1973-74 energy crisis, but it wasn't Dearborn's only attempt at downsizing. For 1977, the old Torino was refurbished with cleaner exterior sheetmetal and "badge-engineered" to pass as a new-wave big car. Called LTD II, it was only a little lighter than before, and sales went nowhere. One reason was the simultaneous arrival of a new downsized Thunderbird on this same platform. With much lower prices than before and that magical name, the T-Bird swamped LTD II in sales.

Besides a new Fairmont-based Mustang, 1979 saw the fruition of the "Panther" design project in an LTD that was genuinely downsized. Yet it was less successful than the Fairmont or Mustang—and that was curious. In size and execution this smaller LTD was fully a match for shrunken GM opponents, riding a 114.3-inch wheelbase yet offering more claimed passenger and trunk space than the outsized 1973-78 cars. Styling was boxier and less pretentious, and visibility and fuel economy were better. So were ride and handling, thanks to a new all-coil suspension with more-precise four-bar-link location for the live rear axle. Coupes, sedans, and wagons in two trim levels were offered. With all this, what Ford trumpeted as a "New American Road Car" should have scored even higher output than the 357,000 recorded for '79. The new LTD thus trailed the big Oldsmobiles for second place in full-size car sales and ran far behind Chevrolet's Caprice/Impala.

Two factors seemed to be at work. One was GM's two-year lead in downsizing. The other was a severe downturn in the national economy—abetted by another fuel crisis—that began in the spring of '79 and put a big crimp in all new-car sales. This LTD would enjoy a sales resurgence, but not before Ford and the U.S. auto industry passed through three of their bleakest years ever.

Those years—1980-82—saw Ford Division output drop from 1.16 million cars to just under 749,000. But thanks to an economic recovery and an ever-changing line of ever-improving Fords, the division went back above the 1.1-million mark—and would stay there through decade's end. In the process, Ford overhauled Chevrolet, becoming "USA-1" for 1988.

A division mainstay throughout the '80s was the subcompact Escort, the new front-drive 1981 replacement for Pinto. Billed as the first in a promised fleet of Ford "world cars," it was jointly designed by the firm's U.S., British, and German branches under Project "Erika," but the European version ended up sleeker and faster than its American cousin. The practical, low-priced U.S. Escort set a fast sales pace with at least 320,000 copies in each of its first two years. Volume eased to under a quarter million for '85, then returned to at least 363,000 each year through decade's end. The peak was 1986 at over 430,000.

Numerous refinements marked Escort's evolution through

1976 LTD Landau coupe

1976 Maverick Stallion fastback coupe

1976 Elite coupe

1977 Ford LTD Landau four-door sedan

1976 Pinto Stallion Runabout hatchback coupe

1977 Pinto Runabout hatchback coupe

1990. There were always three-door hatchbacks and four-door wagons, plus hatchback sedans after 1981. All rode a 94.2-inch wheelbase and employed transverse-mounted four-cylinder engines—a new "CVH" single-overhead-cam design with hemispherical combustion chambers—initially teamed with four-speed overdrive manual or three-speed automatic transaxles. An optional five-speed manual came along for 1983. All-coil four-wheel independent suspension persisted throughout, with MacPherson struts and lower control arms fore, modified struts on trailing arms and lower control arms aft. Rack-and-pinion steering and front-disc/rear-drum brakes completed the basic specs.

Escort's original 1.6-liter (98-cid) engine had just 69 horsepower, but by 1983 was up to 72/80 horsepower with two-barrel carb or 88 horsepower in optional throttle-body fuel-injected form. The last was standard for a new three-door GT model, which also came with five-speed, firm suspension, and black exterior trim. An optional 2.0-liter (121-cid) 52-bhp diesel four from Mazda arrived for 1984—just in time for the start of a gas glut that quickly killed most all diesel demand in the U.S. That engine duly vanished after '87. A more-exciting 1984 development was a turbocharged 1.6-liter GT with 120 horsepower and a suitably uprated chassis. It was fast and fun but crude and not very quiet. A more-convenient, restyled dash was featured across the line.

A mid-1985 upgrade brought a larger 1.9-liter (113.5 cid) "CVH" with 86 horsepower in carbureted form or 108 with option electronic port fuel injection. The latter was newly standard for GT, which gained its own asymmetric body-color grille, aluminum wheels, bigger tires, rear spoiler, and rocker panel "skirts." All Escorts were mildly facelifted with smoother noses in the "aero" idiom pioneered by the '83 Thunderbird, marked by flush headlamps.

By 1987, Escort's plethora of alphabet series had been sifted down to a stark three-door called Pony, volume-selling GL (all three body styles), and three-door GT. The base engine was treated to throttle-body injection and moved up to 90 horsepower. Styling became smoother in mid-1988: revamped rear quarters for sedans, a new grille and spoiler for GT, and minor cleanups elsewhere. GL was renamed LX, and the dash was restyled a second time. As with previous midyear model revisions, this one carried into 1989 and then 1990 practically without change.

Escort's high success was not matched by an unhappy sporty coupe offshoot, the EXP. New for 1982, it was Ford's first two-seater since the original Thunderbird, but its "frog-eye" styling wasn't in the same league. And though an Escort underneath, it cost considerably more. Still, first-year sales were respectable at over 98,000. But they plunged ominously to under 20,000 for 1983. The following year, EXP picked up the "bubbleback" hatch of its discontinued Mercury twin, the LN7, as well as Escort's new dash and 120-bhp turbo option. Sales recovered to over 23,000. The little-changed '85s sold some 26,400 early into the calendar year, when Ford suspended production. The car then reemerged in mid-1986 as the Escort EXP, with a similar new flush-headlamp front, revamped dash, and 1.9-liter engines for two models: 86-bhp Luxury Coupe and 108-bhp Sport Coupe. Though nearly 31,000 were sold, EXP was still unequal to Japanese two-seaters like the Honda CRX and Toyota MR2. With base and luxury coupe, EXP eased below 26,000 for '87, then was abandoned in 1988 as a bad bet, though this did free up assembly-line space for regular Escorts.

Another constant of Ford's 1980s fleet was the full-size 1979-vintage LTD, which continued beyond 1990 with just minor yearly alterations to equipment, styling, and engines. The changes are easy to chart: standard four-speed overdrive automatic transmission and 255-cid V-8, a new uplevel series reviving the Crown Victoria name (1980); no more 351 option (1982); standard 302 V-8 with throttle-body fuel injection for all models renamed LTD Crown Victoria (1983); sequential multiport injection for 150 horsepower (versus 140), premium LX series added (1986); two-door coupe canceled, "aero" front and rear styling for remaining four-door sedan and Country Squire wagon (1988); standard driver-side air bag, new-style dash, and revised equipment (1990).

Despite the year-to-year sameness, many buyers still craved big, Detroit-style luxury, and the fact that fewer such cars were available as gas became cheaper again only worked in the

1977 Granada with Sports Coupe option

1978 Granada ESS (European Sports Sedan)

1978 Granada Ghia coupe

1978 LTD II Brougham coupe

1978 Fairmont Squire station wagon

1978 Fairmont Futura coupe

1978 LTD two-door sedan

1979 LTD Country Squire station wagon

1979 Granada ESS four-door sedan

1979 LTD II coupe with Sports Touring package

1979 Pinto Cruising wagon

1980 Granada four-door sedan

Crown Vic's favor. Though sales fluctuated, this line was good for an annual average of well over 118,000—considerably more in some years. As late as 1990, Crown Vic did a healthy 74,000. By that point, though, the cars themselves were sourced mainly from Canada.

While Fairmont continued carrying Ford's banner in the compact segment, two derivatives served as the division's midsize warriors. First was a new 1981 Granada, basically the two- and four-door Fairmont sedans with a square eggcrate grille, bulkier sheetmetal, and somewhat plusher appointments. Fairmont wagons transferred to this line for '82. This Granada sold respectably: about 120,000 a year. Engines were the same as Fairmont's: standard 2.3-liter four, optional 200-cid six, and "fuel crisis" 255 V-8 (the last eliminated after '81).

For 1983, Granada was transformed into a "small" LTD—as opposed to the "big" LTD Crown Victoria. This was also an uptown Fairmont, restyled with a sloped nose, airier "six-light" greenhouse, and modestly lipped trunklid. Along with that year's new Thunderbird, it announced Ford's turn to "aero" styling. By 1984, Granada engines were initially carried over along with a new 232-cid V-6. By 1985, only the four, V-6, and an optional 165-bhp 302 V-8 were fielded, the last reserved for a semisporting LX sedan that sold just 3260 copies. Undoubtedly helped by image rub-off from its big sister, the little LTD sold a

1981 Escort GLX liftgate wagon with Squire Trim

1980 Fairmont four-door with Exterior Decor Group

1981 Granada GL two-door sedan

1982 EXP 2-passenger hatchback coupe

1981 LTD Country Squire station wagon

1983 LTD Crown Victoria four-door sedan

lot better than Granada: nearly 156,000 for '83 and over 200,000 in 1984 and '85—Ford's second-best-seller after Escort.

Fairmont, meantime, finished its run in 1983 after few interim changes from '78. Two sedans, plain and fancy wagons, and a smart "basket-handle-roof" coupe reviving the Futura name were offered through 1981 (after which the wagons became Granadas). Engines were the usual Fox assortment: 2.3-liter four, 200-cid straight six, and small-block V-8s (302 cid for 1978-79, 255 cid for 1980-81). Sales tapered off along with the economy, dropping from the first-year high of nearly 461,000 to less than 81,000 by 1983. Still, that was a fine showing in a turbulent period. The Fairmont had more than done its job.

Filling Fairmont's shoes for 1984 was a new front-drive compact called Tempo, a notchback four-door and coupelike two-door with "jellybean" styling on a 99.9-inch chassis with suspension much like Escort's. Power came from a 2.3-liter four, only it wasn't the Pinto/Fairmont ohc "Lima" unit but a cut-down version of the old overhead-valve Falcon six, rated at 84 horsepower. It didn't work that well, but Ford tried to make it better, fitting throttle-body injection and adding a 100-bhp "H.O." (high-output) option for '85. The latter somehow lost six horsepower by '87, then returned to its original rating. Several trim levels were offered, including better-equipped Sport versions with the more powerful engine and firm suspension. Escort's 2.0-liter diesel option was listed through '86, but generated few sales. The standard manual transaxle shifted from a four- to five-speed after '84, with a three-speed automatic optional all years.

Tempo was treated to a mild flush-headlamp facelift for 1986, when it also became one of the first low-priced cars to offer an optional driver-side air bag. The following year brought another interesting new option: all-wheel drive, a part-time "shift-on-the-fly" setup intended for maximum traction on slippery roads, not dry-pavement driving or off-roading. For 1988, Tempo four-doors were reskinned to look like junior versions of the new midsize Taurus, an effective "nip-and-tuck" operation. A new, rather Japanese-looking dash was shared with unchanged coupe models. Offerings now comprised base GL and sporty GLS coupes and sedans, plus four-door all-wheel drive and luxury LX models. Tempo then marked time for 1989-90 aside from price/equipment shuffles.

Despite prosaic mechanicals and increasingly tough compact competition, Tempo proved another fast-selling Ford. It averaged 371,000 buyers in its first two seasons and another 280,000 for 1986-87. Sales then turned strongly upward for 1988-89, breaking the three-quarter-million mark for the two years combined. Dearborn designers and decision-makers evidently had the inside track on what appealed to American buyers.

Yet, even they were likely surprised by the success of Taurus, the front-drive 1986 replacement for the junior LTD in the all-

1983 Escort GT hatchback coupe

1984 LTD LX four-door sedan

1984 LTD Crown Victoria four-door sedan with Brougham roof

1984 Tempo GL coupe

1984 Escort GT hatchback coupe

1985 LTD four-door sedan

important midsize market. Riding a 106-inch wheelbase, these four-door sedans and four-door wagons represented Ford's strongest-ever claim to Detroit design leadership: clean, smooth, and carefully detailed, yet not lumpy like some other low-drag "aero" cars. Dominating the spacious interiors was an obviously European-inspired dashboard with some controls sensibly copied from the best of BMW, Mercedes-Benz, and Saab.

As expected, Taurus engines mounted transversely in a chassis with all-independent suspension. Sedans used MacPherson struts and coil springs at each corner, supplemented at the rear by parallel control arms. Wagons eschewed rear struts for twin control arms, a system better able to cope with the wider range of load weights wagons carry.

Initial engine choices began with a 2.5-liter 88-bhp four, an enlarged Tempo unit available with standard five-speed manual or, from late '87, optional four-speed overdrive automatic transaxles. Most Tauruses, though, were ordered with the new port-injected 3.0-liter "Vulcan" V-6, a 60-degree overhead-valve design rated at 140 bhp and teamed with automatic only. For 1988, Ford added a reengineered version of its 90-degree 3.8-liter V-6 as a new option. Horsepower here was also 140, but the 3.8's extra torque provided quicker acceleration than the 3.0.

With its ultramodern styling, good performance, and prices far lower than those of certain coveted German sedans, Taurus charged up the sales chart like a bull in a china shop. Ford sold over 236,000 of the '86s and nearly 375,000 for '87—astounding for what was, after all, a very daring departure for a middle-class American car.

But there were still those who wanted a Taurus with performance and mechanical specifications as sophisticated as its styling. They got one, and 1989 was showtime—or rather SHO time: a new "Super High Output" 3.0 V-6 with overhead-cam cylinder heads and four valves per cylinder (instead of two), plus dual exhausts. Engineered with help from Yamaha, the SHO engine turned out 220 horsepower, good for seven seconds 0-60 mph, according to Ford; *Consumer Guide®* managed "only" 7.4—still great going. The SHO came only in a sedan with standard antilock all-disc brakes, a handling package with larger antiroll bars, and 15-inch aluminum wheels wearing high-speed V-rated tires. Lending added styling distinction were unique lower-body extensions and inboard front fog lamps. The interior was special too, boasting multi-adjustable front bucket seats, sport cloth upholstery, center console, and, to match the high-winding engine, an 8000-rpm tachometer.

Nevertheless, the SHO was a very slow mover on the sales chart, mainly because there was no automatic option and the mandatory Mazda-supplied manual five-speed suffered balky, high-effort shift action. Production was thus meager through 1990: about 25,000 or so. But Taurus as a whole kept up its initial rip-snorting pace, besting 387,000 for '88, 395,000 for '89,

1985 Tempo Sports GL coupe

1986 Taurus station wagon prototype

1986½ EXP 2-passenger sport coupe

1987 Taurus LX four-door sedan

1987 EXP 2-passenger sport coupe

and 333,000 for recession-plagued 1990. Thoughtful yearly upgrades helped. Among the most thoughtful: optional anti-lock brakes for sedans and a standard driver-side air bag for all 1990 models.

We shouldn't leave this decade without mentioning the Probe, which was new for 1989. A sporty hatchback coupe based on Mazda's MX-6, it was a high point for Dearborn's then 15-year-old partnership with the Japanese automaker. This had been such a success that Ford not only bought a 25-percent stake in Mazda but decided to entrust it with all of Ford's own small-car development for North America. The Probe was the first fruit of that decision.

The original Probe will ever be remembered as the car that almost replaced the Mustang. Ford changed its name only at the last minute amid howls of protest from Mustang loyalists who'd have no truck with a Japanese design—and with "inferior" front drive at that. The name itself came from Ford's exciting early-'80s series of aerodynamic concept cars, but proved to have unexpectedly offensive connotations. To produce the car, Ford and Mazda set up a new factory in Flat Rock, Michigan, not far from historic River Rouge, as part of a joint venture aptly named Auto Alliance. The plant also turned out MX-6s and 626 sedans for Mazda's U.S. dealers.

With all this, the Probe is at best a "half-American" car despite all-Ford styling and availability of the 3.0-liter Taurus V-6 on midrange LX models for 1990-92. (The base GL used a 2.2-liter Mazda four, the top-line GT a turbocharged version). Probe was redesigned for '93 on a new-generation MX-6 platform with 102.9-inch wheelbase (versus 99), again with much more dramatic styling than its cousin. Power was exclusively Mazda: a 2.0-liter four for the base model, a 2.5 V-6 for the sporty GT.

Probe was a timely Ford weapon against sporty Japanese compacts like Toyota Celica, Honda Prelude, Nissan 200SX—and Mazda MX-6. Sales were good at first—more than 117,000 by 1990—but then fell victim to a sharp drop in sporty coupe demand. The second-generation Probe was the last, with production ending in '97.

Despite its ultimate demise, Probe was as much a symbol as Taurus of Ford's strong '80s resurgence, a phoenixlike renaissance engineered by Donald E. Petersen (president from 1980, chairman after 1984) and his young, enthusiastic executive team. From an automaker that was as near to collapse as Chrysler was in 1980, Dearborn remade itself into a trimmer, more-responsive, and vastly more-efficient outfit while fielding aggressive products that were usually right on target. Ford was still the home of "better ideas," but by 1990 it was also home to some of America's most-popular and respected automobiles.

The same was true of trucks—important given the boom in light-truck demand that began in the mid-'80s and continued into the '90s and beyond. If anything, Ford was even more successful here than it was with cars. For example, 1982 saw the full-size F-Series pickup begin a long reign as America's top-selling vehicle of any kind. Ford's Ranger (a 1982 newcomer) became sales king of compact pickups. Dearborn also scored big in the burgeoning sport-utility field with Explorer, the upscale 1991 four-door replacement for the two-door Ranger-based Bronco II. Ford did fumble with minivans, but not seriously. Though its new-for-'86 rear-drive Aerostar was way outpolled by Chrysler's front-drive models, sales were consistent and high enough that Ford stayed the Aerostar's planned 1994 execution, letting the older minivan run alongside the new front-drive Windstar.

By the mid-'90s, these truck successes added to the continuing popularity of Taurus and Escort to make Ford the sales leader in five vehicle segments: full-size pickups (F-Series), midsize car (Taurus), sporty-utility vehicles (Explorer), sub-

1988 Taurus LX four-door sedan

1989 LTD Crown Victoria LX four-door sedan

1989 Taurus LX station wagon

1990 Taurus SHO four-door sedan

1989 Taurus SHO four-door sedan

1990 Escort GT hatchback coupe

1989 Probe coupe

1990 Probe GT coupe

compact car (Escort), and compact pickup (Ranger). Moreover, Taurus took over as the country's top-selling car line in 1992 to end the Honda Accord's three-year reign, though not without cash rebates and other sales incentives.

With all this, Ford Division remained "USA-1" in the early '90s, selling well over a million cars a year and a like number of light trucks. Chevy did move about 40,000 more domestic cars in calendar '91, but that was the only time it surpassed Ford in these years.

Two different Dearborn regimes presided over this remarkable sales performance. First, Don Petersen handed over the chairman's gavel in 1990 to his one-time number-two, Harold A. "Red" Poling; at the same time, the president's job was reactivated after a two-year lapse for Phillip Benton, Jr. Both these men were Dearborn veterans, but they were merely a transition team, for late 1993 ushered in the worldly wise Alex Trotman as both president and chairman.

As a veteran of Ford Europe, Trotman brought a more-international outlook to the company's "Glass House" headquarters, which was soon populated by many of his European colleagues. One of their first projects was an ambitious corporate reorganization dubbed "Ford 2000." Announced in 1994, this aimed to mobilize all of the firm's global resources to further improve quality, shorten product development times, and achieve greater manufacturing efficiencies. Though it wouldn't be evident on the road until middecade, Ford 2000 seemed a prudent plan in light of the automobile industry's ever increasing globalization.

Meantime, Ford Division had redesigned its Escort for the first time since the 1981 original. Arriving in spring 1990 as an early-'91 model, it was another "world car," though in the same way as Probe. Here, Ford applied "mini-Taurus" styling to the latest version of Mazda's small, front-drive 323/Protege to produce a competent Japanese-style subcompact with much greater sales appeal against rival Toyotas, Hondas, and Nissans.

Initial body styles were the same as before. So was the basic "CVH" engine retained for all Escorts save the sporty GT three-door. That one benefited greatly from a new twincam 1.8-liter Mazda four with 16 valves and 127 lively horses. Though the CVH gained sequential-port fuel injection and distributorless electronic ignition, it remained a gruff and noisy slogger with just 88 horsepower. At least it was cheap, and that combined with more efficient production in Mexico as well as Michigan to make for very low list prices: $7976 for the stark three-door Pony to more than $11 grand for the GT. A crisp four-door notchback bowed for 1992 in mid-range LX trim, and there was a sporty LX-E version with the GT's engine and firm suspension, plus rear disc brakes—a kind of pint-size Taurus SHO.

Only evolutionary changes would occur through 1996, save the admirable adoption of a standard passenger airbag for '95 supplementing the already included driver's restraint. An optional fold-out child safety seat was also added that year. Sales remained strong despite the yearly sameness. A clever new "one price" program helped. Begun in 1992, this offered any of the four LX models with several popular options for just $10,899 with five-speed manual transmission or $11,631 with optional four-speed automatic. Ford was copying the no-hassle price policy of GM's Saturn subsidiary, but it was nonetheless a timely counter to Chevy's Cavalier, which was doing the same thing—not to mention Japanese small cars that were rapidly moving up the scale due to a strengthened yen. Unfortunately, everyday Escorts couldn't match many import-brand competitors for pep and refinement, so it's just as well that the freshened '97s went on sale in early 1996.

Ford modernized two more of its cars for 1992. First up was a replacement for something even older than the original Escort: the big, vintage-'79 Crown Victoria. Reaching showrooms in March 1991, it was virtually all-new despite retaining the basic rear-drive "Panther" platform and wheelbase. There was new styling, of course: smooth and rounded in Dearborn's now-expected "aero" mold, but not "jellybean" chunky. A grilleless Taurus-type face replaced the dated standup eggcrate. Other passe stuff like vinyl roof covers, opera lights, and wire-wheel covers was forgotten, too. So was the LTD name—but also the Crown Vic wagon, Ford having concluded that minivans and sport-utility vehicles had now largely replaced traditional full-size wagons in buyer affections. That left a four-door sedan with airy "six-light" roofline in base and uplevel LX trim; a sportier Touring Sedan was added in the fall.

Like its 1990 makeover of the aged Lincoln Town Car, Ford went much further with this new Crown Victoria than was absolutely needed to satisfy the market. Where GM was content to merely rebody its largest cars, Ford overhauled the chassis, adding standard all-disc brakes with optional antilock control and making numerous tweaks to steering, springs, shocks, and suspension geometry. The result was surprisingly agile and responsive for a traditional full-size Detroiter and a vast improvement over the old Crown Vic. It was also a more-potent big Ford with adoption of the 4.6-liter overhead-cam V-8 first seen in the '91 Town Car. The first member of Dearborn's new "modular" engine family, it delivered 190 standard bhp or 210 with dual exhausts, a gain of 40-50 horses over the old pushrod 302. The uprated engine was included in a Handling and Performance package that was standard for the Touring Sedan and optional on other models. As its name implied, this also delivered firmer damping and wider wheels wearing performance tires, as well as ABS and traction control. All models came with a driver-side air bag per Washington's insistence; a passenger-side restraint was also available.

All this plus starting prices in the low $20,000s lit a fire under Crown Victoria sales, which jumped past 152,000 for 1992, the highest since '85. Volume then declined to under 110,000, but remained healthy through decade's end. Buyer requests prompted the addition of conventional grille for '93, when the Touring was dropped. The passenger airbag became standard for '94. The '95s got a mild facelift, "gullwing" taillights, revised climate controls and newly standard rear defroster, heated door mirrors, a radio antenna embedded in the rear window, a

1991 Tempo LX four-door sedan

1991 Taurus SHO four-door sedan

1991 Escort LX hatchback sedan

1992 Escort LX-E four-door sedan

"battery-saver" feature, and displays for outside temperature and "gallons to empty." Even with all these additions, base price was comfortably below $25,000.

Incidentally, the Crown Vic became an "import" for a few years in the early '90s, built north of the border with a high level of Canadian content. The reason was CAFE, the Corporate Average Fuel Economy law that took effect with model-year '78 but had lately been relaxed somewhat. Still, the Crown Vic had fair thirst (about 17 mpg city, 25 highway, as rated by the Environmental Protection Agency) and was thus a drain on Ford's domestic fleet-average economy. As an "import," the Crown Vic counted in Ford's non-domestic CAFE along with the tiny South Korean-built Festiva, whose really high mileage more than offset the big car's. Later, Ford didn't need such tricks to comply with CAFE, so parts and labor were re-sourced to make the Crown Vic truly "American" again. Such is the silliness sometimes wrought by well-meaning regulations.

Ford's other 1992 freshening involved the top-selling Taurus. With competitors pushing hard, the basic '86 design was now in need of an update, so Ford spent a cool $650 million to give it one. Much of the money went toward things that didn't show but made a good car even better, particularly in the areas of noise, vibration, and harshness (NVH). Among these were a stiffer unibody structure, a suspension revised for a smoother ride with no harm to handling, more-responsive power steering, extra sound-deadening in strategic places, engine adjustments for improved drivability, and a more-precise solid-rod shift linkage for the dashing SHO. Ford also dropped the weak four-cylinder engine, which pleased some buyers apart from rent-a-car companies.

Inside, the '92 Taurus presented a redesigned dash with subtle ergonomic refinements and space for a newly optional passenger airbag. Outside was... a disappointment. Though every body panel was new save the doors, the '92 was hard to tell at a glance from previous Tauruses—as critics loved to point out. But buyers didn't seem to care. As mentioned, Taurus took over as America's most-popular car line in '92. Calendar-year sales were smashing at over 397,000, and model-year production was a record 368,000. But that was only a prelude to '93, when model-year output surged to nearly 459,000. The '95 tally was almost as good: just over 410,000.

Like Escort, Taurus wouldn't see another major change until late decade. The most-important interim development was standardizing the passenger air bag for '94. An interesting '95 variation was the SE (Sport Edition) sedan, a kind of budget SHO delivering alloy wheels, rear spoiler, sport front seats, and other extras for about $18-grand with base 3.0-liter V-6 or just under $20,000 with the punchier 3.8. Interestingly, the smaller "Vulcan" V-6 got some needed NVH improvements in preparation for the all-new second-generation Taurus.

Let's not forget the 1992-95 SHO, which gained greater visual distinction through more-aggressive styling front and rear, plus bolder cladding for the lower bodysides. In addition, Ford finally added a four-speed automatic to the SHO's option list for 1993. To maintain performance parity with the five-speed model, the 3.0-liter Yamaha V-6 was enlarged for the shiftless SHO to near 3.2 liters (192 cid), yielding a useful 20 extra pound-feet of torque (220 in all), though no more horsepower. SHO pricing remained unusually steady in these years, but neither that nor the automatic was much help to sales. With base stickers straddling $25,000, the top-line Taurus still faced competition from a host of formidable foreign sports sedans and usually suffered by comparison. But though eclipsed by those cars for image—and ultimately by a V-8 successor for performance, the V-6 SHO was a rewarding driver's car with a pleasing blend of American and European characteristics.

1992 Aerostar Eddie Bauer 4WD extended-length minivan

1993 Probe GT coupe

1993 Tempo GL four-door sedan

1993 Crown Victoria four-door sedan

1994 Taurus LX station wagon

1995 Taurus SE four-door sedan

1995 Contour LX four-door sedan

1996 Windstar LX minivan

1996 Taurus LX four-door sedan

Interest value was definitely not a trait of the early '90s Tempo. Soldiering on with few evident differences from one year to the next, Ford's front-drive compact tended to get lost in the great gray mass of Detroit market-fillers that you were more apt to rent on vacation than put in your driveway. Yet for all its crushing dullness, Tempo remained a decent seller, with steady model-year production of well over 100,000 units through swan-song '94—and the '93s made a surprise spurt to better than 238,000. Tempo's only changes of note in this period were loss of the AWD option after 1991 (when it was called "Four Wheel Drive") and the '92 addition of the 3.0-liter Taurus V-6 as standard for top-line GLS models (which then went away) and an option elsewhere. Base prices remained very attractive, rising no higher than the low $12,000s. While that betrayed an aging design long since paid for, it also helped Ford to keep moving this metal.

Tempo's 1995 replacement stood to be a far easier sell. Called Contour, it was another stab at a "world car," born of "Ford 2000" thinking as an Americanized version of the year-old European Mondeo. But unlike the original compromised U.S. Escort, Contour was very close to its transatlantic cousin, having the same smooth, tightly drawn styling, plus an ultra-stiff structure and a sophisticated all-independent suspension that contributed to crisp, taut handling. Even the Mondeo dash was little altered for the States. Unfortunately, so was its snug interior. Despite a wheelbase half-an-inch longer than Taurus', the Contour was frankly cramped in back, with little underseat footroom and marginal knee-, leg-, and headroom.

Still, this was the closest America had yet come to an affordable European-style sports sedan. Critics raved. *Road & Track* called Contour "a giant step forward in the compact sedan arena." *Car and Driver* termed it "stunningly satisfying." Those verdicts came from road tests of the top-line SE model and its 2.5-liter "Duratec" V-6. A new all-Ford design optional on lesser Contours, this engine made 170 spirited horses—enough for *Consumer Guide*®'s five-speed car to charge from 0 to 60 mph in just 8.9 seconds. GL and midlevel LX models came with another new engine: a 2.0-liter multivalve twincam four called "Zetec," an outgrowth of Ford Europe's recently introduced "Zeta" family of small, high-efficiency powerplants. In line with a fast-growing Detroit trend, both Contour engines could go 100,000 miles without a tune-up. And, of course, either could drive through an optional four-speed automatic.

Ford spent a record $6 billion to introduce Mondeo, Contour, and Mercury's companion '95 Mystique. That was twice the expense of the original Taurus program, but included the high costs of developing two brand-new engines, manufacturing facilities, and the usual new-model tooling. Even so, Ford had bet heavily on these cars (dubbed "CDW127" in the company's new internal code, the letters denoting "World car" in the "C/D" size class), so it was vital they succeed.

Contour did succeed, but not as well as the car it replaced. A minor recall slowed early deliveries, but the real problem was sticker shock. With buyers still flocking to well-equipped Japanese cars, Ford decided to ladle on all kinds of standard features (including dual dashboard airbags), but this only pushed Contour quite a bit upmarket from Tempo, which had been relatively cheap. Many prospects thus balked and walked when Contour arrived at a minimum of $13,300, over $1000 more than a late loaded Tempo. Opt for an SE with desirable extras like ABS and traction control and you were well over $20,000, which was Taurus money. Ford had underestimated the price sensitivity of Contour's target market, as telling a miscalculation as that tight back seat.

Ford tried to correct its mistakes for 1997 by adding a lower-priced low-frills Contour and scooping out the front seatbacks and rear-seat cushion for a little more aft leg room. A modest reskin followed for '98, when the two low-line models were dropped and the LX and SE became better dollar values through careful realigning of prices and standard features. But nothing seemed to help, so Ford pulled the plug on Contour after 2000. Sibling Mondeo continued, however, remaining quite popular in Europe—enough to be accorded a full redesign a few years later.

Before the end, Contour got a megadose of Euro-style performance, courtesy of Ford's Special Vehicle Team. SVT had been formed in the early 1990s as a semi-autonomous part of the Dearborn organization, charged with souping-up various vehicles for sale through selected Ford dealers. Having made its mark with hot Cobra Mustangs and rapid F-150 Lightning pickups, SVT was asked to realize the Contour's full sport sedan potential for 1998. Marketers doubtless hoped the new model's image would boost sales for the rest of the line.

They didn't get that, but enthusiasts got a "stealth" driver's car that could go hunting for BMWs, even on twisty roads. A reworked suspension with stiffer springs and shocks, bigger brakes, and 16-inch rolling stock made cornering nimble and near neutral—a revelation for a domestic front-drive sedan—yet ride was scarcely less supple than in mainstream Contours. To complement the chassis, the 2.5 Duratec V-6 received higher compression, deep-breathing exercises, and other measures to achieve 195 bhp (later 200), delivered through a mandatory short-throw five-speed manual gearbox. Cosmetic alterations were subtle but sufficient for those in the know, and there were plenty of extra niceties such as leather upholstery. The only options, in fact, were a power moonroof and CD player. Even so, the base price was amazingly low at around $23,000. A comparable 3-Series BMW or Mercedes-Benz C-Class cost thousands more, yet the SVT Contour was easily their equal on a road course or a dragstrip, running 0-60 mph in about 7.5 seconds in most road tests. *Collectible Automobile* magazine thought the SVT Contour so good that it would one day be a coveted keepsake. "No doubt about it... Ford has finally produced a genuine European sports sedan right here in the U.S.A. (Hear that, "Buy American" diehards?)" Alas, many enthusiasts either didn't believe their ears or thought the Blue Oval badge too proletarian. In any case, production was slightly more limited than even SVT had planned: about 10,000 in 1998-99, plus a handful more in phaseout 2000.

Ford was somewhat wide of the mark with the erstwhile replacement for its old trucklike Aerostar minivan. Unlike Mercury's two-year-old Villager, which Ford built in Ohio to a Nissan design, the new 1995 Windstar was Dearborn's own front-drive minivan, using a modified Taurus platform and drivetrains to furnish a similarly carlike driving feel. Ford also gave it standard seven-place seating on a 120.7-inch wheelbase, slightly longer than that of Chrysler's extended-length Grand models. Overall, Windstar was eight inches longer than a Grand and nearly a foot longer than Villager. GL and LX price levels were offered in the $20,000-$24,000 range. Nice looks, high utility, and a full range of passenger-car safety features netted healthy sales. Even so, Ford was only catching up, not advancing the art, and Windstar was never a threat to the sales-leading Chrysler/Dodge/Plymouth minivans—not even after being lightly restyled as the 2005 Freestar.

There was nothing half-hearted about the all-new 1996 Taurus. From nose to tail, top to bottom, it was an orgy of ovals on a lozengelike form with concave lower bodysides—what one journalist termed a "predented" look. Chairman Alex Trotman hoped another daring design would grab the public like the original Taurus had and turn the styling spotlight away from the new "cab-forward" Chrysler/Dodge models competing

1996 Taurus LX station wagon

1997 Probe GT coupe

1997 Crown Victoria four-door sedan

1997 Aspire hatchback sedan

1997 Taurus LX four-door sedan

1997 Escort four-door wagon

1998 Escort ZX2 coupe

1998 Contour SVT four-door sedan

1998 Taurus LX four-door sedan

1999 Contour SVT four-door sedan

with Taurus. At one point, Trotman reportedly walked through the styling studio, looked around, and said to those present, "You're not scaring me enough."

Unfortunately for Ford, the result must have scared off some buyers, for Taurus promptly lost its standing as America's top-selling car line and would never get it back. One wag thought the '96 model so odd as to imagine, "If they could have made oval wheels work, they'd have used them." There were ovals aplenty inside too, including a large one in the middle of the dash with oddly curved arrays of look-alike pushbuttons for audio and climate functions. Neither critics nor many consumers were amused.

More's the pity, for the 1996 model represented a major improvement over past Tauruses in many ways. The value-oriented GL sedan and wagon got an updated Vulcan pushrod V-6, while the nicer LXs were treated to a 3.0-liter version of the twincam Duratec V-6 with 200 bhp, considered by many buyers to be well worth its $500 premium. Topping the line was a new SHO with 235 bhp from a 3.4-liter V-8, another Ford-Yamaha collaboration. Wheelbase on all models added 2.5 inches, benefiting rear leg room, as well as handling in concert with a revised suspension. But certain rivals, notably the Honda Accord and Toyota Camry, now had a slight edge in ride quality, a big one in build quality—and were fighting fiercely for Taurus's number-one sales spot. Worse, price hikes of around $1000 chilled early demand, prompting the addition of a detrimmed price-leader G sedan during the '96 season.

Yet for all the controversy, Taurus sales remained strong, actually improving by some 11 percent for 1996 over the prior model year. Volume then held at around 400,000 through 2000. But Taurus still relied far more on fleet sales each year than its leading Japanese-brand rivals, so Ford earned somewhat less on every sale and owners received less at trade-in time.

Ford was more on target with a redesigned Escort that rang up more than 655,000 sales for model years 1997-98 and more than 100,000 each for '99 and 2000. The previous Mazda Protege-based design returned with a smooth new wrapper and a 110-bhp 2.0-liter single-cam Zetec four-cylinder, thus ousting the old CVH engine at last. Models comprised two sedans and a wagon at first, a single sedan after 1999. All aimed to provide nothing more than economical yet stylish transportation at a low price, which was all many people needed. Pricing probably helped close many a sale. Even with a heavy option load, these Escorts seldom broke the $17,000 barrier, yet they were more refined and better built than previous models, enough to stand comparison with some import-brand rivals. But they were only a short-lived bridge to the year 2000 and the debut of a far more ambitious small Ford. Despite its seeming lame-duck status, Escort kept selling well enough that Ford decided to keep it around longer than planned, offering a special fleet sedan to nonretail customers for 2001-02.

For those who missed Escort's spunky GT hatchback, Ford offered the new 1998 Escort ZX2, a sporty coupe with a separate trunk and Taurus-like styling. Appearances notwithstanding, basic architecture and underskin components were shared with other Escorts, while the engine was the same twincam Zetec found in the base Contour. With 130 bhp and relatively low weight (2470 pounds), the ZX2 was frisky, though no neck-snapper. Signaling its mission of wooing younger, cash-short enthusiasts, it initially came in "Cool" and better-equipped "Hot" versions.

Yet once again, Ford's aim was slightly off. *Consumer Guide*® and others thought ZX2 a bit pricey for what it delivered: $12,580 base for a '98 *without* air conditioning. And though Ford trimmed $1000 off the price of a "Cool" model for '99, *CG* repeated that "...ZX2 looks sportier than it performs." This must have sounded all too familiar to Ford folks who remembered the unlovely and unloved EXP. A zippy $1495 SR package was added for 2000 with an extra 13 horses, tuned suspension, four-wheel disc brakes, alloy wheels, performance tires and special seats, but it did nothing to spark sales. By 2002, the ZX2 (minus Escort badging) was down to some 52,000 calendar-year orders, then slid below 25,500, a poor showing for the low-to midteens pricing. Ford stayed the course one more year, then abandoned the sporty-coupe market, which was fast shrinking anyway.

Despite its product fumbles, Ford Motor Company seemed in great shape as the new century opened. Corporate profits hit a record $7.2 billion in 1999 as the stock market and new-vehicle demand stayed strong in an unprecedented boom economy. Ford Division remained "USA-1," owning five of the country's top-10 sellers, including the big F-Series pickup and midsize Explorer SUV. Both were vital high-profit assets in a market gone mad for trucks, and Dearborn gave them yearly improvements to protect their class-leading sales status. The Explorer, for example, was redesigned for 1995 and given optional V-8 power the following year. Answering competitive SUV challenges, Ford soon fielded the F-150-based Expedition and, a bit later, the jumbo Excursion and compact Escape.

Dearborn was no less expansive in the luxury field, pouring major money into new products and plants for Jaguar and Aston Martin, acquired in the 1980s, then adding Land Rover, another British icon, and well-regarded Volvo of Sweden. In 1999 these four makes were combined with Lincoln and Mercury into a new division, Premier Automotive Group (PAG).

Nineteen ninety-nine also witnessed historic changes in top Ford management. Chairman Alex Trotman retired, handing the reins to 42-year-old William Clay Ford, Jr., great-grandson of the company founder and nephew of the late Henry Ford II. At the same time, hard-charging Jacques Nasser was elevated to president and chief executive officer after two years as head of North American operations.

But suddenly it all turned sour. First, the economy unraveled as overpriced "tech stocks" tanked, taking Wall Street and the economy down with them. Then, in 2000, the cash-cow Explorer and its original-equipment Firestone tires were implicated in rollover crashes linked to almost 300 deaths and scores of injuries. Nasser traded charges with Firestone officials in the media and before Congressional investigators, then ponied up $3.5 billion to replace some 6.5 million tires. But months of damning publicity clobbered Dearborn's image—and its stock price. So did a string of recalls and launch glitches involving the new Escape, 2001 Thunderbird, redesigned '02 Explorer, and the small Focus, Ford's latest attempt at a "world car." Other new models like the Lincoln LS and sister Jaguar S-Type didn't sell as expected. Longtime Japanese affiliate Mazda was also in trouble, a further drain on corporate coffers.

And there was worse. After burning through more than $15 billion in 1999-2000, Ford lost a staggering $5.45 billion in 2001 and almost a billion more in '02. Part of that came from having to match the costly zero-percent financing program instituted by GM to jump-start a stunned market after the September 11 terrorist attacks. Equally ominous, Ford's near-term domestic product pipeline looked dry, and Jaguar was gushing red ink.

Many things had obviously gone wrong. Most pundits blamed CEO Nasser. So did the Ford board, who sacked "Jac" in October 2001. A reluctant Bill Ford took command. Nasser had overreached. Buying Volvo and Land Rover was costly enough, but Nasser also splurged on wispy e-commerce ventures, a chain of auto repair shops in Britain, Norwegian-built electric cars, even junkyards. "The plan, theoretically, had promise," said trade weekly *Automotive News*. "[But the] acerbic Nasser

1999 Crown Victoria four-door sedan

1999 Escort ZX2 coupe

1999 Taurus four-door sedan

2000 Ford Explorer four-door wagon

2000 Focus SE four-door wagon

left out a couple of ingredients: building reliable vehicles, and keeping the troops happy."

Some wondered whether Bill Ford could turn the company around, but he silenced many skeptics by moving swiftly to put Ford's "Glass House" in order. From now on, he declared, Ford would build great cars and trucks, period. No more of Nasser's grand vision for a cradle-to-grave "transportation company." After shuffling key executives and drawing up a new organizational chart, Ford announced a recovery plan that aimed to achieve $7 billion in pretax profit by 2006, mainly through "leaner" manufacturing, "smarter" engineering, plant closures, worker layoffs, and supplier concessions. New models were supposed to help, particularly new cars, which Ford heralded by proclaiming 2004 as "The Year of the Car."

But recovery proved stubbornly elusive. By 2006, Dearborn counted five straight years of declining sales representing over a million units lost—Detroit's worst performance by far. Market share, which had been sliding for a full decade, was down to 17.4 percent, the lowest since 1927, and seemed likely to go lower still. *The Economist* in Britain observed that the '02 plan "failed to anticipate rising competition from [import brands] and the impact of soaring health-care costs." Ford was also being squeezed by escalating raw materials costs and—the big hit—a sharp drop in demand for its most profitable SUVs, triggered by a spike in gas prices during 2005 to over $3 a gallon in many places. This "perfect storm" was also battering General Motors. Like Ford, GM still relied too much on truck sales and was trying to "shrink its way back to profitability" in the face of market changes it hadn't foreseen. But more downsizing wasn't the answer. Aside from enormous pension and health-care expenses, both companies had to contend with "job banks" of laid-off workers who still drew most of their former pay, thanks to lush contracts negotiated with management in palmy days. And there was still the thorny problem of weaning buyers off the costly purchase incentives they'd been used to for years.

A final indignity for Ford was an exodus of talented people, a "brain drain" the company could ill-afford in this new crisis. Though not unexpected amid so much turmoil, the constant personnel shuffling only added to the perception that Ford—GM too—was heading toward bankruptcy. As one example, Ford went through no fewer than four executives in five years in the position of president of North American operations.

With all this, Ford was in a fight for its life. As *The Economist* noted: "Now the struggle is simply to make the car business profitable. This could be the last chance to fix Ford this side of the bankruptcy courts." Defiantly, Ford said Chapter 11 was *not* an option and announced a new restructuring effort in January 2006. Though light on many specifics, this "Way Forward" plan called for closing 14 North American plants by 2012, thus erasing some 30,000 jobs and cutting build capacity by more than a fourth. Ford also promised new vehicles that "people will really want." To execute the plan, Ford installed Mark Fields, the architect of a recent turnaround at Mazda, as president of the Americas, with Anne Stevens as his chief operating officer. "We lost our way," Fields admitted. "We lost touch with our customers, particularly our car customers." One result was that Chevrolet became America's top-selling nameplate in 2005, finally wresting the crown from Ford after 19 years.

Though increasingly eclipsed by the likes of Honda and Toyota, several Ford cars did well in the early 2000s. Despite too many recalls, the front-drive Focus was an unqualified success, drawing more than 389,000 orders in debut 2000 and around 300,000 each calendar year from 2001 to '04. This "big and tall" subcompact had a big job, being assigned to fill the market shoes of the Escort, ZX2, and Contour. But Focus was a masterpiece of space utilization, offering more passenger and

2001 Taurus four-door sedan

2001 Taurus SE station wagon

2001 Focus ZTS four-door sedan

2001 ZX2 coupe

2002 Taurus four-door sedan

cargo space than those earlier small Fords, as well as most of its rivals.

Initial engines were the proven 2.0-liter Zetec fours—110-bhp single-cam and 130-bhp twincam—but most everything else was appealingly different. Start with the "New Edge" styling, a parting gift from corporate design chief Jack Telnack. An avant-garde mix of curves and creases, New Edge didn't work on every car, but it did here, lending a visual personality that set Focus apart from every rival. Engineering was no less artful, especially the all-independent suspension that drew rave reviews for delivering both a smooth ride and class-leading handling. It was the sort of small car one expected from Europe. Sure enough, the Focus was developed "over there" and brought to North America with minimal change for local production.

Focus bowed with two-door hatchback, four-door sedan, and four-door wagon body styles, each aimed at a specific audience. The hatchback played both entry-level and sporty roles, offering the widest range of options. The more conventionally styled sedan and wagon emphasized value, practicality, comfort, even luxury with the right options. A hatchback four-door joined the mix for 2002 for even broader market coverage.

To Ford's undoubted delight, the Focus was a critical success most everywhere, winning awards in Europe and the 2000 North American Car of the Year trophy. *Consumer Guide*® gave its "Best Buy" endorsement to the 2001-04 models. The honor was rather remarkable considering that Focus was fending off new import competition with only evolutionary changes, mainly a confusing parade of model names and equipment shuffles.

A notable exception was the SVT Focus, arriving for 2002 as a two-door hatchback pitched toward the fast-growing "sport compact" market. A companion four-door hatch was added for '03. Like other SVT efforts, the "factory tuner" Focus delivered numerous upgrades at a surprisingly modest price, initially $17,480. The twincam Zetec engine, for example, was lifted to 170 bhp via new pistons, revised cylinder head, variable intake-valve timing, and new intake and exhaust manifolds. Also on the menu were a mandatory new six-speed manual gearbox, firm suspension with 17-inch wheels, and larger four-wheel disc brakes. Other Focuses offered ABS, electronic traction control, and front side airbags at extra cost, but these were standard for the SVT. So were unique front and rear fascias, side sills, and a rear spoiler, all *de rigueur* for a "hot hatch." Inside were special SVT gauge graphics and two extra gauges, leather/cloth seats with heavier front bolstering, aluminum pedal caps and shift knob, and a leather-wrapped steering wheel.

Enthusiasts loved it, but the SVT Focus wouldn't be around long, departing after 2004. One reason was that Ford needed to freshen its small car to maintain buyer interest. The result was a refocused 2005 lineup with more orthodox styling inside and out, plus more competitive "value" pricing. The sportiest of the lot was a new ZX4 ST sedan, which was no SVT but had significance for its standard engine: a new 2.3-liter twincam four-cylinder that rated Partial Zero Emissions Vehicle status (PZEV) under the ultratight emissions limits of California and four northeastern states. Available for other Focus models in those five areas, the PZEV four was about as clean as a gasoline engine could be with existing technology—not far behind the gasoline/electric powertrains earning headlines, goodwill, and profits for Toyota and Honda. Even better, a PZEV Focus cost far less than a Toyota Prius or Honda Civic Hybrid, was much simpler and easier to maintain, and possessed noticeably more low-end torque that improved acceleration, especially with automatic transmission. It was quite a coup, yet went all but unnoticed amid Dearborn's deteriorating fortunes.

The big Crown Victoria was all but invisible long before the crisis took hold, a relic of much happier times for Ford and all

2000 Focus ZX3 hatchback coupe

2002 Crown Victoria four-door sedan

2002 ZX2 coupe

2002 Focus SVT hatchback coupe

2002 Explorer four-door wagon

2003 Focus SVT four-door hatchback

2003 Focus SVT hatchback with European Feature Package

2004 Freestar minivan

2004 Taurus four-door sedan

of Detroit. Taxi and law-enforcement fleets were its main buyers as the century turned, sister Mercury Grand Marquis having taken the lead in retail sales. Still, Ford could afford to keep the "Vicky" around and even splurge for occasional changes: a Grand Marquis-like restyle for 1998, standard horsepower bumped to 220 for 2002, and a few new features along the way. Calendar-year sales were down to the high 70,000s by '02, when Ford tried adding a little youth tonic with an LX Sport model. This offered a nostalgic buckets-and-console interior with floorshifter, a dual-exhaust V-8 pumped up to 235 bhp, and the firmer-handling suspension available for the mom-and-pop LX. Extensive revisions occurred for 2003, perhaps because that was Ford's centennial year. A redesigned frame, altered suspension geometry, and a switch from recirculating-ball to rack-and-pinion steering all aimed to improve ride and handling, which they did—a little. No-cost antilock brakes were laudable, as was first-time availability of front side airbags except on the price-leading Standard. Though stickers had inevitably risen over time, the Crown Vic still offered a lot of good old-fashioned American metal for the money at around $24,000-$30,000. But old-fashioned it was, and sales continued trailing off toward oblivion, falling below 64,000 for calendar '05.

Taurus, too, seemed increasingly passé as the new century progressed, the basic 1995 design being left to soldier on while the Honda Accord and Toyota Camry enticed buyers with three clean-sheet makeovers. Such intense competition and a more knowledgeable public made "new or die" imperative even in the family car field, yet Ford had staked its future more on new trucks than new cars.

Not that Taurus was entirely neglected. A 2000-model restyle, much of it patterned on the less radical Mercury Sable, aimed at wider public acceptance, as did a new, more user-friendly dashboard. Airbags and seatbelt pretensioners were improved in line with growing buyer demand for safety features. (Who could have imagined that back in 1956?) But the interesting SHO was canceled for lack of interest, and other Tauruses changed hardly at all over the next six seasons. Given that, calendar-year sales were remarkably good, running in the low 100,000s through 2002, then jumping past 200,000 in 2003-04. Still, one suspects most of these cars went to fleets and skinflint consumers, and then only with heavy "cash on the hood." Taurus was supposed to depart after 2005, when just two varieties of sedan and wagon appeared as a transition to all-new replacements. Yet such was the uncertainty in Dearborn that planners allowed Taurus to hang on through 2006, reduced to just a pair of sedans with the old pushrod V-6.

Hopes were high for the 2005 Five Hundred and '06 Fusion sedans. Bracketing the Taurus in size, price, and character, they represented an end run around the problem of competing head-on with the perennially popular Accord and Camry.

The Five Hundred could have replaced the Crown Victoria: over a foot shorter overall and some 500 pounds lighter, yet no less spacious on a wheelbase just 1.8 inches trimmer. The secret was high-profile styling with an overall height of 61.5 inches, up 3.2 inches on Crown Vic and 5.4 on Taurus. Ford used this to elevate seating some four inches above that in most other cars. The tall body also provided a more natural seating posture front and rear, plus vast trunk space. Another talking point was a new unibody corporate platform. Known within Ford as D3, it was designed in collaboration with Volvo to be very strong except in a crash, when it would absorb energy in a controlled, protective fashion. Optional "passive safety" pluses were front torso side airbags, plus curtain side airbags that deployed from the ceiling above the side windows. Serving "active safety" were standard antilock four-wheel disc brakes and traction control.

Though classed as a large car by *Consumer Guide*®, the EPA, and others, the Five Hundred arrived with a midsize-car engine: a modestly improved "Duratec 30" twincam V-6 with 203 bhp. Drivelines were brand-new, however. Most front-drive models employed a six-speed automatic—Ford's first—and there were all-wheel-drive versions with a "gearless" continuously variable automatic transmission (CVT). The AWD/CVT combination was unique among family cars and thus somewhat risky, but many buyers took a liking to Five Hundreds so equipped for their all-weather traction and promise of good fuel economy. Mileage was at least respectable at 19-20 mpg, but power was lackluster despite respectable 0-60-mph times of 7.5-8.0 seconds with

2005 GT coupe

either powertrain. A new 250-bhp 3.5-liter V-6 was planned for 2007 to address the lack of zip.

Most all the above also applied to Freestyle, essentially a Five Hundred wagon marketed as a "crossover" SUV in a market where "station wagon" rivaled "minivan" as a kiss of death for sales. Slightly larger than Explorer, with lots of room, nice looks, pleasant driving manners, and competitive $25,000-$30,000 pricing, the Freestyle should have sold like 25-cent Starbucks lattes. Instead, it managed fewer than 85,300 orders from launch through the end of 2005. That was so far below expectations that Ford briefly considered dropping the Freestyle after just three model years. Cooler heads prevailed, however, and the twenty-first-century Country Squire was given an indefinite reprieve.

The Five Hundred fared better at more than 122,000 sales for the same period, but that didn't help Ford's bottom line very much. Some critics blamed tepid buyer response on me-too styling, citing a close resemblance with the six-year-old Volkswagen Passat. The similarity was easy to explain. J Mays had succeeded Jack Telnack as Ford design chief in 1997, and Mays had helped shape the Passat in his previous job at VW/Audi.

There was no visual cribbing in the 2006 Fusion, the second prong of Ford's latest assault on the high-volume family car market. A good thing, too, because this "new" midsize sedan was already familiar, amounting to a slightly enlarged Mazda 6 without the "zoom zoom" pretensions. Most everything hidden was the same or very similar: adept all-independent suspension, standard four-wheel disc brakes, even engines: base 2.3-liter four (originated by Mazda) and available Duratec 3.0 V-6. But it wasn't a complete copy. The Mazda, for example, offered both engines with manual and automatic transmissions, while V-6 Fusions were confined to automatic. The Ford also had somewhat softer suspension tuning because it wasn't trying to be as sporty as the Mazda. It also claimed more rear-seat room, thanks to an extra 2.1 inches in wheelbase. Styling, of course, was the most obvious difference, and many thought the Fusion was better looking. It was certainly hard to miss with its bold three-bar grille, a signature destined for future Ford cars (plus an early Five Hundred facelift) and a dim nod to 1966 Galaxies.

2005 GT coupe

Fusion bowed in S, SE, and top-line SEL versions. The last were the nicest inside, with contemporary metal-look accents, tasteful "piano black" panels instead of the usual test-tube wood, easy-read gauges, and convenient, logical controls. Regardless of trim, Fusion showed the same good workmanship as the Five Hundred, the best ever from Ford and fully competitive with Accord and Camry. Even materials were better than expected for the prices. The prices were right, running from just over $17,000 to near $22,000 before options. Ford held back on some standard features to make those numbers, charging extra for traction control, torso and curtain airbags, and antilock brakes, but at least the charges were reasonable.

Though Fusion was just emerging as this book was prepared, first reviews and early sales reports suggested Ford had come up with a winner. *Car and Driver*, for one, thought that with "stylish looks, fine road manners, practical configuration, and aggressive pricing, the Fusion should make a strong impact in the mainstream-sedan segment—and truly put Ford back in the car game." Dearborn must have rejoiced, because upscale Fusions with different styling and feature mixes would have the daunting task of luring new buyers to Lincoln and Mercury, nameplates already given up for dead in many quarters.

Fusion's CD3 platform was the starting point for Ford's first midsize crossover SUV, the 2007 Edge. Though Dearborn was slow to enter this new fast-growing segment, the Edge itself was well-timed, arriving just behind a larger, redesigned Toyota

RAV4 and ahead of a new-generation Honda CR-V. Edge faced those class favorites with bold styling on a 111.2-inch wheelbase, making it larger than the Japanese-brand duo and close in size to the Chevrolet Equinox and Pontiac Torrent.

Being late to game allowed Ford to learn the rules for winning it, so the Edge offered most everything competitors did and a few things they didn't. Prime among the latter was an Advance Trac antiskid system with Roll Stability Control, available with either front-wheel drive or full-time all-wheel drive. Volvo had developed RSC for its XC90 SUV, and Ford fast adopted it for the truck-based Explorer and Expedition. Basically, RSC employed various sensors that monitored vehicle attitude and would automatically activate the stability system to prevent a tip—within the laws of physics, of course. This was a definite sales asset, especially for Ford after the Explorer rollover debacle. Like other Dearborn SUVs, car- and truck-based alike, the Edge also offered optional front torso side airbags and curtain side airbags—what Ford called a "Safety Canopy. " Ford also mined Volvo's deep experience with safety design to design a unibody structure that was tight, strong, and solid. Antilock four-wheel disc brakes were standard.

Edge debuted with a single powerteam comprising Ford's new 250-bhp 3.5-liter V-6 and a six-speed automatic transmission. Interestingly, that gearbox was designed and built in conjunction with GM. Things really *were* tough in Detroit. Ford also hoped to gain a competitive, er, edge with a versatile five-passenger seating package, a center console big enough for a laptop computer, and "lifestyle" options such as a plug-in for digital music players, rear-seat DVD, and satellite radio. Still another class exclusive was a full-length, twin-panel "Vista Roof" with tilt/sliding forward section measuring 2×2.5 feet. With all this and more, the Edge seemed another hopeful sign that Dearborn would eventually find its "Way Forward."

Saving the best for last brings us to the 2004-06 Ford GT. One of the most charismatic roadgoing sports cars ever built, it was nothing less than a modern but faithful, *street-legal* reincarnation of Ford's legendary midengine GT40 endurance racer, four-time winner of the gruelling 24 Hours of Le Mans (1966-69), the ultimate "Total Performance" Ford. Previewed as an engineering prototype at the 2002 North American International Auto Show in Detroit, the GT was developed for production by a small dedicated team. The goal was to have it ready in time for Ford Motor Company's huge June 2003 centennial gala in Dearborn. The team had just 16 months but kept the appointment, and the first three production examples delighted the thousands in attendance. The GT arrived with one major glitch: lower suspension control arms that proved prone to cracking because of faulty casting. Ford swallowed its pride and recalled all 448 GTs built in 2004, the first full production year. The arms were replaced, and a new casting method devised.

The GT looked nearly identical to the GT40, but was built on a foot-longer wheelbase of 106.7 inches. Acceptable road-car passenger space was the rationale, but the cockpit was still race-car cozy for six-footers. Overall length-width-height measured 182.8×76.9×44.3 inches. The GT40 had been named for its rakish 40-inch height, so that designation would have been technically incorrect here. But "GT44" didn't sound right, and another company had legal claim to "GT40" and wouldn't give it up, hence the simple GT moniker.

Despite sharing the same classic lines, the GT was better than the GT40 in many ways, thanks to 40 years of technical progress. Take aerodynamics. Because the basic body shape acted like an inverted wing, the GT40 was infamous for being less-than-stable at racing speeds. Not so the GT, the result of several effective modifications that were very hard to spot. Small front air "splitters" created downforce at the nose, while side splitters beneath the doors worked together with an enclosed bellypan to smooth airflow on the way to rear "venturi" exits. Both cars employed an aluminum space-frame overlaid with aluminum panels, but the GT benefited from manu-

2005 Escape four-door wagon

facturing techniques unknown in the 1960s. As a result, it was claimed to be 40 percent stiffer than Ferrari's formidable F360 Modena, a key rival, yet curb weight was just under 3400 pounds, more than respectable for a fully dressed road car.

Power by Ford was a must, so the GT received a supercharged version of Ford's all-aluminum 5.4-liter V-8. Unique twincam heads with four valves per cylinder, dual fuel injectors at each port, and heavily fortified internals boosted output to rarefied levels: 550 bhp and 500 pound-feet of torque. Ford proudly noted that these numbers were comparable to those of 7.0-liter racing GT40s. A twin-disc clutch and Ricardo six-speed manual transaxle conveyed all the might to the rear wheels through a helical limited-slip differential. Braking was by massive Brembo-brand four-wheel discs of 14 inches across in front, 13.2 in back, all cross-drilled and clamped by four-piston monoblock calipers under antilock control. Rolling stock was suitably beefy but not "bad boy" outrageous, with Goodyear Eagle F1 Supercar tires wrapped on 18 x 9-inch cast-alloy rims fore, 19 x 11.5s aft. Suspension was the same at each end, comprising upper A-arms, lower L-shaped arms, coil-over monotube shocks, and thick antiroll bars.

For all its race-car breeding and heritage, the Ford GT was quite happy to dawdle along at town speeds and could "soak up road imperfections with ease," to quote *Road & Track*. The cockpit was comfortable too, and handsomely appointed with racing-style seats, leather upholstery, and an impressive spread of gauges and toggle-type switches across the dashboard. There were also unexpected conveniences including automatic climate control, power windows/locks/mirrors, tilt steering wheel, and keyless entry. Options were few: a booming 260-watt McIntosh sound system, lightweight BBS forged wheels, painted brake calipers, and the traditional "Le Mans" striping on the nose, roof, tail, and rocker panels. The only drawbacks to commuting in a GT were Thighmaster-high clutch effort and the very limited visibility associated with midships cars.

Such humdrum matters were fast forgotten on the open road, and especially on the racetrack. Acceleration was predictably explosive, with typical 0-60-mph times of just under 4.0 seconds, 0-100 in less than 9.0, standing quarter-miles in the low 12-second area at over 120 mph, and an estimated top speed of around 190. Handling was no less impressive: race-car sharp yet road-car forgiving, with mild understeer changing to power-on oversteer whenever your right foot commanded. Skidpad grip was world-class at near 1g, and *Road & Track*'s test car ran the slalom some 2-mph faster than the much-acclaimed Ferrari Modena. "It is about time that a U.S. automaker enters the supercar ranks," *R&T* concluded. "Watch out. America is roaring back to the top." And so it seemed. Several magazines both at home and abroad drove the GT against Ferrari, Lamborghini, Aston Martin, and other pricey "exoticars," and picked the Ford not only for its stunning abilities but as the best value.

Value in a supercar? At just five bucks shy of $150,000 before destination charge and Gas-Guzzler Tax (triggered by low EPA ratings), the GT was the bargain in its class. Not that many sold at list. After all, supply was limited—about 4000 worldwide max, said Ford—and demand for this thrilling machine was many times greater. With gotta-be-first types waving checkbooks and dealers seeing potential windfalls, market prices soared overnight, reaching a quarter-million or more by some accounts. There were even reports of owners blatantly "flipping" barely used GTs in pursuit of a fat, fast profit.

But all this only adds to the mystique of a fabulous Ford that was gone way too soon, shot down by "Way Forward" cuts along with the Wixom, Michigan, plant that built the cars carefully and largely by hand. Will we ever see its like again? Well, the GT was the starting point for the striking Shelby GR-1 concept coupe of 2005, so that's one possibility.

First, though, Ford Motor Company must get back on its feet. Can it succeed? While we can't say for sure at this writing, we think there's a better-than-even chance. Several planned products hold promise, especially the hybrid-power versions of the Fusion and other models to follow up on the popularity of the 2005 Escape Hybrid, the first gas/electric SUV from an American auto manufacturer.

Ford has lately staked its reputation—and thus its future—on innovation. For the sake of everyone in the company and all who love cars, we hope Ford will come up with the "better ideas" it so urgently needs.

2005 Five Hundred four-door sedan

2005 Five Hundred four-door sedan

2005 Focus four-door hatchback

2005 Focus four-door sedan

2005 Freestyle four-door wagon

2006 Fusion four-door sedan

2006 Fusion four-door sedan

2007 Edge four-door wagon

Specifications

1930

Model A (wb 103.5)	Wght	Price	Prod
rdstr	2,155	435	122,703
rdstr 2-4P	2,230	460	
phtn 5P	2,212	440	39,886
Standard cpe 2P	2,257	495	232,564
spt cpe 2-4P	2,283	525	72,572
cabriolet 2-4P	2,273	625	29,226
Tudor sdn 5P	2,375	495	425,124
Fordor sdn 2W 5P	2,441	600	7,838
Town sdn 5P	2,475	660	122,534
Town Car 5P	2,525	1,200	96
Standard sdn 3W 5P	2,462	600	59,958
DeLuxe rdstr 2-4P	2,230	520	11,629
DeLuxe phtn 5P	2,285	625	4,635
DeLuxe cpe 2P	2,265	545	29,777
victoria 5P	2,265	625	6,447
DeLuxe sdn 5P	2,488	640	13,710
wgn 4d	—	650	3,799
bus cpe 2P	—	—	110

1930 Engine	bore×stroke	bhp	availability
I-4, 200.5	3.88×4.25	40	S-all

1931

Model A (wb 103.5)	Wght	Price	Prod
rdstr 2P	2,155	430	7,793
rdstr 2-4P	2,230	455	
phtn 5P	2,212	435	11,060
Standard cpe 2P	2,257	490	82,885
spt cpe 2-4P	2,283	500	21,272
cabriolet 2-4P	2,273	595	13,706
Tudor sdn 5P	2,375	490	170,645
Standard sdn 3W 5P	2,462	590	25,720
DeLuxe rdstr 2-4P	2,230	475	56,702
DeLuxe phtn 5P	2,285	580	2,875
DeLuxe cpe 2P	2,265	525	23,653
victoria 5P	2,265	580	36,830
DeLuxe Tudor sdn 5P	2,388	525	23,490
DeLuxe Fordor sdn 5P	2,488	630	4,967
DeLuxe town sdn 5P	2,475	630	65,447
conv sdn 5P	2,360	640	5,072
wgn 4d	—	625	3,018

1931 Engine	bore×stroke	bhp	availability
I-4, 200.5	3.88×4.25	40	S-all

1932

Model B (wb 106.5)	Wght	Price	Prod
rdstr 2P	2,077	410	948
rdstr 2-4P	2,119	435	
phtn 5P	2,213	445	593
cpe 2P	2,236	440	20,342
spt cpe 2-4P	2,261	485	739
Tudor sdn 5P	2,353	450	36,553
Fordor sdn 5P	2,388	540	4,116
DeLuxe rdstr 2-4P	2,153	450	3,719
DeLuxe phtn 5P	2,243	495	281
DeLuxe cpe 2P	2,339	525	968
victoria 5P	2,319	550	521
cabriolet 2-4P	2,370	560	427
DeLx Tudor sdn 5P	2,373	500	4,077
DeLx Fordor sdn 5P	2,407	595	2,620
Model B (wb 106.5)			
conv sdn 5P	2,324	600	44
wgn 4D (Incl Model 18)	—	—	1,400
Model 18 V-8 (wb 106.5)			
rdstr	2,217	460	520
rdstr 2-4P	2,258	485	
phtn 5P	2,344	495	483
cpe 2P	2,387	490	28,904
spt cpe 2-4P	2,397	535	1,982
Tudor sdn 5P	2,487	500	57,903
Fordor sdn 5P	2,524	590	9,320
DeLuxe rdstr 2-4P	2,283	500	6,893
DeLuxe phtn 5P	2,350	545	923
DeLuxe cpe 2P	2,477	575	20,506
victoria 5P	2,463	600	7,241
cabriolet 2-4P	2,390	610	5,499
DeLuxe Tudor sdn 5P	2,497	550	18,836
DeLuxe Fordor sdn 5P	2,543	645	18,880
conv sdn 2-4P	2,455	650	842
wgn 4d	—	600	—

1932 Engines	bore×stroke	bhp	availability
I-4, 200.5	3.88×4.25	50	S-Model B
V-8, 221.0	3.06×3.75	65	S-Model 18

1933

Model 40 I-4 (wb 112.0)	Wght	Price	Prod
rdstr	2,021	425	107
rdstr 2-4P	2,064	450	
phtn 5P	2,124	445	457
cpe 3W/5W 2P	2,147	440	189
cpe 3W/5W 2-4P	2,202	465	2,148
Tudor sdn 5P	2,418	450	2,911
Fordor sdn 5P	2,465	510	682
DeLuxe rdstr 2-4P	2,264	460	101
DeLuxe phtn 5P	2,154	495	241
DeLx cpe 3W/5W 2P	2,196	490	24
DeLx cpe 3W/5W 2-4P	2,202	515	28
victoria 5P	2,230	545	25
cabriolet 2-4P	2,181	535	24
DeLuxe Tudor sdn 5P	2,435	500	85
DeLx Fordor sdn 5P	2,505	560	179
wgn 4d	—	590	359
Model 40 V-8 (wb 112.0)			
rdstr 2P	2,337	475	126
rdstr 2-4P	2,420	500	
phtn 5P	2,435	495	232
cpe 3W/5W 2P	2,448	490	6,585
cpe 3W/5W 2-4P	2,380	515	31,797
Tudor sdn 5P	2,536	500	106,387
Fordor sdn 5P	2,590	560	19,602
DeLuxe rdstr 2-4P	2,376	510	4,223
DeLuxe phtn 5P	2,444	545	1,483
DeLx cpe 3W/5W 2P	2,453	540	15,894
DeLx cpe 3W/5W 2-4P	2,450	565	11,244
victoria 5P	2,510	595	4,193
cabriolet 2-4P	2,460	585	7,852
DeLuxe Tudor sdn 5P	2,540	550	48,233
DeLx Fordor sdn 5P	2,599	610	45,443
wgn 4d	—	640	1,654

1933 Engines	bore×stroke	bhp	availability
I-4, 200.5	3.88×4.25	50	S-Mod 40 I-4
V-8, 221.0	3.06×3.75	75	S-Mod 40 V-8

1934

Model 40A Four (wb 112.0)	Wght	Price	Prod
phaeton	—	—	377

Model 40A Four	Wght	Price	Prod
Standard cpe 5W	—	455	20
Tudor sdn 5P	—	470	185
Fordor sdn 5P	—	525	405
DeLuxe rdstr 2-4P	—	475	32
DeLuxe phtn 5P	—	500	412
DeLuxe cpe 3W	—	495	7
DeLuxe cpe 5W	—	520	3
DeLuxe cabriolet 2-4P	—	540	12
DeLuxe Tudor sdn 5P	—	510	12
DeLuxe Fordor sdn 5P	—	565	384
wgn 4d	—	610	95
Model 40A V-8 (wb 112.0)			
roadster 2P	—	—	4
phaeton	—	—	373
Standard cpe 5W	2,448	505	47,623
Deluxe Victoria 5P	2,670	600	20,083
Deluxe cabriolet 2-4P	2,460	590	14,496
Tudor sdn 5P	2,536	520	124,870
Fordor sdn 5P	2,590	575	22,394
DeLuxe rdstr 2-4P	2,376	525	5,038
DeLuxe phtn 5P	2,444	550	3,128
DeLuxe cpe 3W	2,453	545	26,348
DeLuxe cpe 5W	2,450	570	26,879
DeLx Tudor sdn 5P	2,540	560	121,696
DeLx Fordor sdn 5P	2,599	615	102,268
wgn 4d	2,695	660	2,905

1934 Engines	bore×stroke	bhp	availability
I-4, 200.5	3.88×4.25	50	S-Mod 40A Four
V-8, 221.0	3.06×3.75	85	S-Mod 40A V-8

1935

Model 48 (wb 112.0)	Wght	Price	Prod
cpe 5W 2P	2,620	495	78,477
Tudor sdn 5P	2,717	510	237,883
Fordor sdn 5P	2,760	575	49,176
DeLuxe rdstr 2-4P	2,597	550	4,896
DeLuxe phtn 5P	2,667	580	6,073
DeLuxe cpe 3W 2P	2,647	570	31,513
DeLuxe cpe 5W 2P	2,643	560	33,065
DeLuxe cab 2-4P	2,687	625	17,000
DeLuxe Tudor sdn	2,735	575	84,692
DeLx Tudor tour sdn	2,772	595	87,326
DeLuxe Fordor sdn	2,767	635	75,807
DeLx Fordor tour sdn	2,787	655	105,157
DeLuxe conv sdn	2,827	750	4,234
4d station wagon	2,896	670	4,536

1935 Engine	bore×stroke	bhp	availability
V-8, 221.0	3.06×3.75	85	S-all

1936

Model 68 Stndrd (wb 112.0)	Wght	Price	Prod
cpe 5W 2P	2,599	510	78,534 (combined)
cpe 5W 2-4P	2,641	535	
Tudor sdn 5P	2,659	520	174,770
Tudor T/B sdn 5P	2,718	545	165,718
Fordor sdn 5P	2,699	580	31,505
Fordor T/B sdn 5P	2,771	605	39,607
wgn 4d	3,020	670	7,044
Model 68 DeLuxe (wb 112.0)			
rdstr 2-4P	2,561	560	3,862
phtn 5P	2,641	590	5,555
cpe 3W 2P	2,621	570	21,446 (combined)
cpe 3W 2-4P	2,656	595	
cpe 5W 2P	2,641	555	29,938 (combined)
cpe 5W 2-4P	2,666	580	
cabriolet 2-4P	2,649	625	14,068
club cabriolet 2-4P	2,661	675	4,616
Tudor sdn 5P	2,691	565	20,519
Tudor T/B sdn 5P	2,789	590	125,303
Fordor sdn 5P	2,746	625	42,867
Fordor T/B sdn 5P	2,816	650	159,825
conv sdn 5P	2,791	760	5,601 (combined)
conv sdn T/B 5P	2,916	780	

1936 Engine	bore×stroke	bhp	availability
V-8, 221.0	3.06×3.75	85	S-all

1937

Model 74 (wb 112.0)	Wght	Price	Prod
cpe 5W 2P	2,275	529	43,866
Tudor sdn 5P	2,405	579	*
Tudor T/B sdn 5P	2,415	604	51,332
Fordor sdn 5P	2,435	639	18,541
Fordor T/B sdn 5P	2,445	664	13,976
wgn 4d side curtains	2,691	744	193 (combined)
wgn 4d glass wndws	2,776	764	
Model 78 Standard (wb 112.0)			
cpe 5W 2P	2,496	586	46,481
Tudor sdn 5P	2,616	611	308,446*
Tudor T/B sdn 5P	2,648	638	78,895
Fordor sdn 5P	2,649	671	30,521
Fordor T/B sdn 5P	2,666	696	31,555
wgn 4d side curtains	2,906	754	9,111 (combined)
wgn 4d glass wndws	2,991	775	
Model 78 DeLuxe (wb 112.0)			
rdstr 2-4P	2,576	694	1,250
phtn 5P	2,691	749	3,723
cpe 5W 2P	2,506	659	26,783
cabriolet 2-4P	2,616	719	10,184
club cpe 5W 5P	2,616	719	16,992
club cabriolet 4P	2,636	759	8,001
Tudor sdn 5P	2,656	674	33,683
Tudor T/B sdn 5P	2,679	699	73,690
Fordor sdn 5P	2,671	734	22,885
Fordor T/B sdn 5P	2,696	759	98,687
conv sdn 5P	2,861	859	4,378
sdn 7P	—	—	521

1937 Engines	bore×stroke	bhp	availability
V-8, 136.0	2.60×3.20	60	S-74
V-8, 221.0	3.06×3.75	85	S-78

*Combined production.

1938

Model 82A (wb 112.0)	Wght	Price	Prod
cpe 5W 2P	2,354	595	13,712
Tudor sdn 5P	2,455	640	30,850
Fordor sdn 5P	2,481	685	5,878
Model 81A (wb 112.0)			
cpe 5W 2P	2,575	625	20,347
Tudor sdn 5P	2,674	665	75,267
Fordor sdn 5P	2,697	710	24,409
wgn 4d	2,981	825	6,944
DeLuxe phtn 5P	2,748	820	1,169
DeLuxe cpe 5W 2P	2,606	685	22,225
DeLx conv cpe 2-4P	2,679	770	4,702
DeLuxe club cpe 5P	2,688	745	7,171
DeLuxe Tudor sdn 5P	2,742	725	101,647
DeLx Fordor sdn 5P	2,773	770	92,020
DeLuxe conv sdn 5P	2,883	900	2,743
DeLuxe sdn 7P	—	—	449

1938 Engines	bore×stroke	bhp	availability
V-8, 136.0	2.60×3.20	60	S-82A
V-8, 221.0	3.06×3.75	85	S-81A

1939

Model 92A (wb 112.0)	Wght	Price	Prod
cpe 5W 2P	2,463	599	*
Tudor sdn 5P	2,608	640	*
Fordor sdn 5P	2,623	686	*
Model 91A (wb 112.0)			
cpe 5W 2P	2,170	640	*
Tudor sdn 5P	2,830	681	*
Fordor sdn 5P	2,850	727	*
wgn 4d	3,080	840	3,277
DeLuxe cpe 5W 2P	2,752	702	37,326
DeLx conv cpe 2-4P	2,840	788	10,422
DeLuxe Tudor sdn 5P	2,867	742	144,333
DeLx Fordor sdn 5P	2,898	788	90,551
DeLuxe conv sdn 5P	2,935	921	3,561
DeLuxe wgn 4d	3,095	916	6,155
DeLuxe sdn 7P	—	—	192

1939 Engines	bore×stroke	bhp	availability
V-8, 136.0	2.60×3.20	60	S-92A
V-8, 221.0	3.06×3.75	85	S-91A

*Production combined by body style as follows:

coupe	38,197
Tudor sdn	124,866
Fordor sdn	28,151

1940

O1A V-8/85 (wb 112.0)	Wght	Price	Prod
cpe	2,763	660	*
bus cpe	2,801	681	*
Tudor sdn	2,909	701	*
Fordor sdn	2,936	747	*
wgn 4d	3,249	875	4,469
DeLuxe cpe	2,791	722	27,919
DeLuxe bus cpe	2,831	742	20,183
DeLuxe conv cpe	2,956	849	23,704
DeLuxe Tudor sdn	2,927	762	171,368
DeLuxe Fordor sdn	2,966	808	91,756
DeLuxe wgn 4d	3,262	947	8,730
O2A V-8/60 (wb 112.0)			
cpe	2,519	619	*
bus cpe	2,549	640	*
Tudor sdn	2,669	660	*
Fordor sdn	2,696	706	*

1940 Engines	bore×stroke	bhp	availability
V-8, 136.0	2.60×3.20	60	S-V-8/60
V-8, 221.0	3.06×3.75	85	S-V-8/85

*Production combined by body style as follows:

cpe	33,693
bus cpe	16,785
Tudor sdn	150,933
Fordor sdn	25,545

1941

1GA Six (wb 114.0)	Wght	Price	Prod*
Special cpe	2,870	684	—
Special Tudor sdn	2,975	720	—
Special Fordor sdn	3,020	761	—
DeLuxe cpe	2,947	715	—
DeLuxe cpe, A/S	2,970	746	—
DeLuxe Tudor sdn	3,065	756	—
DeLuxe Fordor sdn	3,100	797	—
DeLuxe wgn 4d	3,395	946	—
Super DeLuxe cpe	2,934	761	—
Super DeLx cpe, A/S	2,974	792	—
Super DeLx sdn cpe	3,030	833	—
Super DeLx conv cpe	3,145	931	—
Supr DeLx Tudor sdn	3,096	802	—
Supr DeLx Fordor sdn	3,131	843	—
Supr DeLx wgn 4d	3,400	998	—
11A V-8 (wb 114.0)			
Special cpe	2,878	700	9,823
Special Tudor sdn	2,983	736	27,189
Special Fordor sdn	3,033	777	3,838
DeLuxe cpe	2,953	730	33,598
DeLuxe cpe, A/S	2,981	761	12,844
DeLuxe Tudor sdn	3,095	772	177,018
DeLuxe Fordor sdn	3,121	813	25,928
DeLuxe wgn 4d	3,412	962	6,116
Super DeLuxe cpe	2,969	777	22,878
Super DeLx cpe, A/S	3,001	807	10,796
Super DeLx sdn cpe	3,052	849	45,977
Super DeLx conv cpe	3,187	946	30,240
Supr DeLx Tudor sdn	3,110	818	185,788
Supr DeLx Fordor sdn	3,146	859	88,053
Super DeLx wgn 4d	3,419	1,013	9,485

1941 Engines	bore×stroke	bhp	availability
I-6, 226.0	3.30×4.40	90	S-Six
V-8, 221.0	3.06×3.75	85	S-V-8

*11A V-8 includes 1GA Six.

1942

2GA Six (wb 114.0)		Wght	Price	Prod
70C	Special Tudor sdn	3,053	815	3,187
73C	Special Fordor sdn	3,093	850	27,189
77C	Special cpe	2,910	780	1,606
70A	DeLuxe Tudor sdn	3,122	840	—
72A	DeLx sdn cpe	3,045	865	—
73A	DeLuxe Fordor sdn	3,141	875	—
77A	DeLuxe cpe	2,958	805	—
79A	DeLuxe wgn 4d, 8P	3,405	1,035	—
70B	Supr DeLx Tudor sdn	3,136	885	—
72B	Super DeLux sdn cpe	3,109	910	—
73B	Supr DeLx Fordor sdn	3,179	920	—
76	Supr DeLx conv cpe	3,218	1,080	—
77B	Super DeLuxe cpe	3,030	850	—
79B	Supr DeLx wgn 4d, 8P	3,453	1,115	—
21A V-8 (wb 114.0)				
70A	DeLuxe Tudor sdn	3,141	850	27,302*

21A V-8		Wght	Price	Prod
72A	DeLuxe sdn cpe	3,065	875	5,419*
73A	DeLuxe Fordor sdn	3,161	885	5,127*
77A	DeLuxe cpe	2,978	815	5,936*
79A	DeLuxe wgn 4d, 8P	3,420	1,090	567*
70B	Supr DeLx Tudor sdn	3,159	895	37,189*
72B	Super DeLx sdn cpe	3,120	920	13,543*
73B	Supr DeLx Fordor sdn	3,200	930	24,846*
76	Super DeLx conv cpe	3,238	1,090	2,920*
77B	Super DeLuxe cpe	3,050	860	5,411*
79B	Supr DeLx wgn 4d, 8P	3,468	1,125	5,483*

1942 Engines	bore×stroke	bhp	availability
I-6, 226.0	3.30×4.40	90	S-Six
V-8, 221.0	3.06×3.75	90	S-V-8

*Includes 2GA Six.

1946

6GA Six (wb 114.0)*		Wght	Price	Prod
70A	DeLuxe Tudor sdn	3,157	1,136	—
73A	DeLuxe Fordor sdn	3,187	1,198	—
77A	DeLuxe cpe	3,007	1,074	—
70B	Supr DeLx Tudor sdn	3,157	1,211	—
72B	Super DeLx cpe sdn	3,107	1,257	—
73B	Supr DeLx Fordor sdn	3,207	1,273	—
77B	Super DeLuxe cpe	3,007	1,148	—
79B	Super DeLx wgn 4d	3,457	1,504	—

69A V-8 (wb 114.0)*		Wght	Price	Prod
70A	DeLuxe Tudor sdn	3,190	1,185	—
73A	DeLuxe Fordor sdn	3,220	1,248	—
77A	DeLuxe cpe	3,040	1,123	—
70B	Supr DeLx Tudor sdn	3,190	1,260	—
71	Supr DeLx Sprtsmn conv	3,340	1,982	1,209
72B	Super DeLx cpe sdn	3,140	1,307	—
73B	Super DeLx Fordor sdn	3,240	1,322	—
76	Super DeLx conv cpe	3,240	1,488	—
77B	Super DeLuxe cpe	3,040	1,197	—
79B	Supr DeLx wgn 4d, 8P	3,490	1,533	—

*** Model-year production by body style (Six/V-8):**

DeLuxe (wb 114.0)	Prod
Tudor sdn	74,954
Fordor sdn	9,246
cpe	10,670
chassis	86

Super DeLuxe (wb 114.0)	Prod
Tudor sdn	163,370
Fordor sdn	92,056
sdn cpe	70,826
conv cpe	16,359
cpe	12,249
wgn 4d	16,960
chassis	37

1946 Engines	bore×stroke	bhp	availability
I-6, 226.0	3.30×4.40	90	S-Six
V-8, 239.4	3.19×3.75	100	S-V-8

1947

7GA Six (wb 114.0)*	Wght	Price	Prod
DeLuxe Fordor sdn	3,213	1,270	—
DeLuxe Tudor sdn	3,183	1,212	—
DeLuxe cpe	3,033	1,154	—
Supr DeLx Fordor sdn	3,233	1,372	—
Supr DeLx Tudor sdn	3,183	1,309	—
Super DeLx cpe sdn	3,133	1,330	—
Super DeLuxe cpe	3,033	1,251	—
Supr DeLx wgn 4d, 8P	3,487	1,893	—

79A V-8 (wb 114.0)*	Wght	Price	Prod
DeLuxe Fordor sdn	3,246	1,346	—
DeLuxe Tudor sdn	3,216	1,288	—
DeLuxe cpe	3,066	1,230	—
Supr DeLx Fordor sdn	3,266	1,440	—
Supr DeLx Tudor sdn	3,216	1,382	—
Super DeLx cpe sdn	3,166	1,409	—
Supr DeLx conv cpe	3,266	1,740	22,159
Supr DeLx Sprtsmn conv	3,366	2,282	2,250
Supr DeLx wgn 4d, 8P	3,520	1,972	—

*** Model year production by body style (Six/V-8):**

DeLuxe (wb 114.0)	Prod
Tudor sdn	44,523
Fordor sdn	20
cpe	10,872
chassis	23

Super DeLuxe (wb 114.0)	Prod
Tudor sdn	136,126
Fordor sdn	116,744
cpe sdn	80,830
wgn 4d, 8P	16,104
chassis	23

1947 Engines	bore×stroke	bhp	availability
I-6, 226.0	3.30×4.40	90	S-Six
V-8, 239.4	3.19×3.75	100	S-V-8

1948

87HA Six (wb 114.0)*		Wght	Price	Prod
70A	DeLuxe Tudor sdn	3,183	1,212	—
77A	DeLuxe cpe	3,033	1,154	—
70B	Supr DeLx Tudor sdn	3,183	1,309	—
72B	Super DeLx cpe sdn	3,133	1,330	—
73B	Supr DeLx Fordor sdn	3,233	1,372	—
79B	Supr DeLx wgn 4d, 8P	3,487	1,893	—

89A V-8 (wb 114.0)*		Wght	Price	Prod
70A	DeLuxe Tudor sdn	3,216	1,288	—
77A	DeLuxe cpe	3,066	1,230	—
70B	Supr DeLx Tudor sdn	3,216	1,382	—
71B	Supr DeLx Sprtsmn conv	3,366	2,282	28
72B	Super DeLx cpe sdn	3,166	1,409	—
73B	Supr DeLx Fordor sdn	3,266	1,440	—
76B	Supr DeLx conv cpe	3,266	1,740	12,033
79B	Supr DeLx wgn 4d, 8P	3,520	1,972	—

***Model year production by body style (Six/V-8):**

DeLuxe (wb 114.0)	Prod
Tudor sdn	23,356
cpe	5,048

Super DeLuxe (wb 114.0)	Prod
Tudor sdn	82,161
Fordor sdn	71,358
cpe sdn	44,826
wgn 4d, 8P	8,912

1948 Engines	bore×stroke	bhp	availability
I-6, 226.0	3.30×4.40	95	S-Six
V-8, 239.4	3.19×3.75	100	S-V-8

1949

Standard (wb 114.0)		Wght	Price	Prod
70A	Tudor sdn	2,965	1,425	126,770
72A	club cpe	2,945	1,415	4,170
72C	bus cpe	2,891	1,333	28,946
73A	Fordor sdn	3,010	1,472	44,563
—	chassis	—	—	1

Custom V-8 (wb 114.0)		Wght	Price	Prod
70B	Tudor sdn	2,968	1,511	433,316
72B	club cpe	2,948	1,511	150,254
73B	Fordor sdn	3,013	1,559	248,176
76	conv cpe	3,254	1,886	51,133
79	wgn 2d, 8P	3,543	2,119	31,412
—	chassis	—	—	18

1949 Engines	bore×stroke	bhp	availability
I-6, 226.0	3.30×4.40	95	S-Six
V-8, 239.4	3.19×3.75	100	O-V-8

1950

DeLuxe (wb 114.0)		Wght	Price	Prod
D70	Tudor sdn	3,007	1,424	275,360
D72C	bus cpe	2,949	1,333	35,120
D73	Fordor sdn	3,064	1,472	77,888

Custom (wb 114.0)		Wght	Price	Prod
C70	Tudor sdn	3,015	1,511	398,060
C70C	Crestliner sdn 2d	3,050	1,711	17,601
C72	club cpe	2,981	1,511	85,111
C73	Fordor sdn	3,078	1,558	247,181
C76	conv cpe	3,263	1,948	50,299
C79	Cntry Squire wgn 2d	3,511	2,028	22,929

1950 Engines	bore×stroke	bhp	availability
I-6, 226.0	3.30×4.40	95	S-all exc C70C, C76
V-8, 239.4	3.19×3.75	100	S-C70C, C76; O-others

1951

DeLuxe (wb 114.0)		Wght	Price	Prod
70	Tudor sdn	3,043	1,417	146,010
72C	bus cpe	2,979	1,324	20,343
73	Fordor sdn	3,102	1,465	54,265

Custom (wb 114.0)		Wght	Price	Prod
60	Victoria htp cpe	3,188	1,925	110,286
70	Tudor sdn	3,043	1,505	317,869
70C	Crestliner sdn 2d	3,065	1,595	8,703
72	club cpe	3,015	1,505	53,263
73	Fordor sdn	3,102	1,553	232,691
76	conv cpe	3,268	1,949	40,934
79	Cntry Squire wgn 2d	3,530	2,029	29,017

1951 Engines	bore×stroke	bhp	availability
I-6, 226.0	3.30×4.40	95	S-all exc 60, 70C, 76
V-8, 239.4	3.19×3.75	100	S-60, 70C, 76; O-others

1952

Mainline (wb 115.0)		Wght	Price	Prod
59A	Ranch Wagon 2d	3,212	1,832	32,566
70A	sdn 2d	3,111	1,485	79,931
72C	bus cpe	3,035	1,389	10,137
73A	sdn 4d	3,190	1,530	41,227

Customline (wb 115.0)		Wght	Price	Prod
70B	sdn 2d	3,111	1,570	175,762
72B	club cpe	3,116	1,579	26,550
73B	sdn 4d	3,190	1,615	188,303
79C	Cntry Sdn wgn 4d, 6P	3,617	2,060	11,927

Crestline (wb 115.0)		Wght	Price	Prod
60B	Victoria htp cpe	3,274	1,925	77,320
76B	Sunliner conv cpe	3,339	2,027	22,534
79B	Cntry Sqr wgn 4d, 8P	3,640	2,186	5,426

1952 Engines	bore×stroke	bhp	availability
I-6, 215.3	3.56×3.60	101	S-all exc 79C, Crestline (ohv)
V-8, 239.4	3.19×3.75	110	S-79C, Crest; O-others

1953

Mainline (wb 115.0)		Wght	Price	Prod
59A	Ranch Wagon 2d	3,406	1,917	66,976
70A	sdn 2d	3,092	1,497	152,995
72C	bus cpe	3,018	1,400	16,280
73A	sdn 4d	3,138	1,542	69,463

Customline (wb 115.0)		Wght	Price	Prod
70B	sdn 2d	3,100	1,582	305,433
72B	club cpe	3,084	1,591	43,999
73B	sdn 4d	3,154	1,628	374,487
79B	Cntry Sdn wgn 4d, 6P	3,539	2,076	37,743

Crestline (wb 115.0)		Wght	Price	Prod
60B	Victoria htp cpe	3,250	1,941	128,302
76B	Sunliner conv cpe	3,334	2,043	40,861
79C	Cntry Sqr wgn 4d, 8P	3,609	2,203	11,001
—	chassis	—	—	2

1953 Engines	bore×stroke	bhp	availability
I-6, 215.3	3.56×3.60	101	S-all exc 79B, Crestline
V-8, 239.4	3.19×3.75	110	S-79B, Crest; O-others

1954

Mainline (wb 115.5)		Wght	Price	Prod
59A	Ranch Wagon 2d	3,399	2,029	44,315
70A	sdn 2d	3,147	1,651	123,329
72C	bus cpe	3,082	1,548	10,665
73A	sdn 4d	3,203	1,701	55,371

Customline (wb 115.5)		Wght	Price	Prod
59B	Ranch Wagon 2d	3,405	2,122	36,086
70B	sdn 2d	3,160	1,744	293,375
72B	club cpe	3,141	1,753	33,951
73B	sdn 4d	3,216	1,793	262,499
79B	Cntry Sdn wgn 4d, 6P	3,574	2,202	48,384

Crestline (wb 115.5)		Wght	Price	Prod
60B	Victoria htp cpe	3,245	2,055	95,464
60F	Skyliner htp cpe	3,265	2,164	13,344
73C	sdn 4d	3,220	1,898	99,677
76B	Sunliner conv cpe	3,292	2,164	36,685
79C	Cntry Sqr wgn 4d, 8P	3,624	2,339	12,797

1954 Engines	bore×stroke	bhp	availability
I-6, 223.0	3.62×3.60	115	S-all exc 79B
V-8, 239.4	3.50×3.10	130	S-79B; O-others (ohv)

1955

Mainline (wb 115.5)		Wght	Price	Prod
70A	sdn 2d	3,119	1,707	76,698
70D	bus cpe	3,081	1,606	8,809
73A	sdn 4d	3,161	1,753	41,794
Customline (wb 115.5)				
70B	sdn 2d	3,139	1,801	236,575
73B	sdn 4d	3,181	1,845	235,417
Fairlane (wb 115.5)				
60B	Victoria htp cpe	3,251	2,095	113,372
64A	Crown Vic htp cpe	3,313	2,202	33,165
64B	Crwn Vic htp cpe, gls tp	3,321	2,272	1,999
70C	club sdn 2d	3,155	1,914	173,311
73C	Town Sedan	3,201	1,960	254,437
76B	Sunliner conv cpe	3,315	2,224	49,966
Station Wagon (wb 115.5)				
59A	Ranch 2d, 6P	3,376	2,043	40,493
59B	Cust Ranch 2d, 6P	3,394	2,109	43,671
79B	Cntry Sedan 4d, 8P	3,536	2,287	53,209
79C	Cntry Squire 4d, 8P	3,538	2,392	19,011
79D	Cntry Sedan 4d, 6P	3,460	2,156	53,075

1955 Engines	bore×stroke	bhp	availability
I-6, 223.0	3.62×3.60	120	S-all
V-8, 272.0	3.62×3.30	162	O-all
V-8, 272.0	3.62×3.30	182	O-all
V-8, 292.0	3.75×3.30	198	O-Fair, stn wgn

1956

Mainline (wb 115.5)		Wght	Price	Prod
70A	sdn 2d	3,143	1,850	106,974
70D	bus sdn 2d	3,088	1,748	8,020
73A	sdn 4d	3,183	1,895	49,448
Customline (wb 115.5)				
64D	Victoria htp cpe	3,202	1,985	33,130
70B	sdn 2d	3,163	1,939	164,828
73B	sdn 4d	3,203	1,985	170,695
Fairlane (wb 115.5)				
57A	Victoria htp sdn	3,369	2,249	32,111
64A	Crown Vic htp cpe	3,289	2,337	9,209
64B	Crwn Vic htp cpe, gls tp	3,299	2,407	603
64C	Victoria htp cpe	3,274	2,194	177,735
70C	club sdn 2d	3,179	2,047	142,629
73C	Town Sedan	3,219	2,093	224,872
76B	Sunliner conv cpe	3,384	2,359	58,147
Station Wagon (wb 115.5)				
59A	Ranch 2d, 6P	3,402	2,185	48,348
59B	Cust Ranch 2d, 6P	3,417	2,249	42,317
59C	Parklane 2d	3,432	2,428	15,186
79D	Cntry Sedan 4d, 6P	3,555	2,428	85,374
79B	Cntry Sedan 4d, 8P	3,555	2,428	
79C	Cntry Squire 4d, 8P	3,566	2,533	23,221

1956 Engines	bore×stroke	bhp	availability
I-6, 223.0	3.62×3.60	137	S-all
V-8, 272.0	3.62×3.30	173	O-Mainline, Custom
V-8, 292.0	3.75×3.30	200	O-Fair wgn, (202 bhp w/auto)
V-8, 312.0	3.80×3.44	215	O-all (225 bhp w/auto)

1957

Custom (wb 116.0)		Wght	Price	Prod
70A	sdn 2d	3,211	1,991	116,963
70D	bus sdn 2d	3,202	1,879	6,888
73A	sdn 4d	3,254	2,042	68,924
Custom 300 (wb 116.0)				
70B	sdn 2d	3,224	2,105	160,360
73B	sdn 4d	3,269	2,157	194,877
Fairlane (wb 118.0)				
57B	Victoria htp sdn	3,411	2,357	12,695
58A	Town Sedan 4d	3,376	2,286	52,060
63B	Victoria htp cpe	3,366	2,293	44,127
64A	club sdn 2d	3,331	2,235	39,843
Fairlane 500 (wb 118.0)				
51A	Skyl retrac conv cpe	3,916	2,942	20,766
57A	Victoria htp sdn	3,426	2,404	68,550
58B	Town Sedan 4d	3,384	2,286	193,162
63A	Victoria htp cpe	3,381	2,339	183,202
64B	club sdn 2d	3,346	2,281	93,756
76B	Sunliner conv cpe	3,536	2,505	77,726
Station Wagon (wb 116.0)				
59A	Ranch 2d, 6P	3,455	2,301	60,486
59B	Del Rio 2d, 6P	3,462	2,397	46,105
79C	Cntry Sedan 4d, 9P	3,614	2,556	49,638
79D	Cntry Sedan 4d, 6P	3,525	2,451	137,251
79E	Cntry Squire 4d, 9P	3,628	2,684	27,690

1957 Engines	bore×stroke	bhp	availability
I-6, 223.0	3.62×3.60	144	S-all exc 51A
V-8, 272.0	3.62×3.30	190	S-51A; O-others
V-8, 292.0	3.75×3.30	212	O-Fairlane, Fair 500, wgns
V-8, 312.0	3.80×3.44	245	O-all

1958

Custom (wb 116.0)		Wght	Price	Prod
70A	sdn 2d	3,250	2,055	36,272
70D	bus sdn	3,227	1,967	4,062
73A	sdn 4d	3,278	2,109	27,811
Custom 300 (wb 116.0)				
70B	sdn 2d	3,300	2,305	137,169
73B	sdn 4d	3,328	2,159	135,557
Fairlane (wb 118.0)				
57B	Victoria htp sdn	3,450	2,419	5,868
58A	Town Sedan 4d	3,427	2,275	57,490
63B	Victoria htp cpe	3,373	2,354	16,416
64A	club sdn 2d	3,375	2,221	38,366
Fairlane 500 (wb 118.0)				
51A	Skyl retrac conv cpe	4,069	3,163	14,713
57A	Victoria htp sdn	3,488	2,499	36,509
58B	sdn 4d	3,452	2,428	105,698
63A	Victoria htp cpe	3,390	2,435	80,439
64B	club sdn 2d	3,380	2,374	34,041
76B	Sunliner conv	3,556	2,650	35,029
Station Wagon (wb 116.0)				
59A	Ranch 2d, 6P	3,552	2,397	34,578
59B	Del Rio 2d, 6P	3,734	2,503	12,687
79A	Ranch 4d, 6P	3,608	2,451	32,854
79C	Cntry Sedan 4d, 9P	3,682	2,664	20,702
79D	Cntry Sedan 4d, 6P	3,614	2,557	68,772
79E	Cntry Squire 4d, 9P	3,718	2,794	15,020

1958 Engines	bore×stroke	bhp	availability
I-6, 223.0	3.62×3.60	145	S-all exc 51A
V-8, 292.0	3.75×3.30	205	S-51A; O-others
V-8, 332.0	4.00×3.30	240	O-wgns (265 bhp w/auto)
V-8, 332.0	4.00×3.30	265	O-all
V-8, 352.0	4.00×3.50	300	O-all

1959

Custom 300 (wb 118.0)		Wght	Price	Prod
58E	sdn 4d	3,436	2,273	249,553
64F	sdn 2d	3,360	2,219	228,573
64G	bus sdn	3,334	2,132	4,084
Fairlane (wb 118.0)				
58A	Town Sedan 4d	3,466	2,411	64,663
64A	club sdn 2d	3,382	2,357	35,126
Fairlane 500 (wb 118.0)				
57A	Victoria htp sdn	3,502	2,602	9,308
58B	sdn 4d	3,468	2,530	35,670
63A	Victoria htp cpe	3,416	2,537	23,892
64B	club sdn 2d	3,388	2,476	10,141
Galaxie (wb 118.0)				
51A	Skyl retrac htp cpe	4,064	3,346	12,915
54A	sdn 4d	3,456	2,582	183,108
64H	club sdn 2d	3,388	2,528	52,848
65A	Victoria htp cpe	3,428	2,589	121,869
75A	Victoria htp sdn	3,544	2,654	47,728
76B	Sunliner conv cpe	3,578	2,839	45,868
Station Wagon (wb 118.0)				
59C	Ranch 2d, 6P	3,640	2,567	45,588
59D	Del Rio 2d, 6P	3,664	2,678	8,663
71E	Cntry Sedan 4d, 9P	3,818	2,829	28,811
71F	Cntry Sedan 4d, 6P	3,768	2,745	94,601
71G	Cntry Squire 4d, 9P	3,808	2,958	24,336
71H	Ranch 4d, 6P	3,736	2,634	67,339

1959 Engines	bore×stroke	bhp	availability
I-6, 223.0	3.62×3.60	145	S-all exc 51A
V-8, 292.0	3.75×3.30	200	S-51A; O-others
V-8, 332.0	4.00×3.30	225	O-all
V-8, 352.0	4.00×3.50	300	O-all

1960

Falcon (wb 109.5)		Wght	Price	Prod
58A	sdn 4d	2,288	1,974	167,896
59A	wgn 2d	2,540	2,225	27,552
64A	sdn 2d	2,259	1,912	193,470
71A	wgn 4d	2,575	2,287	46,758
Custom 300 (wb 119.0)				
58F	sdn 4d	3,576	2,284	572
64H	sdn 2d	3,465	2,230	302
Fairlane (wb 119.0)				
58E	sdn 4d	3,656	2,311	109,801
64F	sdn 2d	3,582	2,257	93,256
64G	bus sdn	3,555	2,170	1,733
Fairlane 500 (wb 119.0)				
58A	Town Sedan 4d	3,663	2,388	153,234
64A	club sdn 2d	3,586	2,334	91,041
Galaxie (wb 119.0)				
54A	Town Sedan 4d	3,684	2,603	104,784
62A	club sdn 2d	3,603	2,549	31,866
63A	Starliner htp cpe	3,617	2,610	68,461
75A	Victoria htp sdn	3,692	2,675	39,215
76B	Sunliner conv cpe	3,791	2,860	44,762
Station Wagon (wb 119.0)				
59C	Ranch 2d, 6P	3,881	2,586	27,136
71E	Cntry Sedan 4d, 9P	4,058	2,837	19,277
71F	Cntry Sedan 4d, 6P	4,012	2,752	59,302
71G	Cntry Squire 4d, 6P	4,072	2,967	22,237
71H	Ranch 4d, 6P	3,998	2,656	43,872

1960 Engines	bore×stroke	bhp	availability
I-6, 144.3	3.50×2.50	90	S-Falcon only
I-6, 223.0	3.62×3.60	145	S-all exc Falc
V-8, 292.0	3.75×3.30	185	O-all exc Falc
V-8, 352.0	4.00×3.50	235	O-all exc Falc
V-8, 352.0	4.00×3.50	300/360	O-all exc Falc

1961

Falcon (wb 109.5)		Wght	Price	Prod
58A	sdn 4d	2,289	1,976	159,761
59A	wgn 2d	2,525	2,227	32,045
62A	Futura sdn 2d	2,322	2,162	44,470
64A	sdn 2d (inc 50 Econ sdns)	2,254	1,914	150,032
71A	wgn 4d	2,558	2,270	87,933
Custom 300 (wb 119.0)				
58F	sdn 4d	3,516	—	303
64H	sdn 2d	3,405	—	49
Fairlane (wb 119.0)				
58E	sdn 4d	3,634	2,317	96,602
64F	sdn 2d	3,536	2,263	66,875
58A	sdn 4d	3,642	2,432	98,917
64A	sdn 2d	3,551	2,378	42,468
Galaxie (wb 119.0)				
54A	sdn 4d	3,619	2,592	141,823
62A	sdn 2d	3,537	2,538	27,780
63A	Starliner htp cpe	3,566	2,599	29,669
65A	Victoria htp cpe	3,594	2,599	75,437
75A	Victoria htp sdn	3,637	2,664	30,342
76B	Sunliner conv cpe	3,743	2,849	44,614
Station Wagon (wb 119.0)				
59C	Ranch 2d, 6P	3,865	2,588	12,042
71E	Cntry Sedan 4d, 9P	4,011	2,858	16,356
71F	Cntry Sedan 4d, 6P	3,983	2,754	46,311
71G	Cntry Squire 4d, 9P	4,015	3,013	14,657
71H	Ranch 4d, 6P	3,960	2,658	30,292
71J	Cntry Squire 4d, 6P	3,969	2,943	16,961

1961 Engines	bore×stroke	bhp	availability
I-6, 144.3	3.50×2.50	85	S-Falcon
I-6, 170.0	3.50×2.94	101	S-Fairlane; O-Falcon
I-6, 223.0	3.62×3.30	135	S-all exc Falc, Fairlane
V-8, 292.0	3.75×3.30	175	S-all exc Falc
V-8, 352.0	4.00×3.50	220	O-all exc Falc
V-8, 390.0	4.05×3.78	300	O-all exc Falc
V-8, 390.0	4.05×3.78	375/401	O-all exc Falc (limited)

1962

Falcon (wb 109.5)		Wght	Price	Prod
58A	sdn 4d	2,279	2,047	126,041
58B	Deluxe sdn 4d	2,285	2,133	

Falcon		Wght	Price	Prod
59A	wgn 2d	2,539	2,298	20,025
59B	Deluxe wgn 2d	2,545	2,384	
62C	Futura sdn 2d	2,343	2,273	17,011
64A	sdn 2d	2,243	1,985	143,650
64B	Deluxe sdn 2d	2,249	2,071	
71A	wgn 4d	2,575	2,341	66,819
71B	Deluxe wgn 4d	2,581	2,427	
71C	Squire wgn 4d	2,591	2,603	22,583
Series 30 Fairlane (wb 115.5)				
54A	sdn 4d	2,848	2,216	45,342
62A	sdn 2d	2,815	2,154	34,264
Series 40 Fairlane 500 (wb 115.5)				
54B	500 sdn 4d	2,865	2,304	129,258
62B	500 sdn 2d	2,832	2,242	68,624
62C	500 spt cpe	2,928	2,403	19,628
Galaxie (wb 119.0)				
54B	sdn 4d	3,636	2,507	115,594
62B	sdn 2d	3,554	2,453	54,930
Galaxie 500 (wb 119.0)				
54A	sdn 4d	3,650	2,667	174,195
62A	sdn 2d	3,568	2,613	27,824
65A	Victoria htp cpe	3,568	2,674	87,562
65B	XL Victoria htp cpe	3,672	2,268	28,412
75A	Victoria htp sdn	3,640	2,739	30,778
76A	Sunliner conv cpe	3,730	2,924	42,646
76B	XL Sunliner conv cpe	3,831	3,518	13,183
Station Wagon (wb 119.0)				
71A	Cntry Squire 4d, 9P	4,022	3,088	15,666
71B	Cntry Sedan 4d, 6P	3,992	2,829	47,635
71C	Cntry Sedan 4d, 9P	4,010	2,933	16,562
71D	Ranch 4d, 6P	3,968	2,733	33,674
71E	Cntry Squire 4d, 6P	4,006	3,018	16,114

1962 Engines	bore×stroke	bhp	availability
I-6, 144.3	3.50×2.50	85	S-Falcon
I-6, 170.0	3.50×2.94	101	S-Fair; O-Falc
I-6, 223.0	3.62×3.60	138	S-all exc Falc, Fairlane
V-8, 221.0	3.50×2.87	145	O-Fairlane
V-8, 260.0	3.80×2.87	164	O-Fairlane
V-8, 292.0	3.75×3.30	170	S-76B; O-all exc Falc, Fair
V-8, 352.0	4.00×3.50	220	O-all exc Falc, Fairlane
V-8, 390.0	4.05×3.78	300/340	O-all exc Falc, Fairlane
V-8, 390.0	4.05×3.78	375/401	O-all exc Falc, Fairlane
V-8, 406.0	4.13×3.78	385/405	O-all exc Falc, Fairlane

1963

Series 0 Falcon (wb 109.5)		Wght	Price	Prod
54A	sdn 4d	2,337	2,047	62,365
62A	sdn 2d	2,300	1,985	70,630
Series 10 Falcon Futura (wb 109.5)				
54B	sdn 4d	2,345	2,161	31,736
62B	sdn 2d	2,308	2,116	27,018
63B	htp cpe	2,455	2,198	28,496
63C	Sprint htp cpe	2,490	2,603	10,479
76A	conv cpe	2,655	2,470	31,192
76B	Sprint conv cpe	2,690	2,837	4,602
Series 20 Falcon Wagon (wb 109.5)				
59A	wgn 2d	2,580	2,298	7,322
59B	Deluxe wgn 2d	2,586	2,384	4,269
71A	wgn 4d	2,617	2,341	18,484
71B	Deluxe wgn 4d	2,623	2,427	23,477
71C	Squire wgn 4d	2,639	2,603	8,269
Series 30 Fairlane (wb 115.5)				
54A	sdn 4d	2,930	2,216	44,454
62A	sdn 2d	2,890	2,154	28,984
71D	Ranch Wagon 4d	3,281	2,525	24,006
Series 40 Fairlane 500 (wb 115.5)				
54B	sdn 4d	2,945	2,304	104,175
62B	sdn 2d	2,905	2,242	34,764
65A	htp cpe	2,923	2,324	41,641
65B	htp cpe, bkt sts	2,923	2,504	28,268
71B	Cus Ranch Wagon 4d	3,298	2,613	29,612
71E	Squire Wagon 4d	3,295	2,781	7,983
Series 50 300 (wb 119.0)				
54E	sdn 4d	3,627	2,378	44,142
62E	sdn 2d	3,547	2,324	26,010
Series 50 Galaxie (wb 119.0)				
54B	sdn 4d	3,647	2,507	82,419
62B	sdn 2d	3,567	2,453	30,335
Series 60 Galaxie 500 (wb 119.0)				
54A	sdn 4d	3,667	2,667	205,722
62A	sdn 2d	3,587	2,613	21,137
63B	XL htp cpe, fstbk	3,772	2,674	134,370
65A	htp cpe	3,599	2,674	49,733
75A	htp sdn	3,679	2,739	39,154
76A	Sunliner conv cpe	3,757	2,924	29,713
Series 70 Station Wagon (wb 119.0)				
71A	Cntry Squire 4d, 9P	4,003	3,088	19,567
71B	Cntry Sedan 4d, 6P	3,977	2,829	64,954
71C	Cntry Sedan 4d, 9P	3,989	2,933	22,250
71E	Cntry Squire 4d, 6P	3,991	3,018	20,359

1963 Engines	bore×stroke	bhp	availability
I-6, 144.3	3.50×2.50	85	S-Falcon
I-6, 170.0	3.50×2.94	101	S-Fair; O-Falc
I-6, 200.0	3.68×3.13	116	O-Fairlane
I-6, 223.0	3.62×3.60	138	S-all exc Falc, Fairlane
V-8, 221.0	3.50×2.87	145	O-Fairlane
V-8, 260.0	3.80×2.87	164	S-Falc Sprint; O-others
V-8, 289.0	4.00×2.87	271	O-Fairlane
V-8, 352.0	4.00×3.50	220	O-all exc Falc, Fairlane
V-8, 390.0	4.05×3.78	300/330	O-all exc Falc, Fairlane
V-8, 406.0	4.13×3.78	385/405	O-all exc Falc, Fairlane
V-8, 427.0	4.23×3.78	410/425	O-all exc Falc, Fairlane

1964

Series 0 Falcon (wb 109.5)		Wght	Price	Prod
01	sdn 2d	2,365	1,996	36,441
01	Deluxe sdn 2d	2,380	2,039	28,411
02	sdn 4d	2,400	2,058	27,722
02	Deluxe sdn 4d	2,420	2,101	26,532
Series 10 Falcon Futura (wb 109.5)				
11	htp cpe, bkt seats	2,545	2,325	8,607
12	conv cpe, bkt seats	2,735	2,597	2,980
13	Sprint htp cpe	2,813	2,436	13,830
14	Sprint conv cpe	3,008	2,671	4,278
15	conv cpe	2,710	2,481	13,220
16	sdn 4d	2,410	2,176	38,032
17	htp cpe	2,515	2,209	32,608
19	sdn 2d	2,375	2,127	16,833
Series 20 Falcon Wagon (wb 109.5)				
21	wgn 2d	2,660	2,326	6,034
22	wgn 4d	2,695	2,360	17,779
24	Deluxe wgn 4d	2,715	2,446	20,697
26	Squire wgn 4d	2,720	2,622	6,766
Series 30 Fairlane (wb 115.5)				
31	sdn 2d	2,855	2,194	20,421
32	sdn 4d	2,895	2,235	36,693
38	Ranch wgn 4d	3,290	2,531	20,980
Series 40 Fairlane 500 (wb 115.5)				
41	sdn 2d	2,863	2,276	23,447
42	sdn 4d	2,910	2,317	86,919
43	htp cpe	2,925	2,341	42,733
47	htp cpe, bkt sts	2,945	2,502	21,431
48	Ranch Cus wgn 4d	3,310	2,612	24,962
Series 50 Custom (wb 119.0)				
51	500 sdn 2d	3,559	2,464	20,619
52	500 sdn 4d	3,659	2,518	68,828
53	sdn 2d	3,529	2,361	41,359
54	sdn 4d	3,619	2,415	57,964
Series 60 Galaxie 500 (wb 119.0)				
60	XL htp sdn	3,722	3,298	14,661
61	sdn 2d	3,574	2,624	13,041
62	sdn 4d	3,674	2,678	198,805
64	htp sdn	3,689	2,750	49,242
66	htp cpe	3,584	2,685	206,998
65	Sunliner conv cpe	3,759	2,947	37,311
Series 60 Galaxie 500				
68	XL htp cpe	3,622	3,233	58,306
69	XL conv cpe	3,687	3,495	15,169
Series 70 Station Wagon (wb 119.0)				
72	Cntry Sedan 4d, 6P	3,973	2,840	68,578
74	Cntry Sedan 4d, 9P	3,983	2,944	25,661
76	Cntry Squire 4d, 6P	3,988	3,029	23,570
78	Cntry Squire 4d, 9P	3,998	3,099	23,120

1964 Engines	bore×stroke	bhp	availability
I-6, 144.3	3.50×2.50	85	S-Falc exc conv, Sprnt, Del wgns
I-6, 170.0	3.50×2.94	101	S-Falc conv, Sprnt, Del wgn, Fairlane; O-other Falc
I-6, 200.0	3.68×3.13	116	O-Fairlane, Falcon
I-6, 223.0	3.62×3.60	138	S-all exc Fair, Falcon
V-8, 260.0	3.80×2.87	164	S-Falcon Sprint; O-Other Falc, Fairlane
V-8, 289.0	4.00×2.87	195/271	S-60, 68, 69; O-all
V-8, 352.0	4.00×3.50	250	O-all exc Falc, Fairlane
V-8, 390.0	4.05×3.78	300/330	O-all exc Falc, Fairlane
V-8, 427.0	4.23×3.78	410/425	O-all exc Falc, Fairlane

1965

Series 0 Falcon (wb 109.5)		Wght	Price	Prod
01	sdn 2d	2,366	2,020	35,858
01	Deluxe sdn 2d	2,381	2,120	13,824
02	sdn 4d	2,406	2,082	30,186
02	Deluxe sdn 4d	2,426	2,182	13,850
Series 10 Falcon Futura (wb 109.5)				
13	Sprint htp cpe	2,749	2,437	2,806
14	Sprint conv cpe	2,971	2,671	300
15	conv cpe	2,673	2,481	6,315
16	sdn 4d	2,413	2,192	33,985
17	htp cpe	2,491	2,226	25,754
19	sdn 2d	2,373	2,144	11,670
Series 20 Falcon Wagon (wb 109.5)				
21	wgn 2d	2,611	2,333	4,891
22	wgn 4d	2,651	2,367	14,911
24	Delx wgn 4d (Futura)	2,667	2,506	12,548
26	Squire wgn 4d	2,669	2,665	6,703
Series 30 Fairlane (wb 116.0)				
31	sdn 2d	2,902	2,230	13,685
32	sdn 4d	2,954	2,271	25,378
38	wgn 4d	3,279	2,567	13,911
Series 40 Fairlane 500 (wb 116.0)				
41	sdn 2d	2,901	2,312	16,092
42	sdn 4d	2,959	2,353	77,836
43	htp cpe	2,973	2,377	41,405
47	htp cpe, bkt sts	2,984	2,538	15,141
48	wgn 4d	3,316	2,648	20,506
Series 50 Custom (wb 119.0)				
51	sdn 2d	3,306	2,313	49,034
52	sdn 4d	3,378	2,366	96,393
53	500 sdn 2d	3,336	2,464	19,603
54	500 sdn 4d	3,408	2,518	71,727
Series 60 Galaxie 500 (wb 119.0)				
60	LTD htp sdn	3,578	3,313	68,038
62	sdn 4d	3,440	2,678	181,183
64	htp sdn	3,480	2,765	49,982
65	conv cpe	3,592	2,950	31,930
66	htp cpe	3,380	2,685	157,284
67	LTD htp cpe	3,486	3,233	37,691
68	XL htp cpe	3,497	3,233	28,141
69	XL conv cpe	3,665	3,498	9,849
Series 70 Station Wagon (wb 119.0)				
71	Ranch 4d, 6P	3,869	2,763	30,817
72	Cntry Sedan 4d, 6P	3,879	2,855	59,693
74	Cntry Sedan 4d, 9P	3,893	2,959	32,344
76	Cntry Squire 4d, 6P	3,925	3,104	24,308
78	Cntry Squire 4d, 9P	3,937	3,174	30,502

1965 Engines	bore×stroke	bhp	availability
I-6, 170.0	3.50×2.94	101	S-Falc exc Fut, Sqr 'til 9/25/64
I-6, 200.0	3.68×3.13	120	S-Fut/Squire, Fair; O-Falcon
I-6, 240.0	4.00×3.18	150	S-all exc Falc, Fair, LTD, XL
V-8, 289.0	4.00×2.87	200/271	S-LTD, XL; O-others
V-8, 352.0	4.00×3.50	250	O-all exc Falc, Fairlane
V-8, 390.0	4.05×3.78	300/330	O-all exc Falc, Fairlane
V-8, 427.0	4.23×3.78	425	O-all exc Falc, Fairlane

1966

Ser. 0 Falc (wb 110.9; wgn-113.0)		Wght	Price	Prod
01	club cpe	2,519	2,060	41,432
02	sdn 4d	2,559	2,114	34,685
06	wgn 4d	3,037	2,442	16,653
Series 10 Falcon Futura (wb 110.9; wgn-113.0)				
11	club cpe	2,527	2,183	21,997
12	sdn 4d	2,567	2,237	34,039
13	spt cpe	2,597	2,328	20,289
16	wgn 4d	3,045	2,553	13,574
Series 30 Fairlane (wb 116; wgn-113.0)				
31	club cpe	2,832	2,240	13,498
32	sdn 4d	2,877	2,280	26,170
38	wgn 4d	3,267	2,589	12,379
Series 40 Fairlane 500 (wb 116; wgn-113.0)				
40	XL GT htp cpe, V-8	3,493	2,843	33,015
41	club cpe	2,839	3,317	14,118
42	sdn 4d	2,884	2,357	68,635
43	htp cpe	2,941	2,378	75,947
44	XL GT conv cpe	3,070	3,068	4,327
45	conv cpe	3,169	2,603	9,299
46	XL conv cpe	3,184	2,768	4,560
47	XL htp cpe	2,969	2,533	23,942
48	Deluxe wgn 4d	3,277	2,665	19,826
49	Squire wgn 4d	3,285	2,796	11,558
Series 50 Custom (wb 119.0)				
51	500 sdn 2d	3,397	2,481	28,789
52	500 sdn 4d	3,466	2,533	109,449
53	sdn 2d	3,355	2,380	32,292
54	sdn 4d	3,455	2,432	72,245
Series 60 Galaxie 500 (wb 119.0)				
60	LTD htp sdn	3,649	3,278	69,400
61	7-Litre htp cpe	3,914	3,621	8,705
62	sdn 4d	3,478	2,677	171,886
63	7-Litre conv cpe, V-8	4,059	3,872	2,368
64	htp sdn	3,548	2,762	54,884
65	conv cpe	3,655	2,934	27,454
66	htp cpe	3,459	2,685	198,532
67	LTD htp cpe	3,601	3,201	31,696
68	XL htp cpe	3,616	3,231	25,715
69	XL conv cpe	3,761	3,480	6,360
Series 70 Station Wagon (wb 119.0)				
71	Ranch 4d	3,941	2,793	33,306
72	Cntry Sedan 4d, 6P	3,956	2,882	55,616
74	Cntry Sedan 4d, 9P	3,997	2,999	36,633
76	Cntry Squire 4d, 6P	4,026	3,182	27,645
78	Cntry Squire 4d, 9P	4,040	3,265	41,953

1966 Engines	bore×stroke	bhp	availability
I-6, 170.0	3.50×2.94	105	S-Falcon
I-6, 200.0	3.68×3.13	120	S-Falc Fut/wgn, Fair exc GT, GTA; O-Falc
I-6, 240.0	4.00×3.18	150	S-all exc Falc, Fairlane; O-Falc wgns
V-8, 289.0	4.00×2.87	200/225	S-XL, LTD; O-Falc, Fair exc GT, GTA; 50, 60, 70 exc 7L
V-8, 352.0	4.00×3.50	250	O-all exc 7L, Fairlane, Falc
V-8, 390.0	4.05×3.78	265	O-all exc 7L, Fair GT/GTA, Falcon
V-8, 390.0	4.05×3.78	315	O-all exc 7L, Fairlane, Falc
V-8, 390.0	4.05×3.78	335	S-Fair GT/GTA; O-other Fair
V-8, 427.0	4.23×3.78	410/425	O-all exc 7L, 70, Fairlane, Falc
V-8, 428.0	4.13×3.98	345	S-7L; O-others exc Fair, Falc

1967

Falcon (wb 110.9; wgn-113.0)		Wght	Price	Prod
10	sdn 2d	2,520	2,118	16,082
11	sdn 4d	2,551	2,167	13,554
12	wgn 4d	3,030	2,497	5,553
Falcon Futura (wb 110.9; wgn-113.0)				
20	club cpe	2,528	2,280	6,287
21	sdn 4d	2,559	2,322	11,254
22	spt cpe	3,062	2,437	7,053
23	Squire wgn 4d	2,556	2,609	4,552
Fairlane (wb 116.0; wgns-113.0)				
30	sdn 2d	2,832	2,297	10,628
31	sdn 4d	2,867	2,339	19,740
32	Ranch wgn 4d	3,283	2,643	10,881
33	500 club cpe	2,840	2,377	8,473
34	500 sdn 4d	2,887	2,417	51,522
35	500 htp cpe	2,927	2,439	70,135
36	500 conv cpe	3,244	2,664	5,428
37	Deluxe wgn 4d	3,291	2,718	15,902
38	Cntry Squire wgn 4d	3,302	2,902	8,348
Fairlane 500XL (wb 116.0)				
40	htp cpe	2,955	2,724	14,871
41	conv cpe	3,272	2,950	1,943
42	GT htp cpe	3,301	2,839	18,670
43	GT conv cpe	3,607	3,064	2,117
Series 50 Custom (wb 119.0)				
50	sdn 2d	3,430	2,441	18,107
51	sdn 4d	3,488	2,496	41,417
52	500 sdn 2d	3,482	2,553	18,146
53	500 sdn 4d	3,490	2,595	82,260
Galaxie 500 (wb 119.0)				
54	sdn 4d	3,500	2,732	130,063
55	htp cpe	3,503	2,755	197,388
56	htp sdn	3,571	2,808	57,087
57	conv cpe	3,682	3,003	19,068
58	XL htp sdn	3,594	3,243	18,174
59	XL conv cpe	3,794	3,493	5,161
LTD (wb 119.0)				
62	htp cpe	3,626	3,362	46,036
64	sdn 4d	3,795	3,298	12,491
66	htp sdn	3,676	3,363	51,978
Station Wagon (wb 119.0)				
70	Ranch 4d, 6P	3,930	2,836	23,932
71	Cntry Sedan 4d, 6P	3,943	2,935	50,818
72	Cntry Sedan 4d, 9P	4,023	3,061	34,377
73	Cntry Squire 4d, 6P	3,990	3,234	25,600
74	Cntry Squire 4d, 9P	4,030	3,359	44,024

1967 Engines	bore×stroke	bhp	availability
I-6, 170.0	3.50×2.94	105	S-Falcon exc Fut, wagons
I-6, 200.0	3.68×3.13	120	S-Falcon Futura/wgns, Fair exc GTs
I-6, 240.0	4.00×3.18	150	S-all exc Falc, Fairlane
V-8, 289.0	4.00×2.87	200	S-Fair GT, Gal 500XL LTD; O-others
V-8, 289.0	4.00×2.87	225	O-Falcon
V-8, 390.0	4.05×3.78	270	O-Fairlane
V-8, 390.0	4.05×3.78	315	O-Cus, Gal, LTD, Wgn
V-8, 390.0	4.05×3.78	320	O-Fairlane
V-8, 427.0	4.23×3.78	410/425	O-all exc Falc
V-8, 428.0	4.13×3.98	345	O-all exc Falc, Fairlane

1968

Falcon (wb 110.9; wgn-113.0)		Wght	Price	Prod
10	sdn 2d	2,680	2,252	29,166
11	sdn 4d	2,714	2,301	36,443
12	wgn 4d	3,123	2,617	15,576
Falcon Futura (wb 110.9; wgn-113.0)				
20	sdn 2d	2,685	2,415	10,633
21	sdn 4d	2,719	2,456	18,733
22	spt cpe	2,713	2,541	10,077
23	wgn 4d	3,123	2,728	10,761
Fairlane (wb 116.0; wgn-113.0)				
30	htp cpe	3,028	2,456	44,683
31	sdn 4d	2,986	2,464	18,146
32	wgn 4d	3,333	2,770	14,800
33	500 htp cpe	3,066	2,591	33,282
34	500 sdn 4d	3,024	2,543	42,930
35	500 fstbk htp cpe	3,080	2,566	32,452
36	500 conv cpe	3,226	2,822	3,761
37	500 wgn 4d	3,377	2,880	10,190
Torino (wb 116.0; wgn-113.0)				
38	Squire wgn 4d	3,425	3,032	14,773
40	htp cpe	3,098	2,710	35,964
41	sdn 4d	3,062	2,688	17,962
42	GT fstbk htp cpe	3,208	2,747	74,135
43	GT conv cpe	3,352	3,001	5,310
44	GT htp cpe	3,194	2,772	23,939
Custom (wb 119.0)				
50	sdn 2d	3,471	3,584	18,485
51	sdn 4d	3,498	2,642	45,980
52	500 sdn 2d	3,460	2,669	8,983
53	500 sdn 4d	3,511	2,741	49,398
Galaxie 500 (wb 119.0)				
54	sdn 4d	3,516	2,864	117,877
55	fstbk htp cpe	3,534	2,881	69,760
56	htp sdn	3,562	2,936	55,461
57	conv cpe	3,679	3,108	11,832
58	htp cpe	3,540	2,916	84,332
60	XL fstbk htp cpe	3,588	2,985	50,048
61	XL conv cpe	3,745	3,214	6,066
LTD (wb 119.0)				
62	htp cpe	3,679	3,153	54,163
64	sdn 4d	3,596	3,135	22,834
66	htp sdn	3,642	3,206	61,755
Station Wagon (wb 119.0)				
70	Ranch 4d, 6P	3,925	3,000	18,237
71	Ranch 500 4d, 6P	3,935	3,063	18,181
72	Ranch 500 4d, 9P	3,981	3,176	13,421
73	Cntry Sedan 4d, 6P	3,944	3,184	39,335
74	Cntry Sedan 4d, 9P	4,001	3,295	29,374
75	Cntry Squire 4d, 6P	4,013	3,539	33,994
76	Cntry Squire 4d, 9P	4,059	3,619	57,776

1968 Engines	bore×stroke	bhp	availability
I-6, 170.0	3.50×2.94	100	S-base Falcon cpes, sdns
I-6, 200.0	3.68×3.13	115	S-Fair, Tor, Falcon Fut wgn; O-Falcon
I-6, 240.0	4.00×3.18	150	S-all exc Fut, Tor GT, LTD
V-8, 289.0	4.00×2.87	195	O-Falcon
V-8, 302.0	4.00×3.00	210	S-LTD, Tor GT, O-all
V-8, 302.0	4.00×3.00	230	O-Falc, Fair, Tor
V-8, 390.0	4.05×3.78	265	O-all exc Falc
V-8, 390.0	4.05×3.78	315	O-all exc Falc, Fairlane
V-8, 390.0	4.05×3.78	335	O-Fairlane
V-8, 427.0	4.23×3.78	390	O-Fair/Tor htps
V-8, 428.0	4.13×3.98	340	O-all exc Falc, Fairlane

1969

Falcon (wb 110.9; wgn-113.0)		Wght	Price	Prod
10	sdn 2d	2,700	2,283	29,262
11	sdn 4d	2,735	2,333	22,719
12	wgn 4d	3,100	2,660	11,568
Falcon Futura (wb 110.9; wgn-113.0)				
20	sdn 2d	2,715	2,461	6,482
21	sdn 4d	2,748	2,498	11,850
22	spt cpe	2,738	2,598	5,931
23	wgn 4d	3,120	2,771	7,203

Fairlane (wb 116.0; wgn-113.0)		Wght	Price	Prod
30	htp cpe	3,079	2,499	85,630
31	sdn 4d	3,065	2,488	27,296
32	wgn 4d	3,441	2,841	10,882
33	500 htp cpe	3,090	2,626	28,179
34	500 sdn 4d	3,082	2,568	40,888
35	500 fstbk htp cpe	3,137	2,601	29,849
36	500 conv cpe	3,278	2,851	2,264
37	500 wgn 4d	3,469	2,951	12,869
Torino (wb 116.0; wgn-113.0)				
38	Squire wgn 4d	3,503	3,107	14,472
40	htp cpe	3,143	2,754	20,789
41	sdn 4d	3,128	2,733	11,971
42	GT fstbk htp cpe	3,220	2,840	61,319
43	GT conv cpe	3,356	3,090	2,552
44	GT htp cpe	3,173	2,865	17,951
45	Cobra htp cpe	3,490	3,164	*
46	Cobra fstbk htp cpe	3,537	3,189	*
Custom (wb 121.0)				
50	sdn 2d	3,605	2,649	15,439
51	sdn 4d	3,628	2,691	45,653
52	500 sdn 2d	3,590	2,748	7,585
53	500 sdn 4d	3,640	2,790	45,761
70	Ranch wgn 4d	4,089	3,091	17,489
71	500 wgn 4d, 6P	4,102	3,155	16,432
72	500 wgn 4d, 9P	4,152	3,268	11,563
Galaxie 500 (wb 121.0)				
54	sdn 4d	3,690	2,914	104,606
55	fstbk htp cpe	3,700	2,930	63,921
56	htp sdn	3,725	2,983	64,031
57	conv cpe	3,860	3,159	6,910
58	htp cpe	3,655	2,982	71,920
73	Cntry Sdn wgn 4d, 6P	4,087	3,274	36,387
74	Cntry Sdn wgn 4d, 9P	4,112	3,390	27,517
XL (wb 121.0)				
60	fstbk htp cpe	3,805	3,069	54,557
61	conv cpe	3,955	3,297	7,402
LTD (wb 121.0)				
62	htp cpe	3,745	3,251	111,565
64	sdn 4d	3,745	3,209	63,709
66	htp sdn	3,840	3,278	113,168
75	Cntry Sqr wgn 4d, 6P	4,202	3,661	46,445
76	Cntry Sqr wgn 4d, 9P	4,227	3,738	82,790

1969 Engines	bore×stroke	bhp	availability
I-6, 170.0	3.50×2.94	100	S-Falc exc Fut
I-6, 200.0	3.68×3.13	115	S-Futura
I-6, 240.0	4.00×3.18	150	S-all exc Falc, Fairlane, Tor GT, LTD
I-6, 250.0	3.68×3.91	155	S-Fair, Tor exc GT, Cobra
V-8, 302.0	4.00×3.00	220	S-LTD, Tor GT; O-others
V-8, 351.0	4.00×3.50	250	O-Fair, Tor exc Cobra
V-8, 351.0	4.00×3.50	290	O-Fairlane, Tor exc Cobra
V-8, 390.0	4.05×3.78	265	O-full size
V-8, 390.0	4.05×3.78	320	O-Fairlane, Tor exc Cobra
V-8, 428.0	4.13×3.98	335**	S-Tor Cobra; O-Fairlane
V-8, 429.0	4.36×3.59	320/360	O-full size

* Included with Torino GT models. ** Available in standard and Ram Air versions.

1970

Maverick (wb 103.0)		Wght	Price	Prod
91	sdn 2d	2,411	1,995	578,914
Falcon (wb 110.9, wgn-113.0)				
10	sdn 2d	2,708	2,390	4,373
11	sdn 4d	2,753	2,438	5,301
12	wgn 4d	3,155	2,767	1,624
Falcon Futura (wb 110.9; wgn-113.0)				
20	sdn 2d	2,727	2,542	1,129
21	sdn 4d	2,764	2,579	2,262
23	wgn 4d	3,191	2,878	1,005
"1970½" Falcon (wb 117.0; wgn-114.0)*				
26	sdn 2d	3,100	2,460	26,071
27	sdn 4d	3,116	2,500	30,443
"1970½" Falcon				
40	wgn 4d	3,483	2,801	10,539
Fairlane 500 (wb 117.0; wgn-114.0)				
28	sdn 4d	3,166	2,627	25,780
29	htp cpe	3,178	2,660	70,636
41	wgn 4d	3,558	2,957	13,613
Torino (wb 117.0; wgn-114.0)				
30	htp cpe	3,223	2,722	49,826
31	sdn 4d	3,208	2,689	30,117
32	htp sdn	3,239	2,795	14,312
33	Brougham htp cpe	3,293	3,006	16,911
34	fstbk htp cpe	3,261	2,899	12,490
35	GT htp cpe	3,366	3,105	56,819
36	Brougham htp sdn	3,309	3,078	14,543
37	GT conv cpe	3,490	3,212	3,939
38	Cobra fstbk htp cpe	3,774	3,270	7,675
42	wgn 4d	3,603	3,164	10,613
43	Squire wgn 4d	3,673	3,379	13,166
Custom (wb 121.0)				
51	sdn 4d	3,545	2,850	42,849
52	500 htp cpe	3,510	2,918	2,677
53	500 sdn 4d	3,585	2,872	41,261
70	Ranch wgn 4d	4,079	3,305	15,086
71	500 wgn 4d, 6P	4,049	3,368	15,304
72	500 wgn 4d, 9P	4,137	3,481	9,943
Galaxie 500 (wb 121.0)				
54	sdn 4d	3,601	3,026	101,784
55	fstbk htp cpe	3,610	3,043	50,825
56	htp sdn	3,672	3,096	53,817
58	htp cpe	3,611	3,094	57,059
73	Cntry Sdn wgn 4d, 6P	4,089	3,488	32,209
74	Cntry Sdn wgn 4d, 9P	4,112	3,600	22,645
XL (wb 121.0)				
60	fstbk htp cpe	3,750	3,293	27,251
61	conv cpe	3,983	3,501	6,348
LTD (wb 121.0)				
62	htp cpe	3,727	3,356	96,324
62	Brougham htp cpe	3,855	3,537	
64	sdn 4d	3,701	3,307	78,306
64	Brougham sdn	3,829	3,502	
66	htp sdn	3,771	3,385	90,390
66	Brougham htp sdn	4,029	3,579	
75	Cntry Sqr wgn 4d, 6P	4,139	3,832	39,837
76	Cntry Sqr wgn 4d, 9P	4,185	3,909	69,077

1970 Engines	bore×stroke	bhp	availability
I-6, 170.0	3.50×2.94	105	S-Maverick
I-6, 200.0	3.68×3.13	120	S-Falc; O-Mav
I-6, 240.0	4.00×3.18	150	S-full size exc XL, LTD
I-6, 250.0	3.68×3.91	155	S-Tor exc GT, Brghm, Squire, Cobra
V-8, 302.0	4.00×3.00	220	S-Tor GT/ Brghm/Squire Cobra; O-others
V-8, 351.0	4.00×3.50	250	S-XL, LTD, full-size wgns; O-all exc Falc, Cobra
V-8, 351.0	4.00×3.50	300	O-Tor exc Cob
V-8, 390.0	4.05×3.78	265	O-all full size
V-8, 429.0	4.36×3.59	320	O-all full size
V-8, 429.0	4.36×3.59	360	S-Tor Cobra; O-full-size, Tor
V-8, 429.0	4.36×3.59	370**	O-Tor exc wgns
V-8, 429.0	4.36×3.59	375	O-Tor, Cobra

* Replaced Fairlane 500. ** Available in standard and Ram Air versions.

1970½ Eng.	bore×stroke	bhp	availability
I-6, 250.0	3.68×3.91	155	S-Falcon
V-8, 302.0	4.00×3.00	220	O-Falcon
V-8, 351.0	4.00×3.50	250/300	O-Falcon
V-8, 429.0	4.36×3.59	360	O-Falcon
V-8, 429.0	4.36×3.59	370	O-Falc (no Ram Air)

1971

Pinto (wb 94.2)		Wght	Price	Prod
10	fstbk sdn 2d	1,949	1,919	288,606
11	Rnabout htchbk sdn 2d	1,993	2,062	63,796
Maverick (wb 103.0; 4d-109.9)				
91	fstbk sdn 2d	2,546	2,175	159,726
92	sdn 4d	2,641	2,234	73,208
93	Grabber fstbk sdn 2d	2,601	2,354	38,963
Torino (wb 117.0; wgns-114.0)				
25	formal htp cpe	3,168	2,706	37,518
27	sdn 4d	3,163	2,672	29,501
40	wgn 4d	3,514	3,023	21,570
30	500 formal htp cpe	3,170	2,887	89,966
31	500 sdn 4d	3,160	2,855	35,650
32	500 htp sdn	3,196	2,959	12,724
34	500 fstbk htp cpe	3,179	2,943	11,150
42	500 wgn 4d	3,514	3,170	23,270
33	Brghm frm htp cpe V-8	3,209	3,175	8,593
36	Brghm frm htp sdn V-8	3,256	3,248	4,408
43	Squire wgn 4d V-8	3,583	3,560	15,805
35	GT fstbk htp cpe V-8	3,287	3,150	31,641
37	GT conv V-8	3,428	3,408	1,613
38	Cobra fstbk htp cpe	3,525	3,295	3,054
Ford (wb 121.0)				
51	Custom sdn 4d	3,700	3,288	41,062
70	Cst Rnch Wgn 4d V-8	4,222	3,890	16,696
53	Custom 500 sdn 4d	3,705	3,426	33,765
72	C500 Rnch Wgn 4d 2S V-8	4,231	3,982	25,957
72	C500 Rnch Wgn 4d 3S V-8	4,281	4,097	
54	Galaxie 500 sdn 4d	3,782	3,594	98,130
56	Galaxie 500 htp sdn	3,838	3,665	46,595
58	Galaxie 500 htp cpe	3,783	3,628	117,139
74	G500 Ctry Sdn wgn 4d 2S V-8	4,246	4,074	60,487
74	G500 Ctry Sdn wgn 4d 3S V-8	4,296	4,188	
61	LTD conv V-8	4,053	4,094	5,750
62	LTD htp cpe V-8	3,919	3,923	103,896
63	LTD sdn 4d V-8	3,981	3,931	92,260
64	LTD htp sdn V-8	3,976	3,969	48,166
76	Cntry Sqr wgn 4d 2S V-8	4,306	4,380	130,644
76	Cntry Sqr wgn 4d 3S V-8	4,356	4,496	
66	LTD Brghm sdn 4d V-8	4,111	4,094	26,186
67	LTD Brghm htp sdn V-8	4,016	4,140	27,820
68	LTD Brghm htp cpe V-8	3,945	4,097	43,303

1971 Engines	bore×stroke	bhp	availability
I-4, 98.6	3.19×3.06	75	S-Pinto
I-4, 122.0	3.58×3.03	100	O-Pinto
I-6, 170.0	3.50×2.94	100	S-Maverick
I-6, 200.0	3.68×3.13	115	O-Maverick
I-6, 240.0	4.00×3.18	140	S-Ford Cust
I-6, 250.0	3.68×3.91	145	S-Tor exc GT Cobra; O-Mav
V-8, 302.0	4.00×3.00	210	S-Mav, Ford Cust, Tor exc Cobra
V-8, 351.0	4.00×3.50	240	S-Frd exc Cust
V-8, 351.0	4.00×3.50	285	S-Tor Cobra; O-Torino
V-8, 400.0	4.00×4.00	260	O-Ford
V-8, 429.0	4.36×3.59	320/360	O-Ford
V-8, 429.0	4.36×3.59	370	O-Torino

1972

Pinto (wb 94.2)		Wght	Price	Prod
10	fstbk sdn 2d	2,061	1,960	181,002
11	Rnabout htchbk sdn 2d	2,099	2,078	197,920
12	wgn 2d	2,283	2,265	101,483
Maverick (wb 103.0; 4d-109.9)				
91	fstbk sdn 2d	2,654	2,140	145,931
92	sdn 4d	2,751	2,195	73,686
93	Grabber fstbk sdn 2d	2,708	2,309	35,347
Torino (wb 118.0; 2d-114.0)				
25	formal htp cpe	3,374	2,673	33,530
27	sdn 4d	3,442	2,641	33,486
40	wgn 4d	3,840	2,955	22,204
30	Grn Tor formal htp cpe	3,410	2,878	132,284
31	Gran Torino sdn 4d	3,484	2,856	102,300
42	Gran Torino wgn 4d	3,874	3,096	45,212
35	GT Sprt fstbk htp cpe V-8	3,470	3,094	60,794
38	Grn Tor frml htp cpe V-8	3,466	3,094	31,239
43	Squire wgn 4d V-8	3,938	3,486	35,595
Ford (wb 121.0)				
51	Custom sdn 4d	3,742	3,246	33,014
70	Cust Rnch wgn 5d V-8	4,304	3,852	13,064
53	Cust 500 sdn 4d	3,808	3,377	24,870

Ford		Wght	Price	Prod
72	C500 Rnch wgn 4d 2S V-8	4,314	3,941	16,834
72	C500 Rnch wgn 4d 3S V-8	4,364	4,051	
54	Galaxie 500 sdn 4d	3,848	3,537	104,167
56	Galaxie 500 htp sdn	3,910	3,604	28,939
58	Galaxie 500 htp cpe	3,852	3,572	80,855
74	G500 Ctry wgn 4d 2S V-8	4,349	4,028	55,238
74	G500 Ctry wgn 4d 3S V-8	4,399	4,136	
62	LTD htp cpe V-8	3,999	3,882	101,048
63	LTD sdn 4d V-8	4,065	3,890	104,167
64	LTD htp sdn V-8	4,060	3,925	33,742
61	LTD conv V-8	4,165	4,057	4,234
76	LTD Ctry wgn 4d 2S V-8	4,393	4,318	121,419
76	LTD Ctry wgn 4d 3S V-8	4,443	4,430	
66	LTD Brghm sdn 4d V-8	4,095	4,031	36,909
67	LTD Brghm htp sdn V-8	4,090	4,074	23,364
68	LTD Brhm frml htp cpe V-8	4,031	4,034	50,409

1972 Engines	bore×stroke	bhp	availability
I-4, 98.6	3.19×3.06	54	S-Pinto exc wgn
I-4, 122.0	3.58×3.03	86	S-Pinto wgn; O-Pinto
I-6, 170.0	3.50×2.94	82	S-Maverick
I-6, 200.0	3.68×3.13	91	O-Maverick
I-6, 240.0	4.00×3.18	103	S-Ford exc wgn
I-6, 250.0	3.68×3.91	95	S-Tor exc GT
I-6, 250.0	3.68×3.91	98	O-Maverick
V-8, 302.0	4.00×3.00	140	O-Torino, Ford Custom V-8
V-8, 302.0	4.00×3.00	143	O-Maverick
V-8, 351.0	4.00×3.50	153	S-Ford wgn; O-Ford
V-8, 351.0	4.00×3.50	161	O-Torino
V-8, 351.0	4.00×3.50	248	O-Torino
V-8, 400.0	4.00×4.00	168	O-Torino
V-8, 400.0	4.00×4.00	172	O-Ford
V-8, 429.0	4.36×3.59	205	O-Torino
V-8, 429.0	4.36×3.59	208	O-Ford

1973

Pinto (wb 94.2)		Wght	Price	Prod
10	fstbk sdn 2d	2,115	2,021	116,146
11	Rnabout htchbk sdn 2d	2,145	2,144	150,603
12	wgn 2d	2,386	2,343	217,763
Maverick (wb 103.0; 4d-109.9)				
91	fstbk sdn 2d	2,730	2,248	148,943
92	sdn 4d	2,844	2,305	110,382
93	Grabber fstbk sdn 2d	2,770	2,427	32,350
Torino (wb 118.0; 2d-114.0)				
25	htp cpe	3,548	2,732	28,005
27	sdn 4d	3,620	2,701	37,524
40	wgn 4d V-8	4,063	3,198	23,982
30	Gran Torino htp cpe	3,591	2,921	138,962
30	Grn Tor Brham htp cpe	3,598	3,071	
31	Grn Tor sdn 4d	3,675	2,890	98,404
31	Grn Tor Brham sdn 4d	3,690	3,051	
42	Grn Tori wgn 4d V-8	4,097	3,344	60,738
43	Grn Tor Sqr wgn 4d V-8	4,129	3,559	40,023
35	Grn Tor Spt fstbk htp cpe V-8	3,664	3,154	51,853
38	Grn Tor frm htp cpe V-8	3,650	3,154	17,090
Ford (wb 121.0)				
53	Custom 500 sdn 4d	4,059	3,606	42,549
72	C500 Rnch Wgn 4d 2S	4,529	4,050	22,432
72	C500 Rnch Wgn 4d 3S	4,579	4,164	
54	Galaxie 500 sdn 4d	4,086	3,771	85,654
56	Galaxie 500 htp sdn	4,102	3,833	25,802
58	Galaxie 500 htp cpe	4,034	3,778	70,808
74	G500 Cntry Sdn Wgn 4d 2S	4,555	4,146	51,290
74	G500 Cntry Sdn Wgn 4d 3S	4,605	4,260	
62	LTD htp cpe	4,059	3,950	120,864
63	LTD sdn 4d	4,107	3,958	122,851
64	LTD htp sdn	4,123	4,001	28,606
76	LTD Cntry Sqr wgn 4d 2S	4,579	4,401	142,983
76	LTD Cntry Sqr wgn 4d 3S	4,629	4,515	
66	LTD Brghm sdn 4d	4,130	4,113	49,553
67	LTD Brghm htp sdn	4,148	4,157	22,268
68	LTD Brghm htp cpe	4,077	4,107	68,901

1973 Engines	bore×stroke	bhp	availability
I-4, 98.6	3.19×3.06	54	S-Pinto exc wgn
I-4, 122.0	3.58×3.03	83	S-Pinto wgn; O-Pinto
I-6, 200.0	3.68×3.13	84	S-Maverick
I-6, 250.0	3.68×3.91	88	O-Maverick
I-6, 250.0	3.68×3.91	92	O-Torino
V-8, 302.0	4.00×3.00	137/138	S-Tor 35 & wgns; O-other Torino
V-8, 351.0	4.00×3.50	158/159	S-Ford; O-Tor
V-8, 351.0	4.00×3.50	246	O-Torino cpe
V-8, 400.0	4.00×4.00	168	O-Torino, Ford
V-8, 429.0	4.36×3.59	201	O-Torino, Ford
V-8, 460.0	4.36×3.85	202	O-Ford

1974

Pinto (wb 94.2)		Wght	Price	Prod
10	fstbk sdn 2d	2,372	2,527	132,061
11	Rnabout htchbk sdn 2d	2,406	2,676	174,754
12	wgn 2d	2,576	2,771	237,394
Maverick (wb 103.0; 4d-109.9)				
91	fstbk sdn 2d	2,739	2,790	139,818
92	sdn 4d	2,932	2,824	137,728
93	Grabber fstbk sdn 2d	2,868	2,923	23,502
Torino (wb 118.0; 2d-114.0)				
25	htp cpe	3,709	3,236	22,738
27	sdn 4d	3,793	3,239	31,161
40	wgn 4d	4,175	3,818	15,393
30	Gran Torino htp cpe	3,742	3,411	76,290
31	Gran Torino sdn 4d	3,847	3,454	72,728
42	Gran Torino wgn 4d	4,209	4,017	29,866
32	Grn Tor Brghm htp cpe	3,794	3,975	26,402
33	Grn Tor Brghm sdn 4d	3,887	3,966	11,464
43	Grn Tor Sqr wgn 4d	4,250	4,300	22,837
38	Grn Tor Sprt htp cpe	3,771	3,824	23,142
21	Grn Tor Elite htp cpe	—	4,437	96,604
Ford (wb 121.0)				
53	Custom 500 sdn 4d	4,180	3,982	28,941
72	C500 Rnch Wgn 4d 2S	4,654	4,488	12,104
72	C500 Rnch Wgn 4d 3S	4,687	4,608	
54	Galaxie 500 sdn 4d	4,196	4,164	49,661
56	Galaxie 500 htp sdn	4,212	4,237	11,526
58	Gal 500 htp cpe 4d	4,157	4,211	34,214
74	G500 Cntry Sdn wgn 4d 2S	4,690	4,584	22,400
74	G500 Cntry Sdn wgn 4d 3S	4,722	4,704	
62	LTD htp cpe	4,215	4,389	73,296
63	LTD sdn 4d	4,262	4,370	72,251
64	LTD htp sdn	4,277	4,438	12,375
76	LTD Cntry Sqr wgn 4d 2S	4,752	4,898*	64,047
76	LTD Cntry Sqr wgn 4d 3S	4,785	5,018*	
66	LTD Brghm sdn 4d	4,292	4,647	30,203
67	LTD Brghm htp sdn	4,310	4,717	11,371
68	LTD Brghm htp cpe	4,247	4,669	39,084

* Prices with optional woodgrain bodyside trim. Nonwoodgrain version $136 less.

1974 Engines	bore×stroke	bhp	availability
I-4, 122.0	3.58×3.03	80	S-Pinto
I-4, 140.0	3.78×3.13	82	O-Pinto
I-6, 200.0	3.68×3.13	84	S-Maverick
I-6, 250.0	3.68×3.91	91	S-Tor, O-Mav
V-8, 302.0	4.00×3.00	140	O-Mav, Torino
V-8, 351.0	4.00×3.50	162	S-Ford exc 76; O-Torino
V-8, 400.0	4.00×4.00	170	S-Ford 76; O-Torino other Ford
V-8, 460.0	4.36×3.85	220	O-Torino, Ford

1975

Pinto (wb 94.4; wgns-94.7)		Wght	Price	Prod
10	fstbk sdn 2d	2,495	2,769	64,081
11	Rnabout htchbk sdn 3d	2,528	2,984	68,919
12	wgn 2d	2,692	3,153	90,763
Maverick (wb 103.0; 4d-109.9)				
91	fstbk sdn 2d	2,896	3,025	90,695
92	sdn 4d	3,018	3,061	63,404
93	Grabber fstbk sdn 2d	2,903	3,282	8,473
Granada (wb 109.9)				
81	sdn 4d	3,279	3,756	118,168
82	sdn 2d	3,230	3,698	100,810
83	Ghia sdn 4d	3,392	4,283	43,652
84	Ghia sdn 2d	3,342	4,225	40,028
Torino (wb 118.0; 2d-114.0)				
25	htp cpe	3,981	3,954	13,394
27	sdn 4d	4,053	3,957	22,928
40	wgn 4d	4,406	4,336	13,291
30	Gran Torino htp cpe	3,992	4,314	35,324
31	Gran Torino sdn 4d	4,084	4,338	53,161
42	Gran Torino wgn 4d	4,450	4,673	23,951
43	Grn Tor Sqr wgn 4d	4,490	4,952	
32	Grn Tor Brghm htp cpe	4,081	4,805	4,849
33	Grn Tor Brghm sdn 4d	4,157	4,837	5,929
38	Grn Tor Sport htp cpe	4,038	4,790	5,126
21	Elite htp cpe	4,154	4,767	123,372
Ford (wb 121.0)				
53	Custom 500 sdn 4d	4,377	4,477	31,043
72	Cstm 500 Rnch Wgn 4d	4,787	5,067	6,930
62	LTD htp cpe	4,359	4,753	47,432
63	LTD sdn 4d	4,408	4,712	82,382
74	LTD wgn 4d 2S	4,803	5,158	22,936
74	LTD wgn 4d 3S	4,836	5,283	
66	LTD Brghm sdn 4d	4,419	5,099	32,327
68	LTD Brghm sdn 2d	4,391	5,133	24,005
76	LTD Cntry Sqr wgn 4d 2S	4,845	5,440	41,550
76	LTD Cntry Sqr wgn 4d 3S	4,878	5,565	
64	LTD Landau sdn 4d	4,446	5,453	32,506
65	LTD Landau sdn 2d	4,419	5,484	26,919

1975 Engines	bore×stroke	bhp	availability
I-4, 140.0	3.78×3.13	83	S-Pinto
V6, 170.0	3.66×2.70	97	O-Pinto 11, 12
I-6, 200.0	3.68×3.13	75	S-Mav, Gran exc Ghia
I-6, 250.0	3.68×3.91	72	S-Gran Ghia; O-Mav, Gran
V-8, 302.0	4.00×3.00	122	S-Mav, Gran
V-8, 351.0	4.00×3.50	143	O-Granada
V-8, 351.0	4.00×3.50	148/150	S-Torino
V-8, 400.0	4.00×4.00	144/158	S-Ford 74, 76; O-Torino, other Ford
V-8, 460.0	4.36×3.85	216	O-Torino, Ford

1976

Pinto (wb 94.4; wgns-94.7)		Wght	Price	Prod
10	Pony MPG fstbk sdn 2d I-4	2,450	2,895	92,264
10	MPG fstbk sdn 2d I-4	2,452	3,025	
10	sdn 2d V6	2,590	3,472	
11	MPG htchbk sdn 2d I-4	2,482	3,200	92,540
11	Sqr MPG htchbk sdn 2d I-4	2,518	3,505	
11	Rnabout htchbk sdn 2d V6	2,620	3,647	
11	Sqr htchbk sdn 2d V6	2,656	3,952	
12	MPG wgn 2d I-4	2,635	3,365	105,328
12	Sqr MPG wgn 2d I-4	2,672	3,671	
12	wgn 2d V6	2,773	3,865	
12	Squire wgn 2d V6	2,810	4,171	
Maverick (wb 109.9; 2d-103.0)				
91	fstbk sdn 2d	2,846	3,117	60,611
92	sdn 4d	2,956	3,189	79,076
Granada (wb 109.9)				
81	sdn 4d	3,222	3,798	187,923
82	sdn 2d	3,172	3,707	161,618
83	Ghia sdn 4d	3,392	4,355	52,457
84	Ghia sdn 2d	3,334	4,265	46,786
Torino (wb 118.0; 2d-114.0)				
25	htp cpe	3,976	4,172	34,518
27	sdn 4d	4,061	4,206	17,394
30	Gran Torino htp cpe	3,999	4,461	23,939
31	Gran Torino sdn 4d	4,081	4,495	40,568
32	Grn Tor Brghm htp cpe	4,063	4,883	3,183
33	Grn Tor Brghm sdn 4d	4,144	4,915	4,473
40	wgn 4d	4,409	4,521	17,281
42	Gran Torino wgn 4d	4,428	4,769	30,596
43	Grn Tor Sqr wgn 4d	4,454	5,083	21,144
Elite (wb 114.0)				
21	htp cpe	4,169	4,879	146,475
Ford (wb 121.0)				
52	Custom 500 sdn 2d	—	—	7,037
53	Custom 500 sdn 4d	4,298	4,493	23,447
72	Cst 500 Rnch Wgn 4d	4,737	4,918	4,633
62	LTD sdn 2d	4,257	4,780	62,844
63	LTD sdn 4d	4,303	4,752	108,168
74	LTD wgn 4d 2S	4,752	5,207	30,237
74	LTD wgn 4d 3S	4,780	5,333	

Ford		Wght	Price	Prod
66	LTD Brghm sdn 4d	4,332	5,245	32,917
68	LTD Brghm sdn 2d	4,299	5,299	20,863
76	LTD Cntry Sqr wgn 4d 2S	4,809	5,523	47,379
76	LTD Cntry Sqr wgn 4d 3S	4,837	5,649	
64	LTD Landau sdn 4d	4,394	5,560	35,663
65	LTD Landau sdn 2d	4,346	5,613	29,673

1976 Engines	bore×stroke	bhp	availability
I-4, 140.0	3.78×3.13	92	S-Pinto
V6, 170.8	3.66×2.70	103	O-Pinto
I-6, 200.0	3.68×3.13	81	S-Mav, Gran exc Ghia
I-6, 250.0	3.68×3.91	90	S-Gran Ghia; O-Mav, Gran
V-8, 302.0	4.00×3.00	134/138	O-Gran, Mav
V-8, 351.0	4.00×3.50	152/154	S-Tor, Elite, Ford exc wgns; O-Granada
V-8, 400.0	4.00×4.00	180	S-Ford wgns; O-Torino, Ford, Elite
V-8, 460.0	4.36×3.85	202	O-Tor, Ford, Elite

1977

Pinto (wb 94.4; wgns-94.7)		Wght	Price	Prod
10	Pony sdn 2d I-4	2,313	3,099	48,863*
10	sdn 2d	2,376	3,237	
11	Rnabout htchbk sdn 3d	2,412	3,353	74,237*
12	wgn 2d	2,576	3,548	79,499*
12	Squire wgn 2d	2,614	3,891	
Maverick (wb 109.9; 2d-103.0)				
91	fstbk sdn 2d	2,864	3,322	40,086
92	sdn 4d	2,970	3,395	58,420
Granada (wb 109.9)				
81	sdn 4d	3,222	4,118	163,071
82	sdn 2d	3,172	4,022	157,612
83	Ghia sdn 4d	3,276	4,548	35,730
84	Ghia sdn 2d	3,222	4,452	34,166
LTD II (wb 118.0; 2d-114.0)				
25	S htp cpe	3,789	4,528	9,531
27	S sdn 4d	3,894	4,579	18,775
30	htp cpe	3,789	4,785	57,449
31	sdn 4d	3,904	4,870	57,704
32	Brougham htp cpe	3,898	5,121	20,979
33	Brougham sdn 4d	3,930	5,206	18,851
40	S wgn 4d 2S	4,393	4,806	9,636
40	S wgn 4d 3S	4,410	4,906	
42	wgn 4d 2S	4,404	5,064	23,237
42	wgn 4d 3S	4,421	5,164	
43	Squire wgn 4d 2S	4,430	5,335	17,162
43	Squire wgn 4d 3S	4,447	5,435	
LTD (wb 121.0)				
52	Custom 500 sdn 2d	—	—	4,139
53	Custom 500 sdn 4d	—	—	5,582
62	LTD sdn 2d	4,190	5,128	73,637
63	LTD sdn 4d	4,240	5,152	160,255
64	LTD Landau sdn 4d	4,319	5,742	65,030
65	LTD Landau sdn 2d	4,270	5,717	44,396
72	Cust 500 Rnch Wgn 4d	—	—	1,406
74	LTD wgn 5d 2S	4,635	5,415	90,711
74	LTD wgn 5d 3S	4,679	5,541	
74	Cntry Sqr wgn 4d 2S	4,674	5,866	
74	Cntry Sqr sgn 4d 3S	4,718	5,992	

1977 Engines	bore×stroke	bhp	availability
I-4, 140.0	3.78×3.13	89	S-Pinto
V6, 170.8	3.66×2.70	93	O-Pint, exc Pny
I-6, 200.0	3.68×3.13	96	S-Mav, Gran exc Ghia
I-6, 250.0	3.68×3.91	98	S-Gran Ghia; O-Mav, Gran
V-8, 302.0	4.00×3.00	122	O-Granada
V-8, 302.0	4.00×3.00	130	S-LTD II exc wgns
V-8, 302.0	4.00×3.00	137	O-Maverick
V-8, 351.0	4.00×3.50	135	O-Granada
V-8, 351.0	4.00×3.50	149	S-LTD II wgns; O-other LTD II
V-8, 351.0	4.00×3.50	161	S-LTD exc wgns O-LTD II wgns
V-8, 400.0	4.00×4.00	173	S-LTD wgns; O-LTD II, other LTD
V-8, 460.0	4.36×3.85	197	O-LTD

* Includes some units produced as 1978 models but sold as 1977 models.

1978*

Pinto (wb 94.4; wgns-94.7)		Wght	Price	Prod
10	Pony sdn 2d I-4	2,321	3,139	62,317
10	sdn 2d	2,400	3,629	
11	Rnabt htchbk sdn 2d	2,444	3,744	74,313
12	wgn 2d	2,579	4,028	52,269
12	Squire wgn 2d	2,614	4,343	
Fairmont (wb 105.5)				
91	sdn 2d	2,590	3,624	78,776
92	sdn 4d	2,632	3,710	136,849
93	Futura cpe	2,626	4,103	116,966
94	wgn 4d	2,740	4,063	128,390
94	Squire wgn 4d	2,748	4,428	
Granada (wb 109.9)				
81	sdn 2d	3,132	4,300	110,481
81	Ghia sdn 2d	3,192	4,685	
81	ESS sdn 2d	3,190	4,872	
82	sdn 4d	3,167	4,390	139,305
82	Ghia sdn 4d	3,275	4,776	
82	ESS sdn 4d	3,225	4,962	
LTD II (wb 118.0; 2d-114.0)				
25	S htp cpe	3,746	4,850	9,004
27	S sdn 4d	3,836	4,935	21,122
30	htp cpe	3,773	5,112	76,285
30	Brougham htp cpe	3,791	5,448	
31	sdn 4d	3,872	5,222	64,133
31	Brougham sdn 4d	3,901	5,558	
LTD (wb 121.0)				
62	htp cpe	3,972	5,398	57,466
63	sdn 4d	4,032	5,483	112,392
64	LTD Landau htp cpe	4,029	5,970	27,305
65	LTD Landau sdn 4d	4,081	6,055	39,836
74	wgn 4d 2S	4,532	5,885	71,285
74	wgn 4d 3S	4,567	6,028	
74	Cntry Sqr wgn 4d 2S	4,576	6,304	
74	Cntry Sqr wgn 4d 3S	4,601	6,447	

*Fiesta not included (import).

1978 Engines	bore×stroke	bhp	availability
I-4, 140.0	3.78×3.13	88	S-Pinto, Fair
V6, 170.0	3.66×2.70	90	O-Pinto, exc Pony
I-6, 200.0	3.68×3.13	85	O-Fairmont
I-6, 250.0	3.68×3.91	97	S-Granada
V-8, 302.0	4.00×3.00	134	S-LTD II, LTD exc wgns
V-8, 302.0	4.00×3.00	139	S-Granada; O-Fairmont
V-8, 351.0	4.00×3.50	144/145	S-LTD wgns; O-LTD II, other LTD
V-8, 351.0	4.00×3.50	152	O-LTD II
V-8, 400.0	4.00×4.00	166	O-LTD II, LTD
V-8, 460.0	4.36×3.85	202	O-LTD

1979

Pinto (wb 94.4; wgns-94.7)		Wght	Price	Prod
10	Pony fstbk sdn 2d I-4	2,329	3,434	75,789
10	fstbk sdn 2d	2,396	3,939	
11	Rnabt htchbk sdn 2d	2,442	4,055	69,383
12	Pony wgn 2d I-4	—	3,899	53,846
12	wgn 2d	2,571	4,338	
12	Squire wgn 2d	2,607	4,654	
Fairmont (wb 105.5)				
91	sdn 2d	2,524	4,102	54,798
92	sdn 4d	2,578	4,220	133,813
93	Futura cpe	2,580	4,463	106,065
94	wgn 4d	2,708	4,497	100,691
94	Squire wgn 4d	—	4,856	
Granada (wb 109.9)				
81	sdn 2d	3,088	4,678	76,850
81	Ghia sdn 2d	3,124	5,051	
81	ESS sdn 2d	3,140	5,211	
82	sdn 4d	3,134	4,782	105,526
82	Ghia sdn 4d	3,168	5,157	
82	ESS sdn 4d	3,210	5,317	
LTD II (wb. 118.0; 2d-114.0)				
25	S htp cpe	3,781	5,561	834
27	S sdn 4d	3,844	5,661	9,649
30	htp cpe	3,797	5,799	18,300
30	Brougham htp cpe	3,815	6,135	
31	sdn 4d	3,860	5,924	19,781
31	Brougham sdn 4d	3,889	6,259	
LTD (wb 114.3)				
62	sdn 2d	3,421	6,184	54,005
63	sdn 4d	3,463	6,284	117,730
64	Landau sdn 2d	3,472	6,686	42,314
65	Landau sdn 4d	3,527	6,811	74,599
74	wgn 4d 2S	3,678	6,550	37,955
74	wgn 4d 3S	—	6,699	
76	Cntry Sqr wgn 4d 2S	3,719	7,006	29,932
76	Cntry Sqr wgn 4d 3S	—	7,155	

1979 Engines	bore×stroke	bhp	availability
I-4, 140.0	3.78×3.13	88	S-Pinto, Fairmont
V6, 170.0	3.66×2.70	102	O-Pinto exc Pony
I-6, 200.0	3.68×3.13	85	O-Fairmont
I-6, 250.0	3.68×3.91	97	S-Granada
V-8, 302.0	4.00×3.00	129	S-LTD
V-8, 302.0	4.00×3.00	133	S-LTD II
V-8, 302.0	4.00×3.00	137	O-Granada
V-8, 302.0	4.00×3.00	140	O-Fairmont
V-8, 351.0	4.00×3.50	142	O-LTD
V-8, 351.0	4.00×3.50	151	O-LTD II, LTD

1980

Pinto (wb 94.4; wgns-94.7)		Wght	Price	Prod
10	Pony fstbk sdn 2d	2,377	4,117	84,053
10	fstbk sdn 2d	2,385	4,605	
11	Rnabt htchbk sdn 2d	2,426	4,717	61,842
12	Pony wgn 2d	2,545	4,627	39,159
12	wgn 2d	2,553	5,004	
12/604	Squire wgn 2d	2,590	5,320	
Fairmont (wb 105.5)				
91	sdn 2d	2,576	4,894	45,074
92	sdn 4d	2,610	5,011	137,812
92	Futura sdn 4d	—	5,390	5,306
93	Futura cpe	2,623	5,325	51,878
94	wgn 4d	2,735	5,215	77,035
Granada (wb 109.9)				
81	sdn 2d	3,135	5,541	60,872
81/602	Ghia sdn 2d	3,168	5,942	
81/933	ESS sdn 2d	3,199	6,031	
82	sdn 4d	3,168	5,664	29,557
82/602	Ghia sdn 4d	3,209	6,065	
82/933	ESS sdn 4d	3,240	6,154	
LTD (wb 114.3)				
	S sdn 2d	—	—	553
61	S sdn 4d	3,464	6,875	19,283
62	sdn 2d	3,447	7,003	15,333
63	sdn 4d	3,475	7,117	51,360
64	Crown Vic sdn 2d	3,482	7,628	7,725
65	Crown Vic sdn 4d	3,524	7,763	21,962
72	S wgn 4d 2S	3,707	7,198	3,490
72	S wgn 4d 3S	3,748	7,344	
74	wgn 4d 2S	3,717	7,463	11,718
74	wgn 4d 3S	3,758	7,609	
76	Crown Vic wgn 4d 2S	3,743	7,891	9,868
76	Crown Vic wgn 4d 3S	3,784	8,042	

1980 Engines	bore×stroke	bhp	availability
I-4, 140.0	3.78×3.13	88	S-Pinto, Fairmont
I-6, 200.0	3.68×3.13	91	O-Fairmont
I-6, 250.0	3.68×3.91	90	S-Granada
V-8, 255.0	3.68×3.00	119	O-Fairmont, Granada
V-8, 302.0	4.00×3.00	130	S-LTD
V-8, 302.0	4.00×3.00	134	O-Granada
V-8, 351.0	4.00×3.50	140	O-LTD

1981

Escort (wb 94.2)		Wght	Price	Prod
05	htchbk sdn 2d	1,962	5,158	
05/60Q	L htchbk sdn 2d	1,964	5,494	
05/60Z	GL htchbk sdn 2d	1,987	5,838	192,554
05/602	GLX htchbk sdn 2d	2,029	6,476	
05/936	SS htchbk sdn 2d	2,004	6,139	
08	htchbk sdn 4d	2,074	5,731	
08/60Q	L htchbk sdn 4d	2,075	5,814	
08/60Z	GL htchbk sdn 4d	2,094	6,178	128,173
08/602	GLX htchbk sdn 4d	2,137	6,799	
08/936	SS htchbk sdn 4d	2,114	6,464	
Fairmont (wb 105.5)				
20	S sdn 2d	—	5,701	—
20	sdn 2d	2,590	6,032	23,066
21	sdn 4d	2,640	6,151	104,883
21/605	Futura sdn 4d	2,674	6,361	
22	Futura cpe	2,645	6,347	24,197
23	wgn 4d	2,754	6,384	59,154
23/605	Futura wgn 4d	2,788	6,616	
Granada (wb 105.5)				
26	L sdn 2d	2,752	6,474	
26/602	GL sdn 2d	2,773	6,875	35,057
26/933	GLX sdn 2d	2,777	6,988	
27	L sdn 4d	2,795	6,633	
27/602	GL sdn 4d	2,822	7,035	86,284
27/933	GLX sdn 4d	2,829	7,148	
LTD (wb 114.3)				
31	S sdn 4d	3,490	7,527	17,490
32	sdn 2d	3,496	7,607	6,279
33	sdn 4d	3,538	7,718	35,932
34	Crown Vic sdn 2d	3,496	8,251	11,061
35	Crown Vic sdn 4d	3,538	8,384	39,139
37	S wgn 4d 2S	3,717	7,942	2,465
38	wgn 4d 2S	3,719	8,180	10,554
39	Cntry Sqr wgn 4d 2S	3,737	8,640	9,443

1981 Engines	bore×stroke	bhp	availability
I-4, 97.6	3.15×3.13	69	S-Escort
I-4, 140.0	3.78×3.13	88	S-Fair, Gran
I-6, 200.0	3.68×3.13	88	O-Fair, Gran
V-8, 255.0	3.68×3.00	115/120	S-LTD; O-Fair, Granada
V-8, 302.0	4.00×3.00	130	O-LTD
V-8, 351.0	4.00×3.50	145	O-LTD

1982

Escort (wb 94.2)		Wght	Price	Prod
05	htchbk sdn 2d	1,920	5,462	
05	L htchbk sdn 2d	1,926	6,046	
05	GL htchbk sdn 2d	1,948	6,406	165,660
05	GLX htchbk sdn 2d	1,987	7,086	
05	GT htchbk sdn 2d	1,963	6,706	
06	htchbk sdn 4d	1,926	5,668	
06	L htchbk sdn 4d	2,003	6,263	
06	GL htchbk sdn 4d	2,025	6,622	130,473
06	GLX htchbk sdn 4d	2,064	7,302	
08	L wgn 4d	2,023	6,461	
08	GL wgn 4d	2,043	6,841	88,999
08	GLX wgn 4d	2,079	7,475	
EXP (wb 94.2)				
01	htchbk cpe	2,146	7,387	98,256
Fairmont Futura (wb 105.5)				
20	sdn 2d	2,616	5,985	8,222
21	sdn 4d	2,664	6,419	101,666
22	spt cpe	2,640	6,517	17,851
Granada (wb 105.5)				
26	L sdn 2d	2,732	7,126	
26	GL sdn 2d	2,758	7,543	12,802
26	GLX sdn 2d	2,776	7,666	
27	L sdn 4d	2,764	7,301	
27	GL sdn 4d	2,794	7,718	62,339
27	GLX sdn 4d	2,812	7,840	
28	L wgn 4d I-6	2,965	7,983	45,182
28	GL wgn 4d I-6	2,995	8,399	
LTD (wb 114.3)				
31	S sdn 4d	3,522	8,312	22,182
32	sdn 2d	3,496	8,455	3,510
33	sdn 4d	3,526	8,574	29,776
34	Crown Vic sdn 2d	3,523	9,149	9,287
35	Crown Vic sdn 4d	3,567	9,294	41,405
37	S wgn 4d 2S	3,725	8,783	2,973
38	wgn 4d 2S	3,741	9,073	9,294
39	Cntry Sqr wgn 4d 2S	3,741	9,580	9,626

1982 Engines	bore×stroke	bhp	availability
I-4, 97.6	3.15×3.13	70	S-Escort, EXP
I-4, 97.6	3.15×3.13	80	O-late Esct, EXP
I-4, 140.0	3.78×3.13	86	S-Fairmont, Granada
I-6, 200.0	3.68×3.13	87	S-Gran wgn; O-Fair, Gran
V-6, 232.0	3.80×3.40	112	O-Granada
V-8, 255.0	3.68×3.00	122	S-LTD; O-Fair (police)
V-8, 302.0	4.00×3.00	132	S-LTD wgn; O-LTD
V-8, 351.0	4.00×3.50	165	S-LTD (police)

1983

Escort (wb 94.2)		Wght	Price	Prod
04	L htchbk sdn 2d	2,016	5,639	
05	GL htchbk sdn 2d	1,959	6,384	151,386
06	GLX htchbk sdn 2d	1,993	6,771	
07	GT htchbk sdn 2d	2,020	7,339	
13	L htchbk sdn 4d	2,078	5,846	
14	GL htchbk sdn 4d	2,025	6,601	84,649
15	GLX htchbk sdn 4d	2,059	6,988	
09	L wgn 4d	2,117	6,052	
10	GL wgn 4d	2,052	6,779	79,335
11	GLX wgn 4d	2,083	7,150	
EXP (wb 94.2) - 19,697 built				
01	htchbk cpe	2,156	6,426	—
01/301B	HO htchbk cpe	—	7,004	—
01/302B	HO sport htchbk cpe	—	7,794	—
01/303B	Luxury htchbk cpe	—	8,225	—
01/304B	GT htchbk cpe	—	8,739	—
Fairmont Futura (wb 105.5)				
35	sdn 2d	2,890	6,444	3,664
35/41K	S sdn 2d	2,628	5,985	
36	sdn 4d	2,933	6,590	69,287
36/41K	S sdn 4d	2,672	6,125	
37	spt cpe	2,908	6,666	7,882
LTD (wb 105.6)				
39	L sdn 4d	2,912	7,777	111,813
39/60H	Brougham sdn 4d	2,845	8,165	
40	wgn 4d I-6	3,092	8,577	43,945
LTD Crown Victoria (wb 114.3)				
43	sdn 4d	3,748	10,094	81,859
43/41K	S sdn 4d	3,732	9,130	
42	sdn 2d	3,732	10,094	11,414
44	Cntry Sqr wgn 4d 2S	3,901	10,253	
44/41E	wgn 4d 2S	3,895	10,003	20,343
44/41K	S wgn 4d 2S	3,891	9,444	

1983 Engines	bore×stroke	bhp	availability
I-4, 97.6	3.15×3.13	72	S-Escort, EXP
I-4, 97.6	3.15×3.13	80	O-Escort, EXP
I-4, 97.6	3.15×3.13	88	S-Escort GT; O-Escort, EXP
I-4, 140.0	3.78×3.13	90	S-Fair, LTD
I-4P, 140.0	3.78×3.13	—	O-LTD (prop)
I-6, 200.0	3.68×3.13	92	S-LTD wgn; O-Fair, other LTD
V-6, 232.0	3.80×3.40	110	O-LTD
V-8, 302.0	4.00×3.00	130	S-Crown Vic; O-LTD
V-8, 302.0	4.00×3.00	145	O-Crown Victoria
V-8, 351.0	4.00×3.50	165	S-Crn Vic (pol)

1984

Escort (wb 94.2)		Wght	Price	Prod
04	htchbk sdn 2d	2,016	5,629	
04	L htchbk sdn 2d	2,080	5,885	
05	GL htchbk sdn 2d	2,122	6,382	184,323
07	GT htchbk sdn 2d	2,170	7,593	
07/935	GT turbo sdn 2d	—	8,680	
13	htchbk sdn 4d	2,078	5,835	
13	L htchbk sdn 4d	2,146	6,099	
14	GL htchbk sdn 4d	2,188	6,596	99,444
15	LX htchbk sdn 4d	2,222	7,848	
09	L wgn 4d	2,176	6,313	
10	GL wgn 4d	2,216	6,773	88,756
11	LX wgn 4d	2,249	7,939	
EXP (wb 94.2) - 23,016 built				
01/A80	htchbk cpe	2,212	6,653	—
01/A81	Luxury htchbk cpe	2,235	7,539	—
01/A82	Turbo htchbk cpe	2,243	9,942	—
Tempo (wb 99.9)				
18	L sdn 2d	2,286	6,936	
19	GL sdn 2d	—	7,159	107,065
20	GLX sdn 2d	—	7,621	
21	L sdn 4d	2,348	6,936	
22	GL sdn 4d	—	7,159	295,149
23	GLX sdn 4d	—	7,621	
LTD (wb 105.6)				
39	sdn 4d	2,830	8,605	154,173
39/60H	Brougham sdn 4d	—	9,980	
39/93B	LX sdn 4d V-8	—	11,098	**
40	wgn 4d I-6	3,123	9,102	59,569
LTD Crown Victoria (wb 114.3)				
43	sdn 4d	3,730	10,954	130,164
43/41K	S sdn 4d	3,728	9,826	
42	sdn 2d	3,689	10,954	12,522
44	Cntry Sqr wgn 4d 2S	3,936	11,111	
44/41E	wgn 4d 2S	3,931	10,861	30,803
44/41K	S wgn 4d 2S	3,880	10,136	

** 3,260 LTD LX models built in 1984-85 model years com.

1984 Engines	bore×stroke	bhp	availability
I-4, 97.6	3.15×3.13	70	S-Esc exc LX, GT
I-4, 97.6	3.15×3.13	80	S-EXP; O-Esc
I-4, 97.6	3.15×3.13	84	S-Esc LX, GT; O-Escort, EXP
I-4T, 97.6	3.15×3.13	120	S-Esc GT/EXP Turbo
I-4D, 121.0	3.39×3.39	52	O-Esc, Tempo
I-4, 140.0	3.70×3.30	84	S-Tempo
I-4, 140.0	3.78×3.13	88	S-LTD exc LX
I-4P, 140.0	3.78×3.13	—	O-LTD (prop)
V-6, 232.0	3.80×3.40	120	S-LTD wgn; O-LTD
V-8, 302.0	4.00×3.00	140	S-Crown Vic exc wgn
V-8, 302.0	4.00×3.00	155	S-Crn Vic wgn
V-8, 302.0	4.00×3.00	165	S-LTD LX

1985

Escort First Series (wb 94.2)		Wght	Price	Prod
04/41P	htchbk sdn 2d	1,990	5,620	
04	L htchbk sdn 2d	1,979	5,876	
05	GL htchbk sdn 2d	2,047	6,374	112,406*
07	GT htchbk sdn 2d	2,140	7,585	
07/935	GT trbo htchbk sdn 2d	2,172	8,680	
13	htchbk sdn 4d	2,078	5,835	
13/41P	L htchbk sdn 4d	2,055	5,827	
14	GL htchbk sdn 4d	2,114	6,588	62,709*
15	LX htchbk sdn 4d	2,175	7,840	
09	L wgn 4d	2,071	6,305	
10	GL wgn 4d	2,139	6,765	45,740*
11	LX wgn 4d	2,198	7,931	

* Estimated totals

Escort Second Series 1985½ (wb 94.2)		Wght	Price	Prod
31	htchbk sdn 2d	2,142	5,856	
31	L htchbk sdn 2d	—	6,127	100,554
32	GL htchbk sdn 2d	—	6,642	
36	L htchbk sdn 4d	2,195	6,341	48,676
37	GL htchbk sdn 4d	—	6,855	
34	L wgn 4d	2,223	6,622	36,998
35	GL wgn 4d	—	7,137	
EXP (wb 94.2) - 26,462 built				
01/A80	htchbk cpe	2,098	6,697	—
01/A81	Luxury htchbk cpe	2,124	7,585	—
01/A82	Turbo htchbk cpe	2,232	9,997	—
Tempo (wb 99.9)				
18	L sdn 2d	2,271	7,052	
19	GL sdn 2d	2,302	7,160	72,311
20	GLX sdn 2d	2,372	8,253	
21	L sdn 4d	2,328	7,052	
22	GL sdn 4d	2,358	7,160	266,776
23	GLX sdn 4d	2,428	8,302	

LTD (wb 105.6)		Wght	Price	Prod
39	sdn 4d I-4/V-6	2,852	8,874	
39/60H	Brghm sdn 4d I-4/V-6	2,857	9,262	162,884
39/938	LX sdn 4d V-8	2,904	11,421	**
40	wgn 4d V-6	2,990	9,384	42,642

LTD Crown Victoria (wb 114.3)				
43	sdn 4d	3,588	11,627	
43/41K	S sdn 4d	3,709	10,609	154,612
42	sdn 2d	3,552	11,627	
44	Cntry Sqr wgn 4d 2S	3,763	11,809	
44/41E	wgn 4d 2S	3,758	11,559	30,825
44/41K	S wgn 4d 2S	3,883	10,956	

** 3,260 LTD LX models built in 1984-85 model years com.

1985 Engines	bore×stroke	bhp	availability
I-4, 97.6	3.15×3.13	70	S-Esc exc LX, GT
I-4, 97.6	3.15×3.13	80	S-EXP; O-Esc
I-4, 97.6	3.15×3.13	84	S-Esc LX, GT; O-Escort
I-4T, 97.6	3.15×3.13	120	S-Escort/EXP Turbo
I-4, 113.5	3.23×3.46	86	S-late Escort
I-4D, 121.0	3.39×3.39	52	O-Esc, Tempo
I-4, 140.0	3.70×3.30	86	S-Tempo
I-4, 140.0	3.70×3.30	100	O-Tempo
I-4, 140.0	3.78×3.13	88	S-LTD exc wgn
I-4P, 140.0	3.78×3.13	—	O-LTD (prop)
V-6, 232.0	3.80×3.40	120	S-LTD wgn; O-other LTD
V-8, 302.0	4.00×3.00	140	S-Crown Vic
V-8, 302.0	4.00×3.00	155	O-Crown Vic
V-8, 302.0	4.00×3.00	165	S-LTD LX
V-8, 351.0	4.00×3.50	180	S-Crn Vic (pol)

1986

Escort (wb 94.2)		Wght	Price	Prod
31/41P	Pony htchbk sdn 2d	2,159	6,052	
31	L htchbk sdn 2d	2,153	6,327	
32	LX htchbk sdn 2d	2,238	7,234	228,013
33	GT htchbk sdn 2d	2,364	8,112	
36	L htchbk sdn 4d	2,201	6,541	117,300
37	LX htchbk sdn 4d	2,281	7,448	
34	L wgn 4d	2,233	6,822	84,740
35	LX wgn 4d	2,311	7,729	

EXP (wb 94.2) - 30,978 built				
01	htchbk cpe	2,311	7,186	—
01/931	Luxury htchbk cpe	2,413	8,235	—

Tempo (wb 99.9)				
19	GL sdn 2d	2,339	7,358	69,101
20	GLX sdn 2d	2,461	8,578	
22	GL sdn 4d	2,398	7,508	208,570
23	GLX sdn 4d	2,522	8,777	

Taurus (wb 106.0)				
29	L sdn 4d I-4/V-6	2,979	9,645	
29/934	MT5 sdn 4d I-4	2,878	10,276	178,737
29/60D	GL sdn 4d V-6	3,009	11,322	
29/60H	LX sdn 4d V-6	3,109	13,351	
30	L wgn 4d V-6	3,184	10,763	
30/934	MT5 wgn 4d I-4	3,076	10,741	57,625
30/60D	GL wgn 4d V-6	3,214	11,790	
30/60H	LX wgn 4d V-6	3,306	13,860	

LTD (wb 105.6)				
39	sdn 4d	3,001	10,032	58,270
39/60H	Brougham sdn 4d	3,009	10,420	
40	wgn 4d	3,108	10,132	14,213

LTD Crown Victoria (wb 114.3)				
43	sdn 4d	3,748	12,562	
43/60H	LX sdn 4d	3,781	13,784	97,314
43/41K	S sdn 4d	3,715	12,188	
42	sdn 2d	3,708	13,022	6,559
42/60H	LX sdn 2d	3,754	13,752	
44	Cntry Sqr wgn 4d 2S	3,937	12,655	
44/60H	LX Cntry Sqr wgn 4d 2S	3,829	13,817	
44/41E	wgn 4d 2S	3,930	12,405	20,164
44/41E	LX wgn 4d 2S	3,821	13,567	
44/41K	S wgn 4d 2S	3,921	12,468	

1986 Engines	bore×stroke	bhp	availability
I-4, 113.5	3.23×3.46	86	S-Escort exc GT, EXP
I-4, 113.5	3.23×3.46	108	S-Escort GT; O-Escort, EXP
I-4D, 121.0	3.39×3.39	52	O-Esc, Tempo
I-4, 140.0	3.70×3.30	86	S-Tempo
I-4, 140.0	3.70×3.30	100	O-Tempo
I-4, 153.0	3.70×3.60	88	S-Taurus I-4
V-6, 182.0	3.50×3.15	140	S-Taur LX, wgn; O-other Taurus
V-6, 232.0	3.80×3.40	120	S-LTD
V-8, 302.0	4.00×3.00	150	S-Crown Vic
V-8, 351.0	4.00×3.50	180	S-Crn Vic (pol)

1987

Escort (wb 94.2)		Wght	Price	Prod
20	Pony htchbk sdn 2d	2,180	6,436	
21	GL htchbk sdn 2d	2,187	6,801	206,729
23	GT htchbk sdn 2d	2,516	8,724	
25	GL htchbk sdn 4d	2,222	7,022	102,187
28	GL wgn 4d	2,274	7,312	65,849

EXP (wb 94.2) - 25,888 built				
18	sport htchbk cpe	2,388	8,831	—
17	Luxury htchbk cpe	2,291	7,622	—

Tempo (wb 99.9)'				
31	GL sdn 2d	2,462	8,043	
32	LX sdn 2d	2,562	9,238	70,164
33	Spt GL sdn 2d	2,667	8,888	
34	AWD (4WD) sdn 2d	2,667	9,984	
36	GL sdn 4d	2,515	8,198	
37	LX sdn 4d	2,617	9,444	212,468
38	Spt GL sdn 4d	2,270	9,043	
39	AWD (4WD) sdn 4d	2,720	10,138	

Taurus (wb 106.0)				
50	L sdn 4d I-4/V-6	2,982	10,491	
51	MT5 sdn 4d I-4	2,886	11,966	278,562
52	GL sdn 4d I-4/V-6	3,045	11,498	
53	LX sdn 4d V-6	3,113	14,613	
55	L wgn 4d V-6	3,186	11,722	
56	MT5 wgn 4d I-4	3,083	12,534	96,201
57	GL wgn 4d V-6	3,242	12,688	
58	LX wgn 4d V-6	3,309	15,213	

LTD Crown Victoria (wb 114.3)				
73	sdn 4d	3,741	14,355	
72	S sdn 4d	3,708	13,860	105,789
74	LX sdn 4d	3,788	15,454	
70	cpe 2d	3,724	14,727	5,527
71	LX cpe 2d	3,735	15,421	
78	Cntry Sqr wgn 4d	3,920	14,507	
76	wgn 4d	3,920	14,235	
75	S wgn 4d	3,894	14,228	17,562
79	LX Cntry Sqr wgn 4d	4,000	15,723	
77	LX wgn 4d	4,000	15,450	

1987 Engines	bore×stroke	bhp	availability
I-4, 113.5	3.23×3.46	90	S-Esc exc GT, EXP Luxury
I-4, 113.5	3.23×3.46	115	S-Esc GT, EXP spt; O-other Esc
I-4D, 121.0	3.39×3.39	58	O-Escort
I-4, 140.0	3.70×3.30	86	S-Tem exc 4WD
I-4, 140.0	3.70×3.30	94	S-Tem AWD; O-Tempo
I-4, 153.0	3.70×3.60	90	S-Taurus I-4
V-6, 182.0	3.50×3.15	140	S-Taur LX, wgn; O-other Taurus
V-8, 302.0	4.00×3.00	150	S-Crown Vic
V-8, 351.0	4.00×3.50	180	S-Crn Vic (pol)

1988

Escort First Series (wb 94.2)		Wght	Price	Prod
20	Pony htchbk sdn 2d	2,180	6,632	
21	GL htchbk sdn 2d	2,187	6,949	251,911
23	GT htchbk sdn 2d	2,516	9,055	
25	GL htchbk sdn 4d	2,222	7,355	113,470
28	GL wgn 4d	2,274	7,938	

Escort Second Series 1988½ (wb 94.2)*				
90	Pony htchbk sdn 2d	—	6,747	—
91	LX htchbk sdn 2d	2,258	7,127	—
93	GT htchbksdn 2d	—	9,093	—
95	LX htchbk sdn 4d	2,295	7,457	—
98	LX wgn 4d	2,307	8,058	—

EXP First Series (wb 94.2)				
17	Luxury htchbk cpe	2,291	8,037	—

EXP 2nd Ser. 1988½ (wb 94.2)		Wght	Price	Prod
88	Luxury htchbk cpe	2,359	8,201	—

Tempo (wb 99.9)				
31	GL sdn 2d	2,536	8,658	49,930
33	GLS sdn 2d	2,552	9,249	
36	GL sdn 4d	2,585	8,808	163,409
37	LX sdn 4d	2,626	9,737	
38	GLS sdn 4d	2,601	9,400	263,332
39	AWD (4WD) sdn 4d	2,799	10,413	

Taurus (wb 106.0)				
50	L sdn 4d I-4/V-6	3,005	11,699	
51	MT5 sdn 4d I-4	2,882	12,835	284,576
52	GL sdn 4d I-4/V-6	3,049	12,200	
53	LX sdn 4d V-6	3,119	15,295	
55	L wgn 5d V-6	3,182	12,884	
57	GL wgn 4d V-6	3,215	13,380	93,001
58	LX wgn 4d V-6	3,288	15,905	

LTD Crown Victoria (wb 114.3)				
73	sdn 4d	3,779	15,218	
72	S sdn 4d	3,742	14,653	110,249
74	LX sdn 4d	3,820	16,134	
78	Crown Squire wgn 4d	3,998	15,613	
76	wgn 4d	3,991	15,180	
79	LX Cntry Sqr wgn 4d	4,070	16,643	14,940
77	LX wgn 4d	3,972	16,210	

* Production included in Escort First Series

1988 Engines	bore×stroke	bhp	availability
I-4, 113.5	3.23×3.46	90	S-Escort exc GT, EXP
I-4, 113.5	3.23×3.46	115	S-Escort GT
I-4, 140.0	3.70×3.30	98	S-Tempo exc AWD, GLS
I-4, 140.0	3.70×3.30	100	S-Tempo AWD, GLS
I-4, 153.0	3.70×3.60	90	S-Taurus I-4
V-6, 182.0	3.50×3.15	140	S-Taur LX, wgn; O-other Taurus
V-6, 232.0	3.80×3.40	140	O-Taurus
V-8, 302.0	4.00×3.00	150	S-Crown Vic
V-8, 351.0	4.00×3.50	180	S-Crn Vic (pol)

1989

Escort (wb 94.2)		Wght	Price	Prod
90	Pony htchbk sdn 2d	2,235	6,964	
91	LX htchbk sdn 2d	2,242	7,349	210,795
93	GT htchbk sdn 2d	2,442	9,315	
95	LX htchbk sdn 4d	2,313	7,679	119,582
98	LX wgn 4d	2,312	8,280	32,745

Probe (wb 99.0) - 133,650 built*				
20	GL htchbk cpe	2,715	10,660	—
21	LX htchbk cpe	2,715	11,644	—
22	GT htchbk cpe	2,870	13,794	—

Tempo (wb 99.9)				
31	GL sdn 2d	2,529	9,057	27,705
33	GLS sdn 2d	2,545	9,697	
36	GL sdn 4d	2,587	9,207	
37	LX sdn 4d	2,628	10,156	261,080
38	GLS sdn 4d	2,603	9,848	
39	AWD (4WD) sdn 4d	2,787	10,860	

Taurus (wb 106.0)				
50	L sdn 4d I-4/V-6	3,001	11,778	
52	GL sdn 4d I-4/V-6	3,046	12,202	284,605
53	LX sdn 4d V-6	3,076	15,282	
—	SHO sdn 4d V-6	3,078	19,739	16,561
55	L wgn 5d V-6	3,172	13,143	
57	GL wgn 5d V-6	3,189	13,544	94,095
58	LX wgn 5d V-6	3,220	16,524	

LTD Crown Victoria (wb 114.3)				
73	sdn 4d	3,730	15,851	120,741
74	LX sdn 4d	3,770	16,767	
78	Cntry Sqr wgn 4d	3,935	16,527	
76	wgn 4d	3,941	16,209	13,362
79	LX Cntry Sqr wgn 4d	4,013	17,556	
77	LX wgn 4d	3,915	17,238	

* Calendar-year production

1989 Engines	bore×stroke	bhp	availability
I-4, 113.5	3.23×3.46	90	S-Esc exc GT
I-4, 113.5	3.23×3.46	115	S-Escort GT
I-4, 133.0	3.39×3.70	110	S-Prob GL/LX

1989 Engines	bore×stroke	bhp	availability
I-4T, 133.0	3.39×3.70	145	S-Probe GT
I-4, 140.0	3.70×3.30	98	S-Tempo exc AWD, GLS
I-4, 140.0	3.70×3.30	100	S-Tempo AWD, GLS
I-4, 153.0	3.70×3.60	90	S-Taurus I-4
V-6, 182.0	3.50×3.15	140	S-Taur V-6 exc SHO, LX wgn
V-6, 182.0	3.50×3.15	220	S-Taurus SHO
V-6, 232.0	3.80×3.40	140	S-Taur LX wgn; O-other Taurus
V-8, 302.0	4.00×3.00	150	S-Crown Vic
V-8, 351.0	4.00×3.50	180	S-Crn Vic (pol)

1990

Escort (wb 94.2)		Wght	Price	Prod
90	Pony htchbk sdn 2d	2,242	7,402	
91	LX htchbk sdn 2d	—	7,806	110,534
93	GT htchbk sdn 2d	—	9,804	
95	LX htchbk sdn 4d	2,310	8,136	70,016
98	LX wgn 4d	2,313	8,737	15,760
Probe (wb 99.0) - 109,898 built				
20	GL htchbk cpe	2,731	11,470	—
21	LX htchbk cpe	—	13,006	—
22	GT htchbk cpe	—	14,726	—
Tempo (wb 99.9)				
31	GL sdn 2d	2,462	9,483	9,805
33	GLS sdn 2d	—	10,300	
36	GL sdn 4d	2,515	9,633	
37	LX sdn 4d	—	10,605	256,088
38	GLS sdn 4d	—	10,448	
39	AWD (4WD) sdn 4d	2,720	11,331	
Taurus (wb 106.0)				
50	L sdn 4d I-4/V-6	2,956	12,640	
52	GL sdn 4d I-4/V-6	—	13,113	242,197
53	LX sdn 4d V-6	—	16,180	
—	SHO sdn 4d V-6	—	21,633	8,609
55	L wgn 4d V-6	3,244	14,272	
57	GL wgn 4d V-6	—	14,722	82,195
58	LX wgn 4d V-6	—	17,771	
LTD Crown Victoria (wb 114.3)				
73	sdn 4d	3,821	17,257	68,187
74	LX sdn 4d	—	17,894	
78	Cntry Sqr wgn 4d	3,941	17,921	
76	wgn 4d	3,941	17,668	6,419
79	LX Cntry Sqr wgn 4d	—	18,761	
77	LX wgn 4d	—	18,418	

1990 Engines	bore×stroke	bhp	availability
I-4, 113.5	3.23×3.46	90	S-Esc exc GT
I-4, 113.5	3.23×3.46	110	S-Escort GT
I-4, 133.0	3.39×3.70	110	S-Probe GL
I-4T, 133.0	3.39×3.70	145	S-Probe GT
I-4, 140.0	3.70×3.30	98	S-Tempo exc AWD, GLS
I-4, 140.0	3.70×3.30	100	S-Tempo AWD, GLS
I-4, 153.0	3.70×3.60	90	S-Taurus I-4
V-6, 182.0	3.50×3.15	140	S-Probe LX, Taurus LX sdn; O-other Taurus
V-6, 182.0	3.50×3.15	220	S-Taurus SHO
V-6, 232.0	3.80×3.40	140	S-Taur LX wgn; O-other Taurus
V-8, 302.0	4.00×3.00	150	S-Crown Vic
V-8, 351.0	4.00×3.50	180	S-Crn Vic (pol)

Note: Full-size (Crown Victoria) station wagons in the 1980s could have an optional dual-facing rear seat. Base prices of 1983-87 Escort and Tempo diesel models were higher than amounts shown.

1991

Escort (98.4)		Wght	Price	Prod
61/BM	Pony htchbk sdn 2d	2,287	7,976	136,157
61/AI	LX htchbk sdn 2d	2,312	8,667	
61/AX	GT htchbk sdn 2d	2,364	11,484	58,201
58	LX htchbk sdn 4d	2,355	9,095	126,579
74	LX wgn 4d	2,411	9,680	62,513
Probe (wb 99.0) - 93,737 built				
AF	GL htchbk cpe	2,730	11,691	—
AI	LX htchbk cpe	3,000	13,229	—
AX	GT htchbk cpe	2,970	14,964	—
Tempo (wb 99.9)				
66/HVB	GL sdn 2d	2,532	9,541	8,585
66/HVD	GLS sdn 2d	2,601	10,358	
54/HVB	GL sdn 4d	2,600	9,691	
54/HVD	GLS sdn 4d	2,659	10,506	211,756
54/HVC	LX sdn 4d	2,626	10,663	
39	AWD (4WD) sdn 4d	2,587	11,390	
Taurus (106.0)				
FC/HVS	L sdn 4d	3,049	13,352	
FC/HVD	GL sdn 4d	—	13,582	224,344
FC/HVB	LX sdn 4d	—	17,373	
FC/HVE	SHO sdn 4d	—	22,071	9,136
FF/HVS	L wgn 4d	3,276	14,784	
FF/HVD	GL wgn 4d	—	14,990	69,092
FF/HVB	LX wgn 4d	—	18,963	
Crown Victoria (wb 114.3)				
FC/AB	sdn 4d	3,822	18,227	81,667
FC/AI	LX sdn 4d	—	18,863	
	wgn 4d	4,028	18,083	
	LX wgn 4d	—	18,883	3,865
	Cntry Squire wgn 4d	—	18,335	
	LX Cntry Sqr wgn 4d	—	19,085	

1991 Engines	bore×stroke	bhp	availability
I-4, 109.0	3.27×3.35	127	S-Esc GT (dohc)
I-4, 114.0	3.23×3.46	88	S-Escort
I-4, 133.3	3.39×3.70	110	S-Prob GL/LX
I-4T, 133.3	3.39×3.70	145	S-Probe GT
I-4, 141.0	3.70×3.30	98	S-Tempo
I-4, 141.0	3.70×3.30	100	O-Tempo
I-4, 153.0	3.70×3.60	105	S-Taur exc SHO
V-6, 182.0	3.50×3.15	140	O-Taur exc SHO
V-6, 182.0	3.50×3.10	145	O-Probe
V-6, 182.0	3.50×3.15	220	S-Taur SHO (dohc)
V-6, 232.0	3.80×3.40	140	O-Taur exc SHO
V-8, 302.0	4.00×3.00	150	S-Crown Vic
V-8, 302.0	4.00×3.00	160	O-Crown Vic
V-8, 351.0	4.00×3.50	180	O-Crn Vic (pol)

1992

Escort (98.4)		Wght	Price	Prod
61/BM	Pony htchbk sdn 2d	2,287	8,355	36,568
61/AI	LX htchbk sdn 2d	2,312	9,055	
61/AX	GT htchbk sdn 2d	2,458	11,871	14,241
54/AI	LX sdn 4d	2,364	9,795	37,400
54/AX	LX-E sdn 4d	2,464	11,933	6,771
58/AI	LX htchbk sdn 4d	2,355	9,483	34,880
74/AI	LX wgn 4d	2,411	10,067	39,749
Probe (wb 99.0) - 50,517 built				
AF	GL htchbk cpe	2,730	12,257	—
AI	LX htchbk cpe	3,000	13,257	—
AX	GT htchbk cpe	2,970	14,857	—
Tempo (wb 99.9)				
66/HVB	GL sdn 2d	2,532	9,987	37,364
66/HVD	GLS sdn 2d	2,601	12,652	
54/HVB	GL sdn 4d	2,600	10,137	
54/HVD	GLS sdn 4d	2,659	12,800	301,606
54/HVC	LX sdn 4d	2,626	11,115	
Taurus (106.0)				
FC/HVS	L sdn 4d	3,111	14,980	
FC/HVD	GL sdn 4d	3,117	15,280	286,090
FC/HVB	LX sdn 4d	3,193	17,775	
FC/HVE	SHO sdn 4d	3,309	23,889	8,000
FF/HVS	L wgn 4d	3,262	16,013	
FF/HVD	GL wgn 4d	3,264	16,290	73,964
FF/HVB	LX wgn 4d	3,388	19,464	
Crown Victoria (wb 114.3) - 152,373 built				
FC/AB	sdn 4d	3,748	19,563	—
FC/AI	LX sdn 4d	3,769	20,887	—
FC/A3	Touring Sdn sdn 4d	3,850	23,832	—

1992 Engines	bore×stroke	bhp	availability
I-4, 109.0	3.27×3.35	127	S-Esc GT (dohc)
I-4, 114.0	3.23×3.46	88	S-Escort
I-4, 133.3	3.39×3.70	110	S-Prob GL/LX
I-4T, 133.3	3.39×3.70	145	S-Prob GT (ohc)
I-4, 141.0	3.70×3.30	98	S-Temp exc GLS
I-4, 153.0	3.70×3.60	105	S-Taur exc SHO
V-6, 182.0	3.50×3.15	140	O-Taur exc SHO
V-6, 182.0	3.50×3.10	135	S-Tempo GLS, O-other Tempo
V-6, 182.0	3.50×3.10	145	O-Probe
V-6, 182.0	3.50×3.15	220	S-Taurus SHO (dohc)
V-6, 232.0	3.80×3.40	140	O-Taur exc SHO
V-8, 281.0	3.60×3.60	190	S-Crown Vic
V-8, 281.0	3.60×3.60	210	O-Crown Vic

1993

Escort (98.4)		Wght	Price	Prod
61/BM	Std. htchbk sdn 2d	2,285	8,355	
61/AI	LX htchbk sdn 2d	2,306	9,364	104,827
61/AX	GT htchbk sdn 2d	2,440	11,871	
54/AI	LX sdn 4d	2,359	10,041	78,905
54/AX	LX-E sdn 4d	2,440	11,933	
58/AI	LX htchbk sdn 4d	2,354	9,797	66,021
74/AI	LX wgn 4d	2,403	10,367	175,354
Probe (wb 102.9) - 89,701 built				
AB	htchbk cpe	2,619	12,845	—
AX	GT htchbk cpe	2,815	15,174	—
Tempo (wb 99.9)				
66/HVB	GL sdn 2d	2,511	10,267	56,250
54/HVB	GL sdn 4d	2,569	10,267	182,043
54/HVC	LX sdn 4d	2,613	12,135	
Taurus (106.0)				
FC/HVD	GL sdn 4d	3,083	15,491	350,487
FC/HVB	LX sdn 4d	3,201	18,300	
FC/HVE	SHO sdn 4d	3,354	24,829	21,991
FF/HVD	GL wgn 4d	3,255	16,656	86,231
FF/HVB	LX wgn 4d	3,368	19,989	
Crown Victoria (wb 114.4) - 108,201 built				
FC/AB	sdn 4d	3,793	19,972	—
FC/AI	LX sdn 4d	3,799	21,559	—

1993 Engines	bore×stroke	bhp	availability
I-4, 109.0	3.27×3.35	127	S-Esc GT (dohc)
I-4, 114.0	3.23×3.46	88	S-Escort
I-4, 122.0	3.27×3.62	115	S-Prob (dohc)
I-4, 141.0	3.70×3.30	96	S-Tempo
V-6, 153.0	3.33×2.92	164	S-Prob GT (dohc)
V-6, 182.0	3.50×3.15	140	S-Taur exc SHO
V-6, 182.0	3.50×3.10	135	O-Tempo
V-6, 182.0	3.50×3.15	220	S-Taurus SHO (man) (dohc)
V-6, 195.0	3.60×3.15	220	S-Taurus SHO (auto) (dohc)
V-6, 232.0	3.80×3.40	140	O-Taur exc SHO
V-8, 281.0	3.60×3.60	190	S-Crown Vic
V-8, 281.0	3.60×3.60	210	O-Crown Vic

1994

Escort (98.4)		Wght	Price	Prod*
61/BM	Std. htchbk sdn 2d	2,304	9,035	
61/AI	LX htchbk sdn 2d	2,325	9,890	96,434
61/AX	GT htchbk sdn 2d	2,447	12,300	
54/AK	LX sdn 4d	2,371	10,550	50,786
61/AI	LX htchbk sdn 4d	2,419	10,325	116,321
74/AI	LX wgn 4d	2,419	10,880	47,278
Probe (wb 102.8) - 83,872 built				
AB	htchbk cpe	2,690	13,685	—
AX	GT htchbk cpe	2,921	16,015	—
Tempo (wb 99.9)				
66/HVB	GL sdn 2d	2,511	10,735	35,445
54/HVB	GL sdn 4d	2,569	10,735	145,625
54/HVC	LX sdn 4d	2,613	12,560	
Taurus (106.0)				
FC/HVD	GL sdn 4d	3,104	16,140	225,532
FC/HVB	LX sdn 4d	3,177	18,785	
FC/HVE	SHO sdn 4d	3,395	24,715	13,698
FF/HVD	GL wgn 4d	3,272	17,220	70,966
FF/HVB	LX wgn 4d	3,349	20,400	
Crown Victoria (wb 114.4) - 109,545 built				
FC/AB	sdn 4d	3,786	19,300	—
FC/AI	LX sdn 4d	3,794	20,715	—

*Includes production for export.

1994 Engines	bore×stroke	bhp	availability
I-4, 109.0	3.27×3.35	127	S-Esc GT (dohc)
I-4, 114.0	3.23×3.46	88	S-Escort
I-4, 122.0	3.27×3.62	115	S-Probe (dohc)

1994 Engines	bore×stroke	bhp	availability
I-4, 141.0	3.70×3.30	96	S-Tempo
V-6, 153.0	3.33×2.92	164	S-Prob GT (dohc)
V-6, 182.0	3.50×3.15	140	S-Taur exc SHO
V-6, 182.0	3.50×3.10	135	O-Temp exc SHO
V-6, 182.0	3.50×3.15	220	S-Taurus SHO (man) (dohc)
V-6, 195.0	3.60×3.15	220	S-Taurus SHO (auto) (dohc)
V-6, 232.0	3.80×3.40	140	O-Taur exc SHO
V-8, 281.0	3.60×3.60	190	S-Crown Vic
V-8, 281.0	3.60×3.60	210	O-Crown Vic

1995

Escort (98.4)		Wght	Price	Prod
P10	Std. htchbk sdn 2d	2,316	9,580	
P11	LX htchbk sdn 2d	2,355	10,435	91,785
P12	GT htchbk sdn 2d	2,459	12,720	
P13	LX sdn 4d	2,385	11,040	62,713
P14	LX htchbk sdn 4d	2,404	10,870	50,233
P15	LX wgn 4d	2,451	11,425	115,960
Probe (wb 102.8) - 52,226 built				
T20	htchbk cpe	2,690	14,180	—
T22	GT htchbk cpe	2,921	16,545	—
Contour (wb 106.5) - 178,832 built				
P65	GL sdn 4d	2,769	13,310	—
P66	LX sdn 4d	—	13,995	—
P67	SE sdn 4d	3,040	15,695	—
Taurus (106.0)				
P52	GL sdn 4d	3,118	17,585	
P52/SE	SE sdn 4d	—	18,630	345,244
P53	LX sdn 4d	—	19,400	
P54	SHO sdn 4d	—	25,140	
P57	GL wgn 4d	3,285	18,680	50,494
P58	LX wgn 4d	—	21,010	
Crown Victoria (wb 114.4) - 98,309 built				
P73	sdn 4d	3,762	20,160	—
P74	LX sdn 4d	—	21,970	—

1995 Engines	bore×stroke	bhp	availability
I-4, 109.0	3.27×3.35	127	S-Esc GT (dohc)
I-4, 114.0	3.23×3.46	88	S-Escort
I-4, 121.0	3.34×3.46	125	S-Contour GL/LX(dohc)
I-4, 122.0	3.27×3.62	118	S-Prob (dohc)
V-6, 153.0	3.33×2.92	164	S-Prob GT (dohc)
V-6, 155.0	3.24×3.13	170	S-Cntr SE (dohc); O-Contour LX
V-6, 182.0	3.50×3.15	140	S-Taur exc SHO
V-6, 182.0	3.50×3.15	220	S-Taurus SHO (man) (dohc)
V-6, 195.0	3.60×3.15	220	S-Taurus SHO (auto) (dohc)
V-6, 232.0	3.80×3.40	140	O-Taur exc SHO
V-8, 281.0	3.60×3.60	190	S-Crown Victoria
V-8, 281.0	3.60×3.60	210	O-Crown Victoria

1996

Escort (wb 98.4)		Wght	Price	Prod
P10	htchbk sdn 2d	2,323	10,065	
P11	LX htchbk sdn 2d	3,356	10,910	71,626
P12	GT htchbk sdn 2d	2,455	13,205	
P13	LX sdn 4d	2,378	11,515	17,019
P14	LX htchbk sdn 4d	2,398	11,345	15,056
P15	LX wgn sdn 4d	2,444	11,900	42,708
Probe (wb 102.8) - 30,125 built				
T20	SE htchbk cpe	2,690	13,930	—
T22	GT htchbk cpe	2,921	16,450	—
Contour (wb 106.5) - 186,263 built				
P65	GL sdn 4d	2,769	13,785	—
P66	LX sdn 4d	2,815	14,470	—
P67	SE sdn 4d	3,040	16,170	—
Taurus (wb 108.5)				
P51	G sdn 4d	3,329	17,995	
P52	GL sdn 4d	3,326	18,600	
P53	LX sdn 4d	3,358	20,980	378,577
P54	SHO sdn 4d	3,544	25,140	
P57	GL wgn 4d	3,480	19,680	60,672
P58	LX wgn 4d	3,531	22,000	
Crown Victoria (wb 114.4) - 115,547 built				
P73	sdn 4d	3,780	20,955	
P74	LX sdn 4d	3,791	22,675	

1996 Engines	bore × stroke	bhp	availability
I-4, 109.0	3.27 × 3.35	127	S-Esc GT (dohc)
I-4, 114.0	3.23 × 3.46	88	S-Escort
I-4, 121.0	3.34 × 3.46	125	S-Cntr GL, LX
I-4, 122.0	3.27 × 3.62	118	S-Probe
V-6, 153.0	3.33 × 2.92	164	S-Probe GT
V-6, 155.0	3.24 × 3.13	170	S-Contour SE
V-6, 181.0	3.50 × 3.10	200	S-Taur LX (dohc)
V-6, 182.0	3.50 × 3.15	145	S-Taur G, GL
V-8, 207.0	3.20 × 3.10	240	S-Taurus SHO
V-8, 281.0	3.60 × 3.60	190	S-Crown Vic
V-8, 281.0	3.60 × 3.60	210	O-Crown Vic

1997

Escort (wb 98.4)		Wght	Price	Prod
P10	sdn 4d	2,457	11,015	251,894
P13	LX sdn 4d	2,503	11,515	
P15	LX wgn sdn 4d	2,571	12,065	71,610
Probe (wb 102.8) - 16,821 built				
T20	htchbk cpe	2,690	14,280	—
T22	GT htchbk cpe	2,921	16,780	—
Contour (wb 106.5)—79,951 built				
P65	sdn 4d	2,769	13,460	—
P65	GL sdn 4d	2,769	14,285	—
P66	LX sdn 4d	2,769	14,915	—
P67	SE sdn 4d	2,994	16,615	—
Taurus (wb 108.5)				
P51	G sdn 4d	3,329	17,995	
P52	GL sdn 4d	3,329	18,985	384,844
P53	LX sdn 4d	3,326	21,610	
P54	SHO sdn 4d	3,440	26,460	
P57	GL wgn 4d	3,480	20,195	13,958
P58	LX wgn 4d	3,480	22,715	
Crown Victoria (wb 114.4) - 123,833 built				
P73	sdn 4d	3,776	21,475	—
P74	LX sdn 4d	3,780	23,195	—

1997 Engines	bore × stroke	bhp	availability
I-4, 121.0	3.34 × 3.46	110	S-Escort
I-4, 121.0	3.34 × 3.46	125	S-Contour exc SE (dohc)
I-4, 122.0	3.27 × 3.62	118	S-Probe
V-6, 153.0	3.33 × 2.92	164	S-Probe GT
V-6, 155.0	3.24 × 3.13	170	S-SE; O-Contour GL/LX
V-6, 181.0	3.50 × 3.10	200	S-Taur LX (dohc)
V-6, 182.0	3.50 × 3.15	145	S-Taurus G, GL
V-8, 207.0	3.20 × 3.10	235	S-Taurus SHO
V-8, 281.0	3.60 × 3.60	190	S-Crown Vic

1998

Escort (wb 98.4)-331,860 blt		Wght	Price	Prod*
P10	LX sdn 4d	2,468	11,280	—
P13	SE sdn 4d	—	12,580	—
P15	LX wgn sdn 4d	2,531	13,780	—
P11	ZX2 Cool cpe 2d	2,478	12,580	—
P11	ZX2 Hot cpe 2d	—	13,080	—
Contour (wb 106.5) - 147,783 built				
P66	LX sdn 4d	2,811	14,460	—
P67	SE sdn 4d	3,030	15,785	—
P68	SVT sdn 4d	3,068	22,405	—
Taurus (wb 108.5) - 400,652 built				
P52	LX sdn 4d	3,353	18,245	—
P52/60E	SEsdn 4d	3,294	19,445	—
P54	SHO sdn 4d	—	28,920	—
P57	SE wgn 4d	3,457	21,105	—
Crown Victoria (wb 114.4) - 134,905 built				
P73	sdn 4d	3,917	20,935	—
P74	LX sdn 4d	—	23,135	—

1998 Engines	bore × stroke	bhp	availability
I-4, 121.0	3.34 × 3.46	110	S-Esc exc ZX2
I-4, 121.0	3.34 × 3.46	125	S-Contour exc SVT (dohc)
I-4, 121.0	3.34 × 3.46	130	S-Esc ZX2 (dohc)
V-6, 155.0	3.24 × 3.13	170	O-Cntr exc SVT
V-6, 155.0	3.24 × 3.13	195	S-Contour SVT
V-6, 181.0	3.50 × 3.10	200	O-Taurus exc SHO (dohc)
V-6, 182.0	3.50 × 3.15	145	S-Taur exc SHO
V-8, 207.0	3.20 × 3.10	235	S-Taurus SHO
V-8, 281.0	3.60 × 3.60	200	S-Crown Vic
V-8, 281.0	3.60 × 3.60	215	O-Crown Vic

* Calendar-year production

1999

Escort (wb 98.4)-114,171 blt		Wght	Price	Prod*
P10	LX sdn 4d	2,468	11,455	—
P13	SE sdn 4d	—	12,935	—
P15	LX wgn sdn 4d	2,531	14,135	—
P11	ZX2 Cool cpe	2,478	11,610	—
P11	ZX2 Hot cpe	—	13,290	—
Contour (wb 106.5) - 110,146 built				
P66	LX sdn 4d	2,769	14,460	—
P67	SE sdn 4d	—	15,955	—
P68	SVT sdn 4d	—	22,665	—
Taurus (wb 108.5) - 380,337 built				
P52	LX sdn 4d	3,329	17,745	—
P52/60E	SEsdn 4d	3,353	18,445	—
P54	SHO sdn 4d	—	29,000	—
P57	SE wgn 4d	3,480	19,445	—
Crown Victoria (wb 114.4) - 125,624 built				
P73	sdn 4d	3,917	21,905	—
P74	LX sdn 4d	3,927	23,925	—

1999 Engines	bore × stroke	bhp	availability
I-4, 121.0	3.34 × 3.46	110	S-Esc exc ZX2
I-4, 121.0	3.34 × 3.46	125	S-Contour exc SVT (dohc)
I-4, 121.0	3.34 × 3.46	130	S-Esc ZX2 (dohc)
V-6, 155.0	3.24 × 3.13	170	O-Cntr exc SVT
V-6, 155.0	3.24 × 3.13	200	S-Contour SVT
V-6, 181.0	3.50 × 3.10	200	O-Taurus exc SHO (dohc)
V-6, 182.0	3.50 × 3.15	145	S-Taur exc SHO
V-8, 207.0	3.20 × 3.10	235	S-Taurus SHO
V-8, 281.0	3.60 × 3.60	200	S-Crown Vic
V-8, 281.0	3.60 × 3.60	215	O-Crown Vic

* Calendar-year production

2000

Escort (wb 98.4)-107,005 blt		Wght	Price	Prod*
P13	sdn 4d	2,468	12,070	—
P11	ZX2 cpe	2,478	11,760	—
Focus (wb 103.0)				
P31	ZX3 htchbk cpe	2,551	11,865	63,538
P33	LX sdn 4d	2,564	12,125	
P34	SE sdn 4d	2,564	13,565	
P38	ZTS sdn 4d	—	15,165	325,879
P36	SE wgn 4d	2,717	15,380	
Contour (wb 106.5) - 17,410 built				
P66	Sport sdn 4d	2,603	16,845	—
P68	SVT sdn 4d	3,065	22,905	—
Taurus (wb 108.5) - 440,678 built				
P52	LX sdn 4d	3,326	17,885	—
P53	SE sdn 4d	3,355	18,935	—
P55	SES sdn 4d	3,392	19,810	—
P56	SEL sdn 4d	3,408	21,085	—
P57	SE wgn 4d	3,519	20,090	—
Crown Victoria (wb 114.4) - 102,911 built				
P73	sdn 4d	3,946	22,005	—
P74	LX sdn 4d	3,968	24,120	—

2000 Engines	bore × stroke	bhp	availability
I-4, 121.0	3.34 × 3.46	110	S-Escort sdn, Focus LX/SE
I-4, 121.0	3.34 × 3.46	130	S-Escort ZX2, Foc ZX3, ZTS; O-other Foc (dohc)
V-6, 155.0	3.24 × 3.13	170	S-Contour Sport
V-6, 155.0	3.24 × 3.13	200	S-Contour SVT
V-6, 181.0	3.50 × 3.10	200	O-Taurus (dohc)
V-6, 182.0	3.50 × 3.15	155	S-Taurus
V-8, 281.0	3.60 × 3.60	200	S-Crown Vic
V-8, 281.0	3.60 × 3.60	215	O-Crown Vic

* Calendar-year production

2001

ZX2 (wb 98.4)		Wght	Price	Prod*
P11	cpe 2d	2,478	12,050	89,850

▲ 1950 Ford club coupe

▼ 1956 Ford Crown Victoria two-door

▲ 1966 Ford LTD hardtop sedan

▼ 1972 Ford Gran Torino hardtop coupe

▲ 2005 Ford GT coupe

▼ 1965 Ford Mustang GT convertible coupe

▲ 1969 Ford Mustang Mach I fastback coupe

▼ 1973 Ford Mustang notchback coupe

▲ 2007 Ford Shelby Cobra GT500 convertible coupe

▼ 1957 Ford Thunderbird convertible coupe

▲ 1959 Ford Thunderbird convertible coupe

▼ 1964 Ford Thunderbird convertible coupe

▲ 1983 Ford Thunderbird coupe

▼ 2002 Ford Thunderbird convertible coupe

▲ 1949 Frazer Manhattan four-door sedan

▼ 1951 Frazer Manhattan hardtop sedan

▲ 1939 Graham four-door sedan

▼ 1941 Graham Hollywood four-door sedan

▲ 1951 Henry J Deluxe two-door sedan

▼ 1937 Hudson Country Club four-door sedan

▲ 1949 Hudson Commodore Six Brougham convertible coupe

▼ 1954 Hudson Hornet club coupe

▲ 1932 Hupmobile 222F sport coupe

▼ 1955 Imperial Newport hardtop coupe

▲ 1960 Imperial Crown convertible coupe

▼ 1968 Imperial Crown hardtop sedan

▲ 1947 Kaiser Special four-door sedan

▼ 1951 Kaiser Golden Dragon four-door sedan

▲ 1954 Kaiser-Darrin convertible coupe

▼ 1955 Kaiser Manhattan two-door sedan

▲ 1930 LaSalle 340 convertible coupe

▼ 1934 LaSalle coupe

Focus (wb 103.0)		Wght	Price	Prod*
P31	ZX3 htchbk cpe	2,551	12,125	55,529
P33	LX sdn 4d	2,564	12,385	
P34	SE sdn 4d	2,564	14,040	249,879
P38	ZTS sdn 4d	—	15,260	
P36	SE wgn 4d	2,717	16,235	
Taurus (wb 108.5) - 350,076 built				
P52	LX sdn 4d	3,326	18,260	—
P53	SE sdn 4d	3,355	19,035	—
P55	SES sdn 4d	3,392	20,050	—
P56	SEL sdn 4d	3,408	21,535	—
P57	SE wgn 4d	3,519	20,190	—
Crown Victoria (wb 114.4) - 101,409 built				
P73	sdn 4d	3,946	22,005	—
P74	LX sdn 4d	3,968	24,120	—

2001 Engines	bore × stroke	bhp	availability
I-4, 121.0	3.34 × 3.46	110	S-Foc LX/SEs
I-4, 121.0	3.34 × 3.46	130	S-ZX2, Foc ZX3, ZTS; O-other Focus (dohc)
V-6, 181.0	3.50 × 3.10	200	O-Taurus (dohc)
V-6, 182.0	3.50 × 3.15	155	S-Taurus (ohc)
V-8, 281.0	3.60 × 3.60	220	S-Crown Vic
V-8, 281.0	3.60 × 3.60	235	O-Crown Vic

2002

ZX2 (wb 98.4) - 52,709 built		Wght	Price	Prod*
P11	Deluxe cpe 2d	—	13,545	—
P11	Premium cpe 2d	—	14,000	—
Focus (wb 103.0) - 344,928 built				
P31	ZX3 htchbk cpe	2,551	12,445	—
P31	ZX3 Prem htchbk cpe	—	13,540	—
P31	ZX3 Pwr Prem htchbk cpe	—	14,480	—
P39	SVT htchbk cpe	2,770	17,505	—
P33	LX sdn 4d	2,551	12,760	—
P33	LX Premium sdn 4d	—	13,605	—
P34	SE sdn 4d	—	14,350	—
P34	SE Comfort sdn 4d	—	14,695	—
P34	SE Cmft/Zetec sdn 4d	—	14,945	—
P38	ZTS sdn 4d	—	15,270	—
P37	ZX5 htchbk sdn 4d	2,600	15,645	—
P36	SE wgn 4d	2,551	16,555	—
P36	SE Comfort wgn 4d	—	16,900	—
P36	ZTW wgn 4d	—	17,735	—
Taurus (wb 108.5) - 375,219 built				
P52	LX sdn 4d	3,326	18,750	—
P53	SE sdn 4d	3,355	19,560	—
P55	SES Standard sdn 4d	3,392	20,575	—
P55	SES Deluxe sdn 4d	—	21,675	—
P56	SEL Deluxe sdn 4d	3,408	22,445	—
P56	SEL Premium sdn 4d	—	23,015	—
P58	SE Standard wgn 4d	3,519	21,495	—
P58	SE Deluxe wgn 4d	—	22,120	—
P58	SE Premium wgn 4d	—	22,810	—
P59	SEL Deluxe wgn 4d	—	22,695	—
Crown Victoria (wb 114.4) - 100,192 built				
P73	sdn 4d	3,942	22,855	—
P74	LX sdn 4d	—	26,445	—
P74	LX Sport sdn 4d	—	28,060	—

2002 Engines	bore × stroke	bhp	availability
I-4, 121.0	3.34 × 3.46	110	S-Focus LX/SE
I-4, 121.0	3.34 × 3.46	130	S-ZX2, Foc ZX3, ZTS, ZTW; O-Focus (dohc)
I-4, 121.0	3.34 × 3.46	170	S-Foc SVT (dohc)
V-6, 181.0	3.50 × 3.10	200	O-Taurus (dohc)
V-6, 182.0	3.50 × 3.15	155	S-Taurus
V-8, 281.0	3.60 × 3.60	220	S-Crown Vic
V-8, 281.0	3.60 × 3.60	235	O-Crown Vic

2003

ZX2 (wb 98.4) - 12,404 built		Wght	Price	Prod*
P11	Standard cpe 2d	2,478	12,940	—
P11	Deluxe cpe 2d	2,478	14,090	—
P11	Premium cpe 2d	2,478	14,545	—
Focus (wb 103.0) - 263,289 built				
P31	ZX3 htchbk cpe	2,551	12,680	—
P31	ZX3 Prem htchbk cpe	2,551	14,075	—
P31	ZX3 Pwr Prem htchbk cpe	2,551	14,965	—
P39	SVT htchbk cpe	2,551	18,380	—

Focus		Wght	Price	Prod*
P33	LX sdn 4d	2,564	12,990	—
P33	LX Premium sdn 4d	2,564	13,835	—
P34	SE sdn 4d	2,564	14,660	—
P34	SE Comfort sdn 4d	2,564	15,005	—
P34	SE Comf/Zetec sdn 4d	2,564	15,260	—
P38	ZTS sdn 4d	2,564	15,580	—
P37	ZX5 htchbk sdn 4d	2,600	15,385	—
P37	ZX5 Comf htchbk sdn 4d	2,600	15,735	—
P37	ZX5 Prem htchbk sdn 4d	2,600	16,485	—
P37	SVT htchbk sdn 4d	2,600	19,085	—
P36	SE wgn 4d	2,717	17,010	—
P36	ZTW wgn 4d	2,717	17,355	—
Taurus (wb 108.5) - 294,326 built				
P52	LX sdn 4d	3,336	19,180	—
P53	SE sdn 4d	3,336	19,695	—
P55	SES Standard sdn 4d	3,316	21,020	—
P55	SES Deluxe sdn 4d	3,316	22,120	—
P56	SEL Deluxe sdn 4d	3,316	22,920	—
P56	SEL Premium sdn 4d	3,316	23,490	—
P58	SE Standard wgn 4d	3,502	21,345	—
P58	SE Premium wgn 4d	3,502	22,780	—
P59	SEL Deluxe wgn 4d	3,502	23,170	—
Crown Victoria (wb 114.7) - 82,541 built				
P73	Standard sdn 4d	3,942	23,805	—
P74	LX sdn 4d	3,964	27,075	—
P74	LX Sport sdn 4d	3,964	28,795	—

2003 Engines	bore×stroke	bhp	availability
I-4, 121.0	3.34×3.46	110	S-Focus
I-4, 121.0	3.34×3.46	130	S-ZX2, O-Foc (dohc)
I-4, 121.0	3.34×3.46	170	S-Foc SVT (dohc)
V-6, 181.0	3.50×3.10	200	O-Taur (dohc)
V-6, 182.0	3.50×3.15	155	S-Taurus
V-8, 281.0	3.60×3.60	220	S-Crown Vic
V-8, 281.0	3.60×3.60	235	O-Crown Vic

2004

Focus (wb 103.0) - 244,149 blt		Wght	Price	Prod*
P31	ZX3 htchbk cpe	2,551	12,795	—
P31	ZX3 Comft htchbk cpe	2,551	14,325	—
P31	ZX3 Prem htchbk cpe	2,551	15,340	—
P39	SVT htchbk cpe	2,551	18,660	—
P33	LX sdn 4d	2,564	13,255	—
P34	SE sdn 4d	2,564	14,985	—
P38	ZTS sdn 4d	2,564	15,605	—
P37	ZX5 htchbk sdn 4d	2,600	15,105	—
P37	ZX5 Cmft htchbk sdn 4d	2,600	16,050	—
P37	ZX5 Prem htchbk sdn 4d	2,600	16,860	—
P30	SVT htchbk sdn 4d	2,600	18,660	—
P36	SE wgn 4d	2,717	17,200	—
P35	ZTW wgn 4d	2,717	17,815	—
Taurus (wb 108.5) - 254,842 built				
P52	LX sdn 4d	3,336	19,660	—
P53	SE sdn 4d	3,336	20,195	—
P55	SES sdn 4d	3,316	22,120	—
P55	SES Duratec sdn 4d	3,316	22,075	—
P56	SEL sdn 4d	3,316	23305	—
P58	SE wgn 4d	3,502	21,630	—
P58	SE Duratec wgn 4d	3,502	22,325	—
P59	SEL wgn 4d	3,502	23,455	—
Crown Victoria (wb 114.7) - 82,826 built				
P73	Standard sdn 4d	3,942	23,620	—
P74	LX sdn 4d	3,964	26,645	—
P74	LX Sport sdn 4d	3,964	29,590	—

2004 Engines	bore×stroke	bhp	availability
I-4, 121.0	3.34×3.46	110	S-Focus
I-4, 121.0	3.34×3.46	130	O-Focus (dohc)
I-4, 121.0	3.34×3.46	170	S-Foc SVT (dohc)
I-4, 138.0	3.44×3.70	145	O-Focus (dohc)
V-6, 181.0	3.50×3.10	201	O-Taurus (dohc)
V-6, 182.0	3.50×3.15	155	S-Taurus
V-8, 281.0	3.60×3.60	224	S-Crown Vic
V-8, 281.0	3.60×3.60	239	O-Crown Vic

2005

Focus (wb 102.9) - 189,323 blt		Wght	Price	Prod*
P31	ZX3 S htchbk cpe	2,621	13,090	—
P31	ZX3 SE htchbk cpe	2,651	14,590	—
P31	ZX3 SES htchbk cpe	2,694	15,690	—
P34	ZX4 S sdn 4d	2,647	13,690	—
P34	ZX4 SE sdn 4d	2,685	15,190	—
P34	ZX4 SES sdn 4d	2,725	16,290	—
P38	ST sdn 4d	2,738	17,790	—

Focus		Wght	Price	Prod*
P37	ZX5 S htchbk sdn 4d	2,696	14,390	—
P37	ZX5 SE htchbk sdn 4d	2,685	15,890	—
P37	ZX5 SES htchbk sdn 4d	2,745	16,990	—
P36	ZXW SE wgn 4d	2,771	16,890	—
P35	ZTW SES wgn 4d	2,775	17,990	—
Taurus (wb 108.5) - 180,494 built				
P53	SE sdn 4d	3,306	20,485	—
P56	SEL sdn 4d	3,313	22,395	—
P58	SE wgn 4d	3,497	22,355	—
P59	SEL wgn 4d	3,497	23,345	—
Five Hundred (wb 112.9) - 118,740 built				
P23	SE sdn 4d	3,643	22,145	—
P26	SE AWD sdn 4d	3,814	23,845	—
P24	SEL sdn 4d	3,643	24,145	—
P27	SEL AWD sdn 4d	3,814	25,845	—
P25	Limited sdn 4d	3,643	26,145	—
P28	Limited AWD sdn 4d	3,814	27,845	—
Crown Victoria (wb 114.7) - 71,320 built				
P73	Standard sdn 4d	4,101	24,085	—
P74	LX sdn 4d	4,134	27,220	—
P74	LX Sport sdn 4d	4,134	30,165	—
GT (wb 106.7) - 1,898 built				
P90	cpe 2d	3,350	149,995	—

2005 Engines	bore×stroke	bhp	availability
I-4, 121.0	3.44×3.27	136	S-Focus
I-4, 138.0	3.44×3.70	151	O-Focus
V-6, 181.0	3.50×3.10	201	S-Five Hundrd, O-Taurus (dohc)
V-6, 182.0	3.50×3.15	153	S-Taurus
V-8, 281.0	3.60×3.60	224	S-Crown Vic
V-8, 281.0	3.60×3.60	239	O-Crown Vic
V-8S, 330.0	3.55×4.17	550	S-GT

2006

Focus (wb 102.9)		Wght	Price	Prod**
P31	ZX3 S htchbk cpe	2,621	13,450	—
P31	ZX3 SE htchbk cpe	2,651	14,715	—
P31	ZX3 SES htchbk cpe	2,694	15,475	—
P34	ZX4 S sdn 4d	2,647	13,750	—
P34	ZX4 SE sdn 4d	2,685	15,015	—
P34	ZX4 SES sdn 4d	2,725	15,775	—
P38	ST sdn 4d	2,738	17,040	—
P37	ZX5 S htchbk sdn 4d	2,696	14,450	—
P37	ZX5 SE htchbk sdn 4d	2,685	15,720	—
P37	ZX5 SES htchbk sdn 4d	2,745	16,485	—
P36	ZXW SE wgn 4d	2,771	16,735	—
P36	ZTW SES wgn 4d	2,775	17,495	—
Fusion (wb 107.4)				
P06	S sdn 4d	3,151	17,145	—
P07	SE sdn 4d I-4	3,151	17,900	—
P07	SE sdn 4d V-6	3,354	20,625	—
P08	SEL sdn 4d I-4	3,151	18,985	—
P08	SEL sdn 4d V-6	3,354	21,710	—
Taurus (wb 108.5)				
P53	SE sdn 4d	3,306	21,315	—
P56	SEL sdn 4d	3,313	23,245	—
Five Hundred (wb 112.9)				
P23	SE sdn 4d	3,643	22,230	—
P26	SE AWD sdn 4d	3,814	24,080	—
P24	SEL sdn 4d	3,643	24,230	—
P27	SEL AWD sdn 4d	3,814	26,080	—
P25	Limited sdn 4d	3,643	26,380	—
P28	Limited AWD sdn 4d	3,814	28,230	—
Crown Victoria (wb 114.7)				
P73	Standard sdn 4d	4,101	24,510	—
P74	LX sdn 4d	4,134	28,055	—
P74	LX Sport sdn 4d	4,134	30,830	—
GT (wb 106.7)				
P90	cpe 2d	3,350	149,995	—

2006 Engines	bore×stroke	bhp	availability
I-4, 121.0	3.44×3.27	136	S-Focus
I-4, 138.0	3.44×3.70	151	O-Focus
I-4, 139.0	3.44×3.70	160	S-Fusion
V-6, 181.0	3.50×3.10	201	S-500 (dohc)
V-6, 181.0	3.50×3.10	220	O-Fusion (dohc)
V-6, 182.0	3.50×3.15	153	S-Taurus
V-8, 281.0	3.60×3.60	224	S-Crown Vic
V-8, 281.0	3.60×3.60	239	O-Crown Vic
V-8S, 330.0	3.55×4.17	550	S-GT

* Calendar-year production

** Prod figures not available at time of publication

Ford Mustang

Mustang, the original "ponycar," was Detroit's greatest single success of the '60s. Announced six months ahead of model-year 1965, it lifted Ford volume by well over half a million units and set an all-time record for first-year new-model sales. No fewer than 680,989 were sold between the April 1964 introduction (at the New York World's Fair) and August 1965 (when production switched to '66 models). Truckers accidentally drove through showroom windows while staring at them, housewives entered contests to win them, and dealers auctioned them off because initial demand exceeded supply by a 15-to-1 ratio. No doubt about it: Everyone loved the Mustang.

Spearheading this remarkable achievement was Lee A. Iacocca, the plain-talking car salesman who in five years worked his way from an obscure Ford outpost in Pennsylvania to vice-president and general manager of Ford Division. In 1970, he became president of Ford Motor Company, only to be fired eight years later by chairman Henry Ford II. As is now well known, that celebrated debacle sent Iacocca off to take over as board chairman at Chrysler Corporation, where he'd become a legend all over again.

The Mustang idea was simplicity itself: a low-cost "personal car" derived from a high-volume compact. People had pleaded with Ford to revive the two-seat Thunderbird ever since its demise in 1957. Iacocca and company briefly considered doing that very thing with the "XT-Bird" prototype, a reengineered '57 proposed by the Budd Company in 1961. Ultimately, though, they opted for a new young-person's car that would seat four, be inexpensive to build, peppy, sporty-looking, and priced to sell for less than $2500. Sales volume was modestly projected at 100,000 units a year.

The very first Mustang was a low, two-seat fiberglass roadster with a 90-inch wheelbase and a midships 2.0-liter German Ford V-4 developing 90 brake horsepower. This experiment was pretty but impractical. After looking at those who drooled over it at various venues, Iacocca concluded, "That's sure not the car we want to build, because it can't be a volume car. It's too far out." Accordingly, many more prototypes were drawn, developed, and debated, culminating in the 108-inch-wheelbase "1964½" Mustang based on Ford's popular Falcon compact. From a marketing standpoint, it couldn't have been better.

Through 1973, Mustang was offered as a hardtop coupe, convertible, and fastback coupe. Convertible sales started at the 100,000-unit annual level, but declined to fewer than 15,000 by 1969. The crisp notchback hardtop was the best-seller by far. The fastback, initially a semi-notch style called 2+2, arrived in autumn 1964 with the rest of the '65 Ford line. It soon outsold the convertible, averaging about 50,000 a year through 1970.

Standard power at first came from the Falcon's sturdy and simple 170-cubic-inch 101-bhp straight six; optional was the lively 260-cid "Challenger" V-8 from Ford's midsize Fairlane, good for 164 ponies. After the first six months of production, Mustangs got a standard 200-cid six with 120 bhp and bored-out 289-cid V-8 options with 200-271 bhp. Increasingly hairy big-block engines were offered before government rules put an end to Ford's "Total Performance" program: a 320-horse 390 for '67; a 390-bhp 427 for '68, a 335-bhp 428 for '69.

Much of Mustang's appeal stemmed from the myriad options allowing customers to personalize the car to taste. Depending on use of the order form, you could have a stylish economy car, a thundering drag racer, a deceptively nimble sporty car, or a small luxury liner. Transmission choices comprised automatic, three- and four-speed manuals, and stick-overdrive. Handling packages, power steering, front-disc brakes, air conditioning, and tachometer were all available. So was a bench seat in lieu of the standard front buckets, though few buyers chose it. A GT package option delivered a pleasant assortment of goodies including firm suspension, full-gauge instrument panel, and special badges. A variety of interior trims was available, as

1965 convertible coupe

1965 GT 2+2 fastback coupe

1965 GT 2+2 fastback coupe

were exterior accent stripes and extra chrome moldings.

The Mustang was an inspired piece of design created by Joe Oros, L. David Ash, and Gale L. Halderman of the Ford Division styling studio. Its long-hood/short-deck proportions quickly became Detroit *de rigueur*. The inevitable imitators began showing up for 1967, hoping to cash in on the public mania for what came to be called "ponycars." General Motors fielded two, the Chevrolet Camaro and Pontiac Firebird, which would be Mustang's most serious competition for many years.

The basic '65 styling saw careful refinement in Mustang's first four seasons. The '66s changed only in detail. A deeper grille and sculptured side panels ending in twin simulated air scoops marked the '67s, when the 2+2 adopted a full-fastback roofline. The '68s had a revised grille with a bright inner ring around the by-now-familiar galloping-horse emblem.

But this relative sameness, plus increasing competition and a steady decline in ponycar demand, took its toll in Mustang production. After an impressive 607,500 units for '66, volume dropped to 472,000 in 1967, then to 317,000 for '68.

Mustang was more extensively revised for 1969, becoming lower, longer, and wider to suit much more flamboyant styling. New features included ventless side glass, quad headlamps, and a more-imposing dash. A new Mach 1 fastback with firm suspension and a standard 250-bhp 351-cid V-8 joined the line at $3139. It stood apart from the standard "SportsRoof" via a special grille with driving lamps, matte-black center-hood section with functional air scoop, quick-fill gas cap, and black honeycomb rear appliqué. Catering to the luxury market was a new Grandé hardtop priced at $2866 with standard six-cylinder engine and offering landau-style black or white vinyl roof, racing-type mirrors, special I.D., and bright wheelwell moldings.

Making an even bigger splash for mid-1969 was the fastback Boss 302, a $3588 roadgoing version of the Mustangs then cleaning up in the Sports Car Club of America's Trans-American racing series. Its exclusive 302 small-block delivered an alleged 290 bhp, but actual output was more like 350. Only 1934 were built for '69, another 6319 for 1970. All had special striping, front "chin" spoiler, Mach 1-style rear wing, and distinctive rear-window louvers.

A horse of a different color was the Boss 429, another mid-'69 debut but tagged at $4798. The number referred to what was shoehorned under the hood: a 429 "Cobra Jet" big-block wearing aluminum heads with semi-hemispherical combustion chambers. The big Boss was an obvious drag racer and did well as such, but only 858 were built for '69 and another 498 to 1970 specs. All were largely custom-crafted, as the stock front end required much reworking to accommodate the bulky V-8.

The 1969 package was mildly facelifted for '70 with recessed taillamps and a return to dual headlamps, plus standard high-back bucket seats for all models (as on the '69 Mach 1). As before, available Mach 1 V-8s ran from a 351 to a four-barrel-equipped 428 with optional "Ram Air" induction. Convertibles were becoming quite scarce by now, thanks to growing buyer preference for air conditioning and closed body styles. This year's total was off nearly 50 percent from 1969's, dropping from 14,700 to about 7700. Overall Mustang volume was down, too. The '69s garnered just under 300,000 sales; the '70s sank to a bit less than 191,000.

In late 1970, Ford abandoned most of its Trans-Am, USAC, NASCAR, and international competition efforts. Meantime, future Mustangs were being planned with an eye to the plunging market for hot cars in general and ponycars in particular.

But that wasn't evident in the third-generation Mustang of 1971, conceived in the ponycar's late-'60s heyday. Heavily influenced by Semon E. "Bunkie" Knudsen, the GM executive who briefly served as Ford Motor Company president, the '71 aimed to answer a frequent criticism of early ponycars—namely insufficient passenger room. The result was the most-changed

1966 hardtop coupe

1966 convertible coupe

1967 convertible coupe

1967 GTA 2+2 fastback coupe

1967 hardtop coupe

1968 GT/SC (later California Special)

Mustang yet: larger, heavier, and thirstier—as fat as Mustang would ever get. Though wheelbase grew only an inch, the '71 was eight inches longer overall, six inches wider, and close to 600 pounds heavier than the '65 original. Styling was more-massive, too, with busier sheetmetal; aggressive noses; and a sweeping, near-horizontal roofline on the "SportsRoof" 2+2, inspired by Ford's international GT endurance racers.

There was now plenty of room for big-block V-8s, so the performance-focused Mach 1 got an optional 429 Cobra Jet packing 370 bhp. But with the market's growing preference for luxury and convenience, this engine could now be ordered with air conditioning, power steering, tilt wheel, and other niceties. Yet a '71 Mustang could be blindingly quick. With automatic and 3.25:1 final drive, the 429 Mach 1 could do 0-60 mph in 6.5 seconds and the standing quarter-mile in 14.5 seconds.

A more-balanced '71 performer was the Boss 351 fastback, replacing both previous Bosses. Though its efficient, highly tuned small-block delivered 330 bhp and ample go, high price—$4124, nearly $1000 more than a Mach 1—limited sales, and the model vanished after one year.

Other Mustangs fared little better. Total 1971 production dropped below 150,000, with the compact Maverick and other Ford products cannibalizing a good many potential sales. The '72s were little changed, but engine options were fewer, horsepower and performance were down, and colors and trim got most of the marketing emphasis. Reflecting the last was a new Sprint decor option sporting white paint set off by broad blue racing stripes edged in red; complementary colors were used inside, and mag wheels, raised-white-letter tires, and competition suspension were all available. But nothing seemed to help much, and production bottomed out at a bit over 125,000.

Mustang remained its hefty self for one more year and again saw little change. But Ford was well along on a more-practical successor by 1973—and more willing to admit its error. Said design vice president Eugene Bordinat: "We started out with a secretary's car and all of a sudden we had a behemoth." Most '73 changes were prompted by the latest federal regulations: 5-mph front bumpers (optional color-keyed covers helped keep them from looking like clumsy afterthoughts), rubber-sheathed control knobs, flame-retardant upholstery, and exhaust-gas recirculation to help curb emissions. Volume recovered to nearly 135,000 units, the increase likely coming from buyers who'd heard that a "downsized" Mustang was due and feared what it might be like.

Yet the all-new 1974 Mustang II was a turning point for the original ponycar. Much trimmer and thriftier than the 1971-73 generation, it couldn't have been better timed, arriving just as the nation was being rocked by its first energy crisis. Sales boomed with an impressive model-year production of nearly 400,000.

With an eye on the fast-growing popularity of sporty import coupes, Iacocca specified that Mustang II have a wheelbase of 96-100 inches—it ended up at 96.2—plus a scaled-down version of the familiar long-hood/short-deck styling. Compared to the "fat" Mustangs, the II was 20 inches shorter, four inches slimmer, an inch lower and a sizable 400-500 pounds lighter. A good many components were shared with Ford's three-year-old subcompact Pinto, which benefitted from some upgrades developed for Mustang II. Both had unit construction and a conventional short/long-arm coil-spring front suspension. But instead of being bolted directly to the main structure, the Mustang's lower arms attached to a rubber-mounted subframe that supported the rear of the engine/transmission assembly. This added to production costs, but was deemed necessary to provide more-precise steering and a smoother, quieter ride than Pinto. Also, Mustang's rear leaf springs were longer than

Pinto's, and its shock absorbers were staggered for better handling and grip. These and other refinements made for what Iacocca called "the little jewel."

There was no Mustang II convertible, but notchback and fastback coupe body styles continued. The former was now a fixed-pillar style, the latter a hatchback. And for the first time, there was no V-8, engines being limited to a 2.3-liter inline four with overhead camshaft and 88 bhp, and a 2.8-liter pushrod V-6 (sourced from Ford Germany) with 105 bhp (like other makes, Ford was by now quoting horsepower in more realistic SAE net measure, rather than gross). The V-6 was standard for a new hatchback Mach 1, which could do 0-60 mph in 13-14 seconds and reach 100 mph with standard four-speed manual gearbox.

The Mustang II continued for five years without significant change. The Mach 1 and luxury four-cylinder and V-6 Ghia notchbacks continued throughout. So did numerous options, per Mustang tradition. Air conditioning, power steering and brakes, a raft of audio systems, fancy trim, a vinyl top for notchbacks, sunroof, and forged-aluminum wheels were among the available items. For 1975, a sliding-glass moonroof and a luxury package became optional for the already posh Ghia.

Subsequent Mustang II sales never came near the 1974 level, but were a lot better than 1971-73. The total fell by over half for '75, to just short of 189,000, then held steady.

Ford gave a nod to performance by reviving a V-8 option for 1975. Not surprisingly, it was the workhorse 302 small-block,

1969 Boss 302 fastback hardtop coupe prototype

1969 Mach 1 CJ 428 fastback hardtop coupe

1970 Boss 302 fastback hardtop coupe

1971 Boss 351 fastback hardtop coupe

1969 Grandé hardtop coupe

1972 Sprint fastback hardtop coupe

1973 convertible coupe

1972 hardtop coupe

1973 Mach 1 fastback hardtop coupe

1974 Mustang II Mach 1 hatchback coupe

initially rated at 122 bhp and requiring quite a bit of front-end reengineering. Following at mid-'76 was a "Cobra II" trim package for hatchbacks. This delivered a sports steering wheel, dual remote-control door mirrors, brushed-aluminum dash and door-panel appliqués, black grille, styled steel wheels, flip-out rear side windows with louvered appliques, front airdam, rear spoiler, and simulated hood scoop. Cobra II was first available only with blue stripes against white paint, then added other color combinations. It was flashy, but a far cry from the great Shelby Mustangs it strained to emulate. Ford again tried "paint-on performance" with the 1978 King Cobra. This package had many Cobra II items, plus a gaudy snake decal on the hood and tape stripes from stem to stern. Also included were the 302 V-8, power steering, and a handling suspension with 70-series radial tires. With a typical 17-second quarter-mile, the King was far from muscle-car fast, but was decent for the day.

A "New Breed" arrived for 1979, and in many ways it was the best Mustang to date. From some angles it looked vaguely like a BMW—clean, taut, and tight—and its surface execution, downswept nose, ample glass area, and lack of needless ornamentation combined the best of contemporary American and European design. It was the sort of restrained, efficient, and elegant ponycar Ford had built in the first place.

Many styling proposals were considered for the '79. The one chosen for production originated with a team headed by Jack Telnack, then executive director of Ford North American Light Truck and Car Design, later corporate design chief. Greater use of lightweight materials—including plastics, low-alloy steel, and aluminum—made the '79 roughly 200 pounds lighter than a comparable Mustang II, despite the fact that the new car was larger in almost every dimension. A wheelbase lengthened to 100.4 inches upped rear legroom by five inches. Other interior measurements gained too: for example, shoulder room by 3.5/5.0 inches front/rear, cargo volume by two cubic feet.

The '79 was planned around a cut-down version of the "Fox" platform of the previous year's new Ford Fairmont/Mercury Zephyr compacts. Suspension involved modified MacPherson-strut geometry in front, a four-bar-link live rear axle, antisway bars at both ends, and coil springs all around. A handling package with firmer springs,. shocks and bushings was available with mandatory 14-inch tires. There was also a premium setup that improved roadability via Michelin's new TRX tires, special metric-sized forged-aluminum wheels, and appropriately tuned chassis pieces. The engine lineup was expanded with addition of a 140-bhp turbocharged version of the standard 2.3-liter four, good for 0-60 times of 10 seconds or so and fuel economy in the low to mid-20s. Late in the model year, the 200-cid six returned to supplant the V-6, which Ford's German branch couldn't supply in adequate numbers.

Mustang paced the 1979 Indianapolis 500, and a pace-car replica was duly issued at midyear. For 1980, this model's slatted grille showed up on a revived Cobra package offering front and rear spoilers, integral fog lamps, nonfunctional hood scoop, and the TRX suspension. The 302 vanished that year,

1974 Mustang II "Grandé" prototype

1977 Mustang II hatchback coupe

1975 Mustang II Ghia V-8 notchback coupe

1978 Mustang II Ghia V-8 notchback coupe

1976 Mustang II Stallion hatchback coupe

1978 Mustang II King Cobra hatchback coupe

1979 Cobra Turbo hatchback coupe

1979 Ghia notchback coupe

replaced by a debored 255 version with 118 bhp as an option for all models.

With the overall market strong and Ford's ponycar all-new, Mustang volume soared for '79, reaching almost 370,000. Sales plunged by almost 100,000 the next year, but then recovered, remaining healthy throughout the '80s despite difficult market conditions bookending the decade. Of course, it helped that Mustang became more exciting as time passed, part of the vanguard for renaissance in Detroit performance.

Announcing this trend was a revived Mustang GT for 1982, a hatchback packing a reborn 302 with 157 bhp. Looking much like the Cobra it replaced, though without the cartoonish body decoration, the GT came only with four-speed manual transmission and was one of the year's hotter Detroit cars. Arrayed below were L, GL, and GLX notchbacks and hatchbacks, all with carryover power save the turbo-four, which temporarily vanished. A five-speed overdrive manual, introduced at mid-1980, remained optional with the normally aspirated base four.

Ford turned up the wick again for '83. A deft facelift brought bigger taillamps and a more-aggressive face with a sloping nose per Dearborn's newly embraced "aero" styling philosophy. But the big news was the first Mustang convertible in 10 years, offered only in top GLX trim. Performance fans applauded a more-potent 302 with a big four-barrel carb (replacing a two-barrel) and 175 bhp. The "blown" four returned with improvements and 142 bhp for a new GT Turbo hatchback. But that satisfied far less than the smooth, torquey V-8 GT, so sales were very low. The non-turbo four and a new 232-cid pushrod V-6 (replacing the old straight six) were offered for slow-laners. Unlike some other new-era ragtops, the Mustang was a "factory" job from the first, built by Ford itself. It was also quite practical for a convertible, with standard features like power top, glass rear window, and roll-down rear side windows.

Perhaps as a hedge against another energy crisis, Ford massaged its turbo-four even more for 1984, wrapping the result in a new performance Mustang, the SVO. Named for the company's Special Vehicle Operations unit, which engineered it, the SVO boasted 175 bhp via a new electronically controlled port-fuel-injection system and turbo intercooler. Also included were four-wheel disc brakes—a first for Mustang—and a fortified suspension with 16-inch wheels and meaty 225-section tires. Outside were a specific grilleless nose and a controversial "biplane" double-wing rear spoiler. But though it seemed an enthusiast's dream, the SVO was fussier to drive than the V-8

1979 Cobra hatchback coupe

GT, a little slower, and over $5000 more expensive, all of which dampened demand. Ford persisted with it through 1986, when it coaxed the engine to an impressive 200 bhp, then gave up on the SVO Mustang after total production of just 9844.

The rest of the '84 line was rearranged into two- and three-door L and LX models (the latter merging the previous GL and GLX) plus hatchback and convertible V-8 and Turbo GTs. The Turbos succumbed to slow sales a couple years before the SVO, disappearing after 1984. A second 302 with fuel injection and 165 horses was newly available for non-GTs or with automatic. Ford halfheartedly observed Mustang's 20th birthday in '84 with a modest paint-and-tape special called, for no particular reason, GT-350. Carroll Shelby, who by now had joined Lee Iaccoca at Chrysler, had used the title for his first modified Mustangs of 1965, and made a fuss over Ford's using it here.

For 1985, the cheap L models were dropped and remaining LX and GT Mustangs acquired a new nose similar to the SVO's. The high-output GT V-8 was booted to 210 bhp via a wilder camshaft and low-friction roller valve lifters; similar changes lifted the injected 302 to 180 bhp. The GT remained five-speed only, with revised internal ratios enhancing performance even further. Though a GT now cost some three times more in raw dollars than its predecessor of 20 years before, it was a far more-balanced performer. Better equipped, too. This year, for instance, it picked up beefier 60-series "gatorback" tires on seven-inch-wide cast-aluminum wheels, plus gas-pressurized front shock absorbers.

Mustangs saw few changes for '86. The main one was adoption of port fuel injection and lower compression for a single 302 V-8 rated at 200 bhp and available with either five-speed or automatic. Continuing attention to details was evident in such practical matters as a longer anti-corrosion warranty, increased sound-deadening, and a single-key lock system.

The clean fifth-generation Mustang got its first major facelift for '87, announced by newly allowed Euro-style flush-mounted headlamps. GT appearance ended up rather busy, with heavily sculpted rocker-panel extensions and "cheese-grater" tail panel. The more-sedate-looking LXs could be ordered with most key GT features, including V-8 and handling suspension. The venerable 302 was more potent than ever, gaining 25 bhp via new cylinder heads and manifolding. Strangely, the midrange V-6 option was canceled, leaving the veteran four-cylinder as the only other engine choice. Still standard for LXs, this now had port injection, too. But with only 90 bhp, it left a huge gap with V-8 performance.

Though Mustang ended the decade with no further changes of great consequence, offerings expanded for '89 to include an "LX 5.0L" series—notchback, hatchback, and convertible that amounted to GTs in conservative LX dress. But wait: 1989 marked Mustang's 25th birthday. Time for another commemorative special, right? Well, no. Ford considered one, but was distracted by several issues—including Mustang enthusiasts who objected to the new Mazda-based, American-made 1989 Probe, the smaller front-drive sporty coupe originally devised to replace Mustang. But Ford didn't neglect the original ponycar, ponying up $200 million that year to upgrade Mustang production facilities as the company's historic River Rouge plant.

And there *was* a commemorative of sorts in 3800 special Emerald Green V-8 LX convertibles offered from mid-January 1990—appropriate, as Ford sometimes regarded the first Mustang as a '65 model, not a "1964½." It was a poor substitute for the much hotter Silver Anniversary special that had been

1980 Cobra hatchback coupe

1984 SVO hatchback coupe

1982 GT 5.0 hatchback coupe

1986 GT 5.0 convertible coupe

1988 GT 5.0 hatchback coupe

1990 LX 5.0 hatchback coupe

rumored, but at least the Mustang was still alive.

And Ford kept on upgrading the venerable fifth generation. The 1990s gained a driver-side air bag in the steering-wheel hub to meet a new federal rule for front "passive restraints," plus door map pockets, clearcoat paint, and newly optional leather interior trim (as on the green '89 ragtops). Prices remained attractive: under $9500 for a four-cylinder LX two-door, less than $19,000 for the GT ragtop. Even so, production plunged to just over 128,000. The reason had less to do with Mustang's advancing age than a national economy being crippled again by a sharp recession.

Sales dropped below 99,000 for 1991, the lowest Mustang figure anyone could remember. Changes were again few. The anemic four was boosted to 105 horses via a new eight-plug cylinder head, but only rental-car fleet managers cared. Convertible tops were redesigned to fold closer to the body, and the automatic transmission met another new federal edict by adding a safety interlock that required pushing the brake pedal to move the shifter out of Park. Prices rose a bit, the base LX two-door now just over $10,000, though V-8 convertibles again stickered below $20,000.

A few more details were changed for '92, when Mustang sales hit an all-time model-year low of 79,280. An optional four-way power driver's seat arrived, but extra-cost whitewalls and wire-wheel covers departed, a blow for good taste.

With the economy perking up by model-year '93, Mustang sales rebounded to some 114,200—which was a bit surprising. For one thing, GM had a swoopy new Chevrolet Camaro and Pontiac Firebird with up to 275 bhp from the latest 5.7-liter Corvette V-8. Ford, meantime, had to downgrade Mustang's V-8 to more "realistic" ratings of 205 bhp and 275 pound-feet of torque. Even without that, Mustang should have lost sales in this final year for the fifth generation. Perhaps the rumored debut of a new '94 Mustang was an incentive to buy for those who still loved the old warhorse.

Ford provided its own incentive with a hot hatchback that might have appeared with 25th Anniversary badges. But it wore the Cobra name and snake insignia of Carroll Shelby's legendary '60s sports cars, mainly so Ford could keep its legal claim to both from expiring for lack of use. *Road & Track* called it the "best of an aging breed," and by most measures it was. Developed by Dearborn's new Special Vehicle Team (SVT, supplementing a refocused SVO department), the '93 Cobra boasted 235 bhp from a tweaked 302 with special big-port "GT40" heads, tuned-runner intake manifold, revised cam, and other muscle-building enhancements. Torque, a stout 280 pound-feet, was delivered through a beefier (and mandatory) manual five-speed transmission and thick 245/45ZR17 performance tires. Standard rear disc brakes were a first for a volume Mustang, and new "balanced" suspension tuning went against conventional wisdom with softer damping and a smaller front stabilizer. Outside were a neater nose, taillamps from the late SVO, seven-blade alloy wheels, oversized rear spoiler—and, finally, the return of the nostalgic running-horse grille emblem. In all, it was a speedy, sophisticated package.

How speedy? *R&T*'s Cobra clocked 5.9 seconds 0-60 mph, 14.5 at 98 mph in the standing quarter-mile, and under 16 seconds in the 0-100 dash. As for sophisticated, *Car and Driver* termed it "a nicer-riding, more-supple car [than the GT]. Although it can feel less buttoned down... the Cobra makes better use of its tires and rewards coordinated hands and feet with clearly higher limits and cornering speeds..."

Although cynics viewed the '93 Cobra as a ploy to keep Ford's old ponycar from being overshadowed by GM's new ones, it was a grand send-off for the old fifth generation. And with only some 5000 built, this Cobra stands to be the most collectible of a long-lived breed.

Except for 1993's 107 Cobra Rs. The "R" meant "racing," so this one came with competition-grade front brakes, cooling system and chassis tuning, plus bigger wheels and tires, and strategic structural reinforcements. Omitting the stock Cobra's back seat, air conditioning, and power accessories saved 60 pounds—not much on the road but critical on the track. Ford sold every R-model for the full $25,692 sticker price, versus about $20-grand for a regular Cobra, itself a bona fide bargain.

But it was past time to move on, and a mostly new Mustang rode in for 1994 on a tidal wave of anticipation and nostalgia. Announcement ads pictured it with the classic '65 to declare, "It is what it was." Actually, it almost wasn't at all.

The uproar over the Probe had shown that ponycar diehards wouldn't take a Japanese-style substitute. Trouble was, demand for "real" ponycars was lagging again by the early '90s, leading some in Dearborn to question if another new Mustang might ever be needed. Even if it were, Ford had more-profitable fish to fry, and Mustang sales were still decent, so why rush? With that, planning floundered for a good two years while the car's future was debated. Then Ford learned GM was abandoning a planned front-drive Camaro/Firebird for a new rear-drive 1993 concept. Corporate pride demanded a proper reply, and Ford authorized work on a new Mustang in 1991.

Because Ford had become a much leaner outfit, and with the "team concept" now gospel in Detroit, the new SN95 project developed quite differently from earlier Mustang efforts. The big departure was forming a fairly small, independent multidiscipline group to herd the new pony from drawing board to showroom. Money matters dictated a slim $700 million budget, with only $200 million earmarked for design and engineering. The deadline was equally tight: just 36 months.

Echoing past Mustangs was the trio of mock-ups considered for production SN95 styling. All had the requested "retro" appearance cues, including a big galloping steed in the grille, plus a smooth, muscular, slightly wedgy shape. Tamest of the three was the "Bruce Jenner," a "trim, athletic" design that scored low in consumer polls for looking too "soft." At the other extreme was "Rambo," an aggressively exaggerated version that failed as too macho. This left the in-between "Arnold Schwarzenegger" proposal to carry the day. All three finalists were modeled as "trunked" coupes. Though a new convertible was never in doubt, Americans no longer cared much for hatchbacks, so that body style was forgotten despite its importance to fifth-generation Mustang sales.

Interior designers also strove for a "classic" feel while building in new government-mandated safety features like dual dashboard airbags and anti-intrusion door beams. What emerged was the usual 2+2 package with a wildly sculpted "twin-cowl" instrument panel paying faint homage to the '60s.

Because time and money precluded a full redesign, SN95 made do with a much-modified version of the old '79 platform dubbed "Fox-4." Body engineers worked hard to increase rigidity without appreciable weight gain, and succeeded. Against the previous notchback, the SN95 coupe was some 56-percent stiffer in bending resistance and 44 percent better in torsional strength; comparable convertible numbers were 76 percent and a startling 150 percent. Despite these impressive gains, curb weights rose by only some 280 pounds from equivalent '93s. Chassis engineers decreed softer damping, much-revised suspension geometry, and a 1.8-inch longer wheelbase. Wheel/tire packages were upgraded. So were brakes, with larger front discs, newly standard rear discs, a bigger booster, and Bosch antilock control as a first-time option. Powerteams were familiar fare. Base models, no longer called LX, traded the anemic standard four-cylinder for the 3.8-liter V-6 last offered in '86 Mustangs, retuned for 145 bhp. The LX 5.0L package was also dropped, leaving V-8 power the sole province of GT models. Though the venerable small-block was little changed from '93, it somehow gained 10 horses and a like number of pound-feet, perhaps by the stroke of a pen. Transmissions again comprised five-speed manual or optional four-speed automatic, but the latter was Ford's latest "AOD-E" unit with electronic shift control.

Overall, the '94 Mustang seemed the same kind of thorough makeover just accorded the big Ford Crown Victoria, Mercury Grand Marquis and Lincoln Town Car sedans. Still, some were disappointed that the long-awaited new Mustang wasn't ground-up new, especially as some prices rose to the point of "sticker shock." The base coupe, for instance, jumped $2646 to $13,365, though that included a bigger engine, better brakes and dual airbags, plus a tilt steering wheel and power driver-side seat, both options before. The GT coupe was up $1533 to $17,280, though it, too, claimed the same improvements, plus expected standards like foglights, rear spoiler, and sport seats. At least the base convertible looked a fine value at $20,160, and the GT edition was a reasonable $21,970. Both ragtops were again factory-built with standard power roof and glass rear window, which now included a rear defogger. An optional 80-pound lift-off hardtop was announced as a $1500 convertible option, but was never actually sold due to production glitches.

To Ford's undoubted dismay, the rejuvenated Mustang earned decidedly mixed reviews. While road-testers rightly lauded the many upgrades, there was general head-scratching over the GT's 60-bhp deficit with the latest Camaro Z28 and Firebird Trans Am. "The carryover power may challenge the loyalty of some...fans," mused *Car and Driver*, "[though] with substantial improvements in braking and body structure, the Mustang [GT still] offers tremendous performance for the dollar." As if to prove the point, *C/D*'s five-speed coupe clocked 0-60 mph in just 6.1 seconds and the standing quarter-mile in 14.9 at 93 mph—not bad for a 30-year-old engine. The automatic version was no slouch either, *Consumer Guide*®'s coupe running 0-60 in a brisk 7.4 seconds.

Still, the power/performance gap with GM suggested sights had not been set very high. And indeed, Dearborn admitted the '94 was designed mainly to please the 6.1 million people who'd bought Mustangs since day one. From a sales standpoint, that wasn't a bad plan. As *Motor Trend* observed: "Mustang fans have been deprived of a new platform for so long they would've accepted almost anything with a chrome horse on it." And, of

1991 LX 5.0L convertible coupe

1993 Cobra hatchback coupe

1995 Cobra R coupe

1996 Cobra coupe

course, they *did* accept it—certainly more enthusiastically than some of the press. And why not? They had, after all, helped to design it. As a thank you, Ford hosted regional parties for Mustang clubs on Sunday, April 17, 1994, exactly 30 years since the original Mustang's smash debut.

But the celebrating didn't end there. Again recalling '60s doings, Ford got a special Cobra convertible named pace car for the '94 Indianapolis 500. Sure enough, Dearborn wasn't entirely conceding the power issue to GM, and by model year's end it had built 6009 new-design Cobras—5009 coupes, and 1000 ragtops, the latter sold as replica Pace Cars.

Another SVT project, the '94 Cobra wore a unique front fascia, low-profile rear spoiler, chrome 17-inch five-spoke wheels with extra-wide Z-rated tires, discreet front-fender snake emblems, and a leather-lined interior with snazzy white-faced gauges. Underneath were bigger brakes with twin front calipers and standard ABS, a GT suspension again made slightly softer for "controlled compliance" handling, and a 302-cid V-8 massaged for... 240 horsepower. Motor-noters heaved more sighs. Even this new Cobra was still 35 horses shy of a standard V-8 Camaro/Firebird.

Car and Driver found the performance gap narrowed, but not much. Though its five-speed coupe ran 0-60 in 5.9 seconds and the standing-quarter in 14.7 at 96 mph, both clockings were a good half-second adrift of a Z28's. The Cobra "is undoubtedly the most muscular Mustang available," *C/D* concluded, "and at $21,240 for the coupe and $24,010 for the convertible, the most expensive. At those prices... we have a hard time imagining that a new breed of customers will be flocking into SVT showrooms [some 750 carefully selected Ford dealers]."

But if Mustang remained runner-up in a drag race, it still easily won the sales race. In fact, with model-year output of just over 137,000, the '94 Mustang came close to outselling Camaro and Firebird combined. Ford also built more ponycars for the calendar year: some 199,000 versus GM's 192,000. Only a bit less impressive, Mustang's showing marked a 16-percent gain on 1993, itself a good year despite the new GM competition.

Though little change was expected for '95, Ford expanded the herd at midseason with the GTS, essentially a GT coupe with base-model trimmings and a friendlier $16,910 price. The year also introduced a new limited-edition Cobra R coupe with a 351-cid V-8. Borrowed from the hot-rod F-150 Lightning pickup, it was Mustang's first 351 since 1973. With 300 bhp and 365 pound-feet of torque, it looked a scorcher on paper, helped by a domed fiberglass hood and another stripped-out interior. But despite more power and less weight, this R would only keep pace with an everyday Z28, *Car and Driver* timing a so-so 5.4 seconds to 60 mph and a 14-second/99-mph quarter-mile. Perhaps it's just as well that only some 250 were built, again mainly for competition.

Making headlines for 1996 were big changes beneath the hood—and to the hood itself. After 40 years of faithful service, the GT's pushrod V-8 was honorably retired in favor of Ford's "modular" 4.6-liter overhead-cam unit. The new iron-block, aluminum-head engine claimed no more power or torque, though, so performance remained on par with the '95 GT. But the 4.6 was smoother than the old "five-point-oh" and ran cleaner, too. It was also taller, prompting a bulged hoodline and structural changes in the engine bay. V-6 models got those too, plus five more horses for 150 total. The only other visual distinctions were a mesh insert for the front air intake and—in a '60s flashback—three-lens taillamps turned from horizontal to vertical.

SVT Cobras also went "mod" for '96, but they got a "premium" V-8 with aluminum block, forged crankshaft, specific dual-overhead-cam cylinder heads, and other upgrades. Horsepower checked in at 305, a solid 90 bhp more than the sohc GT and 65

1996 GT convertible coupe

1997 Cobra coupe

1997 GT convertible coupe

1998 Cobra coupe

1999 35th Anniversary Edition convertible coupe

1999 Cobra convertible coupe

1999 coupe

2000 convertible coupe

2000 Cobra convertible coupe

2001 GT coupe

better than the '95 Cobra. Torque was 300 pound-feet, matching GM's hottest stock ponycars at last. Still, the twincam engine only leveled the playing field while changing the Cobra's character in a way some disliked. That's because it thrived on revs—"Anything under about 3500 rpm is bogging-down territory," said one tester—with relatively weak low-end torque that demanded liberal use of the mandatory five-speed gearbox. Still, a three-way *Car and Driver* showdown put the SVT ahead of a top-power Firebird Formula and just slightly behind a similarly optioned Camaro SS. The Cobra was "the best daily-driver muscle car," said the editors, "the one car we would most want to drive home at the end of a long day."

Despite the new engines, model-year production dropped a steep 27 percent for '96, skidding to 135,620. Cobras accounted for 10,006 of those units, the most SVT could turn out in a single year. The '97 lineup showed very few changes, but demand dove again, losing 20 percent year-on-year at 108,344, though Cobra volume stayed about the same.

Model-year '98 output jumped 62 percent to 175,522 units. Though that surely pleased Ford, the sales spurt was tough to figure, as changes were again modest. Engineers pulled another 10 bhp from the GT V-8, though performance was scarcely affected, and dealers began selling SVT "off-highway" parts—including a supercharger kit—to speed-seeking customers. All models got safer, "depowered" airbags per federal decree, and GTs added a $595 Sport Group with 17-inch wheels, engine oil cooler, and stripes on the hood and fenders. A new $345 V-6 Sport Appearance Group bundled 16-inch alloy wheels and a rear spoiler with body accent stripes and a leather-wrapped steering wheel.

A reskin highlighted an extensive 1999 makeover intended to keep the S95 going a few more years. Described by *Road & Track* as "Ford's New Edge goes retro," the freshened exterior combined traditional Mustang cues with elements then being applied to other Blue Oval cars. Body lines went from softly rounded to knife-edge crisp, head- and taillamps were reshaped to suit, and there was new emphasis on air slots, both functional (grille, lower front-fascia intake) and fake (vertical appliqués ahead of the rear wheels, an indented "sugar scoop"on the hood). Even the grille's galloping horse was put back in its "corral." Another nod to the past appeared on the front fenders: "pony tricolor" badges celebrating Mustang's 35th year. But it wasn't all about visuals. Fully boxed chassis rails increased structural stiffness, and GT spring rates were recalibrated to improve handling.

More power was also on the '99 agenda, and in useful doses. The 3.8-liter V-6 gained a sizable 40 bhp to reach 190 total, thanks to a new intake manifold, freer-flowing cylinder heads, and lower-friction pistons. It also added five pound-feet of torque, plus a vibration-damping "balance shaft" that was just as welcome as the extra grunt. The 4.6-liter GT V-8 also muscled-up, swelling by 35 bhp to 260 via bigger valves, higher-lift camshaft, freer-flow intake and exhaust, and other measures. A laudable new option for GT performance and safety was electronic traction control, which could apply the rear brakes and/or reduce engine power to minimize wheelspin. Priced at $230, it was a great supplement to the antilock brakes (ABS) that remained standard for GTs and optional for V-6 models.

The 1999 Mustangs got a mostly thumbs-up reception. All models earned praise for melding a tighter driving feel and meatier steering with a more supple ride and less cabin noise. *R&T* pronounced the fortified V-6 "a respectable performer. It's not as quick or smooth as the GT, but it's no slouch." As for the GT itself, *Motor Trend* judged the '99 edition "as good or better than any stock Mustang we've ever tested, Cobra or not." Its manual coupe dispatched 0-60 mph in a swift 5.4 seconds, the

2001 GT Bullitt coupe

2002 coupe

2002 GT convertible coupe

quarter-mile in 14 seconds at 100.2 mph.

Styling drew the most criticism. Design VP Jack Telnack had developed "New Edge" as both a follow-on and an antidote to his aerodynamic "jellybean" look, which had been so widely imitated it now seemed stale. But the new geometric lines fit uneasily on the SN95 bodies. *AutoWeek*, in fact, likened the '99 coupe as "akin to putting a baseball cap on a shoebox."

Buyers might have felt uneasy too, as model-year volume dropped by nearly a fourth from 1998 to 133,367 units. The "dot-bomb" debacle and other bad economic news didn't help, nor did higher prices for the many '99 upgrades: up $500 on V-6 models, $900 on GTs, lifting the range to $16,500-$25,000.

As usual, the SVT Cobra coupe and convertible bowed a few months after the mainstream models. The '99s naturally shared all the latest improvements and offered a few of their own. New "tumble-port" cylinder heads and other tweaks added 15 bhp to bring the twincam V-8 to 320 bhp, the same as the top-option Camaro/Firebird. Traction control and ABS were standard here, joined by big new Brembo-brand disc brakes.

But the most talked about SVT innovation for 1999 was Mustang's first independent rear suspension. IRS had been an on-and-off rumor since 1965. Now it was reality, consisting of high-rate coil springs, lower control arms, and upper toe-control links, plus a thicker-than-stock antiroll bar. It was all mounted to a welded-up tubular subframe along with an aluminum-case differential (purloined from the late Lincoln Mark VII coupe) and Cobra-specific halfshafts. Cleverly, SVT engineered this assembly as an easy bolt-in on the regular Mustang line; the existing floorpan and body structure required drilling only two holes for bolts and "weld nuts."

Yet for all its wizard engineering, the '99 Cobra was a puzzle. To be sure, the IRS erased 110 pounds of curb weight and 125 in unwanted unsprung weight, so the Cobra was now more balanced and "pointable" than the live-axle GT. It was also less prone to bump-steer on its softer springs, which also furnished a more compliant ride. But these benefits weren't usually manifest on the road and were hard to discern on the track. In fact, the Cobra did little better than the GT in *Motor Trend*'s skidpad and slalom tests. "Viewed in this way," the magazine concluded, "the SVT superpony seems hardly worth [its] extra $7000."

The fortified engine was a mystery, too. Testers found the Cobra slower than its 320 bhp implied, and some owners found with dynamometer tests that some 30 horsepower were AWOL. The explanation turned out to be a batch of improperly made intake runners and exhaust components delivered by a Ford supplier. To its credit, SVT recalled all '99 Cobras on the ground for free repairs. But it was a time-consuming effort for the small team, enough that they decided to skip a 2000 model. But they did manage a "consolation prize" in another Cobra R, this time with 385-bhp *5.4-liter* V-8. It was the fastest factory Mustang yet, capable of 0-60 in under 5.0 seconds, a 13-second quarter-mile, and a stunning 1g on the skidpad. The 2000 R was costly for a 'Stang—$54,995—but included a high-flying rear spoiler, deep front air dam, huge Brembo brakes, and genuine Recaro seats. Only 300 were built, all red coupes. They sold in a trice.

While the SVT episode played out, Ford happily observed Mustang's 35th birthday in April 1999, hosting huge gatherings of the faithful at Charlotte Motor Speedway and in Southern California (as it had five years before). Also honoring the occasion was a $2695 35th Anniversary trim package applied to about 5000 GTs, marked by a raised scoop on a black-striped hood, black/silver interior, and other unique touches. At year's end, the U.S. Postal Service issued a stamp honoring Mustang as one of 15 American icons of the 1960s. Pictured thereon was—what else?—a red '65 convertible.

With the parties over, regular Mustangs saw predictably little change for 2000. GTs gained standard ABS, while V-6 models were granted a trim option that gave them most of the GT's appearance features, plus the same wheels and tires. Prices were hiked a modest $50-$150. Despite a worsening economy and little new to show, sales turned up on a *calendar-year* basis, rising 4.1 percent to nearly 173,700.

The 2001 total was just over 169,000 despite some encouraging developments. For starters, the Cobra returned with all 320 horses accounted for. *Car and Driver* put two on a dynamometer just to be sure, then reeled off 0-60 mph in 4.8 seconds and a satisfying 13.5-second quarter-mile at 105 mph. Even better, *C/D* decided "the Cobra has left its crude ponycar roots and joined the ranks of competent sports coupes... Now you can point [it] exactly where you want and assume it will go there." The result, *C/D* said, was nothing short of a Cobra transformation... a superb all-rounder."

Only a bit less thrilling was the midyear "Bullitt" coupe, a specially equipped GT previewed by a concept in 2000. It was the brainchild by J Mays, who'd come to Ford in late 1997 to succeed the retiring Jack Telnack as corporate design chief. Mays, who is credited with the ultraclean Audi TT, saw problems with '99 Mustang styling and tried to "correct" them here, omitting the rear spoiler and adding a unique hood scoop, side scoops, rear-roof trim and rocker moldings, plus an aluminum fuel-filler flap. Inside were specific leather-covered seats, an aluminum shift knob and pedal trim, '60s-style gauge graphics, and chrome doorsill plates with "Bullitt" in art deco type. The entire package paid homage to the 1968 cult film in which Steve McQueen raced a dark-green Mustang 390 fastback against a bad guy's Dodge Charger through the streets of San Francisco in one of the most exciting car chases in Hollywood history.

But the Bullitt was more than cosmetics. It had to be for "street credibility" in evoking such a famed forebear. Upgrades began with the engine, which gained a larger throttle body, cast-aluminum intake manifold, smaller accessory-drive pulleys, and a freer-flowing exhaust system. The result was 265 bhp, only 5 more than the stock GT, but with a slightly fatter torque curve and a subtle but noticeable difference in the engine's sound and feel. Ride height lowered by ¾-inch combined with specific strut/shock units, antiroll bars, and what Ford called "frame rail connectors" to deliver the best ride and handling of any non-Cobra Mustang. Brawny 13-inch front brake rotors clamped by red-painted calipers gave first-rate stopping power.

The Bullitt cost $3500 more than a stock GT coupe, yet was little, if any quicker. But it was quick to move out of showrooms, and dealers reportedly had no trouble selling the planned 6500-unit one-year run at or above sticker price ($28,230). Most Bullitts were painted Highland Green Metallic, just like McQueen's movie Mustang, though a somber black and blue were available for less-sentimental types.

Motor Trend reported that the Bullitt was to be "the first in a series of short-term specials designed to bring extra excitement and collectibility into the current [line]." Excitement was surely needed for 2002. The Cobra was a no-show, while the only other news involved turning popular option groups into separate models with dull names: Base Standard, Deluxe, and Premium with V-6, plus Deluxe and Premium GTs. Calendar-year sales duly dropped again, falling to some 138,400, a worrisome 18.2-percent slide in a year when zero-percent financing had stoked the general market to red hot. The one consolation was GM's announcement that 2002 would the last year for the slow-selling Camaro/Firebird so long outpaced by Mustang.

Happily for Ford Motor Company, its 2003 centennial year saw Mustang sales hold steady, aided in part by two new sizzlers. Arriving first, in spring '02, was an SVT Cobra packing a huge new supercharged wallop of 390 bhp and 390 pound-feet of torque. Accommodating the blower dictated numerous changes to the twincam V-8. Chief among them were an iron block to ensure durability under pressure, a water-to-air intercooler, new heads, and different pistons with suitably lower compression (8.5:1). The only transmission was a Tremec six-speed manual, a legacy of the '00 Cobra R. The suspension was naturally retuned, and rolling stock was upgraded to inch-wider cast-alloy wheels with high-speed 275/40ZR rubber. Other modifications included a vented hood (to counter the blower's added engine-bay heat), revised front fascia and rocker panels, an air diffuser beneath the back bumper, and a lower-profile spoiler. With all this, SVT's latest Mustang delivered near 2000 Cobra R thrust at a much friendlier price: $33,460 to start. The stats told the tale: 0-60 mph in 4.5-4.9 seconds, quarter-mile ETs around 13 seconds, 0.90g skidpad stick. Yet this Cobra was also quite happy to be your daily commuter. "You might not call it refined, said *Road & Track*, but "it's refined enough for those who elevate performance and affordability...above ultimate sophistication."

Even more affordable was the Bullitt's 2003 follow-up, a new Mach 1, the first in 25 years. Another variation on the GT coupe, it carried an unblown Cobra V-8 tuned for 300 bhp and topped

2003 Mach I coupe

2003 Premium Centennial Edition convertible coupe

2003 SVT Cobra convertible coupe

2004 GT 40th Anniversary Edition coupe

by a functional "shaker" hood scoop straight out of the '60s. It cost a stout $3715 more than a GT Premium coupe, but the extra money also bought a six-speed manual gearbox, slightly lowered suspension, Brembo brakes, unique exterior touches and "comfort weave" leather upholstery.

Reaction was fairly predictable. Despite a dated basic design, the revived Mach 1 earned the runner-up spot in a *Car and Driver* comparison with three high-tech import-brand sporty cars. Why? "Brute fun. Drop the hammer [and] 60 mph is yours in a scalding 5.2 seconds...the fastest time in this test...[It] is an ode to the past. Perhaps Henry Ford was wrong. History isn't bunk. It's a hoot."

History figured into three more blasts from Mustang's past

2004 SVT Cobra coupe

2005 GT coupe

for 2003. The GT-style appearance group for V-6 models was retitled Pony Package, recalling a popular 1965-66 option. Joining it later in the season was a $995 GT Centennial Package with two-tone leather interior, mandatory black paint, and special badging. A similar ensemble made up a $1495 Cobra 10th Anniversary group for the SVT.

Still, the trusty old steed was obviously marking time, and everyone knew a frisky new filly was on the way. Ford heralded the next Mustang in January 2003 by unveiling a pair of "modern retro" concepts, an eye-grabbing convertible and a fastback coupe, at the Los Angeles and Detroit Auto Shows.

The SN95 thus made one last run for 2004. Pundits didn't expect much change—and didn't get it. Still, the Mach 1 added 10 horses and V-6 models three, and the Cobra got striking "Mystichrome" paint—a high-tech finish that seemed to change color depending on ambient light and the beholder's vantage point—as an exclusive $3650 option.

But wasn't 2004 Mustang's 40th anniversary year? Yes indeed, Ford said, notwithstanding its inconsistency over the years as to whether the first ponycar was a 1964 or a very early '65. No matter. The obligatory gilding was duly laid on, an $895 kit for Premium-grade V-6s and GTs. This bundled the stand-alone Interior Upgrade Package with unique wheels, fold-in mirrors, and special birthday trim while deleting the stock rear spoiler. All very low-key for such a milestone event, but announced in time for another. On November 20, 2003, a 40th Anniversary ragtop came off the Dearborn line as Ford Motor Company's 300-millionth vehicle.

With that, the stage was set for the history-making 2005 Mustang, the first new Ford ponycar in a quarter-century and the first *not* based on an existing Dearborn car. Interestingly, Ford had first slated a replacement for 2001 or early '02, but steady SN95 sales prompted designers and engineers to take their time. It was a smart move. After 25 years, Mustangers

2005 GT coupe

would be satisfied with nothing less than a blockbuster.

They got one, and more. Developed as project S197, the 2005 was all-Mustang: Visually arresting, mechanically straightforward, and affordable most of all, but also familiar, yet thoroughly modern. Styling, finalized under design manager Larry Erickson and design VP J Mays, was a masterful mix of early Mustang hallmarks—the '65 C-scoop, the '67 dashboard, the '70 nose—reinterpreted for a new era. Significantly, there were no intramural contests this time, and the only consumer clinics were held at Mustang club events. "We did one [styling prototype]," Mays told one of this book's editors. "We knew what we wanted. I said, 'If we don't know how to design a Mustang, then we should go home.'"

Engineers were no less mindful of the icon entrusted to them. Led by a young Mustang fan named Hau Thai-Tang, they first envisioned adapting the DEW98 platform introduced with the 2000 Lincoln LS. But that came with an independent rear suspension deemed too expensive for Mustang's price range; besides, Mustangers told Ford they *wanted* to keep a solid rear axle. Moreover, "Due 98" was too narrow for Mustang's V-8, and modifications to accommodate that engine—as well as the required four-seat convertible—would have cost a bundle. Most of all, the Lincoln platform didn't work with the change in production venue decreed for the '05 Mustang. For better quality and to align build costs more closely to anticipated sales, Ford decided to move Mustang production from the old Rouge plant to AutoAlliance, the facility it operated with Japanese partner Mazda, where the new ponycars would roll down the same line as Mazda 6 sedans. In the end, it was just easier and cheaper to start fresh.

Nonetheless, the S197 Mustang did inherit a few things from DEW98, and Ford said the finished car shared some 35 percent of its components with other Dearborn products. But the sharing wasn't obvious, and the car drove beautifully—light years better than SN95. Key figures in making it all work so well were project engineering manager Bob Johnson, driving dynamics manager Mark Rushbrook, packaging supervisor Keith Knudsen, and interior design manager Kevin George. Besides their talents, development relied on the most extensive use of computerized simulation in Ford's long history. This not only helped save time and money, it ensured all team members were always literally on the same page. Another benefit was that the very first running prototypes were right on spec. Even so, the team spent more than a year fine-tuning some 6000 different variables in on-road trials from Arizona to Sweden, including a nonstop 24-hour tour of Ohio's Nelson Ledges race course.

2005 convertible coupe

The new-millennium Mustang launched in late 2004 with four fastback coupes: V-6 Base and V-8 GT, each in Deluxe and Premium versions. Lower-priced Base Standards joined in for 2006. Base models dumped the old pushrod 3.8 V-6 for the overhead-cam 4.0-liter unit familiar from the Explorer SUV and other Ford trucks. In the Mustang it furnished 210 bhp—up 20 horses—and 240 pound-feet of torque. A 4.6-liter sohc V-8 continued for GTs, but acquired new heads with three valves per cylinder, variable cam timing, and a computer-controlled intake flap that effectively varied port size for better cylinder filling and more efficient combustion. These and other measures combined to add 40 bhp, bring the horse count to a nice round 300, not a startling output by contemporary standards but a new high for a mainstream Mustang. Torque also improved, swelling 13 pound-feet to 320. Both engines arrived with electronic "drive-by-wire" throttle control, a state-of-the-art aid to enhance fuel economy and lower emissions. A revised five-speed manual gearbox was standard with both mills, but the optional automatic was also a five-speed now, the same transmission used in the Ford Thunderbird and Lincoln LS.

To the engineers' credit, S197 ended up larger but little heavier than SN95, coupes scaling 3300-3500 pounds depending on

2006 coupe with V-6 Pony Package

2007 Shelby Cobra GT500 coupe

2007 Shelby Cobra GT500 convertible coupe

powertrain. Wheelbase had been lengthened nearly six inches, and the front wheels were moved ahead five inches. This made for more even front/rear weight distribution (53/47 percent), which, in turn, worked with 2.4-inch-wider tracks to benefit handling. Overall, S197 stood 4.4 inches longer than SN95, 1.4 inches taller, and 0.8 inch wider. Most interior dimensions expanded as a result, but this was still a two-adults-plus-two-kids car. Coupes added 1.4 cubic feet of trunk space, plus fold-down rear seatbacks.

Though a solid rear axle seemed downright antique in 2005, it was better controlled with twin lower trailing links, a single upper link, and a lateral Panhard rod. Coil springs continued at both ends, as did standard antiroll bars for all models. Struts reprised at the front, but were now located by L-shaped lower arms, while springs remounted from the arms to the struts gave a more precise feel to the power rack-and-pinion steering. All models came with four-wheel disc brakes. ABS with traction control remained standard for GTs and available for V-6s. A new plus for "passive safety" were optional front side airbags providing both head and torso protection.

As expected, convertibles joined the new herd for a timely spring 2005 rollout, offered in the same trim levels as coupes. S197 had been engineered from the get-go for open-air fun, and it paid off with the tightest, most solid-feeling ragtop Mustangs ever—a match for even many vaunted European convertibles. So, too, the fabric roof with its full interior lining and a new compact "Z-fold" mechanism, plus standard power operation and electrically defrosted glass window. Convertibles got slightly softer suspension tuning than coupes in the interest of ride comfort, yet they handled virtually as well, with crisp turn-in, modest cornering lean, and poised, predictable moves.

All told, the 2005 Mustang looked a surefire sales hit, but even Ford was surprised by the overwhelming public response. The new models almost flew out of showrooms—nearly 161,000 for the calendar year—and mostly without the profit-draining incentives that automakers hated and consumers had come to expect. So great was the clamor that some early buyers willingly paid above sticker, especially for GTs, which sold faster than Ford expected and were in short supply for a time.

Not that pricing was an issue for most folks. If anything, it made the new pony even more of a "gotta-have." The V-6 coupe started under $19,000, the GT coupe at around $25,000. Equivalent ragtops ran some $4800 higher. Considering what that money bought in twenty-ought-five, any model was darn near irresistible. Then again, high "bang for the buck" has always been Mustang's stock-in-trade.

Inevitably, a few things were sacrificed on the altar of affordability. Most every road-tester complained about cut-rate interior materials, and the "new" V-6 was really a very old basic design with nowhere near the refinement of most rival sixes. There was also general carping about sundry ergonomic details, steering both too light and too quick for best control—and, as ever, rear-axle hop under full power, especially in GTs, though it was less irksome than before.

But no car is perfect, and the new Mustang's virtues made it easy to forgive its vices. *Car and Driver* did, lauding a V-6 coupe for doing a brisk 6.9 seconds 0-60 mph—with *automatic*. The same journal compared a GT coupe with the sophomore edition of Pontiac's reborn GTO, both manually shifted. When the dust settled, the editors picked the Mustang, even though it trailed in the 0-60 mph dash (by 0.3-second at 5.1) and in the quarter-mile sprint (13.8 seconds at 103 mph, 0.5-sec and 4 mph in arrears). Styling and"character" had a lot to do with their choice, but "the Mustang wins because... as a total package [it] makes better sense. Pick apart the Mustang's laundry list of simple components and it will seem to be less of a car than the GTO, but drive the Mustang, and it feels like far more than the sum of its parts. That is the draw... It makes the most of what it has, doesn't suffer for what it doesn't have, charges you less than you'd expect, and beckons [you to] take it home." *Consumer Guide*® waited a year before naming Mustang a Best Buy, but its reasoning was not unlike *C/D*'s. "[It's] mainly for the GT versions, but V-6 Mustangs don't lack bang-for-the-buck appeal... GTs deliver great go for relatively little dough, and all convertibles blend value, verve, and nominal four-seat practicality. Mustang's main letdowns are low-rent cabin appointments and occasional workmanship lapses."

Few changes occurred for 2006; not that many were needed. Ford still couldn't build new Mustangs fast enough. Still, GTs added extra-cost 18-inch wheels, and an optional Pony package returned for Premium-grade V-6s, bundling ABS and traction control with GT-style visuals for $1195.

Meanwhile, leadfoots were drooling at the scheduled summertime release of the most potent production Mustang ever, the 2007 Shelby Cobra GT500. Developed by SVT to replace the Cobra, and previewed with an undisguised coupe "concept" in April 2005, it was an unabashed throwback to the rip-roaring days of Carroll Shelby's Mustang GTs (see *Shelby*), only with far more actual power and speed than the best of that legendary breed possessed. Ol' Shel even helped SVT keep the new GT500 true to his principles, having resumed his relationship with Dearborn a few years before as an advisor on the midengine Ford GT supercar (see *Ford*).

If classic Shelby-Mustangs were liberally dosed with Vitamin HP, this new one was a full-blown steroid case. Lurking within was a supercharged 5.4-liter twincam V-8, basically the 550-bhp Ford GT unit with a less-expensive Roots-type blower and milder tuning. Milder? Not really. Horsepower was a thundering 475, torque a stump-pulling 475 pound-feet, according to SVT estimates. This muscle was too much for any automatic on the Ford shelf, so the only transmission was a heavy-duty six-speed manual, familiar from recent Cobras and the race-winning FR Mustangs developed by Ford Racing. Thrust control also dictated a beefed-up suspension, big Brembo disc brakes with pizza-size 14-inch four-caliper rotors up front, and sticky high-performance tires sized at 255/45ZR18 up front and a massive 285/40ZR18 out back.

Aerodynamics received special attention. What else for a car able to reach 160 mph—with a speed governor? The wind-tunnel work was extensive, though not easily discerned. The unique "powerdome" hood, for example, had small built-in "heat extractors" near its leading edge, which served to cool the engine bay—vital with a "blown" engine—without disrupting air flow. Competition experience also brought forth a modest "air splitter" at the base of the nose, an air "diffuser" below the rear bumper, and a carefully shaped "ducktail" decklid spoiler, all designed to optimize high-speed stability. Optimizing visual impact at any speed were a menacing "big mouth" grille and Shelby-traditional rocker-panel stripes, wide dorsal "Le Mans" striping, large "Shelby" lettering on the tail, and chrome snake insignia on the grille and fuel-filler cap. More, er, vipers showed up inside, along with heavily bolstered front seats and leather upholstery in black or black/crimson. Other unique cockpit touches included satin-finish aluminum trim to replace chrome, white-faced gauges per SVT custom, and swapped speedometer and tachometer positions so drivers could more easily see when to shift.

Recalling 1968 Shelbys, the new GT500 was offered in both coupe and convertible form. The development program was led by none other than Hau Thai-Tang, recently promoted to director of Advanced Product Creation and head of SVT. "Our goal was to build the most powerful, most capable Mustang *ever*," he declared. *Car and Driver*'s first impressions, gleaned from brief runs granted in a late GT500 prototype, suggested that was no idle boast. The magazine demurred on instrumented tests, as some details weren't yet final. However, it found Ford's performance claims quite credible, estimating 0-60 mph in four seconds flat, a 12.5-second quarter-mile at 116 mph, and at least 0.94g of skidpad grip. With that, the reborn Shelby Mustang looked at least the equal of a new C6 Chevrolet Corvette, yet would likely sell for thousands less, perhaps as low as $39,000. *C/D*'s reporter also praised the muscle Mustang's swift braking, agile handling, and surprisingly supple ride motions. The one dynamic demerit cited was slightly overboosted steering, especially in exuberant cornering.

So Mustang gallops on, better than ever and with an apparently bright future, notwithstanding the many challenges facing Ford Motor Company as of press time. But whatever lies ahead, it's safe to say that everybody still loves the Mustang, and that's reassuring in an ever-more uncertain automotive world.

Specifications

1965

(wb 108.0)		Wght	Price	Prod
07	htp cpe	2,583	2,372	501,965
08	conv cpe	2,789	2,614	101,945
09	fstbk cpe	2,633	2,589	77,079

1965 Engines	bore×stroke	bhp	availability
I-6, 170.0	3.50×2.94	101	S-all thru 9/24/64
I-6, 200.0	3.68×3.13	120	S-all aft 9/24/64
V-8, 260.0	3.80×2.87	164	O-all thru 9/24/64
V-8, 289.0	4.00×2.87	200	O-all aft 9/24/64
V-8, 289.0	4.00×2.87	225/271	O-all

Note: 1965 production totals include 121,538 early (4/64-9/24/64) models.

1966

(wb 108.0)		Wght	Price	Prod
01	htp cpe	2,488	2,416	499,751
02	fstbk cpe	2,519	2,607	35,698
03	conv cpe	2,650	2,653	72,119

1966 Engines	bore×stroke	bhp	availability
I-6, 200.0	3.68×3.13	120	S-all
V-8, 289.0	4.00×2.87	200	O-all
V-8, 289.0	4.00×2.87	225/271	O-all

1967

(wb 108.0)		Wght	Price	Prod
01	htp cpe	2,568	2,461	356,271
02	fstbk cpe	2,605	2,592	71,042
03	conv cpe	2,738	2,698	44,808

1967 Engines	bore×stroke	bhp	availability
I-6, 200.0	3.68×3.13	120	S-all
V-8, 289.0	4.00×2.87	200	O-all
V-8, 289.0	4.00×2.87	225/271	O-all
V-8, 390.0	4.05×3.78	320	O-all

1968

(wb 108.0)		Wght	Price	Prod
01	htp cpe	2,635	2,602	249,447
02	fstbk cpe	2,659	2,712	42,581
03	conv cpe	2,745	2,814	25,376

1968 Engines	bore×stroke	bhp	availability
I-6, 200.0	3.68×3.13	115	S-all
I-6, 250.0	3.68×3.91	155	O-all (late)
V-8, 289.0	4.00×2.87	195	O-all
V-8, 302.0	4.00×3.00	220	O-all
V-8, 390.0	4.05×3.78	335	O-all
V-8, 427.0	4.23×3.78	390	O-all
V-8, 428.0	4.13×3.98	335	O-all (late)

1969

(wb 108.0)		Wght	Price	Prod
01	htp cpe	2,798	2,635	128,458
02	fstbk cpe	2,822	2,635	60,046
02	Boss 302 fstbk cpe,V-8	3,210	3,588	1,628
02	Boss 429 fstbk cpe,V-8	—	4,798	858
03	conv cpe	2,908	2,849	14,746
04	Grandé htp cpe	2,873	2,866	22,182
05	Mach 1 fstbk cpe	3,175	3,139	72,458

1969 Engines	bore×stroke	bhp	availability
I-6, 200.0	3.68×3.13	115	S-all exc Mach 1, Boss
I-6, 250.0	3.68×3.91	155	O-all exc Mach 1, Boss
V-8, 302.0	4.00×3.00	220	O-all exc Mach 1, Boss
V-8, 302.0	4.00×3.00	290	S-Boss 302
V-8, 351.0	4.00×3.50	250	S-Mach 1; O-others exc Boss
V-8, 351.0	4.00×3.50	290	O-all
V-8, 390.0	4.05×3.78	320	O-all
V-8, 428.0	4.13×3.98	335	O-Mach 1 (Ram Air avail)
V-8, 429.0	4.36×3.59	360/375	S-Boss 429

1970

(wb 108.0)		Wght	Price	Prod
01	htp cpe	2,822	2,721	82,569
02	fstbk cpe	2,846	2,771	39,316
02	Boss 302 fstbk cpe,V-8	3,227	3,720	7,013
02	Boss 429 fstbk cpe,V-8	—	4,798	498
03	conv cpe	2,932	3,025	7,673
04	Grandé htp cpe	2,907	2,926	13,581
05	Mach 1 cpe	3,240	3,271	40,970

1970 Engines	bore×stroke	bhp	availability
I-6, 200.0	3.68×3.13	115	S-all exc Mach 1, Boss
I-6, 250.0	3.68×3.91	155	O-all exc Mach 1, Boss
V-8, 302.0	4.00×3.00	220	O-all exc Mach 1, Boss
V-8, 302.0	4.00×3.00	290	S-Boss 302
V-8, 351.0	4.00×3.50	250	S-Mach 1; O-others exc Boss
V-8, 351.0	4.00×3.50	300	O-all exc Boss
V-8, 428.0	4.13×3.98	335	O-Mach 1 (Ram Air avail)
V-8, 429.0	4.36×3.59	375	S-Boss 429, O-Mach 1

1971

(wb 109.0)		Wght	Price	Prod
01	htp cpe	2,982	2,911	65,696
02	fstbk cpe	2,950	2,973	23,956
02	Boss 351 fstbk cpe V-8	3,281	4,124	
03	conv	3,102	3,227	6,121
04	Grandé htp cpe	3,006	3,117	17,406
05	Mach 1 fstbk cpe V-8	3,220	3,268	36,499

1971 Engines	bore×stroke	bhp	availability
I-6, 250.0	3.68×3.91	145	S-all exc Mach 1, Boss 351
V-8, 302.0	4.00×3.00	210	O-all exc Boss 351
V-8, 351.0	4.00×3.50	240	O-all exc Boss 351
V-8, 351.0	4.00×3.50	285	O-all exc Boss 351
V-8, 351.0	4.00×3.50	330	S-Boss 351; O-others
V-8, 429.0	4.36×3.59	370	O-all

1972

(wb 109.0)		Wght	Price	Prod
01	htp cpe	2,983	2,729	57,350
02	fstbk cpe	2,952	2,786	15,622
03	conv	3,099	3,015	6,401
04	Grandé htp cpe	3,008	2,915	18,045
05	Mach 1 fstbk cpe V-8	3,046	3,053	27,675

1972 Engines	bore×stroke	bhp	availability
I-6, 250.0	3.68×3.91	99	S-all exc Mach 1
V-8, 302.0	4.00×3.00	141	S-Mach 1; O-others
V-8, 351.0	4.00×3.50	177/275	O-all

1973

(wb 109.0)		Wght	Price	Prod
01	htp cpe	3,040	2,760	51,480
02	fstbk cpe	3,053	2,820	10,820
03	conv	3,171	3,102	11,853
04	Grandé htp cpe	3,059	2,946	25,274
05	Mach 1 fstbk cpe V-8	3,115	3,088	35,440

1973 Engines	bore×stroke	bhp	availability
I-6, 250.0	3.68×3.91	95	S-all exc Mach 1
V-8, 302.0	4.00×3.00	136	S-Mach 1; O-others
V-8, 351.0	4.00×3.50	154/156	O-all

Ford Mustang

1974

II (wb 96.2)		Wght	Price	Prod
02	cpe 2d	2,654	3,134	177,671
03	htchbk cpe 3d	2,734	3,328	74,799
04	Ghia cpe 2d	2,820	3,480	89,477
05	Mach 1 htchbk cpe 3d V-6	2,778	3,674	44,046

1974 Engines	bore×stroke	bhp	availability
I-4, 140.0	3.78×3.13	88	S-all exc Mach 1
V-6, 170.0	3.66×2.70	105	S-Mach 1; O-others

1975

II (wb 96.2)		Wght	Price	Prod
02	cpe 2d	2,718	3,529	85,155
03	htchbk cpe 3d	2,754	3,818	30,038
04	Ghia cpe 2d	2,762	3,938	52,320
05	Mach 1 htchbk cpe 3d V-6	2,879	4,188	21,062

1975 Engines	bore×stroke	bhp	availability
I-4, 140.0	3.78×3.13	83	S-all exc Mach 1
V-6, 170.0	3.66×2.70	97	S-Mach 1; O-others
V-8, 302.0	4.00×3.00	122	O-all

1976

II (wb 96.2)		Wght	Price	Prod
02	cpe 2d	2,717	3,525	78,508
03	htchbk cpe 3d	2,745	3,781	62,312
04	Ghia cpe 2d	2,768	3,859	37,515
05	Mach 1 htchbk cpe V-6 3d	2,822	4,209	9,232

1976 Engines	bore×stroke	bhp	availability
I-4, 140.0	3.78×3.13	92	S-all exc Mach 1
V-6, 170.0	3.66×2.70	103	S-Mach 1; O-others
V-8, 302.0	4.00×3.00	134	O-all

1977

II (wb 96.2)		Wght	Price	Prod
02	cpe 2d	2,688	3,702	67,783
03	htchbk cpe 3d	2,734	3,901	49,161
04	Ghia cpe 2d	2,728	4,119	29,510
05	Mach 1 htchbk cpe V-6 3d	2,785	4,332	6,719

1977 Engines	bore×stroke	bhp	availability
I-4, 140.0	3.78×3.13	89	S-all exc Mach 1
V-6, 170.0	3.66×2.70	93	S-Mach 1; O-others
V-8, 302.0	4.00×3.00	139	O-all

1978

II (wb 96.2)		Wght	Price	Prod
02	cpe 2d	2,656	3,555	81,304
03	htchbk cpe 3d	2,702	3,798	68,408
04	Ghia cpe 2d	2,694	3,972	34,730
05	Mach 1 htchbk cpe V-6 3d	2,733	4,253	7,968

1978 Engines	bore×stroke	bhp	availability
I-4, 140.0	3.78×3.13	88	S-all exc Mach 1
V-6, 170.0	3.66×2.70	90	S-Mach 1; O-others
V-8, 302.0	4.00×3.00	139	O-all

1979

(wb 100.4)		Wght	Price	Prod
02	cpe 2d	2,471	4,071	156,666
03	htchbk cpe 3d	2,491	4,436	120,535
04	Ghia cpe 2d	2,579	4,642	56,351
05	Ghia htchbk cpe 3d	2,588	4,824	36,384

1979 Engines	bore×stroke	bhp	availability
I-4, 140.0	3.78×3.13	88	S-all
I-4T, 140.0	3.78×3.13	140	O-all
V-6, 170.0	3.66×2.70	109	O-all
I-6, 200.0	3.68×3.13	91	O-all (late)
V-8, 302.0	4.00×3.00	140	O-all

1980

(wb 100.4)		Wght	Price	Prod
02	cpe 2d	2,514	4,884	128,893
03	htchbk cpe 3d	2,548	5,194	98,497
04	Ghia cpe 2d	2,582	5,369	23,647
05	Ghia htchbk cpe 3d	2,606	5,512	20,285

1980 Engines	bore×stroke	bhp	availability
I-4, 140.0	3.78×3.13	88	S-all
I-4T, 140.0	3.78×3.13	140	O-all
I-6, 200.0	3.68×3.13	91	O-all
V-8, 255.0	2.68×3.00	118	O-all

1981

(wb 100.4)		Wght	Price	Prod
10	cpe 2d	2,537	6,171	77,458
15	htchbk cpe 3d	2,557	6,408	77,399
12	Ghia cpe 2d	2,571	6,645	13,422
13	Ghia htchbk cpe 3d	2,606	6,729	14,273

1981 Engines	bore×stroke	bhp	availability
I-4, 140.0	3.78×3.13	88	S-all
I-4T, 140.0	3.78×3.13	140	O-all
I-6, 200.0	3.68×3.13	88/94	O-all
V-8, 255.0	3.68×3.00	115	O-all

1982

(wb 100.4)		Wght	Price	Prod
10	L cpe 2d	2,568	6,345	45,316
10	GL cpe 2d	2,585	6,844	
16	GL htchbk cpe 3d	2,622	6,979	45,901
16	GT htchbk cpe 3d V-8	2,597	8,308	23,447
12	GLX cpe 2d	2,600	6,980	5,828
13	GLX htchbk cpe 3d	2,636	7,101	9,926

1982 Engines	bore×stroke	bhp	availability
I-4, 140.0	3.78×3.13	88	S-all
I-6, 200.0	3.68×3.13	88	O-all
V-8, 255.0	3.68×3.00	120	O-all
V-8, 302.0	4.00×3.00	157	S-GT; O-all

1983

(wb 100.4)		Wght	Price	Prod
26	L cpe 2d	2,684	6,727	
26/60C	GL cpe 2d	2,743	7,264	33,201
26/602	GLX cpe 2d	2,760	7,398	
28/60C	GL htchbk cpe 3d	2,788	7,439	
28/602	GLX htchbk cpe 3d	2,801	7,557	64,234
28/932	GT htchbk cpe 3d V-8	2,969	9,328	
28/932	Trb GT htchbk cpe 3d	—	9,714	
27/602	GLX conv cpe V-6	2,807	12,467	23,438
27/932	GT conv cpe V-8	—	13,479	

1983 Engines	bore×stroke	bhp	availability
I-4, 140.0	3.78×3.13	90	S-all exc conv, GT
I-4T, 140.0	3.78×3.13	142	S-Turbo GT
V-6, 232.0	3.80×3.40	112	S-conv; O-all exc GT
V-8, 302.0	4.00×3.00	175	S-GT; O-others exc Turbo GT

1984

(wb 100.4)		Wght	Price	Prod
26	L cpe 2d	2,736	7,098	37,780
26/602	LX cpe 2d	2,757	7,290	
28	L htchbk cpe 3d	2,782	7,269	
28/602	LX htchbk cpe 3d	2,807	7,496	
28/932	GT htchbk cpe 3d V-8	3,013	9,578	86,200
28/932	Tro GT htchbk cpe 3d	2,869	9,762	
28/939	SVO trb htchbk cpe 3d	2,992	15,596	
27/602	LX conv cpe V-6	3,020	11,849	
27/932	GT conv cpe V-8	3,124	13,051	17,600
27/932	Turbo GT conv cpe	3,004	13,245	

1984 Engines	bore×stroke	bhp	availability
I-4, 140.0	3.78×3.13	88	S-all exc conv, GTs/SVO
I-4T, 140.0	3.78×3.13	145	S-Turbo GT
I-4T, 140.0	3.78×3.13	175	S-SVO
V-6, 232.0	3.80×3.40	120	S-conv; O-all exc GTs, SVO
V-8, 302.0	4.00×3.00	165	O-all exc GTs, SVO
V-8, 302.0	4.00×3.00	175	S-GT

1985

(wb 100.4)		Wght	Price	Prod
26/602	LX cpe 2d	2,657	6,885	56,781
28/602	LX htchbk cpe 3d	2,729	7,345	
28/932	GT htchbk cpe 3d V-8	3,063	9,885	84,623
28/939	SVO trb htchbk cpe 3d	2,991	14,521	
27/602	LX conv cpe V-6	2,907	11,985	15,110
27/932	GT conv cpe V-8	3,165	13,585	

1985 Engines	bore×stroke	bhp	availability
I-4, 140.0	3.78×3.13	88	S-all exc conv, GT, SVO
I-4T, 140.0	3.78×3.13	175	S-SVO
V-6, 232.0	3.80×3.40	120	S-conv; O-all exc GT, SVO
V-8, 302.0	4.00×3.00	180	O-all exc SVO
V-8, 302.0	4.00×3.00	210	S-GT

1986

(wb 100.4)		Wght	Price	Prod
26	LX cpe 2d	2,795	7,189	
27	LX conv cpe V-6	3,044	12,821	106,720
27	GT conv cpe V-8	3,269	14,523	
28	LX htchbk cpe 3d	2,853	7,744	
28	GT htchbk cpe V-8	3,139	10,691	117,690
28/937	SVO trb htchbk cpe 3d	3,140	15,272	

1986 Engines	bore×stroke	bhp	availability
I-4, 140.0	3.78×3.13	88	S-all exc conv, GTs, SVO
I-4T, 140.0	3.78×3.18	200	S-SVO
V-6, 232.0	3.80×3.40	120	S-conv; O-all exc GT, SVO
V-8, 302.0	4.00×3.00	200	S-GT

1987

(wb 100.5) - 159,145 built		Wght	Price	Prod
40	LX cpe 2d	2,862	8,043	
44	LX conv cpe	3,059	12,840	64,704*
45	GT conv cpe V-8	3,214	15,724	
41	LX htchbk cpe 3d	2,920	8,474	94,441*
42	GT htchbk cpe V-8	3,080	11,835	

*Some industry sources state that 58,100 two-doors, 80,717 hatchbacks, and 20,328 convertibles were built.

1987 Engines	bore×stroke	bhp	availability
I-4, 140.0	3.78×3.13	90	S-LX
V-8, 302.0	4.00×3.00	225	S-GT; O-LX

1988

(wb 100.4) - 211,225 built		Wght	Price	Prod
40	LX cpe 2d	2,894	8,726	—
44	LX conv cpe	3,081	13,702	—
45	GT conv cpe V-8	3,341	16,610	—
41	LX htchbk cpe 3d	2,961	9,221	—
42	GT htchbk cpe V-8	3,193	12,745	—

1988 Engines	bore×stroke	bhp	availability
I-4, 140.0	3.78×3.13	90	S-LX
V-8, 302.0	4.00×3.00	225	S-GT; O-LX

1989

(wb 100.4)—209,769 built*		Wght	Price	Prod
40	LX cpe 2d I-4	2,754	9,050	—
40	LX 5.0L cpe 2d V-8	3,045	11,410	—
44	LX conv cpe I-4	2,966	14,140	—
44	LX 5.0L conv cpe V-8	3,257	17,001	—
45	GT conv cpe V-8	3,333	17,512	—
41	LX htchbk cpe 3d I-4	2,819	9,556	—
41	LX 5.0L htchbk 3d V-8	3,110	12,265	—
42	GT htchbk cpe V-8	3,194	13,272	—

* Total includes 42,244 convertibles.

1989 Engines	bore×stroke	bhp	availability
I-4, 140.0	3.78×3.13	90	S-LX
V-8, 302.0	4.00×3.00	225	S-GT, LX 5.0L

1990

(wb 100.4) - 128,189 built*		Wght	Price	Prod
40	LX cpe 2d I-4	2,759	9,456	—
40	LX 5.0L cpe 2d V-8	—	12,164	—
44	LX conv cpe I-4	2,960	15,141	—
44	LX 5.0L conv cpe V-8	—	18,183	—
45	GT conv cpe V-8	—	18,805	—
41	LX htchbk cpe 3d I-4	2,824	9,962	—
41	LX 5.0L htchbk 3d V-8	—	13,007	—
42	GT htchbk cpe V-8	—	13,986	—

* Total includes 26,958 convertibles.

1990 Engines	bore×stroke	bhp	availability
I-4, 140.0	3.78×3.13	88	S-LX
V-8, 302.0	4.00×3.00	225	S-GT, LX 5.0L

1991

(wb 100.5)		Wght	Price	Prod
66/HVS	LX cpe 2d	2,759	10,157	19,447
66/HVS	LX 5.0L cpe 2d	—	13,270	
61/HVS	LX cpe 3d	2,824	10,663	
61/HVS	LX 5.0L cpe 3d	—	14,055	57,777
61/HVB	GT cpe 3d	—	15,034	
66/HVS (B2L)	LX conv cpe 2d	2,960	16,222	
66/HVS (B2I)	LX 5.0L conv cpe 2d	—	19,242	21,513
66/HVS (B2L)	GT conv cpe 2d	—	19,864	

1991 Engines	bore×stroke	bhp	availability
I-4, 140.0	3.78×3.12	105	S-LX
V-8, 302.0	4.00×3.00	225	S-LX 5.0, GT

1992

(wb 100.5)	Wght	Price	Prod
66/HVS LX cpe 2d	2,775	10,215	15,717
66/HVS LX 5.0L cpe 2d	3,010	13,422	
61/HVS LX cpe 3d	2,834	10,721	40,093
61/HVS LX 5.0L cpe 3d	3,069	14,207	
61/HVB GT cpe 3d	3,144	15,243	
66/HVS (B2L) LX conv cpe 2d	2,996	16,899	23,470
66/HVS (B2l) LX 5.0L conv cpe 2d	3,231	19,644	
66/HVS (B2L) GT conv cpe 2d	3,365	20,199	

1992 Engines	bore×stroke	bhp	availability
I-4, 140.0	3.78×3.12	105	S-LX
V-8, 302.0	4.00×3.00	225	S-LX 5.0, GT

1993

(wb 100.5)	Wght	Price	Prod
66/HVS LX cpe 2d	2,751	10,719	24,851
66/HVS LX 5.0L cpe 2d	3,035	13,926	
61/HVS LX cpe 3d	2,812	11,224	56,978
61/HVS LX 5.0L cpe 3d	3,096	14,710	
Cobra cpe 3d	3,255	19,990	5,099
61/HVB GT cpe 3d	3,144	15,747	
66/HVS (B2L) LX conv cpe 2d	2,973	17,548	27,300
66/HVS (B2l) LX 5.0L conv cpe 2d	3,259	20,293	
66/HVS (B2L) GT conv cpe 2d	3,365	20,848	

1993 Engines	bore×stroke	bhp	availability
I-4, 140.0	3.78×3.12	105	S-LX
V-8, 302.0	4.00×3.00	205	S-LX 5.0, GT
V-8, 302.0	4.00×3.00	235	S-Cobra

1994

(wb 101.3)		Wght	Price	Prod
63	cpe 2d	3,065	13,365	84,010
63	GT cpe 2d	3,276	17,280	
	Cobra cpe 2d	3,365	20,765	5,009
76	conv cpe 2d	3,245	20,160	47,055
76	GT conv cpe 2d	3,452	21,970	
	Cobra conv cpe 2d	3,567	23,535	1,000

1994 Engines	bore×stroke	bhp	availability
V-6, 232.0	3.80×3.40	145	S-base
V-8, 302.0	4.00×3.00	215	S-GT
V-8, 302.0	4.00×3.00	240	S-Cobra

1995

(wb 101.3)		Wght	Price	Prod
P40	cpe 2d	3,077	14,330	167,880
P44	conv cpe 2d	3,257	20,795	
—	GTS cpe 2d	—	16,910	
P42	GT cpe 2d	3,280	17,905	
P45	GT conv cpe 2d	3,451	22,595	
P42	Cobra cpe 2d	3,354	21,300	4,005
P45	Cobra conv cpe 2d	3,524	25,605	1,003

1995 Engines	bore×stroke	bhp	availability
V-6, 232.0	3.80×3.40	145	S-base
V-8, 302.0	4.00×3.00	215	S-GT
V-8, 302.0	4.00×3.00	240	S-Cobra

1996

(wb 101.3)		Wght	Price	Prod
P40	cpe 2d	3,065	15,180	99,947
P42	GT cpe 2d	3,278	17,610	
P42	Cobra cpe 2d	3,393	24,810	
P44	conv cpe 2d	3,264	21,060	33,173
P45	GT conv cpe 2d	3,471	23,495	
P45	Cobra conv cpe 2d	3,565	27,580	2,500

1996 Engines	bore×stroke	bhp	availability
V-6, 232.0	3.80×3.40	150	S-base
V-8, 281.0	3.60×3.60	215	S-GT
V-8, 281.0	3.60×3.60	305	S-Cobra (dohc)

1997

(wb 101.3)		Wght	Price	Prod
P40	cpe 2d	3,084	15,355	75,760
P42	GT cpe 2d	3,288	18,000	
P44	conv cpe 2d	3,264	20,755	24,490
P45	GT conv cpe 2d	3,422	23,895	
P42	Cobra cpe 2d	3,404	25,335	7,475
P45	Cobra conv cpe 2d	3,540	28,135	2,525

1997 Engines	bore × stroke	bhp	availability
V-6, 232.0	3.80 × 3.40	150	S-base
V-8, 281.0	3.60 × 3.60	215	S-GT
V-8, 281.0	3.60 × 3.60	305	S-Cobra (dohc)

1998

(wb 101.3) - 149,129 built		Wght	Price	Prod*
P40	cpe 2d	3,065	15,970	—
P42	GT cpe 2d	3,227	19,970	—
P44	conv cpe 2d	3,210	20,470	—
P45	GT conv cpe 2d	3,400	23,970	—
P42	Cobra cpe 2d	3,364	26,400	—
P45	Cobra conv cpe 2d	3,506	30,200	—

1998 Engines	bore×stroke	bhp	availability
V-6, 232.0	3.80×3.40	150	S-base
V-8, 281.0	3.60×3.60	225	S-GT
V-8, 281.0	3.60×3.60	305	S-Cobra (dohc)

* Calendar-year production

1999

(wb 101.3) - 192,889 built		Wght	Price	Prod*
P40	cpe 2d	3,069	16,470	—
P42	GT cpe 2d	—	20,870	—
P44	conv cpe 2d	3,211	21,070	—
P45	GT conv cpe 2d	—	24,870	—
P42	Cobra cpe 2d	—	27,470	—
P45	Cobra conv cpe 2d	—	31,470	—

1999 Engines	bore×stroke	bhp	availability
V-6, 232.0	3.80×3.40	190	S-base
V-8, 281.0	3.60×3.60	260	S-GT
V-8, 281.0	3.60×3.60	320	S-Cobra (dohc)

* Calendar-year production

2000

(wb 101.3) - 181,209 built		Wght	Price	Prod*
P40	cpe 2d	3,066	16,805	—
P42	GT cpe 2d	3,241	22,440	—
P44	conv cpe 2d	3,208	22,220	—
P45	GT conv cpe 2d	3,479	26,695	—

2000 Engines	bore×stroke	bhp	availability
V-6, 232.0	3.80×3.40	190	S-base
V-8, 281.0	3.60×3.60	260	S-GT

* Calendar-year production

2001

(wb 101.3) - 160,964 built		Wght	Price	Prod*
P40	cpe 2d	3,066	16,805	—
P42	GT cpe 2d	3,241	22,440	—
P44	conv cpe 2d	3,208	22,220	—
P45	GT conv cpe 2d	3,379	26,695	—
P42	Cobra cpe 2d	—	28,605	—
P45	Cobra conv cpe 2d	—	32,605	—

2001 Engines	bore×stroke	bhp	availability
V-6, 232.0	3.80×3.40	190	S-base
V-8, 281.0	3.60×3.60	260/265	S-GT/Bullitt
V-8, 281.0	3.60×3.60	320	S-Cobra (dohc)

* Calendar-year production

2002

(wb 101.3) - 171,262 built		Wght	Price	Prod*
P40	Standard cpe 2d	3,066	17,305	—
P40	Deluxe cpe 2d	—	17,910	—
P40	Premium cpe 2d	—	19,025	—
P42	GT Deluxe cpe 2d	3,241	22,965	—
P42	GT Premium cpe 2d	—	24,135	—
P44	Deluxe conv cpe 2d	3,208	22,745	—
P44	Premium conv cpe 2d	—	25,330	—
P45	GT Delx conv cpe 2d	3,379	27,220	—
P45	GT Prem conv cpe 2d	—	28,390	—

2002 Engines	bore×stroke	bhp	availability
V-6, 232.0	3.80×3.40	190	S-base
V-8, 281.0	3.60×3.60	260	S-GT

* Calendar-year production

2003

(wb 101.3) - 154,937 built		Wght	Price	Prod*
P40	Standard cpe 2d	3,114	17,475	—
P40	Deluxe cpe 2d	3,114	18,205	—
P40	Premium cpe 2d	3,114	19,320	—
P42	GT Deluxe cpe 2d	3,273	23,345	—
P42	GT Premium cpe 2d	3,273	24,515	—
P42	Mach I Prem cpe 2d	—	28,705	—
P48	Cobra cpe 2d	—	33,125	—
P44	Deluxe conv cpe 2d	3,254	18,205	—
P44	Prem conv cpe 2d	—	25,730	—
P45	GT Delx conv cpe 2d	3,429	27,620	—
P45	GT Prem conv cpe 2d	3,429	27,770	—
P49	Cobra conv cpe 2d	—	37,370	—

2003 Engines	bore×stroke	bhp	availability
V-6, 232.0	3.80×3.40	190	S-base
V-8, 281.0	3.60×3.60	260	S-GT
V-8, 281.0	3.60×3.60	300	S-Mach I
V-8S, 281.0	3.60×3.60	390	S-Cobra

* Calendar-year production.

2004

(wb 101.3) - 69,704 built		Wght	Price	Prod*
P40	Standard cpe 2d	3,114	17,720	—
P40	Deluxe cpe 2d	3,114	18,450	—
P40	Premium cpe 2d	3,114	19,105	—
P42	GT Deluxe cpe 2d	3,273	23,245	—
P42	GT Premium cpe 2d	3,273	24,415	—
P42	Mach I Prem cpe 2d	—	28,820	—
P48	Cobra cpe 2d	—	33,575	—
P44	Deluxe conv cpe 2d	3,254	23,455	—
P44	Prem conv cpe 2d	—	25,580	—
P45	GT Delx conv cpe 2d	3,429	27,585	—
P45	GT Prem conv cpe 2d	3,429	28,755	—
P49	Cobra conv cpe 2d	—	37,950	—

2004 Engines	bore×stroke	bhp	availability
V-6, 232.0	3.80×3.40	193	S-base
V-8, 281.0	3.60×3.60	260	S-GT
V-8, 281.0	3.60×3.60	310	S-Mach I
V-8S, 281.0	3.60×3.60	390	S-Cobra

* Calendar-year production.

2005

(wb 107.1) - 198,416 built		Wght	Price	Prod*
T80	Deluxe cpe 2d	3,300	18,785	—
T80	Premium cpe 2d	3,300	19,370	—
T82	GT Deluxe cpe 2d	3,450	24,370	—
T82	GT Premium cpe 2d	3,450	25,705	—
T84	Deluxe conv cpe 2d	3,476	23,940	—
T84	Prem conv cpe 2d	3,476	24,815	—
T85	GT Delx conv cpe 2d	3,614	29,565	—
T85	GT Prem conv cpe 2d	3,614	30,745	—

2005 Engines	bore×stroke	bhp	availability
V-6, 245.0	3.95×3.32	210	S-base
V-8, 281.0	3.60×3.60	300	S-GT

* Calendar-year production.

2006

(wb 107.1)		Wght	Price	Prod**
T80	Standard cpe 2d	3,352	19,115	—
T80	Deluxe cpe 2d	3,352	19,215	—
T80	Premium cpe 2d	3,352	20,090	—
T82	GT Deluxe cpe 2d	3,356	25,140	—
T82	GT Premium cpe 2d	3,356	26,320	—
T84	Standard conv cpe 2d	3,477	23,940	—
T84	Deluxe conv cpe 2d	3,477	24,040	—
T84	Prem conv cpe 2d	3,477	24,915	—
T85	GT Delx conv cpe 2d	3,612	29,965	—
T85	GT Prem conv cpe 2d	3,612	31,145	—

2006 Engines	bore×stroke	bhp	availability
V-6, 245.0	3.95×3.32	210	S-base
V-8, 281.0	3.60×3.60	300	S-GT

** Production figures not available at time of publication.

Ford Thunderbird

Legend says the Thunderbird was born in October 1951, when Ford Division general manager Louis Crusoe visited the Paris Auto Show with styling consultant George Walker. America had a love affair with European sports cars in the early postwar years, and both men were taken by what they saw in Paris—especially the curvy Jaguar XK-120 and GM's experimental two-seat LeSabre. "Why don't we have something like that?" Crusoe asked. "Oh, but we do!" replied Walker—who then hurried to phone Dearborn to get his troops cracking.

But like many apocryphal stories, this one isn't true. Frank Hershey, who headed the team that styled the original '55 T-Bird, said Ford had been conjuring two-seaters well before this, but never felt rushed to build one because sports-car sales only amounted to a minuscule 0.27 percent of the total U.S. market. But in January 1953, GM threw down a gauntlet Ford couldn't ignore: the Chevrolet Corvette. Barely a month later, Ford was hard at work on the car that would ultimately be named for the god worshiped by America's Southwest Native Americans as the bringer of rain and prosperity.

First displayed as a wood mock-up at the Detroit show in early 1954, the Thunderbird was a "personal" car, not a pure sports car. It rode the same wheelbase as the first-generation Corvette—102 inches—but was far more luxurious and practical. In place of creaking fiberglass and clumsy side curtains was a sturdy steel body with convenient roll-up windows. Instead of an ill-fitting soft top was a snug convertible top, a detachable hardtop, or both. And there was no plodding six-cylinder engine but a burly 292-cubic-inch Mercury V-8 delivering 193 bhp with stickshift or 198 bhp with optional self-shift Ford-O-Matic.

Bill Burnett supervised the engineering, which relied heavily on passenger-Ford components. Styling, conceived by Walker lieutenant Hershey and executed by a young Bill Boyer, couldn't have been better: simple and smooth yet clearly Ford, with rakish long-hood/short-deck proportions recalling the classic early-'40s Lincoln Continental.

With European style and American comfort, convenience, and go, the Thunderbird proved well-nigh irresistible at just under $3000 without options. It whipped the rival Chevy in 1955 production by nearly 24-to-1—16,155 for the model year.

You don't mess with success in Detroit, and Ford didn't with the '56 T-Bird. Changes were limited to a larger 312 V-8 option with 215/225 bhp (nonoverdrive stickshift cars retained the 292, now up to 202 bhp), plus exterior-mounted spare (answering

1955 2-passenger convertible coupe

1955 convertible coupe

1956 2-passenger convertible coupe

1957 with and without removable hardtop

cries for more trunk space), softer suspension (for a smoother ride), and no-cost portholes for the hardtop (a Boyer idea inspired by vintage coachwork). Porthole hardtops heavily outsold the nonporthole kind in 1956, and virtually all '57 Thunderbirds had them. Production eased to 15,631, but was still five times Corvette's. Trouble was, Robert S. McNamara, who'd replaced Crusoe as head of Ford Division, wanted much higher volume. Also, market surveys indicated much greater demand for a four-seater. So for 1958 and beyond, that's what the T-Bird would be.

The '57 was thus the last two-seat T-Bird—and arguably the best. A handsome facelift brought a prominent bumper/grille and a longer deck (again enclosing the spare) wearing modest bladelike tailfins. There was more power than ever. Stickshift models still had a 292, but uprated to 212 bhp, and there was now a trio of 312s offering 245, 270, or 285 bhp, the last being a

1957 2-passenger convertible coupe with hardtop

1957 2-passenger convertible with hardtop

1958 convertible coupe

1958 hardtop coupe

twin-four-barrel version with 10.0:1 compression. Ford also built 208 supercharged "F-Birds" with 300/340 bhp courtesy of Paxton-McCulloch blowers, mainly for racing.

And race the early T-Birds did, though with limited success. A '55 sponsored by *Mechanix Illustrated* magazine's Tom McCahill swept the production sports-car class at that year's Daytona Speed Weeks, Joe Ferguson clocking a two-way average of 124.633 mph to best every Austin-Healey, Porsche, and all but one Jaguar XK-120. Chuck Daigh did even better in '56 with a T-Bird prepped by Pete DePaolo; he did 88.779 mph in the standing mile, though a 'Vette modified by Zora Arkus-Duntov proved faster (at 89.735 mph). Daigh returned in '57 to score 93.312 mph, and a privately entered T-Bird ran the flying-mile at 146.282 mph one way, 138.775 mph both ways. Then the Automobile Manufacturers Association issued its infamous racing "ban" and development stopped.

With a base price still under $3500 for 1957, the T-Bird remained an attractive buy. Production ran through the end of the calendar year, so production was the highest for the three two-seater years at 21,380.

As expected, the all-new four-seater arrived for 1958 (though Ford briefly considered retaining a two-seater with updated styling). A dramatic design with unibody construction; all-coil suspension; and a low, rakish stance, the second-generation Thunderbird rode a compact 113-inch wheelbase, yet had ample interior room. Only one engine was available, a new 300-bhp, 352-cid big-block V-8, linked to Ford Division's three-speed Cruise-O-Matic self-shift transmission, also new that year. Joining the familiar convertible was a fixed-roof hardtop that popularized the square "formal-look" wide-quarter roofline that would soon spread throughout the Ford line—and to other automakers. (A rumored retractable hardtop like the 1957-59 Ford Skyliner was canceled in the design stage. The '59 convertible used a similar top-stowing arrangement in that the power top folded beneath a rear-hinged decklid.) A new interior feature—a central control console atop the transmission

1959 convertible coupe

1960 hardtop coupe with sunroof

1960 hardtop coupe

1961 hardtop coupe

1961 convertible coupe

tunnel—would also be widely imitated.

With all this, the 1958 Thunderbird was a solid hit despite higher base prices of $3600-$3900. Nearly 38,000 were built for the model year, about twice as many as any of the previous two-seaters. The '59s changed only in detail: a honeycomb, instead of horizontal-bar, motif for grille; nonfunctional hood air-scoop and taillight appliqué; "bullet" moldings on the sculptured lower-body "bombs"; reworked Thunderbird script; a bird emblem instead of a round emblem on hardtop C-pillars. Lincoln's huge 350-bhp, 430-cid V-8, listed the previous year but likely never installed, became a full-fledged Thunderbird option. Owing to production over a full model year, the '59 bested the '58 at some 67,500 units.

The 1960 edition marked the end of the planned three-year "squarebird" styling cycle. Though substantially the same as its predecessor, it wore a new grille with a main horizontal bar bisecting three vertical bars ahead of a fine grid, plus triple tail-lights (replacing dual-lamp clusters), and detail-trim changes. Engines were untouched. Returning to U.S. production for the first time before World War II was a slide-back metal sunroof as a new hardtop option. Volume continued climbing, reaching nearly 91,000 units. Included were 2536 limited-edition hardtops with gold-color roofs and other special touches. Hardtops as a whole, outsold convertibles nearly 8-to-1, suggesting that T-Bird buyers wanted luxury first and sportiness second.

A new third-generation Thunderbird bowed for 1961 on an unchanged wheelbase and would see mostly minor alterations through 1963. Distinctive styling was highlighted by severely pointed front profiles, modest "blade" tailfins, big circular taillamps (a sometimes Ford hallmark), and outward-curving bodysides bereft of sheetmetal sculpturing. There was again just one engine: Ford Division's new 390 V-8, a stroked 352 but delivering the same 300 horsepower. An optional power package offered 40 more bhp for 1962-63. With minor alterations, the 390 would be the basic Thunderbird powerplant through 1968, joined by big-block options beginning with '66. Base prices for '61 stood at $4172 for the hardtop and $4639 for the ragtop.

Third-generation engineering was conservative but sound. Ford had contemplated front-wheel drive, but felt it too unorthodox for this market. Instead, engineers stressed quality control, solid construction, ride comfort, and minimum noise at speed. Extensive use of rubber bushings for the coil-spring independent front and leaf-spring rear suspensions made the 1961-63 Thunderbirds among the best-riding cars of the day.

Two derivative models were added for '62: the Sports Roadster and the Landau. The former was the only production four-seat car to become a two-seater. (Of course, there are many examples of the opposite—including the '58 T-Bird.) It was approved by new Ford Division chief Lee A. Iacocca largely because dealers had been besieged with requests for a car like the 1955-57 T-Bird. While Iacocca knew there was no

1962 Sports Roadster convertible coupe

1963 Sports Roadster convertible coupe

1964 convertible coupe

1965 convertible coupe

1965 convertible coupe

1966 Landau hardtop coupe

significant market for anything like that, he felt a semisports model couldn't hurt.

The designer most responsible for the Sports Roadster was Bud Kaufman, who developed a fiberglass tonneau to cover the normal convertible's rear seat, thus creating a "two-seater." When installed, the cover formed twin headrests for the front seats and blended neatly with the rear deck. Kaufman overcame fitting problems so that the soft top could be raised and lowered with the tonneau in place. Completing the package were Kelsey-Hayes chrome wire wheels with knock-off hubs that dictated omitting the stock rear fender skirts (due to inadequate clearance).

But stunning though it was, the Sports Roadster didn't sell. The problem was price: initially $5439, a hefty $650 above the standard convertible. Ford built only 1427 of the '62s and just 455 of the '63s before canceling the model. Ford dealers offered a similar tonneau and wire wheels as accessories for 1964 convertibles, but these are even scarcer today.

The Landau was far more popular. At $4398 it cost only $77 more than the standard hardtop, yet delivered a vinyl-covered roof with a fake landau or "S" bar on each rear pillar, plus a spiffier interior. Despite these minor touches, buyers flocked to the Landau. By 1966, it was outselling the plain hardtop; three years after that it was generating the bulk of T-Bird sales. There were also 2000 examples of a Limited Edition 1963 Landau. Introduced in the spring of that year, it came with a special numbered plaque on the console, plus all-white interior, special paint, and spinner wheel covers.

Though Thunderbird production was down in these years, it remained far higher than it had been in the two-seater days. The respective totals for model years 1961-63 were 73,000, 78,000, and about 63,300.

Following the now customary three-year cycle, and with wheelbase again unchanged, the 1964 Thunderbird arrived with completely new sheetmetal marked by busy bodyside sculpturing. This fourth design generation would carry on without major change through 1966. Quiet, refined luxury was again increasingly emphasized as convertible sales declined markedly. The open T-Bird, which accounted for only 7.5 percent of production in '66, didn't return for '67. The '64s set a T-Bird production record with close to 92,500 units. Volume eased to around 75,000 for '65, then to just over 69,000.

Among features introduced with this generation were a cockpit-style passenger compartment and "Silent-Flo" ventilation (1964); standard front-disc brakes (1965); full-width taillight housings, including backup lights and sequential turn signals, and a "Town" (formal) roofline for the Landau and hardtop (all for '66). A popular accessory offered since 1961 was the "Swing-Away" steering wheel. With the transmission in Park, it could be shifted about 10 inches inboard to facilitate driver entry/exit. The 300-bhp 390 remained the only engine through 1965, after which it gained 15 horsepower, plus an alternative

1967 Landau four-door sedan

1968 Landau hardtop coupe

1968 Landau four-door sedan

1969 Landau hardtop coupe

428-cid big-block option rated at 345 bhp.

The pros and cons of offering a Thunderbird sedan were debated by Ford officials throughout the '60s. By middecade, Iacocca was satisfied that sporty-car buyers were being catered to by other Fords—namely the new Mustang and an attractive array of Falcons and Fairlanes. Market studies indicated that the T-Bird, now firmly entrenched as a personal-luxury car, no longer needed even a semisporting image.

Reflecting this conclusion was a completely restyled group of 1967 Thunderbirds headlined by a new $4825 four-door Landau on a 117.2-inch wheelbase. The hardtop and two-door Landau continued on a 114.7-inch span, priced at $4600/$4700. Front ends featured a handsome recessed loop grille with honeycomb insert, plus headlamps covered by matching flip-up sections; a hefty bumper wrapped underneath. Rear-quarter windows on two-doors now retracted horizontally into the roof pillars. Engines were unchanged.

This fifth-generation series would continue through 1971 despite sales that trended mostly downward as prices went upward (reaching $5500 for the '71 four-door). The Landau sedan wasn't very practical—especially its rear-hinged back doors, a throwback to the '30s—and it declined from almost 25,000 sales for '67 to just over 8400 by 1970. Volume as a whole sank from 78,000 to just above 49,000 for '69, then recovered to just over 50,000.

Styling changes were minor through decade's end. The '68s bore narrowed rocker moldings and an eggcrate grille pattern. For '69, the grille was composed of horizontal louvers and three vertical dividers, the full-width taillamp ensemble gave way to divided units, and rear-quarter windows were eliminated on the Landau coupe. Returning for the first time since 1960 was a sliding sunroof, albeit electrically operated, as an option for any vinyl-top model.

In its first departure from a three-year design cycle, the Thunderbird received a heavy facelift of its '67 shell for 1970, marked by a more-prominent thrust-forward snout. Radio antenna and windshield wipers were newly concealed (the latter via an extended hood) and two-door models had a "faster" roofline. The customary three-model lineup returned for '71 with wheel covers, grille insert, and minor trim the only revisions. However, two-door Landaus were newly available sans the dummy S-bars (a T-Bird emblem substituted).

Big-block V-8s were the order of the day but very mildly tuned, the T-Bird no longer having a performance image to uphold. For 1968, the optional 428 gave way to Ford's new 429. Rated at 360 bhp, it was more easily adaptable to the new emissions standards that took effect that year. It would be standard T-Bird power from 1969 through 1973.

Following a '71 sales slide to some 36,000, Thunderbird was completely redesigned for 1972. Riding a new 120.4-inch wheelbase, it was larger and heavier than any T-Bird before—or since. The plain coupe and slow-selling sedans were dropped, leaving a single Landau hardtop to share basic structure with that year's new Continental Mark IV. Besides list prices starting around $5300, some $2500 below Lincoln, a big selling point for this bigger T-Bird was a plusher-riding, new all-coil suspension with four-bar-link location for the live rear axle.

Not surprisingly, greater size and weight conspired with more-restrictive emissions tuning to hurt both performance and economy. This explains why a second engine option returned: the big Lincoln 460-cid V-8, though it was scarcely more powerful than the still-standard 429: 224 bhp versus 212, both in newly proscribed SAE net measure. Either way, the '72 T-Bird needed 12 seconds for the 0-60 mph sprint and returned a dismal 11-12 mpg of increasingly more-expensive gas.

Yet buyers apparently didn't care. Perhaps because of its

1969 Landau hardtop coupe with sunroof

1970 hardtop coupe

1971 Landau hardtop coupe

1972 Landau hardtop coupe

closer similarity with the prestigious Mark, the '72 posted a healthy 60-percent sales gain, followed by over 87,000 for '73—the T-Bird's third-best yearly total yet. Then came the Middle East oil embargo, which put a big dent in big-car sales. Thunderbird was no exception, dropping below 59,000 for '74, then to just under 43,000 for '75. The last of this generation, the '76, managed a slight recovery—to near 53,000—mainly because the economy had mostly recovered from the 1973-74 gas crisis. Yet if these figures were disheartening to Ford, the Thunderbird at least maintained a solid lead over its Buick Riviera and Oldsmobile Toronado rivals.

Relatively few changes attended the heavyweight sixth-generation T-Bird. Federal bumper standards took effect for 1973, which meant withstanding a five-mph frontal impact (and a five-mph rear shunt for '74s) without damage to safety-related components. The Thunderbird met this requirement with bigger bumpers that only aggravated its weight problem. Styling changes involved headlights set in square chrome bezels, a gaudy eggcrate instead of horizontal bars for the grille, a stand-up hood ornament, and, instead of dummy landau irons, optional "opera" windows—contrived little oblong panes in the still ultrawide rear-roof pillars.

The '74 had to be the least pleasant of all Thunderbirds to live with. The infamous, short-lived seatbelt interlock system, mandated by the feds, forced strapping in anything on the right front seat—even a bag of groceries—before the car could be started. Heftier rear bumpers added to overall length with no gain in interior space. With weight up and emissions standards stricter, the whopping Lincoln 460-cid V-8 with 220 bhp became standard that year, along with vinyl roof, opera windows, solid-state ignition, AM radio, air conditioning, power windows, and tinted glass. There were eight variations of metalflake paint available, and a glass moonroof appeared as an optional alternative to the steel sunroof.

Aside from details, such as segmented taillights for 1974, this series saw few appearance changes after '73. Emissions tuning continued to strangle the big 460-cid V-8. Rated horsepower was 218/202 for 1975-76—ridiculously low for such a large engine, and this despite the adoption of the catalytic converter. Ford went all-out to promote the '75 as "the best luxury car buy," trumpeting "new softness, new ease, with ample room for six... rich, lavish fabrics... 24-oz. cut-pile carpeting... wood-tone appliqués." More-practical options included four-wheel disc brakes (available since '72), "Sure-Track" antilock braking system (ditto), and a fuel-monitor warning light. The last was really needed, because these T-Birds were among the thirstiest cars ever seen from Dearborn.

Ford had long since become a master at keeping interest alive in an aging model via special editions, and the mid-'70s Thunderbird offered its share. An optional gold-tint moonroof was announced at mid-1974, along with Burgundy and White-and-Gold Luxury Groups color-keyed to a fare-thee-well inside and out. Copper and Silver Luxury Groups replaced them for '75, each offering velour or leather upholstery; a Jade LG was added in April. All of these wore a padded vinyl rear half-roof with opera windows, the latter being deleted when a moonroof was specified. The '76 LGs were Creme-and-Gold, Bordeaux, and "Lipstick." The last was far less gaudy than its name implied.

For 1977, Thunderbird marked a first in its history by being smaller than it was the year before. This "downsized" model was nothing more than a new derivative of Ford's existing mid-size platform as suggested by the 1974-76 Gran Torino Elite, which tested whether the public would accept a Thunderbird sized like Chevy's Monte Carlo. Though the Elite had sold quite well, this "new" T-Bird would put it in the shade.

Compared to the 1972-76 models, the '77 was lighter and more-economical, reflecting big reductions in almost every dimension: nearly 10 inches in overall length, 6.4 inches in wheelbase (to 114), three inches in width, and up to 900 pounds of "road-hugging weight." There were big reductions in price, too: some $2700 for the base model, which now started at just over $5000. Of course, the old big-blocks were gone. Standard power was now a 130-bhp version of the trusty 302-cid V-8—except for California, where only a 135-bhp 351 was sold. Optional was a 400-cid V-8, rated at 173 bhp for '77 and 166 bhp the following year, after which it was canceled.

1973 coupe

1974 coupe

1974 coupe

1975 coupe with Copper Luxury Group

1976 coupe with power glass Moonroof

Downsizing the T-Bird this way was expedient given that Washington's new corporate average fuel economy standards (CAFE) would be in force for 1978. But it was that much lower price and the Thunderbird name that sent sales soaring; better fuel efficiency was merely incidental. T-Bird thus enjoyed 300,000-unit years for 1977 and '78, better than three times the previous model-year record set in distant 1960. And it easily outsold sibling LTD II (see Ford) despite fewer model choices.

Though the 1977 model was smaller and less-singular than previous T-Birds, it had many of the same style overtones and brash trim touches. Prices soon started climbing to where they had been. January 1977 brought a new top-line Town Landau with a near $8000 base price and numerous standard luxuries, plus a dubious brushed-aluminum "tiara" roof band echoing the old mid-'50s Crown Victoria.

There was little change for 1978, but a Diamond Jubilee edition was issued to commemorate Ford Motor Company's 75th anniversary. Tagged at close to $10,000, it was painted in Diamond Blue or Ember metallics and came with the owner's initials near the outside door handles and on a 22-carat-gold dashboard nameplate. This package proved so popular that Ford retained it for 1979 as the Heritage, finished in either special maroon or light blue. There were few other changes that year except for volume, which was down again but hardly bad at about 284,000 units.

Thunderbird was further downsized, and in much the same manner, for 1980. Instead of an intermediate, its foundation this time was a compact, the practical "Fox" platform developed for the 1978 Ford Fairmont/Mercury Zephyr. But the size reductions for this eighth generation were just as dramatic as they'd

1977 coupe

1977 Town Landau coupe

1978 coupe with T-Roof Convertible option

1978 coupe with Sports Decor Group

1978 coupe

been for the seventh: 16 inches in overall length, 4.5 inches in width, 5.6 inches in wheelbase (now 108.4). Next to the '76, the 1980 looked positively tiny: two feet shorter, eight inches narrower, a foot less between wheel centers, and nearly a ton lighter. Yet it was no less comfortable or luxurious than its immediate predecessors.

The adoption of the Fox platform returned Thunderbird from body-on-frame to unitized construction for the first time since 1966, which contributed to both weight efficiency and interior-space utilization. The interior blended opulence and convenience, and a split front-bench seat, buckets, and purpose-designed Recaro bucket seats were all available. The 302 V-8, now rated at 131 bhp, shifted to the options column and its debored 255-cid relative moved in as standard with 115 bhp. At mid-model year, Ford made its 200-cid six available as a credit option, the first six in Thunderbird history.

Other 1980 developments included a new four-speed overdrive automatic transmission, providing the traditional economy benefit of OD without the hassle of shifting; rack-and-pinion steering, for precision unknown in previous T-Birds; and the all-coil suspension system so well-proven in the Fairmont/Zephyr. A midyear offering expected in that 25th Thunderbird year was a Silver Anniversary special, again featuring a tiara roof appliqué plus a standard 302, the overdrive automatic, and gray-and-silver upholstery with complementing paintwork.

This more-efficient T-Bird should have sold well, but the market turned sour as another energy crisis began in late '79; then too, the boxy, overdecorated 1980 styling did not appeal to potential buyers. As a result, production slid below 157,000, then dropped by 50 percent a year for the 1981s and '82s.

But help was on the way for '83 in the form of a stunning new ninth-generation T-Bird that announced a new direction for Dearborn styling: the clean, no-frills "aero look." Though still built on the faithful Fox platform, the '83 employed a new 104-inch-wheelbase "S-shell" whose rounded "organic" shape cheated the wind with a rakish 60-degree windshield angle and a three-inch reduction in overall width, reducing the drag coefficient to a slick 0.35. The only vestige of recent Thunderbirds was a modest eggcrate grille curved snugly on the nose.

The startlingly different and handsome 1983 T-Bird arrived in base and upmarket Heritage models with a choice of Ford's aluminum-head 232-cid "Essex" V-6 or an equally new 140-bhp, 302-cid V-8 with single-point fuel injection. But the real surprise came at mid-model year with the Turbo Coupe, the sportiest Thunderbird in 20 years. As the name implied, it carried a reengineered 142-bhp version of Mustang's 2.3-liter turbo-four from recent Mustangs, now with port fuel injection among numerous improvements. Initially, it linked exclusively to a five-speed overdrive manual gearbox. A standard handling package, optional for other '83s, brought high-rate springs and shocks; a second pair of rear shocks, horizontally mounted to resist axle patter (Ford termed this "Quadra-Trac"); "Traction-Lok" limited-slip differential; and beefy performance radials on handsome aluminum wheels. Completing this enthusiasts' Thunderbird were black exterior moldings, fog lamps, and a well-furnished interior with shapely multiadjustable front bucket seats featuring variable thigh and lumbar supports.

Roundly applauded by "buff books" and even *Consumer Guide®*, the Turbo Coupe was a bit crude mechanically, but the most-roadable T-Bird anyone could remember. It was quick, too: 0-60 mph took 9.6 seconds. Yet it could return an honest 23 mpg in city/suburban driving—impressive for a 3000-pound luxury midsize. Workmanship was also better than anyone could recall (or dared to). All the '83s were tight and solid, thoroughly detailed, and beautifully finished.

Buyers were quick to recognize the excellence of what Ford

1979 Heritage coupe

1979 coupe with T-Roof Convertible option

1980 Town Landau coupe

1980 Town Landau coupe with Exterior Decor Group

1981 coupe

1981 Heritage coupe

1982 Town Landau coupe

1983 coupe

had wrought, snapping up nearly 122,000 of the 1983 T-Birds—a sensational 250 percent gain over depressed 1982-model sales. The Turbo Coupe made up only about 10 percent of Thunderbird sales but, as T-Birds always have, lured many people into showrooms who left in one of the tamer versions or another Ford model.

Indeed, the market was fast pulling out of its early decade slump, and T-Bird shared in the renewed prosperity with some 170,500 sales for 1984. Changes that year were modest but useful. The V-6 discarded its carburetor for throttle-body injection that gave a slight power increase, and both it and the 302 V-8 took on Ford's EEC-IV electronic control system, as already used on the Turbo Coupe engine. The TC itself was unchanged save newly available three-speed automatic transmission. Heritage was renamed Elan, and a new Fila "designer" model was added with special colors and trim inspired by the Italian sportswear maker.

More refinements followed for '85: altered grille texture, full-width wraparound taillamps, counterbalanced hood (thus banishing a cheap, awkward prop-rod), restyled dash with new fully electronic instrumentation (one of the more-informative and legible such setups) and wider standard tires (meaty 225/60VR-15s on Turbo Coupe, 205/70-14s elsewhere). Model-year volume remained healthy at close to 152,000.

The '86 figure was even better, reflecting the fact that it was one of Detroit's strongest sales years of the decade. The Fila

1983½ Turbo coupe

1983½ Turbo coupe

1984 Fila coupe

1985 30th Anniversary coupe

1985 Turbo coupe

1986 coupe

1987 Turbo coupe

1988 coupe

model was dropped, but sequential-port injection and friction-reducing internal changes lifted the 302 V-8 to 150 bhp. A power moonroof was newly optional. Gas was again cheap, so the V-8 was ordered in the bulk of that year's nearly 164,000 Thunderbirds in spite of its so-so 20-mpg thirst. Judicious use of the options sheet made it possible to order the V-8 with most Turbo Coupe features. Many buyers did just that, enjoying more-relaxed performance and far greater refinement. Even in the late '80s, there was still no substitute for cubic inches.

Recognizing this trend, Ford issued a rearranged group of '87 Thunderbirds with all-new sheetmetal. The reskin didn't much change silhouette, but did make a slick car look even slicker. Glass areas were larger (though not the actual window openings) and both headlamps and side glass were fully flush-mounted to further reduce air drag. The Turbo Coupe wore twin functional hood scoops behind a unique grilleless nose. Other models displayed a rather gaudy chrome eggcrate between the headlamps. Replacing Elan were two new offerings: luxury LX and the Sport. The latter combined the V-8 with a TC-style chassis, interior and exterior, but was otherwise equipped like the base T-Bird. At just over $15,000, it cost some $1800 less than a Turbo Coupe, which made it a terrific performance buy—second only perhaps to the Mustang GT.

The '87s had mechanical and equipment improvements aplenty. The TC acquired the intercooled four of the recently departed Mustang SVO, here rated at 190 bhp. Even more laudable were its newly standard four-wheel disc brakes with electronic antilock control (developed with the German Alfred Teves company), plus a new variable-rate shock-absorber system (called Automatic Ride Control) and standard 225/60VR16 unidirectional performance tires. Air conditioning and tinted glass were standard across the board, and the overdrive automatic took over entirely for the less-efficient three-speeder. Yet for all this, volume dipped, sinking to near 128,000.

The same lineup—V-6 base and LX, V-8 Sport and four-cylinder Turbo Coupe—sold somewhat better for '88: over 147,000. The V-6 was heavily revised, gaining 20 horsepower via multipoint injection, plus a "balancer" shaft mounted in the vee between cylinder banks to help quell secondary vibrations. TC appointments were slightly upgraded, and the Sport changed from digital/graphic to analog gauges as standard.

A striking new 10th-generation T-Bird was Ford's big attraction for 1989. And new it was: smoother, slightly wider and lower, and nearly 3.5 inches shorter on a wheelbase stretched to 113 inches—longer than that of even the overblown early-'70s cars. Overall appearance reminded some of BMW's classic 6-Series coupe, but it nevertheless managed to be distinctively Ford—proving, perhaps, that the '83 T-Bird and the equally striking '86 Taurus sedan weren't flukes after all.

Surprisingly, both the V-8 and turbo-four were gone, replaced by a brace of reworked 232 V-6s. The familiar 140-bhp unit with sequential-port injection continued in the base Thunderbird and luxury LX, offered only with automatic. But all eyes were on the hot new Super Coupe with a supercharged and intercooled 210-bhp V-6, teamed with standard five-speed manual (automatic was optional). The engine-driven supercharger was a '30s idea which enjoyed a revival at several European and Japanese automakers. With the SC, Ford joined them in offering its well-known advantages over the exhaust-driven turbocharger—mainly smoother, more-progressive power delivery at a slight sacrifice in noise and efficiency.

Chassis engineering was equally new. Though the front suspension retained MacPherson-style coil-over-shock units, geometry now involved an A-arm atop each strut and a transverse arm at the base connected by a long, sickle-shaped member integrated with the hub carrier. Rear suspension was fully independent—a first for Thunderbird—and quite compact with variable-rate coil springs sandwiched between an upper lateral link and a wide H-shaped lower member. Vertical shocks rode ahead of the hub carriers. Steering remained power rack-and-pinion, but with new speed-sensitive variable assist as standard. Though base and LX carried front-disc/rear-drum power brakes, they offered the SC's all-disc ABS system as a first-time option. The SC itself came with a more-sophisticated version of the Turbo Coupe's electronic variable-damping system.

Inside the '89s was a logically ordered, very "Euro-looking" instrument panel with digital/graphic or analog instruments (the latter standard on Super Coupe). Maintaining tradition was a functional center console on all models.

But no car is perfect, and the '89 T-Birds ended up much too heavy in the opinion of many critics: a minimum of 3500 pounds. As a result, an unblown LX took a sluggish 10.4 seconds in *Consumer Guide*®'s 0-60 test. The magazine's five-speed SC was far livelier at just 7.8, but would have been faster still without so many extra pounds. The '89 also ended up way over budget, prompting Ford to fire some development engineers.

More disturbing for an all-new model, production dropped again. The '89 total was below 115,000, and the little-changed 1990 models were 1000 units under that. Higher prices undoubtedly played a part: some $15,000 for the base 1990 model, over $20,000 for the Super Coupe. The deep new national recession that began in 1990 didn't help. Still, those produc-

1988 Turbo coupe

1989 Super Coupe (SC)

1989 Super Coupe (SC)

1989 LX coupe

1989 LX coupe

1990 Super Coupe (SC)

1990 Super Coupe (SC)

tion numbers were respectable given a worsening economy and a far more crowded luxury-performance field.

T-Bird volume became even less respectable for '91, then sank to just under 78,000 for model-year '92 before turning up again along with the economy. Only one notable change occurred: the return of V-8 power as a 1991 option for base and LX models. It was the familiar pushrod 5.0-liter last offered for 1988, but it now made 200 bhp, 45 more than before. On the other hand, that was 25 less than the same engine in a '91 Mustang or Lincoln Mark VII, the result of a more-restrictive exhaust system. Still, the V-8 was welcome, being slower, but less-thirsty, than the supercharged V-6, and it quickly accounted for the bulk of T-Bird sales. Two minor '91 improvements involved automatic climate control as a new linewide option and availability of the SC's analog gauges for base and LX.

Expanding the 1992 lineup was a revived Sport model. This time, it was a slightly detrimmed Super Coupe with the V-8 and narrower tires (but on unique alloy wheels). The price was attractive at $18,611, a good $3500 below that year's blown Thunderbird. All '92s wore full-width taillamps nestled under a reshaped "gullwing" trunklid, and both the Sport and LX adopted the SC's distinctive aero front-bumper and driving lamps as standard equipment.

Only the LX and SC returned for '93. The former lost a few standard frills to undercut the previous base model by over $500. It was all for sales, of course, and it worked, T-Bird model-year volume nearly doubling to over 133,000. To no one's surprise, the vast majority were LXs. The SC was lowered a token $16 that year, which only underscored how good a value it was at $22,030 to start. But affordable luxury was now overwhelmingly preferred to high-tech potency, and the Super Coupe continued to decline as a percentage of total T-Bird sales.

The LX and SC looked nearly identical for 1994, when a timely freshening occurred, starting with a minor facelift announced by large oval cutouts in the front bumper. The dash was revised to contain a passenger air bag. Dual cupholders were added, too, but electronic gauges were deleted. The big news was in the engine room. Internal changes boosted the blown V-6 to 230 bhp, a gain of 20, while the LX switched optional V-8s, ditching the pushrod 5.0-liter for Ford's new 4.6-liter "modular" unit with single overhead camshaft.

Reduced V-8 displacement implied reduced V-8 torque. Sure enough, the 4.6 made 10 fewer pound-feet than the 5.0, 265 in all, though it did bring a nominal gain of five horsepower. It did not, however, bring a noticeable improvement in smoothness or quietness, and performance was predictably little changed, *Consumer Guide*® clocking 0-60 mph in a decent 8.8 seconds. Like the old V-8, the new one teamed exclusively with four-speed automatic, which gained an overdrive lockout button (to give better around-town performance at the driver's discretion)

1991 LX coupe

1992 Sport coupe

1993 LX coupe

1994 Super Coupe (SC)

and electronic shift control. The latter was noticeable, but mostly in the negative, as it made some shifts slurred, others sharp, and both often tardy.

Despite such fumbles, Thunderbird output eased only a little for '94, dropping some 7000 units to just over 126,000. Continued aggressive pricing certainly helped stem the loss in a rougher-than-ever market where buyers often "cross-shopped" the T-Bird against luxury sedans. In that light, the $22,240 SC looked an even better buy in luxury-performance, its base price having risen only $2400 over five model years. The LX was up to $16,830, less than $1900 higher than the less-well-equipped base model of 1990. Unfortunately, the basic '89 design was showing its age, and little was done to freshen it in '95. Sales continued to decline. Even new bumper fascias front and rear, headlamps, hood and taillamp clusters, and spark plugs guaranteed to last 100,000 miles couldn't spark much interest from the public. If the picture was bleak in '96, it grew positively dismal when the '97 T-Birds were introduced. The only change of any consequence was the deletion of two gauges from the instrument panel. Rumors swirled through the industry that a new T-Bird was imminent, perhaps a smaller, lighter car with front-wheel drive. Such speculation certainly didn't help dealers shift their remaining '97s.

And then there were none—except in NASCAR Winston Cup racing, where the Thunderbird had been Ford's warrior since the early 1980s. It remained so in '98, as teams were allowed to run '97-bodied cars for one last season while Ford developed a new racer. (It materialized as a two-door Taurus, a mythical beast with no showroom counterpart.) As for the rumored front-drive T-Bird, the idea was apparently given serious consideration, said Ford insiders, but the car itself emerged for 1999 as a small new Mercury Cougar, a sporty front-drive coupe spinoff of the compact Ford Contour/Mercury Mystique sedans.

As it turned out, the Thunderbird was only on vacation. Even while journalists were writing obituaries, Ford was finishing up an all-new T-Bird—a two-seater in the mold of the classic originals. To hold down costs, it was planned for a modified version of Ford's new rear-wheel-drive DEW98 corporate platform, set to premiere beneath Lincoln's 2000 LS sedan and a companion S-Type four-door from Ford-owned Jaguar. Leading new-T-Bird development were product planner Rich Kisler, engineer Don Werneke, and Ted Finney, chief designer for all of Dearborn's "large/luxury" rear-wheel-drive cars. Styling, supervised by Dave Turner and Ford design VP Jack Telnack, rejected both a clean-sheet approach and a near-copy of 1955-57 for what Ford called a "modern heritage" look. Everyone else called it "retro," but it worked, reimagining the original two-seaters in a contemporary way. The design came together quickly, and the new T-Bird was all but finished by the time Telnack retired in late 1997. But Telnack's successor, J Mays, a *wunderkind* recruited from Volkswagen/Audi, wasn't entirely happy with what he found, and allegedly did a little tweaking.

The end result broke cover in January 1999 as a "concept" at the Detroit Auto Show. Though Ford officials were coy about production, the shiny car on the turntable looked suspiciously showroom-ready, so few were surprised a little over a year later when Ford confirmed plans to put it on sale in 2001 as an early '02 model. Soon afterward, and with deposits in hand from many eager customers, Ford announced that its Wixom, Michigan, plant would turn out Job 1 at the end of July.

It was all part of a planned, protracted rollout intended to build buzz for the new T-Bird. So, too, was giving Neiman Marcus customers a shot at 200 advance copies. In a arrangement with the luxury-goods retailer, Ford presented a special black-and-silver NM Edition in August 2000, fittingly at the 50th annual staging of the tony Concours d'Elegance classic-car fest in Pebble Beach, California. Listed in the store's "Christmas Book" at $41,995, the NM special was offered for sale on September 23, 2000. All 200 were snapped up in a phone blitz lasting just a little over two hours.

Regular deliveries didn't begin until September 2001, delayed by unforeseen problems that had cropped up in preproduction. Cooling-system and other woes required replacing components that had been thought acceptable. This was another black eye for Dearborn's image, coming after the Explorer/Firestone tire debacle and a rash of recalls involving early examples of Ford's Focus subcompact. Fortunately, the T-Bird bugs were squashed with fair dispatch, and full production began in autumn 2001.

1995 LX coupe

1997 LX coupe

1996 LX coupe

2002 Premium convertible coupe with removable hardtop

Essentially, the new T-Bird was a shortened Lincoln LS with a convertible body. Wheelbase was trimmed 7.3 inches to 107.2, though that was more than five inches longer than the 1955-57 dimension. The new two-seater also stretched 11 inches longer overall than the original and was about an inch wider but no taller. It was much heavier, though, by a whopping 744 pounds, weighing nearly 3600 at the curb. But some of that reflected much stronger unibody construction (versus the old body-on-frame), plus built-in "crumple zones," airbags, and other modern safety musts unimaginable in the '50s. Interestingly, all of the body panels, save the rear fenders, were made of sheet-molding-compound plastic. Any weight savings these panels provided was at least partly offset by steel underbody bracing, deemed necessary for rigidity.

There was only one powertrain, with a 3.9-liter/240-cid twin-cam V-8 sending 292 bhp through a five-speed automatic transmission. Both came from the LS, as did the basic all-independent coil-spring suspension with twin A-arms at each end, plus rear toe-control links. Brakes were four-wheel discs with antilock control nestled within 17-inch alloy wheels. The dashboard was another Lincoln lift, though customized for the T-Bird with turquoise gauge needles.

For full-on nostalgia, an extra $600-$800 put body-color accents on the seats, center console, door panels, lower dash, even the standard tilt/telescope steering wheel. Another "happy days" echo was the $2500 detachable hardtop, complete with rear-quarter porthole windows. It weighed 83 pounds and thus usually took two people to manage, but came with a tube-frame rack for safe above-floor storage. Per tradition, the cloth roof folded electrically beneath a lift-up cover behind the cockpit.

Initial reviews were largely positive. Some taller testers felt the cockpit a bit tight, and rough roads could induce unwanted body flex and cowl shake. The biggest gripe was lack of sports-car-level handling. But as Ford repeatedly emphasized, the '02 T-Bird was never intended to be a pure sports car. Rather, it was built for "relaxed sportiness" just like the "personal" '55: two-seat jaunty, but also comfortable and well-appointed. Viewed in that light, it was excellent, with more than enough performance to make a fun drive. Indeed, *Road & Track* reported a respectable 0.83g on the skidpad and only moderate understeer in corners. "Dynamically, this is the best T-Bird ever," said *R&T*, "by no means just a... stylish cruiser. Hustled down a twisty canyon road, [it] responds well to driver inputs. Sure, its soft spring rates translate to a comfort-oriented ride with a fair amount of body roll and even a bit of floatiness at high speeds, but neither is excessive as the Thunderbird hangs on in corners, aided by good overall balance, communicative steering, and ample grip from [standard V-rated P235/50 tires]." Acceleration wasn't lacking either, with most testers timing 0-60 mph in a brisk 7.0 seconds or so.

The reborn T-Bird came two ways: a Deluxe model initially pegged at $34,965 and a Premium version with standard traction control and chrome wheels for $1000 more. Of course, buyers expected a load of equipment at such prices, and Ford didn't disappoint. Besides those already mentioned, the no-cost features list showed leather-covered power seats, in-dash CD changer, dual-zone automatic climate control, tachometer, and remote keyless-entry door locks with antitheft alarm.

Yet for all its feel-good qualities, the retro T-Bird would prove something of a flop. At launch, Ford promised to build no more than 20,000 a year, hoping that an "exclusive" aura would preclude the need for profit-draining incentives and prop up resale values. But only in 2002 did sales come close to that mark: 19,085 for the calendar year. And though some "early adopters" willingly paid well over sticker, transaction prices soon dropped right along with orders. Sales fell to 18,100 for '03, to just under 12,000 the year after, and finally to 9548. One problem was a growing band of like-priced import-brand droptops, some of which had more speed and/or greater cachet. Upward price creep did nothing to help, especially as there was little to justify it. A few useful changes did occur for 2003, Ford Motor Company's centennial year. Higher compression and variable intake-valve timing added 28 bhp, trimming 0-60-mph runs to 6.5 seconds. Ford also installed more-legible gauges and added a $130 Select Shift option, a manual shift gate that could be used to delay upshifts to max rpm, when a rev limiter cut in.

But it was already too late. Come 2004, Ford was saying the T-Bird name could soon go into limbo again, though it might return on a different limited-edition vehicle—emphasize *might*. It was a subtle admission that Ford Motor Company was back in crisis mode. The underperforming T-Bird was doomed.

Sure enough, the 2005s were the last of this flock, unchanged from '04 except for an expected 50th Anniversary Edition. Impudently priced at $44,355, the birthday memento should have been more special—like one of the slick-looking 400-bhp supercharged concept T-Birds Ford had shown in 2003-04. Instead, it was just a gilded Premium model with Select Shift and the hardtop included, plus specific trim—a sad farewell for a car that had seemed so promising a mere four years earlier.

The Thunderbird name is still too good to lose, but does it have a future? Hard to say just now. But if there is another Thunderbird, we hope it meets a better fate than the last one.

2002 Neiman Marcus Edition convertible coupe with hardtop

2002 convertible coupe with hardtop

2003 convertible coupe

2004 convertible coupe

2005 50th Anniversary Limited Edition convertible coupe

Specifications

1955

(wb 102.0)		Wght	Price	Prod
40A	conv 2S	2,980	2,944	16,155

1955 Engines	bore×stroke	bhp	availability
V-8, 292.0	3.75×3.30	193	S-stickshift
V-8, 292.0	3.75×3.30	198	S-automatic

1956

(wb 102.0)		Wght	Price	Prod
40A	conv 2S	3,038	3,151	15,631

1956 Engines	bore×stroke	bhp	availability
V-8, 292.0	3.75×3.30	202	S-3-speed trans
V-8, 312.0	3.80×3.44	215	S-overdrive
V-8, 312.0	3.80×3.44	225	S-automatic

1957

(wb 102.0)		Wght	Price	Prod
40	conv 2S	3,145	3,408	21,380

1957 Engines	bore×stroke	bhp	availability
V-8, 292.0	3.75×3.30	212	S-3-speed trans
V-8, 312.0	3.80×3.44	245	S-ovrdrv, auto
V-8, 312.0	3.80×3.44	270/285	O-all (3-sp briefly)
V-8S, 312.0	3.80×3.44	300/340	O-auto; few od/3sp

1958

(wb 113.0)		Wght	Price	Prod
63A	htp cpe	3,876	3,631	35,758
76A	conv cpe	3,944	3,929	2,134

1958 Engines	bore×stroke	bhp	availability
V-8, 352.0	4.00×3.50	300	S-all
V-8, 430.0	4.30×3.70	350	O-prod. uncertain

1959

(wb 113.0)		Wght	Price	Prod
63A	htp cpe	3,813	3,696	57,195
76A	conv cpe	3,903	3,979	10,261

1959 Engines	bore×stroke	bhp	availability
V-8, 352.0	4.00×3.50	300	S-all
V-8, 430.0	4.30×3.70	350	O-all

1960

(wb 113.0)		Wght	Price	Prod
63A	htp cpe	3,799	3,755	76,447
63B	htp cpe, gold top	3,799	3,900*	2,536
76A	conv cpe	3,897	4,222	11,860

1960 Engines	bore×stroke	bhp	availability
V-8, 352.0	4.00×3.50	300	S-all
V-8, 430.0	4.30×3.70	350	O-all

* Estimated

1961

(wb 113.0)		Wght	Price	Prod
63A	htp cpe	3,958	4,172	62,535
76A	conv cpe	4,130	4,639	10,516

1961 Engine	bore×stroke	bhp	availability
V-8, 390.0	4.05×3.78	300	S-all

1962

(wb 113.0)		Wght	Price	Prod
63A	htp cpe	4,132	4,321	69,554*
63B	Landau htp cpe	4,144	4,398	
76A	conv cpe	4,370	4,788	7,030*
76B	Sprts Rdstr conv cpe	4,471	5,439	1,427*

* Some sources list total of 68,127 hardtops/Landaus and 9,884 convertibles.

1962 Engines	bore×stroke	bhp	availability
V-8, 390.0	4.05×3.78	300	S-all
V-8, 390.0	4.05×3.78	340	O-all

1963

Series 80 (wb 113.0)		Wght	Price	Prod
63A	htp cpe	4,195	4,445	42,806*
63B	Landau htp cpe	4,203	4,548	14,139*
76A	conv cpe	4,322	4,912	5,913*
76B	Sprts Rdstr conv cpe	4,396	5,563	455*

* Some sources list total of 59,000 hrdtps/Landaus and 5,457 convs. Model 63B incl. 2,000 Lim Ed Landaus with spec trim; model 76B incl. 37 units with 340-bhp eng.

1963 Engines	bore×stroke	bhp	availability
V-8, 390.0	4.05×3.78	300	S-all
V-8, 390.0	4.05×3.78	340	O-all

1964

Series 80 (wb 113.2)		Wght	Price	Prod
83	htp cpe	4,431	4,486	60,552
85	conv cpe	4,586	4,953	9,198
87	Landau htp cpe	4,441	4,589	22,715

1964 Engine	bore×stroke	bhp	availability
V-8, 390.0	4.05×3.78	300	S-all

1965

Series 80 (wb 113.2)		Wght	Price	Prod
83	htp cpe	4,470	4,486	42,652
85	conv cpe	4,588	4,953	6,846
87	Landau htp cpe	4,478	4,589	20,974
87	Lim Ed Spec Landau	4,500	4,639	4,500

1965 Engine	bore×stroke	bhp	availability
V-8, 390.0	4.00×3.78	300	S-all

1966

Series 80 (wb 113.2)		Wght	Price	Prod
81	Town Hardtop cpe	4,359	4,483	15,633
83	htp cpe	4,386	4,426	13,389
85	conv cpe	4,496	4,879	5,049
87	Landau htp cpe	4,367	4,584	35,105

1966 Engines	bore×stroke	bhp	availability
V-8, 390.0	4.00×3.78	315	S-all
V-8, 428.0	4.13×3.98	345	O-all

1967

Series 80 (wb 114.7; 4d-117.2)		Wght	Price	Prod
81	htp cpe	4,248	4,603	15,567
82	Landau htp cpe	4,256	4,704	37,422
84	Landau sdn 4d	4,348	4,825	24,967

1967 Engines	bore×stroke	bhp	availability
V-8, 390.0	4.00×3.78	315	S-all
V-8, 428.0	4.13×3.98	345	O-all

1968

Series 80 (wb 114.7; 4d-117.2)		Wght	Price	Prod
83	htp cpe	4,366	4,716	9,977
84	Landau htp cpe	4,372	4,845	33,029
87	Landau sdn 4d	4,458	4,924	21,925

1968 Engines	bore×stroke	bhp	availability
V-8, 390.0	4.00×3.78	315	S-all
V-8, 429.0	4.36×3.59	360	O-all

1969

Series 80 (wb 114.7; 4d-117.2)		Wght	Price	Prod
83	htp cpe	4,348	4,824	5,913
84	Landau htp cpe	4,360	4,964	27,664
87	Landau sdn 4d	4,460	5,043	15,695

1969 Engine	bore×stroke	bhp	availability
V-8, 429.0	4.36×3.59	360	S-all

1970

Series 80 (wb 114.7; 4d-117.2)		Wght	Price	Prod
83	htp cpe	4,354	4,961	5,116
84	Landau htp cpe	4,630	5,104	36,847
87	Landau sdn 4d	4,464	5,182	8,401

1970 Engine	bore×stroke	bhp	availability
V-8, 429.0	4.36×3.59	360	S-all

1971

Series 80 (wb 115.0; 4d-118.0)		Wght	Price	Prod
83	htp cpe	4,399	5,295	9,146
84	Landau htp cpe	4,370	5,438	20,356
87	Landau sdn 4d	4,509	5,516	6,553

1971 Engine	bore×stroke	bhp	availability
V-8, 429.0	4.36×3.59	360	S-all

1972

Series 80 (wb 120.4)		Wght	Price	Prod
87	htp cpe	4,420	5,293	57,814

1972 Engines	bore×stroke	bhp	availability
V-8, 429.0	4.36×3.59	212	S-all
V-8, 460.0	4.36×3.85	224	O-all

1973

Series 80 (wb 120.4)		Wght	Price	Prod
87	htp cpe	4,505	6,437	87,269

1973 Engines	bore×stroke	bhp	availability
V-8, 429.0	4.36×3.59	208	S-all
V-8, 460.0	4.36×3.85	219	O-all

1974

Series 80 (wb 120.4)		Wght	Price	Prod
87	htp cpe	4,825	7,330	58,443

1974 Engine	bore×stroke	bhp	availability
V-8, 460.0	4.36×3.85	220	S-all

1975

Series 80 (wb 120.4)	Wght	Price	Prod
87 htp cpe	4,893	7,701	42,685

1975 Engine	bore×stroke	bhp	availability
V-8, 460.0	4.36×3.85	218	S-all

1976

Series 80 (wb 120.4)	Wght	Price	Prod
87 htp cpe	4,808	7,790	52,935*

1976 Engine	bore×stroke	bhp	availability
V-8, 460.0	4.36×3.85	202	S-all

* Includes 30 commemorative editions.

1977

(wb 114.0)	Wght	Price	Prod
87 htp cpe	3,907	5,063	318,140
87 Town Landau cpe	4,104	7,990	

1977 Engines	bore×stroke	bhp	availability
V-8, 302.0	4.00×3.00	130	S-all
V-8, 351.0	4.00×3.50	135	S-in Calif.; O-all
V-8, 400.0	4.00×4.00	173	O-all

1978

(wb 114.0)	Wght	Price	Prod
87 htp cpe	3,907	5,411	333,757
87 Town Landau cpe	4,104	8,420	
87 Diamond Jubilee cpe	4,200	10,106	18,994

1978 Engines	bore×stroke	bhp	availability
V-8, 302.0	4.00×3.00	134	S-all
V-8, 351.0	4.00×3.50	152	O-all
V-8, 400.0	4.00×4.00	166	O-all

1979

(wb 114.0)	Wght	Price	Prod
87 cpe	3,893	5,877	
87/607 Town Landau cpe	4,284	8,866	284,141
87/603 Heritage cpe	4,178	10,687	

1979 Engines	bore×stroke	bhp	availability
V-8, 302.0	4.00×3.00	133	S-all
V-8, 351.0	4.00×3.50	135/151	O-all

1980

(wb 108.4)	Wght	Price	Prod
87 cpe	3,118	6,432	
87/607 Town Landau cpe	3,357	10,036	156,803
87/603 Silver Ann cpe	3,225	11,679	

1980 Engines	bore×stroke	bhp	availability
I-6, 200.0	3.68×3.13	88	O-all(late)
V-8, 255.0	3.68×3.00	115	S-all
V-8, 302.0	4.00×3.00	131	S-Silver Ann, O-others

1981

(wb 108.4)	Wght	Price	Prod
42 cpe	3,064	7,551	
42/60T Town Landau cpe	3,127	8,689	86,693
42/607 Heritage cpe V-8	3,303	11,355	

1981 Engines	bore×stroke	bhp	availability
I-6, 200.0	3.68×3.13	88	S-all exc Heritage
V-8, 255.0	3.68×3.00	115	S-Herit; O-others
V-8, 302.0	4.00×3.00	130	O-all

1982

(wb 108.4)	Wght	Price	Prod
42 cpe I-6/V-8	3,068	8,492	
42/60T Twn Lndu cpe I-6/V-8	3,131	9,703	45,142
42/607 Heritage cpe V-6/V-8	3,303	12,742	

1982 Engines	bore× stroke	bhp	availability
I-6, 200.0	3.68×3.13	88	S-all exc Heritage
V-6, 232.0	3.80×3.40	112	O-all exc Heritage
V-8, 255.0	3.68×3.00	120	S-Herit; O-others

1983

(wb 104.0)	Wght	Price	Prod
46 cpe V-6/V-8	3,076	9,197	
46/607 Heritage cpe V-6/V-8	3,076	12,228	121,999
46/934 Turbo cpe I-4T	—	11,790	

1983 Engines	bore×stroke	bhp	availability
I-4T, 140.0	3.78×3.13	142	S-turbo cpe
V-6, 232.0	3.80×3.40	110	S-all exc trb cpe
V-8, 302.0	4.00×3.00	140	O-all exc trb cpe

1984

(wb 104.0)	Wght	Price	Prod
46 cpe V-6/V-8	3,155	9,633	
46/607 Elan cpe V-6/V-8	3,221	12,661	
46/606 Fila cpe V-6/V-8	3,326	14,471	170,553
46/934 Turbo cpe I-4T	3,073	12,330	

1984 Engines	bore ×stroke	bhp	availability
I-4T, 140.0	3.78×3.13	145	S-turbo cpe
V-6, 232.0	3.80×3.40	120	S-all exc trb cpe
V-8, 302.0	4.00×3.00	140	O-all exc trb cpe

1985

(wb 104.0)	Wght	Price	Prod
46 cpe V-6/V-8	3,004	10,249	
46/607 Elan cpe V-6/V-8	3,041	11,916	151,851
46/606 Fila cpe V-6/V-8	3,108	14,974	
46/934 Turbo cpe I-4T	2,990	13,365	

1985 Engines	bore×stroke	bhp	availability
I-4T, 140.0	3.78×3.13	155	S-turbo cpe
V-6, 232.0	3.80×3.40	120	S-all exc trb cpe
V-8, 302.0	4.00×3.00	140	O-all exc trb cpe

1986

(wb 104.0)	Wght	Price	Prod
46 cpe V-6/V-8	3,182	11,020	
46 Elan cpe V-6/V-8	3,238	12,554	163,965
46 Turbo cpe I-4T	3,172	14,143	

1986 Engines	bore× stroke	bhp	availability
I-4T, 140.0	3.78×3.13	145/155	S-turbo cpe
V-6, 232.0	3.80×3.40	120	S-all exc trb cpe
V-8, 302.0	4.00×3.00	150	O-all exc trb cpe

1987

(wb 104.2)	Wght	Price	Prod
60 cpe V-6/V-8	3,202	12,972	
61 Sport cpe V-8	3,346	15,079	128,135
62 LX cpe V-6/V-8	3,245	15,383	
64 Turbo cpe I-4T	3,380	16,805	

1987 Engines	bore×stroke	bhp	availability
I-4T, 140.0	3.78×3.13	190	S-turbo cpe
I-4T, 140.0	3.78×3.13	150	S-trb cpe (auto)
V-6, 232.0	3.80×3.40	120	S-all exc trb cpe
V-8, 302.0	4.00×3.00	150	O-all exc trb cpe

1988

(wb 104.2)	Wght	Price	Prod
60 cpe V-6/V-8	3,280	13,599	
61 Sport cpe V-8	3,450	16,030	147,243
62 LX cpe V-6/V-8	3,324	15,585	
64 Turbo cpe I-4T	3,415	17,250	

1988 Engines	bore×stroke	bhp	availability
I-4T, 140.0	3.78×3.13	190	S-turbo cpe
I-4T, 140.0	3.78×3.13	150	S-trb cpe (auto)
V-6, 232.0	3.80×3.40	140	S-all exc trb cpe
V-8, 302.0	4.00×3.00	155	S-Sport; O-all exc trb cpe

1989

(wb 113.0)	Wght	Price	Prod
— cpe V-6	3,542	14,612	101,906
— LX cpe V-6	3,554	16,817	
— Super cpe S/C V-6	3,701	19,823	12,962

1989 Engines	bore×stroke	bhp	availability
V-6, 232.0	3.80×3.40	140	S-all exc Spr cpe
V-6S, 232.0	3.80×3.40	210	S-Super cpe

1990

(wb 113.0)	Wght	Price	Prod
— cpe V-6	3,581	14,980	90,247
— LX cpe V-6	—	17,283	
— Super cpe S/C V-6	—	20,390	23,710

1990 Engines	bore×stroke	bhp	availability
V-6, 232.0	3.80×3.40	140	S-all exc Spr cpe
V-6S, 232.0	3.80×3.40	210	S-Super cpe

1991

(wb 113.0)	Wght	Price	Prod
63/HVD cpe 2d	3550	15,318	75,547
— LX cpe 2d	—	17,374	
63/HVC SC cpe 2d	—	20,999	7,267

1991 Engines	bore×stroke	bhp	availability
V-6, 232.0	3.80×3.40	140	S-Base, LX
V-6S, 232.0	3.80×3.40	210	S-Super Coupe
V-8, 302.0	4.00×3.00	200	O-Base, LX

1992

(wb 113.0)	Wght	Price	Prod
BA/VS-AB cpe 2d	3,772	16,345	
BA/VS Sport cpe 2d	3,738	18,611	73,175
BA/VS-AI LX cpe 2d	3,719	18,778	
BA/VS-BB/SC cpe 2d	3,686	22,046	4,614

1992 Engines	bore×stroke	bhp	availability
V-6, 232.0	3.80×3.40	140	S-Base, LX
V-6S, 232.0	3.80×3.40	210	S-Super Coupe
V-8, 302.0	4.00×3.00	200	O-Base, LX

1993

(wb 113.0)	Wght	Price	Prod
BA/VS-AI LX cpe 2d	3,536	15,797	128,931
BA/VS-BB SC cpe 2d	3,760	22,030	4,178

1993 Engines	bore×stroke	bhp	availability
V-6, 232.0	3.80×3.40	140	S-LX
V-6S, 232.0	3.80×3.40	210	S-Super Coupe
V-8, 302.0	4.00×3.00	200	O-LX

1994

(wb 113.0)	Wght	Price	Prod
BA/VS-AI LX cpe 2d	3,570	16,830	123,283
BA/VS-BB SC cpe 2d	3,758	22,240	2,973

1994 Engines	bore×stroke	bhp	availability
V-6, 232.0	3.80×3.40	140	S-LX
V-6S, 232.0	3.80×3.40	230	S-Super Coupe
V-8, 281.0	3.60×3.60	205	O-LX

1995

(wb 113.0)	Wght	Price	Prod
P62 LX cpe 2d	3,536	17,400	115,165
P64 SC cpe 2d	—	22,910	

1995 Engines	bore×stroke	bhp	availability
V-6, 232.0	3.80×3.40	140	S-LX
V-6S, 232.0	3.80×3.40	230	S-Super Coupe
V-8, 281.0	3.60×3.60	205	O-LX

1996

(wb 113.0)	Wght	Price	Prod
P62 LX cpe 2d	3,536	17,485	86,549

1996 Engines	bore×stroke	bhp	availability
V-6, 232.0	3.80×3.40	140	S-LX
V-8, 281.0	3.60×3.60	205	O-LX

1997

(wb 113.0)	Wght	Price	Prod
P62 LX cpe 2d	3,561	17,885	73,814

1996 Engines	bore×stroke	bhp	availability
V-6, 232.0	3.80×3.40	145	S-LX
V-8, 281.0	3.60×3.60	205	O-LX

2002

(wb 107.2) - 25,722 built	Wght	Price	Prod*
P60 Deluxe conv cpe 2d	3,775	34,965	—
P60 Prem conv cpe 2d	—	35,965	—

2002 Engines	bore×stroke	bhp	availability
V-8, 241.0	3.39×3.35	252	S-all

2003

(wb 107.2) - 18,837 built	Wght	Price	Prod*
P60 Deluxe conv cpe 2d	3,775	36,340	—
P60 Prem conv cpe 2d	3,775	37,385	—

2003 Engines	bore×stroke	bhp	availability
V-8, 240.0	3.39×3.35	280	S-all

2004

(wb 107.2) - 10,716 built	Wght	Price	Prod*
P60 Deluxe conv cpe 2d	3,775	36,295	—
P60 Prem conv cpe 2d	3,863	37,970	—
P63 Pac Cst conv cpe 2d	—	43,390	—

2004 Engines	bore×stroke	bhp	availability
V-8, 240.0	3.39×3.35	280	S-all

2005

(wb 107.2) - 4,868 built	Wght	Price	Prod*
P60 Deluxe conv cpe 2d	3,775	37,605	—
P60 Prem conv cpe 2d	3,780	38,650	—
P69 50th Ann conv cpe 2d	3,869	44,355	—

2005 Engines	bore×stroke	bhp	availability
V-8, 240.0	3.39×3.35	280	S-all

* Calendar-year production

Franklin

Franklin has the special distinction in being one of the few U.S. automakers to achieve real success with air-cooled power. It was featured on the very first Franklins of 1902, which immediately won a reputation for high quality and innovation that would carry on right to the end of the company in 1934.

Weight-saving construction received particular emphasis. In an age when cast iron was the standard stuff of engine blocks, pistons, and cylinder heads, Franklin used high-grade, light-weight aluminum. At one time, Franklin was the world's largest consumer of aluminum. Equally unusual were the cars' all-around full-elliptic springs, which provided a smoother ride and much reduced tire wear than most competitors' half-elliptic suspensions. A flexible wood frame also softened the ride. By 1920, other advanced technical features such as full-pressure lubrication, automatic spark control, and electric choke were long-familiar Franklin fare. So too were six-cylinder engines; Franklin abandoned fours after 1914.

Franklin's commitment to "aircooling" got a boost when Charles A. Lindbergh made his historic transatlantic flight in 1927. After all, the *Spirit of St. Louis* had an air-cooled engine, and Franklin advertising eagerly pointed up the parallel. The company then began using the name "Airman" on some 1928 models to honor the Lone Eagle. All Franklins that year adopted four-wheel Lockheed hydraulic brakes and a steel chassis. Standard "silent second" synchromesh was further innovation for 1929.

Like many Detroit producers, Franklin entered the '30s with optimism despite Wall Street's recent, ominous crash. That was understandable. The company had enjoyed record sales in 1929, and interest in both aviation and air-cooling was at an all-time high.

Reflecting Franklin's rosy outlook was its 1930 line of "145" and "147" models with new styling and power on respective wheelbases of 125 and 132 inches. Both were announced by a handsome new radiator, which Franklin always termed a "hood front," believing that a conventional radiator was essential to sales. This now had shutters governing the amount of incoming air, with shutter opening controlled automatically by a thermostat connected to the number-one cylinder. Per company tradition, the new engine had six individually cast cylinders and overhead valves, but differed in having cooling air directed to the sides of the block from left to right—an arrangement soon known as "side-blast" cooling. The six delivered 95 horsepower from 274 cubic inches.

Franklin had always been a luxury make, so its chassis were a logical basis for many custom bodies, typically by Derham, Dietrich, Locke, and Brunn. Among the more memorable 1930 open styles was Dietrich's four-door Pirate, available as either a five-passenger phaeton or seven-seater touring. Its most striking feature was running boards fully concealed by flared door bottoms. Also new that year was the Pursuit, a dual-cowl phaeton that lacked external door handles in the interest of cleaner appearance. Upholstery in the Pursuit's front compartment wrapped up and over the outer edge of the doors *a la* aircraft cockpits of the day. Dietrich also conjured a popular four-door, four-seat speedster with an abbreviated body ending midway over the rear wheels. Most of these were closed styles with permanent canvas tops, but a full-convertible option was offered at extra cost.

As you might expect, famous pioneer aviators like Lindbergh, Amelia Earhart, and Frank Hawks chose Franklins as their personal cars, something else the company was only too eager to publicize. But though Franklin had its sporty models, it never sold cars on that basis. Most of its customers were physicians, attorneys, business executives, and other professionals, so paint colors were usually conservative and blackwall tires were the norm. Franklin was ahead of the industry by selling more sedans than open cars before 1920, and sedans remained the models of choice in the '30s. Franklins may thus be described as conservative, elegant, and fairly expensive. The owners were loyal, and Franklin had many repeat customers.

Franklin claimed its share of the "fine car business" was up 100 percent in the first quarter of 1930 versus the comparable 1928 period. Trouble was, the Great Depression had all but killed the "fine car business," so Franklin's 1930 calendar-year sales came to less than half its 1929 total. Seeking desperately to maintain production levels, Franklin introduced the "Transcontinent Six" (Series 141) in May 1930. Like the "145," it offered a closed coupe, convertible coupe, victoria brougham, and four-door sedan on the 125-inch chassis. The sedan was the cheapest car Franklin offered, but even its $2395 price was four times the cost of a new Model A Ford. In those days, remember, such sums equaled a nice annual salary. With all this, model-year production was dismal: just 5744.

1930 Series 147 Six Town Car by Derham

1930 Series 147 Six Pirate dual-cowl phaeton

1930 Pirate Touring

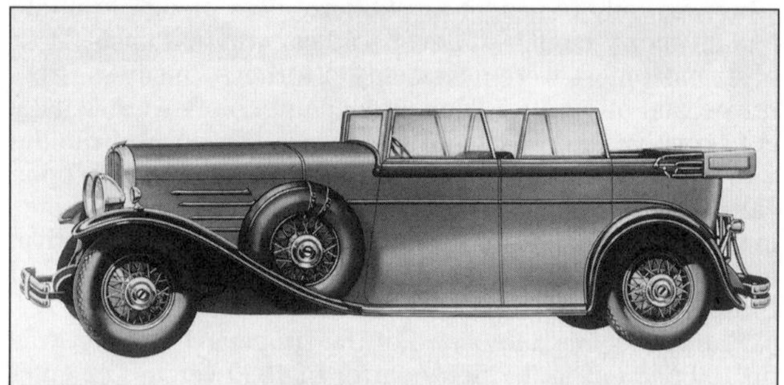

1930 Series 147 Six Pirate 7-passenger phaeton

1931 Series 153 DeLuxe Six Pirate touring

Offerings were promptly pared for 1931. Transcontinent returned with its previous body styles at prices trimmed to just $1800-$1900. Up in the $2400-$2700 area was the DeLuxe Six, a four-model group sporting rakish clamshell fenders and beautiful flowing body lines by Ray Dietrich on the 132-inch wheelbase. The six was coaxed up to 100 brake horsepower for all models. Advertising continued to stress engineering links with aviation via florid phrases such as "riding like gliding." But the Great Depression had set in with a vengeance, and Franklin's model-year production withered to 2851.

Then Franklin hatched a startling idea: an air-cooled V-12—a mighty thing with 398 cid and 150 bhp. Franklin advertised its V-12 as "supercharged," but in reality it had a ram-air effect, courtesy of a duct from the cooling fan. The Twelve was originally planned for the 1931 DeLuxe Six chassis, but was delayed to '32 by financial problems. Franklin had failed to meet payment on certain notes, and the banks sent in managers to protect their investment. Company president Edwin McEwen also decided some changes were needed, so the Twelve bowed as an entirely new and larger car for 1932.

It resembled previous Franklins only in being air-cooled. The traditional full-elliptics and tubular front axle gave way to semi-elliptics and an I-beam. Instead of bodies built by Walker of Massachusetts, Franklin's longtime supplier, Twelve coach-work was hand-crafted at the company's own Syracuse factory. LeBaron was responsible for the styling, distinguished by a sharply Vee'd "hood cover" extending back to a jaunty angled windshield. By the standards of 1932, the Franklin Twelve was truly exotic and magnificent to the eye. On a 144-inch wheelbase chassis, its size alone was impressive.

But sales were far from that: an estimated 200 for the model year, plus another 1700 or so six-cylinder Airmans on the 132-inch wheelbase chassis. Franklin's situation was now quite desperate.

Accordingly, the firm issued an even cheaper line for 1933. Dubbed Olympic, it resulted from a hasty agreement with Reo (*see entry*), another automaker facing imminent demise. Basically it was Reo's new 118-inch-wheelbase Flying Cloud with a Franklin six installed by Franklin in Syracuse, New York. Reo shipped 30 bodies a day from its Lansing, Michigan, factory; a like number of Olympics rolled out of Syracuse the following day. Franklin's investment was modest, so the Olympic's retail price was attractively low: $1385 for either the coupe or sedan, and $1500 for a convertible coupe.

The Olympic was a very good car, but it was too late to save Franklin. Just 1218 were built for 1933, and a mere 109 for swan-song '34. Franklin also offered mechanically unchanged Twelves and Airman Sixes in those final two years, each with four body styles, but production was minuscule. Combined totals were only 98 and 468 units, respectively.

The Franklin story didn't end with bankruptcy. The company was bought by a firm led by former Franklin engineers and began manufacturing Franklin air-cooled airplane engines. Helicopter engines were added in the '40s. In '48 water-cooling was added to a Franklin helicopter engine to power the Tucker (*see entry*) car. Aircraft engine production continued into the 1970s.

1931 Series 153 DeLuxe Six Speedster sedan

1933 Series 18 Olympic four-door sedan

1932 Airman Six convertible coupe

1933 Series 17-A Twelve four-door sedan

Specifications

1930 - 5,744 built

145 Six (wb 125.0)	Wght	Price	Prod
cpe 3-5P	3,880	2,610	—
conv cpe 3-5P	3,790	2,710	—
victoria brghm 4-6P	3,790	2,695	—
sdn 4d	3,930	2,585	—
147 Six (wb 132.0)			
rdstr 2-4P	3,950	2,885	—
Pirate phtn 5P	4,120	2,885	—
Pirate touring 7P	4,050	2,885	—
Salon spdstr sdn 5P	4,130	2,715	—
sdn 7P	4,230	2,875	—
Pursuit phtn	4,120	2,885	—
141 Transcontinent Six (wb 125.0)*			
cpe 3-5P	3,850	2,445	—
conv cpe 3-5P	3,775	2,495	—
victoria brougham 4P	3,845	2,495	—
sdn 4d	3,930	2,395	—

* Production combined with 1931 Series 151.

1930 Engine	bore × stroke	bhp	availability
I-6, 274.0	3.50 × 4.75	95	S-all

1931 - 2,851 built

151 Transcon Six (wb 125.0)*	Wght	Price	Prod
cpe 3-5P	3,850	1,845	—
conv cpe 3-5P	3,775	1,895	—
victoria brougham 4P	3,845	1,895	—
sdn 4d	3,930	1,795	—
153 DeLuxe Six (wb 132.0)			
Cstm conv spdstr 4P	4,110	2,695	—
conv cpe 3-5P	4,185	2,465	—
victoria brougham 5P	4,200	2,495	—
sdn 4d	4,220	2,395	—

* Includes 1930 Series 141.

1931 Engine	bore × stroke	bhp	availability
I-6, 274.0	3.50 × 4.75	100	S-all

1932

16 Airman Six (wb 132.0) - 1,700 built*

	Wght	Price	Prod
cpe 3-5P	4,210	2,345	—
conv cpe 3-5P	4,285	2,390	—
victoria brougham 4P	4,390	2,445	—
sdn 4d	4,420	2,345	—
17 Twelve (wb 144.0) - 200 built*			
sdn 4d	5,600	3,885	—
club brougham	5,515	3,885	—
sdn 7P	5,900	3,985	—
limo 7P	5,890	4,185	—

* Estimated.

1932 Engines	bore × stroke	bhp	availability
I-6, 274.0	3.50 × 4.75	100	S-16
V-12, 398.0	3.25 × 4.00	150	S-17

1933

18 Olympic (wb 118.0) - 889 blt	Wght	Price	Prod
cpe 3-5P	3,500	1,385	—
conv cpe 3-5P	3,425	1,500	—
sdn 4d	3,625	1,385	—
16-B Airman Six (wb 132.0) - 171 built			
sdn 4d	4,420	1,936	—
Oxford sdn 4d	4,420	1,995	—
club sdn 5P	4,425	1,985	—
sdn 7P	4,500	2,135	—
17-A Twelve (wb 144.0) - 98 built*			
sdn 4d	5,630	2,885	—
club brougham 5P	5,515	2,885	—
sdn 7P	5,900	2,985	—
limo 7P	5,890	3,185	—
18-B Olympic (wb 118.0) - 329 blt	**Wght**	**Price**	**Prod**
cpe 3-5 P	3,500	1,435	—
conv cpe 3-5P	3,425	1,550	—
sdn 4d	3,625	1,435	—

* Includes 1934 Series 17-B.

1933 Engines	bore × stroke	bhp	availability
I-6, 274.0	3.50 × 4.75	100	S-18, 18-B, 16-B
V-12, 398.0	3.25 × 4.00	150	S-17-B

1934

18-C Olympic (wb 118.0) - 109 blt	Wght	Price	Prod
cpe 3-5P	3,500	1,435	—
conv cpe 3-5P	3,425	1,550	—
sdn 4d	3,625	1,435	—
19A Airman (wb 132.0) - 186 built			
cpe 3-5P	4,270	2,185	—
sdn 4d	4,500	2,185	—
club sdn 5P	4,610	2,285	—
sdn 7P	4,710	2,385	—
19-B Airman (wb 132.0) - 111 built			
cpe 3-5P	4,270	2,185	—
sdn 4d	4,500	2,185	—
club sdn 5P	4,610	2,285	—
sdn 7P	4,710	2,385	—
17-B Twelve (wb 144.0) - 98 built*			
sdn 4d	5,630	2,885	—
club brougham 5P	5,515	2,885	—
sdn 7P	5,900	2,985	—
limo 7P	5,890	3,185	—

* Includes 1933 Series 17-A.

1934 Engines	bore × stroke	bhp	availability
I-6, 274.0	3.50 × 4.75	100	S-18-C, 19, 19-B
V-12, 398.0	3.25 × 4.00	150	S-17-B

Frazer

1948 Standard four-door sedan

Frazer was one of the few genuinely new post World War II American cars, but managed only a short, somewhat unhappy life. The name honored Joseph Washington Frazer, the high-born aristocrat (descended from the Virginia Washingtons) who loved motorcars and became a super-salesman through stints at Packard, Pierce-Arrow, and General Motors. Frazer also worked with Walter P. Chrysler in the 1920s and resuscitated moribund Willys-Overland in the late '30s.

In the early '40s, Frazer was looking to build a new postwar car, an idea that also occurred to Henry J. Kaiser, the West Coast metals and construction tycoon who'd turned out wartime Liberty ships double-quick. Frazer and Kaiser met, hit it off, and formed Kaiser-Frazer Corporation in July 1945, with Frazer as president, Kaiser as board chairman. It seemed a match made in automotive heaven: Joe's redoubtable sales acumen married to Henry J.'s vast manufacturing resources.

After considering several proposals (including a radical front-drive design), they settled on a conventional rear-drive four-door sedan with modern flush-fender styling by renowned custom-body designer Howard A. "Dutch" Darrin. The end product wasn't all Darrin's work—nor entirely to his satisfaction—but it was smooth and fairly stylish for the period, with the arguable exception of the high blunt hood.

Two versions were planned: a medium-price Kaiser and a luxury Frazer. Henry J, thinking big as usual, geared up for Kaisers by buying Ford's huge, wartime bomber plant at Willow Run, Michigan. Frazers were to be built by Graham-Paige in Detroit, lately acquired by Joe and his associates. But G-P was foundering and sold out to K-F in 1947, so all but the earliest Frazers were built alongside Kaisers.

Both makes began production in June 1946 (for model-year '47). Each offered basic and upmarket models. Frazers were nameless "Standards" and Manhattans. There was only one engine: a long-stroke 226.2-cubic-inch flathead six, basically the Continental "Red Seal" design improved upon and mostly built by K-F. Frazer advertised it as the "Supersonic Six," but with only 100/110 horsepower to push over 3300 pounds, no K-F car acted jet-propelled. At least the "Darrin-styled" body offered exceptional passenger room—including the industry's widest front seat—64 inches—and the rugged box-section chassis boasted modern front-coil/rear-leaf suspension.

Initially, K-F built two Kaisers to each Frazer, reflecting the latter's higher $2295 starting price—close to Cadillac territory. The Manhattan was some $400 more, but also elegantly upholstered in nylon and fine Bedford cord cloth keyed to

1949-50 Manhattan convertible sedan

1949-50 Manhattan four-door sedan

exterior colors, which were typically two-tones. Full leather upholstery was also available. Unfortunately, this Cadillac price rival lacked an automatic transmission of any kind, let alone one to match ultrasmooth Hydra-Matic: just a three-speed manual or the same with optional Borg-Warner overdrive ($80).

Yet despite the stiff prices, lack of automatic, and no eight-cylinder engine in sight, K-F enjoyed strong initial sales to earn the press sobriquet of "postwar wonder company." Still, some observers doubted the dynamic managerial duo. Henry Kaiser, they said, didn't know an automobile from a motorboat, while Frazer had only sold cars, not built them.

Even so, K-F succeeded despite postwar materials shortages, forming a crack team of expediters who foraged the country for everything from sheet steel to copper wire. They usually got what they wanted—though at a price, the main reason the cars cost so much. Still, K-F racked up the highest output of any independent in 1947-48, with total volume sufficient for ninth place in the production race.

And why not? Both the Kaiser and Frazer had the advantage of being all-new cars with no prewar links, and both were readily available (though competitors were fast returning to prewar production levels). They also looked good: very clean, with modest horizontal grilles (Frazer's was a bit more ornate than Kaiser's) and little decorative chrome or sculptured sheetmetal, reflecting Darrin's design ideals. A long 123.5-inch wheelbase provided a smooth ride, and the six-cylinder engine, though plodding, delivered excellent fuel economy. But this was a heady age when buyers wanted all the performance and chrome they could get. Though Frazer ultimately got around to optional hood ornaments and more-glittery interiors, the lack of eight-cylinder power would prove an increasing sales liability for the prices charged.

In fact, the Frazer never really went much beyond its original formula. Indeed, the '48 models changed only in detail yet cost even more: $2483-$2746. So though the postwar seller's market was still in full swing, Frazer volume dropped ominously for model-year '48, from 68,775 to 48,071.

Then, a gross miscalculation. Knowing his firm could field only facelifts against all-new models from the Big Three and Nash, Joe Frazer recommended cutting 1949 production, then coming back with all-new designs for 1950. But Henry Kaiser wouldn't hear of it, declaring, "The Kaisers never retrench!" Predictably, Henry won. In protest, Joe stepped down to the meaningless position of board vice-chairman, and Henry appointed his own son, Edgar, as president. K-F duly tooled for 200,000 cars, but ended up selling just 58,000 for '49. A long downhill slide had begun.

The '49 Frazers took on an eggcrate grille, prominent rectangular parking lamps, and large two-lens vertical taillamps. There was also a new four-door Manhattan convertible, but it was a makeshift job at best. Directed to do or die, engineers John Widman and Ralph Isbrandt sheared the top off a sedan, retained B-pillars with little inset glass panes, and purchased

1949 Standard prototype (with Kaiser hubcaps)

1949-50 Standard four-door sedan

1951 Standard Vagabond utility sedan

1951 Standard four-door sedan

1951 Manhattan hardtop sedan

1951 Manhattan hardtop sedan

beefed-up X-member frames at an inordinate price. But at over $3000, the four-door flop-top Frazer simply couldn't sell in viable numbers.

Nor could any '49 Frazer. As a result, some 5000 '49 leftovers were reserialed for a brief 1950 run that ended in the spring of that year. Production for the two seasons came to just under 25,000 units, including a mere 70 Manhattan convertibles. It's estimated that only 15 percent of the total were sold as 1950 models.

Frazer's 1951 was abbreviated, too, but the cars looked startlingly different, thanks to an effective front and rear redo by Herb Weissinger of K-F Styling. The intent was to use up remaining 1949-50 bodyshells. Thus, leftover Kaiser Vagabond utility sedans (with double hatchback and folding rear seat) became standard-trim '51 Frazer Vagabonds, while Kaiser Virginian four-door "hardtops" were made into '51 Frazer Manhattans. Pillared sedans were assigned to Frazer's standard line, but trimmed like 1950 Manhattans. Encouraged by the belated arrival of Hydra-Matic as a $159 option, dealers ordered 55,000 of the '51 Frazers, but received only 10,214. The Frazer was dead.

K-F stylists had created numerous renderings for future Frazers based on Darrin's sleek and low 1951 "Anatomic" Kaiser. But these and other plans were rendered stillborn when Joe Frazer left the company in early '49. Two years later, the Kaisers were busy with their new small car, the Henry J—and leftover '51 Kaisers. In retrospect, they really should have listened to Joe.

Specifications

1947

Standard (wb 123.5)		Wght	Price	Prod
F47	sdn 4d	3,340	2,295	36,120
Manhattan (wb 123.5)				
F47C	sdn 4d	3,375	2,712	32,655

1947 Engines	bore × stroke	bhp	availability
I-6, 226.2	3.31 × 4.38	100	S-all
I-6, 226.2	3.31 × 4.38	112	O-Manhattan

1948

F485 Standard (wb 123.5)		Wght	Price	Prod
4851	sdn 4d	3,340	2,483	29,480
F486 Manhattan (wb 123.5)		**Wght**	**Price**	**Prod**
4861	sdn 4d	3,375	2,746	18,591

1948 Engines	bore × stroke	bhp	availability
I-6, 226.2	3.31 × 4.38	100	S-all
I-6, 226.2	3.31 × 4.38	112	O-Manhattan

1949-50

F495/505 Stndrd (wb 123.5)	Wght	Price	Prod
4951/5051 sdn 4d	3,386	2,395	14,700*
F496/506 Manhattan (wb 123.5)			
4961/5051 sdn 4d	3,391	2,595	9,950*
4962/5052 conv sdn	3,726	3,295	70*

* Estimated: actual total 24,923. Years were combined by factory; estimated breakdown 85% 1949, 15% 1950.

1949-50 Eng	bore × stroke	bhp	availability
I-6, 226.2	3.31 × 4.38	112	S-all

1951

F515 Standard (wb 123.5)		Wght	Price	Prod
5151	sdn 4d	3,456	2,359	6,900*
5155	Vagabond util sdn 4d	3,556	2,399	3,000*
F516 Manhattan (wb 123.5)				
5161	htp sdn	3,771	3,075	152
5162	conv sdn	3,941	3,075	131

* Estimated from actual total of 9,931.

1951 Engine	bore × stroke	bhp	availability
I-6, 226.2	3.31 × 4.38	115	S-all

Graham

Brothers Joseph, Robert, and Ray Graham were "Indiana sharpies," to quote auto historian Jeffrey Godshall—farm boys with "dreams beyond the bucolic life." Sharp they were. After starting a glassmaking business that grew to become Libbey-Owens-Ford in 1930, the brothers built trucks for Dodge. They did so well that by 1926 they were running Dodge's entire truck organization. Then, suddenly, they left and bought the declining Paige Motor Company in 1927 to build their own cars. The first appeared the following year under the Graham-Paige banner, which continued through 1930. The name was then changed to simply Graham, though Paige remained in the company name and on its commercial vehicles.

The Grahams prospered with cars as quickly as they had with trucks, volume soaring to more than 77,000 in calendar 1929. By that time they'd set up a vast new factory in Dearborn, Michigan, plus facilities in Indiana and Florida. However, 1929 would be the firm's production peak.

Graham's 1930 line was expansive, comprising Standard and Special Sixes on a 115-inch wheelbase and Standard, Special, and Custom Eights on spans of 122, 134, 127, and 137 inches. Engines were conventional L-heads: 207- and 224-cubic-inch inline-sixes with 66/76 horsepower as well as 298.6- and 322-cid straight-eights with 100/120 bhp. Among numerous body styles were beautiful long-wheelbase Custom Eight town cars and limousines by the LeBaron studios at Briggs Manufacturing Company. All models featured Graham-Paige's famous four-speed transmission.

This basic lineup continued through early 1932, joined in the spring of 1931 by the hopefully named "Prosperity Six," a cheap four-model series priced as low as $785. But the Depression was on, and Graham-Paige failed to prosper. Model-year 1930 car production sank to about 24,000, then slid to 20,000 for '31.

Undaunted, the Grahams came back for 1932 with the Blue Streak Eight. This mounted a generous 123-inch wheelbase that perfectly suited magnificent new styling by Amos Northup of the Murray Corporation. Northup had just created the 1931 Reo Royale and was also responsible for the earlier Hupp Century. The Blue Streak was no less stunning. Smooth, ultraclean bodies hid unsightly chassis components, windshields tilted jauntily back, a radiator with tapered vertical bars and no cap fit flush with the hood, and fenders were artfully drawn down to hug the wheels—the "skirted" treatment was a first for a production car.

The Blue Streak bowed with only a coupe, four-door sedan, and convertible coupe. All carried a 90-bhp 245.4-cid eight with an aluminum head and pistons. Beneath the trend-setting bodies was an equally advanced chassis with straight side rails, outboard rear springs, and "banjo" rear-axle mounting. The result was exceptional handling stability combined with great ride comfort, abetted by adjustable shock absorbers and, a bit later, low-pressure tires. Standard and Deluxe trim was offered at attractively low prices ranging from $1095 to $1270.

In good times, the Blue Streak would have sold well. But 1932 wasn't a good year for anyone in Detroit, and Graham's calendar-year volume slid to 12,967. Most were Blue Streaks and conventionally styled Sixes.

The Blue Streak was renamed Custom Eight for 1933, when its little-changed basic design spread to all "second-series" Grahams. Competitors' styling began mimicking the Blue Streak, so Graham proclaimed itself "the most imitated car on the road." With almost every '33 American car wearing fender skirts, they were right. Below the Custom were a new 113-inch-wheelbase Standard Six and 119-inch Standard Eight. All models rode stronger frames with front K-brace and sported gracefully vee'd front bumpers. Yet for all this quality and appeal, Graham-Paige production sank again, hitting 11,000 for the calendar year, though the firm somehow eked out a tiny $67,000 profit.

Still hoping for better times, Graham sprang a surprise for 1934: the Supercharged Custom Eight. Tagged as low as $1295, it was America's first moderate-cost supercharged car. Boosting its newly bored 265.4-cid engine was a Graham-built centrifugal blower that helped deliver 135 bhp—good for lively midrange urge and 90 mph all-out. Daredevil driver "Cannonball" Baker drove a Supercharged Custom cross-country in 53 hours, 30 minutes; a solo record that would stand until 1975. Baker's feat also testified to the utter relia-

1932 Model 57 Blue Streak Eight 3-window coupe

1932 Model 57 Blue Streak Eight four-door sedan

1933 Model 64 Standard Eight four-door sedan (Second Series)

1933 Model 65 Standard Six four-door sedan (Second Series)

1934 Model 67 Standard Eight trunkback sedan (Second Series)

bility of the Graham blower. Over the next six years, Graham would build more supercharged cars than any company ever had before.

Other Grahams saw little change through the "first-series" 1935 models, though the lineup was juggled several times and built-in trunks were a notable new option for sedans (at $35). With calender 1934 output rising to 15,745 cars, things seemed to be looking up.

Offerings shuffled again for 1935's "second series." Coupes and convertibles looked much as before, but sedans began backing away from Blue Streak styling, which was becoming a bit dated anyway. A smaller new Standard Six arrived with a 60-bhp, 169.6-cid engine and Blue Streak styling on a trim 111-inch wheelbase. It lacked some big-Graham technical features, but sold well. A good thing, as eight-cylinder sales declined sharply. So even though model-year volume went up to near 18,500, Graham was now feeling a severe financial pinch.

Accordingly, the firm abandoned Eights for 1936 but offered America's first supercharged six: a 217.8-cid unit that would be Graham's mainstay engine right to the end. It arrived in 115-inch-wheelbase Supercharged and unblown Cavalier series sharing Hayes-built coupe, sedan, and convertible bodies with Reo's 1935-36 Flying Cloud, an arrangement worked out during 1935. The two companies never "married," but Graham used Reo bodies through 1937, which resulted in some very ordinary looking cars. Graham's price-leading 1936-37 Crusader used 1935 tooling, which was later sold to Nissan of Japan to bring in needed cash. And Graham needed that, losing $1 million in 1936 despite higher calendar-year sales of over 16,400.

Hoping for a miracle, Graham unleashed the radical "Spirit of Motion" for 1938, a blown and unblown four-door sedan with a sharply undercut front that soon earned the dubious nickname "sharknose." It was Northup's last design before his untimely death in 1936. (Ray Graham had passed away in 1932; he was only 45.) Graham was trying to be the style leader it had been with the Blue Streak, but the public didn't buy it—literally, as model-year production ended at 5020. A "sharknose" two-door sedan and "Combination" club coupe arrived for 1939, when running boards were eliminated. Horsepower remained 116 supercharged, 90 unblown, and all models offered Deluxe and better Custom trim. Despite impressive supercharged performance (10.9 seconds 0-50) and fuel economy of up to 25 mpg, the "sharknose" remained a poor seller. It thus departed after 1940, seeing little further change save slight horsepower gains (to 120 and 93). Respective 1939-40 model-year production was 5392 and an estimated 1000.

By now, company president Joseph Graham had spent a half-million dollars of his own money to keep his firm going. He needed something new, but how to pay for it? The answer came in 1939 with Norman De Vaux, who'd failed with auto-

1935 Model 69 Supercharged Custom Eight sedan (First Series)

mobiles marketed under his own name. De Vaux had bought up the tooling for the late 1936-37 Cord 810/812 Westchester sedan, and had talked equally struggling Hupp Motors into building a modified version with rear-wheel drive instead of front drive. Joe Graham proposed building the bodies, provided his company could sell its own version of the car with Graham power. Aside from that and minor trim differences, the resulting Graham Hollywood and Hupp Skylark were identical. The Skylark was announced first, in April 1939 at the New York World's Fair, though that proved premature. Gearing up for production took longer than expected, so neither model was built in significant numbers until May 1940.

Like Hupp, Graham planned to offer a sedan and convertible, but only one Hupp convertible was ever built and maybe up to five Grahams. Production Hollywoods carried Graham's own 120-bhp supercharged six, and thus cost a bit more than Hupp's unblown Skylark: initially $1250 versus $1145. Both models rode a 115-inch wheelbase, 10 inches shorter than the parent Cord's. To fit their tall engine beneath the Cord's lower hoodline, Graham engineers offset both carburetor and air cleaner. Both versions wore a handsomely reworked face (by the renowned John Tjaarda) with a double grille (fully chromed on Hollywoods), exposed bullet headlamps, and nicely shaped front fenders.

Unfortunately, the old tooling was simply unsuitable for volume production—the same thing that had tripped up the Cord. The roof alone comprised seven separate panels. Joe Graham hoped to simplify matters, but was distracted when he agreed to take over Skylark production, which necessitated a complete overhaul of Graham's assembly line and added further cost and delay.

Though Hupp called it quits in the summer of 1940, Graham pressed on for '41, adding an unblown Hollywood priced at just $968 and cutting the price of the supercharged model to $1065. Horsepower was upped slightly on both engines. But it was all to no avail, and Graham finally gave up the auto business, too, in September 1940.

Ironically, departing the car business proved quite timely, as Graham prospered through World War II on $20 million of government defense contracts. Joseph W. Frazer then bought the firm in 1944. His namesake Frazer car was built as a "Graham-Paige" product in 1946-47, though at Kaiser's Willow Run factory rather than G-P's old Dearborn plant. In early 1947, Graham-Paige sold its remaining automotive interests to Kaiser-Frazer, and in 1952 quit farm equipment as well. G-P then dropped "Motors" from its name and became a closed investment corporation. It later operated Madison Square Garden and owned several professional New York athletic teams. All these endeavors proved far more profitable than carmaking had ever been.

1935 Model 75 Supercharged Eight four-door sedan

1936 Series 110 Supercharged two-door touring sedan

1937 Series 120 Custom Supercharged business coupe

1939 Series 96 Special Combination coupe

1940 Series 107 Supercharged Custom four-door sedan

1941 Custom Hollywood Supercharged four-door sedan

Specifications

Note: All production figures approximate, based on assigned serial number spans.

1930

Stndrd Six (wb 115)-18,000 blt	Wght	Price	Prod
rdstr 2-4P	2,865	995	—
phtn 5P	2,910	1,015	—
cpe 2P	2,940	845	—
cpe 2-4P	2,995	895	—
cabriolet 2-4P	2,950	1,065	—
sdn 2d	3,015	895	—
Universal sdn 3W 5P	3,160	895	—
DeLuxe sdn 3W 5P	3,175	995	—
Town sdn 2W 5P	3,145	845	—
DeLuxe cpe 2P	2,940	895	—
DeLuxe cpe 2-4P	2,995	945	—
DeLx Town sdn 5P	3,145	945	—

Special Six (wb 115.0) - 2,600 built	Wght	Price	Prod
cpe 2P	3,230	1,195	—
cpe 2-4P	3,355	1,225	—
sdn 4d	3,390	1,225	—

Standard Eight (wb 122.0; 7P-134.0) - 925 built	Wght	Price	Prod
cpe 2-4P	3,735	1,445	—
sdn 4d	3,795	1,445	—
conv sdn 5P	3,725	1,985	—
sdn 7P	4,040	1,745	—

Special Eight (wb 122.0; 7P-134.0) - 2,025 built	Wght	Price	Prod
cpe 2-4P	3,805	1,595	—
sdn 4d	3,875	1,595	—
conv sdn 5P	3,785	2,085	—
sdn 7P	4,120	1,845	—

Custom Eight (wb 127.0; lwb-137.0) - 575 built	Wght	Price	Prod
rdstr 2-4P	4,009	2,225	
phtn 5P	3,975	2,295	
cpe 2-4P	4,105	2,225	250
cabriolet 2-4P	4,075	2,245	
sdn 4d	4,300	2,025	
lwb phtn 7P	4,200	2,295	
lwb sdn 4d	4,405	2,445	
Town sdn 4d (lwb)	4,465	2,455	
lwb sdn 7P	4,340	2,525	325
limo 7P (lwb)	4,590	2,595	
LeBrn limo sdn 7P (lwb)	4,535	3,940	
LeBrn town car 7P (lwb)	4,545	4,255	
LeBrn limo 7P (lwb)	4,545	4,505	

1930 Engines	bore×stroke	bhp	availability
I-6, 207.0	3.13×4.50	66	S-Standard 6
I-6, 224.0	3.25×4.50	76	S-Special 6
I-8, 298.6	3.25×4.50	100	S-Stndrd 8, Sp 8
I-8, 322.0	3.38×4.50	120	S-Custom 8

1931

Stndrd Six (wb 115) - 9,000 blt	Wght	Price	Prod
rdstr 2-4P	2,865	995	—
phtn 5P	2,910	1,015	—
bus cpe 2P	2,940	845	—
cpe 2-4P	2,995	895	—
spt cpe 2-4P	2,995	1,045	—
sdn 2d	3,015	895	—
Town sdn 5P	3,145	845	—
Univ sdn 5P	3,160	895	—
DeLuxe sdn 5P	3,175	995	—
DeLuxe Town sdn 5P	3,145	945	—

Special Six (wb 115.0) - 1,400 built	Wght	Price	Prod
bus cpe 2P	3,230	1,195	—
cpe 2-4P	3,355	1,225	—
sdn 5P	3,390	1,225	—

621 Six (wb 121.0)	Wght	Price	Prod
rdstr 2-4P	3,835	1,795	—
phtn 5P	3,805	1,865	—
victoria cpe 4P	3,905	1,595	—
cpe 2-4P	3,935	1,795	—
sdn 5P	4,130	1,595	—

Standard Eight (wb 122.0; lwb-134.0)	Wght	Price	Prod
cpe 2-4P	3,735	1,445	—
sdn 5P	3,795	1,445	—
conv sdn 5P	3,725	1,985	—
lwb sdn 7P	4,040	1,745	—
lwb sdn 5P	3,980	1,695	—
limo 7P (lwb)	4,090	1,945	—

Special Eight (wb 122.0; lwb-134.0) - 2,025 built	Wght	Price	Prod
822 cpe 2-4P	3,805	1,595	
822 sdn 5P	3,875	1,635	1,125
822 conv sdn 5P	3,785	1,635	
lwb sdn 7P	4,120	1,845	
lwb sdn 5P	4,060	1,795	900
limo 7P (lwb)	4,110	2,045	

Custom Eight (wb 127.0; lwb-137.0)	Wght	Price	Prod
rdstr 2-4P	4,005	2,225	—
phtn 5P	3,975	2,295	—
victoria cpe 4P	4,075	2,025	—
cabriolet 2-4P	4,075	2,245	—
sdn 5P	4,300	2,025	—
lwb phtn 7P	4,270	2,595	—
lwb sdn 5P	4,470	2,455	—
LeBaron limo 7P (lwb)	4,620	4,505	—

1931 Engines	bore×stroke	bhp	availability
I-6, 207.0	3.13×4.50	66	S-Standard 6
I-6, 224.0	3.25×4.50	76	S-Special 6
I-6, 228.0	3.50×5.00	97	S-621
I-8, 298.6	3.25×4.50	100	S-Standard 8, Special 8
I-8, 322.0	3.38×4.50	120	S-Custom 8

1931 Second Series (Production began Jan. 1, 1931)

Stndrd Six (wb 115)-11,600 blt	Wght	Price	Prod
rdstr 2-4P	2,930	895	—
sdn 5P	3,265	955	—
bus cpe 2P	3,120	845	—
cpe 2-4P	3,170	895	—
Town sdn 5P	3,220	895	—

Special Six (wb 115.0) - 2,000 built	Wght	Price	Prod
bus cpe 2P	3,175	925	—
cpe 2-4P	3,235	975	—
sdn 4d	3,330	1,035	—
Town sdn 5P	3,270	975	—

820 Special Eight (wb 120.0) - 2,800 built	Wght	Price	Prod
bus cpe 2P	3,445	1,155	—
cpe 2-4P	3,500	1,195	—
spt sdn 5P	3,565	1,195	—
sdn 5P	3,560	1,245	—

834 Custom Eight (wb 134.0) - 200 built	Wght	Price	Prod
sdn 4d	4,100	1,845	—
sdn 7P	4,190	1,895	—
limo 7P	4,245	2,095	—

Prosperity Six (wb 113.0) - 1,000 built	Wght	Price	Prod
cpe 2P	3,015	785	—
cpe 2-4P	3,070	825	—
sdn 5P	3,100	825	—
Town sdn 5P	3,100	795	—

1931(2) Eng	bore×stroke	bhp	availability
I-6, 207.0	3.13×4.50	70	S-Prosp Six
I-6, 224.0	3.25×4.50	76	S-Std 6, Sp 6
I-8, 245.4	3.13×4.50	85	S-820
I-8, 298.6	3.25×4.50	100	S-834

1932

Prosp Six (wb 113) - 700 built	Wght	Price	Prod
cpe 2P	3,015	785	—
cpe 2-4P	3,070	825	—
sdn 5P	3,100	825	—
Town sdn 5P	3,100	795	—

Standard Six (wb 115.0)	Wght	Price	Prod
rdstr 2-4P	2,930	945	—
bus cpe 2P	3,120	934	—
cpe 2-4P	3,170	985	—
sdn 5P	3,265	995	—
Town sdn 5P	3,220	975	—

Special Six (wb 115.0)	Wght	Price	Prod
rdstr 2-4P	2,995	985	—
bus cpe 2P	3,175	985	—
cpe 2-4P	3,235	1,025	—
sdn 4d	3,330	1,035	—
Town sdn 5P	3,270	1,015	—

820 Special Eight (wb 120.0)	Wght	Price	Prod
bus cpe 2P	3,445	1,185	—
cpe 2-4P	3,500	1,225	—
spt sdn 5P	3,565	1,235	—
sdn 5P	3,560	1,285	—

822 Special Eight (wb 122.0)	Wght	Price	Prod
sdn 5P	3,875	1,635	—
conv sdn 5P	3,785	1,635	—

834 New Custom Eight (wb 134.0)	Wght	Price	Prod
sdn 4d	4,100	1,895	—
sdn 7P	4,190	1,945	—
limo 7P	4,245	2,145	—

57 Blue Streak Eight (wb 123.0) - 9,714 built	Wght	Price	Prod
cpe 2P	3,600	1,095	—
cpe 2-4P	3,675	1,145	—
sdn 5P	3,665	1,145	—
DeLuxe cpe 2P	3,620	1,170	—
DeLuxe cpe 2-4P	3,685	1,220	—
DeLuxe conv cpe	3,730	1,270	—
DeLuxe sdn 5P	3,690	1,220	—

Six (wb 113.0) - 700 built	Wght	Price	Prod
sdn 5P	3,205	795	—
Town sdn 5P	3,190	765	—

1932 Engines	bore×stroke	bhp	availability
I-6, 207.0	3.13×4.50	70	S-Six, Prosp Six
I-6, 224.0	3.25×4.50	76	S-Standard 6, Special 6
I-8, 245.4	3.13×4.50	85	S-820
I-8, 245.4	3.13×4.50	90	S-57
I-8, 298.6	3.25×4.50	100	S-822, 834

1933

Six(a) (wb 118.0)	Wght	Price	Prod
bus cpe 2P	3,480	825	—
cpe 2-4P	3,545	875	—
conv cab 2-4P	3,590	895	—
sdn 5P	3,570	875	—

Six(b) (wb 113.0)	Wght	Price	Prod
sdn 5P	3,205	710	—
Town sdn 5P	3,190	680	—

57A Eight (wb 123.0)	Wght	Price	Prod
cpe 2P	3,600	925	—
cpe 2-4P	3,675	975	—
sdn 5P	3,665	975	—
DeLuxe cpe 2P	3,620	1,000	—
DeLuxe 2-4P	3,685	1,050	—
DeLx conv cpe 2-4P	3,730	1,070	—
DeLuxe sdn 5P	3,690	1,050	—

65 Standard Six (wb 113.0) - 4,000 built	Wght	Price	Prod
bus cpe 2P	3,230	745	—
cpe 2-4P	3,295	795	—
conv cpe 2-4P	3,255	835	—
sdn 5P	3,265	795	—

64 Standard Eight (wb 119.0) - 2,000 built	Wght	Price	Prod
bus cpe 2P	3,455	845	—
cpe 2-4P	3,510	895	—
conv cpe 2-4P	3,470	935	—
sdn 5P	3,500	895	—

57A Custom Eight (wb 123.0) - 1,000 built	Wght	Price	Prod
cpe 2P	3,625	1,045	—
cpe 2-4P	3,680	1,095	—
sdn 5P	3,695	1,095	—

1933 Engines	bore×stroke	bhp	availability
I-6, 207.0	3.13×4.50	70	S-Six(b)
I-6, 224.0	3.25×4.50	80	S-Six(a)
I-6, 224.0	3.25×4.50	85	S-Std Six
I-8, 245.4	3.13×4.50	90	S-57A Eight
I-8, 245.4	3.13×4.50	95	S-64, 57A Custom Eight

1934

65 Stndrd Six (wb 113) - 6,000 blt	Wght	Price	Prod
cpe 2P	3,205	745	—
cpe 2-4P	3,275	795	—
conv cpe 2-4P	3,230	835	—
sdn 5P	3,240	795	—

64 Standard Eight (wb 119) - 3,000 built	Wght	Price	Prod
cpe 2P	3,415	845	—
cpe 2-4P	3,485	895	—
conv cpe 2-4P	3,430	935	—
sdn 5P	3,460	895	—

57A Custom Eight (wb 123.0) - 4,000 built	Wght	Price	Prod
cpe 2P	3,600	1,045	—
cpe 2-4P	3,640	1,095	—
sdn 5P	3,670	1,095	—

68 Six (wb 116.0) - 8,550 blt	Wght	Price	Prod
Standard bus cpe 2P	3,135	695	
Standard cpe 2-4P	3,190	765	
Standard sdn 5P	3,165	775	
Standard sdn T/B 5P	3,260	810	
DeLuxe bus cpe 2P	3,165	805	5,320
DeLuxe cpe 2-4P	3,210	855	
DeLx conv cpe 2-4P	3,195	845	
DeLuxe sdn 5P	3,215	855	
DeLuxe sdn T/B 5P	3,300	890	
later production (from April 1934)			
Standard bus cpe 2P	3,100	745	
Standard cpe 2-4P	3,165	795	
Stndrd conv cpe 2-4P	3,165	845	3,230
Standard sdn 5P	3,120	795	
Standard sdn T/B 5P	3,210	830	
67 Eight (wb 123.0) - 915 built			
Special bus cpe 2P	3,365	875	—
Special cpe 2-4P	3,450	925	—
Special sdn 5P	3,490	925	—
Special sdn T/B 5P	3,500	960	—
Standard bus cpe 2P	3,415	965	—
Standard cpe 2-4P	3,475	1,015	—
Stndrd conv cpe 2-4P	3,445	995	—
Standard sdn 5P	3,470	1,015	—
Standard sdn T/B 5P	3,555	1,050	—
69 Custom Eight (wb 123.0) - 89 built			
bus cpe 2P	3,505	1,245	—
cpe 2-4P	3,590	1,295	—
conv cpe 2-4P	3,535	1,295	—
sdn 5P	3,600	1,295	—
sdn T/B 5P	3,660	1,330	—
71 Custom Eight (wb 138.0)			
sdn 7P	—	1,695	—
sdn T/B 7P	—	1,730	—

1934 Engines	bore×stroke	bhp	availability
I-6, 224.0	3.25×4.50	85	S-65, 68
I-8, 245.4	3.13×4.50	95	S-57A, 64, 67
I-8, 265.4	3.25×4.50	135	S-69, 71

1935

68 Stndrd Six (wb 116) - 4,000 blt	Wght	Price	Prod
bus cpe 3P	3,105	695	—
cpe 3-5P	3,165	765	—
conv cpe 3-5P	3,155	845	—
sdn 6P	3,135	775	—
sdn T/B 6P	3,225	810	—
67 Special Eight (wb 123.0)			
cpe 3P	3,365	875	—
cpe 3-5P	3,450	925	—
conv cpe 3-5P	3,445	995	—
sdn 6P	3,385	925	—
sdn T/B 6P	3,480	960	—
69 Special Eight (wb 123) - 2,419 built			
bus cpe 3P	3,445	1,045	—
cpe 3-5P	3,505	1,095	—
conv cpe 3-5P	3,490	1,165	—
sdn 6P	3,475	1,095	—
sdn T/B 6P	3,560	1,130	—
69 Sprchrgd Custom Eight (wb 123.0) - 1,862 built			
cpe 3P	3,505	1,245	—
cpe 3-5P	3,590	1,295	—
conv cpe 3-5P	3,535	1,295	—
sdn 6P	3,560	1,295	—
sdn T/B 6P	3,640	1,330	—
74 Standard Six (wb 111.0) - 11,470 built			
touring sdn 2d	2,620	595	—
touring sdn 4d	2,655	635	—
DeLx touring sdn 2d	2,645	645	—
DeLx touring sdn 4d	2,680	685	—
73 Special Six (wb 116.0) - 4,903 built			
cpe 2P	3,130	795	—
cpe 2-4P	3,215	845	—
conv cpe 2-4P	3,190	915	—
touring sdn 4d	3,265	845	—
72 Eight (wb 123.0) - 1,020 built			
cpe 2P	3,385	925	—
cpe 2-4P	3,445	975	—
conv cpe 2-4P	3,425	1,045	—

72 Eight	Wght	Price	Prod
touring sdn 4d	3,530	975	—
75 Supercharged Eight (wb 123.0) - 1,252 built			
cpe 2P	3,480	1,095	—
cpe 2-4P	3,585	1,145	—
conv cpe 2-4P	3,545	1,215	—
touring sdn 4d	3,640	1,145	—

1935 Engines	bore×stroke	bhp	availability
I-6, 169.6	3.00×4.00	60	S-74
I-6, 224.0	3.25×4.50	85	S-68, 73
I-8, 245.4	3.13×4.50	95	S-67, 72
I-8, 265.4	3.25×4.50	135	S-69 Sp 8
I-8, 265.4	3.25×4.50	140	S-69 Spchrgd, 75

1936

80/80A Crusadr (wb 111) - 3,220 blt	Wght	Price	Prod
touring sdn 2d	2,665	640	—
touring sdn 2d T/B	2,690	655	—
touring sdn 4d	2,700	680	—
touring sdn 4d T/B	2,735	695	—
90 Cavalier (wb 115.0) - 2,755 built			
bus cpe 3P	2,815	725	—
cpe 3-5P	2,880	710	—
conv cpe 3-5P	2,960	775	—
touring sdn 2d	2,930	720	—
touring sdn 2d T/B	2,930	825	—
touring sdn 4d	3,015	750	—
touring sdn 4d T/B	3,015	825	—
90A Cavalier (wb 115.0) - 7,750 built			
bus cpe 3P	2,730	750	—
cpe 3-5P	2,795	735	—
conv cpe 3-5P	2,875	800	—
touring sdn 2d	2,785	745	—
touring sdn 2d T/B	2,785	850	—
touring sdn 4d	2,870	775	—
touring sdn 4d T/B	2,870	850	—
110 Supercharged (wb 115) - 5,500 built			
bus cpe 2P	2,930	865	—
cpe 2-4P	2,995	875	—
conv cpe 3-5P	3,075	910	—
touring sdn 2d	3,060	850	—
touring sdn 2d T/B	3,060	880	—
touring sdn 4d	3,080	895	—
touring sdn 4d T/B	3,080	925	—
Cst touring sdn 4d T/B	3,200	1,170	—

1936 Engines	bore×stroke	bhp	availability
I-6, 169.6	3.00×4.00	70	S-80/80A
I-6, 199.1	3.25×4.00	80	S-90A
I-6, 217.8	3.25×4.38	85	S-90
I-6, 217.8	3.25×4.38	112	S-110

1937

85 Crusadr (wb 111) - 4,218 blt	Wght	Price	Prod
touring sdn 2d	2,660	690	—
touring sdn 2d T/B	2,675	720	—
touring sdn 4d	2,695	770	—
touring sdn 4d T/B	2,715	795	—
95 Cavalier (wb 116.0) - 8,250 built			
bus cpe 3P	2,815	850	—
cpe 3-5P	2,880	900	—
conv cpe 3-5P	2,960	945	—
touring sdn 2d	2,930	875	—
touring sdn 2d T/B	2,930	905	—
touring sdn 4d	2,960	905	—
touring sdn 4d T/B	2,945	935	—
116 Supercharged (wb 116.0) - 5,551 built			
bus cpe 3P	2,975	1,015	—
cpe 3-5P	3,040	1,045	—
conv cpe 3-5P	3,120	1,080	—
touring sdn 2d	3,105	1,020	—
touring sdn 2d T/B	3,105	1,050	—
touring sdn 4d	3,125	1,050	—
touring sdn 4d T/B	3,125	1,080	—
120 Cust Supercharged (wb 116.0; lwb-120.0) - 200 built			
bus cpe 3P	3,020	1,105	—
cpe 3-5P	3,055	1,135	—
conv cpe 3-5P	3,135	1,170	—
lwb touring sdn 4d	3,200	1,160	—
lwb tour sdn 4d T/B	3,200	1,190	—

1937 Engines	bore×stroke	bhp	availability
I-6, 169.6	3.00×4.00	70	S-85
I-6, 199.1	3.25×4.00	85	S-95
I-6, 199.1	3.25×4.00	106	S-116
I-6, 217.8	3.25×4.38	116	S-120

1938

96 Six (wb 120.0) - 2,610 blt	Wght	Price	Prod
Standard sdn 4d T/B	3,250	1,025	—
Special sdn 4d T/B	3,275	1,075	—
97 Supercharged (wb 120.0) - 2,410 built			
sdn 4d T/B	3,345	1,198	—
Custom sdn 4d T/B	3,350	1,320	—

1938 Engines	bore×stroke	bhp	availability
I-6, 217.8	3.25×4.38	90	S-96
I-6, 217.8	3.25×4.38	116	S-97

1939

96 Special (wb 120.0) - 2,913 blt*	Wght	Price	Prod
Combination cpe 5P	3,185	940	—
sdn 2d T/B	3,230	940	—
sdn 4d T/B	3,240	965	—
Cust Comb cpe 5P	3,200	1,070	—
Custom sdn 2d T/B	3,245	1,070	—
Custom sdn 4d T/B	3,255	1,095	—
97 Supercharged (wb 120.0) - 2,479 built*			
Combination cpe 5P	3,260	1,070	—
sdn 2d T/B	3,285	1,070	—
sdn 4d T/B	3,295	1,095	—
Custom Comb cpe 5P	3,290	1,200	—
Custom sdn 2d T/B	3,315	1,200	—
Custom sdn 4d T/B	3,325	1,225	—

1939 Engines	bore×stroke	bhp	availability
I-6, 217.8	3.25×4.38	90	S-96
I-6, 217.8	3.25×4.38	116	S-97; O-96 Cust

* Production totals based on published serial number spans. Total calendar-year production: 3,876.

1940

107 Supercharged (wb 120.0) - 1,000 built (estimated) (includes Standard)	Wght	Price	Prod
Deluxe cpe	3,245	1,160	—
Deluxe sdn 2d	3,250	1,135	—
Deluxe sdn 4d	3,250	1,160	—
Custom cpe	3,370	1,295	—
Custom sdn 2d	3,365	1,265	—
Custom sdn 4d	3,370	1,295	—
108 Standard (wb 120.0)			
Deluxe cpe	3,190	1,020	—
Deluxe sdn 2d	3,195	995	—
Deluxe sdn 4d	3,195	1,015	—
Custom cpe	3,315	1,160	—
Custom sdn 2d	3,315	1,135	—
Custom sdn 4d	3,320	1,160	—
Hollywood Custom Supercharged (wb 115.0)			
sdn 4d	2,965	1,250	*
conv cpe (prototype)	3,075	—	1-2

1940 Engines	bore×stroke	bhp	availability
I-6, 217.8	3.25×4.38	93	S-Unsuprchrgd
I-6, 217.8	3.25×4.38	120	S-Superchrgd

1941

109 Hollywood Custom Supercharged (wb 115)	Wght	Price	Prod
sdn 4d	2,965	1,065	*
113 Custom Hollywood (wb 115.0)			
sdn 4d	2,915	968	*

1941 Engines	bore×stroke	bhp	availability
I-6, 217.8	3.25×4.38	95	S-Unsuprchrgd
I-6, 217.8	3.25×4.38	124	S-Superchrgd

*Total 1940-41 Hollywood production: 1,859 (some sources claim 1,597).

Henry J

Kaiser-Frazer went from being the "postwar wonder" of 1947 and '48 to looking like a postwar blunder in 1949, falling from ninth to fourteenth in Detroit production. Determined to press on, chairman Henry J. Kaiser borrowed $44 million from the Reconstruction Finance Corporation to maintain inventories, then tooled up for new models. One result was the abrupt departure of co-founder Joseph W. Frazer. Kaiser promised the RFC that part of its money would go toward a new small car that any American could afford. With no little modesty, he named it the Henry J.

Designer Howard A. "Dutch" Darrin had proposed a short-wheelbase compact car derived from his beautiful 1951 Kaiser, which was already locked up during Henry J planning. But the head man, wanting something all-new, went with a proposal from American Metal Products, a Detroit supplier of frames and springs for car seats. Darrin reluctantly tried to improve this ungainly little two-door fastback sedan, applying his trademark "dip" to the beltline, windshield, and rear window—plus little tailfins. Though the result was still pretty weird, The New York Fashion Academy named Henry J its 1951 "Fashion Car of the Year."

Power was provided by Willys L-head engines: a 134 cubic-inch four and a 161-cid six. Incredible economy was promised for the 68-horsepower Four. The 80-horsepower Six turned out to be something of a hot rod, with 0-60 times of around 14 seconds, helped largely by low curb weight (around 2300 pounds). Though built on a compact 100-inch wheelbase, the Henry J could handle four passengers along with a considerable amount of luggage.

K-F began its '51 model year in March 1950. For awhile, the Henry J was quite popular, and nearly 82,000 were sold for the model year. But that evidently satisfied demand, for sales went down sharply through 1952. One reason was price. At $1363, even the four-cylinder model was only $200 cheaper than a full-size six-cylinder Chevrolet—and far more basic. The Henry J Six offered "DeLuxe" trim starting at $1499, but it was only slightly less stark.

A mild facelift gave 1952-54 models a smart new full-width grille, taillights moved from the body to the fins, and nicer interiors. An interim '52 measure designed to use up leftover stock was the Vagabond—a '51 wearing "continental" outside spare tire, identifying script, and a hood ornament of black plastic and chrome. After this, Henry Js were called Corsair or Corsair DeLuxe, priced around $1400 for the four, $1560 with the six.

But nothing seemed to work, so the Henry J departed in 1954. An estimated 1100 were sold that year, all of which were reserialed '53 leftovers. Some 30,000 were built altogether. Left stillborn were plans for a hardtop, wagon, four-door sedan, and even a convertible.

Many felt the original approach was wrong. Lacking gloveboxes, trunklids, and other expected features, the '51s were simply too plain for most buyers. As Joe Frazer later comment-

1951 Standard two-door fastback sedan

1951 DeLuxe two-door fastback sedan

1951 DeLuxe two-door fastback sedan

1952 Vagabond two-door fastback sedan

ed: "I would have brought it out dressed up." And indeed, that's what Sears did with its short-lived Allstate derivative (*see* Allstate). Then, too, the market wasn't quite ready for compacts (though it soon would be), and K-F was looking increasingly terminal, which surely kept some buyers away.

In all, this was a classic case of too little, too soon. Like Hudson's equally ill-starred Jet, the Henry J was the wrong car at the wrong time.

1953 Corsair DeLuxe two-door fastback sedan

1953 Corsair two-door fastback sedan

1953 Corsair two-door fastback sedan

Specifications

1951

K513 Standard (wb 100.0)	Wght	Price	Prod
5134 sdn 2d	2,293	1,363	38,500*
K514 DeLuxe (wb 100.0)			
5144 sdn 2d	2,341	1,499	43,400*

1951 Engines	bore×stroke	bhp	availability
I-4, 134.2	3.13×4.38	68	S-K513
I-6, 161.0	3.13×3.50	80	S-K514

1952

K523 Vagabond (wb 100.0)	Wght	Price	Prod
5234 sdn 2d	2,365	1,407	3,000*
K524 Vagabond DeLuxe (wb 100.0)			
5244 sdn 2d	2,385	1,552	4,000*
K523 Corsair (wb 100.0)	**Wght**	**Price**	**Prod**
5234 sdn 2d	2,370	1,517	7,600*
K524 Corsair DeLuxe (wb 100.0)			
5244 sdn 2d	2,405	1,664	8,900*

1952 Engines	bore×stroke	bhp	availability
I-4, 134.2	3.13×4.38	68	S-K523
I-6, 161.0	3.13×3.50	80	S-K524

1953

K533 Corsair (wb 100.0)	Wght	Price	Prod
5334 sdn 2d	2,395	1,399	8,500*
K534 Corsair DeLuxe (wb 100.0)			
5344 sdn 2d	2,445	1,561	8,100*

1953 Engines	bore×stroke	bhp	availability
I-4, 134.2	3.13×4.38	68	S-K533
I-6, 161.0	3.13×3.50	80	S-K534

1954

K543 Corsair (wb 100.0)	Wght	Price	Prod
5434 sdn 2d	2,405	1,404	800*
K544 Corsair DeLuxe (wb 100.0)			
5444 sdn 2d	2,455	1,566	300*

1954 Engines	bore×stroke	bhp	availability
I-4, 134.2	3.13×4.38	68	S-K543
I-6, 161.0	3.13×3.50	80	S-K544

* Estimates based on highest serial numbers found.
Total model-year production:

1951 all	81,942
1952 Vagabond	7,017
1952 Corsair	23,568
1953 all	16,672
1954 all	1,123

Hudson

Eight Detroit businessmen pooled resources to found the Hudson Motor Car Company in February 1909. Among them was retailing magnate Joseph L. Hudson. Another was Roy D. Chapin, Sr., who led the new firm to high prosperity as its president from 1910 to 1923.

Hudson built some of America's fleetest and finest cars during its 48-year history and was often among the industry's sales leaders through 1950. A key early success was the low-priced four-cylinder Essex introduced in 1919. By 1925, it had boosted Hudson to third place behind Ford and Chevrolet. Hudson then ran third, fourth, or fifth on volume that reached 300,000 cars by 1929. Unfortunately, total sales fell sharply in the devastated Depression market. Had it not been for the speedy, inexpensive Essex Terraplane (*see* Essex and Terraplane), Hudson might have folded by 1940.

The firm forged an enviable reputation in the 1920s largely with its Super and Special Sixes: big, smooth, solid cars offering good performance for the money and fine reliability. But with the advent of an Essex Six in 1924, Hudson decided to move upmarket. The result was a single 1930 line called Great Eight. Great it wasn't. At 213.5 cubic inches, its engine was actually smaller than previous Hudson sixes, had just 80 horsepower to move a heavy chassis, and wasn't as sturdy. It did boast an integrally cast block and crankcase, and was the first straight eight with a counterweighted crankshaft, but its splash lubrication system was outmoded. Hudson stayed with this engine for the optimistically named Greater Eights of 1931-32—in retrospect it was a mistake for a depressed market where sixes would surely have sold better. Displacement was increased each year: first to 233.7 cid and 87 bhp, then to 254 cid and 101 bhp.

Another 1930 setback was the Depression-related closure of Biddle and Smart, Hudson's longtime supplier of magnificent open bodies. The company thus turned to Murray and Briggs for phaeton and speedster bodies. A few eight-cylinder Hudsons of this period also sported dashing coachwork by the renowned firm LeBaron.

Through 1933, Hudson Eights offered numerous body styles on wheelbases of 119-132 inches: roadsters, Victorias, convertibles, sedans, town sedans, coupes, and Broughams (two-door sedans). It was an attractive line that would have done justice to far-costlier brands, but it wasn't successful. The Greater Eight managed only 22,250 sales for 1931. The '32 total was below 8000, despite unchanged prices and lush new Sterling and Major series.

Seeing the error of its ways, Hudson launched a new Super Six for its 1933 "Pacemaker" line—the car was essentially the 73-bhp 193-cid Essex Terraplane engine in the 113-inch Hudson chassis. That year's Eights comprised four 119-inch-wheelbase standard models and five luxurious Majors on a 132-inch platform. But production bottomed out at under 3000. Interestingly, Eights outsold Sixes nearly 2-to-1. For 1934, Hudson again abandoned sixes, reserving them for the new Terraplane line that replaced Essex as the firm's "companion" marque.

Like most other Detroit producers in the early '30s, Hudson began moving away from classic four-square styling, rooted in Greek architecture, to embrace streamlining. The 1934 and '35 models were transitional: still rather boxy but less-angular, helped by skirted front fenders. The all-new '36s looked something like the previous year's Chrysler/DeSoto Airstreams: modern, but not Airflow-radical. Highlights included tall, rounded,

1930 Great Eight four-door town sedan

1931 Greater Eight DeLuxe Brougham four-door

1931 Greater Eight convertible sedan by Murphy

1932 Greater Eight Major Brougham four-door sedan

Plymouth-like diecast grilles and all-steel bodies with rather dowdy lines. Engines remained dowdy, too. The straight eight was little changed through 1936, variously sold in Standard, DeLuxe, and Custom series. For '35 came a new six: a 212.1-cid unit that made 93 bhp through 1936, then 101/107. The 1937-38 Eights delivered 122/128 bhp.

A reduced 1935-36 market share suggests Hudson was late in shifting to the popular "potato look." Though the firm managed 85,000 units and fifth place for 1934, some two-thirds were low-priced Terraplanes. Output then rose to average 100,000 units per year in 1935-37, but that was good for only eighth—and Terraplane still garnered the lion's share of sales. Worse, Hudson likely cut prices below the profit point, as it kept losing money despite this increased volume. From less than $1 million in earnings for 1937, Hudson lost nearly $5 million in recession year 1938.

After serving in the Hoover Administration, Roy Chapin returned as Hudson president in 1933. He departed again three years later after making some key product decisions inaugurated under his successor, A. E. Barit. These involved a consolidated line emphasizing economy rather than performance. Thus, after four years as a separate marque, Terraplane was put back under the Hudson banner for 1938. Bowing that same year was a new low-priced senior series, the "112" (named for its wheelbase length). With only a small 175-cid six making just 83 bhp, the 112 was sluggish next to the speedy 96-bhp Terraplane: 35 seconds 0-60 mph, top speed barely 70 mph. But it returned up to 24 mpg and was attractively priced as low as $700. The 212 Terraplane engine also powered that year's Custom Six, again tuned for 101/107 bhp. An unchanged eight was reserved for a single Custom line.

The national economy was looking up by 1939, when Hudson dropped Terraplane, trimmed the 112 to a single DeLuxe series, and unveiled new 101-bhp Pacemaker and Country Club Sixes on respective wheelbases of 118 and 122 inches. The 212 six also returned in large, comfortable five- and seven-passenger sedans curiously tagged "Big Boy." Custom Eight became Country Club Eight, but power and wheelbases were untouched. This was the final year for Hudson's 1936 bodies, and some deft design work alleviated much of their former bulkiness. Long-chassis models were especially graceful, but all of the '39s wore more-horizontal grilles with thick bars that made for a nicer "face" than the controversial "waterfall" ensemble of 1937-38.

Hudson's 1940 line was rearranged, rebodied, and restyled. Though not innovative, the new look was pleasing and clean, with little side ornamentation and a trendy "prow front" dividing a lower horizontal-bar grille. Hudson added another page to its book of durability triumphs by running more than 20,000 miles at an average speed of 70.5 mph, setting a new American

1934 DeLuxe Eight 2/4-passenger coupe

1935 Custom Eight Brougham four-door sedan

1936 Custom Six Brougham two-door

1937 Custom Eight convertible Brougham

1938 Custom Eight Country Club touring sedan

1939 Pacemaker Six touring sedan

Automobile Association record.

Offerings spanned seven series, three wheelbases, and three engines. Smallest were the new 113-inch Traveler and DeLuxe: coupes, Victoria coupes, two- and four-door sedans, a convertible, and convertible sedan. All carried the 175-cid six, now rated at 92 bhp. The 212 engine with 98/102 bhp powered the Country Club Six and a new 118-inch-wheelbase Super Six, plus the two Big Boys. The old 254 straight-eight was still around, now producing 128 bhp. Standard Eights shared the Super Six chassis and full range of body styles. Country Club Eights remained on the 125-inch span but were down to one six-passenger and two seven-passenger sedans. Yet for all this, Hudson volume changed little—just under 88,000 for the model year—and red ink flowed again with a calendar-year loss of some $1.5 million.

A mild facelift was performed for 1941, when wheelbases were juggled once more: 116 inches for DeLuxe and new entry-level Traveler Sixes, 121 and 128 for Super Six and new Commodore Six and Eight. All series listed two coupes and two sedans. DeLuxe, Super Six, and Commodores also offered convertible sedans. Hudson had held onto that body style longer than most makes, but buyers didn't much want it anymore, and only 200 or so were built this year in each series. Rarer still were the new Super Six and Commodore Eight wagons, Hudson's first: only about 100 of each. Prices ranged from $754 for the Traveler coupe to $1537 for the long-wheelbase Commodore Eight seven-place sedan. As it had for many years, Hudson continued selling a fair number of commercial vehicles. Among seven offerings for '41 was a car-style pickup that now inherited the Big Boy name.

Perhaps because many people suspected war was coming, Hudson recorded 1941-model production of close to 92,000 cars, good for nearly $4 million in earnings. But that profit came mainly from defense contracts, which began materializing in early '41—a badly needed breather.

The 1942 models arrived in August 1941 looking smoother, if chubbier. Running boards were newly hidden, the grille was again lowered and simpler, and fenders became more stylishly fulsome. Hudson's famous white-triangle logo graced each side of the prow, and lit up with the headlamps to aid after-dark identification. Offerings were broadly the same, but wagons were departing, and a new Commodore Custom Eight listed a lush 121-inch-wheelbase coupe and 128-inch six-seater sedan in the $1300-$1400 range. All prices nudged upward, the minimum now above $800. The government-ordered turn to war production in February 1942 ended the firm's model-year car output at just under 41,000. Among them were a handful of Hudson's last four-door convertibles.

Hudson's contributions to winning World War II included "Helldiver" aircraft, "Invader" landing-craft engines, sections

1939 Country Club Eight convertible Brougham

1940 Eight two-door convertible sedan

1941 Super Six station wagon

1941 Commodore Eight two-door convertible sedan

1941 Super Six four-door touring sedan

1942 Commodore Eight four-door sedan

1942 Commodore Six convertible coupe

1946 Commodore Eight four-door sedan

1947 Commodore Eight four-door sedan

1948 Commodore Six four-door sedan

1948 Commander convertible coupe

for B-29 bombers and Aircobra helicopters, and a variety of naval munitions. The company made small wartime profits, then quickly resumed production after V-J Day. A total of 4735 cars put Hudson fifth for calendar 1945, a spot it hadn't held since 1934—and would not hold again.

Like most other Detroit cars, the 1946-47 Hudsons were just '42s with new wrinkles—mainly a less-elegant front sans prow. However, the small 175-cid six was forgotten, and a vastly simplified lineup offered fewer models spread among Super and Commodore Six and Eight, all on a 121-inch chassis. But there were no fewer than three transmission options: $88 stick/overdrive, $40 "Vacumotive Drive," and $98 "Drive-Master" (with Vacumotive). Vacumotive operated the clutch automatically, while Drive-Master eliminated both clutch and shift motions. By putting the shifter in third gear, the car would start in second gear and upshift to third when the accelerator was lifted. Slowing to a stop, Drive-Master would shift to second again. Hudson built over 91,000 of its '46 models, two-thirds of which were Super Sixes.

The 1947s were unchanged save details like a chrome trunklid nameplate, right- and left-side exterior door locks, and a small lip on the housing of the prominent triangle medallion above the grille. Hudson produced some 92,000 cars for the model year, but fell from ninth to 11th on the industry board. Other makes were doing better in the unprecedented postwar seller's market. Still, Hudson sales exceeded $120 million in 1946, and the firm netted over $2.3 million. Two years later, Hudson made more money than it ever would again, earning $13.2 million on gross sales of $274 million.

The reason was a brand-new car, the now-famous "Step-Down." Named for its innovative recessed or dropped floorpan, it completely surrounded passengers with strong frame girders in one of the safest packages of the day—maybe one of the safest ever. It also offered rattle-free unitized construction and a radically low center of gravity that made for great handling. The long 124-inch wheelbase provided a smooth ride and king-size interior space. The Step-Down was even beautiful in its way: a long "torpedo" with clean flush-fender sides, modest taillamps, fully skirted rear wheels, and a low, horizontal grille. The design evolved from wartime doodles of aerodynamic forms by a design team under Frank Spring, who went way back with Hudson and was way ahead of the times with the Step-Down.

Though Hudson stuck with a four-series lineup for 1948-49, it violated an old Detroit caution about not restyling and re-engineering in the same year. Thus, Super and Commodore Sixes carried a new 262-cid inline six-cylinder engine with 121 bhp, only seven less than the unchanged 254-cid straight eight. It had only four main bearings instead of five, but was as smooth and durable as the eight. Hudson finally joined the rest of the industry and replaced its outdated splash lubrication with full pressure for the new six. It also delivered surprising performance: 0-40 mph in 12 seconds with Drive-Master; stick-shift cars were even faster. With this gutsy new six in the advanced Step-Down platform, Hudson was transformed almost overnight from an also-ran performer into one of America's quickest, most-roadworthy cars.

Dealers cheered the Step-Down upon its mid-1948 introduction. Here was precisely what they needed for great sales in a heady market where customers sometimes outnumbered available cars. Sure enough, Hudson surged not only in profits but also in production, selling 117,200 of the '48s and 159,100 of the near-identical '49s (only the serial numbers were different).

But there was one big problem. As a unitized design, the Step-Down couldn't be greatly changed without great expense, and Hudson sales wouldn't be sufficient to cover the cost once the postwar seller's market ended in 1950. A slow-selling '53-54 compact only accelerated the depletion of cash reserves. As a result, the Step-Down wouldn't be updated much until 1954, by which time it was way too late, forcing Hudson to seek refuge with Nash under the American Motors banner. Nor would Hudson be able to afford a station wagon or V-8 engine, two very popular '50s commodities. In fact, Hudson offered only sixes in 1953-54, and though the "fabulous" Hornet engine dominated stock-car racing in that period, sixes were a tough sell in the mostly eight-cylinder medium-price field where Hudson competed.

Sales executive Roy D. Chapin, Jr., the son of the famous Hudson founders (and a future chairman of American Motors), later explained things this way: "If you don't have enough money to do something... and if you haven't learned to specialize in a given thing... sooner or later you find you just can't do everything. [Hudson was] usually reacting, rather than anticipating." To a large extent, Hudson's postwar plight was shared by all the independents: too little money for enough changes to keep buyers interested, resulting in fewer sales and even less money for new products.

Hudson entered the 1950s in excellent shape, selling more than 120,000 Step-Downs for the first model year. A big hit—more than 39,000 orders—was the new low-priced Pacemaker with a 119-inch wheelbase and a destroked 232-cid Super Six. Though horsepower was only 112, performance was as good as that of Nash's top-line Ambassador and well ahead of most similarly priced rivals.

Both Pacemaker and the 1950 Super Six offered fastback four-door sedans, long-deck club coupe, and a convertible and fastback two-door sedan called Brougham. Pacemaker also listed a three-passenger coupe, the 1950 price-leader at $1807. Other standard Pacemakers cost under $2000 except the convertible ($2428). A few dollars more bought a Pacemaker DeLuxe in the same body types save the long-deck coupe. These used the 262 Super Six engine, which was a bit more potent now at 123 bhp. Commodore Six and Eight deleted two-door sedans, Super Eight the convertible. The main appearance change from 1948-49 involved adding twin diagonal grille bars—the make's traditional triangle motif.

Hudson also added yet another transmission choice for 1950. Though called Supermatic, this was just a semiautomatic like Drive-Master. Supermatic added an overdrive that automatically engaged at 22 mph when selected by a dashboard button. Price was $199, versus $105 for Drive-Master. Of course, neither was a proper substitute for a fully automatic transmission, which belatedly arrived for 1951: a proprietary GM Hydra-Matic at $158. At that point, Supermatic was dropped.

But Hudson's big '51 news was the powerful six-cylinder Hornet, a four-model line priced the same as Commodore Eight ($2543-$3099). At 308 cubic inches, the Hornet engine was the largest American six offered after World War II, and though it made just 145 bhp in initial form, it was capable of far more in the hands of precision tuners.

Undoubtedly the most famous of Hudson wrench-spinners was Marshall Teague, who claimed he could get 112 mph from an AAA- or NASCAR-certified stock Hornet. An enthusiastic cadre of Hudson engineers helped by conjuring a raft of "severe usage" options—thinly disguised racing parts. By late 1953, they'd cooked up a hot "7-X" racing engine with about 220 bhp via 0.020-inch overbored cylinders, special cam and head, larger valves, higher compression, and "Twin-H Power" with dual carbs and manifolds—which Hudson claimed were the first twin manifolds on a six.

The Hornet proved near-invincible in stock-car racing. Teague finished his 1952 AAA season with a 1000-point lead

1950 Pacemaker four-door sedan

1950 Commodore Eight Custom convertible Brougham

1951 Hornet convertible Brougham

1951 Commodore Eight Custom Hollywood hardtop coupe

1951 Commodore Eight Custom Hollywood hardtop coupe

1952 Hornet four-door sedan

1952 Pacemaker Brougham two-door sedan

1952 Hornet club coupe

1952 Wasp convertible Brougham

1952 Wasp Hollywood hardtop coupe

1953 Super Wasp four-door sedan

over his closest rival, winning 12 of the 13 scheduled events. NASCAR aces Herb Thomas, Dick Rathmann, Al Keller, and Frank Mundy drove Hornets to 27 victories in 1952, another 21 in '53, and 17 in '54.

Hornets kept on winning after that, but none of their competition successes affected production Hudsons, and sales continued to fall. Though the company kept adding and subtracting series through 1954, it couldn't alter styling much, nor add new body styles after the Hollywood hardtop coupe bowed as a Hornet, Super Six, and Commodore Six/Eight for 1951. Super Eight and the standard Pacemaker were dropped that year, when another facelift brought more-massive, full-width grilles, plus larger rear windows for nonhardtop closed models.

More trim was shuffled for '52, when Super Six was renamed Wasp and gained a slightly more-potent 127-bhp 262 engine that it shared with Commodore Six. Pacemaker and both Commodores vanished for '53, leaving 119-inch-wheelbase Wasp coupe and sedans, the same plus Hollywood and convertible in new upmarket Super Wasp trim, and four Hornets on the 124-inch platform. One bright spot: The Hornet six was now offered in a 160-bhp version, and the 170-bhp Twin-H Power (7-X) mill was a regular factory option.

But Step-Down production diminished in each of these years, falling from about 93,000 in 1951 to 45,000 in 1953. Though government-ordered Korean War cutbacks didn't help civilian sales, military contracts earned Hudson an $8.3 million profit in 1952. Unfortunately, that was more than wiped out by staggering 1953 losses totaling more than $10.4 million.

Part of that was reflected in the $12 million bill for Hudson's first compact, the ill-fated 1953 Jet. Bowing as a standard-trim notchback four-door and nicer "Super Jet" two- and four-door sedans, the Jet carried a 202-cid inline six carved from the old Commodore eight. Only 104 bhp was standard, but optional "Twin-H" and high-compression head improved that to 114, which made the little 105-inch-wheelbase Hudsons fairly speedy. Jets were also as roadable and well-built as any Hudson, but they were not pretty. Over the objections of chief designer Spring, company president A. E. Barit insisted on bolt-upright, slab-sided styling that failed to impress. Hudson tried harder for 1954, adding a cheap Family club sedan at $1621 and luxury Jet-Liners at around $2050. Still, sales went from bad to worse, dropping from 21,143 to only 14,224.

But the Jet did spark a project that might have become the much-needed Step-Down replacement. Called Italia, this was a four-place *gran turismo* designed by Spring and bodied on the Jet chassis by Carrozzeria Touring of Milan. Advanced features abounded: *de rigueur* wrapped windshield, doors cut into the roof, fender scoops that fed cooling air to the brakes, flow-through ventilation, form-fitting leather seats, and a 10-inch lower stance than '54 Step-Downs. But the Italia was too heavy for the 114-bhp Jet inline six-cylinder engine, and its aluminum bodywork was fragile. Of course, these problems might have been licked if Hudson had the money, but by now it didn't. As a result, only 25 "production" Italias were built, plus the prototype and an experimental four-door derivative called X-161 (Spring's 161st design project, evidently intended for '57). Project sales manager Roy Chapin, Jr., booted Italias out the door as fast as he could at $4800 apiece. "I got rid of them," he said later, "[but] it wasn't one of my greatest accomplishments."

Nor, for that matter, was the last-gasp Step-Down of 1954. Somehow, Hudson found money for a one-piece windshield and a below-the-belt reskin that imparted fashionable GM squareness—and an unfortunate resemblance to the dumpy Jet. Cheap Hornet Specials—club coupe and two fastback four-doors—were added at around $2600, but the Step-Down was just too old to sell anymore. Model-year production ended at just 36,436 units.

The 1954 Hudsons had bowed amid rumors of a Hudson-Nash merger. The talk was true, and Nash couldn't have come calling at a better time. From January 1, 1954, to its demise as an independent in April, Hudson lost more than $6 million on sales of just $28.7 million. However, Nash president George Mason insisted on one condition: The Jet had to go. Hudson chief A. E. Barit resisted, but not for long. He was in no position to bargain.

The merger amounted to a Nash takeover. Mason had hoped to add just-married Studebaker and Packard to make his new American Motors Corporation into Detroit's "Big Fourth," but that was forever forestalled by his untimely death in October 1954. Mason lieutenant George Romney succeeded to the president's chair, and soon put all of AMC's eggs into the compact car basket.

Meantime, Hudson's Detroit plant was closed and the Nash factory in Kenosha, Wisconsin, retooled for an "all-new" '55 Hudson. Of course, everyone knew what it was: a restyled Nash. Still, it wasn't all bad. Hudson could not only continue to tout unit construction but also Nash's all-coil suspension in lighter, trimmer cars that promised better fuel economy.

AMC stylists hid the Nash origins well, giving Hudsons a handsome eggcrate grille, distinct trim, a different rear end, full front-wheel openings (instead of semiskirted), plus Nash's new '55 wrapped windshield. One direct link to the Step-Down was carried-over 1954 gauges.

Offerings began with Wasp Super and Custom sedans and Custom Hollywood hardtop with 114.3-inch Nash Statesman wheelbase and a 202 "Hi-Torque" six from the now-departed Jet. Hornet Six rode Nash's 121.3-inch Ambassador platform and offered the same three models with 160/170-bhp 308-cid engines. Topping the line were a trio of 208-bhp Hornets powered by Packard's new 320-cid V-8 (a legacy of Mason's planned four-way merger). Twin-H Power was again available for sixes, and Nash's tiny Metropolitans and compact Ramblers gained Hudson badges to give the make broader market coverage. Yet for all this—and a banner Detroit sales year—big-Hudson volume continued sliding, reaching just over 20,000.

Fewer models and horrendous "V-Line Styling" arrived for '56. AMC design chief Edmund E. Anderson gets blamed for the ugliest Hudsons in a generation. These really did look like a

1954 Italia coupe

1954 Italia coupe

1954 Super Jet club sedan

1954 Wasp four-door sedan

1954 Hornet Brougham convertible coupe

1955 Wasp Custom Hollywood hardtop coupe

1955 Hornet Custom Hollywood hardtop coupe

1955 Wasp Custom four-door sedan

"Hash," as some latterday wags refer to post-'54 Hudsons. The Hornet Six was otherwise unchanged, but the Wasp was down to a lone four-door, and Hornet V-8s gave way in March to downpriced Hornet Specials with AMC's own new 250-cid V-8—which had only 190 bhp. An anemic engine and terrible looks only depressed demand, and AMC built just 10,671 non-Rambler '56 Hudsons.

Styling didn't improve in '57, but horsepower did. The AMC V-8 was newly bored to 327 cid, netting a more-respectable 255 bhp for a four-Hudson line of Hornet Super and Custom sedans and Hollywoods. But buyers had long since branded Hudson a

1956 Hornet V-8 Hollywood hardtop coupe

1956 Wasp four-door sedan

1957 Hornet four-door sedan

loser, and all but 3876 stayed away from the '57s. With that, Hudson was put out of its misery, as was Nash. In their place for '58 was a new Rambler Ambassador line with cleaner new styling originally intended for Hudson and Nash.

In retrospect, dropping these venerable makes was just common sense. As Roy Chapin, Jr., later recalled: "... [T]he decision really was one that said we've got to spend our money and our effort and our concentration on the Rambler..." Thus expired two once-great names, with Hudson perhaps the greater, sadder loss. Given the Hornet's great performance record and the Step-Down's engineering legacy, one can only guess what Hudson might have become had things been different.

1957 Hornet V-8 Hollywood hardtop coupe

Specifications

1930

Grt Eight (wb 119.0; lwb-126.0)	Wght	Price	Prod
rdstr 2-4P	2,870	995	
phtn 5P	2,940	965	
cpe 2P	3,010	885	
cpe 2-4P	3,060	925	74,891
coach 5P	3,080	895	
sdn 4d	3,200	1,025	
Sun sdn 5P	3,100	1,045	
lwb phtn 7P	3,080	1,160	
lwb Brougham 4d	3,210	1,195	10,516
lwb touring sdn 5P	3,270	1,145	
lwb sdn 7P	3,385	1,295	

1930 Engine	bore×stroke	bhp	availability
I-8, 213.5	2.75×4.50	80	S-all

1931

Grt Eight (wb 119.0; lwb-126.0)	Wght	Price	Prod
rdstr 2-4P	2,675	995	
phtn 5P	2,745	1,095	
cpe 2P	3,865	875	
cpe 2-4P	2,955	925	16,477
coach 5P	2,975	895	
Town sdn 5P	3,055	945	
Standard sdn 4d	3,115	995	
spt cpe 2-4P	3,145	1,065	
lwb phtn 7P	3,055	1,295	
lwb touring sdn 5P	3,190	1,145	
lwb Family sdn 5-7P	3,230	1,195	
lwb Brougham 5P	3,190	1,225	5,769
lwb club sdn 5P	3,225	1,445	
lwb sdn 7P	3,305	1,450	
lwb DeLx Brghm 5P	3,480	1,375	
lwb Special sdn 5P	3,430	1,325	

1931 Engine	bore×stroke	bhp	availability
I-8, 233.7	2.88×4.50	87	S-all

1932 (Total calendar-year production: 7,777)

Greater Eight-Standard (wb 119.0) - 5,933 built	Wght	Price	Prod
cpe 2P	3,145	995	—
cpe 2-4P	3,175	1,045	—
conv cpe 2-4P	3,085	1,195	—
Special cpe 2-4P	3,215	1,195	—
coach 5P	3,190	1,025	—
Town sdn 5P	3,270	1,050	—
Std sdn 5P	3,285	1,095	—
Greater Eight-Sterling (wb 126.0)			
Suburban 5P	3,350	1,275	—
Special sdn 5P	3,415	1,295	—
Greater Eight-Major (wb 132.0) - 1,116 built			
phtn 7P	3,350	1,395	—
touring sdn 5P	3,475	1,445	—
club sdn 5P	3,555	1,495	—
Brougham 5P	3,560	1,495	—
sdn 7P	3,590	1,595	—

1932 Engine	bore×stroke	bhp	availability
I-8, 254.5	3.00×4.50	101	S-all

1933

Super Six Pacemaker (wb 113.0) - 962 built	Wght	Price	Prod
phtn 5P	2,700	765	—
bus cpe 2P	2,780	695	—
cpe 2-4P	2,845	735	—
conv cpe 2-4P	—	845	—
coach 5P	2,900	695	—
sdn 4d	2,980	765	—
Pcmkr Eight (wb 119.0; Major-132.0) - 1,890 built			
Standard cpe 2-4P	3,190	995	—
Stand conv cpe 2-4P	3,145	1,145	—
Standard coach 5P	3,245	975	—
Standard sdn 4d	3,345	1,045	—
Major phtn 7P	—	1,250	—
Major sdn 4d T/B	3,485	1,250	—
Major Brougham 5P	3,650	1,350	—
Major club sdn 5P	3,630	1,350	—
Major sdn 7P	3,605	1,350	—

1933 Engines	bore×stroke	bhp	availability
I-6, 193.1	2.94×4.75	73	S-Six
I-8, 254.5	3.00×4.50	101	S-Eight
I-8, 254.5	3.00×4.50	110	O-Eight

1934

LT/LU Eight (wb 116.0)-18,679 blt	Wght	Price	Prod
Special bus cpe 2P	2,720	695	—
Special cpe 2P	2,750	725	—
Special cpe 2-4P	2,795	775	—
Special conv cpe 2-4P	2,815	835	—
Spec comp Victoria 5P	2,880	785	—
Special coach 5P	2,855	745	—
Special sdn 4d	2,905	805	—
Special sdn 4d T/B	2,930	845	—
DeLuxe cpe 2P	2,805	815	—
DeLuxe cpe 2-4P	2,850	855	—
DeLx comp Victoria 5P	2,895	875	—
DeLuxe coach 5P	2,870	835	—
DeLuxe sdn 4d	2,930	895	—
DeLuxe sdn 4d T/B	2,955	935	—
LL/LLU Major Eight (wb 123.0) - 4,158 built			
Spec sdn 4d touring	2,950	970	—
Spec sdn 4d T/B tour	2,975	1,000	—
DeLuxe club sdn 4P	3,085	1,070	—
DeLx 5P Brougham	3,075	1,145	—
DeLx club sdn 4P T/B	3,110	1,125	—
LTS Challenger Eight (wb 116.0) - 4,217 built			
cpe 2P	2,720	685	—
cpe 2-4P	2,765	735	—
conv cpe 2-4P	2,785	800	—
coach 5P	2,860	705	—
sdn 4d	2,910	765	—

1934 Engines	bore×stroke	bhp	availability
I-8, 254.5	3.00×4.50	108	S-Eight, Chalgr
I-8, 254.5	3.00×4.50	113	S-Major
I-8, 254.5	3.00×4.50	121	O-All

1935

GH Big Six (wb 116.0)-7,624 blt	Wght	Price	Prod
cpe 2P	2,600	695	—
cpe 2-4P	2,665	740	—
conv cpe 2-4P	2,640	790	—
touring Brougham 5P	2,735	742	—
coach 5P	2,720	710	—
sdn 4d	2,780	770	—
Suburban sdn 5P	2,795	802	—

	Eight (wb 117.0)	Wght	Price	Prod
HT	Special cpe 2P	2,740	760	
HT	Special cpe 2-4P	2,810	810	
HT	Spec conv cpe 2-4P	2,765	860	
HT	Spec tour Brghm 5P	2,855	812	7,150
HT	Special coach 5P	2,840	780	
HT	Special sdn 4d	2,890	840	
HT	Suburban sdn 5P	2,905	872	
HU	DeLuxe cpe 2P	2,790	845	
HU	DeLuxe cpe 2-4P	2,855	895	
HU	DeLx conv cpe 2-4P	2,805	955	
HU	DeLx tour Brghm 5P	2,895	907	3,097
HU	DeLuxe coach 5P	2,880	875	
HU	DeLuxe sdn 4d	2,945	935	
HU	DeLx Suburb sdn 5P	2,960	967	
	HHU Custom Eight (wb 124.0) - 1,460 built			
	Brougham 5P	3,055	1,095	—
	touring Brougham 5P	3,070	1,127	—
	club sdn 5P	3,130	1,025	—
	Suburban sdn 5P	3,145	1,057	—
	Eight (wb 124.0)			
HTL	Spec Brougham 5P	2,995	930	
HTL	Spec tour Brghm 5P	3,010	962	
HTL	club sdn 5P	2,975	880	968
HTL	Spec Suburb sdn 5P	2,990	912	
HUL	DeLux Brougham 5P	3,055	1,025	
HUL	DeLx tour Brghm 5P	3,070	1,057	
HUL	DeLuxe club sdn 5P	3,015	975	721
HUL	DeLx Suburb sdn 5P	3,030	1,007	

1935 Engines	bore×stroke	bhp	availability
I-6, 212.0	3.00×5.00	93	S-Big Six
I-6, 212.0	3.00×5.00	100	O-Big Six
I-8, 254.5	3.00×4.50	113	S-all Eights
I-8, 254.5	3.00×4.50	124	O-all Eights

1936

	63 Cust Six (wb 120) - 9,720 blt	Wght	Price	Prod
63	cpe 2P	2,730	710	—
63	cpe 2-4P	2,810	755	—
63	conv cpe 2-4P	2,870	810	—
63	Brougham 2d 5P	2,830	730	—
63	touring 2d 5P	2,830	755	—
63	sdn 4d	2,880	785	—
63	touring sdn 4d	2,880	810	—
	64/66 DeLuxe Eight (wb 120.0; lwb-127.0)*			
64	cpe 2P	2,865	760	—
64	cpe 2-4P	2,965	810	—
64	conv cpe 2-4P	3,000	875	—
64	Brougham 2d 5P	2,985	790	—
64	tour Brougham 2d 5P	2,985	815	—
64	sdn 4d	3,045	830	—
64	touring sdn 4d	3,045	855	—
66	lwb sdn 4d	3,110	855	—
66	lwb touring sdn 4d	3,110	880	—
	65/67 Custom Eight (wb 120.0; lwb-127.0)*			
65	cpe 2P	2,915	845	—
65	cpe 2-4P	3,000	895	—
65	conv cpe 2-4P	3,045	970	—
65	Brougham 2d 5P	3,034	885	—
65	tour Brougham 2d 5P	3,034	910	—
65	sdn 4d	3,075	925	—
65	touring sdn 4d	3,075	950	—
67	lwb sdn 4d	3,140	950	—

65/67 Custom Eight		Wght	Price	Prod
67	lwb touring sdn 4d	3,140	975	—

* Total Eight production: 16,627

1936 Engines	bore×stroke	bhp	availability
I-6, 212.0	3.00×5.00	93	S-63
I-6, 212.0	3.00×5.00	100	O-63
I-8, 254.5	3.00×4.50	113	S-Eights
I-8, 254.5	3.00×4.50	124	O-Eights

1937

73 Cust Six (wb 122) - 6,813 blt		Wght	Price	Prod
73	bus cpe 2P	2,760	865	—
73	cpe 3P	2,805	905	—
73	Victoria cpe 3P	2,865	950	—
73	conv cpe 2P	2,870	1,005	—
73	Brougham 2d 5P	2,925	930	—
73	tour Brougham 2d 5P	2,925	955	—
73	sdn 4d	2,990	980	—
73	touring sdn 4d	2,990	1,005	—
73	conv Brougham 4P	2,945	1,000	—
74/76 DeLuxe (wb 122.0; lwb-129.0)				
74	cpe 3P	3,010	950	
74	Victoria cpe 3P	3,055	1,015	
74	conv cpe 2P	3,020	1,080	
74	Brougham 2d 5P	3,105	1,000	5,628
74	tour Brougham 2d 5P	3,105	1,025	
74	sdn 4d	3,135	1,040	
74	touring sdn 4d	3,135	1,065	
74	conv Brougham 4P	3,125	1,165	
76	lwb sdn 4d	3,205	1,065	1,097
76	lwb touring sdn 4d	3,205	1,090	
75/77 Custom Eight (wb 122.0; lwb-129.0)				
75	cpe 3P	3,055	1,050	
75	Victoria cpe 3P	3,085	1,100	
75	conv cpe 2p	3,070	1,175	
75	Brougham 2d 5P	3,135	1,090	3,274
75	tour Brougham 2d 5P	3,135	1,115	
75	sdn 4d	3,195	1,140	
75	touring sdn 4d	3,195	1,165	
75	conv Brougham 4P	3,160	1,260	
77	lwb sdn 5P	3,260	1,165	3,652
77	lwb touring sdn 5P	3,260	1,190	

1937 Engines	bore×stroke	bhp	availability
I-6, 212.0	3.00×5.00	101	S-73
I-6, 212.0	3.00×5.00	107	O-73
I-8, 254.5	3.00×4.50	122	S-Eights
I-8, 254.5	3.00×4.50	128	O-Eights

1938

80/88 Terraplane Six (wb 117; lwb-124)		Wght	Price	Prod
80	Util cpe 3P	2,840	789	—
80	Util coach 6P	2,835	779	—
80	Util tour cabriolet 6P	2,840	799	—
80	Util wgn 4d	3,055	965	—
88	lwb sdn 6P	2,965	974	—
88	lwb touring sdn 6P	2,970	995	—
81 Terraplane DeLuxe Six (wb 117.0)				
81	cpe 3P	2,725	789	—
81	Victoria cpe 3-5P	2,775	835	—
81	conv cpe 3P	2,780	926	—
81	Brougham 6P	2,820	822	—
81	tour Brougham 6P	2,825	843	—
81	sdn 6P	2,885	864	—
81	touring sdn 6P	2,890	884	—
81	conv Brougham 6P	2,860	990	—
82 Terraplane Super Six (wb 117.0)				
82	cpe 3P	2,755	845	—
82	Victoria cpe 3-5P	2,805	886	—
82	conv cpe 3P	2,835	971	—
82	Brougham 6P	2,865	878	—
82	tour Brougham 6P	2,870	899	—
82	sdn 6P	2,925	915	—
82	touring sdn 6P	2,930	935	—
82	conv Brougham 6P	2,880	1,034	—
89 "112" Six (wb 112.0)				
	Standard cpe 3P	2,500	694	
	Stand Victoria cpe 4P	2,540	740	
	Stand conv cpe 3P	2,545	835	
	Stand Brougham 6P	2,595	724	

89 "112" Six		Wght	Price	Prod
	Stand tour Brghm 6P	2,600	743	
	Standard sdn 4d	2,600	755	24,475
	Standard tour sdn 5d	2,625	775	
	Stand conv Brghm 6P	2,610	886	
	Utility cpe 3P	2,660	724	
	Utility coach 6P	2,600	697	
	Utility coach T/B 6P	2,605	716	
	Deluxe cpe 3P	2,500	704	—
	Delx Victoria cpe 4P	2,540	750	—
	Deluxe conv cpe 3P	2,545	840	—
	Deluxe Brougham 6P	2,595	734	—
	Delx tour Brghm 6P	2,600	753	—
	Deluxe sdn 4d	2,620	765	—
	Deluxe tour sdn 4d	2,625	785	—
	Delx conv Brghm 6P	2,610	891	—
83 Custom Six (wb 122.0)				
	cpe 3P	2,825	909	—
	Victoria cpe 3-5P	2,880	955	—
	conv cpe 3P	2,895	1,041	—
	Brougham 6P	2,935	948	—
	touring Brougham 6P	2,940	968	—
	sdn 4d	3,005	984	—
	touring sdn 4d	3,010	1,005	—
	conv Brougham 6P	2,975	1,104	—
84 Deluxe Eight (wb 122.0)				
	cpe 3P	3,010	990	—
	Victoria cpe 3-5P	3,060	1,031	—
	conv cpe 3P	3,060	1,121	—
	Brougham 6P	3,115	1,028	—
	touring Brougham 6P	3,120	1,049	—
	sdn 4d	3,155	1,060	—
	touring sdn 4d	3,160	1,080	—
	conv Brougham 6P	3,140	1,185	—
85/87 Custom Eight (wb 122.00; lwb-129.0)				
85	cpe 3P	3,020	1,080	—
85	Victoria cpe 3-5P	3,080	1,131	—
85	Brougham 6P	3,140	1,134	—
85	touring Brougham 6P	3,145	1,155	—
85	sdn 4d	3,190	1,171	—
85	touring sdn	3,195	1,191	—
87	Cntry Clb sdn 4d (lwb)	3,270	1,199	—
87	Cntry Clb vic sdn 4d (lwb)	3,275	1,299	—

1938 Engines	bore×stroke	bhp	availability
I-6, 175.0	3.00×4.13	83	S-89
I-6, 212.0	3.00×5.00	96	S-80, 81, 88
I-6, 212.0	3.00×5.00	101	S-82, 83
I-6, 212.0	3.00×5.00	107	O-83
I-8, 254.5	3.00×4.50	122	S-84, 85, 87

1939 (Total calendar-year production: 81,521)

90 "112" Delx Six (wb 112.0)		Wght	Price	Prod
	Traveler cpe 3P	2,544	695	—
	cpe 3P	2,587	745	—
	Victoria cpe 4P	2,622	791	—
	conv cpe 3P	2,627	886	—
	tour Brougham 6P	2,682	775	—
	conv Brougham 6P	2,732	936	—
	touring sdn 4d	2,712	806	—
	Utility coach 6P	2,634	725	—
	Utility cpe 3P	2,714	750	—
	Utility wgn 4d	2,880	931	—
91 Pacemaker Six (wb 118.0)				
	cpe 3P	2,717	793	—
	Victoria cpe 5P	2,752	844	—
	touring Brougham 6P	2,832	823	—
	touring sdn 4d	2,867	854	—
92 Six (wb 118.0)				
	cpe 3P	2,757	833	—
	Victoria cpe 5P	2,787	879	—
	conv cpe 3P	2,782	982	—
	touring Brougham 6P	2,847	866	—
	conv Brougham 6P	2,892	1,042	—
	touring sdn 4d	2,897	908	—
93 Country Club Six (wb 122.0)				
	cpe 3P	2,848	919	—
	Victoria cpe 5P	2,893	967	—
	conv cpe 3P	2,898	1,052	—
	touring Brougham 6P	2,968	960	—
	conv Brougham 6P	2,983	1,115	—

93 Country Club Six		Wght	Price	Prod
	touring sdn 4d	3,023	995	—
98 Big Boy Six (wb 119.0)				
	sdn 4d	2,909	884	—
	sdn 7P	3,022	1,114	—
95/97 Country Club Eight (wb 122.0; lwb-129.0)				
95	cpe 3P	3,003	1,009	—
95	Victoria cpe 5P	3,053	1,051	—
95	conv cpe 3P	3,033	1,138	—
95	touring Brougham 6P	3,138	1,049	—
95	conv Brougham 6P	3,123	1,201	—
95	touring sdn 4d	3,193	1,079	—
97	lwb touring sdn 4d	3,268	1,174	—
97	lwb sdn 7P	3,378	1,430	—

1939 Engines	bore×stroke	bhp	availability
I-6, 175.0	3.00×4.13	86	S-90, 98 sedan 4d
I-6, 212.0	3.00×5.00	96/101	S-91, 92, 93, 98 sedan 7P
I-8, 254.5	3.00×4.50	122	S-95, 97

1940 (Total model-year production: 87,915; Sixes: 77,295; Eights: 10,620)

40-T Traveler (wb 113.0)	Wght	Price	Prod
cpe 3P	2,800	670	—
Victoria cpe 4P	2,830	750	—
sdn 2d	2,895	735	—
sdn 4d	2,940	763	—
40-P Deluxe (wb 113.0)			
cpe 3P	2,840	745	—
Victoria cpe 4P	2,865	791	—
conv cpe	2,860	930	—
sdn 2d	2,930	775	—
sdn 4d	2,965	808	—
conv sdn	2,920	955	—
41 Super (wb 118.0)			
cpe 3P	2,950	809	—
Victoria cpe 4P	2,980	860	—
conv cpe	2,980	995	—
sdn 2d	3,020	839	—
sdn 4d	3,050	870	—
conv sdn 2d	3,020	1,030	—
43 Country Club (wb 125.0)			
sdn 4d	3,240	1,018	—
Special sdn 4d	3,240	1,044	—
sdn 4d, 7P	3,355	1,230	—
44 Eight (wb 118.0)			
cpe 3P	3,040	860	—
Victoria cpe 4P	3,075	942	—
conv cpe	3,065	1,087	—
sdn 2d	3,140	918	—
sdn 4d	3,185	952	—
conv sdn 2d	3,130	1,122	—
47 Cntry Club Eight (wb 125.0)			
sdn 4d	3,285	1,118	—
Special sdn 4d	3,285	1,144	—
sdn 4d, 7P	3,400	1,330	—
48 Big Boy (wb 125.0)			
Carry-all sdn 4d	3,245	989	—
sdn 4d, 7P	3,140	1,095	—

1940 Engines	bore×stroke	bhp	availability
I-6, 175.0	3.00×4.13	92	S-40
I-6, 212.0	3.00×5.00	98	S-48
I-6, 212.0	3.00×5.00	102	S-41, 43
I-8, 254.5	3.00×4.50	128	S-44, 47

1941 (Total model-year production: 91,769; Sixes: 82,051; Eights: 9,718)

10-T Traveler (wb 116.0)	Wght	Price	Prod
cpe 3P	2,790	695	—
club cpe 4P	2,840	788	—
sdn 2d	2,850	765	—
sdn 4d	2,900	793	—
10-P Deluxe (wb 116.0)			
cpe 3P	2,840	801	—
club cpe 4P	2,895	848	—
sdn 2d	2,900	822	—
sdn 4d	2,950	856	—
conv sdn 2d	2,980	1,063	140 est

11 Super (wb 121.0)	Wght	Price	Prod
cpe 3P	2,935	881	—
club cpe 4P	2,980	936	—
sdn 2d	3,000	901	—
sdn 4d	3,050	932	—
conv sdn 2d	3,125	1,156	300 est
wgn 4d	3,315	1,297	100 est
12 Commodore Six (wb 121.0)			
cpe 3P	3,000	935	—
club cpe 4P	3,045	997	—
sdn 2d	3,050	966	—
sdn 4d	3,100	994	—
conv sdn 2d	3,160	1,204	200 est
14 Commodore Eight (wb 121.0)			
cpe 3P	3,135	978	—
club cpe 4P	3,210	1,040	—
sdn 2d	3,210	1,003	—
sdn 4d	3,260	1,035	—
conv sdn	3,350	1,254	200 est
wgn 4d	3,400	1,383	80 est
15-17 Commodore Eight (wb 128.0; cpe-121.0)			
15 cpe 3P	3,185	1,064	—
15 club cpe 4P	3,235	1,127	—
17 sdn 4d	3,370	1,232	—
17 sdn 4d 7P	3,440	1,438	—
18 Big Boy (wb 128.0)			
sdn 4d, 7P	3,155	1,223	—

1941 Engines	bore×stroke	bhp	availability
I-6, 175.0	3.00×4.13	92	S-10
I-6, 212.0	3.00×5.00	98	S-18
I-6, 212.0	3.00×5.00	102	S-11, 12
I-8, 254.5	3.00×4.50	128	S-14, 15, 17

1942 (Total model-year production: 40,661; Sixes: 34,069; Eights: 6,592)

20T Traveler (wb 116.0)	Wght	Price	Prod
cpe 3P	2,795	893	—
club cpe 4P	2,845	965	—
sdn 2d	2,895	945	—
sdn 4d	2,940	973	—
20P Deluxe (wb 116.0)			
cpe 3P	2,845	981	—
club cpe 4P	2,900	1,034	—
sdn 2d	2,935	1,012	—
sdn 4d	2,975	1,045	—
conv sdn	3,140	1,292	—
21 Super (wb 121.0)			
cpe 3P	2,950	1,102	—
club cpe 4P	3,010	1,159	—
sdn 2d	3,035	1,132	—
sdn 4d	3,080	1,162	—
conv sdn 2d	3,200	1,414	—
wgn 4d	3,315	1,486	—
22 Commodore Six (wb121.0)			
cpe 3P	2,995	1,176	—
club cpe 5P	3,090	1,239	—
sdn 2d	3,090	1,216	—
sdn 4d	3,145	1,246	—
conv sdn	3,280	1,481	—
24 Commodore Eight (wb 121.0)			
cpe 3P	3,130	1,220	—
club cpe 5P	3,205	1,282	—
sdn 2d	3,230	1,252	—
sdn 4d	3,280	1,291	—
conv sdn 2d	3,400	1,533	—
25 Commodore Custom Eight (wb 121.0)			
cpe 3p	3,160	1,318	—
club cpe 4P	3,235	1,380	—
27 Commodore Custom Eight (wb 128.0)			
sdn 4d, 8P	3,395	1,510	—

1942 Engines	bore×stroke	bhp	availability
I-6, 175.0	3.00×4.13	92	S-20
I-6, 212.0	3.00×5.00	102	S-21, 22
I-8, 254.5	3.00×4.50	128	S-24, 25, 27

1946

51 Super Six (wb121)-61,787 blt	Wght	Price	Prod
sdn 4d	3,085	1,555	—
Brougham sdn 2d	3,030	1,511	—
club cpe	3,015	1,553	—
cpe 3P	2,950	1,481	—
Brougham conv cpe	3,195	1,879	1,035*
52 Commodore Six (wb 121.0) - 17,685 built			
sdn 4d	3,150	1,699	—
club cpe	3,065	1,693	—
53 Super Eight (wb 121.0) - 3,961 built			
sdn 4d	3,235	1,668	—
club cpe	3,065	1,664	—
54 Commodore Eight (wb 121.0) - 8,193 built			
sdn 4d	3,305	1,774	—
club cpe	3,235	1,760	—
Brougham conv cpe	3,410	2,050	140*

* Estimated; total convertibles: 1,177

1946 Engines	bore×stroke	bhp	availability
I-6, 212.0	3.00×5.00	102	S-51, 52
I-8, 254.5	3.00×4.50	128	S-53, 54

1947

171 Spr Six (wb 121)-49,276 blt	Wght	Price	Prod
sdn 4d	3,110	1,749	—
Brougham sdn 2d	3,055	1,704	—
club cpe	3,040	1,744	—
cpe 3P	2,975	1,628	—
Brghm conv cpe	3,220	2,021	1,460*
172 Commodore Six (wb 121.0) - 25,138 built			
sdn 4d	3,175	1,896	—
club cpe	3,090	1,887	—
173 Super Eight (wb 121.0) - 5,076 built			
sdn 4d	3,260	1,862	—
club cpe	3,210	1,855	—
174 Commodore Eight (wb 121.0) - 12,593 built			
sdn 4d	3,330	1,972	—
club cpe	3,260	1,955	—
Brougham conv cpe	3,435	2,196	360*

* Estimated; total convertibles: 1,823

1947 Engines	bore×stroke	bhp	availability
I-6, 212.0	3.00×5.00	102	S-171, 172
I-8, 254.5	3.00×4.50	128	S-173, 174

1948

481 Spr Six (wb124)-49,388 blt	Wght	Price	Prod
sdn 4d	3,500	2,222	—
Brougham sdn 2d	3,470	2,172	—
club cpe	3,480	2,219	—
cpe 3P	3,460	2,069	—
Brougham conv cpe	3,750	2,836	88*
482 Commodore Six (wb 124.0) - 27,159 built			
sdn 4d	3,540	2,399	—
club cpe	3,550	2,374	—
Brougham conv cpe	3,780	3,057	48*
483 Super Eight (wb 124.0) - 5,338 built			
sdn 4d	3,525	2,343	—
club cpe	3,495	2,340	—
484 Commodore Eight (wb 124.0) - 35,315 built			
sdn 4d	3,600	2,514	—
club cpe	3,570	2,490	—
Brougham conv cpe	3,800	3,138	64*

* Estimated; total convertibles: 200

1948 Engines	bore×stroke	bhp	availability
I-6, 262.0	3.56×4.38	121	S-481, 482
I-8, 254.5	3.00×4.50	128	S-483, 484

1949

491 Spr Six (wb124)-91,333 blt	Wght	Price	Prod
sdn 4d	3,555	2,207	—
Brougham sdn 2d	3,515	2,156	—
club cpe	3,480	2,203	—
cpe 3P	3,485	2,053	—
Brougham conv cpe	3,750	2,799	1,870*
492 Commodore Six (wb 124.0) - 32,715 built			
sdn 4d	3,625	2,383	—
club cpe	3,585	2,359	—
Brougham conv cpe	3,780	2,952	655*
493 Super Eight (wb 124.0) - 6,365 built			
sdn 4d	3,565	2,296	—
Brougham sdn 2d	3,545	2,245	—
493 Super Eight	**Wght**	**Price**	**Prod**
club cpe	3,550	2,292	—
494 Commodore Eight (wb 124.0) - 28,687 built			
sdn 4d	3,650	2,472	—
club cpe	3,600	2,448	—
Brougham conv cpe	3,800	3,041	595*

* Estimated; total convertibles: 3,119

1949 Engines	bore×stroke	bhp	availability
I-6, 262.0	3.56×4.38	121	S-491, 492
I-8, 254.5	3.00×4.50	128	S-493, 494

1950

500 Pacmkr (wb 119)-39,455 blt	Wght	Price	Prod
sdn 4d	3,510	1,933	—
Brougham sdn 2d	3,475	1,912	—
club cpe	3,460	1,933	—
cpe 3P	3,445	1,807	—
Brougham conv cpe	3,655	2,428	1,100*
50A Pacemaker Deluxe (wb 119.0) - 22,297 built			
sdn 4d	3,520	1,959	—
Brougham sdn 2d	3,485	1,928	—
club cpe	3,470	1,959	—
Brougham conv cpe	3,665	2,444	630*
501 Super Six (wb 124.0) - 17,246 built			
sdn 4d	3,590	2,105	—
Brougham sdn 2d	3,565	2,068	—
club cpe	3,555	2,102	—
Brougham conv cpe	3,750	2,629	465*
502 Commodore Six (wb 124.0) - 24,605 built			
sdn 4d	3,655	2,282	—
club cpe	3,640	2,257	—
Brougham conv cpe	3,840	2,809	700*
503 Super Eight (wb 124.0) - 1,074 built			
sdn 4d	3,605	2,189	—
Brougham sdn 2d	3,575	2,152	—
club cpe	3,560	2,186	—
504 Commodore Eight (wb 124.0) - 16,731 built			
sdn 4d	3,675	2,366	—
club cpe	3,655	2,341	—
Brougham conv cpe	3,865	2,893	425*

* Estimated; total convertibles: 3,322

1950 Engines	bore×stroke	bhp	availability
I-6, 232.0	3.56×3.88	112	S-500
I-6, 262.0	3.56×4.38	123	S-50A, 501, 502
I-8, 254.5	3.00×4.50	128	S-503, 504

1951

4A Pacemaker Cust (wb 119.0) - 34,495 built	Wght	Price	Prod
sdn 4d	3,460	2,145	—
Brougham sdn 2d	3,430	2,102	—
club cpe	3,410	2,145	—
cpe 3P	3,380	1,965	—
Brougham conv cpe	3,600	2,642	430*
5A Super Six Custom (wb 124.0) - 22,532 built			
sdn 4d	3,565	2,287	—
Brougham sdn 2d	3,535	2,238	—
club cpe	3,525	2,287	—
Hollywood htp cpe	3,590	2,605	1,100*
Brougham conv cpe	3,720	2,827	280*
6A Commodore Six Custom (wb 124.0) - 16,979 built			
sdn 4d	3,600	2,480	—
club cpe	3,585	2,455	—
Hollywood htp cpe	3,640	2,780	820*
Brougham conv cpe	3,785	3,011	210*
7A Hornet (wb 124.0) - 43,656 built			
sdn 4d	3,600	2,568	—
club cpe	3,580	2,543	—
Hollywood htp cpe	3,630	2,869	2,100*
Brougham conv cpe	3,780	3,099	550*
8A Commodore Eight Cust (wb 124.0) - 14,243 built			
sdn 4d	3,620	2,568	—
club cpe	3,600	2,543	—
Hollywood htp cpe	3,650	2,869	670*
Brougham conv cpe	3,800	3,099	180*

* Production estimated; total convertibles: 1,651; total hardtops: 4,689

1951 Engines	bore×stroke	bhp	availability
I-6, 232.0	3.56×3.88	112	S-Pacemaker
I-6, 262.0	3.56×4.38	123	S-Super & Commodr Six
I-6, 308.0	3.81×4.50	145	S-Hornet
I-8, 254.5	3.00×4.50	128	S-Commodr Eight

1952

4B Pacemaker (wb 119)-7,486 blt	Wght	Price	Prod
sdn 4d	3,390	2,311	—
Brougham sdn 2d	3,355	2,264	—
club cpe	3,335	2,311	—
cpe 3P	3,305	2,116	—
5B Wasp (wb 119.0) - 21,876 built			
sdn 4d	3,485	2,466	—
Brougham sdn 2d	3,470	2,413	—
club cpe	3,435	2,466	—
Hollywood htp cpe	3,525	2,812	1,320*
Brougham conv cpe	3,635	3,048	220*
6B Commodore Six (wb 124.0) - 1,592 built			
sdn 4d	3,595	2,674	—
club cpe	3,550	2,647	—
Hollywood htp cpe	3,625	3,000	100*
Brougham conv cpe	3,750	3,247	20*
7B Hornet (wb 124.0) - 35,921 built			
sdn 4d	3,600	2,769	—
club cpe	3,550	2,742	—
Hollywood htp cpe	3,630	3,095	2,160*
Brougham conv cpe	3,750	3,342	360*
8B Commodore Eight (wb 124.0) - 3,125 built			
sdn 4d	3,630	2,769	—
club cpe	3,580	2,742	—
Hollywood htp cpe	3,660	3,095	190*
Brougham conv cpe	3,770	3,342	30*

* Est.; total convertibles: 636; total hardtops: 3,777

1952 Engines	bore×stroke	bhp	availability
I-6, 232.0	3.56×3.88	112	S-Pacemaker
I-6, 262.0	3.56×4.38	127	S-Wasp, Commodr Six
I-6, 308.0	3.81×4.50	145	S-Hornet
I-8, 254.5	3.00×4.50	128	S-Commodr Eight

1953

1C Jet (wb 105.0)-21,143 blt (Includes Super Jet)	Wght	Price	Prod
sdn 4d	2,650	1,858	—
2C Super Jet (wb 105.0)			
sdn 4d	2,700	1,954	—
sdn 2d	2,695	1,933	—
4C Wasp (wb 119.0) - 17,792 built (Includes Super Wasp)			
sdn 4d	3,380	2,311	—
sdn 2d	3,350	2,264	—
club cpe	3,340	2,311	—
5C Super Wasp (wb 119.0)			
sdn 4d	3,480	2,466	—
sdn 2d	3,460	2,413	—
club cpe	3,455	2,466	—
Hollywood htp cpe	3,525	2,812	590*
Brougham conv cpe	3,655	3,048	50*
7C Hornet (wb 124.0) - 27,208 built			
sdn 4d	3,570	2,769	—
club cpe	3,530	2,742	—
Hollywood htp cpe	3,610	3,095	910*
Brougham conv cpe	3,760	3,342	—

* Estimated; total hardtops: 1,501

1953 Engines	bore×stroke	bhp	availability
I-6, 202.0	3.00×4.75	104	S-Jet
I-6, 202.0	3.00×4.75	106/114	O-Jet
I-6, 232.0	3.56×3.88	112	S-Wasp
I-6, 262.0	3.56×4.38	127	S-Super Wasp
I-6, 308.0	3.81×4.50	145	S-Hornet
I-6, 308.0	3.81×4.50	160	O-Hornet
I-6, 308.0	3.81×4.50	170	O-Hornet (7-X)

1954

1D Jet (wb 105.0)-14,224 blt (Includes Super Jet and Jet-Liner)	Wght	Price	Prod
sdn 4d	2,675	1,858	—
Utility sdn 2d	2,715	1,837	—
Family club sdn 2d	2,635	1,621	—
2D Super Jet (wb 105.0)			
sdn 4d	2,725	1,954	—
club sdn 2d	2,710	1,933	—
3D Jet-Liner (wb 105.0)			
sdn 4d	2,760	2,057	—
club sdn 2d	2,740	2,046	—
4D Wasp (wb 119.0) - 11,603 blt (Incl. Super Wasp)			
sdn 4d	3,440	2,256	—
club sdn 2d	3,375	2,209	—
club cpe	3,360	2,256	—
5D Super Wasp (wb 119.0)			
sdn 4d	3,525	2,466	—
club sdn 2d	3,490	2,413	—
club cpe	3,475	2,466	—
Hollywood htp cpe	3,570	2,704	—
Brougham conv cpe	3,680	3,004	—
6D Hornet Spec (wb 124.0) - 24,833 blt (Incl. Hornet)			
Brougham conv cpe	3,680	3,004	—
sdn 4d	3,560	2,619	—
club sdn 2d	3,515	2,571	—
club cpe	3,505	2,619	—
7D Hornet (wb 124.0)			
sdn 4d	3,620	2,769	—
club cpe	3,570	2,742	—
Hollywood htp cpe	3,655	2,988	—
Brougham conv cpe	3,800	3,288	—
Italia (wb 105.0)			
cpe	2,710	4,800	26

1954 Engines	bore×stroke	bhp	availability
I-6, 202.0	3.00×4.75	104	S-Jet
I-6, 202.0	3.00×4.75	106/114	S-Italia; O-Jet
I-6, 232.0	3.56×3.88	126	S-Wasp
I-6, 262.0	3.56×4.38	140	S-Super Wasp
I-6, 308.0	3.81×4.50	160	S-Hornet
I-6, 308.0	3.81×4.50	170	O-Horn (Twin-H)

1955

54 Metro (wb 85) - 3,000* blt	Wght	Price	Prod
1 conv cpe 3P	1,803	1,469	—
2 htp cpe	1,843	1,445	—
55 Rambler (wb 100.0)			
12 Deluxe bus sdn	2,400	1,457	34
14-1 Super Suburb wgn 2d	2,532	1,869	1,335
16-1 Super club sdn	2,450	1,683	2,970
17-2 Cust Cntry Club htp cpe	2,518	2,098	1,601
55 Rambler (wb 108.0)			
15 Deluxe sdn 4d	2,567	1,695	
15-1 Super sdn 4d	2,570	1,798	7,210
15-2 Custom sdn 4d	2,606	1,989	
18-1 Spr Cross Cntry wgn 4d	2,675	1,975	12,023
18-2 Cust Cross Cntry wgn 4d	2,685	1,995	
3554 Wasp (wb 114.3)			
5-1 Super sdn 4d	3,254	2,290	5,551
5-2 Custom sdn 4d	3,347	2,460	
7-2 Cust Hollywood htp cpe	3,362	2,570	1,640
3556 Hornet 6 (wb 121.3)			
5-1 Super sdn 4d	3,495	2,565	5,357
5-2 Custom sdn 4d	3,562	2,760	
7-2 Cust Hollywood htp cpe	3,587	2,880	1,554
3558 Hornet V-8 (wb 121.3)			
5-1 Super sdn 4d	3,806	2,825	4,449
5-2 Custom sdn 4d	3,846	3,015	
7-2 Cust Hollywood htp cpe	3,878	3,145	1,770
Italia (wb 105.0)			
cpe	2,710	4,800	5

* Estimated; total Nash & Hudson, 3,849.

1955 Engines	bore×stroke	bhp	availability
I-4, 73.2	2.56×3.50	42	S-Metropolitan
I-6, 195.6	3.13×4.25	90	S-Rambler
I-6, 195.6	3.13×4.25	100	S-Rambler fleet model
I-6, 202.0	3.00×4.75	110	S-Wasp
I-6, 202.0	3.00×4.75	114	S-Italia

1955 Engines	bore×stroke	bhp	availability
I-6, 202.0	3.00×4.75	120	O-Wasp
I-6, 308.0	3.81×4.50	160	S-Hornet 6
I-6, 308.0 (Twin-H)	3.81×4.50	170	O-Hornet 6
V-8, 320.0	3.81×3.50	208	S-Hornet V-8

1956

54 Metro (wb 85) - 3,000* blt	Wght	Price	Prod
1 conv cpe 3P	1,803	1,469	—
2 htp cpe 3P	1,843	1,445	—
56 Rambler DeLuxe (wb 108.0) - 5,000 built (Includes Super and Custom)			
15 sdn 4d	2,891	1,829	—
56 Rambler Super (wb 108.0)			
15-1 sdn 4d	2,096	1,939	—
18-1 Cross Cntry wgn 4d	2,992	2,233	—
56 Rambler Custom (wb 108.0)			
13-2 Cross Cntry htp wgn 4d	3,095	2,494	—
15-2 sdn 4d	2,929	2,059	—
18-2 Cross Cntry wgn 4d	3,110	2,329	—
19-2 htp sdn	2,990	2,224	—
3564 Wasp (wb 114.3)			
5-1 sdn 4d	3,264	2,416	2,519
3565 Hornet Special (wb 114.3)			
5-1 sdn 4d	3,467	2,626	1,528
7-1 Hollywood htp cpe	3,486	2,741	229
3566 Hornet 6 (wb 121.3)			
5-1 Super sdn 4d	3,545	2,777	3,022
5-2 Custom sdn 4d	3,636	3,019	
7-2 Hollywood htp cpe	3,646	3,136	358
3568 Hornet V-8 (wb 121.3)			
5-2 sdn 4d	3,862	3,286	1,962
7-2 Hollywood htp cpe	3,872	3,429	1,053

* Estimated; total Nash & Hudson: 7,645

1956 Engines	bore×stroke	bhp	availability
I-4, 73.2	2.56×3.50	42	S-Metropolitan
I-6, 195.6	3.13×4.25	120	S-Rambler
I-6, 202.0	3.00×4.75	120	S-Wasp
I-6, 202.0	3.00×4.75	130	O-Wsp (Twn-H)
I-6, 308.0	3.81×4.50	165	S-Hornet 6
V-8, 352.0	4.00×3.50	220	S-Hornet V-8 (thru 3/56)
V-8, 250.0	3.50×3.25	190	S-Hornet Spec (3/56 on)

1957

357-1 Hornet Super (wb 121.3)	Wght	Price	Prod
sdn 4d	3,631	2,821	1,103
Hollywood htp cpe	3,655	2,911	266
357-2 Hornet Custom (wb 121.3)			
sdn 4d	3,678	3,011	2,256
Hollywood htp cpe	3,693	3,101	483

1957 Engine	bore×stroke	bhp	availability
V-8, 327.0	4.00×3.25	255	S-all

Hupmobile

Robert C. Hupp was an engineer who worked with Ransom Eli Olds and Henry Ford before setting up his own car company in November 1909. His first product, developed with help from several colleagues he hired away from Olds, was the Model 20, a little 16.9-horsepower four-cylinder job on an 86-inch wheelbase. Hupp priced it at a modest $750, a full $75 below Ford's recently introduced Model T. With features like high-tension magneto and two-speed sliding-gear transmission, this first Hupmobile garnered 1618 sales. By 1913, Hupp production was over 12,000.

Hupp left in a huff during 1911 (his next venture would be the unsuccessful RCH), but Hupp Motor Car Company prospered through the Teens and '20s. A straight-eight debuted in 1925, and six-cylinder models replaced fours in 1926. By that point the firm had inked a favorable contract with the Murray Body Corporation, and the considerable talents of its chief designer, Amos Northup, were evident by 1928 in Hupp's stylish new Century line of Sixes and Eights. Buyers responded, and registrations that year totaled some 55,500.

But that would be the peak, and Hupp never built more than 9500 cars a year after 1932. Though its post-1933 "Aerodynamic" cars were among the better examples of period streamlining, the public didn't go for them. As a result, Hupp closed down midway through 1936, reopened to produce a handful of 1937-38 cars, then struggled on without much success into 1939.

After a second straight year of healthy sales, Hupp volume plunged to 22,183 for 1930. That year's line began with the six-cylinder S, a six-model line with 111-inch wheelbase and a 70-bhp, 211.6-cubic-inch engine. Prices were $995-$1160, which made it a medium-priced car. Then came three straight-eight series designated C, H, and U, which were assembled in Detroit; the S was produced in Cleveland at the former Chandler plant that Hupp had acquired. The S and C were Hupp's bread-and-butter cars. The latter mounted a 121-inch chassis and carried a 268.6-cid engine with 100 bhp. H and U used a larger 365.6-cid eight with 133 bhp and included some luxurious limousines on a 137-inch wheelbase.

The next year brought more of the same, plus a new L-series Century Eight with a 90-bhp 240.2-cid engine. A two-door victoria, one of the most-handsome Hupps ever, arrived in the U-Series, and freewheeling was a sales point across the line. With the Depression exerting its death grip, Hupp flew buyers to Detroit and Cleveland to help stimulate orders, but sales remained sluggish at 17,456 for the model year.

For 1932, Hupp series codes indicated model year and wheelbase. That year's B-216 thus rode a 116-inch wheelbase; it also carried a new 75-bhp 228.1-cid engine. Hupp now secured the services of designer Raymond Loewy, who styled the eight-cylinder F-222 and I-226 with tire-hugging, cycle-type fenders; Vee'd radiators; sloped windshields; and chrome wheel discs. Fs had 250.7- or 261.5-cid engines with about 95 bhp. A 103-bhp, 279.9-cid unit powered the I-models. These graceful, handsome cars (issued after a brief run of "first-series" '31 carry-overs) won many awards for Loewy but few sales for Hupp, and production dropped again, this time to just under 10,500.

1930 Model C Standard Eight coupe with rumble seat

The 1933 Hupps were essentially '32 reruns, with a more-sloping grille the most obvious visual change. The 250 eight departed, while the 279 engine was bored out to 303.2 cid and 109 bhp for the I-326. Expanding the line were a cycle-fendered Six, the K-321, plus a cheaper K-321A with stationary hood louvers and single windshield wiper and taillight. But none of this helped, and Hupp's total volume dropped to just 7316.

For 1934, Hupp hitched its falling star to the radical Loewy-designed J-421 Six and T-427 Eight. Advertised as the "Hupp Aerodynamic," these wore three-piece windshields with mild wraparound effect, headlights neatly faired-in between radiator and front fenders, and flush-mounted spare tire. More-orthodox looks graced the W-417 Six, which had a good many body parts borrowed from Ford. Power came from a small 224-cid engine with just 80 bhp. J-models introduced a 245.3-cid engine with 93 bhp, while the T-Series offered 116 horses from an improved 303 eight. This overall formula had evident appeal, for sales rose to 9420. It continued with little change for 1935. However, Hupp enhanced it by introducing the D-518 Aerodynamic Six with flat windshield and 101-bhp 245 engine, and the O-521 Eight with a 120-bhp 303. Production recovered to 1932 levels, nearing 10,800.

But the big news about Hupp in this period concerned a fight for company control. Archie Andrews, promoter of the unsuccessful front-drive 1930 Ruxton, gained control of Hupp in late 1934. He was forced out a year later, but not before the firm was in ruins. Hupp was thus obliged to close its doors in early 1936, keeping them shut for over 18 months. Hupp returned for 1938 with 245 and 303 engines in conventionally styled E-822 Six and H-825 Eight models—just in time for a brief but sharp national recession. As a result, total model-year production came to just 2001 units.

Meanwhile, Norman De Vaux had become Hupp general manager, and had just purchased the body tooling from the late front-drive Cord 810/812. Offering a rear-drive version in fair numbers would revive Hupp—or so he thought. And indeed, De Vaux reportedly took 6000 advance orders for what was announced in 1939 as the "Junior Six," later renamed Skylark. But with funds critically low, Hupp wasn't able to move the project beyond 30 odd prototypes (or pilot models), all hand-built before year's end. Included in the run was one Skylark Corsair convertible.

Undaunted, De Vaux approached Graham-Paige president Joseph Graham, who agreed to produce Skylark bodies if G-P could sell its own version of the car. This deal gave Hupp a ready supplier and Graham a new model to supplement its languishing "sharknose" line. Hupp president J.W. Drake said it did "not mean a merger of the two corporations. The Hupp-Graham contract is a most favorable one for both of us, as careful checking of all production costs demonstrated that great savings could be made." In reality, this was a partnership born of desperation.

Like Graham's Hollywood, the Hupp Skylark was identical to the defunct Cord from the cowl back, but wheelbase was trimmed 10 inches, to 115, via a new front end designed by John Tjaarda. Both versions wore a double grille and "bullet" headlamps nestled inboard of the front fenders, but the upper grille was painted on Skylarks, chromed on Hollywoods. Each firm naturally used its own engines. For Skylark this meant the 101-bhp, 245 six from 1935. Hollywoods carried a 217.8-cid Graham six with 120 bhp supercharged or 95 unsupercharged. The Skylark was thus a bit livelier than an unblown Hollywood, but slower than the blown model. It was also a bit cheaper: $1145 to the Graham's initial $1250.

But the Skylark/Hollywood was delayed by the same tooling problems and cost overruns that had plagued the Cord. Worse, a full nine months were lost in transferring Skylark tools to the Graham assembly line in Dearborn, which had to be reconfigured for the "new" models, so production didn't begin in earnest until May 1940—by which time most of the advance orders had been canceled. Graham, which grabbed the publicity spotlight with its blown engine, ended up building six times as many of these cars. Hupp gave up at the end of July 1940, just three weeks after the start of '41-model production. Only some 300 Skylarks were built in all.

Hupp recovered somewhat with military contracts during World War II, but elected not to return to the auto manufacturing business when peace returned. Eventually, Hupp began making accessories for other auto companies as well as kitchen and electronics equipment.

1932 Series F-222 Eight sport coupe with rumble seat

1934 Series J-421 Six "Aerodynamic" four-door sedan

1932 "second series" Eight four-door sedan

1935 W-517 coupe

1933 Series K-321 cabriolet roadster

1936 Series O-621 Eight DeLuxe touring sedan

1936 D-618 Six four-door sedan

1939 Skylark Corsair convertible coupe

1938 Series E-822 Six four-door sedan

1941 Skylark Custom four-door sedan

Specifications

1930 - 22,183 built

S Standard Six (wb 111.0)	Wght	Price	Prod
phaeton 5P	2,690	1,135	—
bus cpe 2P	2,710	995	—
cabriolet 2-4P	2,690	1,110	—
sdn 4d	2,885	1,095	—
cpe 2-4P	2,740	1,095	—
DeLuxe sdn 4d	—	1,160	—
C Standard Eight (wb 121.0)			
touring div sdn 7P	3,600	1,785	—
cpe 2-4P	3,560	1,695	—
cabriolet 2-4P	3,500	1,770	—
victoria cpe 5P	3,535	1,715	—
sdn 4d	3,640	1,695	—
Town div sdn 5P	—	1,805	—
H Standard Eight (wb 125.0)			
touring div sdn 7P	3,870	2,190	—
cpe 2-4P	3,915	2,080	—
cabriolet 2-4P	3,880	2,155	—
victoria cpe 5P	3,830	2,100	—
sdn 4d	3,995	2,080	—
Town div sdn 4d	3,995	2,190	—
U Standard Eight (wb 137.0)			
sdn 7P	4,225	2,495	—
sdn limo 7P	4,390	2,645	—

1930 Engines	bore×stroke	bhp	availability
I-6, 211.6	3.25×4.25	70	S-S
I-8, 268.6	3.00×4.75	100	S-C
I-8, 365.6	3.50×4.75	133	S-H, U

1931 - 17,456 built

S Century Six (wb 114.0)	Wght	Price	Prod
rdstr 2-4P	2,855	1,075	—
phtn 5P	2,900	1,050	—
comp cpe 2P	2,825	995	—
cpe 2-4P	2,865	995	—
cabriolet 2-4P	2,855	1,050	—
sdn 4d	2,985	995	—
L Century Eight (wb 118.0)			
rdstr 2-4 P	3,055	1,375	—
phaeton 5P	3,330	1,350	—
cpe 2P	3,100	1,295	—
cpe 2-4P	3,165	1,295	—
cabriolet 2-4P	3,125	1,350	—
sdn 4d	3,275	1,295	—
C Standard Eight (wb 121.0)			
touring sdn 7P	3,715	1,685	—
cpe 2-4P	3,650	1,595	—
cabriolet 2-4P	3,610	1,595	—
victoria cpe 5P	3,695	1,615	—
cpe 4P	3,695	1,615	—
sdn 4d	3,730	1,595	—
Town sdn 4d	3,785	1,705	—
H Standard Eight (wb 125.0)			
touring sdn 7P	3,975	2,005	—
cpe 2-4P	4,015	1,895	—
cabriolet 2-4P	3,975	1,895	—
victoria cpe 5P	4,010	1,915	—
cpe 4P	4,010	1,915	—
sdn 4d	4,095	1,895	—
Town sdn 4d	4,230	2,005	—
U Standard Eight (wb 137.0) - 474 built			
victoria cpe 5P	4,165	2,295	—
sdn 7P	4,360	2,295	—
sdn limo 7P	4,400	2,445	—

1931 Engines	bore×stroke	bhp	availability
I-6, 211.6	3.25×4.25	70	S-S
I-8, 240.2	2.88×4.63	90	S-L
I-8, 268.6	3.00×4.75	100	S-C
I-8, 365.6	3.50×4.75	133	S-H, U

1932 First Series

S "214" Six (wb 114.0) - 2,210 blt	Wght	Price	Prod
rdstr 2-4P	2,855	875	—
phaeton 5P	2,900	850	—
cpe 2P	2,825	795	—
cpe 2-4P	2,865	795	—
cabriolet 2-4P	2,855	850	—
sdn 4d	2,985	795	—

L "218" Eight (wb 118.0) - 1,096 blt	Wght	Price	Prod
rdstr 2-4P	3,055	1,075	—
phaeton 5P	3,330	1,050	—
cpe 2P	3,100	995	—
cpe 2-4P	3,165	995	—
cabriolet 2-4P	3,125	1,050	—
sdn 4d	3,275	995	—
C "221" Eight (wb 121.0) - 675 built			
phaeton 7P	3,715	1,305	—
cpe 2-4P	3,650	1,195	—
cpe 4P	3,695	1,215	—
victoria cpe 5P	3,695	1,215	—
sdn 4d	3,730	1,195	—
Town sdn 4d	3,825	1,195	—
H "225" Eight (wb 125.0) - 446 built			
phaeton 7P	3,985	1,585	—
cpe 2-4P	4,015	1,455	—
cpe 4P	4,010	1,475	—
victoria cpe 5P	4,010	1,475	—
sdn 4d	4,095	1,455	—
Town sdn 4d	4,300	1,430	—
U "237" Eight (wb 137.0)—132 built			
victoria cpe	4,165	1,795	—
sdn 7P	4,360	1,895	—
limo 7P	4,400	1,955	—

1932(1) Eng	bore×stroke	bhp	availability
I-6, 211.6	3.25×4.25	70	S-S
I-8, 240.2	2.88×4.63	90	S-L
I-8, 268.6	3.00×4.75	100	S-C
I-8, 365.6	3.50×4.75	133	S-H, U

1932 Second Series (from Jan. 1)

B "216" Six (wb 116.5) - 3,500 blt	Wght	Price	Prod
rdstr 2-4P	2,825	795	—
phaeton 5P	2,925	795	—
cpe 2-4P	2,975	895	—
cpe 2P	2,935	895	—
conv cabriolet 2-4P	2,985	895	—
sdn 4d	3,095	895	—
F "222" Eight (wb 122.0) - 3,755 built			
rdstr cab 2-4P	3,415	1,395	—

F "222" Eight	Wght	Price	Prod
cpe 2-4P	3,505	1,295	—
victoria cpe	3,585	1,360	—
sdn 4d	3,550	1,295	—
I "226" Eight (wb 126.0) - 713 built			
rdstr cab 2-4P	3,650	1,695	—
cpe 2-4P	3,740	1,595	—
victoria cpe 5P	3,820	1,660	—
sdn 4d	3,785	1,595	—

1932(2) Eng	bore×stroke	bhp	availability
I-6, 228.1	3.38×4.25	75	S-B
I-8, 250.7	2.94×4.63	93	S-F thru #6905
I-8, 261.5	3.00×4.63	—	S-F from #6906
I-8, 279.9	3.06×4.75	103	S-I

1933

B "316" Six (wb 116.0) - 1,463 blt	Wght	Price	Prod
rdstr 2P	2,825	795	—
phaeton 5P	2,925	795	—
cpe 2P	2,935	895	—
cpe 2-4P	2,975	895	—
cabriolet 2-4P	2,965	895	—
sdn 4d	3,095	895	—
K "321" Six (wb 121.0) - 4,600 built			
cab rdstr 2-4P	3,235	1,095	—
cpe 2-4P	3,235	995	—
victoria cpe 5P	3,250	1,060	—
sdn 4d	3,290	995	—
F "322" Eight (wb 122.0) - 700 built			
cab rdstr 2-4P	3,600	1,295	—
cpe 2-4P	3,545	1,195	—
victoria cpe 5P	3,605	1,260	—
sdn 4d	3,650	1,195	—
I "326" Eight (wb 126.0) - 250 built			
cab rdstr 2-4P	3,810	1,545	—
cpe 2-4P	3,795	1,445	—
victoria cpe 5P	3,830	1,510	—
sdn 4d	3,845	1,445	—
KK "321-A" Six (wb 121.0) - 300 built			
cpe 2-4P	3,135	895	—
victoria cpe 5P	3,150	960	—
sdn 4d	3,190	895	—

1933 Engines	bore×stroke	bhp	availability
I-6, 228.1	3.38×4.25	75	S-B
I-6, 228.1	3.38×4.25	90	S-K, KK
I-8, 261.5	3.00×4.63	96	S-F
I-8, 303.2	3.19×4.75	109	S-I

1934 - 9,420 built

KK "421-A" Six (wb 121) - 300 blt	Wght	Price	Prod
cpe 2-4P	3,160	795	—
victoria cpe 5P	3,165	860	—
sdn 4d	3,200	795	—
K "421" Six (wb 121.0)			
rdstr cab 2-4P	3,235	895	—
cpe 2-4P	3,250	795	—
victoria cpe 5P	3,255	860	—
sdn 4d	3,290	895	—
F "422" Eight (wb 122.0)			
rdstr cab 2-4P	3,600	1,045	—
cpe 2-4P	3,545	945	—
victoria cpe 5P	3,630	1,010	—
sdn 4d	3,665	1,045	—
I "426" Eight (wb 126.0)			
rdstr cab 2-4P	3,810	1,145	—
cpe 2-4P	3,795	1,045	—
victoria cpe 5P	3,830	1,110	—
sdn 4d	3,845	1,145	—
W "417" Six (wb 117.0)			
cpe 2-4P	2,940	795	—
sdn 4d	3,040	795	—
touring sdn 4d T/B	3,075	845	—
DeLuxe cpe 2-4P	2,940	845	—
DeLuxe sdn 4d	3,040	845	—
DeLx tour sdn 4d T/B	3,075	895	—
J "421" Six (wb 121.0)			
cpe 3-5P	3,230	1,195	—
victoria cpe 5P	3,325	1,195	—
sdn 4d	3,325	1,095	—
T "427" Eight (wb 127.0)			
cpe 3-5P	3,675	1,345	—
victoria cpe 5P	3,700	1,265	—
sdn 4d	3,700	1,245	—

1934 Engines	bore×stroke	bhp	availability
I-6, 224.0	3.50×3.88	80	S-W
I-6, 228.1	3.38×4.25	90	S-K, KK
I-6, 245.3	3.50×4.25	93	S-J
I-8, 261.5	3.00×4.63	96	S-F
I-8, 303.2	3.19×4.75	109	S-I
I-8, 303.2	3.19×4.75	116	S-T

1935

W "517" Six (wb 117.0) - 2,586 blt	Wght	Price	Prod
cpe 2P	2,900	695	—
cpe 2-4P	2,940	695	—
sdn 4d	3,040	695	—
touring sdn 5P	3,075	745	—
DeLuxe cpe 2P	2,900	745	—
DeLuxe cpe 2-4P	2,940	745	—
DeLuxe sdn 4d	3,040	745	—
DeLuxe tour sdn 4d	3,075	795	—
D "518" Six (wb 118.0) - 5,900 built			
sdn 4d	2,930	795	—
touring sdn 4d	2,945	845	—
DeLuxe sdn 4d	2,930	835	—
DeLuxe tour sdn 4d	2,945	885	—
J "521" Six (wb 121.0) - 993 built			
cpe 3-5P	3,230	1,095	—
victoria sdn 4d	3,325	1,095	—
sdn 4d	3,325	1,095	—
DeLuxe cpe 3-5P	3,230	1,170	—
DeLuxe vic sdn 4d	3,325	1,170	—
DeLuxe sdn 4d	3,325	1,170	—
T "527" Eight (wb 127.0) - 902 built			
cpe 3-5P	3,625	1,395	—
victoria sdn 4d	3,700	1,395	—
sdn 4d	3,700	1,395	—
DeLuxe cpe 3-5P	3,625	1,445	—
DeLuxe vic sdn 4d	3,700	1,445	—
DeLuxe sdn 4d	3,700	1,445	—
O "521" Eight (wb 121.0) - 400 built			
cpe 3-5P	3,300	1,195	—
victoria cpe 5P	3,432	1,195	—
sdn 4d	3,432	1,195	—
touring vic cpe 5P	3,447	1,195	—
touring sdn 4d	3,447	1,195	—
DeLuxe cpe 3-5P	3,330	1,245	—
DeLuxe vic cpe 5P	3,432	1,245	—
DeLuxe sdn 4d	3,432	1,245	—
DeLuxe touring vic 5P	3,447	1,245	—
DeLuxe touring sdn 4d	3,447	1,245	—

1935 Engines	bore×stroke	bhp	availability
I-6, 224.0	3.50×3.88	91	S-W
I-6, 245.3	3.50×4.25	101	S-D, J
I-8, 303.2	3.19×4.75	120	S-T, O

1936

D "618" Six (wb 118.0) - 1,873 blt	Wght	Price	Prod
sdn 4d	2,930	795	—
touring sdn 4d	2,945	845	—
DeLuxe sdn 4d	2,930	835	—
DeLuxe tour sdn 4d	2,945	885	—
O "621" Eight (wb 121.0) - 298 built			
cpe 3-5P	3,330	1,195	—
victoria 5P	3,432	1,195	—
sdn 4d	3,432	1,195	—
touring victoria 5P	3,447	1,195	—
touring sdn 4d	3,447	1,195	—
DeLuxe cpe 3-5P	3,330	1,245	—
DeLuxe victoria 5P	3,432	1,245	—
DeLuxe sdn 4d	3,432	1,245	—
DeLx tour victoria 5P	3,447	1,245	—
DeLuxe tour sdn 4d	3,447	1,245	—

1936 Engines	bore×stroke	bhp	availability
I-6, 245.3	3.50×4.25	101	S-D
I-8, 303.2	3.19×4.75	120	S-O

1937

Note: Hupp closed in early 1936 and remained closed for 18 months. Most sources state no 1937 models were produced, but industry records do quote the following model listings (production based on announced serial number spans):

G Six (wb 118.0) - 199 built	Wght	Price	Prod
bus cpe 3P	3,010	795	—
cpe 3-5P	3,060	840	—
sdn 2d	2,980	815	—
touring sdn 2d	3,030	850	—
sdn 4d	3,000	855	—
touring sdn 4d	3,040	890	—
N Eight (wb 121.0) - 39 built			
cpe 3-5P	3,565	1,035	—
sdn 2d	3,535	995	—
touring sdn 2d	3,565	1,035	—
sdn 4d	3,535	1,035	—
touring sdn 4d	3,550	1,075	—

1937 Engines	bore×stroke	bhp	availability
I-6, 245.3	3.50×4.25	101	S-G
I-8, 303.2	3.19×4.75	120	S-N

1938

E "822" (wb 122.0) - 1,804 blt	Wght	Price	Prod
Standard sdn 4d T/B	3,320	1,045	—
Regular sdn 4d T/B	3,370	1,180	—
DeLuxe sdn 4d T/B	3,400	1,222	—
Custom sdn 4d T/B	3,440	1,340	—
H "825" (wb 125.0) - 197 built			
Regular sdn 4d T/B	3,955	1,325	—
DeLuxe sdn 4d T/B	4,085	1,365	—
Custom sdn 4d T/B	4,125	1,485	—

1938 Engines	bore×stroke	bhp	availability
I-6, 245.3	3.50×4.25	101	S-E
I-8, 303.2	3.19×4.75	120	S-H

1939

E "922" Senior Six (wb 122) - 800 built		Wght	Price	Prod
EQ	DeLuxe tour sdn 4d	3,400	995	—
EQD	Custom tour sdn 4d	3,440	1,095	—
H "925" Senior Eight (wb 125.0) - 200 built				
HQ	DeLuxe tour sdn 4d	4,085	1,145	—
HQD	Custom tour sdn 4d	4,215	1,245	—
Skylark (wb 115.0)				
	Custom sdn 4d	3,000	1,145	35*
	Corsair conv 2d	—	—	1

* Estimated handbuilt prototypes or pilot models

1939 Engines	bore×stroke	bhp	availability
I-6, 245.3	3.50×4.25	101	S-922, Skylark
I-8, 303.2	3.19×4.75	120	S-925 Eight

Note: 1939 production estimates are based on published serial number spans. Total calendar-year prod.: 1,400.

1940

R-015 Skylark Cust (wb 115.0)		Wght	Price	Prod*
RQK	sdn 4d	3,000	1,145	—

1940 Engine	bore×stroke	bhp	availability
I-6, 245.3	3.50×4.25	101	S-all

1941

R-115 Skylark Cust (wb 115.0)		Wght	Price	Prod*
RQK	sdn 4d	3,000	1,095	—

1941 Engine	bore×stroke	bhp	availability
I-6, 245.3	3.50×4.25	101	S-all

*Total 1940-41 Skylark production: 319. Total registrations: 211 in 1940, 103 in 1941.

Imperial

Imperial became a distinct make for 1955 and continued as such for the next 20 years. The name, of course, had been familiar since the late '20s on the most-luxurious Chryslers (*see entry*)—and that was a problem. Somehow, Imperial could never shake its image as a Chrysler, and it was this, more than any other factor, that hampered sales in the prestige-conscious luxury field.

Nevertheless, some of Imperial's best years as a separate make were its first. The beautiful 1955 models, based extensively on Virgil Exner's period Parade Phaeton show cars, are still regarded as the most-desirable Imperials of all. Elegantly trimmed inside and out, this big 130-inch-wheelbase sedan and Newport hardtop coupe wore a distinctive split grille, unique "gunsight" taillights, modestly wrapped windshield, and circular rear-wheel openings, making them among the best-looking of Chrysler Corporation's all-new '55 fleet. Chrome was abundant but tastefully applied; two-toning was limited to the roof.

Naturally, the '55s inherited the brilliant 331-cubic-inch Chrysler hemi-head V-8 used since 1951, now with 250 brake horsepower and mated to the firm's new fully automatic two-speed PowerFlite transmission. At nearly 11,500 units for the model year, volume was about double that of the 1954 Chrysler Imperial, an auspicious beginning. Still, Cadillac's '55 output was 10 times as great, Lincoln's five times as high.

Wheelbase was stretched three inches for 1956. (It would shrink back to 129 inches for '57.) The Newport was renamed Southampton and joined by a pillarless four-door. Still topped by "gunsights," rear fenders were raised into fins, but no other Chrysler product that year wore them more attractively. Frontal styling was unchanged. Following Chrysler, the Hemi was bored to 354 cid for a gain of 30 bhp (helped by higher 9:1 compression), and the PowerFlite switched from a dashboard lever to pushbutton control, which would be featured on Chrysler automatics through 1963. Though not in the same league as a Chrysler 300, the 1955-56 Imperials were lively performers yet surprisingly thrifty, winning luxury-class laurels in the Mobilgas Economy Runs. They were also impeccably built—really the last Imperials that could make that claim. The one major option in these years was air conditioning, priced at $567. List prices ranged from the mid-$4000s to just over $5000.

Also available in 1955-56 were long-wheelbase Crown Imperial sedans and limousines. Built in Detroit, these took over for the long, eight-seat Dodge, DeSoto, and Chrysler sedans offered through '54. Styling and engineering followed that of standard Imperials, but prices were much higher—$7100-$7700—and availability was limited. Just 172 were built for '55; another 226 for '56. Reflecting the industry's general decline from record-setting '55, Imperial's 1956 volume dropped to just below 11,000 units.

Imperial was all-new for 1957, bearing second-generation "Forward Look" styling from design chief Exner, marked by huge tailfins (with vestigial gunsights in the trailing edges), airier rooflines with curved side glass (an industry first), a finely checked full-width grille, and, where law allowed, quad headlamps in lieu of conventional dual units (where law didn't allow). The last was not a first, however, as that year's Chrysler, DeSoto, Nash, Lincoln, and Cadillac Eldorado Brougham also offered "quadrilights." Seeking higher sales,

1955 four-door sedan

1956 four-door sedan

1955 Newport hardtop coupe

1957 Crown convertible coupe

1967 LeBaron hardtop sedan

1958 Crown Southampton hardtop sedan

1958 LeBaron four-door sedan

1959 Crown Southampton hardtop coupe

1960 Crown convertible coupe

Imperial expanded from one series to three, adding more elaborately trimmed Crown and LeBaron versions of the standard pillared sedan and Southampton hardtops. The Crown also offered the line's only convertible—the first soft-top Imperial since 1951. Arriving in January was a pair of LeBaron models, recalling the famed prewar coachworks closely associated with Chrysler—a pillared sedan and four-door Southampton. Both new series were priced considerably higher than the standard Imperials: $5400-$5600 for Crown, and $5743 for either LeBaron.

Standard for '57 Imperials was Chrysler's superb new three-speed TorqueFlite automatic transmission, plus a Hemi enlarged to 392 cid for 325 bhp with 9.25:1 compression. Also shared with other '57 Highland Park cars was torsion-bar front suspension (called "Torsion-Aire Ride"). It made for fine roadability, the best in the luxury field. With all this, Imperial showed surprising sales strength. Volume more than tripled from '56, reaching near 35,000 units. That was still far behind Cadillac's 122,000.

Though the Crown Imperial sedan vanished for '57, the limo returned at a breathtaking $15,075—which largely stemmed from the fact that the car was now built by Ghia in Turin, Italy. With such low sales, Chrysler could no longer justify the time and space necessary to build such cars itself, especially with projected tooling costs of some $3.3 million.

Each Ghia Crown limo began as an unfinished two-door hardtop body mounted on the more-rigid convertible chassis and shipped with all body panels intact. Ghia cut the car apart, added 20.5 inches to the wheelbase, reworked the structure above the beltline, fitted and trimmed the luxurious interior, and finished off the exterior with 150 pounds of lead filler. Each car took a month to complete, and initial delays made the Crown Imperial a very late '57 introduction. Sales were not impressive: only 132 Ghia Crowns would be built by the time production was ended in 1965, but all were impeccably tailored. Exactly 36 were built to '57 specifications, followed by 31 of the '58s and only 7 for '59.

A predictably minor facelift was ordained for '58. The main differences were circular parking lights, standard quad headlamps (by now legal everywhere), and a simpler grille. Prices were marginally higher across an unchanged lineup, and the 392 was tweaked to 345 brake horsepower. Reflecting Exner's fondness for "Classic" styling themes was an optional round decklid hump suggesting a spare tire, a 1957 option that continued to find favor in '58. But this proved a poor year for the industry in general and Chrysler in particular, so only about 16,000 Imperials were built for the model year. To the frustration of dealers, people still thought of these cars as "Chrysler Imperials"—and a Chrysler, though prestigious, didn't have the charisma of a Cadillac.

In time for the 1959 model run, Imperial production left Chrysler's Jefferson Avenue plant for its own assembly plant in Dearborn. Imperial could brag that it was not only a distinct make, but had its own facilities where it could take time for handcrafting and strict quality control. The '59s received a more extensive facelift of the basic '57 styling, highlighted—for some, anyway—by a toothy grille and broad brushed-finish appliqués on the lower rear flanks. Standard models finally got a name—Custom—but the lineup was otherwise again unchanged. As at other Highland Park divisions, Imperial switched from Hemi to wedgehead V-8s: a new 350-bhp 413-cid unit shared with '59 Chrysler New Yorkers. It provided comparable performance, but was more economical to build and maintain than the fabled Hemi. Production inched up to about 17,000. Imperial would outsell Lincoln in 1959 and '60, but would never do so again.

1960 LeBaron Southampton hardtop sedan

1961 LeBaron Southampton hardtop sedan

1962 LeBaron Southampton hardtop sedan

After 1960, Imperial was strictly an also-ran among the Big Three luxury makes. As ever, Cadillac was the overwhelming sales leader, Lincoln a distant second, Imperial an even more distant third.

Though other Highland Park cars adopted "unibody" construction for 1960, Imperial retained a separate body and frame, mainly because it was more amenable to isolation from noise and road shock, necessary for the level of smoothness and silence luxury buyers demanded. Returning unchanged was a lone 413 wedgehead V-8, whose 10:1 compression required premium fuel.

Imperial model choices were also unchanged, but styling became cartoonish for 1960, with swollen fins, a florid grille, and an even larger windshield. Interiors were ornate, dominated by an impressively bright, complicated dash with a plethora of pushbuttons; a squarish steering wheel was merely odd. Emphasizing comfort was a new high-back driver's seat padded in thick foam rubber. Options by now had grown to include adjustable "spot" air conditioning, six-way power seat with single rotary control, "Auto-Pilot" cruise control, and automatic headlamp dimmer. Customs were upholstered in pretty crown-pattern nylon. Upholstery for Crown was wool, leather, or nylon and vinyl. Wool broadcloth lined LeBarons. Model-year production held at the '59 level.

The new 1960 bodyshell was considerably changed for 1961—and not for the better. Fins were the most blatant ever

1962 Custom hardtop coupe

1963 Crown Imperial limousine by Ghia

1963 Crown hardtop sedan

1964 Crown convertible coupe

1965 Crown Imperial limousine by Ghia

1965 Crown convertible coupe

to appear on an Imperial—high and gull-like, with the trademark gunsight taillamps suspended from them. And there was a new gimmick: freestanding headlamps, individual chrome bullets on tiny pedestals pocketed in severely concave front fenders—another of Exner's "classic" throwbacks. This strange idea would persist through 1963, but rear styling became much more tasteful. Four-door pillared sedans were eliminated for '61, but other offerings returned along with an unchanged powerteam. Sci-fi styling; Chrysler's now-widespread reputation for indifferent workmanship; and a handsome, more-compact new Lincoln Continental conspired to dampen demand, and model-year production dropped to around 12,250—less than half of Lincoln's total. Unfortunately that wasn't enough to justify a separate factory, and '62 Imperial assembly rejoined Chrysler at Jefferson Avenue.

Exner left Chrysler during 1961, but not before fashioning a completely new, truncated "S-Series" Imperial as part of an entirely downsized corporate line for 1962. It didn't reach production, which was fortunate because his downsized Dodges and Plymouths did—and met a poor reception. Instead, the '61 Imperial was reissued but with the ugly fins planed off, leaving straight-top rear fenders capped by cigar-like gunsights. The 413 was detuned by 10 bhp, and would continue in this form through 1965. Production rose to a bit over 14,250, but was still only about 50 percent of Lincoln's. Cadillac remained far ahead of both.

Another facelift gave the '63s a new grille insert composed of elongated rectangles, plus a crisper rear roofline and restyled rear deck. The stylist responsible for much of this revision was Elwood Engel, who'd come over from Ford—where he designed the aforementioned Continental—to replace Exner in mid-1961. The lineup was again unchanged, and model-year production was about the same as for '62.

Clean, all-new Engel styling completely banished the old Exner silhouette for 1964 as Imperial became very much like his square-lined Continental. The beltline was edged with full-length bright moldings, a divided grille appeared (recalling 1955-56), and the freestanding headlamps gave way to integral units within the grille. One Exner touch remained, however: the simulated trunklid spare, though it was also squarish now, carried down into the bumper as on the 1956-57 Continental Mark II. A less-contrived dash with strong horizontal format was featured inside. Modelwise, the slow-sell-

1966 Crown convertible coupe

1967 convertible coupe

1968 Crown hardtop sedan

1969 LeBaron hardtop sedan

1970 LeBaron hardtop coupe

1971 LeBaron hardtop sedan

1972 LeBaron hardtop coupe

1973 LeBaron hardtop sedan

ing Custom was eliminated along with the Southampton name for pillarless styles, leaving Crown convertible and hardtops, LeBaron hardtop sedan, and the Ghia Crown limo. Model-year sales were exceedingly good at over 23,000, a level that wouldn't be approached again until 1969.

Good sales and the big '64 redesign dictated a stand-pat 1965. The only significant changes were prominent crossed grille bars on a mesh background, glass-covered headlights, and prices bumped up \$100-\$200. Displayed at that year's New York Auto Show was the exotic LeBaron D'Or, a customized hardtop coupe. The "D'Or" part referred to gold-tint exterior striping and interior embellishments, as well as special "Royal Essence Laurel Gold" paint.

Ghia stopped building Crown limousines in 1965, but 10 more were constructed in Spain using '66 grilles and rear decks. When Imperial finally went to unit construction for '67, Chrysler worked out a limousine program with Stageway Coaches of Fort Smith, Arkansas. Built through 1971 at the rate of about six per year, these cars, simply called LeBaron, were much larger, riding an unbelievable 163-inch wheelbase, by far the longest in the American industry. Prices ranged from \$12,000 to \$15,000, depending on equipment.

Regular Imperials again saw mostly detail changes for 1966. The grille now carried an eggcrate motif, each "crate" containing tiny elongated rectangles, and the decklid was cleaned up by deleting the fake spare tire. A literal big change involved boring the wedge V-8 to 440 cid, which returned horsepower to 350. Model-year production went the other way, though, dropping from 1965's 18,500—itself a considerable decline from '64—to fewer than 13,750.

The '67 Imperials were all-new. Chrysler engineers were by now sufficiently experienced with unit construction to use it for their most-expensive product, and newer technology allowed computerized stress testing of a given shape before it was ever built. Unibody construction also promised weight savings. And indeed, the '67s were about 100 pounds lighter than comparable '66s.

But the real reason for this switch was lackluster sales that had made a completely separate Imperial platform just too costly to sustain. Thus, as it had been before 1960, Imperial again shared basic architecture with Chrysler in the interest of reduced production costs.

Still, this was not readily apparent from 1967 styling. Up front was a high grille with a prominent nameplate, flanked by squarish Lincolnesque fenders containing the parking lights. The rear bumper was a broad U below a full-width taillamp panel with a large Imperial eagle medallion in a central circle. Sides were still flat, but relieved a little by full-length moldings above the rocker panels. Wheelbase contracted to 127 inches, though that was still three inches longer than Chrysler's. A four-door pillared sedan returned without a series name at \$5374, the most-affordable '67 Imperial. Other models soldiered on. Sales moved up to near 18,000, but Imperial was still far adrift of Lincoln, let alone Cadillac.

Volume dropped below 15,400 the following year and prompted a far-reaching decision: From 1969, Imperial would share most Chrysler sheetmetal as well as structure. One casualty of this move was the Crown convertible, which made its last appearance as a '68. Style changes from '67 were slight: A new grille wrapped around the fenders to enclose parking and cornering lights; side marker lights front and rear, newly required by Washington; narrow paint stripes along the beltline; dual lower-bodyside moldings. Newly optional dual exhausts and twin-snorkel air cleaner coaxed 360 bhp from the 440 V-8, but only for this one year.

The Chrysler-like 1969-70 models were among the tidiest

1973 LeBaron hardtop sedan

1974 LeBaron hardtop sedan

1975 LeBaron hardtop coupe

1975 LeBaron hardtop sedan

1981 coupe

Imperials ever, with rounded, low-roof "fuselage styling" announced by a full-width eggcrate face with newly concealed headlamps (behind flip-up doors matched to grille texture). Ventless side glass was featured on air-conditioned coupes. Overall length stretched by five inches with no change in wheelbase, yet curb weights ran about 100 pounds less. Model choices were pared to a hardtop coupe and sedan in Crown and LeBaron trim, plus a pillared Crown sedan priced identically to the Crown hardtop. LeBaron was no longer the $7000 semicustom it had once been, its list price being slashed by about $800 to the $5900-$6100 level. Despite fewer models, LeBaron bested the Crown in sales for the first time. The overall '69 total exceeded 22,000 units, the third-best showing in Imperial history.

However, the return to a close resemblance with Chrysler and increasing buyer preference for more-manageable cars contributed to a sales decline that would end Imperial's life as a separate make. As if to forecast the bitter days ahead, 1970-model production dropped by almost half from '69, to about 11,800 units.

Imperial retained its basic '69 design through 1973. Styling modifications were confined to easy-change items like grilles, taillamps, and minor trim, plus modest sheetmetal alterations at each end and year-to-year price/equipment shuffles. Offerings slimmed to just the pair of LeBarons after 1971. Emissions tuning dropped the big 440 V-8 to 335 bhp for '71, then to 225 bhp—in newly adopted SAE *net* measure—and ultimately to 215 bhp. Horsepower recovered to 230 for 1974 with the adoption of catalytic converters. A laudable new '71 exclusive was a Bendix antiskid brake system, priced at $250; it was extended to the entire Chrysler line for 1972.

Not surprisingly, Imperial suffered more than its rivals from the effects of the first energy crisis. The brand-new 1974 models had crisper lines and bold upright grillework, plus a three-inch shorter wheelbase and about 100 pounds less weight. But these modest reductions had less to do with the fuel shortage—which Chrysler hadn't dreamed of—than the need to realize further economies of scale through even closer sharing with that year's redesigned New Yorker.

Still, these Imperials were good-looking in their way, and distinctly different from the Chryslers. But with prices rapidly moving upward—now $7700-$7800—they were none too successful. At just over 14,000, model-year volume for '74 was the lowest since '71; the following year it sank to fewer than 10,000 cars. Seeking to cut losses, Chrysler decided it was time to forget Imperial, and the last '75 Imperial left the Jefferson Avenue plant in Detroit on June 12, 1975: a LeBaron hardtop sedan bearing serial number YM43-T5C-182947. But only the nameplate vanished immediately; the basic '75 package continued through model-year 1978 as the Chrysler New Yorker Brougham.

By 1980, however, Chrysler thought it was time for another stab at a separate luxury line. Though facing imminent bankruptcy, and having staked their future on the sensible front-drive K-car compacts and planned derivatives, Chrysler executives led by president (and soon-to-be-chairman) Lee Iacocca felt a new flagship would assure the public that Chrysler had a future.

The result appeared for 1981 in a revived Imperial that amounted to little more than the world's most-expensive Dodge Aspen/Plymouth Volare. Actually, it was a reskinned version of Chrysler's second-generation 1980 Cordoba coupe, built on the same 112.7-inch-wheelbase "M-body" platform, complete with odd transverse-torsion-bar front suspension and an ordinary live rear axle on longitudinal leaf springs. The company's veteran 318 V-8 was inevitable, but Imperial

1981 coupe

1982 Frank Sinatra Edition coupe

1983 coupe

received a newly developed fuel-injected version as an exclusive, with mild 8.5:1 compression and a modest 140 bhp. It naturally teamed with the TorqueFlite automatic.

Styling was handsome. Up front was a square, Lincolnlike vertical-bar grille flanked by concealed headlamps inboard of knife-edge fenders. A distinctive "bustleback" rear end evoked razor-edge British custom coachwork from the early '50s—and Cadillac's second-generation Seville, which had arrived the previous year with something very similar. Of course, there was no way Chrysler could have "stolen" the Cadillac's treatment, and the Imperial's bustle was arguably more attractive, but the sameness was still embarrassing.

Chrysler marketed the reborn Imperial as what it called a "one-price" car. Standard equipment was predictably lavish—but then the base price was a steep $18,311. Still, you got clearcoat paint, choice of Mark Cross leather or rich velour upholstery, electronic digital instruments (a dubious feature), full power equipment, and various choices of tires and factory sound systems. The sole option was an electric sliding sunroof priced at a hefty $1044. Production was assigned to Chrysler's Windsor, Ontario, plant, which took pains to ensure that quality would rank with the world's best. Among special measures taken were several post-assembly checks, plus a 5.5-mile road test and a final polish before shipment. Chrysler announced first-year production would be limited to "just" 25,000 units, also in the interest of high quality—not to mention snob appeal.

Unfortunately, the new Imperial got lost in Highland Park's much-publicized financial crisis and an equal amount of ballyhoo surrounding the make-or-break K-cars. Promotional funds were limited. Frank Sinatra helped his friend Iacocca by singing "It's time for Imperial" in television commercials, but even Ol' Blue Eyes couldn't persuade buyers, and model-year production ended up at just 7225 cars.

The following year brought no changes save an "FS" package option—special emblems outside, a set of tapes with Frankie's greatest hits inside—and a base price hiked to nearly $21,000. Though the Imperial still cost thousands less than the rival Cadillac Eldorado and Lincoln Mark VI, sales remained tough, so despite heavy dealer discounts, production sank to just 2329. The '83s were also little changed—the Sinatra option was dropped, price lowered to $18,688—and fared even worse: just 1427. Having now turned the financial corner, but in no need of money-losers, Chrysler put Imperial out to pasture a second time.

Imperial came back, in a way, as the 1990-93 Chrysler Imperial (*see* Chrysler). This was a luxury version of the Chrysler New Yorker sedan. The name died a third time when the LH platform sedans of '93 didn't include an Imperial.

At the 2006 Detroit Auto Show, Chrysler displayed an Imperial concept car. The Imperial was 17 inches longer and six inches taller than the Chrysler 300 on which it was based. The four-place interior featured leather, suede, and wood veneers, while freestanding headlamps recalled Imperials of the early '60s. Despite its roller coaster career, the Imperial name still has meaning to both Chrysler and the public. With luck, Imperial will once again be Chrysler's flagship.

Specifications

1955

C69 (wb 130.0)	Wght	Price	Prod
sdn 4d	4,565	4,483	7,840
Newport htp cpe	4,490	4,720	3,418
conv cpe (proto)	4,600	—	1
chassis	—	—	1
C70 Crown Imperial (wb 149.5)			
sdn 4d, 8P	5,180	6,973	45
limo 4d	5,230	7,095	127

1955 Engine	bore×stroke	bhp	availability
V-8, 331.0	3.81×3.63	250	S-all

1956

C73 (wb 133.0)	Wght	Price	Prod
sdn 4d	4,575	4,832	6,821
Southampton htp sdn	4,680	5,225	1,543
Southampton htp cpe	4,555	5,094	2,094

C70 Crown Imp (wb 149.5)	Wght	Price	Prod
sdn 4d, 8P	5,145	7,603	51
limo 4d	5,205	7,737	175

1956 Engine	bore×stroke	bhp	availability
V-8, 354.0	3.94×3.63	280	S-all

1957

IM1-1 (wb 129.0)	Wght	Price	Prod
sdn 4d	4,640	4,838	5,569
Southampton htp sdn	4,780	4,838	7,157
Southampton htp cpe	4,640	4,736	4,595
IM1-2 Crown (wb 129.0)			
sdn 4d	4,740	5,406	3,472
Southampton htp sdn	4,920	5,406	7,429
Southampton htp cpe	4,755	5,269	3,888
conv cpe	4,830	5,598	1,167
IM1-4 LeBaron (wb 129.0)			
sdn 4d	4,765	5,743	1,659
Southampton htp sdn	4,900	5,743	821

Crown Imperial (wb 149.5)	Wght	Price	Prod
limo 4d	5,960	15,075	36

1957 Engine	bore×stroke	bhp	availability
V-8, 392.0	4.00×3.90	325	S-all

1958

LY1-L (wb 129.0)		Wght	Price	Prod
23	Southampton htp cpe	4,640	4,839	1,801
41	sdn 4d	4,590	4,945	1,926
43	Southampton htp sdn	4,795	4,945	3,336
LY1-M Crown (wb 129.0)				
23	Southampton htp cpe	4,730	5,388	1,939
27	conv cpe	4,820	5,729	675
41	sdn 4d	4,755	5,632	1,240
43	Southampton htp sdn	4,915	5,632	4,146
LY1-H LeBaron (wb 129.0)				
41	sdn 4d	4,780	5,969	501
43	Southampton htp sdn	4,940	5,969	538

Crown Imperial (wb 149.5)		Wght	Price	Prod
	limo 4d	5,960	15,075	31

1958 Engines	bore×stroke	bhp	availability
V-8, 392.0	4.00×3.90	345	S-all exc Crown Imperial
V-8, 392.0	4.00×3.90	325	S-Crown Imp

1959

MY1-L Custom (wb 129.0)		Wght	Price	Prod
612	Southampton htp cpe	4,675	4,910	1,743
613	sdn 4d	4,735	5,016	2,071
614	Southampton htp sdn	4,745	5,016	3,984
MY1-M Crown (wb 129.0)				
632	Southampton htp cpe	4,810	5,403	1,728
633	sdn 4d	4,830	5,647	1,335
634	Southampton htp sdn	4,840	5,647	4,714
635	conv cpe	4,850	5,774	555
MY1-H LeBaron (wb 129.0)				
653	sdn 4d	4,865	6,103	510
654	Southampton htp sdn	4,875	6,103	622
Crown Imperial (wb 149.5)				
	limo 4d	5,960	15,075	7

1959 Engines	bore×stroke	bhp	availability
V-8, 413.0	4.18×3.75	350	S-all exc Crown Imperial
V-8, 392.0	4.00×3.90	325	S-Crown Imp

1960

PY1-L Custom (wb 129.0)		Wght	Price	Prod
912	Southampton htp cpe	4,655	4,923	1,498
913	sdn 4d	4,700	5,029	2,335
914	Southampton htp sdn	4,760	5,029	3,953
PY1-M Crown (wb 129.0)				
922	Southampton htp cpe	4,720	5,403	1,504
923	sdn 4d	4,770	5,647	1,594
924	Southampton htp sdn	4,765	5,647	4,510
925	conv cpe	4,820	5,774	618
PY1-H LeBaron (wb 129.0)				
933	sdn 4d	4,860	6,318	692
934	Southampton htp sdn	4,835	6,318	999
Crown Imperial (wb 149.5)				
	limo 4d	5,960	16,500	16

1960 Engine	bore×stroke	bhp	availability
V-8, 413.0	4.18×3.75	350	S-all

1961

RY1-L Custom (wb 129.0)		Wght	Price	Prod
912	Southampton htp cpe	4,715	4,923	889
914	Southampton htp sdn	4,740	5,109	4,129
RY1-M Crown (wb 129.0)				
922	Southampton htp cpe	4,790	5,403	1,007
924	Southampton htp sdn	4,855	5,647	4,769
925	conv cpe	4,865	5,774	429
RY1-H LeBaron (wb 129.0)				
934	Southampton htp sdn	4,875	6,426	1,026
Crown Imperial (wb 149.5)				
	limo 4d	5,960	16,500	9

1961 Engine	bore×stroke	bhp	availability
V-8, 413.0	4.18×3.75	350	S-all

1962

SY1-L Custom (wb 129.0)		Wght	Price	Prod
912	Southampton htp cpe	4,540	4,920	826
914	Southampton htp sdn	4,620	5,106	3,587
SY1-M Crown (wb 129.0)				
922	Southampton htp cpe	4,650	5,400	1,010
924	Southampton htp sdn	4,680	5,644	6,911
925	conv cpe	4,765	5,770	554
SY1-H LeBaron (wb 129.0)				
934	Southampton htp sdn	4,725	6,422	1,449

1962 Engine	bore×stroke	bhp	availability
V-8, 413.0	4.18×3.75	340	S-all

1963

TY1-L Custom (wb 129.0)		Wght	Price	Prod
912	Southampton htp cpe	4,640	5,058	749
914	Southampton htp sdn	4,690	5,243	3,264
TY1-M Crown (wb 129.0)				
922	Southampton htp cpe	4,720	5,412	1,067

TY1-M Crown		Wght	Price	Prod
924	Southampton htp sdn	4,740	5,656	6,960
925	conv cpe	4,795	5,782	531
TY1-H LeBaron (wb 129.0)				
934	Southampton htp sdn	4,830	6,434	1,537
Crown Imperial (wb 149.5)				
	limo 4d	6,100	18,500	13

1963 Engine	bore×stroke	bhp	availability
V-8, 413.0	4.18×3.75	340	S-all

1964

VY1-M Crown (wb 129.0)		Wght	Price	Prod
922	htp cpe	4,950	5,739	5,233
924	htp sdn	4,970	5,581	14,181
925	conv cpe	5,185	6,003	922
VY1-H LeBaron (wb 129.0)				
934	htp sdn	5,005	6,455	2,949
Crown Imperial (wb 149.5)				
	limo 4d	6,100	18,500	10

1964 Engine	bore×stroke	bhp	availability
V-8, 413.0	4.18×3.75	340	S-all

1965

AY1-M Crown (wb 129.0)		Wght	Price	Prod
922	htp cpe	5,075	5,930	3,974
924	htp sdn	5,015	5,772	11,628
925	conv cpe	5,345	6,194	633
AY1-H LeBaron (wb 129.0)				
934	htp sdn	5,080	6,596	2,164
Crown Imperial (wb 149.5)				
	limo 4d	6,100	18,500	10

1965 Engine	bore×stroke	bhp	availability
V-8, 413.0	4.18×3.75	340	S-all

1966

BY3-M Crown (wb 129.0)		Wght	Price	Prod
23	htp cpe	5,000	5,887	2,373
27	conv cpe	5,315	6,164	514
43	htp sdn	4,990	5,733	8,977
BY3-H LeBaron (wb 129.0)				
43	htp sdn	5,090	6,540	1,878

1966 Engine	bore×stroke	bhp	availability
V-8, 440.0	4.32×3.75	350	S-all

1967

CY1-M (wb 127.0)		Wght	Price	Prod
23	Crown htp cpe	4,780	6,011	3,235
27	conv cpe	4,815	6,244	577
41	sdn 4d	4,830	5,374	2,193
43	Crown htp sdn	4,860	5,836	9,415
CY1-H LeBaron (wb 127.0)				
43	htp sdn	4,970	6,661	2,194
LeBaron, Stageway body (wb 163.0)				
	limo 4d	6,300	15,000	6

1967 Engine	bore×stroke	bhp	availability
V-8, 440.0	4.32×3.75	350	S-all

1968

YM Crown (wb 127.0)		Wght	Price	Prod
23	htp cpe	4,660	5,722	2,656
27	conv cpe	4,795	6,497	474
41	sdn 4d	4,685	5,654	1,887
43	htp sdn	4,715	6,115	8,492
YH LeBaron (wb 127.0)				
43	htp sdn	4,815	6,940	1,852
LeBaron, Stageway body (wb 163.0)				
	limo 4d	6,300	15,000	6

1968 Engines	bore×stroke	bhp	availability
V-8, 440.0	4.32×3.75	350	S-all
V-8, 440.0	4.32×3.75	360	O-all (dual exh)

1969

Crown (wb 127.0)		Wght	Price	Prod
YL23	htp cpe	4,555	5,592	244
YL43	htp sdn	4,690	5,770	823
YM41	sdn 4d	4,620	5,770	1,617
LeBaron (wb 127.0)				
YM23	htp cpe	4,610	5,898	4,572
YM43	htp sdn	4,710	6,131	14,821

LeBrn, Stgwy body (wb 163.0)		Wght	Price	Prod
	limo 4d	6,300	16,000	6 est

1969 Engine	bore×stroke	bhp	availability
V-8, 440.0	4.32×3.75	350	S-all

1970

YL Crown (wb 127.0)		Wght	Price	Prod
23	htp cpe	4,610	5,779	254
43	htp sdn	4,735	5,956	1,333
YM LeBaron (wb 127.0)				
23	htp cpe	4,660	6,095	1,803
43	htp sdn	4,805	6,328	8,426
LeBaron, Stageway body (wb 163.0)				
	limo 4d	6,500	16,500	6 est

1970 Engine	bore×stroke	bhp	availability
V-8, 440.0	4.32×3.75	350	S-all

1971

YM LeBaron (wb 127.0)		Wght	Price	Prod
23	htp cpe	4,800	6,632	1,442
43	htp sdn	4,950	6,864	10,116

1971 Engine	bore×stroke	bhp	availability
V-8, 440.0	4.32×3.75	335	S-all

1972

YM LeBaron (wb 127.0)		Wght	Price	Prod
23	htp cpe	4,790	6,550	2,322
43	htp sdn	4,955	6,778	13,472

1972 Engine	bore×stroke	bhp	availability
V-8, 440.0	4.32×3.75	225	S-all

1973

YM LeBaron (wb 127.0)		Wght	Price	Prod
23	htp cpe	4,905	6,829	2,563
43	htp sdn	5,035	7,057	14,166

1973 Engine	bore×stroke	bhp	availability
V-8, 440.0	4.32×3.75	215	S-all

1974

YM LeBaron (wb 124.0)		Wght	Price	Prod
23	htp cpe	4,825	7,673	3,850
43	htp sdn	4,965	7,804	10,576

1974 Engine	bore×stroke	bhp	availability
V-8, 440.0	4.32×3.75	230	S-all

1975

YM LeBaron (wb 124.0)		Wght	Price	Prod
23	htp cpe	4,965	8,698	2,728
43	htp sdn	5,065	8,844	6,102

1975 Engine	bore×stroke	bhp	availability
V-8, 440.0	4.32×3.75	215	S-all

Note: Chrysler built no cars under the Imperial name from 1975 to 1980.

1981 - 7,225 built

(wb 112.7)		Wght	Price	Prod
YS22	cpe	3,968	18,311	—

1981 Engine	bore×stroke	bhp	availability
V-8, 318.0	3.91×3.31	140	S-all

1982 - 2,329 built

(wb 112.7)		Wght	Price	Prod
YS22	cpe	3,945	20,988	—

1982 Engine	bore×stroke	bhp	availability
V-8, 318.0	3.91×3.31	140	S-all

1983 - 1,427 built

(wb 112.7)		Wght	Price	Prod
YS22	cpe	4,019	18,688	—

1983 Engine	bore×stroke	bhp	availability
V-8, 318.0	3.91×3.31	140	S-all

Kaiser

Henry J. Kaiser and Joseph W. Frazer literally parted company in 1949, but they'd been at loggerheads once before. In 1942, Kaiser was experimenting with plastic-bodied cars, hinting that he just might sell them for $400-$600 once World War II was over. He also suggested that auto companies announce their postwar plans immediately. Industry-veteran Frazer was incensed: "I resent a West Coast shipbuilder asking us if we have the courage to plan postwar automobiles when the President has asked us to forego all work which would take away from the war effort. Kaiser has done a great job as a shipbuilder... but I think his challenge to automobile men is as half-baked as some of his other statements... I think the public is being misled by all these pictures of plastic models with glass tops, done by artists who probably wouldn't want to sit under those tops in the summer and sweat."

This public brouhaha was long forgotten by July 1945, when Henry and Joe joined forces to form Kaiser-Frazer. Both men compromised, and their relationship was amicable, at least for a time. Though Henry discovered that his plastic car for the common man was just wishful thinking, he had high hopes for a more-radical Kaiser than what ultimately emerged.

It would have stemmed from the 1946 K-85 prototype, which looked like the conventional Frazer then already locked up, but employed unit construction on a shorter 117-inch wheelbase. Suspension and the "Packaged Power" drivetrain, worked out by engineer Henry C. McCaslin, were very different. For one thing, an 85-horsepower Continental six drove the front wheels, not the rears. A conventional three-speed transmission sent power via a helical-gear transfer case to a front differential, then to the wheels by U-jointed halfshafts. Equally novel was four-wheel independent "Torsionetic" suspension: a pair of longitudinal torsion bars, each 1.3 inches thick by 44.5 inches long. The steel bars twisted to provide spring action like conventional coils or semi-elliptics. McCaslin wanted unit construction because "we needed to use more of the operation in the plant. We had the welding equipment but lacked large dies and cranes. It was a compromise to get the car into production."

But the front-drive K-85 didn't have a chance. Aside from exorbitant tooling expense, technical problems such as heavy steering, gear whine, and wheel shimmy proved insurmountable. With so much weight over the front wheels, the K-85 would have needed power steering and that would have added $900 to the retail price. So in May 1946, K-F decided to abandon this idea for a conventional rear-drive Kaiser priced below the Frazer.

Production for both new makes began that June at Ford's huge wartime bomber plant in Willow Run, Michigan, near Detroit, that K-F had leased from the federal government's Reconstruction Finance Corporation. Like the Frazer, the new Kaiser Special was a 1947 model. Initial price was $1868, though postwar inflation quickly boosted it above $2000.

It was very much like the Frazer, of course: a roomy flush-fender four-door sedan with 123.5-inch wheelbase, styling by the eminent Howard A. "Dutch" Darrin, and a "stroker" six making 100 bhp from 226 cubic inches. The Kaiser wore a multipiece grille that was cheaper to make than the Frazer's because the pieces were smaller. Furnishings were naturally more-basic, in line with the lower price. Perhaps inevitably, a fancier Kaiser Custom was added late in the model year at about $350 above the Special and $150 more than the standard Frazer, but some $250 less than the top-line Frazer Manhattan. A bit later, Customs were offered with optional dual intake and exhaust manifolds that boosted bhp to 112. But Kaiser would have no automatic transmission through 1950 (after which proprietary GM Hydra-Matic was offered); only a standard three-speed manual available with overdrive as an $80 option.

1947½-48 Special four-door sedan

1949 DeLuxe "Glass Green" four-door sedan

1949 DeLuxe Vagabond utility sedan

1949-50 Special Traveler utility sedan

1949-50 DeLuxe Virginian hardtop sedan

1949 DeLuxe four-door sedan prototype

1951 DeLuxe two-door sedan

Though plans called for building two Kaisers to every Frazer, the 1947 ratio was 1:1 so as to fill initial orders. Both lines were basically unchanged for 1948, when very few Customs were built, though Kaiser volume far outpaced Frazer's. These were outstanding years for what came to called the "postwar wonder company." Kaiser production totaled more than 70,000 for '47 and nearly 92,000 for '48. All told, K-F made a healthy $30 million profit on 1947-48 volume that put it ninth in production—the highest independent.

A scheduled facelift gave the 1949 Kaisers a broader, shinier grille and larger taillights. Custom was retitled DeLuxe, and gained the 112-bhp engine as standard. Four new models arrived. Two were utility sedans, an idea from Henry Kaiser himself. They were much like the standard article save a double-door rear hatch and fold-down back seat. The economical Special Traveler arrived at $2088, the leather-upholstered Custom Vagabond at $200 more. In effect, these were a cost-saving substitute for a true station wagon, one of many things K-F never would get around to building.

Kaiser's other two '49 newcomers were a four-door convertible and the Virginian four-door hardtop, the first postwar use of those body types. Both were richly appointed DeLuxe offerings with excellent visibility thanks to the lack of steel B-posts, though both retained vestigial pillars with glass panes. The convertible also carried fixed side-window frames and a heavily braced X-member frame for added structural strength. Unfortunately, the Kaisers cost as much as some Cadillacs—$3000-$3200—so only a handful were produced: an estimated 946 Virginians and just 54 convertible sedans. Those that didn't sell as '49s were given new serial numbers for 1950.

From the first, K-F offered an unusually wide range of paint, trim, and upholstery variations. This was the work of Carleton Spencer, who took some initial cues from research on home interiors done by *House & Garden* magazine. The results were hues like Indian Ceramic (a vivid pink), Crystal Green, Caribbean Coral, and Arena Yellow. These and other color names were actually written in chrome script on the front fenders of '49 Kaiser Customs. Detroit, as a whole, listed 218 exterior colors for '49; 37 were K-F's. Of the industry's 150 different 1949 interior fabrics, K-F owned 62.

The original Kaiser dashboard was an inexpensive design with horizontal gauges. For 1949, this gave way to a more-ornate panel with a giant speedometer ahead of the driver and a matching clock on the passenger's side. DeLuxe dashboards sparkled with chrome, stainless steel, and a massive ivory steering wheel with a big semicircular chrome horn ring. Such flash combined with colorful paint and fashion upholstery did much to doll up what was otherwise an unchanged and surprisingly fast-aging design.

And therein lay the seeds of disaster. Chairman Henry Kaiser boldly tooled up for 1949 volume of 200,000 cars—against the advice of his marketwise partner. Joe Frazer realized the company couldn't sell nearly that many against all-new 1949 Big Three competition, and had urged a holding action until K-F released its own new models, then scheduled for 1950. But Henry wouldn't have it. "The Kaisers never retrench," he stormed. By now, Kaiser's people had far more influence in company affairs than Frazer's, so Joe yielded the presidency to Kaiser's son Edgar, remaining on the board only for appearance sake. By year's end, he was gone.

Henry should have listened. Instead, K-F's 1949 calendar-year sales were a fraction of the number planned: only some 58,000. About 20 percent couldn't be sold, and were thus recycled with new serial numbers as 1950 models. Though it's impossible to separate model-year "production," 1949 units account for about 84 percent of the total, according to experts.

Meantime, Dutch Darrin and K-F Styling had prepared a real blockbuster: a slender, beautiful new Kaiser with "Anatomic Design." Though scheduled for 1950, it didn't arrive until March of that year as a 1951 offering (delayed until those '49 leftovers were cleared). But it sold like no Kaiser before: close to 140,000 for the model year. From 17th in Detroit for '49, Kaiser promptly shot up to 12th.

Looking unlike any other car of its day, the 1951 Kaiser boasted 700 square inches more glass area than its nearest competitor and a lower beltline than any Detroit car offered through 1956. Though wheelbase slimmed to 118.5 inches, the '51 looked miles sleeker than first-generation Kaisers. Complementing its artful styling was another bewildering array of bright exterior colors and high-fashion interiors by "color engineer" Spencer.

The '51 Kaiser was also the first car that actually sold at least partly on safety features: offering a padded dash, recessed gauges and controls, slim roof pillars for good visibility, and a windshield that popped out if struck with a force of more than 35 pounds per square inch. Though chief engineers John Widman and Ralph Isbrandt shunned unit construction, they designed a rigid separate body for a strong frame weighing but 200 pounds. They also provided a low center of gravity that ensured fine handling, and a suspension that delivered a terrific ride despite curb weights averaging

1952 Manhattan four-door sedan

1953 "Hardtop" Dragon four-door sedan

1953 Carolina two-door sedan

1954 Kaiser-Darrin roadster

only 3100 pounds. Said one Chrysler engineer who later sampled a '51 Kaiser: "It rides like one of our 4500-pound cars."

Still in the lower medium-price field, Kaiser's '51 prices ranged from just under $2000 to a bit over $2400. Special and DeLuxe series returned, each offering regular and utility Traveler sedans with two or four doors, plus the long-deck club coupe; there was also a stripped Special business coupe. But hardtops, convertibles, and station wagons were conspicuously absent, as was a V-8. Though K-F had plans for all of these, it would never have the money to market them. The old six was lifted to 115 bhp via two-barrel carburetor and dual exhausts, but the missing V-8 would prove an increasing sales liability.

1954 Special four-door sedan

1955 Manhattan four-door sedan

A scheduled 1952 facelift wasn't ready on time, so Virginian models, basically leftover '51s with "Continental kits," were sold in the interim—about 5500 in all. The "real" '52s arrived with bulbous taillights and a more prominent, heavier-looking grille. Two-door Travelers and the business coupe departed, Specials became DeLuxes, and previous DeLuxes—a coupe and two sedans—were now retitled Manhattan (borrowing the old Frazer name). The "second-series" '52s are fairly rare: only 7500 DeLuxes and 19,000 Manhattans.

Kaiser had pitched the "fashion market" in 1951 with its $125 Dragon trim options: limited-edition four-door sedans available in Golden, Silver, Emerald, and Jade editions. All sported alligator-look "Dragon" vinyl inside and color-keyed exteriors with padded vinyl tops.

This idea was tried again with 1953's "Hardtop" Dragon sedan, the most-luxurious Kaiser of all. It was easily spotted by a gold-plated hood ornament, badges, and even keyhole covers, plus a padded roof usually covered in "bambu" vinyl—a tough, oriental-style material that also adorned the dash and parts of seats and door panels. Seat inserts were done in "Laguna" cloth, a fabric with an oblong pattern created by fashion consultant Marie Nichols. Standard amenities were plentiful: tinted glass, Hydra-Matic Drive, whitewalls, twin-speaker radio, and Calpoint custom carpet. The finishing touch was a gold-plated dash plaque engraved with the owner's name. The Dragon was spectacular, but a high $3924 price—nearly as much as a Cadillac Coupe de Ville—limited sales to just 1277, a few of which almost had to be given away.

Otherwise, the '53 Kaisers were little changed. A pair of stripped Carolina sedans was fielded in the $2300 range, an effort to build showroom traffic, but only 1800 were sold. Club coupes were cut, the six was persuaded up to 118 bhp, and power steering bowed late in the season as a $122 option.

But Kaiser sales were falling fast: only 32,000 for '52 and just 28,000 for '53. The compact Henry J (*see entry*) had squandered development funds that would have been better spent on new styling, new body types, or a V-8. Cash reserves were further depleted in 1954 when Henry Kaiser decided to buy Willys-Overland, which was no better off.

Seeking to slash overhead, Kaiser transferred production

from Willow Run to W-O's Toledo, Ohio, facilities, and hoped for a sales miracle with a clever facelift by stylist Arnott "Buzz" Grisinger. From the front, the '54 Kaisers looked much like the Buick XP-300 show car (a favorite of company president Edgar Kaiser), with a wide concave grille, dummy hood scoop, and headlights "floating" within oval housings. Out back were "Safety-Glo" taillights: the existing units given finned housings and a lighted strip atop the fenders.

Remaining Travelers were canceled for '54, but Manhattans were boosted to a maximum 140 horsepower by bolting on a McCulloch centrifugal supercharger that cut in at full throttle. Also offered that year were unsupercharged Specials in two "series." The first involved '53 Manhattans warmed over with '54 front ends—yet another effort to use up leftovers. Second-series Specials were genuine '54s with wrapped rear windows, as on all of that year's Manhattans.

But sales didn't improve, and 1954 Kaiser production was a dismal 8539, including 4110 Manhattans, 3500 "early" Specials, and a paltry 929 "late" Specials. With that, only Manhattans returned for '55, distinguished by a higher fin on the hood scoop and little else. Just 270 were sold. Another 1021 were exported, most to Argentina, where Kaiser Motors hoped to continue production for South America at a subsidiary plant. It's a tribute to the design's durability that the '55 was built there through 1962 as the little-altered Kaiser Carabella.

A memorable last-gasp U.S. effort was the 1954 Kaiser-Darrin sliding-door sports car. Dutch had designed it in late 1952 for the 100-inch-wheelbase Henry J chassis, and talked Henry Kaiser into selling it for $3668. Only 435 were built before Kaiser ceased U.S. production.

The Darrin was beautifully styled, and still looks good today. Besides a then-novel fiberglass body, it boasted unique sliding doors, a patented Darrin idea first tried on an unrelated 1946 prototype. The DKF-161 (the official designation) also offered a three-position landau convertible top with intermediate half-up position, plus full instrumentation and, usually, a three-speed floorshift transmission with overdrive. This plus the 90 bhp of the Henry J's 161-cid Willys six gave economy of around 30 mpg, but also 0-60 sprints of about 13 seconds and near-100 mph flat out.

But the Kaiser-Darrin affair greatly disappointed Dutch, who bought up about 100 leftovers, fitted many with Cadillac V-8s, and sold them for $4350 apiece at his Los Angeles showroom. The V-8 Darrins were potent indeed, capable of speeds up to 140 mph.

Kaiser came to an end in America during 1955 after 10 years and $100 million in losses. They were usually good cars and often innovative, but they never seemed to make it with the public. Edgar Kaiser liked to say, "Slap a Buick nameplate on it and it would sell like hotcakes." He was probably right.

Specifications

1947

K100 Special (wb 123.5)		Wght	Price	Prod
1005	sdn 4d	3,295	2,104	65,062
K101 Custom (wb 123.5)				
1015	sdn 4d	3,295	2,456	5,412

1947 Engines	bore×stroke	bhp	availability
I-6, 226.2	3.31×4.38	100	S-all
I-6, 226.2	3.31×4.38	112	O-Custom

1948

K481 Special (wb 123.5)		Wght	Price	Prod
4815	sdn 4d	3,295	2,244	90,588
K482 Custom (wb 123.5)				
4825	sdn 4d	3,295	2,466	1,263

1948 Engines	bore×stroke	bhp	availability
I-6, 226.2	3.31×4.38	100	S-all
I-6, 226.2	3.31×4.38	112	O-Custom

1949-50

K491 Special (wb 123.5)		Wght	Price	Prod
4911	sdn 4d	3,311	1,995	29,000*
4915	Traveler util sdn 4d	3,456	2,088	22,000*
K492 DeLuxe (wb 123.5)				
4921	sdn 4d	3,341	2,195	38,250*
4922	conv sdn	3,726	3,195	54*
4923	Virginian htp sdn	3,541	2,995	946*
4925	Vagabond util sdn 4d	3,501	2,288	4,500*

* 1949-50 prod. comb. by factory; approx. breakdown 84% 1949, 16% 1950. Est. for body styles based on body numbers in extant vehicles. Actual 1949-50 prod: 95,175.

1949-50 Eng.	bore×stroke	bhp	availability
I-6, 226.2	3.31×4.38	100	S-Special
I-6, 226.2	3.31×4.38	112	S-DeLuxe

1951

K511 Special (wb 118.5)		Wght	Price	Prod
5110	Traveler util sdn 2d	3,210	2,265	1,500*
5111	sdn 4d	3,126	2,212	43,500*
5113	bus cpe	3,061	1,992	1,500*
5114	sdn 2d	3,106	2,160	10,000*
5115	Traveler util sdn 4d	3,270	2,317	2,000*
5117	club cpe	3,066	2,058	1,500*
K512 DeLuxe (wb 118.5)				
5120	Traveler util sdn 2d	3,285	2,380	1,000*
5121	sdn 4d	3,171	2,328	70,000*

K512 DeLuxe		Wght	Price	Prod
5124	sdn 2d	3,151	2,275	11,000*
5125	Traveler util sdn 4d	3,345	2,433	1,000*
5127	club cpe	3,111	2,296	6,000*

* Est. based on extant vehicles. Total model-year prod.: 139,452.

1951 Engine	bore×stroke	bhp	availability
I-6, 226.2	3.31×4.38	115	S-all

1952

K521 Virginian Spec (wb 118.5)*		Wght	Price	Prod
5110	Traveler util sdn 2d	3,210	2,085	—
5111	sdn 4d	3,126	2,036	—
5113	bus cpe	3,061	1,832	—
5114	sdn 2d	3,106	1,988	—
5115	Traveler util sdn 4d	3,270	2,134	—
K522 Virginian DeLuxe (wb 118.5)*				
5120	Traveler util sdn 2d	3,285	2,192	—
5121	sdn 4d	3,171	2,143	—
5124	sdn 2d	3,151	2,095	—
5125	Traveler util sdn 4d	3,345	2,241	—
5127	club cpe	3,111	2,114	—
K521 DeLuxe (wb 118.5)				
5211	sdn 4d	3,195	2,537	5,000**
5214	sdn 2d	3,145	2,484	2,000**
5215	Traveler util sdn 4d	3,369	2,643	***
5217	club cpe	3,045	2,296	500**
K522 Manhattan (wb 118.5)				
5221	sdn 4d	3,220	2,654	16,500**
5224	sdn 2d	3,185	2,601	2,000**
5227	club cpe	3,185	2,622	500**

* Total Virginian production: 5,579. ** Est. based on extant vehicles. Total DeLuxe/Manhattan production: 26,552. *** Actual production questionable.

1952 Engine	bore×stroke	bhp	availability
I-6, 226.2	3.31×4.38	115	S-all

1953

K530 "Hrdtp" Dragon (wb 118.5)		Wght	Price	Prod
5301	sdn 4d	3,320	3,924	1,277
K531 DeLuxe (wb 118.5)				
5311	sdn 4d	3,200	2,513	5,800*
5314	sdn 2d	3,150	2,459	1,500*
5315	Traveler util sdn 4d	3,315	2,619	1,000*
K532 Manhattan (wb 118.5)				
5321	sdn 4d	3,265	2,650	15,450*

K532 Manhattan		Wght	Price	Prod
5324	sdn 2d	3,235	2,597	2,500*
5325	Traveler util sdn 4d	3,371	2,755	**
K538 Carolina (wb 118.5)				
5381	sdn 4d	3,185	2,373	1,400*
5384	sdn 2d	3,135	2,313	400*

1953 Engine	bore×stroke	bhp	availability
I-6, 226.2	3.31×4.38	118	S-all

* Est. based on extant vehicles. Model-year production:

K531	DeLuxe	7,883
K532	Manhattan	17,957
K538	Carolina	1,182

** One example found; volume production questionable.

1954

161 Darrin (wb 100.0)		Wght	Price	Prod
161	conv rdstr	2,175	3,668	435
K542 Manhattan (wb 118.5)				
5421	sdn 4d	3,375	2,670	3,860*
5424	sdn 2d	3,265	2,334	250*
K545 Special, early (wb 118.5)**				
5451	sdn 4d	3,265	2,389	3,000*
5454	sdn 2d	3,235	2,334	500*
K545 Special, late (wb 118.5)				
5451	sdn 4d	3,305	2,389	800*
5454	sdn 2d	3,265	2,334	125*

1954 Engines	bore×stroke	bhp	availability
I-6, 161.0	3.13×3.50	90	S-Darrin
I-6, 226.2	3.31×4.38	118	S-Special
I-6S, 226.2	3.31×4.38	140	S-Manhattan

* Est. based on extant vehicles. Model year prod.:

K542	Manhattan	4,110
K545	Special, early**	3,500
K545	Special, late	929

** Converted leftover 1953 Manhattans.

1955

Manhattan (wb 118.5)		Wght	Price	Prod
51363	sdn 4d (export)	3,350	—	1,021
51367	sdn 4d	3,375	2,670	226
51467	sdn 2d	3,335	2,617	44

1955 Engine	bore×stroke	bhp	availability
I-6S, 226.2	3.31×4.38	140	S-all

LaSalle

Cadillac's romantic companion make stemmed from the desire of legendary General Motors president Alfred P. Sloan to offer a car for every pocketbook, the basic philosophy that made GM the giant it is today. In the mid-'20s, Sloan detected a price gap between Buick and Cadillac, and assigned the latter to fill it with a second model line. The division chose the name LaSalle, honoring another French explorer like Cadillac, and introduced its junior series in 1927 on a wheelbase shorter than that of its senior cars. It was all part of the great period of expansion that brought forth a host of such cars to satisfy a market that looked like it would grow forever.

A big attraction of that first LaSalle was elegant body design by Harley Earl, a talented young West Coast designer reared in the "carriage trade," whom Sloan hired specifically to shape the new line. LaSalle amply fulfilled GM's hopes, and launched Earl on an illustrious 30-year career as the company's dean of design. In its first year, LaSalle accounted for 25 percent of Cadillac sales. By 1929, it was outselling its big sister.

In the Depression-racked '30s, LaSalle provided the sales volume that helped Cadillac survive. Though the division's total yearly production rarely exceeded Packard's, LaSalle's share was often substantial and sometimes critical. In rock-bottom 1933, for example, Cadillac's model-year output slid to 6700 units, but LaSalle accounted for fully half of it. In 1937, when Cadillac built 46,000 cars, 32,000 were LaSalles. Even so, LaSalle sales never really satisfied GM managers, who wanted much more.

The 1930 LaSalles, designated Series 340, followed general industry thinking of the times in being longer, heavier, and more expensive than the 1929 offerings. Wheelbase was now 134 inches as all models were put on the "long" chassis, and the original 125-inch "standard" platform was dropped. As before, the mainstay sellers carried bodies from the Fisher Brothers concern acquired by GM some years earlier. These comprised two coupes, two four-door sedans, a convertible coupe, and a pair of seven-passenger sedans in the $2500-$3000 range. Up in the $2400-$4000 area were six semicustom styles by Fleetwood, another respected GM-acquired coachbuilder: a roadster, two

1930 Series 340 convertible coupe

1932 Series 345B convertible coupe

1931 Series 345A town sedan

1933 Series 345C town coupe

1931 Series 345A 5-passenger sedan

1933 Series 345B town sedan

1934 Series 350 coupe

1934 Series 350 club sedan

1935 Series 50 2-passenger convertible coupe

1935 Series 50 two-door touring sedan

phaetons, a seven-seat touring, and two five-passenger sedans. By comparison, 1930 Cadillac prices started at $3295 and went to more than $10,800.

Not surprisingly for a Cadillac product, LaSalle bowed with a V-8, a 303-cubic-inch unit making close to 80 horsepower. This was bored out for 1928 to 328 cid and 86 bhp. To match the increased size and weight of the 1930 models, the V-8 was enlarged once more, this time to 340 cid, good for 90 bhp.

LaSalle styling in 1930 still owed much to Earl's original 1927 concepts: low silhouette, long and sweeping "clamshell" fenders, a tall and round-shouldered radiator inspired by that of the fabled Hispano-Suiza, and two-tone paint, then a novelty. The most obvious change for 1930 was a taller radiator that enhanced an already impressive styling package. The public continued to buy, and LaSalle recorded model-year production of some 15,000. Though that was about 75 percent of Cadillac's volume, it was nonetheless respectable in the aftermath of the Wall Street crash.

The fast-deepening Depression forced Cadillac to adopt cost-cutting measures for 1931-33. As a result, the 1931 Series 345A gained the senior line's 95-bhp 353-cid V-8, while that year's Cadillac Eights were put on the LaSalle chassis. Power improved to 115 for 1932-33. Model choices remained broadly the same for '31, then reduced for the 345B- and C-series of 1932-33, when seven-passenger sedans were upgraded to a 136-inch chassis and standard models were demoted to a 130-inch platform.

LaSalle prices were also reduced in 1931-33—down to $2200-$2800. Though that was about $500 below Cadillac Eights, the latter evidently looked like better buys, for they matched LaSalle in sales and actually beat the junior line in '31. LaSalle volume was well down anyway, dropping from 10,000 to just under 3400 for '32; the 1933 total was scarcely better.

Seeking to turn things around, Cadillac issued an all-new 1934 Series 350 with a look exclusive to LaSalle. Prices were again slashed, this time to $1000 under the senior Eights. Models were also slashed, leaving just a coupe, four-door sedan, club sedan, and convertible coupe. All rode a trim 119-inch wheelbase shared with Oldsmobile, as were basic bodyshells. Still cutting costs, Cadillac replaced LaSalle's V-8 with a 240.3-cid Olds L-head straight eight, albeit with Cadillac-supplied aluminum pistons and other changes. Still, horsepower withered to 95. But "Knee-Action" independent front suspension was a new talking point, and a first at GM (shared with Olds). Stylewise, the transitional 1933 look gave way to full streamlining, highlighted by a rounded grille and curious portholes on the hood sides.

This design/price formula persisted for two more years, but it didn't work well enough and sales remained well below those of rival junior editions. Still, LaSalle improved from just under 7200 for 1934 to over 8600 for the eight-model 1935 range, then to 13,000 for 1936, when offerings were again trimmed to four. Prices for '36 were the lowest ever: $1175 for the two-passenger coupe, $1255 for the convertible coupe. Interim changes included a 105-bhp 248 option for '35 that was made standard for '36, plus the phasing-in of "trunkback" sedans to replace outmoded trunkless styles. All LaSalles were designated Series 50 from 1935 to '39.

Cadillac tried a new formula for 1937, making LaSalles much like its 1936 Series 60—predictable perhaps, given the high success of that low-priced senior line. Power came from the same new 125-bhp 322 "monobloc" V-8, and deftly revised styling on a unique 124-inch wheelbase made LaSalles arguably more attractive than that year's Caddys. Buyers responded, and LaSalle sales reached a record 32,000 for the model year. Few major changes occurred for 1938, but a four-door sedan with a sliding-steel "Sunshine Turret Roof" joined the existing two-and four-door sedans, convertible sedan, and rumble-seat coupe and convertible. Sadly, a short but sharp recession shrank sales by half, to the chagrin of GM accountants. LaSalle was floundering, yet its cars were still bargains at 1938 prices ranging from $1300 to $1900.

But Cadillac was determined, so LaSalle was completely reworked for 1939. The V-8 was untouched, but a new midrange GM B-body brought a smart new shape with greater glass area and no running boards (except on convertibles, where they were optional). Wheelbase, which was shared with senior Oldsmobiles, was trimmed to 120 inches (as for '36). Despite all this, output was

1936 Series 50 four-door touring sedan

1938 Series 50 convertible coupe

1937 Series 50 four-door touring sedan

1939 Series 50 coupe

disappointing once more: only about 21,000 for the model year.

The 1940 model year brought modified styling that marked a high point in LaSalle's 14-year history, plus the make's first two-series lineup in a decade. The design leader was the plush new Series 52 Special bearing Harley Earl's latest "torpedo" look. While Cadillacs retained bullet-pod headlamps on the hood sides, the 52's new sealed beams (shared with other 1940 Detroiters) moved down into the fenders. Body lines were gently rounded and clean, interiors were more spacious on a three-inch longer wheelbase, and windows became even larger. The trademark LaSalle grille arguably reached its pinnacle: still slimmer than Cadillac's but artfully shaped. Like the '39s, the 1940 models wore vertical brightwork in the "catwalk" areas between grille and headlamps (another Earl idea), but the catwalks were now wider and fully integrated with the fenders.

Along with the 1940 Series 50, the new 52 Special offered a coupe and four-door sedan, now with fully integral trunks. The 50s, which included a two-door sedan, retained the basic '39 appearance. Though boxy next to the new Specials, they were nonetheless attractive, with the longer wheelbase and smoother front. The season's most-elegant LaSalles were unquestionably the Special convertible coupe and sedan that arrived midyear. Minor changes added five horsepower to the 322 L-head V-8, lifting output to 130.

But by now, LaSalle had been crowded out of its once-exclusive price niche. True, its 1940 spread was fairly broad, running from the $1240 Series 50 coupe to the $1895 Special convertible sedan. But a genuine Series 62 Cadillac could be had for as little as $1685 that year; Buicks listed at $895-$2199. And although LaSalle accounted for almost two-thirds of Cadillac's total 1940 volume—24,130 out of some 37,000—it ranked only slightly ahead of Lincoln and remained far behind Packard. It now

1940 Series 52 Special four-door sedan

seemed more logical to offer a lower-priced Cadillac rather than a junior line with less prestige. The division did precisely that for 1941, replacing LaSalle with the new entry-level Cadillac, Series 61.

The decision to drop LaSalle ultimately proved correct. Spanning a $1350-$1535 range, the Series 61 sold 29,250 copies its first year, then was gradually outpaced by the costlier 62s. But the 61 remained in premium-price territory to prevent a cheapening of Cadillac's image. Postwar prosperity rendered it unnecessary after 1951. By that point, Cadillac had become America's luxury sales leader by far.

Before the decision to drop LaSalle, GM Styling had prepared a prototype 1941 design. A torpedo-style fastback four-door sedan, it was a pretty car with the traditional slim grille and "catwalk" fender trim, plus thin horizontal parking lights, spinner hubcaps, and a revival of the early LaSalle radiator badge—an "LaS" monogram in a circle.

Memories of LaSalle's distinction, refinement, and class continued to exert considerable magic within GM Design long after World War II, and the name popped up in connection with several projects that led some to believe a revival was imminent. The first of these were the "LaSalle II" hardtop sedan and two-seat roadster created for the 1955 Motorama. Though strictly for show, they wore grilles composed of vertical slats reminiscent of the 1940 catwalks, plus traditional LaSalle heraldry. The name surfaced again for what became the 1963 Buick Riviera, and only at the last minute was LaSalle rejected for Seville as the moniker for Cadillac's new compact sedan of mid-1975.

Will LaSalle ever be reborn? Probably not, but it's a nice thought.

1940 Series 52 Special convertible coupe

1940 Series 52 Special convertible sedan

Specifications

1930 - 14,986 built

340 Fisher (wb 134.0)		Wght	Price	Prod
	cpe 2P	4,465	2,490	—
	conv cpe 2P	4,435	2,590	—
	cpe 5P	4,485	2,590	—
	sdn 4d	4,465	2,565	—
	Town sdn 4d	4,660	2,590	—
	sdn 7P	4,745	2,775	—
	Imperial sdn 7P	4,820	2,925	—
340 Fleetwood Custom (wb 134.0)				
	rdstr 2P	4,340	2,450	—
	phtn 5P	4,380	2,385	—
	touring 7P	4,435	2,525	—
	phtn A/W 5P	4,670	3,995	—
	sdnt cab 5P	4,600	3,725	—
	sdnt 5P	4,600	3,825	—

1930 Engine	bore×stroke	bhp	availability
V-8, 340.0	3.31×4.94	90	S-all

1931-10,095 built

345A (wb 134.0)		Wght	Price	Prod
	rdstr 2-4P	4,345	2,245	—
	touring 7P	4,440	2,345	—
	cpe 2P	4,470	2,195	—
	conv cpe 2P	4,440	2,295	—
	cpe 5P	4,490	2,295	—
	sdn 4d	4,650	2,295	—
	Town sdn 4d	4,665	2,345	—
	phtn A/W 5P	4,675	3,245	—
	sdn 7P	4,750	2,475	—
	Imperial sdn 7P	4,825	2,595	—
	sdnt cab 5P	4,675	3,245	—
	sdnt 5P	4,650	3,245	—

1931 Engine	bore×stroke	bhp	availability
V-8, 353.0	3.38×4.94	95	S-all

1932 - 3,386 built

345B (wb 130.0); lwb-136.0)		Wght	Price	Prod
	cpe 2P	4,660	2,395	—
	conv cpe 2P	4,630	2,545	—
	Town cpe 5P	4,695	2,545	—
	sdn 4d	4,840	2,495	—
	Town sdn 4d (lwb)	4,895	2,645	—
	lwb sdn 7P	5,025	2,645	—
	Imp 7P (lwb)	5,065	2,795	—

1932 Engine	bore×stroke	bhp	availability
V-8, 353.0	3.38×4.94	115	S-all

1933 - 3,482 built

345C (wb 130.0; lwb-136.0)		Wght	Price	Prod
	cpe 2P	4,730	2,245	—
	conv cpe 2P	4,675	2,395	—
	Town cpe 5P	4,695	2,395	—
	sdn 4d	4,805	2,245	—
	Town sdn 4d (lwb)	4,915	2,495	—
	lwb sdn 7P	4,990	2,495	—
	Imperial sdn 7P	5,020	2,645	—

1933 Engine	bore×stroke	bhp	availability
V-8, 353.0	3.38×4.94	115	S-all

1934 - 7,195 built

350 (wb 119.0)		Wght	Price	Prod
6330S	sdn 4d	3,960	1,695	—
633S	club sdn 5	3,960	1,695	—
6335	conv cpe 2-4P	3,780	1,695	—
6376	cpe 2P	3,815	1,595	—

1934 Engine	bore×stroke	bhp	availability
I-8, 240.3	3.00×4.25	95	S-all

1935 - 8,651 built

Series 50 (wb 119.0)		Wght	Price	Prod
6330S	sdn 4d	3,960	1,545	—
633S	club sdn 5P	3,960	1,545	—
6335	conv cpe 2-4P	3,780	1,545	—
6376	cpe 2P	3,185	1,445	—
35-5011	sdn 2d T/B	3,620	1,255	—
35-5019	sdn 4d T/B	3,650	1,295	—
35-5067	conv cpe 2-4P	3,510	1,325	—
35-5077	cpe 2P	3,475	1,225	—

1935 Engines	bore×stroke	bhp	availability
I-8, 240.3	3.00×4.25	95	S-6300 series
I-8, 248.0	3.00×4.38	105	S-5000 series

1936 - 13,004 built

Series 50 (wb 120.0)		Wght	Price	Prod
5011	sdn 2d T/B	3,605	1,185	—
5019	sdn 4d T/B	3,635	1,225	—
5067	conv cpe 2-4P	3,540	1,255	—
5077	cpe 2P	3,460	1,175	—

1936 Engine	bore×stroke	bhp	availability
I-8, 248.0	3.00×4.38	105	S-all

1937 - 32,000 built*

Series 50 (wb 124.0)		Wght	Price	Prod
5011	sdn 2d T/B	3,780	1,275	—
5019	sdn 4d T/B	3,810	1,320	—
5027	cpe 2-4P opt seats	3,675	1,155	—
5049	conv sdn 5P	3,850	1,680	—
5067	conv cpe 2-4P	3,715	1,350	—

* Incl. some comm. chassis on 160.0" whlbs and some CKD.

1937 Engine	bore×stroke	bhp	availability
V-8, 322.0	3.38×4.50	125	S-all

1938

Series 50 (wb 124.0)		Wght	Price	Prod
5011	sdn 2d T/B	3,800	1,345	700
5019	sdn 4d T/B	3,830	1,385	9,993
5019A	Sunroof sdn 4d T/B	3,850	1,435	72
5027	cpe 2-4P opt seats	3,745	1,295	2,710
5029	conv sdn 5P	3,870	1,825	265
5067	conv cpe 2-4P	3,735	1,420	855
	chassis	—	—	80

1938 Engine	bore×stroke	bhp	availability
V-8, 322.0	3.38×4.50	125	S-all

1939

Series 50 (wb 120.0)		Wght	Price	Prod
5011	sdn 2d T/B	3,710	1,280	977
5011A	Sunroof sdn 2d T/B	3,780	1,320	23
5019	sdn 4d T/B	3,740	1,320	15,928
5019A	Sunroof sdn 4d T/B	3,810	1,380	404
5027	cpe 2-4P, opt seats	3,635	1,240	2,525
5029	conv sdn 5P	3,780	1,800	185
5067	conv cpe 2-4P	3,715	1,395	1,056
	chassis	—	—	29

1939 Engine	bore×stroke	bhp	availability
V-8, 322.0	3.38×4.50	125	S-all

1940

40-50 (wb 123.0)		Wght	Price	Prod
5011	sdn 2d	3,760	1,280	375
5019	sdn 4d	3,790	1,320	6,722
5027	cpe, A/S	3,700	1,240	1,527
5029	conv sdn	4,000	1,800	125
5067	conv cpe	3,805	1,395	599
50	chassis	—	—	1,032
40-52 Special (wb 123.0)				
5219	sdn 4d	3,900	1,440	10,250
5227	cpe	3,810	1,380	3,000
5229	conv sdn	4,110	1,895	75
5267	conv cpe	3,915	1,535	425

1940 Engine	bore×stroke	bhp	availability
V-8, 322.0	3.38×4.50	130	S-all

Lincoln

Lincoln and Cadillac had a common founder: the stern, patrician Henry Martyn Leland, "Master of Precision." Leland and his associates formed Cadillac in 1902 from the remains of the Henry Ford Company—which is why his first Cadillac and the first production Ford, both named Model A, are so similar. William C. Durant bought Cadillac in 1909 for his burgeoning General Motors. Leland, meantime, went off to build Liberty aircraft engines during World War I. Then, with son Wilfred, he returned to the car business by forming Lincoln—named for the U.S. president, one of his heroes. When this enterprise ran into financial trouble, Leland came full circle by selling out to Henry Ford in 1922.

At first, Ford Motor Company did little to alter or update the Lincoln Model L that Leland had designed around 1920. Powered by a 385-cid V-8 with 90 brake horsepower, it was beautifully built and handsomely furnished. But by 1930 it was an anachronism: unfashionably upright and sluggish next to contemporary Cadillacs, Packards, and Chrysler Imperials.

Then Henry and son Edsel brought forth the 1931 Model K (why they went backward in the alphabet remains a mystery). Its new 145-inch-wheelbase chassis carried a modernized, 120-bhp V-8 that retained "fork-and-blade" rods and three-piece cast-iron block/crankcase assembly, Leland engineering features that let ads dwell lovingly on "precision-built" quality.

The new chassis was massive, with nine-inch-deep side rails and six crossmembers with cruciform bracing. The transmission gained synchromesh on second and third gears. Like the L, the K employed torque-tube drive and a floating rear axle. Other features included worm-and-roller steering, hydraulic shock absorbers by Houdaille, and mechanical brakes by Bendix. Stylewise, a slightly peaked radiator led a far longer hood, punctuated by twin-trumpet horns and bowl-shaped headlamps. The K was also longer, lower, and sleeker than the L, and it offered an improved ride, greater stability and, with its extra power, faster acceleration and higher top speed.

The K-chassis had been designed for an all-new V-12 that arrived for 1932 in a new KB-Series. This was a smooth 448-cid engine with 150 bhp—Ford's answer to the 12- and 16-cylinder giants from Cadillac, Packard, and others. The V-12 provided better performance than the K's V-8, yet KBs sold for slightly

1930 Series L 3-window town sedan

1933 Series KB 2-window Berline by Judkins

1931 Series K sport phaeton

1935 3-window Berline by Judkins

1932 Series KB convertible sedan by Dietrich

1935 Series K convertible sedan by Brunn

1936 Series K 3-window four-door sedan

1936 Lincoln-Zephyr four-door sedan

1939 Continental ("Special Lincoln-Zephyr")

1939 Series K LeBaron convertible sedan

1940 Lincoln-Zephyr Continental cabriolet

less and came in a wider range of body types. A magnificent around-town car and a fast open-road tourer, the KB was an extraordinary machine that stood far above most contemporary automobiles.

Accompanying the 1932 V-12 was the V-8 KA-Series on a 136-inch wheelbase. Its chassis was dimensionally the same as the old Model L's but structurally equal to the new KB's. The bodies were less lavishly furnished than on 12-cylinder models, but the KA was high-class, not a middle-priced product. Still, this V-8 wasn't as smooth as the engines from Cadillac, Packard, or Pierce-Arrow.

That changed the following year when the KA exchanged its V-8 for a smaller bore 381.7-cid V-12 with the same 125 bhp. This was also installed in the shorter Lincoln chassis, topped by Murray-built bodies made of wood, steel, and aluminum. KB continued as the senior line.

Meantime, the artistic Edsel Ford had been transforming Lincoln styling, updating the standard factory-built bodies and securing a plethora of custom and semicustom styles from the cream of America's coachbuilders, including Brunn, Dietrich, Judkins, LeBaron, Murphy, and Willoughby. The result was some of the finest expressions of Classic-era design. A cautious move toward streamlining began with the 1932 models and was more evident on the '33s, which wore a rakish Vee'd radiator with a chrome grille. Also new that year were hood louvers (replacing shutters), drawn-down "skirted" fenders, Vee'd front bumper, and redesigned trunk racks.

With sales slow in the Depression-ravaged market, Lincoln consolidated for 1934 around a single 414-cid V-12, a bored-out KA unit with the same 150 bhp as the old 448. Differences included aluminum cylinder heads and 6.3:1 compression. The latter was unheard of at the time, but made possible by the advent of 70-octane gasoline, which was nearly as potent as contemporary aviation fuel.

Most 1934 Lincolns could reach 95 mph, helped by the 414's broader rev range compared to the 448. Chassis specs were virtually unchanged, but Murray custom bodies were eliminated and radiators were now lacquered in body color. Smaller headlamps, parking lamps, and color-matched metal spare-tire covers helped clean up appearance. Sedans and limousines also received sloped tails, fairly radical for the day. Like Pierce, Packard, and Stutz, Lincoln was reluctant to abandon the graceful "oh gee" fenders so characteristic of the period—but it would after 1935.

By that point, big-Lincoln engineering was in the essential form it would carry through 1940. The slightly smoother-looking 1935s were all called Model K, and a vast array of body types was still available on the previous two wheelbases. Semi-teardrop fenders appeared for '36, along with a simpler radiator, new disc wheels, and larger hubcaps.

The 1937s emphasized absolute styling simplicity, possibly influenced by the Cord 810. Headlamps were integrated into the fenders, belt moldings were erased, and doors were extended down almost to the running boards. Spare tires lived within new built-in trunk compartments (unless sidemount spares were ordered), and factory bodies received their first Vee'd windshields. As ever, standard Model K interiors were done with rich broadcloth and curly-maple garnish moldings; rarer woods and fabrics were available in custom styles. The V-12 gained hydraulic lifters and moved further forward, which improved ride. Nominal horsepower remained 150, but post-1936 models probably had more usable power because of a different cam contour.

The lush luxury-car market of the 1920s had long since dried up in the economic drought of the '30s, and Lincoln suffered as much as any premium make. Annual sales hovered around 3500 from 1930 through '33, then dropped by about half in 1934. After that, the K-Series would see no more than 2000 units per year. By 1940 it was available only by special order, built on chassis completed during 1939. (The largest of these, the 160-inch-wheelbase "Sunshine Special," served as the parade car of presidents Roosevelt and Truman.)

What pulled Lincoln through the Depression was the Zephyr. It burst on the scene for 1936 as a medium-price product of the sort Cadillac and Packard also relied upon for survival, but was far more advanced. Its major design concepts evolved from a series of radical unit-body prototypes designed by John Tjaarda along aircraft principles and built with help from Briggs Manufacturing Company, eager to win some volume body business from Lincoln. Tjaarda's original design featured a rear-engine layout, but this was switched to a conventional front-engine/rear-drive format.

The rest of the Zephyr was unconventional. Tjaarda claimed this was the first car in which aircraft-type stress analysis proved the superiority of unit construction. And indeed, at around 3300 pounds, the Zephyr was lighter than Chrysler's body-on-frame Airflow, yet much stiffer. Best of all, unit construction offered important cost savings.

A modified Ford flathead V-8 with about 100 bhp was initially slated, but company president Edsel Ford decided that, as a Lincoln, the Zephyr had to have a V-12. As the existing 414 was too large for this smaller package, engineer Frank Johnson, one the ablest in the industry, was told to add four cylinders to the Ford V-8. Cost pressures, however, compromised the result. A four-main-bearing L-head unit of 267 cid, the Zephyr V-12 employed a "monobloc" casting similar to the V-8's, with an exhaust cored between the cylinders. Initial horsepower was unimpressive for a twelve at only 110. The rest of the drivetrain was also derived from Ford V-8 components.

Zephyr styling was similar to that of Tjaarda's prototypes, but a pointy rear-hinged "alligator" hood and matching Vee'd radiator were grafted on under Edsel's direction by Ford stylist E.T. "Bob" Gregorie. The changes made for a much prettier car than either Tjaarda's prototypes or the curved-nose Airflow, yet the essential shape remained more slippery than the Airflow's even though it wasn't "styled in the wind tunnel" like portions of the Chrysler design.

Briggs built most of the Zephyr. Ford only installed the drivetrain, added front sheetmetal, and saw to trimming and painting. Edsel laughingly told Tjaarda that Briggs might as well build the whole thing, as the Zephyr assembly line was only 40 feet long!

Designated Model H, the Zephyr bowed as a two- and four-door sedan on a 122-inch wheelbase. Prices were attractive at around $1300, and performance was at least decent. Top speed was over 87 mph, and a 4.33:1 rear axle, chosen for low-end acceleration over all-out speed, made for 0-50 mph in 10.8 seconds and 30-50 mph in six seconds flat. Yet mileage consistently averaged 16-18 miles per gallon.

With all this, the Zephyr was an immediate hit. Nearly 15,000 were sold for '36, better than 80 percent of Lincoln's total model-year output. That boosted the make to 18th on the industry production card—the first time Lincoln broke into the top 20. Sales for the 1937 HB models came to nearly 30,000 despite few changes, though a three-passenger coupe and division-window Town Limousine were added.

The 1938 Zephyrs bowed with a three-inch-longer wheelbase and revised styling announced by a "mouth organ" grille that beat everyone to the next design trend: the horizontal front-end format. Two- and four-door convertibles arrived. A Custom interior option provided additional model variations for 1939. A deep recession limited 1938 sales to just over 19,000—though

1940 Lincoln-Zephyr 3-passenger coupe

1941 Continental cabriolet

1942 Custom limousine

1942 Continental cabriolet

1947 Continental club coupe

1947 Continental club coupe

1947 Lincoln convertible coupe

1949 Cosmopolitan convertible coupe

1949 Cosmopolitan fastback town sedan

1950 Cosmopolitan four-door sport sedan

1950 Lincoln four-door sport sedan

1951 Cosmopolitan four-door sport sedan

1951 Lincoln four-door sport sedan

1951 Cosmopolitan Capri coupe

1951 Lincoln Lido coupe

that was still some 5500 more than Cadillac managed with its LaSalle. The '39 total was more encouraging at nearly 21,000, but might have been higher had it not been for intramural competition from the new medium-priced Mercury.

Zephyr mechanical alterations before 1940 followed those of other Ford Motor Company cars. Old Henry's stubbornness precluded hydraulic brakes until '39. An optional two-speed Columbia rear axle came along, reducing engine speed by 28 percent in its higher cruising ratio. The V-12 was modified to cure several persistent problems. Water passages, for example, proved inadequate, leading to overheating, bore warpage, and excessive ring wear. Inadequate crankcase ventilation created oil sludge buildup, and oil flow was poor. Yet despite the addition of hydraulic valve lifters for 1938 and cast-iron heads after '41, the powerplant never shed its poor reliability image. Had World War II not intervened, it might have been fully reengineered. But it wasn't, and many collector/owners have since replaced the V-12 with L-head or later overhead-valve V-8s.

With no change in wheelbase or basic appearance, Zephyr was fully rebodied for 1940, gaining sealed-beam headlamps, larger windows and trunk, bodysides bulged out to cover the running boards, and a more-conventional dash. A larger bore brought the V-12 to 292 cid and 120 bhp. The slow-selling convertible sedan was discarded. Among Custom-interior closed models was a special five-passenger "town limousine," a four-door-sedan conversion by Briggs. Brunn also built 10 Zephyr town cars in 1940-41 (three of which went to the Ford family); all were heavy-looking rigs with rooflines that didn't match well with the chiseled lower body. Zephyr production again inched upward, reaching just over 21,750.

But Lincoln had bigger 1940 news. It was, of course, the Zephyr-based Continental, one of the most-stunning automobiles of all time. Though executed by Gregorie, its styling was conceived by Edsel Ford, who directed him to make it "thoroughly continental," complete with outside spare tire. The design originated with a one-off convertible that Edsel used on his annual winter vacation in Palm Beach during 1938-39. Everyone who saw it thought it sensational, which encouraged Ford to offer production models scarcely a year later. A coupe and cabriolet debuted at about $2850 and brought customers into Lincoln dealerships by the thousands.

Continental was broken out from the Zephyr line for 1941, and received its own badges. Model-year production increased from 404 to 1250. Meantime, Lincoln maintained a semblance of K-Series coachbuilt tradition with a Zephyr-based Custom sedan and limousine on a 138-inch wheelbase. But at about $2800, only 650 were called for. The Briggs town limo was scratched for '41, but other Zephyrs returned with minor mechanical improvements, including power tops for convertibles and optional Borg-Warner overdrive in place of the two-speed Columbia axle. Styling changes were slight: fender-mounted parking/turn-indicator lights and, for Continentals, pushbutton exterior door releases (replacing handles). In all, Lincoln built about 18,250 cars for the last full model year before World War II.

War-shortened 1942 brought significant engineering and design changes. The V-12 was bored out to its limit for 305 cid and yielded 10 additional horsepower. A flashy facelift forecast immediate postwar styling. All models now had longer and higher fenders, a busy two-tier horizontal-bar grille, and headlamps flanked by parking lights on either side. Overall height was a bit lower, curb weights a bit higher. Lincoln built 6547 of these cars by early February 1942, when the government ordered a halt to civilian production for the duration.

Despite the dictates of war, Ford stylists found time to experiment, making hundreds of renderings and dozens of scale models. Most involved the "bathtub" look that materialized on several makes for 1948-49. Some Lincoln concepts bordered on the grotesque. Many looked as if they'd been "carved out of a bar of soap," as one stylist put it.

Like most other makes, Lincoln resumed peacetime production with warmed-over '42 models that would not change much through 1948. However, the prewar Customs and three-passenger coupe did not come back, and the Zephyr name was abandoned for just plain Lincoln. The V-12 reverted to its pre-1942 displacement and horsepower dropped to 125. The larger bore had created casting problems for the factory and mechanics found it difficult to rebore for overhauls. Because of the V-12's design flaws, overhauls were all too frequent—especially if the maintenance schedule wasn't rigidly followed. Custom interiors were still available for closed standard-model Lincolns.

The main design difference between 1946 and '42 was grillework composed of vertical and horizontal bars, with a Lincoln emblem in the upper segment, plus a new winged-globe hood ornament. The 1947s carried "Lincoln" lettering on the hubcaps, plus pullout door handles, "pocket" interior armrests, and a hood ornament with a longer wing. There were no visual changes for 1948.

Lincoln's first new postwar cars arrived in mid-1948, but a Continental wasn't among them. One had been planned, but was shelved due to low projected sales. It would have looked clumsy anyway, and some Ford designers, respectful of the late Edsel Ford (who died in 1943) were thankful it didn't appear.

Concentrating instead on high-volume models, Lincoln issued two series for 1949: a 121-inch-wheelbase standard line and the costlier 125-inch Cosmopolitan. The former, sharing basic bodyshells with that year's new Mercury, comprised sedan, coupe, and convertible; Cosmo added a Town Sedan, a massive six-window fastback. The aged V-12 was replaced at last by a 152-bhp 337-cid L-head V-8 originally designed for Ford trucks. Overdrive was a $96 extra.

Dearborn's original '49 planning called for a 118-inch-wheelbase Ford and a 121-inch Mercury. What emerged as the Cosmopolitan was conceived as a Zephyr. At the last minute, Ford's policy committee, led by Ernest Breech and Harold Youngren, mandated a smaller 114-inch-wheelbase Ford, so the proposed Mercury became the '49 standard Lincoln and the 118-inch Ford was made a Mercury—hence the latter's change from "senior Ford" to "junior Lincoln" in this period. The ex-Mercury Lincolns were thus much cheaper than the Cosmos, spanning a $2500-$3100 range versus $3200-$3950.

Predictably, given its wartime design exercises, Lincoln's '49 styling was of the "bar-of-soap" school, but clean and dignified nonetheless. Fadeaway front fenderlines marked base models. Cosmos had fully flush fenders, plus one-piece (instead of two-piece) windshields, broad chrome gravel deflectors over the front wheel arches, and thin window frames. All models wore conservative grilles, sunken headlamps (glass covers were planned), and "frenched" taillamps. Model-year volume set a record at 73,507 units.

Lincoln's first new postwar generation continued for the next two years with no major alteration. Offerings, however, were shuffled for 1950, as the standard convertible and the tubby Cosmo Town Sedan were deleted. This left a notchback coupe and a four-door sport sedan (with throwback "suicide" rear doors) in each series, plus a Cosmopolitan convertible. There were also two newcomers for 1950: the $2721 Lido and $3406 Cosmo Capri. These were limited-edition coupes with custom interiors and padded canvas tops offered in lieu of a true pillarless hardtop to answer Cadillac's 1949 Coupe de Ville. Few were sold through 1951. All 1950 Lincolns sported a restyled dashboard by chief designer Tom Hibbard. It was an attractive

1952 Capri hardtop coupe

1955 Capri hardtop coupe

1953 Capri hardtop coupe

1955 Capri four-door with air conditioning

1954 Capri convertible coupe

1955 Capri convertible coupe

"rolled-top" design with an oblong instrument cluster, a format that would continue through 1957. A self-shifting Hydra-Matic transmission, bought from archrival GM, arrived as a new 1950 option; it would be standard in 1952-54. The '51 models were spruced up by longer rear fenders with upright taillamps (versus the previous round units), plus a simpler grille and different wheel covers.

While not known for performance, Lincoln had enough of the right stuff to place ninth in the 1950 *Carrera Panamericana*—the first of the legendary Mexican Road Races. Lincoln then won the 1951 Mobilgas Economy Run with an average 25.5 mpg. Neither of these feats helped sales, which were well down from record '49. The totals were just over 28,000 for 1950 and a more gratifying 32,500 for '51.

All Ford Motor Company cars were completely new for '52 but though sales rose—to nearly 41,000 by '53—Lincoln was still miles behind Cadillac. One problem may have been sedate, square styling through 1955: again very much like Mercury—and also Ford. Uniformity may have caused trouble, too, with only the same five models offered through '54. Cosmopolitan became the lower series in this period, Capri the upper. Both listed four-door sedan and a belated hardtop coupe (three years behind Cadillac's); Capri added a convertible.

Nevertheless, 1952-54 was a significant period in Lincoln history. The most notable mechanical development was the make's first overhead-valve V-8: a new short-stroke design of 318 cid, good for 160 bhp at first and 205 bhp for 1953-54. It was superior in many ways. Its crankshaft, for example, had eight counterweights versus most competitors' six. Intake valves were oversized for better breathing and higher specific output. (Among '53 engines, it produced 0.64 bhp per cubic inch against 0.63 for Cadillac and 0.54 for the Chrysler Hemi.) The crankcase extended below the crankshaft centerline to form an extremely stiff shaft support, hence this engine's family nickname of "Y-block."

Model-year 1952 also introduced ball-joint front suspension to Lincoln. Together with the new V-8, it made for taut, powerful road machines that would dominate their class in the Mexican Road Race. Other new features included recirculating-ball power steering, oversized drum brakes, liberal sound insulation, optional four-way power seat and, with the extra-cost factory air conditioning, flow-through ventilation (when the compressor was idle). Fabrics, leathers, and fit-and-finish were all top-notch, far above those of lesser Dearborn products.

Despite a rather short 123-inch wheelbase, the 1952-54 Lincolns were roomier inside than previous models—and some later ones. Visibility was better than on any other contemporary U.S. car save Kaiser, and exteriors were notably free of period excesses. Fluted taillamps shed water and dirt, just like those Mercedes would adopt in the '70s.

Lincoln turned in some spectacular performances at the *Carrera Panamericana*—virtually unrivaled in the International Standard Class. Lincolns took the first five places in 1952, the top four in '53, and first and second in 1954. Race preparation was largely owed to Clay Smith, a gifted mechanic who was tragically killed in a pit accident in 1954. Of great help were publicity-conscious Dearborn engineers who supplied stiff "export" suspension pieces, Ford truck camshafts, mechanical valve lifters, special front spindles and hubs, and rear-axle ratios that enabled a "stock" Lincoln to top 130 mph. The 1952 race winner, Chuck Stevenson, finished the 2000-mile grind from Juarez to the Guatemala border nearly an hour ahead of the Ferrari that had won the year before.

Lincoln wasn't ready with a total redesign for 1955, so its cars were among the most conservative in that banner Detroit sales year, despite an extensive facelift. Still, they were crisp, clean, and elegant. Though the wrapped windshield held sway most everywhere else, the '55 Lincolns didn't have one, and were thus more practical. Interiors remained luxurious combinations of high-quality fabrics and top-grain leather.

Wheelbase was unchanged for '55, but the restyle added extra sheetmetal (mostly in back) and 50-100 pounds in curb weight. A good thing, then, that the V-8 was bored to 341 cid and gained 20 bhp. Elsewhere, Cosmopolitan was retagged Custom, and Lincoln finally offered its own automatic transmission. Called Turbo Drive, it was basically the four-year-old Ford/Merc-0-Matic unit enlarged and strengthened to withstand the greater torque of Lincoln's V-8. But likely because its '55s weren't "new" enough, Lincoln was one of the few makes to suffer in Detroit's best sales season of the decade, dropping from nearly 37,000 for '54 to a bit over 27,000.

The '56s were new—really new. Ads proclaimed them "Unmistakably Lincoln," but there was scarcely a trace of the trim '55s. Wheelbase grew by three inches, overall length by seven, width by three inches. Capri now signified the lower series, Premiere the costlier models. Body-style assignments were unchanged, though pillared four-doors were made to look much like hardtops. Styling, partly previewed by the 1954 Mercury XM-800 show car, was fully up to date, with a wraparound windshield, clean grille, and peaked headlamps. Rakish vertical taillights capped long exhaust ports flanking a "grille" motif that echoed the front-end design. Ornamentation was simple, with two-toning confined to the roof.

Matching the expansive new '56 styling was an expanded engine, a Y-block enlarged to 368 cid and 285 bhp. "True power that works for your safety at every speed," blared one ad. Despite their greater bulk, the '56s didn't weigh much more than the '55s. But they cost a whopping $500-$700 more, the range now running from $4120 to about $4750. Yet as the only make with a major restyle instead of a mere facelift, Lincoln did well for '56, moving more than 50,000 cars. Still, even that was only about a third of Cadillac's total.

Prices rose another $500-$700 for 1957, when Lincoln joined a popular Detroit trend by offering its first four-door hardtops, dubbed "Landau" and available in each series. Huge tailfins sprouted, and the front gained "Quadra-Lites": conventional seven-inch-diameter headlamps above 5¾-inch "road" lamps. Though not a true four-light system, it put Lincoln ahead of most rivals. Compression went to 10:1, horsepower to 300. Overall, 1957 was a good, but not great, Lincoln year. At just over 41,000, model-year volume was slightly higher than for Chrysler's Imperial but still less than a third of Cadillac's.

Lincoln pinned hopes for 1958 on yet another all-new design. But '58 proved to be a horrible year for Detroit and a devastating one for Ford's finest, considering the millions invested in new tooling. A flash recession sent the economy reeling and buyers rushing off to buy more-economical cars as industry sales fell 50 percent from 1957. Ford trailed Chevrolet by a quarter-million units, Dearborn's new Edsel began a rapid slide to nowhere, and Mercury ran 46 percent behind its '57 pace.

1956 Premiere hardtop coupe

1956 Premiere four-door sedan with air conditioning

1957 Capri four-door sedan

1957 Premiere convertible coupe

1958 Capri Landau hardtop sedan

1959 Premiere four-door sedan

1960 Lincoln Landau hardtop sedan

1960 Continental Mark V hardtop sedan

1961 Continental four-door sedan

1961 Continental convertible sedan

The '58 Lincolns were longer, lower, and wider in a year when even luxury-car buyers were starting to think about more-sensible size. As a result, model-year production tumbled.

At the bottom of this avalanche was a square-lined giant stretching six inches longer overall than the '57 Lincoln on a 131-inch wheelbase. It was easily recognized, for there was nothing else like it: heavily sculpted sides, a wide grille flanked by true quad headlamps in garish slanted recesses, enormous flared bumpers. Under a hood not much smaller than a Ping-Pong table was 1958's largest American passenger-car engine: a new big-block 430-cid V-8 making 375 bhp. Frameless unibody construction was an unexpected departure for the luxury field.

Of course, this package had been conceived in the far healthier market of 1955. And recession or not, most luxury buyers still wanted big cars like this. Despite appearances and 2½-ton curb weights, the '58 Lincolns were surprisingly quick in a straight line and not that clumsy in curves. But they were too large and ornate for a public that was tiring of blatant excess. Cadillac did better business with a heavy, if still glittery, facelift, and Imperial offered a mild restyle of its tasteful, though heroically befinned, '57s. Both rivals also had lately expanded offerings, and comparable '58 Cadillacs cost several hundred dollars less than Lincolns. No wonder 1958 was a debacle for Dearborn's prestige make. At least it ushered in a three-year program that would culminate in a more-compact—and vastly more-successful—new Lincoln for 1961.

Meantime, there was nothing to do but offer more of the same, so Lincolns and the companion Continentals were little-changed for '59. The Premiere convertible had transferred to the separate 1958 Continental Mark III line, leaving a four-door sedan and two- and four-door hardtops in Capri and Premiere trim. All returned for '59, when Continental was absorbed as a Lincoln subseries and Capris became simply Lincolns.

It bears mentioning that although the 1956-57 Mark II and 1958 Mark III were products of a separate Continental Division, and thus "non-Lincolns," all later Marks and Continentals are properly regarded as Lincolns. The reason is the collapse of Ford's grand scheme for a GM-like five-division structure following the '58 recession, and the particular failure of Edsel and the Mark II to sell as planned. The Continental marque was thus merged with Lincoln for the 1959 model year. In January of 1958, the Edsel and Mercury Divisions were combined into a short-lived M-E-L structure as a cost-cutting move. Ford's upper division then reverted to its original status as just plain Lincoln-Mercury, which continues to this day.

The '59 Mark IV was just a facelifted Mark III, but added a formal-roof Town Car and limousine priced about the same as the short-lived $10,000 Mark II. Likewise, '59 Lincolns were lightly touched-up '58s. Horsepower was reduced to 350 for all models in a faint sop to a now mileage-minded public. Though the division desperately held prices close to previous levels—$4900-$5500 for Lincolns and Premieres, $6600-$7000 for standard Marks—Imperial surged ahead in 1959 model-year volume—and would win again the following year. Lincoln's '59 total was dismal at 15,780, plus 11,126 Mark IVs.

Lincoln and Continental styling was lightly touched up for 1960. Grilles gained new inserts, the massive front bumper guards moved inboard of the canted headlamps, and rear ends were reworked. Lincolns also sported a reshaped roofline and rear window, plus new full-length upper-body moldings. Horsepower dropped to 315. Prices stayed much the same, and standard equipment was as comprehensive as ever, but Lincoln sales withered to just under 14,000, though Continental held steady at about 11,000.

A much happier chapter opened for 1961 with an all-new "downsized" Continental. Replacing all the old behemoths, it bowed in just two models: a thin-pillar four-door sedan and America's first four-door convertible since the abortive Frazer Manhattan model of a decade before. Both rode a 123-inch wheelbase, same as on the trim mid-'50s Lincolns, and featured a '30s throwback in rear-hinged "suicide" back doors. Prices were in the middle of what had been Mark V territory: an announced $6067 for the hardtop, $6713 for the convertible.

With its classic beauty and superb engineering, the '61 was arguably the most-satisfying Lincoln since the V-12 K-Series. It was certainly one of the '60s best Detroit cars. Enhancing both its image and sales was fortuitous timing, the '61 arriving just as a youthful new First Family was occupying the White House. The new Continentals were soon seen in newspaper and magazine photos as the new Administration's transport of choice, personal and official, which is why these cars have since become known in some circles as the "Kennedy Continentals."

Their chiseled good looks reflected the efforts of seven Ford stylists: Eugene Bordinat (corporate design chief), Don DeLaRossa, Elwood P. Engel, Gale L. Halderman, John Najjar, Robert M. Thomas, and George Walker. They were collectively honored with an award from the Industrial Design Institute—unusual, as the IDI rarely bothers with cars. But the '61 Lincoln, it said, was an "outstanding contribution of simplicity and design elegance." Interestingly, the basic cowl structure was shared with Ford's new '61 Thunderbird, which halved tooling costs for two low-volume models, even though the 'Bird was very different aft of the cowl and rode a 113-inch wheelbase.

The '61 introduced a basic Lincoln look that would continue into the late 1980s. The original was naturally the purest: smooth, gently curved bodysides topped by straight-through fenderlines edged in bright metal; a modest grille with outboard horizontal quad headlamps; a simple tail (not unlike the Mark II's) with a panel repeating the grille texture and taillamps set in the trailing edges of the fenders. All corners were easily seen from behind the wheel, handy for parking. Side windows curved inward toward the top were a first for mass production, matched by a greenhouse with the greatest degree of "tumblehome" yet seen on a large American luxury car. Door glass would remain curved through '63, became flat for 1964-70, then be curved again. Unlike the old Frazer, the convertible sedan's window frames slid completely out of sight. So did its fabric top, stowing beneath the rear deck via 11 relays connecting mechanical and hydraulic linkages. (Much of this design stemmed from Ford engineering for the 1957-59 Skyliner "retrac" hardtops and 1958-60 Thunderbird convertibles.)

Styling aside, these Lincolns were renowned for quality. This was mostly due to the efforts of Harold C. MacDonald, then chief engineer of Ford's Car and Truck Group. The '61s had the most-rigid unit body/chassis ever produced, the best sound insulation and shock damping in series production, and extremely close machining tolerances. The model year also brought an unprecedented number of long-life components, including a completely sealed electrical system, and superior rust and corrosion protection.

The 1961 Lincolns were also among the most thoroughly tested cars in Detroit history. Each engine—still a 430-cid V-8, though detuned to 300 bhp—was run three hours on a dynamometer at 3500 rpm (equal to about 98 mph), torn down for inspection, then reassembled. Automatic transmissions were tested for 30 minutes before installation. Each car was given a final 12-mile road test and checked for nearly 200 individual items, after which an ultraviolet light was used to visualize a fluorescent dye in lubricants as a check for leaks. Backing these measures was an unprecedented (for 1961) two-

1962 Continental convertible sedan

1964 Continental convertible sedan

1963 Continental convertible sedan

1965 Continental four-door sedan

year, 24,000-mile warranty.

Response to the '61s was immediate and satisfying. Sales exceeded 25,000, and Lincoln surged ahead of Imperial for keeps. Styling changes for the second and third year were minimal, Lincoln having promised to concentrate on functional improvements, at least for awhile. The '62s had a tidier grille with narrowed central crossbar and headlamps no longer recessed; the '63s gained a finely checked grille, matching backpanel appliqué, and increased trunk space, plus engine tuning that yielded an extra 20 bhp.

Wheelbase grew to 126 inches for 1964, where it would stay through '69. But the essential look was unchanged. The main alterations, aside from the aforementioned flat door glass, were a slightly convex vertical-bar grille, broader rear window, and a lower-profile convertible top. The '65s received a horizontal grille motif, parking/turn-signal lights in the front fenders, and ribbed taillamps.

A body change for 1966 restored a two-door hardtop model as Lincoln sought higher volume, the convertible having accounted for only 10 percent of sales. Body lines became less rectilinear as a slightly larger fender "hop-up" appeared just ahead of larger rear-wheel cutouts. An extended front added some five inches to overall length, the grille acquired fine horizontal bars and a bulged center section (carried through in the sheetmetal above), and the front bumper wrapped all the way back to the front wheel openings. The V-8 was bored and stroked to 462 cid and 340 bhp.

All this plus lower prices—as little as $5485 for the hardtop coupe—pushed 1966 Lincoln sales to nearly 55,000 units, though that was still only 25 percent of Cadillac's model-year volume. A segmented grille, shuffled emblems and taillamps, and a spring-loaded hood emblem appeared for '67, when the convertible sedan took a final bow with only 2276 copies sold. Overall production remained strong, however, at over 45,500 for the model year.

Lincoln's most intriguing development for 1968 was the $6585 Continental Mark III. Not a revival of the leviathan '58 Mark III, this was the putative successor to the charismatic 1956-57 Mark II. It bore the personal stamp of company president Henry Ford II, just as his brother, William Clay, had influenced the Mark II and their father, Edsel, had hatched the original 1940 "Mark I" Continental. Why "Mark III" instead of the expected "Mark VI?" Because HF II didn't view the heavyweight 1958-60 Mark III/IV/V as true Continentals.

But this new one was true to its heritage, at least in spirit. The project had begun in late 1965 as a personal-luxury coupe with long-hood/short-deck proportions in the Continental tradition. Exterior styling was naturally supervised by corporate design chief Gene Bordinat. Hermann Brunn, scion of the great coachbuilding family and a member of Bordinat's staff, was chiefly responsible for the interior, endowing it with large, comfortable bucket seats and a dashboard with simulated woodgrain trim and easy-to-reach controls. Henry Ford II himself selected both the interior and exterior designs from numerous proposals submitted in early 1966.

The result was actually a structural cousin to the new-for-'67 Thunderbird sedan, set on the same 117.2-inch wheelbase (some nine inches shorter than the Mark II's). Overall length was identical with that of Cadillac's new 1967 front-wheel-drive Eldorado. Though slightly baroque, the Mark III was handsome, helped by America's longest hood—more than six feet. It also offered a wide choice of luxury interiors and 26 exterior colors, including four special "Moondust" metallic paints. The 1969-71 models cost a fair bit more: ultimately over $8800. Standard equipment ran to Select-Shift Turbo-Drive automatic, power brakes (discs in front, drums in back), concealed headlamps,

1966 Continental hardtop coupe

1966 Continental convertible sedan

1967 Continental four-door sedan

ventless door windows, power seats and windows, flow-through ventilation, and 150 pounds of sound insulation. Beneath that long hood was a new 460 cid V-8—one of Detroit's largest—with 10.5:1 compression and 365 bhp. Also adopted for standard '68 Continentals, it would remain Lincoln's mainstay powerplant for the next 10 years.

Because of a late introduction (in April), the Mark III saw only 7770 units for model-year '68. But there was no question that it was right for its market. As proof—and despite no major change—more than 23,000 were sold for '69, another 21,432 for 1970, and over 27,000 for '71. The front-drive Eldorado may have been more technically advanced, but the Mark III seemed to have more magic, for it nearly matched Eldorado sales each year through 1971 and never trailed by more than 2000. This was a great achievement considering Lincoln's annual volume had never come close to Cadillac's.

Aside from the larger engine, the '68 Continental sedan and hardtop updated their basic '66 look with a new horizontal grille texture and matching rear-panel applique, beefier bumpers, and large "star" ornaments on the nose and trunklid. A multifunction lamp at each corner imparted a cleaner look by combining turn signals, side-marker lamps (newly required by Washington), and parking lamps (front) or brake/taillamps. Also new were a government-required dual hydraulic brake system with warning light, a four-way emergency flasher, and an energy-absorbing steering column and instrument panel.

1968 Continental Executive Limousine by Lehmann-Peterson

1968 Continental hardtop coupe

1969 Continental hardtop coupe

1969 Continental Mark III hardtop coupe

1970 Continental four-door sedan

1971 Continental hardtop coupe

Model-year volume for this line totaled more than 39,000.

Announcing the 1969 Continentals was a square, finely checked Vee'd grille more-distinct from the headlamps. A new Town Car interior option for the sedan provided "unique, super-puff leather-and-vinyl seats and door panels, luxury wood-tone front seat back and door trim inserts, extra plush carpeting and special napped nylon headlining." Series production eased once again, settling at about 38,300.

The 1970 Continentals carried new bodies on a "torque-box" chassis inspired by Mercury, with coil-link rear suspension (Lincoln's first since 1959), an inch-longer wheelbase and wider rear track. Styling was freshened with hidden headlamps, a more prominently bulged slat grille, plus ventless front-door glass, concealed wipers, and full-width taillamps—all popular period features. Less obvious were wider doors, with the rears now front-hinged on sedans, and a slightly smaller fuel tank (though still ample at 24.1 gallons). The hardtop, again advertised as the Coupe, gained a sweeping roofline with huge C-pillars that made over-the-shoulder vision dodgy. The powertrain was essentially a carryover. Prices were still about what they'd been back in 1961: $5976 for the hardtop, $6211 for the sedan.

This heavier, bulkier-looking Lincoln continued through 1974 with relatively few changes—most dictated by federal, not market, requirements. Prices did change, pushed by inflation past $7000 for 1971 and a little beyond $8000 by 1974. Horsepower numbers changed, too, but only because more-realistic SAE *net* measures replaced gross figures after 1971. Thus, the big 460-cid V-8 suffered a paper drop from 365 gross bhp to 212/224 (Mark/Continental). An even bigger Continental arrived for '75 with a fractionally longer wheelbase and some eight inches added to overall length. Curb weight, though, was slightly lower at around 5000 pounds.

Continental styling remained resolutely blocky and formal throughout the '70s as Ford designers sought to maintain a family resemblance with the Mark. Sales moved up smartly for 1972—to nearly 95,000, including Marks—then to a record 128,000-plus for '73. A decline followed the energy crisis touched off by the OPEC oil embargo, but it was only temporary, and Lincoln rallied along with most other big Detroiters in 1975. Output was more than 190,000 by '77, a new Lincoln high, though still only slightly more than half of Cadillac volume.

Longer-lower-wider was the formula that had traditionally worked well for luxury makes, and it worked well for Lincoln with the new Continental Mark IV of 1972. Sales nearly doubled over those of the '71 Mark III and would average 50,000 or so each year through the final 1976 models. Remarkably, the Mark IV offered less passenger room than the III and was predictably thirstier and less agile. It, too, shared a basic structure and wheelbase (now 120.4 inches) with the concurrent Ford Thunderbird, but it wasn't immediately apparent.

Lincoln enjoyed good success with the Continental Town Car option. The 1970 package consisted of special leather inserts

1971 Continental four-door sedan

1972 Continental Town Car four-door sedan

1973 Continental Mark IV coupe

1974 Continental Mark IV coupe

1974 Continental Town Car four-door sedan

1975 Continental Town coupe

and vinyl bolsters for seats, woodlike panels on the backs of the front seats, deeper cut-pile carpeting and a soft nylon headliner, all color-keyed in a choice of five hues. For 1971, Lincoln offered an extra-special Town Car with dash and front-fender nameplates plus a set of keys and door-mounted owner initials all done in 22-carat gold—which made for a Golden Anniversary Continental to celebrate Lincoln's 50th birthday. For 1972, the Town Car became a Continental submodel. The hardtop got the same treatment for 1973 to become the Town Coupe.

There was little new for '74. Heavier bumpers sprouted at the rear to match the beefier front units adopted the previous year per federal mandate, and the Mark added a brace of Luxury Group interior/exterior options. The revamped big-car line for '75 exchanged pure "hardtop styling" for "opera window" rooflines with fixed B-posts and heavily padded vinyl coverings. These models continued largely intact through 1979.

For 1977, the Mark IV was restyled inside and out to become the Mark V, distinguished by a crisper, lighter appearance. And appearances were not deceiving. Though it rode the same wheelbase and was little changed mechanically, the Mark V weighed some 500 pounds less than the Mark IV. It also boasted 21 percent more trunk space—which seemed like a large gain only because the IV had so little. Engineers paid belated attention to fuel economy by standardizing the corporate 400-cid V-8 with 179 net bhp. The old reliable 460-cid V-8 continued as an option except in California, where it could no longer meet the state's tougher emissions hurdles.

Model-year 1977 also saw Lincoln move into the luxury-compact class, its first response to the radically changed market left behind by the energy crisis. Called Versailles, this was a hastily contrived reply to Cadillac's remarkably successful 1975-76 Seville. It was little more than an everyday Ford Granada/Mercury Monarch adorned with a Continental-style square grille, a stand-up hood ornament and humped trunklid, plus more standard equipment. Established Lincoln buyers looked askance at the plebeian origins (which the press never failed to mention), while buyers balked at the $11,500 price. You can only fool some of the people some of the time, and Lincoln didn't fool many with this one. Versailles' 1977-model sales were a mere 15,434, a fraction of Seville's.

This basic three-car squad held the fort for 1978-79 while Lincoln readied a troop of downsized 1980 models. Amazingly, the big cars continued to sell well, defying the combined threat of further fuel shortages and a fleet of luxury intermediates from lesser makes. Part of this was due to circumstance. By 1979, anyone who wanted a truly large luxury car—"traditional-size," Lincoln called it—had precious few choices.

One of Lincoln's most successful marketing ploys in the '70s was the Designer Series. American Motors had tried something similar with Gucci Hornets and Pierre Cardin Javelins. As a luxury make, however, Lincoln was in a much better position to exploit the snob appeal of *haute couture* brands. First seen for

1975 Continental Mark IV hardtop coupe

1977 Continental Town coupe

1975 Continental Town Car four-door sedan

1978 Continental Mark V Diamond Jubilee Edition coupe

1977 Continental Mark V hardtop coupe

1979 Versailles four-door sedan

1976, these extra-cost packages were decorated inside and out with colors and materials specified by well-known high-fashion designers. The schemes varied somewhat from package to package and year to year, but the results were invariably striking and usually pleasing. Perhaps the most consistently tasteful was the Bill Blass edition, a nautically inspired blend of navy-blue paint and eggshell-white vinyl top outside and navy velour or dark blue-and-cream leather upholstery inside. Other combinations were created by Hubert Givenchy (generally turquoise or jade), Emilio Pucci (maroon and gunmetal grey), and Cartier (champagne/grey). The last, of course, was not a designer but the famous jeweler.

Following a spate of limited-edition 1978 packages to mark Ford Motor Company's 75th anniversary, Lincoln devised a "Collector Series" option group for the '79 Continental and Mark. Both were adorned with appropriate nameplates, gold grille accents, special midnight-blue metallic paint, and a host of "custom" accoutrements such as color-keyed umbrella and leather-bound owner's manual and tool kit. It marked the end of an era: The day of oversized Lincolns was over.

So, too, it seemed, any differences between Continentals and Marks. The 1980s were much more alike, but also much more sensible. Lincoln now adopted the "Panther" platform introduced for '79 with the full-size Ford LTD and Mercury Marquis as the basis for a substantially smaller Continental and an upmarket Mark VI sibling, thus resuming its 1958-60 practice of fielding two versions of one basic design. Compared to their immediate predecessors, these cars were up to 10 inches shorter between the wheels and significantly lighter. Yet they were nearly as spacious, thanks to only marginal reductions in width, plus taller, boxier styling.

Each line retained its usual appearance cues, but not the usual big-block engines. Standard for both was the corporate 302-cid small-block V-8 in new 129-bhp fuel-injected form; a 140-bhp 351 was the only option. It was all for the sake of economy, as was Ford Motor Company's new four-speed overdrive automatic transmission, basically a three-speed unit with a super-tall fourth gear added (0.67:1). Handling was more competent, thanks to a revised suspension, and refinement was emphasized with retuned body mounts and suspension bushings, plus standard high-pressure radial tires, which also helped eke out slightly more mpg. A pillared four-door Mark returned for the first time since 1960, and the various designer editions were bolstered by a new Signature Series much like the previous Collector option.

A second fuel shock occurred in 1979, touching off a deep national recession that drastically reduced 1980 volume throughout the industry. Lincoln suffered more than most, its model-year total skidding to just under 75,000—nearly 115,000 below '79. The underwhelming Versailles was in its final year and found fewer than 5000 buyers.

The 1981 result was even worse, falling to about 69,500. But

1979 Continental Collector's Series four-door sedan

1979 Continental Mark V Bill Blass Edition coupe

1980 Versailles four-door sedan

1980 Continental Town Car four-door sedan

1980 Continental Town coupe

that would be the decade low, and Lincoln followed the overall market in making a strong recovery. By 1985, it was up to some 166,500. Output dipped the following two years, then rebounded to over 215,000 through 1990. More important to proud division managers, Lincoln passed Cadillac in 1988, only to lose that position, but Ford's finest remained competitive with its arch-rival despite offering just three distinct models to Cadillac's five.

Remarkably, much of this success was owed to a single 1980-vintage four-door that saw only one major change through 1989: a rounded-corner "aero" facelift for 1985. Called Town Car after 1980, it soldiered on following the cancellation of the 114.3-inch-wheelbase Town Coupe after '81 and the Mark VI duo after '83. The throttle-body fuel-injected 302-cid V-8 was the only engine available after 1980, but it would be upgraded. After an '84 boost to 140 bhp came more sophisticated multi-point fuel injection that lifted horsepower to 155. Trim and equipment shuffles were the only alterations in most years.

But it didn't matter: At 50,000-100,000 units annually, this series outsold other Lincolns by margins of 2-to-1 or more—sometimes upwards of 5-to-1. Yes, the Town Car was smaller than its late-'70s predecessor, but it proved that traditional Detroit biggies still had a place in the '80s. As Mark Twain would have said, reports of their demise (in the wake of "Energy Crisis II") were greatly exaggerated.

Such consistent popularity was remarkable for this large, relatively old-fashioned car. Though Cadillac remained the luxury sales champ, its lead over Lincoln dwindled as the '80s progressed. One reason: An increasing portion of Cadillac sales depended on smaller "big" cars that looked too much like cheaper GM models and lacked the Town Car's sheer presence. Lincoln was quick to play up its rival's "lookalike" problem in snobbish TV commercials designed to pull in more and more "conquest" sales. Chrysler, meantime, had nothing remotely like a traditional full-size car after 1981, though its midsize Fifth Avenue found a steady market for the same reasons Town Car did: plentiful creature comforts in a package that "mature" buyers could relate to, all at reasonable prices. Of course, stickers swelled a lot on all cars from 1981 to '89--in the Town Car's case from about $14,000 to about $25,000. But relatively speaking, this Lincoln remained a good buy, and the public's "pocketbook vote" confirmed it.

If the late-'70s Versailles was a hasty reply to Cadillac's Seville, the new compact Continental sedan of 1982 was a more-considered response. It even had "bustleback" styling like that of the new 1980 front-drive Seville, plus a Mark-type grille and the usual base, Signature Series, and designer-edition trim and equipment variations.

Underneath, though, it was just a heavily modified Ford Fairmont with an extended-wheelbase version of the same rear-drive "Fox" platform—and it was really none the worse for it, except perhaps for rear-seat room, which was limited. A 232-cid V-6 was offered in the debut '82s, but proved somewhat weak for their weight, so most left the factory with injected 302 V-8s of 130, 140, or 150 bhp (the last adopted after 1985). The front and rear ends were smoothed out for '84 *a la* Town Car, the only appearance change for this design generation.

A noteworthy mechanical development was an antilock brake system (ABS), a 1985 option that became standard equipment for all Lincolns the following year. Developed jointly by Ford and the German company Alfred Teves, ABS greatly improved steering control in panic stops and shortened stopping distances on slick surfaces, a laudable safety advance.

The compact Continental was far more successful than the Versailles it effectively replaced, selling an average 21,000-26,000 a year through 1987. If not a vast aesthetic improvement, the bustleback sedan was more roadable and enjoyable, well put together, and as posh as any Lincoln. And at $21,000-$26,000, it, too, represented good luxury value.

After years of square-lined formality, Lincoln's premium coupe took a dramatic new direction with the 1984 Mark VII. Though it shared a platform with the bustleback Continental, this swoopy semifastback was derived from the new-for-'83 Ford Thunderbird/Mercury Cougar. The result was smooth, distinctive, and more visually aerodynamic than any previous Mark. A humped trunklid, modest taillamps in the rear fender trailing edges, and a toned-down Mark grille were stylistic links with the past, but the car was clearly aimed at a very different clientele: younger, affluent buyers who'd been defecting to high-dollar, high-status imports, a group Lincoln had never courted before. It was also a bold challenge to Cadillac's Eldorado, which was still relatively overblown.

The Mark VII was an instant critical success, especially the performance-oriented LSC (Luxury Sport Coupe)—the fabled "Hot Rod Lincoln" come to life. Enthusiast magazines even thought it a credible rival to the vaunted BMW 6-Series and Mercedes-Benz SEC. No wonder. Where the base and Designer models had a soft ride and traditional appointments, the LSC boasted a firmer suspension with fat performance tires on handsome cast-aluminum wheels, plus multiadjustable sport bucket seats and Lincoln's best cloth or leather upholstery. For 1985 it adopted the Mustang GT's high-output V-8 with 165 bhp (versus 140 for other models). The '86 got an even hotter port-injected engine with 200 bhp (versus 150 bhp on other Marks), plus standard ABS four-wheel disc brakes and a nice set of analog gauges (replacing the digital/graphic electronic display retained for its linemates). Engine refinements extracted another 25 bhp for 1988-90.

With all this, the LSC was the most overtly sporting Lincoln since the very first Continental and the most roadable Lincoln since the "Mexican Road Race" days. It was also one terrific buy at initial prices of $23,700—about half the cost of erstwhile German competitors. Lincoln-Mercury planners thought lesser VIIs would outsell it, but buyers confounded them by ordering more LSCs—enough that by 1988, the original four models had been cut to just LSC and Bill Blass. Overall Mark VII sales were good: 30,000-plus in the first season 15,000-38,000 thereafter. Prices inevitably escalated, reaching the $27,000 level by decade's end, but standard equipment also kept growing even as trim variations thinned. The 1990s boasted an important new safety feature in a standard driver-side airbag, which also brought a reworked, slightly more ergonomic dash.

Perhaps even more daring than the Mark VII was the all-new Continental sedan that bowed for 1988. Essentially a stretched version of the excellent midsize Ford Taurus/Mercury Sable, it was the first Lincoln with front-wheel drive and the first with all-independent suspension, both of which contributed to a noticeable increase in cabin room despite a wheelbase only half an inch longer than its bustleback predecessor's. In appearance, which L-M described as "aero limousine," this new Continental departed even more from tradition than the Mark VII: squarish but carefully detailed for efficient "airflow management." The old humped trunklid was abandoned at last, leaving only a vertical-bar grille to echo the past—and even that was low and smoothly curved to match the nose and modern flush-fit Euro-style headlamps.

Powering the new Continental was the 140-bhp 3.8-liter V-6 made optional for the '88 Taurus/Sable, mounted transversely (in typical front-drive fashion) and teamed with a four-speed overdrive automatic transaxle. It didn't provide much snap in the heavier Conti (which was little lighter than its rear-drive forebear), and even L-M officials later admitted the car was underpowered for its class. At least quietness was a strength. A

1980 Continental Mark VI Signature Series coupe

1983 Continental Signature Series sedan with carriage roof

1983 Continental Givenchy Designer Series four-door sedan

1983 Town Car Cartier Designer Series four-door sedan

1984 Continental Mark VII coupe

MacPherson-strut suspension employing dual-rate shock absorbers and LSC-style air springs, both computer-controlled, sounded great on paper. Unfortunately, this complicated design failed to provide a truly outstanding ride/handling balance in the real world. The standard all-disc brakes with ABS were superb, however, and interior decor was a blend of Euro-trendy and American traditional. For 1989, the dash and steering wheel were redesigned to accommodate dual airbags. Though just a driver-side airbag would have satisfied the government's new passive-restraint rule, Lincoln got the jump on Cadillac by providing inflatable cushions to protect both front occupants.

Arriving at dealers in December 1987, the front-drive Continental proved a strong seller, thanks partly to an attractive $26,000 base price—again, thousands less than comparable European sedans. Model-year production totaled about 41,000 for '88, rose to 57,775 for '89, then climbed above 64,000 for 1990. The Continental wouldn't fare this well again, but the mere fact that Lincolns could now stand comparison with high-buck foreigners spoke volumes about how far Lincoln had come in the '80s and where it hoped to go in the '90s.

A faint hint of that future arrived for 1990 in the first fully restyled Town Car in a decade. Actually, it was little more than the old model in new aerodynamic clothes. Dimensions, weight, and powertrain were all little changed. Not everyone liked the more rounded new look—but then, Lincoln had the unenviable task of needing to modernize its top-seller without making it look too different.

Indeed, designers tried hard to satisfy Town Car loyalists by retaining opera windows and a square "formal" grille, though both were tastefully muted. Also continued were the expected lush interiors with cushy bench seats, tufted upholstery, pseudo-wood dash trim and power everything. Base, Signature, and Cartier models were still available to ease the minds of troubled traditionalists. Yet the 1990s did advance the Town Car with high-tech features such as speed-sensitive power steering, self-leveling rear air springs, and airbags for both driver and front passenger—all standard at base prices in the $27,000-$32,000 range. Antilock brakes were optional at $936.

With all this, the rejuvenated Town Car was another sales hit on a lengthening Dearborn list. Model-year volume topped 147,000, a healthy gain of almost 20,000 over the still-popular '89. L-M must have heaved a big sigh of relief, for the Town Car still accounted for more than 60 percent of total Lincoln sales. For 1990 it outpolled the four-door Continental by over 2-to-1 and the Mark VIII by almost 7-to-1. It was thus a key factor in boosting Lincoln volume so much closer to Cadillac's.

But "closer" can still leave an unbridgeable gap, and Lincoln sales continued to trail Cadillac's into the early '90s by 22,000 to 78,000 units. Then again, Cadillac *should* have had the edge with its much broader lineup, so Lincoln did very well in run-

1985 Continental Mark VII LSC coupe

1986 Continental four-door sedan

1985 Continental four-door sedan

1987 Mark VII LSC coupe

1985 Town Car four-door sedan

1987 Continental Givenchy Designer Series four-door sedan

ning so consistently close with just three models. Evidently, a good many buyers agreed with the make's ad slogan of the time: "What a Luxury Car Should Be."

Even so, a sharp new recession and increasing luxury competition diminished Lincoln's yearly volume after 1990, pushing it down to the 160,000-197,000 range through middecade. But the Town Car kept rolling on, accounting for fewer buyers in this period but an even bigger piece of Lincoln's total sales pie, around two-thirds in this period.

Considered improvements played a part in this performance. The biggest one occurred for 1991, when Town Car introduced the first in a new Dearborn family of modern overhead-cam engines: the so-called "modular" (sometimes "mod") V-8. The name referred to a basic block that could also be used for V-6s and even slant-fours built on the same tooling and assembly lines. The core V-8 allotted to Town Car was a single-cam 4.6-liter unit with electronic multiport fuel injection and cast-iron block and heads. Standard horsepower was 190, up 40 from the ousted pushrod 302/5.0-liter, or 210 bhp with optional dual exhausts. Though not a huge advance for smoothness or quietness, the "mod" V-8 was more easily tuned than the old 302 for the tighter emissions limits then coming on the scene.

The '91 Town Car also boasted a revised front suspension for slightly crisper handling, plus better stopping ability via standard four-wheel disc brakes (versus rear drums). A new option also enhanced "active safety." Called Traction Assist, it was a simple form of traction control that relied on the ABS wheel-speed sensors and was thus tied to the available antilock brakes. When the sensors detected wheel slip, the system would automatically apply gentle pressure to the rear brakes until grip was restored. Other Lincolns would get this, too.

Town Car then stood pat for a few years, though there were notable minor changes. For example, 1992 brought more-responsive electronic shift control to the four-speed automatic transmission, plus a safety interlock that prevented shifting from Park without depressing the brake pedal, a legacy of the late '80s furor over "unintended acceleration." Research determined that unintended acceleration was caused by mistaking the accelerator for the brake pedal. Subtle grille and taillight revisions arrived for '93, as did a handling package option with somewhat firmer damping and wider tires on alloy wheels. The latter was welcome, if paradoxical for such a big cruiser. There was also a new "designer edition" for '93, this one inspired by golfing great Jack Nicklaus. It was offered only this one year for the midline Signature Series. The dual-exhaust engine became standard for '94, as did high-tech "solar-tint" glass for all windows. The '95s got a few cosmetic touchups, and the Signature and top-line Cartier gained a new three-mode power steering system that allowed choosing low, medium, or high steering effort with the push of a dashboard button.

If the Town Car was relatively static in this period, prices weren't, rising to a minimum $41,200 for a '95 Cartier. Despite this, sales held up well at some 125,000 for '91, over 113,000 for '92, and 117,000-118,000 for 1993-94. Though not a sales factor, Town Car was affected by a shortage of airbags in 1991-92, owing to tight supplies of airbag propellant. Indeed, some '91s had to be built without the planned passenger-side restraint. When supplies improved, however, Lincoln did the right thing by retrofitting airbags to those cars at no cost.

The Mark VII also marked time before closing out after the 1992 model year. The only interim change was upgrading the Bill Blass model to the same steering, suspension, tires, and alloy wheels as the sporty LSC. Mark sales plunged from more than 22,000 for model-year 1990 to just 15,000 for 1991 and '92 combined. There were two reasons for the decline. First, the Mark VII had been around nearly a decade—and looked it.

1988 Mark VII LSC coupe

1988 Continental Signature Series four-door sedan

1990 Town Car Cartier Designer Series four-door sedan

1990 Continental Signature Series four-door sedan

1990 Mark VII LSC coupe

Second, a brand-new Mark was waiting in the wings.

Arriving for 1993 as a single well-equipped coupe, the Mark VIII was even sleeker, smoother, and more "aero." It made the VII seem almost stodgy. Styling nodded to Mark heritage with a vertical-bar grille and trunklid tire hump, but both were sized and shaped to complement the overall design. Though certain design elements were debatable—especially the "predented" bodyside concavities—this was the most exciting Lincoln yet.

Structurally, the Mark VIII owed much to the latest MN12 Ford Thunderbird/Mercury Cougar, but was different enough to merit its own internal code, FN10. Compared to the Mark VII, it was 4.5 inches longer in wheelbase (using the 113-inch Thunderbird/Cougar span), 4.1 inches longer overall, and 3.7 inches wider, yet was actually 30 pounds lighter at the curb despite dual airbags and other added features. Engineering was more sophisticated than ever, with all-independent air-spring suspension *a la* Continental, speed-variable power steering and optional Traction Assist. Under the hood lurked a potent new engine: the promised twincam version of the "mod" V-8. Displacement was still 4.6 liters (281 cid), but a 32-valve aluminum cylinder head helped deliver a smashing 280 bhp and 285 pound-feet of torque. A four-speed automatic remained the only transmission, but gained electronic shift control. And for the first time, Mark drivers worked the shifter from a center console, part of a sweeping new "cockpit" dash wrapped in from the center to give a "fighter plane" feel.

The Mark VIII could almost fly like a jet. Despite giving away 15 horses to Cadillac's Northstar-powered Eldorado Touring Coupe, the Lincoln proved decisively quicker in *Consumer Guide®* tests, posting a 0-60-mph time of just 6.9 seconds versus 7.7 for the Eldo. But more than just straightline go, the new Mark set a new high for Lincoln roadability. Cornering was flat and stable, steering fast and informative, braking swift and sure. It also featured a unique air suspension that lowered the car at highway speeds for greater stability. About the only things not to like were certain ergonomic details and less total space than expected in a car of this bulk.

In all, the Mark VIII was a revelation: fast, supremely capable, quiet, luxurious, and comfortable. It was a very different Mark, but also even more of a match for BMW, Mercedes, and Japanese upstart Lexus. Considering that, price was a real eye-opener at well under $37,000 to start, thousands less than comparable *grand luxe* imports. Buyers responded by taking nearly 32,400 of the '93s and 28,000-plus for '94. The '95 tally was lower, but so was overall demand for luxury coupes.

Hoping to buck that trend, Lincoln revived the LSC badge for an even hotter Mark VIII, announced for 1995 but not available until model-year '96. Dual exhausts netted 290 bhp, while a firmed-up chassis gave more tenacious handling and roadholding. But this did nothing for Mark sales, which slipped again.

The tally went up slightly for '97, when the Mark got a serious freshening. A new hood and grille (flanked by high-intensity xenon headlamps) tilted the visual effect from "aero" back to "formal," and a reshaped tail sported a full-width neon light bar instead of incandescent bulbs. Among other changes were reshaped seats, standard power tilt/telescope steering column, brighter dashboard lighting, and the addition of wood cabin trim, which seemed at odds with the original "high-tech" design theme. The chassis gained uprated shock absorbers, larger antiroll bars and standard traction control. The LSC got even sportier calibrations and an extra 10 bhp. But the luxury-coupe market kept shrinking, so Lincoln decided to cancel the Mark VIII after 1998, when production was down to just 6100 units.

The Continental sedan carried through 1994 with considered yearly improvements but no great alterations to the successful front-drive formula of 1988. The base model was renamed Executive Series for '91, when the pushrod 3.8 V-6 gained standard dual exhausts and 10 bhp for 155 total. Another five bhp arrived the following year via internal engine changes. Like Town Car, the Continental picked up electronic transmission control ('91), shift interlock ('92), the usual trim and appearance shuffles, and a few extra standard features, plus new optional items like front bucket seats (for Executive from '93) and remote keyless-entry system. Also prevailing here were spotty passenger-side airbag availability for 1990-92 models, and steady price escalation that lifted base stickers into the mid-$30,000 range by 1994. Production went the other way, falling to 26,798 by '93, less than half the 1990 total—which made the '94 tally of more than 52,000 a real surprise.

An all-new Continental debuted for 1995, appearing just ahead of Lincoln's 75th birthday. Though still front-drive, it was rather like a Mark VIII in more conservative four-door dress. It even had the same twincam V-8, though transverse mounting and a more restrictive exhaust robbed 20 horses to leave "just" 260. Wheelbase was unchanged, and width and height were up only an inch apiece, but weight ballooned nearly 400 pounds despite the use of plasticlike sheet-molding compound to replace steel in the hood, trunklid, and fenders. Some of the extra weight reflected a stiffer unitized structure with more sound-deadening. Other pounds came from added standard features like the full automatic climate control with pollen microfilter. Dual airbags and ABS were again included, and there was a no-cost choice of front seating: three-place bench with column shift or buckets with console shift.

Trying more than most cars to be all things to all people, the '95 Continental came with a dazzling bit of electronic trickery called the Memory Profile System (MPS). This provided "his and her" adjustments for many functions including the position of the power mirrors, driver's seat, and steering wheel (the last an electric tilt/telescopic affair); as well as personalized radio presets, power window and alarm operation, and—most novel of all—suspension and steering calibrations.

1992 Town Car Signature Series four-door sedan

1993 Mark VIII coupe

Like its predecessor, the '95 Continental rode an all-independent air-spring suspension, but with a second, horizontal pair of shock absorbers added in back. All shocks were electronically controlled, like the air springs and now the steering, too. All this allowed rigging the system to allow choosing Firm, Normal, or Plush damping via the MPS control panel. Steering assist still decreased as road speed increased, but overall effort could be varied through Low, Medium, and High modes. Dearborn's computer nerds widely prohibited a combination of Plush damping and Low steering effort, but differences weren't that great among the many possible settings. In fact, the car felt best in the Normal/Medium "default" mode. Firm/High only made the ride more fidgety and helm work more tiring.

With all its new gadgetry, the '95 Continental cost a good $5000 more than the last of the V-6 generation, the lone sedan running higher in the "near-luxury" class at $40,750. Options were restricted to chrome wheels, voice-activated cell phone (complete with a dashboard display for signal strength and call duration), power moonroof, all-speed traction control, CD changer, and a novel wheeled "cart" that moved back and forth in the trunk and could be partitioned for carrying smaller items so they wouldn't tip over.

And so the battle was joined: front-drive V-8 Lincoln versus front-drive V-8 Cadillacs. On paper, the Continental covered all the bases. (Company marketers even coined the snappy name "InTech" for the dohc engine used here and in later Mark VIIIs, a reply to Cadillac's Northstar V-8.) The only question involved styling: Would buyers prefer the Conti's lozenge look or the more formal sharp-edged Cadillacs? The answer came quickly. Continental sales started slowly, about 45,000 in 1995, and continued at a modest pace that was well below expectations.

Added during the first full production year was a Personal Security Package comprising Lincoln's RESCU System—a cell phone link to a special emergency operator—and Michelin run-flat tires. But that didn't help turn the tide. Neither did a considerable $4600 price cut for '96, when a traction-control system became standard. It was clear to all concerned that stronger measures were needed.

They arrived with a 1998 redesign that made a substantial change in the Continental's character. Realizing a heavily sculpted look was no less controversial here than on parent Ford's latest Taurus, Lincoln designers went conservative, applying simple rounded sides and a more upright frontal aspect, plus shorter front and rear overhangs. The driver-adjustable suspension was relegated to the options list, where it was paired with a few minor features to make a Driver Select System. Otherwise, it was conventional shocks and simple rear load-leveling suspension, though the three-mode power steering remained standard. Model-year production rose by some 4000 units from '97, but that qualified as disappointing.

After gaining 15 horses for 1999, the front-drive Conti cruised on without major change. The RESCU option was dropped for 2001, then returned as a Vehicle Communications System. Also for 2002, as with other Dearborn products, major options were repackaged as "models": in this instance base, Driver Select, Personal Security, and Luxury Appearance (a gussied-up Driver Select). Signing on later was a $1550 Collector's Edition package with leather/suede interior and chrome wheels.

That suggested the Continental was about to exit. Sure enough, it didn't return for 2003, mourned no more than the Mark VIII was. Sales had been declining each year since 1998, and were down to less than 15,500 by calendar '02. Several factors were at work, including a broad ongoing buyer shift from cars to sport-utility vehicles all across the price spectrum. But the main problem was ever-stronger competition from import-brand cars with more prestigious nameplates. In the end, the front-drive Continental was a competent upscale sedan that ultimately couldn't cut it in a very cutthroat market.

SUVs were storming that market. Most every one posted impressive sales gains each year, prompting even more entries as the '90s progressed. Significantly, many people began buying SUVs as replacements for cars, and some splurged for high-end models with all the trappings they could get. Taking stock of this lucrative action, Lincoln fielded the Navigator for 1998. Though based on Ford's popular full-size Expedition SUV, it stood apart with a Lincoln grille, a few new body panels, a much dressier interior, and a number of standard features that were options on the Ford, including a 230-bhp 5.4-liter "Triton" V-8 with single overhead camshaft. At first, executives worried that people might balk at a gilded Ford costing some $10,000 more. "At least we won't be out too much money if it doesn't work," one Lincoln honcho said privately. But the Navigator did work, immediately zooming to the number-two spot in Lincoln sales with nearly 44,000 units for calendar '98. Cadillac, caught by surprise, rushed out a luxury GMC Yukon as the 1999 Escalade. Lincoln replied by adding 30 horses to that year's Navigator, then substituting an exclusive twincam 5.4-liter InTech V-8 with 300 bhp.

As Lincoln's first truck, the Navigator attracted buyers who had never looked at a Lincoln before, just what planners had hoped. Though it lost some sales momentum once Escalade arrived, Navigator remained vital to Lincoln sales into the new century, good for roughly 32,000 to 39,000 orders per year, each one a high-margin payday. After adding a few conveniences through 2002, Navigator was fully redesigned with a ride-enhancing independent rear suspension and power-operating standard third-row bench seat, both class firsts shared with Expedition. The makeover also introduced Ford's Advance

1995 Town Car Signature Series four-door sedan

1996 Continental four-door sedan

1997 Town Car four-door sedan

1998 Continental four-door sedan

1998 Town Car four-door sedan

1998 Navigator four-door wagon

1999 Continental four-door sedan

Trac antiskid/traction-control system as an option and standard curtain side airbags to protect the heads of those in the first- and second-row bucket seats. Two other new extras were unique to Navigator among SUVs: a power-operated liftgate and power running-board side steps that automatically moved in or out when opening or closing a door. Sales finally weakened in calendar 2005, sliding below 26,000, though that was mainly due to a sharp spike in gas prices—in some places to an unheard-of $3-plus a gallon.

But Lincoln was still a novice with trucks, and proved it with the 2002-03 Blackwood. This full-zoot take on the Ford F-150 Super Crew four-door pickup mated the Navigator's 300-bhp V-8 and front-end sheetmetal with a special four-foot, eight-inch cargo box with a power-operated front-hinged hard cover. Lincoln hoped to sell 18,000 Blackwoods in the first two model years, mainly to trailer-towing horse owners and other landed gentry, but moved less than a quarter of that number before giving up. This failure was easy to explain: Blackwood was pricey for a pickup—no less than $52,000—yet woefully impractical. Serious truckers laughed at the lack of a four-wheel-drive option, the beautifully trimmed but coffin-small load bed, and the swing-out tail doors instead of a swing-down gate. If nothing else, the Blackwood is rare enough that it may interest collectors someday.

Lincoln was little more successful with its second SUV. A 2003 debut, the Aviator applied Navigator-like styling and trappings to the familiar Ford Explorer and related Mercury Mountaineer. Included were that pair's optional 4.6-liter V-8 with a bit more power, curtain side airbags, power-adjustable pedals, rear-obstacle-detection system, and an uptown interior. A laudable 2004 option became standard for model-year '05: the Advance Trac antiskid system with new Roll Stability Control. Developed by Volvo, now owned by Dearborn (see Ford), RSC employed special sensors that could detect an impending rollover and would automatically activate the antiskid system to help prevent it. But despite numerous standard goodies and fair pricing, the Aviator never took off, and Lincoln bailed after 2005. Buyers were demanding more "car" in their SUVs, and Aviator was still too much a truck.

By contrast, the old Town Car kept cruising on as the most valuable player in the franchise, accounting for at least 50 percent of Lincoln calendar-year car sales from 1998 through 2005. Trouble is, if the star goes into a slump, the whole team suffers, and that's what happened. For those eight model years, Town Car and total Lincoln car sales tailed off in almost perfect unison. Things would have been worse without the Navigator's help, but they were bad enough, car volume plunging more than 50 percent for the period from 150,000 units to just over 71,000. In this, Lincoln symbolized the steady decline of Ford Motor Company itself (see Ford).

In what must have been an "uh-oh" moment for Lincoln planners, Town Car sales were flat for 1998 despite heavy surgery that replaced dated boxiness with a massive rounded form. One wag termed it "a bloated copy of [a 1950s] Mark IX Jaguar"—rather damning given that Lincoln and Jaguar were now corporate cousins. At least the restyle trimmed a helpful three inches from overall length and some 200 pounds from heft. Engine retuning added 10 horses to the Executive and midlevel Signature models. The dual-exhaust V-8 returned with 220 bhp for the top-line Cartier and a $500 Signature Touring Package. Traction control, leather upholstery, and a 40/20/40 split front bench seat were all newly standard.

The addition of front side airbags was Town Car's main news for 1999. The 2000s were mostly reruns, but the following year brought more power, with the base V-8 hiked to 225 bhp, the dual-exhaust version to 240. Also new for 2001 was the Cartier L, a "stretch" job of the sort limousine builders had been doing for years. The stretch here was a modest six inches, all in the wheelbase to provide king-size rear leg room. Rear doors were elongated to match. Fittingly, in a literal sense, Lincoln hired the towering Shaquille O'Neill of L.A. Lakers basketball fame to introduce the L to the press.

Another extensive makeover occurred for Lincoln's 90th-anniversary year and Ford Motor Company's centennial. In a modest nod to new-century expectations, the 2003 Town Car received more coherent styling via new sheetmetal at each end, plus a stiffer frame, revised suspension, and more precise rack-and-pinion steering to replace recirculating ball. Brakes added a "panic assist" feature that automatically kicked in full hydraulic power on a rapid push of the pedal, even without full force. Front side airbags and 17-inch wheels became standard, as did a dual-exhaust V-8 with 239 bhp, up 14 horses. Rear obstacle detection also joined the features array. Lincoln hoped all this would prompt luxury-class buyers to put Town Car on their short lists along with the Lexus LS 430 and comparable big German sedans. But though the '03s were the most roadable Town Cars yet, they did nothing to change the model's yesteryear image, and sales kept sliding through 2005.

Lincoln was now struggling to redefine itself for a new era. If Town Car and "American luxury" no longer ensured profits, what would? Affluent younger buyers hooked on high-status imports mostly associated Lincoln with the Town Car, which made a fine limousine but wasn't something they'd want in their driveways. Lincoln needed to win over such folks, who now dominated the luxury market, but how? These were tough questions, and finding answers was complicated by mounting problems and shifting tactics in Dearborn.

As one telling example, Ford decided to move Lincoln and Mercury sales and marketing staff to the company's Irvine, California, campus in July 1998. Southern California, so the reasoning went, was a hotbed of automotive talent and innovation; planting two wilted brands in such fertile soil would surely help them blossom anew. Three years later, L-M was folded into the Premier Automotive Group, a Southern California-based subsidiary formed in 1999 as an umbrella for Ford's high-end marques: Aston Martin and Jaguar, purchased in the early '90s, and newly acquired Volvo and Land Rover. But it fast became clear that Lincoln and Mercury were out of place at PAG, each beset by daunting challenges that couldn't be resolved by simply soaking up "SoCal" culture. Accordingly, both brands were reabsorbed into Ford North American Operations in April 2002; personnel were ordered back to Michigan seven months later. One top executive said it was only "good business sense" for L-M "to co-locate with Ford Division" again, but many thought the explanation lame.

While that drama played out, Lincoln introduced a youthful replacement for the Continental aimed boldly at high-buck imports. Simply called LS—for "luxury sport"—this midsize sedan employed a new rear-drive "DEW98" platform developed with Jaguar and shared with the British brand's midrange S-Type sedan. Both models arrived for 2000, but looked nothing alike. Where the curvy S-Type recalled Jaguar's beloved "Mark II" series of the 1950s, the LS referenced no previous Lincoln. It was crisp, clean, and contemporary, though not a groundbreaking design. Marketing dictates required the S-Type be imported from Britain with higher-grade trim and equipment than the American-made Lincoln. The Jag also had somewhat more power, though each version used the same basic twincam multivalve engines: Ford's own 3.0-liter "Duratec" V-6 and a Jaguar-designed V-8 billed as a 4.0-liter in the S-Type, a 3.9 in the LS. Because Jaguar buyers

2000 Continental four-door sedan

2001 Town Car Cartier L four-door sedan

2001 LS four-door sedan

2002 LS four-door sedan

2002 Continental four-door sedan

2003 Aviator four-door wagon

2003 LS four-door sedan

2003 Town Car four-door sedan

2004 LSE four-door sedan

2006 Zephyr four-door sedan

were typically wealthier than Lincoln folk, S-Types ran some $10,000 higher than comparable LSes, making the Lincolns quite a buy at an introductory starting price of $31,000. Indeed, strong "near-luxury" value was a prime reason the LS copped *Motor Trend* magazine's 2000 Car of the Year award.

Yet this was no poor Yankee relation. Like the S-Type, the LS had such requisite sport sedan credentials as a taut all-independent suspension (with no electronic tricks), powerful four-wheel antilock disc brakes, traction control, firm rack-and-pinion steering, and front torso side airbags. And though less sumptuous inside, the Lincoln had enough wood and leather to suit a Jaguar, plus all the comforts and conveniences Americans expected. Advance Trac antiskid system and a Sport suspension/appearance package were also offered. And where S-Types came only with five-speed automatic transmission, the V-6 LS offered a five-speed manual too. Not many buyers opted for it, but it indicated that Lincoln was serious about the enthusiast market.

The driver-focused LS was a radical break with Town Car tradition, but necessary and overdue. "Lincoln has taken a pronounced risk with the very Euro-themed LS," said Motor Trend. "...[T]he result fortunately justifies the gamble. The LS not only brings a new dimension to Lincoln... it's simply a blast to drive." Indeed it was: agile and assured on twisty roads and quick on the straights, with 0-60 mph taking around 7.4 seconds for a manual V-6, 7.2 for an automatic V-8. "Simply put," MT concluded, "the LS is the car that wholly changes the image of what an American luxury sedan can be."

But the LS did little to change Lincoln's fuzzy image or bottom line. A sporty four-door was a showroom oddity among Town Cars and "lux trucks," and buyers could find more status for similar money elsewhere. Sales waned quickly as a result, dropping from a first-year 61,000 to the high 30,000s in 2001-03, then skidding below 20,000 in calendar '05. Lincoln tried hard to lure buyers en route, juggling features and options each season; boosting V-6 power two years straight; and muscling up the V-8 for 2003, when all models received a mild restyle and changes to "more than 500 components and systems." *Car and Driver* found lots to like in its test '03 V-8 Sport—including a quicker 6.7-second 0-60 mph dash—but bemoaned steady price creep that had pushed a well-equipped LS to near $50,000. "...Lincoln thinks it can compete without a price advantage. Good luck. As exemplary as it may be, the LS lacks the reputation of its rivals—Lexus for its antiseptic perfection, Mercedes for its unassailable pedigree, and BMW for its arrogant dash. Intangibles, to be sure, but in this class, perceptions count."

With Dearborn fast approaching the brink, the LS rolled on through 2004-06 with no further changes of note. It then died as an early casualty of Ford's "Way Forward" belt-tightening program, announced in early '06. The LS was a bold step for Lincoln, but it was only a first step. Had it been quickly followed by a similarly sporty compact sedan, Lincoln might be in much better shape as we write.

Still, it may not too late for Lincoln to transform its image and near-term prospects, as vital new products are now reaching showrooms or soon will be. Though all have Ford and/or Mercury counterparts, Lexus has succeeded handsomely with various tarted-up Toyotas, giving hope that Lincoln's newest can do likewise.

Two of them bowed for 2006. First up was the Mark LT, a "proper" luxury pickup based on the redesigned 2005 F-150 SuperCrew. The Lincolnized truck avoided the old Blackwood's foibles with a work-ready 5.5-foot-long cargo bed and available four-wheel drive with low-range gearing. A 300-bhp 5.4-liter V-8 and four-speed automatic transmission were

2007 MKX four-door wagon

2007 MKZ four-door sedan

familiar (also mandatory), but most everything else was inherited from the well-regarded new F-Series. *Consumer Guide®* thought Lincoln should have splurged for a more upscale interior, a unique engine, and safety features like curtain side airbags and antiskid system, the last available on the corporate shelf but not offered even as options. But Lincoln may correct those oversights in time, and fewer specific components allowed pricing the LT lower than the Blackwood: just under $39,000 with two-wheel drive, a bit over $42,000 with 4WD. One thing didn't change: Lincoln was still the only luxury brand to offer a full-size pickup—a "difference to sell" that could yet pay off.

Also arriving for '06 was Lincoln's smallest car ever, a front-wheel-drive midsize sedan reviving the historic Zephyr name. The basic design was shared with that year's new Ford Fusion/Mercury Milan and owed much to Japanese partner Mazda, but the Zephyr had all the essentials of a modern near-luxury car, including antilock disc brakes, front and curtain side airbags, dual-zone climate control, and a reasonably roomy leather-upholstered cabin. Fusion/Milan charged extra for a 221-bhp 3.0-liter Duratec V-6 and six-speed automatic transmission, but both were standard for Zephyr. So was a unique twin-cowl instrument panel recalling the dashboards of classic early '60s Continentals. Competitively priced at $29,000 to start, the Zephyr aimed at first-time luxury-class customers seeking a comfortable, well-appointed tourer, though it had sport sedan potential that Lincoln could exploit one day. Meanwhile, Lincoln focused on higher "brand recognition" by discarding model names for "MK" labels—which is why the Zephyr was rebadged MKZ for 2007.

For the same reason, a totally different Aviator appeared for 2007 as the MKX. A sister to that year's new Ford Edge, it was Lincoln's first shot at the lucrative luxury "crossover" market exemplified by the popular Lexus RX wagon. Ford followed a similar formula, employing a car-type platform (designated CD3 and developed with Volvo) with front drive and optional all-wheel drive. The powertrain was fresh, too, comprising a 250-bhp 3.5-liter V-6 and a six-speed automatic transmission codeveloped with General Motors. Predictably, the main differences with Edge involved more standard features and available luxuries, plus a fine-checked grille reminiscent of '60s Lincolns. Though the MKX was just emerging as this book was prepared, it suggests that Dearborn is prepared to give Lincoln whatever it takes to ensure a successful future.

Part of that future rides with the so-called MKS, a new large sedan expected for 2008. It's the smaller of two such Lincoln models based on the corporate "D3" platform, another Volvo collaboration that premiered with the 2005 Ford Five Hundred/Mercury Montego. The apparent plan is to have this pair replace the LS and the venerable Town Car. The MKS was previewed in early 2006 with a "teaser" concept distinguished by crisp, tightly drawn styling and a 315-bhp 4.4-liter V-8 driving all four wheels through a six-speed automatic transmission. "What that concept does for us," declared one Dearborn exec, "is say, 'OK, we're not stopping. [Lincoln is] going to be back. That is very, very important."

We couldn't agree more. The American auto industry seemed down for the count by 2005. Some of its problems were self-inflicted, some the result of forces it couldn't control or have anticipated. Whether Lincoln and the rest of Detroit can rise again remains to be seen, but we, at least, are hopeful. Stranger things have happened.

Specifications

1930

Model L (wb 136.0)	Wght	Price	Prod
conv rdstr 2-4P	4,740	4,500	12
spt phtn 4P	4,840	4,200	53
spt phtn 4P, tonnu-cwl	4,850	4,400	90
spt touring 7P	4,940	4,200	79
cpe 5P	4,940	4,400	275
Town sdn 2W 4P	5,010	4,400	169
Town sdn 3W 4P	5,010	4,400	285
sdn 4d 2-3W	5,180	4,500	541
sdn 7P	5,245	4,700	458
limo 7P	5,190	4,900	329
chassis	—	3,500	47
Custom bodies:			
Locke spt rdstr	—	—	15
Judkins cpe 2P	4,790	5,000	65
Judkins brline 4P 2W	5,280	5,600	72
Judkins brline 4P 3W	4,930	5,600	100
Brunn brghm A/W 7P	5,045	7,000	68
Brunn cab s.c. A/W 7P	4,985	7,200	44
LeBaron conv rdstr	—	—	100
LeBaron cab 7P	5,370	7,200	—
LeBaron A/W cab 7P	5,045	6,900	29
LBrn cab 7P semi-clpsble	5,190	7,100	20
LeBaron cpe-sdn 4P	5,030	5,300	8
Willoughby limo 6P	5,180	5,900	244
Willghby brghm A/W	5,900	NA	5
Dietrich conv cpe 4P	5,180	6,200	42
Dietrich conv sdn 5P	5,235	6,600	40
Derham conv cpe 4P	4,850	6,400	1
Derham phaeton	6,000	NA	21

1930 Engine	bore×stroke	bhp	availability
V-8, 385.0	3.50×5.00	90	S-all

1931

201 Model K (wb 145.0)		Wght	Price	Prod
202A	dual-cowl spt phtn 5P	4,970	4,600	77
202B	spt phaeton 5P	4,960	4,400	60
203	spt tourer 7P	5,060	4,400	45
204A	Town sdn 5P 2W	5,130	4,600	195
204B	Town sdn 5P 3W	5,130	4,600	447
205	sdn 5P	5,300	4,700	552
206	cpe 5P	5,060	4,600	225
207A	sdn 7P	5,365	4,900	521
207B/C	limo 7P	5,310	5,100	401
208A	Brunn cab A/W	5,280	7,400	30
209	Brunn brghm A/W	5,165	7,200	34
210	Dietrich conv cpe 4P	5,300	6,400	25
211	Dietrich sdn 4d	5,355	6,800	65
212	Derham phtn 4P	4,970	6,200	11
213A	Judkins brlin 4P 3W	5,050	5,800	171
214	LBrn conv rdstr 2-4P	4,860	4,700	275
215	Willoughby limo 6P	5,300	6,100	151
216	Willghby panel brghm 7P	5,340	7,400	15
217A	LeBaron Cab A/W 7P	5,165	7,100	21
217B	LBrn Cab 7P semi-clpsble	5,100	7,300	
218	Judkins cpe 2P	4,910	5,200	86
219	Dietrich cpe 2P	5,050	—	35
201	chassis, 145" wb	—	—	61
220	chassis, 150" wb	—	—	3
221	chassis, 155" wb	—	—	3
—	misc. specials	—	—	47

1931 Engine	bore×stroke	bhp	availability
V-8, 385.0	3.50×5.00	120	S-all

1932

501 Model KA (wb 136.0)		Wght	Price	Prod
502A	cpe 2P	5,335	3,200	86
502B	cpe 2-4P	5,205	3,245	
504	Town sdn 5P	5,330	3,100	147
505	sdn 4d	5,300	3,200	921
506	victoria 5P	5,345	3,200	265
507A	sdn 7P	5,435	3,300	508
507B	limo 7P	5,520	3,350	122
508	phaeton	5,270	3,000	29
510A	rdstr 2P	5,050	2,900	12
510B	rdstr 2-4P	5,180	2,945	
501	chassis	—	—	7
—	misc. & unaccounted	—	—	127

231 Model KB (wb 145.0)		Wght	Price	Prod
232A	Mrphy dual-cwl spt phtn 4P	5,625	4,500	30
232B	Murphy spt phtn 4P	5,250	4,300	13
233	spt touring 7P	5,720	4,300	24
234A	Town sdn 5P 2W	5,740	4,500	123
234B	Town sdn 5P 3W	5,740	4,500	200
235	sdn 4d	5,975	4,600	216
236	cpe 5P	5,600	4,400	83
237A	sdn 7P	5,975	4,700	266
237B	limo 7P	5,990	4,900	41
237C	limo 7P	5,900	4,000	135
238	Brunn cab A/W 5P	5,855	7,200	14
239	Brunn brghm A/W 7P	5,920	7,000	13
240	Dietrich spt brlin 5P	5,605	6,500	8
241	Dietrich conv sdn 5P	5,720	6,400	20
242A	Dietrich cpe 2-4P	5,745	5,150	17
242B	Dietrich cpe 2P	5,710	5,000	
243A	Jdkns berline 5P 2W	5,860	5,700	74
243B	Jdkns berline 5P 3W	5,860	5,700	
244A	Judkins cpe 2-4P	5,610	5,350	23
244B	Judkins cpe 2P	5,595	5,100	
245	Willoughby limo 7P	5,950	5,900	64
246	Willghby pnl brghm 4P	5,855	7,100	4
247	Wtrhouse conv vic 5P	5,470	5,900	10
248	LeBaron rdstr 2-4P	5,535	4,600	112
249	Murphy spt rdstr 2P	5,605	6,800	5
231	chassis, 145" wb	—	—	18
250	chassis, 150" wb	—	—	1
—	misc. specials	—	—	13

1932 Engines	bore×stroke	bhp	availability
V-8, 385.0	3.50×5.00	125	S-KA
V-12, 448.0	3.25×4.50	150	S-KB

1933

511 Model KA (wb 136.0)		Wght	Price	Prod
512A	cpe 2-4P	4,929	3,145	44
512B	cpe 2P	4,909	3,100	
513A	conv rdstr 2-4P	4,769	3,200	85
514	Town sdn 5P	4,954	3,100	201
515	sdn 4d	4,989	3,200	320
516	victoria 5P	4,919	3,200	109
517A	sdn 7P	5,159	3,300	190
517B	limo 7P	5,184	3,350	111
518A	dual-cowl phaeton 5P	4,759	3,200	12
518B	phaeton 5P	4,749	3,000	12
519	phaeton 7P	4,759	3,200	10
520A	rdstr 2-4P	4,739	2,745	12
520B	rdstr 2P	4,719	2,700	
511	chassis	—	—	7
—	misc. specials	—	—	5

251 Model KB (wb 145.0)		Wght	Price	Prod
252A	dual-cowl phtn 5P	5,310	4,400	9
252B	spt phaeton 4P	5,220	4,200	6
253	spt touring 7P	5,310	4,300	6
254A	Town sdn 2W	5,401	4,300	39
254B	Town sdn 3W	5,401	4,400	41
255	sdn 4d	5,491	4,500	52
256	victoria cpe 5P	5,511	4,300	18
257A	sdn 7P	5,521	4,600	110
257B	limo 7P	5,571	4,800	105
258C	Brunn cab 5P	5,685	6,900	8
258D	Brunn cab semi-clpsble 5P	5,386	6,900	
259B	Brunn brougham 7P	5,431	6,900	13
260	Brunn conv cpe 5P	5,171	5,700	15
260	Dietrich spt berline 5P	—	—	—

251 Model KB		Wght	Price	Prod
261	Dietrich conv sdn 5P	5,410	6,100	15
263A	Judkins brlin 2W 4P	5,411	5,500	36
263B	Judkins brlin 3W 4P	5,411	5,500	
264D	Judkins cpe 2P	5,530	5,000	12
265B	Willoughby limo 7P	5,541	5,700	40
267B	LeBrn conv rdstr 2-4P	5,191	4,500	37
2197	Dietrich cpe 2P	—	4,900	8
251	chassis	—	—	4
—	chassis, 155" wb	—	—	1
—	misc. specials	—	—	19

1933 Engines	bore×stroke	bhp	availability
V-12, 381.7	3.00×4.50	125	S-KA
V-12, 448.0	3.25×4.50	150	S-KB

1934

521 Model KA (wb 136.0)		Wght	Price	Prod
522A	cpe 2-4P	4,879	3,250	60
522B	cpe 2P	5,210	3,200	
523	conv rdstr 2-4P	5,050	3,400	75
524	Town sdn 5P	5,140	3,450	450
525	sdn 4d	5,044	3,400	425
526	victoria cpe 5P	5,029	3,400	115
527A	sdn 7P	5,203	3,500	275
527B	limo 7P	5,228	3,550	175
531	conv sdn phtn 5P	5,029	3,900	75
521	chassis	—	—	21
—	misc. specials	—	—	8

271 Model KB (wb 145.0)		Wght	Price	Prod
273	touring 7P	5,720	4,200	20
277A	sdn 7P	5,510	4,500	210
277B	limo 7P	5,570	4,700	215
278A	Brunn cb 5P sm-clpsbl	5,315	6,800	13
278B	Brunn cab 5P	5,615	6,800	
279	Brunn brougham 7P	5,480	6,800	15
280	Brunn conv cpe 5P	5,045	5,600	25
281	Dietrich conv sdn 5P	5,330	5,600	25
282	Judkins sdn limo 7P	5,570	5,700	27
283A	Judkins berlin 4P 2W	5,710	5,400	37
283B	Judkins berlin 4P 3W	5,710	5,400	17
285	Willoughby limo 7P	5,605	5,600	77
287	LeBrn conv rdstr 2-4P	5,085	4,400	45
271	chassis	—	—	12
—	misc. specials	—	—	14

1934 Engine	bore×stroke	bhp	availability
V-12, 414.0	3.13×4.50	150	S-all

1935

541 Model K (wb 136.0)		Wght	Price	Prod
542	LeBrn conv rdstr 2-4P	5,030	4,600	30
543	sdn 4d 2W	5,385	4,300	170
544	sdn 4d 3W	5,375	4,300	278
545	cpe 5P	5,230	4,200	44
546	LeBrn cnv sdn phtn 5P	5,360	5,000	20
547	Brunn conv vic 5P	5,135	5,500	15
548	LeBaron cpe 2P	5,030	4,600	23
541	chassis	—	—	1
—	misc. specials	—	—	5

301 Model K (wb 145.0)		Wght	Price	Prod
302	touring 7P	5,225	4,200	15
303A	sdn 7P	5,535	4,600	351
303B	limo 7P	5,630	4,700	282
304A	Brunn cab 5P	5,505	6,600	13
304B	Brunn cb 5P sm-clpsbl	5,415	6,700	13
305	Brunn brougham 7P	5,530	6,700	10
307	LeBaron conv sdn 5P	5,325	5,500	20
308	Judkins limo 7P	5,645	5,700	18
309A	Judkins berline 2W	5,545	5,500	34
309B	Judkins berline 3W	5,555	5,500	13
310	Willoughby limo 7P	5,695	5,700	40
311	Willoughby spt sdn	5,075	6,800	5
301	chassis	—	—	8
—	misc. specials	—	—	26

1935 Engine	bore×stroke	bhp	availability
V-12, 414.0	3.13×4.50	150	S-all

1936

Series H Zephyr (wb 122.0)		Wght	Price	Prod
902	sdn 4d	3,349	1,320	13,180
903	sdn 2d	3,289	1,275	1,814

Model K (wb 136.0)		Wght	Price	Prod
324A	sdn 5P 2W	5,426	4,300	103
324B	sdn 5P 3W	5,476	4,300	297
326	cpe 5P	5,266	4,200	36
328	Brunn conv vic 5P	5,176	5,500	10
330	LeBrn conv rdstr 2-4P	5,136	4,700	20
332	LeBaron cpe 2-4P	4,700	5,126	25
334	LeBrn cnv sdn phtn 5P	5,296	5,000	15

Model K (wb 145.0)		Wght	Price	Prod
323	touring 7P	5,276	4,200	8
327A	sdn 7P	5,591	4,600	368
327B	limo 7P	5,641	4,700	370
329A	Brunn cab 5P	5,511	6,600	10
329B	Brunn cb 5P sm-clpsbl	5,491	6,700	10
331	Brunn brougham 7P	5,571	6,700	20
333	LeBaron conv sdn 5P	5,381	5,500	30
335	Judkins sdn limo 7P	5,671	5,800	26
337A	Judkins berline 5P 2W	5,561	5,500	51
337B	Judkins berline 5P 3W	5,581	5,600	13
339	Willoughby limo 7P	5,661	5,700	62
341	Willoughby spt sdn	5,561	6,800	11
321	chassis	—	—	9
—	misc. specials	—	—	30
322	chassis	—	—	6
—	misc. specials	—	—	4

1936 Engines	bore×stroke	bhp	availability
V-12, 267.3	2.75×3.75	110	S-Zephyr
V-12, 414.0	3.13×4.50	150	S-K

1937

Series HB Zephyr (wb 122.0)		Wght	Price	Prod
700	cpe sdn	3,289	1,245	1,500
720	cpe	3,323	1,165	5,199
730	sdn 4d	3,349	1,265	23,159
737	Town sdn	3,507	1,425	139

Model K (wb 136.0; lwb-145.0)		Wght	Price	Prod
353	Willghby tour 7P (lwb)	5,950	5,550	7
354A	sdn 5P 2W	5,700	4,450	48
354B	sdn 5P 3W	5,700	4,450	136
356	Willoughby cpe 5P	5,790	5,550	6
357A	lwb sdn 7P	5,905	4,750	212
357B	limo 7P (lwb)	5,905	4,850	248
358	Brunn conv vic 5P	5,660	5,550	13
359A	Brunn lwb cab 5P	—	6,650	10
359B	Brunn lwb cb sm-clpsbl 5P	5,960	6,750	7
360	LeBrn conv rdstr 2-4P	5,490	4,950	15
361	Brunn lwb brghm 7P	5,995	6,750	29
362	LeBaron cpe 2P	5,380	4,950	24
363A	LeBrn lwb cnv sdn/part	5,880	5,650	37
363B	LeBrn lwb conv sdn	5,980	5,850	12
365	Jdkns sdn limo 7P (lwb)	5,940	5,950	27
367A	Jdkns lwb brlin 5P 2W	5,880	5,650	47
367B	Jdkns lwb brlin 5P 3W	5,890	5,750	19
369	Willghby limo 7P (lwb)	6,115	5,850	60
371	Willghby lwb spt sdn 5P	5,915	6,850	6
373	Willghby pnl brghm 7P (lwb)	—	7,050	4
375	Brunn lwb tour cab 5P	6,020	6,950	10

1937 Engines	bore×stroke	bhp	availability
V-12, 267.3	2.75×3.75	110	S-Zephyr
V-12, 414.0	3.13×4.50	150	S-K

1938

Series 86H Zephyr (wb 125.0)		Wght	Price	Prod
700	cpe sdn	3,409	1,355	800
720	cpe 3P	3,294	1,295	2,600
730	sdn 4d	3,444	1,375	14,520
737	Town limo	3,474	1,550	130
740	conv sdn 5P	3,724	1,790	461
760B	conv cpe 3P	3,489	1,700	600

Model K (wb 136.0; lwb-145.0)		Wght	Price	Prod
403	Willghby lwb tour 7P	5,557	5,900	5
404A	sdn 5P 2W	5,527	4,900	9
404B	sdn 5P 3W	5,532	4,900	49
406	Willoughby cpe 5P	5,407	5,900	4
407A	lwb sdn 7P	5,672	5,100	78
407B	limo 7P (lwb)	5,762	5,200	91
408	Brunn conv vic 5P	5,322	5,900	8
409A	Brunn cab 5P	5,696	6,900	6
409B	Brunn cb 5P sm-clpsbl (lwb)	5,716	7,000	5
410	LeBrn conv rdstr 2-4P	5,297	5,300	8
411	Brunn lwb brghm 7P	5,806	7,000	13
412	LeBaron cpe 2P	5,462	5,300	12

Model K		Wght	Price	Prod
413A	LeBrn lwb conv sdn/part	5,572	5,800	15
413B	LeBaron lwb conv sdn	5,572	6,000	7
415	Jdkns lwb sdn limo 7P	5,742	6,300	11
417A	Jdkns lwb brlin 5P 2W	5,562	6,000	19
417B	Jdkns lwb brlin 5P 3W	5,632	6,100	11
419	Willghby limo 7P (lwb)	5,826	6,200	46
421	Willghby lwb spt sdn 5P	5,716	7,000	4
423	Willghby pnl brghm 7P	—	7,400	6
425	Brunn lwb tour cb 5P	5,662	7,200	9

1938 Engines	bore × stroke	bhp	availability
V-12, 267.3	2.75 × 3.75	110	S-Zephyr
V-12, 414.0	3.13 × 4.50	150	S-K

1939

Series 96H Zephyr (wb 125.0)		Wght	Price	Prod
700	cpe sdn	3,600	1,369	800
720	cpe 3P	3,520	1,358	2,500
730	sdn 4d	3,620	1,399	16,663
737	Town limo	3,670	1,747	95
740	conv sdn 5P	3,900	1,839	302
760B	conv cpe 2-4P	3,790	1,747	640

Model K (wb 136.0; lwb-145.0)		Wght	Price	Prod
403	Willghby lwb tour 7P	5,870	5,932	1
404A	sdn 5P 2W	5,735	4,905	2
404B	sdn 5P 3W	5,740	4,905	12
406	Willoughby cpe 5P	5,615	5,926	1
407A	lwb sdn 7P	5,880	5,109	25
407B	limo 7P (lwb)	5,970	5,211	58
408	Brunn conv vic 5P	5,530	5,926	2
409A	Brunn lwb cab 5P	6,010	6,947	1
409B	Brunn lwb cb 5P sm-clpsbl	6,030	7,049	1
410	LeBrn conv rdstr 2-4P	5,050	5,313	2
411	Brunn lwb brghm 7P	6,120	7,049	2
412	LeBaron cpe 2P	5,435	5,313	4
413A	LeBrn lwb conv sdn	5,670	5,828	3
413B	LeBrn lwb conv sdn/part	5,780	6,028	6
415	Jdkns sdn limo 7P (lwb)	5,950	6,334	2
417A	Jdkns lwb brlin 5P 2W	5,770	6,028	2
417B	Jdkns lwb brlin 5P 3W	5,840	6,130	1
419	Willghby limo 7P (lwb)	6,140	6,232	4
421	Willghby lwb spt sdn 5P	6,300	7,049	1
423	Willghby pnl brghm 7P	—	—	1
425	Brunn lwb tour cab 5P	5,870	7,253	2

1939 Engines	bore×stroke	bhp	availability
V-12, 267.3	2.75×3.75	110	S-Zephyr
V-12, 414.0	3.13×4.50	150	S-Model K

1940

06H Zephyr (wb 125.0)		Wght	Price	Prod
56	Continental conv cpe	3,740	2,916	350
57	Continental club cpe	3,850	2,783	54
72A	cpe 3P	3,500	1,399	1,256
72A	cpe 3P, Custom intr	3,500	1,506	
72B	cpe, A/S	3,480	1,429	316
73	sdn 4d	3,660	1,439	15,764
73	sdn 4d, Custom intr	3,660	1,547	
76	conv cpe	3,760	1,818	700
77	club cpe	3,590	1,439	3,500
77	club cpe, Custom intr	3,590	1,547	
22	Custom Town Limo	3,700	1,787	4
26	Custom Town Car	3,650	1,750	4

K Series (wb 136.0)*		Wght	Price	Prod
404A	sdn 4d	5,735	4,905	—
406	Willoughby cpe	5,615	5,926	—
408	Brunn conv Victoria	5,530	5,926	—
410	LeBaron rdstr	5,505	5,313	—
412	LeBaron statnry cpe	5,415	5,313	—

K Series (wb 145.0)*		Wght	Price	Prod
407A	sdn 4d, 7P	5,880	5,109	—
407B	limo	5,970	5,211	—
409	Brunn cabriolet	6,010	6,947	—
411	Brunn brougham 7P	6,120	7,049	—
413	LeBaron conv sdn	5,670	5,823	—
415	Judkins sdn limo 7P	5,950	6,334	—
417A	Judkins berline 2W	5,770	6,028	—
417B	Judkins berline 3W	5,840	6,130	—
419	Willoughby limo	6,140	6,232	—
421	Willoughby spt sdn	6,300	7,049	—
425	Brunn cabriolet 2P	5,870	7,253	—

*Total K Series model-year production: 133

1940 Engines	bore×stroke	bhp	availability
V-12, 292.0	2.88×3.75	120	S-Zephyr
V-12, 414.0	3.13×4.50	150	S-K Series

1941

16H Zephyr (wb 125.0)		Wght	Price	Prod
72A	cpe 3P	3,560	1,478	972
72A	cpe 3P, Custom intr	3,560	1,557	
72B	cpe 5P	3,580	1,464	178
73	sdn 4d	3,710	1,541	14,469
73	sdn 4d, Custom intr	3,710	1,641	
76	conv cpe	3,840	1,858	725
77	club cpe	3,640	1,541	3,750
77	club cpe, Custom intr	3,640	1,541	

16H Continental (wb 125.0)		Wght	Price	Prod
56	conv cpe ("cabriolet")	3,860	2,865	400
57	club cpe	3,890	2,812	850

168H Custom (wb 138.0)		Wght	Price	Prod
31	sdn 4d 8P	4,250	2,704	355
32	limo	4,270	2,836	295

1941 Engine	bore×stroke	bhp	availability
V-12, 292.0	2.88×3.75	120	S-all

1942

26H Zephyr (wb 125.0)		Wght	Price	Prod
72A	cpe 3P	3,730	1,650	273
72A	cpe 3P, Custom intr	3,730	1,735	
73	sdn 4d	3,920	1,700	4,418
73	sdn 4d, Custom intr	3,920	1,795	
76	conv cpe	4,130	2,150	191
77	club cpe	3,810	1,700	1,236
77	club cpe, Custom intr	3,810	1,795	

26H Continental (wb 125.0)		Wght	Price	Prod
56	conv cpe ("cabriolet")	4,020	3,000	136
57	club cpe	4,000	3,000	200

268H Custom (wb 138.0)		Wght	Price	Prod
31	sdn 4d 8P	4,380	2,950	47
32	limo	4,400	3,075	66

1942 Engine	bore×stroke	bhp	availability
V-12, 305.0	2.94×3.75	130	S-all

1946

66H (wb 125.0) - 16,179 built		Wght	Price	Prod
73	sdn 4d	3,980	2,337	—
73	sdn 4d, Custom intr	3,980	2,486	—
76	conv cpe	4,210	2,883	—
77	club cpe	3,915	2,318	—
77	club cpe, Custom intr	3,915	2,467	—

66H Continental (wb 125.0)		Wght	Price	Prod
56	conv cpe ("cabriolet")	4,090	4,474	201
57	club cpe	4,100	4,392	265

1946 Engines	bore×stroke	bhp	availability
V-12, 292.0	2.88×3.75	120	S-all late
V-12, 305.0	2.94×3.50	130	S-all early

1947

76H (wb 125.0) - 19,891 built		Wght	Price	Prod
73	sdn 4d	4,015	2,554	—
73	sdn 4d, Custom intr	4,015	2,722	—
76	conv cpe	4,245	3,142	—
77	club cpe	3,915	2,533	—
77	club cpe, Custom intr	3,915	2,701	—

76H Continental (wb 125.0)		Wght	Price	Prod
56	conv cpe ("cabriolet")	4,135	4,746	738
57	club cpe	4,125	4,662	831

1947 Engine	bore×stroke	bhp	availability
V-12, 292.0	2.88×3.75	125	S-all

1948

876H (wb 125.0)—6,470 built		Wght	Price	Prod
73	sdn 4d	4,015	2,554	—
73	sdn 4d, Custom intr	4,015	2,722	—
76	conv cpe	4,245	3,142	—
77	club cpe	3,915	2,533	—
77	club cpe, Custom intr	3,915	2,701	—

876H Continental (wb 125.0)		Wght	Price	Prod
56	conv cpe ("cabriolet")	4,135	4,746	452
57	club cpe	4,125	4,662	847

1948 Engine	bore×stroke	bhp	availability
V-12, 292.0	2.88×3.75	125	S-all

1949

9EL (wb 121.0) - 38,384 built		Wght	Price	Prod
	cpe	3,959	2,527	—
	sport sedan 4d	4,009	2,575	—
	conv cpe	4,224	3,116	—

9EH Cosmopolitan (wb 125.0) - 35,123 built		Wght	Price	Prod
	cpe	4,194	3,186	—
	sport sedan 4d	4,259	3,238	—
	town sdn 4d	4,272	3,238	—
	conv cpe	4,419	3,948	—

1949 Engine	bore×stroke	bhp	availability
V-8, 336.7	3.50×4.38	152	S-all

1950

OEL (wb 121.0)		Wght	Price	Prod
L-72	cpe	4,090	2,529	5,748
L-72C	Lido cpe	4,145	2,721	
L-74	sport sedan 4d	4,115	2,576	11,741

OEH Cosmopolitan (wb 125.0)		Wght	Price	Prod
H-72	cpe	4,375	3,187	1,824
H-72C	Capri cpe	4,385	3,406	
H-74	sport sedan 4d	4,410	3,240	8,341
H-76	conv cpe	4,640	3,950	536

1950 Engine	bore×stroke	bhp	availability
V-8, 336.7	3.50×4.38	152	S-all

1951

1EL (wb 121.0)		Wght	Price	Prod
L-72B	cpe	4,065	2,505	4,482
L-72C	Lido cpe	4,100	2,702	
L-74	sport sedan 4d	4,130	2,553	12,279

1EH Cosmopolitan (wb 125.0)		Wght	Price	Prod
H-72B	cpe	4,340	3,129	2,727
H-72C	Capri cpe	4,360	3,350	
H-74	sport sedan 4d	4,415	3,182	12,229
H-76	conv cpe	4,615	3,891	857

1951 Engine	bore×stroke	bhp	availability
V-8, 336.7	3.50×4.38	154	S-all

1952

2H Cosmopolitan (wb 123.0)		Wght	Price	Prod
60C	Spt htp cpe	4,155	3,293	4,545
73A	sdn 4d	4,125	3,198	*

2H Capri (wb 123.0)		Wght	Price	Prod
60A	htp cpe	4,235	3,518	5,681
73B	sdn 4d	4,140	3,331	*
76A	conv cpe	4,350	3,665	1,191

* Combined sedan production: 15,854.

1952 Engine	bore×stroke	bhp	availability
V-8, 317.5	3.80×3.50	160	S-all

1953

8H Cosmopolitan (wb 123.0)		Wght	Price	Prod
60C	Sport htp cpe	4,155	3,322	6,562
73A	sdn 4d	4,135	3,226	7,560

8H Capri (wb 123.0)		Wght	Price	Prod
60A	htp cpe	4,165	3,549	12,916
73B	sdn 4d	4,150	3,453	11,352
76A	conv cpe	4,310	3,699	2,372

1953 Engine	bore×stroke	bhp	availability
V-8, 317.5	3.80×3.50	205	S-all

1954

Cosmopolitan (wb 123.0)		Wght	Price	Prod
60C	Sport htp cpe	4,155	3,625	2,994
73A	sdn 4d	4,135	3,522	4,447

Capri (wb 123.0)		Wght	Price	Prod
60A	htp cpe	4,250	3,869	14,003
73B	sdn 4d	4,245	3,711	13,598
76A	conv cpe	4,310	4,031	1,951

1954 Engine	bore×stroke	bhp	availability
V-8, 317.5	3.80×3.50	205	S-all

1955

Custom (wb 123.0)		Wght	Price	Prod
60C	Sport htp cpe	4,185	3,666	1,362
73A	sdn 4d	4,235	3,563	2,187

Capri (wb 123.0)		Wght	Price	Prod
60A	htp cpe	4,305	3,910	11,462
73B	sdn 4d	4,245	3,752	10,724
76A	conv cpe	4,415	4,072	1,487

1955 Engine	bore×stroke	bhp	availability
V-8, 341.0	3.94×3.50	225	S-all

1956

Capri (wb 126.0)		Wght	Price	Prod
60E	Sport htp cpe	4,305	4,119	4,355
73A	sdn 4d	4,315	4,212	4,436
Premiere (wb 126.0)				
60B	htp cpe	4,357	4,601	19,619
73B	sdn 4d	4,347	4,601	19,465
76B	conv cpe	4,452	4,747	2,447

1956 Engine	bore×stroke	bhp	availability
V-8, 368.0	4.00×3.66	285	S-all

1957

Capri (wb 126.0)		Wght	Price	Prod
57A	Landau htp sdn	4,460	4,794	1,451
58A	sdn 4d	4,349	4,794	1,476
60A	htp cpe	4,373	4,649	2,973
Premiere (wb 126.0)				
57B	Landau htp sdn	4,538	5,294	11,223
58B	sdn 4d	4,527	5,294	5,139
60B	htp cpe	4,451	5,149	15,185
76B	conv cpe	4,676	5,381	3,676

1957 Engine	bore×stroke	bhp	availability
V-8, 368.0	4.00×3.66	300	S-all

1958

Capri (wb 131.0)		Wght	Price	Prod
53A	sdn 4d	4,799	4,951	1,184
57A	Landau htp sdn	4,810	4,951	3,084
63A	htp cpe	4,735	4,803	2,591
Premiere (wb 131.0)				
53B	sdn 4d	4,802	5,505	1,660
57B	Landau htp sdn	4,798	5,505	5,572
63B	htp cpe	4,734	5,318	3,043

1958 Engine	bore×stroke	bhp	availability
V-8, 430.0	4.30×3.70	375	S-all

1959

(wb 131.0)		Wght	Price	Prod
53A	sdn 4d	4,823	5,090	1,312
57A	Landau htp sdn	4,824	5,090	4,417
63A	htp cpe	4,741	4,902	2,200
Premiere (wb 131.0)				
53B	sdn 4d	4,887	5,594	1,282
57B	Landau htp sdn	4,880	5,594	4,606
63B	htp cpe	4,798	5,347	1,963
Continental Mark IV (wb 131.0)				
23A	limo	5,061	10,230	49
23B	formal sdn	5,190	9,208	78
54A	sdn 4d	5,061	6,845	955
65A	htp cpe	4,967	6,598	1,703
68A	conv cpe	5,076	7,056	2,195
75A	htp sdn	5,050	6,845	6,146

1959 Engine	bore×stroke	bhp	availability
V-8, 430.0	4.30×3.70	350	S-all

1960

(wb 131.0)		Wght	Price	Prod
53A	sdn 4d	5,016	5,441	1,093
57A	Landau htp sdn	5,012	5,441	4,397
63A	htp cpe	4,917	5,253	1,670
Premiere (wb 131.0)				
53B	sdn 4d	5,064	5,945	1,010
57B	Landau htp sdn	5,060	5,945	4,200
63B	htp cpe	4,965	5,696	1,365
Continental Mark V (wb 131.0)				
23A	limo	5,481	10,230	34
23B	formal sdn	5,272	9,208	136
54A	sdn 4d	5,143	6,845	807
65A	htp cpe	5,044	6,598	1,461
68A	conv cpe	5,180	7,056	2,044
75A	Landau htp sdn	5,139	6,845	6,604

1960 Engine	bore×stroke	bhp	availability
V-8, 430.0	4.30×3.70	315	S-all

1961

Continental (wb 123.0)		Wght	Price	Prod
53A	htp sdn	4,927	6,067	22,303
57C	htp sdn, spec model	—	—	4
74A	conv sdn	5,215	6,713	2,857

1961 Engine	bore×stroke	bhp	availability
V-8, 430.0	4.30×3.70	300	S-all

1962

Continental (wb 123.0)		Wght	Price	Prod
53A	htp sdn	4,966	6,074	27,849
74A	conv sdn	5,370	6,720	3,212

1962 Engine	bore×stroke	bhp	availability
V-8, 430.0	4.30×3.70	300	S-all

1963

Continental (wb 123.0)		Wght	Price	Prod
53A	htp sdn	4,936	6,270	28,095
74A	conv sdn	5,340	6,916	3,138

1963 Engine	bore×stroke	bhp	availability
V-8, 430.0	4.30×3.70	320	S-all

1964

Continental (wb 126.0)		Wght	Price	Prod
82	htp sdn	5,055	6,292	32,969
86	conv sdn	5,393	6,938	3,328

1964 Engine	bore×stroke	bhp	availability
V-8, 430.0	4.30×3.70	320	S-all

1965

Continental (wb 126.0)		Wght	Price	Prod
82	htp sdn	5,075	6,292	36,824
86	conv sdn	5,475	6,938	3,356

1965 Engine	bore×stroke	bhp	availability
V-8, 430.0	4.30×3.70	320	S-all

1966

Continental (wb 126.0)		Wght	Price	Prod
82	sdn 4d	5,085	5,750	35,809
86	conv sdn	5,480	6,383	3,180
89	htp cpe	4,985	5,485	15,766

1966 Engine	bore×stroke	bhp	availability
V-8, 462.0	4.38×3.83	340	S-all

1967

Continental (wb 126.0)		Wght	Price	Prod
82	sdn 4d	5,049	5,795	32,331
86	conv sdn	5,505	6,449	2,276
89	htp cpe	4,940	5,553	11,060

1967 Engine	bore×stroke	bhp	availability
V-8, 462.0	4.38×3.83	340	S-all

1968

Continental (wb 126.0)		Wght	Price	Prod
81	htp cpe	4,883	5,736	9,415
82	sdn 4d	4,978	5,970	29,719
Continental Mark III (wb 117.2)				
89	htp cpe	4,739	6,585	7,770

1968 Engines	bore×stroke	bhp	availability
V-8, 462.0	4.38×3.83	340	S-all early
V-8, 460.0	4.36×3.85	365	S-all late

1969

Continental (wb 126.0)		Wght	Price	Prod
81	htp cpe	4,910	5,830	9,032
82	sdn 4d	5,005	6,063	29,258
Continental Mark III (wb 117.2)				
89	htp cpe	4,762	6,758	23,088

1969 Engine	bore×stroke	bhp	availability
V-8, 460.0	4.36×3.85	365	S-all

1970

Continental (wb 126.0)		Wght	Price	Prod
81	htp cpe	4,669	5,976	9,073
82	sdn 4d	4,719	6,211	28,622
Continental Mark III (wb 117.2)				
89	htp cpe	4,675	7,281	21,432

1970 Engine	bore×stroke	bhp	availability
V-8, 460.0	4.36×3.85	365	S-all

1971

Continental (wb 127.0)		Wght	Price	Prod
81	htp cpe	5,032	7,172	8,205
82	sdn 4d	5,072	7,419	27,346
Continental Mark III (wb 117.2)				
89	htp cpe	5,003	8,813	27,091

1971 Engine	bore×stroke	bhp	availability
V-8, 460.0	4.36×3.85	365	S-all

1972

Continental (wb 127.0)		Wght	Price	Prod
81	htp cpe	4,906	7,068	10,408
82	sdn 4d	4,958	7,302	36,561
Continental Mark IV (wb 120.4)				
89	htp cpe	4,792	8,640	48,591

1972 Engines	bore×stroke	bhp	availability
V-8, 460.0	4.36×3.85	224	S-81, 82
V-8, 460.0	4.36×3.85	212	S-89

1973

Continental (wb 127.0)		Wght	Price	Prod
81	htp cpe	5,016	7,230	13,348
82	sdn 4d	5,049	7,474	45,288
Continental Mark IV (wb 120.4)				
89	htp cpe	4,908	8,984	69,437

1973 Engines	bore×stroke	bhp	availability
V-8, 460.0	4.36×3.85	219	S-81, 82
V-8, 460.0	4.36×3.85	208	S-89

1974

Continental (wb 127.2)		Wght	Price	Prod
81	htp cpe	5,366	8,053	7,318
82	sdn 4d	5,361	8,238	29,351
Continental Mark IV (wb 120.4)				
89	htp cpe	5,362	10,194	57,316

1974 Engines	bore×stroke	bhp	availability
V-8, 460.0	4.36×3.85	215	S-81, 82
V-8, 460.0	4.36×3.85	220	S-89

1975

Continental (wb 127.2)		Wght	Price	Prod
81	cpe	5,219	9,214	21,185
82	sdn 4d	5,229	9,656	33,513
Continental Mark IV (wb 120.4)				
89	htp cpe	5,145	11,082	47,145

1975 Engines	bore×stroke	bhp	availability
V-8, 460.0	4.36×3.85	206	S-81, 82
V-8, 460.0	4.36×3.85	194	S-89

1976

Continental (wb 127.2)		Wght	Price	Prod
81	cpe	5,035	9,142	24,663
82	sdn 4d	5,083	9,293	43,983
Continental Mark IV (wb 120.4)				
89	htp cpe	5,051	11,060	56,110

1976 Engines	bore×stroke	bhp	availability
V-8, 460.0	4.36×3.85	202	S-all

1977

Versailles (wb 109.9)		Wght	Price	Prod
84	sdn 4d	3,800	11,500	15,434
Continental (wb 127.2)				
81	cpe	4,836	9,474	27,440
82	sdn 4d	4,880	9,636	68,160
Continental Mark V (wb 120.4)				
89	htp cpe	4,652	11,396	80,321

1977 Engines	bore×stroke	bhp	availability
V-8, 351.0	4.00×3.50	135	S-Versailles
V-8, 400.0	4.00 ×4.00	179	S-81, 82, 89
V-8, 460.0	4.36×3.85	208	O-81, 82, 89

1978

Versailles (wb 109.0)		Wght	Price	Prod
84	sdn 4d	3,759	12,529	8,931
Continental (wb 127.2)				
81	cpe	4,659	9,974	20,977
82	sdn 4d	4,660	10,166	67,110
Continental Mark V (wb 120.4)				
89	htp cpe	4,567	12,099	72,602

1978 Engines	bore×stroke	bhp	availability
V-8, 302.0	4.00×3.00	133	S-Versailles
V-8, 400.0	4.00×4.00	166	S-81, 82, 89
V-8, 460.0	4.36×3.85	210	O-81, 82, 89

1979

Versailles (wb 109.9)		Wght	Price	Prod
84	sdn 4d	3,684	12,939	21,007
Continental (wb 127.2)				
81	cpe	4,639	10,985	16,142
82	sdn 4d	4,649	11,200	76,458

Continental Mark V (wb 120.4)		Wght	Price	Prod
89	htp cpe	4,589	13,067	75,939

1979 Engines	bore×stroke	bhp	availability
V-8, 302.0	4.00×3.00	130	S-Versailles
V-8, 400.0	4.00×4.00	159	S-81, 82, 89

1980

Versailles (wb 109.9)		Wght	Price	Prod
84	4d	3,661	14,674	4,784

Continental (wb 117.3; 2d-114.3)		Wght	Price	Prod
81	cpe	3,843	12,555	7,177
82	sdn 4d	3,919	12,884	24,056

Continentl Mark VI (wb 117.3; 2d-114.3) - 38,891 built		Wght	Price	Prod
89	sdn 2d	3,892	15,424	—
90	sdn 4d	3,988	15,824	38,891
96	Signature sdn 2d	3,896	20,940	—
96	Signature sdn 4d	3,993	21,309	—

1980 Engines	bore×stroke	bhp	availability
V-8, 302.0	4.00×3.00	132	S-Versailles
V-8, 302.0	4.00×3.00	129	S-Contl, Mk VI
V-8, 351.0	4.00×3.50	140	O-Contl, Mk VI

1981

Town Car (wb 117.3)		Wght	Price	Prod
93	sdn 2d	3,884	13,707	4,935
94	sdn 4d	3,958	14,068	27,904

Continental Mark VI (wb 117.3; 2d-114.3)		Wght	Price	Prod
95	cpe 2d	3,899	16,858	18,740
95	Signature cpe 2d	3,990	22,463	
96	sdn 4d	3,944	17,303	17,958
96	Signature sdn 4d	4,035	22,838	

1981 Engines	bore×stroke	bhp	availability
V-8, 302.0	4.00×3.00	130	S-all

1982

Contintl (wb 108.5) - 23,908 blt		Wght	Price	Prod
98	sdn 4d	3,512	21,302	—
98/603	Signature sdn 4d	3,610	24,456	—
98/60H	Givenchy sdn 4d	3,610	24,803	—

Mark VI (wb 117.3; 2d-114.3)		Wght	Price	Prod
95	cpe 2d	3,879	19,452	11,532
95/603	Signature cpe 2d	3,888	22,252	
95/60M	Givenchy cpe 2d	3,910	22,722	
95/60N	Bill Blass cpe 2d	3,910	23,594	
96	sdn 4d	3,976	19,924	14,804
96/603	Signature sdn 4d	3,985	22,720	
96/60P	Pucci sdn 4d	3,970	23,465	

Town Car (wb 117.3) - 35,069 built		Wght	Price	Prod
94	sdn 4d	3,936	16,100	—
94/60U	Signature sdn 4d	3,952	17,394	—
94/605	Cartier sdn 4d	3,944	18,415	—

1982 Engines	bore×stroke	bhp	availability
V-6, 232.0	3.80×3.40	112	O-Continental
V-8, 302.0	4.00×3.00	130	S-Continental
V-8, 302.0	4.00×3.00	134	S-Mark, Twn Car

1983

Contintl (wb 108.5) - 16,831 blt		Wght	Price	Prod
97	sdn 4d	3,719	20,985	—
98/60R	Valentino sdn 4d	3,757	22,576	—
97/60M	Givenchy sdn 4d	3,757	22,576	—

Mark VI (wb 117.3; 2d-114.3)		Wght	Price	Prod
98	cpe 2d	4,004	20,229	12,743
98/603	Signature cpe 2d	4,013	23,124	
98/60N	Bill Blass cpe 2d	4,035	24,533	
98/60P	Pucci cpe 2d	NA	24,345	
99	sdn 4d	4,105	20,717	18,113
99/603	Signature sdn 4d	4,114	23,612	
99/60P	Pucci sdn 4d	4,099	24,407	

Town Car (wb 117.3) - 53,381 built		Wght	Price	Prod
96	sdn 4d	4,062	16,923	—
96/60U	Signature sdn 4d	4,078	18,265	—
96/605	Cartier sdn 4d	4,070	19,601	—

1983 Engines	bore×stroke	bhp	availability
V-8, 302.0	4.00×3.00	130	S-all
V-8, 302.0	4.00×3.00	145	O-Mark

1984

Contintl (wb 108.5) - 30,468 blt		Wght	Price	Prod
97	sdn 4d	3,750	21,769	—
97/60R	Valentino sdn 4d	—	24,217	—
97/60M	Givenchy sdn 4d	—	24,242	—

Mark VII (wb 108.5) - 33,344 built		Wght	Price	Prod
98	cpe 2d	3,625	21,707	—
98/938	LSC cpe 2d	—	23,706	—
98/60N	Bill Blass cpe 2d	—	24,807	—
98/60P	Versace cpe 2d	—	24,406	—

Town Car (wb 117.3) - 93,622 blt		Wght	Price	Prod
96	sdn 4d	4,062	18,071	—
96/60U	Signature sdn 4d	4,078	20,040	—
96/605	Cartier sdn 4d	4,070	21,706	—

1984 Engines	bore×stroke	bhp	availability
I-6TD, 149.0	3.15×3.19	115	O-Cont, Mark VII
V-8, 302.0	4.00×3.00	140	S-all
V-8, 302.0	4.00×3.00	155	O-Town Car

1985

Contintl (wb 108.5) - 28,253 blt		Wght	Price	Prod
97/850A	sdn 4d	3,790	22,573	—
97/865A	Valentino sdn 4d	—	26,078	—
97/860A	Givenchy sdn 4d	—	25,783	—

Mark VII (wb 108.5) - 18,355 built		Wght	Price	Prod
98/800A	cpe 2d	3,615	22,399	—
98/805A	LSC cpe 2d	—	24,332	—
98/810A	Bill Blass cpe 2d	—	26,659	—
98/815A	Versace cpe 2d	—	26,578	—

Town Car (wb 117.3) - 119,878 built		Wght	Price	Prod
96/700A	sdn 4d	4,027	19,047	—
96/705A	Signature sdn 4d	—	22,130	—
96/710A	Cartier sdn 4d	—	23,637	—

1985 Engines	bore×stroke	bhp	availability
I-6TD, 149.0	3.15×3.19	115	O-Cont, Mark VII
V-8, 302.0	4.00×3.00	140	S-all exc LSC
V-8, 302.0	4.00×3.00	155	O-Town Car
V-8, 302.0	4.00×3.00	165	S-Mark VII LSC

Note: 1984-85 Lincolns with turbodiesel engine were priced higher than amounts shown.

1986

Contintl (wb 108.5)-19,012 blt		Wght	Price	Prod
97/850A	sdn 4d	3,778	24,556	—
97/860A	Givenchy sdn 4d	3,808	26,837	—

Mark VII (wb 108.5) - 20,056 built		Wght	Price	Prod
98/800A	cpe 2d	3,667	22,399	—
98/805B	LSC cpe 2d	3,718	23,857	—
98/810B	Bill Blass cpe 2d	3,732	23,857	—

Town Car (wb 117.3) - 117,771 built		Wght	Price	Prod
96/700B	sdn 4d	4,038	20,764	—
96/705B	Signature sdn 4d	4,121	29,972	—
96/710B	Cartier sdn 4d	4,093	25,235	—

1986 Engines	bore×stroke	bhp	availability
V-8, 302.0	4.00×3.00	150	S-all exc LSC
V-8, 302.0	4.00×3.00	200	S-Mark VII LSC

1987

Contintl (wb 108.5) - 17,597 blt		Wght	Price	Prod
97	sdn 4d	3,799	26,402	—
98	Givenchy sdn 4d	3,826	28,902	—

Mark VII (108.5) - 15,286 built		Wght	Price	Prod
91	cpe 2d	3,722	24,216	—
93	LSC cpe 2d	3,772	25,863	—
92	Bill Blass cpe 2d	3,747	25,863	—

Town Car (wb 117.3) - 76,483 built		Wght	Price	Prod
81	sdn 4d	4,051	22,549	—
82	Signature sdn 4d	4,106	25,541	—
83	Cartier sdn 4d	4,086	26,868	—

1987 Engines	bore×stroke	bhp	availability
V-8, 302.0	4.00×3.00	150	S-all exc LSC
V-8, 302.0	4.00×3.00	200	S-Mark VII LSC

1988

Contintl (wb 109.0) - 41,287 blt		Wght	Price	Prod
97	sdn 4d	3,628	26,078	—
98	Signature sdn 4d	3,618	27,944	—

Mark VII (wb 108.5) - 38,259 built		Wght	Price	Prod
93	LSC cpe 2d	3,772	25,016	—
92	Bill Blass cpe 2d	3,747	25,016	—

Town Car (wb 117.3) - 201,113 built		Wght	Price	Prod
81	sdn 4d	4,093	23,126	—
82	Signature sdn 4d	4,119	25,990	—
83	Cartier sdn 4d	4,107	27,273	—

1988 Engines	bore×stroke	bhp	availability
V-6, 232.0	3.80×3.40	140	S-Continental
V-8, 302.0	4.00×3.00	150	S-Town Car
V-8, 302.0	4.00×3.00	225	S-Mark VII

1989

Contintl (wb 109.0) - 57,775 blt		Wght	Price	Prod
97	sdn 4d	3,635	27,468	—
98	Signature sdn 4d	3,633	29,334	—

Mark VII (wb 108.5) - 29,658 built		Wght	Price	Prod
93	LSC cpe 2d	3,743	27,218	—
92	Bill Blass cpe 2d	3,783	27,218	—

Town Car (wb 117.3) - 128,533 built		Wght	Price	Prod
81	sdn 4d	4,044	25,205	—
82	Signature sdn 4d	4,070	28,206	—
83	Cartier sdn 4d	4,059	29,352	—
—	Gucci sdn 4d	4,059	—	—

1989 Engines	bore×stroke	bhp	availability
V-6, 232.0	3.80×3.40	140	S-Continental
V-8, 302.0	4.00×3.00	150	S-Town Car
V-8, 302.0	4.00×3.00	225	S-Mark VII

1990

Contintl (wb 109.0) - 64,257 blt		Wght	Price	Prod
97	sdn 4d	3,663	29,258	—
98	Signature sdn 4d	—	31,181	—

Mark VII (wb 108.5) - 22,313 built		Wght	Price	Prod
93	LSC cpe 2d	3,779	29,437	—
92	Bill Blass cpe 2d	—	29,215	—

Town Car (wb 117.3) - 147,160 built		Wght	Price	Prod
81	sdn 4d	4,025	27,315	—
82	Signature sdn 4d	—	30,043	—
83	Cartier sdn 4d	—	32,137	—

1990 Engines	bore×stroke	bhp	availability
V-6, 232.0	3.80×3.40	140	S-Continental
V-8, 302.0	4.00×3.00	150	S-Town Car
V-8, 302.0	4.00×3.00	225	S-Mark VII

1991

Contintl (wb 109.0) - 53,109 blt		Wght	Price	Prod
54/HVS	Executive sdn 4d	3,633	30,211	—
54/HVB	Signature sdn 4d	3,635	32,120	—

Mark VII (wb 108.5) - 9,299 built		Wght	Price	Prod
63/HVC	Bill Blass cpe 2d	3,782	30,238	—
63/HVB	LSC cpe 2d	3,807	30,362	—

Town Car (wb 117.4) - 124,919 built		Wght	Price	Prod
AB/FC	sdn 4d	4,035	29,458	—
BR/FC	Signature sdn 4d	—	32,416	—
BS/FC	Cartier sdn 4d	—	34,504	—

1991 Engines	bore×stroke	bhp	availability
V-6, 232.0	3.80×3.40	155	S-Continental
V-8, 281.0	3.60×3.60	190	S-Twn Car (ohc)
V-8, 281.0	3.60×3.60	210	O-Twn Car (ohc)
V-8, 302.0	4.00×3.00	225	S-Mark VII

1992

Contintl (wb 109.0) - 40,822 blt		Wght	Price	Prod
54/HVS	Executive sdn 4d	3,628	32,263	—
54/HVB	Signature sdn 4d	3,623	34,253	—

Mark VII (wb 108.5) - 5,732 built		Wght	Price	Prod
63/HVC	Bill Blass cpe 2d	3,768	32,032	—
63/HVB	LSC cpe 2d	3,781	32,156	—

Town Car (wb 117.4) - 113,458 built		Wght	Price	Prod
AB/FC	sdn 4d	4,024	31,211	—
BR/FC	Signature sdn 4d	4,025	34,252	—
BS/FC	Cartier sdn 4d	4,035	36,340	—

1992 Engines	bore ×stroke	bhp	availability
V-6, 232.0	3.80×3.40	160	S-Continental
V-8, 281.0	3.60×3.60	190	S-Twn Car (ohc)
V-8, 281.0	3.60×3.60	210	O-Twn Car (ohc)
V-8, 302.0	4.00×3.00	225	S-Mark VII

1993

Contintl (wb 109.0) - 26,798 blt		Wght	Price	Prod
54/HVS	Executive sdn 4d	3,595	33,328	—
54/HVB	Signature sdn 4d	3,634	35,319	—

Mark VIII (wb 113.0)		Wght	Price	Prod
63/HVB	cpe 2d	3,752	36,640	32,370

Town Car (wb 117.4)-118,040 blt		Wght	Price	Prod
AB/FC	Executive sdn 4d	4,040	34,190	—
BR/FC	Signature sdn 4d	4,046	35,494	—
BS/FC	Cartier sdn 4d	4,084	37,581	—

1993 Engines	bore×stroke	bhp	availability
V-6, 232.0	3.80×3.40	160	S-Continental
V-8, 281.0	3.60×3.60	190	S-Twn Car (ohc)
V-8, 281.0	3.60×3.60	210	O-Twn Car (ohc)
V-8, 281.0	3.60×3.60	280	S-Mrk VIII (dohc)

1994

Contintl (wb 109.0) - 52,107 blt		Wght	Price	Prod
54/HVS	Executive sdn 4d	3,576	33,750	—
54/HVB	Signature sdn 4d	3,613	35,600	—
Mark VIII (wb 113.0)				
63/HVB	cpe 2d	3,768	38,050	28,164
Town Car (wb 117.4)				
AB/FC	Executive sdn 4d	4,039	34,750	62,865 (Executive and Cartier combined)
BS/FC	Cartier sdn 4d	4,095	38,100	
BR/FC	Signature sdn 4d	4,057	36,050	54,583

1994 Engines	bore×stroke	bhp	availability
V-6, 232.0	3.80×3.40	160	S-Continental
V-8, 281.0	3.60×3.60	210	S-Twn Car (ohc)
V-8, 281.0	3.60×3.60	280	S-Mrk VIII (dohc)

1995

Continental (wb 109.0)		Wght	Price	Prod
M97	sdn 4d	3,969	40,750	44,854
Mark VIII (wb 113.0				
M91	cpe 2d	3,768	38,800	18,390
Town Car (wb 117.4) - 119,109 built				
M81	Executive sdn 4d	4,031	36,400	—
M82	Signature sdn 4d	—	38,500	—
M83	Cartier sdn 4d	—	41,200	—

1995 Engines	bore×stroke	bhp	availability
V-8, 281.0	3.60×3.60	210	S-Twn Car (ohc)
V-8, 281.0	3.60×3.60	260	S-Contntl (dohc)
V-8, 281.0	3.60×3.60	280	S-Mrk VIII (dohc)

1996

Continental (wb 109.0)		Wght	Price	Prod
M97	sdn 4d	3,911	41,800	29,455
Mark VIII (wb 113.0)				
M91	cpe 2d	3,768	39,650	13,625
Town Car (wb 117.4) - 93,616 built				
M81	Executive sdn 4d	4,040	36,910	—
M82	Signature sdn 4d	4,040	38,960	—
M83	Cartier sdn 4d	4,103	41,960	—

1996 Engines	bore×stroke	bhp	availability
V-8, 281.0	3.60×3.60	210	S-Town Car
V-8, 281.0	3.60×3.60	260	S-Contntl (dohc)
V-8, 281.0	3.60×3.60	280	S-Mrk VIII (dohc)
V-8, 281.0	3.60×3.60	290	O-Mrk VIII (dohc)

1997

Continental (wb 109.0)		Wght	Price	Prod
M97	sdn 4d	3,884	37,280	32,245
Mark VIII (wb 113.0) - 16,365 built				
M91	cpe 2d	3,765	37,280	—
M92	LSC cpe 2d	3,785	38,880	—
Town Car (wb 117.4) - 104,533 built				
M81	Executive sdn 4d	3,997	37,280	—
M82	Signature sdn 4d	3,977	39,640	—
M83	Cartier sdn 4d	3,977	43,200	—

1997 Engines	bore×stroke	bhp	availability
V-8, 281.0	3.60×3.60	210	S-Town Car
V-8, 281.0	3.60×3.60	260	S-Contntl (dohc)
V-8, 281.0	3.60×3.60	280	S-Mrk VIII (dohc)
V-8, 281.0	3.60×3.60	290	O-Mrk VIII (dohc)

1998

Continental (wb 109.0)		Wght	Price	Prod*
M97	sdn 4d	3,868	37,830	36,328
Mark VIII (wb 113.0) - 6,103 built				
M91	cpe 2d	3,765	37,830	—
M92	LSC cpe 2d	3,785	39,320	—
Town Car (wb 117.7) - 110,718 built				
M81	Executive sdn 4d	3,860	37,830	—
M82	Signature sdn 4d	—	39,480	—
M83	Cartier sdn 4d	—	41,830	—

1998 Engines	bore×stroke	bhp	availability
V-8, 281.0	3.60×3.60	200	S-Town Car
V-8, 281.0	3.60×3.60	220	O-Town Car
V-8, 281.0	3.60×3.60	260	S-Contntl (dohc)
V-8, 281.0	3.60×3.60	280	S-Mrk VIII (dohc)
V-8, 281.0	3.60×3.60	290	O-Mrk VIII (dohc)

* Calendar-year production

1999

Continental (wb 109.0)		Wght	Price	Prod*
M97	sdn 4d	3,868	38,325	27,682
Town Car (wb 117.7) - 83,235 built				
M81	Executive sdn 4d	4,015	38,325	—
M82	Signature sdn 4d	—	40,325	—
M83	Cartier sdn 4d	—	42,825	—

1999 Engines	bore×stroke	bhp	availability
V-8, 281.0	3.60×3.60	200	S-Town Car
V-8, 281.0	3.60×3.60	220	O-Town Car
V-8, 281.0	3.60×3.60	275	S-Contntl (dohc)

* Calendar-year production

2000

LS (wb 114.5) - 60,066 built		Wght	Price	Prod*
M86	V-6 automatic sdn 4d	3,593	30,915	—
M86	V-6 manual sdn 4d	3,598	31,715	—
M87	V-8 sdn 4d	3,692	34,690	—
Continental (wb 109.0)				
M97	sdn 4d	3,868	38,880	23,440
Town Car (wb 117.7) - 83,517 built				
M81	Executive sdn 4d	4,015	38,630	—
M82	Signature sdn 4d	—	40,630	—
M83	Cartier sdn 4d	—	43,130	—

2000 Engines	bore×stroke	bhp	availability
V-6, 181.0	3.50×3.13	210	S-LS (dohc)
V-8, 240.0	3.39×3.35	252	O-LS (dohc)
V-8, 281.0	3.60×3.60	200	S-Twn Car (ohc)
V-8, 281.0	3.60 × 3.60	220	O-Twn Car (ohc)
V-8, 281.0	3.60 × 3.60	275	S-Contntl (dohc)

* Calendar-year production

2001

LS (wb 114.5) - 38,946 built		Wght	Price	Prod*
M86	V-6 automatic sdn 4d	3,593	31,665	—
M86	V-6 manual sdn 4d	3,598	33,445	—
M87	V-8 sdn 4d	3,692	35,695	—
Continental (wb 109.0)				
M97	sdn 4d	3,848	39,380	17,873
Town Car (wb 117.7, L-123.7) - 67,380 built				
M81	Executive sdn 4d	4,015	39,145	—
M82	Signature sdn 4d	4,020	41,315	—
M83	Cartier sdn 4d	4,095	43,700	—
M85	Cartier L sdn 4d	4,215	48,510	—

2001 Engines	bore×stroke	bhp	availability
V-6, 181.0	3.50×3.13	210	S-LS (dohc)
V-8, 240.0	3.39×3.35	252	O-LS (dohc)
V-8, 281.0	3.60×3.60	225	S-Twn Car (ohc)
V-8, 281.0	3.60×3.60	240	O-Twn Car (ohc)
V-8, 281.0	3.60×3.60	275	S-Contntl (dohc)

* Calendar-year production

2002

LS (wb 114.5) - 39,081 built		Wght	Price	Prod*
M86	V-6 auto sdn 4d	3,593	33,045	—
M86	V-6 Cnvnc auto sdn 4d	—	34,230	—
M86	V-6 Sport auto sdn 4d	—	35,030	—
M86	V-6 Sport man sdn 4d	—	35,055	—
M86	V-6 Prem auto sdn 4d	—	36,335	—
M87	V-8 sdn 4d	3,692	37,220	—
M87	V-8 Sport sdn 4d	—	38,075	—
M87	V-8 Premium sdn 4d	—	39,395	—
Continental (wb 109.0) - 17,923 built				
M97	sdn 4d	3,848	38,010	—
M97	Driver Select sdn 4d	—	38,615	—
M97	Personal Sec sdn 4d	—	39,600	—
M97	Lxry Appear sdn 4d	—	39,720	—
Town Car (wb 117.7, L-123.7) - 67,579 built				
M81	Executive sdn 4d	4,015	39,995	—
M82	Signature sdn 4d	4,020	42,165	—
M82	Signature Tour sdn 4d	—	42,875	—
M82	Sign Prem sdn 4d	—	44,295	—

Town Car		Wght	Price	Prod*
M82	Sign Prem Tour sdn 4d	—	45,005	—
M83	Cartier sdn 4d	4,095	44,550	—
M83	Cartier Prem sdn 4d	—	46,680	—
M85	Cartier L sdn 4d	4,215	49,060	—

2002 Engines	bore×stroke	bhp	availability
V-6, 181.0	3.50×3.13	220	S-LS (dohc)
V-8, 240.0	3.39×3.35	252	O-LS (dohc)
V-8, 281.0	3.60×3.60	225	S-Twn Car (ohc)
V-8, 281.0	3.60×3.60	235	O-Twn Car (ohc)
V-8, 281.0	3.60×3.60	275	S-Contntl (dohc)

* Calendar-year production

2003

LS (wb 114.5) - 39,579 built		Wght	Price	Prod*
M86	V-6 sdn 4d	3,674	33,860	—
M86	Premium V-6 sdn 4d	—	37,260	—
M87	Sport V-8 sdn 4d	—	40,060	—
M87	Prem Sprt V-8 sdn 4d	—	43,360	—
Town Car (wb 117.7, L-123.7) - 54,458 built				
M81	Executive sdn 4d	4,308	40,370	—
M82	Signature sdn 4d	—	42,830	—
M82	Sign Prem sdn 4d	—	44,960	—
M83	Cartier sdn 4d	—	45,340	—
M83	Cartier Prem sdn 4d	—	47,470	—
M85	Cartier L sdn 4d	4,428	50,800	—

2003 Engines	bore×stroke	bhp	availability
V-6, 181.0	3.50×3.13	232	S-LS
V-8, 240.0	3.39×3.35	280	O-LS
V-8, 281.0	3.60×3.60	225	S-Town Car

* Calendar-year production

2004

LS (wb 114.5) - 27,146 built		Wght	Price	Prod*
M86	Luxury V-6 sdn 4d	3,719	31,860	—
M86	Premium V-6 sdn 4d	3,719	36,260	—
M87	Sport V-8 sdn 4d	3,772	39,460	—
M87	Ultimate V-8 sdn 4d	3,772	42,860	—
Town Car (wb 117.7, L-123.7) - 53,958 built				
M81	Signature sdn 4d	4,359	41,020	—
M83	Ultimate sdn 4d	4,413	44,130	—
M85	Ultimate L sdn 4d	4,502	49,675	—

2004 Engines	bore×stroke	bhp	availability
V-6, 181.0	3.50×3.13	232	S-LS
V-8, 240.0	3.39×3.35	280	O-LS
V-8, 281.0	3.60×3.60	239	S-Town Car

* Calendar-year production

2005

LS (wb 114.5) - 15,675 built		Wght	Price	Prod*
M86	Luxury V-6 sdn 4d	3,719	32,330	—
M86	Appear V-6 sdn 4d	3,719	36,050	—
M86	Premium V-6 sdn 4d	3,719	36,680	—
M87	Sport V-8 sdn 4d	3,772	39,880	—
M87	Ultimate V-8 sdn 4d	3,772	43,280	—
Town Car (wb 117.7, L-123.7)- 50,284 built				
M81	Signature sdn 4d	4,345	41,675	—
M82	Sign Limited sdn 4d	4,445	44,515	—
M85	Signature L sdn 4d	4,518	50,120	—

2005 Engines	bore×stroke	bhp	availability
V-6, 181.0	3.50×3.13	232	S-LS
V-8, 240.0	3.39×3.35	280	O-LS
V-8, 281.0	3.60×3.60	239	S-Town Car

* Calendar-year production

2006

Zephyr (wb 107.4)		Wght	Price	Prod**
M26	V-6 sdn 4d	3,406	28,895	—
LS (wb 114.5)				
M87	Sport V-8 sdn 4d	3,772	39,285	—
Town Car (wb 117.7, L-123.7)				
M81	Signature sdn 4d	4,345	42,055	—
M82	Sign Limited sdn 4d	4,345	44,920	—
M83	Designer sdn 4d	4,345	46,435	—
M85	Signature L sdn 4d	4,518	50,525	—

2006 Engines	bore×stroke	bhp	availability
V-6, 182.0	3.50×3.13	220	S-Zephyr
V-8, 240.0	3.39×3.35	280	S-LS
V-8, 281.0	3.60×3.60	239	S-Town Car

** Figures not available at time of publication.

Marmon

Howard Marmon was a mechanical genius who strove to build the perfect automobile. By some accounts, he did exactly that with his magnificent 1931-33 Sixteen. But the Depression was not a time for perfectionists or super-expensive luxury giants, so Marmon Motor Car Company went out in a blaze of V-16 glory after only a few years of significant production.

Marmon grew up around his father's Indianapolis milling-machine business, Nordyke and Marmon, said to be the world's largest by the turn of the century. In 1902, after earning a mechanical-engineering degree from the University of California at Berkeley, Howard returned to the family firm as its chief engineer. He was only 26. That same year, he tinkered up his first car: an air-cooled V-twin with pressure lubrication, then a revolutionary development.

Following in 1904 was the 50-cubic-inch V-4 Model A, another air-cooled ohv design but with an embryonic form of independent front suspension. Only six were built. The next year brought a similar Model B, a 2000-pound four-seater with a 90-inch wheelbase. Marmon sold 25 of those at $2500 each. After the derivative C35 and D36 came the ambitious M37 of 1906, a $5000 seven-seat touring car with a 128-inch wheelbase and a 65-horsepower air-cooled V-8 with a massive 707 cid. Yet the car scaled a svelte 3500 pounds, reflecting Howard's passion for low weight through extensive use of aluminum and various alloys.

The M37 didn't sell at all, so Marmon turned to conventional water-cooled inline-fours in 1909. At the same time, he devised his first Six, the Model 32. Marmon had already discovered the sales value of racing, but the 32 propelled him to the publicity pinnacle when a modified version called the "Wasp" won the first Indianapolis 500 in 1911. (Other racing Marmons racked up 51 competition victories in 1909-12.) This encouraged Howard to sell a road version, which arrived as the 1913 Model 48. But it sold poorly at $5000—then a king's ransom. So, too, did the successor 41 of 1914-15. Then came the advanced 1916 Model 34. Its 340-cid six was virtually all-aluminum, as were the transmission and differential housings, body, fenders, hood, even the radiator. The 34 was an outstanding performer and its balanced chassis gave good handling. Durable, too. Driven by a relay team, one trekked from New York to San Francisco in only five days to break Cannonball Baker's record run in a Cadillac by a substantial 41 hours. Sales more than tripled.

Nordyke and Marmon was contracted to build 5000 Liberty aircraft engines during World War I. Howard, meantime, joined the Army Air Corps, rising to the rank of lieutenant-colonel. He then returned home to usher in an improved Model 34, but sales were difficult due to the 1924 economic downturn. With that, Howard's older brother, Walter, resigned as company president in 1924 (to become board chairman) and hired George M. Williams to put the firm back on its feet. New president Williams thought the solution was lower-priced Marmons with conventional small-displacement straight-eights. He was right: Sales improved through 1926, when Nordyke and Marmon became Marmon Motor Company. By 1929, volume had risen to 22,300. Meanwhile, Howard set up a "front" firm called Midwest Aircraft, where he developed a V-16.

Marmon Motors continued with Williams' Eights, issuing new examples of that engine type almost yearly. This activity peaked in 1930 with a facelifted Marmon-Roosevelt, revised straight-eight models designated 69 and 79, and a luxurious new Big Eight with 315 cid and 125 bhp. Prices now stretched from $995 to $3170. But this expansion was too soon and too rapid, and Marmon's image became confused. The Roosevelt (named for President Teddy) was a low-priced "junior edition" typical of the optimistic late '20s, but it failed to sell well and also tarnished the high-class aura of senior Marmons. As a result, registrations plunged nearly 50 percent to 12,369.

1932 Sixteen Touring Cabriolet

Amid this bad news came one result of five years' research and dreaming by Howard Marmon: the unbelievable 1931 Sixteen. Packing 200 bhp from 490.8 cid, this amazing giant was guaranteed to do 100 mph. But it carried a giant-size price: $5100-$5400. Worse, the Cadillac Sixteen, which had arrived a year earlier—much to Howard's dismay—was draining off what little demand still existed for such extraordinary machines in extraordinarily hard times.

Marmon advertised the Sixteen as "The World's Most Advanced Car," and not without reason. Beside overhead valves actuated by pushrods from a single camshaft, the engine employed all-aluminum construction that was a triumph of the foundry art. Both the block and crankcase were cast as a single unit, the block actually being a "Y" in section. One dual-throat downdraft carburetor fed the fuel, and a single cast manifold served both cylinder banks. Despite its size, the engine weighed a relatively light 930 pounds fully dressed, some 370 pounds less than Cadillac's slightly smaller V-16. This contributed to a weight-to-power ratio of just 4.65 pounds per horsepower, an impressive figure for the day, likely rivaled only by Duesenberg.

Howard's passion for minimal weight was naturally evident elsewhere. The hood, front and rear splash aprons, running-board aprons, spare-wheel mounts, headlamp and taillamp brackets, and even the fuel-filler pipe were all made of aluminum. Because of this, few cars could approach the Marmon for sheer speed or through-the-gears acceleration. It accelerated faster than even the mighty Duesenberg Model J, though the Duesie had a higher top speed due to the superior breathing of its twin-cam engine. But while the Marmon was certainly pricey, it cost little more than half as much as a Duesenberg *chassis*.

The body design caused as much stir as the engine. This wasn't Howard's work, but he deserves credit for hiring an industrial designer at a time when that profession was in its infancy. The designer was 47-year-old Walter Dorwin Teague, Sr., though he admitted that his son did all the original sketches and drawings, as well as the full-size renderings and some interior concepts, including the unusual aircraft-type instrument panel. W. D. Teague, Jr., then a student at MIT, completed these tasks on weekends and in summer school. Since the name of the youngster's father carried considerably more prestige, Marmon publicity gave credit to Teague, Sr. Indeed, he handled the contract work with Marmon and translated the concept into production form.

With no resemblance to any previous Marmon, the Sixteen looked modern but not radical. A raked Vee'd radiator devoid of ornament or badge led to a hood concealing the water filler. The doors extended down almost to the running boards. The fenders were designed to hide chassis components. Further accenting a low-slung profile were a prominent beltline that ran absolutely straight around the body, a windshield raked to match the radiator, and ultralow rooflines.

The Sixteen was touted as a "new concept in fine cars," with styling and engineering given equal emphasis. All but three of the 390 Sixteens ultimately built carried "standard" bodies built by LeBaron: five sedans, two coupes, and a victoria. The only custom bodies known are two Waterhouse tourers and a very individual victoria built by Hayes to a design by Alexis de Sakhnoffsky. These were likely artifacts of Howard's plan to offer 32 "regular" custom styles by the likes of Murphy, Waterhouse, and Judkins: town cars, all-weather phaetons, limousines, speedsters, and "sunshine-roof" sedans. Minuscule sales precluded this grand idea (announced in September 1931).

As if the Sixteen weren't enough, Marmon offered five different Eights in two 1931 series. The first series, announced in August 1930, comprised the 120-inch wheelbase Model 79 with the 110-bhp, 303.2-cid engine; the 114-inch Model 69 with an 84-bhp, 211.2-cid engine; and the 136-inch Big Eight, still with a 125-bhp, 315.2-cid powerplant. The last became the Model 88 for the "second series" issued in January 1931, and was reduced some $450 to spark sales—which it didn't. At the same time came a new Model 70 to replace both the model 79 and the 69; it used the 69's engine but sold for $950-$1045, far less than its predecessors.

Despite this weeding out of less-popular models, Marmon sales dropped by over half. Registrations (the only reliable figures available) totaled 5687 for calendar '31, good for only 25th in the industry between LaSalle and struggling Reo. Sixteen sales were hobbled by a long delay. Prototypes attracted much attention at the winter auto shows, but deliveries didn't begin until April 1931. By that point, most prospects had opted for a Cadillac Sixteen or something less conspicuous. As a result, Cadillac's Sixteen outsold Marmon's by a 10-to-1 margin.

Besides plummeting sales, Marmon was also now contending with wracking internal problems. The engineering department split into two warring camps, production people had trouble getting out the Sixteens, and the sales force was struggling to overcome the Roosevelt's low-bucks image.

Retrenchment seemed the only course, so the 1932 line was pared to just the Sixteen, the 70, and the 125. The last was a two-model line offered on a 125-inch wheelbase to replace the Big Eight/88, and it gave away nothing but a shorter distance between the wheel centers and many dollars in price. Both the sedan and coupe listed for just $1420 versus $2220-$2920 for comparable predecessor models. Yet for all this, registrations were the lowest yet, just 1365.

Those price and model reductions left some feeling that Marmon was about to leave the fine-car field. Actually, it was preparing to do just the opposite. For 1933, the Sixteen was the only Marmon you could buy, and you could get one for about $1000 less on average. The coupe and sedan dropped to $4825, the seven-passenger sedan fell to $4975, and the convertible sedan eased to $5075.

1932 Sixteen close-coupled four-door sedan

1932 HCM Special prototype

Specifications were unchanged.

The price cuts didn't solve the big problem. Marmon Motor Car Company was broke. It was duly sold in January 1934 to the American Automotive Corporation, organized and backed by Harry Miller, the famed Indy race-car designer, and a hotshot promoter named Preston Tucker, whose own postwar car would win both fame and infamy. But they couldn't get things moving again, so Marmon was liquidated by receivers in 1937. The new company produced Marmon-Herrington trucks into the 1980s and truck components, such as four-wheel-drive conversions, after that.

Left stillborn was the HCM Special, a revolutionary V-12 car designed by Howard Marmon and chassis engineer George Freers. This envisioned a cut-down Sixteen with four-wheel independent suspension, tubular "backbone" frame, and an aluminum body with new Teague styling highlighted by slab sides, pontoon fenders, and integral headlamps and trunk. A prototype was built for $160,000, financed out of necessity from Howard's personal fortune, but it never had a chance. It was stored on the Marmon estate in North Carolina until Howard's death in 1943, eventually it made its way to industrial designer Brooks Stevens' automotive museum in Mequon, Wisconsin.

Like so many other makes, Marmon fell victim to the Depression for lack of corporate strength and a strong market base. All it had was brilliant engineering and bold visions. Too bad they weren't enough for any car company in those very hard times.

Specifications

1930

Big Eight (wb 136.0)	Wght	Price	Prod
touring 7P	4,200	3,170	37
cpe 2-4P	4,100	2,850	123
sdn 4d	4,210	2,720	473
sdn 7P	4,307	2,920	270
Model 79 (wb 120.0)			
spdstr phtn 5P	3,800	2,020	40
cpe 2-4P	3,805	1,995	124
sdn 4d	3,900	2,020	958
Model 69 (wb 114.0)			
spdstr phtn 5P	3,025	1,610	32
cpe 2-4P	3,011	1,495	196
sdn 4d	3,100	1,520	1,605
Roosevelt (wb 112.8) - 9,000 built*			
sdn 4d	2,695	995	—
cpe	—	—	—
Victoria 2d	—	—	—
conv cpe	—	—	—

*Approximate

1930 Engines	bore×stroke	bhp	availability
I-8, 201.9	2.75×4.25	72	S-Roosevelt
I-8, 211.2	2.81×4.25	84	S-69
I-8, 303.2	3.19×4.75	110	S-79
I-8, 315.2	3.25×4.75	125	S-Big Eight

1931

Big Eight (wb 136.0)	Wght	Price	Prod*
touring 7P	4,200	3,170	—
cpe 2-4P	4,100	2,850	—
sdn 4d	4,210	2,720	—
sdn 7P	4,307	2,920	—
Model 79 (wb 120.0)			
phtn 5P	3,800	2,020	—
cpe 2-4P	3,805	1,995	—
brougham 5P	3,884	2,070	—
sdn 4d	3,900	2,020	—
Model 69 (wb 114.0)			
phtn 5P	3,025	1,610	—
cpe 2-4P	3,011	1,495	—
brougham 4d	3,153	1,565	—
sdn 4d	3,103	1,520	—
Model 70 (wb 112.8) - second series			
cpe 2-4P	2,694	950	—
conv cpe 2-4P	2,586	1,045	—
victoria cpe 2-4P	2,678	995	—
sdn 4d	2,823	995	—
Model 88 (wb 130.0; lwb-136.0) - second series			
cpe 2-4P	4,290	2,275	—
sdn 4d	4,375	2,220	—
club sdn 5P	4,398	2,345	—
lwb sdn 7P	4,504	2,495	—
Sixteen (wb 145.0)**			
cpe 2-4P	5,090	5,220	—
sdn, cl coupled 4d	5,335	5,270	—
sdn 4d	5,360	5,200	—
sdn 7P	5,440	5,400	—

1931 Engines	bore×stroke	bhp	availability
I-8, 211.2	2.81×4.25	84	S-69, 70
I-8, 303.2	3.19×4.75	110	S-79
I-8, 315.2	3.25×4.75	125	S-Big Eight, 88
V-16, 490.8	3.13×4.00	200	S-Sixteen

1932

Model 70 (wb 112.8)	Wght	Price	Prod*
cpe 2-4P	2,694	950	—
sdn 4d	2,823	995	—
Model 125 (wb 125.0)			
cpe 2-4P	3,625	1,420	—
sdn 4d	3,653	1,420	—
Sixteen (wb 145.0)**			
cpe 2-4P	5,090	5,700	—
sdn 4d, close-coupld	5,335	5,800	—
sdn 4d	5,360	5,700	—
sdn 7P	5,440	5,900	—

1932 Engines	bore×stroke	bhp	availability
I-8, 211.2	2.81×4.25	84	S-70
I-8, 315.2	3.25×4.75	125	S-125
V-16, 490.8	3.13×4.00	200	S-Sixteen

1933

Sixteen (wb 145.0)**	Wght	Price	Prod*
cpe 2-4P	5,090	4,825	—
sdn 4d	5,360	4,825	—
conv sdn 5P	5,285	5,075	—
sdn 7P	5,440	4,975	—

1933 Engine	bore×stroke	bhp	availability
V-16, 490.8	3.13×4.00	200	S-all

*Because of its size and limited volume, Marmon did not record model year production per se. Calendar year registrations were as follows:

1930:	12,369
1931:	5,687
1932:	1,365
1933:	86

(source: *The Production Figure Book for U.S. Cars*)

** Total 1931-33 Sixteen production: 390

Mercury

Mercury was conceived largely by Edsel Ford, who saw a place for it in the Ford Motor Company lineup some time before his father Henry did. It arrived for 1939 in the same price league as the Pontiac Eight but somewhat below Oldsmobile—precisely where Edsel wanted it and Dearborn needed it. While Mercury would take many years to approach those GM makes in volume, it was successful from the start. Production averaged about 80,000 per year in the early '40s, good for 12th or 13th in the industry, thus winning important new business for Dearborn by filling the huge price gap between Ford and the Lincoln Zephyr.

The original Mercury engine would remain in production through 1948. A 239-cid L-head V-8, it was a slightly larger version of the Ford "V-8/85," having the same stroke but a larger bore. Brake horsepower was 95 through '41, then 100. Mercury quickly gained a reputation for performance appropriate to its name (after the winged messenger god in Greek mythology). Well-tuned stock models were quicker than V-8 Fords, and were usually capable of turning close to 100 mph.

Mercury bowed on a 116-inch wheelbase, four inches longer than the '39 Ford's and sufficient to give its similar styling a "more-important" look. A dashboard with strip-type instruments was also like Ford's, but Mercury's column-mounted gearshift was a talking point at the time. Styling for 1939-40 featured a crisply pointed "prow," beautifully curved fenders, and rounded body lines. Initial offerings comprised two- and four-door "beetleback" sedans, a notchback sedan coupe, and a convertible coupe spanning a price range of $916-$1018. A $1212 convertible sedan was added for 1940, that year's heaviest and most-expensive Mercury. But four-door ragtops had waned in popularity, so this one was dropped for 1941. Only about 1150 were built.

Models expanded to seven for '41 with a two/four-passenger coupe, business coupe, and wood-bodied station wagon. Styling, again in the Ford mold, was chunkier and less graceful despite a two-inch longer wheelbase; with higher, bulkier fenders; a divider-bar grille; and fender-top parking lights.

Mercury tried harder for 1942 with a serious facelift, the aforementioned 100-bhp engine, and a new extra-cost semi-automatic transmission called "Liquamatic." The last proved

1939 Series 99A convertible coupe

1942 Series 29A station wagon

1940 Series 09A convertible coupe

1946 Series 69M Sportsman convertible coupe

1941 Series 19A 3-passenger coupe

1947½ 69M station wagon

very troublesome, though, and was quickly canceled. America's entry into World War II limited model-year production to fewer than 23,000 units. Chrome was "in," at least before the government diverted it to war use. All '42 Mercs wore a broad, glittery two-section horizontal-bar grille, double chrome bands on each fender, and a bright full-perimeter molding at the beltline. Parking lights shifted inboard to flank a still-pointy hood. The general effect was busier than '41, which had been busier than 1940. Like other '42s, the mostly chromeless, late-production "blackout" Mercurys are now prized by collectors.

Before war's end, Henry Ford II, Edsel's son and old Henry's grandson, returned from the Navy to run Ford Motor Company. Edsel had died in 1943 of complications due to stomach cancer. Old Henry would live until 1947. HF II quickly resumed civilian production, and Mercury placed 10th in the 1946 industry race with about 86,600 units. As Dearborn delayed its first all-new postwar models to 1949, interim Mercurys were similar to the '42 editions. The inboard parking lights and two-band fender moldings remained, but the hood was blunted above a new vertical-bar grille carrying a large "Mercury Eight" nameplate. Mechanicals were unchanged except the fact that Liquamatic didn't return. Ford's adoption of the 239 V-8 for 1946 was hardly to Mercury's advantage.

Mercury's prewar lineup also carried over into 1946 with a single exception: The business coupe was replaced by the novel Sportsman convertible. Comparable to the like-named Ford model, Mercury's Sportsman was adorned with maple or yellow birch framing with mahogany inserts. The wood was structural, not merely decorative. This created a problem at the rear, where standard fenders wouldn't fit. Both Sportsmans thus used 1941 sedan delivery fenders and wood shaped to suit. The solid-wood framing was beautifully mitred and finished with multiple coats of varnish. But with only 205 sold, the Mercury Sportsman was dropped after '46. The likely reason for the low sales was high price: $2209, some $200 more than Ford's version, which did better business and continued into 1948.

Ford's most-important 1947 corporate development was the organization of the Lincoln-Mercury Division. Henry II decided that the two makes could be more competitive as an autonomous operation *a la* the various General Motors units. That year's Mercurys used more of the raw materials that had been scarce during wartime: mainly aluminum (for pistons and hood ornament) and chrome (interior hardware and grille frame). Belt moldings now ended just ahead of the cowl. Postwar inflation boosted prices an average of $450, lifting the range to $1450-$2200. Production of the '47 models didn't begin until February of that year, so Mercury's output was about the same as its 1946 tally.

Except for serial numbers and deletion of the two-door sedan, the '48s were unchanged. They were sold from November 1947

1949 Series SCM two-door station wagon

1951 Series 1CM two-door station wagon

1949 Series 9CM convertible coupe

1952 Series 2M station wagon

1950 Series 0CM convertible coupe

1952 Series 2M Custom hardtop sport coupe

1953 Monterey convertible coupe

1954 Monterey Sun Valley hardtop coupe

1955 Montclair hardtop coupe

1955 Montclair convertible coupe

1956 Medalist phaeton hardtop sedan

through mid-April 1948, when the '49s appeared. As a result, model-year production ended at only about 50,250.

The '49 Mercurys bowed with flush-fender "inverted bathtub" styling like that of the 1948-49 Packards and Hudsons. Mercury's new look stemmed from sporadic wartime work by Dearborn designers. Wheelbase was unchanged, but bodyshells were shared with a new standard Lincoln line instead of Ford, the result of a last-minute change in postwar plans. Styling was good: massive, yet clean and streamlined. The grille looked something like the '48 affair, but was lower and wider. A single bright molding ran full-length at midflank. As before, a single series offered four body styles: coupe, four-door Sport Sedan (with "suicide" rear-hinged back doors), convertible, and a new two-door wagon with less structural wood than the superseded four-door style.

Like '49 Fords, Mercurys were treated to a new chassis with fully independent front suspension, weight-saving Hotchkiss drive (replacing torque-tube), and a live axle on parallel longitudinal leaf springs, ousting at last old Henry's cherished single transverse leaf. Resuming its power lead over Ford, Mercury got a stroked V-8 with 255.4 cid, dual downdraft Holley carburetors and 110 bhp to become a genuine 100-mph performer for the first time. Also introduced was an automatic-overdrive option priced at $97, teamed with a 4.27:1 rear axle instead of the standard 3.90:1.

The 1949 Mercury was an attractive buy with its Lincoln-like looks, lower prices ($1979-$2716), and a V-8 more-potent than Ford's (necessary to offset some 100 extra pounds in curb weight). Buyers responded by taking over 301,000 of the '49s—more than three times the volume of Mercury's previous best year and good for sixth in the industry, another all-time high.

Despite few major changes, sales continued strong for the next two seasons: close to 294,000 for 1950 and a record-setting 310,000-plus for '51, when Mercury again claimed sixth. The 1950 models gained a hood-front chrome molding bearing the Mercury name; the '51s combined this with a large semicircular crest and also sported more-prominent grille bars, larger parking lights (swept back to the front wheel wells), and longer rear fenders with rounded corners and vertical trailing edges. Horsepower rose a nominal two for '51, when a significant new option arrived in Merc-O-Matic Drive. This was, of course, the new three-speed fully automatic transmission developed with the Warner Gear Division of Borg-Warner (and also offered for '51 by Ford as Ford-O-Matic).

A couple of new models were added for 1950: a stripped price-leader coupe ($1875) and the interesting Monterey. The latter was a spiffy limited edition with upgraded interior and a top covered in canvas or vinyl. At around $2150, it cost some $160 more than the standard coupe, but it wasn't the costliest 1950-51 Merc: The wagon was over $400 more. Monterey's purpose, as with the Ford Crestliner and Lincoln Lido/Capri of those years, was to stand in for the pillarless "hardtop-convertibles" being offered by GM and Chrysler rivals.

Hardtops arrived in force for 1952, when Ford Motor Company was the only Big Three maker with all-new styling. Mercury got a pair of hardtops: a Sport Coupe and a more-deluxe Monterey version (*sans* covered roof). Monterey also offered a convertible and a four-door sedan (now minus the "suicide" doors). Following an industry trend, wagons were all-steel four-doors with simulated wood trim. Base-trim two- and four-door sedans completed the lineup. Bodyshells were again shared with Ford, though Mercury retained a three-inch longer wheelbase, all of it ahead of the cowl. Also shared with Ford was tight, clean styling, though the resemblance with that year's equally new Lincoln didn't hurt. Higher compression boosted the flathead V-8 to 125 bhp on unchanged displace-

1956 Medalist hardtop coupe

1957 Montclair hardtop coupe

1957 Turnpike Cruiser hardtop sedan

1958 Montclair Turnpike Cruiser hardtop coupe

1958 Colony Park hardtop station wagon

1959 Colony Park Country Cruiser hardtop station wagon

1959 Montclair Cruiser hardtop coupe

1960½ Comet four-door sedan

ment. The Korean war limited 1952 production throughout Detroit, so Mercury built only 172,087 cars to finish eighth in the annual race.

Mercury bowed its first formal two-series line for 1953: the Custom series offered a hardtop and two- and four-door sedans, while the Monterey line listed a convertible, hardtop, wagon, or four-door sedan. Retained from '52 was a trendy dashboard with big aircraft-type levers flanking a large half-moon gauge cluster. Business picked up with the end of Korean war restrictions, and Mercury moved nearly 305,000 cars, though it once again ran eighth. Prices ranged from $2000 for the Custom two-door to nearly $2600 for the Monterey wagon.

A significant engineering change for 1954 was Mercury's first overhead-valve V-8, a bigger version of the new "Y-Block" design featured on that year's Ford. Though little larger than Mercury's previous L-head at 256 cid, the ohv had modern short-stroke dimensions, a five-main-bearing crankshaft, and much more horsepower—161 with the standard four-barrel carburetor. With a low 3.90 rear axle and standard transmission, the V-8 made any '54 Merc quick off the line. Equally noteworthy was a ball-joint front suspension, another development shared with Ford.

Styling improved for '54 via wraparound taillights and a clean but more-aggressive grille with larger bullet guards. Joining

1960 Montclair Cruiser hardtop sedan

1962 Monterey Custom convertible coupe

1961 Monterey convertible coupe

1963 Comet Custom Sportster hardtop coupe

1962 Meteor Custom four-door sedan

1963 Meteor S-33 hardtop coupe

previous models was a new top-line hardtop, the Monterey Sun Valley (a name that must have amused Californians), which is more famous now than it was then. An outgrowth of Dearborn's experiments with plastic-topped cars (as was Ford's similar '54 Skyliner), the Sun Valley was nice in theory: the airiness of a convertible combined with closed-car comfort and practicality. In practice, though, it was something else. Though the Plexiglas front half-roof was tinted and a snap-in shade was provided for hot weather, customers complained the interior heated up like a sauna. Sales were unimpressive: just 9761 of the '54s and a mere 1787 for the follow-up 1955 Montclair version.

At about 260,000 units in all, 1954 wasn't Mercury's greatest sales year, but hopes were high for '55. With colorful new styling on the basic 1952-54 shell, Mercury's first wheelbase increase since 1941—to 119 inches except on wagons, which remained at 118—and a more-potent V-8, the '55s couldn't miss. They didn't: Model-year production was a record 329,000-plus.

Topping the '55 fleet was the new Montclair line: four-door sedan, hardtop, convertible, and Sun Valley. All wore a slim contrast-color panel outlined in bright metal beneath the side windows. A step below were the Monterey sedan, hardtop, and wagon, followed by the Custom series with the same body styles plus a two-door sedan. Common to all were Mercury's first wrapped windshield, an evolutionary form of the '54 grille, hooded headlamps, and eye-catching surface ornamentation. A Y-block V-8 swelled to 292 cid was offered in two forms: 188 bhp for Custom and Monterey and 198 bhp for Montclair. The higher output version was also available as an option for lesser models with the optional Merc-O-Matic.

Four-door Phaeton hardtops arrived for 1956's "Big M" line, which represented an ambitious expansion into somewhat uncharted territory. To stay competitive in the face of rising prices, Mercury fielded a cut-rate group of Medalist two- and four-door hardtops and sedans at the bottom end of the medium-price ladder. But inflation made these "low-price" Mercs more expensive than 1955 Customs ($2250-$2460)—and not that much cheaper than the better-trimmed '56 Customs ($2350-$2800). Dealers pushed hard with two-door sedans, but Medalist sales came to only 45,812 in all. Custom, Monterey, and Montclair all beat the price-leader by more than 2-to-1. With that, Medalist was duly dropped, only to resurface for '58, when it interfered in a price bracket that should have been reserved exclusively for the new Edsel.

Mercury's '56 styling was a good update of its '55 look. All models save Medalists wore jazzy Z-shaped side moldings that delineated the contrast color area with optional two-toning (the area below was generally matched to the roof). Monterey and Montclair added Phaeton hardtop sedans at mid-season, replacements for their low-roof pillared Sport Sedans held over from mid-1955. Mercury also offered a second convertible for

1963 Monterey Custom "Breezeway" hardtop sedan

1965 Comet Caliente hardtop coupe

1964 Comet Cyclone hardtop coupe

1965 Park Lane Marauder hardtop coupe

1964 Montclair Marauder hardtop sedan

1965 Montclair Marauder hardtop coupe

the first time, a Custom. The Y-block was enlarged again, this time to 312 cid, good for 210 bhp that could be tuned to 235; the latter was standard for Monterey and Montclair.

Though 1956 was a "breather" for the industry as a whole, Mercury was an exception with some 328,000 sales, slightly off its '55 pace. An encouraging sign was the premium Montclair, which proved almost as popular as it had in frantic '55. The midline Monterey was still the big breadwinner, though.

The '57s were all-new, trumpeted as "a dramatic expression of dream car design." They were previewed in 1956 by the XM-Turnpike Cruiser show car, which also had direct showroom counterparts in new top-line Turnpike Cruiser two- and four-door hardtops.

The Turnpike Cruiser had glitz and gimmicks galore: "skylight dual curve windshield," drop-down reverse-slant rear window, and dual air intakes over the A-posts housing little horizontal antennae. If that wasn't enough, there was optional "Seat-O-Matic," which automatically powered the front seat to one of 49 possible positions at the twist of two dials. Mercury also joined Chrysler in offering pushbutton automatic transmission controls, another "space-age" Cruiser standard. Arriving late in the season was a Convertible Cruiser, honoring Mercury's selection as the 1957 Indy 500 pace car, and supplied with replica regalia decals. Yet for all their gadgets—and likely because of them—the Cruisers failed miserably. They were not just expensive—$3760-$3850 for the hardtops, $4100 for the ragtop—they were too far out, even for the dawning space age.

Significantly, the '57s had their own bodyshells on a new 122-inch-wheelbase chassis—the first time Mercurys were neither "senior Fords" nor "junior Lincolns." Like that year's all-new Ford, this was done partly to prepare for the '58 Edsel line that borrowed some from both makes. Monterey and Montclair were bereft of station wagons, which were split off as a separate series with six models. Offered, from the top, were a woody-look Colony Park, a four-door nine-seater; metal-sided two- and four-door Voyagers; and three Commuters with the various seat and door combinations. All had pillarless-hardtop rooflines, the new rage in Big Three wagons.

Styling matched the "Big M's" more-expansive '57 dimensions, looking square, heavy, and contrived. Up front, a massive dual-oblong bumper nestled beneath a slim concave grille of vertical bars. Headlights were quads where legal, regular duals otherwise. Long scallops, typically contrast-colored, carried the beltline from midbody through the upper rear fenders to huge pie-slice taillamps. Weight was up, but so was horsepower. A 255-bhp 312 was newly standard except on Cruisers, which carried a 290-bhp, 368-cid Lincoln V-8 that was optional elsewhere.

The 1957 Mercurys did fairly well, but less so than the '56s. Volume dropped to about 286,000 and the make's production rank fell from seventh to eighth—not encouraging for an all-

1966 Colony Park station wagon

1966 Comet Caliente convertible coupe

1967 Monterey hardtop coupe

1967 Comet Cyclone GT hardtop coupe

1967 Cougar hardtop coupe

new design in a fairly strong sales year.

A minor facelift yielded slightly quieter styling for 1958, but production plunged to 153,000 in a disastrous industry year. The Convertible Cruiser was abandoned (after only 1265 of the '57s) and the two closed Cruisers became Montclair submodels. Lower prices failed to perk up sales (barely 6400 between them). The cheap Medalist returned for a brief encore with two- and four-door sedans, but again proved disappointing: Only 18,732 were sold. Topping the line was the new Park Lane series of two hardtops and a convertible (also available as Montclairs and Montereys). These were ostensibly Cruiser replacements with less hoke and a giant 360-bhp 430-cid V-8 shared with that year's Lincolns. A new automatic transmission called Multi-Drive debuted (basically Ford Division's Cruise-O-Matic), as did a 383-cid V-8—the same size as one of Chrysler's new '58 wedgehead engines but with more-oversquare dimensions. The 383 was standard for all '58 Mercs, save Medalists (which came with a 235-bhp 312) and Park Lane, and delivered 312 or 330 bhp depending on model.

Although the bottom dropped out of the medium-price market in '58, Mercury remained eighth despite building only 40 percent of its 1957 volume. But significantly, Rambler passed the Big M in sales and was fast gaining on Pontiac, Olds, and Buick. Mercury would join the rush to compacts and intermediates soon enough. In the meantime, it could only offer more of the same.

More the '59 Mercurys definitely had, with even bigger bodies on a four-inch longer wheelbase. Styling was still square but more sculpted, marked by a mile-wide grille, huge bumpers at each end, enormous windshields and rear windows, and a more sharply creased version of the odd 1957-58 rear-fender scallops. The Medalist and Turnpike Cruiser models were forgotten, and Montclair and wagons each slimmed from six models to four. Engines were detuned in a faint nod to a newly economy-conscious public. The '59 slate listed a 210-bhp 312 for Monterey, a 345-bhp 430 for Park Lane, and 280- and 322-bhp 383s for others. Despite the retrenchment, model-year volume failed to top 150,000 units—hardly the hoped-for recovery.

Looking back, Mercury sales stumbled after 1956 at least in part because the fleet, good-looking cars of earlier years were abandoned for shiny, begadgeted behemoths that couldn't hope to sell well in a down economy. But the make would return to "hot cars" in the '60s and, with them, achieve new success.

Indeed, volume went up substantially for 1960—to over 271,000—though that was owed mainly to the new compact Comet. The four-series big-car line (which might have been Edsels had things gone better there) remained two-ton heavyweights with huge compound-curve windshields, but a handsome facelift removed a little chrome while adding a tidy concave grille and more-discreet "gullwing" rear fenders. Model choices were mostly as before: Cruiser two- and four-door hardtops in each series, four-door Monterey/Montclair sedans, Monterey two-door sedan, Park Lane convertible and, still a distinct series, four-door Commuter and wood-sided Colony Park hardtop wagons.

Mercury offered three V-8s for 1960, all with lower compression for the sake of economy (such as it was). The 312 was cut to 205 bhp for Monterey and Commuter, the 383 returned as a single 280-bhp option, and a 310-bhp Lincoln 430 was standard elsewhere. Production rose slightly to some 155,000.

The "Big M" shrunk noticeably in both size and price for 1961. In fact, it was again a "deluxe Ford," though on an inch-longer, 120-inch wheelbase. This was done in the interest of production economies as well as fuel economy, and the resulting cars were indeed lighter, thriftier, and more maneuverable. Of course, this also ended four years of unique Mercury chassis and bodyshells, reflecting the collapse of Dearborn's grand mid-'50s "divisionalization" scheme, a stab at a GM-style five-make structure that had spawned separate Edsel, Continental, Lincoln, and Mercury Divisions. Dismal sales since '57 had rendered a separate Mercury platform unacceptably expensive, hence this return to the make's original concept.

Beginning with the 1960 Comet, Mercury followed the growing industry trend of adding models in new sizes, with name changes sometimes confusing buyers. The latter was perhaps symbolic of the make's mixed fortunes in the '60s. Still, Comet and Monterey spanned the entire decade. A new name was Meteor, long the brand of a Canadian-made Mercury derivative, which appeared on two quite different U.S. Mercurys.

The first arrived at the low end of the 1961 full-size line: two- and four-door sedans and hardtops in "600" and nicer "800" trim, offered at vastly reduced prices beginning at $2535. In effect, they filled the gap left by Edsel's demise the previous year. Monterey resumed as the premium Mercury, listing a four-door sedan and hardtop, a two-door hardtop, and a convertible. The separate Station Wagon series reverted to conventional pillared four-doors: six- and nine-passenger Commuters and Colony Parks. Styling was even more conservative than in 1960. The grille remained concave and fins vestigial, but flanks were rounded and '50s gimmicks were mere memories. Meteors carried a standard 223-cid Ford six with 135 bhp; the optional V-8, included on Montereys, was a 175-bhp 292. Across-the-board options comprised a 220-bhp 352 and new big-block 390s with 300 or 330 bhp.

Although Meteor actually outsold Monterey, sales were not spectacular. Accordingly, the line was replaced for '62 by a "Monterey 6," and the name moved to Mercury's version of the new intermediate Ford Fairlane.

Most everything said about the 1962-63 Fairlane (see *Ford*) applies equally to the second Meteor. Its styling was busier and model names were different, but bodies were shared. So were powertrains, including Ford's fine new small-block V-8 with 221 cid and 145 bhp or 260 cid and 164 bhp. Custom denoted the upmarket midsize Meteors, S-33 the sportier bucket-seaters—a two-door sedan for '62, a hardtop coupe for '63. Wagons—woody-look Country Cruiser and plain-sided Villagers (a name transferred from the Edsel line)—joined hardtops as 1963 additions. For all that, this Meteor didn't sell nearly as well as the Fairlane, and Mercury dropped it for 1964 in favor of an extensively upgraded Comet.

Once planned as an Edsel, the first Comet was basically Ford's hugely successful 1960 Falcon compact with squared-up rooflines, a double-row concave grille, and an extended stern with canted fins and oval taillamps. Wheelbase was 114 inches on two- and four-door sedans; wagons used Falcon's 109.5-inch span. Comet wasn't exciting, but it sold well: over 116,000 for the abbreviated debut season. Sales set a record for '61 at 197,000 and were strong for '62, which hurt Meteor. In fact, one reason Meteor didn't sell well is that Comet was comparably sized yet more affordable. Mercury was thus wise to make Comet its only small car after '63. Sales jumped by 55,000 units for '64 and remained high into '67.

Early Comets ran less than $100 above comparable Falcons, yet were more elaborately trimmed. S-22, a $2300 bucket-seat two-door sedan, responded to the sporty-compact craze beginning in 1961, when all Comets gained an optional 101-bhp six. Custom sedans and wagons and a posh Villager wagon with imitation wood trim aided '62 sales. The following year brought Custom and S-22 convertibles and Sportster hardtop coupes. A squarish facelift arrived for 1964, when S-22 was renamed Caliente and any Comet could be ordered with the outstanding 260-cid small-block. A midseason Caliente offshoot, the $2655

1967 Cougar XR-7 hardtop coupe

1968 Park Lane convertible coupe

1968 Cougar XR-7 7.0 Litre GT-E hardtop coupe

1968 Montego MX station wagon

1968 Cyclone fastback hardtop coupe

1969 Cougar CJ 428 hardtop coupe

1969 Marquis Brougham hardtop sedan

1969 Marauder X-100 hardtop coupe

1970 Montego MX Brougham hardtop sedan

1970 Cougar hardtop coupe

1970 Cyclone Spoiler 429 hardtop coupe

1971 Cougar XR-7 hardtop coupe

1972 Marquis Brougham hardtop sedan

Cyclone hardtop, offered even higher performance from a standard 210-bhp 289.

Comet received its first major overhaul for 1966, going from compact to intermediate by shifting to that year's new Fairlane platform. This underlined a basic marketing assumption: Mercury buyers were wealthier than Ford's, and thus probably wanted a compact larger than Falcon.

This 116-inch-wheelbase platform continued on Comets through 1969, but sales waned. By 1967, the Comet line started with a pair of very basic "202" sedans. The rest of that year's line comprised Capri (borrowed from Lincoln to replace "404"), Caliente, Cyclone, and Station Wagon. All gave way for 1968 to a three-series Montego line on the same wheelbase. This offered a standard sedan and hardtop coupe; MX sedan, hardtop coupe, convertible, and wagon; and top-line MX Brougham sedan and hardtop. The last was furnished with a high-quality cloth interior and other luxuries. The Comet name was retained for one price-leading two-door hardtop, then was temporarily shelved after 1969.

Mercury jumped into the midsize muscle-car market with both feet and won several racing laurels. Model-year 1966 brought a smooth Cyclone GT hardtop coupe and convertible powered by Ford's 335-bhp 390 and offered with a variety of useful suspension upgrades. The '67 was even more thrilling with optional 427s delivering 410-425 bhp.

Similar street racers were available for '68, though the 427 was detuned to 390 bhp. Besides Montego, that year's midsize line included new base and GT Cyclone hardtop coupes with curvy new lower-body contours and racy full-fastback rooflines *a la* Ford Mustang/Torino. There was also a one-year-only GT notchback hardtop. For 1969, Mercury unleashed the Cyclone CJ with Ford's 428-cid big-block Cobra Jet engines. GTs and CJs had black grilles, special emblems, bodyside paint stripes, and unique rear-end styling. CJs carried a functional hood scoop when equipped with optional Ram-Air induction. Although Ford won the 1968-69 NASCAR championship, Cyclones turned in some of the most notable performances. A memorable highlight was Cale Yarborough's win in the '68 Daytona 500 at an average speed of 143.25 mph.

For all its activity in compacts and intermediates, big cars remained Mercury's bread-and-butter in the '60s. Annual production averaged around 100,000, though there were back-to-back records for 1965-66—over 165,000 each year. Of all the big-Merc model names, only Monterey lasted the entire decade. The upper-echelon Montclair and Park Lane returned for 1964-68, then vanished again, replaced by a full-range Marquis line.

With Meteor an intermediate, the 1962 full-size fleet was reorganized around Monterey, Monterey Custom, and Station Wagon. The lone convertible shifted to the Custom series. Joining Mercury's bucket-seat brigade at midyear were the S-55 hardtop coupe and convertible. Styling was busier on all the big '62s, with tunneled taillights and a complex convex grille. All V-8s returned, as did the faithful "big six" as standard power for base Montereys and Commuter wagons.

A similar array on the same 120-inch wheelbase returned for 1963, when a heavy reskin introduced "Breezeway Styling" for nonwagon closed models: reverse-slant rear windows that dropped down for ventilation as on the old Turnpike Cruiser (and 1958-60 Continental Marks). Wagons were pared to a pair of Colony Parks. Joining the S-55 subseries at midyear was a handsome "slantback" two-door like Ford's Galaxie Sports Hardtop. Engines remained strictly V-8s: 390s with 250-330 bhp, a new 406-cid enlargement packing 385/405 bhp, and, as a late-season option, a high-performance 427 with 410 bhp.

Tradition returned for Silver Anniversary year 1964 in a revived four-series line of Monterey, Montclair, Park Lane, and Commuter/Colony Park wagons. The first three listed Breezeway two- and four-door hardtops and four-door sedans (Monterey still included a pillared two-door), plus slantback "Marauder" hardtop coupes and sedans. A toothy convex grille replaced the concave '63 unit. The previous 390 V-8s continued, but the 406s didn't, giving way to 427s with 410/425 optional bhp for all models save wagons. Big-inch Marauders were awesome performers.

The record 1965 model year brought a larger full-size body with crisp, rectilinear lines "in the Lincoln Continental tradition," as well as a new "torque box" frame (tuned for each body to minimize noise, vibration, and harshness). Wagons now rode the 119-inch Ford wheelbase; other models were up to 123. Breezeways thinned to a trio of four-door sedans, all hardtops were now slantbacks, and the Marauder name was de-emphasized amid calls for greater automotive safety. V-8s now comprised a quartet of 390s with 250-330 bhp, plus a single 425-bhp 427. The basic '65 look carried into 1966 with a new diecast "electric-shaver" grille and, for hardtop coupes, a "sweep-style roof" with a concave backlight.

More-rounded bodysides mixed well with sharp-edged fenders for '67. Sedans adopted conventional rooflines but still offered an optional drop-down backlight. Hardtop coupes received "faster" roof profiles. Three new limited-production line-top-

1972 Cougar XR-7 hardtop coupe

1972 Montego MX hardtop coupe prototype

1973 Cougar XR-7 hardtop coupe

1974 Marquis Brougham four-door sedan

1974 Cougar XR-7 coupe

pers arrived: Marquis, a two-door hardtop with broad C-pillars and standard vinyl-roof covering, a similar Park Lane Brougham hardtop sedan, and a Park Lane Brougham Breezeway four-door sedan. Intermediates were waging Mercury's sporty-car wars, so the bucket-seat S-55 ragtop and hardtop were in their final year—and just a Monterey option package now. Respective production was minuscule: just 145 and 570.

After a minor '68 facelift, the big Mercs were fully revised for 1969. Wheelbases grew to 121 inches on wagons and 124 on other models (except Marauder), sizes that would persist until their first downsizing for 1979. Series regrouped around base Monterey, revived Monterey Custom, and a full Marquis line comprising Colony Park wagon, convertible, and base and Brougham sedans, hardtop coupes, and hardtop sedans. Riding the shorter 121-inch wheelbase was a new Marauder, a high-performance "tunnelback" hardtop that garnered 14,666 sales. Offered in standard and spiffier X-100 trim, it shared Marquis' hidden-headlamp front and the ventless side glass used by most other models. V-8s comprised the usual 390s and a new 429-cid big-block with 360 bhp, the latter being standard for Marauder X-100, optional elsewhere. The 1970s were basically reruns save minor trim and equipment revisions. Sporty big cars had mostly disappeared by now, and so would the Marauder after just 6043 sales that model year.

After a minor '68 facelift, the big Mercs were fully revised for 1969. Wheelbases grew to 121 inches on wagons and 124 on other models, sizes that would persist until their first downsizing for 1979. Series regrouped around base Monterey, revived Monterey Custom, and a full Marquis line comprising Colony Park wagon, convertible, and base and Brougham sedans, hardtop coupes, and hardtop sedans. Riding the shorter wheelbase was a new Marauder, a high-performance "tunnelback" hardtop that garnered 14,666 sales. Offered in standard and spiffier X-100 trim, it shared Marquis' hidden-headlamp front and the ventless side glass used by most other models. V-8s comprised the usual 390s and a new 429-cid big-block with 360 bhp, the latter being standard for Marauder X-100, optional elsewhere. The 1970s were basically reruns save minor trim and equipment revisions. Sporty big cars had mostly disappeared by now, and so would the Marauder after just 6043 sales that model year.

One of the most interesting and desirable '60s Mercurys was the Cougar. An upscale rendition of Ford's wildly successful Mustang ponycar concept, it premiered for 1967 as a two-door hardtop in three basic permutations. Convertibles were added for 1969. Riding a three-inch-longer wheelbase than Mustang—111 in all—Cougar offered more luxury and standard power for about $200 extra (prices started at $2851). Where Mustang's base engine was a six, Cougar had a lively 200-bhp 289-cid V-8. The big

1975 Monarch Ghia four-door sedan

1976 Monarch Ghia coupe

1975 Bobcat Villager two-door station wagon

1976 Marquis Brougham station wagon

1976 Cougar XR-7 coupe

1976 Montego MX Brougham four-door sedan

335-bhp, 428-cid CJ became an extra-cost option for 1969-70.

The 1967-68 Cougars arguably looked best with their crisply tailored lines, hidden headlamps in an "electric-shaver" grille, and a matching back panel with sequential turn signals, a gimmick borrowed from Ford Thunderbirds. Length and width increased on the '69s, which sported Buick-like sweepspear bodyside contours, ventless side glass, less-distinctive "faces," and full-width taillights. The '70s adopted a divided vertical-bar grille with a slightly bulged nose.

Early Cougars came in several forms. The most luxurious was the XR-7, boasting a rich interior with leather accents and full instrumentation in a simulated walnut dashboard. A GT option delivered a firmer suspension for more-capable roadholding and a standard 320-bhp 390 V-8 for extra go. For 1968 came a GTE package with several unique appearance features and a 390-bhp 427. The hottest '69 Cougar was the Eliminator hardtop, with 428 power and a standard rear-deck spoiler. Convertibles saw very low sales: fewer than 10,000 total for 1969 and less than 4300 for 1970.

Cougar never approached Mustang in popularity, though it was more solid and elegant, and just as roadable. Production was still more than respectable: 150,000 in the first year, about 114,000 in '68, close to 100,000 in '69, then about 72,000 in '70. All are now collector's items.

Cougar was the crowning touch to a decade that saw Mercury move into luxury cars rivaling Lincoln even as it recaptured the performance aura it established in the late '40s and early '50s. But the good times of the '60s couldn't last. As the '70s rolled along, Mercurys became more like equivalent Fords, while government mandates and the vagaries of petroleum power-politics conspired to sacrifice performance on the twin altars of safety and fuel economy. By 1980, Mercury had once again resumed its original role as a plusher, costlier, and sometimes larger Ford. The only differences were that the parallel model lines encompassed five or six different size classes instead of one or two, and that Mercury styling often related more to Lincoln's than to Ford's.

The ponycar field was one area where Ford and L-M divisions parted company in the '70s. Actually, Cougar began diverging from Mustang as early as 1971, when both models were redesigned. The Mercury swelled by two inches in wheelbase instead of one (to 113 inches) and looked considerably bulkier. Standard and XR-7 convertibles remained through the end of this generation in 1973, and have become minor collector's items, primarily by dint of low annual production: fewer than 2000 of each type, except for the 3165 XR-7s in '73.

Of course, this only reflected the abrupt drop in demand for all ponycars after 1970, and it prompted Mercury to chart a new course for Cougar. While Mustang became a smaller, lighter, Pinto-based sporty car for 1974, Cougar grew into a kind of

1977 Bobcat Runabout with Sports Accent Group

1978 Zephyr ES two-door sedan

1977 Cougar Villager station wagon

1978 Cougar XR-7 with Midnight/Chamois Decor Group

1977 Cougar XR-7 coupe

1978 Zephyr Z-7 coupe

1978 Zephyr four-door sedan

1979 Monarch coupe

1979 Marquis Brougham Colony Park station wagon

1979 Capri RS hatchback coupe

1979 Cougar XR-7 coupe

alternative Thunderbird, adopting the 114-inch-wheelbase two-door platform of Mercury's midsize Montego models. Oddly, the L-M studio created the design chosen for the production Mustang II. But rather than field a badge-engineered clone of that car, the division opted to continue with the German-built Ford Capri it had been selling successfully since 1970—a "mini ponycar" like Mustang II, but better-built and more roadable.

The Thunderbirdesque Cougar continued through 1976 as Mercury's marker in the midsize personal-luxury segment dominated by the Chevrolet Monte Carlo and Pontiac Grand Prix. The name was diluted for 1977, when it replaced Montego as the sole intermediate line (including a wagon), with the XR-7 label reserved for a single top-shelf coupe. Things were temporarily sorted out again for 1980, when Cougar really *was* a Thunderbird, a twin to that year's new downsized model on a special 108.4-inch version of the "Fox" corporate platform.

In between, Ford again redesigned the Mustang, and this time Mercury wanted in. The result was a new American-made Capri for 1979. The direct descendent of the genuine Cougar ponycar, it was virtually identical with that year's new-generation Mustang save somewhat busier styling on the Ford's three-door hatch coupe body style, the only one available. Capri offered the same four engines as Mustang in base and luxury Ghia models (the latter honoring the famed Italian coachbuilder that Ford had purchased in 1970). More enthusiastic types could order a sporty RS package roughly comparable to the Mustang Cobra option (Mercury never called it "Rally Sport," likely for fear of objections from Chevrolet).

One of the last cars of this era with a distinctly Mercury character was the Cyclone, which bowed out after 1971. Offered that year with standard 351 and optional 429-cid V-8s, this muscular midsize was impressively fast. Swoopier sheetmetal set it clearly apart from run-of-the-mill Montego linemates and Ford's corresponding Torino GT and Cobra, particularly the protruding nose and "gunsight" grille that appeared with the midsize line's 1970-71 facelift. Reflecting the muscle-car market's sad state of affairs at the time, Cyclone sold poorly in its farewell season, especially the desirable low-production Spoiler hardtop (just 353 of the '71s were built).

Elsewhere, Mercury's new-model development story in the '70s was primarily one of "badge engineering." It began when the Comet name was revived for a restyled version of Ford's new-for-1970 compact Maverick, distinguished mainly by a Montego-style nose. Announced for 1971, this Comet soldiered on through '74 as the division's sole representative in a size and price sector that took on urgent new importance in the wake of the 1973-74 Middle East oil embargo.

Help arrived for 1975 in the form of two new entries. One was the Comet's once-and-future replacement, the slightly larger Granada-based Monarch. The other was Mercury's belated, if inevitable, rendition of the subcompact Ford Pinto, bearing the cute name Bobcat and a pretentious little stand-up grille. Ford replaced Maverick with the more-able Fairmont for 1978, so Mercury got a look-alike derivative, the Zephyr. If none of these moves was exactly original, they at least combined to leave Mercury much more competitive in a market that had been forever changed by an unprecedented combination of forces.

As with Buick and Oldsmobile, intermediate and full-size cars remained Mercury's mainstay through the '70s, and it was here that the changes were most dramatic—and most needed. Mercury's midsize contender was a near duplicate of the Ford Torino/LTD II, under the Montego name for 1972-76, then, as noted, with the Cougar badge from 1977 through the last of this body-on-frame design for 1979. Like the Fords, there was little praiseworthy about these Mercurys, though they arguably looked nicer.

1980 Zephyr Z-7 turbo sports coupe

1980 Cougar XR-7 coupe

1980 Grand Marquis four-door sedan

1981 Lynx LS hatchback coupe

1980 Cougar XR-7 coupe

1982 LN7 2-passenger hatchback coupe

Up in what was loosely called the "standard" class sat the big two-ton Marquis and Monterey. Neither changed much through 1978. Model names centered on Marquis exclusively after 1974, and styling became progressively more like that of the big Lincoln Continental, particularly up front. These Mercs were mammoths, but good ones: smooth and reliable, powered by reasonably potent V-8s (400s, 429s, and Lincoln 460s), and fully equipped (if not always tasteful). Pillarless hardtops gave way to pillared styling after 1974. Like Ford's LTD, the Marquis underwent the "big shrink" for '79, losing 10 inches in wheelbase and about 700 pounds in curb weight. The result would prove amazingly long-lived, though no one could see that at the time, least of all Ford Motor Company.

In retrospect, the '70s were not very good years for Mercury. The make again abandoned performance, and not all the fault lay with Washington and OPEC. A succession of heavier, clumsier Cougars and confusingly named intermediates hardly helped, while moves into the compact and subcompact arenas were blunted by higher prices on cars that offered little more than the Fords they so obviously were. Meantime, Mercury's traditional big-car foundation was rocked by the new economic order of a more energy-conscious world. Yet by 1980, Mercury was turning the corner with cars like the exciting Capri, the practical Zephyr, and reborn Cougar and Marquis.

Mercury decisively completed that maneuver in the '80s, benefiting from the same astute management and timely product introductions that made Ford Motor Company the industry's profit leader by 1986. Though no one Mercury line was among Detroit's top-selling nameplates, the make's total production rose rapidly from 347,700 for 1980 to a decade high of nearly half a million U.S.-built cars for '84—an impressive recovery, though still far below record '79 (669,000-plus). On the model-year board, Mercury sat anywhere from sixth to ninth, as it had since the '50s, but managed fifth for 1983, its best finish ever.

As before, the Mercury line paralleled Ford's except for somewhat higher prices and different model/equipment mixes. Styling also remained similar through 1982, but the following year saw the return of a more-distinctive Mercury look. Much sooner than GM, Dearborn had correctly concluded that too many clones spoil the sales broth. With the 1983 models, Mercurys again began standing more clearly apart from parent Fords—and GM rivals—to the undoubted benefit of sales.

Still, volume throughout the '80s remained much lower than Ford's model-for-model, and Mercury didn't have the same relative success with some of the same products. The Capri ponycar was one telling example. Like Mustang, it received almost annual power increases and higher performance, commencing with 1982's "high-output" 157-bhp 302-cid V-8. But then Mustang got a handsome facelift and a revived convertible, while Capri soldiered on for '83 with just a hatchback coupe and basic '79

▲ 1932 Lincoln KB four-door sedan

▼ 1940 Lincoln Continental coupe

▲ 1938 Lincoln Model K coupe by Judkins

▼ 1961 Lincoln Continental convertible sedan

▲ 2006 Lincoln Zephyr four-door sedan

▼ 1940 Mercury convertible club coupe

▲ 1946 Mercury station wagon

▼ 1957 Mercury Commuter two-door station wagon

▲ 1963 Mercury Comet Custom station wagon

▼ 1967 Mercury Monterey S-55 hardtop coupe

▲ 2006 Mercury Milan four-door sedan

▼ 1954 Muntz Jet hardtop coupe

▲ 1932 Nash coupe

▼ 1948 Nash Ambassador Brougham convertible coupe

▲ 1950 Nash Ambassador Super four-door sedan

▼ 1957 Nash Ambassador Country Club hardtop coupe

▲ 1939 Oldsmobile 70 business coupe

▼ 1942 Oldsmobile 98 four-door sedan

▲ 1950 Oldsmobile Futuramic 88 convertible coupe

▼ 1965 Oldsmobile 4-4-2 coupe

▲ 1967 Oldsmobile Toronado hardtop coupe

▼ 1998 Oldsmobile Aurora four-door sedan

▲ 1934 Packard Twelve Dietrich convertible coupe

▼ 1937 Packard Twelve convertible victoria

▲ 1947 Packard Custom Super Clipper four-door sedan

▼ 1952 Packard 250 convertible coupe

▲ 1956 Packard Caribbean hardtop coupe

▼ 1933 Pierce-Arrow Silver Arrow four-door sedan

▲ 1935 Pierce-Arrow Silver Arrow V-12 coupe

▼ 1934 Plymouth coupe

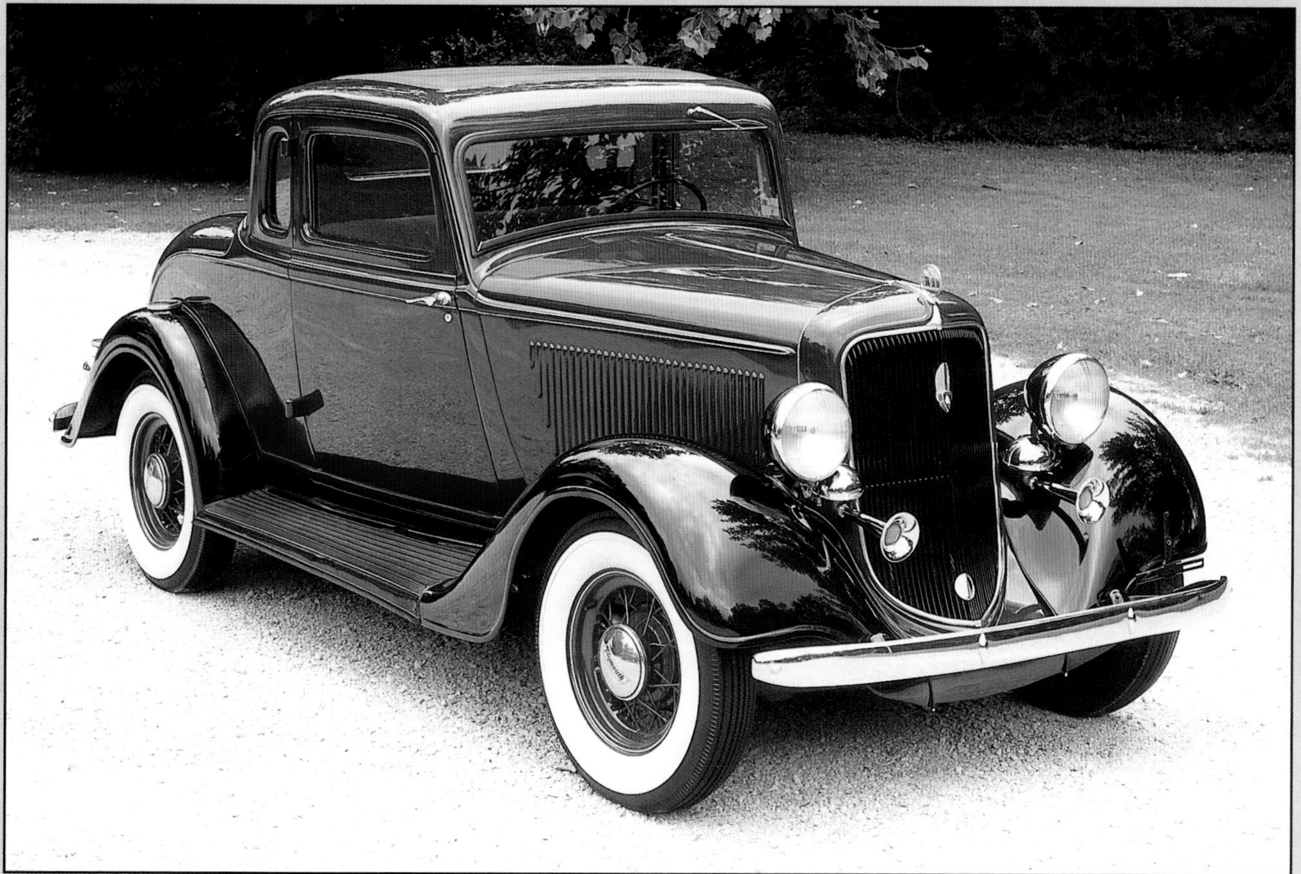

▲ 1947 Plymouth Special Deluxe business coupe

▼ 1955 Plymouth Belvedere four-door sedan

1982 Capri RS 5.0 hatchback coupe

1983 Marquis Brougham four-door sedan

1983 Zephyr four-door sedan

1983 LN7 2-passenger hatchback coupe

1984 Topaz LS four-door sedan

1983 Cougar LS coupe

appearance except for a huge "bubbleback" rear window of dubious aesthetic merit. It's almost as if L-M was ashamed of Capri, and it showed in half-hearted promotion that aggravated the lack of overt change. Production thus steadily waned, from nearly 80,000 for 1980 to only some 18,500 of the '85s (compared with over 156,000 Mustangs). At that level, Capri was too costly to sustain, and it was banished after '86.

The same fate awaited another "bubbleback" Merc: the two-seat LN7, introduced in early 1982 alongside the related Ford EXP. Both were sporty coupes derived from the front-drive Ford Escort/Mercury Lynx subcompacts, which had scored big sales since replacing the old Pinto/Bobcat twins for 1981. Unfortunately, the coupes were anything but lovely, and no match for a number of Japanese competitors in performance, refinement, or workmanship. Perhaps buyers didn't expect a two-seater in L-M showrooms, for the LN7 attracted a middling 40,000 customers before being retired after 1983. A facelifted EXP then took on its bulbous backlight and proved somewhat more popular.

Lynx was Mercury's entry in the increasingly tough small-car market, and it sold respectably, racking up over 100,000 units in its first two seasons and about 85,000 a year thereafter. Like Escort, it started life with a three-door hatchback sedan and a neat five-door wagon in trim levels from plain to fancy. These were bolstered for 1982 by five-door sedans, a sporty three-door RS, and a posh five-door LTS (for Luxury Touring Sedan).

Through mid-'85, Lynx was powered by the Escort's 1.6-liter "CVH" four, also offered in H.O. and turbocharged guises. In mid-'85, both of the latter were dropped and a normal-tune 1.9-liter enlargement took over. A 2.0-liter diesel four supplied by Mazda in Japan was also offered beginning with the '84s, though it attracted few buyers as gas prices fell in an improving national economy. Appearance was cleaned up for "1985½" with a smoother nose and flush headlamps in line with Dearborn's strong turn to aerodynamic styling. An even sportier three-door, called XR3, bowed the following year.

But here, too, Ford planners would conclude that one clone was one too many, though a falling dollar and lower offshore production costs also figured in the decision to drop Lynx during 1987. Taking over was the Mexican-built Tracer, a badge-engineered version of Mazda's similarly sized 323. Yet despite generating less than half of Escort's volume in most years, the Lynx can be judged a success, as it rung up crucial business for L-M dealers during some very difficult times.

The same holds for Mercury's compacts and intermediates of this decade. For 1981-82 these comprised the familiar (and largely unchanged) Zephyr line and a new upmarket Cougar sedan series, both built on the proven rear-drive '78-vintage "Fox" platform. Weighing some 350-400 pounds less than the Monarchs they replaced, these Cougars were twins to Ford's

1983 Capri GS hatchback coupe

1984 Topaz LS coupe with TR Performance Group

1984 Cougar XR-7 coupe

1985 Capri RS 5.0 hatchback coupe

1986 Sable LS station wagon

1986 Sable LS four-door sedan

redesigned '81 Granadas. Styling was similarly squared up and more formal than Zephyr's, appropriate for the higher prices. Though the origins of these models were obvious, there was evidently some magic left in the Cougar name. Between them, Cougar and Zephyr netted well over 80,000 annual sales for 1981-82, not bad considering the sorry state of the market.

Mercury did somewhat better by replacing the Fox-platform Cougars with a midsize Marquis for 1983. This was yet another Fairmont/Zephyr variation, but its cleaner styling was a big improvement, even if it looked rather too much like the downsized 1983 LTD that took over for Granada at Ford. Still, the name link with a full-size Merc didn't hurt, and Marquis sales by 1984 totaled some 108,000, half again as much as the previous Cougar series.

To avoid confusion, the biggest Mercurys were renamed Grand Marquis after 1982, one of their few important changes during the entire decade. Not that many changes were needed. Roomy, quiet, and comfortable, they remained traditional V-8 American family cruisers whose sales rebounded strongly once the economy began to recover and an oil glut pushed gas prices down to more-reasonable levels. Chrysler Corporation and the Buick, Olds, and Pontiac divisions of GM lent a helping hand by canceling most of their old rear-drive biggies by '85, leaving the Grand Marquis all but alone in the medium-price full-size field.

Grand Marquis thus journeyed through the '80s with only the barest of updates. Two-door coupes were dropped after 1985, the mainstay four-door sedan and wagon gained smoother noses and tails for 1988, and fuel injection replaced carburetors on the 302-cid V-8, but that was about it. Once their original '79 tooling was amortized, the big Mercurys (and Fords) became the darlings of corporate accountants and dealers alike, earning more profit per unit than any other model in the line. Consumers kept on buying despite the lack of change. Grand Marquis sales totaled nearly 96,000 for '83, over 148,000 for '84, then 110,000-160,000 each year all the way through 1989. Obviously, the "Big M" still offered what a lot of folks wanted.

Cougar was Mercury's most-dramatic success of these years—not the aforementioned sedan series but L-M's version of the Ford Thunderbird. Blocky and ornate, the downsized XR-7 was little changed through 1982, and laid a gigantic sales egg, dropping below 20,000 units. But then came 1983's handsome aerodynamic redesign, and volume more than tripled, reaching nearly 76,000 units. Sales rose by another 55,000 for '84, then held above 100,000 through 1988.

This Cougar had almost everything the latest T-Bird did—which was plenty. Aiming for a more-conservative clientele, Mercury gave it a near-vertical rear roofline and offered a standard 232-cid V-6 or optional 302 V-8. The essential Fox chassis of 1980-82 was retained, but more finely tuned for a better ride/handling balance, and interiors could be downright luxuri-

1986 Lynx XR3 hatchback coupe

1986 Cougar XR-7 coupe

1986 Sable GS station wagon

1987 Cougar LS coupe

1987 Sable LS four-door sedan

ous with just a modicum of options. No XR-7 model was offered at first, but it returned for '84 as a counterpart to the Thunderbird Turbo Coupe, with the same hyperaspirated 145-cid four, appropriately beefed-up suspension, and standard five-speed manual transmission. The last was an item that hadn't been seen on Cougars since the '60s.

In all, it was a most pleasing package, made even more so by an interim facelift for 1987, Cougar's 20th anniversary. This involved larger-appearing windows and a shapelier nose bearing flush headlamps and a more-rakish grille. At the same time, the XR-7 swapped its turbo four-cylinder for a newly fuel-injected 302 V-8 with 155 horses. For '88 came a hotter XR-7 with monochrome exterior and dual exhausts for the V-8, plus 20 more horsepower for the base V-6 (now at 140 total).

But all this was merely a warm-up for the spectacular '89 Cougar. Based on another all-new T-Bird, it emerged lower and wider but no longer despite a 113-inch wheelbase (previously 104.2). Styling was even more smoothly aerodynamic, but a vertical backlight and upright grille again lent visual distinction.

The new Cougar followed the '89 Thunderbird in forsaking both a V-8 and the old turbo-four for a pair of fuel-injected 232 V-6s: a normally aspirated 140-bhp unit for the base LS model and a 210-bhp supercharged version with intercooler for the high-performance XR-7—America's first supercharged six since the 1954-55 Kaiser Manhattan. It was mounted in a sophisticated new chassis with all-independent suspension, variable-rate shock absorbers, and other technical features that made the new Cougar a road car worthy of comparison with premium European coupes.

No doubt about it: Cougar had been fully transformed in a satisfying way. Sales remained satisfying too, though volume was down somewhat: to about 97,000 for '89, then to a more-worrisome 81,500. Higher prices were undoubtedly a factor: nearly $16,000 for the 1990 LS, a bit over $20,000 for the XR-7. Still, those price tags looked reasonable against the far loftier stickers of imported sports-luxury coupes.

Mercury was well represented in the hard-fought compact and midsize battles of the '80s, its respective warriors being the Topaz and Sable. Topaz, arriving for 1984 as the front-drive replacement for Zephyr, was a predictable kissin' cousin of Ford's new Tempo and thus evolved in parallel with it. Included in developments through decade's end were an available high-output 2.3-liter four, sporty two-doors, 1987's new all-wheel-drive option, a stem-to-stern makeover for 1988 sedans, and an optional driver-side airbag starting in 1986 (one of the earliest domestic cars to offer that feature). Dearborn designers tried to make Topaz look somewhat different from Tempo at each end and by deleting the Tempo sedan's rearmost side windows—not huge distinctions, but another small sign that Mercurys were becoming individual once more.

A pleasant and capable compact, though not state-of-the-art, Topaz followed Lynx in generating lower volume than its Ford counterpart: 80,000-128,000 a year, about half of Tempo's sales. But again, that volume was helpful to L-M dealers.

Sable, replacing the midsize Marquis, was far more helpful. Arriving with base prices in the $11,000-$13,000 range, it immediately commanded almost 96,000 sales for debut '86, then shot up to over 121,000 for '87 and a resounding 130,000-plus for 1989. Sable was Mercury's version of the acclaimed front-drive Ford Taurus, and thus shared most of its widely praised basic design. There were exceptions, though. Where Taurus had three trim levels, Sable offered two: GS and upmarket LS. Mercury also decided it didn't need Ford's small 2.5-liter four after '86—wise, as most Taurus buyers decided they didn't need it either. This left 3.0-liter and, from 1988, 3.8-liter "Vulcan" V-6s. Both produced 140 bhp, but the 3.8 was the engine of choice for all-around driving due to its larger displacement and commensurately greater torque (215 pound-feet vs. 160). Sable also had more simulated wood on the dash and door panels.

But the real distinction was outside. Where the four-door Taurus sedan wore a "six-light" roof treatment, the Sable version had a rear window wrapped fully around to the rear-door trailing edges for a sleek hidden-pillar effect. Also, Sable's rear wheel arches were flat-topped, versus rounded on Taurus. Even more dramatic was Sable's unique front "light bar," a set of running lights behind a wide central white lens that illuminated with the headlamps to make both the sedans and five-door wagons unmistakable at night. The net effect of these simple but clever differences was to give Sable an identity quite apart from that of Taurus. Seldom in recent times had a Mercury been more its "own car"—or more handsome.

Sable didn't get anything like the high-performance '89 Taurus SHO, but this was a reasonable marketing decision given Mercury's more luxury-oriented clientele. Those folks no doubt appreciated useful 1990 upgrades such as optional antilock brakes for sedans, a standard driver-side airbag for all Sables, a dash reworked to be more ergonomic, and new features like an optional compact-disc player and standard tilt steering wheel.

1987 Cougar LS coupe

1988 Grand Marquis LS four-door sedan

1988 Cougar XR-7 coupe

1988 Cougar XR-7 coupe

1989 Cougar XR7 coupe

1990 Grand Marquis Colony Park LS station wagon

1990 Cougar LS coupe

1991 Capri 2+2 convertible coupe

With a stunning new Cougar to carry the performance banner, plus the updated Topaz, evergreen Grand Marquis, and strong-selling Sable, Mercury could take justifiable pride during Golden Anniversary 1989, when total domestic volume (excluding "outsourced" products like Tracer) approached a smashing 500,000. Despite occasional mistakes and some rough periods in its first 50 years. Mercury had produced some of America's best-liked automobiles. Now, on the eve of its second half-century, it was doing so again.

But calendar-year domestic sales plunged to around 309,000 in 1991, reflecting the onset of a deep new national recession that would last a good three years. Even so, Mercury was able to claim sixth from Dodge in 1993, then held the spot on steadily rising volume that reached nearly 387,000 units in 1994. It was a quite credible performance considering that Mercury had only two products in this period not shared with Ford—and that only one was a real success.

The product in question was the Villager, arriving for 1993 as Mercury's first minivan. At first glance, it seemed just a belated copy of the Dodge Caravan/Plymouth Voyager that had been around for a decade and still dominated minivan sales by a wide margin. Indeed, Villager followed their lead by being a front-wheel-drive design sized about halfway between their standard and extended Grand models, riding a 112.2-inch wheelbase and stretching 189.9 inches overall.

But Villager had its attractions, starting with neat, trim styling that was arguably more-fashionable than Chrysler's, plus standard (instead of optional) four-wheel antilock brakes. Mercury also avoided the sham of price-leader models with four-cylinder power and manual transmission, opting for GS and luxury LS editions with a 3.0-liter 150-bhp single-overhead-cam V-6 and four-speed overdrive automatic. Villager's chassis was more sophisticated, too, its modern all-coil suspension making for even more carlike ride and handling than Chrysler had. It even had a clever novelty in a sliding three-place third-row bench seat that could be moved up on built-in floor tracks to substitute for the removable two-place middle bench; it could also be slid halfway up to open up extra cargo space behind.

Trouble was, Villager was all but identical with Nissan's new Quest, built to the same design that borrowed liberally from the Japanese firm's Maxima sedan. The Mercury differed only in having an illuminated front "light bar" *a la* Sable, plus minor trim and equipment distinctions. At least these twins were built in the U.S., produced under Ford auspices in Ohio. It was another joint venture of the sort increasingly common in the industry, but Ford's influence here was confined to minor areas like switchgear and interior materials.

Fortunately for L-M, buyers weren't at all bothered by Villager's Asian origins, especially with high-value base prices of $16,500-$22,000. In fact, thanks to a deliberate production bias in Mercury's favor, Villager outsold Quest by more than 2-to-1 for debut '93 at nearly 109,000. While that was only about a quarter of combined Caravan/Voyager sales, it was hardly bad for such a Johnny-come-lately. And, of course, it was all "plus" business for L-M dealers.

For 1994, Villager added a top-line Nautica model with standard leather interior, front and middle "captain's chair" bucket seats, and a blue/cream color scheme inspired by Nautica sportswear. Nissan was accorded more Quests that season, which partly explains why Villager volume dropped to just under 62,000 for the model year. Both versions added a standard driver-side airbag, but still lacked a passenger-side restraint like Chrysler's minivans. Production sank a bit further for 1995, reflecting stiffer price and product competition in this fast-moving market.

Mercury wasn't at all successful with its other unique product

1991 Topaz GS four-door sedan

1991 Cougar LS coupe

1991 Sable LS station wagon

1992 Grand Marquis LS four-door sedan

1992 Sable GS four-door sedan

1992 Capri XR2 convertible coupe

1992 Tracer LTS four-door sedan

1993 Topaz GS four-door sedan

1993 Tracer four-door sedan

1993 Villager minivan

of this period, which was American only in the market it targeted. This was an Australian-built two-seat convertible that appeared in mid-1990 as yet another Capri. Like Tracer, it was based on the small 323 platform from Japanese affiliate Mazda, with the same proven front-drive mechanicals plus four-wheel-disc brakes, independent rear suspension, driver-side airbag, and an optional liftoff hardtop. A 1.6-liter four delivered 100 bhp in the base model or 132 turbocharged ponies in the uplevel XR2. Yet despite open-air allure and affordable pricing in the $13,000-$15,000 range, this Capri just didn't sell. Dumpy styling hurt as much as indifferent workmanship, and Mazda's own Miata offered a prettier, "more authentic" sports car with superior Japanese build quality for not many more dollars. With all this, Capri sales peaked at about 21,200 for calendar '91, then plummeted to nowhere. Mercury gave up after 1994, when it instituted a mild facelift and standard passenger-side airbag. Perhaps the Capri name had been cursed.

As ever, other Mercs of the early-'90s generally evolved like counterpart Fords. Thus, the subcompact Tracer aped Escort with a full redesign for 1991, while '92 brought a Grand Marquis revamped like Crown Victoria and a Sable reworked *a la* Taurus.

But Mercury didn't follow Ford in every way. The '91 Tracer, for example, offered no hatchback sedans, just a five-door wagon and a four-door notchback. The latter was a full year ahead of Escort's, though, and was the basis for a sporting model called LTS. Though it had twincam Mazda power like the Escort GT hatchback, the LTS stood apart by wearing the front "light bar" motif now used as a Mercury hallmark, though it didn't light up on this lower-cost car. Base models got this and other LTS appearance cues for 1993, when Tracer followed Escort to "one-price" marketing: base models with air conditioning and automatic transmission selling at $11,665. Also like Escort, Tracer added a driver-side airbag for '94 and optional ABS for the LTS. The following year brought a standard passenger airbag, plus a low-cost "Trio" trim package that added a rear spoiler and alloy wheels to the base sedan. One thing Mercury couldn't seem to change was relative sales, and Tracer volume remained only a fraction of Escort's. Then again, with so many small cars to choose from, some buyers likely forgot that L-M dealers even had one.

Sable sales held generally steady, both in absolute numbers and as a proportion of Taurus', but Mercury's midsize was quicker than Ford's to offer a passenger-side airbag: first as an option with the '92 redesign, then standard. Though Sable still had no counterpart to the high-power Taurus SHO, Mercury did offer front buckets and console as new '93 extras for the uplevel LS sedan. These became standard for the '94 version, which was joined late in the season by a sportier LTS edition with leather inside and a "more Euro" look outside. Overall Sable production remained strong in this period, running 116,000-137,000 in all years save recessionary '91, when sales dipped to just above 96,000.

The full-size Grand Marquis showed surprising sales strength with its '92 redesign, accounting for much of Mercury's increased overall volume through middecade. In fact, the newly aerodynamic "Big M" outpolled its Ford sister in '92 model-year production by some 10,000 units with a relatively amazing 163,000-plus. It then settled down to around 100,000 yearly sales except for 1993 (a bit over 90,000).

Grand Marquis still eschewed any pretense of sport, but its '92 makeover was the same considered update accorded Crown Victoria. Highlights included Dearborn's new 4.6-liter "modular" V-8, standard all-disc brakes, available ABS, a thoroughly reworked rear-drive chassis, and a firm-ride Handling and Performance option with dual exhausts adding 20 bhp to the regular 190. Like Ford, Mercury now bailed out of big wagons,

1994 Capri XR2 convertible coupe

1994 Cougar XR7 coupe

1994 Grand Marquis LS four-door sedan

1995 Tracer station wagon

but the GS and uplevel LS sedans were nicely tailored to stand more clearly apart from Crown Vics. Differences included a modest grille, a conventional "four-light" roofline, and Sable-inspired taillight treatment. Considering the conservative character of both the car and its clientele, the rejuvenated Grand Marquis showed a lot of sales life in the early '90s.

The same could not be said for Cougar, which lost interest value after 1990—and a lot of customers. In a way, this was probably inevitable. Like Thunderbird buyers, Cougar prospects were now mainly those who cared less about sporty performance than getting the most luxury per buck. Since there was no point in giving people something they didn't want, Mercury swapped engines for the uplevel '91 XR7, yanking out the supercharged V-6 (and its five-speed manual transmission) for a good old 5.0-liter/302 V-8 with 200 bhp (and mandatory automatic). At the same time, the V-8 became a first-time option for the base LS, replacing its unblown (and unchanged) 3.8 V-6. Both Cougars also wore a minor facelift involving the hood, headlamps, grille, and back panel.

Cougar changed little for 1992, a disappointing way for the model to observe its 25th anniversary. So was the midseason birthday special based not on the XR7 but the everyday LS, with distinctions limited to just a monochrome exterior and fancy BBS-brand alloy wheels. Model-year sales plunged by more than 13,000 to just over 49,000, which was only about half of what Cougar had tallied with its 1989 redesign. Then again, Mercury wasn't pushing the car too hard, and there were other, more-tempting coupes available in Cougar's $16,000-$22,000 price bracket. All the more surprising, then, that sales leaped to nearly 81,500 for 1993 despite only a single, little-changed XR7 without so much as a driver-side airbag.

A substantial '94 freshening made the XR7 look a bit different at each end without really improving it. But there were genuine improvements elsewhere: standard dual airbags within a reworked dashboard, newly optional traction control (with ABS required), and a switch in V-8 options from pushrod 5.0-liter to new single-cam 4.6 "mod." Even with all this, the base price was held to just $16,260—which must have angered all those folks who'd bought '93s. But fewer folks bought '94s, model-year output easing to around 76,000. Fewer still opted for the little-changed '95s, which were pared down to just the XR7. By that point, Cougar again looked like just another stray cat in the personal-luxury jungle, with nothing of substance to stand out in the competitive herd. It was certainly a long way from the exciting luxury ponycar of the '60s.

Excitement was never a trait of Mercury's compact Topaz, and still wasn't when the line ended after 1994. The high point, such as it was, came with '92, when all Topazes got a Sable-type "light bar" face and the sporty LTS sedan and XR5 coupe got the Sable's 3.0-liter 135-bhp V-6 as standard (optional elsewhere). But the V-6 didn't do that much for performance, and a lack of buyer interest finally killed off the useful all-wheel-drive option that year. Topaz was further diluted for '93, down to just a two-door and four-door GS with "value" pricing but little standard equipment. Even a driver-side airbag cost extra, and then only with the base four and optional automatic transmission (the V-6 remained available). Like Ford's related Tempo, this Mercury had come to have more appeal for rental fleets than retail buyers, which might well explain why sales for 1990-93 were relatively strong at 80,000-100,000 a year. Like vanilla ice cream, the Topaz was far from memorable, but offered enough to satisfy many people.

A much tastier compact Mercury arrived for 1995. Called Mystique, it was essentially that year's new Ford Contour with a slightly more-conservative look and somewhat higher prices. The last stemmed from the inclusion of several features that were optional on the Ford. Thus, the $13,855 Mystique GS cost $545 more than the counterpart Contour GL, but gave buyers a full console, tachometer, and power mirrors without asking. The uplevel LS boasted still nicer trim, a few more goodies, and a starting price of $15,230.

To its credit, L-M Division didn't monkey with the basic design originated for Ford's European Mondeo, so this front-drive Merc had a genuine "sports sedan" mystique. That was particularly true for handling and roadholding, which set new standards for small domestic four-doors. Workmanship was also in a higher league: tight, solid and thorough. Performance was rather tame with the base 2.0-liter 125-bhp four-cylinder, but bordered on exhilarating with the optional, new 170-bhp 2.5-liter "Duratec" twincam V-6. The back seat was cramped enough for grown-ups to feel like sardines, but that was about the only serious complaint. Overall, Mystique was vast improvement over the tepid Topaz.

Yet despite mostly positive early reviews, buyers just didn't take to Mystique. Contour sold better, but also wasn't attracting as many buyers as its predecessor. Dearborn did what it could, reshaping the front seatbacks and rear seat cushions to gain a precious inch of aft leg room, touching up the exterior appearance, and reworking the front suspension to more closely match that of the European Mondeo. But nothing seemed to help, and Contour/Mystique bowed out after model-year 2000. Hindsight suggests Mystique suffered more from its nameplate than from any inherent flaws, a factor that would increasingly bedevil Mercury in years to come.

The compact Tracer was reskinned for 1997 to emerge as a handsome, efficient little car, nicely equipped and sensibly priced. Like sibling Ford Escorts, these four-door sedans and wagons appealed for competent road manners, a higher standard of finish than many rivals, and a 110-bhp single-cam inline four that delivered decent performance, even with the optional four-speed automatic transmission. But when Escort began phasing out for 2000 to make way for Focus, Tracer stepped aside to be replaced by...nothing. Mercury sales had mostly been trending down of late, and Dearborn product wizards decided the entry-level Merc wouldn't be missed.

Similar reasoning felled the vintage-1989 Cougar, canceled after 1997 sales of just over 35,000, less than half the volume of four years before. There was no surprise in this. Buyers had been turning away from big coupes, and the basic Thunderbird-based package looked quite dated after nine model years. Though the old 5.0-liter V-8 option was replaced for '94 by the modern 4.6-liter "mod" unit, it was a decidedly mixed blessing that netted only 10 more horses and perceptibly less low-end torque. And whatever buyers still expected of the XR7 name, they were surely disappointed in the base version with its coarse pushrod V-6 dating from the 1980s.

But while Ford went to working up a new T-Bird, Mercury had a new Cougar at the ready, a model with no Blue Oval counterpart. It arrived for 1999 as a front-wheel-drive hatchback coupe based on the Contour/Mystique platform. Wearing the most adventuresome Mercury styling in many years, this "cub" Cougar, the smallest ever, opened to mixed reviews, but benefited from fortuitous timing, as demand for compact performance coupes was on the rise. A relatively long wheelbase gave it a decent ride, and adept suspension calibrations gave it fine handling. Though Mystique's 125-bhp 2.0-liter twincam-four engine was standard, the optional 170-bhp Duratec V-6 proved far more popular, delivering excellent performance for only $500 extra. So equipped, the new small cat was a budget-pleasing match for most Japanese competitors. Not everyone was thrilled. *Consumer Guide®*, for one, found plenty to criticize, though others reacted more favorably.

A Cougar S with a 195-bhp V-6 was in the works for 2000, but never appeared. There was no point. As often happens with trendy cars, Cougar sales peaked early—at nearly 57,000 for calendar '99—then tailed off. The model was thus abolished after 2002 with no interim changes of note save a minor '01 facelift. Offered throughout the run was a desirable V-6 Sport, a package option through 2001, and a separate model for '02. The V-6 Sport delivered such worthwhile upgrades as wider tires on 16-inch wheels (versus 15s), four-wheel disc brakes (made standard for all '02s), fog lights, grippier seats, and a rear spoiler. Antilock brakes, traction control, and front side airbags were available, but only with V-6. So, too, a few late-game cosmetic

1996 Grand Marquis LS four-door sedan

1997 Mystique four-door sedan

1997 Sable GS four-door sedan

1999 Cougar V-6 coupe

1999 Villager minivan

2001 Grand Marquis four-door sedan

2002 Sable station wagon

packages: C2 and Zn for 2001, XR and 35th Anniversary for '02. The last pair was interesting. The $950 XR option comprised 17-inch wheels, high-speed tires, special interior trim, and body add-ons attributed to veteran Ford racing specialist Jack Roush. The $1195 35th Anniversary Package also featured a specific rear spoiler and dummy hood scoop, plus chrome wheels and firmer sport suspension. It wasn't much of a birthday present, but at least Cougar hung on long enough to mark the occasion.

Mercury seemed to lose interest in the small Cougar soon after the press introduction (for which it secured the services of late-night TV host and genial car guy Jay Leno). That was perhaps understandable given the early sales slide and strong new competition, especially the Honda-built Acura RSX. But the main reason this Cougar died early was cancellation of the parent Contour/Mystique after 2000, which rendered it a platform orphan with insufficient sales to cover manufacturing costs.

Another dropout was the Villager minivan, which had been redesigned for 1999 after little change since its '93 debut. The makeover was extensive, adding fresh looks, 4.5 inches to overall length, 140 pounds, and a needed left-side rear sliding door as standard. A new 170-bhp V-6 helped offset the weight gain, but the revamped Villager was actually heavier than the newer, somewhat longer Ford Windstar and the top-selling Chrysler minivans. And while buyers were flocking to new features like power sliding doors and front-seat side airbags, Villager didn't have them and never would. The result was an also-ran that was easy to lose when Ford and Nissan decided to dissolve their minivan joint venture in late 2001.

By that point, Mercury itself seemed to be dissolving. Though the make's combined car and truck sales were a robust 438,000 in calendar '99, the 2000 tally fell some 60,000 units, and the '01 figure was under 311,000. Shocking world events and a boom economy gone bust were partly to blame, but many analysts felt that Mercury had seriously lost focus and would soon land in the celestial junkyard next to Plymouth (canned after 2001) and Oldsmobile (already announced for phaseout after '04).

Dearborn hotly denied such talk and made several moves to demonstrate its commitment to Mercury. First, Lincoln-Mercury sales and marketing staff were moved to Southern California to soak up that area's celebrated creative sunshine. Soon afterward, Mercury and Lincoln were rolled into the recently formed Premier Automotive Group, joining the illustrious ranks of Aston Martin, Jaguar, Volvo, and Land Rover, all recent Dearborn acquisitions. In 2002, Mercury got its own design chief for one of the few times in its history. And he reported to one Elena Ford, cousin of chairman and CEO William C. Ford, Jr., newly installed as Mercury group manager.

Besides their PR value, these and other efforts aimed to define a strong new image for Mercury and develop winning products to go with it. But the mission was soon derailed by a

2002 Cougar coupe with 35th Anniversary Package

2004 Monterey minivan

variety of problems that increasingly threatened Ford Motor Company's very existence (see *Ford*). Thus, by 2003, Mercury was again "colocated" with Ford Division in Michigan—and back to selling just retrimmed Fords developed on very lean budgets. Mercury was on the same perilous path that led Plymouth to its demise, gradually losing unique products to become just a "feeder" line for a more profitable, higher-status brand in the same showroom.

And even shared products were sometimes granted with a curious reluctance. Mercury's first sport-utility vehicle was a case in point. Called Mountaineer, it made an early 1997 debut as a gussied-up four-door Ford Explorer whose basic design was then eight years old. Given the booming demand for Explorer and most other midsize SUVs, it's amazing Dearborn didn't do the Mercury sooner. Appropriate for its higher prices, Mountaineer had nicer furnishings and more standard equipment, including a 215-bhp 5.0-liter/302 V-8 with four-speed automatic transmission, both options for Explorer. Two years later, the siblings adopted a new base powerteam comprising a 205-bhp 4.0-liter V-6 and a first-in-class five-speed automatic transmission. A 2002 redesign improved both versions with standard antilock brakes, class-first independent rear suspension, and new options including curtain side airbags and a 240-bhp 4.6-liter overhead-cam V-8 with five-speed automatic. Mountaineer finally got real visual distinction (mostly up front), plus standard three-row seating for seven (optional on the Ford) and available all-wheel drive instead of dual-range four-wheel drive. Offered a bit later was an antiskid system with rollover sensors, shared with Explorer. But Mountaineer's differences weren't that compelling, and sales oozed along at between 40,000 and 50,000 a year. While this was welcome "plus" business for L-M dealers, it was only a tenth of Explorer's volume and unimpressive in a market crazy for SUVs.

Mercury endured shorter waits for two other hoped-for sales-boosters. A replacement minivan with the nostalgic Monterey name bowed for 2004 as a close copy of that year's new Ford Freestar, which was largely the old Windstar updated. Sailing in the following year was Mariner, an upscale take on Ford's four-year-old Escape compact SUV. L-M dealers also cheered these additions, however belated, but Mariner sales were modest and Monterey didn't break four figures in its first 12 months. Meanwhile, total Mercury sales kept shriveling, reduced to fewer than 194,000 units by calendar '05.

Needless to say, the car side of Mercury's business was also faltering, especially after 2002, when only the Sable and Grand Marquis were left to carry the load. Significantly, Sable ceded its spot as Mercury's best-selling car just one year after its 1996 redesign. All the underskin particulars were naturally the same as for that year's new lozenge-shaped, oval-bedecked Ford Taurus, including a more powerful base V-6 and a more refined optional V-6, the new 200-bhp twincam Duratec. Sable was again more conservatively styled than its Ford counterpart, but evidently not enough for Mercury buyers. Accordingly, the Y2K editions got an unscheduled early facelift to look more conventional, plus a more orthodox dashboard. But after that, Sable followed Taurus in making only detail changes each year, thus falling further and further behind import-brand competitors that were freshened more often. Sales, which reliably topped 100,000 in the late 1990s, waned quickly after 2001, thudding to below 43,000 in calendar 2004. By that point, Mercury had a replacement ready, so Sable was unceremoniously dumped after an abbreviated 2005 run.

The Grand Marquis fell on hard times too, but entered the new century as the best-selling Mercury, car or truck. It had become as indispensible to the make as sister Town Car had become to Lincoln. And that was the trouble. Like Ford's Crown Victoria, which shared the 1979-vintage "Panther" platform, the big L-M sedans were relics of a bygone era. And though considered updating helped them keep pace with changing technology, they still appealed mainly to older folks whose numbers were dwindling. The only reasons the Panthers were able to become so gray were that they remained prof-

2004 Sable four-door sedan

itable—basic tooling had been paid for ages ago—and as full-size V-8 cars with rear-wheel drive they had no domestic competition between 1996 and 2005.

Nevertheless, Grand Marquis stymied Mercury in the same way Town Car befuddled Lincoln. Both were too vital to lose, yet the longer they stayed around, the more their "geezer" image inhibited each make from forging a more youthful identity as a way back to prosperity. Neither brand had resolved this dilemma by 2005, and there seemed little time left to do so. The crisis was particularly dire at Mercury, where Grand Marquis accounted for an increasing percentage of car sales between 2001 and '05 even as its own calendar-year sales volume plunged from over 198,000 to less than 65,000 in that period.

The car itself evolved nicely. The '98 Grand Marquis received a few styling tweaks and 10 extra horses for each V-8, taking the base engine to 200 bhp, the optional dual-exhaust version to 215. A second tune-up added 20 horses apiece for 2001. The 2003s got a surprisingly extensive underskin update involving a stiffer new-design frame, revised suspension geometry, and more precise rack-and-pinion steering to replace the outmoded recirculating-ball setup. Optional front side airbags arrived, joining the antilock brakes and traction control that had been standard for several years. And power went up again, with the base V-8 now at 224 bhp, the dual-exhaust version at 239. Otherwise, the Grand Marquis story through 2006 was one of yearly shuffles in trim, equipment, model names, and pricing.

The sole exception was a hot rod Grand Marquis resurrecting the Marauder name. Created to liven up Mercury's dull image, it was displayed as a concept at the 2001 Chicago Auto Show, but hit the streets as a 2003 model to take advantage of that year's Grand Marquis chassis upgrades. Apart from its four-door format, the new Marauder followed the classic '60s muscle car formula of more power, tight suspension, and a sporty buckets-and-console interior (recently pioneered with an LSE package option). Horses numbered 302, courtesy of a 4.6 V-8 with a new four valves per cylinder head, plus a specific intake manifold devised by tuner Jack Roush. Also specified were standard limited-slip differential, eye-catching three-inch-diameter twin exhaust tips, polished five-spoke 18-inch alloy wheels (versus stock 16s), fat Z-rated tires (235/50 front, 245/55 rear), silver-faced gauges (including tachometer and console-mounted oil-pressure and amps dials), and a leather-trimmed cabin with "dot-matrix" appliqués and metal-look accents instead of the usual Grand Marquis pseudo wood. Paint was anything you liked so long as it was black, though dark blue and other colors were promised. Mercury charged just under $34,000 for the reborn Marauder, which looked a bargain.

America hadn't seen such a car since the last of Chevy's rear-drive SS Impalas, yet the Marauder proved a very tough sell. Mercury hoped to move 18,000 a year, but had to reset the goal to 12,000 after just 2910 sales in the first six months. There were several problems. Only fifty-somethings still remembered Mercury's "hot car" days, and even they must have thought the Marauder akin to a grandpa dressed for a biker bar. Worse, performance didn't live up to the "bad boy" persona. While most every road test praised the car's dynamic balance and mechanical finesse, *Car and Driver* was disappointed by a 7.5-second 0-60-mph time and a so-what quarter-mile run of 15.5 seconds at 91 mph. "It is, in character, more 'disciplined sedan' than 'delinquent hot rod,'" *C/D* concluded. Some industry watchers weren't so tactful. Consultant Jim Wangers of Pontiac GTO fame told trade weekly *Automotive News* that "While in concept it's a good idea, in execution the car is woefully short of anything they have any right to promote as a serious enthusiasts' car." Another analyst dismissed the Marauder as "just a half-hearted attempt at nostalgia. They would have been much better off doing it the right way." Another embarrassment was the last thing Dearborn needed, so the Marauder struggled through model-year '04, then quietly vanished after estimated sales of under 8000 over some 24 months.

A better idea might have been to produce the two-door Marauder convertible presented as a concept in early 2002. It looked good, and no one else had anything like it. But as was becoming all too familiar for Mercury, the accountants just couldn't get the numbers to add up. Too bad. Many observers agreed that Mercury couldn't turn itself around without some kind of "difference to sell."

Mercury is still on the critical list as we write in 2006, and nothing on the horizon seems likely to alter that. The brand did get two appealing new sedans at middecade, the 2005 full-size Montego (another name from yesteryear) and the 2006 compact Milan, but the former is basically a Ford Five Hundred, the latter a Ford Fusion, both with only minimal differences from their parents (see *Ford*). The similarly conceived Mountaineer SUV and Monterey minivan are going nowhere fast, and it's unclear when or even if the geriatric Grand Marquis will be retired. In addition, Mercury has yet to field a "crossover" wagon—a dubious distinction given that fast-growing new market—having been so far denied a version of the new-for-'05 Ford Freestyle and the 2007 Ford Edge/Lincoln MKX duo. Even more telling is word from Dearborn that Lincoln will be further favored over Mercury in new-product development and sales emphasis. Talk about a role reversal.

Some suggest that Mercury, like Plymouth and Oldsmobile, has simply outlived its usefulness. Times have changed, they argue, and these grand old nameplates just couldn't keep up. That's true enough, but it's also true that they weren't given a fair chance after a certain point, becoming self-fulfilling prophecies of corporate indifference, incompetence, or both. Perhaps Mercury will be the exception to this twenty-first-century pattern. We certainly hope so.

2005 Montego four-door sedan

2005 Montego four-door sedan

2006 Milan four-door sedan

Specifications

1939 - 75,000 built*

Series 99A (wb 116.0)	Wght	Price	Prod
conv club cpe 5P	2,995	1,018	—
sdn 2d 5P	2,997	916	—
cpe sdn 2d 5P	3,000	957	—
Town Sedan 4d 5P	3,103	957	—

1939 Engine	bore×stroke	bhp	availability
V-8, 239.4	3.19×3.75	95	S-all

*Estimated.

1940

Series 09A (wb 116.0)-81,128 blt*	Wght	Price	Prod
conv cpe	3,107	1,079	—
sdn 2d	3,068	946	—
cpe-sdn 2d 5P	3,030	978	—
town sedan 4d	3,103	987	—
conv sdn	3,249	1,212	—

*Estimated (see note below 1942).

1940 Engine	bore×stroke	bhp	availability
V-8, 239.4	3.19×3.75	95	S-all

1941

Series 19A (wb 118.0) - 82,391* blt		Wght	Price	Prod
67	cpe, A/S	3,049	936	—
70	sdn 2d	3,184	946	—
72	cpe-sdn 2d 5P	3,118	977	—
73	town sedan 4d	3,221	987	—
76	conv cpe	3,222	1,100	—
77	cpe 3P	3,008	910	—
79	wgn 4d	3,468	1,141	—

*Estimate (see note below 1942).

1941 Engine	bore×stroke	bhp	availability
V-8, 239.4	3.19×3.75	95	S-all

1942

Series 29A (wb 118.0) - 22,186 blt*		Wght	Price	Prod
70	sdn 2d	3,228	1,030	—
72	cpe-sdn 2d 5P	3,148	1,055	—
73	town sedan 4d	3,263	1,065	—
76	conv cpe	3,288	1,215	—
77	cpe 3P	3,073	995	—
79	wgn 4d 8P	3,528	1,260	—

* Estimate (see below).

1942 Engine	bore×stroke	bhp	availability
V-8, 239.4	3.19×3.75	100	S-all

Note: Factory records provide only calendar-year production during 1940-41. Estimates are calculated by adding 25% of previous year's calendar production to 75% of current year's production. Model-year production began in October each year.

1946

Series 69M (wb 118.0)		Wght	Price	Prod
70	sdn 2d	3,240	1,448	13,108
71	Sportsman conv cpe	3,407	2,209	205
72	cpe-sdn 2d 5P	3,190	1,495	24,163
73	town sedan 4d	3,270	1,509	40,280
76	conv cpe	3,340	1,711	6,044
79	wgn 4d	3,540	1,729	2,797
—	chassis	—	—	11

1946 Engine	bore×stroke	bhp	availability
V-8, 239.4	3.19×3.75	100	S-all

1947

Series 79M (wb 118.0)		Wght	Price	Prod
70	sdn 2d	3,268	1,592	34
72	cpe-sdn 2d 5P	3,218	1,645	29,284
73	town sedan 4d	3,298	1,660	43,281
76	conv cpe	3,368	2,002	10,221
79	wgn 4d	3,571	2,207	3,558
—	chassis	—	—	5

1947 Engine	bore×stroke	bhp	availability
V-8, 239.4	3.19×3.75	100	S-all

1948

Series 89M (wb 118.0)		Wght	Price	Prod
72	cpe-sdn 2d 5P	3,218	1,645	16,476
73	town sedan 4d	3,298	1,660	24,283
76	conv cpe	3,368	2,002	7,586
79	wgn 4d	3,571	2,207	1,889
—	chassis	—	—	34

1948 Engine	bore × stroke	bhp	availability
V-8, 239.4	3.19 × 3.75	100	S-all

1949

Series 9CM (wb 118.0)		Wght	Price	Prod
72	cpe	3,321	1,979	120,616
74	sport sedan 4d	3,386	2,031	155,882
76	conv cpe	3,591	2,410	16,765
79	wgn 2d, 8P	3,626	2,716	8,044
—	chassis	—	—	12

1949 Engine	bore×stroke	bhp	availability
V-8, 255.4	3.19×4.00	110	S-all

1950

Series OCM (wb 118.0)		Wght	Price	Prod
M-72A	cpe (economy)	3,345	1,875	
M-72B	club cpe	3,430	1,980	151,489
M-72C	Montry cpe, cnvs top	3,480	2,146	
M-72C	Montry cpe, vinyl top	3,480	2,157	
M-74	sport sedan 4d	3,470	2,032	132,082
M-76	conv cpe	3,710	2,412	8,341
M-79	wgn 2d 8P	3,755	2,561	1,746

1950 Engine	bore×stroke	bhp	availability
V-8, 255.4	3.19×4.00	110	S-all

1951

Series 1CM (wb 118.0)		Wght	Price	Prod
M-72B	cpe	3,485	1,947	
M-72C	Montry cpe, cnvs top	3,485	2,116	142,168
M-72C	Montry cpe, vinyl top	3,485	2,127	
M-74	sport sedan 4d	3,550	2,000	157,648
M-76	conv cpe	3,760	2,380	6,759
M-79	wgn 2d 8P	3,800	2,530	3,812

1951 Engine	bore×stroke	bhp	availability
V-8, 255.4	3.19×4.00	112	S-all

1952

Series 2M (wb 118.0)		Wght	Price	Prod
60B	Monterey htp cpe	3,520	2,225	24,453
60E	sport coupe htp	3,435	2,100	30,599
70B	sdn 2d	3,335	1,987	25,812
73B	sdn 4d	3,390	2,040	83,475
73C	Monterey sdn 4d	3,375	2,115	
76B	Monterey conv cpe	3,635	2,370	5,261
79B	wgn 4d 6P	3,795	2,525	2,487
79D	wgn 4d 8P	3,795	2,570	

1952 Engine	bore×stroke	bhp	availability
V-8, 255.4	3.19×4.00	125	S-all

1953

3M Custom (wb 118.0)		Wght	Price	Prod
60E	sport coupe htp	3,465	2,117	39,547
70B	sdn 2d	3,405	2,004	50,183
73B	sdn 4d	3,450	2,057	59,794
3M Monterey (wb 118.0)				
60B	htp cpe	3,465	2,244	76,119
73C	sdn 4d	3,425	2,133	64,038
76B	conv cpe	3,585	2,390	8,463
79B	wgn 4d 8P	3,765	2,591	7,719

1953 Engine	bore×stroke	bhp	availability
V-8, 255.4	3.19×4.00	125	S-all

1954

Custom (wb 118.0)		Wght	Price	Prod
60E	sport coupe htp	3,485	2,315	15,234
70B	sdn 2d	3,435	2,194	37,146
73B	sdn 4d	3,480	2,251	32,687
Monterey (wb 118.0)				
60B	htp cpe	3,520	2,452	79,533
60F	Sun Valley htp cpe	3,535	2,582	9,761
73C	sdn 4d	3,515	2,333	65,995
76B	conv cpe	3,620	2,610	7,293
79B	wgn 4d 8P	3,735	2,776	11,656

1954 Engine	bore×stroke	bhp	availability
V-8, 256.0	3.62×3.10	161	S-all

1955

Custom (wb 119.0; wgn-118.0)		Wght	Price	Prod
60E	htp cpe	3,480	2,341	7,040
70B	sdn 2d	3,395	2,218	31,295
73B	sdn 4d	3,450	2,277	21,219
79B	wgn 4d	3,780	2,686	14,134
Monterey (wb 119.0; wgn-118.0)				
60B	htp cpe	3,510	2,465	69,093
73C	sdn 4d	3,500	2,400	70,392
79C	wgn 4d	3,770	2,844	11,968
Montclair (wb 119.0)				
58A	sdn 4d	3,600	2,685	20,624
64A	htp cpe	3,490	2,631	71,588
64B	Sun Valley htp cpe	3,560	2,712	1,787
76B	conv cpe	3,685	2,712	10,668

1955 Engines	bore×stroke	bhp	availability
V-8, 292.0	3.75×3.30	188	S-Cust, Montry
V-8, 292.0	3.75 × 3.30	198	S-Montclair; O-others

1956

Medalist (wb 119.0)		Wght	Price	Prod
57D	Phaeton htp sdn	3,530	2,458	6,685
64E	Sport htp cpe	3,545	2,398	11,892
70C	sdn 2d	3,430	2,254	20,582
73D	sdn 4d	3,500	2,313	6,653
Custom (wb 119.0; wgn-118.0)				
57C	Phaeton htp sdn	3,550	2,555	12,187
64D	Sport htp cpe	3,560	2,485	20,857
70B	sdn 2d	3,505	2,351	16,343
73B	sdn 4d	3,520	2,410	15,860
76A	conv cpe	3,665	2,712	2,311
79B	wgn 4d 8P	3,860	2,819	9,292
79D	wgn 4d 6P	3,790	2,722	8,478
Monterey (wb 119.0; wgn-118.0)				
57B	Phaeton htp sdn	3,800	2,700	10,726
58B	sport sedan 4d	3,550	2,652	11,765
64C	Sport htp cpe	3,590	2,630	42,863

Monterey		Wght	Price	Prod
73C	sdn 4d	3,570	2,555	26,735
79C	wgn 4d 8P	3,885	2,977	13,280
Montclair (wb 119.0)				
57A	Phaeton htp sdn	3,640	2,835	23,493
58A	sport sedan 4d	3,610	2,786	9,617
64A	Sport htp cpe	3,620	2,765	50,562
76B	conv cpe	3,725	2,900	7,762

1956 Engines	bore×stroke	bhp	availability
V-8, 312.0	3.80×3.44	210	S-all (manual)
V-8, 312.0	3.80×3.44	225	S-all (auto.)
V-8, 312.0	3.80×3.44	235	O-all (auto.)

1957

Monterey (wb 122.0)		Wght	Price	Prod
57A	Phaeton htp sdn	3,915	2,763	22,475
58A	sdn 4d	3,890	2,645	53,839
63A	Phaeton htp cpe	3,870	2,693	42,199
64A	sdn 2d	3,875	2,576	33,982
76A	Phaeton conv cpe	4,035	3,005	5,033
Montclair (wb 122.0)				
57B	Phaeton htp sdn	3,925	3,317	21,567
58B	sdn 4d	3,905	3,188	19,836
63B	Phaeton htp cpe	3,900	3,236	30,111
76B	Phaeton conv cpe	4,010	3,430	4,248
Turnpike Cruiser (wb 122.0)				
65A	htp cpe	4,005	3,758	7,291
75A	htp sdn	4,015	3,849	8,305
76S	conv cpe	4,125	4,103	1,265
Station Wagon (wb 122.0)				
56A	Commuter 2d 6P	4,115	2,903	4,885
56B	Voyager 2d 6P	4,240	3,403	2,283
77A	Commuter 4d 6P	4,195	2,973	11,990
77B	Colony Park 4d 9P	4,165	3,677	7,386
77C	Commuter 4d 9P	4,155	3,070	5,752
77D	Voyager 4d 9P	4,280	3,570	3,716

1957 Engines	bore×stroke	bhp	availability
V-8, 312.0	3.80×3.44	255	S-all exc Turnpike Cruiser
V-8, 368.0	4.00×3.66	290	S-Trnpk Cruiser; O-others

1958

Medalist (wb 122.0)		Wght	Price	Prod
58C	sdn 4d	3,875	2,617	10,982
64B	sdn 2d	3,790	2,547	7,750
Monterey (wb 122.0)				
57A	Phaeton htp sdn	4,150	2,840	6,909
58A	sdn 4d	4,160	2,721	28,892
63A	Phaeton htp cpe	4,075	2,769	13,693
64A	sdn 2d	4,080	2,652	10,526
76A	conv cpe	4,225	3,081	2,292
Montclair (wb 122.0)				
57B	Phaeton htp sdn	4,165	3,365	3,609
58B	sdn 4d	4,155	3,236	4,801
63B	Phaeton htp cpe	4,085	3,284	5,012
65A	Trnpk Cruiser htp cpe	4,150	3,498	2,864
75A	Trnpk Cruiser htp sdn	4,230	3,577	3,543
76B	conv cpe	4,295	3,536	844
Park Lane (wb 125.0)				
57C	Phaeton htp sdn	4,390	3,944	5,241
63C	Phaeton htp cpe	4,280	3,867	3,158
76C	conv cpe	4,405	4,118	853
Station Wagon (wb 122.0)				
56A	Commuter 2d 6P	4,400	3,035	1,912
56B	Voyager 2d 6P	4,435	3,535	568
77A	Commuter 4d 6P	4,485	3,105	8,601
77B	Colony Park 4d 6-9P	4,605	3,775	4,474
77C	Commuter 4d 9P	4,525	3,201	4,227
77D	Voyager 4d 6-9P	4,540	3,635	2,520

1958 Engines	bore×stroke	bhp	availability
V-8, 312.0	3.80×3.44	235	S-Medalist
V-8, 383.0	4.30×3.30	312	S-Monterey, Commuter
V-8, 383.0	4.30×3.30	330	S-Montclair, Voygr, Col Park
V-8, 430.0	4.30×3.70	360	S-Park Lane; O-others
V-8, 430.0	4.30×3.70	400	O-all, exc. Medal

1959

Monterey (wb 126.0)		Wght	Price	Prod
57A	Cruiser htp sdn	4,013	2,918	11,355
58A	sdn 4d	3,985	2,832	43,570
63A	Cruiser htp cpe	3,932	2,854	17,232
64A	sdn 2d	3,914	2,768	12,694
76A	conv cpe	4,074	3,150	4,426
Montclair (wb 126.0)				
57B	Cruiser htp sdn	4,234	3,437	6,713
58B	sdn 4d	4,205	3,308	9,514
63B	Cruiser htp cpe	4,146	3,357	7,375
Park Lane (wb 128.0)				
57C	Cruiser htp sdn	4,386	4,031	7,206
63C	Cruiser htp cpe	4,311	3,955	4,060
76C	conv cpe	4,455	4,206	1,257
Station Wagon (wb 126.0)				
56A	Commuter 2d 6P	4,334	3,145	1,051
77A	Commuter 4d 6P	4,405	3,215	15,122
77B	Colony Park 4d 6P	4,535	3,932	5,929
77D	Voyager 4d 6P	4,483	3,793	2,496

1959 Engines	bore×stroke	bhp	availability
V-8, 312.0	3.80×3.44	210	S-Monterey
V-8, 383.0	4.30×3.30	280	S-Commuter; O-Monterey
V-8, 383.0	4.30×3.30	322	S-Mont, Voygr, Col Park
V-8, 430.0	4.30×3.70	345	S-Park Lane

1960

Comet (wb 114.0; wgn-109.5)		Wght	Price	Prod
54A	sdn 4d	2,432	2,053	47,416
59A	wgn 2d	2,548	2,310	5,115
62A	sdn 2d	2,399	1,998	45,374
71A	wgn 4d	2,581	2,365	18,426
Monterey (wb 126.0)				
57A	Cruiser htp sdn	4,011	2,845	9,536
58A	sdn 4d	3,981	2,730	49,594
63A	Cruiser htp cpe	3,931	2,781	15,790
64A	sdn 2d	3,901	2,631	21,557
76A	conv cpe	4,131	3,077	6,062
Montclair (wb 126.0)				
57B	Cruiser htp sdn	4,285	3,394	5,548
58B	sdn 4d	4,255	3,280	8,510
63B	Cruiser htp cpe	4,205	3,331	5,756
Park Lane (wb 126.0)				
57F	Cruiser htp sdn	4,380	3,858	5,788
63F	Cruiser htp cpe	4,300	3,794	2,974
76D	conv cpe	4,500	4,018	1,525
Station Wagon (wb 126.0)				
77A	Commuter 4d 6-9P	4,301	3,127	14,949
77B	Colony Park 4d 9P	4,558	3,837	7,411

1960 Engines	bore×stroke	bhp	availability
I-6, 144.3	3.50×2.50	90	S-Comet
V-8, 312.0	3.80×3.44	205	S-Mont, Comm
V-8, 383.0	4.30×3.30	280	O-Mont, Comm
V-8, 430.0	4.30 3.70	310	S-Mont, Pk Lane, Col Park

1961

Comet (wb 114.0; wgn-109.5)		Wght	Price	Prod
54A	sdn 4d	2,411	2,055	85,332
59A	wgn 2d	2,548	2,312	4,199
62A	sdn 2d	2,376	2,000	71,563
62C	S-22 sdn 2d	2,441	2,284	14,004
71A	wgn 4d	2,581	2,355	22,165
Meteor (wb 120.0)				
58A	600 sdn 4d	3,714	2,589	18,117
64A	600 sdn 2d	3,647	2,535	
54A	800 sdn 4d	3,762	2,767	
62A	800 sdn 2d	3,680	2,713	35,005
65A	800 htp cpe	3,694	2,774	
75A	800 htp sdn	3,780	2,839	
Monterey (wb 120.0)				
54B	sdn 4d	3,777	2,871	22,881
65B	htp cpe	3,709	2,878	10,942
75B	htp sdn	3,795	2,943	9,252
76A	conv cpe	3,872	3,128	7,053
Station Wagon (wb 120.0)				
71A	Commuter 4d 6P	4,115	2,924	8,945
71B	Colony Park 4d 6P	4,131	3,120	7,887
71B	Colony Park 4d 9P	4,171	3,191	
71C	Commuter 4d 9P	4,155	2,994	6

1961 Engines	bore×stroke	bhp	availability
I-6, 144.3	3.50×2.50	85	S-Comet
I-6, 170.0	3.50×2.94	101	O-Comet
I-6, 223.0	3.62×3.60	135	O-Metr, Comm
V-8, 292.0	3.75×3.30	175	S-all exc Comet
V-8, 352.0	4.00×3.50	220	O-all exc Comet
V-8, 390.0	4.05×3.78	300	O-Metr 800, Montry
V-8, 390.0	4.05×3.78	330	O-all exc Comet

1962

Comet (wb 114.0; wgn-109.5)		Wght	Price	Prod
54A	sdn 4d	2,457	2,139	70,227
54B	Custom sdn 4d	2,468	2,226	
59A	wgn 2d	2,626	2,396	2,121
59B	Custom wgn 2d	2,642	2,483	
62A	sdn 2d	2,420	2,084	
62B	Custom sdn 2d	2,431	2,171	73,880
62C	S-22sdn 2d	2,458	2,368	
71A	wgn 4d	2,662	2,439	16,759
71B	Custom wgn 4d	2,679	2,526	
71C	Villager wgn 4d	2,712	2,710	2,318
Meteor (wb 116.5)				
54A	sdn 4d	2,956	2,340	18,708
54B	Custom sdn 4d	2,964	2,428	23,484
62A	sdn 2d	2,922	2,278	11,550
62B	Custom sdn 2d	2,930	2,366	9,410
62C	S-33 sdn 2d	2,960	2,509	5,900
Monterey (wb 120.0)				
54A	sdn 4d	3,772	2,726	18,975
62A	sdn 2d	3,695	2,672	5,117
65A	htp cpe	3,712	2,733	5,328
75A	htp sdn	3,781	2,798	2,691
Monterey Custom (wb 120.0)				
54B	sdn 4d	3,836	2,965	27,591
65B	htp cpe	3,772	2,972	10,814
65C	S-55 htp cpe	4,802	3,488	2,772
75B	htp sdn	3,851	3,037	8,932
76A	conv cpe	3,938	3,222	5,489
76B	S-55 conv cpe	3,968	3,738	1,315
Station Wagon (wb 120.0)				
71A	Commuter 4d 6P	4,120	2,920	8,389
71C	Commuter 4d 9P	4,132	2,990	
71B	Colony Park 4d 6P	4,186	3,219	9,596
71D	Colony Park 4d 9P	4,198	3,289	

1962 Engines	bore×stroke	bhp	availability
I-6, 144.3	3.50×2.50	85	S-Comet
I-6, 170.0	3.50×2.94	101	S-Metr; O-Comt
I-6, 223.0	3.62×3.60	138	S-Mont, Comm
V-8, 221.0	3.50×2.87	145	O-Meteor
V-8, 260.0	3.80×2.87	164	O-Meteor
V-8, 292.0	3.75×3.30	170	S-Cust, Col Prk; O-Mont, Cmm
V-8, 352.0	4.00×3.50	220	O-all exc Comet, Meteor
V-8, 390.0	4.05 × 3.78	300	S-S55; O-all exc Comet, Meteor
V-8, 390.0	4.05 × 3.78	330	O-all exc Comt, Meteor
V-8, 406.0	4.13 × 3.78	385	O-all exc Comt, Meteor

1963

Comet (wb 114.0; wgn-109.5)		Wght	Price	Prod
54A	sdn 4d	2,499	2,139	24,230
54B	Custom sdn 4d	2,508	2,226	27,498
59A	wgn 2d	2,644	2,440	623
59B	Custom wgn 2d	2,659	2,527	272
62A	sdn 2d	2,462	2,084	24,351
62B	Custom sdn 2d	2,471	2,171	11,897
62C	S-22 sdn 2d	2,512	2,368	6,303
63B	Cust Sprtstr htp cpe	2,572	2,605	9,432
63C	S-22 htp cpe	2,613	2,635	5,807
71A	wgn 4d	2,681	2,483	4,419
71B	Custom wgn 4d	2,696	2,570	5,151
71C	Villager wgn 4d	2,736	2,754	1,529
76A	Custom conv cpe	2,784	2,557	7,354
76B	S-22 conv cpe	2,825	2,710	5,757
Meteor (wb 116.5; wgn-115.5)				
54A	sdn 4d	3,025	2,340	9,183
54B	Custom sdn 4d	3,031	2,428	14,498
62A	sdn 2d	2,986	2,278	3,935
62B	Custom sdn 2d	2,992	2,366	2,704
65A	Custom htp cpe	3,010	2,448	7,565
65B	S-33 htp cpe	3,030	2,628	4,865
71B	wgn 4d 6P	3,303	2,631	2,904
71D	Cnty Crsr wgn 4d 6-9P	3,319	2,886	1,485
71E	Custom wgn 4d 6-9P	3,311	2,719	3,636
Monterey (120.0)				
54A	sdn 4d	3,944	2,887	18,177
62A	sdn 2d	3,854	2,834	4,640
65A	htp cpe	3,869	2,930	3,879
75A	htp sdn	3,959	2,995	1,692
Monterey Custom (wb 120.0)				
54B	sdn 4d	3,956	3,075	39,542
63B	Mraudr fstbk htp cpe	3,887	3,083	7,298
63C	S-55 Mraudr fstbk htp cpe	3,900	3,650	2,319
65B	htp cpe	3,881	3,083	10,693
65C	S-55 htp cpe	3,894	3,650	3,863
75B	htp sdn	3,971	3,148	8,604
75C	S-55 htp sdn	3,984	3,715	1,203
76A	conv cpe	4,043	3,333	3,783
76B	S-55 conv cpe	4,049	3,900	1,379
Station Wagon (wb 120.0)				
71B	Colony Park 4d 6P	4,306	3,295	6,447
71D	Colony Park 4d 9P	4,318	3,365	7,529

1963 Engines	bore×stroke	bhp	availability
I-6, 144.3	3.50×2.50	85	S-Comet early
I-6, 170.0	3.50×2.94	101	S-Comet later, Meteor
I-6, 200.0	3.68×3.15	116	O-Meteor
V-8, 221.0	3.50×2.87	145	O-Comt, Meteor
V-8, 260.0	3.80×2.87	164	O-Meteor Cus, S-33, Comet
V-8, 390.0	4.05×3.78	250	S-all full-size except S-55
V-8, 390.0	4.05×3.78	300	S-S55; O-other full size
V-8, 390.0	4.05×3.78	330	O-all full size
V-8, 406.0	4.13×3.78	385	O-Monterey, Mont Custom
V-8, 406.0	4.13×3.78	405	O-Monterey, Mont Custom
V-8, 427.0	4.23×3.78	410	O-late Monterey, Mont Custom

1964

Comet 202 (wb 114.0; wgn-109.5)		Wght	Price	Prod
01	sdn 2d	2,539	2,126	33,824
02	sdn 4d	2,580	2,182	29,147
32	wgn 4d	2,727	2,463	5,504
Comet 404 (wb 114.0; wgn-109.5)				
11	sdn 2d	2,551	2,213	12,512
12	sdn 4d	2,588	2,269	25,136
34	Custom wgn 4d	2,741	2,550	6,918
36	Villager wgn 4d	2,745	2,734	1,980
Comet Caliente (wb 114.0)				
22	sdn 4d	2,668	2,350	27,218
23	htp cpe	2,688	2,375	31,204
25	conv cpe	2,861	2,636	9,039
Comet Cyclone (wb 114.0)				
27	htp cpe	2,860	2,655	7,454
Monterey (wb 120.0)				
41	sdn 2d	3,895	2,819	3,932
42	sdn 4d	3,985	2,892	20,234
43	htp cpe	3,910	2,884	2,926
45	conv cpe	4,027	3,226	2,592
47	Maraudr fstbk htp cpe	3,916	2,884	8,760
48	Maraudr fstbk htp sdn	3,914	2,957	4,143
Montclair (wb 120.0)				
52	sdn 4d	3,996	3,116	15,520
53	htp cpe	3,921	3,127	2,329
57	Maraudr fstbk htp cpe	3,927	3,127	6,459
58	Maraudr fstbk htp sdn	4,017	3,181	8,655
Park Lane (wb 120.0)				
62	sdn 4d	4,035	3,348	6,230
63	htp cpe	3,960	3,359	1,786

Park Lane		Wght	Price	Prod
64	htp sdn	4,050	3,413	2,402
65	conv cpe	4,066	3,549	1,967
67	Maraudr fstbk htp cpe	3,966	3,359	2,721
68	Maraudr fstbk htp sdn	4,056	3,413	4,505
Station Wagon (wb 120.0)				
72	Commuter 4d 6P	4,259	3,236	3,484
72	Commuter 4d 9P	4,271	3,306	1,839
76	Colony Park 4d 6P	4,275	3,434	4,234
76	Colony Park 4d 9P	4,287	3,504	5,624

1964 Engines	bore×stroke	bhp	availability
I-6, 170.0	3.50 ×2.94	101	S-Comet
I-6, 200.0	3.68×3.15	116	O-Comet
V-8, 260.0	3.80×2.87	164	O-Comet
V-8, 289.0	4.00×2.87	210	S-Cycl; O-other Comet
V-8, 390.0	4.05×3.78	250	S-all exc Comet, Park Lane
V-8, 390.0	4.05×3.78	266	O-all exc Comt, Park Lane
V-8, 390.0	4.05×3.78	300	S-Park Lane
V-8, 390.0	4.05 × 3.78	330	O-Park Lane
V-8, 427.0	4.23 × 3.78	410	O-Monterey, Montcl, P Lane
V-8, 427.0	4.23 × 3.78	425	O-Monterey, Montcl, P Lane

1965

Comet 202 (wb 114.0; wgn-109.5)		Wght	Price	Prod
01	sdn 2d	2,584	2,154	32,425
02	sdn 4d	2,624	2,210	23,501
32	wgn 4d	2,784	2,491	4,814
Comet 404 (wb 114.0; wgn-109.5)				
11	sdn 2d	2,594	2,241	10,900
12	sdn 4d	2,629	2,294	18,628
34	Custom wgn 4d	2,789	2,578	5,226
36	Villager wgn 4d	2,789	2,762	1,592
Comet Caliente (wb 114.0)				
22	sdn 4d	2,659	2,378	20,337
23	htp cpe	2,684	2,403	29,247
25	conv cpe	2,869	2,664	6,035
Comet Cyclone (wb 114.0)				
27	htp cpe	2,994	2,683	12,347
Monterey (wb 123.0)				
42	Breezeway sdn 4d	3,898	2,904	19,569
43	sdn 2d	3,788	2,767	5,775
44	sdn 4d	3,853	2,839	23,363
45	conv cpe	3,928	3,230	4,762
47	htp cpe	3,823	2,902	16,857
48	htp sdn	3,893	2,978	10,047
Montclair (wb 123.0)				
52	Breezeway sdn 4d	3,933	3,137	18,924
57	htp cpe	3,848	3,135	9,645
58	htp sdn	3,928	3,210	16,977
Park Lane (wb 123.0)				
62	Breezeway sdn 4d	3,988	3,369	8,335
65	conv cpe	4,013	3,599	3,006
67	htp cpe	3,908	3,367	6,853
68	htp sdn	3,983	3,442	14,211
Station Wagon (wb 119.0)				
72	Commuter 4d 6P	4,178	3,235	5,453
72	Commuter 4d 9P	4,213	3,312	2,628
76	Colony Park 4d 6P	4,228	3,434	6,910
76	Colony Park 4d 9P	4,263	3,511	8,384

1965 Engines	bore×stroke	bhp	availability
I-6, 200.0	3.68×3.15	120	S-Comet
V-8, 289.0	4.00×2.87	200	S-Cycl; O-other Comet
V-8, 289.0	4.00×2.87	225	O-Comet
V-8, 390.0	4.05×3.78	250	S-Mont, Comm
V-8, 390.0	4.05×3.78	266	S-Montclair, Colony Park
V-8, 390.0	4.05 × 3.78	300	S-Park Lane; O-all exc Comt
V-8, 390.0	4.05 × 3.78	330	O-all exc Comet
V-8, 427.0	4.23 × 3.78	425	O-all exc Comet

1966

Comet 202 (wb 116.0; wgn-113.0)		Wght	Price	Prod
01	sdn 2d	2,864	2,206	35,964
02	sdn 4d	2,908	2,263	20,440
06	Voyager wgn 4d	3,282	2,553	7,595
Comet Capri (wb 116.0; wgn-113.0)				
12	sdn 4d	2,928	2,378	15,635
13	htp cpe	2,960	2,400	15,031
16	Villager wgn 4d	3,319	2,790	3,880
Comet Caliente (wb 116.0)				
22	sdn 4d	2,930	2,453	17,933
23	htp cpe	2,966	2,475	25,862
25	conv cpe	3,228	2,735	3,922
Comet Cyclone (wb 116.0)				
27	htp cpe	3,078	2,700	6,889
27	GT htp cpe	3,315	2,891	13,812
29	conv cpe	3,321	2,961	1,305
29	GT conv cpe	3,595	3,152	2,158
Monterey (wb 123.0)				
42	Breezeway sdn 4d	3,966	2,917	14,174
43	sdn 2d	3,835	2,783	2,487
44	sdn 4d	3,903	2,854	18,998
45	conv cpe	4,039	3,237	3,279
47	fstbk htp cpe	3,885	2,915	19,103
48	fstbk htp sdn	3,928	2,990	7,647
S-55 (wb 123.0)				
46	conv cpe	4,148	3,614	669
49	fstbk htp cpe	4,031	3,292	2,916
Montclair (wb 123.0)				
54	sdn 4d	3,921	3,087	11,856
57	fstbk htp cpe	3,887	3,144	11,290
58	fstbk htp sdn	3,971	3,217	15,767
Park Lane (wb 123.0)				
62	Breezeway sdn 4d	4,051	3,389	8,696
65	conv cpe	4,148	3,608	2,546
67	fstbk htp cpe	3,971	3,387	8,354
68	fstbk htp sdn	4,070	3,460	19,204
Station Wagon (wb 119.0)				
72	Commuter 4d 6P	4,280	3,240	3,970
72	Commuter 4d 9P	4,331	3,336	2,877
76	Colony Park 4d 6P	4,332	3,502	7,190
76	Colony Park 4d 9P	4,383	3,598	11,704

1966 Engines	bore×stroke	bhp	availability
I-6, 200.0	3.68×3.15	120	S-Comt exc Cycl
V-8, 289.0	4.00×2.87	200	S-Cyclone; O-other Comt
V-8, 390.0	4.05×3.78	265	S-Cyclone GT, full-size w/man
V-8, 390.0	4.05×3.78	275	S-full-size w/auto; O-Cyclone GT
V-8, 390.0	4.05×3.78	335	O-Cyclone GT
V-8, 410.0	4.05×3.98	330	S-Prk Ln; O-other full-size exc. S55
V-8, 428.0	4.13×3.98	345	S-S55; O-other full-size

1967

Comet 202 (wb 116.0)		Wght	Price	Prod
01	sdn 2d	2,868	2,284	14,251
02	sdn 4d	2,906	2,336	10,281
Comet Capri (wb 116.0)				
06	sdn 4d	2,940	2,436	9,292
07	htp cpe	2,970	2,459	11,671
Comet Caliente (wb 116.0)				
10	sdn 4d	2,952	2,535	9,153
11	htp cpe	2,982	2,558	9,966
12	conv cpe	3,250	2,818	1,539
Comet Station Wagon (wb 113.0)				
03	Voyager 4d	3,310	2,604	4,930
08	Villager 4d	3,332	2,841	3,140
Comet Cyclone (wb 116.0)				
15	htp cpe	3,075	2,737	2,682
15	GT htp cpe	3,372	3,372	3,419
16	conv cpe	3,632	2,997	431
16	GT conv cpe	3,350	3,632	378
Cougar (wb 111.0)				
91	htp cpe	2,988	2,851	116,260
91	GT htp cpe	3,000	3,175	7,412
93	XR-7 htp cpe	3,015	3,081	27,221
Monterey (wb 123.0)				
44	sdn 4d	3,798	2,904	15,177
44	Breezeway sdn 4d	3,847	2,967	5,910
45	conv cpe	3,943	3,314	2,673
46	S-55 conv cpe	3,960	3,837	145
47	htp cpe	3,820	2,985	16,910
48	htp sdn	3,858	3,059	8,013
49	S-55 fstbk htp cpe	3,837	3,511	570
Montclair (wb 123.0)				
54	sdn 4d	3,863	3,187	5,783
54	Breezeway sdn 4d	3,881	3,250	4,151
57	htp cpe	3,848	3,244	4,118
58	htp sdn	3,943	3,316	5,870
Park Lane (wb 123.0)				
61	Brghm Breezwy sdn 4d	3,980	3,896	3,325
62	Brougham htp sdn	4,000	3,986	4,189
64	Breezeway sdn 4d	4,011	3,736	4,163
65	conv cpe	4,114	3,984	1,191
67	htp cpe	3,947	3,752	2,196
68	htp sdn	3,992	3,826	5,412
Marquis (wb 123.0)				
69	htp cpe	3,995	3,989	6,510
Station Wagon (wb 119.0)				
72	Commuter 4d 6P	4,178	3,289	3,447
72	Commuter 4d 9P	4,297	3,384	4,451
76	Colony Park 4d 6P	4,258	3,657	5,775
76	Colony Park 4d 9P	4,294	3,752	12,915

1967 Engines	bore×stroke	bhp	availability
I-6, 200.0	3.68×3.15	120	S-Comt exc Cycl
V-8, 289.0	4.00×2.87	200	S-Cougar, Cycl; O-other Comet
V-8, 289.0	4.00×2.87	225	O-Cougar
V-8, 390.0	4.05×3.78	270	S-Mntry, Mntclr, S Wgn; O-Comt
V-8, 390.0	4.05×3.78	320	S-Cycl/Cgr GT; O-other Cougar
V-8, 410.0	4.05×3.98	330	S-Park Lane, Marquis; O-Mont, Montclair
V-8, 427.0	4.23×3.78	410	O-Comet htps and 2d sedans
V-8, 427.0	4.23×3.78	425	O-Comet htps and 2d sedans
V-8, 428.0	4.13×3.98	345	S-S55; O-other full-size

1968

Comet (wb 116.0)		Wght	Price	Prod
01	htp cpe	3,166	2,477	16,693
Montego (wb 116.0; wgn-113.0)				
06	sdn 4d	3,062	2,504	18,492
07	htp cpe	3,138	2,552	15,002
08	MX wgn 4d	3,460	2,876	9,328
10	MX sdn 4d*	3,088	2,657	18,413
11	MX htp cpe*	3,162	2,676	25,827
12	MX conv cpe	3,374	2,935	3,248
Cyclone (wb 116.0)				
15	fstbk htp cpe	3,407	2,768	6,165
15	GT fstbk htp cpe	3,430	2,936	6,105
17	htp cpe	3,361	2,768	1,034
17	GT htp cpe	3,380	2,936	334
Cougar (wb 111.0)**				
91	htp cpe	3,134	2,933	81,014
93	XR-7 htp cpe	3,174	3,232	32,712
Monterey (wb 123.0)				
44	sdn 4d	3,895	3,052	30,727
45	conv cpe	3,977	3,436	1,515
47	htp cpe	3,854	3,133	18,845
48	htp sdn	3,892	3,207	8,927
Montclair (wb 123.0)				
54	sdn 4d	3,897	3,331	7,255
57	htp cpe	3,882	3,387	3,497
58	htp sdn	3,907	3,459	4,008
Park Lane (wb 123.0)				
64	sdn 4d*	4,019	3,552	6,408
65	conv cpe	4,122	3,822	1,112
67	htp cpe	3,955	3,575	2,584
68	htp sdn*	4,000	3,647	10,390

Marquis (wb 123.0)		Wght	Price	Prod
69	htp cpe	3,987	3,685	3,965
Station Wagon (wb 119.0)				
72	Commuter 4d 6P	4,212	3,441	3,497
72	Commuter 4d 9P	4,331	3,569	5,191
76	Colony Park 4d 6P	4,259	3,460	5,674
76	Colony Park 4d 6P	4,295	3,888	15,505

*Includes cars with Brougham trim option.

**Includes cars with GT and GTE package options.

1968 Engines	bore×stroke	bhp	availability
I-6, 200.0	3.68×3.15	115	S-Comt, Montgo
V-8, 289.0	4.00×2.87	195	S-base Cougar; O-Comet
V-8, 302.0	4.00×3.00	210	S-Cougar XR-7, Cycl, O-Montgo
V-8, 302.0	4.00×3.00	230	O-Cougr, Montgo
V-8, 390.0	4.05×3.78	265	S-full-size w/man; O-Montgo, Cycl
V-8, 390.0	4.05×3.78	280	S-full size w/auto; O-Cougar
V-8, 390.0	4.05×3.78	315	S-Pk Ln, Marq; O-other full size
V-8, 390.0	4.05×3.78	325	S-Cougar GT; O-Montego exc MX wgn, Cycl, Cougr (exc. GTE)
V-8, 390.0	4.05×3.78	335	O-Montego exc wgn, Cyclone
V-8, 427.0	4.23×3.78	390	S-Cougr GTE; O-Cycl, Montgo hardtops
V-8, 428,0	4.13×3.98	335	O-Montgo, Cyclone, Cougar
V-8, 428.0	4.13×3.98	340	O-full size only

1969

Comet (wb 116.0)		Wght	Price	Prod
01	htp cpe	3,175	2,532	14,104
Montego (wb 116.0; wgn-113.0)				
06	sdn 4d	3,140	2,556	21,950
07	htp cpe	3,154	2,605	17,785
08	MX wgn 4d	3,504	2,979	10,590
10	MX sdn 4d	3,174	2,718	16,148
10	MX Brghm sdn 4d	3,198	2,808	1,590
11	MX htp cpe	3,186	2,736	23,160
11	MX Brghm htp cpe	3,210	2,826	1,226
12	MX conv cpe	3,356	2,979	1,725
Cyclone (wb 116.0)				
15	fstbk htp cpe	3,273	2,771	5,882
16	CJ fstbk htp cpe	3,634	3,224	3,261
Cougar (wb 111.0)				
91	htp cpe	3,219	3,016	66,331
92	conv cpe	3,343	3,382	5,796
93	XR-7 htp cpe	3,221	3,315	23,918
94	XR-7 conv cpe	3,343	3,595	4,024
—	Eliminator htp cpe	3,250	—	—
Monterey (wb 124.0, wgn-121.0)				
44	sdn 4d	3,948	3,158	23,009
45	conv cpe	4,093	3,540	1,297
46	htp cpe	3,970	3,237	9,865
48	htp sdn	4,008	3,313	6,066
72	wgn 4d 6-9P	4,277	3,536	5,844
Monterey Custom (wb 124.0; wgn-121.0)				
54	sdn 4d	4,013	3,377	7,103
56	htp cpe	3,998	3,459	2,898
58	htp sdn	4,023	3,533	2,827
74	wgn 4d 6-9P	4,342	3,757	1,920
Marauder (wb 121.0)				
60	htp cpe	4,044	3,368	9,031
61	X-100 htp cpe	4,191	4,091	5,635
Marquis (wb 124.0; wgn-121.0)				
63	sdn 4d	4,226	3,857	16,787
63	Brougham sdn 4d	4,295	4,129	14,601
65	conv cpe	4,359	4,124	2,319
66	htp cpe	4,192	3,919	9,907
66	Brougham htp cpe	4,215	4,191	8,395
68	htp sdn	4,237	3,990	14,423
68	Brougham htp sdn	4,436	4,262	14,966
76	Clny Prk wgn 4d 6-9P	4,376	3,895	25,604

1969 Engines	bore×stroke	bhp	availability
I-6, 250.0	3.68×3.91	155	S-Comt, Montgo
V-8, 302.0	4.00×3.00	220	S-Cyclone; O-Comet, Montego
V-8, 302.0	4.00 × 3.00	290	O-Cougar (Elim)
V-8, 351.0	4.00 × 3.50	250	S-Cougar; O-Montgo, Comet, Cyclone
V-8, 351.0	4.00 × 3.50	290	O-Coug, Comet, Cycl, Montego
V-8, 390.0	4.05 × 3.78	265	S-Montry, Maurdr, SW w/manual
V-8, 390.0	4.05 × 3.78	280	O-Montry, Maurdr, SW w/man
V-8, 390.0	4.05 × 3.78	320	O-Cougr, Montgo, Cyclone, Comet
V-8, 428.0	4.13 × 3.98	335	S-Cyclone CJ; O-Cougr; Montgo exc Brghm, SW, conv/sdns w/4 spd
V-8, 428,0	4.13 × 3.98	335	O-Cougr, Cycl, Cycl CJ (ram air)
V-8, 429.0	4.36 × 3.59	320	S-Marq; O-other full-size
V-8, 429.0	4.36 × 3.59	360	S-X100; O-other full-size

1970

Montego (wb 117.0; wgn-114.0)		Wght	Price	Prod
01	htp cpe	2,859	2,645	21,298
02	sdn 4d	3,208	2,631	13,988
06	MX sdn 4d	3,215	2,728	16,708
07	MX htp cpe	3,228	2,740	15,533
08	MX wgn 4d 6P	3,653	3,091	5,094
10	MX Brghm sdn 4d	3,238	2,896	3,315
11	MX Brghm htp cpe	3,248	2,915	8,074
12	MX Brghm htp sdn	3,268	3,037	3,685
18	MX Brghm wgn 4d 6P	3,668	3,304	2,682
Cyclone (wb 117.0)				
15	htp cpe	3,721	3,238	1,695
16	GT htp cpe	3,462	3,226	10,170
17	Spoiler htp cpe	3,773	3,759	1,631
Cougar (wb 111.1)				
91	htp cpe*	3,285	3,114	49,479
92	conv cpe	3,382	3,480	2,322
93	XR-7 htp cpe	3,311	3,413	18,565
94	XR-7 conv cpe	3,408	3,692	1,977
Monterey (wb 124.0; wgn-121.0)				
44	sdn 4d	3,926	3,248	29,432
45	conv cpe	4,071	3,668	581
46	htp cpe	3,890	3,329	9,359
48	htp sdn	3,961	3,406	5,032
72	wgn 4d 6P	4,235	3,682	1,657
72	wgn 4d 9P	4,327	3,774	3,507
Monterey Custom (wb 124.0)				
54	sdn 4d	3,931	3,520	4,823
56	htp cpe	3,922	3,600	1,357
58	htp sdn	3,973	3,676	1,194
Marauder (wb 121.0)				
60	htp cpe	3,972	3,503	3,397
61	X100 htp cpe	4,128	4,136	2,646
Marquis (wb 124.0; wgn-121.0)				
62	Brougham sdn 4d	4,166	4,367	14,920
63	sdn 4d	4,121	4,052	14,394
64	Brougham htp cpe	4,119	4,428	7,113
65	conv cpe	4,337	4,318	1,233
66	htp cpe	4,072	4,113	6,229
67	Brougham htp sdn	4,182	4,500	11,623
68	htp sdn	4,141	4,185	8,411
74	wgn 4d 6P	4,347	3,930	959
74	wgn 4d 9P	4,393	4,022	1,429
76	Clny Prk wgn 4d 6P	4,442	4,123	4,655
76	Clny Prk wgn 4d 9P	4,488	4,215	14,549

1970 Engines	bore×stroke	bhp	availability
I-6, 250.0	3.68×3.91	155	S-Montego
V-8, 302.0	4.00×3.00	220	O-Montego
V-8, 302.0	4.00×3.00	290	O-Cougr Elim
V-8, 351.0	4.00×3.50	250	S-Cycl, Cougar exc Eliminator; O-Montego
V-8, 351.0	4.00×3.50	300	S-Cougr Elim; O-Cougr, Montgo
V-8, 390.0	4.05×3.78	265	S-Montry, Mrdr, Col Park w/man
V-8, 390.0	4.05×3.78	280	S-above models w/auto
V-8, 428.0	4.13×3.98	335	O-Cougar
V-8, 429.0	4.36×3.59	320	S-Marquis exc Colony Park
V-8, 429.0	4.36×3.59	360	S-Cycl exc Splr, Marauder X100; O-Mntgo, Mntry, Mrdr, Col Park
V-8, 429.0	4.36×3.59	370	S-Spoiler; O-Cycl, GT**
V-8, 429.0	4.36×3.59	375	O-all Cyclone
V-8, 429.0	4.36 × 3.59	375	O-all Cycl, Cougr Elim ("Boss")

*Includes models with Eliminator performance option.

**Available in Ram Air and non-Ram Air versions.

1971

Comet (wb 109.9; 2d-103.0)		Wght	Price	Prod
30	sdn 4d	2,789	2,446	28,116
31	fstbk sdn 2d	2,700	2,387	54,884
Montego (wb 117.0; wgns-114.0)				
01	htp cpe	3,229	2,893	9,623
02	sdn 4d	3,228	2,888	5,718
06	MX sdn 4d	3,235	2,994	13,559
07	MX htp cpe	3,236	3,007	13,719
08	MX wgn	3,651	3,331	3,698
10	MX Brghm sdn 4d	3,258	3,189	1,565
11	MX Brghm htp cpe	3,275	3,201	2,851
12	MX Brghm htp sdn	3,302	3,273	1,156
18	MX Villager wgn	3,666	3,572	2,121
Cyclone (wb 117.0)				
15	fstbk htp cpe	3,595	3,369	444
16	GT fstbk htp cpe	3,492	3,680	2,287
17	Spoiler fstbk htp cpe	3,585	3,801	353
Cougar (wb 113.0)				
91	htp cpe	3,331	3,289	34,008
92	conv	3,461	3,681	1,723
93	XR-7 htp cpe	3,360	3,629	25,416
94	XR-7 conv	3,480	3,877	1,717
Monterey (wb 124.0; wgns-121.0)				
44	sdn 4d	4,029	3,858	22,744
46	htp cpe	3,959	3,900	9,099
48	htp sdn	4,024	3,968	2,483
72	wgn 3S	4,451	4,410	4,160 (3S and 2S combined)
72	wgn 2S	4,401	4,283	
54	Custom sdn 4d	4,144	4,030	12,411
56	Custom htp cpe	4,074	4,113	4,508
58	Custom htp sdn	4,140	4,185	1,397
Marquis (wb 124.0; wgns-121.0)				
63	sdn 4d	4,346	4,474	16,030
66	htp cpe	4,276	4,557	7,726
68	htp sdn	4,341	4,624	5,491
74	wgn 3S	4,501	4,674	2,158 (3S and 2S combined)
74	wgn 2S	4,451	4,547	
62	Brougham sdn 4d	4,346	4,880	25,790
64	Brougham htp cpe	4,276	4,963	14,570
67	Brougham htp sdn	4,341	5,033	13,781
76	Colony Park wgn 3S	4,562	4,933	20,004 (3S and 2S combined)
76	Colony Park wgn 2S	4,512	4,806	

1971 Engines	bore×stroke	bhp	availability
I-6, 170.0	3.50×2.94	100	S-Comet
I-6, 200.0	3.68×3.13	115/155	O-Comet
I-6, 250.0	3.68×3.91	145	S-Montego
V-8, 302.0	4.00×3.00	210	O-Comt, Mntgo, Cyclone
V-8, 351.0	4.00×3.50	240	S-Cycl GT, Cougr, Cougr XR-7, Montry exc Cust and sta wag; O-Montgo, Cycl
V-8, 351.0	4.00 × 3.50	280	O-Cougar
V-8, 351.0	4.00 × 3.50	285	S-Cycl exc GT, Monterey; O-Montgo, Cougr

1971 Engines	bore×stroke	bhp	availability
V-8, 400.0	4.00 × 4.00	260	S-Montry Cust and sta wag; O-Marq, Montry
V-8, 429.0	4.36 × 3.59	320	S-Marquis; O-Monterey
V-8, 429.0	4.36 × 3.59	360	O-Marq, Montry
V-8, 429.0	4.36 × 3.59	370	O-Montgo, Cycl, Marq, Montry
V-8, 429.0	4.36 × 3.59	375	O-Montgo, Cycl, Cougar

1972

Comet (wb 109.9; 2d-103.0)		Wght	Price	Prod
30	sdn 4d	2,674	2,398	29,092
31	fstbk sdn 2d	2,579	2,342	53,267
Montego (wb 118.0; 2d-114.0)				
02	sdn 4d	3,454	2,843	8,658
03	htp cpe	3,390	2,848	9,963
04	MX sdn 4d	3,485	2,951	23,387
07	MX htp cpe	3,407	2,971	25,802
08	MX wgn	3,884	3,264	6,268
10	MX Brghm sdn 4d	3,512	3,127	17,540
11	MX Brghm htp cpe	3,433	3,137	28,417
18	MX Villager wgn	3,907	3,438	9,237
16	GT fstbk htp cpe	3,517	3,346	5,820
Cougar (wb 113.0)				
91	htp cpe	3,282	3,016	23,731
92	conv	3,412	3,370	1,240
93	XR-7 htp cpe	3,298	3,323	26,802
94	XR-7 conv	3,451	3,547	1,929
Monterey (wb 124.0; wgns-121.0)				
44	sdn 4d	4,136	3,793	19,012
46	htp cpe	4,086	3,832	6,731
48	htp sdn	4,141	3,896	1,416
72	wgn 3S	4,545	4,334	4,644
72	wgn 2S	4,495	4,212	
54	Custom sdn 4d	4,225	3,956	16,879
56	Custom htp cpe	4,175	4,035	5,910
58	Custom htp sdn	4,230	4,103	1,583
Marquis (wb 124.0; wgns-121.0)				
63	sdn 4d	4,386	4,493	14,122
66	htp cpe	4,236	4,572	5,507
68	htp sdn	4,391	4,637	1,583
74	wgn 3S	4,589	4,567	2,085
74	wgn 2S	4,539	4,445	
62	Brougham sdn 4d	4,436	4,890	38,242
64	Brougham htp cpe	4,386	4,969	20,064
67	Brougham htp sdn	4,441	5,034	12,841
76	Colony Park wgn 3S	4,629	4,672	20,192
76	Colony Park wgn 2S	4,579	4,550	

1972 Engines	bore×stroke	bhp	availability
I-6, 170.0	3.50×2.94	82	S-Comet
I-6, 200.0	3.68×3.13	91	O-Comet
I-6, 250.0	3.68×3.91	95	O-Montego
I-6, 250.0	3.68×3.91	98	O-Comet
V-8, 302.0	4.00×3.00	140	S-Montego
V-8, 302.0	4.00×3.00	143	S-Comet
V-8, 351.0	4.00×3.50	161	O-Montego
V-8, 351.0	4.00×3.50	163	S-Montry exc Cust wgn
V-8, 351.0	4.00×3.50	164	S-Cougar
V-8, 351.0	4.00×3.50	262/266	O-Cougar
V-8, 400.0	4.00×4.00	168	O-Montego
V-8, 400.0	4.00×4.00	172	S-Montry Cust & Marq wgns
V-8, 429.0	4.36×3.59	205	O-Montego
V-8, 429.0	4.36×3.59	208	S-Marq exc wgn
V-8, 460.0	4.36×3.85	224	O-Montry, Marq

1973

Comet (wb 109.9; 2d-103.0)		Wght	Price	Prod
30	sdn 4d	2,904	2,489	28,984
31	fstbk sdn 2d	2,813	2,432	55,707
Montego (wb 118.0; 2d-114.0)				
02	sdn 4d	3,719	2,916	7,459
03	htp cpe	3,653	2,926	7,082
04	MX sdn 4d	3,772	3,009	25,300
07	MX htp cpe	3,683	3,041	27,812
08	MX wgn	4,124	3,417	7,012
10	MX Brghm sdn 4d	3,813	3,189	24,329

Montego		Wght	Price	Prod
11	MX Brghm htp cpe	3,706	3,209	40,951
18	MX Villager wgn	4,167	3,606	12,396
16	GT fstbk htp cpe	3,662	3,413	4,464
Cougar (wb 113.0)				
91	htp cpe	3,396	3,372	21,069
92	conv	3,524	3,726	1,284
93	XR-7 htp cpe	3,416	3,679	35,110
94	XR-7 conv	3,530	3,903	3,165
Monterey (wb 124.0; wgns-121.0)				
44	sdn 4d	4,225	3,961	16,622
46	htp cpe	4,167	4,004	6,452
72	wgn 3S	4,673	4,501	4,275
72	wgn 2S	4,623	4,379	
54	Custom sdn 4d	4,295	4,124	20,873
56	Custom htp cpe	4,239	4,207	6,962
Marquis (wb 124.0; wgns-121.0)				
63	sdn 4d	4,477	4,648	15,250
66	htp cpe	4,411	4,727	5,973
68	htp sdn	4,453	4,782	2,185
74	wgn 3S	4,745	4,730	2,464
74	wgn 2S	4,695	4,608	
62	Brougham sdn 4d	4,547	5,072	46,624
64	Brougham htp cpe	4,475	5,151	22,770
67	Brougham htp sdn	4,565	5,206	10,613
76	Colony Park wgn 3S	4,780	4,835	23,283
76	Colony Park wgn 2S	4,730	4,713	

1973 Engines	bore×stroke	bhp	availability
I-6, 200.0	3.68×3.13	84	S-Comet 6
I-6, 250.0	3.68×3.91	88	O-Comet 6
I-6, 250.0	3.68×3.91	92	O-Montego
V-8, 302.0	4.00×3.00	137/138	S-Montgo, Comt
V-8, 351.0	4.00×3.50	159/161	S-Montry exc Cust wgn; O-Montego
V-8, 351.0	4.00×3.50	168	S-Cougar
V-8, 351.0	4.00×3.50	246	O-Montego cpes
V-8, 351.0	4.00×3.50	264	O-Cougar (CJ)
V-8, 400.0	4.00×4.00	168/171	S-Montry Cust wgn; O-Montego
V-8, 429.0	4.36×3.59	171	S-Marq exc wgn; O-Marq wgn
V-8, 429.0	4.36×3.59	198/200	O-Montry, Montgo
V-8, 460.0	4.36×3.85	202/267	O-Montry, Marq

1974

Comet (wb 109.9; 2d-103.0)		Wght	Price	Prod
30	sdn 4d	2,969	3,042	60,944
31	fstbk sdn 2d	2,861	3,008	64,751
Montego (wb 118.0; 2d-114.0)				
02	sdn 4d	4,062	3,360	5,674
03	htp cpe	3,977	3,327	7,645
04	MX sdn 4d	4,092	3,478	19,446
07	MX htp cpe	3,990	3,443	20,957
08	MX wgn	4,426	4,083	4,085
10	MX Brghm sdn 4d	4,143	3,680	13,467
11	MX Brghm htp cpe	4,010	3,646	20,511
18	MX Villager wgn	4,463	4,307	6,234
Cougar (wb 114.0)				
93	XR-7 htp cpe	4,255	4,706	91,670
Monterey (wb 124.0; wgns-121.0)				
44	sdn 4d	4,559	4,367	6,185
46	htp cpe	4,506	4,410	2,003
72	wgn 3S	4,966	4,853	1,669
72	wgn 2S	4,916	4,731	
54	Custom sdn 4d	4,561	4,480	13,113
56	Custom htp cpe	4,504	4,523	4,510
Marquis (wb 124.0; wgns-121.0)				
63	sdn 4d	4,757	5,080	6,910
66	htp cpe	4,698	5,080	2,633
68	htp sdn	4,753	5,080	784
74	wgn 3S	5,023	5,082	1,111
74	wgn 2S	4,973	4,960	
62	Brougham sdn 4d	4,833	5,519	24,477
64	Brougham htp cpe	4,762	5,519	10,207
67	Brougham htp sdn	4,853	5,519	4,189
76	Colony Park wgn 3S	5,056	5,188	10,802
76	Colony Park wgn 2S	5,006	5,066	

1974 Engines	bore×stroke	bhp	availability
I-6, 200.0	3.68×3.13	84	S-Comet
I-6, 250.0	3.68×3.91	91	O-Comet
V-8, 302.0	4.00×3.00	140	S-Comt, Montgo
V-8, 351.0	4.00×3.50	162	S-Cougar; O-Montego
V-8, 351.0	4.00×3.50	246/264	O-Monetgo, Cougar (CJ)
V-8, 400.0	4.00×4.00	170	S-Monterey; O-Montgo, Cougr
V-8, 460.0	4.36×3.85	195	S-Marq; O-Montgo, Monterey
V-8, 460.0	4.36×3.85	220	O-Cougar
V-8, 460.0	4.36×3.65	275	O-Montry, Marq

1975

Bobcat (wb 94.5; wgn-94.8)		Wght	Price	Prod
20	Runbt htchbk sdn 2d	2,535	3,189	20,651
22	Villager wgn 2d	2,668	3,481	13,583
Comet (wb 109.9; 2d-103.0)				
30	sdn 4d	3,193	3,270	31,080
31	fstbk sdn 2d	3,070	3,236	22,768
Monarch (wb 109.9)				
34	sdn 4d	3,195	3,822	34,307
35	sdn 2d	3,142	3,764	29,151
37	Ghia sdn 4d	3,281	4,349	22,723
37	Grand sdn 4d	3,432	5,375	
38	Ghia sdn 2d	3,231	4,291	17,755
Montego (wb 118.0; 2d-114.0)				
02	sdn 4d	4,066	4,128	4,142
03	htp cpe	4,003	4,092	4,051
04	MX sdn 4d	4,111	4,328	16,033
07	MX htp cpe	4,030	4,304	13,666
08	MX wgn	4,464	4,674	4,508
10	MX Brghm sdn 4d	4,130	4,498	8,235
11	MX Brghm htp cpe	4,054	4,453	8,791
18	MX Villager wgn	4,522	4,909	5,754
Cougar (wb 114.0)				
93	XR-7 htp cpe	4,108	5,218	62,987
Marquis (wb 124.0; wgns-121.0)				
63	sdn 4d	4,513	5,115	20,058
66	htp cpe	4,470	5,049	6,807
74	wgn 3S	4,930	5,538	1,904
74	wgn 2S	4,880	5,411	
62	Brougham sdn 4d	4,799	6,037	19,667
64	Brougham htp cpe	4,747	5,972	7,125
60	Grnd Marquis sdn 4d	4,815	6,469	12,307
61	Grnd Marquis htp cpe	4,762	6,403	4,945
76	Colony Park wgn 2S	5,003	5,725	11,652
76	Colony Park wgn 2S	4,953	5,598	

1975 Engines	bore×stroke	bhp	availability
I-6, 140.0	3.78×3.13	83	S-Bobcat
V-6, 170.8	3.66×2.70	97	O-Bobcat
I-6, 200.0	3.68×3.13	75	S-Comt, Monrch exc Ghia
I-6, 250.0	3.68×3.91	72	S-Monrch Ghia; O-Comt, Montry
V-8, 302.0	4.00×3.00	122	O-Comet
V-8, 302.0	4.00×3.00	129	O-Monarch
V-8, 351.0	4.00×3.50	148/150	S-Cougr, Montgo
V-8, 351.0	4.00×3.50	143	O-Monarch
V-8, 400.0	4.00×4.00	158	S-Marq exc wgn & Brougham; O-Montgo, Cgr
V-8, 460.0	4.36×3.85	216	S-Gr Marq, wgn & Marq Brghm; O-Montego, Cougar, Marq

1976

Bobcat (wb 94.5; wgn-94.8)		Wght	Price	Prod
20	MPG Runbt htchbk sdn 2d	2,535	3,338	28,905
22	MPG Villager wgn 2d	2,668	3,643	18,731
Comet (wb 109.9; 2d-103.0)				
30	sdn 4d	3,058	3,465	21,006
31	fstbk sdn 2d	2,952	3,398	15,068
Monarch (wb 109.9)				
34	sdn 4d	3,195	3,864	56,351
35	sdn 2d	3,142	3,773	47,466
37	Ghia sdn 4d	3,218	4,422	27,056
37	Grand sdn 4d	3,432	5,740	

Monarch		Wght	Price	Prod
38	Ghia sdn 2d	3,231	4,331	14,950
Montego (wb 118.0; 2d-114.0)				
02	sdn 4d	4,133	4,343	3,403
03	htp cpe	4,057	4,299	2,287
04	MX sdn 4d	4,133	4,498	12,666
07	MX htp cpe	4,085	4,465	12,367
08	MX wgn	4,451	4,778	5,012
10	MX Brghm sdn 4d	4,150	4,670	5,043
11	MX Brghm htp cpe	4,097	4,621	3,905
18	MX Villager wgn	4,478	5,065	6,412
Cougar (wb 114.0)				
93	XR-7 htp cpe	4,168	5,125	83,765
Marquis (wb 124.0; wgns-121.0)				
63	sdn 4d	4,460	5,063	28,212
66	htp cpe	4,436	5,063	10,450
62	Brougham sdn 4d	4,693	6,035	22,411
64	Brougham htp cpe	4,652	5,955	10,431
60	Grd Marquis sdn 4d	4,723	6,528	17,650
61	Grd Marquis htp cpe	4,679	6,439	9,207
74	wgn 3S	4,824	5,401	2,493
74	wgn 2S	4,796	5,275	
76	Colony Park wgn 3S	4,906	5,716	15,114
76	Colony Park wgn 2S	4,878	5,590	

1976 Engines	bore×stroke	bhp	availability
I-4, 140.0	3.78×3.13	92	S-Bobcat
V-6, 170.8	3.66×2.70	100	O-Bobcat
I-6, 200.0	3.68×3.13	81	S-Monarch exc Ghia; O-Comet
I-6, 250.0	3.68×3.91	90	S-Monrch Ghia; O-Comt, Monrch
V-8, 302.0	4.00×3.00	143	O-Monarch
V-8, 302.0	4.00×3.00	138	O-Comet
V-8, 351.0	4.00×3.50	154	S-Montgo exc wgn
V-8, 351.0	4.00×3.50	152	S-Montego wgn, Cougr; O-Mnrch
V-8, 400.0	4.00×4.00	180	S-Marquis; O-Montgo, Cougr
V-8, 460.0	4.36×3.85	202	O-Montgo, Cougr, Marquis

1977

Bobcat (wb 94.5; wgn-94.8)		Wght	Price	Prod
20	Runbt htchbk sdn 2d	2,369	3,438	18,405*
22	wgn 2d	2,505	3,629	13,047*
22	Villager wgn 2d	—	3,771	
Comet (wb 109.9; 2d-103.0)				
30	sdn 4d	3,065	3,617	12,436
31	fstbk sdn 2d	2,960	3,544	9,109
Monarch (wb 109.9)				
34	sdn 4d	3,250	4,154	55,952
35	sdn 2d	3,200	4,076	44,509
37	Ghia sdn 4d	3,382	4,722	16,545
38	Ghia sdn 2d	3,321	4,643	11,051
Cougar (wb 118.0; 2d-114.0)				
90	sdn 4d	3,893	4,832	15,256
91	htp cpe	3,811	4,700	15,910
92	wgn	4,434	5,104	4,951
93	XR-7 htp cpe	3,909	5,274	124,799
94	Brougham sdn 4d	3,946	5,230	16,946
95	Brougham htp cpe	3,852	4,990	8,392
96	Villager wgn	4,482	5,363	8,569
Marquis (wb 124.0; wgns-121.0)				
63	sdn 4d	4,326	5,496	36,103
66	htp cpe	4,293	5,496	13,242
62	Brougham sdn 4d	4,408	6,324	29,411
64	Brougham htp cpe	4,350	6,229	12,237
60	Grd Marquis htp sdn	4,572	6,975	31,231
61	Grd Marquis htp cpe	4,516	6,880	13,445
74	wgn 3S	4,678	5,794	20,363
74	wgn 2S	4,628	5,631	

1977 Engines	bore×stroke	bhp	availability
I-4, 140.0	3.78×3.13	89	S-Bobcat
V-6, 170.8	3.66×2.70	93	O-Bobcat
I-6, 200.0	3.68×3.13	96	S-Monarch exc Ghia; O-Comt
I-6, 250.0	3.68×3.91	98	S-Mnrch Ghia; O-Mnrch, Comt
V-8, 302.0	4.00×3.00	122/134	O-Monarch
V-8, 302.0	4.00×3.00	130	S-Cougr exc wgn
V-8, 302.0	4.00×3.00	137	O-Comet
V-8, 351.0	4.00×3.50	149	O-Cougr exc wgn
V-8, 351.0	4.00×3.50	161	S-Cougr wgn; O-Monrch Ghia
V-8, 400.0	4.00×4.00	173	S-Marq exc Grd; O-Cougar
V-8, 460.0	4.36×3.85	197	S-Grd Marquis; O-Marquis

* Incl. some cars built as 1978 models but sold as '77s.

1978

Bobcat (wb 94.5; wgn-94.8)		Wght	Price	Prod
20	Runbt htchbk sdn 2d	2,389	3,830	23,428
22	wgn 2d	2,532	4,112	8,840
22	Villager wgn 2d	—	4,244	
Zephyr (wb 105.5)				
31	sdn 2d	2,594	3,777	27,673
32	sdn 4d	2,636	3,863	47,334
35	Z-7 spt cpe	2,630	4,154	44,569
36	wgn	2,744	4,216	32,596
Monarch (wb 109.9)				
33	sdn 2d	3,094	4,366	38,939
34	sdn 4d	3,138	4,457	52,775
Cougar (wb 114.0; 4d-118.0)				
91	htp cpe	3,761	5,052	21,398
92	sdn 4d	3,848	5,179	25,364
93	XR-7 htp cpe	3,865	5,720	166,508
Marquis (wb 124.0; wgns-121.0)				
61	htp cpe	4,296	5,897	27,793
62	sdn 4d	4,328	5,949	11,176
63	Brougham htp cpe	4,317	6,525	10,368
64	Brougham sdn 4d	4,346	6,638	26,030
65	Grd Marquis htp cpe	4,342	7,290	15,624
66	Grd Marquis sdn 4d	4,414	7,399	37,753
74	wgn 3S	4,606	6,292	16,883
74	wgn 2S	4,578	6,106	

1978 Engines	bore×stroke	bhp	availability
I-4, 140.0	3.78×3.13	88	S-Bobct, Zephyr
V-6, 170.6	3.66×2.70	90	O-Bobcat
I-6, 200.0	3.68×3.13	85	O-Zephyr
I-6, 250.0	3.68×3.91	97	S-Monarch
V-8, 302.0	4.00×3.00	134	S-Cougar
V-8, 302.0	4.00×3.00	139	O-Zphyr, Mnrch
V-8, 351.0	4.00×3.50	144/145	O-Cougr, S-Marq
V-8, 351.0	4.00×3.50	152	O-Cougar
V-8, 400.0	4.00×4.00	160	O-Marquis
V-8, 400.0	4.00×4.00	166	O-Cougar
V-8, 460.0	4.36×3.85	202	O-Marquis

1979

Bobcat (wb 94.5; wgn-94.8)		Wght	Price	Prod
20	Runbt htchbk sdn 2d	2,424	4,104	35,667
22	wgn 2d	2,565	4,410	9,119
22	Villager wgn 2d	—	4,523	
Capri (wb 100.4)				
14	htchbk cpe	2,548	4,872	92,432
16	Ghia htchbk cpe	2,645	5,237	17,712
Zephyr (wb 105.5)				
31	sdn 2d	2,518	4,253	15,920
32	sdn 4d	2,582	4,370	41,316
35	Z-7 spt cpe	2,553	4,504	42,923
36	wgn	2,683	4,647	25,218
Monarch (wb 109.9)				
33	sdn 2d	3,110	4,735	28,285
34	sdn 4d	3,151	4,841	47,594
Cougar (wb 114.0; 4d-118.0)				
91	htp cpe	3,792	5,379	2,831
92	sdn 4d	3,843	5,524	5,605
93	XR-7 htp cpe	3,883	6,430	163,716
Marquis (wb 114.3)				
61	htp cpe	3,507	6,292	10,035
62	sdn 4d	3,557	6,387	32,289
63	Brougham htp cpe	3,540	6,986	10,627
64	Brougham sdn 4d	3,605	7,176	24,682
65	Grd Marquis htp cpe	3,592	7,721	11,066
66	Grd Marquis sdn 4d	3,659	7,909	32,349

Marquis		Wght	Price	Prod
74	wgn 3S	3,825	6,894	5,994
74	wgn 2S	3,775	6,701	
76	Colony Park wgn 3S	3,850	7,688	13,758
76	Colony Park wgn 2S	3,800	7,495	

1979 Engines	bore ×stroke	bhp	availability
I-4, 140.0	3.78×3.13	88	S-Bobcat, Zephyr, Capri
I-4T, 140.0	3.78×3.13	140	O-Capri (Trb RS)
V-6, 170.6	3.66×2.70	102	O-Bobcat
V-6, 170.6	3.66×2.70	109	O-Capri
I-6, 200.0	3.68×3.13	85	O-Zephyr
I-6, 250.0	3.68×3.91	97	S-Monarch
V-8, 302.0	4.00×3.00	129/133	S-Marq, Cougar
V-8, 302.0	4.00×3.00	137	O-Monarch
V-8, 302.0	4.00×3.00	140	O-Capri, Zephyr
V-8, 351.0	4.00×3.50	135	S-Cougar XR-7
V-8, 351.0	4.00×3.50	138	O-Marquis
V-8, 351.0	4.00×3.50	151	O-Cougar

1980

Bobcat (wb 94.5; wgn-94.8)		Wght	Price	Prod
20	Runbt htchbk sdn 2d	2,445	4,764	28,103
22	wgn 2d	2,573	5,070	5,547
22	Villager wgn 2d	—	5,183	
Capri (wb 100.4)				
14	htchbk cpe	2,566	5,672	72,009
16	Ghia htchbk cpe	2,651	5,968	7,975
Zephyr (wb 105.5)				
31	sdn 2d	2,607	5,041	10,977
32	sdn 4d	2,649	5,158	40,399
35	Z-7 spt cpe	2,646	5,335	19,486
36	wgn	2,771	5,364	20,341
Monarch (wb 109.9)				
33	sdn 2d	3,126	5,628	8,772
34	sdn 4d	3,180	5,751	21,746
Cougar (wb 108.4)				
93	XR-7 cpe	3,191	7,045	58,028
Marquis (wb 114.3)				
61	sdn 2d	3,450	7,075	2,521
62	sdn 4d	3,488	7,185	13,018
63	Brougham sdn 2d	3,476	7,860	2,353
64	Brougham sdn 4d	3,528	8,057	8,819
65	Grd Marquis sdn 2d	3,504	8,631	3,434
66	Grd Marquis sdn 4d	3,519	8,824	15,995
74	wgn 3S	3,747	7,782	2,407
74	wgn 2S	3,697	7,583	
76	Colony Park wgn 3S	3,793	8,676	5,781
76	Colony Park wgn 2S	3,743	8,477	

1980 Engines	bore×stroke	bhp	availability
I-4, 140.0	3.78×3.13	88	S-Bobct, Zphyr, Capri
I-4T, 140.0	3.78×3.13	140	O-Capri, Zphyr*
I-6, 200.0	3.68×3.13	91	O-Capri, Zephyr
I-6, 250.0	3.68×3.91	90	S-Monarch
V-8, 255.0	3.68×3.00	115	S-Cougar
V-8, 255.0	3.68×3.00	118/119	O-Capri, Zephyr, Monarch
V-8, 302.0	4.00×3.00	130/131	S-Marquis; O-Cougar
V-8, 302.0	4.00×3.00	134	O-Monarch
V-8, 351.0	4.00×3.50	140	O-Marquis

* Withdrawn for Zephyr after announced; prod. doubtful.

1981

Lynx (wb 94.2)		Wght	Price	Prod
63	htchbk sdn 2d	—	5,603	72,786
63	L htchbk sdn 2d	1,935	5,665	
63/60Z	GL htchbk sdn 2d	1,957	5,903	
63/602	GS htchbk sdn 2d	1,996	6,642	
63/603	LS htchbk sdn 2d	2,004	7,127	
63/936	RS htckbk sdn 2d	1,980	6,223	
65	htchbk 4d	—	5,931	39,192
65	L htchbk 4d	2,059	6,070	
65/60Z	GL htchbk 4d	2,074	6,235	
65/602	GS htchbk 4d	2,114	6,914	
65/936	RS htchbk 4d	2,098	6,563	
Capri (wb 100.4)				
67	htchbk cpe	2,589	6,685	51,786
68	GS htchbk cpe	2,636	6,867	7,160

Zephyr (wb 105.5)		Wght	Price	Prod
70	sdn 2d	2,558	6,103	5,814
—	S sdn 2d	—	5,769	—
71	sdn 4d	2,623	6,222	34,334
73	wgn	2,698	6,458	16,283
72	Z-7 cpe	2,610	6,252	10,078
Cougar (wb 105.5; XR-7-108.4)				
76	sdn 2d	2,727	6,535	10,793
77	sdn 4d	2,771	6,694	42,860
90	XR-7 cpe	3,068	7,799	37,275
Marquis (wb 114.3)				
81	sdn 4d	3,493	7,811	10,392
82	Brougham sdn 2d	3,513	8,601	2,942
83	Brougham sdn 4d	3,564	8,800	11,744
84	Grd Marquis sdn 2d	3,533	9,228	4,268
85	Grd Marquis sdn 4d	3,564	9,459	23,780
87	wgn 2S	3,745	8,309	2,219
88	Colony Park 4d 2S	3,800	9,304	6,293

1981 Engines	bore×stroke	bhp	availability
I-4, 97.6	3.15×3.13	65	S-Lynx
I-4, 140.0	3.78×3.13	88	S-Capri, Zephyr, Cougar
I-4T, 140.0	3.78×3.13	—	O-Capri
I-6, 200.0	3.68×3.13	88/95	S-XR-7; O-Cpr, Zephyr, other Cougar
V-8, 255.0	3.68×3.00	115/120	S-Marquis; O-Capri, Zphyr, Cougar
V-8, 302.0	4.00×3.00	130	O-Cougar XR-7, Marquis
V-8, 351.0	4.00×3.50	145	O-Marquis
V-8, 351.0	4.00×3.50	165	S-Marq (police)

1982

Lynx (wb 94.2)		Wght	Price	Prod
63	htchbk sdn 2d	1,924	5,502	
63	L htchbk sdn 2d	1,927	6,159	
63/60Z	GL htchbk sdn 2d	1,950	6,471	54,611
63/602	GS htchbk sdn 2d	1,987	7,257	
63/603	LS htchbk sdn 2d	1,952	7,762	
63/936	RS htchbk sdn 2d	1,961	6,790	
64	htchbk sdn 4d	1,984	5,709	
64	L htchbk sdn 4d	1,989	6,376	
64/60Z	GL htchbk sdn 4d	2,012	6,688	40,713
64/602	GS htchbk sdn 4d	2,049	7,474	
64/603	LS htchbk sdn 4d	2,014	7,978	
65	L wgn	2,028	6,581	
65/60Z	GL wgn	2,049	6,899	23,835
65/602	GS wgn	2,087	7,594	
65/603	LS wgn	2,052	8,099	
LN7 (wb 94.2)				
61	htchbk cpe	2,059	7,787	35,147
Capri (wb 100.4) - 36,134 built				
67	htchbk cpe	2,554	6,711	—
67	L htchbk cpe	2,627	7,245	—
67	Black Magic cpe 2d	—	7,946	—
67	RS htchbk cpe V-8	—	8,107	—
68	GS htckbk cpe 2d	2,637	7,432	—
Zephyr (wb 105.5)				
71	sdn 4d	2,690	6,411	31,698
71/602	GS sdn 4d	2,703	6,734	
72/Z-7	spt cpe	2,687	6,309	7,394
72/602	Z-7 GS spt cpe	2,697	6,670	
Cougar (wb 105.5)				
76	GS sdn 2d	2,939	7,983	6,984
76	LS sdn 2d	2,974	8,415	
77	GS sdn 4d	2,981	8,158	30,672
77	LS sdn 4d	3,023	8,587	
78	GS wgn	3,114	8,216	19,294
Cougar XR-7 (wb 108.4) - 16,867 built				
90	GS cpe	3,220	9,094	—
90/60H	LS cpe	3,229	9,606	—
Marquis (wb 114.3)				
81	sdn 4d	3,734	8,674	9,454
82	Brougham sdn 2d	3,693	9,490	2,833
83	Brougham sdn 4d	3,776	9,767	15,312
84	Grd Marquis sdn 2d	3,724	10,188	6,149
85	Grd Marquis sdn 4d	3,809	10,456	32,918
87	wgn 2S	3,880	9,198	2,487
88	Colony Park wgn 2S	3,890	10,252	8,004

1982 Engines	bore×stroke	bhp	availability
I-4, 97.6	3.15×3.13	70	S-Lynx, LN7
I-4, 140.0	3.78×3.13	86	S-Capri, Zephyr
I-6, 200.0	3.68×3.13	87	S-Cgr, XR-7; O-Capri, Zphyr
V-6, 232.0	3.80×3.40	112	O-Cougar, XR-7
V-8, 255.0	3.68×3.00	120-122	S-Marq; O-Cpr, XR-7, Zephyr
V-8, 302.0	4.00 × 3.00	132	S-Marq Brghm, Grd Marquis 4d; O-Marquis
V-8, 302.0	4.00 × 3.00	157	O-Capri
V-8, 351.0	4.00 × 3.50	165	S-Marq (police)

1983

Lynx (wb 94.2)		Wght	Price	Prod
54	L htchbk sdn 2d	1,922	5,751	
55	GS htchbk sdn 2d	1,948	6,476	40,142
58	LS htchbk sdn 2d	1,950	7,529	
57	RS htchbk sdn 2d	1,997	7,370	
55	L htchbk sdn 4d	1,984	5,958	
66	GS htchbk sdn 4d	2,010	6,693	28,461
68	LS htchbk sdn 4d	2,012	7,746	
65/934	LTS htchbk sdn 4d	1,920	7,334	
60	L wgn	2,026	6,166	
61	GS wgn	2,050	6,872	19,192
63	LS wgn	2,050	7,909	
LN7 (wb 94.2) - 4,528 built				
51/A80	htchbk cpe	2,076	7,398	—
51/A8C	RS htchbk cpe	—	8,765	—
51/A8A	Sport htchbk cpe	—	8,084	—
51/ABB	Grand Sport cpe 2d	—	8,465	—
Capri (wb 100.4) - 25,376 built				
79/41P	htchbk cpe	2,643	7,156	—
79	L htchbk cpe	2,669	7,711	—
79	Black Magic cpe 2d	2,651	8,629	—
79	Crimson Cat cpe 2d	—	8,525	—
79/602	GS htckbk cpe 2d	—	7,914	—
79	RS htchbk cpe	—	9,241	—
Cougar (wb 104.0) - 75,743 built				
92	cpe	2,997	9,521	—
92/603	LS cpe	2,911	10,850	—
Zephyr (wb 105.5)				
86	sdn 4d	2,690	6,545	21,732
86/602	GS sdn 4d	2,756	7,311	
87	Z-7 spt cpe	2,687	6,442	3,471
87/602	Z-7 GS spt cpe	2,750	7,247	
Marquis (wb 105.5)				
89	sdn 4d	2,778	7,893	50,169
89	Brougham sdn 4d	—	8,202	
90	wgn	2,978	8,693	17,189
90	Brougham wgn	—	8,974	
Grand Marquis (wb 114.3)				
93	sdn 2d	3,607	10,654	11,117
93/60H	LS sdn 2d	3,607	11,209	
95	sdn 4d	3,761	10,718	72,207
95/60H	LS sdn 4d I-6	3,761	11,273	
94	Colony Pk wgn 2S I-6	3,788	10,896	12,394

1983 Engines	bore×stroke	bhp	availability
I-4, 97.6	3.15×3.13	70	S-Lynx, LN7
I-4, 97.6	3.15×3.13	80	O-Lynx, LN7
I-4, 97.6	3.15×3.13	88	O-Lynx, LN7
I-4, 140.0	3.78×3.13	90	S-Capri, Zephyr, Marquis sdns
I-4T, 140.0	3.78×3.13	142	O-Capri
I-4P, 140.0	3.78×3.13	—	O-Marq (prop)
I-6, 200.0	3.68×3.13	92	S-Marq wgns; O-Zephyr, Marquis sdns
V-6, 232.0	3.80×3.40	110-112	S-Cougr; O-Cpr, Marquis
V-8, 302.0	4.00×3.00	130	S-Grand Marq; O-Cougar
V-8, 302.0	4.00×3.00	145	O-Grd Marquis
V-8, 302.0	4.00×3.00	175	O-Capri
V-8, 351.0	4.00×3.50	165	S-Grd Marq (pol)

1984

Lynx (wb 94.2)		Wght	Price	Prod
54	htchbk sdn 2d	2,176	5,758	
54	L htchbk sdn 2d	2,087	6,019	
55	GS htchbk sdn 2d	2,128	6,495	38,208
57	RS htchbk sdn 2d	2,177	7,641	
57	RS Trb htchbk sdn 2d	1,997	8,728	
65	htchbk sdn 4d	2,241	5,965	
65	L htchbk sdn 4d	2,152	6,233	21,090
66	GS htchbk sdn 4d	2,193	6,709	
68/934	LTS htchbk sdn 4d	—	7,879	
60	L wgn	2,181	6,448	16,142
61	GS wgn	2,220	6,887	
Topaz (wb 99.9)				
72	GS sdn 2d	2,357	7,477	32,749
73	LS sdn 2d	—	7,880	
75	GS sdn 4d	2,415	7,477	96,505
76	LS sdn 4d	2,447	7,880	
Capri (wb 100.5) - 20,642 built				
79	GS htchbk cpe I-4/V-6	2,827	7,758	—
79	RS htchbk cpe V-8	—	9,638	—
79	RS Trb htchbk cpe I-4T	2,775	9,822	—
Cougar (wb 104.0) - 131,190 built				
92	cpe	3,151	9,978	—
92/603	LS cpe	3,180	11,265	—
92/934	XR-7 cpe I-4T	3,053	13,065	—
Marquis (wb 105.5)				
89	sdn 4d	2,966	8,727	91,808
89	Brougham sdn 4d	—	9,003	
90	wgn V-6	3,128	9,224	16,004
90	Brougham wgn V-6	—	9,498	
Grand Marquis (wb 114.3)				
93	sdn 2d	3,734	11,576	13,657
93/60H	LS sdn 2d	—	12,131	
95	sdn 4d	3,780	11,640	117,739
95/60H	LS sdn 4d	—	12,195	
94	Colony Park wgn 2S	3,981	11,816	17,421

1984 Engines	bore×stroke	bhp	availability
I-4, 97.6	3.15×3.13	70	S-Lynx exc RS Trb
I-4, 97.6	3.15×3.13	80	O-Lynx exc RS Trb
I-4, 97.6	3.15×3.13	88	S-Lynx RS Trb; O-Lynx
I-4D, 121.0	3.39×3.39	52	O-Lynx, Topaz
I-4, 140.0	3.70×3.30	84	S-Topaz
I-4, 140.0	3.78×3.13	88	S-Cpr GS, Marq
I-4T, 140.0	3.78×3.13	145	S-Cougar XR-7
I-4T, 140.0	3.78×3.13	175	S-Capri RS Trb
I-4P, 140.0	3.78×3.13	—	O-Marq (prop)
V-6, 232.0	3.80×3.40	120	S-Cougar, Marq wgn; O-Cpri GS, Marquis
V-8, 302.0	4.00×3.00	140	S-Grand Marq; O-Cougar
V-8, 302.0	4.00×3.00	155	O-Grd Marquis
V-8, 302.0	4.00×3.00	165/175	O-Capri GS/RS
V-8, 351.0	4.00×3.50	180	S-Grd Marq (pol)

1985

Lynx (wb 94.2)		Wght	Price	Prod
54/41P	htchbk sdn 2d	1,980	5,750	
54	L htchbk sdn 2d	2,000	6,170	26,653*
55	GS htchbk sdn 2d	2,070	6,707	
65	L htchbk sdn 4d	2,060	6,384	11,658*
66	GS htchbk sdn 4d	2,125	6,921	
60	L wgn	2,080	6,508	7,948*
61	GS wgn	2,155	6,973	

*Estimated totals for First Series.

Lynx Second Series 1985½ (wb 94.2)		Wght	Price	Prod
51	htchbk sdn 2d	2,158	5,986	
51	L htchbk sdn 2d	—	6,272	20,515
52	GS htchbk sdn 2d	—	6,962	
63	L htchbk sdn 4d	2,206	6,486	11,297
64	GS htchbk sdn 4d	—	7,176	
58	L wgn	—	6,767	6,721
59	GS wgn	—	7,457	
Topaz (wb 99.9)				
72	GS sdn 2d	2,395	7,767	18,990
73	LS sdn 2d	2,445	8,931	
75	GS sdn 4d	2,450	7,767	82,366
76	LS sdn 4d	2,500	8,980	

Capri (wb 100.5) - 18,657 blt		Wght	Price	Prod
79	GS htchbk cpe I-4/V-6	2,885	7,944	—
79	RS/5.0L htchbk cpe V-8	3,290	10,223	—
Cougar (wb 104.0) - 117,274 built				
92	cpe 2d	3,010	10,650	—
92/603	LS cpe 2d	3,040	11,850	—
92/934	XR-7 cpe 2d I-4T	2,978	13,599	—
Marquis (wb 105.6)				
89	sdn 4d	2,915	8,996	91,465
89/60H	Brougham sdn 4d	2,923	9,323	
90	wgn V-6	2,993	9,506	12,733
90/60H	Brougham wgn V-6	3,000	9,805	
Grand Marquis (wb 114.3)				
93	sdn 2d	3,619	12,240	10,900
93/60H	LS sdn 2d	—	12,789	
95	sdn 4d	3,657	12,305	136,239
95/60H	LS sdn 4d	—	12,854	
94	Colony Park wgn 2S	3,828	12,511	14,119

1985 Engines	bore×stroke	bhp	availability
I-4, 97.6	3.15×3.13	70	S-Lynx base, L
I-4, 97.6	3.15×3.13	80	S-Lynx GS; O-Lynx
I-4, 113.0	3.23×3.46	86	S-late Lynx
I-4D, 121.0	3.39×3.39	52	O-Lynx, Topaz
I-4, 140.0	3.70×3.30	86	S-Topaz
I-4, 140.0	3.70×3.30	100	O-Topaz
I-4, 140.0	3.78×3.13	88	S-Cpr GS, Marq
I-4T, 140.0	3.78×3.13	155	S-Cougar XR-7
V-6, 232.0	3.80×3.40	120	S-Cougr; O-Cpr, Marquis
V-8, 302.0	4.00×3.00	140	S-Grd Marquis; O-Cougar
V-8, 302.0	4.00×3.00	155	O-Grd Marquis
V-8, 302.0	4.00×3.00	180	O-Capri GS
V-8, 302.0	4.00×3.00	210	S-Capri RS; O-Capri GS

1986

Lynx (wb 94.2)		Wght	Price	Prod
51	htchbk sdn 2d	2,156	6,182	45,880
51	L htchbk sdn 2d	2,158	6,472	
52	GS htchbk sdn 2d	2,246	7,162	
53	XR3 htchbk sdn 2d	2,374	8,193	
63	L htchbk sdn 4d	2,206	6,686	26,512
64	GS htchbk sdn 4d	2,289	7,376	
58	L wgn	2,238	6,967	13,580
59	GS wgn	2,312	7,657	
Topaz (wb 99.9)				
72	GS sdn 2d	2,377	8,085	15,757
73	LS sdn 2d	2,464	9,224	
75	GS sdn 4d	2,440	8,235	62,640
76	LS sdn 4d	2,531	9,494	
Capri (wb 100.5) - 20,869 built				
79	GS htchbk cpe I-4/V-6	2,877	8,331	—
79	5.0L htchbk cpe V-8	3,183	10,950	—
Cougar (wb 104.0) - 135,909 built				
92	GS cpe 2d	3,178	11,421	—
92	LS cpe 2d	3,214	12,757	—
92	XR-7 cpe 2d I-4T	3,158	14,377	—
Marquis (wb 105.6)				
89	sdn 4d	2,969	9,660	24,121
89/60H	Brougham sdn 4d	2,994	10,048	
90	wgn V-6	3,112	10,254	4,461
90/60H	Brougham wgn V-6	3,139	10,613	
Sable (wb 106.0)				
87	GS sdn 4d I-4/V-6	2,983	10,700	71,707
87	LS sdn 4d V-6	3,135	12,574	
88	GS wgn V-6	3,210	11,776	23,931
88	LS wgn V-6	3,225	13,068	
Grand Marquis (wb 114.3)				
93	sdn 2d	3,782	13,480	5,610
93/60H	LS sdn 2d	3,782	13,929	
95	sdn 4d	3,818	13,504	93,919
95/60H	LS sdn 4d	3,818	13,952	
94	Colony Park wgn 2S	3,993	13,724	9,891

1986 Engines	bore×stroke	bhp	availability
I-4, 113.5	3.23×3.46	86	S-Lynx exc XR3
I-4, 113.5	3.23×3.46	108	S-Lynx XR3; O-other Lynx
I-4D, 121.0	3.39×3.39	52	O-Lynx, Topaz
I-4, 140.0	3.70×3.30	86	S-Topaz
I-4, 140.0	3.70×3.30	100	O-Topaz
I-4, 140.0	3.78×3.13	88	S-Cpr GS, Marq
I-4T, 140.0	3.78×3.13	145/155	S-Cougar XR-7
I-4, 153.0	3.70 × 3.60	88	S-late Sable GS sdn
V-6, 182.0	3.50 × 3.15	140	S-Sble, LS/wgn; O-other Sable
V-6, 232.0	3.80 × 3.40	120	S-Cougar, Marq wgn; O-Capri GS, Marquis
V-8, 302.0	4.00 × 3.00	150	S-Grand Marq; O-Cougar GS
V-8, 302.0	4.00 × 3.00	200	S-Capri 5.0L

1987

Lynx (wb 94.2)		Wght	Price	Prod
20	L htchbk sdn 2d	2,183	6,569	20,930
21	GS htchbk sdn 2d	2,202	6,951	
23	×R3 htchbk sdn 2d	2,396	8,808	
25	GS htchbk sdn 4d	2,258	7,172	12,124
28	GS wgn	2,277	7,462	6,985
Topaz (wb 99.9)				
31	GS sdn 2d	2,503	8,562	19,738
33	GS Spt sdn 2d	2,565	9,308	
36	GS sdn 4d	2,557	8,716	78,692
38	GS Spt sdn 4d	2,621	9,463	
76	LS sdn 4d	2,631	10,213	
Cougar (wb 104.2) - 104,526 built				
60	LS cpe	3,202	13,595	—
62	XR-7 cpe V-8	3,355	15,832	—
Sable (wb 106.0)				
50	GS sdn 4d	3,054	12,240	91,001
53	LS sdn 4d	3,138	14,522	
55	GS wgn	3,228	12,793	30,312
58	LS wgn	3,311	15,054	
Grand Marquis (wb 114.3)				
72	LS sdn 2d	3,764	15,323	4,904
74	GS sdn 4d	3,794	15,198	115,599
75	LS sdn 4d	3,803	15,672	
78	Clny Prk GS wgn 2S	3,975	15,462	10,691
79	Clny Prk LS wgn 2S	4,015	16,010	

1987 Engines	bore×stroke	bhp	availability
I-4, 113.5	3.23×3.46	90	S-Lynx exc XR3
I-4, 113.5	3.23×3.46	115	S-Lynx XR3
I-4D, 121.0	3.39×3.39	58	O-Lynx
I-4, 140.0	3.70×3.30	86	S-Topz exc Sprt
I-4, 140.0	3.70×3.30	94	O-other Topaz
V-6, 182.0	3.50×3.15	140	S-Sable
V-6, 232.0	3.80×3.40	120	S-Cougar LS
V-8, 302.0	4.00×3.00	150/155	S-XR-7, Grd Marq; O-Cougar LS

1988

Topaz (wb 99.9)		Wght	Price	Prod
31	GS sdn 2d	2,565	9,166	16,001
33	XR5 sdn 2d	2,560	10,058	
36	GS sdn 4d	2,608	9,323	95,885
37	LS sdn 4d	2,651	10,591	
38	LTS sdn 4d	2,660	11,541	
Cougar (wb 104.2) - 119,162 built				
60	LS cpe	3,314	14,134	—
62	XR-7 cpe V-8	3,485	16,266	—
Sable (wb 106.0)				
50	GS sdn 4d V-6	3,097	14,145	94,694
53	LS sdn 4d V-6	3,165	15,138	
55	GS wgn V-6	3,208	14,665	26,591
58	LS wgn V-6	3,268	15,683	
Grand Marquis (wb 114.3)				
74	GS sdn 4d	3,828	16,100	11,611
75	LS sdn 4d	3,839	16,612	
78	Clny Prk GS wgn 2S	4,019	16,341	9,456
79	Clny Prk LS wgn 2S	4,025	16,926	

1988 Engines	bore×stroke	bhp	availability
I-4, 140.0	3.70×3.30	98/100	S-Topaz
V-6, 182.0	3.50×3.15	140	S-Sable
V-6, 232.0	3.80×3.40	140	S-Cgr LS; O-Sbl
V-8, 302.0	4.00×3.00	150/155	S-XR-7, Grd Marq; O-Cougar LS

1989

Topaz (wb 99.9)		Wght	Price	Prod
31	GS sdn 2d	2,567	9,577	10,015
33	XR5 sdn 2d	2,544	10,498	
36	GS sdn 4d	2,606	9,734	118,120
37	LS sdn 4d	2,647	11,030	
38	LTS sdn 4d	2,706	11,980	
Sable (wb 106.0)				
50	GS sdn 4d	3,054	14,101	102,571
53	LS sdn 4d	3,168	15,094	
55	GS wgn	3,228	14,804	28,086
58	LS wgn	3,252	15,872	
Cougar (wb 113.0)				
60	LS cpe	3,553	15,448	92,163
60	XR7 cpe	3,710	19,650	5,149
Grand Marquis (wb 114.3)				
74	GS sdn 4d	3,763	16,701	130,248
75	LS sdn 4d	3,774	17,213	
	50th anniv sdn 4d	3,887	—	
78	Clny Prk GS wgn 2S	3,995	17,338	8,665
79	Clny Prk LS wgn 2S	3,913	17,922	

1989 Engines	bore×stroke	bhp	availability
I-4, 140.0	3.70×3.30	98/100	S-Topaz
V-6, 182.0	3.50×3.15	140	S-Sable
V-6, 232.0	3.80×3.40	140	S-Cougar LS; O-Sable
V-6S, 232.0	3.80×3.40	210	S-Cougar XR7
V-8, 302.0	4.00×3.00	150	S-Grand Marq

1990

Topaz (wb 99.9)		Wght	Price	Prod
31	GS sdn 2d	2,567	10,027	2,512
33	XR5 sdn 2d	—	10,988	
36	GS sdn 4d	2,602	10,184	104,367
37	LS sdn 4d	—	11,507	
38	LTS sdn 4d	—	12,514	
Sable (wb 106.0)				
50	GS sdn 4d	3,131	15,009	80,423
53	LS sdn 4d	—	16,011	
55	GS wgn	3,260	15,711	23,326
58	LS wgn	—	16,789	
Cougar (wb 113.0)				
60	LS cpe	3,608	15,911	76,174
60	XR7 cpe	—	20,217	5,246
Grand Marquis (wb 114.3)				
74	GS sdn 4d	3,833	17,633	72,945
75	LS sdn 4d	—	18,133	
78	Clny Prk GS wgn 2S	4,006	18,348	4,450
79	Clny Prk LS wgn 2S	—	18,920	

1990 Engines	bore×stroke	bhp	availability
I-4, 140.0	3.70×3.30	98/100	S-Topaz
V-6, 182.0	3.50×3.15	140	S-Sable
V-6, 232.0	3.80×3.40	140	S-Cougar LS; O-Sable
V-6S, 232.0	3.80×3.40	210	S-Cougar XR7
V-8, 302.0	4.00×3.00	150	S-Grand Marq

Note: 1981-89 Colony Park wagons could have optional dual-facing rear seats. Base prices of 1984-87 Lynx and Tempo models with diesel engines were higher than figures shown above.

1991

Tracer (wb 98.4)		Wght	Price	Prod
54/AB	sdn 4d	2,356	9,386	59,825
54/AK	LTS sdn 4d	2,464	11,636	
74/AB	wgn	2,468	10,407	13,999
Topaz (wb 99.9)				
66/HVB	GS sdn 2d	2,546	10,065	2,789
66/HVD	XR5 sdn 2d	—	11,064	
54/HVB	GS sdn 4d	2,602	10,222	77,663
54/HVE	LS sdn 4d	—	11,601	
54/HVC	LTS sdn 4d	—	12,626	
Sable (wb 106.0)				
FC/HVS	GS sdn 4d	3,131	15,311	77,471
FC/HVB	LS sdn 4d	—	16,154	
FF/HVS	GS wgn	3,260	16,256	18,806
FF/HVB	LS wgn	—	17,124	
Cougar (113.0)				
BA/VS-AJ	LS cpe	3,587	15,629	59,329
BA/VS-AW	XR7 cpe	—	20,905	3,104

Grand Marquis (wb 114.3)	Wght	Price	Prod
74 GS sdn 4d	3,836	18,741	79,329
75 LS sdn 4d	—	19,241	
78 Colony Park GS wgn	4,032	18,918	3,104
79 Colony Park LS wgn	—	19,490	

1991 Engines	bore×stroke	bhp	availability
I-4, 109.0	3.27×3.35	127	S-Trcr LTS (dohc)
I-4, 114.0	3.23×3.46	88	S-Tracer (ohc)
I-4, 141.0	3.70×3.30	98	S-Topaz
I-4, 141.0	3.70×3.30	100	O-Topaz
V-6, 182.0	3.50×3.15	140	S-Sable
V-6, 232.0	3.80×3.40	140	S-Cougar LS, O-Sable
V-8, 302.0	4.00×3.00	150	S-Grand Marq
V-8, 302.0	4.00×3.00	225	S-Cougar XR7; O-Cougar LS

1992

Tracer (wb 98.4)	Wght	Price	Prod
54/AB sdn 4d	2,356	9,773	21,060
54/AK LTS sdn 4d	2,464	12,023	
74/AB wgn	2,468	10,794	4,660

Topaz (wb 99.9)	Wght	Price	Prod
66/HVB GS sdn 2d	2,544	10,512	20,567
66/HVD ×R5 sdn 2d	2,608	13,452	
54/HVB GS sdn 4d	2,600	10,678	80,655
54/HVE LS sdn 4d	2,625	12,057	
54/HVC LTS sdn 4d	2,763	14,244	

Sable (wb 106.0)	Wght	Price	Prod
FC/HVS GS sdn 4d	3,147	16,418	104,054
FC/HVB LS sdn 4d	3,186	17,368	
FF/HVS GS wgn	3,292	17,396	23,476
FF/HVB LS wgn	3,331	18,395	

Cougar (113.0)	Wght	Price	Prod
BA/VS-AJ LS cpe	3,587	16,460	47,821*
BA/VS-AW XR7 cpe	3,800	22,054	1,433

Grand Marquis (wb 114.3) - 163,262 built	Wght	Price	Prod
FA/AG GS sdn 4d	3,768	20,216	—
FA/AJ LS sdn 4d	3,780	20,644	—

*Includes 4,800 Cougar 25th Anniversary models.

1992 Engines	bore×stroke	bhp	availability
I-4, 109.0	3.27×3.35	127	S-Trcr LTS (dohc)
I-4, 114.0	3.23×3.46	88	S-Tracer (ohc)
I-4, 141.0	3.70×3.30	98	S-Topaz
V-6, 182.0	3.50×3.15	135	S-Topz XR5, LTS O-other Topaz
V-6, 182.0	3.50×3.15	140	S-Sable
V-6, 232.0	3.80×3.40	140	S-Cougar LS, O-Sable
V-8, 281.0	3.60×3.60	190	S-Grd Marq (ohc)
V-8, 281.0	3.60×3.60	210	O-Grd Marq (ohc)
V-8, 302.0	4.00×3.00	200	S-Cougar XR7, O-Cougar LS

1993

Tracer (wb 98.4)	Wght	Price	Prod
54/AB sdn 4d	2,348	10,155	53,985
54/AK LTS sdn 4d	2,460	12,023	
74/AB wgn	2,462	10,982	24,162

Topaz (wb 99.9)	Wght	Price	Prod
66/HVB GS sdn 2d	2,546	9,831	20,400
54/HVB GS sdn 4d	2,602	10,976	78,305

Sable (wb 106.0)	Wght	Price	Prod
FC/HVS GS sdn 4d	3,122	17,480	114,457
FC/HVB LS sdn 4d	3,165	18,430	
FF/HVS GS wgn	3,271	18,459	22,876
FF/HVB LS wgn	3,314	19,457	

Cougar (113.0)	Wght	Price	Prod
BA/VS-AW XR7 sdn 2d	3,512	14,855	81,450

Grand Marquis (wb 114.3) - 90,367 built	Wght	Price	Prod
FA/AG GS sdn 4d	3,794	21,973	—
FA/AJ LS sdn 4d	3,805	22,500	—

1993 Engines	bore×stroke	bhp	availability
I-4, 109.0	3.27×3.35	127	S-Trcr LTS (dohc)
I-4, 114.0	3.23×3.46	88	S-Tracer (ohc)
I-4, 141.0	3.70×3.30	98	S-Topaz
V-6, 182.0	3.50×3.15	135	O-Topaz
V-6, 182.0	3.50×3.15	140	S-Sable
V-6, 232.0	3.80×3.40	140	S-Cougr, O-Sble
V-8, 281.0	3.60×3.60	190	S-Grd Marq (ohc)
V-8, 281.0	3.60×3.60	210	O-Grd Marq (ohc)
V-8, 302.0	4.00 × 3.00	200	O-Cougar

1994

Tracer (wb 98.4)*	Wght	Price	Prod
54/AB sdn 4d	2,393	10,250	31,632
54/AK LTS sdn 4d	2,458	12,560	
74/AB wgn	2,476	10,520	14,701

Topaz (wb 99.9)	Wght	Price	Prod
66/HVB GS sdn 2d	2,531	11,270	12,344
54/HVB GS sdn 4d	2,588	11,270	69,615

Sable (wb 106.0)	Wght	Price	Prod
FC/HVS GS sdn 4d	3,126	17,740	98,536
FC/HVB LS sdn 4d	3,177	20,000	
FF/HVS GS wgn	3,275	18,900	17,915
FF/HVB LS wgn	3,323	21,110	

Cougar (113.0)	Wght	Price	Prod
BA/VS-AW XR7 cpe	3,564	16,260	75,792

Grand Marquis (wb 114.3) - 107,894 built	Wght	Price	Prod
FA/AG GS sdn 4d	3,787	20,330	—
FA/AJ LS sdn 4d	3,796	21,500	—

1994 Engines	bore×stroke	bhp	availability
I-4, 109.0	3.27×3.35	127	S-Trcr LTS (dohc)
I-4, 114.0	3.23×3.46	88	S-Tracer (ohc)
I-4, 141.0	3.70×3.30	96	S-Topaz
V-6, 182.0	3.50×3.15	135	O-Topaz
V-6, 182.0	3.50×3.15	140	S-Sable
V-6, 232.0	3.80×3.40	140	S-Cougr, O-Sble
V-8, 281.0	3.60×3.60	190	S-Grd Marquis
V-8, 281.0	3.60×3.60	205	O-Cougar (ohc)
V-8, 281.0	3.60×3.60	210	O-Grd Marquis

*Includes production for export.

1995

Tracer (wb 98.4) - 44,682 blt*	Wght	Price	Prod
M10 sdn 4d	2,418	11,280	—
M15 wgn	2,498	11,800	—
M14 LTS sdn 4d	2,472	13,140	—

Mystique (wb 106.5) - 66,742 built	Wght	Price	Prod
M65 GS sdn 4d	2,824	13,855	—
M66 LS sdn 4d	3,040	15,230	—

Sable (wb 106.0)	Wght	Price	Prod
M50 GS sdn 4d	3,144	18,210	90,197
M53 LS sdn 4d	—	20,470	
M53 LTS sdn 4d	—	21,715	
M55 GS wgn	3,292	19,360	12,300
M58 LS wgn	—	21,570	

Cougar (113.0)	Wght	Price	Prod
M62 XR7 cpe	3,533	16,860	60,201

Grand Marquis (wb 114.3) - 94,202 built	Wght	Price	Prod
M74 GS sdn 4d	3,761	21,270	—
M75 LS sdn 4d	—	22,690	—

1995 Engines	bore×stroke	bhp	availability
I-4, 109.0	3.27×3.35	127	S-Trcr LTS (dohc)
I-4, 114.0	3.23×3.46	88	S-Tracer (ohc)
I-4, 121.0	3.34×3.46	125	S-Mystq (dohc)
V-6, 155.0	3.24×3.13	170	O-Mystq (dohc)
V-6, 182.0	3.50×3.15	140	S-Sable
V-6, 232.0	3.80×3.40	140	S-Cougr, O-Sble
V-8, 281.0	3.60×3.60	190	S-Grd Marquis
V-8, 281.0	3.60×3.60	205	O-Cougar
V-8, 281.0	3.60×3.60	210	O-Grd Marquis

*Tracer calender-year production.

1996

Tracer (wb 98.4)	Wght	Price	Prod
M10 sdn 4d	2,409	11,755	10,790
M14 LTS sdn 4d	2,460	13,625	
M15 wgn	2,485	12,285	2,500

Mystique (wb 106.5) - 62,207 built	Wght	Price	Prod
M65 GS sdn 4d	2,833	14,330	—
M66 LS sdn 4d	2,855	15,075	—

Sable (wb 108.5)	Wght	Price	Prod
M51 G sdn 4d	—	18,360	121,203
M50 GS sdn 4d	3,358	18,995	
M53 LS sdn 4d	3,359	21,295	
M55 GS wgn	3,502	20,015	17,211
M58 LS wgn	3,525	22,355	

Cougar (wb 113.0)	Wght	Price	Prod
M62 XR7 cpe	3,559	17,430	39,749

Grand Marquis (wb 114.3)	Wght	Price	Prod
M74 GS sdn 4d	3,796	21,975	104,433
M75 LS sdn 4d	—	23,385	

1996 Engines	bore×stroke	bhp	availability
I-4, 109.0	3.27×3.35	127	S-Trcr LTS (dohc)
I-4, 114.0	3.23×3.46	88	S-Tracer (ohc)
I-4, 121.0	3.34×3.46	125	S-Mystique
V-6, 155.0	3.24×3.13	170	O-Mystique
V-6, 181.0	3.50×3.10	200	O-Sable (dohc)
V-6, 182.0	3.50×3.15	145	S-Sable (ohv)
V-6, 232.0	3.80×3.40	145	S-Cougar
V-8, 281.0	3.60×3.60	190	S-Grd Marquis
V-8, 281.0	3.60×3.60	205	O-Cougar
V-8, 281.0	3.60×3.60	210	O-Grd Marquis

1997

Tracer (wb 98.4)	Wght	Price	Prod
M10 GS sdn 4d	2,457	11,145	58,662
M14 LS sdn 4d	2,503	11,950	
M15 LS wgn	2,569	12,605	7,250

Mystique (wb 106.5) - 23,321 built	Wght	Price	Prod
M65 sdn 4d	—	13,960	—
M65 GS sdn 4d	2,861	14,775	—
M66 LS sdn 4d	2,884	16,150	—

Sable (wb 108.5)	Wght	Price	Prod
M51 G sdn 4d	—	18,505	89,108
M50 GS sdn 4d	3,333	19,495	
M53 LS sdn 4d	3,360	22,080	
M55 GS wgn	3,476	19,495	25,132
M58 LS wgn	3,502	22,080	

Cougar (wb 113.0)	Wght	Price	Prod
M62 XR7 cpe	3,536	17,830	35,267

Grand Marquis (wb 114.3) - 127,949 built	Wght	Price	Prod
M74 GS sdn 4d	3,792	22,495	127,949
M75 LS sdn 4d	3,796	23,905	

1997 Engines	bore×stroke	bhp	availability
I-4, 121.0	3.34×3.46	110	S-Tracer
I-4, 121.0	3.34×3.46	125	S-Mystiq (dohc)
V-6, 155.0	3.24×3.13	170	O-Mystique
V-6, 181.0	3.50×3.10	200	O-Sable (dohc)
V-6, 182.0	3.50×3.15	145	S-Sable
V-6, 232.0	3.80×3.40	145	S-Cougar
V-8, 281.0	3.60×3.60	190	S-Grd Marquis
V-8, 281.0	3.60×3.60	205	O-Cougar

1998

Tracer (wb 98.4) - 29,616 blt	Wght	Price	Prod*
M10 GS sdn 4d	2,469	11,355	—
M14 LS sdn 4d	—	12,710	—
M15 LS wgn	2,532	14,205	—

Mystique (wb 106.5) - 47,128 built	Wght	Price	Prod
M65 GS sdn 4d	2,808	16,235	—
M66 LS sdn 4d	—	17,645	—

Sable (wb 108.5) - 111,676 built	Wght	Price	Prod
M50 GS sdn 4d	3,299	19,445	—
M50/60 LS sdn 4d	—	20,445	—
M55 LS wgn	3,462	22,285	—

Grand Marquis (wb 114.3) - 134,155 built	Wght	Price	Prod
M74 GS sdn 4d	3,917	21,890	—
M75 LS sdn 4d	3,922	23,790	—

1998 Engines	bore×stroke	bhp	availability
I-4, 121.0	3.34×3.46	110	S-Tracer
I-4, 121.0	3.34×3.46	125	S-Mystiq (dohc)
V-6, 155.0	3.24×3.13	170	O-Mystique
V-6, 181.0	3.50×3.10	200	O-Sable (dohc)
V-6, 182.0	3.50×3.15	145	S-Sable
V-8, 281.0	3.60×3.60	200	S-Grd Marquis
V-8, 281.0	3.60×3.60	215	O-Grd Marquis

*Calendar-year production.

1999

Tracer (wb 98.4) - 14,691 blt	Wght	Price	Prod*
M10 GS sdn 4d	2,469	11,530	—
M14 LS sdn 4d	—	13,070	—
M15 LS wgn	2,532	14,275	—

Mystique (wb 106.5) - 36,791 built	Wght	Price	Prod
M65 GS sdn 4d	2,805	16,390	—
M66 LS sdn 4d	—	17,745	—

Sable (wb 108.5)-110,700 blt		Wght	Price	Prod*
M50	GS sdn 4d	3,302	18,445	—
M50/60	LS sdn 4d	—	19,545	—
M55	LS wgn	3,470	20,645	—
Cougar (wb 106.4)				
T60	htchbk cpe I-4	2,892	16,195	—
T61	htchbk cpe V-6	—	16,695	—
Grand Marquis (wb 114.3) - 142,372 built				
M74	GS sdn 4d	3,917	22,220	—
M75	LS sdn 4d	—	24,120	—

1999 Engines	bore×stroke	bhp	availability
I-4, 121.0	3.34×3.46	110	S-Tracer
I-4, 121.0	3.34×3.46	125	S-Mystiq, Cougr
I-4, 121.0	3.34×3.46	130	O-Tracer (dohc)
V-6, 155.0	3.24×3.13	170	O-Mystiq, Cougr
V-6, 181.0	3.50×3.10	200	O-Sable (dohc)
V-6, 182.0	3.50×3.15	145	S-Sable
V-8, 281.0	3.60×3.60	200	S-Grd Marquis
V-8, 281.0	3.60×3.60	215	O-Grd Marquis

* Calendar-year production

2000

Mystique (wb 106.5) - 5006 blt		Wght	Price	Prod*
M65	GS sdn 4d	2,805	16,145	—
M66	LS sdn 4d	—	17,445	—
Sable (wb 108.5) - 114,511 built				
M50	GS sdn 4d	3,302	18,845	—
M53	LS sdn 4d	—	19,545	—
M55	LS Premium sdn 4d	—	21,245	—
M58	GS wgn	3,470	20,835	—
M59	LS Premium wgn	3,470	22,345	—
Cougar (wb 106.4)				
T60	htchbk cpe I-4	2,892	16,195	—
T61	htchbk cpe V-6	—	16,695	—
Grand Marquis (wb 114.3) - 132,870 built				
M74	GS sdn 4d	3,917	22,220	—
M75	LS sdn 4d	—	24,120	—

2000 Engines	bore×stroke	bhp	availability
I-4, 121.0	3.34×3.46	125	S-Mystiq, Cougr
V-6, 155.0	3.24×3.13	170	O-Mystiq, Cougr
V-6, 181.0	3.50×3.10	200	O-Sable (dohc)
V-6, 182.0	3.50×3.15	153	S-Sable
V-8, 281.0	3.60×3.60	200	S-Grd Marquis
V-8, 281.0	3.60×3.60	215	O-Grd Marquis

* Calendar-year production

2001

Sable (wb 108.5) - 97,366 blt		Wght	Price	Prod*
M50	GS sdn 4d	3,302	19,185	—
M53	LS sdn 4d	—	20,285	—
M55	LS Premium sdn 4d	—	21,585	—
M58	GS wgn	3,470	20,985	—
M59	LS Premium wgn	—	22,685	—
Cougar (wb 106.4) - 25,016 built				
T60	htchbk cpe I-4	2,861	16,700	—
T61	htchbk cpe V-6	3,013	17,200	—
Grand Marquis (wb 114.3) - 100,774 built				
M74	GS sdn 4d	3,957	22,805	—
M75	LS sdn 4d	3,970	24,705	—

2001 Engines	bore×stroke	bhp	availability
I-4, 121.0	3.34×3.46	125	S-Cougar (dohc)
V-6, 155.0	3.24×3.13	170	O-Cougar
V-6, 181.0	3.50×3.10	200	O-Sable (dohc)
V-6, 182.0	3.50×3.15	155	S-Sable
V-8, 281.0	3.60×3.60	220	S-Grd Marquis
V-8, 281.0	3.60×3.60	235	O-Grd Marquis

* Calendar-year production

2002

Sable (wb 108.5) - 97,690 blt		Wght	Price	Prod*
M50	GS sdn 4d	3,366	19,630	—
M50	GS Plus sdn 4d	—	20,690	—
M55	LS Premium sdn 4d	—	22,055	—
M58	GS wgn	3,531	21,040	—
M58	GS Plus wgn	—	21,930	—
M59	LS Premium wgn	—	23,220	—
Cougar (wb 106.4)-18,321 blt		**Wght**	**Price**	**Prod**
T60	htchbk cpe I-4	2,861	16,520	—
T61	htchbk cpe V-6	3,013	17,020	—
T61	Sport htchbk cpe	—	17,520	—
T61	Sprt Prem htchbk cpe	—	18,520	—
T61	Sprt Ultim htchbk cpe	—	19,920	—
Grand Marquis (wb 114.3) - 96,034 built				
M74	GS sdn 4d	3,966	23,645	—
M74	GS Convnc sdn 4d	—	24,065	—
M75	LS Premium sdn 4d	3,988	27,120	—
M75	LS Ultimate sdn 4d	—	28,300	—
M75	LS Ultimate sdn 4d	—	28,300	—
M75	LSE sdn 4d	—	28,625	—

2002 Engines	bore×stroke	bhp	availability
I-4, 121.0	3.34×3.46	125	S-Cougar (dohc)
V-6, 155.0	3.24×3.13	170	O-Cougar
V-6, 181.0	3.50×3.10	200	O-Sable (dohc)
V-6, 182.0	3.50×3.15	155	S-Sable
V-8, 281.0	3.60×3.60	220	S-Grd Marquis
V-8, 281.0	3.60×3.60	235	O-Grd Marquis

* Calendar-year production

2003

Sable (wb 108.5)-55,215 blt		Wght	Price	Prod*
M50	GS sdn 4d	3,338	20,280	—
M50	GS Plus sdn 4d	3,338	21,340	—
M55	LS Premium sdn 4d	3,313	22,655	—
M58	GS wgn 4d	3,501	21,690	—
M58	GS Plus wgn 4d	3,501	22,580	—
M59	LS Premium wgn 4d	3,484	23,820	—
Grand Marquis (wb 114.7) - 92,140 built				
M74	GS sdn 4d	3,957	23,950	—
M74	GS Convnc sdn 4d	3,957	24,690	—
M75	LS Premium sdn 4d	3,970	28,645	—
M75	LS Ultimate sdn 4d	3,970	29,850	—
Marauder (wb 114.7)**				
M75	sdn 4d	4,195	33,770	—

2003 Engines	bore×stroke	bhp	availability
V-6, 181.0	3.50×3.10	200	O-Sable (dohc)
V-6, 182.0	3.50×3.15	155	S-Sable
V-8, 281.0	3.60×3.60	224	S-Grd Marquis
V-8, 281.0	3.60×3.60	302	S-Mrdr (dohc)

* Calendar-year production
** Included in Marquis production

2004

Sable (wb 108.5) - 44,216 blt		Wght	Price	Prod*
M50	GS sdn 4d	3,338	20,925	—
M55	LS Premium sdn 4d	3,313	23,255	—
M58	GS wgn 4d	3,501	21,925	—
M59	LS Premium wgn 4d	3,484	24,125	—
Grand Marquis (wb 114.7) - 87,583 built				
M74	GS sdn 4d	3,957	23,970	—
M74	GS Convnc sdn 4d	3,957	24,970	—
M75	LS Premium sdn 4d	3,970	28,870	—
M75	LS Ultimate sdn 4d	3,970	30,170	—
Marauder (wb 114.7)**				
M79	sdn 4d	4,195	33,770	—

2004 Engines	bore×stroke	bhp	availability
V-6, 181.0	3.50×3.10	201	O-Sable (dohc)
V-6, 182.0	3.50×3.15	155	S-Sable
V-8, 281.0	3.60×3.60	224	S-Grd Marquis
V-8, 281.0	3.60×3.60	239	O-Grd Marquis
V-8, 281.0	3.60×3.60	302	S-Mrdr (dohc)

* Calendar-year production
** Included in Marquis production

2005

Sable (wb 108.5) - 13,065 blt		Wght	Price	Prod*
M50	GS sdn 4d	3,318	20,855	—
M55	LS sdn 4d	3,325	23,820	—
M59	LS wgn 4d	3,325	25,130	—
Montego (wb 112.9) - 32,622 built				
M40	Luxury sdn 4d	3,680	24,345	—
M41	Luxury AWD sdn 4d	3,930	26,045	—
M42	Premier sdn 4d	3,680	26,545	—
M43	Premier AWD sdn 4d	3,930	28,245	—
Grand Marquis (wb 114.7) - 66,133 built				
M74	GS sdn 4d	3,970	24,370	—
Grand Marquis		**Wght**	**Price**	**Prod***
M74	GS Convnc sdn 4d	3,970	25,520	—
M75	LS Premium sdn 4d	3,957	29,425	—
M75	LSE sdn 4d	3,957	30,640	—
M75	LS Ultimate sdn 4d	3,970	30,725	—

2005 Engines	bore×stroke	bhp	availability
V-6, 181.0	3.50×3.10	201	O-Sable (dohc)
V-6, 181.0	3.50×3.10	203	S-Montgo (dohc)
V-6, 182.0	3.50×3.15	153	S-Sable
V-8, 281.0	3.60×3.60	224	S-Grd Marquis
V-8, 281.0	3.60×3.60	239	O-Grd Marquis

* Calendar-year production

2006

Milan (wb 107.4)		Wght	Price	Prod***
M07	sdn 4d I-4	3,117	18,345	—
M07	sdn 4d V-6	3,303	21,345	—
M08	Premier sdn 4d I-4	3,117	20,240	—
M08	Premier sdn 4d V-6	3,303	22,845	—
Montego (wb 112.9)				
M40	Luxury sdn 4d	3,680	24,430	—
M41	Luxury AWD sdn 4d	3,930	26,280	—
M42	Premier sdn 4d	3,680	26,800	—
M43	Premier AWD sdn 4d	3,930	28,730	—
Grand Marquis (wb 114.7)				
M74	GS sdn 4d	4,135	24,780	—
M74	GS Convnc sdn 4d	4,135	25,930	—
M75	LS Premium sdn 4d	4,117	30,065	—
M75	LS Ultimate sdn 4d	4,117	31,135	—

2006 Engines	bore×stroke	bhp	availability
I-4, 139.0	3.40×3.70	160	S-Milan
V-6, 181.0	3.50×3.10	203	S-Montego
V-6, 182.0	3.50×3.13	220	O-Milan
V-8, 281.0	3.60×3.60	224	S-Grd Marquis
V-8, 281.0	3.60×3.60	239	O-Grd Marquis

*** Prod figures not available at time of publication.

Muntz

The Muntz Jet was one of those interesting "shoestring" cars that sprang up in the late '40s and early '50s, when many believed that a dream and a little money were all it took to make it big in the auto business. The dreamer here was Earl "Madman" Muntz, an irrepressible radio/television manufacturer whose wild-and-woolly advertising also made him Southern California's largest—and most-flamboyant—used-car dealer.

Muntz's car actually originated with Frank Kurtis, the famed designer of winning race cars (especially dirt-track midgets) who turned his enormous talent to a street sports car in 1948. The resulting Kurtis Sport was a slab-sided two-seat convertible that was unusual for the day in having a unit body/chassis with just ten outer panels, all aluminum except for a fiberglass hood and rear deck. Appearance was bulbous but pleasing on a tight 100-inch wheelbase. Side windows were clumsy, clip-in Plexiglas affairs, but a removable rigid top was provided along with the soft top.

Like interior hardware, the Kurtis' suspension and running gear were mostly proprietary components, though Frank Kurtis tuned spring and damper rates for optimum handling and roadholding. The powerteam was anything the buyer wanted, though 239-cid Ford flathead V-8s with Edelbrock manifolds were fitted to most examples. The Sport was also offered as a kit at $1495-$3495, depending on completeness.

Light weight gave the Sport good acceleration despite the flathead's meager 100 horsepower, and reviewers loved the car's nimbleness and stability. But Kurtis-Kraft was a small company building cars mostly by hand, so sales were as slow and sparse as profits. Thus, after building just 36 Sports through 1950, Kurtis sold his Glendale, California, operation to the "Madman" for $200,000.

Muntz set about making the Sport more salable, retaining its basic styling but adding 13 inches to the wheelbase, a back seat, and more conveniences. This meant extra weight, so Cadillac's new 160-horsepower, 331-cid overhead-valve V-8 was substituted for the Ford flathead. The result was America's first high-performance personal-luxury car. Muntz called it the Jet.

Working out of the former Kurtis plant, Muntz built 28 Jets before moving operations to his hometown of Evanston, Illinois, just north of Chicago, and making more substantial changes. The aluminum body—"It would dent if you leaned against it," he told *Collectible Automobile*® magazine in 1985—gave way to a steel shell on a new 116-inch wheelbase. Curiously, the modern Cadillac V-8 was ditched for Lincoln's old 336.7-cid flathead, albeit modified to produce 154 bhp via solid lifters (replacing hydraulics) from the Ford truck version. GM Hydra-Matic transmission was made standard, though Borg-Warner stick-overdrive was optionally available.

"We tooled that car for $75,000," Muntz recalled. But labor costs were a monumental $2000 per car because body panels had to be carefully fitted, then leaded-in. Meticulous detailing was required elsewhere.

1951-54 Muntz Jet convertible coupe

1954 Muntz Jet convertible coupe

The Evanston cars weighed 3780 pounds, about 400 more than the Glendale Jets, but were more durable. Both versions were fairly quick. Lincoln-powered models could do 0-60 in a tick over 12 seconds and see nearly 108 mph. Toward the end, Muntz switched to fiberglass fenders and Lincoln's 317.5-cid ohv V-8, which began at 160 bhp and was later rated at 205 bhp.

Unfortunately, Muntz lost money from the start on his cars, and when his television business hit hard times in 1954, he shut down his car-manufacturing business.

Even the "Madman" didn't know for sure, but it's estimated that 394 Jets were built; of these, at least 49 survive today.

Specifications

1951

Jet (wb 113.0)	Wght	Price	Prod
conv cpe	3,380*	5,500*	**

1951 Engine	bore×stroke	bhp	availability
V-8, 331.0	3.81×3.63	160	S-all

1952

Jet (wb 116.0)	Wght	Price	Prod
conv cpe	3,780*	5,500*	**

1952 Engine	bore×stroke	bhp	availability
V-8, 336.7	3.50×4.38	154	S-all

1953

Jet (wb 116.0)	Wght	Price	Prod
conv cpe	3,780*	5,500*	**

1953 Engine	bore×stroke	bhp	availability
V-8, 336.7	3.50×4.38	154	S-all

1954

Jet (wb 116.0)	Wght	Price	Prod
conv cpe	3,700*	5,500*	**

1954 Engine	bore×stroke	bhp	availability
V-8, 317.5	3.80×3.50	205	S-all

Note: Chassis and engine changes did not necessarily occur on a model-year basis, so some vehicles of a given model year may have different engines or specifications than those listed.

* Approximate figures

** First-series Jet production with Cadillac V-8 is estimated at 28; total 1951-54 Jet production is estimated at 394.

Nash

Crusty Charles W. Nash resigned as president of General Motors in 1916 to build a car under his own name. Two years later, he bought the Thomas B. Jeffery Company of Kenosha, Wisconsin, which manufactured the slow-selling Jeffery and an earlier model called Rambler. Renamed Nash Motors, the firm charged up the sales charts, reaching as high as eighth place in industry production during the 1920s. Along the way, Nash introduced the low-cost six-cylinder Ajax and expanded by absorbing Mitchell and LaFayette. But none of these marques were as successful as the Nash itself and were gone by 1930.

Nash suffered in the general economic malaise following the 1929 Wall Street crash but found financial salvation by merging with the Kelvinator appliance company in 1937. Kelvinator president George Mason, a burly man described by many as "cigar-chomping," continued as president of the new concern; Charles Nash was chairman of the board. By 1940, Nash-Kelvinator had turned the corner and was profitable once more.

Many early-'30s Nashes were sumptuous, beautifully styled automobiles with numerous special features. But the firm also sold low-priced cars with an ordinary side-valve six. For 1930-32, this was a 201.3-cubic-inch engine with 60-70 horsepower; for 1933, it grew to 217.8 cid and 75 bhp. Series were variously titled Single Six (1930), 660 (1931), 960 (1932), and Big Six (1932-33). Prices started at around $1000 in 1930 but were later lowered to the $800-$900 range to spur sales in the Depression-crushed market. A side-valve straight eight was added for the 870/970 of 1931-32, with 227.2 cid and 78 bhp. In 1932-33 came a bored-out 247.4-cid engine with 85 horsepower for Standard and Special Eights (Series 1070/1080), listing at $1000-$1500. The smaller eights generally sold for just below $1000.

More interesting were Nash's "Twin Ignition" cars, also variously titled. As the name implied, these employed two sets of spark plugs and points plus dual condensers and coils, all operating from a single distributor. The Twin Ignition Six arrived in 1928 as a 242-cid engine with 74 bhp. It continued through 1930, then stepped aside in '31 for a 240-cid straight eight with 88-94 bhp. The Twin Ignition Eight arrived for 1930, delivering 100-115 bhp from 298.6 cid. That powerplant persisted through the 1932 model year, when it was bracketed by new 260.8- and 322-cid engines with respective bhp of 100 and 125. The 322 was canceled after 1934, but the 260.8 would carry on all the way through 1942, although it lost twin ignition that final year.

Charlie Nash was president of Buick in 1910-11, a make that espoused overhead valves, so it wasn't surprising that all these Nash engines were ohv, too. The eights also boasted nine main bearings for smooth operation. Cost factors and rising public demand for greater fuel economy prompted Nash to abandon eight-cylinder engines after 1942; they wouldn't return until 1955.

Nash persisted with classically upright styling through 1934 even though other makes were shifting to a rounder streamlined look. Body styles in all early-'30s series encompassed the most-popular period types: closed sedans, touring car, victoria, rumble-seat coupe, roadster, and convertible cabriolet. Seven-passenger sedans and limousines on wheelbases of 133 and 142 inches were cataloged for the six- and eight-cylinder Twin Ignition lines. A notable addition for 1932 was the Ambassador—a nicely proportioned, luxuriously trimmed five-seat sedan priced at $1855. A four-door brougham sedan was also offered, as were two seven-seaters priced $100-$200 higher. Additional choices arrived for 1933.

Charles Nash believed in offering a lot for the money, and his cars bristled with innovations. The Twin Ignition Eight, for example, sported cowl ventilation, a dashboard starter button (instead of a floor pedal), shatterproof glass, and automatic radiator vents in 1930; downdraft carburetors and Bijur automatic chassis lubrication for '31; "Syncro-Safety Shift" and optional freewheeling for 1932 (a device built into the transmission that allowed the car to coast when the driver's foot was off the accelerator; it was ultimately determined to be dangerous because it eliminated engine braking); ignition/steering-wheel lock for '33; and aircraft-type instruments for '34. Many of these features also appeared on the cheaper side-valve Eights.

Like most automakers, Nash was damaged badly by the Depression. Though it regularly built over 100,000 cars a year in the late '20s, it wouldn't repeat that figure in the '30s, and thus ranked 11th, 12th, or 13th in industry production, with the exception of 1932, when it placed seventh in a down year for the industry. Also like many others, Nash hit bottom in 1933, output totaling less than 15,000. With a new approach desperately needed, a planned 1934 restyle was postponed a year while Nash pinned its hopes—and resources—on new low-priced LaFayettes.

Nash built its millionth car in 1934 while trying to summon better times with a drastically reduced line consisting of the 116-inch-wheelbase Big Six, 121-inch Advanced Eight, and 133/142-inch Ambassador Eight, all with ohv Twin Ignition engines. But production didn't improve much, and Nash lost over $1.6 million. Hydraulic brakes arrived for 1935 models, reduced to just a four-door sedan and six-passenger victoria in each series. Ambassador also lost its smooth 322-cid

1930 Twin Ignition Eight 7-passenger (lwb) touring

1931 Series 880 two-door convertible sedan

1932 Special Eight coupe

1933 Advanced Eight convertible roadster

1932 Ambassador Eight four-door sedan

1934 Ambassador Eight Brougham four-door sedan

1935 Ambassador Eight four-door sedan

1936 400 New Six trunkback touring sedan

engine, sharing the Advanced Eight's 260.8-cid unit.

But the belated restyle appeared that year as "Aeroform Design," and it was good. Highlights included sweeping skirted fenders, a handsome Vee'd radiator, and a louvered hood. Prices spanned a range of $825-$1220. Happily for Nash, sales turned up. Registrations for the calendar year went from just under 24,000 to a bit over 35,000. Things were even better for 1936, reaching 43,000 with the help of new low-priced six-cylinder "400" models, standard and Deluxe. That year's Ambassadors comprised two Sixes and one eight-cylinder "trunkback" sedan, all on a 125-inch wheelbase. Prices were $835-$995. Sixes shared the "400" engine: the 234.8-cid unit introduced back in '34, now with 90 or 93 bhp.

Hopes for the revived LaFayette weren't entirely realized. An ostensibly separate make, it was, of course, planned as a junior-edition Depression-beater. Trouble was, the Great Depression was easing by the time the car debuted in 1934, which made the line far less necessary. Indeed, LaFayette attracted only 5000 first-year buyers and another 9400 for '35 before unexpectedly sky-rocketing to 27,860. They had ordinary styling on a 113-inch wheelbase, and popular body styles were offered at $585-$715. But the cars were "built down" to achieve those prices. Their powerplant, for instance, was the old 75-83 bhp 217.8-cid six from 1931-33.

Accordingly, LaFayette was made the lowest-priced 1937 Nash, taking over an unchanged chassis from the previous year's "400s." The Ambassador Six returned on a 121-inch platform and was increased to 105 bhp. Ambassador Eight continued with its 125-inch chassis and a 260.8-cid Twin Ignition eight that now made 115 bhp. This range of engines and wheelbases continued through decade's end. Styling was cautious, even imitative. The '37s, for instance, were much like Chrysler/DeSoto Airstreams: slightly lumpy, with similar barrel grilles. But they seemed to satisfy buyers. Nash had its best year of the decade in 1937, building 77,000 cars to earn $3.4 million.

Kenosha lost some of this hard-won sales ground as 1938 production stumbled to 41,543 cars and the new Nash-Kelvinator Corporation lost $7.7 million. A severe facelift changed Nash's resemblance from Chrysler to the dumpier GM products, but the sales drop was primarily due to that year's sharp recession. A noteworthy innovation was the "Weather-Eye" heating/ventilation system, a pioneering "climatizer" that would remain one of the best in Detroit for the next 20 years.

A total 1939 restyle ushered in handsome Ford-like styling announced by flush-fit headlamps astride a narrow prow bearing horizontal bars; fine vertical bars adorned the "catwalks" on either side. The rest of the package was neat, trim, and coherent, combining all the best elements of late "art-deco" design. Production rebounded strongly to 63,000 cars. Significantly, LaFayette accounted for over 50 percent of pro-

1937 Ambassador Eight trunkback sedan

1938 Lafayette DeLuxe trunkback sedan

1939 LaFayette DeLuxe four-door sedan

1940 Ambassador Eight All-Purpose cabriolet

1941 600 DeLuxe trunkback four-door sedan

1942 600 trunkback four-door sedan

1946 Ambassador fastback four-door sedan

duction. Although Nash-Kelvinator lost $1.6 million in 1939, its future looked brighter than it had in a decade.

LaFayette made its final appearance for 1940, when all models were cautiously facelifted, mainly via applied trim. The veteran 234.8-cid six, as smooth and quiet as ever with its seven main bearings, was up to 99 horsepower for LaFayette. Ambassador Sixes still offered 105 bhp from the same engine, plus a four-inch-longer wheelbase, for about $110 more model-for-model. Ambassador Eights again delivered 115 bhp, as they had since 1937. Body styles were the same in all three series: business coupe, two- and four-door fastback sedans, trunkback four-door, and "All-Purpose" coupe and cabriolet. Model-year output was down slightly from '39 but still fairly healthy at 62,131.

For 1941, Nash joined future partner Hudson in advocating "single-unit" construction with the new 600, which signified 600 miles on a 20-gallon tank of gas. A handsome package on a 112-inch wheelbase, the 600 offered eight models powered by a new 75-bhp, 172.6-cid six. These included sedans and coupes in Spécial or Deluxe trim, all priced remarkably low. The Special fastback four-door, for instance, cost $805, less than a comparable Ford V-8. *Time* magazine called the 600 "the only completely new car in 1941," and demand was strong. Styling, evolved from the '40 look, was shared by senior Nashes, which also gained new unitized bodies, though the Ambassador Eight was demoted to the shorter chassis of its six-cylinder sister. More-horizontal front end styling was featured across the board. Altogether, 1941 proved very profitable for Nash-Kelvinator, which closed the fiscal year with $4.6 million in earnings on total volume of just over 84,000 cars.

Production slimmed to only 31,780 for war-shortened 1942. Following an industry trend, Nash heavily facelifted with a low wraparound grille composed of three horizontal bars, a motif repeated as fender trim on some models. A slightly blunted prow hood rode above a small upper grille with four short horizontal bars, and parking lights appeared atop the front fenders. The same three series continued, but with fewer body and trim variations. Nash-Kelvinator then dug in

1947 Ambassador Suburban four-door sedan

1948 Ambassador Super four-door sedan

1948 Ambassador Custom Brougham two-door

1949 Ambassador Custom fastback four-door sedan

for war production, turning out $600 million worth of aircraft engines and parts, munitions, cargo trailers, and other goods.

Despite severe postwar materials shortages, Nash returned to civilian operations earlier than most automakers and built 6148 cars during late 1945. That was good for third in the calendar-year race, but amounted to only four months of production. For 1946, the first full postwar model year, Nash built about 94,000 cars to finish eighth. Its 1947-48 totals were 101,000 and 110,000, good for only tenth and 11th. Still, these were good years, with strong profits. As if to celebrate, Nash opened a new 204-acre proving grounds near Burlington, Wisconsin, in 1946.

In June 1948, Nash president George Mason became board chairman, succeeding the venerable Charles Nash, who died that month at age 84. Nash was able to share in the 1946 celebration of the auto industry's Golden Jubilee, one of only a dozen pioneers still living at the time.

Mason was among the postwar era's most visionary industry executives, certainly the most prophetic outside the Big Three. Believing the independents would have to merge for survival against the Detroit giants, he soon began working to put Nash together with Hudson and hoped to combine with Studebaker and Packard as well. More immediately, he presided over the development of a radical all-new Nash for the 1949 model year.

In the interim, Nash followed most other makes by fielding renovated 1942 models for 1946-48. Ambassador Eights were dropped, the 600's horsepower was boosted to 82, and the Ambassador Six was pushed to 112 bhp. Styling alterations were relatively minor, yet the cars managed to appear fresh enough. The 1946-47s had inboard parking lamps; the '47s gained a wider upper grille and raised-center hubcaps. For '48, Nash erased the side moldings below the beltline, a cheap change that inadvertently made for a higher, less-streamlined appearance.

The postwar 600 line comprised fastback and trunkback four-door sedans and a notchback Brougham two-door. The lineup was expanded for '48 with the addition of DeLuxe, Super, and Custom trim variations, Nash anticipating a major sales upsurge that year. Ambassador Six offered the same choices save for DeLuxe-trim '48s.

Unique to Ambassador was the Sedan Suburban, lavishly trimmed in wood like the contemporary Chrysler Town & Country and Ford/Mercury Sportsman. Extensive hand labor necessitated stiff prices ($1929-$2227), so Nash built only 272 Suburbans for '46, 595 for '47, and a mere 130 of the '48s (which came only with Super trim). But they played the same role as the nonwagon Ford and Chrysler woodies, attracting buyers to showrooms with the promise of something new. Suburbans are now coveted collectibles, mainly because only 10-15 are thought to survive. Only slightly less rare was the Custom-trim cabriolet added to the 1948 Ambassador line. It was the first open Nash since the war, but only 1000 or so were built. (Nash also built a small number of trucks with sedan-type front ends beginning with the 1947 model year, but most were exported.)

Meantime, Nash's independent rivals had restyled for 1947-48, as had Olds and Cadillac. Remaining Big Three makes targeted 1949 for their first all-new postwar models. But so had Nash, and it weighed in with a stunner: the radical Airflyte. Continued through '51, it looks rather strange now, yet in its day the Airflyte was one of the most-advanced cars on the road. It was unquestionably the boldest Nash ever.

The Airflyte was cooked up during World War II by engineers Ted Ulrich and Nash veteran Nils Erik Wahlberg. Ulrich had worked on the prewar "600" while at The Budd Company, and was hired by Wahlberg on the strength of its success. The way-out "bathtub" styling was the work of Holden "Bob" Koto, who, with partner Ted Pietsch in 1943, had shown Wahlberg a small scale model much like the eventual production Airflyte. Wahlberg must have liked it, for he'd already experimented with streamlined cars in wind-tunnel tests. The Airflyte was thus very slick aerodynamically, with only 113 pounds of drag at 60 mph versus up to 171 pounds for the similar-looking '49 Packard.

Maintaining Nash's two-series lineup, the '49 Airflyte came as a "600," still on a 112-inch wheelbase, and as a 121-inch Ambassador (with the extra wheelbase length again entirely

1950 Rambler Custom Landau convertible coupe

1950 Ambassador Super club coupe

1951 Nash-Healey roadster

1951 Rambler Custom Country Club hardtop coupe

1952 Ambassador Custom Country Club hardtop coupe

ahead of the firewall). Each series listed two- and four-door sedans and Brougham club coupes, all bulbous fastbacks. Engines were unchanged from 1946-48. Novelties abounded: one-piece curved windshield, "Uniscope" gauge cluster (in a pod atop the steering column), reclining front seatbacks that met the rear seat to form a bed (dealers sold pneumatic mattresses as accessories), dual inward-facing rear seats on Broughams (separated by a "card table" armrest) and, after '49, optional seatbelts. Form-a-bed seats, plus the acclaimed "Weather-Eye" system, made Airflytes the most habitable long-distance cars in America.

With the postwar seller's market still strong, the Airflyte sold very well—better than any big Nashes had before. Some 135,000 were built for '49, rocketing Nash into the industry's top ten. The 1950 total was over 160,000—a company record, and that didn't include Nash's new compact Rambler introduced that year.

Optional Hydra-Matic Drive (purchased from GM) arrived for 1950, along with three more horsepower for each engine. The 600 was renamed Statesman. The rear windows were enlarged to improve visibility, though it was still pretty poor. Prices remained competitive: under $2000 for Statesmans, $2060-$2200 for Ambassadors. New for '51 were extended and raised rear fenders that softened the "beetleback" look, plus new grilles. As in 1950, trim levels comprised base Deluxe, midrange Super, and top-shelf Custom, an arrangement Nash would keep for most of the rest of its days. Prices again changed little, but the public was tiring of "bathtubs", so production eased to about 153,000, again minus Rambler.

The new 100-inch-wheelbase 1950 Rambler was the very antithesis of the huge Airflyte. Though several Detroit automakers had attempted smaller cars before World War II, Rambler was the first to sell in significant numbers. Interestingly, Ford and Chevrolet briefly considered compacts after the war, but their concepts were quite different from Nash's. As George Romney, then Mason's top assistant, once said: "It's one thing for a small company—a marginal firm—to pioneer a new concept like that and really push it. But it's another thing for people who already have a big slice to begin pushing something that undercuts their basic market." Still, the Rambler's early sales success didn't go unnoticed at the Big Three, who would follow Nash's lead—though they'd take ten years to do so.

Small cars fascinated George Mason, who knew that the independents couldn't hope to survive in the postwar market without offering types of cars that the Big Three didn't. Together with chief engineer Meade Moore, Mason hammered away until the Rambler (and later the Metropolitan) was a reality. It arrived just as the sell-anything era was ending, and it would keep Nash's head above water through its 1954 merger with Hudson. Three years later, the resulting American Motors Corporation would be selling Ramblers almost exclusively.

The 1950 Rambler saw little change through 1952. Only two models were offered initially: a Custom two-door wagon and the interesting Custom Landau convertible with fixed side-window frames. A pretty hardtop coupe called Country Club was added for '51, but most sales came from the practical, attractive wagons (called Suburban after '51). In those early days of all-steel models, Rambler accounted for 22 percent of total U.S. wagon sales. All these Ramblers carried Nash's smaller 82-bhp L-head six, good for a claimed 25-30 mpg. The '52s maintained the 1950-51 pace, recording just over 53,000 total sales.

Quotable road-tester Tom McCahill of *Mechanix Illustrated* magazine once wrote that Mason and Nash were "busier than a mouse in a barrel of hungry cats." As proof, Mason busied himself with a sports car in these years. Called Nash-Healey, it started with a chance meeting aboard the *Queen Elizabeth* between Mason and famed British sports-car builder Donald Healey, then looking to buy American engines. Their meeting led directly to a low, slab-sided, two-seat roadster appearing in 1951 with a 102-inch wheelbase, British-crafted aluminum body, and an Ambassador six tuned for 125 bhp. Healey built it at his small works in Warwick, England.

The Nash-Healey perfectly expressed Mason's "be different or die" attitude, but it cost a bunch—over $4000 at first—and thus didn't sell well: 104 of the '51s, 150 for '52, 162 of the '53s, and just 90 for '54 (including a few leftovers reserialed as '55 models). Even so, the N-H became better as it went along. Handsome steel bodywork shaped by Italy's Pinin Farina bowed for 1952. The next year brought a six-inch longer wheelbase for a companion coupe called Le Mans (honoring high N-H finishes at the French 24-hour race in 1951-52). Nash also offered a 140-bhp dual-carburetor option, but canceled the roadster after '53. The high cost of transatlantic shipping pushed the price over $6000 by the end, but every Nash-Healey was a genuine dual-purpose sports car: quick and nimble on the road, yet strong enough for the track.

Mason so liked Farina's N-H restyle that he asked the designer to shape a new big Nash for 1952. Farina submitted two proposals, but the end product was mostly the doing of Nash's own Edmund A. Anderson. The only surviving Farina elements were a simple, square grille and a three-element wraparound rear window. Still, the 1952 Statesmans and Ambassadors were good-looking notchbacks that wore "Pinin Farina" badges, just like post-'51 Nash-Healeys. Nash called them "Golden Airflytes," honoring the firm's 50th birthday that year. Unfortunately, integral front-fender skirts, as on the 1949-51 "bathtubs," made for huge turning circles and difficult tire-changing.

Big-Nash offerings for '52 comprised Super and Custom two- and four-door sedans plus a new Custom Country Club hardtop in each line. Statesmans now rode a 114.3-inch wheelbase and carried a stroked 195.6-cid six with 88 bhp. Prices moved up: $2150-$2400 for Statesmans, $2520-$2830 for Ambassadors.

The '53s were identified only by small chrome spacers on their cowl air scoops (part of "Weather-Eye"). Nash still billed itself as "America's travel car" with things like a drawer-type glovebox and a full-width parcel net above the windshield, but those were just masks for tepid performance. To perk things up for '53, Nash boosted the Statesman to 100 bhp and offered the Ambassadors with dual carburetors and a high-compression aluminum head in a 140-bhp "Le Mans" option *a la* Nash-Healey.

An attractive new "floating" grille appeared for '54, when Custom two-door sedans were scratched and the Statesman got its own dual-carb engine: a 110-bhp setup dubbed "Dual Powerflyte." That surely raised eyebrows at Chrysler, which had a new PowerFlite automatic transmission that year, but Nash probably got away with it because sales had been steadily dropping: from about 143,000 for '52, to 109,000 for '53, and finally 77,000 for '54. More ominously, the low-profit Ramblers—nicely updated for '53 via a clean single-bar grille—accounted for a continuously growing percentage of this dwindling pie.

And Nash had something even smaller for '54: a tiny two-seater on an 85-inch wheelbase. Called Metropolitan, it originated in a prototype by freelance designer Bill Flajole that was displayed to select audiences during 1950 as the NXI (for "Nash Xperimental International"). Response was favorable,

1953 Rambler Custom Country Club hardtop coupe

1953 Ambassador Custom Country Club hardtop coupe

1952-53 Nash-Healey roadster by Pinin Farina

1954 Statesman Custom two-door sedan

1955½ Rambler Custom Cross Country station wagon

1955 Ambassador Eight Custom Country Club hardtop coupe

1956 Ambassador Eight Custom four-door sedan

1956 Rambler Custom hardtop sedan

1957 Ambassador Custom Country Club hardtop coupe

1957 Rambler V-8 Custom Cross Country hardtop station wagon

but Mason didn't arrange for production until late 1953. The bodies were contracted to the well-known Fisher & Ludlow works in Birmingham, England, and final assembly to Austin in Longbridge, England. Austin also donated a four-cylinder engine from its A40 model, an elderly long-stroke bit of ironmongery that extracted 42 bhp from 73.8 cid.

The Metropolitan arrived in hardtop and convertible models priced around $1450. Weight was just over 1800 pounds, so mileage was good: up to 40 mpg. At first, sales were pretty good too, Austin shipping 13,095 through late '54. But demand fell to just under 6100 the next year, prompting some changes for '56.

Mason achieved a portion of his goal on May 1, 1954, when Nash and Hudson merged, forming American Motors Corporation (AMC). He still wanted Studebaker and Packard to join the fold so the resulting company could enjoy the economies of scale of the Big Three, and therefore be competitive with them. Studebaker and Packard did merge with each other (also in '54), but Mason died late that year, and his dream of a large company made up of several independents was never fully realized.

Meanwhile, the big "Farina" Nashes were facelifted for 1955, acquiring raised front wheel arches at last, plus a wrapped windshield and a smart new oval grille encircling the headlights. Cooperation between the new AMC and Studebaker-Packard (another '54 merger) gave Nash its first eight-cylinder cars since 1942: Ambassadors with a new 208-bhp Packard-built V-8 of 320 cid. The Ambassador Eight was much quicker than the Six, but cost $300 more. Remaining two-door sedans departed, but other models stayed. As in '54, Statesmans had 100 standard bhp, Ambassador Sixes 130, and both again offered power-packs adding 10 bhp.

For '54 Rambler got its first four-doors: sedans and Cross Country *wagons* on a new 108-inch platform (unitized, of course). Two-doors retained the original 100-inch chassis. Rambler had adopted larger six-cylinder engines in '53: the old 184- and 195.6-cid engines with 85 and 90 bhp, respectively. The smaller engine disappeared for 1955, but the larger one now came in 90- and 100-bhp guises. Fifty-five styling featured exposed front wheels and an eggcrate grille

With Ramblers still popular and Nash newly married to moribund Hudson, the 1955 Ramblers were sold through both dealer chains—with appropriate badges, naturally. The same would apply to 1955-56 Metropolitans. But this tended to obscure the fact that the big Nashes were failing as much as the big Hudsons. In a model year when almost every Detroit make did well, Statesman/Ambassador managed only slightly over 40,000 sales—lower even than the '54 tally.

Accordingly, Rambler got all the emphasis for '56 under new AMC president Romney (who took over upon Mason's death). A full outer-body reskin brought a wrapped windshield, squared eggcrate grille with inboard headlamps, blocky body lines, and colorful exteriors with optional two-tone and even three-tone paint. What's more, all Ramblers were now on the 108-inch wheelbase and had four doors. Some lacked B-posts, though, as airy hardtop sedans and Detroit's first hardtop wagons were added. Horsepower was boosted to 120 across the board. Prices were higher too, but still reasonable: $1830-$2330. Once more, Ramblers wore Nash or Hudson badges depending on which network they were sold through. About 10,000 were built for the model year, after which Rambler became a separate make (*see* Rambler).

An improved Metropolitan, the 1500, was introduced in mid-'56. That referred to the metric displacement of a 90.9-cid Austin four churning out 52 bhp, 24 percent more than the old "1200." Where early Mets did only about 70 mph tops, the 1500 could approach 80, though it was still hardly a sports

1957 Rambler Rebel hardtop sedan

1958 Metropolitan convertible coupe

car. Styling was updated by a mesh grille with a prominent new "M" medallion, a hood shorn of its dummy air scoop, and zigzag side moldings that delineated loud two-tone paint schemes. Though prices were hiked to $1500-$1600, the Met would continue to find favor through decade's end. Sales averaged 14,000 a year for 1957-58, then jumped to 22,300 for '59. But that would prove the peak. Sales dropped to 13,000 for 1960, then plunged below 1000. The Met thus departed in 1962, when a mere 412 were sold—all leftovers (production ceased in mid-1960). These cute little cars have since become "cult collectibles." Who would have thought it?

Far less unthinkable in 1956 was the end of the big Nash. That year's lineup was cut to Statesman and Ambassador Six Super sedans, plus V-8 Ambassador Super and Custom sedans and Custom Country Club. The V-8s retained Packard power through April, then became Ambassador Specials by switching to AMC's own new 250-cid with 190 bhp. Ed Anderson devised big "lollipop" taillights, extra chrome for the sides and front, and splashy duo-tone and tri-tone paint schemes, but they were little help. Model-year production plunged by two-thirds.

Nash got one more chance, but 1957 was anticlimactic. Side trim was shuffled, and headlamps not only moved back to the fenders but multiplied to stack in pairs astride a busy oval grille. Models were limited to Super and Custom Ambassador sedans and Country Clubs, with Customs often heroically overcolored. All carried a 327-cid V-8 lifted to 255 bhp by a four-barrel carb, dual exhausts, and 9:1 compression.

But the bell had been tolling for some time, so after 1957 production of under 3600 big cars, Nash was laid to rest alongside Hudson. It was purely a survival move. AMC was still digging out from the debts incurred with the Nash-Hudson merger, and the Rambler name had become a far more salable commodity—to say nothing of the cars. At least the Ambassador didn't die, returning as a 1958 line of stretched Ramblers once planned for Nash and Hudson.

Specifications

1930

450 Single Six (wb 114.3) - 33,118 blt		Wght	Price	Prod
456	rdstr 2-4P	2,550	975	—
458	touring 5P	2,650	995	—
452	cpe 2P	2,650	940	—
452R	cpe 2-4P	2,700	980	—
451	cabriolet 2-4P	2,600	1,005	—
453	sdn 2d	2,750	935	—
450	sdn 4d	2,850	1,005	—
457	Deluxe sdn 4d	2,900	1,095	—
455	landaulet	2,900	1,155	—
480 Twin Ign Six (wb 118.0; lwb-128.3) - 17,346 built				
486	rdstr 2-4P	3,250	1,365	—
488S	touring, d.c. 5P	3,540	1,595	—
488	lwb touring 7P	3,450	1,475	—
482	cpe 2P	3,400	1,345	—
482R	cpe 2-4P	3,450	1,395	—
481	cabriolet 2-4P	3,350	1,385	—
489	victoria 4P	3,400	1,410	—
483	sdn 2d	3,500	1,325	—
480	sdn 4d	3,535	1,415	—
484	lwb sdn 7P	3,750	1,745	—
485	limo 7P (lwb)	3,760	1,920	—
490 Twin Ign Eight (wb 124.0; lwb-133.0) - 12,801 blt				
498	lwb touring 7P	3,770	1,845	—
498S	lwb touring, d.c. 5P	3,840	1,975	—
492	lwb coupe 2P	3,900	1,915	—
4012R	lwb coupe 2-4P	3,945	1,975	—
401	lwb cabriolet 2-4P	3,840	1,875	—
493	sdn 2d	3,950	1,675	—
490	sdn 4d	4,000	1,795	—
492	Ambassador lwb sdn	4,050	2,095	—
497B	lwb Amb. Brghm trpdo sdn	4,050	2,095	—
494	lwb sedan 7P	4,170	2,195	—
495	limo 7P (lwb)	4,210	2,385	—
499	lwb victoria 5P	3,950	2,045	—

1930 Engines	bore×stroke	bhp	availability
I-6, 201.3	3.13×4.38	60	S-Single Six
I-6, 242.0	3.38×4.50	74	S-T.I. Six
I-8, 298.6	3.25×4.50	100	S-T.I. Eight

1931

660 (wb 114.3) - 12,241 built		Wght	Price	Prod
662	cpe 2d	2,600	795	—
662R	cpe 2-4P	2,650	825	—
663	sdn 2d	2,740	795	—
660	sdn 4d	2,800	845	—
668	touring 5P	2,640	895	—
870 (wb 116.3) - 12,116 built				
872	cpe 2P	2,870	945	—
872R	cpe 2-4P	2,920	975	—
870	sdn 4d	3,000	995	—
877	Special sdn 4d	3,000	955	—
871	conv sdn 2d	2,950	1,075	—
880 (wb 121.0) - 6,830 built				
882	cpe 2P	3,200	1,245	—
882R	cpe 2-4P	3,250	1,285	—
880	sdn 4d	3,360	1,295	—
887	Town sdn 4d	3,400	1,375	—
881	conv sdn 2d	3,275	1,325	—
890 (wb 124.0; lwb-133.0) - 6,199 built				
892	cpe 2P	3,900	1,695	—
892R	cpe 2-4P	3,950	1,745	—
891	cabriolet 2-4P	3,850	1,695	—
890	lwb sedan 4d	4,000	1,565	—
897	Ambassador sdn 4d	4,050	1,825	—
894	lwb sdn 7P	4,170	1,925	—
895	limo 7P (lwb)	4,210	2,025	—
899	victoria 5P	3,950	1,765	—
898	lwb touring 7P	3,880	1,595	—

1931 Engines	bore×stroke	bhp	availability
I-6, 201.3	3.13×4.38	65	S-660
I-8, 227.2	2.88×4.38	78	S-870
I-8, 240.0	3.00×4.25	88	S-880 (T. Ign.)
I-8, 298.6	3.25×4.50	115	S-890 (T. Ign.)

1932

960 (wb 114.3) - 5,787 built		Wght	Price	Prod
968	phaeton 5P	2,640	895	—
962	cpe 2P	2,600	795	—
962R	cpe 2-4P	2,650	825	—
963	sdn 2d	2,740	795	—
960	sdn 4d	2,800	845	—
970 (wb 116.3) - 8,201 built				
972	cpe 2P	2,870	945	—
972R	cpe 2-4P	2,920	975	—
970	sdn 4d	3,000	995	—
977	Special sdn 4d	3,000	955	—
971	conv sdn 2d	2,950	1,075	—
980 (wb 121.0) - 5,204 built				
982	cpe 2P	3,200	1,245	—
982R	cpe 2-4P	3,250	1,285	—
980	sdn 4d	3,360	1,295	—
987	Town sdn 4d	3,400	1,375	—
981	conv sdn 2d	3,275	1,325	—
990 (wb 124.0; lwb 133.0) - 3,900 built				
998	lwb touring 7P	3,880	1,595	—
992	cpe 2P	3,900	1,695	—
992R	cpe 2-4P	3,950	1,745	—
991	cabriolet 2-4P	3,840	1,695	—
999	victoria 5P	3,950	1,765	—
990	lwb sdn 4d	4,000	1,565	—
996	sdn 4d	4,100	1,825	—
997	Ambassador sdn 4d	4,050	1,825	—
994	lwb sdn 7P	4,170	1,925	—
995	limo 7P (lwb)	4,210	2,025	—
1060 Big Six (wb 116.0) - 6,564 built				
1061	conv rdstr 2-4P	3,120	895	—
1062	cpe 2P	3,050	777	—
1062R	cpe 2-4P	3,100	825	—
1060	sdn 4d	3,200	840	—
1063	conv sdn 2d	3,125	935	—
1067	Town sdn 4d	3,150	825	—
1070 Standard Eight (wb 121.0) - 4,069 built				
1071	conv rdstr 2-4P	3,270	1,055	—

1070 Standard Eight		Wght	Price	Prod
1072	cpe 2P	3,250	1,072	—
1072R	cpe 2-4P	3,300	1,015	—
1070	sdn 4d	3,400	1,015	—
1073	conv sdn 2d	3,275	1,095	—
1077	Town sdn 4d	3,400	975	—
1080 Spec Eight (wb 128.0)-3,221 built				
1081	conv rdstr 2-4P	3,750	1,395	—
1082	cpe 2P	3,710	1,270	—
1082R	cpe 2-4P	3,800	1,320	—
1089	victoria cpe 2d	3,840	1,395	—
1080	sdn 4d	3,870	1,320	—
1083	conv sdn 4d	4,000	1,475	—
1090 Advanced Eight (wb 133.0) - 1,891 built*				
1091	conv rdstr 2-4P	4,270	1,795	—
1092R	cpe 2-4P	4,300	1,695	—
1099	victoria cpe 2d	4,300	1,785	—
1090	sdn 4d	4,350	1,595	—
1093	conv sdn 4d	4,470	1,875	—
1090 Ambassador Eight (wb 142.0)*				
1096	sdn 4d	4,510	1,855	—
1097	brougham 4d	4,470	1,855	—
1094	sdn 7P	4,600	1,955	—
1095	limo 7P	4,650	2,055	—

* Includes Ambassador Eight.

1932 Engines	bore×stroke	bhp	availability
I-6, 201.3	3.13×4.38	65	S-960
I-6, 201.3	3.13×4.38	70	S-1060
I-8, 227.2	2.88×4.38	78	S-970
I-8, 240.0	3.00×4.25	94	S-980 (T. Ign.)
I-8, 247.4	3.00×4.38	85	S-1070
I-8, 260.8	3.13×4.25	100	S-1080 (T. Ign.)
I-8, 298.6	3.25×4.50	115	S-990 (T .Ign.)
I-8, 322.0	3.38×4.50	125	S-1090 (T. Ign.)

1933

1120 Big Six (wb 116.0) - 4,600 blt		Wght	Price	Prod
1120	sdn 4d	3,125	745	—
1121	conv rdstr 2-4P	3,000	810	—
1122	cpe 2P	3,000	725	—
1122R	cpe 2-4P	3,050	745	—
1127	Town sdn 4d	3,125	695	—
1130 Standard Eight (wb 116.0)*				
1130	sdn 4d	3,200	845	—
1131	conv rdstr 2-4P	3,050	900	—
1132	cpe 2P	3,050	830	—
1132R	cpe 2-4P	3,100	845	—
1137	Town sdn 4d	3,175	830	—
1170 Special Eight (wb 121.0)*				
1170	sdn 4d	3,400	1,015	—
1171	conv rdstr 2-4P	3,270	1,055	—
1172	cpe 2P	3,250	965	—
1172R	cpe 2-4P	3,300	1,015	—
1173	conv sdn 2d	3,275	1,095	—
1177	Town sdn 4d	3,400	975	—
1180 Advanced Eight (wb 128.0) - 780 built				
1180	sdn 4d	3,870	1,320	—
1181	conv rdstr 2-4P	3,750	1,395	—
1182	cpe 2P	3,710	1,255	—
1182R	cpe 2-4P	3,800	1,275	—
1183	conv sdn 4d	4,000	1,575	—
1189	victoria 5P	3,840	1,395	—
1190 Amb Eight (wb 133.0; lwb 142.0) - 610 built				
1190	sdn 4d	4,350	1,575	—
1191	conv rdstr 2-4P	4,270	1,645	—
1192R	cpe 2-4P	4,300	1,545	—
1193	conv sdn 4d	4,470	1,875	—
1194	lwb sdn 7P	4,600	1,955	—
1195	limo 7P (lwb)	4,650	2,055	—
1196	lwb sdn 4d	4,510	1,855	—
1197	lwb brougham 4d	4,470	1,820	—
1199	victoria 5P	4,300	1,785	—

* Production not available.

1933 Engines	bore×stroke	bhp	availability
I-6, 217.8	3.25×4.38	75	S-1120
I-8, 247.4	3.00×4.38	80	S-1130
I-8, 247.4	3.00×4.38	85	S-1170
I-8, 260.8	3.13×4.25	100	S-1180 (T. Ign.)
I-8, 322.0	3.38×4.50	125	S-1190 (T. Ign.)

1934 - 23,616 built*

1220 Big Six (wb 116.0)		Wght	Price	Prod
1220	sdn 4d	3,370	755	—
1222	cpe 2P	3,290	735	—
1222R	cpe 2-4P	3,340	755	—
1223	brougham 5P T/B	3,400	745	—
1227	Town sdn 4d	3,370	715	—
1228	brougham 5P	3,400	785	—
1280 Advanced Eight (wb 121.0)				
1280	sdn 4d	3,540	995	—
1282	cpe 2P	3,460	965	—
1285R	cpe 2-4P	3,510	985	—
1283	brougham 5P T/B	3,570	995	—
1287	Town sdn 4d	3,540	965	—
1288	brougham 5P	3,370	1,025	—
1290 Ambassador Eight (wb 133.0; lwb-142.0)				
1290	sdn 4d	4,330	1,475	—
1293	sdn 4d T/B	4,360	1,505	—
1294	lwb sdn 7P	4,590	1,805	—
1295	limo 7P (lwb)	4,640	1,905	—
1297	lwb brougham 5P	4,460	1,670	—

1934 Engines	bore×stroke	bhp	availability
I-6, 234.0	3.38×4.38	88	S-1220 (T. Ign.)
I-8, 260.8	3.13×4.25	100	S-1280 (T. Ign.)
I-8, 322.0	3.38×4.50	125	S-1290 (T. Ign.)

* Calendar-year registrations.

1935 - 35,184 built*

3520 Adv Six (wb 120.0)		Wght	Price	Prod
3520	sdn 4d 6W	3,630	875	—
3525	victoria 6P	3,540	825	—
3580 Advanced Eight (wb 125.0)				
3580	sdn 4d 6W	3,750	1,095	—
3585	victoria 6P	3,660	1,045	—
3580 Ambassador Eight (wb 125.0)				
3588	sdn 4d 6W	3,750	1,220	—
3589	victoria 6P	3,660	1,170	—

1935 Engines	bore×stroke	bhp	availability
I-6, 234.8	3.38×4.38	90	S-3520
I-8, 260.8	3.13×4.25	102	S-3580 (T. Ign.)

* Calendar-year registrations.

1936 - 43,070 built*

3640 "400" New Six (wb 117.0)		Wght	Price	Prod
3640	sdn 4d	2,970	765	—
3642	bus cpe 3P	2,900	675	—
3642R	cpe 3-5P	2,960	725	—
3643	touring vic 6P T/B	2,970	745	—
3645	victoria 6P	2,950	715	—
3648	touring sdn 4d T/B	3,000	790	—
3640A "400" Deluxe (wb 117.0)				
3640A	sdn 4d	3,020	765	—
3641A	special cab 3-5P	3,800	800	—
3642A	bus cpe 3P	2,950	675	—
3642A-R	cpe 3-5P	3,010	725	—
3643A	touring vic 6P T/B	3,020	745	—
3645A	victoria 5P	3,000	715	—
3648	sdn 4d T/B	3,050	790	—
3620 Ambassador Six (wb 125.0)				
3620	sdn 4d T/B	3,710	885	—
3625	victoria 6P	3,710	835	—
3680 Ambassador Super Eight (wb 125.0)				
3680	sdn 4d T/B	3,820	995	—

1936 Engines	bore×stroke	bhp	availability
I-6, 234.8	3.38×4.38	90	S-3640, 3640A
I-8, 234.8	3.38×4.38	93	S-3620
I-8, 260.8	3.13×4.25	102	S-3680 (T. Ign.)

*Calendar-year registrations

1937 - 85,949 built

3710 Lafayette 400 (wb 117.0)		Wght	Price	Prod
3711	cabriolet 3-5P	3,180	885	—
3712	bus cpe 3P	3,140	740	—
3712A	All-Purpose cpe	3,160	805	—
3712R	cpe 3-5P	3,190	795	—
3713	victoria 2d 6P	3,200	800	—
3718	sdn 4d T/B	3,240	845	—
3720 Ambassador Six (wb 121.0)				
3721	cabriolet 3-5P	3,320	1,040	—

3720 Ambassador Six		Wght	Price	Prod
3722	bus cpe 3P	3,290	935	—
3722A	All-Purpose cpe	3,310	990	—
3722R	cpe 3-5P	3,320	975	—
3723	victoria 2d 6P	3,380	975	—
3728	sdn 4d T/B	3,400	1,025	—
3780 Amb Eight (wb 125.0)				
3781	cabriolet 3-5P	3,640	1,180	—
3782	bus cpe 3P	3,590	1,075	—
3782A	All-Purpose cpe	3,610	1,130	—
3782R	cpe 3-5P	3,640	1,115	—
3783	victoria 2d 6P	3,690	1,115	—
3788	sdn 4d T/B	3,720	1,165	—

1937 Engines	bore×stroke	bhp	availability
I-6, 234.8	3.38×4.38	90	S-3710
I-6, 234.8	3.38×4.38	105	S-3720
I-8, 260.8	3.13×4.25	115	S-3780 (T. Ign.)

1938 - 32,017 built

3810 Lafayette (wb 117.0)		Wght	Price	Prod
3811	Deluxe cab 3-5P	3,240	940	—
3812	Delx All-Purpose cpe	3,230	860	—
3813	Deluxe victoria 6P	3,290	855	—
3814	Deluxe bus cpe 2P	3,160	820	—
3815	Master bus cpe 3P	3,120	770	—
3816	Master victoria 2d 6P	3,190	805	—
3817	Master sdn 4d T/B	3,200	850	—
3818	Deluxe sdn 4d T/B	3,300	900	—
3820 Ambassador Six (wb 121.0)				
3821	cabriolet 3-5P	3,340	1,099	—
3822	All-Purpose cpe	3,360	1,015	—
3823	victoria 6P	3,450	1,000	—
3825	bus cpe 3P	3,300	970	—
3828	sdn 4d T/B	3,460	1,050	—
3880 Ambassador Eight (wb 125.0)				
3881	cabriolet 3-5P	3,620	1,240	—
3882	All-Purpose cpe	3,640	1,165	—
3883	victoria 6P	3,780	1,150	—
3885	bus cpe 3P	3,580	1,120	—
3888	sdn 4d T/B	3,790	1,200	—

1938 Engines	bore ×stroke	bhp	availability
I-6, 234.8	3.38×4.38	95	S-3810
I-6, 234.8	3.38×4.38	105	S-3820
I-8, 260.8	3.13×4.25	115	S-3880 (T. Ign.)

1939

3910 Lafayette (wb117.0) - 37,302 blt*		Wght	Price	Prod
3910	Deluxe sdn 4d T/B	3,350	885	—
3911	Delx All-Purp cab 5P	3,340	950	—
3912	Delx All-Purp cpe 5P	3,260	860	—
3913	Deluxe sdn 2d	3,320	855	—
3914	Deluxe bus cpe 3P	3,270	825	—
3915	Special bus cpe 3P	3,200	770	—
3916	Special sdn 2d	3,250	810	—
3917	Special sdn 4d	3,290	840	—
3918	Deluxe sdn 4d	3,350	855	—
3919	Special sdn 4d I/B	3,285	840	—
3920 Ambassador Six (wb 121.0) - 8,500 built*				
3920	sdn 4d T/B	3,470	985	—
3921	All-Purpose cab 5P	3,430	1,050	—
3922	All-Purpose cpe 5P	3,360	960	—
3923	sdn 2d	3,420	955	—
3925	bus cpe 3P	3,370	925	—
3928	sdn 4d	3,450	985	—
3980 Ambassador Eight (wb 125.0) - 17,052 built*				
3980	sdn 4d T/B	3,820	1,235	—
3981	All-Purpose cab 5P	3,740	1,295	—
3982	All-Purpose cpe 5P	3,710	1,210	—
3983	sdn 2d	3,770	1,205	—
3985	bus cpe 3P	3,720	1,175	—
3988	sdn 4d	3,800	1,235	—

1939 Engines	bore×stroke	bhp	availability
I-6, 234.8	3.38×4.38	99	S-3910
I-6, 234.8	3.38×4.38	105	S-3920
I-8, 260.8	3.13×4.25	115	S-3980 (T. Ign.)

* Maximum possible production, derived from published serial number spans.

1940

Lafayette (wb 117.0)		Wght	Price	Prod
4010	T/B sdn 4d	3,280	875	17,748

Lafayette		Wght	Price	Prod
4011	All-Purpose cabriolet	3,310	975	901
4012	All-Purpose cpe	3,190	850	1,699
4013	fstbk sdn 2d	3,235	845	9,670
4014	bus cpe	3,190	795	3,865
4018	fstbk sdn 4d	3,275	875	12,369
Ambassador Six (wb 121.0)				
4020	T/B sdn 4d	3,385	985	7,248
4021	All-Purpose cabriolet	3,410	1,085	206
4022	All-Purpose cpe	3,295	960	516
4023	fstbk sdn 2d	3,350	955	554
4025	bus cpe	3,290	925	323
4028	fstbk sdn 4d	3,380	985	3,653
Ambassador Eight (wb 125.0)				
4080	T/B sdn 4d	3,660	1,195	2,086
4081	All-Purpose cabriolet	3,640	1,295	93
4082	All-Purpose cpe	3,575	1,170	123
4083	fstbk sdn 2d	3,620	1,165	26
4085	bus cpe	3,555	1,135	44
4088	fstbk sdn 4d	3,655	1,195	878

1940 Engines	bore×stroke	bhp	availability
I-6, 234.8	3.38×4.38	99	S-Lafayette
I-6, 234.8	3.38×4.38	105	S-Amb Six
I-8, 260.8	3.13×4.25	115	S-Amb Eight (T. Ign.)

1941 - 84,007 built

600 (wb 112.0)		Wght	Price	Prod
4140	DeLuxe T/B sdn 4d	2,655	860	—
4142	DeLuxe bus cpe	2,500	783	—
4143	DeLuxe Brghm 2d	2,575	810	—
4145	Special bus cpe	2,490	731	—
4146	Special fstbk cpe	2,630	745	—
4147	Special fstbk sdn 4d	2,615	780	—
4148	DeLuxe fstbk sdn 4d	2,630	810	—
4149	DeLuxe fstbk sdn 2d	2,640	777	—
Ambassador Six (wb 121.0)				
4160	T/B sdn 4d	3,300	1,065	—
4161	All-Purpose cabriolet	3,430	1,130	—
4162	bus cpe	3,180	940	—
4163	Brougham 2d	3,235	1,009	—
4165	Special bus cpe	3,310	890	—
4167	Special fstbk sdn 4d	3,300	970	—
4168	fstbk sdn 4d	3,300	1,020	—
4169	Special sdn 2d	3,320	933	—
Ambassador Eight (wb 121.0)				
4180	T/B sdn 4d	3,475	1,186	—
4181	All-Purpose cabriolet	3,580	1,250	—
4183	DeLuxe Brougham 2d	3,400	1,116	—
4187	Special fstbk sdn 4d	3,465	1,091	—
4188	DeLuxe fstbk sdn 4d	3,455	1,141	—

1941 Engines	bore×stroke	bhp	availability
I-6, 172.6	3.13×3.75	75	S-600
I-6, 234.8	3.38×4.38	105	S-Amb Six
I-8, 260.8	3.13×4.25	115	S-Amb Eight (T. Ign.)

1942 - 31,780 built

600 (wb 112.0)		Wght	Price	Prod
4240	T/B sdn 4d	2,655	993	—
4242	bus cpe	2,540	918	—
4243	Brougham 2d	2,580	958	—
4248	fstbk sdn 4d	2,650	968	—
4249	fstbk sdn 2d	2,605	948	—
Ambassador Six (wb 121.0)				
4260	T/B sdn 4d	3,335	1,069	—
4262	bus cpe	3,200	994	—
4263	Brougham 2d	3,230	1,034	—
4268	fstbk sdn 4d	3,335	1,044	—
4269	sdn 2d	3,285	1,024	—
Ambassador Eight (wb 121.0)				
4280	T/B sdn 4d	3,485	1,119	—
4282	bus cpe	3,350	1,035	—
4283	Brougham 2d	3,385	1,084	—
4288	fstbk sdn 4d	3,485	1,094	—
4289	fstbk sdn 2d	3,435	1,065	—

1942 Engines	bore×stroke	bhp	availability
I-6, 172.6	3.13×3.75	75	S-600
I-6, 234.8	3.38×4.38	105	S-Amb Six
I-8, 260.8	3.13×4.25	115	S-Amb Eight

1946

600 (wb 112.0)		Wght	Price	Prod
4640	T/B sdn 4d	2,740	1,342	7,300
4643	Brougham 2d	2,685	1,293	8,500
4648	fstbk sdn 4d	2,780	1,298	42,300
Ambassador (wb 121.0)				
4660	T/B sdn 4d	3,335	1,511	3,875
4663	Brougham 2d	3,260	1,453	4,825
4664	Suburban sdn 4d	3,470	1,929	275
4668	fstbk sdn 4d	3,360	1,469	26,925

1946 Engines	bore×stroke	bhp	availability
I-6, 172.6	3.13×3.75	82	S-600
I-6, 234.8	3.38×4.38	112	S-Ambassador

1947

600 (wb 112.0)		Wght	Price	Prod
4740	T/B sdn 4d	2,740	1,464	21,500
4743	Brougham 2d	2,685	1,415	12,100
4748	fstbk sdn 4d	2,780	1,420	27,700
Ambassador (wb 121.0)				
4760	T/B sdn 4d	3,335	1,809	15,927
4763	Brougham 2d	3,260	1,751	8,673
4764	Suburban sdn 4d	3,420	2,227	595
4788	fstbk sdn 4d	3,360	1,767	14,505

1947 Engines	bore×stroke	bhp	availability
I-6, 172.6	3.13×3.75	82	S-600
I-6, 234.8	3.38×4.38	112	S-Ambassador

1948

600 (wb 112.0)		Wght	Price	Prod
4840	Super T/B sdn 4d	2,786	1,587	25,103
4842	DeLuxe bus cpe	2,635	1,478	925
4843	Super Brougham 2d	2,731	1,538	11,530
4848	Super fstbk sdn 4d	2,826	1,543	25,044
4850	Custom T/B sdn 4d	2,786	1,776	346
4853	Custom Brghm 2d	2,731	1,727	170
4858	Custom fstbk sdn 4d	2,826	1,732	332
Ambassador (wb 121.0)				
4860	Super T/B sdn 4d	3,387	1,916	14,248
4863	Super Brougham 2d	3,312	1,858	7,221
4864	Super Subrbn sdn 4d	3,522	2,239	130
4868	Super fstbk sdn 4d	3,412	1,874	14,777
4870	Custom T/B sdn 4d	3,387	2,105	4,102
4871	Cust cabriolet (conv)	3,465	2,345	1,000
4873	Custom Brghm 2d	3,312	2,047	929
4878	Custom fstbk sdn 4d	3,412	2,063	4,143

1948 Engines	bore×stroke	bhp	availability
I-6, 172.6	3.13×3.75	82	S-600
I-6, 234.8	3.38×4.38	112	S-Ambassador

1949

600 (wb 112.0)		Wght	Price	Prod
4923	Super Spec Brghm 2d	2,960	1,846	2,564
4928	Super Special sdn 4d	2,950	1,849	23,606
4929	Super Special sdn 2d	2,935	1,824	9,605
4943	Super Brougham 2d	2,960	1,808	2,954
4948	Super sdn 4d	2,950	1,811	31,194
4949	Super sdn 2d	2,935	1,786	17,006
4953	Custom Brghm 2d	2,970	1,997	17
4958	Custom sdn 4d	2,985	2,000	199
4959	Custom sdn 2d	2,985	1,975	29
Ambassador (wb 121.0)				
4963	Super Brougham 2d	3,390	2,191	1,541
4968	Super sdn 4d	3,385	2,195	17,960
4969	Super sdn 2d	3,365	2,170	4,602
4973	Custom Brghm 2d	3,415	2,359	1,837
4978	Custom sdn 4d	3,415	2,363	6,539
4979	Custom sdn 2d	3,400	2,338	691
4993	Super Spec Brghm 2d	3,390	2,239	807
4998	Super Special sdn 4d	3,385	2,243	6,777
4999	Super Special sdn 2d	3,365	2,218	2,072

1949 Engines	bore×stroke	bhp	availability
I-6, 172.6	3.13×3.75	82	S-600
I-6, 234.8	3.38×4.38	112	S-Ambassador

1950

Rambler (wb 100.0)		Wght	Price	Prod
5021	Cust Landau conv cpe	2,430	1,808	9,330
5024	Custom wgn 2d	2,515	1,808	1,712
Statesman (wb 112.0)				
5032	DeLuxe bus cpe	2,830	1,633	1,198

Statesman		Wght	Price	Prod
5043	Super club cpe	2,940	1,735	1,489
5048	Super sdn 4d	2,965	1,738	60,090
5049	Super sdn 2d	2,930	1,713	34,196
5053	Custom club cpe	2,965	1,894	132
5058	Custom sdn 4d	2,990	1,897	11,500
5059	Custom sdn 2d	2,950	1,872	2,693
Ambassador (wb 121.0)				
5063	Super club cpe	3,335	2,060	716
5068	Super sdn 4d	3,350	2,064	27,523
5069	Super sdn 2d	3,325	2,039	7,237
5073	Custom club cpe	3,385	2,219	108
5078	Custom sdn 4d	3,390	2,223	12,427
5079	Custom sdn 2d	3,365	2,198	1,045

1950 Engines	bore×stroke	bhp	availability
I-6, 172.6	3.13×3.75	82	S-Rambler
I-6, 184.0	3.13×4.00	85	S-Statesman
I-6, 234.8	3.38×4.38	115	S-Ambassador

1951

Rambler (wb 100.0)		Wght	Price	Prod
5114	Super Subrbn wgn 2d	2,515	1,885	5,568
5121	Custom conv cpe	2,430	1,993	15,259
5124	Custom wgn 2d	2,517	1,993	28,618
5127	Cust Cntry Clb htp cpe	2,420	1,968	19,317
Statesman (wb 112.0)				
5132	DeLuxe bus cpe	2,835	1,841	52
5143	Super club cpe	2,935	1,952	152
5148	Super sdn 4d	2,970	1,955	52,325
5149	Super sdn 2d	2,930	1,928	22,261
5153	Custom club cpe	2,950	2,122	38
5158	Custom sdn 4d	2,990	2,125	18,846
5159	Custom sdn 2d	2,940	2,099	2,141
Ambassador (wb 121.0)				
5163	Super club cpe	3,370	2,326	40
5168	Super sdn 4d	3,410	2,330	34,935
5169	Super sdn 2d	3,370	2,304	4,382
5173	Custom club cpe	3,395	2,496	37
5178	Custom sdn 4d	3,445	2,501	21,071
5179	Custom sdn 2d	3,380	2,474	1,118

1951 Engines	bore×stroke	bhp	availability
I-6, 172.6	3.13×3.75	82	S-Rambler
I-6, 184.0	3.13×4.00	85	S-Statesman
I-6, 234.8	3.38×4.38	115	S-Ambassador

1952

Rambler (wb 100.0)		Wght	Price	Prod
5214	Super Subrbn wgn 2d	2,515	2,003	2,970
5221	Custom conv cpe	2,430	2,119	3,108
5224	Custom wgn 2d	2,515	2,119	19,889
5227	Cust Cntry Clb htp cpe	2,420	2,094	25,784
Statesman (wb 114.3)				
5245	Super sdn 4d	3,045	2,178	27,304
5246	Super sdn 2d	3,025	2,144	6,795
5255	Custom sdn 4d	3,070	2,332	13,660
5256	Custom sdn 2d	3,050	2,310	1,872
5257	Cust Cntry Clb htp cpe	3,095	2,433	869
Ambassador (wb 121.3)				
5265	Super sdn 4d	3,430	2,557	16,838
5266	Super sdn 2d	3,410	2,521	1,871
5275	Custom sdn 4d	3,480	2,716	19,585
5276	Custom sdn 2d	3,450	2,695	1,178
5277	Cust Cntry Clb htp cpe	3,550	2,829	1,228

1952 Engines	bore×stroke	bhp	availability
I-6, 172.6	3.13×3.75	82	S-Rambler
I-6, 195.6	3.13×4.25	88	S-Statesman
I-6, 252.6	3.50×4.38	120	S-Ambassador

1953

Rambler (wb 100.0)		Wght	Price	Prod
5314	Super Subrbn wgn 2d	2,555	2,003	1,114
5321	Custom conv cpe	2,590	2,150	3,284
5324	Custom wgn 2d	2,570	2,119	10,571
5327	Cust Cntry Clb htp cpe	2,550	2,125	16,809
Statesman (wb 114.3)				
5345	Super sdn 4d	3,045	2,178	28,445
5346	Super sdn 2d	3,025	2,143	7,999
5355	Custom sdn 4d	3,070	2,332	11,476
5356	Custom sdn 2d	3,050	2,310	1,305
5357	Cust Cntry Clb htp cpe	3,095	2,433	7,025

Ambassador (wb 121.3)		Wght	Price	Prod
5365	Super sdn 4d	3,430	2,557	12,489
5366	Super sdn 2d	3,410	2,521	1,273
5375	Custom sdn 4d	3,480	2,716	12,222
5376	Custom sdn 2d	3,450	2,695	428
5377	Cust Cntry Clb htp cpe	3,550	2,829	6,438

1953 Engines	bore×stroke	bhp	availability
I-6, 184.0	3.13×4.00	85	S-Ramb man
I-6, 195.6	3.13×4.25	90	S-Ramb auto
I-6, 195.6	3.13×4.25	100	S-Statesman
I-6, 252.6	3.50×4.38	120	S-Ambassador
I-6, 252.6	3.50×4.38	140	O-Ambassador

1954

Rambler (wb 100.0; 4d-108.0)		Wght	Price	Prod
5406	DeLuxe sdn 2d	2,425	1,550	7,273
5414	Super Subrbn wgn 2d	2,520	1,800	504
5415	Super sdn 4d	2,570	1,795	4,313
5416	Super sdn 2d	2,425	1,700	300
5417	Spr Cntry Clb htp cpe	2,465	1,800	1,071
5421	Custom conv cpe	2,555	1,980	221
5424	Custom wgn 2d	2,535	1,950	2,202
5425	Custom sdn 4d	2,630	1,965	7,640
5427	Cust Cntry Clb htp cpe	2,515	1,950	3,612
5428	Cust Crs Cntry wgn 4d	2,715	2,050	9,039
Statesman (wb 114.3)				
5445	Super sdn 4d	3,045	2,158	11,401
5446	Super sdn 2d	3,025	2,110	1,855
5455	Custom sdn 4d	3,095	2,332	4,219
—	Custom sdn 2d	3,050	2,310	24
5457	Cust Cntry Clb htp cpe	3,120	2,423	2,276
Ambassador (wb 121.3)				
5465	Super sdn 4d	3,430	2,417	7,433
5466	Super sdn 2d	3,410	2,365	283
5475	Custom sdn 4d	3,505	2,600	10,131
5477	Cust Cntry Clb htp cpe	3,575	2,735	3,581

1954 Engines	bore×stroke	bhp	availability
I-6, 184.0	3.13×4.00	85	S-Ramb 2d man
I-6, 195.6	3.13×4.25	90	S-Rambler 4d, 2d auto
I-6, 195.6	3.13×4.25	110	S-Statesman
I-6, 252.6	3.50×4.38	130	S-Ambassador
I-6, 252.6	3.50×4.38	140	O-Ambassador

1955

Rambler (wb 100.0; 4d-108.0) - 56,000 built*		Wght	Price	Prod
5512	Fleet bus sdn 2d	2,400	—	—
5514	DeLx Subrbn wgn 2d	2,528	1,771	—
5514-1	Super Subrbn wgn 2d	2,532	1,869	—
5515	DeLuxe sdn 4d	2,567	1,695	—
5515-1	Super sdn 4d	2,570	1,798	—
5515-2	Custom sdn 4d	2,606	1,989	—
5516	DeLuxe sdn 2d	2,432	1,585	—
5516-1	Super sdn 2d	2,450	1,683	—
5517-2	Cust Cntry Clb htp cpe	2,518	1,995	—
5518-1	Flt Crs Cntry wgn 4d	2,675	—	—
5518-2	Cust Crs Cntry wgn 4d	2,685	2,098	—
2504	Fleet util wgn 2d	2,500	—	—
Statesman (wb 114.3) - 14,300 built*				
5545-1	Super sdn 4d	3,134	2,215	—
5545-2	Custom sdn 4d	3,204	2,385	—
5547-2	Cust Cntry Clb htp cpe	3,220	2,495	—
Ambassador Six (wb 121.3) - 15,200 built*				
5565-1	Super sdn 4d	3,538	2,480	—
5565-2	Custom sdn 4d	3,576	2,675	—
5567-2	Cust Cntry Clb htp cpe	3,593	2,795	—
Ambassador Eight (wb 121.3) - 10,600 built*				
5585-1	Super sdn 4d	3,795	2,775	—
5585-2	Custom sdn 4d	3,827	2,965	—
5587-2	Cust Cntry Clb htp cpe	3,839	3,095	—

*To nearest 100.

1955 Engines	bore×stroke	bhp	availability
I-6, 195.6	3.13×4.25	90	S-Rambler exc Fleet
I-6, 195.6	3.13×4.25	100	S-Ramb Fleet, States manual
I-6, 195.6	3.13×4.25	110	S-States auto
I-6, 252.6	3.50×4.38	130	S-Amb Six
I-6, 252.6	3.50×4.38	140	O-Amb Six
V-8, 320.0	3.81×3.50	208	S-Amb Eight

1956

Rambler (wb 108.0)*		Wght	Price	Prod
5613-2	Cust Crs Cntry htp wgn 4d	3,095	2,494	—
5615	DeLuxe sdn 4d	2,891	1,829	—
5615-1	Super sdn 4d	2,906	1,939	—
5615-2	Custom sdn 4d	2,929	2,059	—
5618-1	Supr Crs Cntry wgn 4d	2,992	2,233	—
5618-2	Cust Crs Cntry wgn 4d	3,110	2,329	—
5619-1	Custom htp sdn	2,990	2,224	—
Statesman (wb 114.3)*				
5645-1	Super sdn 4d	3,134	2,139	—
Ambassador Special (wb 114.3) - 4,145 built*				
5657-1	sdn 4d	3,397	2,355	—
5657-2	Country Club htp cpe	3,418	2,462	—
5657-3	Custom sdn 4d	3,567	2,541	—
Ambassador Six (wb 121.3)*				
5665-1	Super sdn 4d	3,555	2,425	—
Ambassador Eight (wb 121.3)*				
5685-1	Super sdn 4d	3,748	2,716	—
5685-2	Custom sdn 4d	3,846	2,939	—
5687-2	Cust Cntry Clb htp cpe	3,854	3,072	—

* Estimated Rambler production: 10,000; total Statesman/Ambassador: 14,352.

1956 Engines	bore×stroke	bhp	availability
I-6, 195.6	3.13×4.25	120	S-Rambler, Statesman
I-6, 252.6	3.50×4.38	130	S-Amb Six
I-6, 252.6	3.50×4.38	140	O-Amb Six
V-8, 250.0	3.50×3.25	190	S-Amb Special
V-8, 352.0	4.00×3.33	200	S-Amb Eight

1957*

Amb Super (wb 121.3)		Wght	Price	Prod
5785-1	sdn 4d	3,639	2,586	—
5787-1	Country Club htp cpe	3,655	2,670	—
Ambassador Custom (wb 121.3)				
5785-2	sdn 4d	3,701	2,763	—
5787-2	Country Club htp cpe	3,722	2,847	—

* Approximate model-year production: 3,600.

1957 Engine	bore×stroke	bhp	availability
V-8, 327.0	4.00×3.25	255	S-all

Note: See Rambler listing for 1957 and later models.

Nash Metropolitan Specifications

1954

Series 54 (wb 85.0) - 11,198 blt*		Wght	Price	Prod
541	conv cpe 3P	1,803	1,469	—
542	cpe 3P	1,843	1,445	—

* Includes 571 shipments in 1953.

1954 Engine	bore×stroke	bhp	availability
I-4, 73.8	2.56×3.50	42	S-all

1955

Series 54 (wb 85.0) - 3,849 blt		Wght	Price	Prod
541	conv cpe 3P	1,803	1,469	—
542	cpe 3P	1,843	1,445	—

1955 Engine	bore×stroke	bhp	availability
I-4, 73.8	2.56×3.50	42	S-all

1956 - 7,645 built

Series 54 (wb 85.0)		Wght	Price	Prod
541	conv cpe 3P	1,803	1,469	—
542	cpe 3P	1,843	1,445	—
Series 56 "1500" (wb 85.0)				
561	conv cpe 3P	1,803	1,551	—
562	cpe 3P	1,843	1,527	—

1956 Engines	bore×stroke	bhp	availability
I-4, 73.8	2.56×3.50	42	S-Ser 54 (1200)
I-4, 90.9	2.88×3.50	52	S-Ser 56 (1500)

1957

Ser 56 "1500" (wb 85.0) - 13,425 blt		Wght	Price	Prod
561	conv cpe 3P	1,803	1,591	—
562	cpe 3P	1,843	1,567	—

1957 Engine	bore×stroke	bhp	availability
I-4, 90.9	2.88×3.50	52	S-all

1958

Ser 56 "1500" (wb 85.0) - 11,951 blt		Wght	Price	Prod
561	conv cpe 3P	1,835	1,650	—
562	cpe 3P	1,875	1,626	—

1958 Engine	bore×stroke	bhp	availability
I-4, 90.9	2.88×3.50	52	S-all

1959

Ser 56 "1500" (wb 85.0) - 20,435 blt		Wght	Price	Prod
561	conv cpe 3P	1,835	1,650	—
562	cpe 3P	1,875	1,626	—

1959 Engine	bore×stroke	bhp	availability
I-4, 90.9	2.88×3.50	55/52	S-all

1960

Ser 56 "1500" (wb 85.0) - 13,103 blt		Wght	Price	Prod
561	conv cpe 3P	1,850	1,697	—
562	cpe 3P	1,890	1,673	—

1960 Engine	bore×stroke	bhp	availability
I-4, 90.9	2.88×3.50	55/52	S-all

1961

Series 56 "1500" (wb 85.0) - 853 blt		Wght	Price	Prod
561	conv cpe 3P	1,850	1,697	—
562	cpe 3P	1,890	1,673	—

1961 Engine	bore×stroke	bhp	availability
I-4, 90.9	2.88×3.50	55/52	S-all

1962

Series 56 "1500" (wb 85.0) - 412 blt		Wght	Price	Prod
561	conv cpe 3P	1,850	1,697	—
562	cpe 3P	1,890	1,673	—

1962 Engine	bore×stroke	bhp	availability
I-4, 90.9	2.88×3.50	55/52	S-all

Note: Metropolitans were built in England but marketed by American Motors as Nash and Hudson models. See 1955-57 Hudson listings for additional Metropolitan models. Sold with "Metropolitan" badge 1958-62.

Oldsmobile

There was a time when Oldsmobile, not Chevy or Ford, was America's leading car producer. That time was 1903-05, when Lansing rolled to success with Ransom Eli Olds' little curved-dash runabout, which was then selling in the thousands each year. Ransom had cobbled up his first car in 1891, strictly as an experiment. Regular production got under way in 1897, the same year the Olds Motor Vehicle Company was formed. (The concern was reorganized as Olds Motor Works two years later.) Ultimately, Oldsmobile became the only American automaker founded in the 19th century to survive into the 21st.

A decline set in soon after Ransom left to form Reo in 1904 (see *Reo*). General Motors bought Olds Motor Works four years later, but that didn't help sales right way. Not until its side-valve V-8 of 1916 did Oldsmobile again do healthy business. The make's best pre-Depression years were 1919, 1921, and 1929, when it finished ninth on the industry chart. Its worst model year during the Depression was 1932: only 18,846 cars. But the division recovered rapidly, notching more than 191,000 sales for 1936. A recession cut 1938 output to 85,000, but Olds rallied quickly, then reached a new high with 1941 domestic volume of nearly 266,000. It would do far better in the '50s, '60s, and '70s.

Innovation was an Olds hallmark in the 1930s, the make (among others) pioneering Dubonnet-type "Knee-Action" independent front suspension for '34, a semiautomatic transmission for 1937-39, and completely automatic Hydra-Matic Drive for 1940. Features like these earned Olds its longtime reputation as GM's "experimental" division, a role it would play through the late '60s.

Much of Oldsmobile's technical daring in the '30s was spurred by Charles L. McCuen, who had been chief engineer before becoming division general manager in 1933. To take his place as chief engineer, he recruited another innovator, Harold T. Youngren. Working under him were experimental engineering manager Jack Wolfram and dynamometer wizard Harold Metzel. The last two became division chiefs in later years. Youngren left in 1946 to help develop Ford's engineering department.

Oldsmobile suffered less from the Depression than most other makes, thanks to conservative but salable styling and a fairly consistent lineup of six- and eight-cylinder models. Its L-head six began the decade at 197.5 cubic inches and 62-65

1930 Series F-30 DeLuxe Six four-door sedan

1932 Series L-32 Eight four-door sedan

1931 Series F-31 DeLuxe convertible roadster

1933 Series F-33 Six four-door sedan

1932 L-32 Eight two-door sedan

1934 Series F-34 Six 2/4-passenger sport coupe

brake horsepower. Olds' first straight-eight, another orthodox side-valve design, arrived for 1932 with 240 cubic inches and 87 bhp. These smooth, quiet, and reliable powerplants received important improvements as the decade wore on, such as aluminum pistons for 1936. The eight was otherwise unchanged, but the six grew to 213.3 cid and 74 bhp for 1932.

A major redesign for 1937 took the six to 230 cid and 95 bhp, the eight to 257 cid and 110 bhp. Additional changes that year comprised full-length water jackets, stiffer piston skirts and crankshaft, stronger cams and valve lifters, and longer valve guides. The eight continued in this form through '48, after which it was retired for the history-making overhead-valve "Rocket" V-8. The six would remain unchanged through 1940.

Oldsmobile's 1930s styling followed general industry trends: classically square through '32; slightly streamlined, with angled radiator and skirted fenders for 1933-34; "potato" shapes for 1935-36. After that, the pace of change picked up. Though the division used the same GM B-body as Cadillac's junior-edition LaSalle and the smaller Buicks, its cars managed to look quite individual. More-massive fronts with cross-hatched or horizontal-bar grilles appeared for 1937; the 1938-39s had GM design chief Harley Earl's flanking "catwalk" auxiliary grilles, plus headlamp pods partly faired into the front-fender aprons.

Prices in these years were carefully contrived to target a precise area above Pontiac and below Buick and LaSalle. The range was $900-$1100 through 1932, after which Depression-prompted cuts lowered Sixes to as little as $650 by '34. Prices then inched upward again, returning to the initial spread by '38.

1935 Series F-35 Six station wagon

1936 Series F-36 Six 2/4-passenger convertible coupe

1937 Series F-37 Six 2/4-passenger convertible coupe

Beside choices in wheelbase, engine, and trim, Olds offered styling options such as sidemount spare tires and—a bit ahead of most rivals—a choice of trunkless or "trunkback" sedans starting in 1933. Two notable innovations were Fisher Body's "No-Draft" front-door ventwing windows from 1934 and all-steel "Turret-Top" roof construction from 1935. Convertible coupes were always low-production items. Oddly enough, considering its pioneer ways, Olds was relatively slow to abandon sidemounts and rumble-seat body styles, persisting doggedly with both through 1938.

Lansing's 1930-31 line comprised popular period body styles in Standard, Special, and Deluxe trim, all on a 113.5-inch wheelbase. Trim variations then disappeared for 1932, when the Eight arrived and wheelbase grew to 116.5 inches across the board. Thereafter, Eights were mounted on chassis of 119 inches (1933-34), 121 inches (1935-36), and 124 inches (1937-38). Sixes rode a 115-inch platform from 1933 through 1936 except for '34, when they mysteriously lost an inch; they then graduated to a 117-inch length.

The two transmission innovations noted earlier deserve special comment. The first was "Automatic Safety Transmission" for 1937. This was a semiautomatic four-speed unit for eight-cylinder models that was similar in operation—but not mechanically identical to—Chrysler's subsequent Fluid Drive. Before moving off, the driver depressed the customary clutch pedal and selected Low or High range. The transmission then shifted between first and second in Low; or first, third, and fourth in High. Changes within each range were automatic via oil pressure and two planetary gearsets. Shift points were preset according to vehicle speed.

Olds said AST delivered up to 15-percent-better gas mileage than regular manual shift, but that was due to the numerically lower rear-axle ratio specified. The "safety" aspect referred to the claim that, with less shifting to do, the driver could keep both hands on the wheel more of the time. AST was an option for all 1938-39 Oldsmobiles, and some 28,000 were installed. But its real significance was in leading to Hydra-Matic for 1940.

Though Hydra-Matic also had four speeds, it was fully automatic, using a fluid coupling and a complex system of clutches and brake bands. It arrived at only $57 extra. That surely didn't reflect its true manufacturing or development costs, but both would be offset by high volume. Indeed, by the early '50s, Hydra-Matic had become not only a popular Olds option, but was also being offered by Cadillac and Pontiac as well as Lincoln and independents Nash, Hudson, and Kaiser-Frazer.

Oldsmobile's 1939 line boasted newly styled bodies in three groups: 115-inch-wheelbase Series 60, new 120-inch Series 70, and the similarly sized eight-cylinder Series 80. The 70 was powered by the 230 six; a 90 bhp 216-cid six drove the 60. All three series listed business and club coupes and two- and four-door sedans, the latter pair available in the 70 and 80 lines with "Sunshine Turret Top," an optional sliding metal sunroof that saw few installations. The 70 and 80 also included a convertible coupe. Prices ranged from $777 to $1119.

This basic lineup repeated for 1940 with slightly higher prices, reassigned wheelbases, somewhat smoother looks, and two new models. The 60 now rode a 116-inch platform, adopted the 230-cube six, and included a structural-wood station wagon bodied by Hercules. Replacing the 80 was a new 124-inch-wheelbase Series 90 that included Oldsmobile's first convertible sedan—called "phaeton" per GM practice—an odd latecomer, considering this body type was fast waning at other automakers. At $1570, the Series 90 phaeton was the costliest 1940 Olds, and production was predictably limited: just 50 in all. Styling throughout the line was typical of GM that year, with wider grilles and front fenders, semi-integrated headlights, and, on the 90s, smoother tails and rear rooflines.

A more massive look arrived for 1941. Grillework was lower and wider, and headlights now firmly resided within even wider front fenders that blended more smoothly into the bodysides. Series doubled as Olds offered both six and straight-eight models in two trim levels spanning a narrower $852-$1575 price range. Series designations denoted cylinders. The low-end Special 66 and 68 rode a new 119-inch wheelbase, while the Dynamic Cruiser 76 and 78 shared a 125-inch chassis with the top-line Custom Cruiser 96 and 98. The six was bored out to 238.1 cid for 100 bhp.

The same body styles returned for '41, but most were now available with either engine. The sole exception was the phaeton convertible sedan, which came only as a Custom Cruiser 98. Its production was again minuscule at only 119 for the model year, after which the division followed everyone else by dropping four-door convertibles. Fastback styling bowed in new Dynamic Cruiser four-door and club sedans. Four-door Custom Cruiser sedans again sported a handsome notchback profile with semi-closed rear-roof quarters. In March, the 66/68 expanded by adding a four-door Town Sedan with styling like the Series 90 model. Despite record model-year production, Olds finished sixth in the annual industry race. Though the division had risen as high as fifth for '36, it would usually run sixth or seventh into the mid-'50s.

Olds slipped to seventh for war-shortened 1942, but enjoyed respectable volume of just under 68,000 units. Styling for that year's "B-44" line featured "Fuselage Fenders"—elongated pontoon types faired into the front doors—and a busy, two-tier "double-duty" grille bisected by a prominent horizontal bar. Longer rear fenders tapered beyond the deck, but remained bolt-on components. Engines stayed the same, but not models. The six-cylinder 96 departed and the 98 was cut to convertible coupe, club sedan, and four-door sedan on a new 127-inch wheelbase. All series now offered "torpedo-style" club sedans, with plain and Deluxe versions for 76/78.

To help win World War II, Oldsmobile turned out 350,000 precision aero-engine parts, 175 million pounds of gun forgings, 140,000 machine guns, and millions of rounds of ammunition. It officially became the Oldsmobile Division of General Motors on New Year's Day 1942, thus ousting the Olds Motor Works title dating from 1899.

Like most everyone else, Olds returned to peacetime with warmed-over prewar cars. Business was good in the sell-anything market of the day—close to 118,000 for 1946 and about 200,000 for '47—yet Olds again ran seventh. Most '42 offerings returned with no changes in wheelbase, engines, or body styles. An exception was the Series 68, which wasn't reinstated until

1938 Series L-38 Eight trunkback touring sedan

1940 Series 90 convertible phaeton

1939 Series 70 2/4-passenger club coupe

1941 Custom Cruiser Series 90 convertible

1940 Series 60 station wagon

1941 Series 78 Dynamic Cruiser two-door club sedan

1947. Prices did change in a big way, thanks to postwar inflation. The cheapest '47 Olds, the 66 club coupe, sold for $1407, and the 98 convertible topped the line at more than $2000.

Styling was cleaned up via a four-bar grille shaped like a wide, upside-down U; a shield-type hood medallion rode above it. Front fender moldings were enlarged for '47. Hydra-Matic was increasingly popular, and Olds began producing more self-shift cars as a percentage of total volume than any other make.

Though called "Dynamic," the 1948 Oldsmobiles saw only detail changes: round hood medallion, "Oldsmobile" spelled in block letters below, and full-length chrome rocker-panel moldings. Then, in February, Olds got a jump on most rivals with the "Futuramic" 98, arriving simultaneously with similar styling from Cadillac as GM's first all-new postwar cars. Both were created by Harley Earl's Art & Colour staff with inspiration from the Lockheed P-38 fighter aircraft (well-known for having prompted Cadillac's 1948 tailfins). The 98s comprised a convertible, four-door sedan, and fastback club sedan that were beautifully shaped to look longer and lower despite a slightly trimmer 125-inch wheelbase. Sedans offered a choice of standard and deluxe trim. Prices ranged from $1920 for the base two-door to $2466 for the Deluxe-only convertible. The public responded strongly to the '48s, particularly the 98s, which saw better than 65,000 sales. More than half were four-door sedans.

Olds followed up with Futuramic styling for all 1949 models, plus two new innovations. One was the landmark overhead-valve "Rocket" V-8 designed by Gilbert Burrell. Again, Olds shared honors with Cadillac, which also had a new high-compression V-8 that year, though it was developed independently of Lansing's. Both divisions had been encouraged to outdo each other, and Cadillac actually raised displacement to maintain a "proper distance" from Oldsmobile's V-8. The Rocket arrived at 303.7 cid; Cadillac had started at 309, then went to 331 cid.

A five-main-bearing unit with oversquare cylinder dimensions, the Rocket was initially rated at 135 bhp. Putting it in the lighter 119.5-inch chassis of the six-cylinder 76 created a Futuramic 88 with power-to-weight ratios of about 22.5 pounds/horsepower—quite good for the time. Torque was also impressive at 263 pound-feet. Initial compression was a mild 7.25:1, but the Rocket was designed for ratios as high as 12:1. Engineers had anticipated postwar fuels with ultra-high octane, though levels never became quite high enough to make such ratios practical.

Management had originally planned the Rocket only for the 98, but dropping it into the smaller B-body was a natural move, and the 88 soon began rewriting the stock-car racing record book. Meanwhile, the Olds six was enlarged to the old eight's 257.1 cid for 105 bhp. It continued through 1950, after which Olds offered nothing but V-8s.

Oldsmobile's other '49 innovation was the 98 Holiday, a new $2973 pillarless coupe that bowed alongside the Buick Riviera and Cadillac Coupe de Ville as America's first volume-production

1942 Series 68 Special two-door club sedan

1946 Series F-46 Special 66 convertible coupe

1947 Series L-47 Custom Cruiser 98 convertible coupe

1947 Series J-47 Dynamic Cruiser 76 two-door club sedan

1948 Futuramic 98 DeLuxe convertible coupe

1948 Futuramic 98 DeLuxe four-door sedan

"hardtop convertibles." Presaging another industry trend was Lansing's first all-steel station wagon, offered in 76 and 88 guise. As at Chevy and Pontiac, it appeared at midyear to replace an existing part-wood wagon, and looked much like it. Not predictive at all were fastback Town Sedan four-doors added to the 76 and 88 lines. None sold that well, and would be dropped after this one year.

With so much new, Olds had a rollicking 1949, with home-market production soaring from the 172,500 of 1948 to a record 288,000-plus. The 1950 tally was nearly 408,000, helped by new 76 and 88 Holidays.

Weighing 300-500 pounds less than a comparable 98, the Rocket-engine 88 wowed race-goers in 1949. Oldsmobile was the winningest make in NASCAR that year, taking five of eight races. Red Byron won the '49 NASCAR "Strictly Stock" title by driving an 88. In 1950, an 88 broke the class speed record at Daytona with a two-way average of 100.28 mph. That same year, an 88 won the first Mexican Road Race, besting such formidable competitors as Alfa Romeo, Cadillac, and Lincoln. Back on the stock-car ovals, Olds won 10 of 19 NASCAR contests in 1950 (when young Olds pilot Bill Rexford copped the driving title) and 20 of 41 in '51. Though displaced by Hudson's amazing six-cylinder Hornets in 1952-54, 88s continued to show their mettle. Paul Frere, for example, drove one to victory in a 1952 stock-car race at Spa in Belgium, and a 1950 model nicknamed "Roarin' Relic" was still winning the occasional modified race as late as 1959.

Such goings-on kept sales going strong even after the postwar seller's market went bust around 1950. Olds tapered off to 213,500 orders for '52, but was back up to 354,000 by 1954, when it finished fifth in the model-year production race. Interestingly, Olds managed these triumphs with only three basic series and no station wagons for 1951-56.

Not content to rest on its styling laurels, Olds took advantage of GM's new 1950 B-body to give 98s a one-piece windshield, plus a general look that was again lower and more massive despite another wheelbase cut, this time to 122 inches. The junior 88 and 76 lines received a mild update of their new '49 styling and were granted Holiday hardtops of their own. Fastback sedans were in their final year. Curiously, the lower level ragtops—76 and 88—were now offered in standard trim only.

The big event of 1951 was the Super 88 with a new 120-inch wheelbase and a styling resemblance to that year's facelifted 98. Prices were in the $2200-$2700 bracket. Canceling the 76 left the 88 as the entry-level Olds, with models pared to just two- and four-door sedans, each around $2000. Those repeated as Super 88s along with a notchback club coupe, convertible, and Holiday hardtop. The 98 was trimmed to a Deluxe sedan and convertible and standard/Deluxe Holidays. The Futuramic label was abandoned as styling became more "important," though the grille was formed by simple bars and side decoration was minimal. This basic appearance continued for '52, when the 88 became a detrimmed Super with a retuned 145-bhp Rocket V-8; horsepower on other models moved up to 160. Also, the 98 now had its name spelled out: "Ninety-Eight."

Along with the Cadillac Eldorado and Buick Skylark, 1953 brought a limited-production Olds convertible, the Fiesta, a $5717 midyear addition to the Ninety-Eight line. Custom leather interior, wraparound "panoramic" windshield, and a special 170-bhp V-8 distinguished it from the normal Ninety-Eight ragtop. Hydra-Matic, power brakes and steering, and hydraulic servos for windows and seat were all standard. So were distinctive "spinner" wheel covers soon copied by most every accessory house, appearing on scores of hot rods and custom cars. Though only 458 were built for this one model year, the Fiesta did serve as a styling preview of the next-generation Olds.

1949 Futuramic 98 DeLuxe Holiday hardtop coupe

1950 Futuramic 98 Deluxe Holiday hardtop coupe

1950 Futuramic 88 DeLuxe Holiday hardtop coupe

1951 98 Holiday DeLuxe four-door sedan

That duly arrived for 1954 with a new B-body bearing squared-up below-the-belt sheetmetal, fully wrapped windshields, curved back windows, and distinctive L-shaped bodyside moldings that delineated contrast color areas on some two-tone models. This was arguably the most-attractive Olds of the decade. Happily, its basic look would persist through 1956.

So would body styles: 88 and Super 88 two- and four-door sedans and hardtop coupe; Super 88 convertible; Ninety-Eight Holiday, Deluxe Holiday, Deluxe sedan, and Starfire convertible. Holiday four-door hardtops bowed in all three lines in mid-1955, half a year ahead of other make's offerings save the Buick

1951 Super 88 convertible coupe

1952 88 DeLuxe two-door sedan

1953 Ninety-Eight Holiday hardtop coupe

1953 Ninety-Eight Fiesta convertible coupe

Special and Century (introduced along with Oldsmobile's). Wheelbases shifted to 122 inches for 88/Super 88 and to 126 for Ninety-Eight. The Rocket was bored out for '54 to 324 cid, good for 170 bhp in 88s, 185 in Super 88s and Ninety-Eights. But the "horsepower race" was escalating throughout Detroit, so power was bumped to 185 and 202 for 1955, then to 230 and 240 for '56.

Olds set another record by building about 40 percent more cars for '55 than '54—some 583,000—and held onto fifth in a booming industry. A substantial facelift gave the '55s a bold oval grille and jazzier two-toning. The '56s gained a large "fish-mouth" front like that of the 1953 Starfire show car. Despite a general industry sales retreat, the division did quite well to turn out some 485,000 of its '56s.

Another new body arrived for 1957 with sleeker styling and the first Olds wagons since 1950. Called Fiesta, the revived wagons comprised a pillared 88 four-door and pillarless 88 and Super 88 versions, the latter reflecting the public's evident passion for hardtop styling. Both 88 lines were subtitled Golden Rocket (after a 1956 show car) to mark Oldsmobile's 60th anniversary; Ninety-Eights gained Starfire as a first name. The Rocket was enlarged again, going to 371.1 cid and 277 bhp. Also new was a three-by-two-barrel carburetor option called J-2, good for 300 bhp. With the high-profile exception of driver Lee Petty, Olds was by now largely absent from stock-car tracks, but the J-2 made it a force to be reckoned with on the street: A J-2-equipped 88 could do 0-60 mph in less than nine seconds.

Priced in the $2700-$4200 range, the '57 Oldsmobiles were rather cleanly styled for GM cars that year. The wide-mouth grille was mildly reshaped; windshield pillars were more rakishly angled; a broad, stainless-steel sweepspear dropped down from the middle of the beltline, then shot straight back to the tail to define a two-toning area; and there were finless rear fenders ending in peaked, oval taillamps. But GM styling was beginning to seem a bit passé next to Virgil Exner's "Forward Look" at Chrysler; Harley Earl's reign as America's automotive styling arbiter was at an end. Still, Olds built nearly 385,000 U.S.-market cars for the model year to finish fifth once again.

While most makes faltered badly in recessionary 1958, Olds moved up to fourth, though on lower volume near the 315,000 mark. Offerings stood pat except that two-door sedans were now restricted to the base series, renamed Dynamic 88. Wheelbases stretched a nominal half-inch across the board. Styling, as most observers declared, was atrocious. Ford designer Alex Tremulis satirized Oldsmobile's four horizontal rear-fender chrome strips by drawing in a clef and a few musical notes on a photograph. And indeed, Dearborn's '58s were somewhat more attractive than GM's, while Chrysler's mildly facelifted cars were in another league entirely. Yet for all the overchromed dazzle, Oldsmobiles sold pretty well for '58—aided, no doubt, by more power choices: 265 bhp for 88s (a nod to buyers suddenly concerned with fuel economy), 305 bhp standard on Supers and Ninety-Eights, and an optional 312-bhp J-2 setup for all.

The '59s might have looked even worse, but GM responded to Chrysler's 1957 initiative with a crash restyling program that produced generally cleaner cars than first envisioned—plus a significant divisional body realignment. Chevy and Pontiac would now share the corporate A-body, the junior Buicks and Oldsmobiles a new B-body, and senior models a slightly different C-body with Cadillac. Olds and Buick wheelbases were set at 123 and 126.3 inches, respectively; Pontiac's was slightly shorter, Chevy's shorter still. This program had repercussions. Chevy and Pontiac, for example, had to drop their all-new '58 platforms after only a year; Olds, Buick, and Cadillac after two years. Still, this change helped hold down production costs, thus enabling the company to put that much more time and money into developing a squadron of new compacts.

As ever, divisional styling strived for distinct looks, though the '59 Olds ended up more like Pontiac than Lansing might have liked. With a new emphasis on "Wide-Track" handling, Pontiac outpaced Oldsmobile in production, something it hadn't done since 1953.

But Lansing's '59s were hardly slim, swelling nine inches in width on a new "Guard-Beam" chassis and 10 inches in overall length. Naturally, they shared basic elements of the new corporate styling: vastly enlarged "Vista-Panoramic" windshields, curving non-dogleg A-posts, big rear windows (fully wrapped on new Holiday Sport Sedan hardtops), thin-section coupe rooflines, narrow pillars, and fuller lower body sheetmetal. To

1954 Ninety-Eight DeLuxe Holiday hardtop coupe

1954 88 four-door sedan

1955 Ninety-Eight DeLuxe Holiday hardtop sedan

1955 Ninety-Eight Starfire convertible coupe

1955 Super 88 four-door sedan

1956 Super 88 Holiday hardtop sedan

1957 Golden Rocket 88 Holiday hardtop coupe

1957 Super 88 Fiesta station wagon prototype

1957 Golden Rocket Super 88 convertible coupe

1958 Ninety-Eight convertible coupe

this Olds added a simple dumbbell-shaped grille with four widely spaced headlights and straight-topped rear fenders with vestigial fins above elliptical taillights. Division ad types called all this "The Linear Look."

No matter: The '59s were a vast improvement on the sparkly '58s. But there were still gadgets aplenty, including "New-Matic Ride," Lansing's year-old version of air suspension that was costly, unpopular, and about to disappear. At least power was still plentiful. Dynamic 88s retained a 371 V-8 with 270 bhp standard, 300 optional. New for Ninety-Eights and Super 88s was a bored-out 394 making 315 bhp with four-barrel carb but slightly reduced compression (9.75:1). Not at all obvious were many internal changes made to this year's Rocket as well as the "Jet-Away" Hydra-Matic long ordered by most Olds customers. For 1959, buyers could choose from a convertible, two- and four-door Holidays, and a pillared Celebrity sedan in each line, plus Dynamic 88 two-door sedan, and four-door Dynamic and Super Fiesta wagons. Prices were higher than ever. Only three Dynamics started below $3000, while the ragtop Ninety-Eight was now close to $4400.

Even so, 1959 was a good Olds year on balance, the division notching another fifth-place finish on slightly improved volume of nearly 383,000. Though it had come a long way from the first 88s, Olds still retained something of a performance image (aided by Lee Petty's photo-finish win in the first Daytona 500), which it would shine anew to great success in the '60s.

The market began fragmenting soon after the new decade's dawn, and Lansing responded with other makes by issuing a variety of new models. Most sold very well. The division never fell below seventh in industry output during these years and ran as high as fourth, rising from about 347,000 cars produced for 1960 to 635,000 by decade's end.

Olds jumped on the 1961 bandwagon for upscale compacts by fielding the F-85, which together with its later Cutlass variations saw steadily higher annual production through 1968. This reflected an astute matching of product with customer tastes: small V-8s for 1961-62, larger compacts with an optional V-6 for 1964-65, the high-performance 4-4-2 series from 1964. Each year's junior Olds line was invariably right on the money. The division's standard-size cars also sold consistently well.

F-85 was one of GM's "second-wave" compacts, evolved along with the Buick Special and Pontiac Tempest from Chevrolet's rear-engine 1960 Corvair. All thus shared the first-generation Corvair's basic Y-body platform, albeit reworked for an orthodox front-engine/rear-drive format. Tempest, with its curved driveshaft and rear transaxle, was the most radical of the B-O-P trio. Special and F-85 were resolutely conventional. Both carried an all-new, all-aluminum Buick-built V-8 of 215 cid and 155 bhp, which gave reasonable go (typical 0-60 mph: 13 seconds) and fuel economy (18 mpg). In appearance, the Olds was a bit cleaner than the Buick, with a simpler front end (a small-scale rendition of that year's big-Olds face) but the same sculpted bodysides and crisp roofline.

Naming the F-85 had been a small problem. Starfire was the first choice, but seemed to denote a big sporty car, as it had in the past (and ultimately would again for '61.) "Rockette" was rejected for projecting an unwanted image of the Radio City Music Hall dancers. The final choice looked to the Corvette-like F-88 show car of 1954, with "85" selected to avoid confusion with the big 88s.

F-85 initially offered a four-door sedan and hatchback four-door wagon in standard and Deluxe trim with a $2300-$2900 price spread. All rode a trim 112-inch wheelbase. At midyear came a pair of coupes, including a $2621 job with bucket seats and luxury interior called Cutlass, a name that would eventually supplant F-85. Base and Cutlass convertibles bowed for 1962.

1958 Super 88 Fiesta hardtop station wagon

1959 Dynamic 88 hardtop coupe

1960 Super 88 convertible coupe

1961 F-85 Cutlass DeLuxe sports coupe

All '62 Cutlasses offered a 185-bhp "Power-Pack" V-8, but greater interest surrounded another new derivation. This was the turbocharged Jetfire hardtop coupe, which shared honors with Chevy's 1962 Corvair Monza Spyder as America's first high-volume turbocar. With blower, the Jetfire V-8 churned out a healthy 215 bhp—the long-hallowed "1 hp per cu. in." ideal—but carbon buildup with certain grades of fuel necessitated an unusual water-injection system (actually, a water/alcohol mix). While the Jetfire was remarkably fast (0-60 mph in about 8.5 seconds, top speed around 107 mph), the water-injection proved unreliable. As a result, Olds abandoned turbos for 1964 in favor of a conventional 330-cid V-8 of 230-290 bhp; at the same time, Buick's new 155-bhp 225-cid V-6 became base power for the F-85 line.

The compact Oldsmobiles grew to intermediate size after 1963, GM taking note of the huge sales generated by Ford's 1962-63 Fairlane. Wheelbase went to 115 inches, when Cutlass Holiday hardtop coupes were added. For '68, the line was split into 112-inch-wheelbase two-door models and 116-inch-wheelbase four-doors. Styling improved over time. The original look became squarer and more "important" for '63. The '64s were bulkier but still very clean, with an even closer resemblance to big Oldsmobiles. Straight beltlines yielded to more-flowing "Coke-bottle "contours for '66, when models again expanded via hardtop sedans in Cutlass and F-85 Deluxe trim. Appearance began getting cluttered again after '68, with busier grilles and sometimes clumsy vinyl tops.

The most-exciting F-85s were called 4-4-2, which meant four speeds (or 400 cubic inches beginning with '65), four-barrel carburetor, and dual exhausts. The debut 1964 edition was a package option for any F-85 except wagons, comprising a 310-bhp 330 V-8, heavy-duty suspension, and four-speed manual gearbox. The '65 (confined to two-door models) was hotter still with a 345-bhp 400—a debored version of the full-size Olds' then-new 425-cid V-8—plus heavy-duty wheels, shocks, springs, rear axle, driveshaft, engine mounts, steering and frame; front/rear stabilizer bars; fat tires; special exterior and interior trim; 11-inch clutch; and a 70-amp battery—all for about $250. Performance was terrific: 0-60 mph in 7.5 seconds, the standing quarter-mile in 17 seconds at 85 mph, top speed of 125 mph. The 4-4-2 proved, as *Motor Trend* magazine said, "that Detroit can build cars that perform, handle, and stop, without sacrificing road comfort."

Each year's 4-4-2 was eagerly awaited. Though the 400 V-8 wasn't pushed much beyond 350 bhp, Oldsmobile's hot middleweights remained handsome, fast, and fun. They were also better-balanced overall than rival muscle machines that had too much power for their chassis. The '69s wore large "4-4-2" numerals on front fenders, rear deck, and on a body-color vertical divider ahead of a black-finish grille, plus a unique "bi-level" hood with contrasting paint stripes. If a bit outlandish, the '69 was no less a performance car than the first 4-4-2. It was also a fine value at base prices as low as $3141.

Debuting for 1966 was the most innovative Olds in a generation. This, of course, was the intriguing front-wheel-drive Toronado, a hardtop coupe offered in $4617 standard guise or as a nicer Deluxe model priced $200 higher. Toronado represented a clean break with the past—and a commitment to front drive that would involve every GM nameplate by 1980. Toronado was also a big surprise for a company that had once panned the front-drive Cord, but GM planned it well.

The goals for Toronado were traditional American power combined with outstanding handling and traction. Its 425 V-8 came from full-size Oldsmobiles, but delivered an extra 10 horsepower—385 total—and teamed with a new "split" automatic transmission. A torque converter mounted behind the engine connected via chain drive and sprocket to a Turbo Hydra-Matic transmission located remotely beneath the left cylinder bank. The chain drive, flexible yet virtually unbreakable, saved weight and cut costs. It also resulted in a very compact drivetrain that opened up extra cabin room. (A generous

1961 Super 88 Starfire convertible coupe

1962 F-85 DeLuxe Jetfire hardtop sports coupe

1961 Ninety-Eight Holiday hardtop sport sedan

1963 F-85 DeLuxe Jetfire hardtop sports coupe

1962 Starfire hardtop coupe

1963 Starfire hardtop coupe

119-inch wheelbase helped, too.) Most previous front-drive systems had put the engine behind a transmission slung out ahead of the axle. Toronado's split transmission allowed the engine to be placed directly over the front wheels for a front/rear weight distribution of 54/46 percent, good for a big front-driver that some said could never work simply because it was so large and heavy (over 4300 pounds).

Toronado's styling was as sophisticated as its engineering. The C-pillars spilled gently down from the roof, there was no beltline "break" behind the rear side windows, the rakish fastback roofline terminated in a neatly cropped tail, the curved fuselage was set off by boldly flared wheel arches, and there was a distinctive front end with hidden headlamps. *Automobile Quarterly* editor Don Vorderman termed the result "logical, imaginative, and totally unique."

It was just as superb on the road. Understeer wasn't excessive for a front-driver, 100 mph was a quiet business, and top speed was near 135 mph even with the fairly rangy standard final-drive ratio. Unquestionably, Toronado was the most outstanding single Olds of the '60s. It would also prove to be the last truly innovative product that Lansing could call its own.

Toronado improved for '67 by offering optional front-disc power brakes and radial tires. Save detail changes, styling was mercifully left alone. Sales, unfortunately, took a big dive, dropping from 41,000 to about 21,800.

The 1968 Toro looked heavier in front, gaining a simple but massive combination bumper/grille. The following year brought added rear-end sheetmetal, an apparent effort to create a more conventional notchback appearance. The same reasoning prompted an optional vinyl roof cover that didn't work at all with the clean C-pillar line. Horsepower declined by 10 for '68 despite a switch to the giant new 455 V-8 offered in that year's full-size Olds line. However, an optional W-34 version served up an even 400 bhp thanks to dual exhausts, special cam, and other modifications. Little else but exposed headlamps distinguished the 1970 model, last of the first-generation Toros. Sales were erratic in these years. The total was near 26,500 for '68, an encouraging gain over dismal '67, then rose to almost 28,500 before easing back to 25,400 for 1970.

Despite the likes of Toronado and 4-4-2, big cars remained Oldsmobile's stock-in-trade in the '60s. The 1960 models were basically the expansive "Linear Look" '59s with simpler, more-dignified lines from a below-the-belt reskin. Pointy "rocket" rear fenders and busier bodysides marked the '61s, followed by more-involved grilles and rear-end treatments for '62. Wheelbases and series remained unchanged: 123 inches for price-leader Dynamic 88 and extra-performance Super 88, 126.3 for the luxury Ninety-Eight. A 1961 newcomer was the bucket-seat Starfire convertible on the Super 88 chassis. A companion hardtop coupe was added for '62.

1963 Ninety-Eight convertible coupe

1965 Cutlass 4-4-2 convertible coupe

1964 Starfire hardtop coupe

1965 Jetstar sports coupe

1964 Cutlass Holiday hardtop coupe

1966 Cutlass 4-4-2 Holiday hardtop coupe

1966 Cutlass 4-4-2 Holiday hardtop coupe

1966 Toronado DeLuxe hardtop coupe

1966 Toronado hardtop coupe

1966 Starfire hardtop coupe

1967 Ninety-Eight Holiday hardtop coupe

1967 Delta 88 Custom Holiday hardtop coupe

Further full-size expansion occurred for 1964, when the Dynamic moved up a notch in price to make room for Jetstar 88s. Among them was the bucket-seat Jetstar I sports coupe with a concave backlight *a la* Pontiac's Grand Prix. Super 88 was renamed Delta 88 for 1965; two years later, Dynamics and standard Jetstars were rolled into a single Delmont 88 series. But Delmont would be short-lived, giving way for 1969 to standard, Custom, and Royale Deltas, all on a 124-inch wheelbase. That year's Ninety-Eight moved up to a 127-inch platform.

Despite complete body changes for 1961, '65, and '69, big-Olds styling was remarkably consistent. The dumbbell grille shape persisted through '66, after which the first of Oldsmobile's split grilles appeared. Lines were crisp and straight through 1964, then progressively curvier and bulkier. Body styles were the usual assortment through '64, after which big station wagons were dropped in deference to new F-85/Cutlass-based haulers, including a Vista Cruiser with a raised, glassed-in rear superstructure (shared by Buick's contemporary Skylark-based Sportwagons) and a 120-inch wheelbase. For 1968, the Vista Cruiser chassis grew to 121 inches, though lesser Cutlass wagons were five inches shorter.

After a carryover 1960, big-Olds power through 1964 was provided by 394 V-8s delivering from 250 bhp in base 88s to 345 bhp in the 1962-64 Starfire. The low-priced '64 Jetstar used the F-85's 330 V-8. The 394 was stroked to 425 cid for 1965, and power rose gradually, reaching 375 bhp by 1967. A still longer stroke created 1968's massive 455, but it made only 365 bhp, with some power lost to the advent of emission controls and necessary detuning. The '67 Delmont offered both the 425- and 330-cid engines. The latter was boosted to 350 cid and 250 bhp for 1968.

Of Oldsmobile's two big bucket-seat performance cars, only the Starfire had any success. Production zoomed from 7600 for debut '61 to almost 42,000 for '62. But that would be the peak, output tapering fast through the end of the series in 1966. Jetstar I was the same idea at a more-popular price, but it didn't catch on; only about 22,600 were built for 1964-65. Though neither was anything like a true sports car (despite Oldsmobile's claims), they were distinctive and handled well for their size.

Like sister GM divisions, Oldsmobile's responses to the tumultuous events of the 1970s were quick and usually correct. The 1973-74 OPEC oil embargo and the resulting energy crisis dramatically highlighted the need for smaller, thriftier cars in every size and price range, and Olds needed them as much as any medium-price make. At the start of the decade, its smallest models were two-door intermediates. Yet by 1980, it was offering no fewer than three model lines on wheelbases of less than 110 inches, plus more sensibly sized full-size cars and the trimmest Toronado yet. Still, GM's decision to downsize its entire fleet came well in advance of the fuel shortage. That the first of

1967 4-4-2 Holiday hardtop coupe

1967 Toronado Deluxe hardtop coupe

1968 Toronado Custom hardtop coupe

1968 4-4-2 Holiday hardtop coupe

1969 4-4-2 Holiday hardtop coupe

1969 Ninety-Eight Luxury Sedan four-door

the new breed appeared barely two years after the crisis had passed was merely happy coincidence.

Oldsmobile's great sales success in the '70s was not a coincidence but the result of canny, calculated marketing. In fact, Olds usually ranked third behind Ford and Chevrolet—remarkable considering its products were basically corporate designs available under other nameplates for the same or less money. What undoubtedly attracted buyers was the extra prestige of the Olds badge on more nicely trimmed cars priced only a little above comparable Chevys and Pontiacs and slightly below equivalent Buicks. The full-size B-body Delta 88 and the midsize A-body Cutlass were far and away the division's biggest money spinners in these years.

Cutlass firmly established itself in the 1970s as one of America's favorites, often topping the individual model-line sales charts. Although it remained essentially an upmarket Chevrolet Chevelle/Malibu, Cutlass always offered a broad range of model and trim choices at competitively attractive prices. Another plus was more-august Oldsmobile styling.

Among the most popular of this popular line was the posh range-topping Cutlass Supreme, which debuted as a single 1966 hardtop sedan, then became a separate full-range series (bolstered by a convertible for 1970-72). By 1973, the two-door alone accounted for nearly 220,000 sales, greater than the combined total for all other Cutlasses. Most buyers specified V-8s, especially early in the decade, though sixes were available beginning with the '75s. Coupes far outsold sedans and wagons in most years.

Given this popularity, the downsized 108.1-inch-wheelbase Cutlass/Cutlass Supreme of 1978 seemed very brave at the time, but buyers took to it with no less enthusiasm. The sole exception was the 1978-80 "aeroback" two- and four-door sedans, which were too dumpy-looking even for Oldsmobile's mostly conservative clientele. Conventional notchback styling was thus applied to the four-door after '79, and was greeted with immediate acceptance.

The enthusiast's Cutlass fell on hard times in the '70s, as did every other Detroit muscle car. The last of the traditional high-power 4-4-2s appeared for 1971, a convertible and Holiday hardtop coupe packing the division's big 455 V-8. Sales dropped fast: from 19,000 for 1970 to less than 7600. After this, the 4-4-2 was reduced to a mere option package and a shadow of its original performance self. With GM's redesigned "Colonnade" intermediates of 1973, Olds tried a new approach in the Cutlass Salon, an American-style sporty sedan series somewhat akin to Pontiac's Grand Am. Though it failed to catch on, the name kept popping up on later midsize and compact models. As for the 4-4-2, you could still get a car so badged in 1979, but it was far more show than go.

Olds followed Buick back to compacts in 1973—and with the

1969 Delta 88 Royale Holiday hardtop coupe

1969 Vista Cruiser station wagon

1970 Toronado Custom hardtop coupe

1970 4-4-2 Official Pace Car convertible coupe

1971 Toronado hardtop coupe

same basic car. Omega was Lansing's version, one of three badge-engineered derivatives of the 111-inch-wheelbase X-body platform introduced with the 1968 Chevy Nova. Though it managed a respectable 60,000 first-season sales, Omega was never a big winner. Sales actually fell for 1975 despite a handsome new outer skin and an improved chassis. When the X-body was shrunk around more space-efficient front-wheel-drive mechanicals for 1980, Omega vied with Pontiac's counterpart Phoenix for low spot on the sales totem pole, though an avalanche of highly publicized reliability and safety problems severely hurt all of these corporate cousins.

A similar fate befell another "company car," the subcompact Starfire. Introduced for 1975, this was Oldsmobile's edition of the Vega-based Chevrolet Monza 2+2, with the same hatchback coupe body and the 231-cid V-6 used in Buick's near-identical Skyhawk. Though the name once attached to Lansing's largest and most opulent cars, this 97-inch-wheelbase Starfire was the smallest Olds ever, and thus should have done well in the post-energy crisis market. But big cars were on the rise again, and Starfire captured a mere six percent of division sales in its first year. It wouldn't do much better through the final 1980 models.

Upper-middle-class luxury remained Oldsmobile's mainstay in the '70s, and its big cars never strayed from it. What they did stray from, eventually, was needless bulk, which had become an increasing liability in the more-energy-conscious climate of late decade. GM bowed the largest full-size cars in its history for 1971, so Oldsmobile's B-body Delta 88 and C-body Ninety-Eight acquired extra inches and pounds on wheelbases unchanged from '69. Big-block 455 V-8s prevailed, but were progressively detuned to meet ever-stricter emissions standards. Wagons in this design generation had an interesting "clamshell" rear window/tailgate that retracted electrically into the body like a rolltop desk. The big Chevy, Pontiac, and Buick wagons all had it too, but it worked none too well.

As with Cutlass, the full-size Olds lost none of its appeal when downsized for 1977. If anything, these smaller big cars sold even better than the bigger old ones, doubtless due to improved fuel economy and maneuverability with no sacrifice in passenger room and ride comfort. Wheelbases contracted to 116 inches for Delta 88 and the Custom Cruiser wagon, and to 119 for Ninety-Eight, sizes that would persist through the mid-'80s. Substantial weight reductions allowed the use of 350- and 403-cid V-8s without compromising performance. Diesel V-8s and Buick's 231 gas V-6 were standard or optional from 1978 on. Model choices changed several times, but sedans and coupes usually ran to base, Royale, and Royale Brougham Deltas, and Luxury and Regency Ninety-Eights. The Custom Cruiser hung on in this form all the way through 1990, mainly because GM elected not to replace it with a smaller front-drive model that would have been less useful as a full-size wagon.

The personal-luxury Toronado evolved through the '70s more or less in step with the full-size Oldsmobiles. For 1971, it also became as large as it would ever be, going from mild sportiness to outsized opulence on a 123-inch wheelbase. Styling also changed—mostly for the worse—becoming more contrived and Cadillac-like through the end of this second generation in 1978.

Two Toronado styling developments in these years bear mention. One was a throwback to the early-postwar Studebaker Starlight coupes: a huge rear window wrapped around to the sides in a near unbroken sweep on the XS model of 1977 and XSC of 1978. More laudable was a second set of brake lights just below the rear window, the precursor to an idea that would later be mandated by Washington for all cars sold in the U.S.

Despite its innovative engineering, the Toronado had no direct technical bearing on GM's linewide switch to front drive that began with the 1980 X-body compacts. In fact, it would probably have sold just as well with rear drive—as indeed did Buick's Riviera, which used a rear-drive version of the Toronado platform after 1965 but was always more popular. Save 1973, when sales neared 56,000, second-series Toronado volume was hardly exceptional: about 23,000 in most years. The new downsized generation of 1979 was smaller than even the 1966 original, with a 114-inch-wheelbase E-body platform and adequately potent small-block V-8s. It immediately garnered a bit more than 50,000 orders, then pulled in from 34,000 to 48,000 a year through 1985.

Oldsmobile's fortunes in the 1980s were decidedly mixed. Lansing had sold a record 1.14 million cars for '77 and nearly as many for '78 and '79. With the second energy crisis that began in late '79 came a deep national recession that held division sales well below the one-million mark through 1983. But then Olds bounced back to set another record: a smashing 1.17 million for 1985. In the yearly production derby the division continued to run its usual third, just ahead of Buick, but it also managed to beat Ford for second spot in 1983 and '85. Yet by 1987, Olds was down below 671,000, its worst total since the mid-'70s, and Pontiac had regained third. The decline continued, Olds averaging but 534,000 for 1988-89, then dipping under half a million for 1990.

What happened? One problem was that Oldsmobile's role and image became confused with Buick's—no surprise given similar model lines that had evolved pretty much in lockstep since the mid-'70s at least. Another problem was Pontiac, which in the early '80s began offering the kind of performance-oriented machinery that had served it so well in the '60s. By that point, Oldsmobile's one real marketing asset seemed to be the Cutlass name, and even that had lost much of its appeal by being indiscriminately tacked onto too many models. Olds also suffered from GM's policies of "identicar" styling and divisional duplicates of most every platform in the corporate stable.

Then, too, there was the wholesale corporate reorganization hatched by chairman Roger Smith in 1984. This was a well-intentioned attempt at addressing many ills, including blurred divisional identities, but it only squandered valuable time and untold employee morale. Compounding this confusion was Smith's headlong rush to buy Hughes Electronics and the

1971 Delta 88 Royale hardtop coupe

1971 4-4-2 convertible coupe

1972 Delta 88 Royale hardtop coupe

1972 Toronado Custom hardtop coupe

1973 Cutlass Supreme Colonnade coupe

1973 Ninety-Eight Luxury Coupe hardtop

1973 Omega hatchback coupe

1973 Toronado hardtop coupe

Electronic Data Systems company of one H. Ross Perot, in the mistaken belief that expensive computerized-manufacturing systems would increase both productivity and profitability. Instead, the acquisitions only sapped funds that might have been more wisely spent on much-needed new models. Meantime, the hastily installed automation only worsened the build quality of existing products. Symbolic of the near-chaos that then reigned was the highly touted "Poletown" plant opened in the mid-'80s in Hamtramck, near Detroit, where robots painted each other instead of cars and driverless parts carts scurried around aimlessly.

A final problem, and perhaps the most telling, was the inability—or was it the refusal?—of top GM managers to see they had any problems at all. Of course, some executives were quite insulated by GM's size, and their "business-as-usual" attitude was not harmful as long as the market remained healthy. But when the market turned weak in 1990, GM began hemorrhaging cash like it hadn't done even in its earliest days. Huge losses continued to pile up over the next three years. By that point, rumors were circulating that Oldsmobile—then about to celebrate its 95th anniversary—might have to be sacrificed as part of saving the corporation.

With all this, the 1980s was not one of Oldsmobile's happiest decades. For a time, Lansing tried swapping roles with Flint, emphasizing sporty luxury as a sort of "American BMW" while Buick reasserted its traditional blend of substantial size and smooth-riding softness in what it now called "premium American motorcars." But this game plan worked only for Buick. By decade's end, Olds seemed hopelessly lost and increasingly unnecessary, squeezed by an aggressive Pontiac from below and a resurgent Buick from above. It was all eerily reminiscent of what happened to DeSoto in the late '50s—and, come to that, the Edsel.

The cars that carried Olds to this uncertain state of affairs were workaday intermediates and full-size models. Surprisingly perhaps, given the difficult early-'80s market, the big rear-drive Delta 88 and Ninety-Eight took over as the division's top-sellers through middecade. Together, they attracted a quarter-million buyers a year through 1982 and more than 340,000 in 1983 and '84. Both soon moved to smaller front-drive platforms (except, as noted, the Custom Cruiser wagon) as part of a second-wave GM downsizing program. The 1985 Ninety-Eight was thus put on a new C-body, shared with Buick's Electra; the 88 was similarly transformed for '86 on the related new H-body also used for the Buick LeSabre and Pontiac Bonneville. Like the first-wave '77s, these smaller big cars sold just as well as their predecessors. But aside from styling and equipment details, all these Oldsmobiles, rear-drive and front-drive, differed little from counterpart Buicks.

Number-two on Lansing's 1980s hit parade was the midsize

1973 Ninety-Eight Luxury Coupe hardtop

1973 Hurst/Olds W-30 Official Pace Car

1974 Ninety-Eight Regency coupe

1975 Hurst/Olds W-30 T-top coupe

1976 Delta 88 Royale Crown Landau hardtop coupe

1976 Toronado Brougham coupe

Cutlass, which involved two distinct lines: continuations of the 1978-vintage rear-drive series and its erstwhile front-drive successor, the A-body Cutlass Ciera, new for '82. Each accounted for upward of 200,000-300,000 sales in their best years. Rear-drive Cutlass coupes received a sloped-nose "aero" facelift for 1981 (similar to the full-size cars' 1980 redo). Model years 1983 and '87 saw the end of Cutlass wagons and sedans, respectively. Two-doors adopted flush-mounted "composite" headlamps for '86. Signaling the imminent arrival of a new front-drive Cutlass Supreme, the rear-drive '88s—produced in a short run—were renamed Supreme Classic.

Of interest to collectors is the trio of low-volume, period muscle-car revivals based on the rear-drive Cutlass coupe: a 15th anniversary Hurst/Olds commemorative for 1983, a similar 1984 followup, and a reborn 4-4-2 option package offered for 1985-87. The H/Os wore special badging and modest decklid spoilers. All three packed a four-barrel, 180-bhp version of Oldsmobile's 307-cid small-block V-8 (170 bhp in 1987) and were quite fast. Their mild engine tuning would have seemed laughable in the '60s, but nobody had to be concerned with corporate average fuel economy (CAFE) in those days.

CAFE was a definite motivation for the smaller midsize Olds, the Cutlass Ciera. It was, predictably, much like Buick's new-wave Century, derived from the front-drive corporate X-car compact and initially offered as a notchback coupe and sedan; glass-hatch wagons arrived for 1984. Engine choices included a standard Pontiac-built 151-cid four-cylinder, 181-cube gas V-6, and a 262 diesel V-6. For mid-1986, the Ciera coupe gained a smoother, slightly abbreviated roofline. Sedans got a similarly rounded backlight for 1989, when a new 160-bhp 3.3-liter V-6 replaced the 231-cid Buick V-6 optional since '85.

The rear-drive Cutlass and front-drive Ciera typically offered a choice of plain and fancy trim (the latter usually dubbed Brougham). There were also sporting versions: GT and Euro-style ES Cieras through 1987, plus Calais and Salon Cutlass coupes—all with fortified suspensions and less-traditional interiors. From 1988, the enthusiast's Ciera was retitled International Series, but retained the usual black-finish exterior trim, bigger wheel/tire package, and special body addenda (front and rear spoilers, later matched by rocker-panel skirts).

Somehow, Oldsmobile was less successful with small cars than Buick, let alone Chevrolet. Perhaps they weren't sufficiently different enough, or maybe Oldsmobile customers just couldn't resist the bigger jobs. Whatever the reason, Lansing's smallest cars were slow movers. The front-drive X-body Omega, for example, peaked at nearly 148,000 for 1981, then tailed off to less than 54,000 by '83. Lack of change didn't help, and it was summarily dismissed after 1984.

Firenza fared even worse. Arriving in March 1982 to replace Starfire, Lansing's version of the front-drive 101.2-inch-wheelbase

1976 Cutlass S 4-4-2 coupe (option W-29)

1976 Starfire GT hatchback coupe

1977 Cutlass S 4-4-2 coupe

1977 Toronado XS coupe

1977 Delta 88 Royale town sedan four-door

1978 Cutlass Calais coupe

1978 Starfire GT hatchback coupe

1979 Cutlass Salon diesel four-door sedan

1979 Delta 88 Royale four-door sedan

1979 Starfire Firenza hatchback coupe

1979 Cutlass Salon 4-4-2 fastback coupe

corporate J-body subcompact failed to attract more than about 45,000 customers in most years—except for 1984, when it garnered a creditable 82,500—even though Olds tried most everything it could think of to sell it. By 1988 the Firenza had offered all the J body styles, sporty GT and SX variants, overhead-valve and overhead-cam fours, optional V-6, and a confusing procession of price-leader and luxury models. But nothing seemed to work, and Olds gave up after '88.

Firenza was no great loss, though, because 1985 brought a more-saleable small Olds in the N-body Calais, called Cutlass Calais after 1988. Sized between Firenza and Omega on a 103.4-inch wheelbase, it bowed as a rounded, short-deck coupe in two versions: base and—just to confuse things—Supreme. Four-door sedans were added for 1986. There was a lot of J-car engineering under the "modern formal" styling, and initial engine choices were the Ciera's familiar Pontiac-built four and 3.0-liter Buick V-6. Even so, customers generally liked this new bottle of old wine, snapping up 100,000-plus in the first year and better than 150,000 of the '86s—about midway between the similar Pontiac Grand Am and Buick Skylark/Somerset.

For 1988, Calais coupes and sedans grouped into base, luxury SL, and sporty International Series (the last replacing a GT package option), but the big news was the first twincam, 16-valve four-cylinder engine in American production, the Quad-4. Designed and built by Olds and offered as an across-the-board Calais option, it delivered 150 rather rough and noisy horses, but was claimed capable of much more. Olds proved it by adding a tuned 180-bhp version for 1989. A more-useful option that year was a new 3.3-liter derivative of the 173-cid Chevrolet-sourced V-6. Replacing the Buick-built 3.0, it also produced 160 bhp—and more torque than even the "High Output" Quad-4. To fill in for the departed Firenza, prosaically named Value Leader Calais models appeared for '89 with less standard equipment and restricted options but lower prices.

Enthusiasts surely shuddered when the 442 returned (*sans* hyphens) as a performance option for the base 1990 Calais coupe. Olds said the name now designated "Quad-4, 4 valves per cylinder and 2 camshafts." Included in the $1667 package were the 180-horse Quad-4, five-speed manual transaxle, a specific version of Oldsmobile's FE3 sport suspension, meaty 215/60R14 performance tires on alloy wheels, full instrumentation, a cute rear-deck spoiler, and bold "442" exterior I.D. "Buff books" gave this latest 442 a lot of ink, but customers mostly gave it the cold shoulder. Even a hallowed name on an honestly speedy little car couldn't convince many that Olds still specialized in high performance the way it had in the '50s and '60s.

Olds observed 20 years of Toronados with a new fourth-generation design for 1986, which should have been cause for celebration. In many ways it was: 18 inches trimmer and 550 pounds slimmer on a new 108-inch wheelbase; just as quick despite switching from V-8s to the Buick 231-cid V-6 (making it the first Toro without eight cylinders); clean and contemporary styling, with hidden headlamps for the first time since 1969. In early '87 came a companion model aimed straight at enthusiasts: the Trofeo (pronounced tro-FAY-oh, "trophy" in Spanish and Italian), with a more subdued exterior, standard leather interior, and FE3 "handling" suspension.

Yet for all that, buyers didn't respond. Toronado had long been eclipsed in sales by cousins Buick Riviera and Cadillac Eldorado. The '86 was no different, except that sales were less than half of what they had been: fewer than 16,000 in the debut season versus 42,000-plus for the last of the third-generation cars. The Riv and Eldo fared little better. Critics blamed this poor performance on styling uncomfortably close to that of the much cheaper Calais, and a package that was evidently downsized a little *too* much for most personal-luxury buyers.

Sadly, there was little Olds could do to improve matters right away. The '87s thus received only new engine mounts plus roller valve lifters that helped lift the V-6 from 140 to 150 bhp. For 1988 came a revised "3800" engine with another 15 bhp, a new antilock brake system (ABS) devised by GM and the German Alfred Teves company became optional, and there were minor mechanical and ergonomic changes. More details were attended to for '89, when Trofeo picked up extra standard equipment, including ABS.

Cadillac and Buick had made their E-bodies more-impressive looking for 1988 and '89. Olds was finally able to do the same for the 1990 Toronado, adding 12.4 inches to overall length, mainly at the rear, complemented by minor facial surgery. The result was handsome, and the extra length yielded an extra 2.5 cubic feet of trunk space. Olds also threw in a standard driver-side airbag and larger wheels and tires for both the Toro and Trofeo (the latter increasingly marketed as a separate model). Nevertheless, sales remained a fraction of what they'd once been, although the 1990 total of just over 15,000 was a heartening gain on the previous year's dismal 9900.

By now, GM had learned the folly of fielding too many cars that looked too much like each other. The all-new front-drive Cutlass Supreme that bowed for 1988 provided striking proof. Though it shared the W-body/GM10 platform with that year's Buick Regal and Pontiac Grand Prix, this newest Supreme had its own roofline and outer sheetmetal so it would not be confused with the others (nor they with Supreme). Hallmarks included a low, tapered nose; slim Olds-trademark split grille; curvy flanks; large wheel openings; crisply clipped tail; and a glassy notchback superstructure with semi-concealed C-posts and thin A- and B-pillars.

The front-drive Supreme's initial powerteam was a five-speed manual transaxle driven by the workhorse 173-cid Chevy V-6 in 125-bhp port-injected form; for 1989, cars with optional automatic received a 3.1-liter/191-cid enlargement boasting 135 bhp. At the same time, optional ABS arrived to fortify the standard all-disc brakes. Model choices through '89 comprised Oldsmobile's now-usual range of base, SL, and sporty International Series—all coupes. The I-Series came with quick-ratio power steering, tuned exhaust, full instrumentation, and, for '89, cassette tape player, power door mirrors, and central locking.

Buyers had been conditioned to expect rebates or low-interest financing offers even on new models. The front-drive Supreme bowed without them, and thus got off to a relatively slow sales start: a little less than 95,000 made despite the extra-long 1988 model year. Olds took the hint, offered incentives, and watched sales pass 100,000 for '89, then 119,000 for '90. But what really made the difference was the belated 1990 arrival of four-door Supremes, which critics said should have been introduced first. At the same time, the engine lineup was curiously juggled. Base power with five-speed manual was now the 180-bhp H.O. Quad-4, with the 160-bhp version reserved for cars with optional three-speed automatic. The 3.1 V-6 again teamed solely with extra-cost four-speed automatic, but that combination was no longer available for the I-Series, which could have used it just as much.

A happier 1990 surprise was the first Supreme convertible in 18 years. Patterned on a prototype that paced the 1988 Indy 500, it was announced at $20,995 with SL trim and, sensibly, the 3.1 V-6 and four-speed autobox. What Olds called a "structural top bar" partly made up for lost rigidity in what was basically a roofless Supreme coupe. The bar didn't add rollover protection, as PR types took pains to note, but it did make for a clumsy top-down appearance. Actually, this evil was necessary because of the W-body coupe's B-pillar-mounted exterior door handles, which would have cost too much to change given the convert-

1980 Omega Brougham four-door sedan

1981 Cutlass Supreme Brougham coupe

1981 Toronado Custom Brougham coupe

1982 Omega Brougham four-door sedan

1982 Cutlass Ciera Brougham two-door sedan

1982 Firenza SX hatchback coupe

1984 Firenza GT hatchback coupe

1984 Calais Hurst/Olds coupe

1984 Toronado Caliente coupe

1985 Ninety-Eight Regency Brougham two-door sedan

ible's low planned production. Also, the bar was needed to provide convenient anchors for the mandatory front shoulder belts. At least the Supreme came with a power top, which was more than a Cadillac Allanté or ragtop Corvette could claim, and lowering the top automatically lowered all four side windows with it, another boon for convenience. Also featured were a glass rear window with electric defroster and a low, tidy top stack.

These and other engineering details reflected the expertise of noted convertible converter C&C Inc., of Brighton, Michigan, which was tapped to build the reborn sunny-days Supreme. Brochures said it was "the first Oldsmobile that can go from zero to wide-open in 12 seconds." Deliveries, however, took considerably longer, as C&C didn't begin production until April, mainly in the interest of highest possible workmanship. As a result, fewer than 500 of the 1990s were built.

Convertibles are always nice, but Olds looked to be in big trouble by now, partly because GM was, too. Where Ford and Chrysler had taken painful steps in the '80s to become leaner and more efficient, GM merely redrew its organizational chart to enter the '90s with the highest overhead and lowest per-unit profit in the U.S. industry. When the bottom dropped out of the market in a deep new recession, GM began gushing red ink. By 1993, it had piled up a towering four-year net loss of $18 billion—a U.S. business record. With cost-cutting imperative, some thought GM might take the easy way out and eliminate its weakest division, hence a spate of rumors that Olds would be killed. (The speculation wasn't wrong, just premature.)

But apart from corporate pride, losing Olds was unthinkable, given the political impact of laying off its thousands of workers—and putting some 3000 Olds dealers out of business. Also, there were far less drastic ways to save money, even if chairman Bob Stempel wasn't moving fast enough in those areas to satisfy an increasingly worried GM board. In fact, after just two years in office, Stempel was ousted in an unprecedented 1992 "palace coup." This set the stage for yet another reorganization under John Smale, the one-time CEO of Proctor & Gamble who became the first GM chairman not chosen from company ranks. John F. "Jack" Smith returned from GM Europe to take over as president. This dynamic new duo achieved fast results, and GM was making money again by 1994.

Olds may have been wounded in this period, but it was far from dead. Granted, calendar-year sales slid fast after 1989, going from more than a half-million to only 381,000 in 1993. And yes, Olds sustained these losses despite entering the two hottest segments of the market: minivans, with the 1990 Silhouette, and sport-utility vehicles, with the '91 Bravada. Yet as grim as all this was, Olds ran a consistent fifth in domestic production (behind Ford, Chevy, Pontiac, and Buick) and sixth among all U.S.-based producers (after American Honda). What's more, model-year output turned solidly upward for 1994 to 478,872 units. The '95 tally was better still at nearly 481,000 vehicles. Though even that was a long way from the million-car years of the '70s and '80s, Olds was still generating sizable business that GM couldn't afford to give up.

Important to the future of that business was John D. Rock, who took over as division general manager in 1992 after a successful stint heading GMC Truck. A straight-talking "cowboy" type, Rock worked feverishly to restore employee morale and to burnish the confused, yet generally stodgy, Olds image that was hurting sales as much as all those rumors about the make's imminent demise. He also began implementing some successful ideas borrowed from GM's new Saturn subsidiary, including "no-haggle" pricing (you paid what the sticker said) and "kid-gloves" customer service. At the same time, Olds looked beyond its historic 100th birthday in 1997 with the "Centennial Plan," a business and product road map through the year 2005.

Rock wanted nothing less than to "completely re-create" Olds, a task he likened to "overhauling the engines of a 747 in mid-flight . . . [T]here's no place at the GM table for the 'old' Oldsmobile. No place for a division hell-bent on being a 'Me-Too Pontiac' or a 'Buick-Lite,'" he declared.

Unfortunately, Rock couldn't do much about existing models and a couple of new ones in the pipeline. Thus, the Toronado and its Trofeo offshoot were left to languish through 1992, then dropped for lack of sales (a mere 6436 that last season). Both finished out with the improved "3800" V-6 and electronic transmission controls adopted for '91, the year antilock brakes became standard for Toro as well Trofeo. It was a sad end for a car once so innovative and compelling.

Likewise, the big rear-wheel-drive Custom Cruiser vanished after 1992 and a two-year stand as a clone of Chevy's restyled '91 Caprice wagon. Just slightly more than 12,000 were made. Nineteen-ninety marked the last use of the 307 V-8 descended from the original '49 "Rocket." It was another sad ending for Olds, but the engine was simply no longer needed. With GM down to a handful of rear-drive cars, economics dictated that all but the Cadillacs use Chevy power. And in fact, Chevy's 5.0-liter V-8 was made standard, and its 180-bhp 5.7-liter V-8 was added as a '92 Custom Cruiser option. Both were too late to help sales, but the bigger engine's bountiful torque and 10 extra

1986 Cutlass Salon coupe

1986 Toronado Brougham coupe

1987½ Toronado Trofeo coupe

1988 Cutlass Ciera International Series coupe

1988 Cutlass Calais International Series four-door sedan

1988 Cutlass Supreme Official Pace Car convertible coupe

1988 Cutlass Supreme Classic Brougham coupe

1988 Cutlass Supreme coupe

1990 Silhouette minivan

1990 Cutlass Supreme convertible coupe

1990 Cutlass Supreme International Series coupe

1990 Toronado Trofeo coupe

bhp were appreciated in the weighty wagon.

The Ninety-Eight observed its 50th anniversary with a substantial 1991 makeover. Wheelbase was unchanged, but the new four-door styling was handsome in its chunky way. Both the Touring Sedan and new Regency Elite boasted ample interior space, all kinds of no-cost amenities, and a smooth new "3800" V-6 with 170 bhp. Like Toronado, however, sales were but an echo of Oldsmobile's best days. Though some 55,000 buyers were persuaded for '91, demand tapered off despite the '92 addition of a lower-priced standard Regency (at $24,595) and a 205-bhp supercharged V-6 option for the Touring Sedan. By 1994, sales were down to around 26,600.

The Eighty-Eight, also still front-wheel drive, got its own redesign for 1992. Coupes were gone, but Royale and uplevel Royale LS sedans wore attractive new styling to stand crisply apart from H-body cousins Buick LeSabre and Pontiac Bonneville. Here, too, was a "3800" V-6 and, for LS, newly optional traction control. Arriving in spring was the suave LSS (Luxury Sport Sedan) option package with front bucket seats and a handling-oriented chassis with 16-inch wheels and performance tires. Overall sales were good: some 115,000 for the model year.

All Eighty-Eights got a bit more torque for '93, plus standard antilock brakes (formerly optional). The '94s sported minor cosmetic changes and a tidier dash with a passenger-side airbag to complement the already included driver-side restraint. For '95 came an improved "Series II" V-6 with 35 extra bhp, and the LSS was available with a 225-bhp supercharged "Series I." Sales see-sawed despite the rising technical progress, falling to about 62,400 for '93, then swinging up past 82,000 before easing back to some 75,400. But this was still one of the most pleasant and practical of family cars, and the Eighty-Eight remained the third-most-popular Olds after Cutlasses Ciera and Supreme.

Once the country's best-selling car line, the Supreme wasn't even in the top 25 after 1989, a huge comedown for a mainstream midsize. There were two likely reasons: the increasingly negative image of the Olds name and wave after wave of new, highly appealing competitors. Regardless, Supreme hit a modern sales low with model-year '93 and barely 83,000 units—at best, only a fourth of what it had done as recently as the mid-'80s. Lansing was thus surely relieved when volume went solidly over the 100,000 level for 1994 and '95.

In a way, it's a wonder sales didn't fall further, for aside from a mild '92 facelift and annual powertrain shuffles, the Supreme saw no notable change through middecade. At least the convertible was still around as a customer lure. Though it was always peripheral to overall sales, production climbed steadily, reaching 1515 for '91, then zooming to 4306 for '92 and 6751 for troubled '93. Recovery 1994 saw a healthy 8638 units, but even that wasn't enough for GM accountants, so the droptop Supreme was dropped after 1995 and a final 4490 examples. Many dealers were sad to see it go; it had done much to brighten Olds showrooms during a dreary time.

An interesting new standard engine arrived for Supreme's 1991 I-Series coupe and sedan: a 3.4-liter V-6 with dual overhead camshafts and four-valve cylinder heads. Quaintly named "Twin Dual Cam," it delivered 210 bhp with five-speed manual or 200 with optional four-speed automatic. Though a much more satisfying performer than any Quad-4, it wasn't nearly as racy as its specifications implied. The following year's restyle was a good one, announced by a tidier version of the trademark split-theme Olds grille. New "mini-quad" headlamps flanked square parking lights for a Pontiac-like "six-lamp" visage, and additional body-color components gave some Supremes a more-integrated look. Sensibly, the Quad-4 was axed for '92, and no one missed it. A car of this class with four-cylinder power, no matter how "advanced" on paper, just wasn't what the market wanted. Also that year, the I-Series got an aircraft-type Head-Up Display (HUD): Readouts of speed and other information projected onto the windshield for easy viewing. Olds offered this as an option in the search for "a difference to sell." Like the Quad-4, though, it mainly drew blank stares.

Supreme marked time for '93, though the 3.4 V-6 was now optional for the ragtop and all models gained automatic power door locks and a front cupholder. The '94s benefited from a standard driver-side airbag and antilock brakes, but the I-Series vanished and SL trim became a package option as Olds turned to emphasizing value with a new "one-price" Special Edition coupe and sedan starting at $16,995. Internal improvements added 20 bhp to the mainstay 3.1 pushrod V-6 (still hanging on). Besides a swan-song convertible, the '95 lineup offered just SL coupe and sedan (replacing S) in "Series I" and "Series II" trim/equipment levels. Prices again spanned a narrow $1000 range ($17,500-$18,500), with the convertible way upstream at $25,460. A more-ergonomic dash with standard dual airbags then carried Supreme through a quiet 1996, after which both car and name finally stepped aside for a better midsize Olds.

Lansing's most-popular car of the early '90s was something far older than the W-body Supreme. Against all odds, it was the hoary Cutlass Ciera, whose surprising sales stamina was probably as much an embarrassment to Olds as it was a relief. This was, after all, a very old car by now and quite at odds with the more "with it" image Olds was trying to project. But Olds needed every sale it could get, and every Ciera made money, as GM had long since amortized the cost of the vintage-'82 design.

What kept Ciera going were steadily improved quality and dollar value. The former reflected a gradual but wholesale reengineering effort that put this Olds (and Buick's related Century) near the top of GM's internal quality audits by 1993—and on a few independent surveys, too. As for value, Ciera discarded its I-Series after 1990 and coupes after '91 to focus on workaday sedans and wagons in basic S and nicer SL guise. SLs alone carried on for '94 "one-price" Special Editions as part of the effort. A decent supply of standard features included driver-side airbag (optional before) and GM's low-cost "ABS VI" antilock brake system. By that point, Ciera had exchanged the old "Iron Duke" base four for a 2.2-liter Chevy-sourced engine with 120 bhp; for '94, the 3.3 Buick V-6 gave way to a similar 3.1 Chevy unit with 160 bhp. Respective transmissions were three- and four-speed automatics. The game plan changed for '95, when the SLs returned in Series I and V-6 Series II price levels.

Despite inflationary pressures, Ciera prices rose only as far as $17,000 by middecade, making this Olds a tempting buy even for a relic of a bygone age. Volume fell substantially after 1990, but the old soldier rebounded with 140,000 or more per year for 1992-'94. Though more "rental car" than driveway dream, the Ciera did more than its share to pull Olds through some very rough years.

There was far less help from Achieva, the redesigned 1992 replacement for Cutlass Calais. The name was a last-minute decision prompted by surveys showing that buyers were confused by three different cars called Cutlass. Besides, Achieva had a modern upscale sound to it—just what Olds wanted.

Unfortunately, Lansing's new N-body compact was rather less than its name implied. Like cousins Buick Skylark and Pontiac Grand Am (also redesigned that year), Achieva owed much to Chevy's L-body Corsica/Beretta, using the same floorpan, inner structure, and suspension. Each model had its own styling, though. Achieva was cautiously inoffensive: more conservative than Grand Am, far less weird than Skylark. Four-door sedans were rather "junior Ninety-Eight," but coupes were disappointingly GM-generic, with elements of Chevy Cavalier and even the new Saturn SC. At the 11th hour, designers determined the two-door looked better with rounded rear wheel arches instead of the sedan's flat-top openings, a change that delayed the start of sales for the entire line by some three months to January 1992.

Like Calais, Achieva emphasized Quad-4 power, including a cheaper new version of the Olds design with a single-cam eight-valve cylinder head. Oddly named Quad OHC, it provided 120 bhp as the standard engine in entry-level S models. Mid-range SLs had the familiar twincam Quad-4 with 160 bhp, while the 180-bhp H.O. unit was reserved for manual-shift versions of a

1991 Cutlass Ciera SL four-door sedan

1991 Ninety-Eight four-door touring sedan

1992 Toronado Trofeo coupe

1992 Eighty-Eight Royale LS four-door sedan

1992 Achieva SC coupe

1992 Cutlass Supreme International Series coupe

1993 Silhouette minivan

1993 Ninety-Eight four-door touring sedan

1993 Cutlass Supreme convertible coupe

1994 Achieva SL four-door sedan

sportier coupe prosaically titled SC. Optional across this board was Buick's 160-bhp 3.3 V-6. Added a bit later was the even hotter SCX. Like the previous Calais Quad 442, the SCX featured a 190-bhp Quad-4, close-ratio manual five-speed, unique 14-inch alloy wheels, rear spoiler, and suitable exterior I.D., plus standard ABS VI as on other models.

Olds pushed Achieva hard, pitting it against the popular Honda Accord and Toyota Camry in a splashy 100,000-mile consumer-comparison test. The SCX provided bonus publicity by scoring major victories in IMSA and SCCA road racing. Yet for all the horn-blowing, Achieva didn't achieve its hoped-for sales. The '92 total was fair at just shy of 80,000 (including a few exports), but Pontiac moved far more Grand Ams, and Olds managed only some 48,000 for 1993 despite adding value-priced Special Editions. Achieva did share in the division's '94 recovery, surging to 62,000, but none were SCXs, as that model was dropped after just 1146 of the '92s and a mere 500 of the '93s.

Achieva really retrenched for 1995, listing just an S coupe and sedan in Series I and II equipment levels respectively tagged at $13,500 and $15,200. The OHC and H.O. engines were also dismissed, but the surviving twincam finally got what it had always needed: twin "balance shafts" to quell inherent rock-and-roll roughness. The result was a somewhat smoother, slightly quieter Quad-4 with five fewer horses. Another belated drivetrain improvement was a four-speed automatic transmission to replace the outmoded non-overdrive three-speed as standard with the V-6 (by now a 155-bhp 3.1 liter) and optional with the four. Olds naturally thought all these changes would help sales, but they didn't, and Achieva model-year output sagged to a bit over 57,000.

As a minivan, Lansing's front-drive Silhouette should have sold like crazy, but it, too, failed to live up to expectations. Befitting an Olds, this was a more-luxurious version of the new plastic-paneled "GM200" design used for the Pontiac Trans Sport and Chevy Lumina APV. The Olds cost the most at an initial $17,195, but came with the novel seven-passenger seating package that was optional for the others, with light, easily movable middle- and third-row buckets. There was even a hint of "grand touring" in an available FE3 handling package. But the 3.1-liter V-6 was a thrashy plodder, and the shared "anteater" styling proved a real turnoff for many buyers. Standard ABS and a 3.8-liter V-6 option didn't turn them on for 1992, nor did a unique power-sliding right-rear door as a new '94 extra. Thus, after finding slightly more than 28,000 buyers for debut 1990, Silhouette settled into the 17,000-26,000 range through mid-decade—not great when Plymouth and Dodge each sold more than 200,000 minivans a year. There was nothing to do but start over, and Olds would with a new all-steel 1997 replacement bearing a more conventional shape.

Announcing a bold course for future Oldsmobiles was the all-new 1995 Aurora, the most exciting car from Lansing in 20 years. Originally planned as the next Toronado, it was built on the same new G-body platform as Buick's latest Riviera coupe, but ambitiously targeted upscale sports sedans with unique four-door styling, state-of-the-art V-8 power, a taut front-drive chassis, and loads of luxury, all for less than $32,000 to start.

Aurora's engine wasn't brand-new, being a smaller-bore 4.0-liter version of Cadillac's two-year-old "Northstar" 4.6. But it was a sweet, strong contemporary V-8 with 250 bhp, so despite fair heft (nearly two tons at the curb), Aurora clocked 0-60 mph at a brisk 8.2 seconds in *Consumer Guide*® tests. A computer-controlled four-speed automatic was the only transmission. Options were limited to power moonroof, cloth upholstery (a no-cost alternative to standard leather), heated front seats, and an "Autobahn" package with firm shocks, high-speed tires, and slightly tighter final gearing.

1996 Ninety-Eight Regency Elite four-door sedan

1996 Cutlass Supreme SL coupe

1996 Achieva SL four-door sedan

1997 Regency four-door sedan

As the first of a new generation for GM's most-troubled division, Aurora naturally drew lots of media interest, and Olds confidently sent out pre-production examples for press drives more than a year before sales began. Initial verdicts were generally quite positive. Enthused *Motor Trend*: "The new Aurora has us believing miracles can still happen." *Car and Driver* called it a "combination of value and sophistication that will make an ideal birthright for the new Oldsmobile," while *Consumer Guide®*'s *Auto '95* termed Aurora a "huge step in a new and better direction for Oldsmobile. It's competitive with Japanese and European sedans that cost thousands more."

How odd, then, that Aurora wore a stylized "A" logo but almost no Olds identification, perhaps a tacit admission of how tarnished the old Rocket badge had become. Then again, Aurora was intended to stand somewhat above the rest of the line as a more exclusive "halo" car. Indeed, the model was sold by only two-thirds of Olds dealers, those who met rigid new divisional standards for everything from showroom display to technical proficiency in the service department. Of course, that was only right for an image-building flagship, and it paid off with strong debut model-year sales of close to 48,000, tops among premium sedans.

Unfortunately for Olds, that would be the peak. Aurora sales plunged about 50 percent for model-year '96 and stayed at roughly that level until 1999, when fewer than 20,000 were built. Why the sudden fall? A big factor was tougher-than-ever luxury-class competition, especially from Japanese rivals Acura and Lexus. Aurora, by contrast, got but one major innovation in its first five years: GM's new OnStar communications and assistance service as a dealer-installed option for '98. While Olds had promised no gratuitous changes, hindsight suggests it might have done more to keep Aurora fresh. Then again, this flagship was never intended to be a high-volume moneymaker. Not so the cars that would follow in its image, with nothing less than Oldsmobile's future riding on their success.

GM as a whole still had too many models that cost too much to build and weren't selling as expected. As a result, the company's market share was down to less than 34 percent by 1995, and would ultimately sink to the low-20-percent range. But GM began cutting costs and was soon making money again, helped by a tech-driven boom economy that fueled an upsurge in demand for profitable trucks. Meanwhile, Olds still struggled. GM bean counters were particularly dismayed by the continuing slide in Olds sales, which were now barely a third of record 1985's nearly 1.2 million units.

Volume was even lower by the time Oldsmobile's centennial rolled around on August 21, 1997—100 years to the day since the formal incorporation of the Olds Motor Vehicle Company. Despite the dreary sales situation, Lansing happily welcomed thousands of celebrants from all over the country, many of whom brought vintage Oldsmobiles for a memorable birthday parade comprising nearly 100 vehicles. Also highlighting the festivities were the next Centennial Plan models, all bearing a "soaring rocket" emblem instituted by John Rock, who felt the old '60s-vintage logo resembled a "chicken track."

Two of the newcomers went on sale before the birthday bash as 1997 entries. Though not central to this book, the second-generation Silhouette bears mention for offering more-conventional minivan looks and construction in regular-length and new extended-body models. All boasted seating for seven, dual sliding rear side doors (the left one optional at first, later standard), a torquier 3.4-liter V-6, and more-upscale furnishings and features than sisters Chevrolet Venture and Pontiac Trans Sport. It was a big improvement. Though performance was just adequate, handling was tops among minivans, with standard antilock brakes and available traction control enhancing "dynamic safety." Versatility, convenience, and value earned high marks, too. But Silhouette and its siblings were visibly narrower than most minivans, and that turned off many buyers. As a result, they never threatened the sales-leading Chrysler Corporation minivans. Of the GM trio, Silhouette was the most-expensive and, thus, the least-popular.

Oldsmobile's other '97 debutante was yet another Cutlass, a replacement for the long-serving Ciera. Though just a dressier version of Chevy's new Malibu sedan, it fit neatly between the compact Achieva and midsize Cutlass Supreme in size and price. Differences from Malibu were confined to Aurora-look wheels, minor trim, and a standard instead of optional V-6. Both the base Cutlass (later GL) and uptown GLS offered good value, delivering for $20,000 or less with air conditioning, ABS, and many other expected amenities. An unexpected bonus was the "Oldsmobile Edge," a comprehensive customer-service program launched a few years earlier for all Olds models. One of its provisions allowed a dissatisfied buyer to return a car within 30 days or 1500 miles for a full refund. That might have won a few sales, but it wasn't nearly enough. Though this Cutlass was a match in most ways for the popular Honda Accord and Toyota Camry it targeted, production was less than 20,000 for '97, poor even discounting the short model year. The '98 tally was also underwhelming at 52,600. With that, Oldsmobile's junior midsize was buried, taking the once-magical Cutlass name with it.

The Centennial Plan envisioned "more-international" Oldsmobiles designed with high appeal for the younger, more affluent customers who typically bought imports. If the Malibu-like Cutlass didn't quite fit that template, the Cutlass Supreme was an even bigger mismatch. Accordingly, the Supreme departed after 1997 with no further changes of substance. A decent car to the end, with *Consumer Guide*® "Recommended" labels to prove it, the W-body Supreme had simply grown too old to be as competitive as Olds needed it to be. Achieva, never that competitive in the hard-fought compact class, also vanished after '97, though Olds ran off some 27,000 carefully equipped 1998 sedans for the rental market—anything to make a sale.

Even less relevant to the emerging new Olds order, the Ninety-Eight was quietly dropped after '96—no great loss, as model-year volume was down to just 15,000, less than even the Aurora's. But Olds was reluctant to abandon traditional full-size luxury, so it retained the old Regency name for a top-line 1997 addition to the Eighty-Eight line. This offered similarly posh trappings and even a bright grille reminiscent of the last Ninety-Eight's, but drew only about half as many orders despite a slightly lower price. To no one's surprise, the Eighty-Eight Regency vanished after just two seasons in another money-saving move aimed at breaking completely with the past.

Other Eighty-Eights got a mild makeover for '96, including a slim twin-nostril grille, reshaped front fenders, and new headlights and taillamps. The sporty LSS became even more so, gaining more-supportive Aurora-style front bucket seats and a massaged supercharged V-6 option with an extra 15 bhp, 240 in all. For 1999, Olds marked a half-century of Eighty-Eights with a limited-production 50th Anniversary Edition, a specially equipped version of the mainstay LS priced $2245 higher. But this gesture soon looked very hollow, because the Eighty-Eight would not be back. Dealers howled once they found out, saying a full-size family car was still vital to their business, but their protests went unheeded.

One reason is that GM had discovered something that seemed sure to cure all its ills. "Brand management" wasn't a new business practice, but it was new to the auto industry. It assumes that products of a given type are all pretty much the same, so consumers tend to choose one over another based on their perception of the label or brand; the better the image of a brand, the better the sales of the products that wear it. Chairman John Smale was a strong believer. So was Jack Smith, Jr., who succeeded him in 1996. Ditto G. Richard Wagoner, Jr., who replaced Smith as president in 1998. But the real push for brand management came from Ronald Zarrella, recruited from optics maker Bausch & Lomb to succeed Wagoner as president of GM's North American operations in 1999. Under Zarrella, GM reorganized—again—and greatly expanded marketing staff and budgets. Meantime, overlapping or underperforming models were pruned from product portfolios, hence the deaths of the Ninety-Eight and Eighty-Eight. But critics said cars don't sell in the same way as "commodity products" like soap and eyeglasses, and in time they were proved right. Not only did brand management do little to improve GM's fortunes, it actually added cost, time, and complexity in getting out new models, which tended to wind up as overly cautious, even bland products.

We mention all this because brand management was bad news for Olds, reducing the make to just three car lines by

1997 Achieva four-door sedan

1997 Eighty Eight LSS four-door sedan

1997 Cutlass Supreme four-door sedan

1998 Regency four-door sedan

1998 Aurora four-door sedan

1998 Cutlass four-door sedan

2000. The most commercially promising was Intrigue, a new import-flavored midsize sedan arriving in May '97 as the 1998 replacement for Cutlass Supreme. Though related to the latest Pontiac Grand Prix and Buick Regal, it was arguably Detroit's strongest challenger yet to the all-conquering Accord and Camry. Intrigue rode a 109-inch wheelbase, the same as the Regal's but shorter than the GP's. Styling, previewed by the 1995 Antares concept, was clean and understated, with more than a hint of Aurora. The interior, also tastefully restrained, featured clear, well-placed gauges and controls; plus comfortable space for four adults, five in a pinch. Roadability was another asset. Said *Car and Driver:* "What's genuinely surprising is how the Intrigue's chassis mimics the behavior and feel of the imports—European imports at that. The structure always feels solid and tight [and] the suspension keeps a very tight rein on body motions." The only engine at first was GM's decidedly un-European "3800" pushrod V-6, but its 195 bhp made for brisk acceleration (just under eight seconds 0-60) despite a mandatory four-speed automatic. For 1999, Olds phased in a new 3.5-liter twincam V-6 derived from the all-aluminum Olds/Cadillac Northstar V-8. Dubbed the "Shortstar" by some, it made 215 bhp despite less displacement, but it had little more torque than the 3800, so performance was comparable. Even so, the 3.5 was quicker to rev, sounded neat, and backed up Intrigue's credentials as a serious alternative to imports.

Intrigue bowed in plain and fancier GL trim, followed by a late-arriving, leather-upholstered GLS. All came with premium features like front bucket seats and console, all-disc antilock brakes, traction control, and 16-inch wheels and tires at low- to mid-$20,000 prices, the heart of the market. A worthy new option for 2000 was an antiskid Precision Control System, which helped the keep the car on course if it started to slide.

Consumer Guide® welcomed Intrigue as "more sophisticated than the brash Grand Prix and more nimble and poised than the Ford Taurus or Camry V-6. If you're looking for a midsize car with a thoughtful blend of features and performance, don't decide until you've driven this pleasant and surprising new Olds." Yet despite that and many other endorsements, Intrigue sales tapered off right away, going from nearly 108,000 for extra long model-year '98 to just under 94,000, then to about 80,500 for 2000. But this wasn't the car's fault. Other factors were at work, as we'll soon see.

Complementing Intrigue for 1999 was a more-competitive Olds compact, the Alero. Pontiac's redesigned Grand Am used the same platform and powertrains, but Alero was very much a junior Intrigue, with similarly handsome Aurora-inspired styling inside and out. A 107-inch wheelbase, rangy for compacts, served sedan and jaunty coupe body styles, each offering GX, GL, and top-drawer GLS trim. A 170-hp 3.4-liter twincam V-6 (with roots in 1980, by the way) was standard for GLS models and available for GLs in lieu of a 150-bhp 2.4-liter "Twin Cam" four-cylinder, a more-civilized version of the Quad-4 and one of the few carryover items from the last Achievas. Like Intrigues, all Aleros had standard all-disc antilock brakes, but also traction control (albeit a simpler setup). GL and GLS added a handy electronic tire-pressure monitor, and a firmer Performance Suspension Package was available for GLS coupes. Alero tilted even more toward sportiness for 2000, when a five-speed manual transmission—supplied by the renowned Getrag of Germany, no less—replaced the four-speed automatic as standard for some four-cylinder models. Olds shuffled prices and some features that year and again for 2001. Model-year 2002 introduced GM's new 2.2-liter "Ecotec" four-cylinder engine, then phasing in for all the company's smaller cars. It made less power than the superseded 2.4, but was more refined and easier on gas.

Like Intrigue, Alero was greeted as another sign that Olds

1998 Intrigue four-door sedan

1999 Cutlass GLS four-door sedan

1999 Alero GLS coupe

1999 Aurora four-door sedan

1999 Eighty-Eight 50th Anniversary Edition four-door sedan

1999 LSS four-door sedan

2000 Alero coupe

2000 Intrigue four-door sedan

2000 Silhouette Premiere minivan

2001 Aurora four-door sedan

2001 Alero coupe

2002 Intrigue GLS four-door sedan

2002 Alero four-door sedan

2002 Aurora four-door sedan

2003 Alero four-door sedan

might just be turning itself around. *Car and Driver* judged its V-6 GLS coupe "downright world-class." *Road & Track*, after testing a similar car, praised "expressive styling, a lively chassis, and...satisfying torque." Being smaller and lighter than Intrigues, V-6 Aleros posted slightly quicker 0-60 times and were even more nimble. Four-cylinder performance was adequate, though also rather noisier. But if not perfect—what car is?—Alero gave value-minded shoppers another reason to visit their local Oldsmobile dealer. As *Consumer Guide*® observed: "This new Olds comes across as a refined car that's not embarrassed by a twisting road. Alero feels more mature than [Grand Am], and with a long list of standard features and competitive prices, shapes up as a good value."

Despite the impressive one-two punch of Intrigue and Alero, Olds sales kept sliding. Buyers were hardly reassured by some journalists' persistent doubts about Oldsmobile's future, a chorus that only grew louder once Chrysler announced termination of once-mighty Plymouth after model-year 2001. Nothing, it seemed, was sacred in Detroit at the turn of the millennium, not even America's oldest surviving nameplate.

Heavy symbolic freight thus attached to the all-new 2001 Aurora that reached dealers in spring 2000. Actually, there were two now: a 4.0-liter V-8 model and a more-affordable companion with Intrigue's snappy 3.5 V-6. Both were slightly smaller in most dimensions than the original Aurora and looked more conservative, but the trusty G-body platform was reengineered to be stiffer and thus more protective in a crash, and quieter with it. Options were few, as both models were lavishly equipped with standard leather-and-wood interior, automatic climate control, all-disc antilock brakes, GM's OnStar assistance system, and much more. V-8s added 17-inch wheels instead of 16s and the antiskid Precision Control System.

At just over $30,000 to start, the V-6 Aurora was basically a stand-in for the departed Eighty-Eight, bringing distinctive style and surprising performance to the family-car market. The uplevel V-8 version was arguably less-special than its predecessor, but it also cost a few thousand less. And true to the Centennial Plan, each was a fine road car. Said *Motor Trend:* "This fresh Aurora is a fun-to-drive, remarkably well-executed sport sedan that nicely balances the luxury-comfort and responsive-agile sides of the driving equation at a reasonable price. Less can be more, after all."

But not for GM managers, who by now were more pressured than ever to boost the company's bottom line and especially its stock price. Olds wasn't the only GM unit in the red, but estimated losses of $120 million a year made it a prime target for cost-cutters. Thus, barely two weeks before Christmas 2000, GM announced plans to phase out the Oldsmobile line over the next several years. All future-model development was stopped (it already had been in some cases) and advertising and marketing were cut to the bone.

Needless to say, Olds dealers were stunned, then angry. So were many within Oldsmobile itself. As it happened, the death notice was issued during the press preview of a new and better 2002 Bravada sport utility, where the news took Olds designers, engineers, and marketers completely by surprise. The following May, Olds supplied 90 or so of the new SUVs for service at the Indianapolis 500—including pace car duty, a first for a truck at the Brickyard. This was no sentimental gesture, however. Olds had signed on as a race-day sponsor some time before its termination was decided. *AutoWeek* reported that dealers were to offer regalia decals for Bravada owners who wished to dress their vehicles like the specially equipped pace truck, but the factory issued no Indy replica. There was no point.

Ironically, Olds car sales finally turned up for 2001, the first year-to-year increase since 1994. It wasn't a big gain—less than five percent on a model-year basis—but it did suggest a nascent turnaround. As Zarella told *AutoWeek*: "Our strategy [with Olds] was starting to work—we ended up with a lot of positive demographics. The problem is, there just weren't enough of them." Public relations director Gus Buenz put it more succinctly: "We've got good product, but not enough people know about it."

At first, GM planned to keep building existing Olds models "until the end of their current life cycles or as long as they remain economically viable." By September 2001, however, the company announced "Oldsmobile production has remained unprofitable," and said the end would come with model-year 2004. Intrigue and the V-6 Aurora were killed off quickly, ending production in June 2002. The V-8 Aurora went to its grave in May 2003. For 2004, Olds sold only Bravadas, Silhouette minivans, and Aleros. As a farewell gesture, the last 500 units of each model rolled out with special "Collector Edition" wheels, badges and interior trim. The very last Oldsmobile, a black Alero, came off the line on Thursday, April 29, 2004. It was immediately sent to the R.E. Olds Transportation Museum in Lansing, the city where the story had begun 106 years before. The one possible consolation for legions of Olds loyalists was that the Bravada was quickly reincarnated (with optional V-8 power) as the 2005 Buick Rainier.

The protracted phaseout gave General Motors plenty of time to settle with Olds dealers, many of whom suddenly found themselves without a business. By some estimates, GM spent over a billion dollars in buyouts and other dealer compensation between 2001 and 2006—proving, perhaps, that one must sometimes spend money to save money. But though killing Olds may have been a necessary, if painful, step, it was far from enough to cure what ailed GM—as subsequent events would show.

2003 Aurora four-door sedan

The final oldsmobile, a 2004 Alero, April 29, 2004

Specifications

1930

F-30 Stnd Six (4 wd whls) (wb 113.5)	Wght	Price	Prod
conv rdstr 4P	2,665	995	822
w/5 wire wheels	2,735	1,050	364
phtn 5P	2,655	965	17
w/5 wire wheels	2,735	1,020	5
cpe 2P	2,755	895	3,726
w/5 wire wheels	2,835	950	343
spt cpe 4P	2,810	965	2,214
w/5 wire wheels	2,890	1,020	584
sdn 2d	2,840	895	9,295
w/5 wire wheels	2,920	950	1,357
sdn 4d	2,940	995	11,841
w/5 wire wheels	3,020	1,050	1,242
Patrician sdn 4d	2,945	1,060	1,015
w/5 wire wheels	3,025	1,140	303
F-30 Special Six (wb 113.5)			
conv rdstr 4P	2,745	1,070	233
phtn 5P	2,730	1,040	5
cpe 2P	2,820	970	633
spt cpe 4P	2,895	1,040	478
sdn 2d	2,920	970	1,598
sdn 4d	3,020	1,070	3,031
Patrician sdn 4d	3,025	1,135	426
F-30 DeLuxe Six (wb 113.5)			
conv rdstr 4P	2,815	1,125	1,560
phtn 5P	2,800	1,095	76
cpe 2P	2,900	1,025	306
spt cpe 4P	2,960	1,095	1,594
sdn 2d	2,990	1,025	615
sdn 4d	3,080	1,125	2,973
Patrician sdn 4d	3,090	1,190	2,525

Export Production:	Prod
conv rdstr 4P	27
phtn 5P	9
cpe 2P	5
sdn 2d	47
sdn 4d	95
Patrician sdn 4d	31

1930 Engine	bore×stroke	bhp	availability
I-6, 197.5	3.19×4.13	62	S-all

1931

F-31 Standard Six (wb 113.5)	Wght	Price	Prod
conv rdstr 4P	2,800	935	357
cpe 2P	2,750	845	2,423
spt cpe 2-4P	2,825	895	1,545
sdn 2d	2,855	845	5,323
sdn 4d	2,935	925	6,736
Patrician sdn 4d	2,950	960	958
F-31 DeLuxe Six (wb 113.5)			
conv rdstr 4P	2,875	1,000	3,144
cpe 2P	2,815	910	1,277
spt cpe 2-4P	2,905	960	3,355
sdn 2d	2,925	910	3,833
sdn 4d	3,000	990	10,486
Patrician sdn 4d	3,020	1,025	7,840

Note: Prices in both series were the same for either wire or wood wheels (five on Standards, six on DeLuxes). In addition, a few Standards were built with disc wheels: sdn 2d (1), sdn 4d (26), Patrician sdn (5). Distribution of wire and wood wheels was approximately equal.

1931 Engine	bore×stroke	bhp	availability
I-6, 197.5	3.19×4.13	65	S-all

1932

F-32 Six (wb 116.5) (5 whls)	Wght	Price	Prod
conv rdstr 2-4P	2,870	955	141
cpe 2P	2,845	875	760
spt cpe 2-4P	2,925	925	366
sdn 2d	2,960	875	1,829
sdn 4d	3,035	955	2,603
Patrician sdn 4d	3,040	990	236
F-32 Six (wb 116.5) (6 wheels)			
conv rdstr 2-4P	2,975	1,000	582
for export, RHD	—	—	21
spt cpe 2-4P	3,025	970	809
sdn 2d	3,060	920	975
sdn 4d	3,135	1,000	3,297
Patrician sdn 4d	3,155	1,035	1,878
D-32 Eight (wb 116.5) (5 whls)			
conv rdstr 2-4P	2,995	1,055	47
cpe 2P	2,970	975	89
spt cpe 2-4P	3,045	1,025	84
sdn 2d	3,080	975	122
sdn 4d	3,165	1,055	525
Patrician sdn 4d	3,165	1,090	181
L-32 Eight (wb 116.5) (6 wheels)			
conv rdstr 2-4P	3,100	1,100	347
cpe 2P	3,075	1,020	127
spt cpe 2-4P	3,145	1,070	392
sdn 2d	3,180	1,020	149
sdn 4d	3,260	1,100	1,205
Patrician sdn 4d	3,275	1,135	2,081

1932 Engines	bore×stroke	bhp	availability
I-6, 213.3	3.31×4.13	74	S-Six
I-8, 240.0	3.00×4.25	87	S-Eight

1933

F-33 Six (wb 115.0)	Wght	Price	Prod
bus cpe 2P	2,945	745	1,547
spt cpe 2P	3,010	780	1,740
conv cpe 2P	2,970	825	317
cpe 5P	3,025	745	4,070
touring cpe 5P	3,090	775	5,464
sdn 4d	3,105	825	7,194
touring sdn 4d	3,165	855	5,720
L-33 Eight (wb 119.0)			
bus cpe 2P	3,090	845	396
spt cpe 2P	3,160	880	827
conv cpe 2P	3,110	925	267
cpe 5P	3,190	845	203
touring cpe 5P	3,230	875	1,901
sdn 4d	3,255	925	2,639
touring sdn 4d	3,305	955	4,357

1933 Engines	bore×stroke	bhp	availability
I-6, 221.4	3.38×4.13	80	S-Six
I-8, 240.3	3.00×4.25	90	S-Eight

1934

F-34 Six (wb 114.0)	Wght	Price	Prod
bus cpe 2P	2,970	650	3,934
spt cpe 2-4P	3,030	695	2,370
cpe 5P	3,040	695	4,679
touring cpe 5P	3,095	725	12,306
sdn 4d	3,100	755	7,014
sdn 4d T/B	3,160	785	20,781
L-34 Eight (wb 119.0)			
bus cpe 2P	3,320	885	900
spt cpe 2-4P	3,370	920	1,278
conv cpe 2-4P	3,325	975	915
cpe 5P	3,400	895	649
touring cpe 5P	3,440	925	4,291
sdn 4d	3,470	965	4,187
sdn 4d T/B	3,520	995	12,272

1934 Engines	bore×stroke	bhp	availability
I-6, 213.3	3.31×4.13	84	S-Six
I-8, 240.3	3.00×4.25	90	S-Eight

1935

F-35 Six (wb 115.0)	Wght	Price	Prod
bus cpe 2P	3,110	675	8,468
spt cpe 2-4P	3,150	725	2,905
conv cpe 2-4P	3,155	800	1,598
cpe 5P	3,225	725	12,785
touring cpe 5P T/B	3,225	755	18,821
sdn 4d	3,285	790	13,009
touring sdn 4d T/B	3,285	820	32,647
L-35 Eight (wb 121.0)			
bus cpe 2P	3,335	860	1,226
spt cpe 2-4P	3,380	895	959
conv cpe 2-4P	3,390	950	910
cpe 5P	3,480	870	870
touring cpe 5P	3,485	900	4,868
sdn 4d	3,530	940	2,976
touring sdn 4d T/B	3,530	970	18,058

1935 Engines	bore×stroke	bhp	availability
I-6, 213.3	3.31×4.13	90	S-Six
I-8, 240.3	3.00×4.25	100	S-Eight

1936

F-36 Six (wb 115.0)	Wght	Price	Prod
bus cpe 2P	3,019	665	19,346
spt cpe 2-4P	3,054	730	2,838
conv cpe 2-4P	3,109	805	2,136
cpe 5P	3,144	730	11,143
touring cpe 5P T/B	3,144	755	45,391
sdn 4d	3,179	795	4,082
touring sdn 4d T/B	3,194	820	66,714
L-36 Eight (wb 121.0)			
bus cpe 2P	3,231	810	2,181
spt cpe 2-4P	3,261	845	959
conv cpe 2-4P	3,321	935	931
cpe 5P	3,376	845	232
touring cpe 5P T/B	3,376	870	6,626
sdn 4d	3,401	910	395
touring sdn 4d T/B	3,421	935	28,373

1936 Engines	bore×stroke	bhp	availability
I-6, 213.3	3.31×4.13	90	S-Six
I-8, 240.3	3.00×4.25	100	S-Eight

1937

F-37 Six (wb 117.0)	Wght	Price	Prod
bus cpe 2P	3,220	810	13,958
club cpe 2-4P	3,210	870	7,426
conv cpe 2-4P	3,350	965	1,619
sdn 2d	3,275	860	9,664
sdn 2d T/B	3,275	895	38,048
sdn 4d	3,310	920	4,020
sdn 4d T/B	3,295	945	62,933
L-37 Eight (wb 124.0)			
bus cpe 2P	3,395	925	2,060
club cpe 2-4P	3,405	985	2,302
conv cpe 2-4P	3,530	1,080	728
sdn 2d	3,480	985	398
sdn 2d T/B	3,480	1,010	5,818
sdn 4d	3,510	1,035	496
sdn 4d T/B	3,495	1,060	30,365

1937 Engines	bore×stroke	bhp	availability
I-6, 230.0	3.44×4.13	95	S-Six
I-8, 257.0	3.25×3.88	110	S-Eight

1938

F-38 Six (wb 117.0)	Wght	Price	Prod
bus cpe 2P	3,205	873	6,538
club cpe 2-4P	3,195	929	3,632
conv cpe 2-4P	3,360	1,046	1,184
sdn 2d	3,275	919	3,975
touring sdn 2d T/B	3,265	944	17,390
sdn 4d	3,285	970	1,477
touring sdn 4d T/B	3,290	995	30,914
L-38 (wb 124.0)			
bus cpe 2P	3,400	989	1,098
club cpe 2-4P	3,385	1,035	1,136
conv cpe 2-4P	3,530	1,163	475
sdn 2d	3,475	1,030	137
touring sdn 2d T/B	3,465	1,056	1,950
sdn 4d	3,490	1,081	200
touring sdn 4d T/B	3,480	1,107	14,939

1938 Engines	bore×stroke	bhp	availability
I-6, 230.0	3.44×4.13	95	S-Six
I-8, 257.0	3.25×3.88	110	S-Eight

1939

F-39 Series 60 (wb 115.0)	Wght	Price	Prod
bus cpe 2P	2,870	777	5,575
club cpe 2-4P	2,915	833	2,273
sdn 2d	2,965	838	16,910
sdn 4d	3,000	889	15,958
G-39 Series 70 (wb 120.0)			
bus cpe 2P	3,040	840	5,211
club cpe 2-4P	3,080	891	4,795
conv cpe 2-4P	3,230	1,045	1,714
sdn 2d (incl. 17 Sun sdns)	3,140	901	19,442
sdn 4d (incl. 81 Sun sdns)	3,180	952	38,224
L-39 Series 80 (wb 120.0)			
bus cpe 2P	3,190	920	738
club cpe 2-4P	3,230	971	1,147
conv cpe 2-4P	3,390	1,119	472
sdn 2d (incl. 7 Sun sdns)	3,290	992	1,571
sdn 4d (incl. 85 Sun sdns)	3,340	1,043	13,197

1939 Engines	bore×stroke	bhp	availability
I-6, 216.0	3.44×3.88	90	S-60
I-6, 230.0	3.44×4.13	95	S-70
I-8, 257.1	3.25×3.88	110	S-80

1940

F-40 Series 60 (wb 116.0)	Wght	Price	Prod
bus cpe	3,030	807	2,752
club cpe	3,015	848	7,664
conv cpe	3,110	1,021	1,347
sdn 2d	3,065	853	27,220
sdn 4d	3,100	899	24,422
wgn 4d	3,255	1,042	633

G-40 Series 70 (wb 120.0)	Wght	Price	Prod
bus cpe	3,100	865	4,337
club cpe	3,105	901	8,505
conv cpe	3,240	1,045	1,070
sdn 2d	3,170	912	21,486
sdn 4d	3,220	963	41,467

L-40 Series 90 (wb 124.0)	Wght	Price	Prod
club cpe	3,440	1,069	10,836
conv cpe	3,590	1,222	290
sdn 4d	3,555	1,131	33,075
conv phaeton 4d	3,750	1,570	50

1940 Engines	bore×stroke	bhp	availability
I-6, 230.0	3.44×4.13	95	S-60, 70
I-8, 257.1	3.25×3.88	110	S-90

1941 Production includes exports

66 Special 6 (wb 119.0)	Wght	Price	Prod
bus cpe	3,299	852	6,455
club cpe	3,335	893	24,027
conv cpe	3,503	1,048	2,897
sdn 2d	3,338	898	30,506
sdn 4d	3,384	945	27,125
town sedan 4d	3,377	945	11,963
wgn 4d	3,692	1,104	609
chassis	—	642	644

68 Special 8 (wb 119.0)	Wght	Price	Prod
bus cpe	3,429	893	188
club cpe	3,461	935	2,703
conv cpe	3,633	1,089	789
sdn 2d	3,471	940	500
sdn 4d	3,512	987	3,885
town sedan 4d	3,511	987	2,193
wgn 4d	3,790	1,217	96
chassis	—	683	2

76 Dynamic Cruiser 6 (wb 125.0)	Wght	Price	Prod
bus cpe	3,418	908	353
club sdn	3,466	954	47,098
sdn 4d	3,527	1,010	41,409
chassis	—	737	3

78 Dynamic Cruiser 8 (wb 125.0)	Wght	Price	Prod
bus cpe	3,525	944	51
club sdn	3,571	989	13,641
sdn 4d	3,637	1,045	15,702

96 Custom Cruiser 6 (wb 125.0)	Wght	Price	Prod
club cpe	3,475	1,043	2,196
conv cpe	3,677	1,191	332
sdn 4d	3,558	1,099	4,248

98 Custom Cruiser 8 (wb 125.0)	Wght	Price	Prod
club cpe	3,575	1,079	6,372
conv cpe	3,786	1,227	1,300
conv sdn 4d	3,939	1,575	125
sdn 4d	3,668	1,135	22,509
chassis	—	822	127

1941 Engines	bore×stroke	bhp	availability
I-6, 238.1	3.50×4.13	100	S-66, 76, 96
I-8, 257.1	3.25×3.88	110	S-68, 78, 98

1942 Production includes exports

66 Special 6 (wb 119.0)	Wght	Price	Prod
bus cpe	3,385	972	1,085
club cpe	3,410	1,015	3,803
conv cpe	3,714	1,257	669
club sdn	3,421	1,030	9,493
sdn 2d	3,436	1,020	3,557
sdn 4d	3,469	1,068	7,615
town sedan 4d	3,460	1,068	3,253
wgn 4d	3,875	1,356	744

68 Special 8 (wb 119.0)	Wght	Price	Prod
bus cpe	3,519	1,015	90
club cpe	3,550	1,057	477
conv cpe	3,850	1,299	211
club sdn	3,566	1,073	1,357
sdn 2d	3,571	1,063	137
sdn 4d	3,603	1,110	1,054
town sedan 4d	3,596	1,110	707
wgn 4d	3,995	1,398	56

76 Dynamic Cruiser 6 (wb 125.0)	Wght	Price	Prod
club sdn	3,549	1,073	10,142
sdn 4d	3,610	1,131	8,871

78 Dynamic Cruiser 8 (wb 125.0)	Wght	Price	Prod
club sdn	3,685	1,116	3,674
sdn 4d	3,736	1,174	4,129

98 Custom Cruiser 8 (wb 127.0)	Wght	Price	Prod
conv cpe	4,124	1,536	230
club sdn	3,806	1,294	1,795
sdn 4d	3,885	1,351	4,799
chassis	—	—	51

1942 Engines	bore×stroke	bhp	availability
I-6, 238.1	3.50×4.13	100	S-66, 76
I-8, 257.1	3.25×3.88	110	S-68, 78, 98

1946 Production includes exports

Special 66 (wb 119.0)	Wght	Price	Prod
conv cpe	3,697	1,327	1,409
club cpe	3,436	1,108	4,537
club sdn 2d	3,455	1,134	11,721
sdn 4d	3,488	1,169	11,053
wgn 4d	3,892	1,795	140
chassis	—	—	1,695

Dynamic Cruiser 76 (wb 125.0)	Wght	Price	Prod
club sdn 2d	3,570	1,184	30,929
Deluxe club sdn 2d	—	1,284	1,923
sdn 4d	3,665	1,234	18,425
Deluxe sdn 4d	—	1,334	2,179

Dynamic Cruiser 78 (wb 125.0)	Wght	Price	Prod
club sdn 2d	3,704	1,264	8,723
Deluxe club sdn 2d	—	1,364	2,188
sdn 4d	3,780	1,313	7,103
Deluxe sdn 4d	—	1,413	2,939

Custom Cruiser 98 (wb 127.0)	Wght	Price	Prod
club sdn 2d	3,837	1,442	2,459
conv cpe	4,185	1,840	874
sdn 4d	3,933	1,492	11,031
chassis	—	—	51

1946 Engines	bore×stroke	bhp	availability
I-6, 238.1	3.50×4.13	100	S-66, 76
I-8, 257.1	3.25×3.88	110	S-78, 98

1947 Production includes exports

Special 66 (wb 119.0)	Wght	Price	Prod
club sdn 2d	3,330	1,433	23,960
club cpe	3,315	1,407	11,669
conv cpe	3,520	1,742	3,947
sdn 4d	3,375	1,471	21,015
wgn 4d	3,715	2,319	968
chassis	—	1,075	134

Special 68 (wb 119.0)	Wght	Price	Prod
club sdn 2d	3,405	1,490	6,759
club cpe	3,390	1,463	2,996
conv cpe	3,595	1,798	2,581
sdn 4d	3,450	1,527	5,128
wgn 4d	—	2,375	492

Dynamic Cruiser 76 (wb 125.0)	Wght	Price	Prod
club sdn 2d	3,460	1,497	28,067
sdn 4d	3,525	1,568	21,644

Dynamic Cruiser 78 (wb 125.0)	Wght	Price	Prod
club sdn 2d	3,535	1,554	16,782
sdn 4d	3,600	1,624	17,181

Custom Cruiser 98 (wb 127.0)	Wght	Price	Prod
club sdn	3,690	1,762	8,475
conv cpe	3,765	2,188	3,940
sdn 4d	3,775	1,812	24,733

1947 Engines	bore×stroke	bhp	availability
I-6, 238.1	3.50×4.13	100	S-66, 76
I-8, 257.1	3.25×3.88	110	S-68, 78, 98

1948 Production includes exports

Dynamic 66 (wb 119.0)	Wght	Price	Prod
club sdn 2d	3,439	1,513	19,029
club cpe	3,386	1,488	7,159
conv cpe	3,695	1,845	1,801
sdn 4d	3,471	1,556	16,614
wgn 4d	3,653	2,456	840
Deluxe wgn 4d	—	—	553
chassis	—	1,134	808

Dynamic 68 (wb 119.0)	Wght	Price	Prod
club sdn 2d	3,570	1,572	6,672
club cpe	3,519	1,546	2,415
conv cpe	3,818	1,903	2,091
sdn 4d	3,602	1,614	4,379
wgn 4d	3,880	2,514	760
Deluxe wgn 4d	—	—	554

Dynamic 76 (wb 125.0)	Wght	Price	Prod
club sdn 2d	3,571	1,584	14,945
sdn 4d	3,634	1,659	14,222

Dynamic 78 (wb 125.0)	Wght	Price	Prod
club sdn 2d	3,701	1,643	10,227
sdn 4d	3,764	1,717	10,424

Futuramic 98 (wb 125.0)	Wght	Price	Prod
club sdn 2d	3,795	1,920	2,311
Deluxe club sdn 2d	—	2,024	11,949
sdn 4d	3,866	1,993	5,605
Deluxe sdn 4d	—	2,098	32,456
conv cpe	4,185	2,466	12,914
chassis	—	1,441	1

1948 Engines	bore×stroke	bhp	availability
I-6, 238.1	3.50×4.13	100	S-66, 76
I-8, 257.1	3.25×3.88	110	S-68, 78
I-8, 257.1	3.25×3.88	115	S-98

1949

Futuramic 76 (wb 119.5)	Wght	Price	Prod
club sdn 2d	3,290	1,758	23,059
Deluxe club sdn 2d	3,355	1,900	8,960
club cpe	3,260	1,732	9,403
Deluxe club cpe	3,315	1,873	3,280
conv cpe	3,580	2,148	5,338
town sedan 4d	3,335	1,821	3,741
Delx town sedan 4d	3,400	1,963	2,725
sdn 4d	3,340	1,832	23,631
Deluxe sdn 4d	3,375	1,974	13,874
Deluxe wgn 4d	3,680	2,895	1,545*

Futuramic 88 (wb 119.5)	Wght	Price	Prod
club sdn 2d	3,585	2,170	16,887
Deluxe club sdn 2d	3,615	2,301	11,820
club cpe	3,550	2,143	6,562
Deluxe club cpe	3,590	2,274	4,999
conv cpe	3,845	2,559	5,434
town sedan 4d	3,625	2,233	2,859
Delx town sedan 4d	3,665	2,364	2,974
sdn 4d	3,615	2,244	23,342
Deluxe sdn 4d	3,645	2,375	23,044
Deluxe wgn 4d	3,945	3,296	1,355*

Futuramic 98 (wb 125.0)	Wght	Price	Prod
club sdn	3,835	2,426	3,849
Deluxe club sdn	3,840	2,520	16,200
sdn 4d	3,890	2,500	8,820
Deluxe sdn 4d	3,925	2,594	49,001
Delx Holiday htp cpe	4,000	2,973	3,006
Deluxe conv cpe	4,200	2,973	12,602

1949 Engines	bore×stroke	bhp	availability
I-6, 257.1	3.53×4.38	105	S-76
V-8, 303.7	3.75×3.44	135	S-88, 98

*Includes part-wood and all-steel (midyear) models

1950

Futuramic 76 (wb 119.5)	Wght	Price	Prod
club sdn 2d	3,280	1,745	3,186
Deluxe club sdn 2d	3,285	1,813	1,919
club cpe	3,260	1,719	2,238
Deluxe club cpe	3,280	1,787	1,126
conv cpe	3,585	2,135	973
Holiday htp cpe	3,335	2,003	144
Delx Holiday htp cpe	3,385	2,108	394
sdn 4d	3,320	1,819	7,396
Deluxe sdn 4d	3,340	1,887	9,159
sdn 2d	3,290	1,761	3,865

Futuramic 76	Wght	Price	Prod
Deluxe sdn 2d	3,295	1,829	2,489
wgn 4d	3,610	2,362	121
Deluxe wgn 4d	3,615	2,504	247
Futuramic 88 (wb 119.5)			
club sdn 2d	3,475	1,904	14,705
Deluxe club sdn 2d	3,486	1,982	16,388
club cpe	3,435	1,878	10,684
Deluxe club cpe	3,455	1,956	10,772
conv cpe	3,745	2,294	9,127
Holiday htp cpe	3,510	2,162	1,366
Delx Holiday htp cpe	3,565	2,267	11,316
sdn 4d	3,515	1,978	40,301
Deluxe sdn 4d	3,520	2,056	100,810
sdn 2d	3,485	1,920	23,889
Deluxe sdn 2d	3,500	1,998	26,672
wgn 4d	3,775	2,520	1,830
Deluxe wgn 4d	3,780	2,662	552
Futuramic 98 (wb 122.0)			
club sdn 2d	3,685	2,225	2,270
Deluxe club sdn 2d	3,705	2,319	9,719
Deluxe conv cpe	4,150	2,772	3,925
Holiday htp cpe	3,775	2,383	317
Delx Holiday htp cpe	3,840	2,641	7,946
town sedan 4d	3,710	2,267	255
Delx town sedan 4d	3,755	2,361	1,523
sdn 4d	3,765	2,299	7,499
Deluxe sdn 4d	3,775	2,393	72,766

1950 Engines	bore×stroke	bhp	availability
I-6, 257.1	3.53×4.38	105	S-76
V-8, 303.7	3.75×3.44	135	S-88, 98

1951

88 (wb 119.5)	Wght	Price	Prod
sdn 4d	3,542	2,111	22,848
sdn 2d	3,507	2,049	11,792
Super 88 (wb 120.0)			
club cpe	3,557	2,219	7,328
sdn 4d	3,636	2,328	90,131
sdn 2d	3,579	2,265	34,963
conv cpe	3,831	2,673	3,854
Holiday htp cpe	3,743	2,558	14,180
98 (wb 122.0)			
Deluxe sdn 4d	3,787	2,610	78,122
Holiday htp cpe	3,762	2,545	3,917
Delx Holiday htp cpe	3,857	2,882	14,012
Deluxe conv cpe	4,107	3,025	4,468

1951 Engine	bore×stroke	bhp	availability
V-8, 303.7	3.75×3.44	135	S-all

1952

88 Deluxe (wb 120.0)	Wght	Price	Prod
sdn 4d	3,608	2,327	12,215
sdn 2d	3,565	2,262	6,402
Super 88 (wb 120.0)			
club cpe	3,597	2,345	2,050
sdn 4d	3,649	2,462	70,606
sdn 2d	3,603	2,395	24,963
conv cpe	3,867	2,853	5,162
Holiday htp cpe	3,640	2,673	15,777
Ninety-Eight (wb 124.0)			
sdn 4d	3,765	2,786	58,550
conv cpe	4,111	3,229	3,544
Holiday htp cpe	3,874	3,022	14,150

1952 Engines	bore×stroke	bhp	availability
V-8, 303.7	3.75×3.44	145	S-88
V-8, 303.7	3.75×3.44	160	S-Super 88, 98

1953

88 Deluxe (wb 120.0)	Wght	Price	Prod
sdn 4d	3,642	2,327	20,400
sdn 2d	3,603	2,262	12,400
Super 88 (wb 120.0)			
sdn 4d	3,673	2,462	119,317
sdn 2d	3,628	2,395	36,824
conv cpe	3,905	2,853	8,310
Holiday htp cpe	3,661	2,673	36,881
Ninety-Eight (wb 124.0)			
sdn 4d	3,779	2,786	64,431
conv cpe	4,119	3,229	7,521
Ninety-Eight	**Wght**	**Price**	**Prod**
Holiday htp cpe	3,893	3,022	27,920
Fiesta conv cpe	4,453	5,717	458

1953 Engines	bore×stroke	bhp	availability
V-8, 303.7	3.75×3.44	150	S-88
V-8, 303.7	3.75×3.44	165	S-Super 88, 98
V-8, 303.7	3.75×3.44	170	S-Fiesta

1954

88 (wb 122.0)	Wght	Price	Prod
sdn 4d	3,719	2,337	29,028
sdn 2d	3,699	2,272	18,013
Holiday htp cpe	3,721	2,449	25,820
Super 88 (wb 122.0)			
sdn 4d	3,780	2,477	111,326
sdn 2d	3,729	2,410	27,882
conv cpe	4,003	2,868	6,452
Delx Holiday htp cpe	3,775	2,688	42,155
Ninety-Eight (wb 126.0)			
Deluxe sdn 4d	3,895	2,806	47,972
Holiday htp cpe	3,851	2,826	8,865
Delx Holiday htp cpe	3,938	3,042	29,688
Starfire conv cpe	4,193	3,249	6,800

1954 Engines	bore×stroke	bhp	availability
V-8, 324.3	3.88×3.44	170	S-88
V-8, 324.3	3.88×3.44	185	S-Super 88, 98

1955

88 (wb 122.0)	Wght	Price	Prod
sdn 4d	3,707	2,362	57,777
sdn 2d	3,688	2,297	37,507
Holiday htp sdn	3,768	2,548	41,310
Holiday htp cpe	3,707	2,474	85,767
Super 88 (wb 122.0)			
sdn 4d	3,762	2,503	111,316
sdn 2d	3,720	2,436	11,950
conv cpe	3,983	2,894	9,007
Delx Holiday htp sdn	3,825	2,788	47,385
Delx Holiday htp cpe	3,765	2,714	62,534
Ninety-Eight (wb 126.0)			
sdn 4d	3,864	2,833	39,847
Starfire conv cpe	4,159	3,276	9,149
Delx Holiday htp sdn	3,976	3,140	31,267
Delx Holiday htp cpe	3,924	3,069	38,363

1955 Engines	bore×stroke	bhp	availability
V-8, 324.3	3.88×3.44	185	S-88
V-8, 324.3	3.88×3.44	202	S-Super 88, 98; O-88

1956

88 (wb 122.0)	Wght	Price	Prod
sdn 4d	3,748	2,487	57,092
sdn 2d	3,691	2,422	31,949
Holiday htp sdn	3,797	2,671	52,239
Holiday htp cpe	3,741	2,599	74,739
Super 88 (wb 122.0)			
sdn 4d	3,768	2,640	59,728
sdn 2d	3,717	2,574	5,465
Holiday htp sdn	3,869	2,881	61,192
Holiday htp cpe	3,771	2,808	43,054
conv cpe	4,033	3,031	9,561
Ninety-Eight (wb 126.0)			
sdn 4d	4,028	3,298	20,105
Holiday htp sdn	4,167	3,551	42,320
Holiday htp cpe	4,080	3,480	19,433
Starfire conv cpe	4,325	3,740	8,581

1956 Engines	bore×stroke	bhp	availability
V-8, 324.3	3.88×3.44	230	S-88
V-8, 324.3	3.88×3.44	240	S-Super 88, 98; O-88

1957

Golden Rocket 88 (wb 122.0)	Wght	Price	Prod
3611 sdn 2d	3,942	2,733	18,477
3637 Holiday htp cpe	3,963	2,854	49,187
3639 Holiday htp sdn	4,052	2,932	33,830
3667TX conv cpe	4,232	3,182	6,423
3669 sdn 4d	4,000	2,798	53,923
3693 Fiesta wgn 4d	4,281	3,202	5,052
3695 Fiesta htp wgn 4d	4,314	3,313	5,767
Golden Rckt Spr 88 (wb 122.0)	**Wght**	**Price**	**Prod**
3637SD Holiday htp cpe	4,010	3,180	31,155
3639SD Holiday htp sdn	4,117	3,257	39,162
3667DTX conv cpe	4,283	3,447	7,128
3669D sdn 4d	4,044	3,030	42,629
3695SD Fiesta htp wgn 4d	4,364	3,541	8,981
3611D sdn 2d	4,001	2,968	2,983
Starfire Ninety-Eight (wb 126.0)			
3037SDX Holiday htp cpe	4,296	3,937	17,791
3039SDX Holiday htp sdn	4,385	4,013	32,099
3067DX conv cpe	4,572	4,217	8,278
3069D sdn 4d	4,322	3,741	21,525

1957 Engines	bore×stroke	bhp	availability
V-8, 371.1	4.00×3.69	277	S-all
V-8, 371.1	4.00×3.69	300	O-all (J-2)

1958

Dynamic 88 (wb 122.5)	Wght	Price	Prod
3611 sdn 2d	3,961	2,772	11,833
3637 Holiday htp cpe	3,972	2,893	35,036
3639 Holiday htp sdn	4,035	2,971	28,241
3667TX conv cpe	3,987	3,221	4,456
3669 sdn 4d	3,985	2,837	60,429
3693 Fiesta wgn 4d	4,258	3,284	3,249
3695 Fiesta htp wgn 4d	4,297	3,395	3,323
Super 88 (wb 122.5)			
3637SD Holiday htp cpe	4,000	3,262	18,653
3639SD Holiday htp sdn	4,073	3,339	27,521
3667DTX conv cpe	4,010	3,529	3,799
3669D sdn 4d	4,008	3,112	33,844
3695SD Fiesta htp wgn 4d	4,334	3,623	5,175
Ninety-Eight (wb 126.5)			
3037SDX Holiday htp cpe	4,329	4,020	11,012
3039SDX Holiday htp sdn	4,391	4,096	27,603
3067DX conv cpe	4,318	4,300	5,605
3069D sdn 4d	4,316	3,824	16,595

1958 Engines	bore×stroke	bhp	availability
V-8, 371.1	4.00×3.69	265	S-88
V-8, 371.1	4.00×3.69	305	S-Super 88, 98; O-88
V-8, 371.1	4.00×3.69	312	O-all (J-2)

1959

Dynamic 88 (wb 123.0)	Wght	Price	Prod
3211 sdn 2d	4,040	2,837	16,123
3219 Celebrity sdn 4d	4,130	2,902	70,995
3235 Fiesta wgn 4d	4,465	3,365	11,298
3237 Hol SceniCoupe htp	4,085	2,958	38,488
3239 Hol sport sedan htp	4,165	3,036	48,707
3267 conv cpe	4,120	3,286	8,491
Super 88 (wb 123.0)			
3519 Celebrity sdn 4d	4,135	3,178	37,024
3535 Fiesta wgn 4d	4,485	3,669	7,015
3537 Hol SceniCoupe htp	4,090	3,328	20,259
3539 Hol sport sedan htp	4,185	3,405	38,467
3567 conv cpe	4,135	3,595	4,895
Ninety-Eight (wb 126.3)			
3819 Celebrity sdn 4d	4,390	3,890	23,106
3837 Hol SceniCoupe htp	4,360	4,086	13,669
3839 Hol sport sedan htp	4,450	4,162	36,813
3867 conv cpe	4,360	4,366	7,514

1959 Engines	bore×stroke	bhp	availability
V-8, 371.1	4.00×3.69	270	S-88
V-8, 371.1	4.00×3.69	300	O-88
V-8, 394.0	4.13×3.69	315	S-Super 88, 98

1960

Dynamic 88 (wb 123.0)	Wght	Price	Prod
3211 sdn 2d	4,026	2,835	13,545
3219 Celebrity sdn 4d	4,091	2,900	76,377
3235 Fiesta wgn 4d 6P	4,449	3,363	8,834
3237 Hol SceniCoupe htp	4,049	2,956	29,368
3239 Hol sport sedan htp	4,139	3,034	43,761
3245 Fiesta wgn 4d 8P	4,470	3,471	5,708
3267 conv cpe	4,101	3,284	12,271
Super 88 (wb 123.0)			
3519 Celebrity sdn 4d	4,128	3,176	35,094
3535 Fiesta wgn 4d 6P	4,483	3,665	3,765
3537 Hol SceniCoupe htp	4,086	3,325	16,464
3539 Hol sport sedan htp	4,182	3,402	33,285
3545 Fiesta wgn 4d 8P	4,506	3,773	3,475

Super 88		Wght	Price	Prod
3567	conv cpe	4,134	3,592	5,830

Ninety-Eight (wb 126.3)				
3819	Celebrity sdn 4d	4,360	3,887	17,188
3837	Hol SceniCoupe htp	4,322	4,083	7,635
3839	Hol sport sedan htp	4,431	4,159	27,257
3867	conv cpe	4,349	4,362	7,284

1960 Engines	bore×stroke	bhp	availability
V-8, 371.1	4.00×3.69	240	S-88
V-8, 371.1	4.00×3.69	260	O-88
V-8, 394.0	4.13×3.69	315	S-Super 88, 98

1961

F-85 (wb 112.0)		Wght	Price	Prod
3019	sdn 4d	2,541	2,384	19,765
3027	club cpe	2,549	2,330	2,336
3035	wgn 4d 6P	2,716	2,681	6,677
3045	wgn 4d 8P	2,800	2,762	10,087

F-85 Deluxe (wb 112.0)				
3117	Cutlass spt cpe	2,664	2,621	9,935
3119	sdn 4d	2,547	2,519	26,311
3135	wgn 4d 6P	2,731	2,816	526
3145	wgn 4d 8P	2,822	2,897	757

Dynamic 88 (wb 123.0)				
3211	sdn 2d	3,966	2,835	4,920
3235	wgn 4d 6P	4,354	3,363	5,374
3237	Holiday htp cpe	3,981	2,956	19,878
3239	Holiday htp sdn	4,074	3,034	51,562
3245	wgn 4d 8P	4,428	3,471	4,013
3267	conv cpe	4,068	3,284	9,049
3269	Celebrity sdn 4d	4,031	2,900	42,584

Super 88 (wb 123.0)				
3535	wgn 4d 6P	4,382	3,665	2,761
3537	Holiday htp cpe	4,024	3,325	7,009
3539	Holiday htp sdn	4,099	3,402	23,272
3545	wgn 4d 8P	4,445	3,773	2,170
3567	conv cpe	4,099	3,592	2,624
3569	Celebrity sdn 4d	4,065	3,176	15,328
3667	Starfire conv cpe	4,330	4,647	7,600

Ninety-Eight (wb 126.3)				
3819	town sdn 4d	4,208	3,887	9,087
3829	Holiday htp sdn	4,269	4,021	13,331
3837	Holiday htp cpe	4,187	4,083	4,445
3839	sport sedan htp	4,319	4,159	12,343
3867	conv cpe	4,225	4,362	3,804

1961 Engines	bore×stroke	bhp	availability
V-8, 215.0	3.50×2.80	155	S-F-85
V-8, 394.0	4.13×3.69	250	S-88
V-8, 394.0	4.13×3.69	325	S-Super 88, 98; O-88
V-8, 394.0	4.13×3.69	330	S-Starfire

1962

F-85 (wb 112.0)		Wght	Price	Prod
3019	sdn 4d	2,599	2,457	8,074
3027	club cpe	2,607	2,403	7,909
3035	wgn 4d 6P	2,780	2,754	3,204
3045	wgn 4d 8P	2,852	2,835	1,887
3067	conv cpe	2,790	2,760	3,660

F-85 Deluxe (wb 112.0)				
3117	Cutlass spt cpe	2,651	2,694	32,461
3119	sdn 4d	2,634	2,592	18,736
3135	wgn 4d 6P	2,812	2,889	4,974
3167	Cutlass conv cpe	2,830	2,971	9,893
3147	Jetfire htp cpe	2,739	3,049	3,765

Dynamic 88 (wb 123.0)				
3235	Fiesta wgn 4d 6P	4,392	3,460	8,527
3239	Holiday htp sdn	4,080	3,131	53,438
3245	Fiesta wgn 4d 8P	4,428	3,568	6,417
3247	Holiday htp cpe	3,992	3,054	39,676
3267	conv cpe	4,104	3,381	12,212
3269	Celebrity sdn 4d	4,038	2,997	68,467

Super 88 (wb 123.0)				
3535	Fiesta wgn 4d 6p	4,412	3,762	3,837
3539	Holiday htp sdn	4,117	3,499	21,175
3547	Holiday htp cpe	4,022	3,422	9,010
3569	Celebrity sdn 4d	4,069	3,273	24,125

Starfire (wb 123.0)				
3647	htp cpe	4,213	4,131	34,839
3667	conv cpe	4,334	4,744	7,149

Ninety-Eight (wb 126.0)		Wght	Price	Prod
3819	town sedan 4d	4,258	3,984	12,167
3829	Holiday htp sdn	4,306	4,118	7,653
3839	sport sedan htp	4,337	4,256	33,095
3847	Holiday htp cpe	4,231	4,180	7,546
3867	conv cpe	4,298	4,459	3,693

1962 Engines	bore×stroke	bhp	availability
V-8, 215.0	3.50×2.80	155	S-F-85 exc Cutlass, Jetfire
V-8, 215.0	3.50×2.80	185	S-F-85 Cutlass; O-F-85
V-8T, 215.0	3.50×2.80	215	S-F-85 Jetfire
V-8, 394.0	4.13×3.69	260	O-88
V-8, 394.0	4.13×3.69	280	S-88
V-8, 394.0	4.13×3.69	330	S-Super 88, 98
V-8, 394.0	4.13×3.69	345	S-Starfire

1963

F-85 (wb 112.0)		Wght	Price	Prod
3019	sdn 4d	2,629	2,457	8,937
3027	club cpe	2,599	2,403	11,276
3035	wgn 4d 6P	2,812	2,754	3,348

F-85 Deluxe (wb 112.0)				
3117	Cutlass club cpe	2,679	2,694	41,343
3119	sdn 4d	2,659	2,592	29,269
3135	wgn 4d 6P	2,833	2,889	6,647
3147	Jetfire htp cpe	2,774	3,048	5,842
3167	Cutlass conv cpe	2,858	2,971	12,149

Dynamic 88 (wb 123.0)				
3235	wgn 4d 6P	4,322	3,459	9,615
3239	Holiday htp sdn	4,059	3,130	62,351
3245	wgn 4d 8P	4,354	3,566	7,116
3247	Holiday htp cpe	3,839	3,052	39,071
3267	conv cpe	4,039	3,379	12,551
3269	Celebrity sdn 4d	3,998	2,995	68,611

Super 88 (wb 123.0)				
3535	Fiesta wgn 4d 6P	4,347	3,748	3,878
3539	Holiday htp sdn	4,083	3,473	25,387
3547	Holiday htp cpe	3,966	3,408	8,930
3569	Celebrity sdn 4d	4,027	3,246	24,575

Starfire (wb 123.0)				
3657	htp cpe	4,172	4,129	21,148
3667	conv cpe	4,293	4,742	4,401

Ninety-Eight (wb 126.0)				
3819	town sedan 4d	4,240	3,982	11,053
3829	Luxury htp sdn 6W	4,362	4,332	19,252
3839	sport sedan htp 4W	4,347	4,258	23,330
3847	Holiday Sport htp	4,215	4,178	4,984
3867	conv cpe	4,272	4,457	4,267
3947	Custom coupe htp	4,285	4,381	7,422

1963 Engines	bore×stroke	bhp	availability
V-8, 215.0	3.50×2.80	155	S-F-85 exc Cutlass, Jetfire
V-8, 215.0	3.50×2.80	185	S-F-85 Cutlass; O-F-85
V-8T, 215.0	3.50×2.80	215	S-F-85 Jetfire
V-8, 394.0	4.13×3.69	260	O-88
V-8, 394.0	4.13×3.69	280	S-88
V-8, 394.0	4.13×3.69	330	S-Super 88, 98 exc Custom
V-8, 394.0	4.13×3.69	345	S-Starfire, 98 Custom

1964

F-85 (wb 115.0; Vista Crsr-120.0)		Wght	Price	Prod
3027	club cpe*	2,980	2,343	16,298
3035	wgn 4d 2S	3,274	2,689	4,047
3055	Vist Cruisr wgn 4d 2S	3,652	2,938	1,305
3065	Vist Cruisr wgn 4d 3S	3,729	3,072	2,089
3069	sdn 4d*	3,025	2,397	12,106
3127	Deluxe sports coupe*	2,824	2,537	6,594
3135	Deluxe wgn 4d 2S	3,304	2,797	909
3169	Deluxe sdn 4d *	3,055	2,505	7,428

Cutlass (wb 115.0)				
3227	sports coupe*	3,141	2,644	15,440
3237	Holiday htp cpe*	3,180	2,784	36,153
3255	Custom wgn 4d 2S	3,714	3,146	3,320
3265	Custom wgn 4d 3S	3,781	3,270	7,286
3267	conv cpe*	3,263	2,984	12,822

Jetstar 88 (wb 123.0)		Wght	Price	Prod
3339	Holiday htp sdn	3,783	3,069	19,325
3347	Holiday htp cpe	3,701	2,992	14,663
3367	conv cpe	3,754	3,318	3,903
3369	Celebrity sdn 4d	3,729	2,935	24,614

Dynamic 88 (123.0)				
3435	wgn 4d 2S	4,286	3,468	10,747
3439	Holiday htp sdn	4,012	3,139	50,327
3445	wgn 4d 3S	4,324	3,576	6,599
3447	Holiday htp cpe	3,924	3,062	32,369
3457	Jetstar I spt cpe	4,019	3,603	16,084
3467	conv cpe	3,996	3,389	10,042
3469	Celebrity sdn 4d	3,966	3,005	57,590

Super 88 (wb 123.0)				
3539	Holiday htp sdn	4,069	3,486	17,778
3569	Celebrity sdn 4d	4,009	3,256	19,736

Starfire (wb 123.0)				
3657	htp cpe	4,167	4,138	13,753
3667	conv cpe	4,253	4,753	2,410

Ninety-Eight (wb 126.0)				
3819	town sedan 4d	4,234	3,993	11,380
3829	Luxury htp sdn 4d	4,337	4,342	17,346
3839	Hol sports sedan htp	4,323	4,265	24,791
3847	Holiday sports coupe	4,205	4,118	6,139
3867	conv cpe	4,255	4,468	4,004
3947	Cust sprts coupe htp	4,271	4,391	4,594

1964 Engines	bore×stroke	bhp	availability
V-6, 225.0	3.75×3.40	155	S-F-85 exc Vista Cruiser
V-8, 330.0	3.94×3.38	230	S-Vista Crsr; O-F-85, Jtstr 88
V-8, 330.0	3.94×3.38	245	S-Jetstar 88
V-8, 330.0	3.94×3.38	290	S-Cutl; O-F-85, Jetstar 88
V-8, 330.0	3.94×3.38	310	O-F-85/Cutlass (4-4-2 pkg.)
V-8, 394.0	4.13×3.69	260	O-Dynamic 88
V-8, 394.0	4.13×3.69	280	S-Dynamic 88
V-8, 394.0	4.13×3.69	330	S-Super 88, 98; O-Dynamic 88
V-8, 394.0	4.13×3.69	345	S-Jtstr I, Starfire, 98 Cust ; O-Super 88, 98

* Prod. incl. models with 4-4-2 performance package.

1965

F-85 (wb 115.0; Vista Crsr-120.0)		Wght	Price	Prod
3327	club cpe V-6	2,940	2,344	5,289
3335	wgn 4d V-6	3,252	2,689	714
3369	sdn 4d V-6	2,991	2,398	3,089
3427	club cpe V-8	3,146	2,415	7,720*
3435	wgn 4d V-8	3,457	2,760	2,496
3455	Vist Crsr wgn 6P V-8	3,732	2,937	2,110
3465	Vist Crsr wgn 8P V-8	3,809	3,072	3,335
3469	sdn 4d V-8	3,174	2,469	5,661

F-85 Deluxe (wb 115.0; Vista Crsr-120.0)				
3527	sports coupe V-6	2,980	2,538	6,141*
3535	wgn 4d V-6	3,262	2,797	659
3569	sdn 4d V-6	3,016	2,505	4,989
3635	wgn 4d V-8	3,459	2,868	10,365
3669	sdn 4d V-8	3,218	2,576	47,767
3855	Cst Vst Crsr wgn 4d 6P V-8	3,762	3,146	9,335
3865	Cst Vst Crsr wgn 4d 8P V-8	3,864	3,270	17,205

Cutlass (wb 115.0)				
3827	sports coupe V-8	3,221	2,643	26,441*
3837	Holiday htp cpe V-8	3,245	2,784	46,138*
3867	conv cpe V-8	3,338	2,983	12,628*

Jetstar 88 (wb 123.0)				
5237	Holiday htp cpe	3,688	2,995	13,911
5239	Holiday htp sdn	3,775	3,072	15,922
5267	conv cpe	3,741	3,337	2,879
5269	Celebrity sdn 4d	3,726	2,938	22,725

Jetstar I (wb 123.0)				
5457	sports coupe	3,982	3,602	6,552

Dynamic 88 (wb 123.0)				
5637	Holiday htp cpe	3,873	3,065	24,746
5639	Holiday htp sdn	3,961	3,143	38,889
5667	conv cpe	3,946	3,408	8,832
5669	Celebrity sdn 4d	3,908	3,008	47,030

Delta 88 (wb 123.0)		Wght	Price	Prod
5837	Holiday htp cpe	3,924	3,253	23,194
5839	Holiday htp sdn	4,011	3,330	37,358
5869	Celebrity sdn 4d	3,940	3,158	29,915
Starfire (wb 123.0)				
6657	htp cpe	4,152	4,138	13,024
6667	conv cpe	4,247	4,778	2,236
Ninety-Eight (wb 126.0)				
8437	Hol sports coupe htp	4,178	4,197	12,166
8439	Holiday htp sdn	4,286	4,273	28,480
8467	conv cpe	4,250	4,493	4,903
8469	town sedan 4d	4,186	4,001	13,266
8669	Luxury sdn 4d	4,285	4,351	33,591

1965 Engines	bore×stroke	bhp	availability
V-6, 225.0	3.75×3.40	155	V-6
V-8, 330.0	3.94×3.38	250/260	S-F-85 V-8 exc Cutl, Jetstar 88
V-8, 330.0	3.94×3.38	315	S-Cutlass
V-8, 400.0	4.00×3.98	320	O-Cutlass
V-8, 400.0	4.00×3.98	345	O-F-85 (4-4-2 pkg.)
V-8, 425.0	4.13×3.98	310	S-Dlt 88, Dyn 88; O-98
V-8, 425.0	4.13×3.98	360	S-98; O-othr fl-sz
V-8, 425.0	4.13×3.98	370	S-Jtstr I, Starf; O-full-size

* Prod. incl. models with 4-4-2 performance packages.

1966

F-85 (wb 115.0)		Wght	Price	Prod
33307	club cpe I-6	2,951	2,348	6,341
33335	wgn 4d I-6	3,246	2,695	508
33369	sdn 4d I-6	3,001	2,401	2,862
33407	club cpe V-8	3,153	2,418	4,923*
33435	wgn 4d V-8	3,431	2,764	1,652
33469	sdn 4d V-8	3,187	2,471	3,754
F-85 Deluxe (wb 115.0)				
33517	Holiday htp cpe I-6	2,990	2,513	2,974
33535	wgn 4d I-6	3,273	2,793	434
33539	Holiday htp sde I-6	3,077	2,629	1,002
33569	sdn 4d I-6	3,023	2,497	3,568
33617	Holiday htp cpe V-8	3,196	2,583	13,141*
33635	wgn 4d V-8	3,453	2,862	8,058
33639	Holiday htp sde V-8	3,272	2,699	6,911
33669	sdn 4d V-8	3,210	2,567	27,452
Cutlass (wb 115.0)				
33807	sports coupe	3,219	2,633	13,518*
33817	Holiday htp cpe	3,243	2,770	34,580*
33389	Supreme htp sdn	3,296	2,846	30,871
33867	conv cpe	3,349	2,965	9,410*
33869	Celebrity sdn 4d	3,240	2,673	9,017
Vista Cruiser (wb 120.0)				
33455	wgn 4d 2S	3,735	2,935	1,660
33465	wgn 4d 3S	3,806	3,087	1,869
33855	Custom wgn 4d 2S	3,765	3,137	8,910
33865	Custom wgn 4d 3S	3,861	3,278	14,167
4-4-2 (wb 115.0)				
33407	cpe	3,454	2,604	1,430*
33617	htp cpe	3,502	2,769	3,827*
33807	sports coupe	3,506	2,786	3,937*
33817	Holiday htp cpe	3,523	2,923	10,053*
33867	conv cpe	3,629	3,118	2,750*
Jetstar 88 (wb 123.0)				
35237	Holiday htp cpe	3,727	2,983	8,575
35239	Holiday htp sdn	3,823	3,059	7,938
35269	Celebrity sdn 4d	3,776	2,927	13,734
Dynamic 88 (wb 123.0)				
35637	Holiday htp cpe	3,899	3,069	20,768
35639	Holiday htp sdn	3,982	3,144	30,784
35667	conv cpe	3,971	3,404	5,540
35669	Celebrity sdn 4d	3,930	3,013	38,742
Delta 88 (wb 123.0)				
35837	Holiday htp cpe	3,944	3,253	20,857
35839	Holiday htp sdn	4,026	3,328	33,326
35867	conv cpe	4,010	3,588	4,303
35869	Celebrity sdn 4d	3,963	3,160	30,140
Starfire (wb 123.0)				
35457	htp cpe	4,013	3,564	13,019
Ninety-Eight (wb 126.0)				
38437	Holiday htp cpe	4,165	4,158	11,488
38439	Holiday htp sdn	4,266	4,233	23,048
38467	conv cpe	4,233	4,443	4,568
38469	town sedan 4d	4,177	3,966	10,892
38669	Luxury Sedan 4d	4,271	4,308	38,123
Toronado (wb 119.0)				
39487	htp cpe	4,311	4,617	6,333
39687	Deluxe htp cpe	4,366	4,812	34,630

* Prod. combined; numbers given are proportional to prod. of same models in F-85 and Cutlass lines. Total 4-4-2 production: 21,997.

1966 Engines	bore×stroke	bhp	availability
I-6, 250.0	3.88×3.53	155	S-F-85 I-6
V-8, 330.0	3.94×3.38	250	S-F-85 V-8, Vista Crsr; O-Jetstar 88
V-8, 330.0	3.94×3.38	260	S-Jetstar 88
V-8, 330.0	3.94×3.38	310	O-F85/Cutl V-8, Vista Crsr
V-8, 330.0	3.94×3.38	320	S-Cutl; O-Jtstr 88, F-85, Vista Crsr
V-8, 400.0	4.00×3.98	350	S-442
V-8, 425.0	4.13×3.98	300	O-Dlt 88, Dyn 88
V-8, 425.0	4.13×3.98	310	S-Delt 88, Dynamic 88
V-8, 425.0	4.13×3.98	365	S-98; O-Dlt 88, Dynamic 88
V-8, 425.0	4.13×3.98	375	S-Str; O-98, Dlt 88
V-8, 425.0	4.13×3.98	385	S-Toronado

1967

F-85 (wb 115.0)		Wght	Price	Prod
33307	club cpe I-6	3,014	2,410	5,349
33335	wgn 4d I-6	3,295	2,749	2,749
33369	town sedan 4d I-6	3,031	2,457	2,458
33407	club cpe V-8	3,184	2,480	6,700
33435	wgn 4d V-8	3,463	2,818	1,625
33469	town sedan 4d V-8	3,469	2,527	5,126
Cutlass (wb 115.0)				
33517	Holiday htp cpe I-6	3,033	2,574	2,564
33535	wgn 4d I-6	3,308	2,848	365
33539	Holiday htp sdn I-6	3,125	2,683	644
33567	conv cpe I-6	3,125	2,770	567
33569	town sedan 4d I-6	3,055	2,552	2,219
33617	Holiday htp cpe V-8	3,216	2,644	29,799
33635	wgn 4d V-8	3,473	2,917	8,130
33639	Holiday htp sdn V-8	3,292	2,753	7,344
33667	conv cpe V-8	3,306	2,839	3,777
33669	town sedan 4d V-8	3,223	2,622	29,062
Cutlass Supreme (wb 115.0)				
33807	sports coupe	3,238	2,694	13,041*
33817	Holiday htp cpe	3,262	2,831	41,344*
33839	Holiday htp sdn	3,346	2,900	22,571
33867	conv cpe	3,867	3,026	7,793*
33869	town sedan 4d	3,258	2,726	8,346
4-4-2 (wb 115.0)				
33807	sports coupe	3,540	2,788	5,215*
33817	Holiday htp cpe	3,568	3,015	16,514*
33867	conv cpe	4,047	3,210	3,104*
Vista Cruiser (wb 120.0)				
33465	wgn 4d 3S	3,836	3,136	2,748
33855	Custom wgn 4d 2S	3,796	3,228	9,513
33865	Custom wgn 4d 3S	3,907	3,369	15,293
Delmont 88 "330" (wb 123.0)				
35239	Holiday htp sdn	3,932	3,139	10,600
35269	town sedan 4d	3,867	3,008	15,076
35287	Holiday htp cpe	3,819	3,063	10,786
Delmont 88 "425" (wb 123.0)				
35639	Holiday htp sdn	4,007	3,202	22,980
35667	conv cpe	4,010	3,462	3,525
35669	town sedan 4d	3,968	3,071	28,690
35687	Holiday htp cpe	3,914	3,126	16,699
Delta 88 (wb 123.0)				
35839	Holiday htp sdn	4,053	3,386	21,909
35867	conv cpe	4,039	3,646	2,447
35869	town sedan 4d	3,986	3,218	22,770
35887	Holiday htp cpe	3,956	3,310	14,471
Delta 88 Custom (wb 123.0)				
35439	Holiday htp sdn	4,081	3,582	14,306
35487	Holiday htp cpe	3,994	3,522	12,192
Ninety-Eight (wb 126.0)				
38439	Holiday htp sdn	4,323	4,276	17,533
38457	Holiday htp cpe	4,221	4,214	10,476
38467	conv cpe	4,271	4,498	3,769
38469	town sedan 4d	4,242	4,009	8,900
38669	Luxury Sedan 4d	4,309	4,351	35,511
Toronado (wb 119.0)				
39487	htp cpe	4,310	4,674	1,770
39687	Deluxe htp cpe	4,362	4,869	20,020

* Prod. combined; numbers given are proportional to prod. of same models in Cutlass Supreme line. Total 4-4-2 production: 24,833.

1967 Engines	bore ×stroke	bhp	availability
I-6, 250.0	3.88×3.53	155	S-F-85/Cutl I-6
V-8, 330.0	3.94×3.38	250	S-F-85 V-8, Vst Crsr, Dlm 330 man; O-Delm auto
V-8, 330.0	3.94×3.38	260	S-Dlm 330 auto
V-8, 330.0	3.94×3.38	310	O-Sprm, Cutl, F-85, VC
V-8, 330.0	3.94×3.38	320	S-Sprm; O-Delm 330, VC, F-85, Cutl
V-8, 400.0	4.00×3.98	300	O-Sprm cpe/ conv
V-8, 400.0	4.00×3.98	350	S-442; O-Sprm cpe & conv
V-8, 425.0	4.13×3.98	300	S-all 88 man; O-all 88 auto
V-8, 425.0	4.13×3.98	310	S-all 88 auto
V-8, 425.0	4.13×3.98	365	S-98; O-Dlta 88, Delmont 425
V-8, 425.0	4.13×3.98	375	O-98, Delta 88, Delmont 425
V-8, 425.0	4.13×3.98	385	S-Toronado

1968

F-85 (wb 116.0; 2d-112.0)		Wght	Price	Prod
33169	town sedan 4d I-6	3,108	2,560	1,847
33177	club cpe I-6	3,062	2,512	4,052
33269	town sedan 4d V-8	3,304	2,665	3,984
33277	club cpe V-8	3,255	2,618	5,426
Cutlass (wb 116.0; 2d-112.0)				
33535	wgn 4d 2S, I-6	3,473	2,969	354
33539	Holiday htp sdn I-6	3,193	2,804	265
33567	conv cpe I-6	3,161	2,949	410
33569	town sedan 4d I-6	3,143	2,674	1,305
33577	sports coupe I-6	3,064	2,632	1,181
33587	Holiday htp cpe I-6	3,108	2,696	1,492
33635	wgn 4d 2S, V-8	3,649	3,075	9,291
33639	Holiday htp sdn V-8	3,374	2,910	7,839
33667	conv cpe V-8	3,342	3,055	13,667
33669	town sedan 4d V-8	3,325	2,779	25,994
33677	sport coupe V-8	3,271	2,738	14,586
33687	Holiday htp cpe V-8	3,282	2,801	59,577
Cutlass Supreme (wb 116.0; 2d-112.0)				
34239	Holiday htp sdn	3,421	3,057	15,067
34269	town sedan 4d	3,372	2,884	5,524
34287	Holiday htp cpe	3,312	2,982	33,518
4-4-2 (wb 112.0)*				
34467	conv cpe	3,580	3,341	5,142
34477	sports coupe	3,502	3,087	4,282
34487	Holiday htp cpe	3,512	3,150	24,183
Vista Cruiser (wb 121.0)				
34855	Custom wgn 4d 2S	3,917	3,367	13,375
34865	Custom wgn 4d 3S	4,027	3,508	22,768
Delmont 88 (wb 123.0)**				
35439	Holiday htp sdn	3,928	3,278	21,056
35467	conv cpe	3,916	3,515	2,812
35469	town sedan 4d	3,873	3,146	24,365
35487	Holiday htp cpe	3,844	3,202	18,391
Delta 88 (wb 123.0)**				
36439	Holiday htp sdn	4,038	3,525	30,048
36469	town sedan 4d	3,979	3,357	33,689
36487	Holiday htp cpe	3,950	3,449	18,501
36639	Cust Holiday htp sdn	4,059	3,721	10,727
36687	Cust Holiday htp cpe	3,982	3,661	9,540
Ninety-Eight (wb 126.0)				
38439	Holiday htp sdn	4,278	4,422	21,147

Ninety-Eight	Wght	Price	Prod
38457 Holiday htp cpe	4,185	4,360	15,319
38467 conv cpe	4,264	4,618	3,942
38469 town sedan 4d	4,197	4,155	10,584
38669 Luxury Sedan 4d	4,273	4,497	40,755
Toronado (wb 119.0)			
39487 htp cpe	4,322	4,750	3,957
39687 Custom htp cpe	4,374	4,945	22,497

* 4-4-2 production includes 515 Hurst/Olds models.

** Factory records also indicate 54,794 Dynamic 88s, although other sources do not include these models.

1968 Engines	bore×stroke	bhp	availability
I-6, 250.0	3.88×3.53	155	S-F-85/Cutl I-6
V-8, 350.0	4.06×3.38	250	S-Dlmnt, Vst Crsr; O-Ctls, F-85
V-8, 350.0	4.06×3.38	310	S-Supreme; O-F-85, Ctls, VC, Delmont auto
V-8, 400.0	4.00×3.98	290	O-442 & VC auto
V-8, 400.0	4.00×3.98	325	S-442 auto; O-VC auto
V-8, 400.0	4.00×3.98	350	S-442 manual
V-8, 400.0	4.00×3.98	360	O-442 all
V-8, 455.0	4.13×4.25	310	S-Delta/Cust; O-Delmont
V-8, 455.0	4.13×4.25	320	O-above models w/automatic
V-8, 455.0	4.13×4.25	365	S-98; O-all 88 w/automatic
V-8, 455.0	4.13×4.25	375	S-Toronado
V-8, 455.0	4.13×4.25	390	O-442 (Hurst/Olds)
V-8, 455.0	4.13×4.25	400	O-Toronado

1969

F-85 (wb 112.0)	Wght	Price	Prod
33177 sports coupe I-6	3,082	2,561	2,899
33277 sports coupe V-8	3,281	2,672	5,541
Cutlass (wb 116.0; 2d-112.0)			
33535 wgn 4d 2S, I-6	3,537	3,055	180
33539 Holiday htp sdn I-6	3,212	2,853	236
33567 S conv cpe I-6	3,188	2,998	236
33569 town sedan 4d I-6	3,155	2,722	137
33577 S sports coupe I-6	3,093	2,681	483
33587 S Holiday htp cpe I-6	3,118	2,745	566
33635 wgn 4d 2S, V-8	3,736	3,165	8,559
33639 Holiday htp sdn V-8	3,407	2,964	7,046
33667 S conv cpe V-8	3,386	3,109	13,498
33669 town sedan 4d V-8	3,356	2,833	24,521
33677 S sports coupe V-8	3,293	2,792	10,682
33687 S Holiday htp cpe V-8	3,316	2,855	66,495
Cutlass Supreme (wb 116; 2d-112.0)			
34239 Holiday htp sdn	3,421	3,111	8,714
34269 town sedan 4d	3,361	2,938	4,522
34287 Holiday htp cpe	3,331	3,036	24,193
4-4-2 (wb 112.0)*			
34467 conv cpe	3,580	3,395	4,295
34477 sports coupe	3,502	3,141	2,475
34487 Holiday htp cpe	3,512	3,204	19,587

*Includes 914 Hurst/Olds models (2 convertibles).

Vista Cruiser (wb 121.0)	Wght	Price	Prod
34855 wgn 4d 2S	3,952	3,457	11,879
34865 wgn 4d 3S	4,052	3,600	21,508
Delta 88 (wb 124.0)			
35437 Holiday htp cpe	3,812	3,277	41,947
35439 Holiday htp sdn	3,901	3,353	42,690
35467 conv cpe	3,892	3,590	5,294
35469 town sedan 4d	3,859	3,222	49,995
36437 Cust Holiday htp cpe	3,927	3,525	22,083
36439 Cust Holiday htp sdn	4,009	3,600	36,502
36469 Cust town sedan 4d	3,962	3,432	31,012
36647 Royale Hol htp cpe	3,935	3,836	22,564
Ninety-Eight (wb 127.0)			
38439 Holiday htp sdn	4,260	4,523	17,294
38457 Holiday htp cpe	4,150	4,461	27,041
38467 conv cpe	4,223	4,719	4,288
38469 town sedan 4d	4,150	4,255	11,169
38639 Luxury Sedan htp	4,288	4,692	25,973
38669 Luxury Sedan 4d	4,245	4,598	30,643
Toronado (wb 119.0)			
39487 htp cpe	4,316	4,835	3,421
39687 Custom htp cpe	4,368	5,030	25,073

1969 Engines	bore×stroke	bhp	availability
I-6, 250.0	3.88×3.53	155	S-F-85/Cutl I-6
V-8, 350.0	4.06×3.38	250	S-F-85/Cutl V-8, Delta 88 base, VC; O-Supreme
V-8, 350.0	4.06×3.38	310	S-Sprm; O-F-85/Cutl V-8, VC
V-8, 350.0	4.06×3.38	325	O-Cutl S, F-85
V-8, 400.0	4.00×3.98	325	S-442 & VC auto
V-8, 400.0	4.00×3.98	350	S-442 manual
V-8, 400.0	4.00×3.98	360	O-442
V-8, 455.0	4.13×4.25	310	S-Dlta Cus/Royl; O-other Delta
V-8, 455.0	4.13×4.25	365	S-98; O-all Dlta 88
V-8, 455.0	4.13×4.25	375	S-Toronado
V-8, 455.0	4.13×4.25	380	O-442 (Hurst/Olds)
V-8, 455.0	4.13×4.25	390	O-all Delta 88
V-8, 455.0	4.13×4.25	400	O-Toronado

1970

F-85 (wb 112.0)	Wght	Price	Prod
33177 sports coupe I-6	3,190	2,676	2,836
33277 sports coupe V-8	3,401	2,787	8,274
Cutlass (wb 116.0; 2d-112.0)			
33535 wgn 4d 2S, I-6	3,630	3,234	85
33539 Holiday htp sdn I-6	3,326	2,968	238
33569 town sedan 4d I-6	3,257	2,837	1,171
33577 S sports coupe I-6	3,201	2,796	484
33587 S Holiday htp cpe I-6	3,238	2,859	729
33635 wgn 4d 2S, V-8	3,837	3,344	7,686
33639 Holiday htp sdn V-8	3,523	3,079	9,427
33669 town sedan V-8	3,468	2,948	35,239
33677 S sports coupe V-8	3,416	2,907	10,677
33687 S Holiday htp cpe V-8	3,452	2,970	88,578
Cutlass Supreme (wb 116; 2d-112.0)			
34239 Holiday htp sdn	3,558	3,226	10,762
34257 Holiday htp cpe	3,471	3,151	68,309
34267 conv cpe	3,510	3,335	11,354
4-4-2 (wb 112.0)			
34467 conv cpe	3,740	3,567	2,933
34477 sports coupe	3,667	3,312	1,688
34487 Holiday htp cpe	3,713	3,376	14,709
Vista Cruiser (wb 121.0)			
34855 wgn 4d 2S	4,064	3,636	10,758
34865 wgn 4d 3S	4,166	3,778	23,336
Delta 88 (wb 124.0)			
35437 Holiday htp cpe	3,900	3,590	33,017
35439 Holiday htp sdn	3,986	3,666	37,695
35467 conv cpe	3,985	3,903	3,095
35469 town sedan 4d	3,944	3,534	47,067
36437 Cust Holiday htp cpe	3,999	3,848	16,149
36439 Cust Holiday htp sdn	4,087	3,924	28,432
36469 Cust town sedan 4d	4,040	3,755	24,727
36647 Royale Hol htp cpe	4,002	4,159	13,249
Ninety-Eight (wb 127.0)			
38439 Holiday htp sdn	4,329	4,582	14,098
38457 Holiday htp cpe	4,257	4,656	21,111
38467 conv cpe	4,289	4,914	3,161
38469 town sedan 4d	4,263	4,451	9,092
38639 Luxury Sedan htp	4,400	4,888	19,377
38669 Luxury Sedan 4d	4,356	4,793	29,005
Toronado (wb 119.0)			
39487 htp cpe	4,331	5,023	2,351
39687 Custom htp cpe	4,386	5,216	23,082

1970 Engines	bore×stroke	bhp	availability
I-6, 250.0	3.88×3.53	155	S- F-85/Cutl I-6
V-8, 350.0	4.06×3.38	250	S- F-85/Cutlass V-8, VC; O-Sprm
V-8, 350.0	4.06×3.38	310	S-Sprm; O-VC, F-85, Cutlass
V-8, 350.0	4.06×3.38	325	O-F-85, Cutl S auto or 4 spd
V-8, 455.0	4.13×4.25	310	S-Delta 88 man
V-8, 455.0	4.13×4.25	320	O-Cutl w/auto
V-8, 455.0	4.13×4.25	365	S-442, 98; O-Sprm, 88/ VC manual
V-8, 455.0	4.13×4.25	370	O-442 w/auto or close-ratio 4 spd
V-8, 455.0	4.13×4.25	375	S-Toronado
V-8, 455.0	4.13×4.25	390	O-Delta 88
V-8, 455.0	4.13×4.25	400	O-Toronado

1971

F-85 (wb 116.0)	Wght	Price	Prod
33169 town sedan 4d I-6	3,226	2,885	769
33269 town sedan 4d V-8	3,424	3,006	3,650
Cutlass (wb 116.0; 2d-112.0)			
33187 Holiday htp cpe I-6	3,292	2,901	1,345
33536 wgn 4d 2S I-6	3,732	3,454	47
33569 town sedan 4d I-6	3,252	2,999	618
33287 htp cpe V-8	3,398	3,022	32,278
33636 wgn 4d 2S V-8	3,927	3,575	6,742
33669 town sdn 4d V-8	3,438	3,120	31,904
33577 S sports coupe I-6	3,196	2,958	113
33587 S htp cpe I-6	3,228	3,021	169
33677 S sports coupe V-8	3,392	3,079	4,339
33687 S htp cpe V-8	3,398	3,142	63,145
Cutlass Supreme (wb 116.0; 2d-112.0)			
34239 htp sdn	3,541	3,398	10,458
34257 htp cpe	3,429	3,323	60,599
34267 conv	3,513	3,507	10,255
4-4-2 (wb 112.0)			
34467 conv cpe	3,731	3,743	1,304
34487 cpe	3,688	3,552	6,285
Vista Cruiser (wb 121.0)			
34856 wgn 4d 2S	4,163	3,866	5,980
34866 wgn 4d 3S	4,251	4,008	20,566
Delta 88 (wb 124.0; wgns-127.0)			
35439 sdn 4d	4,202	4,103	31,420
35457 htp cpe	4,122	4,041	27,031
35469 town sedan 4d	4,150	3,985	38,298
36439 Custom htp sdn	4,237	4,366	26,593
36457 Custom cpe	4,179	4,291	24,251
36469 Cust town sedan 4d	4,202	4,198	22,209
36647 Royale htp cpe	4,221	4,549	8,397
36667 Royale conv	4,296	4,557	2,883
36835 Cust Crsr wgn 4d 2S	4,880	4,776	4,049
36845 Cust Crsr wgn 4d 3S	5,000	4,917	9,932
Ninety-Eight (wb 127.0)			
38437 htp cpe	4,382	4,790	8,335
38439 htp sdn	4,467	4,852	15,025
38637 Luxury Coupe htp	4,418	5,065	14,876
38639 Luxury Sedan htp	4,504	5,159	45,055
Toronado (wb 123.0)			
39657 htp cpe	4,522	5,457	28,980

1971 Engines	bore×stroke	bhp	availability
I-6, 250.0	3.88×3.53	145	S-F-85/Cutl I-6
V-8, 350.0	4.06×3.38	240	S-F-85/Cutl V-8 Delta, VC
V-8, 350.0	4.06×3.38	260	S-Sprm, O-F-85, Cutlass, VC
V-8, 455.0	4.13×4.25	280	O-Delta
V-8, 455.0	4.13×4.25	320	S-98; O-442, F-85, Cutl, VC, Delta
V-8, 455.0	4.13×4.25	340	S-442; O-F-85, Cutlass, VC
V-8, 455.0	4.13×4.25	350	S-Toronado

1972

F-85 (wb 116.0)	Wght	Price	Prod
3D69 sdn 4d	3,420	2,958	3,792
Cutlass (wb 116.0; 2d-112.0)			
3F87 cpe	3,379	2,973	37,790
3G36 Cruiser wgn 4d 2S	3,919	3,498	7,979
3G69 town sedan 4d	3,443	3,066	38,893
3G77 S spt cpe	3,387	3,027	4,141
3G87 S htp cpe	3,404	3,087	78,461
3J39 Supreme htp sdn	3,530	3,329	14,955
3J57 Supreme htp cpe	3,395	3,258	105,087
3J67 Supreme conv	3,528	3,433	11,571
Vista Cruiser (wb 121.0)			
3K56 wgn 4d 2S	4,150	3,774	10,573
3K66 wgn 4d 3S	4,241	3,908	21,340
Delta 88 (wb 124.0)			
3L39 sdn 4d	4,235	4,060	35,538

Delta 88		Wght	Price	Prod
3L57	htp cpe	4,133	4,001	32,036
3L69	town sedan 4d	4,187	3,948	46,092
3N39	Royale sdn 4d	4,263	4,238	42,606
3N57	Royale htp cpe	4,184	4,179	34,345
3N67	Royale conv	4,257	4,387	3,900
3N69	Royale twn sedan 4d	4,198	4,101	34,150
3R35	Cust Crsr wgn 4d 2S	4,947	4,700	6,907
3R45	Cust Crsr wgn 4d 3S	5,040	4,834	18,087
Ninety-Eight (wb 127.0)				
3U37	htp cpe	4,372	4,748	13,111
3U39	htp sdn	4,448	4,807	17,572
3V37	Luxury Coupe htp	4,428	5,009	24,453
3V39	Luxury Sedan htp	4,533	5,098	69,920
Toronado (wb 122.0)				
3Y57	Custom htp cpe	4,544	5,341	48,900

1972 Engines	bore×stroke	bhp	availability
V-8, 350.0	4.06×3.38	160	S-F-85, Cutl, Dlt exc wgns
V-8, 350.0	4.06×3.38	180	S-Sprm; O-Ctls, F-85, VC, Delta exc wgn
V-8, 455.0	4.13×4.25	225	S-Delta wgn, 98; O-other Delta
V-8, 455.0	4.13×4.25	250	S-Toro; O-Dlt, 98
V-8, 455.0	4.13×4.25	270/300	O-Cutl cpe/conv (Hurst/Olds)

Note: Total of 629 H/O pkgs installed on Cutlass models.

1973

Omega (wb 111.0)		Wght	Price	Prod
B17	htchbk cpe	3,329	2,762	21,433
B27	cpe	3,217	2,613	26,126
B69	sdn 4d	3,280	2,641	12,804
Cutlass (wb 116.0; 2d-112.0)				
G29	Colonnade sdn 4d	3,786	3,137	35,578
F37	Colonnade coupe	3,713	3,049	22,022
G37	Colonnade S coupe	3,721	3,159	77,558
J29	Sprm Clnnde sdn 4d	3,808	3,395	26,099
J57	Sprm Clnnde cpe	3,694	3,324	219,857
Vista Cruiser (wb 116.0)				
J35	wgn 4d 2S	4,240	3,789	10,894
J45	wgn 4d 3S	4,290	3,902	13,531
Delta 88 (wb 124.0)				
L39	htp sdn	4,270	4,108	27,986
L57	htp cpe	4,192	4,047	27,096
L69	town sedan 4d	4,243	3,991	42,476
N39	Royale htp sdn	4,296	4,293	49,145
N57	Royale htp cpe	4,206	4,221	27,096
N67	Royale conv	4,298	4,442	7,088
N69	Royale twn sedan 4d	4,255	4,156	42,672
Q35	Cust Crsr wgn 4d 2S	4,997	4,630	5,275
Q45	Cust Crsr wgn 4d 3S	5,061	4,769	7,341
R35	Cust Crsr wgn 4d 2S	4,999	4,785	7,142
R45	Cust Crsr wgn 4d 3S	5,063	4,924	19,163
Ninety-Eight (wb 127.0)				
T37	htp cpe	4,435	4,799	7,850
T39	htp sdn	4,522	4,860	13,989
V37	Luxury Coupe htp	4,471	5,071	26,925
V39	Luxury Sedan htp	4,560	5,164	55,695
X39	Regency htp sdn	4,594	5,418	34,009
Toronado (wb 122.0)				
Y57	htp cpe	4,654	5,441	55,921

1973 Engines	bore×stroke	bhp	availability
I-6, 250.0	3.88×3.53	100	S-Omega
V-8, 350.0	4.06×3.38	160	S-Dlta exc wgns
V-8, 350.0	4.06×3.38	180	S-Omg, Cutl, VC
V-8, 455.0	4.13×4.25	225	S-Dlta wgns, 98; O-other Dlta
V-8, 455.0	4.13×4.25	250	S-Toro, O-Cutl, VC

1974

Omega (wb 111.0)		Wght	Price	Prod
B17	htchbk cpe	3,423	3,166	12,449
B27	cpe	3,319	3,043	27,075
B69	sdn 4d	3,367	3,071	10,756
Cutlass (wb 116.0; 2d-112.0)				
F37	Colonnade cpe	3,868	3,793	16,063
G29	Colonnade sdn 4d	3,924	3,868	25,718
G37	Colonnade S coupe	3,883	3,890	50,860

Cutlass		Wght	Price	Prod
J29	Sprm Clnnde sdn 4d	3,969	4,142	12,525
J57	Sprm Clnnde cpe	3,872	4,085	172,360
H35	Sprm Crsr wgn 4d 2S	4,369	4,289	3,437
H45	Sprm Crsr wgn 4d 3S	4,406	4,402	3,101
Vista Cruiser (wb 116.0)				
J35	wgn 4d 2S	4,380	4,499	4,191
J45	wgn 4d 3S	4,417	4,612	7,013
Delta 88 (wb 124.0)				
L39	htp sdn	4,428	4,490	11,941
L57	htp cpe	4,375	4,429	11,615
L69	town sedan 4d	4,396	4,373	17,939
N39	Royale htp sdn	4,462	4,650	26,363
N57	Royale htp cpe	4,397	4,584	27,515
N67	Royale conv	4,454	4,799	3,716
N69	Royale twn sedan 4d	4,414	4,513	22,504
Q35	Cust Crsr wgn 4d 2S	5,120	4,981	1,481
Q45	Cust Crsr wgn 4d 3S	5,182	5,120	2,528
R35	Cst Crsr wgn 4d 2S (wdgrn)	5,123	5,136	2,960
R45	Cst Crsr wgn 4d 3S (wdgrn)	5,184	5,275	8,947
Ninety-Eight (wb 127.0)				
T39	htp sdn	4,699	5,303	4,395
V37	Luxury Coupe htp	4,638	5,514	9,236
V39	Luxury Sedan htp	4,730	5,607	21,896
X37	Regency cpe	4,664	5,776	10,719
X39	Regency htp sdn	4,759	5,869	24,310
Toronado (wb 122.0)				
Y57	htp cpe	4,698	5,933	27,582

1974 Engines	bore×stroke	bhp	availability
I-6, 250.0	3.88×3.53	100	S-Omega
V-8, 350.0	4.06×3.38	180	S-Omg, Cutl, VC, Delta exc wgns
V-8, 350.0	4.06×3.38	200	O-Cutl, VC, Delta exc wgns
V-8, 455.0	4.13×4.25	210	S-Dlta wgns, 98; O-other Delta
V-8, 455.0	4.13×4.25	230	S-Toro; O-exc Omg
V-8, 455.0	4.13×4.25	275	O-Cutlass, VC

1975

Starfire (wb 97.0)		Wght	Price	Prod
D37	htchbk cpe	2,914	4,144	31,081
T07	htchbk cpe 2d	2,889	3,873	
Omega (wb 111.0)				
S27	F-85 htchbk cpe	3,250	3,203	15,979
B27	cpe	3,390	3,422	
B17	htchbk cpe	3,482	3,546	6,287
B69	sdn 4d	3,436	3,450	13,971
C17	Salon htchbk cpe	3,566	4,298	1,694
C27	Salon cpe	3,476	4,148	2,176
C69	Salon sdn 4d	3,526	4,192	1,758
Cutlass (wb 116.0; 2d-112.0)				
F37	Colonnade cpe	3,684	3,742	12,797
G29	Colonnade sdn 4d	3,806	3,818	30,144
G37	Colonnade S cpe	3,740	3,840	42,921
J29	Sprm Clnnde sdn 4d	3,852	4,092	15,517
J57	Sprm Clnnde cpe	3,754	4,035	150,874
K29	Sln Clnnde sdn 4d V-8	4,008	4,713	5,810
K57	Sln Clnnde cpe V-8	3,915	4,641	39,050
H35	Sprm Crsr wgn 4d 2S V-8	4,376	4,665	8,329
H45	Sprm Crsr wgn 4d 3S V-8	4,413	4,778	3,096
J35	Vist Crsr wgn 4d 2S V-8	4,380	4,875	7,089
J45	Vist Crsr wgn 4d 3S V-8	4,417	4,988	7,101
Delta 88 (wb 124.0)				
L39	htp sdn	4,404	4,891	9,283
L57	htp cpe	4,343	4,830	8,522
L69	town sedan 4d	4,356	4,778	16,112
N39	Royale htp sdn	4,454	5,051	32,481
N57	Royale htp cpe	4,386	4,985	23,465
N67	Royale conv	4,455	5,200	21,038
N69	Royale twn sedan 4d	4,385	4,914	7,181
Q35	Cust Crsr wgn 4d 2S	5,095	5,413	6,008
R35	Cst Crsr wgn 4d 2S (wdgrn)	5,107	5,568	
Q45	Cust Crsr wgn 4d 3S	5,146	5,552	10,060
R45	Cst Crsr wgn 4d 3S (wdgrn)	5,161	5,707	
Ninety-Eight (wb 127.0)				
V37	Luxury Coupe	4,591	5,950	8,798
V39	Luxury Sedan htp	4,743	6,091	18,091
X37	Regency cpe	4,621	6,212	16,697
X39	Regency htp sdn	4,755	6,353	35,264

Toronado (wb 122.0)		Wght	Price	Prod
Y57	Custom htp cpe	4,647	6,523	4,419
Z57	Brougham htp cpe	4,691	6,753	18,882

1975 Engines	bore×stroke	bhp	availability
V-6, 231.0	3.80×3.40	110	S-Starfire
I-6, 250.0	3.88×3.53	105	S-Omega, Cutl exc wgns
V-8, 260.0	3.50×3.39	110	S-Omega, Cutl exc wgns
V-8, 350.0	4.06×3.38	145	O-Omega
V-8, 350.0	4.06×3.38	165	O-Omega
V-8, 350.0	4.06×3.38	170	S-Cutl wgns, Delta exc wgns; O-other Cutl
V-8, 400.0	4.12×3.75	185	O-Delta, 98
V-8, 455.0	4.13×4.25	190	S-Dlta wgns, 98; O-Cutl, other Dlt
V-8, 455.0	4.13×4.25	215	S-Toronado

1976

Starfire (wb 97.0)		Wght	Price	Prod
D07	SX htchbk cpe	2,864	4,062	20,854
T07	htchbk cpe	2,857	3,882	8,305
Omega (wb 111.0)				
S27	F-85 cpe	3,246	3,390	3,918
B17	htchbk cpe	3,322	3,627	4,497
B27	cpe	3,248	3,485	15,347
B69	sdn 4d	3,270	3,514	20,221
E17	Brghm htchbk cpe	3,332	3,817	1,235
E27	Brougham cpe	3,252	3,675	5,363
E69	Brougham sdn 4d	3,286	3,704	7,587
Cutlass (wb 116.0; cpe-112.0)				
G29	S Colonnade sdn 4d	3,772	4,033	34,994
G37	S Colonnade	3,690	3,999	59,179
J29	Sprm Clnnde sdn 4d	3,812	4,415	37,112
J57	Sprm Clnnde cpe	3,718	4,291	186,647
M57	Sprm Brougham cpe	3,750	4,580	91,312
K29	Sln Clnnde sdn 4d V-8	3,949	4,965	7,921
K57	Sln Clnnde cpe V-8	3,829	4,890	48,440
H35	Sprm Crsr wgn 4d 2S V-8	4,298	4,923	13,964
H35	Sprm Crsr wgn 4d 3S V-8	4,350	5,056	
J35	Vst Crsr wgn 4d 2S V-8	4,304	5,041	20,560
J35	Vst Crsr wgn 4d 3S V-8	4,350	5,174	
Delta 88 (wb 124.0; wgns-127.0)				
L39	sdn 4d	4,336	5,038	9,759
L57	cpe 2d	4,243	4,975	7,204
L69	town sedan 4d	4,279	4,918	17,115
N39	Royale sdn 4d	4,268	5,217	52,103
N57	Royale cpe 2d	4,263	5,146	33,364
N69	Royale town sdn 4d	4,294	5,078	33,268
Q35	Cust Crsr wgn 4d 2S	4,987	5,563	2,572
Q45	wgn 4d 3S	5,060	5,705	3,626
R35	wgn 4d 2S (wdgrn)	5,009	5,719	3,849
R45	CC wgn 4d 3S (wdgrn)	5,071	5,861	12,269
Ninety-Eight (wb 127.0)				
V37	Luxury Coupe	4,501	6,271	6,056
V39	Luxury Sedan htp	4,633	6,419	16,802
X37	Regency cpe	4,535	6,544	26,282
X39	Regency htp sdn	4,673	6,691	55,339
Toronado (wb 122.0)				
Y57	Custom htp cpe	4,694	6,891	2,555
Z57	Brougham htp cpe	4,729	7,137	21,749

1976 Engines	bore×stroke	bhp	availability
V-6, 231.0	3.80×3.40	105	S-Starfire
I-6, 250.0	3.88×3.53	105	S-Omg,Cutlass exc Salon
V-8, 260.0	3.50×3.39	110	S-Omega, Cutl Sln; O-other Cutl
V-8, 350.0	3.80×3.85	140/155	O-Omega
V-8, 350.0	4.06×3.38	170	S-Dlt exc wgn; O-Cutl, Salon
V-8, 455.0	4.13×4.25	190	S-Delta wgn, 98; O-Cutl, other Dlt
V-8, 455.0	4.13×4.25	215	S-Toronado

1977

Starfire (wb 97.0)		Wght	Price	Prod
D07	SX htchbk cpe	2,836	4,140	14,181
T07	htchbk cpe	2,808	3,942	4,910
Omega (wb 111.0)				
S27	F-85 cpe	3,184	3,653	2,241

Omega		Wght	Price	Prod
B17	htchbk cpe	3,270	3,905	4,739
B27	cpe	3,202	3,740	18,611
B69	sdn 4d	3,236	3,797	21,723
E17	Brougham htchbk cpe	3,302	4,105	1,189
E27	Brougham cpe	3,226	3,934	6,478
E67	Brougham sdn 4d	3,262	3,994	9,003
Cutlass (wb 116.0; 2d-112.0)				
G29	S sdn 4d	3,690	4,387	42,923
G37	S cpe	3,608	4,351	70,155
J29	Supreme sdn 4d	3,438	4,734	37,929
J57	Supreme cpe	3,638	4,670	242,874
M29	Sprm Brghm sdn 4d	3,764	5,033	16,738
M57	Sprm Brghm cpe	3,656	4,969	124,712
K57	Salon cpe V-8	3,787	5,269	56,757
H35	Sprm Crsr wgn 4d V-8	4,218	5,243	14,838
H35	Vist Crsr wgn 4d V-8	4,255	5,395	25,816
Delta (wb 116.0)				
L37	cpe	3,496	5,145	8,788
L69	sdn 4d	3,537	5,205	26,084
N37	Royale cpe	3,505	5,363	61,138
N69	Royale sdn 4d	3,561	5,433	117,571
Q35	Cust Crsr wgn 4d 2S V-8	4,064	5,923	32,827
Q35	Cust Crsr wgn 4d 3S V-8	4,095	6,098	
Ninety-Eight (wb 119.0)				
V37	Luxury cpe	3,753	6,609	5,058
V69	Luxury sdn 4d	3,807	6,786	14,323
X37	Regency cpe	3,767	6,949	32,072
X69	Regency sdn 4d	3,840	7,133	87,970
Toronado (wb 122.0)				
W57	XS htp cpe	4,688	10,684	2,714*
Z57	Brougham htp cpe	4,634	8,134	31,371

*Includes one XSR prototype.

1977 Engines	bore×stroke	bhp	availability
I-4, 140.0	3.50×3.63	84	S-Starfire
V-6, 231.0	3.80×3.40	105	S-Omg, Cutl, exc Salon/wgns, Delta; O-Starfire
V-8, 260.0	3.50×3.39	110	S-Cutl Sln; O-Omg, other Cutl, Delta
V-8, 305.0	3.74×3.48	145	O-Omega
V-8, 350.0	4.06×3.38	160	O-Delta
V-8, 350.0	4.06×3.38	170	S-Cutl wgns, CC wgns, 98; O-other Cutlass, Delta
V-8, 403.0	4.35×3.38	185	O-Cutl, Dlt, 98
V-8, 403.0	4.35×3.38	200	S-Toronado

1978

Starfire (wb 97.0)		Wght	Price	Prod
D07	SX htchbk cpe	2,790	4,306	9,265
T07	htchbk cpe 2d	2,786	4,095	8,056
Omega (wb 111.0)				
B17	htchbk cpe	3,250	4,173	4,084
B27	cpe 2d	3,184	4,009	15,632
B69	sdn 4d	3,236	4,094	19,478
E27	Brougham cpe 2d	3,204	4,215	3,798
E69	Brougham sdn 4d	3,246	4,300	7,125
Cutlass (wb 108.1)				
G09	Salon sdn 4d	3,136	4,543	29,509
G87	Salon cpe	3,122	4,433	21,198
J09	Salon Brghm sdn 4d	3,186	4,828	21,902
J87	Salon Brougham cpe	3,082	4,717	10,741
R47	Supreme cpe	3,228	4,873	240,917
K47	Calais cpe	3,212	5,231	40,842
M47	Supreme Brghm cpe	3,204	5,287	117,880
H35	Cruiser wgn 4d 2S	3,308	5,287	44,617
Delta 88 (wb 116.0)				
L37	cpe	3,496	5,549	17,469
L67	sdn 4d	3,541	5,634	25,322
N37	Royale cpe	3,507	5,778	68,469
N69	Royale sdn 4d	3,569	5,888	131,430
Q35	Cust Crsr wgn 4d 2S V-8	4,045	6,419	34,491
Q35	Cust Crsr wgn 4d 3S V-8	4,075	6,605	
Ninety-Eight (wb 119.0)				
V37	Luxury cpe	3,753	7,170	2,956
V69	Luxury sdn 4d	3,805	7,351	9,136
X37	Regency cpe	3,767	7,538	28,573
X69	Regency sdn 4d	3,836	7,726	78,100
Toronado (wb 122.0)				
Z57	Brougham cpe	4,624	9,412	22,362
W57	XSC cpe	4,627	—	2,453

1978 Engines	bore×stroke	bhp	availability
I-4, 151.0	4.00×3.00	85	S-Starfire
V-6, 231.0	3.80×3.40	105	S-Omega, Ctls, Delta; O-Starfire
V-8, 260.0	3.50×3.39	110	O-Cutlass, Delta
V-8, 305.0	3.74×3.48	145	O-Strfr, Omg, Cutl
V-8, 305.0	3.74×3.48	165	O-Cutlass
V-8D, 350.0	4.06×3.38	120	O-Delta, 98
V-8, 350.0	4.06×3.38	170	O-Delta, 98, O-Omega, Cutl
V-8, 403.0	4.35×3.38	185/190	S-Toro; O-Dlt, 98

1979

Starfire (wb 97.0)		Wght	Price	Prod
D07	SX htchbk cpe 2d	2,703	4,475	7,155
T07	htchbk cpe 2d	2,690	4,275	13,144
Omega (wb 111.0)				
B17	htchbk cpe	3,222	4,345	956
B27	cpe	3,145	4,181	4,806
B69	sdn 4d	3,183	4,281	5,826
E27	Brougham cpe	3,156	4,387	1,078
E69	Brougham sdn 4d	3,214	4,487	2,145
Cutlass (wb 108.1)				
G09	Salon sdn 4d	3,138	5,038	20,266
G87	Salon cpe	3,118	4,938	8,399
J09	Salon Brougham sdn	3,185	5,352	18,714
J87	Salon Brougham cpe	3,158	5,227	3,617
R47	Supreme cpe	3,148	5,390	277,944
K47	Calais cpe	3,180	5,828	43,780
M47	Supreme Brghm cpe	3,174	5,829	137,323
G35	Cruiser wgn 4d 2S	3,281	5,223	10,755
H35	Crsr Brghm wgn 4d 2S	3,325	5,775	42,953
Delta 88 (wb 116.0)				
L37	cpe	3,550	6,112	16,202
L69	sdn 4d	3,576	6,212	25,424
N37	Royale cpe	3,560	6,399	60,687
N69	Royale sdn 4d	3,602	6,524	152,526
Q35	Cust Crsr wgn 4d 2S V-8	4,042	7,201	36,648
Q35	Cust Crsr wgn 4d 3S V-8	4,092	7,394	
Ninety-Eight (wb 119.0)				
V37	Luxury cpe	3,806	8,614	2,104
V69	Luxury sdn 4d	3,850	8,795	6,720
X37	Regency cpe	3,810	9,236	29,965
X69	Regency sdn 4d	3,885	9,424	91,962
Toronado (wb 114.0)				
Z57	Brougham cpe	3,731	10,709	50,056

1979 Engines	bore×stroke	bhp	availability
I-4, 151.0	4.00×3.00	85	O-Starfire
I-4, 151.0	4.00×3.00	90	S-Starfire
V-6, 231.0	3.80×3.40	115	S-Omega, Ctls, Delta; O-Starfire
V-8D, 260.0	3.50×3.39	90	O-Cutlass
V-8, 260.0	3.50×3.39	105	S-Cutl, Delta exc wgn
V-8, 301.0	4.00×3.00	135	O-Delta exc wgn
V-8, 305.0	3.74×3.48	130	O-Starfire, Omg
V-8, 305.0	3.74×3.48	160	O-Cutlass
V-8, 350.0	4.06×3.28	160	S-Delta wagons
V-8D, 350.0	4.06×3.38	125	O-Cutl, Dlt, 98, Toronado
V-8, 350.0	4.06×3.38	160	S-98
V-8, 350.0	4.06×3.38	165	S-Toro; O-Omg, Cutl wgn
V-8, 403.0	4.35×3.38	175	O-Dlt wgns, 98

1980

Starfire (wb 97.0)		Wght	Price	Prod
D07	SX htchbk cpe	2,668	4,950	8,237
T07	htchbk cpe	2,656	4,750	
Omega (wb 104.9)				
B37	cpe	2,420	5,501	28,267
B69	sdn 4d	2,446	5,672	42,172
E37	Brougham cpe	2,452	5,858	21,595
E69	Brougham sdn 4d	2,478	6,013	42,289
Cutlass (wb 108.1)				
G69	sdn 4d	3,144	6,124	36,923
G87	Salon cpe	3,140	5,764	3,429
J87	Salon Brougham cpe	3,140	6,054	965
R47	Supreme cpe	3,264	6,655	169,597
R69	LS sdn 4d	3,254	6,780	86,868
K47	Calais cpe	3,276	7,119	26,269
M47	Suprem Brghm cpe	3,276	7,094	77,875
M69	Sprm Brghm sdn 4d	3,280	7,219	52,462
G35	Cruiser wgn 4d 2S	3,343	6,572	7,815
H35	Crsr Brghm wgn 4d 2S	3,380	6,809	22,791
Delta 88 (wb 116.0)				
L37	cpe	3,395	6,808	6,845
L69	sdn 4d	3,428	6,905	15,285
N37	Royale cpe	3,403	7,076	39,303
N69	Royale sdn 4d	3,406	7,228	87,178
P35	Cust Crsr wgn 4d 2S V-8	3,910	7,820	17,067
P35	Cust Crsr wgn 4d 3S V-8	3,940	8,028	
Ninety-Eight (wb 119.0)				
V69	Luxury sdn 4d	3,789	9,517	2,640
X37	Regency cpe	3,811	10,035	12,391
X69	Regency sdn 4d	3,832	10,159	58,603
Toronado (wb 114.0)				
Z57	cpe	3,627	11,934	43,440

1980 Engines	bore×stroke	bhp	availability
I-4, 151.0	4.00×3.00	85/90	S-Starfire, Omg
V-6, 173.0	3.50×3.00	115	O-Omega
V-6, 231.0	3.80×3.40	110	S-Cutl, Delta exc wgns; O-Starfire
V-8, 260.0	3.50×3.39	105	S-Cutlass
V-8, 265.0	3.75×3.00	120	S-Dlt exc wgns
V-8, 305.0	3.74×3.48	155	O-Cutlass
V-8, 307.0	3.80×3.38	150	S-Dlt wgns, 98, Toro; O-Delta
V-8D, 350.0	4.06×3.38	105	O-Cutl, Dlt, 98, Toronado
V-8, 350.0	4.06×3.38	160	O-Cutl, Dlt, 98, Toronado

1981

Omega (wb 104.9)		Wght	Price	Prod
B37	cpe 2d	2,439	6,343	27,323
B69	sdn 4d	2,469	6,514	51,715
E37	Brougham cpe 2d	2,462	6,700	19,260
E69	Brougham sdn 4d	2,499	6,855	49,620
Cutlass (wb 108.1)				
G69	sdn 4d	3,205	6,955	25,580
R47	Supreme cpe	3,213	7,484	187,875
R69	LS sdn 4d	3,236	7,652	84,272
K47	Calais cpe	3,227	8,004	4,105
M47	Supreme Brghm cpe	3,238	7,969	93,855
M69	Sprm Brghm sdn 4d	3,242	8,100	53,952
G35	Cruiser wgn 4d 2S	3,369	7,418	31,926
H35	Crsr Brghm wgn 4d 2S	3,367	7,725	
Delta 88 (wb 116.0)				
L37	cpe	3,485	7,429	3,330
L69	sdn 4d	3,501	7,524	10,806
N37	Royale cpe	3,489	7,693	41,682
Y37	Royale Brghm cpe	3,519	8,058	
N69	Royale sdn 4d	3,530	7,842	104,124
Y69	Royale Brghm sdn 4d	3,564	8,141	
P35	Cust Crsr wgn 4d 2S V-8	3,950	8,452	18,956
Ninety-Eight (wb 119.0)				
V69	Luxury sdn 4d	3,741	9,951	1,957
X37	Regency cpe	3,735	10,440	13,696
X69	Regency sdn 4d	3,794	10,558	74,017
Toronado (wb 114.0)				
Z57	cpe	3,631	12,148	42,604

1981 Engines	bore×stroke	bhp	availability
I-4, 151.0	4.00×3.00	90	S-Omega
V-6, 173.0	3.50×3.00	110	O-Omega
V-6, 231.0	3.80×3.40	110	S-Cutl, Delta exc wgns
V-6, 252.0	3.97×3.40	125	S-98, Toronado
V-8, 260.0	3.50×3.39	105	O-Cutl, Delta 88
V-8, 307.0	3.80×3.39	140	S-Delta wgn; O-Cutlass wgn, Delta, 98, Toro
V-8D, 350.0	4.06×3.39	105	O-Cutl, Delta, 98, Toronado

1982

Firenza (wb 101.2)		Wght	Price	Prod
C77	S htchbk cpe	2,344	7,413	8,894
C69	sdn 4d	2,345	7,448	9,256
D77	SX htchbk cpe	2,379	8,159	6,017
D69	LX sdn 4d	2,370	8,080	5,941
Omega (wb 104.9)				
B37	cpe	2,506	7,388	12,140
B69	sdn 4d	2,538	7,574	29,548
E37	Brougham cpe	2,529	7,722	9,430
E69	Brougham sdn 4d	2,569	7,891	26,351
Cutlass Ciera (wb 104.9)				
G27	cpe	2,618	8,847	5,185
G19	sdn 4d	2,637	8,997	9,717
J27	LS cpe	2,618	8,968	10,702
J19	LS sdn 4d	2,624	9,157	29,322
M27	Brougham cpe	2,620	9,397	12,518
M19	Brougham sdn 4d	2,626	9,599	33,876
Cutlass (wb 108.1)				
R47	Supreme cpe	3,231	8,588	89,617
R69	sdn 4d	3,292	8,712	60,053
K47	Calais cpe	3,304	9,379	17,109
M47	Supreme Brghm cpe	3,258	9,160	59,592
M69	Sprm Brghm sdn 4d	3,317	9,255	34,717
H35	Cruiser wgn 4d 2S	3,433	8,905	20,363
Delta 88 (wb 116.0)				
L69	sdn 4d	3,557	8,603	8,278
N37	Royale cpe	3,534	8,733	41,382 (N37/Y37)
Y37	Royale Brghm cpe	3,572	9,202	
N69	Royale sdn 4d	3,572	8,894	105,184 (N69/Y69)
Y69	Royale Brghm sdn 4d	3,608	9,293	
P35	Cust Crsr wgn 4d 2S V-8	4,026	9,614	19,367
Ninety-Eight (wb 119.0)				
X37	Regency cpe	3,785	12,117	11,832
X69	Regency sdn 4d	3,842	12,294	79,135 (X69/W69)
W69	Rgncy Brghm sdn 4d	3,890	13,344	
Toronado (wb 114.0)				
Z57	Brougham cpe	3,695	14,462	33,928

1982 Engines	bore×stroke	bhp	availability
I-4, 112.0	3.50×2.91	88	S-Firenza
I-4, 121.0	3.50×3.15	90	O-Firenza
I-4, 151.0	4.00×3.00	90	S-Omg, Cutl Ciera
V-6, 173.0	3.50×3.00	112	O-Omega
V-6, 173.0	3.50×3.00	130	O-Omega
V-6, 181.0	3.80×2.66	110	O-Cutlass Ciera
V-6, 231.0	3.80×3.40	110	S-Ctls Supreme, Delta exc wgns
V-6, 252.0	3.97×3.40	125	S-98, Toronado
V-8, 260.0	3.50×3.39	100	O-Cutl Sprm, Delta exc wgns
V-6D, 262.0	4.06×3.39	85	O-Cutl Ciera, Supreme
V-8, 307.0	3.80×3.39	140	S-Delta wgn; O-Cutl Supreme, other Dlt, 98, Toro
V-8D, 350.0	4.06×3.39	105	O-Supreme, Delta, 98, Toro

1983

Firenza (wb 101.2)		Wght	Price	Prod
C77	S htchbk cpe	2,440	7,007	8,208
C69	sdn 4d	2,418	7,094	11,278
D77	SX htchbk cpe	2,478	7,750	3,767
D69	LX sdn 4d	2,438	7,646	5,067
C35	Cruiser wgn 4d	2,496	7,314	7,460
D35	LX Cruiser wgn 4d	2,520	7,866	4,972
Omega (wb 104.9)				
B37	cpe	2,531	7,478	6,448
B69	sdn 4d	2,569	7,676	24,287
E37	Brougham cpe	2,562	7,767	5,177
E69	Brougham sdn 4d	2,594	7,948	18,014
Cutlass Ciera (wb 104.9)				
J27	LS cpe	2,732	8,703	12,612
J19	LS sdn 4d	2,765	8,892	66,731
M27	Brougham cpe	2,754	9,183	17,088
M19	Brougham sdn 4d	2,789	9,385	73,219
Cutlass (wb 108.1)				
R47	Supreme cpe	3,340	8,950	107,946
R69	sdn 4d	3,382	9,103	56,347
M47	Supreme Brghm cpe	3,377	9,589	60,025
M69	Sprm Brghm sdn 4d	3,416	9,719	28,451
K47	Calais cpe	3,357	9,848	16,660
K47/W40	Calais H/O cpe V-8	—	12,069	3,001
H35	Cruiser wgn 4d 2S	3,529	9,381	22,037
Delta 88 (wb 116.0)				
L69	sdn 4d	3,644	9,084	8,297
N37	Royale cpe	3,632	9,202	54,771 (N37/Y37)
Y37	Royale Brghm cpe	3,648	9,671	
N69	Royale sdn 4d	3,679	9,363	132,683 (N69/Y69)
Y69	Royale Brghm sdn 4d	3,689	9,762	
P35	Cust Crsr wgn 4d 2S V-8	4,202	10,083	25,243
Ninety-Eight (wb 119.0)				
X37	Regency cpe	3,910	12,943	13,816
X69	Regency sdn 4d	3,964	13,120	105,948 (X69/W69)
W69	Rgncy Brghm sdn 4d	4,006	14,170	
Toronado (wb 114.0)				
Z57	Brougham cpe	3,816	15,252	39,605

1983 Engines	bore×stroke	bhp	availability
I-4, 112.0	3.34×3.13	84	O-Firenza
I-4, 121.0	3.50×3.15	86	S-Firenza
I-4, 151.0	4.00×3.00	90	S-Omg, Cutl Ciera
V-6, 173.0	3.50×3.00	112	O-Omega
V-6, 173.0	3.50×3.00	130	O-Omega
V-6, 181.0	3.80×2.66	110	O-Cutlass Ciera
V-6, 231.0	3.80×3.40	110	S-Cutl Supreme, Delta exc wgns
V-6, 252.0	3.97×3.40	125	S-98, Toronado
V-6D, 262.0	4.06×3.39	85	O-Cutl Cir, Sprm
V-8, 307.0	3.80×3.39	140	S-Delta wgn; O-Cutl Sprm, other Dlt, 98, Toro
V-8, 307.0	3.80×3.39	180	S-Calais H/O
V-8D, 350.0	4.06×3.39	105	O-Sprm, Delta, 98, Toronado

1984

Firenza (wb 101.2)		Wght	Price	Prod
C77	S htchbk cpe	2,457	7,214	13,811
C69	sdn 4d	2,461	7,301	34,564
D77	SX htchbk cpe	2,505	7,957	4,179
D69	LX sdn 4d	2,505	7,853	11,761
C35	Cruiser wgn 4d	2,507	7,521	12,389
D35	LX Cruiser wgn 4d	2,525	8,073	5,771
Omega (wb 104.9)				
B37	cpe	2,539	7,634	5,242
B69	sdn 4d	2,572	7,832	21,571
E37	Brougham cpe	2,556	7,923	5,870
E69	Brougham sdn 4d	2,593	8,104	20,303
Cutlass Ciera (wb 104.9)				
J27	LS cpe	2,742	9,014	14,887
J19	LS sdn 4d	2,762	9,203	99,182
M27	Brougham cpe	2,768	9,519	22,687
M19	Brougham sdn 4d	2,788	9,721	102,667
J35	LS Cruiser wgn 4d	2,957	9,551	41,816
Cutlass (wb 108.1)*				
R47	Supreme cpe	3,301	9,376	132,913
R69	sdn 4d	3,344	9,529	62,136
M47	Supreme Brghm cpe	3,340	10,015	87,207
M69	Sprm Brghm sdn 4d	3,374	10,145	37,406
K47	Calais cpe	3,377	10,274	21,393
K47/W40	Calais H/O cpe V-8	—	12,644	3,500

* Cutlass totals incl. Canadian prod. for the U.S. market.

Delta 88 (wb 116.0)		Wght	Price	Prod
N37	Royale cpe	3,585	9,939	23,387
Y37	Royale Brghm cpe	3,619	10,408	41,913
N69	Royale sdn 4d	3,624	10,051	87,993
Y69	Royale Brghm sdn 4d	3,654	10,499	89,450
V69	Ryl Brghm LS sdn 4d V-8	3,853	13,854	17,064
P35	Cust Crsr wgn 4d 2S V-8	4,128	10,839	34,061
Ninety-Eight (wb 119.0)				
G37	Regency cpe	4,090	13,974	7,855
G69	Regency sdn 4d	4,126	14,151	26,919
H69	Rgncy Brghm sdn 4d	4,177	15,201	42,059
Toronado (wb 114.0)				
Z57	Brougham cpe	3,795	16,107	48,100

1984 Engines	bore×stroke	bhp	availability
I-4, 112.0	3.34×3.13	82	O-Firenza
I-4, 121.0	3.50×3.15	88	S-Firenza
I-4, 151.0	4.00×3.00	92	S-Omg, Cutl Ciera
V-6, 173.0	3.50×3.00	112	O-Omega
V-6, 173.0	3.50×3.00	130	O-Omega
V-6, 181.0	3.80×2.66	110	O-Cutlass Ciera
V-6, 231.0	3.80×3.40	110	S-Cutl Supreme, Delta exc wgns
V-6, 252.0	3.97×3.40	125	S-Toronado
V-6D, 262.0	4.06×3.39	85	O-Cutl Cir, Sprm
V-8, 307.0	3.80×3.39	140	S-Delta wgn, 98; O-Cutl Sprm, other Delta, Toro
V-8, 307.0	3.80×3.39	180	S-Calais H/O
V-8D, 350.0	4.06×3.39	105	O-Sprm, Delta, 98, Toronado

1985

Firenza (wb 101.2)		Wght	Price	Prod
C77	S htchbk cpe	2,388	7,588	5,842
C69	sdn 4d	2,385	7,679	25,066
D77	SX htchbk cpe	2,438	8,395	1,842
D69	LX sdn 4d	2,441	8,255	7,563
C35	Cruiser wgn 4d	2,450	7,898	6,291
D35	LX Cruiser wgn 4d	2,487	8,492	2,436
Calais (wb 103.4)				
F27	cpe	2,545	8,499	49,545
T27	Supreme cpe	2,547	8,844	56,695
Cutlass Ciera (wb 104.9)				
J27	LS cpe	2,763	9,307	13,396
J19	LS sdn 4d	2,802	9,497	118,575
M27	Brougham cpe	2,784	9,787	20,476
M19	Brougham sdn 4d	2,825	9,998	112,441
J35	LS Cruiser wgn 4d	2,962	9,858	38,225
Cutlass (wb 108.1)				
R47	Supreme cpe	3,277	9,797	75,045
R69	sdn 4d	3,321	9,961	43,085
M47	Supreme Brghm cpe	3,308	10,468	58,869
M69	Supreme sdn 4d	3,341	10,602	28,741
K47	Salon cpe	3,308	10,770	14,512
K47/W42	Salon 4-4-2 cpe V-8	—	12,435	3,500
Delta 88 (wb 116.0)				
N37	Royale cpe	3,584	10,488	15,002
Y37	Royale Brghm cpe	3,584	10,968	31,891
N69	Royale sdn 4d	3,616	10,596	69,641
Y69	Royale Brghm sdn 4d	3,616	11,062	72,103
V69	Ryl Brghm LS sdn 4d V-8	3,515	14,331	30,239
P35	Cust Crsr wgn 4d 2S V-8	4,085	11,627	22,889
Ninety-Eight (wb 110.8)				
X11	Regency cpe	3,261	14,725	4,734
X69	Regency sdn 4d	3,297	14,665	43,697
W11	Regency Brghm cpe	3,261	15,932	9,704
W69	Rgncy Brghm sdn 4d	3,297	15,864	111,297
Toronado (wb 114.0)				
Z57	Brougham cpe	3,853	16,798	42,185

1985 Engines	bore×stroke	bhp	availability
I-4, 112.0	3.34×3.13	82	O-Firenza
I-4, 121.0	3.50×3.15	88	S-Firenza
I-4, 151.0	4.00×3.00	92	S-Clis, Cutl Cir
V-6, 173.0	3.50×3.00	130	O-Firenza
V-6, 181.0	3.80×2.66	110	S-98 exc Brghm; O-Cutlass Ciera
V-6, 181.0	3.80×2.66	125	O-Calais
V-6, 231.0	3.80×3.40	110	S-Cutl, Sprm, Dlt exc LS/wgns
V-6, 231.0	3.80×3.40	125	S-98 Brghm; O-Ciera, 98
V-6D, 262.0	4.06×3.39	85	O-Ciera, Supreme, 98
V-8, 307.0	3.80×3.39	140	S-Delta LS/wgn, Toro; O-Cutl Sprm, other Dlt
V-8, 307.0	3.80×3.39	180	S-Salon 4-4-2
V-8D, 350.0	4.06×3.39	105	O-Sprm, Delta, Toronado

1986

Firenza (wb 101.2)		Wght	Price	Prod
C27	cpe 2d	2,344	7,782	12,003
D27	LC cpe 2d	2,396	8,611	2,867
C77	S htchbk cpe	2,396	7,941	2,531
D77	GT htchbk cpe V-6	2,445	9,774	1,032

Firenza		Wght	Price	Prod
C69	sdn 4d	2,397	8,035	18,437
D69	LX sdn 4d	2,428	8,626	4,415
C35	Cruiser wgn 4d	2,454	8,259	5,416
Calais (wb 103.4)				
F27	cpe	2,531	9,283	52,726
F69	sdn 4d	2,598	9,478	40,393
T27	Supreme cpe	2,542	9,668	33,060
T69	Supreme sdn 4d	2,601	9,863	25,128
Cutlass Ciera (wb 104.9)				
J27	LS cpe	2,761	10,153	9,233
J37	S cpe	2,757	10,619	16,281
J19	LS sdn 4d	2,805	10,354	144,466
M27	Brougham cpe	2,778	10,645	11,534
M37	Brougham SL cpe	2,800	11,154	12,525
M19	Brougham sdn 4d	2,834	10,868	123,027
J35	LS Cruiser wgn 4d	2,964	10,734	35,890
Cutlass (wb 108.1)				
R47	Supreme cpe	3,277	10,698	79,654
R69	sdn 4d	3,320	10,872	41,973
M47	Supreme Brghm cpe	3,307	11,408	55,275
M69	Sprm Brghm sdn 4d	3,341	11,551	24,646
K47	Salon cpe	3,340	11,728	9,608
K47/W42	Salon 4-4-2 cpe V-8	—	14,343	
Delta 88 (wb 110.8)				
N37	Royale cpe	3,141	12,760	13,696
N69	Royale sdn 4d	3,186	12,760	88,564
Y37	Royale Brghm cpe	3,170	13,461	23,697
Y69	Royale Brghm sdn 4d	3,211	13,461	108,344
Custom Cruiser (wb 116.0)				
P35	wgn 4d 2S V-8	4,085	13,416	21,073
Ninety-Eight (wb 110.8)				
X11	Regency cpe	3,268	16,062	803
X69	Regency sdn 4d	3,304	15,989	23,717
W11	Regency Brghm cpe	3,285	17,052	5,007
W69	Rgncy Brghm sdn 4d	3,320	16,979	95,045
Toronado (wb 108.0)				
Z57	cpe	3,304	19,418	15,924

1986 Engines	bore×stroke	bhp	availability
I-4, 112.0	3.34×3.13	84	O-Firnz exc GT
I-4, 121.0	3.50×3.15	88	S-Firnz exc GT
I-4, 151.0	4.00×3.00	92	S-Clis, Cutl Cir
V-6, 173.0	3.50×3.00	112	O-Cutlass Ciera
V-6, 173.0	3.50×3.00	130	S-Firenza GT
V-6, 181.0	3.80×2.66	125	S-Dlt; O-Calais
V-6, 231.0	3.80×3.40	110	S-Cutl Supreme
V-6, 231.0	3.80×3.40	140	S-98, Toronado
V-6, 231.0	3.80×3.40	150	O-Ciera, Delta
V-8, 307.0	3.80×3.39	140	S-Cust Crsr; O-Sprm
V-8, 307.0	3.80×3.39	180	S-Salon 4-4-2

1987

Firenza (wb 101.2)		Wght	Price	Prod
C27	cpe 2d	2,327	8,541	5,335
D27	LC cpe 2d	2,379	9,639	874
C77	S htchbk cpe	2,380	8,976	991
D77	GT htchbk cpe V-6	2,576	11,034	783
C69	sdn 4d	2,381	8,499	12,597
D69	LX sdn 4d	2,412	9,407	2,388
C35	Cruiser wgn 4d	2,438	9,146	2,860
Calais (wb 103.4)				
F27	cpe	2,516	9,741	52,286
F69	sdn 4d	2,584	9,741	35,169
T27	Supreme cpe	2,529	10,397	17,883
T69	Supreme sdn 4d	2,595	10,397	11,676
Cutlass Ciera (wb 104.9)				
J37	S cpe	2,811	10,940	21,904
J19	sdn 4d	2,775	10,940	140,334
M37	Brougham SL cpe	2,822	11,747	11,960
M19	Brougham sdn 4d	2,846	11,747	94,764
J35	Cruiser wgn 4d	2,975	11,433	20,556
M35	Brghm Crsr wgn 4d	2,975	12,095	7,770
Cutlass (wb 108.1)				
R47	Supreme cpe	3,293	11,539	46,343
R47/W42	Sprm 4-4-2 cpe V-8	—	14,706	4,210
R69	sdn 4d	3,345	11,539	21,379
M47	Supreme Brghm cpe	3,252	12,378	28,607
M69	Sprm Brghm sdn 4d	3,427	12,378	17,383
K47	Salon cpe	3,293	12,697	8,862
Delta 88 (wb 110.8)				
N37	Royale cpe	3,176	13,639	4,287
N69	Royale sdn 4d	3,216	13,639	66,214
Y37	Royale Brghm cpe	3,204	14,536	7,907
Y69	Royale Brghm sdn 4d	3,237	14,536	75,129
Custom Cruiser (wb 116.0)				
P35	wgn 4d 2S V-8	4,136	14,420	17,742
Ninety-Eight (wb 110.8)				
X69	Regency sdn 4d	3,307	17,371	18,600
W11	Regency Brghm cpe	3,285	18,388	4,207
W69	Rgncy Brghm sdn 4d	3,320	18,388	58,199
Toronado (wb 108.0)				
Z57	cpe	3,352	19,938	15,040

1987 Engines	bore×stroke	bhp	availability
I-4, 121.0	3.50×3.15	90	S-Firnz exc GT
I-4, 121.0	3.50×3.15	102	O-Firnz exc GT
I-4, 151.0	4.00×3.00	98	S-Clis, Cutl Cir
V-6, 173.0	3.50×3.00	125	S-Firnz GT; O-other Firnz, Ciera
V-6, 181.0	3.80×2.66	125	O-Calais
V-6, 231.0	3.80×3.40	110	S-Cutl Supreme
V-6, 231.0	3.80×3.40	150	S-Dlt, 98, Toro; O-Ciera
V-8, 307.0	3.80×3.39	140	S-Cust Cruiser; O-Supreme
V-8, 307.0	3.80×3.39	170	S-Sprm 4-4-2

1988

Firenza (wb 101.2) - 12,260 blt		Wght	Price	Prod
C27	cpe 2d	2,327	9,295	—
C69	sdn 4d	2,381	9,295	—
C35	Cruiser wgn 4d	2,438	9,995	—
Calais (wb 103.4) - 110,276 built				
F27	cpe	2,500	10,320	—
F69	sdn 4d	2,571	10,320	—
T27	SL cpe	2,518	11,195	—
T69	SL sdn 4d	2,583	11,195	—
K27	International cpe I-4	2,757	13,695	—
K69	Interl sdn 4d I-4	2,830	13,695	—
Cutlass Ciera (wb 104.9) - 21,620 built				
J37	cpe	2,805	10,995	—
J19	sdn 4d	2,769	11,656	—
M37	Brougham SL cpe	2,816	11,845	—
M19	Brougham sdn 4d	2,840	12,625	—
S37	International cpe V-6	2,958	14,995	—
S19	Interl sdn 4d V-6	1,913	15,825	—
J35	Cruiser wgn 4d	2,968	12,320	—
M35	Brghm Cruisr wgn 4d	3,039	12,995	—
Cutlass Supreme FWD (wb 107.7) - 94,723 built				
H47	cpe	2,958	12,846	—
S47	SL cpe	—	13,495	—
R47	International cpe	—	15,644	—
Cutlass Supreme Clsic RWD (wb 108.1) - 27,678 built				
R47	cpe	3,180	13,163	—
M47	Brougham cpe	3,233	13,995	—
Delta 88 (wb 110.8) - 160,913 built				
N37	Royale cpe	3,172	14,498	—
N69	Royale sdn 4d	3,216	14,498	—
Y37	Royale Brghm cpe	3,187	15,451	—
Y69	Royale Brghm sdn 4d	3,220	15,451	—
Custom Cruiser RWD (wb 116.0)				
P35	wgn 4d 2S V-8	4,136	15,655	11,114
Ninety-Eight (wb 110.8) - 79,935 built				
X69	Regency sdn 4d	3,300	17,995	—
W69	Rgncy Brghm sdn 4d	3,316	19,371	—
V69	Touring sdn 4d	3,421	24,470	—
Toronado (wb 108.0) - 16,496 built				
Z57	cpe	3,364	20,598	—
V57	Trofeo cpe	3,426	22,695	—

1988 Engines	bore×stroke	bhp	availability
I-4, 121.0	3.50×3.15	90	S-Firenza
I-4, 121.0	3.50×3.15	96	O-Firenza
I-4, 138.0	3.62×3.35	150	S-Calais Int'l; O-Calais (dohc)
I-4, 151.0	4.00×3.00	98	S-Clis, Cutl Cir
V-6, 173.0	3.50×3.00	125	S-Cutl Supreme; O-Ciera
V-6, 181.0	3.80×2.66	125	O-Calais
V-6, 231.0	3.80×3.40	150	S-Cir Int'l, Delta; O-Ciera
V-6, 231.0	3.80×3.40	165	S-98, Toronado; O-Delta
V-8, 307.0	3.80×3.39	140	S-Cust Cruiser; O-Sprm Classic

1989

Cutlass Calais (wb 103.4)		Wght	Price	Prod
L27	VL cpe	2,512	9,995	11,432
L69	VL sdn 4d	2,573	9,995	14,506
F27	S cpe	2,512	10,895	33,633
F69	S sdn 4d	2,573	10,995	25,592
T27	SL cpe	2,538	11,895	10,350
T69	SL sdn 4d	2,597	11,995	9,443
K27	International cpe I-4	2,740	14,395	3,345
K69	Interntnl sdn 4d I-4	2,804	14,495	1,590
Cutlass Ciera (wb 104.9)				
J37	cpe	2,736	11,695	7,221
J69	sdn 4d	2,764	12,195	140,264
M37	SL cpe	2,767	12,695	2,548
M69	SL sdn 4d	2,791	13,495	65,725
S37	International cpe V-6	—	15,995	1,913
S69	Interntnl sdn 4d V-6	—	16,795	5,132
J35	Cruiser wgn 4d	2,913	12,995	12,368
M35	Brghm Crsr wgn 4d	2,938	13,995	4,431
Cutlass Supreme (wb 107.7)				
H47	cpe	3,084	14,295	49,895
S47	SL cpe	—	15,195	32,015
R47	International cpe	—	16,995	18,116
Eighty-Eight (wb 110.8)				
N37	Royale cpe	3,215	15,195	1,927
N69	Royale sdn 4d	3,265	15,295	81,512
Y37	Royale Brghm cpe	3,236	16,295	3,024
Y69	Royale Brghm sdn 4d	3,285	16,395	65,576
Custom Cruiser (wb 116.0)				
P35	wgn 4d 2S V-8	4,221	16,795	8,929
Ninety-Eight (wb 110.8)				
X69	Regency sdn 4d	3,329	19,295	17,184
W69	Rgncy Brghm sdn 4d	3,353	20,495	48,726
V69	Touring sdn 4d	3,494	25,995	7,193
Toronado (wb 108.0)				
Z57	cpe	3,361	21,995	3,734
V57	Trofeo cpe	3,428	24,995	6,143

1989 Engines	bore×stroke	bhp	availability
I-4, 138.0	3.62×3.35	150	S-Calais Int'l; O-Calais (dohc)
I-4, 138.0	3.62×3.35	180	O-late Calais
I-4, 151.0	4.00×3.00	110	S-Calais, (dohc) Ciera
V-6, 173.0	3.50×3.00	125	O-Ciera
V-6, 173.0	3.50×3.00	130	S-Supreme
V-6, 191.0	3.30×3.27	135	O-late Supreme
V-6, 204.0	3.70×3.16	160	S-Ciera Int'l; O-Calais, Ciera
V-6, 231.0	3.80×3.40	165	S-88, 98, Toro
V-8, 307.0	3.80×3.39	140	S-Cust Cruiser

1990

Cutlass Calais (wb 103.4)		Wght	Price	Prod
L27	VL cpe	2,518	9,995	15,846
L69	VL sdn 4d	2,585	9,995	41,018
F27	S cpe	—	10,895	12,839
F69	S sdn 4d	—	10,995	12,207
T27	SL cpe	—	13,195	2,503
T69	SL sdn 4d	—	13,295	3,971
K27	International cpe I-4	—	14,895	1,454
K69	Interntnl sdn 4d I-4	—	14,995	877
Cutlass Ciera (wb 104.9)				
L69	sdn 4d	2,764	11,995	46,933
J37	S cpe	2,767	12,395	2,203
J69	S sdn 4d	2,791	12,995	54,549
M69	SL sdn 4d	—	14,695	33,229
S37	International cpe V-6	—	15,995	411
S69	Interntnl sdn 4d V-6	—	16,795	959
J35	Cruiser S wgn 4d	2,913	13,395	3,321
M35	Cruiser SL wgn 4d	2,938	15,295	5,576
Cutlass Supreme (wb 107.7)				
H47	cpe	3,133	14,495	15,848

Cutlass Supreme		Wght	Price	Prod
H69	sdn 4d	3,221	14,595	47,043
S47	SL cpe	—	16,095	10,076
S69	SL sdn 4d	—	16,195	32,798
R47	International cpe	—	17,995	5,602
R69	International sdn 4d	—	17,995	7,474
T67	conv cpe	3,501	20,995	464

Eighty-Eight (wb 110.8)				
N37	Royale cpe	3,248	15,895	1,127
N69	Royale sdn 4d	3,293	15,995	65,800
Y37	Royale Brghm cpe	—	17,295	1,585
Y69	Royale Brghm sdn 4d	—	17,395	48,311

Custom Cruiser (wb 116.0)				
P35	wgn 4d 2S V-8	4,221	17,595	3,890

Ninety-Eight (wb 110.8)				
X69	Regency sdn 4d	3,325	19,995	17,914
W69	Brougham sdn 4d	—	21,595	38,915
V69	Touring sdn 4d	—	26,795	5,566

Toronado (wb 108.0)				
Z57	cpe	3,462	21,995	5,596
V57	Trofeo cpe	—	24,995	9,426

1990 Engines	bore×stroke	bhp	availability
I-4, 138.0	3.62×3.35	160	S-Calais SL; O-Calais, Sprm (dohc)
I-4, 138.0	3.62×3.35	180	S-Calais Int'l, Supreme (dohc)
I-4, 151.0	4.00×3.00	110	S-Calais, Ciera
V-6, 191.0	3.30×3.27	135	S-Supreme SL/conv.; O-Supreme
V-6, 204.0	3.70×3.16	160	S-Ciera SL/Int'l; O-Calais, Ciera
V-6, 231.0	3.80×3.40	165	S-88, 98, Toro
V-8, 307.0	3.80×3.39	140	S-Cust Cruiser

1991

Cutlass Calais (wb 103.4)		Wght	Price	Prod
L27	cpe	2,553	10,295	14,978
L69	sdn 4d	2,616	10,295	41,746
F27	S cpe	2,548	11,495	6,906
F69	S sdn 4d	2,613	11,595	7,267
T27	SL cpe	2,665	15,095	1,030
T69	SL sdn 4d	2,725	15,195	2,437
K27	I Series cpe	2,729	16,295	671
K69	I Series sdn 4d	2,798	16,395	379

Cutlass Ciera (104.9)				
L69	sdn 4d	2,771	12,459	63,888
J37	S sdn 2d	2,771	13,395	1,665
J69	S sdn 4d	2,813	12,995	29,307
M69	SL sdn 4d	2,958	15,895	13,700
J35	Cruiser S wgn 4d	2,975	13,895	3,977
M35	Cruiser SL wgn 4d	3,160	19,595	3,247

Cutlass Supreme (wb 107.7)				
H47	cpe	3,187	14,995	16,766
H69	sdn 2d	3,228	15,095	52,241
S47	SL cpe	3,260	16,895	4,253
S69	SL sdn 4d	3,355	16,995	15,653
R47	I Series cpe	3,517	19,695	2,304
R69	I Series sdn 4d	3,597	19,795	7,357
T67	conv cpe	3,602	20,995	1,515

Eighty-Eight (wb 110.8)				
H37	Royale cpe	3,248	17,095	234
N69	Royale sdn 4d	3,292	17,195	33,690
Y37	Brougham cpe	3,276	18,695	458
Y69	Brougham sdn 4d	3,303	18,795	21,865

Ninety-Eight (wb 110.8)				
X69	Regency Elite sdn 4d	3,580	23,695	50,625
V69	touring sedan 4d	3,654	28,595	4,280

Custom Cruiser (wb 115.9)				
P35	wgn 4d	4,435	20,495	7,663

Toronado (wb 108.0)				
Z57	cpe	3,455	23,795	2,705
V57	Trofeo cpe	3,526	26,495	5,348

1991 Engines	bore×stroke	bhp	availability
I-4, 138.0	3.63×3.94	160	S-Supreme; O-Calais (dohc)
I-4, 138.0	3.63×3.94	180	O-Calais (dohc)
I-4, 138.0	3.63×3.94	190	O-Calais (dohc)
I-4, 151.0	4.00×3.00	110	S-Calais, Ciera
V-6, 191.0	3.50×3.30	140	O-Supreme
V-6, 204.0	3.70×3.16	160	O-Calais, Ciera
V-6, 207.0	3.62×3.30	200	S-Supreme I-Series (dohc)
V-6, 207.0	3.62×3.30	210	S-Supreme I-Series (dohc)
V-6, 231.0	3.80×3.40	165	S-Eighty-Eight
V-6, 231.0	3.80×3.40	170	S-Ninety-Eight, Toronado
V-8, 305.0	3.74×3.48	170	S-Cust Cruiser

1992

Achieva (wb 103.4)		Wght	Price	Prod
L37	S cpe	2,696	12,715	24,719*
L69	S sdn 4d	2,778	12,815	38,171
F37	SL cpe	2,795	14,495	2,892
F69	SL sdn 4d	2,868	14,595	11,674

Cutlass Ciera (104.9)				
J69	S sdn 4d	2,886	12,995	123,243
M69	SL sdn 4d	3,048	15,895	8,867
J35	Cruiser S wgn 4d	2,992	13,895	5,861
M35	Cruiser SL wgn 4d	3,226	19,595	1,932

Cutlass Supreme (wb 107.7)				
H47	S cpe	3,221	15,695	20,700
H69	S sdn 4d	3,375	15,795	63,692
R47	I Series cpe	3,385	21,795	1,181
R69	I Series sdn 4d	3,498	21,895	2,066
T67	conv cpe	3,589	21,995	4,306

Eighty-Eight (wb 110.8)				
N69	sdn 4d	3,404	18,495	75,182
Y69	LS sdn 4d	3,468	21,395	40,142

Ninety-Eight (wb 110.8)				
X69	Regency sdn 4d	3,593	24,595	20,076
W69	Regency Elite sdn 4d	—	26,195	24,713
V69	touring sedan 4d	3,697	28,995	2,795

Custom Cruiser (wb 115.9)				
P35	wgn 4d	4,378	20,995	4,347

Toronado (wb 108.0)				
Z57	cpe	3,467	24,695	1,239
V57	Trofeo cpe	3,528	27,295	5,197

*Includes 1,146 SC× models.

1992 Engines	bore×stroke	bhp	availability
I-4, 138.0	3.63×3.94	120	S-Achieva
I-4, 138.0	3.63×3.94	160	O-Achv (dohc)
I-4, 138.0	3.63×3.94	180	O-Achv (dohc)
I-4, 138.0	3.63×3.94	190	S-Achv SCX (dohc)
I-4, 151.0	4.00×3.00	110	S-Ciera
V-6, 191.0	3.50×3.30	140	S-Supreme
V-6, 204.0	3.70×3.16	160	O-Achv, Ciera
V-6, 207.0	3.62×3.30	200	S-Supreme I-Series (dohc)
V-6, 207.0	3.62×3.30	210	O-Supreme I-Series (dohc)
V-6, 231.0	3.80×3.40	170	S-Eighty-Eight, Ninety-Eight, Toronado
V-6S, 231.0	3.80×3.40	205	O-Ninety-Eight V69
V-8, 305.0	3.74×3.48	170	S-Cust Cruiser
V-8, 350.0	4.00×3.48	180	O-Cust Cruiser

1993

Achieva (wb 103.4)		Wght	Price	Prod
L37	S cpe	2,716	13,409	13,525*
L69	S sdn 4d	2,779	13,149	30,837
F37	SL cpe	—	14,849	590
F69	SL sdn 4d	—	14,949	3,283

Cutlass Ciera (104.9)				
J69	S sdn 4d	2,886	14,859	142,552
M69	SL sdn 4d	3,048	18,559	4,304
J35	Cruiser S wgn 4d	2,992	15,559	5,785
M35	Cruiser SL wgn 4d	3,226	19,059	1,084

Cutlass Supreme (wb 107.7)				
H47	S cpe	3,243	15,695	23,544
H69	sdn 4d	3,354	15,795	51,678
R47	I Series cpe	3,376	22,799	395
R69	I Series sdn 4d	3,479	22,899	645
T67	conv cpe	3,651	22,699	6,751

Eighty-Eight (wb 110.8)		Wght	Price	Prod
N69	sdn 4d	3,404	19,549	47,428
Y69	LS sdn 4d	3,468	21,949	14,903

Ninety-Eight (wb 110.8)				
X69	Regency sdn 4d	3,512	24,999	8,906
W69	Regency Elite sdn 4d	3,527	26,999	9,900
V69	touring sedan 4d	3,697	29,699	1,885

*Includes 500 SCX models.

1993 Engines	bore×stroke	bhp	availability
I-4, 133.0	3.50×3.46	110	S-Ciera S
I-4, 138.0	3.63×3.94	115	S-Achieva
I-4, 138.0	3.63×3.94	155	O-Achv (dohc)
I-4, 138.0	3.63×3.94	175	O-Achv (dohc)
I-4, 138.0	3.63×3.94	185	S-Achv SCX (dohc)
V-6, 191.0	3.50×3.30	140	S-Supreme
V-6, 204.0	3.70×3.16	160	S-Ciera SL; O-Achv, Ciera S
V-6, 207.0	3.62×3.30	200	S-Sprm I-Ser (dohc)
V-6, 231.0	3.80×3.40	170	S-Eighty-Eight, Ninety-Eight,
V-6S, 231.0	3.80×3.40	205	O-Ninety-Eight V69

1994

Achieva (wb 103.4)		Wght	Price	Prod
L37	S cpe	2,716	14,075	15,668
L69	S sdn 4d	2,779	14,175	43,329
F37	SC cpe	—	17,475	1,555
F69	SL sdn 4d	—	17,475	1,540

Cutlass Ciera (104.9)				
G69	SL sdn 4d	2,833	15,675	132,351
J35	Cruiser SL wgn 4d	3,086	17,175	9,809

Cutlass Supreme (wb 107.7)				
H47	S cpe	3,307	17,375	35,757
H69	S sdn 4d	3,405	17,475	77,861
T67	conv cpe	3,638	25,275	8,638

Eighty-Eight (wb 110.8)				
N69	sdn 4d	3,439	20,875	60,362
Y69	LS sdn 4d	3,469	22,875	21,664 (Y69 and Y69/R7C combined)
Y69/R7C	LSS sdn 4d	—	22,995	

Ninety-Eight (wb 110.8)				
X69	Regency sdn 4d	3,509	25,875	20,171
W69	Regency Elite sdn 4d	3,585	27,975	6,463

1994 Engines	bore×stroke	bhp	availability
I-4, 133.0	3.50×3.46	120	S-Ciera
I-4, 138.0	3.63×3.94	115	S-Achieva
I-4, 138.0	3.63×3.94	155	O-Achv (dohc)
I-4, 138.0	3.63×3.94	170	O-Achv (dohc)
V-6, 191.0	3.50×3.30	160	S-Supreme; O-Achv, Ciera
V-6, 207.0	3.62×3.30	210	O-Sprm (dohc)
V-6, 231.0	3.80×3.40	170	S-Eighty-Eight, Ninety-Eight
V-6S, 231.0	3.80×3.40	225	O-Ninety-Eight

1995

Achieva (wb 103.4)	Wght	Price	Prod
L37/R7B S cpe (Series I)	2,716	13,500	16,078 (both L37 rows combined)
L37/R7C S cpe (Series II)	—	15,200	
L69/R7B S sdn 4d (Series I)	2,779	13,500	41,185 (both L69 rows combined)
L69/R7C S sdn 4d (Series II)	—	15,200	

Cutlass Ciera (104.9)			
J69/R7B SL sdn 4d (Series I)	2,722	14,460	126,244 (both sdn 4d rows combined)
G69/R7C SL sdn 4d (Series II)	—	16,060	
J35 SL wgn 4d	2,934	17,060	9,102

Cutlass Supreme (wb 107.7)			
H47/R7B SL cpe (Series I)	3,243	17,460	24,809 (both H47 rows combined)
H47/R7C SL cpe (Series II)	—	18,460	
H69/R7B SL sdn 4d (Series I)	3,354	17,460	83,933 (both H69 rows combined)
H69/R7C SL sdn 4d (Series II)	—	18,460	
T67 conv cpe	3,651	25,460	4,490

Eighty-Eight (wb 110.8)			
N69 sdn 4d	3,404	20,410	56,862
Y69 LS sdn 4d	—	22,710	7,106
Y69/R7C LSS sdn 4d	—	24,010	11,513

Ninety-Eight (wb 110.8) - 25,444 built			
X69/R7B Rg Elit sdn 4d (Ser I)	3,593	26,060	—
X69/R7C Rg Elit sdn 4d (Ser II)	—	27,160	—

Aurora (wb 113.0)				
R29	sdn 4d	4,000	31,370	47,831

1995 Engines	bore×stroke	bhp	availability
I-4, 133.0	3.50×3.46	120	S-Ciera
I-4, 138.0	3.63×3.94	150	S-Achv (dohc)
V-6, 191.0	3.50×3.30	155	O-Achieva
V-6, 191.0	3.50×3.30	160	S-Supreme; O-Ciera
V-6, 207.0	3.62×3.30	210	O-Sprm (dohc)
V-6, 231.0	3.80×3.40	205	S-Eighty-Eight, Ninety-Eight
V-6S, 231.0	3.80×3.40	225	O-Eighty-Eight, Nnty-Eight, LSS
V-8, 244.0	3.42×3.31	250	S-Aurora (dohc)

1996

Achieva (wb 103.4)	Wght	Price	Prod
L37/1SA SC cpe (Series I)	2,751	13,495	1,437
L37/1SB SC cpe (Series II)	—	14,495	6,496
L37/1SC SC cpe (Series III)	—	16,495	2,286
L69/1SA SL sdn 4d (Series I)	—	—	34
L69/1SB SL sdn 4d (Series II)	2,813	14,495	9,833
L69/1SC SL sdn 4d (Series III)	—	16,495	17,661
Cutlass Ciera (104.9)			
J69/1SA sdn 4d	—	—	6,710
J69/1SB sdn 4d (Series I)	2,924	14,455	23,744
J69/1SC sdn 4d (Series II)	3,059	16,455	86,721
J35/1SA wgn 4d	—	—	1,851
J35/1SB wgn 4d	3,229	17,455	7,156
Cutlass Supreme (wb 107.7)			
H47/1SA cpe (Series I)	3,283	17,455	5,597
H69/1SA sdn 4d (Series I)	3,388	17,455	9,541
H47/1SB cpe (Series II)	—	18,455	7,194
H69/1SB sdn 4d (Series II)	—	18,455	15,876
H47/1SC cpe (Series III)	—	18,960	9,548
H69/1SC sdn 4d (Series III)	—	18,960	13,597
H47/1SD cpe (Series IV)	—	20,160	8,256
H69/1SD sdn 4d (Series IV)	—	20,160	9,986
Eighty-Eight (wb 110.8)			
N69/1SA sdn 4d	3,455	20,405	12,528
N69/1SB LS sdn 4d	3,459	22,810	33,017
Y69/1SA LSS sdn 4d	3,502	26,010	12,074
Y69/1SB LSS sdn 4d	—	—	1
Ninety-Eight (wb 110.8)			
X69/1SB Reg Elite sdn 4d (Ser I)	3,515	28,160	5,638
X69/1SC Reg Elite sdn 4d (Ser II)	—	29,260	9,469
Aurora (wb 113.8)			
R29 sdn 4d	3,967	34,360	24,133

1996 Engines	bore×stroke	bhp	availability
I-4, 133.0	3.50×3.46	120	S-Ciera
I-4, 146.0	3.54×3.70	150	S-Achv (dohc)
V-6, 191.0	3.50×3.30	155	O-Achieva
V-6, 191.0	3.50×3.30	160	S-Supreme, O-Ciera
V-6, 207.0	3.62×3.30	215	O-Sprm (dohc)
V-6, 231.0	3.80×3.40	205	S-Eighty-Eight, Ninety-Eight
V-6S, 231.0	3.80×3.40	240	O-Egty-Egt LSS
V-8, 244.0	3.42×3.31	250	S-Aurora

1997

Achieva (wb 103.4)	Wght	Price	Prod
L37/1SA SC cpe (Series I)	2,886	15,425	4,951
L37/1SB SC cpe (Series II)	—	16,975	
L69/1SA SL sdn 4d (Series I)	2,917	15,225	47,593
L69/1SB SL sdn 4d (Series II)	—	16,775	
Cutlass (107.0)			
J69 sdn 4d	2,982	17,325	9,973
G69 GLS sdn 4d	—	19,225	8,139
Cutlass Supreme (wb 107.7)			
H47/1SA cpe (Series I)	3,286	18,950	10,197
H47/1SB cpe (Series II)	—	19,850	
H47/1SC cpe (Series III)	—	20,750	
H69/1SA sdn 4d (Series I)	3,388	18,950	49,327
H69/1SB sdn 4d (Series II)	—	19,850	
H69/1SC sdn 4d (Series III)	—	20,750	
Eighty-Eight (wb 110.8)			
N69 sdn 4d	3,465	22,495	51,183
N69 LS sdn 4d	—	23,795	
Y69 LSS sdn 4d	3,547	27,695	11,101
C69 Regency sdn 4d	—	27,995	8,219
Aurora (wb 113.8)			
R29 sdn 4d	3,967	35,795	27,927

1997 Engines	bore×stroke	bhp	availability
I-4, 146.0	3.54×3.70	150	S-Achv (dohc)
V-6, 191.0	3.50×3.310	155	S-Cutl, O-Achv
V-6, 191.0	3.50×3.30	160	S-Cutl Supreme
V-6, 231.0	3.80×3.40	205	S-Eighty-Eight
V-6S, 231.0	3.80×3.40	240	O-Egty-Egt LSS
V-8, 244.0	3.42×3.31	250	S-Aurora

1998

Achieva (wb 103.4)	Wght	Price	Prod
L69 SL sdn 4d	2,917	—	26,922
Cutlass (107.0)			
B69 GL sdn 4d	2,982	17,800	21,428
G69 GLS sdn 4d	—	19,425	31,256
Intrigue (wb 109.0)			
H69 sdn 4d	3,455	20,700	43,840
S69 GL sdn 4d	—	22,100	59,525
X69 GLS sdn 4d	—	24,110	4,303
Eighty-Eight (wb 110.8)			
N69 sdn 4d	3,455	22,795	20,000
N69 LS sdn 4d	—	24,195	34,075
Y69 LSS sdn 4d	3,502	28,095	5,283
C69 Regency sdn 4d	3,813	28,295	7,958
Aurora (wb 113.8)			
R29 sdn 4d	3,967	35,960	25,721

1998 Engines	bore×stroke	bhp	availability
I-4, 146.0	3.54×3.70	150	S-Achv (dohc)
V-6, 191.0	3.51×3.31	150	S-Cutlass
V-6, 191.0	3.51×3.31	155	O-Achieva
V-6, 231.0	3.80×3.40	195	S-Intrigue
V-6, 231.0	3.80×3.40	205	S-Eighty-Eight
V-6S, 231.0	3.80×3.40	240	O-Egty-Egt LSS
V-8, 244.0	3.42×3.31	250	S-Aurora

1999

Alero (wb 107.0)	Wght	Price	Prod
— GX cpe	2,960	16,325	8,730
— GL cpe	—	18,655	22,302
— GLS cpe	—	20,875	11,273
— GX sdn 4d	3,020	16,325	5,711
— GL sdn 4d	—	18,220	71,944
— GLS sdn 4d	—	20,875	22,302
Intrigue (wb 109.0)			
H69 GX sdn 4d	3,465	21,175	38,553
S69 GL sdn 4d	—	22,575	39,321
X69 GLS sdn 4d	—	24,945	16,041
Eighty-Eight (wb 110.8)			
— sdn 4d	—	23,555	11,546
— LS sdn 4d	3,455	25,105	24,091
— LSS sdn 4d	3,500	29,105	597
— 50th Anniv. sdn 4d	—	27,350	4,719
Aurora (wb 113.8)			
R29 sdn 4d	3,965	36,229	19,635

1999 Engines	bore×stroke	bhp	availability
I-4, 146.0	3.54×3.70	150	S-Alero (dohc)
V-6, 207.0	3.62×3.31	170	S-Alero GLS; O-Alero GL
V-6, 212.0	3.52×3.62	215	O-Intrig (dohc)
V-6, 231.0	3.80×3.40	195	S-Intrigue
V-6, 231.0	3.80×3.40	205	S-Eighty-Eight
V-6S, 231.0	3.80×3.40	240	O-Egty-Egt LSS
V-8, 244.0	3.42×3.31	250	S-Aurora

2000

Alero (wb 107.0)	Wght	Price	Prod
K37 GX cpe	3,027	15,675	6,506
L37 GL cpe	3,038	17,650	19,378
F37 GLS cpe	3,051	21,365	8,422
K69 GX sdn 4d	3,078	15,675	11,937
L69 GL sdn 4d	3,089	17,650	71,624
F69 GLS sdn 4d	3,102	21,635	19,273
Intrigue (wb 109.0)			
H69 GX sdn 4d	3,426	22,090	43,249
S69 GL sdn 4d	3,452	23,720	21,564
X69 GLS sdn 4d	3,433	25,720	15,698

2000 Engines	bore×stroke	bhp	availability
I-4, 146.0	3.54×3.70	150	S-Alero (dohc)
V-6, 207.0	3.62×3.31	170	O-Alero
V-6, 212.0	3.52×3.62	215	S-Intrigue (dohc)

2001

Alero (wb 107.0)	Wght	Price	Prod
K37 GX cpe	2,973	17,210	5,026
L37 GL cpe	2,997	18,620	17,044
F37 GLS cpe	3,060	22,190	4,795
K69 GX sdn 4d	3,026	17,210	13,902
L69 GL sdn 4d	3,046	18,620	75,895
F69 GLS sdn 4d	3,108	21,965	13,064
Intrigue (wb 109.0)			
H69 GX sdn 4d	3,493	22,395	26,637
S69 GL sdn 4d	3,420	24,150	12,926
X69 GLS sdn 4d	3,434	26,615	5,104
Aurora (wb 112.2)			
R29 V-6 sdn 4d	3,686	30,469	37,397
S29 V-8 sdn 4d	3,803	34,644	16,243

2001 Engines	bore×stroke	bhp	availability
I-4, 146.0	3.54×3.70	150	S-Alero (dohc)
V-6, 207.0	3.62×3.31	170	O-Alero
V-6, 212.0	3.52×3.62	215	S-Intrig, Aurora V-6 (dohc)
V-8, 244.0	3.42×3.31	250	S-Aurora V-8

2002

Alero (wb 107.0) - 98,979 blt	Wght	Price	Prod
K37 GX cpe 2d	2,946	17,470	—
L37 GL1 cpe 2d	2,961	19,680	—
L37 GL2 cpe 2d	3,042	20,580	—
F37 GLS cpe 2d	3,085	22,315	—
K69 GX sdn 4d	3,021	17,470	—
L69 GL1 sdn 4d	3,016	19,455	—
L69 GL2 sdn 4d	3,103	20,580	—
F69 GLS sdn 4d	3,147	22,090	—
Intrigue (wb 109.0) - 32,727 built			
H69 GX sdn 4d	3,393	22,817	—
S69 GL sdn 4d	3,420	24,402	—
X69 GLS sdn 4d	3,434	27,892	—
Aurora (wb 112.2) - 12,189 built			
R29 V6 sdn 4d	3,686	30,995	—
S29 V8 sdn 4d	3,803	34,990	—

2002 Engines	bore×stroke	bhp	availability
I-4, 134.0	3.38×3.72	140	S-Alero (dohc)
V-6, 207.0	3.62×3.31	170	O-Alero
V-6, 212.0	3.52×3.62	215	S-Intrig, Aurora V-6 (dohc)
V8, 244.0	3.42×3.31	250	S-Aurora V-8

2003

Alero (wb 107.0) - 109,773 blt	Wght	Price	Prod
K37 GX cpe 2d	2,939	17,785	—
L37 GL1 cpe 2d	2,950	19,635	—
L37 GL2 cpe 2d	3,030	21,185	—
F37 GLS cpe 2d	3,065	22535	—
K69 GX sdn 4d	2,996	17,785	—
L69 GL1 sdn 4d	3,008	19,635	—
L69 GL2 sdn 4d	3,088	21,185	—
F69 GLS sdn 4d	3,123	22,285	—
Aurora (wb 112.2) - 4,047 built			
S29 sdn 4d	3,803	34,150	—

2003 Engines	bore×stroke	bhp	availability
I-4, 134.0	3.38×3.72	140	S-Alero
V-6, 207.0	3.62×3.31	170	O-Alero
V-8, 244.0	3.42×3.31	250	S-Aurora

2004

Alero (wb 107.0) - 79,796 blt	Wght	Price	Prod
K37 GX cpe 2d	2,939	18,200	—
L37 GL1 cpe 2d	2,950	20,150	—
L37 GL2 cpe 2d	3,030	20,150	—
F37 GLS cpe 2d	3,065	21,700	—
K69 GX sdn 4d	2,996	18,200	—
L69 GL1 sdn 4d	3,008	20,150	—
L69 GL2 sdn 4d	3,088	21,700	—
F69 GLS sdn 4d	3,123	22,800	—

2004 Engines	borexstroke	bhp	availability
I-4, 134.0	3.38×3.72	140	S-Alero
V-6, 207.0	3.62×3.31	170	O-Alero

Packard

For many people, Packard was, in its heyday, "the supreme combination of all that is fine in motor-cars." It may not have always been the technical "Standard of the World," but it was the social Standard of America, even for millions of would-be buyers who could never afford one. In 1929, more people owned stock in Packard than any other company save General Motors, and there were far more Packard stockholders than Packard owners.

Packard got its start in Warren, Ohio, in 1899, when James Ward Packard figured he could build a better car than the Winton he had purchased. His first was a small one-cylinder model with automatic spark advance. James B. Joy took over the concern in 1901 and moved it to Detroit in 1903, the year of the first four-cylinder Packard.

The car that moved Packard firmly into the industry's front rank was its 48-horsepower Six of 1912. Packard then leap-frogged Cadillac's new 1915 V-8 with a V-12 the following year—the fabled "Twin Six," though that only lasted until 1923. A new straight-eight arrived for the 1924 season. Packard did introduce a less-prestigious Six in 1921, but that was dropped well before 1930. The make then maintained its reputation mainly with eight-cylinder engines right on through its sad death in 1958.

For a company so single-mindedly devoted to luxury, Packard compiled a remarkable production record. It regularly outproduced Cadillac in 1925-30, even though its GM rival had help from LaSalle beginning in 1927. Except for 1931, '32, and '34, Packard continued to out-build Cadillac/LaSalle until WWII.

Like other luxury makes, Packard relied on middle-priced products to survive the Depression, most notably the One Twenty, new for 1935. This, together with the companion One Ten, enabled Packard not only to endure "hard times" but to grow rapidly from low-volume luxury to true mass-market producer. Unfortunately, the firm was far slower to abandon medium-price products after World War II than either Cadillac or Lincoln, thus sowing the seeds of its ultimate demise.

In 1923, Packard began using a "series" number to designate each year's model line, a practice it continued into the '50s. Historians have since converted these to model years for ease of recognition. The Seventh Series, for example, coincides with 1930.

That hierarchy began with a standard Eight, which had the least-pretentious bodies on relatively short wheelbases of 127.5 and 134.5 inches. Power came from a 320-cubic-inch inline engine making 90 bhp. Next up was the dashing Speedster Eight, offering lithe boattail and standard roadsters, plus phaeton, victoria, and sedan, all on a 134-inch chassis. Speedsters cost the world—$5200-$6000—so only 150 were built before the series was canceled after 1930. A 385-cid eight delivered 125-145 bhp in Speedsters. A 106-bhp version powered Custom and DeLuxe Eights on respective wheelbases of 140.5 and 145.5 inches. These were generally built with closed bodies, but were also available in phaeton, roadster, and convertible styles by Packard and various custom coach-builders. Prices here weren't quite the world, ranging from $3200 to over $5000. Then again, such sums bought a rather nice house at the time.

The 1931 Eighth Series comprised standard, Custom, and DeLuxe Eights. The standard line now offered "Individual Customs" on the 134.5-inch chassis. Included were a Dietrich convertible sedan and victoria, plus Packard's own cabriolet, town car, and landaulet styles. Standard models retained the 320 engine, now 10 bhp richer; Custom and DeLuxe again carried the 385 unit, now with 120 bhp. The extra power came from modified intake and exhaust passages similar to those on the 1930 Speedsters. Other linewide mechanical changes included automatic Bijur chassis-lubrication system and a new quick-shift mechanism for the four-speed gearbox to reduce effort.

For 1932's Ninth Series came a more-conventional three-speed all-synchromesh transmission, plus lower, more-streamlined styling that was nonetheless similar to upright 1930-31 appearance. But the big news occurred at the top and bottom of the line. Leading the fleet was a new Twin Six, which was renamed Twelve after this one year. It bore no relationship to the 1916-23 original, with a new 445.5-cid V-12 that had actually been planned for an aborted front-drive chassis. Though a fairly low numerical axle ratio was available, most of these cars got gearsets of 4.41:1 or higher. The result was smooth, relatively shift-free motoring rather than high performance. The factory claimed a sustained 100 mph was well within the new V-12's capabilities, but that was under test conditions; the 160-bhp engine usually ran out of breath at about 90 mph in stock tune. At 60 or 70 mph, though, it was whisper quiet and highly refined.

The 1932-34 V-12s shared the same two wheelbases and most bodies with the upper Eight series, which was again called DeLuxe for '32, then Super. In all cases, the longer chassis was reserved for Individual Customs and a standard seven-passenger sedan and limousine. Despite their prestige as the ultimate Packards, the V-12s arrived at only $100-$200 above counterpart DeLuxes with factory bodywork, but the gap grew as time passed, especially between the various custom-body models. In 1935, when "senior" production was consolidated to make room for the new high-volume One Twenty, the Twelve gained a stroked 473-cid engine with 175 bhp, and shifted to 139- and 144-inch wheelbases. Super Eights offered similar body styles on those same chassis, as well as a trim 132-inch platform. Custom bodies thinned quickly as coachbuilders either went bankrupt or were bought out, but a few were always listed through 1942.

As an independent, Packard couldn't face the Depression with solid financial backing from a big parent, so it tried medium-priced cars well before Cadillac or Lincoln. Its first was the 1932 Light Eight, appearing two years ahead of a smaller, cheaper LaSalle and four years ahead of Lincoln's Zephyr. A quality product built with the same meticulous care as other Packards, the Light Eight was true to its name. It rode a lighter, trimmer 127.8-inch chassis mounting the standard Eight's 320 engine, rated that year at 110 bhp. The Light Eight was thus faster than its bigger sisters. Body styles comprised four-door sedan, five-passenger coupe-sedan, and rumble-seat roadster and coupe.

But the Light Eight looked chunkier than other '32 Packards because it was shorter overall, and its attractively affordable pricing—around $2000—was more liability than asset. A Light Eight cost almost as much to build as a corresponding standard Eight yet sold for $500-$850 less, so Packard was lucky to break even on any Light Eight sold. The line was accordingly dropped after this one year.

Packard lost $7 million in 1932, much of it on the Light Eight, so company president Alvan Macauley began searching the ranks of GM executives for someone wise in the ways of volume production who could help the firm develop a profitable middle-priced car. Ironically, the firm netted $500,000 with 1933 sales that amounted to 38 percent of the high-priced market—well above Cadillac's share. Trouble was, the high-priced market was virtually gone.

But Macauley's search was about to pay big dividends. Soon coming aboard were Max Gilman, "that hardboiled guy in New

1930 Speedster Eight boattail roadster

1932 900 Series Light Eight convertible coupe

1932 DeLuxe Eight sport phaeton

1935 One Twenty 2/4-passenger sport coupe

1936 One Twenty four-door sedan

1937 Twelve convertible victoria

York" (he'd started as a Brooklyn truck salesman in 1919), and George T. Christopher, a production whiz enticed out of retirement from GM. (Gilman replaced Macauley as president in 1938, when the latter became chairman; Christopher replaced Gilman in 1942.) While Gilman astutely set the publicity stage, Christopher modernized Packard's plant end-to-end for much higher volume. The fruit of their combined labors was unveiled on January 6, 1935, as the One Twenty.

It was a dramatic departure for Packard. Bowing in seven models, the One Twenty cost a little more than half as much as the unmourned Light Eight—$1000-$1100—perfect for those who'd always wanted a Packard but had never been able to afford one. There were traditional hallmarks like the "ox-yoke" radiator and red hexagon wheel-hub emblems, but styling was updated, emerging conservative but contemporary with rounded contours, "potato-shape" windows, fullsome fenders, and a radiator raked 30 degrees from vertical—all pretty daring for Packard.

Designed largely by former GM people, the One Twenty engine was a straightforward L-head eight of 257.2 cid and 110 bhp. Features included a heavily ribbed block, individual exhaust ports, ample water jackets, five main bearings, and counterweighted overlapping journals. It was a smooth engine, easy on gas, and granite strong. After 1935, a longer stroke yielded 282 cid and 120 bhp. Most One Twentys could reach 85 mph and do 0-60 in less than 20 seconds—not bad for a 3500-pound prewar car.

For 1936, the One Twenty added a convertible sedan bearing "Dietrich" body plates, though Ray Dietrich personally had nothing to do with it; his name had been owned by the Murray Body Company since the early '30s. The following year brought a station wagon, three DeLuxe closed models, and a 138-inch wheelbase sedan and limousine. The '37 Senior Packards joined the One Twenty in offering independent front suspension, grease fittings (instead of the Bijur automatic chassis-lube system), and hydraulic brakes. For 1938, when the One Twenty was simply called Eight (one year only), the standard wheelbase lengthened to 127 inches.

Though long and unfairly criticized as "cheap," the One Twenty was a genuine Packard in appearance, road behavior, and workmanship. To no one's surprise, it sold like nickel hot dogs. As a result, Packard rocketed to 12th in industry production for 1935, leaping from 8000 to nearly 32,000. And it kept right on soaring, reaching about 61,000 in '36 and 122,000 in '37. A sharp recession held 1938 volume to some 56,000, but the firm soon recovered, and output remained healthy until World War II.

Contributing to that 1937 record was an even less-expensive line, the new Six, called One-Ten for 1940-42. Arriving on a 115-inch wheelbase, it used what was basically an over-bored One Twenty eight with two fewer cylinders, which made for a 237-cid six with 100 bhp. Wheelbase stretched to 122 inches for 1938-39, when displacement went up to 245 cid, though horsepower was

1938 Twelve Brunn all-weather cabriolet

1938 Twelve touring limousine

1938 Eight two-door touring sedan

1939 One Twenty four-door touring sedan

1940 Darrin convertible sedan

unchanged. Offerings basically duplicated the One Twenty's, but prices averaged some $150 lower, so the One Ten outsold the One Twenty by 13-to-10 in 1937. Though its six wasn't as smooth or potent as the One Twenty eight, it did offer excellent mileage and adequate performance.

The One Ten completed Packard's transformation from a purveyor of virtually handmade luxury cars to one of Detroit's top-10 producers. Of course, the firm still sold regular and Super Eights and opulent Twelves through decade's end, but at a rate of only some 6000 a year. The One Twenty was far and away the breadwinning eight, costing some $1200 less than a standard Eight. Testifying to its success, the Super Eight lost its 385 engine after 1936, demoted to the 320 unit of the standard Eight, which itself disappeared after 1937, though not in name.

But the rather small and dumpy One Ten/Six was by no means a Packard in the traditional sense. Perhaps the firm had become too greedy for sales, blinded by George Christopher's push for ever-higher production. Regardless, by the end of the '30s, Cadillac was in firm charge as the sales and prestige leader of the high-dollar class. Many people who previously wouldn't have been seen in a Caddy now bought them instead of big Packards, which had been upstaged by the low-cost One Ten/One Twenty that looked almost the same, at least in front.

A definite factor in Cadillac's leap to luxury-league supremacy was its more-modern Harley Earl styling. True to tradition, Packard maintained a tall, formal look that seemed quite stuffy by 1939, not least because it hadn't changed much since the great design overhaul of four years before.

The line was again anchored for '39 by the Six (soon to be called One Ten), priced as low as $1000 for the business coupe. (Fords and Chevys cost $600-$900 that year.) The One Twenty name returned on entry-level eight-cylinder models, with 127- and 148-inch wheelbases; prices were $1245-$1700. Super Eights offered the same two chassis, but models were reduced to cover a $1650-$2300 spread. The Twelve, however, still ran a very broad gamut of models and prices ($4155-$8355), including custom styles by Rollston and Brunn. However, the magnificent Twelve was in its final year; the Depression had rendered it an unnecessary anachronism. Only 5744 were built during its eight-year reign as queen of the line (including 1932 Twin Sixes).

More major styling adjustments occurred for 1940, when a new 160-bhp 356-cid engine bowed in an expanded Super Eight line divided between One Sixty and Custom One Eighty models. These spanned wheelbases of 127, 138, and 148 inches and a price band of $1500-$2900 with standard bodywork. The new 356 was impressively quiet, what with nine main bearings and a crankshaft that weighed 105 pounds. It was also potent enough to push the lighter models to well over 100 mph. The 356 would power Supers through 1947 and Customs through 1950. Another new feature for 1940 was air conditioning. Packard was the first production car to offer it, though it was bulky and not as effective as later units.

Meantime, the low-priced Six was again a One Ten for 1940, but neither it nor the One Twenty was much changed mechanically. However, rumble-seat models were eliminated, and the One Twenty extended its coverage with four new DeLuxe-trim models: a sedan, club coupe and sedan, and convertible coupe in the $1160-$1300 price range.

A stunning exception to Packard's more-competitive 1940 price structure was a new quartet of rakish custom-built Darrin models, the work of renowned designer Howard A. "Dutch" Darrin. Effectively filling the glamour gap left by the departed Twelve, these comprised a One Twenty convertible victoria, a Custom Super Eight One Eighty version on the same short wheelbase, and a long-chassis Custom Super convertible sedan and closed Sport Sedan. All boasted ground-hugging silhouettes enhanced by the complete absence of running boards (Dutch detested running boards, though they were fast-fading anyway). The victorias were exquisite: smooth, low, ideally proportioned, yet with just the right amount of proper Packard dignity.

The Darrin-Packards evolved from a handful of 1938-39 specials that Dutch had built at his Hollywood works for various celebrities, including actor/crooner Dick Powell. Strong response encouraged Dutch to convince Packard to catalog such wares on a special-order basis. In a clever ploy to do just that, he got the Powell car parked at the Packard Proving Grounds in the summer of 1939, where it was roundly cheered by dealers attending their annual sales meeting.

Save sectioned radiators and hoods, the Darrins wore unique body panels. The Sport Sedan was a handsome "gentleman's" car with a semblance of Bill Mitchell's 1938 Cadillac Sixty Special in its curved, blind-quarter roof, chrome-edged windows, and sharp beltline. But the real eye-catcher was the sleek victoria, with cut-down windshield and an abrupt kickup to the rear flanks from a gradually sloped doorline—the famous "Darrin notch."

The Darrins were naturally Packard's priciest 1940s—$3819 for the One Twenty victoria, $6332 for the Custom Super convertible sedan—so sales were naturally minuscule. Then, too, planned production (at the old Auburn plant in Connersville, Indiana) was deliberately limited. Only 50 victorias were built for 1940 and a mere 12 convertible sedans (of which nine survive today). The Sport Sedan was announced as "virtually a request car—built for those who look to Packard to . . . create the newest, the finest, the most luxurious in motorcar transportation." But it never got going, and was dropped after only two were completed at Dutch's shop. Packard itself built two "Darrinized" sedans with stock 1940 front ends, but they weren't nearly as pretty and led nowhere productwise. As you might expect, all Darrin-Packards have long been deemed "Classics" by the Classic Car Club of America (CCCA).

Also offered for 1940 were an all-weather cabriolet and town car by Rollston, priced at $4473 and $4599, respectively. Only a handful were built. But even some regular models were quite scarce. Of the 98,000 Packards built for 1940, only 5662 were Super Eights and just 1900 were Customs. The rest were One Tens and One Twentys.

Packard finally rebodied its entire line for 1941, though it wasn't blindingly obvious. The main visual clues were slightly larger windows and—in a big styling innovation for Packard—headlamps set firmly within the front fenders. Wheelbases were unchanged, but floors were lowered, suspension was suitably revised, motor mounts were enlarged, and engines benefited from steel-backed rod bearings and an oil-bath air cleaner. These changes also applied to Darrins, but there was only one now: a Custom Super Eight One Eighty Victoria. This retained its general 1940 appearance save minor trim, a slightly different "notch" treatment, and the flush headlamps. One other difference: Its production was transferred to Cincinnati, where ambulance/hearse builder Sayers and Scoville crafted 35 as '41 models and another 15 to little-changed 1942 specifications. Overdrive was still optional throughout the Packard line, but for 1941 it could team with a new $37.50 "Electromatic" clutch. This disengaged by manifold vacuum upon releasing the accelerator to permit "clutchless" driving in second gear, which covered most day-to-day use; the pedal could still be floored to select first.

But Packard saved its biggest '41 news for midseason, when it unveiled the Clipper, a four-door sedan priced at $1420, squarely between the One Twenty and One Sixty. Though built on the One Twenty chassis, it looked like no Packard before: smooth and modern—a bold, unexpected bid for industry design leadership. The Clipper bore the unmistakable Darrin touch but was actually a joint project, with contributions from Packard's own stylists

1940 Darrin convertible victoria

1940 One Twenty four-door touring sedan

1941 One Eighty four-door touring sedan

1941 One Twenty station wagon

1947 Custom Super Clipper two-door club sedan

under Werner Gubitz, plus several stellar consultants. Still, it was mostly Darrin, seen in the descending beltline, tapered tail, and long prow-front with the slimmest Packard radiator yet. Predicting postwar styling at Packard and elsewhere was a nearly flush-sided "envelope" body with front fenders "swept-through" into the doors—and width that exceeded height.

Dutch had dashed off the Clipper in just 10 days to meet Packard's deadline, but never got a promised $10,000 fee. That was poor form, for the Clipper alone garnered some 16,000 sales—22 percent of Packard's total '41 volume, which was down some 25,000 from 1940. Still, this performance encouraged Packard to proceed with making "Clipper styling" virtually linewide for 1942. The sole exceptions were commercial vehicles, One Sixty/One Eighty convertible coupes, and custom bodies. The last again included the Rollston styles as well as new LeBaron-built long sedans and limousines and a beautifully formal Sport Brougham. Like other makes, Packard's 1942 production was cut short by America's entry into World War II, the total ending just shy of 34,000, mostly Clipper-styled 110/120 and One Sixty/One Eighty models.

After building Rolls-Royce Merlin aero engines and power units for military vehicles and PT boats, Packard returned to peacetime as the only independent free of debt. But then came a decision that would ultimately prove fatal. Instead of reverting to luxury cars alone, Packard continued to stress medium-price models in the One Twenty tradition. While such cars had been vital during the Depression, they simply weren't needed in the hectic sell-everything postwar economy, and they severely squandered what remained of Packard's grand-luxe image.

Still, disaster was a long way off in 1946, when Packard followed most other Detroit makes in reprising its final prewar line, though abbreviated. That year's low-priced Clipper Six sedan and coupe looked exactly like the Clipper Eight models, which included DeLuxe versions. All used the familiar 120-inch wheelbase. Clipper Super and Custom sedans and coupes had the equally familiar 127-inch chassis save the seven-passenger Custom sedan and limo (which had a 148-inch wheelbase). Basic Eights retained the 282 engine with 125 bhp, Supers and Customs kept the 165-bhp 356 from '42, and the Six continued with its 105-bhp 245. Overdrive and Electromatic clutch returned as options. Customs were trimmed with plush broadcloth and leather upholstery, special carpeting, and beautiful imitation wood paneling. Packard moved more than 30,000 cars in 1946 and over 50,000 of the '47s, which were identical except for serial numbers.

1950 Eight DeLuxe four-door sedan

1952 Patrician 400 four-door sedan

There was just one problem. Most automakers were able to stretch their prewar tooling through 1948, then issue all-new postwar designs that were ahead of the Clipper in style. But Packard, despite its postwar financial health, couldn't afford to junk its prewar dies so soon because they hadn't been amortized over sufficient production. Accordingly, Packard stylists loaded on heavy chunks of sheetmetal to give the Clipper a modern "flow-through-fender" effect. It also added 200 needless pounds in curb weight. The result looked fatter too, aggravated by a short, squat grille—eggcrate on Customs, bar-type on other models—that was far-less-elegant than the slim prow of 1941-47. All this moved auto writer Tom McCahill to pronounce the '48 Packard fit for "a dowager in a Queen Mary hat." Many simply called it a "pregnant elephant."

Still, in 1948 it didn't matter whether a Packard looked trim or tubby or cost $2500 or $4500. Like most everyone else in the postwar seller's market, Packard could sell every car it built, and it sold a respectable number: some 92,000 for model-year '48 and about 116,000 of the similar '49s—two of its best years ever.

Engine and chassis assignments altered somewhat for the '48 line of standard, DeLuxe, Super, and Custom Eights. Customs retained their 160-bhp 356 engine, but Supers got a new 327 unit with five main bearings and 145 bhp; standard Eights used a much squarer new 288 engine with 130 bhp. These powerplants carried through to May 1949 in the Twenty-Second Series. Then the Twenty-Third series appeared with horsepower raised to 135 for standards and to 150 for Supers.

As before, sedans and coupes were Packard's mainstays in 1948-50. Standards, DeLuxes, and Supers kept to 120-inch wheelbases, Customs to a 127-inch chassis; a 141-inch platform supported four new Super Eight long sedans and limos, while a 148-inch chassis continued under counterpart Customs. Packard also crafted a few long Custom commercial chassis, plus some six-cylinder 1948 platforms for taxi and export use.

Also new for '48 were Custom and Super convertibles and the novel four-door Station Sedan in the standard Eight series. The last, priced at $3425, had a wagonlike body made almost entirely of steel, though it employed structural wood at the tailgate and decorative timber on the doors. It was unusual for a Packard, which may be why it didn't sell too well: just 3864 copies through 1950. The Custom Eight convertible was Packard's priciest standard model tagged at $4295 for 1948-49, then $4520.

Ushered in with the Twenty-Third series of mid-1949 was Ultramatic, the only automatic transmission developed by an independent without outside help. This combined a torque converter with multiple-disc and direct-drive clutches, plus forward/reverse bands. The car started from rest using the torque converter, then shifted into direct mechanical drive at about 15 miles an hour. Though much smoother than GM's rival Hydra-Matic, Ultramatic provided only leisurely acceleration, and frequent use of Low range for faster starts caused premature wear.

Also arriving with the Twenty-Third series was a mild facelift distinguished by a beltline spear on most models, plus new Deluxe-trim Eight and Super Eight sedans and coupes. The Super versions carried a 327-cid engine and the same eggcrate grille as corresponding Customs but cost about $1000 less, so Custom sales suffered mightily. So did Packard as a whole. The seller's market was ending, and production showed it, plunging to just under 42,400 units for the model year.

Packard finally managed a total redesign for 1951, adopting

1953 Caribbean convertible coupe

1954 Clipper DeLuxe Sportster coupe

1953 Patrician four-door sedan

1955 Four Hundred hardtop coupe

John Reinhart's squarish, but praiseworthy, "high-pockets" notchback shape—a complete break with the "elephants." A new 122-inch chassis supported a "200" series of standard and DeLuxe two- and four-door sedans, plus a spiffy "250" convertible and Mayfair hardtop coupe, the latter body style a first for Packard. A 127-inch platform was used for "300" and Patrician 400 sedans. Like the old One Ten, the 200s weren't traditional Packards even though they carried the same 288 engine as the previous standard Eight. The line even included a $2302 business coupe, $529 less than the cheapest '51 Cadillac. But with the market ended, the 200s couldn't hope to do well against established price rivals, and they didn't.

The "real" Packards of 1951 were the 250s, which did sell pretty well, and the regal 300 and Patrician. At just under $3700, the Patrician effectively replaced the broad Custom Eight line. But though very smooth and utterly reliable, the Custom's 356 engine cost too much to build in light of expected sales, so Packard's biggest '51 engine was the destroked 327, previously the middle powerplant and with nearly as much horsepower: 155 for Patricians and Ultramatic 250/300s, 150 otherwise.

Overall, Packard's new '51 package fared quite well—probably because it was new in a year when little else was. Model-year production ended at 101,000, more than twice the dismal 1950 total. (Packard also built 401 "300" chassis that year for the professional car market and what remained of its once-thriving custom-body business.)

Unfortunately, 1952 production was down substantially, sliding to just under 63,000 units. Changes were few. The 200 business coupe was dropped, power brakes arrived as a (postwar) first-time option, and there were colorful new interiors in high-quality fabric and leather by fashion designer Dorothy Draper. Styling was virtually untouched, however. The most-obvious change was a different wing position for the traditional "pelican" hood ornament.

A far more significant change occurred in the executive suite during 1952. In May, aging president Hugh Ferry (who'd replaced George Christopher in 1949) stepped down in favor of James J. Nance, a marketwise hotshot recruited from Hotpoint to turn Packard around. That was sorely needed. By the time Nance arrived, Packard's Detroit plant was working at only 50 percent capacity. Incredibly, several long-time executives felt that was good enough, but Nance saw then what we all see now: At that pace, Packard was doomed.

Nance blew in like a tornado, aggressively seeking new military business while declaring that the firm's continued emphasis on medium-price cars was "bleeding the Packard name white." Accordingly, he made the 200/250 into new Packard Clipper models for 1953, stage-one of his plan to divorce the cheaper cars from the rest of the line in both fact and name. Packard, he decreed, would henceforth build nothing but luxury cars, including the long-wheelbase formal sedans and limousines it had lately neglected.

Lack of time and money precluded a linewide makeover for '53, but Nance did see to the inclusion of an eight-place Executive Sedan and "Corporation Limousine" on a massive 149-inch chassis, priced around $7000. He also contracted with the Derham Body Company for a few formal Patricians with leather-covered tops, tiny rear windows, and $6531 price tags.

Also for the top of the 1953 line, Nance pushed out the Caribbean, a glamorous convertible on the short wheelbase with colorful styling by Richard A. Teague. Inspired by Richard Arbib's 1952 Packard Pan American show car (built by Henney), the Caribbean carried a 180-bhp 327, rakish circular rear-wheel cutouts, jaunty "Continental kit" outside spare tire, and chrome wire wheels, plus most every optional amenity in the book. It cost a lofty $5210 and was deliberately limited to 750 copies—for snob appeal—but the Caribbean was as well-received as Cadillac's new '53 Eldorado.

Anchoring the '53 line were Nance's Clippers: two- and four-door sedans in standard and DeLuxe guise powered by unchanged 288 and 327 engines. Included in the standard group was a snazzy hardtop-styled pillared two-door called Sportster, attractively priced at $2805. The 250-series was defunct, but the Mayfair and standard convertible returned; the cheapest long-wheelbase '53 was a sedan called Cavalier, replacing the 300.

Nance had hoped for all-new '54 Packards, but time and

1955 Caribbean convertible coupe

1956 Clipper Super hardtop coupe

1957 Town Sedan four-door

1958 hardtop coupe

1958 Hawk hardtop coupe

money were again lacking, so a look-alike interim series was fielded with rimmed headlamps and integrated backup lights the only visible differences. The 327 engine was enlarged to 359 cid and 212 bhp for Patrician, Caribbean and standard convertibles, commercial chassis, and a hardtop named Pacific. Air conditioning now returned for the first time since the war. But 1954 was a terrible year, with production of only 31,000 cars. Of these, some 23,000 were Clippers: Specials and DeLuxes as before, plus new Super sedans and a Super Panama hardtop coupe. Specials again used the 288 engine, but the DeLuxe's 327 was bumped up five bhp; the latter also powered Supers. The Cavalier sedan used a 185-bhp version. Chassis production came to 335.

The revolutionary new model Nance wanted for '54 was postponed to '55 partly by the so-called Studebaker-Packard merger, which was actually a Packard buyout. What Nance didn't know when he signed the papers was that Studebaker had huge productivity problems in its high-overhead South Bend, Indiana plant, with a break-even point somewhere over 250,000 cars. Contrary to many accounts, Packard was still a fairly healthy company at this point, but Studebaker was sinking and would eventually drag Packard down with it.

As the all-new '55s neared production, another smoldering problem burst into flame. Back in 1940, Packard had stopped building its own bodies, contracting the work to Briggs Manufacturing Company. But Packard lost this supplier when Chrysler bought Briggs in 1954, and thus had to build its own bodies again. Inexplicably, it settled for a cramped body plant on Conner Avenue in Detroit. Never large enough, this facility caused big production tie-ups and quality-control problems that hampered sales of the '55 Packards and forced immediate cancellation of long models. Though Packard built some 55,000 cars for prosperous '55, it would have done better to assign body production to its old, but adequate, main plant on Detroit's East Grand Boulevard.

Despite these woes, the 1955 Packard was a technological marvel. Prime among its wonders was "Torsion-Level" suspension: long torsion bars connecting front and rear wheels on each side. A complex electrical system enabled the suspension to correct for load weight, and effectively interlinked all four wheels for truly extraordinary ride and handling despite two-ton bulk. And there was more: powerful new short-stroke ohv V-8s, ousting the old-fashioned flathead straight-eights at last. Clipper DeLuxes and Supers (now shorn of two-door sedans) used a 320-cid version with 225 bhp. A bored-out 352 delivered 245 bhp in new Clipper Customs (a sedan and Constellation hardtop), 275 bhp in Caribbeans (via twin four-barrel carbs) and 260 bhp in Patrician sedans and new "Four Hundred" hardtop coupes. Ultramatic was suitably modified to handle the higher V-8 torque.

The engines, improved Ultramatic, and Torsion-Level gave the '55 Packards a fine chassis. Despite their heft, these were impressively fast and roadable cars—real Packards in every sense. Styling was equally impressive. Dick Teague's clever facelift of the old '51 body produced "cathedral" taillights; peaked front fenders; an ornate grille; and that '55 must-have, a wrapped windshield. Clippers gained their own special grille and retained 1954-style taillights.

Production problems at the Conner plant were finally licked, but not in time for '56, when customers were scared away by Studebaker's desperate struggle as well as the '55 Packards' notorious quality and service problems. Ironically, the '56s were better built.

Nance's "divorce action" reached fruition that year in an entirely separate Clipper line. Besides registering the name as a distinct make, he decreed separate Clipper and Packard dealer signs, and changed Packard Division to the Packard-Clipper Division of Studebaker-Packard Corporation. As a final touch,

"Packard" appeared nowhere on '56 Clippers except for tiny decklid script—and some didn't even have that.

Nevertheless, the line again offered five models: DeLuxe, Super, and Custom four-door sedans and Super and Custom Constellation hardtops. Wheelbase was unchanged, but horsepower was lifted to 275 for Customs and 240 for other models. Torsion-Level was again featured too, although a conventional suspension was available on the DeLuxe. Options included overdrive manual transmission ($110), Ultramatic ($199), power steering, power brakes, and air conditioning.

These Clippers were luxuriously trimmed and nicely styled, but sales weren't sufficient to help floundering S-P. The DeLuxe sedan was the most popular, attracting 5715 buyers. Least popular was the handsome Custom Constellation hardtop, garnering under 1500 sales. Though still obvious Packard relatives, the '56 Clippers retained their own grille and taillamp designs, made even more different in line with Nance's aims.

The Packard line still listed Clipper-type models in the 1956 Executive, a sedan and hardtop coupe announced at midyear to bridge the price gap with Clipper. Executives even shared the Clipper's chassis, 275-bhp 352 V-8, and pointy taillights, but wore "senior" '56 front-end styling, plus higher prices in the $3500-$3600 range. The longer 127-inch chassis returned for Patrician, Four Hundred, and two Caribbeans: the familiar convertible and a new hardtop, both with unique seat covers that could be reversed from fabric to leather. All these models were upgraded to a bored-out 374 V-8 packing a mighty 310 bhp in Caribbeans and 290 bhp elsewhere. But none of this helped, and only 10,353 Packards were built for '56, including just 263 Caribbean hardtops and 276 convertibles.

Packard was now sinking fast, being pulled down with Studebaker. Including Clipper, 1956 production totaled 28,835 cars, just slightly more than half of '55 volume.

Studebaker-Packard had planned an all-new 1957 corporate line that included a shared bodyshell but totally different looks for Studebaker and Clipper, plus a much larger separate platform for a group of high-luxury Packards styled in the image of Dick Teague's 1956 Packard Predictor show car. But S-P was on the ropes, so no financial backing could be found, leading Nance to resign in August 1956. (He soon resurfaced at another ill-fated outfit: the new Edsel Division of Ford Motor Company.) Salvation finally arrived in the form of Curtiss-Wright Corporation, which picked up Studebaker-Packard as a dalliance and/or tax write-off. C-W's Roy Hurley began directing S-P's affairs. One of his first decisions was to end Packard production in Detroit and substitute Studebaker-based models built in South Bend.

Thus appeared a new Packard Clipper for 1957: the infamous "Packardbaker," as many have since called it. Though a very good Studebaker, it was hardly in the same league with the '55-56 Packards. It came in just two models: four-door Town Sedan and Country Sedan station wagon. The sedan was on Studebaker's longer 120.5-inch chassis while the wagon was on a 116.5-inch chassis. A supercharged Studebaker 289-cid V-8 delivered the same 275 bhp as on '55 Caribbeans and '56 Executives, but Ultramatic, Torsion-Level, and other "real Packard" features were gone. Styling, at least, played on Packard themes. Prices were higher than for comparable Studeys: $3212/$3384. But everyone recognized this as a charade, and only about 5000 of the '57s, mostly sedans, were bought.

A big-Packard revival was still theoretically possible as the '58s were planned, so S-P again tried a holding action. This time there were four "Packardbakers" priced as high as $3995. Studebaker's shorter 116.5-inch platform carried a two-door hardtop and four-door wagon, the 120-inch chassis a sedan and the Packard Hawk. The last, perhaps the most-famous of this series, was a more-luxurious version of Studebaker's Golden Hawk.

All featured full-leather interiors and bizarre styling announced by low, "fish-mouth" grilles. In defense of stylist Duncan McRae, the Hawk was really built only because of Roy Hurley, who also dictated its long, bolt-on fiberglass nose and gaudy gold-mylar tailfins. McRae, however, gets the blame for the Hawk's outside "armrests" and styling on the other three models: also garishly finned, and with hastily contrived four-headlight systems to keep up with an industry trend. Only the Hawk was supercharged. Other '58 Packards used a stock 289 with 210 bhp. Production was uniformly low: 159 wagons, 588 Hawks, 675 hardtops, and 1200 sedans.

With that, there was no point in going on, and once-proud Packard vanished from the scene (though its name continued in the corporate title until 1962). It was a great loss, but it did give Studebaker a new lease on life, though that make, too, would soon expire.

Specifications

1930

726 Eight (wb 127.5)		Wght	Price	Prod
403	sdn 4d	4,265	3,275	15,731
733 Eight (wb 134.5) - 12,531 built				
400	touring 7P	4,055	2,525	—
401	phtn 4P	3,935	2,425	—
402	rdstr 2-4P	3,945	2,425	—
404	sdn 7P	4,500	2,675	—
405	sdn limo 7P	4,555	2,775	—
406	club sdn 5P	4,325	2,675	—
407	cpe 5P	4,255	2,675	—
408	cpe 2-4P	4,180	2,525	—
409	conv cpe 2-4P	4,100	2,550	—
431	spt phtn 4P	4,130	2,725	—
734 Speedster Eight (wb 134.0) - 113 built				
422	boattail rdstr 2P	4,295	5,210	—
443	sdn 5P	4,660	6,000	—
445	phtn 4P	4,300	5,200	—
447	cpe victoria 5P	4,525	6,000	—
452	rdstr 2-4P	4,435	5,200	—
740 Custom Eight (wb 140.5) - 6,200 built				
410	touring 7P	4,345	3,325	—
411	phtn 4P	4,250	3,190	—
412	rdstr 2-4P	4,245	3,190	—
413	sdn 4d 5P	4,560	3,585	—
414	sdn 7P	4,765	3,785	—
415	sdn limo 7P	4,810	3,885	—

740 Custom Eight		Wght	Price	Prod
416	club sdn 5P	4,580	3,750	—
417	cpe 5P	4,555	3,650	—
418	cpe 2-4P	4,500	3,295	—
419	conv cpe 2-4P	4,425	3,350	—
441	spt phtn	4,450	3,490	—
745 DeLuxe Eight (wb 145.5) - 1,789 built				
420	touring 7P	4,745	4,585	—
421	phtn 4P	4,645	4,585	—
422	rdstr 2-4P	4,695	4,585	—
423	sdn 4d 5P	4,805	4,985	—
424	sdn 7P	5,095	5,185	—
425	sdn limo 7P	5,140	5,350	—
426	club sdn 5P	5,000	5,150	—
427	cpe 5P	4,995	5,100	—
428	cpe 2-4P	4,875	4,785	—
429	conv cpe 2-4P	4,665	4,885	—
451	spt phtn 4P	4,845	4,885	—

1930 Engines	bore×stroke	bhp	availability
I-8, 320.0	3.19×5.00	90	S-726, 733
I-8, 384.8	3.50×5.00	106	S-740, 745
I-8, 384.8	3.50×5.00	125/145	S-734

1931

826 Eight (wb 127.5)		Wght	Price	Prod
463	sdn 4d 5P	4,479	2,385	6,009
833 Eight (wb 134.5) - 6,096 built				
460	touring 7P	4,256	2,525	—

833 Eight		Wght	Price	Prod
461	phtn 4P	4,185	2,425	—
462	rdstr 2-4P	4,140	2,425	—
464	sdn 7P	4,665	2,785	—
465	sdn limo 7P	4,695	2,885	—
466	club sdn 5P	4,488	2,675	—
467	cpe 5P	4,308	2,675	—
468	cpe 2-4P	4,360	2,525	—
469	conv cpe 2-4P	4,290	2,550	—
481	spt phtn 4P	4,285	2,725	—
483	conv sdn 5P	4,555	3,465	—
	Individual custom:			
1879	Dietrich conv vic 4P	4,186	4,275	—
1881	Dietrich conv sdn 4P	4,442	4,375	—
3000	A/W cab 7P	4,684	4,850	—
3001	A/W landaulet 7P	4,684	5,050	—
3002	A/W town car 7P	4,744	4,975	—
3003	A/W Indlt town car 7P	4,744	5,175	—
3004	sdn cab limo 6P	4,485	4,490	—
3008	A/W spt cab 7P	4,614	4,850	—
3009	A/W spt landaulet 7P	4,614	5,050	—
840 Custom Eight (wb 140.5) - 2,035 built				
470	touring 7P	4,507	3,595	—
471	phtn 4P	4,439	3,490	—
472	rdstr 2-4P	4,383	3,490	—
473	sdn 4d 5P	4,955	3,795	—
476	club sdn 5P	4,720	3,950	—
477	cpe 5P	4,673	3,850	—

840 Custom Eight		Wght	Price	Prod
478	cpe 2-4P	4,592	3,545	—
479	conv cpe 2-4P	4,523	3,595	—
491	spt phtn 4P	4,535	3,790	—
	Individual custom:			
1879	Dietrich conv vic 4P	4,418	5,175	—
1881	Dietrich conv sdn 4P	4,674	5,275	—
3000	A/W cab 7P	4,916	5,750	—
3001	A/W landaulet 7P	4,976	5,950	—
3002	A/W town car 7P	4,976	5,875	—
3003	A/W Indlt town car 7P	4,976	6,075	—
3008	A/W spt cab 7P	4,846	5,750	—
3009	A/W spt landaulet 7P	4,846	5,950	—
845 DeLuxe Eight (wb 145.5) -1,310 built				
474	sdn 7P	5,010	4,150	—
475	sdn limo 7P	5,080	4,285	—

1931 Engines	bore×stroke	bhp	availability
I-8, 320.8	3.19×5.00	100	S-826, 833
I-8, 384.8	3.50×5.00	120	S-840, 845

1932

900 Light Eight (wb 127.8)		Wght	Price	Prod
553	sdn 4d	4,115	1,895	4,850*
558	cpe 2-4P	3,990	1,940	510*
559	cpe-rdstr 2-4P	3,930	1,940	1,060*
563	cpe-sdn 5P	4,060	1,940	330*
901 Eight (wb 129.5)				
503	sdn 4d 5P	4,570	2,485	3,922
902 Eight (wb 136.5) - 3,737 built				
500	touring 7P	4,345	2,775	—
501	phtn 4P	4,300	2,650	—
504	sdn 7P	4,735	2,885	—
505	sdn limo 7P	4,770	2,985	—
506	club sdn 5P	4,555	2,775	—
507	cpe 5P	4,505	2,795	—
508	cpe 2-4P	4,475	2,675	—
509	cpe rdstr 2-4P	4,420	2,650	—
521	spt phtn 5P	4,400	2,950	—
523	conv sdn 5P	4,573	3,445	—
527	conv victoria 5P	4,317	3,395	
543	sdn 4d 5P	4,590	3,685	—
903 DeLuxe Eight (wb 142.5) - 955 built				
510	touring 7P	4,760	3,795	—
511	phtn 4P	4,715	3,690	—
513	sdn 4d 5P	5,045	3,845	—
516	club sdn 5P	5,000	3,890	—
517	cpe 5P	4,985	3,850	—
518	cpe 2-4P	4,890	3,725	—
519	cpe rdstr 2-4P	4,825	3,750	—
531	spt phtn 4P	4,795	3,990	—
533	conv sdn 5P	4,985	4,550	—
537	conv victoria 5P	4,727	4,495	—
904 DeLuxe Eight (wb 147.5) - 700 built				
514	sdn 7P	5,195	4,150	—
515	sdn limo 7P	5,240	4,285	—
	Individual custom:			
2060	Dietrich stnry cpe 2-4P	5,000	5,900	—
2069	Dietrich spt phtn 4P	4,800	5,800	—
2070	Dietrich conv sdn 5P	5,100	6,250	—
2071	Dietrich conv cpe 2-4P	4,965	6,050	—
2072	Dietrich conv vic 4P	4,815	6,150	—
4000	A/W cab 7P	5,250	6,850	—
4001	A/W landaulet 7P	5,250	7,250	—
4002	A/W town car 7P	5,310	6,850	—
4003	A/W Indlt town car 7P	5,310	7,250	—
4004	limo sdn cabriolet 6P	5,050	6,850	—
4005	spt sdn 4d 5P	5,030	6,850	—
4006	A/W brougham 7P	5,293	6,850	—
4007	Dietrich limo sdn 6P	5,075	6,850	—
4008	A/W spt cab 7P	5,180	6,850	—
4009	A/W spt landaulet 7P	5,180	7,250	—
905 Twin Six (wb 142.5) - 311 built				
570	touring 7P	5,315	3,895	—
571	phtn 4P	5,275	3,790	—
573	sdn 4d 5P	5,635	3,745	—
576	club sdn 5P	5,585	3,895	—
577	cpe 5P	5,485	3,850	—
578	cpe 2-4P	5,425	3,650	—
579	cpe rdstr 2-4P	5,350	3,750	—
581	spt phtn 4P	5,375	4,090	—

905 Twin Six		Wght	Price	Prod
583	conv sdn 5P	5,255	4,395	—
587	conv victoria 5P	5,180	4,325	—
906 Twin Six (wb 147.5)-238 blt				
574	sdn 7P	5,765	3,995	—
575	sdn limo 7P	5,830	4,195	—
	Individual custom:			
2068	Dietrich cpe 2-4P	5,180	6,600	—
2069	Dietrich spt phtn 4P	4,980	6,500	—
2070	Dietrich conv sdn 5P	5,280	6,950	—
2071	Dietrich conv cpe 2-4P	5,145	6,750	—
2072	Dietrich conv vic 4P	4,995	6,850	—
4000	A/W cabriolet 7P	5,430	7,550	—
4001	A/W landaulet 7P	5,430	7,950	—
4002	A/W town car 7P	5,490	7,550	—
4003	A/W town car Indlt 7P	5,490	7,950	—

* Estimates based on serial number analysis by Jack Triplett (*The Packard Cormorant*, Spring 1979).

1932 Engines	bore ×stroke	bhp	availability
I-8, 320.0	3.19×5.00	110	S-900, 901, 902
I-8, 384.8	3.50×5.00	135	S-903, 904
V-12, 445.5	3.44×4.00	160	S-905, 906

1933

1001 Eight (wb 127.5)		Wght	Price	Prod
602	cpe sdn 5P	4,245	2,190	73*
603	sdn 4d 5P	4,335	2,150	1,465*
608	cpe 2-4P	4,200	2,160	120*
609	cpe rdstr 2-4P	4,150	2,250	215*
—	chassis	—	—	9*
1002 Eight (wb 136.0) - 1,099 built				
610	touring 7P	4,275	2,390	—
611	phtn 5P	4,270	2,370	—
613	sdn 4d 5P	4,590	2,385	—
614	sdn 7P	4,640	2,455	—
615	limo 7P	4,725	2,550	—
616	club sdn 5P	4,545	2,390	—
617	cpe 5P	4,500	2,440	—
618	cpe 2-4P	4,455	2,350	—
623	conv sdn 5P	4,515	2,890	—
627	conv victoria 5P	4,540	2,780	—
5613	formal sdn 4d 5P	4,900	3,085	—
1003 Super Eight (wb 135.0)				
653	sdn 4d 5P	4,815	2,750	512
1004 Super Eight (wb 142.0) - 788 built				
650	touring 7P	4,610	2,980	—
651	phtn 5P	4,490	2,890	—
654	sdn 7P	4,965	3,090	—
655	limo 7P	5,025	3,280	—
656	club sdn 5P	4,795	2,975	—
657	cpe 5P	4,780	2,980	—
658	cpe 2-4P	4,670	2,780	—
659	cpe rdstr 2-4P	4,625	2,870	—
661	spt phtn 2-4P	4,690	3,150	—
663	conv sdn 5P	4,840	3,590	—
667	conv victoria 5P	4,795	3,440	—
673	formal sdn 4d 5P	5,155	3,600	—
1005 Twelve (wb 142.0) - 244 built				
631	phtn 5P	5,095	3,790	—
633	sdn 4d 5P	5,385	3,860	—
636	club sdn 5P	5,400	3,880	—
637	cpe 5P	5,300	3,890	—
638	cpe 2-4P	5,255	3,720	—
639	cpe rdstr 2-4P	5,160	3,850	—
641	spt phtn 5P	5,175	4,090	—
643	conv sdn 5P	5,405	4,650	—
647	conv victoria 5P	5,225	4,490	—
5633	formal sdn 5P	5,690	4,560	—
1006 Twelve (wb 147.0) - 276 built				
634	sdn 7P	5,600	4,085	—
635	limo 7P	5,650	4,285	—
	Individual custom:			
3068	Dietrich stnry cpe 2-4P	5,360	6,000	—
3069	Dietrich spt phtn 4P	5,160	5,875	—
3070	Dietrich conv sdn 5P	5,460	6,570	—
3071	Dtrich conv rnbt 2-4P	5,325	6,085	—
3072	Dietrich conv vic 4P	5,175	6,070	—
3182	Dietrich form sdn 7P	5,735	7,000	—
758	LeBaron A/W cab 7P	5,610	7,000	—
759	LeBrn A/W twn car 7P	5,670	7,000	—

1006 Twelve		Wght	Price	Prod
4000	A/W cab 7P	5,650	6,030	—
4001	A/W landaulet 7P	5,650	6,250	—
4002	A/W town car 7P	5,610	6,080	—
4003	landaulet town car 7P	5,610	6,250	—
4004	landaulet limo 7P	5,650	6,000	—
4005	spt sdn 4d 5P	5,330	6,000	—
4007	limo 7P	5,650	6,045	—

* Estimate based on serial number analysis by Jack Triplett (*The Packard Cormorant*, Spring 1979).

1933 Engines	bore×stroke	bhp	availability
I-8, 320.0	3.19×5.00	120	S-1001, 1002
I-8, 384.8	3.50×5.00	145	S-1003, 1004
V-12, 445.5	3.44×4.00	160	S-1005, 1006

1934

1100 Eight (wb 129.0)*		Wght	Price	Prod
703	sdn 4d 5P	4,640	2,350	—
1101 Eight (wb 136.0)*				
710	touring 7P	4,400	2,590	—
711	phtn 4P	4,359	2,570	—
712	formal sdn 5P	4,760	3,285	—
713	sdn 4d 5P	4,660	2,585	—
716	club sdn 5P	4,730	2,670	—
717	cpe 5P	4,580	2,640	—
718	cpe 2-4P	4,580	2,640	—
719	cpe rdstr 2-4P	4,430	2,580	—
721	spt phtn 4P	4,430	2,830	—
723	conv sdn 5P	4,680	3,090	—
727	conv victoria 5P	4,710	2,980	—
1102 Eight (wb 141.0)*				
714	sdn 7P	4,945	2,655	—
715	limo sdn 7P	5,000	2,790	—
1103 Super Eight (wb 135.0)**				
753	sdn 4d 5P	4,890	2,950	—
1104 Super Eight (wb 142.0)**				
750	touring 7P	4,720	3,180	—
751	phtn 4P	4,645	3,090	—
752	formal sdn 5P	5,010	3,800	—
756	club sdn 5P	4,985	3,255	—
757	cpe 5P	4,885	3,180	—
758	cpe 2-4P	4,800	2,980	—
759	cpe rdstr 2-4P	4,680	3,070	—
761	spt phtn 4P	4,740	3,350	—
763	conv sdn 5P	4,930	3,790	—
767	conv victoria 5P	4,875	3,640	—
773	sdn 4d 5P	4,910	3,200	—
1105 Super Eight (wb 147.0)**				
754	sdn 7P	5,245	3,290	—
755	sdn limo 7P	5,275	3,480	—
	Individual custom:			
280	LeBaron phtn 4P	4,755	7,065	—
858	LeBaron A/W cab 7P	5,205	5,450	—
859	LeBrn A/W twn car 7P	5,265	5,450	—
4068	Dtrich stnry cpe 2-4P	4,955	5,445	—
4070	Dietrich conv sdn 5P	5,055	5,800	—
4071	Dtrich runbt conv 2-4P	4,920	5,365	—
4072	Dietrich conv vic 4P	4,770	5,345	—
4182	Dietrich spt sdn 5P	5,380	6,295	—
1106 Twelve (wb 135.0)***				
275	LeBrn spdstr runbt 2P	5,400	7,746	—
1107 Twelve (wb 142.0)***				
730	touring 7P	5,415	3,980	—
731	phtn 4P	5,325	3,890	—
732	formal sdn 5P	5,630	4,660	—
733	sdn 4d 5P	5,530	3,960	—
736	club sdn 5P	5,660	4,060	—
737	cpe 5P	5,530	3,990	—
738	cpe 2-4P	5,585	3,820	—
739	cpe rdstr 2-4P	5,330	3,850	—
741	spt phtn 4P	5,400	4,190	—
743	conv sdn 5P	5,470	4,750	—
747	conv victoria 5P	5,440	4,590	—
1108 Twelve (wb 147.0)***				
734	sdn 7P	5,700	4,185	—
735	sdn limo 7P	5,750	4,385	—
	Individual custom:			
280	LeBaron spt phtn 4P	5,130	7,065	—
858	Lebaron A/W cab 7P	5,655	6,155	—

1108 Twelve		Wght	Price	Prod
859	LBrn A/W twn car 7P	5,655	6,155	—
4002	Dtrich A/W twn car 7P	5,715	5,695	—
4068	Dtrich stnry cpe 2-4P	5,405	6,185	—
4069	Dietrich spt phtn 4P	5,400	5,180	—
4070	Dietrich conv sdn 5P	5,505	6,555	—
4071	Dtrich conv runbt 2-4P	5,370	6,100	—
4072	Dietrich conv vic 4P	5,220	6,080	—
4182	Dietrich spt sdn 5P	5,130	7,060	—

* Total 1100/1101/1102 production: 5,120 **Total Super Eight production: 1,920

*** Total Twelve production: 960

1934 Engines	bore × stroke	bhp	availability
I-8, 320.0	3.19×5.00	120	S-Eight
I-8, 384.8	3.50×5.00	145	S-Super Eight
V-12, 445.5	3.44×4.00	160	S-Twelve

1935

120A One Twenty (wb 120) - 24,995 built

		Wght	Price	Prod
892	touring sdn 4d	3,550	1,095	—
893	sdn 4d	3,510	1,060	—
894	touring cpe 5P	3,455	1,025	—
895	spt cpe 2-4P	3,435	1,020	—
896	club sdn 5P	3,515	1,085	—
898	bus cpe 2P	3,400	980	—
899	conv cpe 2-4P	3,385	1,070	—
1200 Eight (wb 127.0)*				
803	sdn 4d 4,780	2,385	—	
1201 Eight (wb 134.0)*				
195	LeBaron A/W cab 7P	5,185	5,240	—
807	conv victoria 5P	4,835	3,100	—
811	phtn 5P	4,475	2,670	—
812	formal sdn 4d 5P	5,035	3,285	—
813	sdn 4d 5P	4,935	2,585	—
816	club sdn 5P	4,845	2,580	—
817	cpe 5P	4,700	2,560	—
818	cpe 2-4P	4,625	2,475	—
819	conv cpe 2-4P	4,555	2,580	—
1202 Eight (wb 139.0)*				
194	LBrn A/W twn car 7P	5,225	5,385	—
810	touring 7P	4,400	3,170	—
814	comm sdn 8P	4,985	2,630	—
815	limo 7P	5,125	2,890	—
815	comm limo 8P	5,150	2,765	—
863	conv sdn 5P	4,800	3,200	—
1203 Super Eight (wb 132.0)**				
843	sdn 4d	4,985	2,990	—
1204 Super Eight (wb 139.0)**				
195	LeBaron A/W cab 7P	5,300	5,670	—
841	spt phtn 5P	4,875	3,450	—
847	conv victoria 5P	5,000	3,760	—
851	phtn 5P	4,775	3,190	—
852	formal sdn 5P	5,150	3,800	—
856	club sdn 5P	5,100	3,170	—
857	cpe 5P	5,015	3,080	—
858	cpe 2-4P	4,920	2,880	—
859	conv cpe 2-4P	4,800	3,070	—
1205 Super Eight (wb 144.0)**				
194	LBrn A/W twn car 7P	5,525	5,815	—
850	touring 7P	4,729	3,690	—
854	sdn 7P	5,375	3,390	—
854	comm sdn 8P	5,320	3,265	—
855	limo 7P	5,400	3,580	—
855	comm limo 8P	5,380	3,455	—
883	conv sdn 5P	5,050	3,910	—

1206 Twelve (wb 132.0)***

The "06" series of short-wheelbase Twelve sedans was omitted by Packard for this and subsequent years; there is some conjecture on whether minor production occurred, but this has not been confirmed to date.

1207 Twelve (wb 139.0)***		Wght	Price	Prod
195	LeBaron A/W cab 7P	5,930	6,290	—
821	spt phtn 5P	5,550	4,290	—
827	conv victoria 5P	5,590	4,790	—
831	phtn 5P	5,470	3,990	—
832	formal sdn 7P	5,780	4,660	—
833	sdn 5P	5,700	3,960	—
836	club sdn 5P	5,800	4,060	—
837	cpe 5P	5,680	3,990	—

1207 Twelve		Wght	Price	Prod
838	cpe 2-4P	5,635	3,820	—
839	conv cpe 2-4P	5,480	3,850	—
1208 Twelve (wb 144.0)***				
194	LBrn A/W twn car 7P	5,950	6,535	—
830	touring 7P	5,415	4,490	—
834	sdn 7P	5,800	4,285	—
835	limo 7P	5,900	4,485	—
873	conv sdn 5P	5,620	4,950	—

*Total Eight production: 4,781 **Total Super Eight production: 1,392

***Total Twelve production: 721

1935 Engines	bore × stroke	bhp	availability
I-8, 257.2	3.25×3.88	110	S-120A
I-8, 320.0	3.19×5.00	130	S-1200, 1201, 1202
I-8, 384.8	3.50×5.00	150	S-1203, 1204, 1205
V-12, 473.0	3.44×4.25	175	S-1207, 1208

1936

120B One Twenty (wb 120) - 55,042 built

		Wght	Price	Prod
992	touring sdn 5P	3,560	1,115	—
993	sdn 4d 5P	3,505	1,075	—
994	touring cpe 5P	3,575	1,040	—
995	spt cpe 2-4P	3,455	1,030	—
996	club sdn 5P	3,495	1,090	—
997	conv sdn 5P	3,660	1,395	—
998	bus cpe 2P	3,380	990	—
999	conv cpe 2-4P	3,525	1,110	—
1400 Eight (wb 127.0)*				
903	sdn 4d 5P	4,815	2,385	—
1401 Eight (wb 134.0)*				
294	LeBaron A/W cab 7P	5,185	5,240	—
907	conv victoria 5P	4,810	3,200	—
911	phtn 4P	4,890	3,020	—
912	formal sdn 7P	5,030	3,285	—
913	sdn 4d 5P	4,978	2,585	—
916	club sdn 5P	4,815	2,580	—
917	cpe 5P	4,745	2,560	—
918	cpe 2-4P	4,735	2,470	—
919	cpe rdstr 2-4P	4,740	2,730	—
1402 Eight (wb 139.0)*				
295	LBrn A/W twn car 7P	5,225	5,385	—
910	touring 7P	5,060	3,270	—
914	sdn 7P	4,955	2,755	—
914	bus sdn 8P	4,985	2,630	—
915	limo 7P	5,045	2,890	—
915	bus limo 8P	5,150	2,765	—
963	conv sdn 5P	5,140	3,400	—
1403 Super Eight (wb 132.0)**				
943	sdn 4d	5,080	2,990	—
1404 Super Eight (wb 139.0)**				
294	LeBaron A/W cab 7P	5,300	5,670	—
941	spt phtn 5P	5,200	3,650	—
947	conv victoria 5P	5,122	3,860	—
951	phtn 5P	5,080	3,390	—
952	formal sdn 5P	5,245	3,800	—
956	club sdn 5P	5,178	3,170	—
957	cpe 5P	5,010	3,080	—
958	cpe 2-4P	4,933	2,880	—
959	cpe rdstr 2-4P	4,993	3,070	—
1405 Super Eight (wb 144.0)**				
295	LBrn A/W twn car 7P	5,525	5,815	—
950	touring 7P	5,200	3,690	—
954	sdn 7P	5,300	3,390	—
954	bus sdn 8P	5,320	3,265	—
955	limo 7P	5,380	3,580	—
955	bus limo 8P	5,380	3,455	—
983	conv sdn 5P	5,390	4,010	—
1407 Twelve (wb 139.0)***				
294	LeBaron A/W cab 7P	5,900	6,290	—
921	spt phtn 5P	5,785	4,490	—
927	conv victoria 5P	5,585	4,890	—
931	phtn 5P	5,480	4,190	—
932	formal sdn 5P	5,735	4,660	—
933	sdn 5P	5,695	3,960	—
936	clb sdn 5P	5,640	4,060	—
937	cpe 5P	5,495	3,990	—
938	cpe 2-4P	5,495	3,820	—
939	cpe rdstr 2-4P	5,495	3,850	—

1408 Twelve (wb 144.0)		Wght	Price	Prod
295	LBrn A/W ton car 7P	5,950	6,435	—
934	sdn 7P	5,790	4,285	—
935	limo 7P	5,890	4,483	—
930	touring 7P	5,460	4,490	—
973	conv sdn 5P	5,945	5,050	—

*Total Eight production: 3,973 **Total Super Eight production: 1,330

***Total Twelve production: 682

1936 Engines	bore × stroke	bhp	availability
I-8, 282.0	3.25×4.25	120	S-120B
I-8, 320.0	3.19×5.00	130	S-1400, 1401, 1402
I-8, 384.8	3.50×5.00	150	S-1403, 1404, 1405
V-12, 473.0	3.44×4.25	175	S-1407, 1408

1937

115C Six (wb 115.0) - 65,400 built

		Wght	Price	Prod
1060	wgn 4d 8P	3,380	1,295	—
1082	touring sdn 5P	3,310	910	—
1083	sdn 4d 5P	3,265	895	—
1084	touring cpe 5P	3,235	860	—
1085	spt cpe 2-4P	3,215	840	—
1086	club sdn 5P	3,275	900	—
1088	bus cpe 2P	3,140	795	—
1089	conv cpe 2-4P	3,285	910	—
120C/CD One Twenty (wb 120.0)*				
1070	wgn 4d 8P	3,590	1,485	—
1092	touring sdn 5P	3,520	1,060	—
1093	sdn 4d 5P	3,465	1,045	—
1094	touring cpe 5P	3,435	1,010	—
1095	spt cpe 2-4P	3,415	990	—
1096	club sdn 5P	3,455	1,050	—
1097	conv sdn 5P	3,630	1,355	—
1098	bus cpe 2P	3,340	945	—
1099	conv cpe 2-4P	3,485	1,060	—
1094CD	touring cpe 5P	3,465	1,220	—
1096CD	club sdn 5P	3,485	1,260	—
1098CD	touring sdn 4d	3,550	1,270	—
138CD One Twenty (wb 138.0)*				
1090CD	touring limo 7P	3,900	1,840	—
1091CD	touring sdn 7P	3,835	1,690	—
1500 Super Eight (wb 127.0)**				
1003	touring sdn 5P	4,530	2,335	—
1501 Super Eight (wb 134.0)**				
L394	LeBaron A/W cab 7P	4,965	4,850	—
1007	conv victoria 5P	4,650	3,150	—
1012	formal sdn 5P	4,795	3,235	—
1013	touring sdn 5P	4,670	2,535	—
1016	club sdn 5P	4,600	2,530	—
1017	cpe 5P	4,595	2,510	—
1018	cpe 2-4P	4,585	2,420	—
1019	conv cpe 2-4P	4,580	2,680	—
1502 Super Eight (wb 139.0)**				
L395	LBrn A/W twn car 7P	5,360	4,990	—
1014	touring sdn 7P	4,700	2,705	—
1014B	bus sdn 8P	4,755	2,580	—
1015	touring limo 7P	4,815	2,840	—
1015B	bus limo 8P	4,925	2,715	—
1063	conv sdn 5P	4,945	3,350	—
1506 Twelve (wb 132.0)***				
1023	touring sdn 5P	5,335	3,490	—
1507 Twelve (wb 139.0)***				
L394	LeBaron A/W cab 7P	5,740	5,700	—
1027	conv victoria 5P	5,345	4,490	—
1032	formal sdn 5P	5,550	4,260	—
1033	touring sdn 4d	5,525	3,560	—
1036	club sdn 5P	5,520	3,660	—
1037	cpe 5P	5,415	3,590	—
1038	cpe 2-4P	5,255	3,420	—
1039	conv cpe 2-4P	5,255	3,450	—
1508 Twelve (wb 144.0)***				
L395	LBrn A/W twn car 7P	5,790	5,900	—
1034	touring sdn 7P	5,600	3,885	—
1035	touring limo 7P	5,660	4,085	—
1073	conv sdn 5P	5,680	4,650	—

*Total One Twenty production: 50,100 **Total Super Eight production: 5,793

***Total Twelve production: 1,300

1937 Engines	bore×stroke	bhp	availability
I-6, 237.0	3.44×4.25	100	S-Six
I-8, 282.0	3.25×4.25	120	S-One Twenty
I-8, 320.0	3.19×5.00	135	S-Super Eight
V-12, 473.0	3.44×4.25	175	S-Twelve

1938

1600 Six (wb 122.0) - 30,050 built		Wght	Price	Prod
1182	touring sdn 4d	3,525	1,175	—
1184	touring sdn 2d	3,475	1,145	—
1185	club cpe 2-4P	3,425	1,120	—
1188	bus cpe 2P	3,450	1,075	—
1189	conv cpe 2-4P	3,500	1,235	—
1601 Eight (wb 127.0)*				
1192	touring sdn 4d	3,650	1,525	—
1194	touring sdn 2d	3,600	1,295	—
1195	club cpe 2-4P	3,550	1,270	—
1197	conv sdn 5P	3,775	1,650	—
1198	bus cpe 2P	3,570	1,225	—
1199	conv cpe 2-4P	3,625	1,365	—
1172	DeLuxe tour sdn 4d	3,685	1,540	—
1601 Eight (wb 139.0)*				
1665	Rollston A/W cab 7P	—	4,810	—
1668	Rollstn A/W brghm 4P	—	5,100	—
1669	Rllstn A/W twn car 7P	—	4,885	—
1602 Eight (wb 148.0)*				
1190	limo 7P	4,245	1,955	—
1191	touring sdn 7P	4,195	2,110	—
1603 Super Eight (wb 127.0)**				
1103	touring sdn 4d	4,530	2,790	—
1604 Super Eight (wb 134.0)**				
1107	conv victoria 5P	4,650	3,670	—
1112	formal sdn 5P	4,795	3,710	—
1113	touring sdn 4d	4,670	2,995	—
1116	club sdn 5P	4,600	2,990	—
1117	cpe 5P	4,595	2,965	—
1118	cpe 2-4P	4,585	2,925	—
1119	conv cpe 4P	4,580	3,210	—
1605 Super Eight (wb 139.0)**				
494	Rollston A/W cab 7P	4,945	5,790	—
495	Rllstn A/W twn car 7P	4,940	5,890	—
1114	bus sdn 7P	4,815	3,165	—
1115	bus limo 7P	4,815	3,305	—
1143	conv sdn 5P	4,945	3,970	—
3086	Brunn touring cab 7P	4,990	7,475	—
3087	Brunn A/W cab 7P	4,995	7,475	—
1607 Twelve (wb 134.0)***				
1127	conv victoria 5P	5,345	5,230	—
1132	formal sdn 5P	5,550	4,865	—
1133	touring sdn 4d	5,525	4,155	—
1136	club sdn 5P	5,520	4,255	—
1137	cpe 5P	5,415	4,185	—
1138	cpe 2-4P	5,255	4,135	—
1139	conv cpe 2-4P	5,255	4,370	—
1608 Twelve (wb 139.0)***				
494	Rollston A/W cab 7P	5,740	6,730	—
495	Rllstn A/W twn car 7P	5,735	6,880	—
1134	touring sdn 7P	5,600	4,485	—
1135	touring limo 7P	5,600	4,485	—
1153	conv sdn 5P	5,680	5,390	—
3086	Brunn touring cab 7P	5,725	8,510	—
3087	Brunn A/W cab 7P	5,730	8,510	—

*Total Eight production: 22,624 **Total Super Eight production: 2,478
***Total Twelve production: 566

1938 Engines	bore×stroke	bhp	availability
I-6, 245.0	3.50×4.25	100	S-Six
I-8, 282.0	3.25×4.25	120	S-Eight
I-8, 320.0	3.19×5.00	130	S-Super Eight
V-12, 473.0	3.44×4.25	175	S-Twelve

1939

1700 Six (wb 122.0) - 24,350 built		Wght	Price	Prod
1282	touring sdn 4d	3,400	1,095	—
1283	wgn 4d 7P	3,652	1,404	—
1284	touring sdn 2d	3,390	1,065	—
1285	club cpe 2-4P	3,365	1,045	—
1288	bus cpe 2P	3,295	1,000	—
1289	conv cpe 2-4P	3,385	1,092	—
1701 One Twenty (wb 127.0)*				
1292	touring sdn 4d	3,605	1,295	—
1293	wgn 4d 7P	3,850	1,636	—
1294	touring sdn 2d	3,595	1,265	—
1295	club cpe 2-4P	3,535	1,245	—
1297	conv sdn 5P	3,780	1,700	—
1298	bus cpe 2P	3,490	1,200	—
1299	conv cpe 2-4P	3,545	1,390	—
1702 One Twenty (wb 148.0)*				
1290	touring limo 7P	4,185	1,955	—
1291	touring sdn 7P	4,100	1,805	—
1703 Super Eight (wb 127.0)**				
1272	touring sdn 4d	3,930	1,732	—
1275	club cpe 2-4P	3,860	1,650	—
1277	conv sdn 5P	4,005	2,130	—
1279	conv cpe 2-4P	3,870	1,875	—
1705 Super Eight (wb 148.0)**				
1270	touring limo 7P	4,510	2,294	—
1271	touring sdn 7P	4,425	2,156	—
1707 Twelve (wb 134.0)				
594	Rollston A/W cab 7P	4,950	6,730	—
1227	conv victoria 5P	5,570	5,230	—
1232	formal sdn 5P	5,745	4,865	—
1233	touring sdn 4d	5,670	4,155	—
1236	club cpe 5P	5,590	4,255	—
1237	cpe 5P	5,425	4,185	—
1238	cpe 2-4P	5,400	4,185	—
1239	conv cpe 2-4P	5,540	4,375	—
1708 Twelve (wb 139.0)***				
595	Rllstn A/W twn car 7P	5,075	6,880	—
1234	touring sdn 7P	5,750	4,485	—
1235	touring limo 7P	5,825	4,690	—
1253	conv sdn 5P	5,890	5,395	—
4086	Brunn touring cab 5P	5,845	8,355	—
4087	Brunn A/W cab 6P	5,845	8,355	—

*Total One Twenty production: 17,647 **Total Super Eight production: 3,962
***Total Twelve production: 446

1939 Engines	bore×stroke	bhp	availability
I-6, 245.0	3.50×4.25	100	S-Six
I-8, 282.0	3.25×4.25	120	S-One Twenty
I-8, 320.0	3.19×5.00	130	S-Super Eight
V-12, 473.0	3.44×4.25	175	S-Twelve

1940

1800 One Ten (wb 122) - 62,300 built		Wght	Price	Prod
1382	sdn 4d	3,200	996	—
1383	wgn 4d, 8P	3,380	1,200	—
1384	sdn 2d	3,190	964	—
1385	club cpe	3,165	940	—
1388	bus cpe	3,120	867	—
1389	conv cpe	3,200	1,104	—
1801 One Twenty (wb 127.0) - 28,138 built				
700	conv vic by Darrin	3,826	3,819	—
1392	sdn 4d	3,520	1,166	—
1393	wgn 4d, 8P	3,590	1,404	—
1394	sdn 2d	3,510	1,135	—
1395	club cpe	3,450	1,111	—
1396	club sdn	3,520	1,239	—
1397	conv sdn	3,710	1,573	—
1398	bus cpe	3,340	1,038	—
1399	conv cpe	3,540	1,277	—
DE 1392	Deluxe sdn 4d	3,495	1,246	—
DE 1395	Deluxe club cpe	3,400	1,161	—
DE 1396	Deluxe club sdn	3,480	1,314	—
DE 1399	Deluxe conv cpe	3,470	1,318	—
1803 Super Eight One Sixty (wb 127.0) - 5,662 built (includes all One Sixtys)				
1372	sdn 4d	3,855	1,655	—
1375	club cpe	3,760	1,614	—
1376	club sdn	3,855	1,740	—
1377	conv sdn	4,000	2,075	—
1378	bus cpe	3,735	1,524	—
1379	conv cpe	3,825	1,797	—
1804 Super Eight One Sixty (wb 138.0)				
1362	sdn 4d	4,165	1,919	—
1805 Spr Eght One Sixty (wb 148.0)				
1370	limo 7P	4,500	2,179	—
1371	sdn 4d, 7P	4,425	2,051	—
1806 Custom Super Eight One Eighty (wb 127.0) -1,900 built (includes all One Eightys)				
700	conv vic by Darrin	4,121	4,593	—
1356	club sdn	3,900	2,243	—
1807 Custom Super Eight One Eighty (wb 138.0)				
694	A/W cab by Rollston	4,050	4,473	—
710	conv sdn by Darrin	4,050	6,332	—
1332	formal sdn	4,210	2,855	—
1342	sdn 4d	4,210	2,422	—
1808 Custom Super Eight One Eighty (wb 148.0)				
695	A/W twn car by Rllstn	4,175	4,599	—
1350	limo 7P	4,585	2,683	—
1351	sdn 4d, 7P	4,510	2,554	—

1940 Engines	bore × stroke	bhp	availability
I-6, 245.3	3.50 × 4.25	100	S-One Ten
I-8, 282.0	3.25 × 4.25	120	S-One Twenty
I-8, 356.0	3.50 × 4.63	160	S-Super/Cust Super Eights

1941

1900 One Ten (wb 122) - 34,700 built (est.)		Wght	Price	Prod
1482	sdn 4d	3,260	1,076	—
1483	wgn 4d, 8P	3,460	1,251	—
1484	sdn 2d	3,250	1,010	—
1485	club cpe	3,230	1,020	—
1488	bus cpe	3,190	927	—
1489	conv cpe	3,260	1,195	—
1463DE	Deluxe wgn 4d, 8P	3,470	1,236	—
1482DE	Deluxe sdn 4d	3,280	1,136	—
1484DE	Deluxe sdn 2d	3,270	1,070	—
1485DE	Deluxe club cpe	3,250	1,058	—
1489DE	Deluxe conv cpe	3,280	1,229	—
1901 One Twenty (wb 127.0) - 17,000 built (est.)				
1473	Deluxe wgn 4d, 8P	3,730	1,541	—
1492	sdn 4d	3,535	1,291	—
1493	wgn 4d, 8P	3,720	1,466	—
1494	sdn 2d	3,525	1,260	—
1495	club cpe	3,470	1,235	—
1497	conv sdn	3,725	1,753	—
1498	bus cpe	3,360	1,142	—
1499	conv cpe	3,570	1,407	—
1951 Clipper (wb 127.0)				
1401	sdn 4d	3,725	1,420	16,600
1903 Super Eight One Sixty (wb 127.0) - 3,525 built (includes all One Sixtys)				
1472	sdn 4d	3,995	1,795	—
1475	club cpe	3,900	1,754	—
1477	conv sdn	4,140	2,225	—
1478	bus cpe	3,875	1,639	—
1479	conv cpe	3,965	1,937	—
1477DE	Deluxe conv sdn	4,160	2,450	—
1479DE	Deluxe conv cpe	3,985	2,112	—
1904 Super Eight One Sixty (wb 138.0)				
1462	sdn 4d	4,305	2,054	—
1905 Super Eight One Sixty (wb 148.0)				
1470	limo 7P	4,570	2,334	—
1471	sdn 4d 7P	4,495	2,206	—
1906 Custom Super Eight One Eighty (wb 127.0) -930 built (includes all One Eightys)				
1429	conv vic by Darrin	4,040	4,595	—
1907 Custom Super Eight One Eighty (wb 138.0)				
794	A/W cab by Rollston	4,075	4,695	—
1422	spt sdn by Darrin	4,490	4,795	—
1432	form sdn	4,350	3,090	—
1442	sdn 4d	4,350	2,632	—
1452	Sprt Brghm by LBrn	4,450	3,545	—
1908 Custom Super Eight One Eighty (wb 148.0)				
795	A/W twn car by Rllstn	4,200	4,820	—
1420	limo 7P by LeBaron	4,850	5,595	—
1421	sdn 4d, 7P by LBrn	4,740	5,345	—
1450	limo 7P	4,650	2,913	—
1451	sdn 4d, 7P	4,590	2,769	—

1941 Engines	bore×stroke	bhp	availability
I-6, 245.3	3.50×4.25	100	S-One Ten
I-8, 282.0	3.25×4.25	120	S-One Twenty
I-8, 282.0	3.25×4.25	125	S-Clipper
I-8, 356.0	3.50×4.63	160	S-One Sixtys, One Eightys

1942

2000 Clipper 110 Special (wb 120.0) - 11,325 built (includes all 110s)		Wght	Price	Prod
1582	sdn 4d	3,435	1,232	—
1585	club sdn	3,415	1,199	—
1588	bus cpe	3,365	1,166	—
2010 Clipper 110 Custom (wb 120.0)				
1502	sdn 4d	3,460	1,299	—
1505	club sdn	3,440	1,266	—
2020 Clipper 110 (wb 122.0)				
1589	conv cpe	3,315	1,375	—
2001 Clipper 120 Special (wb 120.0) - 19,199 built (includes all 120s)				
1592	sdn 4d	3,560	1,275	—
1595	club sdn	3,540	1,241	—
1598	bus cpe	3,490	1,208	—
2011 Clipper 120 Custom (wb 120.0)				
1512	sdn 4d	3,585	1,341	—
1515	club sdn	3,565	1,308	—
2021 Clipper 120 (wb 127.0)				
1599	conv cpe	3,585	1,469	—
2003 Clipper One Sixty (wb 127.0) - 2,580 built (includes all One Sixtys)				
1572	sdn 4d	4,005	1,688	—
1575	club sdn	3,985	1,630	—
2023 Clipper One Sixty (wb 127.0)				
1579	conv cpe	3,905	1,786	—
2004 Clipper One Sixty (wb 138.0)				
1562	sdn 4d	4,090	1,893	—
2005 Clipper One Sixty (wb 148.0)				
1570	limo 7P	4,445	2,156	—
1571	sdn 4d, 7P	4,325	2,034	—
2055 Clipper One Sixty (wb 148.0)				
1590	bus limo 7P	4,435	2,010	—
1591	bus sdn 4d, 7P	4,315	1,888	—
2006 Clipper One Eighty (wb 127.0) - 672 built (includes all One Eightys)				
1522	sdn 4d 4,030	2,196	—	
1525	club sdn	4,010	2,099	—
1529	conv vic by Darrin	3,920	4,519	—
2007 Clipper One Eighty (wb 138.0)				
894	A/W cab by Rollston	4,075	4,792	—
1532	form sdn	4,390	3,011	—
1542	sdn 4d	4,280	2,440	—
2008 Clipper One Eighty (wb 148.0)				
895	A/W twn car by Rllstn	4,200	4,889	—
1520	limo 7P by LeBaron	4,850	5,690	—
1521	sdn 4d, 7P by LBrn	4,740	5,446	—
1550	limo 7P	4,540	2,645	—
1551	sdn 4d, 7P	4,525	2,523	—

1942 Engines	bore×stroke	bhp	availability
I-6, 245.3	3.50×4.25	105	S-Clipper 110
I-8, 282.0	3.25×4.25	125	S-Clipper 120
I-8, 356.0	3.50×4.63	165	S-Clipper One Sixty, One Eighty

1946

2100 Clipper Six (wb 120) - 15,982 built		Wght	Price	Prod
1682	sdn 4d	3,495	1,730	—
1685	club sdn	3,450	1,680	—
2101 Clipper Eight (wb 120.0)				
1692	sdn 4d	3,630	1,802	1,500
2111 Clipper Deluxe Eight (wb 120.0) - 5,714 built				
1612	sdn 4d	3,670	1,869	—
1615	club sdn	3,625	1,817	—
2103 Super Clipper (wb 127.0) - 4,924 built				
1672	sdn 4d	3,995	2,290	—
1675	club sdn	3,950	2,241	—
2106 Custom Super Clipper (wb 127.0) - 1,472 built				
1622	sdn 4d	4,060	3,047	—
1625	club sdn	4,000	2,913	—
2126 Custom Super Clipper (wb 148.0) - 1,291 built				
1650	limo 7P	4,900	4,496	—
1651	sdn 4d, 7P	4,870	4,332	—

1946 Engines	bore×stroke	bhp	availability
I-6, 245.3	3.50×4.25	105	S-Clipper Six
I-8, 282.0	3.25×4.25	125	S-Clipper Eight/ DeLuxe Eight
I-8, 356.0	3.50×4.63	165	S-Super/Cust Super Clipper

1947

2100 Clipper Six (wb 120) - 14,949 built		Wght	Price	Prod
2182	sdn 4d	3,520	1,937	—
2185	club sdn	3,475	1,912	—
2111 Clipper DeLuxe Eight (wb 120.0) - 23,855 built				
2112	sdn 4d	3,695	2,149	—
2115	club sdn	3,650	2,124	—
2103 Super Clipper (wb 127.0) - 4,802 built				
2172	sdn 4d	4,025	2,772	—
2175	club sdn	3,980	2,747	—
2106 Custom Super Clipper (wb 127.0) - 7,480 built (includes model 2126)				
2122	sdn 4d	4,090	3,449	—
2125	club sdn	3,384	2,125	—
2126 Cust Spr Clipper (wb 148.0)		**Wght**	**Price**	**Prod**
2150	limo 7P	4,920	4,668	—
2151	sdn 4d, 7P	4,890	4,504	—

1947 Engines	bore×stroke	bhp	availability
I-6, 245.3	3.50×4.25	105	S-Clipper Six
I-8, 282.0	3.25 ×4.25	125	S-Clipper Eight/ DeLuxe Eight
I-8, 356.0	3.50×4.63	165	S-Super/Cust Super Clipper

1948

2201 Eight (wb 120) - 12,782 built		Wght	Price	Prod
2292	sdn 4d	3,815	2,275	—
2293	Station Sdn wgn 4d	4,075	3,425	*
2295	club sdn	3,755	2,250	—
2211 DeLuxe Eight (wb 120.0) - 47,807 built				
2262	sdn 4d	3,840	2,543	—
2265	club sdn	3,770	2,517	—
2202 Super Eight (wb 120.0) - 12,921 built				
2272	sdn 4d	3,855	2,827	—
2275	club sdn	3,790	2,802	—
2222 Super Eight (wb 141.0) - 1,766 built				
2270	DeLuxe limo 7P	4,610	4,000	—
2271	Deluxe sdn 4d, 7P	4,590	3,850	—
2276	limo 7P	4,525	3,650	—
2277	sdn 4d, 7P	4,460	3,500	—
2232 Super Eight (wb 120.0)				
2279	conv cpe	4,025	3,250	7,763
2206 Custom Eight (wb 127.0) - 5,936 built				
2252	sdn 4d	4,175	3,750	—
2255	club sdn	4,110	3,700	—
2226 Custom Eight (wb 148.0) - 230 built				
2250	limo 7P	4,880	4,868	—
2251	sdn 4d, 7P	4,860	4,704	—
2313 Custom Eight (wb 148.0)				
—	chassis	—	—	1,941
2233 Custom Eight (wb 127.0)				
2259	conv cpe	4,380	4,295	1,105

1948 Engines	bore×stroke	bhp	availability
I-8, 288.0	3.50×3.75	130	S-Eight, DeLuxe Eight
I-8, 327.0	3.50×4.25	145	S-Super Eight
I-8, 356.0	3.50×4.63	160	S-Cust Eight

* See note following 1950.

1949 First Series

2201 Eight (wb 120) - 13,553* blt		Wght	Price	Prod
2292-9	sdn 4d	3,815	2,275	—
2293-9	Station Sdn wgn 4d	4,075	3,425	*
2295-9	club sdn	3,755	2,250	—
2211 DeLuxe Eight (wb 120.0) - 27,422 built				
2262-9	sdn 4d	3,840	2,543	—
2265-9	club sdn	3,770	2,517	—
2202 Super Eight (wb 120.0) - 5,879 built				
2272-9	sdn 4d	3,855	2,827	—
2275-9	club sdn	3,790	2,802	—
2222 Super Eight (wb 141.0) - 867 built				
2270-9	DeLuxe limo 7P	4,610	4,000	—
2271-9	DeLuxe sdn 4d, 7P	4,590	3,850	—
2276-9	limo 7P	4,525	3,650	—
2277-9	sdn 4d, 7P	4,460	3,500	—
2232 Super Eight (wb 120.0)				
2279-9	conv cpe	4,025	3,250	1,237
2206 Custom Eight (wb 127.0) - 2,990 built				
2252-9	sdn 4d	4,175	3,750	—
2255-9	club sdn	4,110	3,700	—
2226 Custom Eight (wb 148.0) - 50 built				
2250-9	limo 7P	4,880	4,868	—
2251-9	sdn 4d, 7P	4,860	4,704	—
2213 Custom Eight (wb 148.0)				
—	chassis	—	—	220
2233 Custom Eight (wb 127.0)				
2259-9	conv cpe	4,380	4,295	213

* See note following 1950.

1949 Second Series

2301 Eight (wb 120) - 53,168* blt		Wght	Price	Prod
2362	DeLuxe sdn 4d	3,840	2,383	—
2365	DeLuxe club sdn	3,770	2,358	—
2392	sdn 4d	3,815	2,249	—
2393	Station Sdn wgn 4d	4,075	3,449	*
2395	club sdn	3,740	2,224	—
2302 Super Eight (wb 127.0) - 8,759 built				
2372	DeLuxe sdn 4d	3,925	2,919	—
2375	DeLuxe club sdn	3,855	2,894	—
2382	sdn 4d	3,870	2,633	—
2385	club sdn	3,800	2,608	—
2322 Super Eight (wb 141.0) - 4 built				
2370	DeLuxe limo 7P	4,620	4,100	—
2371	DeLuxe sdn 4d, 7P	4,600	3,950	—
2332 Super Eight (wb 127.0)				
2332	DeLuxe conv cpe	4,260	3,350	685
2306 Custom Eight (wb 127.0)				
2352	sdn 4d	4,310	3,750	973
2313 Custom Eight (wb 148.0)				
—	chassis	—	—	160
2333 Custom Eight (wb 127.0)				
2359	conv cpe	4,530	4,295	68

1949 Engines	bore×stroke	bhp	availability
I-8, 288.0	3.50×3.75	135	S-Eight, DeLuxe Eight
I-8, 327.0	3.50×4.25	150	S-Super/Super DeLuxe Eight
I-8, 356.0	3.50×4.63	160	S-Cust Eight

* See note following 1950.

1950

2301 Eight (wb 120) - 36,471 blt		Wght	Price	Prod
2362-5	DeLuxe sdn 4d	3,840	2,383	—
2365-5	DeLuxe club sdn	3,770	2,358	—
2392-5	sdn 4d	3,815	2,249	—
2393-5	Station Sdn wgn 4d	4,075	3,449	*
2395-5	club sdn	3,740	2,224	—
2302 Super Eight (wb 127.0) - 4,528 built				
2372-5	DeLuxe sdn 4d	3,925	2,919	—
2375-5	club sdn	3,855	2,894	—
2382-5	sdn 4d	3,870	2,633	—
2385-5	club sdn	3,800	2,608	—
2332 Super Eight (wb 127.0)				
2379-5	conv cpe	4,110	3,350	600
2306 Custom Eight (wb 127.0)				
2352-5	sdn 4d	4,310	3,975	707
2313 Custom Eight (wb 148.0)				
—	chassis	—	—	244

2333 Cust Eight (wb 127.0)		Wght	Price	Prod
2359-5	conv cpe	4,530	4,520	77

*See 1950.

1950 Engines	bore×stroke	bhp	availability
I-8, 288.0	3.50×3.75	135	S-Eight, DeLuxe Eight
I-8, 327.0	3.50×4.25	150	S-Super/Super DeLuxe Eight
I-8, 356.0	3.50×4.63	160	S-Cust Eight

* Although Packard did not break down model-year production by body style, some calendar-year figures exist for the Station Sedan. These are: 126 in 1947, 3,266 in 1948, and 472 in 1949, for a total of 3,864. An estimated 75 percent were 1948 models.

1951

2401 200 (wb 122.0)		Wght	Price	Prod
2462	DeLuxe sdn 4d	3,660	2,616	47,052
2465	DeLuxe club sdn	3,605	2,563	
2492	sdn 4d	3,665	2,469	24,310
2495	club sdn	3,600	2,416	
2498	bus cpe	3,550	2,302	
2401 250 (wb 122.0) - 4,640 built				
2467	Mayfair htp cpe	3,820	3,234	—
2469	conv cpe	4,040	3,391	—
2402 300 (wb 127.0)				
2472	sdn 4d	3,875	3,034	15,309
2413 300 (wb 127.0)				
—	chassis	—	—	401
2406 Patrician 400 (wb 127.0)				
2452	sdn 4d	4,115	3,662	9,001

1951 Engines	bore×stroke	bhp	availability
I-8, 288.0	3.50×3.75	135	S-200
I-8, 327.0	3.50×4.25	150	S-250/300 man
I-8, 327.0	3.50×4.25	155	S-Patr 400, 250/300 auto

1952

2501 200 (wb 122.0) - 46,720 blt		Wght	Price	Prod
2562	DeLuxe sdn 4d	3,685	2,695	—
2565	DeLuxe club sdn	3,660	2,641	—
2592	sdn 4d	3,680	2,548	—
2595	club sdn	3,640	2,494	—
2531 250 (wb 122.0) - 5,201 built				
2577	Mayfair htp cpe	3,805	3,318	—
2579	conv cpe	4,000	3,476	—
2502 300 (wb 127.0)				
2572	sdn 4d	3,380	3,116	6,705
2513 300 (wb 127.0)				
—	chassis	—	—	320
2506 Patrician 400 (wb 127.0)				
2552	sdn 4d	4,100	3,797	3,975

1952 Engines	bore×stroke	bhp	availability
I-8, 288.0	3.50×3.75	135	S-200
I-8, 327.0	3.50×4.25	150	S-250/300 man
I-8, 327.0	3.50×4.25	155	S-Patr 400, 250/300 auto

1953

2601 Clipper (wb 122.0)		Wght	Price	Prod
2692	sdn 4d	3,730	2,598	23,126
2695	club sdn	3,700	2,544	6,370
2697	Sportster cpe	3,720	2,805	3,672
—	chassis	—	—	1
2611 Clipper DeLuxe (wb 122.0)				
2662	sdn 4d	3,760	2,745	26,037
2665	club sdn	3,720	2,691	4,678
2633 Clipper commercial (wb 122.0)				
—	chassis (Henney bodies)	—	—	380
2631 (wb 122.0)				
2677	Mayfair htp cpe	3,905	3,278	5,150
2678	Caribbean conv cpe	4,265	5,210	750
2679	conv cpe	4,125	3,486	1,518
2602 Cavalier (wb 127.0)				
2672	sdn 4d	3,975	3,244	10,799
2613 Packard commercial (wb 127.0)				
—	chassis (Henney bodies)	—	—	166
2606 Patrician (wb 127.0)				
2652	sdn 4d	4,190	3,740	7,456
2653	frml sdn by Derham	4,335	6,531	25*
2626 (wb 149.0)				
2650	Corporation limo 8P	4,720	7,100	50
2651	Executive sdn 4d, 8P	4,650	6,900	100
2602-2606-2631				
—	chassis	—	—	9

* Constructed from finished Patricians.

1953 Engines	bore×stroke	bhp	availability
I-8, 288.0	3.50×3.75	150	S-2601
I-8, 327.0	3.50×4.25	160	S-2611
I-8, 327.0	3.50×4.25	180	S-2602, 2631 (5 mn bearing)
I-8, 327.0	3.50×4.25	180	S-2606, 2626 (9 mn bearing)

1954

5400 Clipper Spec (wb 122.0)		Wght	Price	Prod
5482	sdn 4d	3,650	2,594	970
5485	club sdn	3,585	2,544	912
5401 Clipper DeLuxe (wb 122.0)				
5492	sdn 4d	3,660	2,695	7,610
5495	club sdn	3,650	2,645	1,470
5497	Sportster cpe	3,595	2,830	1,336
5411 Clipper Super (wb 122.0)				
5462	sdn 4d	3,695	2,815	6,270
5465	club sdn	3,610	2,765	887
5467	Panama htp cpe	3,765	3,125	3,618
5433 Clipper commercial (wb 122.0)				
—	chassis (Henney bodies)	—	—	120
5402 Cavalier (wb 127.0)				
5472	sdn 4d	3,955	3,344	2,580
5413 Packard commercial (wb 127.0)				
—	chassis (Henney bodies)	—	—	205
5431 (wb 122.0)				
5477	Pacific htp cpe	4,065	3,827	1,189
5478	Caribbean conv cpe	4,660	6,100	400
5479	convertible cpe	4,290	3,935	863
—	chassis	—	—	1
5406 Patrician (wb 127.0)				
5452	sdn 4d	4,190	3,890	2,760
5426 (wb 149.0)				
5450	Corporation limo 8P	4,720	5,960	35
5451	Executive sdn 4d, 8P	4,650	5,610	65

1954 Engines	bore×stroke	bhp	availability
I-8, 288.0	3.50×3.75	150	S-5400
I-8, 327.0	3.50×4.25	165	S-5401, 5411
I-8, 327.0	3.50×4.25	185	S-5402
I-8, 359.0	3.56×4.50	212	S-5406, 5426, 5431 (9 main bearing)

1955

5540 Clipper (wb 122.0)		Wght	Price	Prod
5522	DeLuxe sdn 4d	3,680	2,586	8,309
5542	Super sdn 4d	3,670	2,686	7,979
5547	Supr Panama htp cpe	3,700	2,776	7,016
5560 Clipper Custom (wb 122.0)				
5562	sdn 4d	3,885	2,926	8,708
5567	Constellation htp cpe	3,865	3,076	6,672
5580 (wb 127.0)				
5582	Patrician sdn 4d	4,275	3,890	9,127
5587	Four Hundred htp cpe	4,250	3,930	7,206
5588	Caribbean conv cpe	4,755	5,932	500

1955 Engines	bore×stroke	bhp	availability
V-8, 320.0	3.81×3.50	225	S-Clipper DeLuxe/Super
V-8, 352.0	4.00×3.50	245	S-Clipper Cust
V-8, 352.0	4.00×3.50	260	S-Packard exc Caribbean
V-8, 352.0	4.00×3.50	275	S-Caribbean

1956

Clipper (wb 122.0)*		Wght	Price	Prod
	DeLuxe sdn 4d	3,745	2,733	5,715
	Super sdn 4d	3,800	2,866	5,173
	Supr Panama htp cpe	3,825	2,916	3,999
	Custom sdn 4d	3,860	3,069	2,129
	Cust Constell htp cpe	3,860	3,164	1,466
5670 Executive (wb 122.0)				
5672	sdn 4d	4,185	3,465	1,784
5677	htp cpe	4,185	3,560	1,031
5680 (wb 127.0)				
5682	Patrician sdn 4d	4,045	4,160	3,775
5687	Four Hundred htp cpe	4,080	4,190	3,224
5688 Caribbean (wb 127.0)				
5697	htp cpe	4,590	5,495	263
5699	conv cpe	4,960	5,995	276

1956 Engines	bore×stroke	bhp	availability
V-8, 352.0	4.00×3.50	240	S-Clipper
V-8, 352.0	4.00×3.50	275	S-Exec, Clippr Custom
V-8, 374.0	4.13×3.50	290	S-Patr, Four Hundred
V-8, 374.0	4.13×3.50	310	S-Caribbean

*Clipper was marketed as a separate make for 1956.

1957

57L (wb 120.5; wgn-116.5)		Wght	Price	Prod
Y8	Town Sedan 4d	3,570	3,212	3,940
P8	Country Sdn wgn 4d	3,650	3,384	869

1957 Engine	bore×stroke	bhp	availability
V-8, 289.0	3.56×3.63	275	S-all (sprchrgd)

1958

58L (wb 120.5; wgn/htp-116.5)		Wght	Price	Prod
J8	sdn 4d	3,505	3,212	1,200
Y8	htp cpe	3,480	3,262	675
K9	Hawk htp cpe	3,470	3,995	588
P8	wgn 4d	3,555	3,384	159

1958 Engines	bore×stroke	bhp	availability
V-8, 289.0	3.56×3.63	275	S-Hawk (supercharged)
V-8, 289.0	3.56×3.63	210	S-Others

Note: Final (1957-58) Packards were based on Studebaker models, following the 1954 merger of the two companies.

Panoz

A true "family affair," Panoz Auto Development Company was founded in late 1988 by sports-car and racing enthusiast Daniel Panoz with backing from his billionaire father Donald. The elder Panoz (pronounced "PAY-nose") made a vast fortune from two pharmaceutical companies based in Ireland, where Dan was born in 1962. One of those companies developed the enormously lucrative transdermal patch familiar to many ex-cigarette smokers.

After training as a designer and engineer for the aircraft and aerospace industries, 26-year-old Dan Panoz applied for a job with Frank Costin's Ireland-based Thompson Motor Company, only to find it was going out of business. But Thompson had developed an innovative chassis that Dan saw as a way to realize his dream of building a high-performance low-production sports car in the mold of Caroll Shelby's hallowed Cobra. To keep it affordable and practical, he decided to use off-the-shelf Ford components that could be easily serviced most anywhere.

While setting up a small factory near the family's U.S. estate outside Atlanta, Georgia, he worked with engineer John M. Leverett to develop a two-seater based on the Thompson chassis, though the eventual Panoz Roadster was entirely new. The car included classic cycle-fender styling on a steel frame with a pushrod 5.0-liter Mustang V-8, five-speed manual transmission, solid rear axle, 16-inch wheels, and a 98.5-inch wheelbase. Sixty of these were built in 1990-96, and all were sold at a suggested price of $43,495, including canvas top and side curtains.

In late 1996, Dan invited *Car and Driver* to test an improved Roadster dubbed A.I.V.—"Aluminum Intensive Vehicle." The term referred to a stout new "twin tier" spaceframe chassis made of extruded aluminum. There were many other changes, including a six-inch longer wheelbase, independent rear suspension (with unequal-length A-arms and coil-over shocks as in front), 18-inch wheels, fatter tires, and a big hood air scoop for clearing a taller engine, the 4.6-liter twincam V-8 from the latest Mustang SVT Cobra. *Car and Driver* clocked 0-60 mph in a swift 4.8 seconds and a standing quarter-mile of 13.6 seconds at 101 mph. "It's like driving a Lotus 7 but with fewer rattles, twice the room, and twice the thrust," enthused tester John Phillips.

Despite its elemental nature, the A.I.V. was beautifully crafted. Each took 350 man-hours to build, a big reason why the price eventually reached $63,000. Even so, it came with a three-year/36,000-mile warranty, generous by "exoticar" standards. The factory would even send out a technician to work with a local body shop on a car unlucky enough to be crunched. Such personal customer service remains a PAD specialty.

In 1996, Don Panoz and his son formed Panoz Motor Sports and tapped famed constructor Adrian Reynard to develop two prototype-class coupes for the 1997 Le Mans 24 Hours. Neither car finished, but a prototype Panoz GTR-1 did complete the 1998 event, placing seventh overall. A similar car won the team prize in '98's U.S. Road Racing Championship. Meanwhile, Don purchased Road Atlanta, set up the Panoz Racing School for drivers, and helped instigate two new racing series, the Petit Le Mans and the American Le Mans Series (ALMS). An open-top Panoz LMP 1 Roadster S won both the Team and Manufacturers titles in the '99 ALMS, beating entries from BMW and Audi.

These racers were a thrilling preview of a new roadgoing sports car. Named Esperante—meaning "hope" or "spirit"—it was publicly unveiled at the April 2000 New York Auto Show, but didn't enter production until that August, delaying deliveries until 2001. A luxurious two-seat convertible, Esperante was sized close to the Roadster and used a similar suspension, but featured an all-new spaceframe conceived by Leverett and fellow engineer William McClendon. The design comprised five extruded-aluminum modules that bolted and bonded together instead of being welded or riveted. Panoz claimed extraordinary strength for this chassis while hinting that its modular nature would make additional models easy to realize.

The base price was $79,950, including 24-hour roadside assistance and a 3/36 warranty. Unlike the Roadsters, Esperante was fully equipped, boasting dual dashboard airbags, antilock brakes (again big discs all-around), electronic traction control, power steering, power driver seat, power windows/locks/mirrors, cruise control, and a "semi-rigid" manual top with a folding-fabric rear section and a hard liftoff panel above the seats. Under the hood was the latest Mustang Cobra V-8 with 320 bhp, but hand-assembled by SVT especially for Panoz. A five-speed manual was again the only transmission.

Initial reviews were positive. *Road & Track* termed Esperante "the gentleman's Le Mans racer." Though no magazine was able to do a full road test right away, factory performance numbers seemed entirely credible: 0-60 mph in 5.1 seconds, 0-100 in 12.6, the standing quarter-mile in 13.7 seconds at 103.5 mph. But Dan later admitted to launching the car before it was ready. "I realize it was good to get press early... but by God, they hold your feet to the fire," he told journalist Pete Lyons for an August 2004 *AutoWeek* update. "There was very good response to the car, and it was a very good time in the market... [But because] we're small, people are a little skeptical."

Despite a major plant expansion, Esperante production was slow to get rolling, commencing with a mere 65 cars built in calendar 2001. But the right way was still the only way, and Dan would carefully evolve the Esperante to ever-higher standards of workmanship, technical sophistication, and performance. Volume soon moved higher, too, reaching 100 units in 2002.

Somehow, Dan and his team found time to cook up a "spec

1999 A.I.V. Roadster

2006 Esperante convertible coupe

racer" Esperante coupe, the GTS, as an affordable turnkey competitor for Sports Car Club of America and National Auto Sport Association events, not to mention the recently established Panoz Racing Series. Features included a specific body composed of 15 "thermoformed" alloy panels, plus a 430-bhp Ford Motorsports 5.8-liter racing V-8, an eight-point integrated roll cage, high-speed aerodynamic enhancements, and a race-ready weight of just 2700 pounds. Cars like this competed with distinction all over the land and won Panoz the 2002 B.F. Goodrich Trans-Am Manufacturers Championship. Still available through the small Panoz dealer network (some 50 outlets in major metro areas), the GTS has seen between 50 and 60 copies as of early 2006. The figure is some 200 for another racy early days variation. This is the GTR-A ("Road Atlanta"), a "trainer" for students at the family racing school. It was only to be expected from a company with a Ferrari-like devotion to raceworthy street cars engineered with track-tested technology.

That ethic produced a new Esperante announced in early 2003: the limited-edition, high-performance GTLM—"LM" for LeMans. By this time, the "classic" Esperante was also available as a "carbon-roof" coupe—basically the convertible with its folding roof and mechanism exchanged for a lightweight bonded-and-fastened carbon-fiber canopy. The GTLM also offered this choice, but arrived with its own long-nose/long-tail styling shaped to enhance high-speed stability. That was in order, because the engine was a supercharged 4.6-liter iron-block V-8, basically the latest twincam, 48-valve SVT Mustang Cobra unit tuned for an advertised 420 bhp (versus 390), though the dynamometer showed quite a bit more. There was only one transmission this time, the stout Tremec T56 six-speed manual.

Taking advantage of Esperante's inherent design "modularity," the GTLM introduced an improved rear-suspension assembly. This comprised a new subframe developed with Panoz partner Multimatic, Inc., and featuring lighter, tubular-steel lower control arms bolted to aluminum uprights; new "motorsport-oriented" suspension geometry; and damping by double-isolated coil-over spring/shock units, similar to those up front. Panoz claimed this setup cut unsprung weight for better handling and also reduced noise, vibration, and harshness, this despite an upgrade from 17- to 18-inch alloy wheels (on P255/45ZR tires).

Weighing less than 3400 pounds, the GTLM performed impressively: 4.2 seconds 0-60 mph, 12.8 seconds at 109.4 mph in the standing quarter-mile, no less than 180 mph all out, and 0.98g on the skidpad (versus 0.92). All this plus EPA-rated fuel economy of 17 mpg city/25 highway and the same plush furnishings as the "unblown" version. The LM was also treated to more heavily bolstered seats and purposeful aluminum-billet cockpit trim. Cars like this don't come cheaply. The price tag: some $121,000, reasonable for such an exclusive high-speed *gran tourismo*.

Panoz unveiled the Esperante GT in early 2004. This was basically the GTLM convertible or coupe with the base-model powerteams and an in-between initial price of just over $96,000 to start. Performance was in between too, the factory claiming 4.9 seconds 0-60, 13.4 at 107.3 mph in the quarter-mile, 155 mph tops, and 0.96g lateral acceleration.

Production, meantime, had been inching upward, reaching 110 retail units in calendar 2003, then 135 each in '04 and '05. That might seem low, even for a "exotic" marque, but every Esperante is hand-built by a dedicated workforce of about three dozen employees.

The main news for 2005 was extending the GT/GTLM rear suspension to the standard Esperante, though Panoz also expanded color, trim, and sound-system choices. Also added that year were Recaro's new "Style Top Line" seats—optional for base models and standard otherwise. Prices crept up, partly due to rising materials costs but also because of constant improvements, such as a revised rear-end structure making extensive use of carbon composites.

Meantime, the redesigned 2005 Ford Mustang allowed Dan to redesign his car's firewall/bulkhead/A-pillar structure, again relying on carbon composites to make it lighter yet stronger in concert with a new, integral "backbone" transmission tunnel. "I'm using more expensive material," he told Pete Lyons, "but I'm losing a ton of labor in processes and assemblage, and I'm handing the buyer a better product." Dan also had to contemplate an eventual change of engines, as the SVT V-8s were out of production by 2005, though he had stockpiled enough to get him through for a while. Meantime, he managed to roll out a racing GTLM, which scored its first major win in early 2006 with a class victory in the Mobil-1 Twelve Hours of Sebring.

Last but not least, Panoz has already started thinking about his next car. As Lyons reported in 2004, it's to be called Abruzzi, after the region in Italy that was home to Dan's grandfather. Dan will say nothing more about it and has announced no introduction date.

The Panoz saga is still unfolding, but it bears the hallmarks of a long-running story filled with more high adventure on the track and more high performance for the street.

Specifications

1990-96

Roadster (wb 98.5)	Wght	Price	Prod
conv 2d	2,316	43,495	60

1990-96 Eng.	bore×stroke	bhp	availability
V-8, 302.0	4.00×3.00	205	S-all

1997-2000

A.I.V. Rdstr (wb 104.5)	Wght	Price	Prod
conv 2d	2,698	57,980-62,500	250

1997-2000 Eng.	bore×stroke	bhp	availability
V-8, 281.0	3.55×3.54	305	S-all

2001

Esperante (wb. 106.0)	Wght	Price	Prod*
conv 2d	3,125	79,950	65

2001 Engine	bore×stroke	bhp	availability
V-8, 281.0	3.55×3.54	320	S-all

* Calendar year production.

2002

Esperante (wb. 106.0)	Wght	Price	Prod*
conv 2d	3,125	79,950	100

2002 Engine	bore×stroke	bhp	availability
V-8, 281.0	3.55×3.54	320	S-all

* Calendar year production.

2003 - 110 built (Calendar year prod.)

Esperante (wb. 106.0)	Wght	Price	Prod
conv 2d	3,125	89,000	—
cpe 2d	3,125	94,900	—
GTLM conv 2d	3,384	121,000	—
GTLM cpe 2d	3,384	—	—

2003 Engines	bore×stroke	bhp	availability
V-8, 281.0	3.55×3.54	320	S-Esperante
V-8S, 281.0	3.55×3.54	420	S-GTLM

2004 - 135 built (Calendar year prod.)

Esperante (wb. 106.0)	Wght	Price	Prod
conv 2d	3,125	—	—
cpe 2d	3,125	—	—
GT conv 2d	3,197	96,271	—
GT cpe 2d	3,197	—	—
GTLM conv 2d	3,384	—	—
GTLM cpe 2d	3,384	—	—

2004 Engines	bore×stroke	bhp	availability
V-8, 281.0	3.55×3.54	320	S-exc GTLM
V-8S, 281.0	3.55×3.54	420	S-GTLM

2005 - 135 built (Calendar year prod.)

Esperante (wb. 106.0)	Wght	Price	Prod
conv 2d	3,125	92,256	—
cpe 2d	3,125	98,229	—
GT conv 2d	3,197	97,360	—
GT cpe 2d	3,197	103,040	—
GTLM conv 2d	3,384	121,326	—
GTLM cpe 2d	3,384	128,319	—

2005 Engines	bore×stroke	bhp	availability
V-8, 281.0	3.55×3.54	305	S-exc GTLM
V-8S, 281.0	3.55×3.54	420	S-GTLM

2006

Esperante (wb. 106.0)	Wght	Price	Prod*
conv 2d	3,197	92,256	—
cpe 2d	3,197	98,229	—
GT conv 2d	3,197	97,360	—
GT cpe 2d	3,197	103,040	—
GTLM conv 2d	3,384	121,326	—
GTLM cpe 2d	3,384	128,319	—

2006 Engines	bore×stroke	bhp	availability
V-8, 281.0	3.55×3.54	305	S-exc GTLM
V-8S, 281.0	3.55×3.54	420	S-GTLM

* Prod. figures not available at time of publication.

Pierce-Arrow

Of all the great American classics, none is more famous for meticulous craftsmanship or refined luxury than the noble Pierce-Arrow. Along with Packard and Peerless, it was one of the fabled "three Ps" of U.S. automotive royalty.

Pierce-Arrow Motor Car Company started out in 1901 as an outgrowth of the George N. Pierce Company of Buffalo, New York, a bicycle manufacturer and, earlier, a birdcage maker. By 1918, it reached the pinnacle of preeminence with cars like the Model 66A. This mounted a giant 147.5-inch wheelbase, carried a huge 824.7-cubic-inch T-head six, and sold for upward of $8000 at a time when a Model T Ford cost a paltry $525; even the costliest 1918 Packard, the Twin Six Imperial limousine, seemed modest at $5850. But staunch conservatism led to stagnation, and by the mid-'20s, Pierce-Arrows were technically passé. The firm was soon awash in red ink, its cars hopelessly outdated if still ardently admired.

That Pierce survived to build any cars in the '30s was owed to Albert R. Erskine, the accountant-turned-president of Studebaker who wanted a prestige nameplate for the automotive empire he hoped to erect in South Bend, Indiana. Thus, after months of negotiating, Studebaker acquired Pierce in 1928 through a stock transfer. Pierce remained ostensibly independent with its own general manager, Arthur J. Chanter, though Erskine named himself president. More importantly, Buffalo and not South Bend would retain responsibility for developing new Pierce-Arrows.

Pierce sold its traditional big sixes through 1928. Its first Eight of 1929 did much to restore the make's flagging reputation. Against the Sixes it was better looking, better handling, faster, lower slung—and, remarkably enough, lower priced. As a result, Pierce enjoyed its best year ever: some 8000 built for the model year.

Eights comprised the entire 1930 lineup, which was quite broad for such a low-volume producer. A vast array of body types covered three series, four wheelbases—132, 134, 139, and a regal 144 inches—and three nine-main-bearing inline engines: a 115-horsepower 340 cid, a 125-bhp 366, and a 132-bhp 385. Prices were stiff, ranging from $2700 for the short-chassis Model C club brougham to over $5000 for the long Model A seven-passenger salon town car.

Still, Pierce sales remained healthy through spring despite the stock market crash. Though demand began flagging in the second quarter, there was no immediate concern, for 1930 would be the firm's second-best year with 7670 built. Once again, Pierce viewed a worsening market with a combination of arrogance and naïveté.

The firm forged ahead with an even broader line for 1931. Engines stood pat, but wheelbases shifted: 134/137 inches for the least-expensive Model 43s, 142 for the midrange 42s, and 147 for the top-line Model 41s. The last now included five semi-custom "catalog" styles by LeBaron; and Derham, Dietrich, and Brunn contributed special bodies on a few individual chassis. But production withered to just 3775, a worrisome 53 percent below the high-water mark of just two years before.

Determined to improve sales and prove its mettle, Pierce cut back on Eights for 1932 but cut loose with two new V-12s. Flagship of the fleet was the Model 52, offering five body types on 142- and 147-inch wheelbases at prices in the $4295-$4800 range. All carried a new 150-bhp 429-cid V-12. Designed by chief engineer Karl M. Wise, this was a super-smooth, super-quiet engine with an 80-degree cylinder-bank angle, seven main bearings, and dual downdraft carburetors. A smaller-bore 398 version with 140 bhp powered the Model 53, which listed more choices on 137- and 142-inch wheelbases for some $500 less than comparable 52s. Anchoring the line was the Model 54, essentially the 53 with an improved 366 straight-eight. Common to all '32 Pierce-Arrows were ultrasteady eight-point engine mounting, stronger frames, and "fingertip" adjustable shock absorbers. Yet despite all these worthy developments, production skidded to a disheartening 2100 units and Pierce posted a $3 million loss.

Save skirted fenders, the 1933s showed slight external change. Series rose to four: straight-eight Model 836 and V-12 Models 1236, 1242, and 1247. The smaller twelve was axed for want of performance, the eight gained 10 bhp for 135 total, and the 429 V-12 went to 160 bhp for the 1236 series. The top-line 1242/1247 carried a bored-out 452 V-12 with higher-compression heads giving a majestic 175 bhp. All engines featured hydraulic valve tappets for quiet operation and less maintenance—an industry first.

1931 Model 42 convertible coupe

1932 Model 54 coupe

1933 Silver Arrow four-door sedan

Test driver Ab Jenkins took to the Bonneville Salt Flats in September 1932 with a stripped 452 V-12 roadster prototype that had already done 33,000 miles. It promptly ran 2710 miles in 24 hours at an average speed of 112.91 mph. Jenkins commented: "The car was stable at all speeds, more like a racing chassis." The car was stable enough that Jenkins could write notes to spectators and toss them out at speeds over 110. No mechanical problems were experienced during the run. Fenders, windshield, and other road equipment reinstalled for the 2000 mile drive back to Buffalo—a convincing demonstration of Pierce-Arrow stamina. Jenkins returned to Utah in 1933 with a modified 207-bhp car that set 79 world speed records over 25½ hours, running as high as 128 mph. The road and weather conditions were more-difficult than the first trip, but neither car nor driver seemed to mind. Ab managed to shave during the final laps.

But speed records, multicylinder engines, and high-priced luxury were not enough to survive "hard times," as Cadillac, Marmon, Packard, and Stutz were learning. Pierce had grossly underestimated both the depth and breadth of the Depression, just like its Studebaker owner. Extensive advertising didn't help. By 1933, both firms were dangerously overextended, yet Studebaker continued pumping money into Pierce-Arrow. The two companies soon agreed to standardize several manufacturing processes for their vastly dissimilar cars, but this didn't save much money. Still, Pierce was able to reduce some operating costs in light of its fast-dwindling sales.

Late 1932 brought a new sales manager in Roy Faulkner, the dynamic former president of Auburn, which lent credence to rumors of an impending Pierce/Auburn merger. One of his first acts was the revolutionary Silver Arrow that was displayed at the 1933 Chicago World Fair. Designed by Phil Wright, it was the product of numerous wind-tunnel tests yet a striking aesthetic success. Said company literature: "It gives you in 1933 the car of 1940."

Actually, the Silver Arrow wasn't a literal forecast of future Pierce styling, but it was truly futuristic. A four-door sedan on the 139-inch chassis of the model 1236, it bore a handsomely Vee'd radiator flanked by Pierce's trademark faired-in headlamps now fully integrated with flush-sided fenders. Running boards were absent, and pronounced pontoon rear fenders set off a radically tapered "beetle back" with a narrow Vee'd slit for a rear window. Pierce claimed the Silver Arrow capable of 115 mph, but with over 5700 pounds of heft, even the 175-bhp V12 would be hard pressed to get much over 100. At an announced $10,000 (Faulker evidently planned limited regular sales) this dream car would remain just that for most, and only five were built.

Faulkner, the Silver Arrow, and Jenkin's speed runs briefly lifted Pierce fortunes in early 1933. Twelve-cylinder sales were up by 200 percent in January and by 130 percent in February; even through October they ran 55 percent ahead of the previous year's pace. But this recovery was dashed by strikes at tool-and-die makers, and Pierce lost 300-400 orders late in the year. As a result, production rose only slightly to 2295. Worse, Studebaker went bankrupt in the spring of 1933, leading Erskine to commit suicide that July. Studebaker's receivers ordered Pierce to be sold, so in August the firm passed to a group of Buffalo-area businessmen and bankers who paid $1 million for a chance to turn things around. Faulkner returned to Indiana.

With this, Pierce-Arrow was independent again and, ironically, healthier than Studebaker. With debts canceled, the new owners hoped to break even at 3000 annual sales and to make $1 million at 4000. To achieve that they installed Chanter as president, who began planning for higher volume.

Somehow, Pierce managed a total restyle for 1934, adopting a more-streamlined look that would continue for '35. Offerings were trimmed, but not drastically. The standard 1934 Eight offered four models with a 136-inch wheelbase and 135-bhp 366 engine in the $2500-$2700 range. A new long-stroke 385 eight with 140 bhp powered a more-extensive DeLuxe Eight line on 139- and 144-inch chassis shared with Salon Twelves. Both Salons and that year's 147-inch Custom Twelves carried an unchanged 462 engine. The DeLuxe Eight covered a $2800-$5000 price range. Twelves sold for $3200-$4500 with standard bodywork; six long-wheelbase Brunn "town" models listed for as high as $7000. A notable newcomer was a 144-inch-wheelbase two-door fastback in the image of the Silver Arrow, available as a DeLuxe Eight or Salon Twelve. Other closed bodies sported draft-free ventwing front-door windows, adjustable rear seats, and more head room.

Yet for all this, sales refused to improve, and Pierce kept bleeding cash: $861,000 for the first half of 1934, another $176,000 in July alone. The very next month, Pierce filed for bankruptcy after futile merger talks with Auburn and Reo. Though Chanter managed to raise $1 million from the Buffalo community and New York banks, Pierce had to slash its workforce some 70 percent. With the new capital, a leaner, reorganized company called Pierce-Arrow Motor Corporation began operations in May 1935.

Despite a threadbare budget, Pierce managed an attractive redesign for 1936. Advertised as "The World's Safest Car," it boasted over 30 significant improvements: more fashionably rounded lines with built-in trunks on sedans; standard vacuum brake booster; added cruciform frame member; engines and radiators moved farther forward; and a steering box mounted ahead of the front axle with a trailing drag link. Pierces had always been surprisingly easy to drive, but improved steering, brakes, suspension, and weight distribution gave the 1936s outstanding roadability despite the near three-ton bulk of some models. The previous three wheelbases returned for a reduced line of Eights and Twelves downpriced to $3100-$5600. The 366 eight was dropped, but new high-compression aluminum cylinder heads added ten horsepower to the other two engines.

Registrations climbed 25 percent in the first four months of 1936, suggesting Pierce had finally turned the corner, but production came to just 770. Pierce bravely carried on with little-changed 1937 models, but built only 191 before suspending production. Though new financing was simply unavailable now, the company announced 1938 models in October '37, but built only 40. Their only visual changes were a plastic-rim "banjo" steering wheel, new license-plate lamp, and relocated emergency brake handle.

The success of medium-priced cars at Packard and Lincoln prompted a final reorganization attempt, Pierce announcing a $10.7-million stock issue in August 1937 to produce 25,000 medium-priced cars, 1200 luxury models, and 4800 trailers. It also planned to tap Postmaster General James A. Farley, then about to leave the Roosevelt Administration, as new general manager. But none of this came to pass. Farley had received similar offers from Studebaker and Willys that he also rejected because they meant using his Washington connections, presumably to obtain contract work or federal loans.

Thus, Pierce again filed for bankruptcy in December 1937 after losing nearly $250,000 in the 17 months that followed July 1936. The firm was declared insolvent the following April; a month later, it was summarily liquidated. It was a sad end for a once-great American marque. However, the V-12 engine design was bought by Seagrave and lived on in fire engines until 1970.

1933 Model 1247 V-12 LeBaron convertible sedan

1934 Silver Arrow fastback coupe

1933 Model 1236 V-12 club Brougham

1936 Model 1601 Eight four-door sedan

Specifications

1930

Model A (wb 144.0) - 1,150 blt	Wght	Price	Prod
touring 7P	4,510	3,975	—
conv cpe 2P	4,540	3,975	—
sedan 7P	4,820	4,485	—
salon sdn 7P	4,900	4,835	—
salon town car 7P	5,040	5,035	—
Model B (wb 134.0; lwb-139.0) - 3,640 built			
rdstr 2P	4,290	3,125	—
touring 4-5P	4,375	3,300	—
dual-cwl spt phtn 4-5P	4,470	3,600	—
conv cpe 2-4P	4,420	3,350	—
lwb victoria cpe 5P	4,590	3,475	—
lwb sdn 4d	4,720	3,495	—
lwb salon sdn 4d	4,780	3,795	—
lwb salon club sdn 4d	4,770	3,795	—
lwb sln clb berline 5P	4,840	3,995	—
lwb club sdn 5P	4,730	3,670	—
lwb club berline 7P	4,790	3,870	—
lwb sdn 7P	4,790	3,625	—
limo 7P (lwb)	4,820	3,825	—
lwb salon sdn 7P	4,840	3,925	—
lwb salon limo 7P	4,860	4,125	—
Model C (wb 132.0) - 2,880 built			
cpe 2-4	4,450	2,865	—
club brougham 5P	4,460	2,695	—
sdn 4d	4,525	2,875	—

1930 Engines	bore×stroke	bhp	availability
I-8, 340.0	3.38×4.75	115	S-C
I-8, 366.0	3.50×4.75	125	S-B
I-8, 385.0	3.50×5.00	132	S-A

1931

Model 41 (wb 147.0) - 385 blt	Wght	Price	Prod
touring 7P	4,786	4,275	—
conv cpe 2-4P	4,740	4,275	—
sdn 7P	5,100	4,785	—
limo 7P	5,157	4,985	—
LeBaron cpe 2-4P	—	5,100	—
LeBaron vic cpe 5P	—	5,100	—
LeBaron conv sdn 5P	—	5,200	—
LeBaron spt sdn 5P	—	5,375	—
LeBaron limo 7P	—	5,975	—
town brougham 7P	5,206	6,250	—
town car 7P	5,211	6,250	—
town landau 7P	—	6,400	—
Model 42 (wb 142.0) - 800 built			
spt roadster 2-4P	4,565	3,450	—
touring 5P	4,605	3,450	—
dual-cowl spt phtn 4P	4,734	3,750	—
conv cpe 2-4P	4,698	3,650	—
sdn 4d	4,980	3,695	—
club sdn 5P	4,929	3,745	—
sdn 7P	5,046	3,825	—
club berline 5P	4,953	3,945	—
limo 7P	5,075	3,995	—
Model 43 (wb 134.0; lwb-137.0) - 2,590 built			
rdstr 2-4P	4,332	2,895	—
touring 5P	4,372	2,895	—
cpe 2-4P	4,528	2,685	—
lwb sdn 4d	4,638	2,685	—
lwb club sdn 5P	4,654	2,835	—
lwb sdn 7P	4,717	2,995	—
limo (lwb) 7P	4,819	3,145	—
lwb conv sdn 5P	—	3,650	—

1931 Engines	bore×stroke	bhp	availability
I-8, 366.0	3.50×4.75	125	S-43
I-8, 385.0	3.50×5.00	132	S-41, 42

1932

	Model 54 (wb 137.0; lwb-142.0) - 1,790 built	Wght	Price	Prod
	conv rdstr 2-4P	4,650	3,100	—
	touring 4P	—	3,150	—
	spt phtn 4P	—	3,350	—
	cpe 2-4P	4,735	2,985	—
	club 5P brougham	4,745	2,850	—
	sdn 4d	4,819	2,985	—
	club sdn 5P	—	3,150	—
	conv sdn 5P	4,961	3,450	—
	club berline 5P	—	3,350	—
	lwb touring 7P	—	3,450	—
	lwb sdn 7P	5,024	3,185	—
	limo (lwb) 7P	5,071	3,450	—
Model 52 (wb 142.0; lwb-147.0) - 60 built				
52	sdn 4d	5,395	4,295	—
52	club sdn 5P	—	4,400	—
52	club berline 5P	—	4,600	—
51	lwb sdn 7P	5,465	4,535	—
51	limo 7P (lwb)	5,506	4,800	—
Model 53 (wb 137.0; lwb-142.0) - 250 built				
	conv rdstr 2-4P	—	3,900	—
	touring 4P	—	3,950	—
	spt phtn 4P	—	4,150	—
	cpe 2-4P	—	3,785	—
	club brougham 5P	5,042	3,650	—
	sdn 4d	5,080	3,785	—
	club sdn 5P	5,244	3,950	—

Model 53	Wght	Price	Prod
conv sdn 5P	—	4,250	—
club berline 5P	—	4,150	—
lwb touring 7P	—	4,250	—
lwb sdn 7P	5,301	3,985	—
limo 7P (lwb)	5,366	4,250	—

1932 Engines	bore×stroke	bhp	availability
I-8, 366.0	3.50×4.75	125	S-54
V-12, 398.0	3.25×4.00	140	S-53
V-12, 429.0	3.38×4.00	150	S-52

1933

Model 836 (wb 136.0; lwb-139.0) - 1,525 built	Wght	Price	Prod
conv rdstr 2-4P	4,618	3,100	—
cpe 2-4P	4,663	2,795	—
club brougham 5P	4,622	2,385	—
sdn 4d	4,660	2,575	—
club sdn 5P	4,681	2,695	—
conv sdn 5P	4,958	2,975	—
lwb sdn 7P	4,780	2,850	—
limo 7P (lwb)	4,819	2,975	—
salon conv rdstr 2-4P	4,643	3,265	—
salon cpe 2-4P	4,688	2,960	—
salon club brghm 5P	4,647	2,550	—
salon sdn 4d	4,685	2,740	—
salon club sdn 5P	4,706	2,860	—
salon conv sdn 7P	4,983	3,140	—
lwb salon sdn 7P	4,805	3,015	—
salon limo lwb 7P	4,844	3,140	—

Model 1236 (wb 136.0; lwb-139.0) - 500 built	Wght	Price	Prod
conv rdstr 2-4P	4,729	3,500	—
cpe 2-4P	4,922	3,195	—
club brougham 5P	4,854	2,785	—
sdn 4d	4,892	2,975	—
club sdn 5P	4,929	3,095	—
conv sdn 5P	—	3,375	—
lwb sdn 7P	5,027	3,250	—
limo 7P (lwb)	5,088	3,375	—
salon conv rdstr 2-4P	4,754	3,665	—
salon cpe 2-4P	4,947	3,360	—
salon club brghm 5P	4,879	2,950	—
salon sdn 4d	4,917	3,140	—
salon club sdn 5P	4,954	3,260	—
salon conv sdn 5P	—	3,540	—
lwb salon sdn 7P	5,052	3,415	—
salon limo 7P (lwb)	5,113	3,540	—

Model 1242 (wb 137.0; lwb-142.0) - 120 built	Wght	Price	Prod
conv cpe rdstr	5,107	3,900	—
touring 5P	5,256	3,950	—
spt phtn 5P	5,296	4,150	—
cpe 2-4P	—	3,785	—
club brougham 5P	5,198	3,650	—
sdn 4d	—	3,785	—
club sdn 5P	5,361	3,950	—
conv sdn 5P	5,438	4,250	—
club berline 5P	—	4,150	—
lwb touring 7P	—	4,250	—
lwb sdn 7P	—	3,985	—
limo 7P (lwb)	5,507	4,250	—

Model 1247 (wb 142.0; lwb-147.0) - 145 built	Wght	Price	Prod
sdn 4d	—	4,295	—
club sdn 5P	5,417	4,400	—
club berline 5P	5,421	4,600	—
lwb LeBaron cpe metal-back 2P	5,286	5,300	—
lwb LeBaron cpe leather-back 2P	5,286	5,600	—
lwb LBrn conv vic 5P	5,198	5,200	—
lwb LBrn conv sdn 5P	5,466	5,700	—
lwb LeBaron conv sedan/partition 5P	—	6,100	—
lwb LeBaron club sdn	5,391	5,700	—
lwb LeBaron sdn 7P	5,550	4,535	—
limo 7P (lwb)	5,550	4,800	—
LeBaron limo 7P (lwb)	5,778	6,200	—
lwb Brunn twn brghm	—	6,700	—
lwb Brunn cab	—	7,200	—
lwb Brunn town car	5,768	6,700	—
lwb Brunn brougham	—	7,200	—

Silver Arrow (wb 139.0)	Wght	Price	Prod
sdn 4d	5,729	10,000	5

1933 Engines	bore×stroke	bhp	availability
I-8, 366.0	3.50×4.75	135	S-836
V-12, 429.0	3.38×4.00	160	S-1236
V-12, 462.0	3.50×4.00	175	S-1242, 1247, Silver Arrow

1934

836A Eight (wb 136.0) - 500 blt	Wght	Price	Prod
club brougham 5P	4,780	2,495	—
club brghm salon 5P	4,797	2,595	—
sdn 4d	4,923	2,595	—
salon sdn 4d	4,940	2,695	—

840A DeLuxe Eight (wb 139.0; lwb-144.0) - 655 built	Wght	Price	Prod
conv rdstr	4,817	2,995	—
cpe 4P	4,913	2,895	—
club brougham 5P	4,906	2,795	—
sdn 4d	4,964	2,895	—
club sdn 5P	5,042	2,995	—
Silver Arrow cpe (lwb)	5,046	3,495	—
lwb sdn 7P	5,107	3,200	—
limo 7P (lwb)	5,183	3,350	—
Brunn metro	—	—	—
town brghm 5P (lwb)	5,228	4,995	—

1240A Salon Twelve (wb 139.0; lwb:144.0) - 290 built	Wght	Price	Prod
conv rdstr 4P	5,072	3,395	—
cpe 4P	5,168	3,295	—
club brougham 5P	5,152	3,195	—
sdn 4d	5,227	3,295	—
club sdn 5P	5,315	3,395	—
Silver Arrow cpe (lwb)	5,347	3,895	—
lwb sdn 7P	5,381	3,600	—
limo 7P (lwb)	5,442	3,750	—
Brunn metro town brougham 7P (lwb)	5,529	5,395	—

1248A Custom Twelve (wb 147.0) - 90 built	Wght	Price	Prod
sdn 7P	—	4,295	—
limo 7P	5,494	4,495	—
Brunn limo 7P	—	6,000	—
Brunn twn brghm 7P	—	6,500	—
Brunn town cab 7P	—	7,000	—
Brunn town car 7P	—	6,500	—
Brunn brougham 7P	—	7,000	—

1934 Engines	bore×stroke	bhp	availability
I-8, 366.0	3.50×4.75	135	S-836A
I-8, 385.0	3.50×5.00	140	S-840A
V-12, 462.0	3.50×4.00	175	S-1240A, 1248A

1935

845 Eight (wb 139.0; lwb-144.0) - 525 built	Wght	Price	Prod
conv rdstr 2-4P	—	2,995	—
cpe 2-4P	—	2,895	—
club brougham 5P	—	2,795	—
sdn 4d	4,964	2,895	—
club sdn 5P	—	2,995	—
Silver Arrow cpe (lwb)	—	3,495	—
lwb sdn 7P	—	3,200	—
limo 7P (lwb)	—	3,350	—
Brunn metro town brougham 5P (lwb)	—	4,995	—

1245 Twelve (wb 139.0; lwb-144.0) - 145 built	Wght	Price	Prod
conv rdstr 2-4P	—	3,395	—
cpe 2-4P	—	3,295	—
club brougham 5P	—	3,195	—
sdn 4d	5,433	3,295	—
club sdn 5P	—	3,395	—
Silver Arrow cpe (lwb)	—	3,895	—
lwb sdn 7P	—	3,600	—
limo 7P (lwb)	—	3,750	—
Brunn town brougham 5P (lwb)	—	5,395	—

1255 Twelve (wb 147.0) - 60 built	Wght	Price	Prod
sdn 7P	—	4,295	—
limo 7P	—	4,495	—

1935 Engines	bore×stroke	bhp	availability
I-8, 366.0	3.50×4.75	135	S-836A
I-8, 385.0	3.50×5.00	140	S-845
V-12, 462.0	3.50×4.00	175	S-1245, 1255

1936

1601 Eight (wb 139.0, 144.0, 147.0) - 635 built		Wght	Price	Prod
438C	cpe 2P, 139 in.	—	3,115	—
438E	club berline 5P, 139 in.	5,600	3,495	—
438N	club sdn 5P, 139 in.	5,600	3,295	—
438P	conv rdstr cpe 2P, 139 in.	5,590	3,295	—
438S	sdn 4d, 139 in.	—	3,195	—
444L	limo 7P, 144 in.	—	3,650	—
444M	sdn 7P, 144 in.	—	3,500	—
447L	limo 7P, 147 in.	—	—	—
447M	sdn 7P, 147 in.	—	—	—

1602 Twelve (wb 139.0; lwb-144.0) - 135 built*		Wght	Price	Prod
538	sdn 4d	—	3,900	—
544	lwb sdn 7P	—	4,050	—
538	conv rdstr cpe, 2P	5,800	3,695	—
538	club sdn 5P	5,850	3,795	—

1603 Twelve (wb 147.0)	Wght	Price	Prod
sdn 7P	—	4,795	—
limo 7P	6,145	4,995	—
Brunn met twn car 7P	—	5,795	—

* Includes 1603 Twelve.

1936 Engines	bore×stroke	bhp	availability
I-8, 385.0	3.50×5.00	150	S-Eight
V-12, 462.0	3.50×4.00	185	S-Twelve

1937

1701 (wb 139.0, 144.0, 147.0) - 120 built	Wght	Price	Prod
cpe 2P, 139 in.	—	3,195	—
club berline 5P, 139 in.	5,600	3,495	—
club sdn 5P, 139 in.	5,600	3,295	—
conv rdstr cpe 2P, 139 in.	5,590	3,295	—
sdn 4d, 139 in.	—	3,195	—
conv sdn 5P, 139 in.	—	—	—
formal sdn 4d, 139 in.	—	—	—
limo 7P, 144 in.	—	3,650	—
sdn 7P, 144 in.	—	3,500	—
limo 7P, 147 in.	—	—	—
sdn 7P, 147 in.	—	—	—

1702 Twelve (wb 139.0; lwb-144.0) - 43 built	Wght	Price	Prod
sdn 4d	—	3,900	—
conv rdstr cpe 2P	5,800	3,695	—
club sdn 5P	5,850	3,795	—
club berline 5P	5,850	3,945	—
conv sdn 5P	5,920	4,650	—
formal sdn 4d	—	—	—
lwb sdn 7P	—	4,050	—

1703 Twelve (wb 147.0) - 28 built	Wght	Price	Prod
sdn 7P	6,065	4,845	—
limo 7P	6,145	4,995	—
town car 7P	6,100	6,500	—
Brunn met twn car 7P	6,085	5,795	—

1937 Engines	bore×stroke	bhp	availability
I-8, 385.0	3.50×5.00	150	S-Eight
V-12, 462.0	3.50×4.00	185	S-Twelve

1938

1801 Eight (wb 138.0, 144.0, 147.0) - 18 built	Wght	Price	Prod
Body Styles similar to 1937 "1701"	—	—	—

1802 Twelve (wb 139.0; lwb-144.0) - 12 built	Wght	Price	Prod
Body Styles similar to 1937 "1702"	—	—	—

1803 Twelve (wb 147.0) - 10 built	Wght	Price	Prod
Body Styles similar to 1937 "1703"	—	—	—

1938 Engines	bore×stroke	bhp	availability
I-8, 385.0	3.50×5.00	150	S-Eight
V-12, 462.0	3.50×4.00	185	S-Twelve

Plymouth

When Walter P. Chrysler decided to launch a low-priced car in 1928, his sales manager, Joseph W. Frazer, suggested the name Plymouth, after the storied Massachusetts rock where the Pilgrims landed. WPC wasn't sure people would make that connection, so Frazer mentioned another product well known to the ex-farmboy. That was all Chrysler needed. "Every god damn farmer in America's heard of Plymouth Binder Twine," he replied—so Plymouth it was.

Plymouth was a success from day one. Though it was first sold only through Chrysler dealers, demand was so strong that franchises were extended to Dodge and DeSoto agents by 1930. The strategy excellent and it vastly increased the number of Plymouth dealers while insulating them from the Depression-era sales reversals suffered by costlier Chrysler makes.

Yet despite those "hard times"—or perhaps because of them—Plymouth prospered in the '30s on a formidable combination of low price, attractive styling, and engineering often more advanced than that of Ford or Chevrolet. Though Plymouth never outproduced those rivals, it was firmly established as America's number-three seller as early as 1932, a spot it would hold well into the '50s.

Many key features figured in this meteoric rise: all-steel construction (per Chrysler practice) in an age of wood-framed bodies; four-wheel hydraulic brakes some years before Ford and Chevy had them; "Floating Power" rubber engine mounts that gave the 1931 models "the smoothness of an eight and the economy of a four"; independent coil-spring front suspension for 1934, again beating Ford (and matching Chevrolet); rubber body isolators (1936); standard safety glass, recessed controls, concealed heater blower and defroster vents (1937).

Reflecting these and other pluses, Plymouth was one of the few makes to score higher production in 1930-31 than in the pre-Depression period. It also gained in 1933, one of the roughest industry years on record. Output peaked at nearly 552,000 for 1937, dropped to about 279,000 for recession-year 1938, then recovered beyond the half-million mark by 1941.

A "New Finer Plymouth" was announced in April 1930, but it was much like the 1928-29 Models Q and U, with the same 109-inch wheelbase and a competitive lineup in the $600-$700 range. The big difference was a four-cylinder engine enlarged for the third time in as many years, reaching 196 cid (versus 170 for '28 and 175.4 for 1929). Horsepower stood at 48, up three. Like the Model U, the 30U carried into the succeeding calendar year, but saw lower total production of 76,950 versus 108,350. A likely factor was Ford's enormously popular new Model A.

Plymouth responded in May 1931 with a car that was genuinely new, the fruit of a $2.5-million development program. Designated PA, it kept to the same wheelbase but boasted "Floating Power," as mentioned, plus eight more horses to go with it. There was also a broader lineup with a dashing new sport phaeton and rumble-seat roadster. But mindful of the Depression, Plymouth also fielded two cheap "Thrift" sedans at $495 and $575. Despite the general economic gloom, model-year production soared to nearly 107,000.

Bowing in February 1932 was the last four-cylinder domestic Plymouth for the next 46 years. Styling wasn't greatly altered, but the new PB was more expansive on a three-inch longer standard wheelbase. A convertible sedan was added, Chrysler evidently feeling confident enough to dabble with less-popular body styles even in its price-leader line. Also new was a seven-seat sedan on a 121-inch chassis. That model found only 2200 buyers and was duly dropped—but not for long. Horsepower kept climbing, reaching 65, but prices stayed put. Sales fell sharply in this first year of Ford's milestone V-8, but were still respectable at just under 84,000.

Plymouth offered better value by switching to a six for 1933. The project cost $9 million, but was worth every penny in extra sales, which leaped beyond 298,000 for the model year. No wonder, for the new Six sold for as little as $445, over $300 less than the original 1928 Four. The six naturally had more horses, but from fewer cubic inches. Arriving with 189.8 cid and 70 bhp, it was stroked to 201.3 cid and 77 bhp for 1934. Save an interim push to 82 bhp for 1935, this sturdy four-main-bearing L-head would remain that size through '41, when it spun out 87 bhp.

Like other makes, Plymouth continued "splitting" model years by offering two 1933 series. The first, titled PC, was built from October 1932 through March 1933 in five models on a 107-inch wheelbase. Then came a two-series PD line of standard and DeLuxe Sixes on respective wheelbases of 108 and 112 inches. A convertible coupe was exclusive to DeLuxe. Following another industry trend, Plymouth began a cautious move from four-square to streamlined styling, adopting fully skirted fenders and a rounder hood/radiator ensemble. A winged-lady hood mascot arrived as a new accessory.

Styling was smoother still for 1934, when Plymouth made its aforementioned moves to independent front suspension and a larger six. Offerings grouped into PF Standard and PE DeLuxe, the latter on a still-longer 114-inch wheelbase. A second Standard series designated PG arrived in March with three cheap models priced around $500. DeLuxes now featured safety glass as well as "artillery" steel wheels, which were gaining favor over traditional wires that looked old-hat on streamlined cars. The winged-lady mascot was replaced by an image of the ship *Mayflower*, reminding buyers of the Plymouth Rock connection.

1930 Model 30U convertible coupe

1932 Series PA 2/4-passenger convertible coupe

1933 Series PC Six four-door sedan

1934 Series PE DeLuxe four-door sedan

1935 Series PJ DeLuxe Six 2/4-passenger convertible coupe

1936 Series P-1 Business Series 2-passenger coupe

1937 Series PT-50 commercial sedan

Though a factory Plymouth station wagon wouldn't arrive until 1938, U.S. Body & Forge of Tell City, Indiana, built wagon bodies on modified 1934 Plymouth Standard chassis. The resulting Westchester Suburban was a four-door model made mostly of wood from the cowl back; it thus demanded lots of upkeep. Only 119 were built that year. On August 10, Chrysler built its one-millionth Plymouth, and Walter Chrysler was pleased by even higher model-year volume of over 321,000.

Lumpy but modern "potato" streamlining identified the fully redesigned 1935 PJ Plymouths, which included new "trunk-back" two- and four-door Touring sedans with integral luggage compartments. Standard and DeLuxe continued, but now shared a single 113-inch wheelbase. The one exception was the new DeLuxe Traveler, a five-passenger four-door sedan on its own 128-inch chassis. Only 77 were sold that year. All models boasted new "Chair-Height" seats, improved engine cooling via full-length water jackets, an extra five horsepower, and better handling via a new front stabilizer bar and improved weight distribution. Helped by prices as low as $510, Plymouth moved up in model-year production: nearly 327,500.

Despite relatively few changes, the 1936 Plymouths broke the half-million mark, a first for the make. The long chassis was trimmed three inches between wheel centers, and the Standard line was prosaically retitled Business. The main styling distinction was a fulsome barrellike radiator with thin vertical bars.

Plymouth achieved its decade production high with rebodied 1937 models bearing reduced window areas but standard safety glass on all models. Also as mentioned, Plymouth offered recessed interior knobs, plus a rounded dash bottom and a padded front-seat top, all for safety's sake. Oddly, a right-hand windshield wiper still cost extra. Crank-open windshields were in their final year, but 1937 was the first time Plymouth prices exceeded $1000. That applied to a new seven-seat DeLuxe limousine, which shared a long wheelbase, stretched seven inches from '36, with a similar sedan. Other models lost an inch between wheel centers.

Styling became dumpy for 10th Anniversary 1938; a near-oval radiator didn't help. Models and specifications were mostly carryovers, though there were some changes. For example, a high-compression head was newly optional, lifting bhp to 86, up four from standard. Also available, as it had been since 1936, was a low-compression 65-bhp "economy" engine, a no-charge lure offered to Depression-weary buyers. On the model front, the Business line became the Roadking in March 1938, but was no less spartan for it. A four-door DeLuxe station wagon, the Suburban, bowed as Plymouth's first such "catalog" model, though U.S. Body & Forge built its coachwork, as it had done back in '34. Like some other contemporary wagons, this came with front-door glass only; glazing behind cost extra. There was no rear bumper either, but a tailgate-mounted spare tire provided some protection.

A refreshing facelift arrived for 1939, the work of Raymond H. Dietrich, the great coachbuilder who then headed Chrysler styling. Hallmarks included a strongly peaked "prow" front, perhaps inspired by the Lincoln Zephyr's, plus a Vee'd two-piece windshield instead of the previous single pane. Headlights, now rectangular, nestled within the front fenders, and the gearshift moved from floor to steering column. The canvas convertible top could be power-operated for the first time in any car, a definite selling point—especially in the low-price arena. Offerings largely reprised the '38 line, but Roadking added a Suburban and two-door utility sedan. The former saw just 97 copies. Plymouth's long models were equally slow sellers: only about 2000 for the model year. Such cars would be a Chrysler specialty for many years to come, but none would sell well. Making a final stand in the DeLuxe series was

1938 Series S-6 DeLuxe Westchester Suburban wagon

1939 Series P-8 DeLuxe convertible coupe

1940 Series P-10 DeLuxe convertible coupe

1941 Series P20-12 Special DeLuxe station wagon

1942 Series P-14C Special DeLuxe convertible coupe

1942 Series P-14C Special DeLuxe four-door sedan

the rumble-seat convertible coupe and a 117-inch-wheelbase five-seat convertible sedan. The latter was a Plymouth exclusive at Chrysler Corporation for '39, revived for a 12-month stand. After a big dip below 280,000 for recessionary '38, Plymouth recovered nicely with 1939 volume of over 417,000.

A full body change for 1940 introduced "speedline" fenders and better proportions on three-inch-longer wheelbases. Sealed-beam headlamps appeared, as elsewhere in Detroit, and simple horizontal-bar grilles flanked a less-prominent prow. Sedans were now solely trunked fastbacks, though with more luggage space than the superseded "trunkbacks." Though 1940 prices began as low as $645, Plymouths remained a bit costlier than equivalent Fords. They also remained noticeably slower than Dearborn's V-8/85s despite a token two extra horsepower for 1940. Yet if no speedway threat, the Plymouth six still provided reliable cruising at over 65 mph, and was well-known for economy. A notable manufacturing advance was Chrysler "Superfinish," a special process of giving certain internal engine parts a mirror-smooth surface for reduced friction and decreased wear.

After healthy 1940-model production of 423,000, Plymouth scored a robust 546,000 for '41, thanks mainly to heavy output in the closing months of 1940. Calendar-year figures reflected the turn toward defense work at the end of 1941, running some 50,000 units behind Ford.

The 1941 Plymouths wore an adroit facelift featuring a simple, almost heart-shaped grille and modest bright-metal side accents. Six cheap standard-trim models were added, Roadking became DeLuxe, and the old DeLuxe was now Special DeLuxe. The slow-selling limousine was axed after just 24 were built. Other '41 rarities were the DeLuxe club coupe (204) and the standard club coupe (994), utility sedan (468), and Suburban (217). All models boasted another Chrysler engineering first: the Safety-Rim wheel, with a beaded circumference to prevent tire loss in a blowout. The battery moved under the hood for the first time, and Plymouth offered "Powermatic" shift, a vacuum-transmission assist.

War-shortened 1942 introduced a more massive look via a wider grille and front fenders, plus door sheetmetal extended to cover the running boards. The six was enlarged for the first time since 1934, bored out to 217.8 cid and 95 bhp; it wouldn't be touched again until 1949. Standard-trim models departed, and Special DeLuxe expanded with the town sedan, a new Chrysler style with more formal, closed-in rear roof quarters.

Plymouth Division's 1942 output was close to 152,500 when the government halted civilian automobile production in February for the duration of World War II. While all '42 Detroit cars are quite scarce today, some of these Plymouths are especially rare. For example, only 80 utility sedans, 1136 wagons, and 2806 convertibles were built.

While Plymouth manufactured munitions and military engines during the war, stylists like A. B. "Buzz" Grisinger, John Chika, and Herb Weissinger worked on postwar ideas whenever they could. Typical of Chrysler thinking at the time, these involved smooth, flush-fender bodies with thin door pillars and wraparound grilles. But like most everyone else, Plymouth resumed civilian operations with mildly modified '42s, which the booming seller's market happily consumed into model-year '49. The first all-new postwar Plymouths bowed in March '49 as squarer and more upright than any wartime study. Plymouth built just 770 cars between V-J Day and the end of 1945, then quickly picked up the pace, reaching near 265,000 for 1946 and over half a million by '49.

Plymouth's 1946-48 facelift involved a more modest grille with alternating thick/thin horizontal bars, rectangular parking lights beneath the headlamps, wide front-fender moldings, a new hood ornament, and reworked rear fenders. DeLuxe and Special DeLuxe returned, but without utility models. No styling or mechanical changes would occur through early '49, so serial numbers are the only clue as to model year.

Postwar inflation boosted 1946 prices by $270 over 1942. The '47s ran about $250 more than the '46s, and the '48s were up to $300 costlier than the '47s. While Plymouth readied its first all-new postwar models for spring introduction, the '48s were sold as "interim" '49s with inch-smaller wheels and tires (15s versus 16s), plus other minor alterations, but still at '48 prices.

When the "real" '49s arrived, Grisinger and Weissinger had departed for Kaiser-Frazer and a new styling philosophy was in force. It reflected the tastes of K. T. Keller, who'd taken over as company president following Walter Chrysler's death in 1940. No fan of low "torpedos," Keller preferred what designers termed "three-box styling—one box on top of two others," believing in function over form. "Cars should accommodate people rather than the ideas of far-out designers," he said. What he failed to grasp was how much postwar buyers wanted the long, low look—never mind the reduced headroom or ground clearance. In time, Keller's practical bent would severely hurt company sales.

But the seller's market was at its height in 1949, most everything sold no matter what it looked like, and the new Plymouth offered an efficient, comfortable, and roomy package with good visibility. Wheelbase stretched to 118.5 inches for a DeLuxe notchback coupe and sedan priced in the $1500s, and for Special DeLuxe coupe, sedan, convertible, and wood-trimmed wagon covering a $1600-$2400 spread. A shorter 111-inch chassis supported a DeLuxe fastback two-door, business coupe, and

1946-48 Special DeLuxe four-door sedan

1946-48 DeLuxe coupe

1946-48 Series P-15C Special DeLuxe convertible coupe

1949 Series P-19 DeLuxe Suburban two-door station wagon

1950 Series P-20 Special DeLuxe convertible coupe

1951 Series P-23 Cranbrook four-door sedan

new all-steel Suburban wagon.

Plymouth liked to credit its '49 Suburban as the first "modern" wagon, but Chevy, Olds, and Pontiac also issued all-steel haulers during 1949. Still, the Suburban cost only $1840, quite a bit less than the GM models, and thus sold well: nearly 20,000 for '49. Buyers evidently loved wagons that didn't require costly, time-consuming upkeep. Within four years, other Chrysler makes and the rest of Detroit had put "woodys" to rest. Plymouth kept its wood-framed wagon through 1950.

Oldsmobile's 1949 "Rocket" 88 fired the gun for a "horsepower race" that turned all manner of staid cars into stylish sizzlers. Plymouth was one of them. But even more than Chevrolet, Pontiac, or sister Dodge, Plymouth reinvented itself because it had to. Although the make spent most of the early '50s still entrenched as number-three, it sold fewer and fewer cars after '49, bottoming to fifth in calendar-year sales by 1954.

As continuations of the new '49s, the 1950-54 Plymouths were well-engineered, solid, and reliable; but they were also squarish, stubby-looking, and none too fast. The ancient L-head six was raised to 97 bhp for '49 and would remain there through 1952, after which it went to 100 bhp (probably by the stroke of an ad writer's pen). Plymouths were still thrifty (20-23 mpg wasn't uncommon), but hard-pressed to beat 90 mph. However, automatic electric choke and combined ignition/starter switch arrived as innovations for the low-priced field.

The 1950 line was basically a '49 reprise. An effective facelift brought a simpler square grille with large horizontal bar, slightly longer rear decks (to relieve the boxiness), and taillights placed low within reworked fenders. The Special outsold the plain DeLuxe by about 7-to-5.

After some 611,000 of its 1950s, Plymouth built about the same number of its 1951 models, which gained a modified hood and a lower, wider grille that made frontal appearance a little less blunt. New model names accompanied the fresh face. Short-wheelbase DeLuxes were retitled Concord and now included a two-door Savoy wagon besides the Suburban. The long-chassis DeLuxe and Special DeLuxe were now Cambridge and Cranbrook, respectively. The latter listed a convertible and Plymouth's first hardtop coupe, the Belvedere, which typically wore "saddleback" two-toning with the roof and rear body (but not rear fenders) in a contrast color. Ford also offered its first hardtop for '51, but it, too, was a year behind Chevrolet's Bel Air. The Belvedere trailed both in sales by wide margins, but was still pretty popular, with 51,266 built for 1951-52.

1952 Series P-23 Cranbrook Belvedere hardtop coupe

1953 Series P24-2 Cranbrook club coupe

1954 Belvedere hardtop sport coupe

1955 Belvedere Six hardtop sport coupe

1955 Belvedere Suburban station wagon

1956 Plaza club sedan with Sportone two-tone

Chrysler didn't bother to separate 1951 and '52 production, mainly because its cars changed so little. Plymouth was no exception, though a rear nameplate integrated with the trunk-handle (replacing separate script) was a small spotter's point. Overdrive arrived for '52 as a new option, and all Plymouths continued with an important 1951 improvement: Oriflow shock absorbers, a Chrysler hydraulic-type designed to improve ride and handling. But dumpy looks, a weak old six, and lack of full automatic transmission put Plymouth at a sales disadvantage in '52, when output slid by a substantial 204,000 units to below 400,000, aggravated by government-ordered civilian production cutbacks for the Korean War.

The '53s addressed some of the competitive deficits, starting with an outer-body reskin that brought flow-through fender-lines, a one-piece windshield, and a more aggressive grille. A single new 114-inch wheelbase was used for a revived two-series lineup minus Concord (Cambridge expanded to embrace the business coupe and wagons). Another ploy to boost sales was the midyear introduction of semiautomatic "Hy-Drive," a manual transmission with torque converter that eliminated most clutch work, though you still had to clutch between forward and reverse.

But the '53s still looked small, and so did the facelifted '54s, which were as uninspired as any Chrysler product. Volume dwindled from the previous year's 650,000-plus to around 463,000—less than half of Ford/Chevy output. Models were regrouped again, this time into cheap Plaza, midline Savoy, and top-shelf Belvedere series covering a $1600-$2300 price spread. Plaza and Savoy each listed a club coupe, sedans with two or four doors, and a Suburban wagon; there was also a Plaza business coupe. Belvedere comprised four-door sedan, convertible, Suburban, and Sport Coupe hardtop.

Two important mechanical changes occurred during '54. The old six was enlarged for the first time since 1942, a longer stroke swelling displacement to 230.2 cid and horsepower to 110. Also at about midyear came a fully automatic two-speed PowerFlite transmission as a new option. It would prove to be very popular.

Plymouth repeated this basic lineup for 1955, but with a dramatic difference: all-new styling hatched by Chrysler design chief Virgil Exner and executed under his assistant, Maury Baldwin. Suddenly, Plymouths looked exciting. What's more, they had performance to match, thanks to the first V-8 in Plymouth history—and a new polyspherical design, at that.

Called "Hy-Fire," this new V-8 was an excellent overhead-valve unit in the small-block tradition begun with Studebaker's 232 of 1951. It premiered in two sizes: 241 cid and 157 bhp, and a 260 with 167 standard bhp or 177 with an optional "Power-Pak" of four-barrel carb and dual exhausts. Outstanding features ran to lightweight aluminum pistons and carburetor, and chrome-plated top piston rings for longer life and better oil control. Tuning changes brought the old six, now called "Power-Flow," to 117 bhp.

Other highlights for 1955 included suspended foot pedals, tubeless tires, front shocks enclosed within the front coil springs, and dashboard lever control for the PowerFlite automatic. There were also several options new to Plymouth: factory air conditioning, power windows, and power front seat.

But Plymouth's most-visible '55 attraction was its crisp new styling: pointed front and rear fenders, smooth flanks, shapely tail, a bright but not gaudy grille. Two-toning was confined to the roof and, via optional moldings, broad bodyside sweep panels. Four-door wagons returned for the first time since 1948 as Plaza and Belvedere Suburbans. The line-topping Belvedere convertible came only with V-8, as it would through the end of the decade.

Ads proclaimed the '55 a "great new car for the young in heart." It was certainly a clean break from Plymouth's plodding past. Customers rushed to buy—encouraged by prices little higher than in '54—but production lagged and Plymouth dropped to sixth for the model year at 401,000 units. But volume for calendar '55 was a rousing 742,991 (including some '56s, of course)—a record that would stand well into the '60s.

Plymouth reclaimed fourth for model-year 1956, which introduced "The Forward Look"—essentially tailfins, achieved by raising rear fenderlines a little. Engineers brought forth push-button PowerFlite, a 12-volt electrical system, and an optional "Highway Hi-Fi" record player that used special platters and a tone arm designed to stay in the groove—which it typically did not do on bumpy roads. Suburbans became a separate line with two-door Deluxe, two- and four-door Customs, and four-door Sport models respectively trimmed like Plaza, Savoy, and Belvedere. A Sport Sedan four-door hardtop expanded Belvedere models, and a two-door hardtop did likewise for Savoy. Both Hy-Fire V-8s were larger and more potent, comprising a base 270-cid version with 180 bhp, and a pair of 277s packing 187 and 200 bhp.

An even hotter Plymouth arrived at mid-'56: the limited-edition Fury. An attractive hardtop coupe, it came only in white, set off by bodyside sweepspears of gold anodized aluminum. Power was supplied by a special 303 V-8 with 240 bhp via 9.25:1 compression, solid lifters, stronger valve springs, dual exhausts, and a Carter four-barrel carb. A stock Fury could do 0-60 in about 10 seconds and reach 110 mph, though one modified example approached 145 mph on the sands of Daytona Beach. The Fury gave a big boost to Plymouth's growing performance image, and 4485 of the '56s were sold—not bad for the $2866 price, some $600 above the Belvedere hardtop.

After record-shattering production of nearly 553,000, Plymouth zoomed to better than 762,000 with its stunning all-new '57 line. Ads said, "Suddenly, It's 1960"—and not without reason. Next to its rivals, Plymouth did seem "three full years ahead," with the lowest beltline and highest tailfins of the Low-Priced Three. Wheelbases lengthened to 122 inches for wagons and to 118 inches for others. Offerings were unchanged through midyear, when a Savoy Sport Sedan hardtop was added.

The PowerFlow six had been coaxed up to 132 bhp by 1957, when Plymouth listed no fewer than five V-8s: 197- and 235-bhp 277s, new 301s with 215/235 bhp, and the Fury's even larger new wedgehead 318 with 290 bhp. TorqueFlite, Chrysler's excellent new three-speed automatic, was an optional alternative to PowerFlite. Also shared with other '57 Chrysler cars was new torsion-bar front suspension, whose superior geometry made for the best-handling Plymouth ever.

It's hard to remember how truly different Plymouth seemed in 1957: low and wide with distinctive "shark" fins, a graceful grille, a front bumper raised over a vertically slotted center panel, two-toning on the roof and tasteful bodyside color panels (sometimes the roof alone), huge glass areas (the convertible windshield curved at the top as well as the sides), and a delicate-looking thin-section roofline on hardtop coupes. Suburbans gained load space with an upright spare tire mounted in the right-rear fender, an idea borrowed from the 1956 Plymouth Plainsman show car. The '57 Plymouths were indeed memorable, but their tendency to early rust—reflecting a rushed development program and a consequent decline in quality control—makes good examples fairly rare today.

A predictably mild facelift for '58 brought quad headlamps, a horizontal-bar grille insert (repeated in the under-bumper modesty panel), and small round taillights at the base of the fins (bright metal filled the space above). A trio of 318 V-8s offered 225-290 bhp (the latter standard for Fury), and a newly optional

1956 Belvedere convertible coupe

1956 Fury hardtop sport coupe

1957 Belvedere two-door sedan

1957 Belvedere four-door sedan

1957 Fury hardtop coupe

1958 Belvedere hardtop sport coupe

1958 Belvedere hardtop sport sedan

1959 Sport Fury convertible coupe

1959 Sport Fury hardtop coupe

1960 Fury hardtop sedan

1960 Fury hardtop coupe

1960 Valiant V-200 four-door sedan

1960 Valiant V-100 station wagon

350 "Golden Commando" wedgehead packed 305 bhp or, with that year's ultra-rare fuel-injection option, 315 bhp. Fuel injection proved troublesome and all were probably converted to carburetors. A deep national recession held production to just under 444,000, but most everyone built fewer cars for '58.

Plymouth shared in the industry's modest '59 recovery, turning out a bit more than 458,000 cars that were heavily restyled—and heavy-handed: longer and higher fins, garish eggcrate grille, headlamps with odd "siamesed" eyelids, more prominent bumpers, more plentiful bright trim, and abstract pilgrim-ship emblems. The Plaza vanished and Savoy and Belvedere moved down a notch in price; Fury became a top-line series with two- and four- door hardtops and a four-door sedan in the $2700-$2800 range. Plymouth's high performer was the new Sport Fury, offering a convertible as well as hardtop coupe for around $3000, including a 260-bhp 318 V-8. That year's regular 318 delivered 230 bhp. Fuel injection was no longer offered, but a new 361 "Golden Commando" V-8 with 305 bhp arrived as an $87 extra.

The division's '59 convertibles and hardtop coupes could be ordered with a simulated spare tire on the decklid, a lump of add-on tin reflecting Virgil Exner's love of "classic" design elements. It's since acquired the unflattering nickname "toilet seat." Typical of the gimmick-mad 1950s—and increasingly of Chrysler—was Sport Fury's standard "swivel-action" front seats: individual affairs (separated by a pull-down armrest) that turned outward at the touch of a lever to ease getting in and out. Sturdy latches kept them from swiveling while in use.

Also gimmicky, if occasionally predictive, were the several interesting Plymouth-branded show cars of the 1950s. They started with Ghia's 1950 XX-500, a pretty sedan that won Exner's patronage for the Italian coachworks to build later show cars and limousines. The 1954 Explorer, another Ghia-built Exner design, was a smoothly styled grand tourer. Also in 1954, Briggs Manufacturing, the body maker purchased by Chrysler that year, contributed the two-seat Belmont roadster. The car was supposed to spur Plymouth into offering something similar for the showroom—with Briggs-supplied bodies, of course—thus answering Chevy's Corvette and the Ford Thunderbird. A minuscule sports-car market precluded that, however, which was just as well: The Belmont wasn't much of a looker. The glassy '56 Plainsman, mentioned above, was followed by the even-glassier 1958 Cabana "dream wagon," which sported four-door hardtop styling that would make it to showrooms on 1960-62 Chrysler wagons, but not Plymouth's.

Plymouth built its hottest cars in the '60s—and also began the long slow slide to its demise. Though Plymouth ran its usual third for 1960, it would not do so again for another 11 years. It dropped to eighth for 1962, knocked out by Rambler, Pontiac, and Olds—and its own slow-selling line of smaller big cars with no full-size alternatives. Though it began to recover the next year, Plymouth wouldn't dislodge Pontiac from third until 1971, settling for fourth instead. Much of this trouble reflected management's repeated failure to gauge the market correctly and have the right products at the right time.

Trouble was apparent right away, with 1960 volume easing to just under 448,000 despite support from the compact Valiant, which arrived at Chrysler-Plymouth dealers as an ostensibly separate make. Sport Fury departed but other Plymouths returned with Highland Park's new "Unibody" construction on an unchanged wheelbase. "Misshapen" described the styling. Tailfins strained to mimic the outlandish appendages of '59 Cadillacs, and headlamp hoods stretched awkwardly down and around from a blunt front to the front wheel openings.

Good news began with a new 225-cid ohv "Slant Six" with 145 bhp, essentially a larger version of the Valiant's 170 unit to replace the old L-head six as base power. Exceptionally strong and reliable, this fine engine would be a corporate mainstay for the next 20 years. V-8s were largely '59 reruns and all "wedgeheads": 318s with 230/260 bhp for Savoys and low-line Suburban wagons; 361s with 260/305/310 bhp for Belvederes and midline Suburbans; and top-dog Golden Commando 383 with new "Ram-Induction" manifolding and 330 bhp for Fury/Sport Suburban. Though Rambler's more conservative styling and thriftier sixes scored 2000 more sales for calendar 1960, Plymouth won the model-year race by a substantial 25,000-plus, though that included 194,292 Valiants.

The compact Valiant got Plymouth badges for 1961, and the standard line just got weird. A drastic restyle of the year-old Unibody eliminated fins and Fury's extra-cost "toilet seat," but taillights became ponderous bullets attached to scalloped fenders, while the pinched grille was eerily reminiscent of an old Graham "sharknose." A V-8 reshuffle cut the 260-bhp, while a hotter one arrived with 340 bhp. Chrysler's biggest V-8, the mighty 413 wedge, came to Plymouth with 350/375 bhp. But Plymouth's odd "plucked chicken" styling combined with still-mediocre workmanship reduced model-year volume to around 350,000. Industry standing fell to fourth place behind Rambler.

Then came the division's worst mistake of the '60s. Anticipating strong demand for smaller "standard" cars, Exner sliced standard Plymouths eight inches in overall length, trimmed two inches from wheelbase, slashed curb weights by up to 550 pounds, and applied strange, Valiant-like styling. Existing models returned, and Sport Fury was reborn at midseason as a sporty bucket-seat convertible and hardtop coupe.

These lighter, more maneuverable '62 Plymouths could get away with a smaller standard engine. The 225 Slant Six became the powerplant for more models. Previous V-8s returned, though horsepower ratings fluctuated somewhat. Most significant was the boost given to the big 413, which now packed a whopping 410/420 bhp, making these Plymouths (and sister Dodges) the cars to beat at the dragstrip. But mainstream buyers, not enthusiasts, were what mattered, and they still hungered for "full-size" cars. Ford and Chevrolet had them, and thus prospered as Plymouth's model-year volume plunged below 340,000 (again including Valiant). At least that would be the decade low.

Beating a hasty retreat, Plymouth issued more conservative, squared-up styling for '63, then a Chevy-like '64 facelift. Both were crafted under Ford alumnus Elwood Engel, who replaced Exner in 1962. But this didn't help much. Plymouth rebounded to fourth for '63 mainly on continuing strong demand for Valiants rather than appreciable gains in its "big-car" sales.

Engines in these years stood pretty much pat save a notable '63 newcomer. This was a wedgehead 426, a bored-out 413 with ultra-high compression—11:1 up to 13.5:1—packing 370/375 bhp with twin four-barrel carburetors or 415/425 with Ram Induction. Driver Richard Petty gave Plymouth a big morale boost by winning the '64 NASCAR championship hands down, driving a Fury hardtop whose new "slantback" rear roofline undoubtedly aided aerodynamics on the long-distance "supertracks." But this triumph came with a 426 hemi-head V-8 available only to racers, not the general public. Still, it was heartening to see Chrysler's famed '50s muscle mill revived for a new "horsepower race" that was already well underway.

A full-scale Plymouth renaissance was evident for 1965, largely because the make returned to the full-size fold with big, blocky Furys on a new 119-inch wheelbase (121 for wagons). Fury I and II offered two sedans and a wagon; Fury III added two- and four-door hardtops and a convertible; at the top were a bucket-seat Sport Fury convertible and hardtop coupe. They were the largest Plymouths ever, and naturally far roomier than the '64s. Yet prices were amazingly reasonable: $2400-$3200. Unit construction continued, but a bolt-on subframe carried engine and front suspension. Powerplants ran from 225 Slant Six through 318, 361, 383, and wedgehead 426 V-8s producing 230-365 bhp.

Meanwhile, the advent of intermediates begun with Ford's 1962 Fairlane suggested a new role for the 116-inch-wheelbase "standard" Plymouth of 1962-64. With a blocky reskin to resemble the big Fury, it returned for '65 as the "new midsize" Belvedere and met strong buyer approval. Offerings ran to Belvedere I sedans and wagon; Belvedere II four-door sedan, wagon, hardtop coupe, and convertible; bucket-seat V-8-only Satellite hardtop and convertible; and a much-altered drag-oriented two-door hardtop aptly named Super Stock. A wedgehead 426 with 365 bhp was standard on S/S and optional for other Belvederes. A 426 Hemi with 425 bhp was optional for the Super Stock. S/S rode a special 115-inch chassis and weighed just 3170 pounds, so performance was mighty. But it was neither cheap at $4671, nor readily available as it was built for strip and not practical on the street. Normal Belvederes cost $2200-$2700 and offered mostly the same engines as Furys, though their base V-8 was a new small-block 273 rated at 180 bhp. This was a debored cousin of the 318, which was reengineered for '65 to save weight, yet the result was no less durable or potent.

Scoring points with performance-minded youngbloods,

1961 Fury hardtop coupe

1961 Valiant V-200 hardtop coupe

1962 Sport Fury convertible coupe

Plymouth finally took the incredible Hemi from track to showroom as a limited-production option for the 1966 Belvedere II/Satellite. Heavy-duty suspension and oversize brakes were included to cope with its awesome power, which was 425 advertised but closer to 500 actual. Transmission was initially limited to four-speed manual, but three-speed TorqueFlite automatic was soon added.

Surprisingly docile at low "touring" speeds, Street Hemi Belvederes were electrifying demons when pushed. Correctly set up with proper tires and axle ratio, they could reach 100 mph in 12-13 seconds, making them prime quarter-mile competitors in the National Hot Rod Association's A/Stock and AA/Stock classes, along with Dodge's similar Coronet-based Hemi-Chargers. Chrysler's mighty "B-body" middleweights continued doing well in NASCAR. David Pearson won the '66 championship for Dodge; Richard Petty again did the honors for Plymouth in '67.

Belvedere/Satellite's crisp-lined '66 styling continued with only detail changes for 1967, the last year for the original '62 "standard" platform. Topping the line was the new Belvedere GTX, a lush hardtop coupe ($3178) and convertible ($3418) equipped with a 375-bhp version of the big-block 440 wedge (evolved from the 426) introduced on Chrysler Corporation's full-size '66s. Plymouth reserved its '67 Street Hemi option exclusively for GTX, which was easily spotted: silver-and-black

1963 Fury hardtop sedan

1964 Fury convertible coupe

1963 Valiant Signet 200 convertible coupe

1965 Valiant Signet V-8 convertible coupe

1963 Valiant Signet 200 hardtop coupe

1965 Fury III hardtop coupe

grille and back panel, simulated hood air intakes, sport striping, and dual exhausts.

A new B-body with no change in wheelbases gave Plymouth's 1968 intermediates a more rounded look that was just as pretty. Belvedere was reduced to a low-line coupe, sedan, and wagon. Satellite was now the full-range volume series, and Sport Satellite denoted a top-line wagon, convertible, and hardtop coupe priced just below GTX ($2800-$3240).

Plymouth scored a marketing coup with the 1968 Road Runner, a budget-priced no-frills muscle machine with ingenious tie-ins to the beloved Warner Bros. cartoon character. It bowed as a pillared coupe, but unexpected popularity (2500 first-year sales forecast, almost 45,000 actual) prompted adding a two-door hardtop at mid-year. Exterior badging comprised RR nameplates and cartoon-bird decals inside and out, along with side-facing dummy hood scoops that could be made functional for a little extra money. Power came from a 335-bhp 383 with intake manifold and big-port heads from the 440. The Street Hemi was available, as was a slew of comfort and cosmetic goodies; beefy suspension, four-speed, and a cute "beep-beep" horn were standard. Dynamite on street or track, this finely tuned package of power and performance cost only $2800-$3100—an extraordinary bargain for the day.

The midsize Plymouths continued through 1970 with only minor interim changes. A convertible and more standard equipment bolstered Road Runner's appeal for 1969, though higher prices didn't ($3000-$3300). The ragtop GTX disappeared after '69 and a mere 700 copies.

Following a mild '66 facelift, the big Furys received crisp new lower-body sheetmetal that added inches to length and width. Wheelbases and engines stayed largely the same, with the big-block 440 option returning from '66 with 350/375 bhp. Fury's standard V-8 remained a 230-bhp 318; a brace of optional 383s offered 270/325 bhp. The 225 slant six continued as base power for all models.

Plymouth joined Ford and Chevy in the move up to medium-price territory with the 1966 Fury VIP, a hardtop coupe and sedan offering standard 318 V-8, vinyl top, richly appointed interior, and special badging for around $3100. VIP returned as a separate series for '67 with the same two body styles although the hardtop switched from notchback to that year's "Fast Top" styling, with a slanted backlight and very wide C-pillars that also showed up on a second Sport Fury hardtop. Pillarless Fury coupes offered the same choice of rooflines for 1968, when another mild facelift occurred.

If not exactly head-turners, late-'60s Furys gave away nothing in appearance to rival Fords and Chevys. The 1965-66 models wore conservative full-width grilles, stacked quad headlamps, minimal side decoration, and simple taillights. Sheetmetal was more sculptured for 1967-68—crisper yet somehow more

1966 Barracuda Formula S fastback hardtop coupe

1967 Barracuda hardtop coupe

1966 Valiant Signet four-door sedan

1967 Satellite Hemi hardtop coupe

1967 Valiant Signet four-door sedan

1967 VIP hardtop sedan

imposing than before.

For 1969, the big Plymouths adopted the smoother, more massive "fuselage styling" then in vogue at Chrysler. Beltlines were higher, which made windows shallower, and lower-body contours were more flowing and heavier-looking. Squarish fenderlines were links with the past, but headlamps reverted to horizontal pairs. Model offerings again stood pat, with non-wagon styles on an inch-longer 120-inch wheelbase. Plymouth's big ragtops were now fast-waning sellers. The Fury III saw only 4129 copies for '69, the Sport fury a mere 1579. The latter then disappeared, leaving the bench-seat job as Plymouth's last big convertible; only 1952 of the 1970 models were built.

The car that pulled Plymouth through its early-'60s troubles was Valiant, one of the Big Three's original 1960 compacts. The first design generation ran through 1962: ruggedly built Unibody cars with Exner styling marked by square grilles, pronounced "blade" fenderlines, and short decks adorned by dummy spare tires, all on a 106.5-inch wheelbase. A four-door sedan and wagon were initially offered in V100 and V200 trim for $2000-$2500—cheaper than Chevy's Corvair but quite a bit upstream of Ford's runaway-hit Falcon. A V100 two-door sedan and V200 hardtop coupe arrived for '61. With bucket seats and spiffy trim, the hardtop became 1962's Signet 200, perhaps the most-collectible early Valiant.

A strong point of most every Valiant ever built was its robust Slant Six, so named because the block canted right to permit lower hoodlines, though engineers also claimed certain manufacturing and operational benefits. The initial 170-cid version produced 101 bhp; a 1960-61 four-barrel option called "Hyper-Pack" raised that to 148 bhp. The larger 225 unit from the big Plymouths became optional from 1962.

Exner's departure left Elwood Engel to shape the '63 Valiant, which emerged as clean, rounded, and conventional, if a bit stodgy. Bolstered by appealing new Signet and V200 convertibles, Valiant picked up sales, rising from about 157,000 for '62 to over 225,000. The '64s sold even better, thanks in part to optional availability of the new 273 small-block V-8, which made these sprightly cars indeed.

After two facelift years, Valiant was completely redesigned for 1967, adopting a 108-inch wheelbase and four-square lines reminiscent of some midsize European sedans. Wagons were dropped—they hadn't been huge sellers anyway—as were hardtops and convertibles, leaving two- and four-door sedans in "100" and Signet trim. Yet despite this, and aggressive new Ford and Chevy competition, Valiant remained one of Detroit's most-popular compacts. Except for some interesting interim developments, the basic '67 design would persist through the final Valiants of 1976.

The reason Valiant lost its sporty models was the success of Chevy's Corvair Monza, which prompted Plymouth to refocus

1968 Satellite convertible coupe

1968 Barracuda Formula S hardtop coupe

1968 Sport Satellite hardtop coupe

1968 Sport Barracuda Formula S fastback coupe

1968 Barracuda Formula S hardtop coupe

its sights on the sporty-compact market. The result was Barracuda, launched in mid-1964 as a '65 model. This was not a direct reply to Ford's Mustang "ponycar," though some observers thought otherwise, as the two models appeared almost simultaneously. Actually, Barracuda was the existing Valiant with a new superstructure: a cleverly conceived fastback hardtop coupe with a huge compound-curve backlight and stubby trunklid. A fold-down back seat, then a novelty for Detroit, could be used to create a seven-foot-long cargo deck for hauling things like surfboards and hero sandwiches. Despite its obvious workaday origins, Barracuda offered a pleasing combination of sporty looks, good handling, utility, and room for four. Close to 65,000 were sold for model-year '65—far adrift of Mustang's near 681,000, but welcome added business all the same. And unlike Mustang, Barracuda didn't "cannibalize" sales from sister models.

Predictably, the 225 slant six was standard for the 1964-65 Barracuda, with the 180-bhp 273 V-8 optional. However, a high-performance 235-bhp 273 was also offered with a high-lift, high-overlap camshaft, domed pistons, solid lifters, dual-contact breaker points, unsilenced air cleaner, and a sweet-sounding, low-restriction exhaust system. With "Rallye Suspension" (heavy-duty front torsion bars and antisway bars, stiff rear leaf springs), "Firm-Ride" shocks, and a four-speed gearbox, the 235-bhp job could do 0-60 mph in eight seconds flat.

After a debatable '66 facelift featuring a squarish front (shared with Valiant) and two-piece eggcrate grille, Barracuda was handsomely redesigned for '67. Wheelbase was stretched two inches, overall length five inches, and a shapelier fastback (without the "glassback") was joined by a new convertible and notchback hardtop coupe (the latter with a rather odd, "kinked" rear roofline). A newly available four-barrel 383 with 280 bhp provided better straightline performance, but hurt handling by adding up to 300 extra pounds at the front. The 273 remained the best choice for all-around roadability. As for '66, a Formula S package was offered; it included heavy-duty suspension, tachometer, wide-oval tires, and special stripes and badges.

Happily, the '67 Barracudas continued without drastic change through 1969—except, of course, for the feds' new safety and emissions equipment then appearing on all Detroit cars. A vertical-bar grille insert and small round side-market lights identified the '68s; the '69s gained a checked insert, revamped taillights, and square side-markers. In both years, Plymouth fielded muscle-market "'Cuda" versions offering a choice of Chrysler's new 340 small-block with 275 bhp or the big-block 383 with 300 bhp for '68 and 330 bhp for '69.

Appearing for 1970 was a fully redesigned third-generation Barracuda that donated its basic structure to a new Dodge double, the Challenger. Against the 1967-69 Barracudas, the '70 was two inches lower, three inches wider, a tad shorter, much heavier, and somehow more conventional-looking. Wheelbase remained at 108 inches, but the new "widebody" design had plenty of room for every big-block V-8 in the Chrysler stable, up to and including the 426 Hemi and a new six-barrel 440 that was conservatively rated at 390 bhp. Those two were available with a special "shaker" hood, so-called because a functional scoop attached directly to the carb housing poked through the panel and could be seen a-shakin'. The trademark fastback was no more, but hardtop and convertible returned in three forms: base, performance-oriented 'Cuda, and luxury Gran Coupe (which in ragtop form was thus a Gran Coupe convertible).

Perhaps the most-interesting 1970 Barracuda was the racy, midyear AAR, named for and inspired by the Dan Gurney All-American Racers team cars that contested that year's Trans-Am series in Sports Car Club of America competition. Based on the 'Cuda 340 hardtop, the AAR was easily spotted by its bold body-

1969 GTX hardtop coupe

1970 'Cuda Hemi hardtop coupe

1969 Barracuda 383-S Sports fastback coupe

1970 AAR 'Cuda hardtop coupe

1970 Road Runner Superbird hardtop coupe

1970 Fury III hardtop sedan

1970 Valiant Duster 340 coupe

1970 Fury Gran Coupe two-door

side "strobe" stripes, wide tires, matte-black fiberglass hood with functional scoop, rear spoiler, and long exhaust trumpets peeking out from beneath the rocker panels. The last also made the thing unmistakable to the ear. A modified 340 V-8 carried an Edelbrock intake manifold mounting three two-barrel carbs, plus special heads and a fortified block and valvetrain. Heavy-duty suspension was also included. Planned production was 2800, but the final figure is estimated at no more than 1500.

Giving Valiant a lift for 1970 was a new semifastback pillared coupe called Duster, a pleasant little car of good quality that attracted more than 217,000 first-year sales. Several thousand sported a "Gold Duster" option package with gold accents on grille, body, and interior, plus bucket seats, whitewall tires, and special wheel covers. The Duster 340 was a racy derivation with a mechanical package similar to the 'Cuda 340's. Equipment ran to the 275-bhp small-block, three-speed floor-shift, front disc brakes, wide tires, and tuned suspension.

Among 1970 Plymouth intermediates was a startling newcomer: the Superbird. Part of the Road Runner series, it was an evolution of Dodge's 1969 Charger Daytona, with a similar hidden-headlamp "droop-snoot" and huge struts carrying a stabilizer wing high above the rear deck. The Superbird looked fast—and was: Racing versions recorded over 220 mph. Street models came with a four-barrel 440 and TorqueFlite automatic, but the 440 "Six Pak," 426 Street Hemi, and four-speed manual transmission were all optionally available. Dodge built some 500 Charger Daytonas to qualify it as "production" for NASCAR events; then the sanctioning body increased its minimum to 1500. That was no problem for Plymouth, which ended up building 1920 Superbirds.

The Superbird's greatest moment came at the 1970 Daytona 500, when Pete Hamilton romped home at an average speed of

1971 GTX hardtop coupe

1971 'Cuda 340 hardtop coupe

1971 Sport Fury hardtop coupe

1971 Road Runner 440+6 hardtop coupe

1971 Valiant Duster 340 coupe

1971 Valiant Scamp hardtop coupe

nearly 150 mph to best every Dodge and every Ford. Superbirds then went on to take 21 of Chrysler's 38 Grand National wins that year. But NASCAR changed the rules again for 1971, thus ending the Superbird's dominance on the high-speed ovals—and the car itself.

Full-size Plymouths got their own dose of extra performance for 1970. Most notable was the new Sport Fury GT, a hardtop coupe carrying a 350-bhp 440, heavy-duty suspension, and long-legged rear axle ratios (up to 2.76:1). Also new to the Sport Fury line was the S/23 hardtop. Its standard 230-bhp 318 wasn't in the GT's league, but you did get a tuned chassis and modest "strobe" body stripes. Other Sport Furys were upgraded to take over from the now-departed luxury VIP, and all versions now hid their headlamps within a big new loop bumper/grille worn by all full-size Plymouths. Arriving in February was a plush Gran Coupe pillared two-door boasting most every comfort and convenience feature in the book at $3833 without air conditioning or $4216 with A/C.

For two brief shining moments, 1971 and '74, Plymouth again finished its traditional third in industry production. But after that, it never ran higher than fourth. By decade's end Plymouth had sunk to ninth, even though 1979 was a very healthy Detroit year. By the early '80s, the make was all but invisible.

Several factors contributed to this sorry decline: more wrong products at wrong times, indifferent workmanship even on the few models that were well timed, dwindling public confidence in Chrysler Corporation generally, and decreased styling distinction with related Dodges. Plymouth also suffered from a growing dullness that stemmed from the '60s consolidation of Chrysler's five divisions into two (Dodge and Chrysler-Plymouth). Because this eliminated the need to put all nameplates on all major platforms, glamour assignments like Cordoba went to Chrysler while Dodge increasingly got sportier models all to itself. By 1978, Plymouth was back to peddling basic family transportation—just as it had started out doing 50 years before.

Yet few could have foreseen this diminished role in 1970, when Plymouth countered Ford and Chevy with five separate car lines spanning 44 individual models and about 70 basic variations (counting trim levels and engines). Valiant, the lone survivor of the original Big Three compacts, dominated its market right on through swan-song '76. A key factor was the Duster coupe, which chalked up well over a quarter-million sales for 1974 alone. It was conventional but cute and well-engineered, and at least as well-built as comparable GM and Ford products.

Plymouth kept Duster desirable with a stream of extra-cost packages. The 1971-74 "Twister" option included matte-black hood, Duster 340-type black grille, bodyside tape stripes, and Rallye wheels. The Gold Duster continued through 1975 with a color-keyed pebble-grain vinyl roof. The "Space Duster" of 1973-74 was Plymouth's equivalent of Dodge's Dart Sport "Convertriple," with a wagon-style fold-down rear seatback that gave a 6½-foot-long carpeted cargo deck. (Shades of the original Barracuda.) Even at the end of the line there was a special "Silver Duster" (a handsome combination of silver, red, and black) as well as a "Feather Duster." The latter, a reply to Ford's "MPG" models, had an economy-tuned 225 Slant Six with aluminum intake manifold, and aluminum instead of steel inner panels for hood and decklid. With a manual-overdrive gearbox, which had an aluminum case, the Feather Duster was surprisingly frugal; a prudent driver could nurse one up to 30 mpg.

Further bolstering the Valiant line were the performance-oriented V-8 Duster 340 (through '73) and 360 (1974-75); the 1974-76 Brougham luxury option for sedans and two-door hardtops, offering opulence not usually found in compacts; and the Scamp hardtop, which was new for 1971. Altogether, Valiant and Dodge's similar Dart were impressive sellers right to the

1972 Barracuda 'Cuda 340 hardtop coupe

1973 Road Runner coupe with metal sunroof

1972 Satellite Sebring Plus hardtop coupe

1973 Barracuda hardtop coupe

1972 Gran Fury hardtop coupe

1973 Road Runner coupe

end. In some years Valiant gave Chrysler the compact lead over Ford and Chevy.

Unveiled for mid-'76 was Volare, a more upscale Plymouth compact that replaced Valiant entirely the following year. Though only a bit larger outside, Volare (and its Dodge Aspen cousin) had been designed for maximum interior space, which was quite good for the day. Workmanship, however, was anything but good. Still, this very real problem didn't harm sales right away, mainly because it didn't surface for a few years. Trim levels comprised base, mid-range Custom, and high-line Premier; the last offering unexpected luxury for around $4500. Volare also came as a five-door wagon in addition to the expected coupe and sedan—Plymouth's first compact wagon since 1966.

The Volare was right on target, racking up almost 400,000 sales for '77. Most examples had a 225 Slant Six or 318 V-8, both able veterans of some two decades. Though no trend-setter, Volare appealed mainly for its restrained styling and a decent performance/economy compromise.

Compacts were Plymouth's only real success in the '70s; its intermediates and full-size cars fared poorly. So, too, did the Barracuda, which was of no significance in the steadily declining ponycar market. The all-new 1970 design was warmed over for '71, gaining quad headlamps and a none-too-pretty Vee'd grille with vertical slats. A low-priced pillared hardtop replaced the convertible Gran Coupe and promptly took the lion's share of drastically reduced sales. Convertibles and big-block power were scrubbed for '72, leaving standard and 'Cuda V-8 coupes. These carried on for two more seasons before Plymouth gave up. Low production has thrust 'Cudas and Gran Coupes into the collector limelight—especially convertibles. The '71 droptop 'Cuda saw just 374 copies, and the standard convertible was almost as rare at 1014.

Midsize Plymouths consolidated under the Satellite name for 1971 and were completely revamped, shedding their relatively square 1968-70 look for more radically sculptured sheetmetal and large loop bumper/grilles. In line with a Detroit trend, coupes rode a shorter wheelbase than sedans and wagons (115 vs. 117 inches). Convertibles vanished here too, but Road Runner and GTX were still around, and there was a smart new sports-luxury hardtop called Sebring Plus.

Unfortunately, these Plymouths suffered the same fate as most '70s intermediates, becoming ever-more ponderous, thirsty, and ugly. The GTX was dumped after '71 for lack of sales, and the Road Runner, still ostensibly a separate model, wasn't nearly as fast on its feet as before. An attempt to regroup for 1975 brought the "small Fury," basically the existing platform with squared-up outer sheetmetal and a new name, but sales continued to languish. The last of these cars rolled out the door in 1978.

The big full-size Furys vanished after 1977, but for 1971-73

1973 Gran Fury hardtop coupe

1973 Satellite Sebring Plus hardtop coupe

1974 Barracuda hardtop coupe

1974 Gran Fury hardtop sedan

1974 Valiant four-door sedan

they were restyled continuations of the 1969-70 "fuselage" body/chassis design. They retained the same four-series lineup of Sport Fury and three lower trim levels designated by Roman numerals. Plymouth began whittling away at this group for '72, with Gran Fury taking over at the top and economy Fury I offerings cut from four to one. Meanwhile, Chrysler Corporation was preparing a brand-new design for all its full-size cars, scheduled well in advance of the brewing Middle East oil crisis.

Nevertheless, the hulkier new 1974 Fury (and the corresponding Dodge Monaco and Chrysler Newport/New Yorker) seemed incredibly ill-timed. They were not only heavier, but looked it: square and undistinguished on wheelbases stretched two inches. A Slant Six was available in some models, but made them grossly underpowered. V-8s were the now-usual assortment of 318, 360, midrange 400, and big-block 440. Significantly, sales didn't improve even after gas supplies eased and big-car sales began recovering.

After 1974, the full-size Fury was called Gran Fury to avoid confusion with Plymouth's renamed '75 intermediate Furys. But somehow, Chrysler never seemed to understand that badge shifting seldom (if ever) makes any difference in sales. It sure didn't here. Except for the midrange Custom sedan, not a single Gran Fury model scored more than 10,000 sales for 1976, and production of some Brougham and wagon models was laughably low for a traditional high-volume make.

Hoping to cut such losses, Plymouth trimmed big-car offerings for '76 and again for '77—mainly hardtop sedans and some trim variations. But the losses continued, and Plymouth temporarily fled the full-size field. It halfheartedly returned for 1980 with a bargain-basement version of the pseudo-downsized R-body Chrysler Newport, again bearing the Gran Fury name and intended mainly for the fleet market. But sales, at less than 19,000 for the model year, were disappointing.

The shape of Plymouth's future arrived with the all-new 1978 Horizon, a five-door subcompact sedan whose 99.2-inch wheelbase made it the smallest Plymouth in history. It was virtually identical to Dodge's Omni except for grille insert, taillights, and badges, and thus shared distinction as America's first domestically built front-drive small car.

Horizon sold briskly from the start despite later ill-founded charges that handling wasn't all it should be. In fact, roadability was one of Horizon's strengths. So was fine economy, courtesy of a 70-bhp, Volkswagen-based 104.7-cid four-cylinder engine. Another plus was the practical, space-efficient hatchback body. A sleek 2+2 "fasthatch" coupe called TC3, riding a 96.7-inch wheelbase, added some spice to the line for '79.

But by that point, Plymouth was a mere shadow of its former self, down to just Horizons, TC3s, and Volares. Management tried fostering the illusion that this was still a "full-line" make by slapping Plymouth nameplates on various "captive imports" from Mitsubishi of Japan. These included the little Arrow hatch-back coupe (1976-80), the larger and more luxurious notchback Sapporo (1978-82, sold with a Dodge double reviving the Challenger name), and the front-drive Champ economy hatchback (new for '79 and duplicated as the Dodge Colt). The badging was a good marketing move, providing vital sales support at a crucial time, but it only underscored how low once-prominent Plymouth had fallen.

Though more salable new domestic products soon appeared, Plymouth's record in the '80s was pretty sorry for what used to be Detroit's perennial number-three. After moving slightly more than 500,000 American-made cars for 1977 and again for '78, Plymouth wouldn't exceed 400,000 in any one year through 1986—and was well below 300,000 for 1980, '82, and '83.

Though having fewer domestic models was a definite sales handicap, Plymouth's also-ran status in the '80s stemmed as

1975 Gran Fury Brougham coupe

1976 Volare Premier four-door sedan

1975 Valiant Duster 360 coupe

1977 Gran Fury Brougham coupe

1975 Sport Fury hardtop coupe

1978 Volare Road Runner coupe

1976 Gran Fury Brougham four-door sedan

1978 Horizon hatchback with Premium Woodgrain package

much from a conscious decision to change its role within the corporate lineup. Planners decreed that Chrysler would cater to luxury buyers, per tradition, while Dodge would again go after the performance crowd. This left Plymouth with nothing to emphasize except reliable value-for-money cars that duplicated Dodges but were less interesting and fewer in number.

The Plymouth product story in the '80s is thus basically the same as for the duller Dodges. And a short one it is, too, because the make missed out on reborn convertibles, luxury models, and a latterday ponycar like the front-drive Dodge Daytona. With that, most Plymouth sales came from just two model lines: the L-body Horizon and derivative TC3 coupe (retitled Turismo for 1983-87), and the seminal K-body Reliant, which ousted Volare as the division's compact for 1981. In yearly styling and engineering changes they parallel Dodge's near-identical Omni/Charger and Aries, respectively, except for minor trim and, in line with Plymouth's solid-citizen role, no Shelby-tuned subcompacts.

In most years, Reliant earned honors as Chrysler's single best-selling model line. Wagons departed after 1989, but coupes and sedans finished out Reliant's run as value-equipped "America" models priced at $7595. Plymouth's Horizon also outsold Dodge's Omni, though not by much, averaging 150,000 per year except for about 90,000 managed for 1982-83.

1978 Fury Salon four-door sedan

1978 Horizon TC3 2+2 hatchback coupe

1981 Reliant Special Edition two-door sedan

1981 Gran Fury four-door sedan

1982 Turismo TC3 hatchback coupe

Badge-engineering gave the make token representation in the full-size and intermediate ranks. For the former, Plymouth was doled a "downsized" 1982 Gran Fury, a near-twin of the 112.7-inch-wheelbase M-body Dodge Diplomat to replace the slow-selling 118.5-inch-wheelbase Gran Fury of 1980-81. This sputtered along as a four-door sedan with few interim changes through swan-song 1989. Engines were the expected Slant Six and 318 V-8 (V-8 only after '83), and trim levels were restricted to only one or two. Of course, this was nothing like previous Gran Furys, being the original Aspen/Volare compact as evolved through the midsize 1977 Diplomat/Chrysler LeBaron. Most sold to police and taxi fleets, where the M-body's aging but proven rear-drive design was an asset.

Canadians were offered an M-body Plymouth before 1982 as the Caravelle. For '85, this name came to the U.S. on a restyled, downpriced version of what had been the Chrysler E-Class. All but a copy of Dodge's 103.3-inch-wheelbase 600 four-door sedan, this front-drive Caravelle was nominally Plymouth's midsize family car, and sold in plain and uplevel SE trim at a respectable 35,000-45,000 a year until its 1988 retirement when sales dropped to 17,000. Unlike Dodge with the 600 ES, Plymouth was not allowed a more sporty model or even a five-speed transaxle, but for a time the 146-bhp turbocharged edition of Chrysler's 2.2-liter (135-cid) "Trans-4" engine was optional. Most Caravelles had either a 2.6-liter (156-cid) Mitsubishi four with a balance shaft or, after debut-model 1985, the 2.5-liter (153-cid) enlargement of Chrysler's 2.2. All carried TorqueFlite automatic.

Like Dodge, Plymouth's other big winner in this decade was the practical K-based T-115 minivan, new for '84. The name here was Voyager (retained from Dodge-clone big-Plymouth vans of the '70s), but that and a different grille were about all that separated it from Dodge's Caravan. Added to the K-cars' success, the fast-selling minivans were a big reason why Chrysler Corporation enjoyed record profits by middecade, a mere five years after nearly tumbling into the financial abyss. Because the industry counts minivans as trucks rather than cars, Voyagers don't figure in the Plymouth production totals cited here.

Plymouth got in on the new-for-'87 P-body, the more upscale subcompact originally intended to replace Omni/Horizon. That replacement didn't happen immediately, though, as strong demand for the high-value "America" models announced for 1987 prompted Chrysler to keep the L-bodies through 1990. A surprising number of changes occurred that final year: new dash, standard driver-side air bag, and no America tag. Identically priced at $6995 for 1990, the Omni/Horizon went out as outstanding value for the money.

Plymouth's name for the erstwhile successor P-body was Sundance (recalling an early-'70s Satellite trim option). Though predictably all but identical to Dodge's Shadow, Sundance aimed more at luxury-minded small-car shoppers, offering three- and five-door notchback sedans with only one well-equipped trim level and a suspension tuned more for ride than handling.

But Highland Park hadn't entirely forgotten Plymouth's performance past, because the 1988 Sundance offered a new RS package option with sportier appointments that included integral fog lamps, two-tone paint, wider tires on racier wheels, special bucket seats, and leather-rim steering wheel. An optional 2.2-liter port-injected turbo-four with 146 bhp backed up this brag, then gave way to a blown 150-bhp 2.5 the next year. Also available through 1990 were standard 93-bhp 2.2 and optional 96-bhp 2.5, both normally aspirated engines with electronic throttle-body injection. All could be teamed with standard five-speed manual or optional TorqueFlite transaxles. A new face with flush headlamps cleaned up Sundance's 1989 appearance. The 1990s added a driver-side air bag in the steering-wheel hub as a worthy safety advance.

Like Shadow, Sundance generated nearly 76,000 sales in its first year. Production then settled at around the 80,000-100,000 unit level through 1990. This suggested that Chrysler could still reach small-car buyers, but not nearly as many per year as in Valiant days. Still, many things had changed, and Sundance was arguably just as right for its time and market.

That also applied to the new-for-'89 Acclaim. Like Sundance, this was conceived to replace an older Plymouth, the remarkable Reliant, but the K-car's continuing sales strength prompted corporate planners to let the new and the old run side-by-side that year, as Volare and Valiant did in '76. More immediately, Acclaim replaced Caravelle as Plymouth's midsize sedan. Riding the same wheelbase but sharing the latest corporate A-body with that year's new Dodge Spirit. There was still lots of Reliant in Acclaim styling, but the look was more contemporary: formal yet smooth, and carefully detailed for good aerodynamic efficiency.

Again, Plymouth marketed a shared package less aggressively than Dodge, announcing Acclaim in base, midrange LE, and luxury LX guises with few sporting touches. Engine choices were naturally the same: blown and unblown 2.5 fours and a new 3.0-liter (181-cid) Mitsubishi V-6 with 141 bhp. The last was reserved for LX and teamed only with Chrysler's first four-speed overdrive automatic transaxle, called Ultradrive. Of course, certain sporty features were available, including bucket seats and, for 1990, a Rallye Sport option with uprated chassis, enthusiast-oriented interior, and subtle exterior badging.

But this was only a nod to Plymouth's performance past, and fully 85 percent of Acclaim buyers opted for the workaday base model. That wasn't necessarily bad, of course. After all, Plymouth's value-for-money marketing emphasis stood to pay off big once the economy turned down again in 1990. But two domestic cars and a smattering of rebadged Japanese imports (still from Chrysler affiliate Mitsubishi) were no substitute for the full-range lineup Plymouth had lacked for so long, especially as none of its cars was really tops in class. As a result, Plymouth became an even weaker also-ran in the early '90s, finishing next to last in domestic model-year car sales through middecade. The low point came with 1993, when Plymouth moved some 141,300 domestic cars, after which volume picked up to just over 178,000 for '94. While the make's overall volume in this period wasn't exactly puny at between 365,000 and 424,000, more than half of each year's total came from Voyager minivans, making Plymouth more of a "truck" producer than a carmaker for the first time in its history.

It was just as well, for Plymouth might have died sooner without Voyager's consistently high yearly sales. At one point in late 1991, Chrysler was said to be on the verge of killing Plymouth so as to free up funds for its new upscale Eagle line, of which great things were expected (*see entry*). But where Eagle generated only a third to a sixth of Plymouth's volume (to run dead last in the industry race), Plymouth still accounted for no less than 40 percent of total company sales, thanks mainly to Voyager. On realizing that, management decided Plymouth deserved another chance and approved a heavy infusion of product and promotion money in an attempt to rejuvenate a name that had slipped in public awareness to somewhere between fuzzy and unknown. They even plumped for a nostalgic new Plymouth logo: a stylized sailing vessel reminiscent of the Good Ship *Mayflower* that would be in place by 1996.

Money was one thing, however, and mission quite another. Though any attention was welcome after some 20 years of not-so-benign neglect, Plymouth still had no place in the corporate

1981 Reliant Custom four-door sedan prototype

1982 Horizon Custom hatchback sedan

1982 Gran Fury four-door sedan

1982 Reliant Custom two-door sedan

1983 Turismo coupe

1984 Voyager Limited Edition minivan

1987 Grand Voyager LE minivan

1985 Caravelle four-door sedan

1987 Caravelle SE four-door sedan

1986 Turismo Duster hatchback coupe

1988 Sundance RS Turbo Liftback coupe

1986 Gran Fury sedan with Police Package

1989 Acclaim LX four-door sedan

1987 Horizon America hatchback sedan

1990 Acclaim LX four-door sedan

scheme except as a "value" brand with a limited selection of low-priced, largely low-profile cars. No surprise, then, that Plymouth continued in the '90s exactly as it had in the '80s, except that offerings declined to three with the complete elimination of imports after 1994. This reflected the decision (at the time) of a newly resurgent Chrysler to sever long-standing product and manufacturing ties with Mitsubishi. Among the casualties was arguably the most-interesting Plymouth of this era, the Laser sport coupe, a "badge-engineered" Mitsubishi Eclipse built in the same Illinois plant (as was an Eagle version, the Talon).

Voyager, meantime, kept doing land-office business, helped by the same thoughtful changes accorded Dodge's Caravan. Highlights began with a deft exterior makeover for 1991, which also introduced antilock brakes as a first-time extra, plus a revised dash and, with the optional 3.3-liter V-6, available all-wheel drive. A standard driver-side air bag was added as a '91 running change, followed by the industry's first integrated child safety seat as a 1992 option. For '94 came a standard passenger air bag in another revised dash, plus side-guard door beams and an optional 3.3 V-6 converted to run on compressed natural gas. Environmentalists loved it, even if a $1700 price severely tested their convictions. The basic '84-vintage Voyager then put in a final year. Though Plymouth still trailed Dodge in passenger minivan sales, Voyager volume remained significant after 1990 at well over 200,000 per model year.

By contrast, Acclaim and Sundance mostly withered in both sales and interest value, giving little evidence that Plymouth had ever offered anything so exciting as a Hemi 'Cuda or Superbird. With product plans now dictated by marketing goals and sales trends, Plymouth's midsize line was reduced for 1992 to a single base-trim sedan with an exhaustingly long list of option packages but only two engine choices: 100-bhp 2.5-liter four and 141-bhp 3.0-liter V-6. An eggcrate grille was the main visual change for '93, when an interesting "flex fuel" version of the four became optional. Sold only to fleets for '93 but available to retail customers for '94, this could run on any combination of gasoline or "M85" methanol (an 85-percent methanol/gasoline mix). Also for '94, Acclaim gained a motorized right-front-shoulder belt to meet that year's federal man-date for dual front "passive restraints." The A-body Plymouth then made a last stand with a shortened options list omitting automatic, ABS, and the flex-fuel engine. Production declined steadily after 1991's respectable 97,000-plus, finishing just above 12,000 for the token '95 model run.

Sundance was treated to a few more yearly changes than Acclaim, but not many. Predictably, most were shared with Dodge's Shadow. Sundance never got a convertible like its P-body sister, but it did add budget-priced three- and five-door America models for 1991. Though you could get one for as little as $7699, you had to make do with less sound insulation, fewer options, no cargo area carpeting, and just a 93-bhp version of the veteran 2.2-liter inline four. For '92, Sundance dropped its sporty RS option in favor of a new confection reviving the Duster name from Valiant days. Available for both body styles at about $2100 above base-trim spec, this package delivered sporty paint, applied tape graphics, a slightly firmer suspension, cast aluminum wheels, more aggressive standard tires, and—the big attraction—the same 3.0-liter V-6 available in Acclaim. Ordering the Duster also opened up a new optional transmission: the first four-speed automatic available in a Chrysler subcompact. Though 141 bhp implied a certain speediness, this Duster was no whirlwind, but it was pleasantly swifter than any four-banger Sundance save the rough and raucous turbo models.

Duster stayed on for '93, but America and Highline trim dis-

1990 Horizon hatchback sedan

1991 Acclaim LX four-door sedan

1991 Sundance America hatchback coupe

1992 Grand Voyager LE minivan

1992 Acclaim four-door sedan

1992 Sundance America hatchback coupe

1992 Laser RS Turbo AWD hatchback coupe

1992 Acclaim four-door sedan

1993 Acclaim four-door sedan

1994 Grand Voyager LE minivan

1994 Sundance Duster hatchback coupe

1995 Neon coupe

appeared in favor of a single price level equipped with elements of both. Antilock brakes were newly optional, a laudable addition. Like Acclaim, Sundance added a right front "mouse-belt" to meet 1994's requirement for dual passive restraints, but five-doors exited in January, leaving three-doors to finish out the last model year. Considering its elderly K-car origins and lack of real pizzazz, Sundance sold quite well in this period, falling no further than 62,800 for model-year '91 and hitting nearly 86,000 for '93.

The reason Sundance lost its five-door models early was the advent of a much better small Plymouth, the Neon. Of course, it was all but identical with the 1995 Dodge Neon that arrived at the same time, so everything said about that version applies to this one—save for badges done in Plymouth blue instead of Dodge red. As with minivans, Plymouth's Neon didn't sell quite as well as Dodge's, yet C-P dealers moved some 121,400 Neons for the '95 season. This was strong public acceptance recalling that of Plymouth's first front-drive car, the 1978-79 Horizon, yet Neon was far superior, offering spunky performance, taut handling, and surprising interior room thanks to scaled-down "cab-forward" styling that managed to be winsomely cute. Low prices also spurred sales: under $10,000 to start. About all that needed fixing were undue engine and road noise, patchy workmanship, and obviously low-buck interior materials. Overall, though, Neon represented impressive value, and competitors lost sleep trying to figure out how Chrysler could deliver so much small car for the money. Even vaunted Toyota was moved to take one apart to learn its secrets.

Speaking of cab-forward, Plymouth was denied the car that pioneered the look, Chrysler's full-size LH sedan of 1993—and more's the pity. One suspects a new LH-based "Fury" would have sold well. But Plymouth was always in the loop for the new midsize JA platform, even if its 1996 Breeze was a year behind the similar Chrysler Cirrus and Dodge Stratus.

Per Plymouth's ongoing mission, Breeze was the cheapest of the JA trio, appealingly base-priced at $14,060, about $300 below the last Acclaim. Though inevitably less lavish than its sister "cloud cars," Breeze was no stripper, boasting standard dual air bags, air conditioning, AM/FM stereo radio, tilt steering wheel, tinted glass, and fold-down back seat. An eggcrate grille echoed Acclaim, but attached to a much slicker cab-forward sedan body on a rangy 108-inch wheelbase that again made for relatively generous passenger and cargo space. As the most-affordable JA, Breeze offered the fewest options, though the list included important items like antilock brakes; integrated child safety seat; and power windows, mirrors, and door locks.

Price reasons also dictated but one engine: the new 2.0-liter overhead-cam inline four designed and built by Chrysler for the Neon. Though its 132 bhp promised slow going in the larger, heavier JA, the Breeze proved surprisingly able, running 0-60 in 10 seconds with standard five-speed manual and about 11.5 with optional four-speed automatic—decent if not exactly, er, breezy. Even nicer perhaps, *Consumer Guide*® found this Plymouth a very tight and solid car by any standard, a real revelation for a low-priced Detroiter. And, of course, Breeze was no less fun to drive than a Cirrus or Stratus, inheriting their crisp, responsive front-drive handling; stable, well-planted wide-stance cornering poise; precise power steering; and delightfully "tossable" feel.

For 1998, Chrysler's well-known 2.4-liter four with 150 bhp became optional for Breeze. Automatic was mandatory, so the bigger engine delivered little more zip than the smaller one with manual, but it did reduce driver stress in the daily grind and used little more gas. Any Breeze was more comfortable for '99, thanks to softer damping providing a more absorbent ride.

Together with Neon and an all-new crop of nicely redesigned 1996 Voyagers, the Breeze gave reason to be optimistic about Plymouth's future. So did Chrysler's stated commitment to the make, symbolized by a handsome new "Mayflower" logo. Marketing efforts were stepped up to "reintroduce" Plymouth to those who still remembered, while hammering home the "high value" message to younger folks who didn't. One of the more novel initiatives involved setting up computerized "Plymouth Place" kiosks in selected major shopping malls, where prospective buyers could learn about the various models and even price one to order without fear of being set upon by some salesperson. Chrysler also staked out some cyberspace for Plymouth on the burgeoning Internet, and returned to forceful advertising of more conventional kinds with the slogan "One clever idea after another."

For sheer impact, though, nothing could match the 1997 Prowler, the most-exciting Plymouth in a generation. It was unlike anything ever offered by a mainstream automaker, being a modern reincarnation of the iconic American hot rod. Like the Dodge Viper before it, Prowler began as a concept, premiering at the 1993 Detroit Auto Show amid rabid pleas to "Build it!" Once more, Chrysler president Bob Lutz gave his full endorsement to a fairly outrageous automobile aimed squarely at car buffs like himself. Again sharing his enthusiasm were design chief Tom Gale, long an active hot rod hobbyist, and Advanced Design director Neil Walling, who oversaw the concept's development from an idea suggested by a staffer at the company's California design outpost, Chrysler Pacifica. Though hardly the sort of car expected of a "value brand," Prowler promised to do for Plymouth what Viper had for Dodge—namely, get people talking and change their minds. Indeed, Chrysler viewed its two-seat retro roadster has having just the right "shock value" for resuscitating Plymouth's moribund image and low "brand awareness" among consumers.

There was high-tech seriousness beneath the hot-rod fun, as Prowler became Chrysler's low-volume laboratory for nontraditional construction and materials. For example, aluminum was used not only for an all-independent suspension but the entire chassis and much of the body. In fact, Prowler packed more aluminum than any car in Chrysler history—some 900 pounds of it—construction rivaled only by the exotic Honda-built Acura NSX sports car. The result was a lean machine with about the same length as a Porsche 911 but weighing well under 2900 pounds. Other weight-watching measures included a lateral dashboard brace made of costly magnesium, the industry's first cast aluminum brake rotors (rear only; front discs were iron Voyager parts), and plasticlike sheet molding to shape the quarter panels, vintage cycle-type front fenders, and a pointy nose skimming just 4.5 inches above the pavement.

Helped by a raked-forward profile and broad 76.5-inch beam, the Prowler turned heads like nothing else on the street. The only changes from the stunning concept were more prominent front "bumperettes" and headlights, both to satisfy the feds. Wheels were handsome five-spoke alloys measuring 17×7.5 inches fore and a massive 20×10 aft, and you could have any color at first so long as it was vivid Prowler Purple. The manual top, a black fabric affair, stowed easily beneath a rear-hinged trunklid—and most always was. Prowler, after all, was about lookin' good. There was no room for introverts.

Or much of anything else. The front-tapering '30s-style body left footwells uncomfortably narrow (though wider than on the concept). Standard run-flat tires eliminated the need for a spare, but the trunk was nearly useless, squeezed from below by the fuel tank (itself laughably small at 12 gallons) and a rear transaxle, also new for Chrysler. The latter contributed to front/rear weight distribution of 45/55 percent, making Prowler quite nimble on dry roads despite a long 113-inch wheelbase. And for times when you had to carry more than a couple of pizzas, Chrysler offered a small accessory trailer, shaped like the tail, for about five-grand. But the fat tires with their ultrastiff sidewalls "find every bump," as *Car and Driver* noted, and could be way too slippery in the rain. And like Viper, antilock brakes and traction control weren't available, yet a number of luxuries were standard: air conditioning, power windows and mirrors, leather upholstery, high-power sound system, even a gee-whiz tire-pressure monitor.

Hot-rod purists also shook their heads at Prowler's powertrain: a 3.5-liter V-6 sending a modest 214 bhp through a four-speed automatic transmission. Like much of the interior, these were off-the- shelf components used to keep price reasonable,

1997 Prowler roadster

1998 Neon Expresso four-door sedan

which it was at an initial $38,300. Yet despite that, the lowish weight and standard AutoStick manual-shift feature, Prowler was nowhere near as fast as it looked. *Car and Driver*'s results were typical: 0-60 in 7 seconds flat, a standing quarter-mile of 15.6 at 87 mph—pretty tame.

Overall, *C/D* viewed Prowler as "awash in contradictions. Hot rods have V-8s and manual gearboxes. The Prowler offers neither. Hot rods are supposed to ride badly and handle badly, then set fire to the dragstrip. Instead, the Prowler handles almost like a sports car but is a relative flatliner on the dragstrip. Hot rods are supposed to have individualized exteriors ... [not] one level of trim. Hot rods customarily sport spartan, handmade interiors. The Prowler's is more plush and option laden than a BMW Z3's." On the other hand, "It's a convertible, the drivetrain is dead reliable, it can be driven [every day] as long as there's no snow, there's a three-year/36,000-mile warranty, and the vehicle regularly twists the needle right off... the gawk meter."

Predictably, Chrysler's latest piece of eye candy was always in short supply. Though the long wait from concept to reality stoked demand to a fever pitch, Chrysler wouldn't rush. After all, Prowler was Plymouth's important new image-leader, and thus needed to be well-made and glitch-free from day one. Besides, why risk diluting the car's mystique—and driving down resale values—by building too many too fast? All this echoed Viper experience, and Chrysler sensibly assigned Prowler production to the Viper plant on Detroit's Conner Avenue, which was geared to build semicustom machines at a measured pace with considerable hand labor. As it happened, though, Prowlers didn't begin reaching dealers until August 1997, delayed by last-minute production glitches. As a result, model-year output was only 312 units instead of the 2000-3000 planned, and a bidding war broke out among would-be owners.

Prowler skipped model-year '98 for an early start on 1999. Red, black, and a vibrant yellow expanded the color palette, but the big news was an aluminum-block version of the single-cam 3.5 V-6. Horsepower swelled by 39 to 253, peaking at 6400 rpm instead of 5850. Torque rose by a useful 34 pound-feet to 255, and maxed out at more accessible 3100 rpm (versus 3950). *Car and Driver* lopped a second off the 0-60 dash and timed quarter-mile acceleration at 14.7 seconds at 90 mph. Other magazine tests showed less-dramatic improvements, but the '99 was stronger by most accounts. And though the traditional hot-rod exhaust burble was still missing, so were some of the '97 model's unwanted cowl shake and body quivering. Base price went up $1000, but nobody complained.

Yet for all its high-profile pizzazz, Prowler did nothing to spur sales of workaday Plymouths, and that spelled trouble once Germany's Daimler-Benz absorbed Chrysler Corporation in late 1998. The new DaimlerBenz was troubled from the start, and the mostly German top brass were far more concerned with "shareholder value" than any value Plymouth might have for their American "division." Thus, in late October 1999, after months of mounting rumors, DC's American-born president, James Holden, announced that Plymouth would be terminated after model-year 2001 as irrelevant to the company's new "global growth strategy." It was a sad day for many car lovers, but industry analysts (and even Chrysler-Plymouth dealers) weren't surprised. After all, Prowler was only the first Plymouth since the '69 Barracuda with no direct Dodge duplicate, and Dodge always did better with shared products.

But *C/D*'s Pat Bedard, himself a former Chrysler engineer, begged to differ. In a March 2000 epitaph, he noted that Plymouth sales might still be sliding, but were "hardly dead... Voyager sales not only outnumbered Plymouth cars in 1998, they outgunned the combined minivan efforts of the Chevrolet Venture and Pontiac Montana... There's something odd, too, about DC's notion of global growth. Yeah, Plymouth is only a U.S. brand. So what?... Low-priced brands always slump when people have the dough to buy higher on the status ladder. [When they don't], a trusted budget brand makes a great lifeboat [for an automaker]. Building a fresh one, as GM did with Saturn, costs billions... I think DaimlerChrysler is walking away from sales."

Maybe so, but losing Plymouth was easy for DC, and customers could be steered to other company brands. With that, Breeze was dropped with the 2001 redesign of its Dodge and Chrysler siblings (which would then presumably take up the slack), and rebadging created Chrysler Voyagers even before the company's new minivans arrived, also for '01. The second-generation 2000 Neon was sold as Plymouth, but only for about 18 months and without the sporty options Dodge offered.

Prowler, too, became a Chrysler, swapping nameplates during model-year 2001, but hung on through '02. The 2000 edition got revised damping and adjustable shock absorbers for a more pliant ride, plus a few minor feature additions. Otherwise, only colors were changed.

Left behind in Plymouth's demise was the intriguing Howler concept. Basically a Prowler with a handsome new squared-off tail, it offered usable luggage space at last, achieved by exchanging the rear transaxle for a conventional front-mounted transmission. Even better, though, that gearbox was a five-speed manual bolted to a V-8, a torquey 250 4.7-liter borrowed from the Jeep Grand Cherokee. Enthusiasts cheered, but there was no hope for Howler, a strictly what-if dream unveiled only weeks before Plymouth's announced execution.

Plymouth wasn't Detroit's only historic nameplate to be killed off by new-century corporate tactics. General Motors' Oldsmobile went to the gallows barely a year later. But there's an ironic footnote in that the 2001 PT Cruiser was once planned for Plymouth, as product chief Tom Gale told us. Considering its huge sales success as a low-priced Chrysler, the versatile, "way-cool" Cruiser could have been just the comeback car Plymouth needed, setting the stage for more Plymouth-only models and a true revival of the make. A pity Chrysler walked away from that, too.

2000 Breeze four-door sedan

2001 Prowler Black Tie Edition roadster

Specifications

1930

Model U (wb 109.0)	Wght	Price	Prod*
rdstr 2-4P	2,265	610	—
phaeton 5P	2,355	625	—
cpe 2P	2,380	590	—
Deluxe cpe 2-4P	2,415	625	—
sdn 2d	2,475	610	—
sdn 4d	2,555	625	—
Deluxe sdn 4d	2,590	675	—

Model 30U (wb 109.0)	Wght	Price	Prod*
spt rdstr 2-4P	2,280	610	—
phaeton 5P	2,340	625	—
cpe 2P	2,420	590	—
cpe 2-4P	2,510	625	—
sdn 4d	2,595	625	—
Deluxe sdn 4d	2,590	745	—
conv cpe 2-4P	2,450	695	—
chassis	—	—	—

1930 Engines	bore×stroke	bhp	availability
I-4, 175.4	3.63×4.25	45	S-Model U
I-4, 196.0	3.63×4.75	48	S-Model 30U

* 1930 model-year production was confused by the overlapping of the Model U into 1929 and the Model 30U into 1931.

For the Model U, no serial number spans are recorded for 1929 or 1930, but 1929 calendar-year production was 93,592, and total 1929-30 Model U production was 108,350.

For the 1930-31 Model 30U, total production was 76,950. The 1930-model 30U carried serial numbers 1500001 to 1530244 (30,244 cars), while 1931 models carried serial numbers 1530245 to 1570300 (40,055 cars). This does not add up to the 76,950 total figure, but may serve to provide an approximate breakdown between the two model years. Individual factory production figures for Model 30U body styles are given under 1931. Note that the business roadster and both two-door sedans were not offered during model year 1930.

1931

Model 30U (wb 109.0)	Wght	Price	Prod
bus rdstr 2P	2,245	535	1,609
sdn 2d	2,497	565	7,980
commercial sdn 2d	2,450	750	80
spt rdstr 2-4P	2,280	610	2,884*
spt phaeton 5P	2,340	625	632*
cpe 2P	2,420	565	9,189*
cpe 2-4P	2,510	625	5,850*
sdn 4d	2,595	625	47,152*
conv cpe 2-4P	2,450	695	1,272*
chassis	—	—	302*

* Comb. prod. for 1930-31 models. For approx. breakdown, take 57 percent of total shown for 1931, 43 percent for 1930. See also prod. notes under 1930.

1931 Engine	bore×stroke	bhp	availability
I-4, 196.0	3.63×4.75	48	S-all

1932

Model PA (wb 109.0) blt 5/31-2/32	Wght	Price	Prod
bus rdstr 2P	2,440	535	2,000
spt rdstr 2-4P	2,470	595	2,680
spt phaeton 5P	2,545	595	528
cpe 2P	2,600	565	1,279
cpe 2-4P	2,645	610	9,696
conv cpe 2-4P	2,615	645	2,783
sdn 2d	2,650	575	23,038
sdn 4d	2,730	635	49,465
Deluxe sdn 4d	2,795	690	4,384
Thrift sdn 2d	2,690	495	*
Thrift sdn 4d	2,745	575	*
chassis and taxicabs	—	—	243

Model PB (wb 112.0; lwb-121.0) built 2/32-9/32	Wght	Price	Prod
bus rdstr 2P	2,550	495	3,225
spt rdstr 2-4P	2,600	595	2,163
spt phaeton 5P	2,660	595	259
cpe 2P	2,700	565	11,126
cpe 2-4P	2,755	610	8,159
conv cpe 2-4P	2,735	645	4,853
sdn 2d	2,830	575	13,031
sdn 4d	2,875	635	38,066
conv sdn 5P	2,925	785	690
lwb sdn 7P	3,075	725	2,179
chassis and taxicabs	—	—	159

* Production included with 2d and 4d sedans. Total production of Thrift models was 4,894.

1932 Engines	bore×stroke	bhp	availability
I-4, 196.1	3.63×4.75	56	S-PA
I-4, 196.1	3.63×4.75	65	S-PB

1933

PC Six (wb 107.0)	Wght	Price	Prod
cpe 2P	2,418	495	10,853
cpe 2-4P	2,473	525	8,894
conv cpe 2-4P	2,483	565	2,034
sdn 2d	2,498	505	4,008
sdn 4d	2,553	545	33,815
chassis	—	—	396

PCXX Standard Six (wb 108.0)	Wght	Price	Prod
bus cpe 2P	2,353	445	9,200
cpe 2-4P	2,423	485	2,497
sdn 2d	2,443	464	17,736
sdn 4d	2,523	510	13,661
chassis	—	—	309

PD DeLuxe Six (wb 112.0)	Wght	Price	Prod
cpe 2P	2,485	495	30,728
cpe 2-4P	2,545	545	20,821
conv cpe 2-4P	2,530	595	4,596
sdn 2d	2,560	525	49,826
sdn 4d	2,645	575	88,404
chassis	—	—	779

1933 Engines	bore×stroke	bhp	availability
I-6, 189.8	3.13×4.14	70	S-PC
I-6, 189.8	3.13×4.14	76	S-PCXX, PD

1934

PE DeLuxe (wb 114.0)	Wght	Price	Prod
bus cpe 2P	2,668	595	28,433
cpe 2-4P	2,733	630	15,658
conv cpe 2-4P	2,698	685	4,482
sdn 2d	2,773	610	58,535
sdn 4d	2,848	660	108,407
town sdn 4d 5P	2,898	695	7,049
sdn 7P	—	—	891
chassis	—	—	2,362

PF Standard (wb 108.0)	Wght	Price	Prod
bus cpe 2P	2,513	540	6,980
cpe 2-4P	2,573	570	2,061
sdn 2d	2,603	560	12,562
sdn 4d	2,693	600	16,789
chassis	—	—	1,152

PFXX Special (wb 108.0)	Wght	Price	Prod
bus cpe 2P	2,563	560	3,721
cpe 2-4P	2,608	590	1,746
sdn 2d	2,658	580	12,497
sdn 4d	2,708	620	16,760
town sdn 4d 5P	2,783	655	574

PG Standard (wb 108.0)	Wght	Price	Prod
bus cpe 2P	2,438	485	7,844
sdn 2d	2,538	510	12,603
sdn 4d	—	—	62
chassis	—	—	3

1934 Engines	bore×stroke	bhp	availability
I-6, 201.3	3.13×4.38	77	S-all
I-6, 201.3	3.13×4.38	82	O-all

1935

PJ Six (wb 113.0)	Wght	Price	Prod
bus cpe 2P	2,625	510	16,691
bus sdn 2d	2,670	535	29,942
bus sdn 4d	2,720	570	15,761
bus comm sdn 2d	2,735	635	1,142
cpe 2P	2,665	565	6,664
sdn 2d	2,685	615	7,284

PJ DeLuxe Six (wb 113.0; lwb-128.0)	Wght	Price	Prod
bus cpe 2P	2,675	575	29,190
cpe 2-4P	2,730	630	12,118
conv cpe 2-4P	2,830	695	2,308
sdn 2d	2,720	625	12,424
touring sdn 2d T/B	2,780	650	45,203
sdn 4d	2,790	660	66,083
touring sdn 4d T/B	2,815	685	82,068
Traveler lwb sdn 5P	—	895	77
lwb sdn 7P	3,130	895	350
Wstchstr Sub wgn 4d	—	765	119
chassis (lwb)	—	—	24

1935 Engine	bore×stroke	bhp	availability
I-6, 201.3	3.13×4.38	82	S-all

1936

P1 Business Ser (wb 113.0)	Wght	Price	Prod
cpe 2P	2,650	510	26,856
sdn 2d	2,720	545	39,516
sdn 4d	2,750	590	19,104
wgn 4d	2,920	765	309
commercial sdn 2d	—	605	3,527
touring sdn 4d T/B	—	—	1,544
touring sdn 2d T/B	—	—	768
chassis	—	—	1,211

P2 DeLuxe Series (wb 113.0; lwb-125.0)	Wght	Price	Prod
cpe 2P	2,705	580	54,601
cpe 2-4P	2,775	620	9,663
conv cpe 2-4P	2,830	725	3,297
sdn 2d	2,785	625	6,149
touring sdn 2d T/B	2,815	645	99,373
sdn 4d	2,820	660	10,001
touring sdn 4d T/B	2,850	680	240,136
tour sdn 7P T/B (lwb)	3,155	895	1,504
chassis	—	—	2,775

1936 Engines	bore×stroke	bhp	availability
I-6, 201.3	3.13×4.38	82	S-all
I-6, 201.3	3.13×4.38	65	O-all

1937

P3 Business Ser (wb 112.0)	Wght	Price	Prod
cpe 2P	2,771	580	18,202
cpe 2-4P	2,841	620	540
sdn 2d	2,841	620	28,685
touring sdn 2d T/B	2,871	640	1,350
sdn 4d	2,841	665	16,000
touring sdn 4d T/B	2,871	685	7,842
chassis	—	—	1,025

P4 DeLuxe Series (wb 112.0; lwb-132.0)	Wght	Price	Prod
cpe 2P	2,839	650	67,144
cpe 2-4P	2,884	700	6,877
conv cpe 2-4P	2,994	830	3,110
sdn 2d	2,899	715	7,926
touring sdn 2d T/B	2,914	725	111,099
sdn 4d	2,914	745	9,000
touring sdn 4d T/B	2,944	755	269,062
lwb sdn 7P	3,333	995	1,840
sdn limo 7P (lwb)	3,400	1,095	63
chassis and taxicabs	—	—	2,229

1937 Engines	bore×stroke	bhp	availability
I-6, 201.3	3.13×4.38	82	S-all
I-6, 201.3	3.13×4.38	65	O-all

1938

P5 Bus./Roadking* (wb 112.0)	Wght	Price	Prod
cpe 2P	2,739	645	15,932
sdn 2d	2,764	685	15,393
sdn 4d	2,809	730	6,459
touring sdn 2d T/B	2,779	701	16,413
touring sdn 4d T/B	2,824	746	18,664
cpe 2-4P	2,809	695	338
chassis	—	—	1,586

*Name changed to Roadking March 31, 1938, and touring sedans introduced.

P6 DeLx (wb 112.0; lwb-132.0)	Wght	Price	Prod
cpe 2P	2,804	730	27,181
cpe 2-4P	2,864	770	2,000
conv cpe 2-4P	3,009	850	1,900
sdn 2d	2,874	773	1,222
touring sdn 2d T/B	2,864	785	46,669
sdn 4d	2,894	803	1,446
touring sdn 4d T/B	2,874	815	119,669
Suburban wgn 4d 8P	3,039	880	555
lwb sdn 7P T/B	3,289	1,005	1,824
sdn limo 7P (lwb)	3,300	1,095	75
chassis and taxicabs	—	—	2,062

1938 Engines	bore×stroke	bhp	availability
I-6, 201.3	3.13×4.38	82	S-all
I-6, 201.3	3.13×4.38	65	O-all
I-6, 201.3	3.13×4.38	86	O-all

1939

P7 Roadking (wb 114.0)	Wght	Price	Prod
cpe 2P	2,724	645	22,537
cpe 2-4P	2,784	695	222
sdn 2d	2,824	685	7,499
touring sdn 2d T/B	2,824	699	42,186
sdn 4d	2,839	726	2,553
touring sdn 4d T/B	2,829	740	23,047
util sdn 2d	2,844	685	341
commercial sdn	—	—	2,270
Suburban wgn 4d	—	—	97
chassis	—	—	1,616

P8 DeLuxe (wb 114.0; conv sdn-117.0; lwb-134.0)	Wght	Price	Prod
cpe 2P	2,789	725	41,924
cpe 2-4P	2,874	755	1,322
conv cpe 2-4P	3,044	895	5,976
sdn 2d	2,889	761	2,653
touring sdn 2d T/B	2,894	775	80,981
sdn 4d	2,909	791	2,279
touring sdn 4d T/B	2,919	885	175,054
conv sdn 4d	3,209	1,150	387
Sub wgn 4d 8P (curtains)	3,089	930	1,680
Sub wgn 4d 8P (glass)	3,189	970	
util sd 2d	—	—	13
lwb sdn 7P T/B	3,374	1,005	1,837
sdn limo 7P (lwb)	3,440	1,095	98
chassis and taxicabs	—	—	947

1939 Engine	bore×stroke	bhp	availability
I-6, 201.3	3.13×4.38	82	S-all
I-6, 201.3	3.13×4.38	86	O-all
I-6, 201.3	3.13×4.38	65	O-all

1940

P9 Roadking (wb 117.5)	Wght	Price	Prod
bus cpe	2,769	645	26,745
sdn 2d	2,834	699	55,092
sdn 4d	2,869	740	20,076
util sdn	2,769	699	589
club cpe	2,814	699	360
wgn 4d	3,089	925	80
chassis	—	—	907

P10 DeLuxe (wb 117.5; 7P-137.0)	Wght	Price	Prod
bus cpe	2,804	725	32,244
sdn 2d	2,889	775	76,781
sdn 4d	2,924	805	173,351
util sdn	2,824	775	4
club cpe	2,849	770	22,174
conv cpe	3,049	950	6,986
wgn 4d	3,144	970	3,126
sdn 4d 7P	3,359	1,005	1,179
limo 7P	3,409	1,080	68
chassis	—	—	503

1940 Engines	bore×stroke	bhp	availability
I-6, 201.3	3.13×4.38	84	S-all
I-6, 201.3	3.13×4.38	87	O-all
I-6, 201.3	3.13×4.38	65	O-all

1941

P11 DeLuxe (wb 117.5)	Wght	Price	Prod
bus cpe	2,809	720	23,754
sdn 2d	2,859	769	46,646
sdn 4d	2,889	800	21,175
util sdn	2,794	760	468
club cpe	2,819	764	994
wgn 4d	3,139	1,006	217
DeLuxe bus cpe	2,839	760	15,862
DeLuxe sdn 2d	2,899	809	46,138
DeLuxe sdn 4d	2,924	845	32,336
DeLuxe club cpe	2,859	804	204
DeLuxe util sdn	—	proto	1
chassis	—	—	676

P12 Special DeLuxe (wb 117.5; 7P-137.0)	Wght	Price	Prod
bus cpe	2,859	795	23,851
sdn 2d	2,934	845	84,810
sdn 4d	2,959	877	190,513
util sdn	—	proto	2
club cpe	2,934	842	37,352

P12 Special DeLuxe	Wght	Price	Prod
conv cpe	3,166	1,007	10,545
wgn 4d	3,194	1,031	5,594
sdn 4d, 7P	3,379	1,078	1,127
limo, 7P	3,429	1,153	24
chassis	—	—	321

1941 Engines	bore×stroke	bhp	availability
I-6, 201.3	3.13×4.38	87	S-all
I-6, 201.3	3.13×4.38	92	O-all

1942

P14S DeLuxe (wb 117.5)	Wght	Price	Prod
bus cpe	2,906	812	3,783
sdn 2d	2,961	850	9,350
sdn 4d	3,001	889	11,973
util sdn	2,906	842	80
club cpe	2,966	885	2,458
chassis	—	—	1

P14C Special DeLuxe (wb 117.5)	Wght	Price	Prod
bus cpe	2,931	855	7,258
sdn 2d	2,996	895	24,142
sdn 4d	3,036	935	68,924
Town Sedan	3,061	980	5,821
club cpe	3,011	928	14,685
conv cpe	3,231	1,078	2,806
wgn 4d	3,371	1,145	1,136
chassis	—	—	10

1942 Engine	bore×stroke	bhp	availability
I-6, 217.8	3.25×4.38	95	S-all

1946* See note following 1949 First Series.

P15S DeLuxe (wb 117.5)	Wght	Price	Prod
bus cpe	2,977	1,089	—
sdn 2d	3,047	1,124	—
sdn 4d	3,082	1,164	—
club cpe	3,037	1,159	—
chassis	—	—	—

P15C Special DeLuxe (wb 117.5)	Wght	Price	Prod
bus cpe	2,982	1,159	—
sdn 2d	3,062	1,199	—
sdn 4d	3,107	1,239	—
club cpe	3,057	1,234	—
conv cpe	3,282	1,439	—
wgn 4d	3,402	1,539	—
chassis	—	—	—

1946 Engine	bore×stroke	bhp	availability
I-6, 217.8	3.25×4.38	95	S-all

1947* See note following 1949 First Series.

P15S DeLuxe (wb 117.5)	Wght	Price	Prod
bus cpe	2,977	1,139	—
sdn 2d	3,047	1,164	—
sdn 4d	3,082	1,214	—
club cpe	3,037	1,189	—
chassis	—	—	—

P15C Special DeLuxe (wb 117.5)	Wght	Price	Prod
bus cpe	2,982	1,209	—
sdn 2d	3,062	1,239	—
sdn 4d	3,107	1,289	—
club cpe	3,057	1,264	—
conv cpe	3,282	1,565	—
wgn 4d	3,402	1,765	—
chassis	—	—	—

1947 Engine	bore×stroke	bhp	availability
I-6, 217.8	3.25×4.38	95	S-all

1948* See note following 1949 First Series.

P15S DeLuxe (wb 117.5)	Wght	Price	Prod
bus cpe	2,955	1,346	—
sdn 2d	2,995	1,383	—
sdn 4d	3,030	1,441	—
club cpe	3,005	1,409	—
chassis	—	—	—

P15C Special DeLuxe (wb 117.5)	Wght	Price	Prod
bus cpe	2,950	1,440	—
sdn 2d	3,030	1,471	—
sdn 4d	3,045	1,529	—
club cpe	3,020	1,503	—
conv cpe	3,225	1,857	—
wgn 4d	3,320	2,068	—
chassis	—	—	—

1948 Engine	bore×stroke	bhp	availability
I-6, 217.8	3.25×4.38	95	S-all

1949 First Series* See note following 1949 First Series.

P15S DeLuxe (wb 117.5)	Wght	Price	Prod
bus cpe	2,955	1,346	—
sdn 2d	2,995	1,383	—
sdn 4d	3,030	1,441	—
club cpe	3,005	1,409	—
chassis	—	—	—

P15C Special DeLuxe (wb 117.5)	Wght	Price	Prod
bus cpe	2,950	1,440	—
sdn 2d	3,030	1,471	—
sdn 4d	3,045	1,529	—
club cpe	3,020	1,503	—
conv cpe	3,225	1,857	—
wgn 4d	3,320	2,068	—
chassis	—	—	—

1949(1) Eng.	bore×stroke	bhp	availability
I-6, 217.8	3.25×4.38	95	S-all

*Factory combined production figures for 1946 through 1949 First Series.

Combined 1946-1949 First Series Production

P15S DeLuxe (wb 117.5)	Prod
bus cpe	16,117
sdn 2d	49,918
sdn 4d	120,757
club cpe	10,400
chassis	10

P15C Special DeLuxe (wb 117.5)	Prod
bus cpe	31,399
sdn 2d	125,704
sdn 4d	514,986
club cpe	156,629
conv cpe	15,295
wgn 4d	12,913
chassis	5,361

1949 Second Series

P17 DeLuxe (wb 111.0)	Wght	Price	Prod
bus cpe	2,825	1,371	13,715
sdn 2d	2,951	1,492	28,516
Suburban wgn 2d	3,105	1,840	19,220
chassis	—	—	4

P18 DeLuxe (wb 118.5)	Wght	Price	Prod
sdn 4d	3,059	1,551	61,021
club cpe	3,034	1,519	25,687

P18 Special DeLuxe (wb 118.5)	Wght	Price	Prod
sdn 4d	3,079	1,629	252,878
club cpe	3,046	1,603	99,680
conv cpe	3,323	1,982	15,240
wgn 4d	3,341	2,372	3,443
chassis	—	—	981

1949(2) Eng.	bore×stroke	bhp	availability
I-6, 217.8	3.25×4.38	97	S-all

1950

P19 DeLuxe (wb 111.0)	Wght	Price	Prod
bus cpe	2,872	1,371	16,861
sdn 2d	2,946	1,492	67,584
Suburban wgn 2d	3,116	1,840	34,457
Sub Special wgn 2d	3,155	1,946	
chassis	—	—	1

P20 DeLuxe (wb 118.5)	Wght	Price	Prod
sdn 4d	3,068	1,551	87,871
club cpe	3,040	1,519	53,890

P20 Special DeLuxe (wb 118.5)	Wght	Price	Prod
sdn 4d	3,072	1,629	234,084
club cpe	3,041	1,603	99,361
conv cpe	3,295	1,982	12,697
wgn 4d	3,353	2,372	2,057
chassis	—	—	2,091

1950 Engine	bore×stroke	bhp	availability
I-6, 217.8	3.25×4.38	97	S-all

1951 See note following 1952.**

P22 Concord (wb 111.0)	Wght	Price	Prod
bus cpe	2,919	1,537	—
sdn 2d	2,969	1,673	—
Savoy wgn 2d	3,184	2,182	—

P22 Concord	Wght	Price	Prod
Suburban wgn 2d	3,124	2,064	—
P23 Cambridge (wb 118.5)			
sdn 4d	3,104	1,739	—
club cpe	3,059	1,703	—
P23 Cranbrook (wb 118.5)			
sdn 4d	3,109	1,826	—
club cpe	3,074	1,796	—
conv cpe	3,294	2,222	—
Belvedere htp cpe	3,182	2,114	—

1951 Engine	bore×stroke	bhp	availability
I-6, 217.8	3.25×4.38	97	S-all

1952** See note following 1952.

P22 Concord (wb 111.0)	Wght	Price	Prod
bus cpe	2,893	1,610	14,255
sdn 2d	2,959	1,753	49,139
Savoy wgn 2d	3,165	2,287	76,520 (Savoy and Suburban wgn combined)
Suburban wgn 2d	3,145	2,163	
P23 Cambridge (wb 118.5)			
sdn 4d	3,068	1,822	179,417
club cpe	3,030	1,784	101,784
P23 Cranbrook (wb 118.5)			
sdn 4d	3,088	1,914	388,735
club cpe	3,046	1,883	126,725
Belvedere htp cpe	3,105	2,216	51,266
conv cpe	3,256	2,329	15,650
chassis	—	—	4,171

1952 Engine	bore×stroke	bhp	availability
I-6, 217.8	3.25×4.38	97	S-all

**Factory combined 1951 and 1952 production figures.

1953

P24-1 Cambridge (wb 114.0)	Wght	Price	Prod
bus cpe	2,888	1,618	6,975
sdn 2d	2,943	1,727	56,800
sdn 4d	2,983	1,765	93,585
club cpe	2,950	1,725	1,050
Suburban wgn 2d	3,129	2,064	43,545
P24-2 Cranbrook (wb 114.0)			
sdn 4d	3,023	1,873	298,976
club cpe	2,971	1,843	92,102
Belvedere htp cpe	3,027	2,064	35,185
conv cpe	3,193	2,220	6,301
Savoy wgn 2d	3,170	2,207	12,089
chassis	—	—	843

1953 Engine	bore×stroke	bhp	availability
I-6, 217.8	3.25×4.38	100	S-all

1954

P25-1 Plaza (wb 114.0)	Wght	Price	Prod
bus cpe	2,889	1,618	5,000
club cpe	2,950*	1,700*	1,275
sdn 4d	3,004	1,765	43,077
sdn 2d	2,943	1,727	27,976
Suburban wgn 2d	3,122	2,064	35,937
chassis	—	—	1
P25-2 Savoy (wb 114.0)			
club cpe	2,982	1,843	30,700
sdn 4d	3,036	1,873	139,383
sdn 2d	2,986	1,835	25,396
chassis	—	—	3,588
P25-3 Belvedere (wb 114.0)			
sdn 4d	3,050	1,953	106,601
Sport Coupe htp	3,038	2,145	25,592
conv cpe	3,273	2,301	6,900
Suburban wgn 2d	3,186	2,288	9,241
chassis	—	—	2,031

*Estimated.

1954 Engines	bore×stroke	bhp	availability
I-6, 217.8	3.25 ×4.38	100	S-all to engine #P25-243000
I-6, 230.2	3.25×4.63	110	S-all from eng. #P25-243001

1955

P26-1 Plaza, I-6 (wb 115.0)	Wght	Price	Prod
sdn 4d	3,129	1,781	68,826
club cpe	3,089	1,738	45,561
Suburban wgn 2d	3,261	2,077	23,319

P26-1 Plaza, I-6	Wght	Price	Prod
Suburban wgn 4d	3,282	2,158	10,594
bus cpe	3,025	1,639	4,882
P27-1 Plaza, V-8 (wb 115.0)			
sdn 4d	3,246	1,884	15,330
club cpe	3,202	1,841	8,049
Suburban wgn 2d	3,389	2,180	8,469
Suburban wgn 4d	3,408	2,262	4,828
P26-3 Savoy, I-6 (wb 115.0)			
sdn 4d	3,154	1,880	93,716
club cpe	3,109	1,837	45,438
chassis	—	—	1
P27-3 Savoy, V-8 (wb 115.0)			
sdn 4d	3,265	1,983	69,025
club cpe	3,224	1,940	29,442
P26-2 Belvedere, I-6 (wb 115.0)			
sdn 4d	3,159	1,979	69,128
club cpe	3,129	1,936	19,471
Sport Coupe htp	3,330	2,113	13,942
Suburban wgn 4d	3,312	2,322	6,197
P27-2 Belvedere V-8 (wb 115.0)			
sdn 4d	3,262	2,082	91,856
club cpe	3,228	2,039	22,174
Sport Coupe htp	3,261	2,217	33,433
conv cpe	3,409	2,351	8,473
Suburban wgn 4d	3,475	2,425	12,291

1955 Engines	bore×stroke	bhp	availability
I-6, 230.2	3.25×4.63	117	S-all I-6
V-8, 241.0	3.44×3.25	157	O-all V-8
V-8, 260.0	3.56×3.25	167	S-all V-8
V-8, 260.0	3.56×3.25	177	O-all V-8

1956

P28/29-1 Plaza (wb 115.0)	Wght	Price	Prod
bus cpe	3,100	1,784	3,728
sdn 4d	3,210	1,926	60,197
club sdn	3,175	1,883	43,022
P28/29-2 Savoy (wb 115.0)			
sdn 4d	3,228	2,025	151,762
club sdn	3,190	1,982	57,927
Sport Coupe htp	3,200	2,130	16,473
P28/29-3 Belvedere (wb 115.0)			
sdn 4d	3,248	2,109	84,218
club sdn 2d	3,285	2,170	19,057
Sport Sedan htp	3,343	2,281	17,515
Sport Coupe htp	3,243	2,214	24,723
conv cpe V-8	3,435	2,478	6,735
P28/29 Suburban (wb 115.0)			
DeLuxe wgn 2d	3,373	2,196	23,866
Custom wgn 2d	3,418	2,267	9,489
Custom wgn 4d	3,470	2,314	33,333
Sport wgn 4d	3,513	2,484	15,104
P29-3 Fury (wb 115.0)			
htp cpe	3,650	2,866	4,485

1956 Engines	bore×stroke	bhp	availability
I-6, 230.2	3.25×4.38	125	S-all exc Fury, Belv conv
I-6, 230.2	3.25×4.38	131	O-all exc Fury, Belv conv
V-8, 270.0	3.63×3.26	180	O-Plaza, Savoy, Belvedere
V-8, 277.0	3.75×3.13	187	S-Belv conv; O-Belv, Savoy, Plaza
V-8, 277.0	3.75×3.13	200	O-all exc Fury
V-8, 303.0	3.82×3.31	240	S-Fury

1957

P30/31-1 Plaza (wb 118.0)	Wght	Price	Prod
bus cpe	3,235	1,899	2,874
sdn 4d	3,333	2,050	70,248
sdn 2d	3,245	2,009	49,137
P30/31-2 Savoy (wb 118.0)			
sdn 4d	3,340	2,194	153,093
Sport Sedan htp	3,428	2,317	7,601
sdn 2d	3,263	2,147	55,590
Sport Coupe htp	3,335	2,229	31,373
P30/31-3 Belvedere (wb 118.0)			
sdn 4d	3,373	2,310	110,414

P30/31-3 Belvedere	Wght	Price	Prod
Sport Sedan htp	3,428	2,419	37,446
sdn 2d	3,288	2,264	55,590
Sport Coupe htp	3,348	2,349	67,268
conv cpe V-8	3,585	2,638	9,866
P30/31 Suburban (wb 122.0)			
DeLuxe wgn 2d	3,620	2,330	20,111
Custom wgn 2d	3,668	2,440	11,196
Custom wgn 4d, 6P	3,753	2,494	40,227
Custom wgn 4d, 9P	3,800	2,649	9,357
Sport wgn 4d, 6P	3,748	2,622	15,414
Sport wgn 4d, 9P	3,795	2,777	7,988
P31 Fury (wb 118.0)			
htp cpe	3,595	2,925	7,438

1957 Engines	bore×stroke	bhp	availability
I-6, 230.2	3.25×4.63	132	S-all exc Fury, Belv conv
V-8, 277.0	3.75×3.13	197	O-Plaza
V-8, 301.0	3.91×3.13	215	O-Plaz, Savoy, Belv
V-8, 301.0	3.91×3.13	235	O-all exc Fury
V-8, 318.0	3.91×3.31	290	S-Fury

1958

LP1/2-L Plaza (wb 118.0)		Wght	Price	Prod
21	club sdn	3,253	2,118	39,062
22	bus cpe	3,245	2,028	1,472
41	sdn 4d	3,335	2,169	54,194
LP1/2-M Savoy (wb 118.0)				
21	club sdn	3,290	2,254	17,624
23	Sport Coupe htp	3,320	2,329	19,500
41	sdn 4d	3,310	2,305	67,933
43	Sport Sedan htp	3,393	2,400	5,060
LP1/2H Belvedere (wb 118.0)				
21	club sdn	3,305	2,389	4,229
23	Sport Coupe htp	3,325	2,457	36,043
27	conv cpe V-8	3,545	2,762	9,941
41	sdn 4d	3,343	2,440	49,124
43	Sport Sedan htp	3,425	2,528	18,194
LP1/2 Suburban (wb 122.0)				
—	DeLuxe wgn 4d	3,660	2,486	15,535
25	DeLuxe wgn 2d	3,560	2,432	15,625
25	Custom wgn 2d	3,630	2,553	5,925
45A	Custom wgn 4d, 6P	3,665	2,607	38,707
45B	Custom wgn 4d, 9P	3,763	2,747	17,158
45A	Sport wgn 4d, 6P	3,680	2,760	10,785
45B	Sport wgn 4d, 9P	3,758	2,900	12,385
LP2-H Fury (wb 118.0)				
23	htp cpe	3,510	3,067	5,303

1958 Engines	bore ×stroke	bhp	availability
I-6, 230.2	3.25×4.63	132	S-all exc Fury, Belv conv
V-8, 318.0	3.91×3.31	225	O-all exc Fury
V-8, 318.0	3.91×3.31	250	O-all exc Fury
V-8, 318.0	3.91×3.31	290	S-Fury
V-8, 350.0	4.06×3.38	305	O-all
V-8, 350.0	4.06×3.38	315	O-all (fuel inj.)

1959

MP1/2-L Savoy (wb 118.0)		Wght	Price	Prod
21	club sdn	3,333	2,222	46,979
22	bus cpe	3,130	2,143	1,051
41	sdn 4d	3,333	2,283	84,272
MP1/2-M Belvedere (wb 118.0)				
21	club sdn	3,310	2,389	13,816
23	htp cpe	3,318	2,461	23,469
27	conv cpe	3,580	2,814	5,063
41	sdn 4d	3,353	2,440	67,980
43	htp sdn 4d	3,335	2,525	5,713
MP2-H Fury (wb 118.0)				
23	htp cpe	3,435	2,714	21,494
41	sdn 4d	3,455	2,691	30,149
43	htp sdn	3,505	2,771	13,614
MP2-P Sport Fury (wb 118.0)				
23	htp cpe	3,475	2,927	17,867
27	conv cpe	3,670	3,125	5,990
MP1/2 Suburban (wb 122.0)				
25	DeLuxe wgn 2d	3,625	2,694	15,074
25	Custom wgn 2d, 6P	3,690	2,814	1,852

MP1/2 Suburban		Wght	Price	Prod
45A	DeLuxe wgn 4d	3,675	2,761	35,086
45A	Custom wgn 4d, 6P	3,678	2,881	35,024
45B	Custom wgn 4d, 9P	3,775	2,991	16,993
45A	Sport wgn 4d, 6P	3,760	3,021	7,224
45B	Sport wgn 4d, 9P	3,805	3,131	9,549

1959 Engines	bore×stroke	bhp	availability
I-6, 230.2	3.25×4.63	132	S-all exc Fury, Sport Fury, Del/Cus Sub
V-8, 318.0	3.91×3.31	230	S-Fury, Custom Suburban; O-other exc Sport Fury
V-8, 318.0	3.91×3.31	260	S-Sport Fury; O-others
V-8, 361.0	4.12×3.38	305	O-all

1960

V100 Valiant (wb 106.5)		Wght	Price	Prod
110	sdn 4d	2,635	2,053	52,788
140	wgn 4d, 6P	2,815	2,365	12,018
—	wgn 4d, 9P	2,845	2,488	1,928

V200 Valiant (wb 106.5)		Wght	Price	Prod
130	sdn 4d	2,655	2,130	106,515
170	wgn 4d, 6P	2,855	2,443	16,368
—	wgn 4d, 9P	2,860	2,566	4,675

PP1/2-L Savoy (wb 118.0)		Wght	Price	Prod
21	club sdn	3,410	2,260	26,820
41	sdn 4d	3,433	2,310	51,384

PP1/2-M Belvedere (wb 118.0)		Wght	Price	Prod
21	club sdn	3,423	2,389	6,529
23	htp cpe	3,438	2,641	14,085
41	sdn 4d	3,448	2,439	42,130

PP1/2-H Fury (wb 118.0)		Wght	Price	Prod
23	htp cpe	3,465	2,599	18,079
27	conv cpe	3,630	2,967	7,080
41	sdn 4d	3,475	2,575	21,292
43	htp sdn	3,528	2,656	9,036

PP1/2 Suburban (wb 122.0)		Wght	Price	Prod
25	DeLuxe wgn 2d	3,375	2,721	5,503
45	DeLuxe wgn 4d	3,815	2,787	18,484
45	Custom wgn 4d, 6P	3,890	2,880	17,308
45	Custom wgn 4d, 9P	3,875	2,990	8,116
45	Sport wgn 4d, 6P	3,895	3,024	3,333
45	Sport wgn 4d, 9P	4,020	3,134	4,253

1960 Engines	bore ×stroke	bhp	availability
I-6, 170.0	3.40×3.13	101	S-Valiant
I-6, 170.0	3.40×3.13	148	O-Valiant
I-6, 225.0	3.40×4.13	145	S-full-size
V-8, 318.0	3.91×3.31	230/260	S-full-size V-8 (PP2)
V-8, 361.0	4.12×3.38	305/310	O-all full-size (PP2)
V-8, 383.0	4.25×3.38	330	O-full-size (PP2)

1961

V100 Valiant (wb 106.5)		Wght	Price	Prod
111	sdn 2d	2,565	1,955	22,230
113	sdn 4d	2,590	2,014	25,695
156	wgn 4d	2,745	2,327	6,717

V200 Valiant (wb 106.5)		Wght	Price	Prod
132	htp cpe	2,605	2,137	18,586
133	sdn 4d	2,600	2,110	59,056
176	wgn 4d	2,770	2,423	10,794

RP1/2-L Savoy (wb 118.0)		Wght	Price	Prod
211	sdn 2d, I-6	3,300	2,260	18,729
311	sdn 2d, V-8	3,440	2,379	
213	sdn 4d, I-6	3,310	2,310	44,913
313	sdn 4d, V-8	3,465	2,430	

RP1/2-M Belvedere (wb 118.0)		Wght	Price	Prod
221	sdn 2d, I-6	3,300	2,389	4,740
321	sdn 2d, V-8	3,450	2,508	
222	htp cpe, I-6	3,320	2,461	9,591
322	htp cpe, V-8	3,460	2,580	
223	sdn 4d, I-6	3,315	2,439	40,090
323	sdn 4d, V-8	3,470	2,559	

RP1/2-H Fury (wb 118.0)		Wght	Price	Prod
232	htp cpe, I-6	3,330	2,599	16,141
332	htp cpe, V-8	3,520	2,718	
233	sdn 4d, I-6	3,350	2,575	22,169
333	sdn 4d, V-8	3,515	2,694	
234	htp sdn, I-6	3,390	2,656	8,507
334	htp sdn V-8	3,555	2,775	
335	conv cpe, V-8	3,535	2,967	6,948

RP1/2 Suburban (wb 122.0)		Wght	Price	Prod
255	DeLuxe wgn 2d, I-6	3,675	2,602	2,464
355	DeLuxe wgn 2d, V-8	3,845	2,721	
256	DeLuxe wgn 4d, I-6	3,715	2,668	12,980
356	DeLuxe wgn 4d, V-8	3,885	2,788	
266	Custom wgn 4d, I-6	3,730	2,761	13,553
366	Custom wgn 4d, V-8	3,885	2,880	
367	Cust wgn 4d, 9P, V-8	3,985	2,990	
376	Sprt wgn 4d, 6P, V-8	3,890	3,024	2,844
377	Sprt wgn 4d, 9P, V-8	3,995	3,134	3,088

1961 Engines	bore×stroke	bhp	availability
I-6, 170.0	3.40×3.13	101	S-Valiant
I-6, 170.0	3.40×3.13	148	O-Valiant
I-6, 225.0	3.40×4.13	145	S-full-size
V-8, 318.0	3.91×3.31	230	S-full-size V-8 (RP2)
V-8, 318.0	3.91×3.31	260	O-full-size with TorqueFlite
V-8, 361.0	4.12×3.38	305	O-full-size exc PowerFlite or a/c
V-8, 383.0	4.25×3.38	325/340	O-full-size exc PowerFlite or a/c
V-8, 413.0	4.19×3.75	350/375	O-full-size

1962

SV1-L Valiant V100 (wb 106.5)		Wght	Price	Prod
111	sdn 2d	2,480	1,930	19,679
113	sdn 4d	2,500	1,991	33,769
156	wgn 4d	2,660	2,285	5,932

SV1-H Valiant V200 (wb 106.5)		Wght	Price	Prod
131	sdn 2d	2,500	2,026	8,484
133	sdn 4d	2,510	2,087	55,789
176	wgn 4d	2,690	2,381	8,055

SV1-P Valiant Signet (wb 106.5)		Wght	Price	Prod
142	htp cpe	2,515	2,230	25,586

SP1/2-L Savoy (wb 116.0)		Wght	Price	Prod
211	sdn 2d, I-6	2,930	2,206	18,825
311	sdn 2d, V-8	3,080	2,313	
213	sdn 4d, I-6	2,960	2,262	49,777
313	sdn 4d, V-8	3,115	2,369	

SP1/2-M Belvedere (wb 116.0)		Wght	Price	Prod
221	sdn 2d, I-6	2,930	2,342	3,128
321	sdn 2d, V-8	3,070	2,450	
222	htp cpe, I-6	2,945	2,431	5,086
322	htp cpe, V-8	3,075	2,538	
223	sdn 4d, I-6	2,960	2,399	31,263
323	sdn 4d, V-8	3,095	2,507	

SP1/2-H Fury (wb 116.0)		Wght	Price	Prod
232	htp cpe, I-6	2,960	2,585	9,589
332	htp cpe, V-8	3,105	2,693	
233	sdn 4d, I-6	2,990	2,563	17,531
333	sdn 4d, V-8	3,125	2,670	
334	htp sdn, V-8	3,190	2,742	5,995
335	conv cpe, V-8	3,210	2,924	4,349

SP2-P Sport Fury (wb 116.0)		Wght	Price	Prod
342	htp cpe, V-8	3,195	2,851	4,039
345	conv cpe, V-8	3,295	3,082	1,516

SP1/2 Station Wagon (wb 116.0)*		Wght	Price	Prod
256	Savoy wgn 4d, I-6	3,225	2,609	12,710
356	Savoy wgn 4d, V-8	3,390	2,717	
266	Belv wgn 4d, 6P, I-6	3,245	2,708	9,781
366	Belv wgn 4d, 6P, V-8	3,390	2,815	
367	Belv wgn 4d, 9P, V-8	3,440	2,917	4,168
376	Fury wgn 4d, 6P, V-8	3,395	2,968	2,352
377	Fury wgn 4d, 9P, V-8	3,455	3,071	2,411

*Due to factory numbering in 1962, model names such as "Savoy" were listed as body-style names. This practice occurred in 1962 only.

1962 Engines	bore×stroke	bhp	availability
I-6, 170.0	3.40×3.13	101	S-Valiant
I-6, 225.0	3.40×4.13	145	S-SP1; O-Val
V-8, 318.0	3.91×3.31	230	S-all SP2 exc Sport Fury
V-8, 318.0	3.91×3.31	260	O-all SP2 exc Sport Fury
V-8, 361.0	4.12×3.38	305	S-Sport Fury; O-other SP2 exc w/PowerFlite or a/c
V-8, 383.0	4.25×3.38	330/335	O-SP2
V-8, 413.0	4.19×3.75	365/380/410	O-Fry, Sprt Fry

1963

TV1-Valiant V100 (wb 106.0)		Wght	Price	Prod
111	sdn 2d	2,515	1,910	32,761
113	sdn 4d	2,535	1,973	54,617
156	wgn 4d	2,700	2,268	11,864

TV1-H Valiant V200 (wb 106.0)		Wght	Price	Prod
131	sdn 2d	2,515	2,035	10,605
133	sdn 4d	2,555	2,097	57,029
135	conv cpe	2,640	2,340	7,122
176	wgn 4d	2,715	2,392	11,147

TV1-P Valiant Signet 200 (wb 106.0)		Wght	Price	Prod
142	htp cpe	2,570	2,230	30,857
145	conv cpe	2,675	2,454	9,154

TP1/2-L Savoy (wb 116.0)		Wght	Price	Prod
211	sdn 2d, I-6	2,980	2,206	20,281
311	sdn 2d, V-8	3,200	2,313	
213	sdn 4d, I-6	3,020	2,262	56,313
313	sdn 4d, V-8	3,220	2,369	
256	wgn 4d, 6P, I-6	3,325	2,609	12,874
356	wgn 4d, 6P, V-8	3,475	2,717	
257	wgn 4d, 9P, I-6	3,375	2,710	4,342
357	wgn 4d, 9P, V-8	3,560	2,818	

TP1/2-M Belvedere (wb 116.0)		Wght	Price	Prod
221	sdn 2d, I-6	3,000	2,342	6,218
321	sdn 2d, V-8	3,215	2,450	
222	htp cpe, I-6	3,025	2,431	9,204
322	htp cpe, V-8	3,190	2,538	
223	sdn 4d, I-6	3,020	2,399	54,929
323	sdn 4d, V-8	3,235	2,507	
366	wgn 4d, 6P, V-8	3,490	2,815	10,297
367	wgn 4d, 9P, V-8	3,585	2,917	4,012

TP1/2-H Fury (wb 116.0)		Wght	Price	Prod
232	htp cpe, I-6	3,030	2,585	13,832
332	htp cpe, V-8	3,215	2,693	
233	sdn 4d, I-6	3,075	2,563	31,891
333	sdn 4d, V-8	3,265	2,670	
334	htp sdn, V-8	3,295	2,742	11,887
335	conv cpe, V-8	3,340	2,924	5,221
376	wgn 4d, 6P, V-8	3,545	2,968	3,304
377	wgn 4d, 9P, V-8	3,590	3,071	3,368

TP2-P Sport Fury (wb 116.0)		Wght	Price	Prod
342	htp cpe, V-8	3,235	2,851	11,483
345	conv cpe, V-8	3,385	3,082	3,836

1963 Engines	bore×stroke	bhp	availability
I-6, 170.0	3.40×3.13	101	S-Valiant
I-6, 225.0	3.40×4.13	145	S-all TP1; O-Val
V-8, 318.0	3.91×3.31	230	S-all TP2
V-8, 361.0	4.12×3.38	265	O-all TP2
V-8, 383.0	4.25×3.38	320/330	O-all TP2
V-8, 426.0	4.25×3.75	370/425	O-TP2

1964

VV1-L Valiant V100 (wb 106.0)		Wght	Price	Prod
111	sdn 2d	2,540	1,921	35,403
113	sdn 4d	2,575	1,992	44,208
156	wgn 4d	2,725	2,273	10,759

VV1-H Valiant V200 (wb 106.0)		Wght	Price	Prod
131	sdn 2d	2,545	2,044	11,013
133	sdn 4d	2,570	2,112	63,828
135	conv cpe	2,670	2,349	5,856
176	wgn 4d	2,730	2,388	11,146

VV1-P Valiant Signet 200 (wb 106.0)		Wght	Price	Prod
142	htp cpe	2,600	2,256	37,736
145	conv cpe	2,690	2,473	7,636
149	Barrcud fstbk htp cpe	2,740	2,365	23,443

VP1/2-L Savoy (wb 116.0)		Wght	Price	Prod
211	sdn 2d, I-6	2,990	2,224	21,326
311	sdn 2d, V-8	3,205	2,332	
213	sdn 4d, I-6	3,040	2,280	51,024
313	sdn 4d, V-8	3,210	2,388	
256	wgn 4d, 6P, I-6	3,345	2,620	12,401
356	wgn 4d, 6P, V-8	3,495	2,728	

VP1/2-L Savoy		Wght	Price	Prod
257	wgn 4d, 9P, I-6	3,400	2,721	3,242
357	wgn 4d, 9P, V-8	3,600	2,829	
VP1/2-M Belvedere (wb 116.0)				
221	sdn 2d, I-6	3,000	2,359	5,364
321	sdn 2d, V-8	3,210	2,466	
222	htp cpe, I-6	3,010	2,444	16,334
322	htp cpe, V-8	3,190	2,551	
223	sdn 4d, I-6	3,065	2,417	57,307
323	sdn 4d, V-8	3,225	2,524	
366	wgn 4d, 6P, V-8	3,510	2,826	10,317
367	wgn 4d, 9P, V-8	3,605	2,928	4,207
VP1/2-H Fury (wb 116.0)				
232	htp cpe, I-6	3,040	2,598	26,303
332	htp cpe, V-8	3,212	2,706	
233	sdn 4d, I-6	3,045	2,573	34,901
333	sdn 4d, V-8	3,230	2,680	
334	htp sdn, V-8	3,300	2,752	13,713
335	conv cpe, V-8	3,345	2,937	5,173
376	wgn 4d, 6P, V-8	3,530	2,981	3,646
377	wgn 4d, 9P, V-8	3,630	3,084	4,482
VP2-P Sport Fury (wb 116.0)				
342	htp cpe, V-8	3,270	2,864	23,695
345	conv cpe, V-8	3,405	3,095	3,858

1964 Engines	bore×stroke	bhp	availability
I-6, 170.0	3.40×3.13	101	S-Valiant
I-6, 225.0	3.40×4.13	145	S-VP1; O-Valiant
V-8, 273.0	3.62×3.31	180	O-Valiant
V-8, 318.0	3.91×3.31	230	S-all VP2
V-8, 361.0	4.12×3.38	265	O-all exc Valiant
V-8, 383.0	4.25×3.38	305/330	O-all exc Valiant
V-8, 426.0	4.25×3.75	365	O-all exc Valiant
V-8, 426.0	4.25×3.75	415/425	O-VP2 (Super Stock/Street)

1965

AV1-L Valiant 100 (wb 106.0)*		Wght	Price	Prod
V11	sdn 2d	2,560	2,004	40,434
V13	sdn 4d	2,590	2,075	42,857
V56	wgn 4d	2,750	2,361	10,822
AV1-H Valiant 200 (wb 106.0)*				
V31	sdn 2d	2,570	2,127	8,919
V33	sdn 4d	2,605	2,195	41,642
V35	conv cpe	2,695	2,437	2,769
V78	wgn 4d	2,755	2,476	6,133
AV-1P Valiant Signet (wb 106.0)*				
V42	htp cpe	2,620	2,340	10,999
V45	conv cpe	2,725	2,561	2,578
AV1-P Barracuda (wb 106.0)*				
V89	fstbk htp cpe	2,725	2,487	64,596
AR1/2-L Belvedere I (wb 116.0; SS-115.0)				
R01	Super Stock htp cpe	3,170	4,671	—
R11	sdn 2d	3,088	2,226	12,536
R13	sdn 4d	3,153	2,265	35,968
R56	wgn 4d	3,423	2,562	8,338
AR1/2-H Belvedere II (wb 116.0)				
R32	htp cpe	3,123	2,378	29,924
R33	sdn 4d	3,128	2,352	41,445
R35	conv cpe	3,230	2,597	1,921
R76	wgn 4d, 6P	3,425	2,649	5,908
R77	wgn 4d, 9P	3,488	2,747	3,294
AR2-P Satellite (wb 116.0)				
R42	htp cpe	3,220	2,649	23,341
R45	conv cpe	3,325	2,869	1,860
AP1/2-L Fury I (wb 119.0; wgns-121.0)				
P11	sdn 2d	3,518	2,376	17,294
P13	sdn 4d	3,573	2,430	48,575
P56	wgn 4d	4,030	2,776	13,360
AP1/2-M Fury II (wb 119.0; wgn-121.0)				
P21	sdn 2d	3,525	2,478	4,109
P23	sdn 4d	3,573	2,532	43,350
P66	wgn 4d, 6P	4,135	2,948	12,853
P67	wgn 4d, 9P	4,160	3,051	6,445
AP1/2-H Fury III (wb 119.0; wgns-121.0)				
P32	htp cpe	3,563	2,691	43,251
P33	sdn 4d	3,595	2,684	50,725
P34	htp sdn	3,690	2,863	21,367
P35	conv cpe	3,710	3,048	5,524
P76	wgn 4d, 6P	4,140	3,090	8,931

AP1/2-H Fury III		Wght	Price	Prod
P77	wgn 4d, 9P	4,200	3,193	9,546
AP2-P Sport Fury (wb 119.0)				
P42	htp cpe	3,715	2,960	38,348
P45	conv cpe	3,755	3,209	6,272

* Factory quoted only V-8 Valiant prices this year, which are given along with V-8 weights. For sixes, deduct approximately $128.

1965 Engines	bore×stroke	bhp	availability
I-6, 170.0	3.40×3.13	101	S-Valiant
I-6, 225.0	3.40×4.13	145	S-Barracuda, all AR1/AP1; O-Valiant
V-8, 273.0	3.62×3.31	180	S-all AR2; O-Valiant, Barracuda,
V-8, 273.0	3.62×3.31	235	O-Valiant, Barracuda
V-8, 318.0	3.91×3.31	230	S-AP2; O-AR2
V-8, 361.0	4.12×3.38	265	O-AR2
V-8, 383.0	4.25×3.38	270	O-AP2
V-8, 383.0	4.25×3.38	330	O-AR2, AP2
V-8, 426.0	4.25×3.75	365	S-Belv I SS; O-Sat, Sprt Fry
V-8, 426.0	4.25×3.75	425	O-Belv I SS (hemi)

1966

BV1/2-L Valiant 100 (wb 106.0)		Wght	Price	Prod
21	sdn 2d	2,700	2,025	35,787
41	sdn 4d	2,725	2,095	36,031
45	wgn 4d	2,648	2,387	6,838
BV1/2-H Valiant 200 (wb 106.0)				
41	sdn 4d	2,728	2,226	39,392
45	wgn 4d	2,883	2,502	4,537
BV1/2-H Valiant Signet (wb 106.0)				
23	htp cpe	2,735	2,261	13,045
27	conv cpe	2,830	2,527	2,507
BV1/2-P Barracuda (wb 106.0)				
29	fstbk htp cpe	2,865	2,556	38,029
BR1/2-L Belvedere I (wb 116.0; wgn-117.0)				
21	sdn 2d	3,095	2,277	9,381
41	sdn 4d	3,125	2,315	31,063
45	wgn 4d	3,523	2,605	8,200
BR1/2-H Belvedere II (wb 116.0; wgn-117.0)				
23	htp cpe	3,123	2,430	36,644
27	conv cpe	3,200	2,644	2,502
41	sdn 4d	3,115	2,405	49,941
45	wgn 4d, 6P	3,525	2,695	8,667
46	wgn 4d, 9P	3,618	2,804	4,726
BR2-P Satellite (wb 116.0)				
23	htp cpe	3,255	2,695	35,399
27	conv cpe	3,320	2,910	2,759
BP1/2-L Fury I (wb 119.0; wgn-121.0)				
21	sdn 2d	3,518	2,426	12,538
41	sdn 4d	3,570	2,479	39,698
45	wgn 4d	4,048	2,836	9,690
BP1/2-M Fury II (wb 119.0; wgn-121.0)				
21	sdn 2d	3,530	2,526	2,503
41	sdn 4d	3,573	2,579	55,016
45	wgn 4d, 6P	4,145	2,986	10,718
46	wgn 4d, 9P	4,175	3,087	5,580
BP1/2-H Fury III (wb 119.0; wgn-121.0)				
23	htp cpe	3,578	2,724	36,711
27	conv cpe	3,720	3,074	4,326
41	sdn 4d	3,217	2,718	46,505
43	htp sdn	3,730	2,893	21,864
45	wgn 4d, 6P	4,155	3,115	9,239
46	wgn 4d, 9P	4,165	3,216	10,886
BP2-P Sport Fury (wb 119.0)				
23	htp cpe	3,730	3,006	32,523
27	conv cpe	3,755	3,251	3,418
VP2-H VIP (wb 119.0)				
23	htp cpe	3,700	3,069	5,158
43	htp sdn	3,780	3,133	12,058

1966 Engines	bore×stroke	bhp	availability
I-6, 170.0	3.40×3.13	101	S-Valiant
I-6, 225.0	3.40×4.13	145	S-Brcda, all BR1, BP1; O-Valiant
V-8, 273.0	3.62×3.31	180	S-BR2, Brcda, Valiant
V-8, 273.0	3.62×3.31	235	O-Brcda, Valiant Signet
V-8, 318.0	3.91×3.31	230	S-all BP2; O-BR2
V-8, 361.0	4.12×3.38	265	O-Belvedere, Satellite
V-8, 383.0	4.25×3.38	325	O-BR2, BP2
V-8, 426.0	4.25×3.75	425	O-BR2 (hemi) exc wgn
V-8, 440.0	4.32×3.75	365	O-VIP, Sport Fury

1967

CV1/2-L Valiant 100 (wb 108.0)		Wght	Price	Prod
21	sdn 2d	2,738	2,117	29,093
41	sdn 4d	2,753	2,163	46,638
CV1/2-H Valiant Signet (wb 108.0)				
21	sdn 2d	2,765	2,262	6,843
41	sdn 4d	2,750	2,308	26,395
CV1/2-P Barracuda (wb 108.0)				
23	htp cpe	2,793	2,449	28,196
27	conv cpe	2,903	2,779	4,228
29	fstbk htp cpe	2,878	2,639	30,110
CR1/2-E Belvedere (wb 117.0)				
45	wgn 4d	3,543	2,579	5,477
CR1/2-L Belvedere I (wb 116.0; wgn-117.0)				
21	sdn 2d	3,095	2,318	4,718
41	sdn 4d	3,125	2,356	13,988
45	wgn 4d	3,553	2,652	3,172
CR1/2-H Belvedere II (wb 116.0; wgn-117.0)				
23	htp cpe	3,130	2,457	34,550
27	conv cpe	3,205	2,695	1,552
41	sdn 4d	3,118	2,434	42,694
45	wgn 4d, 6P	3,553	2,729	5,583
46	wgn 4d, 9P	3,595	2,836	3,968
CR2-P Satellite (wb 116.0)				
23	htp cpe	3,265	2,747	30,328
27	conv cpe	3,335	2,986	2,050
CR2-P Belvedere GTX (wb 116.0)*				
23	htp cpe	3,545	3,178	—
27	conv cpe	3,615	3,418	—
CP1/2E Fury I (wb 119.0; wgn-122.0)				
21	sdn 2d	3,493	2,473	6,647
41	sdn 4d	3,533	2,517	29,354
45	wgn 4d	4,000	2,884	6,067
CP1/2L Fury II (wb 119.0; wgn-122.0)				
21	sdn 2d	3,490	2,571	2,783
41	sdn 4d	3,526	2,614	45,673
45	wgn 4d, 6P	4,045	3,021	10,736
46	wgn 4d, 9P	4,110	3,122	5,649
CP1/2-M Fury III (wb 119.0; wgn-122.0)				
23	htp cpe	3,535	2,872	37,448
27	conv cpe	3,670	3,118	4,523
41	sdn 4d	3,555	2,746	52,690
43	htp sdn	3,650	2,922	43,614
45	wgn 4d, 6P	4,080	3,144	9,270
46	wgn 4d, 9P	4,135	3,245	12,533
CP2-H Sport Fury (wb 119.0)				
23	htp cpe	3,630	3,033	28,448
23	fstbk htp cpe	3,705	3,062	
27	conv cpe	3,645	3,279	3,133
CP2-P VIP (wb 119.0)				
23	htp cpe	3,705	3,182	7,912
43	htp sdn	3,660	3,117	10,830

* Included with Satellite.

1967 Engines	bore×stroke	bhp	availability
I-6, 170.0	3.40×3.13	115	S-Valiant
I-6, 225.0	3.40×4.13	145	S-Brcda, CR1, CP1; O-Val
V-8, 273.0	3.62×3.31	180	S-Brcda, Val, CR2 exc GTX
V-8, 273.0	3.62×3.31	235	O-Valiant, Barracuda
V-8, 318.0	3.91×3.31	230	S-CP2,CR2 exc GTX

1967 Engines	bore×stroke	bhp	availability
V-8, 383.0	4.25×3.38	270	O-CP2, CR2, exc GTX
V-8, 383.0	4.25×3.38	280	O-Barracuda
V-8, 383.0	4.25×3.38	325	O-Brcda, Furys, Belv exc GTX
V-8, 426.0	4.25×3.75	425	O-Belv GTX (hemi)
V-8, 440.0	4.32×3.75	350	O-Fury wgns
V-8, 440.0	4.32×3.75	375	S-GTX, O-Furys exc wgns

1968

VL Valiant 100 (wb 108.0)*		Wght	Price	Prod
21	sdn 2d	2,733	2,254	31,178
41	sdn 4d	2,763	2,301	49,446
VH Valiant Signet (wb 108.0)				
21	sdn 2d	2,745	2,400	6,265
41	sdn 4d	2,768	2,447	23,906
VH Barracuda (wb 108.0)				
23	htp cpe	2,810	2,605	19,997
27	conv cpe	2,923	2,907	2,840
29	fstbk htp cpe	2,895	2,762	22,575
RL Belvedere (wb 116.0; wgn-117.0)				
21	cpe	3,050	2,444	15,702
41	sdn 4d	3,080	2,483	17,214
45	wgn 4d	3,553	2,773	8,982
RH Satellite (wb 116.0; wgn-117.0)				
23	htp cpe	3,070	2,594	46,539
27	conv cpe	3,188	2,824	1,771
41	sdn 4d	3,080	2,572	42,309
45	wgn 4d, 6P	3,605	2,891	12,097
46	wgn 4d, 9P	3,625	2,998	10,883
RP Sport Satellite (wb 116.0; wgn-117.0)				
23	htp cpe	3,155	2,822	21,014
27	conv cpe	3,285	3,036	1,523
45	wgn 4d, 6P	3,610	3,131	**
46	wgn 4d, 9P	3,685	3,239	**
RM Road Runner (wb 116.0)				
21	cpe	3,440	2,896	29,240
23	htp cpe	3,455	3,034	15,359
RS GTX (wb 116.0)				
23	htp cpe	3,470	3,355	17,914
27	conv cpe	3,595	3,590	1,026
PE Fury I (wb 119.0)				
21	sdn 2d	3,480	2,617	5,788
41	sdn 4d	3,653	2,660	23,208
PL Fury II (wb 119.0)				
21	sdn 2d	3,488	2,715	3,112
41	sdn 4d	3,533	2,757	49,423
PM Fury III (wb 119.0)				
23	htp cpe	3,538	2,912	60,472
23	fstbk htp cpe "PX"	3,528	2,932	
27	conv cpe	3,680	3,236	4,483
41	sdn 4d	3,545	2,890	57,899
43	htp sdn	3,635	3,067	45,147
PH Sport Fury (wb 119.0)				
23	htp cpe	3,620	3,206	6,642
23	fstbk htp cpe "PS"	3,615	3,225	17,073
27	conv cpe	3,710	3,425	2,489
PP VIP (wb 119.0)				
23	fstbk htp cpe	3,615	3,260	6,768
43	htp sdn	3,655	3,326	10,745
DP Suburban (wb 122.0)				
45	wgn 4d	3,990	3,048	6,749
45	Custom wgn 4d, 6P	4,045	3,252	17,078
46	Custom wgn 4d, 9P	4,090	3,353	9,954
45	Sport wgn 4d, 6P	4,055	3,442	9,203
46	Sport wgn 4d, 9P	4,100	3,543	13,224

* Includes "Valiant 200" trim option.

** Sport Satellite wagon included with Satellite wagon.

1968 Engines	bore×stroke	bhp	availability
I-6, 170.0	3.40×3.13	115	S-Valiant
I-6, 225.0	3.40×4.13	145	S-Brcda, Belv, Sat, FI/II, FIII sdn/htps, Sub; O-Valiant
V-8, 273.0	3.62×3.31	190	O-Val, Belv, Sat, Spt Sat wgn
V-8, 318.0	3.91×3.31	230	S-Spt Sat, Fry III; O-Val, Brcda, Belv, Sat, Spt Sat wgn
V-8, 340.0	4.04×3.31	275	S-Brcda Form S
V-8, 383.0	4.25×3.38	290	O-Belv, Sat, Spt Sat, Furys
V-8, 383.0	4.25×3.38	300	O-Brcda Form S
V-8, 383.0	4.25×3.38	330	O-Belv, Satellite, Furys, Subs
V-8, 383.0	4.25×3.38	335	S-Road Runner
V-8, 426.0	4.25×3.75	425	O-Road Runner, GTX (hemi)
V-8, 440.0	4.32×3.75	375	S-GTX; O-Fury exc DP
V-8, 440.0	4.32 × 3.75	350	O-Suburban

1969

VL Valiant 100 (wb 108.0)*		Wght	Price	Prod
21	sdn 2d	2,740	2,094	29,672
41	sdn 4d	2,760	2,154	49,409
VH Valiant Signet (wb 108.0)				
21	sdn 2d	2,740	2,253	6,645
41	sdn 4d	2,760	2,313	21,492
VH Barracuda (wb 108.0)				
23	htp cpe	2,815	2,780	12,757
27	conv cpe	2,940	3,082	1,442
29	fstbk htp cpe	2,902	2,813	17,788
RL Belvedere (wb 116.0; wgn-117.0)				
21	cpe	3,052	2,509	7,063
41	sdn 4d	3,082	2,548	12,914
45	wgn 4d	3,540	2,879	7,038
RH Satellite (wb 116.0; wgn-117.0)				
23	htp cpe	3,080	2,659	38,323
27	conv cpe	3,200	2,875	1,137
41	sdn 4d	3,087	2,635	35,296
45	wgn 4d, 6P	3,540	2,997	5,837
46	wgn 4d, 9P	3,612	3,106	4,730
RP Sport Satellite (wb 116.0; wgn-117.0)				
23	htp cpe	3,156	2,883	15,807
27	conv cpe	3,276	3,081	818
41	sdn 4d	3,196	2,911	5,836
45	wgn 4d, 6P	3,596	3,241	3,221
46	wgn 4d, 9P	3,666	3,350	3,152
RM Road Runner (wb 116.0)				
21	cpe	3,435	2,945	33,743
23	htp cpe	3,450	3,083	48,549
27	conv cpe	3,790	3,313	2,128
RS GTX (wb 116.0)				
23	htp cpe	3,465	3,416	14,902
27	conv cpe	3,590	3,635	700
PE Fury I (wb 120.0)				
21	sdn 2d	3,501	2,701	4,971
41	sdn 4d	3,533	2,744	18,771
PL Fury II (wb 120.0)				
21	sdn 2d	3,506	2,813	3,268
41	sdn 4d	3,536	2,841	41,047
PM Fury III (wb 120.0)				
23	htp cpe	3,516	3,000	44,168
27	conv cpe	3,704	3,324	4,129
29	formal htp cpe	3,601	3,020	22,738
41	sdn 4d	3,541	2,979	72,747
43	htp sdn	3,643	3,155	68,818
PH Sport Fury (wb 120.0)				
23	htp cpe	3,603	3,283	14,120
27	conv cpe	3,729	3,502	1,579
29	formal htp cpe	3,678	3,303	2,169
PP VIP (wb 120.0)				
23	htp cpe	3,583	3,382	4,740
29	formal htp cpe	3,668	3,402	1,059
43	htp sdn	3,663	3,433	7,982
EP Suburban (wb 122.0)				
45	wgn 4d	4,056	3,231	6,424
45	Custom wgn 4d, 6P	4,103	3,436	15,976
46	Custom wgn 4d, 9P	4,148	3,527	10,216
45	Sport wgn 4d, 6P	4,123	3,651	8,201
46	Sport wgn 4d, 9P	4,173	3,718	13,502

*Includes "Valiant 200" trim option.

1969 Engines	bore×stroke	bhp	availability
I-6, 170.0	3.40×3.13	115	S-Valiant
I-6, 225.0	3.40×4.13	145	S-Brcda, Belv, Sat, Fury I/II; O-Valiant
V-8, 273.0	3.62 × 3.31	190	O-Valiant
V-8, 318.0	3.91 × 3.31	230	S-Brcda, Spt Sat, Fry III, Spt Fry, VIP, Suburban
V-8, 340.0	4.04 × 3.31	275	O-Barracuda
V-8, 383.0	4.25 × 3.38	290	O-Belv, Sat, Spt Sat, Furys, VIP
V-8, 383.0	4.25 × 3.38	330	O-Brcda, Belv, Sat, Spt Sat, Furys, VIP
V-8, 383.0	4.25 × 3.38	335	S-Road Runner
V-8, 426.0	4.25 × 3.75	425	O-Road Runner, GTX (hemi)
V-8, 440.0	4.32 × 3.75	375	S-GTX; O-Furys exc EP
V-8, 440.0	4.32 × 3.75	350	O-Suburban

1970

VL Valiant (wb 108.0)		Wght	Price	Prod
29	Duster fstbk cpe	2,830	2,172	192,375
41	sdn 4d	2,835	2,250	50,810
VS Valiant Duster 340 (wb 108.0)				
29	fstbk cpe	3,110	2,547	24,817
BH Barracuda (wb 108.0)				
23	htp cpe	2,905	2,764	25,651
27	conv cpe	3,071	3,034	1,554
BP Barracuda Gran Coupe (wb 108.0)				
23	htp cpe	3,015	2,934	8,183
27	conv cpe	3,090	3,160	596
BS 'Cuda (wb 108.0)				
23	htp cpe	3,395	3,164	18,880
27	conv cpe	3,480	3,433	635
RL Belvedere (wb 116.0; wgn-117.0)				
21	cpe	3,095	2,603	4,717
41	sdn 4d	3,130	2,641	13,945
45	wgn 4d	3,655	3,075	5,584
RH Satellite (wb 116.0; wgn-117.0)				
23	htp cpe	3,105	2,765	28,200
27	conv cpe	3,225	3,006	701
41	sdn 4d	3,125	2,741	30,377
45	wgn 4d, 6P	3,637	3,101	4,204
46	wgn 4d, 9P	3,747	3,211	3,277
RP Sport Satellite (wb 116.0; wgn-117.0)				
23	htp cpe	3,170	2,988	8,749
41	sdn 4d	3,205	3,017	3,010
45	wgn 4d, 6P	3,675	3,345	1,975
46	wgn 4d, 9P	3,750	3,455	2,161
RM Road Runner (wb 116.0)				
21	cpe	3,450	2,896	15,716
23	htp cpe	3,475	3,034	24,944
23	Superbird htp cpe	3,785	4,298	1,920
27	conv cpe	3,550	3,289	824
RS GTX (wb 116.0)				
23	htp cpe	3,515	3,535	7,748
PE Fury I (wb 120.0)				
21	sdn 2d	3,603	2,790	2,353
41	sdn 4d	3,640	2,825	14,813
PL Fury II (wb 120.0)				
21	sdn 2d	3,583	2,903	21,316
41	sdn 4d	3,643	2,922	27,694
PM Fury III (wb 120.0)				
23	htp cpe	3,610	3,091	21,373
27	conv cpe	3,770	3,415	1,952
29	formal htp cpe	3,645	3,217	12,367
41	sdn 4d	3,645	3,069	50,876
43	htp sdn	3,690	3,246	47,879
PH Sport Fury (wb 120.0)				
23	htp cpe	3,630	3,313	
23	S/23 htp cpe "PS"	3,660	3,379	8,018
23	GT htp cpe "PP"	3,925	3,898	
29	formal htp cpe	3,645	3,333	5,688
41	sdn 4d	3,680	3,291	5,135

PH Sport Fury		Wght	Price	Prod
43	htp sdn	3,705	3,363	6,854
PL Fury Gran Cpe (wb 120.0)				* Incl. with Fury II sdn 2d
21	sdn 2d	3,864	3,833	See note*
FP Suburban (wb 122.0)				
45	wgn 4d, 6P	4,125	3,303	5,300
46	wgn 4d, 9P	4,205	3,518	2,250
45	Custom wgn 4d, 6P	4,155	3,527	8,898
46	Custom wgn 4d, 9P	4,215	3,603	6,792
45	Sport wgn 4d, 6P	4,200	3,725	4,403
46	Sport wgn 4d, 9P	4,260	3,804	9,170

1970 Engines	bore×stroke	bhp	availability
I-6, 198.0	3.40×3.64	125	S-Valiant VL
I-6, 225.0	3.40×4.13	145	S-Brcda, Belv, Sat, Fury I/II; O-Val VL
V-8, 318.0	3.91×3.31	230	S-Spt Sat, Fry III, Spt Fury, Gran Coupe, Sub
V-8, 340.0	4.04×3.31	275	S-Duster 340; O-'Cuda
V-8, 383.0	4.25×3.38	290	O-all exc Valiant
V-8, 383.0	4.25×3.38	330	O-all exc Valiant
V-8, 383.0	4.25×3.38	335	S-Rd Rnr, 'Cuda
V-8, 426.0	4.25×3.75	425	O-Rd Rnr, 'Cuda, GTX (hemi)
V-8, 440.0	4.32×3.75	350	S-Spt Fury GT; O-other Fury
V-8, 440.0	4.32 × 3.75	375	S-GTX, O-'Cuda
V-8, 440.0	4.32 × 3.75	390	O-'Cuda, RR, GTX, PH23

1971

Valiant (wb 108.0; Scamp-111.0)		Wght	Price	Prod
VL29	Duster fstbk cpe	2,825	2,313	173,592
VL41	sdn 4d	2,831	2,392	42,660
VH23	Scamp htp cpe	2,900	2,561	48,253
VS29	Duster 340 fstbk cpe	3,140	2,703	12,886
Barracuda (wb 108.0)				
VH21	cpe 2d	3,040	2,654	9,459
VH23	htp cpe	3,075	2,766	
VH27	conv	3,145	3,023	1,014
VP23	Gran Cpe htp cpe V-8	3,105	3,029	1,615
VS23	'Cuda htp cpe V-8	3,475	3,155	6,228
VS27	'Cuda conv cpe V-8	3,550	3,412	374
Satellite (wb 117.0; 2d-115.0)				
RL41	sdn 4d	3,294	2,734	11,059
RL21	cpe	3,230	2,663	46,807
RH23	Sebring htp cpe	3,256	2,931	
RL45	wgn 4d, 2S	3,770	3,058	7,138
RH41	Custom sdn 4d	3,286	2,908	30,773
RH45	Custom wgn 4d, 2S	3,776	3,235	5,045
RH46	Custom wgn 4d, 3S	3,846	3,315	4,626
RM23	Rd Rnnr htp cpe V-8	3,640	3,147	14,218
RP23	Seb Plus htp cpe V-8	3,300	3,179	16,253
RP41	Brghm sdn 4d, V-8	3,330	3,189	3,020
RP45	Reg wgn 4d, 2S, V-8	3,815	3,558	2,161
RP46	Reg wgn 4d, 3S, V-8	3,885	3,638	2,985
RS23	GTX htp cpe V-8	3,675	3,733	2,942
Fury (wb 120.0; wgn-122.0)				
PE41	I sdn 4d	3,742	3,163	16,395
PE41	I Custom sdn 4d	3,742	3,241	
PE21	I sdn 2d	3,708	3,113	5,152
PE21	I Custom sdn 2d	3,708	3,208	
PL23	II htp cpe	3,710	3,283	7,859
PL41	II sdn 4d	3,746	3,262	20,098
PL45	II Sub wgn 4d, 2S, V-8	4,245	3,758	4,877
PL46	II Sub wgn 4d, 3S, V-8	4,290	3,869	2,662
PM23	III htp cpe	3,716	3,458	21,319
PM41	III sdn 4d	3,752	3,437	44,244
PM29	III formal htp cpe V-8	3,750	3,600	24,465
PM43	III htp sdn V-8	3,820	3,612	55,356
PM45	III Cus Sub wgn 4d, 2S, V-8	4,240	3,854	10,874
PM46	III Cus Sub wgn 4d, 3S, V-8	4,300	3,930	11,702
Sport Fury (wb 120.0; wgn-122.0)				
PH23	htp cpe V-8	3,805	3,677	3,912
PH29	formal htp cpe V-8	3,810	3,710	3,957
PH41	sdn 4d, V-8	3,845	3,656	2,823
PH43	htp sdn V-8	3,865	3,724	4,813
PH45	Sprt Sub wgn 4d, 2S, V-8	4,290	4,071	5,103

Sport Fury		Wght	Price	Prod
PH46	Sprt Sub wgn 4d, 3S, V-8	4,370	4,146	13,021
PP23	GT htp cpe V-8	4,090	4,111	375

1971 Engines	bore×stroke	bhp	availability
I-6, 198.0	3.40×3.64	125	S-Val, Brcda cpe
I-6, 225.0	3.40×4.13	145	S-Brcda exc cpe, Sat, Fury exc GT; O-Val, Brcda cpe
V-8, 318.0	3.91×3.31	230	S-Sat, Fury; O-Val, Brcda
V-8, 340.0	4.04×3.31	275	S-Dstr 340, 'Cuda; O-Barracuda
V-8, 360.0	4.00 × 3.58	255	O-Fury
V-8, 383.0	4.25 × 3.38	275	O-Brcda, RR, Fry
V-8, 383.0	4.25 × 3.38	300	S-'Cuda, Rd Rnr; O-Brcda, Fury
V-8, 426.0	4.25 × 3.75	425	O-Brcda (hemi)
V-8, 440.0	4.32 × 3.75	335	O-Fury
V-8, 440.0	4.32 × 3.75	370	S-GTX, Fry GT; O-Fury
V-8, 440.0	4.32 × 3.75	385	O-Barracuda

1972

Valiant (wb 108.0; Scamp-111.0)		Wght	Price	Prod
VL29	Duster fstbk cpe	2,780	2,287	212,331
VL41	sdn 4d	2,800	2,363	52,911
VH23	Scamp htp cpe	2,825	2,528	49,470
VS29	Duster 340 fstbk cpe	3,100	2,742	15,681
Barracuda (wb 108.0)				
VH23	htp cpe	3,185	2,710	10,622
VS23	'Cuda htp cpe V-8	3,195	3,029	7,828
Satellite (wb 117.0; 2d-115.0)				
RL21	cpe	3,272	2,609	10,507
RL41	sdn 4d	3,312	2,678	12,794
RL45	wgn 4d 2S V-8	3,785	3,167	7,377
RH23	Sebring htp cpe	3,282	2,871	34,353
RH41	Custom sdn 4d	3,318	2,848	34,973
RH45	Custom wgn 2S V-8	3,825	3,340	5,485
RH46	Cus wgn 4d 3S V-8	3,780	3,418	5,637
RP23	Seb Plus htp cpe V-8	3,320	3,127	21,399
RP45	Reg wgn 4d 2S V-8	3,790	3,562	1,893
RP46	Reg wgn 4d 3S V-8	3,830	3,640	2,907
RM23	Rd Rnnr htp cpe V-8	3,495	3,095	7,628
Fury (wb 120.0; wgn-122.0)				
PL41	I sdn 4d	3,840	3,464	14,006
PM23	II htp cpe	3,790	3,605	7,515
PM41	II sdn 4d	3,830	3,583	20,051
PM45	II Sub wgn 4d 2S	4,315	4,024	5,368
PM46	II Sub wgn 4d 3S	4,360	4,139	2,773
PH23	III htp cpe	3,790	3,785	21,204
PH29	III formal htp cpe	3,790	3,818	9,036
PH41	III sdn 4d	3,830	3,763	46,731
PH43	III htp sdn	3,855	3,829	48,618
PH45	III Cus Sub wgn 4d 2S	4,315	4,123	11,067
PH46	III Cus Sub wgn 4d 3S	4,365	4,201	14,041
PP23	Gran Fury htp cpe	3,735	3,941	15,840
PP29	Grn Fry formal htp cpe	3,805	3,974	8,509
PP43	Gran Fury htp sdn	3,865	3,987	17,551
PP45	Sport Sub wgn 4d 2S	4,335	4,389	4,971
PP46	Sport Sub wgn 4d 3S	4,395	4,466	15,628

1972 Engines	bore×stroke	bhp	availability
I-6, 198.0	3.40×3.64	100	S-Valiant
I-6, 225.0	3.40×4.13	110	S-Brcda, Sat; O-Valiant
V-8, 318.0	3.91×3.31	150	S-Sat, Fury; O-Val, Brcda
V-8, 340.0	4.04×3.31	240	S-Duster 340, 'Cuda, Rd Rnnr; O-Barracuda
V-8, 360.0	4.00×3.58	170	O-Fury
V-8, 400.0	4.34×3.38	190/250	O-Fury
V-8, 440.0	4.32×3.75	230/285	O-Fury

1973

Valiant (wb 108.0; Scamp-111.0)		Wght	Price	Prod
VL29	Duster fstbk cpe	2,830	2,376	249,243
VL41	sdn 4d	2,865	2,447	61,826
VH23	Scamp htp cpe	2,885	2,617	53,792
VS29	Duster 340 fstbk cpe	3,175	2,822	15,731
Barracuda (wb 108.0)				
VH23	htp cpe	3,140	2,935	11,587

Barracuda		Wght	Price	Prod
VS23	'Cuda htp cpe	3,235	3,120	10,626
Satellite (wb 117.0; 2d-115.0)				
RL21	cpe	3,408	2,755	13,570
RL41	sdn 4d	3,482	2,824	14,716
RL45	wgn 4d 2S V-8	3,950	3,272	6,906
RH23	Sebring htp cpe	3,425	2,997	51,575
RH41	Custom sdn 4d	3,478	2,974	46,748
RH45	Cus wgn 4d 2S V-8	3,945	3,400	6,733
RH46	Cus wgn 4d 3S V-8	3,990	3,518	7,705
RP23	Seb Plus htp cpe V-8	3,455	3,258	43,628
RP45	Reg wgn 4d 2S V-8	3,950	3,621	2,781
RP46	Reg wgn 4d 3S V-8	4,010	3,740	4,786
RM21	Road Runner cpe V-8	3,525	3,115	19,056
Fury (wb 120.0; wgn-122.0)				
PL41	I sdn 4d	3,865	3,575	17,365
PM41	II sdn 4d	3,845	3,694	21,646
PM45	II Sub wgn 4d 2S	4,410	4,150	5,206
PH23	III htp cpe	3,815	3,883	34,963
PH41	III sdn 4d	3,860	3,866	51,742
PH43	III htp sdn	3,880	3,932	51,215
PH45	III Cus Sub wgn 4d 2S	4,420	4,246	9,888
PH46	III Cus Sub wgn 4d 3S	4,465	4,354	15,671
PP23	Gran Fury htp cpe	3,845	4,064	18,127
PP43	Gran Fury htp sdn	3,890	4,110	14,852
PP45	Sport Sub wgn 4d 2S	4,435	4,497	4,832
PP46	Sport Sub wgn 4d 3S	4,495	4,599	15,680

1973 Engines	bore×stroke	bhp	availability
I-6, 198.0	3.40×3.64	100	S-Valiant
I-6, 225.0	3.40×4.13	110	S-Brcda, Sat; O-Valiant
V-8, 318.0	3.91×3.31	150	S-Sat, Fury; O-Val, Brcda
V-8, 340.0	4.04×3.31	240	S-Duster 340, 'Cuda, Rd Rnnr; O-Barracuda
V-8, 360.0	4.00×3.58	175	O-Fury
V-8, 400.0	4.34×3.38	190/250	O-Fury
V-8, 440.0	4.32×3.75	230/285	O-Fury

1974

Valiant (wb 110.0; fstbk-108.0)		Wght	Price	Prod
VL29	Duster fstbk cpe	2,975	2,829	277,409
VS29	Duster 360 fstbk cpe	3,315	3,288	
VL41	sdn 4d	3,035	2,942	127,430
VP41	Brougham sdn 4d	3,195	3,819	
VP23	Brougham htp cpe	3,180	3,794	2,545
VH23	Scamp htp cpe	3,010	3,077	51,699
Barracuda (wb 108.0)				
VH23	htp cpe	3,210	3,067	6,745
VS23	'Cuda htp cpe	3,300	3,252	4,989
Satellite (wb 117.0; 2d-115.0)				
RL21	cpe	3,470	3,155	10,634
RL41	sdn 4d	3,555	3,226	12,726
RL45	wgn 4d 2S V-8	4,065	3,654	4,622
RH23	Sebring htp cpe	3,490	3,353	31,980
RH41	Custom sdn 4d	3,550	3,329	45,863
RH45	Cus wgn 4d 2S V-8	4,065	3,839	4,354
RH46	Cus wgn 4d 3S V-8	4,110	4,152	5,591
RP45	Reg wgn 4d 2S V-8	4,065	4,066	2,026
RP46	Reg wgn 4d 3S V-8	4,130	4,381	3,132
RP23	Seb Plus htp cpe V-8	3,555	3,621	18,480
RM21	Road Runner cpe V-8	3,615	3,545	11,555
Fury (wb 120.0; wgn-124.0)				
PL41	I sdn 4d	4,185	4,101	8,162
PM41	II sdn 4d	4,165	4,223	11,649
PM45	II Sub wgn 4d 2S	4,745	4,669	2,490
PH23	III htp cpe	4,125	4,418	14,167
PH41	III sdn 4d	4,180	4,400	27,965
PH43	III htp sdn	4,205	4,268	18,778
PH45	III Cus Sub wgn 4d 2S	4,755	4,767	3,877
PH46	III Cus Sub wgn 4d 3S	4,800	4,878	5,628
PP23	Gran Fury htp cpe	4,300	4,627	9,617
PP43	Gran Fury htp sdn	4,370	4,675	8,191
PP45	Sport Sub wgn 4d 2S	4,795	5,025	1,712
PP46	Sport Sub wgn 4d 3S	4,850	5,130	6,047

1974 Engines	bore×stroke	bhp	availability
I-6, 198.0	3.40×3.64	95	S-Val exc Brghm

1974 Engines	bore×stroke	bhp	availability
I-6, 225.0	3.40×4.13	105	S-Val, Brghm, Sat; O-Val
V-8, 318.0	3.91×3.31	150	S-Brcda, Sat; O-Valiant
V-8, 318.0	3.91×3.31	170	S-Road Runner
V-8, 360.0	4.00×3.58	180	S-Fury exc wgn/Gran Fury
V-8, 360.0	4.00×3.58	200	O-Sat, Fury exc wgn/Gran Fury
V-8, 360.0	4.00×3.58	245	S-Duster 360; O-Valiant
V-8, 400.0	4.34×3.38	185	S-Gran Fury, Fury wgns; O-Fury
V-8, 400.0	4.34×3.38	205	O-Satellite, Fury
V-8, 400.0	4.34×3.38	240	O-Fury
V-8, 400.0	4.34×3.38	250	O-Satellite
V-8, 440.0	4.32×3.75	230/250	O-Fury
V-8, 440.0	4.32×3.75	275	O-Satellite

1975

Valiant (wb 111.0; fstbk-108.0)		Wght	Price	Prod
VL29	Duster fstbk cpe	2,970	3,243	79,384
VH29	Duster Cus fstbk cpe	2,970	3,418	38,826
VL41	sdn 4d	3,040	3,247	44,471
VH41	Custom sdn 4d	3,040	3,422	56,258
VH23	Scamp htp cpe	3,020	3,518	23,581
VS29	Dstr 360 fstbk cpe V-8	3,315	3,979	1,421
VP23	Brougham htp cpe	3,240	4,232	5,781
VP41	Brougham sdn 4d	3,250	4,139	17,803
Fury (wb 117.5; 2d-115.0)				
RL21	cpe	3,612	3,542	8,398
RL41	sdn 4d	3,642	3,591	11,432
RL45	wgn 4d V-8	4,180	4,309	4,468
RH23	Custom cpe	3,692	3,711	27,486
RH41	Custom wgn 4d	3,692	3,704	31,080
RH45	Cus wgn 4d 2S V-8	4,230	4,512	3,890
RH46	Cus wgn 4d 3S V-8	4,285	4,632	4,285
RP23	Sport htp cpe V-8	3,790	4,105	17,782
RP45	Sprt Sub wgn 4d 2S V-8	4,230	4,770	1,851
RP46	Sprt Sub wgn 4d 3S V-8	4,295	4,867	3,107
Gran Fury (wb 122.0; wgn-124.0)				
PM41	sdn 4d	4,260	4,565	8,185
PM45	wgn 4d 2S	4,855	5,067	2,295
PH23	Custom htp cpe	4,205	4,781	6,041
PH41	Custom sdn 4d	4,260	4,761	19,043
PH43	Custom htp sdn	4,290	4,837	11,292
PH45	Custom wgn 4d 2S	4,870	5,176	3,155
PH46	Custom wgn 4d 3S	4,915	5,294	4,500
PP29	Brougham htp cpe	4,310	5,146	6,521
PP43	Brougham htp sdn	4,400	5,067	5,521
PP45	Sport Sub wgn 4d 2S	4,885	5,455	1,508
PP46	Sport Sub wgn 4d 3S	4,930	5,573	4,740

1975 Engines	bore×stroke	bhp	availability
I-6, 225.0	3.40×4.13	90	S-Valiant
I-6, 225.0	3.40×4.13	95	S-Fury
V-8, 318.0	3.91×3.31	135	O-Fury, Valiant
V-8, 318.0	3.91×3.31	150	S-Fury; O-Gran Fury exc wgn/Brghm
V-8, 360.0	4.00×3.58	180	S-Gran Fury exc wgn/Brghm; O-Fury, G.F. wgn/Brghm
V-8, 360.0	4.00×3.58	190	O-Fury, Gran Fury
V-8, 360.0	4.00×3.58	230	S-Duster 360
V-8, 400.0	4.34×3.38	165/185	O-Fury
V-8, 400.0	4.34×3.38	175	S-Gran Fury Brougham wgn; O-other
V-8, 400.0	4.34×3.38	190/235	O-Fury
V-8, 400.0	4.34×3.38	195	O-Gran Fury
V-8, 440.0	4.32×3.75	215	O-Gran Fury

1976

Valiant (wb 111.0; fstbk-108.0)		Wght	Price	Prod
VL23	Scamp Spec htp cpe	3,020	3,337	4,018
VL29	Duster fstbk cpe	2,975	3,241	34,681
VL41	sdn 4d	3,050	3,276	40,079
VH23	Scamp htp cpe	3,020	3,510	6,908
Volare (wb 112.5; cpe-108.5)		**Wght**	**Price**	**Prod**
HL29	cpe	3,222	3,324	37,024
HL41	sdn 4d	3,252	3,359	23,058
HL45	wgn 5d	3,622	3,646	46,065
HH29	Custom cpe	3,232	3,506	31,252
HH41	Custom sdn 4d	3,262	3,541	36,407
HP29	Premier cpe	3,438	4,402	31,475
HP41	Premier sdn 4d	3,472	4,389	37,131
HH45	Premier wgn 5d	3,628	3,976	49,507
Fury (wb 117.5; 2d-115.0)				
RL23	htp cpe	3,708	3,699	16,415
RL41	sdn 4d	3,742	3,733	22,654
RL45	wgn 4d 2S V-8	4,285	4,597	4,624
RL46	wgn 4d 3S V-8	4,350	4,739	4,412
RH23	Sport htp cpe	3,712	3,988	28,851
RH41	Salon sdn 4d	3,762	4,022	20,234
RH45	Sprt Sub wgn 2S V-8	4,285	4,986	2,175
RH46	Sprt Sub wgn 3S V-8	4,360	5,128	3,482
Gran Fury (wb 122.0; wgn-124.0)				
PM41	sdn 4d	4,140	4,349	8,928
PM45	wgn 4d 2S	4,880	4,909	1,587
PH23	Custom htp cpe	4,265	4,730	2,733
PH41	Custom sdn 4d	4,305	4,715	14,738
PH45	Cus Sub wgn 4d 2S	4,895	5,193	1,433
PH46	Cus Sub wgn 4d 3S	4,940	5,316	1,998
PP29	Brougham htp cpe	4,400	5,334	2,619
PP41	Brougham sdn 4d	4,435	5,162	2,990
PP46	Sport Sub wgn 4d 3S	4,975	5,761	2,484

1976 Engines	bore×stroke	bhp	availability
I-6, 225.0	3.40×4.13	100	S-Val, Vol, Fury exc wgn
V-8, 318.0	3.91×3.31	150	S-Fury exc wgn, Gran Fury sdn; O-Val, Volare
V-8, 360.0	4.00×3.58	170	S-Fury wagon, Grn Fury Cus; O-Val, Vol, Fury, Gran Fury exc Cus/Brougham
V-8, 360.0	4.00×3.58	220	O-Volare, Fury
V-8, 400.0	4.34×3.38	175	S-Gran Fury wgn/Brougham; O-Fury
V-8, 400.0	4.34×3.38	200/240	O-Gran Fury
V-8, 440.0	4.32×3.75	205	O-Gran Fury

1977

Volare (wb 112.7; cpe-108.7)		Wght	Price	Prod
HL29	cpe	3,235	3,570	42,455
HL41	sdn 4d	3,290	3,619	44,550
HL45	wgn 4d	3,500	3,941	80,180
HH29	Custom cpe	3,240	3,752	34,196
HH41	Custom sdn 4d	3,295	3,801	50,859
HP29	Premier cpe	3,430	4,305	21,979
HP41	Premier sdn 4d	3,496	4,354	31,443
HP45	Premier wgn 5d	3,505	4,271	76,756
Fury (wb 117.5; 2d-115.0)				
RL23	htp cpe	3,742	3,893	16,410
RL41	sdn 4d	3,772	3,944	25,172
RL45	Sub wgn 4d 2S V-8	4,335	4,687	6,765
RL46	Sub wgn 4d 3S V-8	4,390	4,830	5,556
RH23	Sport htp cpe	3,748	4,132	30,075
RH41	Salon sdn 4d	3,782	4,185	25,617
RH45	Sprt Sub wgn 4d 2S V-8	4,330	5,192	2,502
RH46	Sprt Sub wgn 4d 3S V-8	4,400	5,335	4,065
Gran Fury (wb 122.0; wgn-124.0)				
PM23	cpe	4,070	4,692	2,772
PM41	sdn 4d	4,145	4,677	14,242
PM45	Suburban wgn 4d 2S	4,885	5,315	2,055
PH23	Brougham cpe	4,190	4,963	4,846
PH41	Brougham sdn 4d	4,250	4,948	17,687
PH45	Sport Sub wgn 4d 2S	4,880	5,558	1,631
PH46	Sport Sub wgn 4d 3S	4,925	5,681	4,319

1977 Engines	bore×stroke	bhp	availability
I-6, 225.0	3.40×4.13	100	S-Vol exc wgns
I-6, 225.0	3.40×4.13	110	S-Vol wgns; Fury exc wgns
V-8, 318.0	3.91×3.31	145	S-Gran Fury exc Brougham wgn; O-Vol, other Fry
V-8, 360.0	4.00×3.58	155	S-Fury wgns, Grn Fry Brghm; O-Volare, Fury, other Gran Fury
V-8, 360.0	4.00×3.58	170	O-Fry, Grn Fry
V-8, 400.0	4.34×3.38	190	S-Grn Fry wgns; O-Fury, Grn Fry
V-8, 440.0	4.32×3.75	185/195	O-Gran Fury

1978

Horizon (wb 99.2)		Wght	Price	Prod
ML44	htchbk sdn 4d	2,145	3,976	106,772
Volare (wb 112.7; cpe-108.7)				
HL29	cpe	3,200	3,771	74,818
HL41	sdn 4d	3,235	3,899	100,718
HL45	wgn 5d	3,465	4,241	81,242
Fury (wb 117.5; 2d-115.0)				
RL23	htp cpe	3,725	4,236	13,276
RL41	sdn 4d	3,760	4,326	83,649
RL45	Sub wgn 4d 2S V-8	4,310	5,084	4,522
RL46	Sub sgn 4d 3S V-8	4,370	5,227	3,889
RH23	Sport htp cpe	3,735	4,483	13,031
RH41	Salon sdn 4d	3,770	4,568	14,964
RH45	Sprt Sub wgn 4d 2S V-8	4,300	5,545	1,720
RH46	Sprt Sub wgn 4d 3S V-8	4,375	5,688	2,528

1978 Engines	bore×stroke	bhp	availability
I-4, 104.7	3.13×3.40	70	S-Horizon
I-6, 225.0	3.40×4.13	90	O-Vol exc wgn
I-6, 225.0	3.40×4.13	100	S-Vol exc wgn
I-6, 225.0	3.40×4.13	110	S-Vol wgn, Fury
V-8, 318.0	3.91×3.31	140	S-Vol, Fury exc wgns
V-8, 318.0	3.91×3.31	155	O-Vol, Fury exc wgns
V-8, 360.0	4.00×3.58	155	S-Fury wgns; O-Volare, other Fury
V-8, 360.0	4.00×3.58	165/175	O-Volare
V-8, 360.0	4.00×3.58	170	O-Fury
V-8, 400.0	4.34×3.38	190	O-Fury

1979

Horizon (wb 99.2; TC3-96.6)		Wght	Price	Prod
ML24	TC3 htchbk cpe	2,195	4,864	63,715
ML44	htchbk sdn 4d	2,135	4,469	99,048
Volare (wb 112.7; cpe-108.7)				
HL29	cpe	3,110	4,387	63,620
HL41	sdn 4d	3,175	4,504	95,383
HL45	wgn 5d	3,435	5,110	50,683

1979 Engines	bore×stroke	bhp	availability
14, 104.7	3.13×3.40	70	S-Horizon
I-6, 225.0	3.40×4.13	100	S-Volare
I-6, 225.0	3.40×4.13	110	O-Volare
V-8, 318.0	3.91×3.31	135	O-Volare
V-8, 360.0	4.00×3.58	195	O-Volare

1980

Horizon (wb 99.2; TC3-96.6)		Wght	Price	Prod
ML24	TC3 htchbk cpe	2,135	5,681	67,738
ML44	htchbk sdn 4d	2,095	5,526	94,740
Volare (wb 112.7; cpes-108.7)				
HE29	Special cpe I-6	3,155	5,151	16,475
HE41	Special sdn 4d I-6	3,210	5,151	25,509
HL29	cpe	3,170	5,033	17,781
HL41	sdn 4d	3,225	5,150	30,097
HL45	wgn 4d	3,540	5,422	19,910
Gran Fury (wb 118.5)				
JL42	sdn 4d	3,562	6,741	15,469
JH42	Salon sdn 4d	3,438	7,116	3,255

1980 Engines	bore ×stroke	bhp	availability
I-4, 104.7	3.13×3.40	65	S-Horizon
I-6, 225.0	3.40×4.13	90	S-Vol, Grn Fry
V-8, 318.0	3.91×3.31	120	S-Gran Fury O-Volare exc Special
V-8, 360.0	4.00×3.58	130	O-Gran Fury

Note: Plymouth production totals through 1980 include export models, which makes figures in this book higher than some quoted elsewhere.

1981

Horizon (wb 99.1; TC3-96.6)	Wght	Price	Prod
ML24 TC3 htchbk cpe	2,205	6,149	36,312
ME24 Miser TC3 htchbk cpe	2,137	5,299	
ML44 htchbk sdn 4d	2,130	5,690	58,547
ME44 Miser htchbk sdn 4d	2,060	5,299	
Reliant (wb 99.6)			
PL21 sdn 2d	2,305	5,880	58,093
PL41 sdn 4d	2,300	5,980	
PH21 Custom sdn 2d	2,315	6,315	13,587
PH41 Custom sdn 4d	2,310	6,448	
PH45 Custom wgn 5d	2,375	6,721	40,830
PP21 SE sdn 2d	2,340	6,789	28,457
PP41 SE sdn 4d	2,340	6,933	
PP45 SE wgn 5d	2,390	7,254	10,670
Gran Fury (wb 118.5)			
L42 sdn 4d	3,547	7,387	7,719

1981 Engines	bore × stroke	bhp	availability
I-4, 104.7	3.13 × 3.40	63	S-Horizon
I-4, 135.0	3.44 × 3.62	84	S-Reliant, late TC3; O-Horiz
I-4, 156.0	3.59 × 3.86	92	O-Reliant
I-6, 225.0	3.40 × 4.12	85	S-Gran Fury
V-8, 318.0	3.91 × 3.31	130	O-Gran Fury
V-8, 318.0	3.91 × 3.31	165	O-Grn Fry (CA)

1982

TC3 (wb 96.6)	Wght	Price	Prod
MH24 Custom htchbk cpe	2,205	6,421	12,889
ME24 Miser htchbk cpe	2,180	5,799	18,359
MP24 Turismo htchbk cpe	2,285	7,115	6,608
Horizon (wb 99.1)			
MH44 htchbk sdn 4d	2,175	5,927	17,315
ME44 Miser htchbk sdn 4d	2,110	5,499	19,102
MP44 Euro-Sedan sdn 4d	2,285	6,636	779
Reliant (wb 99.6)			
PL21 sdn 2d	2,315	5,990	12,026
PL41 sdn 4d	2,310	6,131	37,488
PH21 Custom sdn 2d	2,320	6,898	12,403
PH41 Custom sdn 4d	2,320	7,053	29,980
PH45 Custom wgn 5d	2,395	7,334	32,501
PP21 SE sdn 2d	2,365	7,575	2,536
PP41 SE sdn 4d	2,385	7,736	4,578
PP45 SE wgn 5d	2,470	8,101	7,711
Gran Fury (wb 112.7)			
BL41 sdn 4d	3,345	7,750	18,111

1982 Engines	bore×stroke	bhp	availability
I-4, 104.7	3.13×3.40	63	S-TC3, Horizon
I-4, 135.0	3.44×3.62	84	S-Reliant, TC3 Turismo; O-TC3, Horizon
I-4, 156.0	3.59×3.86	92	O-Reliant
I-6, 225.0	3.40×4.12	90	S-Gran Fury
V-8, 318.0	3.91 × 3.31	130	O-Gran Fury
V-8, 318.0	3.91 × 3.31	165	O-Grn Fry (CA)

1983

Turismo (wb 96.6)	Wght	Price	Prod
MH htchbk cpe	2,226	6,379	22,527
MP 2.2 htchbk cpe	2,363	7,303	9,538
Horizon (wb 99.1)			
ME44 htchbk sdn 4d	2,175	5,841	35,796
MH Cus htchbk sdn 4d	2,206	6,071	10,675
Reliant (wb 100.1)			
PL21 sdn 2d	2,317	6,577	16,109
PL41 sdn 4d	2,323	6,718	69,112
PH45 Custom wgn 5d	2,372	7,636	38,264
PH21 SE sdn 2d	2,333	7,260	5,852
PH41 SE sdn 4d	2,360	7,417	13,434
PP45 SE wgn 5d	2,432	8,186	3,791
Gran Fury (wb 112.7)			
BL41 Salon sdn 4d	3,478	8,248	15,739

1983 Engines	bore×stroke	bhp	availability
I-4, 97.3	3.17×3.07	62	S-late Turismo, Horizon
I-4, 104.7	3.13×3.40	63	S-early Turismo, Horizon
I-4, 135.0	3.44×3.62	94	S-Relnt, Trsmo 2.2; O-Turismo, Horizon
I-4, 156.0	3.59×3.86	93	O-Reliant
I-6, 225.0	3.40×4.12	90	S-Gran Fury
V-8, 318.0	3.91×3.31	130	O-Gran Fury

1984

Turismo (wb 96.6)	Wght	Price	Prod
MH24 htchbk cpe	2,220	6,494	38,835
MP24 2.2 htchbk cpe	2,327	7,288	10,881
Horizon (wb 99.1)			
ME44 htchbk sdn 4d	2,151	5,830	62,903
MH44 SE htchbk sdn 4d	2,180	6,148	15,661
Reliant (wb 100.3)			
PL21 sdn 2d	2,354	6,837	14,533
PL41 sdn 4d	2,361	6,949	72,595
PH45 Custom wgn 5d	2,450	7,736	39,207
PH21 SE sdn 2d	2,364	7,463	5,287
PH41 SE sdn 4d	2,394	7,589	16,223
PP45 SE wgn 5d	2,501	8,195	4,338
Gran Fury (wb 112.7)			
BL41 Salon sdn 4d	3,558	9,180	14,516

1984 Engines	bore×stroke	bhp	availability
I-4, 97.3	3.17×3.07	64	S-Trsmo, Horizn
I-4, 135.0	3.44×3.62	96	S-Relnt; O-Trsmo, Horizon
I-4, 135.0	3.44×3.62	101	S-Turismo 2.2
I-4, 135.0	3.44×3.62	110	O-Trsmo, Horizn
I-4, 156.0	3.59×3.86	101	O-Reliant
V-8, 318.0	3.91×3.31	130	S-Gran Fury

1985

Turismo (wb 96.6)	Wght	Price	Prod
LMH24 htchbk cpe	2,215	6,584	44,377
LMP24 2.2 htchbk cpe	2,366	7,515	7,785
Horizon (wb 99.1)			
LME44 htchbk sdn 4d	2,154	5,977	71,846
LMH44 SE htchbk sdn 4d	2,174	6,342	16,165
Reliant (wb 100.3)			
KPL21 sdn 2d	2,375	6,924	11,317
KPL41 sdn 4d	2,393	7,039	46,972
KPM21 SE sdn 2d	2,390	7,321	9,530
KPM41 SE sdn 4d	2,424	7,439	27,231
KPH45 SE wgn 5d	2,514	7,909	27,489
KPH21 LE sdn 2d	2,414	7,659	4,110
KPH41 LE sdn 4d	2,446	7,792	7,072
KPP45 LE wgn 5d	2,546	8,348	4,017
Caravelle (wb 103.3)			
EJH41 SE sdn 4d	2,593	9,007	39,971
Gran Fury (wb 112.7)			
MBL41 Salon sdn 4d	3,553	9,658	19,102

1985 Engines	bore×stroke	bhp	availability
I-4, 97.3	3.17×3.07	64	S-Trsmo, Horizn
I-4, 135.0	3.44×3.62	96	S-Relnt, O-Trsmo, Horizon
I-4, 135.0	3.44 × 3.62	99	S-Caravelle
I-4, 135.0	3.44 × 3.62	110	S-Turismo 2.2
I-4T, 135.0	3.44 × 3.62	146	O-Caravelle
I-4, 156.0	3.59 × 3.86	101	O-Reliant, Caravelle
V-8, 318.0	3.91 × 3.31	140	S-Gran Fury

1986

Turismo (wb 96.6)	Wght	Price	Prod
LMH24 htchbk cpe	2,215	6,787	41,899
LMP24 2.2 htchbk cpe	2,366	7,732	4,488
Horizon (wb 99.1)			
LME44 htchbk sdn 4d	2,154	6,209	76,458
LMH44 SE htchbk sdn 4d	2,174	6,558	8,050
Reliant (wb 100.3)			
KPL21 sdn 2d	2,395	7,184	2,573
KPL41 sdn 4d	2,402	7,301	26,220
KPM21 SE sdn 2d	2,412	7,639	10,707
KPM41 SE sdn 4d	2,429	7,759	47,827
KPM45 SE wgn 5d	2,513	8,186	22,154
KPH21 LE sdn 2d	2,427	8,087	2,482
KPH41 LE sdn 4d	2,444	8,207	5,941
KPH45 LE wgn 5d	2,549	8,936	5,101
Caravelle (wb 103.3)			
EJM41 sdn 4d	2,589	9,241	18,698
EJH41 SE sdn 4d	2,589	9,810	15,654
Gran Fury (wb 112.7)			
MBL41 Salon sdn 4d	3,550	9,947	14,761

1986 Engines	bore×stroke	bhp	availability
I-4, 97.3	3.17×3.07	64	S-Trsmo, Horizn
I-4, 135.0	3.44×3.62	96	O-Trsmo, Horizn
I-4, 135.0	3.44×3.62	97	S-Reliant, Crvlle
I-4, 135.0	3.44×3.62	110	S-Turismo 2.2
I-4T, 135.0	3.44×3.62	146	O-Caravelle
I-4, 153.0	3.44×4.09	100	O-Reliant, Crvlle
V-8, 318.0	3.91×3.31	140	S-Gran Fury

1987

Turismo (wb 96.6)	Wght	Price	Prod
LMH24 htchbk cpe	2,290	7,199	24,104
Horizon (wb 99.1)			
LME44 Amer htchbk sdn 4d	2,237	5,799	79,449
Sundance (wb 97.0)			
PPH24 htchbk sdn 2d	2,527	7,599	35,719
PPH44 htchbk sdn 4d	2,565	7,799	39,960
Reliant (wb 100.3)			
KPL21 sdn 2d	2,409	7,655	204
KPL41 sdn 4d	2,415	7,655	5,142
KPM21 LE sdn 2d	2,468	8,134	9,127
KPM41 LE sdn 4d	2,484	8,134	66,575
KPM45 LE wgn 5d	2,588	8,579	22,905
Caravelle (wb 103.3)			
EJM41 sdn 4d	2,589	9,762	23,132
EJH41 SE sdn 4d	2,596	10,355	19,333
Gran Fury (wb 112.7)			
MBL41 Salon sdn 4d	3,599	10,598	10,377

1987 Engines	bore×stroke	bhp	availability
I-4, 135.0	3.44×3.62	96	S-Trsmo, Horizn
I-4, 135.0	3.44×3.62	97	S-Sundance, Reliant, Crvlle
I-4T, 135.0	3.44×3.62	146	O-Sundance, Caravelle
I-4, 153.0	3.44×4.09	100	O-Relnt, Crvlle
V-8, 318.0	3.91×3.31	140	S-Gran Fury

1988

Horizon (wb 99.1)	Wght	Price	Prod
LME44 Amer htchbk sdn 4d	2,225	5,999	61,715
Sundance (wb 97.0)			
PPH24 htchbk sdn 2d	2,513	7,975	34,827
PPH44 htchbk sdn 4d	2,544	8,175	53,521
Reliant (wb 100.3)			
KPH21 America sdn 2d	2,459	6,995	8,543
KPH41 America sdn 4d	2,485	6,995	95,551
KPH45 America wgn 5d	2,537	7,695	21,213
Caravelle (wb 103.3)			
EJM41 sdn 4d	2,594	10,659	9,718
EJH41 SE sdn 4d	2,632	11,628	7,171
Gran Fury (wb 112.7)			
MBE41 sdn 4d	3,576	12,127	238
MBL41 Salon sdn 4d	3,588	11,407	11,183

1988 Engines	bore×stroke	bhp	availability
I-4, 135.0	3.44×3.62	93	S-Horizon, Sndnce, Relnt, Caravelle
I-4T, 135.0	3.44×3.62	146	O-Sundance, Caravelle
I-4, 153.0	3.44×4.09	96	O-Sndnce, Relnt, Caravelle
V-8, 318.0	3.91×3.31	140	S-Gran Fury

1989

Horizon (wb 99.1)	Wght	Price	Prod
LME44 Amer htchbk sdn 4d	2,237	6,595	45,341
Sundance (wb 97.0) - 104,150 built			
PPH24 htchbk sdn 2d	2,520	8,395	—
PPH44 htchbk sdn 4d	2,558	8,595	—
Reliant (wb 100.3) - 36,012 built			
KPH21 America sdn 2d	2,317	7,595	—
KPH41 America sdn 4d	2,323	7,595	—
Acclaim (wb 103.3) - 77,752 built			
APJ41 sdn 4d	2,753	9,920	—
APP41 LE sdn 4d	2,827	11,295	—
APX41 LX sdn 4d	2,968	13,195	—

Gran Fury (wb 112.7)	Wght	Price	Prod
MBL41 Salon sdn 4d	3,599	11,995	4,985

1989 Engines	bore×stroke		availability
I-4, 135.0	3.44×3.62	93	S-Horizon, Sndnce, Relnt
I-4, 153.0	3.44×4.09	100	S-Acclm exc LX; O-Sndnce, Rlnt
I-4T, 153.0	3.44×4.09	150	O-Sundance, Acclaim
V-6, 181.0	3.59×2.99	141	S-Acclaim LX
V-8, 318.0	3.91×3.31	140	S-Gran Fury

1990

Horizon (wb 99.1)	Wght	Price	Prod
LME44 htchbk sdn 4d	2,296	6,995	16,397
Sundance (wb 97.0) - 79,562 built			
PPH24 htchbk sdn 2d	2,513	8,795	—
PPH44 htchbk sdn 4d	2,544	8,995	—
Acclaim (wb 103.3) - 110,330 built			
APJ41 sdn 4d	2,854	10,385	—
APP41 LE sdn 4d	—	11,815	—
APX41 LX sdn 4d	—	13,805	—

1990 Engines	bore×stroke		availability
I-4, 135.0	3.44×3.62	93	S-Hrizn, Sndnce
I-4, 153.0	3.44×4.09	100	S-Acclm exc LX; O-Sundance
I-4T, 153.0	3.44×4.09	150	O-Sundance, Acclaim
V-6, 181.0	3.59×2.99	141	S-Acclaim LX

1991

Sundance (wb 97.0)	Wght	Price	Prod
PPH24 Amer htchbk sdn 2d	2,617	7,699	
Hghlne htchbk sdn 2d	—	8,899	27,909
RS htchbk sdn 2d	—	10,099	
PPH44 Amer htchbk sdn 4d	2,654	7,999	
Hghlne htchbk sdn 4d	—	9,199	34,911
RS htchbk sdn 4d	—	10,425	
Acclaim (wb 103.3) - 97,146 built			
APJ41 sdn 4d	2,789	10,825	—
APP41 LE sdn 4d	—	12,880	—
APX41 LX sdn 4d	—	14,380	—
Laser (wb 97.2) - 30,720 built			
htchbk cpe	2,524	10,864	—
RS htchbk cpe	—	12,770	—
RS Turbo htchbk cpe	2,745	13,954	—

1991 Engines	bore×stroke	bhp	availability
I-4, 107.1	3.17×3.39	92	S-Laser (ohc)
I-4, 122.0	3.35×3.46	135	O-Laser (dohc)
I-4T, 122.0	3.35×3.46	190	O-Laser (dohc)
I-4, 135.0	3.44×3.62	93	S-Sndnce (ohc)
I-4T, 135.0	3.44×3.62	152	O-Sndnce (ohc)
I-4, 153.0	3.44×4.09	100	S-Acclaim; O-Sndnce (ohc)
V-6, 181.4	3.66 × 3.19	141	O-Acclaim (ohc)

1992

Sundance (wb 97.0)	Wght	Price	Prod
PPH24 Amer htchbk sdn 2d	2,617	7,984	
Hghlne htchbk sdn 2d	—	9,246	29,951
Duster htchbk sdn 2d	—	9,849	
PPH44 Amer htchbk sdn 4d	2,654	8,384	
Hghlne htchbk sdn 4d	—	9,646	36,606
Duster htchbk sdn 4d	—	10,249	
Acclaim (wb 103.3)			
APH41 sdn 4d	2,784	11,470	77,105
Laser (wb 97.2)—25,019 built			
htchbk cpe	2,531	11,206	—
RS htchbk cpe	2,690	13,101	—
RS Turbo htchbk cpe	2,756	14,392	—
RS Trb AWD htchbk cpe	3,073	16,368	—

1992 Engines	bore×stroke	bhp	availability
I-4, 107.1	3.17×3.39	92	S-Laser (ohc)
I-4, 122.0	3.35×3.46	135	O-Laser (dohc)
I-4T, 122.0	3.35×3.46	195	O-Laser (dohc)
I-4, 135.0	3.44×3.62	93	S-Sndnce exc Duster
I-4, 153.0	3.44×4.09	100	S-Acclaim; O-Sndnce (ohc) exc Duster
V-6, 181.4	3.66×3.19	141	S-Duster; O-Acclaim (ohc)

1993

Sundance (wb 97.0)	Wght	Price	Prod
PPH24 htchbk sdn 2d	2,613	8,397	42,020
Duster htchbk sdn 2d	—	10,498	
PPH44 htchbk sdn 4d	2,884	8,797	43,736
Duster htchbk sdn 4d	—	10,898	
Acclaim (wb 103.5)			
APH41 sdn 4d	2,784	11,910	55,531
Laser (wb 97.2) - 17,178 built			
htchbk cpe	2,531	11,406	—
RS htchbk cpe	2,690	13,749	—
RS Turbo htchbk cpe	2,756	15,267	—
RS Trb AWD htchbk cpe	3,073	17,371	—

1993 Engines	bore ×stroke	bhp	availability
I-4, 107.1	3.17×3.39	92	S-Laser (ohc)
I-4, 122.0	3.35×3.46	135	O-Laser (dohc)
I-4T, 122.0	3.35×3.46	180	O-Laser (dohc)
I-4T, 122.0	3.35×3.46	195	O-Laser (dohc)
I-4, 135.0	3.44×3.62	93	S-Sndnce (ohc)
I-4, 153.0	3.44×4.09	100	S-Acclaim; O-Sndnce (ohc)
V-6, 181.4	3.66×3.19	141	O-Acclaim, Sundance (ohc)

1994

Sundance (wb 97.0)	Wght	Price	Prod
PPH24 htchbk sdn 2d	2,608	8,806	33,599
Duster htchbk sdn 2d	—	10,946	
PPH44 htchbk sdn 4d	2,643	9,206	36,839
Duster htchbk sdn 4d	—	11,346	
Acclaim (wb 103.5)			
APH41 sdn 4d	2,831	12,470	40,294
Laser (wb 97.2) - 5,067 built			
htchbk cpe	2,531	11,542	—
RS htchbk cpe	2,690	13,910	—
RS Turbo htchbk cpe	2,756	15,444	—
RS Trb AWD htchbk cpe	3,073	17,572	—

1994 Engines	bore×stroke	bhp	availability
I-4, 107.1	3.17×3.39	92	S-Laser (ohc)
I-4, 122.0	3.35×3.46	135	O-Laser (dohc)
I-4T, 122.0	3.35×3.46	180	O-Laser (dohc)
I-4T, 122.0	3.35×3.46	195	O-Laser (dohc)
I-4, 135.0	3.44×3.62	93	S-Sndnce (ohc)
I-4, 153.0	3.44×4.09	100	S-Acclaim; O-Sndnce (ohc)
V-6, 181.4	3.66×3.19	141	O-Sndnce (ohc)
V-6, 181.4	3.66×3.19	142	O-Acclaim (ohc)

1995

Neon (wb 104.0)	Wght	Price	Prod
LPL42 sdn 4d	2,338	9,500	
LPH42 Highline sdn 4d	2,405	11,240	93,187
LPS42 Sport sdn 4d	2,448	13,267	
LPH22 Highline sdn 2d	—	11,240	28,187
LPS22 Sport sdn 2d	—	13,567	
Acclaim (wb 103.5)			
APH41 sdn 4d	2,862	14,323	12,331

1995 Engines	bore×stroke	bhp	availability
I-4, 121.8	3.44×3.27	132	S-Neon (ohc)
I-4, 121.8	3.44×3.27	150	O-Neon (dohc)
I-4, 153.0	3.44×4.09	100	S-Acclaim (ohc)
V-6, 181.4	3.66×3.19	142	O-Acclaim (ohc)

1996

Neon (wb 104.0)	Wght	Price	Prod
LPL42 sdn 4d	2,338	9,995	
LPH42 Highline sdn 4d	2,405	11,500	75,684
LPS42 Sport sdn 4d	2,448	12,700	
LPL22 sdn 2d	—	9,495	
LPH22 Highline sdn 2d	—	11,300	28,129
LPS22 Sport sdn 2d	—	12,500	
Breeze (wb 108.0)			
APH41 sdn 4d	2,931	14,060	46,355

1996 Engines	bore×stroke	bhp	availability
I-4, 121.8	3.44×3.27	132	S-Neon, Breeze
I-4, 121.8	3.44×3.27	150	O-Neon (dohc)

1997

Neon (wb 104.0)	Wght	Price	Prod
LPL42 sdn 4d	2,399	10,595	60,713
LPH42 Highline sdn 4d	2,459	12,670	
LPL22 cpe 2d	2,389	10,395	22,108
LPH22 Highline cpe 2d	2,416	12,470	
Breeze (wb 108.0)			
APH41 sdn 4d	2,931	14,795	70,549
Prowler (wb 113.0)			
RPS27 conv rdstr 2d	2,800	38,300	463*

1997 Engines	bore×stroke	bhp	availability
I-4, 121.8	3.44×3.27	132	S-Neon, Breeze
I-4, 121.8	3.44×3.27	150	O-Neon (dohc)
V-6, 215.0	3.78×3.19	214	S-Prowler

*Calendar-year production.

1998

Neon (wb 104.0)	Wght	Price	Prod
LPL42 Highline sdn 4d	2,507	11,355	
LPH42 Expresso sdn 4d	2,459	13,160	68,521
LPH42 Style sdn 4d	—	14,095	
LPL22 Highline cpe 2d	2,470	11,155	18,545
LPH22 Expresso cpe 2d	—	12,980	
Breeze (wb 108.0)			
APH41 sdn 4d	2,929	14,675	66,620
Prowler (wb 113.0)			
RPS27 conv rdstr 2d	—	—	2,124*

1998 Engines	bore ×stroke	bhp	availability
I-4, 121.8	3.44×3.27	132	S-Neon, Breeze
I-4, 121.8	3.44×3.27	150	O-Neon (dohc)
I-4, 148.0	3.44×3.98	150	O-Breeze
V-6, 215.0	3.78×3.19	214	S-Prowler

* Calendar-year production. Titled as 1997 or 1999.

1999

Neon (wb 104.0) - 63,216 blt	Wght	Price	Prod*
LPL42 Highline sdn 4d	2,507	11,820	—
LPH42 Expresso sdn 4d	—	12,825	—
LPH42 Style sdn 4d	—	13,960	—
LPL22 Highline cpe 2d	2,470	11,735	—
LPH22 Expresso cpe 2d	—	12,740	—
Breeze (wb 108.0)			
APH41 sdn 4d	2,929	15,115	47,911
Prowler (wb 113.0)			
RPS27 conv rdstr 2d	2,838	39,300	2,868

1999 Engines	bore×stroke	bhp	availability
I-4, 121.8	3.44×3.27	132	S-Neon, Breeze
I-4, 121.8	3.44×3.27	150	O-Neon (dohc)
I-4, 148.0	3.44×3.98	150	O-Breeze
V-6, 215.0	3.78×3.19	253	S-Prowler

* Calendar-year production.

2000

Neon (wb 105.0)	Wght	Price	Prod*
LPH41 sdn 4d	2,559	12,490	43,181
Breeze (wb 108.0)			
APH41 sdn 4d	2,945	16,080	2,030
Prowler (wb 113.0)			
RPS27 conv rdstr 2d	2,838	42,800	2,890

2000 Engines	bore×stroke	bhp	availability
I-4, 121.8	3.44×3.27	132	S-Neon, Breeze
I-4, 148.0	3.44×3.98	150	O-Breeze
V-6, 215.0	3.78×3.19	253	S-Prowler

* Calendar-year production

2001

Neon (wb 105.0)	Wght	Price	Prod*
LPH41 sdn 4d	2,559	12,715	21,600
Prowler (wb 113.0)			
RPS27 conv rdstr 2d	2,838	44,225	3,002

2001 Engines	bore×stroke	bhp	availability
I-4, 121.8	3.44×3.27	132	S-Neon
I-4, 121.8	3.44×3.27	150	O-Neon (dohc)
V-6, 215.0	3.78×3.19	253	S-Prowler

*Calendar-year production.

Pontiac

Of the four "companion" makes introduced by General Motors in the 1920s, Pontiac was the only one to survive past 1940. Yet its future was far from certain in the early Depression years. The first Pontiac, the 1926 Six, quickly boosted the popularity of its Oakland parent, pushing combined sales beyond 250,000 units within three years. But sales plummeted with the Great Crash, as elsewhere in Detroit, and Oakland was ditched after 1931 and just 13,408 cars. Pontiac bottomed out in 1932 at a bit over 45,000.

What saved Pontiac were the calm, confident policies of GM president Alfred P. Sloan, who combined Pontiac's manufacturing with Chevrolet's in early 1932, thus saving vast sums in tooling costs through increased sharing of bodies, chassis, and other major components. At the same time he merged Buick, Oldsmobile, and Pontiac sales operations, requiring dealers for each make to sell the other two as well—albeit often unwillingly. These belt-tightening measures continued through mid-1933, effectively reducing GM to three divisions: Cadillac, Chevrolet, and B-O-P.

The well-styled 1933 Eight completely turned Pontiac fortunes around, and production for that model year recovered to more than 90,000. By 1937, the division was back above 200,000, and would go on to rank among the top five or six Detroit nameplates well into the '50s. A group of highly competent people contributed mightily to this resurgence. Among the most notable: former Ford executive William S. "Big Bill" Knudsen, division general manager in 1932-33 and GM president in 1937-40; chief engineer Benjamin H. Anibal, father of the Pontiac eight; and division design chief Franklin Q. Hershey, creator of the handsome 1933 and subsequent models.

Mechanically, Pontiac's 1930-31 cars were virtual reruns of the popular 1929 "Big Six" models, retaining an orthodox inline L-head engine with 200 cubic inches and 60 brake horsepower. Offerings comprised the customary open and closed styles on a 110-inch wheelbase (upped two inches for '31) spread over a $665-$785 price range. Sedans and coupes sold best. For 1932, the rough-running V-8 Oakland became a 117-inch-wheelbase Pontiac, but met with no more success: outsold more than 6-to-1 by "The Chief of the Sixes" on a new 114-inch chassis.

Wheelbase increased to 115 inches for 1933, when Anibal's new straight-eight arrived in a slimmer model group down-priced to the $585-$695 area. Though smaller at 223.4 cid, the inline eight was much smoother than the 85-bhp 251-cid Oakland V-8, and thus far more salable. Horsepower climbed for 1934 from 77 to 84, then to 87 with a bored-out 232 replacement for 1936. The straight-eight was further enlarged for '37, and would continue at that 249-cid size through 1949. A highly reliable engine, it would remain a Pontiac staple until the division's first modern high-compression V-8 of 1955.

Styling in these years followed industry trends. The 1930-32s were boxy and undistinguished, but the transitional '33s and the more fully streamlined '34 models were among the prettiest medium-price cars of the era. The latter jumped to a new 117.5-inch chassis and boasted a notable innovation in GM's "Knee-Action" independent front suspension. Though this was also featured on '34 Chevrolets, components were not interchangeable between the two makes.

Many other parts were shared by then, thanks to Sloan's cor-

1930 Series 6-29A Big Six sport roadster

1933 Series 601 Economy Eight two-door sedan

1931 Series 401 Fine Six two-door sedan

1934 Series 603 Eight 2/4-passenger sport coupe

▲ 1962 Plymouth Fury convertible coupe

▼ 1970 Plymouth (Hemi) 'Cuda hardtop coupe

▲ 1971 Plymouth Road Runner hardtop coupe

▼ 1997 Plymouth Prowler roadster

▲ 1934 Pontiac Eight coupe

▼ 1941 Pontiac Deluxe Six Torpedo coupe

▲ 1950 Pontiac Chieftain Eight Catalina hardtop coupe

▼ 1957 Pontiac Safari two-door station wagon

▲ 1962 Pontiac Catalina convertible coupe

▼ 1967 Pontiac GTO convertible coupe

▲ 1968 Pontiac Firebird coupe

▼ 1974 Pontiac Grand Prix SJ coupe

▲ 2006 Pontiac Solstice roadster

▼ 1959 Rambler Ambassador station wagon

▲ 1936 Reo Flying Cloud two-door sedan

▼ 2001 Saturn SC2 three-door coupe

▲ 2007 Saturn Sky roadster

▼ 1964 (AC) Shelby Cobra roadster

▲ 1969 Shelby GT 500 convertible coupe

▼ 1931 Studebaker President 80R roadster

▲ 1941 Studebaker Commander coupe

▼ 1948 Studebaker Commander convertible coupe

▲ 1956 Studebaker Golden Hawk hardtop coupe

▼ 1961 Studebaker Lark VI convertible coupe

▲ 1963 Studebaker Avanti coupe

▼ 1932 Stutz Super Bearcat convertible coupe

▲ 1932 Stutz DV-32 convertible coupe

▼ 1935 Terraplane DeLuxe coupe

▲ 1948 Tucker Torpedo four-door sedan

▼ 1935 Willys Model 77 coupe

▲ 1941 Willys Americar coupe

▼ 1954 Willys Aero-Eagle hardtop coupe

porate reorganization, yet the 1933-34 Pontiacs looked unique. Credit Hershey and chief body engineer Roy Milner. Hershey convinced GM styling director Harley Earl of the need for more-streamlined Pontiacs, and accordingly designed a Bentley-type radiator and skirted front fenders with horizontal "speed streaks." Milner gave open models (including Pontiac's last roadsters in '33) a smooth deck and beltline moldings different from Chevrolet's. With this, Knee-Action, and Anibal's straight-eight, the Pontiac Eight was a pleasing package. Though it couldn't quite keep pace with a Ford V-8 or Hudson Terraplane, it didn't lag them by much. Pontiac's future was now secure.

After two years of nothing but eight-cylinder cars, and with the market still sluggish, Pontiac reinstated sixes for 1935: Standard and DeLuxe on a 112-inch wheelbase. Sized at 208 cid, their "new" six was really just a bigger-bore version of the old 200. Surprisingly, it made only four fewer horsepower than that year's eight: 80 in all. Standard Sixes cost about $100 less than comparable Eights, which was a lot in those days, and for the rest of the decade they outsold the senior models by a wide margin. Eights were demoted to a slightly shorter 116.6-inch chassis for '35, and all Pontiacs boasted GM's new all-steel "Turret Top" construction that eliminated traditional fabric roof inserts.

"Trunkback" sedans with integral luggage compartments had appeared for 1934. These returned for '35, but bodies were entirely new. Styling was new also, by now of the rounded "potato" school. Pontiac gained added distinction with "Silver Streak" trim, bright-metal bands running forward from the cowl, over the hood, and down the front of the radiator. This has been variously credited to Hershey, "Big Bill" Knudsen, and a young designer named Virgil Exner, who would figure in early-postwar Studebakers and Chrysler's mid-'50s "Forward Look." No matter: Silver Streaks made Pontiacs unmistakable, and would continue as a make hallmark for the next 20 years.

After a mostly stand-pat 1936, Pontiac issued new styling for a trimmer 1937 line of DeLuxe Sixes and Eights on the corporate GM "B" body. Respective wheelbases lengthened five and six inches, which made for better proportions, and a racy reshaped nose with vertical streaks overlaid a more massive wrapped radiator, yielding a rather busy "face." A bore-and-stroke job swelled the six to 222.7 cid, where it would stay through 1940; horsepower stood at 85. The eight was stroked to achieve its aforementioned 249 cid, good for 100 bhp.

After five years of mostly steady gains, sales eased to just over 97,000 in recessionary 1938, pushing Pontiac from fifth to sixth behind Dodge. A four-door station wagon debuted in the DeLuxe Six series. Ads bubbled about all models' "New Silver Streak Beauty," but that was no more than a facelift consisting mainly of a barrel-like radiator with thick horizontal bars and vertical instead of horizontal hood vents.

1935 Series 605 Eight two-door touring sedan

1938 Series 6DA DeLuxe Six two-door touring sedan

1936 Series 6BA DeLuxe Silver Streak Six cabriolet

1939 Series 6EB DeLuxe Six four-door touring sedan

1937 Series 8CA DeLuxe Eight four-door touring sedan

1940 Series 29HB Torpedo Eight four-door sedan

The rebodied '39s were prettier, with wider "pontoon" fenders, reduced overall height, larger glass areas, and smaller pod-style headlamps well inboard of the front-fender crowns. Pontiac's face remained a bit confused, however, as Harley Earl applied his favored "catwalk" vertical trim between the fenders and a radiator bearing four groups of horizontal chrome bands overlaid with Silver Streaks. Still, there was no mistaking Pontiac for Chevrolet.

Rumble-seat styles and four-door convertibles were absent for '39, but a new series anchored the line: the 115-inch-wheelbase Quality Six. Sharing bodies with Chevrolet, it listed coupes, sedans, and a wood-body wagon in the $760-$990 range. Some $55 more bought the same cars (except the wagon) in new DeLuxe 120 guise: a six-cylinder version of that year's 120-inch-wheelbase DeLuxe Eight. Both DeLuxe lines included a convertible. As ever, Pontiac's six was thrifty and reliable, its eight a bit thirstier but more refined, and potent enough. One English magazine opined that a Pontiac Eight "might be borne along by the wind" because it was so impressively quiet and smooth. Depression gloom was lifting, though only because American industry was gearing up for anticipated war production. Still, Pontiac moved a creditable 144,000 cars in the improving 1939 economy to retain sixth behind Chevy, Ford, Plymouth, Buick, and Dodge.

Series expanded to four for 1940: Special and DeLuxe Sixes and DeLuxe and Torpedo Eights. All listed four-passenger coupes and four-door sedans; Special and the DeLuxes added a business coupe and two-door sedan. There were also DeLuxe "cabriolet" convertibles and a Special wagon. All wore a heavy facelift announced by a more coherent face with a painted prow, still Silver Streaked, dividing a lower-profile horizontal-bar grille. Also in evidence were wider front fenders with fully integrated sealed-beam headlamps. Wheelbase extended to 117 inches for Special; DeLuxes returned at 120. Sleekest of all were a new Torpedo coupe and sedan on a 122-inch span. Sixes gained two horsepower via light engine modifications. Volume moved up substantially, reaching 217,000 for the model year.

A corporatewide restyle for 1941 gave Pontiacs higher, wider, crisper fenders embellished with additional Silver Streaks, plus a near full-width horizontal-bar grille with prominent center bulge. Running boards were newly concealed via flared door bottoms (except on wagons). Pontiac's six took the form it would retain through 1954, being bored out to 239.2 cid for 90 bhp. The veteran straight-eight was tweaked to 103 bhp in 1940, where it would remain through '47.

Series now numbered six, all called Torpedo: six- and eight-cylinder DeLuxe, Streamliner, and Custom. DeLuxes, which garnered 155,000 sales, shared a new 119-inch-wheelbase A-body platform with Chevrolet and thus offered the most body styles. Among them was the attractive midseason Metropolitan sedan patterned after the previous four-door Torpedo, with "formal" closed rear-roof quarters. Streamliners and Customs

1941 Series 29JC Custom Torpedo Eight four-door sedan

1941 Custom Torpedo Eight station wagon

1942 Series 27KA Torpedo Eight four-door sedan

1946 Streamliner Eight four-door sedan

1947 Streamliner Eight sedan coupe

1948 Torpedo Eight DeLuxe convertible coupe

1949 Chieftain Eight DeLuxe convertible coupe

1949 Chieftain Eight DeLuxe four-door sedan

1950 Streamliner Eight DeLuxe fastback sedan coupe

1950 Chieftain Eight DeLuxe convertible coupe

1951 Chieftain Eight DeLuxe Catalina hardtop coupe

used the same 122-inch B-body as junior Buicks and Oldsmobiles, and included new fastback four-door sedans and two-door "sedan coupes." Convertibles, again DeLuxes, lacked rear side windows, a treatment that recalled certain Packards but made for awful top-up visibility.

Ever the next step up from Chevy on the GM price/prestige ladder, Pontiac was less luxurious than a Buick or Olds but carefully built to very competitive prices. Its cheapest model cost just $783 in 1940 and only $828 in '41; the costliest was the $1250 Custom Torpedo Eight station wagon of 1941.

After record volume of more than 330,000, Pontiac built about 83,500 of its heavily facelifted '42s, all but 15,400 in the closing months of 1941. Styling again followed GM trends: a gaudy grille, longer front fenders swept back into the front doors, and rounded "drop-off" rear fenders. Series were reduced to four: 122-inch Streamliner and 119-inch Torpedo, each offered as a Six and Eight. The '41 Streamliners had been divided into standard and Super submodels. The '42s came in standard and Chieftain guise, each offering fastback "sedan coupe," fastback four-door sedan, and "woody" wagon. Chieftains cost $50 more than standards, which ran slightly above corresponding Torpedos. Eights delivered for only $25 more than Sixes, yet production split about 50/50.

Like most other makes, Pontiac issued warmed-over '42 models for 1946-48, but stylists made each succeeding version a little different. The '46s, which began streaming from Pontiac, Michigan in September 1945, had a big bell-shaped grille of vertical and horizontal bars. The grille was simplified for '47, then became busier again on the '48s, which adopted round taillights and were the first Pontiacs to carry Silver Streak badges.

Otherwise, the 1946-47 Pontiacs were entirely prewar in design and specifications. A three-speed manual remained the only transmission available. Chieftain submodels did not return, though other prewar offerings did. Eights cost about $30 more than Sixes for 1946, and postwar inflation pushed all prices steadily upward through '48, when the spread reached $1500-$2500. A DeLuxe Torpedo convertible bowed for 1947 at $1853 with the six, $1900 with the eight.

Though still basically '42s, the '48 Pontiacs had some interesting distinctions. A DeLuxe trim option for most models delivered chrome fender moldings, gravel guards, wheel discs (except on wagons), and other embellishments for $78-$90. Also, the eight was inexplicably uprated by one bhp. But the big news that year was the introduction of Hydra-Matic Drive as a $185 option. This was a key factor in boosting Pontiac's model-year volume to near 235,500 because it so well-suited the eight-cylinder models that buyers increasingly preferred. Indeed, Eights outsold Sixes for the first time in 1947, and were far ahead for '48, when Hydra-Matic was ordered on 64 percent of Sixes but 77 percent of Eights.

This activity suggested that Pontiac would grow from a "big Chevy" into a lusher medium-price car—and so it did. Along the way, Pontiacs were transformed from ho-hum to hot.

But that was still some years off when Pontiac unwrapped its 1949 models, which fared quite well in GM's first postwar redesign. All-new A-bodies, now on a single 120-inch wheelbase, were attractively styled under Harley Earl's ever-watchful eye. Highlights began with a lower full-width grille bisected by a modest horizontal bar above little vertical teeth. Silver Streaks still adorned hood and rear deck, but front fenders were now flush with the bodysides and the pontoon rear fenders snugged in closer. Body types divided between Chieftain and Streamliner, the latter with fastback rather than notchback profiles, plus four-door wagons. Exclusive to Chieftain were a business coupe, long-deck sedan coupe (a.k.a. club coupe), and convertible. Both lines offered the usual choices of six- or eight-cylinder power and standard or DeLuxe trim except for the DeLuxe-only convertible. DeLuxes wore chrome headlamp rings, extra side moldings, fender gravel guards, and full wheel covers. Newly optional high-compression heads lofted the six to 93 bhp and the eight to 106. Overall performance was little changed, however, as the '49s weighed a bit more than the '48s.

Continuing postwar inflation pushed prices considerably higher for 1949. The Chieftain DeLuxe Eight convertible jumped by $134; the woody wagon cost more than $2600. As at Chevrolet, the Pontiac wagon switched from part-structural wood to more-practical all-steel construction at mid-'49, though there was no change in price and little change in appearance. Despite the heftier price tags, model-year volume rose to nearly 305,000, the second-highest total in Pontiac history.

Except for larger, taller grille teeth and reshuffled trim, the 1950 models were predictably much like the '49s. However, the long-running eight was bored to 268.4 cid, good for 108 bhp standard or 113 with high-compression head. Chieftain gained an important new body style in Pontiac's first "hardtop-convertible." Called Catalina and sold in DeLuxe or new Super DeLuxe trim, it accounted for 42,305 sales, nine percent of the division's total model-year volume. As in past years, an illuminated countenance of Chief Pontiac continued as a hood mascot; like other such devices of the day, it glowed when the headlights were on. Production rose again, smashing the 1941 record at more than 446,000. Still, Pontiac ran fifth overall, as it

1952 Chieftain Eight DeLuxe convertible coupe

1952 Chieftain Eight DeLuxe station wagon

1953 Chieftain Eight DeLuxe convertible coupe

1954 Star Chief Custom Catalina hardtop coupe

1954 Star Chief Custom four-door sedan

1955 Star Chief convertible coupe

1955 Star Chief Custom Safari two-door station wagon

1955 Star Chief Custom Catalina hardtop coupe

had since '48 and would continue to do until 1959.

Volume sank to about 370,000 for 1951 as all Detroit began feeling the effects of the Korean War, yet that was Pontiac's second-best total ever. Fastbacks were fading from favor, so the Streamliner four-door was dropped, soon followed by the sedan-coupe. The most noticeable change was a "gullwing" grille bar below a prominent medallion. Engines were tweaked: the six to 96/100 bhp, the eight to 116/120 bhp.

A busier grille and new DeLuxe side trim were the main alterations for 1952. Horsepower crept up, too. Korean War restrictions and a nationwide steel strike limited model-year output to only 271,000 units.

A major reskin of the '49 A-body and a two-inch longer wheelbase gave 1953's new all-Chieftain line a more "important" look. Once more, buying patterns had prompted these and other changes. Catalina hardtops, for example, now accounted for nearly 20 percent of sales, and automatic-transmission installations had climbed to 75 percent. The '53s were shinier and larger in most every dimension. Key features of the new look involved kicked-up rear fenders, a lower grille, more prominent bumpers, and a one-piece windshield.

Newly optional power steering made the '53s easier to park; more horsepower made them faster. The six now delivered 115 bhp with manual transmission or 118 with Hydra-Matic; corresponding eight-cylinder outputs were 118/122. A lowish rear axle ratio of 3.08:1 was specified for smooth top-gear performance with Hydra-Matic. A mid-1953 fire in the Hydra-Matic plant hampered supplies, however, so 18,499 Pontiacs were fitted with Chevrolet Powerglide in 1953-54. Overall production remained strong at nearly 419,000.

Nineteen fifty-four brought a minor facelift of 1953's major one. Rearranged side moldings and a narrow oval in the central grille bar were the main changes. The big news was Star Chief, a top-line eight-cylinder hardtop, convertible, and four-door sedan on a new 124-inch chassis. These were the plushest Pontiacs yet—and the priciest ($2300-$2600), another sign of the make's steady push upmarket. Star Chiefs sold well, but Pontiac's total volume slipped to just below 288,000, suggesting it was time for something different.

The all-new '55s were precisely that. Among their claimed 109 new features were fully up-to-date styling, an improved chassis and—the really hot item—a modern overhead-valve V-8, Pontiac's first. Dubbed "Strato-Streak," the new engine bowed at 287.2 cid, but could grow much larger and soon did. Standard horsepower at first was 173/180 (manual/automatic); an optional four-barrel carburetor yielded an even 200. A strong oversquare design with five main bearings, the Strato-Streak was somewhat related to Chevy's all-new 1955 "Turbo-Fire" V-8. Though not quite as advanced, it would serve Pontiac admirably for more than a quarter-century.

As on other '55 GM cars, Pontiac styling was rather boxy but quite trendy, especially the wrapped "Panoramic" windshield taken from recent Harley Earl showmobiles. Equally *au courant* were cowl ventilation; bright solid colors and two-tones; and a longer, lower look despite unchanged wheelbases. A blunt face was the one dubious aspect. As before, Pontiac shared its A-body with Chevrolet, but maintained distinct wheelbases. The shorter one again carried two Chieftain lines: low-priced "860" and midrange "870" sedans and wagons, plus an "870" Catalina hardtop. Star Chief returned on its extended chassis with base-trim convertible and four-door sedan and a Custom sedan and Catalina.

Mounting the Chieftain chassis but officially a Star Chief was an exotic new wagon, the Custom Safari, a "hardtop-style" two-door based on Chevy's new '55 Nomad. Chevy designer Carl Renner recalled that "when Pontiac saw [the Nomad] they felt they could do something with it.... Management wanted it for the Pontiac line, so it worked out." Like Nomad, the original '55 Safari continued with successive facelifts only through 1957, after which both names were applied to conventional four-door wagons. Two-door Safaris naturally cost more than Nomads--a stiff $2962 for '55—and thus sold in fewer numbers: 3760, followed by 4042 for '56, and a final 1292.

1956 Star Chief DeLuxe convertible coupe

1957 Star Chief convertible coupe

1957 Bonneville convertible coupe

1957 Star Chief Custom Safari "Transcontinental" station wagon

On balance, 1955 was a vintage Pontiac year. Its cars were a solid hit with dealers and public alike, and the division built about 554,000 of them, a new record. But some rough times lay ahead, and Pontiac wouldn't better this figure until 1963, after which it set new records. At least three factors figured in the interim slump. Buick's Special and the base Olds 88 were priced more aggressively; demand for lower-medium cars shrank as import sales expanded in the late '50s; and the 1956-58 Pontiacs weren't particularly exciting, though they were competitive in most ways and faster than ever.

The '56s were mildly restyled, and four-door Catalina hardtops arrived in each series. Styling was less distinctive—tester Tom McCahill said the '56 looked like "it was born on its nose"—and ride comfort wasn't the best. A bore job stretched the V-8 to 316.6 cid, but didn't yield much more power: only up

1958 Bonneville Custom convertible coupe

1958 Bonneville Custom hardtop coupe

1959 Star Chief Vista hardtop sedan

1959 Catalina Vista hardtop sedan

1960 Bonneville Custom Safari station wagon

1961 Bonneville convertible coupe

1961 Bonneville Vista hardtop sedan

1961 Tempest sport coupe

to 205 for Chieftains and 227 bhp for Star Chiefs (though at midyear, a 285-bhp option was offered). Pontiac settled for '56 volume that was well down on record-shattering '55, declining to 405,500 and a sixth-place industry finish.

July 1956 ushered in a new Pontiac general manager who would prove crucial to the make's near-term fortunes. This was Semon E. "Bunkie" Knudsen, son of '30s division chief "Big Bill" and the youngest leader in Pontiac history. GM brass told Bunkie to do what he could with the existing design for '57, and he hustled, instituting longer rear springs in rubber shackles, 14-inch wheels and tires (ousting 15-inchers), pedal parking brake, and a V-8 stroked to 347 cid for 227-290 bhp. Stylewise, the grille became a massive bucktooth affair; two-toning switched from 1955-56's half-car patterns to missile-shaped bodyside areas; and Bunkie did the unthinkable by banishing Silver Streak trim as old-hat (it did, after all, hark to his dad's day). Series were reorganized into low-end Chieftain and new mid-price Super Chief on the shorter chassis and Star Chief on the longer 124-inch wheelbase.

Where Bunkie really made his mark was the Bonneville, a flashy Star Chief-based convertible launched in mid-'57. Packing 310 bhp thanks to fuel injection and aggressive cam, this $5782 limited edition was the costliest Pontiac yet. Unfortunately, a hefty curb weight of nearly 4300 pounds dulled performance somewhat. Still it was no slouch: A Bonnie was timed at 18 seconds in the quarter-mile.

Because it was basically a promotional piece for dealers, the '57 Bonneville saw only 630 copies. But it gave Pontiac a whole new performance image even as the Auto Manufacturers Association came down against factory-sponsored racing. (Several '57 "Ponchos" did run well in NASCAR, but they were strictly private entries.) Yet the lack of race wins didn't hamper buyer demand. While Chevy, Olds, and Buick all lost sales to rival 1957 Chrysler products, Pontiac built some 333,500 cars to move within 51,000 units of fifth-place Olds.

Expansive new styling should have helped the '58s sell even better, but a sharp national recession held deliveries to some 217,000. Unlike some '58 GM cars, Pontiacs remained reasonably tasteful, with a simple mesh grille, quad headlights, and side-spears made wider and concave toward the rear. Bodies were lower but not much longer or wider; wheelbases were unchanged. Offerings now included no fewer than seven

1962 Tempest LeMans convertible coupe

1962 Grand Prix hardtop sport coupe

1963 Bonneville convertible coupe

1962 Catalina Vista hardtop sedan

1963 Grand Prix hardtop sport coupe

Catalina hardtops with two or four doors. Bonneville became a regular series, and sold 12,240 convertibles and hardtop coupes. A 370-cid V-8 was now standard across the line, delivering 240 bhp in stickshift Chieftains/Super Chiefs, and up to 285 in Hydra-Matic Star Chiefs and Bonnevilles. Optional across the board were a 300-bhp triple-carb "Tri-Power" unit and a 310-bhp "fuelie."

Then came the first Pontiacs to fully reflect Bunkie's boldness. The '59s were not just startlingly new; they established the performance pattern that would carry Pontiac to undreamed-of glory in the 1960s. Crisp styling on a brand-new body introduced the split-grille theme that remains a Pontiac hallmark to this day, plus modest twin-fin rear fenders and minimal side trim. Wheelbases were again unchanged, but the wheels spread farther apart on a new "Wide-Track" chassis that made Pontiacs among the most-roadable cars in America.

The V-8 was again enlarged, the cube count rising to 389, a number destined for greatness. Horsepower ranged from 345 with Tri-Power down to 245. There was also a detuned 215-bhp "Tempest 420E" for economy-minded buyers, capable of up to 20 mpg. Ridding Pontiac of "that Indian concept" was still part of Bunkie's plan, so Chieftain and Super Chief gave way to a new Catalina line on the shorter wheelbase; Bonneville again shared the longer chassis with Star Chief, which would hang on a good long while. Bonneville, bolstered by new Safari wagons and flat-top Vista hardtop sedans, garnered some 82,000 sales. Total volume for the model year rose to near 383,000, boosting Pontiac into fourth place for the first time.

Pontiac show cars of the '50s were always interesting and often predictive. The smooth 1954 Strato Streak previewed the pillarless four-doors of '56. Also shown in '54 was the first Bonneville, a Corvette-like two-seater with canopy-type cockpit on a 100-inch wheelbase. Both cars carried straight eights. The 1955 Strato Star was a two-door four-seat hardtop forecasting 1956 styling. Wildest of all was the 1956 Club de Mer, with "twin-pod" seating and dual-bubble windshields. Standing only 38.4 inches high, its aluminum body was painted Cerulean blue, one of Harley Earl's favorite colors.

From mostly "also-ran" in the '50s, Pontiac became a consistent front-runner in the '60s, finishing third in the industry race every year from 1962 to 1970. Much of this was owed to three enthusiastic general managers: Knudsen through 1961, then Elliot M. "Pete" Estes (GM president in 1974-81), and finally John Z. DeLorean in 1965-69. These and numerous other "car guys" made Pontiac synonymous with high performance, great looks, superb roadability, innovation, and tasteful, comfortable luxury. No wonder Pontiac did so well.

A minor exception to that was the compact 1961-63 Tempest, significant for having GM's first postwar four-cylinder engine, a flexible driveshaft, and a rear transaxle (transmission in unit with the differential) allied to independent link-type suspension. One enthusiast magazine called Tempest "a prototype of the American car for the '60s," but no other U.S. make would have a rear transaxle and independent rear suspension until the Chevrolet Corvette and Plymouth Prowler of '97. The original Tempests were fairly popular, but Pontiac felt a more orthodox design would sell far better. This appeared for 1964, and it did sell better—much better. At that point, the original Tempest's 195-cid four, basically half of a 389 V-8, was abandoned for an inline six—sensibly cost-effective, but hardly daring.

Like a speedometer cable, the 1961-63 Tempest's "rope" driveshaft carried rotary motion through a long, gently curved bar beneath the floor. Thin, but lightly stressed within a steel case, it was mounted on bearings and permanently lubed. The driveshaft's slight sag allowed a lower transmission tunnel in front, though not in back; it also eliminated the need for U-joints and permitted softer engine mounts for better interior isolation. The rear transaxle, a first for Detroit (but not the world), made Tempest less nose-heavy than conventional cousins Olds F-85 and Buick Special. But though its independent rear suspension was ostensibly superior, it was prone to sudden oversteer that could be alarming, especially on wet roads. Still, the Tempest handled well—more so than Chevy's rear-engine Corvair, even though both used simple but tricky swing axles in back.

The initial 112-inch-wheelbase Pontiac Tempests used a unitized Y-body structure adapted from the first Corvairs, as did the F-85 and Special. The standard slant-four teamed with manual and automatic transaxles, and was offered in tunes to suit regular or premium gas. By 1963, horsepower was 115-166 (versus 110/130 in '61). Optionally available for 1961-62 was the Special's 215-cid aluminum V-8 with 155/185 bhp. This gave way for '63 to a debored 326-cid version of the Pontiac 389 packing 260 bhp. So equipped, a Tempest could scale 0-60 mph in 9.5 seconds and reach 115 mph.

Tempest bowed with a single series listing standard- and Custom-trim four-door notchback sedans and four-door Safari wagons with one-piece rear "liftgate." Coupes arrived at midseason with bench- or bucket-seat interiors, the latter christened LeMans. Custom and LeMans convertibles were added for '62 and proved quite popular, prompting a separate LeMans series for '63. Styling didn't change much. A twin-oval grille was used for '61, a full-width three-section affair for '62, a different split grille and squared-up body lines for '63. Prices also didn't change much, with most models in the $2200-$2500 region.

For 1964, GM redesigned all the B-O-P compacts on a 115-inch wheelbase, which made them intermediates. Pontiac's new Tempest wore taut, "geometric" lines on the resulting A-body shared with Chevrolet's new Chevelle, the Oldsmobile F-85/Cutlass, and Buick's Special/Skylark. But the real excitement came with the midseason debut of the Tempest GTO, the first "muscle car." That nickname was apt. With the right options, a GTO delivered unprecedented performance for a six-passenger American automobile.

Most GTOs were "built" from the order form. For 1964, you started with a Tempest coupe, hardtop coupe, or convertible, then checked off the GTO option: floorshift, 325-horse 389, quick steering, stiff shocks, dual exhaust, and premium tires, all for about $300. From there you ad-libbed: four-speed gearbox ($188); metallic brake linings, heavy-duty radiator, and limited-slip differential ($75 the lot); 348-bhp 389 ($115). Then all you needed was a lead foot and lots of gas.

Sports-car purists took umbrage at Pontiac's use of GTO, short for *gran turismo omologato*, the Italian term for an approved production-based racing car. But the outspoken *Car and Driver* bravely answered them with a mostly on-paper comparison of Pontiac's GTO and Ferrari's GTO. A good Pontiac, they said, would trim the Ferrari in a drag race and lose on a road course. But "with the addition of NASCAR road racing suspension, the Pontiac will take the measure of any Ferrari other than prototype racing cars…The Ferrari costs $20,000. With every conceivable option on a GTO, it would be difficult to spend more than $3800. That's a bargain."

The successful LeMans/Tempest formula saw relatively little change through 1967. Vertical headlights, crisper styling, and three-inch-longer bodies arrived for '65. The '66s had smoother contours, including hopped-up "Coke-bottle" rear fenders and, on coupes and hardtops, "flying buttress" rear roof pillars astride recessed backlights. Standard for the 1967 GTO was a new 400-cid extension of the 389 pumping out 335 bhp; 360 bhp was optional via "Ram-Air," a functional hood scoop.

For 1968 came a redesigned A-body with dual wheelbases: 116 inches on four-doors, 112 on two-doors. Styling borrowed

1963 Tempest LeMans convertible coupe

1964 Catalina 2+2 hardtop sport coupe

1964 Bonneville convertible coupe

1964 Grand Prix hardtop sport coupe

1964 Tempest GTO sport coupe

1965 Tempest LeMans GTO convertible coupe

1965 Grand Prix hardtop sport coupe

1965 Catalina 2+2 421 hardtop sport coupe

1965 Bonneville convertible coupe

1966 Tempest GTO convertible coupe

1966 Grand Prix hardtop sport coupe

1967 Firebird hardtop coupe

1967 Catalina 2+2 428 hardtop sport coupe

1967 Grand Prix convertible coupe

1967 Tempest GTO hardtop coupe

1968 Tempest GTO hardtop coupe

1968 Bonneville convertible coupe

1969 Tempest GTO hardtop coupe with Ram Air IV

1969 Grand Prix Model J hardtop coupe

1969 Firebird Trans Am hardtop coupe

even more big-Pontiac elements such as a large bumper/grille and, on coupes, a more rakish roofline with flush rear window. Exclusive to GTO was a neatly integrated energy-absorbing front bumper sheathed in color-keyed Endura plastic that resisted dings and dents. One TV commercial pointed out its virtues by showing a group of white-coated Pontiac "engineers" happily hammering the proboscis to absolutely no ill effect.

The midsize Pontiacs continued in this basic form through 1972. Among the mildly facelifted '69s was a hotter GTO: "The Judge," actually an option package with colorful striping, loud paint, a 366-bhp Ram-Air V-8, and three-speed manual gearbox with Hurst floorshift. The 1970s received clumsier front ends, bigger rear bumpers, and pronounced longitudinal bodyside bulges above the wheel openings. The result was a heavier-looking Tempest, GTO, LeMans, and LeMans Sport. Collectors have since tended to prefer the tidier 1964-69 models.

The base engine on 1964-65 Tempests was a 215-cid inline six rated at 140 bhp. For 1966 came a surprising replacement engine, a European-style overhead-cam six developed by Pontiac. Sized at 230 cid, it delivered 165 standard bhp or 207 in "Sprint" guise (via Rochester Quadra-Jet carburetor, hotter valve timing, and double valve springs). The crankshaft had seven main bearings. The camshaft was driven by a fiberglass-reinforced notched belt rather than the usual chain.

With that, the '66 Tempest Sprint was a satisfying performer, if hardly in the GTO's league. It could do 0-60 mph in 10 seconds and reach 115 mph. With options like bucket seats, console, and four-on-the-floor, the clean-lined Sprint had the look and feel of a European grand-touring machine. A longer stroke took the ohc engine to 250 cid for 1968, good for 175 bhp or, in Sprint trim, 215 bhp (230 bhp for '69). Sadly, it proved less than reliable and, echoing the Tempest four before it, departed after 1969 in favor of a conventional overhead-valve Chevy engine of the same displacement.

With Pontiac's performance image secure, division brass knew the Firebird "ponycar" had to be special—particularly as it shared a 108.1-inch-wheelbase F-body structure with Chevrolet's new-for-'67 Camaro. But the Firebird was special, sporting a divided grille of the sort now expected on Pontiacs, and offering a "400" model with a 325-bhp V-8 of that size. The base-tune ohc six was initially standard; the optional Sprint version made for a sprightly, yet economical, Firebird Sprint.

Making its debut about five months behind Camaro, Firebird wasn't modified much for 1968. A change of engines made the 326 model a 350, and side-marker lights were added in accordance with a new government decree. The '69s were restyled below the belt and gained a host of federally ordered safety items. Convertibles continued until "1970½," when an all-new coupe-only second generation was introduced.

The hottest and most memorable early Firebird was the '69 Trans Am, a $725 option package announced in March. It was loosely inspired by the Firebirds then half-heartedly contesting the Sports Car Club of America's Trans-American road-racing series. Special badges, white paint, twin blue dorsal racing stripes, and a decklid spoiler identified it. A 335-bhp Ram Air III 400 gave it great performance, and a heavily fortified chassis and brakes made for superb roadability. Only 697 of the '69s were built, including a mere eight convertibles and just nine cars with the optional 345-bhp "Ram Air IV" engine. But the T/A was destined for far greater sales very soon.

Meantime, Pontiac was building some of the best-looking, best-handling standard cars in all of '60s Detroit. The public loved them. Sales were both strong and consistent, starting at about 396,000 for 1960 and reaching near half a million by '65.

Pontiac began the decade with facelifted versions of the successful "Wide Track" '59s, bearing high "twin-tube" taillamps and a Vee'd, full-width horizontal-bar grille. A fourth series was added that year, the Catalina-based Ventura, a hardtop coupe and Vista hardtop sedan priced just below Star Chief at around $3000. Ventura was dropped for '62 in favor of the bucket-seat Grand Prix, an elegantly tailored $3500 hardtop coupe, also on the Catalina chassis. GP sales flirted with the 73,000 mark in 1963, then gradually eased off through '68 with the exception of a tiny spike in 1967, when a convertible was added. Offered only that year, the ragtop has since become a minor collector's item, as only 5856 were built.

Big-Pontiac styling kept improving, at least through '66, thanks to the efforts of William L. Mitchell, who had replaced the legendary Harley Earl as GM design chief back in 1958. Pontiac's distinctive split grille returned to stay for 1961, along with crisp new styling on shorter wheelbases: 119 inches for Catalina/Ventura and all wagons, 123 for Star Chief/Bonneville. Catalina added an inch for '62. Even cleaner machines with stacked quad headlamps and narrow, split grilles were issued for 1963-64. The '65s were well executed but massive, with a bulging front and billowy bodysides. Wheelbase was lengthened to 121 inches for Catalina/Grand Prix/wagons and to 124 for Star Chief/Bonneville. The forceful looks were slightly muted for '66.

Regrettably, the '67s had a heavy look highlighted by bulky, curved rear fenders. Model-year '68 introduced a huge bumper/grille with a prominent vertical center bulge and a return to horizontal headlamps. The snout was toned down for '69, when another inch was tacked on to wheelbases. The following year brought an upright twin-element grille faintly reminiscent of the '30s, but far less graceful.

Full-size model choices in these years were as consistent as their popularity. Catalinas in all the usual body styles were offered throughout, as were the midrange Star Chief sedan, hardtop sedan, and—from '66—hardtop coupe. The latter three types, plus a convertible and four-door Safari wagons, made up the top-line Bonneville group. (A four-door sedan joined in for 1968.) A bucket-seat "2+2" option package bowed for 1964's Catalina convertible and two-door hardtop; it became a distinct series for '66, then vanished after 1967 in the fast-fading market for sporty full-sizers. One change involved Star Chief: It tacked on the Executive name for '66, which then replaced the Star Chief label through 1970.

Big-Pontiac V-8s were equally consistent in the '60s, with numerous horsepower variations but just four basic sizes—two large and two "small"—all based on the original '55 block. The small ones comprised a 389 available through 1966 and a bored-out 400 from '67. These were base equipment for all full-size models. Power ranged from 215 to 350, with the latter standard for Grand Prix starting with '67. The larger mills, optional on most models, were a 421 for 1963-66 and a 428 for 1967-69, after which a huge 455 took over. Horsepower peaked at 390 for 1968-69, then began waning with federally mandated emission

1970 GTO "The Judge" hardtop coupe

1971 LeMans T-37 hardtop coupe

1970 Grand Prix Model SJ hardtop coupe

1971 Bonneville hardtop sedan

1970½ Firebird Formula 400 coupe

1971 Firebird Trans Am coupe

controls. A "Super-Duty" 421 powered a handful of dragstrip-oriented lightweight Catalinas built in 1961. It then became a bit easier to obtain and eventually topped 400 bhp, but it was expensive, rarely ordered, and thus dropped after a few years.

The 1970s was Pontiac's most difficult decade yet. A decision to outproduce and "out-price" Chevrolet (generally ascribed to division head DeLorean) while simultaneously reaching into Buick/Oldsmobile territory contributed to a startling slip in workmanship. These policies also contributed to a confusing succession of models that left many buyers wondering just what a Pontiac was. Not surprisingly, sales sagged. After falling to fourth in the '71 rankings, Pontiac finished fourth or fifth, usually behind Olds, most every year through 1986. Even Buick was often a threat, closing to within 27,000 units for 1972. By 1980, Pontiac trailed both: Buick by nearly 84,000 units and Oldsmobile by more than 140,000.

But not all was gloom. Given the ponycar market's rapid decline after 1969, Firebird was a surprising bright spot, the Trans Am in particular. The brilliant second-generation design of mid-1970 was good enough to last all the way through 1981 with just three styling updates--for 1974, '77, and '79. Through it all, the Trans Am kept Pontiac's "hot car" image simmering—to the point where, as the division later ruefully admitted, Trans Am had higher name recognition than Pontiac itself.

Like Camaro, Firebird almost died after 1972 due to GM's doubts about the future of performance cars, aggravated by a factory strike that severely cut that year's production. But Pontiac kept the faith and reaped the rewards. While Chevy dropped its hottest Camaro, the Z28, for 1975-76, Pontiac retained the T/A as the most-serious model in the line. As a result, the T/A soon moved from peripheral seller (only 1286 for '72) to become the most-popular Firebird of all (more than 117,000 for '79).

Pontiac also helped Firebird's cause by fielding the same four models each year: base coupe, luxury Esprit, roadworthy Formula, and T/A. (Chevy fiddled with the Camaro lineup in this period.) Formula and T/A lost horsepower for 1978 to help Pontiac meet that year's new corporate average fuel economy mandates (CAFE), but they never relinquished their V-8s and never failed to deliver lively motoring. An optional turbocharged 301, issued for 1980, had a bit less go than the big-blocks of old, but was somewhat easier on gas.

Higher-than-ever fuel prices were but one legacy of the 1973-74 Middle East oil embargo, though gas was becoming costlier well before that. Renewed buyer interest in thrifty compacts—and Pontiac's lack of same—prompted the division to put a different nose on Chevrolet's 111-inch-wheelbase Nova to create the Ventura II. Launched in March 1971, it evolved parallel with Nova through 1979 (minus the Roman numeral after '72), but always saw lower volume. One interesting difference is that the hallowed GTO became a Ventura variation for 1974—actually a $195 option package for the workaday pillared two-door com-

1971 Catalina hardtop coupe

1973 Ventura Custom coupe with Sprint package

1972 Grand Prix Model J hardtop coupe

1973 Grand Am SD-455 Colonnade coupe

1972 LeMans GTO hardtop coupe

1973 Firebird Esprit coupe

1973 Le Mans Sport Colonnade coupe with GTO option

1973 Grand Ville convertible coupe

1973 Firebird Trans Am SD-455 coupe

1974 Ventura coupe with GTO package

1974 LeMans Colonnade coupe with GT package

prising hood scoop, a different grille, chassis enhancements, and standard 350 V-8. Purists moaned, but Pontiac moved 7058 of these pretenders before bringing the curtain down on a great tradition—a year too late, many said at the time.

In line with sister X-body compacts, Ventura adopted a more European look for 1975—and promptly withered on the sales vine. Inept marketing and mediocre build quality were as much to blame as competition from within the Pontiac line and elsewhere. An upmarket version called Phoenix arrived for mid-1977, with plusher interiors and a busier front end; the Ventura name vanished the following year. Unhappily, Phoenix was just as much an also-ran, and remained so even after it switched to GM's front-drive X-body for 1980.

Another "lend-lease" deal with Chevrolet produced the subcompact Astre, arriving in the U.S. for 1975 after being marketed in Canada from mid-1973. This was little more than a modestly restyled twin of Chevy's ill-starred Vega, and thus inherited most of its faults. Pontiac varied the model program a bit with base and semi-sporty SJ hatchback coupes and two-door wagons. (A budget S series, which also included a two-door notchback sedan, was added during '75.) There was also a GT package option combining the low-line interior with the SJ's performance and handling features. Astres were confined to a single series for 1976. So were the last-of-the-line '77s, but they were treated to Pontiac's new 151-cid (2.5-liter) "Iron Duke" four, a nickname chosen partly to counter the horrendous durability reputation of the all-aluminum Vega engine it replaced.

Chevy had introduced its sporty Vega-based Monza coupe for 1975, and Pontiac got into this act a year later with the Sunbird. But unlike other editions of this corporate H-Special design, the Pontiac bowed only as a notchback two-door akin to Chevy's Monza Towne Coupe. The 2+2 fastback body style was added for 1977 as the Sunbird Sport Hatch, followed for '78 by the little two-door wagon from the deceased Astre line. Bolstered by various option groups, including a sporty Formula package, Sunbird eventually became Pontiac's top seller, though it was looking old by then. It hung on with no further change of note through 1981; the final cars sold were actually 1980 leftovers.

The story of the larger 1970s Pontiacs is about as exciting as rust—which many of them did all too quickly. Basic designs were inevitably shared with sister GM intermediates and standards, but workmanship often seemed half a notch lower. By late decade, though, both the LeMans/Grand LeMans and Catalina/Bonneville had evolved into more sensible, solid, and saleable cars much better suited to the times than the aging hulks that Chrysler and Ford still peddled.

Midsize Pontiacs quickly turned from their assured roadability of the 1960s to an emphasis on luxury and convenience. One bright exception was the Grand Am. Introduced as part of the redesigned 1973 line with "Colonnade" styling, this LeMans-based coupe and sedan were billed as combining Grand Prix luxury with Trans Am performance, hence the name. The idea was largely owed to assistant chief engineer Bill Collins, who'd been heavily involved with the original GTO, and chassis wizard John Seaton. Their aim was to approximate European sedans like the Mercedes 250/280 and the BMW Bavaria at a third to half the money.

While some features strained at mimicry—a Mercedes-like jumbo-hub steering wheel, for instance—the "G/A" was, on balance, one of the most impressive big Detroiters in a generally dull Detroit decade. But it failed to make a strong impression in a market where most buyers looked for either everyday transport or as much glitz as their money would buy. Grand Am attracted only some 43,000 sales in its debut year—mainly coupes—then plunged to 17,000 for '74 and only 11,000 or so for '75. To no one's surprise, it subsequently disappeared.

Curiously, the name resurfaced on a coupe and sedan in the downsized 1978 LeMans line, but these cars were nowhere near as grand and were similarly short-lived, the sedan canceled after '79, the coupe a year later. But as we'll see, the Grand Am name would be back.

Rivaling Firebird for '70s success was the personal-luxury Grand Prix—in some of these years Pontiac's single best-selling model. It had been reborn for 1969 as a lighter, quicker midsize coupe on a 118-inch-wheelbase "A-Special" platform that Chevrolet would crib for its similarly posh (and popular) Monte Carlo. Offered with both 400 and 428 (later 455) V-8s, the new GP was a handsome brute, with a short-deck notchback profile and a distinctly Pontiac face ahead of a mile-long hood. Inside was an innovative curved instrument cluster bringing all controls within easy driver reach. Cribbing Model J and SJ nomenclature from the revered Duesenberg was a vain attempt at cachet, but the public applauded this Grand Prix, snapping up nearly 112,500 of the '69s. Sales were healthy through the end of this design generation in 1972, when just under 92,000 were retailed. Styling didn't change much, and although horsepower went down a bit after 1970, big-block performance remained quite good.

Pontiac continued this successful formula through GM's 1973-77 Colonnade intermediates, when the GP went to the same 116-inch wheelbase as Monte Carlo. A vertical grille and a roof with a '67 Cadillac Eldorado-like crease through the backlight set these GPs apart. Interestingly, Grand Prix notched a new all-time sales record for 1977, close to 288,500. The '78, unfortunately, was much more like LeMans, downsized to the same new 108.1-inch platform and looking less distinctive. Yet sales weren't vastly affected: some 228,000 for the model year. Clearly, the GP had succeeded in a way that various gussied-up Luxury LeMans and Grand LeMans variations couldn't. Without it, Pontiac wouldn't have weathered the ups and downs of the '70s nearly as well.

Pontiac's troubles were far from over as the 1980s dawned. Workmanship still wasn't all it should have been, and increased model sharing with Chevrolet had only made Pontiac's confused image even fuzzier. Adding insult to these injuries were the deep national recession and accompanying sharp downturn in auto sales that began in late 1979 when the Shah of Iran was deposed, triggering a second "energy crisis." Pontiac suffered as much as any Detroit make. In two years division output plunged by nearly a third, to around 620,500 for '81, then slipped below 500,000 two years later—a sorry situation for a make that had averaged better than 700,000 cars a year since the mid-1960s.

But better times were at hand. Having floundered under four general managers since '69, the division got back on course under William Hoglund, who took the helm in 1980. Taking a cue from history, Hoglund and a bright young team of designers and engineers began steering Pontiac back toward the sort of

1974 Catalina coupe

1975 Grand Am Colonnade coupe

1974 Firebird Trans Am coupe

1975 Grand Le Mans Safari station wagon

1975 Grand Ville Brougham convertible coupe

1976 Firebird Formula coupe

driver-oriented cars that had been the foundation of its high success in the '60s. Events played right into their hands. The economy recovered, the gas shortage became a gas glut, and the market went crazy again for performance. Proclaiming "We Build Excitement," Pontiac turned the corner, and by 1984 it was solidly back over the half-million mark.

Hoglund left in 1984 to head GM's developing Saturn Division, but Pontiac kept picking up steam under a new captain, J. Michael Losh. For 1986 it sailed past 750,000. Then, a year later, it surpassed a bumbling Olds Division to grab third place for the first time in 17 years. Pontiac repeated the performance for '87. The 1989 tally was an impressive 801,600, nearly 300,000 better than a recovering Buick.

The amazing part of Pontiac's resurgence is that it was managed mainly with compacts, intermediates, and the Firebird. Unlike Buick and Olds, big cars were never significant to Pontiac sales in the '80s. In fact, the division's 1982 lineup had no traditional full-size cars at all.

Catalina and Bonneville had been redesigned for 1977 as part of GM's first-wave downsizing program, but didn't sell as well as their B-body cousins at Buick, Olds, and Chevy. Believing buyers were ready to foresake even these smaller biggies in another fuel crunch, Pontiac canceled the line after '81 and substituted a restyled LeMans sedan and wagon called Bonneville Model G (the letter denoting a redesignated A-body platform). But what looked like a smart idea in 1980 seemed just bad timing once big-car sales turned up again, so Pontiac decided to revive a B-body line during 1983. As there was no longer any production room stateside, U.S. dealers got a slightly modified Canadian version—which had never been dropped—under its north-of-the-border name, Parisienne.

If these moves recalled the great Dodge/Plymouth debacle of 20 years before, they weren't nearly so disastrous. But they weren't that successful, either. Bonneville G peaked at about 82,800 sales in '83, then tailed off to around 41,000 by its final appearance for 1986. Parisienne averaged about 83,000 yearly sales for 1985-86, after which the sedan departed (the B-body two-door coupe hadn't returned) and annual sales ran below 13,200 for the lone Safari wagon marketed through 1989. Design, engineering, and yearly changes for both these lines virtually duplicated those for counterpart Chevys, the intermediate Malibu and full-size Caprice/Impala.

Another up-north idea was the subcompact T1000, a Chevette clone by way of Pontiac Canada's Acadian model. Announced in April 1981, it immediately attracted 70,000 buyers, then fell to an annual average of 25,000 or so after 1982, when it was called just plain 1000. Black window frames and a prominent arrowhead grille emblem were the main design elements that set it apart from the littlest Chevy. Naturally, the 1000 evolved in parallel with Chevette through 1987, then gave way to a new front-drive LeMans (which is beyond the scope of this book, being a Korean-built sister of a German Opel Kadett). The 1000 was just a token nod to the econocar market and never a big money-spinner.

The second-generation Phoenix was the least popular of GM's four front-drive X-body compacts, likely because the same package was available with more model/trim choices as a Chevy Citation or with more nameplate prestige as a Buick Skylark or Olds Omega. Pontiac tried to make the downsized Phoenix appealing by offering two-door notchback and four-door hatchback sedans in plain, luxury LJ, and sporty SJ trim (the latter two retagged LE and SE for '84). But nothing seemed to work, and demand fell off rapidly when numerous mechanical bugs began surfacing, with recalls to match. Phoenix never sold better than in its extra-long 1980 debut year: 178,000-plus. Volume dipped below 50,000 units for 1982 and dropped to

1976 Astre hatchback coupe

1976 Grand Prix coupe

1977 LeMans Sport Coupe with Can Am package

1977 Catalina coupe

1977 Grand Prix SJ coupe

1977½ Phoenix four-door sedan

1978 Firebird Trans Am Special Edition coupe

1979 Firebird Trans Am coupe

1979 Sunbird Formula hatchback coupe

1980 Phoenix LJ hatchback sedan

under 23,000 cars by the 1984 finale.

Yet Phoenix was successful in a way, because it spawned a more rational and popular midsize Pontiac, the front-wheel-drive 6000. Arriving for model year '82, it was closely related to that year's new A-body Buick Century, Chevy Celebrity, and Oldsmobile Cutlass Ciera, but wore crisper, more "important" sheetmetal over the shared X-car-based inner structure. Initial offerings comprised base and LE coupe and sedan, but Pontiac went a big step further with the STE (Special Touring Edition). Announced for the 1983 season, this enthusiast-oriented four-door represented a new Pontiac challenge to sporty European sedans from Audi, BMW, Mercedes, Saab, and Volvo.

The STE proved a surprisingly capable challenger. Quick-ratio steering and a fortified suspension with air-adjustable rear shocks and upgraded wheels and tires made the car supremely roadable. Appointments were tastefully understated, and equipment was generous (including even a leather-bound roadside emergency kit). All it lacked was sparkling acceleration; the mandatory three-speed automatic transaxle strained the 135 horses of the standard "high-output" 2.8-liter/173-cid Chevy-built overhead-valve V-6. But the STE served notice that Pontiac was not only back to building driver's cars but could compete on a "best-in-class" basis against many comers.

Other 6000s bathed in the STE's glow, and by 1984 this line was Pontiac's best-selling larger car, bolstered that year by the addition of station wagons. Worthy improvements came almost annually: electronic fuel injection for the base 2.5-liter four (throttle-body, 1983) and V-6 (multipoint for all models by 1987); a more versatile and efficient four-speed automatic for selected models (1986); an S/E sedan and wagon offering much of the STE's panache for less money (1987); an all-wheel-drive option (AWD) and 3.1-liter V-6 for an extensively reengineered STE, plus optional five-speed manual (1988).

After dropping the 6000's coupe models for 1988, Pontiac gave 1989 sedans a restyled rear greenhouse and offered the STE only with AWD. The optional 3.1 V-6 picked up five extra horses for 140 total. By that point, the S/E was what the STE had been, yet was more price-competitive against comparable Japanese sedans at $16,000-$17,000. For 1990, the AWD became an S/E extra. Amazingly, the 6000 was still around for '91, though that was its final year. It had served exceptionally well.

Vying with the 6000 for divisional sales leadership was Pontiac's version of the front-drive J-body subcompact, which succeeded the old rear-drive Sunbird for 1982. At first, the name seemed to change more than the car, which debuted as J2000, then evolved as the 2000 (1983), 2000 Sunbird (1984), and finally just Sunbird again. Pontiac had gotten into "alphamumeric"designations under Hoglund's immediate predecessor, Robert C. Stempel (named GM president in 1987 and chairman in 1990), but eventually backed away from them after buyers found them confusing.

There was no confusion about the cars, which were much like Chevy's Cavaliers down to the same body styles—including a convertible from 1983. Though Chevy's 2.0-liter over- head-valve four was available for a time, Pontiac emphasized an Opel-designed overhead-cam engine imported from GM of Brazil. That engine became standard for 1983, with throttle-body injection and 84 bhp from 1.8 liters (109 cid), followed by a 150-bhp turbocharged option with port injection. Both versions grew to 2.0 liters for 1987, good for respective horsepower of 96 and 165.

Three trims were offered through 1985: base, plush LE, and sporty SE. The LE was canceled for '86, when turbocharged GTs arrived with a new front end highlighted by hidden headlamps. The 1988 GTs were trimmed to just convertible and coupe, the latter a restyled slantback two-door also offered in

1980 Bonneville Brougham four-door sedan

1982 Grand Prix Brougham Landau coupe

1982 J2000 hatchback coupe

1982 Firebird S/E coupe

1983 Firebird S/E coupe

1984 Fiero Official Pace Car coupe

SE form. A new dashboard was the big event for '89. By 1990, Sunbird and Cavalier were the only two J-cars left from the original five, and neither showed signs of going away. Pontiac kept Sunbird going with a handsome restyle featuring a smoother hidden-headlamp nose and various lower-body addenda for SE and GT coupes; the 1990 convertible came only as a cheaper but less-sporting LE. With so much variety, plus attractive prices only a bit above Cavalier's, the 2000/Sunbird garnered well over 100,000 sales in most years, including a record 170,000-plus for '84. Demand remained healthy right through 1990, when output totaled just under 145,000.

As at Buick and Olds, the J-car was the basis for a new compact Pontiac to replace the unloved X-body after 1984. Resurrecting the Grand Am name, this rendition of the 103.4-inch-wheelbase N-body design promptly outsold its divisional cousins by emphasizing handling options and sporty appointments in the European mold. Demand was strong: more than 82,500 of the debut 1985 coupes, a stunning 223,000 coupes and sedans for 1986. This Grand Am was the lifeblood of Pontiac dealers, accounting for better than 235,000 orders each model year through 1989 despite a constant stream of new competition. Not until the market turned difficult in 1990 did Grand Am sales dip below 200,000—and then not by much.

Again seeking individuality, Pontiac proffered a more overtly sporting SE in addition to the expected plain and luxury Grand Ams. The division also varied engines, making Sunbird's turbo-four a 1987 option, then replacing the original 3.0-liter Buick V-6 option with GM's new 150-bhp "Quad-4," America's first postwar production engine with dual overhead camshafts and four valves per cylinder.

Buyers seeking a smaller sports sedan had every reason to look closely at Grand Am SE. Its monochrome exterior with color-keyed wheels, front spoiler, and perimeter lower-body extensions was aggressive but not childish. A well-planned cockpit, assured handling, comfortable ride, and brisk performance completed the package. As with the STE, Pontiac again seemed able to do more with a shared platform than either Buick or Oldsmobile, at least as far as enthusiasts were concerned.

The same could be said for the first front-drive Bonneville, unveiled for 1987 on the 110.8-inch-wheelbase H-body platform of the previous year's new Buick LeSabre and Olds Delta 88. Pontiac designers strove mightily to make this one different, too, and succeeded handsomely. There wasn't much they could do about the boxy roofline, but much smoother front and rear ends set Bonneville cleanly apart from its corporate cousins.

Here, too, there was a sporty SE, an option group with uprated suspension, larger wheels and tires, mellow exhaust, less exterior chrome, console-mount shifter for the mandatory four-speed automatic transaxle, a shorter final drive for snappier step-off, and a full set of large, legible gauges, including tachometer. With all this, you might forget the SE used the same

1984 Fiero 2-passenger coupe

1985 Bonneville Brougham four-door sedan

1984 Grand Prix coupe

1985 Firebird Trans Am coupe

1985 6000 STE four-door sedan

1986 Grand Prix Brougham coupe

150-bhp 3.8-liter (231-cid) V-6 as base and LE Bonnevilles.

An improved 165-bhp engine arrived for 1988, when Pontiac went a bit over the top with a new top-line Bonneville SSE. It was visually contrived, with body-color wheels, grille, decklid spoiler, and rocker skirting set off by a gaudy grille medallion. More-worthy standards ran to GM/Teves antilock brakes (optional on other Bonnevilles for 1989-90), an electronic variable-damping system, and a leather-lined interior with multi-adjustable power bucket seats. Still, most critics felt the more modestly trimmed SE a better buy: less costly, smoother-riding, slightly quieter to both ears and eyes. The public generally agreed, but liked all the new Bonnies to the tune of some 120,000 sales in 1987 and 108,000 in 1988—not far behind LeSabre and Delta despite lacking their coupe body style. Only detail changes occurred for 1990, but the market was sagging and Bonneville demand skidded to just under 86,000 for the model year, down from some 109,000.

Firebird showed surprising sales strength in the '80s, averaging some 100,000 per year through 1986. But that only reflected the renewed interest in performance cars that began around 1982, making that year's all-new Firebird exceedingly well-timed. Inevitably, it shared a redesigned F-body platform with that year's new-generation Chevy Camaro, striding a trimmer, 101-inch wheelbase. Though these ponycars were more alike than ever, Pontiac stylists under John Schinella maintained a distinctive Firebird look via a low-riding nose with shallow twin grilles and hidden headlamps—the latter a first for Firebird—plus full-width taillamps with a smoked lens on some models for a "custom" blackout effect.

Initially, the third-series Firebird was limited to base, midrange S/E, and racy Trans Am, all "glassback" hatch coupes, but the Formula returned as an option package for 1987, along with the "big" 350/5.7-liter V-8 of bygone years. That engine also powered an even meaner-looking Trans Am called GTA. Other developments largely paralleled Camaro's except that Pontiac wouldn't field another Firebird convertible until 1992; it also continued offering specific chassis tuning and trim/equipment mixes. Styling was good enough to last through 1990 with only minor annual tweaks, many of which were exclusive to the Trans Am. Most noticeable was a grilleless "bottom-breather" nose for '84.

Recalling 1976's Limited-Edition T/A (for Pontiac's 50th birthday) and 1979's Tenth Anniversary Trans Am was yet another celebratory Firebird for 1989: the 20th Anniversary Trans Am. This involved a 1500-unit run of GTAs powered by the turbocharged 231-cid/3.8-liter V-6 from Buick's recently departed GNX muscle coupe. Though sold only with four-speed overdrive automatic, the "blown" Bird was the most-potent T/A in more than a decade, packing a quoted 250 bhp and an imposing 340 pound-feet torque (versus the V-8 GTA's 225 bhp and 330 pound-feet). You could have any color as long as it was white, just like the '69 original; no racing stripes, though, just subtle

1986 Grand Prix 2+2 "aero" coupe

1986 Grand Prix 2+2 "aero" coupe

1986 Firebird Trans Am coupe

1986 Grand Am LE four-door sedan

1986 1000 hatchback sedan

"20th Anniversary" cloisonné emblems and "Turbo Trans Am" badges. Performance was straight from "the good old days"—better, really. Would you believe 0-60 in 5.4 seconds? Believe it: This Firebird was chosen pace car for the 1989 Indianapolis 500 and required no engine modifications for the task. Price was reasonable, all told, at about $25,000 with included T-top roof and pace-car decals. In all, this was a glorious reminder that nobody in Detroit still cared more about hot cars than Pontiac.

Unfortunately, Firebird fell on hard times after 1986, with production fading to some 80,000 for '87, then to an average 63,000 a year through '89. The situation grew even more grim for 1990, when fewer than 21,000 were sold. A little-changed basic design and fast-rising prices were mainly to blame (a new F-body wouldn't appear until 1993), but so were intensified import competition, rising hot-car insurance rates (Camaros and Firebirds were long notorious as frequent theft targets), and continuing lackluster workmanship.

By far the most enigmatic 1980s Pontiac was the innovative but ill-starred Fiero. A 1984 newcomer, it was Detroit's first mid-engine production car and the first new series-built U.S. two-seater since the original Ford Thunderbird. Fiero was broached in 1978 as a low-cost, high-mileage "commuter," but that was just a ruse to convince management that the project would help GM fulfill its CAFE obligations. The urge toward something sportier was irresistible, since the plan called for transplanting the front-drive X-body powertrain behind the cockpit to drive the rear wheels.

GM president Elliot Estes approved the concept in 1978, perhaps for sentimental reasons: He had pleaded for a two-seat Pontiac while he was division chief back in the '60s. Corporate cash-flow problems almost killed the Fiero program several times in 1980-82, but engineering director Hulki Aldikacti somehow persuaded decision-makers that this new "P-car" not only made financial sense but could also improve Pontiac's image.

What emerged was definitely sporty; a smooth but chunky notchback coupe on a 93.4-inch wheelbase, evolved under Ron Hill in GM's Advanced Design III section and finalized by John Schinella's production studio. A fully drivable steel space-frame chassis served as a skeleton for supporting body panels made of various plastics—but not fiberglass—making style changes cheap, quick, and easy. To minimize production costs and retail price, steering, front suspension, and brakes were borrowed from the humble Chevy Chevette; rear suspension and disc brakes were retained from the X-car power package.

Announced at base prices carefully pitched in the $8000-$9600 range, the Fiero predictably generated lots of excitement. The division's Pontiac, Michigan home plant, fully retooled as Fiero's exclusive production center, happily cranked out nearly 137,000 of the '84s. But Fiero was flawed—heavy and thus sluggish with the standard 92-bhp, 151-cid Iron Duke four; little faster with the optional 173-cid V-6; low, cramped, noisy, and hard to see out of; hard to shift; stiff-riding; indifferently put together. As it had with the X-cars, GM shot itself in the foot by selling a car before it was fully developed.

Word got around quickly. Fiero sales crumbled by more than 40 percent in the second model year, recovered to near 84,000 for '86, then fell by nearly half for '87. A further blow came in September 1987, when a spate of engine fires implicating some 20 percent of the '84 models occasioned a government-ordered recall. With all this, plus a sharp drop in two-seater demand due to soaring insurance rates, GM announced in early 1988 that Fiero was dead, lamely claiming itself unable to make a profit at 50,000 units a year. Ironically, Pontiac had just spent $30 million for an all-new suspension that greatly improved handling on '88 Fieros. Left stillborn were plans for a 1989 Quad-4 option and the more distant prospect of a lighter aluminum space-

1986 6000 STE four-door sedan

1987 Fiero GT 2-passenger coupe

1987 Firebird Trans Am GTA coupe

1987 Bonneville four-door sedan

1987 Sunbird SE coupe

1987 Firebird Formula coupe

1988 Firebird Trans Am GTA coupe

1988 Grand Prix LE coupe

frame that would have done wonders for performance.

The V-6 S/E and GT models were the most desirable Fieros. The GT bowed for 1985 with a sleek nose inspired by a special 1984 Indy 500 pace car (of which a few thousand replicas were sold). Standard rear spoiler, "ground effects" body addenda, uprated suspension, and a deep-voiced exhaust made it a sort of mini-muscle car. Without the V-6, this package became the midrange S/E model for 1986, bolstered at midseason by a restyled GT with modified rear flanks and "flying buttress" fastback roofline. Arriving in June that year was a five-speed manual transaxle, long promised as an optional alternative to the standard four-speed and extra-cost three-speed automatic. The main changes for '87 involved a reshaped nose for base and S/E, plus a larger fuel tank.

Though compromised in many ways and a relative commercial failure, the Fiero was a useful test bed for General Motors' new Saturn subcompact, which would also use a space-frame skeleton overlaid with dent- and rust-resistant plastic panels. Fiero also symbolized Pontiac's renewed commitment to interesting automobiles. A more successful expression was the all-new front-drive Grand Prix that replaced one of Detroit's dullest cars for 1988.

Pontiac's personal-luxury coupe had become almost invisible since its '78 downsizing, limping along after 1981 with somewhat smoother but still uninspired styling that strained at marrying "aero modern" with "middle-class traditional." Engines

1988 Bonneville SSE four-door sedan

1988 Fiero GT 2-passenger coupe

1988 Grand Am SE coupe

1988 Sunbird GT Turbo coupe

1989 Firebird Trans Am Turbo Official Pace Car

1989 Grand Prix Turbo coupe

were equally uninspired, mostly Buick V-6s and Chevy small-block V-8s, all economy-tuned. The trouble-prone Olds 350 diesel V-8 offered from 1981 to '84 only underlined the old-fogey aura of a car that was less important on the street than on NASCAR circuits (thanks to Richard Petty, and others).

But the GP's role as stock-car standard-bearer did lead to an interesting limited edition reviving the 2+2 handle. Introduced at mid-1986, this wore a wind-cheating body-color front instead of the usual stand-up brightwork, plus a huge "glassback" deck designed for smoother airflow to a bespoilered tail. GM Design concocted this configuration to counter Ford's more slippery new Thunderbirds in long-distance races. As ever, NASCAR approval depended on building a set number of street models, hence this Pontiac and Chevy's similar Monte Carlo SS Aerocoupe. Showroom 2+2s carried a four-barrel, 165-bhp Chevy 305 V-8--fair enough, considering all period GM competitors in NASCAR ran Chevy-based engines. If any Grand Prix built between 1978 and '87 will interest collectors, this is the one, though it's generated scant interest so far.

The all-new '88 was a very different Grand Prix. Though it premiered with the same W-body/GM10 coupe platform as the latest Olds Cutlass Supreme and Buick Regal, its looks were pure Pontiac: sleek, purposeful, and obviously more "aero" than its blocky predecessor. It was more sophisticated, too, with standard all-disc brakes and four-wheel independent suspension. Though 7.8 inches shorter overall than the '87, the '88 rode a wheelbase only 0.5-inch shorter. This, plus a transverse drivetrain (nearly universal with front drive), made for a much-roomier interior than before.

For the base and midrange LE models, that drivetrain involved a 130-bhp 173-cid Chevy V-6 with port fuel injection driving a four-speed automatic transaxle; a five-speed manual designed by Getrag of Germany was optional. The five-speed was standard on the sporty SE, which came with a beefed-up suspension and more comprehensive instruments set in a very busy dash. Automatic GPs were upgraded to a stroked 3.1-liter (191-cid) V-6 during 1989, but the big thrill was a McLaren Turbo model powered by a blown 3.1 producing 200 bhp.

The "McTurbo" was another limited edition, developed with ASC/McLaren and planned for only 2000 copies. Finished in monochrome red or black with gold-color accents, it rolled on sizable 16-inch lacy-spoke wheels fitted with Z-rated high-performance tires (safe at over 149 mph). Wheel openings were suitably flared for clearance via specific lower-body panels with wind-cheating "spats" at each wheel, plus a grooved rub strip carried into the bumpers at each end. Like Ford with its '83 Thunderbird, Pontiac had come up with a car to revitalize a tired name. The McLaren was arguably the best GP yet for all-around performance.

Workaday Grand Prixs made a good sales start with model-year '88 volume of about 86,000. The '89s fared even better at just under 137,000, with optional antilock brakes a new inducement to buy. The 1990 total was a bit lower at 128,000—disturbing, as that included two new sedans, an LE and a reincarnated STE. Each was shapely, but the STE was both sporty and lush. Among its no-cost features were antilock brakes, handling suspension, upgraded rolling stock, analog gauges (replacing contrived digigraphic), buckets-and-console interior, and an available 205-bhp 3.1 turbo V-6 (offered on a Turbo coupe as well). Bodyside cladding cluttered appearance, a bank of running lights between the headlamps looked me-too next to the Mercury Sable (which had this first), and the standard powertrain teamed the unexciting 140-bhp 3.1 V-6 with mandatory four-speed automatic. Still, it was heartening to see the STE continue, and the LE was a fitting replacement for the 6000 as Pontiac's mainstream family four-door.

1989 6000 STE All-Wheel-Drive four-door sedan

1990 Trans Sport SE minivan

1989 Sunbird GT Turbo convertible coupe

1990 Firebird Trans Am GTA coupe

Pontiacs kept evolving more or less in step with related Chevrolets, Oldsmobiles, and Buicks, but contrived to seem sportier, even if driving reality didn't always match the division's new "We Build Excitement" ad slogan. Sales tactics shifted greatly, as Pontiac added a minivan for 1990, then merged with the GMC truck division to create a "full-line" franchise like Chevrolet. The latter move was announced in February 1996 by Ronald Zarrella, recruited four years earlier from optics maker Bausch & Lomb to be GM's group executive for North American vehicle sales, service, and marketing. In a press release, Zarrella touted the new Pontiac-GMC Division as part of a "continuing effort…to configure our organization to achieve the most effective, efficient results for our customers, dealers, and stockholders. Both Pontiac and GMC have long recognized the complimentary [sic] nature of their businesses …and the advantages inherent in a dual franchise." Indeed, some 55 percent of Pontiac dealers already handled GMC at the time. The combined division began with 3736 outlets and total calendar-year sales of over a million units. Of course, the goal for this wedding was plain: fewer but more profitable dealers.

Zarrella, named president of GM North America in 1999, espoused "brand management," long a staple at consumer-products companies like Proctor & Gamble. GM chairman John Smale, who once headed P&G, and president John F. "Jack" Smith were believers, too. Smale and Smith came to power earlier in 1992 in a board-instigated "palace coup" that ignominiously removed chairman Bob Stempel and president Lloyd Reuss, veteran GMers who were blamed for continuing losses in company market share and earnings. Zarrella's mission was to turn things around. Under brand management, that meant sharpening the image of each GM make for more customer appeal and less intramural rivalry, plus weeding out similar and/or underperforming models throughout the corporate fleet.

But Zarrella's efforts, however well-intentioned, produced mixed results. Though recovery was evident by middecade, it stemmed more from a booming tech-driven national economy and fast-growing demand for high-margin trucks than fancy ads and design dictated increasingly by consumer focus groups.

Pontiac was less affected by brand-management antics than other GM makes save Saturn, which was in its own orbit anyway. In fact, Pontiac had been pretty well-managed before Zarrella came in. All it needed to do in the '90s was more of the same—which it did to good effect, sales running at a half-million units or better each calendar year save 1998. Even so, an ominous downtrend set in as the new century neared.

The Trans Sport minivan was a peripheral player, generally drawing fewer than 30,000 yearly sales, a fraction of what the top-selling Dodge Caravan and Plymouth Voyager achieved. GM had missed the minivan mark with its new-for-'85 rear-drive Chevy Astro/GMC Safari, so it drew up a Chrysler-like front-drive platform for Trans Sport, a new Chevrolet Lumina APV, and a luxury-oriented Oldsmobile Silhouette. All placed plastic-like body panels over a steel skeleton like the late Fiero, unique among minivans but debatable here. So, too, was the shared "dustbuster" styling, with a long pointy snout grafted onto a practical minivan box. *Car and Driver* likened the look to something out of "Star Trek." Equally weird was a dashtop that stretched way ahead to a steeply raked windshield flanked by large, fixed triangular side windows ahead of the front doors. Visibility, needless to say, wasn't the best. More useful was available "2+2+2" seating for the uplevel Trans Sport SE. This involved lightweight individual seats for the second and third rows that could be rearranged to suit various passenger- and cargo-carrying requirements—a bright new minivan idea.

At first, Trans Sport and company only had a 120-bhp version of GM's 3.1-liter V-6, with less-efficient throttle-body fuel injection instead of a squirter at each cylinder. That was hardly a selling point for a vehicle that could be loaded with seven people and/or lots of cargo. But GM made amends for '92 by adding an extra-cost 165-bhp 3.8 V-6, plus available antilock brakes. The 3.8 gained five bhp for '93, when a pop-up sunroof, leather upholstery, and steering wheel-mounted audio controls joined Trans Sport's options roster. The next year introduced a standard driver-side airbag and automatic power door locks, plus an optional power sliding right-rear side door—and an oddly blunted nose paring 2.3 inches from overall length, an attempt to silence style critics. Optional traction control arrived late that season. Progress slowed as a planned redesign drew near: just a shift interlock for '95, and a new 180-bhp 3.4-liter V-6 as the sole engine for '96. In all, these minivans were another example of how GM so often stumbles when attempting to innovate.

Though Grand Am and Grand Prix remained Pontiac's top sellers in the '90s, Sunbird contributed important volume, attracting more than 100,000 orders each model year through the end of the original J-car design in 1994. It was looking quite tired by then, but steady updating helped maintain its appeal. The '91s, for example, replaced the gruff, growly turbo-four with the corporate 3.1 V-6, whose modest 140 horses seemed quite lively in this light subcompact. The V-6 was standard for the GT coupe, optional otherwise. A base-trim coupe and sedan were added at nearly $800 less than counterpart LEs, but they didn't get the V-6 or many other options. For '92 came standard antilock brakes—a real plus for the small car class—plus no-cost automatic power door locks and a shift interlock for the automatic transmission. LE now denoted base-trim Sunbirds; SEs expanded to coupe, sedan, and convertible choices. A new fuel-injection system added 15 horsepower to the old 2.0-liter base four. The flock saw even fewer changes for '93, though SE coupes gained an optional Sport Appearance Package that delivered a GT-style nose and bodyside cladding for less money. The '94 line comprised the LE trio and a V-6 SE coupe with Sport Appearance features, basically the departed GT with a lower price.

Everything changed for 1995, name included, as the Sunbird became the Sunfire on a heavily revised J-car platform shared with Chevrolet Cavalier. A curvy new look was common to both, but Sunfire stood apart with Pontiac's signature twin-port grille, plus a busier rear end, plastic-clad lower bodysides—a growing Pontiac fetish at the time—and even different coupe rooflines. An SE coupe and sedan rolled in first, followed at midmodel year by a GT coupe and then an SE convertible with standard power top. SE base power was the 2.2-liter 120-bhp pushrod four that Cavaliers had used for some time already, while the V-6 gave way to the 150-bhp 2.3-liter twincam Quad-4 familiar from recent GM compacts and intermediates. The latter was standard for the GT, optional for the SE coupe. Both engines mated to a standard five-speed manual transmission. Optional automatics were the usual three-speed with the 2.2, a new four-speed with the Quad-4. The latter combination included traction control, which was otherwise unavailable. At least all models finally shed annoying motorized "mouse belts" for twin dashboard airbags to meet the fed's requirement for front "passive restraints."

Sunfire shuffled powerteams for 1996. The 2.2 was now offered with the four-speed automatic and traction control. The Quad-4 got some internal tweaks, a displacement bump to 2.4 liters, and the prosaic name Twin Cam. Horsepower was unchanged, but the big four was newly optional for the four-door SE. Changes for '97 centered on the ragtop SE, which got a four-speed automatic, cruise control, and electric defrosting for its glass rear window as additional no-cost items. There was little news for '98, while the main '99 development was shifting the convertible to GT trim. Modestly freshened year-2000 Sunfires bowed in early '99. The longer model year yielded higher production on that basis, but calendar-year orders declined. The ragtop, never a strong seller, was phased out during the year.

The vintage-1985 Grand Am said goodbye after 1991, when it added base-trim price-leaders, plus standard antilock brakes for top-line SEs. The latter were touted as America's most affordable cars with ABS, even though stickers swelled more than $1300 to $16,000-plus. Engines, carried over from 1990, started with the old 2.5-liter Iron Duke four providing 110 stan-

1991 Sunbird GT coupe

1991 Firebird Trans Am convertible coupe

1991 Bonneville SSE four-door sedan

1991 Grand Prix STE four-door sedan

1992 Grand Am GT coupe

1992 SSEi four-door sedan

1992 Firebird Trans Am convertible coupe

1993 Grand Am SE four-door sedan

1993 Grand Prix LE four-door sedan

1993 Sunbird SE convertible coupe

dard bhp in base and LE models. Available for LEs and included on SEs was the gruff but game Quad-4 with 160 bhp when tied to the optional three-speed automatic, 180 if mated to the linewide-standard five-speed manual. LEs, now midline Grand Ams, offered a Sport Performance option with SE-like styling and Quad-4 power.

A somewhat overdue redesign put 1992 Grand Ams on a fresh N-body platform along with Chevrolet's Corsica/Beretta, redone Buick Skylarks, and Oldsmobile's new Achievas. Wheelbase was untouched, but length grew by more than half a foot. Only SE and GT coupes and sedans returned. Despite the general industry move to airbags, Grand Am persisted with door-mounted "automatic safety belts" and promoted linewide-standard ABS instead. Styling was sleeker but rather exaggerated, with heavy lower-body plastic cladding on GTs—which Skylark and Achieva designers had to work around—and a sleeker profile for coupes.

The redesign also shook things up under Grand Am hoods. The base Iron Duke stepped aside for a single-cam version of the Quad-4 dubbed Quad OHC, tuned for 120 bhp. The Quad-4 itself returned unchanged, but a V-6 was made available for the first time since 1987. This Buick-sourced pushrod 3.3-liter unit had the same 160 bhp as the automatic-transmission Quad-4, but also boasted greater low-speed torque that made a better match with the three-speed slushbox, the only choice offered.

The makeover spurred Grand Am to some 208,500 sales for '92. Second-year changes were predictably minor: an optional remote keyless-entry system, a standard battery-rundown protection feature, and four-cylinder engines made slightly quieter. The fours were still rather unrefined lumps and they managed to lose five bhp. Sales approached 255,000 for 1994, when updates were relatively monumental: a standard driver-side airbag at last—just as most rivals were getting dual airbags—an available four-speed automatic transmission, and a 155-bhp 3.1-liter V-6 to replace the 160-horse 3.3. Leather upholstery was a new extra, and the sometimes-hated automatic door locks could now be set for automatic unlocking, sparing occupants the trouble of flicking a switch.

After a short three-year run, the Quad OHC was canceled for 1995 Grand Ams and a 150-bhp Quad-4 became the new base engine, adding "balance shafts" for smoother running but losing its High-Output variant. Despite being a virtual carryover otherwise, Grand Am continued on a rising sales track, nudging past 291,000 for the model year.

Modest cosmetic tweaks and standard dual airbags in a reworked dash marked the '96 models. As with the Sunfire and other cars that used it, the Quad-4 became a 2.4-liter Twin Cam, gaining internal refinements but no more horsepower. The old three-speed automatic was dropped, and traction control was a new bonus when the four-speed automatic was ordered. Grand Am then stood pat for two full years, awaiting another redesign.

Similar honing marked the midsize Grand Prix through 1996, its basic 1988 design updated as new engines and features emerged from General Motors labs. Of course, the same held for the W-body Buick Regal and Olds Cutlass Supreme. Yet the GP, perhaps because of Pontiac's hipper image, usually sold the best, if not quite as well as Chevrolet's more affordable W-body Lumina. Worrisome, though, were see-saw sales in these years, dropping from more than 197,000 for 1990 to 100,000-150,000 per model year. The exception was swan-song '96, when early release of redesigned '97s held volume below 84,000.

Grand Prix's 1991 program reprised LE, SE, and STE sedans, but not the turbocharged STE. The Turbo coupe was gone too, replaced by a nonturbo GT and uplevel GTP, the latter dressed in aggressive body cladding. (The plastics industry must have loved Pontiac in these years.) While some mourned losing the

1993 Firebird Trans Am coupe

1994 Sunbird SE coupe

1994 Grand Am GT coupe

1994 Firebird Trans Am coupe with 25th Anniversary package

turbocharged V-6, Pontiac consoled them with GM's new normally aspirated Twin Dual Cam V-6, a 24-valve 3.4-liter rated at 210 bhp with five-speed manual or an even 200 with that year's new four-speed automatic option. Standard for GTP, this engine was available for other models save the LE sedan. Also on the card were a base 140-bhp 3.1 V-6 and a 160-bhp 2.3 Quad-4. LE sedans also missed out on the ABS that was newly available on other '91 GPs. The Quad-4 departed for '92, when ABS became standard except on LEs, and all sedans took on the STE's front light bar. Linewide-standard automatic power door locking was the main change for '93.

Catching up with many rivals for 1994, Grand Prix added standard dual airbags in a redesigned interior, the year's only W-body so blessed. More surprising was a lineup pared to just a pair of well-equipped mainstream SEs. The 3.1 V-6 added 20 bhp for 160 total. The five-speed manual transmission was discarded, but the options list still had enough of the right stuff to approximate the sportiness of the discontinued GT and STE. Interestingly, the more overt family focus boosted GP sales by some 31,500 units over model-year '93. The '95s drew only some 4700 fewer orders despite little change. There was even less news for the abbreviated '96 season, though the 3.4 V-6 tacked on five bhp.

A mostly new H-body Bonneville sedan began an eight-year run for 1992, distinguished by a billowy new look that not everyone liked. That might explain why sales followed the Grand Prix pattern, with a first-year peak (some 124,000), a lower midlife plateau (fewer than 100,000 through '94), and a still-lower level through series end (75,000 at best).

The most exciting '92 Bonneville was the new SSEi, offering a supercharged version of GM's evergreen 3.8-liter V-6 with 205 bhp. An unblown 170-bhp standard engine was shared with midrange SSE and base SE models. All boasted a driver-side airbag. The SSE added ABS, buckets-and-console interior, and alloy wheels. The SSEi looked pricey at $28,045 to start, but came with a passenger-side airbag, automatic climate control, 12-way power front seats, and a racy head-up display (HUD) that projected speed and other data onto the windshield ahead of the driver. But the SSEi's most important feature was its standard traction-control system. This helped tame unruly, unwanted front wheelspin by throttling back power and/or applying the brakes in response to signals from the ABS wheel-speed sensors. Sporting owners appreciated traction control. Then again, few cars in this class needed it so much. Indeed, enthusiasts still blanched at any front-drive car with handling compromised by a surplus of power, as this Bonneville was.

Curiously, the SSEi's flagship appeal was diluted for '93 by giving the SE standard ABS and an SLE package option with SSEi-style grille and body addenda, 16-inch "lacy spoke" wheels and other amenities. In addition, the supercharged V-6 was newly available for the SSE. Pontiac was after more competitive price points, a motive that also figured in the SSEi's 1994 demotion from separate model to SSE option. At least that year's blown V-6 got an extra 20 bhp, and all Bonnevilles benefited from included dual airbags. Price pressure also prompted a special SLE option for California-bound '94 SEs, an alleged $4500 value tagged at just $1371. Exclusive to the SSE option list was GM's Computer Command Ride (CCR), basically sensor-linked shock absorbers that automatically changed from soft to firm damping in hard cornering or braking maneuvers.

Tech again dominated news for 1995. An extensive internal revamp evolved the base V-6 into a smoother, quieter "Series II" engine with 205 bhp, and the supercharged mill was newly optional for SLE-equipped SEs. The blown engine became a Series II for '96, adding 15 horses with it, and all models sported a subtle facelift.

But none of this affected sales very much, nor did further fiddling for 1997-99. Though Bonneville still ran a strong second to Buick's LeSabre in H-body sales, it had been eclipsed for style, space, and roadability by the "cab-forward" Dodge Intrepid and Chrysler Concorde/LHS/300. Larger new import-brand sedans were also stealing the big Poncho's thunder—and customers. Indeed, *Consumer Guide*® demoted Bonneville from "Best Buy" to "Recommended" status after 1997. Like Grand Am and Grand Prix, the 1990s Bonnie had slipped into the "rental car" trap: OK for a week's vacation, maybe, but not the top choice for a long-term relationship.

That left Firebird to carry the "excitement" banner. As ever, it was the most stirring thing in Pontiac showrooms, and promptly became even more so—mainly because it had to.

Firebird began its 1991 season in spring '90, about six months early. Base, Formula, Trans Am, and GTA came back with another deft facelift of the familiar vintage-1982 design, announced by a smoother snout recalling the recent Banshee show car. A new Sport Appearance option gave the low-liner much of the T/A's show, but not the go. Engines ranged from a budget-grade 140-bhp 3.1 V-6 to a 240-bhp 350-cid/5.7-liter V-8. Though everyone knew a fresh Firebird was just two years off, Pontiac sprang a surprise at mid-1991 with its first convertible ponycar in more than two decades. Offered in base, Formula, and T/A guise only, the droptop Firebird was naturally much like the rag-roof Chevy Camaro that had been around since 1987. It spurred a modest sales recovery as a bridge to '93.

That season also began early, and why not? Abetted by a recent concept preview and fuzzy spy photos in newspapers and "buff" magazines, Firebird fans were clamoring for the fourth generation of their favorite. They weren't disappointed. Bowing in spring '92 with coupes only, the 1993 Firebird was a real looker: slick, slinky, even a bit menacing. Wheelbase was unchanged, but flowing new contours gave greater visual distinction from F-body cousin Camaro. Fiero experience paid practical dividends in the use of dent-resistant plasticlike material for the front and rear fascias, front fenders, doors, roof, and rear hatchlid. Beneath was a spaceframelike structure that improved rigidity so much that the optional twin T-tops could be replaced by single lift-off panel—the first Firebird "targa" coupe. Powerteams were drastically simplified. Base models came with the corporate 3.4 V-6, here tuned for 160 bhp and linked to five-speed manual or optional four-speed automatic transmissions. Formula and Trans Am shared a new-generation small-block V-8 dubbed LT1, still a 5.7 but chockablock with engineering improvements. Also found in Camaros and Chevrolet Corvettes, it delivered a 275-bhp wallop via the automatic or a newly standard six-speed manual gearbox. Chassis changes were equally extensive, though the all-coil suspension was much the same in concept. The factory changed too, with F-body production moving from Van Nuys, California, to a more modern GM plant in St. Therese, Quebec, Canada.

All 1993 Firebirds came with dual airbags and ABS, a sop to insurance companies and the high premiums that still dampened demand for many sporty cars. Unfortunately, those additions pushed sticker prices much higher. A base Firebird previously listing at $12,505 with automatic now started at $13,995 with manual. Given that, plus surprisingly strong, sustained competition from an aged yet seemingly ageless Ford Mustang, the brand-new Firebird was no sales smash. A slow production ramp-up for the sake of build quality held model-year '93 volume below 15,000 units. Yet even when production did hit stride in 1994, sales recovered only to the 50,000-unit level achieved by the last third-generation cars of 1992.

Firebird started 1994 with a "decontented" and downpriced Trans Am, though the previous T/A was still around as the Trans Am GT. V-8 buyers choosing six-speed manual got CAGS, GM's Computer Aided Gear Selection feature. Long familiar in Corvettes, it basically "forced" a first-to-fourth upshift under light throttle as an aid to fuel economy—and to CAFE numbers. GM refused to build cars that would qualify for the Gas-Guzzler Tax. Purists widely disdained the electronic intrusion, but it was easily avoided with a careful right foot. And its mpg benefit allowed substituting a shorter rear-axle ratio (3.42:1 versus 3.23) for better off-the-line snap.

As planned, Firebird convertibles returned at midseason in base, Formula, and T/A GT trim, now factory-assembled wares with a standard power top. Also appearing in the '94 run was another nostalgic birthday Firebird, the 25th Anniversary Trans Am. An option package for T/A GTs, it was strictly cosmetic: blue dorsal striping, white paint, monogrammed white leather seats, specific body-color five-spoke alloy wheels, and, of course, the requisite celebratory logos. At least the price was right at just $995, and installations were limited to some 1500.

For reasons only Pontiac marketers could explain, the T/A GT was dropped for '95 and the regular Trans Am restored to its former standard-equipment glory. It shared with Formula an appreciated new traction-control system as a $450 extra that was worth every penny. The base Firebird wasn't neglected, gaining a 200-bhp 3.8 V-6 as a late-season option in concert with

1995 Firebird Trans Am coupe

1995 Grand Am GT coupe

1995 Sunfire SE four-door sedan

1995 Bonneville SSE four-door sedan with SSEi package

1996 Trans Sport SE minivan

1996 Sunfire SE four-door sedan

1996 Grand Am GT four-door sedan

1996 Bonneville SE four-door sedan with SLE package

1996 Firebird Trans Am coupe with Ram Air package

automatic transmission. That evergreen engine then replaced the 3.4 V-6 for all base models. V-8s also got more power for '96, going to 285 bhp standard and to a healthy 305 via a new Ram Air package featuring a big hood air scoop (with twin intakes), plus larger tires on five-spoke alloy wheels.

After a quiet 1997, Firebird followed V-8 Camaros by adopting the impressive new aluminum-block LS1 engine from Chevy's C5 Corvette. In the ponycars, it made 305 bhp, up 20 from the final iron-block LT1; the optional Ram Air package (code WS6) upped the count to 320. At the same time, the six-speed manual became a no-cost option to automatic for Formula and Trans Am. All '98 Firebirds wore a modest facelift marked by honeycomb-pattern taillights and a slightly shorter, more rounded nose. A pair of aggressive nasal air slots distinguished Trans Ams—and Ram-Air cars now had four. Changes for '99 were few but worthwhile. V-8s adopted a more effective Torsen limited-slip differential, traction control was newly available for V-6s, and all models got a slightly larger fuel tank.

Another milestone Trans Am birthday rolled around in 1999. Pontiac observed it with a 30th Anniversary Package comprising the WS6 engine, Arctic White paint, more wide blue dorsal striping, unique 17-inch alloy wheels—and even "Screaming Chicken" decals, albeit much less blatant than in the old days. There was the usual logo-bedecked cockpit, this one with a numbered commemorative plaque on the console. Production was restricted, of course: 1065 "targa"coupes (with 65 reserved for Canada), 535 convertibles (35 for up north). Amid all these warm fuzzies, few might have guessed that Firebird had but three years left to live.

Meanwhile, Pontiac began renewing its bread-and-butter models, starting with Grand Prix for 1997. Previewed two years before by the 300 GPX concept, it was one of the handsomest Ponchos since the '60s: purposeful, curvy, near frippery-free. The sedan showed particularly dramatic change in a new coupelike profile. Even better, "Wide Track" was back, as ads loudly proclaimed. Like Buick's latest Regal on the same updated W-body platform, the GP was little longer than before despite a three-inch-longer wheelbase. But Pontiac went for a broader stance, upping track width by two inches fore, three inches aft.

Grand Prix offered three V-6 models for '97: a mom-and-pop 3.1-liter SE sedan with 160 bhp and an enthusiast-oriented GT sedan and coupe with GM's ever-improving "3800" engine and 195 standard bhp. An optional GTP package delivered a muscular 240-bhp supercharged 3800, plus beefier four-speed automatic transmission, somewhat firmer suspension, stickier tires, modest decklid spoiler, and discreet identification. All models boasted standard all-disc antilock brakes and traction control, though the latter was denied GTPs until 1998, when a stouter system was adopted across the board.

Car and Driver had good things to say about the '97 GTP sedan. Topping the list were a zippy 0-60-mph time of 6.8 seconds, fine skidpad grip (0.79g), safe and predictable front-drive moves, a roomy and comfortable cabin with generally sound ergonomics, and lots of features for only about $25,000 delivered. There were faults, to be sure, but *C/D* dismissed them as "relatively minor carping. We were expecting the 1997 Grand Prix to be a better car than the previous model, but we weren't expecting it to be this much better."

Buyers also responded favorably, snapping up about 159,000 GPs for the extended '97 season. Though the extra selling time helped pump up the volume, this was Grand Prix's best model-year performance in two decades. Demand eased for '98 to a bit over 142,000, but the '99 tally was 155,000, and model-year 2000 output climbed to near 173,000. Interim changes helped keep buyers interested. The GTP proved popular enough to win separate-model status for '99, when the base V-6 added five bhp.

1997 Bonneville SSEi four-door sedan

1997 Sunfire GT coupe

1998 Grand Am GT coupe

1998 Grand Prix GTP four-door sedan

1999 30th Anniversary Trans Am coupe

For 2000, GM's useful OnStar communications and assistance system became available, the base V-6 got another 15 bhp, and all models added an engine immobilizer that disabled the ignition if starting was attempted by devious means. Grand Prix was chosen as the pace car for the 2000 Daytona 500, and Pontiac reeled off 2000 replicas, all silver GTP coupes with unique 16-inch aluminum wheels, functional hood vents, special interior, and Daytona insignia inside and out.

Arriving with the 1997 Grand Prix was a redesigned Trans Sport. Like that year's Olds Silhouette and new Chevy Venture, it reverted to conventional all-steel construction with mainstream minivan styling that might be termed "attractively forgettable." Buyers could now opt for five-passenger and extended seven-seat versions on separate wheelbases, a nod to the top-selling Chrysler Corporation minivans, themselves overhauled the previous year. Also aping Chrysler's latest was an available left-side sliding rear door, which later became standard and could be electrically operated like the power right-side door GM had pioneered. All the new GM models were widely judged the best-handling minivans. Trans Sport went furthest with a Montana Package comprising tighter suspension, alloy wheels and traction control, plus jazzy two-tone exterior. Reasonably priced at around \$1000-\$1200 depending on model, this option proved so popular that Montana replaced the Trans Sport name for '99 (except in Canada), though most previous Montana features continued in a Performance and Handling option.

This new blend of minivan practicality, Pontiac flair, and affordable low-\$20,000 pricing more than doubled Trans Sport sales for 1997. But volume went little higher afterward, and Dodge moved more than four times as many Caravans each year. Though all minivans were increasingly regarded as uncool "soccer mom" vehicles, with a consequent softening in overall demand, GM's entries had another problem in being visibly narrower than their rivals. This reflected a basic design created partly for the tight streets of Europe, where it was sold as the Opel/Vauxhall Sintra. Most Americans didn't like their minivans so skinny, and thus shopped elsewhere. A relatively static product didn't help Pontiac's cause, either. Indeed, the only changes of note after '97 were an optional "MontanaVision" rear-seat DVD video system (1999); standard OnStar (2001); and available fold-flat third-row seat, "Versatrak" all-wheel-drive, and ultrasonic rear-obstacle-detection system (2002). The benign neglect was unfortunate. Like other GM efforts approaching the new millennium, the Trans Sport/Montana was basically a good vehicle, just not quite what the market wanted.

The same could said for the redesigned 1999 Grand Ams that started sale in early '98. Coupes and sedans continued, but the lineup was more confusing, with each body style offered in base SE, SE1, and SE2 versions, plus sportier GT and GT1 trim. Wheelbase lengthened 3.6 inches to 107, rangy for a compact. Overall length was little-changed, but width swelled almost three inches (to 70.4). Powertrains, alas, weren't much changed. SE2s and all GTs came with the hoary 3.4-liter pushrod V-6; others used the 2.4-liter Twin Cam until 2002, when they followed Sunbird to the newer 2.2-liter "L850" corporate four-cylinder, eventually known by the "Ecotec" name used in Europe, where it originated. Four-speed automatic remained the only transmission until 2000, after which four-cylinder models got a standard five-speed manual supplied by German gearbox specialist Getrag.

Grand Am styling was now much like Grand Prix's, but on a smaller scale and with lots of geegaws larded on. *Car and Driver* judged appearance "overwrought and exaggerated," especially on GTs. "Only the roof panel is devoid of scoops, spoilers, strakes, and other 'character' lines... Even the GT's five-spoke alloys are cluttered with little cartoonish speedline indentations on each spoke. One or two of these cues might be acceptable, but together they're too much."

The rest of the car wasn't enough. Despite a performance-sapping automatic, *C/D*'s test GT sedan ran 0-60 in a brisk 7.7 seconds and scored well for handling, but lacked the poise and polish of most import rivals. Ride was generally judged good on any model, but noise levels were only average and workmanship needed, well, work. Value was an asset, but that didn't offset all the debits for *Consumer Guide®*. Said *CG's Auto 2000* issue: "Unless sporty looks are your top priority in a family compact, you'd be well advised to scout the competition." Many people did, and Grand Am sales fell steadily thereafter.

A new Bonneville was next on the to-do list, and it arrived for 2000 on an improved version of the GM G-car platform that made the Oldsmobile Aurora such a roadable big four-door. Like the latest GP and Grand Am, Bonneville grew a bit longer in wheelbase, plus a little taller and heavier. Styling turned toward the flamboyant with a more steeply canted windshield, newly downsloped hood, and wheels pushed further toward the corners on slightly wider tracks. Plastics factories worked overtime to supply more flashy body cladding, and Grand Am-type "speed streaks" popped up everywhere.

Y2K Bonnevilles numbered three: volume-selling SE, semi-sporty SLE, and a revived supercharged SSEi. Powertrains stayed broadly the same, but more internal refinements made the trusty V-6 a tad smoother and quieter still. The updated G-platform, GM's stiffest ever, contributed to a solid, satisfying down-the-road feel. Predictably, the hot-shot SSEi was the subject of most "buff book" reviews, which were generally positive. *Car and Driver* clocked 0-60 in 7.8 seconds, which beat Chrysler's Euro-inspired 300M, and judged the ride/handling compromise about right for a sporty big domestic. The dashboard was something else. "Whoever designed it," *C/D* complained, "seemed to have an obsession with gray plastic buttons and knobs—from the driver's seat, we counted 70 of them." For passengers, though, the interior was a spacious, comfortable, pleasant place to be.

If overdone in some respects, the 2000 was clearly a better Bonneville. Buyers initially agreed, lifting model-year sales by some 13 percent from '99. Changes for 2001 included the return of GM OnStar as standard for SLE and SSEi, standard anti-skid/traction control for the top-liner (the Cadillac-pioneered "Stabilitrak" system that also applied brakes to minimize fish-tailing), and optional heated front seats for all models, not just SSEi. As Pontiac expected, the value-priced SE accounted for more than half of Bonneville sales. What Pontiac didn't expect was the steep 27-percent drop in '01 model-year volume to less than 45,500 units, marginal even for a high-profit full-size. By 2002, Detroit's rumor mill was predicting that Bonneville would not see another redesign, having become too costly to continue and out of step with long-range product plans.

"Offbeat" aptly described Aztek, Pontiac's response to the fast-growing popularity of sport-utility vehicles based on car platforms rather than trucks. An early 2001 debut, it was basically a short-wheelbase Montana reconfigured as an "active lifestyle" vehicle. In line with that, Aztek introduced optional Versatrak all-wheel drive, GM's clever new way of adding four-wheel traction to a front-drive powertrain without adding complexity or weight. Instead of a rear propshaft and extra differentials, an electronically controlled clutch pack at each rear wheel could lock up as needed to redirect torque from the front. This also brought a bonus in the form of independent rear suspension to replace the twist-beam axle, plus rear disc brakes instead of drums. Antilock brakes were standard, as on Montanas.

Still, Aztek wasn't a serious off-roader. Pontiac rightly called it a "sport recreational vehicle," meaning it could haul up to five folks and their gear to activities not very far off the beaten path. Naturally, Aztek drove much like its minivan parent, with adequate acceleration and safe but ponderous handling. Its biggest attraction was a versatile five-seat interior with many novel touches. Among them was a totable drinks cooler-cum-CD box that locked in between the front seats, and a slide-out cargo-area storage tray that could double as a table for "tailgate" parties or be folded out to make a wheeled cart. Also available were separate stereo controls and speakers in the cargo bay, washable seat covers, and a camper package with a fitted air mattress and a tent for slipping over the raised rear hatch.

Trouble was, these nifty ideas were wrapped in some pretty

2000 Bonneville SSEi four-door sedan

2000 Sunfire GT coupe

2001 Aztek GT wagon

2001 Grand Prix GTP Special Edition four-door sedan

odd styling. *Motor Trend* described Aztek as "minivan meets creature from the black lagoon." The Los Angeles *Times* simply wondered, "Who let the dog out?" Said *Road & Track*: Aztek is trying way too hard to be hip. That's understandable if you're trying to hide its minivan roots, [but] Pontiac has gone to extremes. The overall length was shortened and the rear hatch chopped into a fastback while the hood was raised and sliding doors were replaced with conventional portals... The styling [is] ungainly [despite] hood nostrils that recall the Ram Air look of the Trans Am and enough body cladding for a fleet of surfboards." There were kinder, gentler reviews, but hardly anyone bought an Aztek for its looks.

Early sales suggested as much. Pontiac planned on moving 60,000 Azteks every 12 months, but managed just slightly over 38,000 for the 18 months of the extra-long 2001 model year. Beyond questionable styling, some faulted Aztek as too pricey for the younger buyers it targeted. Pontiac addressed both issues for 2002. Body-color cladding without molded-in "speed streaks" cleaned up the exterior, and making some standard features optional allowed cutting base prices by a few thousand dollars to around $20,000 minimum. But the unforgiving public had already branded Aztek an unhip loser, and sales remained at well under half the original projection through 2004. Pontiac made more price adjustments and added appealing options including satellite radio, rear DVD entertainment, and a sporty Rally Edition package with lowered suspension and 17-inch wheels. But Aztek couldn't be saved without a total redesign, which wasn't in the cards, so Pontiac gave up after '05 to avoid further embarrassment. Sales that calendar year: a paltry 5020.

Firebird also seemed beyond saving as the new century opened, but only because buyer tastes had changed. Ponycars and muscle machines had given way to big-engine trucks and highly tuned "sport compacts" as America's performance icons. The Chevrolet Camaro was also falling from favor because of this shift, but not the Ford Mustang, which by now outsold the two GM ponycars combined.

It was thus no great shock that Firebird and Camaro were terminated after 2002. For a time it seemed that neither had a prayer of ever returning, but GM had second thoughts once an all-new Mustang began generating huge buzz and rip-roaring sales. By early 2006, GM was all but promising a new Camaro in two to three years time—shades of 1967. But there was no mention of a new Firebird. That's because its performance role at Pontiac had already passed to another car, described later.

True to its tradition, Firebird did not go quietly. The Formula, for example, celebrated Pontiac's 75th birthday with a like-named package option at mid-2001. Priced at $2550 with manufacturer discount, it bundled unique cosmetics with traction control, a tighter axle ratio, and performance tires on chrome alloy wheels. Arriving with it was a separate $1170 NHRA group honoring the National Hot Rod Association and Firebird's continued drag-racing successes. This option delivered similar gearing and rolling stock, plus a six-speed manual with Hurst-brand shifter and linkage (recently added as a stand-alone option). The NHRA package returned for '02, when the WS6 engine added five bhp to reach 325. Also back was the SLP Firehawk, a show-and-go package that Pontiac first cataloged in 2001 after securing sales rights from SLP Engineering, an outside company that had been putting more fire in Firebirds for some 10 years. Available for '01 Formulas and Trans Ams and for '02 T/As, the Firehawk option comprised a forced-air induction system that upped the WS6 to 330/345 bhp, plus stiffened suspension, fat low-profile tires on 17-inch wheels, and many exclusive trim items. Power junkies happily ponied up the $4000/$4300 asking price. Last but not least was 2002's tellingly named Collector Edition Trans Am, another ensemble

2001 Montana minivan

2002 Aztek four-door wagon

2002 Bonneville SE four-door sedan

2002 Grand Am coupe

2002 Firebird Collector Edition coupe

2002 Grand Prix four-door sedan

2003 Grand Prix GTP four-door sedan

2003 Sunfire coupe

2003 Vibe GT four-door wagon

2004 Bonneville GXP four-door sedan

option. It largely duplicated the 30th Anniversary Package, but wore black accents on bright yellow paint, plus unique wheels and interior trim. With that, Firebird was history.

Pontiac's ponycar was tough to lose, but it was strictly a business decision. Times were tough for General Motors and about to get much tougher. By 2005, the company was desperate for cash, posting a $10.6 billion loss that year, most all of it sustained by North American Operations (NAO). More ominously, GM faced enormous near-term health-care and pension costs not only for its own still-sizable workforce but also the employees at Delphi, the money-losing parts unit spun off in 1999 as a quasi-independent concern. Yet years of withering sales, market share, and stock price had left GM hard-pressed to borrow needed funds, banks having cut its credit rating to undesirable "junk" status.

Fortunately, 2001 had ushered in new managers determined to do whatever was needed to restore GM's health. Company veteran G. Richard "Rick" Wagoner, Jr., took over from Ron Zarrella (who returned to Bausch & Lomb to be CEO). Wagoner soon moved up to chairman, then took charge of the floundering NAO unit. In a surprise early days move, he persuaded former Chrysler Corporation president Bob Lutz out of retirement to be GM "product czar," charged with spearheading smash-hit new models—and avoiding another Aztek. Lutz immediately began dismantling brand management and its bloated, confusing bureaucracy, while putting new emphasis on stand-out styling and scrutinizing the competition with the eye of a "car guy." As part of streamlining product development, he aimed for closer links between Detroit and GM's overseas branches to avoid profit-sapping duplication, increase manufacturing flexibility, and quicken GM's responsiveness in the super-competitive twenty-first-century market. Lutz was rewarded for his efforts by being named vice chairman in early 2005.

Wagoner, meantime, made some wrenching decisions under pressure from restive shareholders and an increasingly impatient GM board. Among the toughest were phasing out Oldsmobile after 2004; selling stakes in once-promising "alliance" partners Fiat, Isuzu, Subaru, and Suzuki; seeking more concessions from the United Auto Workers and other unions; and planning a "right size" dealer body in which Buicks would be sold through many Pontiac-GMC outlets. But the drama had just begun. In early 2006, GM said it would lay off some 30,000 workers and close a dozen North American plants by 2010. A few weeks later, the company announced it had found a buyer for a 51-percent share of its profitable financing arm, General Motors Acceptance Corporation (GMAC), another divestiture to pad cash reserves against looming disaster. Yet even with all this, some financial gurus gave only 50/50 odds that GM could avoid filing for bankruptcy within five years. For a company that once ruled the U.S. auto industry with a giant's strength, this was a stunning state of affairs.

Pontiac's turn of the century record mirrored the deepening crisis. Calendar-year sales, which began wobbling in the 1990s, headed south once the boom economy ended, plunging from more than 616,000 cars and trucks in 1999 to just under 438,000 in 2005. Most of the losses naturally came on the car side, which dropped more than 28 percent in those six years from 552,000 units to some 395,000.

What happened? Like most GM brands, Pontiac had lost focus. As *Business Week* noted in 2003, "Pontiac's recent history has been based on a fabrication. It markets itself as GM's excitement division while offering a lineup of glammed-up Chevrolets and Buicks that fool no one with their faux sportiness." Bob Lutz swept in vowing to change all that, ordering an end to silliness like plastic cladding and fast-tracking new, "gotta have" models. "We want to make Pontiac an affordable, American

BMW," he told *BW* (understandable, perhaps, as he once worked at the German automaker). But the magazine was skeptical, predicting "it could be years before enough new cars arrive to make a difference."

Business Week was right, and real change wasn't evident until 2005. But that proved a watershed Pontiac year, bringing the curtain down on Sunfire, Bonneville, Grand Am, and Aztek. At the same time, a genuine sports car arrived, something John DeLorean had lobbied for back in the mid-1960s.

But getting there wasn't easy. For example, the little Sunfire and sister Chevy Cavalier would have been all-new for 2000 or 2001, but a prototype design bombed with consumer focus groups and was duly shelved. That left the existing Sunfire to carry on with few noteworthy changes. An exception was 2002, when the passé three-speed automatic transmission option was finally junked (the four-speed continued, of course) and the old Twin Cam four-cylinder was replaced in Sunfire GTs by a tuned 140-bhp version of the newer 2.2 "Ecotec." Despite costing 10 bhp, the swap had little affect on performance or refinement. This engine became standard for 2003, when the sedan and GT left and a lone SE coupe got satellite radio and front side airbags as first-time options. A bare-bones coupe was added for 2004, sold only with manual shift and no options for under $11,000, a meek response to new value-priced small cars from South Korea. Moving in the other direction was a pair of 2005 SE Sport Appearance Packages providing firm suspension, 16-inch wheels and various interior dressings for $600 or $800.

Interestingly, there was no direct replacement for Sunfire in the U.S., but there was in Canada: the Pursuit sedan, built on the Delta platform of the two-year-old Saturn Ion and the 2005 Cobalt. But GM evidently had second thoughts here too, as a Delta-based U.S.-market G5 coupe was rumored for 2007 as this book was prepared.

Yet none of this seemed vital when Pontiac already had an appealing small car called Vibe. Beginning sale in 2002 as an early '03 model, this compact four-door wagon was close kin to Toyota's new Japan-sourced Matrix. It was built at the joint-venture GM/Toyota plant in California called NUMMI (New United Motor Manufacturing, Inc., still going strong after nearly 20 years). Basic engineering came from Toyota's latest Corolla

2004 Grand Prix GTP four-door sedan

2004 GTO coupe

2005 G6 GT four-door sedan

2005 Grand Prix GXP four-door sedan

2005 GTO coupe

2005 Montana SV6 minivan

2005 Vibe GT four-door wagon

subcompact sedan. Pontiac influenced the styling. All models used four-cylinder 1.8-liter twincam engines. The base Vibe offered front-wheel drive and 130 bhp or all-wheel drive and 123 bhp. (A more realistic rating method adopted for 2006 netted 126/118 bhp, though the engines themselves were unchanged.) A sporty GT came with 180 bhp (later 164), front-drive, and six-speed manual gearbox. Other models listed five-speed manual and optional four-speed automatic. Vibe was noisy but fun to drive. It was practical, too, with a versatile interior and good people space, thanks to a high-profile body. Though younger buyers tended to favor Matrix for the many virtues associated with Toyotas, Pontiac's version was quite popular. Sales in the long debut season topped 84,000, followed by nearly 57,000 in calendar '04 and 72,000 in '05, this despite only detail changes. Though the GT and AWD were dropped after '06 for various reasons, Vibe was one of Pontiac's few bright spots in this period.

Bonneville sales, by contrast, were stuck in reverse, suffering more double-digit losses in calendar 2002-03—hence the above-mentioned rumors of the model's imminent demise. But the big front-driver had a final fling with the GXP, the first V-8 Bonneville in nearly two decades. A mid-2004 replacement for the supercharged V-6 SSEi, it targeted fancy V-8 European sports sedans with a 275-bhp version of Cadillac's ever-impressive 4.6-liter twincam Northstar engine. Also on hand were uprated suspension and brakes, Stabilitrak antiskid/traction control, performance tires on 18-inch wheels (versus 16s or 17s), plus a suave leather/suede cabin with pseudo "satin nickel" accents, 12-way power front seats with side airbags, and everything else marketers could stuff in. Contrived styling was out now that Bob Lutz was calling the shots, so the GXP was the cleanest Bonneville in years. Price was attractive, too—initially $35,270 to start—and Pontiac claimed credible 0-60-mph performance of 6.8 seconds. Yet for all this, the GXP didn't feel very different from the SSEi, and everyone knew "real" sports sedans had rear-wheel or all-wheel drive—and a more prestigious badge. But it was all academic. GM had already signed Bonneville's death warrant.

Montana got a reprieve through a 2005 makeover. This was initially labeled Montana SV6 to mark a transition from the out-

2006 G6 GTP hardtop convertible

going minivan, then just SV6. "SV" meant "sport van," which in turn meant an extended-body model with squared-up snout and other styling cues intended to make buyers think "SUV" or "crossover." Though minivans were still big business, marketers everywhere now tried to avoid the "minivan image." GM's whizzers thought a new Montana costume would work sales magic. It didn't. Instead, sales fell sharply despite some nice new interior touches, added safety features, a larger V-6, and little-changed prices. There were two problems. First, SV6 was just more old wine in another new bottle, obviously built to GM's basic 1997 minivan design. Second, there were more wine bottles on the corporate shelf, with a new Buick Terraza and Saturn Relay joining a renamed Chevrolet Uplander. As differences among the four were superficial, this was '80s-style "badge engineering," and it still didn't work. In fact, demand was so weak that just a year after launch, Pontiac said SV6 would bow out early, probably by 2007. The entire exercise was likely a write-off, money GM could ill-afford to squander.

More badge engineering produced a nicer midsize Pontiac crossover, the 2006 Torrent. Replacing Aztek, this was a somewhat sportier rendition of Chevrolet's popular Equinox wagon, though differences here, too, were mostly skin deep. Still, Torrent quickly drew a fair number of new customers to Pontiac dealers, who'd been pleading to get in on the fast-rising sales action for untrucky SUVs. How it ultimately fares still remains to be seen, but Pontiac needed sales help as this book was prepared, and Torrent provided timely assistance.

Pontiac's midsize *car* gave up little sales ground despite take-no-prisoners competition and GM's mounting troubles. The vintage-'97 Grand Prix drew some 130,000 calendar-year orders from 2001 through 2003, then got a heavy makeover to stay at roughly that level—a modest feat in the old days, but now a cause for rejoicing at embattled fortress GM.

After a stand-pat 2001, Grand Prix marked its 40th anniversary with a cosmetic package for GT and GTP coupes and sedans. It wasn't much—Dark Cherry paint, specific red/grey interior, hood ducts, chrome wheels, rear spoiler, aerodynamic "roof fences"—but it cost a bit much: $2400 even with a built-in manufacturer discount. Such cars might be minor collector's items in the far-distant future, but they may not. Grand Prix gave up coupes for 2003—a first for this Pontiac—but sales had been waning for years. There was little other news that season, which was shortened anyway. The remodeled '04s were ready.

Remodeled they were: purged of plastic paneling and given a more rakish sedan roofline imparting coupelike sportiness in concert with a dramatic beltline upsweep at the rear doors. The overall look was curvier and more sculpted, emphasized by deeper fascias, slightly pinched nose and deck contours, and larger headlamps and taillights. The dashboard was naturally redone too, and became much more driver friendly, with an orderly layout and large, legible gauges. Hard to believe that beneath this new finery lurked the basic W-body platform first seen in the late 1980s.

Grand Prix reprised three sedans for 2004, but under new name management: GT1, GT2, and top-line GTP. Powerteams, alas, were not new, with a 200-hp 3.8 V-6 for GTs and the supercharged edition for GTP, though the latter now puffed out an extra 20 bhp. ABS/traction control was available for GT1, standard otherwise, and curtain side airbags at last came to Pontiac's midsize car as a GT2/GTP option. A nice surprise was the GTP's available Competition Group, aka the "Comp G" package. This aimed at maximum driver involvement with a specially calibrated "Stabilitrak Sport" antiskid system, power steering whose assist varied with cornering force as well as straightline speed, numerically higher final drive for quicker takeoffs, plus higher-speed tires and performance suspension tuning. The

2006 G6 GTP coupe

2006 Torrent four-door wagon

$1395 package price also included an import-style "TAPShift" allowing manual control of the mandatory four-speed automatic transmission (still) via "paddle" switches on the steering wheel. A head-up display, trip computer, and red-painted brake calipers completed the enhancements.

Predictably, the Comp G GTP got the most early press, and most of it was good. *Car and Driver* judged the redesign underdone in some ways, overdone in others, but liked the Comp G's lively acceleration—6.6 seconds to 60, just 0.1 second off the factory claim. Steering feel wasn't the best, but adept road manners compensated. "Understeer rules the Grand Prix's high-speed life," *C/D* reported. "At least the car's electronic safety net is an excellent one. [It] quietly and unobtrusively works individual calipers to keep the car on course with minimal power-killing throttle intervention... In that respect, Stabilitrak Sport outsmarts the jumpy, heavy-handed stability computers fitted to more pricey rides from Mercedes, BMW, and Lexus." Though lesser GPs were less impressive, the general view was that Pontiac had done a remarkable job of bringing its elderly W-car up to twenty-first-century standards. As *Consumer Guide®* summarized: "It trails our top-rated Honda Accord and Toyota Camry in quality of interior materials, and rear-seat comfort is substandard. But Grand Prix delivers good performance, a comfortable ride, cargo versatility, and plenty of features."

More features arrived as 2005 options: a remote engine-start system operable from the door-lock keyfob—great for pretrip wintertime warm-ups—plus an onboard navigation system (an industrywide must by now) and dual-zone automatic climate control. But the real news was the midyear GXP, the first V-8 Grand Prix in two decades. This packed a 5.3-liter pushrod engine first seen in GM midsize trucks, lately enhanced with an "Active Fuel Management" system that would deactivate four cylinders under light throttle loads to eke out a few more mpg. Horsepower was listed at 303, and the number rang true. *Car and Driver* clocked just 5.7 seconds for the 0-60 dash.

This GXP was an early replacement for the soon-to-depart Bonneville, as well as the new top-dog Grand Prix. As such, it relegated the GTP to midline status, where the name was now GT. It still had a blown V-6, but a Comp G option was nowhere in sight. Not to worry, though, because the Comp G's TAPShift, antiskid system, and other features passed to the GXP. Unusually, the GXP also included 18-inch wheels with tires that were wider at the front—deemed necessary for putting the V-8's power down effectively. Many still wondered why GM persisted at all with high-power front-drive cars when rear drive was dynamically superior. Nevertheless, some critics judged the GP GXP a tempting alternative to certain import-brand sports sedans—BMWs included—especially given a heavily discounted mid-$20,000 delivered price.

Overshadowing Grand Prix's renewal for 2004 was the surprising return of the fabled GTO. Aside from rear-wheel drive and thumping V-8 power, it shared nothing with the legendary "Goats" of yore, being an Americanized version of the four-seat Holden Monaro coupe at GM's Australian branch. Bob Lutz had taken a close look at the Monaro and decided it was just the thing to liven up Pontiac's image and sales. And with Firebird recently deceased, what better name for a new performance Poncho in the classic mold? About the only changes needed were a twin-port Pontiac face, plus a better-protected fuel tank and other adjustments to satisfy U.S. regulations.

The new GTO wasn't that new. Though Holden had devised the two-door Monaro as an Aussie-market exclusive, it started with the GM V-car platform originated with the German Opel Omega sedan, which had come to the U.S. as the 1997-2001 Cadillac Catera. But Americans were generally unaware of this lineage, and it didn't matter anyway. In all respects but two, the Australian-built GTO lived up to its hallowed name.

It was rather large for a new-century intermediate, standing 189.8 inches long, 72.5 inches wide, and 54.9 inches tall on a 109.8-inch wheelbase. Curb weight was a burly 3770 pounds, but that was no strain for the mandatory 5.7-liter LS1 V-8 packing 350 bhp and 365 pound-feet of torque on 10.1:1 compression. A four-speed automatic transmission was standard; $695 bought a sturdy Tremec T56 six-speed manual, the sole option for debut '04. The automatic GTO was saddled with a $1000 Gas-Guzzler Tax, but Lutz waved it through, figuring muscle car die-hards wouldn't be denied. Suspension was coil-spring independent with front struts, rear semitrailing arms and stout antiroll bars, all specially tuned. Handsome 18-inch five-spoke alloy wheels wearing 245/45ZR performance rubber enclosed big disc brakes with antilock control. Traction control was also standard, but no antiskid system was offered, nor were side airbags. But the $32,000 list price included most everything else: leather upholstery, power seats, remote keyless locking, trip computer, premium Blaupunkt audio with CD changer, rear-deck spoiler and more. In all, the reborn GTO was, a high-performance bargain.

Acceleration was predictably vivid. *Road & Track*'s manual-equipped '04 clocked 0-60 mph in 5.3 seconds, 0-100 in 12.9, and a standing quarter-mile of 13.8 seconds at 103.8 mph, stats worthy of the fastest showroom Goats of the muscle car era. Yet this was no cart-sprung, limp-wristed rocket that went to pieces on twisty roads. On the contrary, the new GTO provided assured Euro-style handling with little cornering lean, fine grip—0.81g on the *R&T* skidpad—and clear, properly weighted steering, plus braking power and mechanical refinement the old "Great Ones" never knew. In fact, this car felt like a posh big BMW coupe that played a '60s-style Detroit soundtrack.

With all this, the new GTO couldn't miss, yet it did. For those old enough to remember the originals and even for some critics, this reincarnation was just too quiet, too comfortable, too cultured to be a bona fide American performance car. And most everyone thought the styling was nowhere—"Lusty performance disguised in a phone-company fleet car," as *Car and Driver* huffed. Even Jim Wangers, who'd helped father the first GTO and generally liked the new one, had reservations. As he told *AutoWeek*: "It isn't what I call an 'Oh, my God.' The fact that they don't have a hood scoop is critical. According to GM, [that] would have interrupted the airflow, which would mean [costly] certification on its own [with the EPA]. Somebody said, 'We were thinking of putting a decal hood scoop on it,' which would be flat. That would be asking for criticism."

The criticism was abundant enough, and Pontiac strained to move fewer than 14,000 GTOs from the autumn '03 launch

2006 Solstice convertible coupe

through calendar '04, a bummer given an 18,000 per-annum target. Hefty rebates were applied mere weeks after introduction, but they didn't work. For all his global industry experience and undoubted taste, Lutz had misread the market. Not so Pontiac's old friend SLP Engineering, which in late 2003 announced a trio of "tuner" kits with 370, 389, or 421 bhp, plus a twin-scoop hood and other visual testosterone added. SLP wanted to market these under the Judge name, recalling the like-named 1969 GTO option, but GM fought the idea.

Answering the chorus of complaints, Pontiac gave the 2005 GTO not one hood scoop but two. They didn't connect to a power-boosting Ram Air setup, but they did help cool a more potent V-8: the 6.0-liter/364-cid LS2 from the brand-new C6 Corvette. Outputs rose to 400 bhp and 395 pound-feet, numbers that also applied with the scoopless engine lid available as a no-cost option. The bigger engine trimmed a few tenths from acceleration times but did nothing for sales, which dropped below 11,600 for the calendar year. The 2006 edition was unchanged save a few cosmetic details and newly optional 18-inch wheels. Demand remained sluggish and higher gas prices didn't help. With saving cash now imperative for GM, the GTO was dropped at the end of the model year. By that point, planners were eyeing a new Holden-developed platform intended for a variety of future rear-drive cars, giving hope that GTO will rise again, perhaps sharing underpinnings with a new Camaro.

As noted, the compact Grand Am departed after 2005 and four final years of declining sales. Changes in this period were remedial. Body cladding, which Pontiac once thought oh-so European, began fading away for 2002, when a 140-bhp 2.2-liter Ecotec four took over as the base engine. For '03, ABS/traction control moved from standard to optional for SE models. The '04s were virtual reruns. Grand Am bid a not-so-grand farewell with a pair of V-6 coupes, which made a last gesture to sportiness with an SC/T package comprising a twin-scoop hood, rear spoiler, chrome wheels, satellite radio, and special logos.

Grand Am's 2006 replacement began sale in mid-2005 with a pair of sedans called G6. The name change was meant to signal a complete break with Pontiac's compact-car past, and the G6 was precisely that, being large enough to qualify as a midsize. Pontiac went its own way with GM's global front-drive Epsilon platform, putting G6s on the longer-wheelbase version recently introduced with Chevrolet's hatchback Malibu Maxx "extended sedan." Unhappily, the extra inches combined with abbreviated overhangs to make G6 styling a bit awkward from some angles. At least it was different.

G6 rolled in with base and uplevel GT sedans using a 200-bhp 3.5-liter pushrod V-6 and mandatory four-speed automatic transmission. A GT coupe was added for the formal '06 selling season. So were a "Base 4-Cylinder Sedan" (that's what they called it) and an even cheaper "1SV" version, both powered by a 2.4-liter engine. Completing the lineup were a sporty GTP coupe and sedan sharing a 240-bhp 3.9-liter V-6 and available six-speed manual gearbox. GT and GTP convertibles had been announced with the latest thing in open-air motoring, a power-retractable hardtop, but were delayed many months by apparent teething troubles with the complex roof mechanism. Perhaps a simple old cloth canopy would have been wiser.

To build buzz for "the first-ever" G6, Pontiac arranged for Oprah Winfrey to give away 276 sedans on her top-rated TV talk show in September 2003—one for each person in the audience. Pontiac said the publicity was worth $20 million, at least four times the retail value of the cars, but some analysts thought the stunt did more to promote Oprah than it did the G6. And though the recipients must have been delighted to get a new car for nothing, road-testers mostly yawned. The G6 might have debuted as a roomier, more attractive, and better built car than

2007 Solstice GXP convertible coupe

2007 G6 GXP four-door sedan

the Grand Am, but it was also another modest, mainstream GM offering. It was "... a car with many good pieces that don't quite realize their potential as a whole," as *Road & Track* said. *Consumer Guide*® put the matter more directly: "G6 lacks the well-toned feel of a Honda Accord, the isolating comfort of a Toyota Camry, or the ready-to-rock energy of a Nissan Altima. But it undercuts them all on price, especially with a V-6 engine. Frequent discounts and a wide selection of safety and convenience features add to its appeal." Which was a nice way of saying that despite its good points, this new Pontiac had a whiff of "rental car" about it. But let's not be too harsh or hasty. The G6 was still new in town as this book was prepared, so perhaps all it needs is seasoning to become an impressive class competitor.

Impressive certainly described Pontiac's first sports car, the 2006 Solstice. It hit the streets less than four years after rabid public response to a we-might-build-it concept, itself whipped up in just 18 weeks—unheard-of speed for lumbering GM. Of course, this was Bob Lutz's doing, a demonstration that GM could get out fresh, exciting cars as fast as anyone in the world, and with world-class levels of performance and quality. He had to break all sorts of internal rules to get it done so quickly, so Solstice was just as much an example to GM people of what they could achieve when given half a chance.

Solstice was a lot like the ever-popular Mazda MX-5 Miata, which had been maturing since 1990 as the very definition of the modern "affordable sports car." Like the Japanese automaker, GM had to improvise in many areas to do something so very different from its usual fare, but the Solstice came together beautifully, an artful blend of some things old and some things new. When it was all over, GM had created a whole new platform called Kappa, with all sorts of possibilities for the future.

The concept was little-changed for production, and the Solstice emerged as larger and heavier than a redesigned Miata that made its debut at about the same time. Solstice hewed to the same classic formula, though, of a small and light two-seat convertible with manual-folding fabric top, rear-wheel drive, and four-cylinder power. Solstice offset its greater weight with a larger, torquier engine, an evolved 2.4-liter twincam with 177 bhp and 166 pound-feet or torque. Both cars boasted manual and optional automatic transmissions, four-wheel independent suspension, all-disc brakes, and equally obligatory rack-and-pinion power steering. Solstice offered optional ABS, by now a Miata standard, but not the Mazda's available antiskid system or no-cost side airbags. On the other hand, the Pontiac came on 18-inch wheels versus 16s or 17s, and matched its rival's "weekend racer" appeal with a $1095 Club Sport package and available limited-slip differential. Both listed options like air conditioning, cruise control, and power windows, but only Solstice offered satellite radio and the GM OnStar system. Lutz promised a sub-$20,000 price, and kept his word by a slim $5, including destination charge, though the minimum soon rose to $20,490. But even that virtually level-pegged the least expensive '06 Miata, and Mazda's broader lineup stretched to nearly $27,000, thousands more than a Solstice with every possible option.

If Solstice and Miata were a close match on paper, they ran a virtual dead heat on the road. Most magazine comparisons decided the Mazda was just a little bit better, but the judgements were highly subjective, and most all reviews said you couldn't go wrong with the Pontiac. It all came down to "horses for courses," with the Solstice winning points for eye appeal, a smoother ride, superior cornering stability, appreciated extra cockpit space, and stronger low-end pull. The Miata had the edge in handling, braking, fuel economy, and overall execution, plus a long record of reliability and a more convenient top.

But the Solstice had one advantage Miata could never match: It was all-American, a big emotional tug for many folks at a time when General Motors (Ford Motor Company, too) seemed fast headed for ruin. With all this, Solstice was as hard to get as a straight answer from a politician. Pontiac booked some 13,000 presale orders, but could fill only about half for model-year '06. That's because GM's refurbished Wilmington, Delaware, plant also had to build an upscale Saturn version, the 2007 Sky, plus variants for GM Europe. But people seemed happy to wait. Solstice was worth waiting for.

Pontiac spent some $4 million to promote Solstice with a "product placement" on the hit TV show "The Apprentice," but they needn't have bothered. The press had been breathlessly reporting every stage of the car's swift progress from auto-show concept to showroom reality. By the time it was ready, most all America knew about the Solstice.

The Solstice wait list may grow even longer with the 2007 addition of a GXP version with no less than 260 bhp from a new turbocharged 2.0-liter twincam four. Designated LNF, this engine is significant, marking GM's first use of high-efficiency direct fuel injection in North American production. Other premium features included a twin-scroll turbo that starts boosting sooner than conventional units, oil-cooled low-friction cast-aluminum pistons, and variable timing for both intake and exhaust valves that are sodium-filled for cooler running and less reciprocating weight. Though not yet released in time for this book, the Solstice GXP was expected to start around $26,000, which also encompassed expected chassis upgrading, special trim, and added equipment. Pontiac projects 0-60 to fall from 6.7 seconds to 5.5, throwing down the performance gauntlet to Miata.

Solstice closes the Pontiac story thus far on a happy note—a small sign that better days finally might be at hand for Pontiac and all of GM. Let's hope that's the case. The thought this saga could be in its final chapter is unsettling, to say the least.

Specifications

1930

6-29 Big Six (wb 110.0)	Wght	Price	Prod*
rdstr 4P	2,394	775	—
phaeton 5P	2,407	825	—
std cpe 2P	2,532	745	—
sdn 2d	2,595	745	—
sdn 4d	2,717	845	—
6-30 Big Six (wb 110.0)			
rdstr 2-4P	2,410	665	—
phaeton 5P	2,475	695	—
std cpe 2P	2,580	665	—
spt cpe 2-4P	2,655	725	—
sdn 2d	2,695	665	—
sdn 4d	2,745	725	—
Custom sdn 4d	2,785	785	—

* Total 1930 production: 62,888. Pontiac does not state whether this is model or calendar year.

1930 Engine	bore×stroke	bhp	availability
I-6, 200.0	3.31×3.88	60	S-all

1931

401 Six (wb 112.0)	Wght	Price	Prod*
cpe 2P	2,670	675	—
spt cpe 2-4P	2,730	715	—
conv cpe 2-4P	2,710	745	—
sdn 2d	2,765	675	—
sdn 4d	2,845	745	—
Custom sdn 4d	2,855	785	—

* Total 1931 production: 84,708. Pontiac does not state whether this is model or calendar year.

1931 Engine	bore×stroke	bhp	availability
I-6, 200.0	3.31×3.88	60	S-all

1932

402 Six (wb 114.0) - 39,059 blt	Wght	Price	Prod
std cpe 2P	2,765	635	—
spt cpe 2-4P	2,810	715	—
conv cpe 2-4P	2,770	765	—
sdn 2d	2,870	645	—

402 Six	Wght	Price	Prod
sdn 4d	2,960	725	—
Custom sdn 4d	2,965	795	—
302 V-8 (wb 117.0) - 6,281 built			
std cpe 2P	3,145	845	—
spt cpe 2-4P	3,205	925	—
conv cpe 2-4P	3,165	945	—
sdn 2d	3,225	845	—
sdn 4d	3,310	945	—
Custom sdn 4d	3,335	1,025	—

1932 Engines	bore×stroke	bhp	availability
I-6, 200.0	3.31×3.88	65	S-402
V-8, 251.0	3.44×3.38	85	S-302

1933

601 Eight (wb 115.0)-90,198 blt	Wght	Price	Prod
rdstr 2-4P	2,675	585	—
cpe 2P	2,865	635	—
spt cpe 2-4P	2,930	670	—
conv cpe 2-4P	2,905	695	—
touring sdn 4d	2,995	675	—
sdn 2d	2,945	635	—
sdn 4d	3,020	695	—

1933 Engine	bore×stroke	bhp	availability
I-8, 223.4	3.19×3.50	77	S-all

1934

603 Eight (wb 117.5)-78,859 blt	Wght	Price	Prod
cpe 2P	3,185	675	—
spt cpe 2-4P	3,260	725	—
cabriolet 2-4P	3,225	765	—
sdn 2d	3,280	705	—
sdn 2d T/B	3,300	745	—
sdn 4d	3,350	765	—
sdn 4d T/B	3,405	805	—

1934 Engine	bore×stroke	bhp	availability
I-8, 223.4	3.19×3.50	84	S-all

1935

701-B Std Six (wb 112.0)-49,302 blt	Wght	Price	Prod
cpe 2P	3,065	615	—

701-B Standard Six	Wght	Price	Prod
sdn 2d T/B	3,195	695	—
sdn 2d	3,195	665	—
touring sdn 4d T/B	3,245	745	—
sdn 4d	3,245	715	—
701-A DeLuxe Six (wb 112.0) - 36,032 built			
cpe 2P	3,125	675	—
spt cpe 2-4P	3,150	725	—
cabriolet 2-4P	3,180	775	—
sdn 2d T/B	3,245	745	—
sdn 2d	3,245	715	—
touring sdn 4d T/B	3,300	795	—
sdn 4d	3,300	765	—
605 Eight (wb 116.6) - 44,134 built			
cpe 2P	3,260	730	—
spt cpe 2-4P	3,290	780	—
cabriolet 2-4P	3,305	840	—
sdn 2d T/B	3,400	805	—
sdn 2d	3,400	775	—
touring sdn 4d T/B	3,450	860	—
sdn 4d	3,450	830	—

1935 Engines	bore×stroke	bhp	availability
I-6, 208.0	3.38×3.88	80	S-Sixes
I-8, 223.4	3.19×3.50	84	S-Eight

1936

6BB Master Six (wb 112.0) - 93,475 built	Wght	Price	Prod
cpe 2P	3,085	615	—
spt cpe 2-4P	3,120	675	—
cabriolet 2-4P	3,125	760	—
sdn 2d	3,195	675	—
touring sdn 2d T/B	3,195	700	—
sdn 4d	3,235	720	—
touring sdn 4d T/B	3,245	745	—
6BA DeLuxe Six (wb 112.0) - 44,040 built			
cpe 2P	3,130	665	—
spt cpe 2-4P	3,165	720	—
cabriolet 2-4P	3,200	810	—
sdn 2d	3,265	720	—

6BA DeLuxe Six	Wght	Price	Prod
touring sdn 2d T/B	3,270	745	—
sdn 4d	3,300	770	—
touring sdn 4d T/B	3,300	795	—

8BA DeLuxe Eight (wb 116.6) - 38,755 built	Wght	Price	Prod
cpe 2P	3,250	730	—
spt cpe 2-4P	3,285	785	—
cabriolet 2-4P	3,335	855	—
sdn 2d	3,390	770	—
touring sdn 2d T/B	3,390	795	—
sdn 4d	3,415	815	—
touring sdn 4d T/B	3,420	840	—

1936 Engines	bore×stroke	bhp	availability
I-6, 208.0	3.38×3.88	80	S-Sixes
I-8, 232.3	3.25×3.50	87	S-Eight

1937

6CA DeLuxe Six (wb 117.0) - 179,244 built	Wght	Price	Prod
cpe 2P	3,165	781	—
spt cpe 2-4P	3,165	853	—
cabriolet 2-4P	3,250	945	—
sdn 2d	3,240	830	—
touring sdn 2d T/B	3,240	855	—
sdn 4d	3,265	881	—
touring sdn 4d T/B	3,275	906	—
conv sdn 5P	3,375	1,197	—
wgn 4d	3,340	992	—

8CA DeLuxe Eight (wb 122.0) - 56,945 built	Wght	Price	Prod
cpe 2P	3,305	857	—
spt cpe 2-4p	3,305	913	—
cabriolet 2-4P	3,360	985	—
sdn 2d	3,385	893	—
touring sdn 2d T/B	3,380	919	—
sdn 4d	3,410	939	—
touring sdn 4d T/B	3,400	965	—
conv sdn 5P	3,505	1,235	—

1937 Engines	bore×stroke	bhp	availability
I-6, 222.7	3.44×4.00	85	S-Six
I-8, 248.9	3.25×3.75	100	S-Eight

1938

6DA DeLx Six (wb117.0)-77,713 blt	Wght	Price	Prod
cpe 2P	3,190	835	—
spt cpe 2-4P	3,200	891	—
cabriolet 2-4P	3,285	993	—
sdn 2d	3,265	865	—
touring sdn 2d T/B	3,265	891	—
sdn 4d	3,295	916	—
touring sdn 4d T/B	3,280	942	—
conv sdn 5P	3,410	1,310	—
wgn 4d	3,420	1,110	—

8DA DeLuxe Eight (wb 122.0) - 19,426 built	Wght	Price	Prod
cpe 2P	3,320	898	—
spt cpe 2-4P	3,325	955	—
cabriolet 2-4P	3,390	1,057	—
sdn 2d	3,395	934	—
touring sdn 2d T/B	3,385	960	—
sdn 4d	3,415	980	—
touring sdn 4d T/B	3,410	1,006	—
conv sdn 5P	3,530	1,353	—

1938 Engines	bore×stroke	bhp	availability
I-6, 222.7	3.44×4.00	85	S-Six
I-8, 248.9	3.25×3.75	100	S-Eight

1939

6EA QltySix (wb115.0)-55,736 blt	Wght	Price	Prod
cpe 3P	2,875	758	—
spt cpe 5P	2,920	809	—
touring sdn 2d T/B	2,965	820	—
touring sdn 4d T/B	3,000	866	—
wgn 4d	3,175	990	—

6EB DeLuxe Six (wb 120.0) - 53,830 built	Wght	Price	Prod
cpe 3P	3,020	814	—
spt cpe 5P	3,055	865	—
conv cpe 5P	3,155	993	—
touring sdn 2d T/B	3,115	871	—
touring sdn 4d T/B	3,165	922	—

8EA DeLuxe Eight (wb 120.0) - 34,774 built	Wght	Price	Prod
cpe 3P	3,105	862	—
spt cpe 5P	3,165	913	—

8EA DeLuxe Eight	Wght	Price	Prod
conv cpe 5P	3,250	1,046	—
touring sdn 2d T/B	3,225	919	—
touring sdn 4d T/B	3,265	970	—

1939 Engines	bore×stroke	bhp	availability
I-6, 222.7	3.44×4.00	85	S-Sixes
I-8, 248.9	3.25×3.75	100	S-Eight

1940

25HA Spec Six (wb117.0)-106,892 blt	Wght	Price	Prod
cpe 3P	3,060	783	—
spt cpe 4P	3,045	819	—
sdn 2d	3,095	830	—
wgn 4d, 8P	3,295	1,015	—
sdn 4d	3,125	876	—

26HB DeLuxe Six (wb 120.0) - 58,452 built	Wght	Price	Prod
cpe 3P	3,115	835	—
spt cpe 4P	3,105	876	—
cabriolet (conv cpe)	3,190	1,003	—
sdn 2d	3,170	881	—
sdn 4d	3,210	932	—

28HA DeLuxe Eight (wb 120.0) - 20,433 built	Wght	Price	Prod
cpe 3P	3,180	875	—
spt cpe 4P	3,195	913	—
cabriolet (conv cpe)	3,280	1,046	—
sdn 2d	3,250	919	—
sdn 4d	3,300	970	—

29HB Torpedo Eight (wb 122.0) - 31,224 built	Wght	Price	Prod
spt cpe 4P	3,390	1,016	—
sdn 4d	3,475	1,072	—

1940 Engines	bore×stroke	bhp	availability
I-6, 222.7	3.44×4.00	87	S-Sixes
I-8, 248.9	3.25×3.75	100	S-DeLuxe Eight
I-8, 248.9	3.25×3.75	103	S-Torpedo Eight

1941

25JA DeLuxe Torpedo Six (wb 119.0) - 117,976 built	Wght	Price	Prod
cpe 3P	3,145	828	—
sdn cpe	3,180	864	—
conv cpe	3,335	1,023	—
sdn 2d	3,190	874	—
sdn 4d 6W	3,235	921	—
Metro sdn 4d 4W	3,230	921	—

26JB Strmlnr Torpedo Six (wb 122.0) - 82,527 built	Wght	Price	Prod
sdn cpe	3,305	923	—
Super sdn cpe	3,320	969	—
sdn 4d	3,365	980	—
Super sdn 4d	3,400	1,026	—

24JC Custom Torpedo Six (wb 122.0) - 8,257 built	Wght	Price	Prod
sdn cpe	3,260	995	—
sdn 4d	3,355	1,052	—
wgn 4d, 8P	3,650	1,175	—
DeLuxe wgn 4d 8P	3,665	1,225	—

27JA DeLuxe Torpedo Eight (wb 119.0) - 37,823 blt	Wght	Price	Prod
cpe 3P	3,220	853	—
sdn cpe	3,250	889	—
conv cpe	3,390	1,048	—
sdn 2d	3,250	899	—
sdn 4d 6W	3,285	946	—
Metro sdn 4d 4W	3,295	946	—

28JB Strmlnr Torpedo Eight (wb 122.0) - 66,287 blt	Wght	Price	Prod
sdn cpe	3,370	948	—
Super sdn cpe	3,385	994	—
sdn 4d	3,425	1,005	—
Super sdn 4d	3,460	1,051	—

29JC Custom Torpedo Eight (wb 122.0) - 17,191 built	Wght	Price	Prod
sdn cpe	3,325	1,020	—
sdn 4d	3,430	1,077	—
wgn 4d, 8P	3,715	1,200	—
DeLuxe wgn 4d, 8P	3,730	1,250	—

1941 Engines	bore×stroke	bhp	availability
I-6, 239.2	3.56×4.00	90	S-Sixes
I-8, 248.9	3.25×3.75	103	S-Eights

1942

25KA Torpedo Six (wb 119.0) - 29,886 built	Wght	Price	Prod
cpe 3P	3,210	895	—
sdn cpe	3,255	950	—

25KA Torpedo Six	Wght	Price	Prod
spt cpe	3,260	935	—
conv cpe	3,535	1,165	—
sdn 2d	3,265	940	—
sdn 4d 6W	3,305	985	—
Metro sdn 4d 4W	3,295	985	—

26KB Streamliner Six (wb 122.0)	Wght	Price	Prod
sdn cpe	3,355	980	
sdn 4d	3,415	1,035	10,284
wgn 4d, 8P	3,810	1,265	
Chieftain sdn cpe	3,400	1,030	
Chieftain sdn 4d	3,460	1,085	2,458
Chieftain wgn 4d 6P	3,785	1,315	

27KA Torpedo Eight (wb 119.0) - 14,421 built	Wght	Price	Prod
cpe 3P	3,270	920	—
sdn cpe	3,320	975	—
spt cpe	3,320	960	—
conv cpe	3,605	1,190	—
sdn 2d	3,325	965	—
sdn 4d 6W	3,360	1,010	—
Metro sdn 4d 4W	3,355	1,010	—

28KB Streamliner Eight (wb 122.0)	Wght	Price	Prod
sdn cpe	3,430	1,005	
sdn 4d	3,485	1,060	15,465
wgn 4d, 8P	3,885	1,290	
Chieftain sdn cpe	3,460	1,055	
Chieftain sdn 4d	3,515	1,110	11,041
Chieftain wgn 4d 6P	3,865	1,340	

1942 Engines	bore×stroke	bhp	availability
I-6, 239.2	3.56×4.00	90	S-Sixes
I-8, 248.9	3.25×3.75	103	S-Eights

1946

25LA Torpedo Six (wb 119.0) - 26,636 built	Wght	Price	Prod
sdn 4d	3,361	1,427	—
sdn 2d	3,326	1,368	—
sdn cpe	3,326	1,399	—
spt cpe	3,311	1,353	—
cpe 3P	3,261	1,307	—
conv cpe	3,591	1,631	—

26LB Streamliner Six (wb 122.0) - 43,430 built	Wght	Price	Prod
sdn 4d	3,490	1,510	—
sdn cpe	3,435	1,438	—
wgn 4d 8P	3,790	1,942	—
DeLuxe wgn 4d 8P	3,735	2,019	—

27LA Torpedo Eight (wb 119.0) - 18,273 built	Wght	Price	Prod
sdn 4d	3,436	1,455	—
sdn 2d	3,396	1,395	—
sdn cpe	3,391	1,428	—
spt cpe	3,376	1,381	—
cpe 3P	3,331	1,335	—
conv cpe	3,651	1,658	—

28LB Streamliner Eight (wb 122.0) - 49,301 built	Wght	Price	Prod
sdn 4d	3,550	1,538	—
sdn cpe	3,495	1,468	—
wgn 4d 8P	3,870	1,970	—
DeLuxe wgn 4d 8P	3,850	2,047	—

1946 Engines	bore×stroke	bhp	availability
I-6, 239.2	3.56×4.00	90	S-Sixes
I-8, 248.9	3.25×3.75	103	S-Eights

1947

6MA Torpedo Six (wb 119.0) - 67,125 built	Wght	Price	Prod
sdn 4d	3,320	1,512	—
sdn 2d	3,295	1,453	—
sdn cpe	3,300	1,484	—
spt cpe	3,295	1,438	—
cpe 3P	3,245	1,387	—
conv cpe	3,560	1,811	—
DeLuxe conv cpe	3,560	1,853	—

6MB Streamliner Six (wb 122.0) - 42,336 built	Wght	Price	Prod
sdn 4d	3,450	1,598	—
sdn cpe	3,400	1,547	—
wgn 4d 8P	3,775	2,235	—
DeLuxe wgn 4d 8P	3,715	2,312	—

8MA Torpedo Eight (wb 119.0) - 34,815 built	Wght	Price	Prod
sdn 4d	3,405	1,559	—
sdn 2d	3,370	1,500	—

8MA Torpedo Eight	Wght	Price	Prod
sdn cpe	3,370	1,531	—
spt cpe	3,360	1,485	—
cpe 3P	3,310	1,434	—
conv cpe	3,635	1,854	—
DeLuxe conv cpe	3,635	1,900	—
8MB Streamliner Eight (wb 122.0) - 86,324 built			
sdn 4d	3,515	1,645	—
sdn cpe	3,455	1,595	—
wgn 4d 8P	3,845	2,282	—
DeLuxe wgn 4d 8P	3,790	2,359	—

1947 Engines	bore×stroke	bhp	availability
I-6, 239.2	3.5×4.00	90	S-Six
I-8, 248.9	3.25×3.75	103	S-Eight

1948

6PA Torpedo Six (wb 119.0) - 39,262 built	Wght	Price	Prod
sdn 4d	3,320	1,641	—
sdn 2d	3,280	1,583	—
sdn cpe	3,275	1,614	—
spt cpe	3,220	1,552	—
bus cpe	3,230	1,500	—
DeLuxe sdn 4d	3,340	1,731	—
DeLuxe sdn cpe	3,275	1,704	—
DeLuxe spt cpe	3,230	1,641	—
DeLuxe conv cpe	3,525	2,025	—
6PB Streamliner Six (wb 122.0) - 37,742 built			
sdn 4d	3,450	1,727	—
sdn cpe	3,365	1,677	—
wgn 4d 8P	3,755	2,364	—
DeLuxe sdn 4d	3,455	1,817	—
DeLuxe sdn cpe	3,370	1,766	—
DeLuxe wgn 4d 6P	3,695	2,442	—
8PA Torpedo Eight (wb 119.0) - 35,300 built			
sdn 4d	3,395	1,689	—
sdn 2d	3,360	1,630	—
sdn cpe	3,340	1,661	—
spt cpe	3,295	1,599	—
bus cpe	3,295	1,548	—
DeLuxe sdn 4d	3,395	1,778	—
DeLuxe sdn cpe	3,340	1,751	—
DeLuxe spt cpe	3,305	1,689	—
DeLuxe conv cpe	3,600	2,072	—
8PB Streamliner Eight (wb 122.0) - 123,115 built			
sdn 4d	3,525	1,775	—
sdn cpe	3,425	1,724	—
wgn 4d 8P	3,820	2,412	—
DeLuxe sdn 4d	3,530	1,864	—
DeLuxe sdn cpe	3,455	1,814	—
DeLuxe wgn 4d 6P	3,765	2,490	—

1948 Engines	bore×stroke	bhp	availability
I-6, 239.2	3.56×4.00	90	S-Six
I-8, 248.9	3.25×3.75	103	S-Eight

1949

6R Strmlnr Six (wb 120.0) - 69,654 blt (incl. 6R Chieftain)	Wght	Price	Prod
sdn 4d	3,385	1,740	—
sdn cpe	3,360	1,689	—
wgn 4d 8P wd bdy	3,745	2,543	—
wgn 4d 8P mtl bdy	3,650	2,543	—
DeLuxe sdn 4d	3,415	1,835	—
DeLuxe sdn cpe	3,375	1,784	—
Dlx wgn 4d 6P wd bdy	3,730	2,622	—
Dlx wgn 4d 6P mtl bdy	3,580	2,622	—
6R Chieftain Six (wb 120.0)			
sdn 4d	3,385	1,761	—
sdn 2d	3,355	1,710	—
sdn cpe	3,330	1,710	—
bus cpe	3,280	1,587	—
DeLuxe sdn 4d	3,415	1,856	—
DeLuxe sdn 2d	3,360	1,805	—
DeLuxe sdn cpe	3,345	1,805	—
DeLuxe conv cpe	3,600	2,138	—
8R Strmlnr Eight (wb 120.0) - 235,165 blt (incl. 8R Chieftain)			
sdn 4d	3,470	1,808	—
sdn cpe	3,435	1,758	—
wgn 4d 8P wd bdy	3,835	2,611	—
wgn 4d 8P mtl bdy	3,690	2,611	—

8R Streamliner Eight	Wght	Price	Prod
DeLuxe sdn 4d	3,500	1,903	—
DeLuxe sdn cpe	3,445	1,853	—
Dlx wgn 4d 6P wd bdy	3,800	2,690	—
Dlx wgn 4d 6P mtl bdy	3,640	2,690	—
8R Chieftain Eight (wb 120.0)			
sdn 4d	3,475	1,829	—
sdn 2d	3,430	1,779	—
sdn cpe	3,390	1,779	—
bus cpe	3,355	1,656	—
DeLuxe sdn 4d	3,480	1,924	—
DeLuxe sdn 2d	3,430	1,874	—
DeLuxe sdn cpe	3,415	1,874	—
DeLuxe conv cpe	3,670	2,206	—

1949 Engines	bore×stroke	bhp	availability
I-6, 239.2	3.56×4.00	90	S-Sixes
I-6, 239.2	3.56×4.00	93	O-Sixes
I-8, 248.9	3.25×3.75	104	S-Eights
I-8, 248.9	3.25×3.75	106	O-Eights

1950

6T Strmlnr Six (wb 120.0) - 115,542 blt (incl. 6T Chieftain)	Wght	Price	Prod
fstbk sdn 4d	3,414	1,724	—
fstbk sdn cpe	3,379	1,673	—
wgn 4d 8P	3,714	2,264	—
DeLuxe fstbk sdn 4d	3,419	1,819	—
DeLuxe fstbk sdn cpe	3,399	1,768	—
DeLuxe wgn 4d 6P	3,649	2,343	—
6T Chieftain Six (wb 120.0)			
sdn 4d	3,409	1,745	—
sdn 2d	3,384	1,694	—
sdn cpe	3,359	1,694	—
bus cpe	3,319	1,571	—
DeLuxe sdn 4d	3,414	1,840	—
DeLuxe sdn 2d	3,389	1,789	—
DeLuxe sdn cpe	3,364	1,789	—
DeLx Catalina htp cpe	3,469	2,000	—
DeLuxe conv cpe	3,624	2,122	—
Spr DeLx Cat htp cpe	3,469	2,058	—
8T Strmlnr Eight (wb 120.0) - 330,997 blt (incl. 8T Chieftain)			
fstbk sdn 4d	3,499	1,792	—
fstbk sdn cpe	3,464	1,742	—
wgn 4d 8P	3,799	2,332	—
DeLuxe fstbk sdn 4d	3,509	1,887	—
DeLuxe fstbk sdn cpe	3,469	1,837	—
DeLuxe wgn 4d 6P	3,739	2,411	—
8T Chieftain Eight (wb 120.0)			
sdn 4d	3,494	1,813	—
sdn 2d	3,454	1,763	—
sdn cpe	3,444	1,763	—
bus cpe	3,399	1,640	—
DeLuxe sdn 4d	3,499	1,908	—
DeLuxe sdn 2d	2,464	1,858	—
DeLuxe sdn cpe	3,454	1,858	—
DeLx Catalina htp cpe	3,549	2,069	—
DeLuxe conv cpe	3,704	2,190	—
Spr DeLx Cat htp cpe	3,549	2,127	—

1950 Engines	bore×stroke	bhp	availability
I-6, 239.2	3.56×4.00	90	S-Sixes
I-6, 239.2	3.56×4.00	93	O-Sixes
I-8, 268.4	3.38×3.75	108	S-Eights
I-8, 268.4	3.38 × 3.75	113	O-Eights

1951

6U Strmlnr Six (wb 120.0) - 53,748 blt (incl. 6U Chieftain)	Wght	Price	Prod
fstbk sdn cpe	3,363	1,824	—
wgn 4d 8P	3,718	2,470	—
DeLuxe fstbk sdn cpe	3,378	1,927	—
DeLuxe wgn 4d 6P	3,638	2,556	—
6U Chieftain Six (wb 120.0)			
sdn 4d	3,388	1,903	—
sdn 2d	3,358	1,848	—
sdn cpe	3,338	1,848	—
bus cpe	3,308	1,713	—
DeLuxe sdn 4d	3,388	2,006	—
DeLuxe sdn 2d	3,358	1,951	—
DeLuxe sdn cpe	3,343	1,951	—
DeLx Catalina htp cpe	3,458	2,182	—
DeLuxe conv cpe	3,603	2,314	—

6U Chieftain Six	Wght	Price	Prod
Spr DeLx Cat htp cpe	3,468	2,244	—
8U Strmlnr Eight (wb 120.0) - 316,411 blt (incl. 8U Chieftain)			
fstbk sdn cpe	3,458	1,900	—
wgn 4d 8P	3,813	2,544	—
DeLuxe fstbk sdn cpe	3,463	2,003	—
DeLuxe wgn 4d 6P	3,743	2,629	—
8U Chieftain Eight (wb 120.0)			
sdn 4d	3,478	1,977	—
sdn 2d	3,443	1,922	—
sdn cpe	3,418	1,922	—
bus cpe	3,388	1,787	—
DeLuxe sdn 4d	3,488	2,081	—
DeLuxe sdn 2d	3,448	2,026	—
DeLuxe sdn cpe	3,433	2,026	—
DeLx Catalina htp cpe	3,543	2,257	—
DeLuxe conv cpe	3,683	2,388	—
Spr DeLx Cat htp cpe	3,548	2,320	—

1951 Engines	bore×stroke	bhp	availability
I-6, 239.2	3.56×4.00	96	S-Sixes
I-6, 239.2	3.56×4.00	100	S-Sixes
I-8, 268.4	3.38×3.75	116	S-Eights
I-8, 268.4	3.38×3.75	120	S-Eights

1952

6W Chieftain Six (wb 120.0) - 19,809 built	Wght	Price	Prod
sdn 4d	3,403	2,014	—
sdn 2d	3,378	1,956	—
wgn 4d 8P	3,718	2,615	—
DeLuxe sdn 4d	3,403	2,119	—
DeLuxe sdn 2d	3,378	2,060	—
DeLx Catalina htp cpe	3,483	2,304	—
DeLuxe conv cpe	3,603	2,444	—
DeLuxe wgn 4d 6P	3,653	2,699	—
Spr DeLx Cat htp cpe	3,493	2,370	—
8W Chieftain Eight (wb 120.0) - 251,564 built			
sdn 4d	3,503	2,090	—
sdn 2d	3,458	2,031	—
wgn 4d 8P	3,813	2,689	—
DeLuxe sdn 4d	3,503	2,194	—
DeLuxe sdn 2d	3,458	2,136	—
DeLx Catalina htp cpe	3,568	2,380	—
DeLuxe conv cpe	3,683	2,518	—
DeLuxe wgn 4d 6P	3,758	2,772	—
Spr DeLx Cat htp cpe	3,573	2,446	—

1952 Engines	bore×stroke	bhp	availability
I-6, 239.2	3.56×4.00	100/102	S-Six man/auto
I-8, 268.4	3.38×3.75	118/122	S-Eight man/auto

1953

6X Chieftain Six (wb 122.0) - 38,914 built	Wght	Price	Prod
sdn 4d	3,506	2,015	—
sdn 2d	3,466	1,956	—
wgn 4d 6P	3,713	2,450	—
wgn 4d 6P (wdgrn)	3,713	2,530	—
wgn 4d 8P	3,791	2,505	—
wgn 4d 8P (wdgrn)	3,791	2,585	—
DeLuxe sdn 4d	3,521	2,119	—
DeLuxe sdn 2d	3,481	2,060	—
DeLx Catalina htp cpe	3,546	2,304	—
DeLuxe conv cpe	3,696	2,444	—
DeLuxe wgn 4d 6P	3,751	2,590	—
DeLx 4d 6P (wdgrn)	3,751	2,670	—
Cus Catalina htp cpe	3,546	2,370	—
8X Chieftain Eight (wb 122.0) - 379,705 built			
sdn 4d	3,581	2,090	—
sdn 2d	3,546	2,031	—
wgn 4d 6P	3,811	2,525	—
wgn 4d 6P (wdgrn)	3,811	2,605	—
wgn 4d 8P	3,881	2,580	—
wgn 4d 8P (wdgrn)	3,881	2,660	—
DeLuxe sdn 4d	3,596	2,194	—
DeLuxe sdn 2d	3,561	2,136	—
DeLx Catalina htp cpe	3,621	2,380	—
DeLuxe conv cpe	3,751	2,518	—
DeLuxe wgn 4d 6P	3,841	2,664	—
DeLx wgn 4d 6P (wdgrn)	3,841	2,744	—
Cus Catalina htp cpe	3,621	2,446	—

1953 Engines	bore×stroke	bhp	availability
I-6, 239.2	3.56×4.00	115	S-Six man
I-6, 239.2	3.56×4.00	118	S-Six auto
I-8, 268.4	3.38×3.75	118	S-Eight man
I-8, 268.4	3.38×3.75	122	S-Eight auto

1954

6Z Chieftain Six (wb 122.0) - 22,670 built	Wght	Price	Prod
Special sdn 4d	3,391	2,027	—
Special sdn 2d	3,331	1,968	—
Special wgn 4d 8P	3,691	2,419	—
Special wgn 4d 6P	3,601	2,364	—
DeLuxe sdn 4d	3,406	2,131	—
DeLuxe sdn 2d	3,351	2,072	—
DeLx Catalina htp cpe	3,421	2,316	—
DeLuxe wgn 4d 6P	3,646	2,504	—
Cus Catalina htp cpe	3,421	2,382	—
8Z Chieftain Eight (wb 122.0) - 149,986 built			
Special sdn 4d	3,451	2,102	—
Special sdn 2d	3,396	2,043	—
Special wgn 4d 8P	3,771	2,494	—
Special wgn 4d 6P	3,676	2,439	—
DeLuxe sdn 4d	3,466	2,206	—
DeLuxe sdn 2d	3,416	2,148	—
DeLx Catalina htp cpe	3,491	2,392	—
DeLuxe wgn 4d 6P	3,716	2,579	—
Cus Catalina htp cpe	3,491	2,458	—
8Z Star Chief (wb 124.0) - 115,088 built			
DeLuxe sdn 4d	3,536	2,301	—
DeLuxe conv cpe	3,776	2,630	—
Custom sdn 4d	3,536	2,394	—
Cus Catalina htp cpe	3,551	2,557	—

1954 Engines	bore×stroke	bhp	availability
I-6, 239.2	3.56×4.00	115	S-Six man
I-6, 239.2	3.56×4.00	118	S-Six auto
I-8, 268.4	3.38×3.75	122	S-Eights
I-8, 268.4	3.38×3.75	127	S-Eights

1955

860 Chieftain (wb 122.0)	Wght	Price	Prod
sdn 4d	3,511	2,164	65,155
sdn 2d	3,476	2,105	58,654
wgn 4d 8P	3,686	2,518	6,091
wgn 2d 6P	3,626	2,434	8,620
870 Chieftain (wb 122.0)			
sdn 4d	3,511	2,268	91,187
sdn 2d	3,476	2,209	28,950
Catalina htp cpe	3,521	2,335	72,608
wgn 4d 6P	3,676	2,603	19,439
Star Chief (wb 124.0; wgn-122.0)			
sdn 4d	3,556	2,362	44,800
conv cpe	3,791	2,691	19,762
Custom sdn 4d	3,557	2,455	35,153
Cus Catalina htp cpe	3,566	2,499	99,629
Cus Safari wgn 2d 6P	3,636	2,962	3,760

1955 Engines	bore×stroke	bhp	availability
V-8, 287.2	3.75×3.25	173	S-all (manual)
V-8, 287.2	3.75×3.25	180	S-all (automatic)
V-8, 287.2	3.75×3.25	200	O-all

1956

860 Chieftain (wb 122.0)	Wght	Price	Prod
sdn 4d	3,512	2,298	41,987
Catalina htp sdn	3,577	2,443	35,201
sdn 2d	3,452	2,240	41,908
Catalina htp cpe	3,512	2,370	46,335
wgn 4d 9P	3,707	2,653	12,702
wgn 2d 6P	3,612	2,569	6,099
870 Chieftain (wb 122.0)			
sdn 4d	3,512	2,413	22,082
Catalina htp sdn	3,577	2,534	25,372
Catalina htp cpe	3,512	2,480	24,744
wgn 4d 6P	3,657	2,749	21,674
Star Chief (wb 124.0; wgn-122.0)			
sdn 4d	3,577	2,527	18,346
conv cpe	3,797	2,857	13,510
Cus Catalina htp sdn	3,647	2,735	48,035
Cus Catalina htp cpe	3,567	2,665	43,392
Cus Safari wgn 2d 6P	3,642	3,129	4,042

1956 Engines	bore×stroke	bhp	availability
V-8, 316.6	3.94×3.25	192	O-Chieftain
V-8, 316.6	3.94×3.25	205	S-Chieftain
V-8, 316.6	3.94×3.25	216	O-Str Chf, Chftn
V-8, 316.6	3.94×3.25	227	S-Str Chf; O-Chftn
V-8, 316.6	3.94×3.25	285	O-all

1957

Chieftain (wb 122.0)	Wght	Price	Prod
sdn 4d	3,560	2,527	35,671
Catalina htp sdn	3,635	2,614	40,074
sdn 2d	3,515	2,463	21,343
Catalina htp cpe	3,555	2,529	51,017
Safari wgn 4d 9P	3,835	2,898	11,536
Safari wgn 2d 6P	3,690	2,841	2,934
Super Chief (wb 122.0)			
sdn 4d	3,585	2,664	15,153
Catalina htp sdn	3,640	2,793	19,758
Catalina htp cpe	3,570	2,735	15,494
Safari wgn 4d 6P	3,765	3,021	14,095
Star Chief (wb 124.0; wgn-122.0)			
sdn 4d	3,630	2,839	3,774
conv cpe	3,860	3,105	12,789
Custom sdn 4d	3,645	2,896	8,874
Cus Catalina htp sdn	3,710	2,975	44,283
Cus Catalina htp cpe	3,640	2,901	32,862
Cus Safari wgn 4d 6P	3,810	3,636	1,894
Cus Safari wgn 2d 6P*	3,750	3,481	1,292
Bonneville (wb 124.0)			
conv cpe	4,285	5,782	630

* All 1957 Pontiac wagons were called Safari. The model indicated is the "hardtop-styled" Safari offered 1955-1957 only.

1957 Engines	bore×stroke	bhp	availability
V-8, 347.0	3.94×3.56	227	S-Chieftain man
V-8, 347.0	3.94×3.56	252	S-Chieftain auto
V-8, 347.0	3.94×3.56	244	S-Super, Star Chief manual
V-8, 347.0	3.94×3.56	270	S-Spr Chf, Str Chf auto
V-8, 347.0	3.94×3.56	290	O-all exc Bonn
V-8, 347.0	3.94×3.56	310	S-Bonn (fuel inj)

1958

	Chieftain (wb 122.0)	Wght	Price	Prod
2567	conv cpe	3,850	3,019	7,359
2731	Catalina htp cpe	3,650	2,707	26,003
2739	Catalina htp sdn	3,785	2,792	17,946
2741	sdn 2d	3,640	2,573	17,394
2749	sdn 4d	3,735	2,638	44,999
2793	Safari wgn 4d 6P	4,025	3,019	9,701
2794	Safari wgn 4d 9P	4,070	3,088	5,417
	Super Chief (wb 124.0)			
2831D	Catalina htp cpe	3,690	2,880	7,236
2839D	Catalina htp sdn	3,810	2,961	7,886
2849D	sdn 4d	3,770	2,834	12,006
	Star Chief (wb 124.0; wgn-122.0)			
2793SC	Cus Safari wgn 4d 6P	4,065	3,350	2,905
2831SD	Catalina htp cpe	3,735	3,122	13,888
2839SD	Catalina htp sdn	3,850	3,210	21,455
2849SD	Custom sdn 4d	3,825	3,071	10,547
	Bonneville (wb 122.0)			
2547SD	Sport Coupe htp	3,710	3,481	9,144
2567SD	conv cpe	3,925	3,586	3,096

1958 Engines	bore×stroke	bhp	availability
V-8, 370.0	4.06×3.56	240	S-Chf/Super Chief manual
V-8, 370.0	4.06×3.56	255	S-Str Chf/Bonn man
V-8, 370.0	4.06×3.56	270	S-Chf/Super Chief auto
V-8, 370.0	4.06×3.56	285	S-Str Chief/ Bonn auto
V-8, 370.0	4.06×3.56	300	O-all (Tri-Power)
V-8, 370.0	4.06×3.56	310	O-all (fuel inj.)

1959

	Catalina (wb 122.0)	Wght	Price	Prod
2111	Sport sdn 2d	3,870	2,633	26,102
2119	sdn 4d	3,955	2,704	72,377
2135	Safari wgn 4d 6P	4,345	3,101	21,162
2137	Sport Coupe htp	3,900	2,768	38,309
2139	Vista Sedan htp	4,005	2,844	45,012
2145	Safari wgn 4d 9P	4,405	3,209	14,084
2167	conv cpe	3,970	3,080	14,515
	Star Chief (wb 124.0)			
2411	Sport sdn 2d	3,930	2,934	10,254
2419	sdn 4d	4,005	3,005	27,872
2439	Vista Sedan htp	4,055	3,138	30,689
	Bonneville (wb 124.0; wgn-122.0)			
2735	Cus Safari wgn 4d 6P	4,370	3,532	4,673
2837	Sport Coupe htp	3,985	3,257	27,769
2839	Vista Sedan htp	4,085	3,333	38,696
2867	conv cpe	4,070	3,478	11,426

1959 Engines	bore×stroke	bhp	availability
V-8, 389.0	4.06×3.75	215	O-all auto
V-8, 389.0	4.06×3.75	245	S-Catalina/Star Chief man
V-8, 389.0	4.06×3.75	260	S-Bonn manual
V-8, 389.0	4.06×3.75	280	S-Cat/Str Chf auto
V-8, 389.0	4.06×3.75	300	S-Bonn auto
V-8, 389.0	4.06×3.75	300/303	O-all (4bbl)
V-8, 389.0	4.06×3.75	315/345	O-all (Tri-Pwr)

1960

	Catalina (wb 122.0)	Wght	Price	Prod
2111	Sport sdn 2d	3,835	2,631	25,504
2119	sdn 4d	3,935	2,702	72,650
2135	Safari wgn 4d 6P	4,310	3,099	21,253
2137	Sport Coupe htp	3,850	2,766	27,496
2139	Vista Sedan htp	3,990	2,842	32,710
2145	Safari wgn 4d 9P	4,365	3,207	14,149
2167	conv cpe	3,940	3,078	17,172
	Ventura (wb 122.0)			
2337	Sport Coupe htp	3,865	2,971	27,577
2339	Vista Sedan htp	3,990	3,047	28,700
	Star Chief (wb 124.0)			
2411	Sport sdn 2d	3,910	2,932	5,797
2419	sdn 4d	3,995	3,003	23,038
2439	Vista Sedan htp	4,040	3,136	14,856
	Bonneville (wb 124.0; wgn-122.0)			
2735	Cus Safari wgn 4d 6P	4,360	3,530	5,163
2837	Sport Coupe htp	3,965	3,255	24,015
2839	Vista Sedan htp	4,065	3,331	39,037
2867	conv cpe	4,030	3,476	17,062

1960 Engines	bore×stroke	bhp	availability
V-8, 389.0	4.06×3.75	215	O-all auto
V-8, 389.0	4.06×3.75	245	S-Str Chf/Cat/ Vent manual
V-8, 389.0	4.06×3.75	283	S-Str Chf/Cat/ Vent auto
V-8, 389.0	4.06×3.75	281	S-Bonn man
V-8, 389.0	4.06×3.75	303	S-Bonn auto
V-8, 389.0	4.06×3.75	318/348	O-all (Tri-Power)

1961

	Tempest (wb 112.0)	Wght	Price	Prod
2117	Custom spt cpe	2,795	2,297	7,455
2119	sdn 4d	2,800	2,167	22,557
2120	Custom sdn 4d	2,810	2,351	40,082
2127	spt cpe	2,785	2,113	7,432
2135	Safari wgn 4d	2,980	2,438	7,404
2136	Cus Safari wgn 4d	2,990	2,622	15,853
	Catalina (wb 119.0)			
2311	Sport sdn 2d	3,650	2,631	9,846
2335	Safari wgn 4d 6P	4,135	3,099	12,595
2337	Sport Coupe htp	3,680	2,766	14,524
2339	Vista Sedan htp	3,785	2,842	17,589
2345	Safari wgn 4d 9P	4,175	3,207	7,783
2367	conv cpe	3,805	3,078	12,379
2369	sdn 4d	3,725	2,702	38,638
	Ventura (wb 119.0)			
2537	Sport Coupe htp	3,685	2,971	13,297
2539	Vista Sedan htp	3,795	3,047	13,912
	Star Chief (wb 123.0)			
2639	Vista Sedan htp	3,870	3,136	13,557
2669	sdn 4d	3,840	3,003	16,024
	Bonneville (wb 123.0; wgn-119.0)			
2735	Cus Safari wgn 4d	4,185	3,530	3,323

Bonneville		Wght	Price	Prod
2837	Sport Coupe htp	3,810	3,255	16,906
2839	Vista Sedan htp	3,895	3,331	30,830
2867	conv cpe	3,905	3,476	18,264

1961 Engines	bore×stroke	bhp	availability
I-4, 194.5	4.06×3.75	110	S-Tempest man
I-4, 194.5	4.06×3.75	130	S-Tempest auto
V-8, 215.0	3.50×2.80	155	O-Tempest
V-8, 389.0	4.06×3.75	215	S-Str Chf/Cat/ Vent man
V-8, 389.0	4.06×3.75	230	O-all auto exc Tmpst
V-8, 389.0	4.06×3.75	235	S-Bonn man; O-other man
V-8, 389.0	4.06×3.75	267	S-Cat/Vntra auto
V-8, 389.0	4.06×3.75	283	S-Str Chf auto
V-8, 389.0	4.06×3.75	287	O-Cat/Vntra auto
V-8, 389.0	4.06×3.75	303	S-Bonn auto; O-Str Chf auto
V-8, 389.0	4.06×3.75	318/348	O-all exc Tmpst (Tri-Power)
V-8, 389.0	4.06×3.75	333	O-full-size (4bbl)
V-8, 421.0	4.09×4.00	363/373	O-all (Spr Dty ltd)

1962

Tempest (wb 112.0)*		Wght	Price	Prod
2117	spt cpe	2,800	2,294	51,981
2119	sdn 4d	2,815	2,240	37,430
2127	cpe	2,785	2,186	15,473
2135	Safari wgn 4d	2,995	2,511	17,674
2167	conv cpe	2,955	2,564	20,635
Catalina (wb 120.0; wgn-119.0)				
2311	Sport sdn 2d	3,705	2,725	14,263
2335	Safari wgn 4d 6P	4,180	3,193	19,399
2339	Vista Sedan htp	3,825	2,936	29,251
2345	Safari wgn 4d 9P	4,220	3,301	10,716
2347	Sport Coupe htp	3,730	2,860	46,024
2367	conv cpe	3,855	3,172	16,877
2369	sdn 4d	3,765	2,796	68,124
Star Chief (wb 123.0)				
2639	Vista Sedan htp	3,925	3,230	18,882
2669	sdn 4d	3,875	3,097	27,760
Bonneville (wb 123.0; wgn-119.0)				
2735	Cus Safari wgn 4d	4,255	3,624	4,527
2839	Vista Sedan htp	4,005	3,425	44,015
2847	Sport Coupe htp	3,900	3,349	31,629
2867	conv cpe	4,005	3,570	21,582
Grand Prix (wb 120.0)				
2947	htp cpe	3,835	3,490	30,195

* Tempest includes DeLuxe and LeMans trim options. Factory records incl. the following prod. breakdowns:

	Standard	Deluxe	LeMans
cpe	15,473	—	—
spt cpe	—	12,319	39,662
sdn 4d	16,057	21,373	—
Safari wgn 4d	6,504	11,170	—
conv cpe	—	5,076	15,559

1962 Engines	bore×stroke	bhp	availability
I-4, 194.5	4.06×3.75	110	S-Tempest man
I-4, 194.5	4.06×3.75	115	S-Tempest auto
V-8, 215.0	3.50×2.80	185	O-Tempest
V-8, 389.0	4.06×3.75	215	S-Cat/Str Chf man
V-8, 389.0	4.06×3.75	230	O-all full-size
V-8, 389.0	4.06×3.75	235	S-Bonn man; O-Cat/Str Chf man
V-8, 389.0	4.06×3.75	267	S-Catalina auto
V-8, 389.0	4.06×3.75	283	S-Str Chf auto
V-8, 389.0	4.06×3.75	303	S-Bonn auto, GP; O-others
V-8, 389.0	4.06×3.75	318	O-all full-size (Tri-Power)
V-8, 389.0	4.06×3.75	333	O-all fl-sz (4bbl)
V-8, 389.0	4.06×3.75	348	O-all full-size (Tri-Power)
V-8, 421.0	4.09×4.00	405	O-all (Spr Dty)

1963

Tempest (wb 112.0)		Wght	Price	Prod
2117	DeLuxe spt cpe	2,820	2,294	13,157
2119	sdn 4d (incl DeLuxe)	2,835	2,241	28,221
2127	cpe	2,810	2,188	13,307
2135	Saf wgn 4d (incl DeLx)	2,995	2,512	10,135
2167	DeLuxe conv cpe	2,980	2,564	5,012
Tempest LeMans (wb 112.0)				
2217	spt cpe	2,865	2,418	45,701
2267	conv cpe	3,035	2,742	15,957
Catalina (wb 120.0; wgn-119.0)				
2311	Sport sdn 2d	3,685	2,725	14,091
2335	Safari wgn 4d 6P	4,175	3,193	18,446
2339	Vista Sedan htp	3,815	2,934	31,256
2345	Safari wgn 4d 9P	4,230	3,300	11,751
2347	Sport Coupe htp	3,725	2,859	60,795
2367	conv cpe	3,835	3,179	18,249
2369	sdn 4d	3,755	2,795	79,961
Star Chief (wb 123.0)				
2639	Vista Sedan htp	3,915	3,229	12,448
2669	sdn 4d	3,885	3,096	28,309
Bonneville (wb 123.0; wgn-119.0)				
2835	Cus Safari wgn 4d 6P	4,245	3,623	5,156
2839	Vista Sedan htp	3,985	3,423	49,929
2847	Sport Coupe htp	3,895	3,348	30,995
2865	conv cpe	3,970	3,568	23,459
Grand Prix (wb 120.0)				
2957	htp cpe	3,915	3,489	72,959

1963 Engines	bore×stroke	bhp	availability
I-4, 194.5	4.06×3.75	115	S-Tempest
I-4, 194.5	4.06×3.75	120	O-Tempest man
I-4, 194.5	4.06×3.75	140	O-Tempest auto
I-4, 194.5	4.06×3.75	166	O-Tempest
V-8, 326.0	3.72×3.75	260	O-Tempest
V-8, 389.0	4.06×3.75	215	S-Cat/Str Chf man
V-8, 389.0	4.06×3.75	230	O-all fl-sz auto
V-8, 389.0	4.06×3.75	235	S-Bonn man; O-Cat/Str Chf man
V-8, 389.0	4.06×3.75	267	S-Catalina man
V-8, 389.0	4.06×3.75	283	S-Str Chf man
V-8, 389.0	4.06×3.75	303	S-GP, Bonn auto; O-SC/Cat auto
V-8, 389.0	4.06×3.75	318	O-all full-size (Tri-Power)
V-8, 421.0	4.09×4.00	353	O-all full-size
V-8, 421.0	4.09×4.00	370	O-all full-size
V-8, 421.0	4.09×4.00	390/410	O-all (Spr Dty)

1964

Tempest (wb 115.0)		Wght	Price	Prod
2027	spt cpe	2,930	2,259	6,365
2035	Safari wgn 4d	3,245	2,605	6,834
2069	sdn 4d	2,970	2,313	19,427
2127	Custom spt cpe	2,955	2,345	25,833
2135	Cus Safari wgn 4d	3,260	2,691	10,696
2167	Custom conv cpe	3,075	2,641	7,987
2169	Custom sdn 4d	2,990	2,399	29,948
2227	LeMans spt cpe	2,975	2,491	31,317
2237	LeMans htp cpe	2,995	2,556	31,310
2267	LeMans conv cpe	3,125	2,796	17,559
Tempest GTO (wb 115.0)				
2227	spt cpe	3,000	3,200	7,384
2237	htp cpe	3,020	3,250	18,422
2267	conv cpe	3,150	3,500	6,644
Catalina (wb 120.0; wgn-119.0)*				
2311	sdn 2d	3,695	2,735	12,480
2335	Safari wgn 4d 6P	4,190	3,203	20,356
2339	Vista Sedan htp	3,835	2,945	33,849
2345	Safari wgn 4d 9P	4,235	3,311	13,140
2347	Sport Coupe htp*	3,750	2,869	74,793
2367	conv cpe*	3,825	3,181	18,693
2369	sdn 4d	3,770	2,806	84,457
Star Chief (wb 123.0)				
2639	Vista Sedan htp	3,945	3,239	11,200
2669	sdn 4d	3,885	3,107	26,453
Bonneville (wb 123.0; wgn-119.0)				
2835	Cus Safari wgn 4d	4,275	3,633	5,844
2839	Vista Sedan htp	3,995	3,433	57,630
2847	Sport Coupe htp	3,920	3,358	34,769
2867	conv cpe	3,985	3,578	22,016
Grand Prix (wb 120.0)				
2957	htp cpe	3,930	3,499	63,810

* Includes models equipped with 2+2 option package.

1964 Engines	bore×stroke	bhp	availability
I-6, 215.0	3.75×3.25	140	S-Tmpst exc GTO
V-8, 326.0	3.72×3.75	250	O-Tempest
V-8, 326.0	3.72×3.75	280	O-Tempest
V-8, 389.0	4.06×3.75	230	O-all fl-sz auto
V-8, 389.0	4.06×3.75	235	S-Cat/Str Chf man
V-8, 389.0	4.06×3.75	267	S-Cat/Str Chf auto
V-8, 389.0	4.06×3.75	283	S-Cat 2+2 opt; O-Cat/SC auto
V-8, 389.0	4.06×3.75	303	S-GP/Bonn auto; O-Cat/SC auto
V-8, 389.0	4.06×3.75	306	S-GP/Bonn man; O-Cat/SC man
V-8, 389.0	4.06×3.75	325	S-GTO; O-Tmpst
V-8, 389.0	4.06×3.75	330	O-full-size
V-8, 389.0	4.06×3.75	348	O-GTO
V-8, 421.0	4.09×4.00	320/350	O-full-size
V-8, 421.0	4.09×4.00	370	O-full size

1965

233 Tempest (wb 115.0)		Wght	Price	Prod
27	spt cpe	2,930	2,260	18,198
35	Safari wgn 4d	3,220	2,605	5,622
69	sdn 4d	2,975	2,313	15,705
235 Tempest Custom (wb 115.0)				
27	spt cpe	2,975	2,346	18,367
35	Safari wagn 4d	3,215	2,691	10,792
37	htp cpe	2,975	2,411	21,906
67	conv cpe	3,080	2,641	8,346
69	sdn 4d	2,980	2,400	25,242
237 Tempest LeMans (wb 115.0)				
27	spt cpe	3,020	2,491	18,881
27	GTO spt cpe	3,468	2,751	8,319
37	htp cpe	3,030	2,556	60,548
37	GTO htp cpe	3,478	2,816	55,722
67	conv cpe	3,115	2,797	13,897
67	GTO conv cpe	3,563	3,057	11,311
69	sdn 4d	3,020	2,551	14,227
252 Catalina (wb 121.0)				
11	sdn 2d	3,695	2,734	9,526
35	Safari wgn 4d 6P	4,165	3,202	22,399
37	Sport Coupe htp*	3,750	2,868	92,009
39	Vista Sedan htp	3,855	2,945	34,814
45	Safari wgn 4d 9P	4,210	3,309	15,110
67	conv cpe*	3,815	3,196	18,347
69	sdn 4d	3,750	2,805	78,853
256 Star Chief (wb 124.0)				
39	Vista Sedan htp	3,925	3,238	9,132
69	sdn 4d	3,860	3,106	22,183
262 Bonneville (wb 124.0; wgn-121.0)				
35	Cus Safari wgn 4d	4,310	3,632	6,460
37	Sport Coupe htp	3,890	3,357	44,030
39	Vista Sedan htp	3,990	3,433	62,480
67	conv cpe	3,950	3,594	21,050
266 Grand Prix (wb 121.0)				
57	htp cpe	3,940	3,498	57,881

* Includes models equipped with 2+2 option package.

1965 Engines	bore×stroke	bhp	availability
I-6, 215.0	3.75×3.25	140	S-Tmpst exc GTO
V-8, 326.0	3.72×3.75	250	O-Tempest
V-8, 326.0	3.72×3.75	285	O-Tempest
V-8, 389.0	4.06×3.75	256	S-Cat/SC man; O-other full-size
V-8, 389.0	4.06×3.75	290	S-Cat/Str Chf auto
V-8, 389.0	4.06×3.75	325	S-Bonn/GP auto
V-8, 389.0	4.06×3.75	333	S-Bonn/GP man
V-8, 389.0	4.06×3.75	335	S-GTO
V-8, 389.0	4.06×3.75	360	O-GTO
V-8, 421.0	4.09×4.00	338	S-Cat 2+2; O-other full-size
V-8, 421.0	4.09×4.00	356	O-all full-size
V-8, 421.0	4.09×4.00	376	O-all full-size

1966

233 Tempest (wb 115.0)		Wght	Price	Prod
07	spt cpe	3,040	2,278	22,266
35	Safari wgn 4d	3,340	2,624	4,095
69	sdn 4d	3,075	2,331	17,392
235 Tempest Custom (wb 115.0)				
07	spt cpe	3,060	2,362	17,182

235 Tempest Custom		Wght	Price	Prod
17	htp cpe	3,075	2,426	31,322
35	Safari wgn 4d	3,355	2,709	7,614
39	htp sdn	3,195	2,547	10,996
67	conv cpe	3,170	2,665	5,557
69	sdn 4d	3,100	2,415	23,988

237 LeMans (wb 115.0)				
07	spt cpe	3,090	2,505	16,654
17	htp cpe	3,125	2,568	78,109
39	htp sdn	3,195	2,701	13,897
67	conv cpe	3,220	2,806	13,080

242 Tempest GTO (wb 115.0)				
07	spt cpe	3,445	2,783	10,363
17	htp cpe	3,465	2,847	73,785
67	conv cpe	3,555	3,082	12,798

252 Catalina (wb 121.0)				
11	sdn 2d	3,715	2,762	7,925
35	Safari wgn 4d 6P	4,250	3,217	21,082
37	Sport Coupe htp	3,835	2,893	79,013
39	Vista Sedan htp	3,910	2,968	38,005
45	Safari wgn 4d 9P	4,315	3,338	12,965
67	conv cpe	3,860	3,219	14,837
69	sdn 4d	3,785	2,831	80,483

254 2+2 (wb 121.0) - 6,383 built*				
37	Sport Coupe htp	4,005	3,298	—
67	conv cpe	4,030	3,602	—

256 Star Chief Executive (wb 124.0)				
37	Sport Coupe htp	3,920	3,170	10,140
39	Vista Sedan htp	3,980	3,244	10,583
69	sdn 4d	3,920	3,114	24,489

262 Bonneville (wb 124.0; wgn-121.0)				
37	Sport Coupe htp	4,020	3,354	42,004
39	Vista Sedan htp	4,070	3,428	68,646
45	Cus Safari wgn 4d 3S	4,390	3,747	8,452
67	conv cpe	4,015	3,586	16,299

266 Grand Prix (wb 121.0)				
57	htp cpe	4,015	3,492	36,757

*Included with equivalent Catalina body styles.

1966 Engines	bore×stroke	bhp	availability
I-6, 230.0	3.88×3.25	165	S-Tmpst, LeMns
I-6, 230.0	3.88×3.25	207	O-Tmpst, LeMns
V-8, 326.0	3.72×3.75	250	O-Tmpst, LeMns
V-8, 326.0	3.72×3.75	285	O-Tmpst, LeMns
V-8, 389.0	4.06×3.75	256	S-Cat/SC man; O-other full-size
V-8, 389.0	4.06×3.75	290	O-Cat, Str Chf
V-8, 389.0	4.06×3.75	325	S-Bonn/GP auto; O-Cat, Str Chf
V-8, 389.0	4.06×3.75	333	S-Bonn/GP manual, GTO
V-8, 389.0	4.06×3.75	360	O-GTO
V-8, 421.0	4.09×4.00	338	S-2+2; O-other full-size
V-8, 421.0	4.09×4.00	356	O-all full-size
V-8, 421.0	4.09×4.00	376	O-all full-size

1967

223 Firebird (wb 108.1)		Wght	Price	Prod
37	htp cpe	2,955	2,666	67,032
67	conv cpe	3,247	2,903	15,528

233 Tempest (wb 115.0)				
07	cpe	3,110	2,341	17,978
35	wgn 4d	3,370	2,666	3,495
69	sdn 4d	3,140	2,388	13,136

235 Tempest Custom (wb 115.0)				
07	cpe	3,130	2,437	12,469
17	htp cpe	3,140	2,494	30,512
35	wgn 4d	3,370	2,760	5,324
39	htp sdn	3,240	2,608	5,493
67	conv cpe	3,240	2,723	4,082
69	sdn 4d	3,145	2,482	17,445

237 LeMans (wb 115.0)				
07	cpe	3,155	2,586	10,693
17	htp cpe	3,155	2,648	75,965
39	htp sdn	3,265	2,771	8,424
67	conv cpe	3,250	2,881	9,820

239 Tempest Safari (wb 115.0)				
35	wgn 4d	3,390	2,936	4,511

242 Tempest GTO (wb 115.0)		Wght	Price	Prod
07	cpe	3,425	2,871	7,029
17	htp cpe	3,430	2,935	65,176
67	conv cpe	3,515	3,165	9,517

252 Catalina (wb 121.0)				
11	sdn 2d	3,735	2,807	5,633
35	wgn 4d 6P	4,275	3,252	18,305
39	htp sdn	3,960	3,020	37,256
45	wgn 4d 9P	4,340	3,374	11,040
67	conv cpe*	3,910	3,276	10,033
69	sdn 4d	3,825	2,866	80,551
87	htp cpe*	3,860	2,951	77,932

256 Executive (wb 124.0; wgn-121.0)				
35	wgn 4d 6P	4,290	3,600	5,903
39	htp sdn	4,020	3,296	8,699
45	wgn 4d 9P	4,370	3,722	5,593
69	sdn 4d	3,955	3,165	19,861
87	htp cpe	3,925	3,227	6,931

262 Bonneville (wb 124.0; wgn-121.0)				
39	htp sdn	4,110	3,517	56,307
45	wgn 4d 9P	4,415	3,819	6,771
67	conv cpe	4,010	3,680	8,902
87	htp cpe	3,975	3,448	31,016

266 Grand Prix (wb 121.0)				
57	htp cpe	4,005	3,549	37,125
67	conv cpe	4,040	3,813	5,856

* Includes models equipped with 2+2 option package.

1967 Engines	bore×stroke	bhp	availability
I-6, 230.0	3.88×3.25	165	S-Frbrd, LeMns, Temp exc GTO
I-6, 230.0	3.88×3.25	215	O-Frbrd, LeMns, Temp exc GTO
V-8, 326.0	3.72×3.75	250	O-Frbrd, LeMns, Temp exc GTO
V-8, 326.0	3.72×3.75	285	O-Frbrd, LeMns, Temp exc Temp Sfr wgn
V-8, 400.0	4.12×3.75	255	O-GTO auto
V-8, 400.0	4.12×3.75	265	S-Cat/Exc man; O-auto
V-8, 400.0	4.12×3.75	290	S-Cat/Exec auto
V-8, 400.0	4.12×3.75	325	S-Bonn auto, Frbrd 400; O-Cat, Exec
V-8, 400.0	4.12×3.75	333	S-Bonn man; O-Cat, Exec
V-8, 400.0	4.12×3.75	335	S-GTO
V-8, 400.0	4.12×3.75	350	S-Grand Prix
V-8, 400.0	4.12 ×3.75	360	O-GTO
V-8, 428.0	4.12×4.00	360	S-2+2; O-Cat, Exec, Bonn, Grand Prix
V-8, 428.0	4.12×4.00	376	O-Cat, Exec, Bonn, Grnd Prix

1968

223 Firebird (wb 108.1)		Wght	Price	Prod
37	htp cpe	3,061	2,781	90,152
67	conv cpe	3,346	2,996	16,960

233 Tempest (wb 116.0; 2d-112.0)				
27	spt cpe	3,242	2,461	19,991
69	sdn 4d	3,309	2,509	11,590

235 Tempest Custom (wb 116.0; 2d-112.0)				
27	spt cpe	3,252	2,554	10,634
35	wgn 4d	3,667	2,906	8,253
37	htp cpe	3,277	2,614	40,574
39	htp sdn	3,384	2,728	6,147
67	conv cpe	3,337	2,839	3,518
69	sdn 4d	3,297	2,602	17,304

237 LeMans (wb 116.0; 2d-112.0)				
27	spt cpe	3,287	2,724	8,439
37	htp cpe	3,302	2,786	110,036
39	htp sdn	3,407	2,916	9,002
67	conv cpe	3,377	3,015	8,820

239 Tempest Safari (wb 116.0)				
35	wgn 4d	3,677	3,107	4,414

242 Tempest GTO (wb 112.0)				
37	htp cpe	3,506	3,101	77,704
67	conv cpe	3,590	3,227	9,980

252 Catalina (wb 121.0)		Wght	Price	Prod
11	sdn 2d	3,839	2,945	5,247
35	wgn 4d 6P	4,327	3,390	21,848
39	htp sdn	4,012	3,158	41,727
45	wgn 4d 9P	4,408	3,537	13,363
67	conv cpe	3,980	3,391	7,339
69	sdn 4d	3,888	3,004	94,441
87	htp cpe	3,943	3,089	92,217

256 Executive (wb 124.0; wgn-121.0)				
35	wgn 4d 6P	4,378	3,744	6,195
39	htp sdn	4,077	3,439	7,848
45	wgn 4d 9P	4,453	3,890	5,843
69	sdn 4d	4,022	3,309	18,869
87	htp cpe	3,975	3,371	5,880

262 Bonneville (wb 124.0; wgn-121.0)				
39	htp sdn	4,171	3,660	57,055
45	wgn 4d 9P	4,485	3,987	6,926
67	conv cpe	4,090	3,800	7,358
69	sdn 4d	4,122	3,530	3,499
87	htp cpe	4,054	3,592	29,598

266 Grand Prix (wb 121.0)				
57	htp cpe	4,075	3,697	31,711

1968 Engines	bore×stroke	bhp	availability
I-6, 250.0	3.88×3.53	175	S-Frbrd exc Sprint, LeM, Tmpst exc GTO
I-6, 250.0	3.88×3.53	215	S-Frbrd Sprint; O-as above exc wgns
V-8, 350.0	3.88×3.75	265	S-Frbrd 350; O-Tmpst exc GTO, LeM
V-8, 350.0	3.88×3.75	320	S-Frbrd HO; O-Tmpst, LeM exc wgns
V-8, 400.0	4.12×3.75	265	O-GTO, all fl-sz
V-8, 400.0	4.12×3.75	290	S-Cat, Exec
V-8, 400.0	4.12×3.75	330	S-Firebird 400
V-8, 400.0	4.12×3.75	335	O-Frbrd 400 (Ram-Air)
V-8, 400.0	4.12×3.75	340	S-Bonn; O-Cat, Exec
V-8, 400.0	4.12×3.75	350	S-Grnd Prx, GTO
V-8, 400.0	4.12×3.75	360	O-GTO
V-8, 428.0	4.12×4.00	375	O-Cat, Exc, Bonn, GP
V-8, 428.0	4.12×4.00	390	O-Cat, Exec, Bonn, GP (HO)

1969

223 Firebird (wb 108.0)*		Wght	Price	Prod
37	htp cpe	3,080	2,821	76,059
67	conv cpe	3,330	3,045	11,649

233 Tempest (wb 116.0; 2d-112.0)				
27	spt cpe	3,180	2,510	17,181
69	sdn 4d	3,250	2,557	9,741

235 Tempest Custom (wb 116.0; 2d-112.0)				
27	spt cpe	3,210	2,603	7,912
35	wgn 4d	3,595	2,956	6,963
37	htp cpe	3,220	2,663	46,886
39	htp sdn	3,315	2,777	3,918
67	conv cpe	3,265	2,888	2,379
69	sdn 4d	3,235	2,651	16,532

237 LeMans (wb 116.0; 2d-112.0)				
27	spt cpe	3,225	2,773	5,033
37	htp cpe	3,245	2,835	82,817
67	conv cpe	3,290	3,064	5,676
69	htp sdn	3,360	2,965	6,475

239 LeMans Safari (wb 116.0)				
36	wgn 4d	3,690	3,198	4,115

242 Tempest GTO (wb 112.0)				
37	htp cpe	3,503	3,156	64,851
67	conv cpe	3,553	3,382	7,436

252 Catalina (wb 122.0)				
36	wgn 4d 6P	4,455	3,519	20,352
37	htp cpe	3,925	3,174	84,006
39	htp sdn	4,005	3,244	38,819
46	wgn 4d 9P	4,520	3,664	13,393
67	conv cpe	3,985	3,476	5,436

252 Catalina		Wght	Price	Prod
69	sdn 4d	3,945	3,090	84,590

256 Executive (wb 125.0; wgn-122.0)				
36	wgn 4d 6P	4,475	3,872	6,411
37	htp cpe	3,970	3,456	4,492
39	htp sdn	4,065	3,525	6,522
46	wgn 4d 9P	4,545	4,017	6,805
69	sdn 4d	4,045	3,394	14,831

262 Bonneville (wb 125.0; wgn-122.0)				
37	htp cpe	4,080	3,688	27,773
39	htp sdn	4,180	3,756	50,817
46	wgn 4d 9P	4,600	4,104	7,428
67	conv cpe	4,130	3,896	5,438
69	sdn 4d	4,180	3,626	4,859

276 Grand Prix (wb 118.0)				
57	htp cpe	3,715	3,866	112,486

* Prod. incl. 689 Trans Am hardtop cpes, 8 convs.

1969 Engines	bore×stroke	bhp	availability
I-6, 250.0	3.88×3.53	175	S-Frbrd, LeM, Tmpst exc GTO (ohc)
I-6, 250.0	3.88×3.53	230	S-Frbrd Sprint; O-LeM, Tmpst exc GTO (ohc)
V-8, 350.0	3.88×3.75	265	S-Frbrd 350; O-Tmpst, LeM
V-8, 350.0	3.88×3.75	325	S-Frbrd 350 HO
V-8, 350.0	3.88×3.75	330	O-Frbrd, Tmpst, LeM exc wgns/GTO
V-8, 400.0	4.12×3.75	265	O-GTO/fl-sz auto
V-8, 400.0	4.12×3.75	290	S-Cat, Vntra, Exec
V-8, 400.0	4.12×3.75	330	S-Firebird 400
V-8, 400.0	4.12×3.75	335	O-Frbrd 400 (Ram Air)
V-8, 400.0	4.12×3.75	345	O-Frbrd 400 (Ram Air)
V-8, 400.0	4.12×3.75	350	S-GTO, Grd Prix
V-8, 400.0	4.12×3.75	360	S-Bonn; O-Cat, Exec
V-8, 400.0	4.12×3.75	366	O-GTO (Ram Air)
V-8, 400.0	4.12×3.75	370	O-GTO (Ram Air)
V-8, 428.0	4.12×4.00	370/390	O-GP, full size

1970

223 Firebird (wb 108.0)		Wght	Price	Prod
87	cpe	3,140	2,875	18,874
87	Formula 400 cpe	3,470	3,370	7,708
87	Trans Am cpe	3,550	4,305	3,196
87	Esprit cpe	3,435	3,241	18,961

233 Tempest (wb 116.0; 2d-112.0)				
27	cpe	3,225	2,623	11,977
37	htp cpe	3,250	2,683	20,883
69	sdn 4d	3,295	2,670	9,187

235 LeMans (wb 116.0; 2d-112.0)				
27	cpe	3,240	2,735	5,565
35	wgn 4d	3,585	3,092	7,165
37	htp cpe	3,265	2,795	52,304
39	htp sdn	3,385	2,921	3,872
69	sdn 4d	3,315	2,782	15,255

237 LeMans Sport (wb 116.0; 2d-112.0)				
27	cpe	3,265	2,891	1,673
36	wgn 4d	3,775	3,328	3,823
37	htp cpe	3,290	2,953	58,356
39	htp sdn	3,405	3,083	3,657
67	conv cpe	3,330	3,182	4,670

242 GTO (wb 112.0)*				
37	htp cpe	3,641	3,267	36,366
67	conv cpe	3,691	3,492	3,783

252 Catalina (wb 122.0)				
36	wgn 4d 6P	4,517	3,646	16,944
37	htp cpe	3,952	3,249	70,350
39	htp sdn	4,042	3,319	35,155
46	wgn 4d 9P	4,607	3,791	12,450
67	conv cpe	4,027	3,604	3,686
69	sdn 4d	3,997	3,164	84,795

256 Executive (wb 125.0; wgn-122.0)				
36	wgn 4d 6P	4,552	4,015	4,861
37	htp cpe	4,042	3,600	3,499

256 Executive		Wght	Price	Prod
39	htp sdn	4,132	3,669	5,376
46	wgn 4d 9P	4,632	4,160	5,629
69	sdn 4d	4,087	3,538	13,061

262 Bonneville (wb 125.0; wgn-122.0)				
37	htp cpe	4,111	3,832	23,418
39	htp sdn	4,226	3,900	44,241
46	wgn 4d 9P	4,686	4,247	7,033
67	conv cpe	4,161	4,040	3,537
69	sdn 4d	4,181	3,770	3,802

276 Grand Prix (wb 118.0)				
57	htp cpe	3,784	3,985	65,750

* Includes models equipped with "The Judge" option (3,629 coupes and 168 convertibles).

1970 Engines	bore×stroke	bhp	availability
I-6, 250.0	3.88×3.53	155	S-Tmpst, LeM, Firebird (ohv)
V-8, 350.0	3.88×3.75	255	S-Frbrd Esprt; O-above models, Cat exc conv and wgns
V-8, 400.0	4.12×3.75	265	O-all auto exc GTO, Bonn
V-8, 400.0	4.12×3.75	290	S-Cat conv/wgn, Exec; O-other Cat
V-8, 400.0	4.12×3.75	330	S-Frbrd 400; O-Tmpst/LeM/Cat/Exec auto
V-8, 400.0	4.12×3.75	345	S-Frbrd Trns Am; O-Tmpst/LeM man
V-8, 400.0	4.12×3.75	350	S-GTO, Grnd Prx
V-8, 400.0	4.12×3.75	366	S-GTO Judge; O-GTO (Ram Air)
V-8, 400.0	4.12×3.75	370	O-GTO (Ram Air) O-GTO Judge
V-8, 455.0	4.15×4.21	360	S-Bonn; O-Cat, Exec, GTO
V-8, 455.0	4.15×4.21	370	S-Bonn wgn, GP SJ; O-GP J, Cat, Exec, Bonn

1971

Ventura II (wb 111.0)		Wght	Price	Prod
21327	cpe	3,010	2,458	34,681
21369	sdn 4d	3,050	2,488	13,803

Firebird (wb 108.0)				
22387	cpe	3,292	3,047	23,021
22487	Esprit cpe V-8	3,423	3,416	20,185
22687	Formula 400 cpe V-8	3,473	3,445	7,802
22887	Trans Am cpe V-8	3,578	4,595	2,116

LeMans (wb 116.0; 2d-112.0)				
23327	T-37 cpe	3,317	2,747	7,184
23337	T-37 htp cpe	3,322	2,807	29,466
23369	T-37 sdn 4d	3,347	2,795	8,336
23527	cpe	3,327	2,877	2,374
23536	wgn 4d 2S	3,867	3,353	6,311
23537	htp cpe	3,327	2,938	40,966
23539	htp sdn	3,442	3,064	3,186
23546	wgn 4d 3S	3,917	3,465	4,363
23569	sdn 4d	3,357	2,925	11,979
23737	Sport htp cpe	3,327	3,125	34,625
23739	Sport htp sdn	3,442	3,255	2,451
23767	Sport conv cpe	3,417	3,359	3,865
24237	GTO htp cpe V-8	3,619	3,446	9,497
24237	GTO Judge htp cpe	3,650	3,840	357
24267	GTO conv cpe	3,664	3,676	661
24267	GTO Judge conv cpe	3,700	4,070	17

Catalina (wb 123.5; wgn-127.0)				
25235	Safari wgn 4d 2S	4,815	4,315	10,332
25239	htp sdn	4,107	3,939	22,333
25245	Safari wgn 4d 3S	4,905	4,462	9,283
25257	htp cpe	4,042	3,870	46,257
25267	conv cpe	4,081	4,156	2,036
25269	sdn 4d	4,077	3,770	59,355
25839	Brougham htp sdn	4,179	4,154	9,001
25857	Brougham htp cpe	4,119	4,084	8,823
25869	Brougham sdn 4d	4,149	4,000	6,069

Bonneville (wb 126.0; wgn-127.0)				
26235	Grnd Saf wgn 4d 2S	4,843	4,643	3,613
26239	htp sdn	4,273	4,340	16,393

Bonneville		Wght	Price	Prod
26245	Grnd Saf wgn 4d 3S	4,913	4,790	5,972
26257	htp cpe	4,188	4,272	8,778
26269	sdn 4d	4,213	4,210	6,513

Grand Ville (wb 126.0)				
26847	htp cpe	4,223	4,497	14,017
26849	htp sdn	4,303	4,566	30,524
26867	conv cpe	4,266	4,706	1,789
	chassis	—	—	194

Grand Prix (wb 118.0)				
27657	htp cpe	3,863	4,557	58,325

1971 Engines	bore×stroke	bhp	availability
I-6, 250.0	3.88×3.53	145	S-LeM exc GTO; Firebird exc Fmla & T/A
I-6, 250.0	3.88×3.53	185	S-Ventura
V-8, 307.0	3.88×3.25	235	O-Ventura
V-8, 350.0	3.88×3.75	250	S-Cat exc Br/Saf; O-LeM exc GTP, Firebird exc T/A
V-8, 400.0	4.12×3.75	265	S-Cat Br/Saf; O-Firebird exc Frmla & T/A, Cat
V-8, 400.0	4.12 × 3.75	300	S-GTO, Firebird Frmla, GP; O-LeM, Frbrd Esp
V-8, 455.0	4.15 × 4.21	280	S-Bonn; O-Cat
V-8, 455.0	4.15 × 4.21	325	S-GV; O-LeM, Firebird T/A, Catalina, GP
V-8, 455.0	4.15 × 4.21	335	S-Trans Am; O-LeMans

1972

Ventura II (wb 111.0)		Wght	Price	Prod
2Y27	cpe	3,019	2,426	51,203
2Y69	sdn 4d	3,054	2,454	21,584

Firebird (wb 108.0)				
2S87	cpe	3,263	2,828	12,000
2T87	Esprit cpe V-8	3,359	3,194	11,415
2U87	Formula cpe V-8	3,424	3,221	5,250
2V87	Trans Am cpe V-8	3,564	4,256	1,286

LeMans (wb 116.0; 2d-112.0)*				
2D27	cpe	3,402	2,722	6,855
2D36	wgn 4d 2S	3,907	3,271	8,332
2D37	htp cpe	3,342	2,851	80,383
2D46	wgn 4d 3S	3,947	3,378	5,266
2D67	conv cpe	3,392	3,228	3,438
2D69	sdn 4d	3,377	2,814	19,463
2G37	Luxury htp cpe V-8	3,488	3,196	37,615
2G39	Luxury htp sdn V-8	3,638	3,319	8,641

Catalina (wb 123.5; wgn-127.0)				
2L35	Safari wgn 4d 2S	4,743	4,232	14,536
2L39	htp sdn	4,179	3,874	28,010
2L45	Safari wgn 4d 3S	4,818	4,372	12,766
2L57	htp cpe	4,129	3,808	60,233
2L67	conv cpe	4,204	4,080	2,399
2L69	sdn 4d	4,154	3,713	83,004
2M39	Brougham htp sdn	4,238	4,062	8,762
2M57	Brougham htp cpe	4,158	3,996	10,545
2M69	Brougham sdn 4d	4,188	3,916	8,007

Bonneville (wb 126.0; wgn-127.0)				
2N35	Grnd Saf wgn 4d 2S	4,918	4,581	5,675
2N39	htp sdn	4,338	4,293	15,806
2N45	Grnd Saf wgn 4d 3S	4,938	4,721	8,540
2N57	htp cpe	4,238	4,228	10,568
2N69	sdn 4d	4,288	4,169	9,704

Grand Ville (wb 126.0)				
2P47	htp cpe	4,262	4,442	19,852
2P49	htp sdn	4,378	4,507	41,346
2P67	conv cpe	4,333	4,640	2,213
	chassis	—	—	320

Grand Prix (wb 118.0)				
2K57	htp cpe	3,898	4,472	91,961

* Prod. incl. models w/Sport ($164), GTO ($344), and GT ($231) option packages. GTO production: 5,807.

1972 Engines	bore×stroke	bhp	availability
I-6, 250.0	3.88×3.53	110	S-Vntra, LeM, Firebird exc T/A

1972 Engines	bore×stroke	bhp	availability
V-8, 307.0	3.88×3.25	130	O-Vent exc CA
V-8, 350.0	3.88×3.75	160	S-Cat exc Saf, Br; O-Vent (CA), LeM, Firebird exc T/A
V-8, 400.0	4.12×3.75	175	S-Cat Saf, Br; O-LeM, Cat, Frbrd exc T/A
V-8, 400.0	4.12×3.75	250	S-GP; O-Frbrd exc T/A
V-8, 455.0	4.15 × 4.21	185	S-Bonn, GV, GSaf; O-Cat
V-8, 455.0	4.15 × 4.21	220	O-Bonn, GV, GSaf, Cat
V-8, 455.0	4.15 × 4.21	230	O-LeMans
V-8, 455.0	4.15 × 4.21	250	O-LeM, GP
V-8, 455.0	4.15 × 4.21	300	S-Frbrd T/A; O-LeM, Frbrd

1973

Ventura (wb 111.0)		Wght	Price	Prod
Y17	htchbk cpe	3,276	2,603	26,335
Z17	Custom htchbk cpe	3,309	2,759	
Y27	cpe	3,170	2,452	49,153
Z27	Custom cpe	3,203	2,609	
Y69	sdn 4d	3,230	2,481	21,012
Z69	Custom sdn 4d	3,263	2,638	
Firebird (wb 108.0)				
S87	cpe	3,270	2,895	14,096
T87	Esprit cpe V-8	3,309	3,249	17,249
U87	Formula cpe V-8	3,318	3,276	10,166
V87	Trans Am cpe V-8	3,504	4,204	4,802
LeMans (wb 116.0; 2d-112.0)				
D29	Colonnade sdn 4d	3,713	2,918	26,554
D35	Safari wgn 4d 2S	4,064	3,296	10,446
D37	Colonnade sdn 2d	3,687	2,920	68,230
D45	Safari wgn 4d 3S	4,101	3,429	6,127
F37	Sport Col sdn 2d*	3,702	3,008	50,999
G29	Lxry Col sdn 4d V-8	3,867	3,344	9,377
G37	Lxry Col sdn 2d V-8	3,799	3,274	33,916
Grand Am (wb 116.0; 2d-112.0)				
H29	Col sdn 4d V-8	4,018	4,353	8,691
H37	Col sdn 2d V-8	3,992	4,264	34,445
Catalina (wb 124.0; wgn-127.0)				
L35	Safari wgn 4d 2S	4,791	4,311	15,762
L39	htp sdn	4,270	3,938	31,663
L45	Safari wgn 4d 3S	4,873	4,457	14,654
L57	htp cpe	4,190	3,869	74,394
L69	sdn 4d	4,234	3,770	100,592
Bonneville (wb 124.0)				
N39	htp sdn	4,369	4,292	17,202
N57	htp cpe	4,292	4,225	13,866
N69	sdn 4d	4,333	4,163	15,830
Grand Ville/Grand Safari (wb 124.0/127.0)				
P35	Grnd Saf wgn 4d 2S	4,823	4,674	6,894
P45	Grnd Saf wgn 4d 3S	4,925	4,821	10,776
P47	Grand Ville htp cpe	4,321	4,524	23,963
P49	Grand Ville htp sdn	4,376	4,592	44,092
P67	Grand Ville conv	4,339	4,766	4,447
	chassis	—	—	240
Grand Prix (wb 116.0)				
K57	htp cpe	4,025	4,583	153,899

* Production includes models with GT ($246) and GTO ($368) option packages. GTO production: 4,806.

1973 Engines	bore×stroke	bhp	availability
I-6, 250.0	3.88×3.53	100	S-Vent, LeM, Firebird exc T/A
V-8, 350.0	3.88×3.75	150	S-Cat exc wgn; O-Vent, LeM, Firebird exc T/A
V-8, 350.0	3.88×3.75	175	O-Vent, LeM, Firebird exc T/A
V-8, 400.0	4.12×3.75	170	S-GA, Bonn, Cat wgn; O-LeM, other Catalina
V-8, 400.0	4.12×3.75	185	O-GA, LeM, Bonn, Cat
V-8, 400.0	4.12×3.75	200	S-Grnd Saf
V-8, 400.0	4.12×3.75	230	S-GA, LeM, Firebird exc T/A, GSaf, Cat, Bonn
V-8, 400.0	4.12×3.75	250	S-Grand Prix
V-8, 455.0	4.15×4.21	215	S-GV; O-GSaf, Cat, Bonn
V-8, 455.0	4.15×4.21	250	S-Frbrd T/A; O-Frbrd, GSaf, GV, Bonn, GP
V-8, 455.0	4.15×4.21	310	O-Firebird

1974

Ventura (wb 111.0)		Wght	Price	Prod
Y17	htchbk cpe	3,372	3,018	16,694
Z17	Custom htchbk cpe	3,376	3,176	
Y27	cpe*	3,262	2,892	47,782
Z27	Custom cpe*	3,298	3,051	
Y69	sdn 4d	3,284	2,921	17,323
Z69	Custom sdn 4d	3,332	3,080	
Firebird (wb 108.0)				
S87	cpe	3,394	3,335	26,372
T87	Esprit cpe V-8	3,540	3,687	22,583
U87	Formula cpe V-8	3,548	3,659	14,519
V87	Trans Am cpe V-8	3,655	4,446	10,255
LeMans (wb 116.0; 2d-112.0)				
D29	Colonnade sdn 4d	3,736	3,236	17,266
D37	Colonnade sdn 2d	3,660	3,216	37,061
D35	Safari wgn 4d 2S V-8	4,333	4,052	4,743
D45	Safari wgn 4d 3S V-8	4,371	4,186	3,004
F37	Sport Colonnade cpe	3,688	3,300	37,955
G35	Lxry Saf wgn 4d 2S V-8	4,363	4,326	952
G29	Lxry Col sdn 4d V-8	3,904	3,759	4,513
G37	Luxury Col cpe V-8	3,808	3,703	25,882
G45	Lxry Saf wgn 4d 3S V-8	4,401	4,459	1,178
Grand Am (wb 116.0; 2d-112.0)				
H29	Colonnade sdn 4d	4,073	4,623	3,122
H37	Colonnade cpe	3,992	4,534	13,961
Catalina (wb 124.0; wgn-127.0)				
L35	Safari wgn 4d 2S	4,973	4,692	5,662
L39	htp sdn	4,352	4,347	11,769
L45	Safari wgn 4d 3S	5,037	4,834	6,486
L57	htp cpe	4,279	4,278	40,657
L69	sdn 4d	4,294	4,190	46,025
Bonneville (wb 124.0)				
N39	htp sdn	4,444	4,639	6,151
N57	htp cpe	4,356	4,572	7,639
N69	sdn 4d	4,384	4,510	6,770
Grand Ville/Grand Safari (wb 124.0/127.0)				
P35	Grnd Saf wgn 4d 2S	5,011	5,099	2,894
P45	Grnd Saf wgn 4d 3S	5,112	5,256	5,255
P47	Grand Ville htp cpe	4,432	4,871	11,631
P49	Grand Ville htp sdn	4,515	4,939	21,714
P67	Grand Ville conv	4,476	5,113	3,000
	chassis	—	—	113
Grand Prix (wb 116.0)				
K57	htp cpe	4,096	4,936	99,817

* GTO option package ($195) for Ventura coupe only. GTO production: 7,058.

1974 Engines	bore×stroke	bhp	availability
I-6, 250.0	3.88×3.53	100	S-Vent, LeMans, Firebird S87
V-8, 350.0	3.88×3.75	155	S-Frbrd T87; O-Vent, LeM, Firebird S87
V-8, 350.0	3.88×3.75	170	S-Firebird U87; O-LeMans
V-8, 350.0	3.88×3.75	200	O-LeMans
V-8, 400.0	4.12×3.75	175	S-GA, Cat, Bonn, GSaf, GV
V-8, 400.0	4.15×3.75	190	O-Grand Am
V-8, 400.0	4.12×3.75	200	O-Cat, Bonn, GSaf, GV
V-8, 400.0	4.12×3.75	225	S-Frbrd T/A, GP; O-GA, other Frbrd
V-8, 455.0	4.15×4.21	215	S-GV; O-GA, Cat, Bonn
V-8, 455.0	4.15×4.21	250	O-GA, Frbrd T/A, GP
V-8, 455.0	4.15×4.21	255	O-all full-size
V-8, 455.0	4.15×4.21	290	O-Frbrd Form/ Trans Am

1975

Astre (wb 97.0)		Wght	Price	Prod
C11	S sdn 2d	2,416	2,841	8,339
C15	S Safari wgn 2d	2,519	3,071	15,322
V15	Safari wgn 2d	2,545	3,175	
X15	SJ Safari wgn 2d	2,602	3,686	
C77	S htchbk cpe	2,487	2,954	40,809
V77	htchbk cpe	2,499	3,079	
X77	SJ htchbk cpe	2,558	3,610	
Ventura (wb 111.1)				
E27	S cpe	3,360	3,162	34,023
Y27	cpe	3,382	3,293	
Z27	Custom cpe	3,442	3,449	
B27	SJ cpe	3,424	3,829	
Y17	htchbk cpe	3,466	3,432	10,463
Z17	Custom htchbk cpe	3,482	3,593	
B17	SJ htchbk cpe	3,484	3,961	
Y69	sdn 4d	3,418	3,304	22,068
Z69	Custom sdn 4d	3,462	3,464	
B69	SJ sdn 4d	3,454	3,846	
Firebird (wb 108.0)				
S87	cpe	3,498	3,713	22,293
T87	Esprit cpe	3,543	3,958	20,826
U87	Formula cpe V-8	3,631	4,349	13,670
W87	Trans Am cpe V-8	3,716	4,740	27,274
LeMans (wb 116.0; 2d-112.0)				
D29	Colonnade sdn 4d	3,838	3,612	15,065
D35	wgn 4d 2S V-8	4,401	4,555	3,988
D37	Colonnade sdn 2d	3,766	3,590	20,636
D45	wgn 4d 3S V-8	4,439	4,688	2,393
F37	Sport cpe	3,978	3,708	23,817
G35	Grnd wgn 4d 2S V-8	4,462	4,749	1,393
G29	Grand Col sdn 4d	3,896	4,157	4,906
G37	Grand Col sdn 2d	3,832	4,101	19,310
G45	Grnd wgn 4d 3S V-8	4,500	4,882	1,501
Grand Am (wb 116.0; 2d-112.0)				
H29	Colonnade sdn 4d	4,055	4,976	1,893
H37	Colonnade sdn 2d	4,008	4,887	8,786
Catalina (wb 123.4; wgn-127.0)				
L35	Safari wgn 4d 2S	4,933	5,149	3,964
L45	Safari wgn 4d 3S	5,000	5,295	4,992
L57	cpe	4,334	4,700	21,644
L69	sdn 4d	4,347	4,612	40,398
Bonneville (wb 123.4; wgn-127.0)				
P35	Grnd Saf wgn 4d 2S	5,035	5,433	2,568
P45	Grnd Saf wgn 4d 3S	5,090	5,580	4,752
P47	cpe	4,370	5,085	7,854
P49	htp sdn	4,503	5,153	12,641
Grand Ville Brougham (wb 123.4)				
R47	cpe	4,404	5,729	7,477
R49	htp sdn	4,558	5,896	15,686
R67	conv	4,520	5,858	4,519
	chassis	—	—	60
Grand Prix (wb 116.0)				
K57	cpe	4,032	5,296	86,582

1975 Engines	bore×stroke	bhp	availability
I-4, 140.0	3.50×3.63	78	S-Astre exc SJ
I-4, 140.0	3.50×3.63	87	S-Astre SJ; O-Astre
I-6, 250.0	3.88×3.53	105	S-Vent, LeM exc Saf, GA, Frbrd S87/T87
V-8, 260.0	3.50×3.39	110	O-Ventura
V-8, 350.0	3.88×3.75	145/165	O-Ventura
V-8, 350.0	3.88×3.75	155	S-LeM exc Saf; Frbrd S87/T87
V-8, 350.0	3.88×3.75	175	S-Frbrd U87; O-LeM exc Saf
V-8, 400.0	4.12×3.75	170	S-LeM Saf, GA, exc wgn; O-LeM, GP
V-8, 400.0	4.12×3.75	185	S-T/A, Cat wgn; GSaf, GV; O-LeM, GA, U87
V-8, 455.0	4.15×4.21	200	O-all exc Ast, Vent

1976

Astre (wb 97.0)		Wght	Price	Prod
C11	sdn 2d	2,439	3,064	18,143
C15	Safari wgn 2d	2,545	3,306	13,125
C77	htchbk cpe	2,505	3,179	19,116
Sunbird (wb 97.0)				
M27	cpe	2,653	3,431	52,031
Ventura (wb 111.1)				
Y17	htchbk cpe	3,428	3,503	6,428
Z17	SJ htchbk cpe	3,460	3,775	1,823
Y27	cpe	3,358	3,326	28,473
Z27	SJ cpe	3,370	3,612	4,815
Y69	sdn 4d	3,350	3,361	27,773
Z69	SJ sdn 4d	3,406	3,637	4,804
Firebird (wb 108.0)				
S87	cpe	3,473	3,906	21,209
T87	Esprit cpe	3,521	4,162	22,252
U87	Formula cpe V-8	3,625	4,566	20,613
W87	Trans Am cpe V-8	3,640	4,987	46,701
LeMans (wb 116.0; 2d-112.0)				
D29	sdn 4d	3,848	3,813	22,199
D37	sdn 2d	3,738	3,768	21,130
D35	Safari wgn 4d 2S V-8	4,336	4,687	3,988
D45	Safari wgn 4d 3S V-8	4,374	4,820	2,393
F37	Sport cpe	3,756	3,916	15,582
G29	Grand LeM sdn 4d	3,948	4,433	8,411
G37	Grand LeM sdn 2d	3,834	4,330	14,757
G35	Gd LeM Saf wgn 5d 2S V-8	4,389	4,928	1,393
G45	Gd LeM Saf wgn 5d 3S V-8	4,427	5,061	3,964
Catalina (wb 123.4; wgn-127.0)				
L35	Safari wgn 4d 2S	4,944	5,324	4,735
L45	Safari wgn 4d 3S	5,000	5,473	5,513
L57	cpe	4,256	4,844	15,262
L69	sdn 4d	4,276	4,767	47,235
Bonneville (wb 123.4; wgn-127.0)				
P35	Grnd Saf wgn 4d 2S	5,035	5,746	3,462
P45	Grnd Saf wgn 4d 3S	5,091	5,895	6,176
P47	cpe	4,308	5,246	9,189
P49	htp sdn 4d	4,460	5,312	14,942
R47	Brougham cpe	4,341	5,734	10,466
R49	Brougham htp sdn 4d	4,514	5,906	20,236
Grand Prix (wb 116.0)				
J57	cpe	4,048	4,798	110,814
—	LJ cpe*	—	—	29,045
K57	SJ cpe	4,052	5,223	88,232

* Option package ($625) for J57.

1976 Engines	bore×stroke	bhp	availability
I-4, 140.0	3.50×3.63	70	S-Astre, Sunbird
I-4, 140.0	3.50×3.63	84	O-Astre, Snbrd
V-6, 231.0	3.80×3.40	105	O-Sunbird
I-6, 250.0	3.88×3.53	110	S-Vent, LeM, Firebird exc T/A
V-8, 260.0	3.50×3.39	110	O-Vent, LeMans
V-8, 350.0	3.88×3.75	140/155	O-Ventura
V-8, 350.0	3.88×3.75	160	S-Frbrd exc T/A, GP exc SJ; O-LeMans
V-8, 350.0	3.88×3.75	165	O-LeM, Frbrd exc T/A, GP exc SJ
V-8, 400.0	4.12×3.75	170	S-all G LeMans, Cat, Bonn
V-8, 400.0	4.12×3.75	185	S-Frbrd T/A, GP SJ; O-LeM, Fbd, Cat, Bonn, GP
V-8, 455.0	4.15×4.21	200	S-Cat/Bonn wgns; O-LeM, Frbrd T/A, Cat, Bonn, GP

1977

Astre (wb 97.0)		Wght	Price	Prod
C11	sdn 2d	2,480	3,305	10,327
C15	Safari wgn 2d	2,608	3,595	10,341
C77	htchbk cpe	2,573	3,430	12,120
Ventura (wb 111.1)				
Y17	htchbk cpe	3,292	3,792	4,015
Y27	cpe	3,170	3,596	26,675
Y69	sdn 4d	3,210	3,650	27,089
Z17	SJ htchbk cpe	3,336	4,165	1,100
Z27	SJ cpe	3,248	3,985	3,418
Z69	SJ sdn 4d	3,278	4,012	4,339
Sunbird (wb 97.0) - 55,398 blt				
M07	Sport Hatch cpe	2,693	3,784	—
M27	cpe	2,662	3,659	—
Phoenix (wb 111.1)				
X27	cpe	3,283	4,075	10,489
X69	sdn 4d	3,331	4,122	13,639
Firebird (wb 108.0)				
S87	cpe	3,306	4,270	30,642
T87	Esprit cpe	3,354	4,551	34,548
U87	Formula cpe V-8	3,411	4,977	21,801
W87	Trans Am cpe V-8	3,526	5,456	68,745
LeMans (wb 116.0; 2d-112.0)				
D29	sdn 4d	3,680	4,105	23,060
D37	cpe	3,592	4,057	16,038
D35	wgn 4d 2S V-8	4,135	4,889	10,081
D35	wgn 4d 3S V-8	4,167	5,041	
F37	Sport cpe	3,600	4,216	12,277
G29	Grand LeM sdn 4d	3,782	4,742	5,584
G37	Grand LeMans cpe	3,630	4,614	7,581
G35	Gd LeM wgn 4d 2S V-8	4,179	5,144	5,393
G35	Gd LeM wgn 4d 3S V-8	4,211	5,296	
Catalina (wb 124.0; wgn-127.0)				
L37	cpe	3,521	5,053	14,752
L69	sdn 4d	3,555	5,050	46,926
L35	Safari wgn 4d 2S V-8	4,024	5,492	13,058
L35	Safari wgn 4d 3S V-8	4,056	5,657	
Bonneville (wb 124.0; wgn-127.0)				
N35	Grnd Saf wgn 4d 2S	4,066	5,772	18,304
N35	Grnd Saf wgn 4d 3S	4,098	5,937	
N37	cpe	3,579	5,411	37,817
N69	sdn 4d	3,616	5,457	13,697
Q37	Brougham cpe	3,617	5,897	15,901
Q69	Brougham sdn 4d	3,680	5,992	47,465
Grand Prix (wb 116.0)				
J57	cpe	3,804	5,120	168,247
K57	LJ cpe	3,815	5,483	66,741
H57	SJ cpe	3,976	5,753	53,442

1977 Engines	bore×stroke	bhp	availability
I-4, 140.0	3.50×3.63	84	S-Astre sdn
I-4, 151.0	4.00×3.00	87	S-Ast wgn/htch bk, Sbd; O-Astre sdn, Phnx, Vent
V-6, 231.0	3.80×3.40	105	S-Phnx, Vent, LeM, Frbrd exc T/A, Cat; O-Snbrd
V-8, 301.0	4.00×3.00	135	S-Vent, LeM, Frbrd exc T/A, Cat, Bonn, GP exc SJ
V-8, 305.0	3.74×3.48	145	S-Phnx, Vent, Frbrd exc T/A
V-8, 350.0	3.88×3.75	170	O-Phnx, Vent, LeM, Frbrd exc T/A, GP
V-8, 400.0	4.12×3.75	180/200	S-Frbrd T/A, GP SJ; O-LeM, Sbd, GP
V-8, 350.0	3.88×3.75	180	O-Catalina, Bonneville
V-8, 403.0	4.36×3.39	185	O-Firebird, Cat, Bonnville

1978

Sunbird (wb 97.0)		Wght	Price	Prod
E27	cpe	2,662	3,590	20,413
M07	Sport Hatch cpe	2,694	3,962	25,380
M15	Safari wgn 2d	2,610	3,741	8,424
M27	Sport Coupe	2,662	3,823	32,572
Phoenix (wb 111.1)				
Y17	htchbk cpe	3,250	4,103	3,252
Y27	cpe	3,167	3,907	26,143
Y69	sdn 4d	3,217	3,992	32,529
Z27	LJ cpe	3,276	4,399	6,210
Z69	LJ sdn 4d	3,325	4,484	8,393
Firebird (wb 108.0)				
S87	cpe	3,316	4,593	32,672
T87	Esprit cpe	3,346	4,897	36,926
U87	Formula cpe V-8	3,452	5,533	24,346
W87	Trans Am cpe V-8	3,511	5,889	93,341
LeMans (wb 108.1)				
D19	sdn 4d	3,108	4,512	22,728
D27	cpe	3,098	4,427	20,581
D35	Safari wgn 4d	3,298	4,980	15,714
F19	Grand LeM sdn 4d	3,158	4,915	21,252
F27	Grand Lemans cpe	3,130	4,801	18,433
F35	G LeM Safari wgn 4d	3,316	5,310	11,125
G19	Grnd Am sdn 4d V-8	3,239	5,634	2,841
G27	Grand Am cpe V-8	3,209	5,520	7,767
Catalina (wb 116.0)				
L35	Safari wgn 4d 2S V-8	3,976	6,011	12,819
L37	cpe	3,498	5,439	9,224
L69	sdn 4d	3,530	5,484	39,707
Bonneville (wb 116.0)				
N35	Grnd Saf wgn 4d 2S	4,002	6,319	13,847
N37	cpe	3,581	5,913	22,510
N69	sdn 4d	3,637	6,023	48,647
Q37	Brougham cpe	3,611	6,674	17,948
Q69	Brougham sdn 4d	3,667	6,784	36,192
Grand Prix (wb 108.1)				
J37	cpe V-6/V-8	3,162	4,880	127,253
K37	LJ cpe V-8	3,216	5,815	65,122
H37	SJ cpe V-8	3,229	6,088	36,069

1978 Engines	bore×stroke	bhp	availability
I-4, 151.0	4.00×3.00	85	S-Sbd; O-Phnx
V-6, 231.0	3.80×3.40	105	S-Phnx, LeM exc GA, Frbrd S87/T87, Cat, GP J37; O-Sbd
V-8, 301.0	4.00×3.00	140	S-LeM GA, Cat, Bonn, GP LJ
V-8, 301.0	4.00×3.00	150	O-LeM GA, GP SJ
V-8, 305.0	3.74×3.48	145	S-Frbrd Fmla; O-Sbd, Phnx, LeM, Firebird exc U/W87
V-8, 350.0	3.80×3.85	160	O-Phnx, Firebird
V-8, 350.0	3.80×3.85	155/170	O-Cat, Bonn
V-8, 400.0	4.12×3.75	180	S-Firebird T/A; O-Frbrd Fmla, Cat, Bonn
V-8, 403.0	4.36×3.38	185	O-Firebird, Cat, Bonnville

1979

Sunbird (wb 97.0)		Wght	Price	Prod
M07	cpe	2,642	3,899	24,221
M15	Safari spt wgn 2d	2,651	4,321	2,902
M27	Sport Coupe	2,774	4,148	30,087
E27	Sport Hatch cpe	2,774	4,248	40,560
Phoenix (wb 111.1)				
Y17	htchbk cpe	3,319	4,239	923
Y27	cpe	3,236	4,089	9,233
Y69	sdn 4d	3,286	4,189	10,565
Z27	LJ cpe	3,345	4,589	1,826
Z69	LJ sdn 4d	3,394	4,689	2,353
Firebird (wb 108.0)				
S87	cpe	3,294	5,260	38,642
T87	Esprit cpe	3,324	5,638	30,853
U87	Formula cpe V-8	3,460	6,564	24,851
W87	Trans Am cpe V-8	3,551	6,883	109,609
X87	T/A Limited Edition	3,551	10,620	7,500
LeMans (wb 108.1)				
D19	sdn 4d	3,082	5,134	26,958
D27	cpe	3,076	5,031	14,197
D35	Safari wgn	3,240	5,587	27,517
F19	Grand LeM sdn 4d	3,126	5,430	28,577
F27	Grand LeMans cpe	3,098	5,302	13,020
F35	Grand LeM Saf wgn	3,274	5,931	20,783
G19	Grand Am sdn 4d	3,124	5,529	1,865
G27	Grand Am cpe	3,120	5,530	4,021
Catalina (wb 116.0)				
L35	Safari wgn 4d 2S V-8	3,997	6,681	13,353
L35	Safari wgn 4d 3S V-8	4,029	6,864	
L37	cpe	3,534	6,020	5,410
L69	sdn 4d	3,566	6,076	28,121
Bonneville (wb 116.0)				
N35	Safari wgn 4d 2S	4,022	7,050	16,925
N35	Safari wgn 4d 3S	4,054	7,233	

Bonneville		Wght	Price	Prod
N37	cpe	3,616	6,593	34,127
Q37	Brougham cpe	3,659	7,395	39,094
N69	sdn 4d	3,672	6,718	71,906
Q69	Brougham sdn 4d	3,726	7,584	17,364
Grand Prix (wb 108.1)				
J37	cpe	3,166	5,454	124,815
K37	LJ cpe V-8	3,285	6,555	61,175
H37	SJ cpe V-8	3,349	6,814	24,060

1979 Engines	bore×stroke	bhp	availability
I-4, 151.0	4.00×3.00	85	S-Sunbird; O-Phoenix
V-6, 231.0	3.74×3.48	115	S-Phnx,Firebird S87/T87, LeM, GP exc SJ, Cat; O-Sunbird
V-8, 301.0	4.00×3.00	140	S-Bonn, GP exc SJ; O-Phoenix, LeM, Firebird S87/T87, Cat
V-8, 301.0	3.80×3.85	150	S-Frbrd Fmla, GP SJ; O-Phnx, Frbrd S87/T87, LeM, Cat, Bonn
V-8, 305.0	3.80×3.85	145	O-Sunbird, Phnx, LeM, Firebird S/T87
V-8, 350.0	3.88×3.75	160	O-Phnx, Firebird
V-8, 350.0	3.88×3.75	155/170	O-Cat, Bonn
V-8, 400.0	4.12×3.75	180	S-Frbrd T/A; O-Frbrd Fmla, Cat, Bonn
V-8, 400.0	4.12×3.75	220	O-Frbrd Fmla, T/A
V-8, 403.0	4.36×3.38	185	O-Frbrd, Fmla

Note: Because 350-cid V-8s from several GM divisions were used in the late 1970s, bore/stroke may differ from dimensions shown.

1980

Sunbird (wb 97.0)		Wght	Price	Prod
E07	htchbk cpe	2,651	4,808	27,910
M07	Sport Hatch cpe	2,657	4,731	25,042
E27	cpe	2,603	4,371	105,847
M27	Sport Coupe	2,609	4,620	29,180
Phoenix (wb 104.9)				
Y37	cpe	2,516	5,465	49,485
Y67	htchbk sdn 4d	2,558	5,656	72,875
Z37	LJ cpe	2,550	5,936	23,674
Z68	LJ htchbk sdn 4d	2,610	6,127	32,257
Firebird (wb 108.0)				
S87	cpe	3,306	5,948	29,811
T87	Esprit cpe	3,360	6,311	17,277
V87	Formula cpe V-8	3,410	7,256	9,356
W87	Trans Am cpe V-8	3,429	7,480	50,896
LeMans (wb 108.0)				
D19	sdn 4d	3,080	5,758	20,485
D27	cpe	3,064	5,652	9,110
D35	Safari wgn 4d	3,296	6,257	12,912
F19	Grand LeM sdn 4d	3,129	6,120	18,561
F27	Grand LeMans cpe	3,090	5,947	6,477
F35	Gd LeM Saf wgn 4d	3,328	6,682	14,832
G27	Grand Am cpe V-8	3,299	7,504	1,647
Catalina (wb 116.0)				
L35	Safari wgn 4d 2S V-8	3,939	7,362	2,931
L35	Safari wgn 4d 3S V-8	3,961	7,561	
L37	cpe	3,448	6,703	3,319
L69	sdn 4d	3,474	6,761	10,408
Bonneville (wb 116.0)				
N35	Safari wgn 4d 2S V-8	3,939	7,958	5,309
N35	Safari wgn 4d 3S V-8	3,981	8,157	
N37	cpe	3,486	7,034	16,771
R37	Brougham cpe	3,525	7,968	12,374
N69	sdn 4d	3,532	7,167	26,112
R69	Brougham sdn 4d	3,610	8,160	21,249
Grand Prix (wb 108.1)				
J37	cpe	3,201	6,621	72,659
K37	LJ cpe	3,342	7,000	34,968
H37	SJ cpe V-8	3,291	7,597	7,087

1980 Engines	bore ×stroke	bhp	availability
I-4, 151.0	4.00×3.00	90	S-Sunbird, Phnx
V-6, 173.0	3.50×3.00	115	O-Phoenix
V-6, 229.0	3.74×3.48	115	S-LeMans
V-6, 231.0	3.80×3.40	110/115	S-Frbrd S/T87, Cat/Bonn exc wgn, GP; O-Sbd
V-8, 265.0	3.75×3.00	120	O-LeMans
V-8, 301.0	4.00×3.00	140	S-GA, Frbrd V/W, Cat/Bonn wgn, GP SJ; O-LeM, Frbrd, other Cat/ Bonn, other GP
V-8T, 301.0	4.00×3.00	210	O-Frbrd V/W
V-8, 305.0	3.70×3.48	150	O-LeM, Frbrd S/T, GP
V-8D, 350.0	3.88×3.75	105	O-Cat, Bonn wgn/Brghm
V-8, 350.0	4.06×3.39	155/160	O-Cat, Bonn

1981

T1000 (wb 94.3; 4d-97.3)		Wght	Price	Prod
M08	htchbk sdn 2d	2,058	5,358	26,415
M68	htchbk sdn 4d	2,122	5,504	43,779
Phoenix (wb 104.9)				
Y37	cpe	2,477	6,307	31,829
Y68	htchbk sdn 4d	2,524	6,498	62,693
Z37	LJ cpe	2,519	6,778	11,975
Z68	LJ htchbk sdn 4d	2,579	6,969	21,372
Firebird (wb 108.2)				
S87	cpe	3,312	6,901	20,541
T87	Esprit cpe	—	7,645	10,938
V87	Formula cpe	—	7,854	5,927
W87	Trans Am cpe V-8	—	8,322	33,493
X87	Trans Am trb SE cpe	—	12,257	
LeMans (wb 108.1)				
D27	cpe	3,093	6,689	2,578
D69	sdn 4d	3,110	6,797	22,186
D69/Y83	LJ sdn 4d	—	7,100	
D35	Safari wgn 4d	3,313	7,316	13,358
F27	Grand LeMans cpe	3,121	6,976	1,819
F69	Grand LeM sdn 4d	3,166	7,153	25,241
F35	Gd LeM Saf wgn 4d	3,352	7,726	16,683
Catalina (wb 116.0)				
L35	Safari wgn 4d 2S V-8	3,924	8,666	2,912
L37	cpe	3,480	7,367	1,074
L69	sdn 4d	3,488	7,471	6,456
Bonneville (wb 116.0)				
N35	Safari wgn 4d 2S V-8	3,949	9,205	6,855
N37	cpe	3,502	7,649	14,940
R37	Brougham cpe	3,502	8,580	14,317
N69	sdn 4d	3,520	7,776	32,056
R69	Brougham sdn 4d	3,520	8,768	23,395
Grand Prix (wb 108.1)				
J37	cpe	3,226	7,424	74,786
K37	LJ cpe	3,255	7,803	46,842
P37	Brougham cpe	3,281	8,936	26,083

1981 Engines	bore×stroke	bhp	availability
I-4, 97.6	3.23×2.98	70	S-T1000
I-4, 151.0	4.00×3.00	84	S-Phoenix
V-6, 173.0	3.50×3.00	110	O-Phoenix
V-6, 231.0	3.80×3.40	110	S-Frbrd S/T, LeM, Cat, Bonn, GP
V-8, 265.0	3.75×3.00	120	S-Frbrd Frmla; O-Frbrd S/T, LeM, Cat, Bonn, GP
V-8, 301.0	4.00×3.00	135	O-Frbrd S/T, Cat, Bonn, LeM wgn
V-8, 301.0	4.00×3.00	150	S-Firebird T/A; O-Firebird
V-8T, 301.0	4.00×3.00	200	O-Frbrd Frmla, TA
V-8, 305.0	3.74×3.48	145	O-Frbrd Frmla, Trans Am
V-8, 307.0	3.80×3.39	145	S-Bonn/Cat wgn; O-Cat, Bonn
V-8D, 350.0	4.06×3.39	105	O-Cat, Bonn, Safari, GP

1982

T1000 (wb 94.3; 4d-97.3)		Wght	Price	Prod
L08	htchbk sdn 2d	2,034	5,782	21,053
L68	htchbk sdn 4d	2,098	5,945	23,416
J2000 (wb 101.2)				
B27	cpe	2,295	6,999	15,865
B77	htchbk cpe	2,353	7,275	21,219
B69	sdn 4d	2,347	7,203	29,920
B35	wgn 4d	2,418	7,448	16,014
E27	S cpe	2,295	6,734	2,722
E69	S sdn 4d	2,353	6,902	2,760
E35	S wgn 4d	2,355	7,208	1,245
C27	LE cpe	2,302	7,372	6,313
C69	LE sdn 4d	2,353	7,548	14,268
D77	SE htchbk cpe	2,362	7,654	8,533
Firebird (wb 101.0)				
S87	htchbk cpe I-4/V-6	—	7,996	41,683
S87	htchbk cpe V-8	—	8,291	
X87	S/E htchbk cpe V-6/V-8	—	9,624	21,719
W87	TA htchbk cpe V-8	—	9,658	52,960
Phoenix (wb 104.9)				
Y37	cpe	2,395	6,964	12,282
Y68	htchbk sdn 4d	2,503	7,172	24,026
Z37	LJ cpe	2,494	7,449	4,436
Z68	LJ htchbk sdn 4d	2,527	7,658	7,161
T37	SJ cpe V-6	2,562	8,723	994
T68	SJ htchbk sdn 4d V-6	2,612	8,884	268
6000 (wb 104.9)				
F27	cpe	2,531	8,729	6,505
F19	sdn 4d	2,676	8,890	17,751
G27	LE cpe	2,636	9,097	7,025
G19	LE sdn 4d	2,682	9,258	26,253
Bonneville G (wb 108.1)				
N69	sdn 4d	3,203	8,527	44,378
R69	Brougham sdn 4d	3,213	8,985	20,035
N35	wgn 4d	3,380	8,694	16,100
Grand Prix (wb 108.1)				
J37	cpe	3,226	8,333	37,672
K37	LJ cpe	3,248	8,788	29,726
P37	Brougham cpe	3,264	9,209	12,969

1982 Engines	bore×stroke	bhp	availability
I-4, 97.6	3.23×2.98	70	S-T1000
I-4, 112.0	3.50×2.91	88	S-J2000 (ohc)
I-4, 151.0	4.00×3.00	90	S-Phnx exc SJ, Firebird, 6000
V-6, 173.0	3.50×3.00	105	S-Frbrd S/E; O-Firebird
V-6, 173.0	3.50×3.00	112	O-Phoenix exc SJ, 6000
V-6, 173.0	3.50×3.00	135	O-Phoenix SJ
V-6, 231.0	3.80×3.40	110	S-Bonn, Gd Prix
V-6, 252.0	3.96×3.40	125	O-Bonn, Gd Prix
V-6D, 262.0	4.06 × 3.39	85	O-6000, Bonn
V-8, 305.0	3.74 × 3.48	145	S-Frbrd TA; O-Firebird
V-8, 305.0	3.74 × 3.48	165	O-Frbrd TA
V-8D, 350.0	4.06 × 3.39	105	O-Bonn, Gd Prix

1983

1000 (wb 94.3; 4d-97.3)		Wght	Price	Prod
L08	htchbk sdn 2d	2,081	5,582	13,171
L68	htchbk sdn 4d	2,130	5,785	12,806
2000 (wb 101.2)				
B27	cpe	2,353	6,499	22,063
B77	htchbk cpe	2,413	6,809	7,331
B69	sdn 4d	2,412	6,621	24,833
B35	wgn 4d	2,487	6,926	10,214
C27	LE cpe	2,385	7,020	2,690
C67	LE conv cpe	—	—	626
C69	LE sdn 4d	2,436	7,194	6,957
C35	LE wgn 4d	2,517	7,497	1,780
D77	SE htchbk cpe	2,470	8,393	1,835
Firebird (wb 101.0)				
S87	htchbk cpe I-4/V-6	2,937	8,399	32,020
S87	htchbk cpe V-8	3,117	8,774	
X87	S/E hbk cpe V-6/V-8	3,055	10,322	10,934
W87	TA htchbk cpe V-8	3,107	10,396	31,930
Phoenix (wb 104.9)				
Y37	cpe	2,512	6,942	7,205
Y68	htchbk sdn 4d	2,569	7,087	13,377
Z37	LJ cpe	2,553	7,489	2,251

Phoenix		Wght	Price	Prod
Z68	LJ htchbk sdn 4d	2,601	7,698	3,635
T37	SJ cpe V-6	2,581	8,861	853
T68	SJ htchbk sdn 4d V-6	2,642	8,948	172
6000 (wb 104.9)				
F27	cpe	2,719	8,399	3,524
F19	sdn 4d	2,757	8,569	20,267
G27	LE cpe	2,732	8,837	4,278
G19	LE sdn 4d	2,771	8,984	33,676
H19	STE sdn 4d V-6	2,823	13,572	6,719
Bonneville (wb 108.1)				
N69	sdn 4d	3,252	8,899	47,003
R69	Brougham sdn 4d	3,248	9,399	19,335
N35	wgn 4d	3,313	9,112	17,551
Grand Prix (wb 108.1)				
J37	cpe	3,261	8,698	41,511
K37	LJ cpe	—	9,166	33,785
P37	Brougham cpe	—	9,781	10,502
Parisienne (wb 115.9)				
L69	sdn 4d	3,409	9,609	9,279
T69	Brougham sdn 4d	—	9,779	5,139
L35	wgn 4d V-8	3,963	9,927	3,027

1983 Engines	bore×stroke	bhp	availability
I-4, 97.6	3.23×2.98	65	S-1000
I-4, 109.0	3.34×3.13	84	S-2000 (ohc)
I-4D, 111.0	3.31×3.23	51	O-1000
I-4, 121.0	3.50×3.15	88	O-2000 (ohv)
I-4, 151.0	4.00×3.00	90	S-Phnx, Frbrd, 6000
V-6, 173.0	3.50×3.00	107/112	O-Phnx, Frbrd S87, 6000
V-6, 173.0	3.50×3.00	125/135	S-Phnx SJ, Frbrd S/E, 6000 STE
V-6, 231.0	3.80×3.40	110	S-Bonn, GP, Parisienne
V-6D, 262.0	4.06×3.39	85	O-6000
V-8, 305.0	3.74×3.48	150	S-Frbrd T/A; O-other Frbrd, Bonn, GP
V-8, 305.0	3.74×3.48	175	O-Firebird TA
V-8D, 350.0	4.06×3.39	105	O-Bonn, GP, Paris

1984

Fiero (wb 93.4)		Wght	Price	Prod
E37	cpe	2,437	7,999	7,099
M37	Sport Coupe	2,465	8,499	62,070
F37	SE cpe	2,465	9,599	67,671
1000 (wb 94.3; 4d-97.3)				
L08	htchbk sdn 2d	2,078	5,621	19,628
L68	htchbk sdn 4d	2,138	5,824	17,118
2000 Sunbird (wb 101.2)				
B27	cpe	2,347	6,675	53,070
B77	htchbk cpe	2,424	6,995	12,245
B69	sdn 4d	2,406	6,799	59,312
B35	wgn 4d	2,483	7,115	15,143
C27	LE cpe	2,384	7,333	5,189
C67	LE conv cpe	2,514	11,749	5,458
C69	LE sdn 4d	2,436	7,499	11,183
C35	LE wgn 4d	2,504	7,819	2,011
D27	SE cpe	2,469	9,019	2,141
D77	SE htchbk cpe	2,477	9,489	2,165
D69	SE sdn 4d	2,528	9,185	1,373
Firebird (wb 101.0)				
S87	htchbk cpe I-4/V-6	2,955	8,349	62,621
S87	htchbk cpe V-8	3,157	9,024	
X87	S/E hbk cpe V-6/V-8	3,072	10,649	10,309
W87	TA htchbk cpe V-8	3,189	10,699	55,374
Phoenix (wb 104.9)				
Y37	cpe	2,518	7,090	7,461
Y68	htchbk sdn 4d	2,587	7,165	11,545
Z37	LE cpe	2,578	7,683	1,357
Z68	LE htchbk sdn 4d	2,615	7,816	1,783
T37	SE cpe V-6	2,681	9,071	701
6000 (wb 104.9)				
F27	cpe	2,707	8,699	4,171
F19	sdn 4d	2,748	8,873	35,202
G27	LE cpe	2,731	9,142	4,731
G19	LE sdn 4d	2,772	9,292	41,218
F35	wgn 4d	2,909	9,221	8,423

6000		Wght	Price	Prod
G35	LE wgn 4d	2,924	9,612	9,211
H19	STE sdn 4d V-6	2,990	14,437	19,236
Bonneville (wb 108.1)				
N69	sdn 4d	3,213	9,131	40,908
R69	Brougham sdn 4d	3,247	9,835	15,030
S69	LE sdn 4d	3,221	9,358	17,451
Grand Prix (wb 108.1)				
J37	cpe	3,258	9,145	36,893
K37	LE cpe	3,278	9,624	31,037
P37	Brougham cpe	3,319	10,299	9,514
Parisienne (wb 115.9)				
L69	sdn 4d	3,535	9,881	18,713
T69	Brougham sdn 4d	3,575	10,281	25,212
L35	wgn 4d V-8	4,080	10,394	16,599

1984 Engines	bore×stroke	bhp	availability
I-4, 97.6	3.23×2.98	65	S-1000
I-4, 109.0	3.34×3.13	84	S-2000 (ohc)
I-4T, 109.0	3.34×3.13	150	O-2000 (ohc)
I-4, 121.0	3.50×3.15	88	O-2000 (ohv)
I-4, 151.0	4.00×3.00	92	S-Fiero, Phnx, Frbrd, 6000
V-6, 173.0	3.50×3.00	107/112	O-Phnx, Frbrd, 6000
V-6, 173.0	3.50×3.00	125/130	S-Phnx SE, Frbrd S/E, 6000 STE; O-Phnx
V-6, 231.0	3.80×3.40	110	S-Bonn, GP, Parisienne
V-6D, 262.0	4.06×3.39	85	O-6000
V-8, 305.0	3.74×3.48	150	S-TA, Paris wgn; O-other Frbrd, Bonn, GP, Paris
V-8, 305.0	3.74×3.48	190	O-Firebird TA
V-8D, 350.0	4.06×3.39	105	O-Bonn, GP, Prs

1985

Fiero (wb 93.4)		Wght	Price	Prod
E37	cpe	2,454	8,495	5,280
M37	Sport Coupe	2,500	8,995	23,823
F37	SE cpe	2,525	9,995	24,734
G37	GT cpe	—	11,795	22,534
1000 (wb 94.3; 4d-97.3)				
L08	htchbk sdn 2d	2,083	5,445	8,647
L68	htchbk sdn 4d	2,142	5,695	8,216
Sunbird (wb 101.2)				
B27	cpe	2,316	6,875	39,721
B77	htchbk cpe	2,392	7,215	5,235
B69	sdn 4d	2,372	6,995	44,553
B35	wgn 4d	2,446	7,335	7,371
C27	LE cpe	2,349	7,555	3,424
C67	LE conv cpe	2,534	12,035	2,114
C69	LE sdn 4d	2,435	7,725	6,287
C35	LE wgn 4d	2,468	8,055	1,036
D27	SE cpe I-4T	2,422	9,295	965
D77	SE htchbk cpe I-4T	2,500	9,765	535
D69	SE sdn 4d I-4T	2,479	9,455	658
Firebird (wb 101.0)				
S87	htchbk cpe I-4/V-6	2,933	8,763	46,644
S87	htchbk cpe V-8	3,135	9,357	
X87	SE hbk cpe V-6/V-8	3,124	11,063	5,208
W87	TA htchbk cpe V-8	3,213	11,113	44,028
Grand Am (wb 103.4)				
E27	cpe	2,575	7,995	40,275
V27	LE cpe	2,595	8,485	42,269
6000 (wb 104.9)				
F27	cpe	2,766	8,899	4,493
F19	sdn 4d	2,809	9,079	54,424
G27	LE cpe	2,777	9,385	3,777
G19	LE sdn 4d	2,821	9,539	54,284
F35	wgn 4d	2,931	9,435	8,491
G35	LE wgn 4d	2,937	9,869	8,025
H19	STE sdn 4d V-6	3,065	14,829	22,728
Bonneville (wb 108.1)				
N69	sdn 4d	3,267	9,549	34,466
R69	Brougham sdn 4d	3,308	10,280	8,425
S69	LE sdn 4d	3,281	9,789	10,503
Grand Prix (wb 108.1)				
J37	cpe	3,276	9,569	30,365

Grand Prix		Wght	Price	Prod
K37	LE cpe	3,296	10,049	21,195
P37	Brougham cpe	3,314	10,749	8,223
Parisienne (wb 116.0)				
I69	sdn 4d	3,573	10,395	25,638
T69	Brougham sdn 4d	3,586	11,125	38,831
L35	wgn 4d V-8	4,095	10,945	17,638

1985 Engines	bore×stroke	bhp	availability
I-4, 97.6	3.23×2.98	65	S-1000
I-4, 109.0	3.34×3.13	82	S-Sunbird (ohc)
I-4T, 109.0	3.34×3.13	150	S-Snbrd SE (ohc)
I-4, 121.0	3.50×3.15	88	O-Sunbird (ohv)
I-4, 151.0	4.00×3.00	88/92	S-Fiero, G Am, Firebird, 6000 exc STE
V-6, 173.0	3.50×3.00	112	O-6000 exc STE
V-6, 173.0	3.50×3.00	125/135	S-Firebird S/E, 6000 STE; O-Fiero, other Firebird, 6000
V-6, 181.0	3.80×2.70	125	O-Grand Am
V-6, 231.0	3.80×3.40	110	S-Bonn, Gd Prix
V-6, 262.0	4.00×3.48	130	S-Parisienne
V-6D, 262.0	4.06×3.39	85	O-6000
V-8, 305.0 O-other	3.74×3.48	165	S-TA, Paris wgn; Frbrd, Bonn, GP, Paris
V-8, 305.0	3.74×3.48	190/205	O-Firebird TA
V-8D, 350.0	4.06×3.39	105	O-Parisienne

1986

Fiero (wb 93.2)		Wght	Price	Prod
E37	cpe I-4	2,490	8,949	9,143
M37	Sport Coupe I-4	2,504	9,449	24,866
F37	SE cpe I-4/V-6	2,531	10,595	32,305
G97	GT fstbk cpe V-6	2,696	12,875	17,660
1000 (wb 94.3; 4d-97.3)				
L08	htchbk sdn 2d	2,076	5,749	12,266
L68	htchbk sdn 4d	2,135	5,969	9,423
Sunbird (wb 101.2)				
B69	sdn 4d	2,383	7,495	60,080
B35	wgn 4d	2,456	7,879	7,445
D27	SE cpe	2,365	7,469	37,526
D77	SE htchbk cpe	2,405	7,829	3,822
D67	SE conv cpe	2,549	12,779	1,598
U27	GT cpe	2,488	9,459	18,118
U67	GT conv cpe	2,645	14,399	1,268
U77	GT htchbk cpe	2,564	9,819	2,442
U69	GT sdn 4d	2,540	9,499	2,802
Firebird (wb 101.0)				
S87	htchbk cpe I-4/V-6	2,909	9,279	59,334
S87	htchbk cpe V-8	2,995	10,029	
X87	SE hbk cpe V-6/V-8	2,991	11,995	2,259
W87	TA htchbk cpe V-8	3,227	12,395	48,870
Grand Am (wb 103.4)				
E27	cpe	2,529	8,549	69,545
E69	sdn 4d	2,605	8,749	49,166
V27	LE cpe	2,565	9,079	48,530
V69	LE sdn 4d	2,631	9,279	31,790
W27	SE cpe V-6	2,686	11,499	15,506
W69	SE sdn 4d V-6	2,756	11,749	8,957
6000 (wb 104.9)				
F27	cpe	2,781	9,549	4,739
F19	sdn 4d	2,817	9,729	81,531
G27	LE cpe	2,799	10,049	4,803
G19	LE sdn 4d	2,836	10,195	67,697
E19	SE sdn 4d V-6	2,914	11,179	7,348
F35	wgn 4d	2,954	10,095	10,094
G35	LE wgn 4d	2,972	10,579	7,556
E35	SE wgn 4d V-6	3,067	11,825	1,308
H19	STE sdn 4d V-6	3,122	15,949	26,299
Bonneville (wb 108.1)				
N69	sdn 4d	3,276	10,249	27,801
R69	Brougham sdn 4d	3,305	11,079	5,941
S69	LE sdn 4d	3,285	10,529	7,179
Grand Prix (wb 108.1)				
J37	cpe	3,283	10,259	21,668
J37	2+2 cpe V-8	3,530	18,214	1,118
K37	LE cpe	3,305	10,795	13,918
P37	Brougham cpe	3,328	11,579	4,798

Parisienne (wb 116.0)		Wght	Price	Prod
L69	sdn 4d	3,639	11,169	27,078
T69	Brougham sdn 4d	3,667	11,949	43,540
L35	wgn 4d V-8	4,102	11,779	14,464

1986 Engines	bore×stroke	bhp	availability
I-4, 97.6	3.23×2.98	65	S-1000
I-4, 109.0	3.34×3.13	84	S-Sunbird (ohc)
I-4T, 109.0	3.34×3.13	150	S-Snbrd GT (ohc)
I-4, 151.0	4.00×3.00	88/92	S-Fiero, GA, Frbrd, 6000
V-6, 173.0	3.50×3.00	112	O-6000
V-6, 173.0	3.50×3.00	130/140	S-Firebird SE, 6000 STE, Fiero GT; O-Fiero SE, Firebird
V-6, 181.0	3.80×2.70	125	S-Grand Am SE; O-other Gd Am
V-6, 231.0	3.80×3.40	110	S-Bonn, Grd Prx
V-6, 262.0	4.00×3.48	130	S-Parisienne
V-8, 305.0	3.74×3.48	150/165	S-TA, Paris wgn; O-Frbrd, Bonn, GP, Parisienne
V-8, 305.0	3.74×3.48	190/205	O-Firebird TA

1987

Fiero (wb 93.4)		Wght	Price	Prod
E37	cpe I-4	2,542	8,299	23,603
M37	Sport Coupe I-4	2,546	9,989	3,135
F37	SE cpe I-4/V-6	2,567	11,239	3,875
G97	GT fstbk cpe V-6	2,708	13,489	15,968
1000 (wb 94.3; 4d-97.3)				
L08	htchbk sdn 2d	2,114	5,959	3,246
L68	htchbk sdn 4d	2,173	6,099	2,382
Sunbird (wb 101.2)				
B69	sdn 4d	2,366	7,999	41,248
B35	wgn 4d	2,427	8,529	4,637
D27	SE cpe	2,339	7,979	41,825
D77	SE htchbk cpe	2,385	8,499	1,069
D67	SE conv cpe	2,511	13,799	2,470
U27	GT cpe	2,412	10,299	12,060
U67	GT conv cpe	2,551	15,569	1,505
U77	GT htchbk cpe	2,427	10,699	415
U69	GT sdn 4d	2,427	10,349	1,540
Firebird (wb 101.0)				
S87	htchbk cpe V-6/V-8	3,186	10,359	42,558
S87/W66	Frmla hbk cpe V-8	3,350	11,829	13,164
W87	TA htchbk cpe V-8	3,274	13,259	32,890
W87/Y84	T/A GTA hbk cpe V-8	3,435	14,104	—
Grand Am (wb 103.4)				
E27	cpe	2,525	9,299	90,146
E69	sdn 4d	2,598	9,499	52,177
V27	LE cpe	2,561	9,999	47,414
V69	LE sdn 4d	2,623	10,199	21,196
W27	SE cpe	2,641	12,659	23,142
W69	SE sdn 4d	2,719	12,899	10,653
6000 (wb 104.9)				
F27	cpe	2,764	10,499	3,161
F19	sdn 4d	2,797	10,499	72,645
G19	LE sdn 4d	2,731	11,099	33,939
E19	S/E sdn 4d V-6	2,986	12,089	6,649
F35	wgn 4d	2,943	10,095	7,740
G35	LE wgn 4d	2,867	11,499	3,797
E35	S/E wgn 4d V-6	3,162	13,049	1,756
H19	STE sdn 4d V-6	3,101	18,099	8,802
Grand Prix (wb 108.1)				
J37	cpe	3,286	11,069	8,599
K37	LE cpe	3,306	11,799	6,226
P37	Brougham cpe	3,308	12,519	1,717
Bonneville (wb 110.8)				
X69	sdn 4d	3,316	13,399	53,912
Z69	LE sdn 4d	3,355	14,866	69,904
Safari (wb 116.0)				
L35	Brghm wgn 4d V-8	4,109	13,959	13,154

1987 Engines	bore×stroke	bhp	availability
I-4, 97.6	3.23×2.98	65	S-1000
I-4, 121.0	3.39×3.39	96	S-Sunbird (ohc)
I-4T, 121.0	3.39×3.39	165	O-Sunbird SE/GT, Grand Am SE (ohc)
I-4, 151.0	4.00×3.00	98	S-Fiero exc GT, Grand Am, 6000
V-6, 173.0	3.50×3.00	125/135	S-Fiero GT, 6000 S/E, 6000 STE; O-Fiero SE, Frbrd, other 6000
V-6, 181.0	3.80×2.70	125	S-Grand Am SE; O-other Gd Am
V-6, 231.0	3.80×3.40	110	S-GP exc 2+2
V-6, 231.0	3.80×3.40	150	S-Bonneville
V-6, 262.0	4.00×3.48	140	O-Grand Prix
V-8, 305.0	3.74×3.48	140	S-Safari wgn
V-8, 305.0	3.74×3.48	150	S-Gd Prix 2+2; O-other GP
V-8, 305.0	3.74×3.48	155	O-Firebird
V-8, 305.0	3.74×3.48	165/205	O-Firebird TA
V-8, 350.0	4.00×3.48	210	S-Frbrd GTA; O-Frbrd Frm, T/A

1988

Fiero (wb 93.4) - 26,402 blt		Wght	Price	Prod
E37	cpe I-4	2,597	8,999	—
E37/W66	Form cpe V-6	—	10,999	—
G97	GT fstbk cpe V-6	2,783	13,999	—
Sunbird (wb 101.2) - 93,694 built				
B69	sdn 4d	2,366	8,499	—
D37	SE cpe	2,339	8,599	—
D69	SE sdn 4d	2,427	8,799	—
D35	SE wgn 4d	2,427	9,399	—
U37	GT cpe I-4T	2,412	10,899	—
U67	GT conv cpe I-4T	2,551	16,199	—
Firebird (wb 101.0) - 62,467 built				
S87	htchbk cpe V-6/V-8	3,102	10,999	—
S87/W66	Form htchbk cpe V-8	—	11,999	—
W87	TA htchbk cpe V-8	3,355	13,999	—
W87/Y84	T/A GTA hbk cpe V-8	—	19,299	—
Grand Am (wb 103.4) - 235,371 built				
E27	cpe	2,493	9,869	—
E69	sdn 4d	2,568	10,069	—
Y27	LE cpe	2,519	10,569	—
Y69	LE sdn 4d	2,591	10,769	—
W27	SE cpe I-4T	2,713	12,869	—
W69	SE sdn 4d I-4T	2,781	13,099	—
6000 (wb 104.9) - 61,446 built				
F19	sdn 4d	2,828	11,999	—
G19	LE sdn 4d	2,846	11,839	—
E19	S/E sdn 4d V-6	2,888	12,739	—
F35	wgn 4d	2,964	11,639	—
G35	LE wgn 4d	2,982	12,299	—
E35	S/E wgn 4d V-6	3,041	13,639	—
H19	STE sdn 4d V-6	3,109	18,699	—
—	STE AWD sdn 4d V-6	3,409	—	—
Grand Prix (wb 107.6) - 86,357 built				
J37	cpe	3,038	12,539	—
K37	LE cpe	3,056	13,239	—
P37	SE cpe	3,113	15,249	—
Bonneville (wb 110.8) - 108,580 built				
X69	LE sdn 4d	3,275	14,099	—
Z69	SE sdn 4d	3,341	16,299	—
Y69	SSE sdn 4d	3,481	21,879	—
Safari (wb 116.0) - 6,397 built				
L35	wgn 4d V-8	4,109	14,519	—

1988 Engines	bore×stroke	bhp	availability
I-4, 121.0	3.39×3.39	96	S-Sunbird (ohc)
I-4T, 121.0	3.39×3.39	165	S-Sunbird GT, G Am SE; O-GA LE (ohc)
I-4, 138.0	3.62×3.35	150	O-GA (dohc)
I-4, 151.0	4.00×3.00	98	S-Fiero, GA, 6000
V-6, 173.0	3.50×3.00	125/130	S-6000 S/E, STE, GP; O-6000
V-6, 173.0	3.50×3.00	135	S-Fiero Frmla/GT, Firebird base
V-6, 191.0	3.50×3.31	135	S-6000 STE AWD
V-6, 231.0	3.80×3.40	150	S-Bonneville LE
V-6, 231.0	3.00×3.40	165	S-Bonneville SE/SSE
V-8, 305.0	3.74×3.48	140	S-Safari wgn
V-8, 305.0	3.74×3.48	170	S-Firebird TA/ Frmla; O-Frbrd
V-8, 305.0	3.74×3.48	190/215	O-Frbrd TA/ Formula
V-8, 350.0	4.00×3.48	225/235	S-Frbrd GTA; O-Formula, T/A

1989

Sunbird (wb 101.2) - 60,019 blt		Wght	Price	Prod
B37	LE cpe	2,418	8,849	—
B69	LE sdn 4d	2,433	8,949	—
D37	SE cpe	2,376	9,099	—
U37	GT cpe I-4T	2,422	11,399	—
U67	GT conv cpe I-4T	2,577	16,899	—
Firebird (wb 101.0)				
S87	htchbk cpe V-6/V-8	3,083	11,999	49,048 (S87 and S87/W66)
S87/W66	Form hbk cpe V-8	3,318	13,949	
W87	TA htchbk cpe V-8	3,337	15,999	15,358* (W87 and W87/Y84)
W87/Y84	T/A hbk GTA cpe V-8	3,486	20,339	
Grand Am (wb 103.4)				
E27	LE cpe	2,508	10,469	137,121
E69	LE sdn 4d	2,592	10,669	87,385
W27	SE cpe I-4T	2,739	13,599	13,410
W69	SE sdn 4d I-4T	2,826	13,799	8,502
6000 (wb 104.9)				
F69	LE sdn 4d	2,760	11,969	83,014
J69	S/E sdn 4d V-6	2,762	15,399	7,539
F35	LE wgn 4d	2,897	13,769	7,790
J35	S/E wgn 4d V-6	2,899	16,699	887
H69	STE AWD sdn 4d V-6	3,036	22,599	1,376
Grand Prix (wb 107.5) - 136,748 built**				
J37	cpe	3,167	13,899	—
K37	LE cpe	3,188	14,849	—
P37	SE cpe	3,217	15,999	—
Bonneville (wb 110.8)				
X69	LE sdn 4d	3,275	14,829	71,339
Z69	SE sdn 4d	2,327	17,199	20,238
Y69	SSE sdn 4d	3,481	22,899	17,076
Safari (wb 116.0) - 5,146 built				
L35	wgn 4d V-8	4,225	15,659	—

* Includes 1,555 20th Anniversary Trans Ams

** Includes approx. 2,000 McLaren Turbo coupes

1989 Engines	bore×stroke	bhp	availability
I-4, 121.0	3.39×3.39	96	S-Sunbird (ohc)
I-4T, 121.0	3.39×3.39	165	S-Sbd GT, GA SE; O-Sunbird SE (ohc)
I-4, 138.0	3.62×3.35	150	O-GA, (dohc)
I-4, 138.0	3.62×3.35	185	O-late GA (dohc)
I-4,151.0	4.00 × 3.00	110	S-GA LE, 6000
V-6, 173.0	3.50 × 3.00	130	S-6000 S/E, GP; O-6000
V-6, 173.0	3.50 × 3.00	135	S-Firebird
V-6, 191.0	3.50 × 3.31	140	S-6000 STE AWD, late GP
V-6T, 191.0	3.50 × 3.31	200	S-McLaren Turbo GP
V-6, 231.0	3.00 × 3.40	165	S-Bonneville
V-6T, 231.0	3.00 × 3.40	250	S-20th An TA
V-8, 305.0	3.74 × 3.48	140	S-Safari wgn
V-8, 305.0	3.74 × 3.48	170	S-TA/Formula; O-Firebird
V-8, 305.0	3.74 × 3.48	215	O-Firebird TA/ Formula
V-8, 350.0	4.00 × 3.48	225	S-Frbrd GTA; O-Formula T/A

1990

Sunbird (wb 101.2)		Wght	Price	Prod
B37	LE cpe	2,420	8,799	56,151
B69	LE sdn 4d	2,487	8,899	57,911
D37	SE cpe	—	9,204	12,860
U37	GT cpe I-4T	—	11,724	4,813
U67	LE conv cpe	2,662	13,934	13,197
Firebird (wb 101.0)				
S87	htchbk cpe V-6	3,210	11,320	18,046 (S87 and S87/W66)
S87/W66	Form hbk cpe V-8	—	14,610	
W87	TA htchbk cpe V-8	—	16,510	2,507 (W87 and W87/Y84)
W87/Y84	T/A GTA hbk cpe V-8	—	23,320	

Grand Am (wb 103.4)		Wght	Price	Prod
E27	LE cpe	2,508	10,544	104,950
E69	LE sdn 4d	2,592	10,744	80,815
W27	SE cpe	2,739	14,894	6,877
W69	SE sdn 4d	2,826	15,194	4,378
6000 (wb 104.9)				
F69	LE sdn 4d	2,843	12,149	55,290
NA	LE wgn 4d	3,162	15,309	5,086
J69	S/E sdn 4d V-6	—	16,909	5,599
J35	S/E wgn 4d V-6	—	18,509	423
Grand Prix (wb 107.5)				
K37	LE cpe	3,186	14,564	49,492
NA	LE sdn 4d	3,250	14,564	56,410
P37	SE cpe	—	17,684	16,398
NA	Turbo cpe	—	26,016	
NA	STE sdn 4d	—	18,539	5,773
NA	STE Turbo sdn 4d	—	23,775	
Bonneville (wb 110.8)				
X69	LE sdn 4d	3,325	15,744	55,926
Z69	SE sdn 4d	—	19,144	13,064
009	SSE sdn 4d	—	23,994	16,854

1990 Engines	bore×stroke	bhp	availability
I-4, 121.0	3.39×3.39	96	S-Sunbird (ohc)
I-4T, 121.0	3.39×3.39	165	S-Sunbird GT; O-Snbrd conv (ohc)
I-4, 138.0	3.62×3.35	160	S-Grd Prix LE; O-GA (dohc)
I-4, 138.0	3.62×3.35	180	S-GA SE (dohc)
I-4, 151.0	4.00×3.00	110	S-GA LE, 6000
V-6, 191.0	3.50×3.31	140	S-Firebird, Gd Prix SE/STE, 6000 S/E; O-6000 LE, GP LE
V-6T, 191.0	3.50 × 3.31	205	S-Gd Prix Turbo
V-6, 231.0	3.00 × 3.40	165	S-Bonneville
V-8, 305.0	3.74 × 3.48	170	S-Frbrd Frm; O-Firebird
V-8, 305.0	3.74 × 3.48	225	S-Firebird TA; O-Frbrd Frm
V-8, 350.0	4.00 × 3.48	235	S-Frbrd GTA; O-Frbrd Frm, T/A

1991

Sunbird (wb 101.2) - 155,429 blt		Wght	Price	Prod
	cpe 2d	2,570	8,684	—
	sdn 4d	2,592	8,784	—
C37	LE cpe 2d	2,484	9,444	—
C69	LE sdn 4d	2,502	9,544	—
B37	SE cpe 2d	2,484	10,694	—
D37	GT cpe 2d	2,502	12,444	—
B67	LE conv cpe 2d	2,775	14,414	—
Firebird (wb 101.0)—50,247 built				
S87	htchbk cpe	3,121	12,690	—
S67	conv cpe 2d	3,280	19,159	—
S87/W66	Form hbk cpe	3,370	15,530	—
W87	Trans Am htchbk cpe	3,343	17,530	—
W67	Trans Am conv cpe	3,441	22,980	—
W87/Y84	GTA htchbk cpe	3,456	24,530	—
Grand Am (wb 103.4) - 178,150 built				
	cpe 2d	2,508	10,174	—
	sdn 4d	2,592	10,374	—
E27	LE cpe 2d	2,728	11,124	—
E69	LE sdn 4d	2,777	11,324	—
W27	SE cpe 2d	2,804	16,344	—
W69	SE sdn 4d	2,846	16,544	—
6000 (wb 104.9) - 34,721 built				
F69	LE sdn 4d	2,843	12,999	—
J69	S/E sdn 4d	—	18,399	—
F35	LE wgn 4d	3,162	16,699	—
Grand Prix (wb 107.5) - 101,211 built				
H19	LE sdn 4d	3,188	14,294	—
J37	SE cpe 2d	3,252	14,894	—
J19	SE sdn 4d	3,282	15,284	—
P37	GT cpe 2d	3,390	19,154	—
T19	STE sdn 4d	3,434	19,994	—
Bonneville (wb 110.8) - 46,603 built				
X69	LE sdn 4d	3,323	16,834	—
Z69	SE sdn 4d	3,362	20,464	—
009	SSE sdn 4d	3,507	25,264	—

1991 Engines	bore×stroke	bhp	availability
I-4, 121.0	3.38×3.38	96	S-Sunbird (ohc)
I-4, 138.0	3.63×3.35	160	S-GP; O-GA (dohc)
I-4, 138.0	3.63×3.35	180	O-GA (dohc)
I-4, 151.0	4.00×3.00	110	S-GA, 6000
V-6, 191.0	3.50×3.31	140	S-Frbrd, Snbrd GT; O-Snbrd, 6000, Gd Prix
V-6, 207.0	3.62×3.31	200	O-GP (dohc)
V-6, 207.0	3.62×3.31	210	O-GP (dohc)
V-6, 231.0	3.80×3.40	165	S-Bonneville
V-8, 305.0	3.74×3.48	170	S-Frbrd Fmla; O-Firebird
V-8, 305.0	3.74×3.48	230	S-Firebird T/A; O-Frbrd, Frmla
V-8, 350.0	4.00×3.48	240	S-Frbrd GTA; O-T/A, Formula

1992

Sunbird (wb 101.2) - 100,402 blt		Wght	Price	Prod
C37	LE cpe	2,484	9,620	—
C69	LE sdn 4d	2,502	9,720	—
B37	SE cpe	2,484	10,380	—
B69	SE sdn 4d	2,502	10,480	—
B67	SE conv cpe	2,694	15,345	—
D37	GT cpe	2,682	12,820	—
Firebird (wb 101.0) - 52,405 built (est.)				
S87	htchbk cpe	3,121	12,505	—
S67	conv cpe	3,280	19,375	—
S87/W66	Form hbk cpe	3,370	16,205	—
W87	Trans Am htchbk cpe	3,343	18,105	—
W67	TA conv cpe 2d	3,441	23,875	—
W87/Y84	GTA htchbk cpe	3,456	25,880	—
Grand Am (wb 103.4) - 208,568 built				
E37	SE cpe 2d	2,728	11,899	—
E69	SE sdn 4d	2,777	11,999	—
W37	GT cpe 2d	2,804	13,699	—
W69	GT sdn 4d	2,846	13,799	—
Grand Prix (wb 107.5) - 119,319 built				
H19	LE sdn 4d	3,243	14,890	—
J37	SE cpe 2d	3,214	15,390	—
J19	SE sdn 4d	3,282	16,190	—
P37	GT cpe 2d	3,357	20,340	—
T19	STE sdn 4d	3,434	21,635	—
Bonneville (wb 110.8) - 124,511 built				
X69	SE sdn 4d	3,362	18,599	—
Z69	SSE sdn 4d	3,507	23,999	—
Y69	SSEi sdn 4d	3,607	28,045	—

1992 Engines	bore×stroke	bhp	availability
I-4, 121.0	3.38×3.38	111	S-Sunbird (ohc)
I-4, 138.0	3.63×3.35	120	S-GA (ohc)
I-4, 138.0	3.63×3.35	160	O-GA (dohc)
I-4, 138.0	3.63×3.35	180	O-GA (dohc)
V-6, 191.0	3.50×3.31	140	S-Frbrd, Snbrd GT; O-Snbrd SE
V-6, 204.0	3.70×3.16	160	O-Grand Am
V-6, 207.0	3.62×3.31	210	O-Gd Prix (dohc)
V-6, 231.0	3.80×3.40	170	S-Bonn exc SSEi
V-6S, 231.0	3.80×3.40	205	S-Bonn SSEi
V-8, 305.0	3.74×3.48	170	S-Frbrd Frml; O-Firebird
V-8, 305.0	3.74×3.48	205	S-Firebird T/A; O-Formula
V-8, 350.0	4.00×3.48	240	S-Firebird GTA; O-T/A, Formula

1993

Sunbird (wb 101.2) - 98,811 blt		Wght	Price	Prod
C37	LE cpe	2,484	9,382	—
C69	LE sdn 4d	2,502	9,382	—
B37	SE cpe	2,484	10,380	—
B69	SE sdn 4d	2,502	10,380	—
B67	SE conv cpe	2,694	15,403	—
D37	GT cpe	2,682	12,820	—
Firebird (wb 101.1) - 14,475 built				
S87	htchbk cpe	3,241	13,995	—
V87	Formula htchbk cpe	—	17,995	—
V87/Y82	Trans Am htchbk cpe	—	21,395	—
Grand Am (wb 103.4) - 247,498 built				
E37	SE cpe	2,728	12,524	—
E69	SE sdn 4d	2,777	12,624	—
Grand Am				
W37	GT cpe	2,804	13,924	—
W69	GT sdn 4d	2,846	14,024	—
Grand Prix (wb 107.5) - 116,885 built				
H19	LE sdn 4d	3,243	14,890	—
J37	SE cpe	3,189	15,390	—
J19	SE sdn 4d	3,312	16,190	—
P37	GT cpe	3,357	20,340	—
T19	STE sdn 4d	3,434	21,635	—
Bonneville (wb 110.8) - 104,806 built				
X69	SE sdn 4d	3,362	19,444	—
Z69	SSE sdn 4d	3,507	24,844	—
Y69	SSEi sdn 4d	3,607	29,444	—

1993 Engines	bore×stroke	bhp	availability
I-4, 121.0	3.38×3.38	110	S-Sunbird (ohc)
I-4, 138.0	3.63×3.35	115	S-GA (ohc)
I-4, 138.0	3.63×3.35	155	O-GA (dohc)
I-4, 138.0	3.63×3.35	175	O-GA (dohc)
V-6, 191.0	3.50×3.31	140	S-GP, Snbrd GT; O-Sunbird SE
V-6, 204.0	3.70×3.16	160	O-Grand Am
V-6, 207.0	3.62×3.31	160	S-Firebird
V-6, 207.0	3.62×3.31	210	O-GP (dohc)
V-6, 231.0	3.80×3.40	170	S-Bonneville
V-6S, 231.0	3.80×3.40	205	S-Bonn SSEi; O-Bonn SSE
V-8, 350.0	4.00 × 3.48	275	S-Firebird Formula/TA

1994

Sunbird (wb 101.2) - 103,738 blt		Wght	Price	Prod
B37	LE cpe	2,484	9,764	—
B69	LE sdn 4d	2,502	9,764	—
B67	LE conv cpe	2,661	15,524	—
L37	SE cpe	2,682	12,424	—
Firebird (wb 101.1) - 51,523 built				
S87	htchbk cpe	3,232	14,099	—
S67	conv cpe	3,346	21,179	—
V87	Formula htchbk cpe	3,425	18,249	—
V87	Formula conv cpe	3,489	24,279	—
V87/Y82	Trans Am htchbk cpe	3,447	20,009	—
V87/Y83	TA GT htchbk cpe	3,494	21,509	—
V87/Y83	TA GT conv cpe	3,610	26,479	—
Grand Am (wb 103.4) - 254,919 built				
E37	SE cpe	2,736	12,514	—
E69	SE sdn 4d	2,793	12,614	—
W37	GT cpe	2,822	15,014	—
W69	GT sdn 4d	2,882	15,114	—
Grand Prix (wb 107.5) - 148,405 built				
J37	SE cpe	3,275	16,174	—
J19	SE sdn 4d	3,370	16,770	—
Bonneville (wb 110.8) - 87,926 built				
X69	SE sdn 4d	3,446	20,424	—
Z69	SSE sdn 4d	3,587	25,884	—

1994 Engines	bore×stroke	bhp	availability
I-4, 121.0	3.38×3.38	110	S-Sunbird (ohc)
I-4, 138.0	3.63×3.35	115	S-GA (ohc)
I-4, 138.0	3.63×3.35	155	O-GA (dohc)
I-4, 138.0	3.63 × 3.35	175	O-GA (dohc)
V-6, 191.0	3.50 × 3.31	140	S-Sunbird SE; O-Sunbird LE
V-6, 191.0	3.50 × 3.31	155	O-Grand Am
V-6, 191.0	3.50 × 3.31	160	S-Grand Prix
V-6, 207.0	3.62 × 3.31	160	S-Firebird
V-6, 207.0	3.62 × 3.31	210	O-GP (dohc)
V-6, 231.0	3.80 × 3.40	170	S-Bonneville
V-6S, 231.0	3.80 × 3.40	225	O-Bonn SSE
V-8, 350.0	4.00 × 3.48	275	S-Firebird Formula/TA

1995

Sunfire (wb 104.1)		Wght	Price	Prod
B37	SE cpe	2,679	11,074	42,313
B69	SE sdn 4d	2,723	11,224	32,481
B67	SE conv cpe	2,835	16,764	990
D37	GT cpe	2,829	12,834	5,313
Firebird (wb 101.1)				
S87	htchbk cpe	3,230	14,859	
V87	Formula htchbk cpe	3,372	19,099	49,191
V87/Y82	Trans Am hbk cpe	3,345	21,069	

Firebird		Wght	Price	Prod
S67	conv cpe	3,346	21,939	
V67	Formula conv cpe	3,489	25,129	7,532
V67/Y82 Trans Am conv cpe		3,610	27,139	
Grand Am (wb 103.4)				
E37	SE cpe	2,824	12,904	77,655
E69	SE sdn 4d	2,881	13,004	163,991
W37	GT cpe	2,888	14,854	28,343
W69	GT sdn 4d	2,941	14,954	21,155
Grand Prix (wb 107.5)				
J37	SE cpe	3,243	16,634	60,397
J19	SE sdn 4d	3,318	17,384	83,332
Bonneville (wb 110.8)				
X69	SE sdn 4d	3,446	20,804	84,362
Z69	SSE sdn 4d	3,587	25,804	12,399

1995 Engines	bore×stroke	bhp	availability
I-4, 133.0	3.50×3.46	120	S-Sunfire (ohv)
I-4, 138.0	3.63×3.35	150	S-GA, Snfr GT; O-Snfr SE (dohc)
V-6, 191.0	3.50 × 3.31	155	O-Grand Am
V-6, 191.0	3.50 × 3.31	160	S-Grand Prix
V-6, 207.0	3.62 × 3.31	160	S-Firebird
V-6, 207.0	3.62 × 3.31	210	O-GP (dohc)
V-6, 231.0	3.80 × 3.40	200	S-Firebird*
V-6, 231.0	3.80 × 3.40	205	S-Bonneville
V-6S, 231.0	3.80 × 3.40	225	O-Bonneville
V-8, 350.0	4.00 × 3.48	275	S-Frbrd Frml/Trans Am

* Intro. in midyear. Standard only on California models.

1996

Sunfire (wb 104.1)-131,759 blt		Wght	Price	Prod
B37	SE cpe	2,679	11,504	—
B69	SE sdn 4d	2,723	11,674	—
B67	SE conv cpe	2,835	17,734	—
D37	GT cpe	2,829	13,214	—
Firebird (wb 101.1) - 32,799 built				
S87	htchbk cpe	3,481	15,614	—
S67	conv cpe	3,546	22,444	—
V87	Formula htchbk cpe	3,512	19,464	—
V67	Formula conv cpe	3,689	25,284	—
V87/Y82 Trans Am htchbk cpe		3,605	21,414	—
V67/Y82 Trans Am conv cpe		3,710	27,364	—
Grand Am (wb 103.4) - 229,117 built				
E37	SE cpe	2,881	13,499	—
E69	SE sdn 4d	2,954	13,499	—
W37	GT cpe	2,932	15,499	—
W69	GT sdn 4d	3,011	15,499	—
Grand Prix (wb 107.5) - 83,587 built				
J37	SE cpe	3,243	17,089	—
J19	SE sdn 4d	3,318	18,359	—
Bonneville (wb 110.8) - 74,191 built				
X69	SE sdn 4d	3,446	21,589	—
Z69	SSE sdn 4d	3,587	26,559	—

1996 Engines	bore×stroke	bhp	availability
I-4, 133.0	3.50×3.46	120	S-Sunfire
I-4, 146.0	3.54×3.70	150	S-GA, Snfr GT; O-Snfr SE (dohc)
V-6, 191.0	3.51×3.31	155	O-Grand Am
V-6, 191.0	3.51×3.31	160	S-Grand Prix
V-6, 207.0	3.62×3.31	215	O-GP (dohc)
V-6, 231.0	3.80×3.40	200	S-Firebird
V-6, 231.0	3.80×3.40	205	S-Bonneville
V-6S, 231.0	3.80 × 3.40	240	O-Bonneville
V-8, 350.0	4.00 × 3.48	285	S-Frbrd Frml/Trans Am
V-8, 350.0	4.00 × 3.48	305	O-Frbrd Fmla/TA

1997

Sunfire (wb 104.1)		Wght	Price	Prod
B37	SE cpe	2,627	12,059	80,740
B69	SE sdn 4d	2,670	12,199	46,370
B67	SE conv cpe	2,868	18,899	8,002
D37	GT cpe	2,791	13,719	16,911
Firebird (wb 101.1)				
S87	htchbk cpe	3,311	17,124	17,463
S67	conv cpe	3,481	23,034	1,310
V87	Formula htchbk cpe	3,452	20,654	12,068
V87/Y82 Trans Am hbk cpe		3,477	22,814	
V-67	Formula conv cpe	3,512	26,454	1,851
V-67/Y82 Trans Am conv cpe		3,605	28,374	
Grand Am (wb 103.4)				
E37	SE cpe	2,835	14,634	44,592
E69	SE sdn 4d	2,877	14,634	133,735
W37	GT cpe	2,945	15,874	33,613
W69	GT sdn 4d	2,987	15,874	23,798
Grand Prix (wb 110.5)				
J69	SE sdn 4d	—	18,029	66,427
P37	GT cpe	3,396	18,809	52,237
P69	GT sdn 4d	3,414	19,809	40,369
Bonneville (wb 110.8)				
X69	SE sdn 4d	3,446	22,114	67,007
Z69	SSE sdn 4d	3,587	27,164	12,385

1997 Engines	bore ×stroke	bhp	availability
I-4, 133.0	3.50×3.46	120	S-Sunfire
I-4, 146.0	3.54×3.70	150	S-GA, Snfr GT; O-Snfr SE (dohc)
V-6, 191.0	3.51 × 3.31	155	O-Grand Am
V-6, 191.0	3.51 × 3.31	160	S-Grand Prix SE
V-6, 231.0	3.80 × 3.40	195	S-GP GT
V-6, 231.0	3.80 × 3.40	200	S-Firebird
V-6, 231.0	3.80 × 3.40	205	S-Bonneville
V-6S, 231.0	3.80 × 3.40	240	O-GP, Bonn
V-8, 350.0	4.00 × 3.48	285	S-Frbrd Frml/Trans Am
V-8, 350.0	4.00 × 3.48	305	O-Frbrd Frml/Trans Am

1998

Sunfire (wb 104.1)		Wght	Price	Prod
B37	SE cpe	2,637	12,495	65,416
B69	SE sdn 4d	2,674	12,495	46,024
B67	SE conv cpe	2,870	19,495	6,147
D37	GT cpe	2,822	15,495	15,532
Firebird (wb 101.1)				
S87	htchbk cpe	3,340	17,124	15,909
S67	conv cpe	3,492	24,305	911
V87	Formula htchbk cpe	3,455	22,865	14,946
V87/Y82 Trans Am htchbk cpe		3,477	25,975	
V-67/Y82 Trans Am conv cpe		3,605	29,715	1,532
Grand Am (wb 103.4)				
E37	SE cpe	2,835	14,874	21,410
E69	SE sdn 4d	2,877	15,024	59,785
W37	GT cpe	2,945	16,324	16,781
W69	GT sdn 4d	2,987	16,474	13,633
Grand Prix (wb 110.5)				
J69	SE sdn 4d	—	18,795	50,733
P37	GT cpe	3,396	20,415	35,841
P69	GT sdn 4d	3,414	20,665	55,772
Bonneville (wb 110.8)				
X69	SE sdn 4d	3,446	22,390	48,778
Z69	SSE sdn 4d	3,587	29,390	19,551

1998 Engines	bore×stroke	bhp	availability
I-4, 133.0	3.50×3.46	115	S-Sunfire
I-4, 146.0	3.54×3.70	150	S-GA, Snfr GT; O-Snfr SE (dohc)
V-6, 191.0	3.51×3.31	155	O-Grand Am
V-6, 191.0	3.51×3.31	160	S-Grand Prix SE
V-6, 231.0	3.80×3.40	195	S-GP GT; O-GP SE
V-6, 231.0	3.80×3.40	200	S-Firebird
V-6, 231.0	3.80×3.40	205	S-Bonneville
V-6S, 231.0	3.80×3.40	240	O-GP, Bonn
V-8, 346.0	3.90 × 3.62	305	S-Frbrd Frml/Trans Am
V-8, 346.0	3.90 × 3.62	320	O-Frbrd Frml/TA

1999

Sunfire (wb 104.1)		Wght	Price	Prod
B37	SE cpe	2,630	12,745	52,115
B69	SE sdn 4d	2,670	12,745	47,695
B67	GT conv cpe	2,998	21,145	9,367
D37	GT cpe	2,822	15,745	12,648
Firebird (wb 101.1)				
S87	htchbk cpe	3,340	18,165	15,088
S67	conv cpe	3,492	24,785	1,859
V87	Formula htchbk cpe	3,455	23,065	17,520
V87/Y82 Trans Am hbk cpe		3,477	26,175	
V-67/Y82 Trans Am conv cpe		3,605	30,245	1,752
Grand Am (wb 107.0)				
E37	SE cpe	3,066	15,870	43,339
E69	SE sdn 4d	3,116	16,470	195,190
W37	GT cpe	—	19,070	48,803
W69	GT sdn 4d	—	19,470	43,864
Grand Prix (wb 110.5)				
J69	SE sdn 4d	—	19,415	47,399
P37	GT cpe	3,396	20,995	30,327
P69	GT sdn 4d	3,414	21,145	44,767
R37	GTP cpe	—	23,760	11,329
R69	GTP sdn 4d	—	23,910	21,242
Bonneville (wb 110.8)				
X69	SE sdn 4d	3,446	22,800	49,064
Z69	SSE sdn 4d	3,587	29,880	5,320

1999 Engines	bore×stroke	bhp	availability
I-4, 133.0	3.50×3.46	115	S-Sunfire
I-4, 146.0	3.54×3.70	150	S-GA, Snfr GT; O-Snfr SE (dohc)
V-6, 191.0	3.51 × 3.31	160	S-Grand Prix SE
V-6, 207.0	3.62 × 3.31	170	O-Grand Am
V-6, 231.0	3.80 × 3.40	200	S-Frbrd, GP GT
V-6, 231.0	3.80 × 3.40	205	S-Bonneville
V-6S, 231.0	3.80 × 3.40	240	S-GP GTP; O-Bonneville
V-8, 346.0	3.90 × 3.62	305	S-Frbrd Frml/Trans Am
V-8, 346.0	3.90 × 3.62	320	O-Frbrd Frml/Trans Am

2000

Sunfire (wb 104.1)		Wght	Price	Prod
B37	SE cpe	2,606	13,910	64,335
B69	SE sdn 4d	2,644	14,010	54,670
B67	GT conv cpe	2,906	21,610	3,958
D37	GT cpe	2,771	16,210	11,251
Firebird (wb 101.1)				
S87	htchbk cpe	3,323	18,410	14,958
S67	conv cpe	3,402	25,110	1,373
V87	Formula htchbk cpe	3,341	23,520	13,685
V87/Y82 Trans Am hbk cpe		3,397	26,630	
V-67/Y82 Trans Am conv cpe		3,514	30,700	1,910
Grand Am (wb 107.0)				
E37	SE cpe	3,066	15,920	33,126
E69	SE sdn 4d	3,116	16,220	155,866
W37	GT cpe	—	19,550	30,771
W69	GT sdn 4d	—	19,850	36,092
Grand Prix (wb 110.5)				
J69	SE sdn 4d	—	19,815	61,993
P37	GT cpe	3,396	21,395	23,482
P69	GT sdn 4d	3,414	21,545	59,082
R37	GTP cpe	—	24,160	10,497
R69	GTP sdn 4d	—	24,310	17,718
Bonneville (wb 112.2)				
X69	SE sdn 4d	3,590	23,680	40,698
Y69	SLE sdn 4d	3,650	27,380	
Z69	SSEi sdn 4d	3,790	31,635	21,765

2000 Engines	bore×stroke	bhp	availability
I-4, 133.0	3.50×3.46	115	S-Sunfire
I-4, 146.0	3.54×3.70	150	S-GA, Snfr GT; O-Snfr SE (dohc)
V-6, 191.0	3.51×3.31	175	S-Grand Prix SE
V-6, 207.0	3.62×3.31	170	O-Grand Am SE
V-6, 207.0	3.62×3.31	175	S-Grand Am GT
V-6, 231.0	3.80×3.40	200	S-Frbrd, GP GT; O-GP SE
V-6, 231.0	3.80×3.40	205	S-Bonneville
V-6S, 231.0	3.80×3.40	240	S-GP GTP, Bonneville SSEi
V-8, 346.0	3.90 × 3.62	305	S-Frbrd Frml/Trans Am
V-8, 346.0	3.90 × 3.62	320	O-Frbrd Frml/Trans Am
V-8, 346.0	3.90 × 3.62	327	O-Frbrd Frml/TA

2001

Sunfire (wb 104.1)		Wght	Price	Prod
B37	SE cpe	2,606	14,175	53,551
B69	SE sdn 4d	2,644	14,430	57,933

Sunfire		Wght	Price	Prod
D37	GT cpe	2,771	16,295	7,543
Firebird (wb 101.1)				
S87	htchbk cpe	3,323	18,725	7,172
S67	conv cpe	3,402	25,345	2,360
V87	Formula htchbk cpe	3,341	23,905	10,716
V87/Y82	Trans Am hbk cpe	3,397	27,015	
V67/Y82	Trans Am conv cpe	3,514	31,085	1,189
Grand Am (wb 107.0)				
E37	SE cpe	3,066	16,410	8,584
F37	SE1 cpe	—	17,870	19,793
E69	SE sdn 4d	3,116	16,440	25,471
F69	SE1 sdn 4d	—	18,170	99,926
W37	GT cpe	3,099	20,235	16,646
V37	GT1 cpe	—	21,655	6,338
W69	GT sdn 4d	3,118	20,535	25,724
V-69	GT1 sdn 4d	—	21,805	7,854
Grand Prix (wb 110.5)				
K69	SE sdn 4d	3,384	20,300	46,898
P37	GT cpe	3,429	21,865	14,484
P69	GT sdn 4d	3,496	22,015	55,180
R37	GTP cpe	—	25,335	4,816
R69	GTP sdn 4d	3,559	25,535	9,149
Bonneville (wb 112.2)				
X69	SE sdn 4d	3,590	25,075	29,329
Y69	SLE sdn 4d	3,650	28,045	9,322
Z69	SSEi sdn 4d	3,790	32,415	6,787

2001 Engines	bore×stroke	bhp	availability
I-4, 133.0	3.50×3.46	115	S-Sunfire
I-4, 146.0	3.54×3.70	150	S-GA, Snfr GT; O-Snfr SE (dohc)
V-6, 191.0	3.51×3.31	175	S-Grand Prix SE
V-6, 207.0	3.62×3.31	170	O-GA SE1
V-6, 207.0	3.62×3.31	175	S-GA GT/GT1
V-6, 231.0	3.80×3.40	200	S-Frbrd, GP GT
V-6, 231.0	3.80×3.40	205	S-Bonneville
V-6S, 231.0	3.80×3.40	240	S-GP GTP, Bonneville SSEi
V-8, 346.0	3.90×3.62	310	S-Frbrd Frml/ Trans Am
V-8, 346.0	3.90×3.62	325	O-Firebird TA
V-8, 346.0	3.90×3.62	330	O-Frbrd Frml/ Trans Am

2002

Sunfire (wb 104.1) - 128,208 blt		Wght	Price	Prod
B37	SE cpe	2,606	14,540	—
B69	SE sdn 4d	2,644	15,040	—
D37	GT cpe	2,771	16,855	—
Firebird (wb 101.1) - 30,690 built				
S87	htchbk cpe	3,319	19,715	—
S67	conv cpe	3,484	26,630	—
V87	Formula htchbk cpe	3,541	25,660	—
V87/Y82	Trans Am hbk cpe	3,495	27,690	—
V-67/Y82	Trans Am conv cpe	3,605	31,760	—
Grand Am (wb 107.0) - 181,882 built				
E37	SE cpe	3,066	16,800	—
F37	SE1 cpe	—	18,240	—
E69	SE sdn 4d	3,116	16,950	—
F69	SE1 sdn 4d	—	18,390	—
W37	GT cpe	3,099	20,690	—
V37	GT1 cpe	—	21,960	—
W69	GT sdn 4d	3,118	20,840	—
V69	GT1 sdn 4d	—	22,110	—
Grand Prix (wb 110.5) - 160,543 built				
K69	SE sdn 4d	3,384	20,965	—
P37	GT cpe	3,429	22,935	—
P69	GT sdn 4d	3,496	23,085	—
R37	GTP cpe	3,495	25,625	—
R69	GTP sdn 4d	3,559	25,805	—
Bonneville (wb 112.2) - 44,152 built				
X69	SE sdn 4d	3,590	25,530	—
Y69	SLE sdn 4d	3,650	28,720	—
Z69	SSEi sdn 4d	3,790	32,950	—

2002 Engines	bore×stroke	bhp	availability
I-4, 133.0	3.50×3.46	115	S-Sunfire
I-4, 146.0	3.54×3.70	150	S-GA, Snfr GT; O-Sunfire SE (dohc)*
I-4, 134.0	3.39×3.72	140	S-GA, Snfr GT; O-Snfr SE (dohc)**
V-6, 191.0	3.51×3.31	175	S-Grand Prix SE
V-6, 207.0	3.62×3.31	170	O-GA SE1
V-6, 207.0	3.62×3.31	175	S-GA GT/GT1
V-6, 231.0	3.80 × 3.40	200	S-Frbrd, GP GT
V-6, 231.0	3.80 × 3.40	205	S-Bonneville
V-6S, 231.0	3.80 × 3.40	240	S-GP GTP, Bonneville SSEi
V-8, 346.0	3.90 × 3.62	310	S-Frbrd Frml/ Trans Am
V-8, 346.0	3.90 × 3.62	325	O-Firebird TA
V-8, 346.0	3.90 × 3.62	345	O-Firebird TA

* Early production. ** Late production.

2003

Vibe (wb 102.4) - 84,274 blt		Wght	Price	Prod
L26	wgn 4d	2,700	16,365	—
M26	AWD wgn 4d	2,980	19,615	—
N26	GT wgn 4d	2,780	19,365	—
Sunfire (wb 104.1)				
B37	SE cpe 2d	2,771	14,910	76,009
Grand Am (wb 107.0) - 167,866 built				
W37	GT cpe 2d	3,091	21,085	—
V37	GT1 cpe 2d	3,168	22,385	—
E69	SE sdn 4d	3,066	17,085	—
F69	SE1 sdn 4d	3,066	18,535	—
G69	SE2 sdn 4d	3,066	20,885	—
W69	GT sdn 4d	3,091	21,085	—
V69	GT1 sdn 4d	3,168	22,385	—
Grand Prix (wb 110.5) - 81,300 built				
K69	SE sdn 4d	3,384	21,645	—
P69	GT sdn 4d	3,496	23,495	—
R69	GTP sdn 4d	3,559	26,295	—
Bonneville (wb 112.2) - 35,688 built				
X69	SE sdn 4d	3,633	26,115	—
Y69	SLE sdn 4d	3,678	29,315	—
Z69	SSEi sdn 4d	3,716	33,565	—

2003 Engines	bore×stroke	bhp	availability
I-4, 109.4	3.11×3.60	123	S-AWD Vibe
I-4, 109.4	3.11×3.60	130	S-FWD Vibe
I-4, 109.5	3.23×3.35	170	S-Vibe GT
I-4, 134.0	3.39×3.72	140	S-Sunfire, GA
V-6, 191.0	3.51×3.31	175	S-Grand Prix SE
V-6, 207.0	3.62×3.31	170	O-Grand Am
V-6, 207.0	3.62×3.31	175	S-GA GT/GT1
V-6, 231.0	3.80×3.40	200	S-GP GT
V-6, 231.0	3.80×3.40	205	S-Bonneville
V-6S, 231.0	3.80×3.40	240	S-GP GTP, Bonn SSEi

2004

Vibe (wb 102.4) - 72,044 blt		Wght	Price	Prod
L26	wgn 4d	2,700	16,485	—
M26	AWD wgn 4d	2,980	19,785	—
N26	GT wgn 4d	2,780	19,435	—
Sunfire (wb 104.1) - 64,558 built				
B37	1SV cpe 2d	2,771	10,895	—
B37	SE cpe 2d	2,771	14,930	—
Grand Am (wb 107.0) - 190,815 built				
W37	GT cpe 2d	3,091	21,825	—
V37	GT1 cpe 2d	3,168	23,075	—
E69	SE sdn 4d	3,066	17070	—
F69	SE1 sdn 4d	3,066	19,020	—
G69	SE2 sdn 4d	3,066	21,375	—
W69	GT sdn 4d	3,091	21,825	—
V69	GT1 sdn 4d	3,168	23,075	—
Grand Prix (wb 110.5) - 194,408 built				
P69	GT1 sdn 4d	3,477	21,760	—
S69	GT2 sdn 4d	3,484	23,660	—
R69	GTP sdn 4d	3,583	25,860	—
Bonneville (wb 112.2) - 21,920 built				
X69	SE sdn 4d	3,633	27,185	—
Y69	SLE sdn 4d	3,678	30,035	—
Z69	GXP sdn 4d	3,790	35,270	—
GTO (wb 109.8)				
X37	cpe 2d	3,725	31,795	15,784

2004 Engines	bore×stroke	bhp	availability
I-4, 109.4	3.11×3.60	123	S-AWD Vibe
I-4, 109.4	3.11×3.60	130	S-FWD Vibe
I-4, 109.5	3.23×3.35	170	S-Vibe GT
I-4, 134.0	3.39×3.72	140	S-Sunfire, GA
V-6, 207.0	3.62×3.31	170	O-Grand Am
V-6, 207.0	3.62×3.31	175	S-GA GT/GT1
V-6, 231.0	3.80×3.40	200	S-Grand Prix
V-6, 231.0	3.80×3.40	205	S-Bonneville
V-6S, 231.0	3.80×3.40	260	S-GP GTP
V-8, 278.0	3.66×3.31	275	S-Bonn GXP
V-8, 346.0	3.90×3.62	350	S-GTO

2005

Vibe (wb 102.4) - 84,607 blt		Wght	Price	Prod
L26	wgn 4d	2,700	17,000	—
M26	AWD wgn 4d	2,980	20,325	—
N26	GT wgn 4d	2,780	19,975	—
Sunfire (wb 104.1) - 67,325 built				
B37	1SV cpe 2d	2,771	10,895	—
B37	SE cpe 2d	2,771	15,085	—
Grand Am (wb 107.0) - 73,182 built				
W37	GT cpe 2d	3,091	22,365	—
V37	GT1 cpe 2d	3,168	23,615	—
G6 (wb 112.3) - 73,019 built				
G69	sdn 4d	3,420	20,675	—
H69	GT sdn 4d	3,425	23,300	—
Grand Prix (wb 110.5) - 118,225 built				
P69	sdn 4d	3,477	22,900	—
S69	GT sdn 4d	3,484	24,800	—
R69	GTP sdn 4d	3,583	26,650	—
C69	GXP sdn 4d	3,600	29,335	—
Bonneville (wb 112.2) - 21,920 built				
X69	SE sdn 4d	3,633	27,775	—
Y69	SLE sdn 4d	3,678	30,160	—
Z69	GXP sdn 4d	3,790	35,395	—
GTO (wb 109.8)				
X37	cpe 2d	3,725	32,295	10,838

2005 Engines	bore×stroke	bhp	availability
I-4, 109.4	3.11×3.60	123	S-AWD Vibe
I-4, 109.4	3.11×3.60	130	S-FWD Vibe
I-4, 109.5	3.23×3.35	170	S-Vibe GT
I-4, 134.0	3.39×3.72	140	S-Sunfire
V-6, 204.0	3.62×3.31	175	S-Grand Am
V-6, 213.0	3.70×3.31	200	S-G6
V-6, 231.0	3.80×3.40	200	S-Grand Prix
V-6, 231.0	3.80×3.40	205	S-Bonneville
V-6S, 231.0	3.80×3.40	260	S-GP GTP
V-8, 278.0	3.66×3.31	275	S-Bonn GXP
V-8, 364.0	4.00×3.62	400	S-GTO

2006

Vibe (wb 102.4)		Wght	Price	Prod*
L26	wgn 4d	2,700	16,430	—
M26	AWD wgn 4d	2,980	20,105	—
N26	GT wgn 4d	2,780	20,455	—
G6 (wb 112.3)				
H37	GT cpe 2d	3,415	21,165	—
M37	GTP cpe 2d	3,525	22,865	—
H67	GT conv cpe	—	27,865	—
M67	GTP conv cpe	—	29,365	—
F69	1SV sdn 4d I-4	—	16,365	—
F69	sdn 4d I-4	—	17,865	—
G69	sdn 4d V-6	3,420	19,065	—
H69	GT sdn 4d	3,425	21,365	—
M69	GTP sdn 4d	—	23,065	—
Grand Prix (wb 110.5)				
P69	sdn 4d	3,477	22,435	—
R69	GT sdn 4d	3,484	26,085	—
C69	GXP sdn 4d	3,600	28,735	—
Solstice (wb 95.1)				
B67	conv cpe	2,860	19,420	—
GTO (wb 109.8)				
X37	cpe 2d	3,725	32,295	—

2006 Engines	bore×stroke	bhp	availability
I-4, 109.4	3.11×3.60	118	S-AWD Vibe
I-4, 109.4	3.11×3.60	126	S-FWD Vibe
I-4, 109.5	3.23×3.35	164	S-Vibe GT
I-4, 145.0	3.46×3.85	167	S-G6
I-4, 145.0	3.46×3.85	177	S-Soltice
V-6, 213.0	3.70×3.31	201	O-G6
V-6, 231.0	3.80×3.40	200	S-Grand Prix
V-6, 231.0	3.80×3.40	205	S-GP GT
V-6S, 231.0	3.80×3.40	260	S-GP GT
V-6, 237.0	3.90×3.31	240	S-G6 GTP
V-8, 325.0	3.78×3.62	303	S-GP GXP
V-8, 364.0	4.00×3.62	400	S-GTO

* Figures not available at time of publication.

Rambler

Rambler, the successful compact begun by Nash in 1950, became a separate make after introducing larger four-door models for '55 and new styling for '56. These and subsequent events reflected the changing fortunes of American Motors Corporation, founded in April 1954 with the Nash-Hudson merger instigated by Nash president George Mason.

Mason had long dreamed of combining Nash with Hudson, then bringing in Studebaker and Packard to form a new company with the same economies of scale as the Big Three. Without this, he warned, none of these four independents could survive over the long term. As a halfway measure, he persuaded Packard president James Nance to take over ailing Studebaker, which was also accomplished in 1954 (at Packard's ultimate peril). But when Mason died suddenly that October, so did his dream of a "Big Four." His assistant, George Romney, became AMC president, completely forgot about linking with S-P, and bet the farm on Rambler to lift AMC from the financial hole dug by its parents.

It was really all Romney could do, but events worked in his favor. Rambler bounded from strength to strength, helped like no other make by the flash economic recession of 1958. By decade's end, AMC was making serious money and Rambler was firmly established as Detroit's best-selling compact.

The 1957 Ramblers were continuations of the reskinned '56 models sold with Nash and Hudson badges. Besides new "R" hood medallions, cosmetic changes were limited to reshuffled trim and a T-shaped grille ornament to fill the void above the eggcrate section. The big news was V-8 power: AMC's 250-cid, 190-bhp engine, introduced in '56 (a derivative was bored out for 1957's new AMC 327). V-8 Ramblers were available in four body styles, each of these unit-construction four-doors on the 108-inch wheelbase introduced for '55. Variations involved sedans and Cross Country station wagons with and without B-pillars—making Rambler the first in Detroit with hardtop wagons. As before, all offered a choice of Super or Custom trim. So did a parallel six-cylinder line retaining the 195.6-cid engine familiar from Nash days. However, that engine was tweaked quite a bit, going from 120 bhp to 125/135. Sixes also included a price-leader DeLuxe sedan at $1961. Other '57 Ramblers sold in the low-to-mid $2000s.

These were solid, reliable, smaller cars that could be quite stylish with optional two-toning. As in the Nash era, exterior "continental" spare tires were available for sedans. Wagons boasted a roll-down tailgate window instead of a clumsy liftgate, something Ford and GM wagons didn't have. Future AMC chairman Roy D. Chapin, Jr., later recalled: "We just rolled with those cars. We couldn't get enough." Indeed, of the roughly 119,000 cars AMC built in calendar '57, all but 7816 were Ramblers. The rest, of course, were Nashes and Hudsons, which would not return for '58—at least not as they had been.

Romney liked to assail Detroit's "gas-guzzling dinosaurs" while preaching the smaller-is-better virtues of Rambler. All the more surprising, then, that AMC had a performance Rambler for '57, a special Custom Country Club four-door hardtop aptly branded Rebel. Arriving at midyear with flashes of anodized aluminum on its flanks, Rebel carried the same 255-bhp 327-cid V-8 as the final Nashes and Hudsons, but was much quicker because it weighed significantly less than those cars. The extra power made Rebel more of a handler than other Ramblers, so AMC included stiff Gabriel shocks, a front antiroll bar, heavy-duty springs, power steering, and power brakes. Performance was impressive by most any standard, let alone for a Rambler. In one test at Daytona Beach, a Rebel covered 0-60 mph—and 50-80—in scarcely more than seven seconds. It might have been quicker still with Bendix mechanical fuel injection, but that promised option never materialized.

No matter. With 9.75:1 compression, the Rebel drank premium fuel and a fair bit of it, which hardly fit Rambler's economy image. And at $2786 it was the costliest '57 Rambler, which was another likely factor that kept production to just 1500 units.

During this period, economy imports were quickly climbing the sales charts, led by Volkswagen's already antiquated Beetle. AMC noted the trend and replied with an unprecedented move for 1958, a revival of the 100-inch-wheelbase 1955 Rambler two-door sedan. Renamed Rambler American and wearing a new mesh-type grille and full wheel openings, it offered DeLuxe, Super, and stripped "business" models at a low prices ranging from $1775 to $1874. With those prices in a recession year, the American couldn't help but sell, and over 30,000 were registered for the model year.

Regular Ramblers weren't ignored for '58, receiving a complete reskin that made the '56 bodies look a bit bulkier on unchanged wheelbases. Little canted tailfins and dual headlamps (moved from within the grille back to the fenders) were new styling touches. Hardtop wagons were omitted. AMC also adopted then-trendy pushbuttons for its optional Borg-Warner "Flash-O-Matic" self-shift transmission. Though V-8 cars were now called Rebel, they retained the 250 engine, which was boosted to 215 bhp. Sixes, now with 127 or 138 bhp, remained nameless, and were again far more popular—no real surprise.

What *did* surprise observers was a new 117-inch-wheelbase line called Rambler Ambassador. AMC brochures implied you should think of it as a distinct make ("Ambassador by Rambler"), but this was simply the 108-inch-wheelbase platform with nine extra inches ahead of the cowl, plus a standard four-barrel 327 V-8 with 270 bhp. Offerings comprised the usual four-door sedans, Country Club hardtop sedans, and pillared and pillarless wagons in Super and Custom trim. Visually, these Ambassadors were nothing like their Nash forebears and everything like regular '58 Ramblers. The only differences, other than the added length, were nameplates, a fine-checked grille, broad swathes of anodized aluminum on Customs, plusher interiors, and arguably better proportions. This is what the '58 Nash and Hudson would have been had those brands not been dropped at the last minute. In fact, the Vee'd front bumper guard of the '58 Ambassador was taken directly from the stillborn Hudson, which had been all but locked up by late 1956 along with a more nearly identical Nash.

Interestingly, the '58 Ambassador virtually doubled full-size '57 Nash/Hudson volume, model-year production totaling 14,570. Rarest of the breed—just 294 total—was the Custom Cross Country hardtop wagon, the only such model in AMC's '58 line. Despite Ambassador's modest sales, Rambler's '58 total of 162,182 was up 77 percent from '57—a fine showing in a generally disastrous industry year. The success ended four straight years of losses for AMC, which scored a $26 million profit on sales of $470 million.

This winning formula netted another $60 million profit on 1959 Rambler volume of nearly 375,000—a new record for the fledgling firm. Ramblers and Ambassadors received more complicated body trim, plus a beltline that curved up gently at the rear doors to blend more smoothly with the finned fenders.

1958 American Super two-door sedan

1958 Rebel V-8 Custom Cross Country station wagon

1960 Ambassador Custom Country Club hardtop sedan

1962 American 400 convertible coupe

1962 Classic Custom two-door sedan

Ambassadors got a more ornate grille with a big "floating" horizontal bar. Powertrains were unchanged. Unlike most competitors, AMC had evidently decided the horsepower race was over.

Indisputably, the rush to compacts was on, and both Americans and the standard Ramblers had new competition in Studebaker's pert '59 Lark. Perhaps anticipating this, AMC expanded that year's American line by reviving the old two-door 100-inch-wheelbase wagon. Also offered in DeLuxe and Super trim, the compact hauler helped the smallest Rambler rack up 91,000 model-year sales. The bigger Ramblers also did very well in 1959's modest industrywide recovery. Ambassador took a satisfying leap to 23,769; standards attracted over a quarter-million sales. The latter were again mostly sixes, as Rebel V-8s found just 16,399 customers.

In all, AMC's 1957-59 sales performance was a remarkable comeback from nail-biting 1954-56. And the good times kept on rolling. For 1960, Rambler recorded about 450,000 sales—the highest annual output ever tallied by an independent manufacturer. Rambler ranked third in the 1961 production race despite volume that was 17 percent lower. Though production for 1962 increased substantially, Rambler ran fifth that year as Pontiac and Olds swept by. The following year found Rambler dropping to eighth place. Output continued to be healthy, yet Rambler/AMC kept slipping: down to ninth for '65 and tenth by 1968.

Two management changes greatly affected Rambler in this period. First, the hard-driving George Romney left in 1962 to make his successful run for the Michigan statehouse. His successor, the ebullient Roy Abernethy, was far less loyal to sensible economy cars, and began an ambitious model expansion that ultimately proved misguided. Abernethy stepped aside in 1966 for Roy D. Chapin, Jr., who became board chairman the following year, with William V. Luneberg as president. This team ordered further diversification, including new "make models" like the 1968 Javelin "ponycar." They also killed the Rambler name after the final Americans of 1969. That was probably wise because by that time, Rambler's sensible image had become more of a liability than an asset.

The compact American returned for 1960 with no fundamental change, but new Super and Custom four-door sedans helped lift model-year volume to 120,600. Though prices were slightly higher at $1781-$2235, the American remained one of the country's most-affordable cars. It also remained an anachronism with its '50s "Farina" styling and elderly L-head six. But sales were more than healthy enough to justify a full restyle for 1961.

Larger Ramblers were attractively restyled for 1960, gaining smoother lines, simple full-width grilles (fine-checked on Ambassador, eggcrate on Six/Rebel), less-intrusive sloped-back A-pillars (replacing vertical), shapelier fins (still mercifully modest), and new taillights. Ambassadors also sported a "Scena-Ramic" windshield curved at the top as well as the sides. A three-seat wagon with a novel left-hinged swing-out tailgate was added to all three series. These changes were evidently well-considered, for AMC passed the billion-dollar mark in net sales for the first time and earned a $48-million profit.

The rebodied 1961 American was a rather odd bit of work by AMC chief designer Edmund A. Anderson (a veteran of Nash days). Boxy and truncated, it was three inches narrower and 5.2 inches shorter than the old '55-vintage design. Happily, the ancient six was modernized with an overhead-valve cylinder head (actually a mid-1960 change), which boosted optional bhp to 127. Existing body styles plus a new convertible and four-door wagons were sprinkled among the usual trims. Posh "400" models were added for '62, and Custom moved down to displace Super. Series were retitled for '63—low-end 220, mid-priced 330, and top-end 440—and hardtop coupes arrived, the last a bench-seat 440 and bucket-seat 440H. Styling changed only in detail each year. Though true economy cars with fair interior space, the 1961-63 Americans were hardly beautiful.

The Six/Rebel became Rambler's Classic for '61, announced by headlights moved into a checkerboard grille beneath a lower hood. V-8s departed for '62, but two-door sedans debuted, and all models wore a more involved grille and finless rear fenders. An interesting '62 Classic option (shared with American) was "E-Stick," a manual transmission with "automatic" clutch. Though it cost just $60, it was too complex to sell really well.

Ambassador, meantime, underwent a big change. The '61s carried a dubious facelift with pointy front-fender bottoms, heavily hooded headlamps, and a raked inverted-trapezoid grille. Hardtop sedans and wagons were axed. Returning from 1960 as base power was a two-barrel 250-bhp "economy" version of the 327 V-8; the 270-bhp engine was now optional. The '62 models effectively replaced Classic V-8s, and were demoted to the same 108-inch platform and given near-identical styling. All this reflected sluggish Ambassador sales, which were little-changed for 1960 at 23,798 but only 18,842 for '61. The '62s fared much better at 36,171. Like Classic, the '62 Ambassador offered new two-door sedans, four-doors, and wagons seating six or eight in DeLuxe, Custom, and top-shelf "400" trim; the last came with an automatic transmission. Prices were $2300-$3000.

Richard A. Teague had joined the AMC styling staff by this time and would soon succeed Ed Anderson. But it was Anderson who shaped the Classic that was named *Motor Trend* magazine's 1963 "Car of the Year." Featured was a wholly new 112-inch-wheelbase unibody platform—the first since '56—with a lower silhouette, smoothly rounded flanks, and curved door glass. One-piece "Uniside" door-frame structures were a Detroit first that saved weight, increased rigidity, and reduced squeaks and rattles. Though styling remained a bit chunky, these Ramblers had never looked better.

They also went better thanks to a new 287-cid version of the familiar 327-cid V-8. Rated at 198 bhp, the 287 would remain through 1966. V-8 Classics combined good go with good mileage; even with "Flash-O-Matic" they could run 0-60 mph in about 10 seconds and return 16-20 mpg. Of course, the V-8s weighed more than six-cylinder Ramblers, so understeer was pronounced.

Teague refined the '63 Classic once Anderson left, giving '64 models stainless steel rocker moldings and a flat grille that replaced the concave design. Hardtops returned, but were now two-doors. Two- and four-door sedans and pillared four-door wagons returned in 550, 660, and 770 trim (replacing Deluxe, Custom, and 400). Hardtops comprised the bench-seat 770 and bucket-seat Typhoon. The latter introduced a new short-stroke 232-cid "Typhoon" six (later "Torque Command") that began replacing the old 195.6-cid unit throughout the AMC line. Arriving with 145 bhp, the 232 spawned a destroked 128-bhp

1963 Ambassador 990 station wagon

1965 Marlin fastback hardtop coupe

1964 Classic 770 Typhoon hardtop coupe

1967 American four-door sedan

1965 Ambassador 990-H hardtop coupe

1969 SC/Rambler-Hurst hardtop coupe

199-cid version for '65-model 550s. The Typhoon itself was a year-only limited edition (2520 built) offering a black vinyl roof, Solar Yellow paint, and a sporty all-vinyl interior for $2509.

A new Classic implied a new Ambassador, but the '63 again shared Classic's wheelbase and styling (save the usual extra chrome bits). Series were retitled 800, 880, and 990, each with the previous three body styles. 800s were a tough sell and vanished for '64. So did 880s, leaving just 990s in four-door sedan and wagon body styles, plus a new hardtop coupe with altered styling *a la* Classic. Also listed was a sporty bucket-seat 990H hardtop with a standard 270-bhp 327 V-8.

Teague succeeded Anderson as AMC design chief on the strength of his pretty 1964 American. Ironically, this was a clever adaptation of Anderson's Classic, with Unisides shortened ahead of the cowl to give a 106-inch wheelbase. But that was still half a foot longer than American's previous span, and Teague used it to produce a well-proportioned compact with only modest brightwork. This styling was good enough to continue with only minor yearly changes through 1969 and the end of the Rambler marque.

The '64 American line repeated 1963's, then thinned for '66, when the bucket-seat 440H became a Rogue. A convertible Rogue was added for '67, only to vanish for '68, when the roster showed just a Rogue, two base-trim sedans, and the 440 as a four-door sedan and a wagon. Sixes continued to dominate American sales, with new-generation 199- and 232-cid engines delivering 128/145 bhp for 1967. But that same year brought American's first V-8 options: a new 290-cid small-block, derived from the 287, in 200- and 225-bhp tune. V-8s continued through Rambler's last stand, when American prices still began just shy of the magic $2000 mark.

All 1965 Ramblers were advertised as "The Sensible Spectaculars," but that fuzzy logic applied mainly to a much-revised Classic and Ambassador. The former wore a new convex "dumbbell" grille, recontoured hood, and a longer, squared-up rear deck. A convertible appeared in the 770 series, where Typhoon returned, this time as the 770H. Engine choices widened with an optional 155-bhp, 232-cid six and Ambassador's two 327 V-8s. The 770H became a Rebel for '66, when a light facelift featured new grilles and minor trim, a "crisp line" hardtop roof, and a reworked rear end for wagons.

Because the '64 Ambassador sold no better than the '63, the premium Rambler reverted to its own longer 116-inch wheelbase for 1965. Also back was an 880/990 lineup that included a pillarless 990H. Standard power was now the 155-bhp 232 six. The base V-8 was that year's new 287, with optional 327s, as before. An outer-sheetmetal redo bestowed rectilinear lines reminiscent of the Classic, plus a Vee'd bilevel grille and vertically stacked quad headlights. Ambassador also followed Classic in '65 by offering its first convertible, a 990. Trunk space improved on all nonwagon models, but passenger room didn't because the extra wheelbase length was again ahead of the cowl. There were no huge changes for '66, when Ambassador became a separate AMC "make" (*see* AMC).

Also new for '65 was the Classic-based Marlin, a fastback to battle Ford Mustang and Plymouth Barracuda in the burgeoning sporty compact wars. A sweeping pillarless roof tapered down and inward at the back, and elliptical rear side windows helped keep it light-looking. This treatment had been previewed on a 1964 show car called Tarpon, based on Teague's new American, which carried it much better. Teague suggested a showroom version. Abernethy agreed, but insisted on besting rival 2+2s with a "3+3." Thus was Marlin molded on the Classic instead—and suffered ungainly overall proportions from that car's fairly stubby hood. This likely explains why the new image-maker sold none too well despite decent performance and a reasonable $3100 base price. Only 10,327 were produced for '65, after which Marlin sold with diminishing success as its own "make" for two more years (*see* AMC).

Rebel replaced Classic for an all-new group of midsize '67 Ramblers. A roomier new body/chassis rode a two-inch longer wheelbase (114 inches), and Teague contributed handsome contemporary styling marked by a floating rectangular grille, squarish front fenders flowing into "hippy" rear flanks, and a shapely deck with large, canted taillights. Besides the expected sixes, Rebels offered a new "thinwall" 290-cid V-8 option with 200 bhp; a bigger bore made for two new 343-cid engines packing 235 and 280 bhp. Other new features included extra-cost front-disc power brakes, available floorshift transmissions, and weight-saving Hotchkiss drive in place of Rambler's old torque-tube. Model choices diminished to two sedans and one wagon in 550 trim; midrange 770 sedan, wagon, and hardtop; and the sporty SST convertible and hardtop. Rebel then joined Marlin and Ambassador as a separate AMC "make" (*see* AMC).

Bidding an outrageous farewell to the Rambler name was the limited-edition 1969 SC/Rambler. This was basically a Rogue hardtop carrying a big new 315-bhp, 390-cid V-8, a working hood scoop, a four-speed manual transmission with Hurst shifter, heavy-duty suspension, and a cartoonish red-white-and-blue paint job. Priced at $2998, the "Scrambler," as it was inevitably nicknamed, was hardly sensible in the Rambler tradition, but it was a pretty spectacular junior muscle car. Published road tests confirmed AMC's claim of standing quarter-miles in the low 14s at around 100 mph. From rest, 60 mph came up in a reported 6.3 seconds. Production was only 1512, though that was triple the planned run.

Not many Rambler convertibles were built, no surprise given AMC's much smaller volume versus the Big Three. Though the ragtop American ran a full seven years (1961-67), the open Classic/Rebel lasted only four (1965-68), and the counterpart Ambassador just three (1965-67). AMC's most-productive soft-top year was 1965, when 3882 Americans, 4953 Classics, and 3499 Ambassadors were produced. All stand to grow in collector esteem and dollar value as the years roll by, as do interesting closed models like the '57 Rebel, the '64 Typhoon, and, of course, the "Scrambler."

Specifications

1957*

Six (wb 108.0)		Wght	Price	Prod
5715	DeLuxe sdn 4d	2,911	1,961	9,402
5715-1	Super sdn 4d	2,914	2,123	16,320
5715-2	Custom sdn 4d	2,938	2,213	10,520
5718-1	Spr Crs Cntry wgn 4d	3,042	2,410	14,083
5718-2	Cus Crs Cntry wgn 4d	3,076	2,500	17,745
5719-1	Super htp sdn	2,936	2,208	612
V-8 (wb 108.0)				
5723-2	Cus Crs Cntry htp wgn 4d	3,409	2,715	182
5725-1	Super sdn 4d	3,223	2,253	3,555
5725-2	Custom sdn 4d	3,259	2,343	3,199

V-8		Wght	Price	Prod
5728-1	Spr Crs Cntry wgn 4d	3,359	2,540	2,461
5728-2	Cus Crs Cntry wgn 4d	3,392	2,630	4,560
5729-2	Custom htp sdn	3,269	2,428	485
5739-2	Cus Rebel htp sdn	3,353	2,786	1,500

* Total model-year registrations: 91,469.

1957 Engines	bore × stroke	bhp	availability
I-6, 195.6	3.13×4.25	125/135	S-Six
V-8, 250.0	3.50×3.25	190	S-V-8 exc Rebl
V-8, 327.0	4.00×3.25	255	S-Rebel

1958

American (wb 100.0)		Wght	Price	Prod
5802	bus sdn 3P	2,439	1,775	184

American		Wght	Price	Prod
5806	DeLuxe sdn 2d	2,463	1,789	15,765
5806-1	Super sdn 2d	2,475	1,874	14,691
Six (wb 108.0)				
5815	DeLuxe sdn 4d	2,947	2,047	12,723
5815-1	Super sdn 4d	2,960	2,212	29,699
5815-2	Custom sdn 4d	2,968	2,327	16,850
5818	DeLuxe wgn 4d	3,050	2,370	78
5818-1	Spr Crs Cntry wgn 4d	3,069	2,506	26,452
5818-2	Cus Crs Cntry wgn 4d	3,079	2,621	20,131
5819-1	Spr Cntry Clb htp sdn	2,983	2,287	983
Rebel V-8 (wb 108.0)				
5825	DeLuxe sdn 4d	3,287	2,177	22

Rebel V-8		Wght	Price	Prod
5825-1	Super sdn 4d	3,300	2,342	2,146
5825-2	Custom sdn 4d	3,313	2,457	2,595
5826-1	Spr Crs Cntry wgn 4d	3,410	2,636	1,782
5826-2	Cus Crs Cntry wgn 4d	3,418	2,751	3,101
5829-2	Cus Cntry Clb htp sdn	3,328	2,532	410
Ambassador (wb 117.0)				
5885-1	Super sdn 4d	3,456	2,587	2,772
5885-2	Custom sdn 4d	3,462	2,732	6,369
5888-1	Spr Crs Cntry wgn 4d	3,544	2,881	1,051
5888-2	Cus Crs Cntry wgn 4d	3,568	3,026	2,742
5883-2	Custom htp wgn 4d	3,586	3,116	294
5889-2	Cus Cntry Clb htp sdn	3,475	2,822	1,340

1958 Engines	bore×stroke	bhp	availability
I-6, 195.6	3.13×4.25	90	S-American
I-6, 195.6	3.13×4.25	127	S-Six
I-6, 195.6	3.13×4.25	138	O-Six
V-8, 250.0	3.50×3.25	215	S-Rebel
V-8, 327.0	4.00×3.25	270	S-Ambassador

1959

American (wb 100.0)		Wght	Price	Prod
5902	bus sdn 3P	2,435	1,821	443
5904	DeLuxe wgn 2d	2,554	2,060	15,256
5904-1	Super wgn 2d	2,554	2,145	17,383
5904-7	Glass panel deliv 2d	—	—	3
5904-8	Steel panel deliv 2d	—	—	3
5906	DeLuxe sdn 2d	2,476	1,835	29,954
5906-1	Super sdn 2d	2,492	1,920	28,449
Six (wb 108.0)				
5915	DeLuxe sdn 4d	2,934	2,098	26,157
5915-1	Super sdn 4d	2,951	2,268	72,577
5915-2	Custom sdn 4d	2,956	2,383	35,242
5918	DeLx Crs Cntry wgn 4d	3,047	2,427	422
5918-1	Spr Crs Cntry wgn 4d	3,082	2,562	66,739
5918-2	Cus Crs Cntry wgn 4d	3,097	2,677	38,761
5919-1	Spr Cntry Clb htp sdn	2,961	2,343	2,683
Rebel V-8 (wb 108.0)				
5925	DeLuxe sdn 4d	3,283	2,228	113
5925-1	Super sdn 4d	3,287	2,398	3,488
5925-2	Custom sdn 4d	3,295	2,513	4,046
5928-1	Spr Crs Cntry wgn 4d	3,398	2,692	3,634
5928-2	Cus Crs Cntry wgn 4d	3,407	2,807	4,427
5929-2	Cus Cntry Clb htp sdn	3,338	2,588	691
Ambassador (wb 117.0)				
5983-2	Cus Crs Cntry htp wgn 4d	3,591	3,116	578
5985	DeLuxe sdn 4d	—	—	155
5985-1	Super sdn 4d	3,428	2,587	4,675
5985-2	Custom sdn 4d	3,437	2,732	10,791
5988-1	Spr Crs Cntry wgn 4d	3,546	2,881	1,782
5988-2	Cus Crs Cntry wgn 4d	3,562	3,026	4,341
5989-2	Cus Cntry Clb htp sdn	3,483	2,822	1,447

1959 Engines	bore×stroke	bhp	availability
I-6, 195.6	3.13×4.25	90	S-American
I-6, 195.6	3.13×4.25	127	S-Six
I-6, 195.6	3.13×4.25	138	O-Six
V-8, 250.0	3.50×3.25	215	S-Rebel
V-8, 327.0	4.00×3.25	270	S-Ambassador

1960

American (wb 100.0)		Wght	Price	Prod
6002	DeLuxe bus sdn 3P	2,428	1,781	630
6004	DeLuxe wgn 2d	2,527	2,020	12,290
6004-1	Super wgn 2d	2,549	2,185	15,093
6004-2	Custom wgn 2d	2,606	2,235	1,430
6005	DeLuxe sdn 4d	2,474	1,844	22,593
6005-1	Super sdn 4d	2,490	1,929	21,108
6005-2	Custom sdn 4d	2,551	2,059	3,272
6006	DeLuxe sdn 2d	2,451	1,795	23,960
6006-1	Super sdn 2d	2,462	1,880	17,233
6006-2	Custom sdn 2d	2,523	2,010	2,994
Six (wb 108.0)				
6015	DeLuxe sdn 4d	2,912	2,098	37,666
6015-1	Super sdn 4d	2,930	2,268	88,004
6015-2	Custom sdn 4d	2,929	2,383	38,003
6018	DeLx Crs Cntry wgn 4d	3,051	2,427	24,011
6018-1	Spr Crs Cntry wgn 4d, 6P	3,054	2,562	59,491
6018-2	Cus Crs Cntry wgn 4d, 6P	3,057	2,677	32,092
6018-3	Spr Crs Cntry wgn 4d, 8P	3,117	2,687	8,456

Six		Wght	Price	Prod
6018-4	Cus Crs Cntry wgn 4d, 8P	3,137	2,802	5,718
6019-2	Cus Cntry Clb htp sdn	2,981	2,458	3,937
Rebel V-8 (wb 108.0)				
6025	DeLuxe sdn 4d	3,252	2,217	143
6025-1	Super sdn 4d	3,270	2,387	3,826
6025-2	Custom sdn 4d	3,278	2,502	3,969
6028-1	Spr Crs Cntry wgn 4d, 6P	3,391	2,681	3,328
6028-2	Cus Crs Cntry wgn 4d, 6P	3,395	2,796	3,613
6028-3	Spr Crs Cntry wgn 4d, 8P	3,446	2,806	718
6028-4	Cus Crs Cntry wgn 4d, 8P	3,447	2,921	886
6029-2	Cus Cntry Clb htp sdn	3,319	2,577	579
Ambassador (wb 117.0)				
6083-2	Cus Crs Cntry htp wgn 4d	3,583	3,116	435
6085	DeLuxe sdn 4d	3,384	2,395	302
6085-1	Super sdn 4d	3,395	2,587	3,990
6085-2	Custom sdn 4d	3,408	2,732	10,949
6088-1	Spr Crs Cntry wgn 4d, 6P	3,521	2,881	1,342
6088-2	Cus Crs Cntry wgn 4d, 6P	3,538	3,026	3,849
6088-3	Spr Crs Cntry wgn 4d, 8P	3,581	3,006	637
6088-4	Cus Crs Cntry wgn 4d, 8P	3,592	3,151	1,153
6089-2	Cus Cntry Clb htp sdn	3,465	2,822	1,141

1960 Engines	bore×stroke	bhp	availability
I-6, 195.6	3.13×4.25	90	S-American
I-6, 195.6	3.13×4.25	127	S-Six; O-Amer
I-6, 195.6	3.13×4.25	138	O-Six
V-8, 250.0	3.50×3.25	200	S-Rebel
V-8, 250.0	3.50×3.25	215	O-Rebel
V-8, 327.0	4.00×3.25	250	S-Ambassador
V-8, 327.0	4.00×3.25	270	O-Ambassador

1961

American (wb 100.0)		Wght	Price	Prod
6102	DeLuxe bus sdn 2d	2,454	1,831	355
6104	DeLuxe wgn 2d	2,549	2,080	5,666
6104-1	Super wgn 2d	2,556	2,165	5,749
6104-2	Custom wgn 2d	2,617	2,295	1,417
6105	DeLuxe sdn 4d	2,523	1,894	17,811
6105-1	Super sdn 4d	2,530	1,979	15,741
6105-2	Custom sdn 4d	2,557	2,060	7,549
6106	DeLuxe sdn 2d	2,490	1,845	28,555
6106-1	Super sdn 2d	2,499	1,930	14,349
6106-2	Custom sdn 2d	2,557	2,060	4,883
6107-2	Custom conv cpe	2,712	2,369	12,918
6108	DeLuxe wgn 4d	2,595	2,129	7,260
6108-1	Super wgn 4d	2,602	2,214	10,071
6108-2	Custom wgn 4d	2,660	2,344	3,679
Classic Six (wb 108.0)				
6115	DeLuxe sdn 4d	2,905	2,098	40,398
6115-1	Super sdn 4d	2,923	2,268	62,563
6115-2	Custom sdn 4d	2,863	2,413	26,497
6118	DeLuxe wgn 4d	3,037	2,437	19,848
6118-1	Super wgn 4d, 6P	3,046	2,572	38,370
6118-2	Custom wgn 4d, 6P	2,984	2,717	16,394
6118-3	Super wgn 4d, 8P	3,087	2,697	4,465
6118-4	Custom wgn 4d, 8P	3,023	2,842	2,741
Classic V-8 (wb 108.0)				
6125	DeLuxe sdn 4d	3,237	2,227	121
6125-1	Super sdn 4d	3,255	2,397	2,156
6125-2	Custom sdn 4d	3,262	2,512	2,180
6128-1	Super wgn 4d, 6P	3,372	2,701	1,964
6128-2	Custom wgn 4d, 6P	3,378	2,816	1,777
6128-3	Super wgn 4d, 8P	3,408	2,826	300
6128-4	Custom wgn 4d, 8P	3,420	2,941	382
Ambassador (wb 117.0)				
6185	DeLuxe sdn 4d	3,343	2,395	273
6185-1	Super sdn 4d	3,361	2,537	3,299
6185-2	Custom sdn 4d	3,380	2,682	10,100
6188-1	Super wgn 4d, 6P	3,493	2,841	1,099
6188-2	Custom wgn 4d, 6P	3,495	2,986	3,010
6188-3	Super wgn 4d, 8P	3,560	2,966	277
6188-4	Custom wgn 4d, 8P	3,566	3,111	784

1961 Engines	bore×stroke	bhp	availability
I-6, 195.6	3.13×4.25	90	S-Amer exc Cus
I-6, 195.6	3.13×4.25	125	S-Amer Cus
I-6, 195.6	3.13×4.25	127	S-Classic Six
I-6, 195.6	3.13×4.25	138	O-Classic Six
V-8, 250.0	3.50×3.25	200	S-Classic V-8
V-8, 250.0	3.50×3.25	215	O-Classic V-8
V-8, 327.0	4.00×3.25	250	S-Ambassador
V-8, 327.0	4.00×3.25	270	O-Ambassador

1962

American (wb 100.0)		Wght	Price	Prod
6202	DeLuxe bus sdn 2d	2,454	1,832	283
6204	DeLuxe wgn 2d	2,555	2,081	4,434
6204-2	Custom wgn 2d	2,565	2,141	4,398
6205	DeLuxe sdn 4d	2,500	1,895	17,758
6205-2	Custom sdn 4d	2,512	1,958	13,884
6205-5	400 sdn 4d	2,585	2,089	5,773
6206	DeLuxe sdn 2d	2,480	1,846	29,665
6206-2	Custom sdn 2d	2,492	1,909	12,710
6206-5	400 sdn 2d	2,558	2,040	4,840
6207-5	400 conv cpe	2,735	2,344	13,497
6208	DeLuxe wgn 4d	2,573	2,130	6,304
6208-2	Custom wgn 4d	2,600	2,190	8,998
6208-5	400 wgn 4d	2,692	2,320	3,134
Classic (wb 108.0)				
6215	DeLuxe sdn 4d	2,888	2,050	38,082
6215-2	Custom sdn 4d	2,898	2,200	68,699
6215-5	400 sdn 4d	2,853	2,349	31,255
6216	DeLuxe sdn 4d	2,866	2,000	14,811
6216-2	Custom sdn 2d	2,876	2,150	12,652
6216-5	400 sdn 2d	2,841	2,299	5,521
6218	DeLuxe wgn 4d, 6P	3,041	2,380	28,203
6218-2	Custom wgn 4d, 6P	3,024	2,492	53,671
6218-4	Custom wgn 4d, 8P	3,094	2,614	6,322
6218-5	400 wgn 4d	2,985	2,640	2,1281
Ambassador (wb 108.0)				
6285	DeLuxe sdn 4d	3,249	2,336	421
6285-2	Custom sdn 4d	3,259	2,464	7,398
6285-5	400 sdn 4d	3,283	2,605	15,120
6286	DeLuxe sdn 2d	3,227	2,282	45
6286-2	Custom sdn 2d	3,237	2,410	659
6286-5	400 sdn 2d	3,261	2,551	459
6288	DeLuxe wgn 4d	3,375	2,648	77
6288-2	Custom wgn 4d	3,385	2,760	4,302
6288-5	400 wgn 4d, 6P	3,408	2,901	6,401
6288-6	400 wgn 4d, 8P	3,471	3,023	1,289

1962 Engines	bore×stroke	bhp	availability
I-6, 195.6	3.13×4.25	90	S-American
I-6, 195.6	3.13×4.25	125	O-American
I-6, 195.6	3.13×4.25	127	S-Classic
I-6, 195.6	3.13×4.25	138	O-Classic
V-8, 327.0	4.00×3.25	250	S-Ambassador
V-8, 327.0	4.00×3.25	270	O-Ambassador

1963

American (wb 100.0)		Wght	Price	Prod
6302	220 bus sdn 2d	2,446	1,832	162
6304	220 wgn 2d	2,528	2,081	3,312
6304-2	330 wgn 2d	2,539	2,141	3,204
6305	220 sdn 4d	2,485	1,895	14,419
6305-2	330 sdn 4d	2,500	1,958	9,666
6305-5	440 sdn 4d	2,575	2,089	2,937
6306	220 sdn 4d	2,472	1,846	27,780
6306-2	330 sdn 2d	2,484	1,909	9,572
6306-5	440 sdn 2d	2,556	2,040	1,486
6307-5	440 conv cpe	2,743	2,344	4,750
6308	220 wgn 4d	2,549	2,130	4,436
6308-2	330 wgn 4d	2,561	2,190	6,848
6308-5	440 wgn 4d	2,638	2,320	1,874
6309-5	440 htp cpe	2,550	2,136	5,101
6309-7	440H htp cpe	2,567	2,281	9,749
Classic (wb 112.0)				
6315	550 sdn 4d	2,729	2,105	43,315
6315-2	660 sdn 4d	2,740	2,245	71,646
6315-5	770 sdn 4d	2,686	2,349	35,281
6316	550 sdn 2d	2,720	2,055	14,417
6316-2	660 sdn 2d	2,725	2,195	11,064
6316-5	770 sdn 2d	2,663	2,299	5,496
6318	550 wgn 4d	2,893	2,435	27,261
6318-2	660 wgn 4d, 6P	2,890	2,537	46,282
6318-4	660 wgn 4d, 9P	2,885	2,609	5,752
6318-5	770 wgn 4d	2,828	2,640	19,319
Ambassador (wb 112.0)				
6385	800 sdn 4d	3,140	2,391	437
6385-2	880 sdn 4d	3,145	2,519	7,667
6385-5	990 sdn 4d	3,158	2,660	14,019
6386	800 sdn 2d	3,110	2,337	41

1961 Engines	bore×stroke	bhp	availability
V-8, 327.0	4.00×3.25	270	O-Ambassador

Ambassador		Wght	Price	Prod
6386-2	880 sdn 2d	3,116	2,465	1,042
6386-5	990 sdn 2d	3,132	2,606	1,764
6388	800 wgn 4d	3,270	2,703	113
6388-2	880 wgn 4d	3,275	2,815	4,929
6388-5	990 wgn 4d, 6P	3,298	2,956	6,112
6388-6	990 wgn 4d, 9P	3,305	3,018	1,687

1963 Engines	bore×stroke	bhp	availability
I-6, 195.6	3.13×4.25	90	S-American 220/330; O-440
I-6, 195.6	3.13×4.25	125	S-Amer 440; O-220/330
I-6, 195.6	3.13×4.25	127	S-Classic
I-6, 195.6	3.13×4.25	138	S-Amer 440H; O-Classic
V-8, 287.0	3.75×3.25	198	O-Classic
V-8, 327.0	4.00×3.25	250	S-Ambassador
V-8, 327.0	4.00×3.25	270	O-Ambassador

1964

American (wb 106.0) - 160,321 blt		Wght	Price	Prod
6405	220 sdn 4d	2,527	1,964	—
6405-2	330 sdn 4d	2,526	2,057	—
6405-5	440 sdn 4d	2,572	2,150	—
6406	220 sdn 2d	2,506	1,907	—
6406-2	330 sdn 2d	2,504	2,000	—
6407-5	440 conv cpe	2,752	2,346	8,907
6408	220 wgn 4d	2,661	2,240	—
6408-2	330 wgn 4d	2,675	2,324	—
6409-5	440 htp cpe	2,596	2,133	19,495
6409-7	440H htp cpe 5P	2,617	2,292	14,527
Classic (wb 112.0)				
6415	550 sdn 4d	2,755	2,116	21,310
6415-2	660 sdn 4d	2,758	2,256	37,584
6415-5	770 sdn 4d	2,763	2,360	14,337
6416	550 sdn 2d	2,732	2,066	6,454
6416-2	660 sdn 2d	2,736	2,206	3,976
6416-5	770 sdn 2d	2,740	2,310	1,278
6418	550 wgn 4d	2,915	2,446	13,164
6418-2	660 wgn 4d	2,915	2,548	26,671
6418-5	770 wgn 4d	2,921	2,651	10,523
6419-5	770 htp cpe	2,789	2,397	8,996
6419-7	Typhoon htp cpe	2,818	2,509	2,520
Ambassador 990 (wb 112.0) - 18,519 built				
6485-5	sdn 4d	3,204	2,671	—
6488-5	wgn 4d	3,350	2,985	—
6489-5	htp cpe	3,213	2,736	—
6489	990H htp cpe	3,255	2,917	—

1964 Engines	bore×stroke	bhp	availability
I-6, 195.6	3.13×4.25	90	S-American 220/330; O-440
I-6, 195.6	3.13×4.25	125	S-Amer 440; O-220/330
I-6, 195.6	3.13×4.25	127	S-Classic
I-6, 195.6	3.13×4.25	138	S-Amer 440H; O-Clsc exc Typhoon
I-6, 232.0	3.75×3.50	145	S-Typhoon; O-other Clsc
V-8, 287.0	3.75×3.25	198	O-Classic
V-8, 327.0	4.00×3.25	250	S-Amb exc 990H
V-8, 327.0	4.00×3.25	270	S-Amb 990H; O-other Amb

1965

American (wb 106.0)		Wght	Price	Prod
6505	220 sdn 4d	2,518	2,036	13,700
6505-2	330 sdn 4d	2,522	2,129	15,433
6505-5	440 sdn 4d	2,580	2,222	5,194
6506	220 sdn 2d	2,492	1,979	26,409
6506-2	330 sdn 2d	2,490	2,072	9,065
6507-5	440 conv cpe	2,747	2,418	3,882
6508	220 wgn 4d	2,684	2,312	5,224
6508-2	330 wgn 4d	2,682	2,396	12,313
6509-5	440 htp cpe	2,596	2,205	13,784
6509-7	440H htp cpe	2,622	2,327	8,164
Classic 550 (wb 112.0)				
6515	sdn 4d	2,987	2,192	30,869
6516	sdn 2d	2,963	2,142	7,082
6518	wgn 4d	3,134	2,522	13,759
Classic 660 (wb 112.0)				
6515-2	sdn 4d	3,016	2,332	50,638
6516-2	sdn 2d	2,991	2,282	4,561
6518-2	wgn 4d	3,155	2,624	32,444
Classic 770 (wb 112.0)				
6515-5	sdn 4d	3,029	2,436	23,603
6517-5	conv cpe	3,169	2,696	4,953
6518-5	wgn 4d	3,180	2,727	15,623
6519-5	htp cpe	3,063	2,436	14,778
6519-7	770H htp cpe	3,089	2,548	5,706
Marlin (wb 112.0)				
6559-7	fastbk htp cpe	3,234	3,100	10,327
Ambassador (wb 116.0)				
6585-2	880 sdn 4d	3,120	2,565	10,564
6585-5	990 sdn 4d	3,151	2,656	24,852
6586-2	880 sdn 2d	3,087	2,512	1,301
6587-5	990 conv cpe	3,265	2,955	3,499
6588-2	880 wgn 4d	3,247	2,879	3,812
6588-5	990 wgn 4d	3,268	2,970	8,701
6589-5	990 htp cpe	3,168	2,669	5,034
6589-7	990H htp cpe	3,198	2,837	6,382

1965 Engines	bore×stroke	bhp	availability
I-6, 195.6	3.13×4.25	90	S-Amer 220/330
I-6, 195.6	3.13×4.25	125	S-American 440/440H
I-6, 199.0	3.75×3.00	128	S-Classic 550
I-6, 232.0	3.75×3.25	145	S-Classic 660/770/770H, Marlin; O-Amb, American

1965 Engines	bore×stroke	bhp	availability
I-6, 232.0	3.75×3.25	155	S-Amb; O-Clsc
V-8, 287.0	3.75×3.25	198	O-Clsc, Marlin, Ambassador
V-8, 327.0	4.00×3.25	270	O-Clsc, Marlin, Ambassador

1966

American 220 (wb 106)		Wght	Price	Prod
6605	sdn 4d	2,574	2,086	15,940
6606	sdn 2d	2,554	2,017	24,440
6608	wgn 4d	2,740	2,369	5,809
American 440 (wb 106.0)				
6605-5	sdn 4d	2,582	2,203	14,543
6606-5	sdn 2d	2,562	2,134	5,252
6607-5	conv cpe	2,782	2,486	2,092
6608-5	wgn 4d	2,745	2,477	6,603
6609-5	htp cpe	2,610	2,227	10,255
Rogue (wb 106.0)				
6609-7	htp cpe	2,630	2,370	8,718
Classic 550 (wb 112.0)				
6615	sdn 4d	2,885	2,238	22,485
6616	sdn 2d	2,860	2,189	5,505
6618	wgn 4d	3,070	2,542	9,390
Classic 770 (wb 112.0)				
6615-5	sdn 4d	2,905	2,337	46,044
6617-5	conv cpe	3,070	2,616	1,806
6618-5	wgn 4d	3,071	2,629	24,528
6619-5	htp cpe	2,935	2,363	8,736
Rebel (wb 112.0)				
6618-7	htp cpe	2,950	2,523	7,512

1966 Engines	bore×stroke	bhp	availability
I-6, 199.0	3.75×3.00	128	S-Amer, Rogue
I-6, 232.0	3.75×3.50	145	S-Clsc, Rebel
I-6, 232.0	3.75×3.50	155	O-all
V-8, 287.0	3.75×3.25	198	O-Clsc, Rebel
V-8, 290.0	3.75×3.28	200	O-American
V-8, 290.0	3.75×3.28	225	O-American
V-8, 327.0	4.00×3.25	250	O-Clsc, Rebel
V-8, 327.0	4.00×3.25	270	O-Clsc, Rebel

1967

American 220 (wb 106.0)		Wght	Price	Prod
6705	sdn 4d	2,621	2,142	12,078
6706	sdn 2d	2,591	2,073	26,196
6708	wgn 4d	2,767	2,425	3,667
American 440 (wb 106.0)				
6705-5	sdn 4d	2,613	2,259	10,083
6706-5	sdn 2d	2,586	2,191	3,317
American 440				
6708-5	wgn 4d	2,769	2,533	4,407
6709-5	htp cpe	2,643	2,283	4,994
Rogue (wb 106.0)				
6707-7	conv cpe	2,821	2,611	921
6709-7	htp cpe	2,663	2,426	4,249
Rebel 550 (wb 114.0)				
6715	sdn 4d	3,055	2,319	10,582
6716	sdn 2d	3,089	2,294	9,121
6718	wgn 4d	3,287	2,623	6,845
Rebel 770 (wb 114.0)				
6715-5	sdn 4d	3,053	2,418	27,457
6718-5	wgn 4d	3,288	2,710	18,552
6719-5	htp cpe	3,092	2,443	9,721
Rebel SST (wb 114.0)				
6717-7	conv cpe	3,180	2,872	1,686
6719-7	htp cpe	3,109	2,604	16,663

1967 Engines	bore×stroke	bhp	availability
I-6, 199.0	3.75×3.00	128	S-American
I-6, 232.0	3.75×3.25	145	S-Rbl; O-Amer
I-6, 232.0	3.75×3.25	155	O-Amer, Rebel
V-8, 290.0	3.75×3.28	200	O-Amer, Rebel
V-8, 290.0	3.75×3.28	225	O-American
V-8, 343.0	4.08×3.28	235	O-Rebel
V-8, 343.0	4.08×3.28	280	O-Rebel

1968

American (wb 106.0)		Wght	Price	Prod
6805	sdn 4d	2,638	2,024	15,144
6806	sdn 2d	2,604	1,946	39,480
American 440 (wb 106.0)				
6805-5	sdn 4d	2,643	2,166	11,179
6808-5	wgn 4d	2,800	2,426	10,414
Rogue (wb 106.0)				
6809-7	htp cpe	2,678	2,244	4,765

1968 Engines	bore×stroke	bhp	availability
I-6, 199.0	3.75×3.00	128	S-American
I-6, 232.0	3.75×3.50	145	S-Rge; O-Amer
V-8, 290.0	3.75×3.28	200	O-American
V-8, 290.0	3.75×3.28	225	O-Amer, Rge

1969

American (wb 106.0)		Wght	Price	Prod
6905	sdn 4d	2,638	2,076	16,234
6906	sdn 2d	2,604	1,998	51,062
American 440 (wb 106.0)				
6905-5	sdn 4d	2,643	2,218	11,957
6908-5	wgn 4d	2,800	2,478	13,233
Rogue (wb 106.0)				
6909-7	htp cpe	2,678	2,296	3,543
SC/Rambler-Hurst (wb 106.0)				
6909-7	htp cpe	3,160	2,998	1,512

1969 Engines	bore×stroke	bhp	availability
I-6, 199.0	3.75×3.00	128	S-American
I-6, 232.0	3.75×3.50	145	S-Rge; O-Amer
V-8, 290.0	3.75×3.28	200	O-Rogue, American 440
V-8, 290.0	3.75×3.28	225	O-Rogue
V-8, 390.0	4.17×3.57	315	S-SC/Rambler-Hurst

Note: See Nash listing for Rambler models prior to 1957. See AMC listing for related 1966-69 models, and those built after 1969.

Reo

Reo resulted from a 1904 argument at Olds Motor Works, the first car company founded by the tenacious Ransom Eli Olds. When colleagues began pressuring him to build four- and six-cylinder models that were more substantial than his little Curved-Dash Oldsmobile, Ransom ventured down the street to set up a rival concern. By year's end, this new R.E. Olds Company was called Reo Motor Car Company, after his initials. Ransom got his "revenge": through 1917, Reo outproduced Olds Motor Works.

From the company's beginning to 1919, Reo fielded one-, two-, four-, and six-cylinder cars. The firm's all-time production record, 29,000, came in 1928, by which time Reo was selling sixes only. After seeing car sales fall almost 30 percent in calendar-year 1929, Reo posted a $2 million loss on 1930 volume of about 12,500 cars and a like number of trucks. The Depression had hit, and Reo was mortally wounded. But even though the company never sold more than 5000 cars a year after 1932, some of those it did sell were memorable, and among the handsomest automobiles ever created.

The Flying Cloud Sixes of 1930 were little changed from 1929. That year's junior Reo was the 115-inch-wheelbase Model 15, basically the previous year's low-priced Flying Cloud Mate with the same 60-bhp, 214.7-cubic-inch Continental engine. Senior models, now called Flying Cloud Master, comprised the 120-inch Model 20 and 124-inch "25" powered by a 268.3-cid Reo engine with 80 bhp. Prices were in the upper-middle bracket at $1175-$1870 (after Depression-prompted cuts). Styling, by the talented and once unappreciated Amos Northup, was classic, formal, and finely proportioned. Workmanship was solid, furnishings top-quality.

January 1931 brought an expanded line that ultimately offered two new straight-eights. Model nomenclature denoted cylinders and wheelbase. The larger eight, delivering 125 bhp from 358 cid, was reserved for magnificent new 8-35 Royales on a strong double-drop frame with 135-inch wheelbase. It also powered companion 8-30 Flying Clouds. Anchoring the line was the new 6-25 with 85-bhp 268 six, selling at around $1800.

The Royale premiered at $2495 with three closed Murray-built bodies. All were smooth and truly beautiful, Northup pointing the way for everyone else with skirted fenders, rounded corners, and raked-back radiators. The 8-30 and 6-25 wore a more conservative version of this look. Reo also announced an immense new 152-inch Royale chassis for custom coachwork by Dietrich, comprising an imposing seven-passenger limousine and three convertibles. But apart from show models, few of those opulent Reos were ever built. Though all Royales had effortless performance with their big nine-main-bearing engine, they were hardly appropriate for hard economic times.

Reo spent $6 million on these initial 1931 models, hoping to spark sales. When sales failed to ignite, the firm threw additional variations at the market: a Royale 8-31; the Flying Cloud 8-25, with a new 90-bhp eight not much bigger than Reo's six; and the 6-21, really a 6-25 downpriced to the $995-$1100 region. But none of these caught on either, and Reo lost nearly $3 million on sales of just 6762 cars.

Still trying hard, Reo unveiled a smaller Flying Cloud in January 1932, the 117-inch-wheelbase 6-S. Carrying a debored 230-cid six with 80 bhp, this new entry-level line listed nine open and closed models in Standard and DeLuxe trim for $995-$1205. Eight-cylinder Clouds returned virtually without change. So did Royales, but the 8-31 and 8-35 were now nameless, and 8-52s were retagged Royale Custom. Of course, everything hinged on the 6-S, but it failed to make the needed impression, and Reo car sales fell to 3900 for the calendar year. Desperately seeking cash, the firm agreed to sell 6-S bodies and chassis to equally beleaguered Franklin for that company's 1933 Olympic, which was nearly identical except for grille, hood, and air-cooled Franklin power.

1931/32 Royale four-door sedan

1933 Flying Cloud convertible coupe

1933 S-2 Flying Cloud Elite four-door sedan

1936 Flying Cloud Six four-door sedan

With all this, Reo had no choice but to drastically cut its 1933 line. Thus, Flying Cloud Eights vanished in January. So did the 6-25, though its engine returned in a new low-end S-2 Flying Cloud that replaced the 6-S on an inch-longer wheelbase. The longest chassis was also dropped, leaving N-2 standard and Elite Royales on the 131-inch platform and N-1 Customs on the 135-inch chassis. Prices were cut too, but the cuts weren't enough to matter. Despite smoother styling and sturdier new X-member frames, Reo's calendar-year registrations fell to 3623, the lowest on record.

Most 1934 Reos appeared in July and September of 1933, essentially carryovers save more deeply skirted fenders and an eye-catching array of six vents per hoodside. Headlining the "real" "34s, unveiled in April, was the new S-4 Flying Cloud with nice streamlining and an optional built-in trunk for four-door sedans, though most everything else was continued from the S-2 and interim S-3 models.

Arriving in May 1933 was the "Self-Shifter," a new freebie for Royales and an $85 extra for S-4s. This was a semiautomatic transmission developed at a cost of about $2 million amidst mounting corporate finacial losses. Innovative and dependable, the Self-Shifter replaced the conventional gearlever with an under-dash T-handle. Pushing the handle to "Forward" brought access to a pair of driving gears that changed automatically according to road speed. You pulled the handle halfway out for Neutral, all the way out for "emergency low," which also had two automatic ratios. For Reverse, turn the handle right, then pull out. The clutch pedal was used only for starting off. Nice though this was, the Self-Shifter attracted few buyers. But surprisingly, Reo's calendar-1934 car output was slightly higher at 4460, and truck sales jumped a startling 70 percent.

Some experts cite the Self-Shifter's development cost as a key factor in Reo's demise, but management turmoil since the Great Crash also contributed. When Ransom Olds moved up to board chairman in 1923, new president Richard Scott greatly expanded production, which left Reo with money-losing excess capacity when the Depression severely shrunk the medium-price market. At Old's insistence, Scott was replaced in 1930 by William Wilson, an executive of the Murray Body Company. But when Wilson couldn't halt the sales slide, Scott got another chance. That angered Olds, yet Scott's supporters were entrenched, prompting the founder to resign in December 1933. That shook up embattled Reo stockholders, who persuaded Olds to return the following April and elected Donald E. Bates as president. Hopes were high that things would turn around.

Meanwhile, the S-4 continued into 1935 as the little-changed S-5, and Eights gave way to a lowly S-7 Royale Six coupe and sedan, essentially S-5s with a 95-bhp engine selling for $985. Both were gone by early 1936, a sorry end for the once-mighty Royale.

But somehow, Reo managed yet another new Flying Cloud for 1935. Designated A-6, this offered two- and four-door Hayes-built fastback sedans with 115-inch wheelbase and a superior new 90-bhp 228-cid six with seven main bearings, aluminum head, automatic choke, and external vibration damper. Front styling vaguely recalled Auburn, with flared fenders and vee'd bumper. For all that, Ransom Olds disliked the A-6, calling its $450,000 tooling cost a waste of money. But as at Olds Motor Works long before, his colleagues disagreed, and they pushed ahead for '36. They were doubtless encouraged by Reo's first profit in years, a slim $42,156 for the first half of 1935 on meager sales of cars and trucks. Still seeking to bolster income, the firm shared its body dies with erstwhile rival, Graham-Paige.

Reo announced "America's Finest Six" in November 1935, but it was just an A-6 with fuller fenders, rubber-tipped bumper guards, optional "Zeppelin-style" fender lamps, and a reworked hood and radiator wearing bright trim *a la* Pontiac's "Silver Streaks." The Self-Shifter was canned for conventional overdrive as a $50 extra for standard and DeLuxe models priced at $795-$895. But public confidence in Reo had nearly evaporated, so the firm built a mere 3206 cars that year, versus 4692 for calendar-year 1935.

With trucks now far more profitable than cars (the G-P deal had produced little revenue), the Reo board voted on May 18, 1936, to move truck assembly into the main Lansing plant; on September 3rd, Reo officially left the auto business. Though the company lost nearly $1.4 million on its 1936 cars, it was able to write off $604,000 for terminating its auto operations. Reo then turned exclusively to the truck field. Ironically, it would thrive there far longer than it had with cars, producing for the next 40 or so years under the Reo and Diamond-Reo nameplates.

Specifications

1930

Model C Flying Cloud Master (wb 120)	Wght	Price	Prod
rdstr 2-4P	3,380	1,685	—
cpe 2P	3,465	1,625	—
spt cpe 2-4P	3,615	1,750	—
victoria 4P	3,550	1,695	—
spt victoria 4P	3,715	1,820	—
brougham 2d	3,540	1,595	—
spt brougham 2d	3,675	1,720	—
sdn 4d	3,665	1,745	—
DeLuxe sdn 4d	3,800	1,870	—
spt rdstr 2-4P	3,570	1,810	—
Model B-2 Flying Cloud (wb 115.0)			
phtn 5P	—	1,395	—
spt phtn 5P 6W	—	1,595	—
Standard cpe 2P	3,170	1,375	—
Standard cpe 2P 5W	3,180	1,435	—
Standard cpe 2-4P	3,220	1,395	—
Stand cpe 2-4P 6W	3,230	1,455	—
Model B-2 Flying Cloud			
spt cpe 2-4P	3,325	1,495	—
Standard sdn 4d 5W	3,280	1,395	—
Standard sdn 4d 6W	3,300	1,455	—
spt sdn 4d	3,390	1,495	—
Model 20 Flying Cloud (wb 120.0) - 2,189 built			
Standard cpe 2-4P	3,635	1,595	—

Model 20 Flying Cloud	Wght	Price	Prod
spt cpe 2-4P	3,720	1,705	—
Standard sdn 4d	3,700	1,595	—
spt sdn 4d	3,785	1,705	—
Model 25 Flying Cld Master (wb 124.0) - 2,128 built			
Standard sdn 4d	3,795	1,795	—
spt sdn 4d	3,945	1,905	—
Model 15 Flying Cloud (wb 115.0) - 1,789 built			
Standard phtn 5P	3,050	1,195	—
spt phtn 5P	3,140	1,238	—
Standard cpe 2P	3,110	1,175	—
spt cpe 2P	3,200	1,218	—
Standard cpe 2-4P	3,170	1,195	—
spt cpe 2-4P	3,260	1,238	—
Model 15 Flying Cloud			
Standard sdn 4d	3,300	1,295	—
spt sdn 4d	3,370	1,338	—

1930 Engines	bore×stroke	bhp	availability
I-6, 214.7	3.38×4.00	60	S-B-2, 15
I-6, 268.3	3.38×5.00	80	S-C, 20, 25

1931

Model 15 Flying Cld (wb 115)	Wght	Price	Prod
Standard phtn 5P	3,050	1,195	—
spt phtn 5P	3,140	1,238	—
Standard cpe 2P	3,110	1,175	—
spt cpe 2P	3,200	1,218	—
Standard cpe 2-4P	3,170	1,195	—

Model 15 Flying Cloud	Wght	Price	Prod
spt cpe 2-4P	3,260	1,238	—
Standard sdn 4d	3,300	1,295	—
spt sdn 4d	3,370	1,338	—
Model 20 Flying Cloud (wb 120.0)			
Standard cpe 2-4P	3,635	1,595	—
spt cpe 2-4P	3,720	1,705	—
Standard sdn 4d	3,700	1,595	—
spt sdn 4d	3,785	1,705	—
Model 25 Flying Cloud (wb 124.0)			
Standard sdn 4d	3,795	1,795	—
spt sdn 4d	3,945	1,905	—
Model 21 Flying Cloud Six (wb 121.0)			
cpe 2P	3,645	1,295	—
Custom spt cpe 2-4P	3,800	1,410	—
sdn 4d	3,495	1,295	—
Custom spt sdn 4d	3,630	1,410	—
Model 21 Flying Cloud Eight (wb 121.0)			
cpe 2P	3,740	1,395	—
Custom spt cpe 2-4P	3,845	1,510	—
sdn 4d	3,685	1,395	—
Custom spt sdn 4d	3,725	1,510	—
Model 25 Flying Cloud Six (wb 124.0/125.0)			
cpe 2-4P	3,895	1,695	—
victoria 4P	3,880	1,695	—
sdn 4d	3,950	1,695	—
Model 25 Flying Cloud Eight (wb 125.0)			
cpe 2-4P	3,841	1,745	—

Model 25 Flying Cloud Eight	Wght	Price	Prod
victoria 5P	3,904	1,745	—
sdn 4d	4,050	1,745	—
Model 830 Flying Cloud Eight (wb 130.0)			
cpe 2-4P	4,380	1,995	—
victoria 4P	4,400	1,995	—
sdn 4d	4,500	1,995	—
Model 831 Royale (wb 131.0)			
cpe 2-4P	4,310	2,145	—
victoria 4P	4,320	2,145	—
sdn 4d	4,375	2,145	—
Model 835 Royale (wb 135.0)			
cpe 2-4P	4,500	2,745	—
victoria 4P	4,475	2,745	—
sdn 4d	4,650	2,745	—

1931 Engines	bore×stroke	bhp	availability
I-6, 214.7	3.38×4.00	60	S-15
I-6, 268.3	3.38×5.00	80	S-20, 25
I-6, 268.3	3.38×5.00	85	S-21
I-8, 268.6	3.00×4.75	90	S-21, 25
I-8, 358.0	3.38×5.00	125	S-830, 831, 835

1932

Model 6-21 Flying Cloud (wb 121)	Wght	Price	Prod
cpe 2-4P	3,495	995	—
spt cpe 2-4P	3,630	1,110	—
sdn 4d	3,645	995	—
spt sdn 4d	3,800	1,110	—
Model 6-25 Flying Cloud (wb 125.0)			
victoria 5P	3,880	1,565	—
sdn 4d	3,950	1,565	—
cpe 2-4P	3,895	1,565	—
Model 6-S Flying Cloud (wb 117.0) (from 4/32)			
Standard cpe 2-4P	3,300	995	—
Stand conv cpe 2-4P	3,220	1,045	—
Standard sdn 4d	3,405	995	—
spt cpe 2-4P	3,445	1,070	—
spt conv cpe 2-4P	3,360	1,120	—
spt sdn 4d	3,510	1,070	—
DeLx spt cpe 2-4P	—	1,155	—
DeLx spt conv cpe 2-4P	—	1,205	—
DeLuxe spt sdn 4d	—	1,155	—
Model 8-21 Flying Cloud (wb 121.0)			
cpe 2-4P	3,685	1,195	—
spt cpe 2-4P	3,725	1,310	—
sdn 4d	3,740	1,195	—
spt sdn 4d	3,845	1,310	—
Model 8-25 Flying Cloud (wb 125.0)			
cpe 2-4P	3,841	1,565	—
victoria 5P	3,904	1,565	—
sdn 4d	4,050	1,565	—
Model 8-31 Royale (wb 131.0)			
cpe 2-4P	4,310	1,985	—
victoria 4P	4,320	1,985	—
sdn 4d 4,375	1,985	—	
Model 8-35-52 Royale (wb 135.0; lwb-152.0)			
cpe 2-4P	4,500	2,445	—
victoria 5P	4,475	2,445	—
sdn 4d	4,650	2,445	—
lwb sdn 7P	5,010	3,695	—
lwb sdn 7P partition	5,075	3,895	—
Model RYL Royale (131.0) (from 4/32)			
cpe 2-4P	4,310	1,785	—
victoria 4P	4,320	1,785	—
sdn 4d	4,375	1,785	—
Royale Custom (wb 135.0; lwb-152.0) (from 4/32)			
cpe 2-4P	4,500	2,445	—
victoria 5P	4,475	2,445	—
conv cpe 2-4P	4,440	2,995	—
sdn 4d	4,650	2,445	—
lwb sdn 7P	5,010	3,695	—
lwb berline 7P	5,075	3,895	—

1932 Engines	bore×stroke	bhp	availability
I-6, 230.0	3.13×5.00	80	S-6-S
I-6, 268.3	3.38×5.00	80	S-6-25
I-6, 268.3	3.38×5.00	85	S-6-21
I-8, 268.6	3.00×4.75	90	S-8-21, 8-25
I-8, 358.0	3.38×5.00	125	S-all Royale

1933

Model 6-S Flying Cloud (wb 117) - 615 built	Wght	Price	Prod
cpe 2-4P	3,300	995	—
conv cpe 2-4P	3,220	1,045	—
sdn 4d	3,405	995	—
spt cpe 2-4P	3,445	1,070	—
spt conv cpe 2-4P	—	1,120	—
spt sdn 4d	3,510	1,070	—
DeLuxe spt cpe 2-4P	—	1,155	—
DeLx spt conv cpe 2-4P	—	1,205	—
DeLuxe spt sdn 4d	—	1,155	—
cabriolet 2-4P	3,710	1,250	—
Model S-2 Flying Cloud Six (wb 118.0)			
cpe 2-4P	3,450	995	2,099* (all S-2)
Elite cpe 2-4P	3,515	1,090	
conv cpe 2-4P	3,390	1,045	
Elite conv cpe 2-4P	3,490	1,140	
sdn 4d	3,540	995	
Elite sdn 4d	3,645	1,090	

* Includes 1934 S-2.

Royale (wb 131.0) - 121 built	Wght	Price	Prod
cpe 2-4P	4,310	1,785	—
victoria 5P	4,320	1,785	—
sdn 4d	4,375	1,785	—
Royale Eight (wb 131.0; lwb-135.0)			
N-2 Standard cpe 2-4P	—	1,745	1,150 (all N-2)
N-2 Standard victoria 5P	4,500	1,745	
N-2 Standard sdn 4d	4,725	1,745	
N-2 Elite cpe 2-4P	—	1,845	
N-2 Elite victoria 5P	4,625	1,845	
N-2 Elite sdn 4d	4,850	1,845	
N-1 Custom lwb cpe 2-4P	4,540	2,445	—
N-1 Custom lwb victoria 5P	4,515	2,445	—
N-1 Custom lwb sdn 4d	4,690	2,445	—
Royale Cus Eight (wb 135.0; lwb-152.0) - 127 built			
cpe 2-4P	4,500	2,445	—
conv cpe 2-4P	4,440	2,995	—
victoria 5P	4,475	2,445	—
sdn 4d	4,650	2,445	—
lwb sdn 7P	5,010	3,695	—
lwb sdn brghm 7P	5,075	3,895	—

1933 Engines	bore×stroke	bhp	availability
I-6, 268.3	3.38×5.00	85	S-sixes
I-8, 358.0	3.38×5.00	125	S-eights

1934

S-2 Flying Cld Six (wb 118.0)	Wght	Price	Prod
cpe 2-4P	3,500	845	2,099** (all S-2)
Elite cpe 2-4P	3,563	920	
conv cpe 2-4P	3,440	1,045	
Elite conv cpe 2-4P	3,540	1,140	
sdn 4d	3,590	845	
Elite sdn 4d	3,695	920	

**Includes 1933 S-2.

S-3 Flying Cloud Six (wb 118.0)	Wght	Price	Prod
cpe 2-4P	3,500	795	—
sdn 4d	3,590	795	—
S-4 Flying Cloud Six (wb 118.0) (from April 1934)			
bus cpe 2P	—	795	—
cpe 2-4P	3,510	895	—
conv cpe 2-4P	—	925	—
sdn 4d	3,630	895	—
DeL cpe 2-4P	3,530	945	—
DeL conv cpe 2-4P	—	975	—
DeL sdn 4d	3,650	945	—
DeL cpe 2-4P 6W	3,605	995	—
DeL sdn 4d 6W	3,725	995	—
N-2 Royale Eight (wb 131.0)			
cpe 2-4P	4,640	1,500	—
Elite cpe 2-4P	4,790	1,600	—
victoria 5P	4,730	1,500	—
Elite victoria 5P	4,815	1,600	—
sdn 4d	4,765	1,500	—
Elite sdn 4d	4,955	1,600	—
N-1 Royale Custom Eight (wb 135.0)			
Elite cpe 2-4P	4,825	1,700	—
Elite victoria 5P	4,915	1,700	—
Elite sdn 4d	5,015	1,700	—

1934 Engines	bore×stroke	bhp	availability
I-6, 268.3	3.38×5.00	85	S-sixes
I-8, 358.0	3.38×5.00	125	S-eights

1935

S-5 Flying Cld Six (wb 118.0)		Wght	Price	Prod*
	bus cpe 2P	3,445	795	—
	Standard cpe 2-4P	3,510	895	—
	DeLuxe cpe 2-4P 5W	3,530	945	—
	DeLuxe cpe 2-4P 6W	3,605	995	—
	Stand conv cpe 2-4P	3,495	895	—
	DeLx conv cpe 2-4P 5W	3,515	975	—
	DeLx conv cpe 2-4P 6W	3,590	1,025	—
	Standard sdn 4d	3,630	895	—
	DeLuxe sdn 4d 5W	3,650	945	—
	DeLuxe sdn 4d 6W	3,725	995	—
A-6 Flying Cloud Six (wb 115.0) (from Jan. 1935)				
6AB	sdn 2d	3,190	795	—
6AS	sdn 4d	3,220	845	—
S-7 Royale Six (wb 118.0)				
7SC	cpe 3-5P	3,550	985	—
7SS	sdn 4d	3,595	985	—

* Production not available

1935 Engines	bore×stroke	bhp	availability
I-6, 228.0	3.38×4.25	90	S-A-6
I-6, 268.3	3.38×5.00	85	S-S-5
I-6, 268.3	3.38×5.00	95	S-S-7

1936

Flying Cloud Six (wb 115.0)	Wght	Price	Prod
sdn 2d	3,270	795	—
sdn 4d	3,300	845	—
6-75 Flying Cloud DeLuxe (wb 118.0)			
brougham 2d	3,560	845	—
sdn 4d	3,595	895	—
touring sdn 4d T/B	3,625	895	—

1936 Engines	bore×stroke	bhp	availability
I-6, 228.0	3.38×4.25	90	S-Six
I-6, 268.3	3.38×5.00	95	S-6-75

Reo Calendar-Year Production 1930-1936		
1930.....11,450	1933.....3,623	1935.....4,692
1931.....6,762	1934.....4,460	1936.....3,206
1932.....3,870		

Saturn

General Motors' first new nameplate in over 60 years was born in 1982 as Project Saturn. Conceived in part by then-chairman Roger Smith, it was an all-out effort to stem the growing Japanese dominance of the U.S. small-car market that had begun in the early '70s. Smith realized that although GM was highly successful with traditional American cars, it badly lagged behind Japanese makers for small-car quality, design, and cost. As a result, younger buyers were deserting GM's smaller U.S. products for Hondas, Toyotas, and other Japanese models—and they weren't coming back.

More than eight years passed before the first Saturns were sold. For some, that long gestation reinforced doubts that GM could field a competitive, profitable, all-American small car—especially given recent efforts like the problem-plagued X-body front-drive compacts. Heady pronouncements along the way didn't help. For example, at the November 1983 unveiling of a full-scale sedan prototype (later dubbed "the little red car"), Smith promised Saturn would be a "a quantum leap ahead of the Japanese, including what they have coming in the future. In Saturn we have GM's answer—the American answer—to the Japanese challenge. It's the clean-sheet approach to producing small cars that in time will prove to have historic implications."

Originally, Saturn vehicles were to be sold by Chevrolet, starting with a front-drive four-door sedan somewhat smaller than a contemporary Chevy Cavalier. The projected price was $5000-$7000 and its introduction was vaguely described as sometime in "the late '80s." A two-door coupe and a sport-utility vehicle (SUV) were to follow later. By the time Saturn opened for business, however, it was Saturn Corporation, a wholly owned subsidiary charged with pioneering new ideas in everything from styling to service. The most successful innovations would then spread throughout GM itself, or so it was presumed. Saturn was supposed to make money, of course, preferably by stealing sales from the competition, not other GM makes.

In presenting the prototype, GM served notice that Saturns would be different: Body panels would be made of either metal or plastic and attached to a steel "spaceframe" as on Pontiac's then-new Fiero sporty car. The engine would be a brand-new, fuel-injected four-cylinder with an aluminum block and cylinder heads formed by a precision "lost foam" technique. Oil passages would be designed in instead of drilled in after casting to save both time and material. Astonishing EPA-rated fuel economy was promised: 45 mpg city, 60 mpg highway. Other components need not come from corporate bins, and Saturn was free to devise its own engineering and manufacturing methods. A major goal for this experiment was finding ways to close the cost gap with "Japan, Inc.," then estimated at more than $2000 per car. The resultant savings, Smith said, would finally make GM a small-car power in the U.S. market. In fact, he declared Saturn nothing less than "the key to GM's long-term competitiveness, survival, and success."

As announced in January 1985, Saturn Corporation would have its own plant, its own employees, its own contract with the United Auto Workers union, and a separate dealer network. Initial funding was $150 million, and up to $5 billion was earmarked for future expenditures, including some $3.5 billion for a "greenfield" factory in Spring Hill, Tennessee. Smith hoped production would start by fall 1987, and vowed to drive the first car off the line himself. Oldsmobile general manager Joseph Sanchez was tapped as Saturn president, but died of a heart attack less than three weeks later. Pontiac general manager Bill Hogland was named to replace him.

A prime reason for locating in Tennessee was to distance Saturn from other GM facilities, thus allowing a unique "corporate culture" to flower more easily. Just as important, tiny Spring Hill (population 1400 at the time) was about 35 miles south of Nashville and 30 miles from Smyrna, Tennessee, home of Nissan's North American factory, so vital railroad lines, interstate highways, and suppliers were all conveniently close. Groundbreaking took place in April 1986, by which time fledgling Saturn, barely a year old, had its third president: Richard G. "Skip" LeFauve, transferred from GM's Buick-Olds-Cadillac Group after Hoglund was named to head that unit.

Saturn's self-proclaimed mission was to "market vehicles developed and manufactured in the United States that are world leaders in quality, cost, and customer enthusiasm through the integration of people, technology, and business systems and to exchange knowledge, technology, and experience throughout General Motors." That was a tall order for an established car company, but Saturn was starting from scratch. The job was monumental, and ensuing months witnessed delays, cost overruns, and difficulties in signing up dealers that forced pushing back the production start date to summer 1990, shortly before Smith's scheduled retirement. Yearly volume was first set at a half-million units, then reduced to a more manageable 240,000, and GM's total investment was trimmed to about $3.5 billion.

Smith envisioned the Saturn plant as the last word in automated manufacturing, with computer-guided vehicles delivering parts to robots that did most assembly chores. But like so many GM leaders before him, Smith was a financial manager, not an engineer or manufacturing expert, and he didn't really understand "high tech" or its limits. Spring Hill would use robots for welding, applying adhesives, and painting the cars, but the

1991 SL2 four-door sedan

1991 SC coupe

plant wasn't nearly as futuristic as Smith envisioned. The real innovation came in labor/management relations. As LeFauve noted: "People are going to make the difference for Saturn."

The first employees were recruited from other GM operations. There were just 3800 jobs but more than 16,000 applicants, all evidently intrigued by the Saturn experiment and wanting to be part of it. Candidates were invited to Spring Hill for a two-day screening session, and 90 percent of those who came were hired. The eventual employee roster showed migrants from 46 states with an average of 13 years GM experience. Being so accustomed to GM's old ways, "associates" were required to undergo comprehensive training in the new Saturn way of thinking and working.

UAW members received 350 hours of training on average, though some high-skill positions got twice as much. Base pay for all workers was 80 percent of GM's national average, but there were bonuses for meeting productivity targets and a profit-sharing plan—if Saturn turned a profit.

Saturn's labor agreement had few traditional industry "shop rules" and gave employees more say in how they did their jobs. Workers were organized into teams responsible for monitoring the quality of parts and their own work, and any worker could stop the assembly line to fix safety or quality problems on the spot, a common practice in Japan but unknown in U.S. auto plants. That allowed doing away with separate quality-control inspection areas. In addition, workers sat alongside managers in meetings, helping to make decisions as "team members," and everyone ate in the same dining room. LeFauve even shared the executive office suite with the UAW's Saturn coordinator.

The team approach also figured in Saturn product development. Designers, factory workers, engineers, and outside suppliers came together for what was called "simultaneous engineering." This was in sharp contrast to the old way of having designers, once finished with their part of the car, "throw it over the wall" to engineers, who did their jobs before tossing the project to manufacturing, and so on down the line. Just as important, Saturn planners, some of whom already drove imports, put aside personal preferences to focus on what buyers wanted. Said engineering vice-president Jay Wetzel: "Most great cars in history reflect the personality of one person. In our case, that person just happens to be the consumer."

Despite myriad obstacles and much outside naysaying, Saturn production finally got under way in time for model-year 1991. Job One, a metallic-red sedan, rolled out the door at 10:57 A.M. on July 30, 1990, with Smith at the wheel in one of his last public appearances as GM chairman. With that, attention turned to the car itself.

Saturn greeted the world with four-door sedans and two-door coupes sharing a basic front-drive platform and major components. Each body style had its own styling, but neither drew rave reviews on that score. The sedan was criticized as looking like a scaled-down Oldsmobile Cutlass Supreme. (Some designers apparently worked on both, with the Saturn finished before the Olds but introduced after it.) The coupe, a swoopy 2+2 with hidden headlamps, was more favorably received, though some said it resembled the Geo Storm, an Isuzu-built hatchback coupe then sold by Chevrolet. Despite the shared platform, the sedan rode a 102.4-inch wheelbase, the coupe a 99.2-inch span. Respective overall lengths were 176.3 and 175.8 inches, making Saturns a little shorter than Chevy Cavaliers but seven inches longer than a Honda Civic, a key design benchmark. As promised, body panels bolted to a steel inner skeleton, with fenders, doors, and other vertical panels made of dent- and rust-resistant thermoplastic polymer material. Steel was used for hoods, trunklids, and roofs. Galvanized underbody panels and a standard stainless-steel exhaust system helped reduced corrosion worries, too.

Also as promised, the engine was a new inline-four created expressly for Saturn, with an aluminum block and heads cast by the lost-foam technique. There were two versions of this 1.9-liter (116-cubic inch) design, both fuel-injected and mounted transversely per established front-drive small-car practice. The base 85-horsepower unit had a single overhead camshaft (sohc) and throttle-body injection with a central squirter at the intake manifold. A dual-cam (dohc) derivative with multipoint injection (a squirter for each cylinder) delivered 123 bhp. Each teamed with five-speed manual transmission or optional electronically controlled four-speed automatic. As on some Japanese cars, the automatic had a switch for selecting "normal" or "performance" shift modes; the latter delayed full-throttle upshifts to higher rpm for best acceleration. Alas, no Saturn powertrain delivered anywhere near the economy touted seven years earlier. The best was 27 mpg city and 37 highway for the single-cam/five-speed combination.

Initially, the sedan was offered in price-leader SL and better-equipped SL1 models with the sohc engine and as a dohc-powered SL2 with "Twin Cam" writ large on the rear bumper. The coupe, dubbed SC, was dohc only. Bumpers were black on single-cam cars, body-color on the sportier dual-cam models.

Interior design and features mimicked those of targeted competitors. Climate controls and the steering-column stalk switches for lights and wipers might have been lifted from a Civic or Toyota Corolla, and all models came with reclining cloth front bucket seats, tachometer, tilt steering column, trip odometer, split folding rear seatback, and a rear electric defroster—items found on most all Japanese rivals. Wheel designs emulated Honda's, including the use of four lug nuts instead of GM's usual five. With all this, some people thought Saturns were Japanese cars, but content was actually 95-percent domestic.

Early road-test verdicts were generally positive. Despite automatic transmission, *Consumer Guide*®'s test SL2 ran 0-60 mph in 8.8 seconds, surprisingly brisk for an affordable subcompact. A single-cam car took up to two seconds more, but Saturn's slick-shifting manual transmission was a match for Japan's best and a welcome change from previous GM efforts. All models offered agile handling, a comfortably absorbent ride, good people and cargo space for the exterior size, and, of course, convenient Japanese-style ergonomics. Fuel economy was another asset, but most reviewers judged the engines too loud and rough, especially for a modern four-cylinder under 2.0 liters. Which led to the most-telling judgment of all: Despite all-new engineering and the long gestation, Saturn was not the big breakthrough Roger Smith had promised—competitive with the Japanese, but not clearly superior.

Where Saturn did have an edge was price. At $7995 to start, the Scrooge-special SL was a whopping $1495 less than the base Civic sedan and $1000 less the cheapest Corolla (though the SL didn't offer an automatic transmission or power steering). Saturn's $275 destination charge was in line with those of Japanese makers and $180 less than Cavalier's. The SL1, starting $600 above the SL, swiftly became the volume seller. The SL2 listed at an attractive $10,295, but could be optioned up to around $14,600—a bit steep for the class, though that included antilock brakes (ABS) with rear discs (an $895 option) and CD player, features Civic and Corolla didn't yet offer. The SC2 topped the line at $11,775 and, like most other small coupes, was a tougher sell than the sedans.

Saturn sales officially began on October 25, 1990. Advertising never mentioned a GM connection—arguably wise, considering GM's sullied reputation among the targeted buyers, though also appropriate for Saturn's freewheeling status. Spring Hill was

1991 SL1 four-door sedan

1991 SC coupe

1991 SL1 four-door sedan

still moving slowly on a single shift to assure the highest possible assembly quality, now a must for even entry-level cars. The first Saturns were sold by some 30 dealers in Tennessee and neighboring states as well as on the West Coast, long an import stronghold. Dealers opened in other areas as production ramped up. By the following spring, Saturn counted 130 "retailers" in 33 states, most of them in 70 major urban markets.

It was in the retail area that Project Saturn had its greatest impact. Saturn carefully selected dealers who agreed to build separate showrooms and service facilities and to operate under strict guidelines for customer treatment. Sales personnel were trained in "consultative selling" to replace hard-sell tactics. A "retail associate" would sit down with customers, discuss their needs, explain their options, and arrange a test drive.

Pricing would be just as buyer-friendly. Federal laws on price-fixing prohibit car companies from forcing dealers to sell at a set price. That's why window stickers carry the legend "manufacturer's suggested retail price." But Saturn strongly urged its dealers to avoid the usual haggling, saying no customer should ever wonder about paying too much. Dealers agreed, and Saturns sold at full retail price—no more, no less. With production slowed to solve nagging quality problems, demand quickly exceeded supply during the 1991 model year. A good thing, then, that dealers obeyed another Saturn commandment: Thou shall not gouge. Buyers used to seeing "added dealer profit" signs on popular cars were pleasantly surprised by Saturn's "no ups, no extras" policy.

The red-carpet treatment didn't end there. Buyers were given a tour of their dealer's service area and met the mechanics who would work on their cars. Before driving off, new owners were photographed in their Saturns amid rousing cheers from dealership employees. Most all dealers invited owners in for weekend service clinics and even a free lunch. They also followed up with customers on a regular basis after the sale. If for any reason an owner was unhappy with a Saturn, the car could be returned within the first 30 days or 1500 miles for a full refund, no questions asked. When Saturn announced its first recall in February 1991, dealer technicians drove to where the owners were just to replace a seatback bracket on about 1200 cars. A few months later, Saturn learned a supplier had provided a batch of improperly formulated antifreeze that might cause engine damage. Instead of replacing the antifreeze, Saturn replaced more than 1100 cars.

This extraordinary approach to customer care drew derisive comments from competing dealers, but it worked. With Spring Hill managing only 48,629 units the first model year, dealers sold every one they could get. Most customers were ecstatic. Some even volunteered to help sell Saturns on their days off.

Another key part of Saturn's sales strategy was giving dealers broad "market areas" so they would compete with other brands instead of each other. Thus, a metropolitan region like Chicago might have more than 60 Chevrolet stores but only nine or 10 Saturn dealers. Limiting the number of retail outlets helped Saturn become the industry leader in sales per dealer, and Saturn franchises quickly became both profitable and sought after.

This new way of doing business got an immediate endorsement in the form of J. D. Power and Associates' 1991 surveys of new-car owners. Respondents ranked Saturn third in both customer satisfaction and sales satisfaction. In its very first year, the "different kind of car company" leapfrogged Honda, Toyota, Nissan, and other rivals in two key measurements: how well customers liked their cars and how well they were treated by dealers. Only Lexus and Infiniti, the new Japanese luxury brands whose cars sold for three and four times as much, ranked higher.

And this was no first-year fluke. Saturn again ranked No. 3 in both Power surveys for the '92 and '93 model years, and was No. 1 in sales satisfaction and third in customer satisfaction for '94 and '95. More impressive still, Saturn would remain tops in sales satisfaction each model year through 2001 except for 1999, when it tied for sixth with Lexus and Germany's BMW at a mere four points behind first-place Cadillac and Jaguar. These and other accolades buoyed values of used Saturns, which retained a higher percentage of their original price than other cars in their class. Saturn's own research showed that fully 50 percent of its customers bought primarily for the positive shopping experience, versus 25 percent for the product itself. This led one Saturn executive to remark, "We're not trying to sell people a car. We're helping them buy a car."

Other brands scrambled to "Saturnize," hoping to boost their customer satisfaction and sales with it. Struggling Oldsmobile, in fact, soon implemented many of Saturn's policies in the "Oldsmobile Edge" program. Some other dealers switched to "one-price" and "no-haggle" appeals, but many of those also selling other brands eventually returned to high-pressure tactics. As LeFauve observed, Saturn's success stemmed from many factors, including being true to its mission statement. "You can't just tell your retailers to be nice to people," he said.

Saturn's first big product change occurred late in the 1992

1992 SL four-door sedan

1992 SL1 four-door sedan

1992 SC coupe

model year: an optional driver-side airbag. The cars had been introduced with motorized shoulder belts to meet the federal requirement for dual front-seat "passive restraints," but Japanese rivals were rapidly adding airbags and Saturn needed to match them. The motorized belts continued through model-year '94.

The driver-side cushion became an across-the-board standard for 1993, when four-door wagons and optional traction control arrived. The wagon, striding the same wheelbase as the sedan and otherwise identical to it ahead of the rear doors, came in sohc SW1 and dohc SW2 versions. Also added was a lower-cost coupe, titled SC1, with the single-cam engine and exposed headlamps. The dual-cam coupe retained its hidden-headlamp face as the SC2. The new traction control was available for just $50 on models ordered with ABS and automatic. There was hardly any hardware involved. Saturn simply wrote new software allowing the ABS computer to counteract wheel slip in three stages: retard spark timing to reduce engine power, shift the transmission to a higher gear, and interrupt fuel flow. Traction control was a Saturn class exclusive and thus a big coup for the brand; even many luxury cars didn't have it yet.

Saturn production finally hit full stride during model-year '93. Spring Hill ran two shifts to crank out some 244,000 cars, almost 75,000 more than the year before. But dealers were still short of stock and asking for more, so a third shift was added and all shifts rescheduled to four days a week, 10 hours a day. That had the plant going six days a week to squeeze out nearly 60,000 additional cars each year.

The cars themselves were little changed for '94, but there was big news on the financial front. In January 1994, Saturn announced its first operating profit, achieved in calendar '93, though the amount wasn't made public. The workforce had grown to 8500 by then, and each employee received a profit-sharing check for about $5100.

Though Saturn was still a long way from paying back GM's initial investment, officials hastened to point out several benefits accruing from the new company. On the technology side were the lost-foam engine casting technique, a new water-borne paint process, and team-oriented assembly systems, all being adopted or studied by other GM operations. In addition, Saturn's four-cylinder cars were earning valuable corporate average fuel economy (CAFE) credits for GM as a whole to offset sales of gas-guzzling V-8 models, including a fast-rising number of thirsty full-size light trucks. Most important perhaps, 75 percent of Saturn sales represented "plus business," meaning they came at the expense of non-GM brands. More than half of Saturn owners said they would have bought a Japanese car instead, thus realizing one of Roger Smith's goals—stealing customers from the likes of Honda, Toyota, and Nissan.

To say thanks, Saturn invited its customers—all 700,000 of them—to a "Homecoming" weekend in Spring Hill in late June 1994. It was another extraordinary thing for a car company to do, but even Saturn was surprised when more than 44,000 people showed up. All came at their own expense, some driving in from as far away as Alaska and Hawaii. Drenching rains and muddy fields didn't dampen the family-oriented fun, which included plant tours, picnics, a concert, and sharing the gospel with fellow owners and Spring Hill workers. Two employees from Pennsylvania Saturn retailers got married during the event; Skip LeFauve gave the bride away, plus a 1995 Saturn as a wedding present. Beyond great PR, the Homecoming testified to how well Saturn was making friends and fostering customer loyalty. It was judged a success, despite the soggy weather and other problems, and would be repeated in 1999.

But dark clouds were gathering. Saturn bowed amid huge losses for GM as a whole: $2 billion in 1990, $4.5 billion in 1991, the latter a U.S. business record to that time. New top-level executives came in during 1992, and though they had GM back in the black by mid-decade, the company's total market share continued to shrink and profits were down. With funding tight, sibling rivalry broke out within the GM family. As *AutoWeek* observed in its report on the first Homecoming: "General Motors has already poured $5 billion into Saturn, and there are people at places like Chevrolet, Buick, and Oldsmobile... who would frown upon more of their corporation's dollars heading south. They'd like to see their younger sister pull some of her own weight; that's how families work." Trouble was, Saturn had only small cars to sell, and the small-car market was weakening.

In short, Saturn needed more funding and new models, yet other divisions were needy too, and there wasn't enough money to go around. Some observers recommended that GM cut overhead by merging Saturn with Oldsmobile Division, as both were growing ever closer in products and sales practices. By summer 1995, however, GM decided to delay additional Saturn models and shift development resources to other brands, Olds included. This thinking probably made sense at the time, as Saturn was doing great business. Though sales eased fractionally for calendar '95 to less than 286,000, production for that model year rose 18 percent to a record 303,000. Saturn's lineup would expand, but the fast-changing economics of the auto business meant future models would share more with other GM cars. Tellingly, Skip LeFauve was promoted in 1995 to head all GM small-car programs and "small-car convergence" efforts.

1994 SL1 four-door sedan

1995 SW1 station wagon

GM veteran Don Hudler took over as president and CEO at Saturn Corporation after serving as its vice-president for sales, marketing, and service since 1987.

Several changes marked the 1995 Saturns. A passenger-side airbag in a redesigned dashboard allowed manual three-point seatbelts to replace the never-liked shoulder "mousebelts." Multipoint fuel injection added a welcome 15 bhp to the single-cam engine, coupes got mildly freshened faces, and the SC2 sported a new rear panel and spoiler. A prime rationale for spaceframe construction with bolt-on body panels was to make styling updates relatively easy and cheap, but Saturn said it couldn't afford to redesign the whole car at once, so it focused on the interior first.

Exteriors were updated for '96. Sedans and wagons retained familiar cues, but grew slightly longer and more rounded; a newly arched roofline increased sedan head room fore and aft. But the biggest change was reserved for coupes. After a brief run of '96 carryovers, the '97 models bowed in early 1996 on the sedan/wagon wheelbase to gain a whopping 4.5 inches of rear leg room. All models got additional side-impact protection in advance of 1997 federal standards, plus daytime running lights (inboard of the headlamps), a safety feature spreading throughout GM. Traction control was now available with either transmission as part of the ABS option. Prices had been creeping up, ranging now from $9995 for the basic SL sedan to $12,695 for the top-line SW2 wagon. Despite the restyle, calendar-year sales slipped 2.5 percent to around 278,600—not a good sign.

A widely hailed sign of the future arrived at select Saturn retailers in December 1996. The EV1 wasn't GM's first battery-powered car, but it built on decades of company experiments with electric vehicles. And it wasn't just for fun. California and other states had enacted laws requiring automakers to sell a percentage of zero-emissions vehicles (ZEVs) as a condition for doing business in those states. Though lawmakers kept fiddling with deadlines and sales counts, clean-air mandates were a fact of life demanding alternatives to the internal-combustion engine. Most automakers started with electric cars.

EV1 was built to gain real-world experience with advanced technology and, just as important, to assess consumer interest in electric vehicles. Saturn owners liked new ideas, and the small lozenge-shaped electric coupe had plastic body panels over a steel skeleton, so it was right at home in Saturn showrooms. EV1 was not a Saturn, though, wearing the GM logo as a new one-model "make."

Evolved from the 1989 Impact prototype, the EV1 had a front-mounted AC induction motor driving the front wheels through a "1-speed" transaxle with reduction gear. The juice came from 26 lead-acid batteries arranged in a central T-structure and weighing some 1175 pounds, nearly half the car's curb weight. For maximum driving range, a "regenerative" feature reversed the main motor on braking to replace some of the power used; a transaxle "coastdown" feature gave a similar effect when coasting on flat surfaces or when or descending hills. Recharging was by a 220-volt stand-alone unit or a 110V onboard charger. Recharging took 12-14 hours with the onboard unit, about three hours with the 220V equipment.

The EV1 cost a cool $350 million to develop, and GM said it should have sold each one for at least $35,000 just to break even on the project. That was deemed excessive for a fairly impractical car with unclear market prospects and embryonic technology. So instead, GM offered three-month leases that included all normal servicing, though not the required home charger. Fittingly, EV1s were first leased in smoggy Los Angeles and San Diego, California, and in Phoenix and Tucson, Arizona. The program was extended to Sacramento, California, in 1997 and to San Francisco the following year. "Owners" loved the cars, happily passing gas stations in eerie silence and zipping through traffic or along winding roads with verve. Acceleration was strong—about 8.0 seconds 0-60—but you dare not use full power very often. Even careful drivers were hard-put to get more than 60 miles on a full charge. With that and the rise of more-practical gasoline/electric "hybrids," interest in the EV1 tailed off. GM ended production in late 2000 after fewer than 1000 units, but continued the lease program for a time.

Saturn No. 1,500,000, a blue SC2, rolled out of Spring Hill on January 17, 1997. There was little product news, though: just a standard low-fuel warning light for all '97 models and, with the optional keyless entry system, an antitheft feature that sounded the horn in the event of a break-in.

But in another highly symbolic event, GM's import-fighting brand began selling cars in Japan, something even Roger Smith hadn't planned. Critics had long maintained that American cars weren't good enough for demanding Japanese buyers. But Saturns were selling well against many Japanese cars in the U.S., so why not Japan itself? The export models were reengineered for right-hand drive and equipped to satisfy both local regulations and, it was hoped, the local market. Unfortunately, sales commenced in April 1997 just as the Japanese economy was slipping into recession, and there were only eight dealers for the entire country. But the main difficulty, said one Japanese industry analyst quoted by U.S. trade weekly *Automotive News*, was that "Saturn didn't have any brand appeal. American brands are hard to sell in Japan because some people still have a low-quality image of them." After four tough years and only 4324 sales, Saturn gave up.

It was just as well, for troubles were mounting at home. Calendar-year sales fell nearly 10 percent in 1997, another 7.7 percent in '98. The problem, many observers felt, was that Saturns hadn't changed much and the competition had—and not just import-brand rivals. Meantime, the '98 Saturns appeared with only retuned suspensions, for a smoother ride, and more powertrain refinements—an almost yearly ritual—aimed at reducing noise, vibration, and harshness. Retailers soon found themselves with more cars than buyers for the first time, yet Saturn's one-price policy precluded rebates and other incentives to trim the backlog. The only thing left was to trim production, and Spring Hill scaled back in September 1997 by about 17 percent to some 275,000 cars a year. There were no layoffs, prohibited by the UAW contract, but workers were worried all the same.

Sales were basically flat in calendar 1999, which was relatively good news. And Saturn finally had some real product news that year: three-door coupes. A number of extended-cab pickups had lately sprouted auxiliary rear doors to improve back-seat access, and the idea made even more sense for the small Saturn SCs. New Jersey retailer Stuart Lasser reportedly suggested it after noticing how his son Hal had trouble getting in and out of the regular two-door. Engineers worked fast, and the "back door" coupes were in dealerships by November 1998.

The extra door was on the driver's side, rear-hinged, about 19 inches wide, and could open to near 90 degrees. You had to open the driver's door first, because the rear-door latch was flush-mounted in the front doorjamb for safety's sake. Opening both doors left a spacious unobstructed opening 62 inches wide. The third door changed roof styling slightly—but only on the left—and added a mere 50 pounds despite required structural reinforcing. Unfortunately, it also cut rear hip room by three inches and rear shoulder room by 5.5 inches. Young Hal Lasser might have had an easier scramble in and out, but less space to move around in once inside.

Meanwhile, after several years of dithering, GM had finally decided to fund the additional products Saturn so badly needed. First up was the all-new midsize L-Series, launched in early 1999 for model-year 2000. A $1.2-billion effort, it was loosely based on GM's European Opel/Vauxhall Vectra, and Saturn took pains to make sure reporters understood how loose the relationship was. Though the L-Series used the Vectra's basic architecture and front-drive powertrains, only about 130 parts, mostly fasteners, were said to be interchangeable—as one engineer demonstrated by pouring them out of a small laundry basket at the press preview. "That is literally everything this car has in common with the Vectra," he declared. Saturn took over an older GM plant in Wilmington, Delaware, and retooled it for the L-Series, which was built under a more-traditional labor agreement than existed in Spring Hill.

Despite similar "global GM" styling, the L-Series strode a 2.5-inch longer wheelbase than its Euro cousin and looked recognizably Saturn. It even had plastic fenders and door skins, though they attached to a conventional unibody rather than a spaceframe. Two engines covered five models with familiar Saturn nomenclature. Powering the LS and LS1 sedans and LW1 wagon was a dohc 2.2-liter four-cylinder, part of GM's new "L850" engine family and marketed under the "Ecotec" name. The LS2 sedan and LW2 wagon carried a twincam 3.0-liter V-6, also designed by GM Europe and shared with Saab of Sweden (by now part of the GM empire). The V-6 teamed only with a four-speed automatic transmission, which was also available for four-cylinder models in lieu of five-speed manual. Options included ABS with traction control across the board, leather upholstery except on the base LS sedan, and a rear spoiler for

1995 SL2 four-door sedan

1996 SL1 four-door sedan

1996 SW2 station wagon

LS1/LS2. V-6 models came with rear disc brakes.

Hopes were high for the L-Series, though the odds seemed against it. After all, Saturn was wading into a very crowded and competitive market where the Honda Accord and Toyota Camry were perennial contenders as America's best-selling car line. But with total sales of some 3.5 million units a year, the midsize class offered huge growth potential for Saturn and GM—an irresistible opportunity. What's more, critics found the L-Series had most everything necessary for success. Said *Car and Driver*: "We're not about to bet against the top dogs…but the LS1 covers all the sedan bases very well and could make the others sweat a little if Saturn can persuade Americans to take notice of its new model."

Unfortunately, Saturn fumbled. Unexpected production glitches kept supplies tight in the critical early weeks, and initial advertising touted "the next big thing from Saturn" without giving a clear idea of what the L-Series was. As a result, calendar-2000 deliveries were just over 94,000. Saturn had projected 192,000 the first year and up to 300,000 a year thereafter. Cars started piling up once the factory got cranking, forcing Saturn to slash production twice in quick succession. To jump-start sales, Saturn granted a $1000 per car "advertising allowance" that retailers could use any way they liked. Many simply passed it on to customers as a hidden rebate, but even that didn't help. Zero-down leases were being offered by July, when *Business Week* reported that average incentives for all Saturn models were at a record $1116 per vehicle.

With the L-Series in the lineup, the smaller Saturns were named S-Series for 2000. The SW1 wagon was dropped. Remaining models sported a new gauge cluster and switchgear, redesigned center console, revised front seats with more rearward travel, plus new lower-body panels that increased length by 1.2 inches but were hardly noticeable. Coupes had a short model year, with slightly restyled '01s arriving in early 2000. Powertrains were fiddled with yet again, getting a new induction system and other changes in the continuing quest for smoothness and quietness. *Consumer Guide*® thought a decade of effort had "finally paid off—at least in the '2' models. Their twincam engine now feels coarse and buzzy only at maximum rpm. The changes don't affect [output], so acceleration with either transmission remains slightly better than the class norm." But at age 10, the original Saturn design looked downright old against most rivals, and sales took a beating in calendar 2000, dropping 23.7 percent to a little over 177,000. With that, Spring Hill was put on furlough to give dealers time to clear stocks—including some leftover '99s. Still, Saturn's total sales rose 16.9 percent to 271,800. The L-Series, disappointment though it was, more than made up for the S-Series' decline.

Sounding a hopeful note in 2000 was the April 25 announcement of a $1.5-billion cash infusion for Saturn. Two-thirds would go toward capital improvements at Spring Hill for building Saturn's first SUV, starting in late 2001. Remaining funds were earmarked for equipment needed to build the 2.2-liter four-cylinder engine, which Saturn would supply for all North American GM vehicles using it, as well as a new continuously variable automatic transmission (CVT). Intriguingly, the announcement also mentioned a "yet undisclosed future Saturn" with a Honda V-6. The engine would be supplied under a recently concluded agreement between GM and the Japanese automaker, who was to get diesel engines from GM affiliate Isuzu in exchange. "Our challenge now," said new Saturn president Cynthia Trudell, is to keep up with customer demand for a wider variety of vehicles…and [to] position Saturn as more than just a small-car company."

Actually, it was do-or-die time. In 2000 alone, Saturn lost nearly $840 million, more than $3000 on each sale. The brand created to stop buyers from deserting GM was itself being deserted. With that, nearly half of Saturn's total factory capacity was left idle that year, according to an internal report. By April 2001, GM was nearly out of patience. Saturn was told to double productivity at Spring Hill, boost production there by two-thirds while cutting employment by 18 percent, and to at least break even on operations—or else. Suddenly, everything seemed to depend on the new SUV. If it bombed like the L-Series, reported *Automotive News*, GM would cancel the redesigned S-Series set for model-year 2003. Though Trudell expected to

1997 SL1 four-door sedan

2000 LW2 station wagon

1998 SC1 coupe

2001 SC2 three-door coupe

carry out all of management's marching orders, she admitted, "If we are not successful with [the SUV], no one would put in more products."

But 2001 was another discouraging year. Aggravated by a sharp downturn in the national economy, calendar-year sales slid 4.2 percent from the previous 12 months to just above 260,000. The L-Series was up (to just over 98,000 units), but the S-Series was down (by 8.6 percent to 162,110). Product news was again scant. Both lines added optional curtain side airbags that dropped down from above the doors to cushion occupants' heads in a side impact, but neither yet offered torso side airbags. Midsize model names changed—four-cylinder L100 and L200 sedans, V-6 L300 sedan, and LW200 and LW300 wagons. And that was about it. For 2002, the S-Series lost its remaining wagon, while every L-Series standardized ABS, curtain airbags, and traction control. L-Series also expanded options with an in-dash six-disc CD changer, minivan-style rear-seat DVD video, GM OnStar communications/assistance system, and 16-inch chrome wheels.

The national nightmare of September 11, 2001, was the unforeseen backdrop for the rollout of Saturn's vital SUV, the Vue. Americans were flocking to car-based "crossover" wagons like the Ford Escape, Honda CR-V, and Toyota RAV4. Vue was intended to match or beat them for roominess, versatility, performance, and fuel economy. Significantly, Vue introduced the "Theta" platform destined for similar vehicles at other GM brands, but maintained Saturn tradition by wearing thermoplastic vertical body panels.

Vue initially offered the two L-Series engines. The V-6 came only with a new five-speed automatic transmission and an all-wheel drive system (AWD) with no transfer case or low-range gearing. The four-cylinder teamed with front drive and five-speed manual or with front drive or AWD operating through the promised CVT, called VTi (for "Variable Transmission, intelligent"). Developed by GM's Hydramatic Division and sourced from Europe, the CVT was another Saturn first in American production. Like similar designs at Honda and Audi, it used a special drive belt running between two laterally expandable pulleys to provide a near-infinite number of drive ratios. Electronic control insured the transmission was always in the right "gear" for optimum performance and fuel efficiency. Interestingly, Saturn claimed 0-60 mph acceleration of 10.2 seconds for the front-drive Vue with CVT versus 11.1 with manual. The AWD V-6 was pegged at 8.4 seconds, which *Car and Driver* verified in its first full Vue test. Another class exclusive was electric power steering, with motors replacing power-sapping hydraulics.

Otherwise, Saturn's SUV closely matched its rivals in dimensions, utility, and fuel economy. *Consumer Guide®* found that it "leans more in corners than Escape or CR-V and tends to nose-plow where most compact SUVs feel nimble." Steering was "vague on-center and doesn't impart much road feel." But ride was judged a "strong point. Tires and suspension [four-wheel independent] do a good job of absorbing the worst bumps..." *CG*'s overall assessment: "What Vue lacks in handling it more than makes up for in versatility, ride quality, and interior comfort. Even more attractive are its competitive pricing [about $16,300-$22,600] and the high customer-satisfaction ratings for Saturn's dealership experience and no-haggle price strategy."

Vue got off to a good start, finding more than 75,000 buyers in calendar 2002 and nearly 82,000 in '03. Though that was a modest showing by historic U.S.-industry standards, it was creditable in the far-more diverse and ruthless new-century market. Most buyers preferred the AWD V-6 with its orthodox automatic transmission—a good thing, as the CVT was delayed by teething troubles to mid-2002 and was hard to get even then. *Automotive News* estimated that only 37 percent of Vue production was so equipped. No matter. The V-6 increased its popularity for 2003, when Saturn offered it with front-wheel drive, too. One other change that season was the new option of leather upholstery and heated front seats.

Calendar 2004 deliveries rose six percent to nearly 87,000. Making sense of that 2000 press release, Vue exchanged the 181-bhp 3.0-liter GM V-6 for a 250-bhp 3.5-liter Honda unit, basically the same engine used in Honda's popular Odyssey minivan. Though the swap did wonders for Vue acceleration and mechanical finesse, it was a telling move for the world's largest automaker. Awkward, too, as Saturn now had to sell, service, and warranty a competitor's engine while avoiding mention that it *was* a competitor's engine.

But the Honda V-6 made a fine starting point for the Vue Red

2002 Vue four-door wagon

Line, the first in a planned series of sporty Saturn submodels. Arriving at mid-2004 as a $1995 package for V-6 versions, the Red Line also included a lower-riding firmed-up suspension with 18-inch wheels and tires, plus specific trim inside and out. All '04 Vues received recalibrated steering, chrome-ringed white-face gauges, and available satellite radio; AWDs added standard 17-inch wheels, a new option on mainstream front-drivers.

Vue was a timely tonic for total Saturn sales, which inched up some 20,000 in calendar '02 to exceed 280,000. But the car side was still slipping, and the 2003 total retreated to around 271,000. Though that partly reflected the transition to a new small car, the real culprit was the L-Series: down 17 percent in '02, then by 20 percent more—to just 65,000 or so—despite facelifted '03s with standard curtain side airbags and detail chassis improvements. Worse, as *Consumer Guide*® noted in '03: "A decent midsize car is now less of a value because Saturn charges extra for ABS and traction control, yet increases base prices... except on the manual-transmission L200... At least the L-Series has been a tepid seller, so lease incentives and low financing rates may be available." They were indeed, as Saturn was pushing incentives harder than ever, including zero-percent financing with GM's market-priming "Keep America Rolling" promotion in the wake of 9/11. Yet neither that nor later lures could spark buyer interest in the midsize Saturn, and orders plunged a whopping 70 percent in calendar '04 to less than 19,500. All were L300s with standard ABS/traction control reinstated and no manual shift offered. Not surprisingly, the unloved L-Series faded away during model-year '05, when only

2003 Ion Quad coupe

2003 Ion four-door sedan

2003 LW300 four-door wagon

an unchanged V-6 sedan was available with far fewer options. Just over 5000 were sold.

Saturn by now had a capable new leader in Jill Lajdziak. She reported both to G. Richard "Rick" Wagoner, named GM chairman and CEO in 2001, and to the celebrated "product czar" he quickly brought aboard, former Chrysler Corporation president Robert A. Lutz. Lajdziak enjoyed rather less freedom than her predecessors, however. Bit by bit, Saturn was losing its independence, a shift highlighted by the untimely death of Skip LeFauve in January 2003. As *Automotive News* observed at the time, "LeFauve's Saturn organization [now] looks noticeably different. Decision-making is often conducted higher in the GM organization, and Saturn operates more like a standard GM division with traditional GM practices." But tightening Saturn's orbit was necessary in light of a worsening financial crisis (see *Chevrolet* and *Pontiac*) that would have GM on the brink of bankruptcy by 2006. With Oldsmobile already being phased out as a recovery measure, *Business Week* wondered whether struggling Saturn might soon be dumped, too. "That is out of the question," Lutz told the magazine in mid-2003.

Three years later, Lutz revealed an entirely new game plan for Saturn. From here on, most of the brand's core products would be rebadged versions of select Opel models designed and engineered at GM's German subsidiary. The aim was to save money and get out new product more quickly through the closest ever collaboration among GM's worldwide business units. The pattern, Lutz said, was the British Vauxhall branch, which had been building and selling retrimmed Opels for years. Saturn might advise Opel on design tailoring for the American market, but innovation was no longer a part of its brief. Even Spring Hill was increasingly seen as just another plant supplying all GM makes, not just Saturn.

A tangible early sign of Saturn's shifting status was the 2003 Ion, the belated successor to the subcompact S-Series. This was the first in a planned global family of GM small cars on the new front-drive Delta platform conceived largely by Opel. Ion styling was Saturn's own, however, and plastic was once again used for the front fenders and outer door skins, though the inner structure was a conventional steel unibody. A simple twist-beam axle replaced the S-Series' tri-link rear suspension to keep cost down. Antilock brakes shifted to the options list, but now included traction control. Curtain side airbags were newly available, a plus for Saturn's safety-minded clientele and for the small-car field.

Ion bowed with the all-aluminum "Ecotec" four-cylinder tuned for 145 bhp, a whopping 40 bhp up from the previous single-cam base engine. Sedans launched first with trim levels prosaically named 1, 2 and 3, plus an extra-cost five-speed automatic transmission as another class plus. The two-door Saturn returned in spring '03 as the "Quad Coupe." Sporting rear access doors on *both* sides, it came in 2 and 3 versions with roughly the same features as like-named sedans. The wheelbase of all Ions went up an inch over the S-Series span, while overall length stretched 6.4 inches more on sedans, 4.5 inches on coupes. With that and a two-inch rise in overall height, Ion claimed class-leading interior and cargo space. A bold departure—controversial, too—was a central dashtop gauge cluster canted toward the driver. Only Toyota's subcompact Echo dared something like it. Also brave was making coupes available with the CVT as well as the torque-converter automatic. Unusual, too, was the interchangeable roof-rail trim available through Saturn dealers in colors and patterns to mix and match with paint and interior decor.

As Saturn's most affordable car and the replacement for its top-seller, the Ion was critical for near-term success. Saturn planned to peddle 160,000 a year, yet hardly budged the sales needle from the S-Series' last calendar year: about 114,000 through the end of '03. Reviewers were critical on many counts, none more than *Car and Driver*, which pronounced Ion "probably the most disappointing all-new American car in a decade... Its chassis refinement, advanced safety systems and value for money are impressive"—base prices ran around \$11,600-\$16,000. "But uncomfortable seats, funky ergonomics, cut-rate materials and low-quality engine sounds send the message, 'You should have spent more if you wanted a real car'." *Consumer Guide®* was more charitable, noting that established Saturn virtues made up for the Ion's various vices. But plenty of shoppers thought otherwise. Within seven months, Ion inventory had ballooned to 100 days versus the desired 60-day supply. In all, it was a disheartening and worrisome debut.

To its credit, Saturn went right to work on fixes. Interiors gained visibly better-quality materials for 2004 and again for '05, when an early facelift gave most Ions a simple oblong grille and more exterior chrome, an attempt to add visual class.

Adding visceral appeal at mid-2004 was a racy Ion Red Line coupe with a supercharged 2.0-liter Ecotec pumping out 205 eager horses. The \$21,000 list price included mandatory five-speed manual, a tauter suspension on 17-inch wheels and performance tires, rear disc brakes, big-bolster front seats, snazzy leather/cloth upholstery, and the obligatory "go faster" body addenda, though Saturn wisely left a bulky rear spoiler to the options card. This Ion aimed at the fast-growing youth market for tuned-up, glammed-up "sport compacts." It was mostly on target: nimble, eye-catching, and noisy but quick. *Car and Driver* clocked 0-60 mph at a brisk 6.1 seconds versus a sedate 8.4 for the base 140-bhp manual coupe. Turning up the Red Line's wick for 2006 was a little-promoted \$1375 Competition Package. This delivered a limited-slip differential to get max power to the pavement, dashboard lights to guide gear-swapping, plus a turbo-boost gauge, fog lamps, and unique alloy wheels. The Red Line wasn't the sort of car Saturn customers were used to, but that was the point. After so many years of sensible shoes, it was a refreshing dash of exuberance.

Red Line wasn't, however, a tonic for Ion sales, which slipped in calendar 2004 and again in '05, landing at just under 101,000 despite the availability of a 170-bhp 2.4-liter Ecotec for Ion 3s. Buying a Saturn might still be a first-class experience, but even the beautified Ions seemed second-rate against many import-brand foes. Worse, model-year '05 brought intramural competition in Chevrolet's Delta-based Cobalt, which had no trouble luring buyers with its mainstream styling and superior fit and finish. It was an odd situation for a company founded on small cars, especially as Saturn seemed unsure of what to do about it. In April 2006, *Automotive News* reported that Saturn was scrapping a planned Ion replacement and was looking for another GM car to take over after model-year '07. Trouble was, this substitute couldn't get to market until model-year '08, leaving Saturn dealers with the prospect of having no entry-level car to sell for eight or nine months, an eternity in auto retailing. We'd love to tell you how this drama plays out, but we can't. It was just unfolding as this book was prepared.

Another blow to Saturn's pride came in 2004, when GM decided to scrap the still-troublesome CVT option for both Ion and Vue. This, too, seemed strange, as Audi, Ford, Honda, and Nissan all had vehicles with CVTs that worked like a charm. But maybe it wasn't so strange. GM had made many mistakes since Saturn's birth, and wasn't the company it used to be.

A first-ever minivan should have brightened Saturn's sales picture considerably, but proved another miscalculation. A triumph of marketing style over product substance, the new-for-2005 Relay was basically a rehash of an eight-year-old GM design that had always lagged the class leaders and was no more competitive as a "crossover sport van" with SUV-flavored styling. It even lacked Saturn's trademark plastic body panels, and had little to recommend it over close cousins Chevrolet Uplander, Pontiac Montana SV6, and a first-ever Buick minivan, the Terraza. Buyers saw through the 1980s-style cloning and mostly stayed away from all four models. Relay, though, was particularly disappointing in light of Saturn's still-strong consumer image, drawing a little more than 17,000 orders from late 2004 through the end of '05.

Reflecting the ho-hum response to both Relay and Ion, overall Saturn sales fell a sharp 21.8 percent in calendar 2004 to just over 212,000. The '05 total was just 640 units higher. The one sort of bright spot was Vue, which edged up to some 87,000 in '04, then to nearly 92,000 in '05. Like Ion, Vue got unwanted in-house competition: the 2005 Chevrolet Equinox and Pontiac Torrent built on a stretched Theta platform with different engines. At least tidier size and the available Honda V-6 helped Vue stand apart from that twosome, as well as a thundering herd of class rivals. A modest 2006 facelift and interior sprucing helped keep it looking fresh.

Serving the cause of fresher air was the Vue Green Line, General Motors' first mainstream vehicle with a low-emissions, high-mileage gasoline/electric hybrid powertrain. An early 2007 addition, it employed a 2.4-liter Ecotec four and a nickel-metal-

2004 Ion Red Line coupe

hydride battery pack feeding 10 kilowatts to an electric motor/generator. A four-speed torque-converter automatic transmission channeled a maximum 170 net horsepower to the front wheels. Like Honda's Integrated Motor Assist system, the Vue's hybrid drive used the motor/battery pack to give the gas engine a kick when needed. The motor would charge the battery pack in coasting or braking, so no plug-in charging was required as on the pure-electric EV1. Also like most other hybrids, the engine would automatically shut off on coming to a stop to save gas, then restart on applying the throttle. Projected EPA fuel economy of 27 mpg city and 32 highway was mighty compelling at a time when gas had shot above $3 a gallon and looked to go higher still. Saturn eyed a $23,000 starting price, around $4000 less than Ford's year-old Escape Hybrid and a whopping $10,000 below the new Toyota Highlander Hybrid.

The Vue Green Line arrived in summer 2006, just after this book was prepared, but it promised to generate much needed showroom traffic. So, too, did three more newcomers that made the 2007 line the broadest in Saturn's short history. Though those models also await history's verdict, they looked to give Saturn the competitive reach it had so long been denied.

First on the scene was Sky, a genuine two-seat sports roadster with an even higher fun factor than the Ion Red Line. Starting sale in spring 2006, it was an upscale version of the rear-drive Pontiac Solstice that had launched in late 2005 with a long waiting list. Sky caused the same clamor, orders pouring in before the first one left the Wilmington, Delaware, plant that had been refurbished after finishing with the L-Series.

Sky wore a Saturn face on an all-steel body that was four inches longer than the Pontiac's but with the same general look. It also sported a spiffier cockpit and a $23,000 base price, about $3000 upstream of its sibling. That was owed to no-cost antilock brakes, air conditioning, cruise control, and power windows/door locks, all options for Solstice. Sky also had its own suspension tuning for the plusher-ride Saturn thought its customers would prefer. Otherwise, it was the same appealing package: base 177-bhp 2.4-liter Ecotec four, manual or optional automatic five-speed transmissions, all-disc brakes, 18-inch rolling stock, a manual-folding cloth top with heated rear window, and an options sheet showing limited-slip differential, leather upholstery, satellite radio, rear spoiler, and chrome wheels. Released in fall was a performance-minded Sky Red Line. A counterpart to the Solstice GXP, it packed the same new supercharged 2.0-liter Ecotec with 260 bhp. That was the highest specific output in GM history, abetted by direct fuel injection, a first for a North American GM car. Naturally, Sky Red Line had specific styling touches inside and out, including a deeper front fascia with large brake-cooling ducts. Regular or Red Line, Sky was an exciting symbol of a hoped-for Saturn renaissance.

But the real money is always in mass-market products like midsize sedans, so a lot was riding on the 2007 Aura. Scheduled for release in August 2006, it embodied the new Bob Lutz strategy for Saturn, being a close relation of the European-bred Opel/Vauxhall Vectra, but built at GM's Kansas City plant. On paper—and in the showroom—Aura looked light years ahead of the old L-Series, with crisply honed styling, solid engineering, and most of the features buyers craved. It bowed in two versions, each a front-wheel-drive V-6. The entry-level XE married an iron-block 224-bhp 3.5-liter pushrod engine to a four-speed automatic transmission. The uplevel XR boasted an all-aluminum twincam 3.6 sending 252 bhp through a new six-speed GM automatic. Variable-valve timing enhanced efficiency on both V-6s, and was a claimed first for the "cam in block" 3.5. Headlining a long standard-equipment roster were front torso and curtain side airbags, four-wheel antilock disc brakes, traction control, tilt/telescope steering wheel, and GM OnStar assistance with a year's free service. XR added 18-inch wheels to replace 17s, GM's Stabilitrak antiskid system, remote engine starting, extra interior amenities, and a little more brightwork. Due later in the '07 model year was a Green Line Aura, GM's first hybrid-power passenger car, using the basic Vue Green Line powertrain. With all this, Aura seemed poised to be the sales success the L-Series was not.

No less important to the profit outlook was the aptly named 2007 Outlook, a large crossover SUV. Saturn was entering new territory here, but badly needed a presence in the booming market for new-age family wagons with carlike comfort and road manners. Significantly, Outlook introduced the unibody Lambda platform that had been designed expressly for crossover vehicles and that would soon serve other GM marques. Wheelbase was a generous 118.9 inches, nearly a match for the big truck-based Ford Expedition and more than sufficient to allow for the three-row seating most all shoppers demanded. Like most every class rival, Outlook offered a choice of front-drive or AWD in a four-door package with passenger-car amenities, plus versatile accommodations for seven or eight. A lone powertrain mated GM's new six-speed automatic with a 3.6-liter V-6, basically the Aura engine tuned for 217 bhp and more

2004 Vue Red Line four-door wagon

2005 Ion four-door sedan

2005 Relay minivan

low-end torque. With a full slate of standard safety aids and useful options like power liftgate, remote starting, and rear-obstacle-detection system, Outlook loomed as another big Saturn sales booster upon its scheduled early 2007 showroom debut.

Set to follow Outlook is a new-generation 2008 Vue, likely with bold new styling patterned after the Opel-designed PreVue concept presented in April 2006. That and a fill-in for Ion will complete a remarkable product expansion for a make that seemed to be at death's door just a few years earlier.

Even so, Saturn is hardly of the woods yet, because General Motors itself must still hack through a forest of daunting challenges. But assuming everything works out, Saturn may at last be set for a truly bright, successful, and permanent future—even if it is no longer "a different kind of car company."

2007 Vue Green Line four-door wagon

2007 Outlook four-door wagon

2007 Sky Red Line convertible coupe

2007 Aura four-door sedan

2007 Sky convertible coupe

Specifications

1991 - 48,629 built

Coupe (wb 99.2)		Wght	Price	Prod
G27/H27	SC	2,375	11,775	—
Sedan (wb 102.4)				
F69	SL	2,312	7,995	—
G69/H69	SL1	2,344	8,595	—
J69/K35	SL2	2,408	10,295	—

1991 Engines	bore×stroke	bhp	availability
I-4, 116.0	3.22×3.54	85	S-SL, SL1 (ohc)
I-4, 116.0	3.22×3.54	123	S-SC, SL2 (dohc)

1992 - 169,959 built

Coupe (wb 99.2)		Wght	Price	Prod
G27/H27	SC	2,375	11,875	—
Sedan (wb 102.4)				
F69	SL	2,313	8,195	—
G69/H69	SL1	2,343	8,995	—
J69/K35	SL2	2,407	10,395	—

1992 Engines	bore×stroke	bhp	availability
I-4, 116.0	3.22×3.54	85	S-SL, SL1 (ohc)
I-4, 116.0	3.22×3.54	124	S-SC, SL2 (dohc)

1993 - 244,621 built

Coupe (wb 99.2)		Wght	Price	Prod
E27/F27	SC1	2,304	10,995	—
G27/H27	SC2	2,387	12,795	—
Sedan (wb 102.4)				
F69	SL	2,323	9,195	—
G69/H69	SL1	2,353	9,995	—
J69/K69	SL2	2,425	11,495	—
Wagon (wb 102.4)				
G35/H35	SW1	2,368	10,895	—
J35/K35	SW2	2,475	12,195	—

1993 Engines	bore×stroke	bhp	availability
I-4, 116.0	3.22×3.54	85	S-SC1, SL, SL1, SW1 (ohc)
I-4, 116.0	3.22×3.54	124	O-SC2, SL2, SW2 (dohc)

1994 - 267,518 built

Coupe (wb 99.2)		Wght	Price	Prod
E27/F27	SC1	2,280	11,695	—
G27/H27	SC2	2,376	12,895	—
Sedan (wb 102.4)				
F69	SL	2,314	9,995	—
G69/H69	SL1	2,349	10,795	—
J69/K69	SL2	2,405	11,795	—
Wagon (wb 102.4)				
G35/H35	SW1	2,362	11,695	—
J35/K35	SW2	2,448	12,595	—

1994 Engines	bore×stroke	bhp	availability
I-4, 116.0	3.22×3.54	85	S-SC1, SL, SL1, SW1 (ohc)
I-4, 116.0	3.22×3.54	124	O-SC2, SL2, SW2 (dohc)

1995

(wb 102.4; cpe wb 99.2)		Wght	Price	Prod
E27/F27	SC1 cpe	2,284	11,895	62,434
G27/H27	SC2 cpe	2,360	12,995	
F69	SL sdn 4d	2,345	9,995	
G69/H69	SL1 sdn 4d	2,353	10,995	221,102
J69/K69	SL2 sdn 4d	2,405	11,995	
G35/H35	SW1 wgn 4d	2,380	11,695	19,452
J35/K35	SW2 wgn 4d	2,448	12,695	

1995 Engines	bore×stroke	bhp	availability
I-4, 116.0	3.22×3.54	100	S-SC1, SL, SL1, SW1 (ohc)
I-4, 116.0	3.22×3.54	124	O-SC2, SL2, SW2 (dohc)

1996 - 294,198 built

(wb 102.4; cpe wb 99.2)		Wght	Price	Prod
E27/F27	SC1 cpe	2,282	12,195	—
G27/H27	SC2 cpe	2,363	13,295	—
F69	SL sdn 4d	2,348	10,495	—
G69/H69	SL1 sdn 4d	2,378	11,395	—
J69/K69	SL2 sdn 4d	2,421	12,295	—
G35/H35	SW1 wgn 4d	2,437	11,995	—
J35/K35	SW2 wgn 4d	2,507	12,895	—

1996 Engines	bore×stroke	bhp	availability
I-4, 116.0	3.22×3.54	100	S-SC1, SL, SL1, SW1 (ohc)
I-4, 116.0	3.22×3.54	124	O-SC2, SL2, SW2 (dohc)

1997

(wb 102.4)		Wght	Price	Prod
B27	SC1 cpe	2,309	12,495	70,711
C27	SC2 cpe	2,386	13,695	
B69	SL sdn 4d	2,321	10,595	
B69	SL1 sdn 4d	2,321	11,595	213,182
D69	SL2 sdn 4d	2,390	12,495	
B35	SW1 wgn 4d	2,390	12,195	31,099
D35	SW2 wgn 4d	2,454	13,095	

1997 Engines	bore×stroke	bhp	availability
I-4, 116.0	3.22×3.54	100	S-SC1, SL, SL1, SW1 (ohc)
I-4, 116.0	3.22×3.54	124	O-SC2, SL2, SW2 (dohc)

1998

(wb 102.4)		Wght	Price	Prod
B27	SC1 cpe	2,309	12,595	38,591
C27	SC2 cpe	2,380	13,895	
B69	SL sdn 4d	2,326	10,595	
B69	SL1 sdn 4d	2,326	11,595	160,759
D69	SL2 sdn 4d	2,392	12,495	
B35	SW1 wgn 4d	—	12,295	20,415
D35	SW2 wgn 4d	2,454	13,295	

1998 Engines	bore×stroke	bhp	availability
I-4, 116.0	3.22×3.54	100	S-SC1, SL, SL1, SW1 (ohc)
I-4, 116.0	3.22×3.54	124	O-SC2, SL2, SW2 (dohc)

1999

(wb 102.4)		Wght	Price	Prod
B27	SC1 cpe 3d*	2,320	12,445	52,965
C27	SC2 cpe 3d*	2,390	15,505	
B69	SL sdn 4d	2,327	10,595	
B69	SL1 sdn 4d	2,327	11,295	203,578
D69	SL2 sdn 4d	2,389	12,755	
B35	SW1 wgn 4d	2,391	12,295	19,090
D35	SW2 wgn 4d	2,449	14,225	

1999 Engines	bore×stroke	bhp	availability
I-4, 116.0	3.22×3.54	100	S-SC1, SL, SL1, SW1 (ohc)
I-4, 116.0	3.22×3.54	124	O-SC2, SL2, SW2 (dohc)

* Midyear introduction of left-side rear door.

2000

S-Series (wb 102.4)		Wght	Price	Prod
N27/P27	SC1 cpe 3d	2,368	12,535	8,517
R27/Y27	SC2 cpe 3d	2,436	15,145	8,724
F69	SL sdn 4d	2,332	10,685	74,085
G69/H69	SL1 sdn 4d	2,332	11,485	
J69/K69	SL2 sdn 4d	2,399	12,895	68,907
J35/N35	SW2 wgn 4d	2,452	14,290	9,633
L-Series (wb 106.5)				
R19/S19	LS sdn 4d	2,910	15,010	7,140
T19/U19	LS1 sdn 4d	2,943	16,750	45,953
W19	LS2 sdn 4d	3,152	20,135	35,099
U35	LW1 wgn 4d	3,075	18,835	6,041
W35	LW2 wgn 4d	3,229	21,360	9,573

2000 Engines	bore×stroke	bhp	availability
I-4, 116.0	3.22×3.54	100	S-SC1, SL, SL1, SW1 (ohc) (dohc)
I-4, 134.0	3.39×3.72	137	S-LS, LS1, LW1
V-6, 183.0	3.39×3.35	182	S-LS2, LW2

2001

S-Series (wb 102.4)		Wght	Price	Prod
N27/P27	SC1 cpe 3d	2,368	12,535	23,584
R27/Y27	SC2 cpe 3d	2,436	15,645	17,414
F69	SL sdn 4d	2,332	10,570	
G69/H69	SL1 sdn 4d	2,332	11,485	73,428
J69/K69	SL2 sdn 4d	—	12,895	
J35/N35	SW2 wgn 4d	2,452	14,290	3,416
L-Series (wb 106.5)				
R19/S19	L100 sdn 4d	2,944	14,495	4,023
T19/U19	L200 sdn 4d	2,964	16,750	54,968
W19	L300 sdn 4d	3,182	19,495	23,339
U35	LW200 wgn 4d	3,375	18,835	4,673
W35	LW300 wgn 4d	3,257	21,360	5,283

2001 Engines	bore×stroke	bhp	availability
I-4, 116.0	3.22×3.54	100	S-SC1, SL, SL1, SW1 (ohc)
I-4, 116.0	3.22×3.54	124	O-SC2, SL2, SW2 (dohc)
I-4, 134.0	3.39×3.72	135	S-L100, L200, LW200
V-6, 183.0	3.39×3.35	182	S-L300, LW300

2002

S-Series (wb 102.4) - 213,041 blt		Wght	Price	Prod
N27/P27	SC1 cpe 3d	2,367	12,900	—
R27/Y27	SC2 cpe 3d	2,429	16,080	—
F69	SL sdn 4d	2,341	10,570	—
G69/H69	SL1 sdn 4d	2,341	11,850	—
J69/K69	SL2 sdn 4d	2,393	13,335	—
L-Series (wb 106.5) - 100,752 built				
R19/S19	L100 sdn 4d	2,948	14,495	—
T19/U19	L200 sdn 4d	2,989	16,750	—
W19	L300 sdn 4d	3,197	19,495	—
U35	LW200 wgn 4d	3,070	18,835	—
W35	LW300 wgn 4d	3,272	21,360	—

2002 Engines	bore×stroke	bhp	availability
I-4, 116.0	3.22×3.54	100	S-SC1, SL, SL1 (ohc)
I-4, 116.0	3.22×3.54	124	O-SC2, SL2, (dohc)
I-4, 134.0	3.39×3.72	135	S-L100, L200, LW200
V-6, 183.0	3.39×3.35	182	S-L300, LW300

2003

Ion (wb 103.2) - 107,987 blt		Wght	Price	Prod
M37	2 cpe 4d	2,756	14,030	—
V37	3 cpe 4d	2,778	15,530	—
F69	1 sdn 4d	2,653	11,510	—
Z69	2 sdn 4d	2,686	13,510	—
K69	3 sdn 4d	2,729	15,010	—
L-Series (wb 106.5) - 81,238 built				
T19	L200 sdn 4d	2,989	17,620	—
W19	L300 sdn 4d	3,197	20,645	—
U35	LW200 wgn 4d	3,086	20,240	—
W35	LW300 wgn 4d	3,256	22,575	—

2003 Engines	bore×stroke	bhp	availability
I-4, 134.0	3.39×3.72	135	S-L200
I-4, 134.0	3.39×3.72	140	S-Ion
V-6, 183.0	3.39×3.35	182	S-L300

2004

Ion (wb 103.2) - 132,330 blt		Wght	Price	Prod
M37	2 cpe 4d	2,751	14,285	—
V37	3 cpe 4d	2,751	15,785	—
Y37	Red Line cpe 4d	2,590	20,385	—
F69	1 sdn 4d	2,692	10,430	—
Z69	2 sdn 4d	2,692	13,735	—
K69	3 sdn 4d	2,692	15,260	—
L300 (wb 106.5) - 21,322 built				
C19	1 sdn 4d	3,033	16,370	—
D19	2 sdn 4d	3,197	20,785	—
L19	3 sdn 4d	3,197	22,685	—
C35	1 wgn 4d	3,107	18,420	—
D35	2 wgn 4d	3,272	22,935	—
L35	3 wgn 4d	3,272	24,735	—

2004 Engines	bore×stroke	bhp	availability
I-4S, 122.0	3.39×3.39	205	S-Ion Red Line
I-4, 134.0	3.39×3.72	140	S-Ion, L300
V-6, 183.0	3.39×3.35	182	O-L300

2005

Ion (wb 103.2) - 83,707 built		Wght	Price	Prod
M37	2 cpe 4d	2,784	14,930	—
V37	3 cpe 4d	2,812	16,680	—
Y37	Red Line cpe 4d	2,933	20,885	—
F69	1 sdn 4d	2,722	11,430	—
Z69	2 sdn 4d	2,743	14,380	—
K69	3 sdn 4d	2,772	15,905	—
L300 (wb 106.5) - 7,110 built				
D19	sdn 4d	3,237	21,370	—

2005 Engines	bore×stroke	bhp	availability
I-4S, 122.0	3.39×3.39	205	S-Ion Red Line
I-4, 134.0	3.39×3.72	140	S-Ion
V-6, 183.0	3.39×3.35	182	S-L300

2006

Ion (wb 103.2)		Wght	Price	Prod*
M37	2 cpe 4d	2,796	12,925	—
V37	3 cpe 4d	2,813	15,625	—
Y37	Red Line cpe 4d	2,945	19,425	—
Z69	2 sdn 4d	2,752	11,925	—
K69	3 sdn 4d	2,788	14,325	—

2006 Engines	bore×stroke	bhp	availability
I-4S, 122.0	3.39×3.39	205	S-Ion Red Line
I-4, 134.0	3.39×3.72	140	S-Ion
I-4, 145.0	3.46×3.85	170	O-Ion

* Figures not available at time of publication.

2007

Ion (wb 103.2)		Wght	Price	Prod*
B67	conv cpe	2,860	23,115	—

2007 Engines	bore×stroke	bhp	availability
I-4, 145.0	3.46×3.85	177	S-Sky

* Figures not available at time of publication.

Shelby

When heart trouble forced Carroll Shelby to retire from driving race cars after he won the LeMans 24 Hours in 1959, the one-time Texas chicken rancher turned to building stark, incredibly fast road cars to suit himself and other like-minded enthusiasts. The first were the legendary Shelby-Cobras. Starting with lithe, lightweight Ace roadsters from A.C. Cars in England, Carroll replaced a plodding small six-cylinder engine with potent Ford V-8s: initially 260- and 289-cubic-inch engines with up to 306 horsepower, then mammoth 427s making up to 425 bhp. The result was a hairy thrill on the road and nearly unbeatable in major-league sports-car racing. Even the "little" 289 could scale 0-60 mph in 5.5 seconds and exceed 135 mph. The otherworldly 427s needed just 4.2 seconds 0-60 on the way to 165 mph.

Shelby built 654 small-block Cobras and some 350 big-block versions from 1962 to '68. All have since become prized collector's items fetching six-figure prices (sometimes more), thanks to a fabled competition record (seven U.S. national road-racing championships, the World Manufacturer's title in 1965) and a raw, elemental nature unmatched by other sports cars. Those same factors explain the numerous Cobra "replicars" that appeared after them and which Shelby fiercely fought against. Shelby also contributed to the mid-engine GT40 and Mark IV prototypes that took Ford to the racing pinnacle by winning the 24 Hours of LeMans in 1966-69.

Equally famous, but more popular and practical, was the series of limited-edition Shelby Mustang GTs built in 1965-69. The first, named GT 350 for no particular reason, was a race-inspired conversion of Ford's new 1965-66 "ponycar" carried out by the small Shelby American shop in Los Angeles. Early Shelby Mustangs were uncompromising grand tourers equally at home on the track. Post-1967 models were planned and built by Ford and were thus "softer," though still plenty exciting.

Ford Division chief Lee Iacocca had asked Shelby to modify the Mustang so it could win the Sports Car Club of America's national B-production championship. The GT 350 did just that in 1965-67, virtually running away from the field to give showroom Mustangs a "competition-proved" aura.

The 1965-66 GT 350 began as a white, blue-striped Mustang fastback supplied with the excellent small-block 289 in 271-bhp "Hi-Performance" guise. "Hi-rise" manifold, bigger four-barrel carburetor, free-flow exhaust, and other Shelby changes lifted output to 306 bhp at 6000 rpm. Carroll also specified the Mustang's optional Borg-Warner T-10 four-speed gearbox, plus a stronger rear axle from the full-size Ford Galaxie to replace the stock Mustang's Falcon unit. Other component swaps included Koni adjustable shocks, Shelby-cast 15-inch alloy wheels wearing high-performance Goodyear tires, metallic friction surfaces for both rear-drum and front-disc brakes, and fast-ratio steering (with relocated front suspension mounting points). A hefty steel tube linked the tops of the front shock towers to reduce body flex in hard cornering. The result of all this was near-neutral handling instead of the stock Mustang's strong understeer, plus 0-60 mph acceleration of just 6.8 seconds—impressive even today—and over 120 mph all-out. An optional Paxton supercharger, offered during 1966, boosted horsepower beyond 400 and cut the 0-60 time to just five seconds. Shelby built only such 11 cars, though a handful of stock GT 350s received owner-installed "blower" kits.

As planned, Carroll also developed a race-ready GT 350R with the same engine as competition Cobra 289s. That meant a nominal 350 bhp—an outstanding 1.21 bhp per cubic inch. To minimize weight, the gearbox got an aluminum case and the interior was stripped down to a single racing seat with safety harness, plus protective roll bar. Competition tires and super-duty suspension were specified, too. The front bumper was replaced by a fiberglass air dam with a large central slot for feeding in extra air. A few GT 350Rs were built with all-disc brakes, 400-bhp 289s, and wide tires under flared fenders.

As if all that weren't enough, Shelby devised a special GT 350H for Hertz Rent-A-Car, which ordered 936 examples. All carried Ford's three-speed Select-Shift Cruise-O-Matic transmission and black paint set off by gold stripes. Hertz rented them for $17 a day and 17 cents a mile. Some customers violated

1965 GT 350 fastback coupe

their contracts by racing the cars, but probably not as many as once thought. In any case, Hertz lost money on the venture and bailed out after one year.

In all, Shelby built 562 GT 350s for '65 and another 2378 to '66 specs, including R-model racers and Hertz cars, plus six prototype '66 convertibles. That was good production for such a specialized machine, but profit-minded Ford wanted far more. As a result, the original Shelby concept began to be watered down.

Ford bowed a heavier, restyled ponycar for 1967 with a first-time 390-cid V-8 big-block option. Typical of the man, Carroll went one better by offering Dearborn's new 428-cid V-8 for a second Shelby Mustang, the GT 500. Horsepower was conservatively advertised at 335, mainly so insurance companies wouldn't worry, but was closer to 400 actual. The GT 350 returned with its previous power rating, but the true figure was now under 300 because the original steel-tube headers were eliminated to satisfy noise regulations. Both Shelbys sported a longer, more-aggressive new fiberglass nose, crisply clipped "Kamm" tail with prominent spoiler, and other appearance departures from regular Mustangs, plus small chassis refinements. Interiors gained a large black-finish roll bar with built-in inertia-reel seatbelts. Shelby built 3225 of his '67 GTs, which sold for around $4000, down some $500 from the 1965-66 cars that were themselves incredible high-performance buys.

The 350 and 500 returned for '68 in convertible as well as fastback form, but all were somewhat less special than the '67s. Interiors, for instance, were stock Mustang save a console-mounted ammeter and oil-pressure gauge, and there were cushy new options like air conditioning, power steering, and automatic transmission. Styling was modified via a wider hood scoop and wide taillights with sequential turn signals (lifted from the Mercury Cougar). The new convertibles listed about $100 above comparable fastbacks. At midseason, the GT 500 became the GT 500KR—"King of the Road"—denoting Ford's latest 428 "Cobra Jet" engine with jumbo ports and a new intake manifold fed by a huge four-barrel Holley carb. Fastbacks rose to $4117 for the 350, $4317 for the 500, and $4473 for the KR. The costliest '68 Shelby was the KR ragtop, at $4594.

With Ford now calling the shots, the '69 Shelbys became even more like that year's fully redesigned stock Mustangs. Styling remained distinctive but was busier, with a big loop bumper/grille, scoops and ducts most everywhere, and reflective tape stripes midway up the flanks. GT 350s were demoted to Ford's new 351 "Cleveland" V-8 with 290 bhp; GT 500s, no longer KRs, stayed with the Cobra Jet, still at a nominal 335 bhp. But after just 3150 of the '69s, plus 636 leftovers sold as 1970 models, Shelby and Iacocca agreed to end the Mustang GT program in the face of blossoming government regulations, spiraling insurance rates (the cars' accident record was staggering), and sales interference from hot new production Mustangs like the Mach I and Boss 302. Like the Cobras, however, these Shelbys quickly became high-priced, highly sought after collector cars.

The Mustang experience had soured Shelby on being an auto manufacturer, so he turned to tending his other businesses. Iacocca, meantime, was promoted to Ford Motor Company president in 1970. He continued as such until the summer of '78,

1966 GT 350 fastback coupe

1967 GT 350 fastback coupe

1968 GT 500 fastback coupe

1968 GT 500 convertible coupe

1969 GT 500 fastback coupe

1969 GT 500 convertible coupe

1986 GLH-S four-door hatchback

when he was abruptly fired by chairman Henry Ford II in a celebrated row that was as personal as it was public. (HFII was reportedly jealous of Iacocca's growing prominence and power in Dearborn). Later that year, Iacocca made his equally celebrated move to the presidency of then-moribund Chrysler Corporation, where he was named board chairman in 1979.

After helping pull Chrysler from the financial brink, Iacocca called on old friend Shelby to add some needed pizzazz to the corporate lineup—timely, as performance was starting to make a comeback throughout Detroit. Carroll agreed, and Chrysler duly announced his arrival in 1982 as a "performance consultant" who promised to "bring excitement back to the auto industry."

The first fruit of the renewed Shelby/Iacocca partnership was the Chrysler Shelby California Development Center. Set up in Santa Fe Springs, near Los Angeles, CSCDC was assigned to work with Chrysler engineers in exploring new technology for future models and to devise specific performance packages for Chrysler's "excitement" division, Dodge. Two immediate results were the 1983-86 Shelby Charger coupe and Omni GLH ("Goes Like Hell") hatchback, essentially "Shelbyized" versions of those workaday front-drive subcompacts. Both offered extra power, tight suspensions, distinctive styling touches, and attractively low prices (see *Dodge*). Things went a step further in February 1986, when Shelby and Chrysler Motors chairman Gerald Greenwald announced the formation of Shelby Automobiles, Inc. (SAI) in nearby Whittier, California, to build high-performance Dodge-based limited editions.

With that, March 1, 1986, introduced the first Shelby-marque car since the final Mustang GTs: a quicker, more-powerful GLH called GLH-S ("Goes Like Hell—Some more"). It had a 2.2-liter (135 cid) turbocharged Chrysler four-cylinder engine that Shelby tweaked to 175 bhp via an air-to-air intercooler, equal-length intake runners, and other alterations. Helped by a mandatory five-speed manual transmission, the GLH-S offered brisk eight-second 0-60 mph performance—and truly horrendous front-drive torque-steer.

In February 1987, SAI began building a Shelby Lancer based on Dodge's recently launched "H-body" four-door hatchback sedan. Base-priced at $16,995, it also came with a five-speed and the 175-bhp turbo-four, but offered a tamer 146-bhp turbo 2.2 with TorqueFlite automatic for $1000 extra. The Shelby Lancer took Carroll into a new realm: the high-style European-type sports sedan. Equipment was suitably lavish, with power everything, all-disc brakes (instead of rear drums), and a special Shelby Touring Suspension (good for 0.80g on the skidpad). Handling was sharp and manual-shift acceleration lively—7.7 seconds 0-60 mph in most published road tests—but shift action was clunky, the ride jarring, turbo "lag" annoying, and quietness conspicuously absent.

As ever, though, Shelby wasn't building cars for the masses. After completing 800 Shelby Lancers by July of '87, SAI turned to a similarly modified Dodge Shadow compact called the Shelby CSX. Offered only as a two-door hatchback sedan, it weighed 200 pounds less than the midsize Shelby Lancer and was thus a bit quicker. The factory claimed 0-60 in 7.1 seconds and a standing quarter-mile of 15.1 seconds at 90 mph. Most road tests agreed.

Meanwhile, Carroll wrote two postscripts to his Ford experience. The first involved a dozen GT 350 convertibles built from restored Mustangs, essentially brand-new '66 models identical to Shelby's original six prototypes. All sold quickly despite stiff $40,000 price tags. Shelby sprang a similar surprise in early '93 by announcing that four dozen "continuation" Cobra 427SCs would be assembled from never-used stock parts he had stored away back in the '60s.

A heart transplant forced Shelby to slow down for a while, yet he somehow found the time and energy to be the "spiritual conscience" behind the Cobra-like 1992 Dodge Viper RT/10. In late 1997 he lent his name to something rather unusual for him: a hot-rodded Dodge Durango sport-utility vehicle. Premiered as a concept at the SEMA aftermarket-industry show, the Shelby SP360 was a limited-edition SUV created by several independent tuners hoping to win Carroll's endorsement, which they did. The concept used a supercharged 5.9-liter (360-cid) Dodge V-8 making 360 bhp, plus a fortified suspension and other Shelby-style features, including Cobra Blue paint and broad white dorsal striping. Dodge said only 3000 SP360s would be built, all in 1999, but actual production was minuscule.

By this point, however, Shelby had long since drifted away from Chrysler (his pal Iacocca had left in 1992) and was pursuing various businesses new and old, plus charitable projects. After moving some of his enterprises to new facilities near the recently opened Las Vegas Motor Speedway, he began advertising another "new-old" Cobra, the CSX 4000. This looked much like an original 427, but was sold without an engine as a "component vehicle," again to sidestep pesky "gummint" rules.

Shelby was now in his 70s, but as restless as ever. "I'm tired of imitations," he had told the press. "Folks have put the Cobra name on all sorts of stuff... but none of them were Shelby Cobras. Before they throw the last shovel of dirt on me, I want to take one last shot at an honest-to-goodness Cobra."

Though not exactly a Cobra, the prosaically named Series I (internally designated CSX 5000) would prove the most-vexing car of Shelby's storied career. It entered production—with great difficulty—in 1999 after some five years of second thoughts and false starts. The original plan, revealed in April 1994, was for a twin-turbo V-8 roadster with 500 bhp, a chassis made of high-tech carbon fiber, and a staggering $200,000 price tag. Only 500 would be built. The engine would come from none other than flagging Oldsmobile. Olds general manager John Rock, a cowboy type worthy of Shelby himself, suggested the new 4.0-liter twincam Aurora V-8, hoping an Olds-powered "Cobra for the '90s" would do for his brand what the Viper had done for Dodge. But market realities soon forced downshifting to a less-ambitious $50,000 machine.

The Series I premiered as a "pushmobile" at the Greater Los Angeles Auto Show in January 1997. A running prototype was tested the following October, by which time the chassis was a steel-tube structure supporting a carbon-fiber body. Initial deliveries were planned for 1998. But uncharacteristically, Shelby American underestimated production costs by a whopping $60,000 a car. That, plus unforeseen development glitches and construction delays with the new Las Vegas plant, pushed production back to mid-1999. By that point the price had soared to near $100,000 and soon went to nearly $114-grand. Despite sizable deposits from 300 would-be owners and a handful of Olds dealers who would sell the car, the project was almost bankrupt by year's end, when only 20 Series Is had been built.

1987 Shelby Lancer hatchback sedan

1987 Charger GLH-S hatchback coupe

1987 CSX hatchback coupe

Just when all seemed lost, Venture Industries, which supplied the carbon-fiber bodies, rode to the rescue, offering some $10 million for a 60-percent stake in Shelby American. By late April, Shelby American was honoring original contracts with dealers, depositers, and suppliers; lingering engineering bugs were fast being squashed; and production was up to 1.2 cars a day, thanks to more-efficient methods. But about 250 Series Is were still unsold, and price had to be hiked again—first to $160,000, then to near $175,000—close, ironically, to the original 1994 figure.

For the few who got to drive it, the Series I was a genuine Shelby with all the thrills that name implied. Riding a tight 96.2-wheelbase, it was three inches wider than a C5 Corvette yet scaled a feathery 2650 pounds. The carbon-fiber body weighed only 130 pounds, yet was stronger than steel. So, too, the chassis, made up from extruded-aluminum members and boasting a resonance frequency of 52 hertz, more than double the best then attained in production cars. Suspension was also mostly aluminum, with four-wheel independent geometry by upper and lower control arms, adjustable shocks, and coil springs attached to Formula 1-style pushrod-operated inboard rocker arms. This layout not only reduced undesirable unsprung weight, but could be easily custom-tuned. An antiroll bar lived at each end. Brakes were contemporary Corvette discs of 13-inch diameter fore, 12 inches aft. As with the Viper, though, Shelby felt no need for antilock control. Steering was the expected power rack-and-pinion. Rolling stock comprised five-spoke 18-inch alloys wearing Z-rated Goodyear Eagle F1 Supercar tires sized at P265/40 front, P315/40 rear. A Corvette six-speed manual gearbox was sited in the tail, helping achieve the ideal 50/50 weight distribution. The Aurora V-8 got new camshafts, intake manifold, exhaust system, and control chip, modest changes that nevertheless yielded 320 bhp—up 70 from stock—and 30 extra pound-feet of torque (290 in all).

With a stump-pulling 4.22:1 rear axle and carrying just 8.3 pounds per horsepower, the Series I was claimed to do 0-60 mph in 4.4 seconds, 0-100 in 11 flat, and a 12.8-second standing quarter-mile at 109.9 mph. *AutoWeek* found those numbers credible, though it couldn't confirm them in testing two prototypes. But the magazine did find the Series I "a blast to drive. It handles like a world-class sports car." Yet this Shelby was no raw-edged Cobra, equipped with standard air conditioning, power windows, leather-trimmed cockpit, and a booming stereo. Some GM bits were obvious inside, but the manual folding top was snug and easy to operate, and workmanship improved to first-class once Venture came aboard. By February 2002, Shelby American had delivered 240 Series Is, with orders for 25 more.

But when a new round of federal regulations required the car to be recertified for sale after 1999, Shelby halted Series I production after 249 units. That seemed to leave the remaining 251 scheduled cars in limbo, but Shelby later marketed them as "component vehicles," like his latter-day Cobras, after securing an outside company to install Olds V-8s postpurchase. And in line with original plans, that engine was finally available in a supercharged version, making the Series I an "honest 3.3-second [0-60] car," according to Shelby. "There's a lot of people that want them as kit cars," he said in August 2004. "We have had 15 or 20 bites and we've [already] sold two or three." The rest will doubtless find homes, too.

Shelby was also far from finished with the Cobra. Indeed, it remained the heart and soul of his business. Though "component vehicles" are beyond the scope of this book, these merit mention as lineal descendants commonly accepted as true *Shelby* Cobras. Not "originals," however. Again typical of the man, Ol' Shel couldn't resist updating his signature car with new technology, components, and materials. Anything to go faster. There were several variations, each carefully built in small numbers, some bodied in fiberglass instead of aluminum. Announced in 2002 were specially trimmed 40th anniversary Cobras, a 40-unit run split between a small-block CSX 8000 and the first 427 model with an aluminum-block supercharged engine. Appearing two years later were an AC 427 S/C (CSX 1000) and AC 289 FIA (CSX 7500). The initials signified bodies supplied by AC Motor Holdings, the Malta-based descendant of Britain's A.C. Cars, which had sold various Cobras of its own through several corporate incarnations. Now Shelby and AC had finally joined forces (after settling an intellectual property dispute), which seemed only right. By the mid-2000s, the Cobra duo had become a trio comprising big-block 427 (still CSX 4000), 289 Street (CSX 8000), and track-ready 289 FIA (CSX 7000). All these "continuations" were sold as rolling chassis ready for installation of Shelby-vetted "crate motors" based on period-correct 1960s Ford engines. Of course, Shelby sold those too, plus all manner of parts and accessories.

There was also another "continuation" Shelby Mustang, the GT 500E "Eleanor," star of the auto-heist film *Gone in 60 Seconds*. Built in Texas, again from pristine restorations, the Eleanors carried a Shelby-tuned 5.4-liter Ford V-8 and carefully updated styling. Only a handful were completed, all in 2003.

Meanwhile, Shelby renewed personal ties with Ford, lending his priceless first-hand experience to the development of the roadgoing midengine Ford GT patterned on the great, late-'60s LeMans-winning racer (see *Ford*). For Shelby, still energetic at 80, it must have been an emotional homecoming. He then served as "spiritual advisor" on Ford's 2004 Cobra concept roadster (a mix of GT components and a mighty new 605-bhp front-mounted V-10) and a rebodied 2005 follow-up, the rakish Shelby GR-1 coupe. More significant to this book were his contributions to showroom models, starting with the muscular 2007 Shelby-Cobra GT 500 based on Ford's newly redesigned Mustang (see *Ford Mustang*).

As ever, though, Shelby couldn't let Ford have all the glory. Bringing history full circle, he teamed with Hertz on a modern "rent-a-racer," the Shelby GT-H. Available at select U.S. airports starting in mid-2006, it began, fittingly, as a Mustang fastback, a V-8 GT with automatic transmission (now a five-speed unit). Shelby shopped Ford Racing Performance Parts for a "cold-air kit," low-restriction "cat back" exhaust system, and a new engine-control chip to realize 325 bhp and 330 pound-feet of torque, up 25 bhp and 10 pound-feet from stock. The same source also supplied special high-rate shocks, low-rise springs, heftier antiroll bars, and a front strut-tower brace, plus a tighter rear-axle ratio. Livery was predictably retro: prominent gold stripes, black paint, thin-bar grille, and racing-style lock pins on a domed Shelby-designed hood, plus a modest rear spoiler and subtle aerodynamic fairings beneath the nose and rocker panels. With all this, the GT-H promised much excitement at Hertz service counters. Disappointment would be inevitable, too, as only 500 cars would be built for rental at 14 far-flung points. The clamor should be no less fierce once GT-Hs reach the collector market, as they inevitably will.

For those who'd rather buy than rent, Shelby had another 2006 surprise, the CS 6 package. This picked up on an idea Ford had toyed with back in the 1960s: a high-performance *six*-cylinder Mustang. In yet another link to the past, Shelby offered a Paxton supercharger (a Novi-1200 centrifigal unit) for the base-Mustang 4.0-liter V-6. When properly installed (by the customer or a shop of his or her choice), horsepower jumped by at least 140 to a stout 350. Also available were a suitably uprated suspension, brakes, custom 20-inch American Racing wheels, exhaust, and body addenda (including hood, front fascia, side scoops, and grille) *a la* GT-H. Shelby sold the CS 6 components separately or as a complete package for $14,999.

A signal event in the business story came in 2004 with the formation of Carroll Shelby International, Inc. as a public stock company. CSBI, to use its ticker symbol, oversees Shelby Automobiles in Las Vegas, which not only builds vehicles but offers consultant services in design, engineering, and prototype construction. The CSI umbrella also covers Los Angeles-based Carroll Shelby Licensing, Inc., established in 1988 as basically a legal clearinghouse for Shelby vehicle designs, trademarks, and other intellectual property.

That's the Shelby saga so far, but it's surely far from finished. Carroll Shelby has been described as having "the unique ability to combine elements so that their sum becomes greater than the total of their parts." Though the same can be said for other automotive geniuses, there's never been one like ol' Shel—and never will be again.

1999 Series I convertible coupe

2004 Cobra concept

2005 GR-1 concept

2006 Ford Mustang with CS 6 package

Specifications

1965

GT 350 (wb 108.0)	Wght	Price	Prod
fstbk cpe	2,800	4,457	562

1965 Engine	bore×stroke	bhp	availability
V-8, 289.0	4.00×2.87	306	S-all

1966

GT 350 (wb 108.0)	Wght	Price	Prod
fstbk cpe	2,800	4,600	2,378

1966 Engines	bore×stroke	bhp	availability
V-8, 289.0	4.00×2.87	306	S-all
V-8S, 289.0	4.00×2.87	400	O-all (limited)

1967

GT 350 (wb 108.0)	Wght	Price	Prod
fstbk cpe	2,800	3,995	1,175
GT 500 (wb 108.0)			
fstbk cpe	3,000	4,195	2,050

1967 Engines	bore×stroke	bhp	availability
V-8, 289.0	4.00×2.87	290	S-GT350
V-8, 428.0	4.13×3.98	400*	S-GT500

* Estimated; advertised bhp: 335

1968

GT 350 (wb 108.0)	Wght	Price	Prod
fstbk cpe	3,000	4,117	1,253
conv cpe	3,100	4,238	404
GT 500 (wb 108.0)			
fstbk cpe	3,100	4,317	1,140
conv cpe	3,200	4,439	402
GT 500KR (wb 108.0)			
fstbk cpe	3,200	4,473	933
conv cpe	3,300	4,594	318

1968 Engines	bore×stroke	bhp	availability
V-8, 302.0	4.00×3.00	250	S-GT 350
V-8, 390.0	4.05×3.78	335	S-GT 500
V-8, 428.0	4.13×3.98	360	S-GT 500
V-8, 428.0	4.13×3.98	400*	S-GT 500KR

* Estimated; advertised bhp: 335

1969

GT 350 (wb 108.0)	Wght	Price	Prod
fstbk cpe	3,000	4,434	1,085
conv cpe	3,100	4,753	194
GT 500 (wb 108.0)			
fstbk cpe	3,100	4,709	1,536
conv cpe	3,200	5,027	335

1969 Engines	bore×stroke	bhp	availability
V-8, 351.0	4.00×3.50	290	S-GT 350
V-8, 428.0	4.13×3.98	400*	S-GT 500

* Estimated; advertised bhp: 335

1970

GT 350 (wb 108.0) - 350 blt	Wght	Price	Prod
fstbk cpe	3,000	4,500*	—
conv cpe	3,100	4,800*	—
GT 500 (wb 108.0) - 286 blt			
fstbk cpe	3,100	4,800*	—
conv cpe	3,200	5,100*	—

* Estimated.

1970 Engines	bore×stroke	bhp	availability
V-8, 351.0	4.00×3.50	290	S-GT 350
V-8, 428.0	4.13×3.98	375*	S-GT 500

* Estimated; advertised bhp: 335

1986

Shelby GLH-S (wb 99.1)	Wght	Price	Prod
htchbk sdn 4d	2,300	10,995	500

1986 Engine	bore×stroke	bhp	availability
I-4T, 135.0	3.44×3.62	175	S

1987

Shelby Chrgr GLH-S (wb 96.5)	Wght	Price	Prod
htchbk cpe	2,483	12,995	1,000
Shelby CSX (wb 97.0)			
htchbk cpe	2,690	13,495	750
Shelby Lancer (wb 103.1)			
htchbk sdn 4d	2,895	16,995*	800

1987 Engines	bore×stroke	bhp	availability
I-4T, 135.0	3.44×3.62	175	S-All
I-4T, 135.0	3.44×3.62	146	O-Shlby Lncr auto

* with 5-speed manual transmission, cloth upholstery; $17,995 with automatic transmission, leather upholstery

1988

Shelby CSX-T (wb 97.0)	Wght	Price	Prod
htchbk cpe	2,675	*	1,000

1988 Engine	bore×stroke	bhp	availability
I-4T, 135.0	3.44×3.62	146	S

* All were sold to Thrifty Car Rental at fleet prices

1989

Shelby CSX (wb 97.0)	Wght	Price	Prod
htchbk cpe	2,790	15,000	500

1989 Engine	bore×stroke	bhp	availability
I-4T, 135.0	3.22×3.62	175	S

1999-2002*

Series 1 (wb 96.2)	Wght	Price	Prod
conv 2d	2,650	175,000	249**

1999-2002 Eng.	bore×stroke	bhp	availability
V-8, 244.0	3.42×3.31	320	S
V-8S, 244.0	3.42×3.31	450-500	O***

* All certified as 1999 models.

** More sold as kit cars after production ended

*** Supercharged engine installed in some kit versions

Studebaker

Studebaker was born in 1852 when brothers Henry and Clem built three covered wagons in South Bend, Indiana. Actually there were five Studebaker brothers, all of whom participated in company affairs over the years. By 1872, Studebaker was the largest horse-drawn vehicle manufacturer in the world.

J. M. "Wheelbarrow Johnny" was president in 1902 when Studebaker began building automobiles. The first were electrics, soon joined (and later replaced) by gas-powered models. Albert Russell Erskine, a one-time company accountant, ran the company from 1915 to 1933. Erskine liked to say "I eat obstacles for breakfast." His energy, optimism, and efficiency multiplied Studebaker's sales and profits. The company was quite successful in the medium-price field, but Erskine wanted expand both down- and upmarket. In 1927, a light six (dubbed Erskine) gave Studebaker a presence in low-priced field. Pierce-Arrow was acquired in '28 and gave Studebaker a strong entry in the luxury market.

Studebaker fared poorly after the 1929 stock market crash. Albert Erskine's optimism worked against him during the Depression. Instead of conserving cash reserves, he paid large dividends to Studebaker shareholders, expecting the economy to recover soon. The Depression only deepened and Erskine's policies put the company in a precarious position.

The Erskine car was a weak performer and sold poorly. It became the Studebaker Model 53 Six during 1930. Having failed with his namesake car, A. R. Erskine tried again with another low-priced "companion," the Rockne, named for then-famous Notre Dame football coach Knute Rockne. This car didn't last as long as the Erskine, with just over 36,000 built in 1932-33. At $585-$735, the Rockne should have sold well in those deep Depression years, but a lack of power was a handicap, compounded by iffy workmanship. Yet another Erskine error was selling a Studebaker called Dictator. The name seemed downright unpatriotic as real-life dictators Hitler and Mussolini consolidated their power, yet it persisted through 1937.

Excluding the Erskine, Studebaker's 1930 line encompassed no fewer than six engines and seven series. A six and eight, both 221-cubic-inch inline units of similar power, featured in that year's 115-inch-wheelbase Dictator and 120-inch Commander series. Low-priced 114-inch-wheelbase Standard Sixes anchored the line. At the top were magnificent President Eights, offered on both a 125-inch-wheelbase chassis and a special 135-inch platform. These were the finest automobiles South Bend built in this decade—perhaps the best ever.

For 1931, Studebaker dropped the Dictator Six, but retained the Dictator Eight. Wheelbases stretched to 124 inches on Commanders and to 130/136 on Presidents. At midyear, the 221 Dictator eight was booted from 70 to 81 bhp, and the long-stroke 250.4-cid Commander unit was pushed to 101. Prices were adjusted to cover a slightly broader range of $795-$2550, versus 1930's $895-$2595.

This same lineup returned for 1932, when either a small 205-cid six or smaller 190-cid six powered the Rockne. The senior-line six, a stroked 230 with 80 bhp, went into a new 117-inch-wheelbase Standard chassis that also served Dictator Eights. The Commander's wheelbase increased an inch. All Presidents had a 135-inch wheelbase.

For 1933, Commanders rode a 117-inch wheelbase with a smaller 235-cid straight eight, but at 100 bhp, it had almost the same power. The President retained its 135-inch chassis and the smooth 337-cid 135-bhp eight. The 125-inch-wheelbase President returned—this time with a smaller 250-cid eight rated at 125 horsepower. The Dictator name was wisely dropped for that year.

Curiously, the Dictator name returned for '34. Comprising Standard, Special, and Deluxe models, Dictators had a 113-inch-wheelbase and were powered by a 205 six with 88 bhp. That year's Commanders rode a 119-inch wheelbase and carried a revived 221 eight, albeit with 103 bhp. Presidents were downgraded to a 110-bhp, 250-cid eight and now rode a 123-inch chassis.

Sales dwindled from over 123,000 for 1930 to under 26,000 for '32, dropping the make from fourth to 11th. Studebaker finished 14th for 1933, when it went into receivership after a hoped-for merger with White Motors fell through. With that, Erskine resigned, then committed suicide soon afterward.

Stepping into this managerial breach were production vice-president Harold S. Vance and sales VP Paul G. Hoffman, who would jointly guide Studebaker through 1949. They quickly got rid of Pierce-Arrow (the luxury market had evaporated), then took steps to get idle production lines moving again. As a result, Studebaker made a small profit in 1934, enough to secure a line of credit and get out of receivership. Production promptly moved up to near 60,000 from 1933's paltry 12,500, lifting the make to eighth in the industry. Output slipped below 44,000 for '35, but recovered to near 56,000 and some 98,000 for 1936-37, respectively, when Studebaker finished 11th and tenth. Part of this success reflected a reversal of Erskine's "full-line" market approach. Studebaker's 1934-35 line comprised just three series: Dictator Six, Commander Eight, and President Eight. Commanders then took a two-year vacation.

For 1934, Studebaker introduced streamlined "Year Ahead" models with pontoon fenders and rounded grilles. Rumble-seat body types departed the following year. "Potato" shapes were evident for 1936-37, as most everywhere else, yet Studebaker managed a handsome, individual appearance. Offerings in both those years comprised 116-inch-wheelbase Dictators and Presidents that rode 125-inch chassis.

For 1938 styling, Hoffmann hired Raymond Loewy, the brilliant industrial designer who'd created the 1932-34 "Aerodynamic" Hupmobiles. This first of many Loewy projects at South Bend produced a prominent prow-type radiator with pod headlights snugged in between it and the fenders, plus GM-style "catwalk" trim on some models. Those offerings involved a revived Commander Six with five body styles, a replacement for the departed Dictator on a slightly longer 116.5-inch chassis. The same platform supported four State Commander Eights, while a newly abbreviated 122-inch chassis appeared under four State Presidents. The 1939 models had headlamps moved out into the fenders and more horizontal grillework to match.

Though Studebaker earned a respectable $2 million for 1936, profits slimmed to just $812,000 for '37, followed by a deficit of $1.76-million in recession-plagued 1938. But things improved markedly in '39, when model-year car production jumped nearly 50 percent to almost 86,000. From there, it went nowhere but up until the war.

The big reason for this roaring success was the cleanly styled Champion, available as a new economy coupe, club sedan, and four-door Cruising Sedan on a 110-inch wheelbase. Pitched in the $660-$800 range, it cost only $25-$40 more than the "Low-Priced Three."

Though carefully weight-engineered by engineering VP Roy Cole and project chief Eugene Hardig, the Champ was no less substantial than a Commander or President. Its new 164.3-cid

1930 President FH four-door sedan

1932 President Eight four-door sedan

1934 Commander 2/4-passenger convertible roadster

1934 Commander Land Cruiser four-door sedan

1936 President Eight four-door sedan

L-head six was smaller than rival engines and made less power—78 bhp initially—but the Champ delivered comparable performance because it weighed an average 500-600 pounds less. Though no match for a V-8/85 Ford, it would run up to 78 mph—equal to or better than Chevy, Plymouth, and the Ford V-8/60. Mileage and durability were fantastic.

With all this, the Champ scored nearly 34,000 model-year sales despite its midseason debut, lofting Studebaker back up to seventh in the industry with total 1939 car production just short of 86,000. Coupled with the much-reduced break-even point of 75,000 cars wrought by Hoffman and Vance, South Bend earned $2.9 million.

You don't mess with a savior, so Champ changes for 1940 were limited to finer grille bars, sealed-beam headlamps per industry practice, new Custom DeLuxe trim, and a second coupe with rear "opera seat." Series production nearly doubled for the model year, hitting 66,264. Commanders and Presidents returned with wheelbases and engines unchanged in 1938-39, but lost their convertible sedans, leaving each with a coupe, Cruising Sedan, and two-door club sedan; Commander still listed a business coupe as well. Front ends were more Lincoln-like than Champion's, with sharper prows and a split, roughly heart-shaped vertical-bar grille. Presidents sold for about $125 more than comparable Commanders, which ranged upward of $200 above the Champs.

Loewy reworked the entire line for 1941, giving the cars slightly sharper noses and lower, wider vertical-bar grilles. The engines were reworked, too. Champ's was stroked to 169.6 cid and 80 bhp, while more-subtle changes lifted Commander's six to 94 bhp and the President's silky nine-main straight-eight to 117.

1941 was another excellent Studebaker sales year, though the make slipped from eighth to ninth in the model-year production race. Still, Champ attracted nearly 85,000 buyers to become the single best-selling line in Studebaker history, and Commander rose from just under 35,000 to nearly 42,000. President maintained its low-volume tradition with just under 7000 model-year sales, up only 500 from 1940.

A wider, heavier-looking, and rather Chevy-like "face" arrived for war-shortened '42, when DeLux-tone models were renamed "Deluxstyle." Studebaker touted a "new, perfected Turbo-matic Drive" as a Commander/President option. This was much like Chrysler's semiautomatic Fluid Drive, a manual transmission with a fluid coupling allowing clutchless changes within two gear ranges. Studebaker returned to eighth for the model year by building some 50,000 cars before February 1942, when the government ended consumer production for the duration of World War II.

Studebaker's military output was numerous and varied, chiefly trucks (where the firm had an equally long and successful record) but also airplane engines and "Weasel" personnel carriers. Thanks largely to the success of the '39 Champion, Studebaker had turned over its styling chores to Loewy Associates, an outside firm not entirely occupied with defense contracts. As a result, Studebaker was able to introduce all-new postwar cars in the spring of 1946—well ahead of everyone else except industry newcomer Kaiser-Frazer.

Earlier that year, Studebaker returned to civilian car sales with Skyway Champions, slightly altered versions of the 1942 Champ three- and five-passenger coupe and two- and four-door sedan. Changes were few and modest: an upper-grille molding that extended beneath the headlamps, optional lamps atop the fenders, and the elimination of hoodside moldings. Only 19,275 were built before South Bend changed over to the all-new '47s.

Costing some $11 million to develop, these appealing new Studebakers had evolved from sketches done as early as 1940 by young Robert E. Bourke. It was that work that prompted

1938 Commander Six 3-passenger business coupe

1948 Commander Regal DeLuxe convertible coupe

1941 President Custom Land Cruiser four-door sedan

1950 Champion Regal DeLuxe coupe

1947 Commander four-door sedan

1950 Commander Starlight coupe

Bourke's hiring at Loewy Associates by Virgil M. Exner, the group's chief stylist. Exner had joined Loewy before the war after a career at Pontiac. Though Exner began the '47 Studebaker program, he left Loewy before the design was finalized, so the end product was a blend of Exner and Bourke ideas.

Postwar Presidents were still some years off in 1947, but Commanders returned along with Champions. The latter, no longer called Skyway, were little changed mechanically, but rode a two-inch-longer wheelbase. A special 123-inch chassis was reserved for a lush new Commander Land Cruiser priced at $2043. Other Commanders retained the prewar 119-inch wheelbase. Both series listed two- and four-door sedans (the latter now with "suicide" back doors), long-deck three-seater coupe, and a new five-passenger "Starlight" coupe with radical three-element wraparound rear window. All were available with base DeLuxe trim or, for about $120 more, in new Regal DeLuxe form. Also new were a pair of Regal convertibles, a $1902 Champ and $2236 Commander. Studebaker returned to profitability in 1947, earning more than $9 million on 58.5-percent higher calendar-year car/truck sales.

The upward trend continued in 1948, with $19 million in earnings on calendar-year output of over a quarter-million cars and trucks—both Studebaker records. Predictably, South Bend's cars changed little for '48, though a winged hood medallion provided instant identification. Another, more significant linewide change was a price hike averaging $200, bringing stickers to $1535-$2430 in reflection of strong postwar inflation. South Bend moved up a notch on the industry roster, finishing seventh for the model year with nearly 185,000 cars.

Though brand-new styling was planned for 1949 to one-up the competition again, lack of time precluded it, so Studebaker settled for refinements. Champs sported a new grille composed of horizontal and vertical louvers forming three rows of rectangular openings, and the Commander six was stroked to 245.6 cid, good for an even 100 bhp. Despite the lack of change, profits soared to $27.5 million.

Studebaker was 98 years young in 1950, which would be its best-ever car year. Model-year production totaled 343,166. Grand preparations were underway for the firm's "second century," about which there were many equally grand predictions. But, of course, that second 100 years would be cut far short—to exactly 14.

Seeking to look fresh against newer-design rivals for 1950, Studebaker gave its basic '47 bodies a dramatic cowl-forward facelift that was controversial at the time. According to designer Bob Bourke, the new "bullet nose" front was ordered by the French-accented Loewy with the words, "Now Bob, eet has to look like zee aeroplane." It did, and had the most-bizarre face of any American car since Graham's abortive 1939-40 "Sharknose."

The new front increased wheelbase a nominal one inch for all 1950 Studebakers, bringing Champs up to 113 inches and Commanders to 120. Engines were unchanged. So was the lineup, except for a quartet of price-leading Champ Customs in the low $1400s. That year's Land Cruiser was tagged at $2187. The

1952 Champion Starlight coupe

1953 Champion Regal Starliner hardtop coupe

1954 Commander Starliner hardtop coupe

1956 Sky Hawk hardtop coupe

1956 Golden Hawk hardtop coupe

1956 President Classic four-door sedan

year's big technical news was "Automatic Drive" as an across-the-board option. Studebaker had designed this excellent new fully self-shifting transmission in cooperation with the Detroit Gear Division of Borg-Warner—the only postwar automatic developed by an independent other than Packard's Ultramatic.

Wheelbases were rearranged again for 1951, thanks to an improved chassis with better brakes, easier "center-point" steering, and a 115-inch wheelbase for all models (up two on Champions, down five on Commanders) except the Land Cruiser, which got a 119-inch spread. Champ power was unchanged, but there was big news in Studebaker's first V-8, a new standard for Commanders. Sized at 232.6 cid, it pumped out 120 bhp by conventional means, although overhead cams and hemispherical combustion chambers had been considered.

Rising production costs forced Studebaker to raise prices a bit for 1951, and again at midyear for a range running $1560-$2380. But buyers seemed happy to pay for South Bend's lively new V-8, which boosted Commander sales no less than 70 percent. Appearance changes for '51 were slight. The bullet nose was toned down by painting its chrome outer ring, the prominent air vents above the sub-grilles were erased, and model names were spelled out on hood leading edges. However you think it looks now, the 1950-51 bullet nose was quite salable. Though Korean War restrictions held 1951 car production to 268,566, Studebaker actually increased its market share from 4.02 to 4.17 percent.

An all-new Studebaker was planned for centennial 1952, with unit construction and evolutionary bullet-nose styling. But though this "N-Series" progressed to a running prototype, it was abandoned due to continuing government restraints on civilian goods and a big upturn in Studebaker's military business.

Accordingly, the '47 platform was facelifted one last time for '52, gaining a low and toothy full-width grille dubbed "the clam digger" by Loewy stylists. Offerings stood pat with the exception of the belated addition of new Starliner hardtop coupes. As in '51, trim levels comprised Custom, DeLuxe, and Regal for Champion; Regal and State for Commander. Starliners were top-liners. To no one's surprise, Studebaker paced the 1952 Indy 500, and a Champ and Commander scored class wins in that year's Mobilgas Economy Run. But Studey's centennial saw production of just 186,239 units.

Studebaker updated its look in literal high style for the first model year of its second century. Headlining the all-new '53 line were the now-legendary "Loewy coupes." These were sleek, low, and clean—triumphs of good taste. There were six in all: pillarless Regal Starliner and pillared Deluxe and Regal Starlights, Commander, and Champion. Despite the "Loewy" nickname, the basic design was actually the work of Bob Bourke. It was first intended only for a show car, but Loewy himself convinced Studebaker management that it should be put into production.

Perfect from every angle, the Loewy coupe mounted a new 120.5-inch Land Cruiser chassis rather than the 116.5-inch platform used for other models. Advertised as the "new European look," it's still widely regarded as America's best automotive design of the decade. Studebaker's 1953 two- and four-door sedans were almost as pretty, bearing coupe lines but necessarily stubbier and more upright on the shorter wheelbase.

Ominously, tooling the '53 line delayed its production, which ended at a disappointing 169,899. Worse, when things finally did get rolling, demand for coupes was four times that for sedans. Management had expected just the reverse, and both time and sales were lost in switching around. On top of that coupe frames were too light and the flexing resulted in squeaks and rattles. Still, Studebaker managed a slim $2.69 million profit for the fiscal year.

Eggcrate grille inserts identified the predictably little-changed '54 models, which again included the "Loewys," a pair of cheap Champ Custom sedans, and Deluxe and Regal sedans in each line. A belated newcomer was the two-door all-steel Conestoga, Studebaker's first station wagon. Named for the famous "prairie schooners" of the firm's infancy, it came as Deluxe and Regal Champs and Commanders. Also new for '54 were seven extra horses for Commanders and larger brakes across the board. More importantly, the coupe's frame was beefed-up, but Studebaker's reputation had already been hurt by the poor quality of the '53s.

But Studebaker's weaknesses were now painfully apparent. On "pricing out" a Commander Starliner using the General Motors cost structure, Bourke found that Chevrolet could have sold it for $1900; Studebaker charged $2500. Meanwhile, the "Ford Blitz" was on, as Dearborn waged a no-holds-barred price war with GM. Though neither giant damaged the other, they wreaked havoc on independents like Studebaker, whose model-year volume plunged to 81,930.

But just as things looked blackest, Nash president George Mason persuaded Packard president James J. Nance to purchase Studebaker as a prelude to combining with Nash and Hudson to form Mason's hoped-for American Motors. The Packard takeover was duly accomplished in October 1954, ushering in the able Nance to preside over a new Studebaker-Packard Corporation. But when Mason died suddenly that same month, so did his dream of a "Big Four."

Meantime, Studebaker hitched hopes for higher sales to a group of facelifted '55s laden with chrome. Among them were the first postwar Presidents: top-line Deluxe and State four-door sedans (replacing Land Cruiser) and pillared and pillarless State coupes. More power was the order of the day. The Champ six was stroked to 185.6 cid and 101 bhp. Commander's V-8 was pumped up to 140 bhp despite a downsizing to 224.3 cid. Presidents arrived with a 232 bored out to 259 cid, good for 175 bhp. Seeking to hold production costs, Studebaker discarded Automatic Drive for Borg-Warner's cheaper "Flight-O-Matic."

But sales still lagged, so a raft of changes were made in January '55. Commander was promoted to a 162-bhp "Bearcat" 259 (an optional "High Power Kit" added 20 bhp more), and Presidents graduated to a 185-bhp "Passmaster" version. At the same time, noncoupe Presidents and Commanders gained trendy "Ultra Vista" wrapped windshields, and a jazzy President Speedster hardtop bowed with "quilted" leather interior, full instrumentation in a tooled-metal dash, and wild two-tone paint schemes like pink and black and "lemon and lime." But because it listed at a pricey $3253, the Speedster was not a big seller (just 2215 built). Neither were its linemates. In a year when most makes set new sales records, Studebaker managed only 133,826 cars. At this point, South Bend needed about 250,000 annual car sales just to break even.

A game reskin for '56 achieved a squarer look announced by large mesh-filled grilles. Commander and Champion gained inexpensive two-door "sedanets" priced under $2000, a spiffy long-chassis Classic sedan joined the President range at $2489, and wagons got new names: Pelham (Champion), Parkview (Commander), and Pinehurst (President).

Coupes were dubbed the Hawk line of "family sports cars." The last '50s Studebakers styled by the Loewy team, they featured an admirably restrained facelift of the original 1953 coupe, with modest tailfins and a large square grille riding high on an elevated hood. Deluxe interiors featured tooled-metal dash trim, as on the '55 Speedster. There were four versions, pillared Flight Hawk and Power Hawk, and hardtop Sky Hawk and Golden Hawk. All were good-looking, competent through curves, and impressive on straights.

Topping Studebaker's '56 engine chart was a 275-bhp 352 V-8 from new partner Packard as exclusive power for the Golden Hawk. Champs, Flight Hawk, and the Pelham wagon carried an unchanged six, while 259 V-8s now delivered 170/185 bhp in Commander/Power Hawk/Parkview. A new long-stroke 289 version offered 195/210/225 bhp in Presidents/Sky Hawk/Pinehurst.

The Flight Hawk listed below $2000 and the Golden Hawk at $3061, so Studebaker's "family sports cars" were good buys in 1956. Trouble was, they were peripheral sellers appealing mainly to enthusiasts, while the bread-and-butter models appealed to few mainstream buyers. Studebaker thus managed just 85,462 of its '56 cars, including 19,165 Hawks. But the worst was yet to come: In 1957-58, Studebaker and Packard combined couldn't sell more than 80,000 cars a year.

In May 1956, Nance arranged with Curtiss-Wright Corporation, through its president, Roy Hurley, for "advisory management services"—in other words, a cash bailout. With that, plans for an expansive new 1957 S-P line were abruptly canceled and Nance resigned along with Studebaker chairman Paul Hoffman and president Harold Vance. This left Hurley to preside over a group of 1957-58 Studebakers restyled in the only possible way—on the cheap.

Duncan McRae did the deed, giving standard '57s a full-width grille and grossly distended rear fenders suggesting fins. Hawks gained prominent fins that didn't seriously detract from overall appearance. Models were cut to Deluxe and Custom Champ and Commander sedans, Pelham and Parkview wagons, three President sedans, Golden Hawk, and a new pillared Silver Hawk available with six or 289 V-8. Somehow, Studebaker also managed four-door wagons, offered as Commander Provincial and President Broadmoor. Higher compression lifted the 259-cid V-8 to 180/195 bhp, and the Golden Hawk exchanged its Packard engine for a Paxton-supercharged Studebaker 289 delivering the same 275 bhp. Another attempt to spark sales produced the midyear Scotsman, a miserly wagon and two sedans offering six-cylinder power—and very little else—for well under $2000. Some 9300 were sold, but overall '57 sales did not spark, and model-year car production ended at only 74,738.

The '58s were uglier still, with hastily contrived four-headlamp fronts and even-more-garish trim. Commander and President introduced new Starlight hardtop coupes on the 116.5-inch chassis, but the overall lineup was thinner. The Scotsmans did well in that recession year with nearly 21,000 sales. A good thing, too, for total volume dropped again, this time to 62,114.

Studebaker might have died right there had it not been for the sudden success of the compact Lark. Replacing all the old standard models for 1959, this retained the basic sedan/wagon inner structure used since '53, but shorn of all the extra sheetmetal hung on it in the intervening years, good for a loss of up to 200 pounds in curb weight. In its place, McRae applied simple, clean, well-formed styling announced by a Hawk-like grille and a return to dual headlamps. The 169.6-cid six also returned, making 90 bhp in "Lark VI" Deluxe and Regal two- and four-door sedans, two-door wagons, and Regal hardtop coupe. A

1957 Commander two-door sedan

1957 Silver Hawk coupe

1958 Commander four-door sedan

1960 Lark VIII convertible coupe

1961 Hawk coupe

Regal four-door, hardtop, and wagon comprised the "Lark VIII" series with standard two-barrel 180-bhp 259 V-8; optional "Power Pack" four-barrel carb and dual exhaust added 15 horses. Wagons rode the familiar 113-inch wheelbase, but other Larks sat on a trim new 108.5-inch span.

With all this, the Lark was lively (0-60 in under 10 seconds with 180-bhp V-8) yet economical (over 22 mpg easy) and surprisingly roomy. Aided by starting prices below $2000, it was a smash hit, garnering 131,078 sales.

Studebaker didn't give up on "family sports cars" for '59, but the only one it offered was a pillared Silver Hawk. Available with six or either Lark V-8, it added only 7788 units to total model-year production. Still, Studebaker found its way out of the financial woods, earning its first profit in six years on a startling sales gain of over 250 percent from abysmal 1958.

Lark was predictably little changed for 1960. Minor trim was shuffled, and the grille went from horizontal bars to mesh. Four-door wagons returned for the first time since 1958, and that year's Lark VIII line offered Studebaker's first convertible in eight years, a $2756 Regal. Prices were bumped up slightly across the line, and this together with new Big Three competition cost some sales. Meantime, South Bend's lone "family sports car" carried on as simply the Hawk. Its main 1960 change involved engines: V-8s were now exclusively 289s with 210 standard bhp or 225 with optional "Power Pack." Though dated, the V-8 Hawk remained a fine value at $2650, and was still a good performer. But model-year sales dropped by almost half from '59, to 3939, owing to a dearth of dealers, continued advertising emphasis on Lark, and steadily diminishing demand.

Ominously, Lark volume also fell by more than half for 1961 despite revised outer sheetmetal imparting a slightly squarer look, quad headlamps on V-8 models, a new overhead-valve head that turned the old six into a new 112-bhp "Skybolt Six," and the addition of a V-8 Lark Cruiser. The last, reviving Studebaker's luxury-sedan idea, rode the wagon chassis and boasted a richly upholstered interior with extra rear legroom. Hawk returned with a narrow contrast-color panel beneath its fins and newly optional four-speed gearbox, but sales slipped to 3340.

Studebaker got a new president in early '61 when the dynamic Sherwood H. Egbert replaced the embattled Harold Churchill, who'd held the job since August 1958. Shortly after he arrived, Egbert asked Milwaukee-based industrial designer Brooks Stevens to rework both the Lark and Hawk for 1962 on a six-month "crash" basis. Company styling chief Randall Faurot stepped aside, and Stevens whipped up cheap but remarkably effective makeovers. All Larks now wore quad headlamps, plus elongated rear quarters, large round taillights, a Mercedes-like grille (Studebaker had been the North American Mercedes-Benz distributor since 1958 via Curtiss-Wright), and crisper nonwagon rooflines. Two-door wagons vanished, but there were four new Daytona models: a six and V-8 convertible and hardtop coupe with bucket seats, deluxe trim, and an available European-type sliding cloth sunroof for the hardtop.

For the '62 Hawk, Stevens resurrected the pillarless "Loewy" body and applied square, Thunderbird-style rear roof quarters, a matching tail bereft of fins, and a thrust-forward grille. He also penned a new dash with a full set of round gauges in a large rectangle with outboard ends canted in toward the driver. Retitled Gran Turismo Hawk and offered only with the previous pair of 289 V-8s, it was a deft piece of work. Quick, too, with the optional 225-bhp engine good for 120 mph all out and under 10 seconds 0-60 mph. Though heavy, the 289 was strong, with far greater power potential than its modest size implied—as we'd soon see.

Helped by an attractive $3095 base price, the GT Hawk attracted nearly 8400 buyers. Total Studebaker car sales jumped by over 30,000 to some 101,400. Regrettably, that would be the firm's only gain of the decade.

Stevens made further refinements for '63. Larks got raked A-pillars and new windshields, thinner door-window frames, a finely checked grille, and a new Hawk-style dash with round gauges, rocker switches, and a "vanity" glovebox with pop-up mirror. Also new, and quite novel, was Steven's "Wagonaire." Offered in Standard, Regal, and Daytona form, this boasted a unique rear roof panel that could be slid forward for unlimited "head room"—perfect for hauling tall loads. But Wagonaires leaked badly even when buttoned up, which likely explains why cheaper fixed-roof Stude wagons were reinstated during the year. Further expanding the '63 line were six and V-8 sedans in Standard and nicer new Custom trim, the latter priced between Regal and Daytona.

The '63 GT Hawk displayed a revised grille similar to Lark's, round parking lights (amber, per new federal law), woodgrain dash trim, and pleated-vinyl seats. By midseason, both Lark and Hawk could be ordered with new "Avanti" 289 V-8s: a 240-bhp R1 and a 290-bhp supercharged R2 respectively priced at $210 and $372. An R2-equipped "Super Hawk" exceeded 140 mph at Bonneville that year; an R2 "Super Lark" did over 132 mph.

Those engines were named for the totally unexpected grand-touring Studebaker that broke cover in early 1962. Easily the most-stunning South Bend product in a decade, the Avanti lived up to its name—"forward" in Italian—brilliantly conceived by Raymond Loewy and his stellar team of John Ebstein, Robert Andrews, and Tom Kellogg. Because Stevens was occupied with updating higher-volume models, Egbert had turned to Loewy Associates for the exotic sporty car he felt would rejuvenate Studebaker's sagging image—a swoopy four-seat coupe of the sort Loewy had been designing for years.

As with Chevrolet's first Corvette of a decade before, fiberglass was chosen for the Avanti bodyshell to minimize both time and tooling costs. Those same factors nixed an all-new chassis, but chief engineer Gene Hardig beefed up a Lark ragtop frame with front/rear antiroll bars, rear radius rods, and the Bendix front-disc power brakes newly optional for the '63 Lark and Hawk (the first caliper discs in U.S. production, by the way). The 289 V-8 was heavily revised to become a "Jet Thrust." The basic R1 employed ¾-race high-lift cam, dual-breaker distributor, four-barrel carb, and dual exhaust. Andy Granatelli's Paxton Products, then part of Studebaker, added a Paxton supercharger to create the R2. They also devised a trio of bored-out, 304.5-cid extensions: blown R3 with 9.6:1 compression and 335 bhp; naturally aspirated R4 with twin four-barrels, 12:1 compression, and 280 bhp; and the experimental R5 with twin blowers (one per cylinder bank), magneto ignition, Bendix fuel injection, and no less than 575 bhp.

Immediately generating high excitement, the Avanti promised to pack Studebaker showrooms like nothing else in years. Calamitously, production was delayed a critical six months by botched bodies from the supplier, Molded Fiber Glass Company (which also built Corvette shells), forcing Studebaker to set up its own fiberglass production. By the time these and other bugs were squashed, most buyers with advance orders had canceled and bought Corvettes. Thus, just 3834 Avantis (including 500 exports) were built for '63.

Overall, Studebaker's 1963 volume was well down from '62, skidding to 81,660. Only Lincoln and Imperial ranked lower among major U.S. makes. Egbert, who'd been repeatedly hospitalized of late, left in November, never to return. (Sadly, he would die of cancer in 1969.) A month later, new president Byers Burlingame announced the closure of Studebaker's historic South Bend plant after failed last-ditch efforts to obtain financing for future models. Operations were consolidated at the Hamilton, Ontario, assembly plant, where management hoped to return to profitability on 20,000 cars a year, all family compacts. With that, the Avanti and GT Hawk were unceremoniously dumped after a token run of little-changed '64 models: just 809 and 1767, respectively (including exports).

1962 Gran Turismo Hawk hardtop coupe

1963 Lark Daytona hardtop coupe

1963 Lark Daytona Wagonaire station wagon

1963 Avanti coupe

Also among the last South Bend Studebakers were the first '64 Larks, with crisply square new outer body panels, again courtesy of Brooks Stevens. Overall length grew six inches; the grille became more horizontal, with an eggcrate center and integral headlights; and a pointy new rear end carried high-set tail/backup lamps. The stripped Standard was retagged Lark Challenger and priced from as low as $1943. The hallowed Commander name returned to oust Custom/Regal, a four-door Daytona sedan arrived, and newly optional Avanti R3 power reduced a Super Lark's 0-60 to 7.3 seconds (though very few such cars were built). The R3 was also listed (and as rarely ordered) for the GT Hawk, which bowed out with "landau" roof styling and optional rear vinyl half-top, plus a smoother rear deck and matte-black dash appliqué. But Studebaker sales kept sliding, to fewer than 20,000 for calendar '64, and to about 44,400 for the model year.

For 1965, the Lark name was dropped as a liability and the line pared to just ten "Common-Sense" models: six and V-8 Cruisers, two- and four-door Commander sedans, and solid-top Commander wagon, plus V-8 Daytona Wagonaire (with and without sliding roof) and a new pillared Daytona sport coupe. Styling was virtually unchanged. Because the closure of South Bend ended production of Studebaker engines, management settled for Chevy substitutes: the 120-bhp 194 six from the compact Chevy II and the legendary 283 small-block V-8 in 195-bhp tune.

Hamilton almost managed 20,000 cars for '65, but without facilities for developing replacement models, Studebaker had no real future as an automaker. Besides, financing was all but gone. The 1966 models thus ended the marque. These were basically '65s warmed over with dual-beam headlamps (replacing quads), a new four-slot grille, and air-extractor vents in place of the upper taillight units. Studebaker built only 8947 of these cars before calling it quits.

In retrospect, Studebaker's death was a classic case of the deadly downward spiral that claimed so many makes in the Depression: insufficient sales to cover development costs for new models to replace increasingly unpopular old ones, thus further depressing sales and spurring talk of a possible demise that becomes a self-fulfilling prophecy. So although losing Studebaker was a greater shame, it was, perhaps, inevitable.

1964 Daytona R1 "Avanti-Powered" convertible coupe

1965 Daytona Sport Sedan two-door

1966 Cruiser four-door sedan

Specifications

1930*

53 Six (wb 114.0) - 22,371 built 11/29-11/30	Wght	Price	Prod
touring 5P	2,840	965	—
Regal touring 5P	2,900	1,065	—
bus cpe 2P	2,835	895	—
cpe 2-4P	2,890	985	—
club sdn 5P	2,875	935	—
sdn 4d	2,950	985	—
Regal sdn 4d	3,100	1,085	—
landau sdn 4d	3,110	1,125	—
GJ Commander Six (wb 120.0) - 16,019 blt 12/28-4/30			
Regal rdstr 2-4P	3,000	1,495	—
touring 5P	3,070	1,395	—
touring 7P	3,095	1,360	—
Regal touring 5P	3,200	1,495	—
Regal touring 7P	3,225	1,460	—
cpe 2P	3,105	1,345	—
cpe 2-4P	3,160	1,425	—
victoria 4P	3,130	1,425	—
conv cab 4P	3,215	1,545	—
sdn 4d	3,235	1,425	—
Regal sdn 4d	3,335	1,545	—
brougham (mohair) 5P	3,415	1,575	—
brghm (broadcloth) 5P	3,390	1,575	—
GL Dictator Six (wb 115.0) - 17,561 blt 6/29-5/30			
touring 5P	2,955	1,145	—
Regal touring 5P	3,075	1,265	—
cpe 2P	2,915	1,135	—
cpe 2-4P	2,980	1,195	—

GL Dictator Six	Wght	Price	Prod
brougham 5P	3,250	1,295	—
club sdn 5P	2,970	1,095	—
sdn 4d	3,080	1,195	—
Regal sdn 4d	3,200	1,295	—
FC Dictator Eight (wb 115.0) - 16,359 blt 5/29-8/30			
touring 5P	2,980	1,285	—
Regal touring 5P	3,100	1,385	—
cpe 2P	2,950	1,255	—
cpe 2-4P	3,010	1,315	—
brougham 5P	3,275	1,415	—
club sdn 5P	2,990	1,195	—
sdn 4d	3,095	1,295	—
Regal sdn 4d	3,230	1,415	—
FD Commander Eight (wb 120.0) - 24,639 blt 12/28-6/30			
Regal rdstr 2-4P	3,040	1,595	—
touring 5P	3,100	1,495	—
Regal touring 5P	3,250	1,595	—
cpe 2P	3,150	1,495	—
cpe 2-4P	3,235	1,545	—
victoria 4P	3,200	1,515	—
conv cab 4P	3,345	1,695	—
sdn 4d	3,310	1,515	—
Regal sdn 4d	3,435	1,695	—
sdn 7P	3,355	1,695	—
Regal sdn 7P	3,480	1,845	—
brougham (mohair) 5P	3,540	1,695	—
brghm (broadcloth) 5P	3,520	1,695	—
FH President Eight (wb 125.0) - 17,527 blt 12/28-6/30			
rdstr 2-4P	3,810	1,795	—
conv cab 4P	4,000	1,995	—

FH President Eight	Wght	Price	Prod
State victoria 4P	4,050	1,995	—
sdn 4d	4,110	1,795	—
State sdn 4d (mohair)	4,235	1,995	—
State sdn 4d (brdclth)	4,225	1,995	—
FE President Eight (wb 135.0) - 8,740 blt 12/28-6/30			
touring 7P	4,020	1,845	—
State touring 7P	4,175	2,145	—
brougham (mohair) 5P	4,440	2,395	—
brghm (broadcloth) 5P	4,425	2,345	—
sdn 7P	4,035	2,095	—
State sdn (mohair) 7P	4,435	2,295	—
State sdn (brdclth) 7P	4,435	2,295	—
limo 7P	4,205	2,295	—
State limo 7P	4,445	2,595	—
State victoria 5P	4,230	2,295	—

* Includes 1929 production; FC also includes 1931.

1930 Engines	bore×stroke	bhp	availability
I-6, 205.3	3.25×4.13	70	S-53
I-6, 221.0	3.38×4.13	68	S-GL
I-6, 248.3	3.38×4.63	75	S-GJ
I-8, 221.0	3.06×3.75	70	S-FC
I-8, 250.4	3.06×4.25	80	S-FD
I-8, 337.0	3.50×4.38	115	S-FH, FE

1931*

53 Six (wb 114.0) - 22,371 built 11/29-11/30	Wght	Price	Prod
rdstr 2P	2,720	795	—
touring 5P	2,840	895	—
Regal touring 5P	2,990	995	—

53 Six	Wght	Price	Prod
bus cpe 2P	2,785	845	—
cpe 2-4P	2,840	895	—
club sdn 5P	2,830	845	—
sdn 4d	2,900	895	—
Regal sdn 4d	3,030	995	—
landau sdn 4d	3,110	995	—
54 Six (wb 114.0) - 23,917 built 12/30-9/31			
rdstr 2P	2,700	895	—
bus cpe 2P	2,790	845	—
cpe 2-4P	2,840	895	—
sdn 4d	2,930	895	—
Regal sdn 4d	3,075	970	—
touring 5P	2,805	895	—
Regal touring 5P	2,960	970	—
FC Dictator Eight (wb 115.0) - 16,359 blt 5/29-8/30			
touring 5P	2,980	1,285	—
Regal touring 5P	3,100	1,385	—
cpe 2P	2,950	1,255	—
cpe 2-4P	3,010	1,315	—
brougham 5P	3,275	1,415	—
club sdn 5P	2,990	1,195	—
sdn 4d	3,095	1,295	—
Regal sdn 4d	3,230	1,415	—
61 Dictator Eight (wb 114.0) - 14,141 built 8/30-9/31			
cpe 2P	2,905	1,095	—
cpe 2-4P	2,955	1,150	—
sdn 4d	3,055	1,150	—
Regal sdn 4d	3,195	1,225	—
70 Commander Eight (wb 124.0) - 10,823 blt 6/30-9/31			
victoria 4P	3,390	1,585	—
cpe 4P	3,400	1,585	—
Rgl brghm (mohair) 5P	3,660	1,685	—
Rgl brghm (brdclth) 5P	3,655	1,685	—
sdn 4d	3,520	1,585	—
Regal sdn 4d	3,660	1,685	—
80 President Eight (wb 130.0) - 6,340 blt 6/30-9/31			
rdstr 4P	4,130	1,900	—
cpe 2P	3,995	1,850	—
State cpe 4P	4,200	1,950	—
sdn 4d	4,230	1,850	—
State sdn (mohair) 4d	4,385	1,950	—
State sdn (brdclth) 4d	4,380	1,950	—
90 President Eight (wb 136.0) - 2,762 blt 6/30-9/31			
State victoria 5P	4,275	2,250	—
St brghm (mohair) 5P	4,460	2,250	—
St brghm (brdclth) 5P	4,450	2,250	—
sdn 7P	4,360	2,150	—
State sdn 7P	4,520	2,250	—
touring 7P	4,125	1,850	—
State touring 7P	4,265	2,050	—
State limo 7P	4,580	2,550	—

* Includes 1930; FC includes 1929-30.

1931 Engines	bore×stroke	bhp	availability
I-6, 205.3	3.25×4.13	70	S-53, 54
I-8, 221.0	3.06×3.75	70	S-FC
I-8, 221.0	3.06×3.75	81	S-61
I-8, 250.4	3.06×4.25	101	S-70
I-8, 337.0	3.50×4.38	122	S-80, 90

1932

55 Six (wb 117.0) - 13,647 blt	Wght	Price	Prod
conv rdstr 2-4P	3,035	915	—
Regal conv rdstr 2-4P	3,135	1,020	—
cpe 2P	3,025	840	—
Regal cpe 2P	3,125	945	—
cpe 2-4P	3,080	890	—
Regal cpe 2-4P	3,165	995	—
St. Regis brghm 2d 5P	3,130	915	—
St. Rgs Rgl brghm 2d 5P	3,215	1,020	—
sdn 4d	3,170	915	—
Regal sdn 4d	3,260	1,020	—
conv sdn 5P	—	985	—
Regal conv sdn 5P	—	1,090	—
62 Dictator Eight (wb 117.0) - 6,021 built			
conv rdstr 2-4P	3,115	1,060	—
Regal conv rdstr 2-4P	3,190	1,155	—
cpe 2P	3,085	980	—
Regal cpe 2P	3,170	1,085	—
cpe 2-4P	3,160	1,030	—

62 Dictator Eight	Wght	Price	Prod
Regal cpe 2-4P	3,225	1,135	—
St. Rgs brghm 2d 5P	3,225	1,050	—
St. Rgs Rgl brghm 2d 5P	3,280	1,155	—
sdn 4d	3,240	1,050	—
Regal sdn 4d	3,330	1,155	—
conv sdn 5P	3,285	1,125	—
Regal conv sdn 5P	3,370	1,230	—
71 Commander Eight (wb 125.0) - 3,551 built			
conv rdstr 2-4P	3,380	1,445	—
Regal conv rdstr 2-4P	3,480	1,550	—
cpe 2P	3,400	1,295	—
Regal cpe 2P	3,475	1,400	—
cpe 2-4P	3,465	1,350	—
Regal cpe 2-4P	3,530	1,455	—
St. Rgs brghm 2d 5P	3,530	1,445	—
St. Rgs Rgl brghm 2d 5P	3,585	1,550	—
sdn 4d	3,545	1,445	—
Regal sdn 4d	3,645	1,550	—
conv sdn 5P	3,690	1,560	—
Regal conv sdn 5P	3,775	1,665	—
91 President Eight (wb 135.0) - 2,399 built			
conv rdstr 2-4P	4,100	1,750	—
State conv rdstr	4,200	1,855	—
cpe 2P	4,120	1,595	—
State cpe 2P	4,220	1,700	—
cpe 2-4P	4,265	1,690	—
State cpe 2-4P	4,365	1,795	—
St. Rgs brghm 2d 5P	4,200	1,750	—
St. Rgs St brghm 2d 5P	4,300	1,855	—
sdn 4d	4,260	1,750	—
State sdn 4d	4,390	1,855	—
conv sdn 5P	4,335	1,880	—
State conv sdn 5P	4,445	1,985	—
sdn 7P	4,365	1,890	—
State sdn 7P	4,475	1,995	—
limo 7P	4,415	1,990	—
State limo 7P	4,525	2,095	—

1932 Engines	bore×stroke	bhp	availability
I-6, 230.0	3.25×4.63	80	S-55
I-8, 221.0	3.06×3.75	85	S-62
I-8, 250.4	3.06×4.25	101	S-71
I-8, 337.0	3.50×4.38	122	S-91

1933

56 Six (wb 117.0) - 6,861 blt	Wght	Price	Prod
rdstr 2-4P	3,165	915	—
Regal rdstr 2-4P	3,260	1,020	—
cpe 2P	3,160	840	—
Regal cpe 2P	3,245	945	—
cpe 2-4P	3,210	890	—
Regal cpe 2-4P	3,300	995	—
St. Rgs brghm 2d 5P	3,300	915	—
St. Rgs Rgl brghm 2d 5P	3,375	1,020	—
sdn 4d	3,310	915	—
Regal sdn 4d	3,435	1,020	—
conv sdn 5P	3,380	1,015	—
Regal conv sdn 5P	3,460	1,120	—
73 Commander Eight (wb 117.0) - 3,841 built			
conv rdstr 2-4P	3,245	1,095	—
Regal conv rdstr 2-4P	3,335	1,200	—
cpe 2P	3,220	1,000	—
Regal cpe 2P	3,345	1,105	—
cpe 2-4P	3,275	1,050	—
Regal cpe 2-4P	3,405	1,155	—
St. Rgs brghm 2d 5P	3,375	1,075	—
St. Rgs Rgl brghm 2d 5P	3,475	1,180	—
sdn 4d	3,385	1,075	—
Regal sdn 4d	3,500	1,180	—
conv sdn 5P	3,475	1,195	—
Regal conv sdn 5P	3,545	1,300	—
82 President Eight (wb 125.0) - 1,194 built			
conv rdstr 2-4P	3,480	1,385	—
State conv rdstr 2-4P	3,560	1,490	—
cpe 2-4P	3,520	1,325	—
State cpe 2-4P	3,600	1,430	—
St. Rgs brghm 2d 5P	3,605	1,385	—
St. Rgs St brghm 2d 5P	3,670	1,490	—
sdn 4d	3,640	1,385	—
State sdn 4d	3,720	1,490	—

82 President Eight	Wght	Price	Prod
State conv sdn 5P	3,745	1,650	—
92 President Eight (wb 135.0) - 635 built			
conv rdstr 2-4P	4,205	1,685	—
State conv rdstr 2-4P	4,285	1,790	—
cpe 2-4P	4,255	1,625	—
State cpe 2-4P	4,335	1,730	—
St. Rgs St brghm 2d 5P	4,400	1,790	—
sdn 4d	4,380	1,685	—
State sdn 4d	4,465	1,790	—
State conv sdn 5P	4,470	1,960	—
sdn 7P	4,470	1,835	—
State sdn 7P	4,565	1,940	—
State limo 7P	4,605	2,040	—

1933 Engines	bore×stroke	bhp	availability
I-6, 230.0	3.25×4.63	85	S-56
I-8, 235.0	3.06×4.00	100	S-73
I-8, 250.0	3.06×4.25	110	S-82
I-8, 337.0	3.50×4.38	132	S-92

1934

A Dictator Six (wb 113.0) - 45,851 blt	Wght	Price	Prod
conv rdstr 2-4P	2,860	790	—
Regal conv rdstr 2-4P	2,935	820	—
cpe 2P	2,795	740	—
Regal cpe 2P	2,860	770	—
cpe 2-4P	2,865	790	—
Regal cpe 2-4P	2,950	820	—
St. Rgs brghm 2d 5P	2,840	760	—
St. Rgs Rgl brghm 2d 5P	2,935	810	—
St. Rgs Cus brghm 2d 5P	2,890	810	—
sdn 4d	2,910	790	—
Regal sdn 4d	3,005	840	—
Custom sdn 4d	2,950	840	—
Special series:			
cpe 2P	2,780	685	—
Regal cpe 2P	2,845	720	—
cpe 2-4P	2,850	740	—
Regal cpe 2-4P	2,935	770	—
St. Rgs brghm 2d 5P	2,825	710	—
St. Rgs Rgl brghm 2d 5P	2,920	760	—
St. Rgs Cus brghm 2d 5P	2,875	760	—
sdn 4d	2,895	740	—
Regal sdn 4d	2,990	790	—
Custom sdn 4d	2,935	790	—
"Year Ahead" series (from Jul/34):			
cpe 3P	2,800	695	—
Regal cpe 3P	2,885	730	—
cpe 5P	2,880	750	—
Regal cpe 5P	2,980	780	—
St. Regis sdn 4d	2,850	720	—
St. Regis Cus sdn 2d	2,910	755	—
St. Regis Rgl sdn 2d	2,970	770	—
sdn 4d	2,915	750	—
Custom sdn 4d	2,960	785	—
Regal sdn 4d	3,020	800	—
Deluxe subseries:			
rdstr 3-5P	2,900	800	—
Regal rdstr 3-5P	2,970	800	—
cpe 3P	2,830	750	—
Regal cpe 3P	2,920	780	—
cpe 3-5P	2,900	800	—
Regal cpe 3-5P	3,020	830	—
St. Regis sdn 2d	2,895	770	—
St. Regis Rgl sdn 2d	2,985	820	—
St. Regis Cus sdn 2d	2,945	805	—
sdn 4d	2,945	800	—
Regal sdn 4d	3,055	850	—
Custom sdn 4d	2,990	835	—
Land Cruiser sdn 4d	3,015	995	—
Rgl Lnd Crsr sdn 4d	3,110	995	—
B Commander Eight (wb 119.0) - 10,315 built			
conv rdstr 2-4P	3,255	970	—
Regal conv rdstr 2-4P	3,335	1,000	—
cpe 2P	3,205	920	—
Regal cpe 2P	3,290	950	—
cpe 2-4P	3,280	970	—
Regal cpe 2-4P	3,350	1,000	—
St. Rgs brghm 2d 5P	3,235	940	—
St. Rgs Rgl brghm 2d 5P	3,355	990	—
St. Rgs Cus brghm 2d 5P	3,295	990	—

B Commander Eight	Wght	Price	Prod
sdn 4d	3,310	970	—
Regal sdn 4d	3,435	1,020	—
Custom sdn 4d	3,360	1,020	—
Land Cruiser sdn 4d	3,385	1,165	—
Rgl Lnd Crsr sdn 4d	3,480	1,165	—
"Year Ahead" series (began Jul/34):			
rdstr 3-5P	3,290	915	—
Regal rdstr 3-5P	3,355	945	—
cpe 3P	3,215	865	—
Regal cpe 3P	3,300	895	—
cpe 3-5P	3,295	915	—
Regal cpe 3-5P	3,375	945	—
St. Rgs Rgl sdn 2d	3,385	935	—
St. Rgs Cus sdn 2d	3,340	920	—
Regal sdn 4d	3,435	965	—
Custom sdn 4d	3,395	950	—
Land Cruiser sdn 4d	3,410	1,135	—
Rgl Lnd Crsr sdn 4d	3,500	1,135	—
C President Eight (wb 123.0) - 3,698 built			
conv rdstr 2-4P	3,435	1,220	—
Regal conv rdstr 2-4P	3,510	1,250	—
cpe 2P	3,370	1,170	—
Regal cpe 2P	3,470	1,200	—
cpe 2-4P	3,410	1,220	—
Regal cpe 2-4P	3,510	1,250	—
sdn 4d	3,490	1,220	—
Regal sdn 4d	3,620	1,270	—
Custom sdn 4d	3,550	1,270	—
Land Cruiser sdn 4d	3,565	1,445	—
Rgl Lnd Crsr sdn 4d	3,655	1,445	—
Custom berline 5P	—	1,420	—
Regal berline 5P	—	1,420	—
***"Year Ahead"* series (began Jul/34)**			
rdstr 3-5P	3,460	1,220	—
Regal rdstr 3-5P	3,520	1,250	—
cpe 3P	3,395	1,170	—
Regal cpe 3P	3,495	1,200	—
cpe 3-5P	3,465	1,220	—
Regal cpe 3-5P	3,535	1,250	—
Regal sdn 4d	3,630	1,270	—
Custom sdn 4d	3,560	1,255	—
Regal berline 6P	3,720	1,420	—
Custom berline 6P	3,660	1,405	—
Land Cruiser sdn 4d	3,595	1,445	—
Rgl Lnd Crsr sdn 4d	3,710	1,445	—

1934 Engines	bore×stroke	bhp	availability
I-6, 205.3	3.25×4.13	88	S-Dictator
I-8, 221.0	3.06×3.75	103	S-Commander
I-8, 250.0	3.06×4.25	110	S-President

1935

1A Dictator Six* (wb 114) - 11,742 blt	Wght	Price	Prod
rdstr 3-5P	2,985	745	—
Regal rdstr 3-5P	3,070	775	—
cpe 3P	2,895	695	—
Regal cpe 3P	3,005	725	—
cpe 3-5P	2,995	745	—
Regal cpe 3-5P	3,070	775	—
St. Regis sdn 4d	2,965	715	—
St. Rgs Rgl sdn 2d	3,085	755	—
St. Regis Cus sdn 2d	3,035	740	—
sdn 4d	3,030	745	—
Regal sdn 4d	3,160	785	—
Custom sdn 4d	3,085	770	—
Land Cruiser sdn 4d	3,100	880	—
Rgl Lnd Crsr sdn 4d	3,220	895	—
2A Dictator Six (wb 114.0) - 23,550 built**			
rdstr 3-5P	3,040	780	—
Regal rdstr 3-5P	3,140	810	—
cpe 3P	2,975	720	—
Regal cpe 3P	3,075	760	—
cpe 3-5P	3,065	780	—
Regal cpe 3-5P	3,135	810	—
St. Regis sdn 4d	3,035	750	—
St. Regis Rgl sdn 2d	3,170	790	—
St. Regis Cus sdn 2d	3,105	775	—
sdn 4d	3,095	780	—
Regal sdn 4d	3,230	820	—
Custom sdn 4d	3,155	805	—
Land Cruiser sdn 4d	3,170	915	—

2A Dictator Six**	Wght	Price	Prod
Rgl Lnd Crsr sdn 4d	3,285	930	—
1B Commander Eight (wb 120.0) - 6,085 built			
rdstr 3-5P	3,510	980	—
Regal rdstr 3-5P	3,570	1,010	—
cpe 3P	3,420	925	—
Regal cpe 3P	3,510	960	—
cpe 3-5P	3,520	980	—
Regal cpe 3-5P	3,570	1,010	—
St. Regis Rgl sdn 2d	3,620	1,000	—
St. Regis Cus sdn 2d	3,550	985	—
Regal sdn 4d	3,685	1,030	—
Custom sdn 4d	3,600	1,015	—
Land Cruiser sdn 4d	3,692	1,115	—
Rgl Lnd Crsr sdn 4d	3,720	1,130	—
1C President Eight (wb 124.0) - 2,305 built			
rdstr 3-5P	3,645	1,295	—
Regal rdstr 3-5P	3,740	1,325	—
cpe 3P	3,600	1,245	—
Regal cpe 3P	3,685	1,275	—
cpe 3-5P	3,660	1,295	—
Regal cpe 3-5P	3,740	1,325	—
Regal sdn 4d	3,900	1,345	—
Custom sdn 4d	3,790	1,330	—
Land Cruiser sdn 4d	3,820	1,430	—
Rgl Lnd Crsr sdn 4d	3,900	1,445	—
Custom berline 5P	3,900	1,430	—
Regal berline 5P	3,970	1,445	—

* Conventional front susp. ** Planar front susp.

Note: DeLuxe version of all Sixes also offered at $40 higher, 15 pounds more weight, and included free-wheeling, Startix, dual windshield wipers, sun visor, taillamp, robe rail, and ash receivers. All Regal models equipped with trunks and six wire wheels all series.

1935 Engines	bore×stroke	bhp	availability
I-6, 205.3	3.25×4.13	88	S-1A, 2A
I-8, 250.0	3.06×4.25	107	S-1B
I-8, 250.0	3.06×4.25	110	S-1C

1936

3A Dictator Six* (wb 116) - 26,634 blt	Wght	Price	Prod
bus cpe 3P	2,910	665	—
Custom cpe 3P	2,965	695	—
Custom cpe 5P	3,020	720	—
St. Regis Cus sdn 2d	3,075	725	—
St. Rgs Crsng Sdn 2d T/B	3,080	745	—
Custom sdn 4d	3,110	755	—
Cruising Sdn 4d T/B	3,120	775	—
4A Dictator Six (wb 116.0) - 22,029 built**			
bus cpe 3P	2,980	685	—
Custom cpe 3P	3,035	705	—
Custom cpe 5P	3,090	740	—
St. Regis Cus sdn 2d	3,145	745	—
St. Rgs Crsng Sdn 2d T/B	3,150	765	—
Custom sdn 4d	3,180	775	—
Cruising Sdn 4d T/B	3,190	795	—
2C President Eight (wb 125) - 7,297 built			
Custom cpe 3P	3,460	965	—
Custom cpe 5P	3,515	995	—
St. Regis Cus sdn 2d	3,560	1,015	—
St. Rgs Crsng Sdn 2d T/B	3,570	1,035	—
Custom sdn 4d	3,600	1,045	—
Cruising Sdn 4d T/B	3,615	1,065	—

* Conventional front susp. ** Planar front susp.

1936 Engines	bore×stroke	bhp	availability
I-6, 218.0	3.25×4.38	90	S-Dictator
I-8, 250.0	3.06×4.25	115	S-President

1937

5A Dictator Six* (wb 116) - 50,000 built***	Wght	Price	Prod
bus cpe 3P	2,695	765	—
Custom cpe 3P	3,005	820	—
Custom cpe 5P	3,045	845	—
St. Regis Cus sdn 2d	3,100	850	—
St. Rgs Crsng Sdn 2d T/B	3,100	850	—
Custom sdn 4d	3,130	880	—
Cruising Sdn 4d T/B	3,140	900	—
6A Dictator Six (wb 116.0) - 39,000 built*****			
bus cpe 3P	2,765	785	—

6A Dictator Six**	Wght	Price	Prod
Custom cpe 3P	3,075	840	—
Custom cpe 5P	3,115	865	—
St. Regis Cus sdn 2d	3,170	870	—
St. Rgs Crsng Sdn 2d T/B	3,170	890	—
Custom sdn 4d	3,200	900	—
Cruising Sdn 4d T/B	3,210	920	—
3C President Eight (wb 125.0) - 9,000 built*			
Custom cpe 3P	3,510	1,087	—
Custom cpe 5P	3,540	1,115	—
St. Regis Cus sdn 2d	3,600	1,135	—
St. Rgs Crsng Sdn 2d T/B	3,610	1,155	—
Custom sdn 4d	3,620	1,165	—
Cruising Sdn 4d T/B	3,635	1,185	—

* Conventional front susp. ** Planar front susp.
*** Estimated.
Note: President State trim option $30 higher

1937 Engines	bore×stroke	bhp	availability
I-6, 218.0	3.25×4.38	90	S-Dictator
I-8, 250.0	3.06×4.25	115	S-President

1938

7A Commander Six (wb 116.5) - 19,260 built	Wght	Price	Prod
bus cpe 3P	3,045	875	—
Custom cpe 3P	3,060	900	—
Club sdn 2d 6P	3,140	955	—
Cruising Sdn 4d	3,140	960	—
conv sdn 6P	3,390	1,315	—
8A State Commander (wb 116.5) - 22,053 built			
Custom cpe 3P	3,095	965	—
Club sdn 2d 6P	3,160	1,030	—
Cruising Sdn 4d 6P	3,215	1,040	—
conv sdn 6P	3,400	1,365	—
4C State President (wb 122.0) - 5,474 built			
cpe 3P	3,315	1,130	—
club sdn 2d 6P	3,400	1,195	—
Cruising Sdn 4d 6P	3,455	1,205	—
conv sdn 6P	3,640	1,555	—

1938 Engines	bore×stroke	bhp	availability
I-6, 226.2	3.31×4.38	90	S-Commander
I-8, 250.0	3.06×4.25	110	S-President

1939

G Champion (wb 110) - 33,905 blt	Wght	Price	Prod
Custom cpe 3P	2,260	660	—
Cus club sdn 2d 5P	2,330	700	—
Cus Cruising Sdn 4d	2,360	740	—
DeLuxe cpe 3P	2,275	720	—
DeLx club sdn 2d 5P	2,345	760	—
DeLx Crsng Sdn 4d	2,375	800	—
9A Commander (wb 116.5) - 43,724 built			
bus cpe 3P	3,045	875	—
Custom cpe 3P	3,080	900	—
club sdn 2d 6P	3,160	955	—
Cruising Sdn 4d	3,200	965	—
conv sdn 6P	3,400	1,290	—
5C President (wb 122.0) - 8,205 built			
Custom cpe 3P	3,300	1,035	—
club sdn 2d 6P	3,390	1,100	—
Cruising Sdn 4d	3,440	1,110	—
conv sdn 6P	3,640	1,460	—

1939 Engines	bore×stroke	bhp	availability
I-6, 164.3	3.00×3.88	78	S-Champion
I-6, 226.2	3.31×4.38	90	S-Commander
I-8, 250.0	3.06×4.25	110	S-President

Note: Some station wagons were built on Commander chassis by Hercules Body Company in 1939. Production figures include chassis.

1940

2G Champion (wb 110) - 66,264 blt	Wght	Price	Prod
cpe 3P	2,290	660	—
cpe 5P	2,335	696	—
club sdn	2,360	700	—
Cruising Sedan 4d	2,390	740	—
DeLuxe cpe 3P	2,315	705	—
DeLuxe cpe 5P	2,360	740	—
DeLuxe club sdn	2,385	745	—
DeLx Crsng Sdn 4d	2,415	785	—

LOA Cmndr (wb 116.5) - 34,477 blt	Wght	Price	Prod
Custom cpe 3P	3,055	895	—
club sdn	3,135	925	—
Cruising Sedan 4d	3,180	965	—
6C President (wb 122.0) - 6,444 built			
cpe 3P	3,280	1,025	—
club sdn	3,370	1,055	—
Cruising Sedan 4d	3,420	1,095	—

1940 Engines	bore×stroke	bhp	availability
I-6, 164.3	3.00×3.88	78	S-Champion
I-6, 226.2	3.31×4.38	90	S-Commander
I-8, 250.0	3.06×4.25	110	S-President

1941

3G Champion (wb 110) - 84,910 blt	Wght	Price	Prod
Custom cpe 3P	2,370	710	—
Custom Opera cpe	2,410	750	—
Custom club sdn	2,450	755	—
Cus Cruising Sdn 4d	2,480	795	—
Cus DeLuxe cpe 3P	2,395	745	—
Cus DeLx Opera cpe	2,425	780	—
Cus DeLuxe club sdn	2,470	785	—
Cus DeLx Crs Sdn 4d	2,500	825	—
DeLux-Tone cpe 3P	2,400	780	—
DeLx-Tone Opera cpe	2,430	815	—
DeLux-Tone club sdn	2,470	820	—
DeLx-Tone Crs Sdn 4d	2,500	860	—
11A Commander (wb 119.0) - 41,996 built			
Custom sdn cpe	3,160	990	—
Cus Crsng Sedan 4d	3,210	1,010	—
Cus Lnd Crsr sdn 4d	3,230	1,055	—
DeLx-Tone Crs sdn 4d	3,225	1,075	—
DeLx-Tone Lnd Crs sdn 4d	3,245	1,120	—
Skyway sdn cpe	3,200	1,080	—
Skywy Crsng Sdn 4d	3,240	1,100	—
Skywy Lnd Crsr sdn 4d	3,260	1,130	—
7C President (wb 124.5) - 6,994 built			
Cus Crsng Sedan 4d	3,450	1,140	—
Cus Lnd Crsr sdn 4d	3,475	1,185	—
DeLx-Tone Crs sdn 4d	3,475	1,205	—
DeLx-Tone Lnd Crs sdn 4d	3,500	1,250	—
Skyway sdn cpe	3,440	1,210	—
Skywy Crsng Sdn 4d	3,500	1,230	—
Skywy Lnd Crsr sdn 4d	3,520	1,260	—

1941 Engines	bore×stroke	bhp	availability
I-6, 169.6	3.00×4.00	80	S-Champion
I-6, 226.2	3.31×4.38	94	S-Commander
I-8, 250.0	3.06×4.25	117	S-President

1942

4G Champion (wb 110) - 29,678 built	Wght	Price	Prod
Custom cpe 3P	2,415	744	—
Cus Dbl Dater cpe 5P	2,455	769	—
Custom club sdn	2,495	774	—
Cus Cruising Sdn 4d	2,520	804	—
DeLuxstyle cpe 3P	2,435	779	—
DeLxstyl Dbl Dtr cpe 5P	2,470	804	—
DeLuxstyle club sdn	2,520	809	—
DeLxstyl Crsng Sdn 4d	2,545	839	—
12A Commander (wb 119.0) - 17,500 built			
Custom sdn cpe	3,195	1,025	—
Cus Cruising Sdn 4d	3,265	1,045	—
Cus Lnd Crsr sdn 4d	3,290	1,080	—
DeLuxstyle sdn cpe	3,210	1,070	—
DeLxstyl Crsng Sdn 4d	3,280	1,090	—
DeLxstyl Lnd Crsr sdn 4d	3,305	1,125	—
Skyway sdn cpe	3,240	1,105	—
Skywy Crsng Sdn 4d	3,300	1,125	—
Skywy Lnd Crsr sdn 4d	3,315	1,160	—
8C President (wb 124.5) - 3,500 built			
Custom sdn cpe	3,440	1,141	—
Cus Cruising Sdn 4d	3,485	1,161	—
Cus Lnd Crsr sdn 4d	3,510	1,196	—
DeLuxstyle sdn cpe	3,455	1,186	—
DeLxstyl Crsng Sdn 4d	3,500	1,206	—
DeLxstyl Lnd Crsr sdn 4d	3,515	1,241	—
Skywy sdn cpe	3,470	1,221	—
Skywy Crsng Sdn 4d	3,540	1,241	—
Skywy Lnd Crsr sdn 4d	3,540	1,276	—

1942 Engines	bore×stroke	bhp	availability
I-6, 169.6	3.00×4.00	80	S-Champion
I-6, 226.2	3.31×4.38	94	S-Commander
I-8, 250.0	3.06×4.25	117	S-President

1946

5G Skywy Chmpn (wb 110.0)	Wght	Price	Prod
cpe 3P	2,456	1,002	2,465
cpe 5P	2,491	1,044	1,285
club sdn	2,541	1,046	5,000
Cruising Sedan 4d	2,566	1,097	10,525

1946 Engine	bore×stroke	bhp	availability
I-6, 169.6	3.00×4.00	80	S-all

1947

6G Champion (wb 112) - 105,097 built	Wght	Price	Prod
DeLuxe sdn 4d	2,735	1,478	—
DeLuxe sdn 2d	2,685	1,446	—
DeLuxe cpe 5P	2,670	1,472	—
DeLuxe cpe 3P	2,600	1,378	—
Regal DeLx sdn 4d	2,760	1,551	—
Regal DeLx sdn 2d	2,710	1,520	—
Regal DeLx cpe 5P	2,690	1,546	—
Regal DeLx cpe 3P	2,620	1,451	—
Rgl DeLx conv cpe	2,875	1,902	—
15A Commander (wb 119.0; LC-123.0) - 56,399 built			
DeLuxe sdn 4d	3,265	1,761	—
DeLuxe sdn 2d	3,230	1,729	—
DeLuxe cpe 5P	3,210	1,755	—
DeLuxe cpe 3P	3,140	1,661	—
Regal DeLx sdn 4d	3,280	1,882	—
Regal DeLx sdn 2d	3,245	1,850	—
Regal DeLx cpe 5P	3,225	1,877	—
Regal DeLx cpe 3P	3,155	1,782	—
Regl DeLx conv cpe	3,420	2,236	—
Land Cruiser sdn 4d	3,340	2,043	—

1947 Engines	bore×stroke	bhp	availability
I-6, 169.6	3.00×4.00	80	S-Champion
I-6, 226.0	3.31×4.38	94	S-Commander

1948

7G Champion (wb 112) - 99,282 built	Wght	Price	Prod
DeLuxe sdn 4d	2,720	1,636	—
DeLuxe sdn 2d	2,675	1,604	—
DeLuxe cpe 5P	2,670	1,630	—
DeLuxe cpe 3P	2,590	1,535	—
Regal DeLx sdn 4d	2,725	1,709	—
Regal DeLx sdn 2d	2,685	1,678	—
Regal DeLx cpe 5P	2,690	1,704	—
Regal DeLx cpe 3P	2,615	1,609	—
Regl DeLx conv cpe	2,865	2,060	—
15A Commander (wb 119.0; LC-123.0) - 85,711 built			
DeLuxe sdn 4d	3,195	1,956	—
DeLuxe sdn 2d	3,165	1,925	—
DeLuxe cpe 5P	3,150	1,951	—
DeLuxe cpe 3P	3,080	1,856	—
Regal DeLx sdn 4d	3,215	2,078	—
Regal DeLx sdn 2d	3,175	2,046	—
Regal DeLx cpe 5P	3,165	2,072	—
Regal DeLx cpe 3P	3,095	1,978	—
Regl DeLx conv cpe	3,385	2,431	—
Land Cruiser sdn 4d	3,280	2,265	—

1948 Engines	bore×stroke	bhp	availability
I-6, 169.6	3.00×4.00	80	S-Champion
I-6, 226.2	3.31×4.38	94	S-Commander

1949

8G Champion (wb 112) - 85,604 built	Wght	Price	Prod
DeLuxe sdn 4d	2,745	1,689	—
DeLuxe sdn 2d	2,720	1,657	—
DeLuxe cpe 5P	2,705	1,683	—
DeLuxe cpe 3P	2,645	1,588	—
Regal DeLx sdn 4d	2,750	1,762	—
Regal DeLx sdn 2d	2,725	1,731	—
Regal DeLx cpe 5P	2,725	1,757	—
Regal DeLx cpe 3P	2,650	1,652	—
Regl DeLx conv cpe	2,895	2,086	—
16A Commander (wb 119.0; LC-123.0) - 43,694 built			
DeLuxe sdn 4d	3,240	2,019	—

16A Commander	Wght	Price	Prod
DeLuxe sdn 2d	3,215	1,988	—
DeLuxe cpe 5P	3,200	2,014	—
DeLuxe cpe 3P	3,130	1,919	—
Regal DeLx sdn 4d	3,245	2,141	—
Regal DeLx sdn 2d	3,220	2,109	—
Regal DeLx cpe 5P	3,205	2,135	—
Regal DeLx cpe 3P	3,135	2,041	—
Regl DeLx conv cpe	3,415	2,468	—
Land Cruiser sdn 4d	3,325	2,328	—

1949 Engines	bore×stroke	bhp	availability
I-6, 169.6	3.00×4.00	80	S-Champion
I-6, 245.6	3.31×4.75	100	S-Commander

1950

9G Champion (wb 113)	Wght	Price	Prod
Custom sdn 4d	2,730	1,519	16,000
Custom sdn 2d	2,695	1,487	19,593
Custom cpe 5P	2,690	1,514	3,583
Custom cpe 3P	2,620	1,419	1,562
DeLuxe sdn 4d	2,750	1,597	46,027
DeLuxe sdn 2d	2,720	1,565	45,280
DeLuxe cpe 5P	2,705	1,592	19,028
DeLuxe cpe 3P	2,635	1,497	2,082
Regal DeLx sdn 4d	2,755	1,676	55,296
Regal DeLx sdn 2d	2,725	1,644	21,976
Regal DeLx cpe 5P	2,715	1,671	29,966
Regal DeLx cpe 3P	2,640	1,576	849
Regl DeLx conv cpe	2,900	1,981	9,362
17A Commander (wb 120.0; LC-124.0)			
DeLuxe sdn 4d	3,255	1,902	11,440
DeLuxe sdn 2d	3,215	1,871	4,588
DeLuxe cpe 5P	3,215	1,897	4,383
Regal DeLx sdn 4d	3,265	2,024	14,832
Regal DeLx sdn 2d	3,220	1,992	2,363
Regal DeLx cpe 5P	3,220	2,018	7,375
Regl DeLx conv cpe	3,375	2,328	2,867
Land Cruiser sdn 4d	3,355	2,187	24,712

1950 Engines	bore×stroke	bhp	availability
I-6, 169.6	3.00×4.00	85	S-Champion
I-6, 245.6	3.31×4.75	102	S-Commander

1951

10G Champion (wb 115)	Wght	Price	Prod
Custom sdn 4d	2,690	1,571	9,972
Custom sdn 2d	2,670	1,540	10,689
Custom cpe 5P	2,650	1,566	2,781
Custom cpe 3P	2,585	1,471	2,429
DeLuxe sdn 4d	2,715	1,649	26,019
DeLuxe sdn 2d	2,690	1,618	18,591
DeLuxe cpe 5P	2,675	1,644	9,444
DeLuxe cpe 3P	2,610	1,549	961
Regal sdn 4d	2,720	1,728	35,201
Regal sdn 2d	2,690	1,697	8,931
Regal cpe 5P	2,675	1,723	14,103
Regal cpe 3P	2,615	1,628	373
Regal conv cpe	2,890	2,034	4,742
H Commander (wb 115.0; LC-119.0)			
Regal sdn 4d	3,065	1,839	29,603
Regal sdn 2d	3,045	1,807	8,034
Regal cpe 5P	3,030	1,833	8,192
Regal cpe 3P	—	1,758	1
State sdn 4d	3,070	1,939	21,134
State sdn 2d	3,045	1,907	3,903
State cpe 5P	3,030	1,933	11,637
State conv cpe	3,240	2,244	3,770
Land Cruiser sdn 4d	3,165	2,071	38,055

1951 Engines	bore×stroke	bhp	availability
I-6, 169.6	3.00×4.00	85	S-Champion
V-8, 232.6	3.38×3.25	120	S-Commander

1952

12G Champion (wb 115) - 101,390 blt	Wght	Price	Prod
Custom sdn 4d	2,695	1,769	—
Custom sdn 2d	2,655	1,735	—
Custom cpe 5P	2,660	1,763	—
DeLuxe sdn 4d	2,720	1,862	—
DeLuxe sdn 2d	2,685	1,828	—
DeLuxe cpe 5P	2,675	1,856	—
Regal sdn 4d	2,725	1,946	—

12G Champion	Wght	Price	Prod
Regal sdn 2d	2,690	1,913	—
Regal cpe 5P	2,695	1,941	—
Rgl Starliner htp cpe	2,860	2,220	—
Regal conv cpe	2,870	2,273	—

3H Commander (wb 115.0; LC-119.0) - 84,849 built			
Regal sdn 4d	3,085	2,121	—
Regal sdn 2d	3,040	2,086	—
Regal cpe 5P	3,030	2,115	—
State sdn 4d	3,075	2,208	—
State sdn 2d	3,055	2,172	—
State cpe 5P	3,025	2,202	—
St Starliner htp cpe	3,220	2,488	—
State conv cpe	3,230	2,548	—
Land Cruiser sdn 4d	3,155	2,365	—

1952 Engines	bore×stroke	bhp	availability
I-6, 169.6	3.00×4.00	85	S-Champion
V-8, 232.6	3.38×3.25	120	S-Commander

1953

14G Champion (wb 116.5; cpes-120.5) - 93,807 built	Wght	Price	Prod
Custom sdn 4d	2,710	1,767	—
Custom sdn 2d	2,690	1,735	—
DeLuxe sdn 4d	2,735	1,863	—
DeLuxe sdn 2d	2,700	1,831	—
DeLuxe Starlight cpe	2,695	1,868	—
Regal sdn 4d	2,745	1,949	—
Regal sdn 2d	2,715	1,917	—
Regal Starlight cpe	2,700	1,955	—
Regl Starliner htp cpe	2,760	2,116	—

4H Commander (wb 116.5; LC/cpes-120.5) - 76,092 blt			
DeLuxe sdn 4d	3,075	2,121	—
DeLuxe sdn 2d	3,055	2,089	—
DeLuxe Starlight cpe	3,040	2,127	—
Regal sdn 4d	3,095	2,208	—
Regal Starlight cpe	3,040	2,213	—
Regl Starliner htp cpe	3,120	2,374	—
Land Cruiser sdn 4d	3,180	2,316	—

1953 Engines	bore×stroke	bhp	availability
I-6, 169.6	3.00×4.00	85	S-Champion
V-8, 232.6	3.38×3.25	120	S-Commander

1954

15G Champion Six (wb 116.5; cpes-120.5)—51,431 blt	Wght	Price	Prod
Custom sdn 4d	2,735	1,801	—
Custom sdn 2d	2,705	1,758	—
DeLuxe sdn 4d	2,765	1,918	—
DeLuxe sdn 2d	2,730	1,875	—
DeLuxe Starlight cpe	2,740	1,972	—
DeLx Cnstga wgn 2d	2,930	2,187	—
Regal sdn 4d	2,780	2,026	—
Regal sdn 2d	2,745	1,983	—
Regal Starlight cpe	2,750	2,080	—
Regl Starliner htp cpe	2,825	2,241	—
Regl Cnstga wgn 2d	2,950	2,295	—

5H Commander (wb 116.5; LC/cpes-120.5) - 30,499 blt			
DeLuxe sdn 4d	3,105	2,179	—
DeLuxe sdn 2d	3,075	2,136	—
DeLuxe Starlight cpe	3,085	2,233	—
DeLx Cnstga wgn 2d	3,265	2,448	—
Regal sdn 4d	3,120	2,287	—
Regal Starlight cpe	3,095	2,341	—
Regl Starliner htp cpe	3,175	2,502	—
Regl Cnstga wgn 2d	3,265	2,556	—
Land Cruiser sdn 4d	3,180	2,438	—

1954 Engines	bore×stroke	bhp	availability
I-6, 169.6	3.00×4.00	85	S-Champion
V-8, 232.6	3.38×3.25	127	S-Commander

1955

16G Champion (wb 116.5; cpes-120.5) - 50,368 built	Wght	Price	Prod
Custom sdn 4d	2,790	1,783	—
Custom sdn 2d	2,740	1,741	—
DeLuxe sdn 4d	2,805	1,885	—
DeLuxe sdn 2d	2,780	1,841	—
DeLuxe cpe	2,790	1,875	—
DeLx Cnstga wgn 2d	2,980	2,141	—
Regal sdn 4d	2,815	1,993	—

16G Champion	Wght	Price	Prod
Regal cpe	2,795	1,975	—
Regal htp cpe	2,865	2,125	—
Regl Cnstga wgn 2d	2,985	2,312	—

6G Commander (wb 116.5; cpes-120.5) - 58,792 blt			
Custom sdn 4d	3,065	1,919	—
Custom sdn 2d	3,105	1,873	—
DeLuxe sdn 4d	3,075	2,014	—
DeLuxe sdn 2d	3,045	1,969	—
DeLuxe cpe	3,065	1,989	—
DeLx Cnstga wgn 2d	3,265	2,274	—
Regal sdn 4d	3,080	2,127	—
Regal cpe	3,065	2,094	—
Regal htp cpe	3,150	2,282	—
Regl Cnstga wgn 2d	3,274	2,445	—

6H President (wb 120.5)			
DeLuxe sdn 4d	3,165	2,311	
State sdn 4d	3,220	2,381	22,451
State cpe	3,210	2,270	
State htp cpe	3,175	2,456	
Speedster htp cpe	3,301	3,253	2,215

1955 Engines	bore×stroke	bhp	availability
I-6, 185.6	3.00×4.38	101	S-Champion
V-8, 224.3	3.56×2.81	140	S-early Comm
V-8, 259.2	3.56×3.25	162	S-late Comm
V-8, 259.2	3.56×3.25	175	S-early Pres
V-8, 259.2	3.56×3.25	185	S-early Spdstr; O-late Pres

1956

56G Six (wb 116.5; Hawk-120.5) - 28,918* built	Wght	Price	Prod
Champion sdn 4d	2,835	1,996	—
Champion sdn 2d	2,800	1,946	—
Champion sedanet	2,780	1,844	—
Pelham wgn 2d	3,000	2,232	—
Flight Hawk cpe	2,780	1,986	—

56B V-8, 259 (wb 116.5; Hawk-120.5) - 30,654* built			
Commander sdn 4d	3,140	2,125	—
Commander sdn 2d	3,110	2,076	—
Commander sedanet	3,085	1,974	—
Parkview wgn 2d	3,300	2,354	—
Power Hawk cpe	3,095	2,101	—

56H V-8, 289 (wb 116.5; Classic/Hawk-120.5)			
President sdn 4d	3,210	2,235	
President sdn 2d	3,180	2,188	18,209
Pres Classic sdn 4d	3,295	2,489	
Pinehurst wgn 2d	3,395	2,529	
Sky Hawk htp cpe	3,215	2,477	3,610

56J V-8, 352 (wb 120.5)			
Golden Hawk htp cpe	3,360	3,061	4,071

* Includes 11,484 Flight Hawks and Power Hawks.

1956 Engines	bore×stroke	bhp	availability
I-6, 185.6	3.00×4.38	101	S-Chmp, Flht Hwk, Plhm
V-8, 259.2	3.56×3.25	170	S-Cmdr, Pwr Hwk Prkvw
V-8, 259.2	3.56×3.25	185	O-Champ, Comm, Pwr/ Flht Hwk, wgns
V-8, 289.0	3.56×3.63	195	S-Pres, Pnhrst
V-8, 289.0	3.56×3.63	210	S-Pres, Clsic, Sky Hwk
V-8, 289.0	3.56×3.63	225	O-Pres, Pnhrst, Sky Hwk
V-8, 352.0	4.00×3.50	275	S-G Hawk

1957*

57G Six (wb 116.5; Hawk-120.5)	Wght	Price	Prod
Scotsman sdn 4d	2,725	1,826	—
Scotsman club sdn	2,680	1,776	—
Scotsman wgn 2d	2,875	1,995	—
Champ Cus sdn 4d	2,785	2,049	—
Champ Cus club sdn	2,755	2,001	—
Champ DeLx sdn 4d	2,810	2,171	—
Champ DeLx clb sdn	2,780	2,123	—
Pelham wgn 2d	3,015	2,382	—
Silver Hawk cpe	2,790	2,142	—

57B V-8, 259 (wb 116.5)			
Comm Cus sdn 4d	3,105	2,173	—

57B V-8, 259	Wght	Price	Prod
Comm Cus club sdn	3,075	2,124	—
Comm DeLx sdn 4d	3,140	2,295	—
Comm DeLx club sdn	3,100	2,246	—
Provincial wgn 4d	3,355	2,561	—
Parkview wgn 2d	3,310	2,505	—

57H V-8, 289 (wb 116.5; Classic/Hawks-120.5)			
Pres Classic sdn 4d	3,270	2,539	—
President sdn 4d	3,205	2,407	—
President club sdn	3,170	2,358	—
Broadmoor wgn 4d	3,415	2,666	—
Silver Hawk cpe	3,185	2,263	—
Golden Hawk htp cpe	3,185	3,182	4,356

* Total 1957 prod.: 74,738; incl. 15,318 Silver Hawks

1957 Engines	bore×stroke	bhp	availability
I-6, 185.6	3.00×4.38	101	S-Scotsman, Champ, Silver Hawk, Pelham
V-8, 259.2	3.56×3.25	180	S-Commander & 57B wgns, O-Silver Hawk
V-8, 259.2	3.56×3.25	195	O-Commander & 57B wgns, Silver Hawk
V-8, 289.0	3.56×3.63	210	S-President, Silver Hawk, 57H wagons
V-8, 289.0	3.56×3.63	225	S-President Clsc; O-Silver Hawk, 57H wgn
V-8S, 289.0	3.56×3.63	275	S-G Hawk

1958

58G Six (wb 116.5; Hawk-120.5)	Wght	Price	Prod
Silver Hawk cpe	2,810	2,291	*
Scotsman sdn 4d	2,740	1,874	
Scotsman sdn 2d	2,695	1,795	20,870
Scotsman wgn 2d	2,870	2,055	
Champion sdn 4d	2,835	2,253	10,325
Champion sdn 2d	2,795	2,189	

58B V-8, 259 (wb 116.5) - 12,249 built			
Commander sdn 4d	3,185	2,378	—
Comm Strlght htp cpe	3,270	2,493	—
Provincial wgn 4d	3,420	2,664	—

58H V-8, 289 (wb 120.5; Starlight htp-116.5)			
President sdn 4d	3,365	2,639	10,442
Pres Starlight htp cpe	3,355	2,695	
Silver Hawk cpe	3,210	2,352	*
Golden Hawk htp cpe	3,470	3,282	878

* Total Silver Hawk; 7,350

1958 Engines	bore×stroke	bhp	availability
I-6, 185.6	3.00×4.38	101	S-Scotsman, Champion, Silver Hawk
V-8, 259.2	3.56×3.25	180	S-Commander, Prov; O-S Hawk
V-8, 259.2	3.56×3.25	195	O-Comm, Prov, S Hawk
V-8, 289.0	3.56×3.63	210	O-Silver Hawk
V-8, 289.0	3.56×3.63	225	S-President; O-Silver Hawk
V-8S, 289.0	3.56×3.63	275	S-G Hawk

1959

59S Lark VI (wb 108.5; wgns-113.0) - 98,744 built	Wght	Price	Prod
DeLuxe sdn 4d	2,605	1,995	—
DeLuxe sdn 2d	2,577	1,925	—
DeLuxe wgn 2d	2,805	2,295	—
Regal sdn 4d	2,600	2,175	—
Regal htp cpe	2,710	2,275	—
Regal wgn 2d	2,815	2,455	—

59V Lark VIII (wb 108.5; wgn-113.0) - 32,334 built			
Regal sdn 4d	2,924	2,310	—
Regal htp cpe	3,034	2,411	—
Regal wgn 2d	3,148	2,590	—

59S/59V Silver Hawk (wb 120.5)			
cpe, I-6	2,795	2,360	2,417
cpe, V-8	3,140	2,495	5,371

1959 Engines	bore×stroke	bhp	availability
I-6, 169.6	3.00×4.00	90	S-Lrk VI, Slvr Hwk I-6
V-8, 259.2	3.56×3.25	180	S-Lrk VIII, Slvr Hwk V-8
V-8, 259.2	3.56×3.25	195	O-Lrk VIII, Slvr Hwk V-8

1960

60S Lark VI (wb 108.5; wgns-113.0) - 70,153 built	Wght	Price	Prod
DeLuxe sdn 4d	2,592	2,046	—
DeLuxe sdn 2d	2,588	1,976	—
DeLuxe wgn 4d	2,792	2,441	—
DeLuxe wgn 2d	2,763	2,366	—
Regal sdn 4d	2,619	2,196	—
Regal htp cpe	2,697	2,296	—
Regal conv cpe	2,961	2,621	—
Regal wgn 4d	2,836	2,591	—
60V Lark VIII (wb 108.5; wgns-113.0) - 57,562 built			
DeLuxe sdn 4d	2,941	2,181	—
DeLuxe sdn 2d	2,921	2,111	—
DeLuxe wgn 4d	3,161	2,576	—
DeLuxe wgn 2d	3,138	2,501	—
Regal sdn 4d	2,966	2,331	—
Regal htp cpe	3,033	2,431	—
Regal conv cpe	3,315	2,756	—
Regal wgn 4d	3,183	2,726	—
60S/60V Hawk (wb 120.5) - 3,939 built			
cpe, V-8	3,207	2,650	—

1960 Engines	bore×stroke	bhp	availability
I-6, 169.6	3.00×4.00	90	S-Lark VI
V-8, 259.2	3.56×3.25	180	S-Lark VIII
V-8, 259.2	3.56×3.25	195	O-Lark VIII
V-8, 289.0	3.56×3.63	210	S-Hawk
V-8, 289.0	3.56×3.63	225	O-Hawk

1961

61S Lark VI (wb 108.5; wgns-113.0) - 41,035 built	Wght	Price	Prod
DeLuxe sdn 4d	2,665	1,935	—
DeLuxe sdn 2d	2,661	2,005	—
DeLuxe wgn 4d	2,865	2,370	—
DeLuxe wgn 2d	2,836	2,290	—
Regal sdn 4d	2,692	2,155	—
Regal htp cpe	2,770	2,243	—
Regal conv cpe	3,034	2,554	—
Regal wgn 4d	2,836	2,520	—
61V Lark VIII (wb 108.5; Crsr/wgns-113.0) - 25,934 blt			
DeLuxe sdn 4d	2,941	2,140	—
DeLuxe sdn 2d	2,921	2,070	—
DeLuxe wgn 4d	3,183	2,505	—
DeLuxe wgn 2d	3,112	2,425	—
Regal sdn 4d	2,956	2,290	—
Regal htp cpe	3,074	2,378	—
Regal conv cpe	3,315	2,689	—
Regal wgn 4d	3,183	2,655	—
Cruiser sdn 4d	3,001	2,458	—
61V Hawk (wb 120.5)			
cpe	3,205	2,650	3,340

1961 Engines	bore×stroke	bhp	availability
I-6, 169.6	3.00×4.00	112	S-Lark VI
V-8, 259.2	3.56×3.25	180	S-Lark VIII
V-8, 259.2	3.56×3.25	195	O-Lark VIII
V-8, 289.0	3.56×3.63	210	S-Hawk
V-8, 289.0	3.56×3.63	225	O-Hawk

1962

62S Lark Six (wb 113.0; 2d-109.0) - 54,397 built	Wght	Price	Prod
DeLuxe sdn 4d	2,760	2,040	—
DeLuxe sdn 2d	2,655	1,935	—
DeLuxe wgn 4d	2,845	2,405	—
Regal sdn 4d	2,770	2,190	—
Regal wgn 4d	2,875	2,555	—
Regal htp cpe	2,765	2,218	—
Regal conv cpe	3,075	2,589	—
Daytona htp cpe	2,765	2,308	—
Daytona conv cpe	3,075	2,679	—
62V Lark Eight (wb 113.0; 2d-109.0) - 38,607 built			
DeLuxe sdn 4d	3,015	2,175	—

62V Lark Eight	Wght	Price	Prod
DeLuxe sdn 2d	2,925	2,070	—
DeLuxe wgn 4d	3,115	2,540	—
Regal sdn 4d	3,025	2,325	—
Regal wgn 4d	3,145	2,690	—
Regal htp cpe	3,015	2,353	—
Regal conv cpe	3,305	2,724	—
Daytona htp cpe	3,015	2,443	—
Daytona conv cpe	3,305	2,814	—
Cruiser sdn 4d	3,030	2,493	—
62V Gran Turismo Hawk (wb 120.5)			
htp cpe	3,230	3,095	8,388

1962 Engines	bore×stroke	bhp	availability
I-6, 169.6	3.00×4.00	112	S-Lark Six
V-8, 259.2	3.56×3.25	180	S-Lark Eight
V-8, 259.2	3.56×3.25	195	O-Lark Eight
V-8, 289.0	3.56×3.63	210	S-GT Hawk; O-Lark Cruiser
V-8, 289.0	3.56×3.63	225	O-GT Hawk, Lark Cruiser

1963

63S Lark Six (wb 113.0; 2d-109.0) - 73,192 blt (incl. 63V)	Wght	Price	Prod
Standard sdn 4d	2,775	2,040	—
Standard sdn 2d	2,650	1,935	—
Standard wgn 4d*	3,285	2,430	—
Regal sdn 4d	2,790	2,160	—
Regal sdn 2d	2,665	2,055	—
Regal wgn 4d*	3,200	2,550	—
Custom sdn 4d	2,800	2,285	—
Custom sdn 2d	2,680	2,180	—
Daytona wgn 4d*	3,245	2,700	—
Daytona htp cpe	2,795	2,308	—
Daytona conv cpe	3,045	2,679	—
63V Lark Eight (wb 113.0; 2d-109.0)			
Standard sdn 4d	2,985	2,175	—
Standard sdn 2d	2,910	2,070	—
Standard wgn 4d*	3,435	2,565	—
Regal sdn 4d	3,000	2,295	—
Regal sdn 2d	2,925	2,190	—
Regal wgn 4d	3,450	2,685	—
Custom sdn 4d	3,010	2,420	—
Custom sdn 2d	2,940	2,315	—
Daytona wgn 4d*	3,490	2,835	—
Daytona htp cpe	3,035	2,443	—
Daytona conv cpe	3,265	2,814	—
Cruiser sdn 4d	3,065	2,595	—
63V Grand Turismo Hawk (wb 120.5)			
htp cpe	3,280	3,095	4,634
63R Avanti (wb 109.0)			
spt cpe	3,140	4,445	3,834

* Note: Lark wagon data for sliding-roof Wagonaire models. Solid-roof versions offered from midmodel year for $100 less than comparable Wagonaires.

1963 Engines	bore×stroke	bhp	availability
I-6, 169.6	3.00×4.00	112	S-Lark Six
V-8, 259.2	3.56×3.25	180	S-Lark Eight
V-8, 259.2	3.56×3.25	195	O-Lark Eight
V-8, 289.0	3.56×3.63	210	S-Hwk, Crsr; O-Lark Eight
V-8, 289.0	3.56×3.63	225	O-Hawk, Lark Eight, Cruiser
V-8, 289.0	3.56×3.63	240	S-Avanti; O-Hawk, Lark Eight (R1)
V-8S, 289.0	3.56×3.63	290	O-Avanti, Hwk, Lark Eight (R2)

1964

64S Six (wb 113.0; 2d-109.0) - 43,884 built (incl. 64V)	Wght	Price	Prod
Challenger sdn 4d	2,780	2,048	—
Challenger sdn 2d	2,660	1,943	—
Challenger wgn 4d*	3,230	2,438	—
Commander sdn 4d	2,815	2,168	—
Commander sdn 2d	2,695	2,063	—
Comm Spec sdn 2d	2,725	2,193	—
Commander wgn 4d*	3,265	2,558	—
Daytona sdn 4d	2,790	2,318	—
Daytona conv cpe	3,040	2,670	—

64S Six	Wght	Price	Prod
Daytona wgn 4d*	3,240	2,708	—
64V Eight (wb 113.0; 2d-109.0)			
Challenger sdn 4d	3,010	2,183	—
Challenger sdn 2d	2,910	2,078	—
Challenger wgn 4d*	3,480	2,573	—
Commander sdn 4d	3,045	2,303	—
Commander sdn 2d	2,945	2,198	—
Comm Spec sdn 2d	2,975	2,328	—
Daytona sdn 4d	3,055	2,453	—
Daytona htp cpe	3,060	2,451	—
Daytona conv cpe	3,320	2,805	—
Daytona wgn 4d*	3,555	2,843	—
Cruiser sdn 4d	3,120	2,603	—
64V Gran Turismo Hawk (wb 120.5)			
htp cpe	3,120	2,966	1,767
64R Avanti (wb 109.0)			
spt cpe	3,195	4,445	809

* Note: All wagons are sliding-roof Wagonaire models.

1964 Engines	bore×stroke	bhp	availability
I-6, 169.6	3.00×4.00	112	S-Six
V-8, 259.2	3.56×3.25	180	S-Eight exc Cruiser
V-8, 259.2	3.56×3.25	195	O-Eight exc Cruiser
V-8, 289.0	3.56×3.63	210	S-Hwk, Crsr; O-other Eight
V-8, 289.0	3.56×3.63	225	O-all Eight exc Avanti
V-8, 289.0	3.56×3.63	240	S-Avanti; O-other Eight (R1)
V-8S, 289.0	3.56×3.63	290	O-all (R2)
V-8S, 304.5	3.65×3.63	335	O-all exc Chllngr (R3)
V-8, 304.5	3.65×3.63	280	O-all exc Chllngr (R4)

1965 - 19,435 built

C-1 Six (wb 113.0; 2d-109.0)	Wght	Price	Prod
Commander sdn 4d	2,815	2,230	—
Commander sdn 2d	2,695	2,125	—
Commander wgn 4d*	3,265	2,620	—
Cruiser sdn 4d	2,820	2,470	—
C-5 Eight (wb 113.0; 2d-109.0)			
Commander sdn 4d	2,995	2,370	—
Commander sdn 2d	2,895	2,265	—
Commander wgn 4d*	3,465	2,760	—
Daytona Sprt Sdn 2d	2,970	2,565	—
Daytona wgn 4d*	3,505	2,890	—
Cruiser sdn 4d	3,070	2,610	—

* Note: All wagons are sliding-roof Wagonaire models.

1965 Engines	bore×stroke	bhp	availability
I-6, 194.0	3.56×3.25	120	S-Six
V-8, 283.0	3.88×3.00	195	S-Eight

1966 - 8,947 built

Six (wb 113.0; 2d-109.0)	Wght	Price	Prod
Commander sdn 4d	2,815	2,165	—
Commander sdn 2d	2,695	2,060	—
Wagonaire wgn 4d	3,246	2,555	—
Daytona sdn 2d	2,755	2,405	—
Cruiser sdn 4d	2,815	2,405	—
Eight (wb 113.0; 2d-109.0)			
Commander sdn 4d	2,991	2,305	—
Commander sdn 2d	2,891	2,200	—
Wagonaire wgn 4d	3,501	2,695	—
Daytona sdn 2d	3,006	2,500	—
Cruiser sdn 4d	3,066	2,545	—

1966 Engines	bore×stroke	bhp	availability
I-6, 194.0	3.56×3.25	120	S-Six
I-6, 230.0	3.88×3.25	140	O-Six
V-8, 283.0	3.88×3.00	195	S-Eight

Postwar Studebaker production includes cars manufactured in South Bend, Indiana, and Hamilton, Ontario, for U.S., Canadian, and export sale. All 1965-66 Studebakers were built in Canada.

Stutz

1930 Model M Weymann Monte Carlo four-door sedan

1932 DV32 Continental coupe by Waterhouse

The first Stutz built finished eleventh in the first Indianapolis 500 and inspired the slogan "The Car That Made Good in a Day." Stutz was soon building its famous Bearcat and, along with the Mercer Raceabout, introduced America to an early form of the sports car. With big engines and not much bodywork, early Bearcats could easily be taken racing. Both private and factory-backed Bearcats did well in competition and Stutz always traded on a sporting reputation. Stutz was never a high-volume producer, rising from 266 cars its first full year of production, 1912, to just 2207 in 1917. But the firm was making its own engines by the early '20s: a big 361-cubic-inch side-valve four with 88 brake horsepower and an overhead-valve 75-bhp six. The latter was bumped up to 80 bhp and 268 cid for 1924's Speedway Six. Fours were discontinued the following year.

Stutz design was old-fashioned by the mid 1920s. European-born, Frederick E. Moskovics arrived in 1925 to take over the presidency of Stutz. Moskovics did for Stutz what Zora Arkus-Duntov would later do for Corvette—add a European influence that improved performance and handling. Moskovics introduced beautiful new open and closed "Safety Stutz" models the following year. These carried Stutz's first eight, a European-inspired inline engine with single overhead camshaft and dual ignition with two plugs per cylinder. Stutz called it the "Vertical Eight." Bowing at 289 cid and 92 bhp, it would be the heart of all Stutzes through the final 1935 models. The sole exception was the 1929-30 Blackhawk, a companion line powered by an L-head Continental eight or overhead-cam Stutz six. Though "cheap" for Stutz at a base price of $2395, the Blackhawk managed just under 1600 units. After 1930, its chassis was used for the least-costly Stutzes.

The Vertical Eight was quickly uprated, going to 298.6 cid for 1927, then to 322 cid and 113 bhp two years later. Advertised horsepower would go no further, although actual horsepower might have reached 140 by the end of the '20s. Stutz added to its racing image by dominating AAA stock car racing in '27 and giving Bentley a run for its money at the 1928 LeMans. Stutz chassis engineering changed remarkably little after 1929. For example, the same three wheelbases persisted to the end: 134.5 inches, 145, and, after Blackhawk's demise, 127.5 inches.

Though Stutz couldn't afford a 12- or 16-cylinder engine, it did experiment with a supercharger that lifted the Vertical Eight to 143 bhp. The blower was a huge affair mounted low, ahead of the radiator. Like most superchargers, it was driven directly from the crankshaft. It did the job, but it was noisy and carburetion was a problem.

Moskovics left the company in 1929, but some of the greatest Stutzes were still to come. Stutz followed Duesenberg's approach for 1931 by offering a new 32-valve twincam cylinder head. This had no room for the dual ignition of what was now called the "SV16" (single-valve) engine, but improved breathing gave the new "DV32" (dual-valve) 161 bhp at 3900 rpm.

At the same time, Stutz tried to stem sliding sales in the deepening Depression with revived six-cylinder models, designated LA for '31 and LAA for 1932-33. Offering a standard coupe and sedan as well as five semicustom body styles, the LA sold for as little as $1995, the LAA for just $1620. Power came from what amounted to a Vertical Eight with two fewer cylinders—or the same 241.5-cid single-cam engine as the departed Blackhawk. But with just 85 bhp to propel better than 4300 pounds, these cars were hardly swift on the road or the sales chart, and Stutz gave up on them after 1933.

That left nothing but high-priced cars, which reflected a no-compromise approach to sporty performance but also made Stutz an odd, slow-selling fish in luxury-car waters. Even standard-body models sold for upward of $3000-$4000—a lot for "hard times"—and some 30 custom styles were available on both SV16 and DV32 chassis from high-buck crafters like LeBaron, Fleetwood, Rollston, Weymann, Brunn, Waterhouse, and Derham. Stutz had offered Weymann's unusual fabric bodies (actually padded leatherette) since 1928; these were light, strong, elastic, and quiet. Compared to steel shells, they soaked up more noise and road shock, and were easier to repair. Weymann bodies didn't last as long as steel or offer much protection in a crash. Also, many people disliked their dull, pebbled finish and dowdy looks. Stutz offered the well-proportioned Weymann Monte Carlo, a five-passenger four-door "sport" sedan. By 1932 the Monte Carlo was available in aluminum on the DV32 platform, priced at $4895 complete. Stutz also revived the Bearcat name with a boattailed speedster and a short chassis convertible coupe—both guaranteed for over 100 mph.

The DV32 itself made its debut in chassis form at the New York Auto Show in the winter of 1930-31. Prices were announced at the end of March 1931, and production was underway by July. At about the same time, Stutz reported net earnings of just $20,000 on gross sales of only $100,000—pitifully meager, but still preferable to the red ink that had flowed since 1929.

Further changes were announced for 1932 SVs and DVs. The four-speed gearbox gave way to a very rugged three-speed synchronized unit, and freewheeling was a new option. The hot-air manifold was replaced with a hot-water heating system, and an oil cooler was provided. A new trunk rack and dust valance were installed at the rear, bodies were dropped down in a curv-

1932 DV32 Super Bearcat convertible coupe

1933 DV32 convertible coupe by LeBaron

ing line to cover the frame, and single-bar bumpers replaced the previous double-bar design.

Stutz lost $315,000 in fiscal 1932, but continued to stumble on with the same basic lineup of SV16s and DV32s, all little changed. It's hardly surprising then that the company dropped a half-million dollars in 1933 and another quarter-million in '34. Though these weren't particularly huge sums even in those days, the losses greatly accelerated the drain on Stutz's already meager resources.

Management sought refuge by contracting to build a line of small delivery trucks called Pak-Age-Cars. George H. Freers was appointed chief engineer for this effort, and the first 28 vehicles in a total order of 340 were completed by the summer of 1936. But this wasn't nearly enough to keep things going, so Stutz was forced to declare bankruptcy in April 1937. By that time, assets totaled $1.2 million and liabilities only $733,000, yet Stutz still couldn't meet its debts. When creditors couldn't agree on a reorganization plan, a federal judge ordered liquidation of all assets in April 1938. That was completed by summer and the Pak-Age-Car production moved to Auburn's idle Connersville plant while Diamond T Truck Company handled sales and service.

Specifications

1930

Model M (wb 134.5; lwb 145) - 1,038 blt		Wght	Price	Prod
	Torpedo speedster 2P	4,595	3,450	—
	cpe 2P	4,850	3,295	—
	sdn 4d	4,918	3,695	—
	Wymnn Vrslls sdn 4d	—	3,945	—
	phaeton 5P	—	3,945	—
	lwb sdn 7P	5,210	3,895	—
	lwb Wymnn MC spt sdn 5P	—	4,495	—
	chassis (both wbs)	—	—	—

1930 Engine	bore×stroke	bhp	availability
I-8, 322.0	3.38×4.50	113	S-all

1931

Model LA (wb 127.5)		Wght	Price	Prod*
	sdn 4d	4,320	2,245	—
	cpe 2P	4,275	1,995	—
	five other body styles	—	—	—
Model MA/MB (wb 134.5; MB-145.0)				
21	MA sdn 4d	4,918	3,195	—
23	MA cpe 2P	4,850	2,995	—
24	MA speedster 2P	4,595	3,495	—
40	MB sdn 7P	5,210	3,895	—
	MB dual-cowl phtn	—	4,495	—
	MB Fltwd trns twn car 7P	—	7,495	—
	chassis (both wbs)	—	—	—
Model DV32 (wb 134.5; lwb-145.0)				
21	sdn 4d	5,035	4,995	—
23	cpe 2P	4,909	4,995	—
24	Bearcat speedster 2P	4,678	4,995	—
40	lwb sdn 7P	5,270	5,395	—
	chassis (both wbs)	—	—	—

*310 built

1931 Engines	bore×stroke	bhp	availability
I-6, 241.5	3.38×4.50	85	S-LA
I-8, 322.0	3.38×4.50	113	S-MA, MB
I-8, 322.0	3.38×4.50	161	S-DV32

1932*

Model LAA (wb 127.5)**		Wght	Price	Prod
	sdn 4d	4,385	1,620	—
	cpe 2P	4,315	1,620	—
	five other body styles	—	—	—
Model SV16 (wb 134.5; lwb-145.0)		**Wght**	**Price**	**Prod**
21	sdn 4d	4,985	2,995	—
23	cpe 2P	4,859	2,995	—
24	Bearcat speedster 2P	4,628	3,495	—
40	lwb sdn 7P	5,220	3,895	—
	chassis (both wbs)	—	—	—
Model DV32 (wb 134.5; lwb-145.0)				
21	sdn 4d	5,185	3,995	—
23	cpe 2P	5,059	3,995	—
24	Bearcat speedster 2P	4,828	4,495	—
40	lwb sdn 7P	5,420	4,895	—
	Spr Brct 2P (wb 116.0)	—	5,895	—
	chassis (both wbs)	—	—	—

*206 built ** Less than 50 built 1932-33

1932 Engines	bore×stroke	bhp	availability
I-6, 241.5	3.38×4.50	85	S-LAA
I-8, 322.0	3.38×4.50	113	S-SV16
I-8, 322.0	3.38×4.50	161	S-DV32

1933*

Model LAA** (wb 127.5)		Wght	Price	Prod
	sdn 4d	4,243	1,895	—
	cabriolet cpe 5P	—	2,185	—
	three other body styles ($1900-2200)	—	—	—
Model SV16 (wb 134.5; lwb-145.0)				
21	sdn 4d	4,845	3,095	—
23	cpe 2P	4,719	3,095	—
24	Bearcat speedster 2P	4,488	3,195	—
40	lwb sdn 7P	5,080	3,560	—
	Spr Brct 2P (wb 116.0)	—	5,095	—
	chassis (both wbs)	—	—	—
Model DV32 (wb 134.5; lwb-145.0)				
21	sdn 4d	5,045	3,795	—
23	cpe 2P	4,919	3,795	—
24	Bearcat speedster 2P	4,688	3,895	—
40	lwb sdn 7P	5,280	4,260	—
	Spr Brct 2P (wb 116.0)	—	5,795	—
	Wymnn MC spt sdn 5P (lwb)	5,120	4,895	—
64	LeBrn lwb sdn 4d 6P	5,346	3,410	—
	chassis (both wbs)	—	—	—

*80 built ** Less than 50 built 1932-33

1933 Engines	bore×stroke	bhp	availability
I-6, 241.5	3.38×4.50	85	S-LAA
I-8, 322.0	3.38×4.50	113	S-SV16
I-8, 322.0	3.38×4.50	161	S-DV32

1934

SV16 (wb 134.5; lwb 145.0)		Wght	Price	Prod*
21	sdn 4d	4,845	3,095	—
23	cpe 2P	4,719	3,095	—
24	Bearcat speedster 2P	4,488	3,195	—
40	lwb sdn 7P	5,080	3,560	—
	chassis (both wbs)	—	—	—
DV32 (wb 134.5; lwb-145.0)				
21	sdn 4d	5,045	3,795	—
23	cpe 2P	4,919	3,795	—
24	Bearcat speedster 2P	4,688	3,895	—
40	lwb sdn 7P	5,280	4,260	—
	chassis (both wbs)	—	—	—

*6 built

1934 Engines	bore×stroke	bhp	availability
I-8, 322.0	3.38×4.50	113	S-SV16
I-8, 322.0	3.38×4.50	156	S-DV32

1935

SV16 (wb 134.5; lwb-145.0)		Wght	Price	Prod*
21	sdn 4d	4,745	3,095	—
23	cpe 2-4P	4,619	3,095	—
24	Bearcat spdstr 2-4P	4,488	3,195	—
40	lwb sdn 7P	4,980	3,560	—
	chassis (both wbs)	—	—	—
DV32 (wb 134.5; lwb-145.0)				
21	sdn 4d	4,895	3,795	—
23	cpe 2-4P	4,769	3,795	—
24	Bearcat spdstr 2-4P	4,538	3,895	—
40	lwb sdn 7P	5,130	4,260	—
	chassis (both wbs)	—	—	—

*2 built

1935 Engines	bore×stroke	bhp	availability
I-8, 322.0	3.38×4.50	113	S-SV16
I-8, 322.0	3.38×4.50	156	S-DV32

Terraplane

The abundant success of the 1932-33 Essex Terraplane (*see* Essex) prompted Hudson president Roy D. Chapin to use just Terraplane for the firm's 1934 junior models. At the same time, the existing 193-cubic-inch six and 244-cid eight gave way to a new long-stroke six with 212 cid and 80-85 horsepower, upped to 88 bhp for 1935-36. Power rose to 96/102 for 1937. Terraplane then became a Hudson, but as a separate make it literally saved the company.

Though Essex Terraplanes sold for as little as $425, their successors were pitched somewhat upmarket in the $565-$880 range. The 1934 Terraplane also offered more variety, with Special and midline Challenger on a 112-inch wheelbase and Major models on a 116-inch chassis. Majors were mustered out for '35, when Challenger was renamed DeLuxe. The 1936 line offered DeLuxes and uplevel Customs on a new 115-inch platform that was stretched two inches for the 1937 DeLuxe and Super models.

Unlike many companion makes, the separate-make Terraplanes followed period design trends but avoided excesses, though the 1936-37 "fencer's mask" grille was debatable. Body styles were the usual sort. Roadsters and phaetons were never listed, but brougham and coach sedans in regular and trunkback "touring" form were always available, as were fixed-roof and convertible coupes. A smart victoria was offered for 1934 only. A DeLuxe wood-bodied station wagon was exclusive to '36, while in '37, a small number of Terraplane chassis were built for commercial applications.

All these cars had fine performance characteristics. A British road test of a 1936 Terraplane sedan showed 0-60 mph in 26.6 seconds and a top speed of 82 mph, both highly creditable for a period car weighing some 2800 pounds. Moreover, as the report observed, "The six-cylinder engine...has that suppleness and quietness in it's running that are characteristic of American design...Even at 70 there is no special fuss...[The Terraplane] can thus be a decidedly swift car for journeying over long distances, and is an easy one to handle, too...[It] gives, and does, much for its price."

Terraplane accounted for the lion's share of Hudson volume in each of its four years as a separate make, garnering nearly 280,000 total sales. Model-year output was around 51,000 for 1934 and '35, rose to almost 87,000 for '36, then reached 90,253 for the 1937 campaign.

With that, plus the demise of most other junior editions, the 1938 Terraplanes received Hudson badges and expanded to include standard, DeLuxe, and Super models with eight extra horsepower. But with that year's new "112" line, Terraplanes were no longer Hudson's smallest or most-affordable cars. Sales proved disappointing, so the name was dropped, though Terraplane continued to live on in spirit as the 1939 Series 91 Pacemaker and Series 92 Six.

1934 K Special Six convertible coupe

1935 DeLuxe Six coupe

1935 DeLuxe Six convertible coupe

1935 DeLuxe Six touring brougham

1936 DeLuxe Six coupe

1937 Series 70 Custom panel delivery (¾-ton)

1937 DeLuxe convertible coupe

Specifications

Note: Production figures based on serial number spans and other calculations; may exceed actual production.

1934

K Special Six (wb 112) - 23,726 blt	Wght	Price	Prod
cpe 2P	2,600	600	—
cpe 2-4P	2,605	645	—
conv cpe 2-4P	2,625	695	—
victoria 5P T/B	2,655	655	—
coach 5P	2,630	615	—
sdn 4d	2,710	675	—
sdn 4d T/B	2,735	715	—
KS Challenger Six (wb 112.0) - 20,265 built			
cpe 2P	2,540	565	—
cpe 2-4P	2,590	610	—
coach 5P	2,600	575	—
sdn 4d	2,670	635	—
KU Major Six (wb 116.0) - 7,093 built			
cpe 2P	2,650	665	—
cpe 2-4P	2,700	710	—
conv cpe 2-4P	2,695	750	—
victoria 5P T/B	2,755	720	—
coach 5P	2,730	680	—
sdn 4d	2,780	740	—
sdn 4d T/B	2,805	780	—

1934 Engines	bore×stroke	bhp	availability
I-6, 212.0	3.00×5.00	80	S-KS, K
I-6, 212.0	3.00×5.00	85	S-KU

1935

G Special Six (wb 112) - 37,772 blt	Wght	Price	Prod
cpe 2P	2,505	585	—
cpe 2-4P	2,555	625	—
touring brghm 5P T/B	2,610	625	—
coach 5P	2,595	595	—
sdn 4d	2,655	655	—
Suburban sdn 4d T/B	2,670	685	—
GU DeLuxe Six (wb 112.0) - 13,362 built			
cpe 2P	2,565	635	—
cpe 2-4P	2,635	675	—
conv cpe 2-4P	2,590	725	—
touring brghm 5P T/B	2,680	675	—
coach 5P	2,665	645	—
sdn 4d	2,710	705	—
Suburban sdn 4d T/B	2,725	735	—

1935 Engine	bore×stroke	bhp	availability
I-6, 212.0	3.00×5.00	88	S-all

1936

61 DeLx Six (wb 115) - 69,750 blt	Wght	Price	Prod
cpe 2P	2,620	595	—
cpe 2-4P	2,690	640	—
conv sdn 2-4P	—	—	—
brougham 5P	2,745	615	—
touring brghm 5P T/B	2,760	635	—
sdn 4d	2,805	670	—
touring sdn 4d T/B	2,820	690	—
wgn 4d	—	700	—
62 Custom Six (wb 115.0) - 17,041 built			
cpe 2P	2,675	650	—
cpe 2-4P	2,745	690	—
conv cpe 2-4P	—	—	—
brougham 5P	2,800	665	—
touring brghm 5P T/B	2,815	685	—
sdn 4d	2,860	720	—
touring sdn 4d T/B	2,875	740	—

1936 Engine	bore×stroke	bhp	availability
I-6, 212.0	3.00×5.00	88	S-all

1937

71 DeLx (wb 117) - 70,346 blt	Wght	Price	Prod
bus cpe 3P	2,370	595	—
cpe 3P	2,715	605	—
victoria 4P	2,765	850	—
conv cpe 3P	2,765	725	—
brougham 6P	2,830	625	—
conv brougham 6P	2,780	800	—
sdn 4d	2,865	675	—
touring sdn 4d T/B	2,865	695	—
chassis	—	—	—
72 Super (wb 117.0) - 19,907 built			
cpe 3P	2,755	880	—
touring sdn 4d T/B	2,905	745	—
victoria 4P	2,795	700	—
conv cpe 3P	2,825	770	—
conv brougham 6P	2,915	845	—
brougham 6P	2,875	680	—
touring brougham 6P	2,875	700	—
sdn 4d	2,905	725	—
chassis	—	—	—

1937 Engine	bore×stroke	bhp	availability
I-6, 212.0	3.00×5.00	96	S-71
I-6, 212.0	3.00×5.00	102	S-72

Tucker

Preston Thomas Tucker was an ebullient, 200-pound, six-footer who dreamed big and could raise big money—fast. He was an industry veteran with sales experience at Studebaker, Dodge, and elsewhere, and an inveterate entrepreneur who secured financing from Henry Ford to build Indy race cars in 1935. He also built a high-speed military scout car in 1937. In 1948, Tucker surprised everyone with "The Most Completely New Car in Fifty Years."

New it was. A torpedo-shaped fastback four-door sedan, the Tucker "48" looked just like the "car of the future" long expected by war-weary Americans. Styled by the forward-thinking Alex Tremulis on a 128-inch wheelbase, it was 219 inches long but only 60 inches high—low for the day. Engineering broke just as sharply from Detroit convention, with all-independent suspension and a rear-mounted flat-six. The latter derived from a wartime air-cooled helicopter unit, but boasted a fully sealed water-cooling system—an industry first. Horsepower was 166 and torque a thumping 372 pound-feet from 335 cubic inches, yet the all-alloy powerplant weighed just 320 pounds. The chassis was a sturdy box-section perimeter type with a subframe at each end.

Lack of time, money, and even technology precluded a curved windshield, disc brakes, "Torsilastic" rubber springs, and other innovations proposed by Preston. But the car still had novelties aplenty: central "cyclops-eye" headlight that turned with the front wheels, doors cut into the roof to ease entry/exit, a roomy six-passenger cabin with "step-down" floor, and interchangeable front/rear seats (to even out upholstery wear). Safety features abounded, too, and included massive bumpers; recessed or protected knobs, buttons, and levers; windshield glass that popped out harmlessly on impact; and a "Safety Chamber" where front passengers could dive "in case of impending collision."

Despite its size and 4200 pounds of heft, the Tucker could manage the 0-60 mph sprint in about 10 seconds. Top speed was at least 120 mph, thanks to the aerodynamic styling with an estimated drag factor of 0.30—good even today. Factory tests showed a creditable 20 mpg at a steady 50-55 mph. Just as nice, the rear-engine layout, all-independent suspension, and center-point steering combined for surprisingly easy handling and secure roadholding.

The Tucker would probably have sold well despite a Cadillac-like projected price of some $4000. But production ended at only 50 cars, plus the famous "Tin Goose" prototype. All were built before August 1948, the last 37 on a short assembly line in a refurbished wartime Dodge plant on Chicago's South Side.

Preston always claimed the Tucker was too good to live, and evidence suggests that the Detroit establishment felt threatened by it. But Tucker himself doomed the venture by moving with suspicious haste in issuing $15 million worth of stock to finance it. This led to charges of "fast-sell" tactics and a probe by the Securities and Exchange Commission that attracted a spate of adverse publicity. With that, Tucker and seven associates went to trial in October 1949 on 31 counts of conspiracy and securities and mail fraud. All were acquitted in January 1950 after what the jury termed a farce proceeding. Ironically, Tucker Corporation still had funds to produce its car, but public confidence was long gone. Receivers briefly considered going ahead before auctioning everything off at 18 cents on the dollar. Tucker's dream was dead.

Tremulis later sketched a stunning fastback coupe called Talisman as a proposed new '50s Tucker, and even Preston apparently still had hopes of building a car after his ordeal in Chicago. Though broken by the experience, Tucker moved to Brazil and was planning a two-seat kit sports car, the Carioca, when he died on December 26, 1956. He was only 53.

The Tucker saga has since been committed to film in *Tucker: The Man and His Dream*, released in 1988. Though the movie is good drama, director/producer Francis Ford Coppola plays fast and loose with some facts—just as Preston occasionally did. For example, the closing "parade" sequence shows most every Tucker built, including two owned by Coppola himself, but those precious few cars never made a triumphant procession right after the Tucker verdict was announced, let alone in unpredictable springtime Chicago weather. At least you shouldn't fret over the Tuckers that get smashed in an earlier scene; they're replicas.

1948 Torpedo "48" four-door sedan

Willys

Willys built passenger cars for nearly 35 years before it ever built a Jeep—and for some years afterward, too. It started when John North Willys, an Elmira, New York, car dealer, bought ailing Overland of Indianapolis in 1907. A year later he renamed the firm Willys-Overland, moved into the old Pope plant in Toledo, Ohio, and began rebuilding the firm's fortunes. He did that in spectacular fashion. For most of the Teens, the four-cylinder Overland was second in sales only to the Model T Ford. By 1918, J.N. Willys owned the world's second-largest auto company.

Willys-Overland entered the 1920s offering four-, six-, and eight-cylinder models spanning the low- and medium-price ranges. Sixes and Eights were temporarily dropped after 1921, the company concentrating on four-cylinder models. Sixes returned in 1925, and fours were dropped the following year to appear under a new Whippet nameplate. Whippet flourished at first, but died after 1931 when Willys elected to concentrate all its dwindling resources on its own four-cylinder model. Meanwhile, an Eight joined the Willys line in mid-1930 carrying a 245.4-cid 75-bhp Continental engine.

An association with visionary engineer Charles Yale Knight led to the Willys-Knight. Knight's engines replaced conventional valves with two sleeves (between the piston and the bore) that moved up and down in the cylinders. When slots in the two sleeves aligned either an exhaust or intake port was opened. The Knight's sleeve-valve engine had a great advantage in smoothness and silence of operation compared to conventional engines of the teens and '20s. As an added bonus carbon buildup made sleeve-valve engines run better, while other engines of the time required frequent "carbon and valve jobs" to remove carbon. Knight engines were offered by European luxury makes such as Daimler in England, Voisin in France, and even Mercedes in Germany. Willys sold more sleeve-valve engines than anyone. Early '30s Willys-Knights were sixes offered in two series. Smaller models had 178 cid, 53-60 bhp, and wheelbases of 113 or 115 inches; the larger ones used a 255-cid engine with 72-87 bhp in 120- and 121-inch chassis. Prices were rather stiff—$975 to around $1900—so demand tailed off quickly as the Depression took hold. Also by that time conventional engines were as smooth and quiet as the more expensive Knight engines.

Willys' production withered to only some 27,000 for '32. With that, J.N. Willys, who had held the largely honorary post of board chairman since 1929, resigned his recent appointment as U.S. ambassador to Poland and returned to rescue his company, something he'd done twice before. J.N. chipped in $2 million of his own money and personally assured dealers and creditors that all would be well, but Willys-Overland was forced to declare bankruptcy. The company was reorganized and resumed production, but managed only about 13,000 units in 1934. It would not emerge from receivership until 1935, days after John North Willys succumbed to heart troubles.

Meantime, Willys-Overland decided to bet its dwindling bank on a new low-priced small car, which it managed to develop for next to nothing. Called the Willys 77, it was unveiled in June 1932 with a 100-inch wheelbase and an ultrathrifty four-cylinder engine making 48 bhp from 134.2 cid. It was the only car Willys would sell from early 1933 through 1936.

The 1933 reorganization ushered in a new chairman, the bespectacled Ward Canaday. A pillar of the Toledo business community with a strong sense of loyalty to his employees, Canaday ached to get things moving again. His first real chance came with the 1937 line, for which he ordered a full restyle. The result was less than ideal, with lumpy looking rounded bodies carrying pontoon fenders and a bizarre bulging front not unlike that of Graham's forthcoming "sharknose." The new sheetmetal increased overall length by over a foot to 175.5 inches. Again, only a coupe and sedan were tried, albeit in standard and DeLuxe variations. Priced from $500 to near $600, these new Model 37s met with some success despite their odd looks, and model-year volume shot up to 63,467. But 1937 was a recovery year for most of the industry, so despite building twice the number of cars it had in '36, Willys only improved from 15th to 14th in the overall standings.

The 1938 recession resulted in dramatically lower sales, pushing Willys back to 16th. Changes for that year's Model 38 were few, but offerings expanded with a pair of two-door sedans called Clipper.

A sharper prow announced "Slip-Stream" styling for 1939, and the lineup again included Overlands: standard, DeLuxe, and Speedway Special sedans and coupes with two extra inches of wheelbase ahead of the cowl. Designated Model 39, Overlands differed from that year's Model 38/48 in having standard hydraulic brakes, larger tires, headlamps carried in fender-top pods rather than within the fenders, and 62 bhp. Overlands cost an average of $100 more than other Willys models, but the extra money bought markedly better performance. Former Studebaker engineer Barney Roos had coaxed extra power out of the old four via higher compression, an improved carburetor, and a new camshaft. Dubbed the "Go-Devil," this engine would impress the Army and power wartime Jeeps. At $596-$689, the Overlands were still some $32 below the cheapest Chevys. As a result, Overland's model-year production was fairly respectable. But total Willys output was only 17,839—a worrisome

1930 Six four-door sedan

1930 Knight roadster

1931 Series 97 Six two-door sedan

1931 Eight DeLuxe Victoria coupe

1933 77 four-door sedan

1936 77 coupe

1937 37 coupe

decline in a year when most automakers did better than the year before.

It was in 1939 that Joseph W. Frazer, the dynamic sales manager of Chrysler Corporation, went to Toledo and W-O as president and general manager; Canaday remained board chairman. Frazer knew how to cut losses, and decreed more orthodox styling for 1940. Still, it's doubtful even he could have saved Willys' passenger cars.

Designated Series 440—for four cylinders, 1940—Frazer's revised models were essentially '39 Overlands with sealed-beam headlamps and a vertical prow (instead of undercut). Model-year production improved to nearly 27,000.

Frazer and company made further improvements for the following year's Series 441. All models were dubbed "Americar," providing patriotic appeal, and gained two more horsepower and two more inches in wheelbase. Models expanded to seven with the addition of a new Plainsman coupe and sedan. Frontal styling was now quite Ford-like, with an even shapelier nose above a small vertical-bar grille. Prices were hiked nearly $100, now ranging from $634 to $916.

Willys had started building military Jeeps by now, so its 1942 model year was even shorter than for most other U.S. automakers. That year's Series 442 Americars were the same as the '41s save a prominent vertical grille bar (carrying a line down from the hood trim) and slightly higher prices. Just under 29,000 of the '41 and '42 models combined were built before W-O shifted entirely to war production. Frazer would leave Toledo in 1943, ultimately to take over Graham-Paige. Taking over as W-O president was Charles E. Sorensen, the famed former production boss at Ford. "Cast-Iron Charlie" then stepped aside in 1946 for James D. Mooney.

Willys postponed returning to passenger cars, resuming peacetime production with Jeep-based vehicles instead. These included the inevitable civilian version of the military Jeep, plus two hybrids. The first was a station wagon introduced in 1946 and destined to live on for 20 years. Though usually considered a truck and not a car, it arguably qualifies as the first modern all-steel wagon. In any case, it was W-O's main civilian product through 1947.

More directly automotive was the Jeepster, a jaunty open tourer designed during the war by Brooks Stevens, who also did the wagon. Announced in 1948, the Jeepster offered seating for four on the 104-inch wagon wheelbase, plus a manual soft top and clip-in side curtains. Initial power was provided by the "Go-Devil" four. A six with 148.5 cid and 72 bhp was added for 1949. Both engines were converted from L-head to F-head configuration during 1950. F-heads had side exhaust valves with overhead intake valves for better breathing and increased power. That year's Jeepsters sported an eggcrate grille (replacing vertical slats), somewhat less-deluxe appointments, and a six enlarged to 161 cid and 75 bhp.

Priced in the $1400-$1800 range, the Jeepster was relatively popular for such a specialized product. First-year sales were strong at 10,326. But this evidently satisfied demand, for 1949 production was just 2960. The 1950 figure was a healthier 5844, but some were unsold at year's end and registered as '51 models. Today, all Jeepsters are avidly sought collectibles.

Willys could likely have lived just fine on Jeeps, Jeep wagons, trucks, and military vehicles. But the high optimism and booming seller's market of the early postwar years made returning to the passenger-car business seem like a no-lose proposition. Ward Canaday, who had taken over as president in 1950, entertained numerous ideas. His final choice was a trim 108-inch-wheelbase unitized proposal engineered by the distinguished Clyde Paton and inventively styled by Phil Wright. It was ready for the road by 1952, when it was trumpeted as "The

Revolutionary New Aero-Willys."

It was a fine effort. Fashionably square and slabsided, the Aero was relatively light (2500-2600 pounds), roomy, and blessed with good handling. There were four models at first: Aero-Eagle hardtop coupe and three two-door sedans. The Aero-Lark used the 75-bhp, 161-cid six-cylinder engine from late Jeepsters; Eagle and the Aero-Wing and Aero-Ace sedans ran an F-head version with 90 bhp. Though small, the 161 six delivered good performance, plus fuel economy on the order of 25 miles per gallon.

Despite high pricing ($2155 for the Eagle), 1952-model production of 31,363 was good, if not great; the midrange Aero-Wing accounted for well over a third.

Offerings expanded for 1953, when appearance changed only in detail—notably red hubcap emblems and a gold-plated "W" in the grille, honoring Willys' 50th anniversary. About 500 Aero-Larks were built for export with the old F-head fours, but engines were otherwise unchanged. Aero-Wing was retitled Aero-Falcon, and a new four-door sedan arrived in Lark, Falcon, and Ace versions. The hardtop Eagle was again rather pricey, though up only $2 from '52. Helped by the end of government-mandated curbs on consumer production instituted because of the Korean War, Willys had another modestly good year, selling about 42,000 cars.

The situation changed in 1954, when Willys-Overland was purchased by Henry Kaiser, who combined it with ailing Kaiser-Frazer to form Kaiser-Willys Sales Corporation. K-F sold its sprawling Willow Run, Michigan, plant to General Motors (which would use it into the 1990s), and Kaiser production was transferred to Toledo.

The Kaiser takeover didn't immediately affect the '54 Aero-Willys, which was little more than a '53 with larger taillights and revised interior. But March 1954 brought a raft of changes. Chief among them was Kaiser's 226-cid L-head six, which was shoehorned in as optional power for Ace and Eagle. There were also new Ace and Eagle Customs, basically the standard articles with a "continental" spare tire.

Though heavier than the Willys 161, the Kaiser 226 engine

1938 Clipper two-door sedan

1939 Series 39 Overland two-door sedan

1941 Americar DeLuxe station wagon

1946-48 two-door station wagon

1948 Jeepster phaeton convertible

1953 Aero-Eagle hardtop coupe

1955 Custom four-door sedan

produced a useful 25 extra horsepower that made the Aero relatively fast. Top speed was little higher at 85 mph, but the big six dropped typical 0-60 mph times to around 14 seconds. As an experiment, a few Aeros were fitted with 140-bhp supercharged Kaiser Manhattan engines, which made the lighter Willys a performance match for many contemporary V-8 cars—or so company engineers claimed.

All '54s handled much better than earlier Aeros, thanks to a revised front suspension. In all, the best Aeros yet failed to convince many customers, and production dropped to 11,717.

By early 1955, Kaiser-Willys decided to abandon the U.S. car market. No longer called Aero, the '55s comprised Custom two- and four-door sedans and a Bermuda hardtop (formerly called Eagle); Willys also built 659 Ace four-doors, again for export. Engine choices did not change save for deletion of the Lark's 134-cid four, but prices were drastically cut in a last-ditch effort to attract sales. The Bermuda, for instance, was slashed to $1895, and was thus honestly advertised as America's lowest-priced hardtop.

Sales considerations also prompted an ambitious '55 facelift by Kaiser stylists Buzz Grisinger and Herb Weissinger. The restyles' main elements were a busy two-tier grille (replacing the simple horizontal-bar motif of prior years) and Z-line side moldings that made for an odd two-toned appearance. In the meantime, a neat hardtop wagon was in the works for 1955-56, and designers "Dutch" Darrin and Duncan McRae were conjuring more ambitious restyles for the years beyond. But Willys wouldn't live to see them, at least not with passenger cars. So after a final 5986 units, most carrying the 226 engine, Willys returned to making nothing but Jeeps.

Happily, the Aero would live a good while longer in South America, where Kaiser's Willys do (of) Brasil subsidiary took over the Aero dies and offered a cleaned-up '55 with F-head Willys power during 1960-62. Designer Brooks Stevens then applied handsome new square-rigged outer panels, and the car continued through '72, first as the Aero-Willys 2600, then the Willys Itamaraty, and finally the Ford Itamaraty (Dearborn acquired Willys do Brasil via American Motors in 1967). That's eloquent testimony to the sound basic design of the original Aero-Willys. A pity it wasn't more appreciated in its native land.

Specifications

Note: production figures based on serial number spans; may exceed actual production.

1930

98B Six (wb 110.0) - 27,870 blt*	Wght	Price	Prod
rdstr 2-4P	2,497	725	—
sdn 4d	2,641	795	—
rdstr 2P	—	695	—
DeLuxe sdn 4d	2,650	850	—
cpe 2P	—	745	—
DeLuxe cpe 5P	—	800	—
DeLuxe rdstr 2P	—	750	—
DeLuxe rdstr 2-4P	—	780	—
8-80 Eight (wb 120.0) - 1,901 built (from 1/30)			
cpe 2P	—	875	—
rdstr 2-4P	—	855	—
sdn 4d	—	895	—
rdstr 2P	—	825	—
DeLuxe cpe 5P	—	900	—
DeLuxe rdstr 2-4P	—	910	—
DeLuxe sdn 4d	—	950	—
DeLuxe rdstr 2P	—	910	—
87-Knight (wb 112.5; sdn-115.0) - 3,627 blt (from 6/30)			
rdstr 2-4P	2,718	975	—
cpe 2-4P	2,922	1,075	—
sdn 4d	2,989	1,075	—
70B-Knight (wb 112.5; sdn 115.0) - 10,723 built			
rdstr 2-4P	2,748	1,045	—
DeLuxe cpe 2-4P	2,916	1,145	—
sdn 4d	3,015	1,145	—
66B-Knight (wb 120.0) - 5,820 built			
rdstr 2-4P	3,592	1,895	—
cpe 2-4P	3,815	1,895	—
sdn 4d	3,934	1,895	—

* Includes 1931 Model 97.

1930 Engines	bore × stroke	bhp	availability
I-6, 177.9	2.94 × 4.38	53	S-70B
I-6, 177.9	2.94 × 4.38	55	S-87
I-6, 193.0	3.25 × 3.88	65	S-98B
I-6, 255.0	3.38 × 4.75	72	S-66B
I-8, 245.4	3.13 × 4.00	75	S-Eight

1931

97 Six (wb 110.0) - 37,678 blt*	Wght	Price	Prod
rdstr 2P	2,407	495	—
cpe 2P	2,528	565	—
sdn 2d	—	595	—
sdn 4d	2,670	675	—
98B Six (wb 110.0) - 27,870 built*			
rdstr 2-4P	2,430	725	—
sdn 4d	2,623	795	—
98D Six (wb 113.0) - 3,653 blt			
victoria cpe 5P	2,656	795	—
sdn 4d	2,706	795	—
8-80D Eight (wb 120.0; lwb-121.0) - 1,686 built			
80 cpe 2-4P	3,061	1,245	—
80 sdn 4d	3,076	1,295	—
80D lwb vict cpe 5P (from 1/31)	3,063	995	—
80D lwb sdn 4d (from 1/31)	3,131	995	—
66B-Knight (wb 120.0) - 2,189 built			
rdstr 2-4P	3,515	1,795	—
cpe 2-4P	3,745	1,795	—
sdn 4d	3,868	1,795	—
66D-Knight (wb 121.0) - 4,982 built (from 1/31)			
victoria cpe 5P	3,336	1,095	—
sdn 4d	3,400	1,095	—
87-Knight (wb 112.5; sdn-115.0) - 2,541 built			
rdstr 2-4P	2,739	975	—
cpe 2-4P	2,882	1,075	—
sdn 4d	3,001	1,075	—

* Includes 1930 Model 98B.

1931 Engines	bore × stroke	bhp	availability
I-6, 177.9	2.94 × 4.38	55	S-87
I-6, 193.0	3.25 × 3.88	65	S-97, 98B, 98D
I-6, 255.0	3.38 × 4.75	87	S-66B, 66D
I-8, 245.4	3.13 × 4.00	80	S-Eight

1932

6-90-Ovrlnd Six (wb 113) - 13,148 blt	Wght	Price	Prod
rdstr 2P	2,570	415	—
cpe 2P	2,749	530	—
sdn 4d	2,814	610	—
97 Six (wb 110.0) - 9,754 built			
rdstr 2P	2,407	495	—
cpe 5P 2W	2,648	595	—
sdn 4d	2,670	675	—
98D Six (wb 113.0) - 245 built			
victoria cpe 4P	2,656	795	—
sdn 4d	2,706	795	—
8-80D Eight (wb 121.0) - 452 built			
victoria cpe 4P	3,100	995	—
sdn 4d	3,131	995	—
8-88-Overland Eight (wb 121.0) - 1,296 built			
rdstr 2P	2,981	730	—
cpe 2P	3,148	780	—
Custom victoria 4P	3,337	1,030	—
sdn 4d	3,250	830	—
95-Knight (wb 113.0) - 1,300 built (est.)			
Silver Ann. cpe 2P	2,915	745	—
Silver Ann. cpe 2-4P	2,994	775	—
Silver Ann. coach 5P	2,982	745	—
Silver Ann. sdn 4d	3,031	795	—
66D-Knight (wb 121.0)			
victoria cpe 5P	3,360	1,095	718
sdn 4d	3,400	1,095	
Slvr Ann. Cus vic 5P	3,664	1,145	900
Slvr Ann. Cus sdn 4d	3,775	1,295	

1932 Engines	bore × stroke	bhp	availability
I-6, 177.9	2.94 × 4.38	60	S-95
I-6, 193.0	3.25 × 3.88	65	S-97, 98D, 6-90
I-6, 255.0	3.38 × 4.75	87	S-66D
I-8, 245.4	3.13 × 4.00	80	S-8-80D, 8-88

1933

6-90A-Overland Streamlined Six (wb 113.0) - 6,775 blt	Wght	Price	Prod
rdstr 2P	2,569	535	—
cpe 2P	2,781	650	—
sdn 4d	2,913	740	—
8-88A-Ovrlnd Streamlined Eight (wb 121.0) - 1,022 blt			
cpe 2P	3,217	955	—
sdn 4d	3,368	995	—
77 (wb 100.0) - 12,820 built			
cpe 2P	2,058	395	—
Custom cpe 2P	2,072	415	—
cpe 2-4P	2,072	425	—
Custom cpe 2-4P	2,105	445	—
sdn 4d	2,136	445	—
Custom sdn 4d	2,156	475	—
66E-Knight Streamlined Six (wb 121.0)			
Custom sdn 4d	3,830	1,420	574

1933 Engines	bore × stroke	bhp	availability
I-4, 134.2	3.13 × 4.38	48	S-77
I-6, 193.0	3.25 × 3.88	65	S-6-90A
I-6, 255.0	3.38 × 4.75	87	S-66E
I-8, 245.4	3.13 × 4.00	80	S-8-88A

1934

77 (wb 100.0) - 13,235 built	Wght	Price	Prod
cpe 2P	2,058	395	—
Custom cpe 2P	2,072	415	—
cpe 2-4P	2,072	425	—
Custom cpe 2-4P	2,105	445	—
sdn 4d	2,131	445	—
Custom sdn 4d	2,156	475	—
Second Series (from 1/34):			
cpe 2P	2,058	430	—
sdn 4d	2,131	450	—

1934 Engine	bore × stroke	bhp	availability
I-4, 134.2	3.13 × 4.38	48	S-all

1935

77 (wb 100.0) - 10,715 built	Wght	Price	Prod
cpe 3P	2,034	475	—
sdn 4d	2,111	495	—

1935 Engine	bore×stroke	bhp	availability
I-4, 134.2	3.13×4.38	48	S-all

1936

77 (wb 100.0) - 30,826 built	Wght	Price	Prod
cpe 2P	2,034	395	—
sdn 4d	2,131	415	—

1936 Engine	bore×stroke	bhp	availability
I-4, 134.2	3.13×4.38	48	S-all

1937

37 (wb 100.0) - 63,467 built	Wght	Price	Prod
cpe 2P	2,146	499	—
DeLuxe cpe 2P	2,146	579	—
sdn 4d	2,200	538	—
DeLuxe sdn 4d	2,306	589	—

1937 Engine	bore×stroke	bhp	availability
I-4, 134.2	3.13×4.38	48	S-all

1938

38 (wb 100.0) - 26,691 built*	Wght	Price	Prod
Standard cpe 2P	2,145	499	—
Deluxe cpe 2P	2,155	574	—
Clipper sdn 2d	2,258	539	—
Standard sdn 4d	2,247	563	—
Delx Clipper sdn 2d	2,258	575	—
Deluxe sdn 4d	2,263	614	—
Custom sdn 4d	2,336	700	—

* Includes 1939 Model 38 production.

1938 Engine	bore×stroke	bhp	availability
I-4, 134.2	3.13×4.38	48	S-all

1939

38 (wb 100.0)*	Wght	Price	Prod
Standard cpe 2P	2,181	499	—
Standard sdn 2d	2,258	539	—
Standard sdn 4d	2,300	563	—
Deluxe cpe 2P	2,181	574	—
Deluxe sdn 2d	2,258	575	—
Deluxe sdn 4d	2,306	614	—
39 Overland (wb 102.0) - 15,214 built			
Std Spdwy cpe 2P	2,137	596	—
Std Spdwy sdn 2d	2,217	616	—
Std Spdwy sdn 4d	2,249	631	—
Deluxe cpe 2P	2,193	646	—
Deluxe sdn 2d	2,262	667	—
Deluxe sdn 4d	2,306	689	—
Spdwy Spec cpe 2P	2,193	610	—
Spdwy Spec sdn 2d	2,262	631	—
Spdwy Spec sdn 4d	2,306	646	—
48 (wb 100.0) - 2,625 built			
cpe 2P	2,181	524	—
sdn 2d	2,258	565	—
sdn 4d	2,300	586	—

* Included in 1938 Model 38 production.

1939 Engines	bore×stroke	bhp	availability
I-4, 134.2	3.13×4.38	48	S-38, 48
I-4, 134.2	3.13×4.38	62	S-39

1940

440 (wb 102.0) - 26,698 built	Wght	Price	Prod
Speedway cpe	2,146	529	—
Speedway sdn 4d	2,238	596	—
DeLuxe cpe	2,190	641	—
DeLuxe sdn 4d	2,255	672	—
DeLuxe wgn 4d	2,124	830	—

1940 Engine	bore×stroke	bhp	availability
I-4, 134.2	3.13×4.38	61	S-all

1941

441 Americar (wb 104.0)*	Wght	Price	Prod
Speedway cpe	2,116	634	—
Speedway sdn 4d	2,230	674	—
DeLuxe cpe	2,135	685	—
DeLuxe sdn 4d	2,265	720	—
DeLuxe wgn 4d	2,483	916	—
Plainsman cpe	2,175	740	—
Plainsman sdn 4d	2,305	771	—

1941 Engine	bore×stroke	bhp	availability
I-4, 134.2	3.13×4.38	63	S-all

1942

442 Americar (wb 104.0)*	Wght	Price	Prod
Speedway cpe	2,142	695	—
Speedway sdn 4d	2,261	745	—
DeLuxe cpe	2,184	769	—
DeLuxe sdn 4d	2,295	795	—
DeLuxe wgn 4d	2,512	978	—
Plainsman cpe	2,242	819	—
Plainsman sdn 4d	2,353	845	—

1942 Engine	bore×stroke	bhp	availability
I-4, 134.2	3.13×4.38	63	S-all

* Total 1941-42 Americar production: 28,935.

1948

463 Four (wb 104.0)	Wght	Price	Prod
Jeepstr phtn conv 2d	2,468	1,765	10,326

1948 Engine	bore×stroke	bhp	availability
I-4, 134.3	3.13×4.38	63	S-all

1949

463 Four/VJ-3 Four (wb 104.0) - 2,307 built	Wght	Price	Prod
Jeepstr phtn conv 2d	2,468	1,495	—
VJ-3 Six (wb 104.0)			
Jeepstr phtn conv 2d	2,392	1,530	653

1949 Engines	bore×stroke	bhp	availability
I-4, 134.2	3.13×4.38	63	S-463 Four
I-4, 134.2	3.13×4.38	72	S-VJ3 Four (F-hd)
I-6, 148.5	3.00×3.50	72	S-Six

1950

443 Four/VJ-3 Four (wb 104.0) - 4,066 built	Wght	Price	Prod
Jeepstr phtn conv 2d	2,459	1,390	—
VJ-3 Four (wb 104.0)			
Jeepstr phtn conv 2d	2,468	1,495	—
673VJ Six (wb 104.0)			
Jeepster phtn conv 2d	2,485	1,490	1,778

1950 Engines	bore×stroke	bhp	availability
I-4, 134.2	3.13×4.38	63	S-Four, 1st sr, L-head
I-4, 134.2	3.13×4.38	72	S-Four, 2nd sr, F-head
I-6, 148.5	3.00×3.50	72	S-Six, 1st sr, L-head
I-6, 161.0	3.13×3.50	75	S-Six, 2nd sr, L-head

1951

473-VJ Four (wb 104.0)	Wght	Price	Prod
Jeepstr phtn conv 2d	2,459	1,426	*
673-VJ Six (wb 104.0)			
Jeepstr phtn conv 2d	2,485	1,529	*

* Combined with 1950 totals; includes 1950 leftovers sold as '51s.

1951 Engines	bore×stroke	bhp	availability
I-4, 134.2	3.13×4.38	72	S-Four
I-6, 161.0	3.13×3.50	75	S-Six

1952

652-K Aero-Lark (wb 108.0)	Wght	Price	Prod
KA2-675 sdn 2d	2,487	1,731	7,474
652-L Aero-Wing (wb 108.0)			
LA1-685 sdn 2d	2,570	1,989	12,819
652-M Aero (wb 108.0)			
MA1-685 Ace sdn 2d	2,584	2,074	8,706
MC1-685 Eagle htp cpe	2,575	2,155	2,364

1952 Engines	bore×stroke	bhp	availability
I-6, 161.0	3.13×4.38	75	S-Lark
I-6, 161.0	3.13×4.38	90	S-Wng, Ace, Egle

1953

653-K Aero-Lark (wb 108.0)	Wght	Price	Prod
KA1-675 sdn 2d	2,487	1,646	8,205
KB1-675 sdn 4d	2,509	1,732	7,692
653-M Aero (wb 108.0)			
MA1-685 Ace sdn 2d	2,584	1,963	4,988
MB1-685 Ace sdn 4d	2,735	2,038	7,475
MC1-685 Eagle htp cpe	2,575	2,157	7,018
653-P Aero-Falcon (wb 108.0)			
PA1-675 sdn 2d	2,507	1,760	3,054
PB1-675 sdn 4d	2,529	1,861	3,117

1953 Engines	bore×stroke	bhp	availability
I-4, 134.2	3.13×4.38	72	S-Lark 4
I-6, 161.0	3.13×4.38	75	S-Lark 6, Falcn
I-6, 161.0	3.13×4.38	90	S-Ace, Eagle

1954

654-K Aero-Lark (wb 108.0)	Wght	Price	Prod
KA2 sdn 2d, (226)	2,740	—	59
KB2 sdn 4d, (226)	2,730	—	282
KA3-685 sdn 2d	2,623	1,737	1,370
KA3-685 Custom sdn 2d	2,678	1,798	1,132
KB3-685 sdn 4d	2,661	1,823	1,482
KB3-685 Custom sdn 4d	2,722	1,878	548
654-M Aero (wb 108.0)			
MA1 Ace DL sdn 2d (226)	2,751	—	1,195
MA1 Ace DL Cus sdn 2d (226)	2,806	—	7
MB1 Ace DL sdn 4d (226)	2,778	—	1,498
MB1 Ace DL Cus sdn 4d (226)	2,833	—	9
MA2-685 Ace sdn 2d	2,682	1,892	2
MA2-685 Ace Custom sdn 2d	2,737	1,947	586
MB2-685 Ace sdn 4d	2,709	1,968	1,380
MB2-685 Ace Custom sdn 4d	2,764	2,023	611
MC1 Eagle htp cpe (226)	2,847	—	660
MC1 Egl Cus htp cpe (226)	2,904	—	11
MC2 Egl Spc htp cpe (226)	—	—	302
MC3-685 Eagle DL htp cpe	—	2,222	84
MC3-685 Egl DL Cus htp cpe	—	2,411	499

1954 Engines	bore×stroke	bhp	availability
I-4, 134.2	3.13×4.38	72	S-Lark 4
I-6, 161.0	3.13×4.38	90	S-Lrk 6, Ace, Egl
I-6, 226.2	3.31×4.38	115	O-Lrk 6, Ace, Egl

1955

522/6 Ace (wb 108.0)	Wght	Price	Prod
52367 sdn 4d (226)	—	—	659
523/4 Custom (wb 108.0)			
52367 sdn 4d (226)	2,778	1,795	2,822
52462 sdn 2d (161)	—	—	2
52467 sdn 2d (226)	2,751	1,725	288
525 Bermuda (wb 108.0)			
52527 htp cpe (161)	—	1,895	59
52567 htp cpe (226)	2,831	1,997	2,156

1955 Engines	bore×stroke	bhp	availability
I-6, 161.0	3.13×3.50	90	S-Cus, Berm
I-6, 226.2	3.31×4.38	115	S-Ace; O-Cus, Bermuda

Willys production does not include steel-bodied station wagons manufactured from 1946 through 1961, or Wagoneers (wagons) manufactured from 1960 onward. Aero production does not include export or taxi models. Aero production continued in Brazil through 1962.

Minor Makes

The following compilation lists American-built automobiles, 1930 onward, not dealt with in the main body of this book. The vast majority of these saw very limited production; some never progressed beyond the prototype stage; a rare few were sold for several years. Facts about some are unavoidably elusive.

We have omitted all unsubstantiated, experimental, racing, and Canadian cars; likewise products designed for children. Only those prototypes that show evidence of serious intent to manufacture vehicles in complete form have been included. Kit cars are included only where fully assembled models were also available from the manufacturer or dealer.

Dates and factory locations are as accurate as possible. A question mark, as in "1965-?," indicates that the editors have not been able to determine when production ceased. When "c." (circa) is shown, it is not possible to determine the precise date company activity began and/or was terminated. "NA" indicates that precise production-figure information is not available.

Aerocar 1948-c.70
Aerocar Inc.; Longview, WA
Production: 7
Developed by Moulton P. Taylor, the Aerocar was a car/airplane powered by a 100-bhp Franklin engine. It was first sold in late 1954 for $7500, and had a top speed of 50 mph on the ground, 110 mph in the air. Wings and propeller assembly were towed in a 14-foot trailer when in road use. The conversion from car to plane took five minutes for one person with a wrench.

Aircar 1970-c.73
Advanced Vehicle Engineers; Van Nuys, CA
Production: NA
This car/airplane conversion had Cessna Skymaster control surfaces placed on a Pontiac Firebird chassis. A later Ford Pinto-based model flew in 1973 as the Mizar.

Airphibian 1946-52
Continental, Inc. (Robert E. Fulton, Jr.); Danbury, CT
Production: NA
Another car/airplane conversion, this one had an aluminum passenger compartment with detachable wings, propeller, and fuselage. The conversion from plane to car took five minutes. It was powered by a six-cylinder, 150-bhp engine that produced a top speed of 45 mph on the ground, 120 in the air.

Airscoot 1947
Aircraft Products Company; Wichita, KS
Production: NA
The Airscoot was intended to be carried in an airplane for ground transportation upon landing. It was foldable and made of lightweight tubing; it weighed 72 pounds and was 37 inches long. Power came from a single-cylinder 2.6-bhp engine that produced a top speed of 25 mph while promising 60 mpg. It apparently never reached production.

Airway 1948-50
Airway Motors, Inc.; San Diego, CA
Production: 2
A two-door fastback sedan was produced in 1948-49; a notchback coupe followed in 1950. Both were powered by a 10-bhp air-cooled aluminum engine with fluid drive. Total weight was 600-775 pounds, with a top speed of 45-50 mph.

American Buckboard 1955
American Buckboard Corp.; Los Angeles, CA
Production: NA
This tiny roadster was powered by a rear-mounted two-cylinder air-cooled motorcycle engine that drove a fifth wheel. It sat on a 70-inch wheelbase and measured 10 feet long overall. Projected price was $750, but production is doubtful, though a version called the Bearcat was built in 1956.

American Steam Car 1929-c.1931
American Steam Automobile Co.; West Newton, MA
Production: NA
Made-to-order steamers that used Hudson components, bodies, and chassis were the product of engineer Thomas Derr. Derr founded the company in 1924 to provide replacements and improvements for Stanley Steamers still on the road.

Amitron 1967-?
Gulton Industries; Metuchen, NJ
Production: NA
Wedge-shaped three-passenger electric vehicle powered by lithium-nickel batteries was a co-operative venture with American Motors Corp. It was claimed to do 0-50 mph in about 20 seconds with a range of about 150 miles.

Apache 1966-?
Interco Development Corp.; New York, NY
Production: NA
Similar to European economy cars in size, engine displacement, and seating, but the Apache had an unusual collapsible roof that transformed it from a fastback coupe to an open roadster.

Apollo 1962-65
International Motor Cars, Inc. (Newt Davis & Milt Brown); Oakland, CA

Production: 88
A high-performance sports car with coachwork by Carrozzeria Intermeccanica of Turin, Italy, built to a Ron Plescia design modified by Scaglione. It was powered by a 215-cid Buick aluminum V-8. Added in 1964 was the 5000 GT with a 300-cid Buick V-8 that could propel the car to 60 mph in 7.5 seconds and had a top speed of 150+ mph. They were never advertised nationally and had a spotty dealer network. Some bodies were later sold to a Dallas, Texas, firm that assembled them as the Vetta Ventura (*see entry*).

Argonaut 1959-63
Argonaut Motor Machine Co.; Cleveland, OH
Production: NA, but doubtful
Aluminum-bodied luxury cars that were built in the Duesenberg/Pierce Arrow mold. Seven models were announced, ranging from the two-seat Steed sports coupe (126.5-inch wheelbase) to a huge limousine (154-inch wheelbase). Overall lengths varied from 218-258 inches. The proposed air-cooled, overhead-cam aluminum V-12 engine was to produce a whopping 1020 horsepower, enough to provide an equally whopping 240-mph top speed. Factory-direct prices ranged from $25,150-$36,000.

Arnolt 1952-c.58
S.H. Arnolt, Inc, (S.H. "Wacky" Arnolt); Chicago, IL
Production: 65 MG; 142 Bristol
These two sports cars carried specially designed bodywork by Bertone of Italy. The Arnolt-MG was a pleasant, square-cut two-seater hampered by an anemic four-cylinder engine and lofty $3195 price. The follow-up Arnolt-Bristol had a 2.0-liter, 130-bhp six built by Bristol in England, and was offered as a closed coupe and a roadster with or without top. Prices varied from $4000 to $6000. The Bristol weighed but 2100 pounds and was quick: 0-60 mph took about nine seconds, the standing quarter-mile passed in 17 seconds at 82 mph. Top speed was 110 mph. Arnolt-Bristol took first, second, and fourth in its class at the 1955 12 Hours of Sebring. Production ended in '58, but sales continued until Arnolt's death in 1963.

Arrowbile/Aerobile c.1937-c.58
Waldo D. Waterman; Santa Monica, CA
Production: 8 (est.)
An early serious attempt to produce a flying car for commercial sale in U.S. The first examples used a Studebaker Commander six-cylinder engine. The final Aerobile used a horizontally opposed, water-cooled Franklin six. Studebaker intended to sell Arrowbile through selected dealers, but backed out because of a downturn in the economy.

1964 Apollo 5000 GT coupe

Asardo 1959
American Special Automotive Research and Design Organization; North Bergen, NJ
Production: NA
This fiberglass sport coupe with an 88-inch wheelbase, 150-inch overall length, and total weight of 1350 pounds was powered by a 91.3-cid Alfa Romeo four with 135 bhp. It could do 0-60 mph in just 6.4 seconds. Top speed was 135. Price: $5875.

Ascot 1955
Glasspar Co.; Santa Ana, CA
Production: NA
Ascot was a 1700-pound fiberglass roadster with a 94-inch wheelbase and a height of 48 inches. It featured butterfly-type fenders, freestanding headlights, a square grille, and an external deck-mounted spare. Engines included a 172-cid Ford industrial unit, a Studebaker six, and others.

Auburn 1967-81
Glenn Pray Co.; Auburn, IN
Production: NA
From the maker of the mid '60s Cord 8/10 replicar came the "866," a fiberglass, 3100-pound replica of the 1935-36 Auburn 851/852 Speedster. It was built on a modified Ford Galaxie frame with a 127-inch wheelbase and stan-

1953 Arnolt-MG coupe

1961 Arnolt-Bristol roadster

1948 Beechcraft Plainsman four-door sedan

dard 365-bhp 428-cid Thunderbird V-8. Top speed was 130 mph. Priced at $8450, options were limited to a choice of exterior colors and upholstery materials. It was later joined by the Model 874, a dual-cowl phaeton with no 1930s counterpart.

Aurora 1954
Father Alfred A. Juliano; Branford, CT
Production: 1
This one-off safety prototype was built at a cost of $30,000. Mounted on a 1954 Buick Roadmaster chassis, it featured a fiberglass body, transparent plastic roof, and forward-raked bubble windshield.

Auto Cub 1956
Randall Products; Hampton, NH
Production: NA
Auto Cub was a single-passenger, tiller-steered runabout with an overall length of just 51 inches. It weighed 115 pounds, and its rear-mounted 1.6-bhp Briggs & Stratton or Clinton engine could push it along at up to 15 mph while getting 75 mpg. It was priced at $169.50, and was a companion to the Daytona (*see entry*).

Autoette 1952-57
Autoette Electric Car Co.; Long Beach, CA
Production: NA
This small, steel-bodied, two-passenger three-wheeler (single wheel at the front) was available in three versions. All carried a 24-volt DC electric motor powered by four heavy-duty six-volt batteries. Prices ranged from $775 to $950.

Bassons Star 1956
Bassons Industries Corp.; Bronx, NY
Production: NA
An open, three-wheeled (single wheel at the front), two-passenger delivery-service car, the Star had a fiberglass body and single-cylinder German J.L.O. two-cycle engine producing 10 bhp. It was 33 inches high, 49 inches wide, 124 inches long, and weighed 400 pounds. Maximum cruising speed was 40 mph; top speed 70. It was advertised at $1000. Bassons also showed the Stationette, an enclosed fiberglass-bodied delivery van based on an earlier wood-body model designed by James V. Martin (*see* Martinette).

Baymont 1955
Baymont Co.; Redwood City, CA
Production: NA
Baymont's Suburban Model 240 was basically a two-passenger electric golf cart modified for local running on city streets. It boasted a top speed of 20 mph, and a range of 60 miles.

Bearcat 1956
American Buckboard Corp.; Los Angeles, CA
Production: NA
Not at all like its Stutz namesake, this unusual five-wheeled vehicle had a rear-mounted fifth wheel that was chain-driven by a two-cylinder engine. With a wheelbase of 70 inches and an overall length of 120 inches, it was claimed to get 50 mpg. Cost: $1000

Beechcraft Plainsman 1948
Beech Aircraft Co.; Wichita, KS
Production: 1
This one-off prototype had a four-cylinder Franklin air-cooled engine that drove an electric generator, which in turn powered four electric motors—one at each wheel. It had a large six-passenger body and all-independent air suspension with air-filled shocks at each wheel. Though its price was projected at $5000, production models would likely have cost more.

Bergermobile 1948
Berger Air-Turbine Car Co.; Mount Vernon, NY
Production: 1
The Bergermobile started life as a Chevrolet. The engine

1974 Bricklin SV-1 coupe

was replaced by a 30-gallon air tank and Ingersoll-Rand compressed-air turbine engine. A 24-volt storage battery supplied electrical power to drive the turbine and run the car's electrical equipment.

Blackhawk 1929-30
Stutz Motor Car Co.; Indianapolis, IN
Production: 1929: 1310; 1930: 280
Stutz's companion make was derived from the parent company's 1928 Model BB. It was built on a 127½-inch wheelbase and offered with open and closed body styles. The four-door sedan sold for $2395. An 85-bhp overhead-cam six was initially available, followed by a 90-bhp Continental L-head eight. Curb weight was nearly two tons, so performance was leisurely.

B.M.C. 1952
British Motor Car Co.; San Francisco, CA
Production: NA
This version of B.M.C. had no connection with British Motor Corporation. Its fiberglass-bodied two-seater was designed around the engine and chassis of a Singer 1500, built by the Rootes Group in England. Plans were to produce 400 units a year, but the venture folded after a few months.

Bobbi-Kar 1945-47
Bobbi Motor Car Corp.; San Diego, CA
Production: NA
A two-passenger roadster with a four-cylinder, 25-horsepower engine, the Bobbi-Kar had a wheelbase of 80 inches and an overall length of 132 inches. Projected price was $500. (*Also see* Keller)

Bocar 1958-60
Bocar Racing Cars, Inc.; Denver, CO
Production: Less than 100
Though occasionally seen on the street, these were sports cars built primarily for racing. The XP-4 had a 90-inch wheelbase, tubular frame, and a Pontiac 370 or Chevrolet 283 V-8; the latter engine was coaxed to an alleged 350 horsepower in 1959. The later XP-5, an evolution of the XP-4, had sleek, aerodynamic lines and a price of $11,000. It was followed by the XP-6, with a Supercharged Chevy 283 with GMC blower claimed to produce 400 horsepower. It was priced at $11,700, weighed 2300 pounds, had a wheelbase of 104 inches, and could top 135 mph.

Bolide 1969-70
Bolide Motor Car Corp.; Huntington, NY
Production: NA
Bolide's Can-Am 2 was a midengine, fiberglass-bodied car that rode a 105-inch wheelbase and used 351-cid Ford power. It was based on the Can-Am 1 prototype shown at the 1969 New York Auto Show and was expected to enter production for $3500. Also offered was an XJ002 two-passenger sports car with four-wheel-drive and a Jeep V-6 engine. Both were the work of Andrew J. Griffith, Jr., who was involved with the Griffith (*see entry*).

Brewster 1934-36
Springfield Manufacturing Co.; Springfield, MA
Production: approximately 300
An attempt to salvage the Brewster coachbuilding company resulted in open and closed bodies on contemporary Ford, Buick, and other chassis. However, the venture was killed by steep prices that started at $3000.

Bricklin 1974-75
Bricklin Vehicle Corp. (Malcolm Bricklin);
St. John, New Brunswick, Canada
Production: 2897
The "Safety sports car," designated SV-1, was a two-seat, fiberglass-bodied coupe with gullwing doors, large impact-resistant front bumper, and wedgelike styling. A grainy paint finish resulted from the color being impregnated into the outer acrylic shell. It was first powered by

a 220-bhp AMC 360 V-8; later a 175-bhp Ford 351. Suspension was basically that of the AMC Javelin. Prices ranged from $7490 to $9775, though each car may have cost at least $15,000 to build. The SV-1 was claimed to exceed all existing crash standards. Although marketed as a safety car, the Bricklin was really seen as a competitor for the Chevrolet Corvette and Datsun Z. Quality problems from both lack of engineering development and manufacturing difficulties sealed the fate of the underfinanced automaker. Malcolm Bricklin went on to import the Yugo from Yugoslavia and more recently has been attempting to import cars from China.

Brogan 1946-c.52
B & B Specialty Co.; Rossmoyne, OH
Production: NA
The first model was a two-seat three-wheeler (single wheel in front) with a 10-bhp rear-mounted air-cooled twin. With a total weight of 450 pounds, the top speed was 45 mph with claimed 65-mpg fuel economy. The later Broganette model was smaller than the first, delivering 85 mpg but a top speed of barely 40 mph. The Brogan name was phased out in 1951, when a revised Broganette was built that moved its single wheel to the rear. This car was 10 feet long and 52 inches wide, delivering a top speed of 50 mph while getting 55-60 mpg. The price was $550. Some 1947 models were sold under the name B&B Three Wheel.

Buckaroo 1957
Manufacturer unknown; Cleveland, OH
Production: NA
Little is known about the Buckaroo, but it was a very small car with a top speed of only 18 mph that sold for about $400.

Buckboard 1956
Don Bruce; Bronx, NY
Production: 1 show car; additional examples unlikely
With a name like Buckboard, it had to be good—if, that is, any were actually sold. This wood-bodied cycle car was powered by an Ariel "Square-4" motorcycle engine, mounted amidships on a Renault 4CV frame. It had a 94-inch wheelbase and an overall length of 143 inches. Curb weight was 738 pounds, top speed 90+ mph. While production is doubtful, construction plans were available for do-it-yourselfers.

1946 Californian convertible

Bugetta c.1968-?
Bugetta, Inc.; Costa Mesa, CA
Production: NA
Bugetta was a fiberglass-bodied two/four-passenger open design with a midengine Ford 302-cid V-8. Its $3695 starting price included fiberglass and fabric tops. The same firm also made off-road vehicles.

Californian 1945-46
California Motor Car Co.; Los Angeles, CA
Production: NA
Three-wheel convertible with 58-bhp engine boasted a top speed of 100 mph with 40-mpg economy. The prototype was built by former race driver Frank Curtis, and was a predecessor of the Davis (*see entry*).

Chadwick 1960
Chadwick Engineering Works; Pottstown, PA
Production: NA
Chadwick was an open car only 87 inches long on a 58-inch wheelbase, which contributed to its overall weight of just 680 pounds. It was powered by a single-cylinder 13-bhp air-cooled BMW motorcycle engine connected to a four-speed BMW transmission with enclosed chain drive. Features included a tubular chassis, independent front suspension, quarter-elliptic rear leaf springs, and four-wheel hydraulic brakes.

Charles Town-About 1958-59
Stinson Aircraft Tool & Engineering Corp.;
San Diego, CA
Production: NA
Electric conversion of a VW Karmann-Ghia with DeSoto fins and taillights. A 3.2-bhp motor was used at each rear wheel; top speed was 58 mph, range 77 miles. A utility model with protruding cargo box was called Van-About.

Chicagoan 1952-54
Triplex Industries, Ltd.; Blue Island, IL
Production: 15 (est.)
Two-passenger fiberglass sports car with six-cylinder Willys engine seemingly got a name change to Triplex around 1954.

CitiCar 1974-76
Sebring Vanguard, Corp.; Sebring, FL
Production: 2225
Small, two-seat runabout with triangular-shaped body made of Cycolac ABS plastic on a wheelbase of 65½ inches and an overall length of 94 inches. Eight General electric six-volt batteries wired in sequence provided six net horsepower. Initial factory price was $2988. It was succeeded by the Comute-Car.

Clenet 1976-86
Clenet Coachworks; Santa Barbara, CA (to 1982) and Carpinteria, CA (from 1985)
Production: NA, but limited
French-born AMC stylist and industry consultant Alain Clenet's entry into the "neoclassic" market appeared as a prototype first shown at the '76 Los Angeles Auto Expo. Several orders were taken for the $24,500 two-seat, steel-bodied convertible. Series I blended a basic MG Midget cabin with a 351-cid V-8 on a Lincoln Continental Mark IV chassis. The longer four-passenger Series II convertible—built around a Volkswagen Super Beetle cowl and 302-cid Ford V-8—debuted in mid '79. The firm closed during 1982, but was revived in '85 by former Clenet employee Alfred DiMora. The renewed Series II ($98,000) was accompanied by the two-seat Series III "Asha" with fixed ($78,500) or folding ($82,500) top. The 118-inch wheelbase Series IV Sportster announced for 1988 (but not built) was an effort to revive the original Clenet concept but with more amenities.

Colt 1958
Colt Manufacturing Co.; Milwaukee, WI, or Colt Motors Corp.; Boston, MA
Production: NA
Fiberglass-bodied, two-passenger car weighed about 700 pounds. It was powered by an air-cooled 23-cid Wisconsin single-cylinder engine that provided a top speed of 50 mph. It was claimed to get 60 mpg with its standard automatic transmission. Price: $995

Comet (i) c.1946-48
General Developing Co.; Ridgewood, NY
Production: NA
Comet was a 114-inch-long three-wheeler (the single wheel mounted at the front) with a tubular frame, a plastic body, and a 4.5-bhp rear-mounted engine. It was claimed to get 100 mpg.

Comet (ii) 1951-55
Comet Manufacturing Co.; Sacramento, CA
Production: NA
The Comet name later appeared on a two-seat roadster, available as a kit or fully assembled. It was offered with a six-horsepower engine, automatic transmission, heavy-duty brakes, and oversized balloon tires. It was said to reach 40 mph and get 60 mpg. The manufacturer (whose bread and butter was micro-midget race cars) claimed running costs of 50 cents per week.

Continental 1933-34
Continental Automobile Co.; Detroit, MI
Production: less than 4200
Four- and six-cylinder cars were produced by the famed engine company. They were based on DeVaux body styles. Fours rode a 101.5-inch wheelbase, with prices starting at $335; Beacon Six and Ace Big Six had 65- and 85-bhp engines and 107- and 114-inch wheelbases.

Convaircar 1941-48
Consolidated-Vultee Aircraft Corp.; San Diego, CA
Production: NA
Car/airplane powered for the road by a 26.5-horsepower Crosley engine; for flight by a 190-bhp Lycoming. It had a four-seat fiberglass body and a 34½-foot wingspan; the wings were attached to the roof at three points. It was known as the Hall Flying Auto by 1950.

Corbin; c 2000-2002
Corbin Motors; Hollister, CA
Production: less than 300
The Sparrow was an electric, single-seat commuter car. With only three wheels, it was licensed as a motorcycle, though it had fully enclosed plastic body. Top speed was around 70 mph. The initial price was $13,900, but rose to around $17,000. Mechanical and financial problems forced the company into bankruptcy, but the design was bought by an Ohio firm and Sparrow returned in 2006 as the NmG (*see entry*)

Cord 1964-66; 1968-70
Cord Automobile Co.; Tulsa, OK
Sports Automobile Manufacturing Co.; Mannford, OK
Production: approximately 100
Front-wheel-drive (with Corvair drivetrain) replicar revival of the 1936-37 Cord 810/812, was just 80 percent of the original's size, and thus named Cord 8/10. It was styled by Gordon Buehrig, who had worked on the original. The car was redesigned in rear-drive form by a new manufacturer in 1968; it got a Ford 302-cid V-8 as standard, with an optional Chrysler 440-cid Magnum V-8.

Cortez c.1947-c.50
North American Motors; Dallas, TX
Production: NA
Full-size car intended for volume sale at $1000 was designed by Lincoln-Zephyr designer John Tjaarda.

Crofton 1959-61
Crofton Marine Engine Co.; San Diego, CA
Production: approximately 200
Jeep-style vehicle with Crosley engine. Had a 63-inch wheelbase and an overall length of 106 inches. The base price was $1350, but a "Brawny Kit" for an additional $450 brought a six-speed transmission, limited-slip differential, crash pan, deluxe seats, and upsize tires.

1980 Clenet Series II convertible coupe

Cubster 1949
Osborn Wheel Co.; Doylestown, PA
Production: NA
The "racing" chassis and a 6.6-horsepower engine sold for $299.50, but there was a Cubster body available at extra cost. The two-passenger, fenderless roadster had a top speed of 35 mph.

Cumberford 1982-84
Cumberfor;, Stanford, CT and Austin, TX
Production: NA
The Martinique featured a aluminum and wood veneer roadster body in a 1930s-European style. The chassis was cast aluminum and used Citroën hydropneumatic suspension. It was powered by a BMW six. Lack of finances stopped production after just a few copies.

Cunningham (i) 1907-33
James Cunningham and Sons Co.; Rochester, NY
Production: NA, but limited
A maker of hearses and ambulances, Cunningham also sold open- and closed-model luxury cars. Wheelbases of 132 and 142 inches were offered. A 355-cid V-8 was introduced in 1916. Rated at 90-110 bhp, it was one of the most powerful American engines of the teens and '20s. Performance and rakish styling made Cunninghams popular with Hollywood stars on the West Coast, while conservative East Coast buyers appreciated the car's reliability and quality construction. Unfortunately, prices that reached $9000 discouraged Depression-era buyers, and the firm returned to coachbuilding after 1933.

Cunningham (ii) 1953-55
B.S. Cunningham Co.; West Palm Beach, FL

1953 Cunningham C-3 coupe

1948 Davis coupe

Production: 27 (C-3 model)
Grand-touring production cars evolved from sportsman Briggs Cunningham's fleet C-1 and C2-R in order to qualify the Le Mans racers as "production cars"—and fend off scrutiny from the IRS. They were designed by Giovanni Michelotti, built by Vignale of Italy on a Cunningham chassis. Power came from a Chrysler 331-cid V-8 rated at 220-235 bhp. Prices ranged from $9000 to $11,422. Though Cunningham could sell more C-3s than he could build, production halted in 1955 when the IRS no longer allowed Cunningham's racing-related costs to serve as business deductions.

Curtis-Wright Air-Car 1959-60
Curtis-Wright Corporation; South Bend, IN
Production: NA
Wheelless, four-passenger vehicle traveled 6-12 inches above land or water on a cushion of low-pressure air, and had a claimed top speed of 60 mph. Planned versions included Air-Bus and Air-Car pickups and trucks.

Cushman 1945-
Cushman Motor Works; Lincoln, NE
Production: NA
Shopper car from the manufacturer of motor scooters and golf carts had a one-cylinder, air-cooled engine; electric models were occasionally available as well. The Town & Fairway model, c. 1969, could be converted from a four-passenger minicar to a golf cart or carryall.

Custer 1959-60
Custer Specialty Co.; Dayton, OH
Production: NA
Two-passenger "buckboard" vehicle was offered with a Custer Special electric motor or a six-horsepower gas engine. Top speed was 18 mph in electric versions, 40 mph in gas models. Custer had offered cars in 1898 or '99 and from 1920 to '46. The company abandoned cars for good after 1960.

Darrin 1946-47
Howard A. "Dutch" Darrin/Lehman Brothers;
New York, NY
Production: 1
This fiberglass-bodied, five-seat convertible from noted prewar designer of custom coachwork rode a 115-inch wheelbase. It was powered by a 100-bhp 226-cid Kaiser six. An elaborate hydraulic system powered the top, front seat, and jacking and hood-raising mechanisms. Sadly, the sole prototype was destroyed by flood some years later.

Davis 1947-49
Davis Motor Co.; Van Nuys, CA
Production: 17
This wide three-wheeler had a single four-passenger bench seat. It was based on the Californian (*see entry*). Early examples had 46-bhp Hercules four-cylinder engines, but later models got a Continental four. Widely read *Mechanix Illustrated* writer Tom McCahill tested a

Davis and declared it "in a class by itself for agility and ease of handling plus good looks." He noted, "It's one car you can actually park on dime. The car is 15 feet 8 inches long and you can park in a space only two inches longer than its overall size." When the enterprise collapsed, owner Glen Gordon "Gary" Davis was convicted of fraud.

Daytona 1956
Randall Products; Hampton, NH
Production: NA
Rich man's version of the Auto Cub (*see entry*) was a two-passenger runabout that was 72 inches long and weighed 235 pounds. It had a steel chassis with Formica body panels. Power came from a rear-mounted two-horsepower Briggs & Stratton engine providing a top speed of 18 mph and up to 75 mpg.

Debonnaire 1955
Replac Corp.; Euclid, OH
Production: NA
It's unclear whether this was a complete car or just a kit. Contemporary accounts price it (with top) at about $1800. The fiberglass body was designed to fit the '41-48 Ford platform.

Delcar 1947-49
American Motors, Inc.; Troy, NY
Production: NA
Delcar specialized in small delivery trucks, but at least one boxy Delcar station wagon was built. Its four-cylinder engine was mounted beneath the front floor. It claimed room for six, despite a short 60-inch wheelbase and 102-inch overall length.

Del Mar 1949
Del Mar Motors, Inc.; San Diego, CA
Production: less than 10 (est.)
Only prototypes exist of this 100-104-inch-wheelbase subcompact. The Hillman-like bodies were made of aluminum, plastic, and steel, and the drivetrain consisted of a 160-cid 63-bhp Continental four and Warner three-speed transmission. It had a claimed 80 mph top speed and 30 mpg. Most had transverse leaf springs front and rear; a few had semi-elliptic rear springs. The planned price was $1200.

Detroit Electric 1907-38
Detroit Electric Car Co.; Detroit, MI
Production: Several hundred (approximately)
Perhaps the best-known and most-successful American electric car was noted for its tall, glassy "china cabinet" bodies, but '30s cars could be had with false fronts that gave Detroits a contemporary look. Cars built on 100- and 112-inch-wheelbases were offered between 1930 and 1935. Innovations included safety glass, balloon tires, and four-wheel brakes, all of which were featured on '30s versions.

Detroiter 1953
Detroit Accessories Co.; St. Clair Shores, MI
Production: NA, but likely minuscule
Fiberglass-bodied convertible conceived by Raymond Russell (*see* Gadabout) was built on a 115-inch Ford or shortened Cadillac chassis. It was powered by a Ford drivetrain, with a 110-bhp 239.4-cid flathead V-8.

DeVaux 1931-32
DeVaux-Hall Motors; Grand Rapids, MI and Oakland, CA
Production: 1931: 4315; 1932-33: 1239
Norman DeVaux had once been Chevrolet's effective West Coast distributor. DeVaux decided to build his own car at the worst possible time. Even though the DeVaux was an attractive car with good performance and features for the price, the company failed in the tough Depression market. The 1931 Model 6-75 had a 113-inch wheelbase and 70-bhp 214.7-cid Continental L-head six, and carried prices of $645-$885. The 1932 Model 6-80 was slightly more expensive, and was marketed as the Continental DeVaux. For 1933, it was just Continental (*see entry*). Norman DeVaux went on to become Hupmobile's general manager and convinced that company to build the Hupmobile Skylark using body dies from the late Cord 810/812.

Devin 1954-64
Devin Motors, Inc. (Bill Devin & Malcolm MacGregor); El Monte, CA
Production: 15 (SS model)
These high-performance, fiberglass-bodied sports cars

1949 Del Mar convertible coupe

1957 Devin SS roadster

were sold fully assembled (few actually built) and as kits (hundreds sold). The original body mold was pulled from an aluminum Scaglietti design mounted on an Ermini 1100 chassis; the body was later modified to fit Malcolm MacGregor's state-of-the-art steel-tube frame, with de Dion rear suspension and all-disc brakes. The drivetrain was a stock Corvette 283 V-8 and Borg-Warner T-10 four-speed manual transmission. Thanks to low weight, they were quick: 0-60 mph in 4.8 seconds; 0-100 in 12 seconds. The 1958 Devin D had the same body but with a VW Beetle powertrain, and the later Devin C was similar but with a Chevy Corvair powertrain; these were not so quick.

Diehlmobile 1962-64
H.L. Diehl, Co.; South Willington, CT
Production: NA
The tiny three-wheeler weighed 225 pounds, and could be folded up and carried in the trunk of a normal car. Powered by a three-bhp Briggs & Stratton engine, it was priced at $299.50.

Die Valkyrie 1952
Brooks Stevens Design Assoc.; Milwaukee, WI, and Spohn Carosserie, Ravensburg, West Germany
Production: 1
Special-order car on contemporary Cadillac chassis was commissioned by a Cleveland syndicate. One model was manufactured; it was shown at the 1952 Paris Salon.

Doble 1924-31
Doble Steam Motors, Corp. (Abner Doble); Emeryville, CA
Production: 26
Luxurious, technically sophisticated steam cars wearing a variety of body styles, most supplied by Murphy. Power came from a 125-bhp 213-cid four-cylinder engine, with automatic-boiler ignition system. They had a 75 mph cruising speed, a 100 mph top speed, and cost up to $12,000—a huge sum in late '20s dollars.

Doray 1950
Doray, Inc.; Miami Springs, FL
Production: NA, production beyond prototype stage unlikely
This steel-bodied three-seat roadster was based on the contemporary Willys Jeepster chassis, with styling similar to the Cord 810/812. Front fenders were hinged to allow wheel turning clearance. Power came from F- and L-head Willys engines that gave mediocre performance at best, and the rock-hard Jeepster suspension made for a rugged ride.

Dow Electric 1960
Dow Testing Laboratory, Inc. (Douglas Dow); Detroit, MI
Production: none
Two-passenger electric minicar weighed 447 pounds and was 74 inches long. It was powered by two 0.3-horsepower motors driven by three 12-volt and four 24-volt batteries providing a top speed of 15-20 mph and a range of 30 miles. The projected price was $500-$800, but no backers could be found.

1931 DeVaux four-door sedan

1931 Doble Series E roadster

1952 Die Valkyrie convertible coupe

1957 Dual Ghia convertible coupe

Dual-Ghia 1956-63
Dual Motors Corp. (Eugene Casaroll); Detroit, MI
Production: 1956-58: 117; 1961-63: 26
Italo-American GT was inspired by the 1952 Dodge Firearrow show car styled by Virgil Exner and built by Ghia. A stock Dodge chassis was modified by Ghia's Giovanni Savonuzzi. Wheelbase was 115 inches with a Hudson-like step-down floor. It was powered by a 315-cid Dodge Red Ram V-8 rated at 230, 260, and 285 bhp, teamed with floorshift PowerFlite automatic. The initial price was $7650. The design was revised for 1960 as a sleek, glassy semifastback coupe called L6.4. That version had a purpose-designed chassis and fewer stock Chrysler parts, and was powered by a Chrysler 325-bhp wedgehead 383-cid V-8. By this time, the price had risen to $15,000. Casaroll's death in the late 1960s scuttled a planned third generation.

Duesenberg (ii) 1966
Duesenberg Corp. ("Fritz" Duesenberg); Indianapolis, IN
Production: 1
A Duesenberg revival with Virgil Exner-inspired neoclassic styling. It was a 5700-pound, 2345-inch long prototype built by Ghia on 137.5-inch wheelbase. Powe came from a Chrysler 440-cid V-8. The announced price was $19,500. Stillborn were a massive brougham sedan with center-opening doors, plus a limousine and a convertible sedan.

Duesenberg (iii) 1970-75
Duesenberg Co.; Gardena and Inglewood, CA
Production: NA
Another Duesie revival attempt, this one a $24,500 replica of the short-wheelbase SJ, but on a 128-inch wheelbase. It tipped the scales at 3600 pounds. Automatic transmission was standard, with a four-speed manual optional; both were coupled to a Chrysler 383 V-8 with a claimed 500 bhp. The firm moved from Gardena to Inglewood in 1974, and the already-steep price was hiked to $41,500 while the engine became a detoxed 440 V-8 rated at 215 net bhp.

Duesenberg (iv) 1979
Duesenberg Brothers Co. (Harlan & Kenneth Duesenberg and Robert Peterson);
Mundelein and Evanston, IL
Production: 1
Yet another Duesie revival, this one based on a thinly disguised Cadillac Fleetwood Brougham with the same 133-inch wheelbase and 195-bhp (net) fuel-injected 425-cid V-8. It carried a projected price of $100,000, which may explain why only one was produced.

DuPont 1920-32
duPont Motors, Inc. (E. Paul duPont); Springfield, MA
Production: less than 100
The Model G featured a 144-inch wheelbase, a 140-bhp Continental side-valve straight eight engine, and bodywork by Merrimac; a few were also bodied by Waterhouse and Derham. E. Paul duPont was a member of the famous duPont family, but the shortlived automobile company was never connected with E.I. du Pont de Nemours and Company. The cars were expensive and glamorous. A four-passenger speedster raced at LeMans, but failed to finish.

Durant 1921-32
Durant Motors of America (William Crapo Durant);
Detroit, MI
Production: 1930: 21,440; 1931: 7229; 1932: 1135
Billy Durant founded General Motors and lost control of the corporation twice. After the second ousting, he founded Durant Motors which he set up to feature multiple brands similar to General Motors. Durant had some success in the early 1920s, but that was short-lived and the company was in steep decline by 1929. Only the Durant car was left by '30. That year, a half-dozen models were built with a 112-inch wheelbase and 58-70-bhp Continental six-cylinder engines. In 1931, the remaining four models were priced between $695-$775. That was cut to just a pair of models for 1932 (the 621 and 622) with a 71-bhp Continental engine and a starting price of $700. The company closed its doors that year, but continued to sell cars in Canada under the Frontenac name through 1933.

Dymaxion 1933-34
Buckminster Fuller; Bridgeport, CT
Production: 3
Inventor Buckminster Fuller, famous for the geodesic dome and Dymaxion house, built three cars in the early 1930s. Lightweight and aerodynamic, they were claimed to be capable of 120 mph and 40 mpg. A Ford V-8 applied

1966 Duesenberg four-door sedan

1930 DuPont Model G town car

power to the front wheels and a single rear wheel steered. A fatal accident on a demonstration run made it difficult to obtain financing.

Edwards 1953-55
Edwards Engineering Co. (Sterling H. Edwards); San Francisco, CA
Production: 5
Edwards America was a slabsided convertible built on a Mercury station wagon chassis. One car had a 303.7-cid Oldsmobile V-8; two had 205-bhp Lincoln engines; the three remaining cars carried 210-bhp Cadillac V-8s. High prices ($8000 by 1955) and factory setup costs prevented volume production.

Elcar 1915-31
Elcar Motor Company; Elkhart, IN
Production: 1930: 900; 1931: 500, including taxis
Thirty-two models in four series were offered in 1930. The Model 75 had a 117-inch wheelbase and was powered by a 61-bhp Lycoming six. The Model 95/96 rode a 123-inch wheelbase and had a 90-bhp Lycoming eight. The Model 130 sat on a 130-inch wheelbase and was fitted with a 140-bhp Continental straight eight. The 1931 Model 100 had a 100-bhp Lycoming straight eight and wheelbases of 123 or 130 inches. The Model 85 was a revised 75. The Model 140 had a 135-inch wheelbase and low rakish lines that made a big hit at the 1930 New York Auto Show, but it failed to reach production.

Electra 1974-76
Die Mech Corp.; Pelham, NY
Production: NA
The Electra was basically a Fiat 850 Sport Spyder converted to electric operation, with 10 horsepower from triple motors. Heavy batteries increased weight from Fiat's 1620 to more than 3000 pounds, resulting in a range of about 40 miles.

Electra King 1961-c.81
B & Z Electric Car Co.; Long Beach, CA
Production: NA
These tall, two-passenger, fiberglass-bodied electric cars were available in three- or four-wheeled models that were usually powered by five six-volt batteries in series, though sometimes by 24-, 30-, and 36-volt systems. The 1970s brought a choice of four motors producing from one to 3.5 bhp, resulting in top speeds of 16-29 mph and ranges from 18 to 36 miles. For electric cars they were light, tipping the scales at just 675 pounds.

Electricar 1950-c.66
Boulevard Machine Works; North Hollywood, CA
Production: NA
Small electric runabouts were offered in three versions. The two-seat Boulevard was 106 inches long, with four ⅙-bhp electric motors, one driving each wheel. The single-seat Cutie had two such motors, one in front and one in back; top speed 25 mph. The Cutie Junior had but one motor giving a top speed of 10 mph.

Electric Shopper 1956-?
Electric Car Co.; Long Beach, CA
Production: NA
This three-wheeled, battery-powered shopping car had a fiberglass body; it was 86 inches long with a 61-inch wheelbase. Powered by a 1.5-bhp 24-volt DC series-wound motor, it had a top speed of 18 mph and a range of 30-35 miles. It was priced at $945, though metal-bodied models were available at about $750.

Electrobile 1951
Manufacturer unknown; probable Chicago location
Production: NA, but doubtful
Three-wheel runabout with a fiberglass body molded over an aluminum framework. A high-speed DC motor and built-in charger gave a range of 25-35 miles. The proposed price was $350, but only sketches of the car were shown; prototype may not have been built.

Electro Master 1962-64(?)
Nepa Manufacturing Co.; Pasadena, CA
Production: NA
Fiberglass-bodied shopping car was powered by a two-bhp motor connected to six six-volt batteries, which gave a top speed of 20 mph and a range of 40 miles. It weighed 680 pounds. Production may have continued past 1964.

Electronic 1955
Electronic Motor Car Corp.; Salt Lake City, UT
Production: 1
An innovative hybrid-power car with gasoline or diesel

1931 Durant coupe

1954 Edwards America hardtop coupe

engine charging an 80-cell battery pack connected to "Dual-Torque" electric motor within the rear axle housing that was far ahead of its time. "Electro-Magnetic Differential" aimed to provide limited-slip effect. Proposed were sedan, station wagon, panel truck, and sports car body styles, all on a 110-inch wheelbase; though, sadly, none materialized.

El Morocco 1956-57
Rueben Allenden; Detroit, MI
Production: approximately 30
A styling conversion that brought Cadillac cues to contemporary Chevrolet convertibles and two- and four-door hardtops. It used altered bumpers, side trim, and fins.

Erskine 1927-30
Studebaker Corp.; South Bend, IN
Production: 22,371
This six-cylinder companion make for Studebaker was named for company president Albert R. Erskine. The final 1930 Model 53 was offered in nine variations, all powered by a 205.3-cid L-head six with 70 bhp.

Fergus 1949
Fergus Motors, Inc.; New York, NY
Production: Prototype stage only
Followup to this firm's 1915-22 attempt to become an automaker was based on a restyled Austin A40 patterned after the relatively uncommon Austin A40 Sports.

Ferrer 1966
Ferrer Motors Corp.; Miami, FL
Production: NA
A steel-reinforced fiberglass body on a VW Beetle chassis carried styling that mimicked contemporary Ford GT endurance racers. It had an overall length of 158 inches, a width of 60 inches, and a height of 42 inches. The basic kit sold for $990; a deluxe kit cost $1750; and a fully assembled version was $2950 with a 50-bhp engine, or $3800 with a reworked 70-bhp VW flat four. The standard model claimed a 90-mph top speed, 0-60 mph in 12.5 seconds, and 29 mpg at a steady 68 mph.

Fibersport 1953-54
Fibersport, Inc.; Bloomington, IN
Production: NA
An unusually well-engineered fiberglass sports roadster, it was based on the Crosley Hot Shot platform. The Fibersport was sold as a kit for $650-$750, or fully assembled for $2850. It weighed 1150 pounds and claimed a top speed of 100 mph. Following the demise of Crosley, Fibersport designed its own new tubular frame and adopted Morris Minor gearboxes.

Fina 1953-c.55
Fina, Inc. (Perry Fina); New York, NY
Production: NA
Fina's Sport was available as a convertible or hardtop on a 115-inch-wheelbase Ford chassis. Its 188-inch-long body was made by Vignale of Italy. The standard powerplant was a 210-bhp Cadillac unit (300-bhp engine available at extra cost), though most any Detroit V-8 could be ordered. GM's Dual-Range Hydra-Matic was the sole transmission. It was priced at about $10,000.

Fitch (i) 1949
Sports and Utility Motors, Inc. (John Fitch);
White Plains, NY
Production: NA; single prototype built
Race-and-ride sports-car prototype was a proposed Type A model. Proposed Type B model would have used a Fiat 1100 chassis with a 96-inch wheelbase, a modified Crosley Hot Shot body, and a tweaked flathead Ford V-8/60 with 105 bhp.

Fitch (ii) 1961-69
John Fitch and Co., Inc.; Falls Village, CT
Production: NA
A modified Chevrolet Corvair, called the Fitch GT, was also offered in separate packages, including an engine kit and an appearance package for '65 Corvairs. The Fitch Phoenix, offered for 1966, was a 2150-pound targa-top two-seater with modified 170-bhp Corvair engine good for 0-60 mph in 7.5 seconds and a top speed of 130 mph. The Phoenix body was built by Intermeccanica in Italy. But the planned Phoenix run of 500 units was scuttled because of the expense involved in meeting federal safety standards. As a result, only a prototype was built.

1956 El Morocco convertible coupe

1955-57 Gaylord coupe

Fletcher 1954
Fletcher Aviation Corp.; Rosemead, CA
Production: NA
The Fletcher Flair was a four-wheel-drive Jeeplike vehicle powered by a 1500cc Porsche flat four. It had a wheelbase of 78 inches, and an overall length of 115-126 inches.

Flintridge-Darrin 1957
Flintridge Motor Manufacturing Corp.; Los Angeles, CA
Production: 15 (est.)
A contemporary German DKW sedan with a two-stroke engine and low-slung fiberglass roadster body (from Woodill; *see entry*) styled by Howard "Dutch" Darrin. It was priced at $3195, contrasted with $2275 for the DKW. It was also known as the Flintridge, Darrin-DKW, or Flintridge-DKW.

Ford 1901 Replica 1968
Horseless Carriage Corp.; Ft. Lauderdale, FL
Production: NA, but limited
Sold as a three-quarter scale replica "of the 1901 Ford," though Henry's first production car, the Model A, was not built until 1903. Specs have been lost, though production lasted only a few months.

France Jet 1961
France Jet Motors, Ltd.; New York, NY
Production: NA, but limited
A fiberglass-bodied two-seater priced at $1595 with a 17-cid four-cycle one-cylinder engine. An optional 66-cid 40-bhp twin was available for an additional $250.

Frazen 1951-62
Ray Green, Co.; Toledo, OH
Production: NA, but limited
Powered by 161-cid Henry J flathead six, this fiberglass sports roadster was available fully assembled ($2795 in 1952) and as a kit.

Frick 1955
Bill Frick Motors; Rockville Centre, NY
Production: NA; beyond single prototype unlikely
Ferrari-like coupe, bodied by Vignale of Italy, based on Cadillac running gear. It sat on a 110-inch-wheelbase box-channel chassis of Bill Frick's own design, with conventional independent front suspension and live-axle/leaf-spring rear suspension. Total weight was 3000 pounds. (*See also* Studillac)

Gadabout 1945
Ray Russell; Grosse Pointe, MI
Production: none
This three-seat roadster on an 80-inch wheelbase was a home workshop project from industrial designer Russell. It had a flush-fender duraluminum body over an MG chassis and running gear. Top speed was 50 mph. Crash protection was provided by an unobtrusive bumper-height steel perimeter tube. An 1100-pound curb weight contributed to a claimed 50 mpg. Front- and rear-engine models were planned, but no backer could be found.

Gardner 1916-31
Gardner Motor Car Co.; St. Louis, MO
Production: NA
1930 Models 136 and 140 used Lycoming 70-bhp six- and 90-bhp eight-cylinder engines, respectively; Model 150 had a Lycoming 126-bhp eight. The 1930 Gardner Front-Drive rode a 133-inch wheelbase and was powered by an 80-bhp Continental six. The firm turned to hearses and ambulances in 1931 and folded a year later.

Gaslight 1960-61
Gaslight Motors Corp.; Detroit, MI
Production: NA
A 640-pound replica of a 1902 Rambler, the Gaslight was built on a 77-inch wheelbase and powered by a four-bhp air-cooled single-cylinder engine. Price: $1495. (*See also* Rambler 1902 Replica)

Gaylord 1955-57
Gaylord Cars, Ltd. (Edward & Jim Gaylord); Chicago, IL
Production: 3
Luxury two-seater in retractable hardtop convertible form was styled by Brooks Stevens and executed by Spohn coachworks in Ravensburg, West Germany. It had a purpose-built chassis with conventional suspension, and was powered by a Chrysler hemi-head V-8. Despite weighing nearly two tons, the Hemi provided decent performance: 120 mph top speed, 0-60 in 8 seconds. The target price was $17,500, but the project fell apart following a quality dispute with the body contractor.

Glassic 1966-72; 1972-75
Glassic Industries, Inc. (Jack & Joel Faircloth); West Palm Beach, FL
Glassic Motor Car Co. (Fred Pro); West Palm Beach, FL
Production: NA
Model A-style fiberglass bodywork was mounted on an International Scout chassis with its 94-bhp four; cars built after 1972 used a 210-bhp Ford 302 V-8. Initial price of $3800 grew to $10,000 by 1972. The firm did business as Replicar in 1976-77.

Glasspar 1950-54
Glasspar, Inc. (Bill Tritt); Santa Ana, CA
Production: 200 (est.; number may include kits)
These sleek, two-seat fiberglass-bodied roadsters usually rode a 100-inch wheelbase. They were typically sold as kits, though a few were sold fully assembled for $3000 and up through 1954; kits only afterward. The G-2 model was fitted with a Ford or Mercury flathead or an ohv V-8.

Goff 1956
Charles Goff; Texarkana, TX
Production: NA; a handful, at most
A five-passenger, fiberglass-bodied sports model, it was conceived around a '39 Ford chassis and running gear; other engines and matching top were available at extra charge. It was priced at $600 for a kit, or $1500 for a fully assembled car.

Gordon c.1947-48
H. Gordon Hansen; San Lorenzo, CA
Production: 1
This 3750-pound one-off was dubbed the "Diamond" because of its unusual, diamond-pattern wheel placement: one in front, one in back, and one on either side. The end wheels were 156 inches apart, with side wheels halfway between. Power was supplied by a 100-bhp Ford truck engine, providing a 95-mph top speed.

Griffith 1964-66
Griffith Motors (Jack Griffith); Syoset, NY
Griffith Motor Car Co. (Jack Griffith); Plainview, NY
Production: 285
These 138-inch-long sports cars, dubbed Series 200, consisted of a modified fiberglass body from the British TVR on a purpose-built tubular chassis. Power came from a Ford 289 V-8 that produced 0-60-mph times of less than four seconds. Price was $3995-$4800. The cutoff of TVR body supplies caused a switch to Vetta Ventura (*see entry and* Apollo *entry*). The new $6095 GT model had a body by Intermeccanica of Italy and power from a 235-bhp Plymouth 273 V-8 with standard Torque-Flite automatic or optional four-speed manual transmission. This car continued after 1966 as the Omega (*see entry*) and Intermeccanica.

Henney Kilowatt 1960-c.64
Henney Motor Co. (C. Russell Feldman); Canastota, NY
Production: 100 (max.)
This electric conversion of a Renault Dauphine was powered by a dozen six-volt batteries and a seven-bhp motor. At 2250 pounds, it weighed 750 pounds more than a Dauphine. Top speed was 40 mph; range 40 miles.

Honey Bee 1959
Swift Manufacturing Co.; El Cajon, CA
Production: NA
This tiny, fiberglass-bodied open three-wheeler (single wheel in front) had a teardrop shape and low, rounded nose. It was powered by a rear-mounted, four-cycle Briggs & Stratton 1.5-bhp engine. The same firm also made replicars under the Swift name (*see entry*).

Hoppenstand 1948-49
Hoppenstand Motors, Inc.; Greenville, PA
Production: NA
This two-passenger, aluminum-bodied open economy car was powered by an 8.5-bhp 21.4-cid air-cooled flat twin mounted at the rear of its 90-inch-wheelbase chassis. It had all-independent suspension and standard automatic torque converter. Top speed was 50 mph with claimed 35-mpg economy. Overall length was 162 inches; weight 684 pounds. Base price was $1000.

Hydramotive c.1960
Hydramotive Corp.; Charlotte, NC
Production: 1
A small, diesel-engine car, designed by Durward Willis, it had no transmission, universal joints, driveshaft, differential, axles, or brakes. Though it was intended to be sold for $1200, the plan failed when the company was the focus of a 1961 SEC stock-fraud investigation.

Imp 1949-51
International Motor Products; Glendale, CA
Production: NA
The 1949 Imp prototype featured a rear-mounted 7.5-horsepower Gladden 75 engine and doorless, fiberglass-laminate body on a 63-inch wheelbase. It was 120 inches long, weighed 475 pounds, had a top speed of 35 mph, and was claimed to run 180-240 miles on a three-gallon tank of gas. The 1951 models were 108 inches long and priced at $500.

Jetmobile 1952
Richard Harp; Frederick, MD
Production: NA
This missile-shaped single-seat three-wheeler (single wheel at the front) was made from an aircraft fuel tank. Its rear-mounted 75-bhp Lycoming engine was later swapped for a 60-bhp Ford flathead V-8.

Jomar c.1954-60
Saidell Sports Racing Cars (Ray Saidell); Manchester, NH
Production: NA
A British TVR chassis mated to a specially designed aluminum body, the Jomar was powered by a 71.5-cid British Ford Anglia four-cylinder engine; optional alter-

1966 Griffith coupe

1931 Jordan Model Z Speedway Ace roadster

natives included a supercharged version and at least three Coventry-Climax units. Price: $2995-$4595.

Jordan 1916-31
Jordan Motor Car Co., Inc.; Cleveland, OH
Production: 1930-31: 2851
Jordan is best known for the ads written by founder Ned Jordan. "Somewhere West of Laramie," touting the Playboy roadster, is considered one of the greatest car ads of all time. Great Line 80 (120-inch wheelbase) and Great Line 90 (125-inch wheelbase) were powered by 80-85-bhp Continental straight eights in a variety of body styles priced from $1495-$2295. Series 90 roadsters and sedans rode a 125-inch wheelbase, while a seven-seat limousine and sedan used a 131-inch wheelbase. The Model Z of 1931 rode a 145-inch wheelbase powered by a 114-bhp 318-cid Continental straight eight. The Sportsman sedan and Speedway Ace roadster with aluminum bodywork were said to be capable of 100 mph. Extensive instrumentation included a tachometer, compass, altimeter, and vacuum gauges. Price: $5500. Perhaps 14 Model Zs were built.

Keen Streamliner c.1955-67; c.1968
Charles F. Keen; Madison, WI
Thermal Kinetics Corp.; Rochester, NY
Production: NA
Original version was a shortened 1946-48 Plymouth converted to steam power; follow-up car was a fiberglass-bodied convertible based on the Victress shell also used for the Williams steamer (*see entry*). Cars carried a V-4 engine of unknown origin. Top-speed claims vary from 60 mph to 100 mph.

Keller 1948-50
Keller Motors Corp. (George D. Keller); Huntsville, AL
Production: 18 (est.)
Outgrowth of Bobbi Motor Car Co. (*see* Bobbi-Kar) was slightly longer and more-powerful than the Bobbi-Kar. It was first offered as a wagon (two-door; 2100 pounds) and convertible (three-seats, with front- or rear-mounted engine; 2400 pounds), in two series: Chief models were powered by a 47-bhp 133-cid Hercules engine; Super Chiefs had a 58-bhp 162-cid Continental unit. The company claimed to have a network of 1150 dealers in 1948, but the hoped-for annual production of 150,000 never came close to being achieved, and the firm went bankrupt in 1950.

1968 Keen Streamliner convertible coupe

King Midget 1946-c.69
Midget Motors Supply Co. and Midget Motors Corp. (Claud Dry & Dale Orcutt); Athens, OH
Production: approximately 5000
Tiny, buckboard-type vehicle, first available as a kit only, was sold fully assembled starting in about 1949. A more carlike replacement was offered from 1951 to '57. A third generation arrived in 1957. Two different engines were used; 1946-66 models had 7.3-8.5-bhp single-cylinder Wisconsin units, while those built from 1967 onward had 9.3-12-bhp Kohlers. Overall length ranged from 96 to 117 inches; all models rode a 76.5-inch wheelbase. Weight ranged from 400 to 700 pounds; prices from $350 to $1000 or more. Overall fuel economy was claimed to be 60 mpg.

Kissel 1906-30
Kissel Motor Company; Hartford, WI
Production: 1930: 391
Best known for its Gold Bug speedster that featured cut-down doors, a rear turtle deck, and cycle fenders. The Gold Bug attracted celebrity owners such as Amelia Earhart. The last production year of these finely crafted cars included the Model 6-73 (on a 117-inch wheelbase

1953 King Midget Deluxe roadster

1946 King Midget racer

1948 Kurtis 500 roadster

powered by a 70-bhp six), Model 95 (125-inch wheelbase with a 246 cid eight and 95 bhp) and Model 8-126 (wheelbases of 132 and 139 inches with a 126-bhp 298-cid eight). All wore the White Eagle model name. Prices extended to almost $4000. The company was reorganized in 1931 and went on to produce outboard motors.

Krim-Ghia 1966
Krim Car Import Co.; Detroit, MI
Carrozzeria Ghia; Turin, Italy
Production: NA, but limited
The 1500 GT was a sports coupe powered by an 86-bhp Fiat four. Also offered was a roadster on a Plymouth Barracuda chassis, powered by that car's 245-bhp V-8.

Kurtis 1948-49
Kurtis-Craft (Frank Curtis); Glendale, CA
Production: fewer than 50
The initial version of this 169-inch sports car was built using stock production pieces and a supercharged L-head Studebaker Champion engine. Later models were powered by Ford flathead V-8s or 160-bhp Cadillac V-8s. The firm was purchased by Earl "Madman" Muntz in 1949 (*see* Muntz).

LaFayette 1934-36
Nash Motors; Kenosha, WI
Production: 1934: 5000; 1935: 9400; 1936: 27,860
Nash's lower-priced "junior" make was priced from $585-$715. They rode a 113-inch wheelbase and were powered by a 217.8-cid 75-83-bhp Nash six.

La Saetta 1955
Testaguzza Brothers; Detroit, MI
Production: approximately 15
This fiberglass-bodied two-passenger roadster was powered by a variety of Hudson and Oldsmobile engines, and no two cars were alike. Wheelbases were about 110 inches, with overall length ranging from 200 to 210 inches. A late-1955 partnership with Electronic Motor Corporation of Salt Lake City resulted in a turbo-electric called Electronic.

Lawler Steamobile 1948-50
James H. Lawler; Huntington Park, CA
Production: NA
Originally a steam-powered conversion of a 1938 Hudson Terraplane. Conversions of other cars may have been carried out at nearby South Gate, California.

MK III 1968
Auto Craft Northwest; Portland, OR
Production: NA
This sports car was built to owner specifications, and was available with a midengine 327- or 427-cid Chevy V-8 or rear-engine 164-cid Corvair flat six. It was also available in kit form.

1934 LaFayette two-door touring sedan

1930 Marquette two-door sedan

Marketour 1964
Marketour Electric Cars; Long Beach, CA
Production: NA
In addition to a boxy, two-passenger, three-wheel electric car (single wheel in front), a quarter-ton pickup model was built. They were fitted with six heavy-duty batteries that powered a 36-volt motor. Range was 35-40 miles. The steel body had a removable leatherette-covered top.

Markette 1967-68
Westinghouse Electric Corp.; Pittsburgh, PA
Production: 1
This boxy electric car was 116 inches long and powered by 12 six-volt batteries that comprised about half the car's 1730-pound weight. Projected price was $2000.

Marquette 1929-30
Buick Motor Division, General Motors Corp.; Flint, MI
Production: 35,007
The 1930 lineup of Buick's "junior" edition offered six body styles on a 114-inch wheelbase, all powered by a 67.5-bhp 213-cid enlargement of the contemporary Olds L-head six. Price: about $1000.

1955 Maverick roadster

Marquis 1954
Plasticar; Doylestown, PA
Production: NA
While the prototype of this two-door fastback sports coupe on a 4CV Renault chassis had an aluminum body, the production cars were to be bodied in "plastic," perhaps fiberglass, and priced at $3100.

Mars II 1966-c.70
Electric Fuel Propulsion, Inc.; Ferndale, MI
Production: NA
Electric car based on the Renault 10 body was powered by four 3-volt battery packs, each consisting of five lead-cobalt batteries. These battery packs accounted for 1900 of the car's 4160 pounds. Five-year or 50,000-mile battery life was claimed. Top speed was 68 mph, and 0-40 mph was claimed to take 12 seconds.

Martinette 1954
Martin Development Laboratories (James Vernon Martin); Rochelle Park, NY
Production: NA
Two- and three-passenger, teardrop-shaped three wheelers (single wheel at the rear) were based on the firm's 1948 prototype; one panel delivery was produced in 1955. Power came from a rear-mounted 24-bhp Hercules engine. Price: $1000. The firm was sold to Bassons Industries Corporation in 1955 or '56 (*see* Bassons Star).

Maverick 1953-55
Maverick Motors; Mountain View, CA
Production: approximately 7
A three-passenger car mounted on a Cadillac chassis had

a 122-128-inch wheelbase with an overall length of 16 feet. A sleek fiberglass body was available with one, two, or three doors. The drivetrain consisted of a Cadillac engine with Borg-Warner overdrive transmission.

Mighty Mite 1953
Mid-America Research Corp.; Wheatland, PA
Production: NA
Full-time 4WD car offered in a wide range of body styles designed by Ben F. Gregory. The prototype was fitted with an air-cooled Porsche engine; production models were to have modified Lycoming 65-bhp aircraft engines.

Minicar 1969
Minicars, Inc.; Goleta, CA
Production: 1
This three-passenger car was 108 inches long overall and powered by a Corvair six. Anticipated price: $2500.

Mohs 1967-78
Bruce Baldwin Mohs; Madison, WI
Production: 3 or 4 cars a year
The company dates to 1948 but did not build its first car until 1967. Huge Ostentatienne Opera coupe weighed 5740 pounds and measured 246 inches overall on a 119-inch wheelbase—meaning there was substantial overhang on each end. International Harvester built the chassis to Mohs' specs, and also supplied its 304-cid 193-bhp V-8; a 549-cid V-8 was optional. Instead of regular doors, entry was gained though a large rear "hatch" that extended from roof to bumper. Features included a water-cooled automatic transmission, butane furnace-heater, ¾-inch Ming Dynasty-style carpet, velvet upholstery, and a walnut-covered instrument panel inlaid with 24-karat gold. By the late 1960s, the base price was $19,600, or $25,600 with the 549 V-8. A second model, the Safarikar, was added in 1971. It was a metal-topped dual-cowl phaeton with side-mounted doors that extended outward on rails, and the body was covered in padded Naugahyde. Its initial base price was $14,500.

Mota 1953
Banning Electric Products Corp.; New York, NY
Production: NA
Little is known about the Mota save for that it was a fiberglass-bodied gas/electric hybrid.

Multiplex 1952-54
Multiplex Manufacturing Co.; Berwick, PA
Production: 3
This two-passenger sports car was built on a tubular truss frame and powered by a modified Willys F-head four- (87 hp) or six-cylinder (124 hp) engine.

Mustang 1948
Mustang Engineering Corp.; Seattle, WA
Production: NA
A six-passenger car (two in front, four in back), the Mustang was designed by Lincoln-Mercury service alumnus Roy C. McCarty. Its aluminum body was mounted on a tubular-steel frame. Power was supplied by a rear-mounted 59-bhp Hercules four, which was accessible by a door on the car's left side. Projected price: $1235.

Navajo c.1954
Navajo Motor Car Co.; New York, NY
Production: NA
This three-passenger sports car, visually similar to a Jaguar XK-120, was powered by a tweaked Mercury flathead V-8 rated at 130 hp. It was good for a claimed 7.8-second 0-60-mph run.

NmG 2005-
Myers Motors; Tallmadge, OH
Production: NA
Dana Myers bought the rights to the defunct Corbin Sparrow electric car (*see entry*) and resumed production in Ohio under the name NmG (no more gas). The three-wheeled commuter car was priced under $25,000. Its makers claimed it could accelerate from 0 to 60 mph in 12.5 sec and go 30 miles on a charge. The single seater was 112 inches long.

Nu-Klea 1959-60
Nu-Klea Automobile Corp.; Lansing, MI
Production: NA
This small, two-passenger electric car with a steel chassis and fiberglass body had leaf springs at the rear, and

1952 Multiplex roadster

1930 Oakland Eight roadster

coil springs in front. It was powered by a separate motor at each rear wheel. Range was claimed to be 75-85 miles.

Oakland 1907-31
Oakland-Pontiac Division, General Motors Corp.; Pontiac, MI
Production: 1930: 21,943; 1931: 13,408
Pontiac, a companion make to Oakland, eventually overshadowed its parent. 1930-31 Oaklands rode a 117-inch wheelbase and were offered in a variety of open and closed body types priced from $895-$1055. All were powered by an 85-bhp 250-cid V-8; oversquare cylinder dimensions and 180-degree crankshaft made for rough running.

Olds 1901 Replica 1968
Horseless Carriage Corp.; Fort Lauderdale, FL
Production: NA
Three-quarter-scale replicar of the famed curved-dash Olds.

Omega 1967-68
Suspensions International Corp.; Manhasett, NY
Production: NA
The stillborn '66 Griffith GT (*see* Griffith) was continued in 1967 as the steel-bodied (by Intermeccanica of Turin, Italy) Omega. It was constructed by Holman and Moody of Charlotte, North Carolina. The Griffith's Plymouth V-8 was replaced by a Ford 289 engine and driveline. Base price was $8950. The car continued after 1968 as the Torino, Italia, and IMX, all presumably assembled by Intermeccanica.

1962 Panther roadster

1953 Paxton Phoenix retractable convertible coupe

Panda 1955-56
Small Cars, Inc.; Kansas City, KS
Production: NA
This two-passenger fiberglass-bodied roadster was styled like a child's pedal car, but built on a 70-inch wheelbase. Two engines were offered: a 44-cid Aerojet four and a 67-cid Kohler flat twin (the '55 prototype had a Crosley engine).

Panther 1962-c.63
Panther Automobile Co.; Bedford Hills, NY
Production: NA
This two-passenger fiberglass sports car was built on a 94-inch wheelbase and powered by a Daimler V-8.

Paxton Phoenix 1951-54
Paxton Engineering Co.; Los Angeles, CA
Production: 1
A five-passenger, fiberglass-body car styled by Brooks Stevens, the Paxton Phoenix featured a power-retractable hardtop. Robert Paxton McCulloch initiated the project, but killed it when he realized Phoenix was taking too much money and engineering talent from his profitable chainsaw and supercharger businesses. Steam pioneer Abner Doble did the key development work on a steam engine. Ultimately, a rear-mounted Porsche 1500 was installed to make the prototype a runner. McCulloch owned the car until his death in 1977.

Peerless 1900-32
Peerless Motor Car Corp.; Cleveland, OH
Production: 1930: 3642; 1931: 1249; 1932: 1
A respected luxury make rivaling the best in America offered straight eights with 85-120 bhp on 118-, 125-, 138-inch wheelbases. Peerless closed out its history with the beautiful, aluminum-bodied (by Murphy) V-16 of 1932, of which only one was completed. Peerless' car-making activities were killed by the Depression, and the company moved into brewing.

1932 Peerless V-16 four-door sedan

1948 Playboy retractable convertible coupe

1955 Powell Sport Wagon pickup

Pioneer 1959-c.60
Nic-L-Silver Battery Co.; Santa Ana, CA
Production: NA
A fiberglass-bodied electric car powered by twin motors that drove the rear wheels. It was 157 inches long, had a curb weight of 1800 pounds, and a range of 40-100 miles. It was also known as the Lippencott Pioneer and the Nic-L-Silver.

Playboy 1947-51
Playboy Motor Car Corp.; Buffalo, NY
Production: approximately 90
This three-passenger convertible minicar with folding steel top was powered by a 40-bhp Hercules four (some cars had a Continental engine of similar power) driving through a three-speed Warner Gear automatic transmission. Built on a 90-inch wheelbase, it measured 155 inches overall and weighed 2035 pounds.

Powell 1954-56
Powell Manufacturing Co.; Compton, CA
Production: approximately 2400
Steel-bodied Powell Sport Wagon (the nose panel was fiberglass) rode on a remanufactured Plymouth chassis with 90-bhp engine. Initial price was $998. A pickup truck was styled along similar lines.

Publix 1947-48
Publix Motor Car Co.; Buffalo, NY
Production: NA
Two-passenger three-wheeler (single wheel at the front) offered with a choice of fabric or Plexiglas top. It had an aluminum tube frame, body, and engine that combined for a total weight of just 150-200 pounds. It was claimed to get 70-80 mpg at speeds up to 60 mph.

Pup 1948-49
Pup Motor Car Co.; Spencer, WI
Production: NA
Two wood-bodied versions were offered: an open two-seat roadster with separate fenders and no doors or top, and an enclosed, slab-sided coupe. Engine choices included a 7.5-bhp single-cylinder Briggs & Stratton or a 10-bhp two-cylinder unit. Top speed was claimed to be 35-40 mph while getting 50-60 mpg. Price: $500-$600.

Quantum 1962-63
Quantum Corp.; Rockland, MA
Production: NA
Rebodied Saab weighed just 900 pounds, and was distributed in the U.S. through individual Saab dealers.

Rambler 1902 Replica c.1959-60
American Air Products; Fort Lauderdale, FL
Production: NA
Replica of the 1902 Rambler continued as the Gaslight (*see entry*).

Roadable 1946
Portable Products Corp.; Garland, TX
Production: 1
Three-wheel car/airplane with a single wheel at the front. When airborne, ailerons and elevators were controlled by the steering wheel. A 130-bhp Franklin engine provided a top ground speed of 60 mph. It had a cruising airspeed of 110 mph and a range of 600 miles. Five minutes were needed to convert the vehicle to road use.

Rockefeller Yankee 1953
Rockefeller Sports Car Corp.; Rockville Centre, NY
Production: NA
Four-passenger, fiberglass- and Vibrin-bodied sports car fitted with a Ford engine and driveline. It had a 100-inch wheelbase, an overall length of 14 feet, and a claimed top speed of 100 mph.

Rocket 1948
Hewson Pacific Corp.; Los Angeles, CA
Production: NA
This aluminum-bodied three-passenger car sat on a 106-inch wheelbase with an overall length of 161 inches. Two engines were available: a 65-bhp four or a 95-bhp six; a torque-converter automatic transmission was standard with either engine. It was priced at about $1500.

Rockne 1932-33
Studebaker Corp.; South Bend, IN
Production: 1932: 22,715; 1933: 13,326
Studebaker's less-expensive companion make was named after Notre Dame's legendary football coach, Knute Rockne. Rockne died in a plane crash shortly before the car was introduced. The car was offered in two series

1967 Rowan coupe

priced from $585-$735. The base Model 65 had a 66-bhp 190-cid flathead six and rode a 110-inch wheelbase; it was redesignated the Model 10 for 1933 when horsepower was increased to 70. The Model 75, designed by Studebaker's Barney Roos, had a 72-bhp 205-cid six and rode a 114-inch wheelbase. The Model 75 was dropped after 1932. Financial conditions forced Studebaker to reduce its model range and drop the Rockne make altogether after the 1933 model year.

Rollsmobile 1958-c.61
Starts Manufacturing Co.; Fort Lauderdale, FL
Production: NA
Replicars of the 1901 Olds and "1901" Ford (the first Ford was a 1903 model) were powered by an air-cooled three-bhp Continental engine, claimed to provide a top speed of 30 mph and economy of over 100 mpg.

Rowan 1967-69
Rowan Controller Co.; Westminster, MD and/or Oceanport, NY
Production: NA
This closed electric runabout with Ghia body borrowed some mechanical parts from DeTomaso. Dynamic-braking regenerated power during coasting and deceleration to help provide a range of 200 miles.

Ruger 1968-c.72
Sturm Ruger & Co., Inc.; Southport, CT
Production: NA
Built by the famous gunmaker and inspired by the 4.5-liter Bentley tourer, the Ruger had fiberglass body panels covered with Naugahyde. Powered by a 427-cid Ford V-8, it could do 0-60 mph in 7.7 seconds despite a 3500-pound curb weight. Price: $13,000.

Ruxton 1930
New Era Motors, Inc. (Archie Andrews); New York, NY
Production: approximately 500
A one-year marvel, yet one of the most-beautiful cars of the 1930s. It featured a ground-hugging front-wheel-drive chassis, ultralow hood and fenders, no running boards, and a Continental 85-bhp straight eight. New York stage designer Joseph Urban created a paint scheme featuring eight horizontal bands of complementary colors. Only a handful of show cars sported the rainbow treatment.

1930 Ruxton four-door sedan

Saleen S7 2002-
Saleen; Irvine, CA
Production: NA
Famous for high-performance modified versions of Mustangs and other Ford vehicles since 1984, Saleen unveiled its own supercar in 2002. Similar to Saleen's GT race car, the S7 had a midengine 428-cid V-8 of Saleen design and manufacture that developed 550 horsepower. *Road & Track* timed the $395,000 two-seater at 3.3 seconds for the 0-60-mph sprint. Saleen claimed a top speed of 200 mph. By 2006, the price had gone up to $589,950 and horsepower was 750 bhp thanks to the addition of twin turbos. *Car and Driver* clocked the quarter-mile in 10.9 seconds at 140 mph. By now, Saleen was quoting a 248-mph top speed.

Saviano Scat 1960
Saviano Vehicles, Inc.; Warren, MI
Production: 4
This two-door, four-passenger Jeep-type car weighed 1700 pounds and was built on an 80-inch wheelbase. It was powered by an air-cooled 25-bhp Kohler engine teamed with a Borg-Warner transmission. A steel body covered a rectangular-tube frame. Price: $1395.

Scooter Car 1947
Manufacturer unknown
Production: NA
A two-passenger vehicle available in several forms, including a five-bhp model with no body and angular mud guards.

Seagrave 1960
Seagrave Fire Apparatus Co.; Columbus, OH
Production: 3
This compact car sat on a 93-inch wheelbase and was powered by a four-cylinder Continental engine. Of the three built, two had fiberglass bodies, the third was bodied in aluminum. Projected price: $3000.

Scootmobile c.1946-52
Norman Anderson, Vernon Servoss, Lester Sworthwood; Corunna, MI
Production: NA, but unlikely
This three-wheeler (using airplane wheels; single wheel at the rear) was built from a modified auxiliary aircraft

fuel tank and was equipped with an automatic transmission. Though claimed to be capable of 70 mph, top speed was probably closer to 40. Price: $350.

Skorpion 1952-54
Wilro Co.; Pasadena, CA
Production: NA
A fiberglass sports car available as a kit ($445) or fully assembled ($1200). It was designed to accept several different chassis and engines; the best combination was a Crosley Hot Shot chassis and Ford flathead V-8.

Skyline c.1953
Skyline, Inc.; Jamaica, NY
Production: NA
A safety-minded two-passenger hardtop-convertible that shared its L-head six, chassis, and most lower body panels with the Henry J. Projected price was less than $3000.

Spook Electric 1968
Dynamic Development; Pasadena, CA
Production: NA
This 99-inch-long electric was powered by six six-volt batteries and a 36-volt DC ball-bearing motor connected to the rear wheels by chain drive. A steel and fiberglass body on a steel-channel frame combined for a total weight of 750 pounds.

Star Dust 1953
Grantham Motor Car Co.; Los Angeles, CA
Production: NA
Built on an altered Ford chassis with a 110-inch wheelbase, this 2650-pound car was powered by a Ford engine located five inches lower and 19 inches farther back in the chassis than normal. Estimated price: $3750.

Starlite c.1959-?
Kish Industries, Inc.; Lansing, MI
Production: NA
An electric "sports" model with a 82-inch wheelbase and measuring 148 inches overall. It was a soft-top convertible, though a clear-plastic hardtop was planned. Approximate price: $3000.

Stearns-Knight 1899-1930
F. B. Stearns Co.; Cleveland, OH
Production: NA
The final (1930) model of this luxury car was powered by a 385-cid 127-bhp sleeve-valve straight-eight engine. Stearns started building sleeve-valve engines in 1911. John North Willys bought Stearns in 1925 as a luxury companion to his popular Willys-Knight (*see* Willys). Eight body styles were offered, including sedans and a cabriolet roadster. Wheelbases were 137 and 145 inches; base price was $5000. Production stopped in December 1929, but cars were sold into 1930.

Storm 1954
Sports Car Development Corp.; Detroit, MI
Production: NA
Little is known about the Storm aside from the fact it had a two-passenger Bertone body and a 250-bhp Dodge V-8.

Stout Project Y 1946
Kaiser-Frazer, Corp.; Detroit, MI
Production: 1
The brainchild of inventor/engineer William B. Stout, who developed the Scarab in 1936, the Project Y had a sleek fiberglass body, Mercury V-8, and 74-inch-wide rear seat. Production expense and a probable $10,000 selling price quickly killed the project.

Stout Scarab 1936
Stout Engineering Laboratories; Detroit, MI
Production: 9
Rear-engine streamliner had a spacious interior that has been compared to today's minivans. A Ford V-8 provided the power.

Stuart 1962
Stuart Motors; Kalamazoo, MI
Production: 1
This two-passenger, fiberglass-bodied electric car was powered by eight six-volt batteries and a four-bhp motor, which provided a 40-mile range at 35 mph. The car was 115 inches long, 64 inches wide, and 56 inches high. It was offered in two forms: a passenger model for $1600, and a commercial version for $1500.

1952 Skorpion roadster

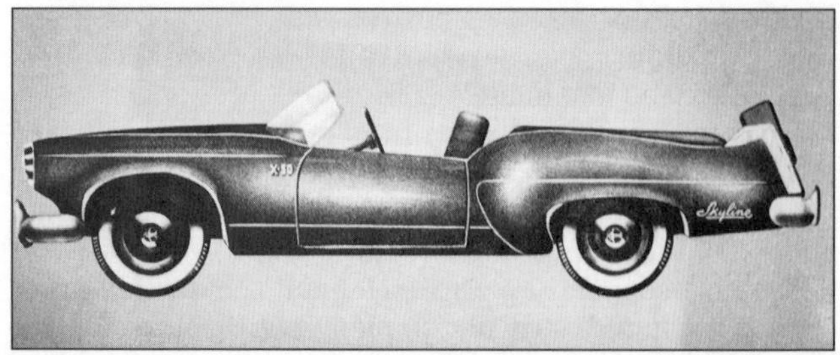
1953 Skyline convertible

Studillac 1953-55
Bill Frick Motors; Rockville Centre, NY
Production: NA
Studebaker hardtops fitted with Cadillac V-8s and three-speed manual ($3695) or Dual-Range Hydra-Matic ($4195) transmissions. They were good for 0-60 mph in 8.5 seconds and a top speed of 125 mph. (*See also* Frick.)

Stutz 1969-91?
Stutz Motor Car of America, Inc.; New York, NY
Production: Less than 1000
A Stutz in name only, this revival, styled by Virgil Exner, was similar in appearance to the '66 Duesenberg (*see* Duesenberg ii *entry*). Initially based on a Pontiac Grand Prix chassis with a 116-inch wheelbase, it was offered as a two-door hardtop and convertible. Later, chassis from various other GM divisions were used. Bodies were built in Italy. Limousines were also constructed. A IV Porte four-door sedan was added in 1979 Prices ranged from $22,500 to more than $200,000.

Super Station Wagon 1954
Henney Motor Co.; Freeport, IL
Production: NA
This 12-passenger wagon, based on the contemporary '54 Packard Cavalier sedan, included an observation-lounge arrangement with a curved rear seat and a table. The projected price was $7500.

Surrey c.1960
E. W. Bliss Co.; Canton, OH
Production: NA
Curved-dash Olds replicar offered a 4.8-bhp standard engine or an eight-bhp air-cooled Cushman unit. It was available fully assembled and as a kit. Top speed was 35 mph, with claimed 65-mpg economy. The base model cost $1045, the DeLuxe $1145.

Swift 1959
Swift Manufacturing Co.; El Cajon, CA
W.M. Manufacturing Co.; San Diego, CA
Production: NA
This trio of ⅝-scale replicars included the Swift-T (styled after a 1910 Model T Ford), Swift Cat (Stutz Bearcat), and Swifter (1903 Cadillac). All were powered by a single-cylinder air-cooled Clinton engine and belt drive. None were actually swift; top speed was 27 mph. The approximate price was $795.

Tasco (The American Sports Car Co.) 1948
Derham Body Co.; Rosemont, PA
Production: NA
Produced by a firm organized by members of the SCCA, the Tasco was designed by Gordon Buehrig, with removable plastic roof panels and front fenders that turned with the wheels. It was powered by a modified Mercury V-8, and the projected price was $7500.

Taylor-Dunn 1948-68
Taylor-Dunn Manufacturing Co.; Anaheim, CA
Production: NA
Two-to-four passenger electric vehicles were built in car and truck form with three or four wheels. Wheelbase ranged from 98 to 101 inches. They had a top speed of 12 mph and a range of 30 miles.

1980-81 Stutz Blackhawk IV Porte sedan

1996 Vector M12 coupe

Thrif-T 1947-55
Tri-Wheel Motor Corp.; Oxford, NC
Production: 50 per month, maximum
These three-wheelers were offered in pickup, closed delivery, and open utility body types on a wheelbase of 85 inches; overall length was 126 inches. They were powered by a 62.6-cid Onan flat-twin mounted on a detachable cradle. Curb weight was 900 pounds, payload about 500 pounds, and top speed about 35-40 mph. Price: $800.

Towne Shopper 1948
International Motor Car Co.; San Diego, CA
Production: NA
Predominantly made of aluminum, this open two-seater was built on a 63-inch wheelbase. A 10.5-bhp Onan twin provided a top speed of 50 mph with 50-mpg fuel economy. A late-1948 variant, the "Town Shopper" from the Carter Motor Corp., had a steel body and frame and 79-inch wheelbase; it's not known if this was a new venture or a revised design from International Motor Car.

Tri-Car 1955
Lycoming Division, Avco Corp.; Williamsport, PA
Tri-Car Co.; Wheatland, PA
Production: NA
Sources disagree on which company built this 117-inch-long, rear-engine three-wheeler (single wheel at the rear), but it had a closed, three-passenger fiberglass body and a Goodrich rubber suspension system. The rear wheel was driven via torque converter by a Lycoming vertical twin. Top speed was 65 mph, and up to 41.5 mpg was claimed.

Triplex c. 1954-55
Kethem's Automotive Corp.; Chicago, IL
Production: NA
This two-place sports car with one-piece fiberglass body was derived from the earlier Chicagoan (*see entry*). Its box-section chassis could accommodate a variety of engines, but was intended to accept a contemporary Ford V-8.

U.S. Mark II 1956
U.S. Fiberglass Co.; Norwood, NJ
Production: NA
A fiberglass-bodied convertible built on wheelbases of 110-118 inches. Sold fully assembled and in kit form.

Valkyrie 1967-69
Fiberfab, Inc.; Los Angeles, CA
Production: NA
Kit-car manufacturer Fiberfab put its Valkyrie body on a ladder-type frame and stuffed in a 450-bhp Chevy 427 V-8 and five-speed ZF transaxle. Not surprisingly, it was very quick: The company claimed 3.9 seconds 0-60 mph and a top speed of 180+. A drag chute was provided for high-speed braking. Price: $12,500.

Vector 1977-97
Vector; Venice, CA
Vector Automotive Group; Jacksonville, FL
Production: 28?
Gerald Wiegart generated much publicity but few vehicles in his attempt to create an American supercar. Only a single midengine V-8 prototype W2 was built from 1977 to 1987. During 1987-93, 18 production W8s were made. An Indonesian group (which later purchased Lamborghini) bought Vector and forced out Wiegart. In 1996, Vector introduced the M12 powered by a 5.7-liter Lamborghini V-12 with 490 bhp. Top speed was 190 mph and its 0-60-mph time was below 4.5 seconds. Approximately eight M12s were built.

Vetta Ventura 1964-66
Vanguard Motors Corp.; Dallas, TX
Production: NA
Identical to the Apollo (*see entry*), the name changed to Vetta Ventura after the Apollo was phased out in 1965. It was offered as a coupe ($6897) or convertible ($7237).

Viking 1929-30
Oldsmobile Motor Division, General Motors Corp.; Lansing, MI
Production: 1390
Introduced as an upmarket extension of Olds, the Viking had styling similar to the "baby Cadillac" LaSalle. Three body styles were offered for 1930, all powered by an 81-bhp 260-cid V-8.

Voltra c.1962
Voltra, Inc.; New York, NY
Production: NA
This compact electric car rode a 106-inch wheelbase, was 170 inches long overall, and weighed 1600 pounds. It was powered by a General Electric DC motor, which provided a top speed of 45 mph.

Warrior 1964
Vanguard Products, Inc.; Dallas, TX
Production: NA
A two-seat targa-roof sports car that sat on a 94-inch-wheelbase rectangular steel-tube chassis. Offered by an air conditioner manufacturer, it was powered by a rear-mounted Ford of Germany V-4.

Westcoaster 1960
Manufacturer unknown
Production: NA
Tiny, three-wheel electric car, suited for golf-cart duty or light shopping, the Westcoaster was powered by a 36-volt GE system with built-in battery charger and automatic voltage relay. The rudimentary fiberglass body was doorless, but a snap-on fiberglass hardtop was optional.

Whippet 1926-31
Willys-Overland Motors; Toledo, OH
Production: 43,422
Whippet was introduced as Willys' "price leader" at $505-$685. The Model 96A had a 103.3-inch wheelbase and a 40-bhp 136-cid four; the Model 98A rode a 112.5-inch wheelbase and had a 50-bhp 179-cid six. Coupes, sedans, and roadsters were offered in both series.

Williams 1957-68
Williams Engine Co. (Calvin Williams & sons); Ambler, PA
Production: NA
Williams built a variety of steam-operated cars with converted gasoline engines. The company's 1963 model used a fiberglass S-4 kit-car body from Victress; a later effort was a converted '66 Chevelle priced at $10,250.

Windsor 1929-1930
Moon Car Co.; St. Louis, MO
Production: 500
Introduced in 1929, Windsor was an eight-cylinder companion to the company's Moon car. For 1930, the six-cylinder Moon adopted the Windsor name. Moons were attractive cars fronted by Rolls-Royce-shaped radiators during the '20s. Moon waned after its 1925 peak production of 10,000 cars. The eight-cylinder Windsor used an 85-horsepower Continental engine and rode a 125-inch wheelbase. The sixes also used Continental engines making 47 or 66 horsepower with a 120-inch wheelbase.

1930 Viking Eight DeLuxe convertible coupe

1953 Woodill Wildfire roadster

1986 Zimmer QuickSilver coupe

1967 Yenko Stinger coupe

1986 Zimmer Golden Spirit coupe

Woodill Wildfire 1952-56
Woodill Motor Co. (B. R. "Woody" Woodill); Downey, CA
Production: 15
America's first fiberglass-bodied production sports car had bodywork by Glasspar (*see entry*). It was conceived as a kit, but was also sold fully assembled for $2900-$4500. The 101-inch-wheelbase frame carried a Willys 90-bhp F-head six with three-speed overdrive manual transmission. Later versions were built to accept Ford V-8s or other engines of the customer's choosing.

Yank 1950
Custom Auto Works; San Diego, CA
Production: NA
This two-seat aluminum-bodied sports car was built on a 100-inch wheelbase and was powered by a Willys four-cylinder engine that provided a top speed of 78 mph. Price: $1000.

Yankee Clipper 1953-54
Strassberger Motor Co.; Menlo Park, CA
Production: NA
This purpose-designed car rode a 101-inch wheelbase chassis, weighed 1900 pounds, and stood but 37 inches high. It used many '54 Ford components, including a 130-bhp V-8.

Yenko Stinger 1965-71?
Yenko Sportscars, Inc. (Don Yenko); Cannonsburg, PA
Production: NA
Five modified versions of the Corvair Corsa coupe were available, all intended mainly for competition. Engines included the 164-cid Corvair flat six or an overbored 176-cid version with ratings of from 160 to 240 bhp. Two Camaro-based cars were offered for 1969 with engines rated at 435 and 450 bhp. The Turbo Stinger, a supercharged version of Chevy's Vega, was announced in 1971.

Zimmer 1980-
Zimmer Motor Cars Co.; Pompano Beach, FL;
Syracuse, NY
Production: Over 14,000
The Golden Spirit was a neoclassic-styled coupe and convertible similar in appearance to later Excaliburs. It was based on Ford Mustang mechanicals. A sedan was added for 1985. For 1986-88, a QuickSilver coupe was based on the Pontiac Fiero. It featured modern styling with an interior more luxurious than offered by Fiero. Bankruptcy of Zimmer's parent company ended production in 1988. Production resumed in '98. Mustang, again, provided the base for coupes and two-door convertibles, with the addition of Lincoln Town Car-based sedans and four-door convertibles. Production is currently 15-20 cars per year.